THE BRITISH ISLES 76
THE LOW COUNTRIES 82
GERMANY 86
NORTHERN CENTRAL EUROPE 92
EUROPE 98
CENTRAL EASTERN EUROPE 100
THE ALPINE NATIONS 88
FRANCE 78
WESTERN BALKANS 94
THE IBERIAN PENINSULA 80
ITALY AND MALTA 90
EASTERN BALKANS 96

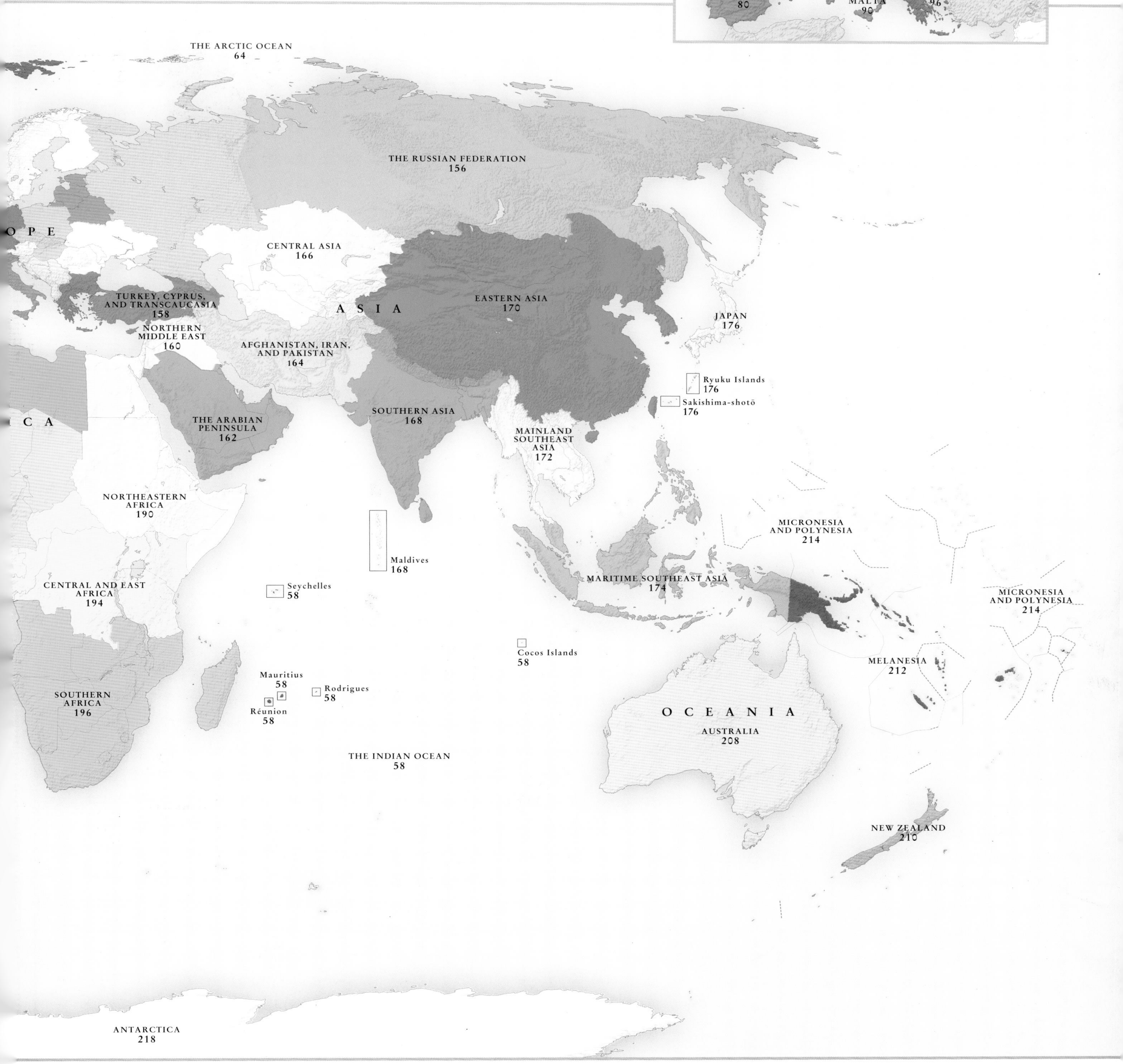

THE ARCTIC OCEAN 64
THE RUSSIAN FEDERATION 156
OPE
CENTRAL ASIA 166
EASTERN ASIA 170
TURKEY, CYPRUS, AND TRANSCAUCASIA 158
ASIA
NORTHERN MIDDLE EAST 160
AFGHANISTAN, IRAN, AND PAKISTAN 164
JAPAN 176
Ryuku Islands 176
Sakishima-shotō 176
CA
THE ARABIAN PENINSULA 162
SOUTHERN ASIA 168
MAINLAND SOUTHEAST ASIA 172
NORTHEASTERN AFRICA 190
MICRONESIA AND POLYNESIA 214
Maldives 168
CENTRAL AND EAST AFRICA 194
Seychelles 58
MARITIME SOUTHEAST ASIA 174
MICRONESIA AND POLYNESIA 214
Cocos Islands 58
MELANESIA 212
Mauritius 58
Rodrigues 58
Réunion 58
SOUTHERN AFRICA 196
OCEANIA
AUSTRALIA 208
THE INDIAN OCEAN 58
NEW ZEALAND 210
ANTARCTICA 218

the **illustrated**
WORLD ATLAS

A comprehensive portrait of planet Earth

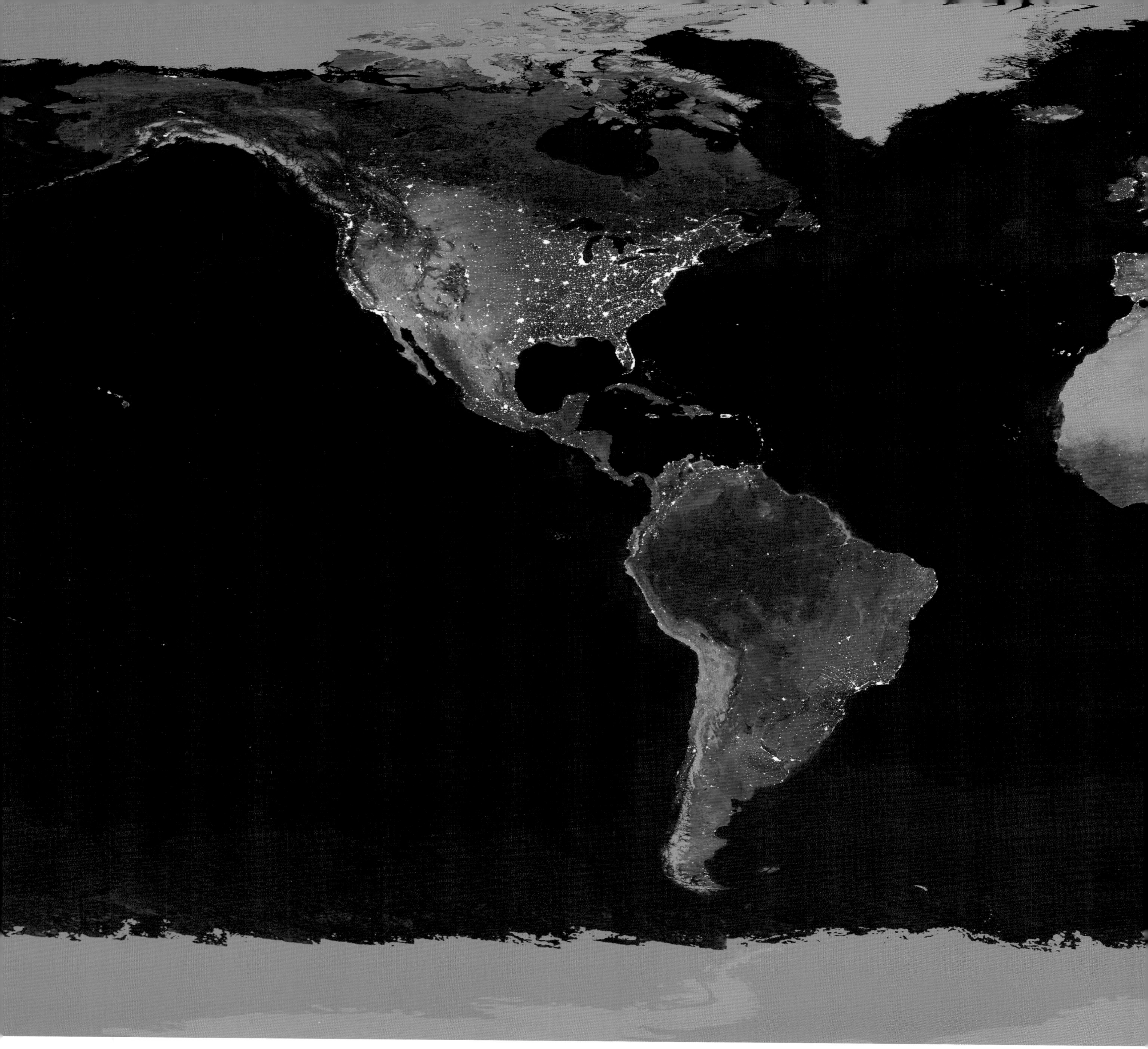

the **illustrated**

WORLD ATLAS

A comprehensive portrait of planet Earth

FOG CITY PRESS

Published by Fog City Press
814 Montgomery Street
San Francisco, CA 94133 USA

Chief Executive Officer John Owen
President Terry Newell
Publisher Sheena Coupe
Creative Director Sue Burk
Vice President International Sales Stuart Laurence
Administrator International Sales Kristine Ravn

Project Manager Sarah Anderson
Art Director Suzanne Tawansi

Project Editors/Text Jenni Bruce, Scott Forbes
Editorial Assistant Karen Penzes

Designers Clare Forte, Liz Murphy
Design Assistant Nika Markovtzev
Initial Design Concept John Bull

Production Manager Caroline Webber
Production Coordinator James Blackman

Systems Administrator Margaret Hilliard
Editorial Coordinator Jennifer Losco

Picture Researcher Jo Collard

Maps Map Illustrations
Chief Cartographer Laurie Whiddon
Cartographic Team Bil Andersen, Andrew Davies,
Kerrie deGruchy, Sydney Gubbay, Ian Faulkner,
Brian Johnston, Brad McLean, Karen Reithmuller

Cityscape Illustrations Murray Zanoni
Information Graphics Andrew Davies, Suzanne Tawansi
Illustrators Richard Bonson/Wildlife Art Ltd,
Tom Connell/Wildlife Art Ltd, Mark A. Garlick, Rob Mancini,
Edwina Riddell, Peter Scott/Wildlife Art Ltd
Flags Flag Society of Australia

ISBN 10: 1-74089-318-2
ISBN 13: 978-1-74089-318-3

First printed in 2004

Color reproduction by Colourscan Overseas Co Pte Ltd
Printed in Singapore by Tien Wah Press (Pte) Limited

A WELDON OWEN PRODUCTION

Cartographic Consultant

Dr William Cartwright
Associate Professor in Multimedia Cartography
School of Mathematical and Geospatial Sciences
RMIT University, Melbourne, Australia
Vice-President, International
Cartographic Association

Regional Mapping Consultants

Imran Ali
Cartographer, Pakistan

M. (John) Balodis
FMSIA Adjunct Professor
Curtin University, Perth, Australia

Professor Jean Carrière
Professeur titulaire
Directeur du Département de géographie
Université du Québec à Montréal, Canada

Prem Chetri
School of Mathematical and Geospatial Sciences
RMIT University, Melbourne, Australia

Professor Benjamin Cohen
Department of Photogrammetry
and Cartography
University of Architecture, Civil Engineering
and Geodesy, Sofia, Bulgaria

Igor Drecki
Geographics Unit Manager
School of Geography and Environmental Science
University of Auckland, Auckland, New Zealand

Dr Francisco Escobar
Profesor Titular de Análisis Geográfico Regional
Departamento de Geografía
Universidad de Alcalá de Henares, Spain

Dr David Fairbairn
School of Civil Engineering and Geosciences
University of Newcastle, Newcastle, U.K.

Steve Foldi
Cartographer, Windsor, Australia

Scott Furey
School of Mathematical and Geospatial Sciences
RMIT University, Melbourne, Australia

Professor Dr Georg Gartner
Institut für Kartographie und Geo-Medientechnik
Technische Universitat Wien, Vienna, Austria

Ibrahim Hanna
Hydrogeologist, Syria

Hashim al Hashimi
Geo-Information Analyst
Environmental Research and Wildlife
Development Agency, United Arab Emirates

Dr Stephen Hutchinson
Southampton Oceanography Centre
University of Southampton, Southampton, U.K.

Dr Simon Jones
School of Mathematical and Geospatial Sciences
RMIT University, Melbourne, Australia

Professor Milan Konecny
Department of Geography, Faculty of Science
Masaryk University, Brno, Czech Republic

Professor Alexandra Koussoulakou
Department of Cadastre, Photogrammetry
and Cartography
The Aristotle University, Thessaloniki, Greece

Colin Kropman
Geographic Consultant, Sydney, Australia

Hyun Jong (David) Lee
Sung Kyun Kwan University, Seoul, South Korea

Antonio Hernández Navarro
Geodetic Coordinator
National Institute of Statistics,
Geography and Informatics (INEGI)
National Mapping Agency of Mexico,
Aguascalientes, Mexico

Professor Ferjan Ormeling,
University of Utrecht, Netherlands
Secretary-General, International
Cartographic Association

Professor Michael P. Peterson
Department of Geography/Geology
University of Nebraska at Omaha, U.S.A.
Chair, International Cartographic Association
Commission on Maps and the Internet

Will Pringle
Cartographic Director
Australian Geographic Pty Ltd,
Sydney, Australia

Professor Patrick Quilty
Honorary Research Professor
School of Earth Sciences
University of Tasmania, Hobart, Australia

Cristhiane da Silva Ramos
School of Mathematical and Geospatial Sciences
RMIT University, Melbourne, Australia

Rushan Gul Rozi
School of Mathematical and Geospatial Sciences
RMIT University, Melbourne, Australia

Afshin Alizadeh Shabini
University of Tehran, Tehran, Iran

Hussein Tawansi
Fellow Member, Institute of Quarrying
Sydney, Australia

Professor Dr Theodor Wintges
Munich University of Applied Sciences,
Munich, Germany

Assistant Professor Hiroyuki Yoshida
Faculty of Policy Management
SFC, Keio University, Endo, Japan

Jason Zhang
School of Mathematical and Geospatial Sciences
RMIT University, Melbourne, Australia

Thematic Mapping Consultants

Kathleen L. Abdalla
Senior Economic Affairs Officer
Division for Sustainable Development
Department of Economic and Social Affairs,
United Nations, New York, U.S.A

Dr Colin Arrowsmith
Senior Lecturer
School of Mathematical and Geospatial Sciences
RMIT University, Melbourne, Australia

Robert Burnham
Senior Editor, *Astronomy* Magazine
Hales Corner, U.S.A

Dr Susan Canney
Department of Zoology
University of Oxford, Oxford, U.K.

Professor Bernard Comrie
Director, Department of Linguistics
Max Planck Institute for Evolutionary
Anthropology, Leipzig, Germany

Professor John Connell
School of Geosciences
University of Sydney, Sydney, Australia

Associate Professor Jim Forrest
Head, Department of Human Geography
Macquarie University, Sydney, Australia

Dr Stephen Gale
School of Geoscience
University of Sydney, Sydney, Australia

Dr Anne Gardner
Director, Religious Studies Programme
La Trobe University, Melbourne, Australia

Dr Stephen Hutchinson
Southampton Oceanography Centre
University of Southampton, Southampton, U.K.

Dr Paul James
Professor of Globalism and Cultural Diversity
Director of the Globalism Institute
RMIT University, Melbourne, Australia

Dr Ian S. McIntosh
Senior Editor, *Cultural Survival*
New York, U.S.A

Dorothy F. Prescott
Senior Fellow
School of Anthropology, Geography
and Environmental Science
University of Melbourne, Melbourne, Australia

Professor John Robert Victor Prescott
Professor Emeritus and Professorial Fellow
School of Anthropology, Geography
and Environmental Studies
University of Melbourne, Melbourne, Australia

Dr John Preston
Reader in Transport Studies
University of Oxford, Oxford, U.K.

Professor Patrick Quilty
Honorary Research Professor
School of Earth Sciences
University of Tasmania, Hobart, Australia

Dr Anne I. Thackeray
Honorary Research Associate
Archaeology Division, School of Geography,
Archaeology and Environmental Studies
University of the Witwatersrand,
Johannesburg, South Africa

David Rains Wallace
Naturalist, Berkeley, U.S.A.

Richard Whitaker
Weathersmart Meteorological Services
Sydney, Australia

Associate Professor Charles Zika
Head, Department of History
University of Melbourne, Melbourne, Australia

Below: The dark-red Namib Desert is clearly visible at bottom center in this satellite photo of the southwestern coast of Africa.

Below left: These abstract patterns are sand beds in The Bahamas that have been carved by the tides and currents.

Contents

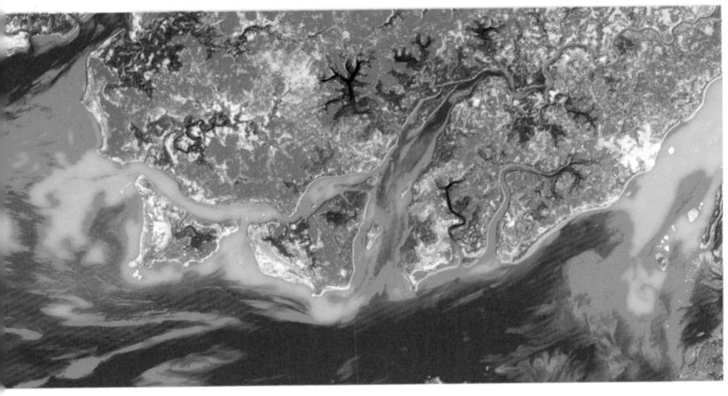
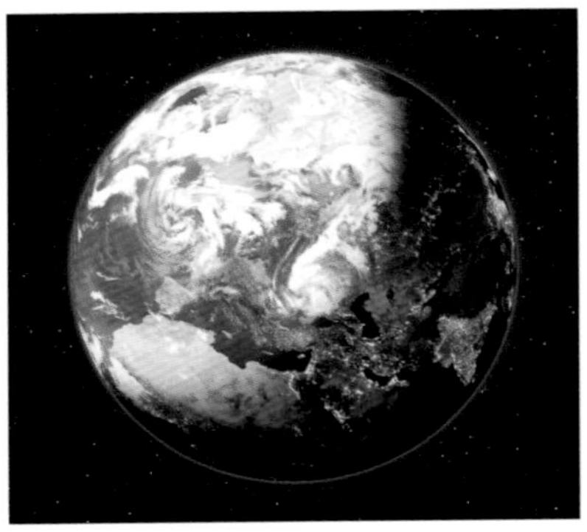

Foreword 8
How to Use this Atlas 10
Index to Map Pages 12

WORLD VIEW 14
Our Place in Space 16
The Changing Earth 18
Climate and Weather 20
The Web of Life 22
The Advance of Humans 24
Exploration 26
Population 28
Natural Resources 30
The Global Environment 32
Languages of the World 34
Religions of the World 36
Indigenous Peoples 38
Rich and Poor 40
States and Borders 42
Transport and Communication 44
Global Connections 46

MAPPING THE WORLD 48
The Physical World 50
The Political World 52

THE OCEANS 54
The Oceans 56
The Indian Ocean 58
The Pacific Ocean 60
The Atlantic Ocean 62
The Arctic Ocean 64

EUROPE 66
The View from Above 68
Land and Environment 70
Peoples and Nations 72
The Human Impact 74
The British Isles 76
Republic of Ireland, United Kingdom
France 78
France, Monaco
The Iberian Peninsula 80
Andorra, Portugal, Spain
The Low Countries 82
Belgium, Luxembourg, Netherlands
Scandinavia 84
Denmark, Finland, Iceland, Norway, Sweden
Germany 86
The Alpine Nations 88
Austria, Liechtenstein, Switzerland
Italy and Malta 90
Italy, Malta, San Marino, Vatican City
Northern Central Europe 92
Czech Republic, Hungary, Poland, Slovakia
Western Balkans 94
Albania, Bosnia and Herzegovina, Croatia, Serbia and Montenegro, Slovenia
Eastern Balkans 96
Bulgaria, Greece, Macedonia
Northeastern Europe 98
Belarus, Estonia, Latvia, Lithuania
Central Eastern Europe 100
Moldova, Romania, Ukraine

NORTH AMERICA 102
The View from Above 104
Land and Environment 106
Peoples and Nations 108
The Human Impact 110
Western Canada and Alaska 112
Alaska, Alberta, British Columbia, Northwest Territories, Nunavut, Saskatchewan, Yukon Territory
Eastern Canada 114
Manitoba, New Brunswick, Newfoundland and Labrador, Nova Scotia, Nunavut, Ontario, Prince Edward Island, Québec, St Pierre and Miquelon
Western United States 116
Arizona, California, Hawaii, Idaho, Nevada, Oregon, Utah, Washington
Central United States 118
Arkansas, Colorado, Iowa, Kansas, Louisiana, Minnesota, Missouri, Montana, Nebraska, New Mexico, North Dakota, Oklahoma, South Dakota, Texas, Wyoming
Northeastern United States 120
Connecticut, Delaware, District of Columbia, Illinois, Indiana, Kentucky, Maine, Maryland, Massachusetts, Michigan, New Hampshire, New Jersey, New York, Ohio, Pennsylvania, Rhode Island, Vermont, Virginia, West Virginia, Wisconsin
Southeastern United States 122
Alabama, Florida, Georgia, Mississippi, North Carolina, South Carolina, Tennessee
Mexico 124
Central America and the West Indies 126
Antigua and Barbuda, The Bahamas, Barbados, Belize, Costa Rica, Cuba, Dominica, Dominican Republic, El Salvador, Grenada, Guatemala, Haiti, Honduras, Jamaica, Nicaragua, Panama, St Kitts and Nevis, St Lucia, St Vincent and the Grenadines, Trinidad and Tobago

SOUTH AMERICA 128

The View from Above 130

Land and Environment 132

Peoples and Nations 134

The Human Impact 136

Northern South America 138
Colombia, Guyana, Suriname, Venezuela

Western South America 140
Bolivia, Ecuador, Peru

Eastern South America 142
Brazil, Paraguay

Southern South America 144
Argentina, Chile, Uruguay

ASIA 146

The View from Above 148

Land and Environment 150

Peoples and Nations 152

The Human Impact 154

The Russian Federation 156

Turkey, Cyprus, and Transcaucasia 158
Armenia, Azerbaijan, Cyprus, Georgia, Turkey

Northern Middle East 160
Iraq, Israel, Jordan, Lebanon, Syria

The Arabian Peninsula 162
Bahrain, Kuwait, Oman, Qatar, Saudi Arabia, United Arab Emirates, Yemen

Afghanistan, Iran, and Pakistan 164

Central Asia 166
Kazakhstan, Kyrgyzstan, Tajikistan, Turkmenistan, Uzbekistan

Southern Asia 168
Bangladesh, Bhutan, India, Maldives, Nepal, Sri Lanka

Eastern Asia 170
China, Mongolia, North Korea, South Korea, Taiwan

Mainland Southeast Asia 172
Cambodia, Laos, Myanmar (Burma), Thailand, Vietnam

Maritime Southeast Asia 174
Brunei, East Timor, Indonesia, Malaysia, Philippines, Singapore

Japan 176

AFRICA 178

The View from Above 180

Land and Environment 182

Peoples and Nations 184

The Human Impact 186

Northwestern Africa 188
Algeria, Libya, Morocco, Tunisia

Northeastern Africa 190
Djibouti, Egypt, Eritrea, Ethiopia, Somalia, Sudan

West Africa 192
Benin, Burkina Faso, Cameroon, Chad, Côte d'Ivoire, Equatorial Guinea, Gambia, Ghana, Guinea, Guinea-Bissau, Liberia, Mali, Mauritania, Niger, Nigeria, Senegal, Sierra Leone, Togo

Central and East Africa 194
Burundi, Central African Republic, Congo, Democratic Republic of Congo, Gabon, Kenya, Rwanda, São Tomé and Príncipe, Tanzania, Uganda

Southern Africa 196
Angola, Botswana, Comoros, Lesotho, Madagascar, Malawi, Mozambique, Namibia, Republic of South Africa, Swaziland, Zambia, Zimbabwe

OCEANIA 198

The View from Above 200

Land and Environment 202

Peoples and Nations 204

The Human Impact 206

Australia 208

New Zealand 210

Melanesia 212
Fiji, Papua New Guinea, Solomon Islands, Vanuatu

Micronesia and Polynesia 214
Federated States of Micronesia, Kiribati, Marshall Islands, Nauru, Palau, Samoa, Tonga, Tuvalu

ANTARCTICA 216

Antarctica 218

Antarctica in Focus 220

REFERENCE 222

Geographical Comparisons 224

Time Zones 226

Fact File 228

Geographic Terms 238

Gazetteer 240

Acknowledgments 304

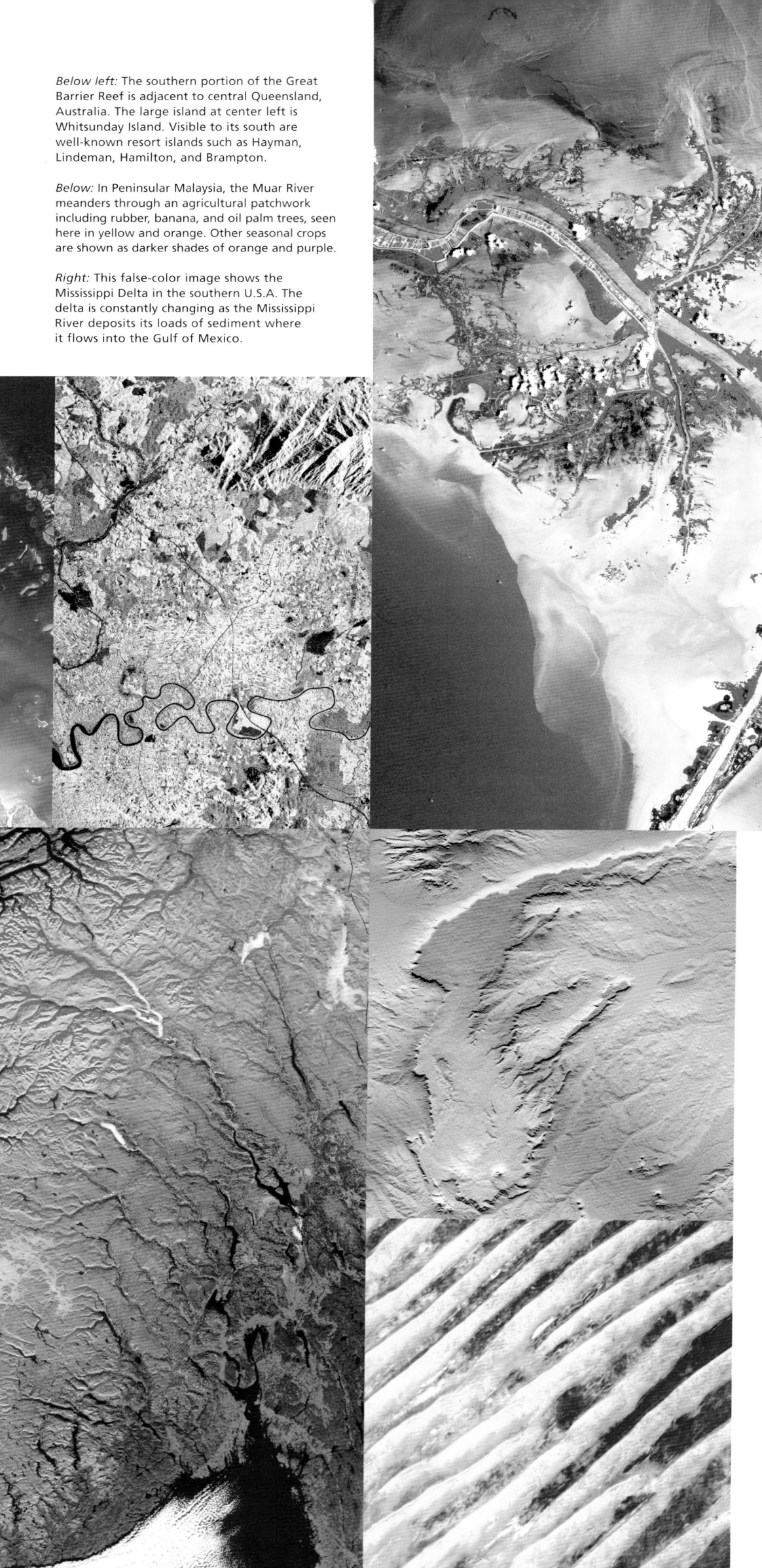

Below left: The southern portion of the Great Barrier Reef is adjacent to central Queensland, Australia. The large island at center left is Whitsunday Island. Visible to its south are well-known resort islands such as Hayman, Lindeman, Hamilton, and Brampton.

Below: In Peninsular Malaysia, the Muar River meanders through an agricultural patchwork including rubber, banana, and oil palm trees, seen here in yellow and orange. Other seasonal crops are shown as darker shades of orange and purple.

Right: This false-color image shows the Mississippi Delta in the southern U.S.A. The delta is constantly changing as the Mississippi River deposits its loads of sediment where it flows into the Gulf of Mexico.

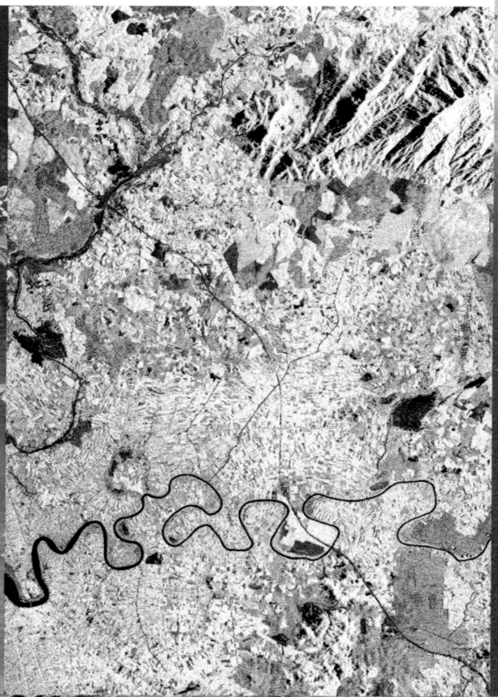

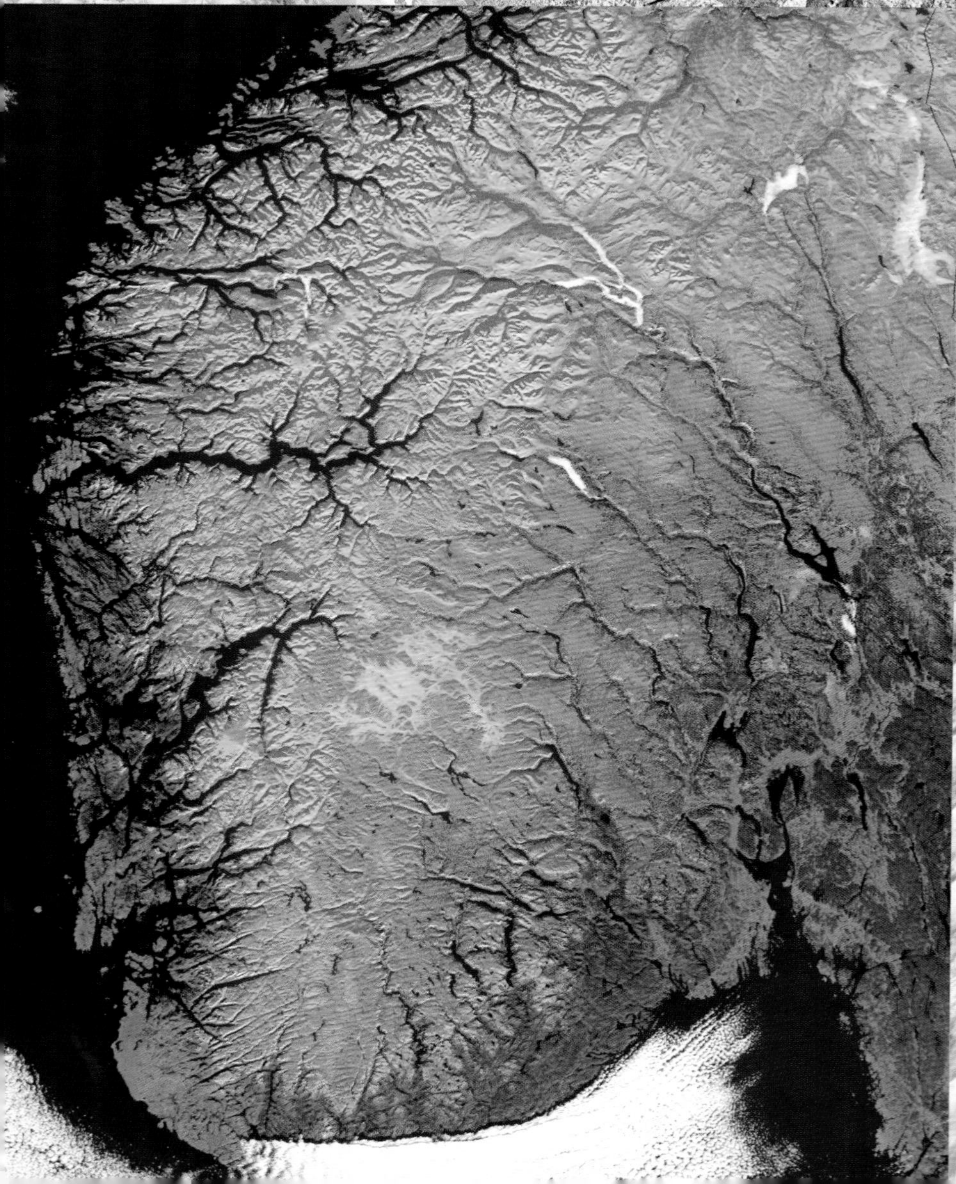

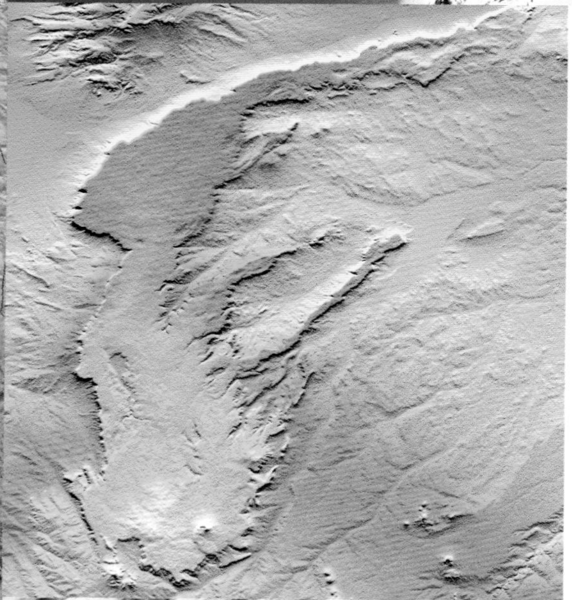

Far left: In this Terra MODIS satellite image, southern Norway is seen surrounded by the Norwegian and North seas. Two of Norway's famous fjords are clearly visible—Sognefjorden at center and Hardangerfjorden at center bottom.

Left: This digitally enhanced image shows a lava plateau near La Esperanza, in Patagonia, Argentina. The ancient stream beds, at bottom, are evidence of the erosion that created this plateau.

Bottom left: These linear dunes lie in one of Earth's driest areas, the Rub' al Khālī in Saudi Arabia. Also know as the Empty Quarter, the Rub' al Khālī, is the world's largest continuous sand desert.

FOREWORD

We live in an increasingly globalized world, in which cultural barriers are breaking down and communication is almost instantaneous. Events and conflicts that in previous eras may have seemed remote now have an immediacy and relevance that demand attention. Although our lives and our view of the world are still centered on a sense of the place where we live, it is now more vital than ever for us to locate ourselves within a global context and to understand clearly the similarities and contrasts between our history, culture, and environment and those of other societies.

An atlas is an indispensable reference tool for all who want to understand the ever-shrinking world of which they are a part. Who are we? Where are we? And where do we fit in a wider perspective? *The Illustrated World Atlas*, with its unique combination of physical and human geography, will enable the reader to gain a better understanding of our remarkable—and fragile—planet. This up-to-the-minute family atlas provides not only clear, contemporary mapping but also encyclopedic information on historical, cultural, social, and environmental themes.

The Illustrated World Atlas is structured in two main parts. Part One, World View, contains a series of global spreads on subjects as diverse as climate and communication, living standards and language, religion and resources. Part Two, Mapping the World, comprises the regional maps. The six largest continents are introduced with four spreads. The first provides a perspective from Earth-orbiting satellites. Then follow three spreads mapping the continent's land and environment, its history and political structure, and the impact of human activity. At the atlas's heart are the physical maps. These beautifully rendered maps are supported by land use and population maps, photographs, illustrations, satellite imagery, and three-dimensional views. The indispensable reference section that concludes the atlas includes illustrated geographical comparisons, a map of time zones, a fact file tabulating each country's essential data, a dictionary of geographical terms, a detailed gazetteer of more than 30,000 place names, and a complete collection of national flags.

The Illustrated World Atlas was developed under the guidance of an international body of cartographic and specialist subject consultants. With more than 330 appealing, easy-to-read maps, engaging text, beautiful illustrations, vivid photographs, intricate detail and wide-ranging scope, it is an essential reference work for every home. Planet Earth has never looked so good.

How to Use this Atlas

The atlas is organized into two major sections. The first, World View, provides an introductory survey of the physical, human, and economic geography of planet Earth. The second section, Mapping the World, contains detailed regional maps, arranged by continent, and includes physical, political, and human impact maps for the six largest continents. A reference section completes the atlas. It includes geographical comparisons, a fact file of the world's nations, a glossary, and a complete gazetteer.

Regional Maps

Each central map is accompanied by economic profile and population pattern maps. Included for selected regions are three-dimensional terrain maps and illustrations of significant cities. Annotated photographs of regional features support the central maps.

Grid reference
The location of each place, as listed in the gazetteer, is referenced against the grid frame.

Regional map
Each regional map includes detailed information on the physical landscape of a region, as well as its human geography.

Photographs
Photographs of natural features and human structures are included, with captions.

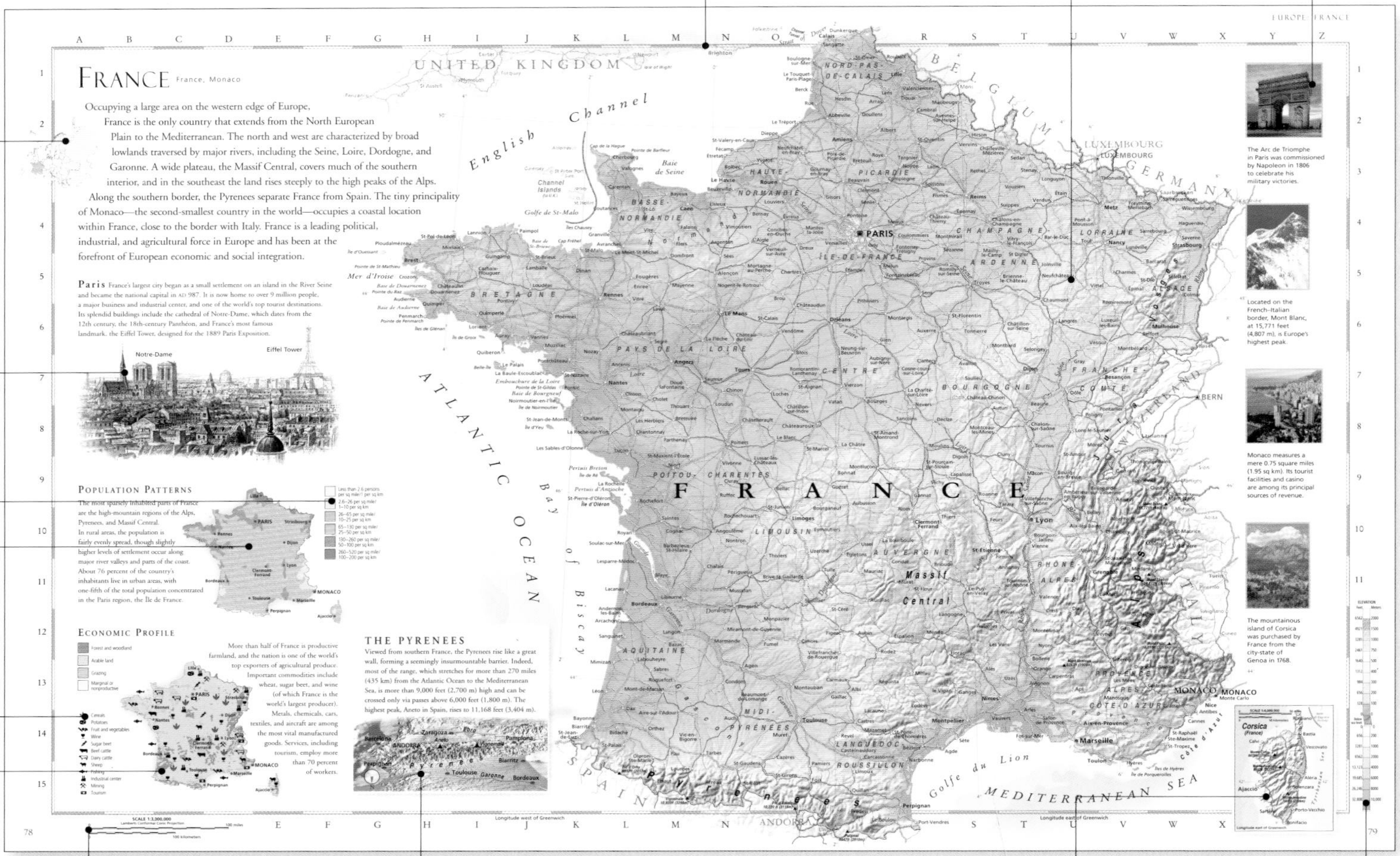

FRANCE
France, Monaco
UNITED KINGDOM
English Channel
ATLANTIC OCEAN
Bay of Biscay
FRANCE
Massif Central
MEDITERRANEAN SEA
Golfe du Lion
BELGIUM
LUXEMBOURG
GERMANY
SWITZERLAND
SPAIN
Population Patterns
Economic Profile
THE PYRENEES
Notre-Dame
Eiffel Tower

Locator map
This map indicates the location of the region within its continent.

Illustration
Illustrations highlight significant areas within a major city.

Population Patterns key

Population Patterns map
The population distribution of the area is plotted on this map.

Economic Profile key

Economic Profile map
The regional land use and economic activity are displayed on this map.

Scale
The scale of the main map, plus a scale bar and projection information, are included here.

Three-dimensional terrain map
This computer-generated map focuses on a specific physical feature.

Inset map
Associated regions that fall outside the area are included as detailed inset maps.

Elevation chart
This chart indicates elevation, the height above sea level, as well as ocean depths.

Thematic Maps

These pages include detailed world maps accompanied by illustrations, diagrams, charts, graphs, and photographs. They cover topics as diverse as our place in space, climate, wildlife, natural resources, exploration, population, religions, languages, indigenous peoples, transport and communications, economics, and governments.

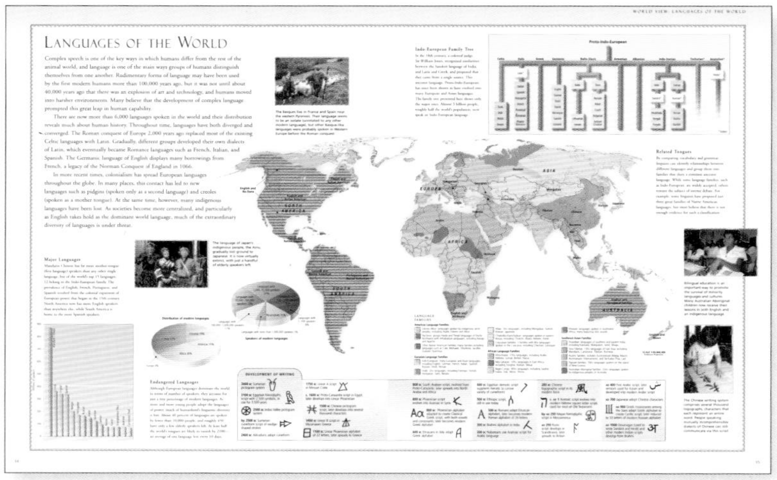

Languages of the World

Satellite Views

Included for the six largest continents are double-page spreads featuring images obtained from the satellites that orbit the globe. The photos reveal the diversity of population patterns, agricultural areas, and concentrations of industry across the continents. From space, the details of landscapes and the impact of human activity are often startlingly clear.

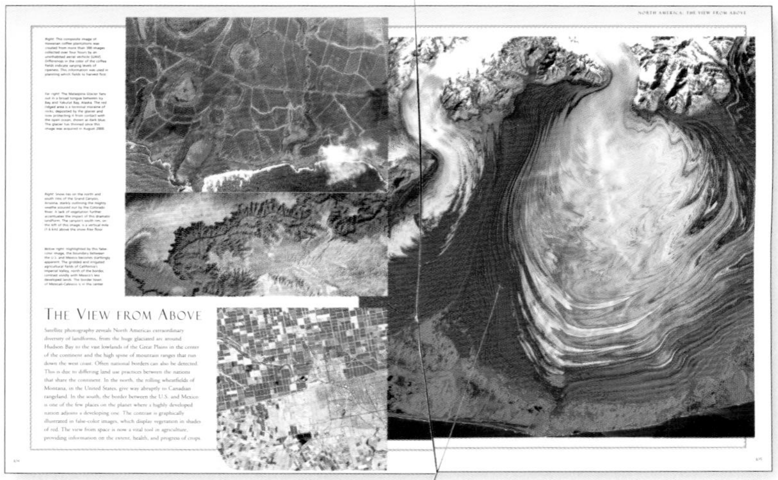

The View from Above

Physical Continent Maps

The central map displays the landform of each continent, including major waterways, mountain ranges, and geographical features. Smaller maps reveal the continental climate and vegetation zones. A side panel, containing a map, diagram, and photograph, reviews a significant natural hazard that occurs on the continent. Satellite photographs highlight major physical features of the continent.

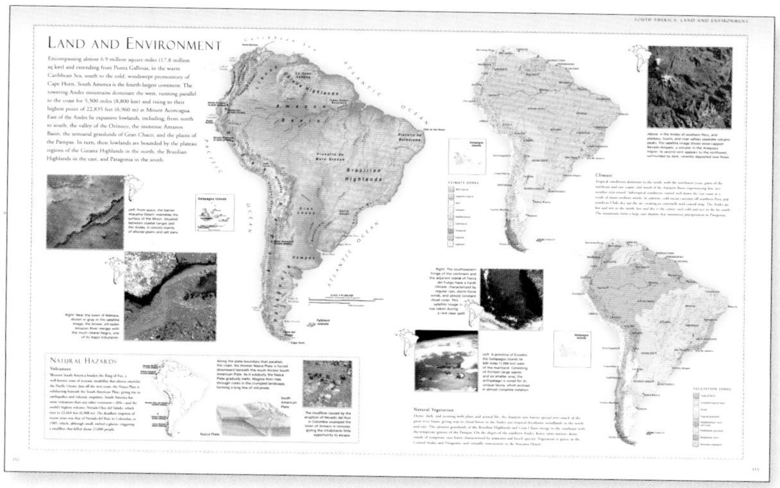

Land and Environment
Natural Hazards

Political Continent Maps

The large political map displays the human geography of the continent. Supporting maps reveal the continental population distribution, and trade or political organizations. A series of historical maps highlight major political and social changes over time. A side panel includes flashpoint maps that focus on areas of current dispute and conflict. The maps are accompanied by a graph indicating the population of the largest cities.

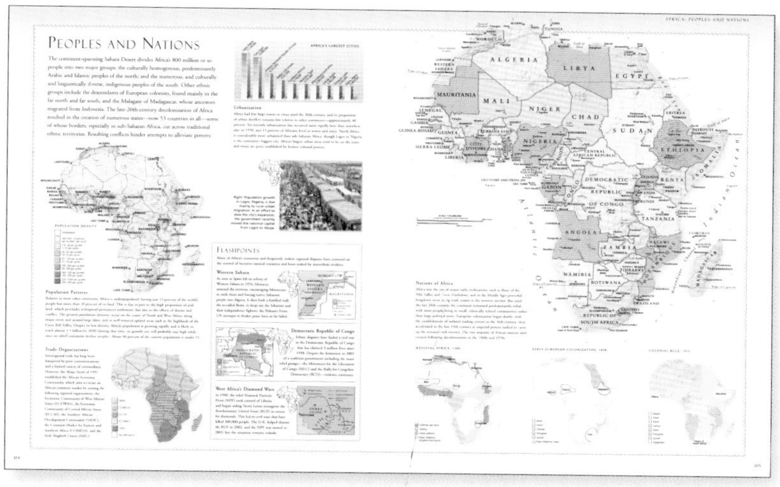

Peoples and Nations
Flashpoints

Human Impact Continent Maps

The main map indicates land use and significant economic activities across the continent. A supporting map, accompanied by photographs, underlines the threats to the continent's environment. A side panel focuses on a dramatic environmental change as a result of human activity. A graph showing protected land illustrates the efforts of selected countries to reverse environmental damage.

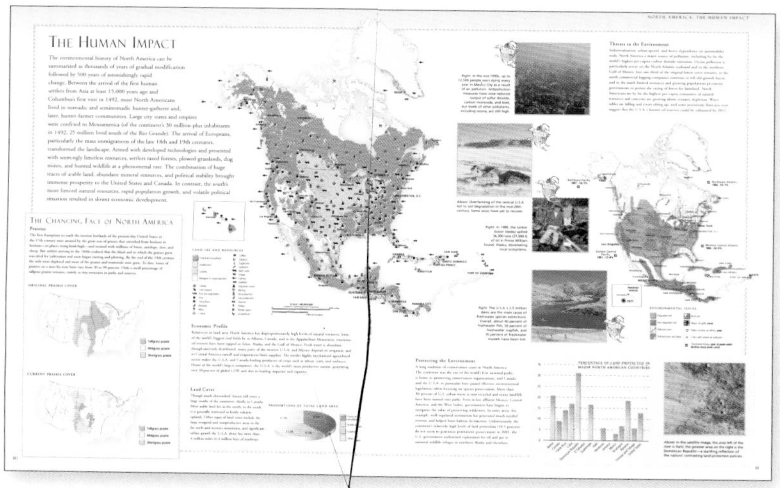

The Human Impact

Key to Regional Maps

PHYSICAL FEATURES

ELEVATION

Feet	Meters
6562	2000
4921	1500
3281	1000
2461	750
1640	500
1312	400
984	300
656	200
328	100
0	0
Below sea level	
0	0
656	200
3281	1000
6562	2000
13,123	4000
19,685	6000
26,246	8000
32,808	10,000

Ice cap

Ice shelf

Mountain peak/volcano Height, feet (meters)

Pole

Geomagnetic Pole

Seamount

Sea trench Depth, feet (meters)

WATER FEATURES

Lake

Salt pan/Dry/Intermittent lake

Coastline

Major river

Minor river

River source

Waterfall

TRANSPORT

Major road

Main road

Minor road

Railway

GRATICULE FEATURE

125° Graticule number

Graticule line

Tropics/polar circle

Equator

BORDERS

International border

Defined maritime boundary

Equidistant lines

Disputed border

Demarcation/line of control/ceasefire line

State/territory border (Australia, Canada, U.S.A.)

International Date Line

NATIONAL/DEPENDENT TERRITORY CAPITAL CITIES

Over 5 million	**LONDON**
1–5 million	**OTTAWA**
100,000–1 million	**HELSINKI**
100,000–1 million	**KINGSTON**
0–100,000	**HONIARA**
0–100,000	**BELMOPAN**

STATE/TERRITORY CAPITAL CITIES (Australia, Canada, U.S.A.)

Over 5 million	**Toronto**
1–5 million	**Sydney**
100,000–1 million	**Québec**
0–100,000	Columbia

OTHER CITIES OR TOWNS

Over 5 million	**São Paulo**
1–5 million	**Calicut**
100,000–1 million	Luxor
0–100,000	Lillehammer

Research base

Built-up area

TYPOGRAPHIC KEY

POLITICAL FEATURES

Country	**BELIZE**
Dependent territory with parent state	**VIRGIN ISLANDS (to U.S.A.)**
Internal administrative region	*UMBRIA*
State/Territory (Australia, Canada, U.S.A.)	**VICTORIA**

PHYSICAL FEATURES

Mountain range	***Allegheny Mountains***
Mountain peak	***Mt Davis***
Geographic feature	***Nullarbor Plain***
Peninsula	***Cape York Peninsula***
Headland/point/cape	*Cabo de São Vincent*
Island group	***Solomon Islands***
Island	***New Caledonia***
Pole	***North Pole***

WATER FEATURES

Ocean	*PACIFIC OCEAN*
Sea	*Irish Sea*
Bay/gulf	*Gulf of Mexico*
Channel/strait	*Bass Strait*
Undersea ridge	***Carlsberg Ridge***
Seamount/Sea trench	***Golden Dragon Seamount***
Lake/Salt pan/Dry/Intermittent lake	*Lake Titicaca*
Major river	*Nile*
Minor river	*Salween*
River source	***Source of the Amazon***
Waterfall	***Angel Falls***

GRATICULE FEATURES

Tropics/polar circle/equator	Tropic of Capricorn
Date line	International Date Line

Index to Map Pages

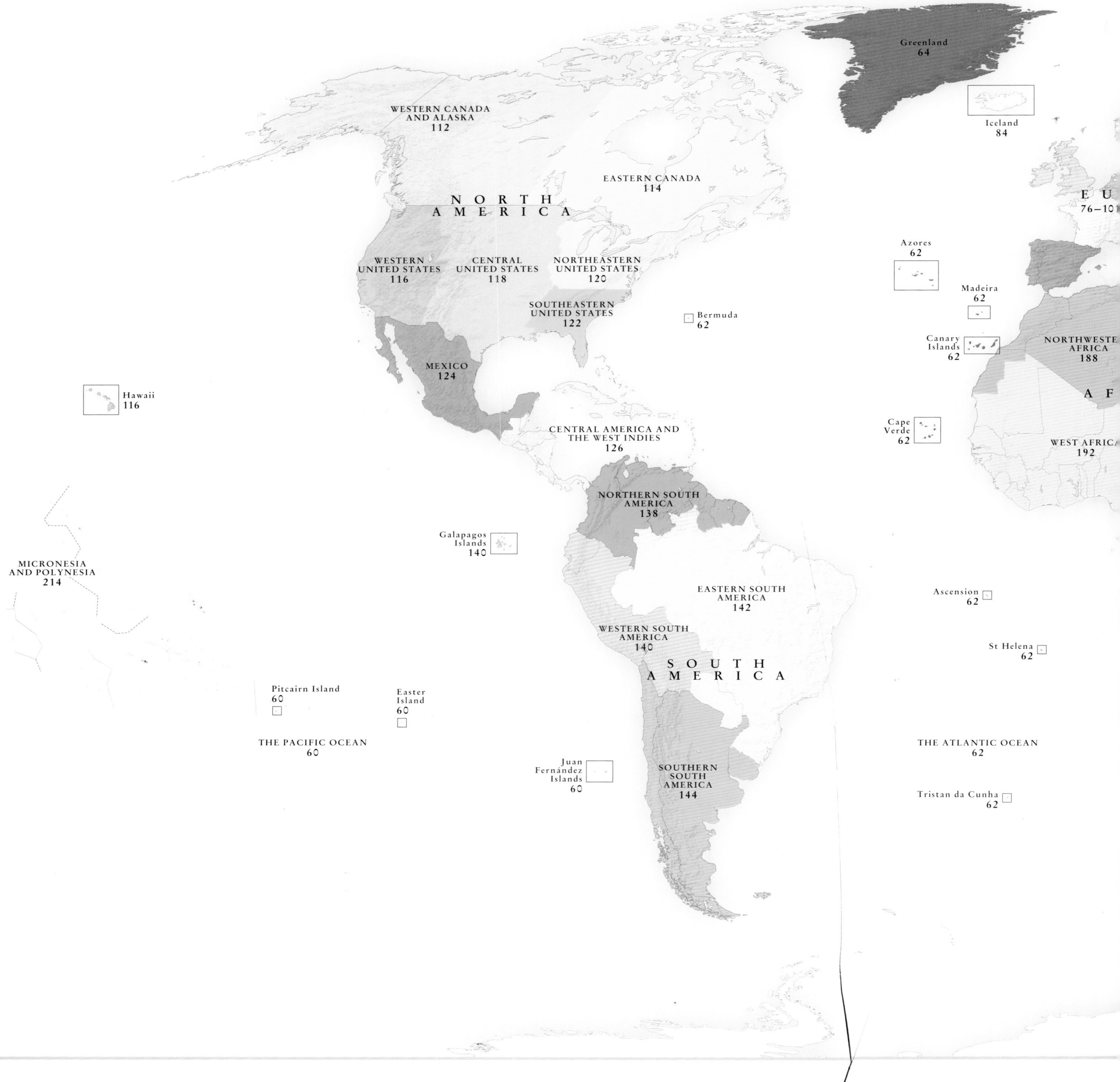
Greenland
64
Iceland
84
WESTERN CANADA AND ALASKA
112
EASTERN CANADA
114
NORTH AMERICA
E U
76–10
WESTERN UNITED STATES
116
CENTRAL UNITED STATES
118
NORTHEASTERN UNITED STATES
120
Azores
62
Madeira
62
SOUTHEASTERN UNITED STATES
122
Bermuda
62
Canary Islands
62
NORTHWESTE AFRICA
188
MEXICO
124
Hawaii
116
A F
Cape Verde
62
CENTRAL AMERICA AND THE WEST INDIES
126
WEST AFRIC
192
NORTHERN SOUTH AMERICA
138
Galapagos Islands
140
MICRONESIA AND POLYNESIA
214
EASTERN SOUTH AMERICA
142
Ascension
62
WESTERN SOUTH AMERICA
140
St Helena
62
SOUTH AMERICA
Pitcairn Island
60
Easter Island
60
THE PACIFIC OCEAN
60
THE ATLANTIC OCEAN
62
Juan Fernández Islands
60
SOUTHERN SOUTH AMERICA
144
Tristan da Cunha
62

SCANDINAVIA
84
NORTHEASTERN EUROPE
98
THE BRITISH ISLES
76
THE LOW COUNTRIES
82
NORTHERN CENTRAL EUROPE
92
GERMANY
86
CENTRAL EASTERN EUROPE
100
THE ALPINE NATIONS
88
FRANCE
78
WESTERN BALKANS
94
THE IBERIAN PENINSULA
80
ITALY AND MALTA
90
EASTERN BALKANS
96

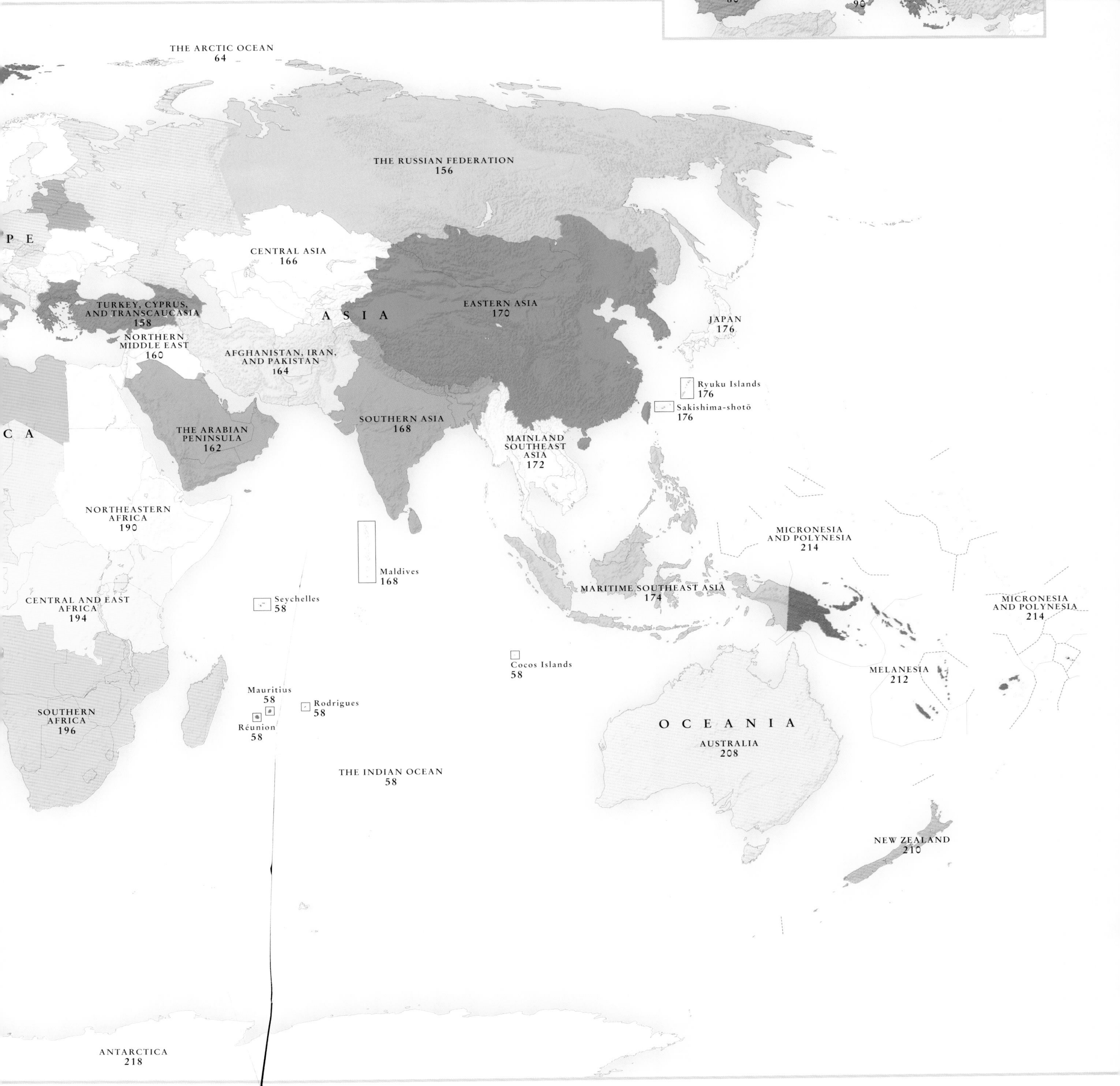
THE ARCTIC OCEAN
64
THE RUSSIAN FEDERATION
156
P E
CENTRAL ASIA
166
TURKEY, CYPRUS, AND TRANSCAUCASIA
158
A S I A
EASTERN ASIA
170
JAPAN
176
NORTHERN MIDDLE EAST
160
AFGHANISTAN, IRAN, AND PAKISTAN
164
Ryuku Islands
176
Sakishima-shotō
176
C A
THE ARABIAN PENINSULA
162
SOUTHERN ASIA
168
MAINLAND SOUTHEAST ASIA
172
NORTHEASTERN AFRICA
190
MICRONESIA AND POLYNESIA
214
Maldives
168
MARITIME SOUTHEAST ASIA
174
CENTRAL AND EAST AFRICA
194
Seychelles
58
MICRONESIA AND POLYNESIA
214
Cocos Islands
58
MELANESIA
212
Mauritius
58
Rodrigues
58
SOUTHERN AFRICA
196
Réunion
58
O C E A N I A
AUSTRALIA
208
THE INDIAN OCEAN
58
NEW ZEALAND
210
ANTARCTICA
218

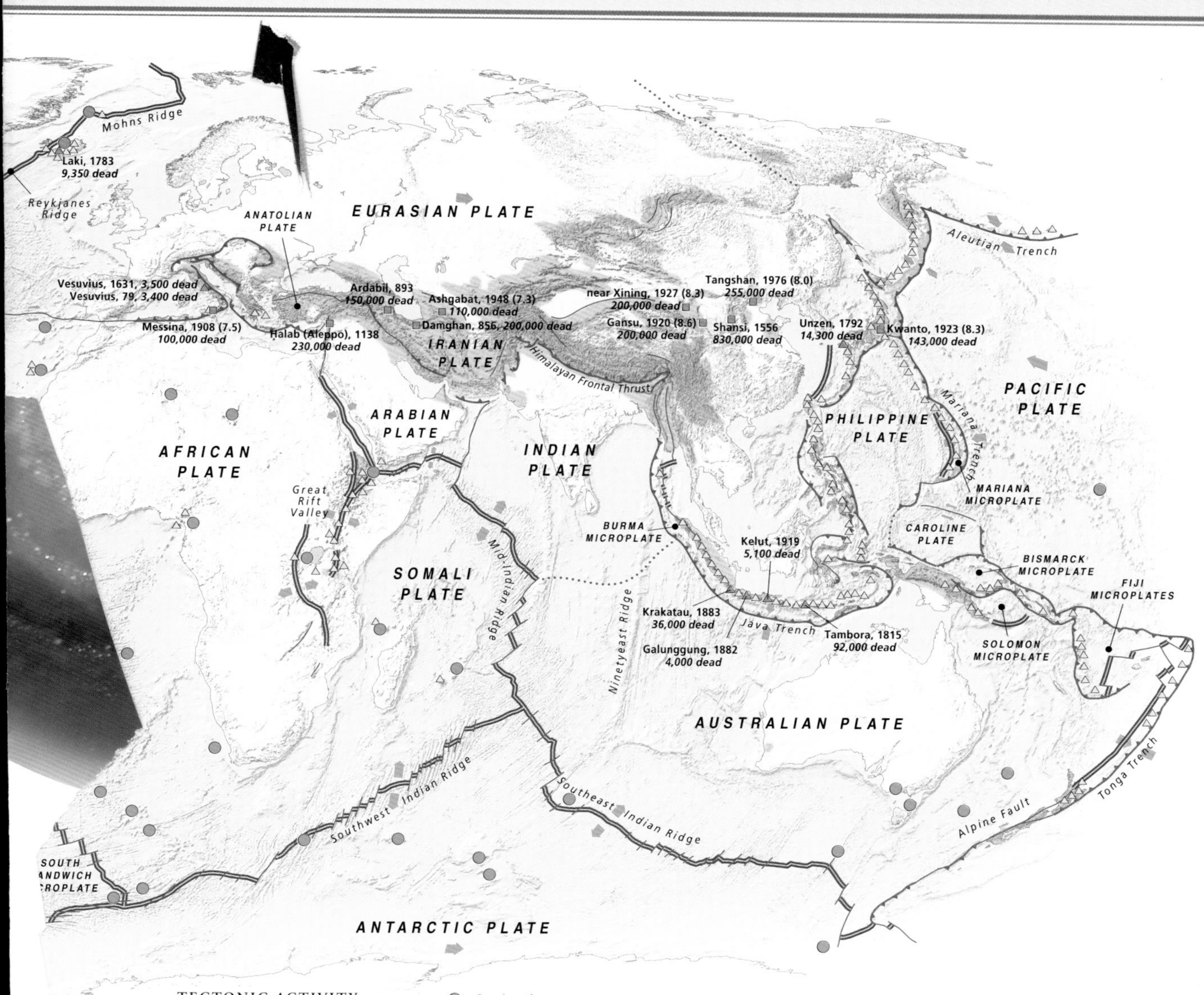

Mohns Ridge
Laki, 1783
9,350 dead
Reykjanes Ridge
ANATOLIAN PLATE
EURASIAN PLATE
Aleutian Trench
Vesuvius, 1631, 3,500 dead
Vesuvius, 79, 3,400 dead
Ardabil, 893
150,000 dead
Ashgabat, 1948 (7.3)
110,000 dead
near Xining, 1927 (8.3)
200,000 dead
Tangshan, 1976 (8.0)
255,000 dead
Messina, 1908 (7.5)
100,000 dead
Halab (Aleppo), 1138
230,000 dead
Damghan, 856, 200,000 dead
Gansu, 1920 (8.6)
200,000 dead
Shansi, 1556
830,000 dead
Unzen, 1792
14,300 dead
Kwanto, 1923 (8.3)
143,000 dead
IRANIAN PLATE
Himalayan Frontal Thrust
PACIFIC PLATE
ARABIAN PLATE
AFRICAN PLATE
INDIAN PLATE
PHILIPPINE PLATE
Mariana Trench
MARIANA MICROPLATE
Great Rift Valley
BURMA MICROPLATE
Kelut, 1919
5,100 dead
CAROLINE PLATE
BISMARCK MICROPLATE
FIJI MICROPLATES
SOMALI PLATE
Mid-Indian Ridge
Ninetyeast Ridge
Krakatau, 1883
36,000 dead
Java Trench
Tambora, 1815
92,000 dead
Galunggung, 1882
4,000 dead
SOLOMON MICROPLATE
AUSTRALIAN PLATE
Tonga Trench
Southwest Indian Ridge
Southeast Indian Ridge
Alpine Fault
SOUTH SANDWICH MICROPLATE
ANTARCTIC PLATE

TECTONIC ACTIVITY

- Earthquake zone
- Deadliest earthquakes: Location, year (magnitude, where known), *number dead*
- Volcanic zone
- Deadliest volcanoes: Location, year, *number dead*
- Prominent hot spot
- Convergent margin
- Divergent margin
- Transform fault
- Diffuse or uncertain
- Direction of movement

50 million years from now
The Atlantic widens, the Mediterranean vanishes as Africa and Europe join up, Australia and Southeast Asia collide, and California slides up to Alaska.

The Story of Earth

About 4.6 billion years ago, Earth formed with the rest of the solar system from a swirling cloud of dust and gas. Since then, our planet has been in a state of flux. The theory of plate tectonics explains how the continents have drifted and altered over millions of years to reach their present state, and how they will continue to change in the future.

The Rock Cycle

Earth's crust features three kinds of rock. Igneous rocks, such as granite and basalt, form when molten magma either cools below ground, or erupts as lava and cools at the surface. Sedimentary rocks, such as sandstone and limestone, are made from mud, silt, or sand broken down from other rocks, or from organic matter such as shells. Metamorphic rocks, such as marble and slate, are rocks that have been altered by heat or pressure. Earth's rocks constantly transform as they are processed through the rock cycle.

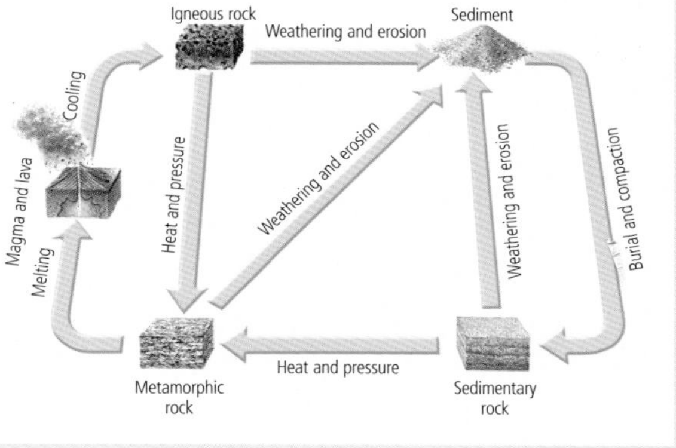

Igneous rock
Weathering and erosion
Sediment
Cooling
Magma and lava
Melting
Heat and pressure
Weathering and erosion
Weathering and erosion
Burial and compaction
Metamorphic rock
Heat and pressure
Sedimentary rock

Sliding plates
At transform boundaries, two plates slide horizontally past each other. California's San Andreas Fault is a transform boundary on land, but most such faults are in the ocean.

Continental rift
When two continental plates move apart at a divergent boundary, a wide valley, such as Africa's Great Rift Valley, is formed. Eventually, such a rift may be flooded by water from a nearby ocean and become a new sea.

Folding crust
When two continental plates collide, neither is subducted. Instead, the crusts buckle, forming high mountains such as the Himalayas.

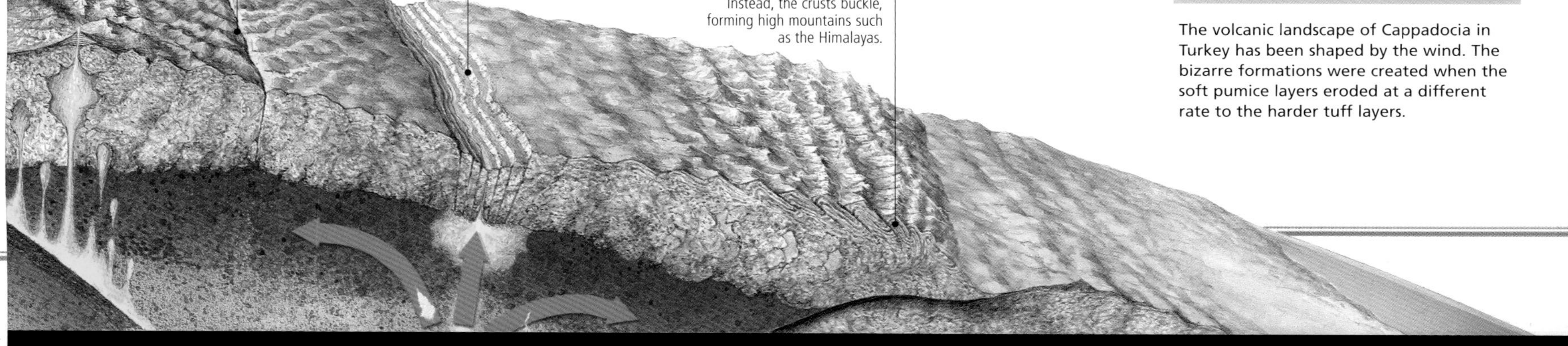

The Forces of Erosion

As wind and water move across the landscape, they wear down rocks and carry away the sediment, gradually reshaping Earth's surface. Water can flow through the terrain in rivers, seep underground through rocks, inch downhill in frozen form as glaciers, or crash along the coast as ocean waves. Winds can pick up loose rock particles, carry them long distances, and blast them at the surface. Temperature can also have a dramatic effect, with extremes of heat and cold both causing rocks to crack and split.

Ruth Glacier is one of many glaciers on North America's highest peak, Mount McKinley in Alaska. The ice has gouged out a U-shaped valley as gravity slowly drags it downhill.

The Goosenecks of the San Juan River in Utah, U.S.A., formed when the region was uplifted, boosting the meandering river's ability to carve its path into the rocks.

Off the coast of Victoria, Australia, ocean waves have carved the Twelve Apostles. These impressive rock stacks are islands of hard limestone that have resisted erosion.

The volcanic landscape of Cappadocia in Turkey has been shaped by the wind. The bizarre formations were created when the soft pumice layers eroded at a different rate to the harder tuff layers.

Climate and Weather

The atmosphere that surrounds Earth is in a constant state of flux, subject to variations in temperature, wind, pressure, humidity, and precipitation that collectively create our weather. The long-term pattern of weather in a particular region is known as its climate and depends on three main factors: latitude, altitude, and proximity to the sea.

The world's weather is fueled by the Sun's uneven heating. Because Earth is a sphere, sunlight is more intense and the air is warmer at the Equator than at the poles. Warm air expands and rises, creating an area of low atmospheric pressure. As it rises, the air cools and its water vapor condenses into clouds, often bringing rain. Cold air is heavier and sinks, forming a high-pressure area with clear skies and settled weather. Wind is created when air flows from areas of high pressure to lower-pressure zones. Sometimes "wedges" of cold air, known as cold fronts, push under existing air, forcing it to rise rapidly and resulting in towering clouds and dramatic storms.

Constantly working toward equilibrium, the atmosphere carries warm air from the Equator toward the poles, and cold air toward the Equator. Earth's rotation deflects these air masses, creating complex patterns that are matched by the warm and cold currents in the ocean. The large-scale air and ocean currents determine the world's various climates, while smaller circulations and individual clouds within them bring our day-to-day weather.

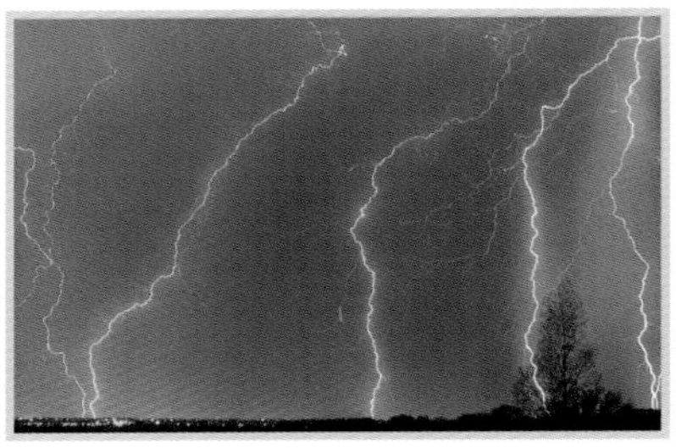

Lightning is an electrical discharge created within a thunderstorm. The heat of the discharge makes the air expand explosively, causing a dramatic clap of thunder.

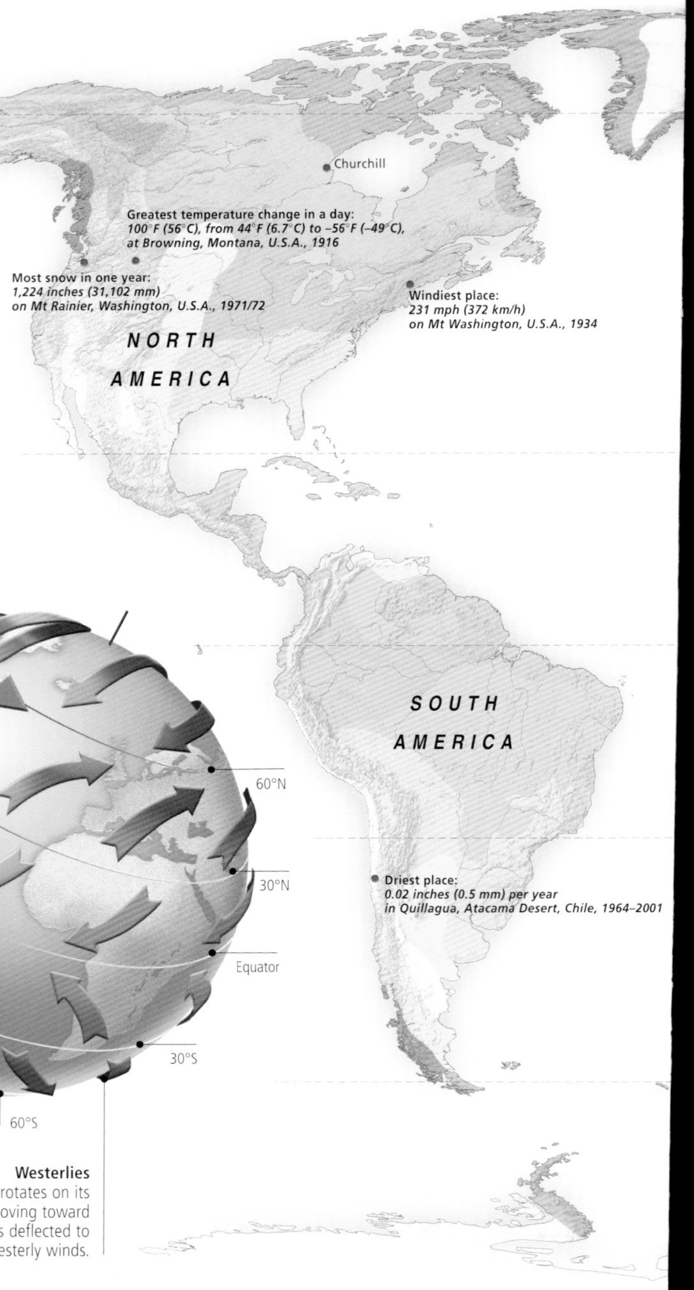

Churchill
Greatest temperature change in a day:
100°F (56°C), from 44°F (6.7°C) to –56°F (–49°C), at Browning, Montana, U.S.A., 1916
Most snow in one year:
1,224 inches (31,102 mm) on Mt Rainier, Washington, U.S.A., 1971/72
Windiest place:
231 mph (372 km/h) on Mt Washington, U.S.A., 1934
NORTH AMERICA
SOUTH AMERICA
Driest place:
0.02 inches (0.5 mm) per year in Quillagua, Atacama Desert, Chile, 1964–2001

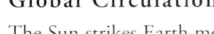

A tornado is a spinning column of air that extends from a thundercloud to the ground. Its powerful winds can exceed speeds of 300 mph (480 km/h).

Global Circulation

The Sun strikes Earth more directly near the Equator than at the poles. The warm air of the tropics rises and moves toward the colder polar regions, then cools and sinks at about 30 degrees north and south latitude. Most of it travels back toward the Equator, but some continues to move poleward until it meets cold polar air at about 60 degrees north and south.

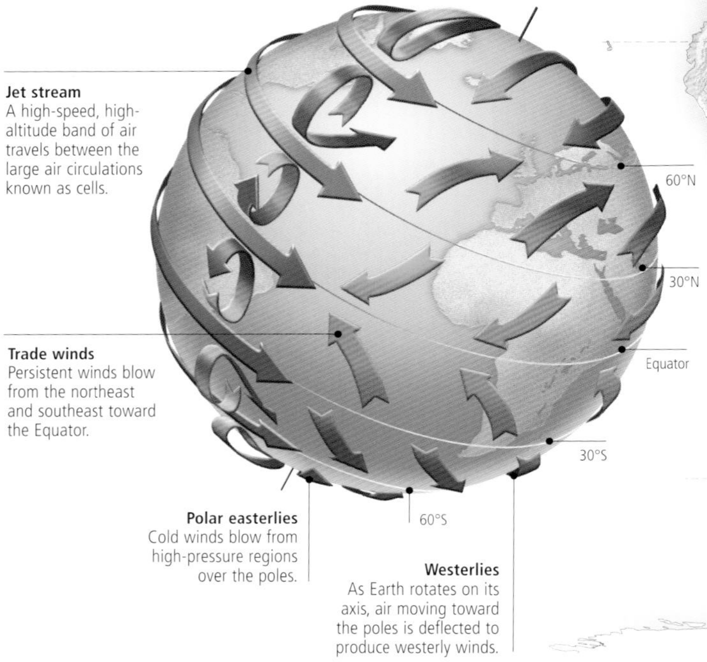

Jet stream
A high-speed, high-altitude band of air travels between the large air circulations known as cells.
60°N
30°N
Equator
30°S
60°S
Trade winds
Persistent winds blow from the northeast and southeast toward the Equator.
Polar easterlies
Cold winds blow from high-pressure regions over the poles.
Westerlies
As Earth rotates on its axis, air moving toward the poles is deflected to produce westerly winds.

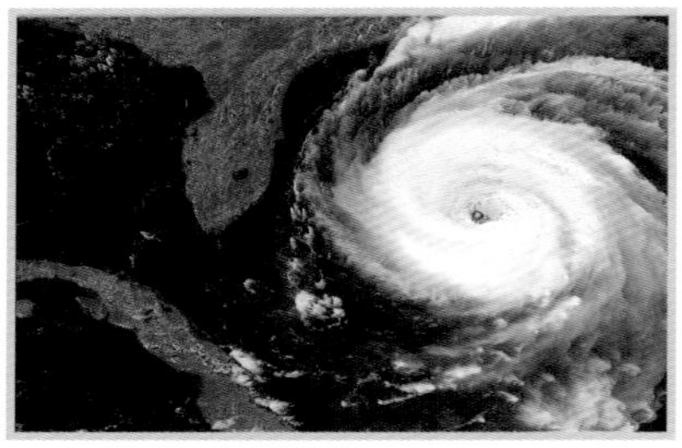

The heat of the tropics can be dispersed to the middle latitudes by tropical storm systems known as cyclones, typhoons, or hurricanes. Hurricane Fran (pictured) hit North Carolina in 1996.

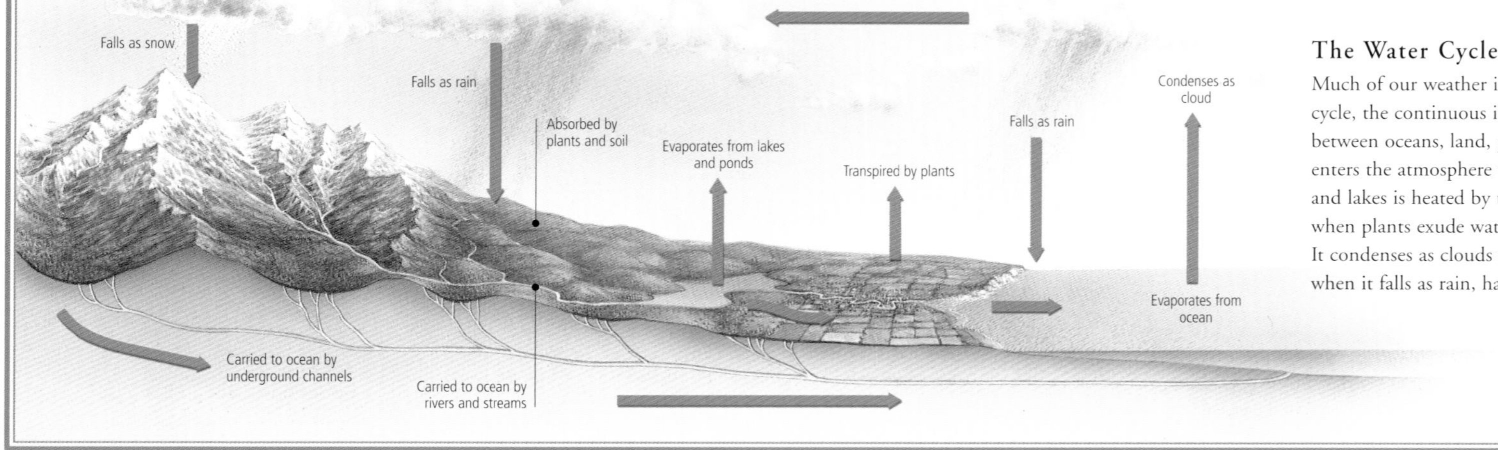

Falls as snow
Falls as rain
Absorbed by plants and soil
Evaporates from lakes and ponds
Transpired by plants
Falls as rain
Condenses as cloud
Evaporates from ocean
Carried to ocean by underground channels
Carried to ocean by rivers and streams

The Water Cycle

Much of our weather is generated by the water cycle, the continuous interchange of moisture between oceans, land, plants, and clouds. Moisture enters the atmosphere when water in oceans, rivers, and lakes is heated by the Sun and evaporates, and when plants exude water as part of photosynthesis. It condenses as clouds and returns to Earth's surface when it falls as rain, hail, or snow.

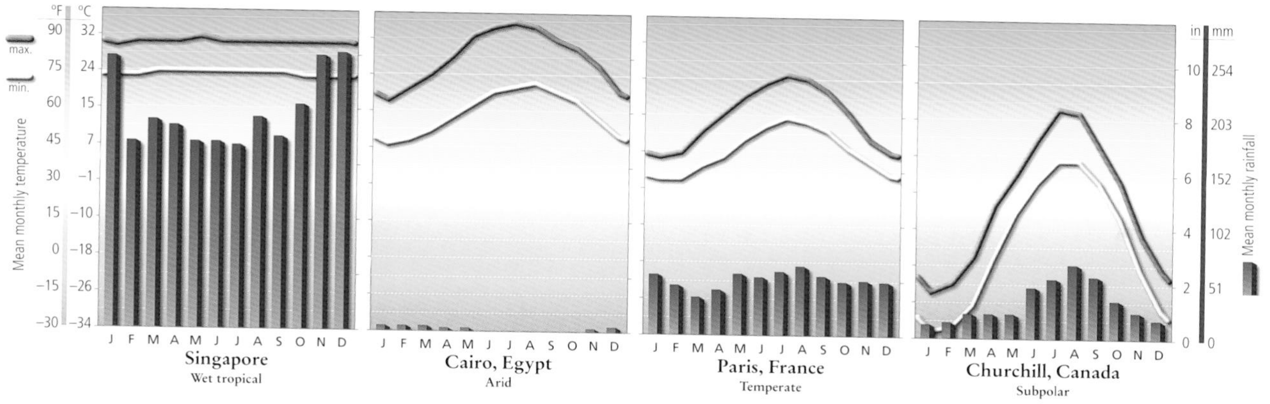
°F °C
max.
min.
Mean monthly temperature
in mm
Mean monthly rainfall
J F M A M J J A S O N D
Singapore
Wet tropical
Cairo, Egypt
Arid
Paris, France
Temperate
Churchill, Canada
Subpolar

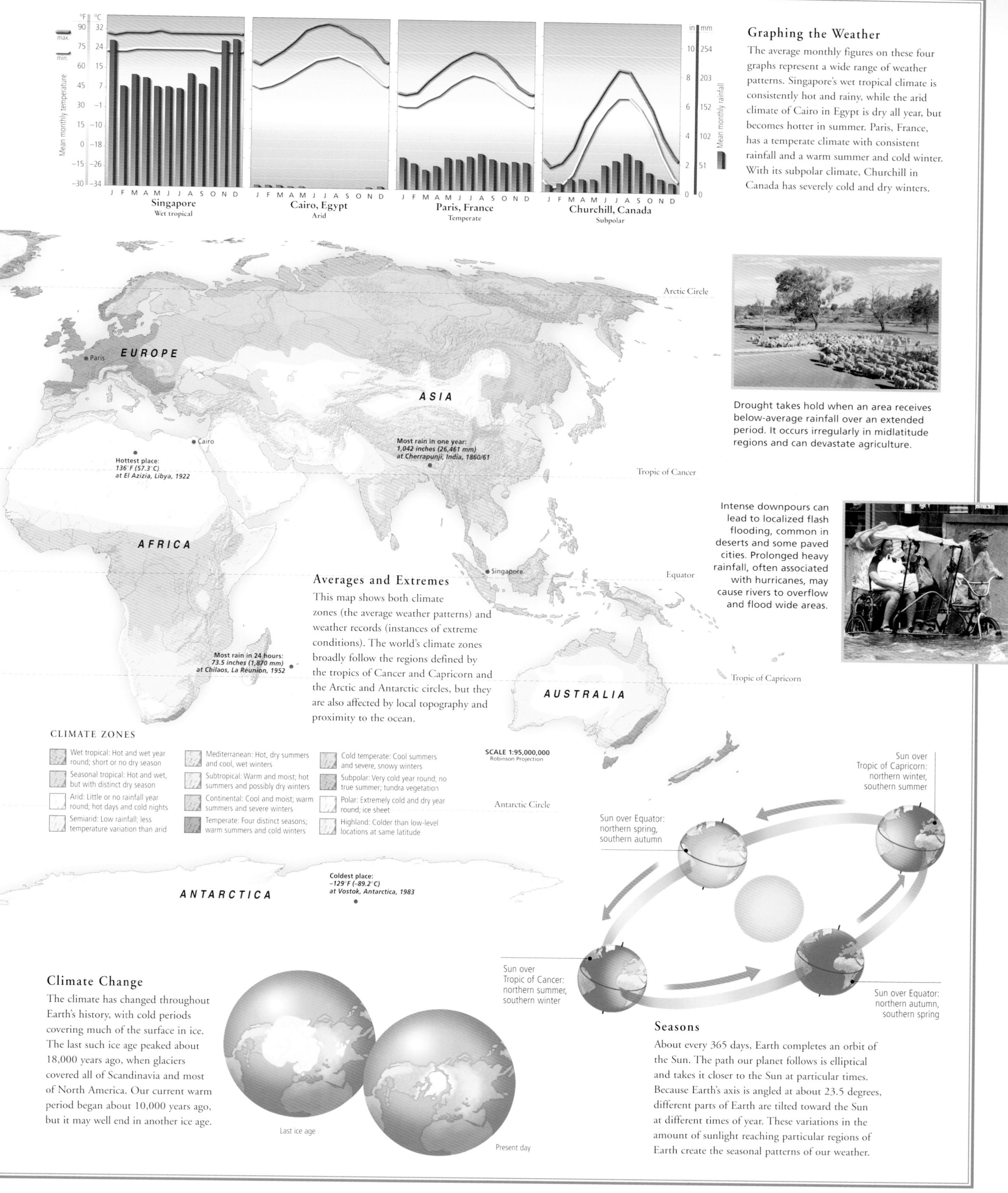

Graphing the Weather

The average monthly figures on these four graphs represent a wide range of weather patterns. Singapore's wet tropical climate is consistently hot and rainy, while the arid climate of Cairo in Egypt is dry all year, but becomes hotter in summer. Paris, France, has a temperate climate with consistent rainfall and a warm summer and cold winter. With its subpolar climate, Churchill in Canada has severely cold and dry winters.

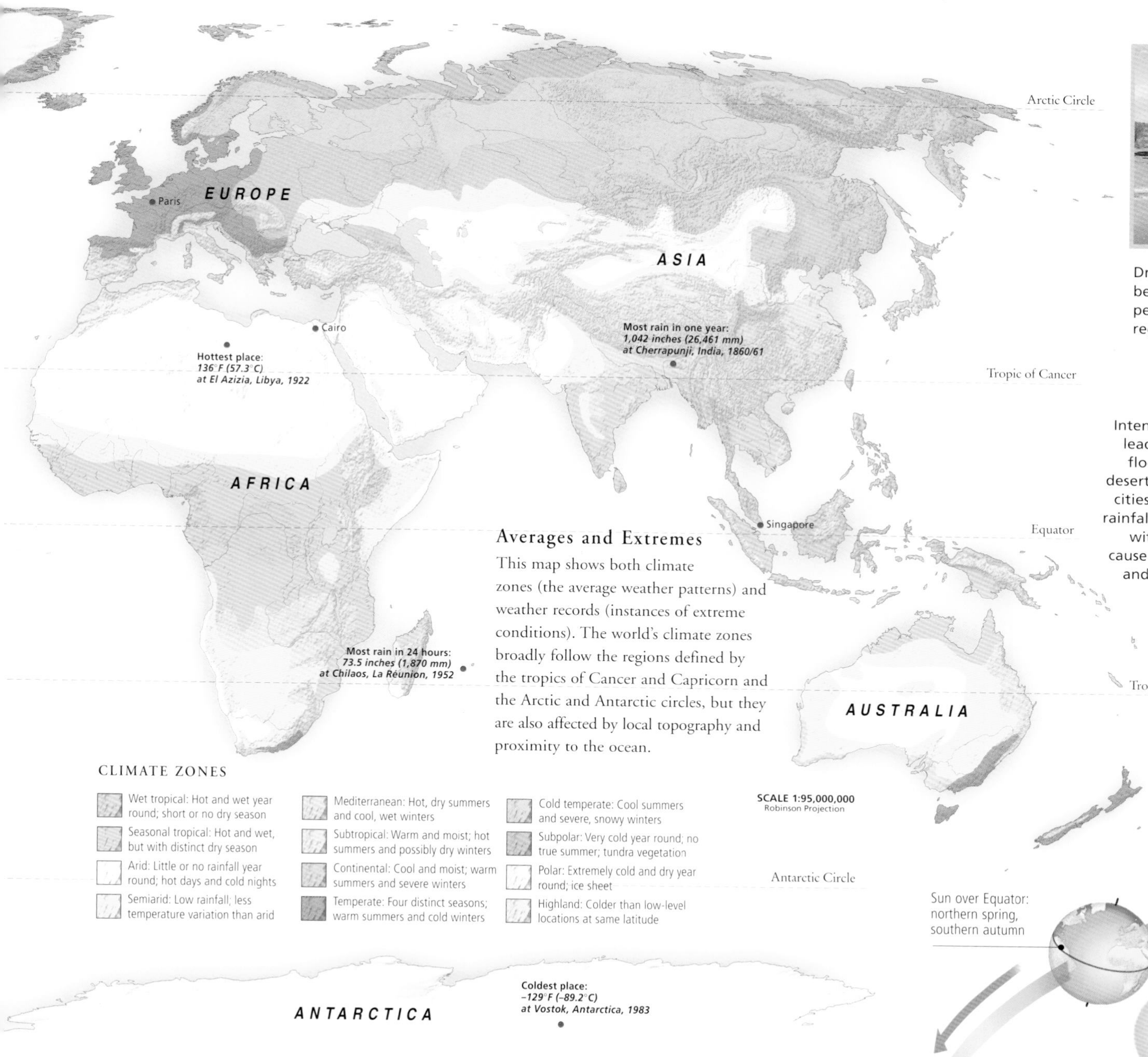
EUROPE
Paris
ASIA
AFRICA
AUSTRALIA
ANTARCTICA
Cairo
Singapore
Arctic Circle
Tropic of Cancer
Equator
Tropic of Capricorn
Antarctic Circle
Hottest place:
136°F (57.3°C)
at El Azizia, Libya, 1922
Most rain in one year:
1,042 inches (26,461 mm)
at Cherrapunji, India, 1860/61
Most rain in 24 hours:
73.5 inches (1,870 mm)
at Chilaos, La Réunion, 1952
Coldest place:
−129°F (−89.2°C)
at Vostok, Antarctica, 1983
SCALE 1:95,000,000
Robinson Projection
CLIMATE ZONES
Wet tropical: Hot and wet year round; short or no dry season
Seasonal tropical: Hot and wet, but with distinct dry season
Arid: Little or no rainfall year round; hot days and cold nights
Semiarid: Low rainfall; less temperature variation than arid
Mediterranean: Hot, dry summers and cool, wet winters
Subtropical: Warm and moist; hot summers and possibly dry winters
Continental: Cool and moist; warm summers and severe winters
Temperate: Four distinct seasons; warm summers and cold winters
Cold temperate: Cool summers and severe, snowy winters
Subpolar: Very cold year round; no true summer; tundra vegetation
Polar: Extremely cold and dry year round; ice sheet
Highland: Colder than low-level locations at same latitude

Averages and Extremes

This map shows both climate zones (the average weather patterns) and weather records (instances of extreme conditions). The world's climate zones broadly follow the regions defined by the tropics of Cancer and Capricorn and the Arctic and Antarctic circles, but they are also affected by local topography and proximity to the ocean.

Drought takes hold when an area receives below-average rainfall over an extended period. It occurs irregularly in midlatitude regions and can devastate agriculture.

Intense downpours can lead to localized flash flooding, common in deserts and some paved cities. Prolonged heavy rainfall, often associated with hurricanes, may cause rivers to overflow and flood wide areas.

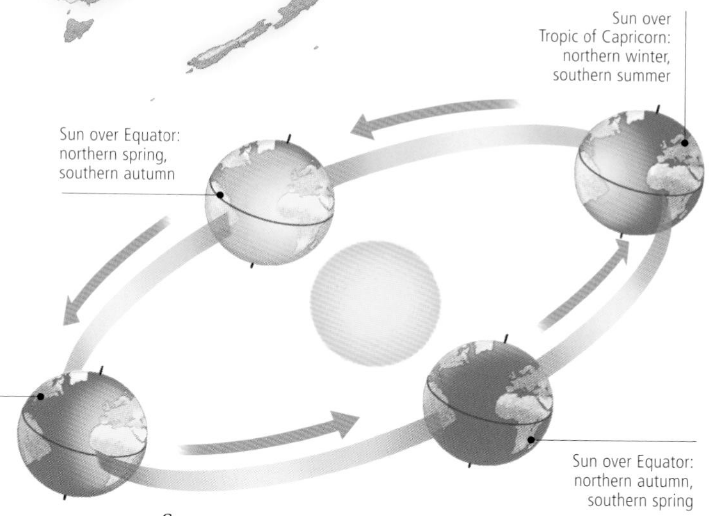
Sun over Tropic of Capricorn: northern winter, southern summer
Sun over Equator: northern spring, southern autumn
Sun over Tropic of Cancer: northern summer, southern winter
Sun over Equator: northern autumn, southern spring

Seasons

About every 365 days, Earth completes an orbit of the Sun. The path our planet follows is elliptical and takes it closer to the Sun at particular times. Because Earth's axis is angled at about 23.5 degrees, different parts of Earth are tilted toward the Sun at different times of year. These variations in the amount of sunlight reaching particular regions of Earth create the seasonal patterns of our weather.

Climate Change

The climate has changed throughout Earth's history, with cold periods covering much of the surface in ice. The last such ice age peaked about 18,000 years ago, when glaciers covered all of Scandinavia and most of North America. Our current warm period began about 10,000 years ago, but it may well end in another ice age.

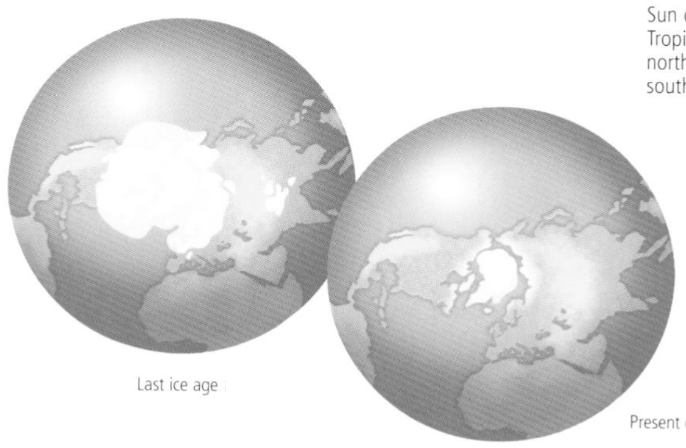
Last ice age
Present day

The Web of Life

Pummeled by comets and meteorites and wracked by volcanic eruptions, the young Earth would have seemed a hostile place. All this activity, however, released chemicals that formed the early atmosphere and oceans, and, eventually, life itself. Scientists believe that life appeared on Earth at least 3.8 billion years ago in the form of anaerobic bacteria, simple cells that can survive without oxygen. Such bacteria still exist around volcanic vents on the deep ocean floor. By about 3.5 billion years ago, cyanobacteria had evolved and were using photosynthesis, the process in which plants convert carbon dioxide and water into food and release oxygen as a by-product. The increased oxygen levels in the oceans and atmosphere allowed more complex organisms to develop and eventually colonize almost every part of our planet's surface.

The biosphere is the space occupied by living organisms. It includes Earth's land, oceans, and atmosphere and contains a great range of environments, from the frigid zones near the poles to the perpetually warm and moist equatorial regions. Life is exceptionally tenacious and has evolved to fill every possible niche within these environments. Charles Darwin's theory of natural selection explains how the individual organisms best suited to their environment survive and pass on the features that favored their survival to the next generation. Over many hundreds of generations, these inherited features are amplified until they create species that seem perfectly adapted to their surroundings. This process is considered responsible for the staggering diversity of life on Earth today.

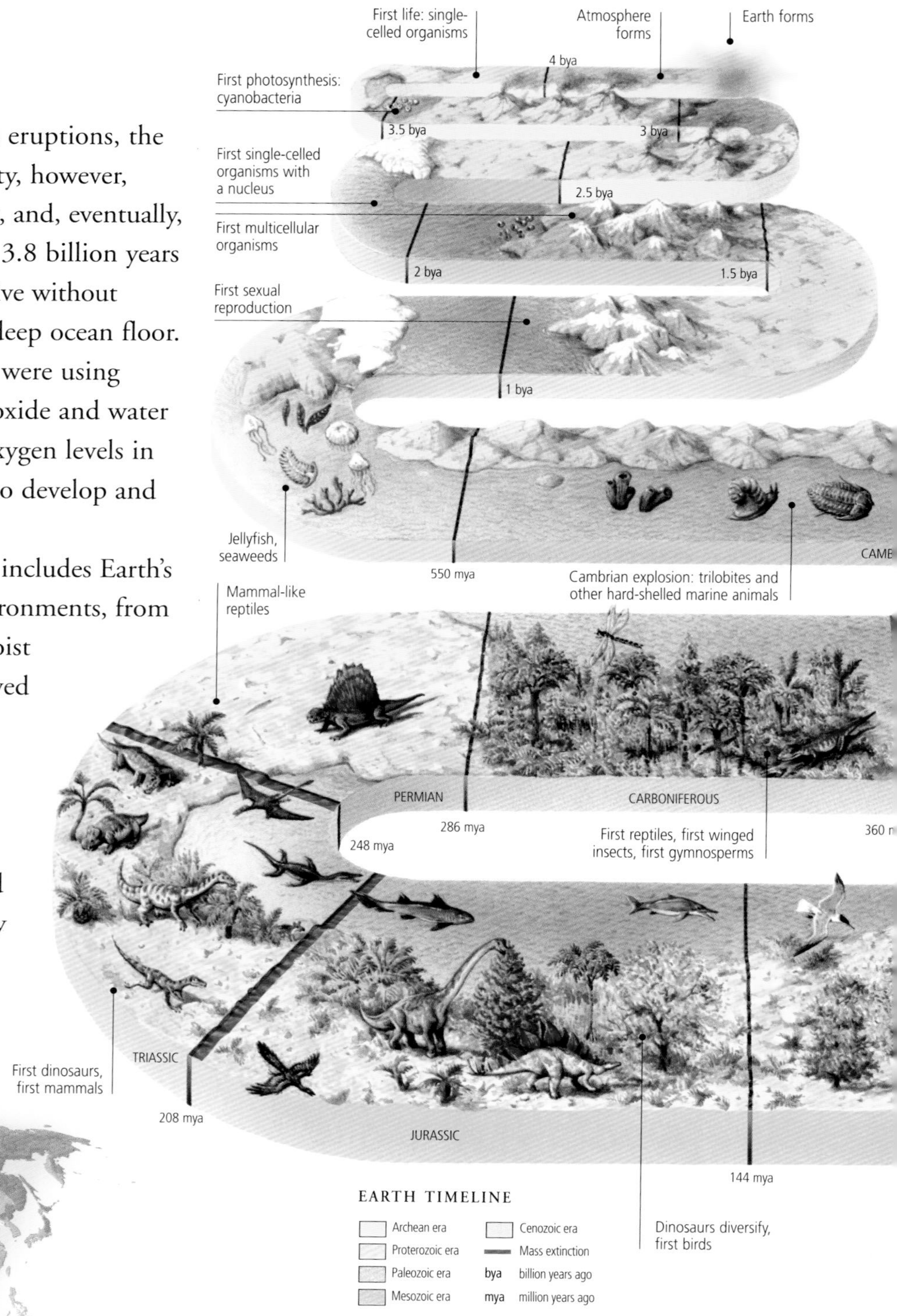
First life: single-celled organisms
Atmosphere forms
Earth forms
4 bya
First photosynthesis: cyanobacteria
3.5 bya
3 bya
First single-celled organisms with a nucleus
2.5 bya
First multicellular organisms
2 bya
1.5 bya
First sexual reproduction
1 bya
Jellyfish, seaweeds
550 mya
Cambrian explosion: trilobites and other hard-shelled marine animals
CAMB
Mammal-like reptiles
PERMIAN
CARBONIFEROUS
286 mya
248 mya
First reptiles, first winged insects, first gymnosperms
360 m
TRIASSIC
First dinosaurs, first mammals
208 mya
JURASSIC
144 mya
Dinosaurs diversify, first birds
EARTH TIMELINE
Archean era
Proterozoic era
Paleozoic era
Mesozoic era
Cenozoic era
Mass extinction
bya billion years ago
mya million years ago

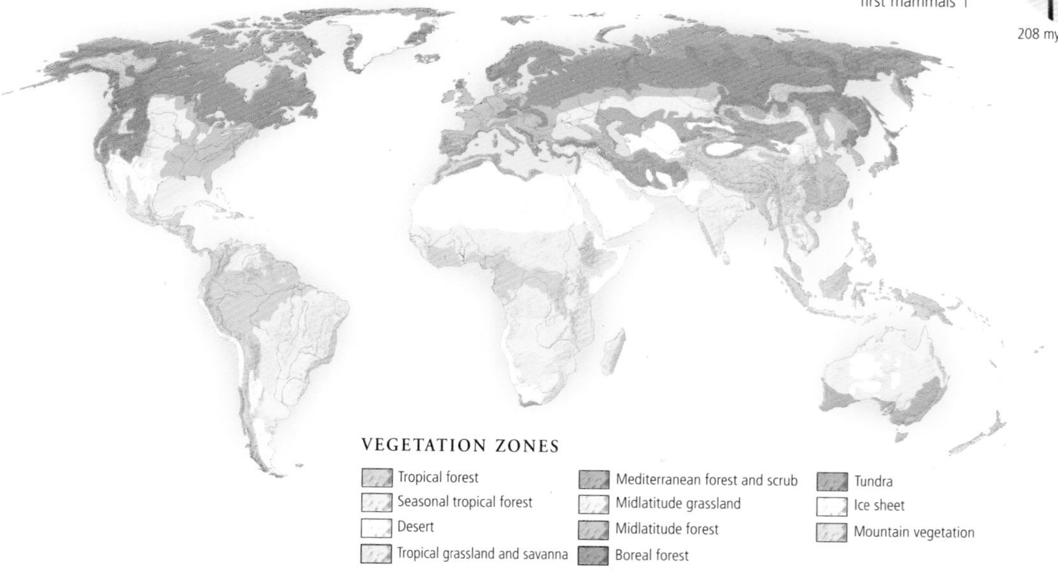
VEGETATION ZONES
Tropical forest
Seasonal tropical forest
Desert
Tropical grassland and savanna
Mediterranean forest and scrub
Midlatitude grassland
Midlatitude forest
Boreal forest
Tundra
Ice sheet
Mountain vegetation

Natural Vegetation

This map (left) shows the vegetation that would occur naturally without human interference. Climate and soil determine the vegetation of an area, and the vegetation, in turn, determines the animal life. Together, the plants and animals of each zone form an ecological community known as a biome. In addition to these terrestrial zones, freshwater and marine biomes contain much of Earth's biodiversity.

Desert species must cope with a scarcity of water, and extremes of heat by day and cold by night. Scorpions can tolerate a body temperature of 122°F (50°C).

Without seasonal fires and grazing by large animals such as elephants, grasslands would be either choked by a build-up of thatch or colonized by woody plants.

The constant warmth and rainfall of the tropics give rise to the world's greatest biodiversity. Amphibians such as tree frogs flourish in lush tropical rain forests.

The temperate climate of midlatitude forests features warm summers and cold winters. To deal with winter, the monarch butterfly migrates to warmer locations.

Freshwater habitats include rivers and streams, ponds and lakes, swamps and marshes. The semi-aquatic false gharial uses water as cover for hunting.

From giant whales to minuscule plankton, the oceans are home to a diverse range of life. The clownfish and the sea anemone protect each other from predators.

Antarctica's emperor penguins deal with the extreme cold of their polar home by huddling together in large colonies and raising their young in summer.

Biodiversity

Life's long history has led to its incredible variety. The map below shows each country's biodiversity level for vertebrates and advanced plants, based on both the total number of species and the number that are endemic (found nowhere else). Species richness increases toward the Equator, with tropical forests home to most of the world's species.

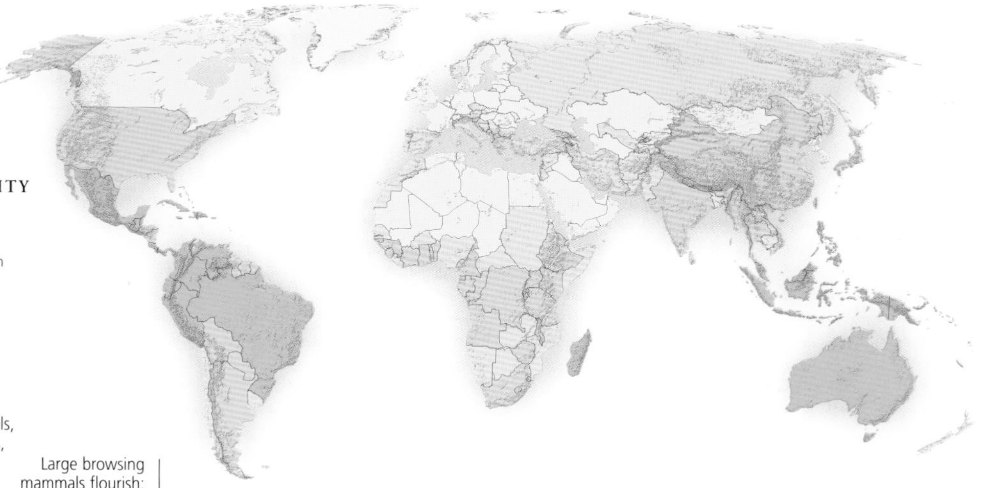

BIODIVERSITY LEVELS
Highest
Medium high
Medium
Medium low
Lowest

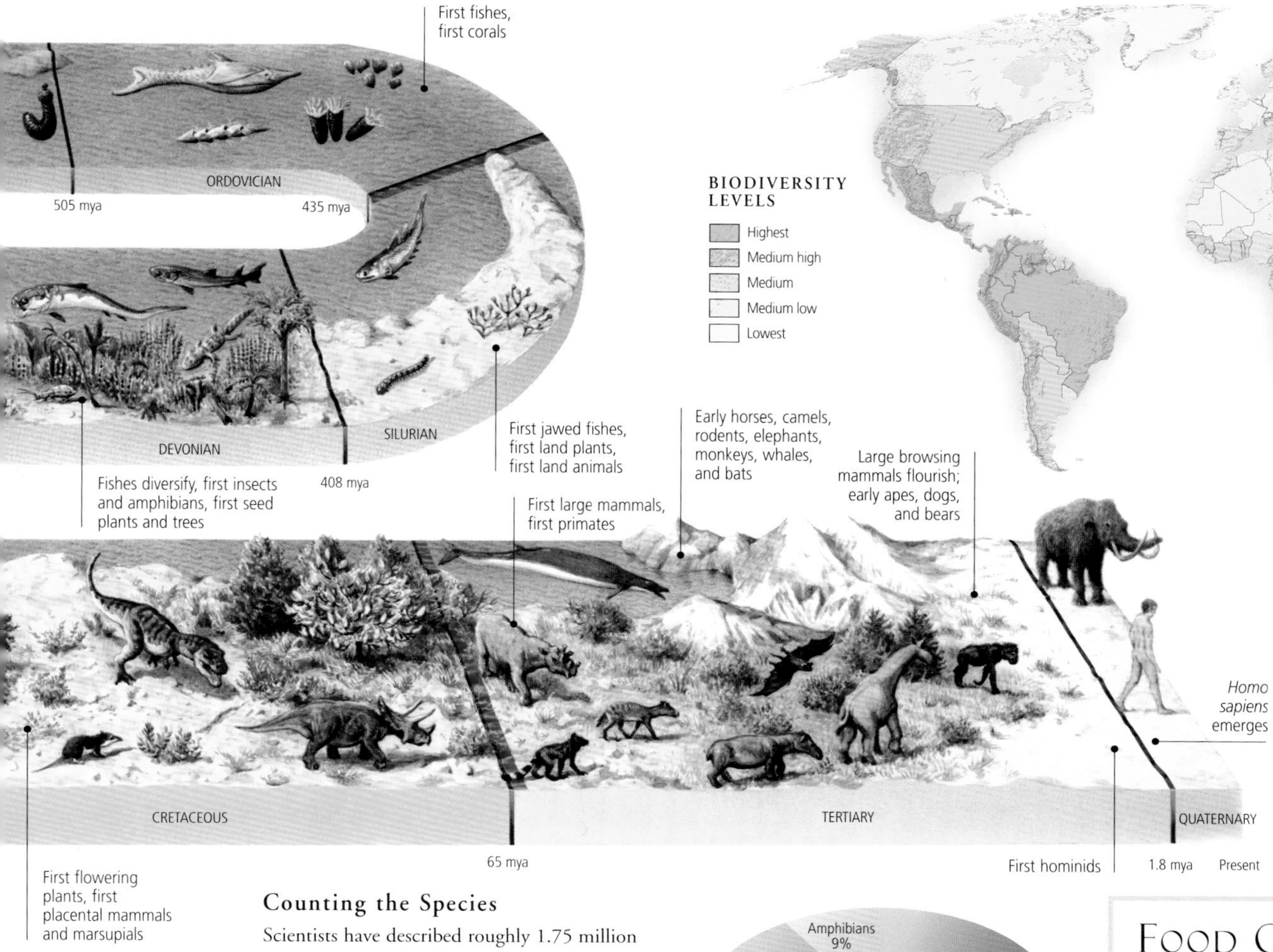

First fishes, first corals
ORDOVICIAN
505 mya
435 mya
DEVONIAN
SILURIAN
408 mya
Fishes diversify, first insects and amphibians, first seed plants and trees
First jawed fishes, first land plants, first land animals
Early horses, camels, rodents, elephants, monkeys, whales, and bats
Large browsing mammals flourish; early apes, dogs, and bears
First large mammals, first primates
Homo sapiens emerges
CRETACEOUS
TERTIARY
QUATERNARY
65 mya
First hominids
1.8 mya
Present
First flowering plants, first placental mammals and marsupials

A History of Life on Earth

Throughout the past 3.8 billion years, many different species have evolved, thrived, and become extinct. Humans are relative latecomers to the scene and represent merely one of the myriad courses evolution has taken. At various times, Earth has experienced a mass extinction involving most of its existing species. The most dramatic occurred at the end of the Permian period, when 96 percent of all species disappeared, while the one at the conclusion of the Cretaceous period included the dinosaurs.

Counting the Species

Scientists have described roughly 1.75 million species, but that is only a small proportion of the estimated 14 million species of life on Earth. Even the figures for the number of known species (below) are hard to pin down because new species are being discovered all the time. Vertebrates (right) are the best described group but make up only about 5 percent of animal species.

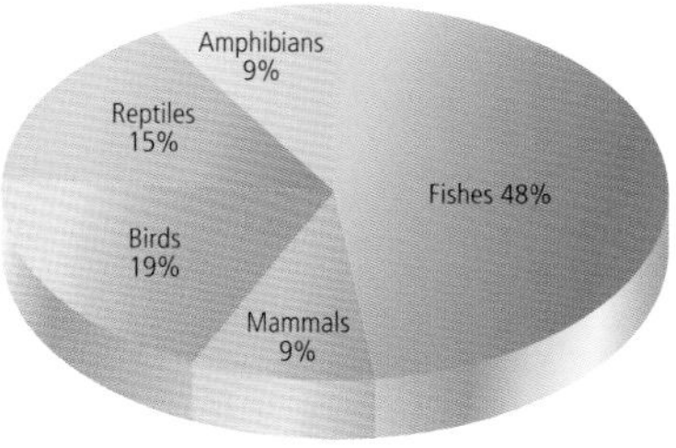

Amphibians 9%
Reptiles 15%
Fishes 48%
Birds 19%
Mammals 9%

Estimated Numbers of Species				
	Estimated number of known species	Working total number of species	Known species as percentage of working total	Estimated accuracy of working total
Viruses	4,000	400,000	1%	Very poor
Bacteria	10,000	1,000,000	1%	Very poor
Protozoa and algae	80,000	600,000	13.3%	Very poor
Vertebrates	52,500	55,000	95.5%	Good
Insects	950,000	8,000,000	12%	Moderate
Arachnids	75,000	750,000	10%	Moderate
Mollusks	70,000	200,000	35%	Moderate
Crustaceans	40,000	150,000	26.7%	Moderate
Roundworms	25,000	400,000	6.3%	Poor
Fungi	72,000	1,500,000	4.8%	Moderate
Plants	270,000	320,000	84.4%	Good

Food Cycle

Within each natural community, energy is transferred among species in a cycle known as a food web. This very simplified food web of an African savanna (below) shows how trees, shrubs, and grasses support herbivores such as the zebra. While alive, the zebra may support parasites such as the tsetse fly, which in turn may be eaten by a bird such as the flycatcher. The zebra may later become prey to a leopard. Scavengers such as the jackal survive on meat left over by carnivores and on the carcasses of herbivores and carnivores that die from illness or injury. Any animal remains not eaten by other animals will decay, slowly broken down by decomposers such as fungi and bacteria into organic matter that enriches the soil and feeds the growth of plants.

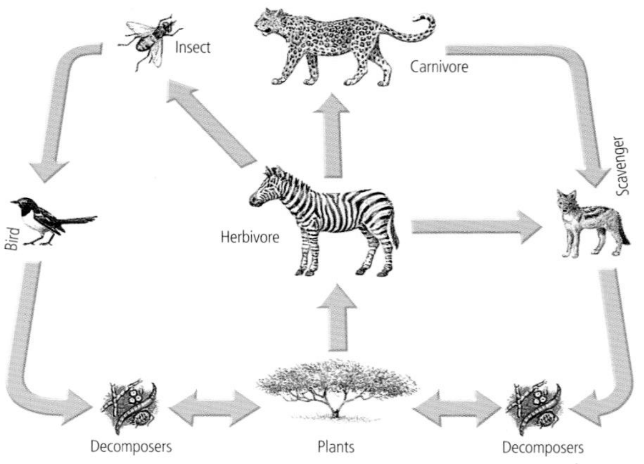

Insect
Carnivore
Scavenger
Bird
Herbivore
Decomposers
Plants
Decomposers

The Advance of Humans

When the world's climate became cooler and drier between 3 million and 2 million years ago, vast areas of grassy plains replaced the lush tropical forests of sub-Saharan Africa. The new environment allowed hominids, a family of upright-walking primates, to evolve and thrive. The first members of the hominid family had branched off from the ape line between 8 million and 6 million years ago, but were probably relatively rare creatures. They walked on two legs, a development that provided a better view of predators and potential meals, and freed the arms to carry young and food and to use tools. The first hominids belonging to our genus, *Homo,* emerged about 2.3 million years ago. The larger brain and toolmaking skills of *Homo* species allowed them to extend their range and move out of Africa perhaps 1.8 million years ago.

Most researchers now agree that our species, modern *Homo sapiens,* evolved in Africa sometime between 200,000 and 100,000 years ago and then gradually migrated to other parts of the world, becoming the first truly global hominids. These anatomically modern humans were distinguished not only by their advanced technology, but perhaps more importantly by their social flexibility, which allowed them to flourish in a wide range of habitats. Recognizably modern behavior emerged at least 40,000 years ago, when evidence for art, ritual, and symbolism begins to accumulate. By 30,000 years ago, *Homo sapiens* was the only remaining hominid species. After the end of the last ice age, about 13,000 years ago, the first transition to settled life and the adoption of agriculture occurred. These developments, in turn, allowed populations to grow and cities and states to form.

Dated to 3.6 million years ago, a trail of footprints at Laetoli, Tanzania, was left by australopithecines walking on two legs.

The spectacular cave paintings of Lascaux, France, were created some 15,000 years ago and represent the peak of ice age art.

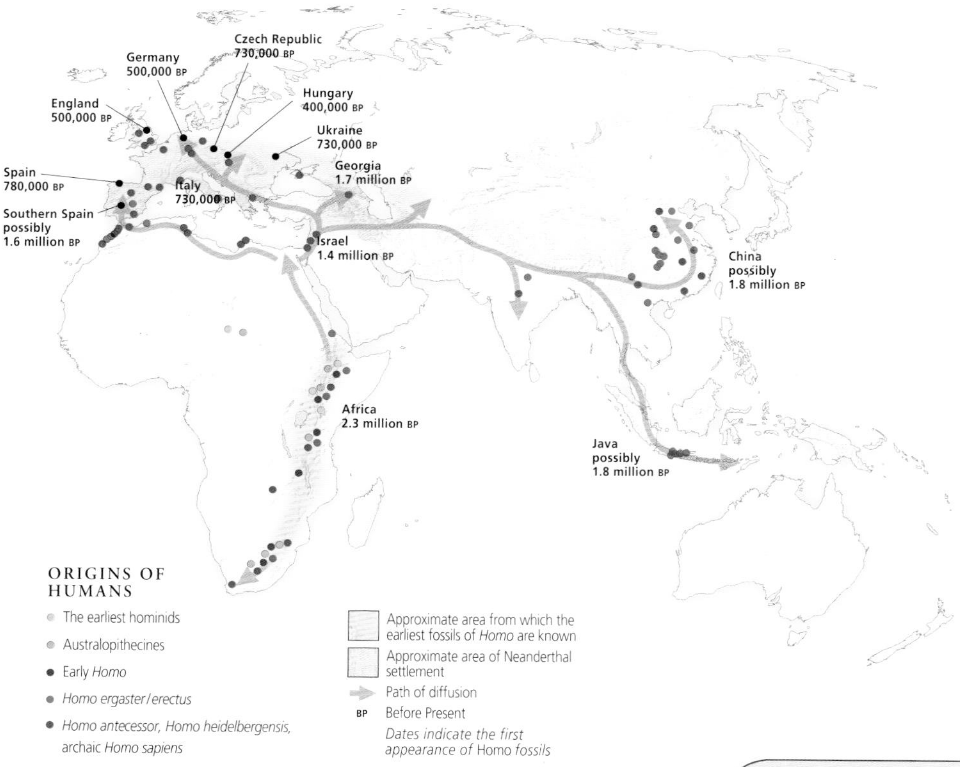

Czech Republic
730,000 BP
Germany
500,000 BP
England
500,000 BP
Hungary
400,000 BP
Ukraine
730,000 BP
Spain
780,000 BP
Italy
730,000 BP
Georgia
1.7 million BP
Southern Spain
possibly
1.6 million BP
Israel
1.4 million BP
China
possibly
1.8 million BP
Africa
2.3 million BP
Java
possibly
1.8 million BP
ORIGINS OF HUMANS
The earliest hominids
Australopithecines
Early *Homo*
Homo ergaster/erectus
Homo antecessor, Homo heidelbergensis, archaic *Homo sapiens*
Approximate area from which the earliest fossils of *Homo* are known
Approximate area of Neanderthal settlement
Path of diffusion
BP Before Present
Dates indicate the first appearance of Homo fossils

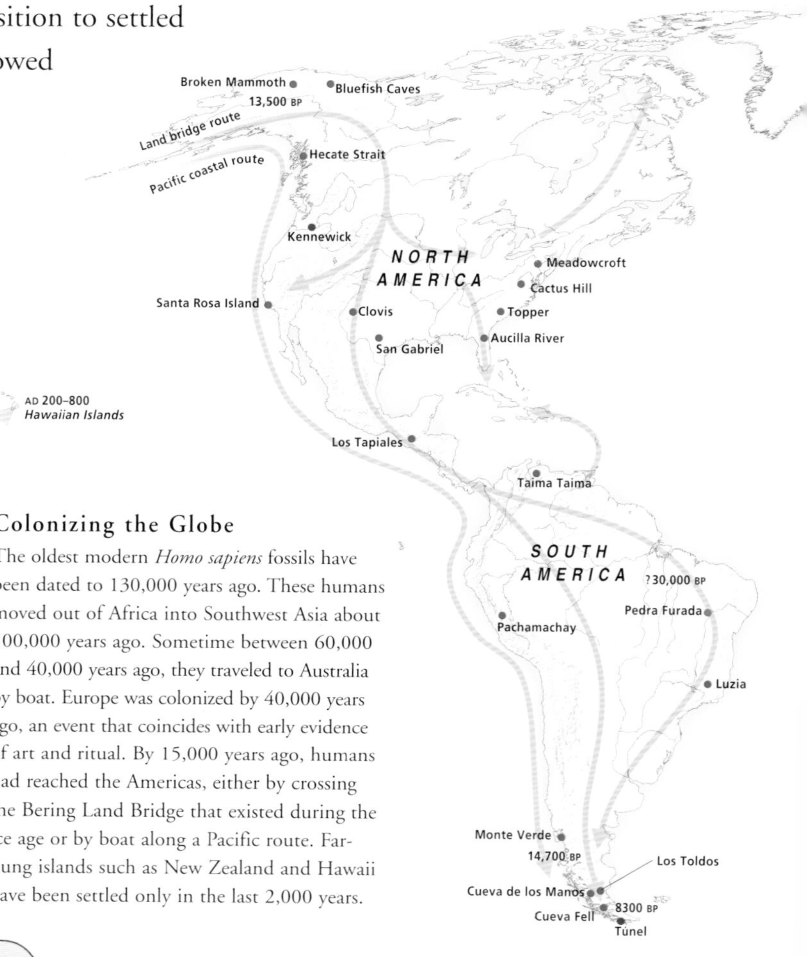

Broken Mammoth
13,500 BP
Bluefish Caves
Land bridge route
Pacific coastal route
Hecate Strait
Kennewick
NORTH AMERICA
Meadowcroft
Cactus Hill
Santa Rosa Island
Clovis
Topper
Aucilla River
San Gabriel
AD 200–800
Hawaiian Islands
Los Tapiales
Taima Taima
SOUTH AMERICA
?30,000 BP
Pedra Furada
Pachamachay
Luzia
Monte Verde
14,700 BP
Los Toldos
Cueva de los Manos
8300 BP
Cueva Fell
Tunel

Colonizing the Globe

The oldest modern *Homo sapiens* fossils have been dated to 130,000 years ago. These humans moved out of Africa into Southwest Asia about 100,000 years ago. Sometime between 60,000 and 40,000 years ago, they traveled to Australia by boat. Europe was colonized by 40,000 years ago, an event that coincides with early evidence of art and ritual. By 15,000 years ago, humans had reached the Americas, either by crossing the Bering Land Bridge that existed during the ice age or by boat along a Pacific route. Far-flung islands such as New Zealand and Hawaii have been settled only in the last 2,000 years.

Hominid Traces

The first hominids evolved in Africa between 8 million and 6 million years ago. Between 4.2 million and 1 million years ago, Africa was home to several kinds of australopithecines, apelike creatures who walked upright and probably used simple tools. The first *Homo* species appeared in Africa about 2.3 million years ago; by 1.8 million years ago, *Homo ergaster* (also known as *Homo erectus*) had moved into Asia. The large-brained *Homo antecessor, Homo heidelbergensis,* and other species of archaic *Homo sapiens* date to between 800,000 and 200,000 years ago. The Neanderthals (*Homo neanderthalensis*) colonized much of Eurasia between 200,000 and 30,000 years ago.

HUMAN DEVELOPMENT

8–6 million BP (BEFORE PRESENT) First hominids

4.2 million BP First australopithecines

Australopithecine "Taung child" *2 million BP*

Oldowan chopper *2 million BP*

2.5 million BP First stone tools (Oldowan)

2.3 million BP Earliest *Homo*

1.9 million BP Early African *Homo ergaster* (also known as *Homo erectus*)

1.8 million BP First early *Homo* outside Africa

1.6 million BP Hand axes (Acheulean)

1.5 million BP *Homo erectus* in Asia

1 million BP First use of fire (Swartkrans Cave, South Africa)

Acheulean hand ax *1.6 million BP*

780,000 BP Archaic *Homo sapiens* (*Homo antecessor*) in Europe

600,000 BP Archaic *Homo sapiens* (*Homo heidelbergensis*) in Africa

500,000 BP Archaic *Homo sapiens* (*Homo heidelbergensis*) in Europe and possibly China

460,000 BP First controlled use of fire (Zhoukoudian, China)

200,000 BP First Neanderthals (*Homo neanderthalensis*)

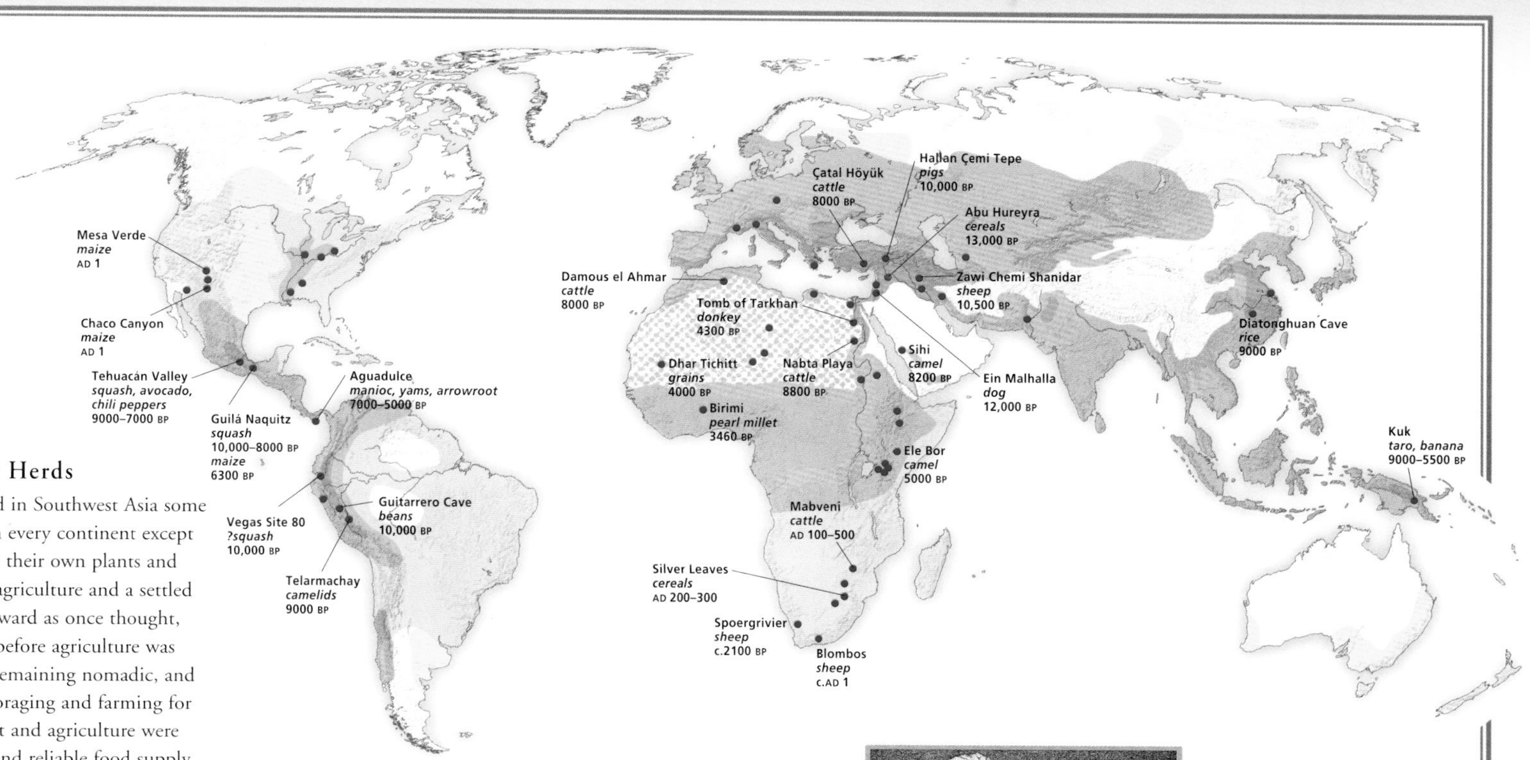

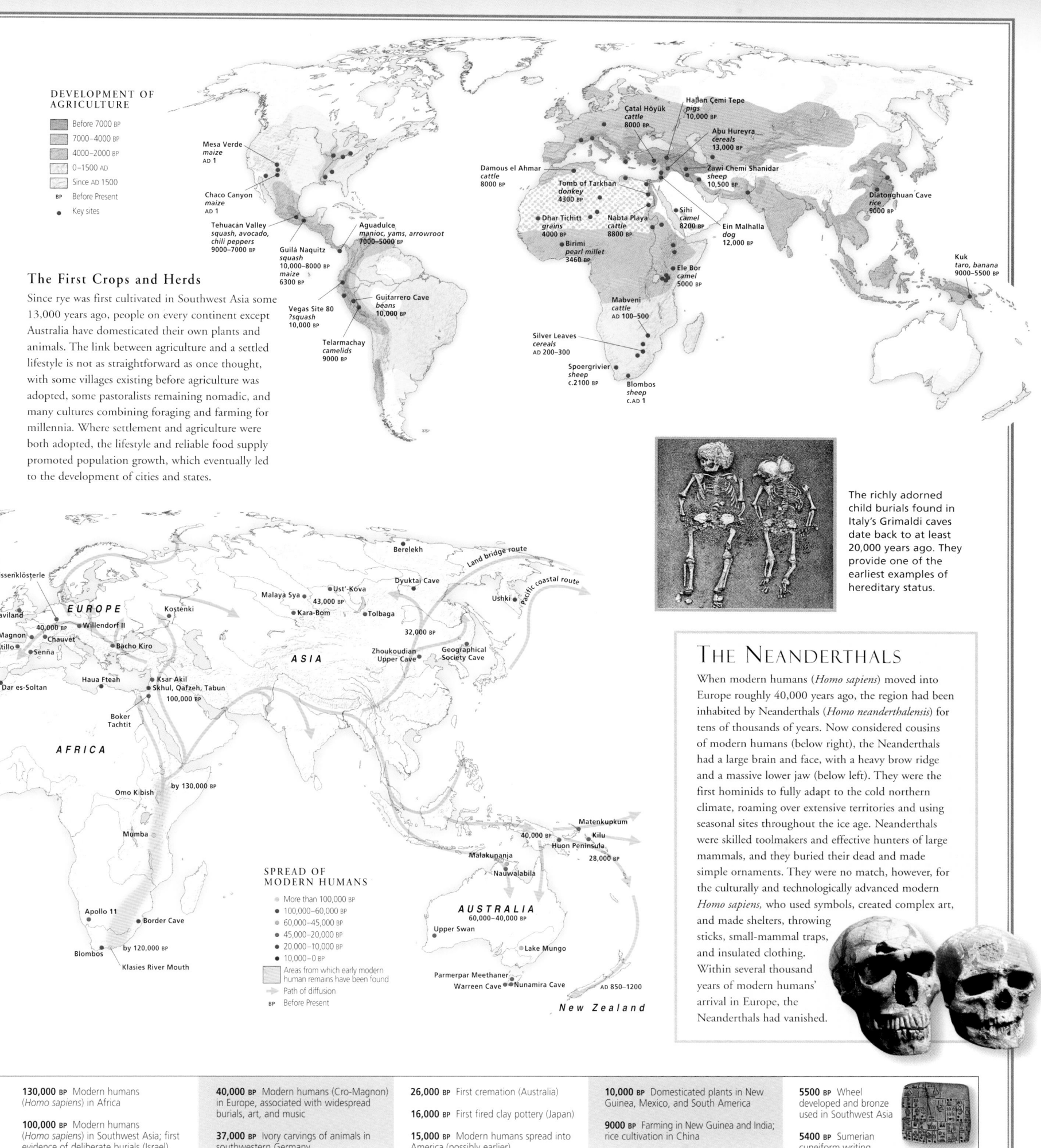

DEVELOPMENT OF AGRICULTURE
Before 7000 BP
7000–4000 BP
4000–2000 BP
0–1500 AD
Since AD 1500
BP Before Present
Key sites
Mesa Verde maize AD 1
Chaco Canyon maize AD 1
Tehuacán Valley squash, avocado, chili peppers 9000–7000 BP
Guilá Naquitz squash 10,000–8000 BP maize 6300 BP
Aguadulce manioc, yams, arrowroot 7000–5000 BP
Vegas Site 80 ?squash 10,000 BP
Guitarrero Cave beans 10,000 BP
Telarmachay camelids 9000 BP
Damous el Ahmar cattle 8000 BP
Tomb of Tarkhan donkey 4300 BP
Dhar Tichitt grains 4000 BP
Nabta Playa cattle 8800 BP
Birimi pearl millet 3460 BP
Çatal Höyük cattle 8000 BP
Hallan Çemi Tepe pigs 10,000 BP
Abu Hureyra cereals 13,000 BP
Zawi Chemi Shanidar sheep 10,500 BP
Sihi camel 8200 BP
Ein Malhalla dog 12,000 BP
Diatonghuan Cave rice 9000 BP
Kuk taro, banana 9000–5500 BP
Ele Bor camel 5000 BP
Mabveni cattle AD 100–500
Silver Leaves cereals AD 200–300
Spoergrivier sheep c.2100 BP
Blombos sheep c.AD 1

The First Crops and Herds

Since rye was first cultivated in Southwest Asia some 13,000 years ago, people on every continent except Australia have domesticated their own plants and animals. The link between agriculture and a settled lifestyle is not as straightforward as once thought, with some villages existing before agriculture was adopted, some pastoralists remaining nomadic, and many cultures combining foraging and farming for millennia. Where settlement and agriculture were both adopted, the lifestyle and reliable food supply promoted population growth, which eventually led to the development of cities and states.

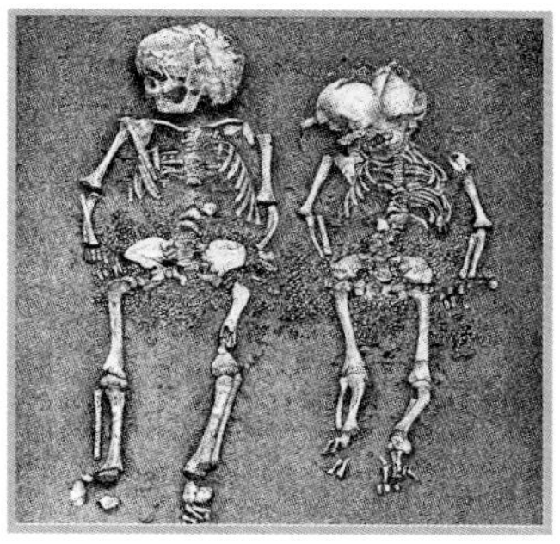

The richly adorned child burials found in Italy's Grimaldi caves date back to at least 20,000 years ago. They provide one of the earliest examples of hereditary status.

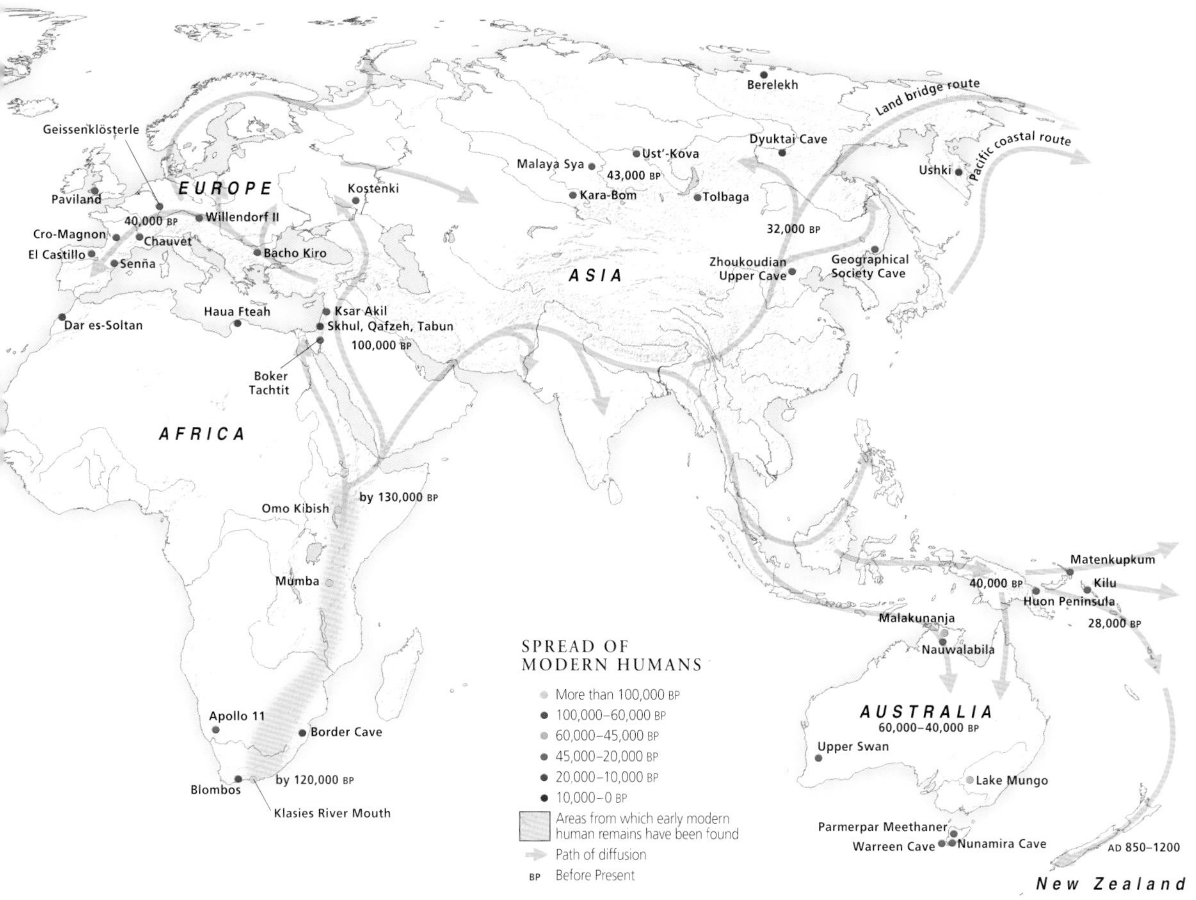

Geissenklösterle
Paviland
EUROPE
40,000 BP
Willendorf II
Kostenki
Cro-Magnon
Chauvet
El Castillo
Senña
Bacho Kiro
Dar es-Soltan
Haua Fteah
Ksar Akil
Skhul, Qafzeh, Tabun
100,000 BP
Boker Tachtit
AFRICA
Omo Kibish
by 130,000 BP
Mumba
Apollo 11
Border Cave
Blombos
by 120,000 BP
Klasies River Mouth
Berelekh
Land bridge route
Pacific coastal route
Dyuktai Cave
Ushki
Malaya Sya
Ust'-Kova
43,000 BP
Kara-Bom
Tolbaga
32,000 BP
Zhoukoudian Upper Cave
Geographical Society Cave
ASIA
Matenkupkum
40,000 BP
Kilu
Huon Peninsula
28,000 BP
Malakunanja
Nauwalabila
AUSTRALIA
60,000–40,000 BP
Upper Swan
Lake Mungo
Parmerpar Meethaner
Warreen Cave
Nunamira Cave
AD 850–1200
New Zealand
SPREAD OF MODERN HUMANS
More than 100,000 BP
100,000–60,000 BP
60,000–45,000 BP
45,000–20,000 BP
20,000–10,000 BP
10,000–0 BP
Areas from which early modern human remains have been found
Path of diffusion
BP Before Present

The Neanderthals

When modern humans (*Homo sapiens*) moved into Europe roughly 40,000 years ago, the region had been inhabited by Neanderthals (*Homo neanderthalensis*) for tens of thousands of years. Now considered cousins of modern humans (below right), the Neanderthals had a large brain and face, with a heavy brow ridge and a massive lower jaw (below left). They were the first hominids to fully adapt to the cold northern climate, roaming over extensive territories and using seasonal sites throughout the ice age. Neanderthals were skilled toolmakers and effective hunters of large mammals, and they buried their dead and made simple ornaments. They were no match, however, for the culturally and technologically advanced modern *Homo sapiens*, who used symbols, created complex art, and made shelters, throwing sticks, small-mammal traps, and insulated clothing. Within several thousand years of modern humans' arrival in Europe, the Neanderthals had vanished.

130,000 BP Modern humans (*Homo sapiens*) in Africa

100,000 BP Modern humans (*Homo sapiens*) in Southwest Asia; first evidence of deliberate burials (Israel)

77,000 BP Rare examples of art (Blombos Cave, South Africa)

70,000 BP Composite tools in Africa (Howieson's Poort industry)

60,000 BP Modern humans in East Asia and Australia—first sea voyages

40,000 BP Modern humans (Cro-Magnon) in Europe, associated with widespread burials, art, and music

37,000 BP Ivory carvings of animals in southwestern Germany

30,000 BP Extinction of Neanderthals

28,000 BP Female statuettes known as "Venus" figurines in Europe

"Venus of Willendorf" *26,000–24,000 BP*

26,000 BP First cremation (Australia)

16,000 BP First fired clay pottery (Japan)

15,000 BP Modern humans spread into America (possibly earlier)

13,000 BP Domesticated plants in Southwest Asia

12,500 BP Settled villages of hunter-gatherers in Southwest Asia

12,000 BP First animal domestication (dogs in the Levant)

10,000 BP Domesticated plants in New Guinea, Mexico, and South America

9000 BP Farming in New Guinea and India; rice cultivation in China

8500 BP Farming in Europe

7000 BP First cities (Southwest Asia); wheat and barley cultivation in Nile Valley; copper work in Balkans

Grain pots from Swiss Alps *6000 BP*

5500 BP Wheel developed and bronze used in Southwest Asia

Sumerian tablet *c. 5000 BP*

5400 BP Sumerian cuneiform writing

5100 BP Hieroglyphic script developed in Egypt

5000 BP Cotton cultivation in Indus valley and Peru

3500 BP Iron smelting developed in Southwest Asia

Exploration

The map of the world that is so familiar today is the legacy of centuries of exploration. Motivated by a desire to discover, conquer, colonize, or trade with other lands, explorers have charted all the continents and their interiors and now look beyond Earth to the realm of space.

The very first explorations were the prehistoric migrations of humankind throughout the globe, but the earliest record of a deliberate expedition dates to 2750 BC, when an Egyptian called Hannu sailed to Arabia. Soon after, Polynesians began exploring the islands of the South Pacific by canoe. Phoenician, Greek, Roman, Chinese, and Arab traders later established extensive networks between East and West, and the Middle Ages saw the great sea voyages of the Vikings.

At the dawn of the 15th century, however, no culture had an accurate knowledge of the world's extent. When the growth of the Ottoman Empire blocked the overland trade routes between Europe and the East, the search for new routes, together with the rise of merchant capitalism and advances in shipbuilding and navigation, prompted the Age of Discovery. By 1600, the Americas had been added to European maps, the globe had been circumnavigated twice, and European trading ports and colonies were being established throughout Africa, Asia, and the Americas. Expeditions during the 18th century charted much of Australia, New Zealand, and the Pacific. By the time explorers reached the South Pole in 1911, the world map was complete.

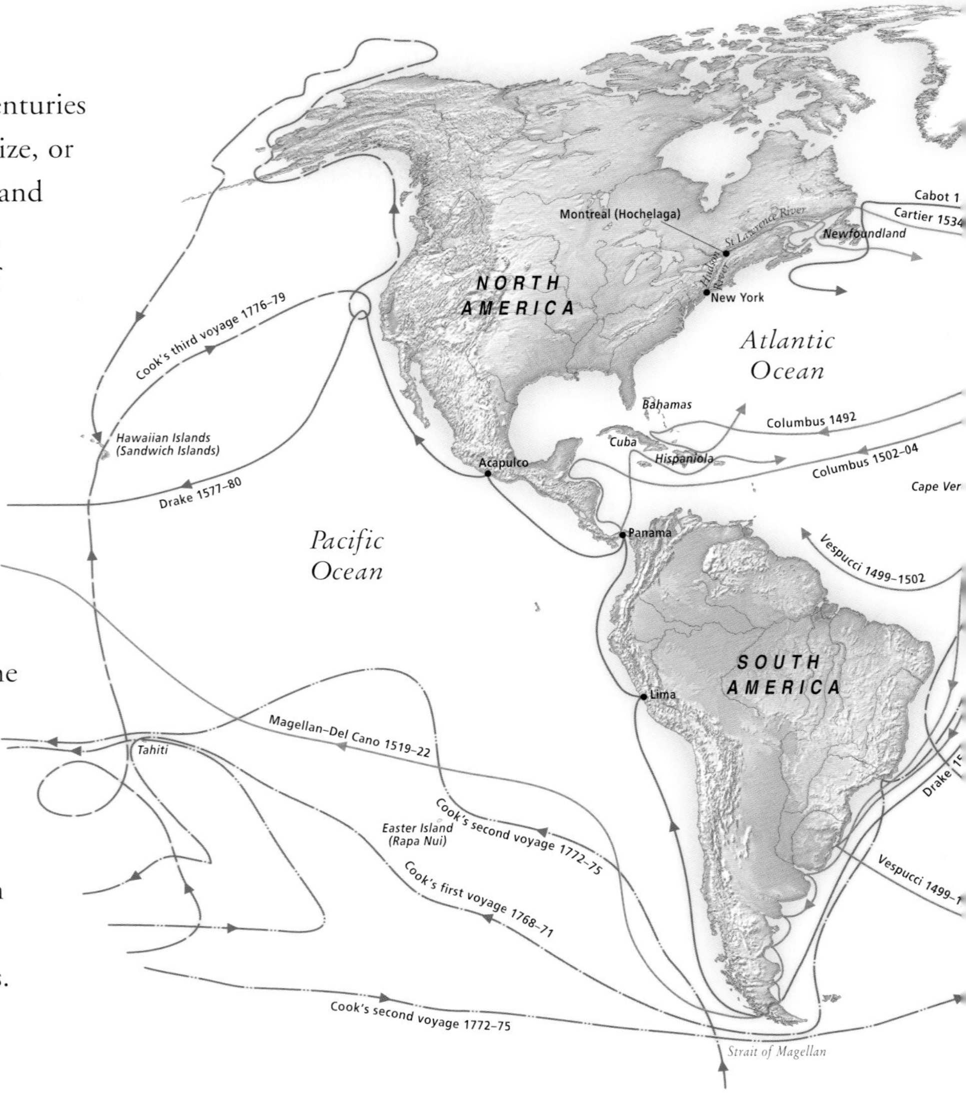
NORTH AMERICA
SOUTH AMERICA
Atlantic Ocean
Pacific Ocean
Montreal (Hochelaga)
St Lawrence River
Newfoundland
New York
Cabot 1
Cartier 1534
Bahamas
Cuba
Hispaniola
Columbus 1492
Columbus 1502–04
Cape Ver
Acapulco
Panama
Vespucci 1499–1502
Lima
Drake
Vespucci 1499–1
Hawaiian Islands
(Sandwich Islands)
Cook's third voyage 1776–79
Drake 1577–80
Tahiti
Magellan–Del Cano 1519–22
Easter Island
(Rapa Nui)
Cook's second voyage 1772–75
Cook's first voyage 1768–71
Cook's second voyage 1772–75
Strait of Magellan

This wall painting from China's Dunhuang caves depicts a caravan on the Silk Road, the main route for trade between East and West before 1450.

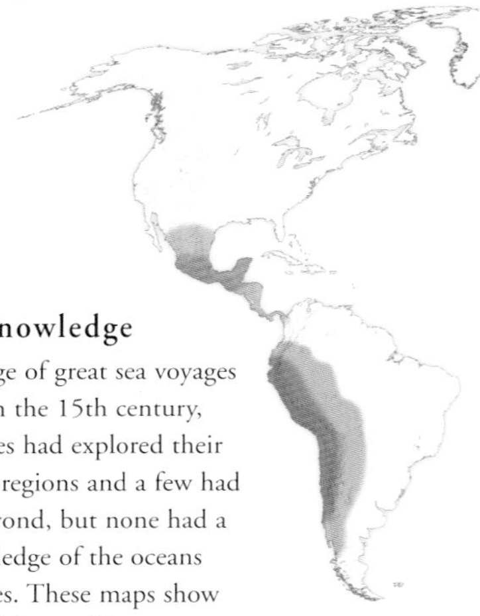

Global Knowledge

Before the age of great sea voyages that began in the 15th century, many cultures had explored their neighboring regions and a few had ventured beyond, but none had a global knowledge of the oceans and coastlines. These maps show the extent of the world as it was known by some of the major cultures around 1500.

The American World

The young empires of the Americas had had little time to expand before the arrival of Europeans. They were also restricted by geography: the Aztecs had deserts to the north and jungle to the south, while the Incas were wedged between the Andes and the Pacific.

THE AMERICAS

- Extent of Aztec empire
- World known to Aztecs c.1500
- Extent of Inca empire
- World known to Incas c.1500

The European World

By the late 15th century, European traders and travelers had compiled a fairly detailed knowledge of what was to them the "Old World," from the west coast of Africa to the East Indies. Columbus's voyage of 1492 would add the Americas to their maps.

EUROPE

- European lands
- World known to Europeans before 1492
- Routes of Carpini 1245–47 and Rubruk 1253–55
- Route of Marco Polo 1271–95

EXPLORATION MILESTONES

2750 BC First recorded exploring expedition, from Egypt to Arabia

2500 BC Polynesians begin migrating throughout South Pacific

Polynesian outrigger canoe

7th c. BC Phoenicians explore the Mediterranean Sea and the Atlantic coasts of Africa and Europe; sent by Egyptian Pharaoh Necho to circumnavigate Africa

510 BC Greek sailor Scylax explores India and Arabia for Persia

500 BC Phoenician Hanno sails along northwestern Africa. Himilco reaches England and establishes tin trade

4th c. BC Greeks travel to England and India

138 BC China's Zhang Qian launches first of several overland expeditions that open up the Silk Road, which becomes the main trade route between China and the West

1st c. AD Chinese invent compass

AD 120 Ptolemy of Egypt invents cartographic projections that allow Earth's curved surface to be represented on a flat drawing

AD 860 Vikings discover Iceland

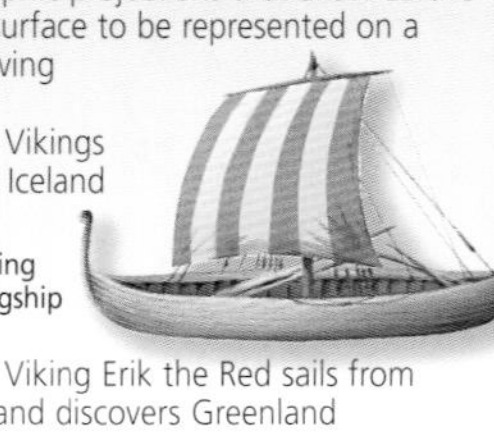

Viking longship

AD 982 Viking Erik the Red sails from Iceland and discovers Greenland

1002 Viking Leif Eriksson finds North America

1050 Asian astrolabes arrive in Europe

1191 Tea first exported from China

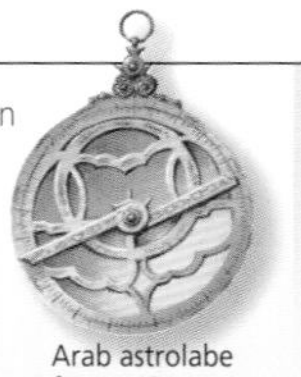

Arab astrolabe from 1131

1271 Marco Polo travels to China via Silk Road, returning in 1295

1325 Arab traveler Ibn Buttuta leaves on a 75,000 mile (120,000 km) journey to Asia and Africa, returning in 1354

1405 Cheng Ho begins voyages for Ming Emperor, dominating South Pacific and Indian Ocean until 1433

1441 Portuguese sail to West Africa and reestablish slave trade

1450 Portugal's Prince Henry the Navigator establishes naval observatory for the teaching of navigation, astronomy, and cartography

1453 Turks overrun Constantinople and shut off the overland trade route between the West and the East

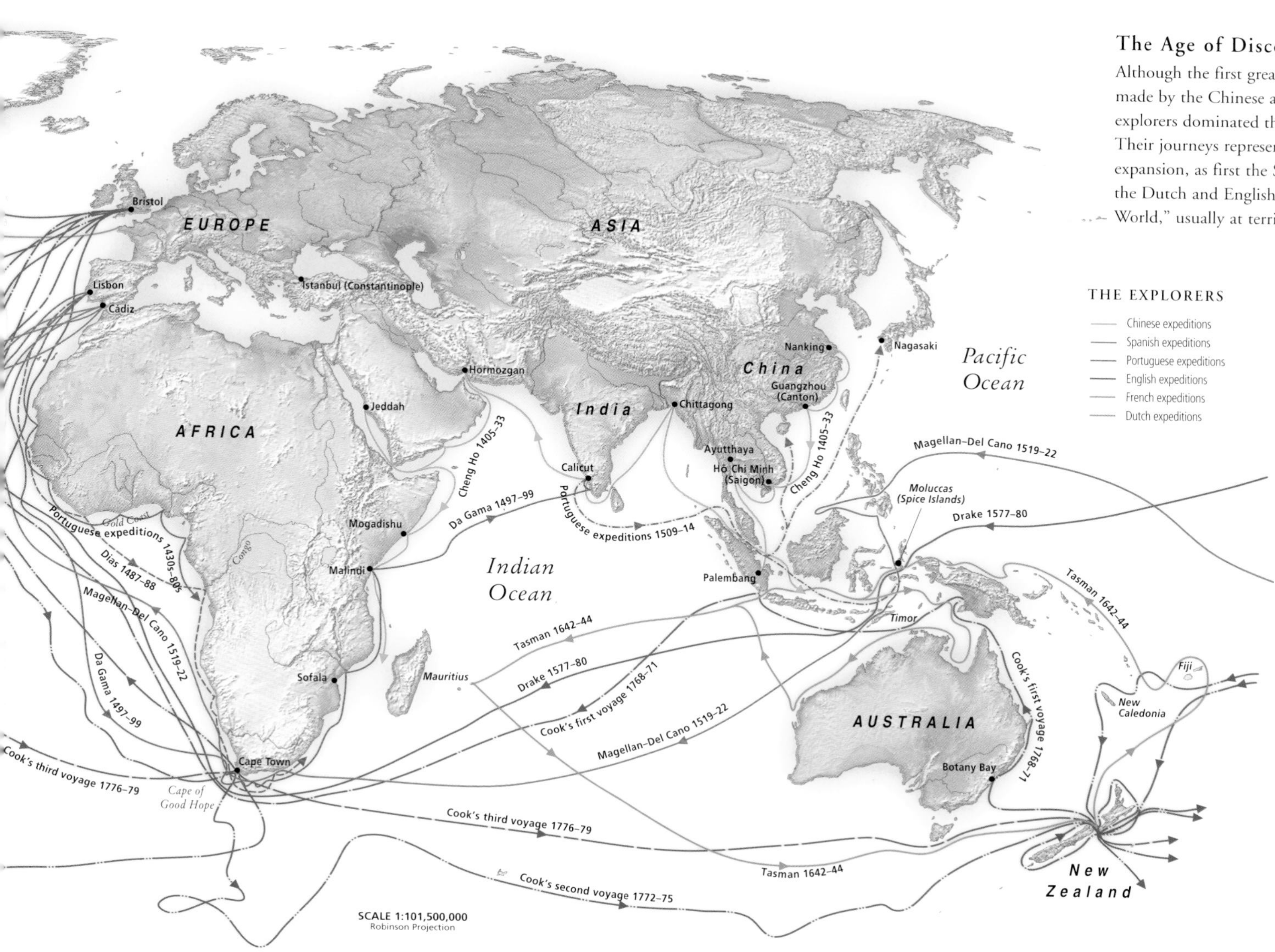
EUROPE
ASIA
AFRICA
AUSTRALIA
India
China
Pacific Ocean
Indian Ocean
New Zealand
Bristol
Lisbon
Cádiz
Istanbul (Constantinople)
Hormozgan
Jeddah
Mogadishu
Malindi
Sofala
Cape Town
Cape of Good Hope
Calicut
Chittagong
Nanking
Nagasaki
Guangzhou (Canton)
Ayutthaya
Ho Chi Minh (Saigon)
Palembang
Moluccas (Spice Islands)
Timor
Mauritius
Botany Bay
New Caledonia
Fiji
Gold Coast
Congo
Cheng Ho 1405–33
Da Gama 1497–99
Portuguese expeditions 1509–14
Portuguese expeditions 1430s–80s
Dias 1487–88
Magellan–Del Cano 1519–22
Drake 1577–80
Tasman 1642–44
Cook's first voyage 1768–71
Cook's second voyage 1772–75
Cook's third voyage 1776–79
THE EXPLORERS
Chinese expeditions
Spanish expeditions
Portuguese expeditions
English expeditions
French expeditions
Dutch expeditions
SCALE 1:101,500,000
Robinson Projection

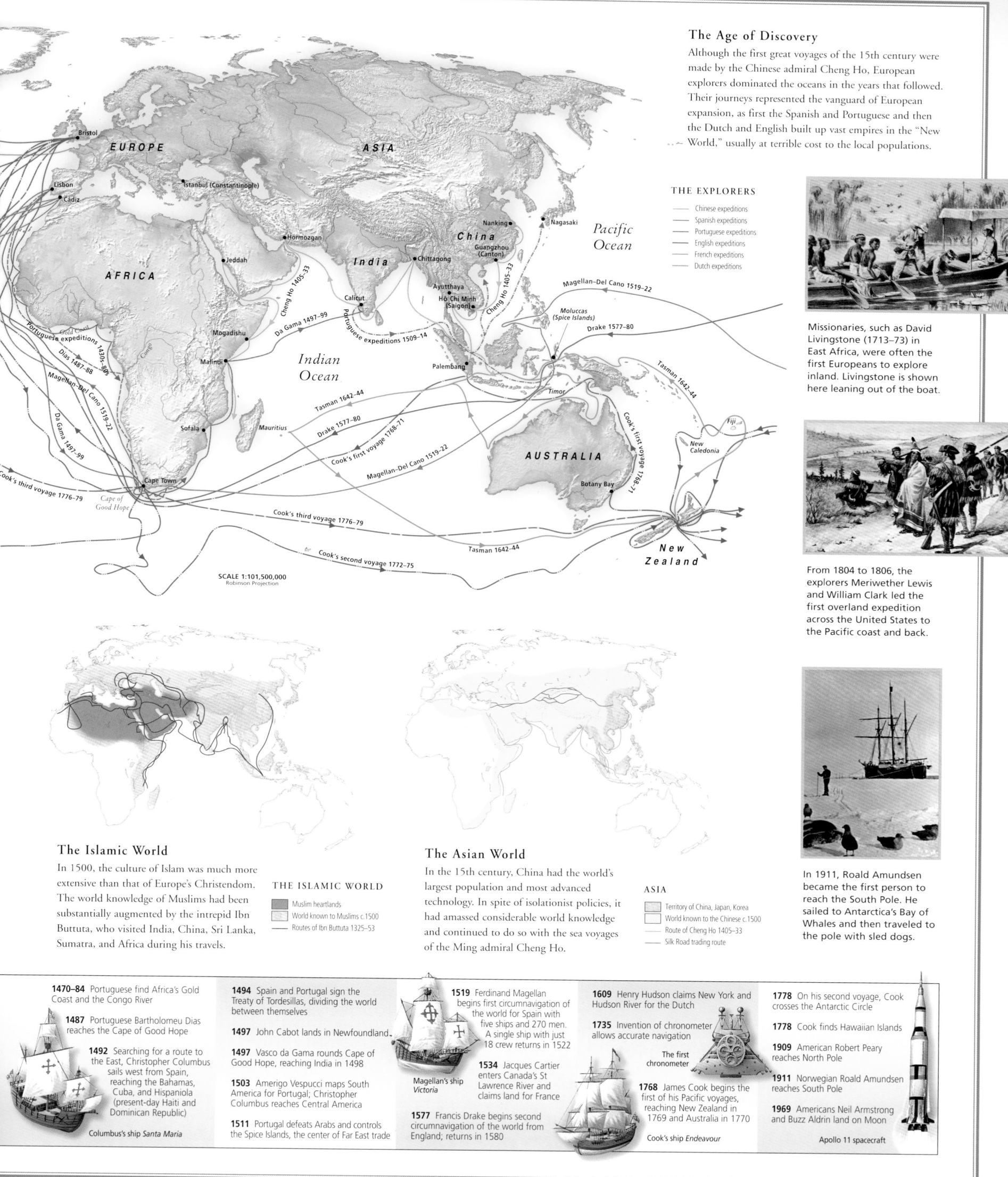

The Age of Discovery

Although the first great voyages of the 15th century were made by the Chinese admiral Cheng Ho, European explorers dominated the oceans in the years that followed. Their journeys represented the vanguard of European expansion, as first the Spanish and Portuguese and then the Dutch and English built up vast empires in the "New World," usually at terrible cost to the local populations.

Missionaries, such as David Livingstone (1813–73) in East Africa, were often the first Europeans to explore inland. Livingstone is shown here leaning out of the boat.

From 1804 to 1806, the explorers Meriwether Lewis and William Clark led the first overland expedition across the United States to the Pacific coast and back.

In 1911, Roald Amundsen became the first person to reach the South Pole. He sailed to Antarctica's Bay of Whales and then traveled to the pole with sled dogs.

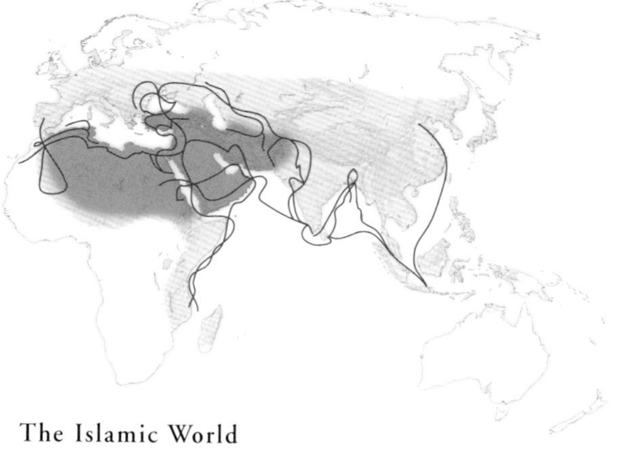

The Islamic World

In 1500, the culture of Islam was much more extensive than that of Europe's Christendom. The world knowledge of Muslims had been substantially augmented by the intrepid Ibn Buttuta, who visited India, China, Sri Lanka, Sumatra, and Africa during his travels.

THE ISLAMIC WORLD
- Muslim heartlands
- World known to Muslims c.1500
- Routes of Ibn Buttuta 1325–53

The Asian World

In the 15th century, China had the world's largest population and most advanced technology. In spite of isolationist policies, it had amassed considerable world knowledge and continued to do so with the sea voyages of the Ming admiral Cheng Ho.

ASIA
- Territory of China, Japan, Korea
- World known to the Chinese c.1500
- Route of Cheng Ho 1405–33
- Silk Road trading route

1470–84 Portuguese find Africa's Gold Coast and the Congo River

1487 Portuguese Bartholomeu Dias reaches the Cape of Good Hope

1492 Searching for a route to the East, Christopher Columbus sails west from Spain, reaching the Bahamas, Cuba, and Hispaniola (present-day Haiti and Dominican Republic)

Columbus's ship *Santa Maria*

1494 Spain and Portugal sign the Treaty of Tordesillas, dividing the world between themselves

1497 John Cabot lands in Newfoundland

1497 Vasco da Gama rounds Cape of Good Hope, reaching India in 1498

1503 Amerigo Vespucci maps South America for Portugal; Christopher Columbus reaches Central America

1511 Portugal defeats Arabs and controls the Spice Islands, the center of Far East trade

Magellan's ship *Victoria*

1519 Ferdinand Magellan begins first circumnavigation of the world for Spain with five ships and 270 men. A single ship with just 18 crew returns in 1522

1534 Jacques Cartier enters Canada's St Lawrence River and claims land for France

1577 Francis Drake begins second circumnavigation of the world from England; returns in 1580

1609 Henry Hudson claims New York and Hudson River for the Dutch

1735 Invention of chronometer allows accurate navigation

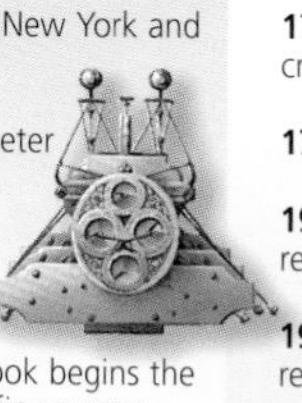

The first chronometer

1768 James Cook begins the first of his Pacific voyages, reaching New Zealand in 1769 and Australia in 1770

Cook's ship *Endeavour*

1778 On his second voyage, Cook crosses the Antarctic Circle

1778 Cook finds Hawaiian Islands

1909 American Robert Peary reaches North Pole

1911 Norwegian Roald Amundsen reaches South Pole

1969 Americans Neil Armstrong and Buzz Aldrin land on Moon

Apollo 11 spacecraft

Population

The number of people in the world has increased tenfold in the past 400 years, but such explosive growth is a very recent phenomenon. World population can expand only when there are more births than deaths, and for most of human history, birth and death rates both remained at high levels. The introduction of farming from around 8000 BC led to the first significant growth in human numbers, but the increase was gradual and it took until AD 1500 to move from 10 million to 500 million people.

In the developed regions, such as Europe and North America, death rates began to decline during the 18th century as revolutions in both agriculture and industry led to improved living conditions and health care. Birth rates stayed high, however, because people had not yet adjusted to the idea that all their children were likely to reach adulthood. Over the next 200 years, population figures exploded, but gradually birth rates started to drop and growth in these regions slowed. Today, some European populations are actually shrinking.

The developing parts of the world, however, are at an earlier stage in the process and are experiencing even more rapid growth. Although the birth rates in much of Asia, Africa, and South America are now falling, it will be many decades before their populations stabilize. Most experts believe that at this point there will be more than 10 billion people on Earth, but nobody knows whether our planet has the capacity to sustain such enormous numbers.

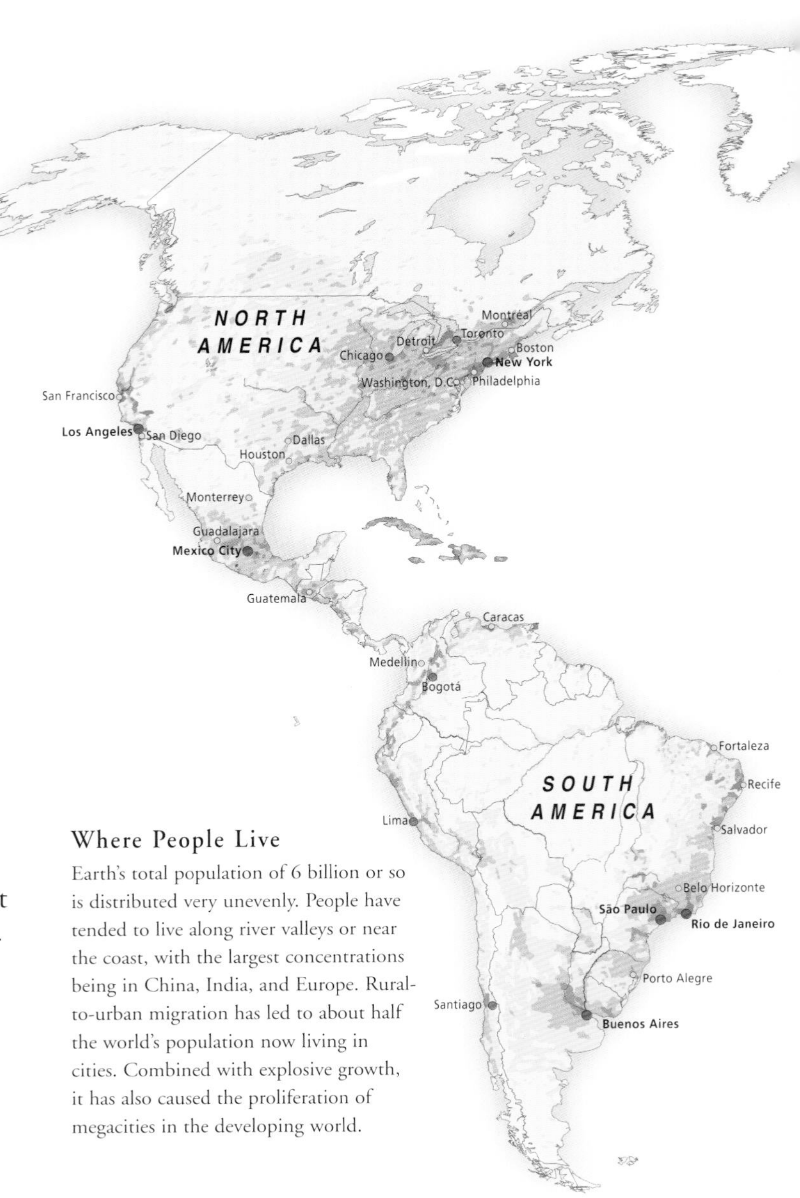

NORTH AMERICA
Montréal
Toronto
Detroit
Chicago
Boston
New York
Washington, D.C.
Philadelphia
San Francisco
Los Angeles
San Diego
Dallas
Houston
Monterrey
Guadalajara
Mexico City
Guatemala
Caracas
Medellín
Bogotá
Fortaleza
Recife
SOUTH AMERICA
Lima
Salvador
Belo Horizonte
São Paulo
Rio de Janeiro
Porto Alegre
Santiago
Buenos Aires

Where People Live

Earth's total population of 6 billion or so is distributed very unevenly. People have tended to live along river valleys or near the coast, with the largest concentrations being in China, India, and Europe. Rural-to-urban migration has led to about half the world's population now living in cities. Combined with explosive growth, it has also caused the proliferation of megacities in the developing world.

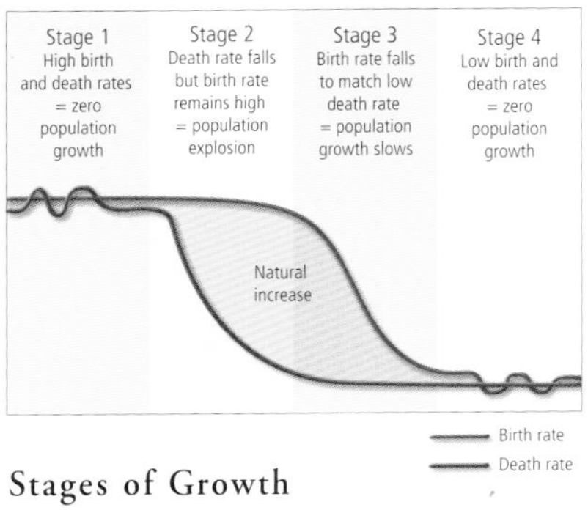

Stage 1
High birth and death rates = zero population growth
Stage 2
Death rate falls but birth rate remains high = population explosion
Stage 3
Birth rate falls to match low death rate = population growth slows
Stage 4
Low birth and death rates = zero population growth
Natural increase
Birth rate
Death rate

Stages of Growth

In Stage 1, birth and death rates are both high and there is little population growth. When health care and living conditions improve, death rates drop but birth rates initially remain high, leading to a natural increase in the population. During Stage 3, the birth rate gradually falls, eventually leading to the zero growth of Stage 4.

Urbanization

In the developed countries, the Industrial Revolution was followed by a massive shift of population from rural to urban areas. With later but more rapid industrialization, developing countries are experiencing a sudden increase in city dwellers. In the coming years, almost all the world's population growth will be in urban areas.

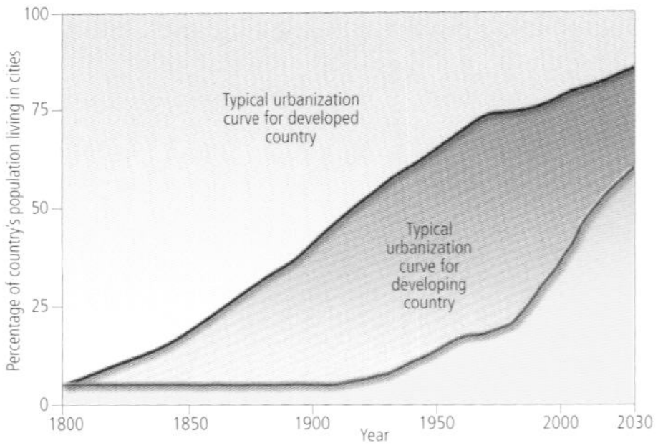

100
75
50
25
0
Percentage of country's population living in cities
Typical urbanization curve for developed country
Typical urbanization curve for developing country
1800
1850
1900
1950
2000
2030
Year

The walled towns of Europe, such as Albarracín, in Spain, reflect a time before technology allowed vast, sprawling cities to become a feature of the modern landscape.

In the Philippines and many other developing countries, extensive shantytowns have grown up, as millions have erected makeshift shelters on the outskirts of cities.

Largest Populations		Most Crowded Countries		Fastest Growing Countries*	
Country	**Population**	**Country**	**Population density**	**Country**	**Annual growth**
China	1,302,207,990	Monaco	26,784 per sq mile (16,620 per sq km)	Liberia	5.53%
India	1,080,264,390	Singapore	11,629 per sq mile (7,219 per sq km)	Sierra Leone	4.54%
United States	295,734,130	Vatican City	5,015 per sq mile (3,111 per sq km)	Eritrea	4.22%
Indonesia	241,973,880	Malta	2,073 per sq mile (1,286 per sq km)	Somalia	4.21%
Brazil	186,112,790	Maldives	1,877 per sq mile (1,164 per sq km)	Yemen	4.07%
Pakistan	156,689,150	Bangladesh	1,735 per sq mile (1,078 per sq km)	Afghanistan	3.68%
Bangladesh	144,319,630	Bahrain	1,667 per sq mile (1,035 per sq km)	Niger	3.63%
Russia	143,736,790	Taiwan	1,143 per sq mile (710 per sq km)	Democratic Republic of Congo	3.34%
Nigeria	140,601,620	Barbados	1,042 per sq mile (648 per sq km)	Oman	3.27%
Japan	127,417,240	Nauru	1,004 per sq mile (621 per sq km)	Uganda	3.11%

** Countries with more than 1 million inhabitants*

Top Ten Countries

The population of a country can be assessed in various ways, including the total number of inhabitants, the ratio of inhabitants to land, and the rate at which it is growing. Many of today's most populous countries are in Asia, but Africa and the Middle East are seeing the highest rates of growth. Apart from Bangladesh, the most densely populated countries listed here all have small land areas.

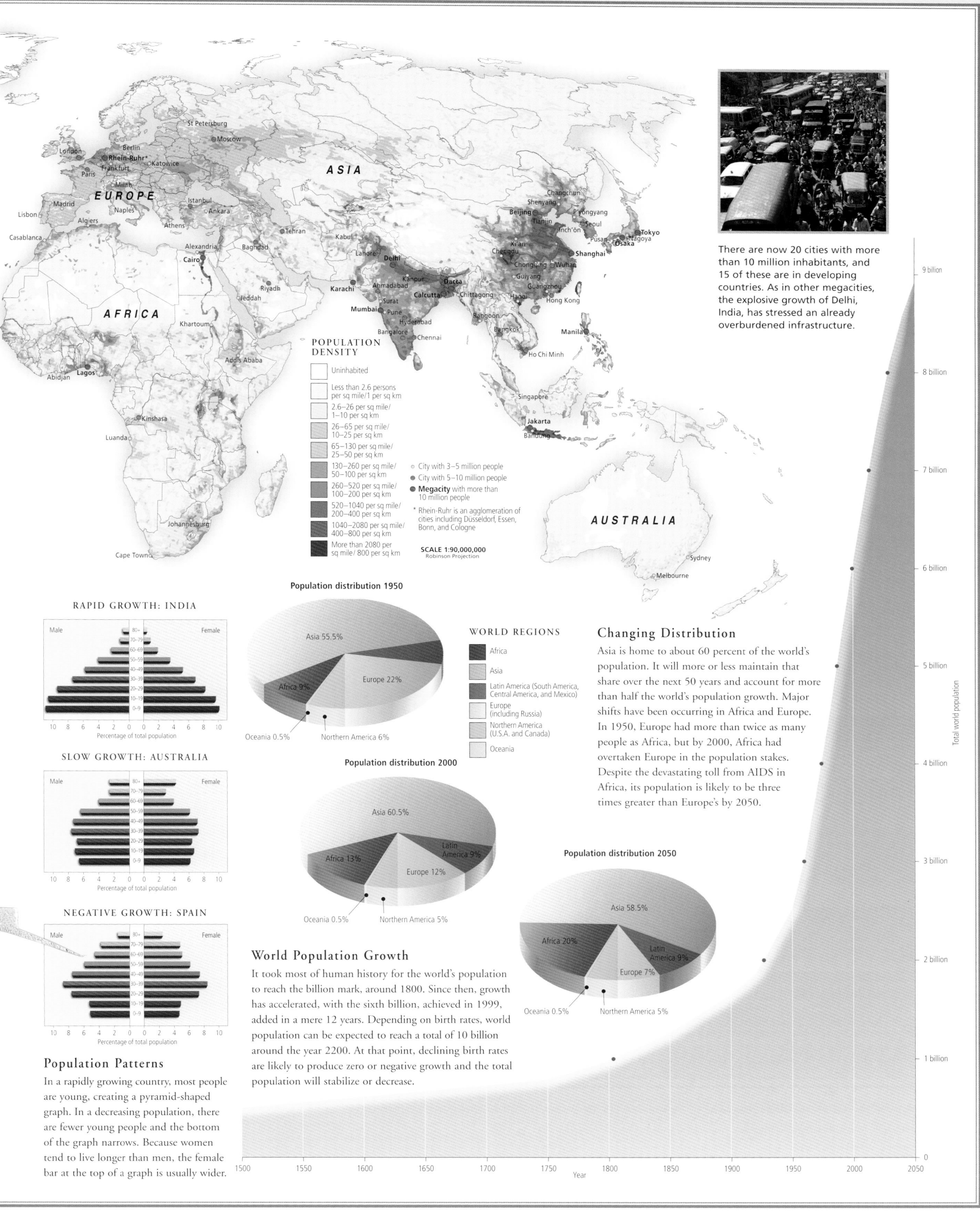

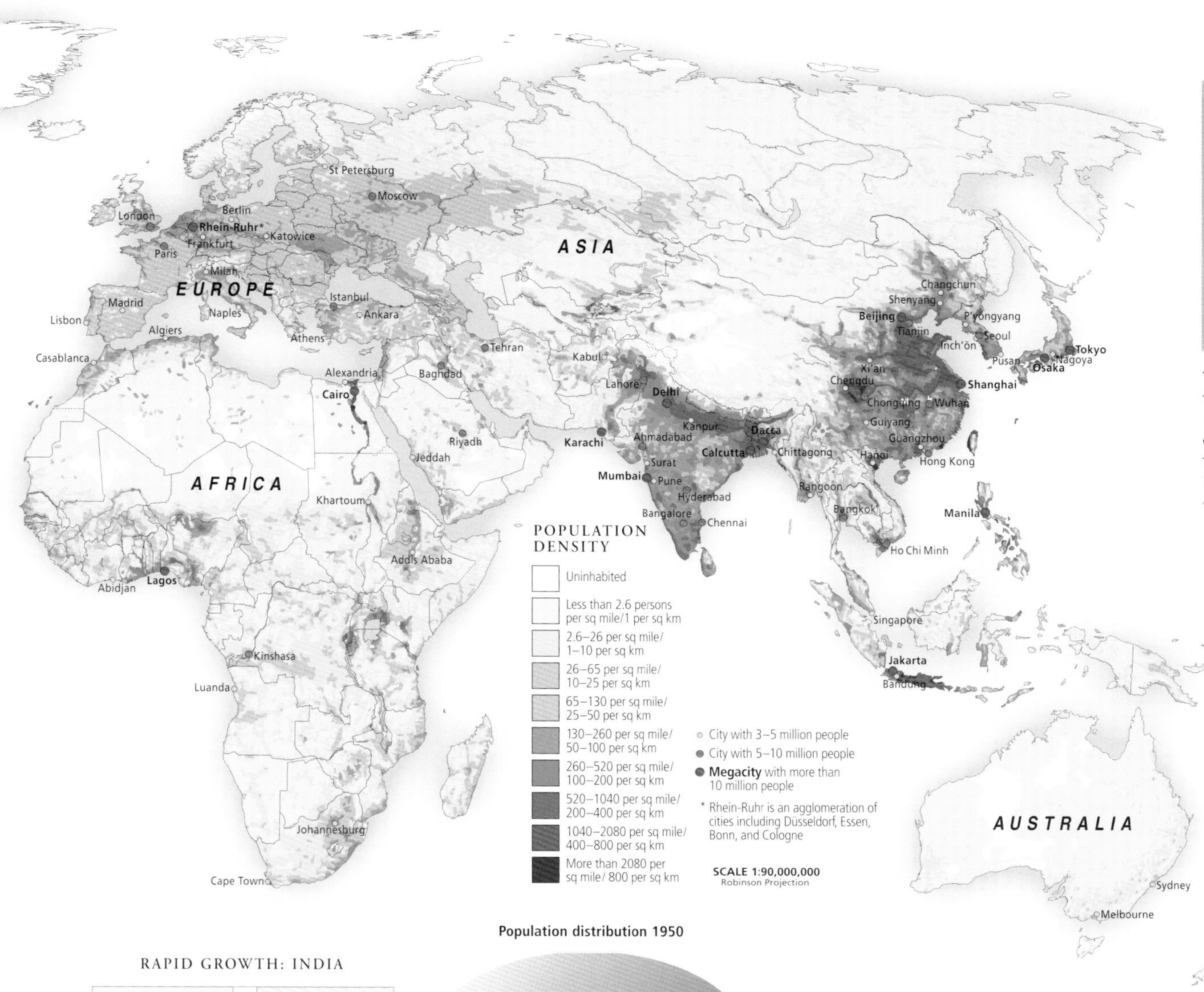
ASIA
EUROPE
AFRICA
AUSTRALIA
St Petersburg
Moscow
London
Berlin
Rhein-Ruhr*
Frankfurt
Katowice
Paris
Milan
Madrid
Lisbon
Naples
Istanbul
Ankara
Algiers
Athens
Casablanca
Tehran
Kabul
Alexandria
Baghdad
Cairo
Lahore
Delhi
Riyadh
Jeddah
Karachi
Ahmadabad
Kanpur
Dacca
Calcutta
Chittagong
Surat
Mumbai
Pune
Hyderabad
Bangalore
Chennai
Khartoum
Addis Ababa
Abidjan
Lagos
Kinshasa
Luanda
Johannesburg
Cape Town
Changchun
Shenyang
Beijing
Tianjin
P'yongyang
Seoul
Inch'on
Pusan
Osaka
Nagoya
Tokyo
Xi'an
Chengdu
Shanghai
Chongqing
Wuhan
Guiyang
Guangzhou
Hanoi
Hong Kong
Rangoon
Bangkok
Manila
Ho Chi Minh
Singapore
Jakarta
Bandung
Sydney
Melbourne
POPULATION DENSITY
Uninhabited
Less than 2.6 persons per sq mile/1 per sq km
2.6–26 per sq mile/ 1–10 per sq km
26–65 per sq mile/ 10–25 per sq km
65–130 per sq mile/ 25–50 per sq km
130–260 per sq mile/ 50–100 per sq km
260–520 per sq mile/ 100–200 per sq km
520–1040 per sq mile/ 200–400 per sq km
1040–2080 per sq mile/ 400–800 per sq km
More than 2080 per sq mile/ 800 per sq km
City with 3–5 million people
City with 5–10 million people
Megacity with more than 10 million people
* Rhein-Ruhr is an agglomeration of cities including Düsseldorf, Essen, Bonn, and Cologne
SCALE 1:90,000,000
Robinson Projection

There are now 20 cities with more than 10 million inhabitants, and 15 of these are in developing countries. As in other megacities, the explosive growth of Delhi, India, has stressed an already overburdened infrastructure.

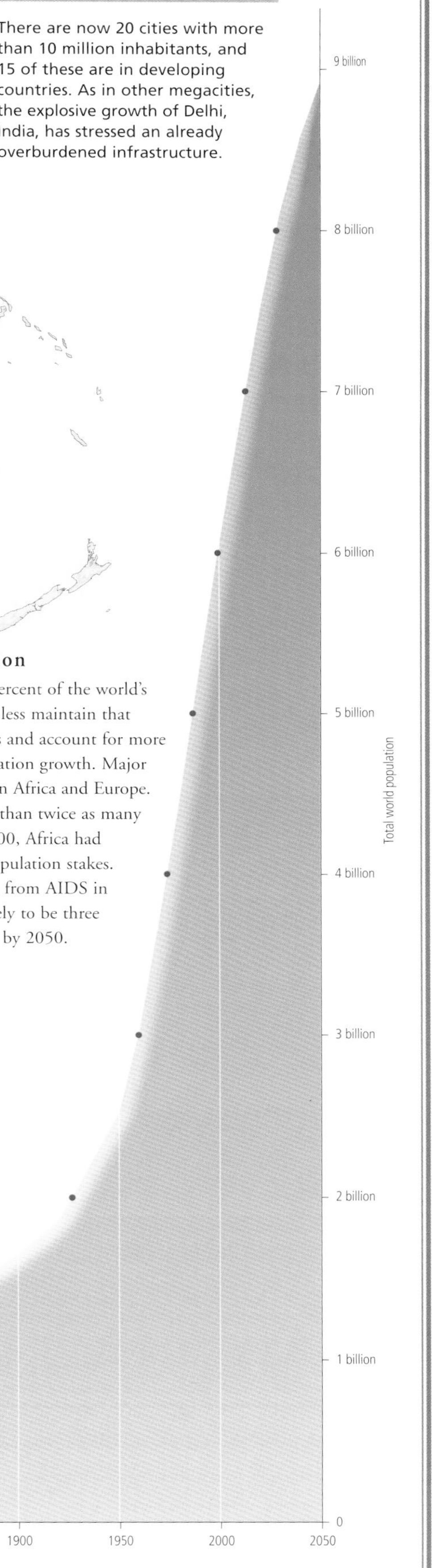
9 billion
8 billion
7 billion
6 billion
5 billion
4 billion
3 billion
2 billion
1 billion
0
Total world population
1500
1550
1600
1650
1700
1750
1800
1850
1900
1950
2000
2050
Year

RAPID GROWTH: INDIA

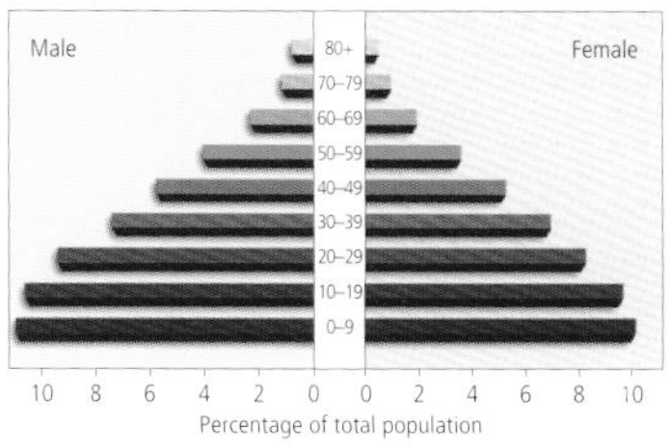
Male
Female
80+
70–79
60–69
50–59
40–49
30–39
20–29
10–19
0–9
10 8 6 4 2 0 0 2 4 6 8 10
Percentage of total population

SLOW GROWTH: AUSTRALIA

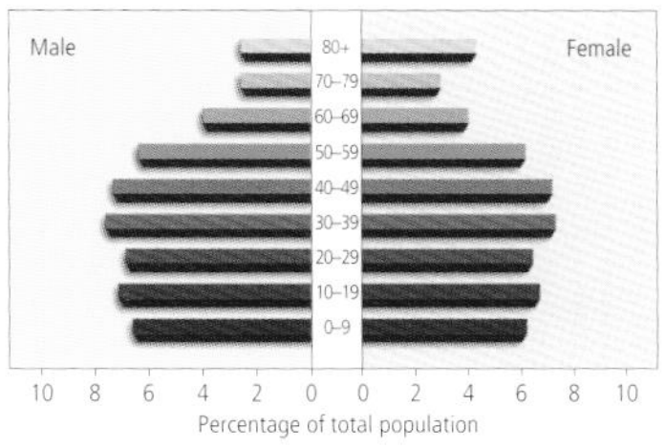
Male
Female
80+
70–79
60–69
50–59
40–49
30–39
20–29
10–19
0–9
10 8 6 4 2 0 0 2 4 6 8 10
Percentage of total population

NEGATIVE GROWTH: SPAIN

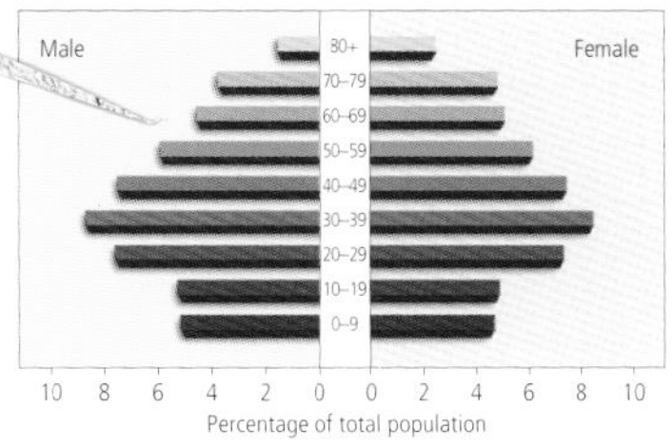
Male
Female
80+
70–79
60–69
50–59
40–49
30–39
20–29
10–19
0–9
10 8 6 4 2 0 0 2 4 6 8 10
Percentage of total population

Population distribution 1950

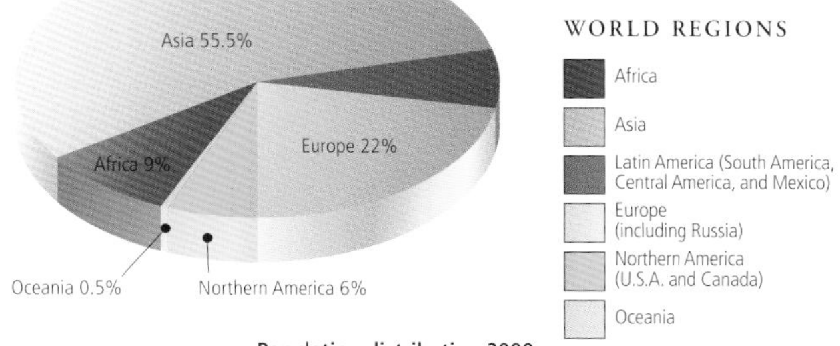
Asia 55.5%
Africa 9%
Europe 22%
Oceania 0.5%
Northern America 6%
WORLD REGIONS
Africa
Asia
Latin America (South America, Central America, and Mexico)
Europe (including Russia)
Northern America (U.S.A. and Canada)
Oceania

Population distribution 2000

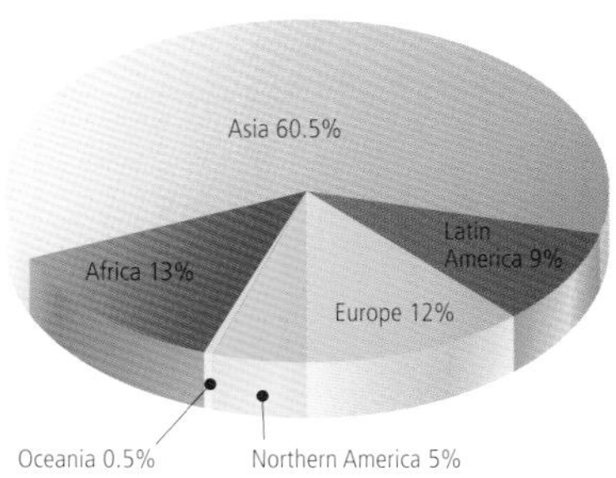
Asia 60.5%
Africa 13%
Latin America 9%
Europe 12%
Oceania 0.5%
Northern America 5%

Population distribution 2050

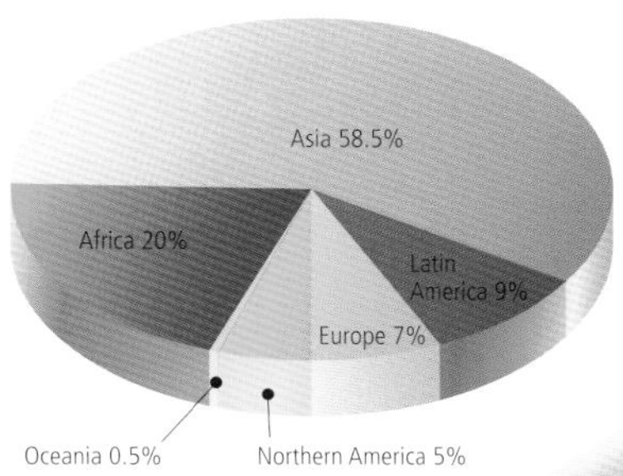
Asia 58.5%
Africa 20%
Latin America 9%
Europe 7%
Oceania 0.5%
Northern America 5%

Changing Distribution

Asia is home to about 60 percent of the world's population. It will more or less maintain that share over the next 50 years and account for more than half the world's population growth. Major shifts have been occurring in Africa and Europe. In 1950, Europe had more than twice as many people as Africa, but by 2000, Africa had overtaken Europe in the population stakes. Despite the devastating toll from AIDS in Africa, its population is likely to be three times greater than Europe's by 2050.

World Population Growth

It took most of human history for the world's population to reach the billion mark, around 1800. Since then, growth has accelerated, with the sixth billion, achieved in 1999, added in a mere 12 years. Depending on birth rates, world population can be expected to reach a total of 10 billion around the year 2200. At that point, declining birth rates are likely to produce zero or negative growth and the total population will stabilize or decrease.

Population Patterns

In a rapidly growing country, most people are young, creating a pyramid-shaped graph. In a decreasing population, there are fewer young people and the bottom of the graph narrows. Because women tend to live longer than men, the female bar at the top of a graph is usually wider.

NATURAL RESOURCES

Humans have shown great ingenuity in using Earth's rich resources. As a species, we have flourished through the exploitation of our planet's wild food supplies, forests, arable and grazing land, freshwater, minerals, and fossil fuels. The phenomenal population growth and industrialization of the 20th century, however, have led to a looming resource crisis, particularly in fossil fuels and metals.

Until the Industrial Revolution began in the 18th century, people relied on human and animal muscle power, wood and other biomass as fuel for heating and cooking, and a limited harnessing of wind and water power by sails, windmills, and watermills. The world was transformed by the invention of coal-fueled steam engines and oil-fueled internal combustion engines. After 1950, natural gas and nuclear power also became important. Much of the globe was electrified, industry boomed, and living standards in industrialized countries rose. Energy use grew spectacularly, as did the pollution caused by fossil fuels. The supply of fossil fuels is finite and the world may face an energy crisis if alternative sources of power are not developed.

Throughout history, people have mined the earth for raw materials and expanded into other territories in search of them. Advanced extraction methods and new uses for metals and minerals have led to rapid growth in the mining industry—copper production, for instance, increased 22-fold during the 20th century. Shortages of some metals, coupled with environmental concerns, have encouraged large-scale recycling schemes.

The most widespread use of solar energy is in domestic hot water systems, with solar panels mounted on individual roofs. Solar power stations, using mirrors to concentrate the Sun's energy, can generate electricity.

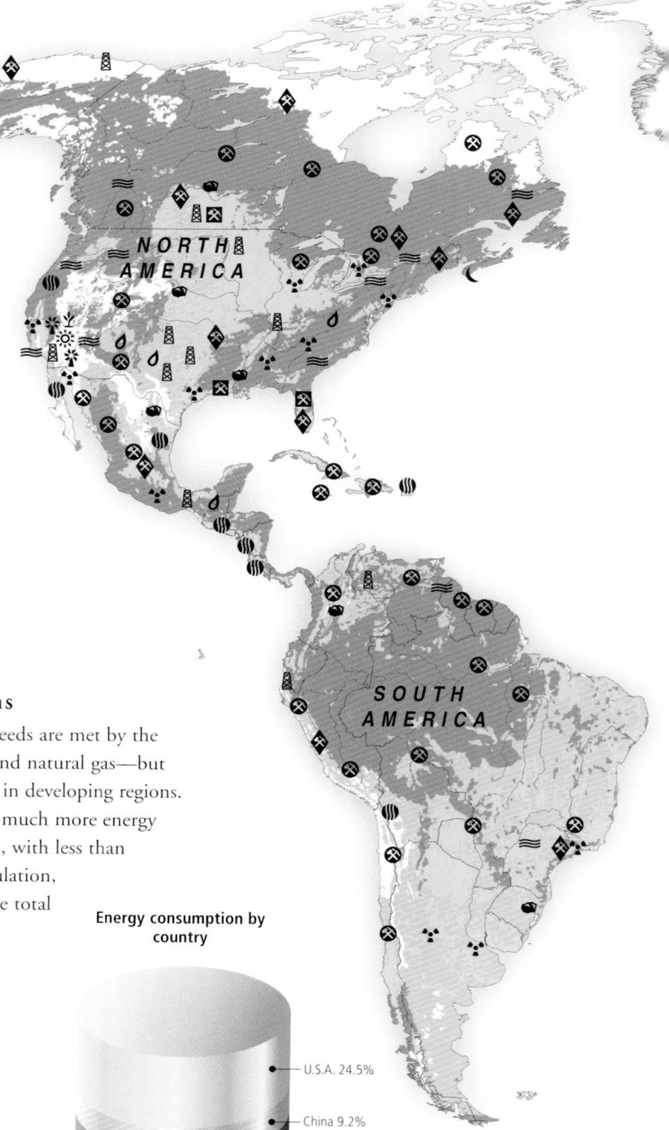

NORTH AMERICA
SOUTH AMERICA

THE WORLD'S WATER

Of all today's resource issues, the scarcity of fresh water may well be the most pressing. Water supplies are distributed very unevenly around the world: arid and semiarid regions make up about 40 percent of land area but receive only 2 percent of global runoff. During the 20th century, as world population grew and more land was irrigated, water consumption increased sixfold and the number of people living without enough water skyrocketed. At least 35 percent of the world's people are now experiencing chronic water shortage, many of them in developing countries such as India, Ethiopia, Nigeria, Kenya, and China (see world map, below). Agricultural irrigation accounts for about 70 percent of water use, but most irrigation schemes are highly wasteful, with 60 percent of the water they use never reaching the crops. Because water is usually heavily subsidized, there is little incentive to conserve it, so one solution may be to price water properly. However, such a strategy may discourage food production and further disadvantage the world's poor.

Water use by sector

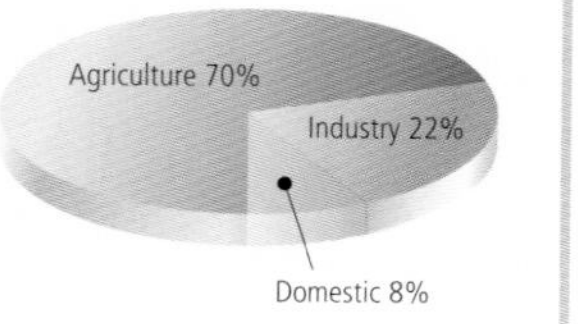

Agriculture 70%
Industry 22%
Domestic 8%

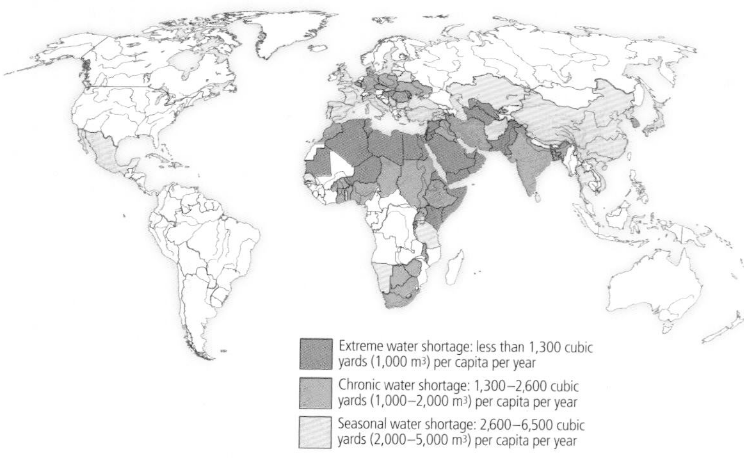

Extreme water shortage: less than 1,300 cubic yards (1,000 m³) per capita per year
Chronic water shortage: 1,300–2,600 cubic yards (1,000–2,000 m³) per capita per year
Seasonal water shortage: 2,600–6,500 cubic yards (2,000–5,000 m³) per capita per year

Consumption Patterns

Most of the world's energy needs are met by the three fossil fuels—oil, coal, and natural gas—but fuelwood remains significant in developing regions. The developed countries use much more energy per capita. The United States, with less than 5 percent of the world's population, uses almost one quarter of the total energy consumed worldwide.

Energy consumption by country

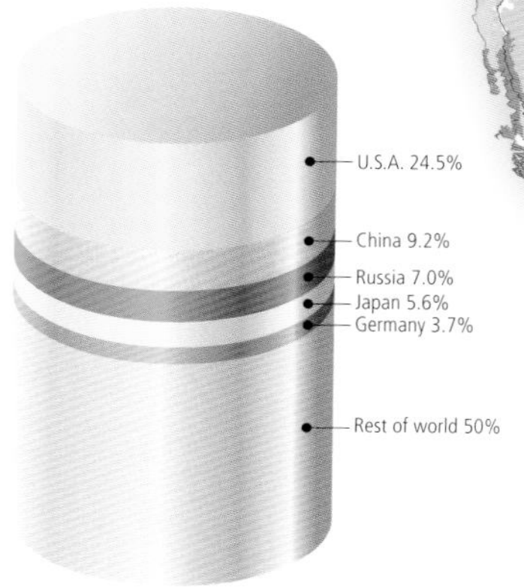

U.S.A. 24.5%
China 9.2%
Russia 7.0%
Japan 5.6%
Germany 3.7%
Rest of world 50%

Energy consumption by source

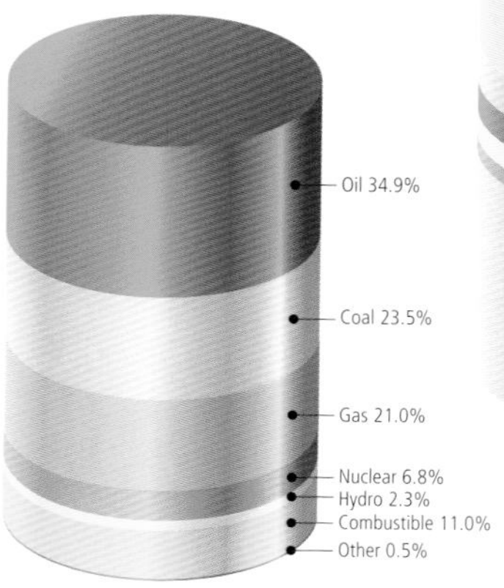

Oil 34.9%
Coal 23.5%
Gas 21.0%
Nuclear 6.8%
Hydro 2.3%
Combustible 11.0%
Other 0.5%

* Combustible includes renewables such as fuelwood and waste

* Other includes geothermal, solar, wind, and heat power

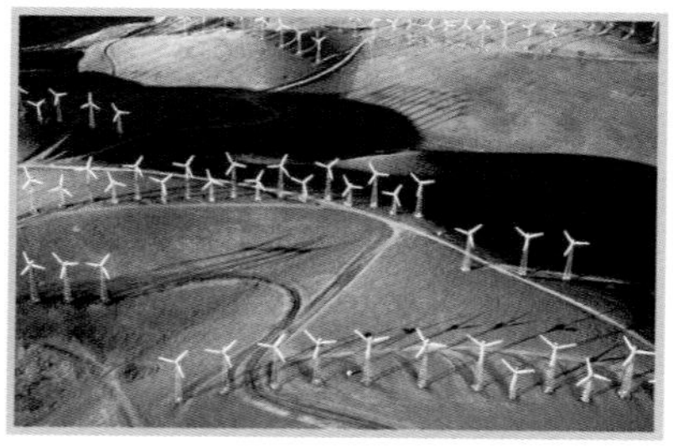

Although it accounts for only 0.03 percent of world energy production, wind power has grown by 52 percent since 1971 and is now becoming more cost effective.

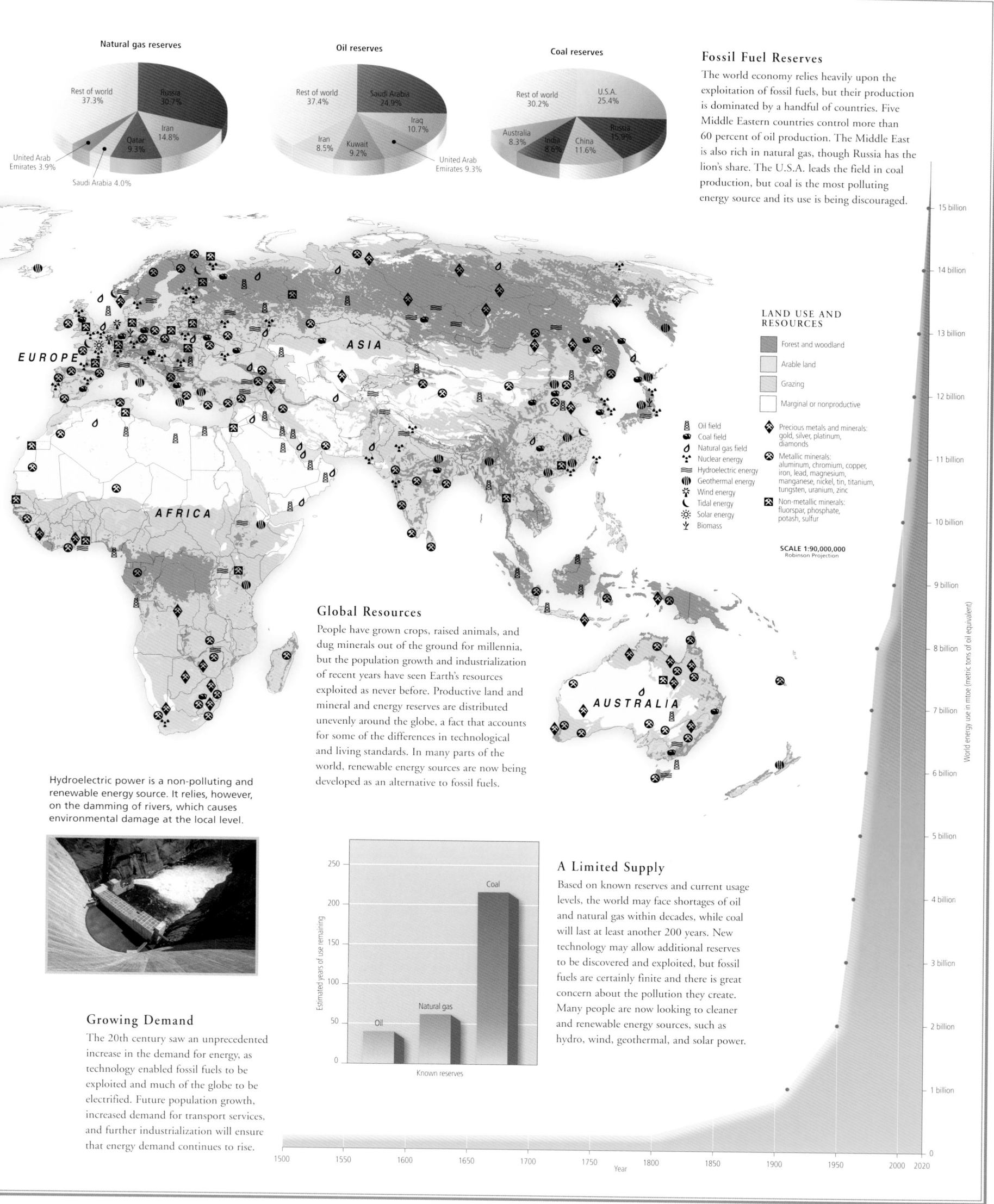

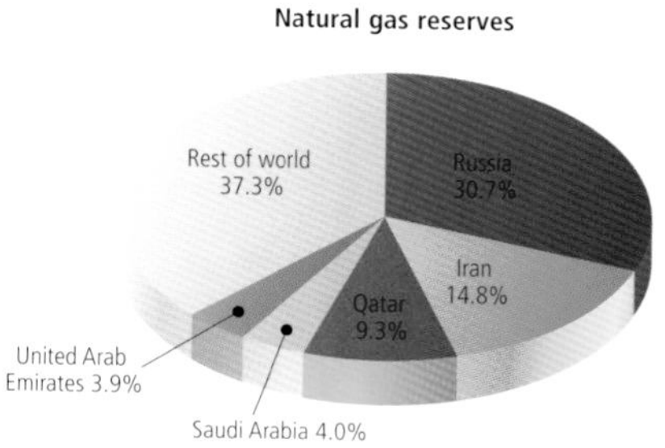
Natural gas reserves
Rest of world 37.3%
Russia 30.7%
Iran 14.8%
Qatar 9.3%
United Arab Emirates 3.9%
Saudi Arabia 4.0%

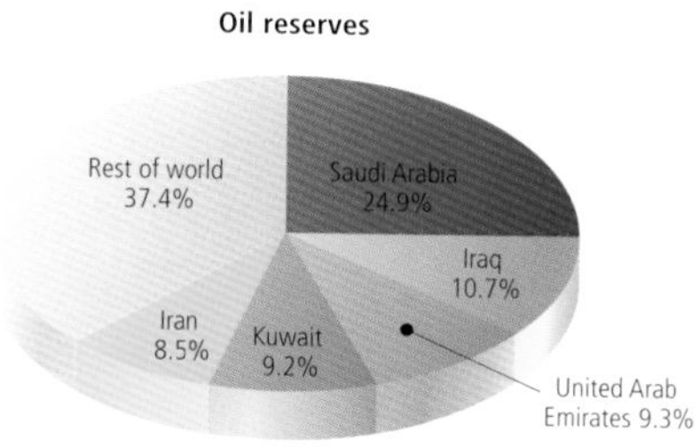
Oil reserves
Rest of world 37.4%
Saudi Arabia 24.9%
Iraq 10.7%
Kuwait 9.2%
Iran 8.5%
United Arab Emirates 9.3%

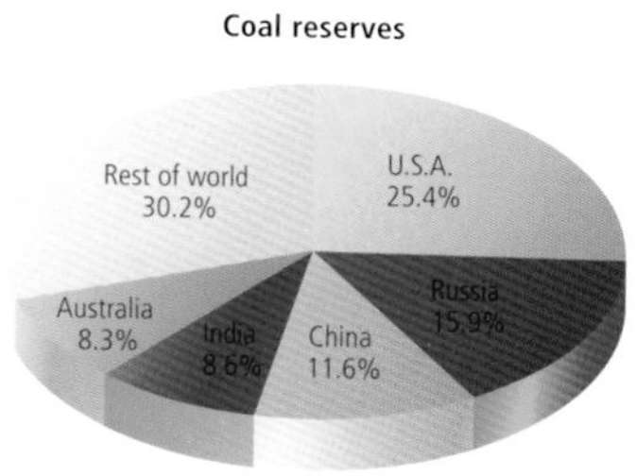
Coal reserves
Rest of world 30.2%
U.S.A. 25.4%
Russia 15.9%
China 11.6%
India 8.6%
Australia 8.3%

Fossil Fuel Reserves

The world economy relies heavily upon the exploitation of fossil fuels, but their production is dominated by a handful of countries. Five Middle Eastern countries control more than 60 percent of oil production. The Middle East is also rich in natural gas, though Russia has the lion's share. The U.S.A. leads the field in coal production, but coal is the most polluting energy source and its use is being discouraged.

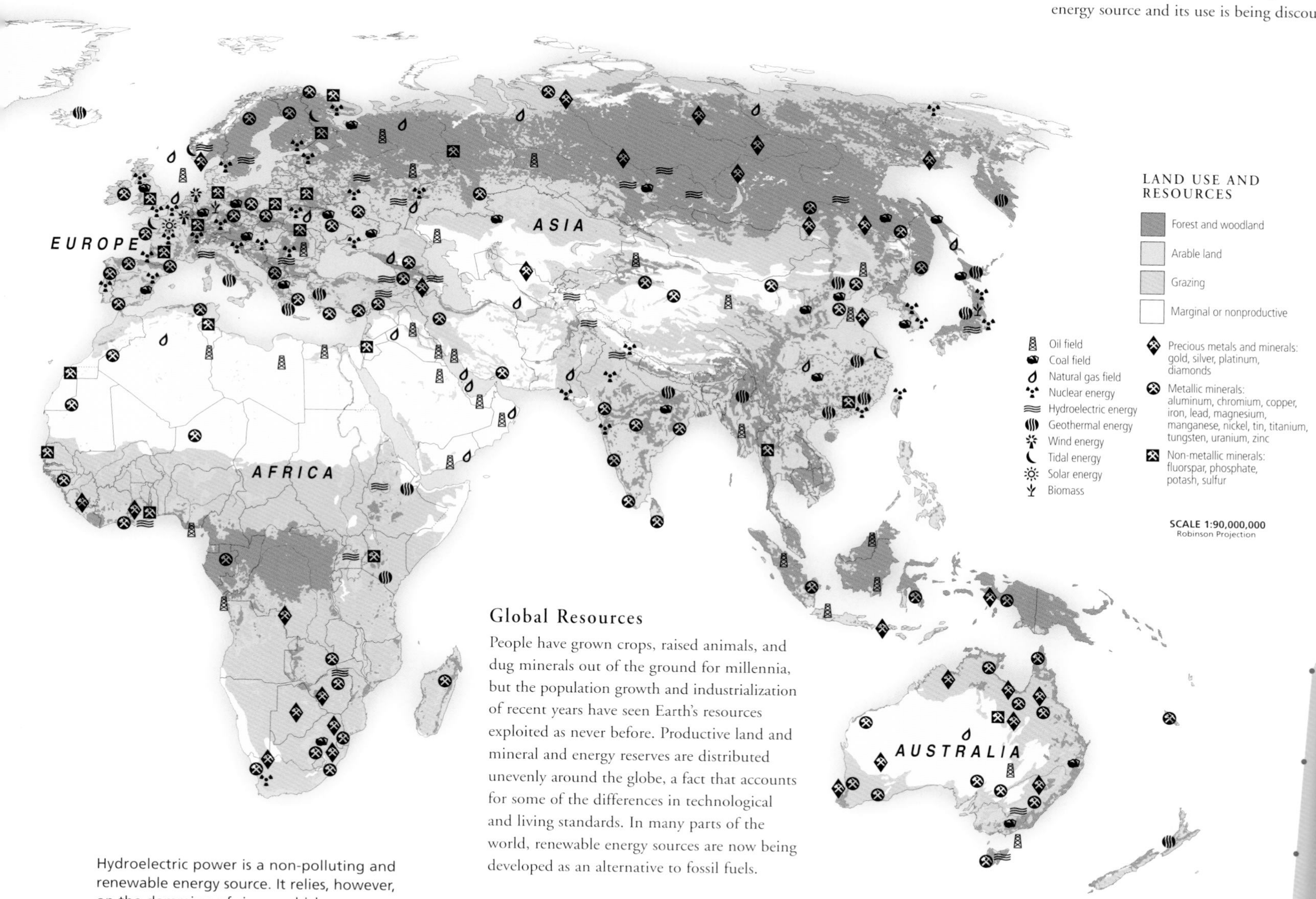
EUROPE
ASIA
AFRICA
AUSTRALIA
LAND USE AND RESOURCES
Forest and woodland
Arable land
Grazing
Marginal or nonproductive
Oil field
Coal field
Natural gas field
Nuclear energy
Hydroelectric energy
Geothermal energy
Wind energy
Tidal energy
Solar energy
Biomass
Precious metals and minerals: gold, silver, platinum, diamonds
Metallic minerals: aluminum, chromium, copper, iron, lead, magnesium, manganese, nickel, tin, titanium, tungsten, uranium, zinc
Non-metallic minerals: fluorspar, phosphate, potash, sulfur
SCALE 1:90,000,000
Robinson Projection

Global Resources

People have grown crops, raised animals, and dug minerals out of the ground for millennia, but the population growth and industrialization of recent years have seen Earth's resources exploited as never before. Productive land and mineral and energy reserves are distributed unevenly around the globe, a fact that accounts for some of the differences in technological and living standards. In many parts of the world, renewable energy sources are now being developed as an alternative to fossil fuels.

Hydroelectric power is a non-polluting and renewable energy source. It relies, however, on the damming of rivers, which causes environmental damage at the local level.

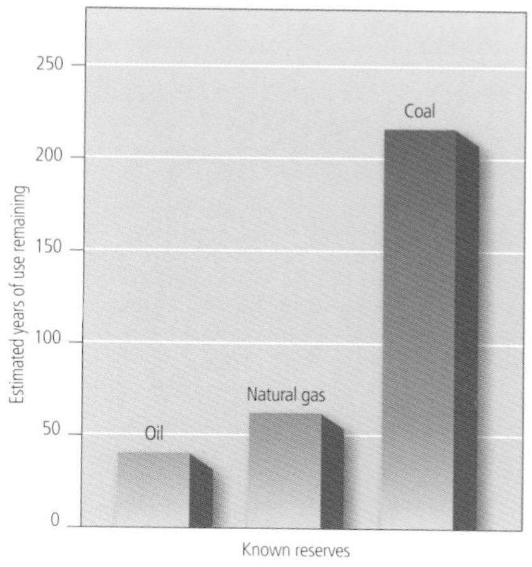
250
200
150
100
50
0
Estimated years of use remaining
Oil
Natural gas
Coal
Known reserves

A Limited Supply

Based on known reserves and current usage levels, the world may face shortages of oil and natural gas within decades, while coal will last at least another 200 years. New technology may allow additional reserves to be discovered and exploited, but fossil fuels are certainly finite and there is great concern about the pollution they create. Many people are now looking to cleaner and renewable energy sources, such as hydro, wind, geothermal, and solar power.

Growing Demand

The 20th century saw an unprecedented increase in the demand for energy, as technology enabled fossil fuels to be exploited and much of the globe to be electrified. Future population growth, increased demand for transport services, and further industrialization will ensure that energy demand continues to rise.

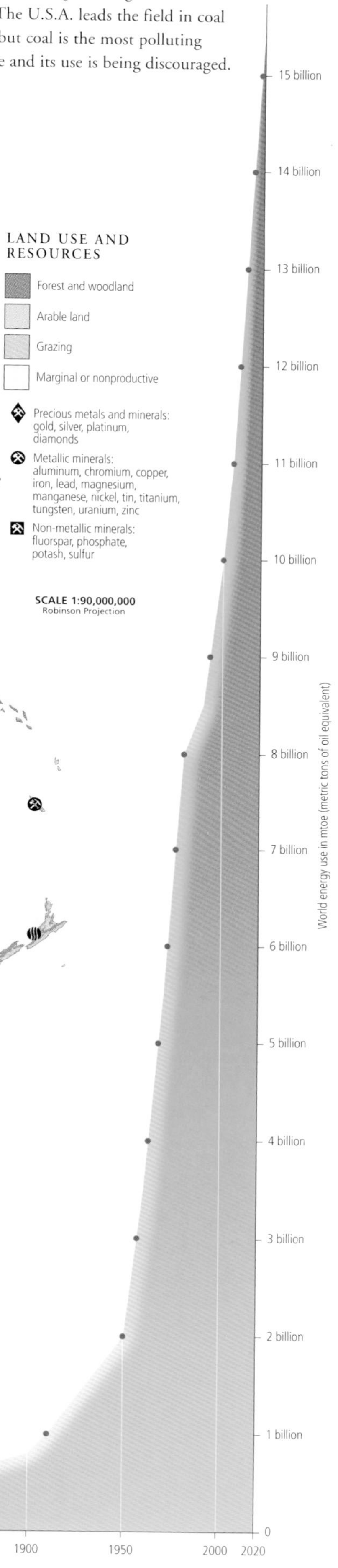
15 billion
14 billion
13 billion
12 billion
11 billion
10 billion
9 billion
8 billion
7 billion
6 billion
5 billion
4 billion
3 billion
2 billion
1 billion
0
World energy use in mtoe (metric tons of oil equivalent)
1500
1550
1600
1650
1700
1750
1800
1850
1900
1950
2000
2020
Year

The Global Environment

The actions of humans have always affected the environment in some way, but never more so than during the industrialization and population explosion of the past 150 years. Almost every part of the world is now suffering from serious environmental problems—from deforestation and soil degradation to air and water pollution—and much of the damage is on a global scale.

The current rate of extinction is unprecedented—between 17,000 and 100,000 species vanish every year, mostly because of habitat destruction. Some biologists believe that a mass extinction caused by human activities is underway and that up to 50 percent of all species could be extinct by 2100.

About 93 percent of materials used in modern production end up as waste. Liquid and gas waste can circulate globally through water and air. Chemicals such as chlorofluorocarbons (CFCs) have depleted the atmosphere's protective ozone layer, leading to a dramatic increase in skin cancers and eye cataracts. Persistent Organic Pollutants (POPs), highly toxic chemicals that accumulate in the fatty tissue of organisms, become more concentrated as they move up the food chain and are now found almost everywhere, even at the poles.

As environmental problems have become more severe, awareness of the impact of human activities has grown. As a result, conservation campaigns aimed at saving threatened species, protecting natural habitat, and curbing pollution have gained broad support in many parts of the world.

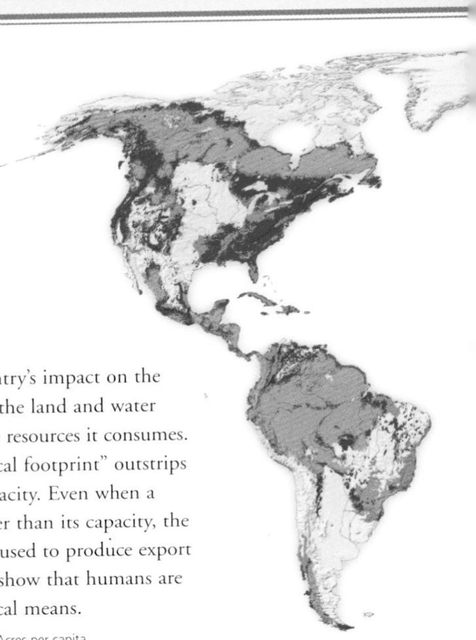

National Footprints

One way to measure a country's impact on the environment is to estimate the land and water area required to produce the resources it consumes. In most cases, this "ecological footprint" outstrips the country's ecological capacity. Even when a country's footprint is smaller than its capacity, the remaining capacity is often used to produce export goods. The world averages show that humans are living beyond their ecological means.

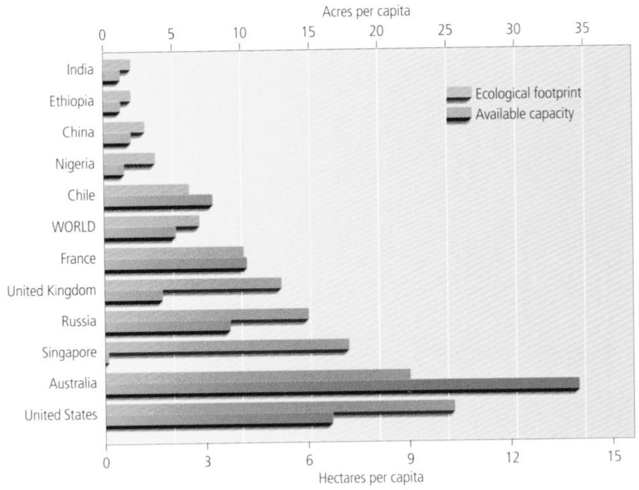
Acres per capita
0
5
10
15
20
25
30
35
India
Ethiopia
China
Nigeria
Chile
WORLD
France
United Kingdom
Russia
Singapore
Australia
United States
Ecological footprint
Available capacity
0
3
6
9
12
15
Hectares per capita

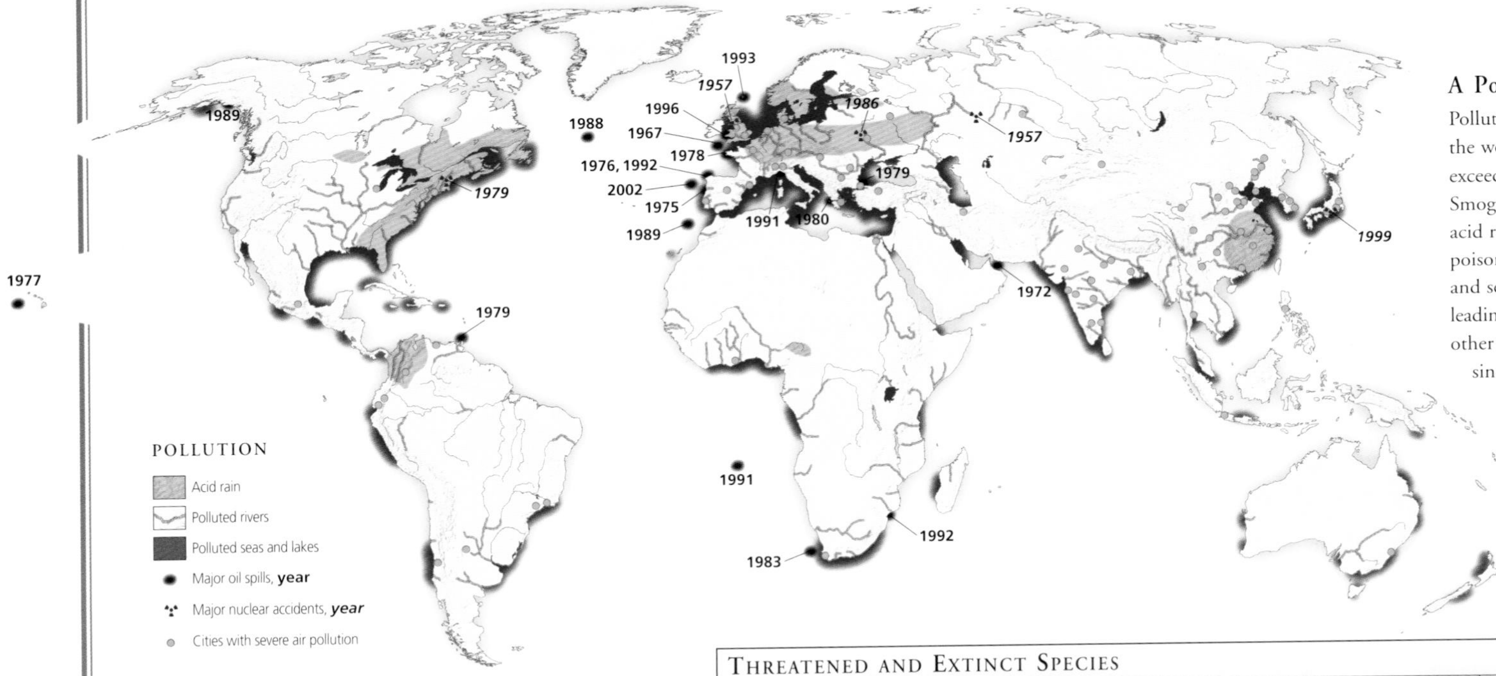
1993
1957
1996
1988
1967
1986
1989
1978
1957
1976, 1992
1979
1979
2002
1975
1991
1980
1989
1999
1977
1972
1979
1991
1992
1983
POLLUTION
Acid rain
Polluted rivers
Polluted seas and lakes
Major oil spills, year
Major nuclear accidents, year
Cities with severe air pollution

A Polluted Planet

Pollution is placing an increasing strain on the world's ecosystems. Air pollution now exceeds safe limits in more than 80 cities. Smogs can travel long distances and deposit acid rain that destroys vegetation and poisons waterways. Runoff carries fertilizers and sewage into lakes, rivers, and oceans, leading to toxic algal blooms that kill off other life. While their incidence has fallen since the 1970s, large oil spills remain a leading cause of marine pollution. Accidents at nuclear power plants can have a global impact when winds transport the radioactive fallout.

About one percent of birds and mammals became extinct in the 20th century. Affected by poaching, habitat loss, and war, gorillas count among the hundreds of mammals threatened today and rely on conservation efforts for survival.

Threatened and Extinct Species

	Known species in group	% assessed for threatened status	Species assessed as threatened	% of assessed species that are threatened	Species known to be extinct	% of described species known to be extinct
Mammals	4,700	100%	1,137	24%	77	1.6%
Birds	9,900	100%	1,192	12%	132	1.3%
Reptiles	8,000	less than 15%	293	25%	23	0.3%
Amphibians	4,900	less than 15%	157	21%	7	0.1%
Fishes	25,000	less than 10%	742	30%	92	0.4%
Insects	950,000	less than 0.1%	557	59%	72	0.004%
Mollusks	70,000	less than 5%	939	27%	304	0.4%
Crustaceans	40,000	less than 5%	409	21%	8	0.02%
Plants	270,000	less than 5%	5,714	49%	92	0.03%

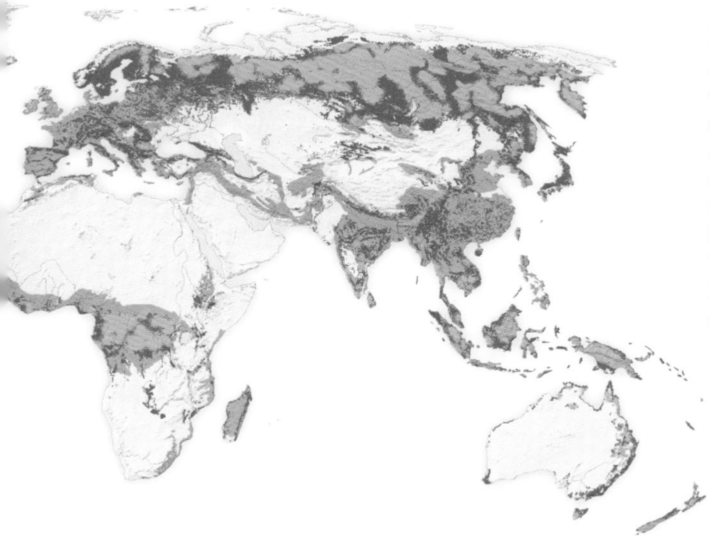
DEFORESTATION
Original forest extent
Current forest cover
Remaining frontier forest

Disappearing Forests

At least 40,000 square miles (100,000 sq km) of forest are lost every year, mainly to logging and land clearing for agriculture. Africa and Asia now have only about one-third of their original forest cover. Frontier forests are areas that have been left undisturbed and remain large enough to maintain their biodiversity. The Amazon basin, Canada and Alaska, and Russia contain the main expanses of frontier forest, but 39 percent of this is under threat.

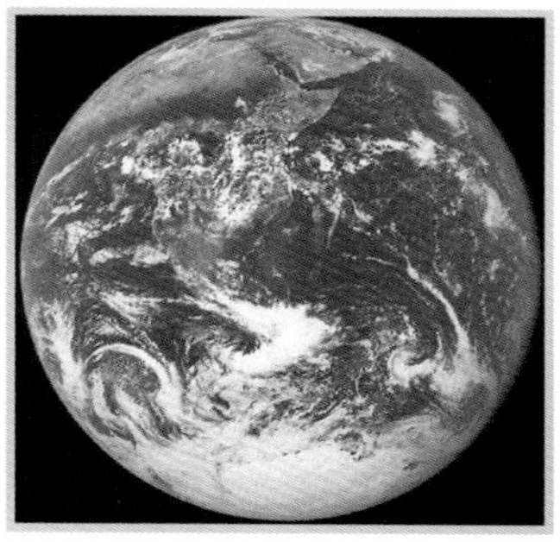

In the 1960s and 1970s, Apollo astronauts photographed Earth from space, allowing many people to see our planet as a single entity. The image both reflected and generated environmental concern.

Like many of the world's major rivers, the Sittang River Delta, in Myanmar (Burma), is choked with silt, a result of widespread deforestation and soil erosion.

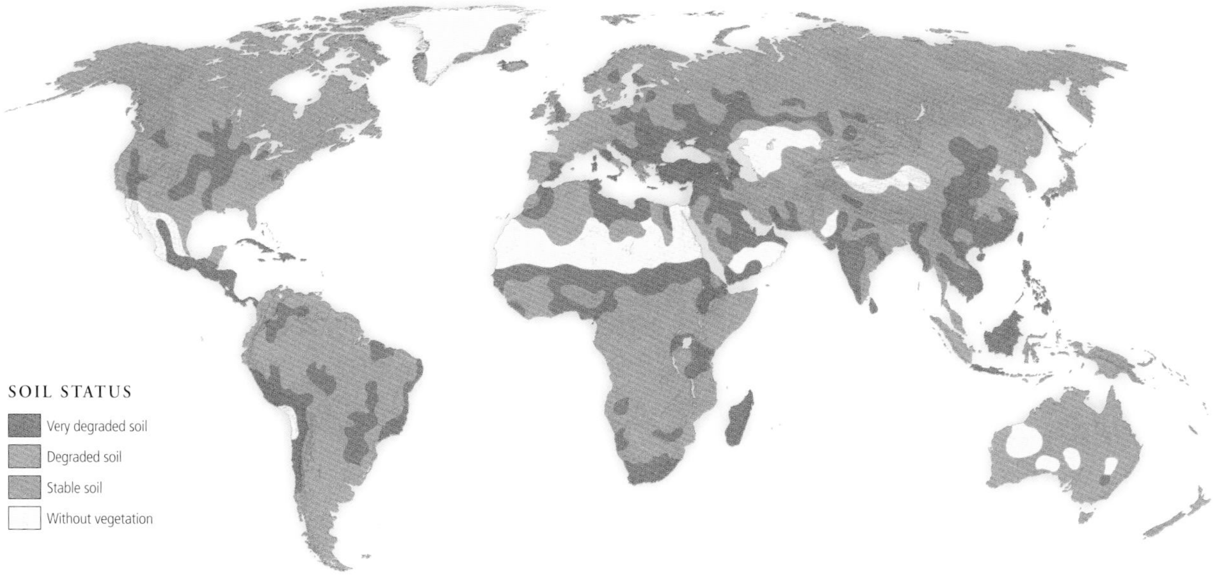
SOIL STATUS
Very degraded soil
Degraded soil
Stable soil
Without vegetation

Degraded Soil

Overgrazing, deforestation, agriculture, and other human activities have degraded about 8 million square miles (20 million sq km) of soil—an area larger than the United States and Mexico combined. Once soil loses its vegetation cover, it becomes particularly susceptible to erosion by water and wind. The problem is acute in many of the world's drylands, where intensified land use has left soils vulnerable to degradation during drought.

Climate Change

Earth is warm enough for life because the atmosphere contains carbon dioxide, methane, and other "greenhouse gases" that trap the Sun's heat (see below). During the past 150 years, fossil fuel combustion and other human activities have dramatically increased the levels of greenhouse gases. Over the same period, Earth has become warmer, with average temperatures rising about 1°F (0.5°C). If this trend continues, the effects could be devastating. As ice sheets and glaciers melt, sea levels will rise and flood many islands and coastal regions of countries such as Bangladesh and China. Rainfall patterns may alter, with widespread drought leading to serious food shortages in Africa and India. The warmer atmosphere will also generate more severe hurricanes and other storms. In response to this threat, most industrialized countries signed the Kyoto Protocol in 1997, agreeing to reduce greenhouse gas emissions.

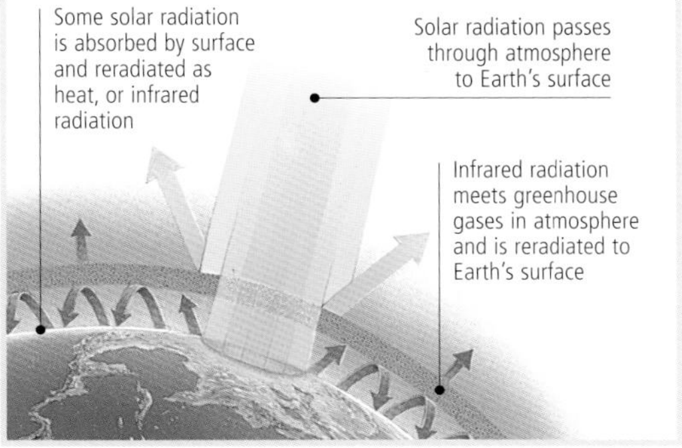
Some solar radiation is absorbed by surface and reradiated as heat, or infrared radiation
Solar radiation passes through atmosphere to Earth's surface
Infrared radiation meets greenhouse gases in atmosphere and is reradiated to Earth's surface

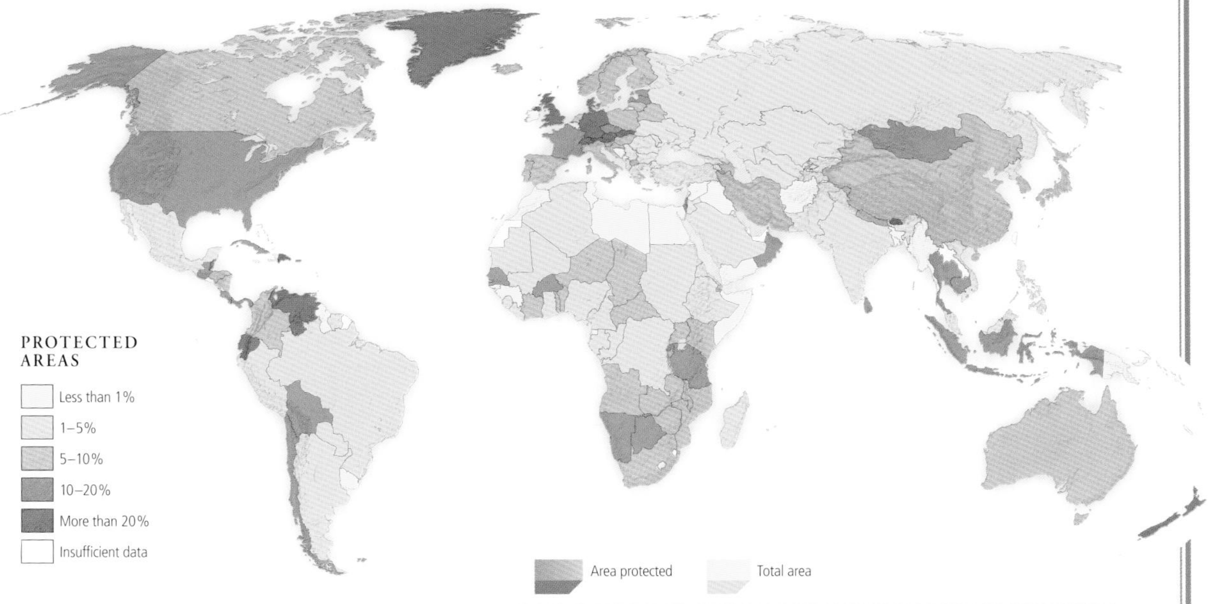
PROTECTED AREAS
Less than 1%
1–5%
5–10%
10–20%
More than 20%
Insufficient data

Nature Conservation

National parks, nature reserves, wildlife sanctuaries, and other protected areas now make up 6.4 percent of Earth's land surface. Some of these, however, are merely "paper parks" that have been severely damaged by human activities. Recent efforts have been aimed at ensuring genuine protection of critical areas, conserving large enough areas to maintain biodiversity, and finding ways for conservation measures to involve and benefit the often impoverished local people.

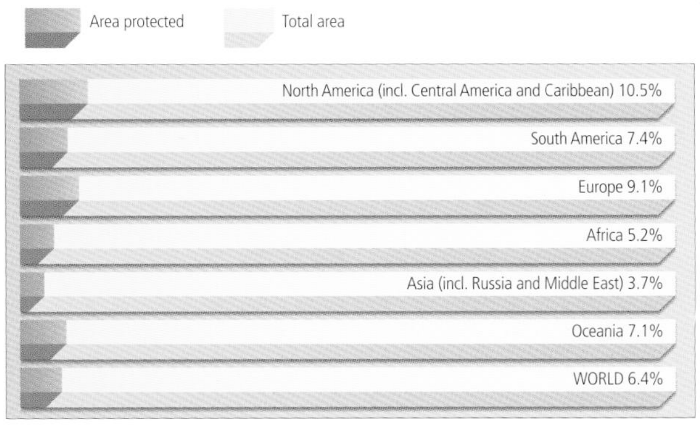
Area protected
Total area
North America (incl. Central America and Caribbean) 10.5%
South America 7.4%
Europe 9.1%
Africa 5.2%
Asia (incl. Russia and Middle East) 3.7%
Oceania 7.1%
WORLD 6.4%

Languages of the World

Complex speech is one of the key ways in which humans differ from the rest of the animal world, and language is one of the main ways groups of humans distinguish themselves from one another. Rudimentary forms of language may have been used by the first modern humans more than 100,000 years ago, but it was not until about 40,000 years ago that there was an explosion of art and technology, and humans moved into harsher environments. Many believe that the development of complex language prompted this great leap in human capability.

There are now more than 6,000 languages spoken in the world and their distribution reveals much about human history. Throughout time, languages have both diverged and converged. The Roman conquest of Europe 2,000 years ago replaced most of the existing Celtic languages with Latin. Gradually, different groups developed their own dialects of Latin, which eventually became Romance languages such as French, Italian, and Spanish. The Germanic language of English displays many borrowings from French, a legacy of the Norman Conquest of England in 1066.

In more recent times, colonialism has spread European languages throughout the globe. In many places, this contact has led to new languages such as pidgins (spoken only as a second language) and creoles (spoken as a mother tongue). At the same time, however, many indigenous languages have been lost. As societies become more centralized, and particularly as English takes hold as the dominant world language, much of the extraordinary diversity of languages is under threat.

The Basques live in France and Spain near the western Pyrenees. Their language seems to be an isolate (unrelated to any other modern language), but other Basque-like languages were probably spoken in Western Europe before the Roman conquest.

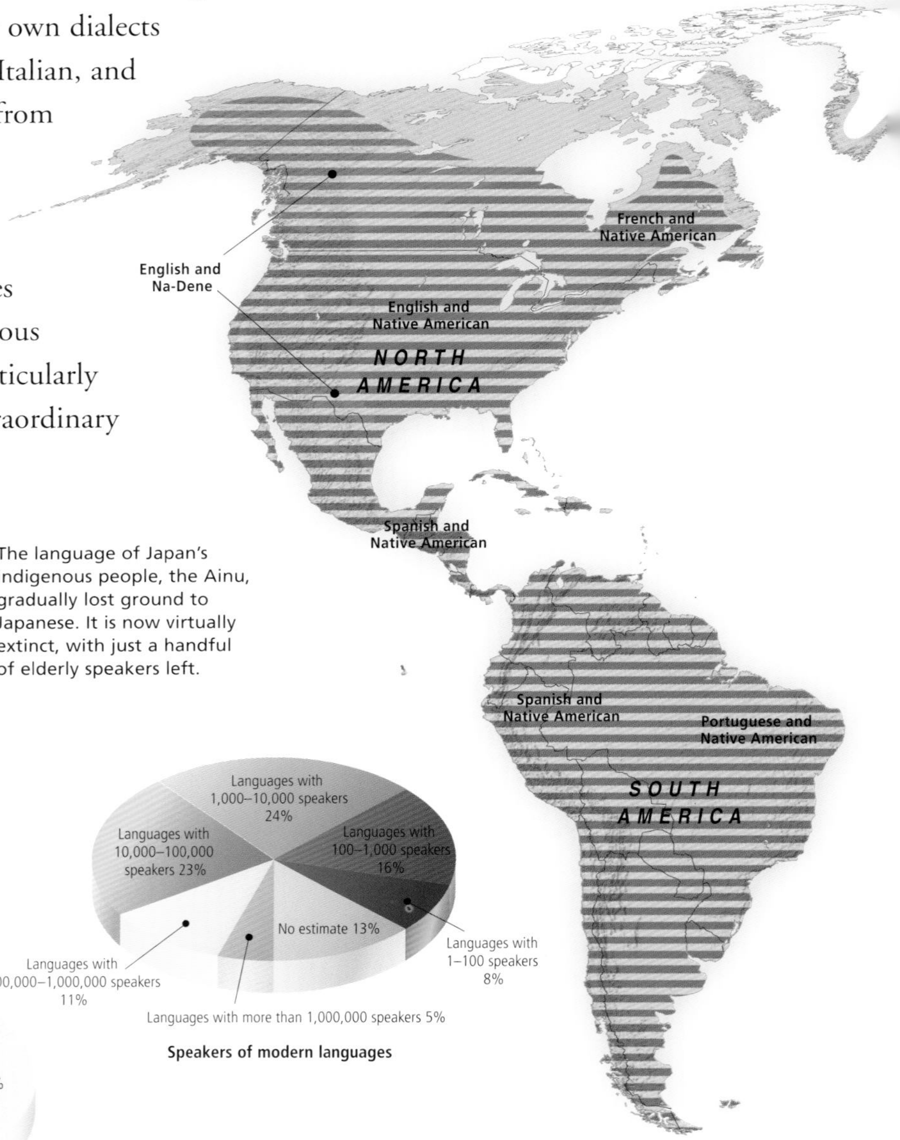

English and Na-Dene
French and Native American
English and Native American
NORTH AMERICA
Spanish and Native American
Spanish and Native American
Portuguese and Native American
SOUTH AMERICA
Languages with 1,000–10,000 speakers 24%
Languages with 10,000–100,000 speakers 23%
Languages with 100–1,000 speakers 16%
No estimate 13%
Languages with 100,000–1,000,000 speakers 11%
Languages with 1–100 speakers 8%
Languages with more than 1,000,000 speakers 5%

The language of Japan's indigenous people, the Ainu, gradually lost ground to Japanese. It is now virtually extinct, with just a handful of elderly speakers left.

Major Languages

Mandarin Chinese has far more mother-tongue (first-language) speakers than any other single language, but of the world's top 15 languages, 12 belong to the Indo-European family. The prevalence of English, French, Portuguese, and Spanish resulted from the colonial expansion of European power that began in the 15th century. North America now has more English speakers than anywhere else, while South America is home to the most Spanish speakers.

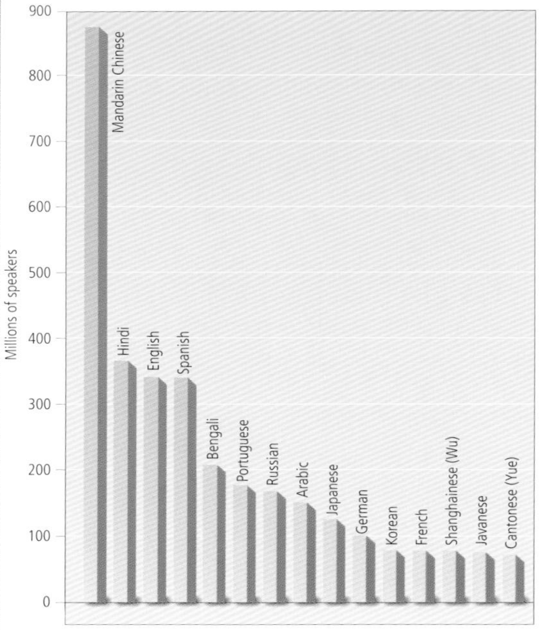

Millions of speakers
900
800
700
600
500
400
300
200
100
0
Mandarin Chinese
Hindi
English
Spanish
Bengali
Portuguese
Russian
Arabic
Japanese
German
Korean
French
Shanghainese (Wu)
Javanese
Cantonese (Yue)

Speakers of modern languages

Distribution of modern languages

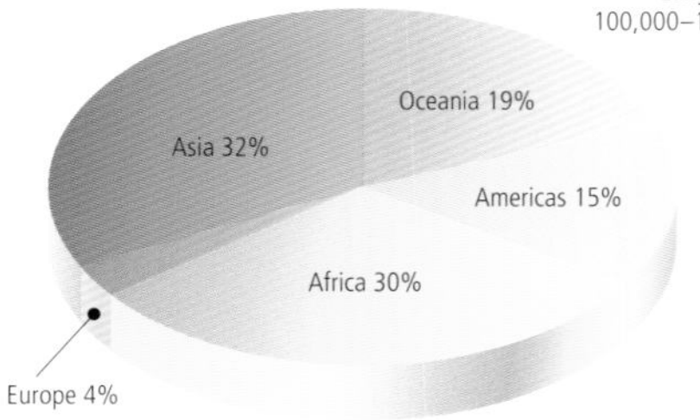

Asia 32%
Oceania 19%
Americas 15%
Africa 30%
Europe 4%

Endangered Languages

Although European languages dominate the world in terms of number of speakers, they account for just a tiny percentage of modern languages. As more and more young people adopt the languages of power, much of humankind's linguistic diversity is lost. About 40 percent of languages are spoken by fewer than 10,000 people, and roughly 450 have only a few elderly speakers left. At least half the world's tongues are likely to vanish by 2100—an average of one language lost every 10 days.

DEVELOPMENT OF WRITING

3400 BC Sumerian pictogram system

3100 BC Egyptian hieroglyphs, script with 2,500 symbols, in use for 3,500 years

2500 BC Indus Valley pictogram system

by 2500 BC Sumerian cuneiform script of wedge-shaped strokes

2400 BC Akkadians adopt cuneiform

1750 BC Linear A script in Minoan Crete

c. 1600 BC Proto-Canaanite script in Egypt, later develops into Linear Phoenician

1500 BC Chinese pictogram script, later develops into several thousand characters

1400 BC Linear B script in Mycenaean Greece

1100 BC Linear Phoenician alphabet of 22 letters, later spreads to Greece

Indo-European Family Tree

In the 18th century, a colonial judge, Sir William Jones, recognized similarities between the Sanskrit language of India, and Latin and Greek, and proposed that they came from a single source. This ancestor language, Proto-Indo-European, has since been shown to have evolved into many European and Asian languages. The family tree presented here shows only the major ones. Almost 3 billion people, roughly half the world's population, now speak an Indo-European language.

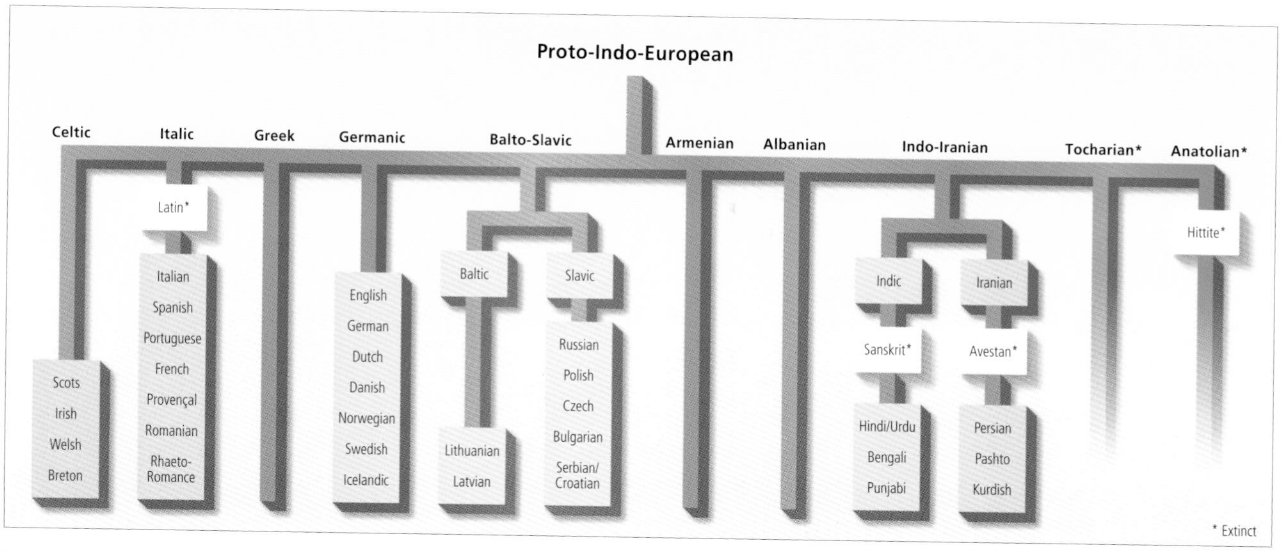
Proto-Indo-European
Celtic
Italic
Greek
Germanic
Balto-Slavic
Armenian
Albanian
Indo-Iranian
Tocharian*
Anatolian*
Scots
Irish
Welsh
Breton
Latin*
Italian
Spanish
Portuguese
French
Provençal
Romanian
Rhaeto-Romance
English
German
Dutch
Danish
Norwegian
Swedish
Icelandic
Baltic
Lithuanian
Latvian
Slavic
Russian
Polish
Czech
Bulgarian
Serbian/Croatian
Indic
Sanskrit*
Hindi/Urdu
Bengali
Punjabi
Iranian
Avestan*
Persian
Pashto
Kurdish
Hittite*
* Extinct

Related Tongues

By comparing vocabulary and grammar, linguists can identify relationships between different languages and group them into families that share a common ancestor language. While some language families, such as Indo-European, are widely accepted, others remain the subject of intense debate. For example, some linguists have proposed just three great families of Native American languages, but most believe that there is not enough evidence for such a classification.

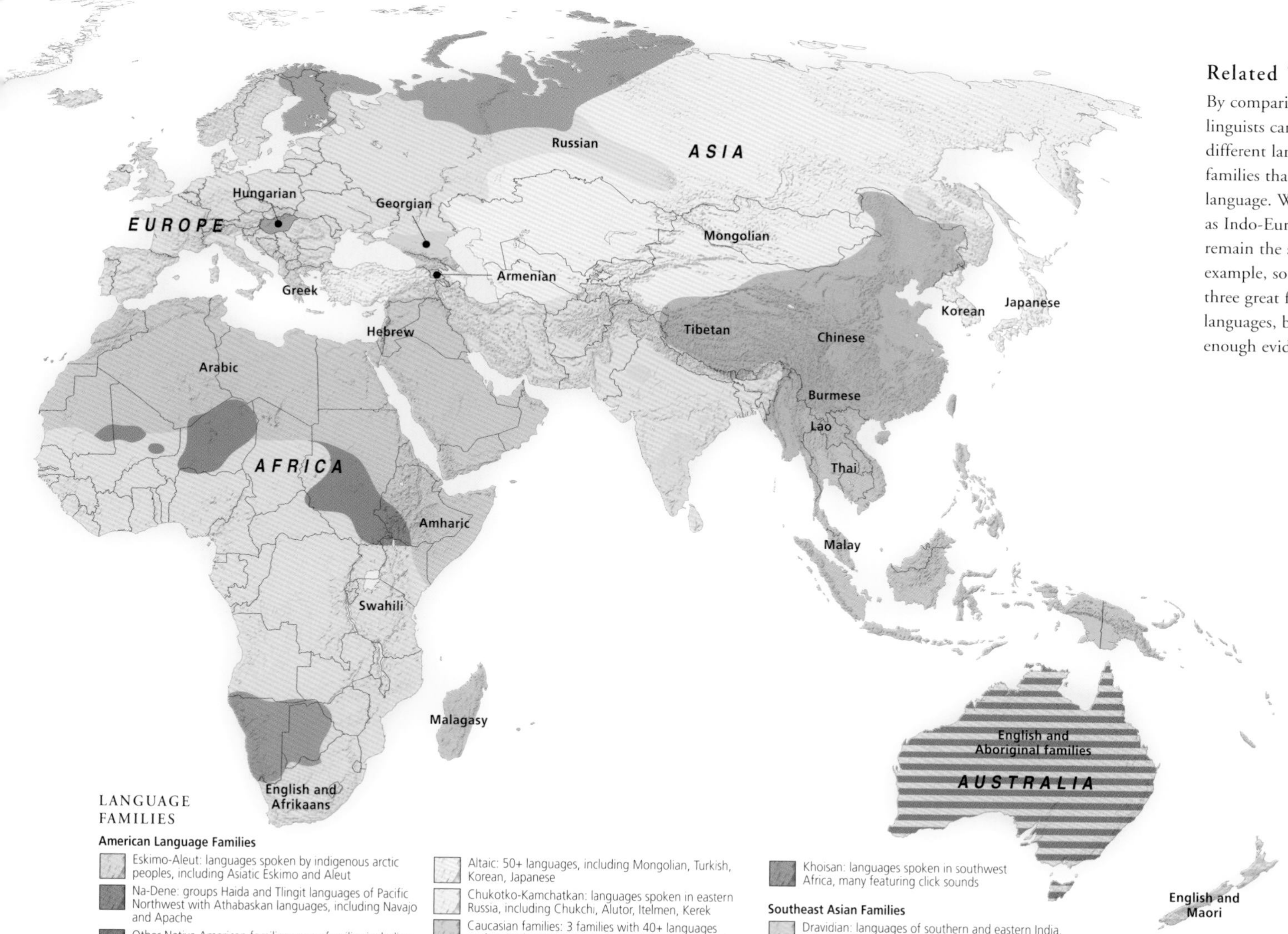
Russian
ASIA
Hungarian
Georgian
EUROPE
Mongolian
Armenian
Greek
Korean
Japanese
Hebrew
Tibetan
Chinese
Arabic
Burmese
Lao
AFRICA
Thai
Amharic
Malay
Swahili
Malagasy
English and Aboriginal families
AUSTRALIA
English and Afrikaans
English and Maori

SCALE 1:90,000,000
Robinson Projection

LANGUAGE FAMILIES

American Language Families

- Eskimo-Aleut: languages spoken by indigenous arctic peoples, including Asiatic Eskimo and Aleut
- Na-Dene: groups Haida and Tlingit languages of Pacific Northwest with Athabaskan languages, including Navajo and Apache
- Other Native American families: many families including languages such as Cree, Mohawk, Shoshone, Jacaltec, Guarani, Quechua

Eurasian Language Families

- Indo-European: many European and Asian languages, including English, German, French, Italian, Spanish, Russian, Hindi, Persian
- Uralic: 20+ languages, including Estonian, Finnish, Hungarian, Sami, Nenets
- Altaic: 50+ languages, including Mongolian, Turkish, Korean, Japanese
- Chukotko-Kamchatkan: languages spoken in eastern Russia, including Chukchi, Alutor, Itelmen, Kerek
- Caucasian families: 3 families with 40+ languages spoken in the Caucasus, including Chechen, Georgian

African Language Families

- Afro-Asiatic: 370+ languages, including Arabic, Hebrew, Somali, Berber, Hausa
- Nilo-Saharan: 100+ languages in East Africa, including Songhai, Nubian, Masai
- Niger-Congo: 900+ languages, including Swahili, Fulani, Zulu, Mossi, Shona
- Khoisan: languages spoken in southwest Africa, many featuring click sounds

Southeast Asian Families

- Dravidian: languages of southern and eastern India, including Kannada, Malayalam, Tamil, Telugu
- Sino-Tibetan: 130+ languages of East Asia, including Mandarin, Cantonese, Tibetan, Burmese
- Austric families: includes Austronesian (Malay, Maori), Austroasiatic (Vietnamese), and Tai-Kadai (Thai, Lao)
- Papuan families: 700+ languages spoken on the island of New Guinea
- Australian Aboriginal families: 250+ languages spoken by indigenous peoples of Australia

Bilingual education is an important way to promote the survival of minority languages and cultures. Many Australian Aboriginal children now receive their lessons in both English and an indigenous language.

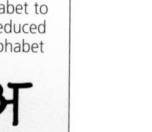

The Chinese writing system comprises several thousand logographs, characters that each represent an entire word. People speaking mutually incomprehensible dialects of Chinese can still communicate via this script.

800 BC South Arabian script, evolved from Proto-Canaanite, later spreads into North Arabia and Africa

800 BC Phoenician script evolves into Aramaic in Syria

800 BC Phoenician alphabet adapted to create Classical Greek script, with both vowels and consonants; later becomes modern Greek alphabet

600 BC Etruscans in Italy adapt Greek alphabet

600 BC Egyptian demotic script supplants hieratic (a cursive variety of cuneiform)

500 BC Ethiopic script, still in use today

500 BC Romans adapt Etruscan alphabet, later becomes modern Roman alphabet of 26 letters

300 BC Brahmi alphabet in India

200 BC Nabateans use Aramaic script for Arabic language

200 BC Chinese logographic script in its modern form

c. AD 1 Aramaic script evolves into modern Hebrew square letter script, used for most of Old Testament

by AD 250 Mayan hieroglyphic script in Mesoamerica

AD 250 Runic script develops in Scandinavia, later spreads to Britain

AD 400 First Arabic script, later versions used for Koran and developed into modern Arabic script

AD 700 Japanese adopt Chinese characters

AD 900 Greek missionaries among the Slavs adapt Greek alphabet to create Cyrillic script, later reduced to 33 letters of modern Russian alphabet

AD 1000 Devanagari (used to write Sanskrit and Hindi) and other modern Indian scripts develop from Brahmi

Religions of the World

Much of history and most national identities have been shaped by religion, and virtually every culture has engaged in some form of religious practice. Prehistoric people depicted gods in artwork and buried their dead with grave goods. Even when religion has been officially abandoned, as in Marxist Communist states, the ruling ideology has tended to take on religious dimensions.

There are now hundreds of different religious traditions in the world, but Hinduism, Buddhism, Judaism, Christianity, and Islam have had the broadest influence. Hinduism and Buddhism both developed in Asia and aim to free followers from the cycle of death and rebirth. Originating in the Middle East, Judaism, Christianity, and Islam are all monotheistic religions, believing in a single god.

History is full of conflicts perpetuated in the name of religion and, in recent years, religious difference has helped fuel disputes in such troublespots as Northern Ireland, the former Yugoslavia, Israel, and India and Pakistan. During the 20th century, advances in science provided new explanations for some of the mysteries traditionally explained by religion and encouraged many to lead increasingly secular lives. In response, fundamentalist movements have arisen in most major religions and some extremists have resorted to violence. New religions have also flourished, with New Age practices, for instance, being widely adopted in the West.

Canada
Black Hills
Salt Lake City
United States of America
Mexico
Chichén Itzá
Cuba
Guatemala
Venezuela
Guyana
Suriname
Colombia
Peru
Machu Picchu
Lake Titicaca
Bolivia
Brazil
Chile
Argentina

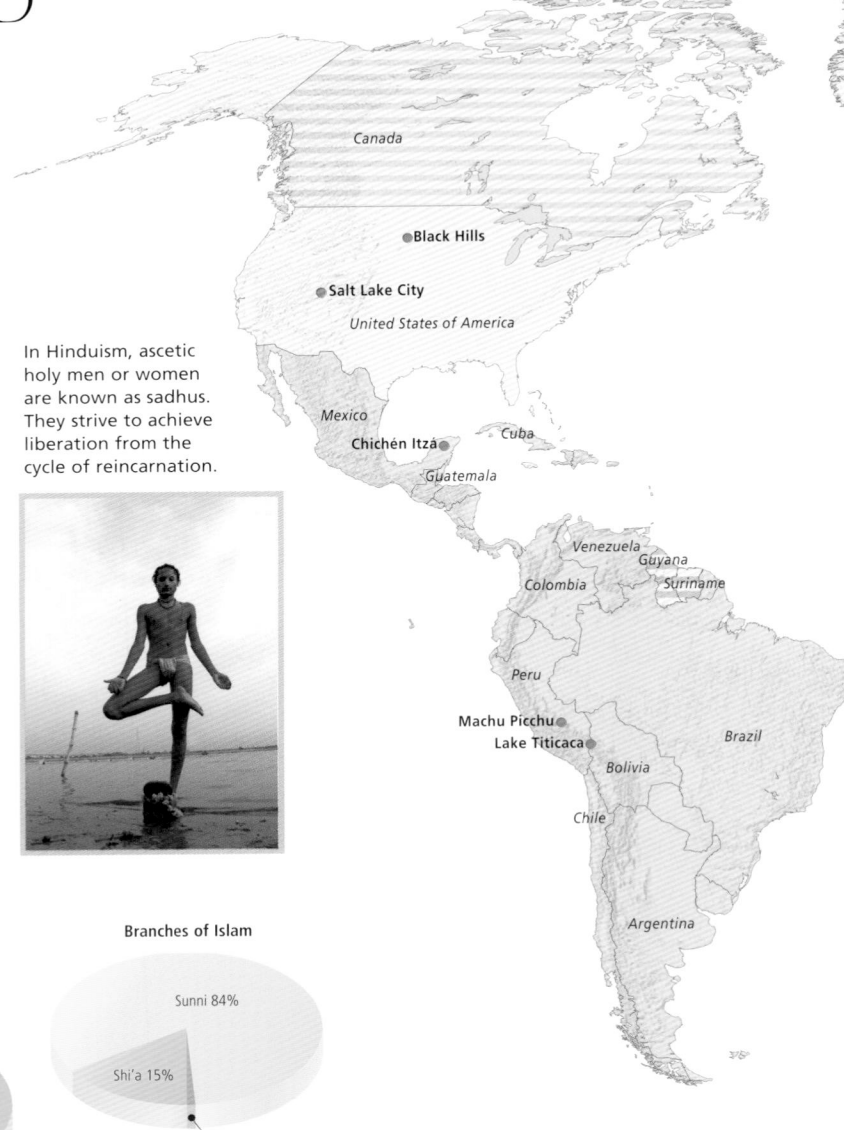

In Hinduism, ascetic holy men or women are known as sadhus. They strive to achieve liberation from the cycle of reincarnation.

Jesus Christ, depicted here in a stained glass window of Bath Abbey, lived in Judaea (present-day Syria and Israel) 2,000 years ago. His teachings form the foundation of the Christian religion.

Branches of Christianity

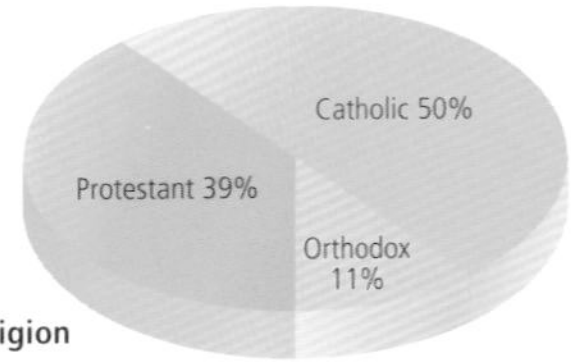

Catholic 50%
Protestant 39%
Orthodox 11%

Branches of Islam

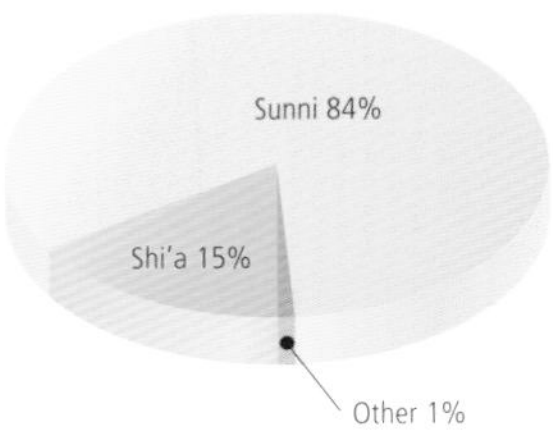

Sunni 84%
Shi'a 15%
Other 1%

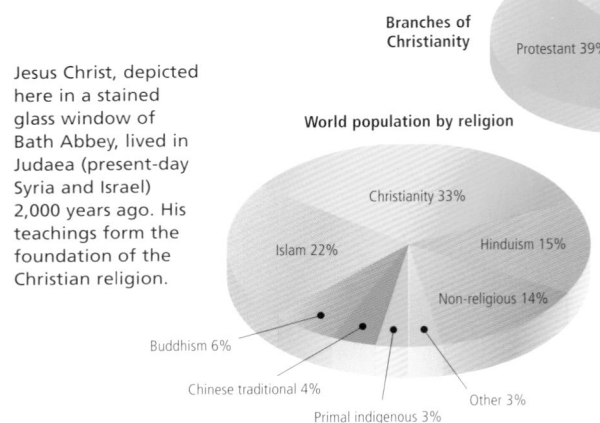

World population by religion

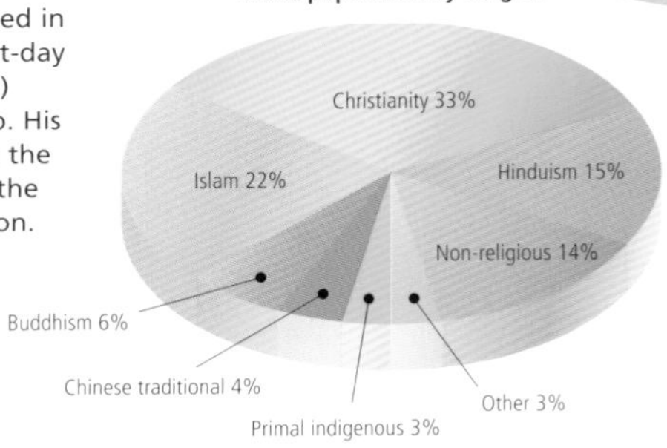

Christianity 33%
Islam 22%
Hinduism 15%
Non-religious 14%
Buddhism 6%
Chinese traditional 4%
Primal indigenous 3%
Other 3%

How the World Worships

The groupings used to divide the world population by religion (left) are all very broad and have many subdivisions. The non-religious group is particularly diverse, with atheists making up a tiny percentage of those claiming no religious preference. The major branches of the two largest religions, Christianity and Islam, are shown in the pie charts above.

Jerusalem, Israel, is a revered place for Jews, Muslims, and Christians. Jews pray at the sacred Western (Wailing) Wall, right next to the third holiest site in Islam, the Dome of the Rock.

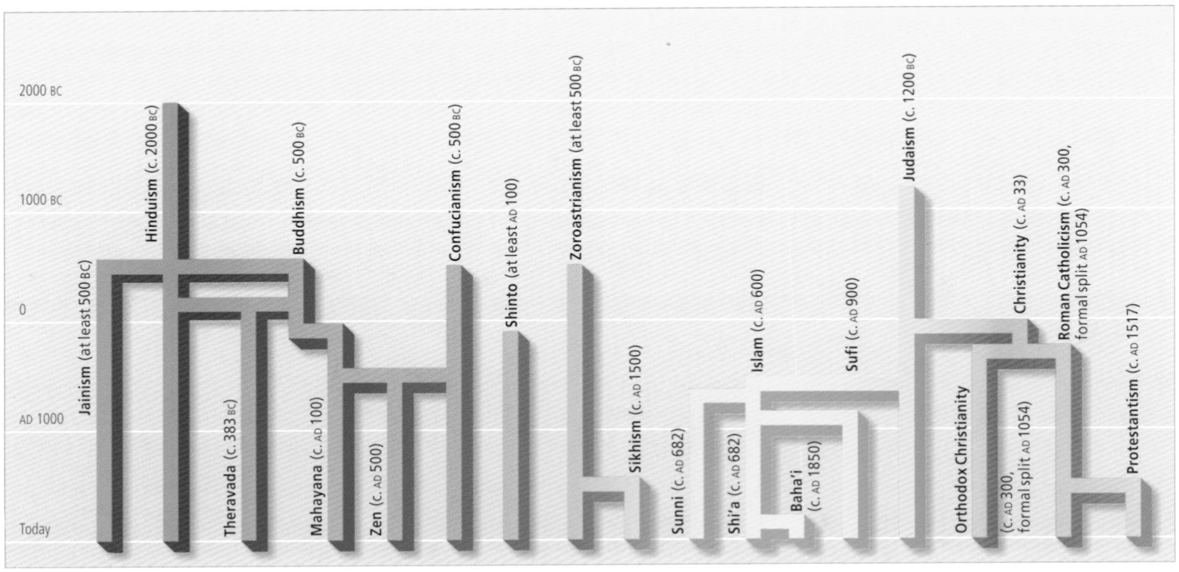

2000 BC
1000 BC
0
AD 1000
Today
Jainism (at least 500 BC)
Hinduism (c. 2000 BC)
Theravada (c. 383 BC)
Buddhism (c. 500 BC)
Mahayana (c. AD 100)
Zen (c. AD 500)
Confucianism (c. 500 BC)
Shinto (at least AD 100)
Zoroastrianism (at least 500 BC)
Sikhism (c. AD 1500)
Sunni (c. AD 682)
Shi'a (c. AD 682)
Islam (c. AD 600)
Baha'i (c. AD 1850)
Sufi (c. AD 900)
Judaism (c. 1200 BC)
Orthodox Christianity
(c. AD 300, formal split AD 1054)
Christianity (c. AD 33)
Roman Catholicism (c. AD 300, formal split AD 1054)
Protestantism (c. AD 1517)

Religious Origins

Although the earliest signs of religious belief date back 60,000 years, the oldest classical religion is Hinduism, which has developed over the past 4,000 years. The newest of the major religions, Baha'i, began only in the 19th century. Many of today's major faiths share common roots: Christianity and Islam can be traced back to earlier forms of Judaism, while Hinduism gave rise to Buddhism and Jainism. Confucianism, Taoism, and Shinto developed independently, but do exhibit similarities that reflect their common link to Asian folklore.

Russian Federation
United Kingdom
Sweden
Canterbury
Germany
Ukraine
Kazakhstan
Mongolia
France
Italy
Bos. & Herz.
Lourdes
Istanbul
The Vatican
Alb.
Mt Athos
Turkey
Greece
Japan
North Korea
South Korea
Fujiyama
Ise Shrine
Kairouan
Tunisia
Syria
Iran
Afghanistan
China
Morocco
Israel
Iraq
Kerbela
Amritsar
Jerusalem, Bethlehem
Nazareth, Haifa
Pakistan
Lumbini
Lhasa
Fai Shan
Algeria
Libya
Mt Sinai
Egypt
Mathura
Nepal
Bhutan
Medina
Saudi Arabia
Mecca
Varanasi,
Ganges River
Bodhgaya
Bangladesh
Myanmar (Burma)
India
Mauritania
Mali
Niger
Chad
Sudan
Yemen
Thailand
Philippines
Mopti
Burkina Faso
Benin
Ghana
Nigeria
Axum
Ethiopia
Central African Republic
Vietnam
Côte d'Ivoire
Liberia
Cameroon
Sri Lanka
Somalia
Uganda
Kenya
Malaysia
Gabon
Congo
Dem. Rep. of the Congo
Tanzania
Indonesia
East Timor
Papua New Guinea
Angola
Mozambique
Namibia
Madagascar
Botswana
Uluru
Australia
South Africa
New Zealand
MAJOR RELIGIOUS GROUPS
Protestant Christianity
Catholic Christianity
Orthodox Christianity
Judaism
Shi'a Islam
Sunni Islam
Chinese religions
Hinduism
Theravada Buddhism
Mahayana Buddhism
Tibetan Buddhism
Primal indigenous
SCALE 1:90,000,000
Robinson Projection

Distribution of Faith

This map shows the predominant religions and key holy sites of each country. In most places, however, multiple religions are actually practiced side by side. Chinese religions include Confucianism, Buddhism, and Taoism, which form a single religious culture in much of China. Primal religions are still strong in many areas, often being incorporated into the local practice of the mainstream religion.

HOLY SITES

- Christian site
- Muslim site
- Hindu site
- Buddhist site
- Primal site
- Shared holy site (Jewish, Muslim, Christian)

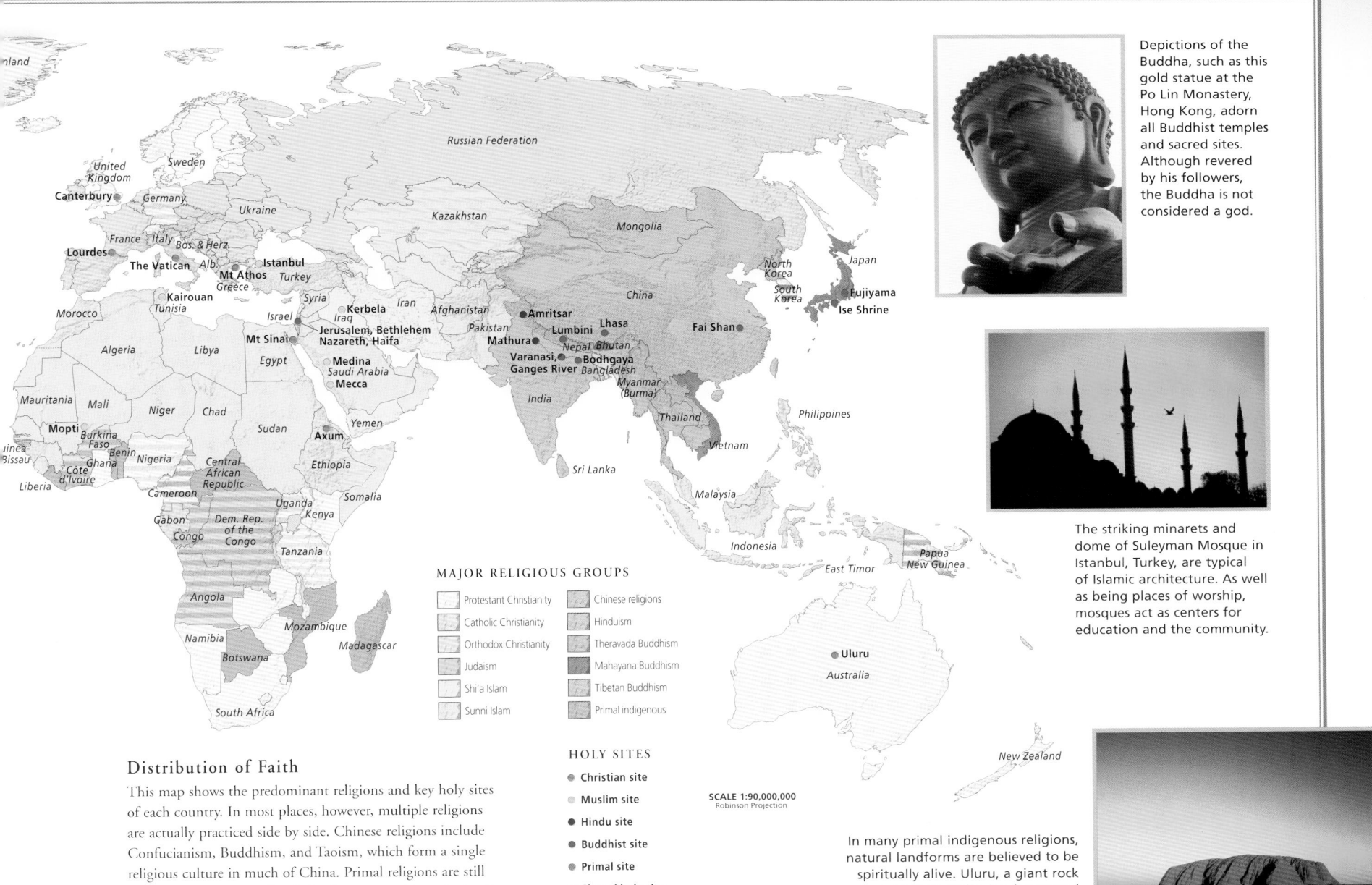

Depictions of the Buddha, such as this gold statue at the Po Lin Monastery, Hong Kong, adorn all Buddhist temples and sacred sites. Although revered by his followers, the Buddha is not considered a god.

The striking minarets and dome of Suleyman Mosque in Istanbul, Turkey, are typical of Islamic architecture. As well as being places of worship, mosques act as centers for education and the community.

In many primal indigenous religions, natural landforms are believed to be spiritually alive. Uluru, a giant rock in central Australia, is a key sacred site for the local Aboriginal people.

The Classical Religions

Religion	Numbers	Deities	Sacred texts	Major festivals	Streams or branches
Christianity	2 billion	God	Bible (Old and New Testaments)	Christmas, Easter	Catholic, Protestant, Orthodox
Islam	1.3 billion	Allah	Koran, Hadith	'Id al-Adha, 'Id al-Fitr, Maulid an-nabi	Sunni, Shi'a, Sufi
Hinduism	900 million	Brahma, Vishnu, Shiva, Mahadevi, and others	Vedas, Gitas	Diwali, Holi, Dusserah	Vaishnavites, Shaivas, Shaktas, and others
Buddhism	360 million	No deity (Buddha paid homage as spiritual guide)	Pali Tripitaka, Suttapitaka and Vinayapitaka, Adhidhammapitaka, Sutras	Wesak day, Esalha, and others	Theravada, Mahayana, Tibetan, Zen
Confucianism	350 million	Ancestor veneration	The Five Classics (including the I Ching)	New Year and others	Han Confucianism, Neo-Confucianism
Taoism	187 million	Shou Hsing, Tsai Shen, Fu Shen	Tao Te Ching, Chuang Tzu	Various annual festivals symbolizing renewal	Religious Taoism
Sikhism	23 million	Sat Guru	Guru Granth Sahib	Gurpurbs (commemorating birth or martyrdom of a Guru)	Khasala (baptised) and non-baptised
Judaism	14 million	God	Tanak (includes Torah), Talmud	Pesach (Passover), Shavuot (Weeks), Sukkoth (Booths), Purim, Hannukah, Rosh Hashanah (New Year)	Sephardim, Ashkenazim, Orthodox, Reform, Hasidic
Baha'i	6 million	Allah	Writings of Baha'u'llah and the Bab	Naw-Ruz, Rivdan	Babi, Baha'i
Jainism	4 million	No deity (various spiritual teachers, Tirthankaras)	Tattvartha Sutra, Kalpa Sutra	Paryushana, Diwali	Digambara, Shvetambara
Shinto	4 million	Amaterasu, Izanami and Izanagi, and others	Kojiki, Nihongi	Various festivals to mark spring planting and autumn harvest and to honor deities of particular shrines	Koshitsu, Jinja, Kyoha/Shinkyoha, Minkan
Zoroastrianism	500,000	Ahura Mazda	Avestas	Nao Raz, Khordad Sal, gahambars (5-day festivals) celebrating Sky, Water, Earth, Plants, Cattle, and Man	Parsism

INDIGENOUS PEOPLES

At least 350 million diverse indigenous individuals—more than 5 percent of the world's population—are spread across the globe, from the Arctic to the South Pacific. Descendants of the people who inhabited a territory before the formation of modern nation-states, they maintain unique and distinctive cultures, but are also among the world's most disadvantaged groups.

When their territories were colonized, indigenous peoples were often treated by the dominant society as inferior and suffered systematic discrimination and oppression. As their land and resources were appropriated, many indigenous peoples lost their livelihood. In some countries, policies of assimilation saw indigenous language and culture suppressed and children separated from their parents. In Africa and Asia, artificial borders divided peoples or turned them into minorities.

Against the odds, a remarkable number of indigenous societies survived, resisting the physical and cultural onslaught—in the United States alone, there are more than 500 federally recognized tribes. Indigenous peoples today range from remote groups maintaining traditional lifestyles to lawyers, doctors, and others working in cities. The way forward for many is marked by the fight for land rights, self-determination, and cultural autonomy. The United Nations provided a measure of recognition when it declared the years 1995–2004 the International Decade of the World's Indigenous People.

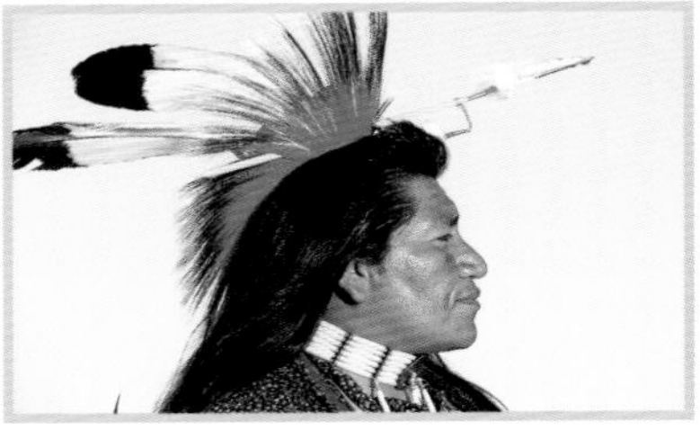

The Ute Indians of Utah and Colorado traditionally consider themselves closely related to bears and perform a Bear Dance known as *Momaqui Mowat.*

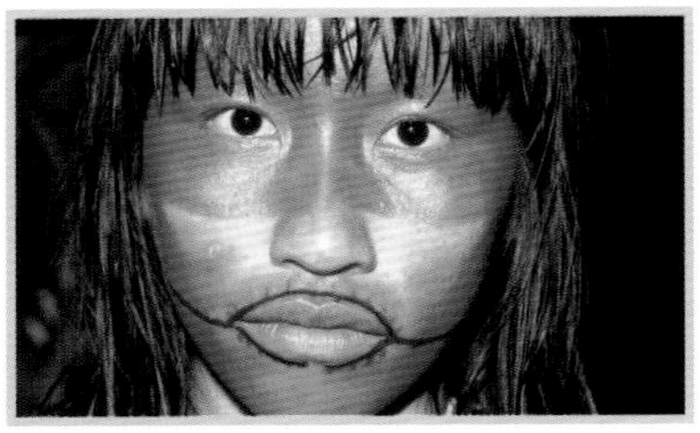

The Matses are seminomadic hunter-gatherers who live in the jungle along the Rio Yavari, Peru. They have names for 47 different types of rain-forest habitat.

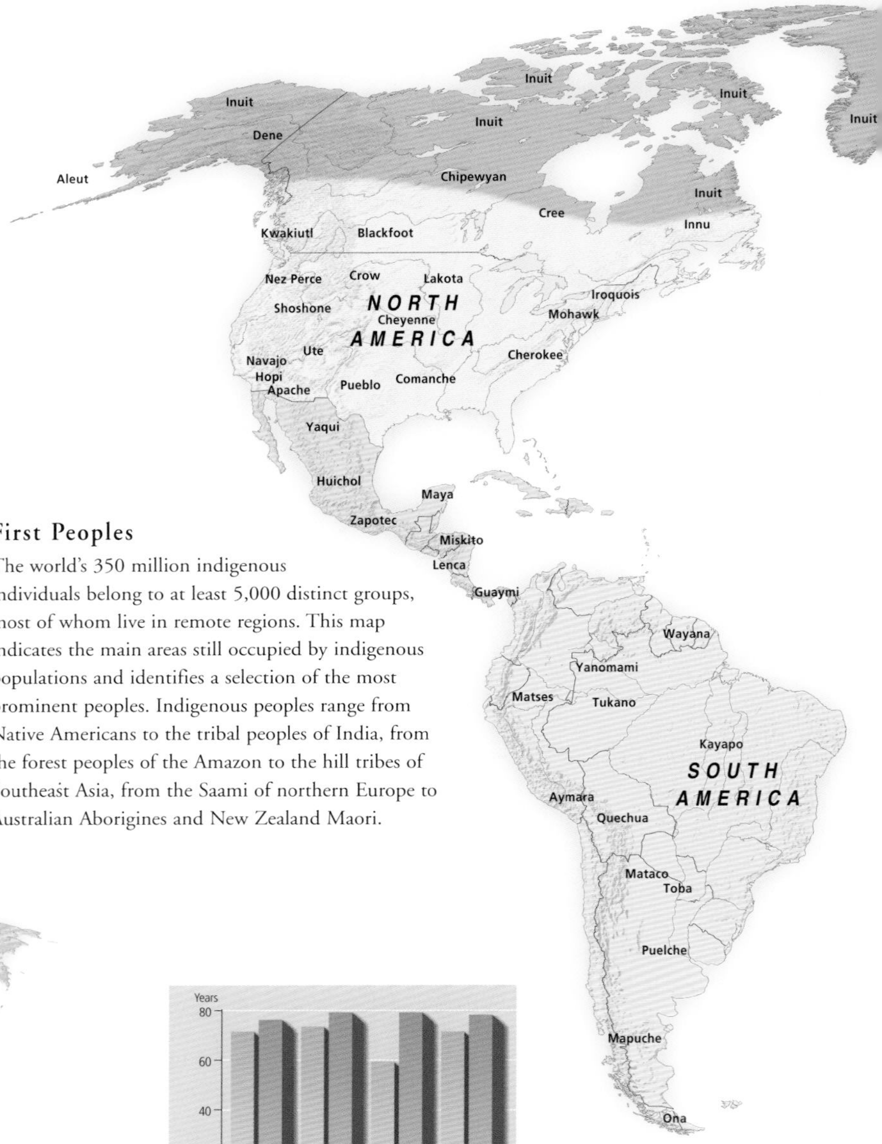

Inuit
Dene
Aleut
Chipewyan
Cree
Innu
Kwakiutl
Blackfoot
Nez Perce
Crow
Lakota
Shoshone
NORTH AMERICA
Cheyenne
Iroquois
Mohawk
Ute
Navajo
Hopi
Apache
Pueblo
Comanche
Cherokee
Yaqui
Huichol
Maya
Zapotec
Miskito
Lenca
Guaymi
Wayana
Yanomami
Matses
Tukano
Kayapo
SOUTH AMERICA
Aymara
Quechua
Mataco
Toba
Puelche
Mapuche
Ona

First Peoples

The world's 350 million indigenous individuals belong to at least 5,000 distinct groups, most of whom live in remote regions. This map indicates the main areas still occupied by indigenous populations and identifies a selection of the most prominent peoples. Indigenous peoples range from Native Americans to the tribal peoples of India, from the forest peoples of the Amazon to the hill tribes of Southeast Asia, from the Saami of northern Europe to Australian Aborigines and New Zealand Maori.

COLONIALISM (c. 1900)

- British
- French
- Belgian
- Dutch
- German
- Danish
- Italian
- Russian
- Spanish
- former Spanish
- Portuguese
- former Portuguese
- Ottoman
- Japanese
- U.S.

The Expansion of European Power

Many empires have been established throughout history, but the European expansion that began in the late 15th century was unprecedented. By 1900, most of the Americas and Oceania and large areas of Africa and Asia had been or were still under foreign control. For the indigenous populations, colonization was usually disastrous. Their land was stolen, its natural resources plundered, and the people were variously exposed to fatal European diseases, forcibly converted to Christianity, forced into slavery, and massacred. At least 10 million African slaves were shipped to the Americas. In North America, the original indigenous population of 5 million was reduced to 1 million by the 1890s, while in Central and South America the numbers fell from 30 million to 5 million.

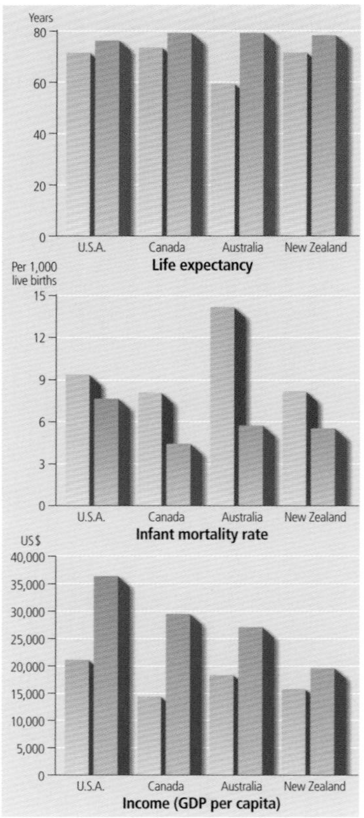

Years
80
60
40
20
0
U.S.A.
Canada
Australia
New Zealand
Life expectancy
Per 1,000 live births
15
12
9
6
3
0
U.S.A.
Canada
Australia
New Zealand
Infant mortality rate
US$
40,000
35,000
30,000
25,000
20,000
15,000
10,000
5,000
0
U.S.A.
Canada
Australia
New Zealand
Income (GDP per capita)

Living Standards

These graphs compare three key standard-of-living indicators in four countries. They demonstrate that, on average, indigenous peoples can expect to lead shorter lives, have more children die in infancy, and earn less money than their non-indigenous compatriots.

- Indigenous
- Total population

The Arctic's Inuit have traditionally relied on hunting and fishing. Their livelihood is threatened by environmental damage from pollution and oil and gas extraction.

This San tribesman of the harsh Kalahari Desert in southern Africa is demonstrating a bow and arrow he has fashioned from a gemsbok horn and springbok hide.

These Karen women in Myanmar (Burma) are among Southeast Asia's indigenous peoples. An elongated neck is considered a sign of great beauty in their society.

The Southern Highlands of Papua New Guinea are home to the Huli people. For dances, they paint their faces with yellow clay and cover their bodies in tree oil.

Saami
Nenet
Evenki
Yakut
Yukagir
Chukchi
Koryak
Tatar
Kazakhs
Dukha
Nivkh
EUROPE
Roma
Roma
ASIA
Manchu
Ainu
Uygurs
Kurds
Pathan
Berber
Tuareg
Naga
Miao
Zhuang
Oraon
Santal
Bhil
Hmong
Gaoshan
AFRICA
Bedouin
Chencha
Meo
Karen
Nuer
Dogon
Dukha
Negrito (Agta)
Fulani
Mende
Yoruba
Toda
Vedda
Negrito (Semang)
Senoi
Batak
Higaonon
Iban
Kenyah
Dayak
Pygmies
Masai
Hutu
Tutsi
Mejprat
Dani
Chambri
Huli
Tolai
Nasioi
Motu
Badui
Atoni
Bemba
Yolngu
Wik
San
Basarwa
!Kung
Warlpiri
Pintubi
Mardu
Pitjantjatjara
AUSTRALIA
Nyungar
Maori
SCALE 1:90,000,000
Robinson Projection

SELECTED INDIGENOUS NUMBERS

- **Arctic Peoples**
  150,000 Inuit in Alaska, Canada, Greenland, Russia
  80,000 Saami in Finland, Norway, Sweden, Russia
- **North American Peoples**
  1.5 million indigenous in U.S.A.
  1 million indigenous in Canada
- **Central American Peoples**
  13 million indigenous in Mexico and Central America
- **South American Peoples**
  15 million indigenous in highlands of Bolivia, Chile, Peru
  1 million indigenous in Amazon forest
  1 million Mapuche in southern Chile
- **European Peoples**
  12 million Roma, mainly in Eastern Europe
- **Asian Peoples**
  5 million Bedouin in Saudi Arabia
  20 million Kurds in Turkey, Iraq, Iran, Syria
  1 million indigenous in Russia
  67 million indigenous in China
  51 million indigenous in India
  30 million indigenous in Southeast Asia
- **African Peoples**
  8 million nomads in West Africa
  250,000 Pygmies in Central Africa
  100,000 San and Basarwa in southern Africa
  6 million nomads in East Africa
- **Peoples of Oceania**
  1.5 million indigenous in the Pacific
  290,000 Aborigines in Australia
  350,000 Maori in New Zealand

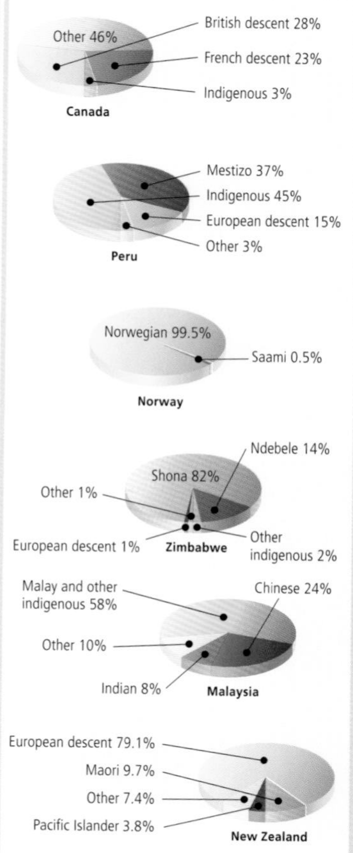

Other 46%
British descent 28%
French descent 23%
Indigenous 3%
Canada
Mestizo 37%
Indigenous 45%
European descent 15%
Other 3%
Peru
Norwegian 99.5%
Saami 0.5%
Norway
Ndebele 14%
Shona 82%
Other 1%
European descent 1%
Zimbabwe
Other indigenous 2%
Malay and other indigenous 58%
Chinese 24%
Other 10%
Indian 8%
Malaysia
European descent 79.1%
Maori 9.7%
Other 7.4%
Pacific Islander 3.8%
New Zealand

Indigenous Proportions

These charts demonstrate the variation in the situation of indigenous peoples around the world. While many groups are outnumbered by the colonizing population, indigenous peoples form the majority in some countries.

Self-Determination

For many indigenous peoples, the key to a positive future is to be able to determine their own future on their own land. In recent years, a number of campaigns for land rights have met with success, but others are still facing significant opposition.

The 'Sea of Hands' display supported Aboriginal native title and reconciliation.

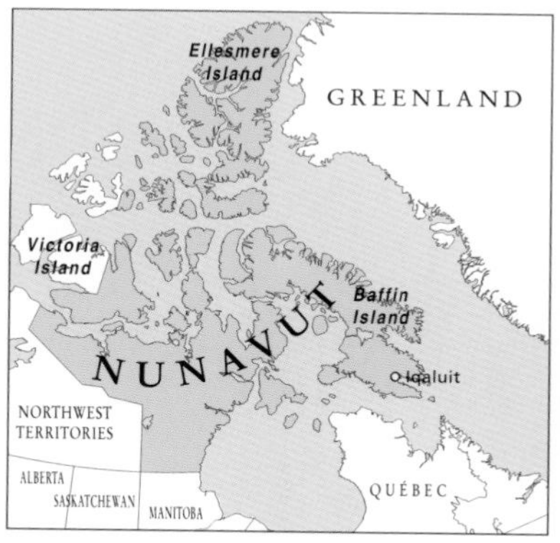

Ellesmere Island
GREENLAND
Victoria Island
Baffin Island
NUNAVUT
Iqaluit
NORTHWEST TERRITORIES
ALBERTA
SASKATCHEWAN
MANITOBA
QUÉBEC

The Nunavut Territory

On April 1, 1999, more than 20 years of negotiations by the Inuit of the Eastern and Central Arctic came to fruition when Nunavut was named Canada's newest province. The Inuit, who make up 85 percent of Nunavut's 25,000 residents, became one of the first indigenous peoples in the Americas to achieve self-government.

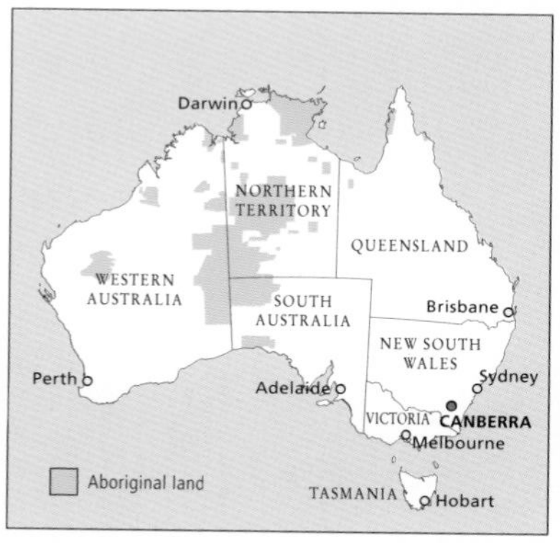

Darwin
NORTHERN TERRITORY
QUEENSLAND
WESTERN AUSTRALIA
SOUTH AUSTRALIA
Brisbane
NEW SOUTH WALES
Perth
Adelaide
Sydney
VICTORIA
CANBERRA
Melbourne
Aboriginal land
TASMANIA
Hobart

Aboriginal Land Rights

Governments had started returning some Crown land to Aboriginal communities in the 1970s, but it wasn't until the landmark *Mabo* decision of 1992 that native title was finally recognized. About 15 percent of Australia is now owned or controlled by indigenous peoples, and many other claims are before the courts.

Saami traditional land
Murmansk
Lappland
SWEDEN
FINLAND
NORWAY
OSLO
HELSINKI
STOCKHOLM
TALLINN
ESTONIA
RUSSIAN FEDERATION
DENMARK
RIGA
COPENHAGEN
LATVIA
LITHUANIA
VILNIUS
GERMANY
BELARUS

Saami Rights

The Nordic Saami Council was formed in 1956 to represent the Saami people. Negotiations are complicated because their traditional lands are now split among Norway, Sweden, Finland, and Russia. The Saami are campaigning to control the land they traditionally use for reindeer-herding, fishing, and hunting.

Rich and Poor

Global industrial output increased 50-fold during the 20th century. The wealth this generated, however, was shared by relatively few and led to an ever greater gap between rich and poor, both within countries and across the world. The richest 1 percent of the world's people receive as much income as the poorest 57 percent. More than 1.2 billion people live on less than US$1 a day, and 2.8 billion live on less than US$2 a day. Developing countries (ones yet to achieve effective industrial production levels) make up much of Asia, Africa, South America, and the Pacific; account for about 75 percent of world population; and share just 20 percent of world income.

During the 1990s, more than 50 developing countries became poorer and many others stagnated, victims of failed economic growth, declining aid from rich countries, rising debt repayments, and falling prices for the raw materials that make up the bulk of their export revenue. The HIV/AIDS epidemic has also been devastating, especially in sub-Saharan Africa, which has 70 percent of the world's 42 million cases.

Even within prosperous countries there can be great disparities in wealth, and in poor countries the brunt of the hardship is borne by disadvantaged groups. On average, men have a larger share of resources than women do, and urban dwellers are far better off than people in rural areas, with greater access to income, education, safe water and sanitation, and health services. On both a national and global level, future stability depends on a fairer distribution of the world's wealth.

Famine can be both a cause and an effect of armed conflict, which prevents farmers from producing and distributing food. While essential during a crisis, food aid does not provide a long-term solution.

Mexico 7.9%
Belize 12.1%
Jamaica 8.3%
St Kitts-Nevis 6.0%
Dominica 6.0%
Honduras 5.3%
Venezuela 6.0%
Guyana 6.3%
Panama 11.6%
Colombia 7.6%
Ecuador 8.6%
Brazil 10.8%
Bolivia 6.8%
Paraguay 5.0%
Uruguay 8.0%
Chile 10.0%
Argentina 9.0%

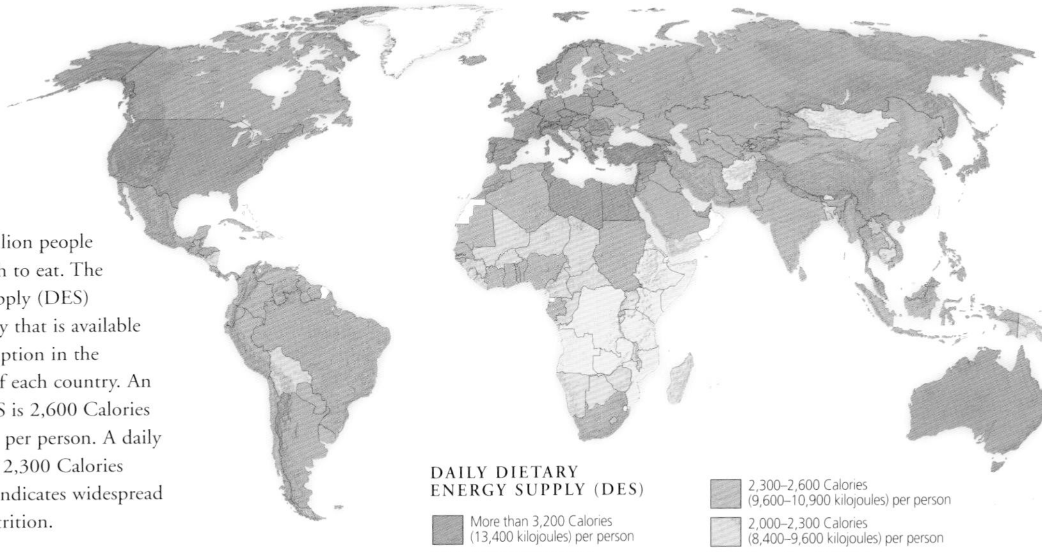

Food Supply

More than 800 million people do not have enough to eat. The Dietary Energy Supply (DES) estimates the energy that is available for human consumption in the total food supply of each country. An adequate daily DES is 2,600 Calories (10,900 kilojoules) per person. A daily DES of fewer than 2,300 Calories (9,600 kilojoules) indicates widespread hunger and malnutrition.

DAILY DIETARY ENERGY SUPPLY (DES)

- More than 3,200 Calories (13,400 kilojoules) per person
- 2,900–3,200 Calories (12,000–13,400 kilojoules) per person
- 2,600–2,900 Calories (10,900–12,000 kilojoules) per person
- 2,300–2,600 Calories (9,600–10,900 kilojoules) per person
- 2,000–2,300 Calories (8,400–9,600 kilojoules) per person
- Fewer than 2,000 Calories (8,400 kilojoules) per person
- Insufficient data

Health Indicators

The gulf between the haves and have-nots is reflected most keenly in a comparison of key health indicators. Most of the risk factors that contribute to the world's major health problems are related to patterns of consumption. Poor countries are home to 170 million underweight children, 3 million of whom die each year. At the same time, obesity contributes to about half a million deaths every year in North America and Western Europe. Unsafe water, sanitation, and hygiene lead to 1.7 million deaths every year. Other leading risk factors in Africa and Asia include unsafe sex, iron deficiency, and indoor smoke from solid fuels.

COUNTRY COMPARISON

- Norway (HDI 0.942)*
- Mexico (HDI 0.796)
- Indonesia (HDI 0.684)
- Pakistan (HDI 0.499)
- Sierra Leone (HDI 0.275)

* HDI Human Development Index

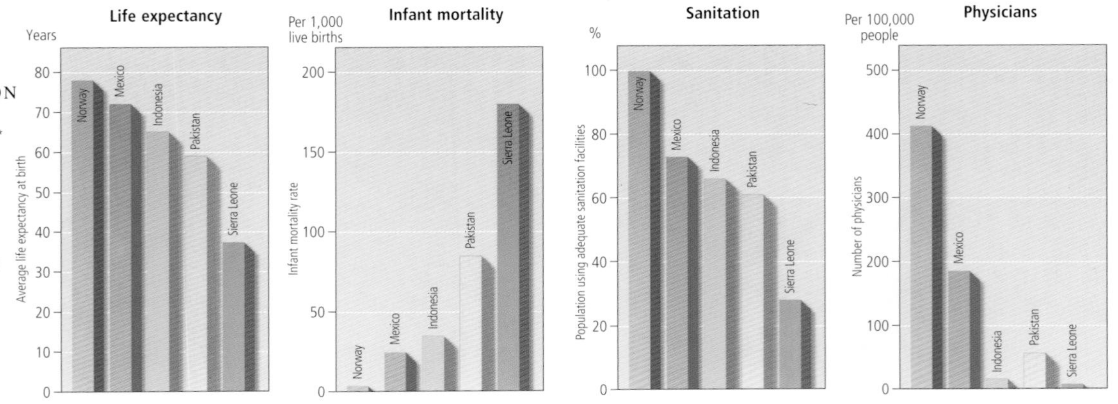

Life expectancy
Years
Average life expectancy at birth
Norway
Mexico
Indonesia
Pakistan
Sierra Leone
Infant mortality
Per 1,000 live births
Infant mortality rate
Sanitation
%
Population using adequate sanitation facilities
Physicians
Per 100,000 people
Number of physicians

RICHEST COUNTRIES: GDP PER CAPITA*	
Luxembourg	US$44,000
United States	US$37,600
San Marino	US$34,600
Norway	US$31,800
Switzerland	US$31,700
Ireland	US$30,500
Canada	US$29,400
Belgium	US$29,000
Denmark	US$29,000
Japan	US$28,000

POOREST COUNTRIES: GDP PER CAPITA*	
East Timor	US$500
Somalia	US$550
Sierra Leone	US$580
Burundi	US$600
Democratic Republic of Congo	US$610
Tanzania	US$630
Malawi	US$670
Afghanistan	US$700
Comoros	US$720
Eritrea	US$740

** All GDP figures are in PPP (Purchasing Power Parity), which takes into account price differences between countries.*

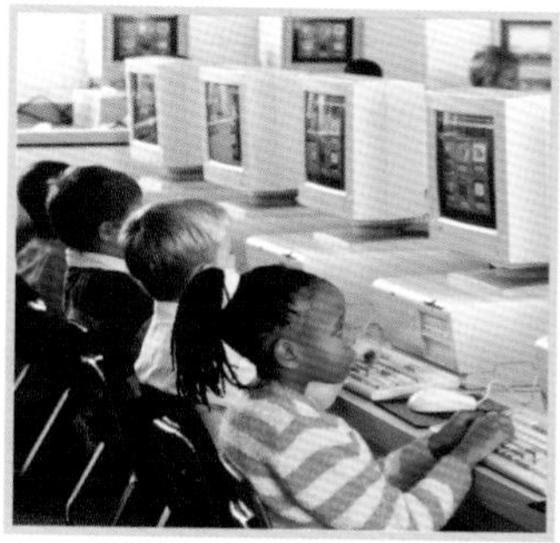

In developed countries, computers are now a feature of classrooms. With only 8 percent of the world connected to the Internet, the "digital divide" is likely to further disadvantage the poorest people.

Although the 1990s saw primary school enrollments increase in every region, less than 60 percent of young children in sub-Saharan Africa attend school.

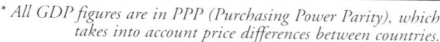

LOWEST ADULT LITERACY RATES**		
COUNTRY	1990	2001
Niger	11.4%	16.5%
Burkina Faso	16.3%	24.8%
Mali	18.8%	26.4%
Gambia	25.6%	37.8%
Senegal	28.4%	38.3%
Benin	26.4%	38.6%
Guinea-Bissau	27.2%	39.6%
Ethiopia	28.6%	40.3%
Bangladesh	34.2%	40.6%
Mauritania	34.8%	40.7%

*** Comparable statistics for several poor countries are not available, but some estimates put Somalia's adult literacy rate at about 25%, Sierra Leone's at about 30%, Guinea's and Afghanistan's at about 35%, and Angola's and Iraq's at about 40%.*

Estonia 6.9%
Latvia 6.8%
Lithuania 16.1%
Poland 8.7%
Ukraine 6.0%
Moldova 12.8%
Romania 6.7%
Bulgaria 10.1%
Turkey 15.2%
Slovakia 12.8%
Czech Republic 8.4%
Hungary 26.4%
Croatia 14.6%
Bosnia and Herzegovina 6.3%
Macedonia 5.7%
Lebanon 8.7%
Jordan 7.6%
Tunisia 6.8%
Morocco 7.7%
Algeria 8.0%
Mauritania 8.9%
Guinea-Bissau 11.7%
Sierra Leone 12.8%
Nigeria 6.2%
Côte d'Ivoire 5.9%
Ghana 6.0%
São Tomé and Príncipe 8.5%
Gabon 10.5%
Angola 19.7%
Lesotho 8.6%
Russian Federation 5.6%
Kazakhstan 14.9%
Uzbekistan 7.4%
Kyrgyzstan 11.6%
Tajikistan 7.6%
Pakistan 5.0%
South Korea 6.2%
Thailand 17.5%
Philippines 10.9%
Malaysia 7.1%
Indonesia 10.7%
Papua New Guinea 9.1%
SCALE 1:90,000,000
Robinson Projection

DEBT REPAYMENTS

- Countries in which debt repayments are 5–10% of the GDP
- Countries in which debt repayments are 10–15% of the GDP
- Countries in which debt repayments are above 15% of the GDP

HUMAN DEVELOPMENT INDEX (HDI) VALUES

- High 0.9–1.0
- High 0.8–0.9
- Medium 0.7–0.8
- Medium 0.6–0.7
- Medium 0.5–0.6
- Low 0.4–0.5
- Low 0.3–0.4
- Low 0.2–0.3
- Insufficient data

Assessing Development

A country's average standard of living can be measured by its Gross Domestic Product (GDP), the total value of all goods and services produced in a year. For a broader assessment of achievement, the Human Development Index (HDI) also takes into account life expectancy, adult literacy, and education enrollments. Many disadvantaged countries are trapped in poverty by the unsustainable debts they owe to wealthier countries, often paying more to service their foreign loans than they receive in foreign aid. In an attempt to address this problem, the United Nations has initiated debt relief schemes.

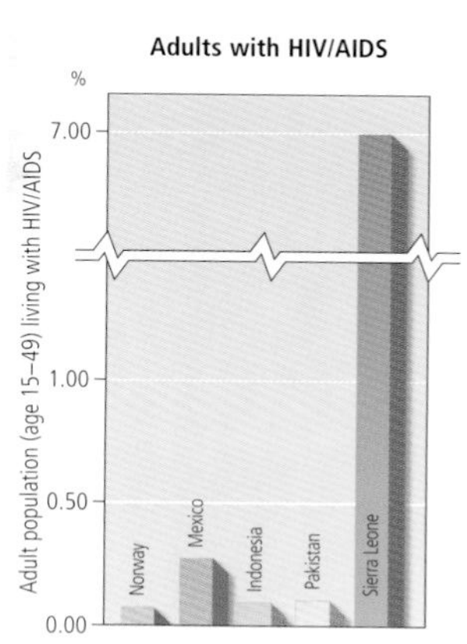
Adults with HIV/AIDS
%
7.00
1.00
0.50
0.00
Adult population (age 15–49) living with HIV/AIDS
Norway
Mexico
Indonesia
Pakistan
Sierra Leone

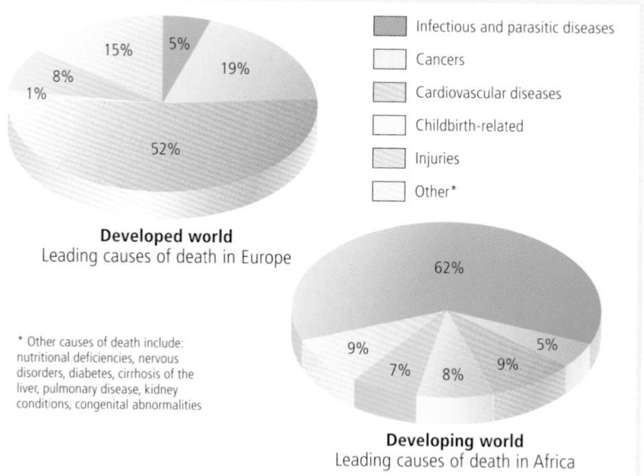
15%
5%
19%
8%
1%
52%
Infectious and parasitic diseases
Cancers
Cardiovascular diseases
Childbirth-related
Injuries
Other*
62%
9%
7%
8%
9%
5%
* Other causes of death include: nutritional deficiencies, nervous disorders, diabetes, cirrhosis of the liver, pulmonary disease, kidney conditions, congenital abnormalities

Developed world
Leading causes of death in Europe

Developing world
Leading causes of death in Africa

WOMEN'S SHARE

Throughout the world, women are poorer than their male compatriots, and three-fifths of the world's 1 billion poorest people are women. Ethiopian women, for example, earn an average of US$550 per year, compared to an average of US$1,074 for men. Education is an important factor—of the nearly 1 billion people who cannot read, two-thirds are women. Even in a country with well-educated women, such as Sweden, the average female income is less than 70 percent of the male income. Other causes of gender inequality include the poor pay that traditionally female work attracts and the lack of women in positions of power in politics and business.

In developed and developing countries alike, women earn significantly less than men.

States and Borders

Of the more than 190 sovereign states that make up today's world map, only about 60 existed at the start of the 20th century, and even by 1950, there were just 82 states. Since then, demands for self-determination and the spread of democracy have seen the proliferation of new states and borders. Some experts predict that these trends will continue, splitting the world into as many as 300 countries within a few decades. At the same time, the globalization of finance and communications, along with regional alliances such as the European Union, are reducing the influence of the individual state.

After the Second World War, many European colonies in Asia sought and achieved independence. This process of decolonization reached Africa in the 1960s and continues today in the Pacific, with island nations such as Palau gaining statehood in the 1990s. The collapse of communism in Europe began with the fall of the Berlin Wall in 1989 and concluded with the dissolution of the Soviet Union in 1991. While some of these transitions have been peaceful, many have involved armed struggles and ethnic or religious conflict.

When the Soviet Union disintegrated, the United States became the world's sole superpower. Following the terrorist attacks of September 11, 2001, the U.S. declared a "war on terror," targeting regimes, such as those of Afghanistan and Iraq, that it perceives as a threat. This strategy is bound to have far-reaching, but largely unpredictable, effects on the world map in years to come.

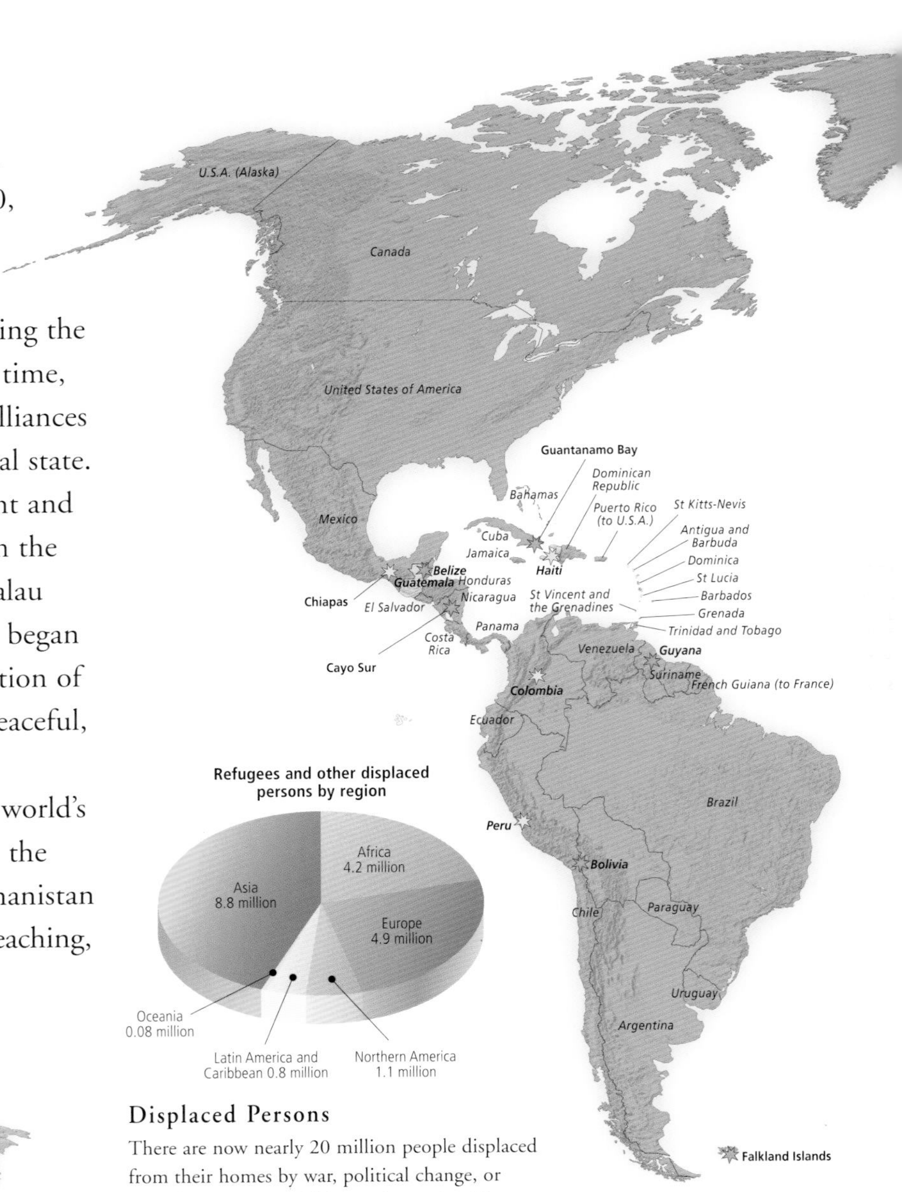

U.S.A. (Alaska)
Canada
United States of America
Guantanamo Bay
Bahamas
Dominican Republic
Puerto Rico (to U.S.A.)
St Kitts-Nevis
Antigua and Barbuda
Dominica
St Lucia
Barbados
Grenada
Trinidad and Tobago
Mexico
Cuba
Jamaica
Haiti
Belize
Guatemala
Honduras
Nicaragua
El Salvador
Chiapas
St Vincent and the Grenadines
Costa Rica
Panama
Cayo Sur
Venezuela
Guyana
Suriname
French Guiana (to France)
Colombia
Ecuador
Peru
Brazil
Bolivia
Chile
Paraguay
Uruguay
Argentina
Falkland Islands
Refugees and other displaced persons by region
Asia 8.8 million
Africa 4.2 million
Europe 4.9 million
Oceania 0.08 million
Latin America and Caribbean 0.8 million
Northern America 1.1 million

Displaced Persons

There are now nearly 20 million people displaced from their homes by war, political change, or fear of persecution. Of these, about 12 million are refugees, people who have fled their countries, while 5 million are internally displaced persons. The remainder include refugees returning home, those seeking permanent asylum in other countries, and "stateless" citizens of the former Soviet Union.

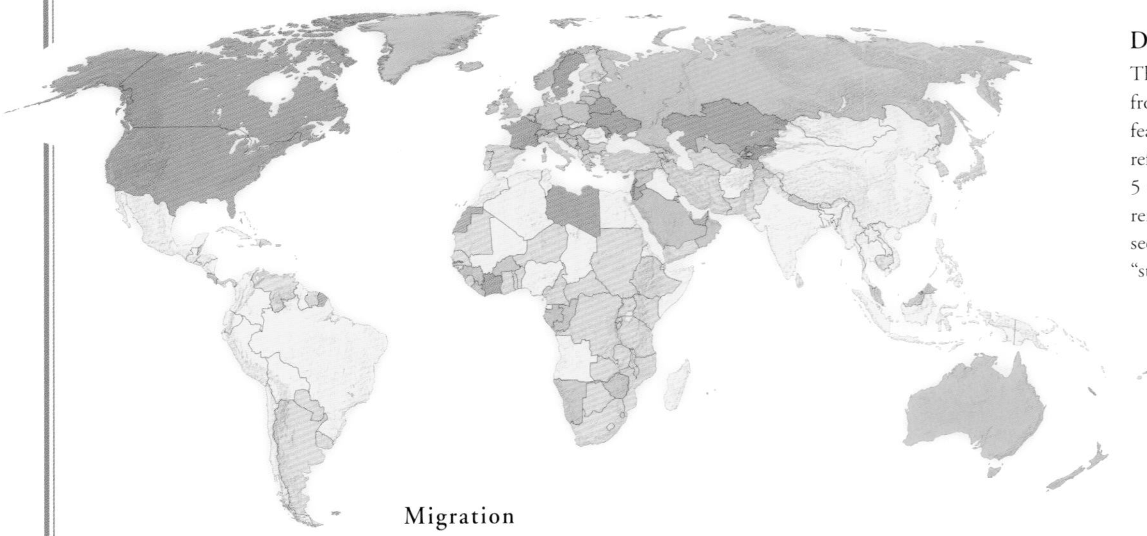

MIGRANT STOCK IN POPULATION

- Less than 1%
- 1–5%
- 5–10%
- 10–20%
- 20–30%
- 30–40%
- More than 40%

Armed conflict in the Democratic Republic of Congo (DRC) has forced thousands of civilians to flee to Tanzania. Meanwhile, refugee camps in DRC itself shelter a similar number of Angolans and Sudanese.

Migration

About 175 million people, or 2.9 percent of the world's population, have left their country of birth and settled in another land. Most migrants have moved to developed countries, where they make up 8.7 percent of the total population. In the developing world, by contrast, migrants account for just 1.5 percent of the population. With 35 million migrants—20 percent of the world total—the United States is the most popular destination.

Top Countries of Origin for Refugees	
Afghanistan	3,810,000
Burundi	554,000
Iraq	530,000
Sudan	490,000
Angola	471,000
Somalia	440,000
Bosnia and Herzegovina	426,000
Democratic Republic of Congo	392,000
Vietnam	353,000
Eritrea	333,000

Top Countries of Asylum for Refugees	
Pakistan	2,001,000
Iran	1,868,000
Germany	906,000
Tanzania	681,000
United States	508,000
Guinea	427,000
Sudan	415,000
Democratic Republic of Congo	333,000
China	294,000
Armenia	281,000

A group of schoolfriends reflects the diversity of Australian society, a consequence of successive waves of migration. About 24 percent of Australia's population was born in another country.

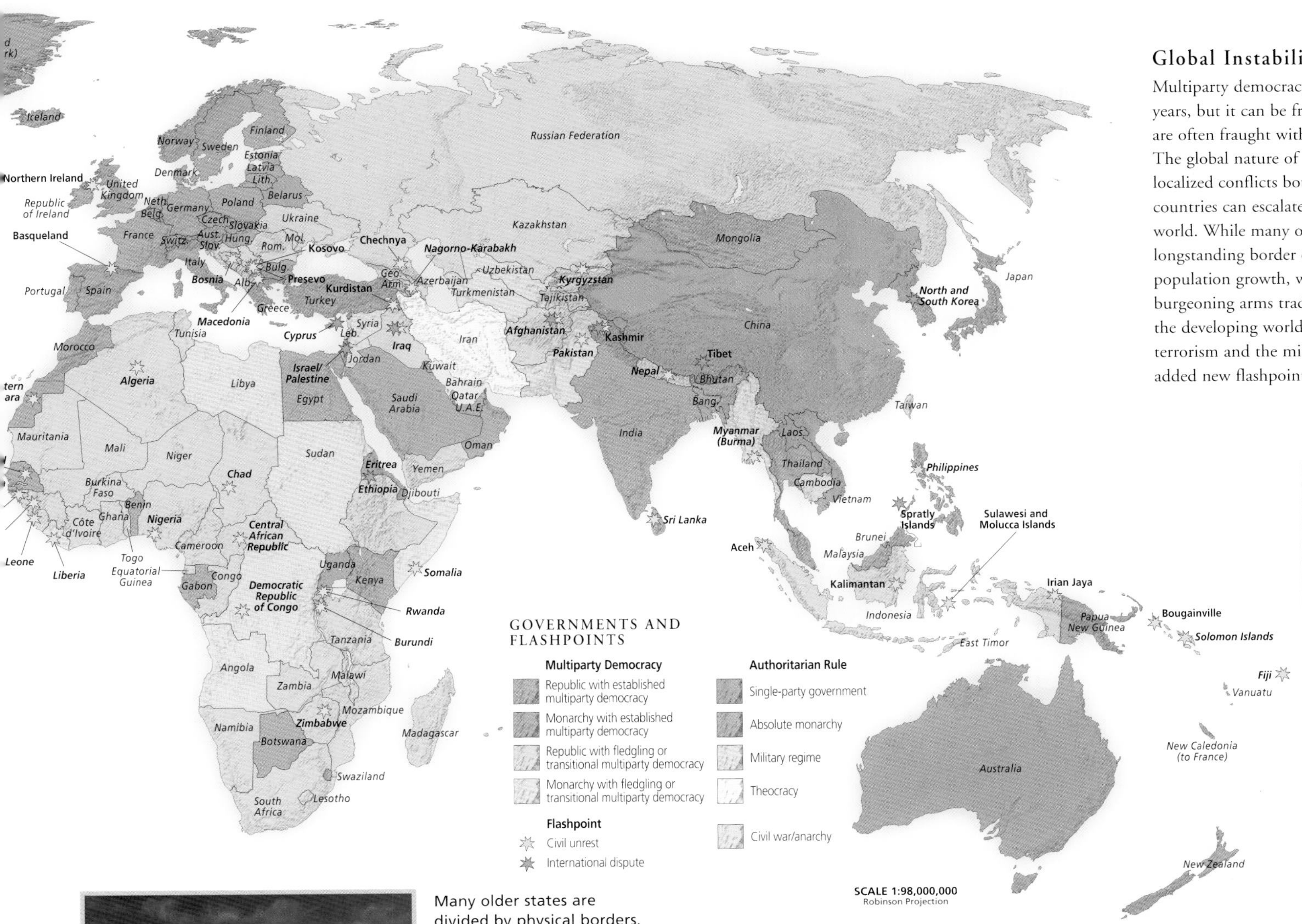

GOVERNMENTS AND FLASHPOINTS
Multiparty Democracy
Republic with established multiparty democracy
Monarchy with established multiparty democracy
Republic with fledgling or transitional multiparty democracy
Monarchy with fledgling or transitional multiparty democracy
Authoritarian Rule
Single-party government
Absolute monarchy
Military regime
Theocracy
Civil war/anarchy
Flashpoint
Civil unrest
International dispute
SCALE 1:98,000,000
Robinson Projection
Iceland
Northern Ireland
Republic of Ireland
Basqueland
Portugal
Spain
France
United Kingdom
Norway
Sweden
Finland
Denmark
Estonia
Latvia
Lith.
Belarus
Poland
Germany
Neth.
Belg.
Czech
Slovakia
Switz.
Aust.
Hung.
Slov.
Ukraine
Mol.
Rom.
Italy
Bosnia
Alb.
Bulg.
Kosovo
Presevo
Greece
Macedonia
Turkey
Kurdistan
Cyprus
Chechnya
Geo.
Arm.
Azerbaijan
Nagorno-Karabakh
Russian Federation
Kazakhstan
Uzbekistan
Turkmenistan
Kyrgyzstan
Tajikistan
Afghanistan
Kashmir
Pakistan
Mongolia
China
Japan
North and South Korea
Taiwan
Tibet
Nepal
Bhutan
Bang.
India
Sri Lanka
Myanmar (Burma)
Laos
Thailand
Cambodia
Vietnam
Philippines
Spratly Islands
Brunei
Malaysia
Aceh
Kalimantan
Indonesia
Sulawesi and Molucca Islands
Irian Jaya
East Timor
Papua New Guinea
Bougainville
Solomon Islands
Fiji
Vanuatu
New Caledonia (to France)
Australia
New Zealand
Syria
Leb.
Iraq
Iran
Jordan
Israel/Palestine
Kuwait
Bahrain
Qatar
U.A.E.
Saudi Arabia
Oman
Yemen
Egypt
Libya
Tunisia
Algeria
Morocco
Mauritania
Mali
Niger
Chad
Sudan
Eritrea
Ethiopia
Djibouti
Somalia
Burkina Faso
Benin
Côte d'Ivoire
Ghana
Nigeria
Togo
Liberia
Leone
Cameroon
Equatorial Guinea
Gabon
Congo
Central African Republic
Democratic Republic of Congo
Uganda
Kenya
Rwanda
Burundi
Tanzania
Angola
Zambia
Malawi
Mozambique
Zimbabwe
Namibia
Botswana
Madagascar
Swaziland
Lesotho
South Africa

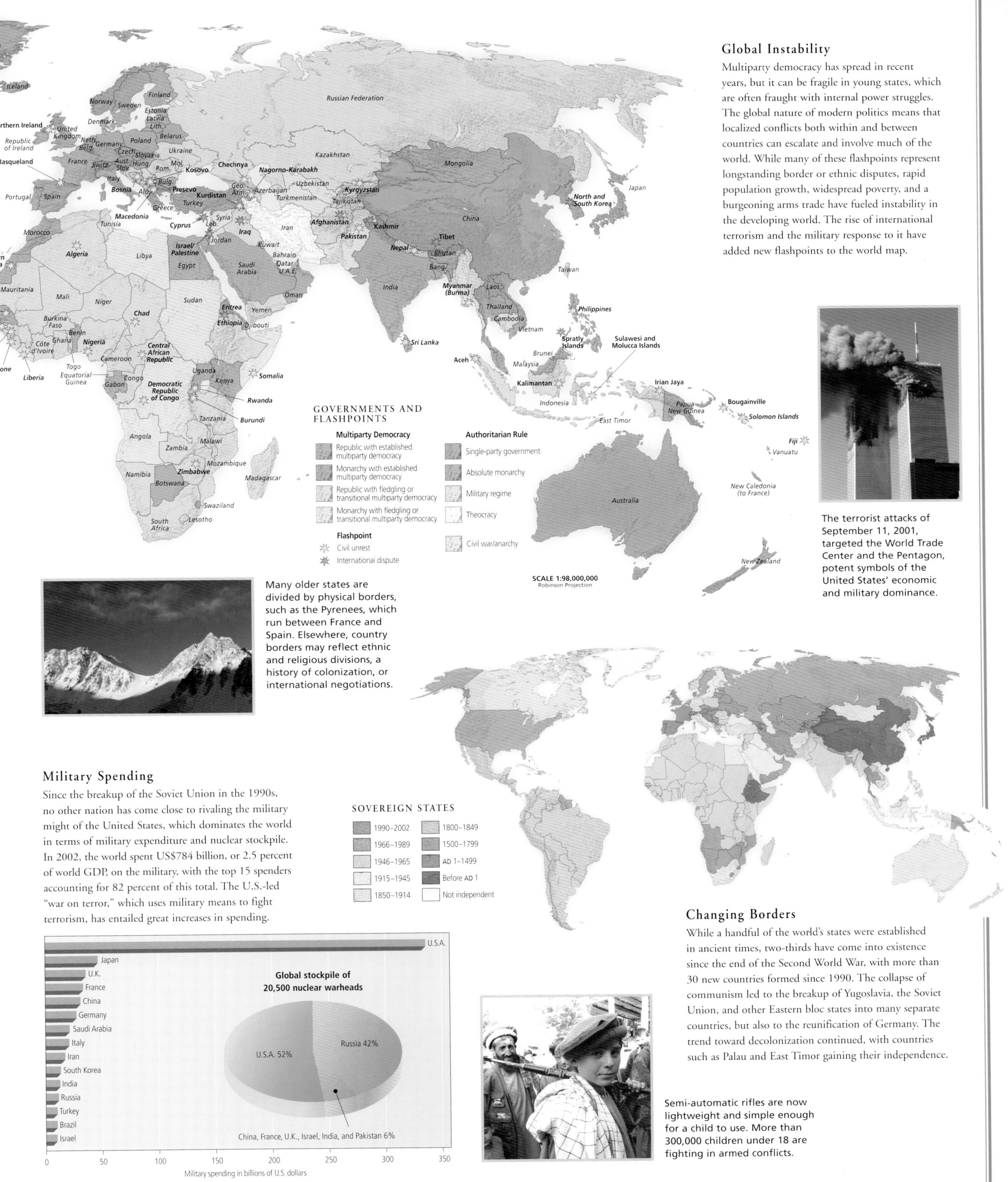

Global Instability

Multiparty democracy has spread in recent years, but it can be fragile in young states, which are often fraught with internal power struggles. The global nature of modern politics means that localized conflicts both within and between countries can escalate and involve much of the world. While many of these flashpoints represent longstanding border or ethnic disputes, rapid population growth, widespread poverty, and a burgeoning arms trade have fueled instability in the developing world. The rise of international terrorism and the military response to it have added new flashpoints to the world map.

The terrorist attacks of September 11, 2001, targeted the World Trade Center and the Pentagon, potent symbols of the United States' economic and military dominance.

Many older states are divided by physical borders, such as the Pyrenees, which run between France and Spain. Elsewhere, country borders may reflect ethnic and religious divisions, a history of colonization, or international negotiations.

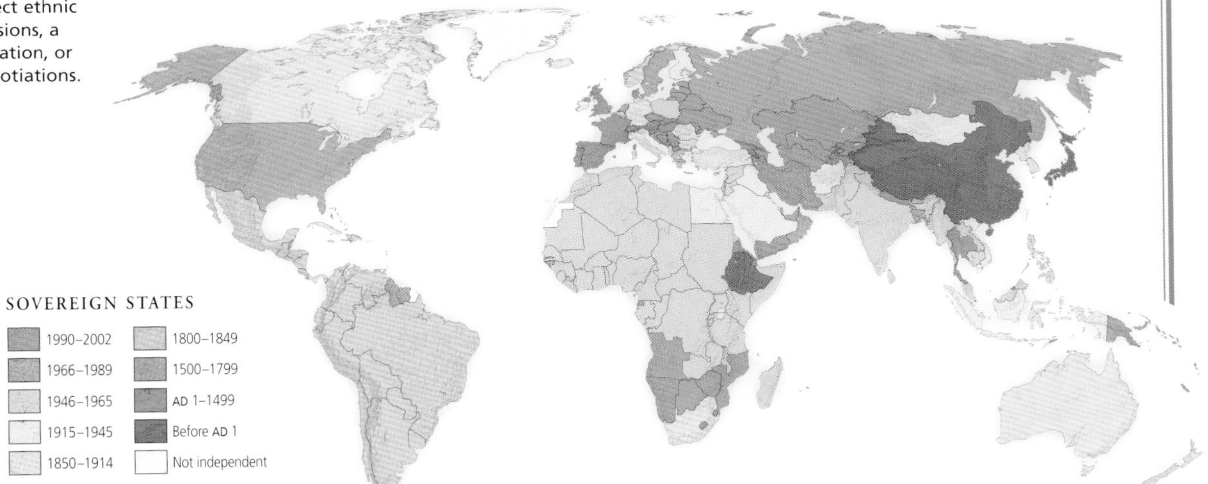

SOVEREIGN STATES
1990–2002
1966–1989
1946–1965
1915–1945
1850–1914
1800–1849
1500–1799
AD 1–1499
Before AD 1
Not independent

Military Spending

Since the breakup of the Soviet Union in the 1990s, no other nation has come close to rivaling the military might of the United States, which dominates the world in terms of military expenditure and nuclear stockpile. In 2002, the world spent US$784 billion, or 2.5 percent of world GDP, on the military, with the top 15 spenders accounting for 82 percent of this total. The U.S.-led "war on terror," which uses military means to fight terrorism, has entailed great increases in spending.

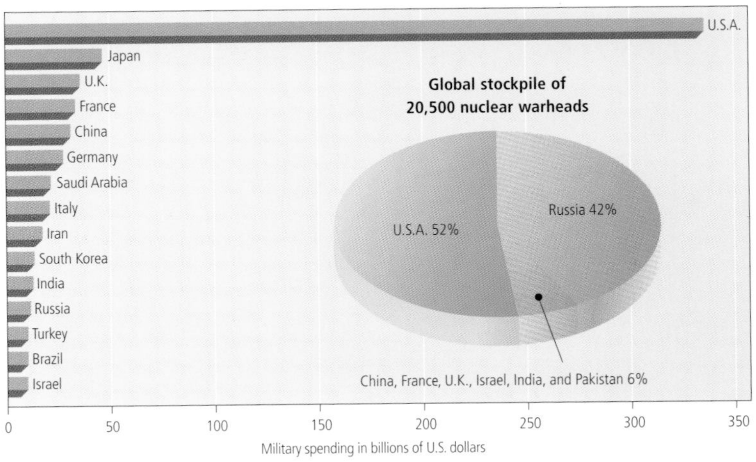

U.S.A.
Japan
U.K.
France
China
Germany
Saudi Arabia
Italy
Iran
South Korea
India
Russia
Turkey
Brazil
Israel
0
50
100
150
200
250
300
350
Military spending in billions of U.S. dollars
Global stockpile of 20,500 nuclear warheads
U.S.A. 52%
Russia 42%
China, France, U.K., Israel, India, and Pakistan 6%

Changing Borders

While a handful of the world's states were established in ancient times, two-thirds have come into existence since the end of the Second World War, with more than 30 new countries formed since 1990. The collapse of communism led to the breakup of Yugoslavia, the Soviet Union, and other Eastern bloc states into many separate countries, but also to the reunification of Germany. The trend toward decolonization continued, with countries such as Palau and East Timor gaining their independence.

Semi-automatic rifles are now lightweight and simple enough for a child to use. More than 300,000 children under 18 are fighting in armed conflicts.

Transport and Communication

During the 20th century, the world's transport and communication networks were utterly transformed. Cars, planes, telephones, and computers are now a feature of daily life for many people. Travel times have been drastically reduced and people on opposite sides of Earth can communicate almost instantaneously, enabling economies and cultures to become increasingly interconnected.

The transport revolution depended on the development of an internal-combustion engine fueled by refined oil. Germany's Karl Benz and Gottlieb Daimler were the first to use this engine in a car, but it was the United States' Henry Ford who introduced mass-production processes in 1913 and made cars affordable for the average person. Meanwhile, an internal-combustion engine allowed the Wright brothers to make the world's first powered flight. In 1952, the first commercial jet service was launched, and many people now take international air travel for granted.

Since the late 1800s, when Alexander Bell invented the telephone and Guglielmo Marconi developed the radio transmitter, distance has become less and less of a barrier to communication. Radio and television broadcasts began in the 1920s, transmitting news and entertainment to ever larger numbers of people. With the development of the microchip in the late 1950s, digital communication became possible and eventually led to an extensive worldwide telephone network and powerful personal computers, which together enabled the Internet to take shape and rework the way the world connects.

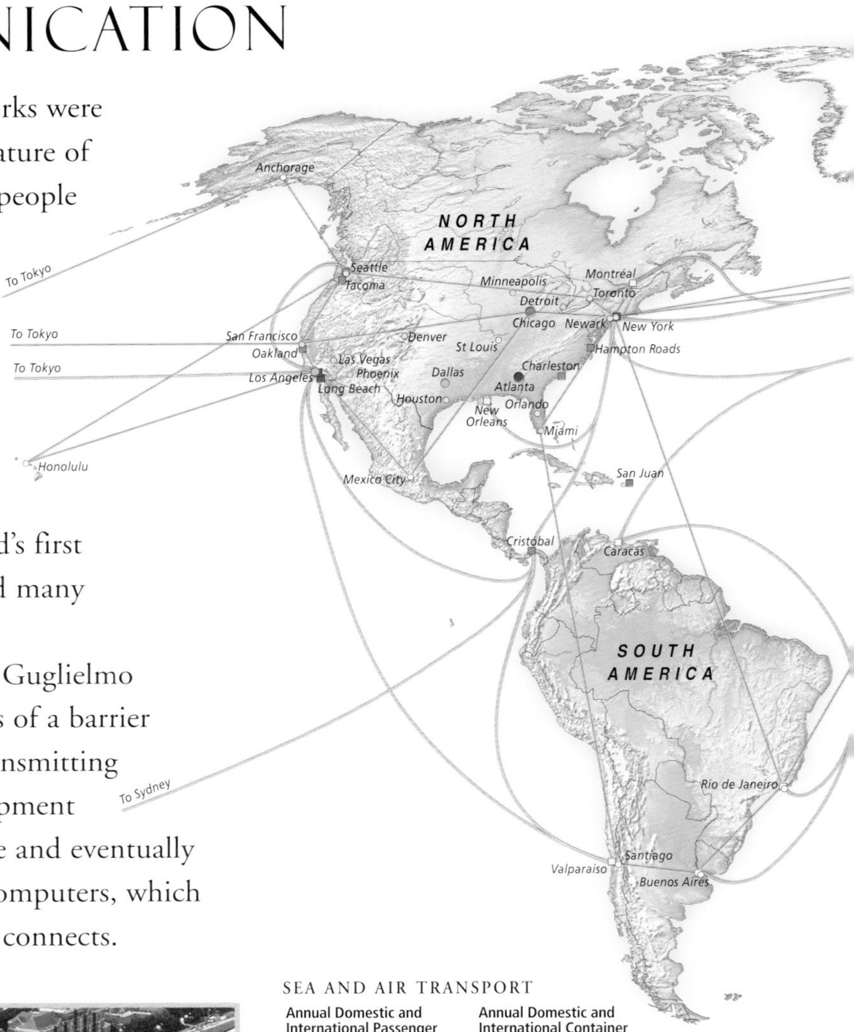

To Tokyo
To Tokyo
To Tokyo
Honolulu
To Sydney
Anchorage
NORTH AMERICA
Seattle
Tacoma
Minneapolis
Montreal
Toronto
Detroit
Chicago
Newark
New York
Hampton Roads
San Francisco
Oakland
Denver
St Louis
Los Angeles
Las Vegas
Phoenix
Long Beach
Dallas
Charleston
Atlanta
Houston
Orlando
New Orleans
Miami
Mexico City
San Juan
Cristobal
Caracas
SOUTH AMERICA
Rio de Janeiro
Santiago
Valparaiso
Buenos Aires

SEA AND AIR TRANSPORT

Annual Domestic and International Passenger Traffic at Busiest Airports
- 70–80 million passengers
- 60–70 million passengers
- 40–60 million passengers
- 30–40 million passengers
- 25.6–30 million passengers
- Other major airport

Annual Domestic and International Container Traffic at Busiest Ports
- 10–20 million TEUs*
- 5–10 million TEUS
- 3–5 million TEUs
- 2–3 million TEUs
- 1.3–2 million TEUs
- Other major port

Selected International Routes
- Air routes
- Sea routes

* TEU Twenty Foot Equivalent Unit (A 20-foot container equals one TEU; a 40-foot container equals two TEUs.)

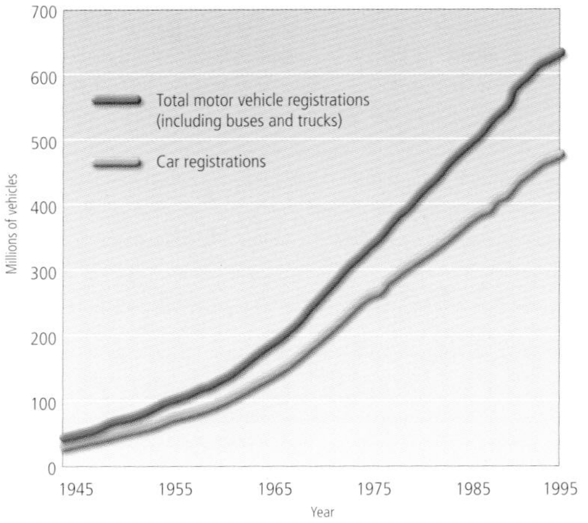

700
600
500
400
300
200
100
0
Millions of vehicles
Total motor vehicle registrations (including buses and trucks)
Car registrations
1945
1955
1965
1975
1985
1995
Year

The Rise of the Motor Vehicle

In 50 years, the number of cars, trucks, and buses on the world's roads rose ninefold. With 750 motor vehicles per 1,000 people, the United States has by far the world's largest fleet. In contrast, China has only 8 vehicles per 1,000 people. As China and other developing countries industrialize, their car ownership is likely to increase. By 2025, there will be more than 1 billion motor vehicles in the world.

Vast networks of roads allow people and goods to travel rapidly and flexibly within and between cities and countries. The world's increasing reliance on cars, however, has led to rising greenhouse gas emissions and urban air pollution.

Top Road Networks	
United States	3,958,000 miles (6,370,000 km)
India	2,063,000 miles (3,320,000 km)
Brazil	1,230,000 miles (1,980,000 km)
China	870,000 miles (1,400,000 km)
Japan	716,000 miles (1,152,000 km)
Russia	592,000 miles (952,000 km)
Australia	567,000 miles (913,000 km)
Canada	561,000 miles (902,000 km)
France	555,000 miles (893,000 km)
Italy	416,000 miles (669,000 km)

Top Rail Networks	
United States	121,000 miles (194,700 km)
Russia	54,200 miles (87,200 km)
China	44,500 miles (71,600 km)
Canada	40,400 miles (65,000 km)
India	39,500 miles (63,500 km)
Germany	28,300 miles (45,500 km)
Australia	25,800 miles (41,600 km)
Argentina	21,400 miles (34,500 km)
France	20,300 miles (32,700 km)
Brazil	19,600 miles (31,500 km)

Technological Breakthroughs

c. 2500 BC Minoans and Mycenaeans build first seagoing cargo ships

AD 1450 First full-rigged ships lead to the European Age of Discovery

1801 First steam train built in England

Richard Trevithick's 1801 locomotive

1837 First oceangoing steamship launched in England

1844 First long-distance telegraph cable operates in U.S.A.

1860 First practical internal-combustion engine built in France

1869 First transcontinental railway in U.S.A.

1869 Suez Canal slashes sailing times between Europe and Asia

1876 Alexander Graham Bell invents the telephone

1878 telephone

1901 First wireless telegraph signal sent from Cornwall to Newfoundland

1903 Wright brothers make world's first powered flight

1913 Henry Ford uses moving assembly line for the Model T, revolutionizing car manufacturing

1913 Model T Ford

1916 Trans-Siberian Railway extends across Russia

1920 First regular radio broadcasts begin in U.S.A. and U.K.

1927 Charles Lindbergh makes first nonstop transatlantic flight

Lindbergh's *Spirit of St Louis*

1928 General Electric in U.S.A. and BBC in U.K. begin first regular television broadcasts

1947 Transistor invented

1948 U.K. develops first storage computer

1952 First jet airliner service launched in Britain

1956 First transatlantic telephone cable laid

1958–59 First microchip allows development of digital communication

1962 First transatlantic transmission of television programs by Telstar satellite

1969 First Concorde flight

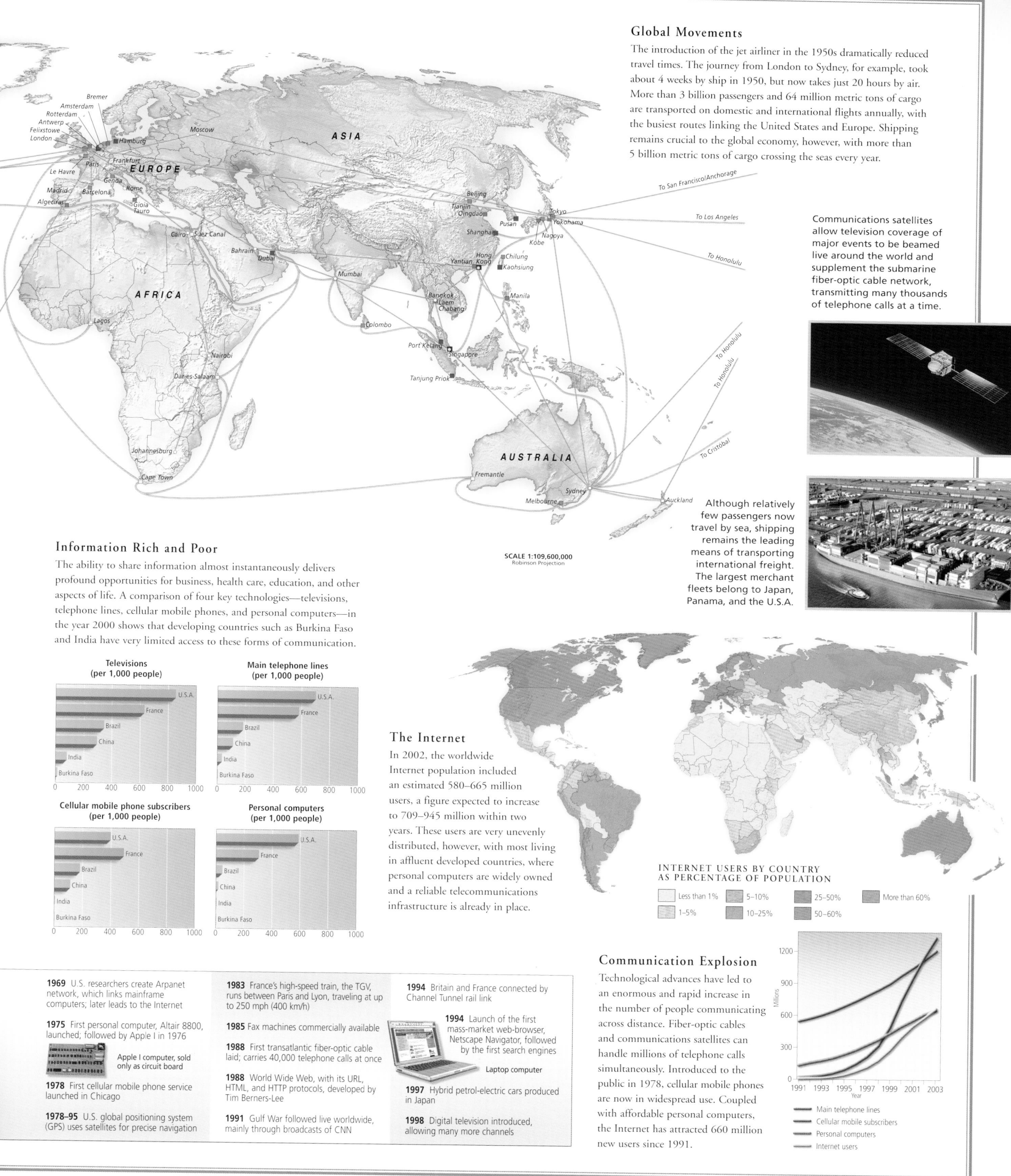

Global Movements

The introduction of the jet airliner in the 1950s dramatically reduced travel times. The journey from London to Sydney, for example, took about 4 weeks by ship in 1950, but now takes just 20 hours by air. More than 3 billion passengers and 64 million metric tons of cargo are transported on domestic and international flights annually, with the busiest routes linking the United States and Europe. Shipping remains crucial to the global economy, however, with more than 5 billion metric tons of cargo crossing the seas every year.

Bremer
Amsterdam
Rotterdam
Antwerp
Felixstowe
London
Hamburg
Moscow
ASIA
Paris
Frankfurt
EUROPE
Le Havre
Genoa
Madrid
Barcelona
Rome
Algeciras
Gioia Tauro
Beijing
Tianjin
Qingdao
Tokyo
Yokohama
Pusan
Shanghai
Nagoya
Kobe
Cairo
Suez Canal
Bahrain
Dubai
Hong Kong
Yantian
Chilung
Kaohsiung
Mumbai
AFRICA
Bangkok
Laem Chabang
Manila
Lagos
Colombo
Port Kelang
Singapore
Nairobi
Dar-es-Salaam
Tanjung Priok
Johannesburg
Cape Town
AUSTRALIA
Fremantle
Sydney
Melbourne
Auckland
To San Francisco/Anchorage
To Los Angeles
To Honolulu
To Honolulu
To Honolulu
To Cristóbal
SCALE 1:109,600,000
Robinson Projection

Communications satellites allow television coverage of major events to be beamed live around the world and supplement the submarine fiber-optic cable network, transmitting many thousands of telephone calls at a time.

Although relatively few passengers now travel by sea, shipping remains the leading means of transporting international freight. The largest merchant fleets belong to Japan, Panama, and the U.S.A.

Information Rich and Poor

The ability to share information almost instantaneously delivers profound opportunities for business, health care, education, and other aspects of life. A comparison of four key technologies—televisions, telephone lines, cellular mobile phones, and personal computers—in the year 2000 shows that developing countries such as Burkina Faso and India have very limited access to these forms of communication.

Televisions (per 1,000 people)

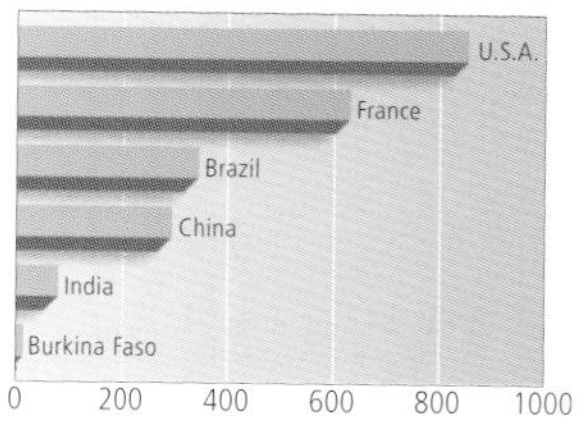
U.S.A.
France
Brazil
China
India
Burkina Faso
0
200
400
600
800
1000

Main telephone lines (per 1,000 people)

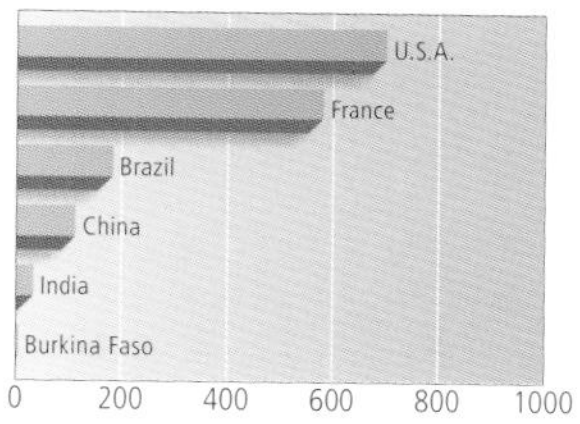
U.S.A.
France
Brazil
China
India
Burkina Faso
0
200
400
600
800
1000

Cellular mobile phone subscribers (per 1,000 people)

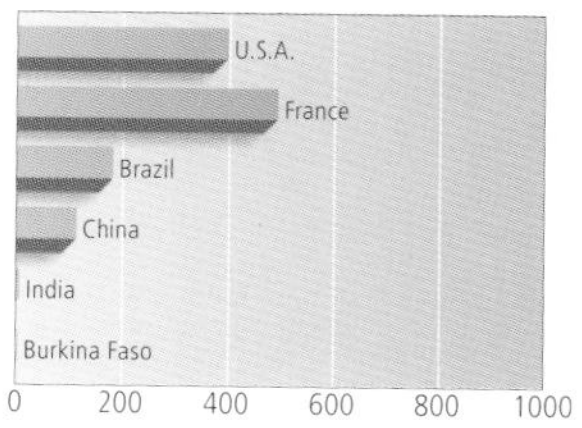
U.S.A.
France
Brazil
China
India
Burkina Faso
0
200
400
600
800
1000

Personal computers (per 1,000 people)

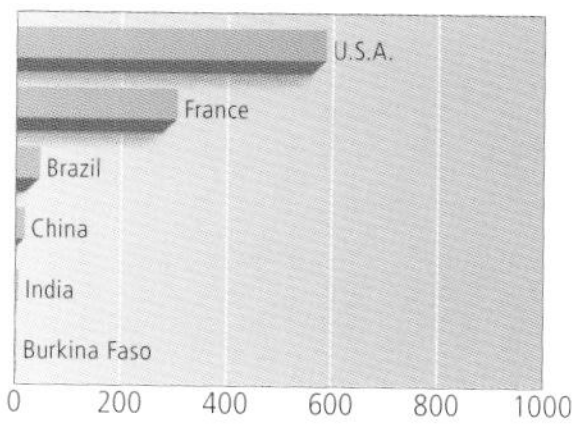
U.S.A.
France
Brazil
China
India
Burkina Faso
0
200
400
600
800
1000

The Internet

In 2002, the worldwide Internet population included an estimated 580–665 million users, a figure expected to increase to 709–945 million within two years. These users are very unevenly distributed, however, with most living in affluent developed countries, where personal computers are widely owned and a reliable telecommunications infrastructure is already in place.

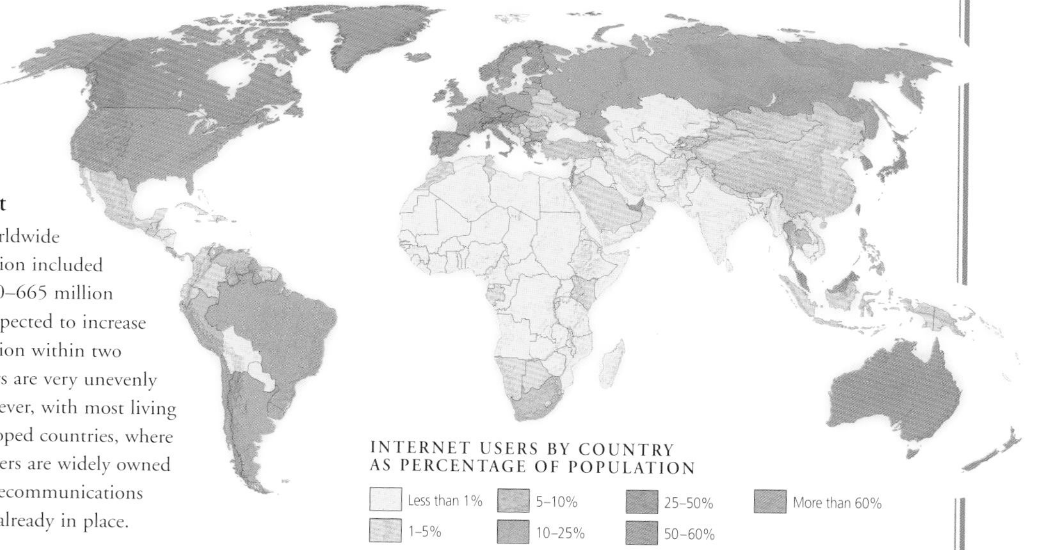
INTERNET USERS BY COUNTRY AS PERCENTAGE OF POPULATION
Less than 1%
1–5%
5–10%
10–25%
25–50%
50–60%
More than 60%

Communication Explosion

Technological advances have led to an enormous and rapid increase in the number of people communicating across distance. Fiber-optic cables and communications satellites can handle millions of telephone calls simultaneously. Introduced to the public in 1978, cellular mobile phones are now in widespread use. Coupled with affordable personal computers, the Internet has attracted 660 million new users since 1991.

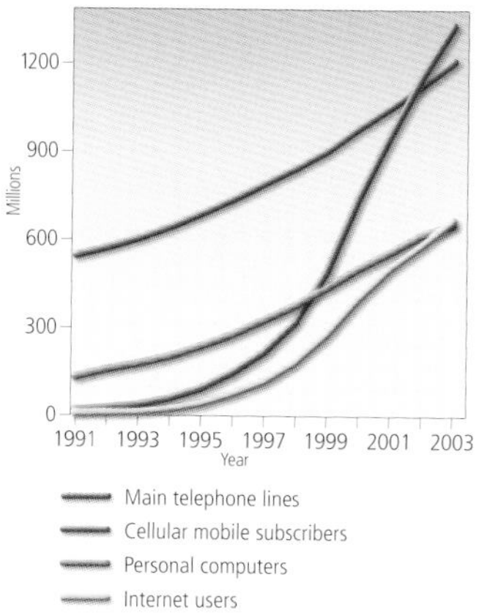
1200
900
600
300
0
Millions
1991
1993
1995
1997
1999
2001
2003
Year
Main telephone lines
Cellular mobile subscribers
Personal computers
Internet users

1969 U.S. researchers create Arpanet network, which links mainframe computers; later leads to the Internet

1975 First personal computer, Altair 8800, launched; followed by Apple I in 1976

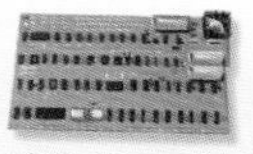

Apple I computer, sold only as circuit board

1978 First cellular mobile phone service launched in Chicago

1978–95 U.S. global positioning system (GPS) uses satellites for precise navigation

1983 France's high-speed train, the TGV, runs between Paris and Lyon, traveling at up to 250 mph (400 km/h)

1985 Fax machines commercially available

1988 First transatlantic fiber-optic cable laid; carries 40,000 telephone calls at once

1988 World Wide Web, with its URL, HTML, and HTTP protocols, developed by Tim Berners-Lee

1991 Gulf War followed live worldwide, mainly through broadcasts of CNN

1994 Britain and France connected by Channel Tunnel rail link

1994 Launch of the first mass-market web-browser, Netscape Navigator, followed by the first search engines

Laptop computer

1997 Hybrid petrol-electric cars produced in Japan

1998 Digital television introduced, allowing many more channels

Global Connections

Throughout the world, people are increasingly connected to each other, and distance and national borders are becoming less significant. Global trade and transnational corporations distribute similar products to many different regions. Tourism is the world's largest single industry, with inexpensive air travel facilitating a growing number of international travelers. Reliable, cheap telephone services and the Internet allow information and money to flow around the globe easily and rapidly. A network of international organizations and alliances ensures that all countries are enmeshed in world politics. This shrinking and interconnecting of the world is known as globalization.

Economic globalization involves the free flow of goods, services, and capital around the world. While some believe that this process offers developing countries their best chance of prosperity, others argue that it favors already wealthy nations and particularly benefits corporate power. Led by the World Trade Organization, global trade has been liberalized, with countries encouraged to remove tariffs and subsidies that favor local goods. At the same time, many trade blocs have been formed, in which countries forge alliances with neighbors to exclude the competition.

Globalization is more than an economic phenomenon. The mechanisms that allow international business to flourish also allow ideas to spread, with social activists, academics, scientists, and others forging international links.

NYSE
NYSE

New York, London, and Tokyo are the world's three most important financial markets. Technological advances have allowed shares and currencies to be traded internationally almost instantly, making national economies vulnerable to sudden fluctuations in the global market.

Toronto
Chicago
New York
Los Angeles
Mexico City
Rio de Janeiro
Buenos Aires

International Exchange

With globalization, countries have become increasingly dependent on the international flow of goods, services, and money. The least developed countries tend to produce raw materials (other than lucrative fuel) and foodstuffs, but the prices for such primary exports have fallen dramatically in recent years, while manufactured goods have captured a larger market share. Countries relying on a single export, such as Zambia (copper), Chad (cotton), or Uganda (coffee), are particularly at risk.

International Organizations			
Name	**Founded**	**Members (in 2004)**	**Description**
United Nations	1945	191	Main international forum for maintaining peace and dealing with global problems; almost every country of the world is a member
World Bank	1945	191	Provides loans and technical assistance to UN members
IMF	1947	191	International Monetary Fund: Promotes monetary cooperation and expansion of trade between nations
WTO	1995	191	World Trade Organization: Promotes less restrictive trade
WHO	1948	191	World Health Organization: Aims to raise health standards
UNESCO	1946	191	United Nations Educational, Scientific and Cultural Organization: Promotes collaboration in science, culture, and heritage protection
EU	1952–93	25	European Union: Promotes economic cooperation among member states, oversaw introduction of the euro currency
Commonwealth	1931	54	Sovereign nations that were once part of the British Empire cooperate to promote democracy and development
OPEC	1960	11	Organization of Petroleum Exporting Countries: Coordinates price and supply policies of oil producers
APEC	1989	21	Asia-Pacific Economic Cooperation: Promotes trade and economic cooperation in the region
ASEAN	1967	10	Association of Southeast Asian Nations: Promotes economic development and trade in the region
NAFTA	1994	3	North American Free Trade Agreement: Trade bloc of U.S.A., Canada, and Mexico
Cairns Group	1986	17	Trade bloc of agricultural exporting nations
Arab League	1945	22	Promotes closer economic, cultural, and security ties in the region
NATO	1949	19	North Atlantic Treaty Organisation: Security alliance of European and North American nations
OECD	1961	30	Organisation for Economic Cooperation and Development: Social and economic alliance of industrialized countries
AU	1963	53	African Union: Supports independence of member states and coordinates political, economic, and defense policies in Africa
OAS	1948	35	Organization of American States: Promotes peace and development

World exports of goods*

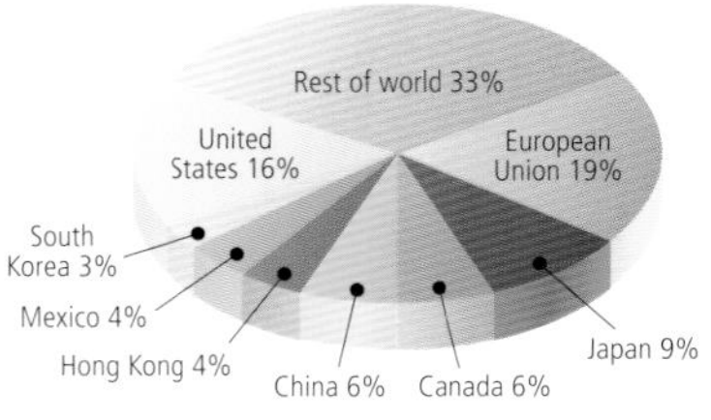
Rest of world 33%
United States 16%
European Union 19%
South Korea 3%
Mexico 4%
Hong Kong 4%
China 6%
Canada 6%
Japan 9%

* Excluding internal European Union trade

World imports of goods*

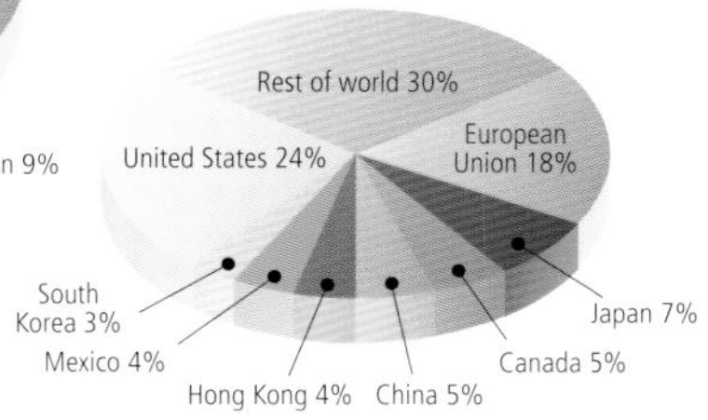
Rest of world 30%
United States 24%
European Union 18%
South Korea 3%
Mexico 4%
Hong Kong 4%
China 5%
Canada 5%
Japan 7%

Trading Partners

In 2001, world exports of goods totaled about US$6,155 billion, or almost US$17 billion a day, an increase of more than 50 percent since 1991. World imports for 2001 were worth US$5,020 billion. The United States and the European Union dominate global trade, accounting for 35 percent of exports and 42 percent of imports. China's economy is growing rapidly, increasing its share of goods exports from 3 percent in 1991 to 6 percent in 2001.

Worldwide Travel

The introduction of the jet airliner, followed by fierce competition among commercial airlines, has made international travel affordable for many people. Every year, there are almost 700 million international tourist arrivals, a figure expected to rise to more than 1.5 billion by 2020. Most travelers originate from and are destined for the developed countries of Europe and North America. France attracted 76.5 million tourists in 2001, far more than any other country.

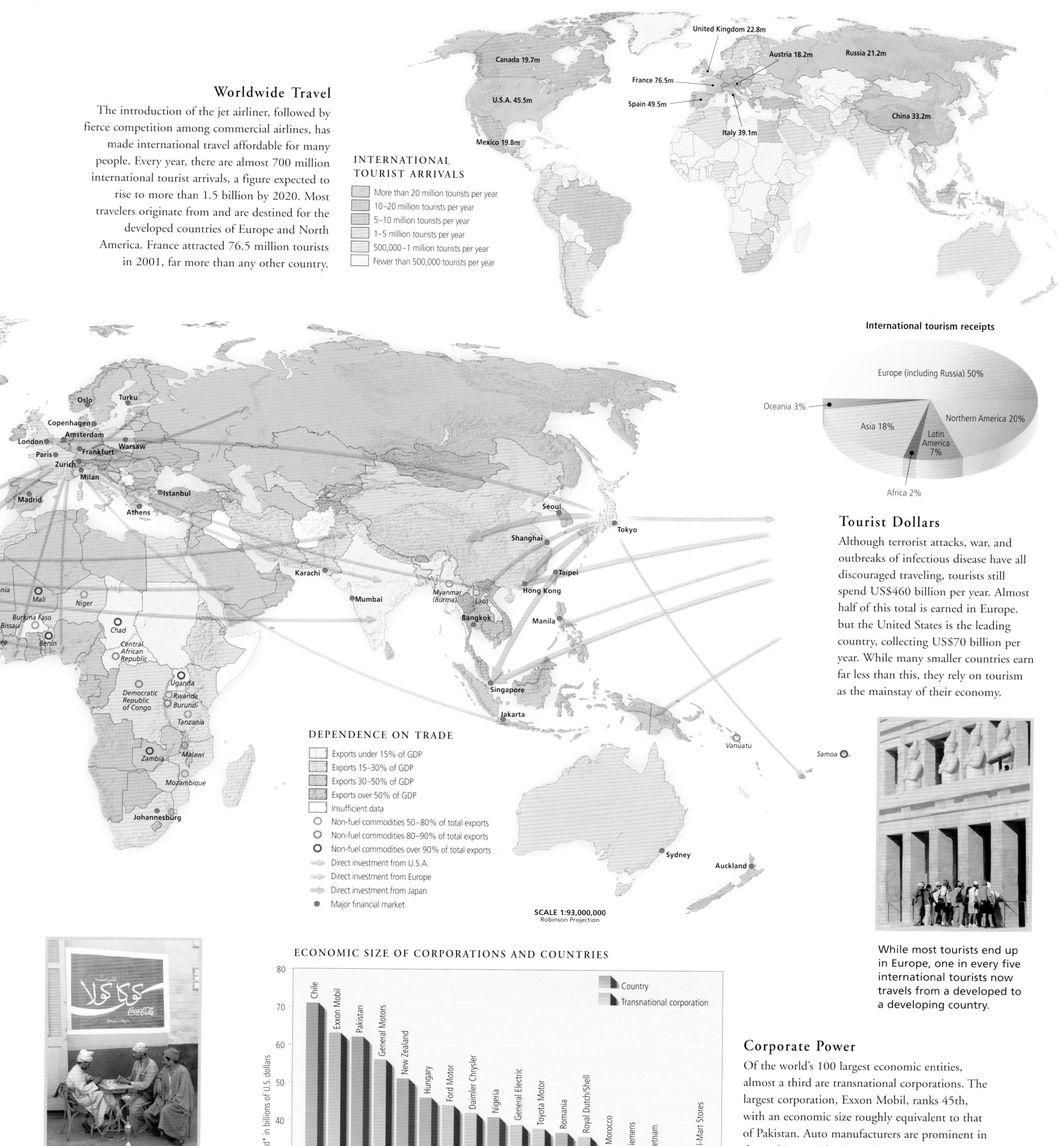

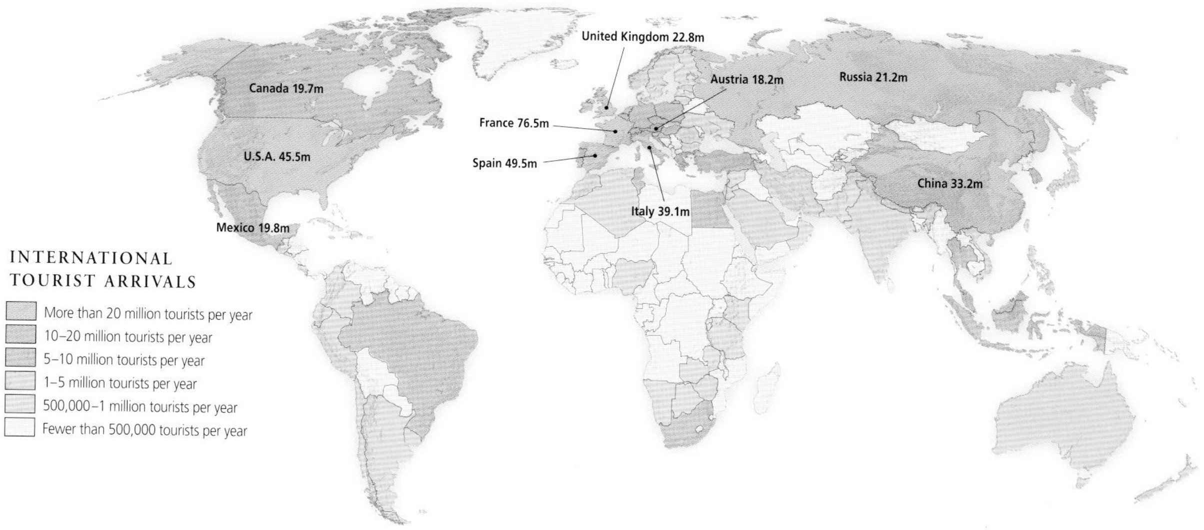
INTERNATIONAL TOURIST ARRIVALS
More than 20 million tourists per year
10–20 million tourists per year
5–10 million tourists per year
1–5 million tourists per year
500,000–1 million tourists per year
Fewer than 500,000 tourists per year
United Kingdom 22.8m
Canada 19.7m
Austria 18.2m
Russia 21.2m
France 76.5m
Spain 49.5m
U.S.A. 45.5m
China 33.2m
Italy 39.1m
Mexico 19.8m

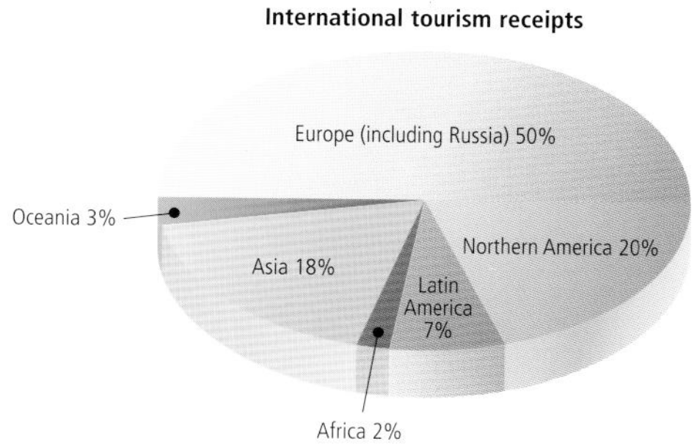
International tourism receipts
Europe (including Russia) 50%
Oceania 3%
Asia 18%
Northern America 20%
Latin America 7%
Africa 2%

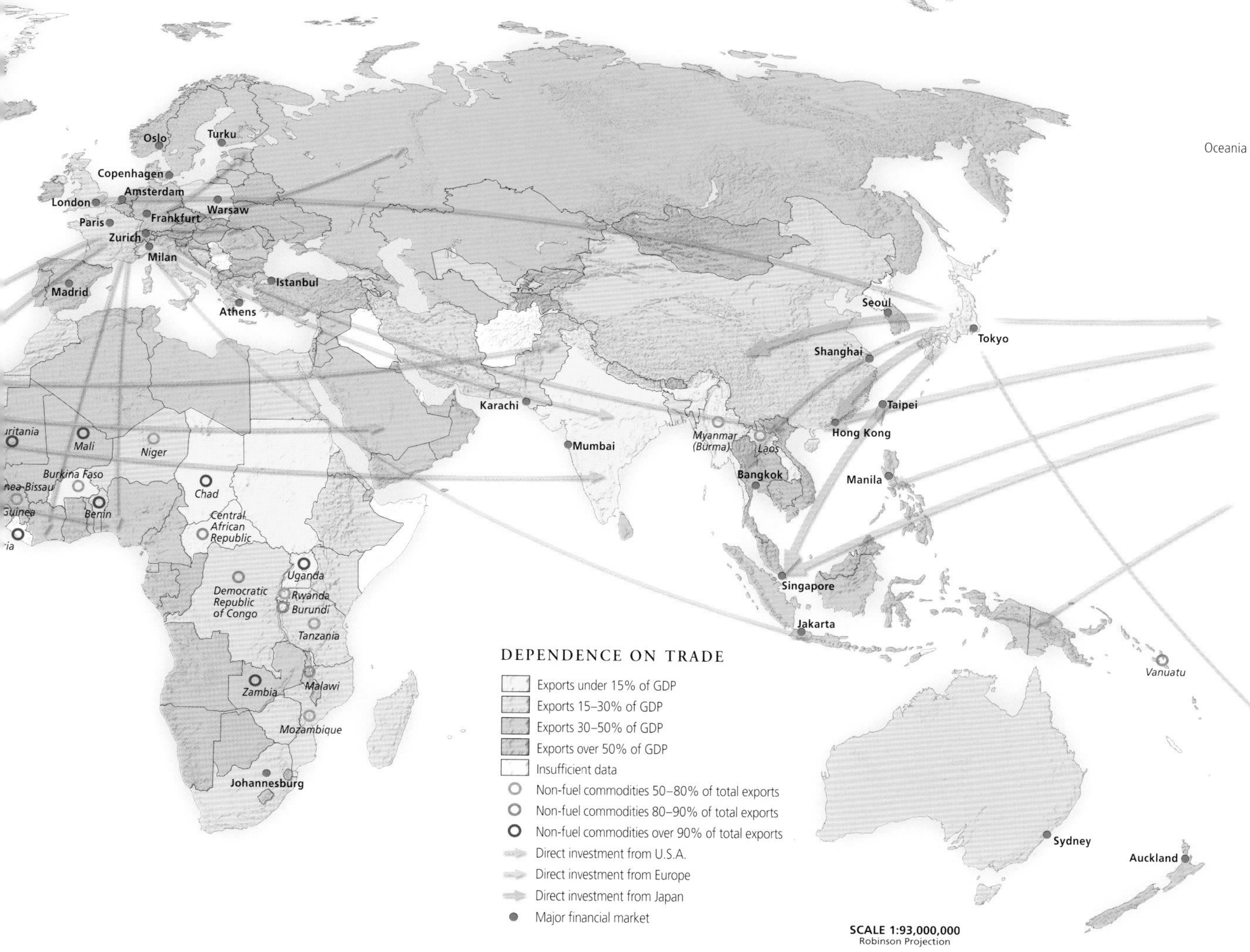
Oslo
Turku
Copenhagen
Amsterdam
London
Warsaw
Paris
Frankfurt
Zurich
Milan
Istanbul
Madrid
Athens
Seoul
Tokyo
Shanghai
Karachi
Taipei
Hong Kong
Mumbai
Myanmar (Burma)
Laos
Bangkok
Manila
Singapore
Jakarta
Mali
Niger
Burkina Faso
Benin
Chad
Central African Republic
Democratic Republic of Congo
Uganda
Rwanda
Burundi
Tanzania
Zambia
Malawi
Mozambique
Johannesburg
Vanuatu
Samoa
Sydney
Auckland
DEPENDENCE ON TRADE
Exports under 15% of GDP
Exports 15–30% of GDP
Exports 30–50% of GDP
Exports over 50% of GDP
Insufficient data
Non-fuel commodities 50–80% of total exports
Non-fuel commodities 80–90% of total exports
Non-fuel commodities over 90% of total exports
Direct investment from U.S.A.
Direct investment from Europe
Direct investment from Japan
Major financial market
SCALE 1:93,000,000
Robinson Projection

Tourist Dollars

Although terrorist attacks, war, and outbreaks of infectious disease have all discouraged traveling, tourists still spend US$460 billion per year. Almost half of this total is earned in Europe, but the United States is the leading country, collecting US$70 billion per year. While many smaller countries earn far less than this, they rely on tourism as the mainstay of their economy.

While most tourists end up in Europe, one in every five international tourists now travels from a developed to a developing country.

Coca-Cola

Developing countries represent both new markets and sources of cheap labor for many transnational corporations. In some places, this has led to a backlash against the westernization of local culture.

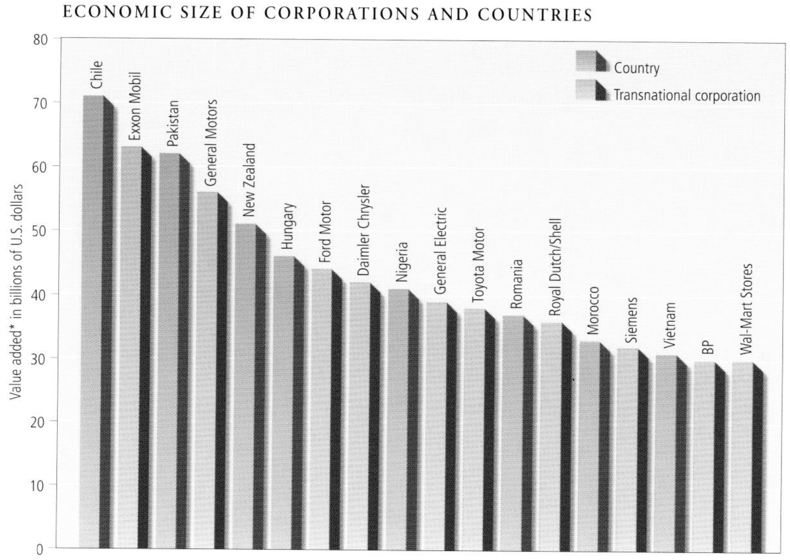
ECONOMIC SIZE OF CORPORATIONS AND COUNTRIES
Country
Transnational corporation
Value added* in billions of U.S. dollars
0
10
20
30
40
50
60
70
80
Chile
Exxon Mobil
Pakistan
General Motors
New Zealand
Hungary
Ford Motor
Daimler Chrysler
Nigeria
General Electric
Toyota Motor
Romania
Royal Dutch/Shell
Morocco
Siemens
Vietnam
BP
Wal-Mart Stores

Corporate Power

Of the world's 100 largest economic entities, almost a third are transnational corporations. The largest corporation, Exxon Mobil, ranks 45th, with an economic size roughly equivalent to that of Pakistan. Auto manufacturers are prominent in the rankings, with General Motors larger than New Zealand; Ford Motor and Daimler Chrysler bigger than Nigeria; and Toyota Motor outstripping Romania. The share of world GDP attributed to the 100 largest transnationals is growing, rising from 3.5 percent in 1990 to 4.3 percent in 2000.

* Value added for countries equals GDP; for corporations, it equals the sum of salaries, pre-tax profits, and depreciation and amortization.

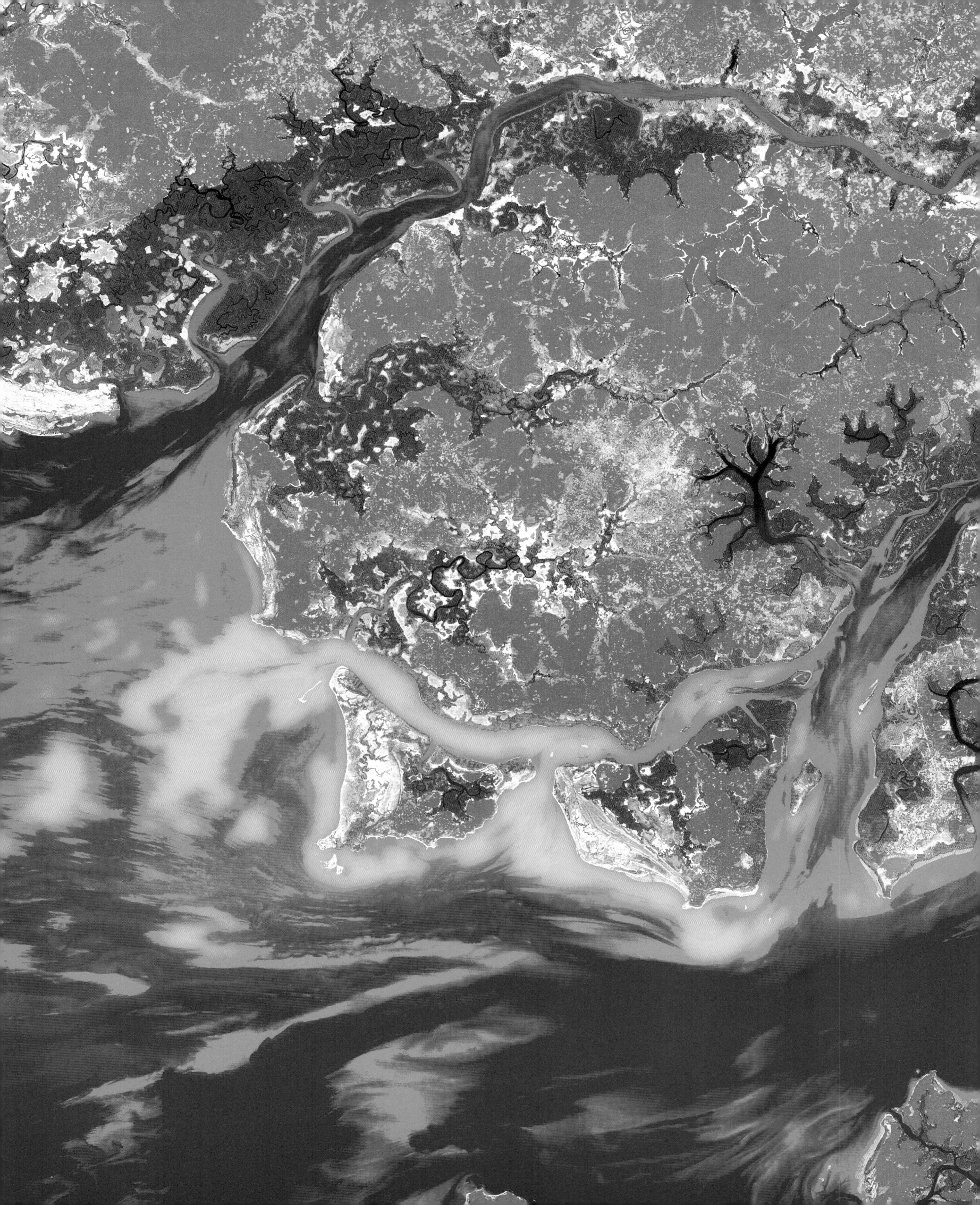

MAPPING THE WORLD

Part of the coastline of Guinea-Bissau in western Africa is visible in this color-enhanced satellite image. It was photographed from Landsat 7 using infrared, red and blue wavelengths. The blue ribbons are river systems; at center right is the River Geba. The light blue areas are silt that has been deposited as rivers flow into the Atlantic Ocean at the bottom of the image.

The Physical World

Oceans and seas dominate the globe, covering 70.8 percent of its surface. The land between these large bodies of water is traditionally divided into seven major landmasses or continents: Europe, Asia, North America, South America, Africa, Australia, and Antarctica. Europe and Asia form a single landmass, known as Eurasia, but are conventionally identified as separate continents because of their distinct peoples and histories. Though technically a continent in itself, Australia is usually considered part of the large region of Oceania, which includes the other islands of the southwestern Pacific Ocean.

Northern Hemisphere

The Northern Hemisphere encompasses more than two-thirds of Earth's land, including all of Europe and North America, and most of Asia and Africa. Its areas of open ocean are further reduced by the presence of a permanent ice cap that surrounds the North Pole, covering most of the Arctic Ocean.

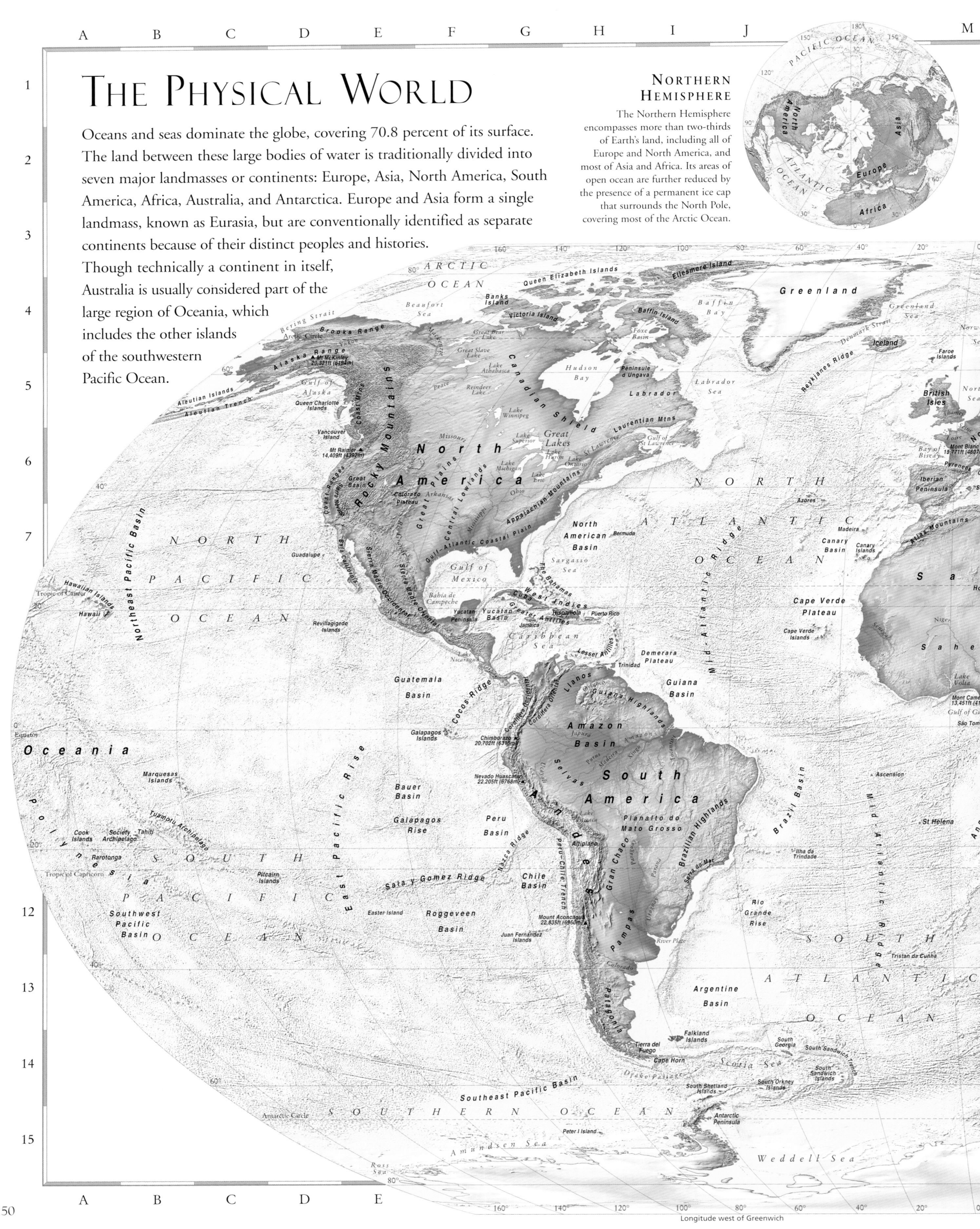

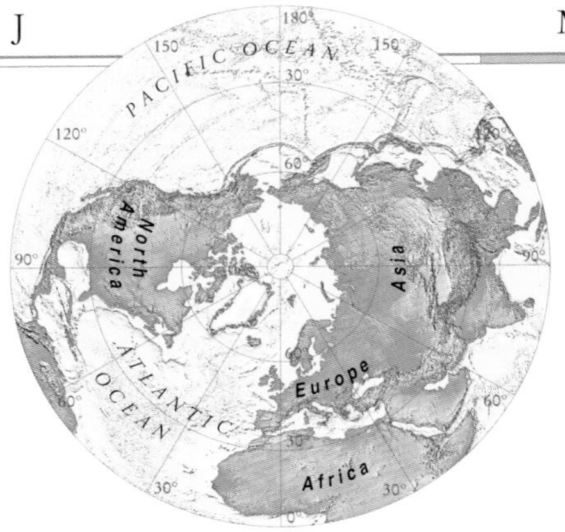

Pacific Ocean
North America
Asia
Atlantic Ocean
Europe
Africa

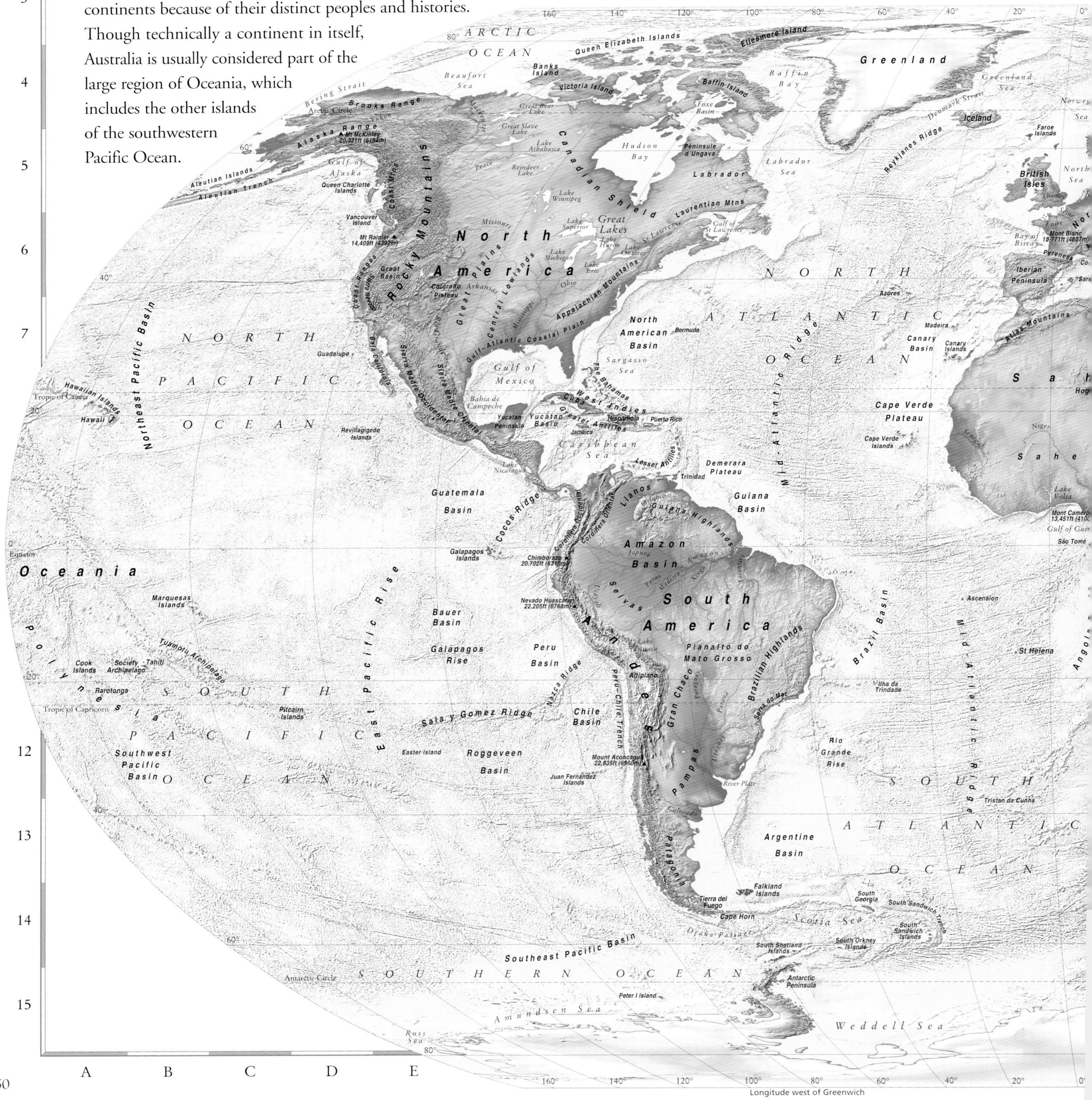

Arctic Ocean
Queen Elizabeth Islands
Ellesmere Island
Greenland
Beaufort Sea
Banks Island
Victoria Island
Baffin Island
Baffin Bay
Greenland Sea
Bering Strait
Brooks Range
Arctic Circle
Alaska Range
Mt McKinley 20,321ft (6194m)
Great Bear Lake
Great Slave Lake
Foxe Basin
Denmark Strait
Iceland
Faroe Islands
Reykjanes Ridge
Hudson Bay
Peninsule d'Ungava
Labrador
Labrador Sea
Lake Athabasca
Reindeer Lake
Canadian Shield
Gulf of Alaska
Aleutian Islands
Aleutian Trench
Queen Charlotte Islands
Coast Mtns
Rocky Mountains
Lake Winnipeg
Laurentian Mtns
Gulf of St Lawrence
British Isles
North Sea
Vancouver Island
Mt Rainier 14,409ft (4392m)
North America
Great Lakes
Lake Superior
Lake Huron
Lake Michigan
Lake Ontario
Lake Erie
Great Plains
Central Lowlands
Great Basin
Colorado Plateau
Appalachian Mountains
Mont Blanc 15,771ft (4807m)
Bay of Biscay
Pyrenees
Iberian Peninsula
North Atlantic Ocean
Azores
North American Basin
Bermuda
Madeira
Canary Basin
Canary Islands
Atlas Mountains
Gulf-Atlantic Coastal Plain
Sargasso Sea
Mid-Atlantic Ridge
Northeast Pacific Basin
North Pacific Ocean
Guadalupe
Sierra Madre Occidental
Sierra Madre Oriental
Gulf of Mexico
The Bahamas
Cuba
West Indies
Greater Antilles
Hispaniola
Puerto Rico
Jamaica
Bahia de Campeche
Yucatan Peninsula
Yucatan Basin
Hawaiian Islands
Tropic of Cancer
Hawaii
Revillagigedo Islands
Cape Verde Plateau
Cape Verde Islands
Caribbean Sea
Lesser Antilles
Trinidad
Demerara Plateau
Lake Nicaragua
Guatemala Basin
Cocos Ridge
Llanos
Guiana Highlands
Guiana Basin
Lake Volta
Mont Cameroon 13,451ft
Gulf of Guinea
São Tomé
Equator
Galapagos Islands
Chimborazo 20,702ft (6310m)
Amazon Basin
Oceania
East Pacific Rise
Marquesas Islands
Nevado Huascaran 22,205ft (6768m)
Selvas
South America
Andes
Brazil Basin
Ascension
Bauer Basin
Polynesia
Tuamotu Archipelago
Galapagos Rise
Peru Basin
Planalto do Mato Grosso
Brazilian Highlands
St Helena
Cook Islands
Society Archipelago
Tahiti
Lake Titicaca
Altiplano
Ilha da Trindade
Rarotonga
South Pacific Ocean
Tropic of Capricorn
Pitcairn Islands
Sala y Gomez Ridge
Nazca Ridge
Chile Basin
Peru-Chile Trench
Gran Chaco
Serra do Mar
Southwest Pacific Basin
Easter Island
Roggeveen Basin
Mount Aconcagua 22,835ft (6960m)
Rio Grande Rise
Juan Fernandez Islands
Pampas
River Plate
South Atlantic Ocean
Tristan da Cunha
Argentine Basin
Patagonia
Falkland Islands
Tierra del Fuego
Cape Horn
South Georgia
South Sandwich Trench
Scotia Sea
South Sandwich Islands
Drake Passage
South Orkney Islands
South Shetland Islands
Southeast Pacific Basin
Antarctic Circle
Southern Ocean
Antarctic Peninsula
Peter I Island
Amundsen Sea
Ross Sea
Weddell Sea
Longitude west of Greenwich

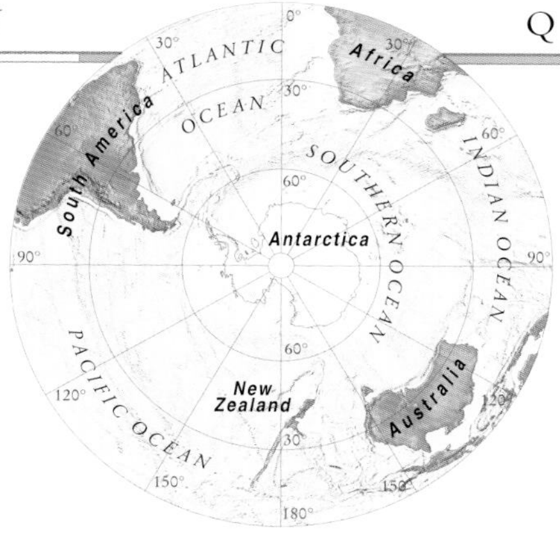
ATLANTIC OCEAN
Africa
South America
SOUTHERN OCEAN
INDIAN OCEAN
Antarctica
PACIFIC OCEAN
New Zealand
Australia
30°
60°
90°
120°
150°
180°

Southern Hemisphere

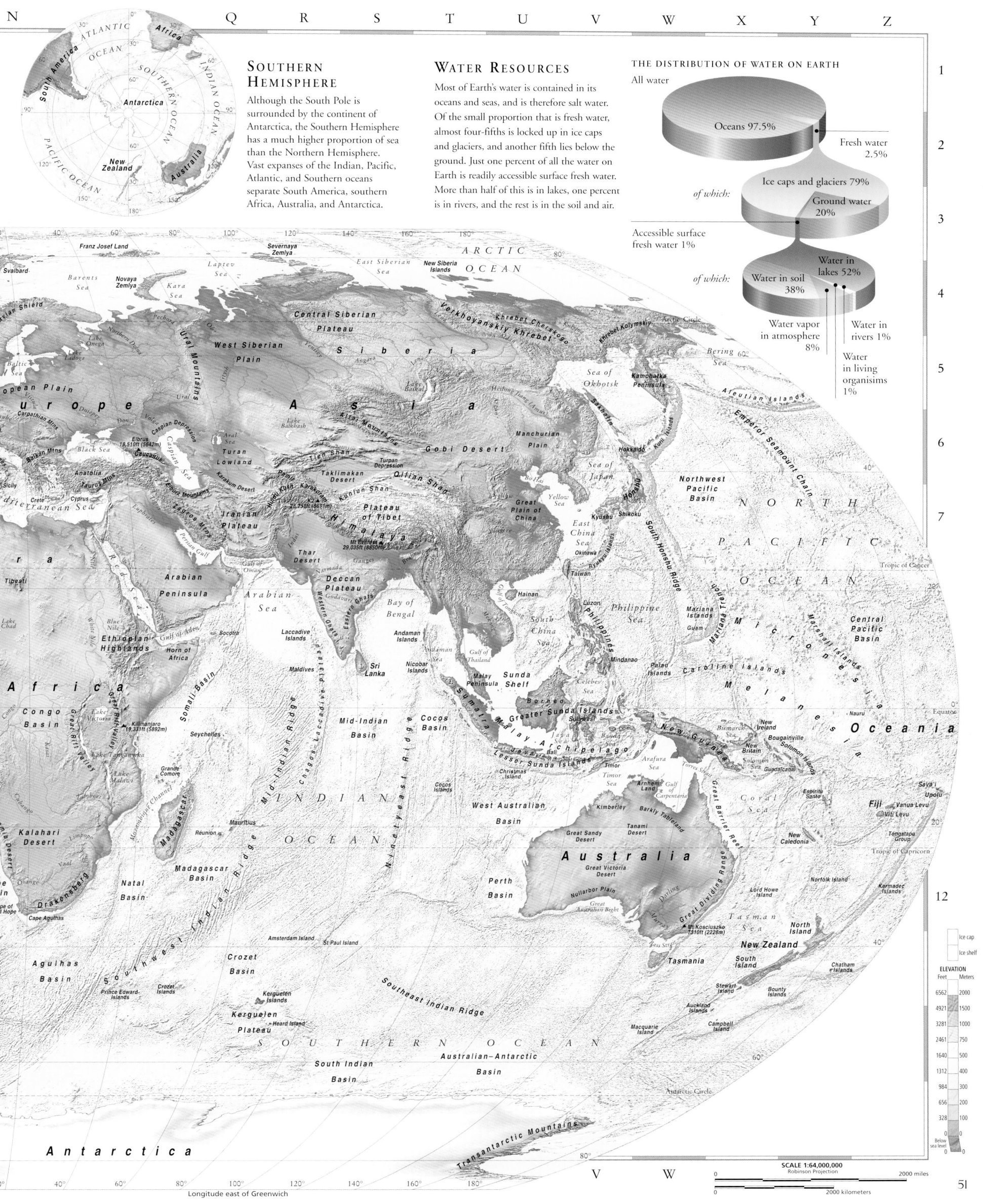

Although the South Pole is surrounded by the continent of Antarctica, the Southern Hemisphere has a much higher proportion of sea than the Northern Hemisphere. Vast expanses of the Indian, Pacific, Atlantic, and Southern oceans separate South America, southern Africa, Australia, and Antarctica.

Water Resources

Most of Earth's water is contained in its oceans and seas, and is therefore salt water. Of the small proportion that is fresh water, almost four-fifths is locked up in ice caps and glaciers, and another fifth lies below the ground. Just one percent of all the water on Earth is readily accessible surface fresh water. More than half of this is in lakes, one percent is in rivers, and the rest is in the soil and air.

The Distribution of Water on Earth

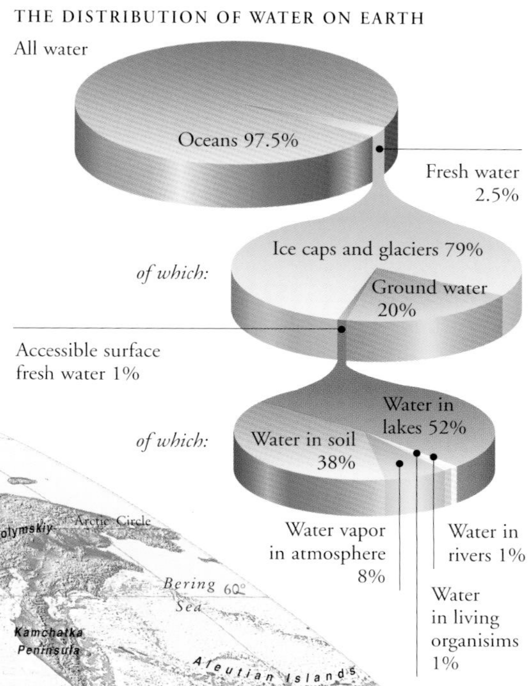
All water
Oceans 97.5%
Fresh water 2.5%
of which:
Ice caps and glaciers 79%
Ground water 20%
Accessible surface fresh water 1%
of which:
Water in soil 38%
Water in lakes 52%
Water vapor in atmosphere 8%
Water in rivers 1%
Water in living organisims 1%

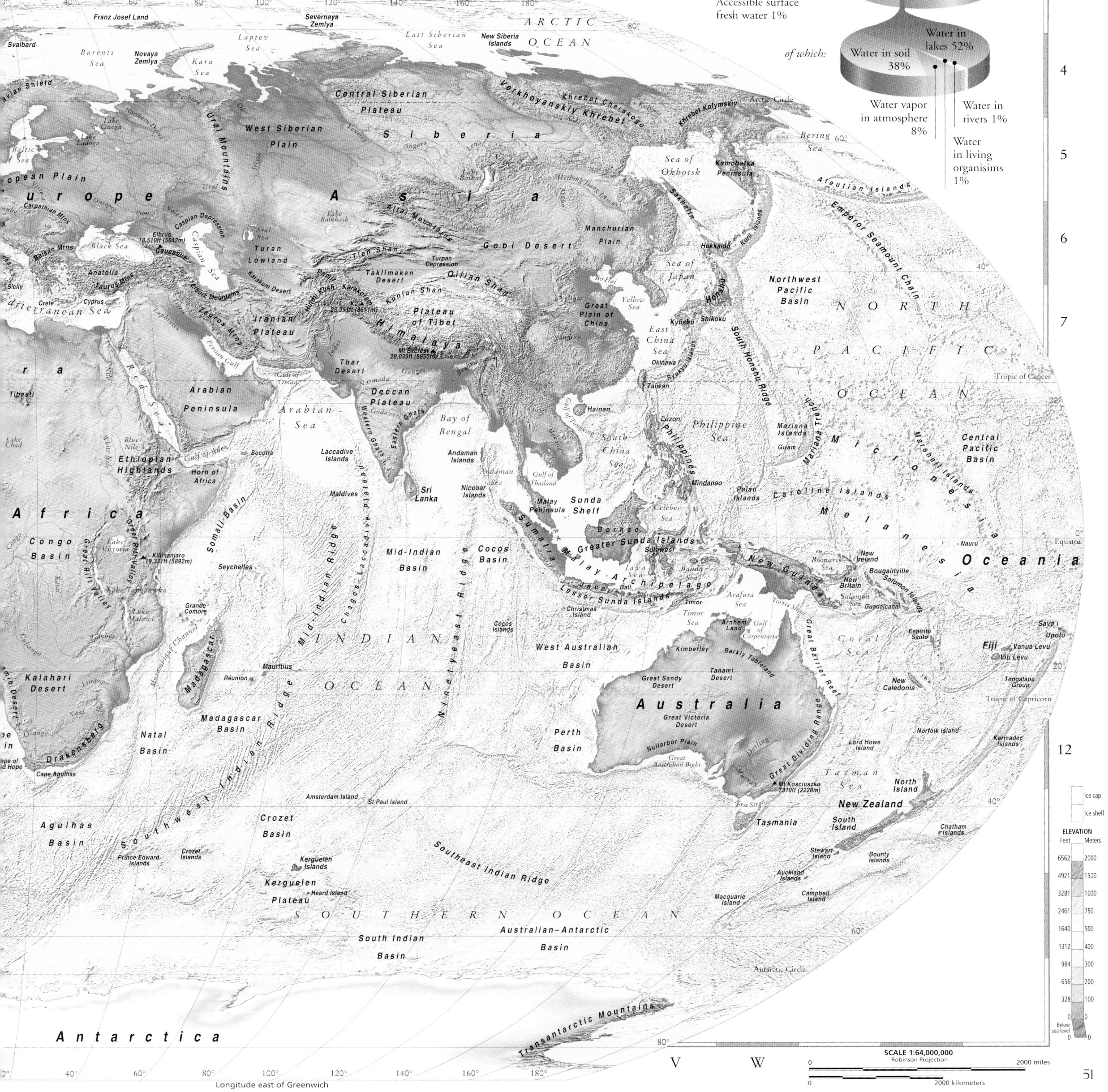
N Q R S T U V W X Y Z
1 2 3 4 5 6 7 12
Franz Josef Land
Severnaya Zemlya
Svalbard
Barents Sea
Novaya Zemlya
Kara Sea
Laptev Sea
East Siberian Sea
New Siberia Islands
ARCTIC OCEAN
Central Siberian Plateau
West Siberian Plain
Ural Mountains
Siberia
Verkhoyanskiy Khrebet
Khrebet Cherskogo
Khrebet Kolymskiy
Arctic Circle
Bering Sea
Sea of Okhotsk
Kamchatka Peninsula
Aleutian Islands
Lake Onega
Lake Ladoga
Baltic Sea
European Plain
Europe
Asia
Carpathian Mtns
Caspian Depression
Elbrus 18,510ft (5642m)
Caucasus
Black Sea
Balkan Mtns
Aral Sea
Turan Lowland
Caspian Sea
Lake Balkhash
Lake Baikal
Altai Mountains
Gobi Desert
Manchurian Plain
Sakhalin
Hokkaido
Kuril Islands
Emperor Seamount Chain
Tien Shan
Turpan Depression
Taklimakan Desert
Qilian Shan
Anatolia
Taurus Mtns
Cyprus
Crete
Sicily
Mediterranean Sea
Elburz Mountains
Zagros Mtns
Karakum Desert
Iranian Plateau
Hindu Kush
Pamir
Karakoram
K2 28,251ft (8611m)
Kunlun Shan
Plateau of Tibet
Himalaya
Mt Everest 29,035ft (8850m)
Sea of Japan
Yellow Sea
Great Plain of China
East China Sea
Honshu
Kyushu
Shikoku
Okinawa
Ryukyu Islands
Taiwan
Northwest Pacific Basin
NORTH PACIFIC OCEAN
South Honshu Ridge
Tropic of Cancer
Tibesti
Lake Chad
Persian Gulf
Gulf of Oman
Arabian Peninsula
Red Sea
Thar Desert
Deccan Plateau
Western Ghats
Eastern Ghats
Arabian Sea
Bay of Bengal
Hainan
Gulf of Tonkin
Luzon
Philippines
Philippine Sea
South China Sea
Mariana Islands
Mariana Trench
Guam
Micronesia
Marshall Islands
Central Pacific Basin
Ethiopian Highlands
Gulf of Aden
Socotra
Horn of Africa
Laccadive Islands
Andaman Islands
Andaman Sea
Gulf of Thailand
Mindanao
Palau Islands
Caroline Islands
Maldives
Sri Lanka
Nicobar Islands
Malay Peninsula
Sunda Shelf
Celebes Sea
Africa
Congo Basin
Lake Victoria
Great Rift Valley
Kilimanjaro 19,331ft (5892m)
Somali Basin
Chagos-Laccadive Plateau
Mid-Indian Ridge
Mid-Indian Basin
Ninetyeast Ridge
Cocos Basin
Sumatra
Borneo
Greater Sunda Islands
Sulawesi
Malay Archipelago
Java
Bali
Lesser Sunda Islands
New Guinea
Bismarck Sea
New Ireland
New Britain
Bougainville
Solomon Islands
Solomon Sea
Guadalcanal
Melanesia
Nauru
Oceania
Equator
Seychelles
Lake Tanganyika
Lake Malawi
Grande Comore
Christmas Island
Cocos Islands
Timor
Timor Sea
Arafura Sea
Torres Strait
Arnhem Land
Gulf of Carpentaria
Great Barrier Reef
Coral Sea
Espiritu Santo
Fiji
Vanua Levu
Viti Levu
Sava'i
Upolu
Mozambique Channel
Madagascar
Mauritius
Réunion
INDIAN OCEAN
West Australian Basin
Kimberley
Barkly Tableland
Tanami Desert
Great Sandy Desert
New Caledonia
Tongatapu Group
Tropic of Capricorn
Kalahari Desert
Limpopo
Namib Desert
Orange
Vaal
Drakensberg
Cape of Good Hope
Cape Agulhas
Natal Basin
Madagascar Basin
Australia
Great Victoria Desert
Perth Basin
Nullarbor Plain
Great Australian Bight
Great Dividing Range
Darling
Murray
Mt Kosciuszko 7310ft (2228m)
Norfolk Island
Lord Howe Island
Kermadec Islands
Tasman Sea
North Island
New Zealand
Bass Strait
Tasmania
South Island
Chatham Islands
Amsterdam Island
St Paul Island
Agulhas Basin
Southwest Indian Ridge
Crozet Basin
Prince Edward Islands
Crozet Islands
Kerguelen Islands
Kerguelen Plateau
Heard Island
Southeast Indian Ridge
Stewart Island
Bounty Islands
Auckland Islands
Campbell Island
Macquarie Island
SOUTHERN OCEAN
Australian-Antarctic Basin
South Indian Basin
Antarctic Circle
Antarctica
Transantarctic Mountains
V W
40° 60° 80° 100° 120° 140° 160° 180°
Longitude east of Greenwich
Ice cap
Ice shelf
ELEVATION
Feet Meters
6562 2000
4921 1500
3281 1000
2461 750
1640 500
1312 400
984 300
656 200
328 100
0 0
Below sea level 0
SCALE 1:64,000,000
Robinson Projection
0 2000 miles
0 2000 kilometers

The Political World

With the exception of Antarctica, where territorial claims have been suspended, all the land on Earth is divided into 192 independent countries and about 60 dependent territories. The countries range in size from the largest, the vast Russian Federation, to the smallest, the Vatican City, which lies entirely within the city of Rome in Italy. Most dependent territories came about as the result of colonization and belong to a few, mainly European nations. Some areas of land, usually on the fringes of countries, are the focus of territorial disputes.

Dividing the World

About 150,000 miles (250,000 km) of land boundaries separate the world's countries and territories. These borders may follow landforms, waterways, the margins of traditional ethnic territories, lines of latitude or longitude, or arbitrary lines plotted by colonial administrators. Many seaboard nations have also established maritime boundaries. A nation's maritime territorial claim extends 12 nautical miles offshore, but exclusive fishing and economic zones are generally recognized up to 200 nautical miles offshore.

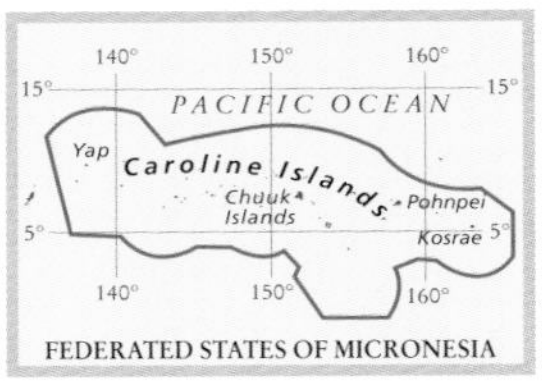

PACIFIC OCEAN
Yap
Caroline Islands
Chuuk Islands
Pohnpei
Kosrae
140°
150°
160°
15°
5°
FEDERATED STATES OF MICRONESIA

The Exclusive Economic Zone (EEZ) of the Federated States of Micronesia encompasses over 1.3 million square miles (3 million sq km) of ocean.

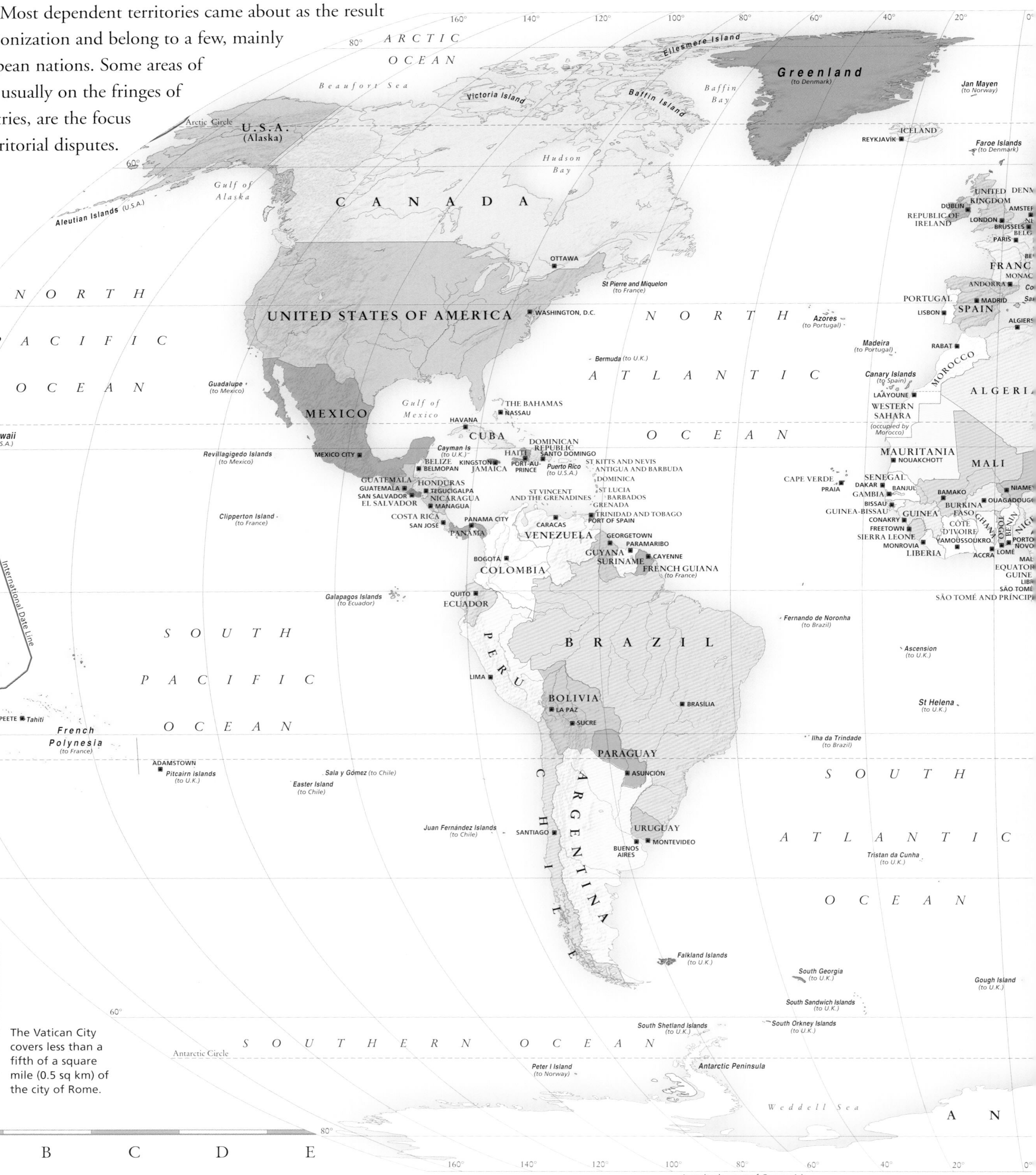

ARCTIC OCEAN
Beaufort Sea
Victoria Island
Baffin Island
Ellesmere Island
Baffin Bay
Greenland
(to Denmark)
Jan Mayen
(to Norway)
ICELAND
REYKJAVIK
Faroe Islands
(to Denmark)
Arctic Circle
U.S.A.
(Alaska)
Hudson Bay
Gulf of Alaska
Aleutian Islands (U.S.A.)
CANADA
OTTAWA
St Pierre and Miquelon
(to France)
UNITED STATES OF AMERICA
WASHINGTON, D.C.
NORTH PACIFIC OCEAN
NORTH ATLANTIC OCEAN
Azores
(to Portugal)
Madeira
(to Portugal)
Bermuda (to U.K.)
Canary Islands
(to Spain)
Guadalupe
(to Mexico)
Gulf of Mexico
MEXICO
MEXICO CITY
THE BAHAMAS
NASSAU
HAVANA
CUBA
Tropic of Cancer
Hawaii
(U.S.A.)
Revillagigedo Islands
(to Mexico)
Cayman Is
(to U.K.)
BELIZE
BELMOPAN
KINGSTON
JAMAICA
HAITI
PORT-AU-PRINCE
DOMINICAN REPUBLIC
SANTO DOMINGO
Puerto Rico
(to U.S.A.)
ST KITTS AND NEVIS
ANTIGUA AND BARBUDA
DOMINICA
ST LUCIA
BARBADOS
ST VINCENT AND THE GRENADINES
GRENADA
TRINIDAD AND TOBAGO
PORT OF SPAIN
GUATEMALA
GUATEMALA
HONDURAS
TEGUCIGALPA
SAN SALVADOR
EL SALVADOR
NICARAGUA
MANAGUA
COSTA RICA
SAN JOSÉ
PANAMA CITY
PANAMA
Clipperton Island
(to France)
CARACAS
VENEZUELA
GEORGETOWN
PARAMARIBO
GUYANA
SURINAME
CAYENNE
FRENCH GUIANA
(to France)
BOGOTÁ
COLOMBIA
QUITO
ECUADOR
Galapagos Islands
(to Ecuador)
0° Equator
International Date Line
KIRIBATI
SOUTH PACIFIC OCEAN
PERU
LIMA
BRAZIL
BRASÍLIA
BOLIVIA
LA PAZ
SUCRE
PARAGUAY
ASUNCIÓN
CHILE
SANTIAGO
ARGENTINA
BUENOS AIRES
URUGUAY
MONTEVIDEO
American Samoa
(to U.S.A.)
Cook Islands
(to N.Z.)
PAPEETE
Tahiti
French Polynesia
(to France)
AVARUA
Tropic of Capricorn
ADAMSTOWN
Pitcairn Islands
(to U.K.)
Sala y Gómez (to Chile)
Easter Island
(to Chile)
Juan Fernández Islands
(to Chile)
Fernando de Noronha
(to Brazil)
Ascension
(to U.K.)
St Helena
(to U.K.)
Ilha da Trindade
(to Brazil)
SOUTH ATLANTIC OCEAN
Tristan da Cunha
(to U.K.)
Falkland Islands
(to U.K.)
South Georgia
(to U.K.)
Gough Island
(to U.K.)
South Sandwich Islands
(to U.K.)
South Shetland Islands
(to U.K.)
South Orkney Islands
(to U.K.)
SOUTHERN OCEAN
Antarctic Circle
Peter I Island
(to Norway)
Antarctic Peninsula
Weddell Sea
UNITED KINGDOM
DUBLIN
REPUBLIC OF IRELAND
LONDON
BRUSSELS
PARIS
FRANCE
ANDORRA
PORTUGAL
LISBON
MADRID
SPAIN
RABAT
MOROCCO
ALGERIA
LAAYOUNE
WESTERN SAHARA
(occupied by Morocco)
MAURITANIA
NOUAKCHOTT
MALI
CAPE VERDE
PRAIA
DAKAR
SENEGAL
BANJUL
GAMBIA
BISSAU
GUINEA-BISSAU
CONAKRY
GUINEA
BAMAKO
BURKINA FASO
OUAGADOUGOU
FREETOWN
SIERRA LEONE
MONROVIA
LIBERIA
CÔTE D'IVOIRE
YAMOUSSOUKRO
GHANA
TOGO
BENIN
ACCRA
LOMÉ
SÃO TOMÉ
SÃO TOMÉ AND PRÍNCIPE
Longitude west of Greenwich

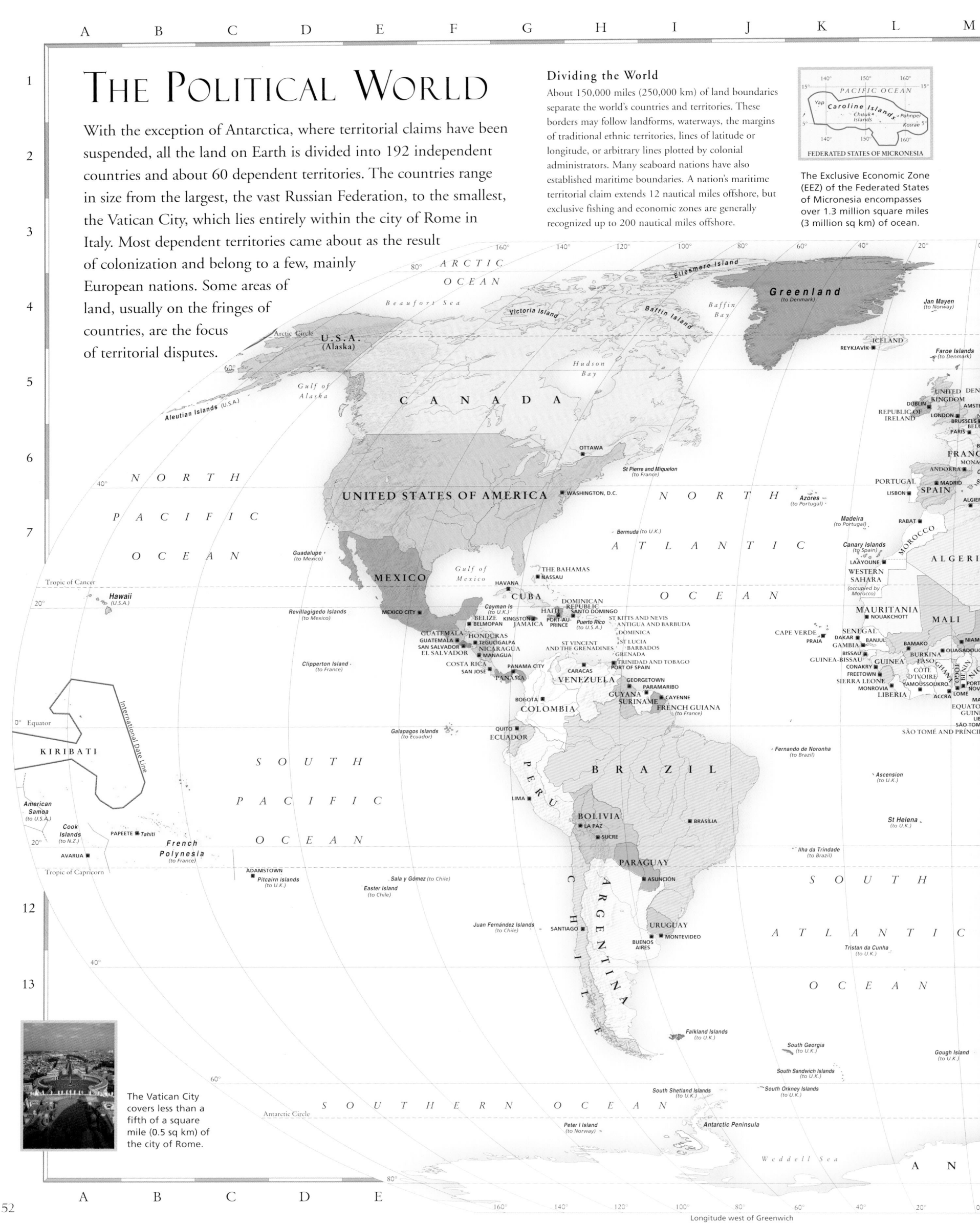

The Vatican City covers less than a fifth of a square mile (0.5 sq km) of the city of Rome.

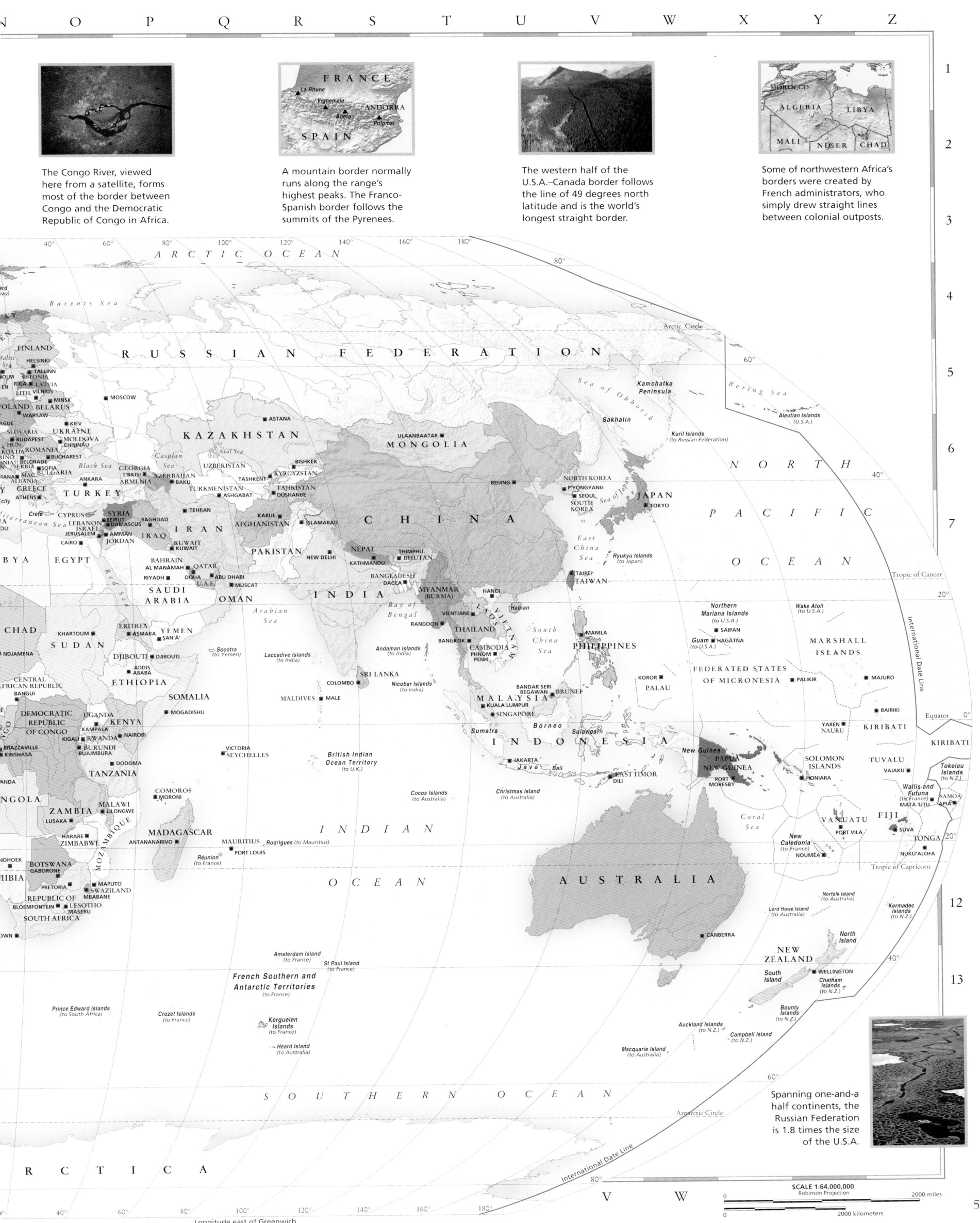

The Congo River, viewed here from a satellite, forms most of the border between Congo and the Democratic Republic of Congo in Africa.

FRANCE
La Rhune
Vignemale
Aneto
ANDORRA
Puigmal
SPAIN

A mountain border normally runs along the range's highest peaks. The Franco-Spanish border follows the summits of the Pyrenees.

The western half of the U.S.A.–Canada border follows the line of 49 degrees north latitude and is the world's longest straight border.

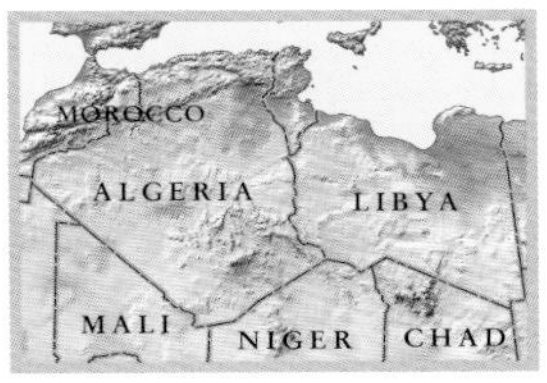

MOROCCO
ALGERIA
LIBYA
MALI
NIGER
CHAD

Some of northwestern Africa's borders were created by French administrators, who simply drew straight lines between colonial outposts.

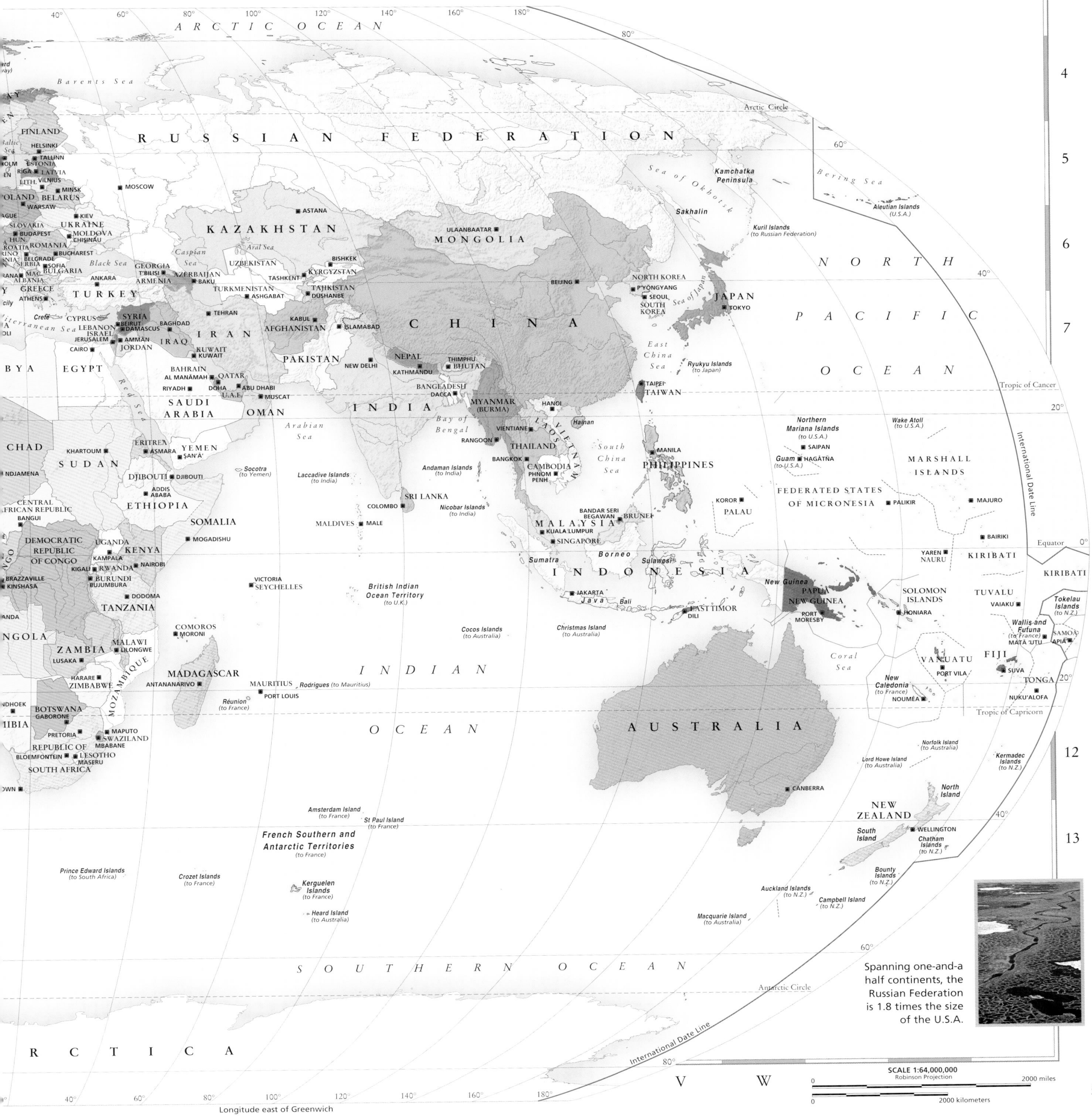

N
O
P
Q
R
S
T
U
V
W
X
Y
Z
1
2
3
4
5
6
7
12
13
ARCTIC OCEAN
Barents Sea
RUSSIAN FEDERATION
FINLAND
HELSINKI
TALLINN
ESTONIA
RIGA
LATVIA
VILNIUS
MINSK
BELARUS
WARSAW
MOSCOW
KIEV
UKRAINE
MOLDOVA
CHIŞINĂU
ROMANIA
BUCHAREST
BELGRADE
SERBIA
SOFIA
BULGARIA
ALBANIA
GREECE
ATHENS
ANKARA
TURKEY
Black Sea
GEORGIA
T'BILISI
ARMENIA
AZERBAIJAN
BAKU
Caspian Sea
Aral Sea
KAZAKHSTAN
ASTANA
UZBEKISTAN
TASHKENT
BISHKEK
KYRGYZSTAN
TURKMENISTAN
ASHGABAT
TAJIKISTAN
DUSHANBE
TEHRAN
IRAN
KABUL
AFGHANISTAN
ISLAMABAD
PAKISTAN
CYPRUS
SYRIA
BEIRUT
DAMASCUS
LEBANON
ISRAEL
JERUSALEM
AMMAN
JORDAN
BAGHDAD
IRAQ
KUWAIT
CAIRO
EGYPT
BAHRAIN
AL MANĀMAH
QATAR
DOHA
ABU DHABI
U.A.E.
MUSCAT
RIYADH
SAUDI ARABIA
OMAN
Red Sea
Arabian Sea
ERITREA
ASMARA
YEMEN
ṢAN'Ā'
KHARTOUM
SUDAN
CHAD
NDJAMENA
DJIBOUTI
ADDIS ABABA
ETHIOPIA
SOMALIA
MOGADISHU
Socotra (to Yemen)
CENTRAL AFRICAN REPUBLIC
BANGUI
DEMOCRATIC REPUBLIC OF CONGO
UGANDA
KAMPALA
KENYA
NAIROBI
KIGALI
RWANDA
BURUNDI
BUJUMBURA
BRAZZAVILLE
KINSHASA
DODOMA
TANZANIA
VICTORIA
SEYCHELLES
COMOROS
MORONI
ZAMBIA
LUSAKA
MALAWI
LILONGWE
MOZAMBIQUE
HARARE
ZIMBABWE
MADAGASCAR
ANTANANARIVO
BOTSWANA
GABORONE
PRETORIA
MAPUTO
SWAZILAND
MBABANE
REPUBLIC OF SOUTH AFRICA
BLOEMFONTEIN
LESOTHO
MASERU
MAURITIUS
PORT LOUIS
Rodrigues (to Mauritius)
Réunion (to France)
MONGOLIA
ULAANBAATAR
CHINA
BEIJING
NORTH KOREA
P'YONGYANG
SEOUL
SOUTH KOREA
Sea of Japan
JAPAN
TOKYO
Sea of Okhotsk
Sakhalin
Kamchatka Peninsula
Kuril Islands (to Russian Federation)
Bering Sea
Aleutian Islands (U.S.A.)
Arctic Circle
NORTH PACIFIC OCEAN
East China Sea
Ryukyu Islands (to Japan)
TAIPEI
TAIWAN
NEPAL
KATHMANDU
THIMPHU
BHUTAN
NEW DELHI
INDIA
BANGLADESH
DACCA
MYANMAR (BURMA)
Bay of Bengal
HANOI
Hainan
VIENTIANE
LAOS
VIETNAM
RANGOON
THAILAND
BANGKOK
CAMBODIA
PHNOM PENH
South China Sea
MANILA
PHILIPPINES
Laccadive Islands (to India)
Andaman Islands (to India)
Nicobar Islands (to India)
SRI LANKA
COLOMBO
MALDIVES
MALE
BANDAR SERI BEGAWAN
BRUNEI
MALAYSIA
KUALA LUMPUR
SINGAPORE
Borneo
Sumatra
Sulawesi
INDONESIA
JAKARTA
Java
Bali
EAST TIMOR
DILI
New Guinea
PAPUA NEW GUINEA
PORT MORESBY
British Indian Ocean Territory (to U.K.)
Cocos Islands (to Australia)
Christmas Island (to Australia)
Tropic of Cancer
Northern Mariana Islands (to U.S.A.)
SAIPAN
Guam (to U.S.A.)
HAGÅTÑA
Wake Atoll (to U.S.A.)
MARSHALL ISLANDS
FEDERATED STATES OF MICRONESIA
PALIKIR
MAJURO
KOROR
PALAU
International Date Line
BAIRIKI
Equator
YAREN
NAURU
KIRIBATI
SOLOMON ISLANDS
HONIARA
TUVALU
VAIAKU
Tokelau Islands (to N.Z.)
Wallis and Futuna (to France)
MATA 'UTU
SAMOA
APIA
FIJI
SUVA
VANUATU
PORT VILA
New Caledonia (to France)
NOUMÉA
TONGA
NUKU'ALOFA
Coral Sea
Tropic of Capricorn
INDIAN OCEAN
AUSTRALIA
CANBERRA
Norfolk Island (to Australia)
Lord Howe Island (to Australia)
Kermadec Islands (to N.Z.)
NEW ZEALAND
North Island
South Island
WELLINGTON
Chatham Islands (to N.Z.)
Bounty Islands (to N.Z.)
Auckland Islands (to N.Z.)
Campbell Island (to N.Z.)
Macquarie Island (to Australia)
Amsterdam Island (to France)
St Paul Island (to France)
French Southern and Antarctic Territories (to France)
Prince Edward Islands (to South Africa)
Crozet Islands (to France)
Kerguelen Islands (to France)
Heard Island (to Australia)
SOUTHERN OCEAN
Antarctic Circle
ANTARCTICA
International Date Line
SCALE 1:64,000,000
Robinson Projection
2000 miles
2000 kilometers
Longitude east of Greenwich

Spanning one-and-a half continents, the Russian Federation is 1.8 times the size of the U.S.A.

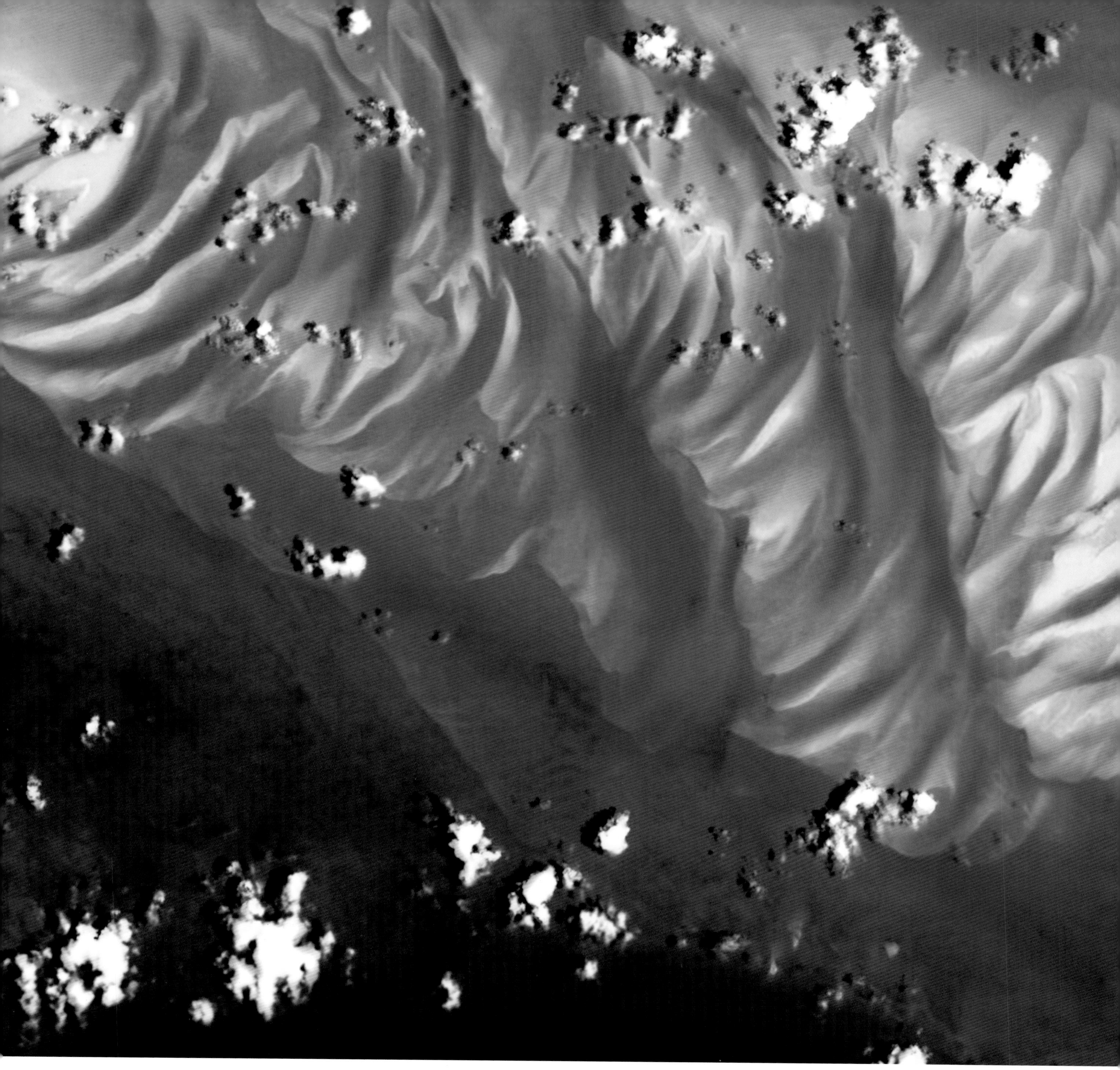

Taken from NASA's Terra satellite, this image shows underwater sand dunes in the waters of Tarpum Bay, southwest of Eleuthera Island in The Bahamas. These dunes, shaped by ocean currents, are made of sand eroded from limestone coral reefs.

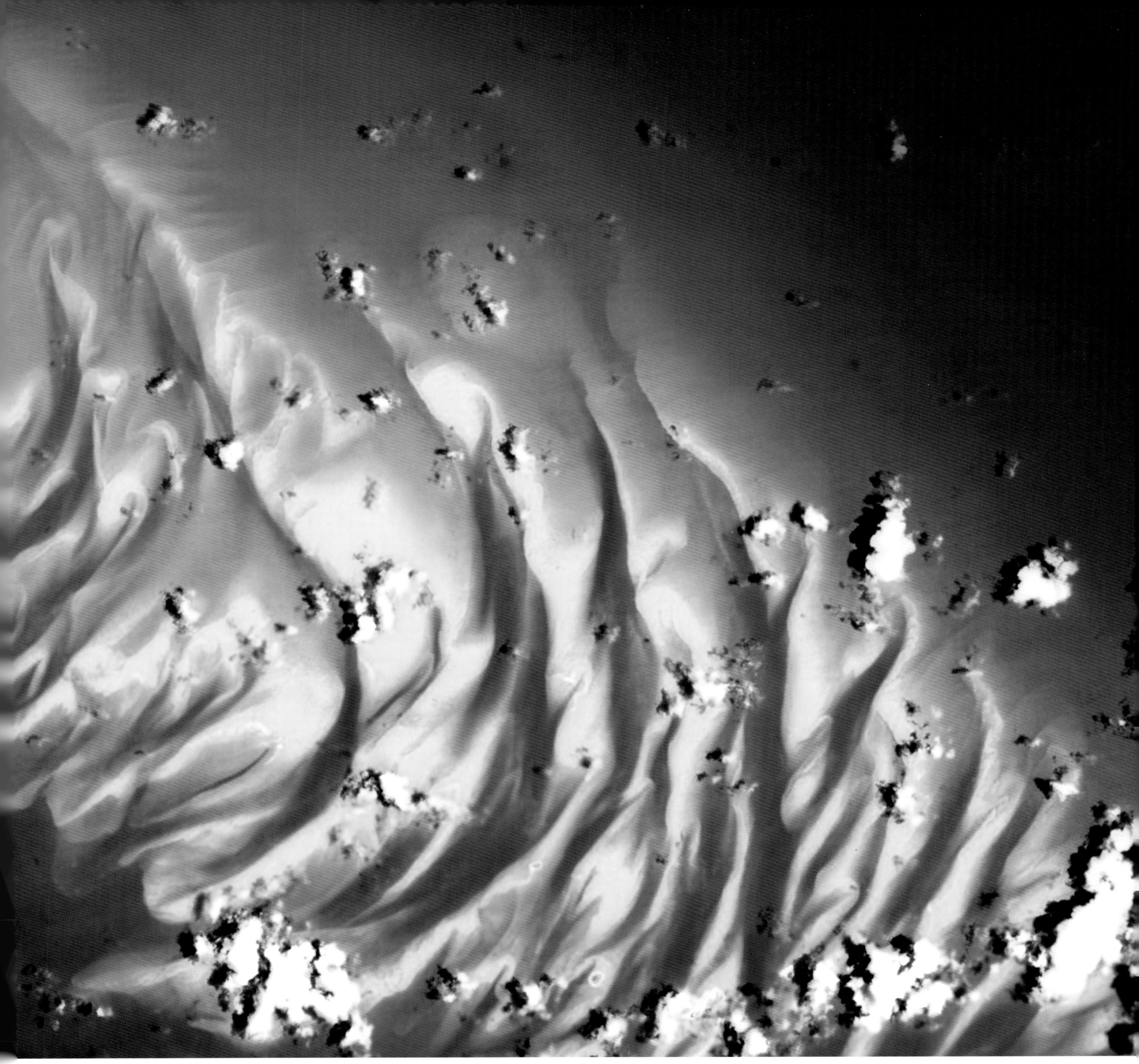

The Oceans

THE OCEANS

More than two-thirds of Earth's surface is covered by its five connected oceans. The Pacific, Atlantic, Indian, and Arctic have been recognized for centuries. The fifth ocean, the Southern, was demarcated by the International Hydrographic Organization only in the year 2000. It encompasses all the waters surrounding Antarctica up to 60 degrees south latitude, taking in areas formerly considered part of the Pacific, Atlantic, and Indian oceans. A region known as the Antarctic Polar Frontal Zone separates the icy waters of the Southern Ocean from the warmer waters to the north.

The oceans absorb more than 80 percent of the solar radiation that reaches Earth, and water has a remarkable capacity for storing heat. Consequently, the uppermost 10 percent of the oceans contains more heat than the entire atmosphere. As ocean currents carry immense quantities of heat around the globe, they modify the climate. The Gulf Stream, for example, carries warm water from the Caribbean past the eastern United States to northern Europe, making northern Europe significantly warmer than northern Canada at the same latitudes.

Recent technologies such as satellites, submersibles, and sounding equipment have dramatically enhanced our understanding of the sea. The underwater landscape contains Earth's greatest canyons and longest mountain chains. Bizarre lifeforms adapted to the cold, dark depths have been discovered. Even so, more than 90 percent of Earth's oceans are still to be explored.

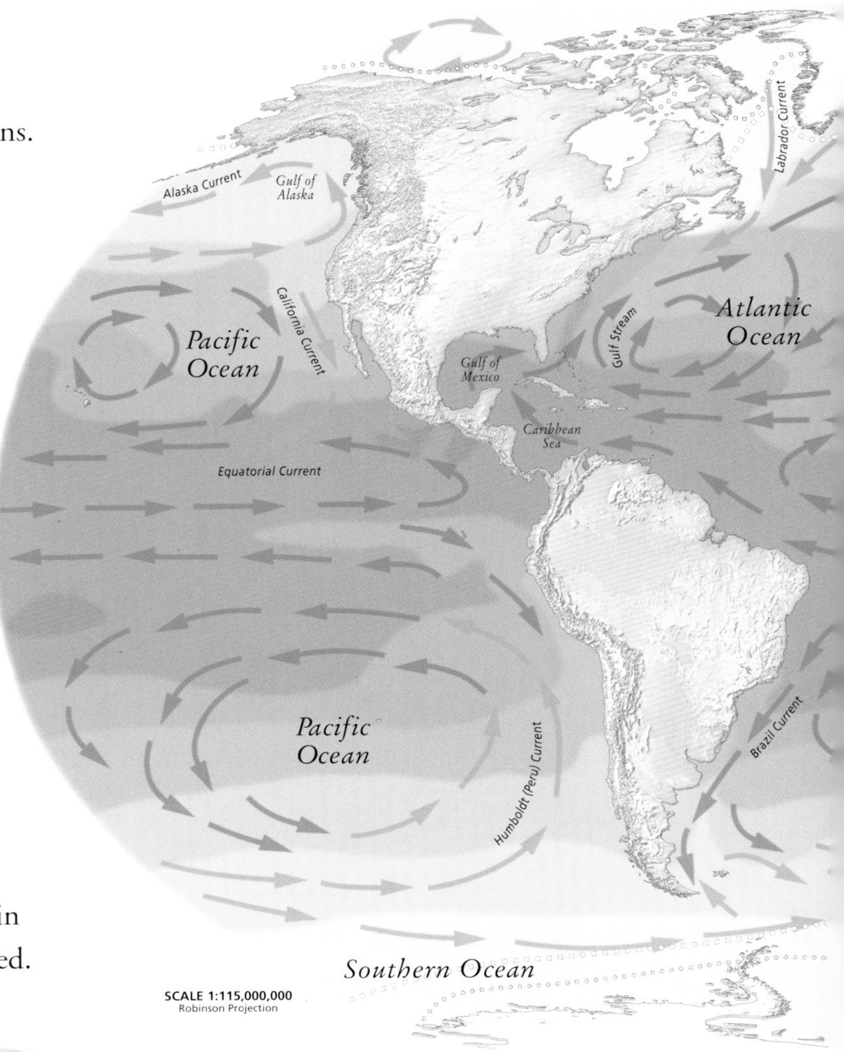

Alaska Current
Gulf of Alaska
Labrador Current
California Current
Pacific Ocean
Gulf Stream
Atlantic Ocean
Gulf of Mexico
Caribbean Sea
Equatorial Current
Pacific Ocean
Humboldt (Peru) Current
Brazil Current
Southern Ocean

SCALE 1:115,000,000
Robinson Projection

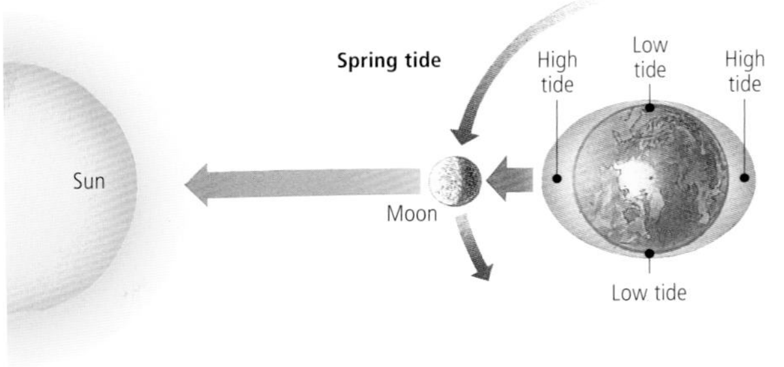

Spring tide
Sun
Moon
High tide
Low tide
High tide
Low tide

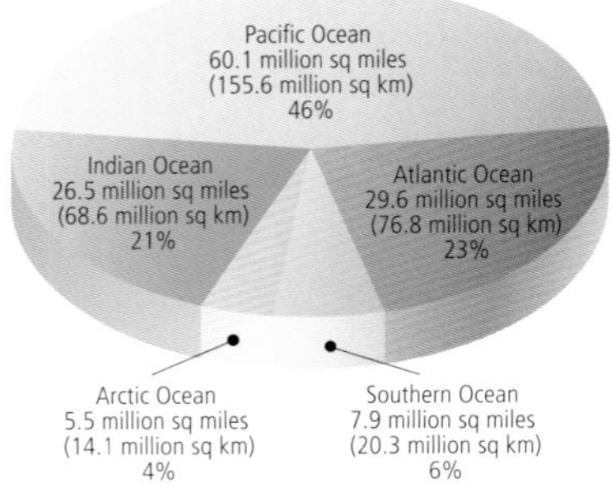

Pacific Ocean
60.1 million sq miles
(155.6 million sq km)
46%
Indian Ocean
26.5 million sq miles
(68.6 million sq km)
21%
Atlantic Ocean
29.6 million sq miles
(76.8 million sq km)
23%
Arctic Ocean
5.5 million sq miles
(14.1 million sq km)
4%
Southern Ocean
7.9 million sq miles
(20.3 million sq km)
6%

Ocean Size

Almost equal in size to the Indian, Atlantic, and Arctic combined, the Pacific is by far the largest ocean. Together, the five oceans cover about 130 million square miles (335 million sq km). They contain 335 million cubic miles (1,400 million cubic km) of water, which makes up 97 percent of all Earth's water and is 18 times greater than the volume of Earth's land.

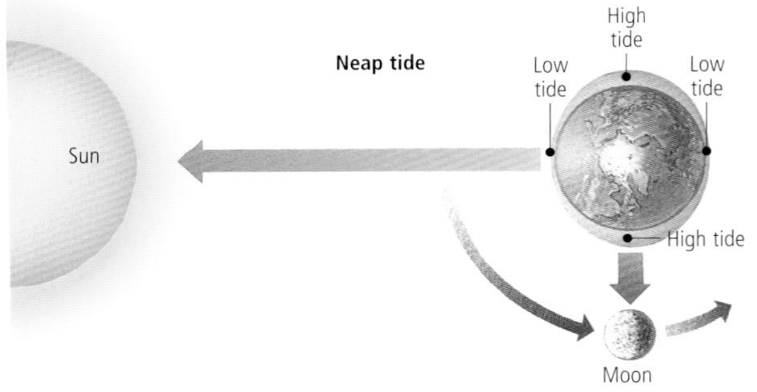

Neap tide
Sun
High tide
Low tide
Low tide
High tide
Moon

Tidal Forces

Every day as Earth rotates, the Moon's gravity pulls on its oceans, creating high tide on the side facing the Moon. Centrifugal force produced by Earth's rotation creates high tide on the opposite side as well. When the Sun and Moon line up, their combined gravitational pull creates especially high tides, known as spring tides. When the Sun and Moon are at right angles to each other, the tidal range is small and neap tides occur.

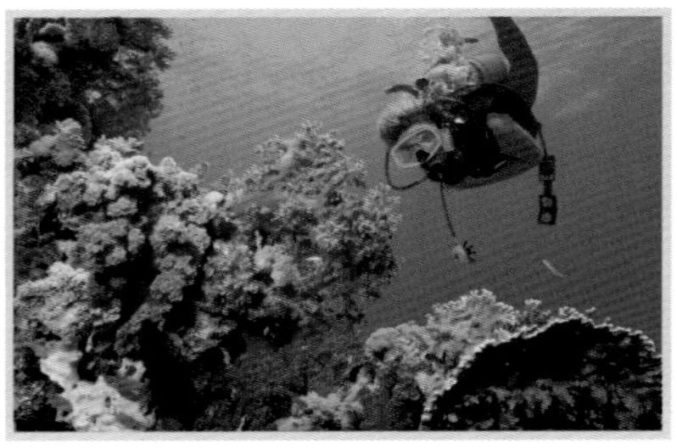

In warm, shallow seas, vast reefs can be built by coral polyps, tiny animals that produce casings of limestone. Referred to as "the rain forests of the sea," coral reefs harbor a rich diversity of life.

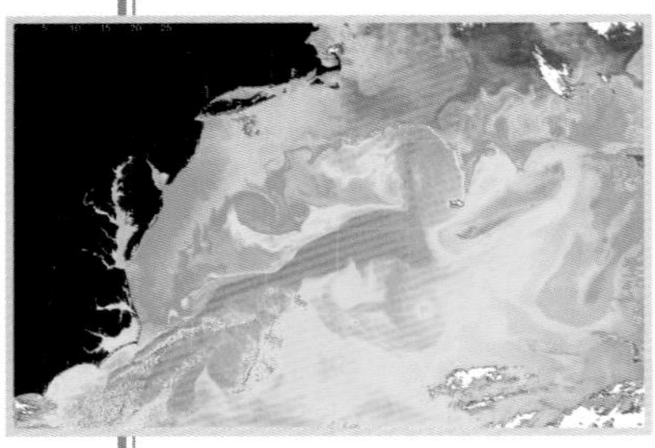

The Gulf Stream is a warm surface current in the Atlantic Ocean off the east coast of the United States. In this false-color satellite image, warmer waters are shown as red, and cooler waters are shown as blue.

Great Ocean Conveyor Belt

A "great ocean conveyor belt" transports heat around the globe. As surface currents carry warm water from the Pacific through the Indian and into the Atlantic, the water cools and evaporation increases its salinity. In the North Atlantic, this denser, colder water sinks, creating a deep current that carries it back to the Indian, Southern, and Pacific oceans. Changes in precipitation and ice melt may affect the belt's strength, which in turn may alter the global climate.

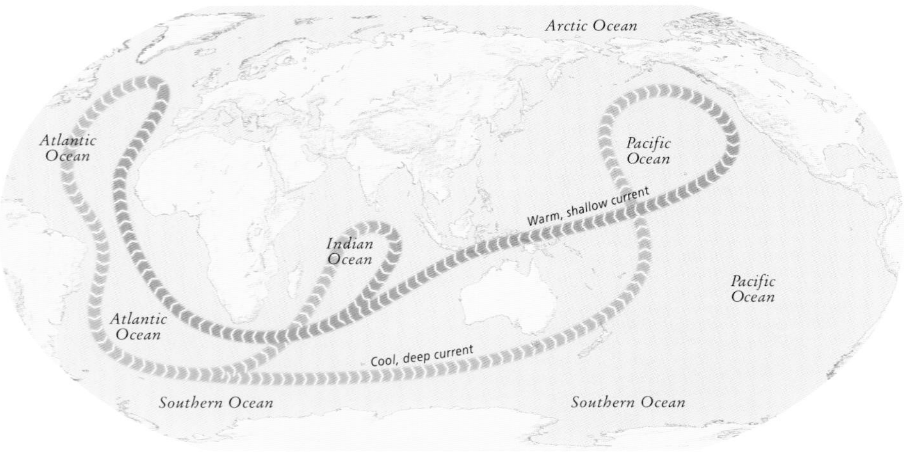

Arctic Ocean
Atlantic Ocean
Pacific Ocean
Warm, shallow current
Indian Ocean
Pacific Ocean
Atlantic Ocean
Cool, deep current
Southern Ocean
Southern Ocean

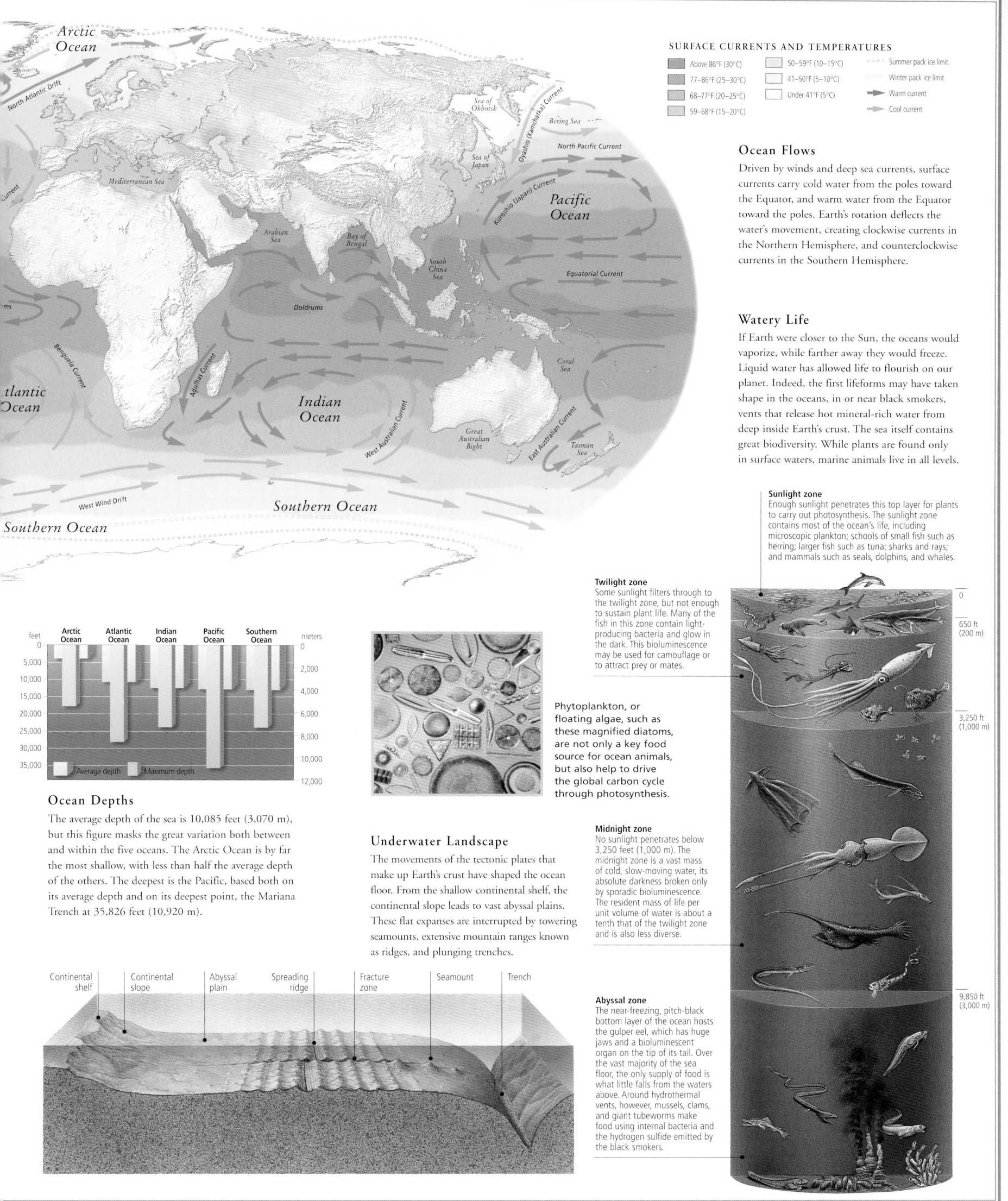

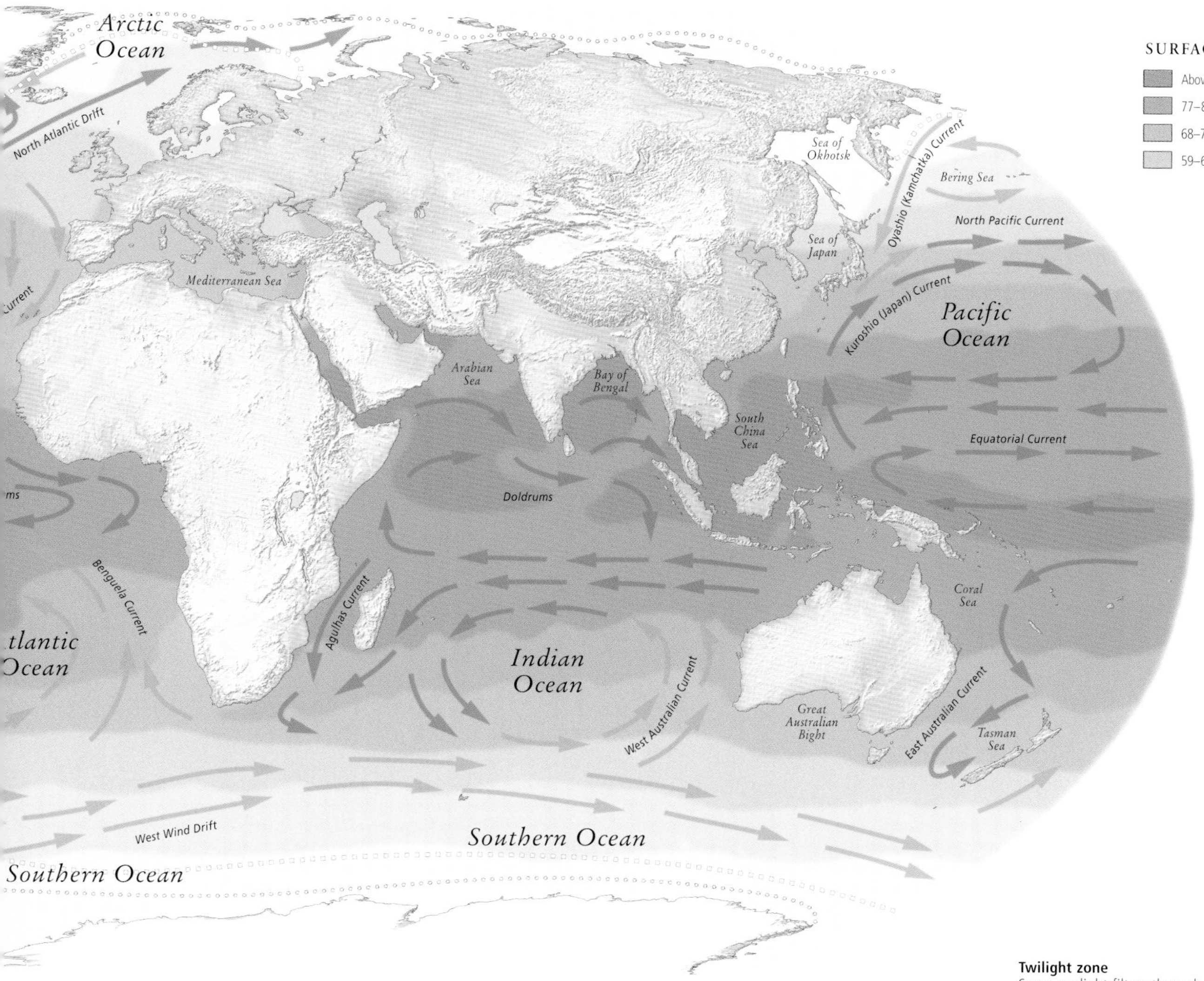
Arctic Ocean
North Atlantic Drift
Sea of Okhotsk
Oyashio (Kamchatka) Current
Bering Sea
North Pacific Current
Sea of Japan
Mediterranean Sea
Kuroshio (Japan) Current
Pacific Ocean
Arabian Sea
Bay of Bengal
South China Sea
Equatorial Current
Doldrums
Benguela Current
Agulhas Current
Coral Sea
Atlantic Ocean
Indian Ocean
West Australian Current
Great Australian Bight
East Australian Current
Tasman Sea
West Wind Drift
Southern Ocean
Southern Ocean

SURFACE CURRENTS AND TEMPERATURES

- Above 86°F (30°C)
- 77–86°F (25–30°C)
- 68–77°F (20–25°C)
- 59–68°F (15–20°C)
- 50–59°F (10–15°C)
- 41–50°F (5–10°C)
- Under 41°F (5°C)
- Summer pack ice limit
- Winter pack ice limit
- Warm current
- Cool current

Ocean Flows

Driven by winds and deep sea currents, surface currents carry cold water from the poles toward the Equator, and warm water from the Equator toward the poles. Earth's rotation deflects the water's movement, creating clockwise currents in the Northern Hemisphere, and counterclockwise currents in the Southern Hemisphere.

Watery Life

If Earth were closer to the Sun, the oceans would vaporize, while farther away they would freeze. Liquid water has allowed life to flourish on our planet. Indeed, the first lifeforms may have taken shape in the oceans, in or near black smokers, vents that release hot mineral-rich water from deep inside Earth's crust. The sea itself contains great biodiversity. While plants are found only in surface waters, marine animals live in all levels.

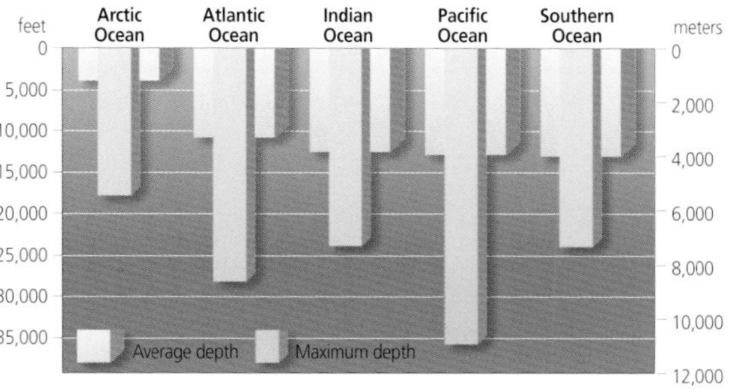
feet
0
5,000
10,000
15,000
20,000
25,000
30,000
35,000
Arctic Ocean
Atlantic Ocean
Indian Ocean
Pacific Ocean
Southern Ocean
meters
0
2,000
4,000
6,000
8,000
10,000
12,000
Average depth
Maximum depth

Ocean Depths

The average depth of the sea is 10,085 feet (3,070 m), but this figure masks the great variation both between and within the five oceans. The Arctic Ocean is by far the most shallow, with less than half the average depth of the others. The deepest is the Pacific, based both on its average depth and on its deepest point, the Mariana Trench at 35,826 feet (10,920 m).

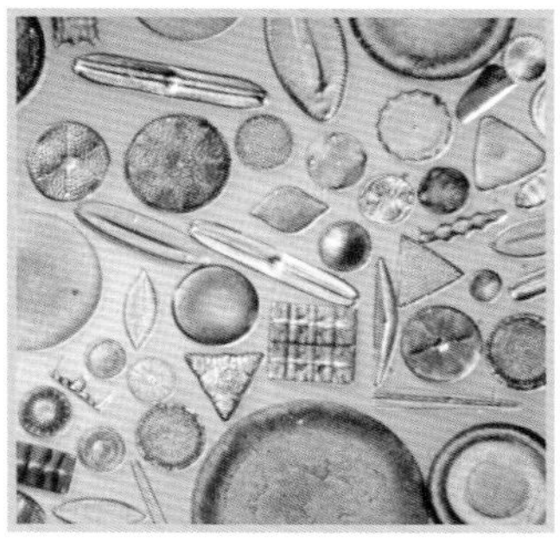

Phytoplankton, or floating algae, such as these magnified diatoms, are not only a key food source for ocean animals, but also help to drive the global carbon cycle through photosynthesis.

Underwater Landscape

The movements of the tectonic plates that make up Earth's crust have shaped the ocean floor. From the shallow continental shelf, the continental slope leads to vast abyssal plains. These flat expanses are interrupted by towering seamounts, extensive mountain ranges known as ridges, and plunging trenches.

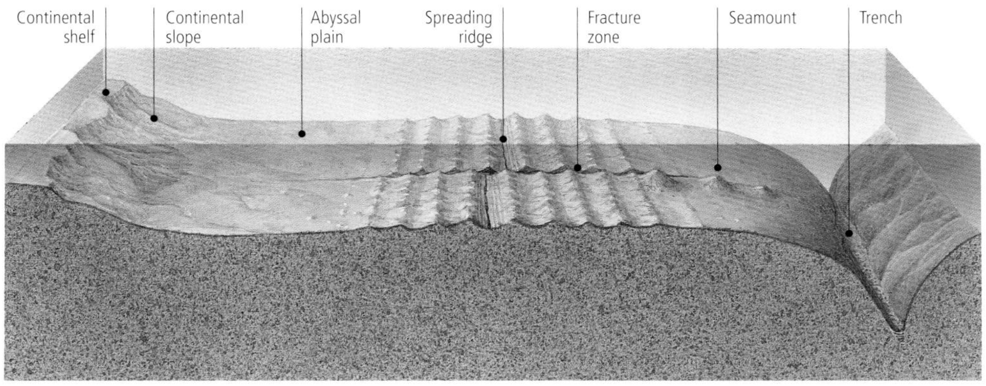
Continental shelf
Continental slope
Abyssal plain
Spreading ridge
Fracture zone
Seamount
Trench

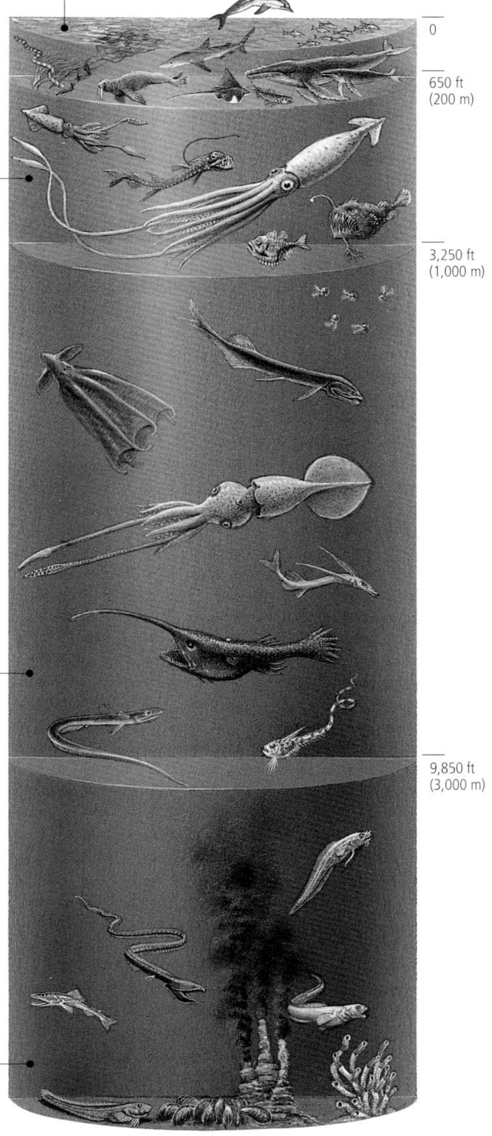
Sunlight zone
Enough sunlight penetrates this top layer for plants to carry out photosynthesis. The sunlight zone contains most of the ocean's life, including microscopic plankton; schools of small fish such as herring; larger fish such as tuna; sharks and rays; and mammals such as seals, dolphins, and whales.
Twilight zone
Some sunlight filters through to the twilight zone, but not enough to sustain plant life. Many of the fish in this zone contain light-producing bacteria and glow in the dark. This bioluminescence may be used for camouflage or to attract prey or mates.
Midnight zone
No sunlight penetrates below 3,250 feet (1,000 m). The midnight zone is a vast mass of cold, slow-moving water, its absolute darkness broken only by sporadic bioluminescence. The resident mass of life per unit volume of water is about a tenth that of the twilight zone and is also less diverse.
Abyssal zone
The near-freezing, pitch-black bottom layer of the ocean hosts the gulper eel, which has huge jaws and a bioluminescent organ on the tip of its tail. Over the vast majority of the sea floor, the only supply of food is what little falls from the waters above. Around hydrothermal vents, however, mussels, clams, and giant tubeworms make food using internal bacteria and the hydrogen sulfide emitted by the black smokers.
0
650 ft (200 m)
3,250 ft (1,000 m)
9,850 ft (3,000 m)

A B C D E F G

THE INDIAN OCEAN

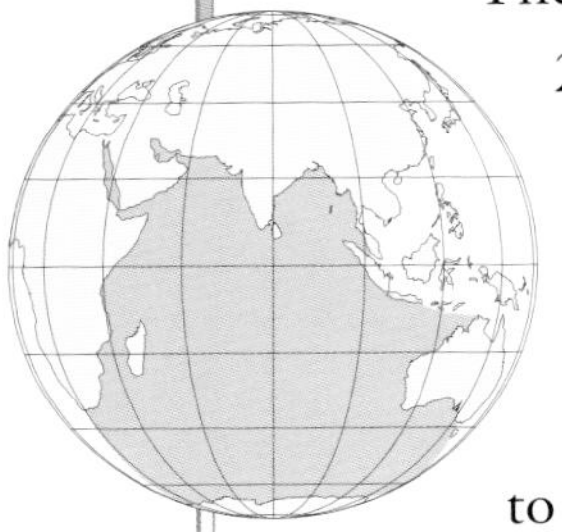

The third-largest ocean on Earth, the Indian Ocean covers 26.5 million square miles (68.6 million sq km), extending from the east coast of Africa to the west coast of Australia, and from the southern shore of Asia to the Southern Ocean. A series of major spreading ridges, including the Mid-Indian Ridge, runs southeast from the Arabian Sea to the center of the ocean, forking to form the Southwest Indian and Southeast Indian ridges. South of these two plate boundaries, broad basins are interrupted by the massive Kerguelen Plateau. To the north lie numerous plateaus and subsidiary, stable ridges, including the Ninetyeast Ridge, the longest straight ridge in the world, named for its location along the 90 degrees east meridian. The deepest part of the Indian Ocean is the Java Trench, south of the Indonesian island of Java, where the ocean floor drops to 23,376 feet (7,125 m) below sea level.

Residents watch a fiery lava flow from Piton de la Fournaise, an active volcano on the island of Réunion.

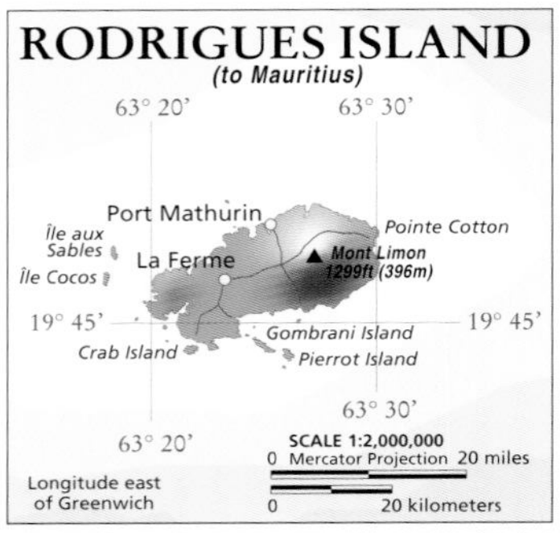

RODRIGUES ISLAND
(to Mauritius)
63° 20'
63° 30'
Port Mathurin
Île aux Sables
Île Cocos
La Ferme
Pointe Cotton
Mont Limon 1299ft (396m)
19° 45'
Crab Island
Gombrani Island
Pierrot Island
Longitude east of Greenwich
SCALE 1:2,000,000
Mercator Projection
20 miles
20 kilometers

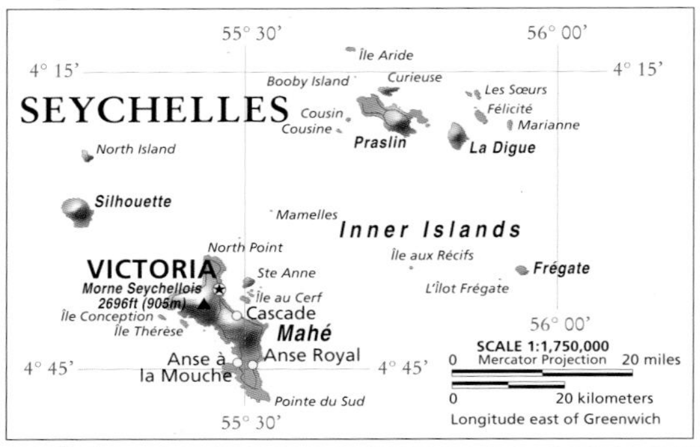

SEYCHELLES
55° 30'
56° 00'
4° 15'
Île Aride
Booby Island
Curieuse
Les Sœurs
Félicité
Marianne
Cousin
Cousine
Praslin
La Digue
North Island
Silhouette
Mamelles
Inner Islands
Île aux Récifs
Frégate
L'Ilot Frégate
North Point
VICTORIA
Ste Anne
Île au Cerf
Morne Seychellois 2696ft (905m)
Île Conception
Cascade
Île Thérèse
Mahé
Anse à la Mouche
Anse Royal
Pointe du Sud
4° 45'
SCALE 1:1,750,000
Mercator Projection
20 miles
20 kilometers
Longitude east of Greenwich

Natural Resources

Busy shipping routes crisscross the ocean, with much of the traffic originating in the Persian Gulf oil fields. Other major oil reserves lie off Saudi Arabia, Iran, India, and Australia; in total, the Indian Ocean generates 40 percent of world offshore production. Sands and placer deposits are mined along the shoreline, and potentially valuable manganese nodules litter the ocean floor, though these have not yet been successfully exploited. Fish stocks, especially shrimps along the coast and tuna in the open ocean, are vital to many seaboard nations. Commercial harvesting occurs on only a modest scale, though fleets come from as far afield as Russia and Japan.

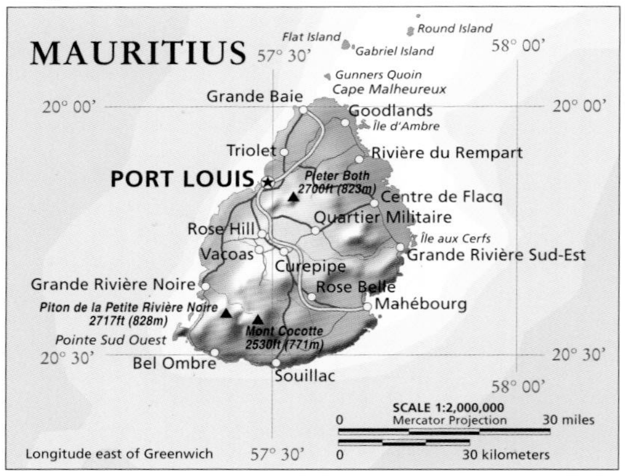

MAURITIUS
Flat Island
Round Island
57° 30'
58° 00'
Gabriel Island
Gunners Quoin
Cape Malheureux
20° 00'
Grande Baie
Goodlands
Île d'Ambre
Triolet
Rivière du Rempart
PORT LOUIS
Pieter Both 2700ft (823m)
Centre de Flacq
Quartier Militaire
Rose Hill
Île aux Cerfs
Vacoas
Curepipe
Grande Rivière Sud-Est
Grande Rivière Noire
Rose Belle
Piton de la Petite Rivière Noire 2717ft (828m)
Mahébourg
Mont Cocotte 2530ft (771m)
Pointe Sud Ouest
20° 30'
Bel Ombre
Souillac
SCALE 1:2,000,000
Mercator Projection
30 miles
30 kilometers
Longitude east of Greenwich

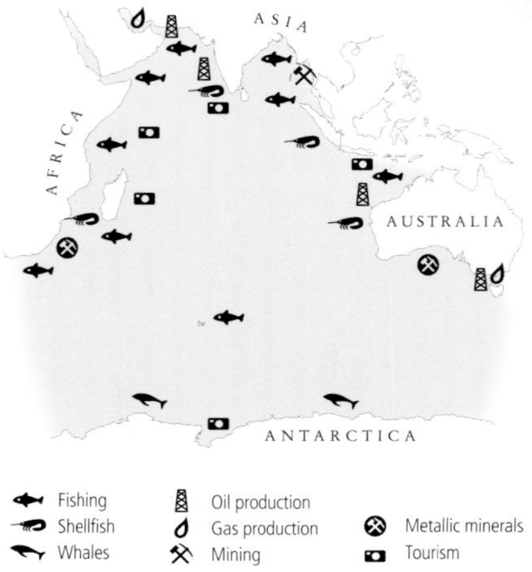

ASIA
AFRICA
AUSTRALIA
ANTARCTICA
Fishing
Shellfish
Whales
Oil production
Gas production
Mining
Metallic minerals
Tourism

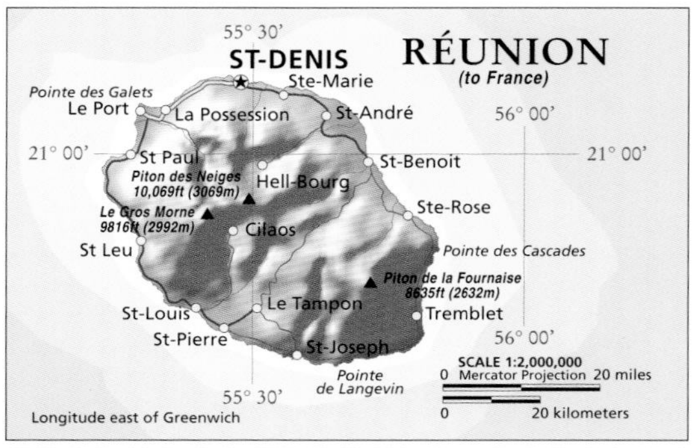

RÉUNION
(to France)
55° 30'
56° 00'
ST-DENIS
Pointe des Galets
Le Port
Ste-Marie
La Possession
St-André
21° 00'
St Paul
St-Benoit
Piton des Neiges 10,069ft (3069m)
Hell-Bourg
Le Gros Morne 9816ft (2992m)
Ste-Rose
St Leu
Cilaos
Pointe des Cascades
Piton de la Fournaise 8635ft (2632m)
Le Tampon
St-Louis
Tremblet
St-Pierre
St-Joseph
Pointe de Langevin
SCALE 1:2,000,000
Mercator Projection
20 miles
20 kilometers
Longitude east of Greenwich

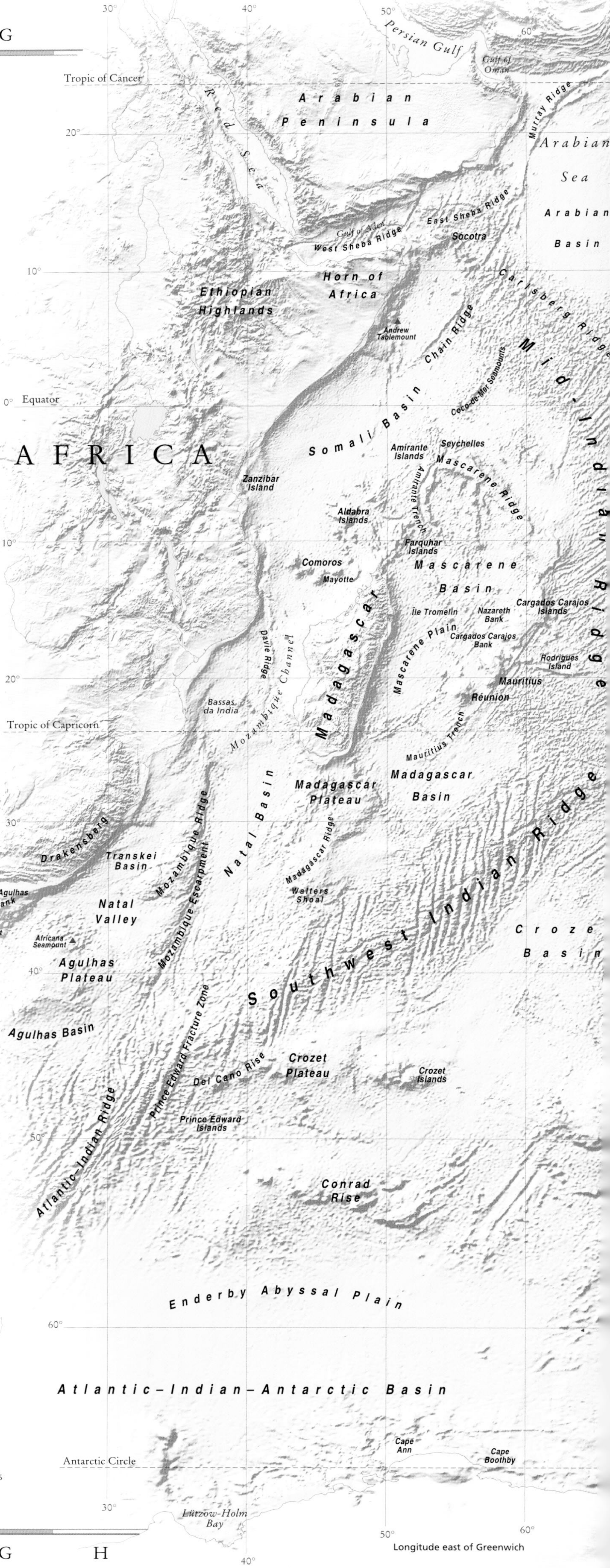

Persian Gulf
Gulf of Oman
Tropic of Cancer
Red Sea
Arabian Peninsula
Murray Ridge
Arabian Sea
Arabian Basin
Gulf of Aden
East Sheba Ridge
West Sheba Ridge
Socotra
Horn of Africa
Carlsberg Ridge
Ethiopian Highlands
Andrew Tablemount
Chain Ridge
Coco-de-Mer Seamounts
Mid-Indian Ridge
Equator
Somali Basin
AFRICA
Amirante Islands
Seychelles
Mascarene Ridge
Zanzibar Island
Amirante Trench
Aldabra Islands
Farquhar Islands
Comoros
Mascarene Basin
Mayotte
Île Tromelin
Nazareth Bank
Cargados Carajos Islands
Madagascar
Davie Ridge
Mozambique Channel
Mascarene Plain
Cargados Carajos Bank
Rodrigues Island
Mauritius
Réunion
Bassas da India
Tropic of Capricorn
Mauritius Trench
Madagascar Plateau
Madagascar Basin
Natal Basin
Mozambique Ridge
Drakensberg
Transkei Basin
Madagascar Ridge
Cape Agulhas
Agulhas Bank
Walters Shoal
Mozambique Escarpment
Natal Valley
Protea Seamount
Africana Seamount
Southwest Indian Ridge
Crozet Basin
Agulhas Plateau
Agulhas Basin
Prince Edward Fracture Zone
Crozet Plateau
Del Cano Rise
Crozet Islands
Atlantic-Indian Ridge
Prince Edward Islands
Conrad Rise
Enderby Abyssal Plain
Atlantic–Indian–Antarctic Basin
Cape Ann
Cape Boothby
Antarctic Circle
Lützow-Holm Bay
Longitude east of Greenwich

1 4 5 6 7

D E F G H

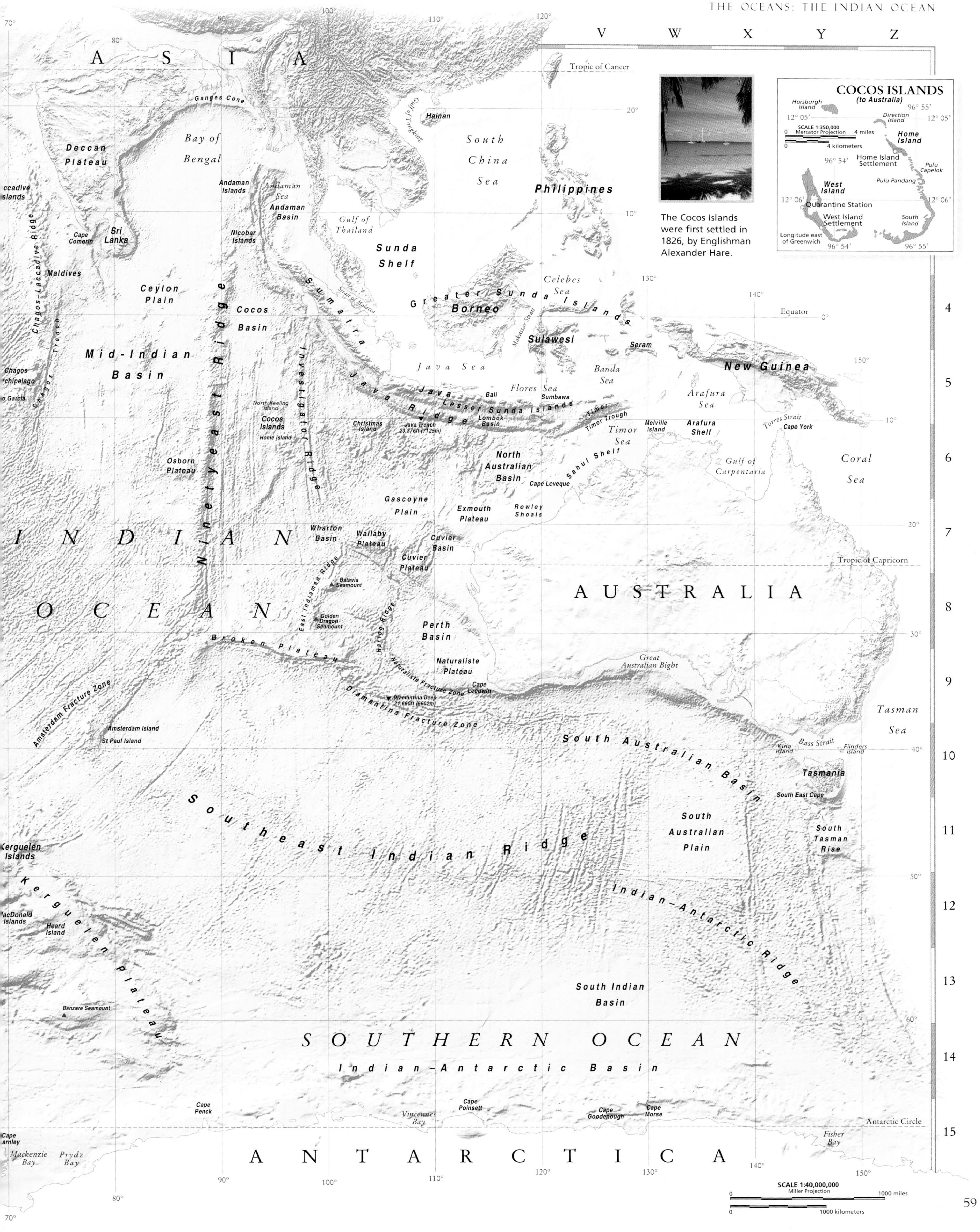

V
W
X
Y
Z
4
5
6
7
8
9
10
11
12
13
14
15
70°
80°
90°
100°
110°
120°
130°
140°
150°
20°
10°
0°
10°
20°
30°
40°
50°
60°
A S I A
Tropic of Cancer
Ganges Cone
Bay of Bengal
Deccan Plateau
Gulf of Tonkin
Hainan
South China Sea
Philippines
ccadive Islands
Chagos-Laccadive Ridge
Cape Comorin
Sri Lanka
Andaman Islands
Andaman Sea
Andaman Basin
Nicobar Islands
Gulf of Thailand
Sunda Shelf
Maldives
Ceylon Plain
Cocos Basin
Chagos Trench
Chagos Archipelago
o Garcia
Mid-Indian Basin
Ninetyeast Ridge
Sumatra
Strait of Malacca
Greater Sunda Islands
Borneo
Celebes Sea
Makassar Strait
Sulawesi
Equator
Seram
New Guinea
Java Sea
Banda Sea
Flores Sea
Java
Bali
Sumbawa
Lesser Sunda Islands
Lombok Basin
Java Ridge
Timor
Timor Trough
Timor Sea
Investigator Ridge
North Keeling Island
Cocos Islands
Home Island
Christmas Island
Java Trench 23,376ft (7125m)
Melville Island
Arafura Sea
Arafura Shelf
Torres Strait
Cape York
Gulf of Carpentaria
Coral Sea
Sahul Shelf
Osborn Plateau
North Australian Basin
Cape Leveque
Gascoyne Plain
Exmouth Plateau
Rowley Shoals
I N D I A N
O C E A N
Wharton Basin
Wallaby Plateau
Cuvier Basin
Cuvier Plateau
Tropic of Capricorn
East Indiaman Ridge
Batavia Seamount
Golden Dragon Seamount
Hartog Ridge
A U S T R A L I A
Perth Basin
Broken Plateau
Naturaliste Plateau
Naturaliste Fracture Zone
Cape Leeuwin
Diamantina Deep 21,680ft (6602m)
Diamantina Fracture Zone
Great Australian Bight
Tasman Sea
Amsterdam Fracture Zone
Amsterdam Island
St Paul Island
South Australian Basin
King Island
Bass Strait
Flinders Island
Tasmania
South East Cape
Southeast Indian Ridge
South Australian Plain
South Tasman Rise
Kerguelen Islands
Kerguelen Plateau
McDonald Islands
Heard Island
Indian-Antarctic Ridge
South Indian Basin
Banzare Seamount
SOUTHERN OCEAN
Indian-Antarctic Basin
Cape Penck
Cape Poinsett
Vincennes Bay
Cape Goodenough
Cape Morse
Antarctic Circle
Cape arnley
Mackenzie Bay
Prydz Bay
Fisher Bay
A N T A R C T I C A
SCALE 1:40,000,000
Miller Projection
0
1000 miles
0
1000 kilometers
COCOS ISLANDS
(to Australia)
Horsburgh Island
96° 55'
12° 05'
Direction Island
12° 05'
SCALE 1:350,000
Mercator Projection
0
4 miles
0
4 kilometers
Home Island
Home Island Settlement
96° 54'
Pulu Capelok
Pulu Pandang
West Island
12° 06'
Quarantine Station
12° 06'
West Island Settlement
South Island
Longitude east of Greenwich
96° 54'
96° 55'

The Cocos Islands were first settled in 1826, by Englishman Alexander Hare.

The Pacific Ocean

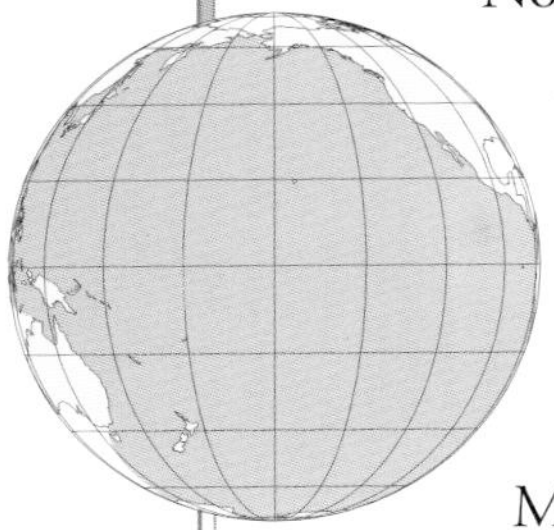

Not only is the Pacific the largest of the oceans, it is twice as large and holds twice as much water as the Atlantic Ocean, and exceeds the combined area of all of Earth's landmasses. Spanning 60.1 million square miles (155.6 million sq km), it separates the continents of Asia and Australia from the Americas. A divergent plate boundary running south from Mexico forms the East Pacific Rise, part of the great chain of mid-ocean ridges that winds round the globe. Trenches formed by subduction border the eastern continental shelves, and volcanic peaks line the shores above. In the west, a complex series of mainly convergent plate boundaries forms a number of deep trenches bordered by volcanic archipelagoes. These zones of volcanic and seismic activity that almost encircle the Pacific Ocean are known as the Ring of Fire. In contrast, the floor of the central Pacific is relatively stable, consisting mainly of wide basins scarred by long, west–east-trending fractures and studded with myriad seamounts, thousands of which breach the sea surface to form islands and atolls.

The Pacific Ocean yields approximately 50 percent of the world's tuna catch.

In the kelp forests off the west coast of North America, the diversity of species rivals that of tropical rain forests.

Natural Resources

The Pacific yields 60 percent of the world's fish catch, with the Northwest Pacific alone providing one-quarter of the entire global catch in recent years. Offshore oil and gas reserves are especially important for China, the U.S.A., Australia, and New Zealand. Sand and gravel are mined in most seaboard nations, and phosphates are extracted off the coasts of Australia, California, and Peru. Metallic nodules are common on the ocean floor, but the high cost of retrieval means that they are not yet mined commercially. The Pacific has by far the most extensive coral reefs of any ocean, which in many regions generate significant revenue from tourism.

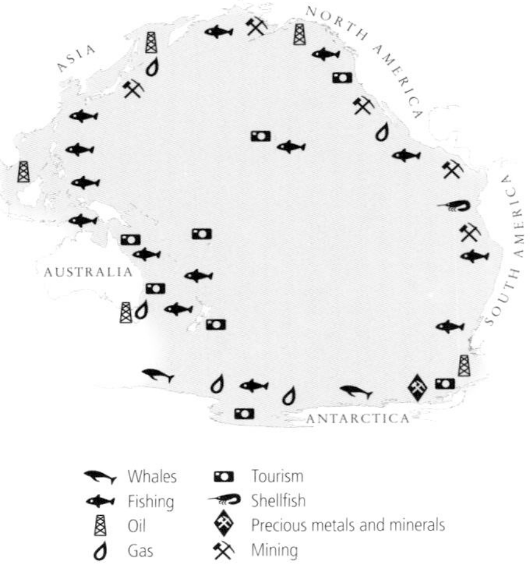

Asia
North America
South America
Australia
Antarctica
Whales
Fishing
Oil
Gas
Tourism
Shellfish
Precious metals and minerals
Mining

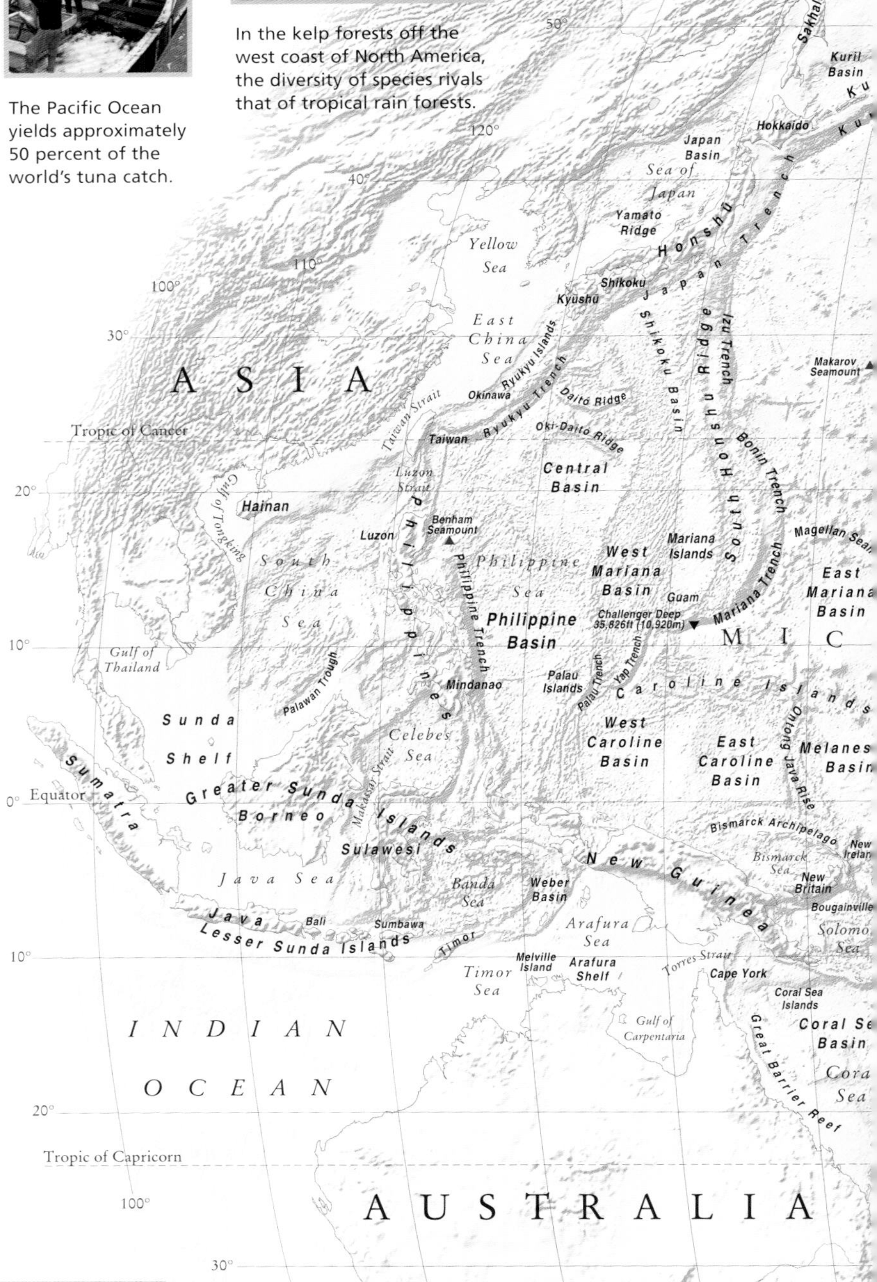

Asia
Indian Ocean
Australia
Southern Ocean
Antarctica
Tropic of Cancer
Equator
Tropic of Capricorn
Antarctic Circle
Sea of Japan
Yellow Sea
East China Sea
South China Sea
Philippine Sea
Philippine Basin
West Mariana Basin
East Mariana Basin
Mariana Trench
Challenger Deep 35,826ft (10,920m)
Caroline Islands
West Caroline Basin
East Caroline Basin
Sunda Shelf
Greater Sunda Islands
Lesser Sunda Islands
Borneo
Sulawesi
Java Sea
Banda Sea
Timor Sea
Arafura Sea
New Guinea
Coral Sea
Coral Sea Basin
Great Barrier Reef
Tasmania
Great Australian Bight
Japan Trench
Izu Bonin Trench
Ryukyu Trench
Philippine Trench
Hokkaido
Honshu
Kyushu
Shikoku
Taiwan
Hainan
Luzon
Mindanao
Sumatra
Guam
Longitude east of Greenwich

In May 2000, Kavachi, an undersea volcano in the Solomon Islands, erupted, giving birth to a new island.

The Mariana Trench

Arcing for 1,580 miles (2,550 km) around the Mariana Islands, the Mariana Trench is the deepest part of the Pacific Ocean and the world's deepest ocean trench. Formed as a result of the Pacific Plate being forced beneath the Philippine Plate—the Mariana Islands are the tips of volcanoes created by this subduction—it reaches 35,826 feet (10,920 m) below sea level at Challenger Deep. This site was named for the British survey ship *Challenger II*, the first vessel to survey the trench, in 1951. In 1960, Jacques Piccard and Donald Walsh descended here in the U.S. bathyscaph *Trieste* to a depth of 35,797 feet (10,911 m), a record that remains unsurpassed.

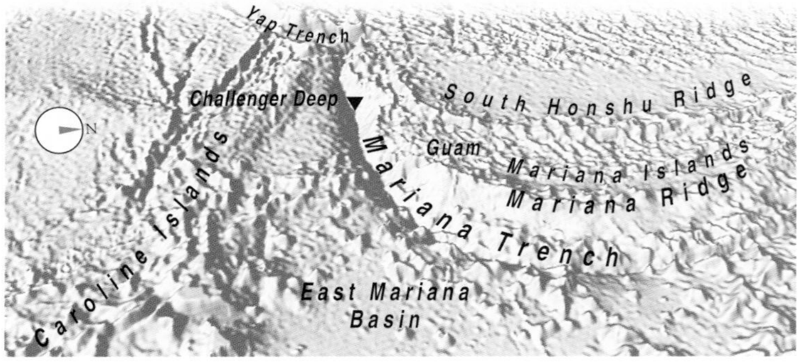

Yap Trench
Challenger Deep
South Honshu Ridge
Guam
Mariana Islands
Mariana Ridge
Mariana Trench
Caroline Islands
East Mariana Basin
N

The humpback whales resident in Alaska in summer migrate to lower latitudes in winter.

The Pacific's coral reefs have six times as many fish species as those of the Caribbean Sea.

SCALE 1:50,000,000
Robinson Projection
0 — 1500 miles
0 — 1500 kilometers

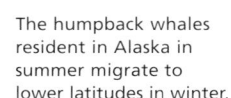

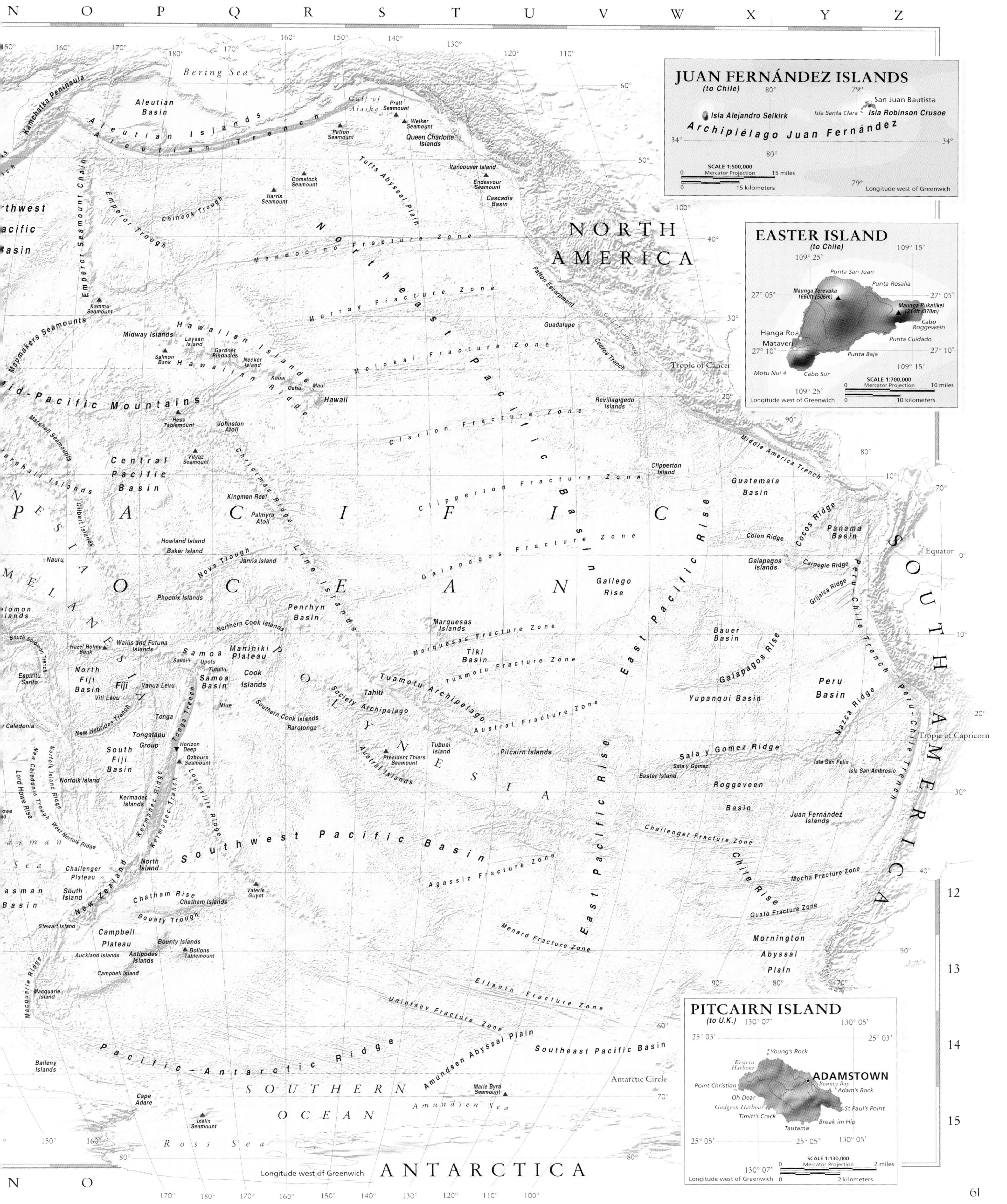
N O P Q R S T U V W X Y Z
JUAN FERNÁNDEZ ISLANDS
(to Chile)
San Juan Bautista
Isla Alejandro Selkirk
Isla Santa Clara
Isla Robinson Crusoe
Archipiélago Juan Fernández
SCALE 1:500,000
Mercator Projection
15 miles
15 kilometers
Longitude west of Greenwich
EASTER ISLAND
(to Chile)
Punta San Juan
Punta Rosalia
Maunga Terevaka 1660ft (506m)
Maunga Pukatikei 1214ft (370m)
Cabo Roggewein
Hanga Roa
Mataveri
Punta Cuidado
Punta Baja
Motu Nui
Cabo Sur
SCALE 1:700,000
Mercator Projection
10 miles
10 kilometers
Longitude west of Greenwich
PITCAIRN ISLAND
(to U.K.)
Young's Rock
Western Harbour
ADAMSTOWN
Bounty Bay
Adam's Rock
Point Christian
Oh Dear
Gudgeon Harbour
Timiti's Crack
St Paul's Point
Break im Hip
Tautama
SCALE 1:130,000
Mercator Projection
2 miles
2 kilometers
Longitude west of Greenwich
Bering Sea
Kamchatka Peninsula
Aleutian Basin
Aleutian Islands
Aleutian Trench
Gulf of Alaska
Pratt Seamount
Welker Seamount
Patton Seamount
Queen Charlotte Islands
Vancouver Island
Endeavour Seamount
Cascadia Basin
Comstock Seamount
Harris Seamount
Tufts Abyssal Plain
Emperor Seamount Chain
Emperor Trough
Chinook Trough
NORTH AMERICA
Mendocino Fracture Zone
Northeast Pacific Basin
Patton Escarpment
Murray Fracture Zone
Kammu Seamount
Mapmakers Seamounts
Midway Islands
Hawaiian Islands
Laysan Island
Gardner Pinnacles
Salmon Bank
Necker Island
Hawaiian Ridge
Kauai
Oahu
Maui
Hawaii
Molokai Fracture Zone
Guadalupe
Gulf of California
Cedros Trench
Tropic of Cancer
Mid-Pacific Mountains
Hess Tablemount
Johnston Atoll
Marshall Seamounts
Marshall Islands
Revillagigedo Islands
Clarion Fracture Zone
Central Pacific Basin
Vityaz Seamount
Christmas Ridge
Middle America Trench
Clipperton Island
Clipperton Fracture Zone
Guatemala Basin
Kingman Reef
Palmyra Atoll
Gilbert Islands
PACIFIC
Cocos Ridge
Panama Basin
Colon Ridge
Howland Island
Baker Island
Nauru
Jarvis Island
Nova Trough
Line Islands
Galapagos Fracture Zone
Galapagos Islands
Equator
Carnegie Ridge
Grijalva Ridge
Peru-Chile Trench
SOUTH AMERICA
MELANESIA
OCEAN
Gallego Rise
East Pacific Rise
Phoenix Islands
Solomon Islands
Penrhyn Basin
Northern Cook Islands
Marquesas Islands
Marquesas Fracture Zone
Bauer Basin
South Solomon Trench
Hazel Holme Bank
Wallis and Futuna Islands
Samoa
Savai'i
Upolu
Tutuila
Samoa Basin
Manihiki Plateau
Tiki Basin
Tuamotu Fracture Zone
Galapagos Rise
North Fiji Basin
Espiritu Santo
Fiji
Vanua Levu
Viti Levu
Cook Islands
POLYNESIA
Society Archipelago
Tahiti
Tuamotu Archipelago
Yupanqui Basin
Peru Basin
Niue
Southern Cook Islands
Rarotonga
Austral Fracture Zone
Nazca Ridge
Tonga
Tonga Trench
New Caledonia
New Hebrides Trench
Tongatapu Group
Horizon Deep
Ozbourn Seamount
Tropic of Capricorn
Tubuai Island
President Thiers Seamount
Austral Islands
Pitcairn Islands
Sala y Gomez Ridge
Sala y Gomez
Isla San Felix
Isla San Ambrosio
South Fiji Basin
Norfolk Island Ridge
Norfolk Island
New Caledonia Trough
Lord Howe Rise
Easter Island
Roggeveen Basin
Kermadec Islands
Kermadec Ridge
Kermadec Trench
Louisville Ridge
Juan Fernández Islands
West Norfolk Ridge
Tasman Sea
Southwest Pacific Basin
Challenger Fracture Zone
Chile Rise
Challenger Plateau
North Island
New Zealand
South Island
Tasman Basin
Valerie Guyot
Agassiz Fracture Zone
Mocha Fracture Zone
Chatham Rise
Chatham Islands
Bounty Trough
Guafo Fracture Zone
Stewart Island
Campbell Plateau
Bounty Islands
Bollons Tablemount
Antipodes Islands
Auckland Islands
Campbell Island
Menard Fracture Zone
Mornington Abyssal Plain
Macquarie Ridge
Macquarie Island
Eltanin Fracture Zone
Udintsev Fracture Zone
Pacific-Antarctic Ridge
Amundsen Abyssal Plain
Southeast Pacific Basin
Balleny Islands
Antarctic Circle
SOUTHERN OCEAN
Marie Byrd Seamount
Cape Adare
Amundsen Sea
Iselin Seamount
Ross Sea
ANTARCTICA
Longitude west of Greenwich
12
13
14
15
N O

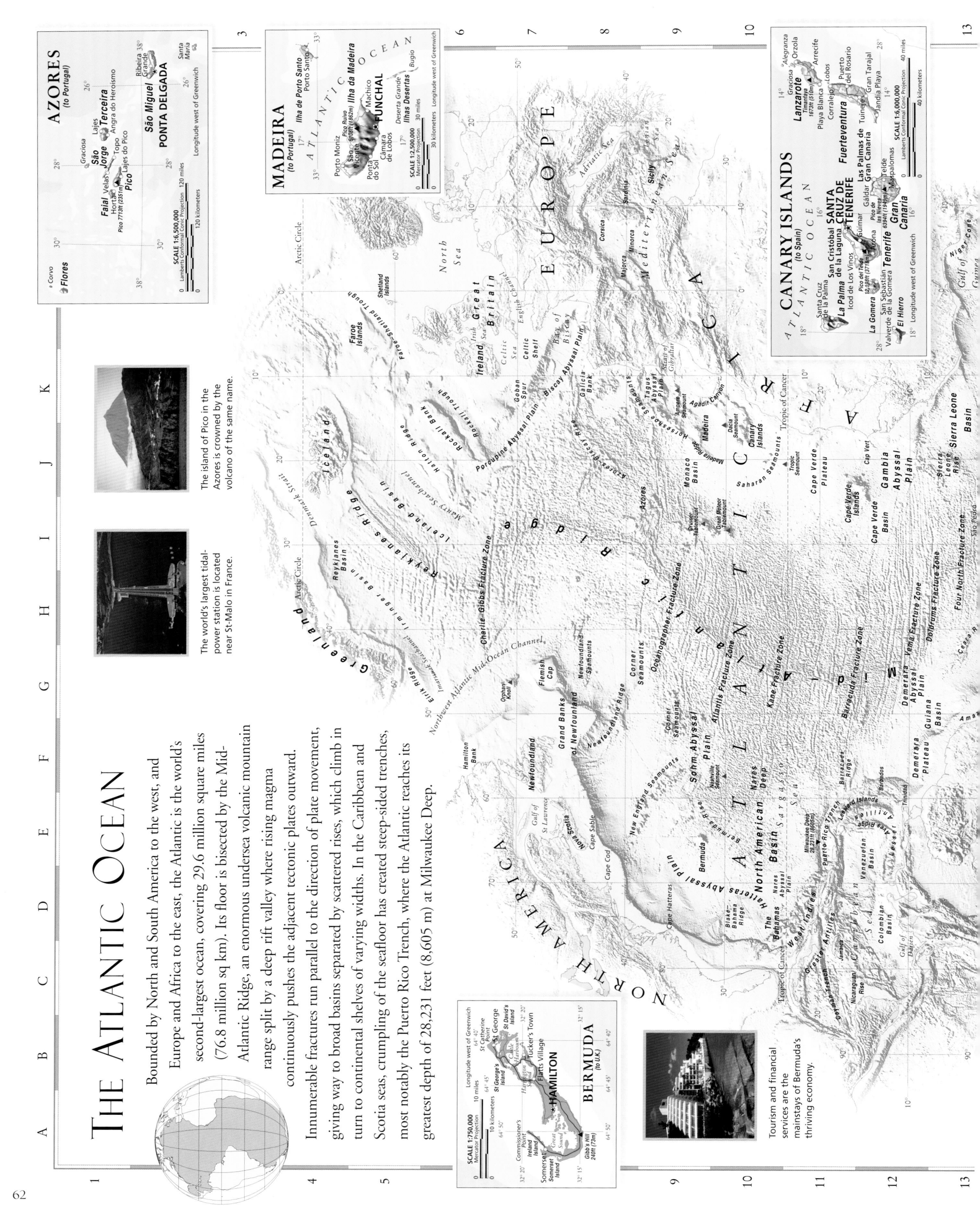

The Atlantic Ocean

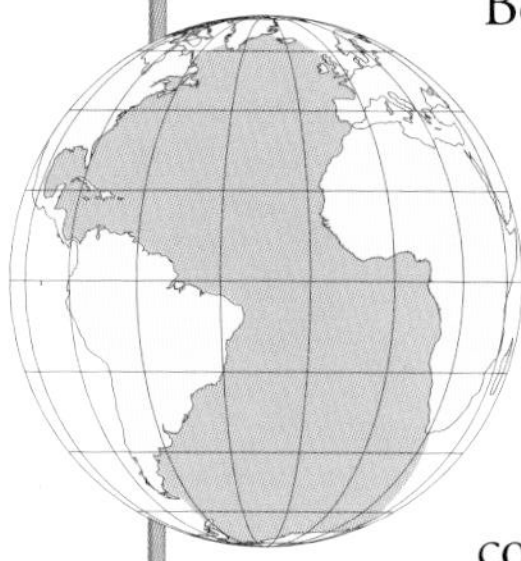

Bounded by North and South America to the west, and Europe and Africa to the east, the Atlantic is the world's second-largest ocean, covering 29.6 million square miles (76.8 million sq km). Its floor is bisected by the Mid-Atlantic Ridge, an enormous undersea volcanic mountain range split by a deep rift valley where rising magma continuously pushes the adjacent tectonic plates outward. Innumerable fractures run parallel to the direction of plate movement, giving way to broad basins separated by scattered rises, which climb in turn to continental shelves of varying widths. In the Caribbean and Scotia seas, crumpling of the seafloor has created steep-sided trenches, most notably the Puerto Rico Trench, where the Atlantic reaches its greatest depth of 28,231 feet (8,605 m) at Milwaukee Deep.

The world's largest tidal-power station is located near St-Malo in France.

The island of Pico in the Azores is crowned by the volcano of the same name.

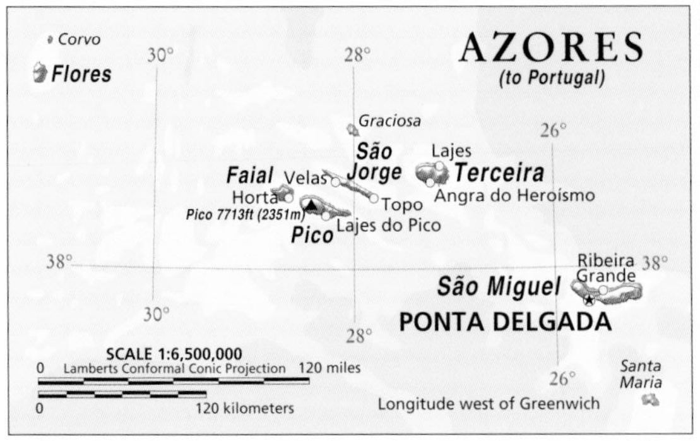
AZORES
(to Portugal)
Corvo
Flores
Graciosa
São Jorge
Lajes
Terceira
Angra do Heroismo
Faial
Velas
Horta
Pico 7713ft (2351m)
Pico
Topo
Lajes do Pico
Ribeira Grande
São Miguel
PONTA DELGADA
Santa Maria
SCALE 1:6,500,000
Lamberts Conformal Conic Projection
120 miles
120 kilometers
Longitude west of Greenwich

MADEIRA
(to Portugal)
Ilha de Porto Santo
Porto Santo
ATLANTIC OCEAN
Porto Moniz
Pico Ruivo 6108ft (1862m)
São Vicente
Ilha da Madeira
Machico
Ponta do Sol
Câmara de Lobos
FUNCHAL
Deserta Grande
Ilhas Desertas
Bugio
SCALE 1:2,500,000
Mercator Projection
30 miles
30 kilometers
Longitude west of Greenwich

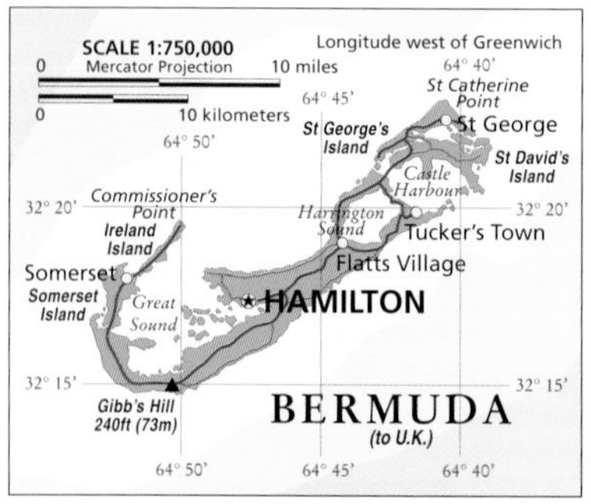
SCALE 1:750,000
Mercator Projection
10 miles
10 kilometers
Longitude west of Greenwich
St Catherine Point
St George's Island
St George
St David's Island
Castle Harbour
Commissioner's Point
Ireland Island
Harrington Sound
Tucker's Town
Somerset
Somerset Island
Great Sound
Flatts Village
HAMILTON
Gibb's Hill 240ft (73m)
BERMUDA
(to U.K.)

Tourism and financial services are the mainstays of Bermuda's thriving economy.

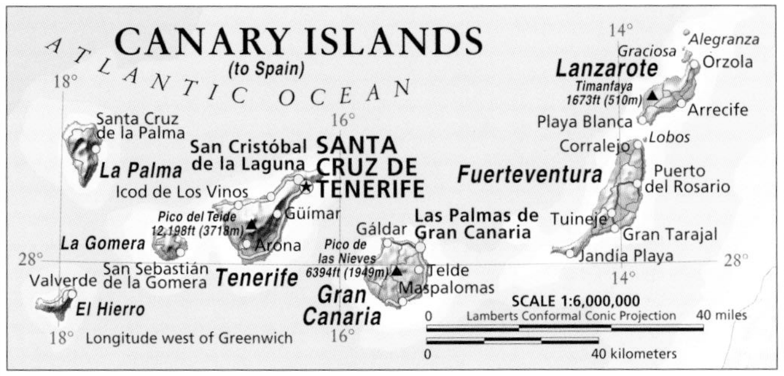
CANARY ISLANDS
(to Spain)
ATLANTIC OCEAN
Alegranza
Graciosa
Orzola
Lanzarote
Timanfaya 1673ft (510m)
Arrecife
Playa Blanca
Lobos
Corralejo
Puerto del Rosario
Fuerteventura
Santa Cruz de la Palma
La Palma
San Cristóbal de la Laguna
SANTA CRUZ DE TENERIFE
Icod de Los Vinos
Pico del Teide 12,198ft (3718m)
Güimar
Arona
Tenerife
La Gomera
San Sebastián de la Gomera
Valverde
El Hierro
Gáldar
Las Palmas de Gran Canaria
Pico de las Nieves 6394ft (1949m)
Telde
Maspalomas
Gran Canaria
Tuineje
Gran Tarajal
Jandia Playa
SCALE 1:6,000,000
Lamberts Conformal Conic Projection
40 miles
40 kilometers
Longitude west of Greenwich

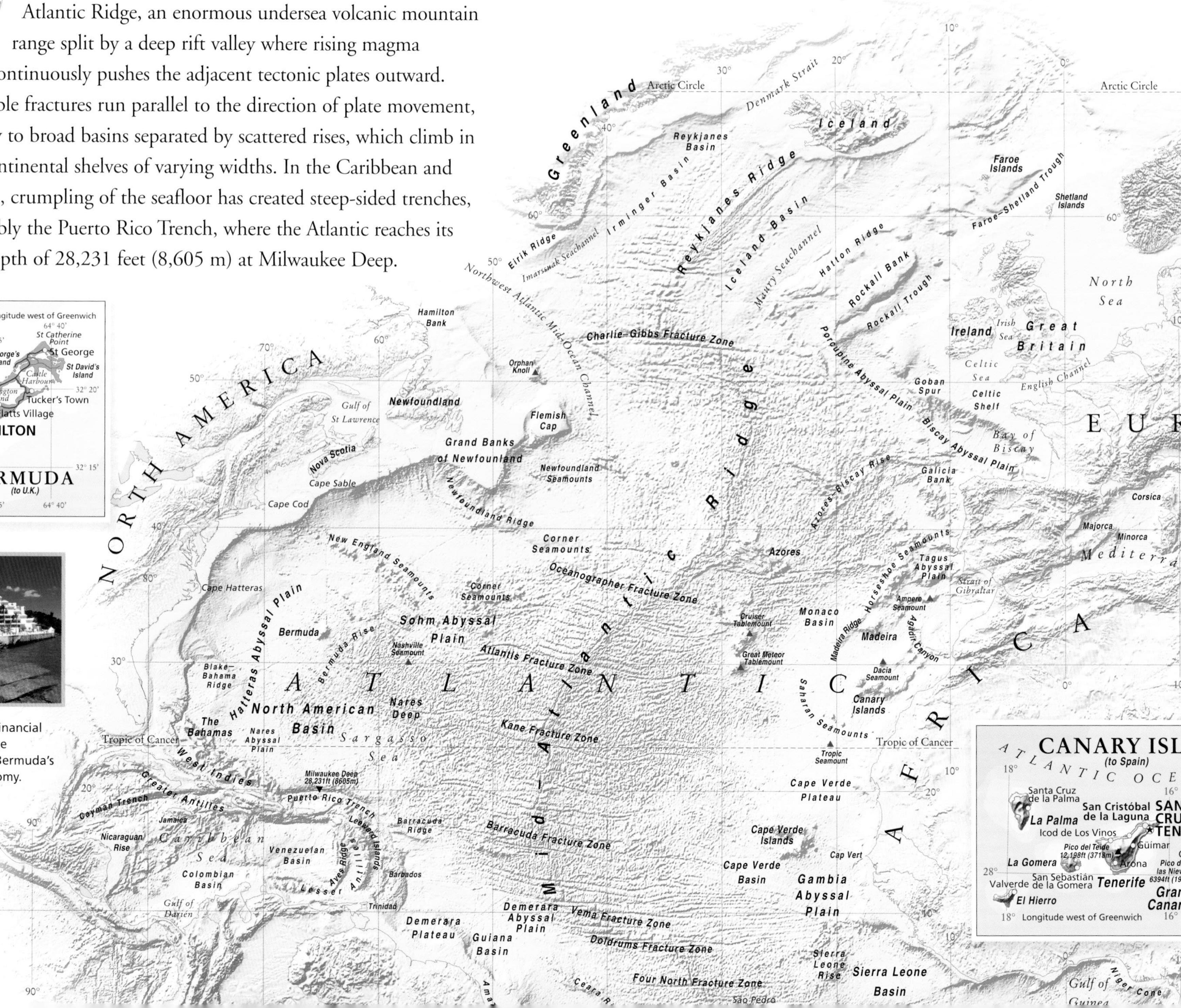
NORTH AMERICA
EUROPE
AFRICA
ATLANTIC
Mid-Atlantic Ridge
Greenland
Iceland
Arctic Circle
Denmark Strait
Reykjanes Basin
Reykjanes Ridge
Irminger Basin
Iceland Basin
Eirik Ridge
Imarssuak Seachannel
Maury Seachannel
Hatton Ridge
Rockall Bank
Rockall Trough
Faroe Islands
Faroe-Shetland Trough
Shetland Islands
North Sea
Ireland
Great Britain
Irish Sea
Celtic Sea
Celtic Shelf
English Channel
Goban Spur
Porcupine Abyssal Plain
Bay of Biscay
Biscay Abyssal Plain
Galicia Bank
Northwest Atlantic Mid-Ocean Channel
Charlie-Gibbs Fracture Zone
Hamilton Bank
Orphan Knoll
Flemish Cap
Newfoundland
Gulf of St Lawrence
Grand Banks of Newfoundland
Newfoundland Seamounts
Newfoundland Ridge
Nova Scotia
Cape Sable
Cape Cod
Corner Seamounts
Azores-Biscay Rise
Azores
Oceanographer Fracture Zone
New England Seamounts
Corner Seamounts
Cape Hatteras
Hatteras Abyssal Plain
Bermuda
Bermuda Rise
Sohm Abyssal Plain
Nashville Seamount
Atlantis Fracture Zone
Blake-Bahama Ridge
The Bahamas
Nares Abyssal Plain
North American Basin
Nares Deep
Sargasso Sea
Kane Fracture Zone
Tropic of Cancer
West Indies
Greater Antilles
Cayman Trench
Jamaica
Nicaraguan Rise
Caribbean Sea
Colombian Basin
Gulf of Darién
Venezuelan Basin
Aves Ridge
Lesser Antilles
Leeward Islands
Milwaukee Deep 28,231ft (8605m)
Puerto Rico Trench
Barracuda Ridge
Barbados
Trinidad
Barracuda Fracture Zone
Demerara Plateau
Guiana Basin
Demerara Abyssal Plain
Vema Fracture Zone
Doldrums Fracture Zone
Four North Fracture Zone
Ceara R
Sao Pedro
Cruiser Tablemount
Great Meteor Tablemount
Monaco Basin
Madeira Ridge
Madeira
Horseshoe Seamounts
Tagus Abyssal Plain
Ampere Seamount
Agadir Canyon
Dacia Seamount
Canary Islands
Saharan Seamounts
Tropic Seamount
Cape Verde Plateau
Cape Verde Islands
Cape Verde Basin
Cap Vert
Gambia Abyssal Plain
Sierra Leone Rise
Sierra Leone Basin
Gulf of Guinea
Niger Cone
Strait of Gibraltar
Mediterranean Sea
Majorca
Minorca
Corsica
Sardinia
Sicily
Adriatic Sea
Ionian Sea

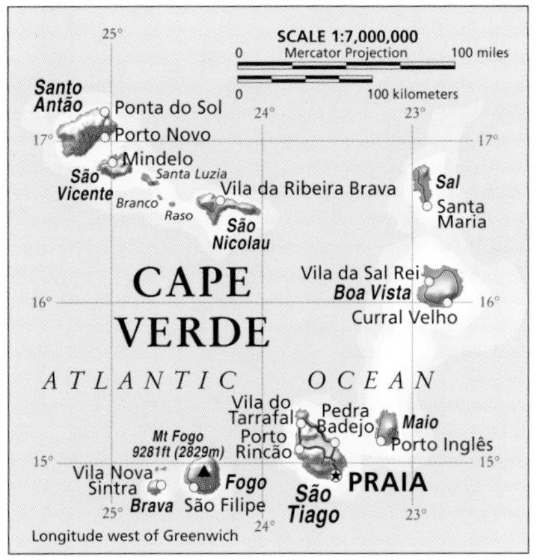
SCALE 1:7,000,000
Mercator Projection
100 miles
100 kilometers
Santo Antão
Ponta do Sol
Porto Novo
Mindelo
Santa Luzia
São Vicente
Branco
Raso
Vila da Ribeira Brava
São Nicolau
Sal
Santa Maria
CAPE VERDE
Vila da Sal Rei
Boa Vista
Curral Velho
ATLANTIC OCEAN
Vila do Tarrafal
Pedra Badejo
Porto Rincão
Maio
Porto Inglês
Mt Fogo 9281ft (2829m)
Vila Nova Sintra
Brava
Fogo
São Filipe
São Tiago
PRAIA
Longitude west of Greenwich

The Atlantic's busiest shipping routes connect Western Europe with the U.S.A.

NORTH AMERICA
EUROPE
AFRICA
SOUTH AMERICA
ANTARCTICA
Fishing
Whales
Shellfish
Precious metals and minerals
Mining
Oil production
Gas production
Tourism

Natural Resources

Upwellings of cold, nutrient-rich water on continental shelves give rise to huge plankton blooms that support large fish stocks, notably of cod and haddock in the north, and hake and tuna in the south. But the formerly productive Atlantic fisheries have been overexploited and many species are depleted. As much as one-third of the world's oil and gas may lie under the Atlantic coastal shelves; large deposits are being exploited in the North Sea and Gulf of Mexico, and off Newfoundland and West Africa. Sand and gravels are mined in U.S. and U.K. waters, and placer deposits of gemstones and other minerals are retrieved from many river mouths. Huge tides in Canada and France are harnessed to generate electricity.

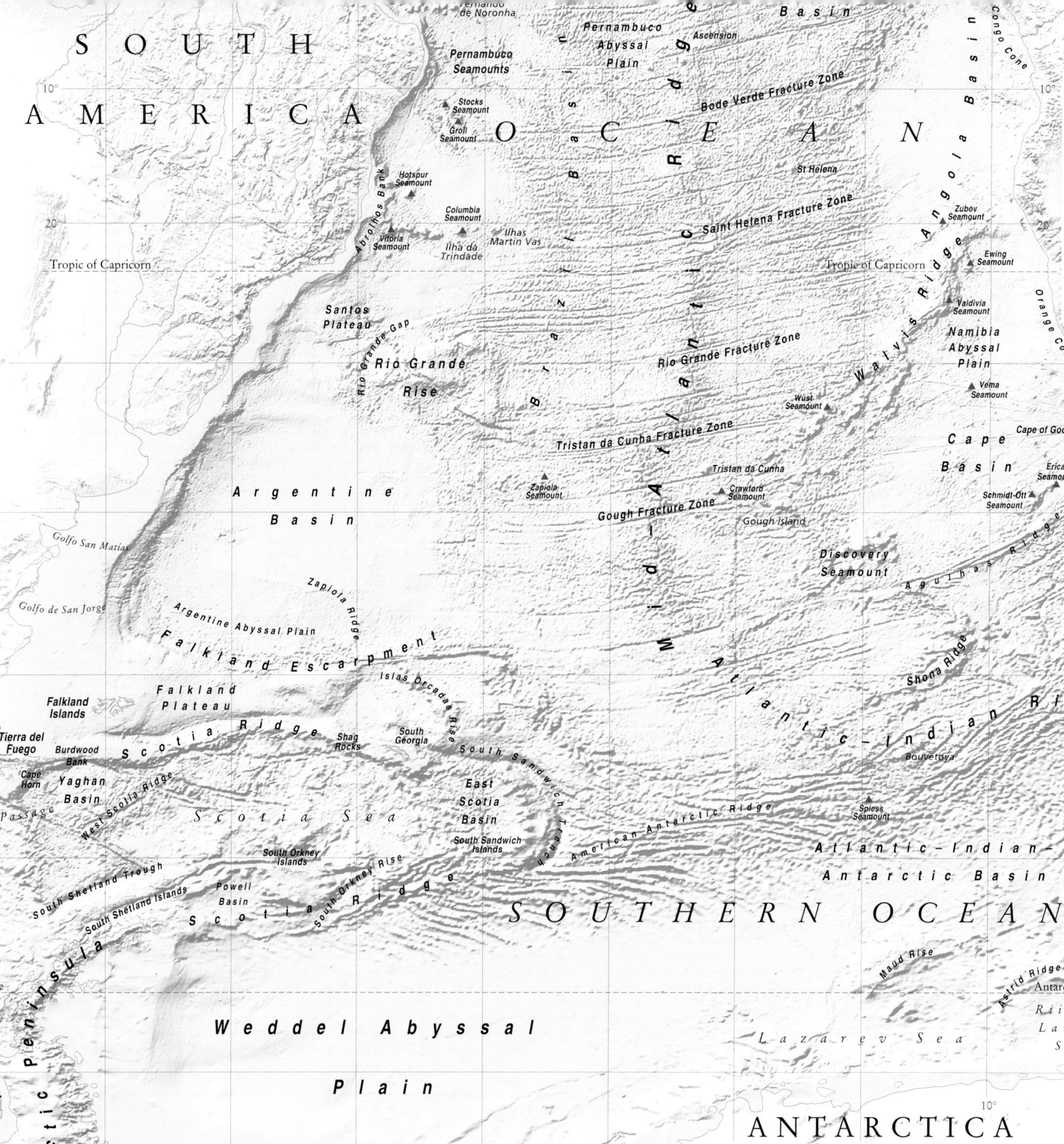
SOUTH AMERICA
ATLANTIC OCEAN
SOUTHERN OCEAN
ANTARCTICA
Pernambuco Seamounts
Pernambuco Abyssal Plain
Ascension
Bode Verde Fracture Zone
Stocks Seamount
Groll Seamount
Hotspur Seamount
Abrolhos Bank
Columbia Seamount
Vitória Seamount
Ilhas Martin Vas
Ilha da Trindade
St Helena
Saint Helena Fracture Zone
Tropic of Capricorn
Santos Plateau
Rio Grande Gap
Rio Grande Rise
Rio Grande Fracture Zone
Brazil Basin
Angola Basin
Zubov Seamount
Ewing Seamount
Walvis Ridge
Valdivia Seamount
Namibia Abyssal Plain
Vema Seamount
Wüst Seamount
Tristan da Cunha Fracture Zone
Tristan da Cunha
Crawford Seamount
Gough Island
Gough Fracture Zone
Zapiola Seamount
Mid-Atlantic Ridge
Cape Basin
Cape of Good Hope
Cape Agulhas
Agulhas Bank
Erica Seamount
Protea Seamount
Schmidt-Ott Seamount
Agulhas Basin
Agulhas Ridge
Discovery Seamount
Argentine Basin
Golfo San Matías
Golfo de San Jorge
Zapiola Ridge
Argentine Abyssal Plain
Falkland Escarpment
Islas Orcadas Rise
Falkland Plateau
Falkland Islands
Shona Ridge
Atlantic-Indian Ridge
Bouvetøya
Tierra del Fuego
Burdwood Bank
Scotia Ridge
Shag Rocks
South Georgia
South Sandwich Trench
Cape Horn
Yaghan Basin
West Scotia Ridge
East Scotia Basin
Drake Passage
Scotia Sea
South Sandwich Islands
American-Antarctic Ridge
Spiess Seamount
South Orkney Islands
Atlantic-Indian-Antarctic Basin
South Shetland Trough
Powell Basin
South Orkney Rise
South Shetland Islands
Antarctic Circle
Maud Rise
Astrid Ridge
Riiser-Larsen Sea
Weddel Abyssal Plain
Lazarev Sea
Antarctic Peninsula
Alexander Island
Weddell Sea
Berkner Island
SCALE 1:48,000,000
Miller Projection
1000 miles
1000 kilometers
Longitude west of Greenwich

TRISTAN DA CUNHA
(to U.K.)
Rookery Point
SETTLEMENT OF EDINBURGH
Queen Mary's Peak 7087ft (2160m)
Tristan da Cunha
Seal Bay
Stonyhill Point
Inaccessible Island
North Point
East Point
SCALE 1:1,250,000
Mercator Projection
15 miles
15 kilometers
Stoltenhoff Island
Middle Island
Nightingale Island
Longitude west of Greenwich

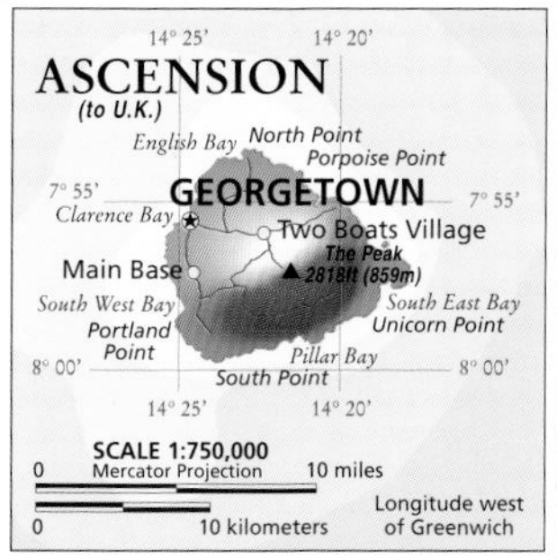
ASCENSION
(to U.K.)
English Bay
North Point
Porpoise Point
Clarence Bay
GEORGETOWN
Two Boats Village
Main Base
The Peak 2818ft (859m)
South West Bay
Portland Point
South East Bay
Unicorn Point
Pillar Bay
South Point
SCALE 1:750,000
Mercator Projection
10 miles
10 kilometers
Longitude west of Greenwich

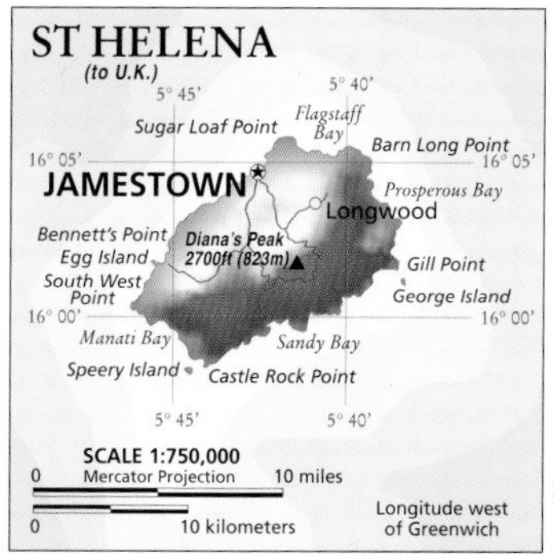
ST HELENA
(to U.K.)
Sugar Loaf Point
Flagstaff Bay
Barn Long Point
JAMESTOWN
Prosperous Bay
Longwood
Bennett's Point
Egg Island
South West Point
Diana's Peak 2700ft (823m)
Gill Point
George Island
Manati Bay
Sandy Bay
Speery Island
Castle Rock Point
SCALE 1:750,000
Mercator Projection
10 miles
10 kilometers
Longitude west of Greenwich

THE ARCTIC OCEAN

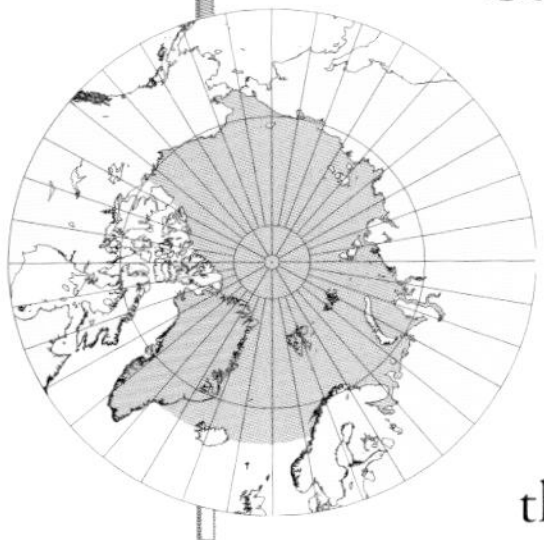

Covering 5.5 million square miles (14.1 million sq km), the Arctic Ocean is the world's smallest ocean. It is ringed by the continental fringes of North America, Europe, and Asia, as well as associated islands, including the largest island on Earth, Greenland. The ocean reaches depths of over 18,000 feet (5,500 m) and is divided into major basins by extensive undersea ranges, the largest of which, the Lomonosov Ridge, surpasses 10,000 feet (3,000 m) in height. Pack ice covers most of the sea surface year-round, expanding to reach most surrounding landmasses in winter. This shoreline has been inhabited by indigenous groups such as the North American Inuit, Asian Yakut, and European Saami for thousands of years. They have learned to cope with the Arctic's extreme climate, including months of darkness in winter, and exploit its restricted range of biological resources. Europeans first explored the Arctic Ocean in the 16th century, searching for a shortcut between Europe and Asia. More recently, outsiders have been lured here by the discovery of potentially vast undersea mineral reserves.

The polar ice pack is 10 feet (3 m) thick on average, but ridges form that may be up to three times that depth.

NORTH POLE
90N

Directly beneath the North Pole, the ocean is 13,410 feet (4,087 m) deep.

NATURAL RESOURCES

The Arctic Ocean's pack ice blocks sunlight, inhibiting photosynthetic processes and limiting marine life, but rich fisheries exist in areas of open ocean such as the Barents, Greenland, and Bering seas. Seals and whales were long a valuable resource for native peoples and, from the late 17th century, the basis of lucrative commercial trades operated by Europeans. Whaling is now banned, but sealing still takes place in Newfoundland and the White Sea. Sparse grazing lands fringe the ocean, providing food for wild caribou in North America and about 3 million domesticated reindeer in Scandinavia and Russia. Huge reserves of oil, coal, and gas have been tapped in northern Siberia and Alaska; even larger supplies are thought to lie offshore, but so far remain inaccessible.

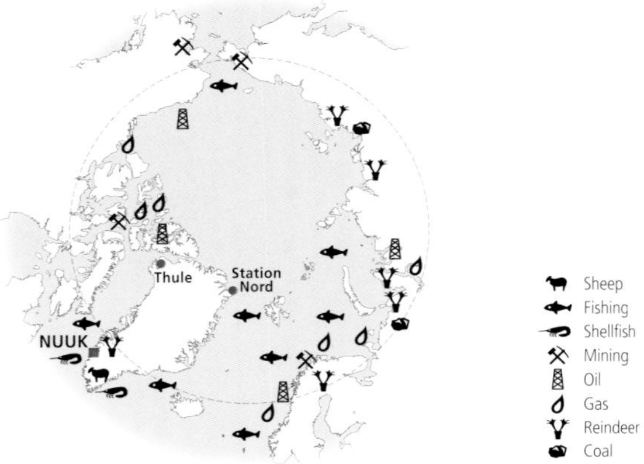
Thule
Station Nord
NUUK
Sheep
Fishing
Shellfish
Mining
Oil
Gas
Reindeer
Coal

GREENLAND AND ICELAND

At the boundary between the Arctic and Atlantic oceans, the narrow Denmark Strait divides Greenland from the much smaller island of Iceland. About two-thirds of Greenland lies within the Arctic Circle, and the northern tip of the island lies just 500 miles (800 km) from the North Pole. More than 80 percent of the landmass is blanketed by the world's second-largest ice sheet. Cupped within a basin encircled by coastal peaks, it has an average thickness of about 5,000 feet (1,500 m). Iceland sits astride the Reykjanes Ridge, part of the Mid-Atlantic Ridge. Divergence of tectonic plates along this boundary steadily tears the island apart, giving rise to great faults as well as volcanoes and geysers.

In winter, the Arctic fox grows a white coat to blend in with the snow.

Baffin Island
Davis Strait
NUUK
Greenland
Ammassalik
Ittoqqortoormiit
Denmark Strait
Iceland
Reykjanes Ridge

About 3,000 people live on Svalbard, working mainly in coal extraction.

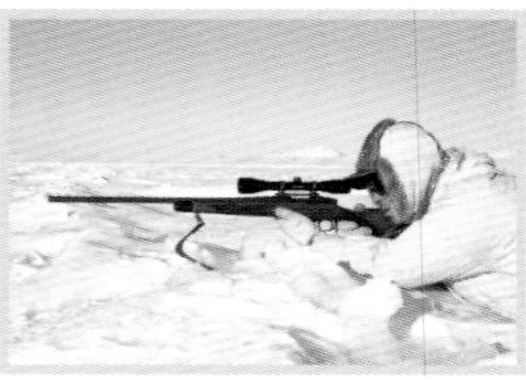

Yakut hunters in the Siberian Arctic employ modern means to catch traditional prey, including seals and walruses.

140°
130°
120°
110°
100°
90°
80°
70°
60°
50°
40°
NORTH AM
Mackenzie
Great Slave Lake
Great Bear Lake
Coronation Gulf
Queen Maud Gulf
King William Island
Booth Penins
Hudson Bay
Southampton Island
Coats Island
Mansel Island
Foxe Basin
Foxe Peninsula
Melville Peninsula
Prince Charles Island
Hudson Strait
Baffin Isla
Ungava Bay
Cape Chidley
Labrador Sea
Labrador Basin
Kangaami
Maniitso
NUUK
J.A.D. Jenson Nunatakker 5472ft (1668m)
Paami
Ivittuut
Narsarsuaq
Apostolens Tommelfinger 7510ft (2289m)
Nanortalik
Kap Fa

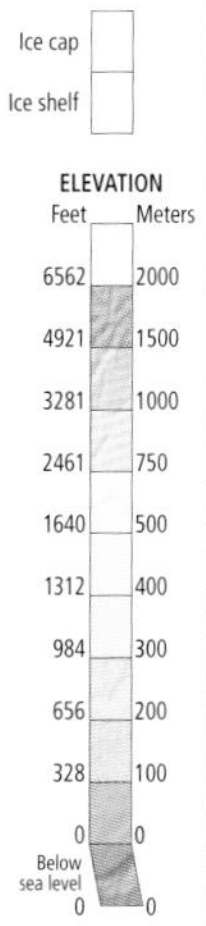
Ice cap
Ice shelf
ELEVATION
Feet Meters
6562 2000
4921 1500
3281 1000
2461 750
1640 500
1312 400
984 300
656 200
328 100
0 0
Below sea level
0 0

SCALE 1:20,000,000
Lamberts Azimuthal Equal Area Projection
0 600 miles
0 600 kilometers

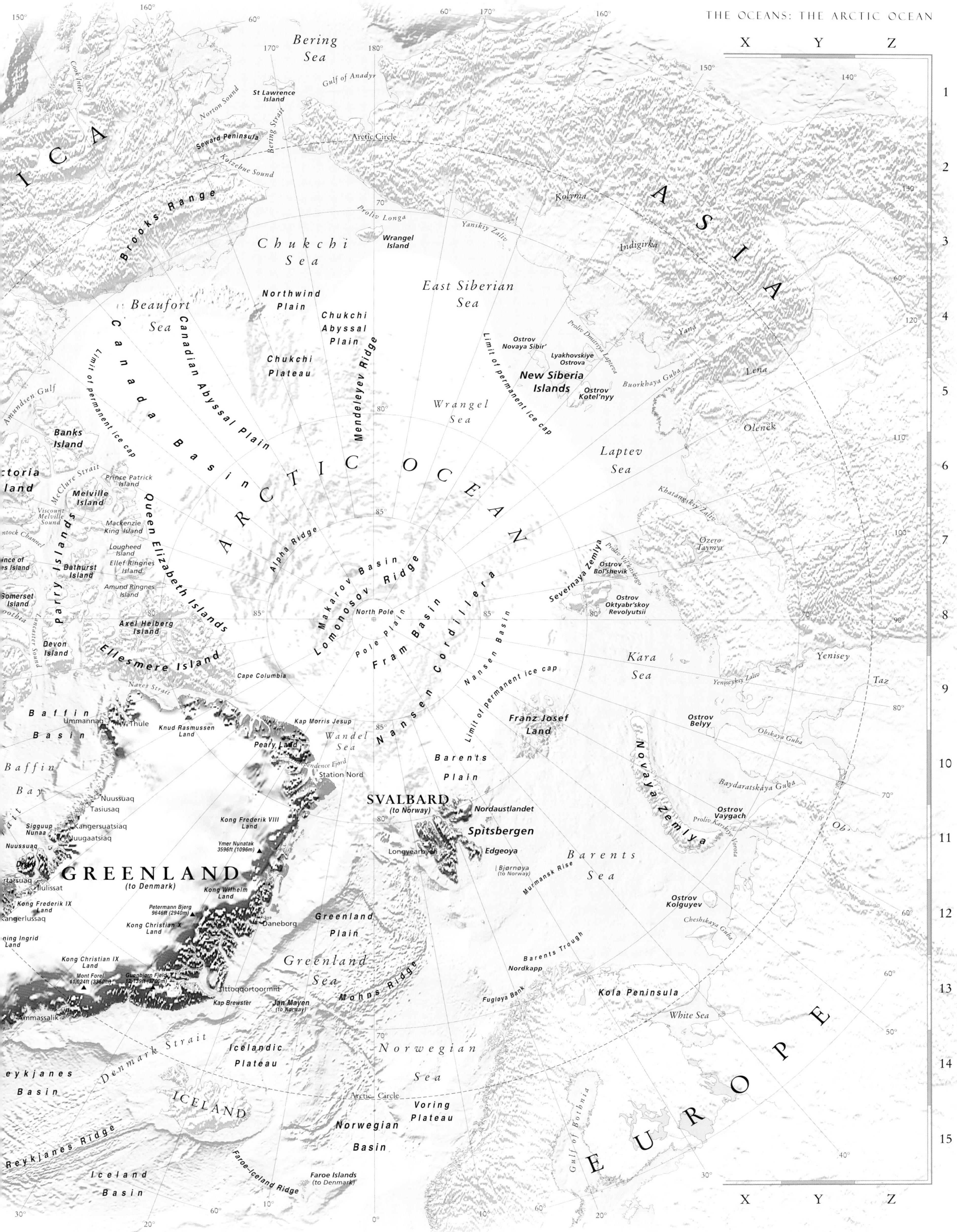
X Y Z
Bering Sea
Gulf of Anadyr
St Lawrence Island
Norton Sound
Cook Inlet
Seward Peninsula
Bering Strait
Kotzebue Sound
Arctic Circle
Brooks Range
Proliv Longa
Wrangel Island
Chukchi Sea
Yanskiy Zaliv
Kolyma
Indigirka
ASIA
East Siberian Sea
Northwind Plain
Chukchi Abyssal Plain
Chukchi Plateau
Mendeleyev Ridge
Beaufort Sea
Canadian Abyssal Plain
Canada Basin
Limit of permanent ice cap
Amundsen Gulf
Banks Island
Ostrov Novaya Sibir'
Lyakhovskiye Ostrova
New Siberia Islands
Ostrov Kotel'nyy
Proliv Dmitriya Lapteva
Buorkhaya Guba
Yana
Lena
Wrangel Sea
ARCTIC OCEAN
Laptev Sea
Olenëk
Victoria Island
McClure Strait
Prince Patrick Island
Melville Island
Viscount Melville Sound
Mackenzie King Island
Queen Elizabeth Islands
Parry Islands
Lougheed Island
Ellef Ringnes Island
Bathurst Island
Amund Ringnes Island
Somerset Island
Lancaster Sound
Axel Heiberg Island
Devon Island
Ellesmere Island
Alpha Ridge
Makarov Basin
Lomonosov Ridge
North Pole
Pole Plain
Fram Basin
Nansen Cordillera
Nansen Basin
Khatangskiy Zaliv
Ozero Taymyr
Severnaya Zemlya
Proliv Vil'kitskogo
Ostrov Bol'shevik
Ostrov Oktyabr'skoy Revolyutsii
Kara Sea
Yenisey
Yeniseyskiy Zaliv
Taz
Cape Columbia
Nares Strait
Baffin Basin
Ummannaq
Thule
Knud Rasmussen Land
Kap Morris Jesup
Peary Land
Wandel Sea
Station Nord
Franz Josef Land
Ostrov Belyy
Obskaya Guba
Novaya Zemlya
Barents Plain
Baffin Bay
Nuussuaq
Tasiusaq
SVALBARD (to Norway)
Nordaustlandet
Spitsbergen
Edgeoya
Longyearbyen
Bjørnøya (to Norway)
Murmansk Rise
Baydaratskaya Guba
Ostrov Vaygach
Proliv Karskiye Vorota
Ob'
Kong Frederik VIII Land
Ymer Nunatak 3596ft (1096m)
Sigguup Nunaa
Kangersuatsiaq
Nuugaatsiaq
GREENLAND (to Denmark)
Ilulissat
Kong Wilhelm Land
Kong Frederik IX Land
Kangerlussuaq
Petermann Bjerg 9646ft (2940m)
Kong Christian X Land
Daneborg
Barents Sea
Ostrov Kolguyev
Cheshskaya Guba
Greenland Plain
Greenland Sea
Barents Trough
Nordkapp
Kong Christian IX Land
Mont Forel 11,024ft (3360m)
Gunnbjørn Fjeld 12,139ft (3700m)
Ittoqqortoormiit
Kap Brewster
Jan Mayen (to Norway)
Mohns Ridge
Fugløya Bank
Kola Peninsula
White Sea
Ammassalik
Denmark Strait
Icelandic Plateau
Norwegian Sea
Reykjanes Basin
EUROPE
ICELAND
Voring Plateau
Norwegian Basin
Reykjanes Ridge
Gulf of Bothnia
Faroe-Iceland Ridge
Iceland Basin
Faroe Islands (to Denmark)
1 2 3 4 5 6 7 8 9 10 11 12 13 14 15

Seen from a satellite, the bright lights of Europe reveal a highly urbanized continent. The pattern of human settlement along the coasts ensures that the outline of much of western Europe is clearly visible from space.

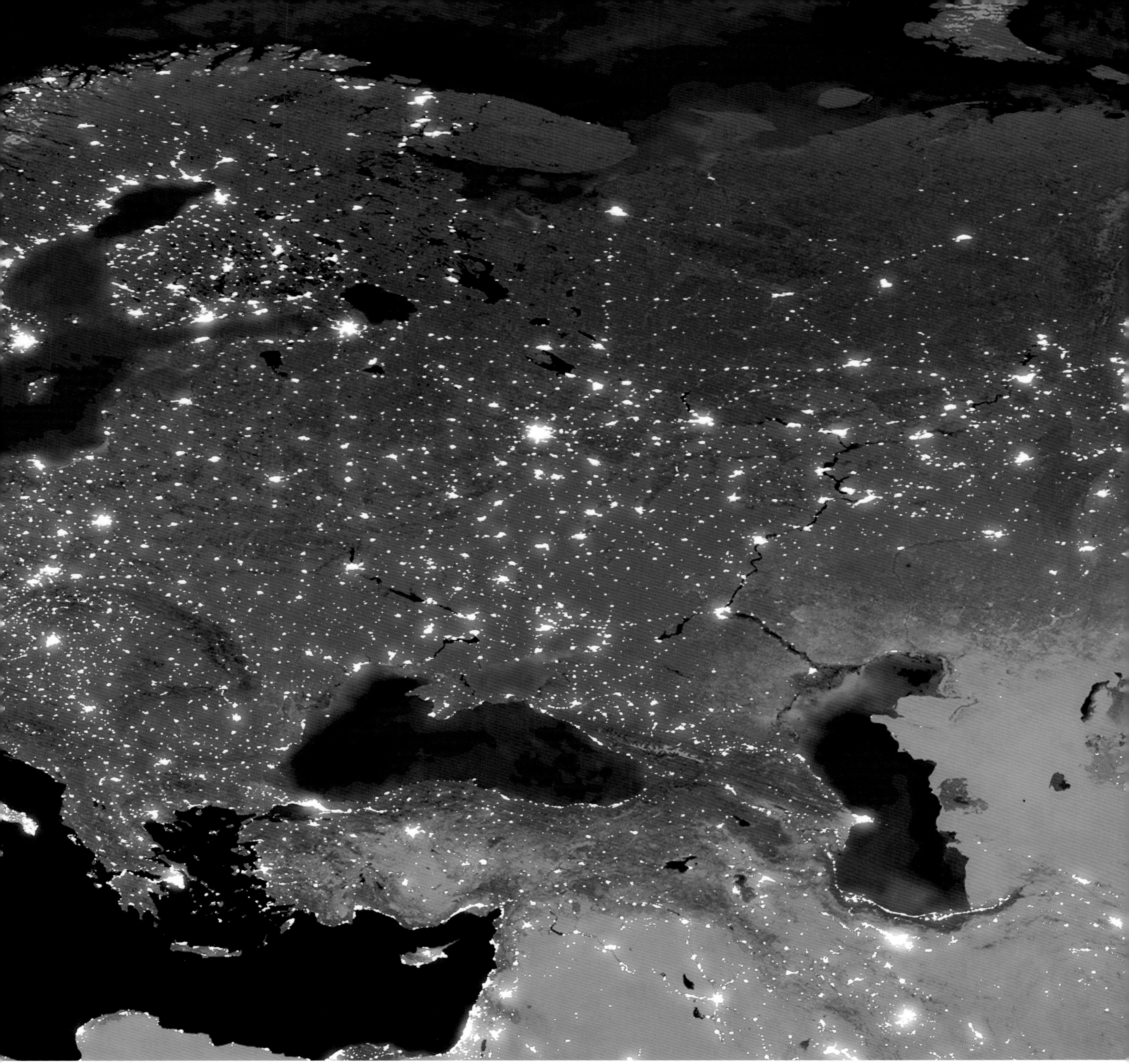

EUROPE

The View from Above

Satellites and space shuttles have been collecting images of our planet from space for more than 40 years. These images are sometimes assigned "false colors" to emphasize particular elements. From above, the patterns of dense populations, concentrations of industry, and vast agricultural areas of Europe emerge in astonishing detail. Revealed also is a surprising amount of natural environment, including the high lands of the Alps and the icy plains that stretch east from the jagged Norwegian coast to the Ural Mountains. Satellites have tracked oil slicks off the Atlantic coasts, captured the eruptions of Mount Etna and Mount Vesuvius, and followed wildfires through the forests of France, Spain, and Portugal. Observations such as these can help civil defense authorities to plan disaster responses. Glaciers, sensitive indicators of global climate change, have also been monitored over decades.

Right: Climate change can be measured by the varying rates of retreat of glaciers such as Switzerland's Aletsch Glacier, seen here curving across the center and upper right of the image. Glacial ice is shown as pale blue, and, from above, the moraine lines that mark its slow-moving path look almost like vehicle tracks.

Far right: The Volga flows 2,291 miles (3,688 km) from near Moscow south to the landlocked Caspian Sea, where it empties its waters through a delta of about 500 outlets. In this false-color image the delta wetlands are shown as bright green. The long thin lines just offshore indicate artificially maintained shipping channels.

Below: Coal mines fan into farmlands in this simulated natural color view of a 19 by 22 mile (30 by 36 km) region of Nordrhein-Westfalen, Germany. The white and dark blue patterns on the right are huge opencast coal mines. The myriad patches are agricultural fields; light green indicates crops, gray is bare soil. The thin dark lines are roads.

Right: Mount Etna, on the Italian island of Sicily, is Europe's largest and most active volcano. Here a dark, thick plume of smoke and ash from its November 2002 eruption is shown blowing southeast toward the city and airport of Catania. The white smoke is from forest fires sparked by ash fall on the slopes of the volcano.

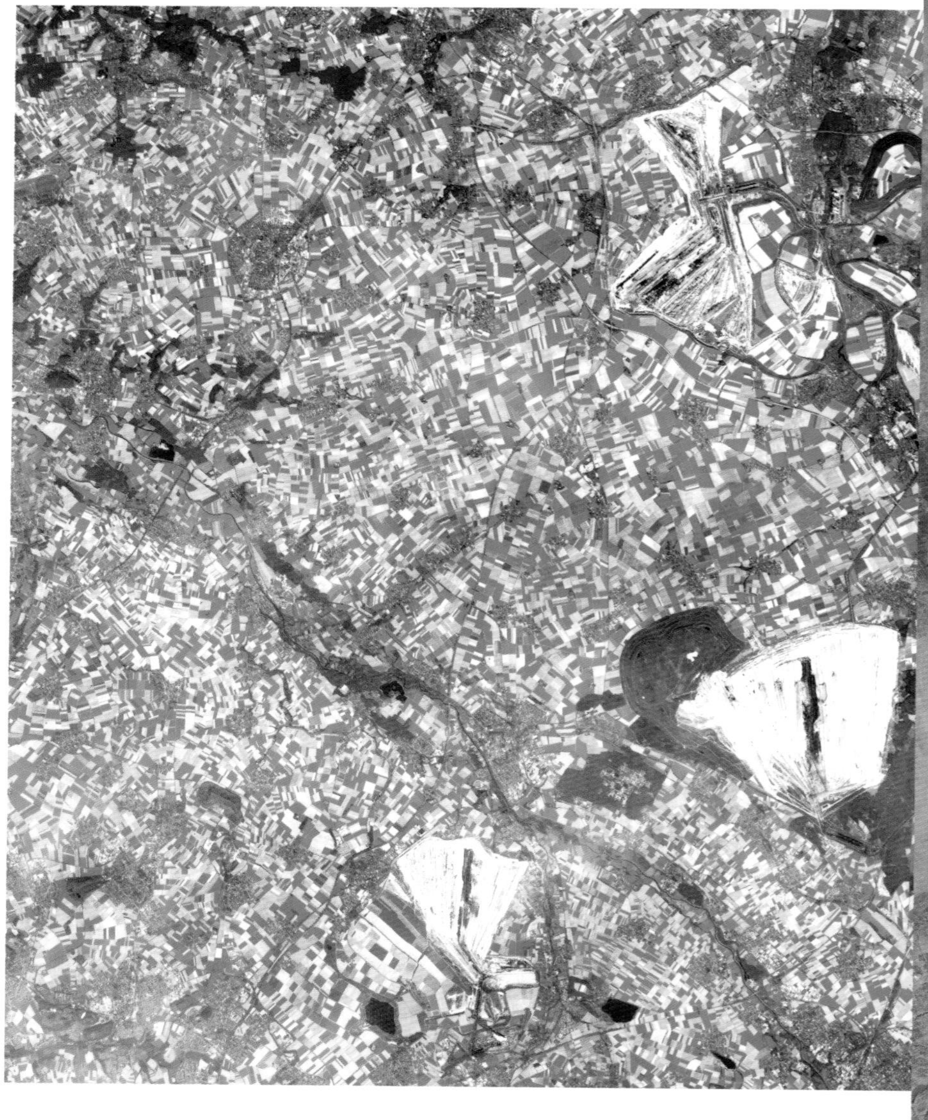

Land and Environment

Covering over 3.8 million square miles (9.8 million sq km), Europe is the second-smallest continent. It is separated from Asia by the Ural Mountains of Russia and bounded by sea to the north, west, and south. A chain of mountain ranges, including the Pyrenees, Alps, and Carpathian Mountains, stretches across the continent from west to east. It separates the rugged lands that fringe the island-studded Mediterranean Sea from the North European Plain, a belt of flat land that extends from the English Channel to the Urals. Farther north lie the broad, glacier-carved Scandinavian Peninsula and the large islands of Great Britain, Ireland, and Iceland.

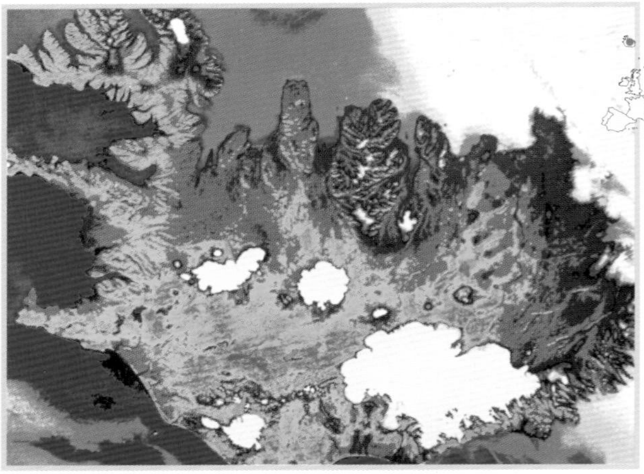

Above: As its name suggests, much of the isolated volcanic island of Iceland is covered by ice. The island's largest ice sheet, Vatnajökull, clearly visible at the bottom right of this satellite image, is bigger than all of mainland Europe's glaciers combined.
Below: The Alps stretch for 650 miles (1,000 km) from southeastern France, through Italy, Switzerland, and Austria to Slovenia. This satellite photograph shows the western end of the chain.

Iceland
Norwegian Sea
Faroe Islands
Atlantic Ocean
Outer Hebrides
British Isles
Orkney Islands
Shetland Islands
Ben Nevis 4406ft (1343m)
Ireland
Irish Sea
Pennines
Great Britain
Thames
North Sea
English Channel
Skagerrak
Kattegat
Jylland
Fyn
Sjaelland
Highlands
Kölen
Scandinavian
Vänern
Vättern
Gulf of Bothnia
Åland
Gotland
Öland
Bornholm
Baltic Sea
Gulf of Riga
Lappland
Elbe
Weser
Rhine
Hartz Mtns
Warta
Oder
Vistula
Bay of Biscay
Seine
Marne
Mosel
Main
Ore Mtns
Bohemian Forest
Loire
Vosges
Black Forest
Danube
Carpathian Mountains
Jura
Geneva
Alps
Dolomites
Mont Blanc 15,771ft (4807m)
Massif Central
Allier
Rhône
Garonne
Great Hungarian Plain
Tisza
Sava
Duero
Tajo
Ebro
Pyrenees
Aneto 11,168ft (3404m)
Iberian Peninsula
Sierra Morena
Guadalquivir
Sistemas Béticos
Majorca
Minorca
Ibiza
Balearic Islands
Po
Ligurian Sea
Corsica
Sardinia
Apennines
Adriatic Sea
Dinaric Alps
Tyrrhenian Sea
Vesuvius 4202ft (1281m)
Ionian Sea
Sicily
Mt Etna 10,902ft (3323m)
Malta
Mediterranean
SCALE 1:20,000,000
Lamberts Conformal Conic Projection
0
500 miles
0
500 kilometers

Natural Hazards

Earthquakes

Europe is located on the western side of the Eurasian Plate. Beneath the Mediterranean Sea, this plate is colliding with the African Plate and the smaller Anatolian Plate. Sudden movements along the plate boundaries create shock waves that are felt regularly in parts of southern Europe as earthquakes. Over the centuries, earthquakes have caused massive destruction and many deaths.

A woman salvages belongings from the remains of her home following the 1980 earthquake in southern Italy.

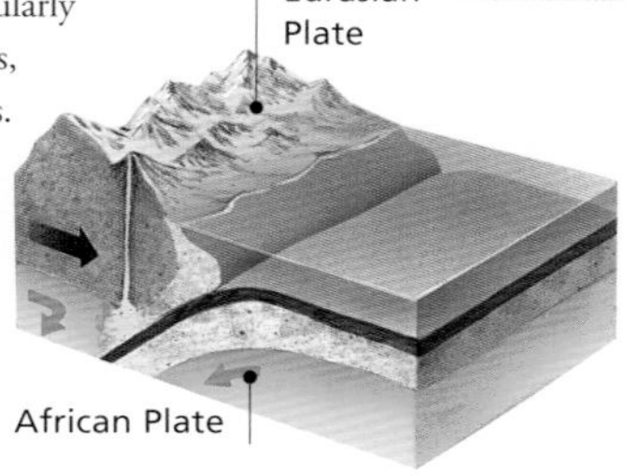

Eurasian Plate
African Plate

Along the plate boundaries that run through the Mediterranean, the thinner African Plate is forced under the thicker Eurasian Plate, buckling the land above and forcing magma to the surface. This creates volcanoes such as Mounts Etna and Vesuvius in Italy.

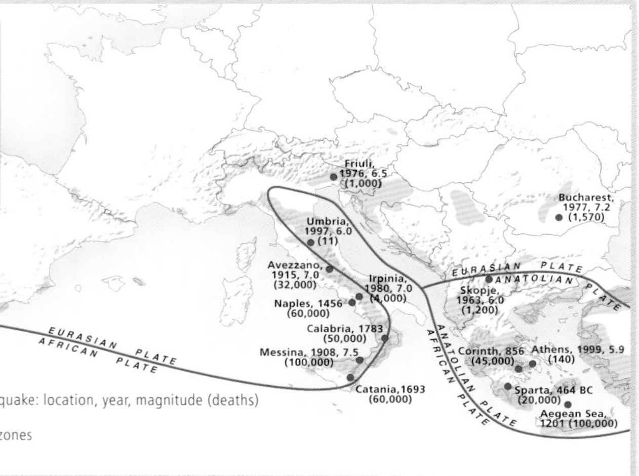

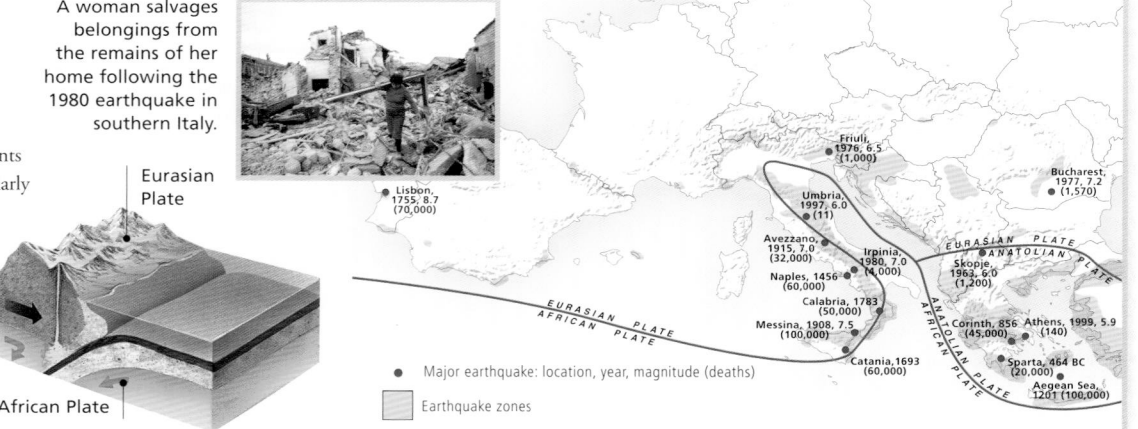

Lisbon, 1755, 8.7 (70,000)
Friuli, 1976, 6.5 (1,000)
Umbria, 1997, 6.0 (11)
Avezzano, 1915, 7.0 (32,000)
Irpinia, 1980, 7.0 (4,000)
Naples, 1456 (60,000)
Calabria, 1783 (50,000)
Messina, 1908, 7.5 (100,000)
Catania, 1693 (60,000)
Bucharest, 1977, 7.2 (1,570)
Skopje, 1963, 6.0 (1,200)
Corinth, 856 (45,000)
Athens, 1999, 5.9 (140)
Sparta, 464 BC (20,000)
Aegean Sea, 1201 (100,000)
EURASIAN PLATE
AFRICAN PLATE
ANATOLIAN PLATE
Major earthquake: location, year, magnitude (deaths)
Earthquake zones

Novaya Zemlya
Kara Sea
Barents Sea
Ostrov Kolguyev
Pechora
Ural Mountains
Kola Peninsula
White Sea
Vychegda
Northern Dvina
Lake Onega
Lake Ladoga
Volga
Kama
Rybinsk Reservoir
European Plain
Kuybyshev Reservoir
Valdai Hills
Volga Uplands
Central Russian Uplands
Dnieper
Kiev Reservoir
Tsimlyansk Reservoir
Caspian Depression
Caspian Sea
Don
Dniester
Sea of Azov
Caucasus
Crimea
Mt Elbrus 18,510ft (5642m)
Black Sea
ASIA
Sea of Marmara
Rhodes
Sea

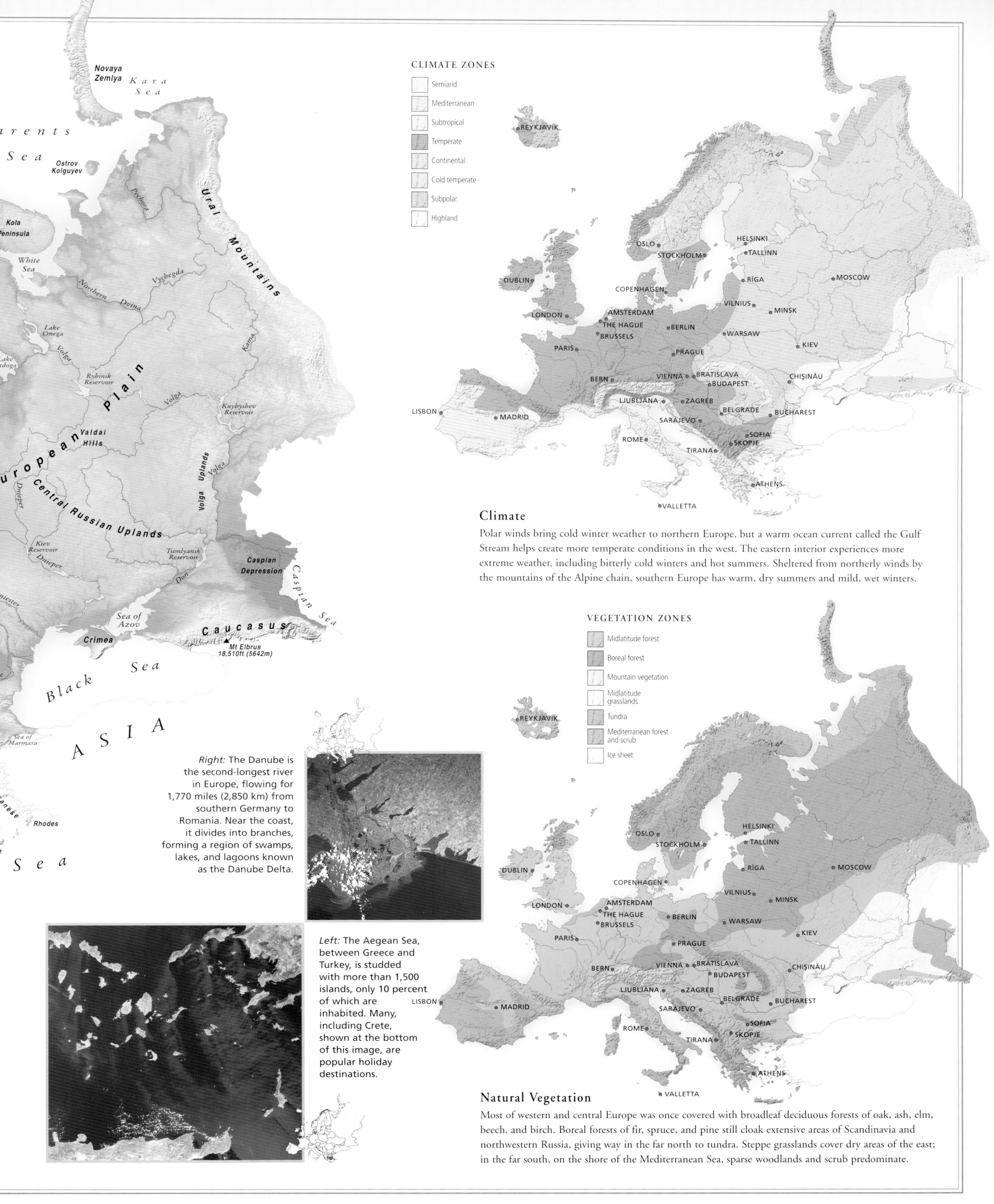

CLIMATE ZONES
Semiarid
Mediterranean
Subtropical
Temperate
Continental
Cold temperate
Subpolar
Highland
REYKJAVÍK
OSLO
STOCKHOLM
HELSINKI
TALLINN
RĪGA
MOSCOW
DUBLIN
COPENHAGEN
VILNIUS
MINSK
LONDON
AMSTERDAM
THE HAGUE
BERLIN
WARSAW
BRUSSELS
KIEV
PARIS
PRAGUE
BERN
VIENNA
BRATISLAVA
BUDAPEST
CHIŞINĂU
LJUBLJANA
ZAGREB
LISBON
MADRID
BELGRADE
BUCHAREST
SARAJEVO
SOFIA
ROME
SKOPJE
TIRANA
ATHENS
VALLETTA

Climate

Polar winds bring cold winter weather to northern Europe, but a warm ocean current called the Gulf Stream helps create more temperate conditions in the west. The eastern interior experiences more extreme weather, including bitterly cold winters and hot summers. Sheltered from northerly winds by the mountains of the Alpine chain, southern Europe has warm, dry summers and mild, wet winters.

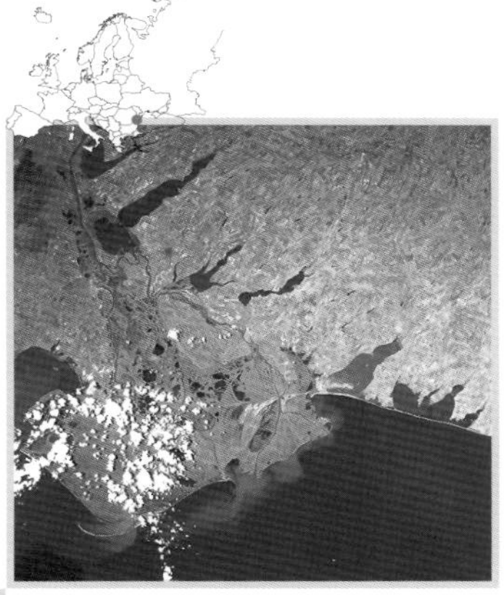

Right: The Danube is the second-longest river in Europe, flowing for 1,770 miles (2,850 km) from southern Germany to Romania. Near the coast, it divides into branches, forming a region of swamps, lakes, and lagoons known as the Danube Delta.

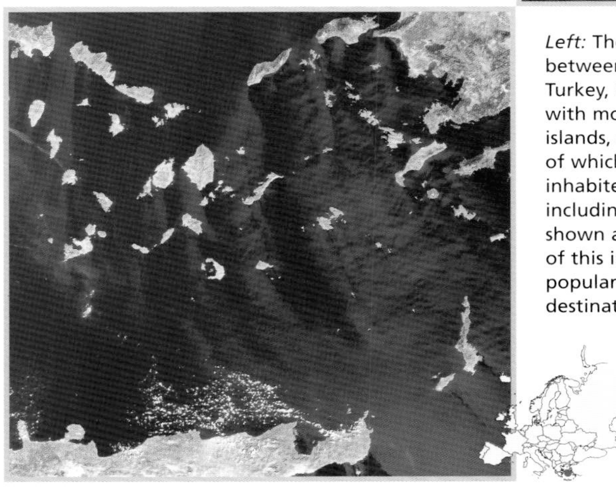

Left: The Aegean Sea, between Greece and Turkey, is studded with more than 1,500 islands, only 10 percent of which are inhabited. Many, including Crete, shown at the bottom of this image, are popular holiday destinations.

VEGETATION ZONES
Midlatitude forest
Boreal forest
Mountain vegetation
Midlatitude grasslands
Tundra
Mediterranean forest and scrub
Ice sheet
REYKJAVÍK
OSLO
STOCKHOLM
HELSINKI
TALLINN
RĪGA
MOSCOW
DUBLIN
COPENHAGEN
VILNIUS
MINSK
LONDON
AMSTERDAM
THE HAGUE
BERLIN
WARSAW
BRUSSELS
KIEV
PARIS
PRAGUE
BERN
VIENNA
BRATISLAVA
BUDAPEST
CHIŞINĂU
LJUBLJANA
ZAGREB
LISBON
MADRID
BELGRADE
BUCHAREST
SARAJEVO
SOFIA
ROME
SKOPJE
TIRANA
ATHENS
VALLETTA

Natural Vegetation

Most of western and central Europe was once covered with broadleaf deciduous forests of oak, ash, elm, beech, and birch. Boreal forests of fir, spruce, and pine still cloak extensive areas of Scandinavia and northwestern Russia, giving way in the far north to tundra. Steppe grasslands cover dry areas of the east; in the far south, on the shore of the Mediterranean Sea, sparse woodlands and scrub predominate.

PEOPLES AND NATIONS

Europe has a population of about 720 million and has long been one of the most densely inhabited parts of the world. It is home to a great diversity of peoples, languages, and cultures—the result of thousands of years of migrations, invasions, wars, and changing allegiances—and its cities are rich in historical, architectural, and artistic treasures. Today, Europe encompasses 42 nations as well as the Eastern Thrace region of Turkey and the eastern part of the Russian Federation, which are sometimes referred to as European Turkey and European Russia. Most European nations have substantial natural resources, and the inhabitants of northwestern Europe, especially, enjoy a high standard of living.

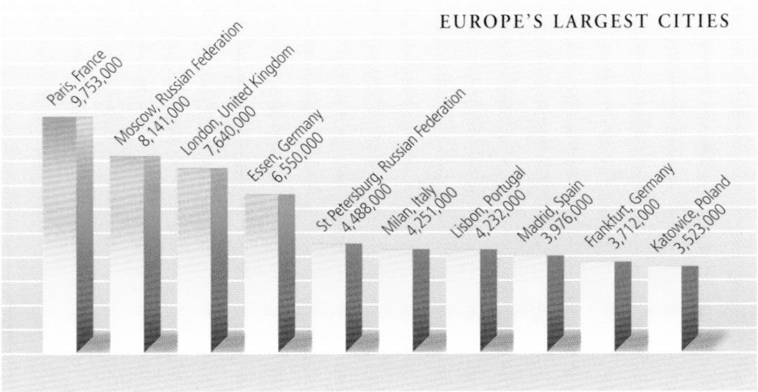
EUROPE'S LARGEST CITIES
Paris, France 9,753,000
Moscow, Russian Federation 8,141,000
London, United Kingdom 7,640,000
Essen, Germany 6,550,000
St Petersburg, Russian Federation 4,488,000
Milan, Italy 4,251,000
Lisbon, Portugal 4,232,000
Madrid, Spain 3,976,000
Frankfurt, Germany 3,712,000
Katowice, Poland 3,523,000

Urbanization

Until the 18th century, relatively few Europeans lived in cities. Following the Industrial Revolution, however, urban areas expanded rapidly. Toward the end of the 18th century, London became the first city in the world to reach a population of 1 million, a figure attained by nine other cities by 1900. Today, approximately 74 percent of Europeans live in urban areas.

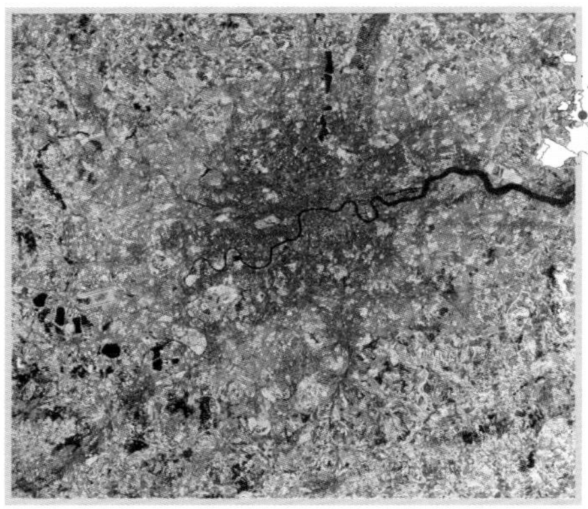

Right: In this false-color satellite image of London, urban areas appear blue, with commercial areas darker than the lighter residential areas. Pale green and orange areas are parklands, and dark orange and red areas indicate arable land. The River Thames is clearly visible as a dark, snaking line.

REYKJAVÍK
OSLO
HELSINKI
STOCKHOLM
TALLINN
RIGA
MOSCOW
DUBLIN
COPENHAGEN
VILNIUS
Kaliningrad
MINSK
AMSTERDAM
LONDON
THE HAGUE
BERLIN
BRUSSELS
WARSAW
KIEV
PARIS
LUXEMBOURG
PRAGUE
BERN
VIENNA
BRATISLAVA
CHIŞINĂU
BUDAPEST
LJUBLJANA
ZAGREB
BELGRADE
BUCHAREST
LISBON
MADRID
SARAJEVO
SOFIA
ROME
TIRANA
SKOPJE
Istanbul
ATHENS
VALLETTA

POPULATION DENSITY
Uninhabited
Less than 2.6 persons per sq mile/1 per sq km
2.6–26 per sq mile/ 1–10 per sq km
26–65 per sq mile/ 10–25 per sq km
65–130 per sq mile/ 25–50 per sq km
130–260 per sq mile/ 50–100 per sq km
260–520 per sq mile/ 100–200 per sq km

Population Density

Europe's early population growth centered on strategically important ports and major rivers. Industrial development in the 19th century attracted large numbers of workers to major manufacturing centers, such as central England, Germany's Ruhr Valley, and northern Italy, and these urban areas are still the most densely populated regions. The least densely populated parts of Europe are the high peaks of the central mountain ranges and the far north, most notably northern Scandinavia, and the Scottish Highlands.

The European Union

Twenty-five European nations belong to the European Union (EU), which seeks to establish common economic, social, and judicial policies across the continent. The EU began to take shape in the early 1950s, when Belgium, France, Germany, Italy, Luxembourg, and the Netherlands agreed to establish a common trading market, the European Economic Community (EEC). Its success led other countries to apply for membership. The EU's major institutions include the Council of the EU, the principal decision-making body located in Brussels, Belgium, and the European Parliament, based in Strasbourg, France.

EU members
Applicant members
Seeking membership

FLASHPOINTS

With so many nations, peoples, and cultures living in close proximity to each other, it is not surprising that Europe is the site of several longstanding disputes.

San Sebastián
Bayonne
Guernica
Bilbao
Pau
Basqueland
FRANCE
SPAIN
Vitoria-Gasteiz
Pamplona
Logroño
Tudela
Zaragoza

Basqueland

The Basque people of northern Spain and southwestern France have a distinct culture and unique language. Since the 1970s, in an attempt to gain independence for their homeland from Spain, Basques belonging to a group called ETA, or Euzkada Ta Askatasuna (Basque Homeland and Liberty), have resorted to terrorism.

Northern Ireland

In 1921, Ireland became self-governing and the six counties of Northern Ireland were incorporated into the United Kingdom (U.K.). Since then, Northern Ireland has been the site of violent conflict between Protestants, who want to remain part of the U.K., and Catholics, who wish to unite with Ireland.

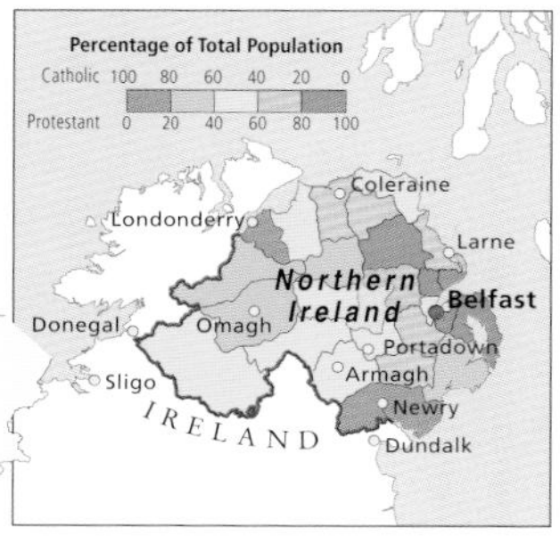
Percentage of Total Population
Catholic 100 80 60 40 20 0
Protestant 0 20 40 60 80 100
Coleraine
Londonderry
Larne
Northern Ireland
Belfast
Donegal
Omagh
Portadown
Armagh
Sligo
Newry
IRELAND
Dundalk

SERBIA and MONTENEGRO
Montenegro
Priština
Serbia
Podgorica
Kosovo
SKOPJE
ALBANIA
MACEDONIA
Albanian majority
TIRANA
Bitola
GREECE

Kosovo

About 90 percent of the inhabitants of the Serbian province of Kosovo are ethnic Albanians, most of whom would like their region to be autonomous or independent. Serbia has violently resisted Kosovar moves toward independence, partly because it fears the unification of Kosovo with neighboring Albania.

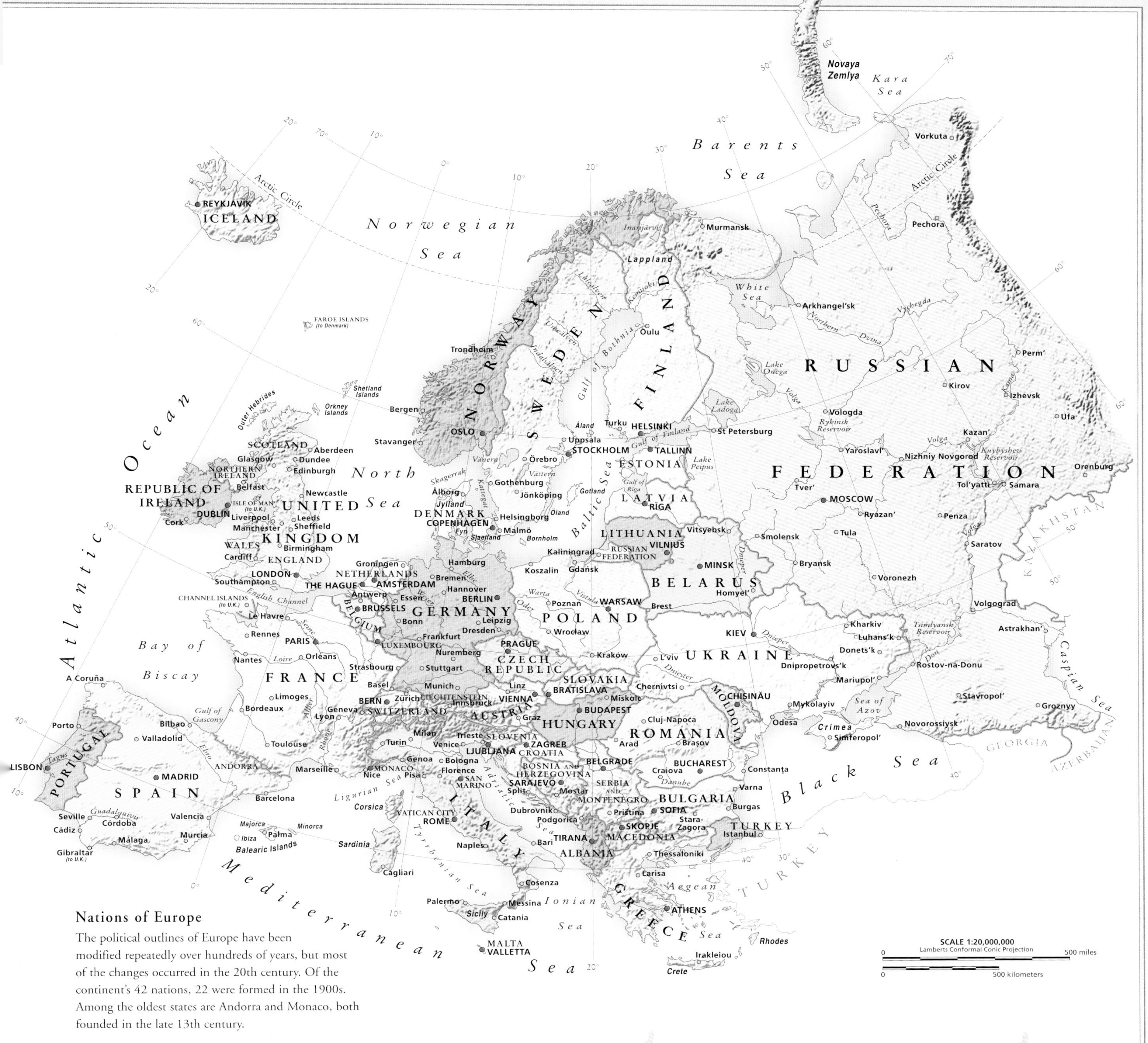
Novaya Zemlya
Kara Sea
Barents Sea
Norwegian Sea
Arctic Circle
REYKJAVIK
ICELAND
FAROE ISLANDS (to Denmark)
Shetland Islands
Orkney Islands
Outer Hebrides
Atlantic Ocean
North Sea
NORWAY
SWEDEN
FINLAND
RUSSIAN FEDERATION
Murmansk
Lappland
White Sea
Arkhangel'sk
Vorkuta
Pechora
Trondheim
Bergen
Stavanger
OSLO
Oulu
Gulf of Bothnia
HELSINKI
Turku
Åland
Uppsala
STOCKHOLM
TALLINN
ESTONIA
St Petersburg
Lake Ladoga
Lake Onega
Vologda
Rybinsk Reservoir
Yaroslavl'
Kirov
Perm'
Izhevsk
Ufa
Kazan'
Nizhniy Novgorod
Kuybyshev Reservoir
Orenburg
Tol'yatti
Samara
Tver'
MOSCOW
Ryazan'
Tula
Penza
Saratov
Smolensk
Bryansk
Voronezh
Volgograd
Astrakhan'
KAZAKHSTAN
Caspian Sea
Örebro
Gothenburg
Jönköping
Gotland
Öland
Bornholm
Malmö
Helsingborg
Ålborg
Jylland
DENMARK
COPENHAGEN
Fyn
Sjælland
Skagerrak
Kattegat
Baltic Sea
Gulf of Riga
Lake Peipus
LATVIA
RIGA
LITHUANIA
VILNIUS
Vitsyebsk
Kaliningrad
RUSSIAN FEDERATION
MINSK
BELARUS
Homyel'
Brest
REPUBLIC OF IRELAND
DUBLIN
Cork
Belfast
NORTHERN IRELAND
SCOTLAND
Glasgow
Aberdeen
Dundee
Edinburgh
Newcastle
ISLE OF MAN (to U.K.)
Liverpool
Leeds
Manchester
Sheffield
UNITED KINGDOM
WALES
Cardiff
Birmingham
ENGLAND
LONDON
Southampton
CHANNEL ISLANDS (to U.K.)
English Channel
Groningen
NETHERLANDS
THE HAGUE
AMSTERDAM
Antwerp
BRUSSELS
BELGIUM
LUXEMBOURG
Hamburg
Bremen
Hannover
Essen
Bonn
BERLIN
GERMANY
Leipzig
Dresden
Frankfurt
Nuremberg
Stuttgart
Munich
Koszalin
Gdańsk
Poznań
WARSAW
POLAND
Wrocław
Kraków
PRAGUE
CZECH REPUBLIC
Le Havre
Rennes
PARIS
Nantes
Orléans
Strasbourg
Basel
Bay of Biscay
FRANCE
Limoges
Bordeaux
Lyon
Geneva
Gulf of Gascony
Toulouse
Marseille
ANDORRA
MONACO
Nice
BERN
Zürich
LIECHTENSTEIN
Innsbruck
SWITZERLAND
AUSTRIA
VIENNA
Linz
Graz
BRATISLAVA
SLOVAKIA
Miskolc
BUDAPEST
HUNGARY
Milan
Turin
Venice
Trieste
SLOVENIA
LJUBLJANA
ZAGREB
CROATIA
Genoa
Bologna
Florence
SAN MARINO
Pisa
Ligurian Sea
Corsica
Adriatic Sea
BOSNIA AND HERZEGOVINA
SARAJEVO
Split
Mostar
BELGRADE
SERBIA AND MONTENEGRO
Dubrovnik
Podgorica
Priština
SKOPJE
MACEDONIA
TIRANA
ALBANIA
VATICAN CITY
ROME
ITALY
Naples
Bari
Tyrrhenian Sea
Sardinia
Cagliari
Cosenza
Palermo
Messina
Sicily
Catania
Ionian Sea
MALTA
VALLETTA
Mediterranean Sea
L'viv
UKRAINE
KIEV
Kharkiv
Luhans'k
Donets'k
Dnipropetrovs'k
Chernivtsi
Dniester
Dnieper
Mariupol'
CHIŞINĂU
MOLDOVA
Mykolayiv
Odesa
Crimea
Simferopol'
Sea of Azov
Rostov-na-Donu
Tsimlyanske Reservoir
Stavropol'
Novorossiysk
Groznyy
GEORGIA
AZERBAIJAN
Cluj-Napoca
Arad
ROMANIA
Braşov
BUCHAREST
Craiova
Danube
Constanţa
Varna
BULGARIA
SOFIA
Burgas
Stara Zagora
Black Sea
TURKEY
Istanbul
Thessaloniki
Larisa
Aegean Sea
GREECE
ATHENS
Rhodes
Irakleiou
Crete
A Coruña
Porto
PORTUGAL
LISBON
Tagus
Bilbao
Valladolid
MADRID
SPAIN
Ebro
Barcelona
Valencia
Seville
Guadalquivir
Córdoba
Cádiz
Málaga
Murcia
Gibraltar (to U.K.)
Majorca
Minorca
Ibiza
Palma
Balearic Islands
SCALE 1:20,000,000
Lamberts Conformal Conic Projection
0
500 miles
500 kilometers

Nations of Europe

The political outlines of Europe have been modified repeatedly over hundreds of years, but most of the changes occurred in the 20th century. Of the continent's 42 nations, 22 were formed in the 1900s. Among the oldest states are Andorra and Monaco, both founded in the late 13th century.

EUROPE IN 1100

Iceland (to Norway)
Norway
Sweden
Scotland
Ireland
England
Estonia
Latvia
Lithuania
Kievan Rus
Denmark
Pomerania
Prussia
Normandy
Poland
France
Holy Roman Empire
Polovtsy
Hungary
León
Castile
Portugal
Navarre
Aragon
Moorish Spain
Byzantine Empire
Norman Principalities

EUROPE IN 1500

Iceland (to Denmark)
Norway (to Denmark)
Sweden (to Denmark)
Scotland
Ireland
England
Denmark
Teutonic Knights
Muscovy
Tartars
Grand Duchy of Lithuania
Holy Roman Empire
France
Swiss Confederation
Hungary
Portugal
Navarre
Andorra
Monaco
Castile and Aragon
Republic of Venice
Papal States
Ottoman Empire
Sardinia (to Aragon)
Naples (to Aragon)
Sicily (to Aragon)
Crete (to Republic of Venice)

EUROPE IN 1914

Iceland (to Denmark)
Faroe Is. (to Denmark)
Norway
Sweden
United Kingdom
Denmark
Russia
Netherlands
Belgium
Luxembourg
Germany
France
Switzerland
Austro-Hungarian Empire
Romania
Portugal
Spain
Andorra
Monaco
Corsica (to France)
San Marino
Kingdom of Italy
Serbia
Montenegro
Albania
Bulgaria
Ottoman Empire
Greece
Dodecanese (to Italy)
Balearic Islands (to Spain)
Sardinia (to Italy)
Sicily (to Italy)
Malta (to Great Britain)
Crete (to Great Britain)

The Human Impact

Along with eastern and southern Asia, Europe was the focus of early population growth. Large-scale modification of the landscape began with the development of subsistence farming around 4000 BC, increased with the introduction of the iron plow and commercial farming in the Middle Ages, then accelerated rapidly with the advent of industry in the 18th century. Humans have now removed more than half of the continent's original forest, along with large areas of natural steppe grasslands. Urban areas, roadways, and railways form a tangled web of concrete, tarmac, and steel covering thousands of square miles. Mines have been excavated, rivers dammed, and swamps drained. Overall, humans are thought to have modified about 65 percent of Europe's surface—double the proportion of any other continent. These transformations have brought significant benefits and enabled Europeans to enjoy a high standard of living. But continuing prosperity could be undermined by damage to the environment caused by depletion of resources and the polluting effects of waste.

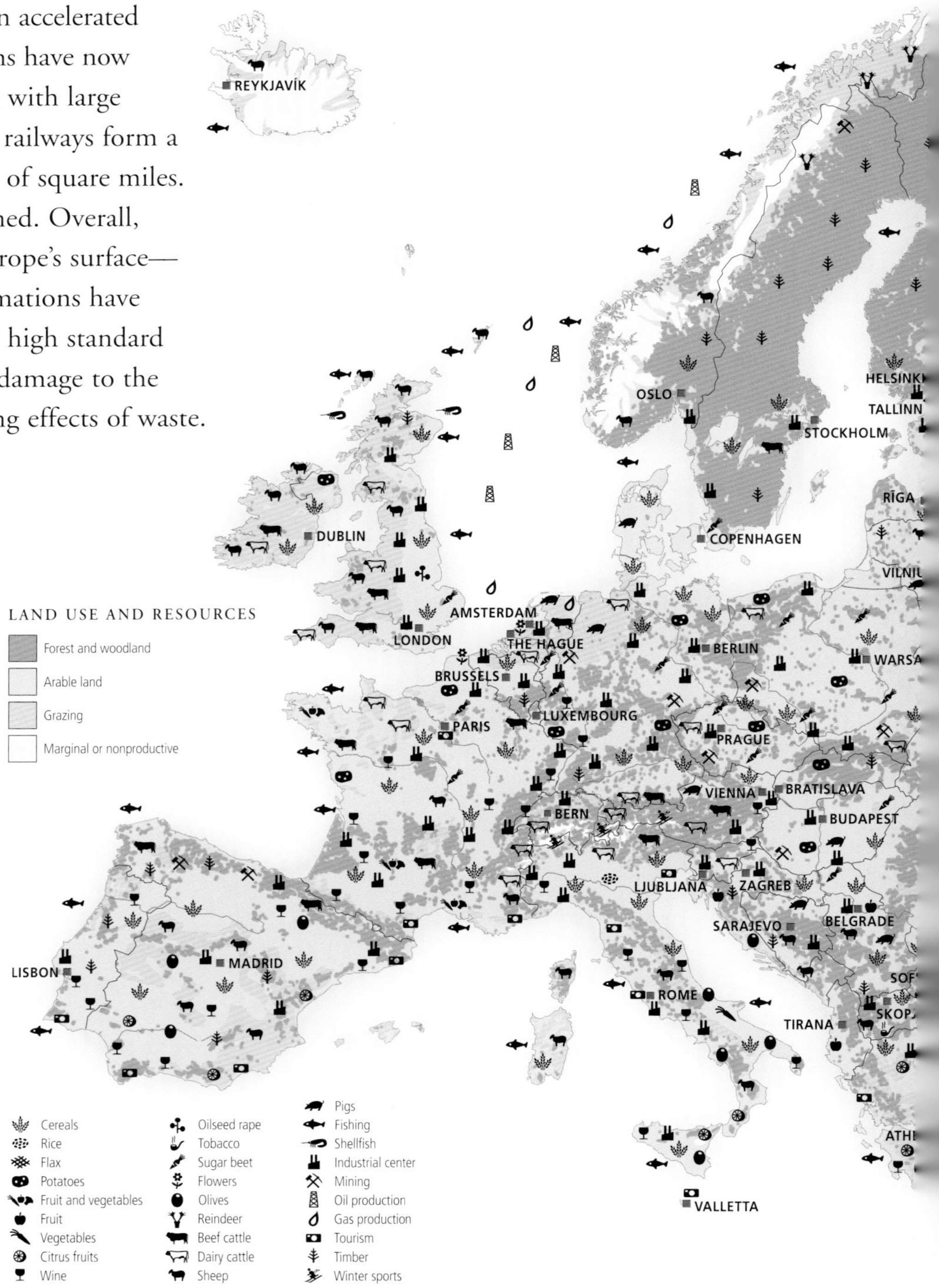

REYKJAVÍK
OSLO
HELSINKI
TALLINN
STOCKHOLM
RIGA
DUBLIN
COPENHAGEN
VILNIU
AMSTERDAM
LONDON
THE HAGUE
BERLIN
WARSA
BRUSSELS
PARIS
LUXEMBOURG
PRAGUE
VIENNA
BRATISLAVA
BERN
BUDAPEST
LJUBLJANA
ZAGREB
SARAJEVO
BELGRADE
LISBON
MADRID
ROME
SOF
SKOP
TIRANA
ATHI
VALLETTA
LAND USE AND RESOURCES
Forest and woodland
Arable land
Grazing
Marginal or nonproductive
Cereals
Rice
Flax
Potatoes
Fruit and vegetables
Fruit
Vegetables
Citrus fruits
Wine
Oilseed rape
Tobacco
Sugar beet
Flowers
Olives
Reindeer
Beef cattle
Dairy cattle
Sheep
Pigs
Fishing
Shellfish
Industrial center
Mining
Oil production
Gas production
Tourism
Timber
Winter sports

The Changing Face of Europe

Forests

About 8,000 years ago, forests covered about 70 percent of Europe, flourishing almost everywhere except for especially high, exposed, or poorly drained land. As populations expanded and technology developed, Europeans cleared ever-larger numbers of trees to provide farmland, fuel, and building materials. Today, excluding Russia, 68 percent of the original forest has disappeared and only one percent of old-growth trees survive. Large stands of forest remain only in northern Europe, European Russia, and subalpine regions. On a more positive note, Europe has increased its forest cover in recent years by 4 percent—more than any other continent.

ORIGINAL FOREST COVER

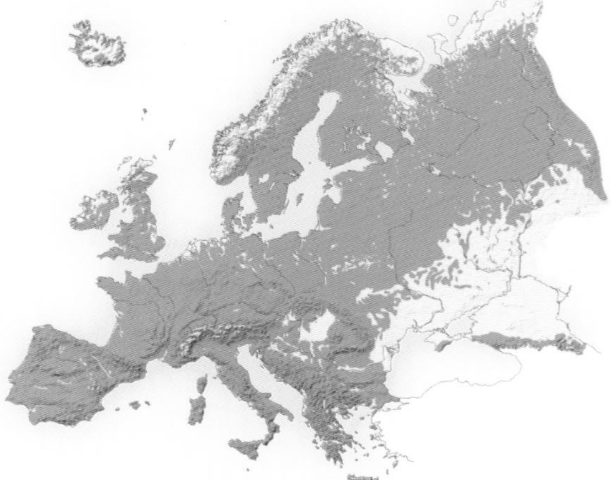

CURRENT FOREST COVER

Economic Profile

Europe's abundant resources include major reserves of fossil fuels, reliable supplies of fresh water, and sizable swathes of arable land. The fertile west, center, and southeast produce large amounts of cereals (20 percent of the world's supply), root crops (including two-thirds of the world's potatoes), fruit, and livestock products. Dairy and beef cattle predominate in the north; the south is better suited to the farming of olives, grapes, citrus fruits, sheep, and goats. European industries make half of the world's steel, one-third of its chemicals, and a plethora of consumer goods, the continent also accounts for half of the world's exports and imports.

Land Cover

Most of Europe's forests and woodlands lie in European Russia and Scandinavia. Western Europe has much higher proportions of arable land and pasture. Large parts of Europe are covered by urban and industrial areas, roads, and railways.

PROPORTIONS OF TOTAL LAND AREA

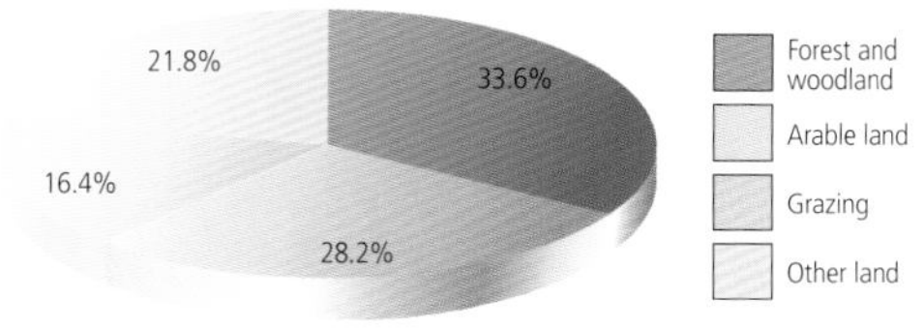

21.8%
33.6%
16.4%
28.2%
Forest and woodland
Arable land
Grazing
Other land

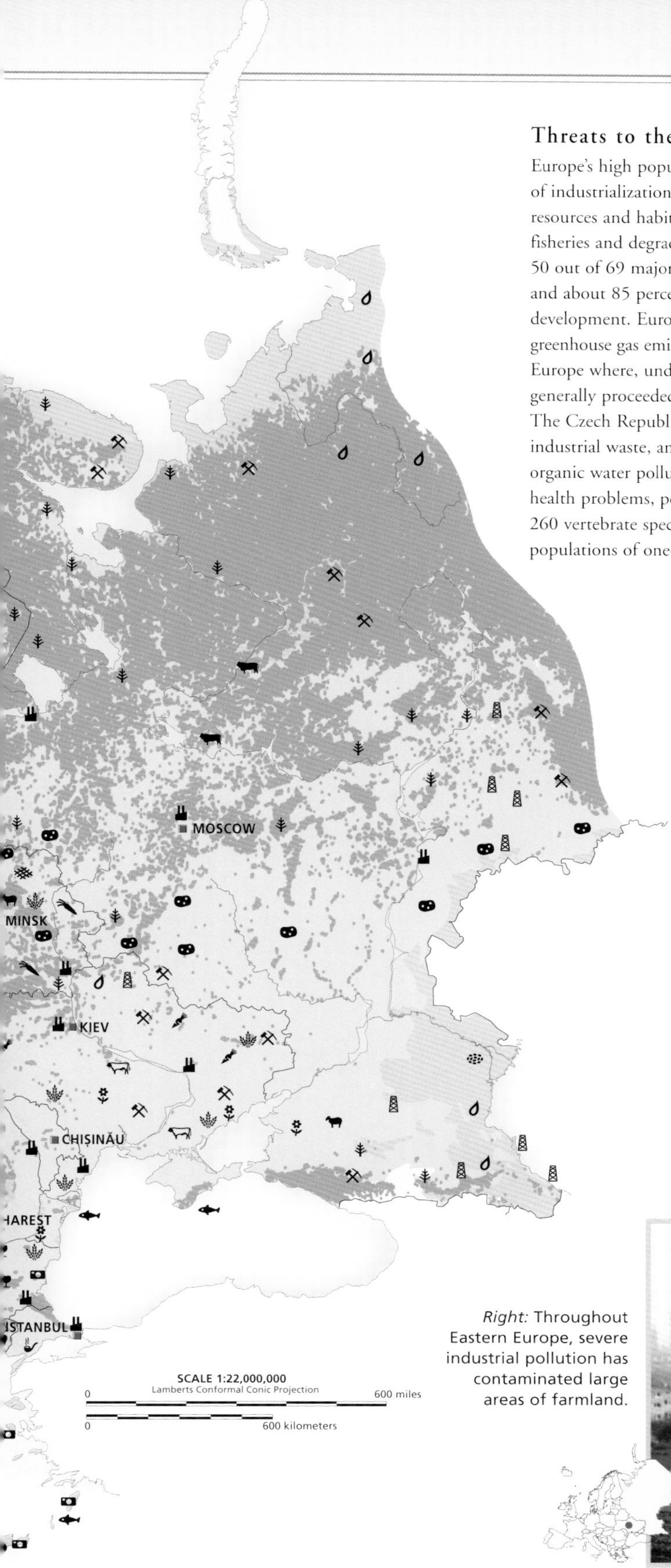
MOSCOW
MINSK
KIEV
CHIŞINĂU
ISTANBUL
SCALE 1:22,000,000
Lamberts Conformal Conic Projection
0
600 miles
0
600 kilometers

Threats to the Environment

Europe's high population density and high level of industrialization have placed great strain on its natural resources and habitats. Overexploitation has depleted fisheries and degraded soils. A recent assessment found 50 out of 69 major rivers to be of poor ecological quality, and about 85 percent of the coastline is threatened by development. Europe is responsible for one-third of global greenhouse gas emissions; pollution is especially bad in Eastern Europe where, under Soviet control, industrialization generally proceeded unchecked by environmental restrictions. The Czech Republic now has the continent's highest levels of industrial waste, and Moldova has the highest levels of organic water pollutants. As well as giving rise to human health problems, pollution has decimated wildlife—about 260 vertebrate species are on the brink of extinction and the populations of one-third of bird species are in decline.

Right: On November 19, 2002, the *Prestige* oil tanker ran aground off the northwest coast of Spain, releasing 24,500 tons (25,000 t) of oil. The spill decimated wildlife and local fishing industries.

ENVIRONMENTAL ISSUES
Degraded soil
Very degraded soil
Polluted rivers
Polluted seas and lakes
Acid rain
Major oil spills, year
Major nuclear accidents, year
Cities with severe air pollution
Overfished fishery, year of peak catch, decline since peak catch
REYKJAVÍK
Northeast Atlantic
1976, -11.9%
1993
OSLO
HELSINKI
TALLINN
STOCKHOLM
MOSCOW
RIGA
DUBLIN
1957
COPENHAGEN
1996
VILNIUS
MINSK
LONDON
AMSTERDAM
1967
THE HAGUE
BERLIN
WARSAW
BRUSSELS
1986
1978
PARIS
KIEV
PRAGUE
1976, 1992
Munich
VIENNA
BRATISLAVA
2002
BERN
BUDAPEST
CHIŞINĂU
1975
LJUBLJANA
Turin
Milan
ZAGREB
BELGRADE
LISBON
MADRID
BUCHAREST
1991
SARAJEVO
SOFIA
1979
Barcelona
ROME
SKOPJE
Istanbul
TIRANA
Mediterranean and Black Seas
1988, -25.0%
ATHENS
1980
VALLETTA

Right: Throughout Eastern Europe, severe industrial pollution has contaminated large areas of farmland.

Right: Chernobyl in the Soviet Union (now Ukraine) was the site of the worst-ever nuclear disaster, in April 1986. It killed 32 people and spread radioactive fallout throughout Europe.

Protecting the Environment

The implementation of recent international legislation has resulted in significant progress in reducing pollution, with greenhouse-gas emissions falling 2 percent between 1990 and 1998, and carbon dioxide emissions declining 8 percent in Eastern Europe between 1990 and 2000. The use of pesticides has dwindled in Eastern Europe, and phosphorous discharges have dropped by 50 to 80 percent in Western Europe in the past 20 years. Levels of the heavy metals cadmium, lindane, and mercury in seas fell by 80 percent in the 1990s. The number of protected areas grows every year and in Western Europe legislation designed to protect biodiversity now covers over 54 million acres (22 million ha) of farmland. However, environmental groups fear that the level of protection offered by many preserves is inadequate.

PERCENTAGE OF LAND PROTECTED IN MAJOR EUROPEAN COUNTRIES

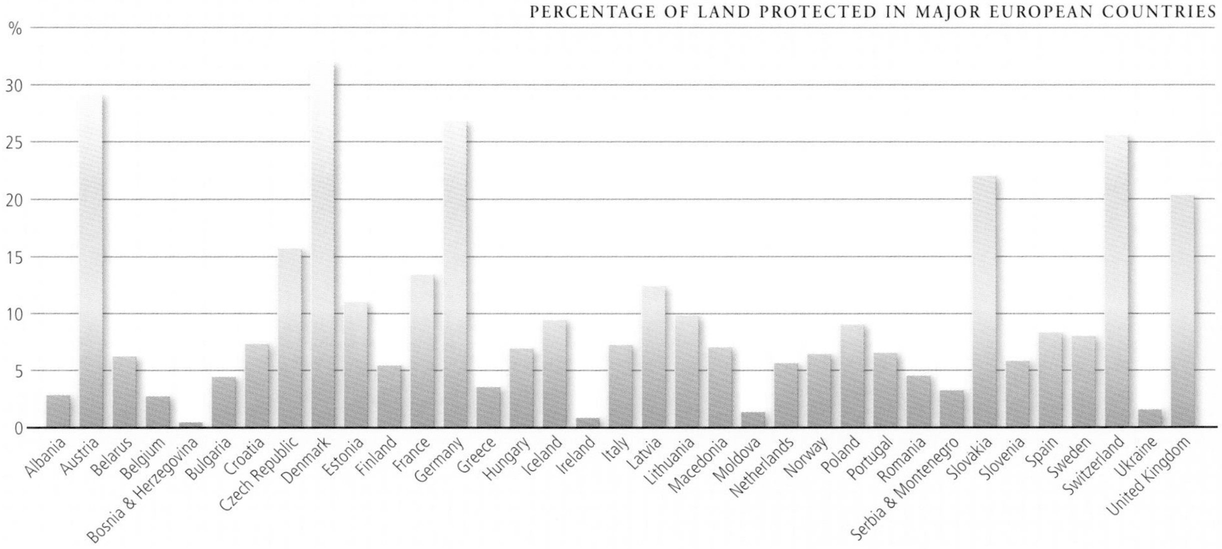
%
30
25
20
15
10
5
0
Albania
Austria
Belarus
Belgium
Bosnia & Herzegovina
Bulgaria
Croatia
Czech Republic
Denmark
Estonia
Finland
France
Germany
Greece
Hungary
Iceland
Ireland
Italy
Latvia
Lithuania
Macedonia
Moldova
Netherlands
Norway
Poland
Portugal
Romania
Serbia & Montenegro
Slovakia
Slovenia
Spain
Sweden
Switzerland
Ukraine
United Kingdom

The British Isles

Republic of Ireland, United Kingdom

The British Isles consist of two large islands, Great Britain and Ireland, and numerous smaller islands located off the northwest coast of mainland Europe. Together with the troubled province of Northern Ireland, the once-independent nations of England, Scotland, and Wales make up the United Kingdom (U.K.).

The southern part of the island of Ireland became self-governing in 1921. Most of southeastern Britain is low, gently undulating terrain, becoming almost entirely flat in the east-coast Fens region. To the north and west the land is more rugged, with hills and mountains dominating central northern England, much of Wales, southern and northern Scotland, and parts of Northern Ireland. In southern Ireland, a well-watered central plain is studded with lakes and peat bogs and ringed by coastal uplands. Both the U.K. and Ireland have recently developed closer social and economic ties with other European nations, and a physical link between Britain and the rest of the continent was forged in 1994 with the completion of the Channel Tunnel.

A distinctive London landmark, Tower Bridge was completed in 1894. The lower platform between its two towers can be opened to allow shipping to pass through.

On the west coast of Ireland, uplands abut the Atlantic Ocean, forming dramatic coastal landforms such as the spectacular Cliffs of Moher, near Hag's Head.

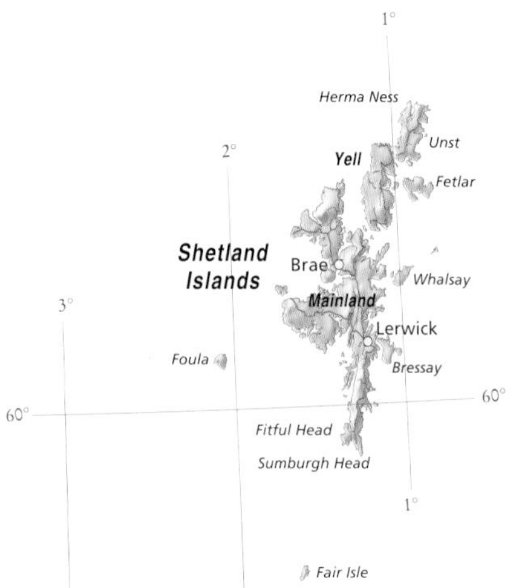
Shetland Islands
Herma Ness
Unst
Yell
Fetlar
Whalsay
Brae
Mainland
Lerwick
Bressay
Foula
Fitful Head
Sumburgh Head
Fair Isle

Orkney Islands
Papa Westray
Nth Ronaldsay
Westray
Sanday
Rousay
Eday
Stronsay
Mainland
Shapinsay
Stromness
Kirkwall
Scapa Flow
Hoy
South Ronaldsay
Pentland Firth
Duncansby Head
John o'Groats
Thurso
Noss Head
Wick
Cape Wrath
Durness
Tongue
Ben Klibreck 2365ft (721m)
Butt of Lewis
Port of Ness
Isle of Lewis
Stornoway
The Minch
Lochinver
Loch Shin
Helmsdale
Golspie
Dornoch Firth
Scarp
Taransay
Tarbert
Shiant Islands
Ullapool
Harris
Tain
Tarbat Ness
Moray Firth
Elgin
Banff
Fraserburgh
Outer Hebrides
North Uist
Uig
Nairn
Inverness
Peterhead
Buchan Ness
Huntly
Benbecula
Portree
Beauly
Spey
Skye
Kyle of Lochalsh
Carn Eighe 3877ft (1182m)
North West Highlands
Ellon
South Uist
Sea of the Hebrides
Broadford
Loch Ness
Aviemore
Grampian Mtns
Don
Fort Augustus
Ben Macdui 4295ft (1309m)
Aberdeen
Girdle Ness
Barra
Eriskay
Canna
Vatersay
Rum
Mallaig
Dee
Braemar
Stonehaven
Eigg
Mingulay
Muck
Fort William
Ben Nevis 4406ft (1343m)
Coll
Tobermory
Ballachulish
Loch Rannoch
Pitlochry
Forfar
Montrose
Arbroath
Carnoustie
Tiree
Tay
Mull
SCOTLAND
Dundee
Iona
Oban
Crieff
Perth
St Andrews
Fife Ness
Firth of Lorn
Inveraray
Colonsay
Jura
Lochgilphead
Loch Lomond
Forth
Stirling
Kirkcaldy
Firth of Forth
Falkirk
Helensburgh
Dumbarton
Edinburgh
Glasgow
Port Glasgow
Islay
Tarbert
Largs
East
Hamilton
St Abb's Head
Berwick-upon-Tweed
Inner Hebrides
OCEAN

Population Patterns

The U.K.'s highly urbanized population—about 90 percent inhabit towns and cities—is heavily concentrated in the southeast and around the industrial centers of Birmingham, Manchester, Leeds, Glasgow, and Belfast. The least densely populated areas are the Scottish Highlands, where sheep far outnumber people, and the uplands of northwest England and Wales. Ireland's population is more evenly distributed, with about 60 percent living in urban areas.

Edinburgh
Glasgow
Belfast
DUBLIN
Manchester
Birmingham
Cardiff
LONDON
Less than 2.6 persons per sq mile/1 per sq km
2.6–26 per sq mile/ 1–10 per sq km
26–65 per sq mile/ 10–25 per sq km
65–130 per sq mile/ 25–50 per sq km
130–260 per sq mile/ 50–100 per sq km
260–520 per sq mile/ 100–200 per sq km

Economic Profile

The decline of the U.K.'s manufacturing industries has been paralleled by the growth in services, which now employ three-quarters of workers. Still-important industries include engineering, chemicals and chemical products, textiles, and food and beverages.

The nation's most abundant food crops are cereals (especially wheat and barley), potatoes, sugar beet, and oilseed rape. Ireland's farming sector is more dependent on livestock. Its industries experienced a boom in the late 20th century, led by textiles, chemicals, machinery, and computer hardware and software.

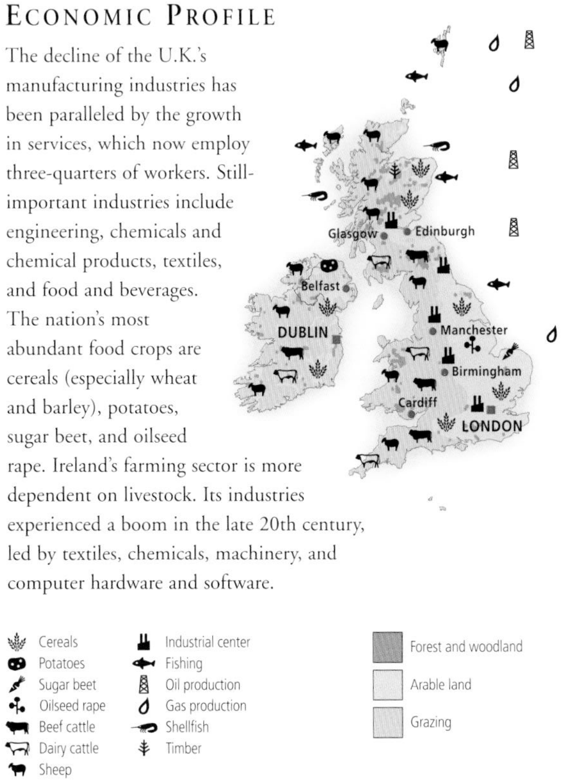
Glasgow
Edinburgh
Belfast
DUBLIN
Manchester
Birmingham
Cardiff
LONDON
Cereals
Potatoes
Sugar beet
Oilseed rape
Beef cattle
Dairy cattle
Sheep
Industrial center
Fishing
Oil production
Gas production
Shellfish
Timber
Forest and woodland
Arable land
Grazing

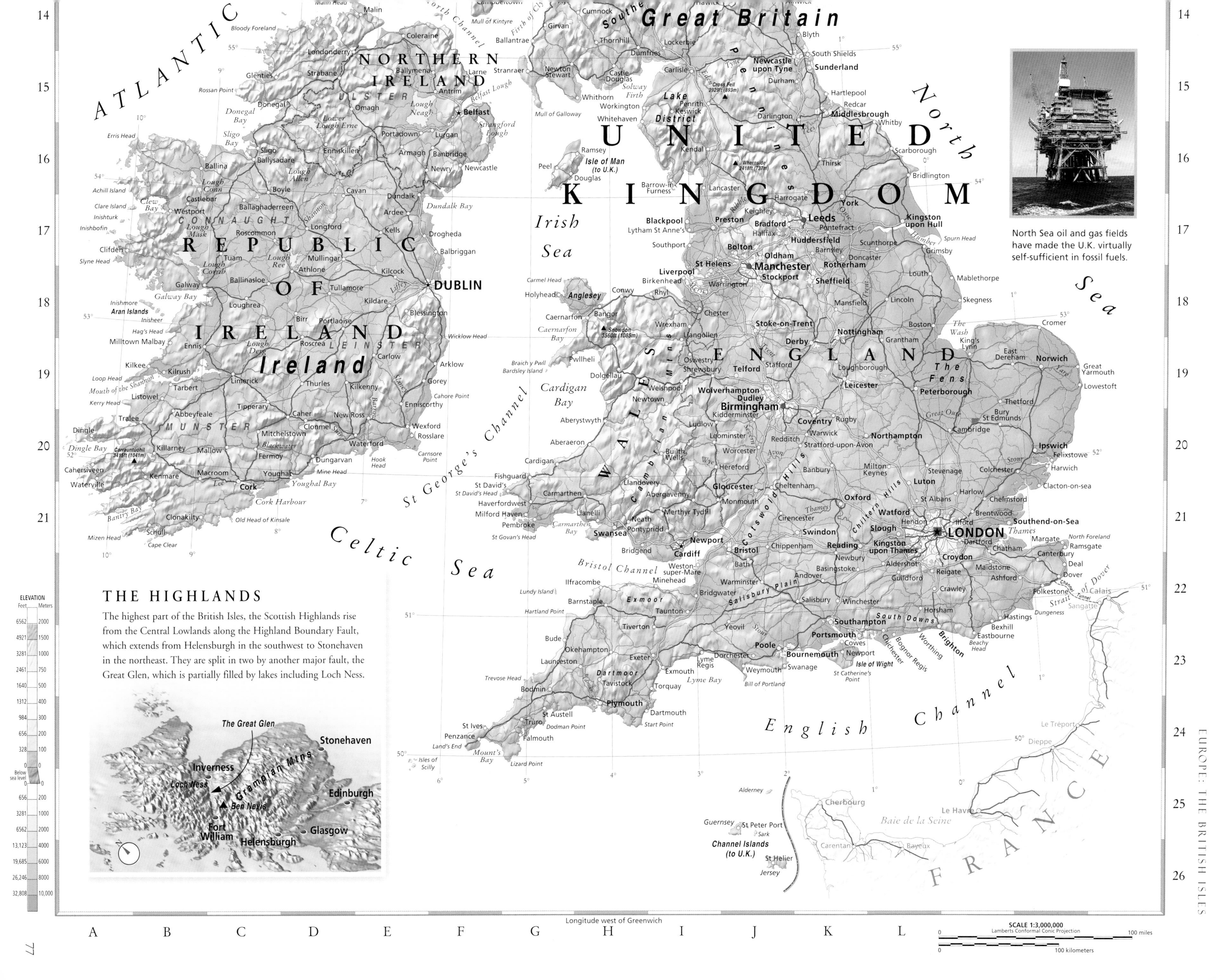
ATLANTIC
North Sea
Irish Sea
Celtic Sea
St George's Channel
English Channel
Bristol Channel
Cardigan Bay
UNITED KINGDOM
Great Britain
NORTHERN IRELAND
REPUBLIC OF IRELAND
Ireland
ENGLAND
WALES
FRANCE
ULSTER
CONNAUGHT
LEINSTER
MUNSTER
DUBLIN
LONDON
Belfast
Cardiff
Isle of Man (to U.K.)
Isle of Wight
Channel Islands (to U.K.)
Anglesey
Lake District
Pennines
Cambrian Mtns
Cotswold Hills
Chiltern Hills
Salisbury Plain
South Downs
The Fens
Exmoor
Dartmoor
Snowdon 3560ft (1085m)
Carrauntuohill 3415ft (1041m)
Cross Fell 2929ft (893m)
Whernside 2418ft (737m)
Manchester
Birmingham
Leeds
Liverpool
Sheffield
Bristol
Newcastle upon Tyne
Plymouth
Southampton
Norwich
Cork
Galway
Limerick
Waterford
Londonderry
Longitude west of Greenwich
ELEVATION
Feet Meters
6562 2000
4921 1500
3281 1000
2461 750
1640 500
1312 400
984 300
656 200
328 100
0 0
Below sea level
0 0
656 200
3281 1000
6562 2000
13,123 4000
19,685 6000
26,246 8000
32,808 10,000
SCALE 1:3,000,000
Lamberts Conformal Conic Projection
0 100 miles
0 100 kilometers

North Sea oil and gas fields have made the U.K. virtually self-sufficient in fossil fuels.

THE HIGHLANDS

The highest part of the British Isles, the Scottish Highlands rise from the Central Lowlands along the Highland Boundary Fault, which extends from Helensburgh in the southwest to Stonehaven in the northeast. They are split in two by another major fault, the Great Glen, which is partially filled by lakes including Loch Ness.

The Great Glen
Stonehaven
Inverness
Loch Ness
Grampian Mtns
Ben Nevis
Edinburgh
Fort William
Glasgow
Helensburgh

FRANCE France, Monaco

Occupying a large area on the western edge of Europe, France is the only country that extends from the North European Plain to the Mediterranean. The north and west are characterized by broad lowlands traversed by major rivers, including the Seine, Loire, Dordogne, and Garonne. A wide plateau, the Massif Central, covers much of the southern interior, and in the southeast the land rises steeply to the high peaks of the Alps. Along the southern border, the Pyrenees separate France from Spain. The tiny principality of Monaco—the second-smallest country in the world—occupies a coastal location within France, close to the border with Italy. France is a leading political, industrial, and agricultural force in Europe and has been at the forefront of European economic and social integration.

Paris France's largest city began as a small settlement on an island in the River Seine and became the national capital in AD 987. It is now home to over 9 million people, a major business and industrial center, and one of the world's top tourist destinations. Its splendid buildings include the cathedral of Notre-Dame, which dates from the 12th century, the 18th-century Panthéon, and France's most famous landmark, the Eiffel Tower, designed for the 1889 Paris Exposition.

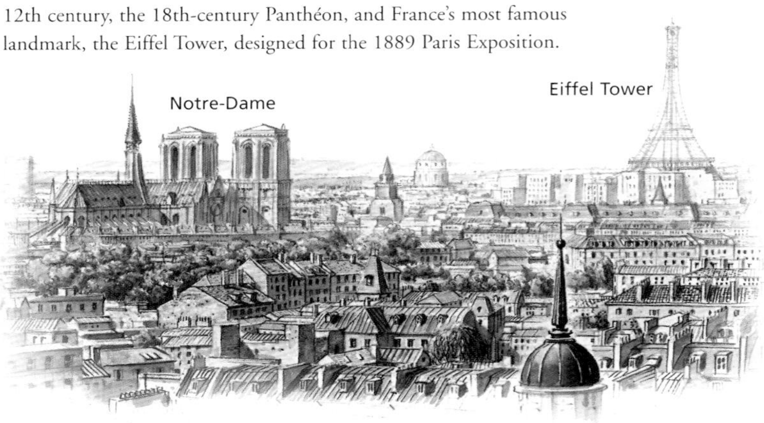

Notre-Dame
Eiffel Tower

Population Patterns

The most sparsely inhabited parts of France are the high-mountain regions of the Alps, Pyrenees, and Massif Central. In rural areas, the population is fairly evenly spread, though slightly higher levels of settlement occur along major river valleys and parts of the coast. About 76 percent of the country's inhabitants live in urban areas, with one-fifth of the total population concentrated in the Paris region, the Île-de-France.

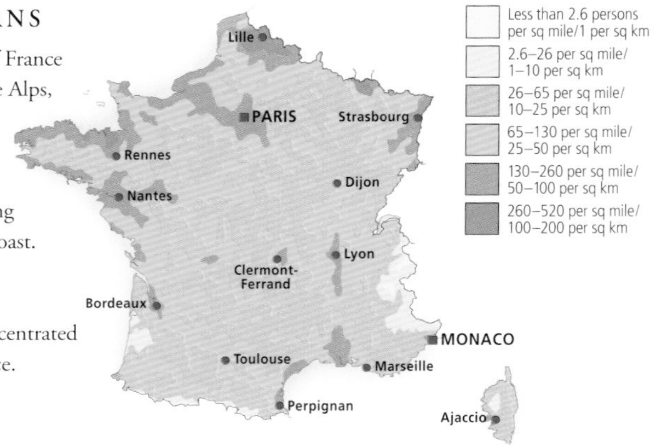

Lille
PARIS
Strasbourg
Rennes
Nantes
Dijon
Lyon
Clermont-Ferrand
Bordeaux
MONACO
Toulouse
Marseille
Perpignan
Ajaccio
Less than 2.6 persons per sq mile/1 per sq km
2.6–26 per sq mile/ 1–10 per sq km
26–65 per sq mile/ 10–25 per sq km
65–130 per sq mile/ 25–50 per sq km
130–260 per sq mile/ 50–100 per sq km
260–520 per sq mile/ 100–200 per sq km

Economic Profile

More than half of France is productive farmland, and the nation is one of the world's top exporters of agricultural produce. Important commodities include wheat, sugar beet, and wine (of which France is the world's largest producer). Metals, chemicals, cars, textiles, and aircraft are among the most vital manufactured goods. Services, including tourism, employ more than 70 percent of workers.

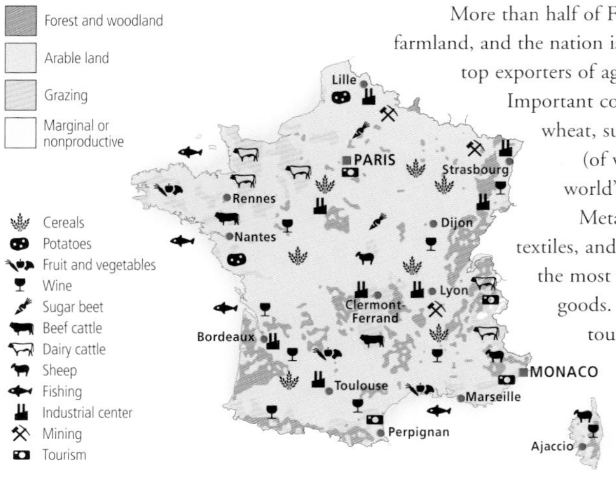

Forest and woodland
Arable land
Grazing
Marginal or nonproductive
Cereals
Potatoes
Fruit and vegetables
Wine
Sugar beet
Beef cattle
Dairy cattle
Sheep
Fishing
Industrial center
Mining
Tourism
Lille
PARIS
Strasbourg
Rennes
Nantes
Dijon
Lyon
Clermont-Ferrand
Bordeaux
MONACO
Toulouse
Marseille
Perpignan
Ajaccio

The Pyrenees

Viewed from southern France, the Pyrenees rise like a great wall, forming a seemingly insurmountable barrier. Indeed, most of the range, which stretches for more than 270 miles (435 km) from the Atlantic Ocean to the Mediterranean Sea, is more than 9,000 feet (2,700 m) high and can be crossed only via passes above 6,000 feet (1,800 m). The highest peak, Aneto in Spain, rises to 11,168 feet (3,404 m).

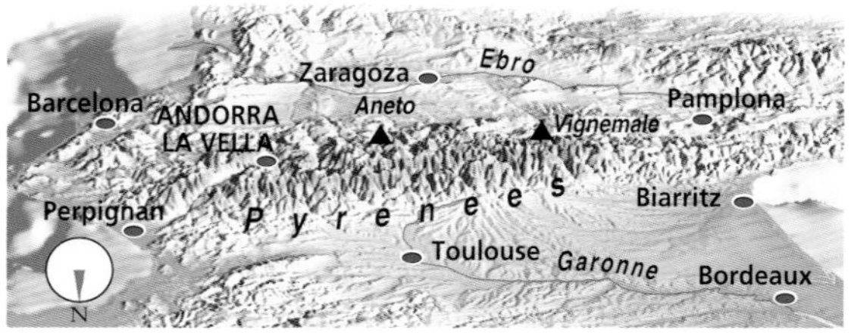

Zaragoza
Ebro
Barcelona
ANDORRA LA VELLA
Aneto
Vignemale
Pamplona
Perpignan
Pyrenees
Biarritz
Toulouse
Garonne
Bordeaux
N

UNITED KINGDOM
Exeter
Newport
Isle of Wight
Torquay
Plymouth
St Austell
Penzance
English Channel
Alderney
Cap de la Hague
Pointe de Barfleur
Cherbourg
Baie de Seine
Guernsey
St Peter Port
Sark
Valognes
Channel Islands (to U.K.)
Jersey
Carentan
Bayeux
St Helier
BASSE-NORMANDIE
Coutances
St-Lô
Golfe de St-Malo
Îles Chausey
Vire
Granville
Avranches
Paimpol
Lannion
St-Pol-de-Léon
Baie de St-Brieuc
Cap Fréhel
St-Malo
Le Mont-St-Michel
Ploudalmézeau
Morlaix
Île d'Ouessant
Brest
Guingamp
St-Brieuc
Pointe de St-Mathieu
Carhaix-Plouguer
Lamballe
Dinan
Fougères
Mer d'Iroise
Crozon
Châteaulin
Baie de Douarnenez
Douarnenez
Pointe du Raz
Loudéac
Ernée
Rennes
Audierne
BRETAGNE
Pontivy
Vitré
Baie de Audierne
Quimper
Laval
Quimperlé
Penmarch
Pointe de Penmarch
Ploërmel
Lorient
Îles de Glénan
Auray
Vannes
Châteaubriant
Îls de Groix
Muzillac
PAYS DE LA LOIRE
Quiberon
Nozay
Pontchâteau
Belle-Île
Le Palais
Ancenis
La Baule-Escoublac
St-Nazaire
Loire
Nantes
Embouchure de la Loire
Pointe de St-Gildas
Pornic
Baie de Bourgneuf
Clisson
Noirmoutier-en-l'Île
Île de Noirmoutier
Cholet
Montaigu
St-Jean-de-Monts
Challans
Les Herbiers
Île d'Yeu
La Roche-sur-Yon
Chantonnay
Les Sables-d'Olonne
Luçon
ATLANTIC OCEAN
Bay of Biscay
Pertuis Breton
Île de Ré
La Rochelle
POITOU
Pertuis d'Antioche
St-Pierre-d'Oléron
Île d'Oléron
Rochefort
Saintes
Royan
Cognac
Soulac-sur-Mer
Gironde
Lesparre-Médoc
Blaye
Lacanau
Libourne
Bordeaux
Andernos-les-Bains
Arcachon
Garonne
Langon
Sanguinet
AQUITAINE
Mimizan
Labouheyre
Sabres
Roquefort
Léon
Mont-de-Marsan
Dax
Aire-sur-l'Adour
Bayonne
Biarritz
Orthez
St-Jean-de-Luz
Bidache
St-Palais
Oloron-Ste-Marie
Pau
Pic d'Orhy 6617ft (2017m)
SPAIN
Vignemale 10,820ft (3298
Longitude west of Greenwich

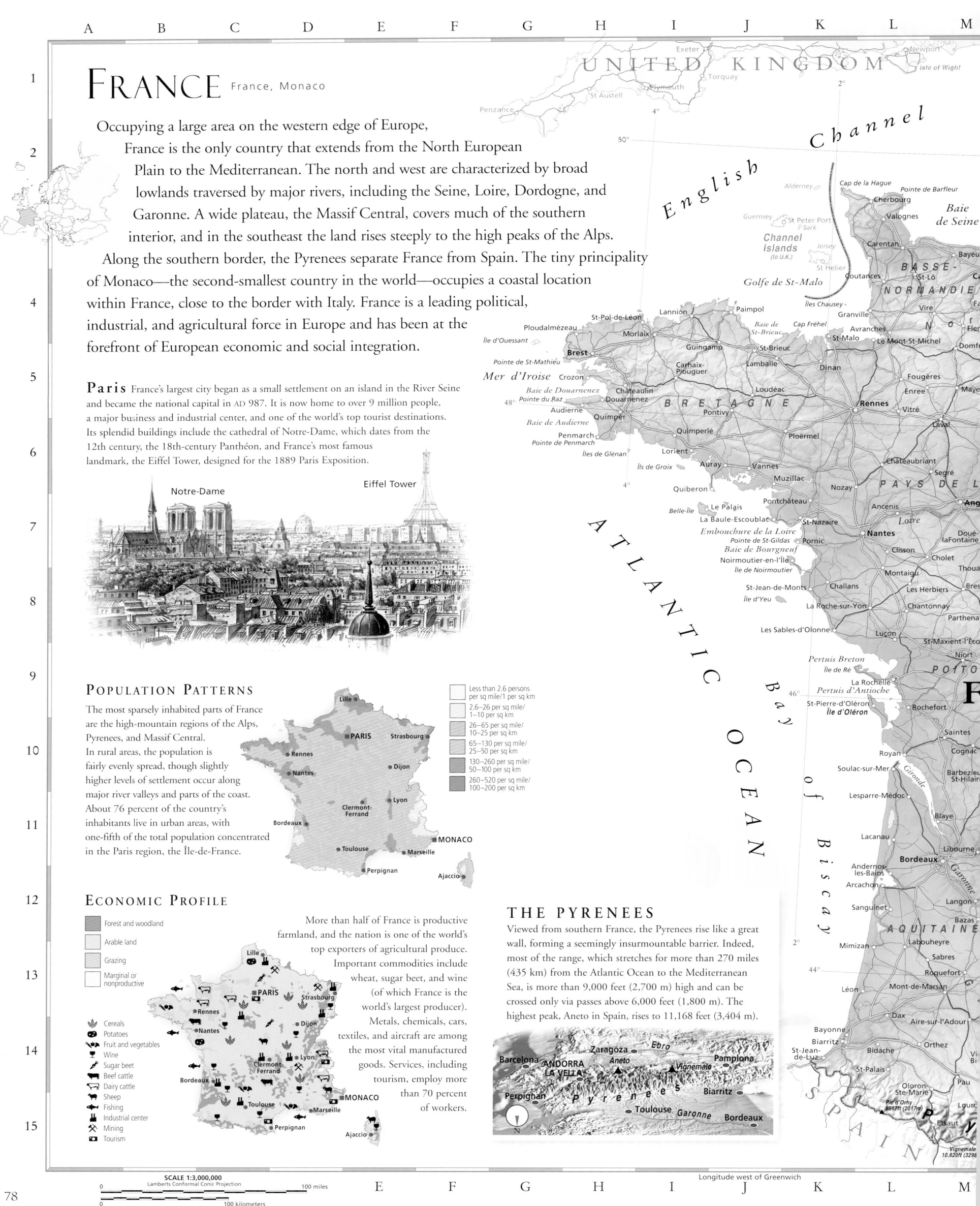

SCALE 1:3,000,000
Lamberts Conformal Conic Projection
0 100 miles
0 100 kilometers

N O R S T U V W X Y Z
1 2 3 4 5 6 7 8 9 10 11
FRANCE
BELGIUM
LUXEMBOURG
GERMANY
SWITZERLAND
ITALY
MONACO
ANDORRA
Strait of Dover
Channel Tunnel
Folkestone
Calais
Dunkerque
Boulogne-sur-Mer
Le Touquet-Paris-Plage
NORD-PAS-DE-CALAIS
Lille
Roubaix
Valenciennes
Mons
St-Omer
Lens
Arras
Douai
Maubeuge
Cambrai
Avesnes-sur-Helpe
Abbeville
Doullens
Le Tréport
Dieppe
Amiens
Albert
St-Quentin
Hirson
Vervins
Charleville-Mézières
Sedan
LUXEMBOURG
PICARDIE
HAUTE-NORMANDIE
Rouen
Beauvais
Compiègne
Noyon
Laon
Soissons
Reims
Rethel
Stenay
Longuyon
Thionville
Metz
Saarbrucken
Sarreguemines
Karlsruhe
Wissembourg
Verdun
Étain
Épernay
Châlons-en-Champagne
CHAMPAGNE-ARDENNE
LORRAINE
Nancy
Toul
Lunéville
Strasbourg
Kehl
Haguenau
Sarrebourg
Saverne
Pont-à-Mousson
Bar-le-Duc
Vitry-le-François
St Dizier
Joinville
Neufchâteau
Chaumont
Langres
Baccarat
St-Dié
Sélestat
ALSACE
Colmar
Mulhouse
Vosges
Rhine
Épinal
Vittel
Remiremont
Luxeuil-les-Bains
Belfort
Basel
Vesoul
Montbéliard
PARIS
Versailles
Orly
Meaux
Coulommiers
Melun
Fontainebleau
ÎLE-DE-FRANCE
Évreux
Pontoise
Senlis
Clermont
Mantes-la-Jolie
Dreux
Chartres
Étampes
Provins
Sézanne
Troyes
Seine
Sens
Auxerre
Tonnerre
Châtillon-sur-Seine
Montbard
Dijon
Beaune
Saône
BOURGOGNE
FRANCHE-COMTÉ
Besançon
Dôle
Gray
Pontarlier
Jura
Lons-le-Saunier
Chalon-sur-Saône
Mâcon
Tournus
Cluny
Autun
Nevers
Moulins
Vichy
Loire
Orléans
Blois
Tours
Vendôme
Châteaudun
Pithiviers
Montargis
Gien
CENTRE
Bourges
Vierzon
Châteauroux
Poitiers
Châtellerault
Chinon
Loches
Le Mans
Limoges
LIMOUSIN
AUVERGNE
Clermont-Ferrand
Massif Central
Aurillac
Le-Puy-en-Velay
St-Étienne
Lyon
Villefranche-sur-Saône
Bourg-en-Bresse
Roanne
Vienne
RHÔNE-ALPES
Grenoble
Chambéry
Annecy
Geneva
Lake Geneva
Lausanne
Thonon-les-Bains
BERN
Mont Blanc 15,771ft (4807m)
Chamonix-Mont-Blanc
Alps
Mont Thabor 10,512ft (3204m)
Briançon
Mont Pelat 10,010ft (3051m)
Mont Ventoux 6263ft (1909m)
Turin
Valence
Rhône
Avignon
Orange
Nîmes
Arles
Montpellier
Marseille
Aix-en-Provence
Toulon
Nice
Cannes
Antibes
MONACO
Monte Carlo
PROVENCE-ALPES-CÔTE-D'AZUR
Côte d'Azur
Îles de Hyères
Île de Porquerolles
Golfe du Lion
MEDITERRANEAN SEA
Sète
Béziers
Narbonne
Perpignan
Carcassonne
LANGUEDOC-ROUSSILLON
Toulouse
MIDI-PYRÉNÉES
Pyrénées
Garonne
Dordogne
Montauban
Albi
Rodez
Cahors
Pic d'Estats 10,220 ft (3115m)
Puigmal 9547ft (2910m)
Port-Vendres
Longitude east of Greenwich

The Arc de Triomphe in Paris was commissioned by Napoleon in 1806 to celebrate his military victories.

Located on the French–Italian border, Mont Blanc, at 15,771 feet (4,807 m), is the Alps' highest peak.

Monaco measures a mere 0.75 square miles (1.95 sq km). Its tourist facilities and casino are among its principal sources of revenue.

The mountainous island of Corsica was purchased by France from the city-state of Genoa in 1768.

SCALE 1:4,000,000
Corsica (to France)
Calvi
Bastia
Rogliano
Vescovato
Monte Cinto 8878ft (2706m)
Monte Rotondo 8602ft (2622m)
Aléria
Ajaccio
Solenzara
Monte Incudine 7008ft (2136m)
Sartène
Porto-Vecchio
Bonifacio
Tyrrhenian Sea
Longitude east of Greenwich

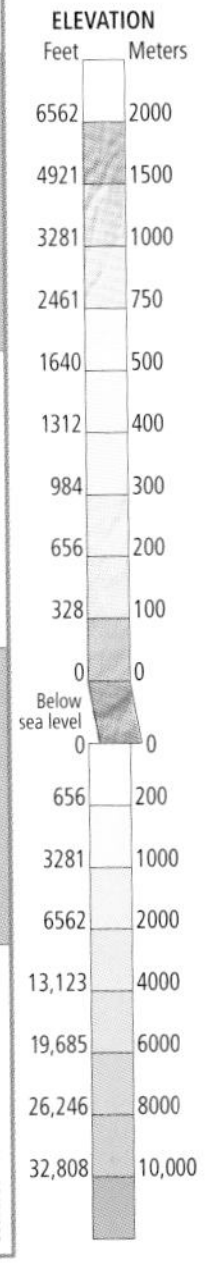
ELEVATION
Feet Meters
6562 2000
4921 1500
3281 1000
2461 750
1640 500
1312 400
984 300
656 200
328 100
0 0
Below sea level
656 200
3281 1000
6562 2000
13,123 4000
19,685 6000
26,246 8000
32,808 10,000

The Iberian Peninsula

Andorra, Portugal, Spain

Located at the southwestern edge of Europe, the wide, almost square-shaped Iberian Peninsula is flanked by the Atlantic Ocean to the west and by the Mediterranean Sea to the east. It is separated from France by the Pyrenees, and from Africa by the Strait of Gibraltar, which is just 8 miles (12.8 km) wide at its narrowest point. Spain occupies more than 80 percent of the landmass, Portugal almost all of the remainder; the tiny principality of Andorra nestles in the eastern Pyrenees. A large plateau, the Meseta, extends across much of the peninsula. It is bisected by the Sistema Central mountain chain and fringed by other ranges. Between the 15th and 17th centuries, Spain and Portugal ruled vast empires. But their 20th-century histories were marred by war and repressive regimes, and their economies are still recovering.

Completed in 1521, the Torre de Belém was built to protect the city of Lisbon.

In Spain's Castilla-La Mancha region, medieval windmills dot flat, semiarid plains.

Population Patterns

In Spain, rapid industrial growth in the late 20th century led to significant urbanization, with the result that 78 percent of the population now live in cities—17 percent in Madrid and Barcelona. The temperate coastal areas are generally more densely inhabited than the less fertile Meseta. In Portugal, the south is more sparsely populated than the north, with the exception of Lisbon and the crowded coastal region of the Algarve.

Bilbao
Donostia-San Sebastián
ANDORRA LA VELLA
Zaragoza
Barcelona
Porto
MADRID
Valencia
LISBON
Murcia
Seville
Cádiz
Málaga
GIBRALTAR

- Less than 2.6 persons per sq mile/1 per sq km
- 2.6–26 per sq mile/1–10 per sq km
- 26–65 per sq mile/10–25 per sq km
- 65–130 per sq mile/25–50 per sq km
- 130–260 per sq mile/50–100 per sq km

Economic Profile

Investment in agriculture is low relative to the European average and small farms are the norm. The region is renowned for its abundant fruit and vegetables; other major crops include cereals, wine grapes, and olives. About one-third of the land is forested, and Portugal is the world's foremost supplier of cork. Textiles and footwear, paper and paper products, chemicals, metals, and tourism are the leading industries; automobile production is also important in Spain. Andorra relies heavily on tourism and its duty-free retail trade.

Bilbao
Donostia-San Sebastián
ANDORRA LA VELLA
Zaragoza
Barcelona
Porto
MADRID
Valencia
LISBON
Murcia
Seville
Cádiz
Málaga
GIBRALTAR

- Forest and woodland
- Arable land
- Grazing
- Cereals
- Citrus fruits
- Wine
- Olives
- Beef cattle
- Sheep
- Industrial center
- Mining
- Timber
- Tourism
- Fishing

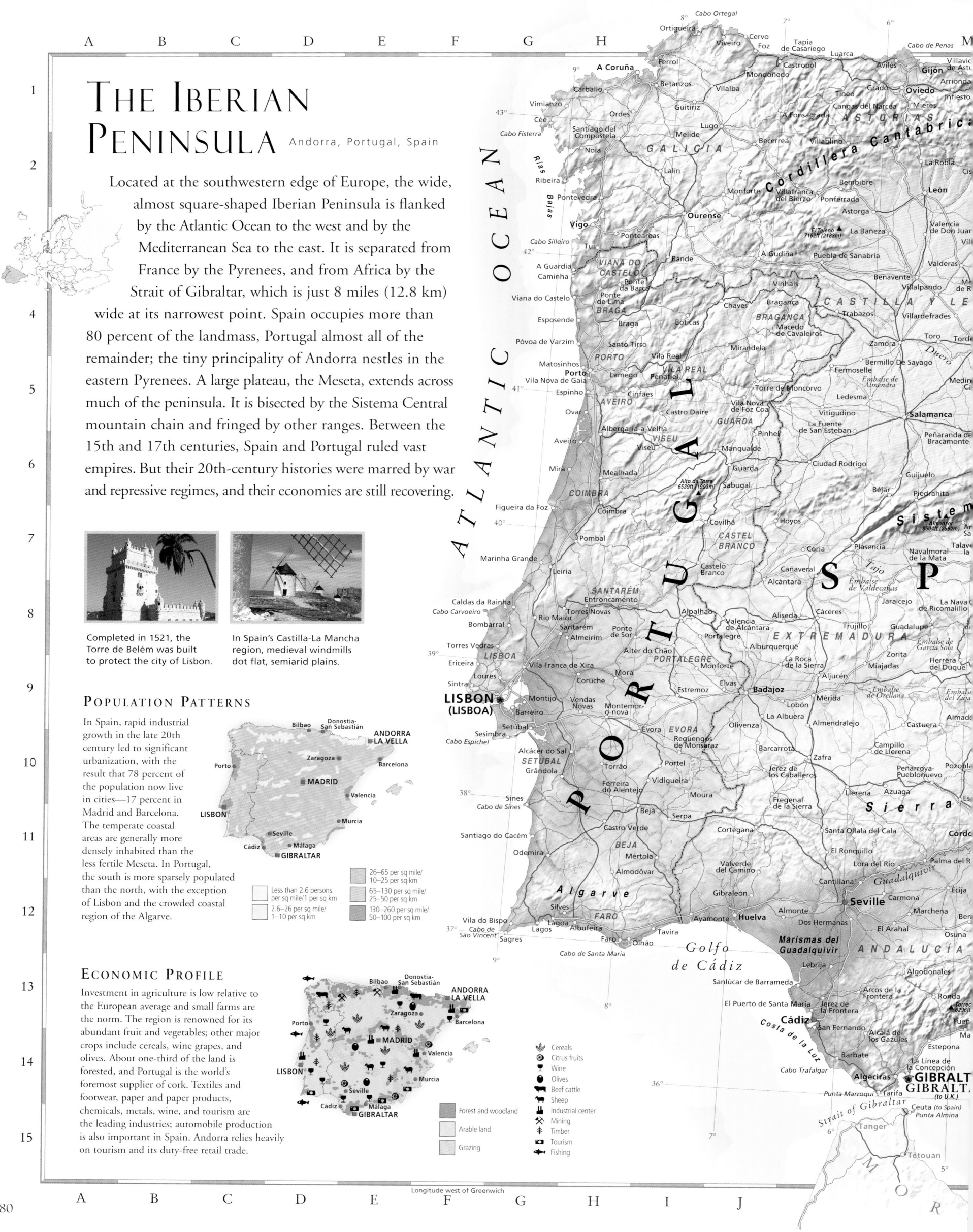

ATLANTIC OCEAN
PORTUGAL
SP
GALICIA
ASTURIAS
Cordillera Cantabrica
CASTILLA Y LE
EXTREMADURA
ANDALUCÍA
Algarve
Golfo de Cádiz
Costa de la Luz
Strait of Gibraltar
Cabo Ortegal
A Coruña
Ferrol
Lugo
Santiago del Compostela
Cabo Fisterra
Rías Baixas
Pontevedra
Vigo
Ourense
Cabo Silleiro
VIANA DO CASTELO
Viana do Castelo
BRAGA
Braga
BRAGANÇA
Bragança
PORTO
Porto
VILA REAL
Vila Real
AVEIRO
VISEU
Viseu
GUARDA
Guarda
COIMBRA
Coimbra
Alto da Torre 6539ft (1993m)
CASTEL BRANCO
Castelo Branco
SANTARÉM
LISBOA
LISBON (LISBOA)
PORTALEGRE
EVORA
Evora
SETÚBAL
Setúbal
Cabo Espichel
Cabo de Sines
BEJA
Beja
FARO
Faro
Cabo de São Vincent
Cabo de Santa Maria
Gijón
Oviedo
León
El Teleno 7162ft (2183m)
Zamora
Duero
Salamanca
Almanzor 8504ft (2592m)
Tajo
Embalse de Valdecañas
Badajoz
Mérida
Sierra
Guadalquivir
Seville
Huelva
Marismas del Guadalquivir
Cádiz
Cabo Trafalgar
Algeciras
GIBRALTAR (to U.K.)
Ceuta (to Spain)
Punta Almina
Tanger
Tétouan
MOR
Longitude west of Greenwich

N O P Q R S T U V W X Y Z
1 2 3 4 5 6 7 8 9 10 11
F R A N C E
Pyrenees
ANDORRA
ANDORRA LA VELLA
Santander
Bilbao
Donostia-San Sebastián
Vitoria-Gasteiz
Pamplona
Logroño
Burgos
Zaragoza
Lleida
Barcelona
L'Hospitalet de Llobregat
Sabadell
Tarragona
Perpignan
Girona
CANTABRIA
PAIS VASCO
NAVARRA
LA RIOJA
CATALUÑA
ARAGÓN
VALENCIA
MURCIA
CASTILLA-LA MANCHA
MADRID
Sistema Ibérico
Sistemas Béticos
Ebro
Costa Brava
Costa Dorada
Costa del Azahar
Costa Blanca
Costa del Sol
Golf de Sant Jordi
Mouth of the Ebro
Golfo de Valencia
Castelló de la Plana
Valencia
Albacete
Alicante
Elche
Murcia
Cartagena
Almería
Granada
Málaga
Jaén
Toledo
Cuenca
Teruel
Balearic Islands
Minorca
Mahón
Majorca
Palma
Ibiza
Eivissa
Formentera
Cabrera
Islas Columbretes
MEDITERRANEAN SEA
Alboran Sea
Isla de Alborán
Melilla (to Spain)
Nador
Al Hoceima
Orhi 6631ft (2021m)
Vignemale 10,820ft (3298m)
Aneto 11,168ft (3404m)
Pic d'Estats 10,220ft (3115m)
Puigmal d'Err 9547ft (2910m)
Cebollera 7041ft (2146m)
Peñalara 7972ft (2430m)
Aitana 5112ft (1558m)
Sagra 7815ft (2382m)
Magina 7110ft (2167m)
Tetica de Becares 6850ft (2088m)
Mulhacén 11,421ft (3481m)
ELEVATION
Feet Meters
6562 2000
4921 1500
3281 1000
2461 750
1640 500
1312 400
984 300
656 200
328 100
0 0
Below sea level
0 0
656 200
3281 1000
6562 2000
13,123 4000
19,685 6000
26,246 8000
32,808 10,000
Longitude east of Greenwich

THE SISTEMAS BÉTICOS

In southeastern Spain, a mountain chain, known as the Sistemas Béticos or Baetic Cordillera, extends from Punta Marroquí on the Strait of Gibraltar to Cabo de la Nao on the Costa Blanca. Incorporating numerous small ranges, it rises to its highest point of 11,421 feet (3,481 m) at Mulhacén, northwest of Almería. East of Cabo de la Nao, the chain continues beneath the Mediterranean Sea—the Balearic Islands of Ibiza, Majorca, and Minorca are the summits of its submerged slopes.

N
MADRID
Valencia
Sistemas Béticos
Mulhacén
Alicante
Balearic Islands
Palma
Majorca
Minorca
Ibiza
GIBRALTAR
Almeria
Oran
ALGIERS

SCALE 1:3,000,000
Lamberts Conformal Conic Projection
0 100 miles
0 100 kilometers

THE LOW COUNTRIES

Belgium, Luxembourg, Netherlands

Situated on the northwestern fringe of mainland Europe, the Low Countries live up to their name. Not only is much of the landscape flat, but one-third of the Netherlands lies *below* sea level. The only large-scale upland formation is the densely wooded plateau of the Ardennes, which spreads across southern Belgium and northern Luxembourg. More than 3,000 square miles (8,000 sq km) of the Low Countries was reclaimed from the sea, mainly by building dikes across shallow estuaries then draining the land behind these barriers. The reclaimed areas are known as polders. The region's three nations have long-established trading, political, and cultural connections. Belgium is divided ethnically between its Dutch-speaking (Flemish) north and French-speaking (Walloon) south. French is also spoken widely in Luxembourg, along with German and the official language of Letzeburgish.

Situated at the junction of several canals, Bruges derives most of its revenue from tourism and light industry.

Every year, 9 billion bulbs are grown in the Netherlands, one-third of which are tulips.

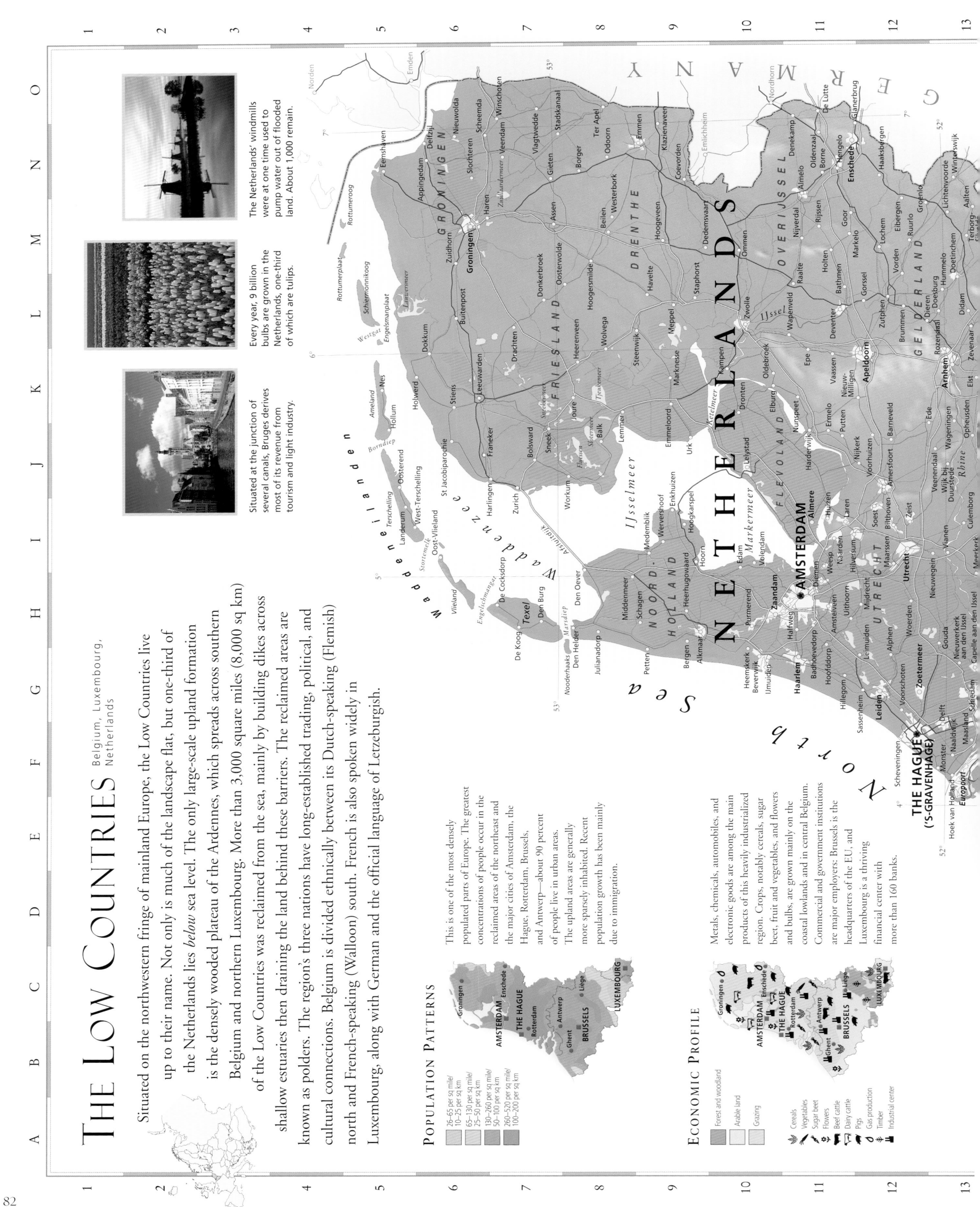

The Netherlands' windmills were at one time used to pump water out of flooded land. About 1,000 remain.

Population Patterns

26–65 per sq mile/ 10–25 per sq km
65–130 per sq mile/ 25–50 per sq km
130–260 per sq mile/ 50–100 per sq km
260–520 per sq mile/ 100–200 per sq km
Groningen
AMSTERDAM
Enschede
THE HAGUE
Rotterdam
Antwerp
Ghent
BRUSSELS
Liège
LUXEMBOURG

This is one of the most densely populated parts of Europe. The greatest concentrations of people occur in the reclaimed areas of the northeast and the major cities of Amsterdam, the Hague, Rotterdam, Brussels, and Antwerp—about 90 percent of people live in urban areas. The upland areas are generally more sparsely inhabited. Recent population growth has been mainly due to immigration.

Economic Profile

Forest and woodland
Arable land
Grazing
Cereals
Vegetables
Sugar beet
Flowers
Beef cattle
Dairy cattle
Pigs
Gas production
Timber
Industrial center
Groningen
AMSTERDAM
Enschede
THE HAGUE
Rotterdam
Antwerp
Ghent
BRUSSELS
Liège
LUXEMBOURG

Metals, chemicals, automobiles, and electronic goods are among the main products of this heavily industrialized region. Crops, notably cereals, sugar beet, fruit and vegetables, and flowers and bulbs, are grown mainly on the coastal lowlands and in central Belgium. Commercial and government institutions are major employers: Brussels is the headquarters of the EU, and Luxembourg is a thriving financial center with more than 160 banks.

NETHERLANDS
GERMANY
North Sea
Waddeneilanden
Waddenzee
IJsselmeer
Markermeer
GRONINGEN
FRIESLAND
DRENTHE
NOORD-HOLLAND
FLEVOLAND
OVERIJSSEL
UTRECHT
GELDERLAND
AMSTERDAM
THE HAGUE ('S-GRAVENHAGE)
Groningen
Leeuwarden
Haarlem
Zaandam
Utrecht
Apeldoorn
Enschede
Arnhem
Zwolle
Almere
Leiden
Zoetermeer
Texel
Vlieland
Terschelling
Ameland
Schiermonnikoog
Afsluitdijk
Rhine
IJssel

BELGIUM
GERMANY
FRANCE
LUXEMBOURG
BRUSSELS (BRUSSEL/BRUXELLES)
ZEELAND
NOORD-BRABANT
LIMBURG
ANTWERPEN
OOST-VLAANDEREN
WEST-VLAANDEREN
VLAAMS BRABANT
BRABANT WALLON
HAINAUT
NAMUR
LIÈGE
LUXEMBOURG
DIEKIRCH
GREVENMACHER
Flanders
Ardennes
Antwerp
Ghent
Bruges
Oostende
Breda
Tilburg
Eindhoven
Maastricht
Aachen
Liège
Namur
Charleroi
Mons
Leuven
Mechelen
Kortrijk
Hasselt
Tournai
Maas
Meuse
Escaut
Sambre
Semois
Ourthe
Westerschelde
Oosterschelde
Signal de Botrange 2277ft (694m)
Baraque de Fraiture 2139ft (652m)
Longitude east of Greenwich
A B C D E F G H I J K L
14 15 16 17 18 19 20 21 22 23 24 25 26
ELEVATION
Feet Meters
6562 2000
4921 1500
3281 1000
2461 750
1640 500
1312 400
984 300
656 200
328 100
0 0
Below sea level
0 0
656 200
3281 1000
6562 2000
13,123 4000
19,685 6000
26,246 8000
32,808 10,000
SCALE 1:1,100,000
Lamberts Conformal Conic Projection
0 30 miles
0 30 kilometers

Amsterdam

In the 13th century, Amsterdam was a fishing village on the Amstel River. By the late 16th century, following an influx of people and funds from other parts of war-ravaged Europe, it had become the world's foremost financial and commercial center. Now one of the Netherlands' two capitals (the Hague is the seat of national government), Amsterdam spreads across 90 islands linked by more than 1,000 bridges. Elegant churches and gabled houses line the canals, which are plied by tourist boats and traditional wooden barges.

The European Parliament meets at this building in Brussels, as well as others in Luxembourg and in Strasbourg, France.

Luxembourg's Grand Ducal Palace has been the home of the head of state (the Grand Duke) since the 1890s.

SCANDINAVIA

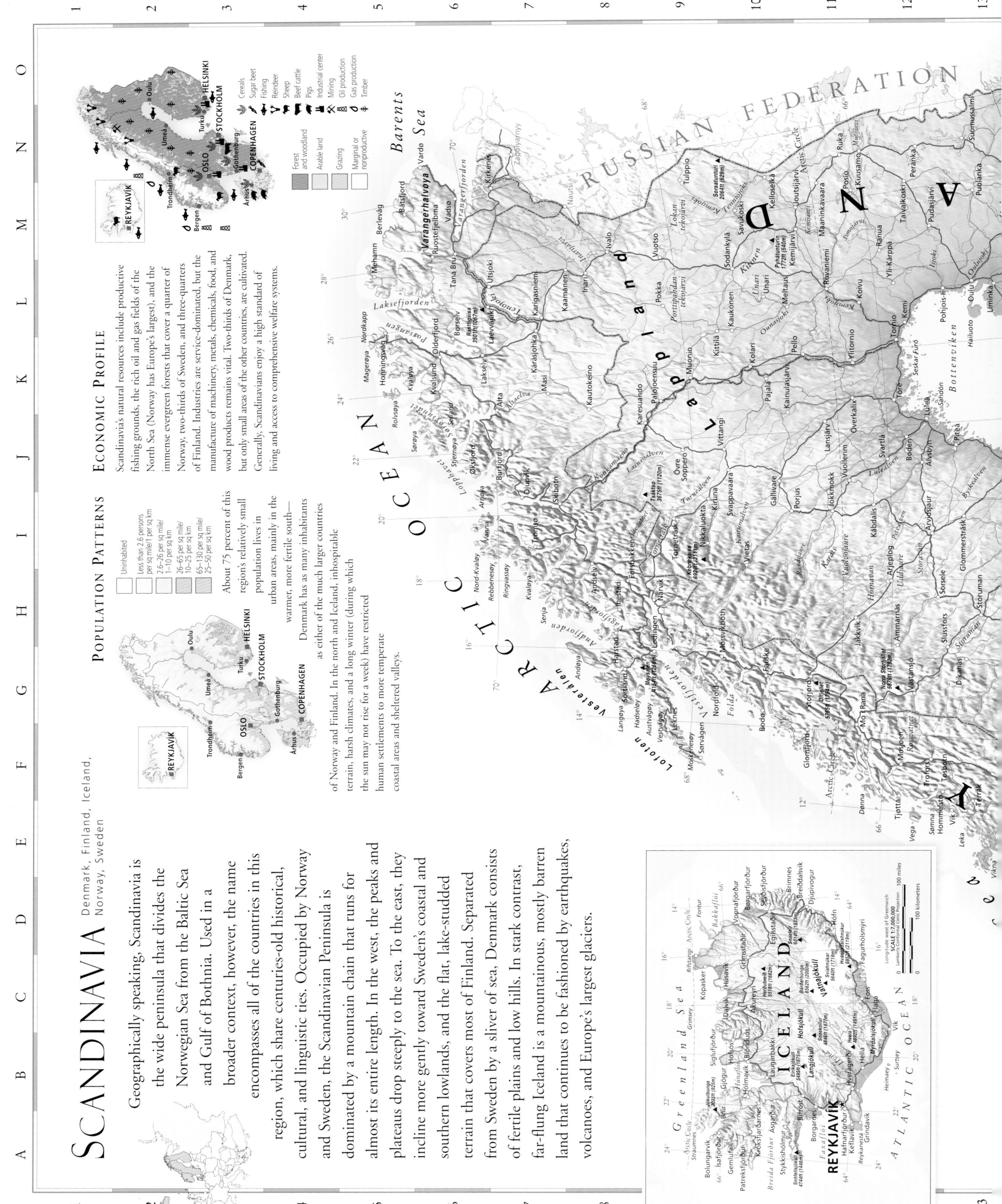

Denmark, Finland, Iceland, Norway, Sweden

Geographically speaking, Scandinavia is the wide peninsula that divides the Norwegian Sea from the Baltic Sea and Gulf of Bothnia. Used in a broader context, however, the name encompasses all of the countries in this region, which share centuries-old historical, cultural, and linguistic ties. Occupied by Norway and Sweden, the Scandinavian Peninsula is dominated by a mountain chain that runs for almost its entire length. In the west, the peaks and plateaus drop steeply to the sea. To the east, they incline more gently toward Sweden's coastal and southern lowlands, and the flat, lake-studded terrain that covers most of Finland. Separated from Sweden by a sliver of sea, Denmark consists of fertile plains and low hills. In stark contrast, far-flung Iceland is a mountainous, mostly barren land that continues to be fashioned by earthquakes, volcanoes, and Europe's largest glaciers.

Population Patterns

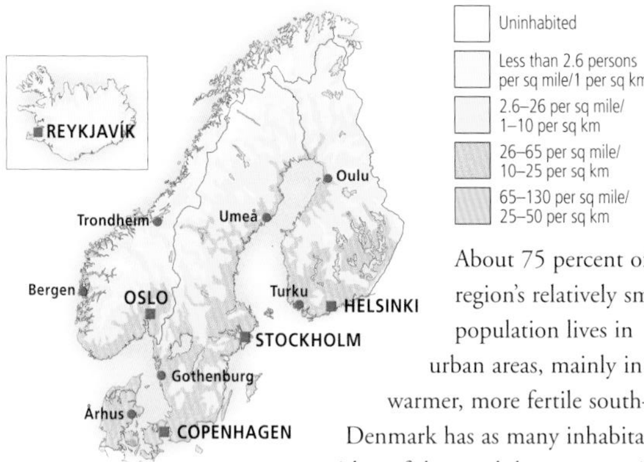
REYKJAVÍK
Trondheim
Umeå
Oulu
Bergen
OSLO
Turku
HELSINKI
STOCKHOLM
Gothenburg
Århus
COPENHAGEN
Uninhabited
Less than 2.6 persons per sq mile/1 per sq km
2.6–26 per sq mile/ 1–10 per sq km
26–65 per sq mile/ 10–25 per sq km
65–130 per sq mile/ 25–50 per sq km

About 75 percent of this region's relatively small population lives in urban areas, mainly in the warmer, more fertile south—Denmark has as many inhabitants as either of the much larger countries of Norway and Finland. In the north and Iceland, inhospitable terrain, harsh climates, and a long winter (during which the sun may not rise for a week) have restricted human settlements to more temperate coastal areas and sheltered valleys.

Economic Profile

Scandinavia's natural resources include productive fishing grounds, the rich oil and gas fields of the North Sea (Norway has Europe's largest), and the immense evergreen forests that cover a quarter of Norway, two-thirds of Sweden, and three-quarters of Finland. Industries are service-dominated, but the manufacture of machinery, metals, chemicals, food, and wood products remains vital. Two-thirds of Denmark, but only small areas of the other countries, are cultivated. Generally, Scandinavians enjoy a high standard of living and access to comprehensive welfare systems.

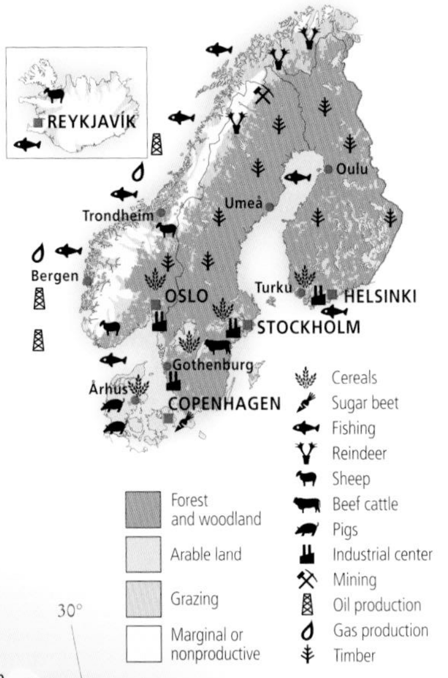
REYKJAVÍK
Trondheim
Bergen
Umeå
Oulu
OSLO
Turku
HELSINKI
STOCKHOLM
Gothenburg
Århus
COPENHAGEN
Forest and woodland
Arable land
Grazing
Marginal or nonproductive
Cereals
Sugar beet
Fishing
Reindeer
Sheep
Beef cattle
Pigs
Industrial center
Mining
Oil production
Gas production
Timber

ARCTIC OCEAN
Barents Sea
RUSSIAN FEDERATION
Lappland
Mageroya
Nordkapp
Honningsvåg
Mehamn
Berlevåg
Båtsfjord
Vardø
Varangerhalvøya
Vadsø
Kirkenes
Tana Bru
Alta
Hammerfest
Tromsø
Narvik
Kiruna
Gällivare
Bodø
Harstad
Lofoten
Vesterålen
Andøya
Senja
Inari
Ivalo
Sodankylä
Rovaniemi
Kemi
Tornio
Oulu
Luleå
Piteå
Boden
Jokkmokk
Arvidsjaur
Mo i Rana
Mosjøen
Kautokeino
Karasjohka
Karesuando
Muonio
Kittilä
Pello
Kemijärvi
Kuusamo
Bottenviken

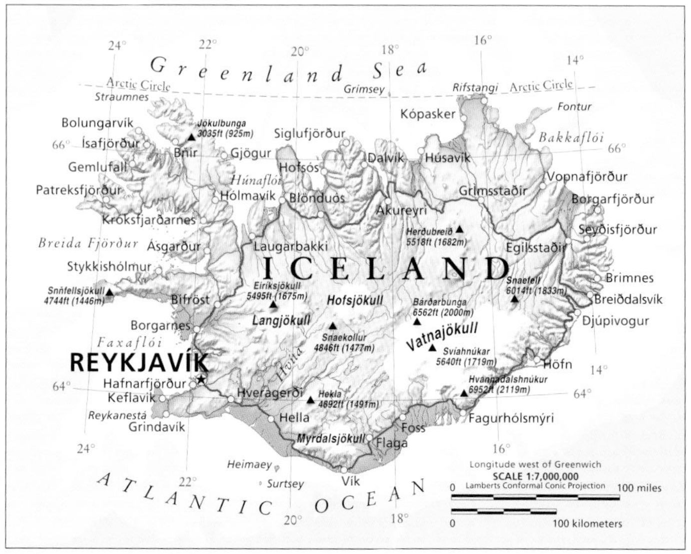
Greenland Sea
ICELAND
REYKJAVÍK
Akureyri
Húsavík
Ísafjörður
Vatnajökull
Langjökull
Hofsjökull
Mýrdalsjökull
Hekla
Keflavík
Hafnarfjörður
Egilsstaðir
Seyðisfjörður
Höfn
Vík
Surtsey
Heimaey
Arctic Circle
ATLANTIC OCEAN
Faxaflói
Breiða Fjörður
SCALE 1:7,000,000
Lamberts Conformal Conic Projection
Longitude west of Greenwich
100 miles
100 kilometers

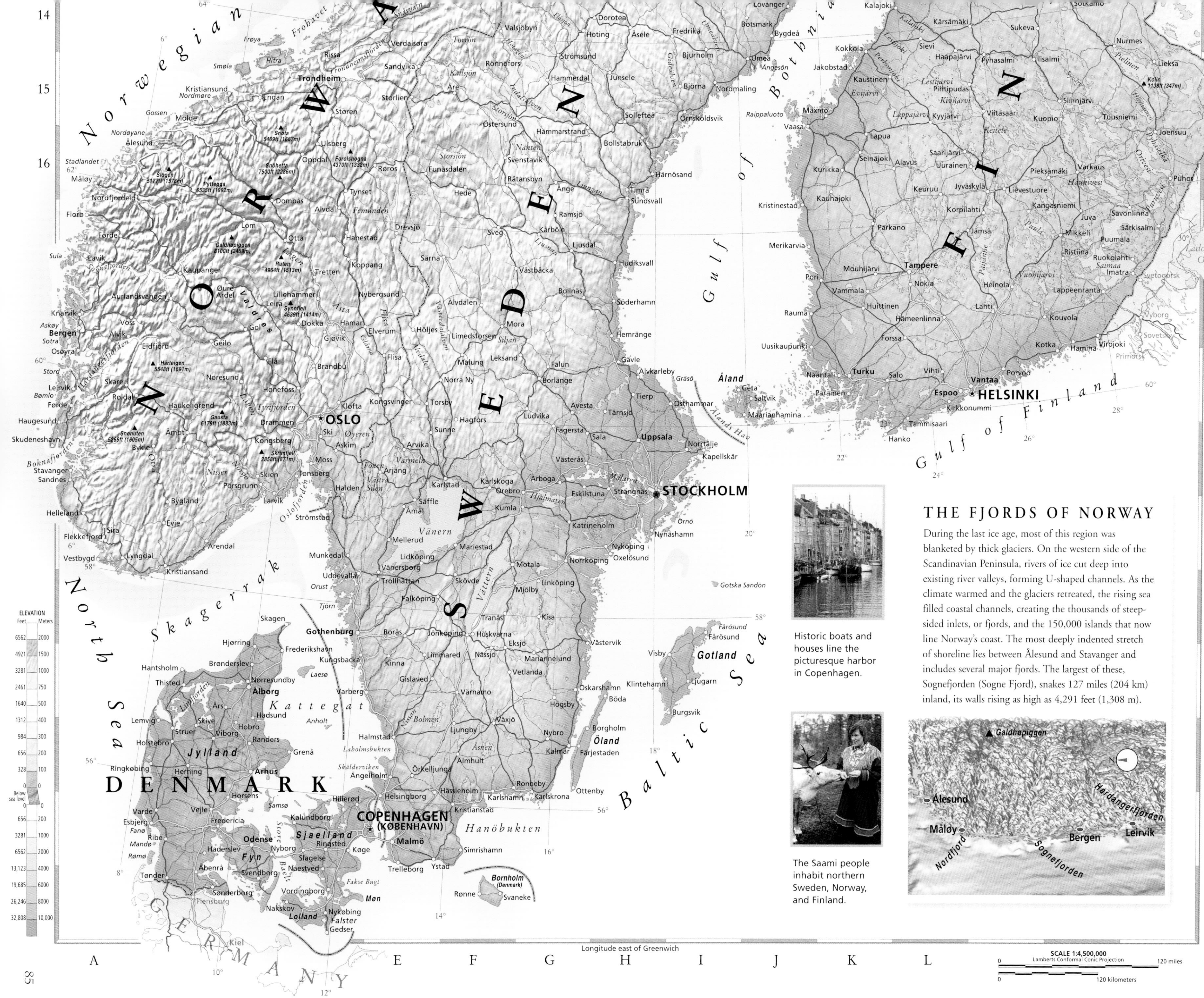
NORWAY
SWEDEN
FINLAND
DENMARK
GERMANY
Norwegian Sea
North Sea
Skagerrak
Kattegat
Baltic Sea
Gulf of Bothnia
Gulf of Finland
OSLO
STOCKHOLM
HELSINKI
COPENHAGEN (KØBENHAVN)
Trondheim
Bergen
Stavanger
Kristiansand
Gothenburg
Malmö
Uppsala
Turku
Tampere
Vantaa
Espoo
Åland
Gotland
Öland
Bornholm (Denmark)
Jylland
Fyn
Sjælland
Lolland
Falster
Møn
Vänern
Vättern
Galdhøpiggen 8100ft (2469m)
Longitude east of Greenwich
ELEVATION
Feet Meters
6562 2000
4921 1500
3281 1000
2461 750
1640 500
1312 400
984 300
656 200
328 100
0 0
Below sea level
0 0
656 200
3281 1000
6562 2000
13,123 4000
19,685 6000
26,246 8000
32,808 10,000
SCALE 1:4,500,000
Lamberts Conformal Conic Projection
0 120 miles
0 120 kilometers

Historic boats and houses line the picturesque harbor in Copenhagen.

The Saami people inhabit northern Sweden, Norway, and Finland.

THE FJORDS OF NORWAY

During the last ice age, most of this region was blanketed by thick glaciers. On the western side of the Scandinavian Peninsula, rivers of ice cut deep into existing river valleys, forming U-shaped channels. As the climate warmed and the glaciers retreated, the rising sea filled coastal channels, creating the thousands of steep-sided inlets, or fjords, and the 150,000 islands that now line Norway's coast. The most deeply indented stretch of shoreline lies between Ålesund and Stavanger and includes several major fjords. The largest of these, Sognefjorden (Sogne Fjord), snakes 127 miles (204 km) inland, its walls rising as high as 4,291 feet (1,308 m).

GERMANY

When East Germany and West Germany merged in October 1990, the reunified nation became the most populous country in Europe. More than 80 million people dwell in this broad land, which stretches south from the North and Baltic seas to the northern flank of the Alps. Germany can be divided into three main physical regions. In the northern lowlands, wide rivers, including the Elbe and Weser, meander seaward across expansive, sandy plains. A complex series of basins, partially wooded plateaus, and mountains extends across the center of the country. In the south, beyond the valley of the Main, stand the nation's highest ranges: the Black Forest, Swabian Alp, and Bavarian Alps. The great Rhine River, a historic artery of trade, defines the nation's southwestern boundaries. Continuing north, it cuts through the central uplands before veering westward across the plains to the Netherlands. Despite the economic and social challenges posed by reunification, Germany has retained its position as Europe's leading industrial power.

Population Patterns

Until the 19th century, Germany was divided into numerous small states with their own capitals and trading centers. As a result, its population is highly urbanized but fairly evenly distributed. Dense concentrations of inhabitants occur at the confluence of the Rhine and Ruhr rivers—the industrial heartland—and around Leipzig and Dresden in the east. Immigration has been the main contributor to recent population growth—10 million incomers settled in West Germany between 1950 and 1990.

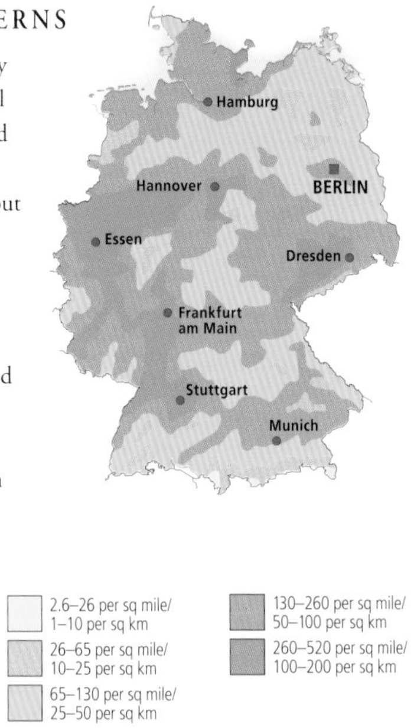

Hamburg
Hannover
BERLIN
Essen
Dresden
Frankfurt am Main
Stuttgart
Munich
2.6–26 per sq mile/ 1–10 per sq km
26–65 per sq mile/ 10–25 per sq km
65–130 per sq mile/ 25–50 per sq km
130–260 per sq mile/ 50–100 per sq km
260–520 per sq mile/ 100–200 per sq km

Economic Profile

West Germany staged a remarkable economic recovery after the Second World War, and Germany is now the third-largest industrial power after the U.S.A. and Japan. The mainstays of manufacturing are machinery, automobiles, iron and steel, chemicals, electrical goods, and food and beverages. Two of the most significant agricultural products are wine and beer; cereals, potatoes, and sugar beet are also grown widely. The largest pastures are in the northwest, but dairying takes place throughout the country.

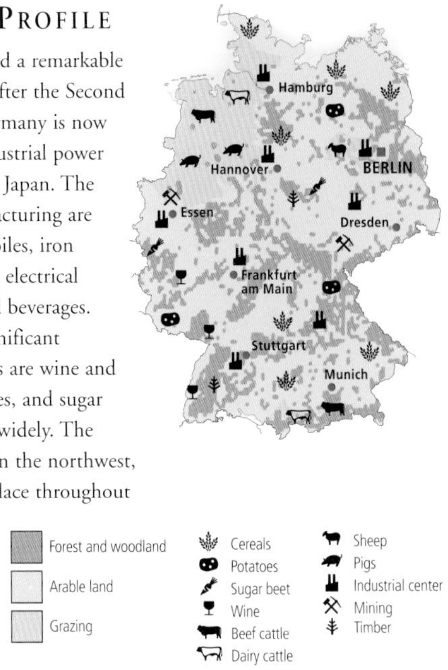

Hamburg
Hannover
BERLIN
Essen
Dresden
Frankfurt am Main
Stuttgart
Munich
Forest and woodland
Arable land
Grazing
Cereals
Potatoes
Sugar beet
Wine
Beef cattle
Dairy cattle
Sheep
Pigs
Industrial center
Mining
Timber

North Sea
Baltic Sea
DENMARK
POLAND
NETHERLANDS
SCHLESWIG-HOLSTEIN
MECKLENBURG-VORPOMMERN
NIEDERSACHSEN
SACHSEN-ANHALT
BREMEN
Nordfriesische Inseln
Ostfriesische Inseln
Helgoländer Bucht
Kieler Bucht
Mecklenburger Bucht
Lübecker Bucht
Fehmarnbelt
Pommersche Bucht
Rügen
Fehmarn
Hamburg
Kiel
Lübeck
Rostock
Schwerin
Bremen
Bremerhaven
Oldenburg
Wolfsburg
BERLIN
Potsdam
Elbe
Weser
Oder

Construction of Cologne Cathedral, the largest Gothic church in Northern Europe, began in 1248 but was not completed until 1880.

GERMANY
BELGIUM
LUXEMBOURG
FRANCE
SWITZERLAND
AUSTRIA
CZECH REPUBLIC
BRANDENBURG
SACHSEN
THÜRINGEN
HESSEN
NORDRHEIN-WESTFALEN
RHEINLAND-PFALZ
SAARLAND
BADEN-WÜRTTEMBERG
BAYERN
Bielefeld
Münster
Essen
Dortmund
Düsseldorf
Cologne
Bonn
Aachen
Koblenz
Frankfurt am Main
Wiesbaden
Mainz
Mannheim
Heidelberg
Karlsruhe
Stuttgart
Freiburg im Breisgau
Ulm
Augsburg
Munich
Nuremberg
Würzburg
Regensburg
Ingolstadt
Erfurt
Jena
Leipzig
Halle
Dresden
Chemnitz
Göttingen
Kassel
Harz
Rothaargebirge
Eifel
Hunsrück
Taunus
Vogelsberg
Rhön
Thüringer Wald
Ore Mountains
Fichtelgebirge
Oberpfälzer Wald
Bohemian Forest
Bayerischer Wald
Fränkische Alb
Swabian Alp
Black Forest
Allgäuer Alpen
Mangfallgebirge
Bavarian Alps
Zugspitze 9721ft (2963m)
Wasserkuppe 3117ft (950m)
Taufstein 2536ft (773m)
Rhine
Elbe
Danube
Main
Mosel
Neckar
ELEVATION
Feet Meters
6562 2000
4921 1500
3281 1000
2461 750
1640 500
1312 400
984 300
656 200
328 100
0 0
Below sea level
0 0
656 200
3281 1000
6562 2000
13,123 4000
19,685 6000
26,246 8000
32,808 10,000
Longitude east of Greenwich
SCALE 1:2,250,000
Lamberts Conformal Conic Projection
0 60 miles
0 60 kilometers

Berlin

Established in the 13th century as a trading post on the Spree River, Berlin first became the capital of Germany in 1871. Though repeatedly ravaged by conflict, the city retains prominent buildings and landmarks from most periods of its history, including the 19th-century Victory Column.

A typical Rhine Valley town, Bacharach is crowned by a castle and surrounded by vineyards.

Linked to the North Sea by the Elbe, Hamburg is one of the world's largest container ports.

THE ALPINE NATIONS

Austria, Liechtenstein, Switzerland

Arcing northeastward from France, the countless peaks and valleys of the Alps sprawl across more than half of Switzerland, the tiny monarchy of Liechtenstein, and two-thirds of Austria. These nations occupy a continental crossroads, their mountain passes permitting the flow of people and goods between north and south, the Danube Valley forming a natural corridor between eastern and western Europe. Despite its strategic importance, Switzerland has remained politically neutral for almost 200 years. This, along with its prosperity and secretive banking practices, has made it a haven for international organizations, businesses, and funds. Austria's more tempestuous past includes periods as the heart of the powerful Holy Roman and Austro-Hungarian empires; its present boundaries were defined after the First World War. Liechtenstein established its independence, and neutrality, in 1866.

Millions of people visit the Alps each year to holiday at winter-sports resorts.

The spectacular Jet d'Eau, a 460-foot (140-m) fountain, is Geneva's best-known landmark.

SWITZERLAND
GERMANY
FRANCE
ITALY
LIECHTENSTEIN
VADUZ
BERN
Basel
Zürich
Lausanne
Geneva
Luzern
St Gallen
Lugano
Locarno
Bellinzona
Chur
Sion
Brig
Zermatt
Interlaken
Thun
Neuchâtel
Fribourg
Schaffhausen
Winterthur
Lake Constance
Lake Geneva
Lac de Neuchâtel
Vierwaldstätter See
Rhine
Rhône
Aare
Jura
Central Plateau
Bernese Alps
Central Alps
Walliser Alpen
VALAIS
VAUD
TICINO
GRAUBÜNDEN
TIROL
Silvretta Gruppe
Allgäuer Alpen
Lechtaler Alpen
Ötztaler Alpen
Stubaier Alpen
Jungfrau 13,642ft (4158m)
Eiger 13,025ft (3970m)
Finsteraarhorn 14,022ft (4274m)
Wildhorn 10,643ft (3244m)
Matterhorn 14,692ft (4478m)
Dufourspitze 15,203ft (4634m)
Mont Blanc 15,771ft (4807m)
Säntis 8209ft (2502m)
Rheinwaldhorn 11,161ft (3402m)
Piz Bernina 13,284ft (4049m)
Zugspitze 9715ft (2961m)
Wildspitze 12,375ft (3772m)
Bregenz
Dornbirn
Feldkirch
Bludenz
Landeck
Innsbruck
Lago Maggiore
Lago di Como
Lago di Lugano
Longitude east of Greenwich

THE CENTRAL ALPS

The Central Alps extend from Lake Geneva in the west to the Rhine Valley in the east. They encompass several ranges including the Bernese Alps—Switzerland's highest—and the valleys of two of Europe's great rivers, the Rhône and Rhine, which form a deep, straight, almost continuous gouge through the mountains. The northern flank of the Central Alps descends to Switzerland's Central Plateau, which is hemmed in to the north by the peaks of the Jura.

Lake Constance
Rhine
St Moritz
Andermatt
Milan
N
Zürich
Finsteraarhorn
Stresa
Bernese Alps
Matterhorn
Turin
Basel
BERN
Rhône
Mont Blanc
Chamonix
Jura
Lake Geneva
Besançon
Geneva

POPULATION PATTERNS

Rugged terrain has always limited the settlement of mountainous areas, so most of the population is concentrated in valleys and lowlands, most notably Switzerland's Central Plateau, site of the nation's major urban centers, and the Danube Valley, where Vienna accommodates one-fifth of the Austrian population. Postindustrial depopulation of upland areas has been slowed by the boom in tourism, which has brought jobs and funds to remote communities.

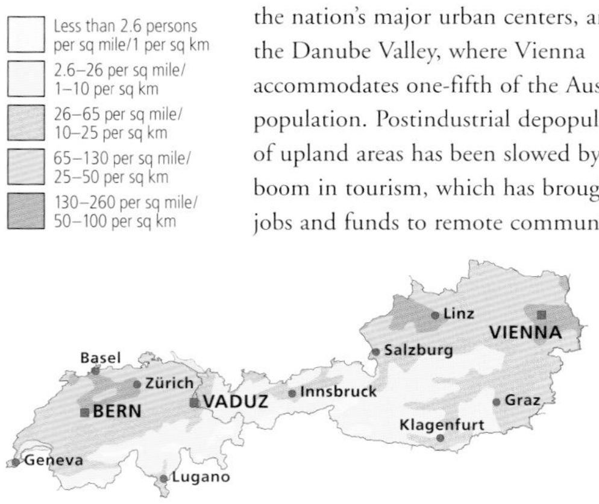

Less than 2.6 persons per sq mile/1 per sq km
2.6–26 per sq mile/ 1–10 per sq km
26–65 per sq mile/ 10–25 per sq km
65–130 per sq mile/ 25–50 per sq km
130–260 per sq mile/ 50–100 per sq km
Linz
VIENNA
Salzburg
Basel
Zürich
BERN
VADUZ
Innsbruck
Graz
Klagenfurt
Geneva
Lugano

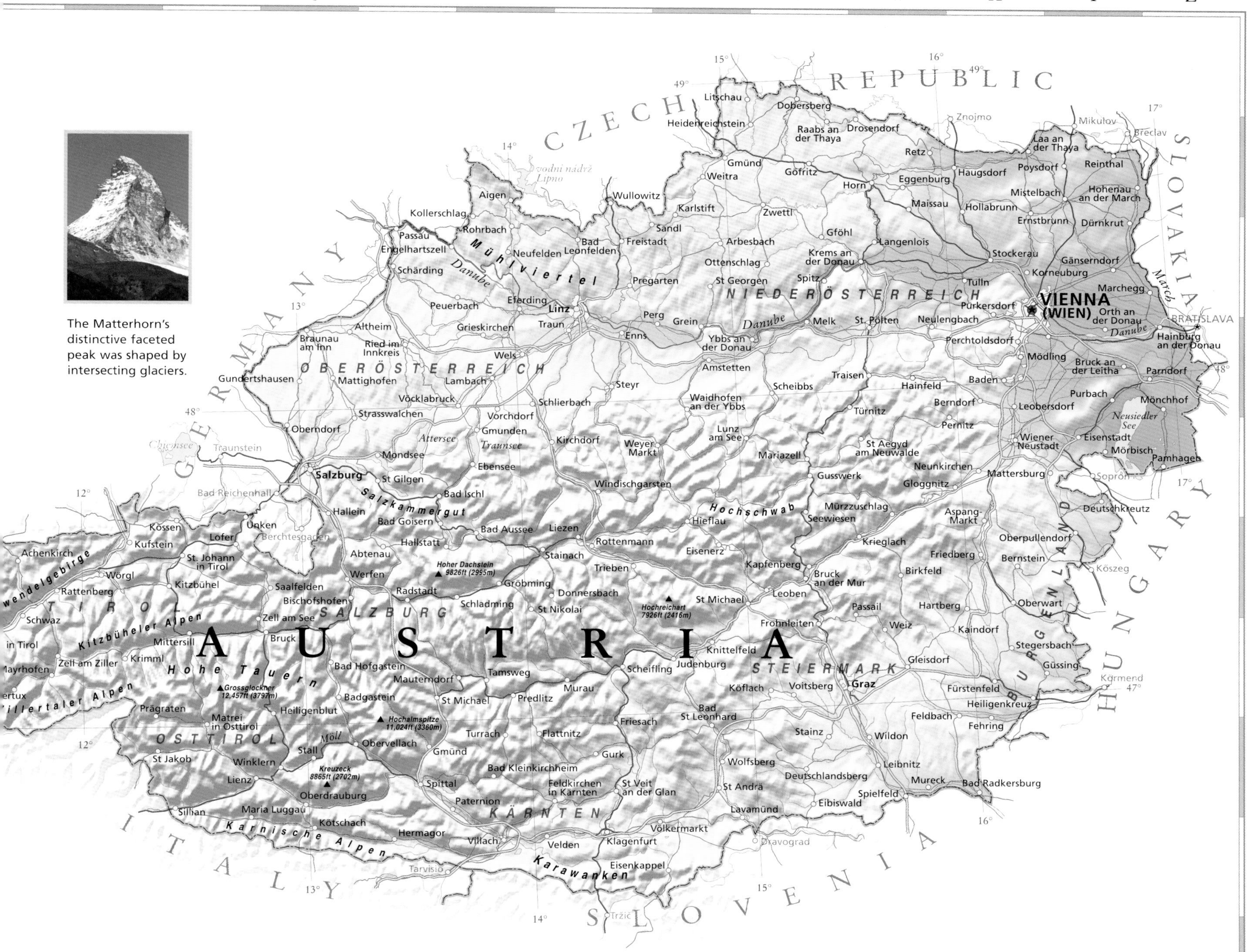
N O P Q R S T U V W X Y Z
1 2 3 4 5 6 7 8 9 10 11
CZECH REPUBLIC
SLOVAKIA
HUNGARY
SLOVENIA
ITALY
GERMANY
AUSTRIA
NIEDERÖSTERREICH
OBERÖSTERREICH
SALZBURG
TIROL
OSTTIROL
STEIERMARK
KÄRNTEN
BURGENLAND
VIENNA (WIEN)
Linz
Salzburg
Graz
Klagenfurt
Villach
Innsbruck
St. Pölten
Wels
Steyr
Leoben
Wiener Neustadt
Mödling
Baden
Krems an der Donau
Melk
Amstetten
Tulln
Stockerau
Korneuburg
Mistelbach
Hollabrunn
Horn
Zwettl
Gmünd
Weitra
Litschau
Heidenreichstein
Dobersberg
Raabs an der Thaya
Drosendorf
Retz
Eggenburg
Maissau
Haugsdorf
Laa an der Thaya
Poysdorf
Reinthal
Hohenau an der March
Ernstbrunn
Dürnkrut
Gänserndorf
Marchegg
Orth an der Donau
Hainburg an der Donau
Bruck an der Leitha
Parndorf
Neusiedler See
Mönchhof
Purbach
Eisenstadt
Mörbisch
Pamhagen
Leobersdorf
Berndorf
Pernitz
Hainfeld
Traisen
Türnitz
St Aegyd am Neuwalde
Neunkirchen
Gloggnitz
Mattersburg
Aspang-Markt
Deutschkreutz
Oberpullendorf
Bernstein
Friedberg
Birkfeld
Hartberg
Oberwart
Kaindorf
Stegersbach
Güssing
Fürstenfeld
Heiligenkreuz
Fehring
Feldbach
Gleisdorf
Weiz
Passail
Bruck an der Mur
Kapfenberg
Mürzzuschlag
Krieglach
Seewiesen
Gusswerk
Mariazell
Lunz am See
Waidhofen an der Ybbs
Scheibbs
Ybbs an der Donau
Grein
Perg
Enns
Pregarten
Freistadt
Bad Leonfelden
Neufelden
Rohrbach
Aigen
Kollerschlag
Passau
Engelhartszell
Schärding
Peuerbach
Grieskirchen
Eferding
Traun
Ried im Innkreis
Altheim
Braunau am Inn
Mattighofen
Gundertshausen
Lambach
Vöcklabruck
Strasswalchen
Oberndorf
Mondsee
Attersee
Traunsee
Vorchdorf
Gmunden
Ebensee
Schlierbach
Kirchdorf
Weyer Markt
Windischgarsten
Bad Ischl
St Gilgen
Hallein
Bad Goisern
Hallstatt
Bad Aussee
Liezen
Rottenmann
Stainach
Trieben
Gröbming
Schladming
Radstadt
Abtenau
Werfen
Bischofshofen
Saalfelden
Zell am See
Bruck
Mittersill
Kitzbühel
St. Johann in Tirol
Lofer
Unken
Kössen
Kufstein
Wörgl
Rattenberg
Schwaz
Achenkirch
Zell am Ziller
Krimml
Mayrhofen
Hohe Tauern
Grossglockner 12,457ft (3797m)
Heiligenblut
Matrei in Osttirol
Prägraten
St Jakob
Winklern
Lienz
Sillian
Maria Luggau
Kötschach
Oberdrauburg
Kreuzeck 8865ft (2702m)
Stall
Möll
Obervellach
Hochalmspitze 11,024ft (3360m)
Bad Hofgastein
Badgastein
Mauterndorf
Tamsweg
St Michael
Murau
Predlitz
Turrach
Gmünd
Flattnitz
Bad Kleinkirchheim
Feldkirchen in Kärnten
Spittal
Paternion
Hermagor
Velden
St Veit an der Glan
Gurk
Friesach
Eisenkappel
Völkermarkt
Lavamünd
Wolfsberg
St Andrä
Bad St Leonhard
Judenburg
Knittelfeld
Scheifling
St Michael
Hochreichart 7926ft (2416m)
Donnersbach
St Nikolai
Hoher Dachstein 9826ft (2995m)
Hieflau
Eisenerz
Hochschwab
Fohnleiten
Köflach
Voitsberg
Stainz
Deutschlandsberg
Eibiswald
Wildon
Leibnitz
Spielfeld
Mureck
Bad Radkersburg
Neulengbach
Purkersdorf
Perchtoldsdorf
Langenlois
Gföhl
Spitz
Ottenschlag
Arbesbach
St Georgen
Sandl
Karlstift
Wullowitz
Göfritz
Mühlviertel
Salzkammergut
Kitzbüheler Alpen
Zillertaler Alpen
Karnische Alpen
Karawanken
Wendelgebirge
Danube
March
Traunstein
Chiemsee
Bad Reichenhall
Berchtesgaden
Tarvisio
Tržič
Dravograd
Kőszeg
Sopron
Körmend
Bratislava
Břeclav
Mikulov
Znojmo
vodní nádrž Lipno
12° 13° 14° 15° 16° 17° 47° 48° 49°

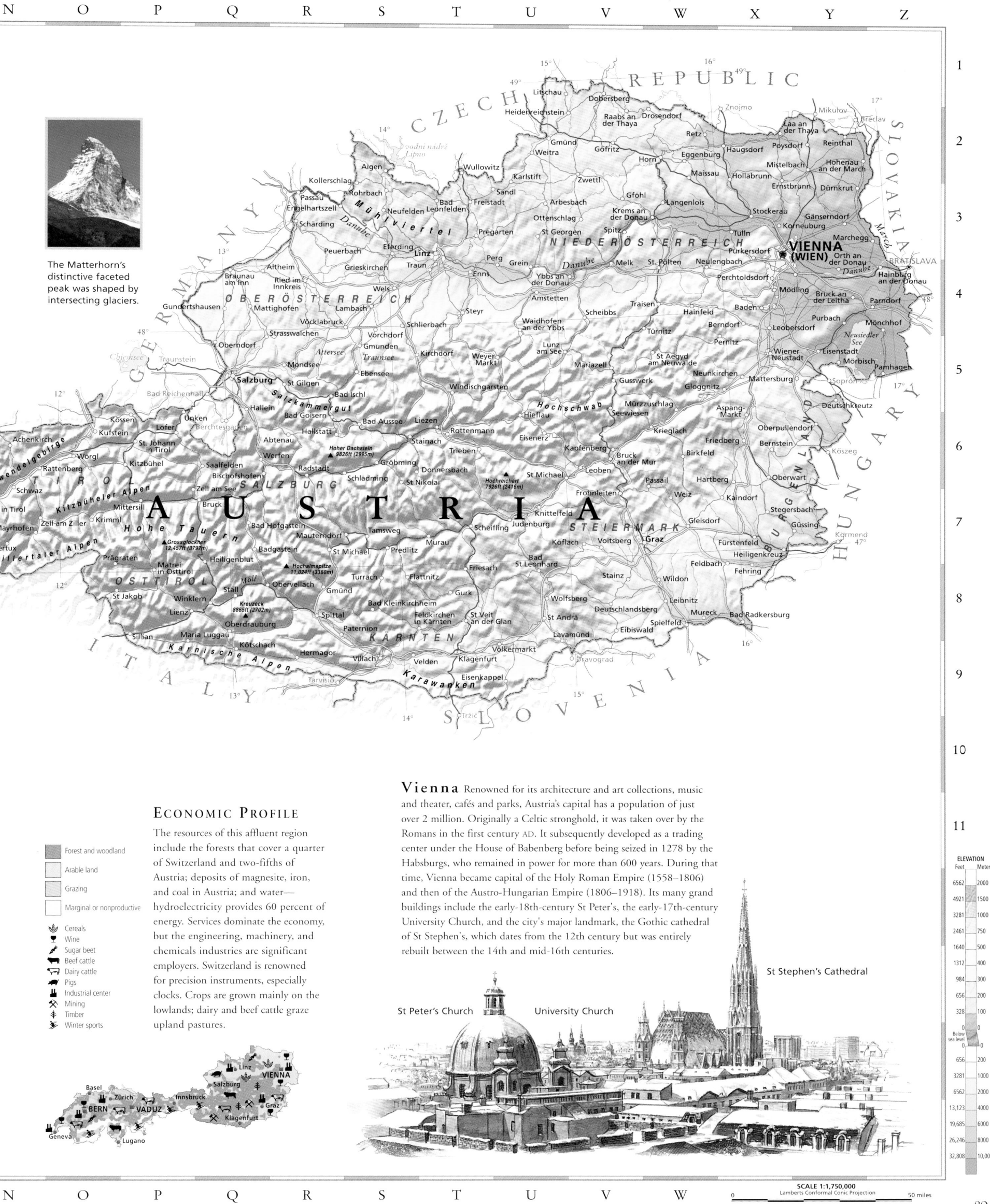

The Matterhorn's distinctive faceted peak was shaped by intersecting glaciers.

Economic Profile

The resources of this affluent region include the forests that cover a quarter of Switzerland and two-fifths of Austria; deposits of magnesite, iron, and coal in Austria; and water—hydroelectricity provides 60 percent of energy. Services dominate the economy, but the engineering, machinery, and chemicals industries are significant employers. Switzerland is renowned for precision instruments, especially clocks. Crops are grown mainly on the lowlands; dairy and beef cattle graze upland pastures.

- Forest and woodland
- Arable land
- Grazing
- Marginal or nonproductive
- Cereals
- Wine
- Sugar beet
- Beef cattle
- Dairy cattle
- Pigs
- Industrial center
- Mining
- Timber
- Winter sports

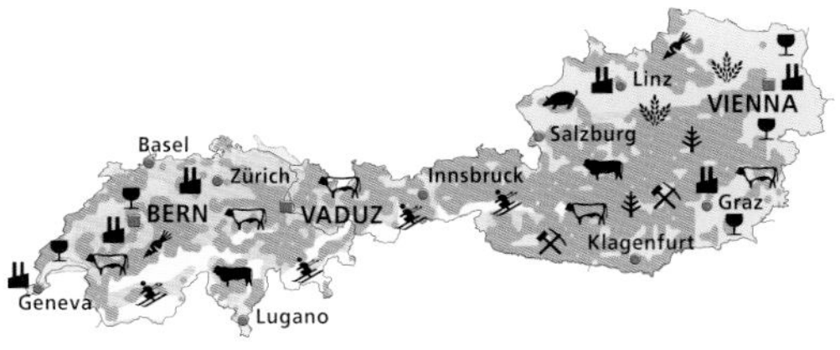
Basel
Zürich
BERN
VADUZ
Geneva
Lugano
Innsbruck
Salzburg
Linz
VIENNA
Graz
Klagenfurt

Vienna Renowned for its architecture and art collections, music and theater, cafés and parks, Austria's capital has a population of just over 2 million. Originally a Celtic stronghold, it was taken over by the Romans in the first century AD. It subsequently developed as a trading center under the House of Babenberg before being seized in 1278 by the Habsburgs, who remained in power for more than 600 years. During that time, Vienna became capital of the Holy Roman Empire (1558–1806) and then of the Austro-Hungarian Empire (1806–1918). Its many grand buildings include the early-18th-century St Peter's, the early-17th-century University Church, and the city's major landmark, the Gothic cathedral of St Stephen's, which dates from the 12th century but was entirely rebuilt between the 14th and mid-16th centuries.

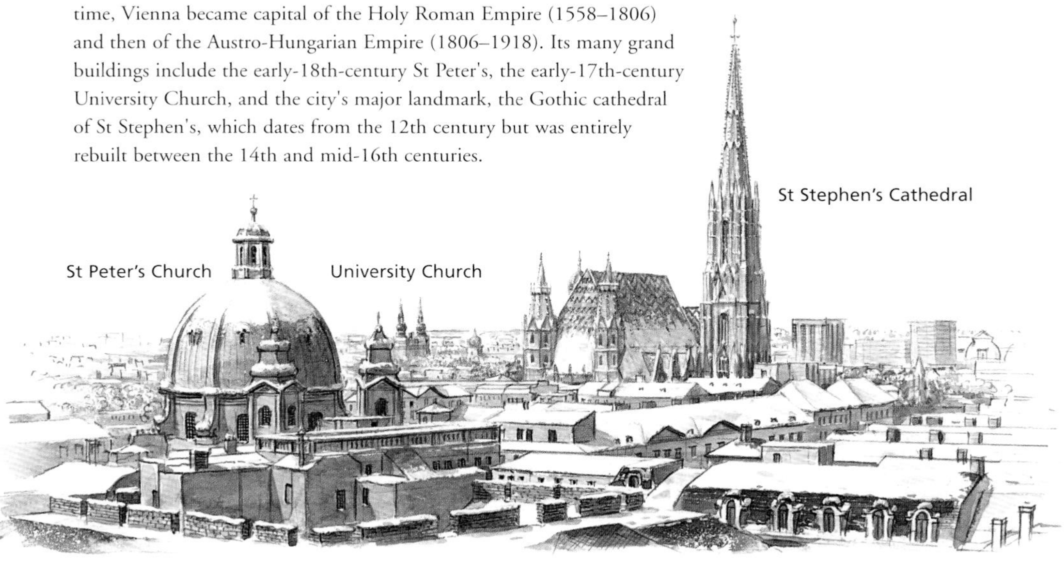
St Stephen's Cathedral
St Peter's Church
University Church

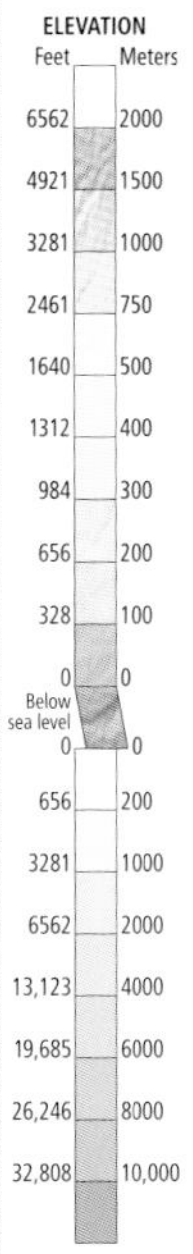
ELEVATION
Feet Meters
6562 2000
4921 1500
3281 1000
2461 750
1640 500
1312 400
984 300
656 200
328 100
0 0
Below sea level
0 0
656 200
3281 1000
6562 2000
13,123 4000
19,685 6000
26,246 8000
32,808 10,000

N O P Q R S T U V W

SCALE 1:1,750,000
Lamberts Conformal Conic Projection
0 50 miles
0 50 kilometers

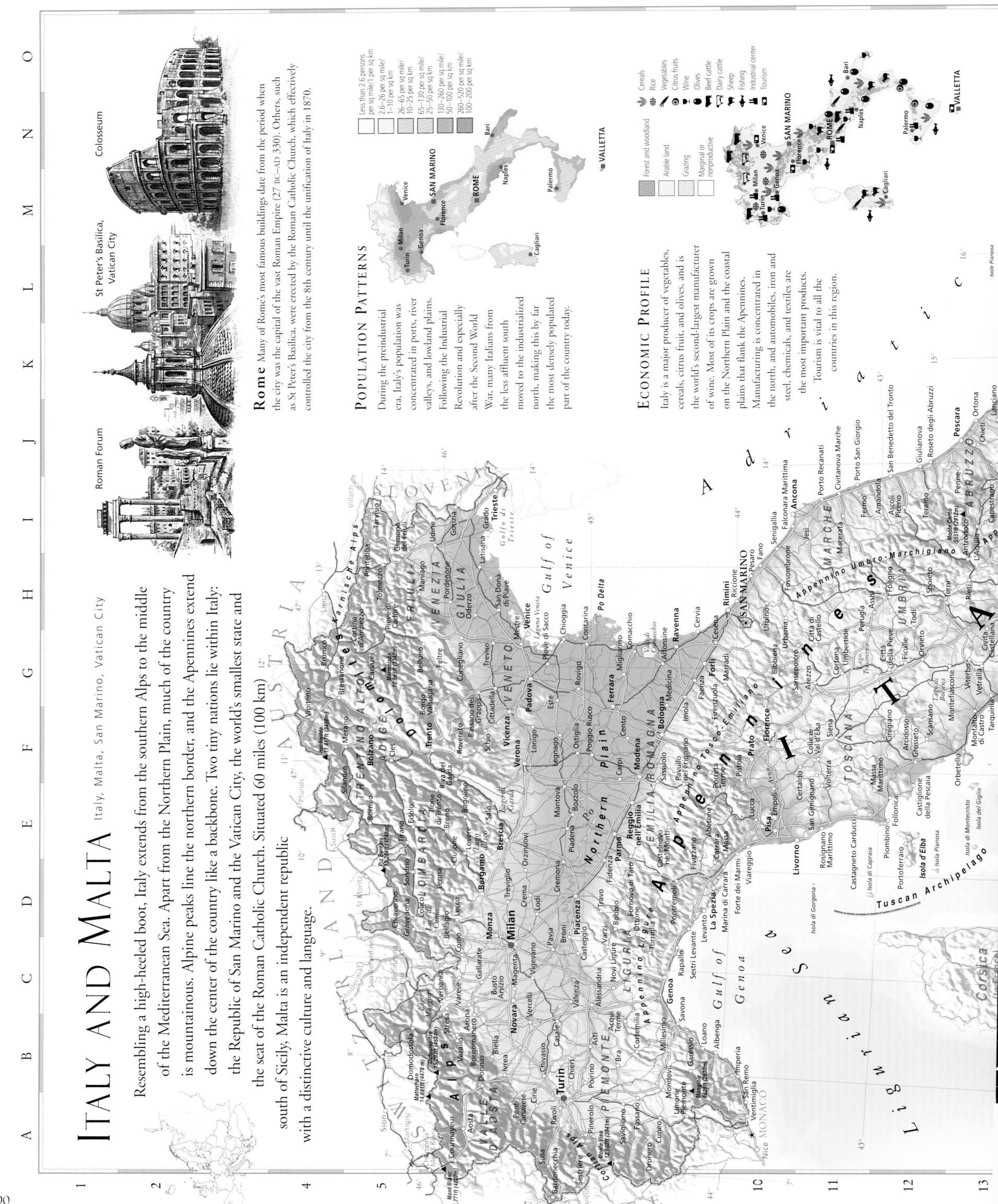

Italy and Malta

Italy, Malta, San Marino, Vatican City

Resembling a high-heeled boot, Italy extends from the southern Alps to the middle of the Mediterranean Sea. Apart from the Northern Plain, much of the country is mountainous. Alpine peaks line the northern border, and the Apennines extend down the center of the country like a backbone. Two tiny nations lie within Italy: the Republic of San Marino and the Vatican City, the world's smallest state and the seat of the Roman Catholic Church. Situated 60 miles (100 km) south of Sicily, Malta is an independent republic with a distinctive culture and language.

Roman Forum
St Peter's Basilica, Vatican City
Colosseum

Rome Many of Rome's most famous buildings date from the period when the city was the capital of the vast Roman Empire (27 BC–AD 330). Others, such as St Peter's Basilica, were erected by the Roman Catholic Church, which effectively controlled the city from the 8th century until the unification of Italy in 1870.

Population Patterns

During the preindustrial era, Italy's population was concentrated in ports, river valleys, and lowland plains. Following the Industrial Revolution and especially after the Second World War, many Italians from the less affluent south moved to the industrialized north, making this by far the most densely populated part of the country today.

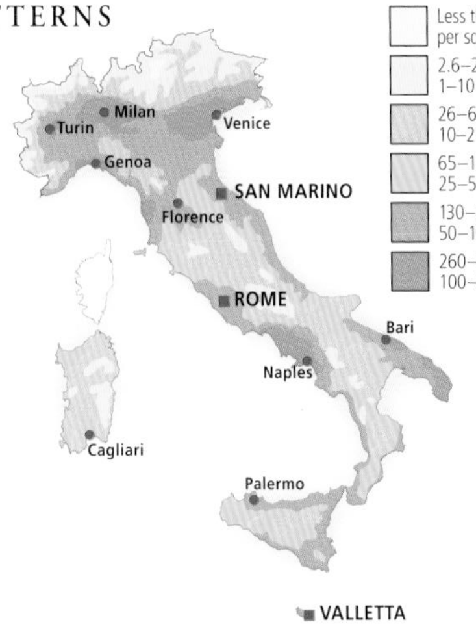
Turin
Milan
Venice
Genoa
SAN MARINO
Florence
ROME
Bari
Naples
Cagliari
Palermo
VALLETTA
Less than 2.6 persons per sq mile/1 per sq km
2.6–26 per sq mile/ 1–10 per sq km
26–65 per sq mile/ 10–25 per sq km
65–130 per sq mile/ 25–50 per sq km
130–260 per sq mile/ 50–100 per sq km
260–520 per sq mile/ 100–200 per sq km

Economic Profile

Italy is a major producer of vegetables, cereals, citrus fruit, and olives, and is the world's second-largest manufacturer of wine. Most of its crops are grown on the Northern Plain and the coastal plains that flank the Apennines. Manufacturing is concentrated in the north, and automobiles, iron and steel, chemicals, and textiles are the most important products. Tourism is vital to all the countries in this region.

Forest and woodland
Arable land
Grazing
Marginal or nonproductive
Cereals
Rice
Vegetables
Citrus fruits
Wine
Olives
Beef cattle
Dairy cattle
Sheep
Fishing
Industrial center
Tourism
Turin
Milan
Venice
Genoa
SAN MARINO
Florence
ROME
Bari
Naples
Cagliari
Palermo
VALLETTA

AUSTRIA
SWITZERLAND
SLOVENIA
FRANCE
MONACO
Alps
Dolomites
Karnische Alps
Cottian Alps
Northern Plain
Po
Po Delta
Apennines
Appennino Ligure
Appennino Tosco-Emiliano
Appennino Umbro-Marchigiano
ITALIA
Gulf of Venice
Golfo di Trieste
Gulf of Genoa
Ligurian Sea
Adriatic
Tuscan Archipelago
Corsica
Mont Blanc 15,771ft (4807m)
Matterhorn 14,691ft (4478 m)
Dufourspitze 15,203ft (4634m)
Piz Bernina 13,284ft (4049m)
Hochwilde 11,417ft (3480m)
Marmolada 10,965ft (3342m)
Monte Viso 12,602ft (3841m)
Mongioie 8629ft (2630m)
Monte Corno 9551ft (2912m)
VALLE D'AOSTA
PIEMONTE
LOMBARDIA
TRENTINO-ALTO ADIGE
VENETO
FRIULI-VENEZIA GIULIA
LIGURIA
EMILIA-ROMAGNA
TOSCANA
MARCHE
UMBRIA
ABRUZZO
Turin
Milan
Venice
Genoa
Bologna
Florence
SAN MARINO
Trieste
Verona
Padova
Brescia
Bergamo
Parma
Modena
Ferrara
Ravenna
Rimini
Ancona
Pisa
Livorno
Lucca
Prato
Perugia
Pescara
Isola d'Elba
Lake Garda
Lago Maggiore
Lago di Como

Tyrrhenian Sea
Ionian Sea
Mediterranean Sea
Sicilian Channel
Malta Channel
Golfo di Taranto
Sardinia
SARDEGNA
Sicily
SICILIA
MALTA
VALLETTA
CAMPANIA
PUGLIA
BASILICATA
CALABRIA
MOLISE
(ROMA)
Naples
Palermo
Messina
Catania
Syracuse
Cagliari
Sassari
Bari
Taranto
Foggia
Lecce
Brindisi
Salerno
Reggio di Calabria
Catanzaro
Cosenza
Isole Lipari
Isole Egadi
Isole Pelagie (to Italy)
Isola di Pantelleria (to Italy)
Strait of Bonifacio
Stretto di Messina
Mount Etna 10,902ft (3323m)
Vesuvius 4202ft (1281m)
Stromboli 3031ft (924m)
Monte Miletto 6726ft (2050m)
ELEVATION
Feet Meters
6562 2000
4921 1500
3281 1000
2461 750
1640 500
1312 400
984 300
656 200
328 100
0 0
Below sea level
656 200
3281 1000
6562 2000
13,123 4000
19,685 6000
26,246 8000
32,808 10,000
Longitude east of Greenwich
SCALE 1:3,000,000
Lamberts Conformal Conic Projection
0 100 miles
0 100 kilometers

THE NORTHERN PLAIN

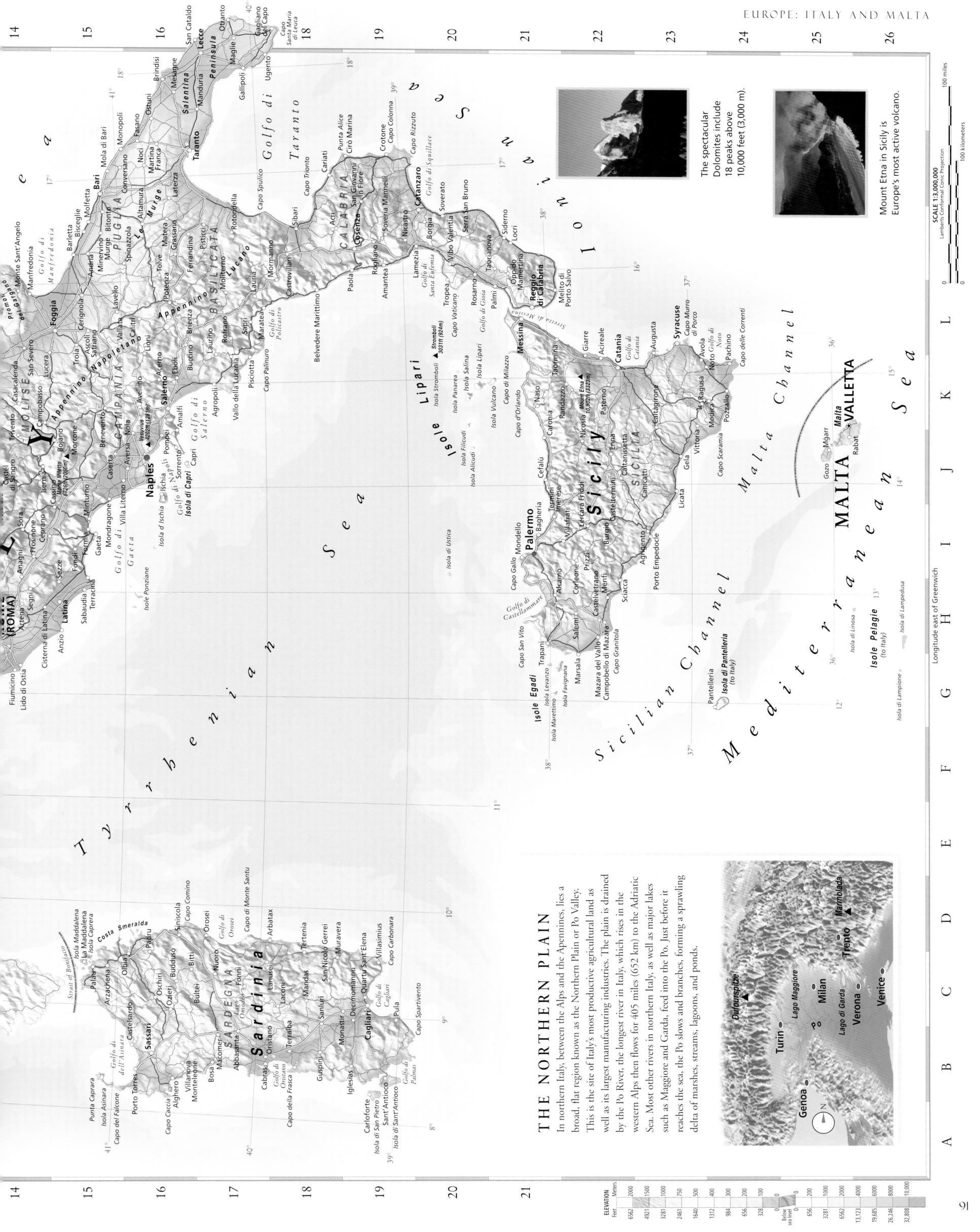

In northern Italy, between the Alps and the Apennines, lies a broad, flat region known as the Northern Plain or Po Valley. This is the site of Italy's most productive agricultural land as well as its largest manufacturing industries. The plain is drained by the Po River, the longest river in Italy, which rises in the western Alps then flows for 405 miles (652 km) to the Adriatic Sea. Most other rivers in northern Italy, as well as major lakes such as Maggiore and Garda, feed into the Po. Just before it reaches the sea, the Po slows and branches, forming a sprawling delta of marshes, streams, lagoons, and ponds.

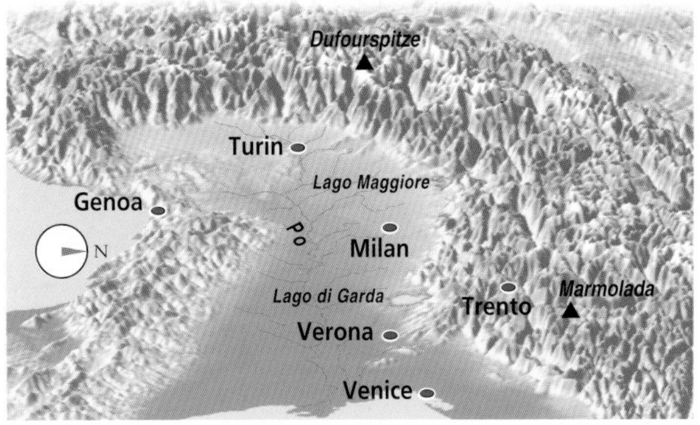
Dufourspitze
Turin
Lago Maggiore
Genoa
Po
Milan
Lago di Garda
Trento
Marmolada
Verona
Venice
N

The spectacular Dolomites include 18 peaks above 10,000 feet (3,000 m).

Mount Etna in Sicily is Europe's most active volcano.

NORTHERN CENTRAL EUROPE

Czech Republic, Hungary, Poland, Slovakia

The Bohemian Massif and the Carpathian Mountains bisect this region from west to east, separating the flatlands of the North European Plain from those of the Great Hungarian Plain in the south. A ring of mountain ranges around a broad central basin, the Bohemian Massif covers most of the Czech Republic. The heavily forested Carpathians—a continuation of the Alps—occupy northern and central Slovakia, giving way to plains in the south and east. Separated from these two nations by the peaks that line its southern border, Poland otherwise has little high land. Rivers meander across its central lowlands and lake-studded coastal plains, many, notably the Oder and Vistula, flowing all the way to the Baltic Sea. Hungary, too, is mostly flat, the Great Hungarian Plain spreading across more than half of its territory. All of these independent, democratic nations were part of the Eastern bloc until the collapse of communism in 1989. In 1992, Czechoslovakia split into two nations, the Czech Republic and Slovakia.

POPULATION PATTERNS

2.6–26 per sq mile/ 1–10 per sq km
26–65 per sq mile/ 10–25 per sq km
65–130 per sq mile/ 25–50 per sq km
130–260 per sq mile/ 50–100 per sq km
260–520 per sq mile/ 100–200 per sq km
Gdańsk
Szczecin
Bydgoszcz
Poznań
Łódź
WARSAW
Wrocław
Radom
PRAGUE
Katowice
Kraków
Plzeň
Ostrava
Brno
Košice
BRATISLAVA
Debrecen
Győr
BUDAPEST
Szeged
Pécs

About 65 percent of the region's inhabitants are urban dwellers, with the highest levels in the Czech Republic and the lowest in less-developed Slovakia (which has half the population of its northwestern neighbor). The most densely populated areas are Poland's industrialized south and its capital Warsaw, the northern Czech Republic, and the Budapest region, home to one-quarter of Hungary's people. Settlements are more scattered in the Slovakian mountains and on the windswept and relatively infertile Baltic Sea coast. More than 5 percent of Hungary's population are ethnic Roma (Gypsy) people.

ECONOMIC PROFILE

Forest and woodland
Arable land
Grazing
Gdańsk
Szczecin
Bydgoszcz
Poznań
Łódź
WARSAW
Wrocław
Radom
PRAGUE
Katowice
Kraków
Plzeň
Ostrava
Brno
Košice
BRATISLAVA
Debrecen
Győr
BUDAPEST
Szeged
Pécs
Cereals
Potatoes
Dairy cattle
Pigs
Industrial center
Mining
Timber
Wine
Sugar beet

Significant natural resources in this region include Poland's rich Silesian coal fields, the more modest but vital mineral reserves of Slovakia's Ore Mountains, and Hungary's large swathes of arable land. Cereals and potatoes are the major crops, along with sugar beet in Poland and Hungary. Leading industries include engineering and the production of automobiles, chemicals, textiles, and food and beverages—the Czech Republic is renowned for its beer and Hungary has a thriving wine industry.

In the mid-18th century, Gdańsk was the largest city in Eastern Europe. Still Poland's main port, it is also a center of shipbuilding.

The jagged Tatra Mountains of northern Slovakia and southern Poland are a refuge for rare animals such as bears and wolves.

Baltic Sea
Gulf of Gdańsk
POLAND
RUSSIAN FEDERATION
LITHUANIA
BELARUS
Zatoka Pomorska
Kaliningrad
Gdańsk
Gdynia
Sopot
Hel
Władysławowo
Elbląg
Szczecin
Koszalin
Kołobrzeg
Słupsk
Ustka
Darłowko
Świnoujście
Bydgoszcz
Toruń
Grudziądz
Olsztyn
Włocławek
Płock
Poznań
Gorzów Wielkopolski
Suwałki
Białystok
Ełk
Łomża
Ostrołęka
Ciechanów
WARSAW (WARSZAWA)
Pomerania
Pojezierze Mazurskie
Vistula
Oder
Warta
Noteć
Narew
Bug
Hrodna
Brest
Frankfurt an der Oder

CZECH REPUBLIC
SLOVAKIA
HUNGARY
GERMANY
AUSTRIA
UKRAINE
ROMANIA
CROATIA
SLOVENIA
SERBIA and MONTENEGRO
PRAGUE (PRAHA)
VIENNA (WIEN)
BRATISLAVA
BUDAPEST
Wrocław
Katowice
Kraków
Brno
Ostrava
Olomouc
Plzeň
Győr
Debrecen
Miskolc
Szeged
Pécs
Kecskemét
Ore Mountains
Bohemian Forest
Bohemian Massif
Bohemia
Moravia
Silesia
Sudeten
Carpathian Mountains
Tatra Mountains
Slovak Ore Mountains
Malé Karpaty
Biele Karpaty
Javorníky
Bakony
Great Hungarian Plain
Wyżyna Lubelska
Wyżyna Małopolska
Góry Świętokrzyskie
Podunajská nížina
Danube
Vistula
Oder
Elbe
Balaton
Longitude east of Greenwich
A B C D E F G H I J K
14 15 16 17 18 19 20 21 22 23 24 25 26
ELEVATION
Feet Meters
6562 2000
4921 1500
3281 1000
2461 750
1640 500
1312 400
984 300
656 200
328 100
0 0
Below sea level
0 0
656 200
3281 1000
6562 2000
13,123 4000
19,685 6000
26,246 8000
32,808 10,000
SCALE 1:2,750,000
Lamberts Conformal Conic Projection
0 100 miles
0 100 kilometers

Prague Undoubtedly the most famous of the many bridges that cross the Vltava River in the city of Prague, the Charles Bridge dates from 1357. At that time, Prague was the capital of Bohemia and the Holy Roman Empire under Charles IV, and a major trading center. Merchants remained central to the development of the economy until the Industrial Revolution, and were responsible for commissioning many of the magnificent Gothic and Baroque buildings and monuments that today attract a steady influx of visitors. Prague became capital of the nation of Czechoslovakia in 1918 and capital of the newly formed Czech Republic in 1992.

Situated on the east bank of the Danube, Budapest's Parliament was completed in 1902.

Western Balkans

Albania, Bosnia and Herzegovina, Croatia, Serbia and Montenegro, Slovenia

Over the centuries, numerous peoples settled in the Balkans, giving rise to a patchwork of ethnically diverse communities. Until the 20th century, these communities remained relatively isolated from each other, partly as a result of the region's rugged terrain—mountains line the coast and spread across much of the interior, yielding to sizable lowlands only in the north. In the mid-20th century, all of the region's nations adopted communism and all but Albania were united as the Republic of Yugoslavia. The breakup of the republic in 1991 brought ethnic and religious rivalries to a head, resulting in a catastrophic civil war between Croats, Serbs, and Bosnian Muslims (Bosniaks). Peace was restored in 1995, but tensions remain high, especially in the culturally distinct and independently oriented provinces of Montenegro and Kosovo.

The Dinaric Alps

Stretching for 350 miles (560 km) along the coast from Slovenia to Albania and rising to 8,274 feet (2,522 m) at Durmitor, the Dinaric Alps form an almost impenetrable barrier between the Adriatic Sea and the Balkan hinterland. A single natural breach, the Neretva River valley, provides Bosnia and Herzegovina with its only coastal access; elsewhere, steep, arid slopes climb directly from the shoreline or narrow coastal plains. In the Dalmatia region of Croatia, the mountains have been partially submerged by the sea, giving rise to a series of long, parallel islands and slender, sheltered channels. The western slopes of the Dinaric Alps consist mainly of porous limestone; in places, the rock is honeycombed with underground channels and pools, and extensive cave systems.

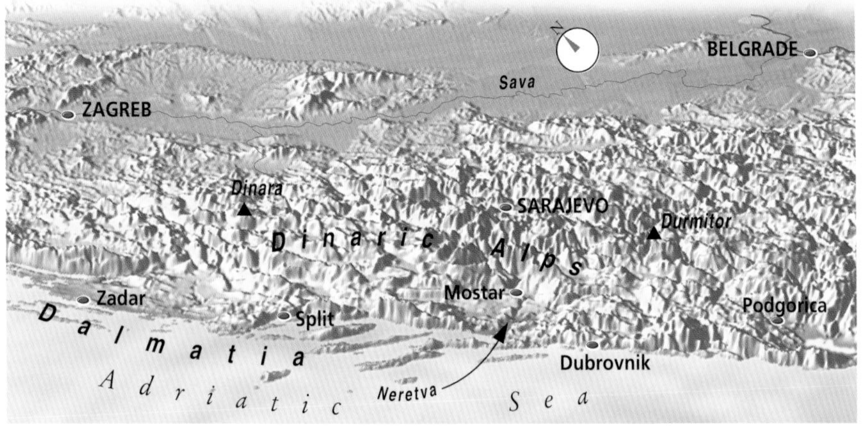

BELGRADE
Sava
ZAGREB
Dinara
SARAJEVO
Durmitor
Dinaric Alps
Zadar
Split
Mostar
Podgorica
Dalmatia
Dubrovnik
Adriatic
Neretva
Sea

AUSTRIA
HUNGARY
ROMANIA
BULGARIA
ITALY
SLOVENIA
CROATIA
BOSNIA and HERZEGOVINA
SERBIA
LJUBLJANA
ZAGREB
SARAJEVO
BELGRADE (BEOGRAD)
VOJVODINA
REPUBLICA SRPSKA
FEDERACIJA BOSNA I HERCEGOVINA
Slavonija
Istra
Dalmatia
Dinaric Alps
Julian Alps
Adriatic
Rijeka
Split
Novi Sad
Banja Luka
Subotica
Maribor
Osijek
Zadar
Danube
Sava
Drava
Tisa
Una

CROATIA
Sea
MONTENEGRO
KOSOVO
ALBANIA
MACEDONIA
GREECE
TIRANA (TIRANË)
SKOPJE
Podgorica
Dubrovnik
Herceg-Novi
Trebinje
Kotor
Budva
Bar
Ulcinj
Shkodër
Lezhë
Durrës
Kavajë
Elbasan
Cërrik
Lushnjë
Fier
Vlorë
Tepelenë
Gjirokastër
Sarandë
Himarë
Korçë
Pogradec
Librazhd
Burrel
Peshkopi
Kukës
Prizren
Priština
Peć
Dečani
Đakovica
Uroševac
Gnjilane
Kačanik
Preševo
Bujanovac
Vranjska Banja
Leskovac
Vlasotince
Dimitrovgrad
Novi Pazar
Bijelo Polje
Mojkovac
Berane
Rožaje
Kolašin
Nikšić
Danilovgrad
Plav
Šavnik
Plana
Bileća
Vis
Hvar
Korčula
Vela Luka
Lastovo
Mljet
Lake Scutari
Lake Ohrid
Lake Prespa
Corfu
Kerkyra
Igoumenitsa
Prokletije
Korab 9068ft (2764m)
Maja e Çikes 6709ft (2045m)
Gjiri i Drinit
Kepi i Rodonit
Bishti i Pallës
Laguna e Karavastasë
Sazan
Kepi i Gjuhëzës

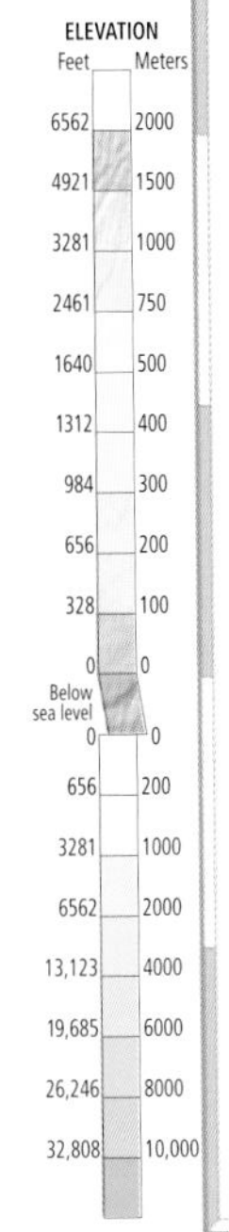

ELEVATION
Feet
Meters
6562 2000
4921 1500
3281 1000
2461 750
1640 500
1312 400
984 300
656 200
328 100
0 0
Below sea level
0 0
656 200
3281 1000
6562 2000
13,123 4000
19,685 6000
26,246 8000
32,808 10,000

Dubrovnik A settlement existed on the site of Dubrovnik at least as far back as the sixth century AD, but the town came to prominence as a trading center only in the 13th century. By the 15th century, Dubrovnik was an independent republic and the most important port in the eastern Adriatic. After falling to Napoleon in 1808, the city became part of Croatia in 1815. During the recent civil war, Dubrovnik was devastated by Serb shelling. However, careful renovation has restored many historic buildings, and tourists are now beginning to return to the city in large numbers.

Mostar is the historical capital of Herzegovina. Its spectacular stone bridge, built in 1566, was destroyed by shelling in 1993.

Site of the pretty Church of St Maria and a dramatic clifftop castle, Lake Bled lies in the foothills of Slovenia's Julian Alps.

Zagreb was originally two medieval cities, Gradec and Kaptol, which merged in the 19th century.

In undeveloped rural Albania, many industrial and agricultural processes are still carried out manually.

The late-19th-century Catholic cathedral is a prominent landmark in Novi Sad, Serbia's second-largest city.

Maribor
LJUBLJANA
ZAGREB
Rijeka
Osijek
Banja Luka
BELGRADE
SARAJEVO
Split
Mostar
Niš
Priština
Podgorica
TIRANA
Less than 2.6 persons per sq mile/1 per sq km
2.6–26 per sq mile/ 1–10 per sq km
26–65 per sq mile/ 10–25 per sq km
65–130 per sq mile/ 25–50 per sq km
130–260 per sq mile/ 50–100 per sq km

Population Patterns

The interior's mountainous terrain and dense forests have long restricted settlement. In contrast, the north's fertile land and developed industries have resulted in higher population densities, especially around Zagreb and along the Sava, Danube, Tisa, and Morava river valleys. However, only about 50 percent of the region's inhabitants are urban dwellers. The civil war displaced huge numbers of people. About 2.5 million inhabitants of Bosnia and Herzegovina left their homes during the conflict; a decade later, one-third had still not returned.

Maribor
LJUBLJANA
ZAGREB
Rijeka
Osijek
Banja Luka
BELGRADE
SARAJEVO
Split
Mostar
Niš
Priština
Podgorica
TIRANA
Forest and woodland
Arable land
Grazing
Cereals
Fruit
Sugar beet
Olives
Dairy cattle
Pigs
Sheep
Industrial center
Timber
Mining

Economic Profile

Economic activity throughout the region was severely disrupted by the civil war, and recovery has been slow. Agriculture is concentrated on the northern plains and the coast; cereals, sugar beet, and vegetables are the leading crops. In the interior, sheep graze hillsides and thick forests provide abundant timber. Sizable mineral resources support the manufacture of metals and machinery in industrial centers. Textile production and food processing are also important, and hydroelectric power stations are widespread.

SCALE 1:2,500,000
Lamberts Conformal Conic Projection
0 80 miles
0 80 kilometers

Longitude east of Greenwich

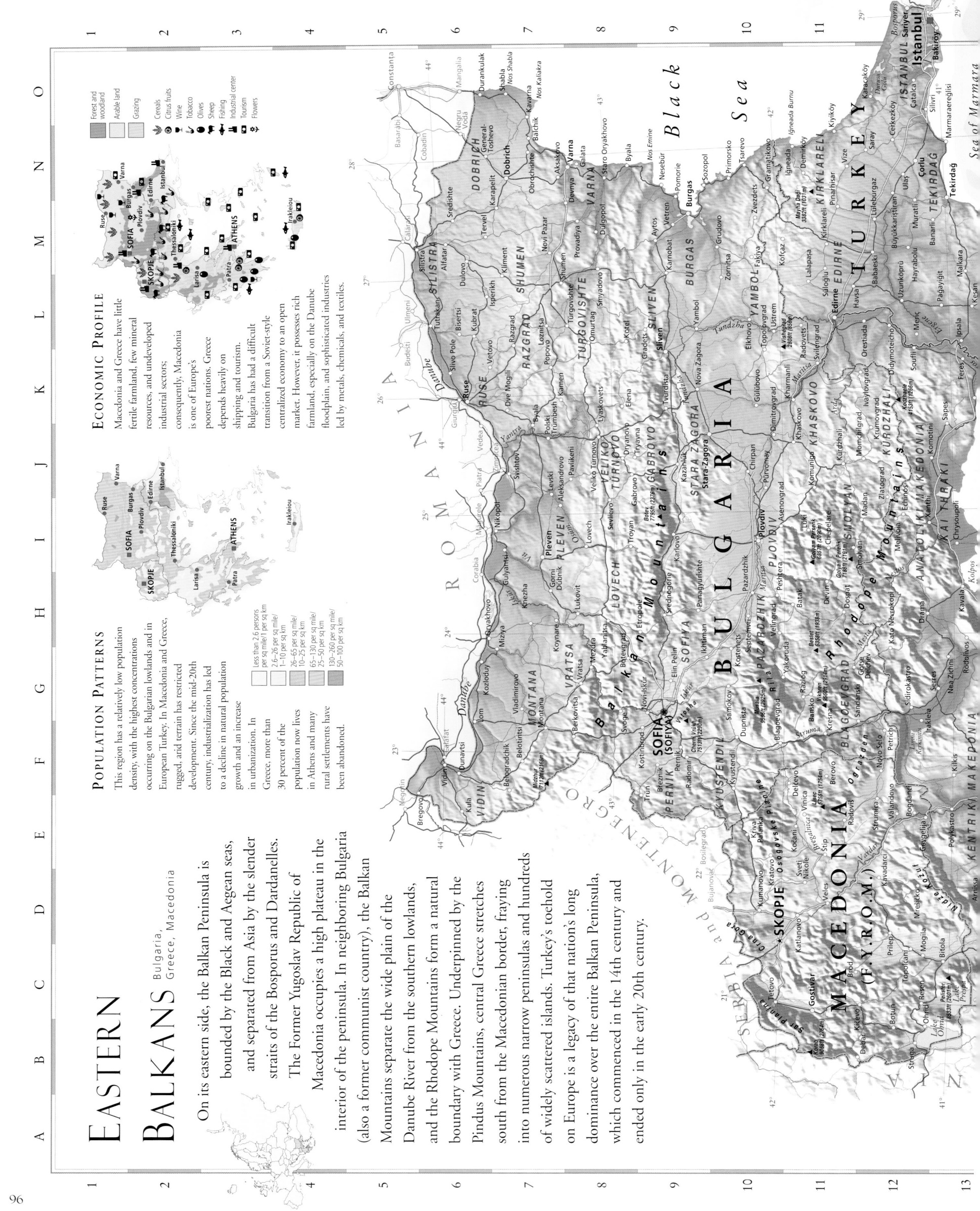

EASTERN BALKANS

Bulgaria, Greece, Macedonia

On its eastern side, the Balkan Peninsula is bounded by the Black and Aegean seas, and separated from Asia by the slender straits of the Bosporus and Dardanelles. The Former Yugoslav Republic of Macedonia occupies a high plateau in the interior of the peninsula. In neighboring Bulgaria (also a former communist country), the Balkan Mountains separate the wide plain of the Danube River from the southern lowlands, and the Rhodope Mountains form a natural boundary with Greece. Underpinned by the Pindus Mountains, central Greece stretches south from the Macedonian border, fraying into numerous narrow peninsulas and hundreds of widely scattered islands. Turkey's toehold on Europe is a legacy of that nation's long dominance over the entire Balkan Peninsula, which commenced in the 14th century and ended only in the early 20th century.

POPULATION PATTERNS

This region has a relatively low population density, with the highest concentrations occurring on the Bulgarian lowlands and in European Turkey. In Macedonia and Greece, rugged, arid terrain has restricted development. Since the mid-20th century, industrialization has led to a decline in natural population growth and an increase in urbanization. In Greece, more than 30 percent of the population now lives in Athens and many rural settlements have been abandoned.

Ruse
Varna
SOFIA
Burgas
Plovdiv
SKOPJE
Edirne
Istanbul
Thessaloniki
Larisa
Patra
ATHENS
Irakleiou

- Less than 2.6 persons per sq mile/1 per sq km
- 2.6–26 per sq mile/ 1–10 per sq km
- 26–65 per sq mile/ 10–25 per sq km
- 65–130 per sq mile/ 25–50 per sq km
- 130–260 per sq mile/ 50–100 per sq km

ECONOMIC PROFILE

Macedonia and Greece have little fertile farmland, few mineral resources, and undeveloped industrial sectors; consequently, Macedonia is one of Europe's poorest nations. Greece depends heavily on shipping and tourism. Bulgaria has had a difficult transition from a Soviet-style centralized economy to an open market. However, it possesses rich farmland, especially on the Danube floodplain, and sophisticated industries led by metals, chemicals, and textiles.

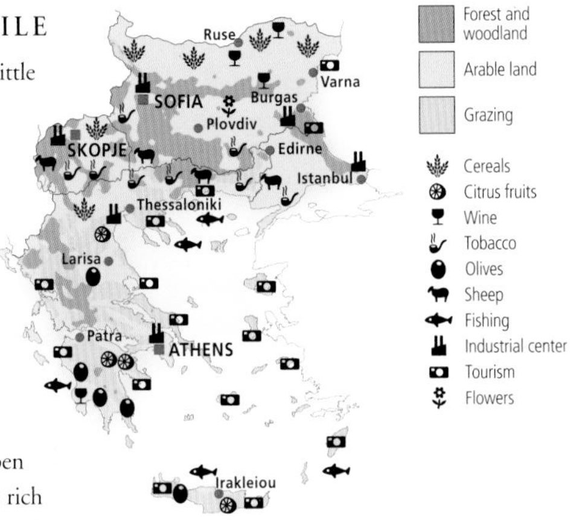

Ruse
Varna
SOFIA
Burgas
Plovdiv
SKOPJE
Edirne
Istanbul
Thessaloniki
Larisa
Patra
ATHENS
Irakleiou
Forest and woodland
Arable land
Grazing
Cereals
Citrus fruits
Wine
Tobacco
Olives
Sheep
Fishing
Industrial center
Tourism
Flowers

ROMANIA
SERBIA and MONTENEGRO
BULGARIA
MACEDONIA (F.Y.R.O.M.)
TURKEY
Black Sea
Sea of Marmara
SOFIA (SOFIYA)
SKOPJE
Istanbul
Plovdiv
Varna
Burgas
Ruse
Danube
Balkan Mountains
Rhodope Mountains

GREECE
TURKEY
Aegean Sea
Ionian Sea
Sea of Crete
Mediterranean Sea
VOREIO AIGAIO
NOTIO AIGAIO
Cyclades
Dodecanese
Voreioi Sporades
Ionian Islands
IONIOI NISOI
Pindus Mountains
Peloponnese
PELOPONNISOS
MAKEDONIA
DYTIKI MAKEDONIA
IPEIROS
THESSALIA
DYTIKI ELLAS
STEREA ELLAS
ATTIKI
KRITI
ÁGION ÓROS
ÇANAKKALE
ATHENS (ATHINA)
Peiraias
Thessaloniki
Larisa
Patra
Ioannina
Kerkyra
Corfu
Kefallonia
Zakynthos
Ithaki
Lefkada
Evvoia
Andros
Tinos
Mykonos
Naxos
Paros
Milos
Thira
Ios
Amorgos
Astypalaia
Kos
Rhodes
Karpathos
Kasos
Samos
Ikaria
Chios
Lesbos
Limnos
Samotharaki
Skyros
Kythira
Crete
Chania
Irakleiou
Rethymno
Gulf of Corinth
Saronic Gulf
Corinth Canal
Thermaikos Kolpos
Argolikos Kolpos
Lakonikos Kolpos
Messiniakos Kolpos
Kyparissiakos Kolpos
Patraikos Kolpos
Mirtoö Pelagos
Karpáthio Pélagos
Kuşadasi Körfezi
Gökova Körfezi
Izmir
Mt Olympus 9551ft (2911m)
Smolikas 8652ft (2637m)
Parnassos 8061ft (2457m)
Pachnes 8045ft (2452m)
Oros Kofinas 4039ft (1231m)
Attavyros 3986ft (1215m)
Longitude east of Greenwich
A B C D E F G L
14 15 16 17 18 19 20 21 22 23 24 25 26
SCALE 1:2,500,000
Lamberts Conformal Conic Projection
0 80 miles
0 80 kilometers
ELEVATION
Feet Meters
6562 2000
4921 1500
3281 1000
2461 750
1640 500
1312 400
984 300
656 200
328 100
0 0
Below sea level
0 0
656 200
3281 1000
6562 2000
13,123 4000
19,685 6000
26,246 8000
32,808 10,000

Built in 1882–93, the Corinth Canal links the Saronic Gulf and the Gulf of Corinth.

Bulgaria provides 80 percent of the world's attar of rose, an oil used in perfumes.

Athens Even after centuries of urban development, civil war, and foreign occupation, Greece's capital is still dominated—physically, economically, and culturally—by the remnants of its great classical civilization. The most prominent of these is the Parthenon, the fifth-century-BC temple to the goddess Athena, which crowns the citadel of the Acropolis.

Northeastern Europe

Belarus, Estonia, Latvia, Lithuania

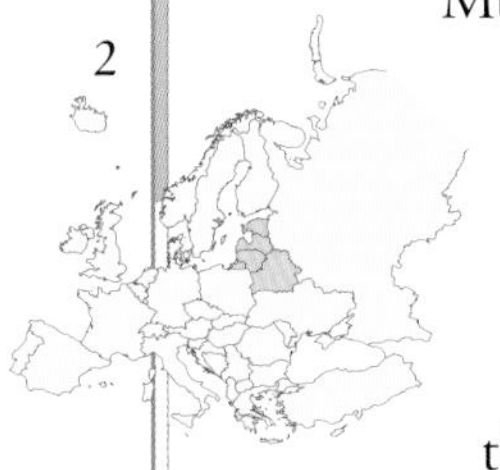

Much of Northeastern Europe's low-lying landscape was fashioned during the last ice age. Across the region, extensive plains, scoured flat by ice, are separated by hills and ridges originally deposited by the wide snouts of glaciers. Innumerable lakes fill hollows, and winding rivers have given rise to some of Europe's largest wetlands. Due to their proximity to the Baltic Sea, the nations of Estonia, Latvia, and Lithuania are often referred to as the Baltic States, even though the three countries are ethnically and linguistically distinct. In common with their southern neighbor Belarus, the Baltic States were, for long periods of their histories, controlled by more powerful nations, including Poland, Russia, Germany, Denmark, and Sweden. In the mid-20th century, all four countries became part of the Soviet Union, but all reasserted their independence soon after the collapse of the Eastern bloc in 1989. The Russian enclave around Kaliningrad is a remnant of the Soviet empire, and a vital Baltic port for the Russian Federation.

Gulf of Finland
ESTONIA
LATVIA
RUSSIAN FEDERATION
Baltic Sea
Gulf of Riga
Irbe Strait
Lake Peipus
Lake Pskov
Narva Bay
TALLINN
RĪGA
Tartu
Pärnu
Narva
Hiiumaa
Saaremaa
Muhu
Liepāja
Ventspils
Daugavpils
Šiauliai
Central Highlands of Vidzemes
Gaiziņkalns 1020ft (311m)
Suur Munamägi 1043ft (318m)
Western Dvina

Population Patterns

Northeastern Europe's population is fairly evenly spread, though it thins out in northern Latvia and on Estonia's chilly Baltic coast—only 14 of Estonia's 1,541 islands are inhabited. About 60 percent of people in Latvia and 70 percent in the other countries are urban dwellers; in both Estonia and Latvia roughly one-third inhabit the capital city. People of Russian origin live throughout the region, but make up 30 percent of the population in Estonia and Latvia, the result of a Soviet policy of encouraging workers from the U.S.S.R. to settle in these states.

TALLINN
Tartu
RĪGA
Liepāja
Daugavpils
Klaipėda
Šiauliai
Kaliningrad
VILNIUS
Vitsyebsk
Mahilyow
MINSK
Hrodna
Baranavichy
Homyel'
Brest

2.6–26 per sq mile/ 1–10 per sq km
26–65 per sq mile/ 10–25 per sq km
65–130 per sq mile/ 25–50 per sq km
130–260 per sq mile/ 50–100 per sq km

Economic Profile

These nations are still dealing with the transition to a market economy, and are still dependent to some extent (especially Belarus) on Russian raw materials and sales. Much of Belarus's arable land was contaminated by fallout from Chernobyl, but it remains a significant supplier of flax as well as potash (widely used for fertilizers), and peat (from its marshlands); its heavy industries produce machinery, tools, tractors, and trucks. Estonia's oil-shale provides much of the Baltic States' energy. The Baltic States are also noted for wood products and textiles, and Lithuania is a major source of amber.

Cereals
Flax
Potatoes
Vegetables
Dairy cattle
Sugar beet
Pigs
Industrial center
Timber
Forest and woodland
Arable land

TALLINN
Tartu
RĪGA
Liepāja
Daugavpils
Klaipėda
Šiauliai
Kaliningrad
VILNIUS
Vitsyebsk
MINSK
Mahilyow
Hrodna
Baranavichy
Homyel'
Brest

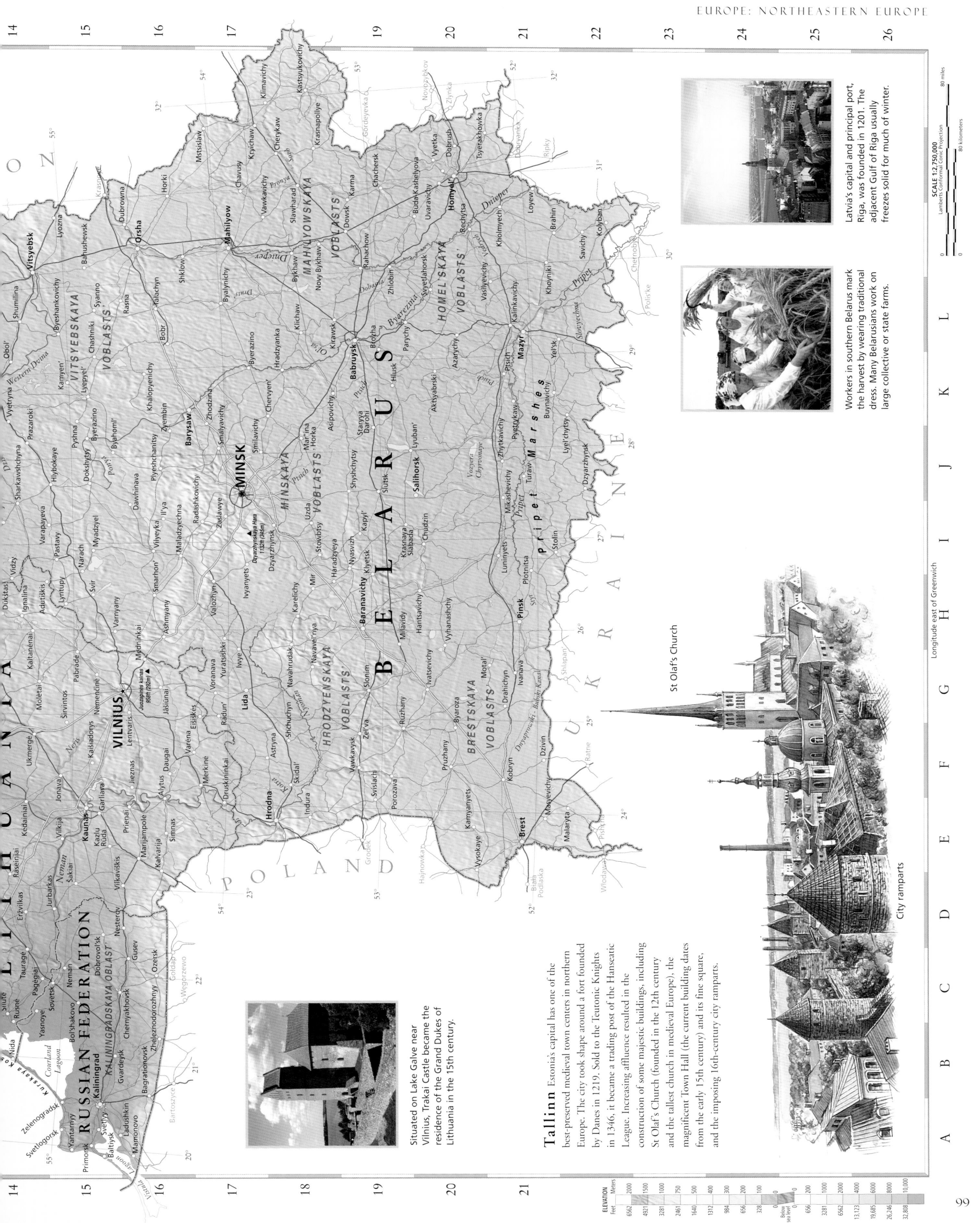

LITHUANIA
RUSSIAN FEDERATION
KALININGRADSKAYA OBLAST'
Kaliningrad
Courland Lagoon
Vistula Lagoon
POLAND
UKRAINE
BELARUS
MINSK
VILNIUS
Juozapinės kalnas 958ft (292m)
Dzyarzhynskaya Hara 1132ft (345m)
VITSYEBSKAYA VOBLASTS'
MAHILYOWSKAYA VOBLASTS'
MINSKAYA VOBLASTS'
HRODZYENSKAYA VOBLASTS'
BRESTSKAYA VOBLASTS'
HOMEL'SKAYA VOBLASTS'
Pripet Marshes
Vitsyebsk
Orsha
Mahilyow
Barysaw
Babruysk
Homyel'
Mazyr
Pinsk
Brest
Hrodna
Lida
Baranavichy
Salihorsk
Kaunas
Western Dvina
Dnieper
Pripet
Neman
Dnyaprowska-Buhski Kanal
14
15
16
17
18
19
20
21
22
23
24
25
26
A
B
C
D
E
F
G
H
I
J
K
L
Longitude east of Greenwich
SCALE 1:2,750,000
Lamberts Conformal Conic Projection
0
80 miles
0
80 kilometers

Situated on Lake Galve near Vilnius, Trakai Castle became the residence of the Grand Dukes of Lithuania in the 15th century.

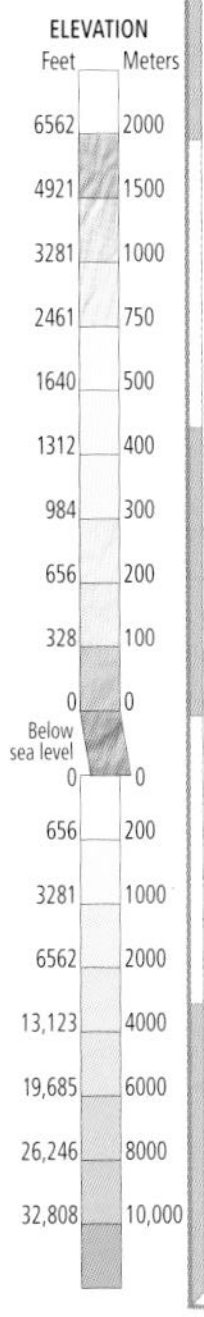
ELEVATION
Feet Meters
6562 2000
4921 1500
3281 1000
2461 750
1640 500
1312 400
984 300
656 200
328 100
0 0
Below sea level
0 0
656 200
3281 1000
6562 2000
13,123 4000
19,685 6000
26,246 8000
32,808 10,000

Tallinn Estonia's capital has one of the best-preserved medieval town centers in northern Europe. The city took shape around a fort founded by Danes in 1219. Sold to the Teutonic Knights in 1346, it became a trading post of the Hanseatic League. Increasing affluence resulted in the construction of some majestic buildings, including St Olaf's Church (founded in the 12th century and the tallest church in medieval Europe), the magnificent Town Hall (the current building dates from the early 15th century) and its fine square, and the imposing 16th-century city ramparts.

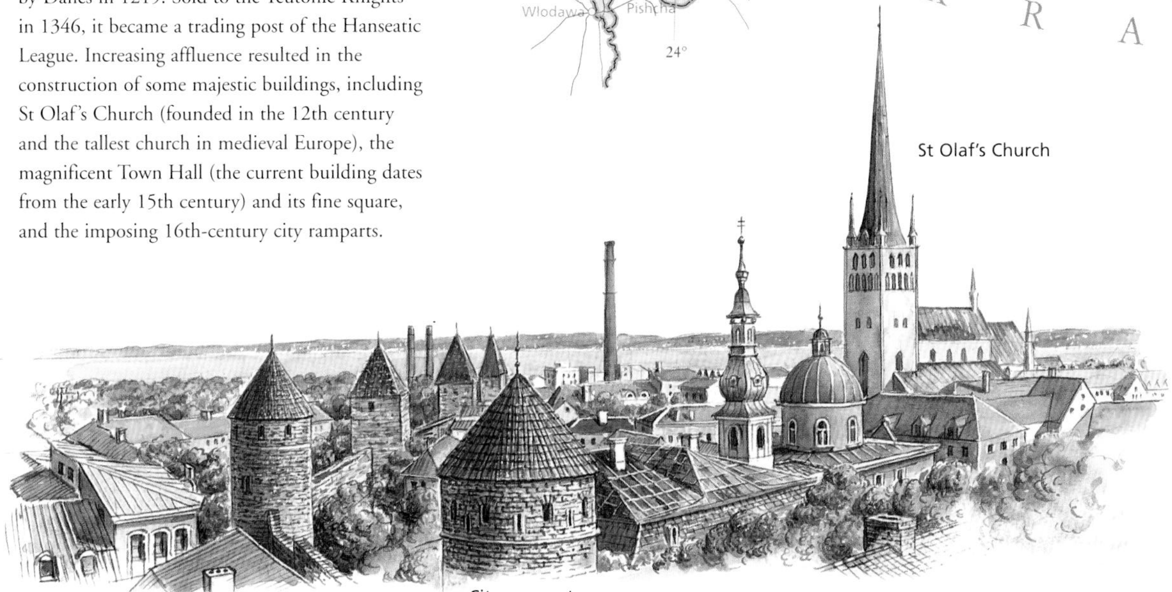
St Olaf's Church
City ramparts

Workers in southern Belarus mark the harvest by wearing traditional dress. Many Belarusians work on large collective or state farms.

Latvia's capital and principal port, Rīga, was founded in 1201. The adjacent Gulf of Riga usually freezes solid for much of winter.

CENTRAL EASTERN EUROPE

Moldova, Romania, Ukraine

Three major rivers flow through Central Eastern Europe to the north shore of the Black Sea. The Danube courses along Romania's southern border, its vast floodplain contrasting with the mountains of the interior. The Dniester runs from the uplands of western Ukraine along the eastern edge of Moldova; in western Moldova, hundreds of other, mainly short, rivers have carved steep ravines and gorges amid low hills. Flowing first south, then east and west in a great S-shape, the Dnieper River snakes through the immense steppe grasslands that cover most of Ukraine. Formerly part of the Soviet Union, Ukraine is now Europe's largest country. Romania and Moldova share strong linguistic and ethnic links, and most of Moldova was incorporated into Romania from 1918 to 1940. In the mid-20th century, both nations were part of the Eastern bloc; like Ukraine, they are now independent fledgling democracies.

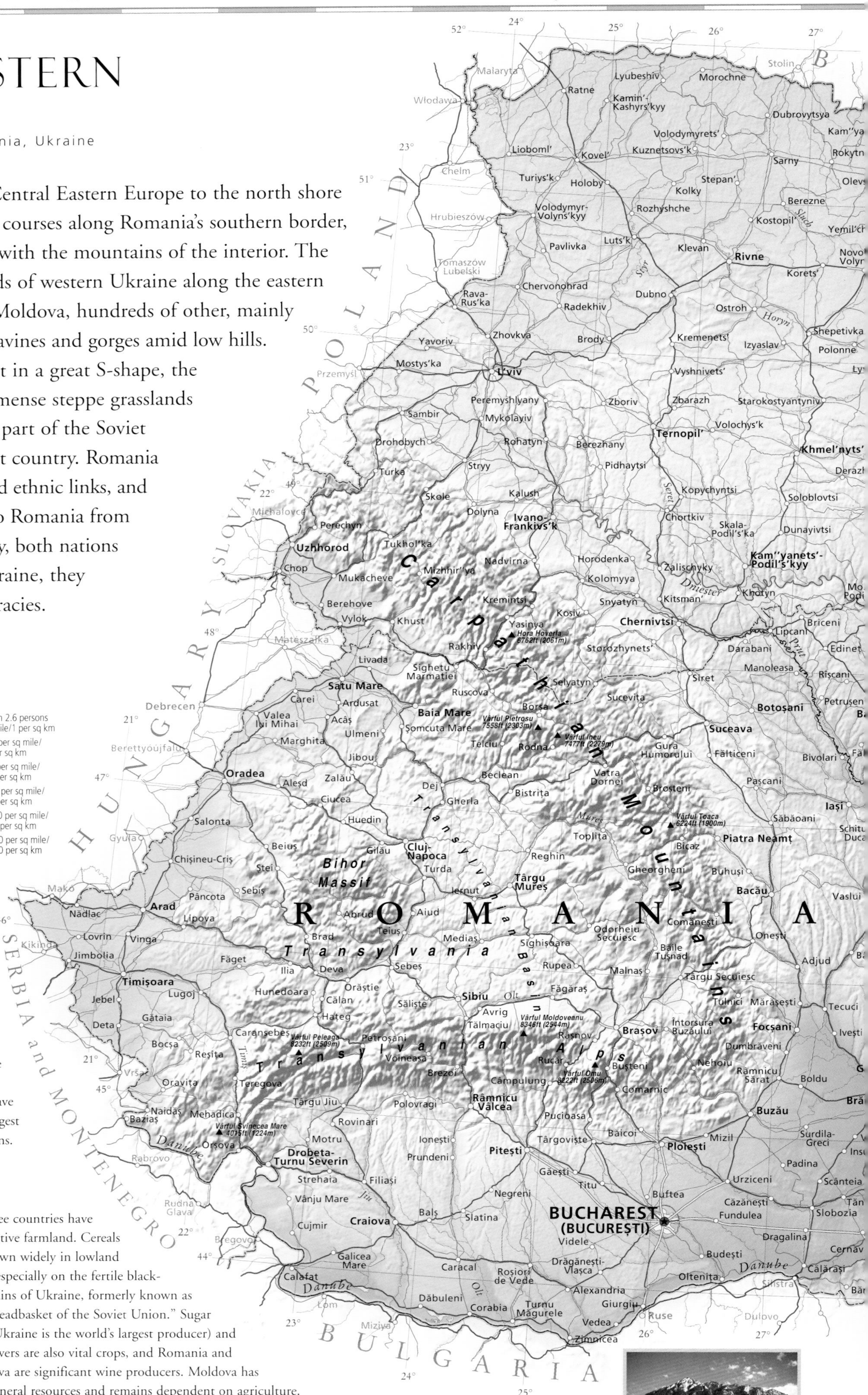

A B C D E F G H I J K L M
1 2 3 4 5 6 7 8 9 10 11 12 13 14 15
POLAND
SLOVAKIA
HUNGARY
SERBIA and MONTENEGRO
BULGARIA
ROMANIA
Carpathian Mountains
Transylvanian Alps
Transylvanian Basin
Transylvania
Bihor Massif
Danube
Dniester
Prut
Mureș
Olt
Jiu
Siret
Horyn
Sluch
Styr
Malaryta
Włodawa
Chełm
Hrubieszów
Tomaszów Lubelski
Przemyśl
Lyubeshiv
Morochne
Stolin
Ratne
Kamin'-Kashyrs'kyy
Dubrovytsya
Volodymyrets'
Kuznetsovs'k
Kam''yans'
Rokytne
Sarny
Liuboml'
Kovel'
Turiys'k
Holoby
Stepan'
Kolky
Rozhyshche
Berezne
Olevs'k
Volodymyr-Volyns'kyy
Kostopil'
Yemil'ch
Pavlivka
Luts'k
Klevan
Rivne
Novohrad-Volyns'kyy
Korets'
Chervonohrad
Rava-Rus'ka
Dubno
Radekhiv
Ostroh
Zhovkva
Kremenets'
Izyaslav
Shepetivka
Polonne
Yavoriv
Brody
Mostys'ka
L'viv
Vyshnivets'
Peremyshlyany
Zboriv
Zbarazh
Starokostyantyniv
Sambir
Mykolayiv
Volochys'k
Drohobych
Rohatyn
Berezhany
Ternopil'
Khmel'nyts'kyy
Turka
Stryy
Pidhaytsi
Derazhnya
Skole
Kalush
Kopychyntsi
Dolyna
Soloblovtsi
Michalovce
Ivano-Frankivs'k
Chortkiv
Perechyn
Skala-Podil's'ka
Dunayivtsi
Uzhhorod
Tukhol'ka
Nadvirna
Horodenka
Kam''yanets'-Podil's'kyy
Chop
Mizhhir''ya
Zalishchyky
Mukacheve
Kolomyya
Khotyn
Berehove
Kremintsi
Sniatyn
Kitsman
Vylok
Khust
Kosiv
Chernivtsi
Briceni
Yasinya
Hora Hoverla 6762ft (2061m)
Lipcani
Mátészalka
Rakhiv
Storozhynets'
Darabani
Edineț
Livada
Sighetu Marmatiei
Selyatyn
Manoleasa
Siret
Rîșcani
Debrecen
Satu Mare
Carei
Ardusat
Ruscova
Suceava
Botoșani
Petrușeni
Valea lui Mihai
Acâș
Baia Mare
Borșa
Vârful Pietrosu 7558ft (2303m)
Șomcuta Mare
Ulmeni
Vârful Ineu 7477ft (2279m)
Berettyóújfalu
Marghita
Teiciu
Rodna
Gura Humorului
Fălticeni
Bivolari
Jibou
Oradea
Aleșd
Zalău
Beclean
Vatra Dornei
Pașcani
Dej
Brosteni
Ciucea
Gherla
Bistrița
Iași
Huedin
Vârful Ceahlău 6224ft (1900m)
Săbăoani
Salonta
Cluj-Napoca
Toplița
Gyula
Beiuș
Gilău
Turda
Reghin
Bicaz
Piatra Neamț
Chișineu-Criș
Ștei
Gheorgheni
Buhuși
Târgu Mureș
Bacău
Makó
Pâncota
Sebiș
Iernut
Vaslui
Nădlac
Arad
Lipova
Abrud
Aiud
Comănești
Teiuș
Odorheiu Secuiesc
Onești
Kikinda
Lovrin
Vinga
Brad
Mediaș
Sighișoara
Băile Tușnad
Jimbolia
Făget
Deva
Sebeș
Rupea
Malnaș
Adjud
Timișoara
Ilia
Orăștie
Făgăraș
Târgu Secuiesc
Lugoj
Hunedoara
Călan
Săliște
Sibiu
Tulnici
Mărășești
Jebel
Hațeg
Avrig
Tecuci
Deta
Gătaia
Tălmaciu
Vârful Moldoveanu 8346ft (2544m)
Râșnov
Brașov
Întorsura Buzăului
Focșani
Caransebeș
Vârful Peleaga 8232ft (2509m)
Petroșani
Dumbrăveni
Bocșa
Reșița
Vulcan
Rucăr
Bușteni
Nehoiu
Ivești
Vršac
Brezoi
Vârful Omu 8222ft (2506m)
Râmnicu Sărat
Oravița
Teregova
Câmpulung
Comarnic
Boldu
Naidăș
Mehadica
Târgu Jiu
Polovragi
Râmnicu Vâlcea
Buzău
Baziaș
Vârful Svinecea Mare 4015ft (1224m)
Rovinari
Pucioasa
Orșova
Motru
Ionești
Târgoviște
Baicoi
Mizil
Surdila-Greci
Drobeta-Turnu Severin
Prundeni
Pitești
Ploiești
Rabrovo
Strehaia
Filiași
Găești
Urziceni
Padina
Titu
Buftea
Scânteia
Rudna Glava
Vânju Mare
Negreni
Cujmir
Craiova
Balș
Slatina
BUCHAREST (BUCUREȘTI)
Căzănești
Fundulea
Slobozia
Brегovo
Videle
Dragalina
Budești
Cernavodă
Calafat
Galicea Mare
Caracal
Roșiori de Vede
Drăgănești-Vlașca
Oltenița
Călărași
Lom
Dăbuleni
Corabia
Turnu Măgurele
Alexandria
Giurgiu
Silistra
Miziya
Ruse
Vedea
Zimnicea
Dulovo
52° 51° 50° 49° 48° 47° 46° 45° 44°
21° 22° 23° 24° 25° 26° 27°
Longitude east of Greenwich

POPULATION PATTERNS

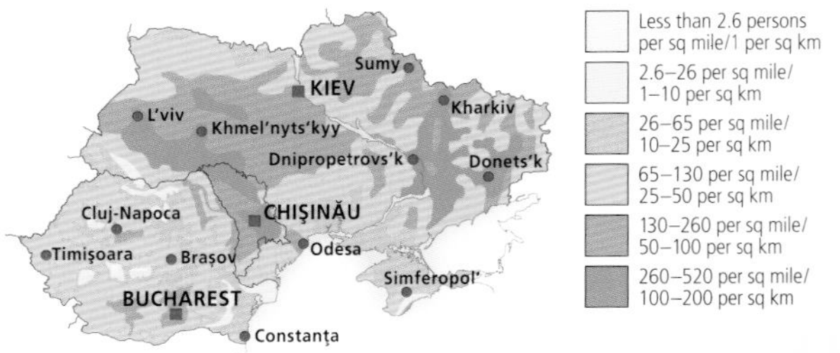

KIEV
Sumy
Kharkiv
L'viv
Khmel'nyts'kyy
Dnipropetrovs'k
Donets'k
Cluj-Napoca
CHIȘINĂU
Odesa
Timișoara
Brașov
Simferopol'
BUCHAREST
Constanța
Less than 2.6 persons per sq mile/1 per sq km
2.6–26 per sq mile/ 1–10 per sq km
26–65 per sq mile/ 10–25 per sq km
65–130 per sq mile/ 25–50 per sq km
130–260 per sq mile/ 50–100 per sq km
260–520 per sq mile/ 100–200 per sq km

Moldova is the most densely populated of the former Soviet republics, yet the majority of its inhabitants still live in rural areas; one-third of the urban population dwells in the capital. More than half of Romanians and Ukrainians live in towns and cities. Romania has areas of low population density in the mountains and swampy Danube Delta; Ukraine's population is a little more evenly spread, with the highest concentrations in the industrial southeast—home to one-third of the population—and the fertile belt that runs eastward from the Dniester. Ukraine and Moldova have many inhabitants of Russian origin, whereas Romania's largest minorities are ethnic Roma (Gypsy) people and Hungarians.

ECONOMIC PROFILE

KIEV
Sumy
Kharkiv
L'viv
Khmel'nyts'kyy
Dnipropetrovs'k
Donets'k
Cluj-Napoca
CHIȘINĂU
Odesa
Timișoara
Brașov
Simferopol'
BUCHAREST
Constanța
Forest and woodland
Arable land
Grazing
Cereals
Sugar beet
Flowers
Dairy cattle
Industrial center
Mining
Oil production
Gas production
Wine
Fishing

All three countries have productive farmland. Cereals are grown widely in lowland areas, especially on the fertile black-soil plains of Ukraine, formerly known as "the breadbasket of the Soviet Union." Sugar beet (Ukraine is the world's largest producer) and sunflowers are also vital crops, and Romania and Moldova are significant wine producers. Moldova has few mineral resources and remains dependent on agriculture. Romania and Ukraine's reserves of oil, coal, and gas support major industries including the manufacture of metals, machinery, and chemicals. Textiles and footwear are important in Romania. Despite some economic progress, these nations remain among Europe's poorest.

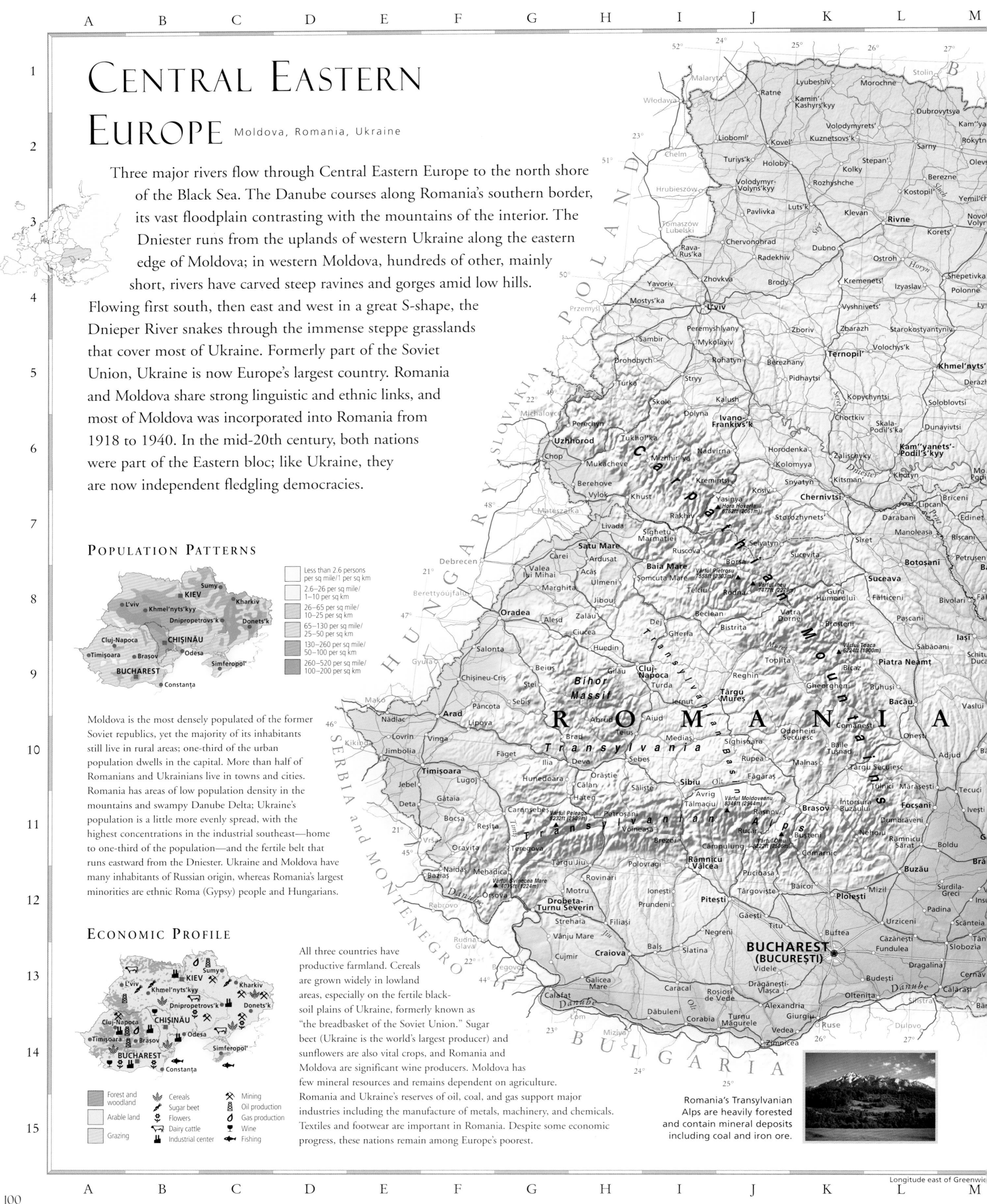

Romania's Transylvanian Alps are heavily forested and contain mineral deposits including coal and iron ore.

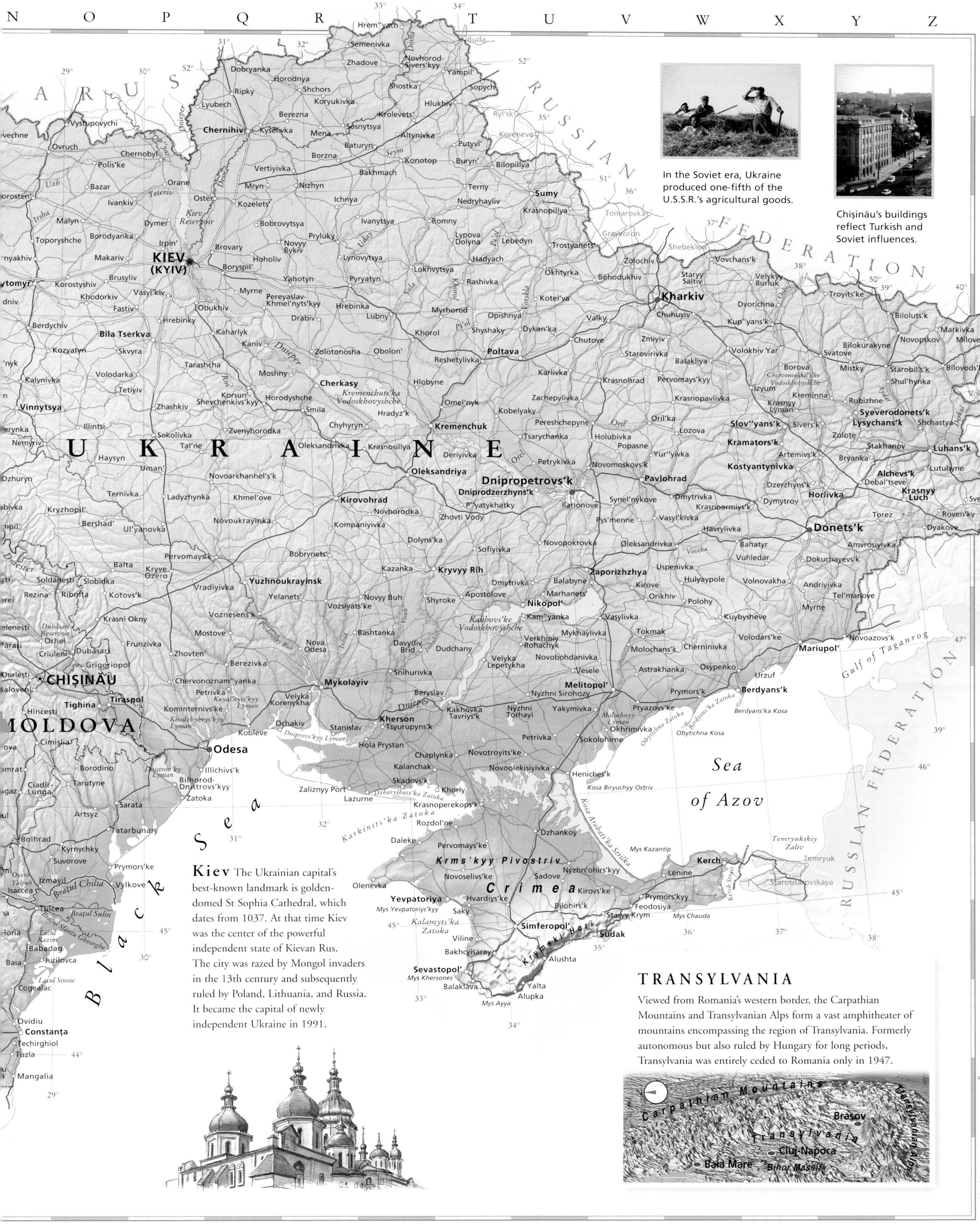
N O P Q R S T U V W X Y Z
UKRAINE
MOLDOVA
RUSSIAN FEDERATION
KIEV (KYIV)
CHIȘINĂU
Kharkiv
Dnipropetrovs'k
Donets'k
Zaporizhzhya
Odesa
Mykolayiv
Kherson
Sumy
Poltava
Luhans'k
Mariupol'
Simferopol'
Sevastopol'
Crimea
Krms'kyy Pivostriv
Black Sea
Sea of Azov
Gulf of Taganrog
Dnieper
1 2 3 8 9 10 11

In the Soviet era, Ukraine produced one-fifth of the U.S.S.R.'s agricultural goods.

Chișinău's buildings reflect Turkish and Soviet influences.

Kiev The Ukrainian capital's best-known landmark is golden-domed St Sophia Cathedral, which dates from 1037. At that time Kiev was the center of the powerful independent state of Kievan Rus. The city was razed by Mongol invaders in the 13th century and subsequently ruled by Poland, Lithuania, and Russia. It became the capital of newly independent Ukraine in 1991.

TRANSYLVANIA

Viewed from Romania's western border, the Carpathian Mountains and Transylvanian Alps form a vast amphitheater of mountains encompassing the region of Transylvania. Formerly autonomous but also ruled by Hungary for long periods, Transylvania was entirely ceded to Romania only in 1947.

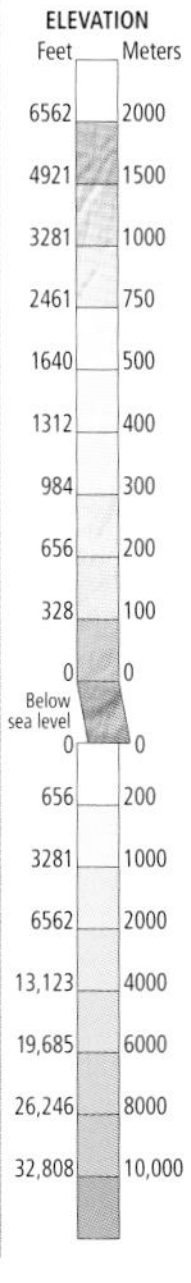
ELEVATION
Feet Meters
6562 2000
4921 1500
3281 1000
2461 750
1640 500
1312 400
984 300
656 200
328 100
0 0
Below sea level
0 0
656 200
3281 1000
6562 2000
13,123 4000
19,685 6000
26,246 8000
32,808 10,000

SCALE 1:3,500,000
Lamberts Conformal Conic Projection
0 100 miles
0 100 kilometers

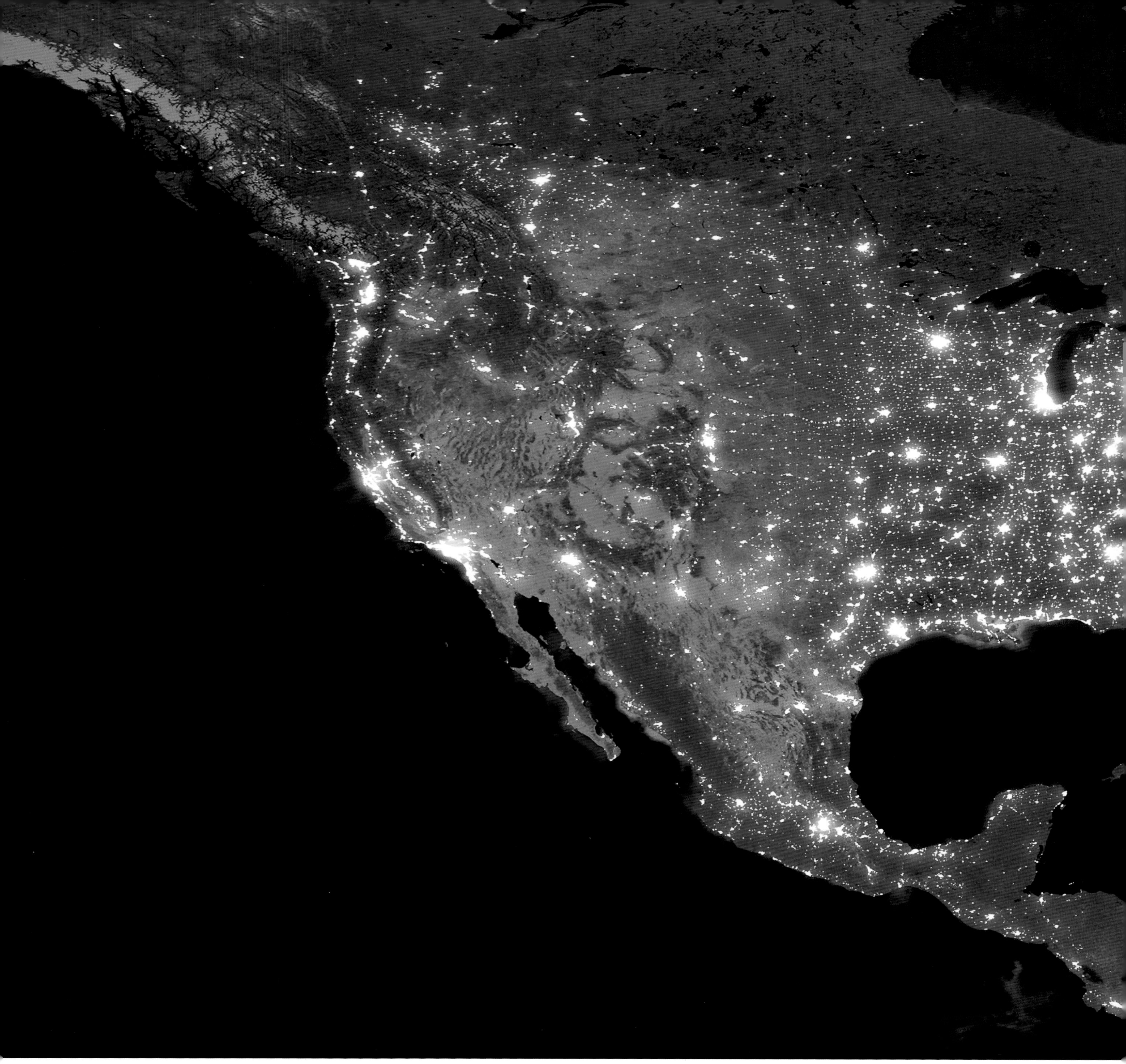

This image from space reveals the concentration of people and infrastructure in the eastern part of the North American continent. The interstate highways create a lattice pattern across the United States, connecting the bright areas of the city centers.

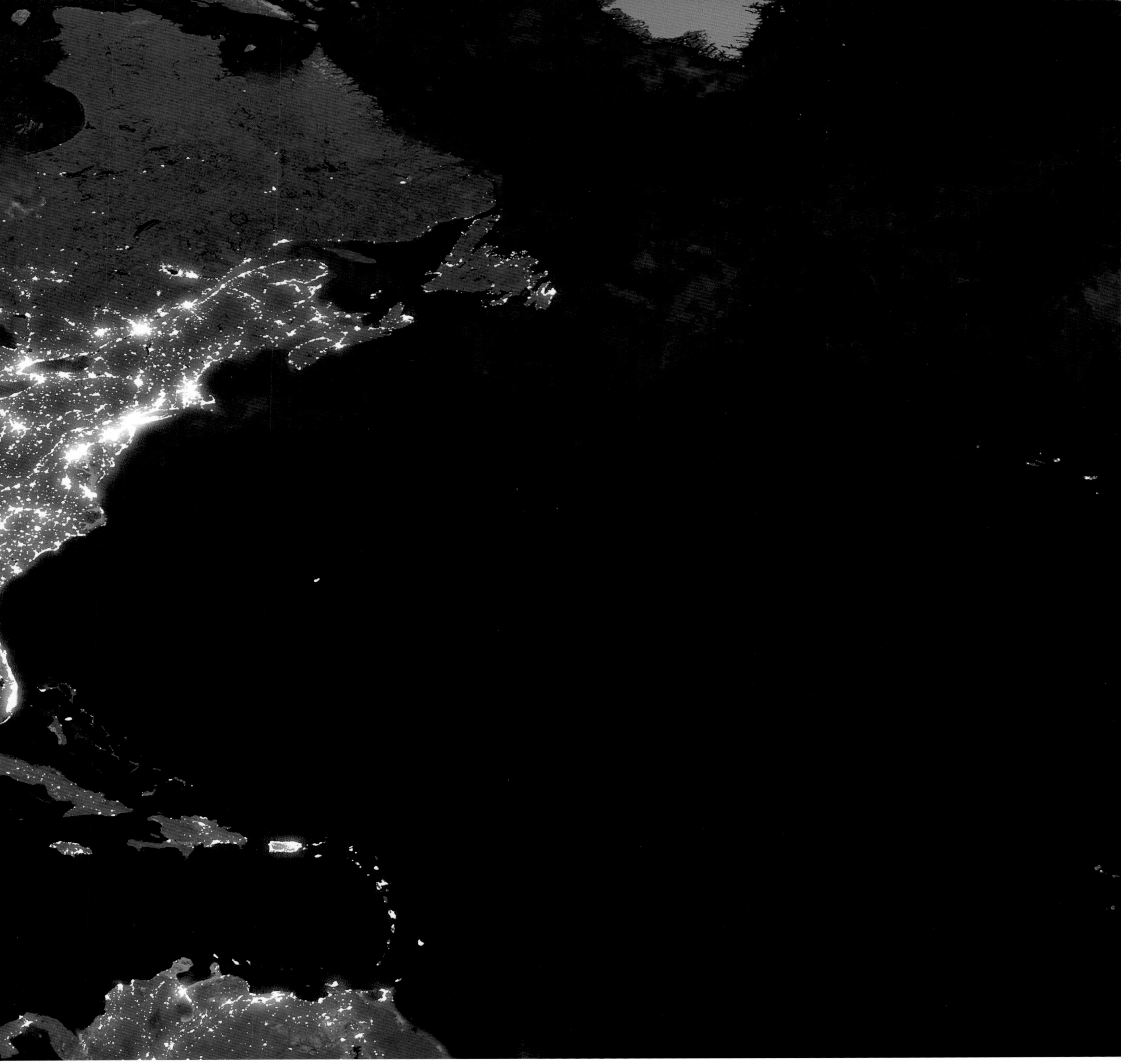

North America

Right: This composite image of Hawaiian coffee plantations was created from more than 300 images collected over four hours by an uninhabited aerial vechicle (UAV). Differences in the color of the coffee fields indicate varying levels of ripeness. This information was used in planning which fields to harvest first.

Far right: The Malaspina Glacier fans out in a broad tongue between Icy Bay and Yakutat Bay, Alaska. The red ridged area is a terminal moraine of rocks, deposited by the glacier and now protecting it from contact with the open ocean, shown as dark blue. The glacier has thinned since this image was acquired in August 2000.

Right: Snow lies on the north and south rims of the Grand Canyon, Arizona, starkly outlining the mighty swathe scoured out by the Colorado River. A lack of vegetation further accentuates the impact of this dramatic landform. The canyon's south rim, on the left of this image, is a vertical mile (1.6 km) above the snow-free floor.

Below right: Highlighted by this false-color image, the boundary between the U.S. and Mexico becomes startlingly apparent. The gridded and irrigated agricultural fields of California's Imperial Valley, north of the border, contrast vividly with Mexico's less developed lands. The border town of Mexicali-Calexico is in the center.

The View from Above

Satellite photography reveals North America's extraordinary diversity of landforms, from the huge glaciated arc around Hudson Bay to the vast lowlands of the Great Plains in the center of the continent and the high spine of mountain ranges that run down the west coast. Often national borders can also be detected. This is due to differing land use practices between the nations that share the continent. In the north, the rolling wheatfields of Montana, in the United States, give way abruptly to Canadian rangeland. In the south, the border between the U.S. and Mexico is one of the few places on the planet where a highly developed nation adjoins a developing one. The contrast is graphically illustrated in false-color images, which display vegetation in shades of red. The view from space is now a vital tool in agriculture, providing information on the extent, health, and progress of crops.

LAND AND ENVIRONMENT

Stretching from the Arctic Circle almost to the Equator, North America covers 9.5 million square miles (24.6 million sq km) and is the third-largest continent. It is bounded by ocean on all sides and linked to South America only by the slender Isthmus of Panama. As well as the mainland, it includes Greenland, the islands of the Caribbean (the West Indies), and the Hawaiian Islands, which lie 2,500 miles (4,000 km) away, in the middle of the Pacific Ocean. Mountains dominate the west and south of the mainland, coastal ranges running from Alaska to Panama and the Rocky Mountains arcing through Canada and the United States. East of the Rockies lie the plateau of the Great Plains and the lowlands of the Canadian Shield and U.S. Midwest. The lowlands extend to the Gulf of Mexico in the south; in the east and north, they are bounded by ancient mountains, including the Appalachian Mountains, the Laurentian Mountains, and the uplands of Labrador.

ASIA
Chukchi Sea
Bering Strait
Bering Sea
Aleutian Islands
Aleutian Range
PACIFIC OCEAN
Gulf of Alaska
Brooks Range
Alaska Range
Mt McKinley 20,321ft (6194m)
Yukon
Beaufort Sea
Queen Elizabeth Islands
Ellesmere Island
Axel Heiberg Island
Ellef Ringnes Island
Parry Islands
Melville Island
Bathurst Island
Devon Island
Banks Island
Somerset Island
Prince of Wales Island
Victoria Island
Boothia Peninsula
Baffin Bay
Baffin Island
Melville Peninsula
Foxe Basin
Hudson Bay
Mackenzie Mountains
Mackenzie
Great Bear Lake
Great Slave Lake
Lake Athabasca
Reindeer Lake
Canadian Shield
Coast Mountains
Rocky Mountains
Peace
Athabasca
North Saskatchewan
South
Lake Winnipeg
Lake Manitoba
Lake Nipigon
Lake Superior
Lake Michigan
Great Lakes
Mt Rainier 14,409ft (4392m)
Cascade Range
Columbia
Snake
Coast Ranges
Sierra Nevada
Great Basin
Great Salt Lake
Mt Elbert 14,432ft (4399m)
Mt Whitney 14,495ft (4418m)
Colorado
Colorado Plateau
Grand Canyon
Mojave Desert
Sonoran Desert
Great Plains
Central Lowlands
Missouri
Mississippi
Ohio
Arkansas
Baja California
Gulf of California
Sierra Madre Occidental
Sierra Madre Oriental
Rio Grande
Gulf-Atlantic Coast
Mississippi Delta
Gulf of Mexico
Yucatan Peninsula
Volcan Popocatepetl 17,887ft (5452m)
Pico de Orizaba 18,405ft (5610m)
Sierra Madre del Sur

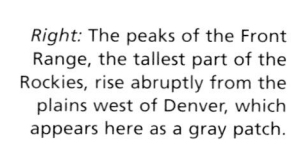

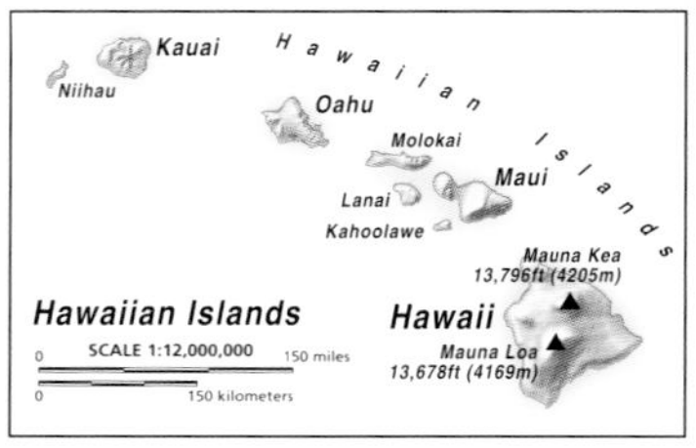

Kauai
Niihau
Hawaiian Islands
Oahu
Molokai
Lanai
Maui
Kahoolawe
Mauna Kea 13,796ft (4205m)
Hawaii
Mauna Loa 13,678ft (4169m)
Hawaiian Islands
SCALE 1:12,000,000
150 miles
150 kilometers

Left: The world's second-largest ice sheet covers 80 percent of Greenland, shown at the bottom of this satellite image. Ellesmere Island appears at top left.

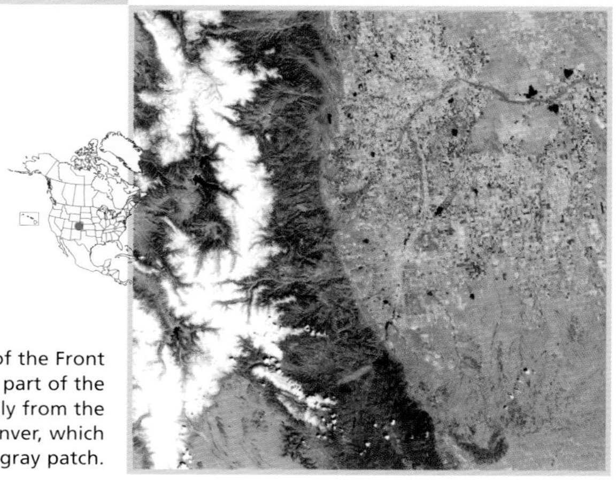

Right: The peaks of the Front Range, the tallest part of the Rockies, rise abruptly from the plains west of Denver, which appears here as a gray patch.

NATURAL HAZARDS

Tornadoes

Tornadoes occur in many parts of the world but are most strongly associated with and most common in the United States—about 1,000 are recorded there each year. At certain times of the year, cold air from the Arctic meets warm, moist air from the tropics over the central and eastern U.S.A., fueling atmospheric instability and thunderstorms. On occasions, wind patterns cause a storm to rotate, creating a spinning column of air, or tornado. Generating powerful updrafts and fearsome winds of up to 300 mph (480 km/h), a tornado can obliterate almost anything in its path.

AVERAGE NUMBER OF TORNADOES PER YEAR PER 10,000 SQUARE MILES (26,000 SQ KM)

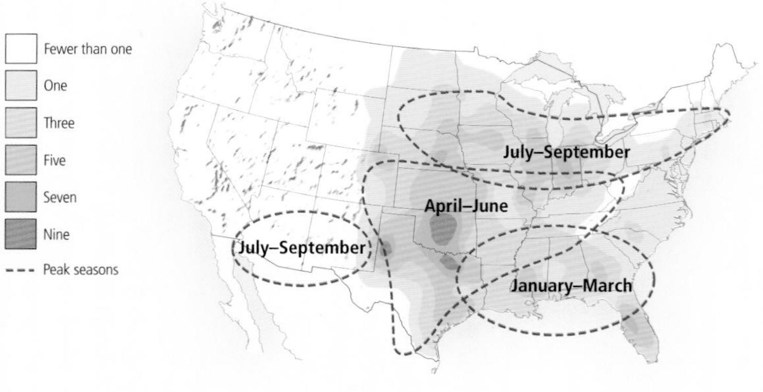

Fewer than one
One
Three
Five
Seven
Nine
Peak seasons
July–September
April–June
July–September
January–March

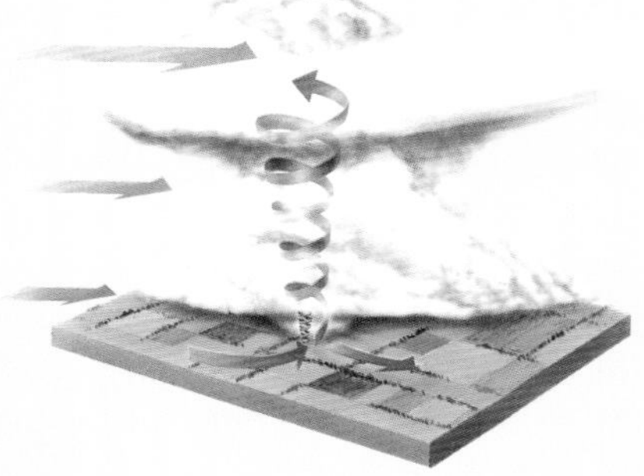

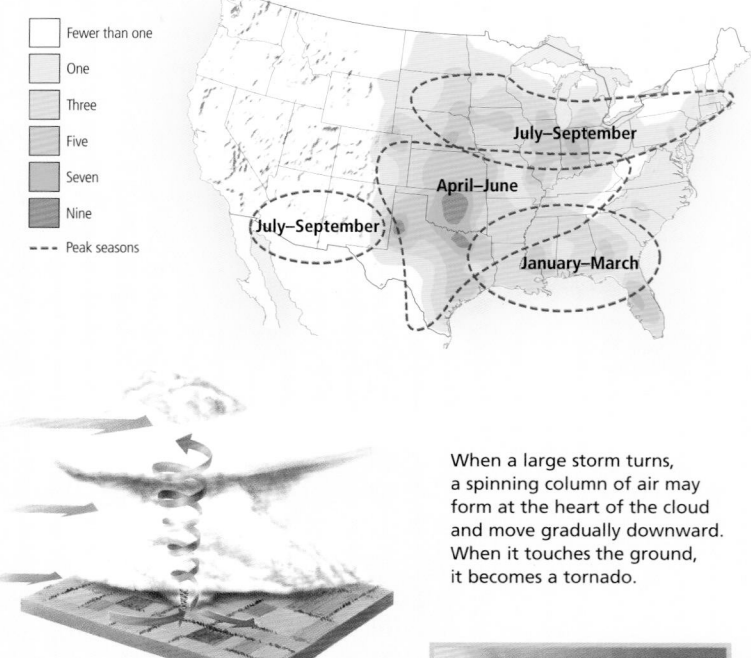

When a large storm turns, a spinning column of air may form at the heart of the cloud and move gradually downward. When it touches the ground, it becomes a tornado.

The outline of a tornado may be enhanced by condensation or the dust and debris it draws skyward.

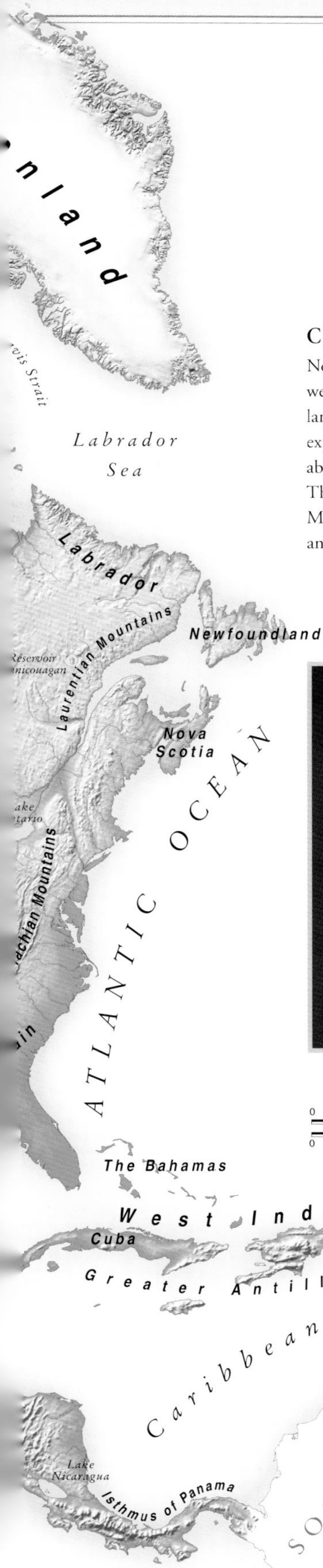
nland
Labrador Sea
Labrador
Newfoundland
Laurentian Mountains
Nova Scotia
ATLANTIC OCEAN
The Bahamas
West Indies
Cuba
Greater Antilles
Leeward Islands
Windward Islands
Caribbean Sea
Lesser Antilles
SOUTH AMERICA
Lake Nicaragua
Isthmus of Panama

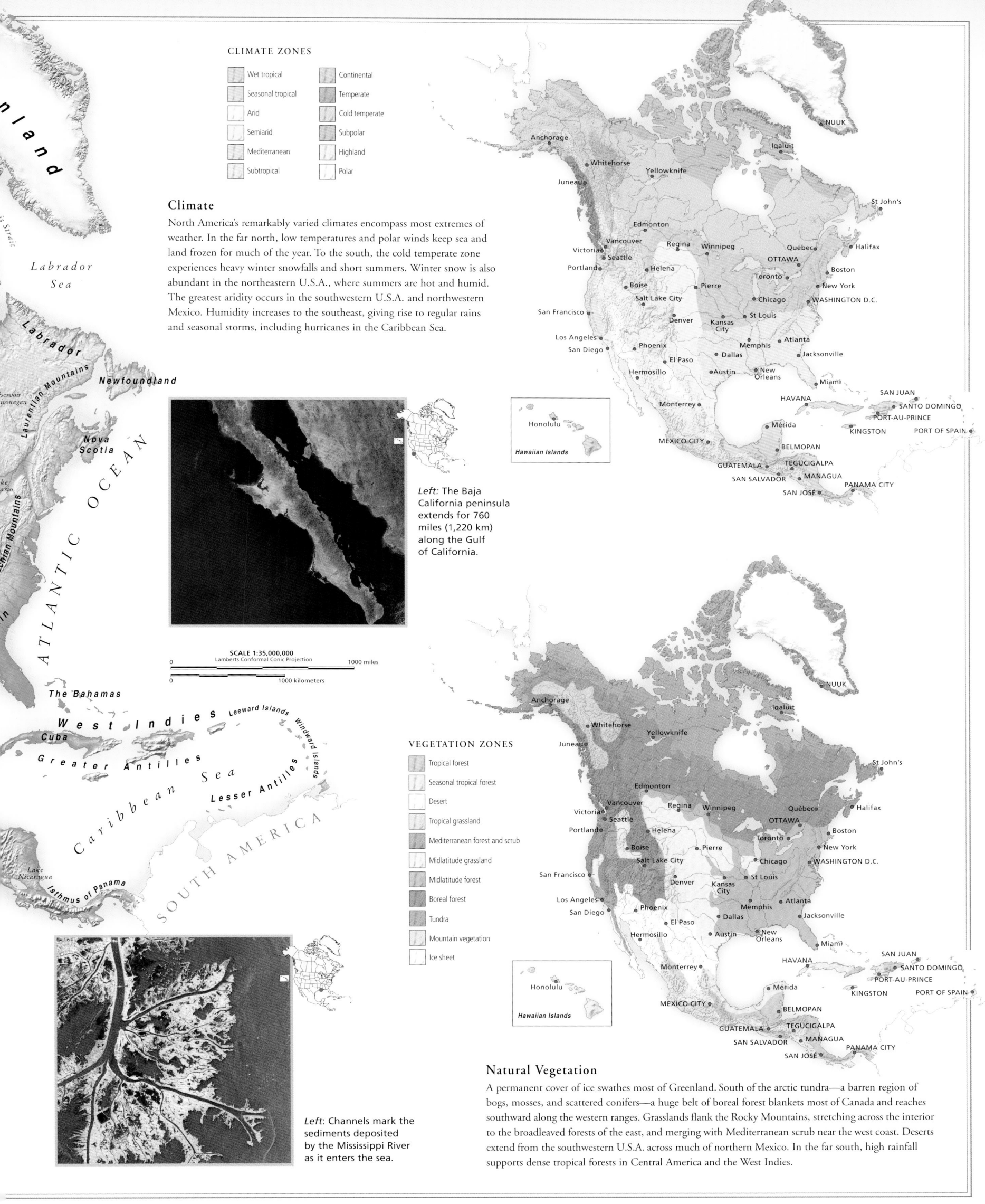

CLIMATE ZONES

- Wet tropical
- Seasonal tropical
- Arid
- Semiarid
- Mediterranean
- Subtropical
- Continental
- Temperate
- Cold temperate
- Subpolar
- Highland
- Polar

NUUK
Anchorage
Iqaluit
Whitehorse
Yellowknife
Juneau
St John's
Edmonton
Vancouver
Victoria
Seattle
Regina
Winnipeg
Québec
Halifax
OTTAWA
Portland
Helena
Boise
Pierre
Toronto
Boston
New York
Salt Lake City
Chicago
WASHINGTON D.C.
San Francisco
Denver
Kansas City
St Louis
Los Angeles
San Diego
Phoenix
Memphis
Atlanta
El Paso
Dallas
Jacksonville
Hermosillo
Austin
New Orleans
Miami
Monterrey
HAVANA
SAN JUAN
SANTO DOMINGO
PORT-AU-PRINCE
KINGSTON
PORT OF SPAIN
Mérida
MEXICO CITY
BELMOPAN
GUATEMALA
TEGUCIGALPA
SAN SALVADOR
MANAGUA
PANAMA CITY
SAN JOSÉ
Honolulu
Hawaiian Islands

Climate

North America's remarkably varied climates encompass most extremes of weather. In the far north, low temperatures and polar winds keep sea and land frozen for much of the year. To the south, the cold temperate zone experiences heavy winter snowfalls and short summers. Winter snow is also abundant in the northeastern U.S.A., where summers are hot and humid. The greatest aridity occurs in the southwestern U.S.A. and northwestern Mexico. Humidity increases to the southeast, giving rise to regular rains and seasonal storms, including hurricanes in the Caribbean Sea.

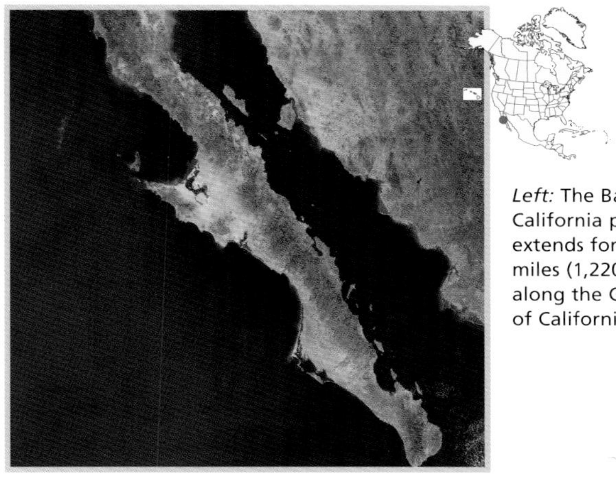

Left: The Baja California peninsula extends for 760 miles (1,220 km) along the Gulf of California.

SCALE 1:35,000,000
Lamberts Conformal Conic Projection
0 — 1000 miles
0 — 1000 kilometers

VEGETATION ZONES

- Tropical forest
- Seasonal tropical forest
- Desert
- Tropical grassland
- Mediterranean forest and scrub
- Midlatitude grassland
- Midlatitude forest
- Boreal forest
- Tundra
- Mountain vegetation
- Ice sheet

NUUK
Anchorage
Iqaluit
Whitehorse
Yellowknife
Juneau
St John's
Edmonton
Vancouver
Victoria
Seattle
Regina
Winnipeg
Québec
Halifax
OTTAWA
Portland
Helena
Boise
Pierre
Toronto
Boston
New York
Salt Lake City
Chicago
WASHINGTON D.C.
San Francisco
Denver
Kansas City
St Louis
Los Angeles
San Diego
Phoenix
Memphis
Atlanta
El Paso
Dallas
Jacksonville
Hermosillo
Austin
New Orleans
Miami
Monterrey
HAVANA
SAN JUAN
SANTO DOMINGO
PORT-AU-PRINCE
KINGSTON
PORT OF SPAIN
Mérida
MEXICO CITY
BELMOPAN
GUATEMALA
TEGUCIGALPA
SAN SALVADOR
MANAGUA
PANAMA CITY
SAN JOSÉ
Honolulu
Hawaiian Islands

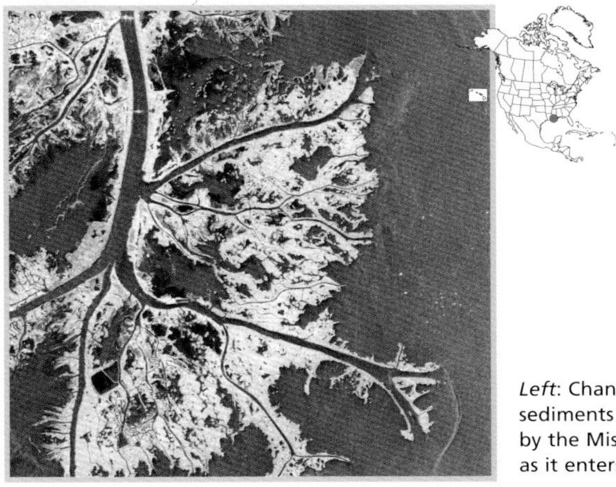

Left: Channels mark the sediments deposited by the Mississippi River as it enters the sea.

Natural Vegetation

A permanent cover of ice swathes most of Greenland. South of the arctic tundra—a barren region of bogs, mosses, and scattered conifers—a huge belt of boreal forest blankets most of Canada and reaches southward along the western ranges. Grasslands flank the Rocky Mountains, stretching across the interior to the broadleaved forests of the east, and merging with Mediterranean scrub near the west coast. Deserts extend from the southwestern U.S.A. across much of northern Mexico. In the far south, high rainfall supports dense tropical forests in Central America and the West Indies.

Peoples and Nations

North America has a population of about 500 million and includes 23 nations and 16 dependencies and territories. These can be divided broadly between the large, affluent, industrialized, predominantly English-speaking nations of Canada and the United States of America (U.S.A.), and the smaller, less affluent, mainly agricultural and Spanish-speaking countries and territories to the south. More than three-quarters of Americans and Canadians are descended from European immigrants, and one-eighth from African slaves; another eighth is of Hispanic origin. Native peoples now account for less than one percent of the population. In the south, Amerindian peoples are significantly outnumbered by mestizos—people of mixed Spanish and Amerindian descent—and also, in the West Indies, by people of African and mixed African–Spanish origin.

The population of Mexico City expanded dramatically in the second half of the 20th century, increasing sixfold between 1950 and 2000. In comparison, New York's population grew by just 25 percent in the same period. Mexico City overtook New York as North America's largest urban center in the mid-1990s and is now the world's third-biggest city.

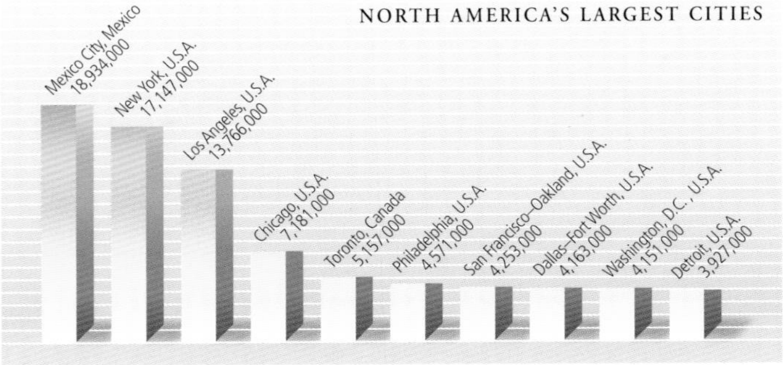
NORTH AMERICA'S LARGEST CITIES
Mexico City, Mexico 18,934,000
New York, U.S.A. 17,147,000
Los Angeles, U.S.A. 13,766,000
Chicago, U.S.A. 7,181,000
Toronto, Canada 5,157,000
Philadelphia, U.S.A. 4,571,000
San Francisco–Oakland, U.S.A. 4,253,000
Dallas–Fort Worth, U.S.A. 4,163,000
Washington, D.C., U.S.A. 4,151,000
Detroit, U.S.A. 3,927,000

Urbanization

Most of North America's largest urban areas are located in the highly industrialized United States and Canada, where four-fifths of inhabitants live in towns and cities. Even in the traditionally agricultural regions of Mexico, Central America, and the West Indies, urbanization has increased dramatically, rising to approximately 65 percent. Many cities in these regions have struggled to cope with the enormous influx of new residents, resulting in widespread social deprivation, most prominent in the form of slums and shanty towns on city fringes.

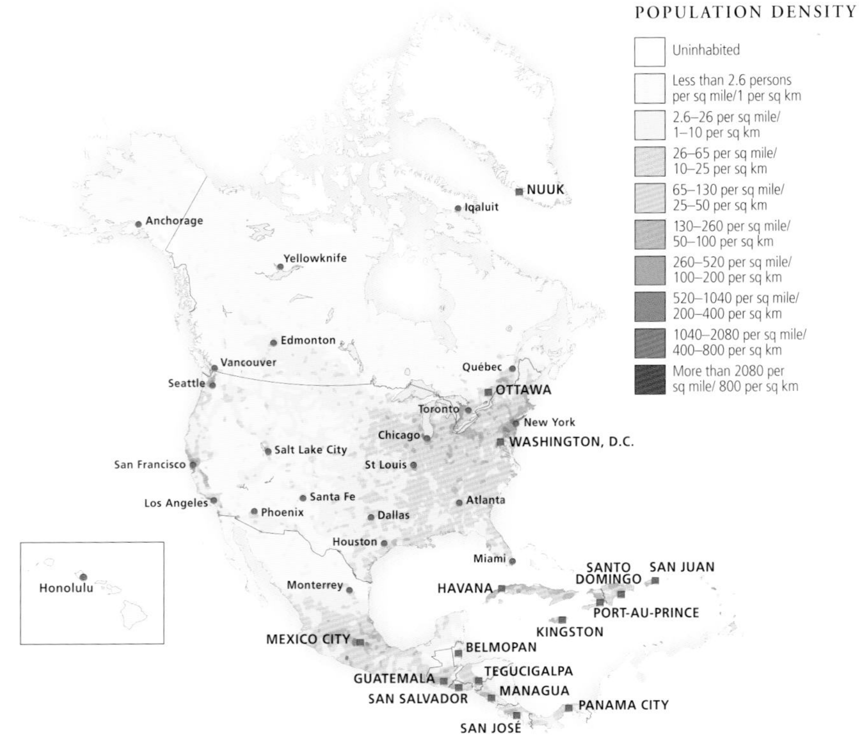
POPULATION DENSITY
Uninhabited
Less than 2.6 persons per sq mile/1 per sq km
2.6–26 per sq mile/ 1–10 per sq km
26–65 per sq mile/ 10–25 per sq km
65–130 per sq mile/ 25–50 per sq km
130–260 per sq mile/ 50–100 per sq km
260–520 per sq mile/ 100–200 per sq km
520–1040 per sq mile/ 200–400 per sq km
1040–2080 per sq mile/ 400–800 per sq km
More than 2080 per sq mile/ 800 per sq km
NUUK
Iqaluit
Anchorage
Yellowknife
Edmonton
Vancouver
Seattle
Québec
OTTAWA
Toronto
New York
WASHINGTON, D.C.
Chicago
Salt Lake City
St Louis
San Francisco
Los Angeles
Santa Fe
Phoenix
Dallas
Atlanta
Houston
Miami
Honolulu
Monterrey
HAVANA
SANTO DOMINGO
SAN JUAN
PORT-AU-PRINCE
KINGSTON
MEXICO CITY
BELMOPAN
GUATEMALA
TEGUCIGALPA
SAN SALVADOR
MANAGUA
PANAMA CITY
SAN JOSE

Population Patterns

Rugged terrain, a harsh climate, and poor soil make the far north one of the world's most sparsely inhabited regions. Canada occupies two-fifths of the continent but, with 35 million inhabitants, has just 7 percent of its population; moreover, about 80 percent of Canadians live within 100 miles (160 km) of the U.S. border. The U.S.A. has almost ten times as many people, who are heavily concentrated in the northeast and on the west coast. Both countries have low population growth by world standards. In contrast, growth is high in Mexico, Central America, and the West Indies, where the most densely settled areas are the uplands of the mainland and the Caribbean islands.

Flashpoints

Central America and the Caribbean have experienced frequent political instability, often as a result of uprisings or military coups. On several occasions, the United States has intervened, overtly and covertly, to protect its interests in the region.

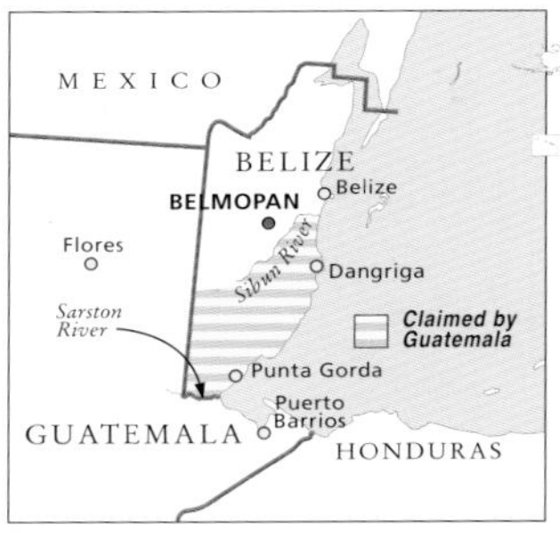
MEXICO
BELIZE
BELMOPAN
Belize
Flores
Sibun River
Dangriga
Sarstoon River
Claimed by Guatemala
Punta Gorda
Puerto Barrios
GUATEMALA
HONDURAS

Belize–Guatemala Border

Since 1821, when it became independent, Guatemala has laid claim to a large area of southern Belize and refused to recognize the latter's western boundary (though it finally recognized its independence in 1991). In recent years, incidents involving alleged illegal settlers and armed forces have led to a number of deaths and increased tension between the two countries.

South Cay

Honduras and Nicaragua have been in dispute over the tiny and uninhabited but potentially oil-rich island of South Cay (Cayo Sur) in the Caribbean Sea since 1999, when Honduras asserted its claim to the island by ratifying the 1986 Caribbean Sea Maritime Limits Treaty with Colombia. This has led to increased military activity on both sides of the common land border.

Nicaraguan boundary claim
South Cay
HONDURAS
Cabo Gracias a Dios
Honduran boundary claim
Laguna Bismuna
NICARAGUA
Cayos Miskitos
Disputed area

Las Lajas
Paraguay
CUBA
Mata Abajo
Bahía de Guantánamo
Caimanera
Boqueron
Guantanamo Bay

Guantanamo Bay, Cuba

Cuba achieved independence from Spain in 1898, following U.S. military intervention. Despite the 1959 communist revolution that brought Fidel Castro to power, the subsequent imposition by the U.S.A. of an embargo on trade with Cuba, and strong Cuban opposition to its presence, an American naval base still operates at Guantanamo Bay.

North American Trade Organizations

Signed by the U.S.A., Canada, and Mexico, the North American Free Trade Agreement (NAFTA) came into effect in 1994, creating the world's largest free-trade zone. The Central American Free Trade Zone (CAFTZ) includes El Salvador, Guatemala, Honduras, and Nicaragua. Mexico also belongs to the Latin American Integration Association (LAIA).

North American Free Trade Agreement (NAFTA)
Latin American Integration Association (LAIA)
Central American Free Trade Zone (CAFTZ)

GREENLAND
(to Denmark)
Ellesmere Island
Axel Heiberg Island
Ellef Ringnes Island
Queen Elizabeth Islands
Parry Islands
Melville Island
Bathurst Island
Devon Island
Banks Island
Somerset Island
Prince of Wales Island
Victoria Island
Boothia Peninsula
Baffin Island
Baffin Bay
Davis Strait
NUUK
Melville Peninsula
Foxe Basin
Iqaluit
Labrador Sea
Hudson Strait
Péninsule d'Ungava
Hudson Bay
Chukchi Sea
Bering Strait
Bering Sea
Aleutian Islands
Beaufort Sea
U.S.A. (ALASKA)
Yukon
Fairbanks
Anchorage
Dawson
YUKON TERRITORY
Whitehorse
Great Bear Lake
NORTHWEST TERRITORIES
NUNAVUT
Yellowknife
Great Slave Lake
Gulf of Alaska
Juneau
SCALE 1:40,000,000
Lamberts Conformal Conic Projection
1000 miles
1000 kilometers
BRITISH COLUMBIA
ALBERTA
Lake Athabasca
Reindeer Lake
Churchill
MANITOBA
CANADA
Edmonton
SASKATCHEWAN
Lake Winnipeg
ONTARIO
QUÉBEC
Réservoir Manicouagan
NEWFOUNDLAND and LABRADOR
St John's
Newfoundland
ST PIERRE and MIQUELON (to France)
PRINCE EDWARD ISLAND
Charlottetown
NEW BRUNSWICK
Fredericton
NOVA SCOTIA
Halifax
Calgary
Saskatoon
Regina
Vancouver
Victoria
Winnipeg
Lake Manitoba
Lake Nipigon
Thunder Bay
Lake Superior
Québec
Montréal
OTTAWA
Kauai
Oahu
Honolulu
Molokai
Maui
Hawaiian Islands
Hawaii
Scale 1:17,000,000
PACIFIC OCEAN
Olympia
Seattle
WASHINGTON
Portland
Salem
OREGON
IDAHO
Boise
Helena
MONTANA
NORTH DAKOTA
Bismarck
MINNESOTA
MICHIGAN
WISCONSIN
Lake Michigan
Lake Huron
Lake Ontario
Lake Erie
St Paul
Madison
Lansing
Toronto
Buffalo
Albany
NEW YORK
MAINE
Augusta
Montpelier VERMONT
Concord NEW HAMPSHIRE
Boston MASSACHUSETTS
Providence RHODE ISLAND
Hartford CONNECTICUT
New York
Trenton NEW JERSEY
Philadelphia
Dover
DELAWARE
WASHINGTON, D.C.
MARYLAND
VIRGINIA
Richmond
STH DAKOTA
Pierre
UNITED STATES OF AMERICA
WYOMING
IOWA
Chicago
Detroit
PENNSYLVANIA
Harrisburg
OHIO
Columbus
NEVADA
Salt Lake City
Cheyenne
NEBRASKA
Des Moines
INDIANA
ILLINOIS
Springfield
Indianapolis
WEST VIRGINIA
Charleston
Sacramento
Reno
Carson City
San Francisco
San Jose
Lincoln
Denver
UTAH
COLORADO
Topeka
KANSAS
Jefferson City
MISSOURI
St Louis
Frankfort
KENTUCKY
Raleigh
NORTH CAROLINA
CALIFORNIA
Las Vegas
Nashville
TENNESSEE
Oklahoma City
OKLAHOMA
ARKANSAS
Memphis
Atlanta
Columbia
SOUTH CAROLINA
Los Angeles
ARIZONA
Santa Fe
NEW MEXICO
Little Rock
ALABAMA
GEORGIA
Savannah
San Diego
Tijuana
Phoenix
Mexicali
Tucson
Dallas
Jackson
MISSISSIPPI
Montgomery
Jacksonville
Tallahassee
El Paso
Ciudad Juárez
TEXAS
LOUISIANA
Baton Rouge
New Orleans
FLORIDA
Austin
Houston
San Antonio
Hermosillo
Chihuahua
Gulf of California
Rio Grande
Gulf of Mexico
Miami
ATLANTIC OCEAN
Tropic of Cancer
West Indies
NASSAU
THE BAHAMAS
TURKS and CAICOS ISLANDS (to U.K.)
VIRGIN ISLANDS (to U.K.)
ANGUILLA (to U.K.)
ANTIGUA and BARBUDA
GUADELOUPE (to France)
PUERTO RICO (to U.S.A.)
SAN JUAN
ST KITTS and NEVIS
DOMINICA
DOMINICAN REPUBLIC
VIRGIN ISLANDS (to U.S.A.)
MONTSERRAT (to U.K.)
MARTINIQUE (to France)
HAVANA
Camagüey
HAITI
SANTO DOMINGO
ST LUCIA
BARBADOS
Monterrey
La Paz
Mazatlán
MEXICO
Tampico
CUBA
Greater Antilles
PORT-AU-PRINCE
ST VINCENT and THE GRENADINES
GRENADA
TRINIDAD and TOBAGO
Mérida
Cancún
Yucatan Peninsula
CAYMAN ISLANDS (to U.K.)
KINGSTON
JAMAICA
Caribbean Sea
NETHERLANDS ANTILLES (to Netherlands)
ARUBA (to Netherlands)
Guadalajara
MEXICO CITY
Veracruz
BELIZE
BELMOPAN
Oaxaca
Acapulco
GUATEMALA
HONDURAS
TEGUCIGALPA
SAN SALVADOR
EL SALVADOR
NICARAGUA
MANAGUA
Lake Nicaragua
PANAMA
Colón
SAN JOSÉ
PANAMA CITY
COSTA RICA
SOUTH AMERICA
Arctic Circle

Nations of North America

In the so-called Pre-Columbian period (prior to the arrival of Christopher Columbus in 1492), North America was home to a variety of indigenous peoples, including nomadic and seminomadic groups in the north and the sophisticated Mesoamerican civilizations of the Toltec, Aztec, and Maya in the south. Spain conquered Mexico, Central America, and parts of the West Indies in the 16th century; Britain gained control of much of the north in the mid-18th century. The United States was the first country to declare independence, in 1776 (formalized in 1783); most other North American nations became independent in the mid-19th or early 20th century.

THE PRE-COLUMBIAN ERA, 1000–1519

Inuit hunters
Inuit hunters
Inuit hunters
Inuit hunters
Northwest coast fishers
Subarctic hunter-gatherers
Plateau hunter-gatherers
Plains hunter-farmers
Desert gatherers
Woodland farmers
Pueblo farmers
Desert gatherers
Toltec (900–1200 AD)
Caribbean farmers
Maya (200–900 AD)
Aztec (1200–1519)
Lowland farmers
Mesoamerican civilizations
Hawaiian Islands
Farming peoples
City states

COLONIAL POSSESSIONS, 1762

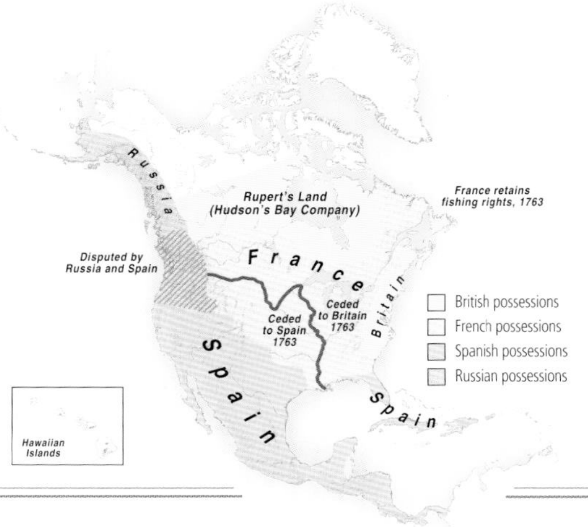
Russia
Rupert's Land (Hudson's Bay Company)
France retains fishing rights, 1763
Disputed by Russia and Spain
France
Britain
Ceded to Spain 1763
Ceded to Britain 1763
Spain
Spain
Hawaiian Islands
British possessions
French possessions
Spanish possessions
Russian possessions

INDEPENDENCE, 1776–1905

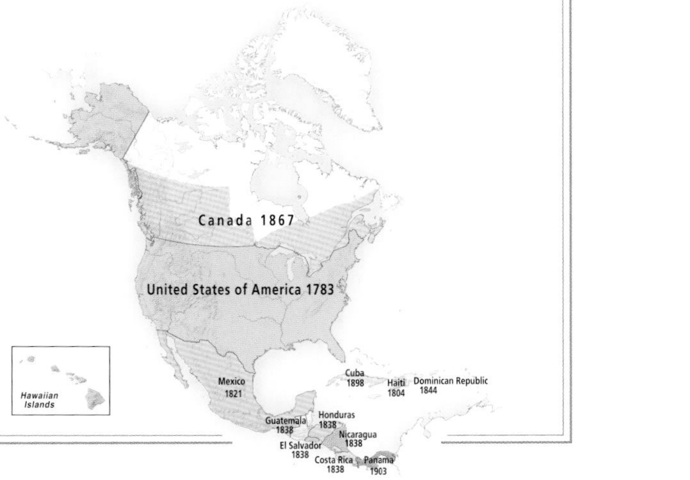
Canada 1867
United States of America 1783
Mexico 1821
Cuba 1898
Haiti 1804
Dominican Republic 1844
Guatemala 1838
Honduras 1838
El Salvador 1838
Nicaragua 1838
Costa Rica 1838
Panama 1903
Hawaiian Islands

The Human Impact

The environmental history of North America can be summarized as thousands of years of gradual modification followed by 500 years of astonishingly rapid change. Between the arrival of the first human settlers from Asia at least 15,000 years ago and Columbus's first visit in 1492, most North Americans lived in nomadic and seminomadic hunter-gatherer and, later, hunter-farmer communities. Large city states and empires were confined to Mesoamerica (of the continent's 30 million-plus inhabitants in 1492, 25 million lived south of the Rio Grande). The arrival of Europeans, particularly the mass immigrations of the late 18th and 19th centuries, transformed the landscape. Armed with developed technologies and presented with seemingly limitless resources, settlers razed forests, plowed grasslands, dug mines, and hunted wildlife at a phenomenal rate. The combination of huge tracts of arable land, abundant mineral resources, and political stability brought immense prosperity to the United States and Canada. In contrast, the south's more limited natural resources, rapid population growth, and volatile political situation resulted in slower economic development.

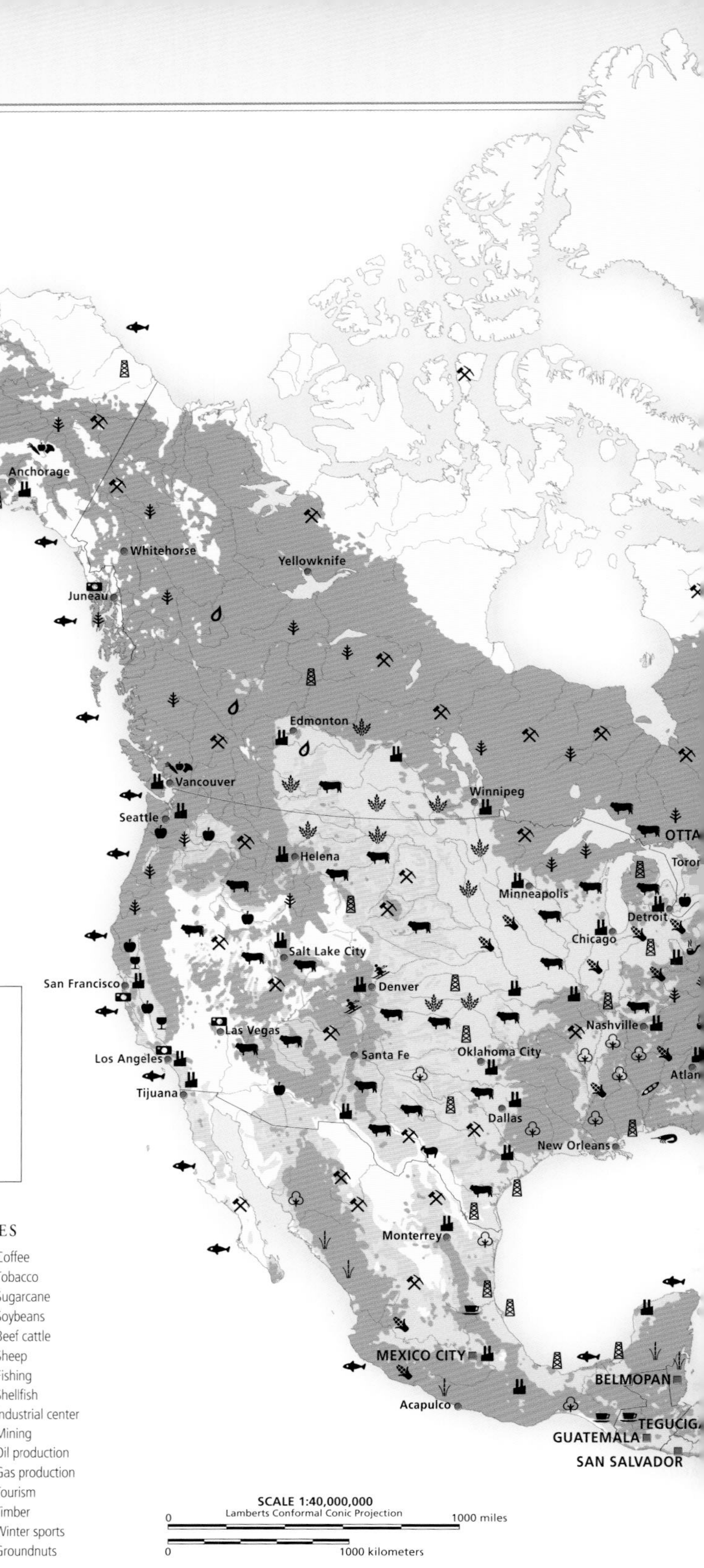

Anchorage
Whitehorse
Yellowknife
Juneau
Edmonton
Vancouver
Seattle
Winnipeg
Helena
Minneapolis
Detroit
Chicago
Salt Lake City
San Francisco
Denver
Nashville
Las Vegas
Los Angeles
Santa Fe
Oklahoma City
Tijuana
Dallas
New Orleans
Monterrey
MEXICO CITY
Acapulco
BELMOPAN
GUATEMALA
SAN SALVADOR
SCALE 1:40,000,000
Lamberts Conformal Conic Projection
0
1000 miles
0
1000 kilometers

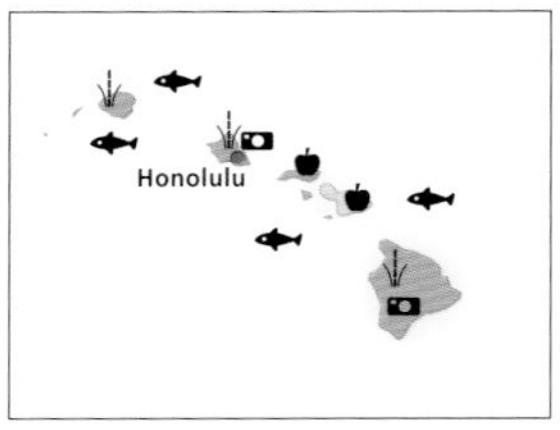

Honolulu

LAND USE AND RESOURCES

Forest and woodland
Arable land
Grazing
Marginal or nonproductive
Cereals
Corn (maize)
Fruit and vegetables
Fruit
Citrus fruits
Bananas
Wine
Cotton
Coffee
Tobacco
Sugarcane
Soybeans
Beef cattle
Sheep
Fishing
Shellfish
Industrial center
Mining
Oil production
Gas production
Tourism
Timber
Winter sports
Groundnuts

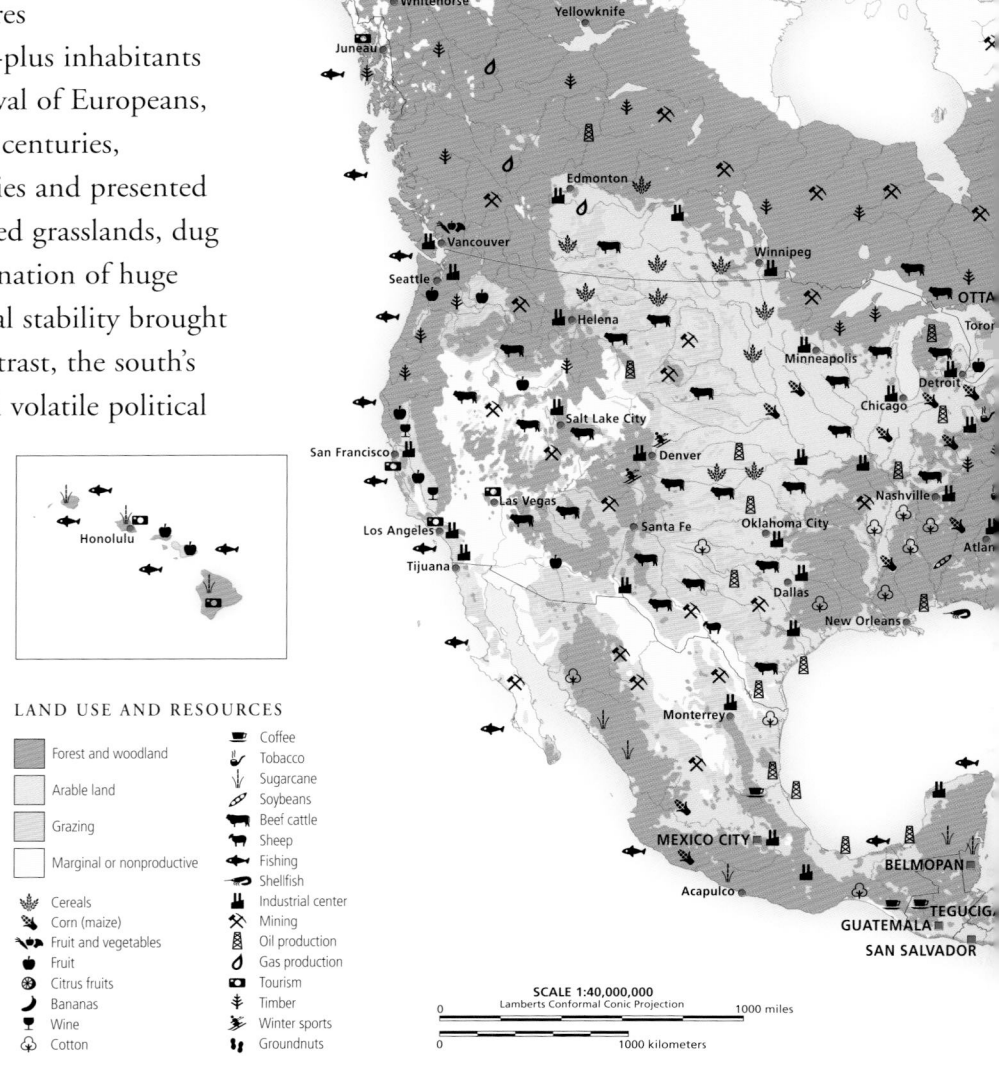

The Changing Face of North America

Prairies

The first Europeans to reach the interior lowlands of the present-day United States in the 17th century were amazed by the great seas of grasses that stretched from horizon to horizon—in places rising head-high—and teemed with millions of bison, antelope, deer, and sheep. But settlers arriving in the 1840s realized that the black soil in which the grasses grew was ideal for cultivation and soon began cutting and plowing. By the end of the 19th century, the soils were depleted and most of the grasses and mammals were gone. To date, losses of prairies on a state-by-state basis vary from 30 to 99 percent. Only a small percentage of tallgrass prairie remains, mainly as tiny remnants in parks and reserves.

ORIGINAL PRAIRIE COVER

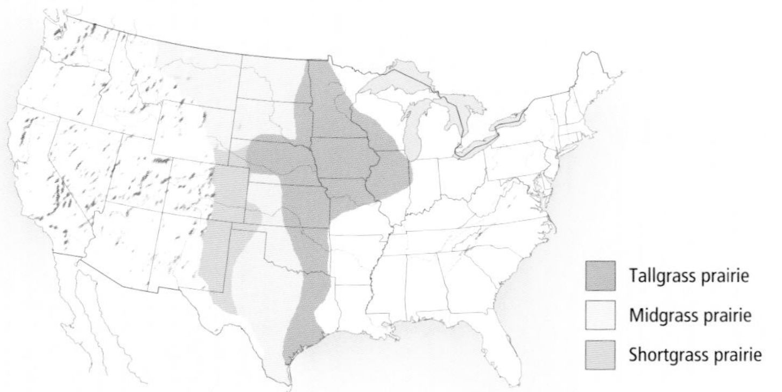

Tallgrass prairie
Midgrass prairie
Shortgrass prairie

CURRENT PRAIRIE COVER

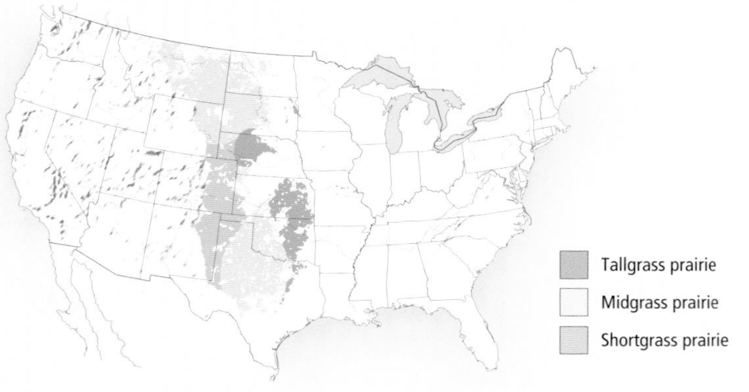

Tallgrass prairie
Midgrass prairie
Shortgrass prairie

Economic Profile

Relative to its land area, North America has disproportionately high levels of natural resources. Some of the world's biggest coal fields lie in Alberta, Canada, and in the Appalachian Mountains; enormous oil reserves have been tapped in Texas, Alaska, and the Gulf of Mexico. Fresh water is abundant, though unevenly distributed: many parts of the western U.S.A. and Mexico depend on irrigation, and in Central America runoff and evaporation limit supplies. The north's highly mechanized agricultural sector makes the U.S.A. and Canada leading producers of crops such as wheat, corn, and soybeans. Home of the world's largest companies, the U.S.A. is the world's most productive nation, generating over 30 percent of global GDP, and also its leading importer and exporter.

Land Cover

Though much diminished, forests still cover a large swathe of the continent, chiefly in Canada. Most arable land lies in the north; in the south it is generally restricted to fertile volcanic uplands. Other types of land cover include the large marginal and nonproductive areas in the far north and western mountains, and significant urban sprawl: the U.S.A. alone has more than 4 million miles (6.4 million km) of roadways.

PROPORTIONS OF TOTAL LAND AREA

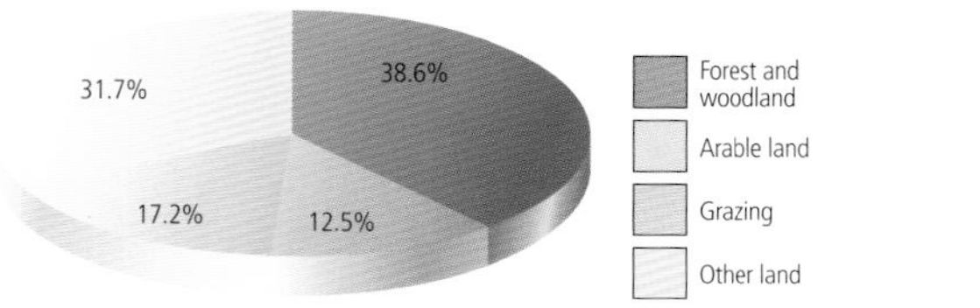

38.6%
31.7%
17.2%
12.5%
Forest and woodland
Arable land
Grazing
Other land

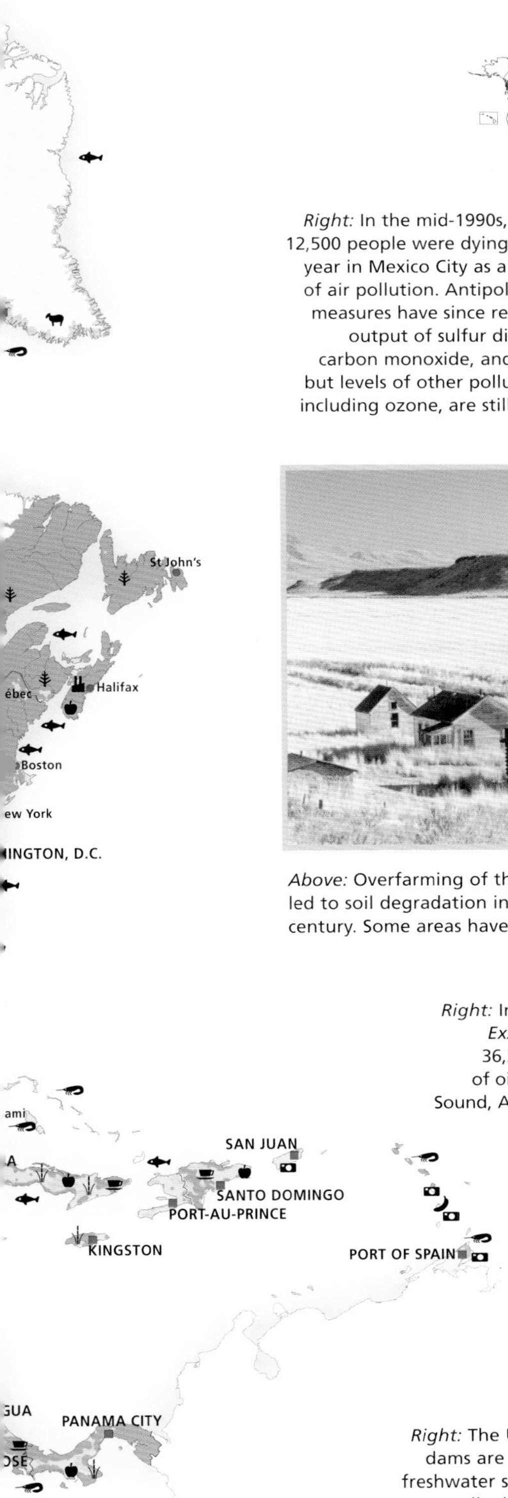
St John's
Halifax
Boston
ew York
INGTON, D.C.
SAN JUAN
SANTO DOMINGO
PORT-AU-PRINCE
KINGSTON
PORT OF SPAIN
PANAMA CITY

Right: In the mid-1990s, up to 12,500 people were dying every year in Mexico City as a result of air pollution. Antipollution measures have since reduced output of sulfur dioxide, carbon monoxide, and lead, but levels of other pollutants, including ozone, are still high.

Threats to the Environment

Industrialization, urban sprawl, and heavy dependence on automobiles make North America a major source of pollution, including by far the world's highest per-capita carbon dioxide emissions. Ocean pollution is particularly severe on the North Atlantic seaboard and in the northern Gulf of Mexico. Just one-third of the original forest cover remains; in the north commercial logging companies continue to fell old-growth forest, and in the south limited resources and growing populations pressurize governments to permit the razing of forest for farmland. North Americans are by far the highest per-capita consumers of natural resources and concerns are growing about resource depletion. Water tables are falling and rivers silting up, and some pessimistic forecasts even suggest that the U.S.A.'s known oil reserves could be exhausted by 2011.

Above: Overfarming of the central U.S.A. led to soil degradation in the mid-20th century. Some areas have yet to recover.

Right: In 1989, the tanker *Exxon Valdez* spilled 36,300 tons (37,000 t) of oil in Prince William Sound, Alaska, devastating local ecosystems.

Right: The U.S.A.'s 2.5 million dams are the main cause of freshwater species extinctions. Overall, about 40 percent of freshwater fish, 50 percent of freshwater crayfish, and 70 percent of freshwater mussels have been lost.

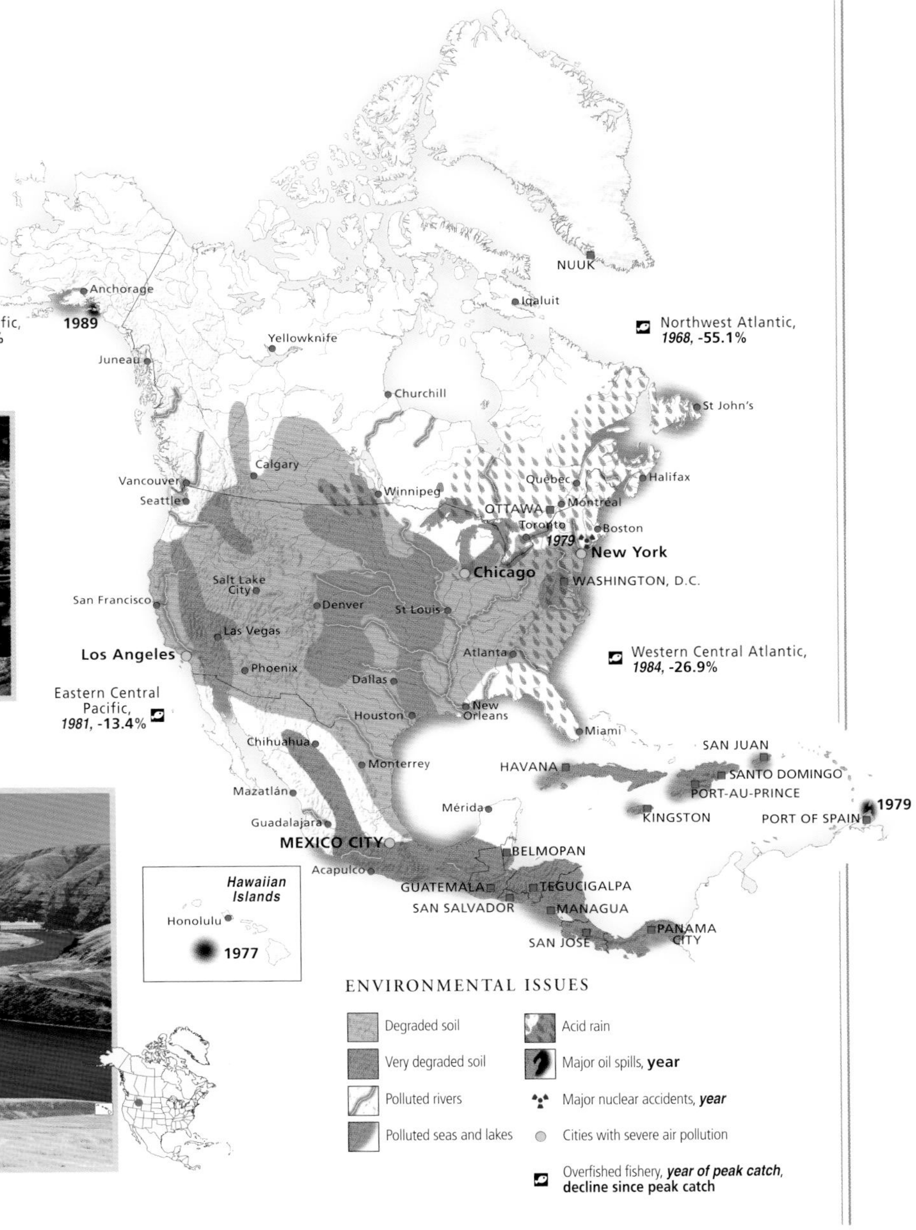
NUUK
Anchorage
1989
Iqaluit
Northeast Pacific, 1987, -18.1%
Northwest Atlantic, 1968, -55.1%
Juneau
Yellowknife
Churchill
St John's
Calgary
Vancouver
Seattle
Winnipeg
Québec
Halifax
OTTAWA
Montréal
Toronto
Boston
1979
New York
Chicago
WASHINGTON, D.C.
Salt Lake City
San Francisco
Denver
St Louis
Las Vegas
Los Angeles
Phoenix
Atlanta
Western Central Atlantic, 1984, -26.9%
Dallas
Eastern Central Pacific, 1981, -13.4%
Houston
New Orleans
Miami
Chihuahua
SAN JUAN
Monterrey
HAVANA
SANTO DOMINGO
PORT-AU-PRINCE
Mazatlán
Mérida
KINGSTON
PORT OF SPAIN
1979
Guadalajara
MEXICO CITY
BELMOPAN
Acapulco
GUATEMALA
TEGUCIGALPA
SAN SALVADOR
MANAGUA
SAN JOSÉ
PANAMA CITY
Hawaiian Islands
Honolulu
1977
ENVIRONMENTAL ISSUES
Degraded soil
Very degraded soil
Polluted rivers
Polluted seas and lakes
Acid rain
Major oil spills, year
Major nuclear accidents, year
Cities with severe air pollution
Overfished fishery, year of peak catch, decline since peak catch

Protecting the Environment

A long tradition of conservation exists in North America. The continent was the site of the world's first national parks, is home to pioneering conservation organizations, and Canada and the U.S.A. in particular have passed effective environmental legislation, often focusing on species preservation. More than 30 percent of U.S. urban waste is now recycled and many landfills have been turned into parks. Even in less affluent Mexico, Central America, and the West Indies, governments have begun to recognize the value of preserving wilderness. In some areas, for example, well-regulated ecotourism has generated much-needed revenue and helped limit habitat destruction. Unfortunately, the continent's relatively high levels of land protection (10.5 percent) do not seem to guarantee permanent preservation: in 2001, the U.S. government authorized exploration for oil and gas in national wildlife refuges in northern Alaska and elsewhere.

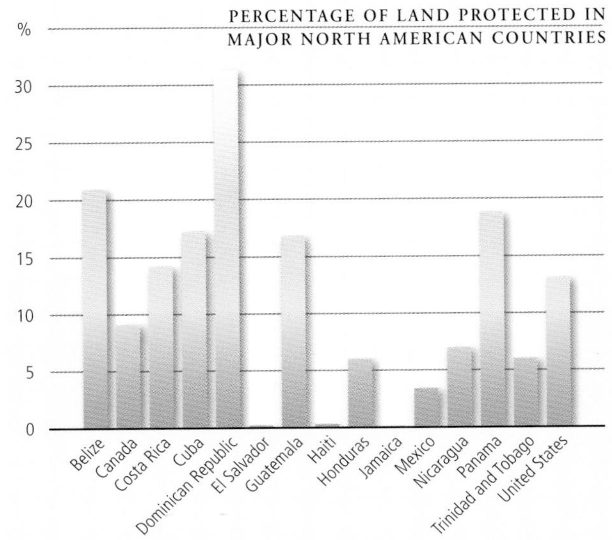
PERCENTAGE OF LAND PROTECTED IN MAJOR NORTH AMERICAN COUNTRIES
%
30
25
20
15
10
5
0
Belize
Canada
Costa Rica
Cuba
Dominican Republic
El Salvador
Guatemala
Haiti
Honduras
Jamaica
Mexico
Nicaragua
Panama
Trinidad and Tobago
United States

Above: In this satellite image, the area left of the river is Haiti; the greener area on the right is the Dominican Republic—a startling reflection of the nations' contrasting land-protection policies.

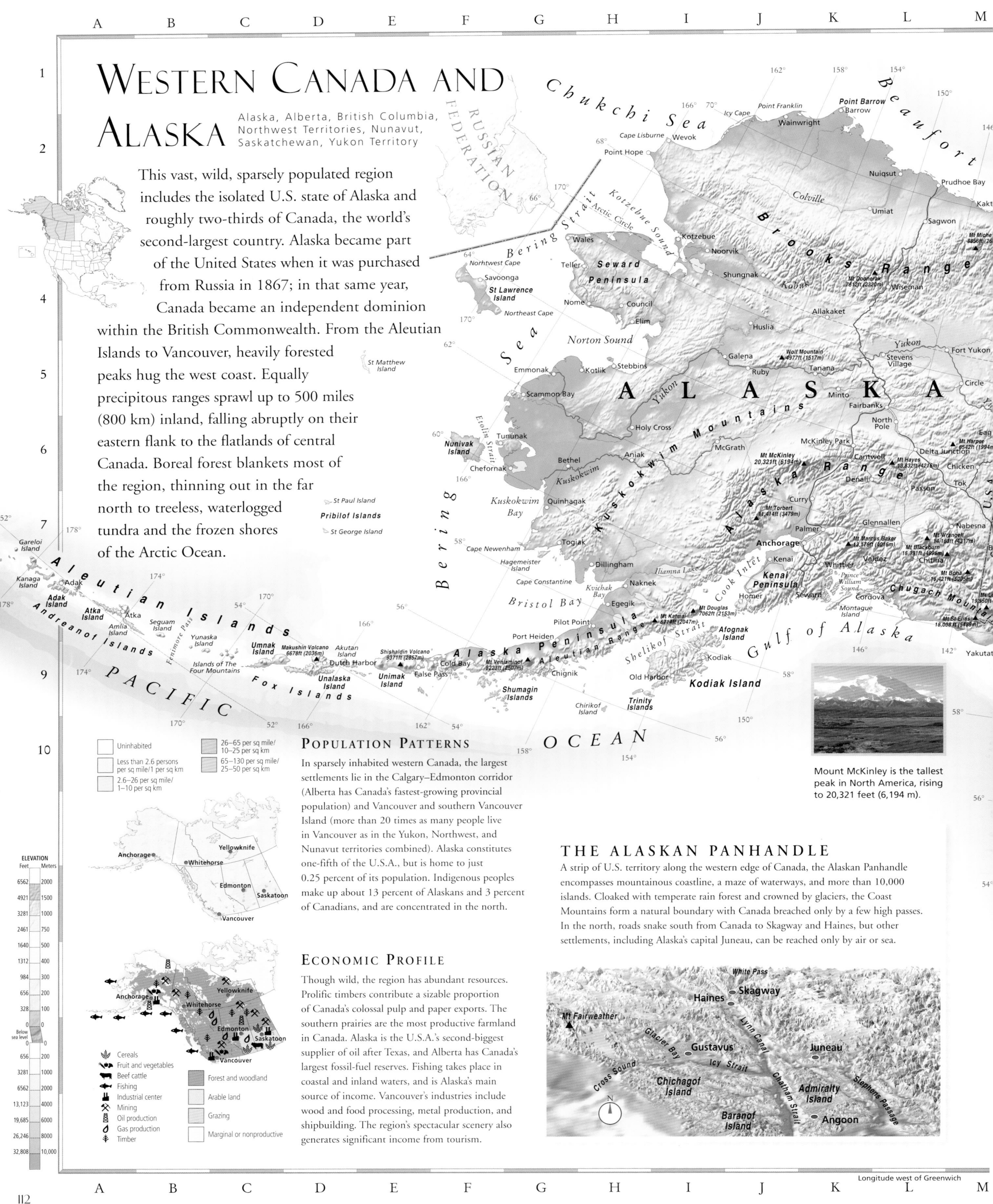

Western Canada and Alaska

Alaska, Alberta, British Columbia, Northwest Territories, Nunavut, Saskatchewan, Yukon Territory

This vast, wild, sparsely populated region includes the isolated U.S. state of Alaska and roughly two-thirds of Canada, the world's second-largest country. Alaska became part of the United States when it was purchased from Russia in 1867; in that same year, Canada became an independent dominion within the British Commonwealth. From the Aleutian Islands to Vancouver, heavily forested peaks hug the west coast. Equally precipitous ranges sprawl up to 500 miles (800 km) inland, falling abruptly on their eastern flank to the flatlands of central Canada. Boreal forest blankets most of the region, thinning out in the far north to treeless, waterlogged tundra and the frozen shores of the Arctic Ocean.

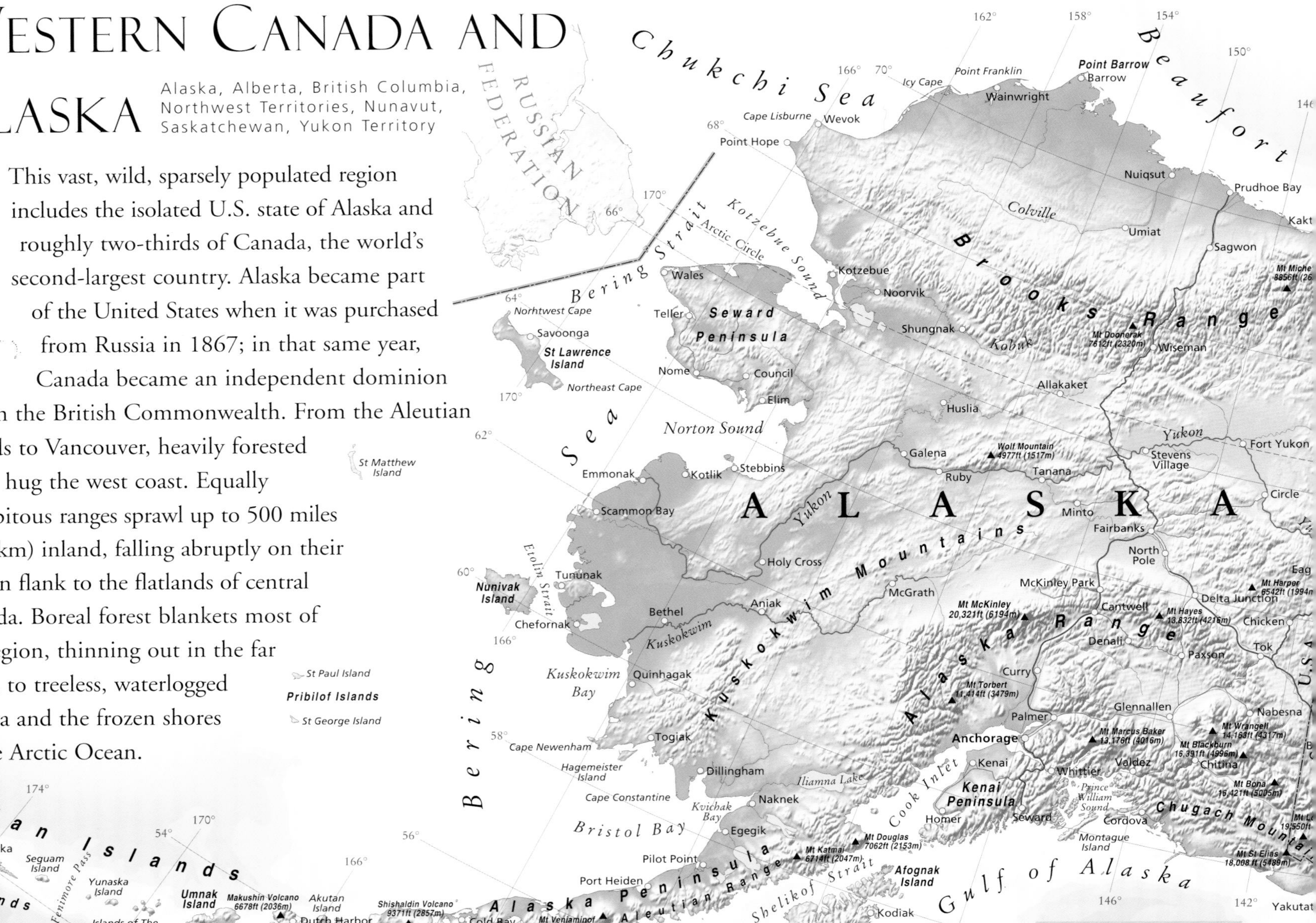

A B C D E F G H I J K L M
1 2 4 5 6 7 9 10
Chukchi Sea
Beaufort
RUSSIAN FEDERATION
Point Barrow
Barrow
Point Franklin
Wainwright
Icy Cape
Cape Lisburne
Wevok
Point Hope
Nuiqsut
Prudhoe Bay
Colville
Umiat
Sagwon
Kotzebue Sound
Arctic Circle
Bering Strait
Wales
Kotzebue
Noorvik
Teller
Seward Peninsula
Shungnak
Brooks Range
Mt Doonerak 7612ft (2320m)
Wiseman
Kobuk
Northwest Cape
Savoonga
St Lawrence Island
Northeast Cape
Nome
Council
Elim
Allakaket
Huslia
Norton Sound
Bering Sea
St Matthew Island
Emmonak
Kotlik
Stebbins
Galena
Ruby
Wolf Mountain 4977ft (1517m)
Tanana
Yukon
Stevens Village
Fort Yukon
Circle
ALASKA
Scammon Bay
Minto
Fairbanks
North Pole
Holy Cross
Kuskokwim Mountains
Etolin Strait
Nunivak Island
Tununak
McGrath
McKinley Park
Delta Junction
Mt Harper 6542ft (1994m)
Mt McKinley 20,321ft (6194m)
Mt Hayes 13,832ft (4216m)
Cantwell
Chicken
Bethel
Aniak
Kuskokwim
Chefornak
Alaska Range
Denali
Paxson
Tok
Kuskokwim Bay
Quinhagak
Curry
Mt Torbert 11,414ft (3479m)
St Paul Island
Pribilof Islands
St George Island
Glennallen
Nabesna
Palmer
Mt Wrangell 14,163ft (4317m)
Mt Marcus Baker 13,176ft (4016m)
Mt Blackburn 16,391ft (4996m)
Togiak
Anchorage
Cape Newenham
Kenai
Valdez
Chitina
Hagemeister Island
Dillingham
Iliamna Lake
Cook Inlet
Whittier
Kenai Peninsula
Prince William Sound
Mt Bona 16,421ft (5005m)
Cape Constantine
Naknek
Kvichak Bay
Homer
Seward
Cordova
Chugach Mountains
Egegik
Bristol Bay
Montague Island
Mt Katmai 6714ft (2047m)
Mt Douglas 7062ft (2153m)
Mt St Elias 18,008ft (5489m)
Pilot Point
Afognak Island
Port Heiden
Alaska Peninsula
Aleutian Range
Shelikof Strait
Gulf of Alaska
Kodiak
Yakutat
Gareloi Island
Kanaga Island
Adak
Adak Island
Aleutian Islands
Atka Island
Atka
Andreanof Islands
Amlia Island
Seguam Island
Fenimore Pass
Yunaska Island
Islands of The Four Mountains
Umnak Island
Makushin Volcano 6678ft (2036m)
Akutan Island
Dutch Harbor
Shishaldin Volcano 9371ft (2857m)
Cold Bay
Mt Veniaminof 8223ft (2507m)
Chignik
Unalaska Island
Unimak Island
False Pass
Fox Islands
Shumagin Islands
Chirikof Island
Trinity Islands
Old Harbor
Kodiak Island
PACIFIC OCEAN

Mount McKinley is the tallest peak in North America, rising to 20,321 feet (6,194 m).

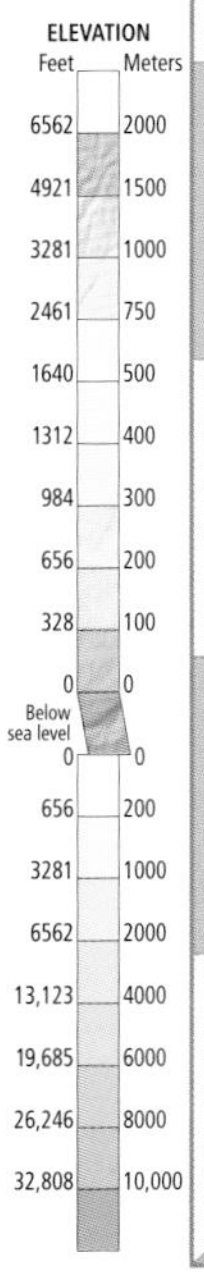

ELEVATION
Feet Meters
6562 2000
4921 1500
3281 1000
2461 750
1640 500
1312 400
984 300
656 200
328 100
0 0
Below sea level
0
656 200
3281 1000
6562 2000
13,123 4000
19,685 6000
26,246 8000
32,808 10,000

- Uninhabited
- Less than 2.6 persons per sq mile/1 per sq km
- 2.6–26 per sq mile/1–10 per sq km
- 26–65 per sq mile/10–25 per sq km
- 65–130 per sq mile/25–50 per sq km

Anchorage
Whitehorse
Yellowknife
Edmonton
Saskatoon
Vancouver

Population Patterns

In sparsely inhabited western Canada, the largest settlements lie in the Calgary–Edmonton corridor (Alberta has Canada's fastest-growing provincial population) and Vancouver and southern Vancouver Island (more than 20 times as many people live in Vancouver as in the Yukon, Northwest, and Nunavut territories combined). Alaska constitutes one-fifth of the U.S.A., but is home to just 0.25 percent of its population. Indigenous peoples make up about 13 percent of Alaskans and 3 percent of Canadians, and are concentrated in the north.

Anchorage
Whitehorse
Yellowknife
Edmonton
Saskatoon
Vancouver

- Cereals
- Fruit and vegetables
- Beef cattle
- Fishing
- Industrial center
- Mining
- Oil production
- Gas production
- Timber
- Forest and woodland
- Arable land
- Grazing
- Marginal or nonproductive

Economic Profile

Though wild, the region has abundant resources. Prolific timbers contribute a sizable proportion of Canada's colossal pulp and paper exports. The southern prairies are the most productive farmland in Canada. Alaska is the U.S.A.'s second-biggest supplier of oil after Texas, and Alberta has Canada's largest fossil-fuel reserves. Fishing takes place in coastal and inland waters, and is Alaska's main source of income. Vancouver's industries include wood and food processing, metal production, and shipbuilding. The region's spectacular scenery also generates significant income from tourism.

The Alaskan Panhandle

A strip of U.S. territory along the western edge of Canada, the Alaskan Panhandle encompasses mountainous coastline, a maze of waterways, and more than 10,000 islands. Cloaked with temperate rain forest and crowned by glaciers, the Coast Mountains form a natural boundary with Canada breached only by a few high passes. In the north, roads snake south from Canada to Skagway and Haines, but other settlements, including Alaska's capital Juneau, can be reached only by air or sea.

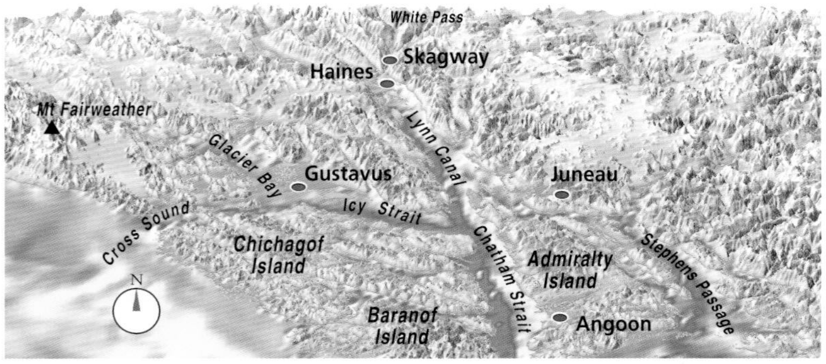

White Pass
Haines
Skagway
Mt Fairweather
Glacier Bay
Lynn Canal
Gustavus
Icy Strait
Juneau
Cross Sound
Chichagof Island
Chatham Strait
Admiralty Island
Stephens Passage
Baranof Island
Angoon
N

Longitude west of Greenwich

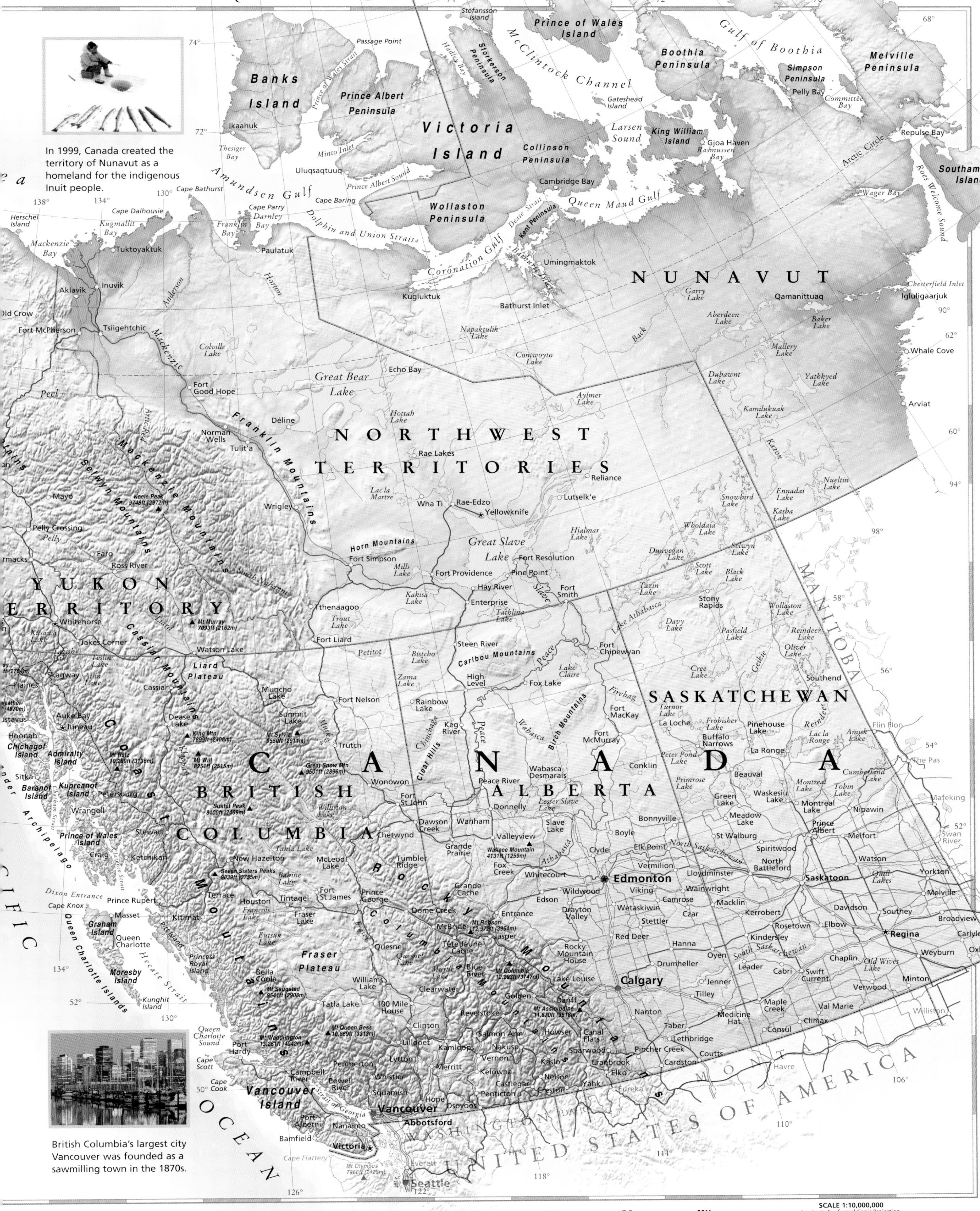
N O P Q R S T U V W X Y Z
1 2 3 4 5 6 7 8 9 10 11 12 13 14 15
Banks Island
Prince Albert Peninsula
Victoria Island
Prince of Wales Island
Boothia Peninsula
Simpson Peninsula
Melville Peninsula
Southampton Island
Stefansson Island
Storkerson Peninsula
McClintock Channel
Gulf of Boothia
King William Island
Gjoa Haven
Larsen Sound
Collinson Peninsula
Cambridge Bay
Wollaston Peninsula
Kent Peninsula
Queen Maud Gulf
Amundsen Gulf
Dolphin and Union Strait
Coronation Gulf
Prince of Wales Strait
Passage Point
Ikaahuk
Uluqsaqtuuq
Minto Inlet
Prince Albert Sound
Thesiger Bay
Cape Bathurst
Cape Dalhousie
Cape Parry
Darnley Bay
Franklin Bay
Paulatuk
Cape Baring
Herschel Island
Kugmallit Bay
Mackenzie Bay
Tuktoyaktuk
Inuvik
Aklavik
Old Crow
Fort McPherson
Tsiigehtchic
Pelly Bay
Committee Bay
Repulse Bay
Rasmussen Bay
Gateshead Island
Arctic Circle
Wager Bay
Roes Welcome Sound
Chesterfield Inlet
Igluligaarjuk
Qamanittuaq
Baker Lake
Garry Lake
Aberdeen Lake
Umingmaktok
Bathurst Inlet
Kugluktuk
NUNAVUT
Whale Cove
Arviat
Mallery Lake
Yathkyed Lake
Dubawnt Lake
Kamilukuak Lake
Napaktulik Lake
Contwoyto Lake
Aylmer Lake
Colville Lake
Echo Bay
Great Bear Lake
Fort Good Hope
Déline
Norman Wells
Tulit'a
Hottah Lake
Rae Lakes
NORTHWEST TERRITORIES
Reliance
Lutselk'e
Lac la Martre
Wha Ti
Rae-Edzo
Yellowknife
Wrigley
Franklin Mountains
Mackenzie Mountains
Selwyn Mountains
Keele Peak 9748ft (2972m)
Mayo
Pelly Crossing
Faro
Ross River
Horn Mountains
Great Slave Lake
Fort Simpson
Fort Resolution
Pine Point
Fort Providence
Mills Lake
Hay River
Enterprise
Fort Smith
Kakisa Lake
Tathlina Lake
YUKON TERRITORY
Whitehorse
Mt Murray 7093ft (2162m)
Tthenaagoo
Trout Lake
Fort Liard
Jakes Corner
Teslin Lake
Atlin Lake
Watson Lake
Skagway
Haines
Cassiar
Cassiar Mountains
Liard Plateau
Petitot
Bistcho Lake
Steen River
Caribou Mountains
Fort Chipewyan
Lake Athabasca
Lake Claire
Fox Lake
High Level
Zama Lake
Fort Nelson
Muncho Lake
Rainbow Lake
Keg River
Dease Lake
Summit Lake
King Mtn 7899ft (2408m)
Mt Sylvia 9550ft (2911m)
Mt Will 8251ft (2515m)
Mt Ratz 10,289ft (3136m)
Great Snow Mtn 9501ft (2896m)
Juneau
Auke Bay
Hoonah
Chichagof Island
Admiralty Island
Sitka
Baranof Island
Kupreanof Island
Petersburg
Wrangell
Stewart
Prince of Wales Island
Craig
Ketchikan
Alexander Archipelago
Trutch
Clear Hills
CANADA
BRITISH COLUMBIA
ALBERTA
SASKATCHEWAN
MANITOBA
Wonowon
Fort St John
Dawson Creek
Chetwynd
Williston Lake
Sustut Peak 8400ft (2469m)
Peace River
Wabasca-Desmarais
Birch Mountains
Fort McMurray
Fort MacKay
Conklin
La Loche
Turnor Lake
Buffalo Narrows
La Ronge
Pinehouse Lake
Beauval
Flin Flon
The Pas
Southend
Lac la Ronge
Amisk Lake
Cumberland Lake
Dunvegan Lake
Scott Lake
Black Lake
Stony Rapids
Wollaston Lake
Reindeer Lake
Pasfield Lake
Davy Lake
Cree Lake
Oliver Lake
Kasba Lake
Ennadai Lake
Nueltin Lake
Snowbird Lake
Wholdaia Lake
Hjalmar Lake
Selwyn Lake
Tazin Lake
Donnelly
Wanham
Grande Prairie
Valleyview
Wallace Mountain 4131ft (1259m)
Slave Lake
Lesser Slave Lake
Athabasca
Boyle
Bonnyville
Cold Lake
Clyde
Elk Point
Vermilion
Lloydminster
St Walburg
Spiritwood
Meadow Lake
Green Lake
Montreal Lake
Prince Albert
Waskesiu Lake
Nipawin
Tobin Lake
Melfort
North Battleford
Saskatoon
Watson
Yorkton
Melville
Quill Lakes
Mafeking
Swan River
Edmonton
Whitecourt
Wildwood
Viking
Wainwright
Macklin
Camrose
Wetaskiwin
Stettler
Czar
Kerrobert
Rosetown
Elbow
Kindersley
Davidson
Southey
Regina
Broadview
Carlyle
Oxbow
Weyburn
Red Deer
Hanna
Drumheller
Oyen
Leader
Chaplin
Old Wives Lake
Calgary
Jenner
Tilley
Cabri
Swift Current
Minton
Verwood
Medicine Hat
Maple Creek
Val Marie
Climax
Consul
Williston
Taber
Lethbridge
Coutts
Cardston
Pincher Creek
Nanton
Havre
MONTANA
UNITED STATES OF AMERICA
Rocky Mountain House
Drayton Valley
Edson
Entrance
Hinton
Jasper
Mt Robson 12,972ft (3954m)
Tête Jaune Cache
Blue River
Mt Columbia 12,293ft (3747m)
Lake Louise
Banff
Golden
Mt Assiniboine 11,870ft (3618m)
Canal Flats
Revelstoke
Salmon Arm
Kamloops
Nakusp
Vernon
Kelowna
Kaslo
Nelson
Castlegar
Creston
Penticton
Cranbrook
Sparwood
Fernie
Elko
Yahk
Eureka
Osoyoos
Merritt
Hope
Rocky Mountains
Columbia Mountains
Grande Cache
McBride
Dome Creek
Prince George
Quesnel
Quesnel Lake
Fort St James
McLeod Lake
Tumbler Ridge
Babine Lake
Takla Lake
New Hazelton
Seven Sisters Peaks 9039ft (2755m)
Terrace
Houston
François Lake
Tintagel
Fraser Lake
Kitimat
Prince Rupert
Dixon Entrance
Cape Knox
Masset
Graham Island
Queen Charlotte
Queen Charlotte Islands
Hecate Strait
Moresby Island
Kunghit Island
Princess Royal Island
Pitt Island
Bella Coola
Mt Saugstad 9541ft (2908m)
Fraser Plateau
Williams Lake
Clearwater
Tatla Lake
100 Mile House
Clinton
Lillooet
Lytton
Mt Queen Bess 10,869ft (3313m)
Mt Waddington 13,261ft (4042m)
Coast Mountains
Queen Charlotte Sound
Port Hardy
Cape Scott
Cape Cook
Vancouver Island
Campbell River
Powell River
Pemberton
Whistler
Squamish
Vancouver
Abbotsford
Strait of Georgia
Nanaimo
Port Alberni
Bamfield
Victoria
Cape Flattery
Mt Olympus 7966ft (2428m)
Everett
Seattle
WASHINGTON
IDAHO
PACIFIC OCEAN
SCALE 1:10,000,000
Lamberts Conformal Conic Projection
0 300 miles
0 300 kilometers

In 1999, Canada created the territory of Nunavut as a homeland for the indigenous Inuit people.

British Columbia's largest city Vancouver was founded as a sawmilling town in the 1870s.

EASTERN CANADA

Manitoba, New Brunswick, Newfoundland and Labrador, Nova Scotia, Nunavut, Ontario, Prince Edward Island, Québec, St Pierre and Miquelon

Underpinned by the ancient Canadian Shield, Eastern Canada consists of a horseshoe-shaped, island-fringed swathe of mostly low-lying land that curls around and inclines gently toward the shores of Hudson Bay. Mountains rise along the eastern edge of the shield, on Baffin Island and in Newfoundland and Labrador, in southeastern Québec and New Brunswick. North America's great belt of lake-studded boreal forest covers most of Manitoba, Ontario, and Québec, separating the cold, windswept northern tundra from the more temperate south. The majority of the region's—and indeed Canada's—people, businesses, and industries, as well as its centers of national government, are based in the Great Lakes–St Lawrence lowlands, where fertile valleys abut navigable waterways. The province of Québec is culturally distinct from the rest of Canada in that the majority of its inhabitants are of French origin and French-speaking. Its demands for greater autonomy constitute Canada's most problematic and potentially disruptive political issue.

In Hudson Bay, polar bears live onshore in summer but hunt seals across the pack ice throughout winter.

Ottawa was selected as Canada's capital in 1857. Its parliament was rebuilt in 1916–27, following a fire.

POPULATION PATTERNS

Reflecting the nation as a whole, Eastern Canada's population is ethnically diverse, highly urbanized, and heavily concentrated in the south. The Great Lakes–St Lawrence lowlands, the center of early European colonization and subsequent industrial expansion, remain the country's most densely populated area and the focus of most immigration—in the 1990s, Ontario absorbed more than half of all Canada's immigrants. Though productive, Manitoba's farmlands are highly mechanized and population density therefore remains relatively low in the west. The sparsely populated and frequently snow-covered far north is home mainly to scattered indigenous communities.

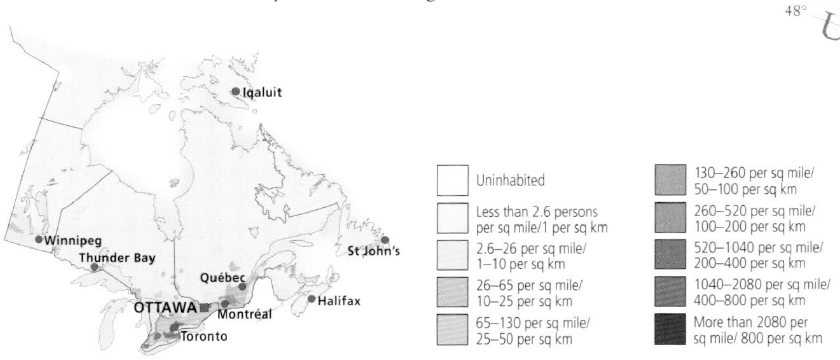

Iqaluit
Winnipeg
Thunder Bay
St John's
Québec
Halifax
OTTAWA
Montréal
Toronto
Uninhabited
Less than 2.6 persons per sq mile/1 per sq km
2.6–26 per sq mile/ 1–10 per sq km
26–65 per sq mile/ 10–25 per sq km
65–130 per sq mile/ 25–50 per sq km
130–260 per sq mile/ 50–100 per sq km
260–520 per sq mile/ 100–200 per sq km
520–1040 per sq mile/ 200–400 per sq km
1040–2080 per sq mile/ 400–800 per sq km
More than 2080 per sq mile/ 800 per sq km

ECONOMIC PROFILE

Agriculture and mining led Canada's early growth, but manufacturing and especially services now dominate the economy. The Canadian Shield holds rich deposits of iron ore, nickel, and other minerals. Fast-flowing rivers have been harnessed to generate hydroelectric power (which provides 60 percent of Canada's energy), and the immense conifer forests help make Canada the world's largest supplier of wood products. Ontario is the industrial heartland, with transportation equipment, metals, chemicals, wood and paper, and foodstuffs among the most vital products. The Grand Banks off Newfoundland are Canada's richest fisheries, though overfishing has significantly reduced catches since the 1970s.

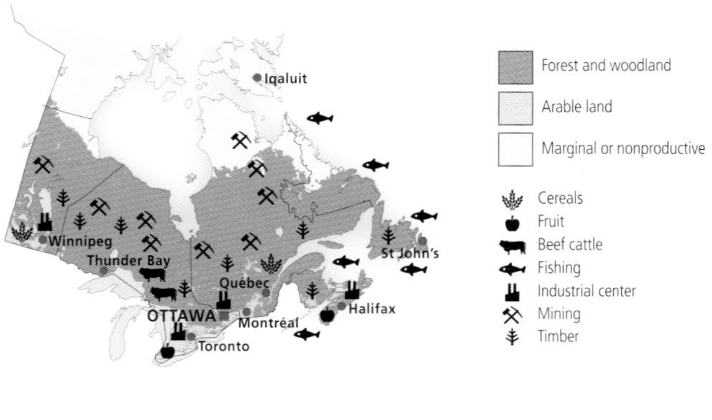

Iqaluit
Winnipeg
Thunder Bay
St John's
Québec
Halifax
OTTAWA
Montréal
Toronto
Forest and woodland
Arable land
Marginal or nonproductive
Cereals
Fruit
Beef cattle
Fishing
Industrial center
Mining
Timber

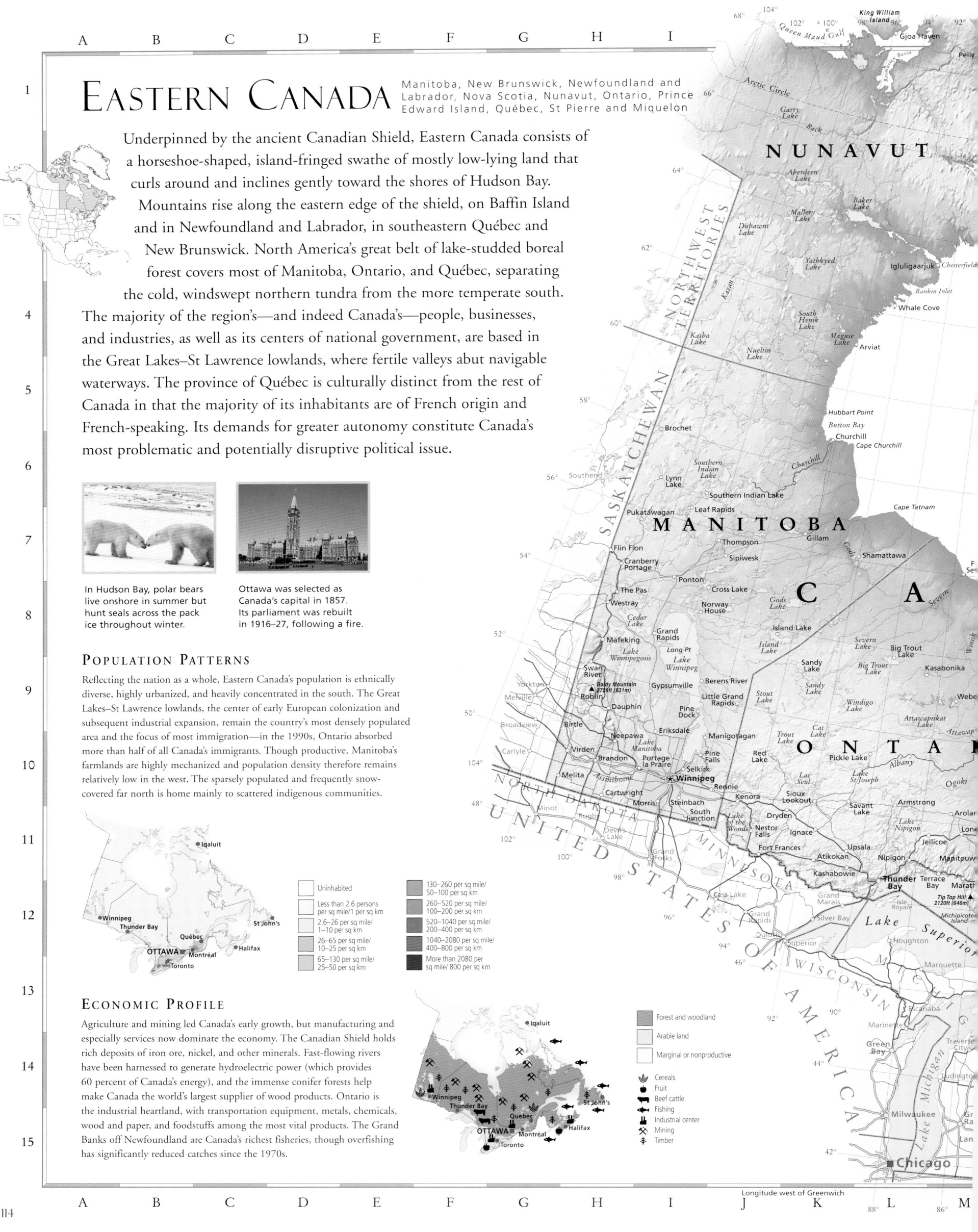

A
B
C
D
E
F
G
H
I
J
K
L
M
1
4
5
6
7
8
9
10
11
12
13
14
15
Queen Maud Gulf
King William Island
Gjoa Haven
Arctic Circle
Garry Lake
NUNAVUT
Aberdeen Lake
Baker Lake
Mallery Lake
Dubawnt Lake
NORTHWEST TERRITORIES
Yathkyed Lake
Igluligaarjuk
Rankin Inlet
Whale Cove
Kazan
South Henik Lake
Kasba Lake
Nueltin Lake
Maguse Lake
Arviat
SASKATCHEWAN
Hubbart Point
Button Bay
Churchill
Cape Churchill
Brochet
Southern Indian Lake
Lynn Lake
Pukatawagan
Leaf Rapids
Cape Tatnam
MANITOBA
Gillam
Thompson
Flin Flon
Shamattawa
Cranberry Portage
Sipiwesk
Ponton
Cross Lake
The Pas
Norway House
Westray
Gods Lake
Cedar Lake
Grand Rapids
Island Lake
Mafeking
Lake Winnipegosis
Long Pt
Lake Winnipeg
Severn Lake
Big Trout Lake
Kasabonika
Swan River
Baldy Mountain 2726ft (831m)
Gypsumville
Berens River
Sandy Lake
Yorkton
Melville
Roblin
Little Grand Rapids
Dauphin
Pine Dock
Broadview
Birtle
Eriksdale
Manigotagan
Neepawa
Lake Manitoba
Carlyle
Virden
Pine Falls
Red Lake
Pickle Lake
Brandon
Portage la Prairie
Selkirk
Melita
Assiniboine
Winnipeg
Rennie
Cartwright
Morris
Kenora
Steinbach
South Junction
Dryden
Sioux Lookout
Savant Lake
Armstrong
NORTH DAKOTA
UNITED STATES OF AMERICA
Minot
Rugby
Devils Lake
Lake of the Woods
Nestor Falls
Ignace
Lake Nipigon
Jellicoe
Fort Frances
Upsala
Atikokan
Nipigon
Grand Forks
MINNESOTA
Kashabowie
Thunder Bay
Terrace Bay
Tip Top Hill 2120ft (646m)
Cass Lake
Grand Marais
Isle Royale
Grand Rapids
Silver Bay
Lake Superior
Duluth
Superior
Houghton
WISCONSIN
Marquette
Escanaba
Marinette
Green Bay
Lake Michigan
Milwaukee
Chicago
Albany
Ogoki
Attawapiskat Lake
ONTARIO
CANADA
Longitude west of Greenwich

S
T
U
V
W
X
Y
Z
1
2
3
4
5
6
7
8
9
10
11
P
Q
R
Igloolik
Rowley Island
Bray Island
Home Bay
Kangeeak Point
Qikiqtarjuaq
Hall Beach
Foley Island
Melville Peninsula
Parry Bay
South Spicer Island
Prince Charles Island
Air Force Island
Baffin Island
Cumberland Peninsula
Cape Dyer
Davis Strait
Repulse Bay
Cape Wilson
Foxe Basin
Arctic Circle
Nettilling Lake
Great Plain of the Koukdjuak
Pangnirtung
Cumberland Sound
Vansittart Island
NUNAVUT
Cape Mercy
Foxe Peninsula
Amadjuak Lake
Southampton Island
Foxe Channel
Hall Peninsula
Lemieux Islands
Coral Harbour
Cape Dorset
Iqaluit
Mill Island
Salisbury Island
Meta Incognita Peninsula
Frobisher Bay
Nottingham Island
Evans Strait
Kimmirut
Loks Land
Big Island
Fisher Strait
Coats Island
Cap Wolstenholme
Hudson Strait
Salluit
Ivujivik
Resolution Island
e Southampton
Mansel Island
Kangiqsujuaq
Cap Hopes Advance
Quaqtaq
Button Islands
Killiniq
Cape Labrador
Akpatok Island
Akulivik
Smith Island
Péninsule d'Ungava
Hudson Bay
Mosquito Bay
Arnaud
Kangirsuk
Ungava Bay
Labrador Sea
Puvurnituq
Lac Payne
Aupaluk
Mt Caubvick 5479ft (1729m)
Cape Uivak
Hebron
Ottawa Islands
Kogaluk
Tasiujaq
Cod Island
Kangiqsualujjuaq
Kuujjuaq
Okak Islands
Inukjuak
Rivière aux Feuilles
Rivière aux Mélèzes
Torngat Mountains
George
Caniapiscau
Nain
Fraser
Davis Inlet
Sleeper Islands
King George Islands
Nastapoka Islands
Lac Minto
Labrador
Hopedale
North Belcher Islands
Makkovik
Mt Benedict 2720ft (829m)
Indian Harbour
Groswater Bay
Nastapoca
Belcher Islands
Sanikiluaq
Lac Guillaume-Delisle
Flaherty Island
Lac à l'Eau Claire
Hamilton Inlet
Black Tickle
Cartwright
N
A
D
A
Winisk
Cape Henrietta Maria
Kuujjuaraapik
Matimekosh
Schefferville
Kanairiktok
Naskaupi
Lake Melville
Mealy Mountains
Eagle
Snug Harbour
Lac Bienville
Smallwood Reservoir
Happy Valley-Goose Bay
Port Hope Simpson
Long Island
Lac Burton
Lac Caniapiscau
Churchill Falls
Esker
Churchill
Belle Isle
James Bay
Réservoir la Grande Deux
Réservoir la Grande Trois
Radisson
NEWFOUNDLAND AND LABRADOR
Red Bay
Cape Bauld
St Anthony
Lac Joseph
Blanc-Sablon
Strait of Belle Isle
Chisasibi
North Twin Island
Labrador City
Mont Wright 2949ft (899m)
Pitaga
Grey Islands
Englee
Attawapiskat
Akimiski Island
South Twin Island
Wemindji
QUÉBEC
St-Augustin
Hawkes Bay
White Bay
Long Range Mountains
Baie Verte
Notre Dame Bay
Fogo Island
Musgrave Harbour
Réservoir Opinaca
Mont Yapeitso 3724ft (1135m)
Gagnon
Laurentian Mountains
Daniel's Harbour
Kashechewen
Eastmain
Mont de Babel 3117ft (950m)
Étamamiou
Musquaro
Springdale
Bonavista Bay
Bonavista
Fort Albany
Charlton Island
Albany
Hannah Bay
Péribonca
Réservoir Manicouagan
Havre-St-Pierre
Natashquan
Gander
Deer Lake
Trinity Bay
Waskaganish
Sheldrake
Grand Lake
Clarenville
St John's
Moosonee
Lac Manouane
Manicouagan
Détroit de Jacques-Cartier
Rivière-aux-Saumons
Corner Brook
Newfoundland
Lac Mistassini
Sept-Îles
Port-Menier
Île d'Anticosti
Stephenville
Buchans
Moose
Harricanaw
Nottaway
Lac Evans
Mistassini
St Alban's
Avalon Peninsula
Rivière-Pentecôte
Détroit d'Honguedo
Chute-des-Passes
Réservoir Pipmuacan
St Georges Bay
Harbour Breton
Placentia Bay
St Mary's Bay
Trepassey
Gulf of St Lawrence
Fortune Bay
Hearst
Fraserdale
Matagami
Chibougamau
Baie-Comeau
Gaspé
Péninsule de Gaspé
Burgeo
Channel-Port-aux-Basques
St Lawrence
Kapuskasing
Bochart
Matane
St Lawrence
ST PIERRE and MIQUELON (to France)
ST-PIERRE
Cochrane
Forestville
Mont-Joli
Notre Dame
New Richmond
Îles de la Madeleine
Grande-Entrée
Cabot Strait
Beattyville
Réservoir Gouin
Lac St-Jean
Saguenay
Chaleur Bay
Miscou Island
Havre Aubert
Dingwall
La Sarre
Roberval
Saguenay
Caraquet
Cape Breton Island
Amos
Timmins
Matheson
St-Siméon
Rivière-du-Loup
Campbellton
Tignish
PRINCE EDWARD ISLAND
White Hill 1745ft (532m)
Elmira
Glace Bay
Foleyet
Kirkland Lake
Rouyn
Val-d'Or
Parent
Baie-St-Paul
Edmundston
Mount Carleton 2690ft (820m)
Newcastle
Prince Edward Island
Sydney
OCEAN
Sultan
New Liskeard
Réservoir Cabonga
La Tuque
Monts Notre Dame
Presque Isle
NEW BRUNSWICK
Northumberland Strait
Charlottetown
St Peter's
Westree
Lac Kempt
Québec
Port Hawkesbury
Canso
Marten River
Depot-Forbes
Réservoir Baskatong
Grand-Mère
Houlton
Fredericton
Moncton
Truro
New Glasgow
Ste Marie
Elliot Lake
Sudbury
North Bay
Trois-Rivières
Victoriaville
St-Georges
MAINE
Windsor
NOVA SCOTIA
Sheet Harbour
North Channel
Lake Nipissing
Maniwaki
Labelle
Joliette
Sorel
Drummondville
Saint John
St George
Bay of Fundy
Manitoulin Island
Parry Sound
Stonecliffe
Pembroke
Ottawa
OTTAWA
Montréal
Sherbrooke
Halifax
Chester
ATLANTIC
Haliburton Highlands
Huntsville
Whitney
Cornwall
St-Jean-sur-Richelieu
Orono
Digby
Georgian Bay
Bancroft
Perth
Smiths Falls
Lake Huron
Owen Sound
Orillia
Kaladar
Brockville
Plattsburgh
Waterville
Liverpool
Yarmouth
Gulf of Maine
Peterborough
Burlington
VERMONT
NEW HAMPSHIRE
Barrington
Kincardine
Oshawa
Trenton
Watertown
Toronto
Lake Ontario
Kitchener
Oswego
Rochester
London
Niagara Falls
St Catharines
NEW YORK
Buffalo
Sarnia
Chatham
St Clair
Windsor
Lake Erie
Erie
Toledo
Cleveland
OHIO
86°
84°
82°
80°
78°
76°
74°
72°
70°
68°
66°
64°
62°
60°
58°
56°
54°
52°
50°
48°
46°
44°
42°

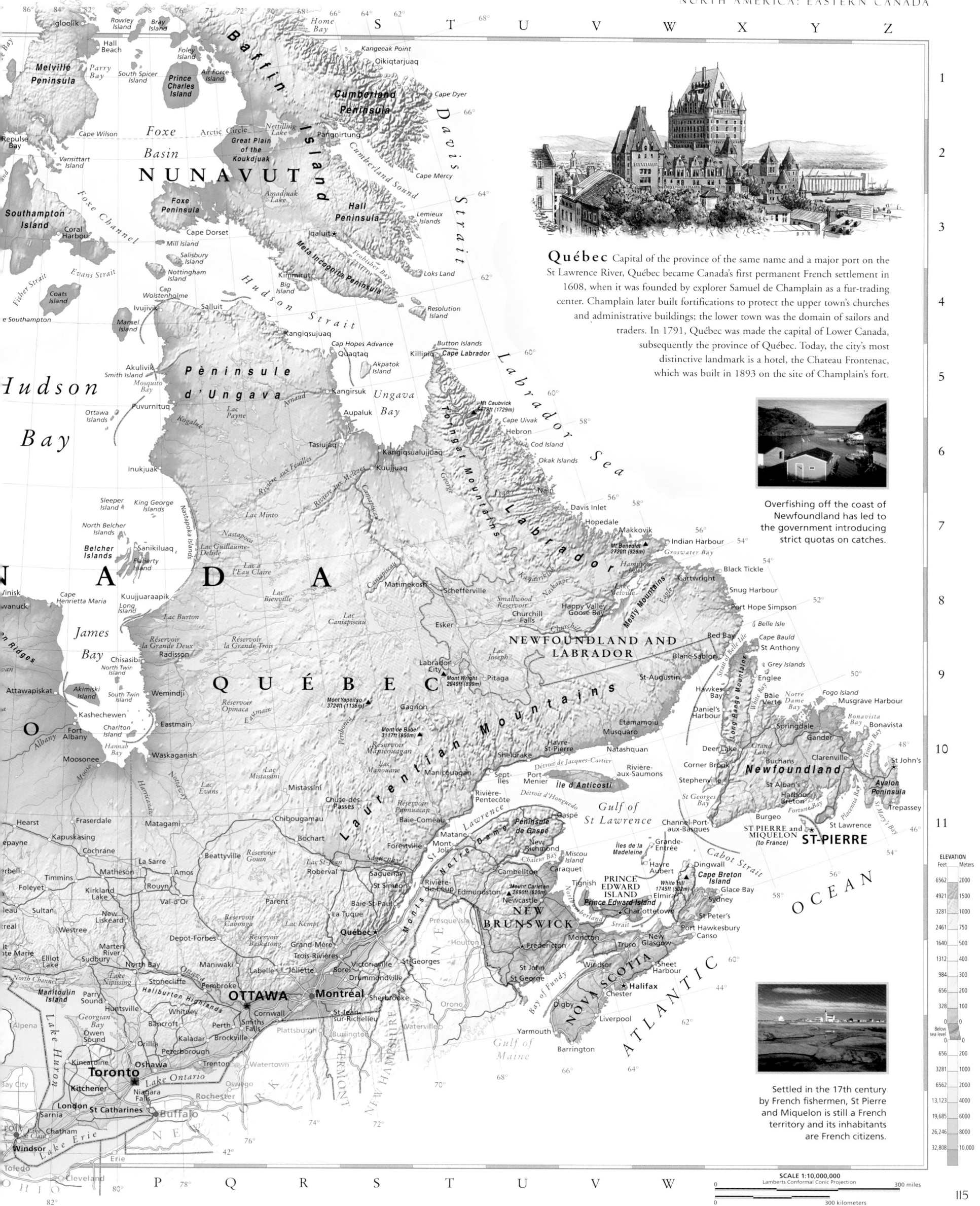

Québec Capital of the province of the same name and a major port on the St Lawrence River, Québec became Canada's first permanent French settlement in 1608, when it was founded by explorer Samuel de Champlain as a fur-trading center. Champlain later built fortifications to protect the upper town's churches and administrative buildings; the lower town was the domain of sailors and traders. In 1791, Québec was made the capital of Lower Canada, subsequently the province of Québec. Today, the city's most distinctive landmark is a hotel, the Chateau Frontenac, which was built in 1893 on the site of Champlain's fort.

Overfishing off the coast of Newfoundland has led to the government introducing strict quotas on catches.

ELEVATION

Feet	Meters
6562	2000
4921	1500
3281	1000
2461	750
1640	500
1312	400
984	300
656	200
328	100
0	0
Below sea level 0	0
656	200
3281	1000
6562	2000
13,123	4000
19,685	6000
26,246	8000
32,808	10,000

Settled in the 17th century by French fishermen, St Pierre and Miquelon is still a French territory and its inhabitants are French citizens.

SCALE 1:10,000,000
Lamberts Conformal Conic Projection
0 — 300 miles
0 — 300 kilometers

Western United States

Arizona, California, Hawaii, Idaho, Nevada, Oregon, Utah, Washington

The north–south-trending ridge formed by the Cascade Range, Sierra Nevada, and San Bernardino Mountains separates this region's temperate, populous coastal zone from its arid, sparsely inhabited hinterland. A jumble of plateaus, basins, and ranges, the interior encompasses volcanic uplands in the north, deserts in the south, and ancient landforms such as the Grand Canyon. In contrast, the coastal zone and the distant Hawaiian Islands are geologically young and active—volcanoes crown the Cascades, earthquakes regularly rock California, and lava flows continually reshape Hawaii. The West's rugged, intimidating terrain deterred early European settlers, who clung to the coast and threaded their way along river valleys before being lured into the uplands by the discovery of gold and other minerals in the mid-19th century.

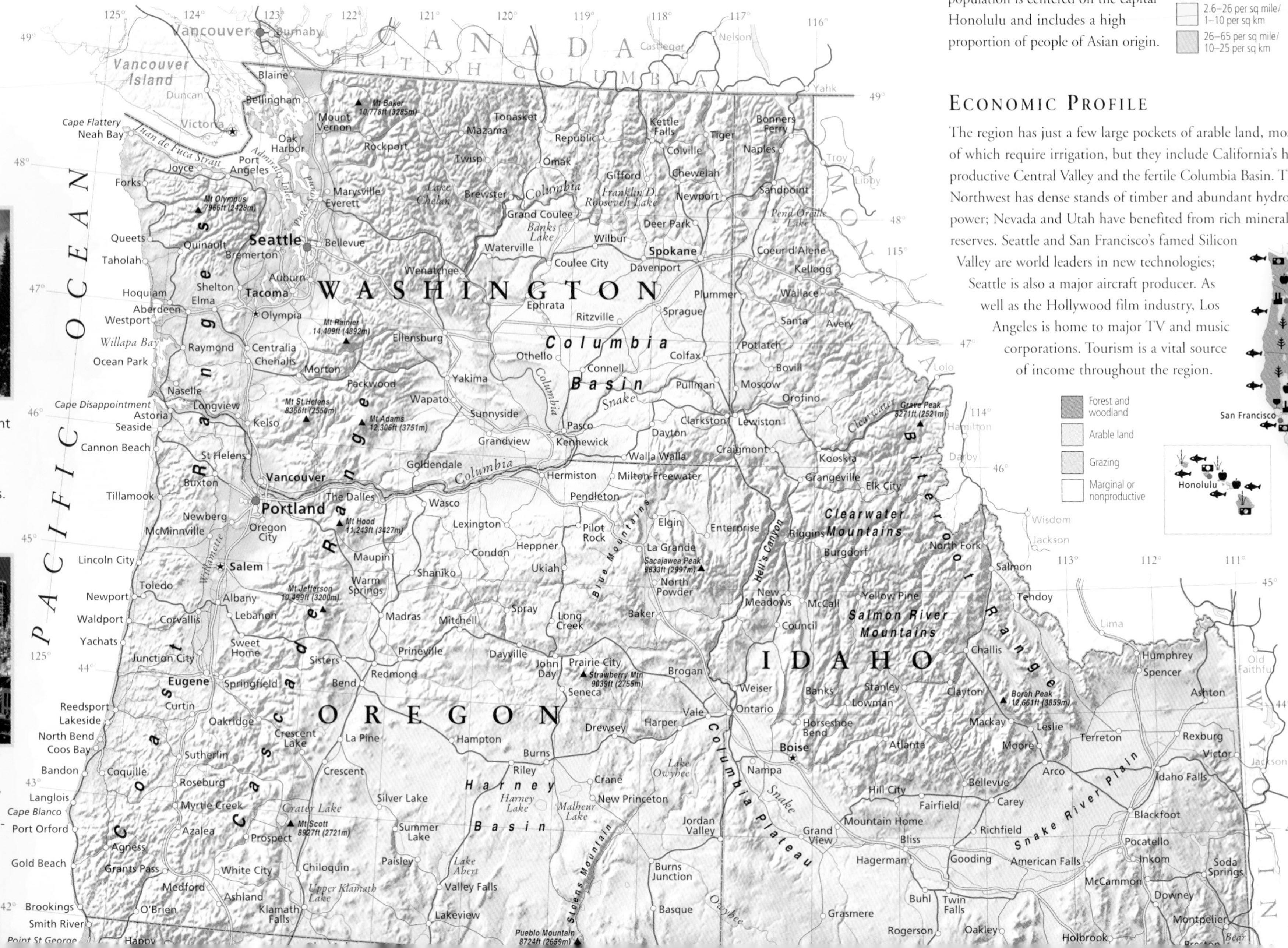
PACIFIC OCEAN
CANADA
BRITISH COLUMBIA
MONTANA
WYOMING
WASHINGTON
OREGON
IDAHO
Vancouver Island
Vancouver
Seattle
Tacoma
Olympia
Spokane
Portland
Salem
Eugene
Boise
Columbia Basin
Columbia Plateau
Snake River Plain
Harney Basin
Cascade Range
Coast Ranges
Clearwater Mountains
Salmon River Mountains
Bitterroot Range
Blue Mountains
Steens Mountain
Mt Baker 10,778ft (3285m)
Mt Olympus 7,965ft (2428m)
Mt Rainier 14,409ft (4392m)
Mt St Helens 8,365ft (2550m)
Mt Adams 12,306ft (3751m)
Mt Hood 11,243ft (3427m)
Mt Jefferson 10,499ft (3200m)
Mt Scott 8,927ft (2721m)
Strawberry Mtn 9,038ft (2755m)
Sacajawea Peak 9,833ft (2997m)
Grave Peak 8,271ft (2521m)
Borah Peak 12,661ft (3859m)
Pueblo Mountain 8,724ft (2659m)

Washington's Mount Rainier is crowned by the largest glacier system in the lower 48 states.

Founded in 1781 by Spanish settlers, Los Angeles is now the U.S.A.'s second-largest city.

Population Patterns

More than 90 percent of the inhabitants of California, the U.S.A.'s most populous state, live in urban areas, mainly around Los Angeles and San Francisco. In the Pacific Northwest, densely populated areas line Puget Sound and Oregon's Willamette Valley. Inland, settlements tend to be small and widely scattered. Notable exceptions include Las Vegas, a desert metropolis founded on gambling and tourism, and Salt Lake City, originally established as a refuge for members of the Mormon religious sect. Hawaii's population is centered on the capital Honolulu and includes a high proportion of people of Asian origin.

Seattle
Portland
Boise
Salt Lake City
San Francisco
Las Vegas
Los Angeles
Phoenix
Honolulu
Less than 2.6 persons per sq mile/1 per sq km
2.6–26 per sq mile/ 1–10 per sq km
26–65 per sq mile/ 10–25 per sq km
65–130 per sq mile/ 25–50 per sq km
130–260 per sq mile/ 50–100 per sq km
260–520 per sq mile/ 100–200 per sq km
520–1040 per sq mile/ 200–400 per sq km

Economic Profile

The region has just a few large pockets of arable land, most of which require irrigation, but they include California's highly productive Central Valley and the fertile Columbia Basin. The Northwest has dense stands of timber and abundant hydroelectric power; Nevada and Utah have benefited from rich mineral reserves. Seattle and San Francisco's famed Silicon Valley are world leaders in new technologies; Seattle is also a major aircraft producer. As well as the Hollywood film industry, Los Angeles is home to major TV and music corporations. Tourism is a vital source of income throughout the region.

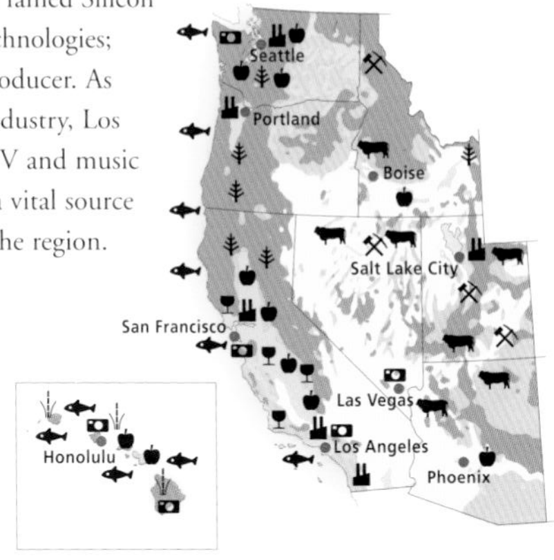
Sugarcane
Fruit
Wine
Beef cattle
Fishing
Industrial center
Mining
Tourism
Timber
Forest and woodland
Arable land
Grazing
Marginal or nonproductive
Seattle
Portland
Boise
Salt Lake City
San Francisco
Las Vegas
Los Angeles
Phoenix
Honolulu

Oregon's Crater Lake fills a caldera that was once part of an enormous volcano, Mount Mazama.

Carved by the Colorado River, the Grand Canyon is more than one mile (1.6 km) deep.

Kilauea, on the island of Hawaii, is the world's largest active crater. Regular eruptions often generate extensive lava flows.

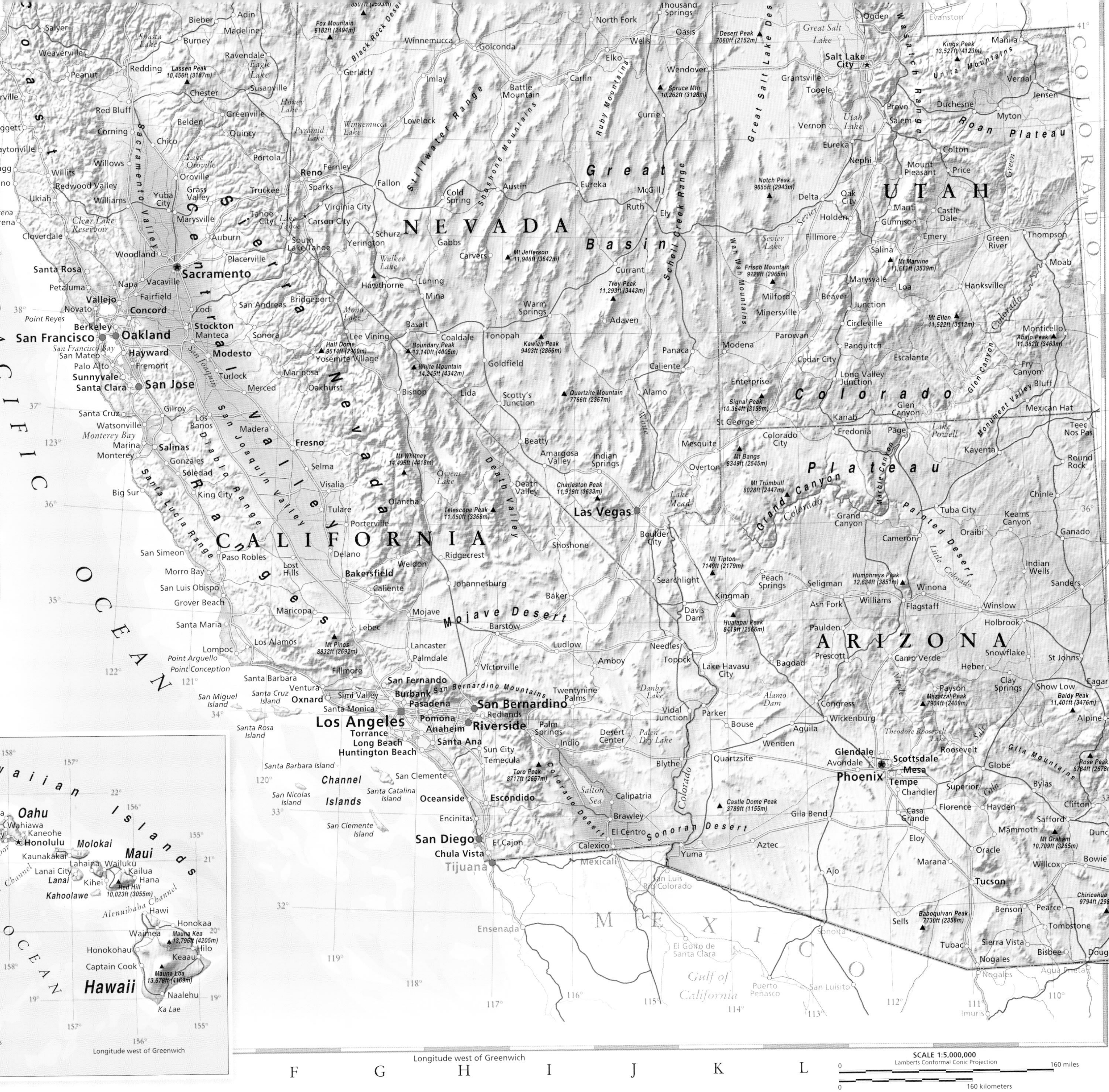
COLORADO
NEW MEXICO
UTAH
NEVADA
ARIZONA
CALIFORNIA
MEXICO
PACIFIC OCEAN
Great Basin
Colorado Plateau
Sierra Nevada
Central Valley
Coast Ranges
Mojave Desert
Sonoran Desert
Colorado Desert
Painted Desert
Grand Canyon
Death Valley
Gulf of California
Salt Lake City
Sacramento
Phoenix
San Francisco
Oakland
San Jose
Los Angeles
San Diego
Las Vegas
Fresno
Reno
Tucson
Tijuana
Mexicali
SCALE 1:5,000,000
Lamberts Conformal Conic Projection
160 miles
160 kilometers
Longitude west of Greenwich
HAWAII
(U.S.A.)
Hawaiian Islands
PACIFIC OCEAN
Kauai
Oahu
Molokai
Maui
Lanai
Kahoolawe
Hawaii
Niihau
Honolulu
Hilo
Mauna Kea 13,796ft (4205m)
Mauna Loa 13,678ft (4169m)
SCALE 1:7,000,000
Lamberts Conformal Conic Projection
100 miles
100 kilometers
Longitude west of Greenwich

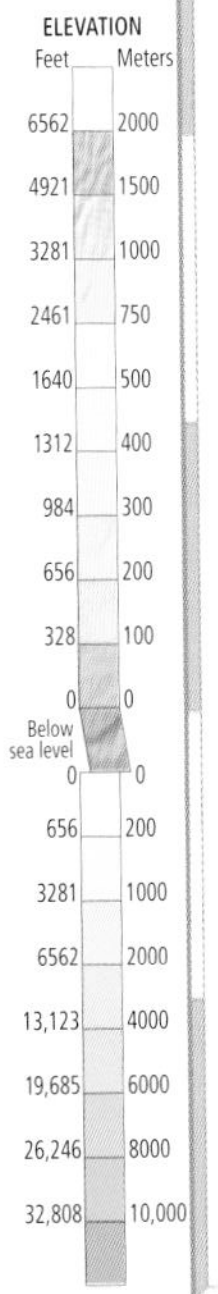
ELEVATION
Feet Meters
6562 2000
4921 1500
3281 1000
2461 750
1640 500
1312 400
984 300
656 200
328 100
Below sea level 0
656 200
3281 1000
6562 2000
13,123 4000
19,685 6000
26,246 8000
32,808 10,000

CENTRAL UNITED STATES

Arkansas, Colorado, Iowa, Kansas, Louisiana, Minnesota, Missouri, Montana, Nebraska, New Mexico, North Dakota, Oklahoma, South Dakota, Texas, Wyoming

The Central United States is bound to the north and south by the Canadian and Mexican borders, to the west by the great spine of the Rocky Mountains, and to the east by North America's longest river, the Mississippi, which winds for 2,340 miles (3,765 km) from northern Minnesota to New Orleans on the Gulf of Mexico. The Rockies form an almost unbroken wall along the edge of the Great Plains, a broad plateau that stretches from southern Canada to the Rio Grande and tilts almost imperceptibly eastward. Numerous rivers follow the plateau's inclination, draining across wide pastures and the rich farmlands of the Central Lowlands into the Mississippi, major tributaries such as the Missouri, and the Gulf of Mexico. The Mississippi and Missouri were vital communications routes for Native American peoples and early European settlers, and became the launching pad for the great wave of westward colonial expansion that occurred in the 1840s.

THE TETON RANGE

Extending for 40 miles (64 km) across northwestern Wyoming, the Teton Range is one of the youngest and most imposing mountain ranges in the Rockies. Its jagged peaks began to form more than 1 million years ago when the land to the east dropped downward along a 50-mile (80-km) fault line. Today, 13,770-foot (4,197-m) Grand Teton, the highest peak in the range, rises 7,000 feet (2,135 m) above the valley of Jackson Hole.

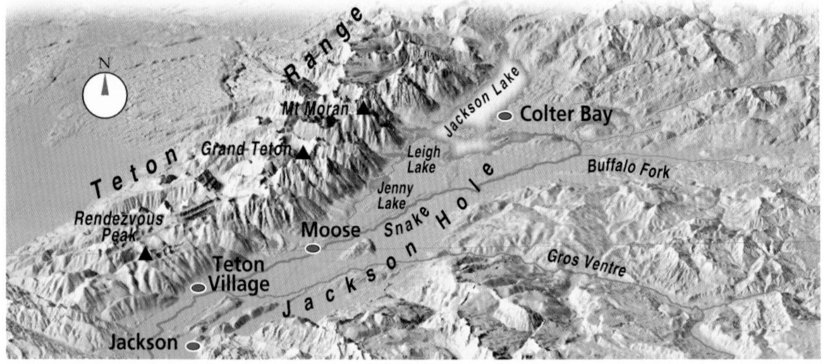
N
Teton Range
Mt Moran
Grand Teton
Jackson Lake
Colter Bay
Leigh Lake
Jenny Lake
Buffalo Fork
Rendezvous Peak
Moose
Snake
Jackson Hole
Teton Village
Gros Ventre
Jackson

C A N A D A
ALBERTA
SASKATCHEWAN
MANITOBA
ONTARIO
MONTANA
NORTH DAKOTA
SOUTH DAKOTA
MINNESOTA
WYOMING
NEBRASKA
IOWA
IDAHO
WISCONSIN
Rocky Mountains
Great Plains
Bitterroot Range
Absaroka Range
Bighorn Mtns
Bighorn Basin
Wind River Range
Wyoming Range
Teton Range
Laramie Mtns
Great Divide Basin
Black Hills
Badlands
Lake Superior
Lake of the Woods
Missouri
Yellowstone
Mississippi
Lake Sakakawea
Lake Oahe
Fort Peck Reservoir
Yellowstone Lake
Helena
Bismarck
Pierre
Cheyenne
Lincoln
Des Moines
St Paul
Minneapolis
Billings
Great Falls
Missoula
Butte
Bozeman
Fargo
Sioux Falls
Rapid City
Casper
Omaha
Duluth
Cedar Rapids
West Butte 6980ft (2128m)
Baldy Mtn 6621ft (2018m)
Big Snow Mtn 8730ft (2661m)
Mt Evans 10,640ft (3243m)
Granite Peak 12,799ft (3901m)
Grand Teton 13,770ft (4197m)
Gannett Peak 13,785ft (4202m)
Devil's Tower 5112ft (1558m)
Mt Rushmore 5725ft (1745m)
Sentinel Butte 3428ft (1045m)
White Butte 3530ft (1076m)
Diamond Peak 9659ft (2944m)
Mt Zirkel 12,178ft (3712m)

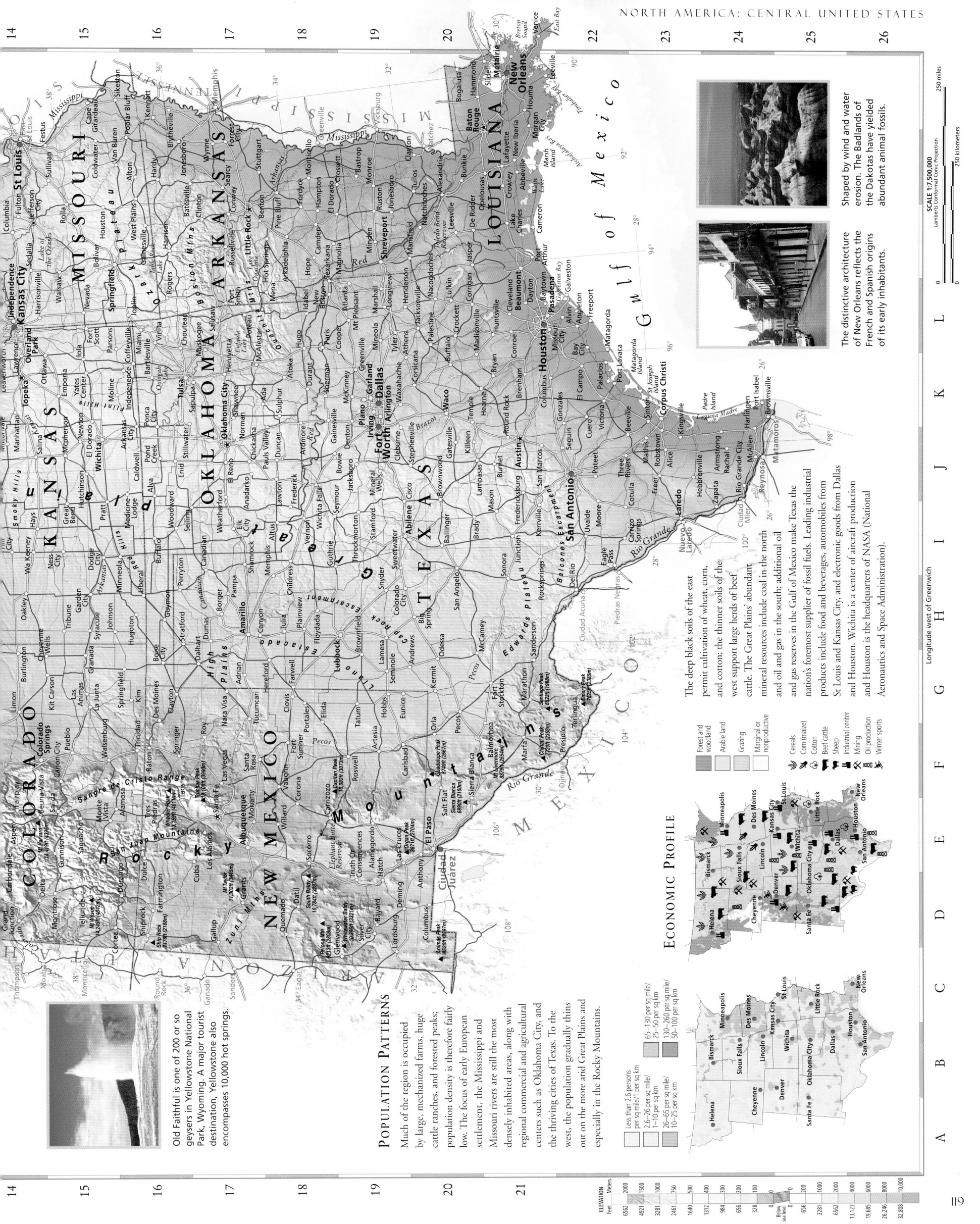

COLORADO
KANSAS
MISSOURI
OKLAHOMA
ARKANSAS
NEW MEXICO
TEXAS
LOUISIANA
MEXICO
Gulf of Mexico
Rocky Mountains
Great Plains
Ozark Plateau
Edwards Plateau
Llano Estacado
High Plains
Kansas City
St Louis
Oklahoma City
Dallas
Fort Worth
Houston
San Antonio
New Orleans
Albuquerque
El Paso
Ciudad Juárez
Little Rock
Baton Rouge
Longitude west of Greenwich
SCALE 1:7,500,000
Lamberts Conformal Conic Projection
250 miles
250 kilometers

Old Faithful is one of 200 or so geysers in Yellowstone National Park, Wyoming. A major tourist destination, Yellowstone also encompasses 10,000 hot springs.

Population Patterns

Much of the region is occupied by large, mechanized farms, huge cattle ranches, and forested peaks; population density is therefore fairly low. The focus of early European settlement, the Mississippi and Missouri rivers are still the most densely inhabited areas, along with regional commercial and agricultural centers such as Oklahoma City, and the thriving cities of Texas. To the west, the population gradually thins out on the more arid Great Plains and especially in the Rocky Mountains.

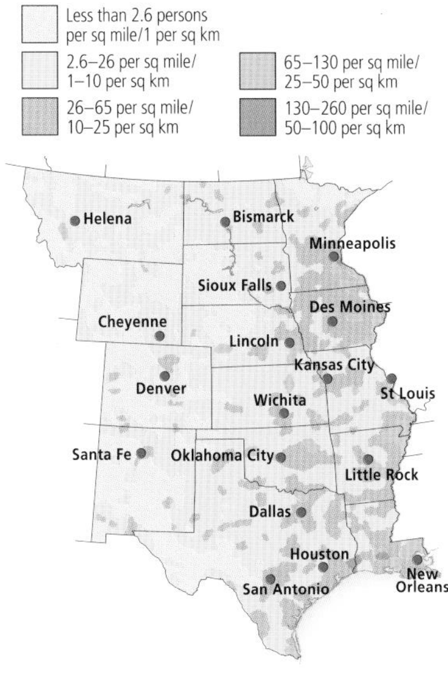
Less than 2.6 persons per sq mile/1 per sq km
2.6–26 per sq mile/ 1–10 per sq km
26–65 per sq mile/ 10–25 per sq km
65–130 per sq mile/ 25–50 per sq km
130–260 per sq mile/ 50–100 per sq km
Helena
Bismarck
Minneapolis
Sioux Falls
Des Moines
Cheyenne
Lincoln
Kansas City
Denver
Wichita
St Louis
Santa Fe
Oklahoma City
Little Rock
Dallas
Houston
San Antonio
New Orleans

Economic Profile

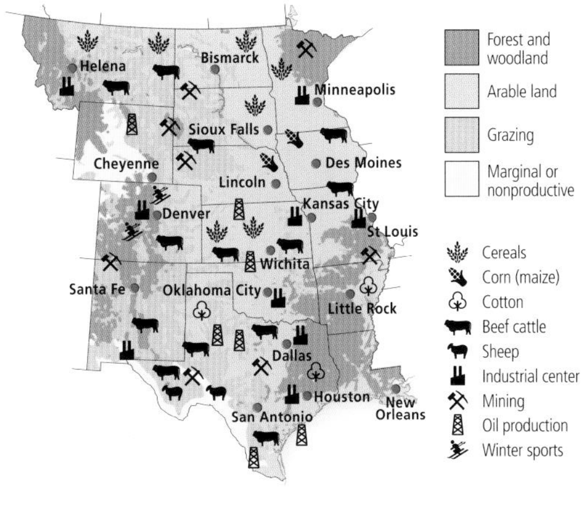
Forest and woodland
Arable land
Grazing
Marginal or nonproductive
Cereals
Corn (maize)
Cotton
Beef cattle
Sheep
Industrial center
Mining
Oil production
Winter sports
Helena
Bismarck
Minneapolis
Sioux Falls
Des Moines
Cheyenne
Lincoln
Kansas City
Denver
Wichita
St Louis
Santa Fe
Oklahoma City
Little Rock
Dallas
Houston
San Antonio
New Orleans

The deep black soils of the east permit cultivation of wheat, corn, and cotton; the thinner soils of the west support large herds of beef cattle. The Great Plains' abundant mineral resources include coal in the north and oil and gas in the south; additional oil and gas reserves in the Gulf of Mexico make Texas the nation's foremost supplier of fossil fuels. Leading industrial products include food and beverages, automobiles from St Louis and Kansas City, and electronic goods from Dallas and Houston. Wichita is a center of aircraft production and Houston is the headquarters of NASA (National Aeronautics and Space Administration).

The distinctive architecture of New Orleans reflects the French and Spanish origins of its early inhabitants.

Shaped by wind and water erosion. The Badlands of the Dakotas have yielded abundant animal fossils.

NORTHEASTERN UNITED STATES

Connecticut, Delaware, District of Columbia, Illinois, Indiana, Kentucky, Maine, Maryland, Massachusetts, Michigan, New Hampshire, New Jersey, New York, Ohio, Pennsylvania, Rhode Island, Vermont, Virginia, West Virginia, Wisconsin

The northeastern seaboard of the United States is where the nation can be said to have begun: the first permanent British colony was established at Jamestown, near present-day Newport News, Virginia, in 1607, and the Pilgrim Fathers arrived on the *Mayflower* at what is now Plymouth, Massachusetts, in 1620. Today, this is the U.S.A.'s most densely populated region and the site of its leading centers of government, industry, and commerce. Tapering to the north, the coastal plain is bounded by the Appalachian Mountains. Formed 400 million years ago, this once-colossal range has been worn down by water and wind into low, rounded peaks. On their western side, the Appalachians descend to the Central Lowlands, a major agricultural region. To its north, a string of industrial cities borders the Great Lakes, the largest system of freshwater lakes in the world.

POPULATION PATTERNS

The line of cities that stretches more than 300 miles from Washington, D.C., to Boston forms one vast urban area known as the Bos–Wash conurbation, or megalopolis. This coastal strip is home to over 44 million people, more than 15 percent of the U.S. population. Smaller but equally dense agglomerations are also taking shape around Chicago, Detroit, and Buffalo, and between Cleveland and Pittsburgh. Settlements are more spread out on the predominantly agricultural plains and relatively sparse in the forested uplands of the Appalachian chain and in northern Michigan and Wisconsin.

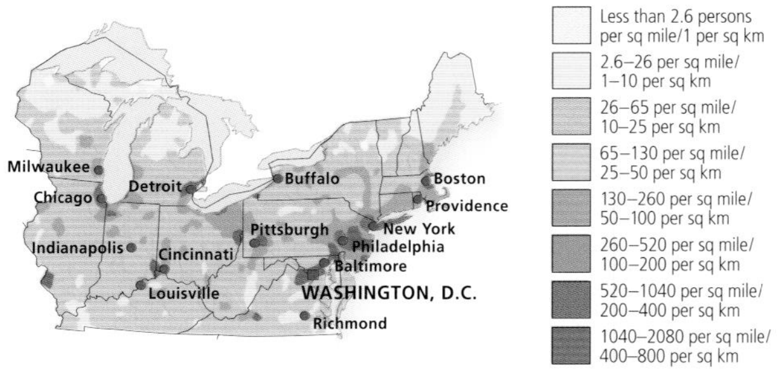
Milwaukee
Chicago
Detroit
Buffalo
Boston
Providence
New York
Philadelphia
Baltimore
Pittsburgh
Indianapolis
Cincinnati
Louisville
WASHINGTON, D.C.
Richmond
Less than 2.6 persons per sq mile/1 per sq km
2.6–26 per sq mile/ 1–10 per sq km
26–65 per sq mile/ 10–25 per sq km
65–130 per sq mile/ 25–50 per sq km
130–260 per sq mile/ 50–100 per sq km
260–520 per sq mile/ 100–200 per sq km
520–1040 per sq mile/ 200–400 per sq km
1040–2080 per sq mile/ 400–800 per sq km

ECONOMIC PROFILE

The northeast is America's commercial and industrial hub. New York, site of the New York Stock Exchange and Wall Street, leads the world in business and finance and has the nation's largest port; Boston is a center of banking, insurance, and electronics; and Washington is the seat of national government. The traditional heavy industries of the Great Lakes, such as automobile manufacture, founded on the region's extensive iron-ore deposits, have begun to give way to high-tech industries and services. The Corn Belt, which stretches west from Ohio, generates half the world's corn; the mountains of Kentucky and West Virginia supply much of the nation's coal.

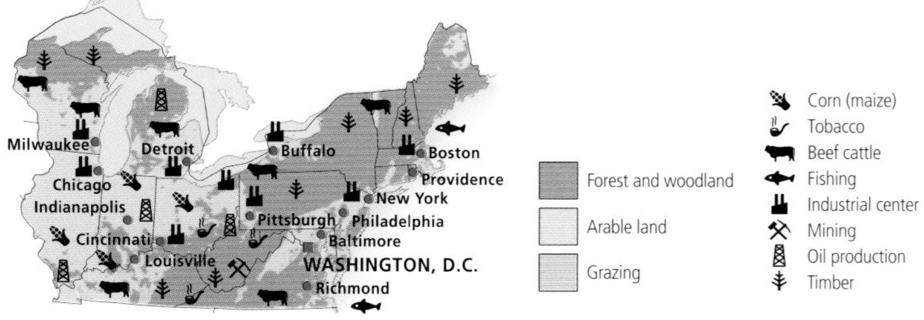
Milwaukee
Detroit
Buffalo
Boston
Providence
Chicago
New York
Indianapolis
Pittsburgh
Philadelphia
Cincinnati
Baltimore
Louisville
WASHINGTON, D.C.
Richmond
Forest and woodland
Arable land
Grazing
Corn (maize)
Tobacco
Beef cattle
Fishing
Industrial center
Mining
Oil production
Timber

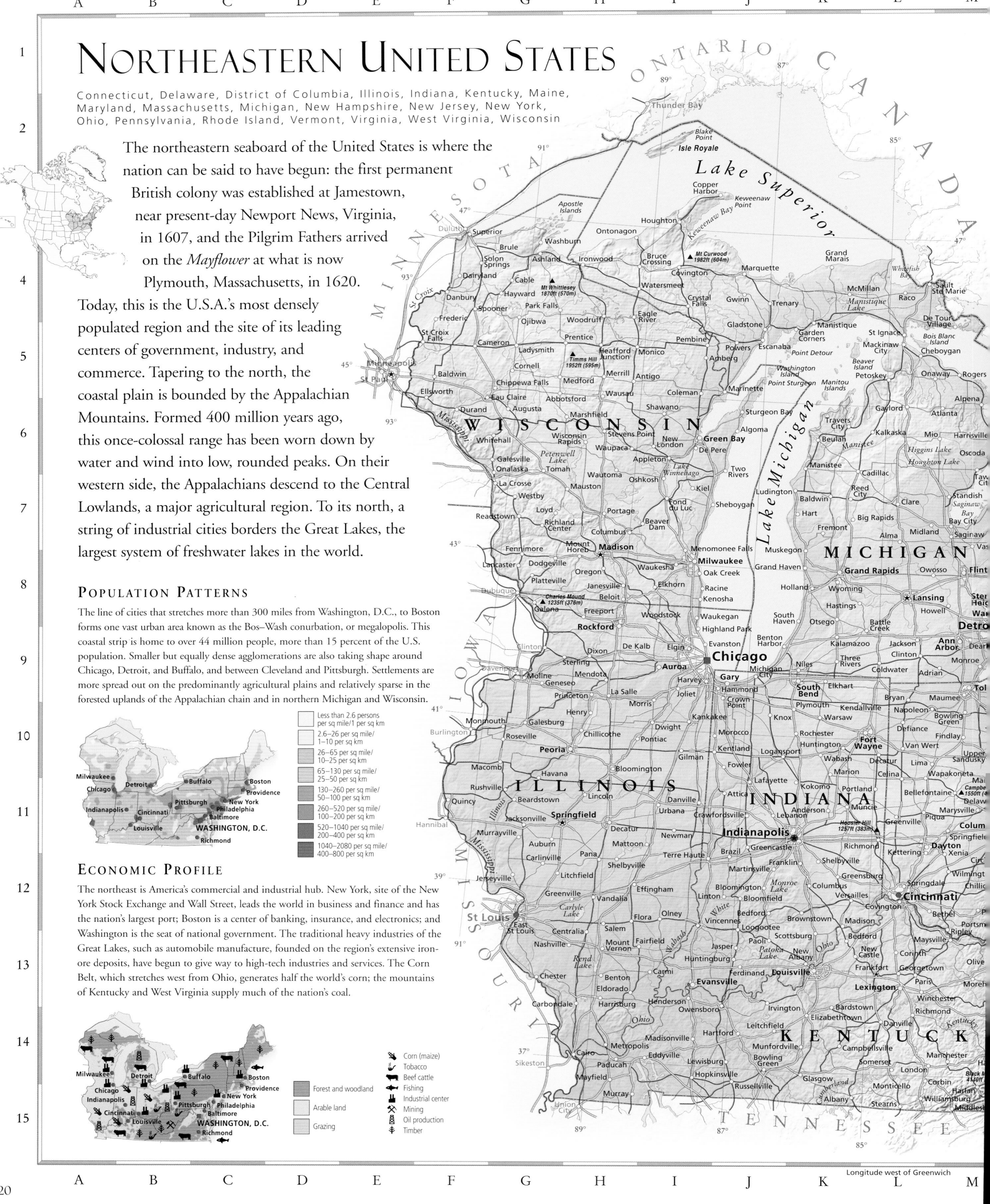

ONTARIO
CANADA
MINNESOTA
IOWA
MISSOURI
TENNESSEE
WISCONSIN
MICHIGAN
ILLINOIS
INDIANA
KENTUCKY
Lake Superior
Lake Michigan
Isle Royale
Thunder Bay
Chicago
Milwaukee
Madison
Green Bay
Grand Rapids
Lansing
Indianapolis
Springfield
Cincinnati
Louisville
Lexington
Evansville
St Louis
Minneapolis
St Paul
Duluth
Fort Wayne
South Bend
Peoria
Rockford
Gary
Mt Curwood 1982ft (604m)
Mt Whittlesey 1870ft (570m)
Timms Hill 1952ft (595m)
Charles Mound 1235ft (376m)
Hoosier Hill 1257ft (383m)
Longitude west of Greenwich

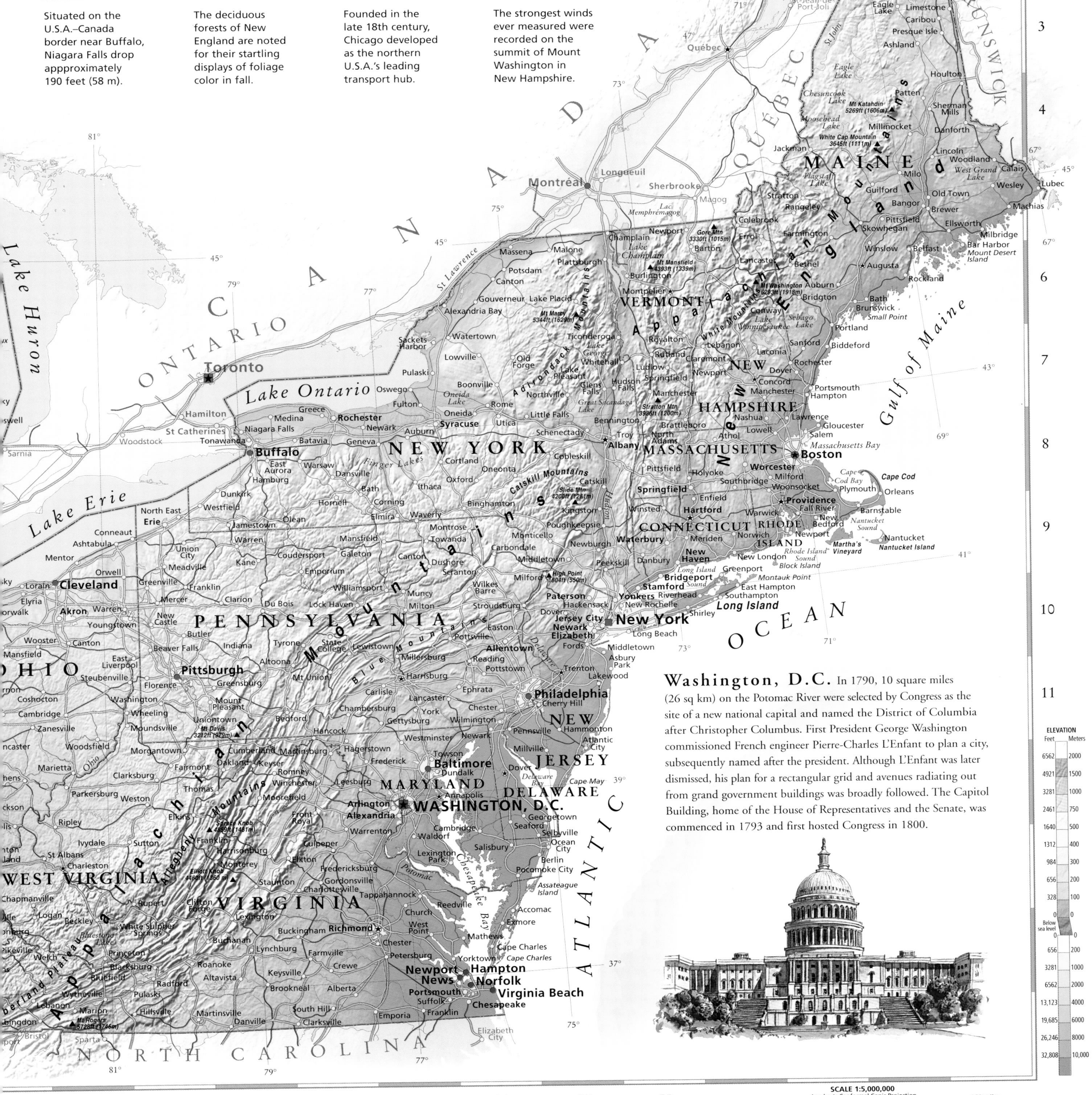
N O P Q R S T U V W X Y Z
1 2 3 4 5 6 7 8 9 10 11
C A N A D A
ONTARIO
QUÉBEC
NEW BRUNSWICK
Lake Huron
Lake Ontario
Lake Erie
Toronto
Hamilton
St Catherines
Niagara Falls
Montréal
Longueuil
Sherbrooke
Québec
Magog
La Malbaie
Rivière-du-Loup
St-Jean-de-Port-Joli
NEW YORK
VERMONT
NEW HAMPSHIRE
MAINE
MASSACHUSETTS
CONNECTICUT
RHODE ISLAND
PENNSYLVANIA
NEW JERSEY
DELAWARE
MARYLAND
WASHINGTON, D.C.
VIRGINIA
WEST VIRGINIA
OHIO
NORTH CAROLINA
ATLANTIC OCEAN
Gulf of Maine
Massachusetts Bay
Cape Cod
Long Island
Chesapeake Bay
Appalachian Mountains
Adirondack Mountains
Catskill Mountains
Blue Mountains
Allegheny Mountains
White Mountains
New England
Finger Lakes
Buffalo
Rochester
Syracuse
Albany
Boston
Providence
Hartford
New Haven
New York
Newark
Jersey City
Philadelphia
Pittsburgh
Cleveland
Baltimore
Richmond
Norfolk
Virginia Beach
Newport News
Hampton
Chesapeake
Portland
Augusta
Bangor
Concord
Manchester
Worcester
Springfield
Burlington
Montpelier
Harrisburg
Trenton
Dover
Annapolis
Arlington
Alexandria
Mt Washington 6293ft (1918m)
Mt Katahdin 5269ft (1606m)
Mt Marcy 5344ft (1629m)
Mt Mansfield 4393ft (1339m)
High Point 1804ft (550m)
Mt Rogers 5728ft (1746m)
ELEVATION
Feet Meters
6562 2000
4921 1500
3281 1000
2461 750
1640 500
1312 400
984 300
656 200
328 100
0 0
Below sea level
0 0
656 200
3281 1000
6562 2000
13,123 4000
19,685 6000
26,246 8000
32,808 10,000

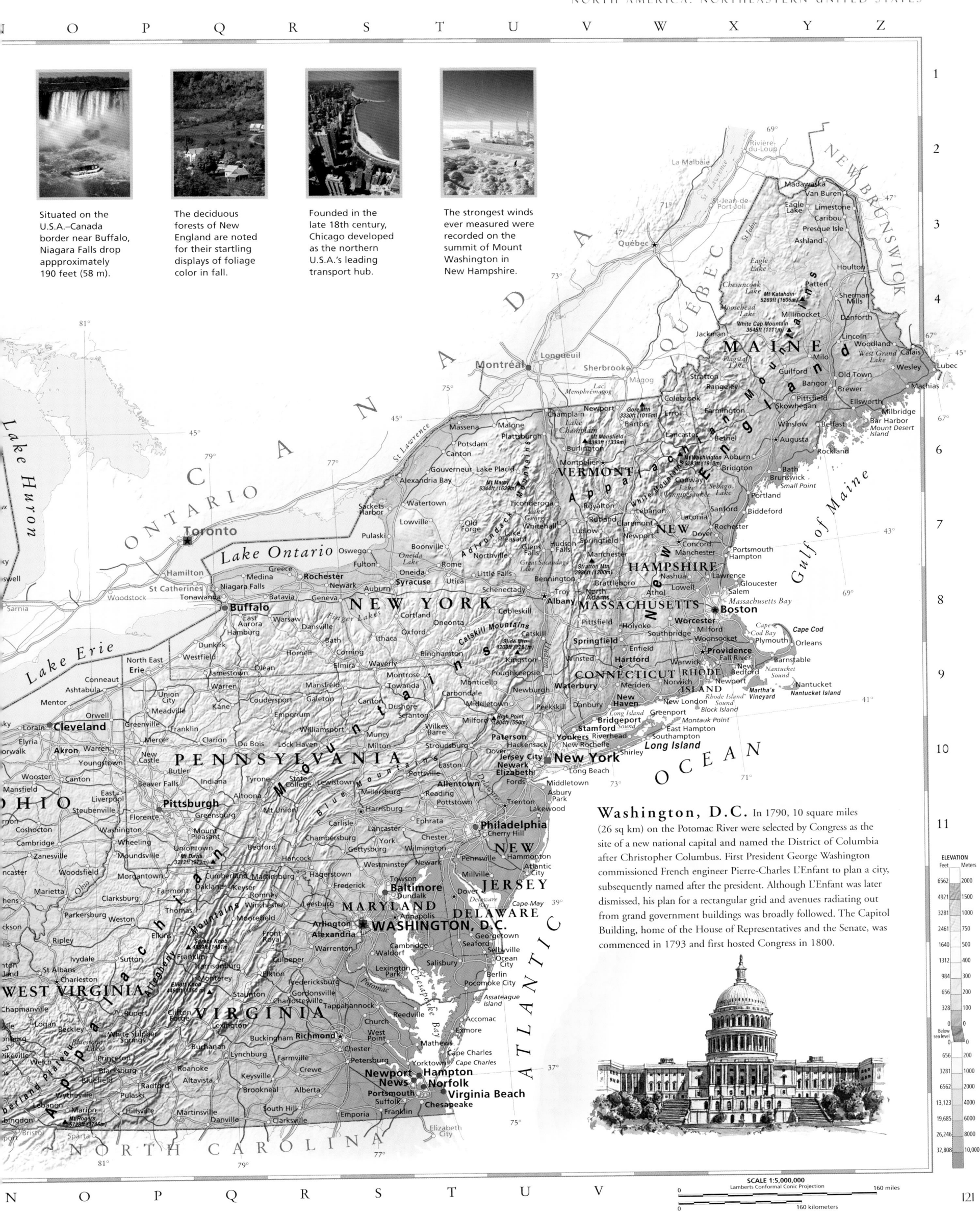

Situated on the U.S.A.–Canada border near Buffalo, Niagara Falls drop appproximately 190 feet (58 m).

The deciduous forests of New England are noted for their startling displays of foliage color in fall.

Founded in the late 18th century, Chicago developed as the northern U.S.A.'s leading transport hub.

The strongest winds ever measured were recorded on the summit of Mount Washington in New Hampshire.

Washington, D.C. In 1790, 10 square miles (26 sq km) on the Potomac River were selected by Congress as the site of a new national capital and named the District of Columbia after Christopher Columbus. First President George Washington commissioned French engineer Pierre-Charles L'Enfant to plan a city, subsequently named after the president. Although L'Enfant was later dismissed, his plan for a rectangular grid and avenues radiating out from grand government buildings was broadly followed. The Capitol Building, home of the House of Representatives and the Senate, was commenced in 1793 and first hosted Congress in 1800.

N O P Q R S T U V

SCALE 1:5,000,000
Lamberts Conformal Conic Projection
0 — 160 miles
0 — 160 kilometers

Southeastern United States

Alabama, Florida, Georgia, Mississippi, North Carolina, South Carolina, Tennessee

In the southeastern corner of the United States, the low-lying peninsula of Florida separates the Gulf of Mexico from the Atlantic Ocean. To the north and west, swamps, sandbars, and barrier islands fringe the broad coastal plain. Lowlands spread across most of the southern interior. In the northeast, rolling, forested terrain known as the Piedmont forms the foothills of the Appalachian Mountain system, which reaches its southern limit in northern Alabama. Spain and France made tentative, mostly unsuccessful, attempts to settle the Southeast in the 16th century. In 1763, the entire region came under British control; 20 years later, the U.S.A. achieved independence. The subsequent development of plantation-based farming, and the practice of importing African slaves to work on these plantations, gave the southern U.S.A. a distinctive economic profile and a sense of independence. This brought it into dispute with the more industrialized and antislavery North, resulting in the American Civil War of 1861–65 and a cultural and political rivalry that endures to this day.

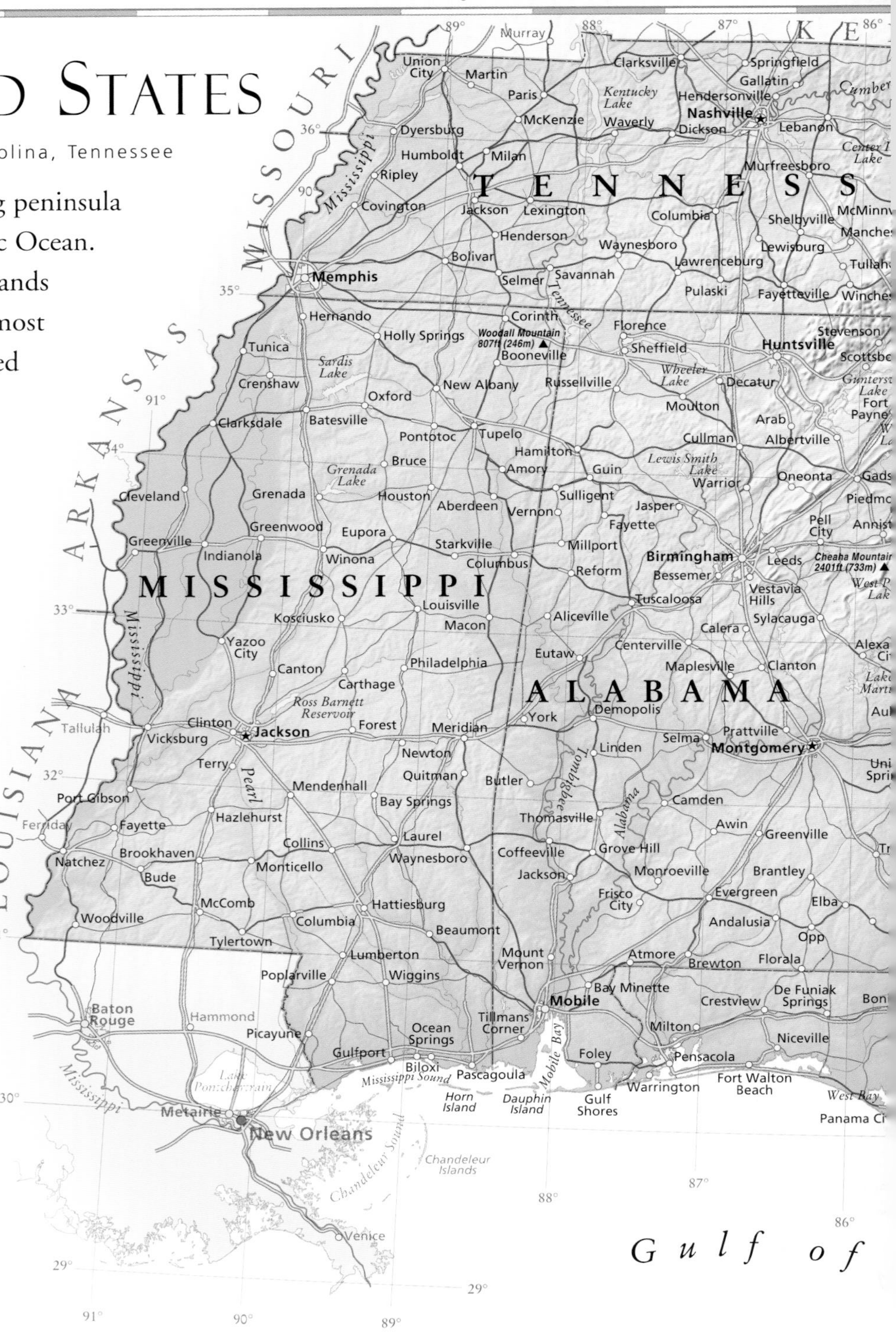

TENNESSEE
MISSISSIPPI
ALABAMA
ARKANSAS
LOUISIANA
MISSOURI
Gulf of
Memphis
Nashville
Jackson
Montgomery
Birmingham
Huntsville
Mobile
New Orleans
Baton Rouge
Tuscaloosa
Gulfport
Biloxi
Pascagoula
Hattiesburg
Meridian
Tupelo
Vicksburg
Natchez
Pensacola
Metairie
Chandeleur Islands
Woodall Mountain 807ft (246m)
Cheaha Mountain 2401ft (733m)
Longitude west of Greenwich

Population Patterns

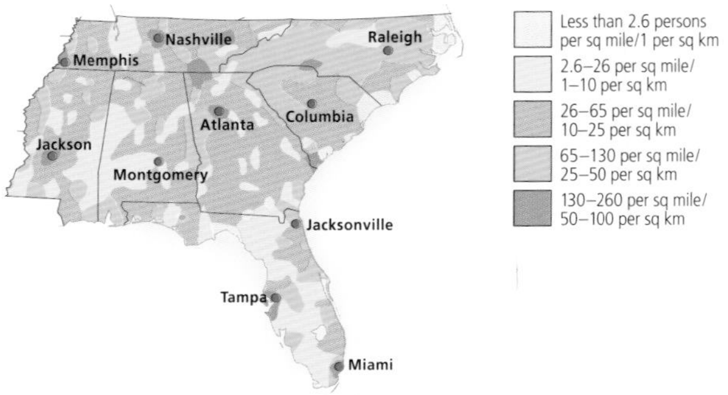

Nashville
Raleigh
Memphis
Atlanta
Columbia
Jackson
Montgomery
Jacksonville
Tampa
Miami
Less than 2.6 persons per sq mile/1 per sq km
2.6–26 per sq mile/ 1–10 per sq km
26–65 per sq mile/ 10–25 per sq km
65–130 per sq mile/ 25–50 per sq km
130–260 per sq mile/ 50–100 per sq km

In the Carolinas, people and industries are concentrated in the Piedmont; nevertheless, the cities here are relatively small and half of North Carolina's inhabitants live in rural areas. Mississippi has similarly low levels of urbanization and the lowest state population (2.4 million). The other southeastern states are more urbanized, with settlement focused on centers such as Memphis, Nashville, Birmingham, Atlanta (home to half of Georgia's people), Tampa, and Miami. The populations of Florida (which is much favored as a place of retirement) and Georgia are growing rapidly, with Florida's projected to reach 20 million by 2010.

Economic Profile

Until the early 20th century, the Southeast was dependent on agriculture, especially the cultivation of cotton and tobacco. These crops remain significant, but farmers have diversified into soybeans, peanuts, and citrus fruits. In addition, the industrial sector has since expanded rapidly, led by food processing, wood products, textiles, transportation equipment, electronics, and the aerospace industry. The Southeast is home to major business corporations—Atlanta is the headquarters of Coca-Cola and CNN (Cable News Network)—and thriving tourist destinations, including Florida's theme parks and the Great Smoky Mountains of Tennessee.

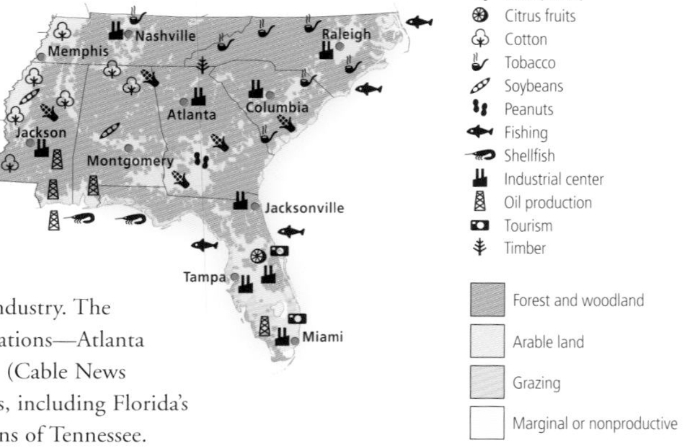

Nashville
Raleigh
Memphis
Atlanta
Columbia
Jackson
Montgomery
Jacksonville
Tampa
Miami
Corn (maize)
Citrus fruits
Cotton
Tobacco
Soybeans
Peanuts
Fishing
Shellfish
Industrial center
Oil production
Tourism
Timber
Forest and woodland
Arable land
Grazing
Marginal or nonproductive

A barrier island separated from the mainland by lagoons, Cape Canaveral in Florida is the site of the U.S. space program's principal launch pad and NASA's John F. Kennedy Space Center.

Nashville is recognized as the home of country music. The Grand Ole Opry, which began as a radio program in 1925, is its leading show.

Hurricanes regularly strike the Southeast. In August 1992, Hurricane Andrew caused U.S.$25 billion worth of damage and 23 deaths.

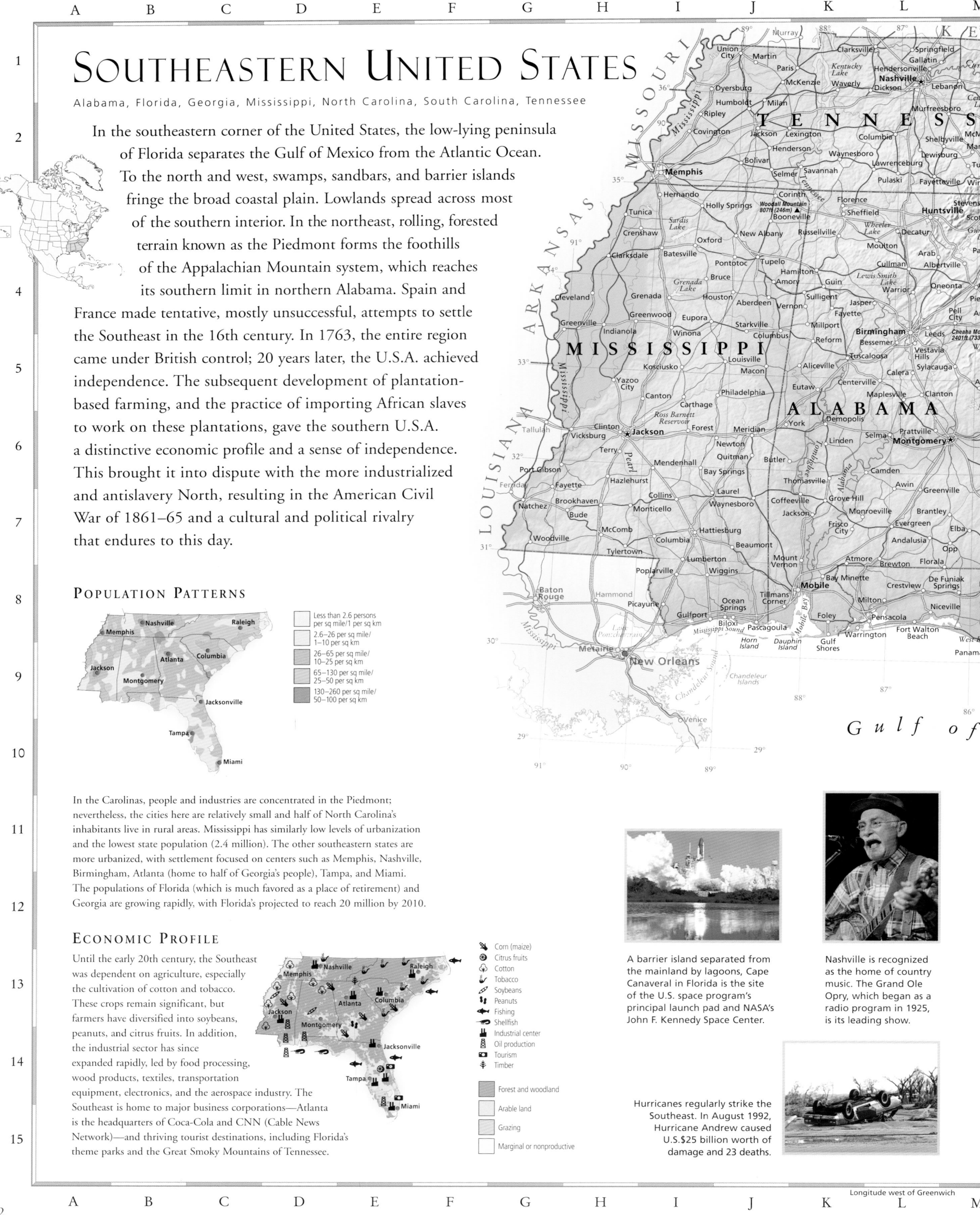

O P Q R S T U V W X Y Z
1 2 3 4 5 6 7 8 9 10 11
N O P Q R S T U V W
VIRGINIA
NORTH CAROLINA
SOUTH CAROLINA
GEORGIA
FLORIDA
ATLANTIC OCEAN
Appalachian Mountains
Blue Ridge Mountains
Great Smoky Mountains
Piedmont
Mt Mitchell 6683ft (2037m)
Mt Guyot 6621ft (2018m)
Albemarle Sound
Pamlico Sound
Raleigh Bay
Onslow Bay
Long Bay
Cape Hatteras
Cape Lookout
Cape Fear
Cape Romain
St Helena Sound
Port Royal Sound
St Andrew Sound
Cape Canaveral
Lake Okeechobee
Everglades
Tampa Bay
Florida Bay
Florida Keys
Straits of Florida
Ten Thousand Islands
Apalachee Bay
Waccasassa Bay
Charlotte Harbor
Bimini Islands
Dry Tortugas
Marquesas Keys
Key West
Raleigh
Charlotte
Columbia
Atlanta
Savannah
Jacksonville
Tallahassee
Orlando
Tampa
Clearwater
St Petersburg
West Palm Beach
Delray Beach
Pompano Beach
Fort Lauderdale
Hollywood
Miami
Knoxville
Charleston
Macon
Columbus
Winston Salem
Wilmington
Myrtle Beach
Augusta
Gainesville
Daytona Beach
Fort Myers
Naples
Key Largo
Islamorada
Marathon

The swamps and bayous of the Gulf Coast are home to abundant wildlife, including thriving populations of American alligators.

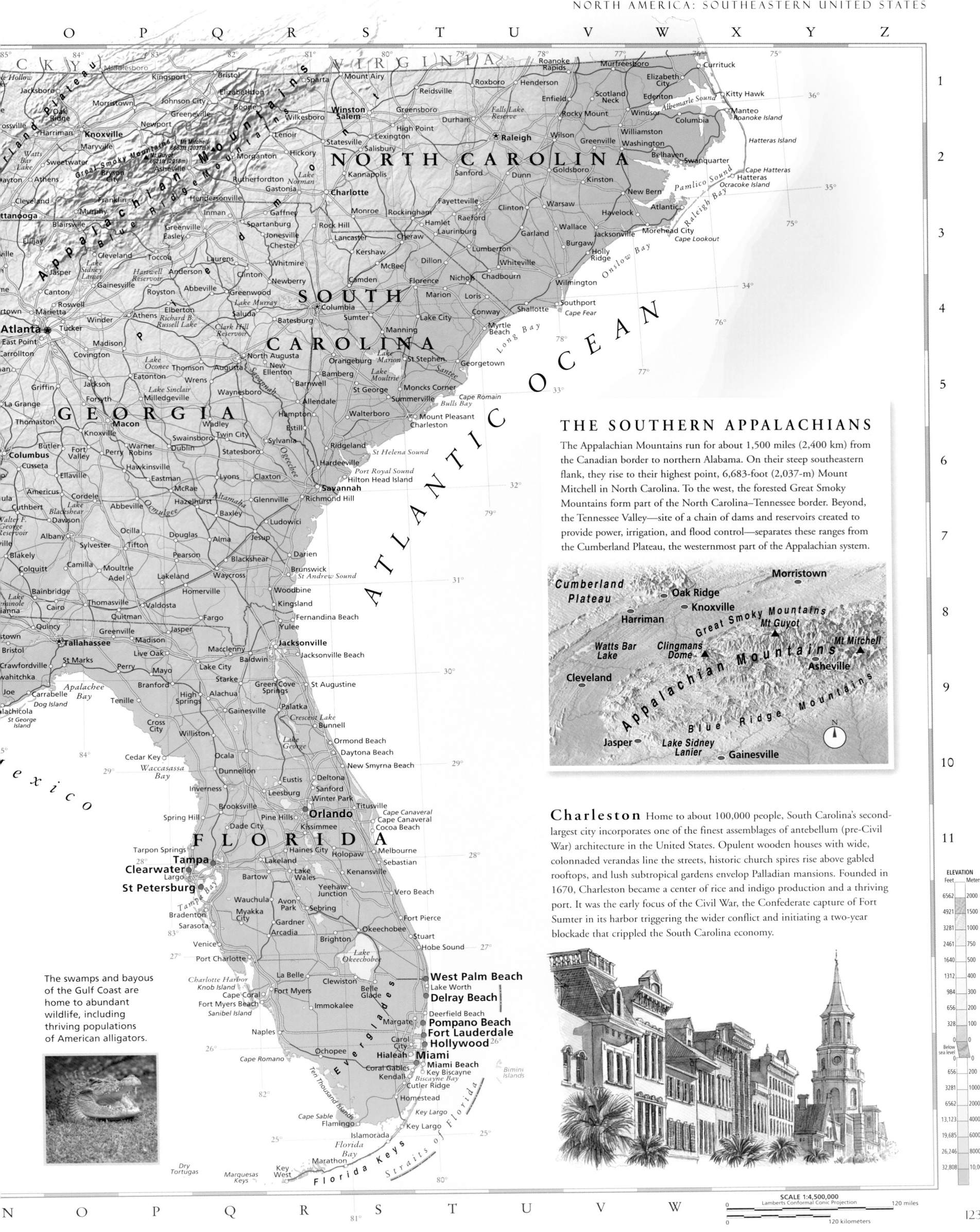

THE SOUTHERN APPALACHIANS

The Appalachian Mountains run for about 1,500 miles (2,400 km) from the Canadian border to northern Alabama. On their steep southeastern flank, they rise to their highest point, 6,683-foot (2,037-m) Mount Mitchell in North Carolina. To the west, the forested Great Smoky Mountains form part of the North Carolina–Tennessee border. Beyond, the Tennessee Valley—site of a chain of dams and reservoirs created to provide power, irrigation, and flood control—separates these ranges from the Cumberland Plateau, the westernmost part of the Appalachian system.

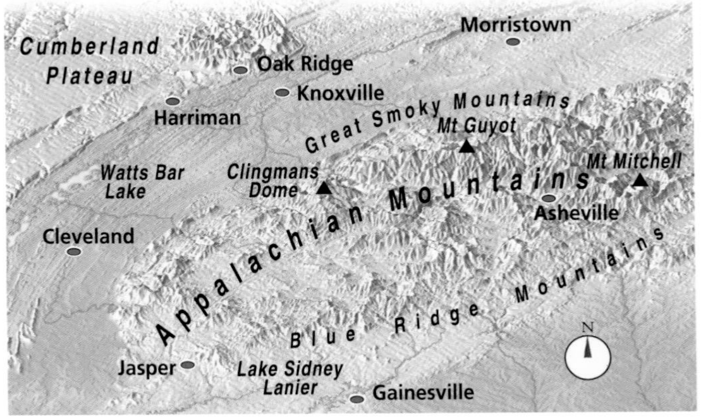
Cumberland Plateau
Oak Ridge
Morristown
Knoxville
Harriman
Great Smoky Mountains
Mt Guyot
Mt Mitchell
Watts Bar Lake
Clingmans Dome
Appalachian Mountains
Asheville
Cleveland
Blue Ridge Mountains
Jasper
Lake Sidney Lanier
Gainesville
N

Charleston Home to about 100,000 people, South Carolina's second-largest city incorporates one of the finest assemblages of antebellum (pre-Civil War) architecture in the United States. Opulent wooden houses with wide, colonnaded verandas line the streets, historic church spires rise above gabled rooftops, and lush subtropical gardens envelop Palladian mansions. Founded in 1670, Charleston became a center of rice and indigo production and a thriving port. It was the early focus of the Civil War, the Confederate capture of Fort Sumter in its harbor triggering the wider conflict and initiating a two-year blockade that crippled the South Carolina economy.

ELEVATION

Feet	Meters
6562	2000
4921	1500
3281	1000
2461	750
1640	500
1312	400
984	300
656	200
328	100
0	0
Below sea level	
0	0
656	200
3281	1000
6562	2000
13,123	4000
19,685	6000
26,246	8000
32,808	10,000

SCALE 1:4,500,000
Lamberts Conformal Conic Projection
0 120 miles
0 120 kilometers

Mexico

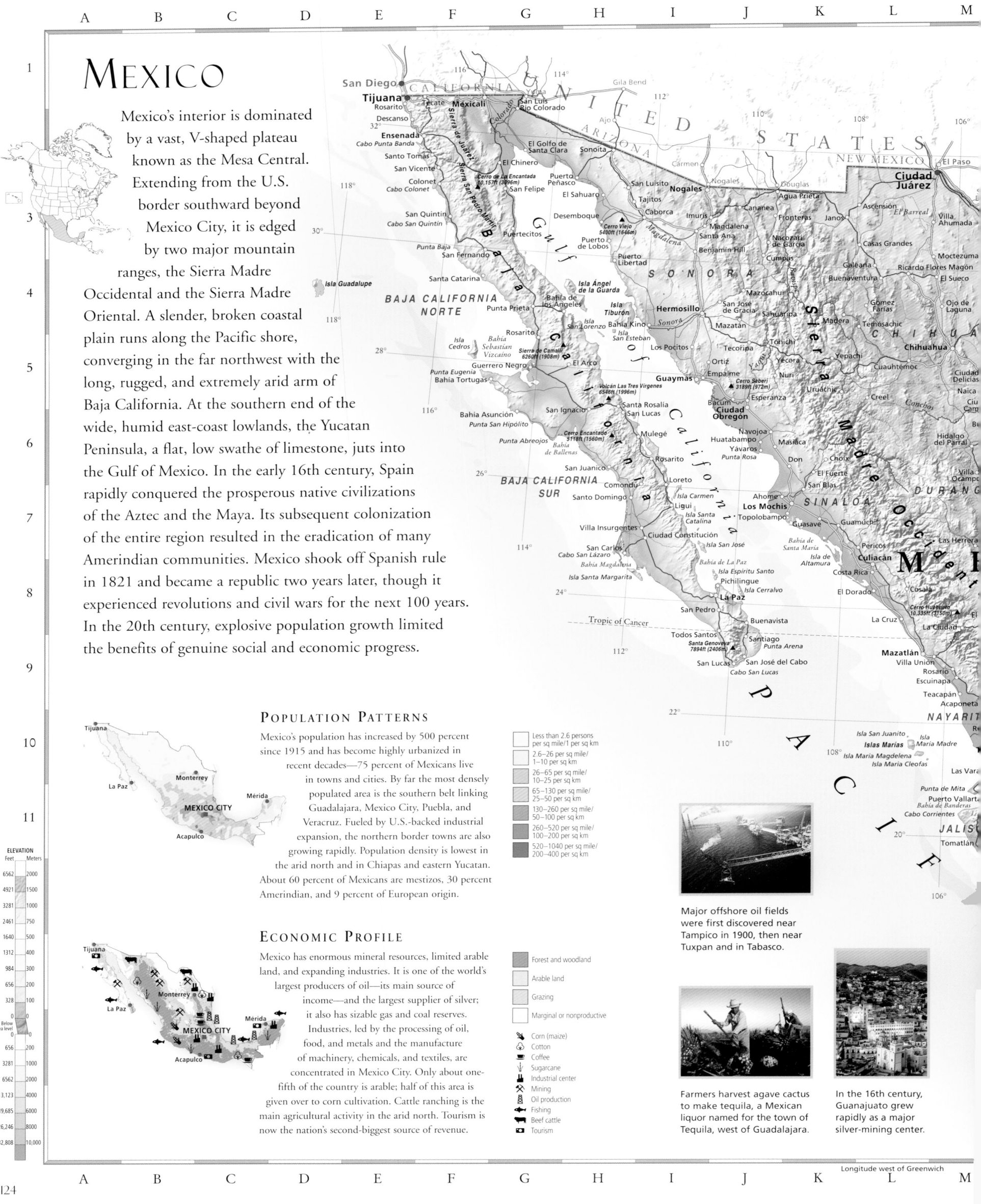

Mexico's interior is dominated by a vast, V-shaped plateau known as the Mesa Central. Extending from the U.S. border southward beyond Mexico City, it is edged by two major mountain ranges, the Sierra Madre Occidental and the Sierra Madre Oriental. A slender, broken coastal plain runs along the Pacific shore, converging in the far northwest with the long, rugged, and extremely arid arm of Baja California. At the southern end of the wide, humid east-coast lowlands, the Yucatan Peninsula, a flat, low swathe of limestone, juts into the Gulf of Mexico. In the early 16th century, Spain rapidly conquered the prosperous native civilizations of the Aztec and the Maya. Its subsequent colonization of the entire region resulted in the eradication of many Amerindian communities. Mexico shook off Spanish rule in 1821 and became a republic two years later, though it experienced revolutions and civil wars for the next 100 years. In the 20th century, explosive population growth limited the benefits of genuine social and economic progress.

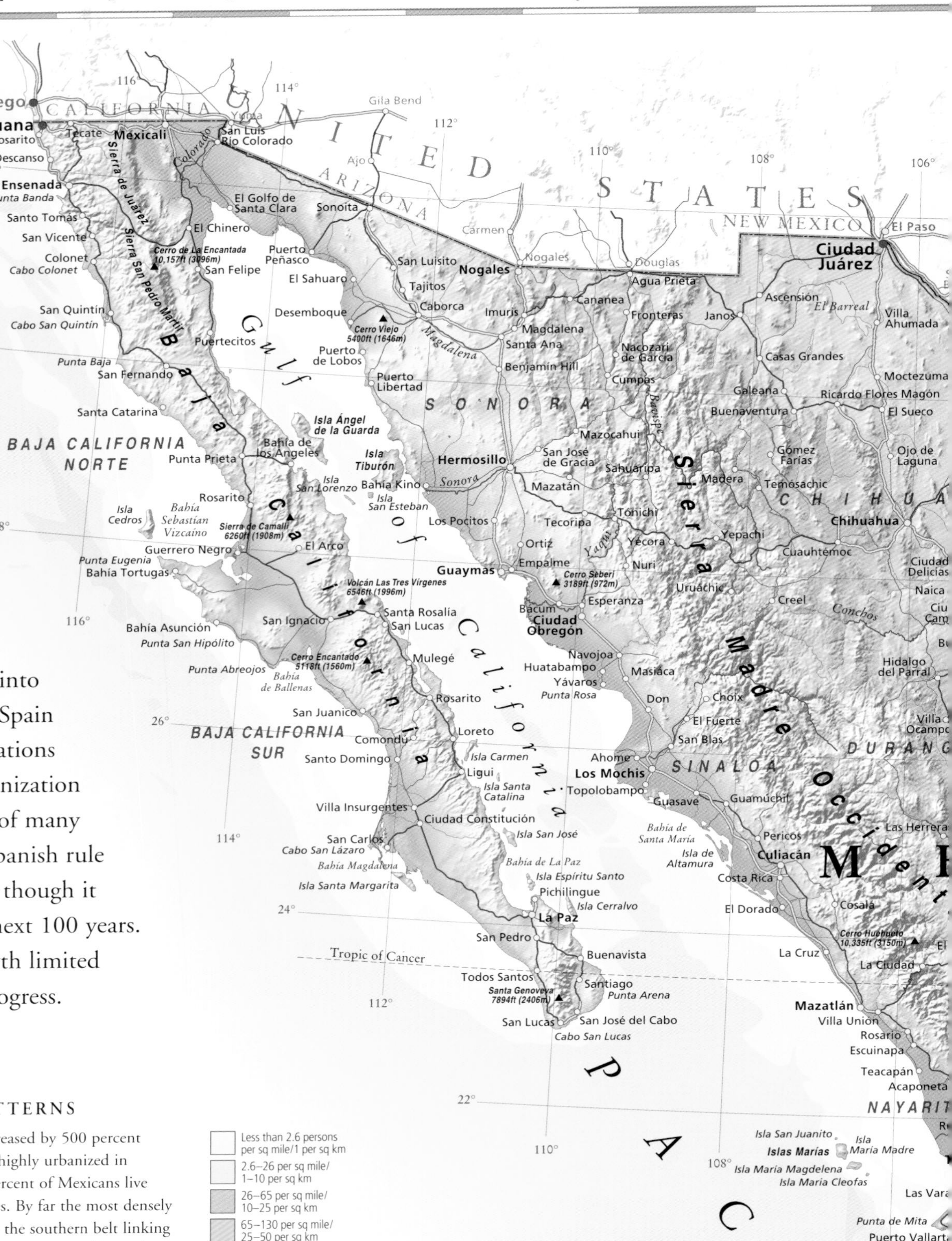

A B C D E F G H I J K L M
1 3 4 5 6 7 8 9 10 11
San Diego
Tijuana
Rosarito
Tecate
Mexicali
Descanso
Ensenada
Cabo Punta Banda
Santo Tomás
San Vicente
Colonet
Cabo Colonet
San Quintín
Cabo San Quintín
Punta Baja
San Fernando
Santa Catarina
Isla Guadalupe
BAJA CALIFORNIA NORTE
Sierra de Juárez
Sierra San Pedro Mártir
Cerro de La Encantada 10,157ft (3096m)
San Felipe
El Chinero
Puertecitos
El Golfo de Santa Clara
Sonoita
Puerto Peñasco
El Sahuaro
Desemboque
Cerro Viejo 5400ft (1646m)
Puerto de Lobos
Puerto Libertad
Isla Ángel de la Guarda
Bahía de los Ángeles
Punta Prieta
Isla Tiburón
Isla San Lorenzo
Bahía Kino
Isla San Esteban
Rosarito
Isla Cedros
Bahía Sebastian Vizcaino
Sierra de Camalli 6260ft (1908m)
El Arco
Guerrero Negro
Punta Eugenia
Bahía Tortugas
Volcán Las Tres Virgenes 6546ft (1996m)
Santa Rosalía
San Lucas
San Ignacio
Bahía Asunción
Punta San Hipólito
Punta Abreojos
Cerro Encantado 5118ft (1560m)
Bahía de Ballenas
Mulegé
Rosarito
San Juanico
BAJA CALIFORNIA SUR
Comondú
Loreto
Santo Domingo
Isla Carmen
Ligui
Isla Santa Catalina
Villa Insurgentes
Ciudad Constitución
San Carlos
Cabo San Lázaro
Bahía Magdalena
Isla Santa Margarita
Isla San José
Bahía de La Paz
Isla Espíritu Santo
Pichilingue
Isla Cerralvo
La Paz
San Pedro
Buenavista
Todos Santos
Santa Genoveva 7894ft (2406m)
Santiago
Punta Arena
San Lucas
San José del Cabo
Cabo San Lucas
Tropic of Cancer
Gulf of California
Baja California
PACIFIC
UNITED STATES
CALIFORNIA
ARIZONA
NEW MEXICO
Yuma
San Luis Río Colorado
Colorado
Gila Bend
Ajo
Carmen
Nogales
Douglas
El Paso
Ciudad Juárez
San Luisito
Tajitos
Caborca
Nogales
Imuris
Cananea
Agua Prieta
Fronteras
Janos
Ascensión
El Barreal
Villa Ahumada
Magdalena
Santa Ana
Nacozari de García
Benjamín Hill
Cumpas
Casas Grandes
Moctezuma
Galeana
Ricardo Flores Magón
Buenaventura
El Sueco
SONORA
Mazocahui
Hermosillo
San José de Gracia
Sahuaripa
Gómez Farías
Ojo de Laguna
Madera
Temosachic
Sonora
Mazatán
CHIHUAHUA
Chihuahua
Los Pocitos
Tecoripa
Tónichi
Yepachi
Ortiz
Yécora
Cuauhtémoc
Empalme
Nuri
Guaymas
Cerro Seberi 3189ft (972m)
Esperanza
Uruáchic
Ciudad Delicias
Creel
Naica
Bácum
Ciudad Obregón
Conchos
Navojoa
Huatabampo
Yávaros
Punta Rosa
Masiaca
Hidalgo del Parral
Don
Choix
Sierra Madre Occidental
El Fuerte
San Blas
Villa Ocampo
DURANGO
Ahome
Los Mochis
SINALOA
Topolobampo
Guasave
Guamúchil
Bahía de Santa María
Isla de Altamura
Pericos
Las Herreras
Culiacán
Costa Rica
El Dorado
Cosalá
Cerro Huehueto 10,335ft (3150m)
La Cruz
La Ciudad
Mazatlán
Villa Unión
Rosario
Escuinapa
Teacapán
Acaponeta
NAYARIT
Isla San Juanito
Islas Marías
Isla María Madre
Isla María Magdelena
Isla María Cleofas
Las Varas
Punta de Mita
Puerto Vallarta
Bahía de Banderas
Cabo Corrientes
JALISCO
Tomatlán
Longitude west of Greenwich

Population Patterns

Tijuana
La Paz
Monterrey
Mérida
MEXICO CITY
Acapulco

Mexico's population has increased by 500 percent since 1915 and has become highly urbanized in recent decades—75 percent of Mexicans live in towns and cities. By far the most densely populated area is the southern belt linking Guadalajara, Mexico City, Puebla, and Veracruz. Fueled by U.S.-backed industrial expansion, the northern border towns are also growing rapidly. Population density is lowest in the arid north and in Chiapas and eastern Yucatan. About 60 percent of Mexicans are mestizos, 30 percent Amerindian, and 9 percent of European origin.

- Less than 2.6 persons per sq mile/1 per sq km
- 2.6–26 per sq mile/ 1–10 per sq km
- 26–65 per sq mile/ 10–25 per sq km
- 65–130 per sq mile/ 25–50 per sq km
- 130–260 per sq mile/ 50–100 per sq km
- 260–520 per sq mile/ 100–200 per sq km
- 520–1040 per sq mile/ 200–400 per sq km

Economic Profile

Tijuana
La Paz
Monterrey
Mérida
MEXICO CITY
Acapulco

Mexico has enormous mineral resources, limited arable land, and expanding industries. It is one of the world's largest producers of oil—its main source of income—and the largest supplier of silver; it also has sizable gas and coal reserves. Industries, led by the processing of oil, food, and metals and the manufacture of machinery, chemicals, and textiles, are concentrated in Mexico City. Only about one-fifth of the country is arable; half of this area is given over to corn cultivation. Cattle ranching is the main agricultural activity in the arid north. Tourism is now the nation's second-biggest source of revenue.

- Forest and woodland
- Arable land
- Grazing
- Marginal or nonproductive
- Corn (maize)
- Cotton
- Coffee
- Sugarcane
- Industrial center
- Mining
- Oil production
- Fishing
- Beef cattle
- Tourism

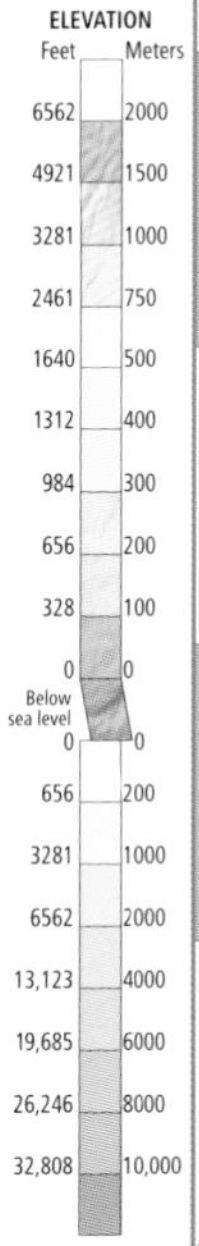

ELEVATION
Feet Meters
6562 2000
4921 1500
3281 1000
2461 750
1640 500
1312 400
984 300
656 200
328 100
0 0
Below sea level
0 0
656 200
3281 1000
6562 2000
13,123 4000
19,685 6000
26,246 8000
32,808 10,000

Major offshore oil fields were first discovered near Tampico in 1900, then near Tuxpan and in Tabasco.

Farmers harvest agave cactus to make tequila, a Mexican liquor named for the town of Tequila, west of Guadalajara.

In the 16th century, Guanajuato grew rapidly as a major silver-mining center.

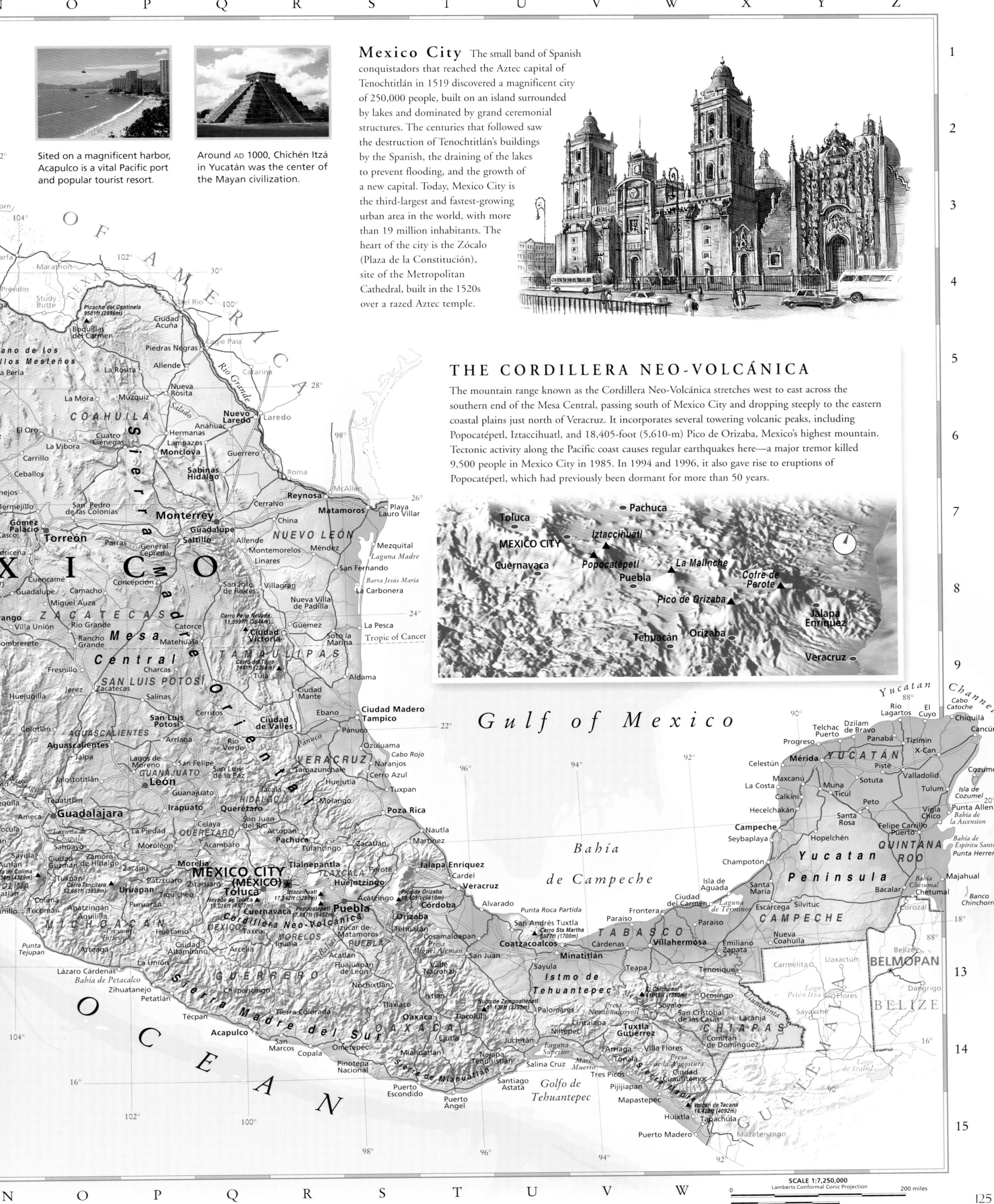

Sited on a magnificent harbor, Acapulco is a vital Pacific port and popular tourist resort.

Around AD 1000, Chichén Itzá in Yucatán was the center of the Mayan civilization.

Mexico City The small band of Spanish conquistadors that reached the Aztec capital of Tenochtitlán in 1519 discovered a magnificent city of 250,000 people, built on an island surrounded by lakes and dominated by grand ceremonial structures. The centuries that followed saw the destruction of Tenochtitlán's buildings by the Spanish, the draining of the lakes to prevent flooding, and the growth of a new capital. Today, Mexico City is the third-largest and fastest-growing urban area in the world, with more than 19 million inhabitants. The heart of the city is the Zócalo (Plaza de la Constitución), site of the Metropolitan Cathedral, built in the 1520s over a razed Aztec temple.

THE CORDILLERA NEO-VOLCÁNICA

The mountain range known as the Cordillera Neo-Volcánica stretches west to east across the southern end of the Mesa Central, passing south of Mexico City and dropping steeply to the eastern coastal plains just north of Veracruz. It incorporates several towering volcanic peaks, including Popocatépetl, Iztaccihuatl, and 18,405-foot (5,610-m) Pico de Orizaba, Mexico's highest mountain. Tectonic activity along the Pacific coast causes regular earthquakes here—a major tremor killed 9,500 people in Mexico City in 1985. In 1994 and 1996, it also gave rise to eruptions of Popocatépetl, which had previously been dormant for more than 50 years.

Pachuca
Toluca
MEXICO CITY
Iztaccihuatl
Popocatépetl
Cuernavaca
Puebla
La Malinche
Cofre de Perote
Pico de Orizaba
Jalapa Enríquez
Tehuacán
Orizaba
Veracruz
N

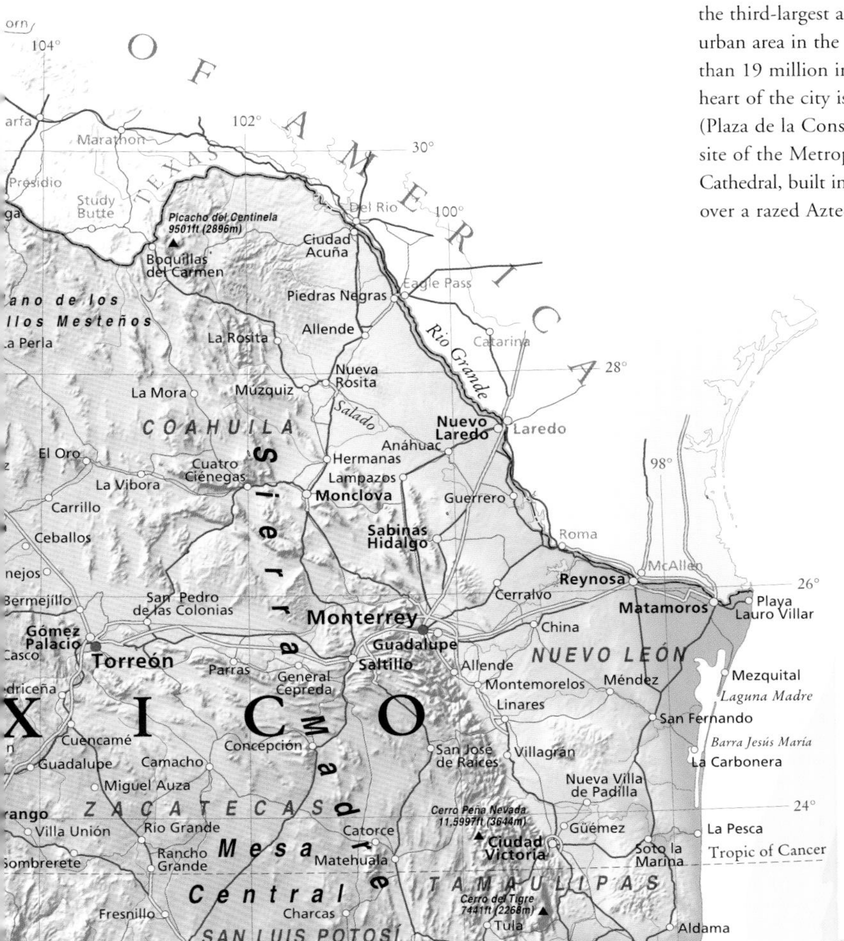

N O P Q R S T U V W X Y Z
1 2 3 4 5 6 7 8 9 10 11 12 13 14 15
OF AMERICA
Marathon
Presidio
Study Butte
TEXAS
Picacho del Centinela 9501ft (2896m)
Boquillas del Carmen
Del Rio
Ciudad Acuña
Eagle Pass
Piedras Negras
Llano de los Llanos Mesteños
La Perla
La Rosita
Allende
Río Grande
Catarina
Nueva Rosita
La Mora
Múzquiz
COAHUILA
Nuevo Laredo
Laredo
Anáhuac
El Oro
Hermanas
Cuatro Ciénegas
Lampazos
La Víbora
Monclova
Guerrero
Carrillo
Sabinas Hidalgo
Roma
Ceballos
McAllen
Reynosa
Matamoros
Playa Lauro Villar
Bermejillo
San Pedro de las Colonias
Cerralvo
Monterrey
China
Gómez Palacio
Torreón
Guadalupe
Saltillo
NUEVO LEÓN
Mezquital
Laguna Madre
Parras
General Cepeda
Allende
Montemorelos
Méndez
MEXICO
Linares
San Fernando
Cuencamé
Concepción
San José de Raíces
Villagrán
Barra Jesús María
La Carbonera
Guadalupe
Camacho
Nueva Villa de Padilla
Miguel Auza
ZACATECAS
Cerro Peña Nevada 11,5991ft (3664m)
La Pesca
Villa Unión
Río Grande
Catorce
Ciudad Victoria
Güémez
Soto la Marina
Tropic of Cancer
Sombrerete
Rancho Grande
Mesa
Matehuala
TAMAULIPAS
Central
Charcas
Cerro del Tigre 7431ft (2265m)
Fresnillo
Tula
Aldama
SAN LUIS POTOSÍ
Huejuquilla
Jerez
Zacatecas
Salinas
Ciudad Mante
Ciudad Madero
Tampico
San Luis Potosí
Cerritos
Ebano
Colotlán
Ciudad de Valles
Pánuco
AGUASCALIENTES
Aguascalientes
Arriaga
Río Verde
Ozuluama
Cabo Rojo
Jalpa
Lagos de Moreno
San Felipe
San Luis de la Paz
VERACRUZ
Naranjos
Tamazunchale
Cerro Azul
GUANAJUATO
León
Huejutla
Tuxpan
Jalostotitlán
Guanajuato
HIDALGO
Molango
Tepatitlán
Irapuato
Querétaro
Poza Rica
Ameca
Guadalajara
Celaya
San Juan del Río
Nautla
La Piedad
QUERÉTARO
Actopan
Laguna de Chapala
Pachuca
Martínez
Sahuayo
Moroleón
Acámbaro
Tulancingo
Zacatlán
Sayula
Ciudad Guzmán
Zamora de Hidalgo
Morelia
Tlalnepantla
Perote
Jalapa Enríquez
Autlán
MEXICO CITY (MÉXICO)
TLAXCALA
Cardel
Huejotzingo
Zacapu
Zitácuaro
Veracruz
Nevado de Colima 14,236ft (4339m)
Tuxpan
Pátzcuaro
Toluca
Iztaccihuatl 17,342ft (5286m)
Puebla
Acatzingo
Pico de Orizaba 18,405ft (5610m)
COLIMA
Cerro Tancítaro 12,661ft (3859m)
Uruapan
Tiquicheo
Nevado de Toluca 15,016ft (4577m)
Popocatépetl 17,887ft (5452m)
Córdoba
Alvarado
Colima
Apatzingán
Puruarán
Cuernavaca
Cordillera Neo-Volcánica
Orizaba
Tecomán
Aguililla
MICHOACÁN
MÉXICO
Izúcar de Matamoros
Tehuacán
Huetamo
Taxco
MORELOS
Cosamaloapan
Punta Tejupan
Presa del Infiernillo
Iguala
PUEBLA
Presa Miguel Alemán
San Juan
Arteaga
Ciudad Altamirano
Arcelia
Acatlán
Huajuapan de León
Valle Nacional
Lázaro Cárdenas
La Unión
Bahía de Petacalco
GUERRERO
Nochixtlán
Zihuatanejo
Petatlán
Chilpancingo
Ixtlán
Tierra Colorada
Tlaxiaco
Técpan
Sierra Madre del Sur
Oaxaca
Tlacolula
Acapulco
OAXACA
Ejutla
San Marcos
Copala
Ometepec
Miahuatlán
Nejapa
Tequisistlán
Pinotepa Nacional
Sierra de Miahuatlán
Santiago Astata
Puerto Escondido
Puerto Ángel
OCEAN
Gulf of Mexico
Bahía de Campeche
Punta Roca Partida
San Andrés Tuxtla
Cerro Sta Martha 5577ft (1700m)
Coatzacoalcos
Minatitlán
Frontera
Paraíso
Cárdenas
TABASCO
Villahermosa
Sayula
Istmo de Tehuantepec
Teapa
El Chichonal 4101ft (1250m)
Nudo de Zempoaltépetl 11,138ft (3395m)
Palomares
Presa Netzahualcóyotl
Ocosingo
Soyalo
Cintalapa
Niltepec
San Cristóbal de las Casas
Tuxtla Gutiérrez
CHIAPAS
Juchitán
Laguna Superior
Salina Cruz
Arriaga
Villa Flores
Comitán de Domínguez
Mar Muerto
Tonalá
Presa de la Angostura
Golfo de Tehuantepec
Tres Picos
Ciudad Cuauhtémoc
Pijijiapan
Mapastepec
Volcán de Tacana 14,429ft (4092m)
Huixtla
Tapachula
Puerto Madero
Mazatenango
GUATEMALA
Yucatan Channel
Cabo Catoche
Río Lagartos
El Cuyo
Chiquilá
Cancún
Dzilam de Bravo
Telchac Puerto
Progreso
Panabá
Tizimín
Mérida
YUCATÁN
X-Can
Celestún
Maxcanú
Pisté
Cozumel
Muna
Sotuta
Valladolid
La Costa
Ticul
Tulum
Isla de Cozumel
Calkiní
Peto
Punta Allen
Hecelchakán
Santa Rosa
Vigía Chico
Bahía de la Ascensión
Campeche
Felipe Carrillo Puerto
Seybaplaya
Hopelchén
QUINTANA ROO
Bahía de Espíritu Santo
Punta Herrero
Yucatan Peninsula
Champotón
Majahual
Isla de Aguada
Santa María
Bahía Chetumal
Bacalar
Chetumal
Banco Chinchorro
Ciudad del Carmen
Laguna de Términos
Escárcega
Silvituc
Corozal
Paraíso
CAMPECHE
Nueva Coahuila
Emiliano Zapata
Belize
Carmelita
Uaxactún
BELMOPAN
Tenosique
Usumacinta
Lago Petén Itzá
Flores
Dangriga
Sayaxché
BELIZE
Lago de Izabal
SCALE 1:7,250,000
Lamberts Conformal Conic Projection
0 200 miles
0 200 kilometers

Central America and the West Indies

Antigua and Barbuda, The Bahamas, Barbados, Belize, Costa Rica, Cuba, Dominica, Dominican Republic, El Salvador, Grenada, Guatemala, Haiti, Honduras, Jamaica, Nicaragua, Panama, St Kitts and Nevis, St Lucia, St Vincent and the Grenadines, Trinidad and Tobago

Together with the north coasts of Colombia and Venezuela, Central America and the West Indies enclose the 1 million square miles (2.6 million sq km) of ocean known as the Caribbean Sea. From the Mexican border, Central America dog-legs and tapers southeastward. Mountain chains form its backbone, narrow plains border the Pacific Ocean, and swampy lowlands fringe the Caribbean. Curving east then south from Florida, the West Indies incorporate two major island groups, the Greater Antilles and the Lesser Antilles. Spain led the European conquest of Central America and the West Indies in the 16th century. Subsequent colonial subjugation is today reflected in the region's cultural diversity and its large number of overseas territories, ranging from U.S.-controlled Puerto Rico to the Netherlands Antilles.

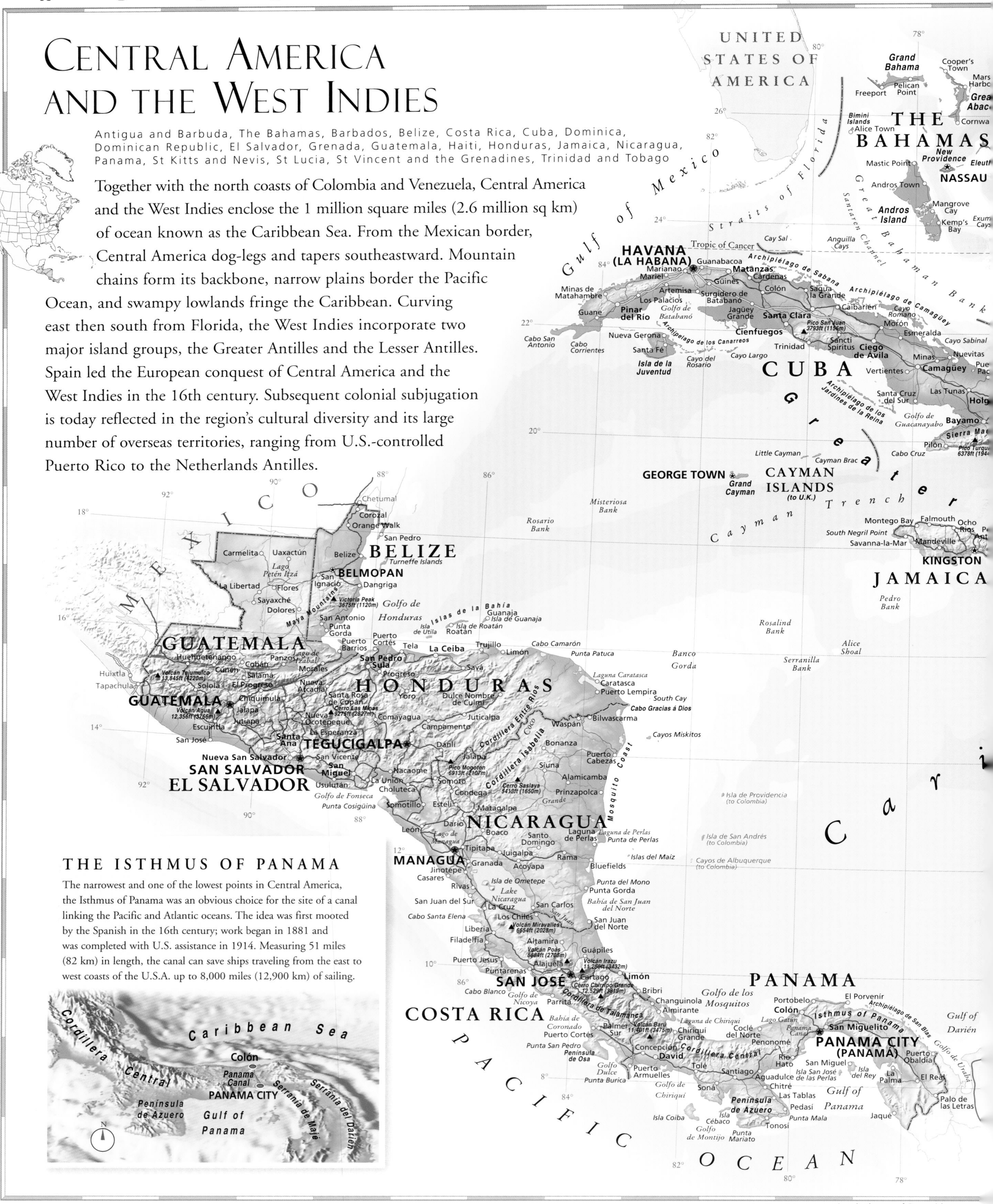

UNITED STATES OF AMERICA
THE BAHAMAS
NASSAU
Gulf of Mexico
Straits of Florida
Tropic of Cancer
HAVANA (LA HABANA)
CUBA
Greater
CAYMAN ISLANDS (to U.K.)
GEORGE TOWN
Cayman Trench
JAMAICA
KINGSTON
MEXICO
BELIZE
BELMOPAN
GUATEMALA
HONDURAS
TEGUCIGALPA
SAN SALVADOR
EL SALVADOR
NICARAGUA
MANAGUA
SAN JOSÉ
COSTA RICA
PANAMA
PANAMA CITY (PANAMÁ)
PACIFIC OCEAN
Caribbean
Longitude west of Greenwich
Cordillera Central
Caribbean Sea
Colón
Panama Canal
PANAMA CITY
Serranía de Majé
Serranía del Darién
Península de Azuero
Gulf of Panama

The Isthmus of Panama

The narrowest and one of the lowest points in Central America, the Isthmus of Panama was an obvious choice for the site of a canal linking the Pacific and Atlantic oceans. The idea was first mooted by the Spanish in the 16th century; work began in 1881 and was completed with U.S. assistance in 1914. Measuring 51 miles (82 km) in length, the canal can save ships traveling from the east to west coasts of the U.S.A. up to 8,000 miles (12,900 km) of sailing.

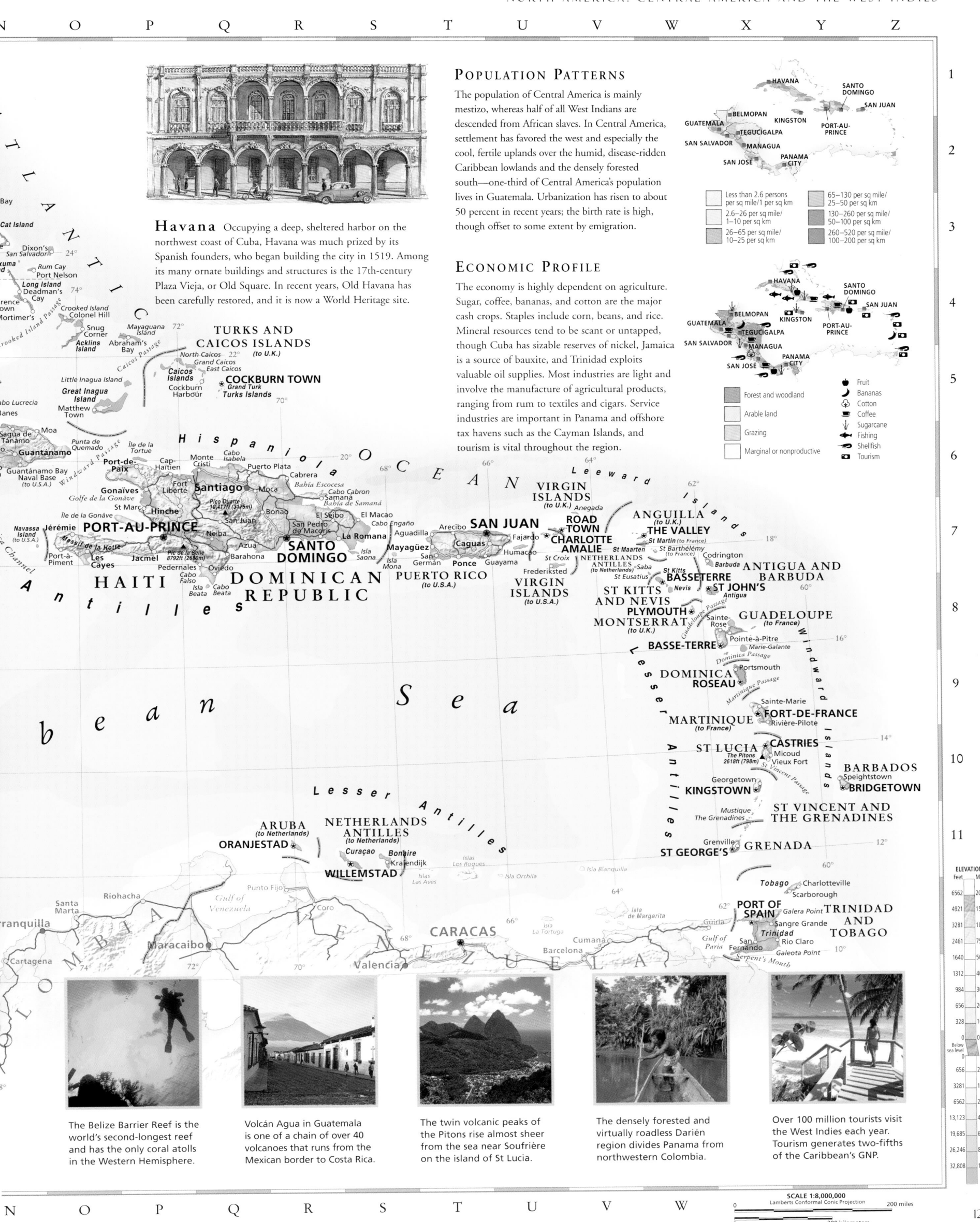

Havana Occupying a deep, sheltered harbor on the northwest coast of Cuba, Havana was much prized by its Spanish founders, who began building the city in 1519. Among its many ornate buildings and structures is the 17th-century Plaza Vieja, or Old Square. In recent years, Old Havana has been carefully restored, and it is now a World Heritage site.

Population Patterns

The population of Central America is mainly mestizo, whereas half of all West Indians are descended from African slaves. In Central America, settlement has favored the west and especially the cool, fertile uplands over the humid, disease-ridden Caribbean lowlands and the densely forested south—one-third of Central America's population lives in Guatemala. Urbanization has risen to about 50 percent in recent years; the birth rate is high, though offset to some extent by emigration.

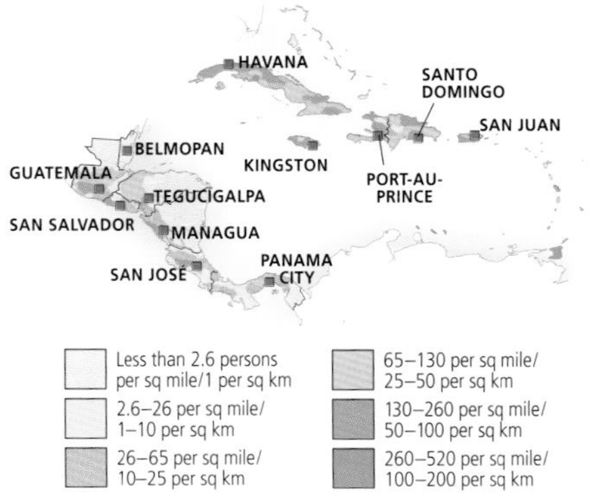
HAVANA
SANTO DOMINGO
SAN JUAN
BELMOPAN
KINGSTON
GUATEMALA
TEGUCIGALPA
PORT-AU-PRINCE
SAN SALVADOR
MANAGUA
PANAMA CITY
SAN JOSÉ
Less than 2.6 persons per sq mile/1 per sq km
2.6–26 per sq mile/ 1–10 per sq km
26–65 per sq mile/ 10–25 per sq km
65–130 per sq mile/ 25–50 per sq km
130–260 per sq mile/ 50–100 per sq km
260–520 per sq mile/ 100–200 per sq km

Economic Profile

The economy is highly dependent on agriculture. Sugar, coffee, bananas, and cotton are the major cash crops. Staples include corn, beans, and rice. Mineral resources tend to be scant or untapped, though Cuba has sizable reserves of nickel, Jamaica is a source of bauxite, and Trinidad exploits valuable oil supplies. Most industries are light and involve the manufacture of agricultural products, ranging from rum to textiles and cigars. Service industries are important in Panama and offshore tax havens such as the Cayman Islands, and tourism is vital throughout the region.

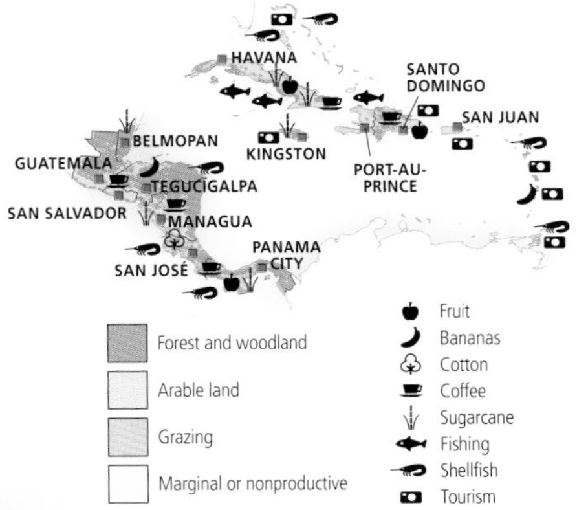
HAVANA
SANTO DOMINGO
SAN JUAN
BELMOPAN
KINGSTON
GUATEMALA
TEGUCIGALPA
PORT-AU-PRINCE
SAN SALVADOR
MANAGUA
PANAMA CITY
SAN JOSÉ
Forest and woodland
Arable land
Grazing
Marginal or nonproductive
Fruit
Bananas
Cotton
Coffee
Sugarcane
Fishing
Shellfish
Tourism

HAITI
PORT-AU-PRINCE
DOMINICAN REPUBLIC
SANTO DOMINGO
Santiago
Hispaniola
OCEAN
PUERTO RICO
(to U.S.A.)
SAN JUAN
VIRGIN ISLANDS
(to U.K.)
ROAD TOWN
VIRGIN ISLANDS
(to U.S.A.)
CHARLOTTE AMALIE
ANGUILLA
(to U.K.)
THE VALLEY
ANTIGUA AND BARBUDA
ST JOHN'S
ST KITTS AND NEVIS
BASSETERRE
MONTSERRAT
(to U.K.)
PLYMOUTH
GUADELOUPE
(to France)
BASSE-TERRE
DOMINICA
ROSEAU
MARTINIQUE
(to France)
FORT-DE-FRANCE
ST LUCIA
CASTRIES
BARBADOS
BRIDGETOWN
ST VINCENT AND THE GRENADINES
KINGSTOWN
GRENADA
ST GEORGE'S
TRINIDAD AND TOBAGO
PORT OF SPAIN
ARUBA
(to Netherlands)
ORANJESTAD
NETHERLANDS ANTILLES
(to Netherlands)
WILLEMSTAD
CARACAS
VENEZUELA
COLOMBIA
Leeward Islands
Windward Islands
Lesser Antilles
Antilles
bean Sea

The Belize Barrier Reef is the world's second-longest reef and has the only coral atolls in the Western Hemisphere.

Volcán Agua in Guatemala is one of a chain of over 40 volcanoes that runs from the Mexican border to Costa Rica.

The twin volcanic peaks of the Pitons rise almost sheer from the sea near Soufrière on the island of St Lucia.

The densely forested and virtually roadless Darién region divides Panama from northwestern Colombia.

Over 100 million tourists visit the West Indies each year. Tourism generates two-fifths of the Caribbean's GNP.

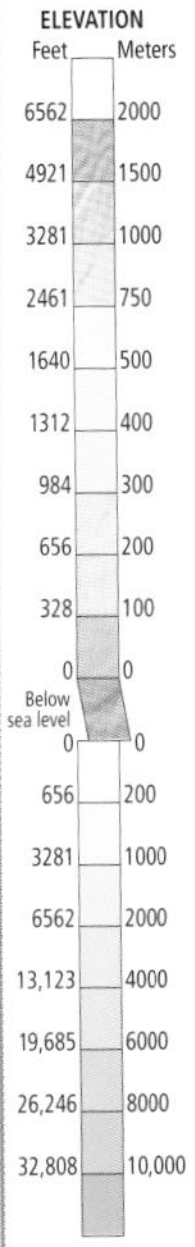
ELEVATION
Feet
Meters
6562 2000
4921 1500
3281 1000
2461 750
1640 500
1312 400
984 300
656 200
328 100
0 0
Below sea level
656 200
3281 1000
6562 2000
13,123 4000
19,685 6000
26,246 8000
32,808 10,000

SCALE 1:8,000,000
Lamberts Conformal Conic Projection
0 200 miles
0 200 kilometers

The lights of South America reveal the focus of development around the continent's edges while the interior jungle remains mostly dark. The three brightest areas on the east coast are the sprawling cities of Rio de Janeiro, Sâo Paulo, and Buenos Aires.

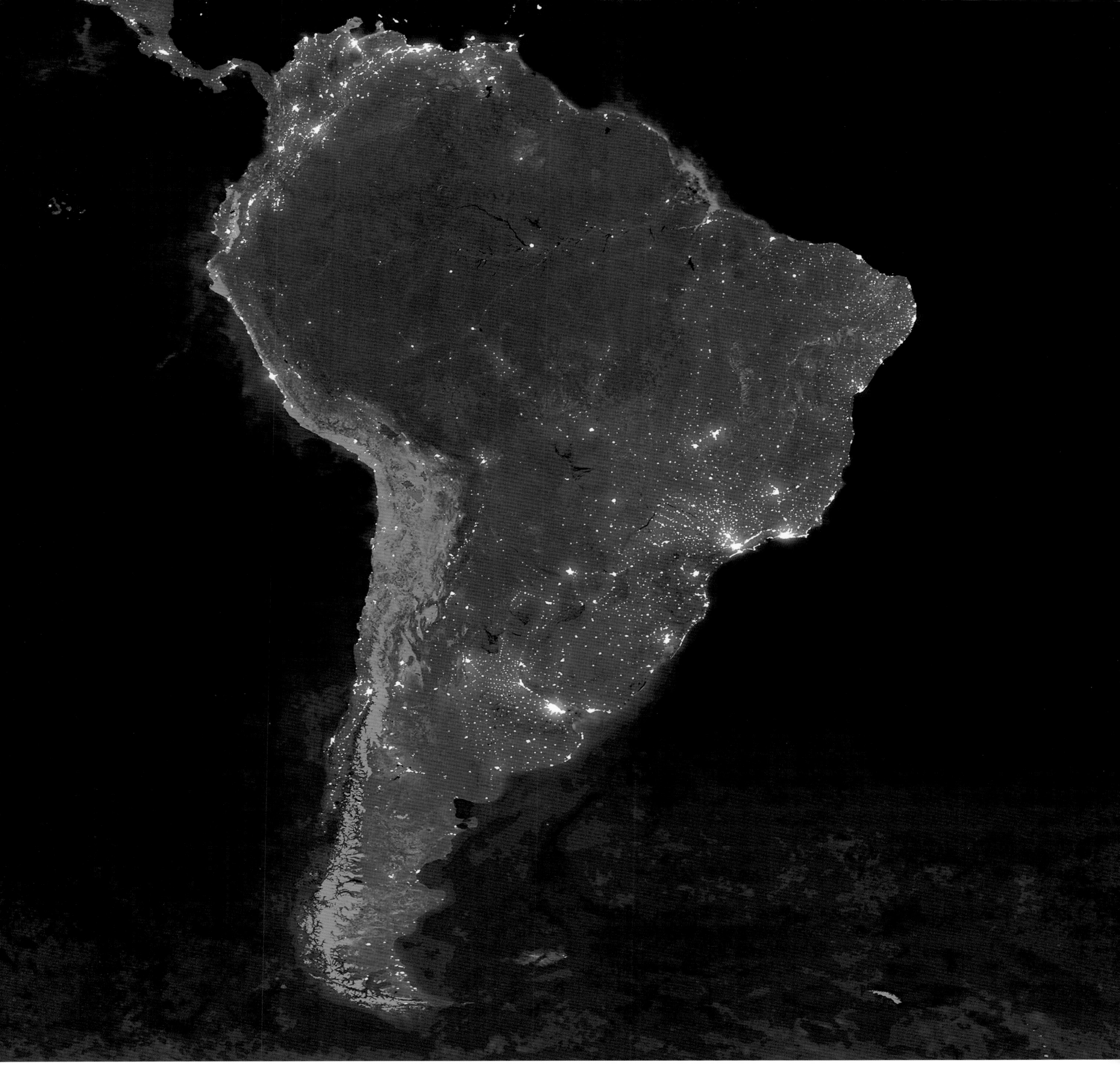

South America

The View from Above

From space, the details of South America's landscapes are revealed. The human impact is startling: many photographs record the scars of logging and burning in the vast tropical rain forests of Brazil; others are dominated by artificial features such as the enormous dams and reservoirs created for irrigation and hydroelectric power. Satellite photography can also help explain natural phenomena. The Andes Mountains run like a spine down the west coast of South America, creating what is known as a rain-shadow effect. Tradewinds from the east carry warm, moist tropical air over the forested interior. As the air climbs the high eastern slopes of the Andes, it cools, condenses, and falls as rain or snow, which runs into the Amazon River and Basin. The air warms again as it descends the western slopes and so holds its moisture as it crosses the Atacama Desert to the coast. This effect contributes to both the extreme dryness of the Atacama Desert, in the rain-shadow area, and the lushness of the Amazon Basin, which dominates the continent's interior and is one of the wettest places on the planet.

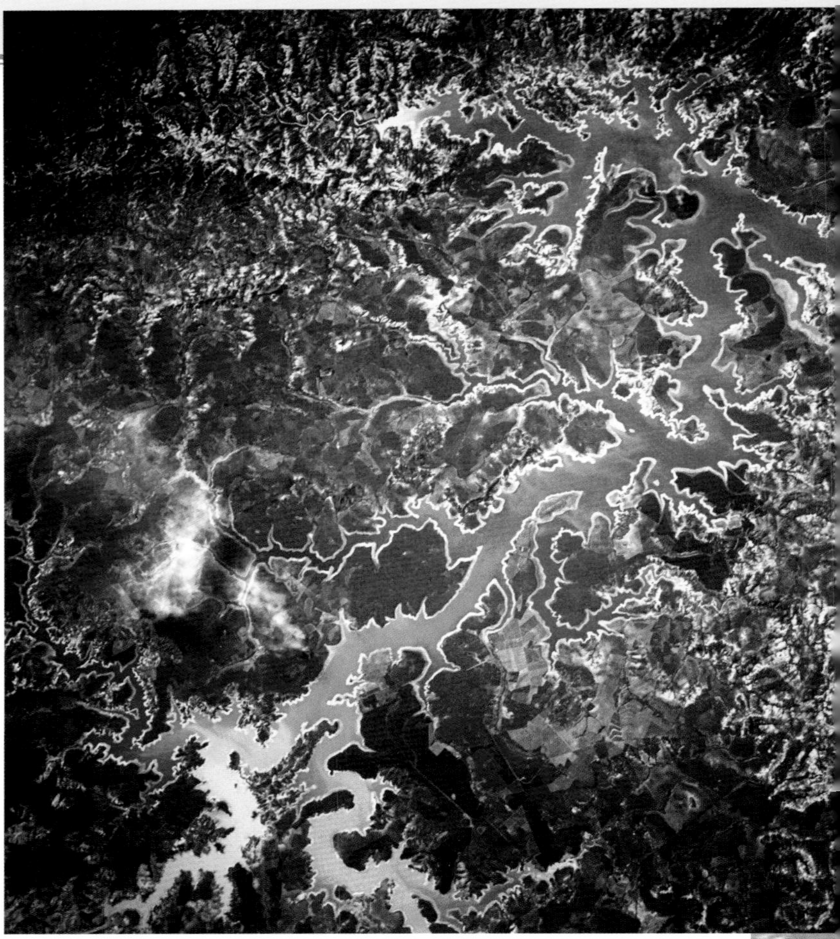

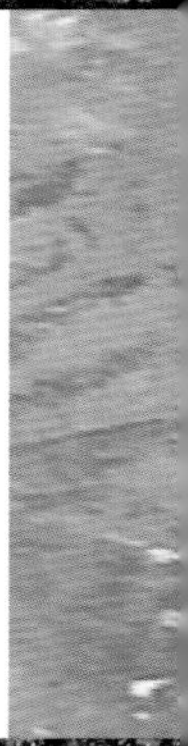

Below: Two banks of clouds flank Chile's Atacama Desert. Those on the left stop at the coast because the cold waters of the Humboldt (Peru) Current, just off shore, cause rain to fall over the ocean. On the right, the Andes stop a line of clouds, forcing rain to fall on the eastern slopes. Parts of the Atacama Desert have never recorded rain.

Below right: The destruction of Brazil's forests is dramatically illustrated in this false-color image. The remaining tropical forest appears as bright red, while darker areas represent cleared land, and black and gray patches are recently burned areas. The vertical lines indicate land cleared along transportation routes.

Above: The serpentine Represa Três Marias winds across this true-color image of southeastern Brazil. This reservoir was built in 1960 to generate hydroelectric power for the state of Minas Gerais. It occupies some 60 miles (95 km) of the São Francisco River, which can be seen carrying sediment into the reservoir's southern end.

Right: In this satellite view of Argentina, the sediment-laden waters filling the bay of the River Plate reflect light and so appear bright. In contrast, the waters stretching north along the coast have absorbed light, perhaps because of a phytoplankton bloom, and so look very dark. Buenos Aires is the gray area at the bay's western end.

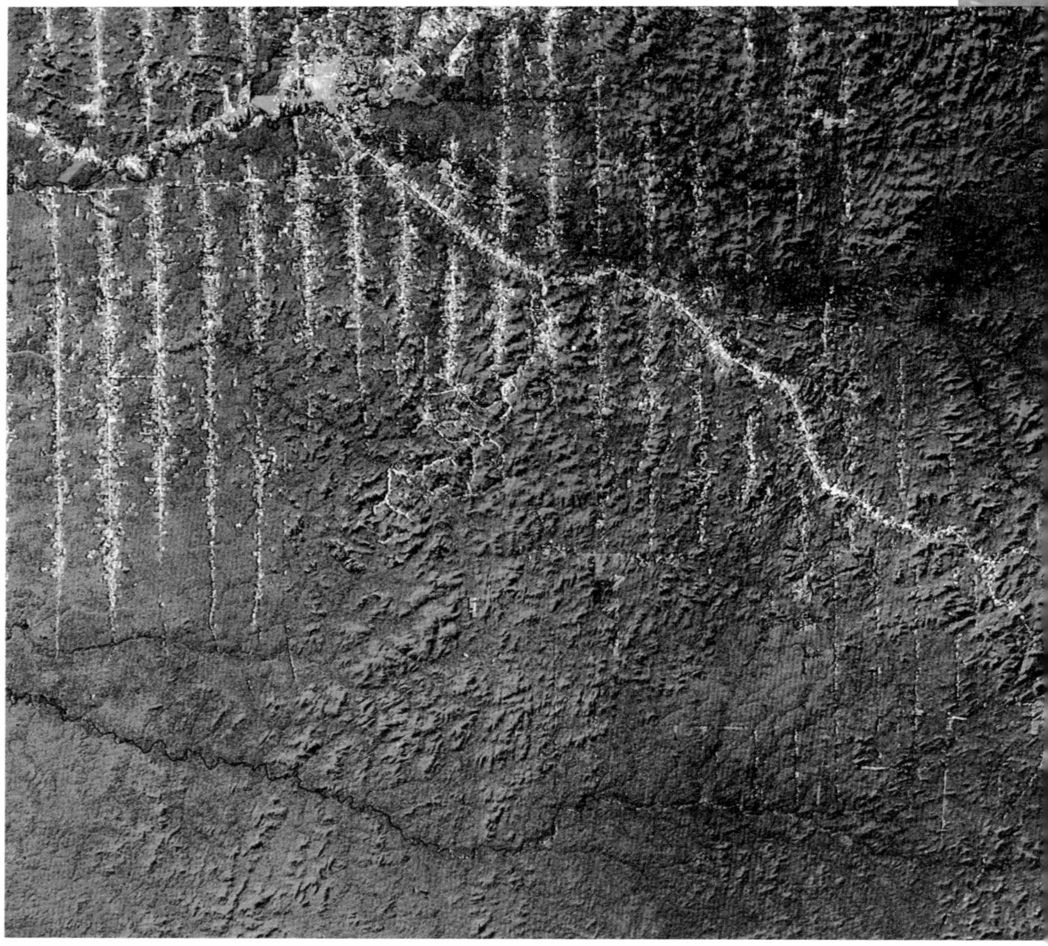

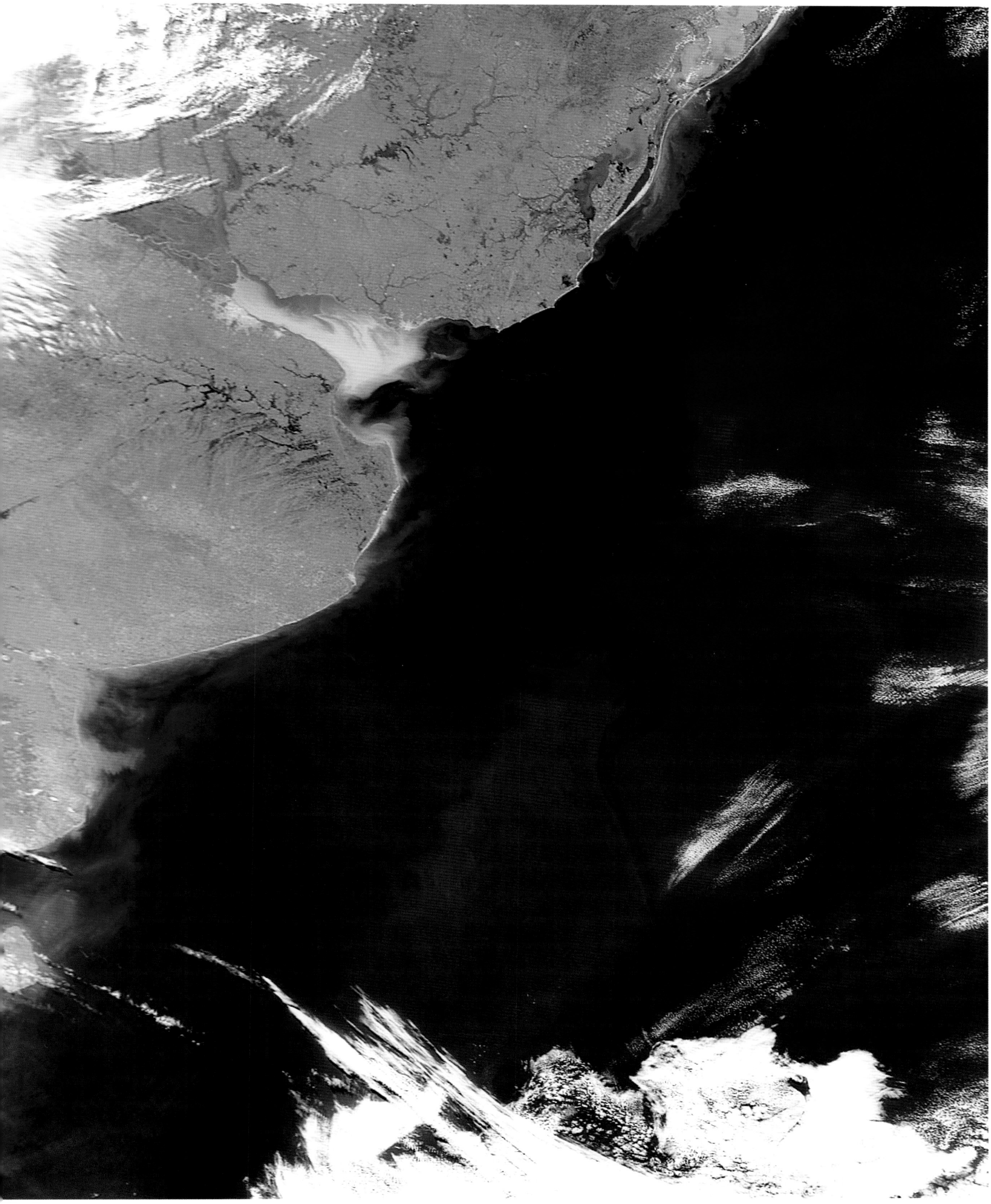

Land and Environment

Encompassing almost 6.9 million square miles (17.8 million sq km) and extending from Punta Gallinas, in the warm Caribbean Sea, south to the cold, windswept promontory of Cape Horn, South America is the fourth-largest continent. The towering Andes mountains dominate the west, running parallel to the coast for 5,500 miles (8,800 km) and rising to their highest point of 22,835 feet (6,960 m) at Mount Aconcagua. East of the Andes lie expansive lowlands, including, from north to south, the valley of the Orinoco, the immense Amazon Basin, the semiarid grasslands of Gran Chaco, and the plains of the Pampas. In turn, these lowlands are bounded by the plateau regions of the Guiana Highlands in the north, the Brazilian Highlands in the east, and Patagonia in the south.

Caribbean Sea
Punta Gallinas
Gulf of Venezuela
Lake Maracaibo
Gulf of Darién
Gulf of Panama
Cordillera Occidental
Cordillera Central
Cordillera Oriental
Llanos
Orinoco
La Gran Sabana
Guiana Highlands
Negro
Branco
Tumuc-Humac Mountains
Amazon
Caquetá
Putumayo
Volcán Cotopaxi 19,344ft (5896m)
Chimborazo 20,702ft (6310m)
Gulf of Guayaquil
Punta Pariñas
Marañón
Amazon Basin
Juruá
Purus
Madeira
Tapajós
Xingu
Ucayali
Nevado Huascarán 22,205ft (6768m)
Tocantins
Araguaia
Planalto do Mato Grosso
Andes
Lake Titicaca
Altiplano
Atacama Desert
Brazilian Highlands
Pilcomayo
Paraguay
Paraná
Gran Chaco
Serra Geral
Serra do Mar
Paraná
Uruguay
Mesopotamia
Lagoa dos Patos
Lagoa Mirim
Mount Aconcagua 22,835ft (6960m)
River Plate
Pampas
Colorado
Negro
Patagonia
Chico
Golfo de San Jorge
Deseado
Golfo de Penas
Bahía Grande
Falkland Islands
Tierra del Fuego
Cape Horn
Pacific Ocean
Atlantic Ocean
Galapagos Islands
Isla San Salvador
Fernandina
Isla Isabela
Isla Santa Cruz
Isla San Cristóbal
SCALE 1:12,500,000
100 miles
100 kilometres
SCALE 1:35,000,000
Lamberts Conformal Conic Projection
1000
1000 kilometers

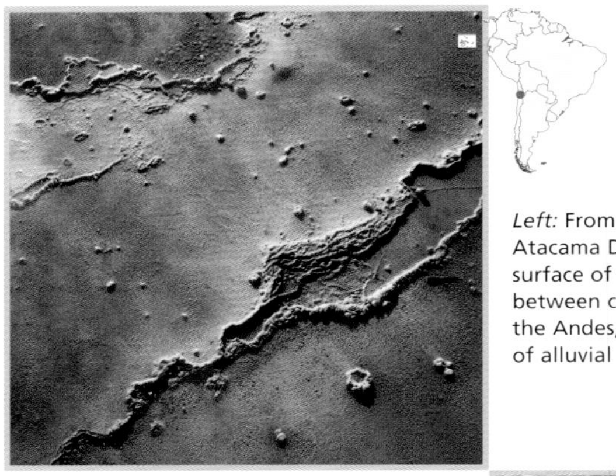

Left: From space, the barren Atacama Desert resembles the surface of the Moon. Situated between coastal ranges and the Andes, it consists mainly of alluvial plains and salt pans.

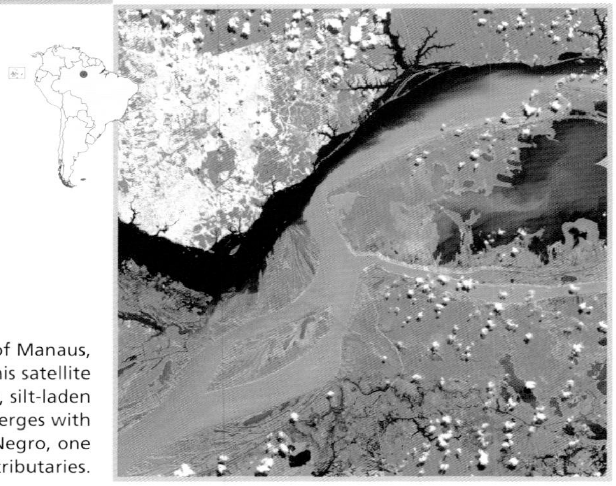

Right: Near the town of Manaus, shown in gray in this satellite image, the brown, silt-laden Amazon River merges with the much clearer Negro, one of its major tributaries.

Natural Hazards

Volcanoes

Western South America borders the Ring of Fire, a well-known zone of tectonic instability that almost encircles the Pacific Ocean. Just off the west coast, the Nazca Plate is subducting beneath the South American Plate, giving rise to earthquakes and volcanic eruptions. South America has more volcanoes than any other continent—204—and the world's highest volcano, Nevado Ojos del Salado, which rises to 22,664 feet (6,908 m). The deadliest eruption of recent years was that of Nevado del Ruiz in Colombia, in 1985, which, although small, melted a glacier, triggering a mudflow that killed about 23,000 people.

Nevado del Ruiz 17,716ft (5400m)
Volcán Cotopaxi 19,344ft (5896m)
Nevado Ojos del Salado 22,664ft (6908m)
Volcán Villarrica 9318ft (2840m)
Cerro Hudson 8530ft (2600m)

Along the plate boundary that parallels the coast, the thinner Nazca Plate is forced downward beneath the much thicker South American Plate. As it subducts, the Nazca Plate gradually melts. Magma then rises through cracks in the crumpled landscape, forming a long line of volcanoes.

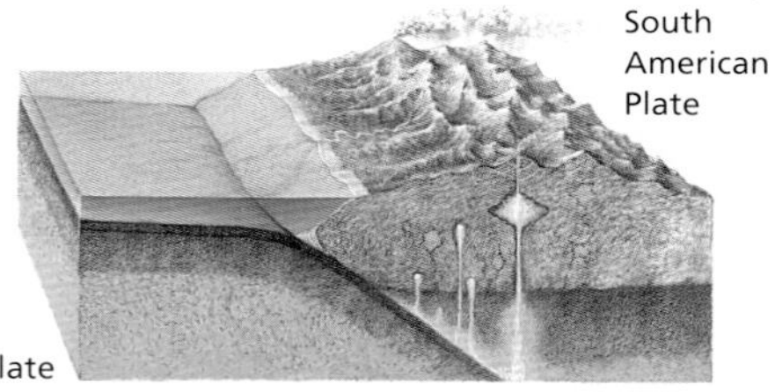

South American Plate
Nazca Plate

The mudflow caused by the eruption of Nevado del Ruiz in Colombia swamped the town of Armero in minutes, giving the inhabitants little opportunity to escape.

OCEAN
Cabo de São Roque
Planalto da Borborema
São Francisco

Barranquilla
Maracaibo
CARACAS
GEORGETOWN
PARAMARIBO
CAYENNE
Medellín
BOGOTÁ
Cali
Boa Vista
Macapá
QUITO
Manaus
Belém
Iquitos
Chiclayo
Fortaleza
Porto Velho
Palmas
Recife
LIMA
Cuzco
Cuiabá
Salvador
LA PAZ
BRASÍLIA
SUCRE
Belo Horizonte
Galapagos Islands
Antofagasta
Salta
São Paulo
Rio de Janeiro
ASUNCIÓN
Coquimbo
Córdoba
Porto Alegre
SANTIAGO
BUENOS AIRES
MONTEVIDEO
Bahía Blanca
Puerto Montt
Rawson
STANLEY
Punta Arenas
CLIMATE ZONES
Wet tropical
Seasonal tropical
Arid
Semiarid
Mediterranean
Subtropical
Temperate
Subpolar
Highland

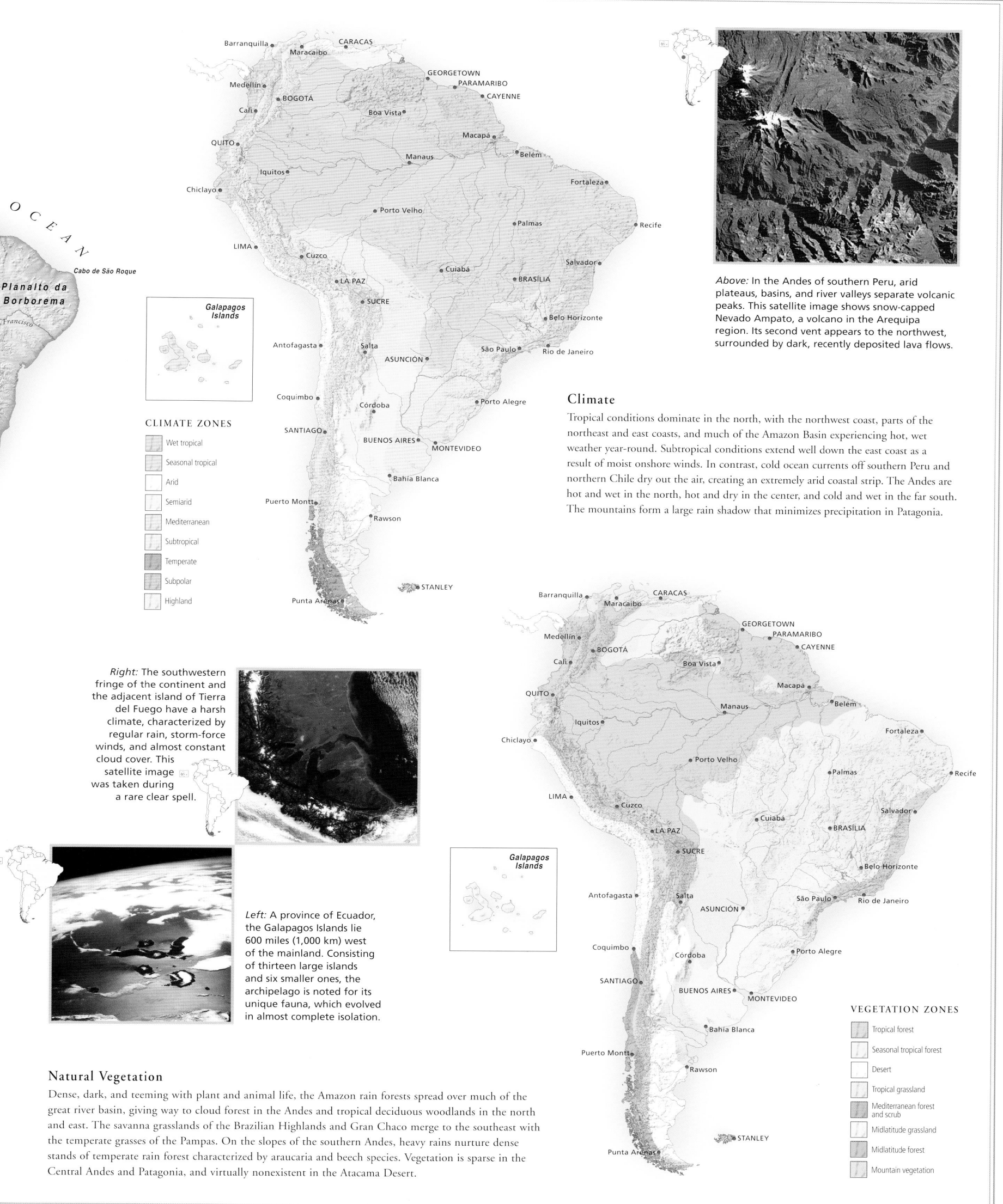

Above: In the Andes of southern Peru, arid plateaus, basins, and river valleys separate volcanic peaks. This satellite image shows snow-capped Nevado Ampato, a volcano in the Arequipa region. Its second vent appears to the northwest, surrounded by dark, recently deposited lava flows.

Climate

Tropical conditions dominate in the north, with the northwest coast, parts of the northeast and east coasts, and much of the Amazon Basin experiencing hot, wet weather year-round. Subtropical conditions extend well down the east coast as a result of moist onshore winds. In contrast, cold ocean currents off southern Peru and northern Chile dry out the air, creating an extremely arid coastal strip. The Andes are hot and wet in the north, hot and dry in the center, and cold and wet in the far south. The mountains form a large rain shadow that minimizes precipitation in Patagonia.

Right: The southwestern fringe of the continent and the adjacent island of Tierra del Fuego have a harsh climate, characterized by regular rain, storm-force winds, and almost constant cloud cover. This satellite image was taken during a rare clear spell.

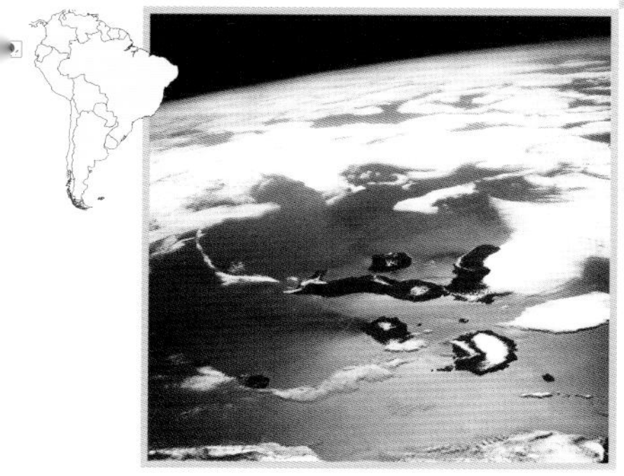

Left: A province of Ecuador, the Galapagos Islands lie 600 miles (1,000 km) west of the mainland. Consisting of thirteen large islands and six smaller ones, the archipelago is noted for its unique fauna, which evolved in almost complete isolation.

Barranquilla
Maracaibo
CARACAS
GEORGETOWN
PARAMARIBO
CAYENNE
Medellín
BOGOTÁ
Cali
Boa Vista
QUITO
Macapá
Manaus
Belém
Iquitos
Chiclayo
Fortaleza
Porto Velho
Palmas
Recife
LIMA
Cuzco
Cuiabá
Salvador
LA PAZ
BRASÍLIA
SUCRE
Galapagos Islands
Belo Horizonte
Antofagasta
Salta
São Paulo
Rio de Janeiro
ASUNCIÓN
Coquimbo
Córdoba
Porto Alegre
SANTIAGO
BUENOS AIRES
MONTEVIDEO
Bahía Blanca
Puerto Montt
Rawson
STANLEY
Punta Arenas
VEGETATION ZONES
Tropical forest
Seasonal tropical forest
Desert
Tropical grassland
Mediterranean forest and scrub
Midlatitude grassland
Midlatitude forest
Mountain vegetation

Natural Vegetation

Dense, dark, and teeming with plant and animal life, the Amazon rain forests spread over much of the great river basin, giving way to cloud forest in the Andes and tropical deciduous woodlands in the north and east. The savanna grasslands of the Brazilian Highlands and Gran Chaco merge to the southeast with the temperate grasses of the Pampas. On the slopes of the southern Andes, heavy rains nurture dense stands of temperate rain forest characterized by araucaria and beech species. Vegetation is sparse in the Central Andes and Patagonia, and virtually nonexistent in the Atacama Desert.

Peoples and Nations

Relative to its size, South America has a modest population of about 350 million. These people inhabit twelve nations and two overseas territories. Their dominant cultures and languages are those of the European colonial powers that, from the early 16th century onward, seized large parts of the continent. Portuguese is the official language in Brazil; Spanish predominates in most other areas. English, Dutch, and French are spoken in, respectively, the Falkland Islands and the former British colony of Guyana; the former Dutch colony of Suriname; and French Guiana, a French territory. Amerindian languages are restricted mainly to the Amazon Basin, the central Andes, and western Paraguay.

CARACAS
Maracaibo
GEORGETOWN
PARAMARIBO
CAYENNE
Bucaramanga
BOGOTÁ
Cali
QUITO
Guayaquil
Manaus
Belém
Fortaleza
Trujillo
Recife
LIMA
Cuzco
Salvador
LA PAZ
BRASÍLIA
SUCRE
Belo Horizonte
Galapagos Islands
São Paulo
Rio de Janeiro
Curitiba
ASUNCIÓN
Porto Alegre
Córdoba
Valparaíso
Rosario
SANTIAGO
BUENOS AIRES
La Plata
MONTEVIDEO
Puerto Montt
STANLEY
Punta Arenas
POPULATION DENSITY
Uninhabited
Less than 2.6 persons per sq mile/1 per sq km
2.6–26 per sq mile/ 1–10 per sq km
26–65 per sq mile/ 10–25 per sq km
65–130 per sq mile/ 25–50 per sq km
130–260 per sq mile/ 50–100 per sq km
260–520 per sq mile/ 100–200 per sq km

Left: São Paulo is the continent's largest city and the second-biggest urban agglomeration in the world after Tokyo in Japan. In 1947, São Paulo's city center had just three high-rise buildings; now it bristles with skyscrapers.

Flashpoints

Though it has been relatively stable since the mid-19th century, South America has recently experienced conflict between guerilla groups and governments, as well as several border disputes.

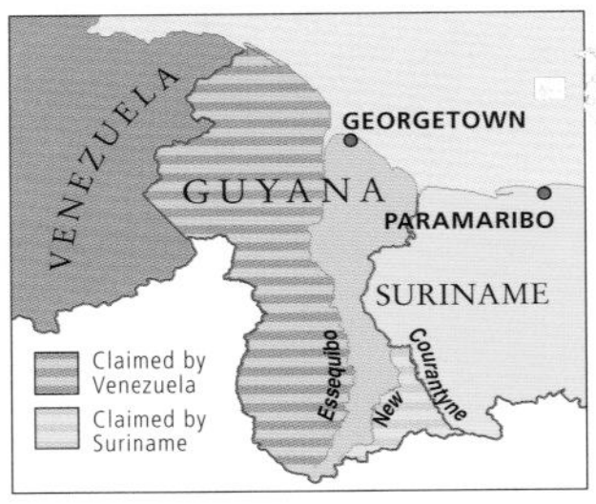
VENEZUELA
GEORGETOWN
GUYANA
PARAMARIBO
SURINAME
Essequibo
New
Courantyne
Claimed by Venezuela
Claimed by Suriname

Guyana

Guyana has long faced significant territorial claims from its western and eastern neighbors, which, if realized, would see its territory drastically reduced. Venezuela disputes ownership of the entire area west of the Essequibo River, asserting that it inherited the land from Spain. Suriname claims the triangular region between the New (Upper Courantyne) and Courantyne rivers.

Northern Chile

In 1879–83, Chile defeated Bolivia and Peru in the War of the Pacific. As a result, it gained much of the Atacama region including southern Peru and coastal Bolivia. Peru regained some territory in 1929 as a result of negotiation, but Chile has refused to consider regular requests from Bolivia for sovereign access to the sea. This has led to repeated breakdowns in diplomatic relations.

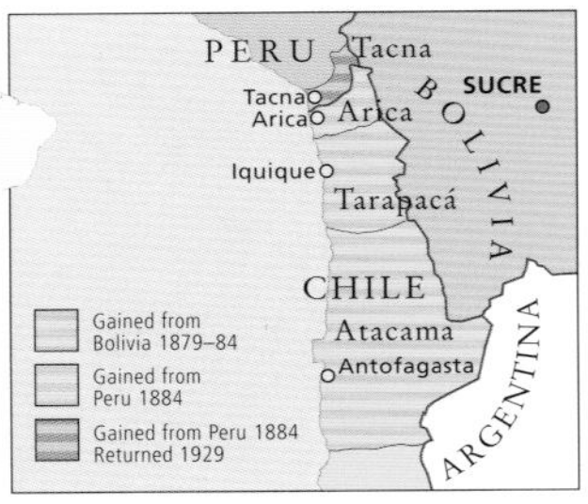
PERU
Tacna
SUCRE
BOLIVIA
Tacna
Arica
Arica
Iquique
Tarapacá
CHILE
Atacama
Antofagasta
ARGENTINA
Gained from Bolivia 1879–84
Gained from Peru 1884
Gained from Peru 1884 Returned 1929

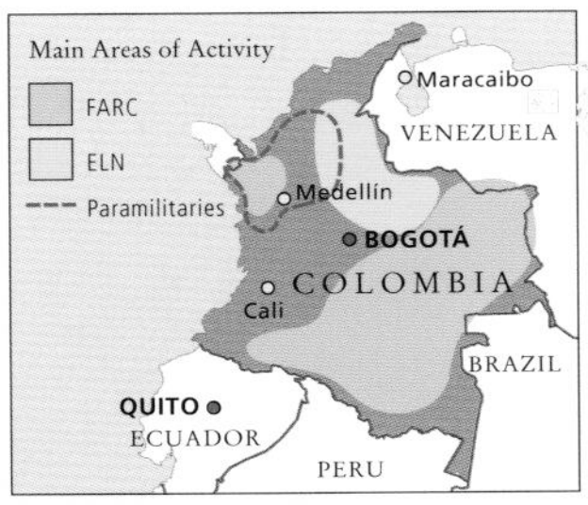
Main Areas of Activity
FARC
ELN
Paramilitaries
Maracaibo
VENEZUELA
Medellín
BOGOTÁ
COLOMBIA
Cali
BRAZIL
QUITO
ECUADOR
PERU

Colombia

Since the mid-1960s, guerillas belonging to the Revolutionary Armed Forces of Colombia (FARC) and the National Liberation Army (ELN) have been attempting to install a socialist government by force, a conflict that has cost 38,000 lives. Although the current government is supported by right-wing paramilitaries and the U.S.A., the guerilla groups control more than half of the country, and have formed alliances with drug traffickers.

Population Patterns

Sometimes referred to as "the hollow continent," South America has a sparsely populated interior ringed by areas of heavy coastal settlement. Among the most densely inhabited areas are the northeast and south coasts of Brazil, the Andean plateaus, and the River Plate region of Argentina and Uruguay. Most South Americans are descended from one or more of four main groups: native Amerindian peoples; early Spanish or Portuguese colonists; African slaves brought to the continent between the 16th and early 19th centuries; and more recent immigrants, especially from Italy, Spain, Portugal, Eastern Europe, and Japan.

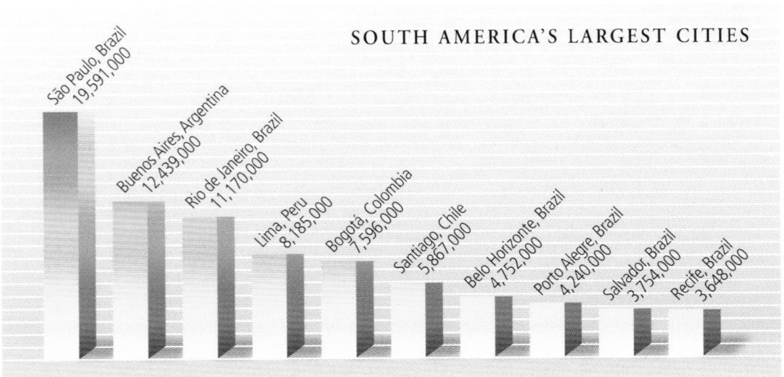
SOUTH AMERICA'S LARGEST CITIES
São Paulo, Brazil 19,591,000
Buenos Aires, Argentina 12,439,000
Rio de Janeiro, Brazil 11,170,000
Lima, Peru 8,185,000
Bogotá, Colombia 7,596,000
Santiago, Chile 5,867,000
Belo Horizonte, Brazil 4,752,000
Porto Alegre, Brazil 4,240,000
Salvador, Brazil 3,754,000
Recife, Brazil 3,648,000

Urbanization

Prior to the early 16th century, major population centers lay on the Pacific Coast, in the Andes, and along the waterways of the Amazon Basin. The arrival by sea of Spanish and Portuguese colonists and traders caused a shift of settlement to seaboard towns. In the mid-20th century, rapid industrialization of these centers, combined with a lack of development, communications, and infrastructure in the interior, spurred large-scale migration to coastal cities. Continent-wide, urbanization has risen from less than 50 percent in 1950 to a current level of around 82 percent.

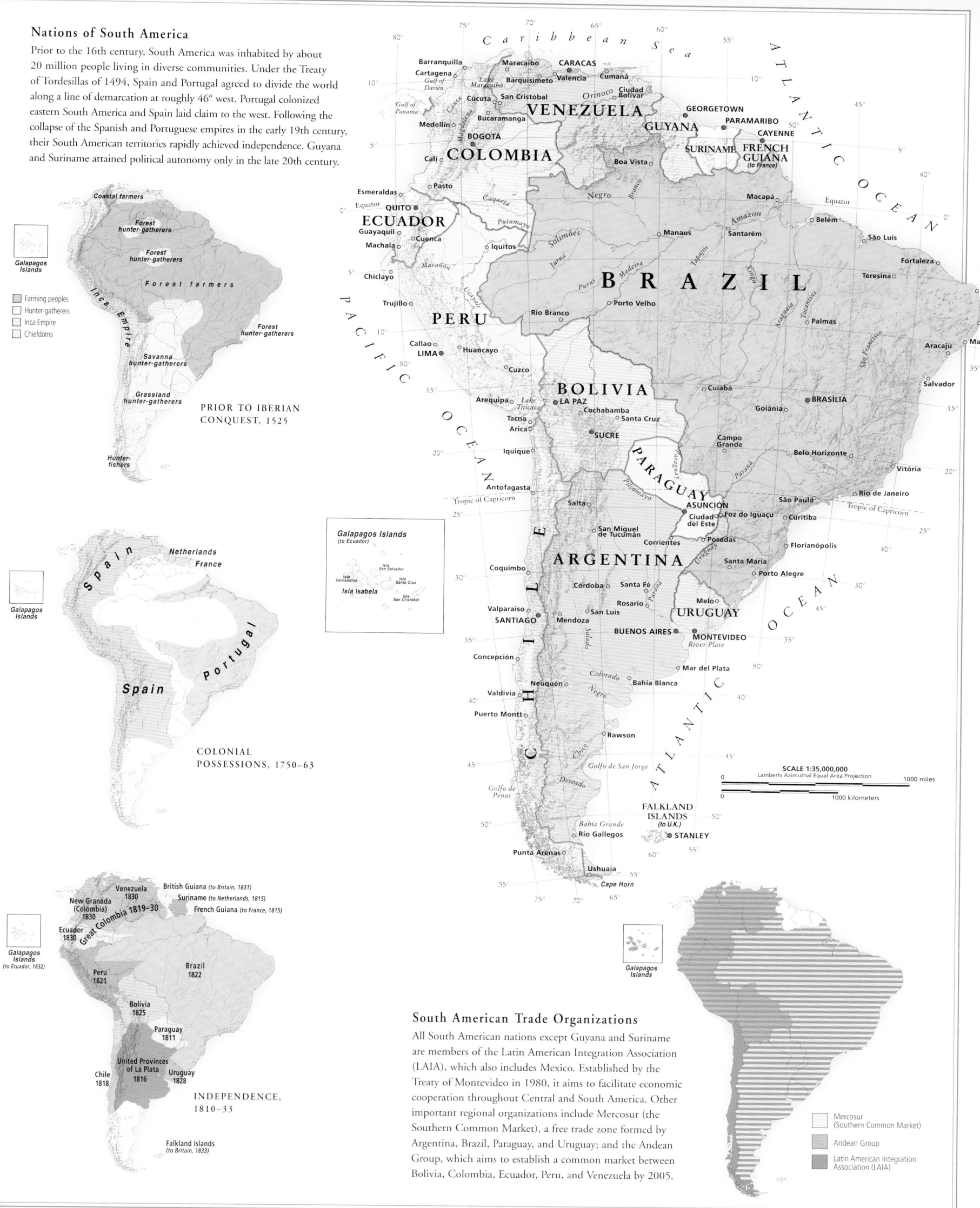

Nations of South America

Prior to the 16th century, South America was inhabited by about 20 million people living in diverse communities. Under the Treaty of Tordesillas of 1494, Spain and Portugal agreed to divide the world along a line of demarcation at roughly 46° west. Portugal colonized eastern South America and Spain laid claim to the west. Following the collapse of the Spanish and Portuguese empires in the early 19th century, their South American territories rapidly achieved independence. Guyana and Suriname attained political autonomy only in the late 20th century.

Coastal farmers
Forest hunter-gatherers
Forest hunter-gatherers
Forest farmers
Inca Empire
Forest hunter-gatherers
Savanna hunter-gatherers
Grassland hunter-gatherers
Hunter-fishers
Galapagos Islands
Farming peoples
Hunter-gatherers
Inca Empire
Chiefdoms

PRIOR TO IBERIAN CONQUEST, 1525

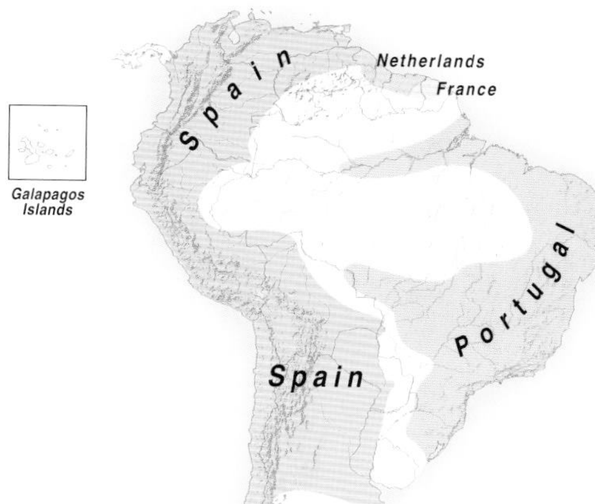
Spain
Netherlands
France
Spain
Portugal
Galapagos Islands

COLONIAL POSSESSIONS, 1750–63

Venezuela 1830
New Granada (Colombia) 1830
Great Colombia 1819–30
British Guiana (to Britain, 1831)
Suriname (to Netherlands, 1815)
French Guiana (to France, 1815)
Ecuador 1830
Galapagos Islands (to Ecuador, 1832)
Peru 1821
Brazil 1822
Bolivia 1825
Paraguay 1811
United Provinces of La Plata 1816
Chile 1818
Uruguay 1828
Falkland Islands (to Britain, 1833)

INDEPENDENCE, 1810–33

Caribbean Sea
ATLANTIC OCEAN
PACIFIC OCEAN
ATLANTIC OCEAN
VENEZUELA
COLOMBIA
GUYANA
SURINAME
FRENCH GUIANA (to France)
ECUADOR
PERU
BRAZIL
BOLIVIA
PARAGUAY
CHILE
ARGENTINA
URUGUAY
FALKLAND ISLANDS (to U.K.)
CARACAS
BOGOTÁ
GEORGETOWN
PARAMARIBO
CAYENNE
QUITO
LIMA
LA PAZ
SUCRE
BRASÍLIA
ASUNCIÓN
SANTIAGO
BUENOS AIRES
MONTEVIDEO
STANLEY
Barranquilla
Cartagena
Maracaibo
Barquisimeto
Valencia
Cumaná
Ciudad Bolívar
Cúcuta
San Cristóbal
Bucaramanga
Medellín
Cali
Pasto
Boa Vista
Esmeraldas
Guayaquil
Cuenca
Machala
Iquitos
Manaus
Macapá
Belém
Santarém
São Luís
Fortaleza
Teresina
Natal
Recife
Maceió
Aracaju
Salvador
Chiclayo
Trujillo
Porto Velho
Rio Branco
Palmas
Callao
Huancayo
Cuzco
Arequipa
Tacna
Arica
Cochabamba
Santa Cruz
Cuiabá
Goiânia
Campo Grande
Belo Horizonte
Vitória
Rio de Janeiro
São Paulo
Curitiba
Iquique
Antofagasta
Salta
Ciudad del Este
Foz do Iguaçu
San Miguel de Tucumán
Corrientes
Posadas
Florianópolis
Santa Maria
Porto Alegre
Coquimbo
Córdoba
Santa Fé
Rosario
Melo
Valparaíso
Mendoza
San Luis
Concepción
Mar del Plata
Neuquén
Bahía Blanca
Valdivia
Puerto Montt
Rawson
Río Gallegos
Punta Arenas
Ushuaia
Cape Horn
Gulf of Darien
Gulf of Panama
Lake Maracaibo
Orinoco
Negro
Branco
Amazon
Caquetá
Putumayo
Solimões
Juruá
Purus
Madeira
Tapajós
Xingu
Araguaia
Tocantins
São Francisco
Marañón
Ucayali
Lake Titicaca
Paraguay
Pilcomayo
Paraná
Uruguay
Salado
Colorado
Negro
Chico
Deseado
Golfo de San Jorge
Golfo de Penas
Bahía Grande
River Plate
Equator
Tropic of Capricorn
Galapagos Islands (to Ecuador)
Isla San Salvador
Isla Fernandina
Isla Santa Cruz
Isla Isabela
Isla San Cristóbal
SCALE 1:35,000,000
Lamberts Azimuthal Equal Area Projection
1000 miles
1000 kilometers

South American Trade Organizations

All South American nations except Guyana and Suriname are members of the Latin American Integration Association (LAIA), which also includes Mexico. Established by the Treaty of Montevideo in 1980, it aims to facilitate economic cooperation throughout Central and South America. Other important regional organizations include Mercosur (the Southern Common Market), a free trade zone formed by Argentina, Brazil, Paraguay, and Uruguay; and the Andean Group, which aims to establish a common market between Bolivia, Colombia, Ecuador, Peru, and Venezuela by 2005.

Galapagos Islands
Mercosur (Southern Common Market)
Andean Group
Latin American Integration Association (LAIA)

The Human Impact

By the time of European colonization, human modification of the South American landscape was already widespread, though uneven. Hunter-gatherer lifestyles still predominated in some areas, but many of the continent's estimated 6 to 9 million inhabitants practiced agriculture, cultivating crops that would become staples worldwide, such as corn, potatoes, and beans. From 1800 BC, large settlements incorporating ceremonial buildings and irrigation systems took shape on the west coast. In the 15th century, the Inca expanded the practice of building terraces to increase agricultural output and constructed a road network covering 13,000 miles (21,000 km). After 1532, the pace of change accelerated. The Portuguese cleared huge swathes of tropical forest on the east coast to make way for sugar and, later, coffee plantations; less than 8 percent of that forest remains. The Andes, too, were stripped of timber, and the woodlands that covered the Pampas were cleared and planted with grasses to feed introduced livestock. Rapid population growth in the second half of the 20th century increased pressure on remaining wilderness areas, and has given rise to overcrowding and severe pollution and waste problems in cities.

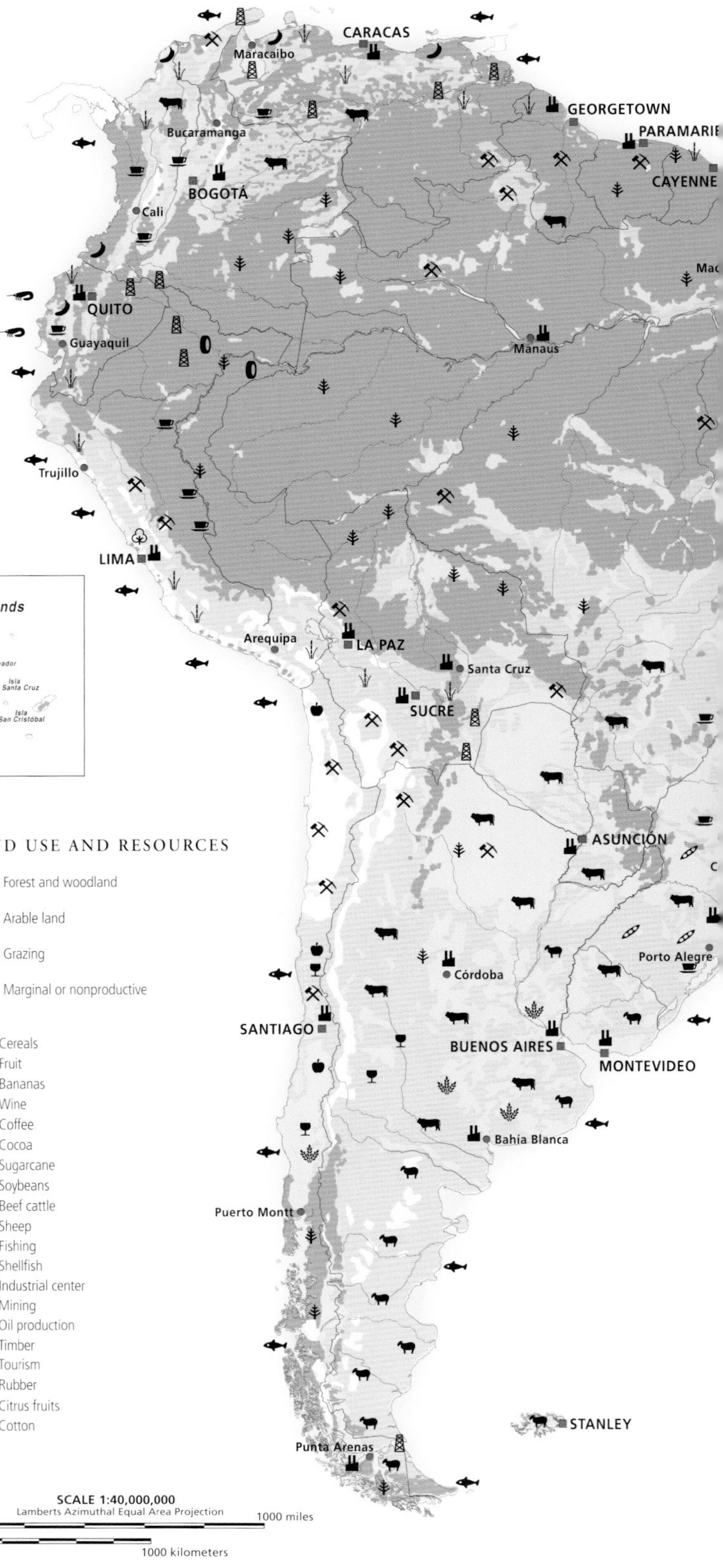

CARACAS
Maracaibo
GEORGETOWN
PARAMARIBO
CAYENNE
Bucaramanga
BOGOTÁ
Cali
QUITO
Guayaquil
Manaus
Trujillo
LIMA
Arequipa
LA PAZ
Santa Cruz
SUCRE
ASUNCIÓN
Córdoba
Porto Alegre
SANTIAGO
BUENOS AIRES
MONTEVIDEO
Bahia Blanca
Puerto Montt
Punta Arenas
STANLEY
LAND USE AND RESOURCES
Forest and woodland
Arable land
Grazing
Marginal or nonproductive
Cereals
Fruit
Bananas
Wine
Coffee
Cocoa
Sugarcane
Soybeans
Beef cattle
Sheep
Fishing
Shellfish
Industrial center
Mining
Oil production
Timber
Tourism
Rubber
Citrus fruits
Cotton
SCALE 1:40,000,000
Lamberts Azimuthal Equal Area Projection
0
1000 miles
0
1000 kilometers

Galapagos Islands
Isla San Salvador
Isla Fernandina
Isla Santa Cruz
Isla Isabela
Isla San Cristobal

Economic Profile

Though unevenly distributed, South America's abundant natural resources help make it a major exporter of primary produce. The continent provides one-quarter of the world's copper and one-fifth of its iron ore, as well as large supplies of tin and bauxite. Oil reserves have been located in areas such as Lake Maracaibo in Venezuela, the western Amazon Basin, and southern Patagonia. The immense pastures of the east and southeast support massive beef-cattle herds, and tropical plantations generate enormous cash crops of sugar, coffee, citrus fruits, and rubber. The southeastern Pacific Ocean is the world's second-most productive fishery. Plentiful metals and hydroelectric power have aided the development of industries, but most remain resource-based and South America is dependent on imports of many manufactured goods.

Land Cover

Forests still swathe more than half of the continent and account for 25 percent of global forest cover. South America has extensive reserves of cultivable land, though most is used as pasture. Other types of land cover include sprawling coastal settlements, wetlands, and the barren Andean uplands and western and southern deserts.

PROPORTIONS OF TOTAL LAND AREA

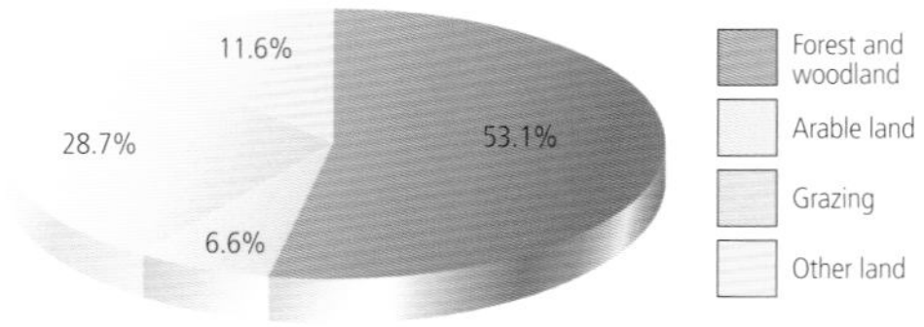

11.6%
28.7%
53.1%
6.6%
Forest and woodland
Arable land
Grazing
Other land

The Changing Face of South America

The Amazon Rain Forest

The Amazon rain forest covers an area as large as the United States and harbors at least 40 percent of the world's plant and animal species, as well as 180,000 indigenous people; it also recycles 10 percent of the world's airborne carbon. Since the mid-20th century, this ecologically vital and once-remote environment has come increasingly under threat. In 1960, faced with mounting pressure from a land-hungry citizenry, the Brazilian government adopted the vote-winning policy of populating the region. Ten percent of the rain forest was cleared within seven years. Currently, an area the size of New Jersey disappears every year and total losses now amount to an area as large as France. Despite this, Brazil recently announced another plan to cover the region with dams, settlements, and thousands of miles of roads. Conservation groups estimate this could result in the loss of between 33 and 42 percent of the remaining Amazon rain forest.

ORIGINAL RAIN FOREST

REMAINING RAIN FOREST

Right: Throughout South America, enormous amounts of domestic waste are deposited in open garbage dumps like this one in Buenos Aires, Argentina. In Bolivia, Ecuador, and Peru, sanitary landfills can be found only in the capital cities.

Right: Hydroelectricity provides much of South America's energy, but it has an environmental cost. Construction of the Itaipu dam, on the Brazil–Paraguay border, the world's largest, destroyed 270 square miles (700 sq km) of forest and wiped out several rare plant species.

Fortaleza
Recife
Salvador
Belo Horizonte
Rio de Janeiro

Below: In 1980, the Brazilian industrial city of Cubatão was so polluted that it reportedly had no birds or insects and one-third of infants died in their first year.

Above: In 1972 in Peru, a combination of overfishing and an El Niño episode saw fish stocks plummet by two-thirds for the next 15 years. More than 80 percent of stocks in South American waters are now fully fished, overfished, or depleted.

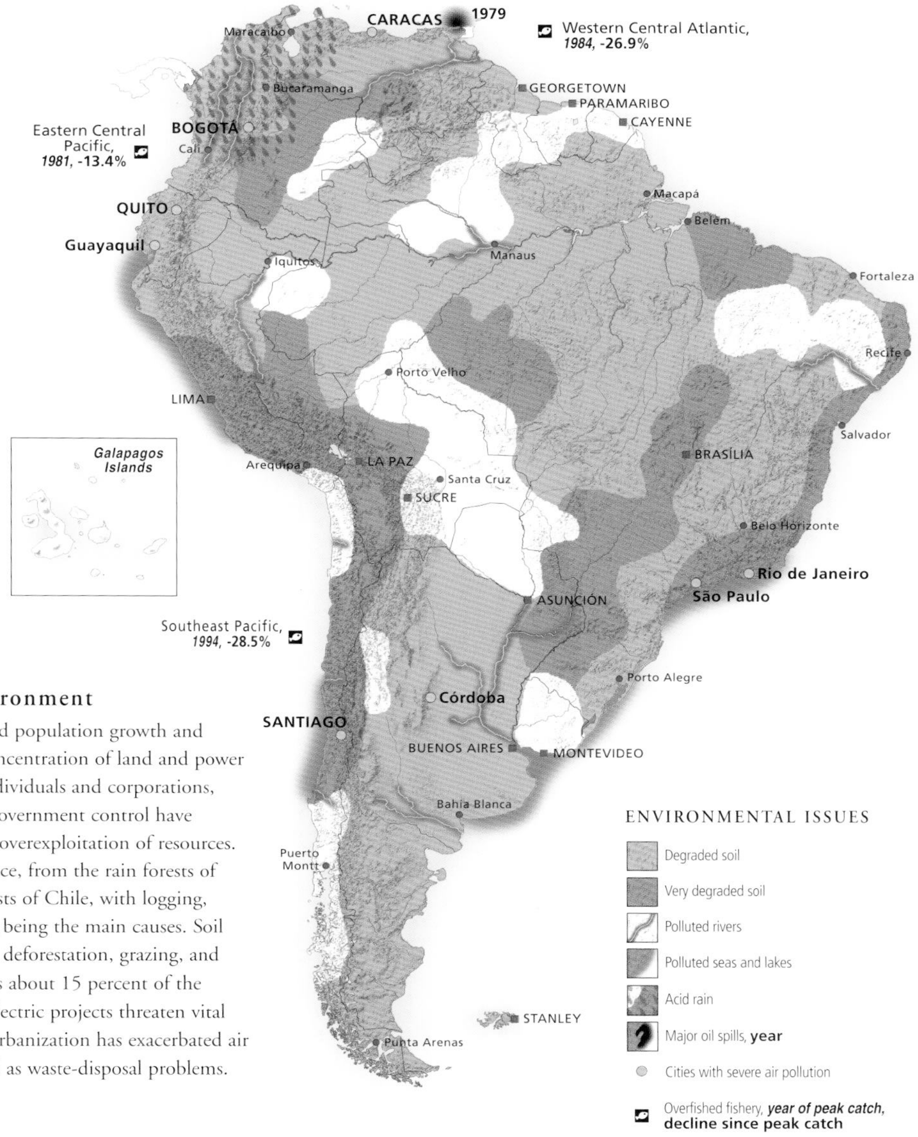

CARACAS
1979
Western Central Atlantic, 1984, -26.9%
Maracaibo
Bucaramanga
GEORGETOWN
PARAMARIBO
CAYENNE
Eastern Central Pacific, 1981, -13.4%
BOGOTÁ
Cali
QUITO
Guayaquil
Macapá
Belém
Manaus
Iquitos
Fortaleza
Recife
Porto Velho
LIMA
Salvador
Galapagos Islands
Arequipa
LA PAZ
Santa Cruz
SUCRE
BRASÍLIA
Belo Horizonte
Rio de Janeiro
São Paulo
ASUNCIÓN
Southeast Pacific, 1994, -28.5%
Porto Alegre
Córdoba
SANTIAGO
BUENOS AIRES
MONTEVIDEO
Bahía Blanca
Puerto Montt
STANLEY
Punta Arenas
ENVIRONMENTAL ISSUES
Degraded soil
Very degraded soil
Polluted rivers
Polluted seas and lakes
Acid rain
Major oil spills, year
Cities with severe air pollution
Overfished fishery, year of peak catch, decline since peak catch

Threats to the Environment

Over the past century, rapid population growth and widespread poverty, the concentration of land and power in the hands of wealthy individuals and corporations, corruption, and a lack of government control have contributed to widespread overexploitation of resources. Deforestation proceeds apace, from the rain forests of Guyana to the conifer forests of Chile, with logging, mining, and road-building being the main causes. Soil degradation resulting from deforestation, grazing, and overuse of chemicals affects about 15 percent of the continent. Massive hydroelectric projects threaten vital wetlands and continuing urbanization has exacerbated air and water pollution as well as waste-disposal problems.

Protecting the Environment

Air pollution has been reduced in several cities, most notably Santiago, and Argentina has led the way in setting voluntary greenhouse-gas emission targets. South America's carbon dioxide emissions per capita are now below the world average. Modest reductions in deforestation rates have been recorded in some countries and government incentives for the creation of plantations have stimulated reforestation (although plantations do not fully compensate for the loss of natural forests, which support specialized ecosystems). Approximately 7.4 percent of the continent is now protected and Ecuador and Venezuela have, respectively, the highest and second-highest proportions of protected areas in the world. However, many South American preserves lack the funds and personnel to prevent degradation.

PERCENTAGE OF LAND PROTECTED IN MAJOR SOUTH AMERICAN COUNTRIES

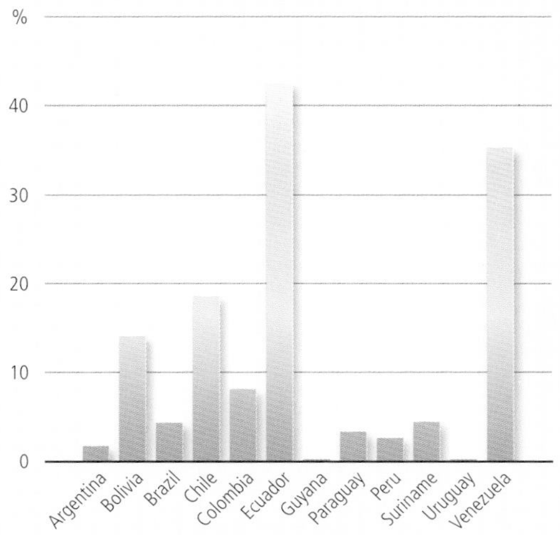

%
40
30
20
10
0
Argentina
Bolivia
Brazil
Chile
Colombia
Ecuador
Guyana
Paraguay
Peru
Suriname
Uruguay
Venezuela

Skillful town planning has made Curitiba in Brazil a model of sustainability. It has dozens of parks, a traffic-free downtown zone, highly efficient public transport, and an effective recycling program.

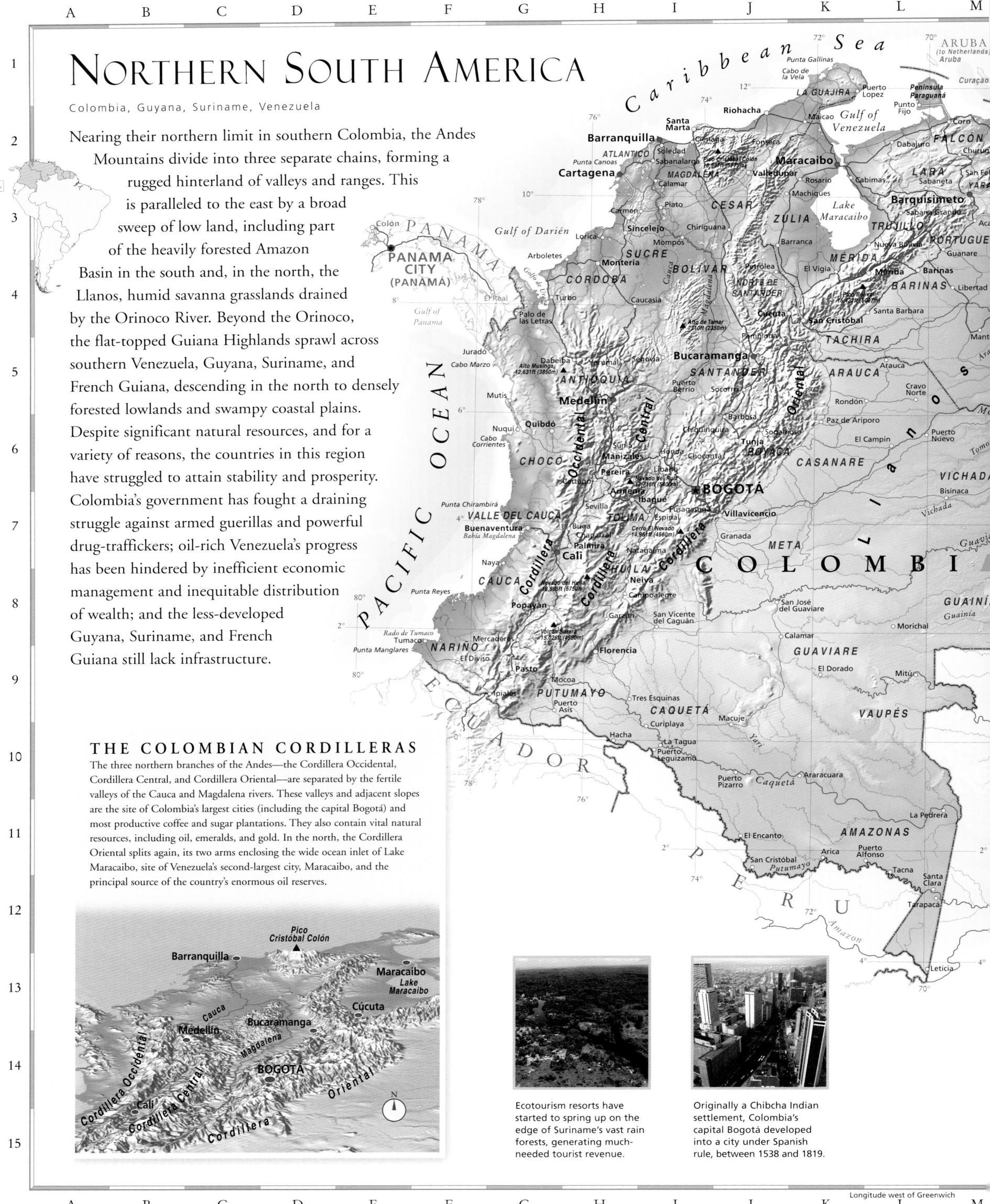

Northern South America

Colombia, Guyana, Suriname, Venezuela

Nearing their northern limit in southern Colombia, the Andes Mountains divide into three separate chains, forming a rugged hinterland of valleys and ranges. This is paralleled to the east by a broad sweep of low land, including part of the heavily forested Amazon Basin in the south and, in the north, the Llanos, humid savanna grasslands drained by the Orinoco River. Beyond the Orinoco, the flat-topped Guiana Highlands sprawl across southern Venezuela, Guyana, Suriname, and French Guiana, descending in the north to densely forested lowlands and swampy coastal plains. Despite significant natural resources, and for a variety of reasons, the countries in this region have struggled to attain stability and prosperity. Colombia's government has fought a draining struggle against armed guerillas and powerful drug-traffickers; oil-rich Venezuela's progress has been hindered by inefficient economic management and inequitable distribution of wealth; and the less-developed Guyana, Suriname, and French Guiana still lack infrastructure.

Caribbean Sea
ARUBA (to Netherlands) Aruba
Curaçao
Punta Gallinas
Cabo de la Vela
LA GUAJIRA
Puerto Lopez
Península Paraguaná
Punto Fijo
Riohacha
Santa Marta
Barranquilla
ATLANTICO
Cartagena
Maicao
Gulf of Venezuela
Maracaibo
Lake Maracaibo
ZULIA
CESAR
MAGDALENA
Valledupar
SUCRE
Sincelejo
Montería
CÓRDOBA
BOLÍVAR
Gulf of Darién
PANAMA
PANAMA CITY (PANAMÁ)
Colón
Gulf of Panama
NORTE DE SANTANDER
Cúcuta
San Cristóbal
TACHIRA
MÉRIDA
Mérida
BARINAS
TRUJILLO
LARA
Barquisimeto
FALCÓN
Bucaramanga
SANTANDER
ANTIOQUIA
Medellín
Quibdó
CHOCÓ
PACIFIC OCEAN
Manizales
Pereira
Armenia
Ibagué
BOGOTÁ
Villavicencio
VALLE DEL CAUCA
Buenaventura
Cali
TOLIMA
HUILA
Neiva
CAUCA
Popayán
NARIÑO
Pasto
PUTUMAYO
Mocoa
CAQUETÁ
Florencia
META
COLOMBIA
Llanos
ARAUCA
Arauca
CASANARE
VICHADA
BOYACÁ
Tunja
GUAVIARE
VAUPÉS
Mitú
GUAINÍA
AMAZONAS
Leticia
ECUADOR
PERU
Amazon
Cordillera Occidental
Cordillera Central
Cordillera Oriental
Pico Cristóbal Colón
Longitude west of Greenwich

The Colombian Cordilleras

The three northern branches of the Andes—the Cordillera Occidental, Cordillera Central, and Cordillera Oriental—are separated by the fertile valleys of the Cauca and Magdalena rivers. These valleys and adjacent slopes are the site of Colombia's largest cities (including the capital Bogotá) and most productive coffee and sugar plantations. They also contain vital natural resources, including oil, emeralds, and gold. In the north, the Cordillera Oriental splits again, its two arms enclosing the wide ocean inlet of Lake Maracaibo, site of Venezuela's second-largest city, Maracaibo, and the principal source of the country's enormous oil reserves.

Pico Cristóbal Colón
Barranquilla
Maracaibo
Lake Maracaibo
Cúcuta
Cauca
Medellín
Bucaramanga
Magdalena
BOGOTÁ
Cordillera Occidental
Cali
Cordillera Central
Cordillera Oriental
N

Ecotourism resorts have started to spring up on the edge of Suriname's vast rain forests, generating much-needed tourist revenue.

Originally a Chibcha Indian settlement, Colombia's capital Bogotá developed into a city under Spanish rule, between 1538 and 1819.

ST GEORGE'S
GRENADA
PORT OF SPAIN
TRINIDAD and TOBAGO
CARACAS
ATLANTIC OCEAN
GEORGETOWN
PARAMARIBO
CAYENNE
VENEZUELA
GUYANA
SURINAME
FRENCH GUIANA (to France)
BRAZIL
Guiana Highlands
Pakaraima Mountains
Tumuc-Humac Mountains
Acarai Mountains
Sierra Parima
Sierra Tapirapecó
Sierra Maigualida
DELTA AMACURO
MONAGAS
ANZOÁTEGUI
GUÁRICO
BOLÍVAR
AMAZONAS
SUCRE
Ciudad Bolívar
Ciudad Guayana
Maturín
Barcelona
Cumaná
Angel Falls
Mt Roraima 9219ft (2810m)
Glendor Mountains
La Gran Sabana
Kourou
St-Laurent-du-Maroni
Boa Vista
Lethem
Linden
New Amsterdam
Nieuw Nickerie

Paramaribo

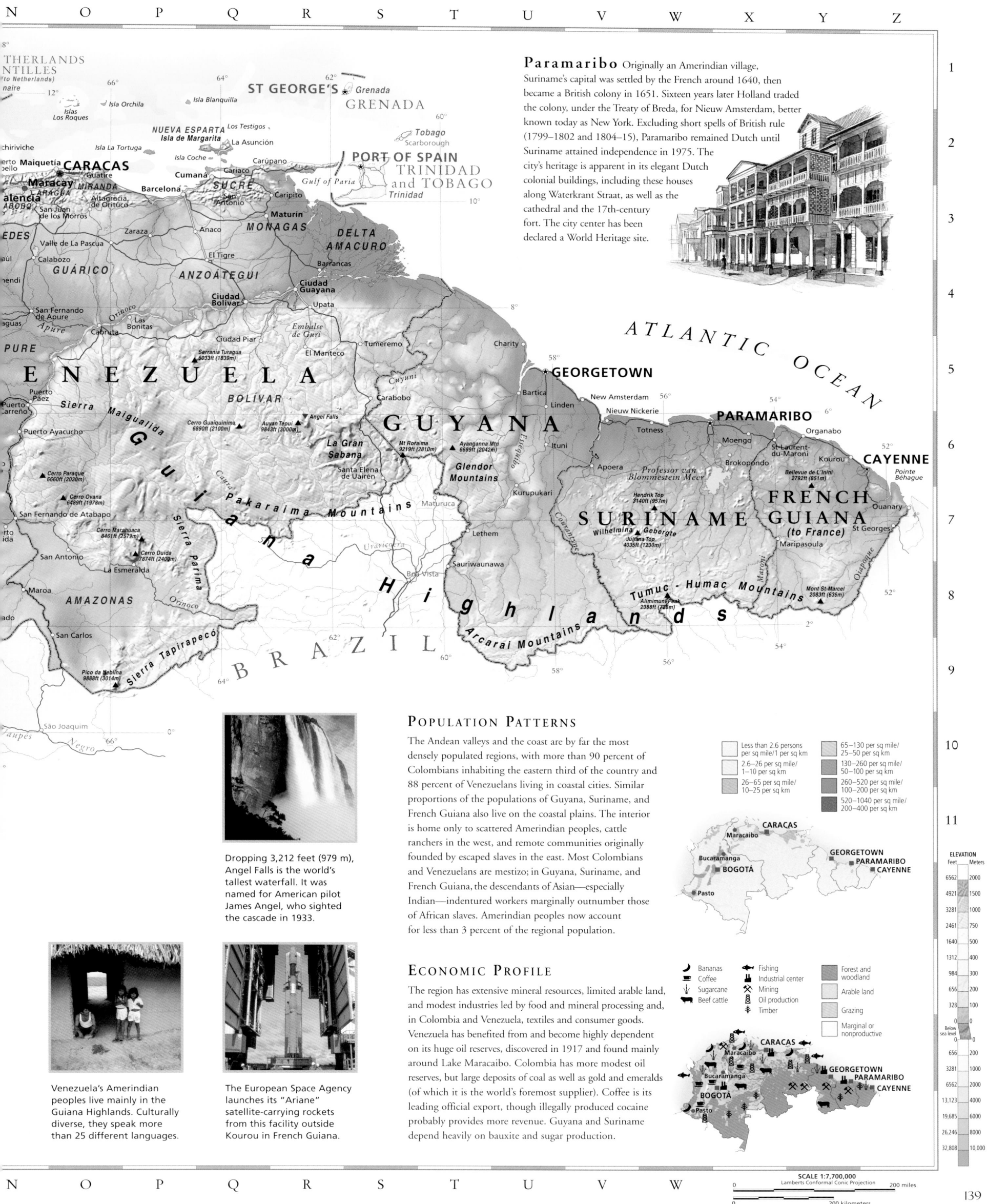

Paramaribo Originally an Amerindian village, Suriname's capital was settled by the French around 1640, then became a British colony in 1651. Sixteen years later Holland traded the colony, under the Treaty of Breda, for Nieuw Amsterdam, better known today as New York. Excluding short spells of British rule (1799–1802 and 1804–15), Paramaribo remained Dutch until Suriname attained independence in 1975. The city's heritage is apparent in its elegant Dutch colonial buildings, including these houses along Waterkrant Straat, as well as the cathedral and the 17th-century fort. The city center has been declared a World Heritage site.

Dropping 3,212 feet (979 m), Angel Falls is the world's tallest waterfall. It was named for American pilot James Angel, who sighted the cascade in 1933.

Population Patterns

The Andean valleys and the coast are by far the most densely populated regions, with more than 90 percent of Colombians inhabiting the eastern third of the country and 88 percent of Venezuelans living in coastal cities. Similar proportions of the populations of Guyana, Suriname, and French Guiana also live on the coastal plains. The interior is home only to scattered Amerindian peoples, cattle ranchers in the west, and remote communities originally founded by escaped slaves in the east. Most Colombians and Venezuelans are mestizo; in Guyana, Suriname, and French Guiana, the descendants of Asian—especially Indian—indentured workers marginally outnumber those of African slaves. Amerindian peoples now account for less than 3 percent of the regional population.

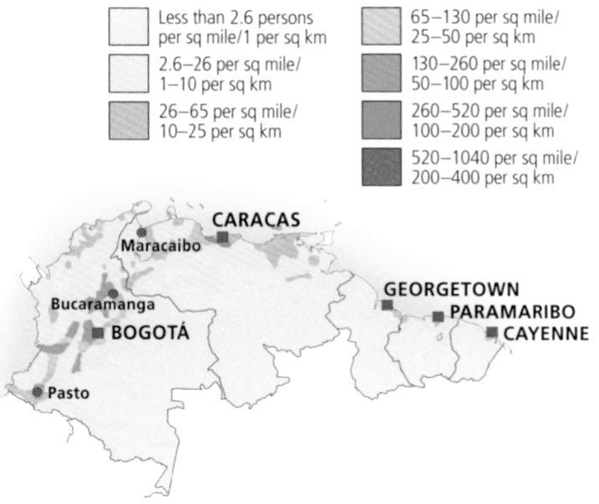
Less than 2.6 persons per sq mile/1 per sq km
2.6–26 per sq mile/ 1–10 per sq km
26–65 per sq mile/ 10–25 per sq km
65–130 per sq mile/ 25–50 per sq km
130–260 per sq mile/ 50–100 per sq km
260–520 per sq mile/ 100–200 per sq km
520–1040 per sq mile/ 200–400 per sq km
CARACAS
Maracaibo
Bucaramanga
BOGOTÁ
Pasto
GEORGETOWN
PARAMARIBO
CAYENNE

Venezuela's Amerindian peoples live mainly in the Guiana Highlands. Culturally diverse, they speak more than 25 different languages.

The European Space Agency launches its "Ariane" satellite-carrying rockets from this facility outside Kourou in French Guiana.

Economic Profile

The region has extensive mineral resources, limited arable land, and modest industries led by food and mineral processing and, in Colombia and Venezuela, textiles and consumer goods. Venezuela has benefited from and become highly dependent on its huge oil reserves, discovered in 1917 and found mainly around Lake Maracaibo. Colombia has more modest oil reserves, but large deposits of coal as well as gold and emeralds (of which it is the world's foremost supplier). Coffee is its leading official export, though illegally produced cocaine probably provides more revenue. Guyana and Suriname depend heavily on bauxite and sugar production.

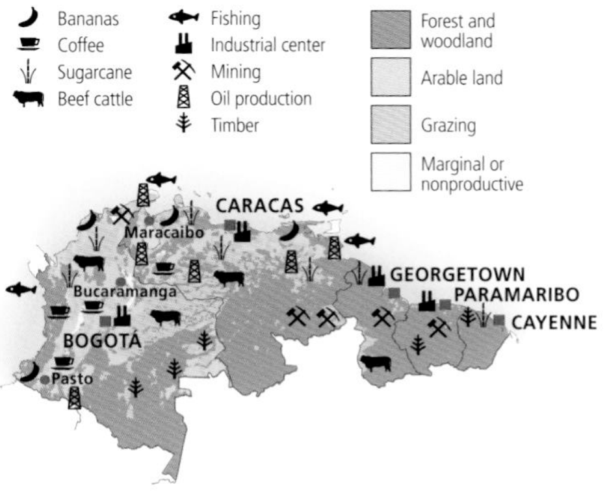
Bananas
Coffee
Sugarcane
Beef cattle
Fishing
Industrial center
Mining
Oil production
Timber
Forest and woodland
Arable land
Grazing
Marginal or nonproductive
CARACAS
Maracaibo
Bucaramanga
BOGOTÁ
Pasto
GEORGETOWN
PARAMARIBO
CAYENNE

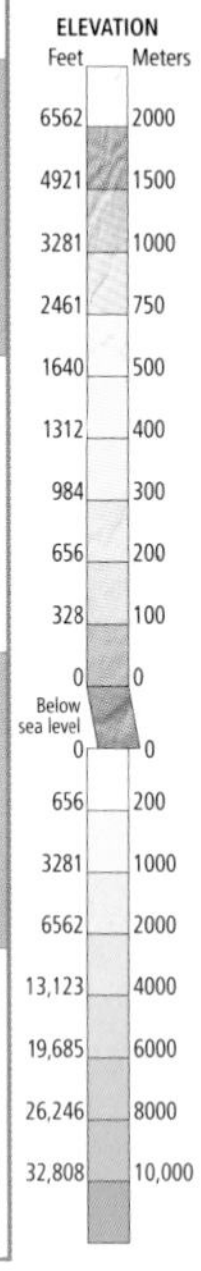
ELEVATION
Feet
Meters
6562 2000
4921 1500
3281 1000
2461 750
1640 500
1312 400
984 300
656 200
328 100
0 0
Below sea level
0 0
656 200
3281 1000
6562 2000
13,123 4000
19,685 6000
26,246 8000
32,808 10,000

SCALE 1:7,700,000
Lamberts Conformal Conic Projection
0 200 miles
0 200 kilometers

WESTERN SOUTH AMERICA Bolivia, Ecuador, Peru

Separated from the Pacific Ocean by a slender coastal plain, the towering peaks of the Andes dominate the entire western side of this region, yielding in the east to well-watered, forest-cloaked lowlands, most of which drain into the vast Amazon Basin. Narrower in the north, the Andes broaden in southern Peru and Bolivia, splitting into two parallel chains, the Cordillera Occidental and the Cordillera Oriental. In the south, these ranges enclose an expansive, arid plateau known as the Altiplano. From around 1200 until shortly after the arrival of the Spanish conquistadors, Cuzco in the northern Altiplano was the capital of the Inca empire, which encompassed virtually the entire Andean sector of this region. Spanish rule left most of the region's wealth and resources in the hands of European-dominated elites. Dissatisfaction with this state of affairs has since fueled indigenous uprisings, labor unrest, Maoist guerilla activity in Peru, and repeated changes of government. In turn, this has hampered economic development, especially in Bolivia, South America's poorest nation.

In the 16th century, the silver-mining center of Potosi in Bolivia was the New World's largest city, with 120,000 inhabitants.

The Galapagos Islands' wildlife includes a host of species unique to the archipelago, including the land iguana.

Quito The world's second-highest capital city after La Paz in Bolivia, Ecuador's capital occupies a narrow valley on the slopes of spectacular Pichincha volcano in the Andes. Little trace remains of the Amerindian and Inca settlements that once stood here, but the city's rich array of buildings from the early period of Spanish settlement in the 16th and 17th centuries, including the elegant Monastery of San Francisco, Ecuador's oldest church, make it the best-preserved capital city in South America.

Less than 2.6 persons per sq mile/1 per sq km
2.6–26 per sq mile/ 1–10 per sq km
26–65 per sq mile/ 10–25 per sq km
65–130 per sq mile/ 25–50 per sq km
130–260 per sq mile/ 50–100 per sq km
QUITO
Guayaquil
Trujillo
LIMA
Arequipa
LA PAZ
Santa Cruz
SUCRE
Galapagos Islands

POPULATION PATTERNS

In Ecuador and Peru, the population is split evenly between coastal and mountain dwellers, with only a minority inhabiting the interior. One-third of Peruvians live in Lima. In Bolivia, the Altiplano is by far the most densely populated region, despite attempts in the late 20th century to encourage people to settle in the east. Relative to other South American nations, all three countries have high proportions of indigenous peoples—25 percent in Ecuador, 45 percent in Peru, and more than 50 percent in Bolivia. They live mainly in the Andean uplands.

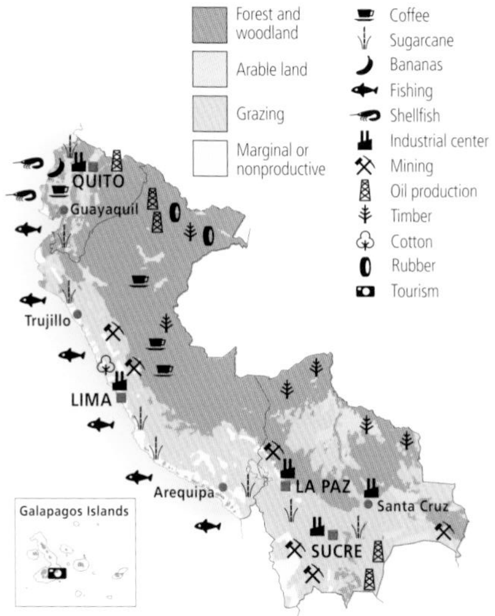
Forest and woodland
Arable land
Grazing
Marginal or nonproductive
Coffee
Sugarcane
Bananas
Fishing
Shellfish
Industrial center
Mining
Oil production
Timber
Cotton
Rubber
Tourism
QUITO
Guayaquil
Trujillo
LIMA
Arequipa
LA PAZ
Santa Cruz
SUCRE
Galapagos Islands

ECONOMIC PROFILE

Subsistence farming involving the cultivation of corn and potatoes and grazing of sheep and llamas takes place in the uplands. On the coast, Ecuador's fertile lowlands yield bananas (of which Ecuador is the world's largest exporter), coffee, and sugar; Peru's irrigated plains produce sugar, cotton, and rice. Peru and Bolivia are the leading producers of coca, the source of cocaine, an illegal but profitable crop. Metals, especially silver, copper, and tin, have long been mainstays of the economy; oil and gas have also become vital. Industries are mainly resource-based and include smelting, oil refining, food processing, and textiles.

ECUADOR
COLOMBIA
BRAZIL
QUITO
Guayaquil
Cuenca
Machala
Portoviejo
Manta
Ambato
Riobamba
Latacunga
Esmeraldas
Tumaco
San Lorenzo
Ibarra
Tulcán
Pasto
Nueva Loja
SUCUMBÍOS
Puerto Francisco de Orellana
NAPO
PICHINCHA
COTOPAXI
Volcán Cotopaxi 19,344ft (5896m)
Cayambe 18,996ft (5790m)
Chimborazo 20,702ft (6310m)
Volcán Sangay 17,159ft (5230m)
TUNGURAHUA
PASTAZA
MORONA-SANTIAGO
Puyo
Tena
Macas
Alausí
Loja
Zamora
Tumbes
Zorritos
Talara
Sullana
Piura
Paita
Sechura
PIURA
Chiclayo
Lambayeque
Cajamarca
CAJAMARCA
AMAZONAS
Chachapoyas
SAN MARTÍN
Moyobamba
Tarapoto
LORETO
Iquitos
Amazon
Napo
Curaray
Tigre
Marañón
Huallaga
Ucayali
Yavari
Caballococha
Pebas
Requena
Nauta
Leticia
Tabatinga
Equator
Gulf of Guayaquil
Andes

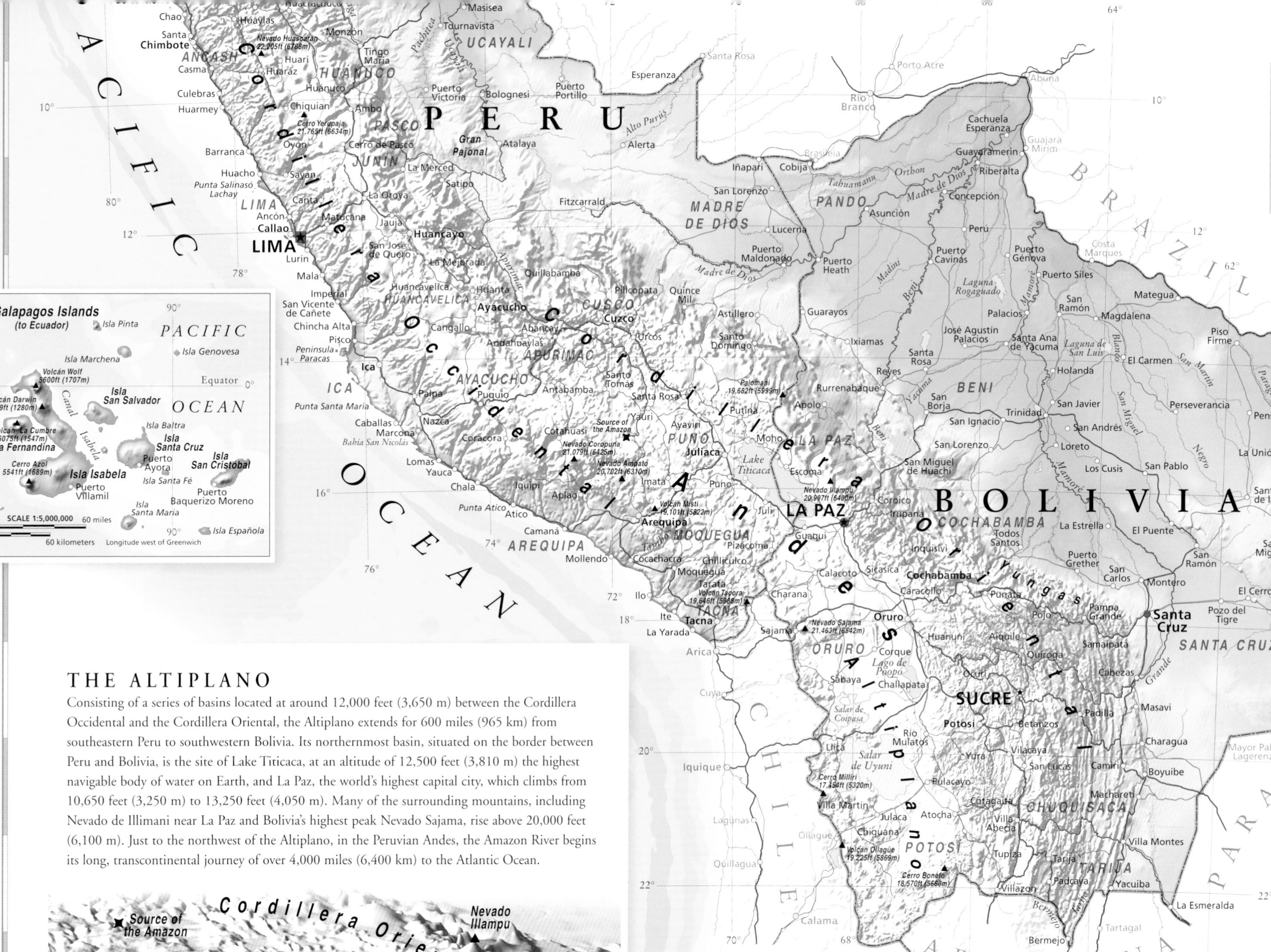
PACIFIC OCEAN
PERU
BOLIVIA
BRAZIL
CHILE
ARGENTINA
PARAGUAY
LIMA
LA PAZ
SUCRE
Cordillera Occidental
Cordillera Oriental
Altiplano
Andes
Lake Titicaca
Arequipa
Cuzco
Cochabamba
Santa Cruz
Oruro
Potosí
Galapagos Islands (to Ecuador)
Longitude west of Greenwich
SCALE 1:8,500,000
Lamberts Conformal Conic Projection
ELEVATION

The mountaintop citadel of Machu Picchu, near Cuzco in southern Peru, was built by the Inca in the mid-15th century.

THE ALTIPLANO

Consisting of a series of basins located at around 12,000 feet (3,650 m) between the Cordillera Occidental and the Cordillera Oriental, the Altiplano extends for 600 miles (965 km) from southeastern Peru to southwestern Bolivia. Its northernmost basin, situated on the border between Peru and Bolivia, is the site of Lake Titicaca, at an altitude of 12,500 feet (3,810 m) the highest navigable body of water on Earth, and La Paz, the world's highest capital city, which climbs from 10,650 feet (3,250 m) to 13,250 feet (4,050 m). Many of the surrounding mountains, including Nevado de Illimani near La Paz and Bolivia's highest peak Nevado Sajama, rise above 20,000 feet (6,100 m). Just to the northwest of the Altiplano, in the Peruvian Andes, the Amazon River begins its long, transcontinental journey of over 4,000 miles (6,400 km) to the Atlantic Ocean.

Cordillera Oriental
Source of the Amazon
Nevado Illampu
Nevado Chachani
Volcán Misti
Arequipa
Juliaca
Puno
Lake Titicaca
Escoma
Juli
Nevado de Illimani
Volcán Tacora
Guaqui
LA PAZ
Charana
Nevado Sajama
Altiplano
Cordillera Occidental
Tacna

La Paz (left) is Bolivia's administrative capital and seat of national government. Sucre is the constitutional capital and home of the supreme court.

The Aymara people are native to the Altiplano. Aymara women wear distinctive derby hats and woollen shawls.

Eastern South America

Brazil, Paraguay

Encompassing more than 2.3 million square miles (6 million sq km) between the Andes and the eastern seaboard, the Amazon Basin is the world's largest drainage system. Cloaked with dense tropical rain forest embroidered by more than 1,000 tributaries, it dominates western and northern Brazil, its great river draining into the Atlantic Ocean near the town of Macapá. To the south rises the extensive plateau region of the Brazilian Highlands, which falls steeply to the coast in the east but descends more gently in the west to the swamps of the Pantanal, the low hills of eastern Paraguay, and the plains of Argentina. Here, the main drainage outlets are the Paraná River, which forms Paraguay's eastern boundary, and its major tributary, the Paraguay, which bisects the nation of the same name, dividing its eastern uplands from its semiarid western plains. Relatively small and landlocked, Paraguay has modest natural resources and a predominantly agricultural economy. In contrast, Brazil is South America's biggest and the world's fifth-largest country, with 5,400 miles (8,700 km) of coastline, the continent's largest population, and immense natural resources.

Population Patterns

Brazil's population is concentrated on the coast, especially around São Paulo and Rio de Janeiro—37 million people inhabit São Paulo state alone. About half of Brazilians are of European origin, 6 percent are of African descent, and 38 percent are of mixed African-European or African-Amerindian descent (so-called mulatos or pardos). Just 0.1 percent are Amerindian. These diverse groups are united by the Portuguese language. In Spanish-speaking Paraguay, 95 percent of the population is mestizo. Many Paraguayans also speak the indigenous Guaraní language. Paraguay is sparsely inhabited, and only 5 percent of the population lives west of the Paraguay River.

Macapá
Manaus
Belém
Fortaleza
Recife
Salvador
BRASÍLIA
Campo Grande
Belo Horizonte
Rio de Janeiro
São Paulo
Curitiba
ASUNCIÓN
Porto Alegre
Less than 2.6 persons per sq mile/1 per sq km
2.6–26 per sq mile/ 1–10 per sq km
26–65 per sq mile/ 10–25 per sq km
65–130 per sq mile/ 25–50 per sq km
130–260 per sq mile/ 50–100 per sq km
260–520 per sq mile/ 100–200 per sq km

Economic Profile

Though hyperinflation, inequitable wealth distribution, and social problems have hampered development, Brazil has enormous economic potential. It is the world's second-largest iron-ore producer and third-biggest bauxite producer and it has the world's second-largest forests. Self-sufficient in food, it is the world's third-biggest meat producer and leading supplier of coffee, sugar, and oranges. Almost 90 percent of its energy comes from hydroelectric power. Industries include the manufacture of automobiles, petrochemicals, steel, shoes and textiles, and wood products. Paraguay generates all of its energy from hydroelectricity. It has a large "informal" or cash economy involving the resale of imported goods, often at street stalls.

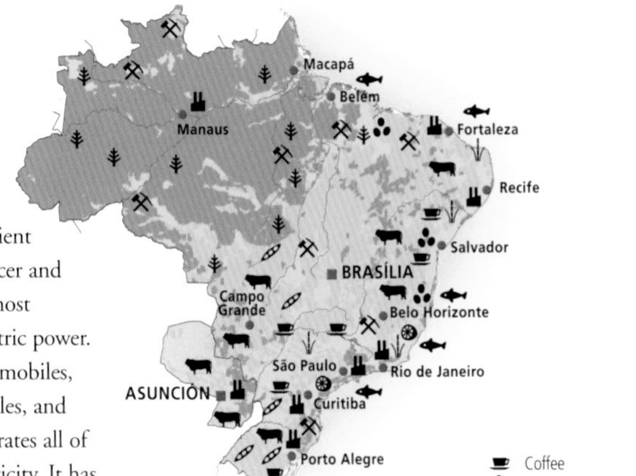

Macapá
Belém
Manaus
Fortaleza
Recife
Salvador
BRASÍLIA
Campo Grande
Belo Horizonte
São Paulo
Rio de Janeiro
ASUNCIÓN
Curitiba
Porto Alegre
Forest and woodland
Arable land
Grazing
Marginal or nonproductive
Coffee
Cocoa
Sugarcane
Soybeans
Beef cattle
Fishing
Industrial center
Mining
Timber
Citrus fruits

VENEZUELA
GUYANA
SURINAME
FRENCH GUIANA (to France)
COLOMBIA
PERU
ATLANTIC OCEAN
BRAZIL
Guiana Highlands
Pakaraima Mountains
Acari Mountains
Tumuc-Humac Mountains
Mt Roraima 9219ft (2810m)
Pico Tamacuari 7677ft (2340m)
Pico da Neblina 9888ft (3014m)
Mitaraka 2264ft (690m)
Planalto de Maracanaquara
Mouths of the Amazon
Ilha de Marajó
Amazon Basin
RORAIMA
AMAPÁ
AMAZONAS
PARÁ
MARANHÃO
PIAUÍ
CEARÁ
RIO GRANDE DO NORTE
PARAÍBA
PERNAMBUCO
ACRE
Serra do Cachimbo
Serra da Ibiapaba
Boa Vista
Macapá
Belém
Manaus
Santarém
São Luís
Fortaleza
Teresina
Natal
João Pessoa
Recife
Porto Velho
Equator

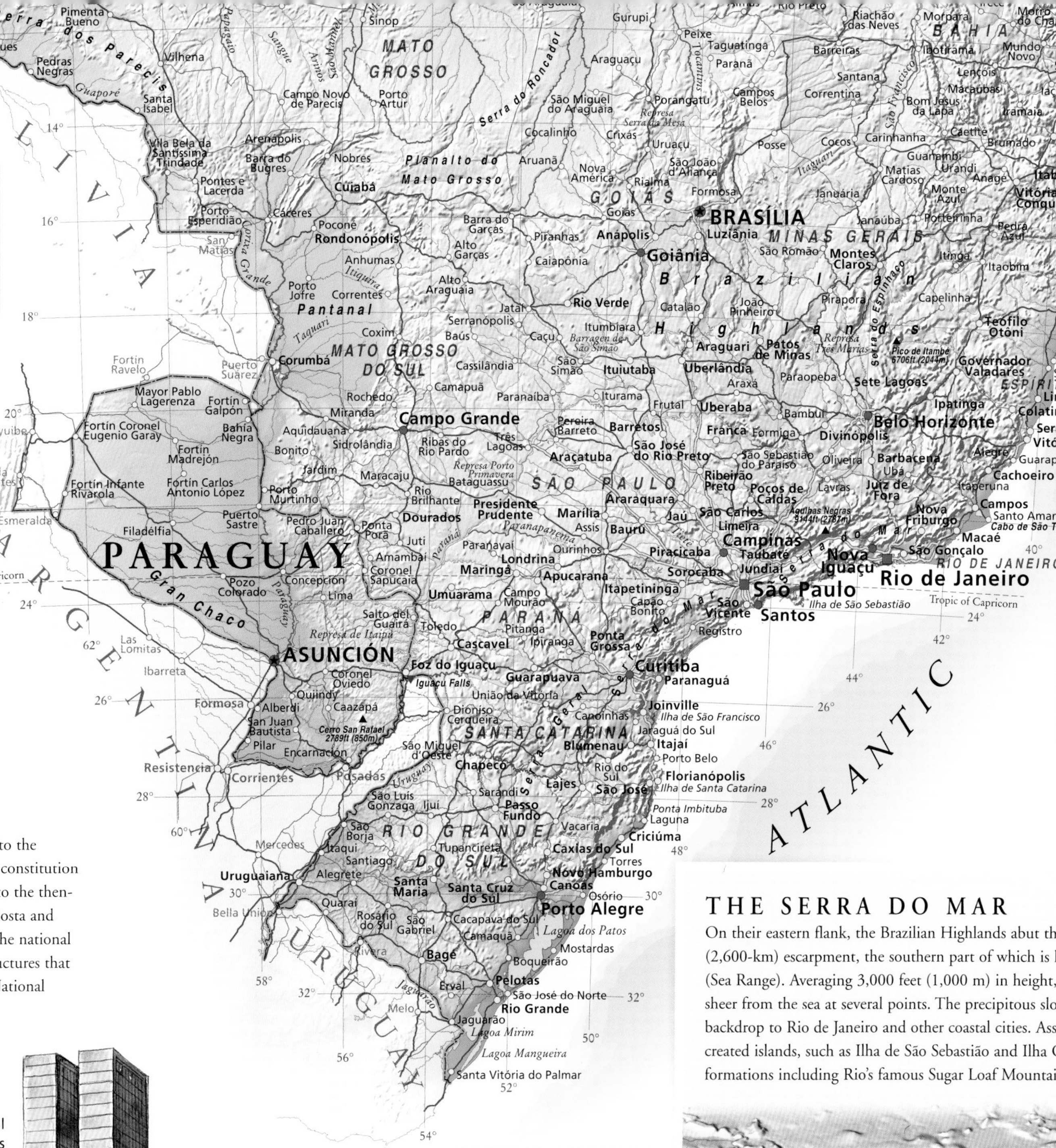
PARAGUAY
ASUNCIÓN
BRASÍLIA
BOLIVIA
ARGENTINA
URUGUAY
PERU
ATLANTIC
OCEAN
MATO GROSSO
MATO GROSSO DO SUL
GOIÁS
MINAS GERAIS
BAHIA
SÃO PAULO
PARANÁ
SANTA CATARINA
RIO GRANDE DO SUL
RIO DE JANEIRO
ESPÍRITO SANTO
Brazilian Highlands
Pantanal
Gran Chaco
Planalto do Mato Grosso
Serra do Espinhaço
Serra do Mar
Serra Geral
Serra do Roncador
Serra dos Parecis
Salvador
Rio de Janeiro
São Paulo
Belo Horizonte
Goiânia
Campo Grande
Curitiba
Porto Alegre
Santos
Campinas
Nova Iguaçu
Florianópolis
Cuiabá
Corumbá
Foz do Iguaçu
Iguaçu Falls
Tropic of Capricorn
Longitude west of Greenwich

Brazil's Iguaçu Falls stand 269 feet (82 m) high and span 1.7 miles (2.7 km)—three times the width of the U.S.A.'s Niagara Falls.

Toucans abound in the rain forests of the Amazon Basin, 4 square miles (10 sq km) of which may harbor more than 400 bird species.

The Pantanal in western Brazil is the world's largest freshwater wetland, covering approximately 40,000 square miles (100,000 sq km).

Founded by Portuguese settlers in 1565, Rio de Janeiro was the capital of Brazil from 1822 until 1960.

Brasília A proposal for a new capital city was first presented to the Brazilian government in 1823 and subsequently incorporated in the constitution of 1891. The site was selected in 1956, partly to entice new settlers to the then-sparsely populated interior. Designed by Brazilian architects Lucio Costa and Oscar Niemeyer in a monumental modernist style, Brasília became the national capital in 1960 and now has over 2 million inhabitants. Notable structures that helped it gain World Heritage status include its Cathedral and the National Congress—both designed by Niemeyer.

Cathedral

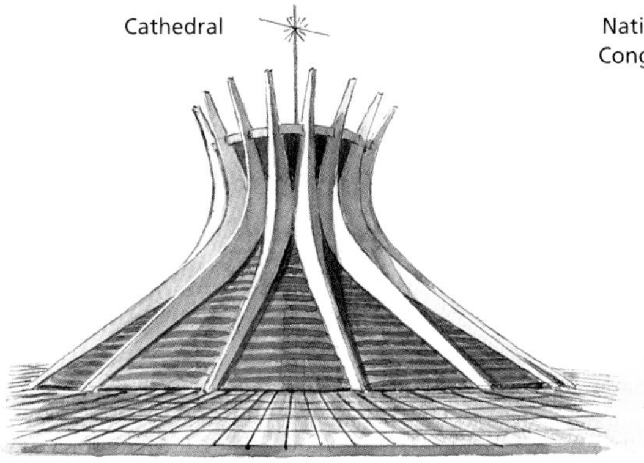

National Congress

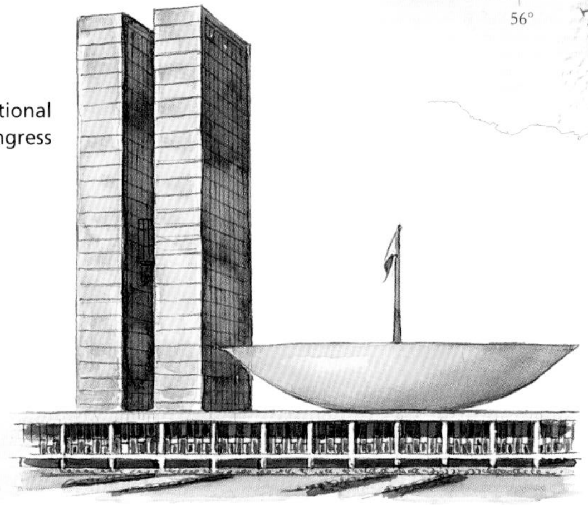

Western Paraguay is home to about 10,000 German-speaking Mennonites, whose forebears arrived in the 1920s from Eastern Europe.

THE SERRA DO MAR

On their eastern flank, the Brazilian Highlands abut the coast along a 1,600-mile (2,600-km) escarpment, the southern part of which is known as the Serra do Mar (Sea Range). Averaging 3,000 feet (1,000 m) in height, this range rises almost sheer from the sea at several points. The precipitous slopes provide a mountainous backdrop to Rio de Janeiro and other coastal cities. Associated outcrops have created islands, such as Ilha de São Sebastião and Ilha Grande, and other coastal formations including Rio's famous Sugar Loaf Mountain.

Represa de Furnas
Serra da Mantiqueira
Paraíba do Sul
Volta Redonda
Serra do Mar
Nova Iguaçu
Rio de Janeiro
São Paulo
Serra do Mar
Ilha Grande
Baía da Ilha Grande
Sugar Loaf Mountain
Cabo Frio
Ubatuba
Ilha de São Sebastião
Santos
N

ELEVATION

Feet	Meters
6562	2000
4921	1500
3281	1000
2461	750
1640	500
1312	400
984	300
656	200
328	100
0	0
Below sea level 0	0
656	200
3281	1000
6562	2000
13,123	4000
19,685	6000
26,246	8000
32,808	10,000

SCALE 1:14,000,000
Lamberts Conformal Conic Projection
0 — 400 miles
0 — 400 kilometers

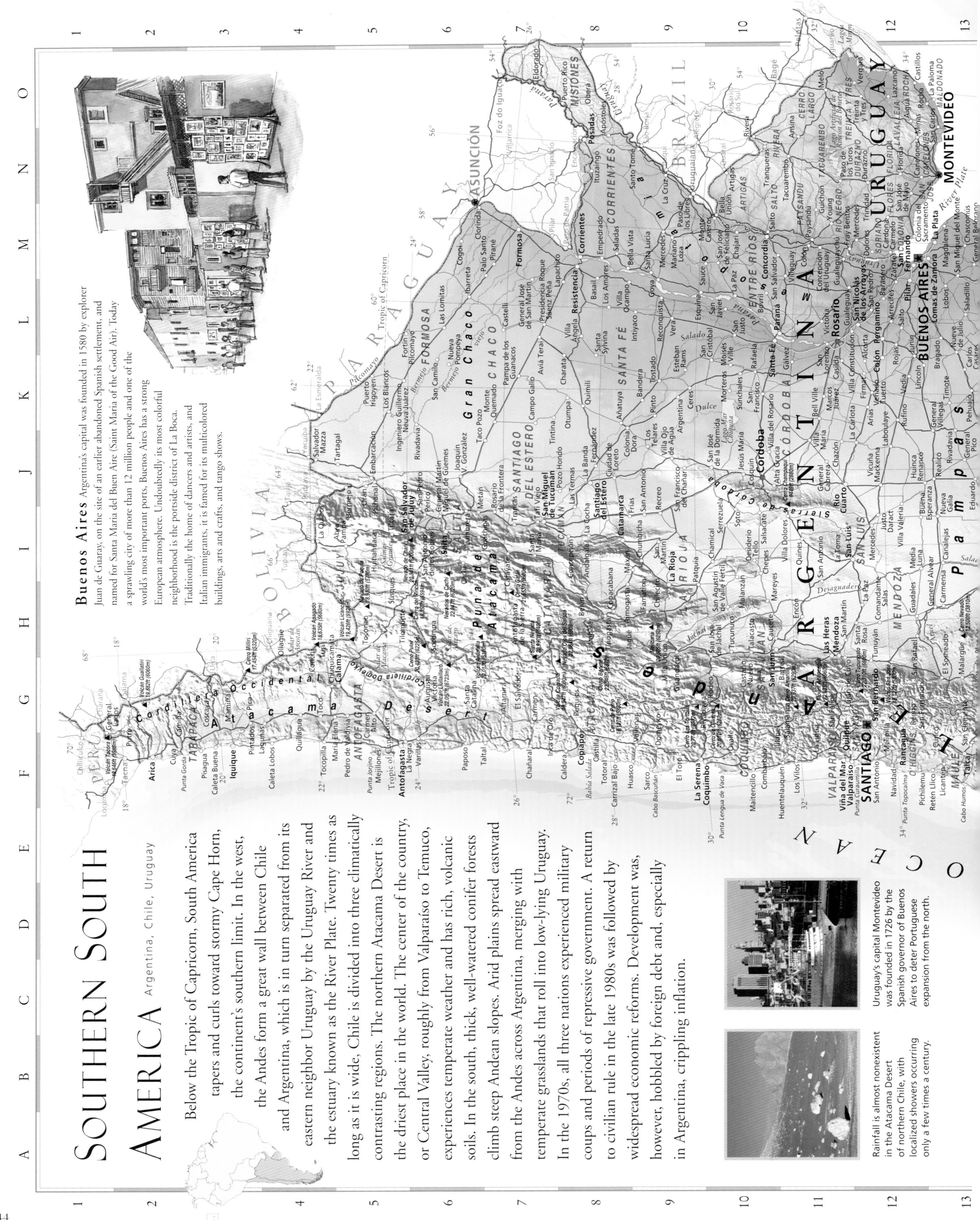

Southern South America

Argentina, Chile, Uruguay

Below the Tropic of Capricorn, South America tapers and curls toward stormy Cape Horn, the continent's southern limit. In the west, the Andes form a great wall between Chile and Argentina, which is in turn separated from its eastern neighbor Uruguay by the Uruguay River and the estuary known as the River Plate. Twenty times as long as it is wide, Chile is divided into three climatically contrasting regions. The northern Atacama Desert is the driest place in the world. The center of the country, or Central Valley, roughly from Valparaíso to Temuco, experiences temperate weather and has rich, volcanic soils. In the south, thick, well-watered conifer forests climb steep Andean slopes. Arid plains spread eastward from the Andes across Argentina, merging with temperate grasslands that roll into low-lying Uruguay. In the 1970s, all three nations experienced military coups and periods of repressive government. A return to civilian rule in the late 1980s was followed by widespread economic reforms. Development was, however, hobbled by foreign debt and, especially in Argentina, crippling inflation.

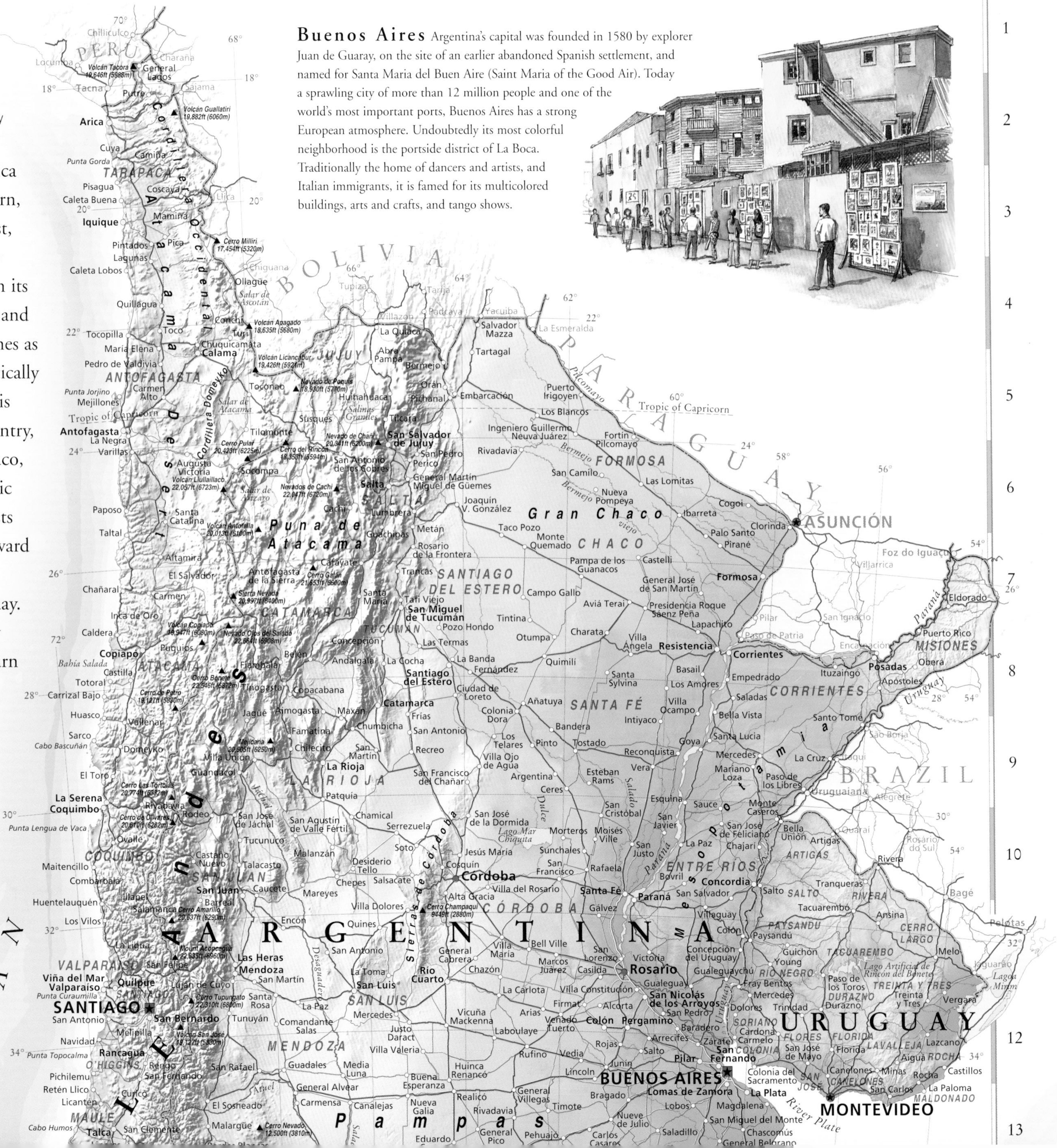
PERU
BOLIVIA
PARAGUAY
BRAZIL
ARGENTINA
URUGUAY
ASUNCIÓN
BUENOS AIRES
MONTEVIDEO
SANTIAGO
Gran Chaco
Puna de Atacama
Atacama Desert
Andes
Pampas
Tropic of Capricorn
River Plate
OCEAN

Buenos Aires Argentina's capital was founded in 1580 by explorer Juan de Guaray, on the site of an earlier abandoned Spanish settlement, and named for Santa Maria del Buen Aire (Saint Maria of the Good Air). Today a sprawling city of more than 12 million people and one of the world's most important ports, Buenos Aires has a strong European atmosphere. Undoubtedly its most colorful neighborhood is the portside district of La Boca. Traditionally the home of dancers and artists, and Italian immigrants, it is famed for its multicolored buildings, arts and crafts, and tango shows.

Rainfall is almost nonexistent in the Atacama Desert of northern Chile, with localized showers occurring only a few times a century.

Uruguay's capital Montevideo was founded in 1726 by the Spanish governor of Buenos Aires to deter Portuguese expansion from the north.

Population Patterns

Almost 90 percent of the region's inhabitants live in cities, mainly in the central temperate belt. Chileans cluster around Santiago, a third of Argentines live in greater Buenos Aires, and half of all Uruguayans inhabit Montevideo. Settlements are sparse on Andean peaks, and in the cold, wet southwest. Chile's population is predominantly mestizo, with a small residual population of mainly Mapuche Indians. Argentina and Uruguay have more varied cultures, influenced by the large numbers of Spanish, Italian, and German immigrants who arrived after 1870. Indigenous groups still inhabit remote parts of Argentina but have almost vanished from Uruguay.

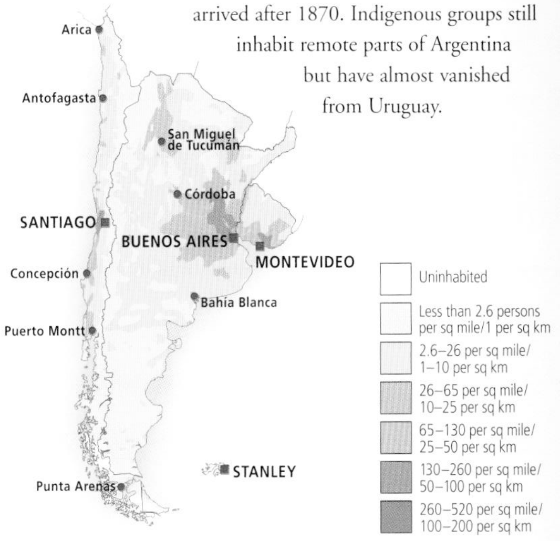

Arica
Antofagasta
San Miguel de Tucumán
Córdoba
SANTIAGO
BUENOS AIRES
MONTEVIDEO
Concepción
Bahía Blanca
Puerto Montt
STANLEY
Punta Arenas
Uninhabited
Less than 2.6 persons per sq mile/1 per sq km
2.6–26 per sq mile/ 1–10 per sq km
26–65 per sq mile/ 10–25 per sq km
65–130 per sq mile/ 25–50 per sq km
130–260 per sq mile/ 50–100 per sq km
260–520 per sq mile/ 100–200 per sq km

Economic Profile

All three countries are strong exporters of primary goods. Chile is the world's leading supplier of copper and in the top five fish producers. Its forests provide abundant timber and the Central Valley yields large quantities of wheat, rice, fruit, and vegetables. Beef and wool from livestock grazed on the Pampas are the traditional mainstays of the Argentine and Uruguayan economies. Uruguay has few mineral resources, but Argentina has sizable oil reserves. Chile and Argentina have thriving wine industries, and Argentina is now the world's fifth-largest producer. All three capital cities are important commercial centers. Leading industries include food processing, chemicals, and textiles.

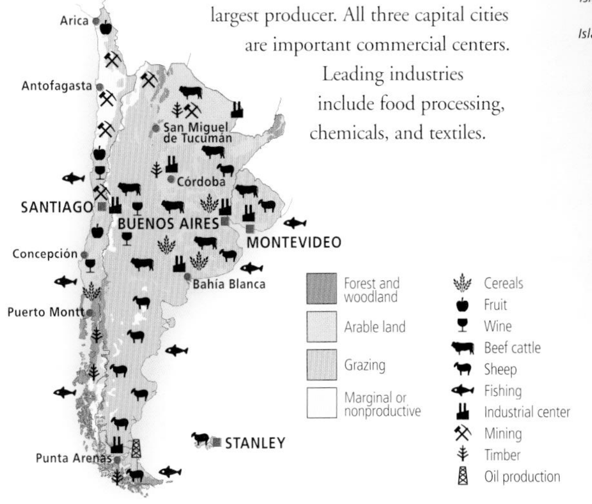

Arica
Antofagasta
San Miguel de Tucumán
Córdoba
SANTIAGO
BUENOS AIRES
MONTEVIDEO
Concepción
Bahía Blanca
Puerto Montt
STANLEY
Punta Arenas
Forest and woodland
Arable land
Grazing
Marginal or nonproductive
Cereals
Fruit
Wine
Beef cattle
Sheep
Fishing
Industrial center
Mining
Timber
Oil production

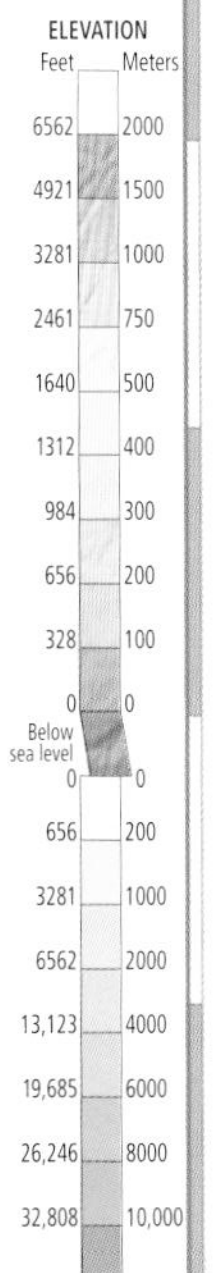

ELEVATION
Feet
Meters
6562 2000
4921 1500
3281 1000
2461 750
1640 500
1312 400
984 300
656 200
328 100
0 0
Below sea level
0 0
656 200
3281 1000
6562 2000
13,123 4000
19,685 6000
26,246 8000
32,808 10,000

PACIFIC
ATLANTIC
OCEAN
Concepción
Los Angeles
Temuco
ARAUCANÍA
NEUQUÉN
Neuquén
General Roca
RÍO NEGRO
Valdivia
Osorno
LOS LAGOS
Puerto Montt
Isla de Chiloé
Archipiélago de los Chonos
Península de Taitao
Golfo de Penas
CHUBUT
Patagonia
Gran Altiplanicie Central
SANTA CRUZ
MAGALLANES
AISÉN
Comodoro Rivadavia
Golfo de San Jorge
Golfo San Matías
Península Valdés
Puerto Madryn
Trelew
Rawson
Viedma
Bahía Blanca
Mar del Plata
Cabo Corrientes
Río Gallegos
Bahía Grande
Puerto Santa Cruz
Archipiélago de la Reina Adelaida
Isla Desolación
Punta Arenas
Isla Grande de Tierra del Fuego
TIERRA DEL FUEGO
Ushuaia
Isla de los Estados
Cape Horn
Drake Passage
Islas Diego Ramírez
FALKLAND ISLANDS (to U.K.)
West Falkland
East Falkland
STANLEY
Longitude west of Greenwich
SCALE 1:9,000,000
Lamberts Conformal Conic Projection
0 300 miles
0 300 kilometers

The Moreno Glacier forms a 200-foot (60-m) wall of ice across an arm of Lago Argentino in the foothills of the Argentine Andes.

Southern Patagonia

On the southern Chile–Argentina border, extensive icefields crown Andean peaks such as Cerro Murallón and Cerro Fitz Roy. Glaciers snake down from these summits, plowing through expansive conifer forests. In the west, they reach the ragged, island-studded coast. In the east, they fall to lakes such as Argentino—site of the huge Moreno Glacier—and Viedma, and fuel mountain streams that drain across the barren Patagonian plateau and feed in turn into major rivers such as the Chico and Gallegos.

Cerro Fitz Roy
Lago San Martín
Lago Cardiel
Isla Wellington
Cerro Murallón
Lago Viedma
Chico
Chalía
Lago Argentino
Calafate
Isla Madre de Dios
Cerro Paine
Santa Cruz
Bahía Grande
Isla Hanover
Lago del Toro
Coig
Isla Jorge Montt
Puerto Natáles
Gallegos
Río Gallegos
Isla Vidal
Isla Desolación
Punta Arenas
Strait of Magellan
Tierra del Fuego
Isla Santa Inés

Argentina has long claimed ownership of the British-ruled Falkland Islands. An Argentine invasion in 1982 led to defeat in a brief war with the U.K.

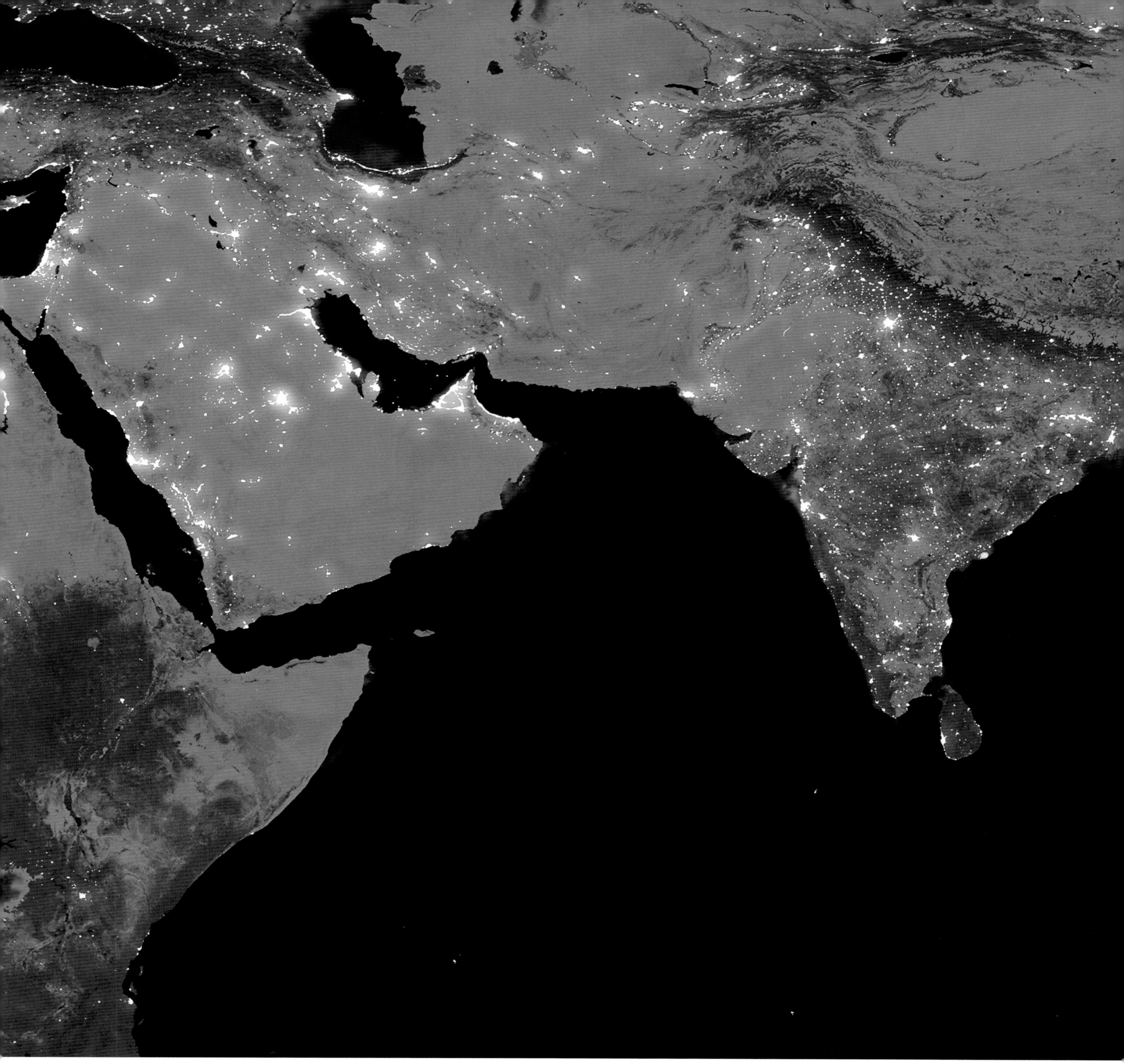

The intensity of light from Japan reflects that nation's high population density and considerable urbanization. The Indian subcontinent and eastern China stand out at night. The Himalayan mountains and the Gobi Desert remain mostly dark.

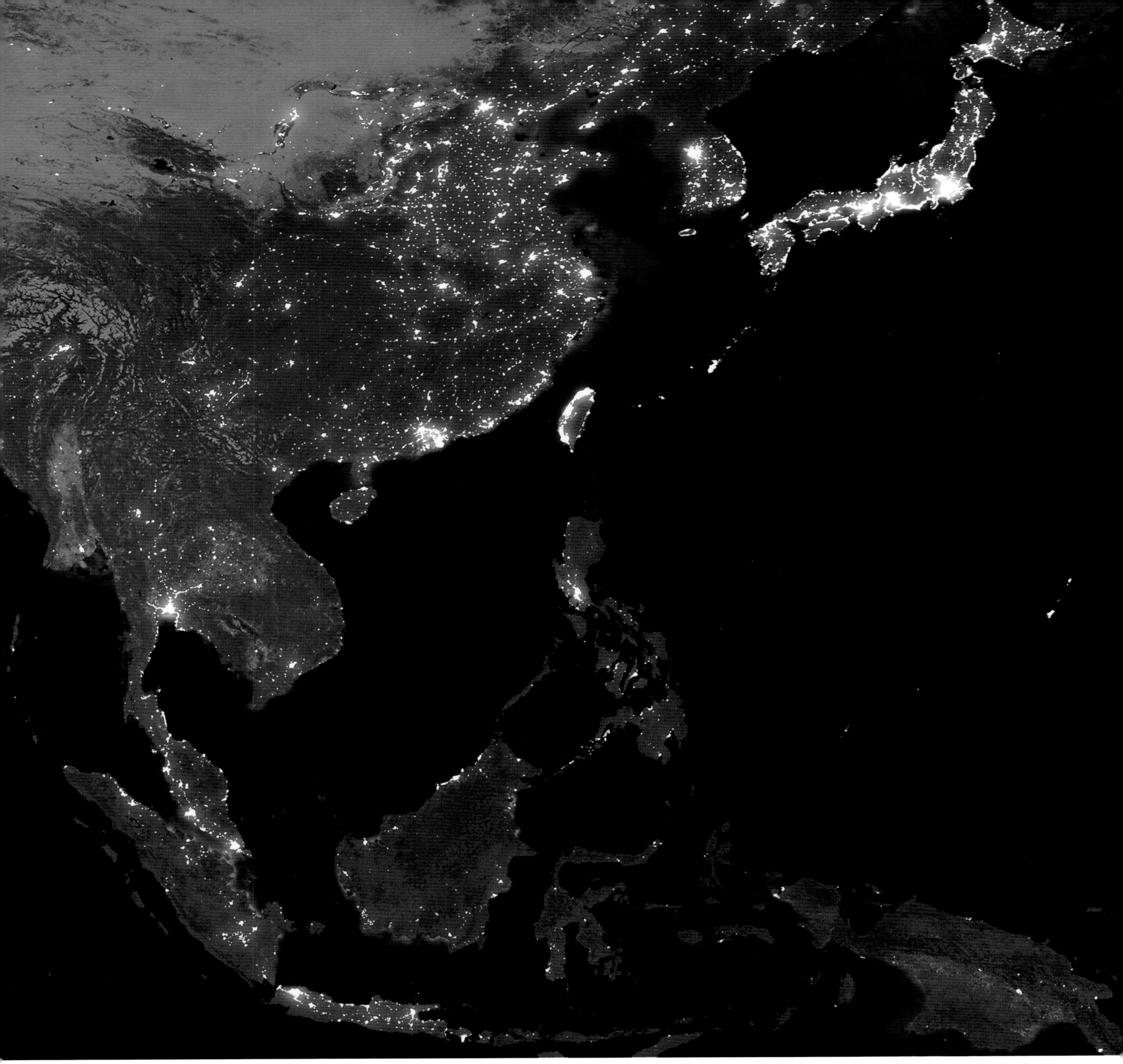

ASIA

The View from Above

Asia's eastern and southern fringes lie near the edge of a mighty tectonic plate called the Eurasian plate. It is one of the constantly shifting pieces of Earth's crust that make up the surface of the planet. The collision zone where the Eurasian plate converges with other plates is marked by the upthrust of massive mountain ranges such as the Himalayas, recurring earthquakes, and numerous active volcanoes, including the chain that runs from Sumatra through Java and north to Japan. Satellites have captured dramatic images of both current activity and the results of past upheavals. Also visible is evidence of climate change. Radar images of China's Taklimakan Desert reveal ancient alluvial fans laid down in wetter times, and changed landforms caused by the Kunlun Shan on the edge of the desert being pushed north by the continuing collision of the Eurasian plate with the Indian plate.

Right: This false-color image shows part of the volcanic chain that crosses the Indonesian island of Java. Old lava flows appear in shades of yellow and green on Gunung Merbabu, center, and Gunung Merapi, lower right. In November 1994, six weeks after this image was collected, Gunung Merapi erupted, killing more than 60 people.

Below: The veined patterns in the center of this radar image of China's Taklimakan Desert are gravel deposits that accumulated at the base of the Kunlun Shan when the climate was wetter. They mark ancient alluvial fans. The large lavender triangles are the modern fans. Yellow areas on the modern fans are vegetated oases.

Left: This false-color view of the Turkish city of Istanbul displays urban areas as blue-green and vegetation as red. The busy shipping channel of the Bosporus divides the city and links the Black Sea in the north with the Sea of Marmara in the south. This image also indicates water temperature, with colder waters shown in deeper shades of blue.

Below: This radar image of a desert area in northern Oman, on the Arabian Peninsula, was collected by the space shuttle Endeavour in 1994. The bright arcs are limestone, formed on the bed of a shallow sea, and worn away into hills after sea levels dropped. The branching patterns are ancient drainage channels cut in wetter times.

Land and Environment

Asia covers 17.4 million square miles (45 million sq km), one-third of the world's landmass. The mainland is separated from Europe by Russia's Ural and Caucasus mountains and the narrow straits of the Bosporus in Turkey, from Africa by the Red Sea and Suez Canal, and from North America by the Bering Strait. Its center is dominated by an immense plateau region ringed by high mountain ranges. The northern ranges ripple across eastern Siberia to the Bering Sea. To the west, the uplands stretch through Afghanistan, Iran, and Turkey, dividing the arid Arabian Peninsula from the plains bordering the Caspian sea. The southern peaks are crowned by the world's highest mountain chain, the Himalaya, which falls steeply to the Gangetic Plain of the Indian Subcontinent but slopes more gently toward the Indochina Peninsula. Islands and archipelagoes fringe Asia's south and east coasts, including Sri Lanka, Japan, and the sprawling Malay Archipelago.

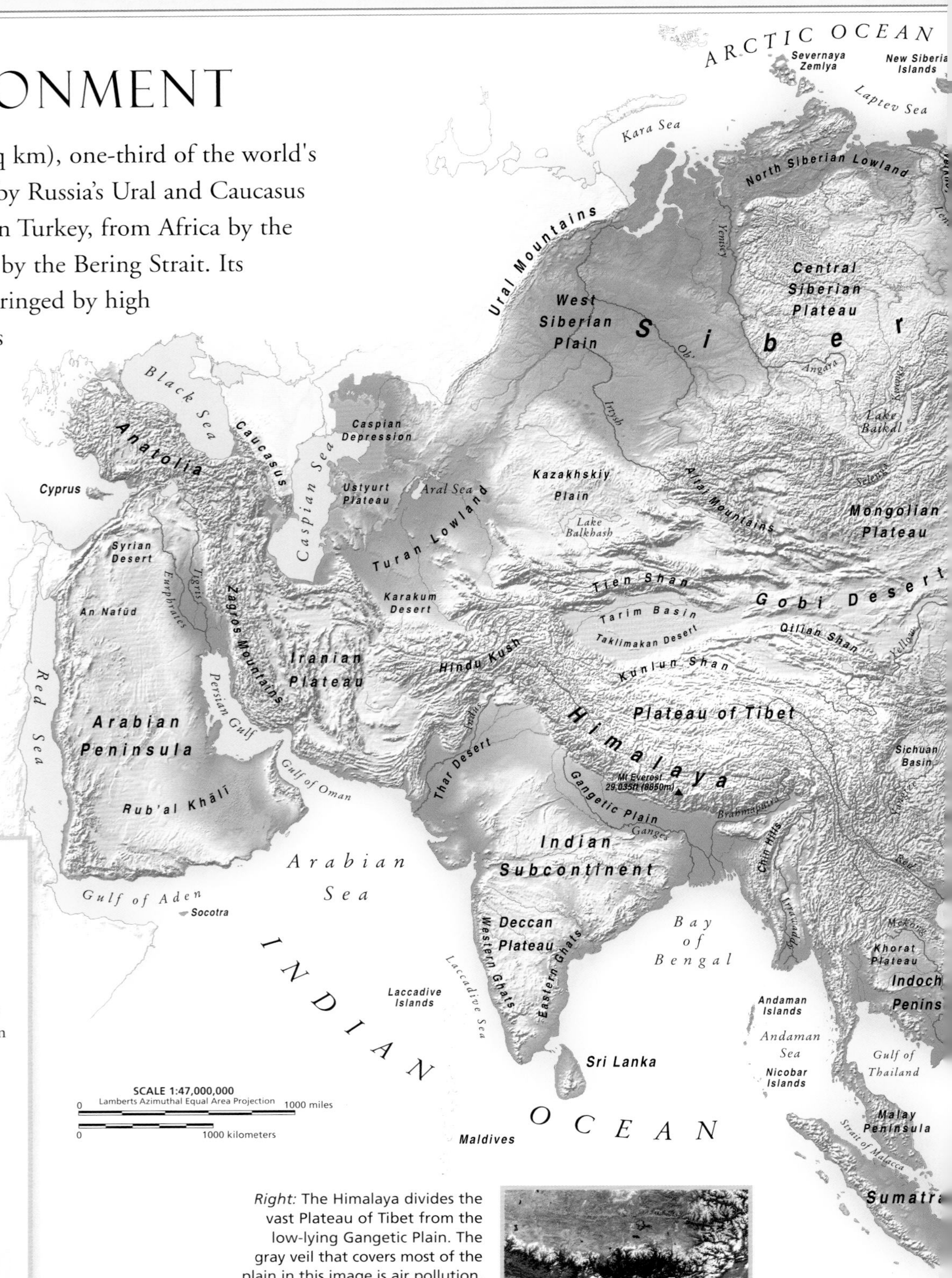

ARCTIC OCEAN
Severnaya Zemlya
New Siberian Islands
Laptev Sea
Kara Sea
North Siberian Lowland
Ural Mountains
Yenisey
West Siberian Plain
Central Siberian Plateau
S i b e r
Ob'
Angara
Lake Baikal
Black Sea
Anatolia
Caucasus
Caspian Depression
Caspian Sea
Cyprus
Ustyurt Plateau
Aral Sea
Kazakhskiy Plain
Irtysh
Altai Mountains
Mongolian Plateau
Lake Balkhash
Turan Lowland
Syrian Desert
Euphrates
Tigris
Zagros Mountains
Karakum Desert
Tien Shan
Tarim Basin
Gobi Desert
An Nafūd
Taklimakan Desert
Qilian Shan
Iranian Plateau
Hindu Kush
Kunlun Shan
Red Sea
Persian Gulf
Plateau of Tibet
Arabian Peninsula
Indus
Thar Desert
Himalaya
Mt Everest 29,035ft (8850m)
Sichuan Basin
Gulf of Oman
Gangetic Plain
Ganges
Brahmaputra
Rub' al Khālī
Arabian Sea
Indian Subcontinent
Chin Hills
Gulf of Aden
Socotra
Deccan Plateau
Western Ghats
Eastern Ghats
Bay of Bengal
Mekong
Khorat Plateau
Indochina Peninsula
INDIAN OCEAN
Laccadive Islands
Laccadive Sea
Andaman Islands
Andaman Sea
Nicobar Islands
Gulf of Thailand
Sri Lanka
Maldives
Malay Peninsula
Strait of Malacca
Sumatra
SCALE 1:47,000,000
Lamberts Azimuthal Equal Area Projection
0 1000 miles
0 1000 kilometers

Right: The Himalaya divides the vast Plateau of Tibet from the low-lying Gangetic Plain. The gray veil that covers most of the plain in this image is air pollution.

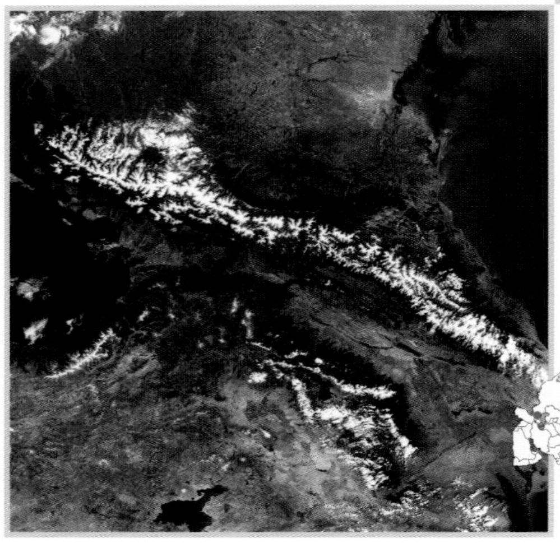

Left: Snow cover highlights the Caucasus Mountains, which divide the Russian Federation from Asia, and the associated Lesser Caucasus, which form the southern boundary of the region known as Transcaucasia.

Natural Hazards

Hurricanes

Known in the western Pacific as typhoons (from the Cantonese *tai-fung*, meaning "great wind") and around the Indian Ocean as tropical cyclones, hurricanes regularly bring devastation to many parts of southern and eastern Asia. They occur when a large cluster of thunderstorms forms over open ocean and begins to spin as a result of Earth's rotation—something that occurs only if the storm system is more than five degrees from the Equator. Once the system starts spinning, it may intensify and grow. It qualifies as a hurricane when its wind speeds reach 74 mph (119 km/h), and it can generate wind gusts of up to 190 mph (305 km/h). One of its most destructive side-effects is a storm surge, a huge wave that can swamp low-lying areas.

HURRICANE DISTRIBUTION

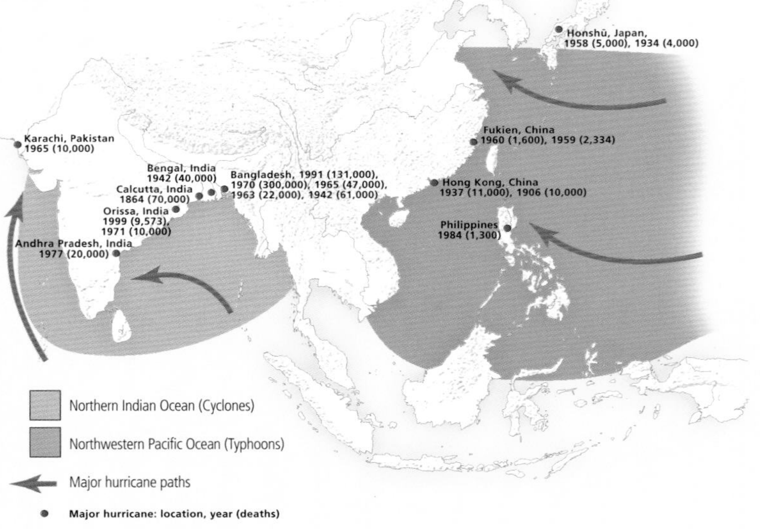

Honshū, Japan, 1958 (5,000), 1934 (4,000)
Karachi, Pakistan 1965 (10,000)
Fukien, China 1960 (1,600), 1959 (2,334)
Bengal, India 1942 (40,000)
Bangladesh, 1991 (131,000), 1970 (300,000), 1965 (47,000), 1963 (22,000), 1942 (61,000)
Calcutta, India 1864 (70,000)
Hong Kong, China 1937 (11,000), 1906 (10,000)
Orissa, India 1999 (9,573), 1971 (10,000)
Philippines 1984 (1,300)
Andhra Pradesh, India 1977 (20,000)
Northern Indian Ocean (Cyclones)
Northwestern Pacific Ocean (Typhoons)
Major hurricane paths
Major hurricane: location, year (deaths)

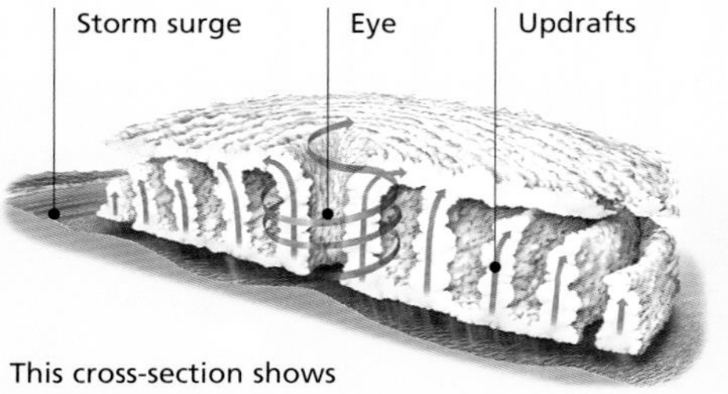

Storm surge
Eye
Updrafts

This cross-section shows how bands of cloud spiral around the eye of the hurricane.

In 1999, floods generated by a cyclone inundated Orissa, India. Over 9,000 people died following the storm.

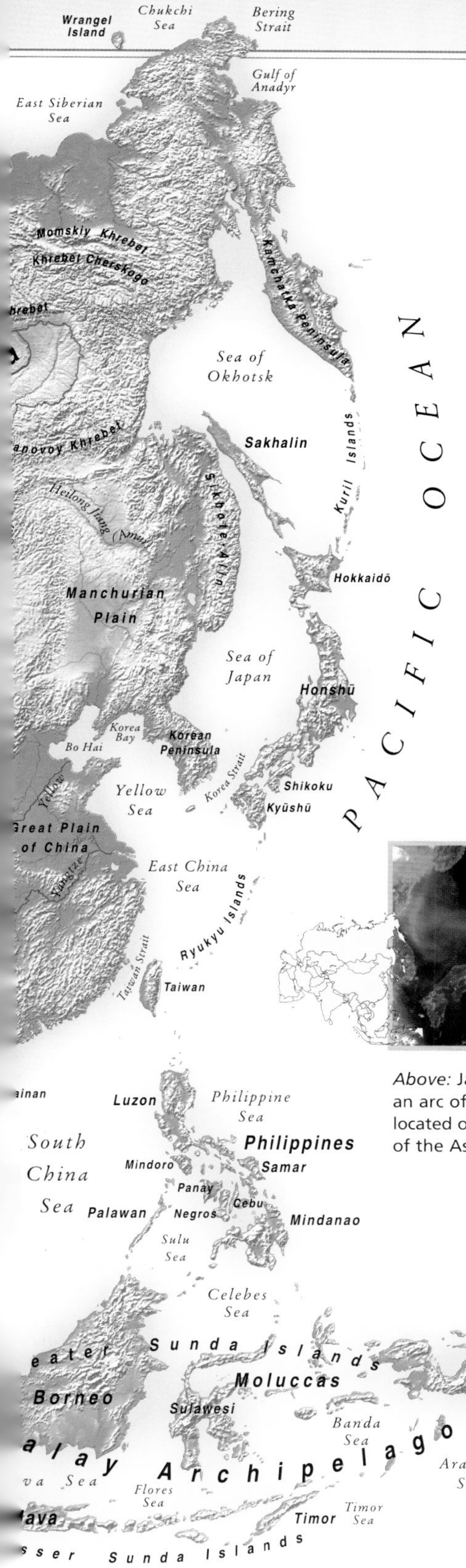

Wrangel Island
Chukchi Sea
Bering Strait
Gulf of Anadyr
East Siberian Sea
Sea of Okhotsk
Sakhalin
Kuril Islands
Kamchatka Peninsula
PACIFIC OCEAN
Hokkaidō
Manchurian Plain
Sea of Japan
Honshū
Korea Bay
Korean Peninsula
Bo Hai
Yellow Sea
Korea Strait
Shikoku
Kyūshū
East China Sea
Ryukyu Islands
Taiwan Strait
Taiwan
Luzon
Philippine Sea
Philippines
South China Sea
Mindoro
Samar
Panay
Cebu
Palawan
Negros
Mindanao
Sulu Sea
Celebes Sea
Sunda Islands
Moluccas
New Guinea
Borneo
Sulawesi
Banda Sea
Malay Archipelago
Arafura Sea
Flores Sea
Timor Sea
Timor
Sunda Islands

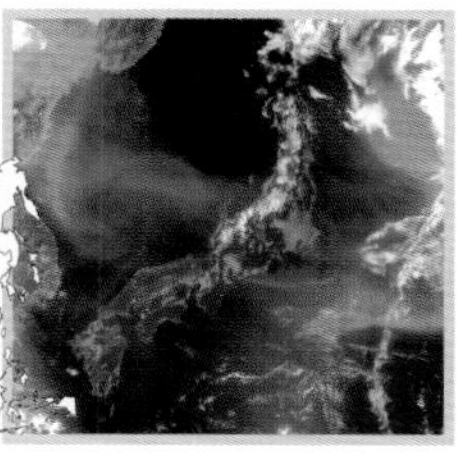

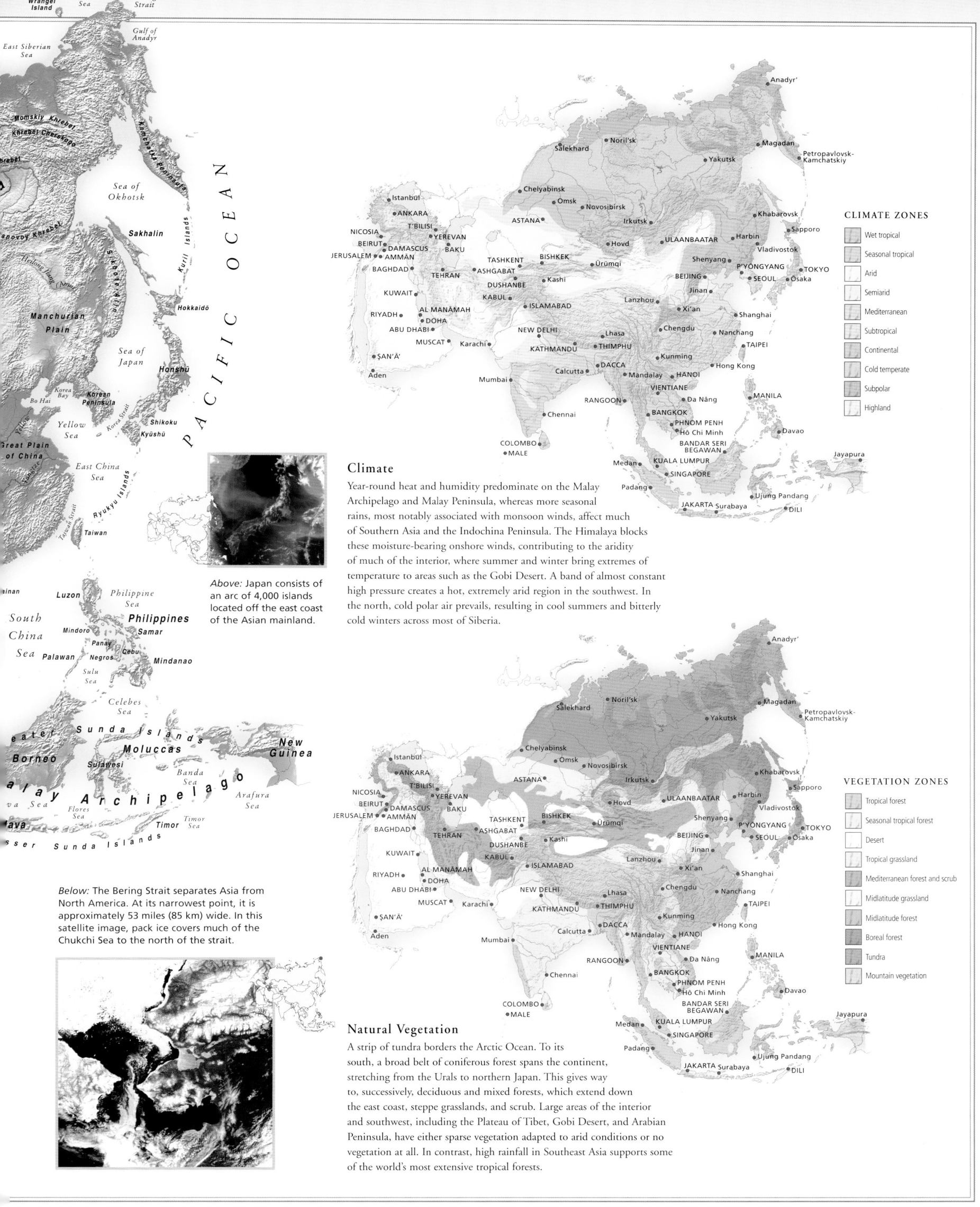

Above: Japan consists of an arc of 4,000 islands located off the east coast of the Asian mainland.

Below: The Bering Strait separates Asia from North America. At its narrowest point, it is approximately 53 miles (85 km) wide. In this satellite image, pack ice covers much of the Chukchi Sea to the north of the strait.

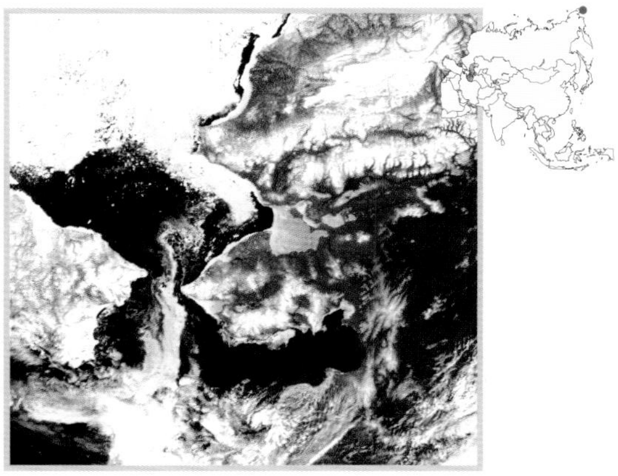

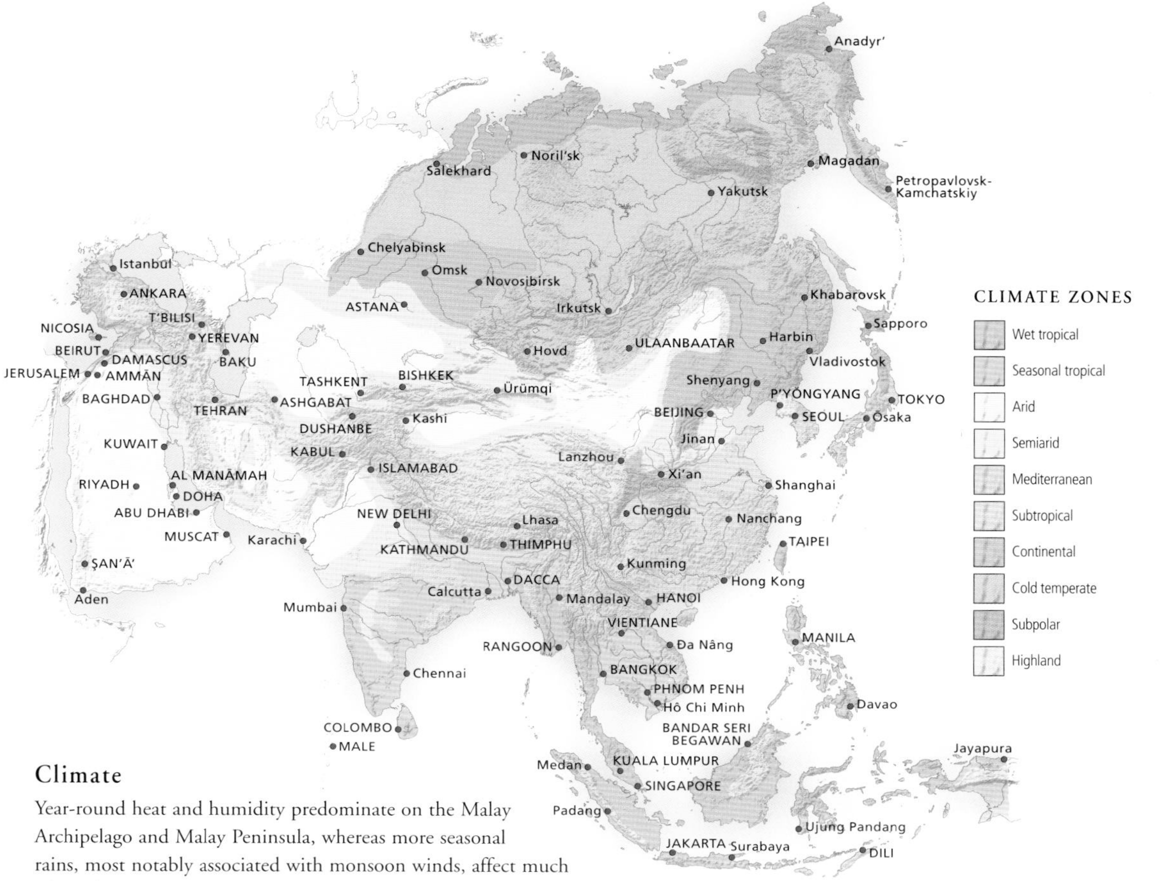

CLIMATE ZONES
Wet tropical
Seasonal tropical
Arid
Semiarid
Mediterranean
Subtropical
Continental
Cold temperate
Subpolar
Highland

Climate

Year-round heat and humidity predominate on the Malay Archipelago and Malay Peninsula, whereas more seasonal rains, most notably associated with monsoon winds, affect much of Southern Asia and the Indochina Peninsula. The Himalaya blocks these moisture-bearing onshore winds, contributing to the aridity of much of the interior, where summer and winter bring extremes of temperature to areas such as the Gobi Desert. A band of almost constant high pressure creates a hot, extremely arid region in the southwest. In the north, cold polar air prevails, resulting in cool summers and bitterly cold winters across most of Siberia.

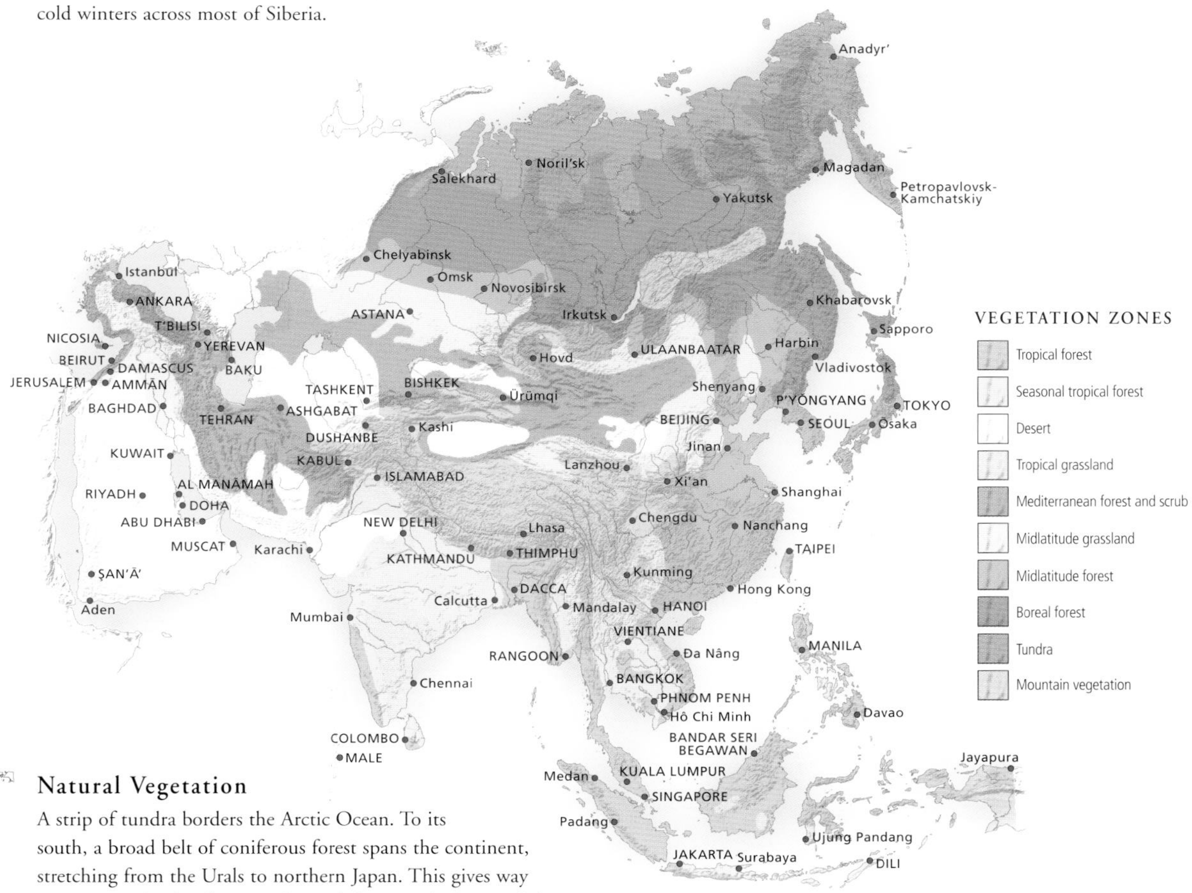

VEGETATION ZONES
Tropical forest
Seasonal tropical forest
Desert
Tropical grassland
Mediterranean forest and scrub
Midlatitude grassland
Midlatitude forest
Boreal forest
Tundra
Mountain vegetation

Natural Vegetation

A strip of tundra borders the Arctic Ocean. To its south, a broad belt of coniferous forest spans the continent, stretching from the Urals to northern Japan. This gives way to, successively, deciduous and mixed forests, which extend down the east coast, steppe grasslands, and scrub. Large areas of the interior and southwest, including the Plateau of Tibet, Gobi Desert, and Arabian Peninsula, have either sparse vegetation adapted to arid conditions or no vegetation at all. In contrast, high rainfall in Southeast Asia supports some of the world's most extensive tropical forests.

Peoples and Nations

In Asia, more than three-fifths of Earth's population—3.7 billion people—occupy one-third of its land. They inhabit 50 nations, ranging in size from the tiny city-state of Singapore to the world's largest country, the Russian Federation. The majority of these are developing nations, and many people lack ready access to clean water, reliable food supplies, and adequate health services. However, several nations, including Japan, South Korea, Singapore, Brunei, the Russian Federation, and Israel, have advanced economies and a relatively high standard of living. Asia has a great diversity of ethnic groups, and was the birthplace of all the world's major religions.

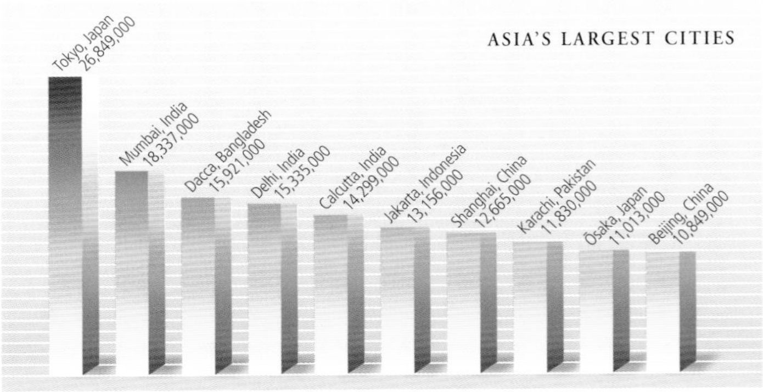

ASIA'S LARGEST CITIES
Tokyo, Japan 26,849,000
Mumbai, India 18,337,000
Dacca, Bangladesh 15,921,000
Delhi, India 15,335,000
Calcutta, India 14,299,000
Jakarta, Indonesia 13,156,000
Shanghai, China 12,665,000
Karachi, Pakistan 11,830,000
Osaka, Japan 11,013,000
Beijing, China 10,849,000

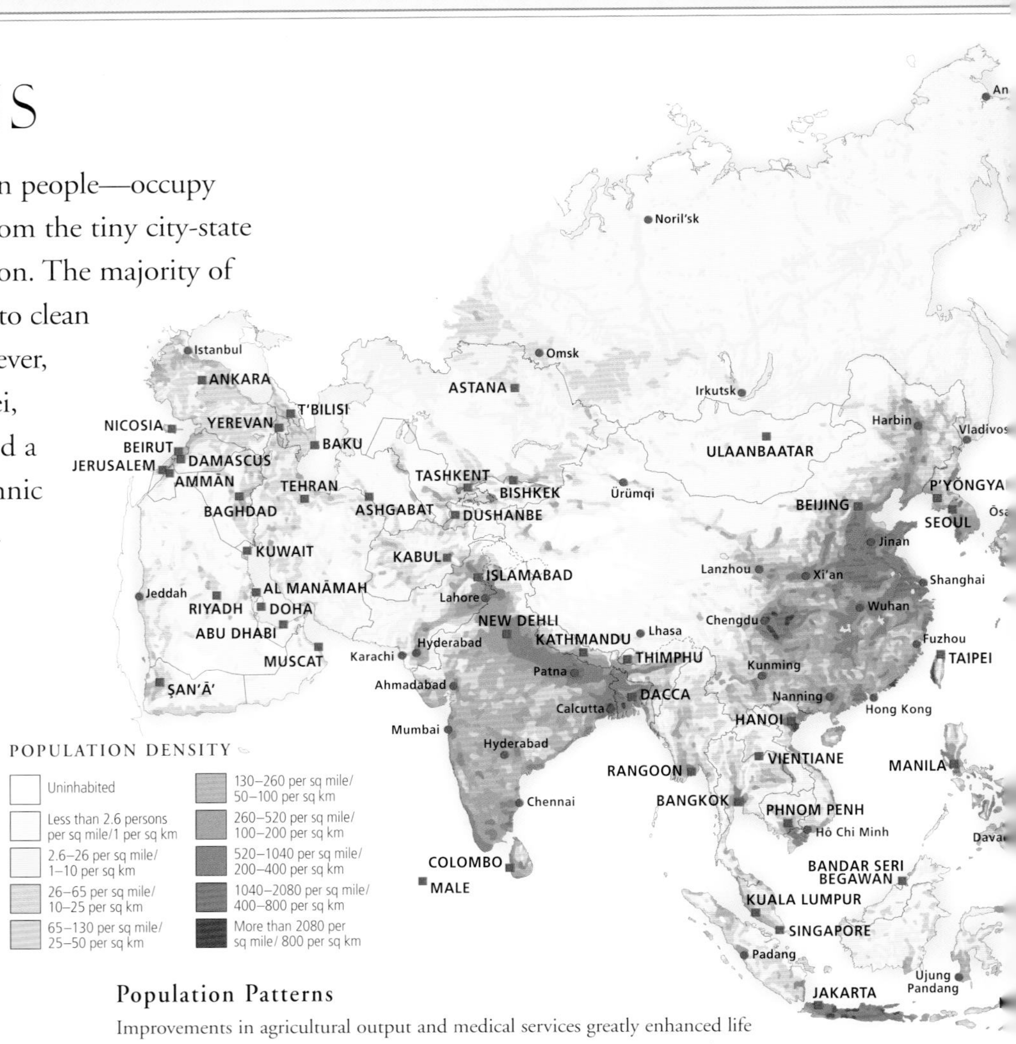

POPULATION DENSITY
Uninhabited
Less than 2.6 persons per sq mile/1 per sq km
2.6–26 per sq mile/ 1–10 per sq km
26–65 per sq mile/ 10–25 per sq km
65–130 per sq mile/ 25–50 per sq km
130–260 per sq mile/ 50–100 per sq km
260–520 per sq mile/ 100–200 per sq km
520–1040 per sq mile/ 200–400 per sq km
1040–2080 per sq mile/ 400–800 per sq km
More than 2080 per sq mile/ 800 per sq km
Noril'sk
Istanbul
ANKARA
Omsk
ASTANA
Irkutsk
NICOSIA
YEREVAN
T'BILISI
BEIRUT
BAKU
JERUSALEM
DAMASCUS
AMMAN
TEHRAN
BAGHDAD
ASHGABAT
TASHKENT
BISHKEK
DUSHANBE
Ürümqi
ULAANBAATAR
Harbin
Vladivos
P'YONGYA
BEIJING
SEOUL
Jinan
KUWAIT
KABUL
ISLAMABAD
Lahore
Jeddah
RIYADH
AL MANĀMAH
DOHA
ABU DHABI
MUSCAT
Karachi
NEW DEHLI
KATHMANDU
Lhasa
THIMPHU
Hyderabad
Ahmadabad
Patna
Lanzhou
Xi'an
Shanghai
Chengdu
Wuhan
Kunming
Fuzhou
TAIPEI
ṢAN'Ā'
Calcutta
DACCA
Nanning
Hong Kong
HANOI
Mumbai
Hyderabad
VIENTIANE
RANGOON
MANILA
BANGKOK
PHNOM PENH
Hô Chi Minh
Chennai
COLOMBO
MALE
BANDAR SERI BEGAWAN
KUALA LUMPUR
SINGAPORE
Padang
JAKARTA
Ujung Pandang

Urbanization

Most Asians are still dependent on subsistence farming and three-fifths live in rural areas. But many regions are becoming rapidly urbanized and industrialized. Singapore, Japan, and Israel are already among the world's most urbanized nations; South Korea's urban population was 21 percent in 1950, has passed 80 percent, and may reach 90 percent around 2025. By then, over half of all Asians are likely to be city dwellers. Already, six of the world's ten largest cities are located in Asia, three of them in India.

Population Patterns

Improvements in agricultural output and medical services greatly enhanced life expectancy in Asia during the 20th century, resulting in a population explosion. Between 1950 and the beginning of the 21st century, the population almost tripled, and it is expected to reach close to 5 billion by 2030. Despite this, great swathes of Asia remain virtually uninhabited, including Siberia, the barren Plateau of Tibet, and the deserts of Central Asia and the Arabian Peninsula. The bulk of the population is concentrated in the south and east, with especially high densities occurring along major rivers such as the Ganges, Yangtze, and Yellow, along the south and east coasts, and on the principal islands of the Japanese and Indonesian archipelagoes. Populations are also dense in fertile pockets of the southwest.

Flashpoints

Religious rivalries underpin many conflicts in Asia. Other causes include ideological schisms, such as the one that divides Korea in two; territorial disputes; independence movements; and internal rebellions against authoritarian governments.

Palestine

Proclaimed in 1948 in predominantly Arab Palestine, the Jewish state of Israel expanded as a result of territorial gains made in a series of wars (in 1948, 1967, and 1973). This displaced thousands of Palestinian people and has led to almost continuous conflict. Palestinians seek restoration of occupied territories and the creation of their own state. Israel has used military might to quash uprisings and often-violent protests.

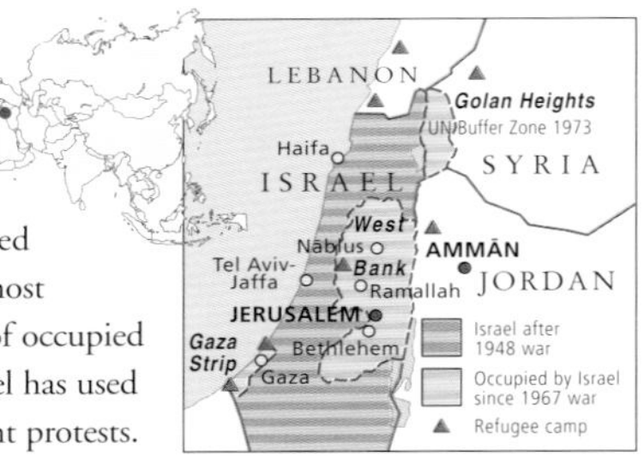

LEBANON
Golan Heights
UN Buffer Zone 1973
Haifa
SYRIA
ISRAEL
West Bank
Nablus
AMMĀN
Tel Aviv-Jaffa
Ramallah
JORDAN
JERUSALEM
Bethlehem
Gaza Strip
Gaza
Israel after 1948 war
Occupied by Israel since 1967 war
Refugee camp

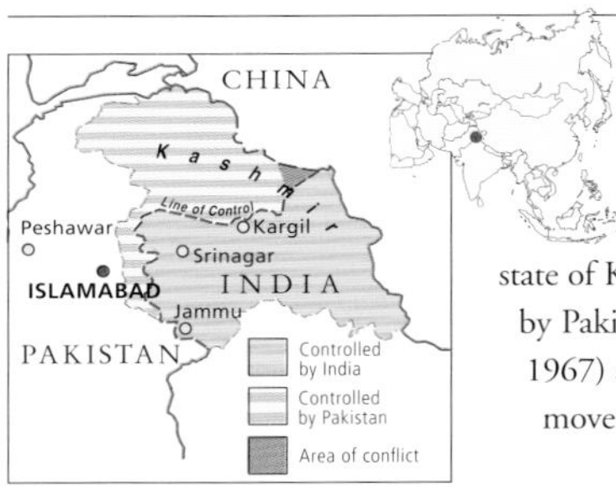

CHINA
Kashmir
Line of Control
Peshawar
Kargil
Srinagar
ISLAMABAD
INDIA
Jammu
PAKISTAN
Controlled by India
Controlled by Pakistan
Area of conflict

Kashmir

In 1947, the partition of British India created the Islamic state of Pakistan and the predominantly Hindu nation of India. The mainly Muslim state of Kashmir became part of India, but has been claimed by Pakistan ever since, resulting in two wars (1947–48 and 1967) and regular border skirmishes. A Kashmiri separatist movement, opposed by both India and Pakistan, has also conducted a guerilla campaign in recent years.

Korea

The Korean War of 1950–53 led to the creation of communist North Korea and democratic South Korea, and the demilitarized zone (DMZ) that separates them. About 151 miles (243 km) long and 2.5 miles (4 km) wide, it is guarded by 1.1 million soldiers on the North Korean side and, to the south, by 650,000 South Korean and 37,000 U.S. troops. Regular military exercises in the area keep tensions high.

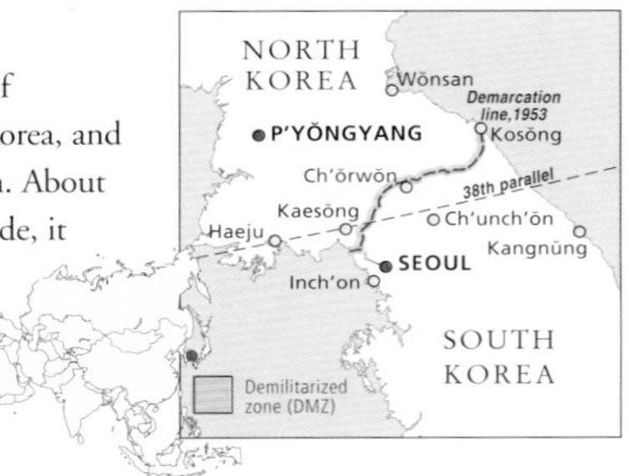

NORTH KOREA
Wŏnsan
Demarcation line, 1953
P'YŎNGYANG
Kosŏng
Ch'ŏrwŏn
38th parallel
Kaesŏng
Haeju
Ch'unch'ŏn
Kangnŭng
SEOUL
Inch'ŏn
SOUTH KOREA
Demilitarized zone (DMZ)

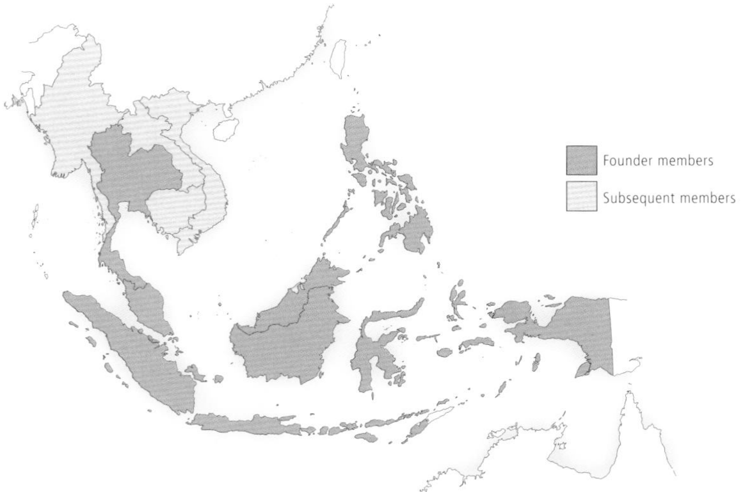

Founder members
Subsequent members

Association of Southeast Asian Nations

Since the mid-19th century, Asian countries have been heavily reliant on exports to Western nations and have often competed for lucrative markets. Greater intraregional economic cooperation has developed only since the 1960s. Aside from international associations formed by traders in the same commodities, few formal bodies have emerged. By far the most significant is the Association of Southeast Asian Nations, or ASEAN. Founded in 1967, it now has ten members—Indonesia, Thailand, Malaysia, the Philippines, Singapore, Brunei, Vietnam, Laos, Myanmar (Burma), and Cambodia. It aims to promote trade between members in order to strengthen economic growth and political stability.

ARCTIC OCEAN
RUSSIAN FEDERATION
KAZAKHSTAN
MONGOLIA
CHINA
INDIA
JAPAN
NORTH KOREA
SOUTH KOREA
TURKEY
IRAN
IRAQ
SYRIA
SAUDI ARABIA
YEMEN
OMAN
AFGHANISTAN
PAKISTAN
TURKMENISTAN
UZBEKISTAN
KYRGYZSTAN
TAJIKISTAN
NEPAL
BHUTAN
BANGLADESH
MYANMAR (BURMA)
THAILAND
LAOS
CAMBODIA
VIETNAM
PHILIPPINES
MALAYSIA
BRUNEI
INDONESIA
EAST TIMOR
SRI LANKA
MALDIVES
TAIWAN
PACIFIC OCEAN
INDIAN OCEAN
Arabian Sea
Bay of Bengal
South China Sea
East China Sea
Sea of Japan
Sea of Okhotsk
Bering Sea
Kara Sea
Laptev Sea
East Siberian Sea
Mediterranean Sea
Black Sea
Caspian Sea
Red Sea
Persian Gulf
Gulf of Aden
Gulf of Oman
Andaman Sea
Java Sea
Banda Sea
Flores Sea
Timor Sea
Arafura Sea
Celebes Sea
Sulu Sea
Philippine Sea
Tropic of Cancer
Arctic Circle
Equator
SCALE 1:49,000,000
Lamberts Azimuthal Equal Area Projection
1000 miles
1000 kilometers

Nations of Asia

From the emergence of the world's first major imperial power, Assyria, in the ninth century BC, to the demise of the Soviet Union in 1990, the history of Asia has been a saga of great empires. The largest of all was fashioned in the 13th century by the Mongol leader Genghis Khan, who subsequently divided his realm into Khanates ruled by his sons. In the 16th century, European empires expanded into Asia. The breakup of these colonial dominions in the 20th century created a clutch of new nations in southern and Southeast Asia during the two decades after World War II; the collapse of the Soviet Union created eight more in Central Asia.

THE MONGOL EMPIRE, C.1300

Mongol Empire
Khanate of the Golden Horde
Chagatai Khanate
Il-Khanate
Empire of the Great Khan
Seljuk States
Rum
Mamluk Empire
Bedouins
Oman
Rasulids
Sultanate of Delhi
Hindu States
Pagan
Annam
Champa
Khmer
Sukothai
Malays
Malay States
Majapahit Empire
Papuans
Koryo
Japan
Samoyeds
Tungus
Palaeosiberians
Mongol Empire under Genghis Khan

EARLY EUROPEAN COLONIZATION, 1700

Russian Empire
Ottoman Empire
Safavid Empire
Khanate of the Dzungars
Qing Empire
Mughal Empire
Tibet
Kazakhs
Khiva
Bukhara
Chukchi
Koryaks
Korea
Japan
Yemen
Oman
Bedouins
Burma
Siam
Laos
Annam
Formosa
Macao
Manila
Philippines
Cambay
Diu
Bombay
Goa
Mangalore
Calicut
Cochin
Masulipatam
Madras
Negapatam
Malacca
Malay States
Malays
Benkulen
Silebar
Mataram
Batavia
Dutch Possessions
Papuans
COLONIAL POSSESSIONS
Dutch
English
Spanish
Portuguese

COLONIAL RULE, 1914

Russian Empire
Ottoman Empire
Persia
Kuwait
Afghanistan
Nejd
Aden
Oman
Mongolia
China
Tibet
Nepal
Bhutan
India
Chandernagore
Diu
Damão
Goa
Mahé
Karikal
Yanaon
Pondicherry
Ceylon
Burma
Siam
French Indochina
Hong Kong
Macao
Philippine Islands
Japanese Empire
North Borneo
Malaya
Sarawak
Borneo
Dutch East Indies
Timor
Dili
COLONIAL POSSESSIONS
British
Dutch
United States of America
Portuguese
French

THE HUMAN IMPACT

Human transformation of the landscape and harnessing of natural resources first occurred on a large scale in Asia. The world's earliest agricultural settlements evolved in the Fertile Crescent region of Southwest Asia, where wheat, olives, peas, goats, and sheep were domesticated more than 10,000 years ago. About 9,000 years ago, farmers in eastern China began to cultivate rice and millet and rear pigs and silkworms. In turn, these settlements became the world's first cities. Southwest Asia and China remained centers of innovation, and from antiquity until the 15th century the flow of ideas and technology was mainly from Asia to Europe. Western interest in Asian technology led to the establishment of arteries of trade such as the Silk Road and the eventual European colonization of much of the continent. The colonial rulers accelerated land clearance, principally to permit the cultivation of plantation crops for export to the West. Steady industrialization and explosive population growth in the 20th century exerted even greater pressure on land and resources, resulting in widespread deforestation, land degradation, and pollution.

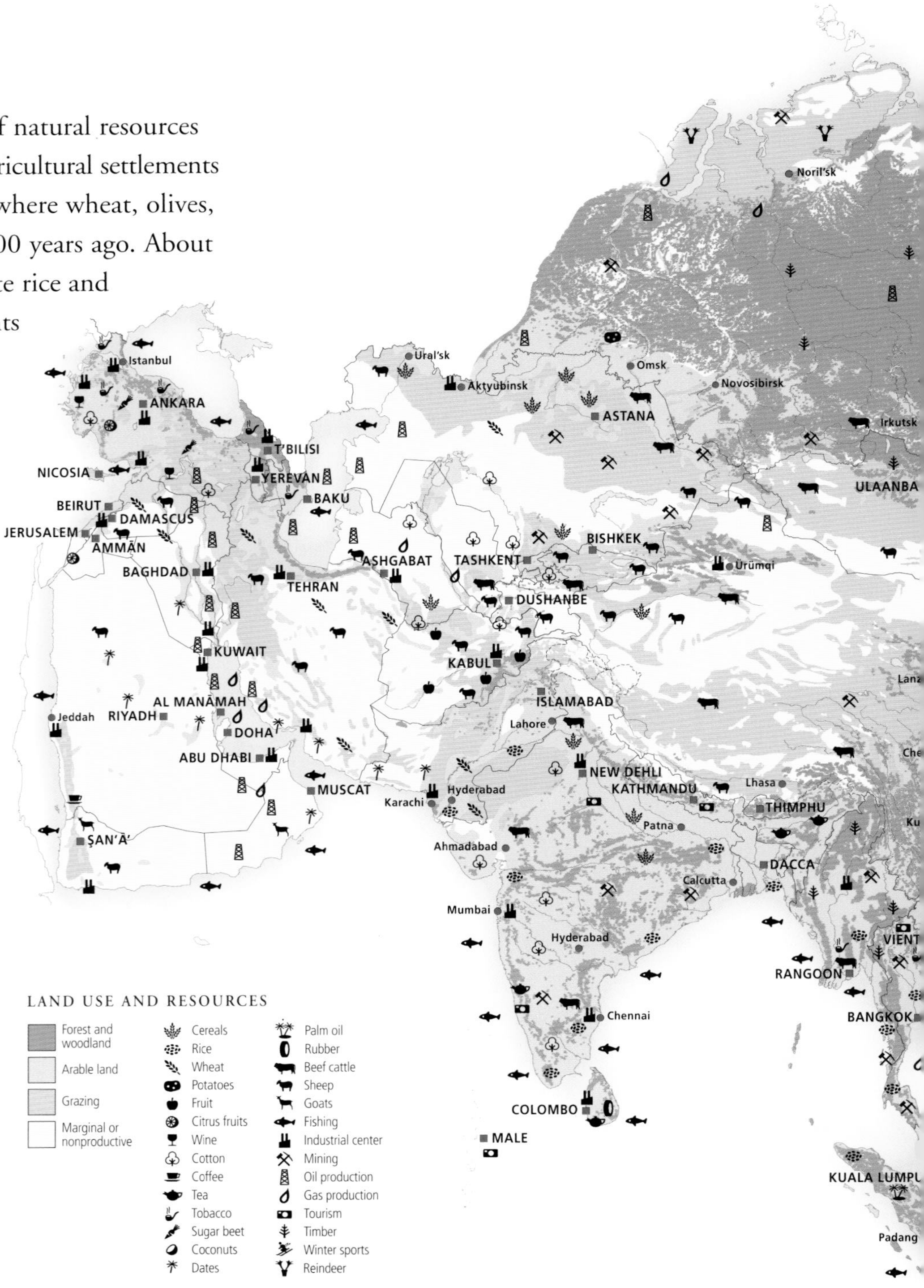

Noril'sk
Ural'sk
Aktyubinsk
Omsk
Novosibirsk
ASTANA
Irkutsk
Istanbul
ANKARA
T'BILISI
NICOSIA
YEREVAN
BAKU
ULAANBA
BEIRUT
DAMASCUS
JERUSALEM
AMMAN
BISHKEK
ASHGABAT
TASHKENT
Urumqi
BAGHDAD
TEHRAN
DUSHANBE
KUWAIT
KABUL
ISLAMABAD
AL MANAMAH
Jeddah
RIYADH
DOHA
Lahore
ABU DHABI
NEW DEHLI
KATHMANDU
Lhasa
MUSCAT
Karachi
Hyderabad
THIMPHU
Patna
ŞAN'Ā'
Ahmadabad
DACCA
Calcutta
Mumbai
Hyderabad
RANGOON
Chennai
BANGKOK
COLOMBO
MALE
KUALA LUMPU
Padang
LAND USE AND RESOURCES
Forest and woodland
Arable land
Grazing
Marginal or nonproductive
Cereals
Rice
Wheat
Potatoes
Fruit
Citrus fruits
Wine
Cotton
Coffee
Tea
Tobacco
Sugar beet
Coconuts
Dates
Palm oil
Rubber
Beef cattle
Sheep
Goats
Fishing
Industrial center
Mining
Oil production
Gas production
Tourism
Timber
Winter sports
Reindeer

THE CHANGING FACE OF ASIA

The Aral Sea

About 85 percent of Asia's water is used for farming and the continent has two-thirds of all irrigated land. The creation of vast irrigation systems has had a catastrophic effect on river basins, most notably in Central Asia. The Aral Sea was once the world's fourth-largest inland sea and had a thriving fishing industry. In the 1960s, the Soviet Union began diverting the rivers that fed the sea, the Amudar'ya and Syrdar'ya, to irrigate cotton fields. Since then, the sea has shrunk to 15 percent of its former volume. Evaporation has raised salinity levels, and pesticides used by farmers have contaminated the remaining waters, decimating marine life. Salt- and chemical-laden sands from the shore have been blown across surrounding land, poisoning plants, animals, and humans. Efforts have been made to raise the sea's water level, but the damage is thought to be irreversible.

DEPLETION OF THE ARAL SEA, 1960–2002

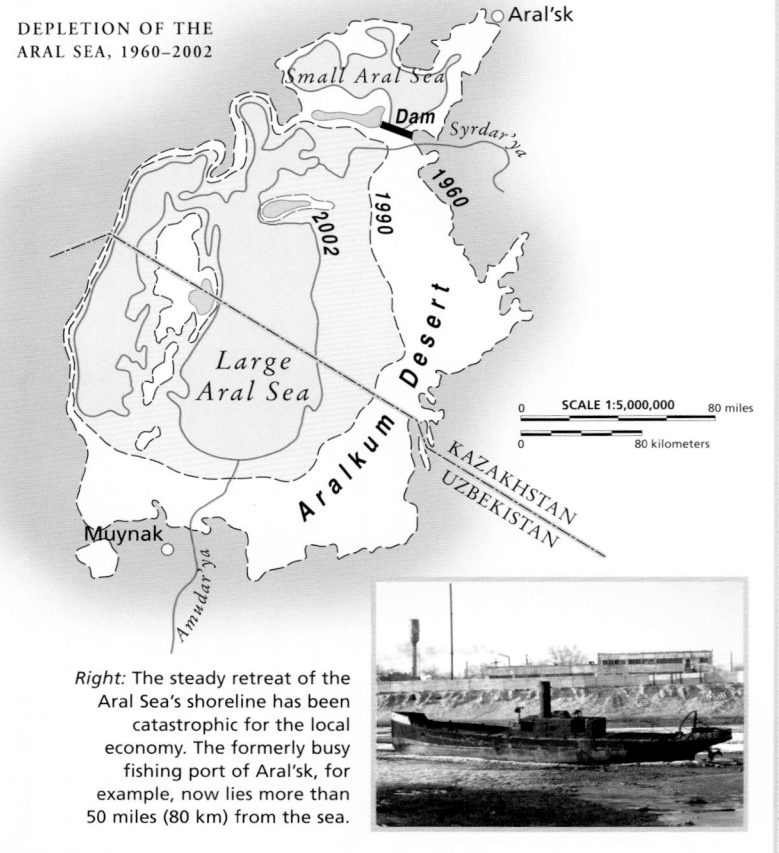

Aral'sk
Small Aral Sea
Dam
Syrdar'ya
1960
1990
2002
Large Aral Sea
Aralkum Desert
KAZAKHSTAN
UZBEKISTAN
Muynak
Amudar'ya
SCALE 1:5,000,000
0
80 miles
0
80 kilometers

Right: The steady retreat of the Aral Sea's shoreline has been catastrophic for the local economy. The formerly busy fishing port of Aral'sk, for example, now lies more than 50 miles (80 km) from the sea.

Economic Profile

From the subsistence-agriculture economies of Afghanistan, Bhutan, and Nepal to the sophisticated, technology-driven societies of Japan and South Korea, Asian countries have attained disparate levels of development. These have been determined by a range of factors, including resource distribution, foreign investment, conflicts, and governing ideologies. Asia harbors two-thirds of the world's known reserves of oil and gas, concentrated in Siberia and the Arabian Peninsula, and 60 percent of the world's coal, found mainly in China, Siberia, and India. It also supplies 60 percent of the world's tin, most of it coming from Southeast Asia. Russia has immense stands of timber and Southeast Asia is endowed with valuable hardwoods such as teak and mahogany, though supplies are dwindling. More than half of the population, however, still depends on farming. Rice is the main staple crop, though wheat predominates in the north. Services and industries are becoming more significant, but heavy industry is confined mainly to Japan, China, and India. More widespread light industries are based on food processing, the manufacture of textiles and pharmaceuticals, and tourism.

Land Cover

The world's largest conifer forests still cloak much of Siberia, though huge swathes of forest have been cleared elsewhere. Arable land covers a large area, but has to support some of the highest population densities on Earth. Extensive barren areas, including the Plateau of Tibet, the deserts of Central Asia, and the arctic shoreline, make a large proportion of the continent unproductive.

PROPORTIONS OF TOTAL LAND AREA

Forest and woodland
Arable land
Grazing
Other land
18.0%
17.6%
35.8%
28.6%

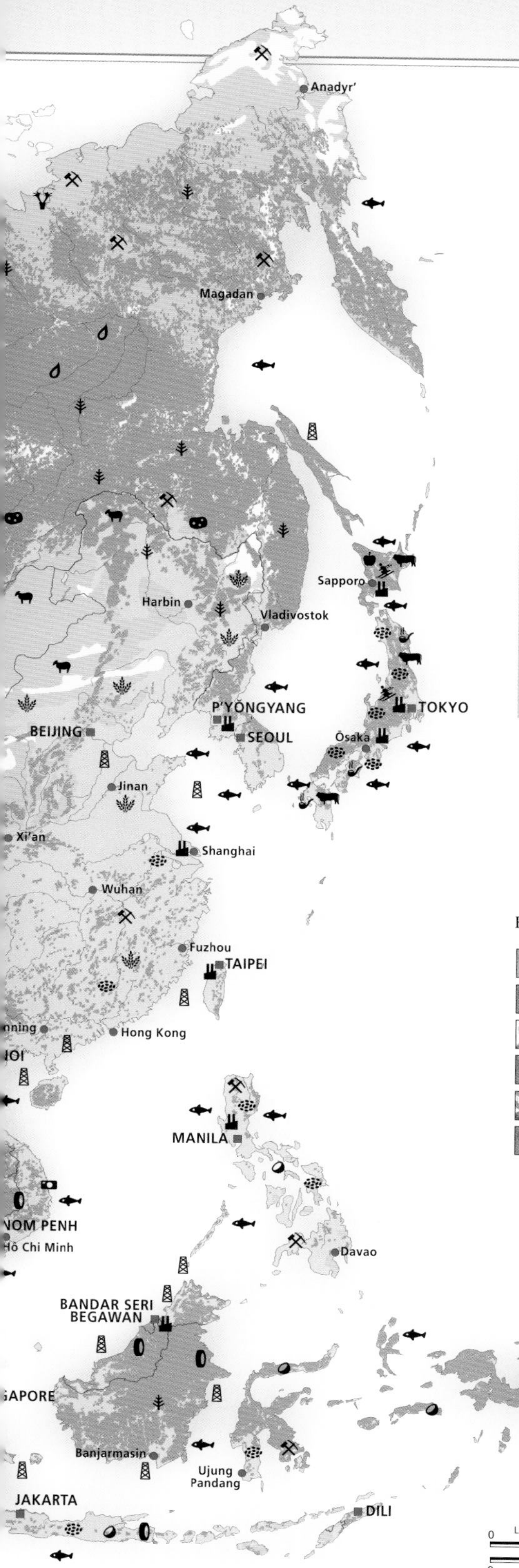

Anadyr'
Magadan
Sapporo
Harbin
Vladivostok
P'YŎNGYANG
TOKYO
BEIJING
SEOUL
Ōsaka
Jinan
Xi'an
Shanghai
Wuhan
Fuzhou
TAIPEI
Hong Kong
MANILA
NOM PENH
Hô Chi Minh
Davao
BANDAR SERI BEGAWAN
Jayapura
APORE
Banjarmasin
Ujung Pandang
JAKARTA
DILI
SCALE 1:47,000,000
Lamberts Azimuthal Equal Area Projection
0
1000 miles
0
1000 kilometers

Above: The growth of aquaculture has led to habitat loss. About 60 percent of Asia's mangroves have been converted to shrimp ponds.

Right: Russia has decommissioned over 150 nuclear submarines. But few have been dismantled and most lie rusting in Arctic and eastern ports, posing a potential threat to the environment.

Above: Heavy use of rivers such as the Ganges reduces water quality. Outside Siberia and Southwest Asia, one-third of people have no access to safe drinking water.

ENVIRONMENTAL ISSUES
Degraded soil
Very degraded soil
Polluted rivers
Polluted seas and lakes
Acid rain
Major oil spills, year
Major nuclear accidents, year
Cities with severe air pollution
Overfished fishery, year of peak catch, decline since peak catch
Anadyr'
Salekhard
Noril'sk
Yakutsk
Magadan
1957
Chelyabinsk
Omsk
1979
Istanbul
ANKARA
ASTANA
Irkutsk
Sapporo
T'BILISI
YEREVAN
BAKU
NICOSIA
BEIRUT
DAMASCUS
JERUSALEM
AMMAN
BAGHDAD
ULAANBAATAR
Harbin
Changchun
Vladivostok
TASHKENT
BISHKEK
Ürümqi
TEHRAN
ASHGABAT
DUSHANBE
Shenyang
Anshan
Dalian
P'YONGYANG
SEOUL
TOKYO
Yokohama
BEIJING
Taiyuan
Tianjin
Zibo
Taegu
Osaka
1999
Pusan
KUWAIT
KABUL
Jinan
Qingdao
Lanzhou
RIYADH
AL MANAMAH
DOHA
ISLAMABAD
Zhengzhou
Shanghai
ABU DHABI
1972
MUSCAT
Karachi
NEW DELHI
Delhi
KATHMANDU
THIMPHU
Chengdu
Chongqing
Wuhan
Nanchang
Pinxiang
SAN'A'
Aden
Kanpur
Lucknow
Lupanshui
Guiyang
TAIPEI
Ahmadabad
DACCA
Kunming
Guangzhou
Mumbai
Pune
Nagpur
Calcutta
HANOI
Hyderabad
RANGOON
VIENTIANE
MANILA
Bangalore
Chennai
BANGKOK
Western Central Pacific,
1995, -0.9%
PHNOM PENH
Hô Chi Minh
Davao
COLOMBO
MALE
BANDAR SERI BEGAWAN
KUALA LUMPUR
SINGAPORE
Jayapura
JAKARTA
Ujung Pandang
DILI

Threats to the Environment

A desire to cater for impoverished, rapidly expanding populations is at the root of much recent environmental degradation in Asia, which has been compounded by neglect and failure to implement protective legislation. Intensive farming practices have increased agricultural output dramatically, but have also led to severe land degradation and water pollution. About 20 percent of vegetated land is degraded and more than half of drylands are affected by desertification. The continent also has some of the world's most polluted rivers. Demand for cultivable land has resulted in the virtual disappearance of Southeast Asia's species-rich lowland rain forests, while heavy logging has begun to threaten the integrity of Siberia's vast frontier forests (which could in turn contribute to global warming). Industrialization has invigorated local economies, especially in Japan, South Korea, Russia, China, Malaysia, Thailand, and India, but has also created some of the world's worst levels of air pollution and given rise to widespread acid rain.

Protecting the Environment

In western and Central Asia, a range of strategies has been implemented to combat the widespread problems of land degradation and desertification, including reforestation, sand-dune stabilization, and soil-fertility restoration programs. Japan has had notable success in reducing air pollution, and other governments are following its lead. In Nepal and Pakistan, for instance, users of gas- or battery-operated vehicles receive tax rebates, and the Indian city of Delhi has converted all its public transport to gas. Asian countries are at the forefront of reforestation: for example, China increased its forest coverage by more than 3.5 percent between 1993 and 2000. Large World Heritage areas have recently been designated in Siberia, and the number of protected areas is growing. However the overall proportion of land protected (3.7%) is low.

PERCENTAGE OF LAND PROTECTED IN MAJOR ASIAN COUNTRIES

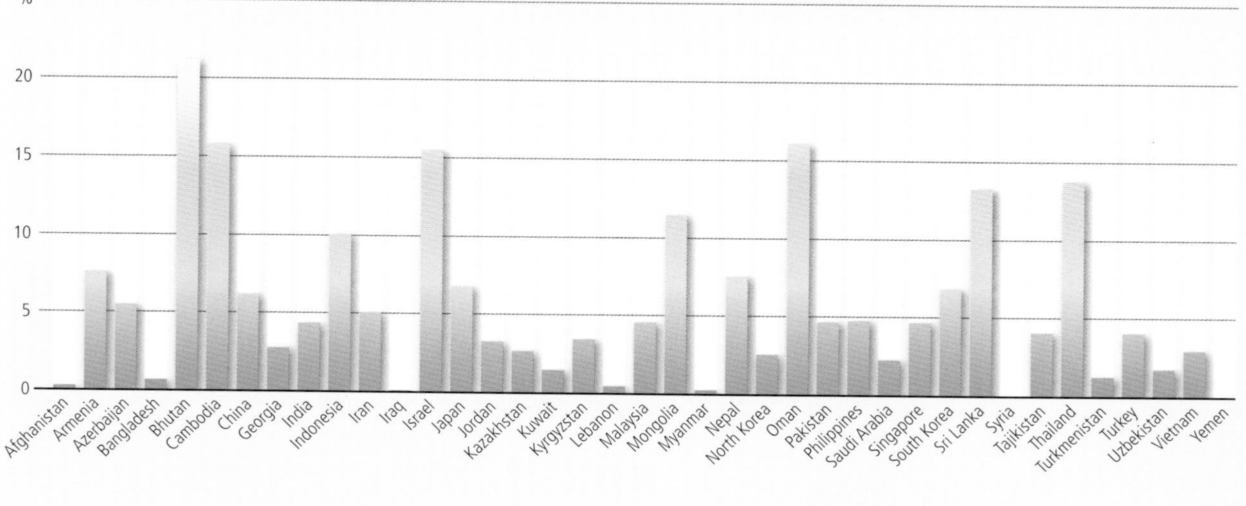

%
20
15
10
5
0
Afghanistan
Armenia
Azerbaijan
Bangladesh
Bhutan
Cambodia
China
Georgia
India
Indonesia
Iran
Iraq
Israel
Japan
Jordan
Kazakhstan
Kuwait
Kyrgyzstan
Lebanon
Malaysia
Mongolia
Myanmar
Nepal
North Korea
Oman
Pakistan
Philippines
Saudi Arabia
Singapore
South Korea
Sri Lanka
Syria
Tajikistan
Thailand
Turkmenistan
Turkey
Uzbekistan
Vietnam
Yemen

THE RUSSIAN FEDERATION

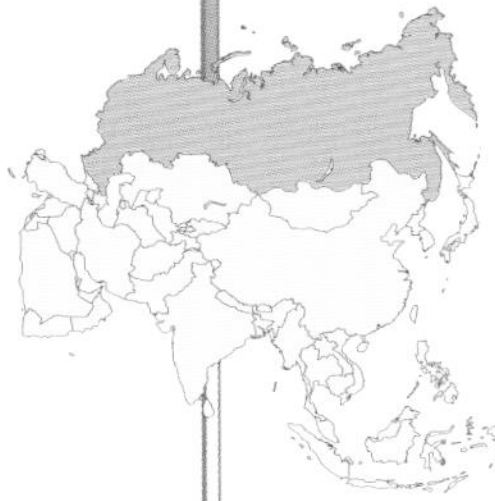

Spanning 11 time zones and most of the Eastern Hemisphere, the Russian Federation is the largest country on Earth. It is divided into European Russia and Asian Russia, or Siberia, by the Ural Mountains, which stretch from the shore of the Kara Sea to Kazakhstan. In European Russia, the site of the nation's largest cities, major rivers divide plains and ranges of low, rolling hills. East of the Urals, an immense, swampy plain stretches to the Yenisey River, where the land climbs to the wide Central Siberian Plateau. High mountains line the Mongolian border and skirt the east coast. An almost unbroken band of boreal forest crosses the entire country, dividing the tundra of the far north from the woodlands and steppe grasslands of the south. In 1917, after a bloody revolution, Russia became a communist state known as the Soviet Union, or Union of Soviet Socialist Republics (U.S.S.R.). Following the collapse of communism in 1991, ten Soviet republics declared independence. The remainder of the union, about 75 percent of its land area, became the Russian Federation.

St Petersburg's Winter Palace is one of a series of buildings constructed in the mid-18th century by Peter the Great.

Local fishermen harvest more than 50 species of fish from Lake Baikal, the deepest lake in the world.

The Chukchi of northeastern Russia live mainly by herding reindeer, fishing, and hunting whales, seals, and walruses.

Moscow The focal point of Russia's capital city, Red Square, dates from the late 15th century and acquired its present name—the Russian word for "red" also means "beautiful"—in the 17th century. It is the site of some of the nation's most important buildings, including the Kremlin, Lenin's Tomb, and the 12-domed Cathedral of St Basil the Blessed (below). The cathedral was built between 1554 and 1560 by Ivan IV ("the Terrible") to celebrate his victory over the Mongols. Legend has it that Ivan then had the architect blinded to prevent him ever building anything to surpass this extraordinary work.

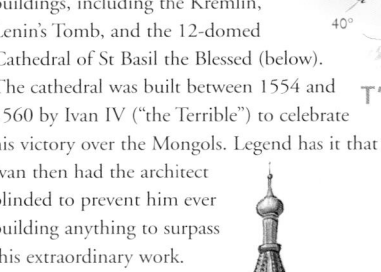

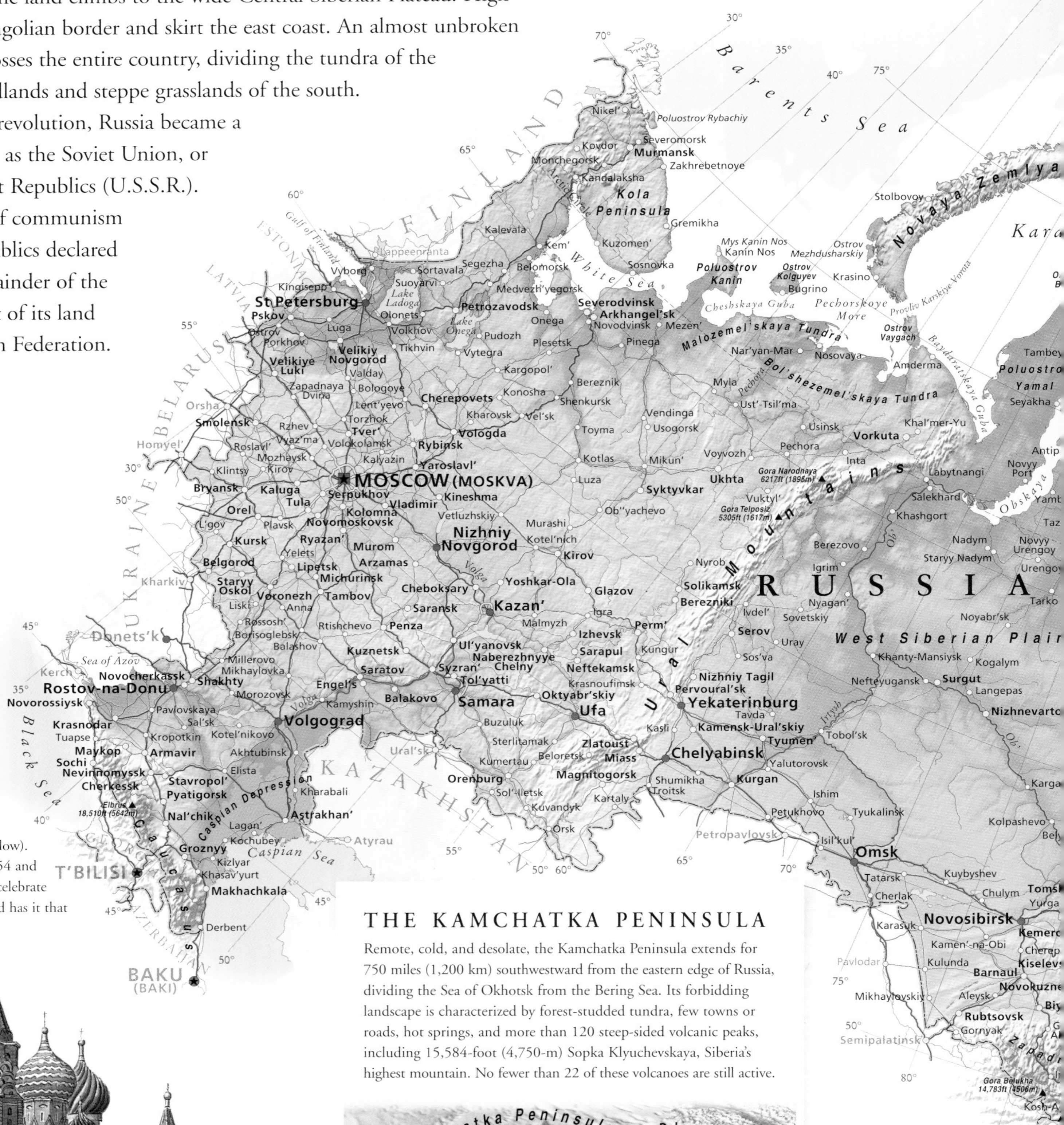
A B C D E F G H I J K L M
1 4 5 6 7 8 9 10 11 12 13 14 15
Barents Sea
FINLAND
ESTONIA
LATVIA
BELARUS
UKRAINE
KAZAKHSTAN
GEORGIA
AZERBAIJAN
Gulf of Finland
Lake Ladoga
Lake Onega
White Sea
Kola Peninsula
Poluostrov Rybachiy
Arctic Circle
Novaya Zemlya
Kara
Sea of Azov
Black Sea
Caspian Sea
Caspian Depression
Caucasus
Ural Mountains
West Siberian Plain
RUSSIA
Volga
Ob'
Irtysh
Pechora
Malozemel'skaya Tundra
Bol'shezemel'skaya Tundra
Pechorskoye More
Cheshskaya Guba
Poluostrov Kanin
Ostrov Kolguyev
Ostrov Vaygach
Proliv Karskiye Vorota
Baydaratskaya Guba
Obskaya
Poluostrov Yamal
Nikel'
Severomorsk
Murmansk
Zakhrebetnoye
Kovdor
Monchegorsk
Kandalaksha
Gremikha
Kalevala
Kem'
Kuzomen'
Sosnovka
Belomorsk
Segezha
Lappeenranta
Vyborg
Sortavala
Suoyarvi
Kingisepp
St Petersburg
Pskov
Ostrov
Porkhov
Luga
Olonets
Volkhov
Tikhvin
Petrozavodsk
Medvezh'yegorsk
Pudozh
Vytegra
Onega
Plesetsk
Severodvinsk
Arkhangel'sk
Novodvinsk
Mezen'
Pinega
Velikiye Luki
Velikiy Novgorod
Valday
Zapadnaya Dvina
Bologoye
Orsha
Smolensk
Rzhev
Vyaz'ma
Tver'
Torzhok
Lent'yevo
Kargopol'
Konosha
Cherepovets
Kharovsk
Vel'sk
Vologda
Rybinsk
Volokolamsk
Kalyazin
Yaroslavl'
Homyel'
Roslavl'
Mozhaysk
Kirov
Klintsy
Bryansk
Kaluga
Tula
MOSCOW (MOSKVA)
Serpukhov
Kineshma
Vladimir
Kolomna
Novomoskovsk
Orel
L'gov
Plavsk
Kursk
Ryazan'
Yelets
Murom
Arzamas
Nizhniy Novgorod
Vetluzhskiy
Belgorod
Lipetsk
Michurinsk
Kharkiv
Staryy Oskol
Voronezh
Anna
Liski
Tambov
Rossosh'
Borisoglebsk
Balashov
Rtishchevo
Penza
Cheboksary
Saransk
Kazan'
Yoshkar-Ola
Donets'k
Millerovo
Mikhaylovka
Kerch
Novocherkassk
Shakhty
Rostov-na-Donu
Novorossiysk
Morozovsk
Kuznetsk
Saratov
Engel's
Kamyshin
Volgograd
Pavlovskaya
Sal'sk
Krasnodar
Tuapse
Kropotkin
Kotel'nikovo
Maykop
Armavir
Akhtubinsk
Sochi
Nevinnomyssk
Cherkessk
Stavropol'
Pyatigorsk
Elista
Kharabali
Elbrus 18,510ft (5642m)
Nal'chik
Astrakhan'
Lagan'
Kochubey
Groznyy
Kizlyar
Khasav'yurt
Makhachkala
Derbent
T'BILISI
BAKU (BAKI)
Atyrau
Ural'sk
Orenburg
Sol'-Iletsk
Kuvandyk
Orsk
Samara
Syzran'
Tol'yatti
Ul'yanovsk
Naberezhnyye Chelny
Balakovo
Buzuluk
Sterlitamak
Kumertau
Beloretsk
Magnitogorsk
Ufa
Oktyabr'skiy
Neftekamsk
Sarapul
Izhevsk
Malmyzh
Kirov
Kotel'nich
Murashi
Glazov
Igra
Perm'
Kungur
Krasnoufimsk
Zlatoust
Miass
Chelyabinsk
Kartaly
Troitsk
Shumikha
Kurgan
Yekaterinburg
Kamensk-Ural'skiy
Kasli
Nizhniy Tagil
Pervoural'sk
Tavda
Tyumen'
Yalutorovsk
Ishim
Petukhovo
Petropavlovsk
Isil'kul'
Omsk
Tyukalinsk
Tobol'sk
Solikamsk
Berezniki
Nyrob
Ivdel'
Serov
Sos'va
Uray
Sovetskiy
Nyagan'
Igrim
Berezovo
Syktyvkar
Ob''yachevo
Mikun'
Kotlas
Luza
Vendinga
Usogorsk
Toyma
Shenkursk
Bereznik
Ukhta
Voyvozh
Pechora
Usinsk
Vorkuta
Inta
Gora Narodnaya 6217ft (1895m)
Gora Telposiz 5305ft (1617m)
Vuktyl'
Myla
Ust'-Tsil'ma
Nar'yan-Mar
Nosovaya
Amderma
Khal'mer-Yu
Labytnangi
Salekhard
Khashgort
Nadym
Staryy Nadym
Novyy Urengoy
Urengoy
Tarko
Noyabr'sk
Kogalym
Khanty-Mansiysk
Surgut
Nefteyugansk
Langepas
Nizhnevartovsk
Kolpashevo
Kuybyshev
Chulym
Tatarsk
Cherlak
Karasuk
Novosibirsk
Kamen'-na-Obi
Kulunda
Barnaul
Pavlodar
Mikhaylovskiy
Aleysk
Rubtsovsk
Gornyak
Semipalatinsk
Gora Belukha 14,783ft (4506m)
Mys Kanin Nos
Kanin Nos
Mezhdusharskiy
Ostrov
Krasino
Bugrino
Stolbovoy
Tambey
Seyakha
Novyy Port
Kiselevsk
Novokuznetsk
Tomsk
Yurga
Kemerovo
Cherepanovo
Zemlya Georga
Nagurskoye
30° 35° 40° 45° 50° 55° 60° 65° 70° 75° 80° 85°
Longitude east of Greenwich

THE KAMCHATKA PENINSULA

Remote, cold, and desolate, the Kamchatka Peninsula extends for 750 miles (1,200 km) southwestward from the eastern edge of Russia, dividing the Sea of Okhotsk from the Bering Sea. Its forbidding landscape is characterized by forest-studded tundra, few towns or roads, hot springs, and more than 120 steep-sided volcanic peaks, including 15,584-foot (4,750-m) Sopka Klyuchevskaya, Siberia's highest mountain. No fewer than 22 of these volcanoes are still active.

Kamchatka Peninsula
Vulkan Ichinskiy
Palana
Sopka Klyuchevskaya
Sredinnyy Khrebet
Sopka Shiveluch
Ozernovskiy
Mil'kovo
Ust'-Kamchatsk
Petropavlovsk-Kamchatskiy
Bering Sea

St Petersburg
MOSCOW
Stavropol'
Novosibirsk
Irkutsk
Magadan
Anadyr'
Vladivostok
Uninhabited
Less than 2.6 persons per sq mile/1 per sq km
2.6–26 per sq mile/ 1–10 per sq km
26–65 per sq mile/ 10–25 per sq km
65–130 per sq mile/ 25–50 per sq km
130–260 per sq mile/ 50–100 per sq km
260–520 per sq mile/ 100–200 per sq km

Population Patterns

European Russia constitutes one-quarter of the country but is home to four-fifths of its inhabitants. Settlement is especially dense around Moscow, along the River Volga, and in the southwest. East of the Urals, Russians cluster around the industrial centers of Omsk and Novosibirsk, the towns strung along the Trans-Siberian railway, and far-flung northern ports and mining centers. Over the past century, Russians have steadily abandoned the countryside for cities; 73 percent now live in urban areas. More than four-fifths are ethnic Russians; the remainder consists of a large number of other ethnic groups, including Ukrainians, Tatars, and Bashkirs.

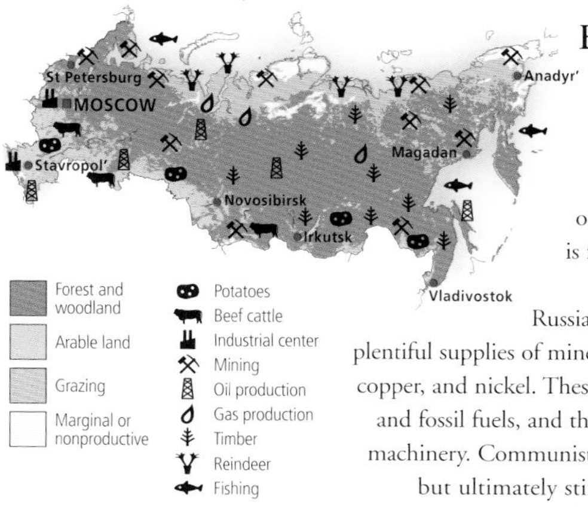
St Petersburg
MOSCOW
Stavropol'
Novosibirsk
Irkutsk
Magadan
Anadyr'
Vladivostok
Forest and woodland
Arable land
Grazing
Marginal or nonproductive
Potatoes
Beef cattle
Industrial center
Mining
Oil production
Gas production
Timber
Reindeer
Fishing

Economic Profile

Much of the Soviet Union's best arable land was located in the now-independent republics of Ukraine and Belarus. Less than one-sixth of the Russian Federation is farmland; wheat, barley, and sugar beet are among the major crops. Russia has the world's largest forests and plentiful supplies of minerals, including coal, oil, gas, gold, copper, and nickel. These support the processing of metals and fossil fuels, and the manufacturing of chemicals and machinery. Communist rule accelerated industrialization, but ultimately stifled development. A shift toward privatization and a more open market is under way.

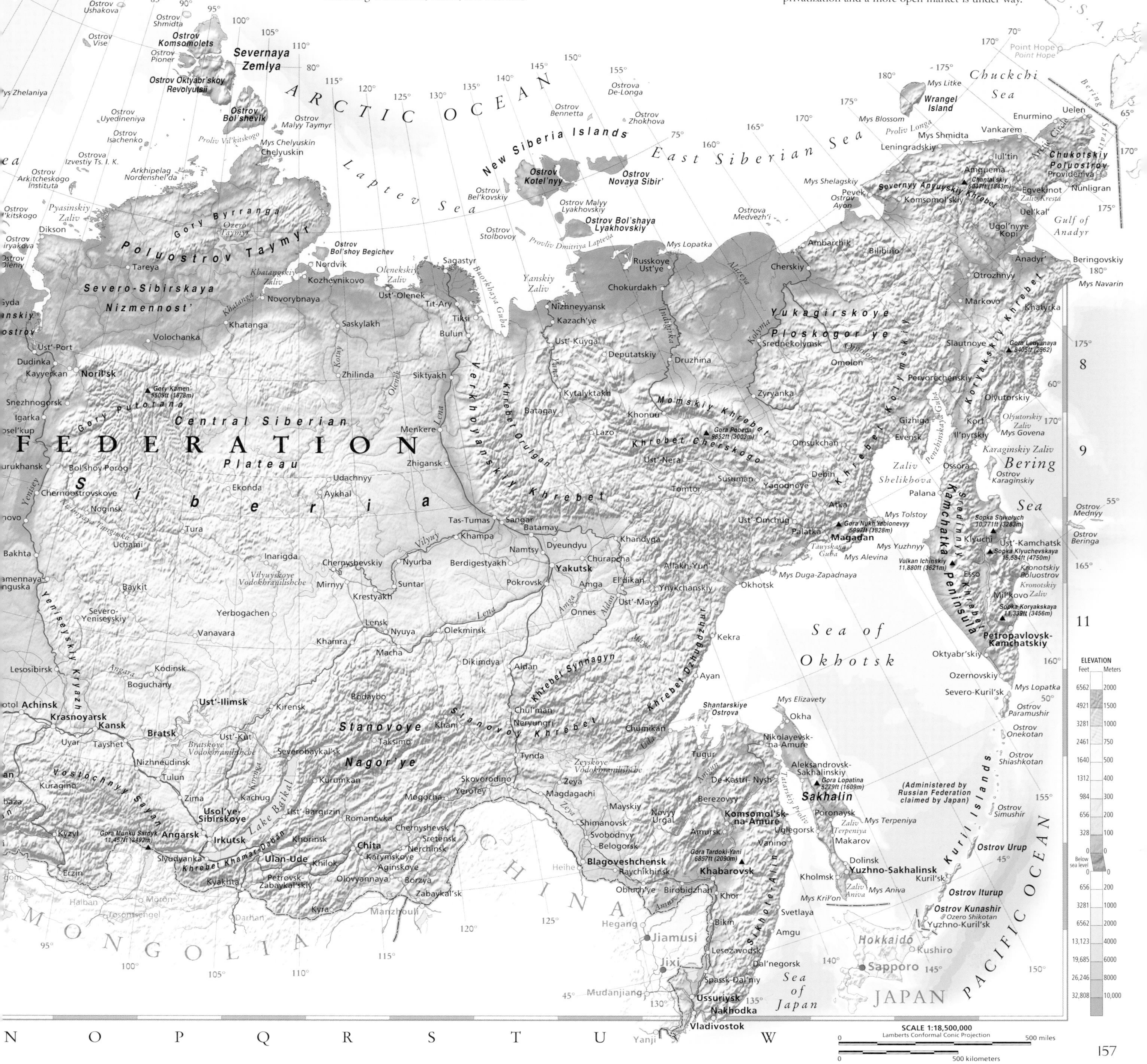
N O P Q R S T U V W X Y Z
1 2 3 8 9 11
ARCTIC OCEAN
Laptev Sea
East Siberian Sea
Chuckchi Sea
Bering Sea
Sea of Okhotsk
Sea of Japan
PACIFIC OCEAN
FEDERATION
Central Siberian Plateau
Siberia
CHINA
MONGOLIA
JAPAN
U.S.A.
Severnaya Zemlya
New Siberia Islands
Poluostrov Taymyr
Severo-Sibirskaya Nizmennost'
Gory Byrranga
Verkhoyanskiy Khrebet
Khrebet Cherskogo
Momskiy Khrebet
Yukagirskoye Ploskogor'ye
Koryakskiy Khrebet
Kamchatka Peninsula
Chukotskiy Poluostrov
Stanovoye Nagor'ye
Stanovoy Khrebet
Vostochnyy Sayan
Lake Baikal
Sakhalin
Kuril Islands
Hokkaido
Wrangel Island
Ostrov Kotel'nyy
Ostrov Novaya Sibir'
Ostrov Bol'shevik
Ostrov Oktyabr'skoy Revolyutsii
Ostrov Komsomolets
Noril'sk
Dudinka
Khatanga
Tiksi
Yakutsk
Lensk
Mirnyy
Bratsk
Irkutsk
Ulan-Ude
Chita
Krasnoyarsk
Achinsk
Kansk
Blagoveshchensk
Khabarovsk
Komsomol'sk-na-Amure
Vladivostok
Nakhodka
Ussuriysk
Magadan
Petropavlovsk-Kamchatskiy
Anadyr'
Yuzhno-Sakhalinsk
Okha
Okhotsk
Ayan
Cherskiy
Bilibino
Providenya
Jiamusi
Jixi
Sapporo
Gora Pobeda 9852ft (3003m)
Sopka Klyuchevskaya 15,584ft (4750m)
(Administered by Russian Federation claimed by Japan)
ELEVATION
Feet Meters
6562 2000
4921 1500
3281 1000
2461 750
1640 500
1312 400
984 300
656 200
328 100
0 0
Below sea level
SCALE 1:18,500,000
Lamberts Conformal Conic Projection
500 miles
500 kilometers

Turkey, Cyprus, and Transcaucasia

Armenia, Azerbaijan, Cyprus, Georgia, Turkey

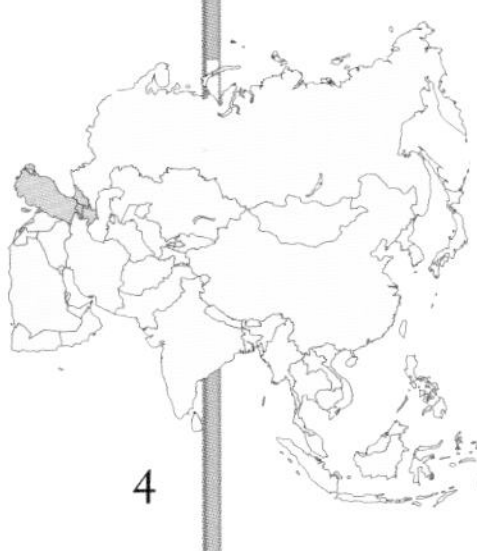

Projecting westward from the Middle East, Turkey forms a land bridge between Europe and Asia. Divided by the Bosporus, it straddles the two continents, its small region of Eastern Thrace lying within Europe and the remainder of the country, Anatolia, forming Asia's westernmost edge. An arid plateau covers much of Anatolia's interior, giving way in the east to a series of ranges that extends into Transcaucasia. Here, the towering Caucasus form another natural boundary between Asia and Europe. Three nations occupy Transcaucasia: Armenia, Azerbaijan, and Georgia. All became Soviet republics in the 20th century before attaining independence in 1991. Turkey was the heart of the Ottoman Empire, which endured from the 12th century to the early 20th century, and from 1573 to 1878 included the mainly Greek island of Cyprus.

The Caucasus

The Caucasus and the associated Lesser Caucasus mountains isolate and define the region known as Transcaucasia. The much higher Caucasus peaks form a great wall that runs from the Black Sea to the shores of the Caspian Sea and reaches Europe's highest point of 18,510 feet (5,642 m) at Elbrus in Russia. The Lesser Caucasus spread to the south across Armenia, merging with the ranges of eastern Turkey. In-between are lowlands and major river valleys, including the Kür–Aras lowlands of Azerbaijan, parts of which lie below sea level.

Black Sea
Elbrus
Aragats Lerr
K'ut'aisi
Mt Ararat
Sevana Lich
T'BILISI
Groznyy
YEREVAN
Gäncä
Caucasus
Caspian Sea
Lesser Caucasus
Yevlax
Bazardüzü Daği
Aras
Kür
Sumqayit
BAKU

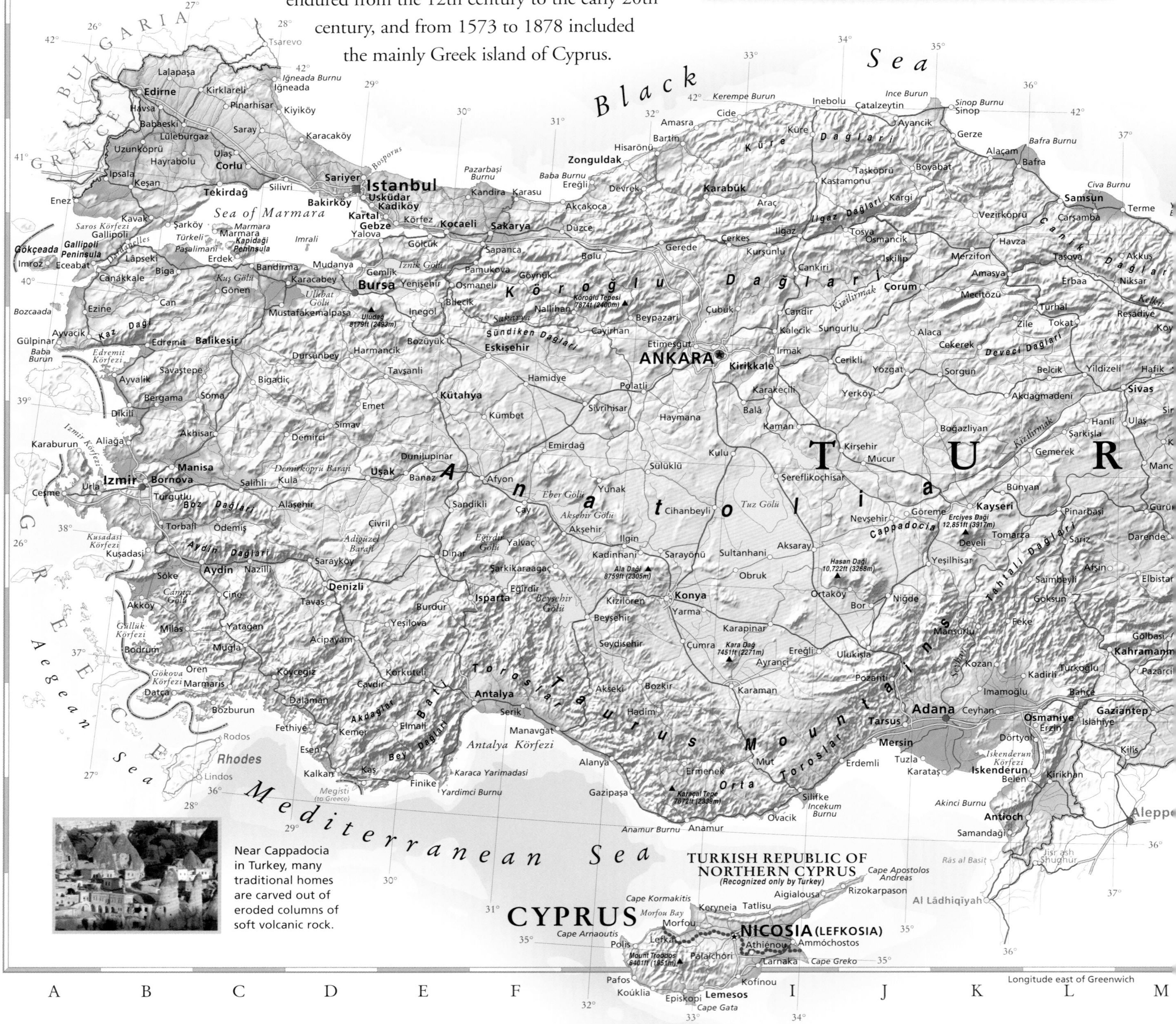

A B C D E F G H I J K L M
1 2 3 4 5 6 7 8 9 10 11 12 13 14 15
BULGARIA
GREECE
Black Sea
Sea of Marmara
Bosporus
Istanbul
Edirne
Bursa
Izmir
ANKARA
Eskişehir
Konya
Kayseri
Adana
Antalya
Samsun
Zonguldak
Köroğlu Dağlari
Küre Dağlari
Anatolia
TURKEY
Tuz Gölü
Cappadocia
Taurus Mountains
Toroslar
Aegean Sea
Mediterranean Sea
Antalya Körfezi
Rhodes
Iskenderun
Antioch
Aleppo
TURKISH REPUBLIC OF NORTHERN CYPRUS
(Recognized only by Turkey)
CYPRUS
NICOSIA (LEFKOSIA)
Lemesos
Larnaka
Pafos
Ammóchostos
Longitude east of Greenwich

Near Cappadocia in Turkey, many traditional homes are carved out of eroded columns of soft volcanic rock.

N O P Q R S T U V W X Y Z

Population Patterns

In Turkey, the interior is less densely inhabited than the Black Sea and Aegean Sea coasts and European Turkey. Transcaucasia's inhabitants cluster on the Black Sea coast, along river valleys, and on foothills, shunning uplands and the Caspian lowlands. Cyprus is more densely populated in the south. Numerous peoples have fought over and settled in this region and ethnic diversity is high, with over 50 different groups in Transcaucasia alone. Turkey and Azerbaijan's populations are predominantly Muslim, whereas Christians are in the majority elsewhere.

Istanbul
T'BILISI
ANKARA
Trabzon
YEREVAN
BAKU
Izmir
Adana
NICOSIA

Less than 2.6 persons per sq mile/1 per sq km
2.6–26 per sq mile/ 1–10 per sq km
26–65 per sq mile/ 10–25 per sq km
65–130 per sq mile/ 25–50 per sq km
130–260 per sq mile/ 50–100 per sq km
260–520 per sq mile/ 100–200 per sq km
520–1040 per sq mile/ 200–400 per sq km

Economic Profile

Metallic minerals, including chromium, manganese, mercury, and copper, are fairly widely distributed; the word Cyprus means "copper" in Greek and the island has long been renowned as a source of this metal. Oil reserves located in the Caspian Sea provide Azerbaijan with energy and valuable export revenue; the nation is also a major supplier of caviar. Traditional agriculture predominates in many areas, though industries and services have expanded rapidly in recent years, especially in Turkey. The production of textiles is important, along with metals, machinery, automobiles, food products, and some electronic goods in Transcaucasia.

Istanbul
T'BILISI
ANKARA
Trabzon
YEREVAN
BAKU
Izmir
Adana
NICOSIA

Forest and woodland
Arable land
Grazing

Citrus fruits
Wine
Cotton
Tobacco
Sugar beet
Fishing
Industrial center
Oil production

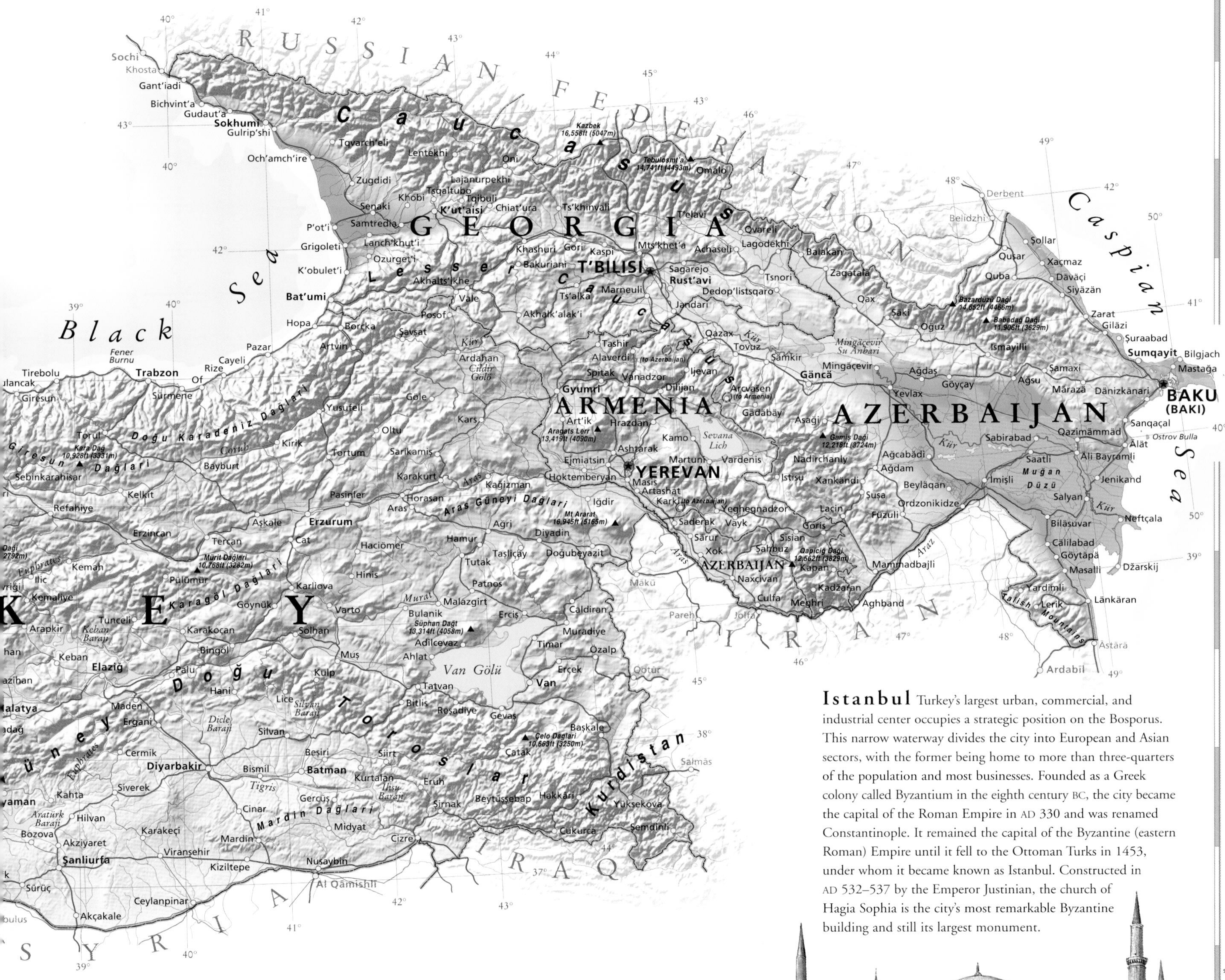

RUSSIAN FEDERATION
Caucasus
GEORGIA
ARMENIA
AZERBAIJAN
Black Sea
Caspian Sea
IRAN
IRAQ
SYRIA
T'BILISI
YEREVAN
BAKU (BAKI)
Sokhumi
Bat'umi
Trabzon
Erzurum
Kars
Gyumri
Gäncä
Sumqayit
Van Gölü
Sevana Lich
Kazbek 16,558ft (5047m)
Mt Ararat 16,945ft (5165m)
Lesser Caucasus
Doğu Toroslar
Kurdistan
Talish Mountains
Diyarbakir
Batman
Şanliurfa
Elazığ
Malatya
Van
Kutaisi
Rust'avi
Naxçivan
Länkäran
Ardabil

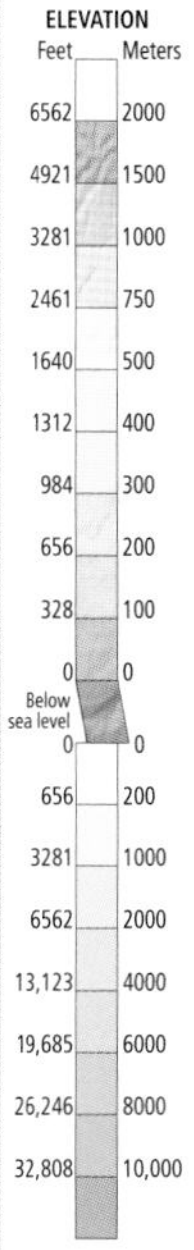

ELEVATION
Feet Meters
6562 2000
4921 1500
3281 1000
2461 750
1640 500
1312 400
984 300
656 200
328 100
0 0
Below sea level
0 0
656 200
3281 1000
6562 2000
13,123 4000
19,685 6000
26,246 8000
32,808 10,000

Istanbul Turkey's largest urban, commercial, and industrial center occupies a strategic position on the Bosporus. This narrow waterway divides the city into European and Asian sectors, with the former being home to more than three-quarters of the population and most businesses. Founded as a Greek colony called Byzantium in the eighth century BC, the city became the capital of the Roman Empire in AD 330 and was renamed Constantinople. It remained the capital of the Byzantine (eastern Roman) Empire until it fell to the Ottoman Turks in 1453, under whom it became known as Istanbul. Constructed in AD 532–537 by the Emperor Justinian, the church of Hagia Sophia is the city's most remarkable Byzantine building and still its largest monument.

A Turkish invasion of Cyprus in 1974 led to the creation of Turkish and Greek sectors divided by a UN buffer zone.

Azerbaijan's oil is not as much in demand as it once was. Around 1900, Baku provided half the world's supplies.

N O P Q R S T U V W

SCALE 1:4,250,000
Lamberts Conformal Conic Projection
0 120 miles
0 120 kilometers

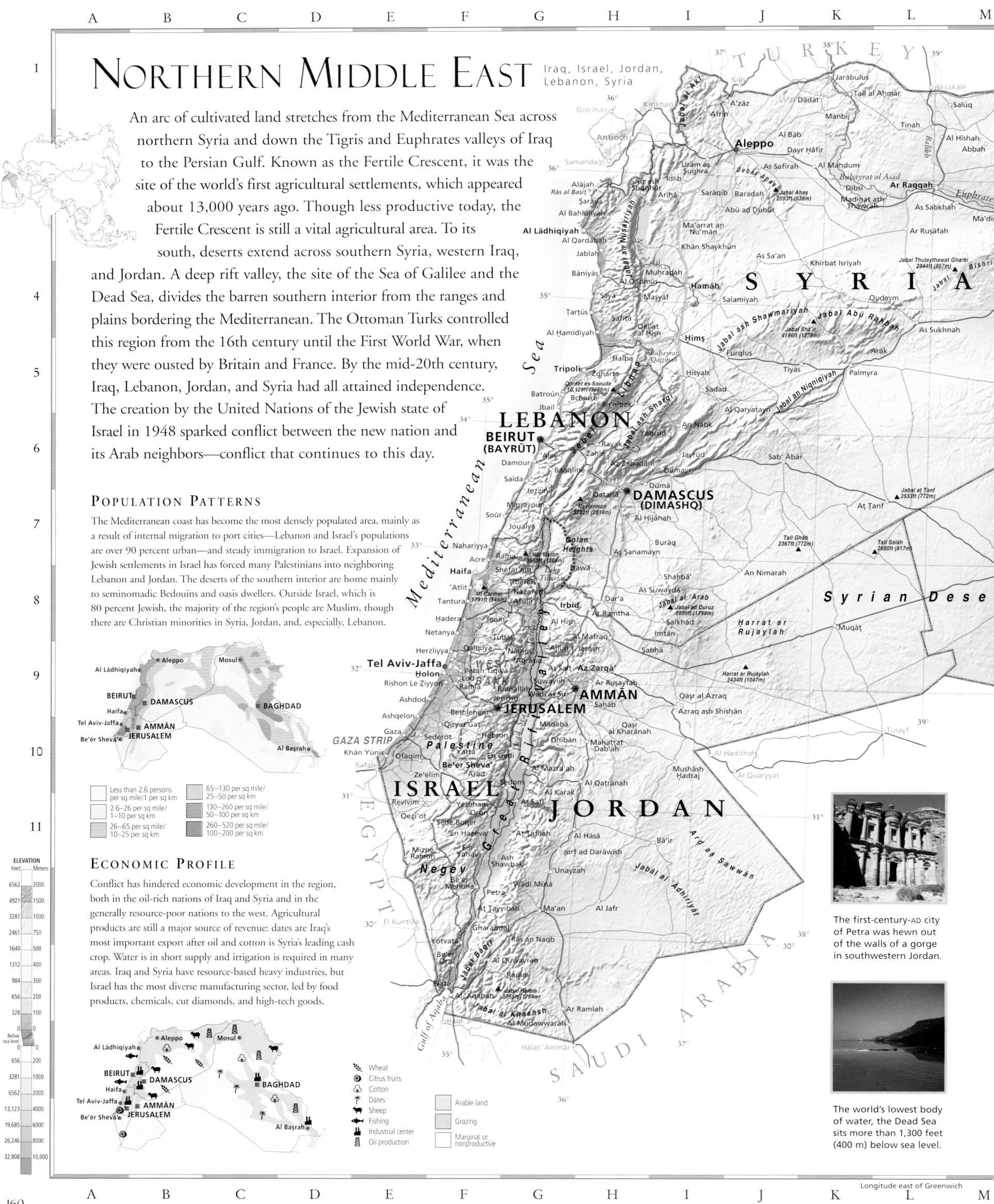

Northern Middle East

Iraq, Israel, Jordan, Lebanon, Syria

An arc of cultivated land stretches from the Mediterranean Sea across northern Syria and down the Tigris and Euphrates valleys of Iraq to the Persian Gulf. Known as the Fertile Crescent, it was the site of the world's first agricultural settlements, which appeared about 13,000 years ago. Though less productive today, the Fertile Crescent is still a vital agricultural area. To its south, deserts extend across southern Syria, western Iraq, and Jordan. A deep rift valley, the site of the Sea of Galilee and the Dead Sea, divides the barren southern interior from the ranges and plains bordering the Mediterranean. The Ottoman Turks controlled this region from the 16th century until the First World War, when they were ousted by Britain and France. By the mid-20th century, Iraq, Lebanon, Jordan, and Syria had all attained independence. The creation by the United Nations of the Jewish state of Israel in 1948 sparked conflict between the new nation and its Arab neighbors—conflict that continues to this day.

A B C D E F G H I J K L M
1 4 5 6 7 8 9 10 11
TURKEY
SYRIA
LEBANON
ISRAEL
JORDAN
Mediterranean Sea
Syrian Desert
SAUDI ARABIA
EGYPT
GAZA STRIP
WEST BANK
Golan Heights
Aleppo
Hamāh
Ḥimṣ
Ar Raqqah
Palmyra
Tripoli
BEIRUT (BAYRŪT)
DAMASCUS (DIMASHQ)
Tel Aviv-Jaffa
Haifa
JERUSALEM
AMMĀN
Irbid
Az Zarqā'
Al Lādhiqīyah
Ṭarṭūs
Euphrates
Great Rift Valley
Dead Sea
Gulf of Aqaba
Negev
Jabal an Nuṣayrīyah
Jebel Liban
Jabal ash Sharqī
Jabal al 'Arab
Qornet es Saouda 10,129ft (3088m)
Mt Hermon 9232ft (2814m)
Har Meron 3963ft (1208m)
Mt Carmel 1791ft (546m)
Jabal Ramm 5755ft (1754m)
Petra
Ma'an
Al 'Aqabah
Elat
Be'ér Sheva'
Longitude east of Greenwich

Population Patterns

The Mediterranean coast has become the most densely populated area, mainly as a result of internal migration to port cities—Lebanon and Israel's populations are over 90 percent urban—and steady immigration to Israel. Expansion of Jewish settlements in Israel has forced many Palestinians into neighboring Lebanon and Jordan. The deserts of the southern interior are home mainly to seminomadic Bedouins and oasis dwellers. Outside Israel, which is 80 percent Jewish, the majority of the region's people are Muslim, though there are Christian minorities in Syria, Jordan, and, especially, Lebanon.

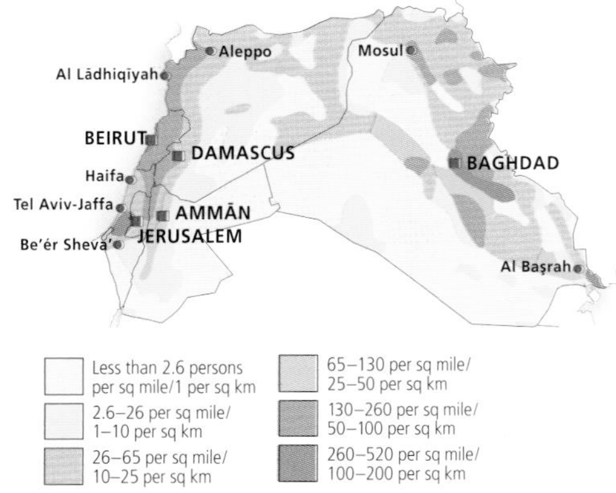

Aleppo
Mosul
Al Lādhiqīyah
BEIRUT
DAMASCUS
BAGHDAD
Haifa
Tel Aviv-Jaffa
AMMĀN
JERUSALEM
Be'ér Sheva'
Al Başrah
Less than 2.6 persons per sq mile/1 per sq km
2.6–26 per sq mile/ 1–10 per sq km
26–65 per sq mile/ 10–25 per sq km
65–130 per sq mile/ 25–50 per sq km
130–260 per sq mile/ 50–100 per sq km
260–520 per sq mile/ 100–200 per sq km

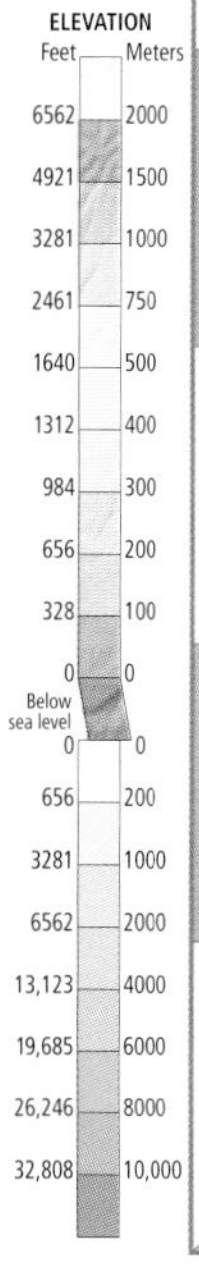

ELEVATION
Feet Meters
6562 2000
4921 1500
3281 1000
2461 750
1640 500
1312 400
984 300
656 200
328 100
0 0
Below sea level

Economic Profile

Conflict has hindered economic development in the region, both in the oil-rich nations of Iraq and Syria and in the generally resource-poor nations to the west. Agricultural products are still a major source of revenue: dates are Iraq's most important export after oil and cotton is Syria's leading cash crop. Water is in short supply and irrigation is required in many areas. Iraq and Syria have resource-based heavy industries, but Israel has the most diverse manufacturing sector, led by food products, chemicals, cut diamonds, and high-tech goods.

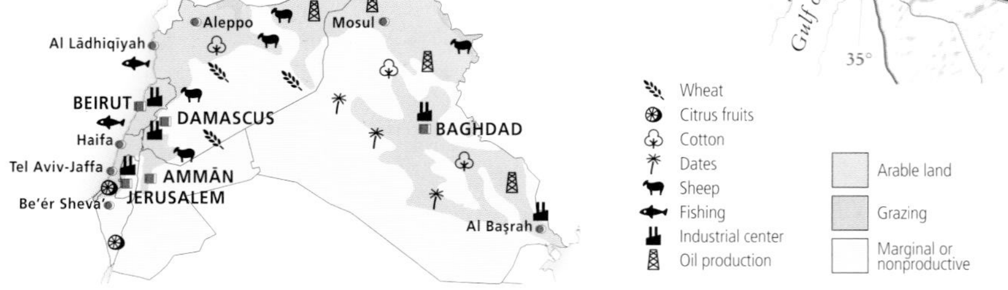

Aleppo
Mosul
Al Lādhiqīyah
BEIRUT
DAMASCUS
BAGHDAD
Haifa
Tel Aviv-Jaffa
AMMĀN
JERUSALEM
Be'ér Sheva'
Al Başrah
Wheat
Citrus fruits
Cotton
Dates
Sheep
Fishing
Industrial center
Oil production
Arable land
Grazing
Marginal or nonproductive

The first-century-AD city of Petra was hewn out of the walls of a gorge in southwestern Jordan.

The world's lowest body of water, the Dead Sea sits more than 1,300 feet (400 m) below sea level.

N O P U V W X Y Z
Q R S T
1 2 3 4 5 6 7 8 9 10 13 14 15
TURKEY
Kurdistan
IRAQ
IRAN
SAUDI ARABIA
KUWAIT
Persian Gulf
BAGHDAD (BAGHDĀD)
KUWAIT (AL KUWAYT)
Mosul
Arbīl
Kirkūk
As Sulaymānīyah
Al Qāmishli
Dayr az Zawr
Al Jazīrah
Jabal Sinjār
Jabal 'Abd al 'Azīz
Jabal Hamrīn
Tigris
Euphrates
Great Zab
Little Zab
Wādī ath Tharthār
Buhayrat ath Tharthār
Hawr al Habbānīyah
Buhayrat ar Razāzah
Hawr as Sa'dīyah
Hawr al Hammār
Wādī Hawrān
Wādī al Bātin
Nahr Diyālā
Shatt al 'Arab
Ar Ramādī
Al Fallūjah
Sāmarrā'
Tikrīt
Ba'qūbah
Karbalā'
Al Hillah
An Najaf
Ad Dīwānīyah
Al Kūt
Al 'Amārah
An Nāsirīyah
Sūq ash Shuyūkh
Al Basrah
Umm Qasr
Al Fāw
Ar Rutbah
Ar Rihab
Ash Shāmīyah
Sahrā' al Hijāra
Zahrat al Batn
Nisāb
Ash Shu'bah
Bubiyān Island
Khorramshahr
Ābādān
Rawāndiz
Zākhō
Dahūk
Sar-i Korawa 10,994ft (3351m)
Kuh-e Haji Ebrahim 11,811ft (3600m)
Jabal Abd al Aziz 3018ft (920m)

Elat in Israel is a popular center for divers exploring the wonders of the Red Sea's extensive coral reefs.

The capital of Lebanon, Beirut was ravaged by civil war between 1975 and 1990, and is just starting to recover.

The Great Ziggurat of Ur is one of the best-preserved parts of the ancient city of Ur, near An Nāṣirīyah in Iraq.

Jerusalem

Situated in a river valley linking the Mediterranean coast and the Dead Sea, the ancient city of Jerusalem is a place of pilgrimage for the adherents of three major faiths: Judaism, Christianity, and Islam. The Old City's many shrines reflect this diversity of beliefs, most notably around the Dome of the Rock. The oldest remaining Islamic temple and said to be the scene of Muhammad's ascension to heaven, it backs onto the Western Wall, the remains of a temple that constitute the most sacred site of Judaism. Nearby is the Church of the Holy Sepulchre, where Jesus is said to have been entombed before rising again.

Dome of the Rock

SCALE 1:3,250,000
Lamberts Conformal Conic Projection
0 100 miles
0 100 kilometers

The Arabian Peninsula

Bahrain, Kuwait, Oman, Qatar, Saudi Arabia, United Arab Emirates, Yemen

Consisting of a broad plateau that slopes downward from a western coastal escarpment to low-lying eastern plains, the Arabian Peninsula is bounded by the Red Sea to the west, the Persian Gulf and Gulf of Oman to the northeast, and the Gulf of Aden and Arabian Sea to the south. Its interior is one of the most arid areas on Earth. Treeless, stony plains and vast sand deserts cover thousands of square miles. Rainfall is meager, and water flows only after seasonal showers along otherwise dry stream beds known as wadis. The Ottoman Turks occupied the western fringe of the peninsula from the 16th century until the early 20th century; by then Britain had established several protectorates on the east coast. An Islamic sect called the Wahhabis, led by the Saudi dynasty, held the interior from the 18th century, eventually founding Saudi Arabia in 1932. The discovery of oil has brought great wealth to that nation, as well as to the so-called Gulf States of Kuwait, Bahrain, Qatar, the United Arab Emirates, and, to a lesser extent, Oman.

Mecca The birthplace of the prophet Muhammad, Mecca is the most sacred site for Muslims, who are obliged by their faith to make at least one visit to the city, a pilgrimage known as the hajj. Two million pilgrims arrive each year, thronging the city and its temples, especially the Al-Haram Mosque. It encircles the Kaaba, a cubic stone shrine said to have been built originally by Abraham and Ishmael as a representation of God's house in heaven.

Population Patterns

The population is concentrated along the shoreline and in the marginally better-watered coastal ranges, with the fertile uplands of Yemen being the most densely inhabited zone. With the exception of the area around the Saudi capital of Riyadh, interior settlements are small and widely dispersed; most center on oases. The urban population is small in Yemen (26 percent) but large elsewhere, ranging from 78 percent in Oman to 96 percent in Kuwait. Culturally, the peninsula is homogenous, the vast majority of the inhabitants being Arab peoples who speak Arabic and follow Islam, which originated here.

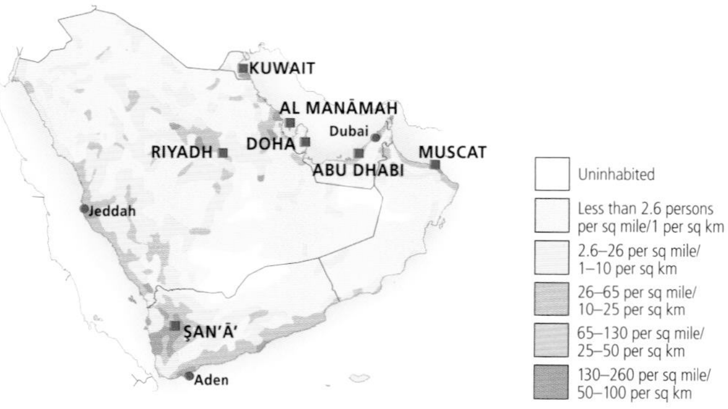
KUWAIT
AL MANĀMAH
Dubai
RIYADH
DOHA
MUSCAT
ABU DHABI
Jeddah
ṢAN'Ā'
Aden
Uninhabited
Less than 2.6 persons per sq mile/1 per sq km
2.6–26 per sq mile/ 1–10 per sq km
26–65 per sq mile/ 10–25 per sq km
65–130 per sq mile/ 25–50 per sq km
130–260 per sq mile/ 50–100 per sq km

Economic Profile

The Arabian Peninsula holds the world's largest petroleum reserves and enormous deposits of natural gas, and the oil and gas industries dominate the local economy. As well as a wide range of services including banking and printing, they support the manufacturing of metals, plastics, fertilizers, cement, and other products. Fossil fuels aside, however, the region is resource-poor. Only small pockets can be cultivated and many of these require irrigation. The major crops are dates and other fruits, coffee, and wheat. Sheep, goats, and camels are widely distributed, but have to graze over large areas to obtain sufficient food.

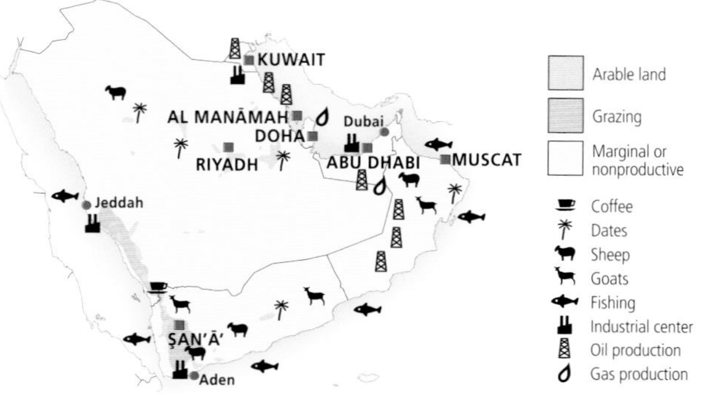
KUWAIT
AL MANĀMAH
Dubai
DOHA
RIYADH
ABU DHABI
MUSCAT
Jeddah
ṢAN'Ā'
Aden
Arable land
Grazing
Marginal or nonproductive
Coffee
Dates
Sheep
Goats
Fishing
Industrial center
Oil production
Gas production

Petroleum was first located in Bahrain in 1932, and soon after in Saudi Arabia.

Tel Aviv-Jaffa
AMMĀN
JERUSALEM
Gaza
Port Said
JORDAN
ISRAEL
Ismâ'iliya
Suez
Ma'an
Turayf
Kāf
Al Ḥamād
Al 'Īsāwiyah
Sakākah
Al Jawf
Elat
Al 'Aqabah
Ḥaql
At Tubayq
Ḥālat 'Ammār
Sinai
Gulf of Suez
Gulf of Aqaba
Al Bi'r
An Nafūd
Jabal al Lawz 8461ft (2579m)
Jabal ash Shifā
Tabūk
Rās ash Shaykh Ḥumayd
Aş Şawrah
Jabal ad Dubbagh 7710ft (2350m)
Al Qalibah
Sharm el Sheikh
Al Muwayliḥ
Taymā'
Ḍubā
Qal'at al Aẓlam
Ḥijāz
EGYPT
Al 'Ulā
Hafirat al'Aydā
Al Wajh
Rās Karkūmā
Jabal Nahr 5249ft (1600m)
Umm Urūmah
Hanak
Khaybar
Shaybārā
Umm Lajj
Rās Abū Madd
Bi'r Naṣīf
Al Ḥanākīyah
Jabal Radwa 6851ft (1814m)
Al 'Uyūn
Medina
Rās Baridi
Yanbu' al Baḥr
Al Musayjīd
Tropic of Cancer
Badr Ḥunayn
Abū Rubā
Red Sea
Masturah
Ḥarrat Rahat
Rābigh
Al Bi'ar
Qaḍimah
Tuwwal
Khulays
Rās Ḥaṭibah
Dahaban
'Usfān
Al Jumūm
Jeddah
Ar Rās al Aswad
Mecca
Aṭ Ṭā'if
Mastābah
SUDAN
Al Līth
Ḥamdānah
Al Qun
ERITREA
ASMARA
ETHIOPIA
Longitude east of Greenwich

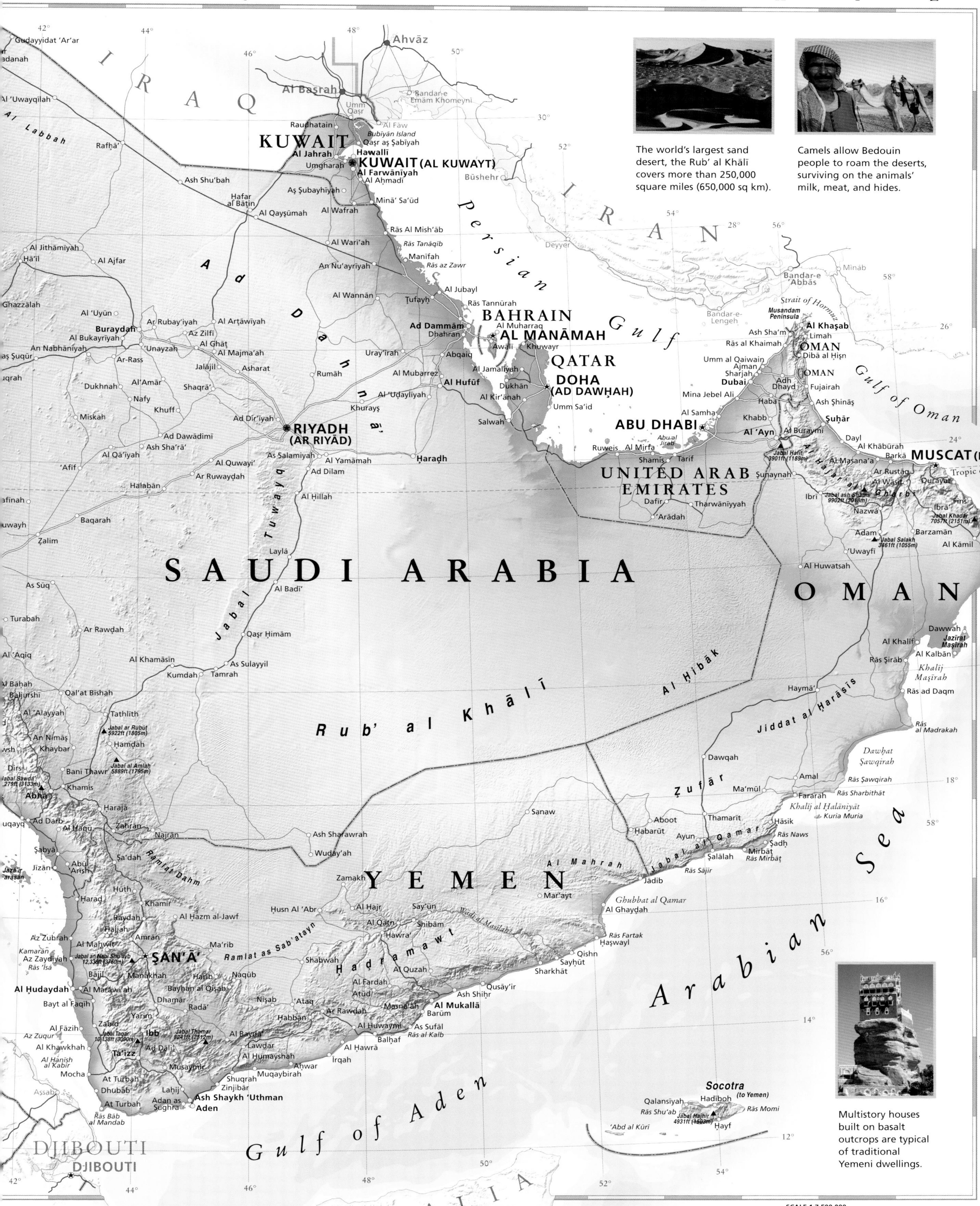
N O P Q R S T U V W X Y Z
1 2 3 4 5 6 7 8 9 10 11
IRAQ
IRAN
KUWAIT
KUWAIT (AL KUWAYT)
BAHRAIN
AL MANĀMAH
QATAR
DOHA (AD DAWḤAH)
ABU DHABI
UNITED ARAB EMIRATES
MUSCAT (MASQAT)
OMAN
SAUDI ARABIA
RIYADH (AR RIYĀḌ)
YEMEN
ṢAN'Ā'
DJIBOUTI
SOMALIA
Persian Gulf
Gulf of Oman
Strait of Hormuz
Arabian Sea
Gulf of Aden
Rub' al Khālī
Ad Dahnā'
Jabal Ṭuwayq
Al Ḥibāk
Jiddat al Ḥarāsīs
Ramlat Dahm
Ramlat as Sab'atayn
Ḥaḍramawt
Al Mahrah
Ẓufār
Jabal al Qamar
Al Ḥajar al Gharbī
Tropic of Cancer
Socotra (to Yemen)
Jabal Ḥajhir 4931ft (1503m)
Jabal Shams 9902ft (3018m)
Jabal Hafīt 3901ft (1189m)
Jabal Akhḍar 7057ft (2151m)
Jabal Salakh 3461ft (1055m)
Jabal ar Rubūt 5922ft (1805m)
Jabal al Amlah 5889ft (1795m)
Jabal an Nabī Shu'ayb 12,336ft (3760m)
Jabal Thamar 8241ft (2512m)
Jabal Ṣabir 10,138ft (3090m)
Ahvāz
Al Başrah
Umm Qaşr
Bandar-e Emām Khomeyni
Būshehr
Deyyer
Bandar-e 'Abbās
Bandar-e Lengeh
Mīnāb
Al Jahrah
Hawallī
Al Farwānīyah
Al Aḥmadī
Mīnā' Sa'ūd
Ad Dammām
Dhahran
Al Hufūf
Al Jubayl
Ḥafar al Bāṭin
Buraydah
Ḥā'il
Abhā
Khamis
Najrān
Al Ḥudaydah
Ta'izz
Ibb
Aden
Al Mukallā
Sayhūt
Salālah
Mirbāṭ
Ṣūr
Ibrā'
Nizwá
Ṣuḥār
Dubai
Sharjah
Ajman
Umm al Qaiwain
Ras al Khaimah
Al Khaṣab
Al 'Ayn
Fujairah
Ruwais
Al Mirfa
Shamis
Tarif
Dafir
'Arādah
Ṭhārwānīyyah
Ash Sharawrah
Haraḍh
Al Kharj
Sanaw
Ḥabarūt
Thamarīt
Ma'mūl
Dawqah
Amal
Haymā'
Duqm
Dawwah
Jazīrat Maṣīrah
Khalīj Maṣīrah
Ras al Madrakah
Dawḥat Şawqirah
Khalīj al Ḥalānīyāt
Kuria Muria
Ghubbat al Qamar
Ras Fartak
Qishn
Shihr
Mar'ayt
Jādib
Ḥadibūh
Qalansīyah
Ḥayf
Rās Momi
'Abd al Kūrī
Al Wajh
Tathlīth
As Sulayyil
Laylā
Qaşr Ḥimām
Al Badī'
Tamrah
Kumdah
Ṣa'dah
Ḥūth
Khamir
Marib
Shibām
Sayun
Tarīm
Ataq
Lahij
Mocha
Zabīd
Bayt al Faqīh
ELEVATION
Feet Meters
6562 2000
4921 1500
3281 1000
2461 750
1640 500
1312 400
984 300
656 200
328 100
0 0
Below sea level
656 200
3281 1000
6562 2000
13,123 4000
19,685 6000
26,246 8000
32,808 10,000
SCALE 1:7,500,000
Lamberts Conformal Conic Projection
0 250 miles
0 250 kilometers

The world's largest sand desert, the Rub' al Khālī covers more than 250,000 square miles (650,000 sq km).

Camels allow Bedouin people to roam the deserts, surviving on the animals' milk, meat, and hides.

Multistory houses built on basalt outcrops are typical of traditional Yemeni dwellings.

AFGHANISTAN, IRAN, AND PAKISTAN

A high, mainly barren plateau dominates the western half of this region, occupying most of Iran and extending into Afghanistan and Pakistan. It is bounded in the northwest by the forested Elburz Mountains and in the west by the Zagros Mountains. In northeastern Afghanistan, it rises to the lofty summits of the Hindu Kush and the Karakorams, offshoots of the Himalaya; in Pakistan, its crumpled eastern fringe abuts the broad, low valley of the Indus River. More than 97 percent of the inhabitants of this rugged and mostly arid land are Muslims, and their religion has profoundly influenced the region's history. Pakistan was founded in 1947 as a home for India's Muslims; Iran has been ruled by Islamic clerics since a revolution in 1979; and in the late 1990s Afghanistan was run by the Taliban, a fundamentalist Islamic regime that was toppled by a U.S.-led invasion in 2001.

A B C D E F G H I J K L M
TURKEY
YEREVAN
ARMENIA
AZERBAIJAN
Kurdistan
Tabrīz
Orūmīyeh
Ardabīl
Rasht
Caspian Sea
Gonbad-e Kavus
Gorgān
Sārī
Bābol
Amol
Elburz Mountains
TEHRAN (TEHRĀN)
Qazvīn
Zanjān
Hamadān
Kermānshāh
Sanandaj
Qom
Kāshān
Dasht-e Kavīr
IRAN
Eşfahān
Yazd
Iranian Plateau
Zagros Mountains
Ahvāz
Ābādān
Khorramshahr
Būshehr
Shīrāz
Kermān
Bandar-e 'Abbās
Strait of Hormuz
Persian Gulf
Gulf of Oman
IRAQ
KUWAIT
SAUDI ARABIA
BAHRAIN
QATAR
UNITED ARAB EMIRATES
OMAN
Kūh-e Shīb
Longitude east of Greenwich

Iran's Dasht-e Kavīr is characterized by vast stony plains and low-lying salt pans (*kavirs*).

Iranian carpets, most of which are still woven by hand, are much in demand overseas.

At 28,251 feet (8,611m), K2, in the Karakoram range, is the world's second-highest peak.

Thriving around 2500 BC, Mohenjo Daro, near Sukkur, Pakistan, was one of Indus Valley's first cities.

THE KHYBER PASS

One of just a few passes permitting travel between Central Asia and the Indian Subcontinent, the Khyber Pass has long been of strategic importance to locals and foreign powers, from the Persians, who used it to reach the Indus in the fifth century BC, to the British, who made it the focus of local operations in the late 19th century. Consisting of a narrow opening in the Safed Koh Range, the pass reaches its highest point of 3,543 feet (1,080 m) at Landi Kotal. Its road and rail links facilitate travel between Kabul in Afghanistan and Peshawar in Pakistan.

KABUL
Hindu Kush
Safed Koh
Jalālābād
Khyber Pass
Landi Kotal
Peshawar
Indus
Bannu
Kohat
Pezu
Kalabagh
Wah
ISLAMABAD

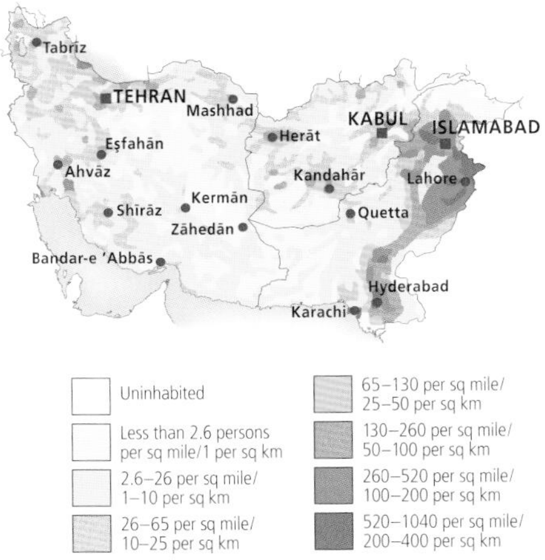
Tabriz
TEHRAN
Mashhad
Eşfahān
Ahvāz
Shīrāz
Kermān
Zāhedān
Bandar-e 'Abbās
Herāt
KABUL
ISLAMABAD
Kandahār
Lahore
Quetta
Hyderabad
Karachi
Uninhabited
Less than 2.6 persons per sq mile/1 per sq km
2.6–26 per sq mile/ 1–10 per sq km
26–65 per sq mile/ 10–25 per sq km
65–130 per sq mile/ 25–50 per sq km
130–260 per sq mile/ 50–100 per sq km
260–520 per sq mile/ 100–200 per sq km
520–1040 per sq mile/ 200–400 per sq km

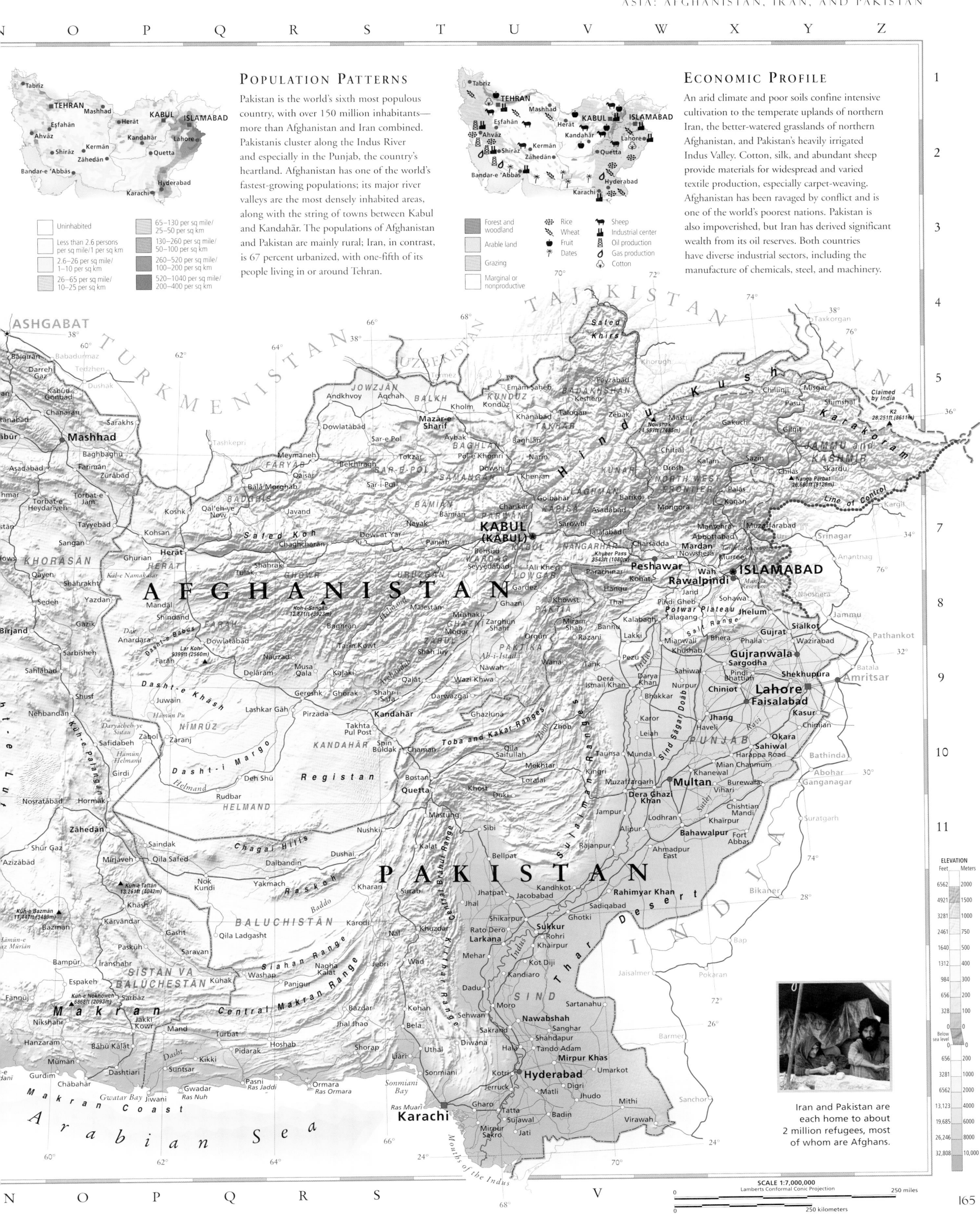

Population Patterns

Pakistan is the world's sixth most populous country, with over 150 million inhabitants—more than Afghanistan and Iran combined. Pakistanis cluster along the Indus River and especially in the Punjab, the country's heartland. Afghanistan has one of the world's fastest-growing populations; its major river valleys are the most densely inhabited areas, along with the string of towns between Kabul and Kandahār. The populations of Afghanistan and Pakistan are mainly rural; Iran, in contrast, is 67 percent urbanized, with one-fifth of its people living in or around Tehran.

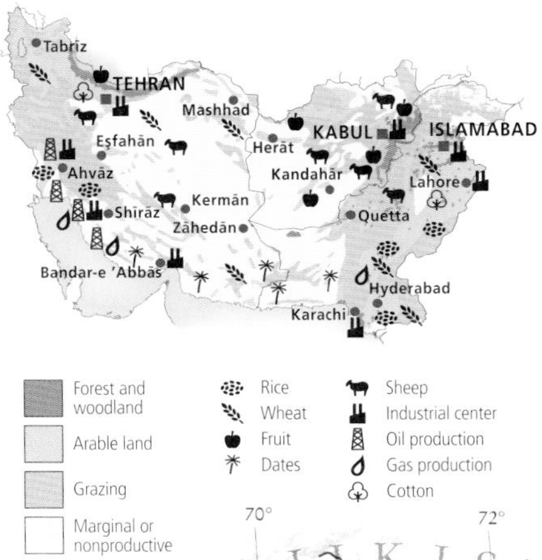
Tabriz
TEHRAN
Mashhad
Eşfahān
Ahvāz
Shīrāz
Kermān
Zāhedān
Bandar-e 'Abbās
Herāt
KABUL
ISLAMABAD
Kandahār
Lahore
Quetta
Hyderabad
Karachi
Forest and woodland
Arable land
Grazing
Marginal or nonproductive
Rice
Wheat
Fruit
Dates
Sheep
Industrial center
Oil production
Gas production
Cotton

Economic Profile

An arid climate and poor soils confine intensive cultivation to the temperate uplands of northern Iran, the better-watered grasslands of northern Afghanistan, and Pakistan's heavily irrigated Indus Valley. Cotton, silk, and abundant sheep provide materials for widespread and varied textile production, especially carpet-weaving. Afghanistan has been ravaged by conflict and is one of the world's poorest nations. Pakistan is also impoverished, but Iran has derived significant wealth from its oil reserves. Both countries have diverse industrial sectors, including the manufacture of chemicals, steel, and machinery.

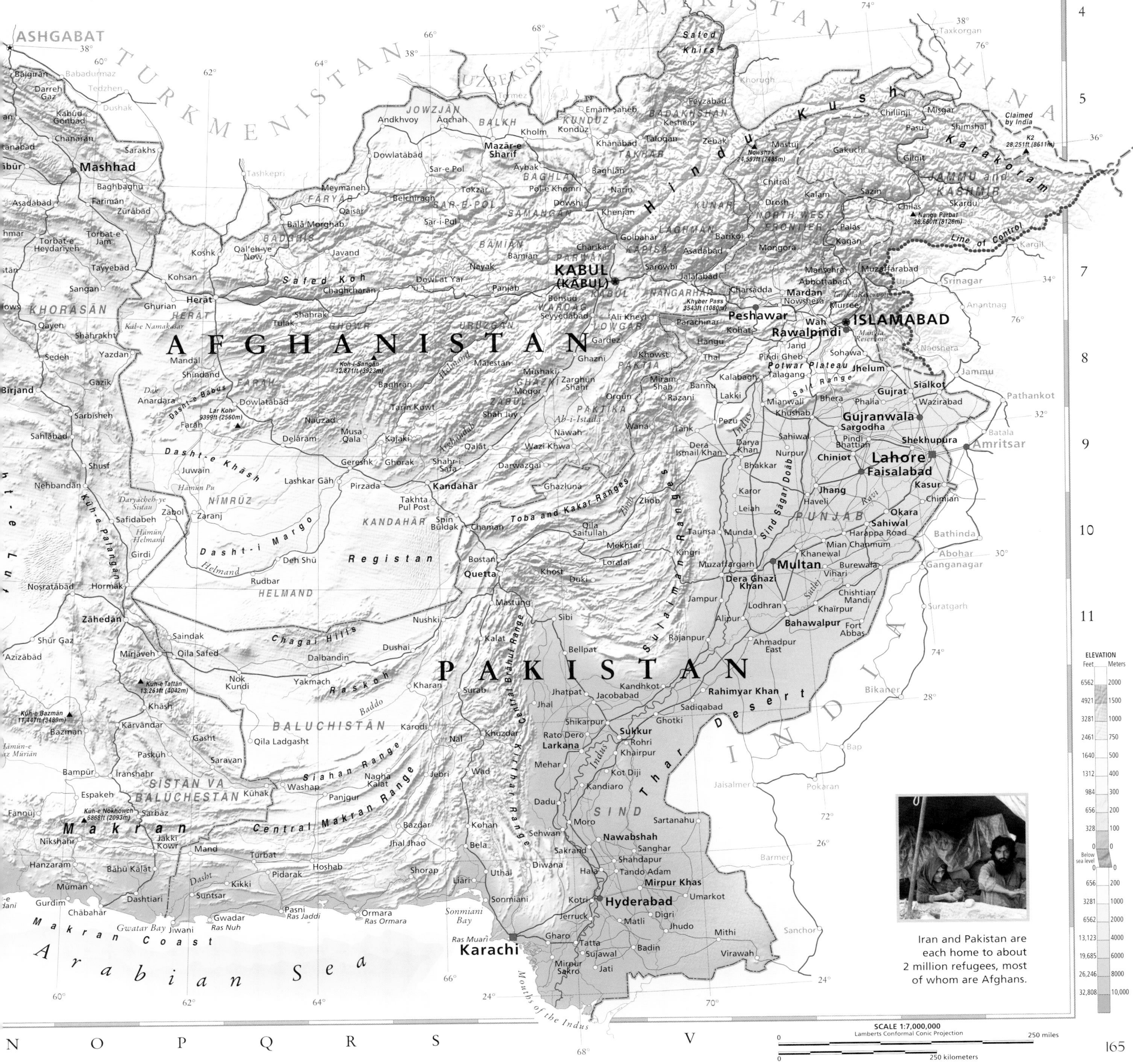
N O P Q R S T U V W X Y Z
1 2 3 4 5 6 7 8 9 10 11
AFGHANISTAN
PAKISTAN
TURKMENISTAN
TAJIKISTAN
UZBEKISTAN
CHINA
INDIA
KABUL (KĀBUL)
ISLAMABAD
ASHGABAT
Arabian Sea
Hindu Kush
Karakoram
JAMMU and KASHMIR
Line of Control
Claimed by India
K2 28,251ft (8611m)
Nanga Parbat 26,660ft (8126m)
Nowshak 24,557ft (7485m)
Khyber Pass 3543ft (1080m)
Safed Koh
Registan
Dasht-i Margo
Dasht-e Khash
Chagai Hills
Toba and Kakar Ranges
Sulaiman Range
Central Brahui Range
Kirthar Range
Central Makran Range
Siahan Range
Thar Desert
Makran
Makran Coast
Mashhad
Herāt
Kandahār
Quetta
Peshawar
Rawalpindi
Lahore
Faisalabad
Gujranwala
Multan
Hyderabad
Karachi
Zāhedān
Mazār-e Sharif
Amritsar
Srinagar
BALUCHISTĀN
SIND
PUNJAB
NORTH WEST FRONTIER
SĪSTĀN VA BALŪCHESTĀN
KHORĀSĀN
HELMAND
NĪMRŪZ
KANDAHĀR
Mouths of the Indus
ELEVATION
Feet Meters
6562 2000
4921 1500
3281 1000
2461 750
1640 500
1312 400
984 300
656 200
328 100
0 0
Below sea level
656 200
3281 1000
6562 2000
13,123 4000
19,685 6000
26,246 8000
32,808 10,000
SCALE 1:7,000,000
Lamberts Conformal Conic Projection
0 250 miles
0 250 kilometers
N O P Q R S V

Iran and Pakistan are each home to about 2 million refugees, most of whom are Afghans.

Central Asia

Kazakhstan, Kyrgyzstan, Tajikistan, Turkmenistan, Uzbekistan

The peoples of Central Asia have long been linked by a shared Islamic religious and cultural heritage, traditionally pastoral and seminomadic lifestyles, and related, mainly Turkic languages. During the 19th century, they were brought even closer together when their lands were annexed by the Russian Empire. Subsequent Soviet control transformed an undeveloped region, rapidly industrializing farming, manufacturing, and mining, turning several villages into cities, and creating separate republics for each of the major ethnic groups—the Uzbeks, Kazaks, Tajiks, Turkmens, and Kyrgyz. After the fall of communism in 1991, all five republics became independent states. These nations occupy a wide, mainly arid and low-lying region. The grasslands of the Kazakh Steppe stretch across its northern third, spreading into Russia. South of the Aral Sea, deserts cover the Turan Lowland. In the east, a series of ranges climbs toward the Pamir and Tien Shan ranges, whose soaring peaks divide Central Asia from China.

Cotton is Turkmenistan's principal crop. Production centers on irrigated areas along the Amudar'ya River.

Russia's spacecraft-launching center is near Baykonur in Kazakhstan.

Population Patterns

The scarcity of fresh water has restricted dense settlement to upland areas and the banks of major rivers, leaving the deserts and grasslands sparsely inhabited. During the Soviet era, Central Asia's population grew rapidly, due partly to an influx of Russians and Ukrainians and partly to improvements in medical services. Despite this, Central Asian society remains predominantly rural; indeed, with the departure of many Russians after the demise of the Soviet Union, the continuing focus on cotton production, and high birth rates in country areas, rural populations have grown recently, against the prevailing world trend.

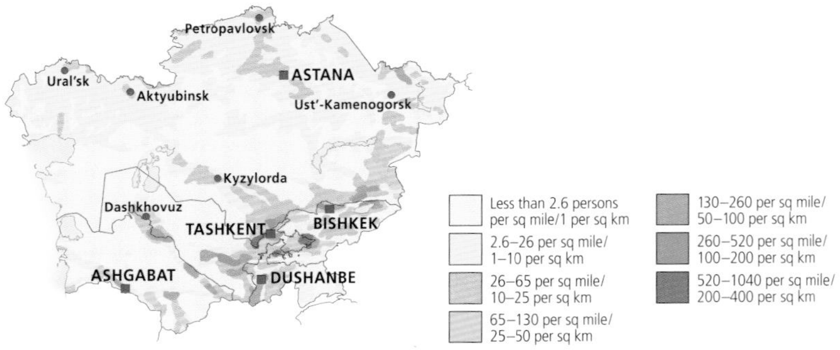

Petropavlovsk
Ural'sk
Aktyubinsk
ASTANA
Ust'-Kamenogorsk
Kyzylorda
Dashkhovuz
TASHKENT
BISHKEK
ASHGABAT
DUSHANBE
Less than 2.6 persons per sq mile/1 per sq km
2.6–26 per sq mile/1–10 per sq km
26–65 per sq mile/10–25 per sq km
65–130 per sq mile/25–50 per sq km
130–260 per sq mile/50–100 per sq km
260–520 per sq mile/100–200 per sq km
520–1040 per sq mile/200–400 per sq km

Economic Profile

Central Asia's mineral reserves include oil and gas deposits near the Caspian Sea and supplies of coal, iron ore, and chromium in Kazakhstan; these support a variety of heavy industries. Three-fifths of the land is desert, and large areas are used for grazing. Crops can be grown only in fertile upland pockets and irrigated areas. Soviet emphasis on the production of coal and oil in Kazakhstan and cotton elsewhere not only created severe environmental problems, but left these nations dependent on just a few commodities. Recent expansion of the gas industry (Turkmenistan has the world's fifth-largest reserves) is part of an attempt to diversify produce and alleviate widespread poverty.

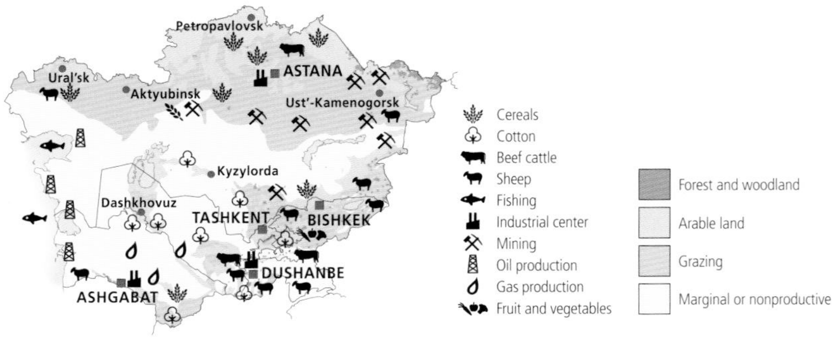

Petropavlovsk
Ural'sk
Aktyubinsk
ASTANA
Ust'-Kamenogorsk
Kyzylorda
Dashkhovuz
TASHKENT
BISHKEK
ASHGABAT
DUSHANBE
Cereals
Cotton
Beef cattle
Sheep
Fishing
Industrial center
Mining
Oil production
Gas production
Fruit and vegetables
Forest and woodland
Arable land
Grazing
Marginal or nonproductive

A B C D E F G H I J K L M
1 2 3 4 5 6 7 8 9 10 11 12 13 14 15
RUSSIAN FEDERATION
Ozinki
Kamenka
Ural'sk
Burlin
Ilek
Kushum
Aksay
Novouzensk
Chingirlau
Sol'-Iletsk
Algabas
ZAPADNYY KAZAKHSTAN
Bitik
Chapayevo
Zhympity
Kransoyar
Martuk
Orsk
Shil'da
Dzhanybek
Kaztalovka
Zhalpaktal
Aktyubinsk
Khobda
Khromtau
Komsomol'sk
Ozero Aralsor
Ural
Ozero Itmurunkol'
Karatobe
Bestamak
Karabutak
Saykhin
Dzhangala
Leninskoye
Taypak
Kandyagash
Zhuryn
Miyaly
Uil
Shubarkuduk
Gory Mugodzhary
Inderborskiy
Ozero Inder
Bayganin
Emba
Shakhty
Kharabali
Caspian Depression
Sagiz
AKTYUBINSK
Makhambet
Zhanterek
Zharkamys
Novobogatinskoye
Dossor
Makat
Chelkar
Zhanbay
Emba
Atyrau
Balykshi
ATYRAU
Astrakhan'
Ganyushkino
Kul'sary
Togu
Karaton
Opornyy
Zaliv Komsomolets
Sarykamys
Ostrova Tyulen'i
Ostrov Kulaly
Mangyshlakskiy Zaliv
Beyneu
Kyushe
Mys Tyub-Karagan
Fort-Shevchenko
Ostrov Vozrozhdeniya
Karakalpakiya
Tauchik
Aral Sea
Shetpe
Say-Utes
Gora Besshoky 1821ft (555m)
Aktau
Ustyurt Plateau
Munayshy
Kyzylsay
QORAQALPOGHISTON RESPUBLIKASI
Mys Peschanyy
Kuryk
Zhanaozen
Muynak
Fetisovo
MANGISTAU
Kungrad
Kazakhskiy Zaliv
Caspian Sea
Mys Sengirli
Shumanay
Nukus
Keneurgench
Mys Suz
Sarykamyshkoye Ozero
Boldumsaz
Bekdash
Akdepe
Dashkhovuz
Zaliv Kara-Bogaz-Gol
Karabogazkel'
Chink Kaplankyr
Gory Koymatdag
Turt
Karshi
DASHKHOVUZSKIY VELAYAT
Urgen
Gory Akkyr
Darta
TURKMENISTAN
Turkmenbashi
Krasnovodskiy Zaliv
Gora Arlang 6169ft (1880m)
Darvaza
Dzhebel
BALKANSKIY VELAYAT
Cheleken
Nebitdag
Turan Lowland
Ostrov Ogurchinskiy
Gumdag
Gazandzhyk
Danata
Turkmenskiy Zaliv
Gyzylarbat
Yerbent
Bugdayli
Gora Khasardag 5302ft (1616m)
Bami
Karakum Desert
Madau
Kopet Dag
Bakherden
Bakhardok
Okarem
Gora Tagarev 7358ft (2243m)
AKHALSKIY VELAYAT
Esenguly
Gyzyletrek
Atrek
ASHGABAT
Bojnurd
Babadurmaz
Tedzhen
Gorgan
IRAN
Quchan
Dushak
Mashhad
Longitude east of Greenwich

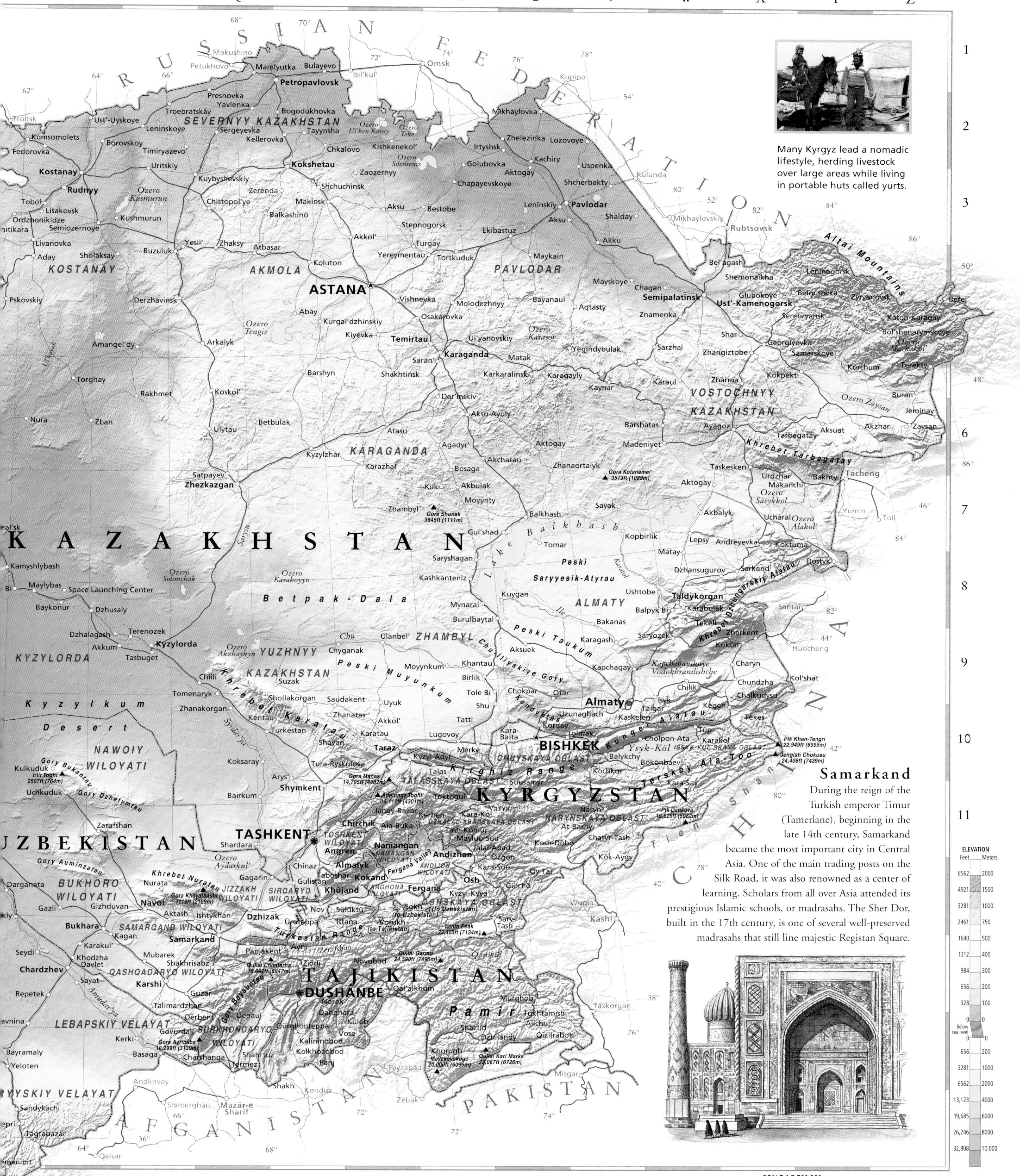
N O P Q R S T U V W X Y Z
1 2 3 4 5 6 7 8 9 10 11
RUSSIAN FEDERATION
KAZAKHSTAN
KYRGYZSTAN
TAJIKISTAN
UZBEKISTAN
AFGANISTAN
PAKISTAN
CHINA
ASTANA
Almaty
BISHKEK
TASHKENT
DUSHANBE
SEVERNYY KAZAKHSTAN
KOSTANAY
AKMOLA
PAVLODAR
KARAGANDA
VOSTOCHNYY KAZAKHSTAN
ALMATY
ZHAMBYL
YUZHNYY KAZAKHSTAN
KYZYLORDA
NAWOIY WILOYATI
BUKHORO WILOYATI
SAMARQAND WILOYATI
QASHQADARYO WILOYATI
SURKHONDARYO WILOYATI
LEBAPSKIY VELAYAT
CHUYSKAYA OBLAST
TALASSKAYA OBLAST
NARYNSKAYA OBLAST
ISSYK-KUL'SKAYA OBLAST
DZHALAL-ABADSKAYA OBLAST
OSHSKAYA OBLAST
Petropavlovsk
Kokshetau
Kostanay
Rudnyy
Pavlodar
Semipalatinsk
Ust'-Kamenogorsk
Karaganda
Temirtau
Zhezkazgan
Balkhash
Kyzylorda
Baykonur
Space Launching Center
Shymkent
Taraz
Taldykorgan
Samarkand
Bukhara
Navoi
Karshi
Chardzhev
Namangan
Andizhan
Osh
Fergana
Khujand
Kokand
Omsk
Rubtsovsk
Lake Balkhash
Ysyk-Köl
Altai Mountains
Khrebet Tarbagatay
Khrebet Dzhungarskiy Alatau
Betpak-Dala
Kyzylkum Desert
Peski Muyunkum
Peski Taukum
Peski Saryyesik-Atyrau
Khrebet Karatau
Kirghiz Range
Terskey Ala-Too
Kungei Alatau
Turkestan Range
Fergana Valley
Pamir
Tien Shan
Syrdar'ya
Amudar'ya
Pik Khan-Tengri 22,949ft (6995m)
Jengish Chokusu 24,406ft (7439m)
Pik Dankova 19,626ft (5982m)
Lenin Peak 23,405ft (7134m)
Qullai Garmo 24,590ft (7495m)
Qullai Karl Marks 22,067ft (6726m)
Gora Kotanemel' 3573ft (1089m)
Gora Shunak 3645ft (1111m)
Gora Manas 14,795ft (4482m)
Gora Ayribaba 10,299ft (3139m)

Many Kyrgyz lead a nomadic lifestyle, herding livestock over large areas while living in portable huts called yurts.

Samarkand

During the reign of the Turkish emperor Timur (Tamerlane), beginning in the late 14th century, Samarkand became the most important trading city in Central Asia. One of the main trading posts on the Silk Road, it was also renowned as a center of learning. Scholars from all over Asia attended its prestigious Islamic schools, or madrasahs. The Sher Dor, built in the 17th century, is one of several well-preserved madrasahs that still line majestic Registan Square.

ELEVATION
Feet / Meters: 6562 2000; 4921 1500; 3281 1000; 2461 750; 1640 500; 1312 400; 984 300; 656 200; 328 100; 0 0; Below sea level; 0 0; 656 200; 3281 1000; 6562 2000; 13,123 4000; 19,685 6000; 26,246 8000; 32,808 10,000

SCALE 1:7,500,000
Lamberts Conformal Conic Projection
0 — 250 miles
0 — 250 kilometers

SOUTHERN ASIA

Bangladesh, Bhutan, India, Maldives, Nepal, Sri Lanka

Sometimes referred to as the Subcontinent, this region is dominated by India, the world's seventh-largest and second-most populous country. It also includes the Himalayan kingdoms of Nepal and Bhutan, low-lying Bangladesh, and the island nations of Sri Lanka and the Maldives. From their dizzy heights, the mountains of the Himalaya drop steeply to the wide, low plain of the Ganges River. West of the Gangetic Plain, the Thar Desert spreads into Pakistan; to the south, the triangular Deccan Plateau occupies most of central and southern India. In the early 16th century, much of Southern Asia was united by the Muslim Mughal dynasty, which ruled until it was undermined by the rise of the Hindu Marathas in the 18th century. Britain controlled most of the region from the early 19th century until 1948; before withdrawing, it created the states of West Pakistan and East Pakistan, which later became Pakistan and Bangladesh, and granted independence to Ceylon, now Sri Lanka.

POPULATION PATTERNS

More than one-sixth of the world's population lives in this region. India alone has more than 1 billion inhabitants and, given its growth rate—48,000 babies are born there every day—could surpass China as the world's most populous nation by 2050. High population densities occur on the Gangetic Plain and in the northeast—Bangladesh is one of the world's most densely populated countries. Just over one-quarter of people live in cities. Most Indians and Nepalis are Hindu, whereas the majority of Bangladeshis are Muslim; Bhutan and Sri Lanka are predominantly Buddhist. Indigenous languages are many and varied, and English functions as a lingua franca.

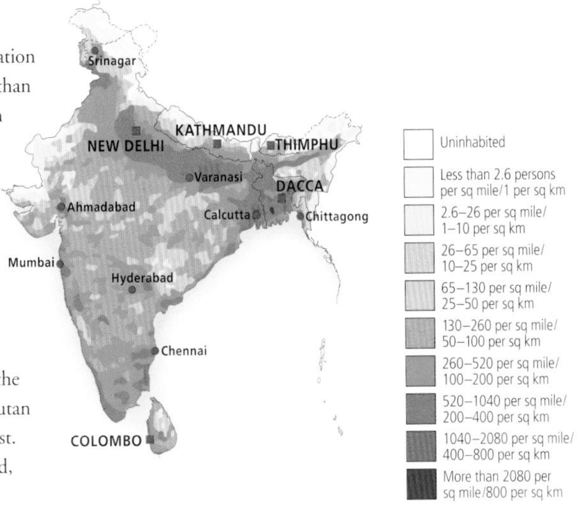
Srinagar
NEW DELHI
KATHMANDU
THIMPHU
Varanasi
DACCA
Ahmadabad
Calcutta
Chittagong
Mumbai
Hyderabad
Chennai
COLOMBO
Uninhabited
Less than 2.6 persons per sq mile/1 per sq km
2.6–26 per sq mile/ 1–10 per sq km
26–65 per sq mile/ 10–25 per sq km
65–130 per sq mile/ 25–50 per sq km
130–260 per sq mile/ 50–100 per sq km
260–520 per sq mile/ 100–200 per sq km
520–1040 per sq mile/ 200–400 per sq km
1040–2080 per sq mile/ 400–800 per sq km
More than 2080 per sq mile/800 per sq km

ECONOMIC PROFILE

The region's enormous population places great strain on its resources, which include large tracts of arable land (including 50 percent of India), forests, and minerals—India has the world's fourth-largest coal reserves, and oil and gas fields have been tapped in many areas. Most people are dependent on agriculture, yet output is insufficient to support the population: half of all Nepalis live below the poverty line and one-quarter of Indians are undernourished. The industrial sector is little developed in Bhutan, Bangladesh, and Nepal, but becoming increasingly sophisticated in India and Sri Lanka, where products include textiles, chemicals, computer software, and machinery.

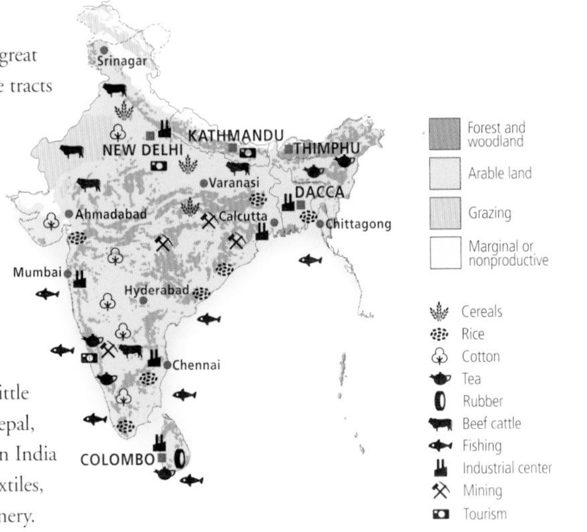
Srinagar
KATHMANDU
NEW DELHI
THIMPHU
Varanasi
DACCA
Ahmadabad
Calcutta
Chittagong
Mumbai
Hyderabad
Chennai
COLOMBO
Forest and woodland
Arable land
Grazing
Marginal or nonproductive
Cereals
Rice
Cotton
Tea
Rubber
Beef cattle
Fishing
Industrial center
Mining
Tourism

In Sri Lanka, Tamil separatists have been waging war on the government since the 1980s.

More than 90 percent of the inhabitants of the landlocked kingdom of Bhutan live in rural areas.

Hindu Kush
Karakoram Range
Ladakh Range
Zaskar Mountains
Pir Panjal Range
Himalaya
Siwalik Range
Mahabharat Range
Thar Desert
Gangetic Plain
PAKISTAN
CHINA
INDIA
NEPAL
BHUTAN
ISLAMABAD
NEW DELHI
KATHMANDU
THIMPHU
JAMMU and KASHMIR
HIMACHAL PRADESH
UTTARANCHAL
UTTAR PRADESH
PUNJAB
HARYANA
RAJASTHAN
SIKKIM
ARUNACHAL PRADESH
ASSAM
MEGHALAYA
NAGALAND
K2 28,251ft (8611m)
Nanga Parbat 26,660ft (8126m)
Mt Everest 29,035ft (8850m)
Kangchenjunga 28,169ft (8586m)
Annapurna 26,545ft (8091m)
Dhaulagiri 26,795ft (8167m)
Nanda Devi 25,646ft (7817m)
Kula Kangri 24,783ft (7554m)
(Administered by China, claimed by India)
(Administered by India, claimed by China)
Lahore
Gujranwala
Amritsar
Ludhiana
Chandigarh
Delhi
Ghaziabad
Faridabad
Meerut
Agra
Jaipur
Jodhpur
Bikaner
Lucknow
Kanpur
Allahabad
Varanasi
Patna
Srinagar
Jammu

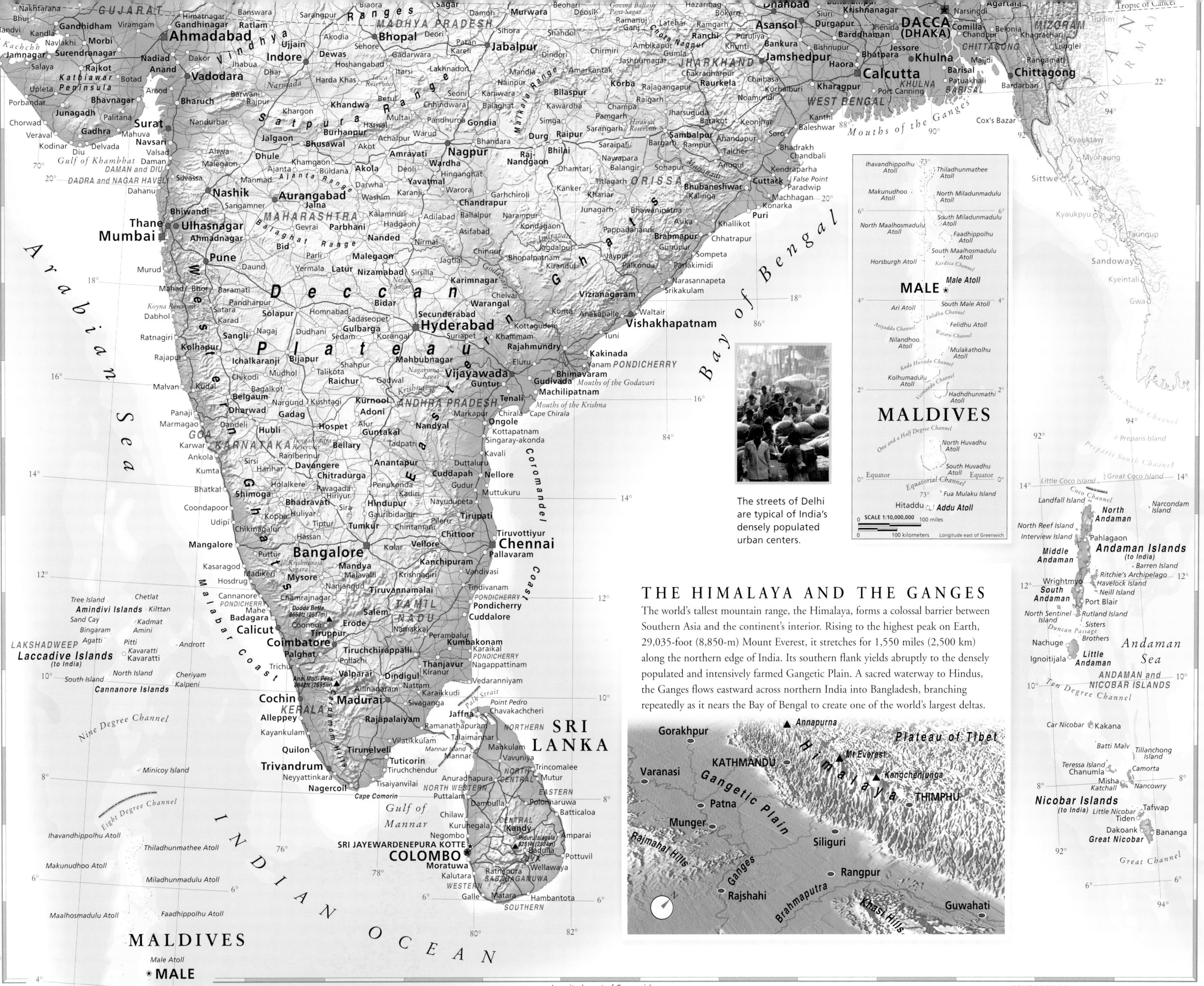
Arabian Sea
Bay of Bengal
INDIAN OCEAN
Deccan Plateau
Western Ghats
Eastern Ghats
Malabar Coast
Coromandel Coast
SRI LANKA
MALDIVES
MALE
Andaman Sea
ANDAMAN and NICOBAR ISLANDS
Andaman Islands (to India)
Nicobar Islands (to India)
Laccadive Islands (to India)
LAKSHADWEEP
Gulf of Mannar
Mouths of the Ganges
Mumbai
Bangalore
Chennai
Hyderabad
Calcutta
DACCA (DHAKA)
SRI JAYEWARDENEPURA KOTTE
COLOMBO
ELEVATION
Feet Meters
Longitude east of Greenwich
SCALE 1:9,000,000
Lamberts Conformal Conic Projection
300 miles
300 kilometers
Gorakhpur
Annapurna
Plateau of Tibet
KATHMANDU
Mt Everest
Kangchenjunga
Himalaya
THIMPHU
Varanasi
Gangetic Plain
Patna
Munger
Siliguri
Rajmahal Hills
Ganges
Rangpur
Rajshahi
Brahmaputra
Khasi Hills
Guwahati

The streets of Delhi are typical of India's densely populated urban centers.

THE HIMALAYA AND THE GANGES

The world's tallest mountain range, the Himalaya, forms a colossal barrier between Southern Asia and the continent's interior. Rising to the highest peak on Earth, 29,035-foot (8,850-m) Mount Everest, it stretches for 1,550 miles (2,500 km) along the northern edge of India. Its southern flank yields abruptly to the densely populated and intensively farmed Gangetic Plain. A sacred waterway to Hindus, the Ganges flows eastward across northern India into Bangladesh, branching repeatedly as it nears the Bay of Bengal to create one of the world's largest deltas.

A B C D E F G H I J K L M

Eastern Asia

China, Mongolia, North Korea, South Korea, Taiwan

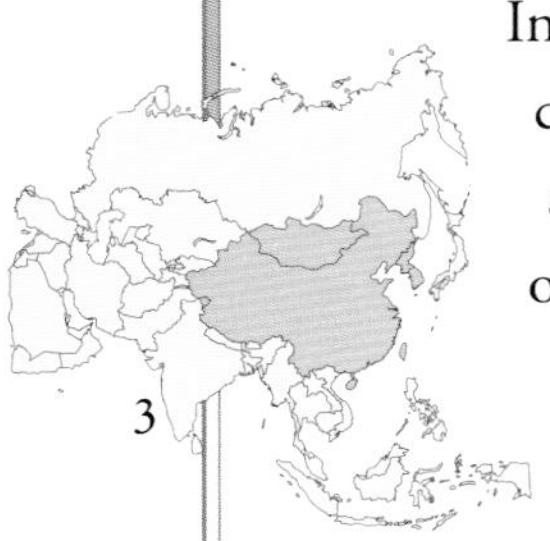

In both size and population, China dwarfs not only its neighbors, but most other countries. The world's third-largest and most populous country, it occupies 3.7 million square miles (9.6 million sq km) and is home to 1.3 billion people. From the Plateau of Tibet, which covers one-quarter of the country, major rivers, including the Yellow and the Yangtze, run eastward through the central ranges to the intensely cultivated coastal plains. Northward-flowing rivers quickly peter out in the belt of arid land that spans northern China and Mongolia. In the northeast, the forested Changbai Mountains separate China from the Korean Peninsula. Early Chinese civilizations led the world in technology, becoming the first to develop products such as paper, cast iron, silk, and gunpowder. The 20th century saw a power struggle within China between the Nationalist Party and the Communist Party. The latter won out, proclaiming the People's Republic of China in 1949, while the Nationalists repaired to Taiwan. That island's subsequent declaration of independence has yet to be recognized by China.

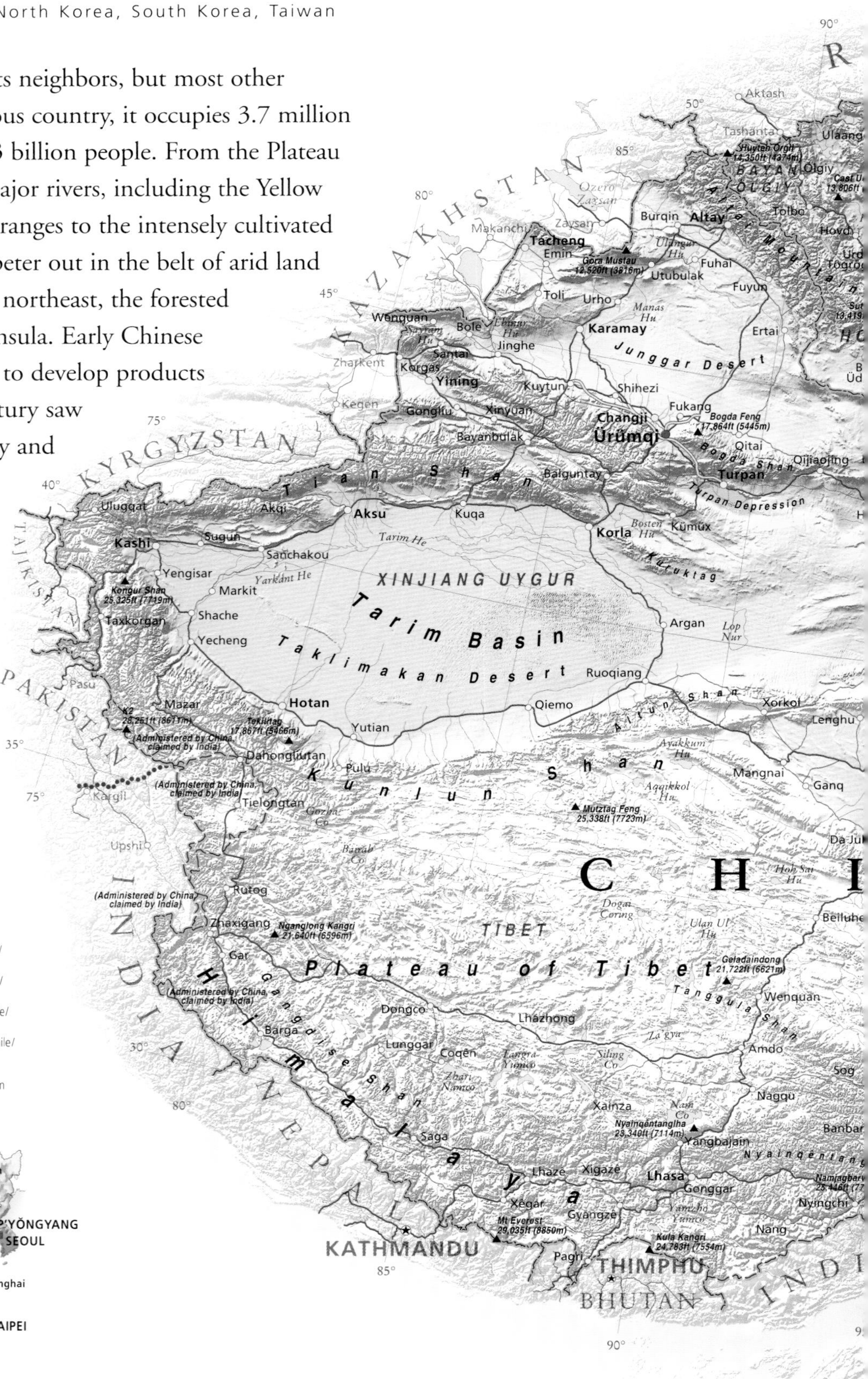

KAZAKHSTAN
KYRGYZSTAN
TAJIKISTAN
PAKISTAN
INDIA
NEPAL
BHUTAN
CHI
XINJIANG UYGUR
Tarim Basin
Taklimakan Desert
Tian Shan
Kunlun Shan
Junggar Desert
Turpan Depression
TIBET
Plateau of Tibet
Himalaya
Kashi
Aksu
Hotan
Karamay
Ürümqi
Turpan
Yining
Korla
Lhasa
KATHMANDU
THIMPHU
Mt Everest 29,035ft (8850m)
K2 28,251ft (8611m)

Cities such as Seoul have absorbed most of the rapid population growth that has occurred in South Korea.

Near Guilin in southeastern China, rice fields form a patchwork between steep, jagged limestone outcrops.

Population Patterns

China's population increases by 10 million every year, a situation that helps explain the government's controversial policy of permitting each family to have only one child. Most Chinese live in small villages and two-thirds occupy the eastern lowlands, which constitute less than one-third of the country. The population dwindles in northern and western China—just 2 million or so inhabit the vast Plateau of Tibet—and in Mongolia. The latter is one of the world's least densely populated countries: its 2.5 million people live in an area bigger than Alaska, with an average of just four people occupying each square mile (1.6 per sq km). Tiny Taiwan has almost ten times the population of Mongolia and, like the similarly crowded Korean Peninsula, is highly urbanized.

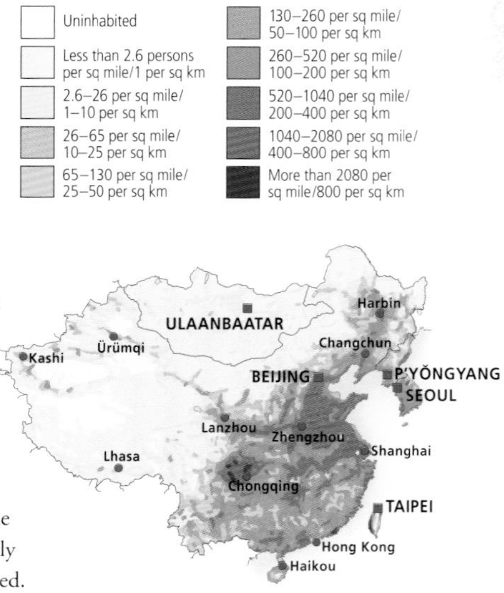

Uninhabited
Less than 2.6 persons per sq mile/1 per sq km
2.6–26 per sq mile/ 1–10 per sq km
26–65 per sq mile/ 10–25 per sq km
65–130 per sq mile/ 25–50 per sq km
130–260 per sq mile/ 50–100 per sq km
260–520 per sq mile/ 100–200 per sq km
520–1040 per sq mile/ 200–400 per sq km
1040–2080 per sq mile/ 400–800 per sq km
More than 2080 per sq mile/800 per sq km
ULAANBAATAR
Harbin
Changchun
Kashi
Ürümqi
BEIJING
P'YÖNGYANG
SEOUL
Lanzhou
Zhengzhou
Lhasa
Shanghai
Chongqing
TAIPEI
Hong Kong
Haikou

Economic Profile

With the world's largest workforce, abundant resources including coal, oil, iron ore, and hydroelectric power, and diverse, developed industries, China has huge economic potential. Until the late 1970s, this was held in check by strict government controls, but recent years have seen a degree of liberalization of production and trade, and consequent rises in productivity. A contrasting reluctance to relax state control has led to recession and food shortages in North Korea. South Korea and Taiwan have taken advantage of U.S. assistance to develop strong, technologically advanced industrial sectors, and both nations are now major producers of electronic goods. Though it has significant mineral reserves, including copper, coal, and oil, Mongolia is still dependent on its pastoral industry.

ULAANBAATAR
Harbin
Changchun
Kashi
Ürümqi
BEIJING
P'YÖNGYANG
SEOUL
Lanzhou
Zhengzhou
Shanghai
Lhasa
Chongqing
TAIPEI
Hong Kong
Haikou
Forest and woodland
Arable land
Grazing
Marginal or nonproductive
Cereals
Rice
Beef cattle
Sheep
Fishing
Industrial center
Mining
Oil production
Timber

Immense dams are being built on the Three Gorges section of the Yangtze River.

About 70 percent of farming in Mongolia involves the rearing of domestic animals.

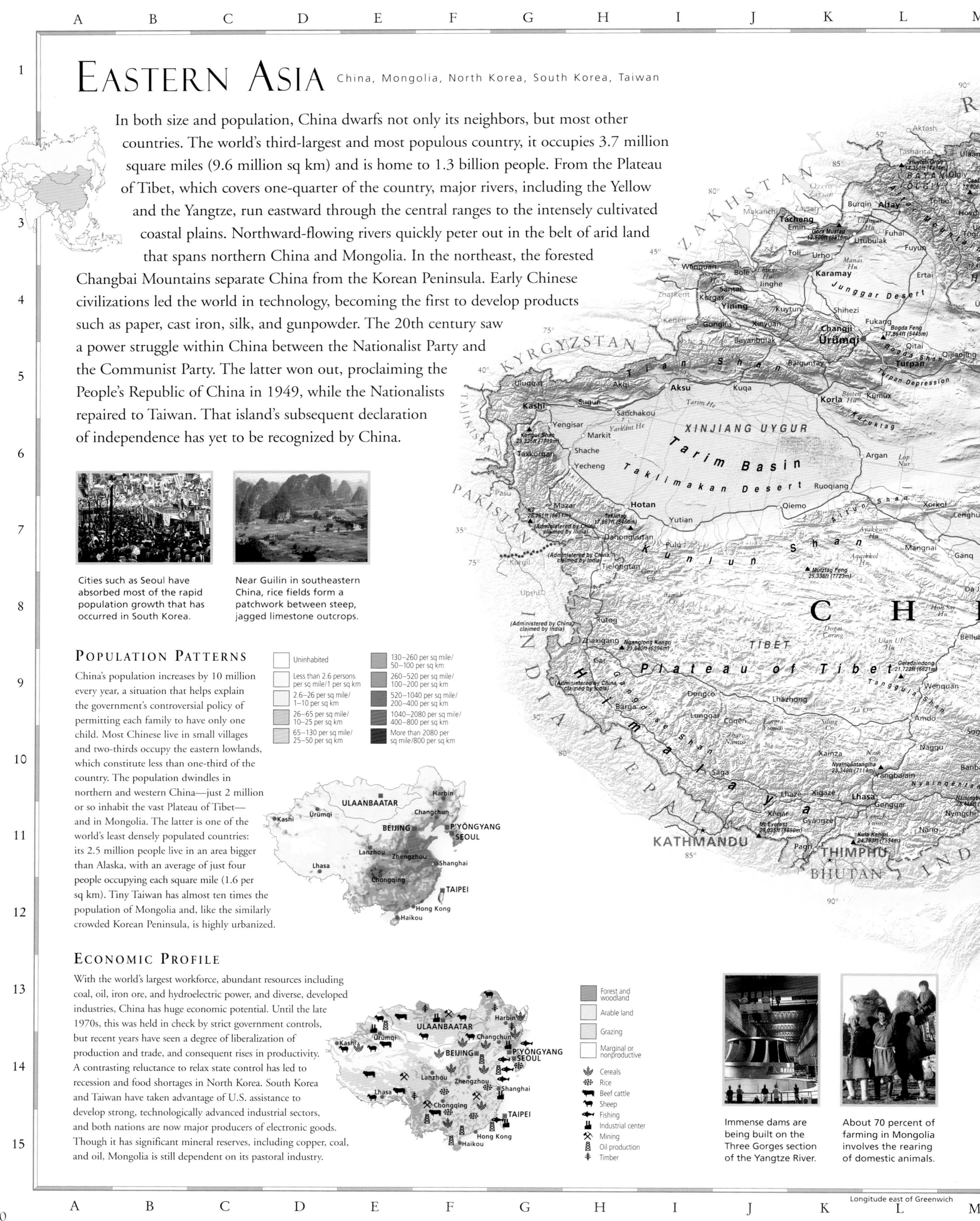

A B C D E F G H I J K L M

Longitude east of Greenwich

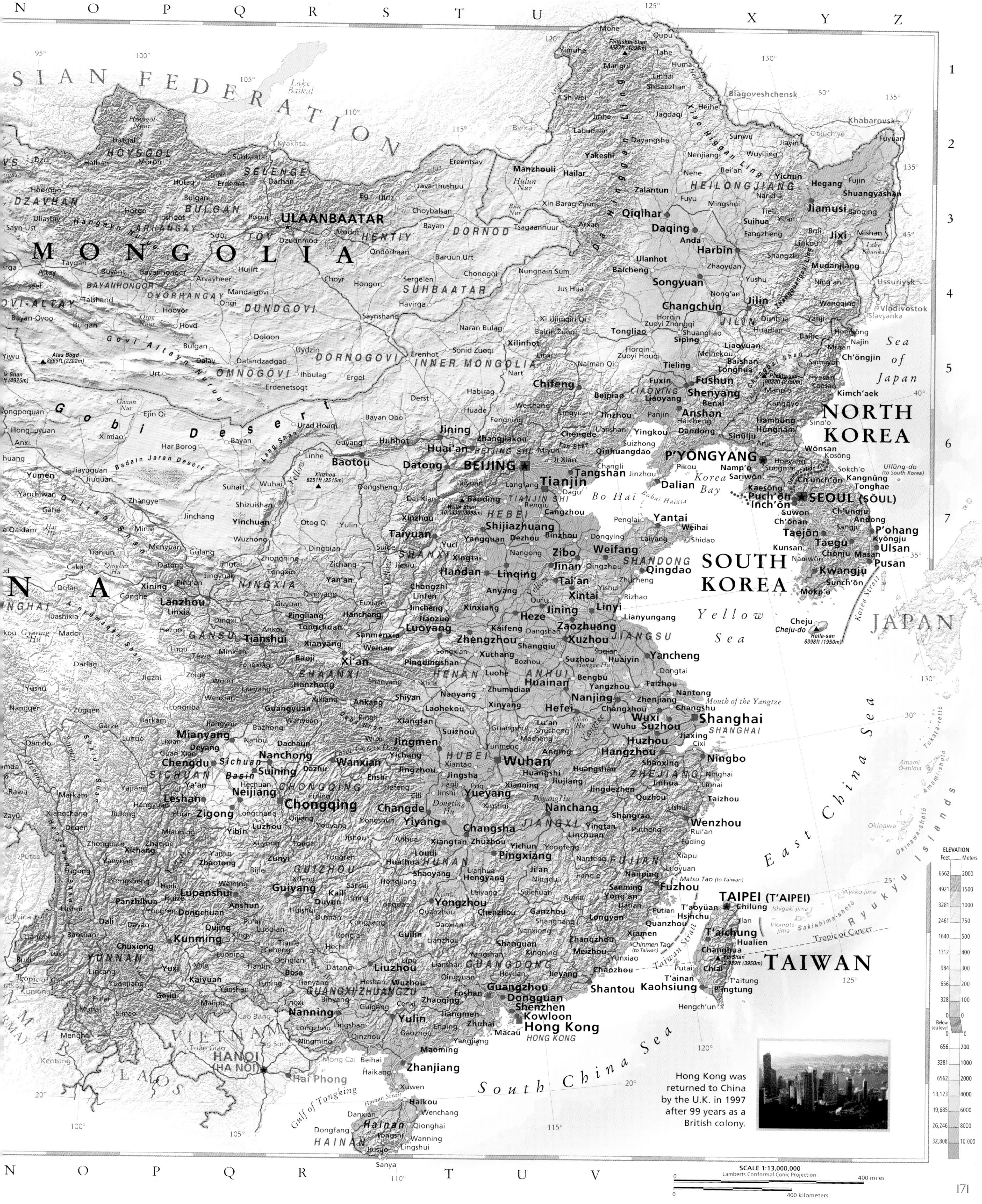
N O P Q R S T U X Y Z
1 2 3 4 5 6 7
RUSSIAN FEDERATION
MONGOLIA
NORTH KOREA
SOUTH KOREA
JAPAN
TAIWAN
ULAANBAATAR
BEIJING
P'YÖNGYANG
SEOUL (SŎUL)
TAIPEI (T'AIPEI)
HANOI (HA NOI)
Hong Kong
HONG KONG
Macau
Gobi Desert
Lake Baikal
Sea of Japan
Yellow Sea
Bo Hai
Korea Bay
East China Sea
South China Sea
Gulf of Tongking
Tropic of Cancer
INNER MONGOLIA
HEILONGJIANG
JILIN
LIAONING
HEBEI
SHANXI
SHANDONG
HENAN
JIANGSU
ANHUI
ZHEJIANG
JIANGXI
FUJIAN
HUBEI
HUNAN
GUANGDONG
GUANGXI ZHUANGZU
HAINAN
GUIZHOU
YUNNAN
SICHUAN
CHONGQING
SHAANXI
NINGXIA
GANSU
SHANGHAI
TIANJIN SHI
BEIJING SHI
Harbin
Changchun
Shenyang
Dalian
Tianjin
Shijiazhuang
Taiyuan
Jinan
Qingdao
Zhengzhou
Xi'an
Lanzhou
Nanjing
Shanghai
Hangzhou
Hefei
Wuhan
Nanchang
Changsha
Fuzhou
Guangzhou
Shenzhen
Kowloon
Nanning
Guiyang
Kunming
Chengdu
Chongqing
Haikou
Kaohsiung
Pusan
Vladivostok
Khabarovsk
Blagoveshchensk
Hong Kong was returned to China by the U.K. in 1997 after 99 years as a British colony.
ELEVATION
Feet Meters
SCALE 1:13,000,000
Lamberts Conformal Conic Projection
0 400 miles
0 400 kilometers

Mainland Southeast Asia

Cambodia, Laos, Myanmar (Burma), Thailand, Vietnam

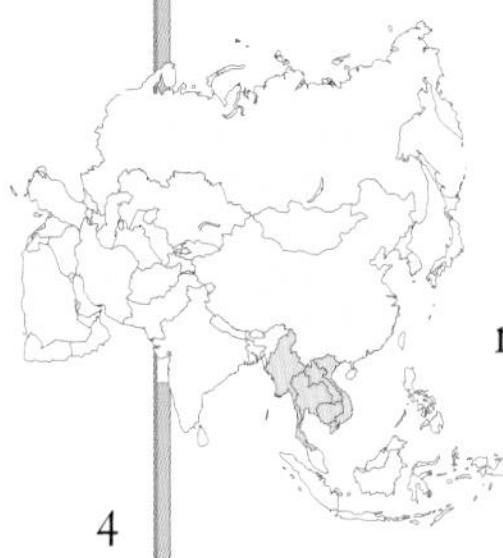

The Southeast Asian mainland consists of a broad peninsula—sometimes referred to as the Indochina Peninsula—that extends southeastward from the borders of Bangladesh, India, and China, as well as part of its narrow offshoot, the Malay Peninsula. From the Chinese Himalaya, a series of mountain ranges divided by rivers fans out over the north. On the southern lowlands, these rivers, which include the Irrawaddy and the Mekong, have formed wide alluvial plains and deltas. In the 16th century, towns along the coast became bases for European traders. By the late 19th century, Britain controlled Burma (now Myanmar) and France ruled Indochina (present-day Laos, Cambodia, and Vietnam). Post-World War II decolonization led to civil wars in Indochina, including the Vietnam War of 1964–75. Only Thailand resisted colonization throughout its history; its independence and political stability have helped it become the region's leading economic power.

Eastern Myanmar is the world's second-biggest source of illegal opium.

Most of the world's high-quality rubies come from mines in northern Myanmar.

Rice is the most widespread crop in Vietnam, covering approximately 80 percent of the country's arable land.

Population Patterns

Ethnically diverse, the inhabitants of Mainland Southeast Asia live mainly in rural villages. They are concentrated along the river valleys and especially the deltas of the Irrawaddy, Chao Phraya, Mekong, and Red rivers; they are sparsest in the heavily forested uplands of Cambodia, Laos, and the Myanmar–Thailand border. Though only about a quarter of the population is urban, the region has several large cities, most notably Bangkok (which is 20 times the size of Thailand's second city, Nonthaburi). Population growth is especially high in Laos and Cambodia; in contrast, Thailand has dramatically slowed its growth through social policies and education.

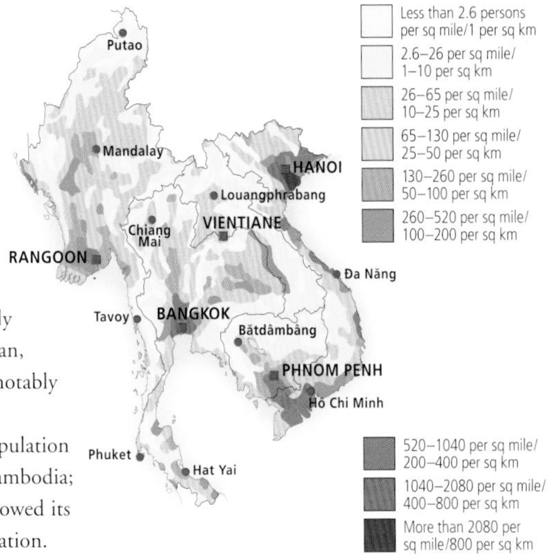

Putao
Mandalay
HANOI
Louangphrabang
Chiang Mai
VIENTIANE
RANGOON
Đa Năng
Tavoy
BANGKOK
Bătdâmbang
PHNOM PENH
Hô Chi Minh
Phuket
Hat Yai
Less than 2.6 persons per sq mile/1 per sq km
2.6–26 per sq mile/ 1–10 per sq km
26–65 per sq mile/ 10–25 per sq km
65–130 per sq mile/ 25–50 per sq km
130–260 per sq mile/ 50–100 per sq km
260–520 per sq mile/ 100–200 per sq km
520–1040 per sq mile/ 200–400 per sq km
1040–2080 per sq mile/ 400–800 per sq km
More than 2080 per sq mile/800 per sq km

Economic Profile

Agriculture is still the principal source of employment and many people, especially in the poorer countries of Cambodia, Laos, Vietnam, and Myanmar, depend on subsistence cultivation, mainly of rice, corn, and vegetables. Cash crops including rubber, palm oil, sugar, and tropical fruits make up the bulk of exports, whereas most manufactured goods are imported. Industrial development is most advanced in Thailand, which produces textiles, foodstuffs, and electrical goods, and has a thriving tourist trade. Cambodia, Laos, and Myanmar continue to exploit their extensive forests for timber, whereas Thailand now limits harvesting following overexploitation. The area where Myanmar, Thailand, and Laos meet, known as the "Golden Triangle," is a major source of opium, from which heroin is derived.

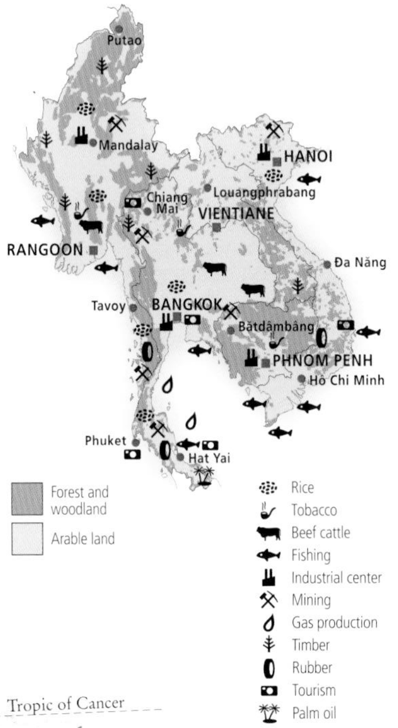

Putao
Mandalay
HANOI
Louangphrabang
Chiang Mai
VIENTIANE
RANGOON
Đa Năng
Tavoy
BANGKOK
Bătdâmbang
PHNOM PENH
Hô Chi Minh
Phuket
Hat Yai
Forest and woodland
Arable land
Rice
Tobacco
Beef cattle
Fishing
Industrial center
Mining
Gas production
Timber
Rubber
Tourism
Palm oil

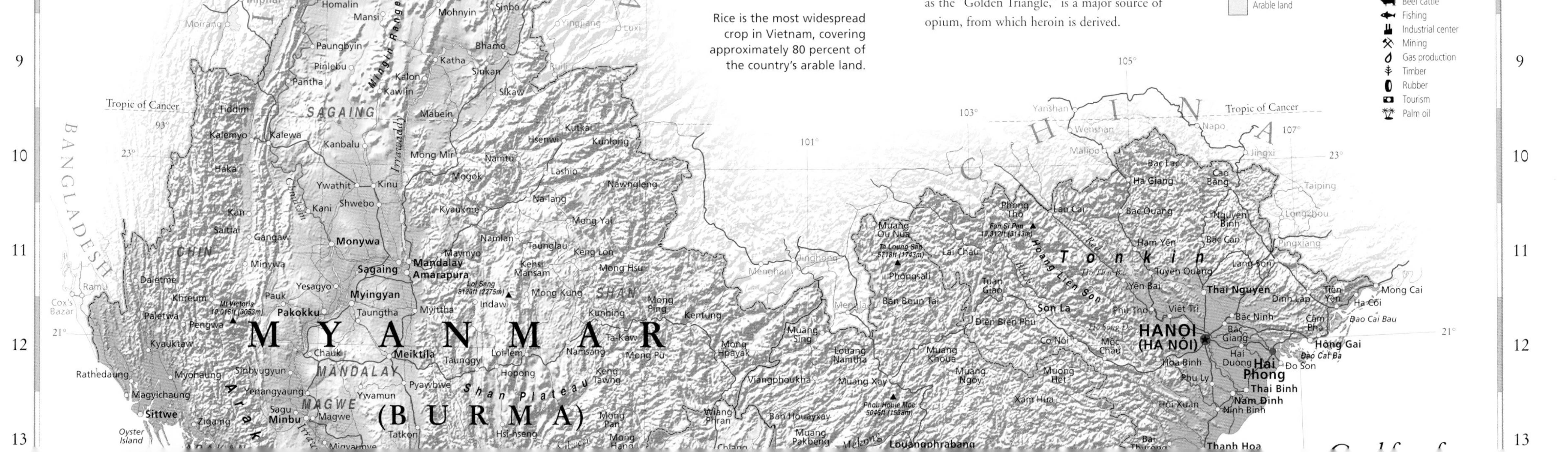

A B C D E F G H I J K L M N O
1 2 3 4 5 6 7 8 9 10 11 12 13
MYANMAR
(BURMA)
CHINA
INDIA
BANGLADESH
Tropic of Cancer
Hkakabo Razi 19,296ft (5881m)
Saramati 12,552ft (3826m)
Mt Victoria 10,016ft (3053m)
Fan Si Pan 10,312ft (3143m)
KACHIN
SAGAING
MANDALAY
MAGWE
CHIN
SHAN
Shan Plateau
The Triangle
Hukawng Valley
Mingin Range
Hoang Lien Son
Tonkin
Irrawaddy
Chindwin
Putao
Myitkyina
Bhamo
Monywa
Sagaing
Mandalay
Amarapura
Meiktila
Pakokku
Sittwe
Lashio
HANOI (HA NOI)
Hai Phong
Thai Nguyen
Nam Dinh
Thai Binh
Hong Gai
Mong Cai
Louangphrabang
Thanh Hoa

Bay of Bengal
Andaman Sea
Gulf of Martaban
Gulf of Thailand
South China Sea
Tongking
Bight of Bangkok
THAILAND
CAMBODIA
LAOS
VIETNAM
Indochina Peninsula
Annam
Cochin
Khorat Plateau
Plateau des Bolovens
Mergui Archipelago
Isthmus of Kra
Bilauktaung Range
Cardamom Range
Chuor Phnum Dângrêk
TENASSERIM
IRRAWADDY
PEGU
KAREN
MON
Mekong
Chao Phraya
Irrawaddy
Mouths of the Irrawaddy
Mouths of the Mekong
Tonlé Sab
BANGKOK (KRUNG THEP)
PHNOM PENH (PHNUM PENH)
VIENTIANE (VIANGCHAN)
RANGOON (YANGON)
Hô Chi Minh
Chiang Mai
Moulmein
Nakhon Ratchasima
Khon Kaen
Ubon Ratchathani
Hat Yai
Songkhla
Da Nang
Huê
Vinh
Qui Nhon
Nha Trang
Da Lat
Buôn Mê Thuôt
Vung Tau
Cân Tho
Rach Gia
Long Xuyên
Batdâmbâng
Kâmpóng Cham
Tavoy
Mergui
Bassein
Pegu
Henzada
Sandoway
Kota Bharu
George Town Pinang
Ko Phuket
Ko Samui
Ko Phangan
Ko Chang
Côn Son
Mui Ca Mau
Longitude east of Greenwich
A B C D E F G K
14 15 16 17 18 19 20 21 22 23 24 25 26
ELEVATION
Feet Meters
6562 2000
4921 1500
3281 1000
2461 750
1640 500
1312 400
984 300
656 200
328 100
0 0
Below sea level
0 0
656 200
3281 1000
6562 2000
13,123 4000
19,685 6000
26,246 8000
32,808 10,000
SCALE 1:6,000,000
Lamberts Conformal Conic Projection
0 200 miles
0 200 kilometers

Bangkok In 1782, Rama I, the King of Siam, as Thailand was then known, decided to relocate his royal court from the existing capital of Ayutthaya to a new site on the Chao Phraya River, 40 miles (64 km) to the south. The new capital, now called Bangkok, covered roughly 1.5 square miles (3.9 sq km), and at its heart, on the east bank of the Chao Phraya, lay the Grand Palace (below). In the second half of the 20th century, Bangkok expanded rapidly and its population grew sixfold. The well-preserved Grand Palace now sits amid a vast sea of modern buildings traversed by an enormous volume of slow-moving traffic and thronged by an evergrowing and increasingly cosmopolitan urban population.

Between the 9th and 15th centuries, Angkor, near Siem Reap, Cambodia, was the capital of the Khmer Empire.

Widely used as draft animals, elephants are also employed to transport tourists.

Maritime Southeast Asia

Brunei, East Timor, Indonesia, Malaysia, Philippines, Singapore

Scattered around the southeastern fringe of the Asian mainland are more than 20,000 islands. Ranging from the massive, rain-forest-cloaked landmass of Borneo—the world's third-largest island—to the tiny atolls of the Banda Sea, they form the largest island group on Earth, the Malay Archipelago. Divided mainly between the large countries of Malaysia (which includes the southern part of the Malay Peninsula), the Philippines, and Indonesia, it also encompasses the small states of Singapore, East Timor, and Brunei. Beginning in the 16th century, intense competition for control of the lucrative spice trade led various European powers to colonize large areas of the region. The British took over the Malay Peninsula, the Dutch seized most of Indonesia, the Portuguese established a foothold in Timor, and the Spanish occupied the Philippines (from where they were ousted by the U.S.A. in 1898). Since decolonization in the second half of the 20th century, Indonesia and Malaysia, in particular, have become major regional powers.

Java's Volcanoes

The islands of southern Indonesia formed as a result of subduction of the Indo-Australian Plate beneath the Eurasian Plate. This process continues to fuel the country's 76 volcanoes (more than any other nation), 22 of which are on Java. Sporadic and sometimes destructive volcanic activity takes place at Gunung Semeru in the east, Gunung Merapi near Yogyakarta, and Galunggung in the west. But the largest recorded eruption occurred on August 28, 1883, when Krakatau (Krakatoa) exploded, unleashing a tidal wave that killed 36,000 people.

Krakatau
JAKARTA
Galunggung
Java Sea
Semarang
Gunung Merapi
Surabaya
Gunung Semeru
Java
Yogyakarta
Indian Ocean
N

Native to Borneo and Sumatra, the orangutan has become endangered due to habitat loss.

A B C D E F G H I J K L M
1 2 3 4 5 6 7 8 9 10 11 12 13 14 15
THAILAND
Songkhla
Hat Yai
Langkawi
PERLIS
KEDAH
Alor Setar
Sungai Petani
Pinang
PINANG
George Town
Butterworth
Kota Bharu
KELANTAN
Kuala Terengganu
TERENGGANU
Taiping
Ipoh
PERAK
PAHANG
MALAYSIA
Kuantan
SELANGOR
KUALA LUMPUR
Kelang
NEGERI SEMBILAN
Seremban
MELAKA
Melaka
JOHOR
Johor Bahru
SINGAPORE
Strait of Malacca
Banda Aceh
ACEH
Gunung Abongabong 9793ft (2985m)
Medan
SUMATERA UTARA
Simeulue
Nias
Kepulauan Batu
Siberut
SUMATERA BARAT
Padang
Sumatra
RIAU
Pekanbaru
JAMBI
Jambi
Gunung Kerinci 12,484ft (3805m)
Sipura
Pagai Utara
Pagai Selatan
BENGKULU
Bengkulu
SUMATERA SELATAN
Palembang
Bangka
Pangkalpinang
Belitung
LAMPUNG
Bandar Lampung
Krakatau 2667ft (813m)
INDIAN OCEAN
Kepulauan Lingga
Kepulauan Anambas
Kepulauan Natuna
Natuna Besar
South China Sea
BANDAR SERI BEGAWAN
BRUNEI
LABUAN
Kota Kinabalu
Mt Kinabalu 13,432ft (4094m)
SABAH
SARAWAK
Kuching
Sibu
Miri
Borneo
KALIMANTAN BARAT
Pontianak
KALIMANTAN TENGAH
Palangkaraya
KALIMANTAN TIMUR
Samarinda
KALIMANTAN SELATAN
Banjarmasin
Bukit Raya 7474ft (2278m)
INDONESIA
Java Sea
JAKARTA RAYA
Serang
JAKARTA
Bogor
Bandung
Cirebon
JAWA BARAT
Java
JAWA TENGAH
Semarang
YOGYAKARTA
Yogyakarta
Surakarta
Madura
Surabaya
Malang
Gunung Semeru 12,060ft (3676m)
JAWA TIMUR
Bali
Denpasar
Lombok
Mataram
NUSA TENGGARA BARAT
Christmas Island (to Australia)
Longitude east of Greenwich

East Timor attained independence in 2002, following almost 25 years of Indonesian rule.

Controlled by the Dutch from 1619 to 1941, Jakarta became the capital of Indonesia in 1949.

N Q R S T U V W X Y Z
1 2 3 4 5 6 7 8 9 10 11
PHILIPPINES
MANILA
Luzon
Mindoro
Samar
Panay
Negros
Cebu
Bohol
Mindanao
Palawan
Philippine Sea
Sulu Sea
Celebes Sea
Sulu Archipelago
PACIFIC OCEAN
Moluccas
Halmahera
Molucca Sea
Sulawesi
SULAWESI UTARA
SULAWESI TENGAH
SULAWESI TENGGARA
INDONESIA
MALUKU
Seram
Buru
Banda Sea
Flores Sea
Flores
Sumba
NUSA TENGGARA TIMUR
Timor
EAST TIMOR
DILI
Timor Sea
IRIAN JAYA
Jayapura
New Guinea
PAPUA NEW GUINEA
Arafura Sea
Torres Strait
Equator
SCALE 1:11,000,000
Lamberts Conformal Conic Projection
0 300 miles
0 300 kilometers

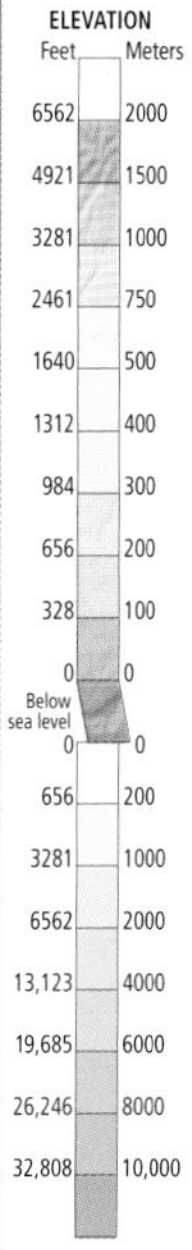

ELEVATION
Feet Meters
6562 2000
4921 1500
3281 1000
2461 750
1640 500
1312 400
984 300
656 200
328 100
0 0
Below sea level
0 0
656 200
3281 1000
6562 2000
13,123 4000
19,685 6000
26,246 8000
32,808 10,000

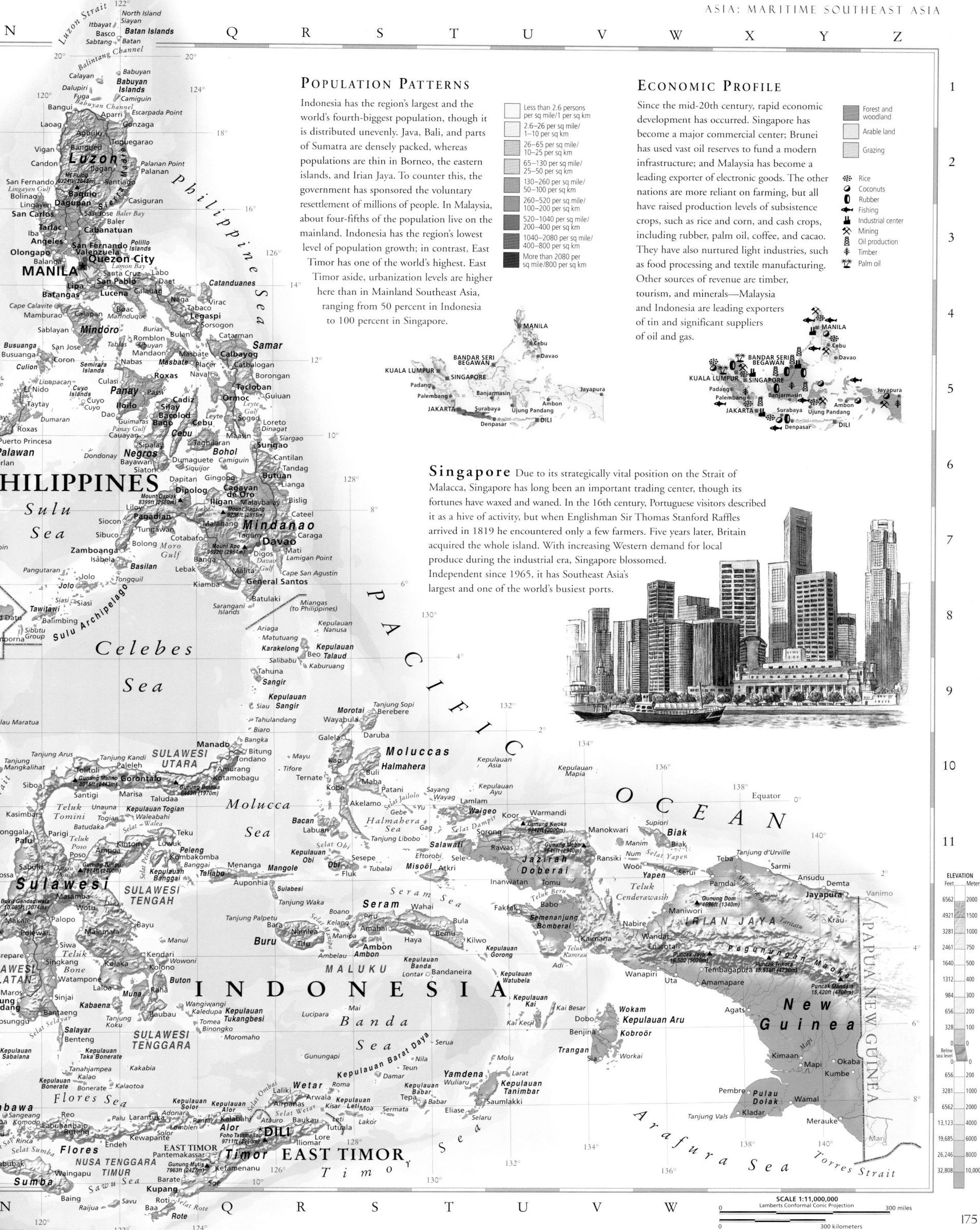

Population Patterns

Indonesia has the region's largest and the world's fourth-biggest population, though it is distributed unevenly. Java, Bali, and parts of Sumatra are densely packed, whereas populations are thin in Borneo, the eastern islands, and Irian Jaya. To counter this, the government has sponsored the voluntary resettlement of millions of people. In Malaysia, about four-fifths of the population live on the mainland. Indonesia has the region's lowest level of population growth; in contrast, East Timor has one of the world's highest. East Timor aside, urbanization levels are higher here than in Mainland Southeast Asia, ranging from 50 percent in Indonesia to 100 percent in Singapore.

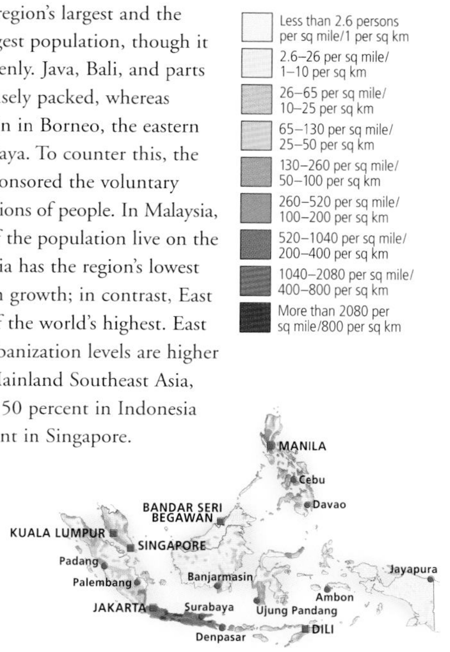

Less than 2.6 persons per sq mile/1 per sq km
2.6–26 per sq mile/ 1–10 per sq km
26–65 per sq mile/ 10–25 per sq km
65–130 per sq mile/ 25–50 per sq km
130–260 per sq mile/ 50–100 per sq km
260–520 per sq mile/ 100–200 per sq km
520–1040 per sq mile/ 200–400 per sq km
1040–2080 per sq mile/ 400–800 per sq km
More than 2080 per sq mile/800 per sq km
MANILA
Cebu
Davao
BANDAR SERI BEGAWAN
KUALA LUMPUR
SINGAPORE
Padang
Palembang
Banjarmasin
JAKARTA
Surabaya
Ujung Pandang
Ambon
Jayapura
Denpasar
DILI

Economic Profile

Since the mid-20th century, rapid economic development has occurred. Singapore has become a major commercial center; Brunei has used vast oil reserves to fund a modern infrastructure; and Malaysia has become a leading exporter of electronic goods. The other nations are more reliant on farming, but all have raised production levels of subsistence crops, such as rice and corn, and cash crops, including rubber, palm oil, coffee, and cacao. They have also nurtured light industries, such as food processing and textile manufacturing. Other sources of revenue are timber, tourism, and minerals—Malaysia and Indonesia are leading exporters of tin and significant suppliers of oil and gas.

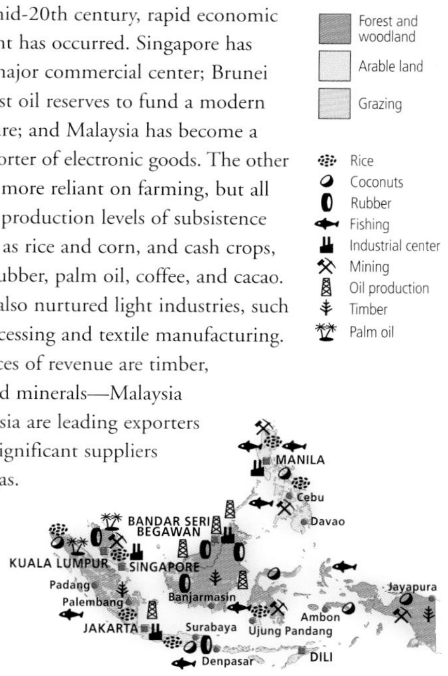

Forest and woodland
Arable land
Grazing
Rice
Coconuts
Rubber
Fishing
Industrial center
Mining
Oil production
Timber
Palm oil
MANILA
Cebu
Davao
BANDAR SERI BEGAWAN
KUALA LUMPUR
SINGAPORE
Padang
Palembang
Banjarmasin
JAKARTA
Surabaya
Ujung Pandang
Ambon
Jayapura
Denpasar
DILI

Singapore Due to its strategically vital position on the Strait of Malacca, Singapore has long been an important trading center, though its fortunes have waxed and waned. In the 16th century, Portuguese visitors described it as a hive of activity, but when Englishman Sir Thomas Stanford Raffles arrived in 1819 he encountered only a few farmers. Five years later, Britain acquired the whole island. With increasing Western demand for local produce during the industrial era, Singapore blossomed. Independent since 1965, it has Southeast Asia's largest and one of the world's busiest ports.

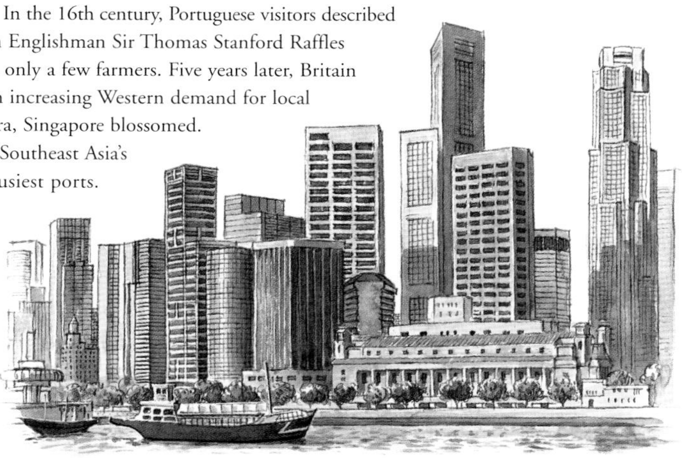

JAPAN

Although it occupies a strategically important position off the northeast coast of Asia, Japan remained isolated from outside influences for long periods of its history. It limited relations with its neighbors from the ninth century and adopted an official policy of isolation in 1639, soon after the arrival of the first Western missionaries and explorers. Only in the mid-19th century did it open up to foreign influences and trade.

Its subsequent attempts to expand its empire led to international conflicts and a devastating defeat in the Second World War. Yet the nation recovered spectacularly to become the world's second-strongest industrial power after the United States and wield an economic and political influence far out of proportion to its small size. Occupying a land area smaller than California, Japan consists of about 4,000 islands, dominated by the large islands of Hokkaidō, Honshū, Shikoku, and Kyūshū. In the interiors of these islands, mountain ranges are separated by river valleys and bounded by narrow coastal plains. Being situated on the Pacific Rim of Fire, the country experiences regular earthquakes and volcanic eruptions, which periodically wreak havoc on the land and its people.

Population Patterns

About 80 percent of Japan is mountainous and has low-to-moderate levels of population density; the other 20 percent, however—mainly valleys and coastal plains—supports the bulk of the population and includes some of the world's most densely inhabited areas. Urban dwellers account for 80 percent of the inhabitants and the capital, Tokyo, is the world's largest urban center. The population is ethnically homogenous, with 99 percent being Japanese. About 84% follow both Buddhist and Shinto traditions. In recent years, a declining birth rate and rapidly aging population have heightened concerns about labor shortages and the cost of maintaining social services.

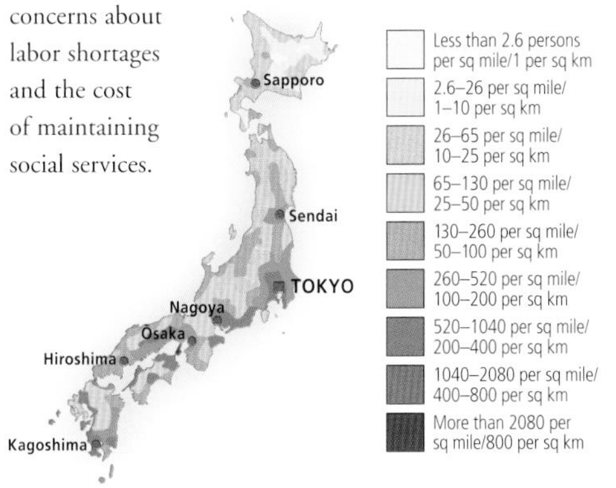
Sapporo
Sendai
TOKYO
Nagoya
Ōsaka
Hiroshima
Kagoshima
Less than 2.6 persons per sq mile/1 per sq km
2.6–26 per sq mile/ 1–10 per sq km
26–65 per sq mile/ 10–25 per sq km
65–130 per sq mile/ 25–50 per sq km
130–260 per sq mile/ 50–100 per sq km
260–520 per sq mile/ 100–200 per sq km
520–1040 per sq mile/ 200–400 per sq km
1040–2080 per sq mile/ 400–800 per sq km
More than 2080 per sq mile/800 per sq km

Economic Profile

Japan is an economic superpower despite having only a small area of cultivable land and modest mineral resources (small deposits of copper, coal, and iron ore and meager reserves of oil and gas). Its success is due mainly to government support and innovation: large subsidies and intensive farming practices have helped it become virtually self-sufficient in rice and produce large quantities of fruit and vegetables; heavy investment in education, research, and technology have created a sophisticated industrial sector renowned for machinery and electronic goods. Even the nation's impressive fish catches, accounting for 15 percent of world totals, are due in part to the use of technology-loaded, wide-ranging fishing boats. This industrial success has greatly increased export revenue; however, a recession in the late 1990s cast a shadow over the nation's economic future.

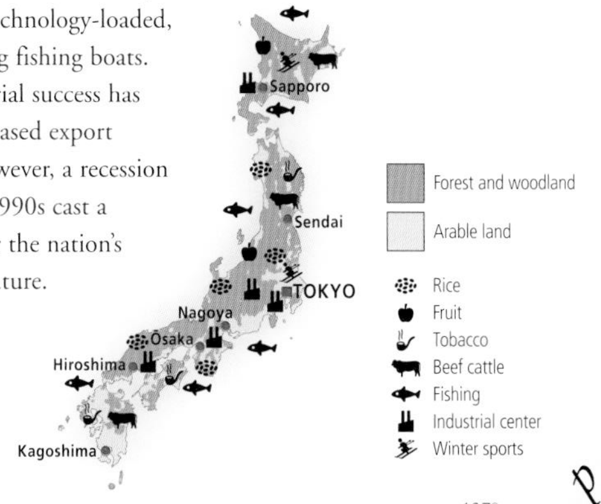
Sapporo
Sendai
TOKYO
Nagoya
Ōsaka
Hiroshima
Kagoshima
Forest and woodland
Arable land
Rice
Fruit
Tobacco
Beef cattle
Fishing
Industrial center
Winter sports

JAPAN
Hokkaidō
PACIFIC OCEAN
Sea of Okhotsk
Sea of Japan
RUSSIAN FEDERATION
Sakhalin
La Pérouse Strait
Kuril Islands
(Administered by Russian Federation claimed by Japan)
Ostrov Iturup
Ostrov Kunashir
Ostrov Shikotan
Yuzhno-Sakhalinsk
Korsakov
Wakkanai
Rebun-tō
Rishiri-tō
Asahikawa
Sapporo
Otaru
Ebetsu
Tomakomai
Muroran
Hakodate
Kitami
Kushiro
Obihiro
Nemuro
Abashiri
Shiretoko-hantō
Oshima-hantō
Okushiri-tō
Shimokita-hantō
Tsugaru-kaikyō
Aomori
Hachinohe
Morioka
Akita
Sakata
Tsuruoka
Yamagata
Sendai
Ishinomaki
Oshika-hantō
Sadoga-shima
Niigata
Ou-sanmyaku
Hidaka-sanmyaku
Kitami-sanchi
Yūbari-sanchi
Teshio-sanchi

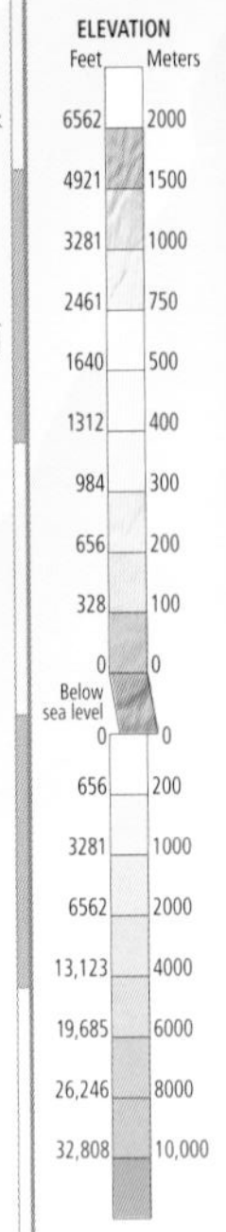
ELEVATION
Feet
Meters
6562
2000
4921
1500
3281
1000
2461
750
1640
500
1312
400
984
300
656
200
328
100
0
0
Below sea level
0
0
656
200
3281
1000
6562
2000
13,123
4000
19,685
6000
26,246
8000
32,808
10,000

In winter, mountain-dwelling macaque monkeys stay warm by sitting in pools fed by hot springs.

Bullet trains began operating in 1964. They now have a top speed of 160 mph (260 km/h).

Sea of Japan
Honshū
Shikoku
Kyūshū
Philippine Sea
East China Sea
Izu-shotō
Ōsumi-shotō
Tokara-rettō
Gotō-rettō
Oki-shotō
Seto Naikai
Chūgoku-sanchi
Kiso-sanmyaku
TOKYO
Kawasaki
Yokohama
Nagoya
Kyōto
Ōsaka
Kōbe
Hiroshima
Fukuoka
Kita-Kyūshū
Kagoshima
Nagasaki
Kumamoto
Sendai
Kōchi
Matsuyama
Takamatsu
Okayama
Niigata
Nagano
Kanazawa
Shizuoka
Hamamatsu
Fuji
Mt Fuji 12,388ft (3776m)
Tsushima
Iki
Yaku-shima
Tanega-shima
Sagami-nada
Suruga-wan
Enshū-nada
Kii-suidō
Bungo-suidō
Tosa-wan
Longitude east of Greenwich
SCALE 1:4,250,000
Lamberts Conformal Conic Projection
120 miles
120 kilometers
14 15 16 17 18 19 20 21 22 23 24 25 26
A D E F G H

In Kiso-sanmyaku of central Honshū, forested valleys separate steep, glacier-carved ridges and peaks.

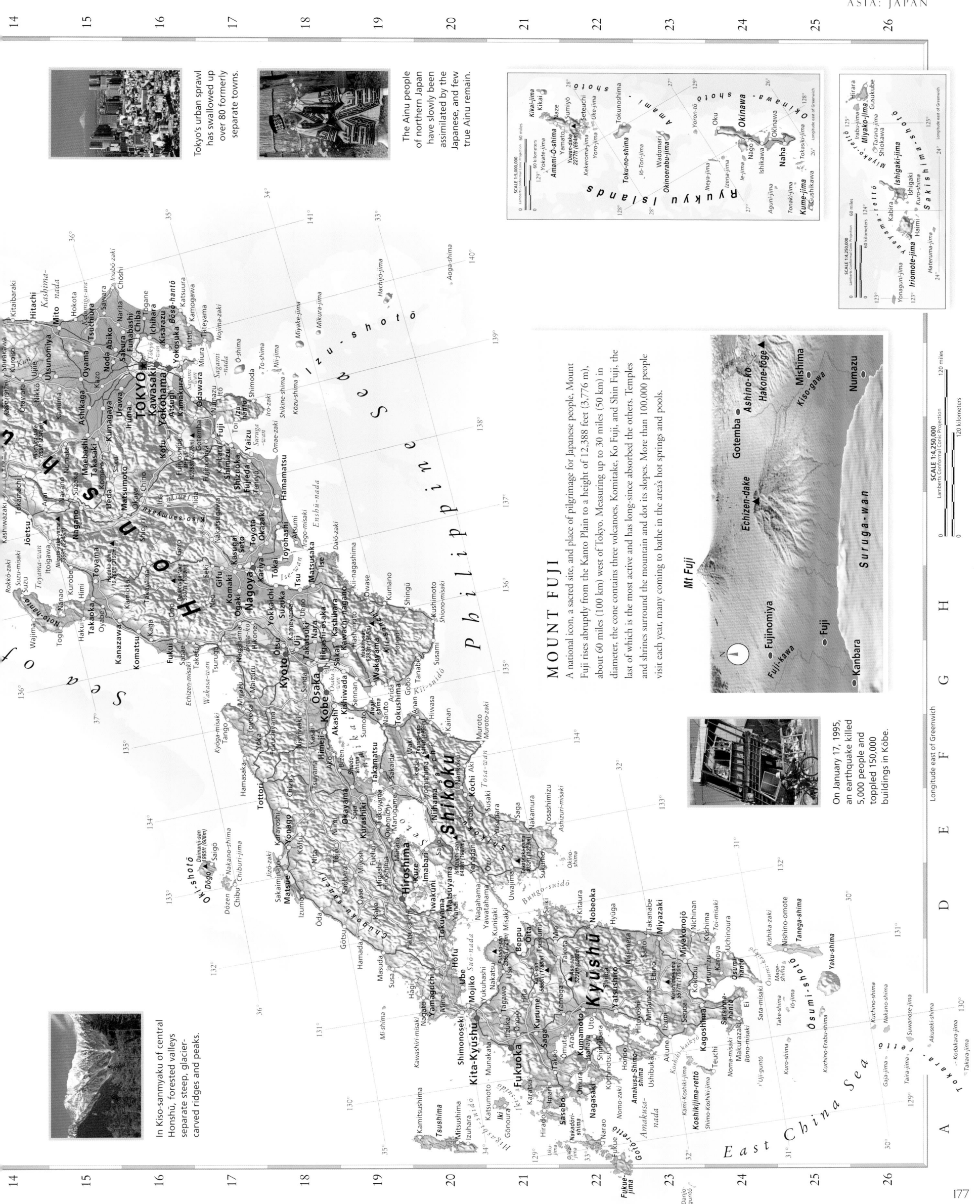

Tokyo's urban sprawl has swallowed up over 80 formerly separate towns.

The Ainu people of northern Japan have slowly been assimilated by the Japanese, and few true Ainu remain.

MOUNT FUJI

A national icon, a sacred site, and place of pilgrimage for Japanese people, Mount Fuji rises abruptly from the Kanto Plain to a height of 12,388 feet (3,776 m), about 60 miles (100 km) west of Tokyo. Measuring up to 30 miles (50 km) in diameter, the cone contains three volcanoes, Komitake, Ko Fuji, and Shin Fuji, the last of which is the most active and has long-since absorbed the others. Temples and shrines surround the mountain and dot its slopes. More than 100,000 people visit each year, many coming to bathe in the area's hot springs and pools.

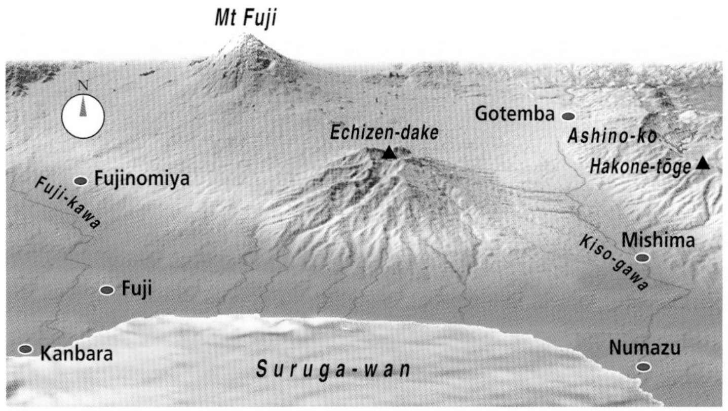

Mt Fuji
N
Echizen-dake
Gotemba
Ashino-ko
Hakone-tōge
Fujinomiya
Fuji-kawa
Mishima
Kiso-gawa
Fuji
Kanbara
Numazu
Suruga-wan

On January 17, 1995, an earthquake killed 5,000 people and toppled 150,000 buildings in Kōbe.

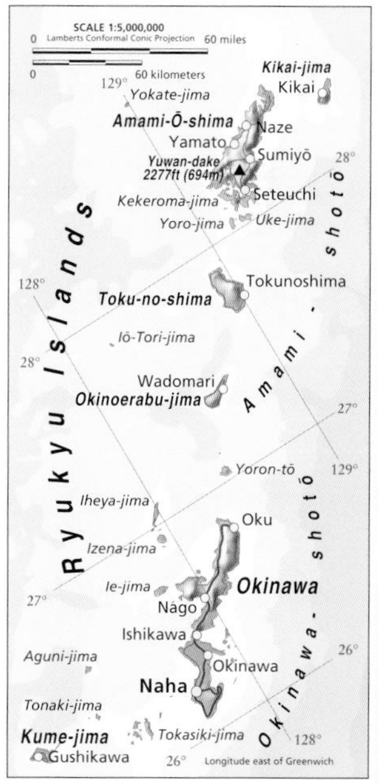

SCALE 1:5,000,000
Lamberts Conformal Conic Projection
60 miles
60 kilometers
Ryukyu Islands
Amami-shotō
Okinawa-shotō
Kikai-jima
Amami-Ō-shima
Tokuno-shima
Okinoerabu-jima
Okinawa
Naha
Kume-jima
Longitude east of Greenwich

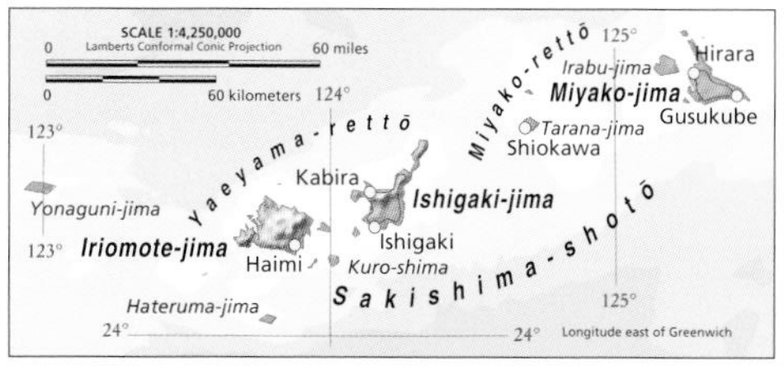

SCALE 1:4,250,000
Lamberts Conformal Conic Projection
60 miles
60 kilometers
Sakishima-shotō
Yaeyama-rettō
Miyako-rettō
Miyako-jima
Ishigaki-jima
Iriomote-jima
Yonaguni-jima
Hateruma-jima
Longitude east of Greenwich

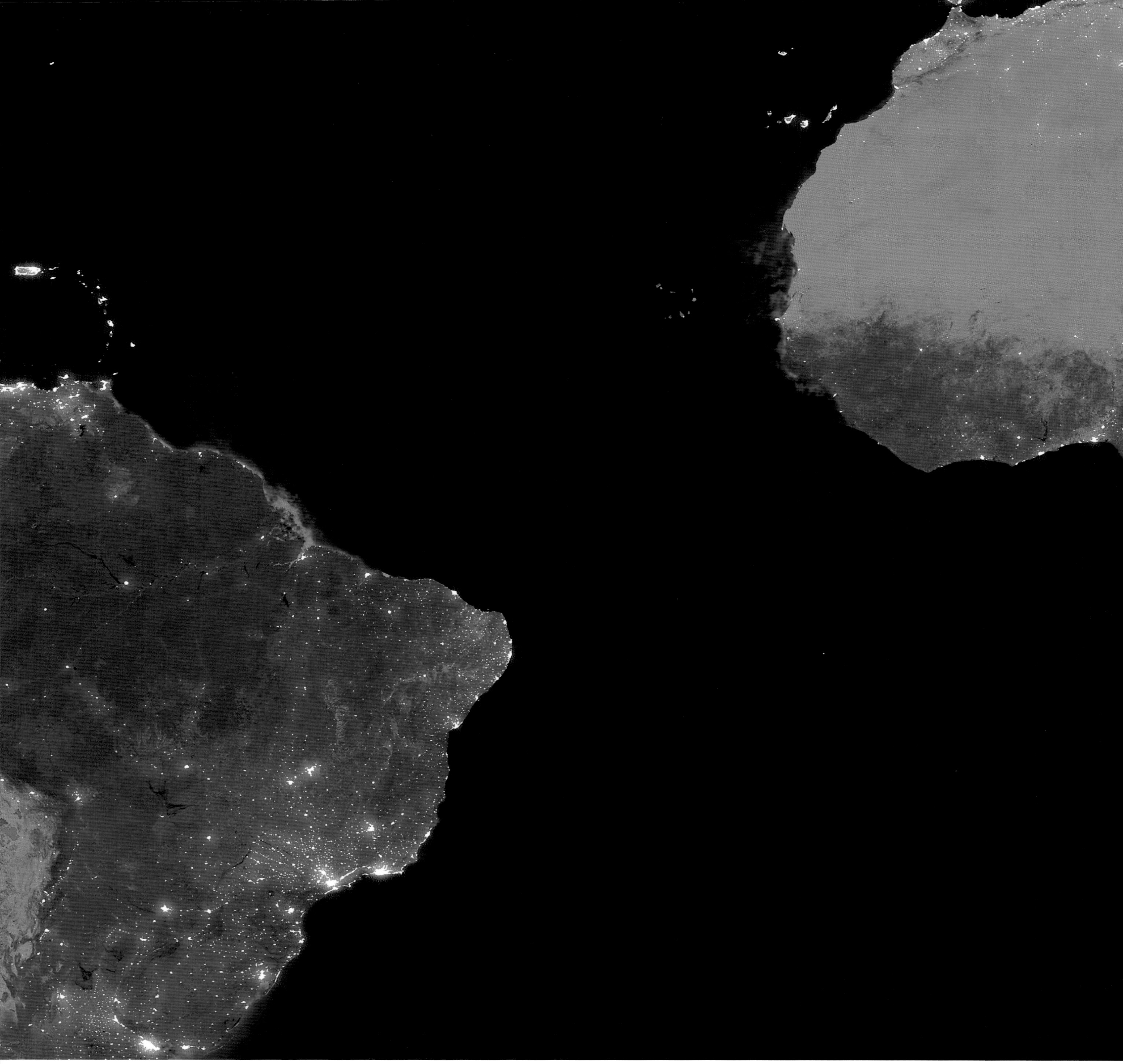

The Nile River, from the Aswan Dam to the Mediterranean, is illuminated at night. This bright thread and the pockets of lights in the north and south indicate urbanized areas. The Sahara Desert and the tropical forests of the Congo Basin show little light.

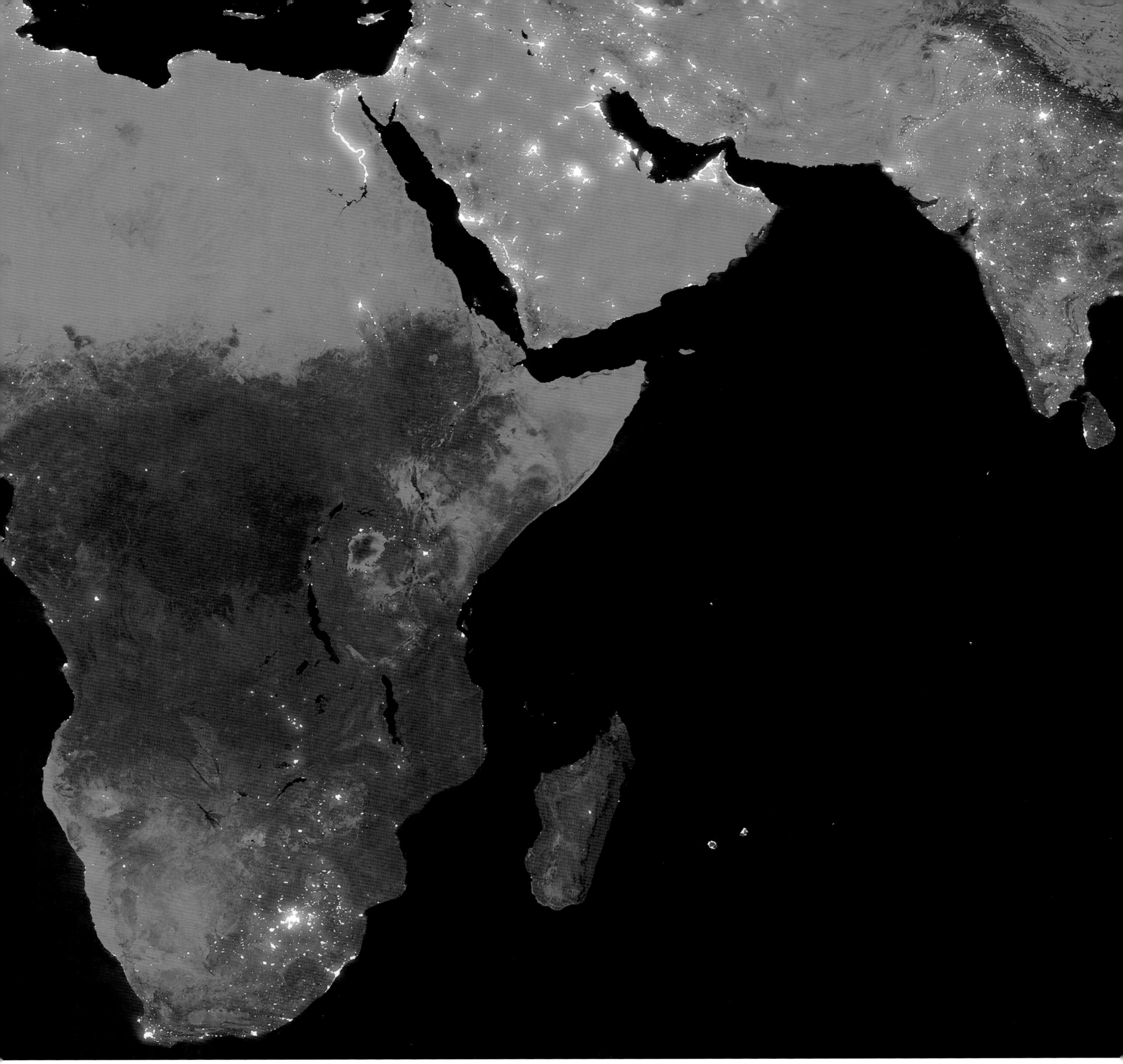

AFRICA

The View from Above

Dominating the top third of the continent of Africa is the mighty Sahara, the largest region of dry land on the planet. Using radar imaging that can penetrate the Sahara's dry sands, satellites can "see" geological features that chronicle past climate changes and events that are not visible at ground level. Revealed are ancient drainage channels, scoured out in wetter times when forests and grasslands covered the region, and long valleys carved by wind-driven sand. Satellites also record ongoing change, such as the effects of the prolonged drought that sent huge clouds of dust billowing across the Atlantic. Africa's few volcanoes are concentrated in the Great Rift Valley, in the east of the continent, where two tectonic plates are slowly pulling apart. The Virunga volcanic chain lies near the southwestern end of the valley, straddling the borders of Rwanda, Democratic Republic of Congo, and Uganda.

Below: Land and ocean seem reversed in this false-color image of the vast Namib Sand Sea, on the west coast of southern Africa. The magenta areas are fields of high, steep sand dunes, while the orange area at the bottom is the South Atlantic Ocean. The bright green features in the upper right are rocky hills poking above the sand sea.

Above right: A comet slamming into the Sahara Desert millions of years ago left the circular scars seen in this radar image.The concentric ring structure left of center is the main impact crater, with a diameter of 10.5 miles (17 km). Scientists believe the comet broke apart before impact, and to the right are two similar, but less distinct, scars.

Right: A dust plume over 1,000 miles (1,600 km) long sweeps past the islands of Cape Verde (lower left), north to the Canary Islands (top center). The dust comes from the savanna lands just south of the Sahara, where long-term drought and overgrazing has stripped the dry soil bare, leading to erosion and catastrophic dust storms.

Far right: The rugged Virunga volcanic chain in Central Africa is home to the endangered mountain gorilla. This false-color image, centered on Mount Karisimbi, graphically illustrates the threat to the gorilla's forest habitat, shown as green, by farmlands, shown as purple. The thin green lines are thought to be agricultural terracing.

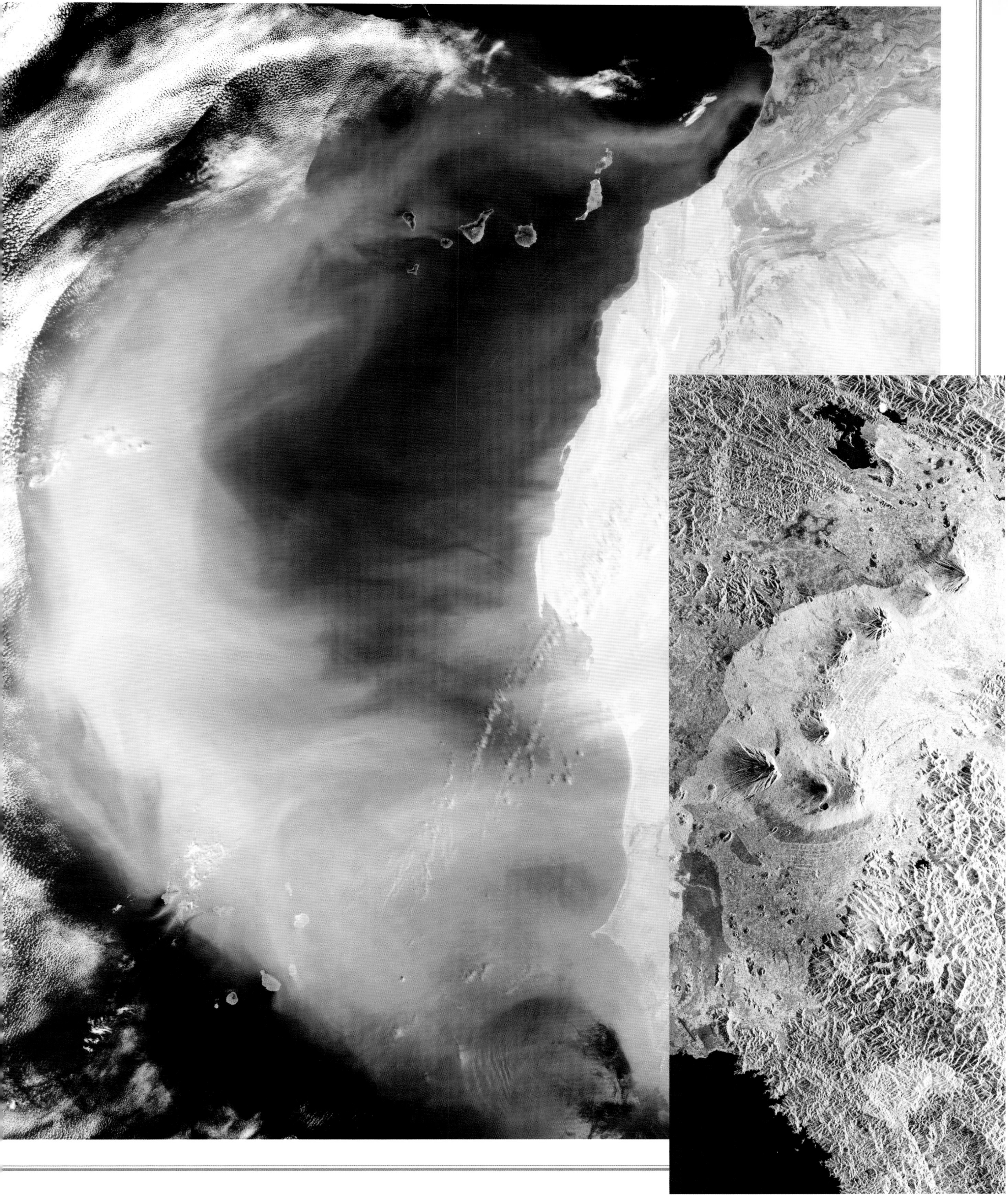

Land and Environment

The second-largest continent after Asia, Africa encompasses 11.7 million square miles (30 million sq km), almost one-fifth of Earth's land. It is separated from Europe by the Mediterranean Sea and from Asia by the Red Sea and Gulf of Aden. From Cap Blanc in the far north, it stretches about 5,000 miles (8,000 km) south to Cape Agulhas in South Africa. The northern half of the continent is far wider than the south, spanning 4,600 miles (7,360 km) between Cap Vert in Senegal and Rās Xaafuun in Somalia. Relative to the other continents, Africa has few extensive lowlands or high mountain ranges. It consists mainly of a huge plateau, rimmed by narrow coastal plains, which slopes gently from southeast to northwest. The highest areas are the Ethiopian Highlands and the East African Plateau, site of Africa's highest peak, Kilimanjaro. These uplands are riven by the Great Rift Valley, an extensive fault that runs for 4,000 miles (6,400 km) from the Red Sea to the Zambezi River.

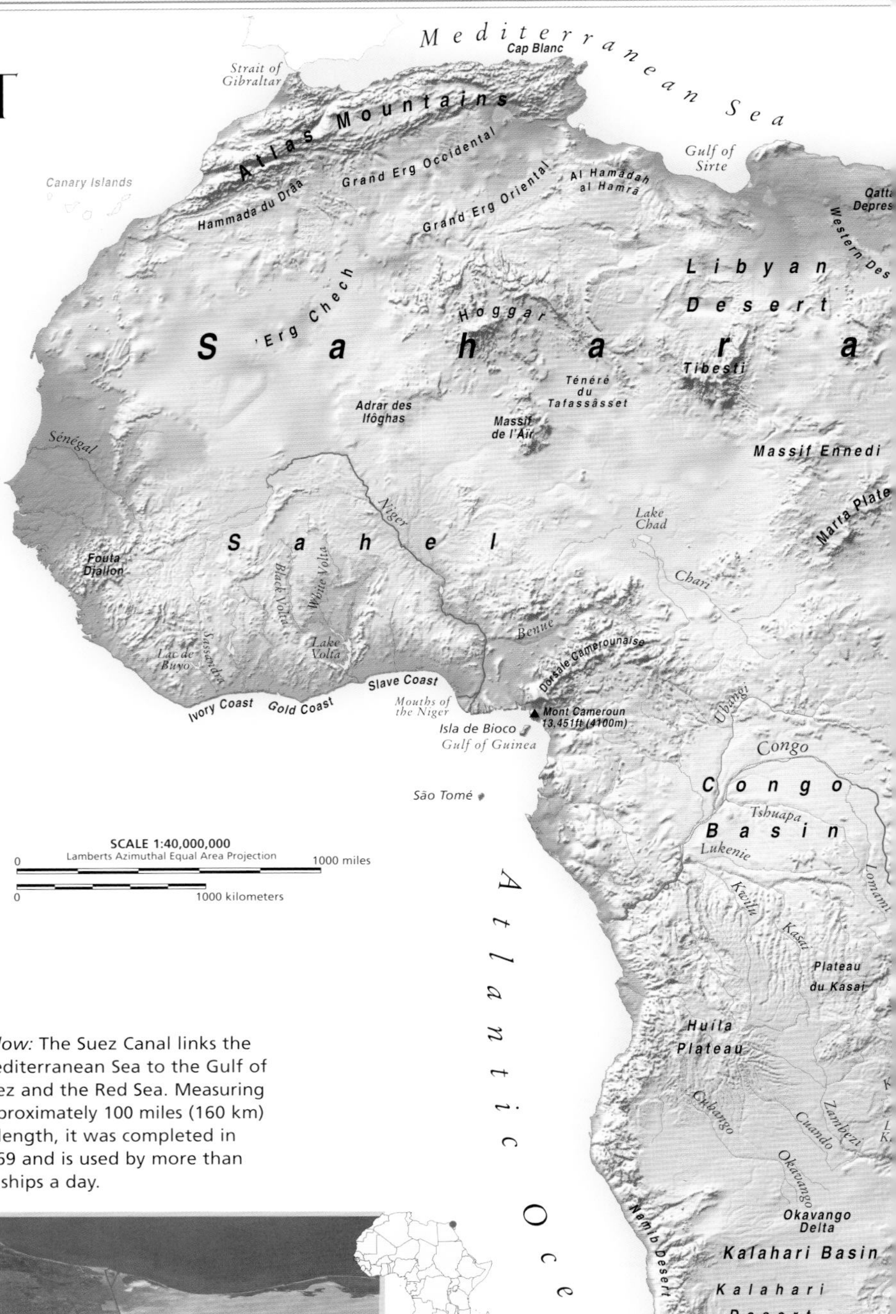

Mediterranean Sea
Cap Blanc
Strait of Gibraltar
Atlas Mountains
Canary Islands
Hammada du Drâa
Grand Erg Occidental
Grand Erg Oriental
Al Hamādah al Hamrā
Gulf of Sirte
Libyan Desert
Western Desert
'Erg Chech
Sahara
Hoggar
Tibesti
Ténéré du Tafassâsset
Adrar des Ifôghas
Massif de l'Aïr
Massif Ennedi
Sénégal
Cap Vert
Niger
Lake Chad
Marra Plateau
Fouta Djallon
Sahel
Black Volta
White Volta
Chari
Lake Volta
Benue
Lac de Buyo
Dorsale Camerounaise
Slave Coast
Ivory Coast
Gold Coast
Mouths of the Niger
Mont Cameroun 13,451ft (4100m)
Isla de Bioco
Gulf of Guinea
Ubangi
Congo
São Tomé
Congo Basin
Tshuapa
Lukenie
SCALE 1:40,000,000
Lamberts Azimuthal Equal Area Projection
0
1000 miles
0
1000 kilometers
Atlantic Ocean
Kasai
Kwilu
Lomami
Plateau du Kasai
Huila Plateau
Cubango
Cuando
Zambezi
Okavango
Okavango Delta
Namib Desert
Kalahari Basin
Kalahari Desert
Orange
Great Karoo
Little Karoo
Cape of Good Hope
Cape Agulhas

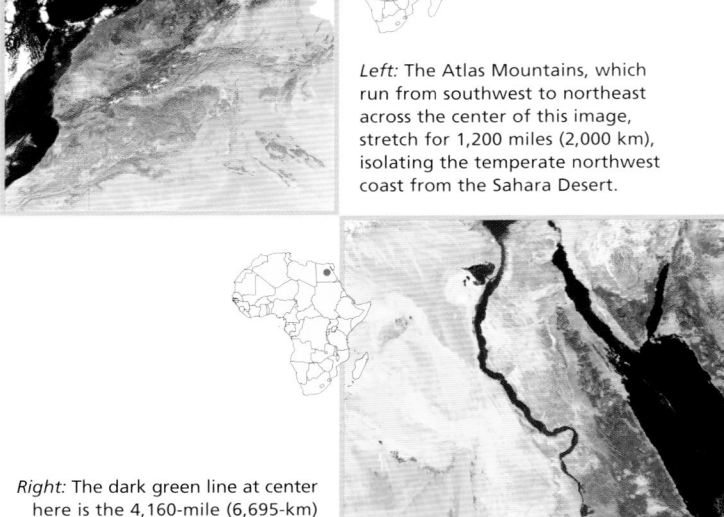

Left: The Atlas Mountains, which run from southwest to northeast across the center of this image, stretch for 1,200 miles (2,000 km), isolating the temperate northwest coast from the Sahara Desert.

Below: The Suez Canal links the Mediterranean Sea to the Gulf of Suez and the Red Sea. Measuring approximately 100 miles (160 km) in length, it was completed in 1869 and is used by more than 50 ships a day.

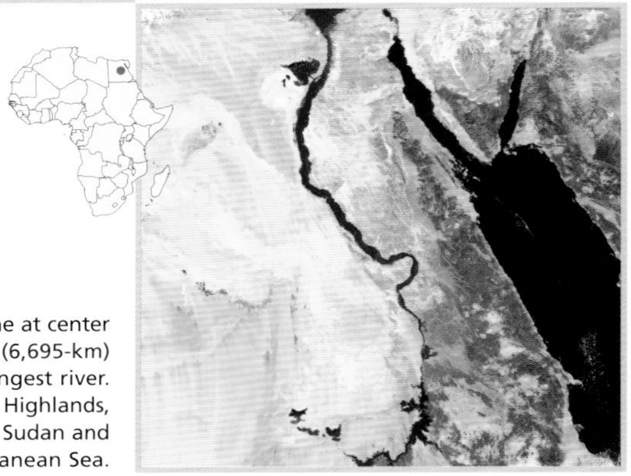

Right: The dark green line at center here is the 4,160-mile (6,695-km) Nile, the world's longest river. Rising in the Ethiopian Highlands, it flows north through Sudan and Egypt to the Mediterranean Sea.

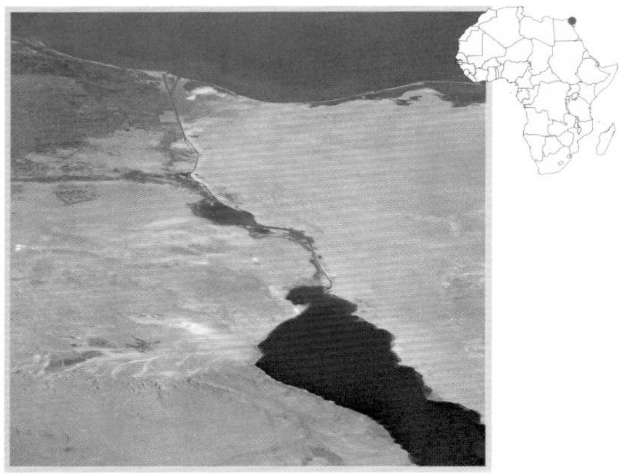

Natural Hazards

Drought

Many parts of Africa receive rain only during an annual wet season. Fluctuations in this seasonal rainfall can result in drought—periods of rainfall well below the long-term average. With so many of the inhabitants of these regions dependent on subsistence agriculture, drought can, in turn, cause great hardship and loss of life. Sometimes, the losses are due to a misreading of natural long-term climatic patterns. In the Sahel region in the 1960s, for example, a succession of years of above-average rainfall (see graph, right) encouraged farmers to cultivate this normally arid region. When rainfall levels returned to the norm, the crops soon failed. By 1973, an estimated 100,000 people had starved to death.

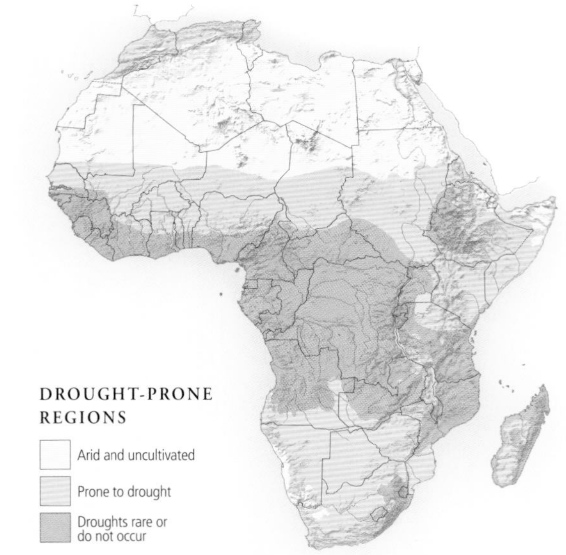

DROUGHT-PRONE REGIONS
Arid and uncultivated
Prone to drought
Droughts rare or do not occur

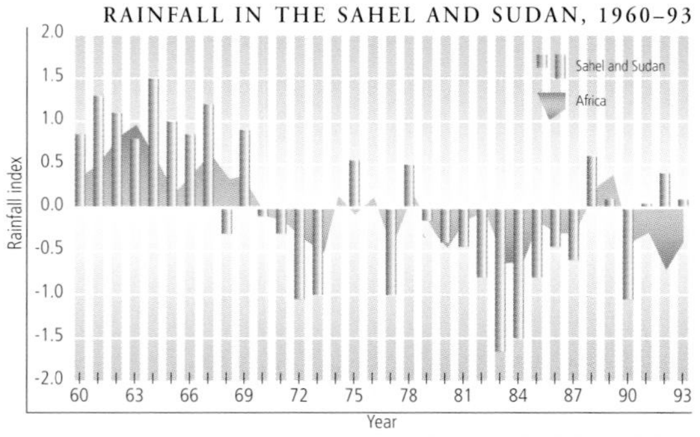

RAINFALL IN THE SAHEL AND SUDAN, 1960–93
Sahel and Sudan
Africa
Rainfall index
2.0
1.5
1.0
0.5
0.0
-0.5
-1.0
-1.5
-2.0
60
63
66
69
72
75
78
81
84
87
90
93
Year

In recent decades, Ethiopia has suffered a number of disastrous droughts, with the most severe one, in 1984, accounting for approximately 300,000 deaths. In 2003, an acute drought left about 11 million people facing severe food shortages.

Climate

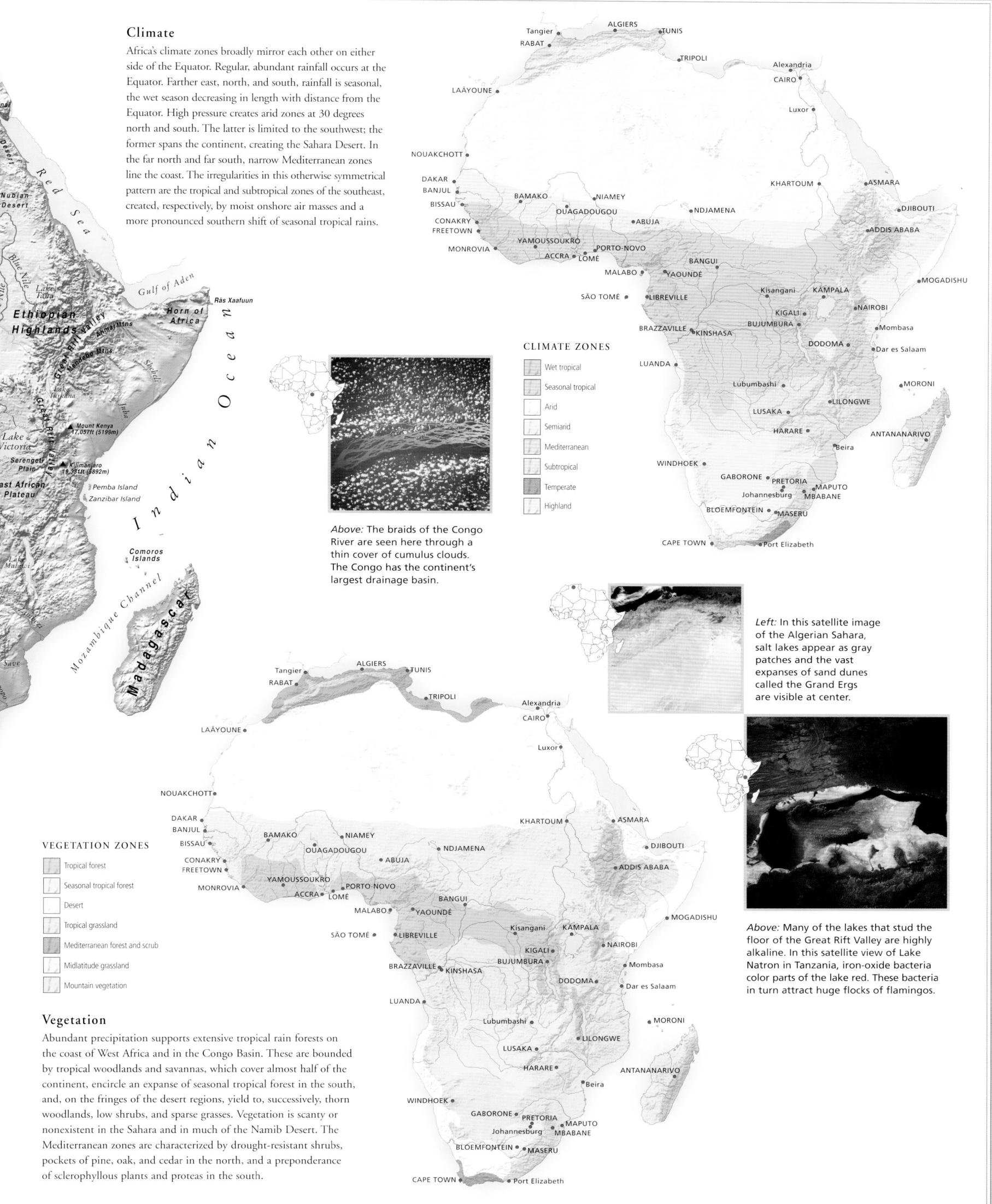

Africa's climate zones broadly mirror each other on either side of the Equator. Regular, abundant rainfall occurs at the Equator. Farther east, north, and south, rainfall is seasonal, the wet season decreasing in length with distance from the Equator. High pressure creates arid zones at 30 degrees north and south. The latter is limited to the southwest; the former spans the continent, creating the Sahara Desert. In the far north and far south, narrow Mediterranean zones line the coast. The irregularities in this otherwise symmetrical pattern are the tropical and subtropical zones of the southeast, created, respectively, by moist onshore air masses and a more pronounced southern shift of seasonal tropical rains.

Red Sea
Nubian Desert
Blue Nile
Lake Tana
Ethiopian Highlands
Great Rift Valley
Ahmar Mts
Gulf of Aden
Rās Xaafuun
Horn of Africa
Shebeli
Lake Turkana
Juba
Mount Kenya 17,057ft (5199m)
Lake Victoria
Serengeti Plain
Kilimanjaro 19,331ft (5892m)
East African Plateau
Pemba Island
Zanzibar Island
Indian Ocean
Comoros Islands
Lake Malawi
Mozambique Channel
Madagascar
Save

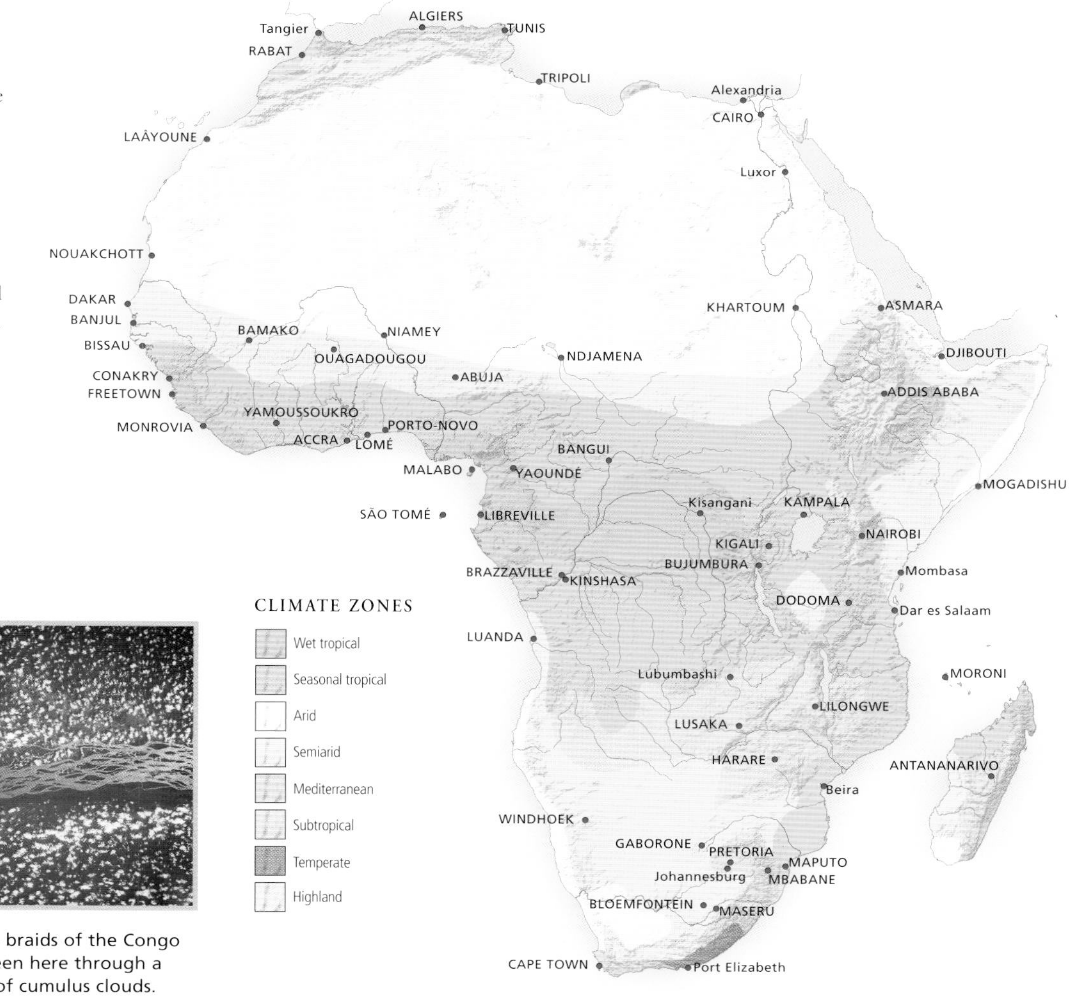

CLIMATE ZONES
Wet tropical
Seasonal tropical
Arid
Semiarid
Mediterranean
Subtropical
Temperate
Highland
Tangier
RABAT
ALGIERS
TUNIS
TRIPOLI
Alexandria
CAIRO
LAÂYOUNE
Luxor
NOUAKCHOTT
DAKAR
BANJUL
BISSAU
CONAKRY
FREETOWN
MONROVIA
BAMAKO
NIAMEY
OUAGADOUGOU
ABUJA
NDJAMENA
KHARTOUM
ASMARA
DJIBOUTI
ADDIS ABABA
YAMOUSSOUKRO
ACCRA
LOMÉ
PORTO-NOVO
BANGUI
MALABO
YAOUNDÉ
SÃO TOMÉ
LIBREVILLE
MOGADISHU
Kisangani
KAMPALA
NAIROBI
KIGALI
BUJUMBURA
BRAZZAVILLE
KINSHASA
Mombasa
DODOMA
Dar es Salaam
LUANDA
Lubumbashi
MORONI
LILONGWE
LUSAKA
HARARE
ANTANANARIVO
Beira
WINDHOEK
GABORONE
PRETORIA
Johannesburg
MAPUTO
MBABANE
BLOEMFONTEIN
MASERU
CAPE TOWN
Port Elizabeth

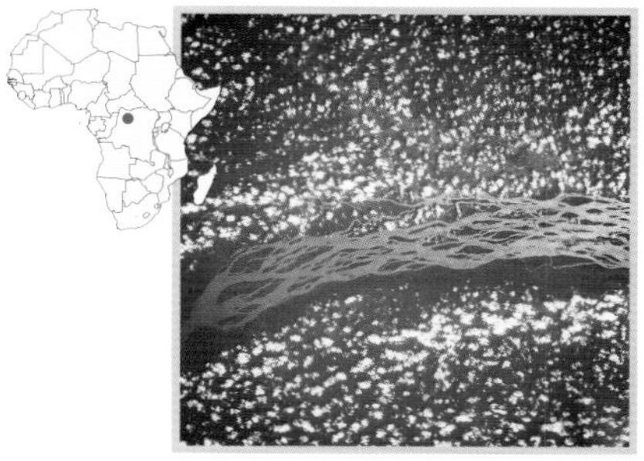

Above: The braids of the Congo River are seen here through a thin cover of cumulus clouds. The Congo has the continent's largest drainage basin.

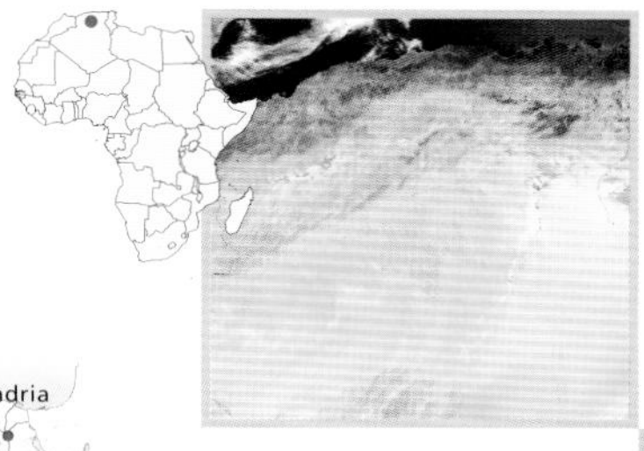

Left: In this satellite image of the Algerian Sahara, salt lakes appear as gray patches and the vast expanses of sand dunes called the Grand Ergs are visible at center.

Above: Many of the lakes that stud the floor of the Great Rift Valley are highly alkaline. In this satellite view of Lake Natron in Tanzania, iron-oxide bacteria color parts of the lake red. These bacteria in turn attract huge flocks of flamingos.

VEGETATION ZONES
Tropical forest
Seasonal tropical forest
Desert
Tropical grassland
Mediterranean forest and scrub
Midlatitude grassland
Mountain vegetation
Tangier
RABAT
ALGIERS
TUNIS
TRIPOLI
Alexandria
CAIRO
LAÂYOUNE
Luxor
NOUAKCHOTT
DAKAR
BANJUL
BISSAU
CONAKRY
FREETOWN
MONROVIA
BAMAKO
NIAMEY
OUAGADOUGOU
ABUJA
NDJAMENA
KHARTOUM
ASMARA
DJIBOUTI
ADDIS ABABA
YAMOUSSOUKRO
ACCRA
LOMÉ
PORTO-NOVO
BANGUI
MALABO
YAOUNDÉ
SÃO TOMÉ
LIBREVILLE
MOGADISHU
Kisangani
KAMPALA
NAIROBI
KIGALI
BUJUMBURA
BRAZZAVILLE
KINSHASA
Mombasa
DODOMA
Dar es Salaam
LUANDA
Lubumbashi
MORONI
LILONGWE
LUSAKA
HARARE
ANTANANARIVO
Beira
WINDHOEK
GABORONE
PRETORIA
Johannesburg
MAPUTO
MBABANE
BLOEMFONTEIN
MASERU
CAPE TOWN
Port Elizabeth

Vegetation

Abundant precipitation supports extensive tropical rain forests on the coast of West Africa and in the Congo Basin. These are bounded by tropical woodlands and savannas, which cover almost half of the continent, encircle an expanse of seasonal tropical forest in the south, and, on the fringes of the desert regions, yield to, successively, thorn woodlands, low shrubs, and sparse grasses. Vegetation is scanty or nonexistent in the Sahara and in much of the Namib Desert. The Mediterranean zones are characterized by drought-resistant shrubs, pockets of pine, oak, and cedar in the north, and a preponderance of sclerophyllous plants and proteas in the south.

Peoples and Nations

The continent-spanning Sahara Desert divides Africa's 800 million or so people into two major groups: the culturally homogenous, predominantly Arabic and Islamic peoples of the north; and the numerous, and culturally and linguistically diverse, indigenous peoples of the south. Other ethnic groups include the descendants of European colonists, found mainly in the far north and far south, and the Malagasy of Madagascar, whose ancestors migrated from Indonesia. The late-20th-century decolonization of Africa resulted in the creation of numerous states—now 53 countries in all—some of whose borders, especially in sub-Saharan Africa, cut across traditional ethnic territories. Resulting conflicts hinder attempts to alleviate poverty.

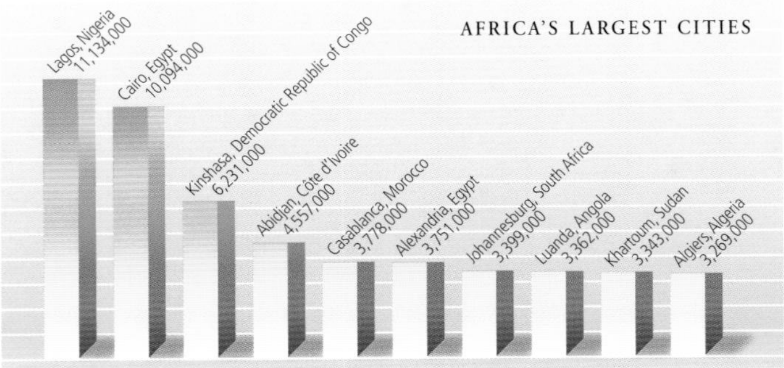
AFRICA'S LARGEST CITIES
Lagos, Nigeria 11,134,000
Cairo, Egypt 10,094,000
Kinshasa, Democratic Republic of Congo 6,231,000
Abidjan, Côte d'Ivoire 4,557,000
Casablanca, Morocco 3,778,000
Alexandria, Egypt 3,751,000
Johannesburg, South Africa 3,399,000
Luanda, Angola 3,362,000
Khartoum, Sudan 3,343,000
Algiers, Algeria 3,269,000

Urbanization

Africa had few large towns or cities until the 20th century, and its proportion of urban dwellers remains low relative to other continents—approximately 40 percent. Yet recently urbanization has occurred more rapidly here than anywhere else: in 1950, just 15 percent of Africans lived in towns and cities. North Africa is considerably more urbanized than sub-Saharan Africa, though Lagos in Nigeria is the continent's biggest city. Africa's largest urban areas tend to be on the coast, and many are ports established by former colonial powers.

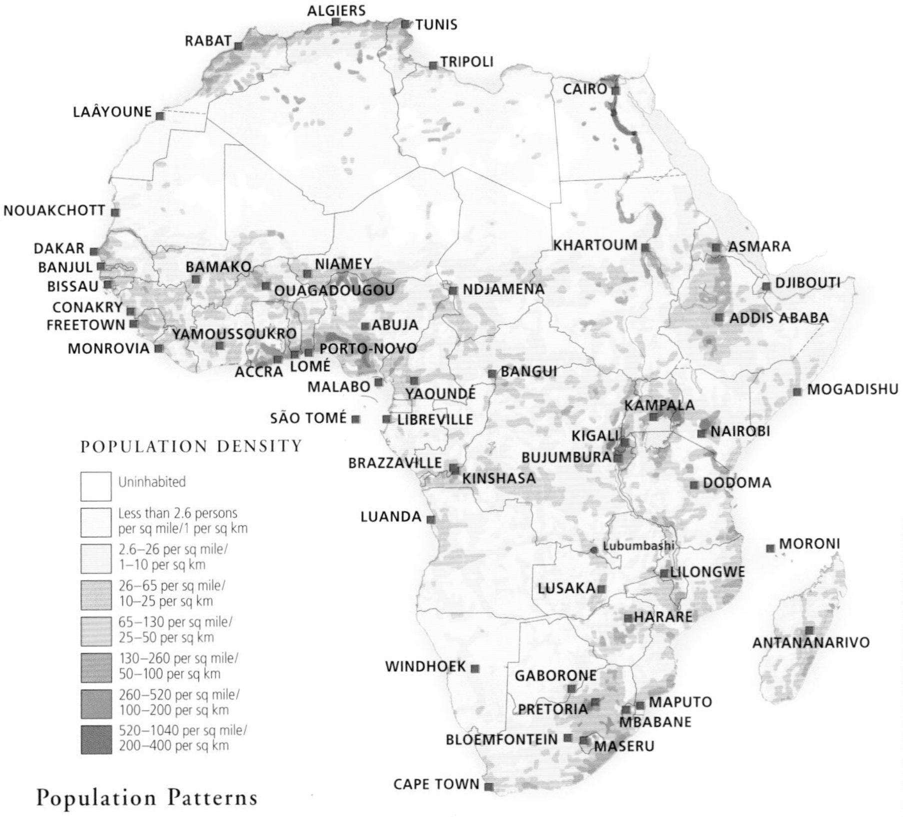
ALGIERS
TUNIS
RABAT
TRIPOLI
CAIRO
LAÂYOUNE
NOUAKCHOTT
DAKAR
BANJUL
BISSAU
CONAKRY
FREETOWN
MONROVIA
BAMAKO
NIAMEY
OUAGADOUGOU
NDJAMENA
KHARTOUM
ASMARA
DJIBOUTI
ADDIS ABABA
YAMOUSSOUKRO
ABUJA
PORTO-NOVO
ACCRA
LOMÉ
MALABO
BANGUI
YAOUNDÉ
SÃO TOMÉ
LIBREVILLE
KAMPALA
MOGADISHU
KIGALI
NAIROBI
BUJUMBURA
BRAZZAVILLE
KINSHASA
DODOMA
LUANDA
Lubumbashi
MORONI
LILONGWE
LUSAKA
HARARE
ANTANANARIVO
WINDHOEK
GABORONE
PRETORIA
MAPUTO
MBABANE
BLOEMFONTEIN
MASERU
CAPE TOWN
POPULATION DENSITY
Uninhabited
Less than 2.6 persons per sq mile/1 per sq km
2.6–26 per sq mile/ 1–10 per sq km
26–65 per sq mile/ 10–25 per sq km
65–130 per sq mile/ 25–50 per sq km
130–260 per sq mile/ 50–100 per sq km
260–520 per sq mile/ 100–200 per sq km
520–1040 per sq mile/ 200–400 per sq km

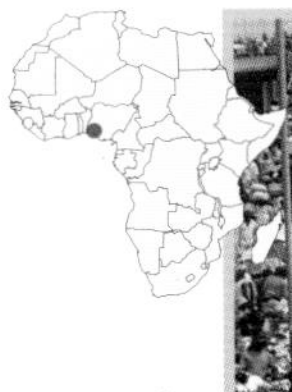

Right: Population growth in Lagos, Nigeria, is due mainly to rural–urban migration. In an effort to slow the city's expansion, the government recently moved the national capital from Lagos to Abuja.

Population Patterns

Relative to most other continents, Africa is underpopulated, having just 13 percent of the world's people but more than 20 percent of its land. This is due in part to the high proportion of arid land, which precludes widespread permanent settlement, but also to the effects of disease and conflict. The greatest population densities occur on the coasts of North and West Africa, along major rivers and around large lakes, and in well-watered upland areas such as the highlands of the Great Rift Valley. Despite its low density, Africa's population is growing rapidly and is likely to reach almost 1.5 billion by 2030 (during that time, its growth rate will probably stay high while rates on other continents decline steeply). About 40 percent of the current population is under 15.

Trade Organizations

Intraregional trade has long been hampered by poor communications and a limited variety of commodities. However, the Abuja Treaty of 1991 established the African Economic Community, which aims to create an African common market by uniting the following regional organizations: the Economic Community of West African States (ECOWAS), the Economic Community of Central African States (ECCAS), the Southern African Development Community (SADC), the Common Market for Eastern and Southern Africa (COMESA), and the Arab Maghreb Union (AMU).

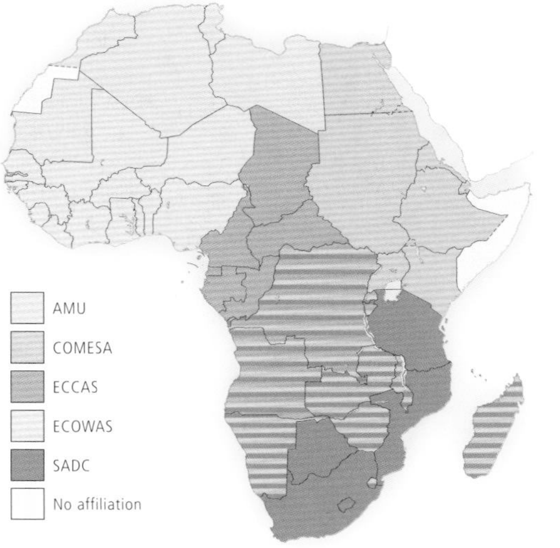
AMU
COMESA
ECCAS
ECOWAS
SADC
No affiliation

Flashpoints

Many of Africa's numerous and frequently violent regional disputes have centered on the control of lucrative natural resources and been stoked by interethnic rivalries.

Western Sahara

As soon as Spain left its colony of Western Sahara in 1976, Morocco annexed the territory, encouraging Moroccans to settle there and forcing native Saharawi people into Algeria. It then built a fortified wall, the so-called Berm, to keep out the Saharawi and their independence fighters, the Polisario Front. UN attempts to broker peace have so far failed.

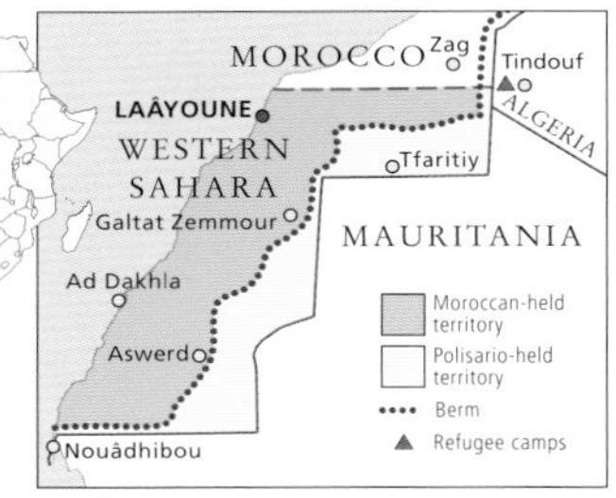
MOROCCO
Zag
Tindouf
ALGERIA
LAÂYOUNE
WESTERN SAHARA
Tfaritiy
Galtat Zemmour
MAURITANIA
Ad Dakhla
Aswerd
Nouâdhibou
Moroccan-held territory
Polisario-held territory
Berm
Refugee camps

Democratic Republic of Congo

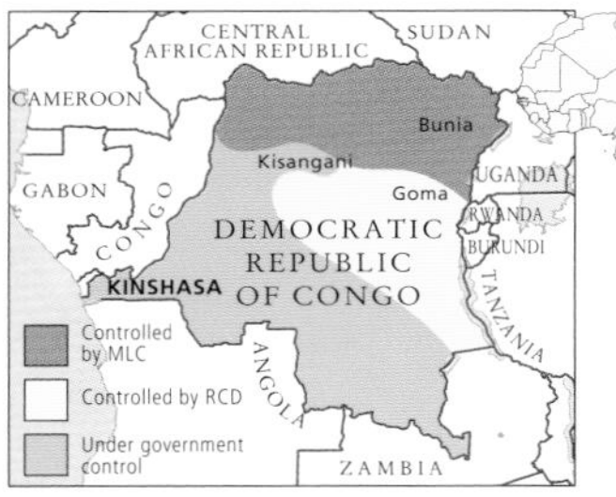
CENTRAL AFRICAN REPUBLIC
SUDAN
CAMEROON
Bunia
Kisangani
UGANDA
GABON
Goma
RWANDA
CONGO
DEMOCRATIC REPUBLIC OF CONGO
BURUNDI
KINSHASA
TANZANIA
ANGOLA
ZAMBIA
Controlled by MLC
Controlled by RCD
Under government control

Ethnic disputes have fueled a civil war in the Democratic Republic of Congo that has claimed 3 million lives since 1998. Despite the formation in 2003 of a coalition government including the main rebel groups—the Movement for the Liberation of Congo (MLC) and the Rally for Congolese Democracy (RCD)—violence continues.

West Africa's Diamond Wars

In 1990, the rebel National Patriotic Front (NPF) took control of Liberia and began aiding Sierra Leone insurgents the Revolutionary United Front (RUF) in return for diamonds. This led to civil wars that have killed 300,000 people. The U.K. helped disarm the RUF in 2002, and the NPF was ousted in 2003, but the situation remains volatile.

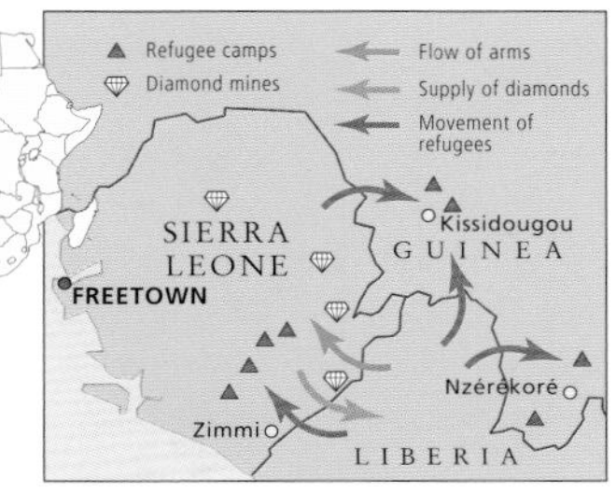
Refugee camps
Diamond mines
Flow of arms
Supply of diamonds
Movement of refugees
SIERRA LEONE
FREETOWN
Kissidougou
GUINEA
Nzérékoré
Zimmi
LIBERIA

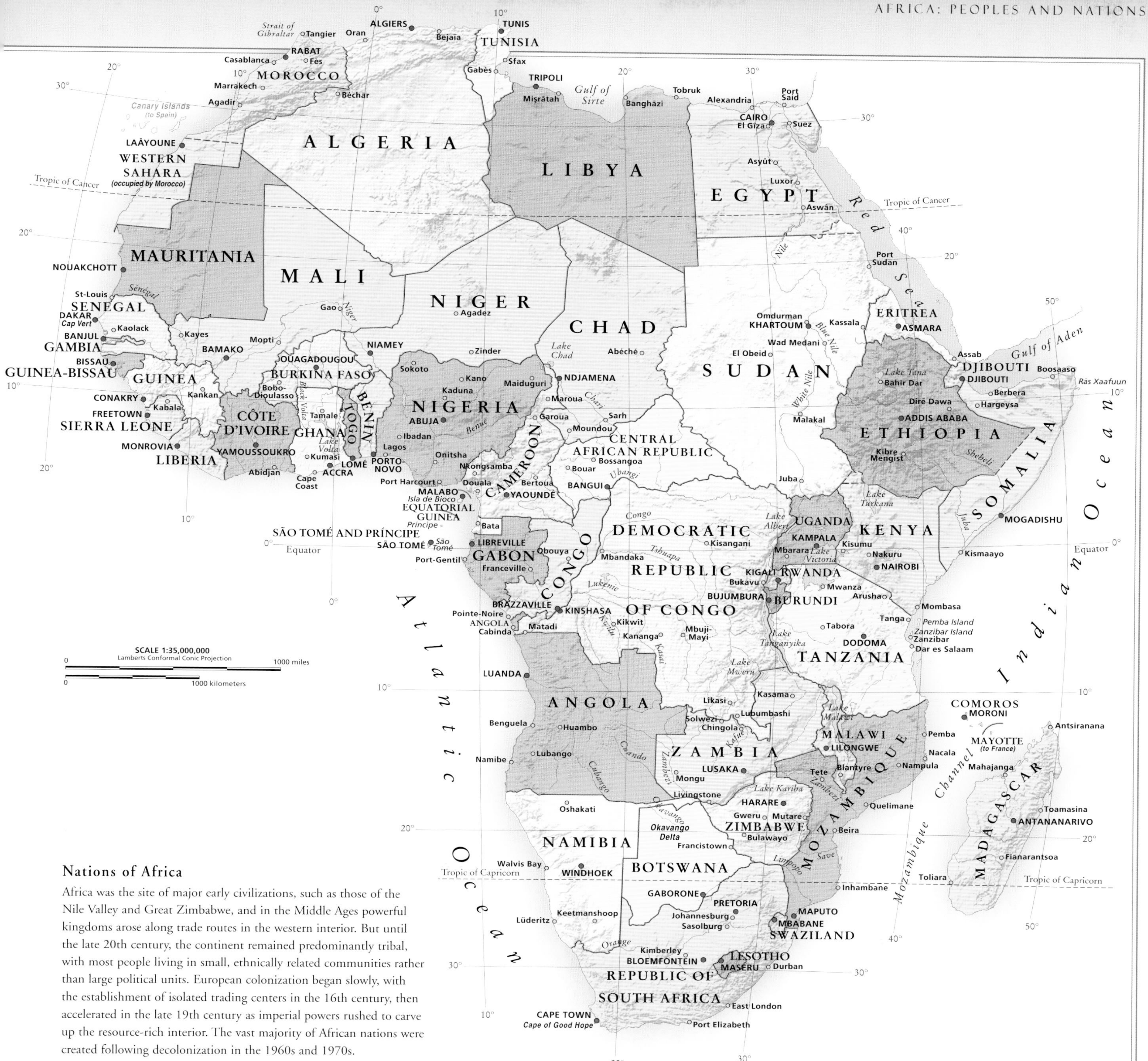
ALGERIA
LIBYA
EGYPT
MOROCCO
TUNISIA
WESTERN SAHARA (occupied by Morocco)
MAURITANIA
MALI
NIGER
CHAD
SUDAN
ERITREA
DJIBOUTI
ETHIOPIA
SOMALIA
SENEGAL
GAMBIA
GUINEA-BISSAU
GUINEA
SIERRA LEONE
LIBERIA
CÔTE D'IVOIRE
BURKINA FASO
GHANA
TOGO
BENIN
NIGERIA
CAMEROON
CENTRAL AFRICAN REPUBLIC
EQUATORIAL GUINEA
SÃO TOMÉ AND PRÍNCIPE
GABON
CONGO
DEMOCRATIC REPUBLIC OF CONGO
UGANDA
KENYA
RWANDA
BURUNDI
TANZANIA
ANGOLA
ZAMBIA
MALAWI
MOZAMBIQUE
ZIMBABWE
NAMIBIA
BOTSWANA
SWAZILAND
LESOTHO
REPUBLIC OF SOUTH AFRICA
MADAGASCAR
COMOROS
MAYOTTE (to France)
Atlantic Ocean
Indian Ocean
Red Sea
Gulf of Aden
Mozambique Channel
Gulf of Sirte
Tropic of Cancer
Equator
Tropic of Capricorn
SCALE 1:35,000,000
Lamberts Conformal Conic Projection
1000 miles
1000 kilometers

Nations of Africa

Africa was the site of major early civilizations, such as those of the Nile Valley and Great Zimbabwe, and in the Middle Ages powerful kingdoms arose along trade routes in the western interior. But until the late 20th century, the continent remained predominantly tribal, with most people living in small, ethnically related communities rather than large political units. European colonization began slowly, with the establishment of isolated trading centers in the 16th century, then accelerated in the late 19th century as imperial powers rushed to carve up the resource-rich interior. The vast majority of African nations were created following decolonization in the 1960s and 1970s.

MEDIEVAL AFRICA, 1300

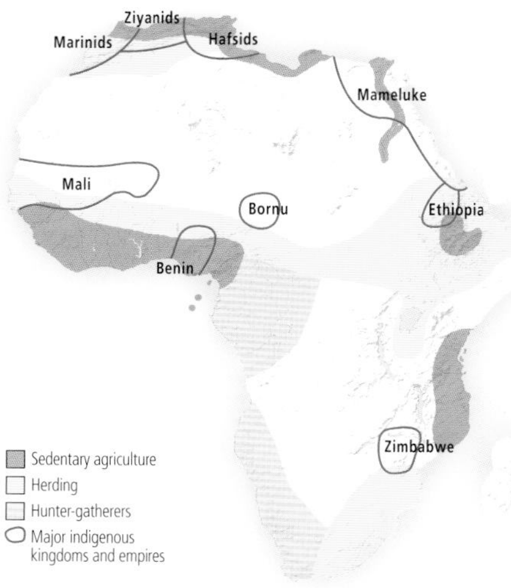
Ziyanids
Marinids
Hafsids
Mameluke
Mali
Bornu
Ethiopia
Benin
Zimbabwe
Sedentary agriculture
Herding
Hunter-gatherers
Major indigenous kingdoms and empires

EARLY EUROPEAN COLONIZATION, 1830

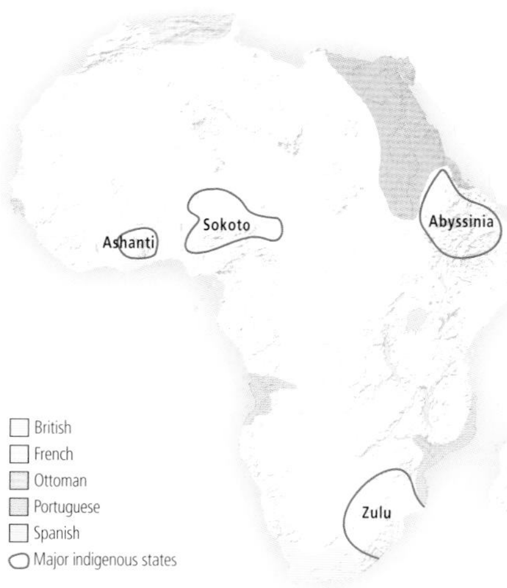
Ashanti
Sokoto
Abyssinia
Zulu
British
French
Ottoman
Portuguese
Spanish
Major indigenous states

COLONIAL RULE, 1914

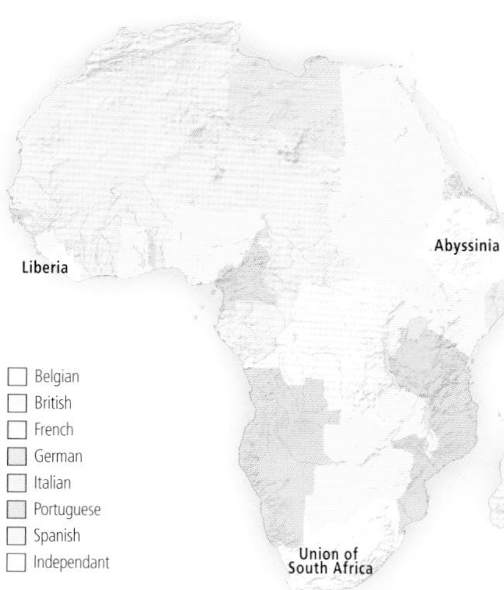
Liberia
Abyssinia
Union of South Africa
Belgian
British
French
German
Italian
Portuguese
Spanish
Independant

The Human Impact

Africa is where humans first evolved, and modification of the land to facilitate hunting and farming, as well as the excavation of minerals, have been happening there for thousands of years. As on most other continents, however, it was the arrival of European colonists that precipitated industrial-scale exploitation of natural resources—including people. An estimated 10 million Africans were deported as slaves between the 16th and 19th centuries. In addition, vast amounts of timber and huge quantities of minerals were shipped to foreign markets. Since decolonization, governments have faced the difficult balancing act of providing for impoverished populations while guarding against the exhaustion of resources. Environmental problems are exacerbated by population growth, inequitable land distribution, foreign penetration of local markets, corruption, weak institutions, and violent conflicts.

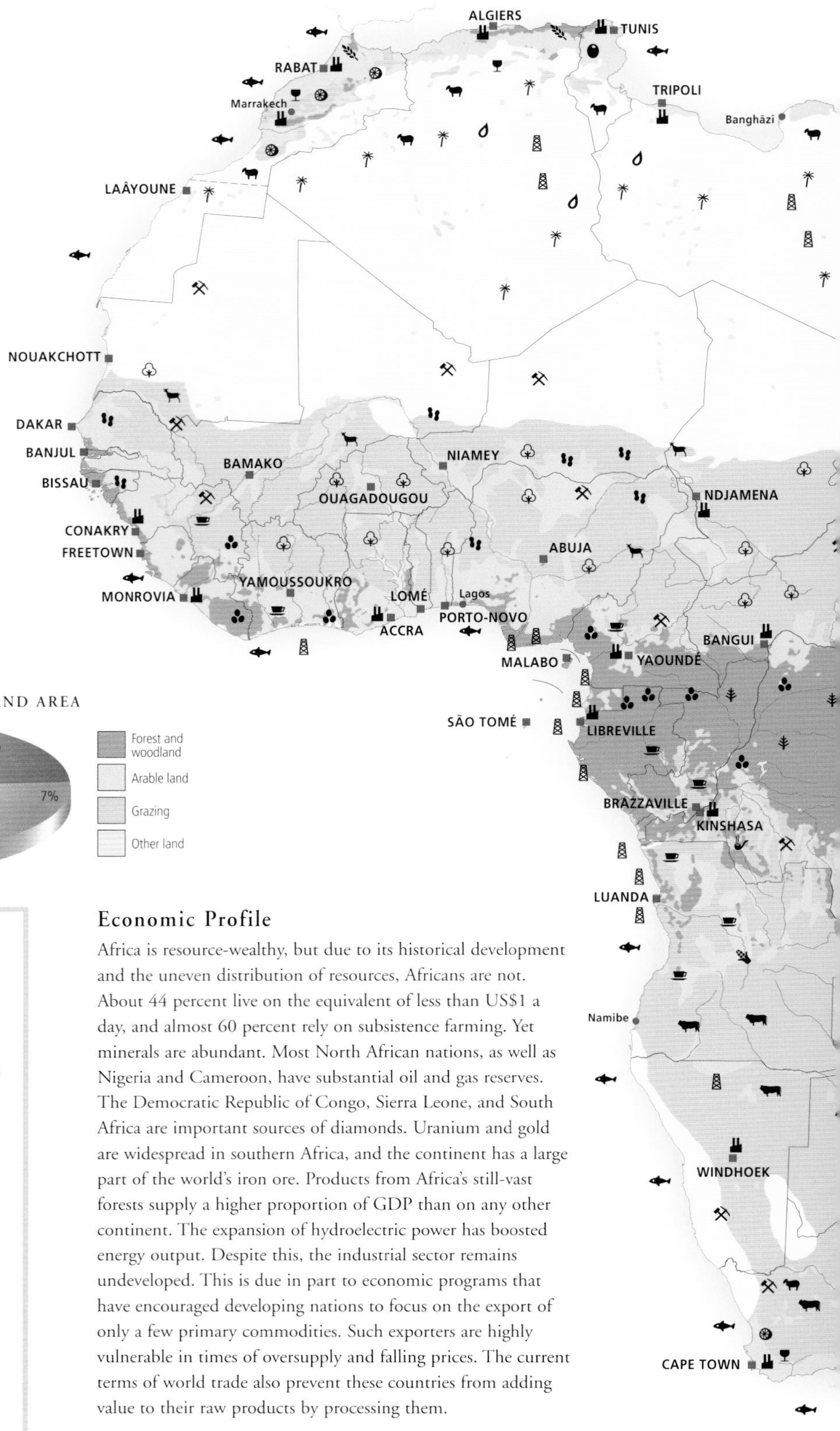

ALGIERS
TUNIS
RABAT
Marrakech
TRIPOLI
Banghāzi
LAÂYOUNE
NOUAKCHOTT
DAKAR
BANJUL
BISSAU
BAMAKO
NIAMEY
OUAGADOUGOU
NDJAMENA
CONAKRY
FREETOWN
ABUJA
YAMOUSSOUKRO
MONROVIA
LOMÉ
Lagos
PORTO-NOVO
ACCRA
BANGUI
MALABO
YAOUNDÉ
SÃO TOMÉ
LIBREVILLE
BRAZZAVILLE
KINSHASA
LUANDA
Namibe
WINDHOEK
CAPE TOWN

Land Cover

Two-thirds of Africa is arid or semiarid; much of this land is used, appropriately, for nomadic grazing. The proportion of arable land is low relative to other continents. Its quality varies, from fertile volcanic and alluvial soils to poor, leached soils in zones of high rainfall. Africa's forests represent 17 percent of global forest cover; one-fifth lies within the Democratic Republic of Congo.

PROPORTIONS OF TOTAL LAND AREA

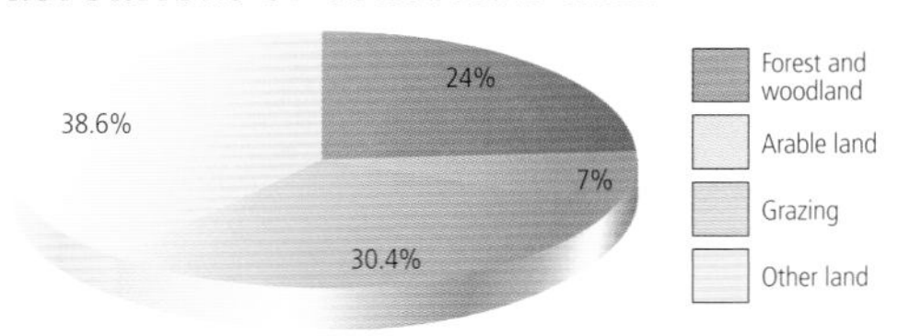

24%
7%
30.4%
38.6%
Forest and woodland
Arable land
Grazing
Other land

The Changing Face of Africa

Desertification

Significant fluctuations in rainfall, including prolonged droughts, periodically reduce vegetation cover in semiarid areas of Africa. The impact of this natural cycle has been intensified by human modification of the land, especially the cultivation and grazing of marginal areas. These activities remove the natural vegetation that binds light soils together, making them vulnerable to erosion, and in turn inhibiting the regeneration of plants. Desertification, as this process is widely known, now threatens 46 percent of Africa, and more than half of this land is at high or very high risk. Around 485 million Africans are affected.

AREAS AT RISK OF DESERTIFICATION

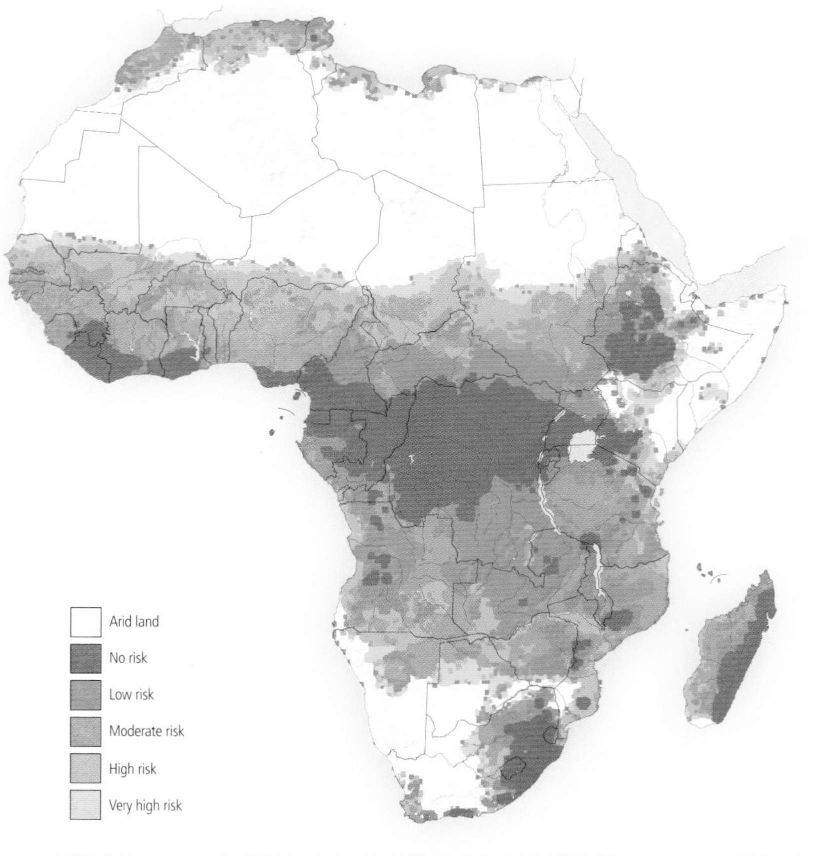

Arid land
No risk
Low risk
Moderate risk
High risk
Very high risk

Economic Profile

Africa is resource-wealthy, but due to its historical development and the uneven distribution of resources, Africans are not. About 44 percent live on the equivalent of less than US$1 a day, and almost 60 percent rely on subsistence farming. Yet minerals are abundant. Most North African nations, as well as Nigeria and Cameroon, have substantial oil and gas reserves. The Democratic Republic of Congo, Sierra Leone, and South Africa are important sources of diamonds. Uranium and gold are widespread in southern Africa, and the continent has a large part of the world's iron ore. Products from Africa's still-vast forests supply a higher proportion of GDP than on any other continent. The expansion of hydroelectric power has boosted energy output. Despite this, the industrial sector remains undeveloped. This is due in part to economic programs that have encouraged developing nations to focus on the export of only a few primary commodities. Such exporters are highly vulnerable in times of oversupply and falling prices. The current terms of world trade also prevent these countries from adding value to their raw products by processing them.

Protecting the Environment

Actions being taken to ameliorate land degradation include a return to the diverse farming systems used by many African farmers before industrial techniques were introduced. Some reforestation is taking place, but mainly in the form of monocultural plantations, which do not support the biological diversity of natural forests. More than 3,000 protected areas have, however, been created, covering 5.2 percent of the continent. Few more are likely to be established in the near future due to pressure on land, but increasing involvement of local people in the management of existing protected areas is helping to improve their effectiveness. Some 48 African countries have signed the Convention on International Trade in Endangered Species (CITES), which strictly controls trade in commodities such as ivory. However, some countries, notably in southern Africa where parks are well managed and elephants consequently abundant, contend that profits from a carefully controlled ivory trade could be used to fund the management of protected areas. Although air pollution is increasing in many cities, Africa emits just 3.5 percent of the world's carbon dioxide and a mere 7 percent of total greenhouse-gas emissions. Leaded petrol has been phased out in Egypt, Sudan, Libya, and Mauritius, and another 22 countries aim to follow suit by 2006.

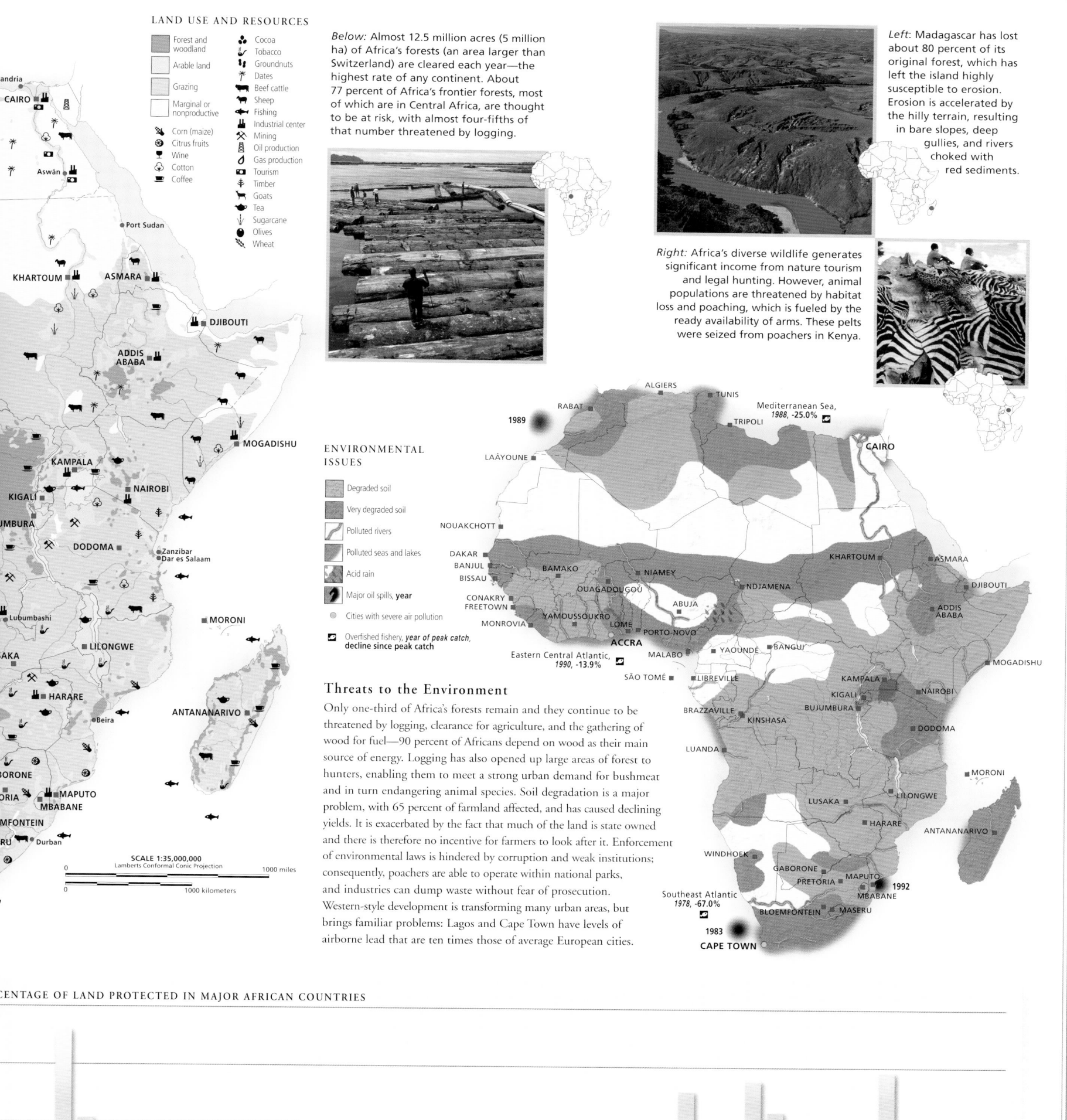

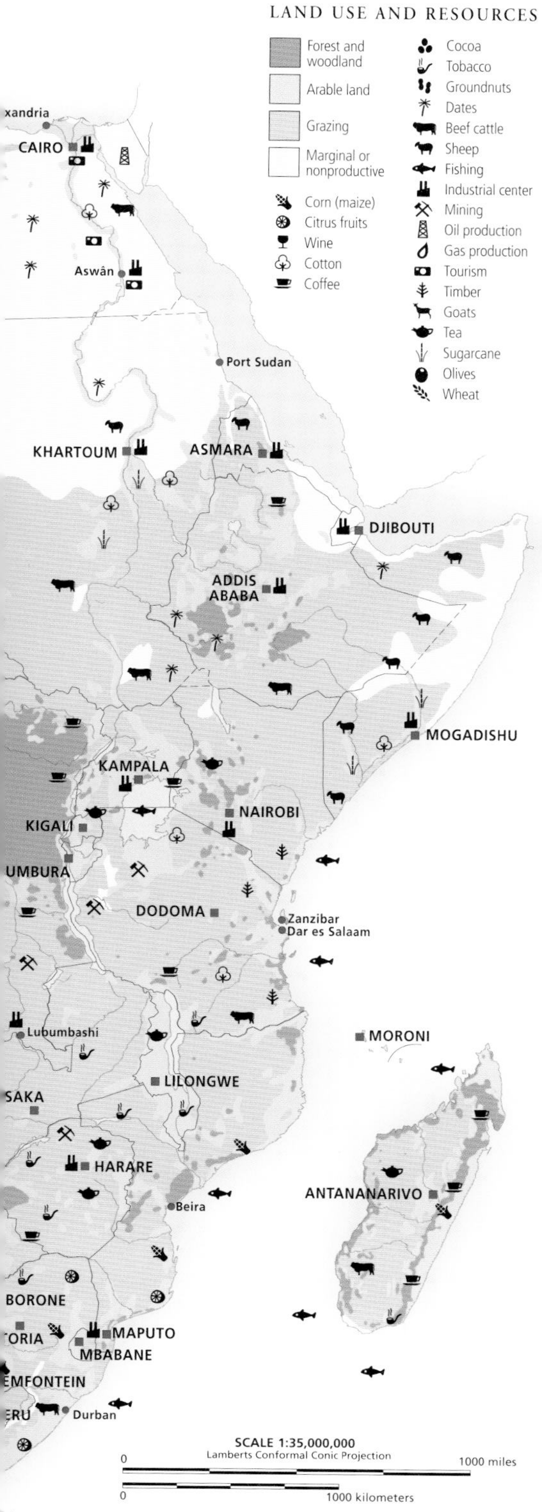
LAND USE AND RESOURCES
Forest and woodland
Arable land
Grazing
Marginal or nonproductive
Corn (maize)
Citrus fruits
Wine
Cotton
Coffee
Cocoa
Tobacco
Groundnuts
Dates
Beef cattle
Sheep
Fishing
Industrial center
Mining
Oil production
Gas production
Tourism
Timber
Goats
Tea
Sugarcane
Olives
Wheat
CAIRO
Aswân
Port Sudan
KHARTOUM
ASMARA
DJIBOUTI
ADDIS ABABA
MOGADISHU
KAMPALA
NAIROBI
KIGALI
DODOMA
Zanzibar
Dar es Salaam
Lubumbashi
MORONI
LILONGWE
HARARE
Beira
ANTANANARIVO
MAPUTO
MBABANE
Durban
SCALE 1:35,000,000
Lamberts Conformal Conic Projection
1000 miles
1000 kilometers

Below: Almost 12.5 million acres (5 million ha) of Africa's forests (an area larger than Switzerland) are cleared each year—the highest rate of any continent. About 77 percent of Africa's frontier forests, most of which are in Central Africa, are thought to be at risk, with almost four-fifths of that number threatened by logging.

Left: Madagascar has lost about 80 percent of its original forest, which has left the island highly susceptible to erosion. Erosion is accelerated by the hilly terrain, resulting in bare slopes, deep gullies, and rivers choked with red sediments.

Right: Africa's diverse wildlife generates significant income from nature tourism and legal hunting. However, animal populations are threatened by habitat loss and poaching, which is fueled by the ready availability of arms. These pelts were seized from poachers in Kenya.

ENVIRONMENTAL ISSUES

- Degraded soil
- Very degraded soil
- Polluted rivers
- Polluted seas and lakes
- Acid rain
- Major oil spills, **year**
- Cities with severe air pollution
- Overfished fishery, ***year of peak catch,*** **decline since peak catch**

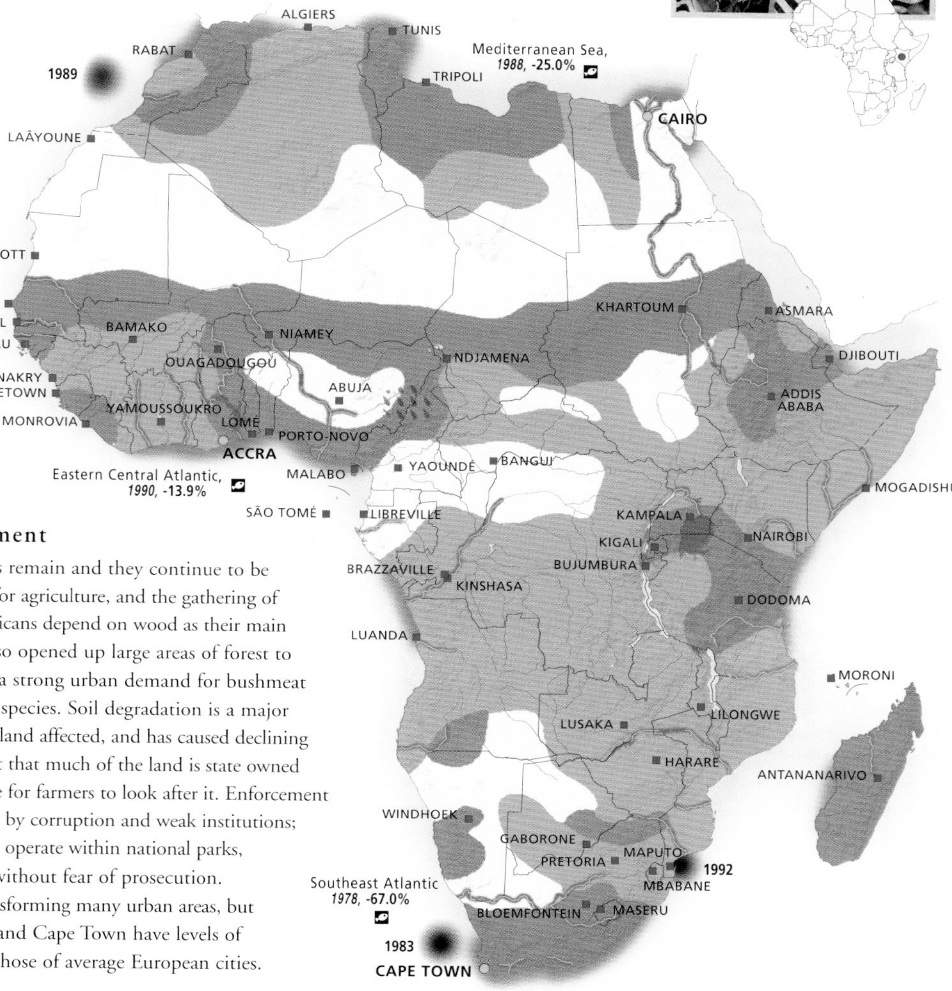
ALGIERS
TUNIS
RABAT
1989
Mediterranean Sea, 1988, -25.0%
TRIPOLI
CAIRO
LAÂYOUNE
NOUAKCHOTT
DAKAR
BANJUL
BISSAU
BAMAKO
NIAMEY
KHARTOUM
ASMARA
DJIBOUTI
OUAGADOUGOU
NDJAMENA
CONAKRY
FREETOWN
ABUJA
ADDIS ABABA
YAMOUSSOUKRO
MONROVIA
LOMÉ
PORTO-NOVO
ACCRA
Eastern Central Atlantic, 1990, -13.9%
MALABO
YAOUNDÉ
BANGUI
MOGADISHU
SÃO TOMÉ
LIBREVILLE
KAMPALA
KIGALI
NAIROBI
BUJUMBURA
BRAZZAVILLE
KINSHASA
DODOMA
LUANDA
MORONI
LUSAKA
LILONGWE
HARARE
ANTANANARIVO
WINDHOEK
GABORONE
PRETORIA
MAPUTO
1992
MBABANE
Southeast Atlantic 1978, -67.0%
BLOEMFONTEIN
MASERU
1983
CAPE TOWN

Threats to the Environment

Only one-third of Africa's forests remain and they continue to be threatened by logging, clearance for agriculture, and the gathering of wood for fuel—90 percent of Africans depend on wood as their main source of energy. Logging has also opened up large areas of forest to hunters, enabling them to meet a strong urban demand for bushmeat and in turn endangering animal species. Soil degradation is a major problem, with 65 percent of farmland affected, and has caused declining yields. It is exacerbated by the fact that much of the land is state owned and there is therefore no incentive for farmers to look after it. Enforcement of environmental laws is hindered by corruption and weak institutions; consequently, poachers are able to operate within national parks, and industries can dump waste without fear of prosecution. Western-style development is transforming many urban areas, but brings familiar problems: Lagos and Cape Town have levels of airborne lead that are ten times those of average European cities.

CENTAGE OF LAND PROTECTED IN MAJOR AFRICAN COUNTRIES

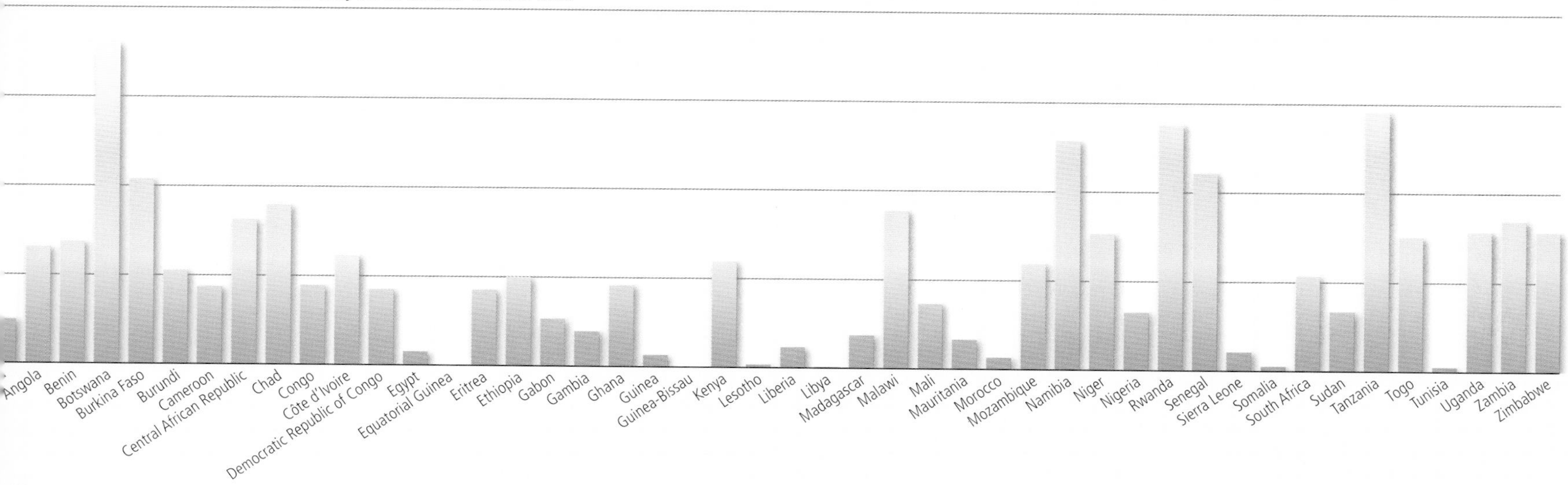
Angola
Benin
Botswana
Burkina Faso
Burundi
Cameroon
Central African Republic
Chad
Congo
Côte d'Ivoire
Democratic Republic of Congo
Egypt
Equatorial Guinea
Eritrea
Ethiopia
Gabon
Gambia
Ghana
Guinea
Guinea-Bissau
Kenya
Lesotho
Liberia
Libya
Madagascar
Malawi
Mali
Mauritania
Morocco
Mozambique
Namibia
Niger
Nigeria
Rwanda
Senegal
Sierra Leone
Somalia
South Africa
Sudan
Tanzania
Togo
Tunisia
Uganda
Zambia
Zimbabwe

Northwestern Africa

Algeria, Libya, Morocco, Tunisia

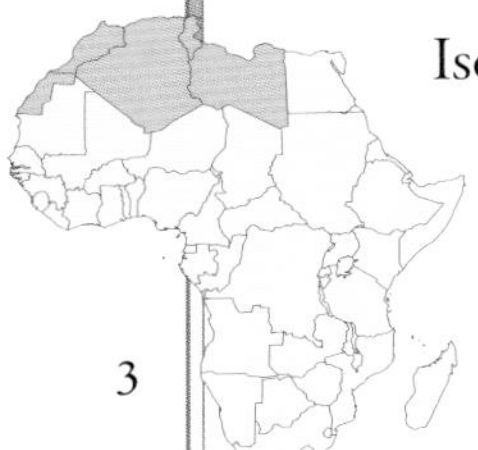

Isolated from the rest of the continent by the Sahara Desert, Northwestern Africa is a transitional zone, between sea and remote interior, Europe and Africa, the West and the Middle East. Its distinctive and relatively homogenous culture was flavored by classical European civilizations and its original, nomadic Berber inhabitants, but derives mainly from the Arab peoples who invaded and settled here in the seventh century AD. This Arabic, Islamic heritage not only withstood subsequent occupation by the Ottoman Empire (between the 16th and 19th centuries), European colonial rule, and a torrid phase of decolonization, but also permeated almost every part of a vast, inhospitable region. Bounded by the Atlas Mountains in the northwest, the Sahara Desert occupies more than 80 percent of the land, confining major population centers and communications routes, sedentary farming, and industries to a narrow coastal strip.

Population Patterns

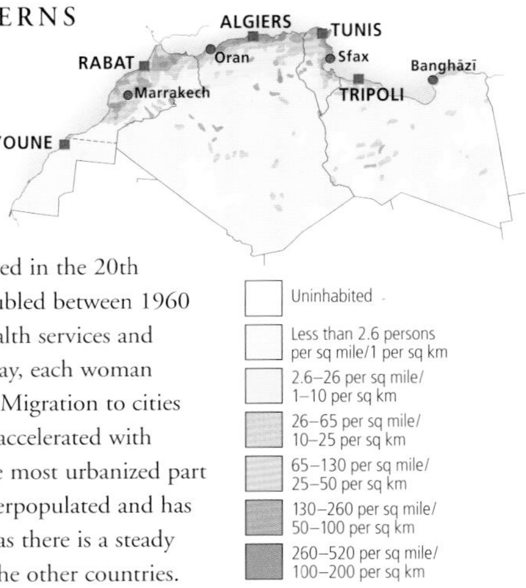

ALGIERS
TUNIS
RABAT
Oran
Sfax
Banghāzī
Marrakech
TRIPOLI
LAÂYOUNE
Uninhabited
Less than 2.6 persons per sq mile/1 per sq km
2.6–26 per sq mile/ 1–10 per sq km
26–65 per sq mile/ 10–25 per sq km
65–130 per sq mile/ 25–50 per sq km
130–260 per sq mile/ 50–100 per sq km
260–520 per sq mile/ 100–200 per sq km

The Sahara contains just a few isolated towns, scattered oases, and groups of nomadic pastoralists; the vast majority of the region's inhabitants dwell on the north coast. The population soared in the 20th century (Algeria's population doubled between 1960 and 1990), due to improving health services and persistent high fertility (even today, each woman has an average of four children). Migration to cities began under European rule and accelerated with industrialization, making this the most urbanized part of Africa. Libya is distinctly underpopulated and has to import skilled workers, whereas there is a steady outward flow of migrants from the other countries.

The seminomadic Tuareg people roam the desert lands of Algeria, Libya, Mali, and Niger.

The Atlas Mountains are home to large numbers of Berbers, the region's original inhabitants.

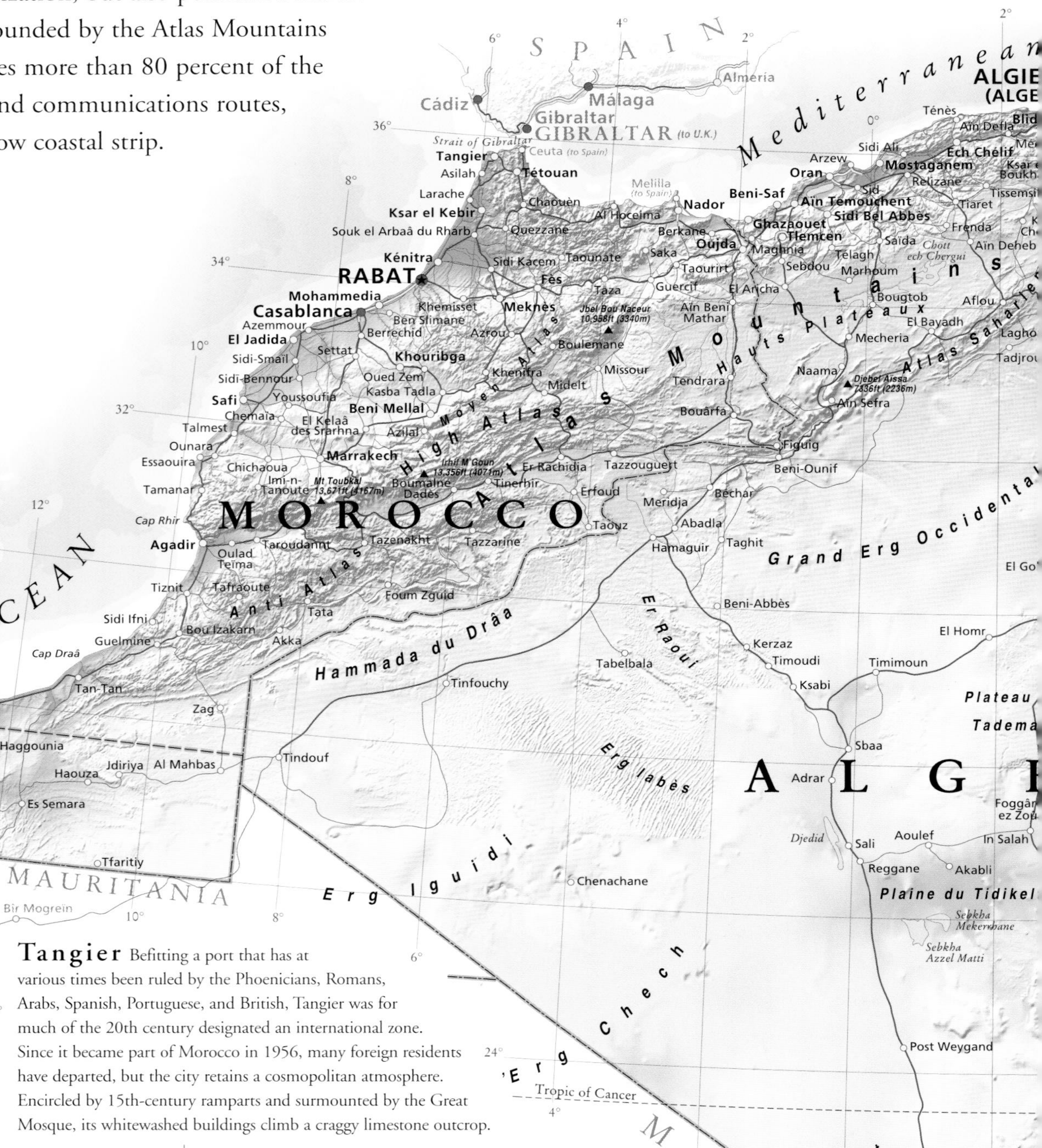
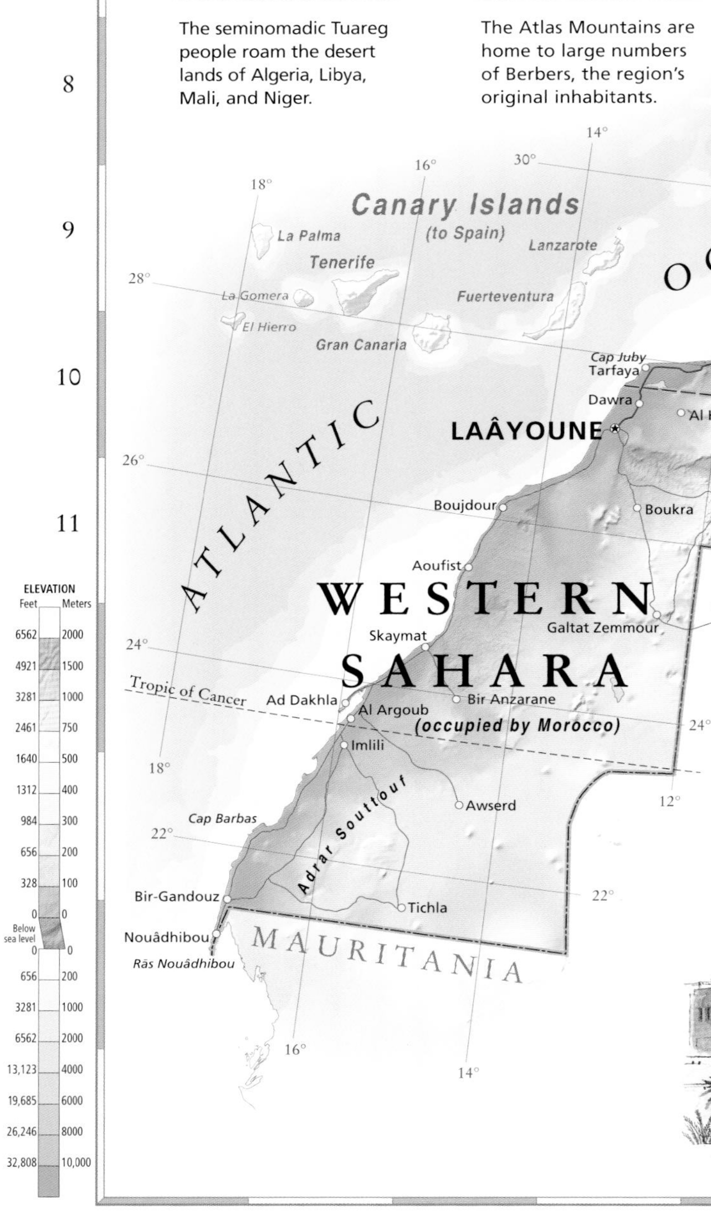

SPAIN
Cádiz
Málaga
Almería
Gibraltar
GIBRALTAR (to U.K.)
Strait of Gibraltar
Ceuta (to Spain)
Tangier
Asilah
Tétouan
Larache
Ksar el Kebir
Chaouèn
Melilla (to Spain)
Nador
Al Hoceïma
Souk el Arbaâ du Rharb
Ouezzane
Kénitra
Sidi Kacem
Taounate
RABAT
Mohammedia
Casablanca
Azemmour
El Jadida
Fès
Taza
Meknès
Khemisset
Ben Slimane
Berrechid
Azrou
Jbel Bou Naceur 10,958ft (3340m)
Oujda
Berkane
Saka
Taourirt
Guercif
El Ancha
Aïn Beni Mathar
Settat
Khouribga
Boulemane
Missour
Khenifra
Midelt
Sidi-Smaïl
Sidi-Bennour
Oued Zem
Kasba Tadla
Safi
Youssoufia
Beni Mellal
Chemaïa
El Kelaâ des Srarhna
Azilal
Talmest
Ounara
Essaouira
Marrakech
Chichaoua
Imi-n-Tanoute
Mt Toubkal 13,671ft (4167m)
Irhil M'Goun 13,356ft (4071m)
Boumalne Dadès
Er Rachidia
Tinerhir
Erfoud
Tazzouguert
Tamanar
MOROCCO
High Atlas
Moyen Atlas
Anti Atlas
Atlas Mountains
Cap Rhir
Agadir
Oulad Teïma
Taroudannt
Tazenakht
Tazzarine
Taouz
Tiznit
Tafraoute
Foum Zguid
Tata
Sidi Ifni
Guelmime
Bou Izakarn
Akka
Cap Draâ
Hammada du Drâa
Tan-Tan
Zag
Cap Juby
Tarfaya
Dawra
LAÂYOUNE
Al Haggounia
Haouza
Jdiriya
Al Mahbas
Tindouf
Es Semara
Boukra
Boujdour
Tfaritiy
Aoufist
WESTERN SAHARA (occupied by Morocco)
Skaymat
Galtat Zemmour
Bir Mogrein
MAURITANIA
Ad Dakhla
Al Argoub
Bir Anzarane
Imlili
Awserd
Cap Barbas
Adrar Souttouf
Tichla
Bir-Gandouz
Nouâdhibou
Râs Nouâdhibou
Tropic of Cancer
ATLANTIC OCEAN
Canary Islands (to Spain)
La Palma
Tenerife
Lanzarote
La Gomera
El Hierro
Fuerteventura
Gran Canaria
Mediterranean
ALGERIA (ALGE
Ténès
Aïn Defla
Blida
Sidi Ali
Arzew
Oran
Mostaganem
Ech Chélif
Relizane
Tissemsilt
Tiaret
Beni-Saf
Aïn Témouchent
Sidi Bel Abbès
Ghazaouet
Tlemcen
Maghnia
Saïda
Frenda
Chott ech Chergui
Aïn Deheb
Telagh
Sebdou
Marhoum
Bougtob
Aflou
El Bayadh
Mecheria
Laghouat
Tadjrout
Naama
Djebel Aïssa 7336ft (2236m)
Aïn Sefra
Hauts Plateaux
Atlas Saharien
Tendrara
Bouârfa
Figuig
Beni-Ounif
Béchar
Meridja
Abadla
Hamaguir
Taghit
Grand Erg Occidental
El Goléa
Beni-Abbès
Er Raoui
Kerzaz
Timoudi
Tabelbala
Tinfouchy
Ksabi
El Homr
Timimoun
Plateau du Tademaït
Sbaa
Erg Iabès
Adrar
ALGERIA
Foggaret ez Zoua
Djedid
Sali
Aoulef
In Salah
Reggane
Akabli
Plaine du Tidikelt
Sebkha Mekerrhane
Sebkha Azzel Matti
Erg Iguidi
Chenachane
Erg Chech
Post Weygand
MALI
Tanezrouft
Bordj Mokhtar
Tessalit
Longitude west of Greenwich
ELEVATION
Feet
Meters
6562
2000
4921
1500
3281
1000
2461
750
1640
500
1312
400
984
300
656
200
328
100
0
Below sea level
200
1000
2000
13,123
4000
19,685
6000
26,246
8000
32,808
10,000

Tangier Befitting a port that has at various times been ruled by the Phoenicians, Romans, Arabs, Spanish, Portuguese, and British, Tangier was for much of the 20th century designated an international zone. Since it became part of Morocco in 1956, many foreign residents have departed, but the city retains a cosmopolitan atmosphere. Encircled by 15th-century ramparts and surmounted by the Great Mosque, its whitewashed buildings climb a craggy limestone outcrop.

Great Mosque

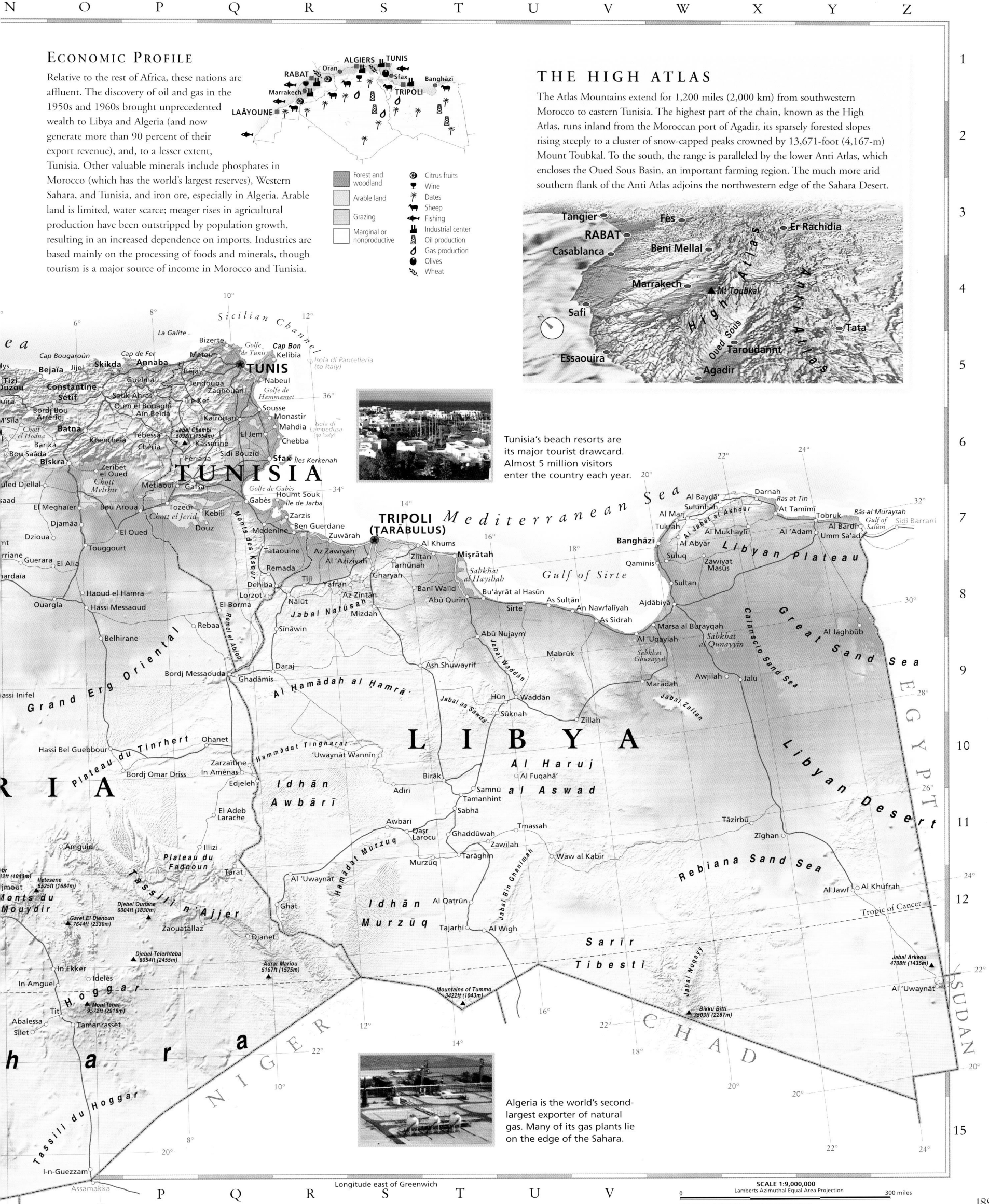

Economic Profile

Relative to the rest of Africa, these nations are affluent. The discovery of oil and gas in the 1950s and 1960s brought unprecedented wealth to Libya and Algeria (and now generate more than 90 percent of their export revenue), and, to a lesser extent, Tunisia. Other valuable minerals include phosphates in Morocco (which has the world's largest reserves), Western Sahara, and Tunisia, and iron ore, especially in Algeria. Arable land is limited, water scarce; meager rises in agricultural production have been outstripped by population growth, resulting in an increased dependence on imports. Industries are based mainly on the processing of foods and minerals, though tourism is a major source of income in Morocco and Tunisia.

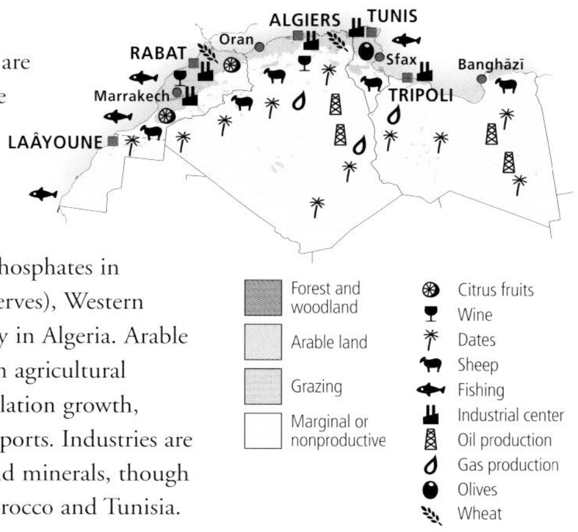
ALGIERS
TUNIS
Oran
RABAT
Sfax
Banghāzī
Marrakech
TRIPOLI
LAÂYOUNE
Forest and woodland
Arable land
Grazing
Marginal or nonproductive
Citrus fruits
Wine
Dates
Sheep
Fishing
Industrial center
Oil production
Gas production
Olives
Wheat

The High Atlas

The Atlas Mountains extend for 1,200 miles (2,000 km) from southwestern Morocco to eastern Tunisia. The highest part of the chain, known as the High Atlas, runs inland from the Moroccan port of Agadir, its sparsely forested slopes rising steeply to a cluster of snow-capped peaks crowned by 13,671-foot (4,167-m) Mount Toubkal. To the south, the range is paralleled by the lower Anti Atlas, which encloses the Oued Sous Basin, an important farming region. The much more arid southern flank of the Anti Atlas adjoins the northwestern edge of the Sahara Desert.

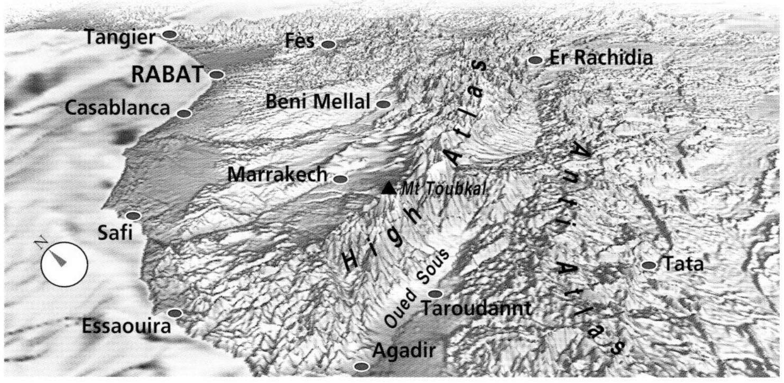
Tangier
RABAT
Casablanca
Fès
Er Rachidia
Beni Mellal
Marrakech
Mt Toubkal
High Atlas
Anti Atlas
Safi
Oued Sous
Tata
Taroudannt
Essaouira
Agadir

Tunisia's beach resorts are its major tourist drawcard. Almost 5 million visitors enter the country each year.

N O P Q R S T U V W X Y Z
1 2 3 4 5 6 7 8 9 10 11 12 15
Sicilian Channel
Mediterranean Sea
TUNISIA
LIBYA
TUNIS
TRIPOLI (TARĀBULUS)
La Galite
Bizerte
Golfe de Tunis
Cap Bon
Kelibia
Cap Bougaroûn
Cap de Fer
Skikda
Annaba
Bejaïa
Jijel
Constantine
Sétif
Guelma
Souk Ahras
Oum el Bouaghi
Aïn Beïda
Bordj Bou Arreridj
Batna
Khenchela
Tébessa
Chéria
Biskra
Barika
Bou Saâda
Chott el Hodna
Mateur
Béja
Jendouba
Zaghouan
Le Kef
Nabeul
Golfe de Hammamet
Sousse
Monastir
Mahdia
Kairouan
Jebel Chambi 5098ft (1554m)
Kasserine
El Jem
Chebba
Sidi Bouzid
Sfax
Îles Kerkenah
Fériana
Isola di Pantelleria (to Italy)
Isola di Lampedusa (to Italy)
Zeribet el Oued
Chott Melrhir
Metlaoui
Gafsa
Golfe de Gabès
Gabès
Houmt Souk
Île de Jarba
Tozeur
Chott el Jerid
Kebili
Douz
Zarzis
Medenine
Ben Guerdane
Zuwārah
Monts des Ksour
Tataouine
Remada
Dehiba
El Meghaïer
Bou Aroua
Djamâa
El Oued
Touggourt
Dzioua
Guerara
El Alia
Haoud el Hamra
Hassi Messaoud
Ouargla
Belhirane
Grand Erg Oriental
Bordj Messaouda
Ghadāmis
Rebaa
Remel el Abiod
El Borma
Lorzot
Nālūt
Jabal Nafūsah
Sīnāwin
Daraj
Az Zāwiyah
Al 'Azīzīyah
Tiji
Yafran
Az Zintān
Mizdah
Gharyān
Tarhūnah
Al Khums
Zlīṭan
Miṣrātah
Sabkhat al Hayshah
Banī Walīd
Abū Qurin
Bu'ayrāt al Hasūn
Sirte
Gulf of Sirte
As Sulṭān
An Nawfalīyah
As Sidrah
Ajdābiyā
Al 'Uqaylah
Sabkhat Ghuzayyil
Marsa al Burayqah
Sabkhat al Qunayyin
Abū Nujaym
Jabal Waddān
Mabrūk
Ash Shuwayrif
Al Ḩamādah al Ḩamrā'
Jabal as Sawdā'
Hūn
Waddān
Sūknah
Zillah
Marādah
Jabal Zaltan
Awjilah
Jālū
Calanscio Sand Sea
Great Sand Sea
Banghāzī
Qaminis
Sulūq
Sultan
Tūkrah
Al Marj
Al Bayḑā'
Sulunṭah
Al Jabal al Akhḑar
Al Abyār
Al Mukhaylī
Zāwiyat Masūs
Darnah
Rās at Tīn
At Tamīmī
Tobruk
Al 'Adam
Al Bardī
Umm Sa'ad
Rās al Muraysah
Gulf of Salūm
Sidi Barrani
Libyan Plateau
Al Jaghbūb
EGYPT
Hammādat Tingharat
'Uwaynāt Wannīn
Idhān Awbārī
Adīrī
Birāk
Samnū
Tamanhint
Sabhā
Al Haruj al Aswad
Al Fuqahā'
Awbārī
Qaṣr Larocu
Ghaddūwah
Tmassah
Zawīlah
Tarāghin
Murzūq
Hamādat Murzuq
Jabal Bin Ghanīmah
Wāw al Kabīr
Al 'Uwaynāt
Ghāt
Idhān Murzūq
Al Qaṭrūn
Tajarhī
Al Wīgh
Sarīr Tibesti
Jabal Nuqayy
Bikku Bitti 7503ft (2287m)
Mountains of Tummo 3422ft (1043m)
Tāzirbū
Zīghan
Rebiana Sand Sea
Libyan Desert
Al Jawf
Al Khufrah
Tropic of Cancer
Jabal Arkenu 4708ft (1435m)
Al 'Uwaynāt
SUDAN
CHAD
NIGER
Grand Erg
Plateau du Tinrhert
Hassi Bel Guebbour
Ohanet
Zarzaïtine
In Aménas
Bordj Omar Driss
Edjeleh
El Adeb Larache
Illizi
Plateau du Fadnoun
Tarat
Tassili n' Ajjer
Zaouatallaz
Djanet
Amguid
Iletesene 5525ft (1684m)
Monts du Mouydir
Djebel Ounane 6004ft (1830m)
Garet El Djenoun 7644ft (2330m)
Djebel Telerhteba 8054ft (2455m)
Adrar Mariou 5167ft (1575m)
In Ekker
Idelès
In Amguel
Hoggar
Mont Tahat 9572ft (2918m)
Tit
Abalessa
Silet
Tamanrasset
Sahara
Tassili du Hoggar
I-n-Guezzam
Assamakka
Longitude east of Greenwich
SCALE 1:9,000,000
Lamberts Azimuthal Equal Area Projection
300 miles
300 kilometers

Algeria is the world's second-largest exporter of natural gas. Many of its gas plants lie on the edge of the Sahara.

Northeastern Africa

Djibouti, Egypt, Eritrea, Ethiopia, Somalia, Sudan

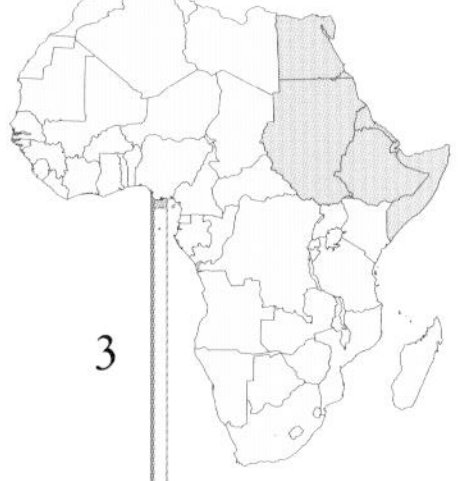

At the northern end of the Great Rift Valley, the Ethiopian Highlands divides the Horn of Africa in the east from the barren expanses of the Sahara in the west. Rivers that descend from the highlands, and from the East African Plateau to the south, are the lifeblood of this predominantly arid and impoverished land.

The Shebeli and Juba are the only permanent rivers in Somalia and supply most of the nation's water. From Lake Tana, the Blue Nile flows east then west to join the White Nile at Khartoum; continuing north, the Nile forms a riverine oasis that constitutes Egypt's only fertile zone. Since decolonization took place after the Second World War, the southern part of this region has been crippled by famines and political instability, including a long civil war that saw Eritrea secede from Ethiopia in 1993.

Population Patterns

The highest population densities occur in the fertile Ethiopian Highlands and along the major rivers—99 percent of Egyptians live in the Nile Valley, an area that constitutes just 3 percent of the country. The deserts of the eastern Sahara, northern Ethiopia, and Somalia, and the swamps of southern Sudan deter settlement. In semiarid zones, many people, including 70 percent of Somalians, maintain a nomadic lifestyle. The Sahara separates the mainly Arabic peoples of the north from the diverse African groups of the south; however, the Middle East has influenced the entire region and most inhabitants are adherents of Islam.

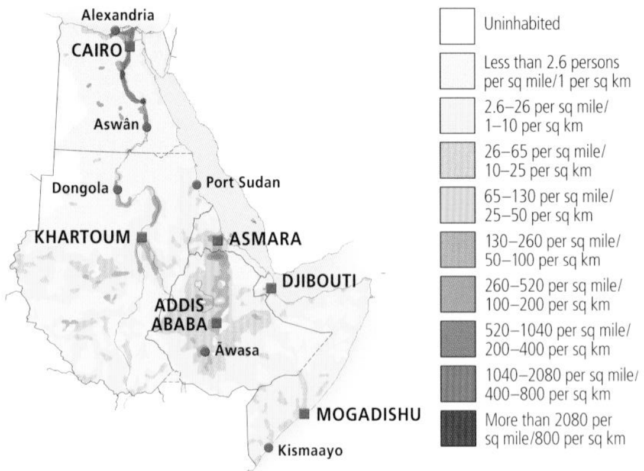
Alexandria
CAIRO
Aswân
Port Sudan
Dongola
KHARTOUM
ASMARA
DJIBOUTI
ADDIS ABABA
Awasa
MOGADISHU
Kismaayo
Uninhabited
Less than 2.6 persons per sq mile/1 per sq km
2.6–26 per sq mile/ 1–10 per sq km
26–65 per sq mile/ 10–25 per sq km
65–130 per sq mile/ 25–50 per sq km
130–260 per sq mile/ 50–100 per sq km
260–520 per sq mile/ 100–200 per sq km
520–1040 per sq mile/ 200–400 per sq km
1040–2080 per sq mile/ 400–800 per sq km
More than 2080 per sq mile/800 per sq km

Economic Profile

The regional economy is undeveloped, and most people rely on subsistence farming of cereals, fruit and vegetables, sheep, cattle, goats, and camels—80 percent of Somalians are dependent on livestock. Cash crops include cotton and sugarcane, grown in the Nile Valley, and coffee from the Ethiopian Highlands (from whose Kaffa region the word "coffee" derives). Only Egypt has a developed industrial sector, based on engineering and the manufacture of metals and electronic goods. It also benefits from modest oil reserves, tourism, and revenue from the Suez Canal.

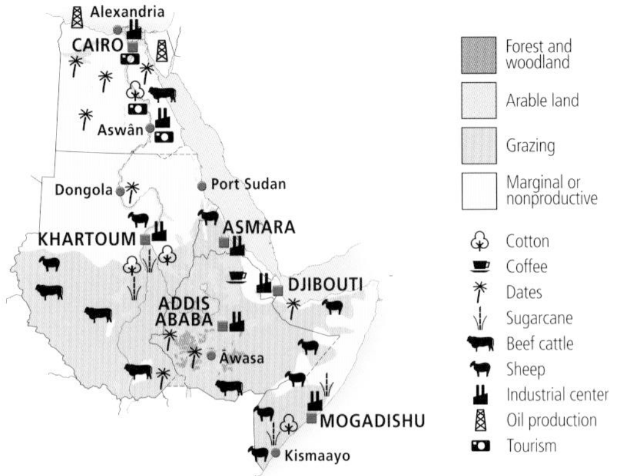
Alexandria
CAIRO
Aswân
Dongola
Port Sudan
KHARTOUM
ASMARA
DJIBOUTI
ADDIS ABABA
Awasa
MOGADISHU
Kismaayo
Forest and woodland
Arable land
Grazing
Marginal or nonproductive
Cotton
Coffee
Dates
Sugarcane
Beef cattle
Sheep
Industrial center
Oil production
Tourism

Mediterranean Sea
Tubruq
Al Bardi
Râs al Muraysah
Gulf of Salûm
Sidi Barrani
Râs el Kanâyis
Marsa Matrûh
Abu Haggag
Alexandria
Khalîg el 'Arab
El 'Alamein
Nile Delta
Damanhûr
Dumyât
Port Said
El 'Arîsh
Tel Aviv-Jaffa
ISRAEL
Gaza
JERUSALEM
Be'er Sheva
El Mansûra
Tanta
Zagazig
Suez Canal
Ismâ'ilîya
Shibîn el Kôm
Benha
CAIRO (EL QÂHIRA)
El Gîza
Helwân
Suez
Nakhl
Libyan Plateau
Qattâra Depression
Siwa Oasis
Siwa
El Faiyûm
El Saff
Sinai
Elat
Al 'Aqabah
Biba
Beni Suef
Abu Zenîma
Gebel Katherina 8668ft (2642m)
Gulf of Suez
Gulf of Aqaba
El Tûr
Maghâgha
Beni Mazâr
El Fashn
Great Sand Sea
Bawiti
Bahariya Oasis
Samalût
El Minya
Eastern Desert
Râs Ghârib
Sharm el Sheikh
Râs Muhammad
Western Desert
Mallawi
Dairût
Manfalût
Nile
Gemsa
Abnûb
Asyût
Hurghada
Dubâ
Qasr Farafra
Tima
Tahta
Akhmim
Sohâg
Girga
Bûr Safâga
EGYPT
El Balyana
Qena
El Qasr
Nag' Hammadi
Quseir
Al Karnak
Luxor
Dakhla Oasis
Mut
El Khârga
Armant
Hanalc
LIBYA
Bûlâq
Isna
Idfu
El Ridisiya Bahari
Marsa Alam
The Great Oasis
Bâris
Kôm Ombo
Daraw
Red
Gebel Hamâta 6486ft (1977m)
Aswân
Berenice
Râs Banâs
Foul Bay
SAUDI ARABIA
Tropic of Cancer
Gilf Kebir Plateau
Badr Hunayn
Lake Nasser
Abu Simbel
Halaib Triangle
(Administered by Sudan)
Halaib
Râs Hardârba
Qadimah
Al 'Uwaynât
Jebel Uweinat 6211ft (1893m)
Lake Nuba
Wadi Halfa
(Administered by Egypt)
Jeddah
Mecca
Libyan

Completed in 1971, the Aswân Dam supplies half of Egypt's electricity.

The Ethiopian Highlands

An enormous plateau, the Ethiopian Highlands cover most of Ethiopia and are bisected by the Great Rift Valley. The western highlands encompass the region's highest peak, 14,872-foot (4,533-m) Rās Dashen, Lake Tana, and Ethiopia's capital Addis Ababa, which sits about 8,000 feet (2,500 m) above sea level. The eastern highlands are narrower but almost as high, reaching 14,176 feet (4,321 m) at Batu. South of Addis Ababa, lakes and volcanic peaks stud the floor of the Great Rift Valley; northeast of the capital, the valley widens, the western wall forming a great escarpment that runs north to the Red Sea, the eastern side arcing toward the Gulf of Aden.

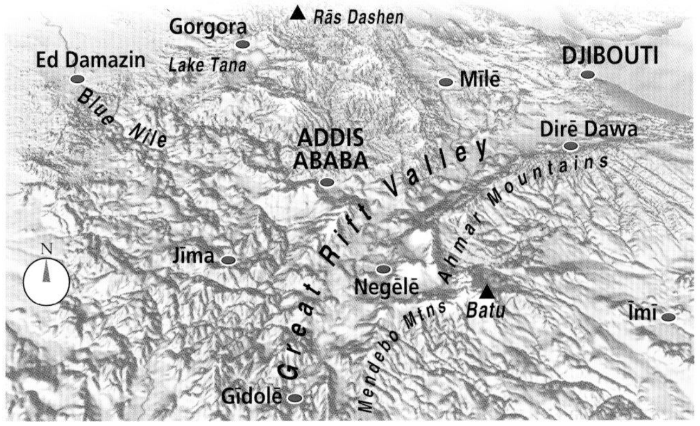
Gorgora
Rās Dashen
Ed Damazin
Lake Tana
DJIBOUTI
Mīlē
Blue Nile
ADDIS ABABA
Dirē Dawa
Great Rift Valley
Ahmar Mountains
Jima
Negēlē
Batu
Mendebo Mts
Imī
Gidolē
N

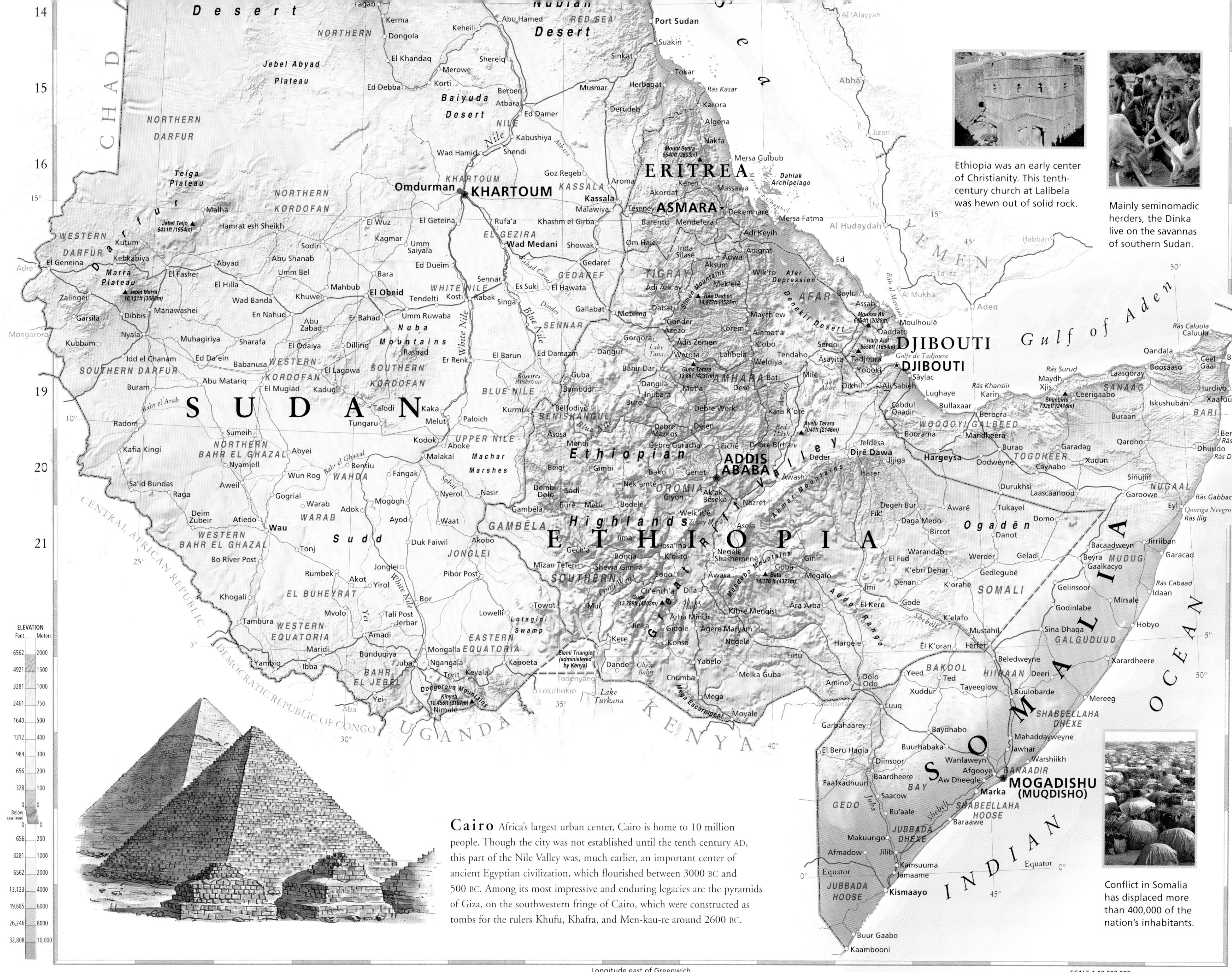
SUDAN
ETHIOPIA
ERITREA
DJIBOUTI
SOMALIA
KHARTOUM
Omdurman
ASMARA
ADDIS ABABA
DJIBOUTI
MOGADISHU (MUQDISHO)
CHAD
CENTRAL AFRICAN REPUBLIC
DEMOCRATIC REPUBLIC OF CONGO
UGANDA
KENYA
YEMEN
Red Sea
Gulf of Aden
INDIAN OCEAN
Nubian Desert
Ethiopian Highlands
Great Rift Valley
Ogadēn
Sudd
Blue Nile
White Nile
Nile
Longitude east of Greenwich
SCALE 1:10,000,000
Lamberts Conformal Conic Projection
300 miles
300 kilometers
ELEVATION
Feet
Meters
Below sea level

Ethiopia was an early center of Christianity. This tenth-century church at Lalibela was hewn out of solid rock.

Mainly seminomadic herders, the Dinka live on the savannas of southern Sudan.

Conflict in Somalia has displaced more than 400,000 of the nation's inhabitants.

Cairo Africa's largest urban center, Cairo is home to 10 million people. Though the city was not established until the tenth century AD, this part of the Nile Valley was, much earlier, an important center of ancient Egyptian civilization, which flourished between 3000 BC and 500 BC. Among its most impressive and enduring legacies are the pyramids of Giza, on the southwestern fringe of Cairo, which were constructed as tombs for the rulers Khufu, Khafra, and Men-kau-re around 2600 BC.

West Africa

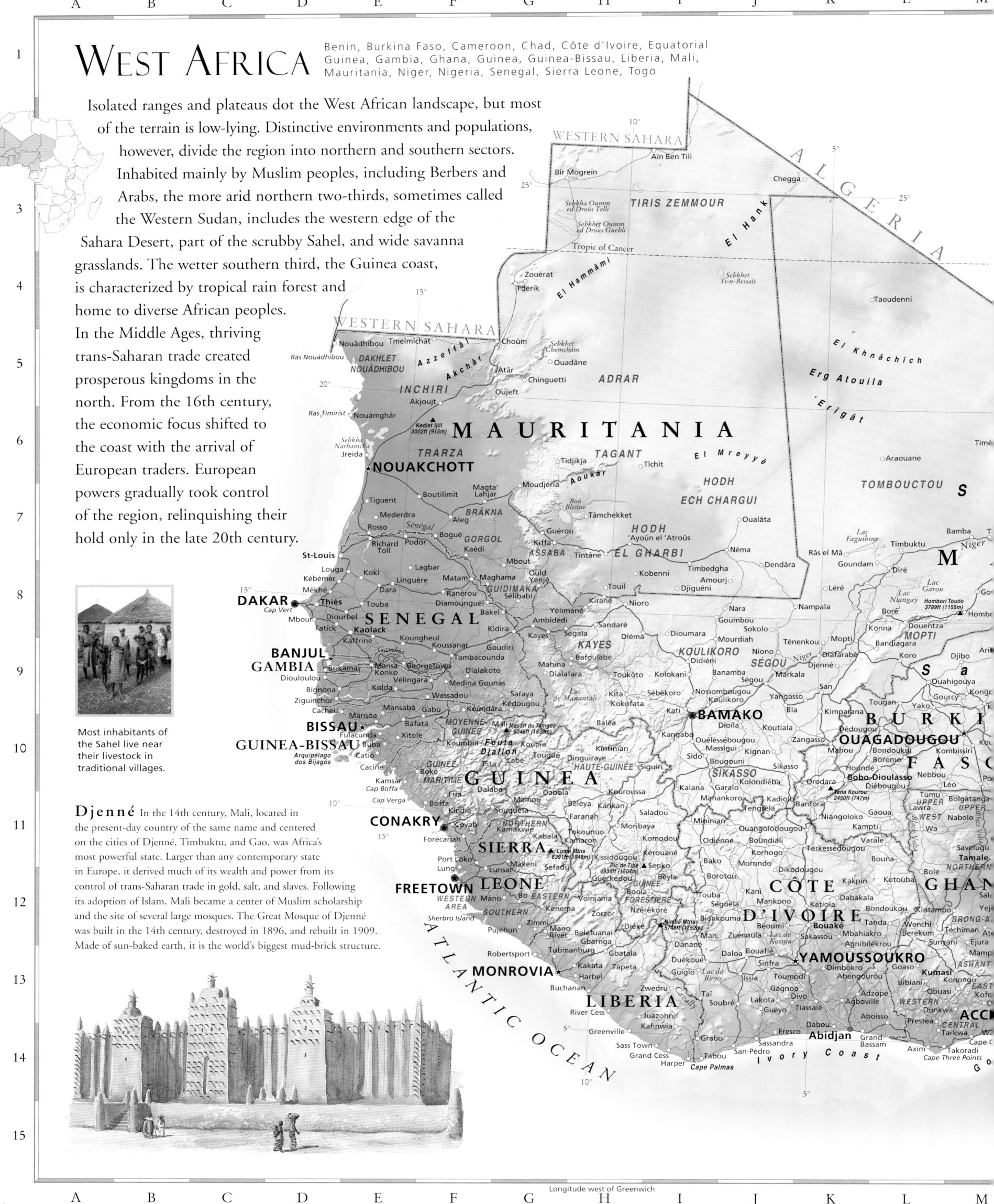

Benin, Burkina Faso, Cameroon, Chad, Côte d'Ivoire, Equatorial Guinea, Gambia, Ghana, Guinea, Guinea-Bissau, Liberia, Mali, Mauritania, Niger, Nigeria, Senegal, Sierra Leone, Togo

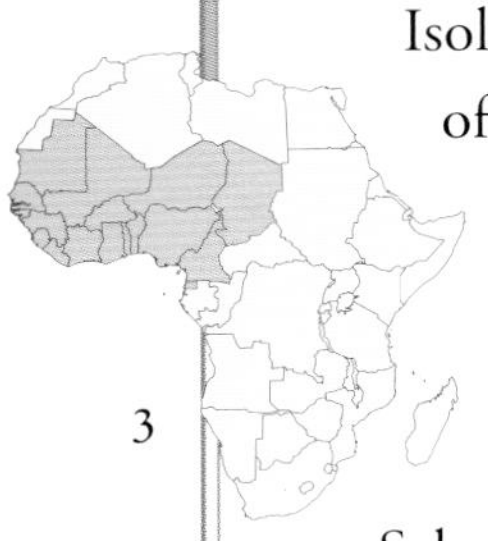

Isolated ranges and plateaus dot the West African landscape, but most of the terrain is low-lying. Distinctive environments and populations, however, divide the region into northern and southern sectors. Inhabited mainly by Muslim peoples, including Berbers and Arabs, the more arid northern two-thirds, sometimes called the Western Sudan, includes the western edge of the Sahara Desert, part of the scrubby Sahel, and wide savanna grasslands. The wetter southern third, the Guinea coast, is characterized by tropical rain forest and home to diverse African peoples. In the Middle Ages, thriving trans-Saharan trade created prosperous kingdoms in the north. From the 16th century, the economic focus shifted to the coast with the arrival of European traders. European powers gradually took control of the region, relinquishing their hold only in the late 20th century.

Most inhabitants of the Sahel live near their livestock in traditional villages.

Djenné In the 14th century, Mali, located in the present-day country of the same name and centered on the cities of Djenné, Timbuktu, and Gao, was Africa's most powerful state. Larger than any contemporary state in Europe, it derived much of its wealth and power from its control of trans-Saharan trade in gold, salt, and slaves. Following its adoption of Islam, Mali became a center of Muslim scholarship and the site of several large mosques. The Great Mosque of Djenné was built in the 14th century, destroyed in 1896, and rebuilt in 1909. Made of sun-baked earth, it is the world's biggest mud-brick structure.

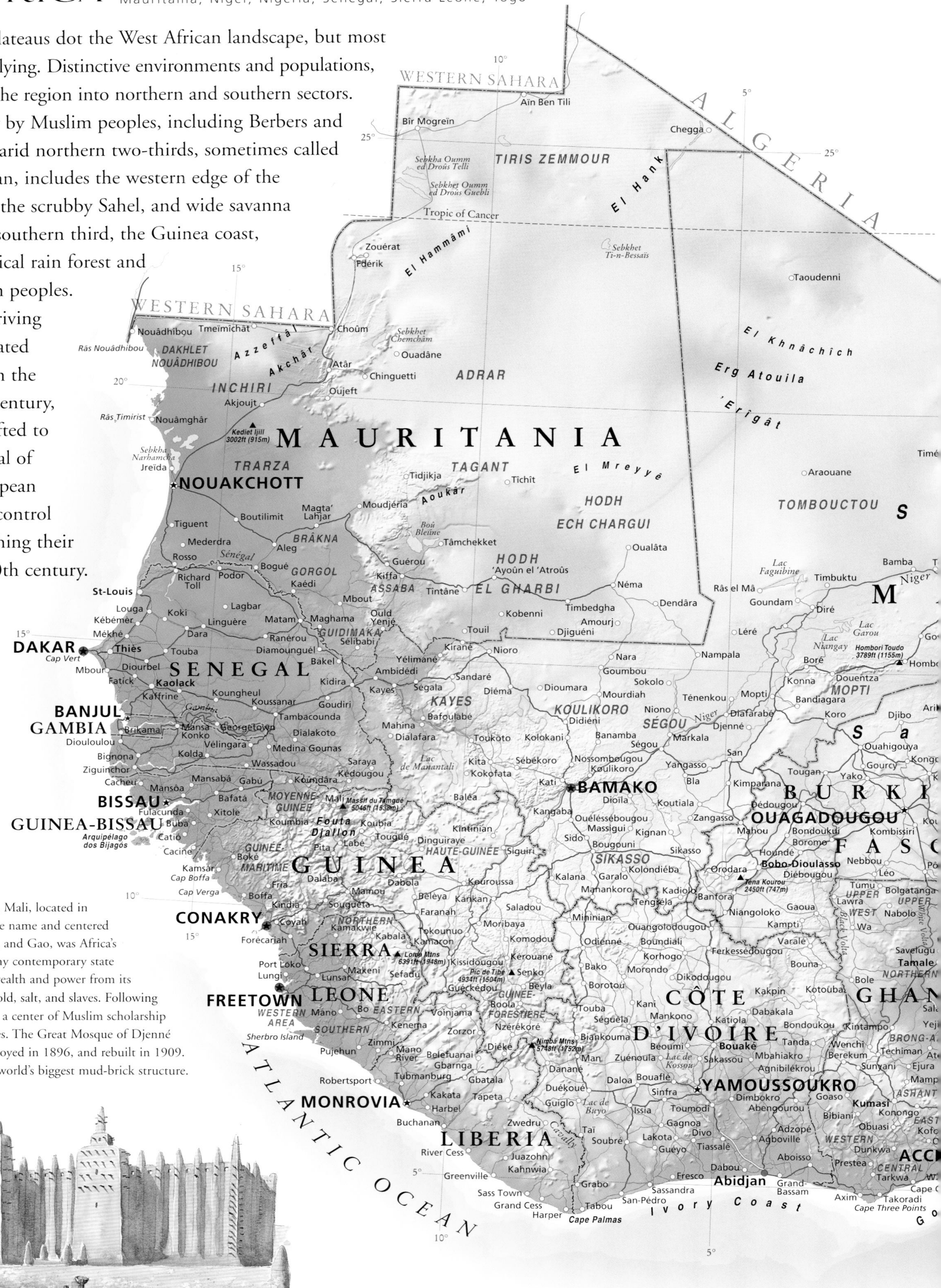

WESTERN SAHARA
ALGERIA
MAURITANIA
SENEGAL
GAMBIA
GUINEA-BISSAU
GUINEA
SIERRA LEONE
LIBERIA
CÔTE D'IVOIRE
BURKINA FASO
ATLANTIC OCEAN
NOUAKCHOTT
DAKAR
BANJUL
BISSAU
CONAKRY
FREETOWN
MONROVIA
BAMAKO
OUAGADOUGOU
YAMOUSSOUKRO
Abidjan
TIRIS ZEMMOUR
ADRAR
INCHIRI
DAKHLET NOUÂDHIBOU
TRARZA
TAGANT
HODH ECH CHARGUI
HODH EL GHARBI
BRÂKNA
GORGOL
ASSABA
GUIDIMAKA
TOMBOUCTOU
KAYES
KOULIKORO
SÉGOU
SIKASSO
MOPTI
Tropic of Cancer
Cap Vert
Cape Palmas
Ivory Coast
Cape Three Points
Erg Atouila
El Khnâchich
El Hank
Nouâdhibou
Zouérat
Atâr
Chinguetti
Ouadâne
Kiffa
Néma
Timbuktu
Dioura
Ségou
Djenné
Mopti
Kayes
Saint-Louis
Thiès
Kaolack
Tambacounda
Ziguinchor
Kindia
Labé
Kankan
Bo
Kenema
Buchanan
Harper
Bouaké
Korhogo
Daloa
San-Pédro
Bobo-Dioulasso
Kumasi
Tamale
Kediet Ijill 3002ft (915m)
Massif du Tamgué 5046ft (1538m)
Loma Mtns 6391ft (1948m)
Nimba Mtns 5748ft (1752m)
Hombori Toudo 3789ft (1155m)
Longitude west of Greenwich

N O P Q R S T U V W X Y Z

Population Patterns

The peoples of the north, many of whom are nomadic, are fewer and more widely dispersed than those of the south, where settlement is focused on river valleys and coastal cities. Urbanization has occurred only recently, but rapidly, rising, for example, in Mauritania from 2 percent in 1950 to 64 percent today. The regional population is expanding quickly—Liberia and Sierra Leone have the world's fastest-growing populations.

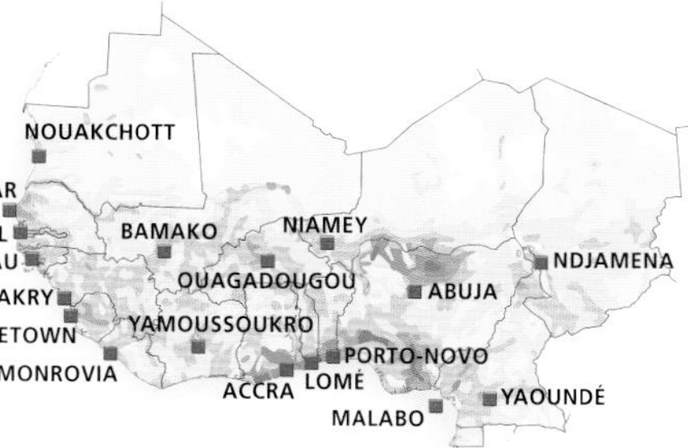
NOUAKCHOTT
DAKAR
BANJUL
BISSAU
BAMAKO
NIAMEY
NDJAMENA
CONAKRY
OUAGADOUGOU
ABUJA
FREETOWN
YAMOUSSOUKRO
MONROVIA
PORTO-NOVO
ACCRA
LOMÉ
YAOUNDÉ
MALABO
Uninhabited
Less than 2.6 persons per sq mile/1 per sq km
2.6–26 per sq mile/ 1–10 per sq km
26–65 per sq mile/ 10–25 per sq km
65–130 per sq mile/ 25–50 per sq km
130–260 per sq mile/ 50–100 per sq km
260–520 per sq mile/ 100–200 per sq km
520–1040 per sq mile/ 200–400 per sq km

Economic Profile

Despite ample resources, most obviously its forests, West Africa has achieved limited development. Grazing predominates in the north. Cash crops include cotton and groundnuts in the interior, palm oil, coffee, and rubber in the south. Industries are mainly limited to food processing and textiles, but mineral resources, including oil (especially in Nigeria and Cameroon), iron ore (Liberia's main export), and bauxite (notably in Guinea), support production of metals, chemicals, and machinery.

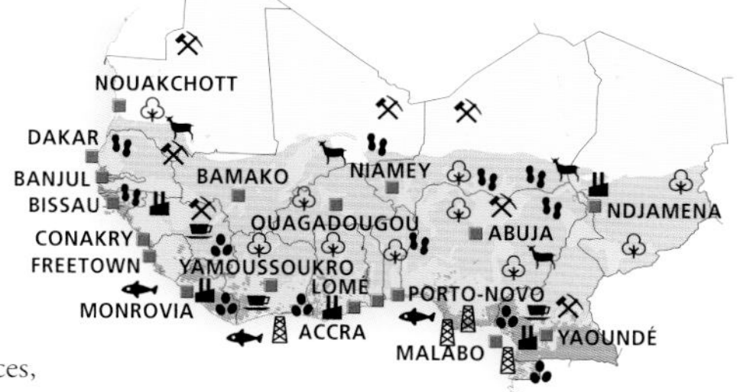
NOUAKCHOTT
DAKAR
BANJUL
BISSAU
BAMAKO
NIAMEY
NDJAMENA
CONAKRY
OUAGADOUGOU
ABUJA
FREETOWN
YAMOUSSOUKRO
LOMÉ
PORTO-NOVO
MONROVIA
ACCRA
YAOUNDÉ
MALABO
Forest and woodland
Arable land
Grazing
Marginal or nonproductive
Cotton
Coffee
Cocoa
Groundnuts
Fishing
Industrial center
Mining
Oil production
Goats

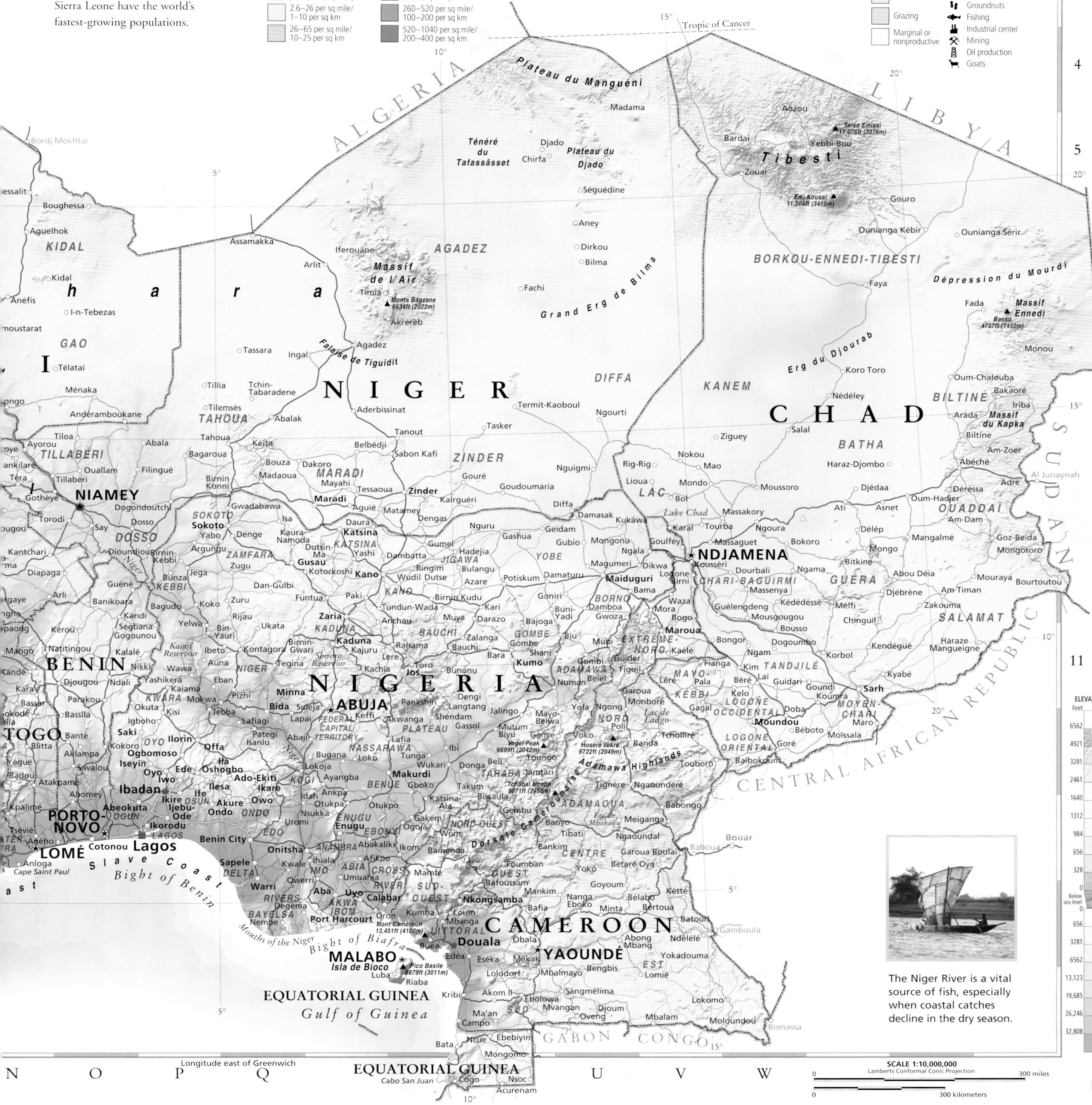
ALGERIA
LIBYA
SUDAN
CENTRAL AFRICAN REPUBLIC
NIGER
CHAD
NIGERIA
BENIN
TOGO
CAMEROON
EQUATORIAL GUINEA
GABON
CONGO
NIAMEY
NDJAMENA
ABUJA
PORTO-NOVO
LOMÉ
YAOUNDÉ
MALABO
Lagos
Ibadan
Kano
Kaduna
Zaria
Maiduguri
Douala
Port Harcourt
Cotonou
Tropic of Cancer
Plateau du Manguéni
Ténéré du Tafassâsset
Plateau du Djado
Tibesti
Tarso Emissi 11,076ft (3376m)
Emi Koussi 11,204ft (3415m)
Massif de l'Aïr
Monts Bagzane 6634ft (2022m)
Grand Erg de Bilma
Falaise de Tiguidit
Erg du Djourab
Dépression du Mourdi
Massif Ennedi
Basso 4757ft (1450m)
Massif du Kapka
AGADEZ
DIFFA
KANEM
BORKOU-ENNEDI-TIBESTI
BILTINE
BATHA
OUADDAÏ
GUÉRA
SALAMAT
CHARI-BAGUIRMI
MAYO-KEBBI
LOGONE OCCIDENTAL
LOGONE ORIENTAL
MOYEN-CHARI
TANDJILÉ
ZINDER
MARADI
TAHOUA
TILLABÉRI
DOSSO
KIDAL
GAO
SOKOTO
KATSINA
ZAMFARA
JIGAWA
YOBE
BORNO
KANO
KEBBI
NIGER
KADUNA
BAUCHI
GOMBE
ADAMAWA
PLATEAU
NASSARAWA
FEDERAL CAPITAL TERRITORY
KWARA
KOGI
BENUE
TARABA
OYO
OSUN
EKITI
ONDO
OGUN
LAGOS
EDO
DELTA
ANAMBRA
ENUGU
EBONYI
CROSS RIVER
ABIA
IMO
AKWA IBOM
RIVERS
BAYELSA
EXTRÊME-NORD
NORD
ADAMAOUA
NORD-OUEST
OUEST
SUD-OUEST
LITTORAL
CENTRE
EST
SUD
Lake Chad
Adamawa Highlands
Dorsale Camerounaise
Vogel Peak 6699ft (2042m)
Hosére Vokre 6722ft (2049m)
Tchabal Mbabo 8071ft (2460m)
Mont Cameroun 13,451ft (4100m)
Pico Basile 9879ft (3011m)
Isla de Bioco
Slave Coast
Bight of Benin
Bight of Biafra
Mouths of the Niger
Gulf of Guinea
Cape Saint Paul
ELEVATION
Feet Meters
6562 2000
4921 1500
3281 1000
2461 750
1640 500
1312 400
984 300
656 200
328 100
0 0
Below sea level
656 200
3281 1000
6562 2000
13,123 4000
19,685 6000
26,246 8000
32,808 10,000
Longitude east of Greenwich
SCALE 1:10,000,000
Lamberts Conformal Conic Projection
300 miles
300 kilometers

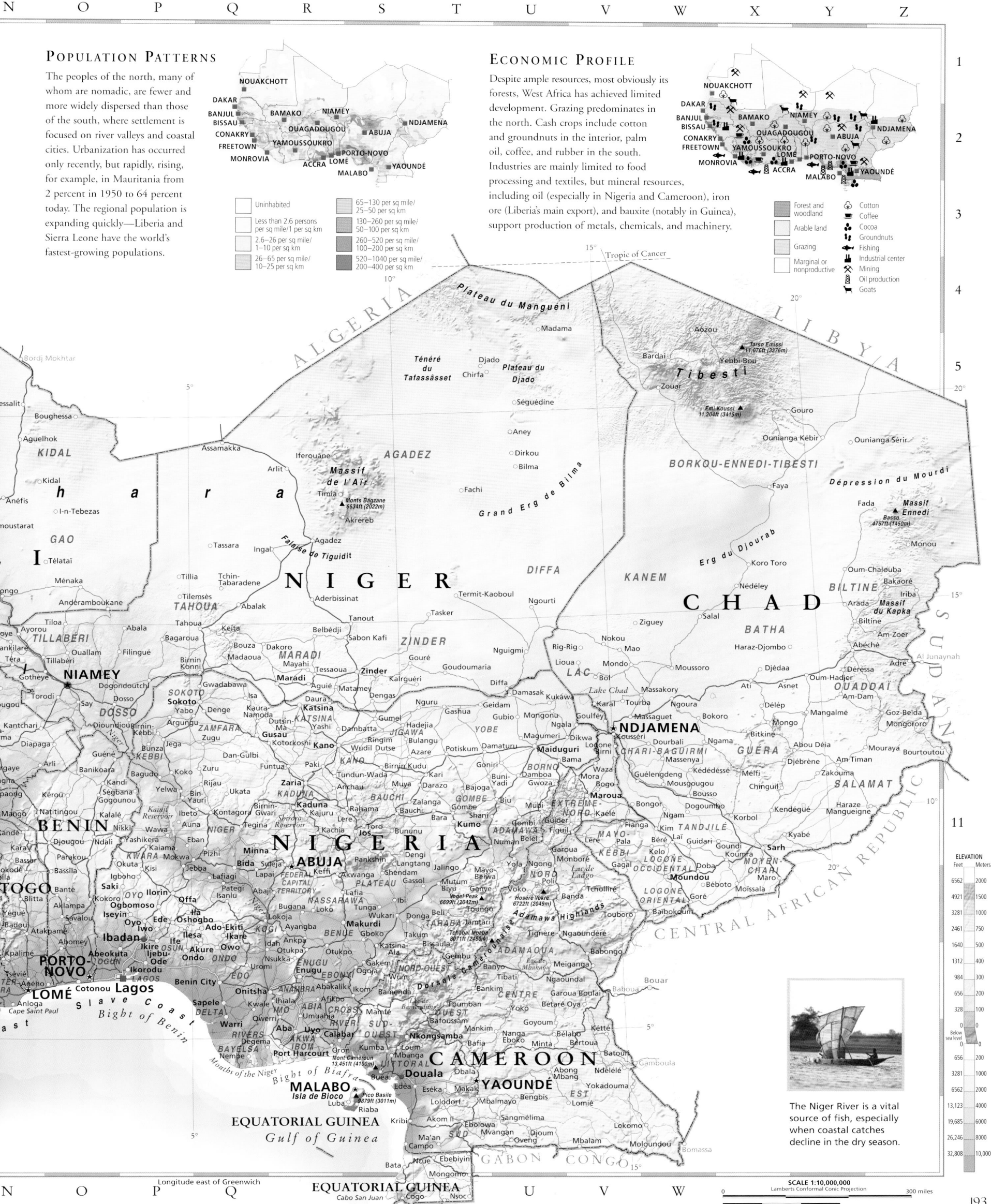

The Niger River is a vital source of fish, especially when coastal catches decline in the dry season.

N O P Q EQUATORIAL GUINEA U V W

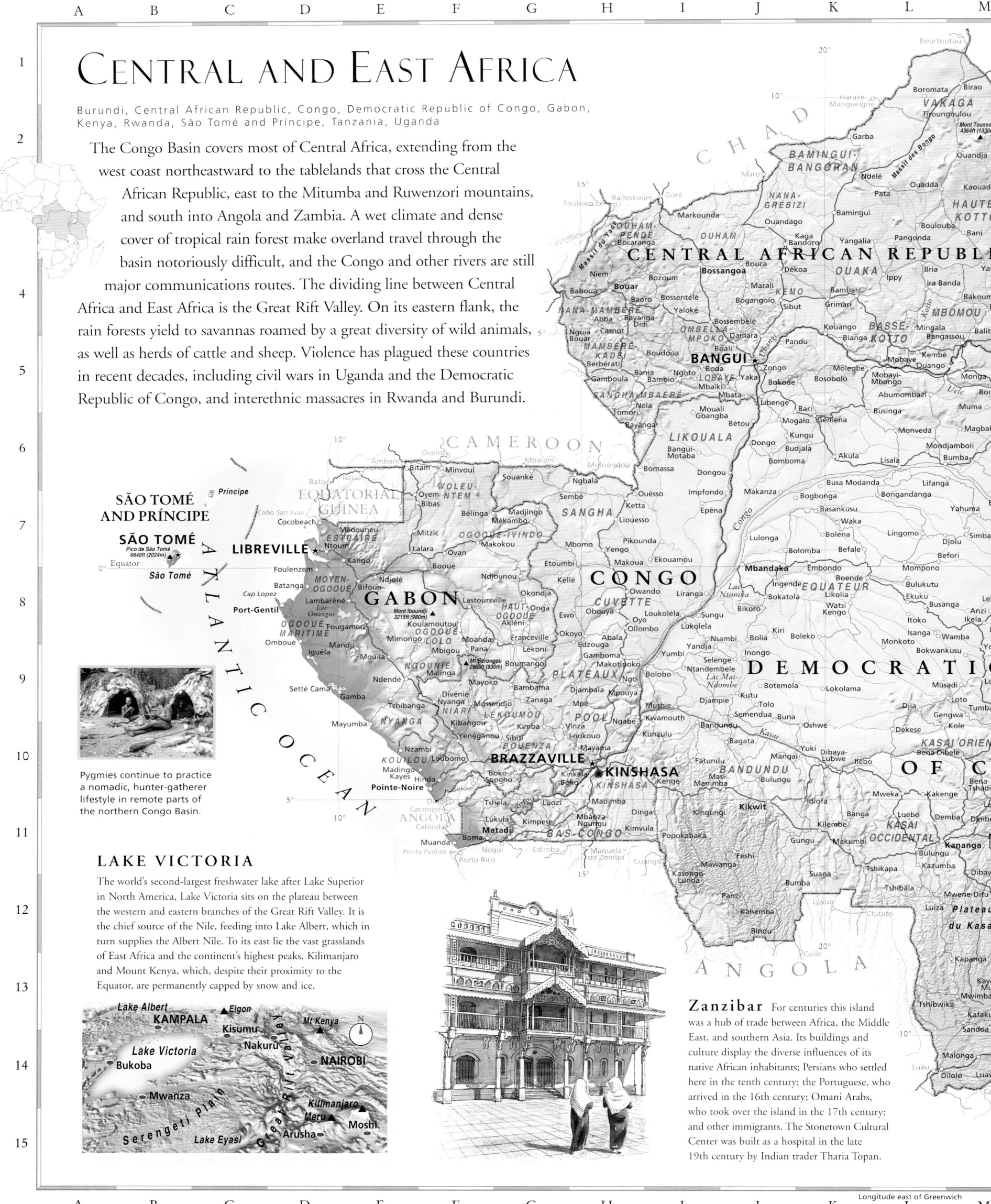

Central and East Africa

Burundi, Central African Republic, Congo, Democratic Republic of Congo, Gabon, Kenya, Rwanda, São Tomé and Príncipe, Tanzania, Uganda

The Congo Basin covers most of Central Africa, extending from the west coast northeastward to the tablelands that cross the Central African Republic, east to the Mitumba and Ruwenzori mountains, and south into Angola and Zambia. A wet climate and dense cover of tropical rain forest make overland travel through the basin notoriously difficult, and the Congo and other rivers are still major communications routes. The dividing line between Central Africa and East Africa is the Great Rift Valley. On its eastern flank, the rain forests yield to savannas roamed by a great diversity of wild animals, as well as herds of cattle and sheep. Violence has plagued these countries in recent decades, including civil wars in Uganda and the Democratic Republic of Congo, and interethnic massacres in Rwanda and Burundi.

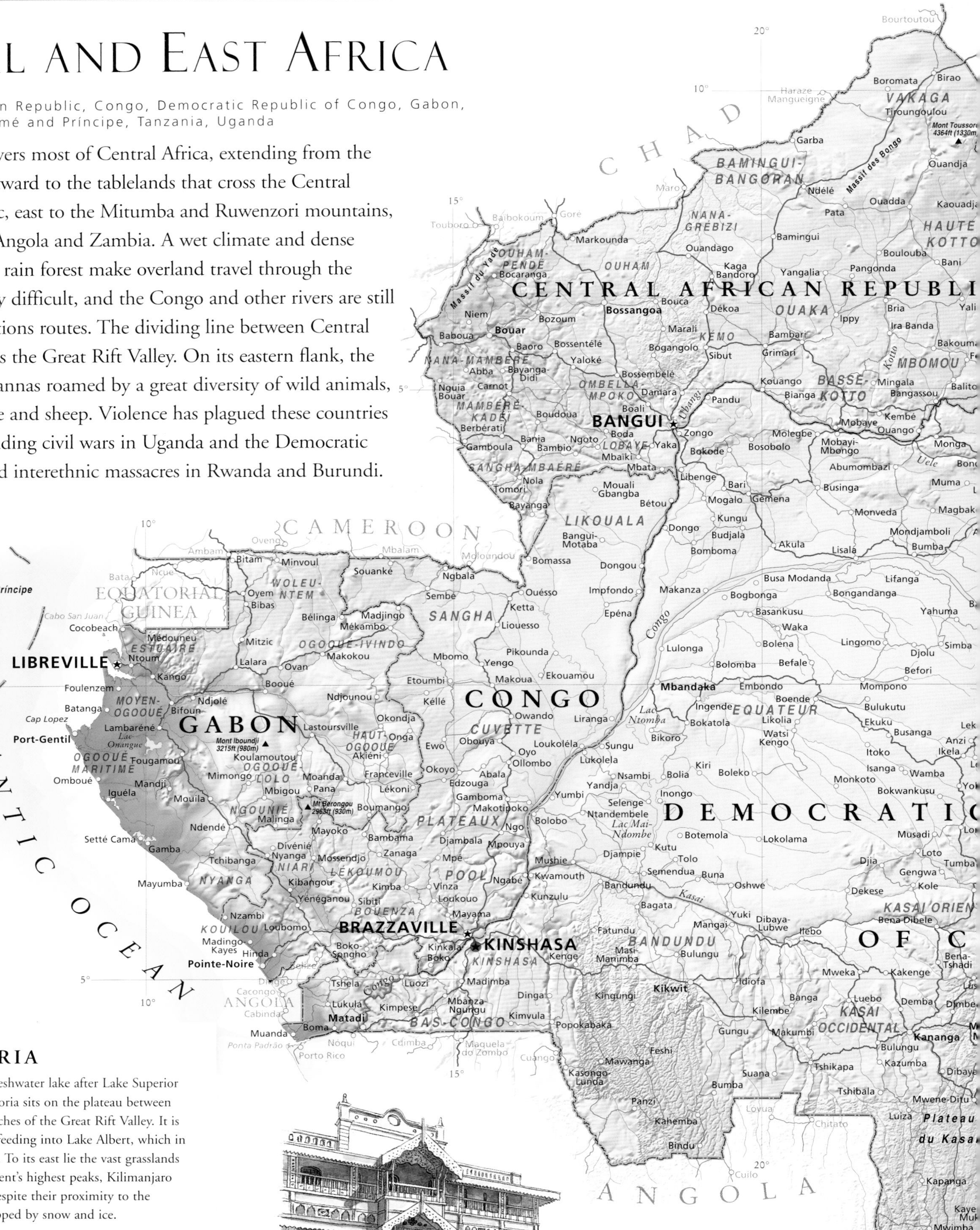

CHAD
CENTRAL AFRICAN REPUBLIC
BANGUI
CAMEROON
EQUATORIAL GUINEA
SÃO TOMÉ AND PRÍNCIPE
Príncipe
SÃO TOMÉ
São Tomé
LIBREVILLE
GABON
CONGO
BRAZZAVILLE
KINSHASA
DEMOCRATIC REPUBLIC OF C
ATLANTIC OCEAN
ANGOLA
Equator
Longitude east of Greenwich

Pygmies continue to practice a nomadic, hunter-gatherer lifestyle in remote parts of the northern Congo Basin.

LAKE VICTORIA

The world's second-largest freshwater lake after Lake Superior in North America, Lake Victoria sits on the plateau between the western and eastern branches of the Great Rift Valley. It is the chief source of the Nile, feeding into Lake Albert, which in turn supplies the Albert Nile. To its east lie the vast grasslands of East Africa and the continent's highest peaks, Kilimanjaro and Mount Kenya, which, despite their proximity to the Equator, are permanently capped by snow and ice.

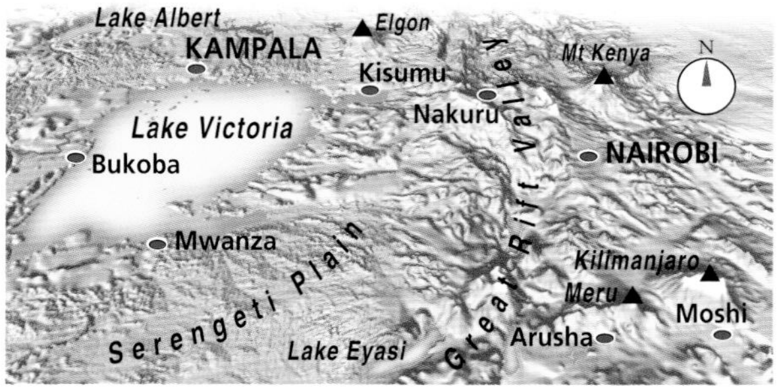

Lake Albert
KAMPALA
Elgon
Kisumu
Mt Kenya
N
Lake Victoria
Nakuru
NAIROBI
Bukoba
Mwanza
Serengeti Plain
Great Rift Valley
Kilimanjaro
Meru
Moshi
Arusha
Lake Eyasi

Zanzibar For centuries this island was a hub of trade between Africa, the Middle East, and southern Asia. Its buildings and culture display the diverse influences of its native African inhabitants; Persians who settled here in the tenth century; the Portuguese, who arrived in the 16th century; Omani Arabs, who took over the island in the 17th century; and other immigrants. The Stonetown Cultural Center was built as a hospital in the late 19th century by Indian trader Tharia Topan.

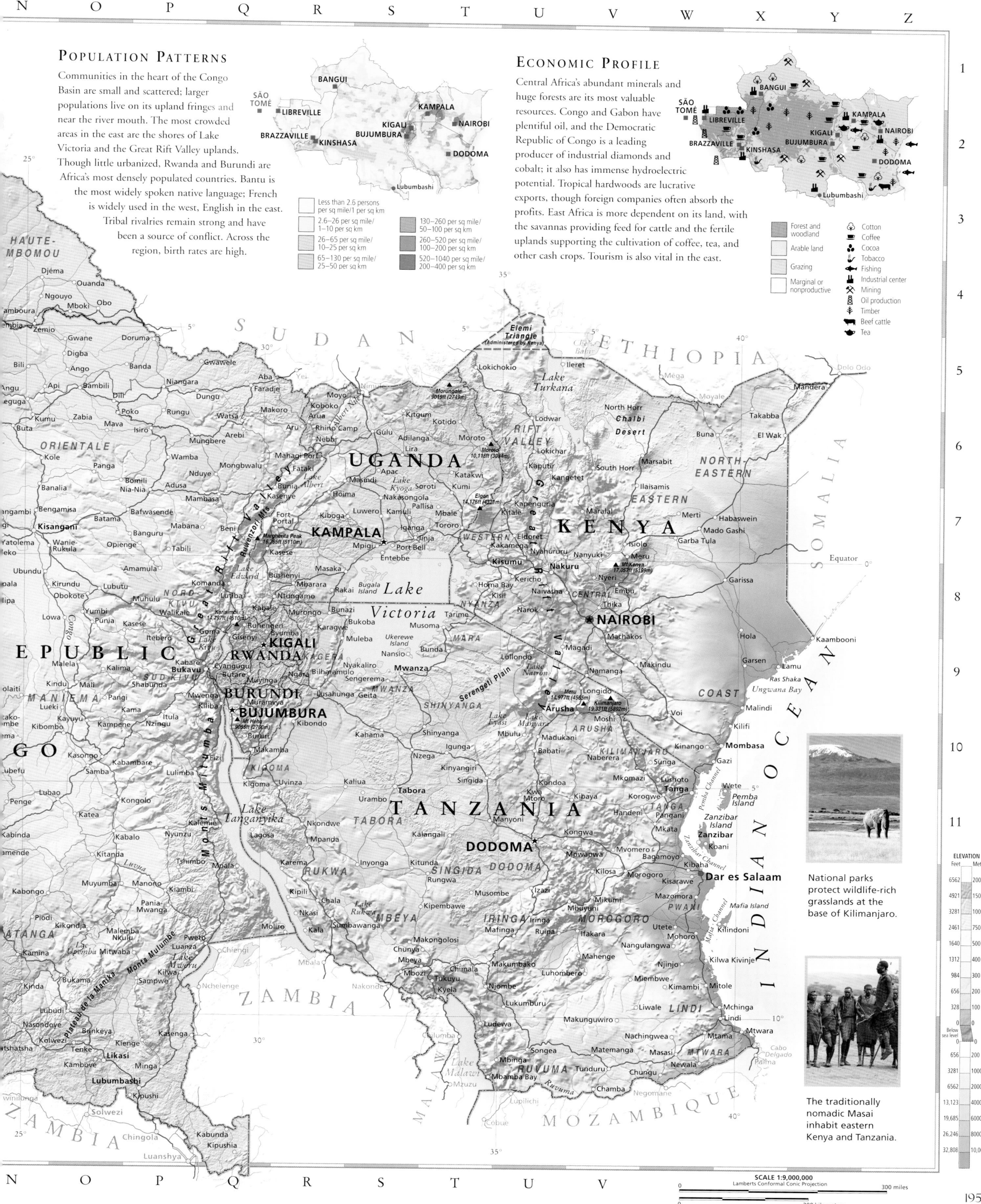

POPULATION PATTERNS

Communities in the heart of the Congo Basin are small and scattered; larger populations live on its upland fringes and near the river mouth. The most crowded areas in the east are the shores of Lake Victoria and the Great Rift Valley uplands. Though little urbanized, Rwanda and Burundi are Africa's most densely populated countries. Bantu is the most widely spoken native language; French is widely used in the west, English in the east. Tribal rivalries remain strong and have been a source of conflict. Across the region, birth rates are high.

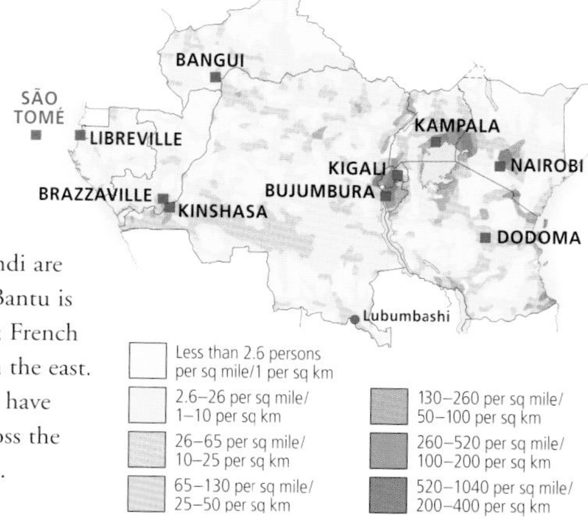
BANGUI
SÃO TOMÉ
LIBREVILLE
KAMPALA
KIGALI
NAIROBI
BUJUMBURA
BRAZZAVILLE
KINSHASA
DODOMA
Lubumbashi
Less than 2.6 persons per sq mile/1 per sq km
2.6–26 per sq mile/1–10 per sq km
26–65 per sq mile/10–25 per sq km
65–130 per sq mile/25–50 per sq km
130–260 per sq mile/50–100 per sq km
260–520 per sq mile/100–200 per sq km
520–1040 per sq mile/200–400 per sq km

ECONOMIC PROFILE

Central Africa's abundant minerals and huge forests are its most valuable resources. Congo and Gabon have plentiful oil, and the Democratic Republic of Congo is a leading producer of industrial diamonds and cobalt; it also has immense hydroelectric potential. Tropical hardwoods are lucrative exports, though foreign companies often absorb the profits. East Africa is more dependent on its land, with the savannas providing feed for cattle and the fertile uplands supporting the cultivation of coffee, tea, and other cash crops. Tourism is also vital in the east.

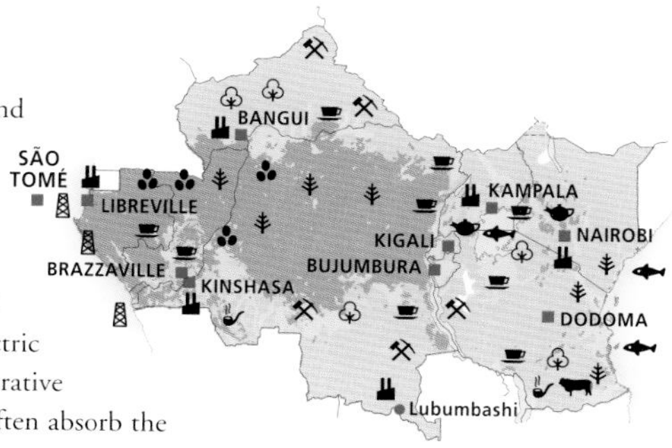
SÃO TOMÉ
BANGUI
LIBREVILLE
KAMPALA
KIGALI
NAIROBI
BRAZZAVILLE
KINSHASA
BUJUMBURA
DODOMA
Lubumbashi
Forest and woodland
Arable land
Grazing
Marginal or nonproductive
Cotton
Coffee
Cocoa
Tobacco
Fishing
Industrial center
Mining
Oil production
Timber
Beef cattle
Tea

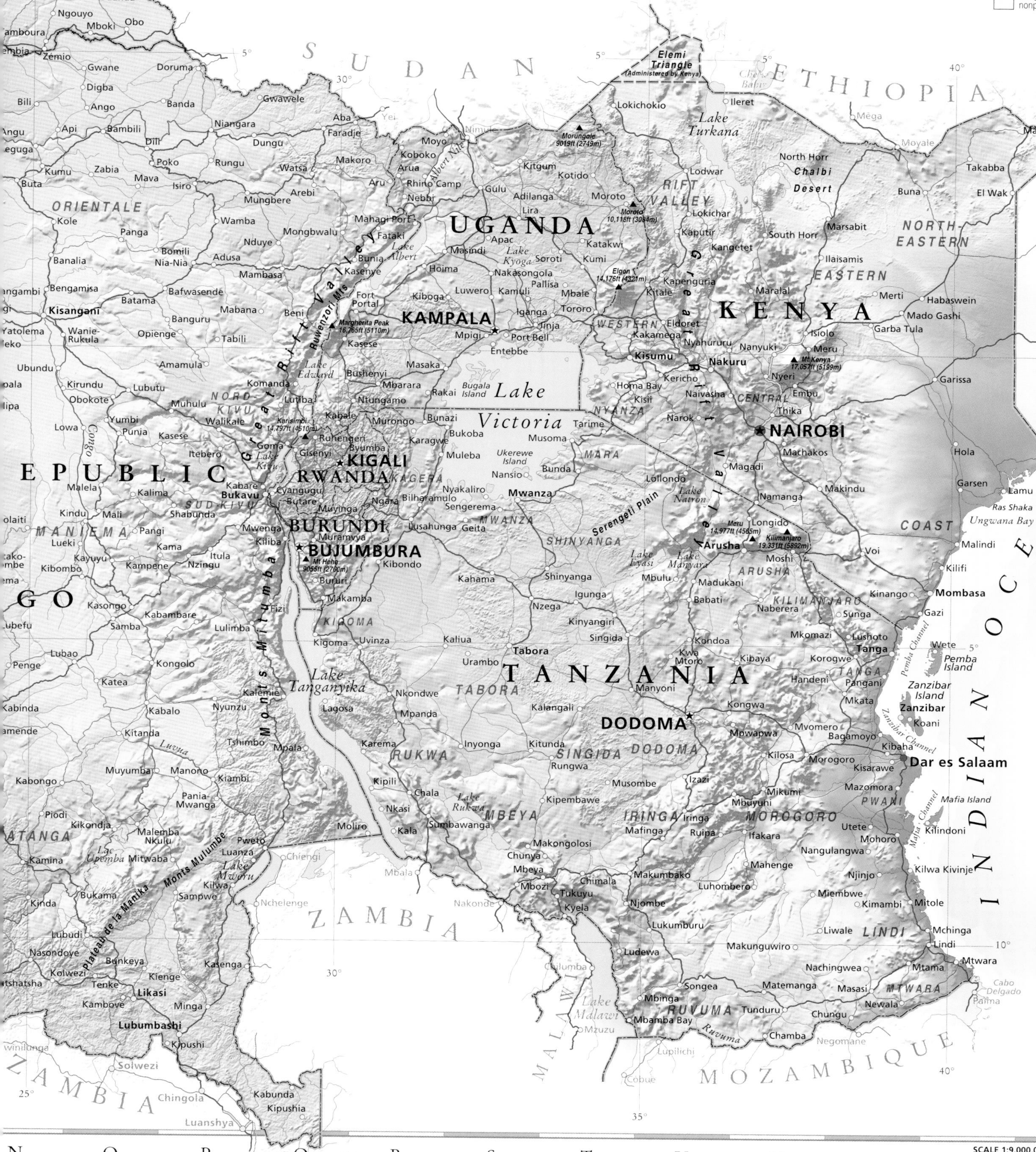
N O P Q R S T U V W X Y Z
1 2 3 4 5 6 7 8 9 10 11
SUDAN
ETHIOPIA
SOMALIA
UGANDA
KENYA
RWANDA
BURUNDI
TANZANIA
ZAMBIA
MALAWI
MOZAMBIQUE
INDIAN OCEAN
KAMPALA
NAIROBI
KIGALI
BUJUMBURA
DODOMA
Dar es Salaam
Mombasa
Zanzibar
Lubumbashi
Kisangani
Lake Victoria
Lake Turkana
Lake Tanganyika
Lake Malawi
Great Rift Valley
Serengeti Plain
Elemi Triangle (Administered by Kenya)
Kilimanjaro 19,331ft (5892m)
Mt Kenya 17,057ft (5199m)
Margherita Peak 16,765ft (5110m)
Equator
ORIENTALE
HAUTE-MBOMOU
NORTH-EASTERN
EASTERN
CENTRAL
COAST
Pemba Island
Zanzibar Island
Mafia Island
SCALE 1:9,000,000
Lamberts Conformal Conic Projection
300 miles
300 kilometers
ELEVATION
Feet Meters

National parks protect wildlife-rich grasslands at the base of Kilimanjaro.

The traditionally nomadic Masai inhabit eastern Kenya and Tanzania.

Southern Africa

Angola, Botswana, Comoros, Lesotho, Madagascar, Malawi, Mozambique, Namibia, Republic of South Africa, Swaziland, Zambia, Zimbabwe

Consisting of an undulating tableland rimmed by escarpments and narrow coastal plains, the southern African mainland takes in contrasting environments, including the Namib and Kalahari deserts, the tropical forests of northern Mozambique, and the "Highveld" grasslands of South Africa. About 250 miles (400 km) off its east coast lie the culturally and ecologically distinct island of Madagascar and the small Comoros archipelago. As in other parts of Africa, colonialism left the region a legacy of instability and inequality. Portugal's efforts to retain Mozambique and Angola initiated devastating wars from the 1960s to the early 1990s. White-minority rule sparked conflict in postcolonial Zimbabwe, in Namibia, and in South Africa, where racial segregation was enshrined in law in 1948 as the system of apartheid, and formally abolished only in 1994.

Population Patterns

The east is more densely populated than the west, with heavy settlement occurring in southern Mozambique, central and southern Zimbabwe, and between Pretoria, Durban, and Port Elizabeth in South Africa. Few people live in the western deserts, and Namibia and Botswana are two of Africa's least densely populated countries. Urbanization remains between 30 and 50 percent in most countries, but reaches 60 percent in South Africa. Most southern Africans belong to Bantu-speaking groups, such as the Zulu, Swazi, and Ndebele (Matabele), but Madagascar's Malagasy peoples originated in Indonesia.

LUANDA
MORONI
Namibe
LUSAKA
LILONGWE
HARARE
ANTANANARIVO
WINDHOEK
GABORONE
PRETORIA
MAPUTO
MBABANE
BLOEMFONTEIN
MASERU
CAPE TOWN
Uninhabited
Less than 2.6 persons per sq mile/1 per sq km
2.6–26 per sq mile/ 1–10 per sq km
26–65 per sq mile/ 10–25 per sq km
65–130 per sq mile/ 25–50 per sq km
130–260 per sq mile/ 50–100 per sq km
260–520 per sq mile/ 100–200 per sq km

Economic Profile

South Africa has by far the most developed and diversified industrial sector in Africa. Led by iron and steel, transport equipment, and chemicals, it accounts for one-third of the continent's total manufacturing output. The country also has huge mineral reserves, including diamonds, gold (half of world reserves), uranium, and iron ore. Uranium and diamonds are also found in Namibia, gold in Zimbabwe. Angola has sizable oil reserves, Madagascar deposits of graphite. The best arable land lies in the east. Cash crops include tobacco, coffee, tea, and citrus fruits—South Africa is the world's largest producer of grapefruit.

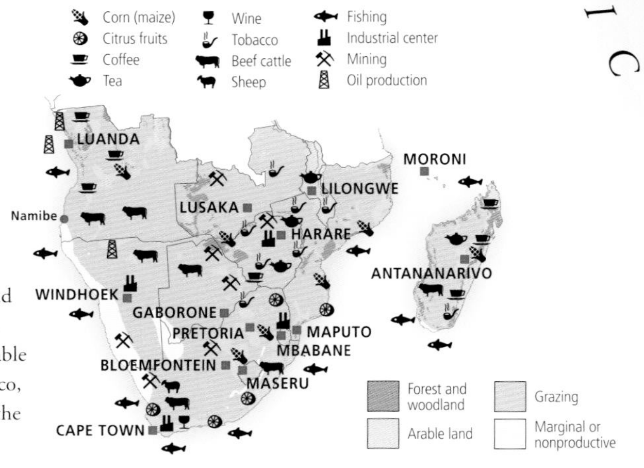

Corn (maize)
Citrus fruits
Coffee
Tea
Wine
Tobacco
Beef cattle
Sheep
Fishing
Industrial center
Mining
Oil production
LUANDA
MORONI
LILONGWE
LUSAKA
Namibe
HARARE
ANTANANARIVO
WINDHOEK
GABORONE
PRETORIA
MAPUTO
MBABANE
BLOEMFONTEIN
MASERU
CAPE TOWN
Forest and woodland
Arable land
Grazing
Marginal or nonproductive

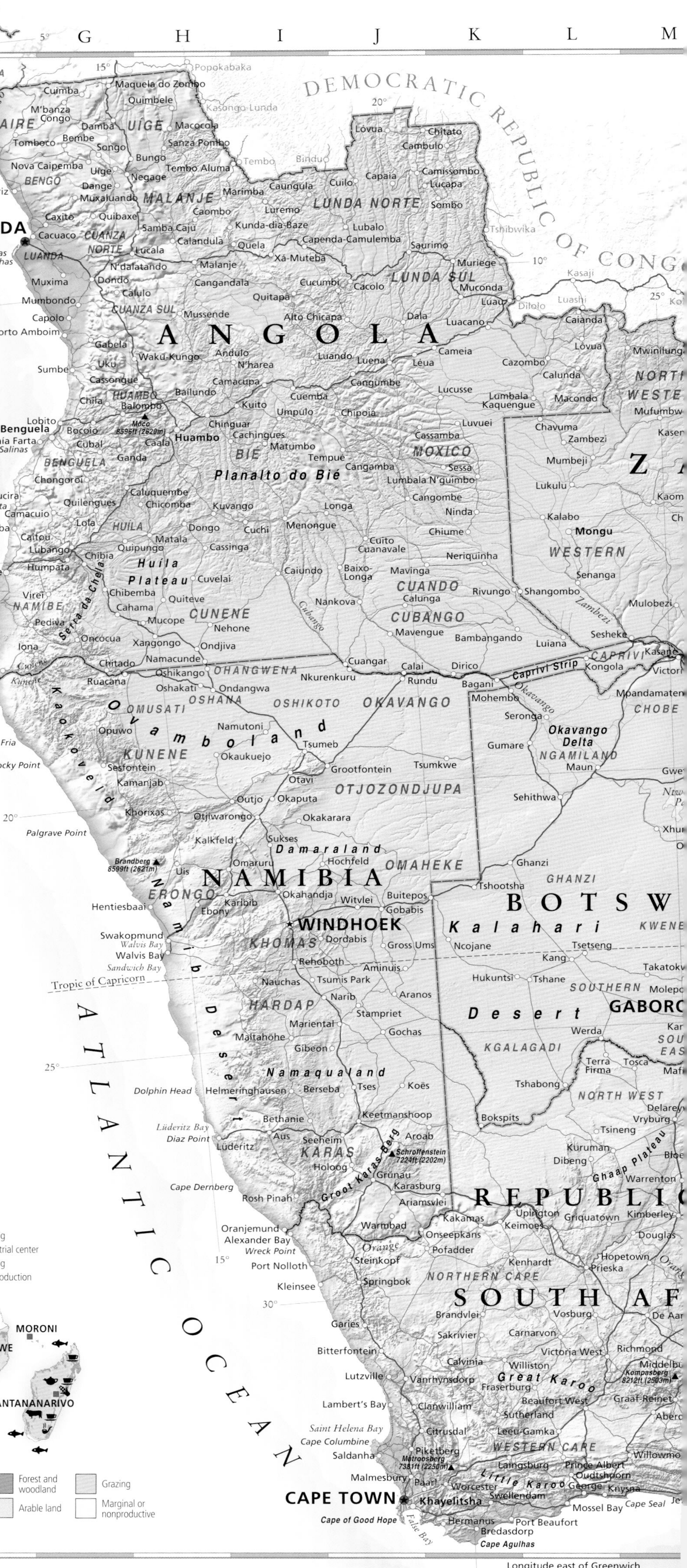

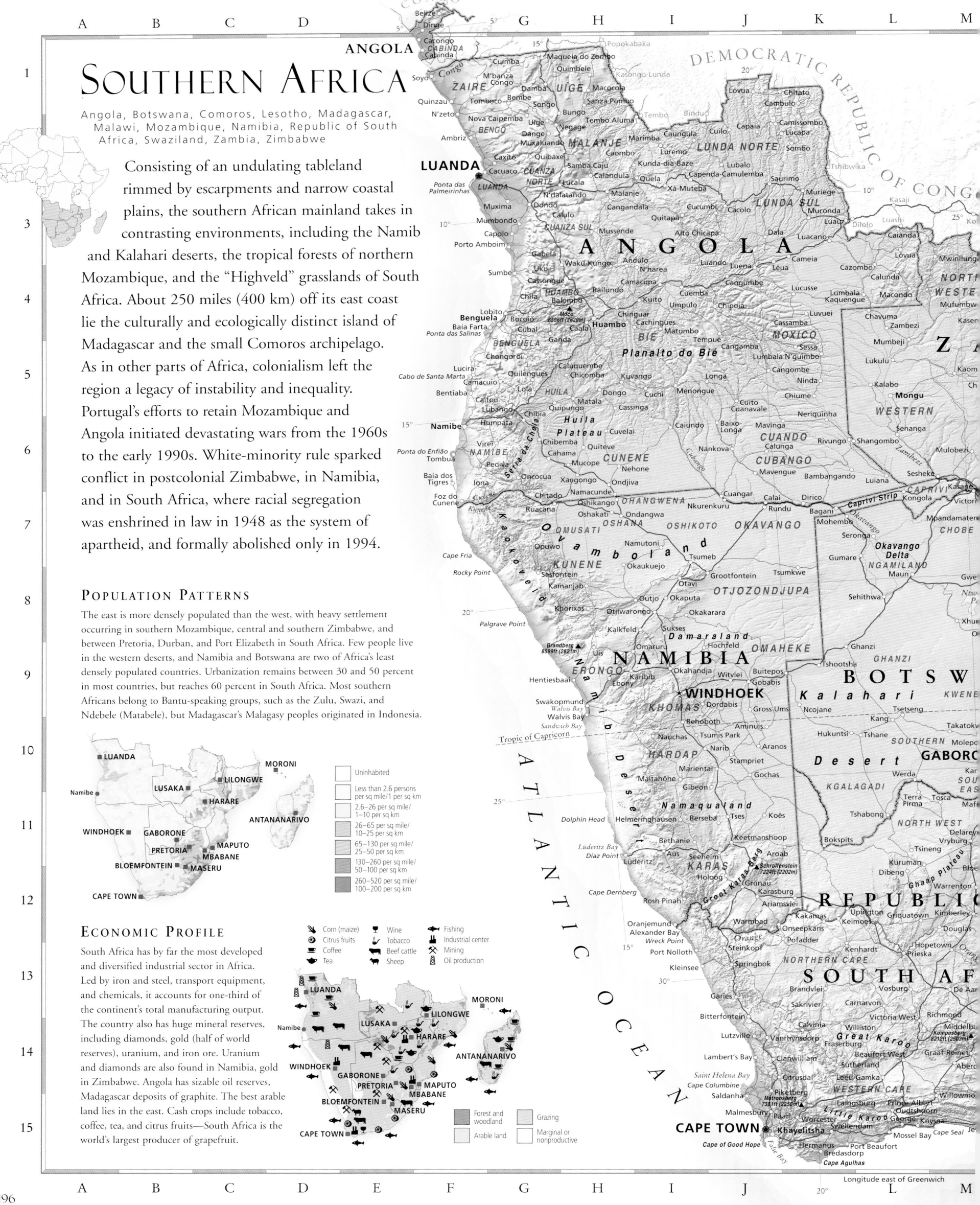

ANGOLA
CABINDA
LUANDA
DEMOCRATIC REPUBLIC OF CONGO
A N G O L A
Planalto do Bié
NAMIBIA
WINDHOEK
Kalahari Desert
BOTSW
ATLANTIC OCEAN
Tropic of Capricorn
Namib Desert
REPUBLIC
SOUTH AF
CAPE TOWN
Cape of Good Hope
Longitude east of Greenwich

N O P Q R S T U V W X Y Z
1 2 3 7 8 9 10 11
TANZANIA
ZAMBIA
MALAWI
LILONGWE
MOZAMBIQUE
ZIMBABWE
HARARE
COMOROS
MORONI
MADAGASCAR
ANTANANARIVO
Madagascar
Mozambique Channel
INDIAN OCEAN
SWAZILAND
MBABANE
LESOTHO
MASERU
MAPUTO
PRETORIA
LUSAKA
Johannesburg
Durban
Beira
Quelimane
Nampula
Nacala
Blantyre
Bulawayo
Toamasina
Mahajanga
Toliara
Fianarantsoa
Tropic of Capricorn
Grande Comore
Anjouan
Mohéli
Mayotte (to France)
Bassas da India (to France)
Île Europa (to France)
Juan de Nova (to France)
Îles Glorieuses (to Seychelles)
ELEVATION
Feet Meters
6562 2000
4921 1500
3281 1000
2461 750
1640 500
1312 400
984 300
656 200
328 100
0 0
Below sea level
0 0
656 200
3281 1000
6562 2000
13,123 4000
19,685 6000
26,246 8000
32,808 10,000

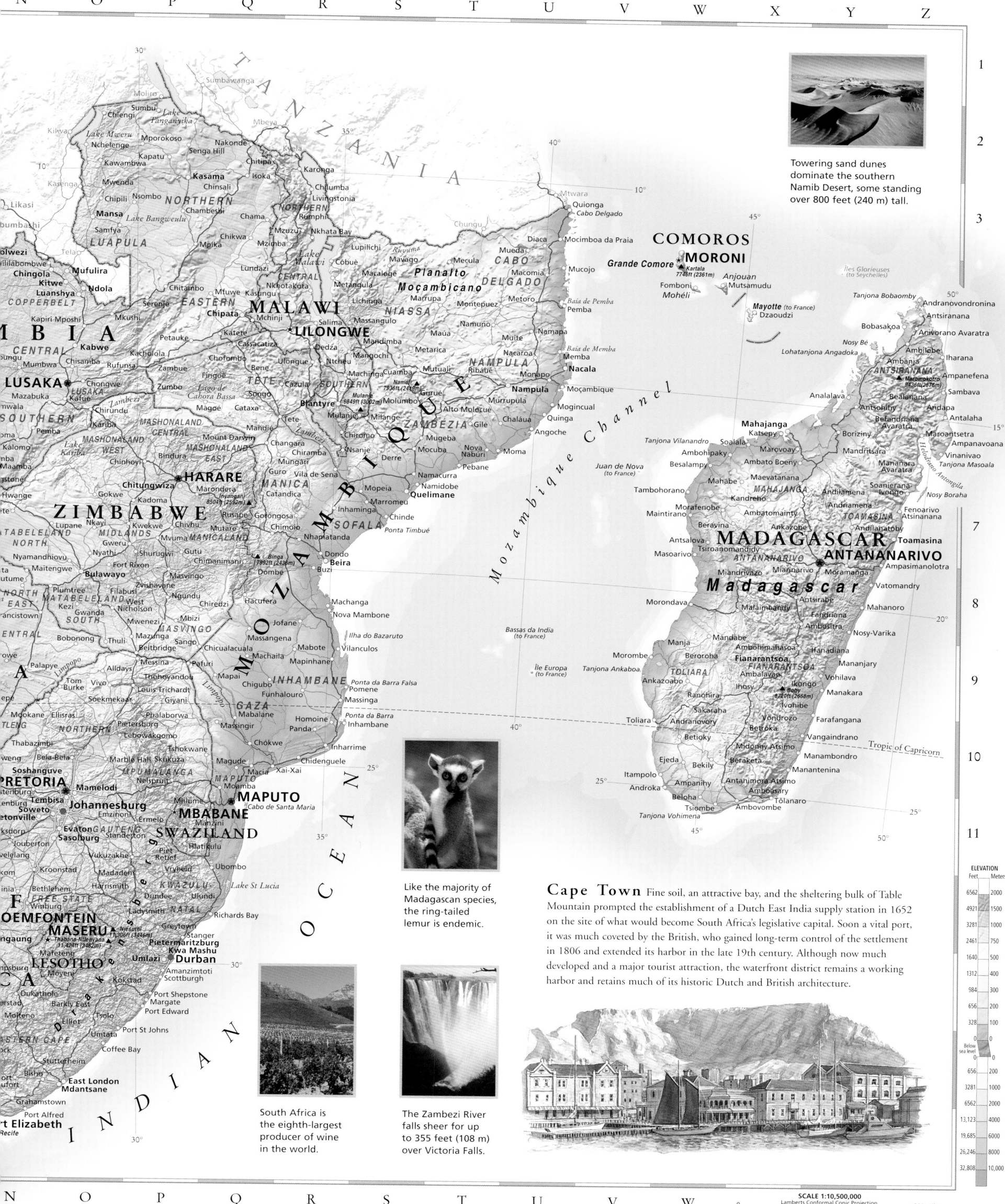

Towering sand dunes dominate the southern Namib Desert, some standing over 800 feet (240 m) tall.

Like the majority of Madagascan species, the ring-tailed lemur is endemic.

Cape Town Fine soil, an attractive bay, and the sheltering bulk of Table Mountain prompted the establishment of a Dutch East India supply station in 1652 on the site of what would become South Africa's legislative capital. Soon a vital port, it was much coveted by the British, who gained long-term control of the settlement in 1806 and extended its harbor in the late 19th century. Although now much developed and a major tourist attraction, the waterfront district remains a working harbor and retains much of its historic Dutch and British architecture.

South Africa is the eighth-largest producer of wine in the world.

The Zambezi River falls sheer for up to 355 feet (108 m) over Victoria Falls.

SCALE 1:10,500,000
Lamberts Conformal Conic Projection
0 300 miles
0 300 kilometers

Australia's eastern seaboard is illuminated at night while the sparsely populated interior remains dark. The north and south islands of New Zealand are clearly visible. The dots of light smattered throughout the Pacific are island nations such as Fiji.

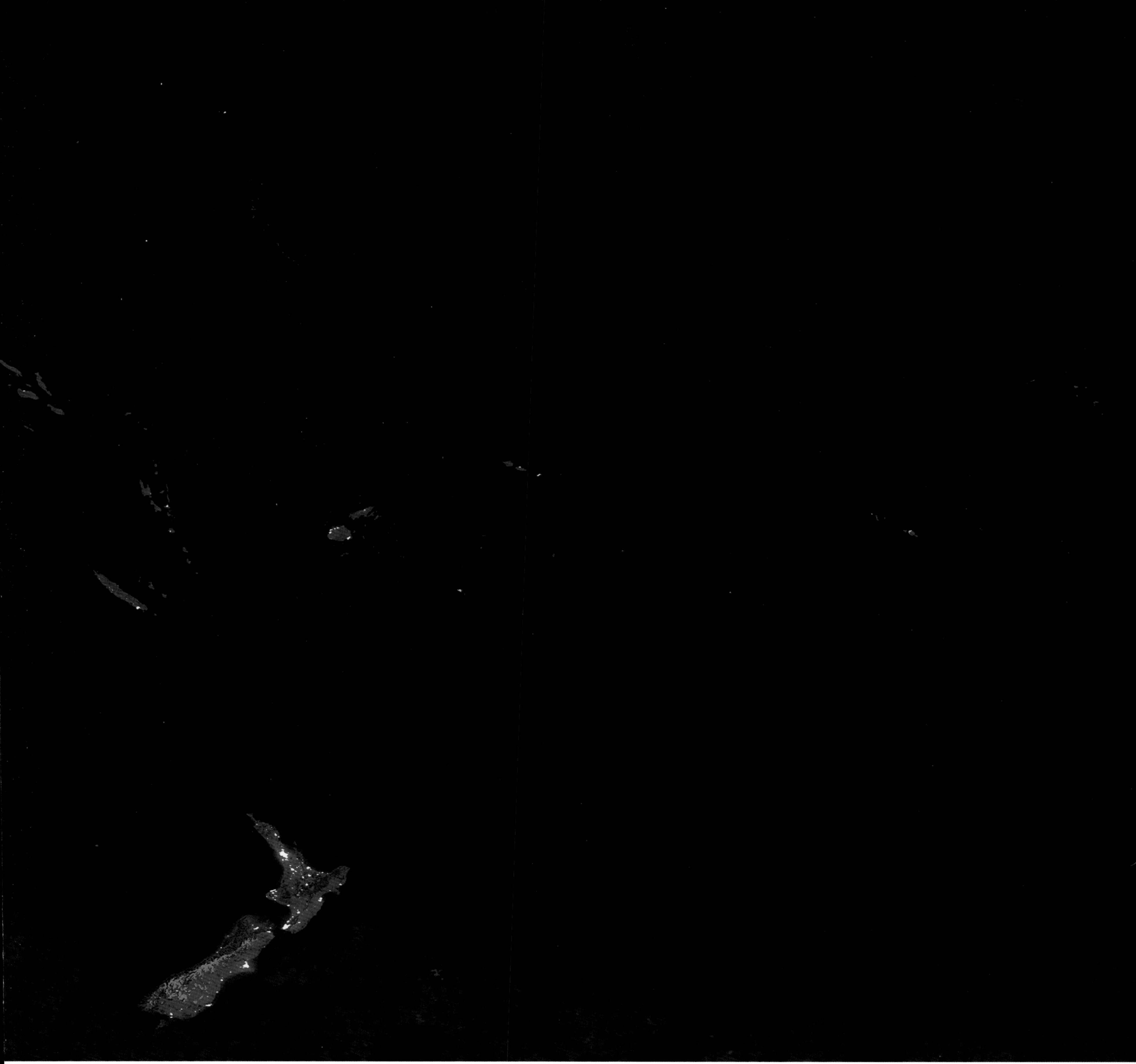

OCEANIA

THE VIEW FROM ABOVE

Satellites can record grand-scale natural happenings, from the calving of a huge iceberg on Antarctica's slowly diminishing Ross Ice Shelf, to devastating wildfires raging across the southeast of Australia. From space, the relative stability of the ancient landmass of Australia is in stark contrast to continuing geological activity in its near neighbors. New Zealand lies in the collision zone between the Indo-Australian and Pacific tectonic plates. Movement of these plates caused the volcanic activity that shaped much of the North Island, and the country's fertile pastures are a legacy of layers of volcanic ash. In the image of Mount Taranaki (Mount Egmont), above, simulated natural color emphasizes the contrast between the lush forests preserved within the circular boundary of Egmont National Park, which extends in a 6-mile (10-km) radius from the volcano's summit, and the bright-colored dairy pastures beyond.

Above: The snow-capped, symmetrical peak of Mount Taranaki (Mt Egmont), 8,261 feet (2,518 m), towers over the forests of Egmont National Park in the west of New Zealand's North Island. Taranaki began forming 70,000 years ago and last erupted in 1755. Nearby are two older volcanoes. The gray area, top right, is the city of New Plymouth.

Right: In January 2003 nearly 100 wildfires were burning in southeastern Australia. This satellite image, gathered on 10 January, shows smoke from fires near Sydney, center, and northeastern Victoria, lower left, streaking the skies above the Tasman Sea. Ten days after this image was taken, the smoke and haze reached beyond New Zealand.

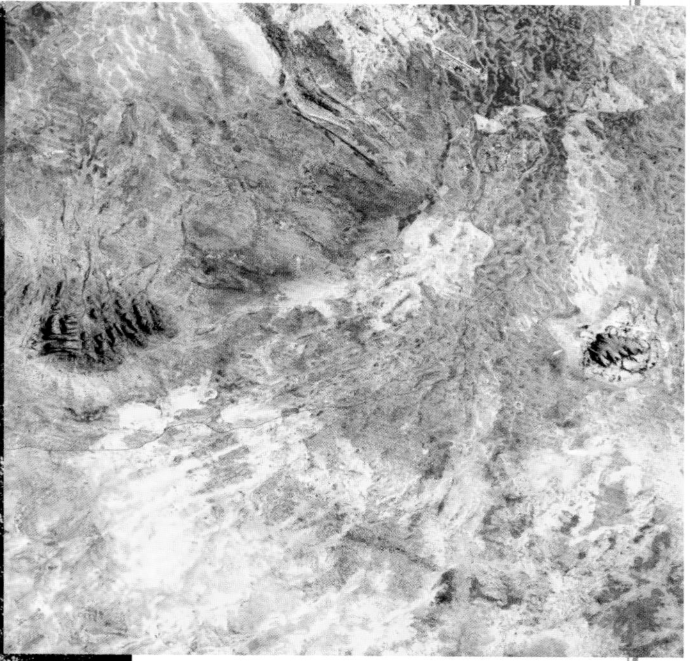

Top: Shown in blue in this false-color image, Uluru, center right, and Kata Tjuta, 30 miles (50 km) to the west, poke through the dry plains of Central Australia. Both are part of an ancient bed of sedimentary rock that has been folded and pushed upward. Uluru is the weathered end of the bed, now standing vertically.

Above: A huge iceberg, center, broke off the Ross Ice Shelf at the end of the Antarctic summer in March 2000, calving along pre-existing cracks in the ice shelf. At 180 miles (300 km) long and 25 miles (40 km) wide it is one of the largest known. It was locked in sea ice until the spring thaw, but began to drift soon after this image was taken.

Land and Environment

Extending from the Indian Ocean to the eastern Pacific, and from the Tropic of Cancer to the remote subantarctic territory of Macquarie Island, Oceania covers a vast area of ocean and about 3.4 million square miles (8.8 million sq km) of land. Of this, almost 3 million square miles (7.7 million sq km) is encompassed by the island continent of Australia; the remainder consists of the eastern half of New Guinea, the large island group of New Zealand, and about 10,000 smaller islands. Oceania is traditionally divided into four subregions named for the ethnic groups that first inhabited them: Australia, Melanesia, Micronesia, and Polynesia (which includes New Zealand). These subregions encompass diverse landscapes. Located in the middle of the Indo-Australian Plate, Australia is an ancient, stable land, with few high mountains and an arid interior. More recently formed, the islands of Melanesia and New Zealand lie on plate margins and have high, young peaks and active volcanoes. Elsewhere in Polynesia, and in Micronesia, most islands are the summits of undersea volcanoes, or tiny atolls.

Agrihan
Pagan
Alamagan
Guguan
Mariana Islands
Anatahan
Saipan
Tinian
Rota
Guam
Micronesia
Hall Islands
Chuuk Islands
Pohnpei
Kosrae
Yap
Palau Islands
Caroline Islands
Ralik Chain
Ratak Chain
Majuro
Tarawa
Nauru
Banaba
Melanesia
Admiralty Islands
Manus Island
Mussau Island
Tabar Islands
Lihir Group
New Ireland
Green Islands
Bismarck Sea
New Britain
Mt Wilhelm 14,793ft (4509m)
New Guinea
Bougainville
Solomon Islands
Choiseul
Santa Isabel
Malaita
Guadalcanal
Rennell
San Cristobal
Ndeni
Santa Cruz Islands
Solomon Sea
Torres Strait
Badu Island
Moa Island
Cape York
Arafura Sea
Coral Sea
Torres Islands
Banks Islands
Espiritu Santo
Malakula
Pentecost
Epi
Éfaté
Erromango
Tanna
Ouvéa
Lifou
Maré
New Caledonia
Île des Pins
Melville Island
Bathurst Island
Arnhem Land
Gulf of Carpentaria
Timor Sea
Bartle Frere 5322ft (1622m)
Great Barrier Reef
Kimberley
Barkly Tableland
Great Dividing Range
Tanami Desert
Great Sandy Desert
Great Artesian Basin
Fraser Island
PACIFIC
Barrow Island
North West Cape
Mt Zeil 5023ft (1531m)
Simpson Desert
Gibson Desert
Pilbara
Mt Meharry 4111ft (1253m)
Australia
Mt Woodroffe 4708ft (1435m)
Lake Eyre
Norfolk Island
Lord Howe Island
INDIAN OCEAN
Great Victoria Desert
Lake Torrens
Lake Frome
Darling
Lachlan
Lake Gairdner
Flinders Ranges
Nullarbor Plain
Great Australian Bight
Murray
Mount Kosciuszko 7310ft (2228m)
Tasman Sea
North Island
New Zealand
Kangaroo Island
Cape Leeuwin
Bass Strait
Flinders Island
Cape Barren Island
King Island
South Island
Mt Ossa 5305ft (1617m)
Tasmania
Mount Cook 12,316ft (3754m)
SOUTHERN OCEAN
Stewart Island
Snares Islands
Bounty
Antipodes I
Macquarie Island

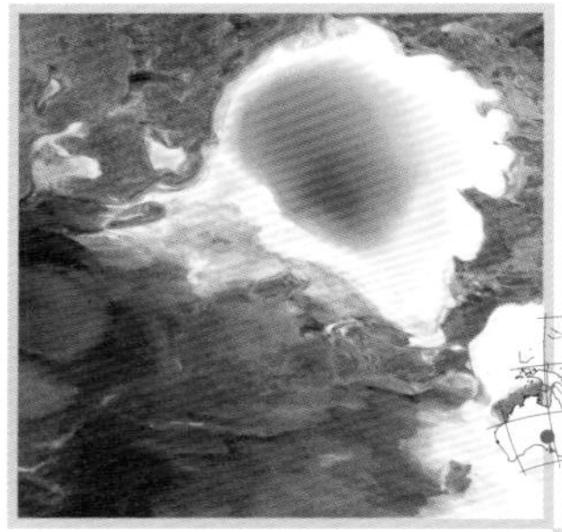

Right: The largest lake in Australia, Lake Eyre is part of a system that drains one-sixth of the continent. But only rarely does the lake fill with water; most of the time, it is dry and encrusted with salt.

Right: This chain of coral reefs is part of the northern end of Australia's Great Barrier Reef. The world's largest coral reef, it extends for over 1,200 miles (2,000 km) down the northeast coast of the continent.

Natural Hazards

Wildfires

Long spells of dry weather combined with inflammable oils produced by widespread eucalypts and acacias make much of Australia highly susceptible to wildfires, or bushfires as they are known locally. Fire is part of the ecology of most Australian environments: many native plants are not only adapted to drought but can also withstand fire; indeed, some require fire to trigger germination. Wildfires are started naturally by lightning strikes. Increasingly, they are also caused by human carelessness or mischief, with the result that they occur regularly in urban areas. In dry, windy conditions, bushfires can move with astonishing speed, rapidly consuming vegetation, leaping roads and waterways, and, in severe cases, causing significant loss of life and property.

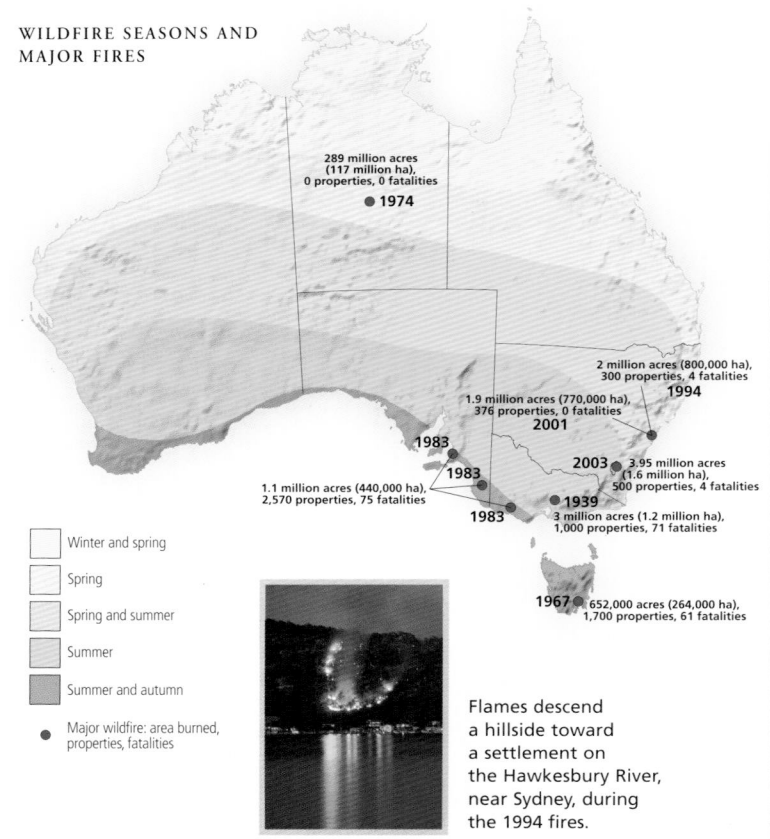

WILDFIRE SEASONS AND MAJOR FIRES

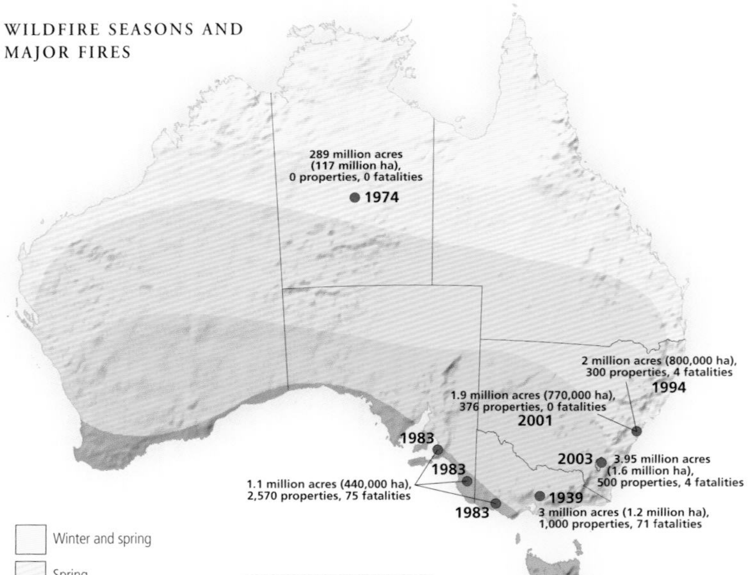

289 million acres (117 million ha), 0 properties, 0 fatalities
1974
2 million acres (800,000 ha), 300 properties, 4 fatalities
1994
1.9 million acres (770,000 ha), 376 properties, 0 fatalities
2001
1983
1983
2003
3.95 million acres (1.6 million ha), 500 properties, 4 fatalities
1.1 million acres (440,000 ha), 2,570 properties, 75 fatalities
1939
1983
3 million acres (1.2 million ha), 1,000 properties, 71 fatalities
1967
652,000 acres (264,000 ha), 1,700 properties, 61 fatalities
Winter and spring
Spring
Spring and summer
Summer
Summer and autumn
Major wildfire: area burned, properties, fatalities

Flames descend a hillside toward a settlement on the Hawkesbury River, near Sydney, during the 1994 fires.

Climate

Most of the countries and territories of Oceania lie close to the Equator and therefore experience warm, humid conditions year-round. Rainfall varies little from month to month at the Equator, but farther north and south pronounced wet and dry seasons occur. During the Southern-Hemisphere summer, hurricanes (known locally as cyclones) occur above 5 degrees north and south. Seasonal tropical conditions—and cyclones—extend to the northern fringe of Australia. In middle latitudes, conditions are cooler, and moist onshore winds keep New Zealand and the east coast of Australia well-watered. The interior of Australia is, however, one of the most arid regions on Earth, and about half of the continent receives less than 12 inches (300 mm) of rain a year. Dry spells occasionally turn to droughts, especially in eastern Australia during El Niño episodes.

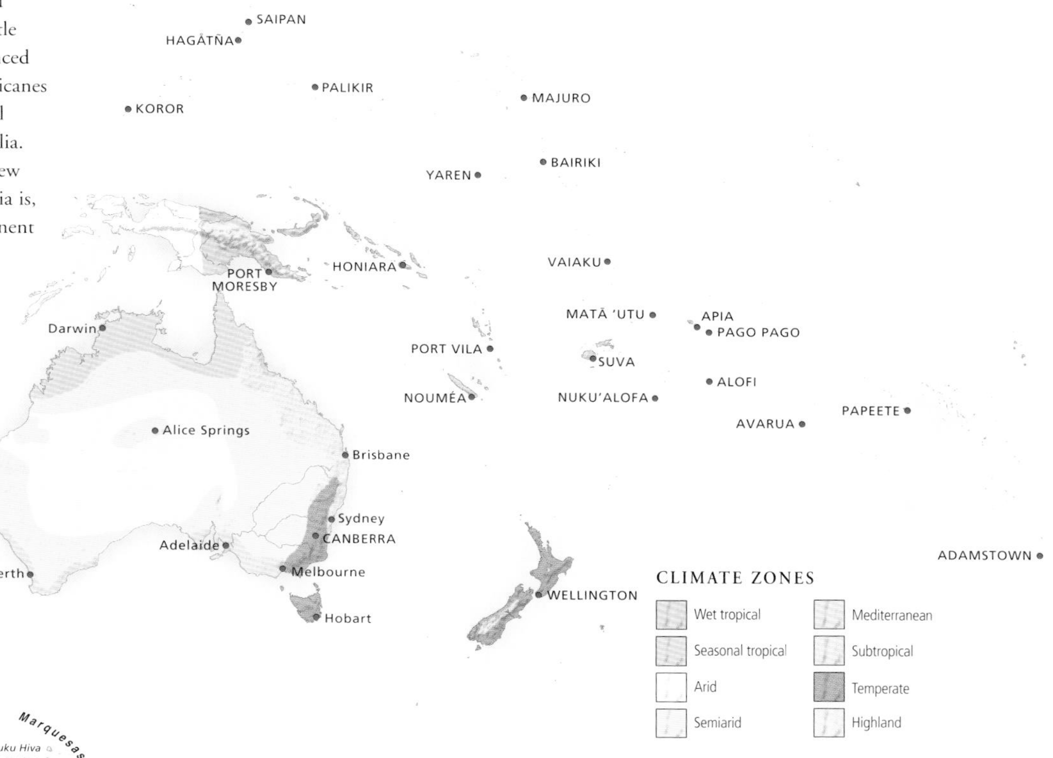
SAIPAN
HAGÅTÑA
PALIKIR
KOROR
MAJURO
BAIRIKI
YAREN
PORT MORESBY
HONIARA
VAIAKU
Darwin
MATĀ 'UTU
APIA
PAGO PAGO
PORT VILA
SUVA
ALOFI
NOUMÉA
NUKU'ALOFA
AVARUA
PAPEETE
Alice Springs
Brisbane
Sydney
CANBERRA
Adelaide
Perth
Melbourne
WELLINGTON
Hobart
ADAMSTOWN
CLIMATE ZONES
Wet tropical
Seasonal tropical
Arid
Semiarid
Mediterranean
Subtropical
Temperate
Highland

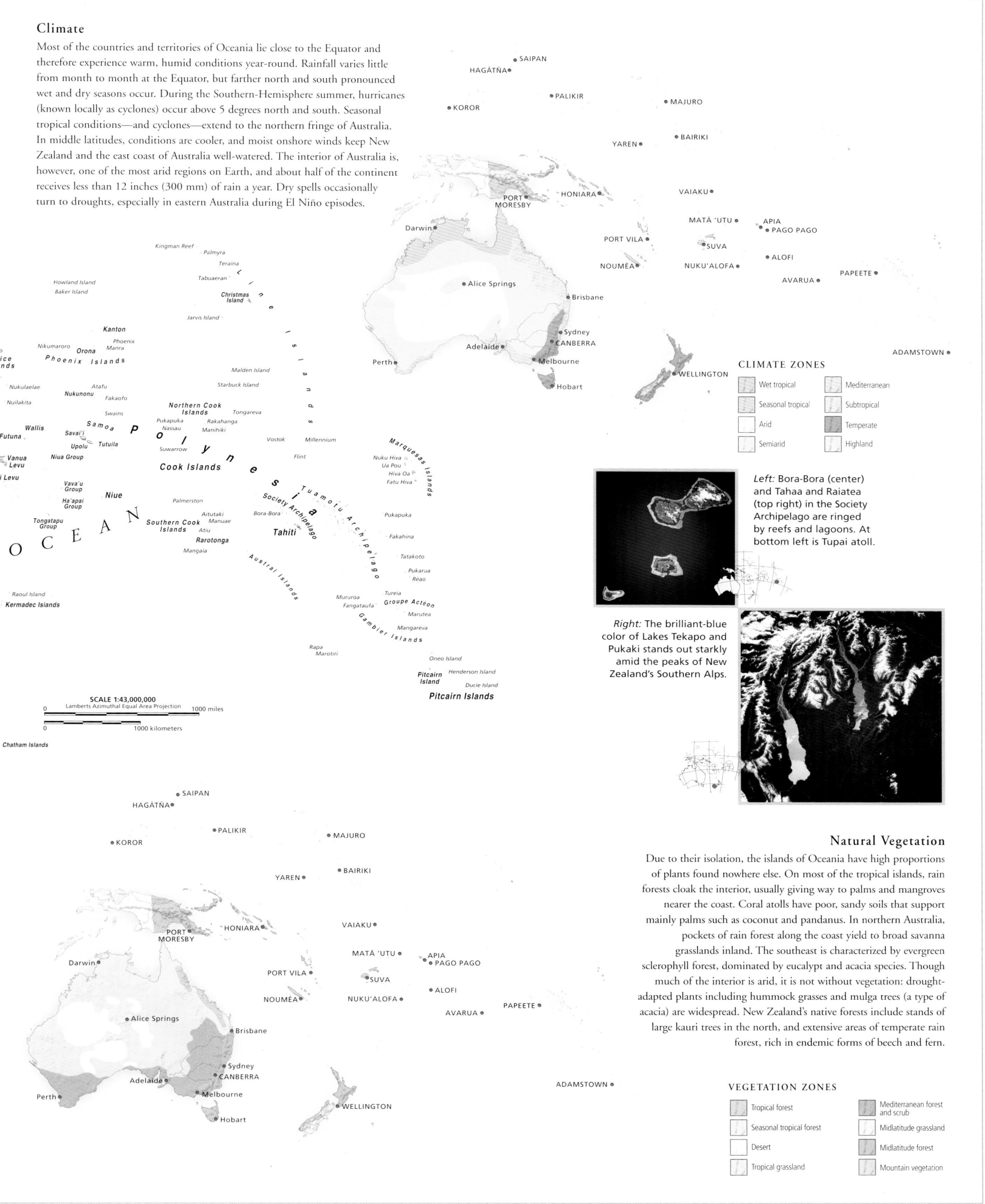

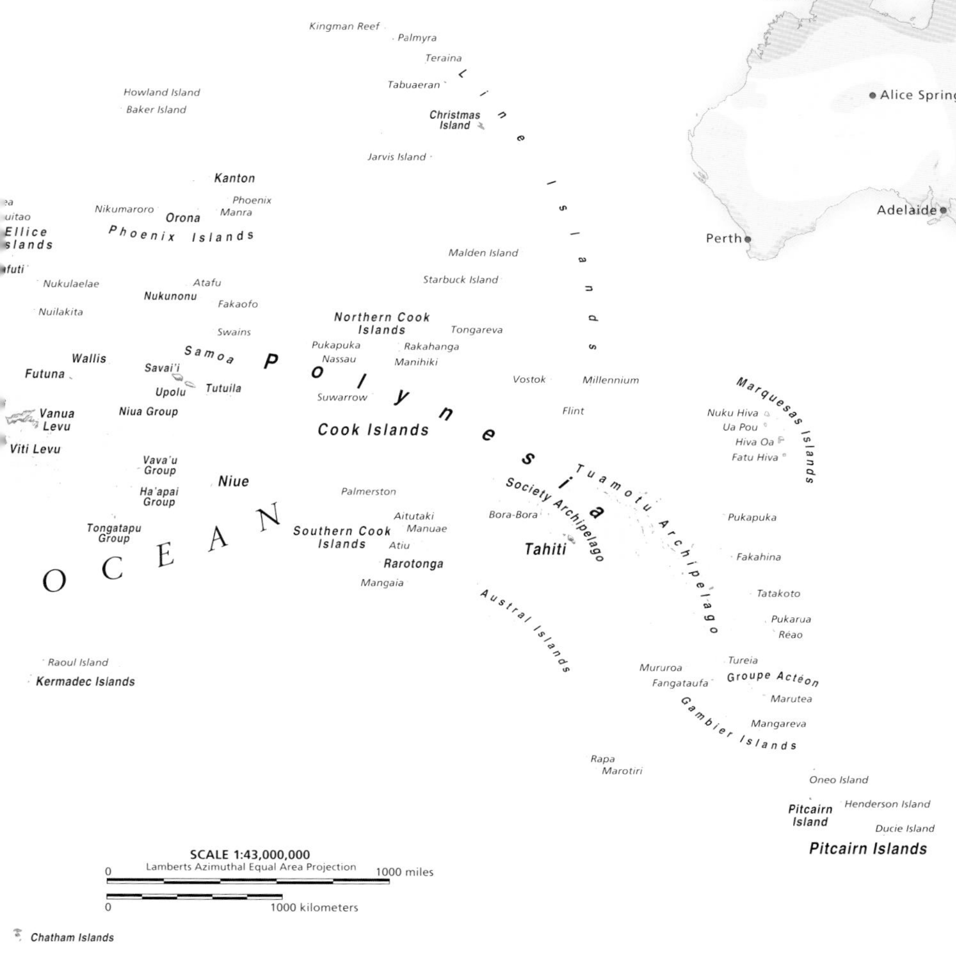
Kingman Reef
Palmyra
Teraina
Tabuaeran
Christmas Island
Line Islands
Howland Island
Baker Island
Jarvis Island
Kanton
Phoenix
Manra
Nikumaroro
Orona
Phoenix Islands
Ellice Islands
Nukulaelae
Nuilakita
Atafu
Nukunonu
Fakaofo
Swains
Malden Island
Starbuck Island
Northern Cook Islands
Tongareva
Pukapuka
Rakahanga
Nassau
Manihiki
Wallis
Futuna
Samoa
Savai'i
Upolu
Tutuila
Polynesia
Suwarrow
Vostok
Millennium
Flint
Marquesas Islands
Nuku Hiva
Ua Pou
Hiva Oa
Fatu Hiva
Vanua Levu
Viti Levu
Niua Group
Cook Islands
Vava'u Group
Ha'apai Group
Niue
Palmerston
Tuamotu Archipelago
Society Archipelago
Tongatapu Group
Southern Cook Islands
Aitutaki
Manuae
Atiu
Bora-Bora
Tahiti
Pukapuka
Fakahina
Rarotonga
Mangaia
OCEAN
Austral Islands
Tatakoto
Pukarua
Reao
Raoul Island
Kermadec Islands
Tureia
Mururoa
Fangataufa
Groupe Acteon
Marutea
Gambier Islands
Mangareva
Rapa
Marotiri
Oneo Island
Pitcairn Island
Henderson Island
Ducie Island
Pitcairn Islands
SCALE 1:43,000,000
Lamberts Azimuthal Equal Area Projection
0
1000 miles
0
1000 kilometers
Chatham Islands

Left: Bora-Bora (center) and Tahaa and Raiatea (top right) in the Society Archipelago are ringed by reefs and lagoons. At bottom left is Tupai atoll.

Right: The brilliant-blue color of Lakes Tekapo and Pukaki stands out starkly amid the peaks of New Zealand's Southern Alps.

SAIPAN
HAGÅTÑA
PALIKIR
KOROR
MAJURO
BAIRIKI
YAREN
PORT MORESBY
HONIARA
VAIAKU
MATĀ 'UTU
APIA
PAGO PAGO
Darwin
PORT VILA
SUVA
ALOFI
NOUMÉA
NUKU'ALOFA
PAPEETE
AVARUA
Alice Springs
Brisbane
Sydney
CANBERRA
Adelaide
Perth
Melbourne
ADAMSTOWN
WELLINGTON
Hobart

Natural Vegetation

Due to their isolation, the islands of Oceania have high proportions of plants found nowhere else. On most of the tropical islands, rain forests cloak the interior, usually giving way to palms and mangroves nearer the coast. Coral atolls have poor, sandy soils that support mainly palms such as coconut and pandanus. In northern Australia, pockets of rain forest along the coast yield to broad savanna grasslands inland. The southeast is characterized by evergreen sclerophyll forest, dominated by eucalypt and acacia species. Though much of the interior is arid, it is not without vegetation: drought-adapted plants including hummock grasses and mulga trees (a type of acacia) are widespread. New Zealand's native forests include stands of large kauri trees in the north, and extensive areas of temperate rain forest, rich in endemic forms of beech and fern.

VEGETATION ZONES

Tropical forest
Seasonal tropical forest
Desert
Tropical grassland
Mediterranean forest and scrub
Midlatitude grassland
Midlatitude forest
Mountain vegetation

Peoples and Nations

Home to about 32 million people, Oceania encompasses 14 nations and numerous dependencies. Its indigenous peoples form four major groups—Australian Aboriginal peoples, Melanesians, Micronesians, and Polynesians—who speak a huge variety of languages. Since the 18th century, large numbers of immigrants have settled in the region, particularly in Australia and New Zealand. Most came from Europe, especially the United Kingdom, making English the most widely spoken language in Australia and New Zealand.

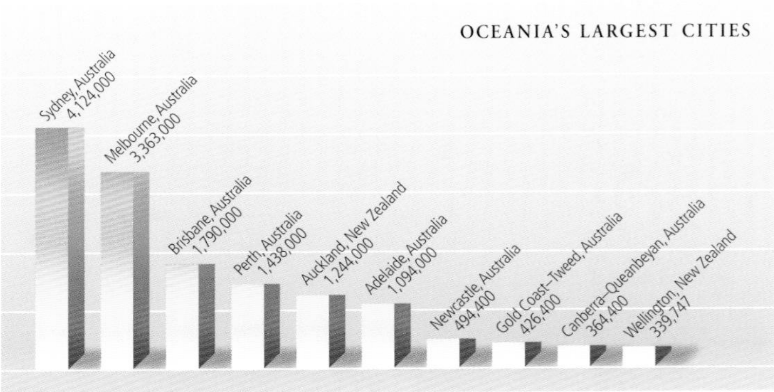

OCEANIA'S LARGEST CITIES
Sydney, Australia 4,124,000
Melbourne, Australia 3,363,000
Brisbane, Australia 1,790,000
Perth, Australia 1,438,000
Auckland, New Zealand 1,244,000
Adelaide, Australia 1,094,000
Newcastle, Australia 494,400
Gold Coast–Tweed, Australia 426,400
Canberra–Queanbeyan, Australia 364,400
Wellington, New Zealand 339,747

Urbanization

There is a stark contrast between Australia and New Zealand, where cities and towns accommodate around 90 percent of the inhabitants, and most of the rest of Oceania, where there are no major cities and the urban population is generally under 60 percent. An exception is the French territory of New Caledonia, where 82 percent of the inhabitants live in urban areas. In Papua New Guinea, just 19 percent of people live in towns and cities, but even here significant change has occurred in recent decades: in 1950, the urban population accounted for less than one percent of the total.

SAIPAN
HAGÅTÑA
PALIKIR
MAJURO
KOROR
BAIRIKI
YAREN
HONIARA
VAIAKU
PORT MORESBY
MATĀ 'UTU
APIA
PAGO PAGO
Darwin
PORT VILA
SUVA
NOUMÉA
NUKU'ALOFA
ALOFI
PAPEETE
AVARUA
Brisbane
Sydney
CANBERRA
Adelaide
Perth
Melbourne
WELLINGTON
Hobart
POPULATION DENSITY
Uninhabited
Less than 2.6 persons per sq mile/1 per sq km
2.6–26 per sq mile/ 1–10 per sq km
26–65 per sq mile/ 10–25 per sq km

Population Patterns

Australia accounts for most of Oceania's population, with about 20 million people. Another 5 million people inhabit New Guinea and about 4 million live in New Zealand. The remainder of Oceania's population is scattered across thousands of small islands. Population density is generally low but varies greatly. The highest concentrations of inhabitants occur on the southeast coast of Australia, in northern New Zealand and the Papua New Guinea highlands, and on the tiny islands of Nauru, the Cook Islands, and Tuvalu (where 11,000 people occupy just 10 square miles [26 sq km] of land). In contrast, the interior of Australia is one of the world's most sparsely populated regions, and many small Pacific islands are uninhabited. Growth rates are high in Micronesia and in Papua New Guinea, where the population is expected to double by 2030.

Flashpoints

Oceania has no major international boundary disputes, but ethnic rivalries have undermined political and economic stability in some countries and sparked a number of regional conflicts.

Fiji

Almost half of the people of Fiji are the descendants of Indian laborers brought to the islands by the British. The accession of a democratically elected, Indo-Fijian-dominated government prompted a military coup in 1987 led by indigenous Fijians, and the introduction of laws to ensure indigenous rule. Continuing Indo-Fijian participation in politics prompted another failed coup by indigenous Fijians in May 2000.

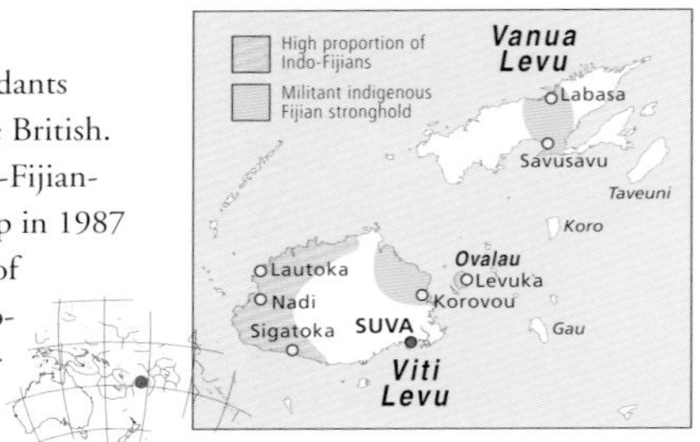

High proportion of Indo-Fijians
Militant indigenous Fijian stronghold
Vanua Levu
Labasa
Savusavu
Taveuni
Koro
Lautoka
Nadi
Sigatoka
SUVA
Ovalau
Levuka
Korovou
Gau
Viti Levu

Solomon Islands

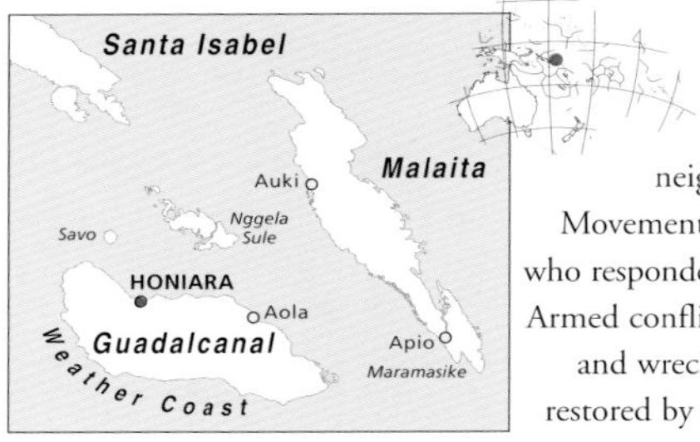

Santa Isabel
Malaita
Auki
Savo
Nggela Sule
HONIARA
Aola
Guadalcanal
Apio
Maramasike
Weather Coast

In 1998, inhabitants of Guadalcanal, resentful of the growing influence of immigrants from neighboring Malaita, founded the Isatabu Freedom Movement (IFM). It began a campaign to oust Malaitans, who responded by setting up the Malaita Eagle Force (MEF). Armed conflict between these groups claimed dozens of lives and wrecked the islands' economy. A degree of order was restored by the arrival of Australian security forces in 2003.

Bougainville

Politically, Bougainville is part of Papua New Guinea, but its inhabitants have strong cultural connections with the people of the Solomon Islands. Discontent among the islanders regarding the distribution of income from mineral reserves led to an armed secessionist revolt that lasted from 1988 to 2001. A peace accord reached in that year, providing an option of independence for Bougainville by 2011–16, has so far held.

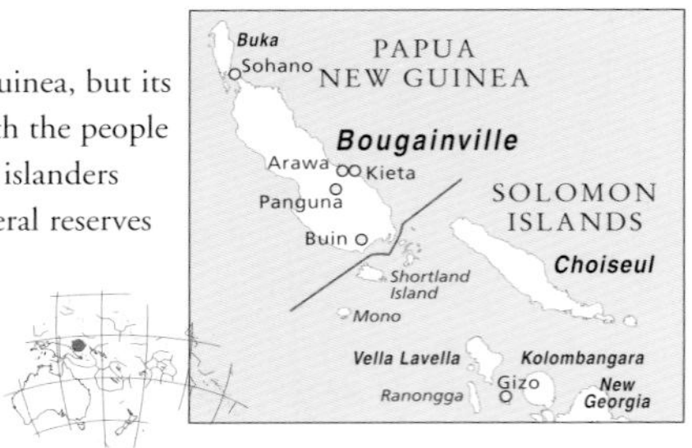

Buka
Sohano
PAPUA NEW GUINEA
Bougainville
Arawa
Kieta
Panguna
SOLOMON ISLANDS
Buin
Shortland Island
Choiseul
Mono
Vella Lavella
Kolombangara
Gizo
Ranongga
New Georgia

Marshall Islands
Federated States of Micronesia
Palau
Kiribati
Nauru
Papua New Guinea
Solomon Islands
Tuvalu
Kiribati
Samoa
Vanuatu
Fiji
Tonga
Niue
Cook Islands
Australia
New Zealand
Pacific Islands Forum

Pacific Islands Forum

The Pacific Islands Forum was founded as the South Pacific Forum in 1971 by Australia, the Cook Islands, Fiji, Nauru, New Zealand, Tonga, and the former Western Samoa (now Samoa) to facilitate trade and economic development in the Oceania region and provide a strong political voice for its member states in international affairs. The forum, which changed its name to the Pacific Islands Forum in October 1999, now includes a total of 16 independent and self-governing states. Its secretariat is based in Suva, Fiji, but annual meetings are hosted by each of the member countries and territories in turn.

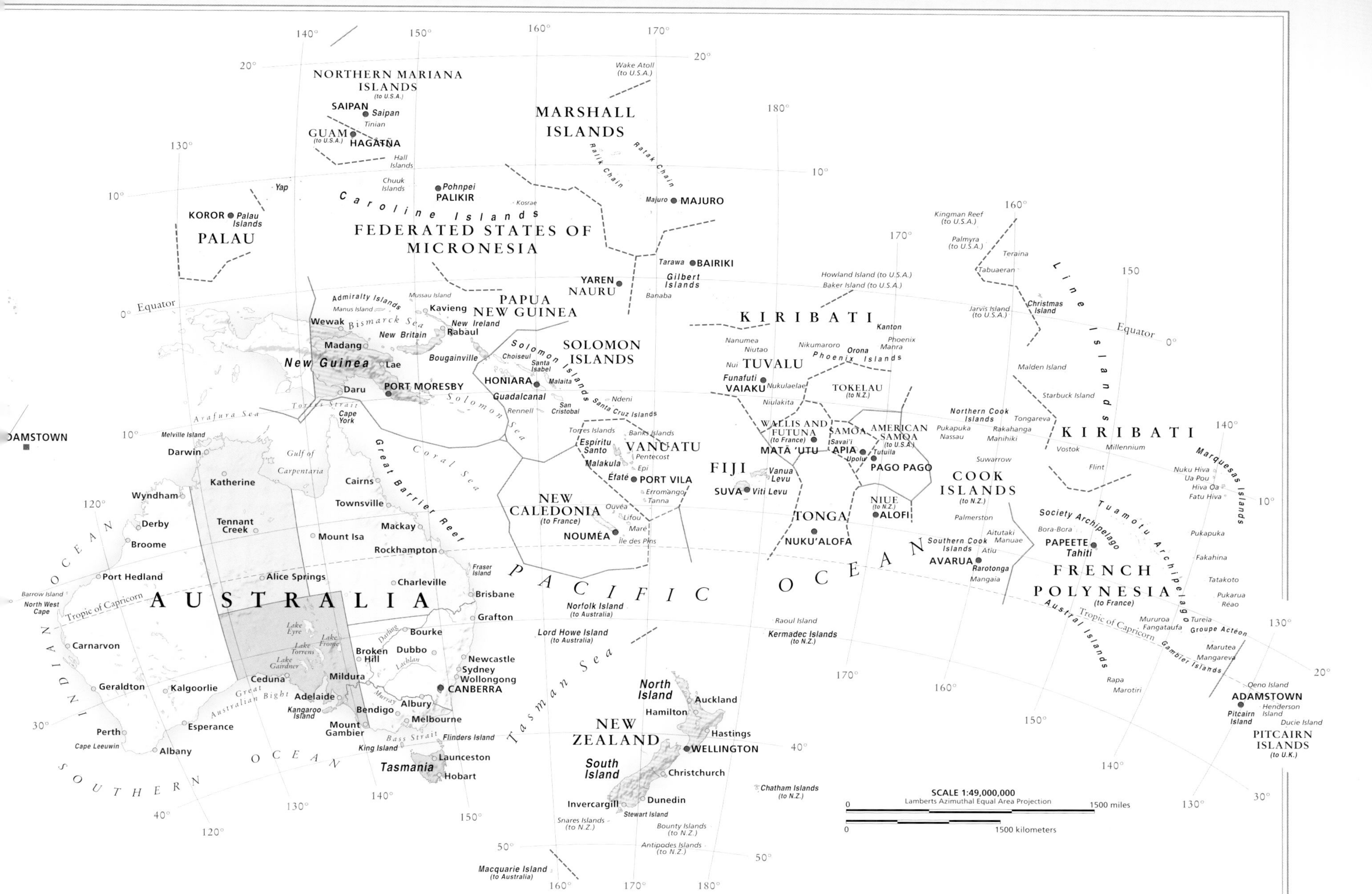

NORTHERN MARIANA ISLANDS (to U.S.A.)
SAIPAN
Saipan
Tinian
GUAM (to U.S.A.)
HAGÅTÑA
Hall Islands
Chuuk Islands
Yap
KOROR
Palau Islands
PALAU
Pohnpei
PALIKIR
Kosrae
Caroline Islands
FEDERATED STATES OF MICRONESIA
Wake Atoll (to U.S.A.)
MARSHALL ISLANDS
Ralik Chain
Ratak Chain
Majuro
MAJURO
Tarawa
BAIRIKI
Gilbert Islands
Banaba
YAREN
NAURU
PAPUA NEW GUINEA
Admiralty Islands
Manus Island
Mussau Island
Wewak
Bismarck Sea
Kavieng
New Ireland
New Britain
Rabaul
Madang
New Guinea
Lae
Daru
PORT MORESBY
Bougainville
Choiseul
Santa Isabel
SOLOMON ISLANDS
Solomon Islands
HONIARA
Malaita
Guadalcanal
Rennell
San Cristobal
Ndeni
Santa Cruz Islands
Solomon Sea
Torres Strait
Arafura Sea
Cape York
Coral Sea
Great Barrier Reef
Gulf of Carpentaria
Melville Island
Darwin
Katherine
Tennant Creek
Mount Isa
Cairns
Townsville
Mackay
Rockhampton
Wyndham
Derby
Broome
Port Hedland
Alice Springs
Charleville
Fraser Island
Brisbane
Grafton
AUSTRALIA
Tropic of Capricorn
Barrow Island
North West Cape
Carnarvon
Lake Eyre
Lake Frome
Lake Torrens
Lake Gairdner
Darling
Bourke
Broken Hill
Dubbo
Lachlan
Newcastle
Sydney
Wollongong
CANBERRA
Geraldton
Kalgoorlie
Ceduna
Mildura
Great Australian Bight
Adelaide
Murray
Albury
Kangaroo Island
Bendigo
Melbourne
Perth
Esperance
Mount Gambier
Bass Strait
Flinders Island
Cape Leeuwin
Albany
King Island
Tasmania
Launceston
Hobart
INDIAN OCEAN
SOUTHERN OCEAN
DAMSTOWN
Torres Islands
Banks Islands
Espiritu Santo
VANUATU
Pentecost
Malakula
Epi
Efaté
PORT VILA
Erromango
Tanna
NEW CALEDONIA (to France)
Ouvéa
Lifou
Maré
NOUMÉA
Île des Pins
Norfolk Island (to Australia)
PACIFIC OCEAN
Lord Howe Island (to Australia)
Tasman Sea
North Island
Auckland
Hamilton
NEW ZEALAND
Hastings
WELLINGTON
South Island
Christchurch
Invercargill
Dunedin
Stewart Island
Snares Islands (to N.Z.)
Bounty Islands (to N.Z.)
Antipodes Islands (to N.Z.)
Macquarie Island (to Australia)
Chatham Islands (to N.Z.)
Raoul Island
Kermadec Islands (to N.Z.)
KIRIBATI
Howland Island (to U.S.A.)
Baker Island (to U.S.A.)
Kanton
Phoenix Islands
Nanumea
Niutao
Nui
Nikumaroro
Orona
Manra
TUVALU
Funafuti
VAIAKU
Nukulaelae
Niulakita
TOKELAU (to N.Z.)
WALLIS AND FUTUNA (to France)
MATA'UTU
SAMOA
Savai'i
APIA
Upolu
AMERICAN SAMOA (to U.S.A.)
Tutuila
PAGO PAGO
FIJI
Vanua Levu
SUVA
Viti Levu
TONGA
NUKU'ALOFA
NIUE (to N.Z.)
ALOFI
COOK ISLANDS (to N.Z.)
Northern Cook Islands
Pukapuka
Nassau
Rakahanga
Manihiki
Tongareva
Suwarrow
Palmerston
Aitutaki
Southern Cook Islands
Manuae
Atiu
AVARUA
Rarotonga
Mangaia
Kingman Reef (to U.S.A.)
Palmyra (to U.S.A.)
Teraina
Tabuaeran
Jarvis Island (to U.S.A.)
Christmas Island
Line Islands
Malden Island
Starbuck Island
Vostok
Millennium
Flint
KIRIBATI
Equator
Marquesas Islands
Nuku Hiva
Ua Pou
Hiva Oa
Fatu Hiva
Tuamotu Archipelago
Society Archipelago
Bora-Bora
PAPEETE
Tahiti
Pukapuka
Fakahina
Tatakoto
Pukarua
Réao
FRENCH POLYNESIA (to France)
Austral Islands
Rapa
Marotiri
Mururoa
Fangataufa
Tureia
Groupe Acteon
Marutea
Mangareva
Gambier Islands
Oeno Island
ADAMSTOWN
Henderson Island
Pitcairn Island
Ducie Island
PITCAIRN ISLANDS (to U.K.)
SCALE 1:49,000,000
Lamberts Azimuthal Equal Area Projection
0
1500 miles
0
1500 kilometers

INDIGENOUS SOCIETIES, 1500

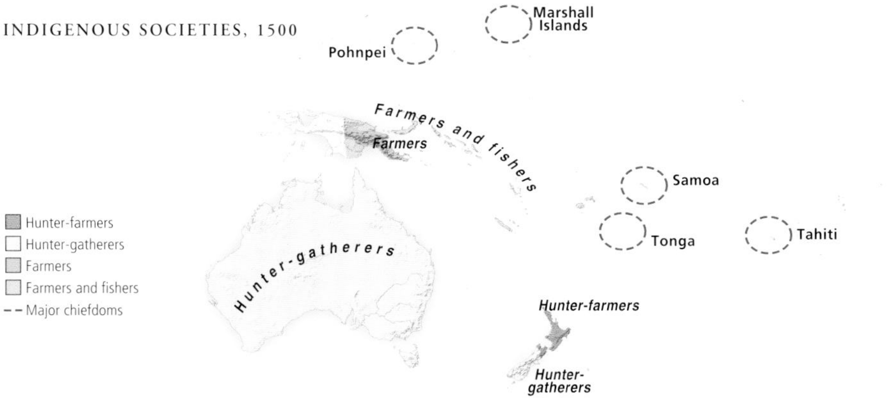

Marshall Islands
Pohnpei
Farmers and fishers
Farmers
Samoa
Tonga
Tahiti
Hunter-gatherers
Hunter-farmers
Hunter-gatherers
Hunter-farmers
Hunter-gatherers
Farmers
Farmers and fishers
-- Major chiefdoms

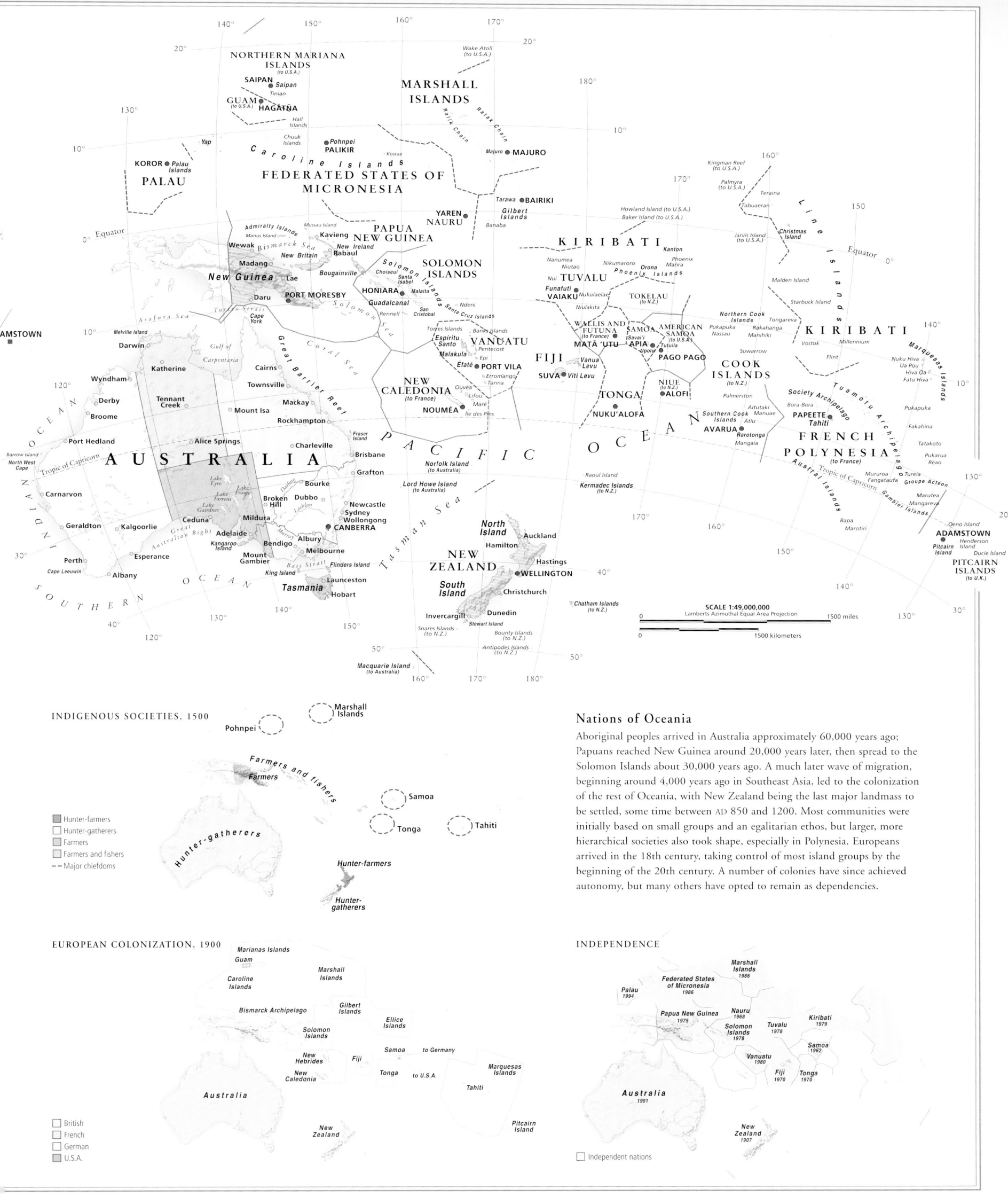

Nations of Oceania

Aboriginal peoples arrived in Australia approximately 60,000 years ago; Papuans reached New Guinea around 20,000 years later, then spread to the Solomon Islands about 30,000 years ago. A much later wave of migration, beginning around 4,000 years ago in Southeast Asia, led to the colonization of the rest of Oceania, with New Zealand being the last major landmass to be settled, some time between AD 850 and 1200. Most communities were initially based on small groups and an egalitarian ethos, but larger, more hierarchical societies also took shape, especially in Polynesia. Europeans arrived in the 18th century, taking control of most island groups by the beginning of the 20th century. A number of colonies have since achieved autonomy, but many others have opted to remain as dependencies.

EUROPEAN COLONIZATION, 1900

Marianas Islands
Guam
Caroline Islands
Marshall Islands
Bismarck Archipelago
Gilbert Islands
Solomon Islands
Ellice Islands
New Hebrides
Fiji
Samoa
to Germany
New Caledonia
Tonga
to U.S.A.
Marquesas Islands
Tahiti
Australia
New Zealand
Pitcairn Island
British
French
German
U.S.A.

INDEPENDENCE

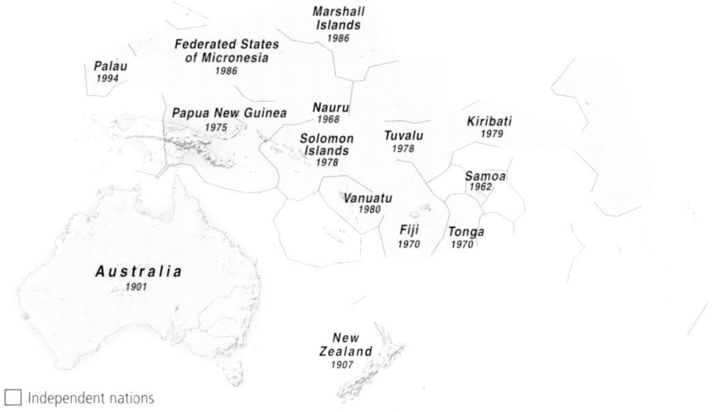

Marshall Islands 1986
Federated States of Micronesia 1986
Palau 1994
Papua New Guinea 1975
Nauru 1968
Solomon Islands 1978
Tuvalu 1978
Kiribati 1979
Samoa 1962
Vanuatu 1980
Fiji 1970
Tonga 1970
Australia 1901
New Zealand 1907
Independent nations

THE HUMAN IMPACT

In well-watered New Guinea, agriculture began as early as 9,000 years ago; by 5,000 years ago, farmers there were clearing forest and digging extensive drainage systems. In Australia, by contrast, an arid climate and poor soils inhibited the development of sedentary agricultural societies. Mainly hunter-gatherers, early Aboriginal peoples did, however, divert waterways to trap fish, and burn woodlands to facilitate hunting, and may have contributed to the extinction of large mammal species, or megafauna. Some of the larger islands export cash crops such as sugar, palm oil, and cocoa, and many Melanesian islands have sizable mineral resources and forests. Europeans arriving in Oceania in the late 18th century imported the livestock, seeds, and technologies to permit rapid conversion of much larger tracts of land to agriculture. Their limited understanding of local conditions meant that they were often unaware of the havoc they were wreaking. In the industrial age, some problems have become acute. Dryland salinity threatens Australian water tables and soil; nuclear testing has contaminated land and ocean; and rising sea levels due to global warming threaten the livelihoods of entire island communities.

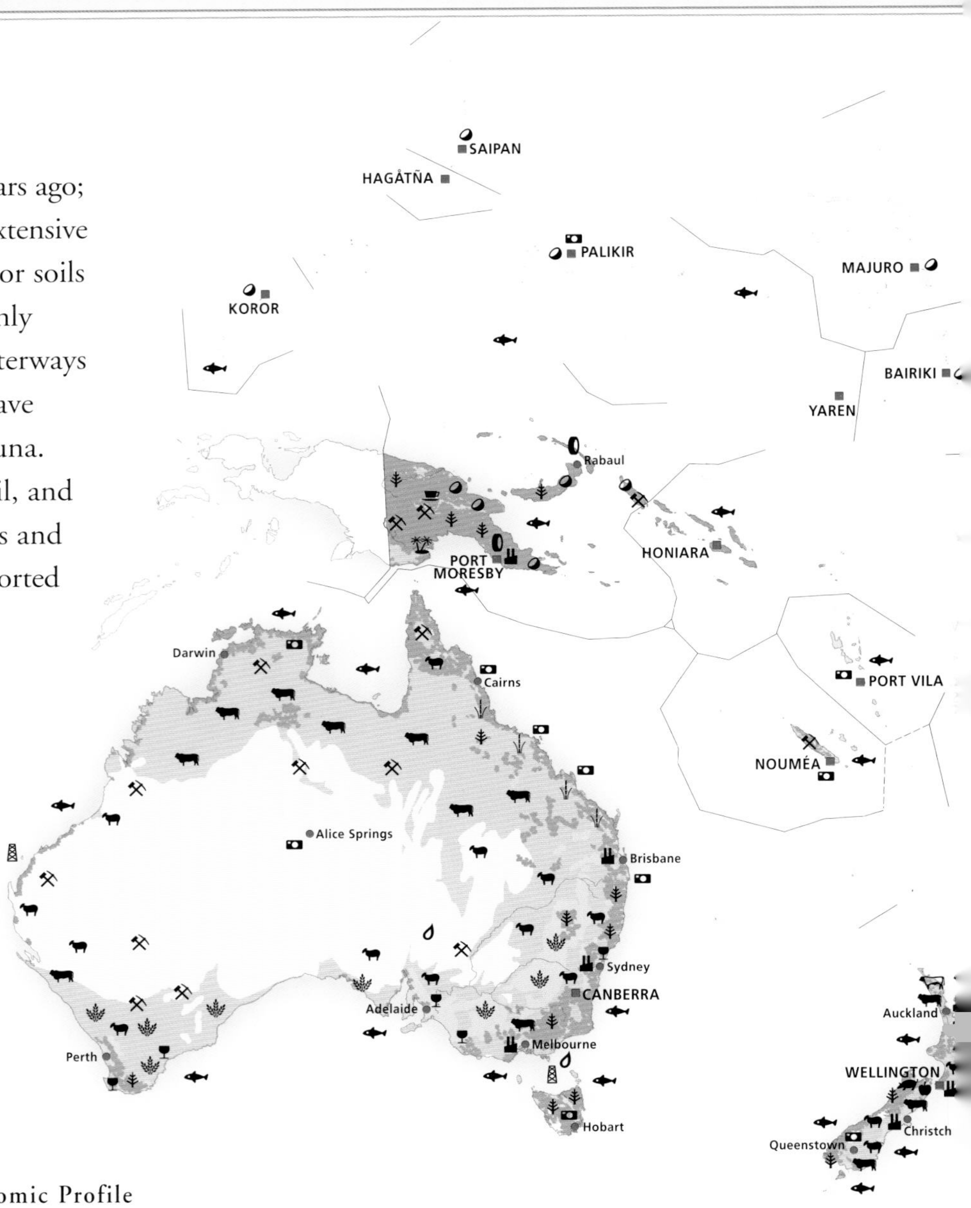
SAIPAN
HAGÅTÑA
PALIKIR
MAJURO
KOROR
BAIRIKI
YAREN
Rabaul
HONIARA
PORT MORESBY
Darwin
Cairns
PORT VILA
NOUMÉA
Alice Springs
Brisbane
Sydney
CANBERRA
Adelaide
Auckland
Melbourne
Perth
WELLINGTON
Hobart
Christch
Queenstown

THE CHANGING FACE OF OCEANIA

Nuclear Testing

To foreign powers, the isolation and sparse populations of many parts of Oceania made them ideal for testing powerful weapons. In 1946, the U.S.A. relocated the inhabitants of Bikini and Enewetak to other other parts of the Marshall Islands, and for the next 12 years used the atolls for setting off nuclear explosions. The U.K. detonated 21 nuclear devices in Australia and the Pacific between 1952 and 1958, and France carried out 193 nuclear tests between 1966 and 1996 in French Polynesia. These tests contaminated the atmosphere and large tracts of land, and exposed service personnel and local people to fallout. Few residents of Bikini and Enewetak have been able to return home, and only in 2000 was the Maralinga site in Australia declared safe enough for its traditional owners to live there. In 1999, a French independent commission reported that radioactivity from French test sites continues to seep into fresh-water supplies, lagoons, and the sea.

NUCLEAR TEST SITES

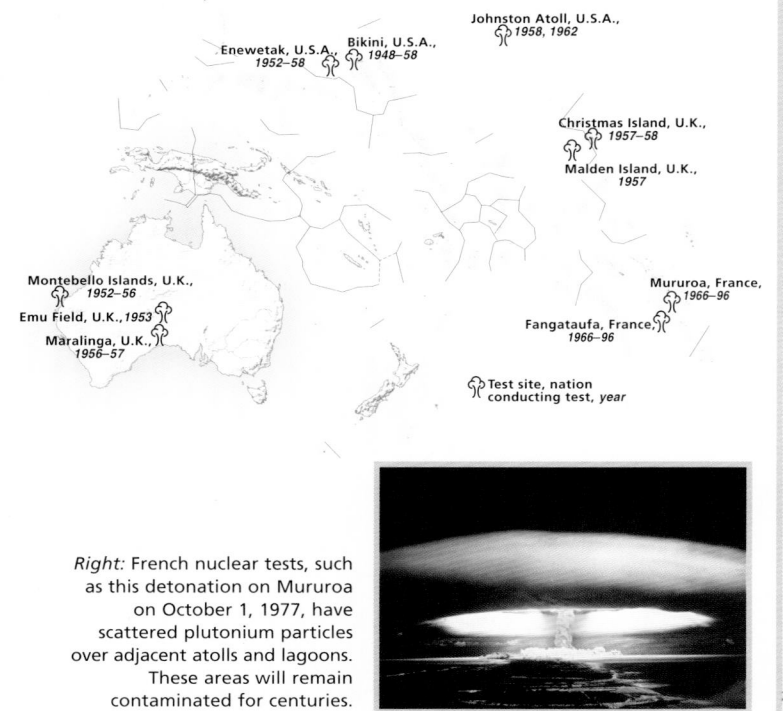

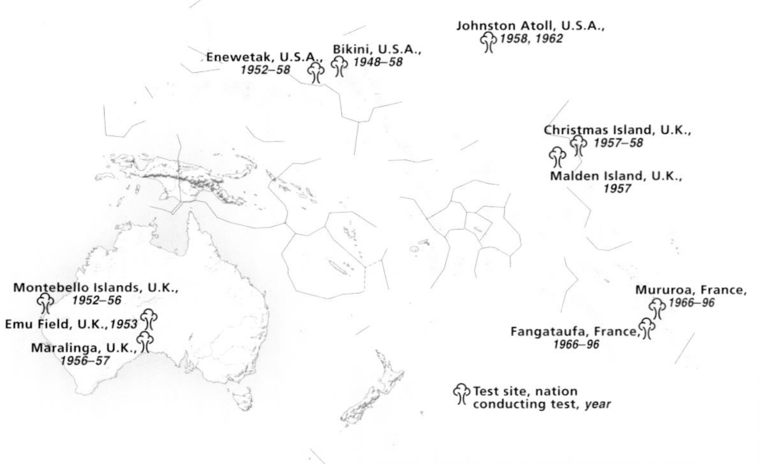
Johnston Atoll, U.S.A., 1958, 1962
Bikini, U.S.A., 1948–58
Enewetak, U.S.A., 1952–58
Christmas Island, U.K., 1957–58
Malden Island, U.K., 1957
Montebello Islands, U.K., 1952–56
Emu Field, U.K., 1953
Maralinga, U.K., 1956–57
Mururoa, France, 1966–96
Fangataufa, France, 1966–96
Test site, nation conducting test, year

Right: French nuclear tests, such as this detonation on Mururoa on October 1, 1977, have scattered plutonium particles over adjacent atolls and lagoons. These areas will remain contaminated for centuries.

Economic Profile

Australia and New Zealand have developed economies, with strong and diverse manufacturing sectors. However, most workers in these countries are employed in services such as the retail trade, banking, and tourism. Primary industries remain important: Australia's top exports are coal, crude oil, iron ore, gold, and wheat; New Zealand relies heavily on sales of dairy produce, meat, and timber. Elsewhere, the industrial sector is little developed, consisting mainly of the processing of raw materials. Many Melanesian islands have sizable mineral reserves and forests, and cash crops such as sugar, palm oil, and cocoa are exported by some of the larger islands. Tourism is a vital source of income for many Pacific communities, and some small islands have benefited from the sale of fishing rights to their disporportionately large maritime zones. However, most people outside Australia and New Zealand make a living from subsistence or small-scale commercial farming and fishing.

Land Cover

Abundant rainfall and volcanic soils make parts of Melanesia agriculturally productive, but arable land is scarce elsewhere. In Australia and New Zealand, in particular, most of the land is better suited to grazing, and in Australia livestock has to roam over large areas to find sufficient food. Though they are still being felled, forests cover almost one-quarter of Oceania. Australia's immense deserts account for much other land cover.

PROPORTIONS OF TOTAL LAND AREA

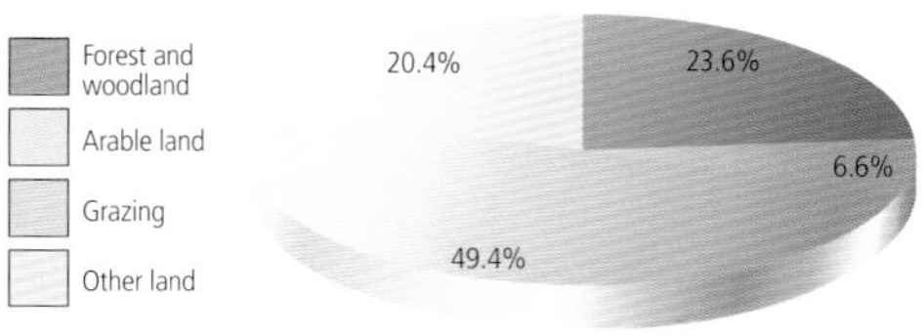
Forest and woodland
Arable land
Grazing
Other land
20.4%
23.6%
6.6%
49.4%

Australia has about 110 million sheep—down from a peak of 180 million in 1970—and their grazing contributes to land degradation. But wool remains an important export.

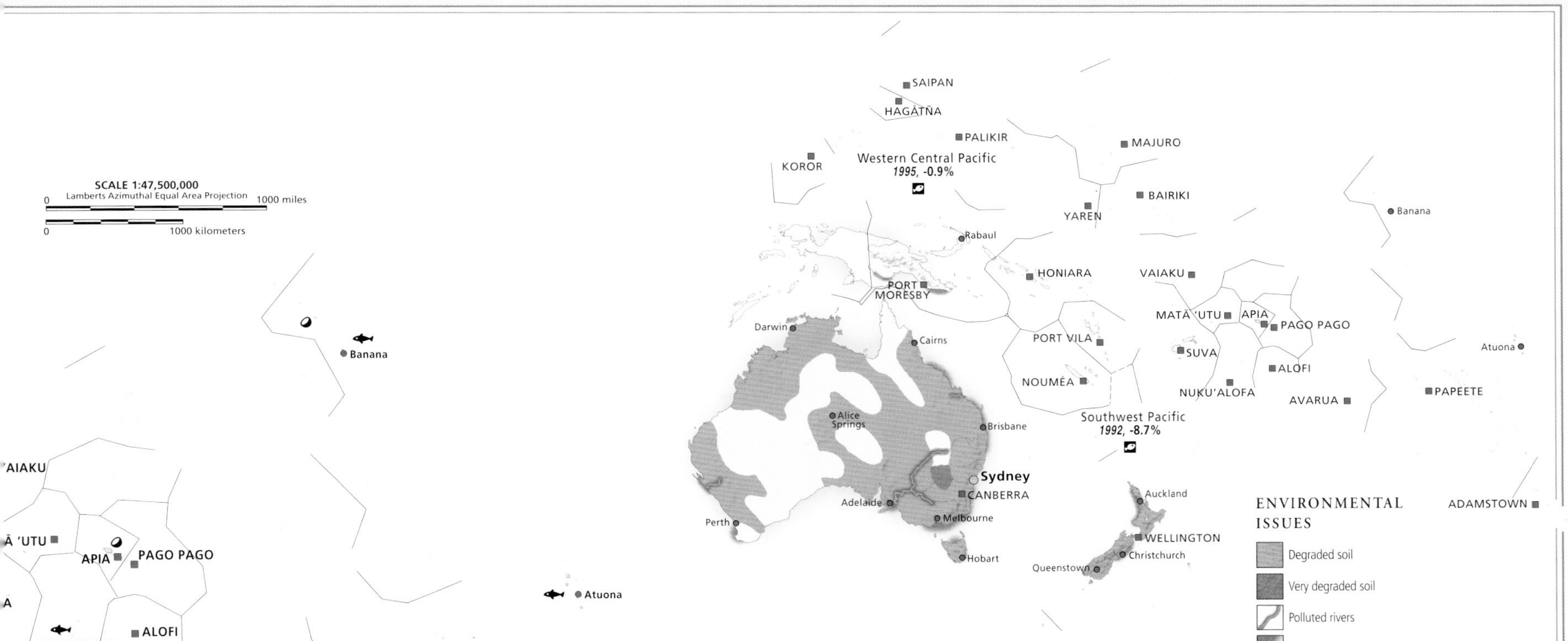
SCALE 1:47,500,000
Lamberts Azimuthal Equal Area Projection
1000 miles
1000 kilometers
SAIPAN
HAGÅTÑA
PALIKIR
MAJURO
KOROR
Western Central Pacific
1995, -0.9%
BAIRIKI
YAREN
Banana
Rabaul
HONIARA
VAIAKU
PORT MORESBY
MATA'UTU
APIA
PAGO PAGO
Darwin
Cairns
PORT VILA
SUVA
Atuona
ALOFI
NOUMÉA
NUKU'ALOFA
AVARUA
PAPEETE
Alice Springs
Brisbane
Southwest Pacific
1992, -8.7%
Sydney
CANBERRA
Auckland
Adelaide
Perth
Melbourne
WELLINGTON
Christchurch
Hobart
Queenstown
ADAMSTOWN
ENVIRONMENTAL ISSUES
Degraded soil
Very degraded soil
Polluted rivers
Polluted seas and lakes
Cities with severe air pollution
Overfished fishery, year of peak catch, decline since peak catch

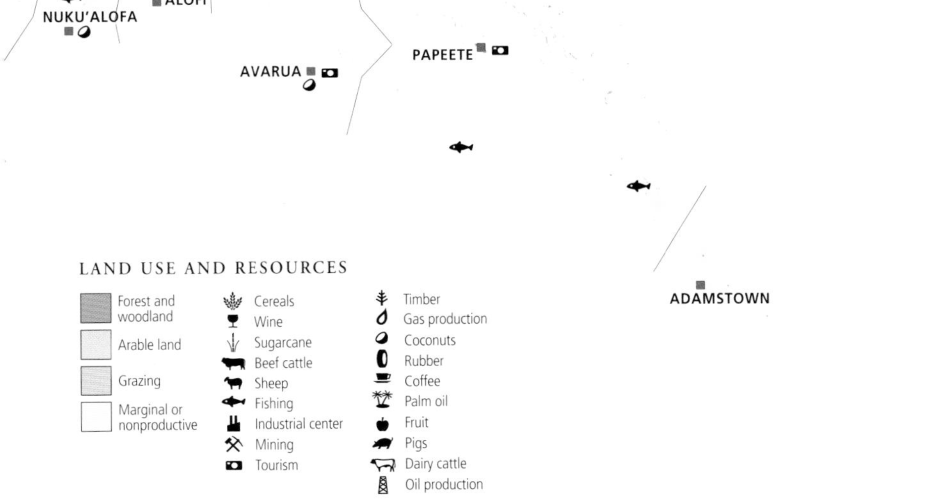
Banana
AIAKU
Ā 'UTU
APIA
PAGO PAGO
ALOFI
NUKU'ALOFA
AVARUA
PAPEETE
Atuona
ADAMSTOWN
LAND USE AND RESOURCES
Forest and woodland
Arable land
Grazing
Marginal or nonproductive
Cereals
Wine
Sugarcane
Beef cattle
Sheep
Fishing
Industrial center
Mining
Tourism
Timber
Gas production
Coconuts
Rubber
Coffee
Palm oil
Fruit
Pigs
Dairy cattle
Oil production

Threats to the Environment

Environmental damage increased greatly following the arrival of Europeans. Forest clearance and the hooves of livestock acclerated erosion; intensive farming of fragile soils resulted in plummeting fertility; and introduced species decimated native ecosystems. Australia now has the world's highest rate of mammalian extinctions; many New Zealand native species survive only on isolated islands; and introduced plant species predominate on many Pacific islands. Since Europeans arrived, more than 40 percent of Australia's original forests have been cleared, and forest cover in New Zealand has fallen from 70 to 16 percent. As a result of corruption, most notably in Papua New Guinea, foreign logging companies have been able to illegally harvest ancient rain forests. Waterways throughout Melanesia have been contaminated by waste from mining operations. Human waste disposal is problematic on remote, densely populated islands: water-borne diseases are the leading cause of death on Kiribati, and in Ebey Lagoon in the Marshall Islands pollution levels are 25,000 times higher than standard safety levels. Due to depletion of stratospheric ozone, ultraviolet levels in Australia and New Zealand are rising by about 10 percent each decade, significantly increasing the risk of skin cancer.

Left: Toxic waste from the Australian-operated Ok Tedi gold mine in Papua New Guinea has destroyed large areas of rain forest and poisoned fish and plants in the Fly, the country's longest river.

Left: Sea levels could rise by up to 3 feet (1 m) over the next century. This would spell disaster for densely inhabited, low-lying island groups such as Tuvalu, which rises just 12 feet (4 m) above sea level.

Right: Over 40 percent of Pacific coral reefs are threatened by pollution, urban development, tourism, and destructive exotic species such as the crown-of-thorns starfish.

Protecting the Environment

In the 1990s, Australian conservation and farming organizations established a coordinated farmland-management program called Landcare, designed to halt degradation. It has now been extended to cover other environments, including bushland, rivers, sand dunes, and coastline. Sustainable forestry practices are now the norm in Australia and New Zealand, and plantation forests are a major source of timber, providing, for example, 99 percent of annual roundwood output in New Zealand. The Pacific Islands Forum Fisheries Agency has had notable success in promoting sustainable fisheries throughout the region. Interest in alternative energy is growing: Vanuatu has declared it will switch to renewable sources by 2020. Overall, Oceania has the lowest proportion of human-dominated land after Antarctica, and the number of protected areas has grown sevenfold since 1960—the proportion of protected land, 7.1 percent, is just above the world average. The majority of states and territories in Oceania have also declared their waters to be whale sanctuaries.

PERCENTAGE OF LAND PROTECTED IN MAJOR COUNTRIES OF OCEANIA

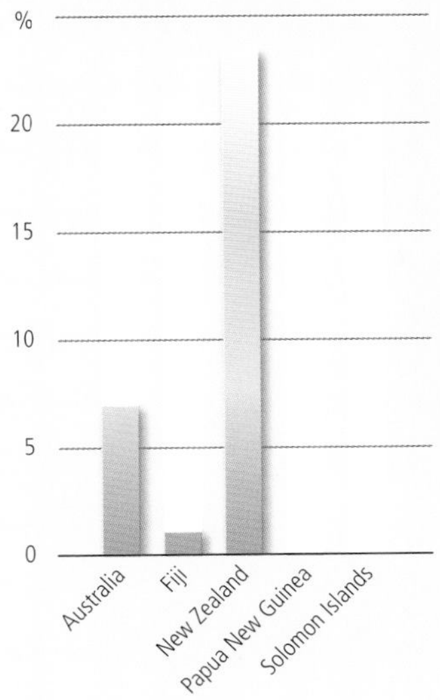
%
20
15
10
5
0
Australia
Fiji
New Zealand
Papua New Guinea
Solomon Islands

New Zealand's national parks help protect remnant populations of native flightless bird species, which have been easy prey for introduced predators. The ground-dwelling kakapo, the world's heaviest parrot, survives only on two small island reserves. As of 2003, just 86 kakapo remained.

AUSTRALIA

The world's sixth-largest country by area, Australia constitutes an entire continent—the world's smallest, flattest, and (after Antarctica) driest. Its massive landmass consists of an ancient western plateau joined by broad sedimentary lowlands to heavily eroded eastern ranges. Known as the Great Dividing Range, the ranges parallel the Pacific coast, separating the better-watered eastern seaboard from the vast, arid interior or "outback." Despite the continent's poor soils and harsh climate, Aboriginal peoples lived off the land for 60,000 years, developing one of the world's most enduring societies. Europeans began arriving only in the late 18th century after the founding of a British penal colony at Port Jackson, now Sydney, in 1788. This and other British colonies drew increasing numbers of free settlers, especially after the discovery of gold in the southeast in the mid-19th century. In 1901, the colonies agreed to federation, resulting in the creation of the independent nation of Australia.

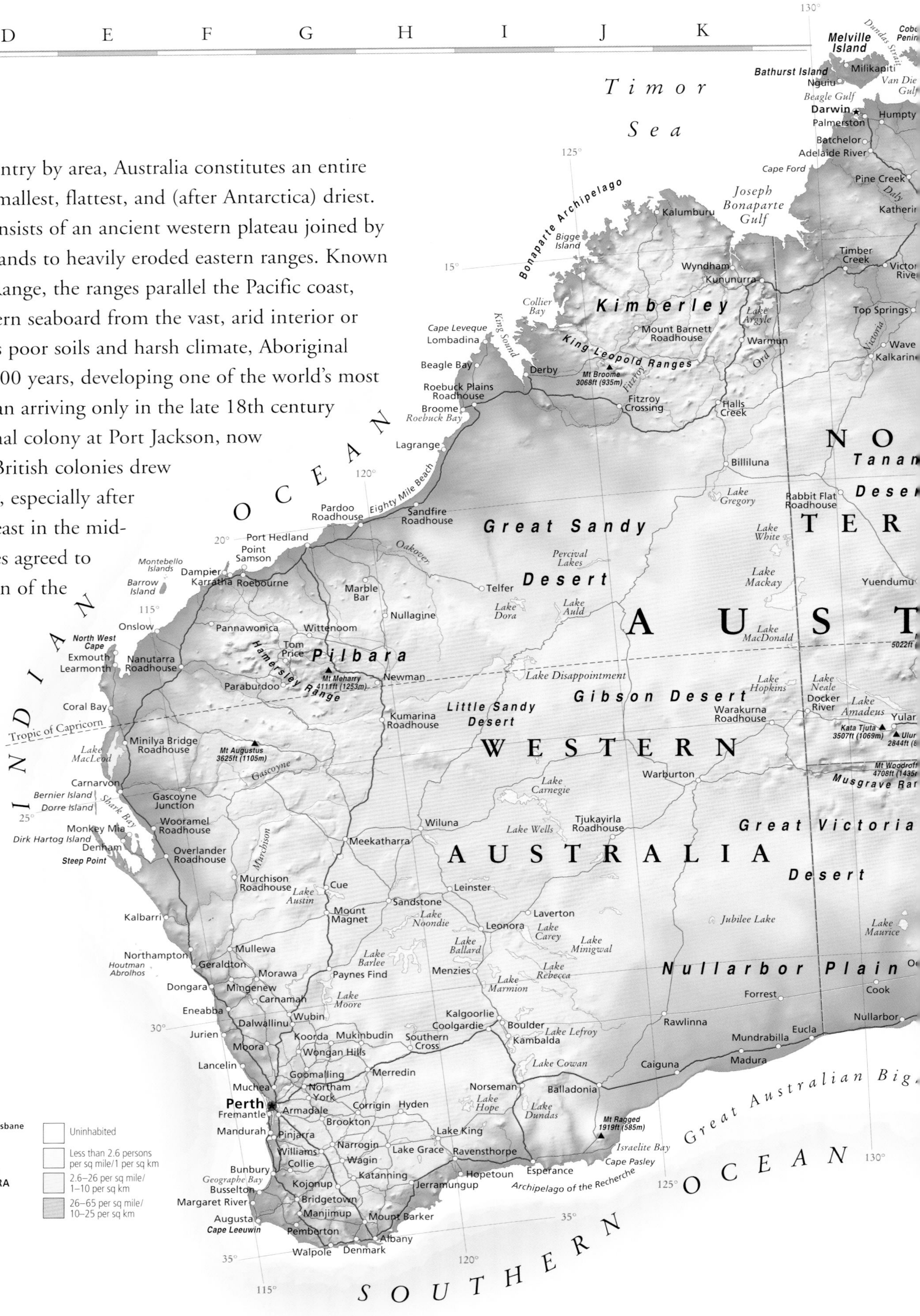

Timor Sea
INDIAN OCEAN
SOUTHERN OCEAN
WESTERN AUSTRALIA
Kimberley
King Leopold Ranges
Great Sandy Desert
Pilbara
Hamersley Range
Gibson Desert
Little Sandy Desert
Great Victoria Desert
Nullarbor Plain
Great Australian Bight
Tropic of Capricorn
Joseph Bonaparte Gulf
Bonaparte Archipelago
Darwin
Perth
Fremantle
Broome
Port Hedland
Kalgoorlie
Esperance
Albany
Geraldton
Carnarvon
Mt Meharry 4111ft (1253m)
Mt Augustus 3625ft (1105m)
Mt Ragged 1919ft (585m)
Longitude east of Greenwich

POPULATION PATTERNS

Recent settlers have shunned the interior, clustering along the temperate east and southwest coasts, where 84 percent of Australians occupy one percent of the land. In the outback, vast areas are devoid of people. Although immigration from Asia has risen in the last 30 years, the majority of Australians are still of European, especially British, origin and English is the official language. Aboriginal and Torres Strait Islander peoples constitute just 2.4 percent of the population. Birth rates are low, and it is estimated that by 2035 immigration will be the country's only source of growth.

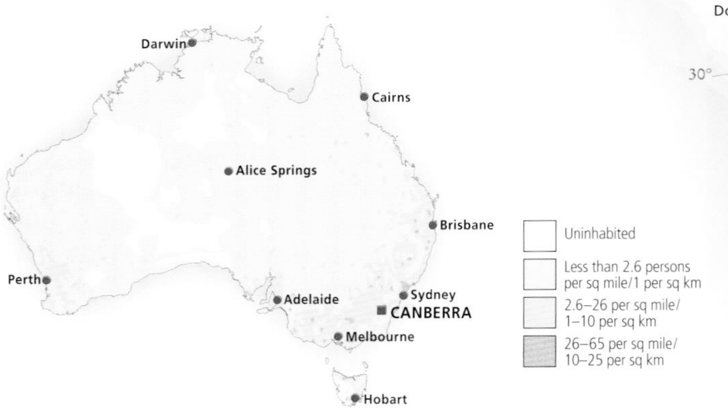

Darwin
Cairns
Alice Springs
Brisbane
Perth
Adelaide
Sydney
CANBERRA
Melbourne
Hobart
Uninhabited
Less than 2.6 persons per sq mile/1 per sq km
2.6–26 per sq mile/ 1–10 per sq km
26–65 per sq mile/ 10–25 per sq km

Darwin
Cairns
Alice Springs
Brisbane
Perth
Adelaide
Sydney
CANBERRA
Melbourne
Hobart
Cereals
Wine
Sugarcane
Beef cattle
Sheep
Fishing
Industrial center
Mining
Tourism
Timber
Gas production
Oil production
Forest and woodland
Arable land
Grazing
Marginal or nonproductive

ECONOMIC PROFILE

Australia's economy was founded on agriculture, especially the wool industry, and mining. Arable land is limited to the temperate zones and irrigated areas along major rivers. Wheat is the largest crop and Australia is the world's third-largest exporter. The country is self-sufficient in natural gas and has the world's largest reserves of lead, uranium, silver, and zinc. It is also estimated to have 40 percent of world bauxite supplies and at least 20 percent of world coal, iron-ore, and diamond reserves. These resources support heavy industries such as the manufacture of steel, machinery, cars, and chemicals, but services, including a thriving retail trade, banking, and tourism, employ 70 percent of the workforce.

Founded in 1939, the Royal Flying Doctor Service provides medical services to people in remote outback communities.

Arafura Sea
Gulf of Carpentaria
Arnhem Land
Cape York Peninsula
Coral Sea
Great Barrier Reef
Great Dividing Range
Barkly Tableland
Gregory Range
Simpson Desert
Sturt Stony Desert
PACIFIC OCEAN
Tasman Sea
Bass Strait
QUEENSLAND
NEW SOUTH WALES
VICTORIA
SOUTH AUSTRALIA
TASMANIA
Tropic of Capricorn
Brisbane
Sydney
CANBERRA
Melbourne
Adelaide
Hobart
Townsville
Cairns
Rockhampton
Newcastle
Wollongong
Alice Springs
Mount Isa
Flinders Ranges
Lake Eyre North
Lake Eyre South
Lake Torrens
Lake Frome
Kangaroo Island
King Island
Flinders Island
Cape York
Fraser Island
Mt Kosciuszko 7310ft (2228m)
Mt Bogong 6516ft (1986m)
Mt Ossa 5305ft (1617m)
Bartle Frere 5322ft (1622m)
St Mary Peak 3838ft (1170m)
Mt Barrington 5105ft (1556m)
ELEVATION
Feet Meters
6562 2000
4921 1500
3281 1000
2461 750
1640 500
1312 400
984 300
656 200
328 100
0 0
Below sea level
656 200
3281 1000
6562 2000
13,123 4000
19,685 6000
26,246 8000
32,808 10,000
SCALE 1:11,500,000
Lamberts Conformal Conic Projection
0 300 miles
0 300 kilometers

THE GREAT DIVIDING RANGE

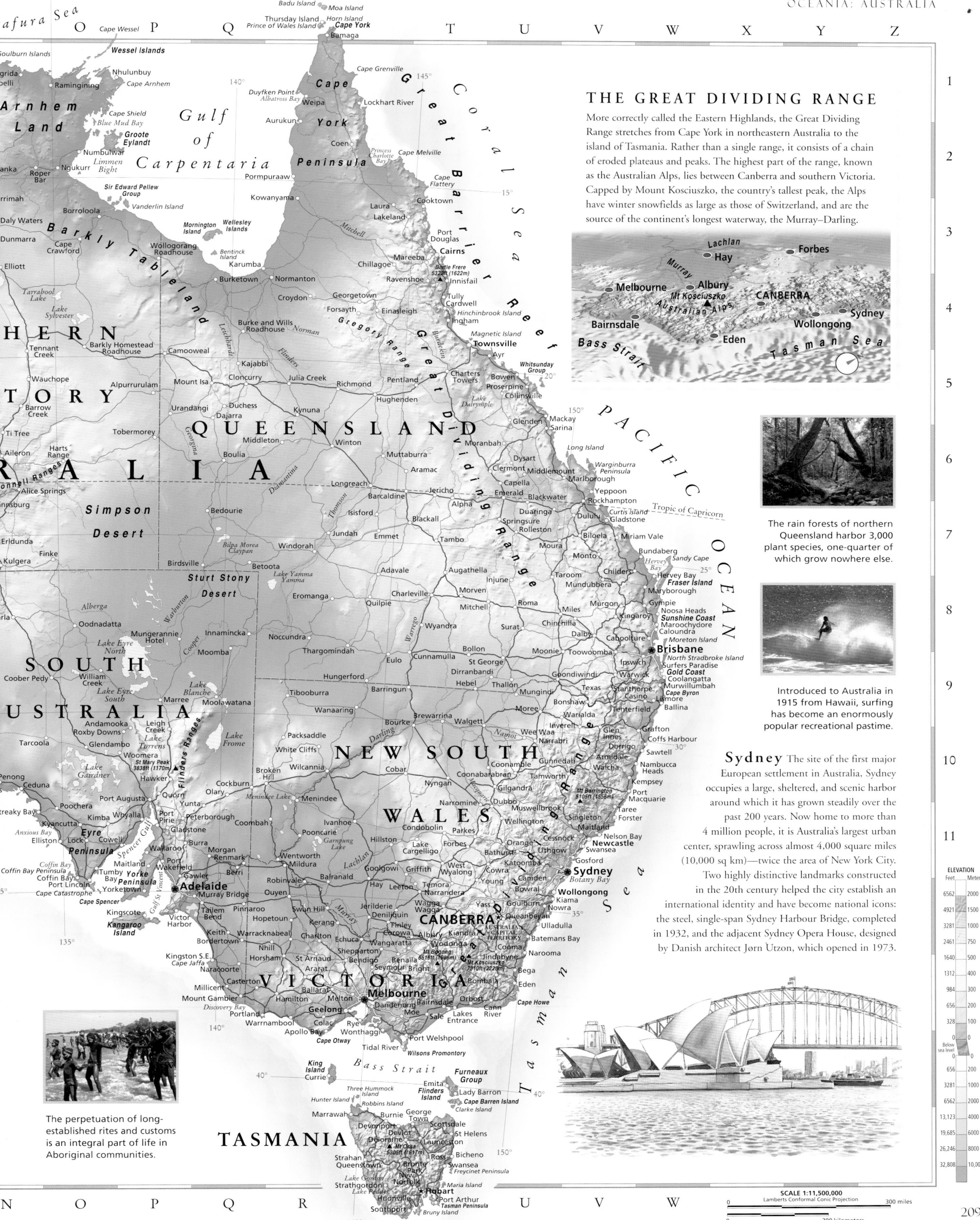

More correctly called the Eastern Highlands, the Great Dividing Range stretches from Cape York in northeastern Australia to the island of Tasmania. Rather than a single range, it consists of a chain of eroded plateaus and peaks. The highest part of the range, known as the Australian Alps, lies between Canberra and southern Victoria. Capped by Mount Kosciuszko, the country's tallest peak, the Alps have winter snowfields as large as those of Switzerland, and are the source of the continent's longest waterway, the Murray–Darling.

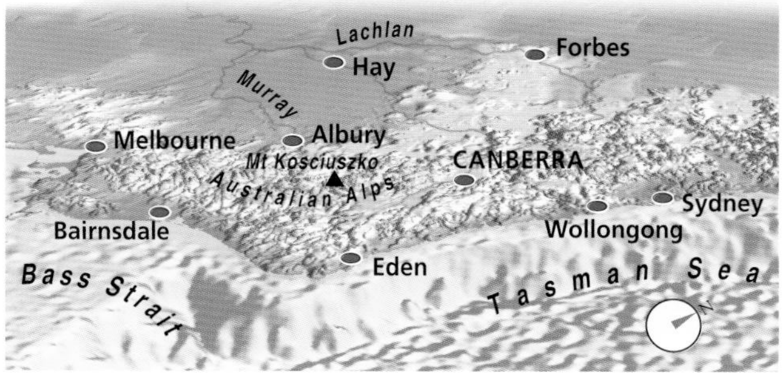

Lachlan
Hay
Forbes
Murray
Albury
Melbourne
Mt Kosciuszko
Australian Alps
CANBERRA
Sydney
Bairnsdale
Wollongong
Eden
Bass Strait
Tasman Sea

The rain forests of northern Queensland harbor 3,000 plant species, one-quarter of which grow nowhere else.

Introduced to Australia in 1915 from Hawaii, surfing has become an enormously popular recreational pastime.

Sydney The site of the first major European settlement in Australia, Sydney occupies a large, sheltered, and scenic harbor around which it has grown steadily over the past 200 years. Now home to more than 4 million people, it is Australia's largest urban center, sprawling across almost 4,000 square miles (10,000 sq km)—twice the area of New York City. Two highly distinctive landmarks constructed in the 20th century helped the city establish an international identity and have become national icons: the steel, single-span Sydney Harbour Bridge, completed in 1932, and the adjacent Sydney Opera House, designed by Danish architect Jørn Utzon, which opened in 1973.

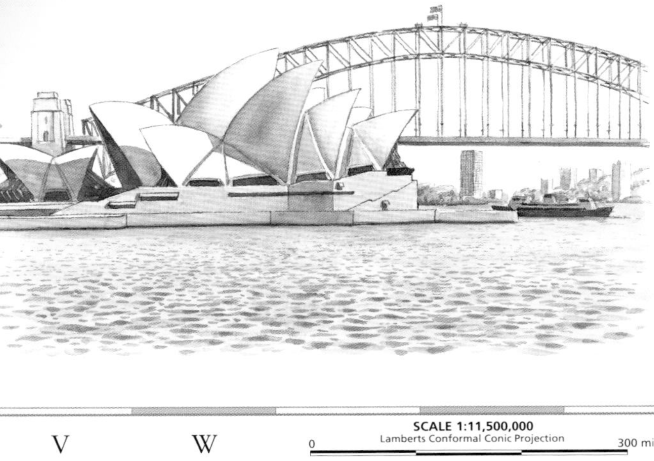

The perpetuation of long-established rites and customs is an integral part of life in Aboriginal communities.

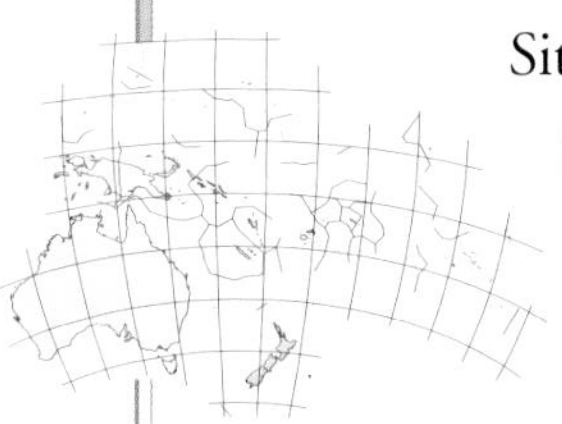

NEW ZEALAND

Situated 1,000 miles (1,600 km) southeast of Australia, its nearest neighbor, New Zealand consists of two large islands and several smaller ones. Both main islands straddle fault lines between the Indo-Australian and Pacific tectonic plates. Movement along these faults causes sporadic earthquakes and has formed active volcanoes and geysers in the North Island; over millions of years, it has also pushed up the steep-sided peaks of the Southern Alps, which form the backbone of the South Island. This rugged interior and the South Island's generally cold, wet climate concentrated the development of modern infrastructure in the North Island and along the drier, more fertile east coast of the South Island. Annexed by Britain in 1840, New Zealand became a self-governing colony in 1856 and a dominion in 1907, but did not achieve full independence until 1947. The descendants of British colonists now far outnumber the indigenous Maori, but Maori remains an official language and in recent years the government has made some reparations to Maori peoples for loss of traditional lands.

Wellington Though Auckland is by far the largest city in New Zealand, Wellington is the country's national capital and major business center. The city occupies a large sheltered harbor—the flooded crater of an ancient volcano—at the southern end of the North Island. Europeans arrived in 1840 and moved their seat of government here in 1865. The foreshore, much of it reclaimed land, is the site of the commercial district and major government buildings including the parliament, with its distinctive executive office building, widely known as the Beehive. Designed by British architect Sir Basil Spence, it was begun in 1969 and completed in 1980.

ELEVATION
Feet Meters
6562 2000
4921 1500
3281 1000
2461 750
1640 500
1312 400
984 300
656 200
328 100
0 0
Below sea level
0 0
656 200
3281 1000
6562 2000
13,123 4000
19,685 6000
26,246 8000
32,808 10,000
PACIFIC OCEAN
North Island
NORTHLAND
AUCKLAND
WAIKATO
BAY OF PLENTY
GISBORNE
TARANAKI
HAWKE'S BAY
Three Kings Islands
Cape Reinga
Cape Maria van Diemen
Spirits Bay
North Cape
Parengarenga Harbour
Great Exhibition Bay
Te Kao
Houhora
Rangaunu Bay
Cape Karikari
Doubtless Bay
Waiharara
Mangonui
Cavalli Islands
Bay of Islands
Cape Brett
Awanui
Kahoe
Kaeo
Ahipara Bay
Tauroa Point
Ahipara
Mangamuka
Kerikeri
Paihia
Herekino
Okaihau
Kawakawa
Oakura
Poor Knights Islands
Whirinaki
Kaikohe
Hokianga Harbour
Te Raupa 2539ft (774m)
Awarua
Whakapara
Hikurangi
Katui
Maungatapere
Whangarei
Otaika
Ocean Beach
Maropiu
Dargaville
Ruakaka
Bream Bay
Waipu
Hen and Chickens Islands
Paparoa
Brynderwyn
Koremoa
Ruawai
Topuni
Mangawhai
Port Fitzroy
Great Barrier Island
Cradock Channel
Jellicoe Channel
Wellsford
Cape Barrier
North Head
Kaipara Harbour
Warkworth
Leigh
Kawau Island
Colville Channel
Moehau 2927ft (892m)
Cape Colville
Great Mercury Island
Mercury Islands
Orewa
Silverdale
Colville
Helensville
Albany
Hauraki Gulf
Waiheke Island
Coromandel
Takapuna
Mercury Bay
Waitakere
Auckland
Howick
Whenuakite
Manukau
Firth of Thames
Coromandel Peninsula
Coromandel Range
Tairua
Manukau Harbour
Pollok
Thames
Pukekohe
Pokeno
Waitakaruru
Whangamata
Waiuku
Tuakau
Mayor Island
Port Waikato
Meremere
Paeroa
Waihi
Rangiriri
Tahuna
Katikati
Matakana Island
Pepepe
Taupiri
Motiti Island
Mount Maunganui
White Island
Bay of Plenty
Cape Runaway
Whangaparaoa
Matakaoa Point
Horotiu
Morrinsville
Raglan
Hamilton
Waharoa
Tauranga
Te Kaha
Te Araroa
East Cape
Matamata
Te Puke
Karamu
Cambridge
Matata
Houpoto
Tikitiki
Ohaupo
Edgecumbe
Whakatane
Ruatoria
Kawhia
Kihikihi
Tirau
Kawhia Harbour
Albatross Point
Lake Rotorua
Mourea
Te Teko
Opotiki
Kutarere
Putaruru
Lake Tarawera
Raukumara Range
Hikurangi 5755ft (1754m)
Rotorua
Otorohanga
Tokoroa
Tokomaru Bay
Kiritehere
Tirua Point
Te Kuiti
Waiotapu
Marau Point
Mangakino
Whakamaru
Kopaki
Piopio
Murupara
Matawai
Te Karaka
Tolaga Bay
Mahoenui
Tihoi
Kinloch
Huiarau Range
Waihau Bay
Awakino
Ruatahuna
Waihirere
Whangara
Tuhua
Ongarue
Taupo
Makaraka
Gisborne
North Taranaki Bight
Ohura
Lake Taupo
Waitahanui
Poverty Bay
Ahititi
Taumarunui
Rangitaiki
Tuai
Muriwai
Motunui
Kotare
Tokirima
New Plymouth
Tahora
Papakai
Turangi
Frasertown
Nuhaka
Oakura
Whangamomona
Mt Tongariro 6457ft (1968m)
Rangipo
Tarawera
Mahia
Inglewood
Mt Ngauruhoe 7503ft (2287m)
Putorino
Wairoa
Mt Taranaki (Mt Egmont) 8261ft (2518m)
Mt Ruapehu 9176ft (2797m)
Kaweka 5656ft (1724m)
Te Pohue
Te Kapu 1214ft (370m)
Mahia Peninsula
Stratford
Raetihi
Ohakune
Tangoio
Hawke Bay
Portland Island
Eltham
Pipiriki
Waiouru
Bay View
Opunake
Napier
Hawera
Taradale
MANAWATU-

VOLCANO COUNTRY

Volcanic activity has fashioned the landscape of the North Island's central plateau and still has the potential to modify it further. Lake Taupo, the country's largest lake, occupies a crater formed by a massive volcanic explosion thought to have taken place in AD 186. To its south stretches a line of active volcanoes—Tongariro, Ngauruhoe, and Ruapehu—all of which erupted in the 20th century. In 1996, in the country's largest eruption in 400 years, Ruapehu spewed great clouds of steam and ash over the surrounding skifields; fortunately, there were no casualties. Farther west, the huge cone of Mount Taranaki (Mount Egmont) looms over the southwestern corner of the island. Now dormant, it last erupted in the 18th century.

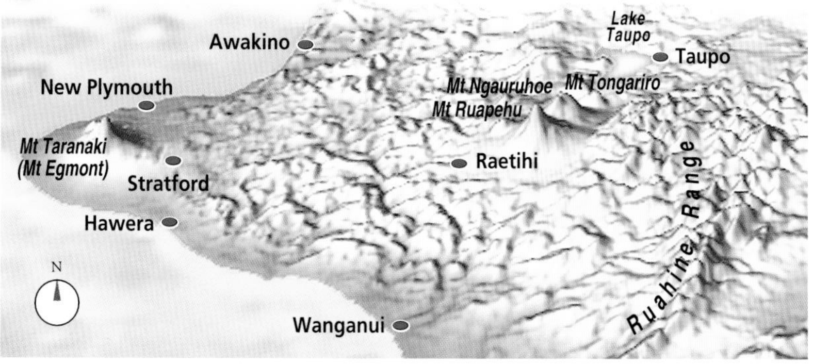

Awakino
Lake Taupo
Taupo
New Plymouth
Mt Ngauruhoe
Mt Tongariro
Mt Ruapehu
Mt Taranaki (Mt Egmont)
Stratford
Raetihi
Hawera
Ruahine Range
N
Wanganui

Geothermal activity is concentrated around Rotorua in the North Island.

Home to approximately 1 million people, Auckland occupies an isthmus between two broad harbors.

NEW ZEALAND

The traditional welcome dance, or powhiri, is still performed for visitors to Maori meeting houses.

In the western South Island, Franz Josef Glacier (above) and Fox Glacier descend as far as the coastal lowlands.

The southwest coast of the South Island is characterized by deep fjords, including spectacular Milford Sound.

South Island
Tasman Sea
PACIFIC OCEAN
Southern Alps
WELLINGTON
Christchurch
Dunedin
Invercargill
Queenstown
Stewart Island
Cook Strait
Foveaux Strait
Canterbury Bight
Canterbury Plains
Fiordland
SOUTHLAND
OTAGO
CANTERBURY
WEST COAST
TASMAN
NELSON
MARLBOROUGH
Mt Cook 12,316ft (3754m)
Cape Farewell
Golden Bay
Tasman Bay
Banks Peninsula
Milford Sound
Longitude east of Greenwich
SCALE 1:3,250,000
Lamberts Conformal Conic Projection
100 miles
100 kilometers

Population Patterns

The North Island constitutes 42 percent of the country but is home to more than three-quarters of the population; indeed, more than 30 percent of New Zealanders live in the Auckland region. About 75 percent of inhabitants live in towns and cities. People of European extraction make up 80 percent of the population, and one in seven New Zealanders is Maori. Ethnic diversity is increasing. The number of residents of Asian origin, for example, climbed 140 percent between 1991 and 2001. Many Pacific Islander people have settled in New Zealand, and Auckland is recognized as the world's largest Polynesian city.

Uninhabited
Less than 2.6 persons per sq mile/1 per sq km
2.6–26 per sq mile/ 1–10 per sq km
26–65 per sq mile/ 10–25 per sq km
Auckland
Hamilton
Napier
WELLINGTON
Christchurch
Queenstown
Dunedin
Invercargill

Cathedral Square is the heart of the South Island's largest city, Christchurch.

Economic Profile

New Zealand has a long association with wool, which was the country's leading agricultural product until the late 1970s. But the sheep population has declined, and dairy products and meat are now the nation's most valuable exports. Forests cover 30 percent of the country and forest products, overwhelmingly from plantations, constitute the third most lucrative export. New Zealand is self-sufficient in all energy sources except oil; two-thirds of its electricity comes from hydroelectric power and over 6 percent from geothermal power. Leading industries include foods and beverages (notably wine), machinery, metals, and textiles. However, services employ 65 percent of workers, with tourism alone generating 10 percent of GDP and supporting one in ten jobs.

Forest and woodland
Arable land
Grazing
Marginal or nonproductive
Fruit
Wine
Beef cattle
Sheep
Pigs
Fishing
Industrial center
Timber
Dairy cattle
Tourism
Auckland
Hamilton
Napier
WELLINGTON
Christchurch
Queenstown
Dunedin
Invercargill

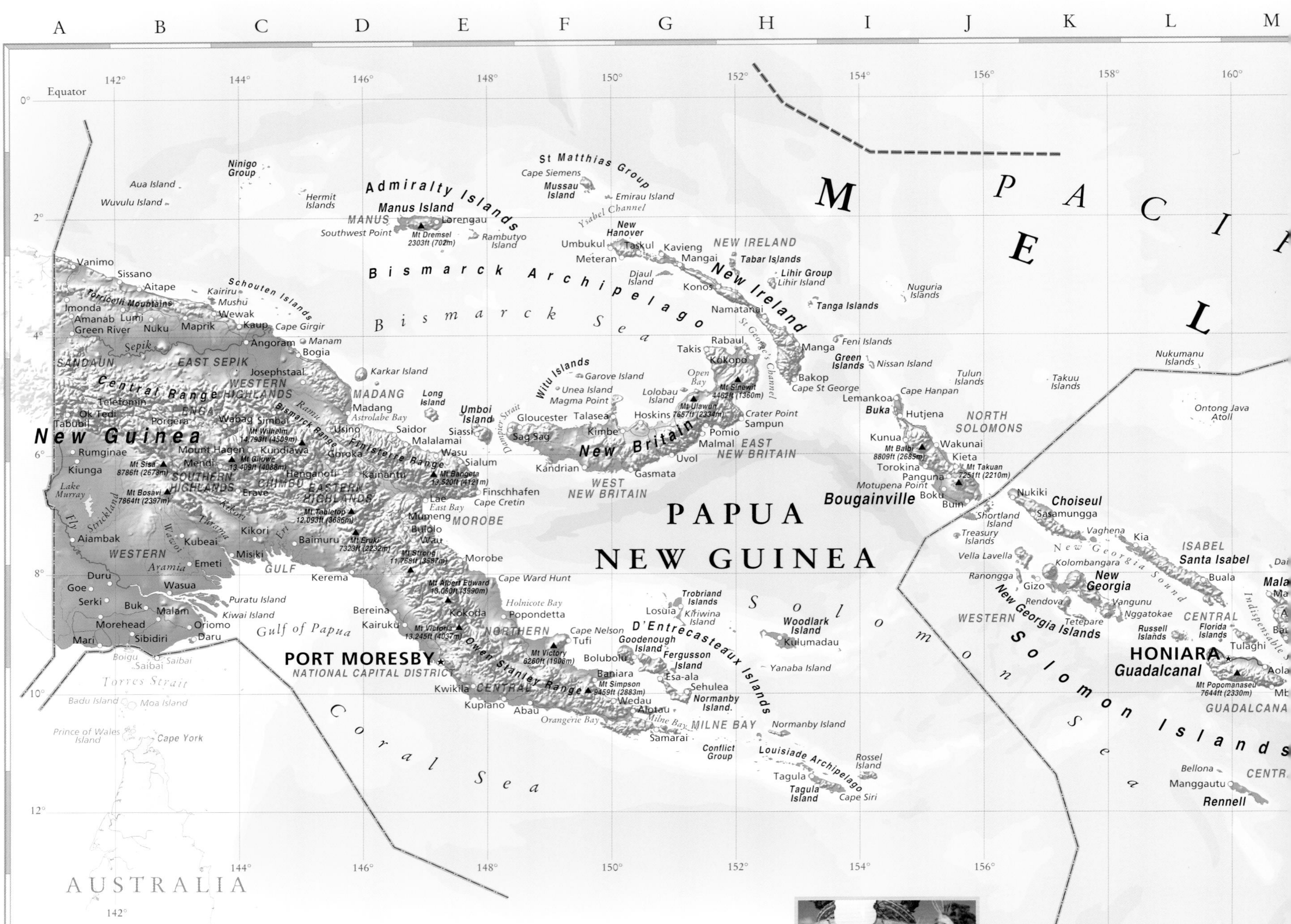

Equator
Aua Island
Wuvulu Island
Ninigo Group
Hermit Islands
Admiralty Islands
Manus Island
MANUS
Lorengau
Southwest Point
Mt Dremsel 2303ft (702m)
Rambutyo Island
St Matthias Group
Cape Siemens
Mussau Island
Emirau Island
Ysabel Channel
New Hanover
Taskul
Umbukul
Meteran
Kavieng
Mangai
NEW IRELAND
Tabar Islands
Lihir Group
Lihir Island
New Ireland
Djaul Island
Konos
Namatanai
Tanga Islands
Nuguria Islands
Bismarck Archipelago
Bismarck Sea
Vanimo
Sissano
Aitape
Schouten Islands
Kairiru
Mushu
Wewak
Torricelli Mountains
Imonda
Amanab
Lumi
Green River
Nuku
Maprik
Kaup
Cape Girgir
Sepik
Angoram
Manam
Bogia
SANDAUN
EAST SEPIK
Karkar Island
Josephstaal
WESTERN HIGHLANDS
Central Range
Telefomin
Ok Tedi
Tabubil
ENGA
Porgera
Wabag
Simbai
Mt Wilhelm 14,793ft (4509m)
MADANG
Madang
Astrolabe Bay
Long Island
Umboi Island
Dampier Strait
Saidor
Malalamai
Usino
Siassi
Gloucester
Talasea
Sag Sag
Kimbe
New Britain
Kandrian
WEST NEW BRITAIN
Gasmata
Uvol
Malmal
EAST NEW BRITAIN
Pomio
Hoskins
Lolobau Island
Witu Islands
Garove Island
Unea Island
Magma Point
Open Bay
Rabaul
Kokopo
Takis
St George's Channel
Mt Ulawun 7657ft (2334m)
Mt Sinewit 4462ft (1360m)
Crater Point
Sampun
Manga
Feni Islands
Green Islands
Nissan Island
Bakop
Cape St George
Lemankoa
Buka
Cape Hanpan
Hutjena
NORTH SOLOMONS
Tulun Islands
Takuu Islands
Nukumanu Islands
Ontong Java Atoll
Kunua
Mt Balbi 8809ft (2685m)
Wakunai
Kieta
Torokina
Panguna
Mt Takuan 7251ft (2210m)
Motupena Point
Bougainville
Boku
Buin
New Guinea
Rumginae
Kiunga
Mount Hagen
Mendi
Kundiawa
Mt Sisa 8786ft (2678m)
Mt Giluwe 14,409ft (4088m)
SOUTHERN HIGHLANDS
CHIMBU
Goroka
EASTERN HIGHLANDS
Henganofi
Kainantu
Bismarck Range
Finisterre Range
Ramu
Wasu
Sialum
Mt Bangeta 13,520ft (4121m)
Finschhafen
Cape Cretin
Lae
East Bay
Lake Murray
Mt Bosavi 7864ft (2397m)
Erave
Strickland
Kikori
Fly
Aiambak
Kubeai
Mt Tabletop 12,093ft (3686m)
Mumeng
Bulolo
Wau
MOROBE
Baimuru
Mt Sruki 7323ft (2232m)
Mt Strong 11,768ft (3587m)
Morobe
WESTERN
Aramia
Emeti
Kikori
Misiki
GULF
Kerema
Duru
Goe
Wasua
Serki
Buk
Malam
Morehead
Mari
Sibidiri
Oriomo
Daru
Purari Island
Kiwai Island
Gulf of Papua
Mt Albert Edward 13,090ft (3990m)
Cape Ward Hunt
Holnicote Bay
Popondetta
Kokoda
Bereina
Kairuku
Mt Victoria 13,245ft (4037m)
NORTHERN
Owen Stanley Range
PORT MORESBY
NATIONAL CAPITAL DISTRICT
Kwikila
CENTRAL
Kupiano
Abau
Orangerie Bay
Cape Nelson
Tufi
Mt Victory 6260ft (1908m)
Bolubolu
Baniara
Mt Simpson 9459ft (2883m)
Wedau
Alotau
Milne Bay
MILNE BAY
Samarai
Boigu
Saibai
Torres Strait
Badu Island
Moa Island
Prince of Wales Island
Cape York
Coral Sea
AUSTRALIA
PAPUA NEW GUINEA
Trobriand Islands
Losuia
Kiriwina Island
D'Entrecasteaux Islands
Goodenough Island
Fergusson Island
Esa-ala
Sehulea
Normanby Island
Woodlark Island
Kulumadau
Yanaba Island
Normanby Island
Conflict Group
Louisiade Archipelago
Rossel Island
Tagula
Tagula Island
Cape Siri
Solomon Sea
MELANESIA
PACIFIC
Nukiki
Choiseul
Sasamungga
Shortland Island
Treasury Islands
Vaghena
Kia
Vella Lavella
Kolombangara
New Georgia Sound
ISABEL
Santa Isabel
Buala
Ranongga
Gizo
New Georgia
Rendova
Vangunu
Tetepare
Nggatokae
New Georgia Islands
WESTERN
Russell Islands
Florida Islands
CENTRAL
Tulaghi
Indispensable Strait
HONIARA
Guadalcanal
Mt Popomanaseu 7644ft (2330m)
GUADALCANAL
Solomon Islands
Bellona
Manggautu
Rennell
Îles Chesterfield
Tropic of Capricorn
Longitude east of Greenwich

MELANESIA

Fiji, Papua New Guinea, Solomon Islands, Vanuatu

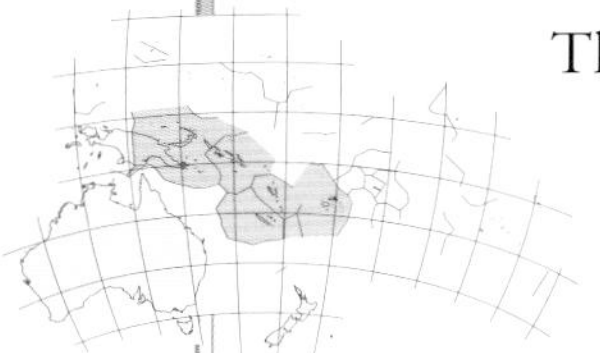

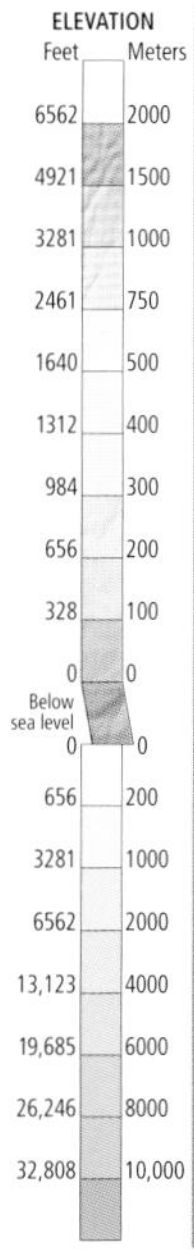

ELEVATION
Feet Meters
6562 2000
4921 1500
3281 1000
2461 750
1640 500
1312 400
984 300
656 200
328 100
0 0
Below sea level
0
656 200
3281 1000
6562 2000
13,123 4000
19,685 6000
26,246 8000
32,808 10,000

The islands of Melanesia arc around the northeast coast of Australia, extend south toward the Tropic of Capricorn and spread east to the edge of the Western Hemisphere. They lie close to the boundary between the Indo-Australian and Pacific plates and have been shaped by relatively recent tectonic activity. Most are mountainous and many have active volcanoes and dark volcanic soil—the word Melanesia derives from the Greek terms *melas* (meaning "black") and *nesoi* ("islands"). Almost all are blanketed with a dense covering of tropical rain forest, though parts of this forest have been cleared. Independence has been achieved by all of the island groups except New Caledonia, which chose to remain part of France. However, many parts of Melanesia have been politically volatile in recent years. In New Caledonia in the 1980s, indigenous Kanak people began a campaign for independence that led to sporadic violence. Coups took place in Fiji in 1987 and 2000, and in Bougainville an armed independence movement fought a war against the Papua New Guinea government from 1988 to 2001.

In the Papua New Guinea highlands, men attending festivals called sing-sings wear paint and headdresses.

Bougainville's giant Panguna copper mine was closed down during the secessionist war and has not reopened.

Fiji's picturesque islands and highly developed tourist facilities attract up to 400,000 visitors a year.

Villagers on the island of Tanna in Vanuatu perform a traditional dance in sight of Yasur, a highly active volcano.

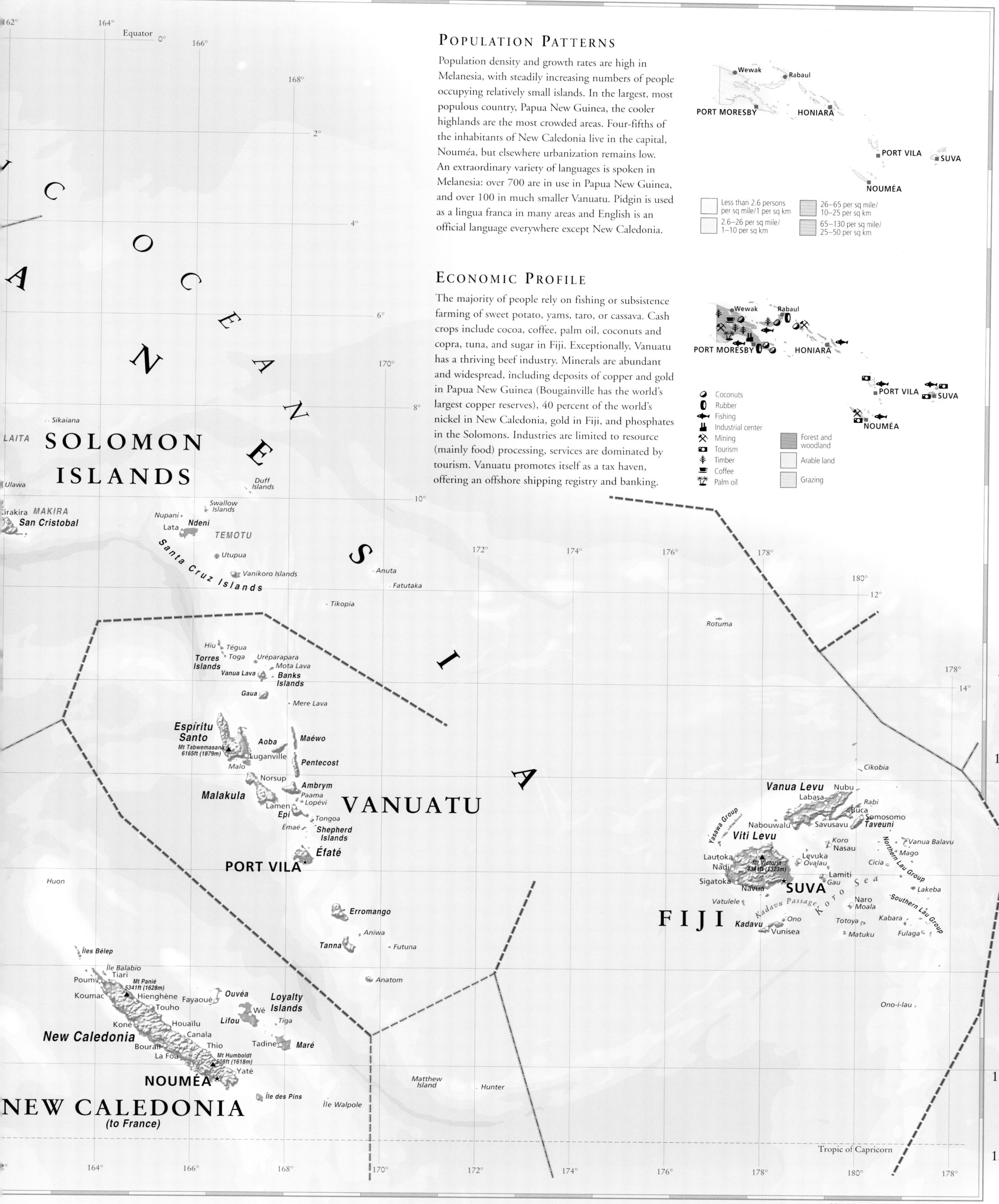

N O P Q R S T U V W X Y Z
OCEANIA
MELANESIA
SOLOMON ISLANDS
Sikaiana
Ulawa
MAKIRA
San Cristobal
Duff Islands
Swallow Islands
Nupani
Lata
Ndeni
TEMOTU
Santa Cruz Islands
Utupua
Vanikoro Islands
Anuta
Fatutaka
Tikopia
Rotuma
Hiu
Tégua
Toga
Torres Islands
Uréparapara
Mota Lava
Vanua Lava
Banks Islands
Gaua
Mere Lava
Espíritu Santo
Mt Tabwemasana 6165ft (1879m)
Aoba
Maéwo
Luganville
Malo
Pentecost
Norsup
Malakula
Ambrym
Paama
Lopévi
Lamen
Epi
Tongoa
Émaé
Shepherd Islands
VANUATU
Éfaté
PORT VILA
Erromango
Aniwa
Futuna
Tanna
Anatom
Huon
Îles Bélep
Île Balabio
Tiari
Poum
Koumac
Mt Panié 5341ft (1628m)
Hienghène
Touho
Fayaoué
Ouvéa
Loyalty Islands
Wé
Lifou
Tiga
Koné
Houaïlu
Canala
New Caledonia
Bourail
Thio
La Foa
Tadine
Maré
Mt Humboldt 5308ft (1618m)
Yaté
NOUMÉA
Île des Pins
NEW CALEDONIA
(to France)
Matthew Island
Hunter
Île Walpole
Cikobia
Vanua Levu
Nubu
Labasa
Rabi
Buca
Somosomo
Taveuni
Yasawa Group
Nabouwalu
Savusavu
Viti Levu
Koro
Nasau
Vanua Balavu
Mago
Northern Lau Group
Lautoka
Nadi
Mt Victoria 4341ft (1323m)
Levuka
Ovalau
Cicia
Sigatoka
Lamiti
Gau
Koro Sea
Lakeba
Navua
SUVA
Vatulele
Naro
Moala
Southern Lau Group
Kadavu Passage
FIJI
Kadavu
Ono
Vunisea
Totoya
Kabara
Matuku
Fulaga
Ono-i-lau
Tropic of Capricorn
Equator
SCALE 1:9,500,000
Mercator Projection
200 miles
200 kilometers
Wewak
Rabaul
PORT MORESBY
HONIARA
Less than 2.6 persons per sq mile/1 per sq km
2.6–26 per sq mile/ 1–10 per sq km
26–65 per sq mile/ 10–25 per sq km
65–130 per sq mile/ 25–50 per sq km
Coconuts
Rubber
Fishing
Industrial center
Mining
Tourism
Timber
Coffee
Palm oil
Forest and woodland
Arable land
Grazing

Population Patterns

Population density and growth rates are high in Melanesia, with steadily increasing numbers of people occupying relatively small islands. In the largest, most populous country, Papua New Guinea, the cooler highlands are the most crowded areas. Four-fifths of the inhabitants of New Caledonia live in the capital, Nouméa, but elsewhere urbanization remains low. An extraordinary variety of languages is spoken in Melanesia: over 700 are in use in Papua New Guinea, and over 100 in much smaller Vanuatu. Pidgin is used as a lingua franca in many areas and English is an official language everywhere except New Caledonia.

Economic Profile

The majority of people rely on fishing or subsistence farming of sweet potato, yams, taro, or cassava. Cash crops include cocoa, coffee, palm oil, coconuts and copra, tuna, and sugar in Fiji. Exceptionally, Vanuatu has a thriving beef industry. Minerals are abundant and widespread, including deposits of copper and gold in Papua New Guinea (Bougainville has the world's largest copper reserves), 40 percent of the world's nickel in New Caledonia, gold in Fiji, and phosphates in the Solomons. Industries are limited to resource (mainly food) processing, services are dominated by tourism. Vanuatu promotes itself as a tax haven, offering an offshore shipping registry and banking.

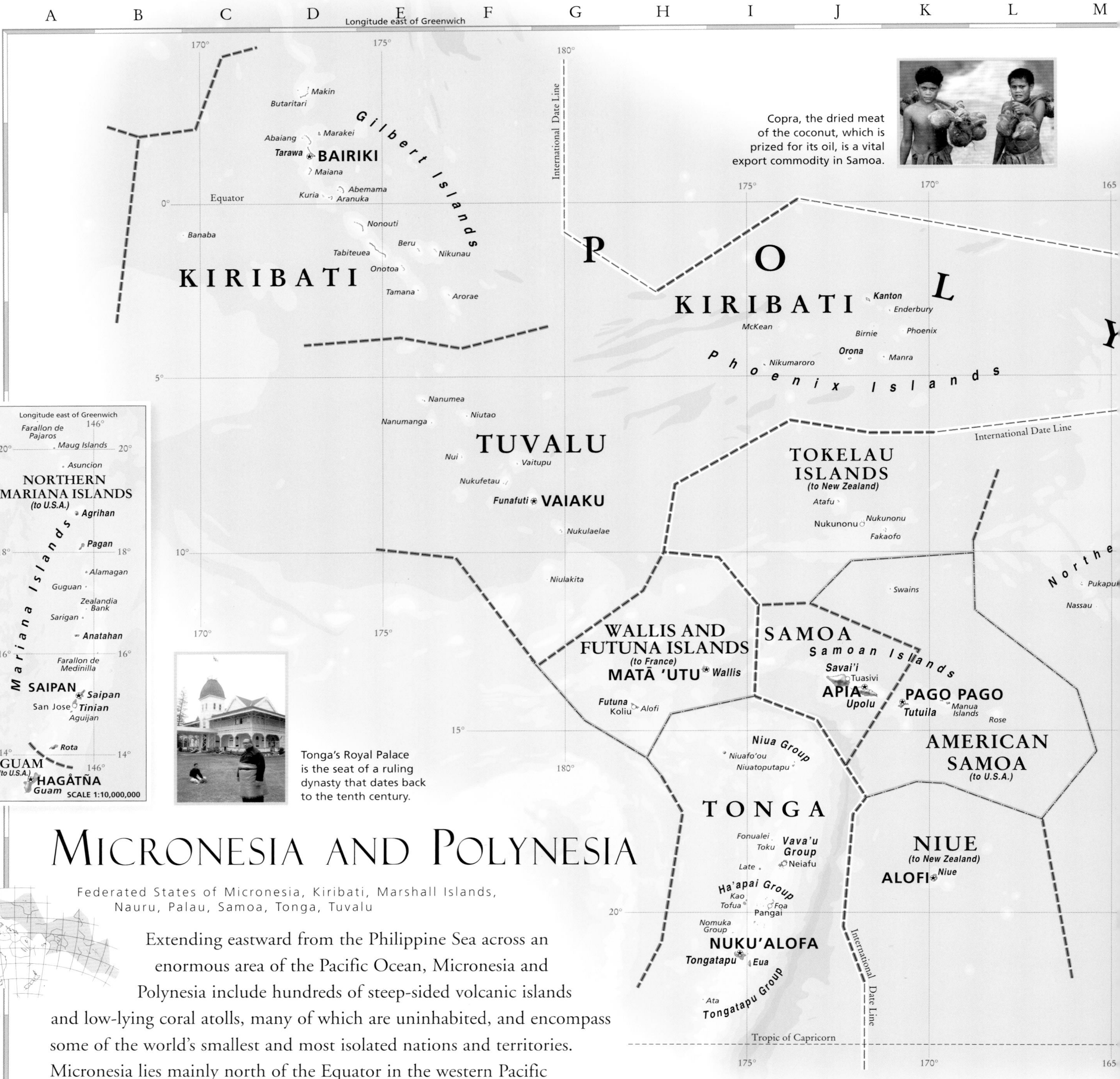

A B C D E F G H I J K L M
1 2 3 4
Longitude east of Greenwich
170° 175° 180° 175° 170° 165°
0° 5° 10° 15° 20°
International Date Line
Equator
Tropic of Capricorn
KIRIBATI
Makin
Butaritari
Gilbert Islands
Abaiang
Marakei
Tarawa
BAIRIKI
Maiana
Abemama
Kuria
Aranuka
Banaba
Nonouti
Beru
Tabiteuea
Nikunau
Onotoa
Tamana
Arorae
P O L Y
KIRIBATI
Kanton
Enderbury
McKean
Birnie
Phoenix
Orona
Nikumaroro
Manra
Phoenix Islands
Nanumea
Niutao
Nanumanga
TUVALU
Nui
Vaitupu
Nukufetau
Funafuti
VAIAKU
Nukulaelae
Niulakita
TOKELAU ISLANDS
(to New Zealand)
Atafu
Nukunonu
Nukunonu
Fakaofo
Swains
Northe
Pukapuk
Nassau
WALLIS AND FUTUNA ISLANDS
(to France)
MATĀ 'UTU
Wallis
Futuna
Koliu
Alofi
SAMOA
Samoan Islands
Savai'i
Tuasivi
APIA
Upolu
PAGO PAGO
Tutuila
Manua Islands
Rose
AMERICAN SAMOA
(to U.S.A.)
Niua Group
Niuafo'ou
Niuatoputapu
TONGA
Fonualei
Toku
Vava'u Group
Neiafu
Late
Ha'apai Group
Kao
Tofua
Foa
Pangai
Nomuka Group
NUKU'ALOFA
Tongatapu
Eua
Ata
Tongatapu Group
NIUE
(to New Zealand)
ALOFI
Niue
Longitude east of Greenwich
146°
Farallon de Pajaros
20°
Maug Islands
Asuncion
NORTHERN MARIANA ISLANDS
(to U.S.A.)
Agrihan
Pagan
18°
Alamagan
Guguan
Zealandia Bank
Sarigan
Anatahan
16°
Farallon de Medinilla
Mariana Islands
SAIPAN
Saipan
San Jose
Tinian
Aguijan
14°
Rota
GUAM
(to U.S.A.)
HAGÅTÑA
Guam
SCALE 1:10,000,000

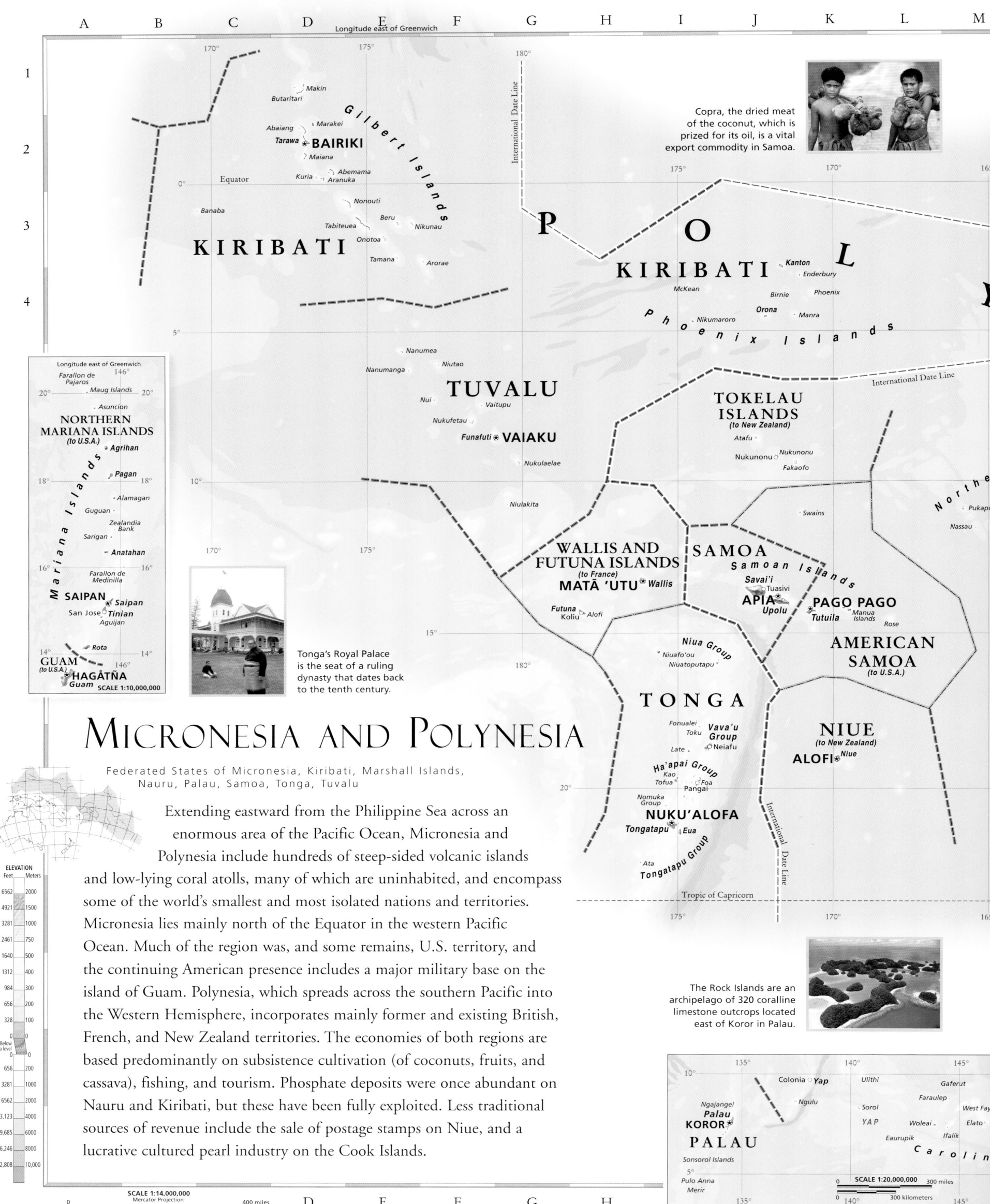

Copra, the dried meat of the coconut, which is prized for its oil, is a vital export commodity in Samoa.

Tonga's Royal Palace is the seat of a ruling dynasty that dates back to the tenth century.

Micronesia and Polynesia

Federated States of Micronesia, Kiribati, Marshall Islands, Nauru, Palau, Samoa, Tonga, Tuvalu

Extending eastward from the Philippine Sea across an enormous area of the Pacific Ocean, Micronesia and Polynesia include hundreds of steep-sided volcanic islands and low-lying coral atolls, many of which are uninhabited, and encompass some of the world's smallest and most isolated nations and territories. Micronesia lies mainly north of the Equator in the western Pacific Ocean. Much of the region was, and some remains, U.S. territory, and the continuing American presence includes a major military base on the island of Guam. Polynesia, which spreads across the southern Pacific into the Western Hemisphere, incorporates mainly former and existing British, French, and New Zealand territories. The economies of both regions are based predominantly on subsistence cultivation (of coconuts, fruits, and cassava), fishing, and tourism. Phosphate deposits were once abundant on Nauru and Kiribati, but these have been fully exploited. Less traditional sources of revenue include the sale of postage stamps on Niue, and a lucrative cultured pearl industry on the Cook Islands.

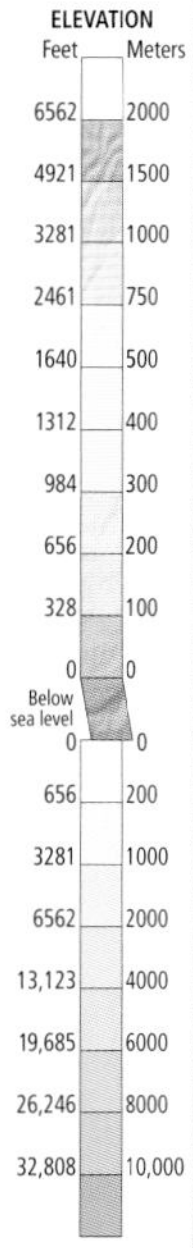

ELEVATION
Feet Meters
6562 2000
4921 1500
3281 1000
2461 750
1640 500
1312 400
984 300
656 200
328 100
0 0
Below sea level
0 0
656 200
3281 1000
6562 2000
13,123 4000
19,685 6000
26,246 8000
32,808 10,000

The Rock Islands are an archipelago of 320 coralline limestone outcrops located east of Koror in Palau.

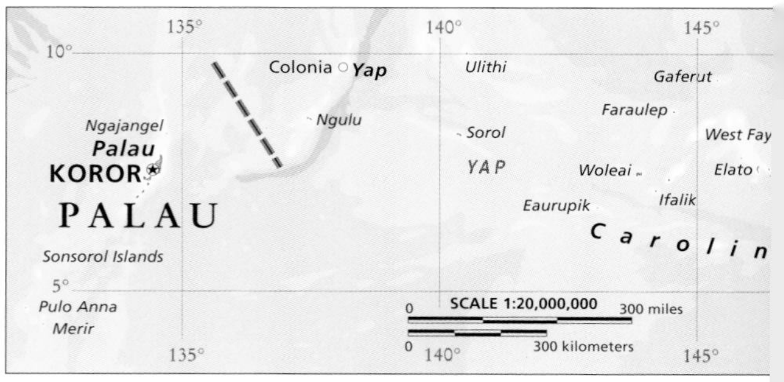

135° 140° 145°
10°
5°
Colonia
Yap
Ulithi
Gaferut
Ngulu
Faraulep
Ngajangel
Palau
KOROR
Sorol
YAP
West Fay
Woleai
Elato
PALAU
Eaurupik
Ifalik
Carolin
Sonsorol Islands
Pulo Anna
Merir
SCALE 1:20,000,000
300 miles
300 kilometers

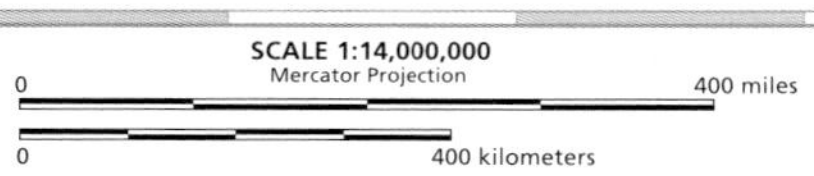

SCALE 1:14,000,000
Mercator Projection
0
400 miles
400 kilometers
D E F G H

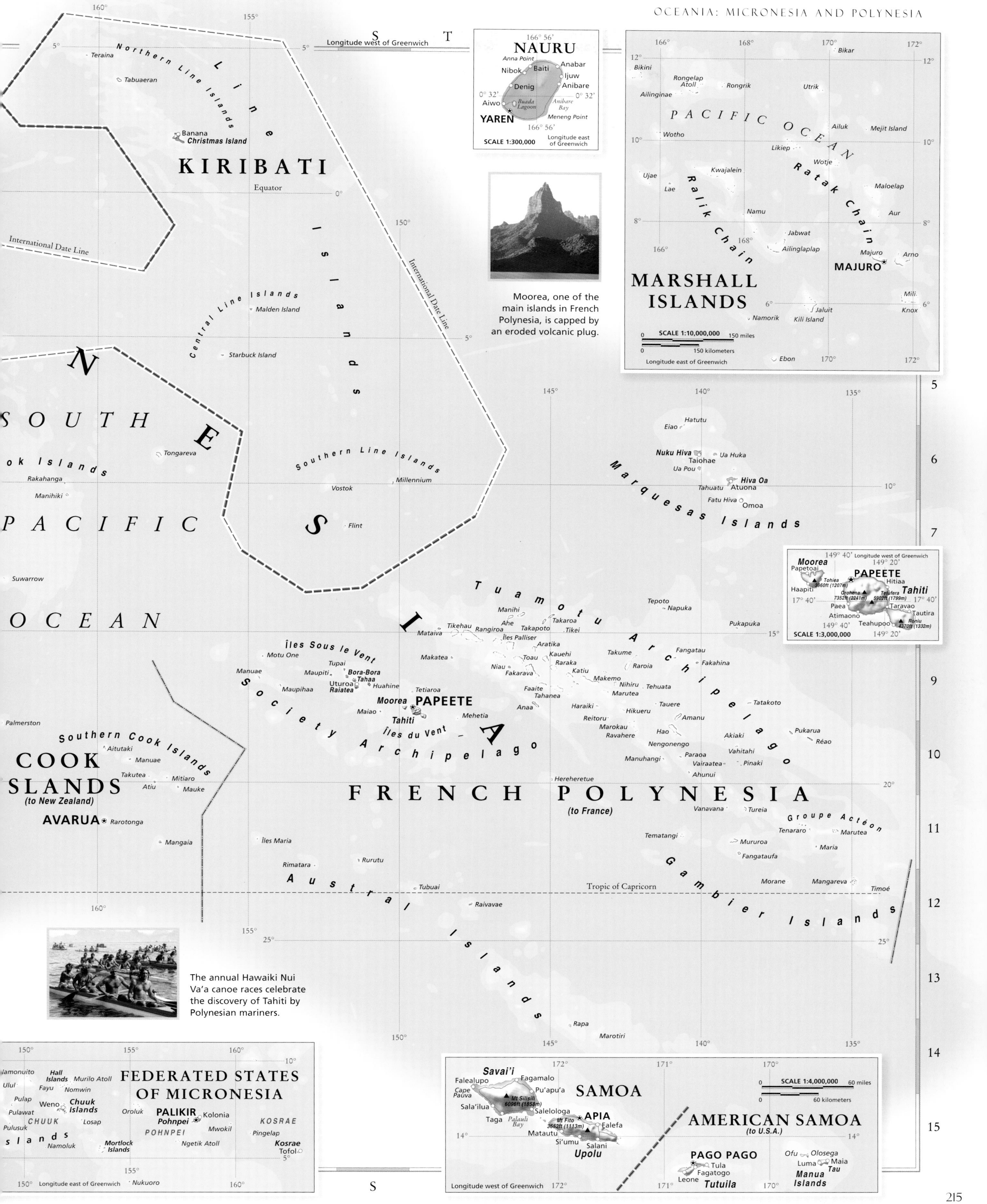

NAURU
Anna Point
Nibok
Baiti
Anabar
Ijuw
Anibare
Denig
Aiwo
Buada Lagoon
Anibare Bay
YAREN
Meneng Point
SCALE 1:300,000
Longitude east of Greenwich
MARSHALL ISLANDS
PACIFIC OCEAN
Bikar
Bikini
Rongelap Atoll
Rongrik
Utrik
Ailinginae
Wotho
Ailuk
Mejit Island
Likiep
Wotje
Ujae
Kwajalein
Lae
Maloelap
Ralik Chain
Ratak Chain
Namu
Aur
Jabwat
Ailinglaplap
Majuro
Arno
MAJURO
Mili
Knox
Jaluit
Namorik
Kili Island
Ebon
SCALE 1:10,000,000
150 miles
150 kilometers
Longitude east of Greenwich
Longitude west of Greenwich
KIRIBATI
Line Islands
Northern Line Islands
Teraina
Tabuaeran
Banana
Christmas Island
Equator
International Date Line
Central Line Islands
Malden Island
Starbuck Island
Southern Line Islands
Vostok
Millennium
Flint
POLYNESIA
SOUTH PACIFIC OCEAN
Tongareva
Cook Islands
Rakahanga
Manihiki
Suwarrow
Palmerston
Southern Cook Islands
Aitutaki
Manuae
Takutea
Mitiaro
Atiu
Mauke
COOK ISLANDS
(to New Zealand)
AVARUA
Rarotonga
Mangaia
Hatutu
Eiao
Nuku Hiva
Ua Huka
Taiohae
Ua Pou
Hiva Oa
Tahuatu
Atuona
Fatu Hiva
Omoa
Marquesas Islands
Tuamotu Archipelago
Manihi
Ahe
Takaroa
Tikehau
Rangiroa
Takapoto
Tikei
Mataiva
Îles Palliser
Aratika
Makatea
Toau
Kauehi
Niau
Raraka
Fakarava
Katiu
Makemo
Faaite
Tahanea
Anaa
Tepoto
Napuka
Pukapuka
Takume
Fangatau
Raroia
Fakahina
Nihiru
Tehuata
Marutea
Tatakoto
Haraiki
Tauere
Hikueru
Reitoru
Amanu
Marokau
Ravahere
Hao
Akiaki
Pukarua
Réao
Nengonengo
Vahitahi
Manuhangi
Paraoa
Vairaatea
Pinaki
Ahunui
Hereheretue
Îles Sous le Vent
Motu One
Tupai
Manuae
Maupiti
Bora-Bora
Tahaa
Huahine
Uturoa
Raiatea
Maupihaa
Tetiaroa
Moorea
PAPEETE
Maiao
Tahiti
Mehetia
Îles du Vent
Society Archipelago
FRENCH POLYNESIA
(to France)
Vanavana
Tureia
Groupe Actéon
Tenararo
Marutea
Tematangi
Mururoa
Fangataufa
Maria
Morane
Mangareva
Timoé
Gambier Islands
Tropic of Capricorn
Îles Maria
Rurutu
Rimatara
Tubuai
Raivavae
Austral Islands
Rapa
Marotiri
Moorea
Papetoai
PAPEETE
Hitiaa
Haapiti
Tohiea 3960ft (1207m)
Orohena 7352ft (2241m)
Tetufera 5902ft (1799m)
Tahiti
Paea
Taravao
Atimaono
Tautira
Teahupoo
Roniu 4370ft (1332m)
SCALE 1:3,000,000
FEDERATED STATES OF MICRONESIA
Hall Islands
Murilo Atoll
Fayu
Nomwin
Ulul
Pulap
Weno
Chuuk Islands
Pulawat
Oroluk
Losap
CHUUK
PALIKIR
Pohnpei
Kolonia
Pulusuk
POHNPEI
Mwokil
KOSRAE
Pingelap
Mortlock Islands
Ngetik Atoll
Namoluk
Kosrae
Tofol
Nukuoro
Longitude east of Greenwich
Savai'i
Falealupo
Fagamalo
Cape Pauva
Pu'apu'a
SAMOA
Mt Silisili 6096ft (1858m)
Sala'ilua
Salelologa
APIA
Taga
Palauli Bay
Mt Fito 3652ft (1113m)
Falefa
Matautu
Si'umu
Salani
Upolu
SCALE 1:4,000,000
60 miles
60 kilometers
AMERICAN SAMOA
(to U.S.A.)
PAGO PAGO
Tula
Fagatogo
Leone
Tutuila
Ofu
Olosega
Luma
Maia
Tau
Manua Islands
Longitude west of Greenwich

Moorea, one of the main islands in French Polynesia, is capped by an eroded volcanic plug.

The annual Hawaiki Nui Va'a canoe races celebrate the discovery of Tahiti by Polynesian mariners.

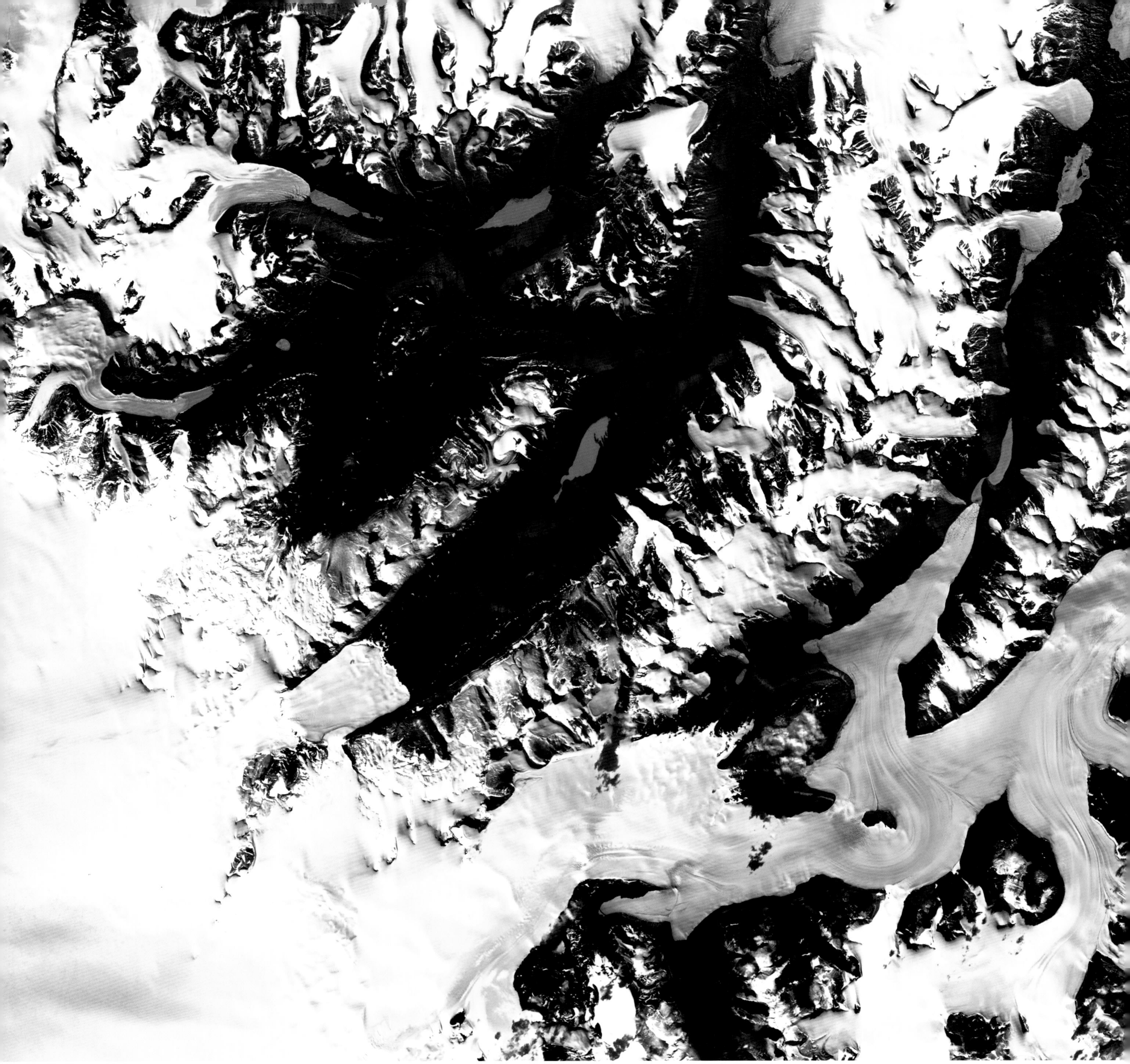

Taken from NASA's Landsat 7 satellite, this image shows part of the Transantarctic Mountains. The glaciers visible at center and center right flow off the Antarctic plateau to the Ross Ice Shelf. The brown areas at left are the McMurdo Dry Valleys.

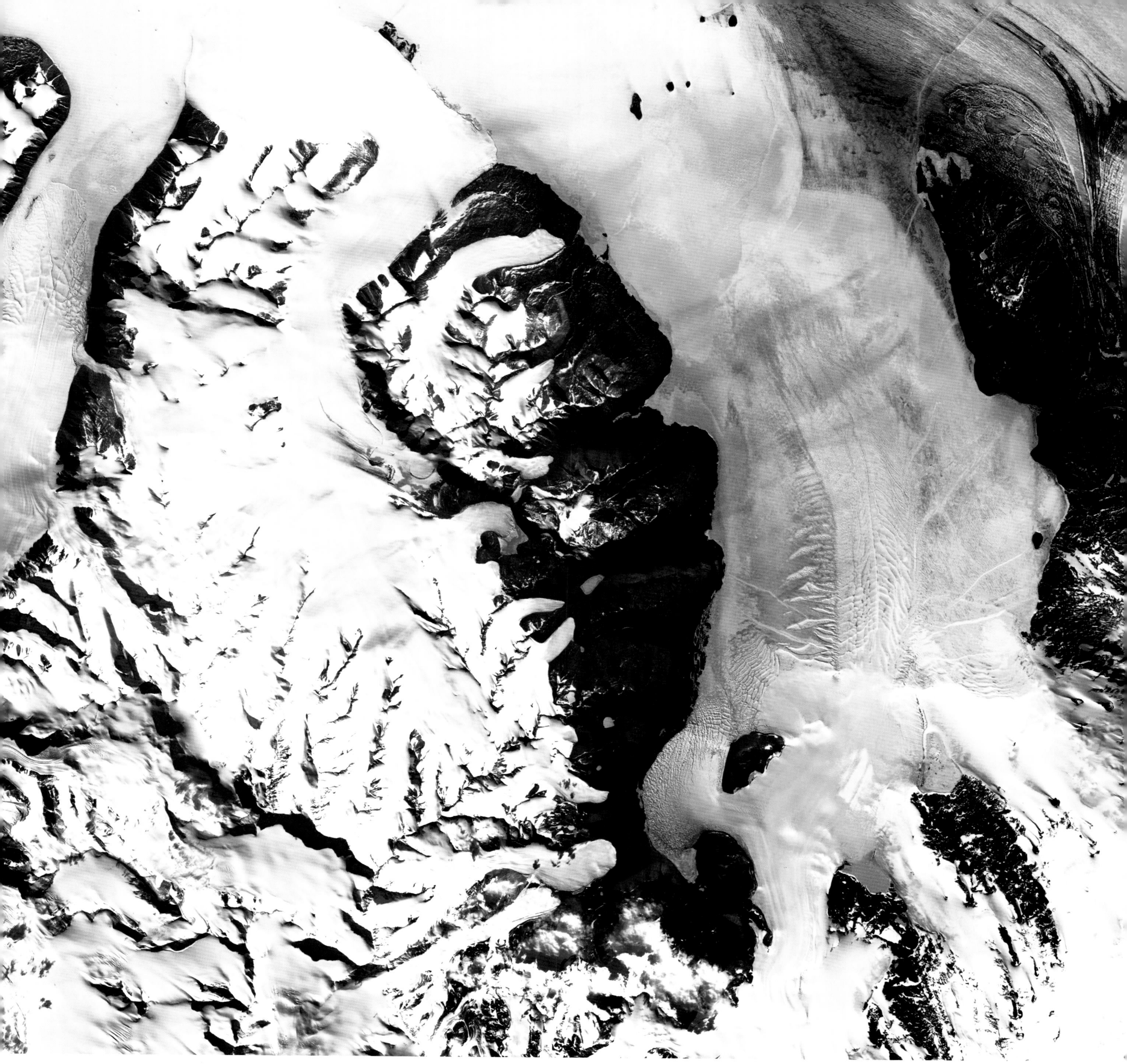

ANTARCTICA

ANTARCTICA

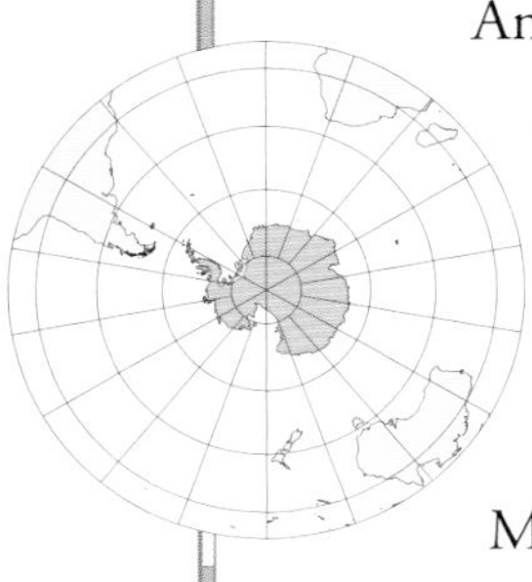

An almost circular landmass centered on the South Pole, Antarctica is the world's fifth-largest as well as its coldest, windiest, driest, and, on average, highest continent. A vast ice sheet covers 98 percent of the land. Among the few topographical features not totally obscured by the ice are the Transantarctic Mountains, which divide the continent into East and West Antarctica. In the east, the ice sheet hides a high plateau; to the west, it conceals a mountainous archipelago. Much of the surrounding ocean freezes in winter, effectively doubling the size of Antarctica, and for much of that season the sun does not rise. These severe conditions drastically restrict animal and plant distribution, and have prohibited permanent human occupation. Nevertheless, Antarctica is home to a fluctuating population of scientists and support staff based at a total of 42 research stations. Their numbers swell annually from around 1,000 in winter to approximately 4,000 in summer.

THE ANTARCTIC PENINSULA

The roughly circular outline of Antarctica is interrupted by the narrow Antarctic Peninsula, which extends 800 miles (1,300 km) toward the southern tip of South America. The peninsula is mountainous—rising to 13,747 feet (4,190 m) at Mount Jackson—capped by ice sheets and glaciers, and fringed by numerous islands, slender channels, and ice shelves. Nevertheless, it experiences the continent's mildest conditions and includes most of its few patches of ice-free land. From the end of the peninsula, an undersea ridge known as the Scotia Arc runs east then west, forming a great loop that eventually connects with Cape Horn in South America.

Bellingshausen Sea
Adelaide Island
Drake Passage
South Shetland Islands
Alexander Island
Graham Land
Joinville Island
Larsen Ice Shelf
James Ross Island
George VI Sound
Hearst Island
Palmer Land
Mt Jackson
Mt Coman
Weddell Sea
Ronne Ice Shelf
N

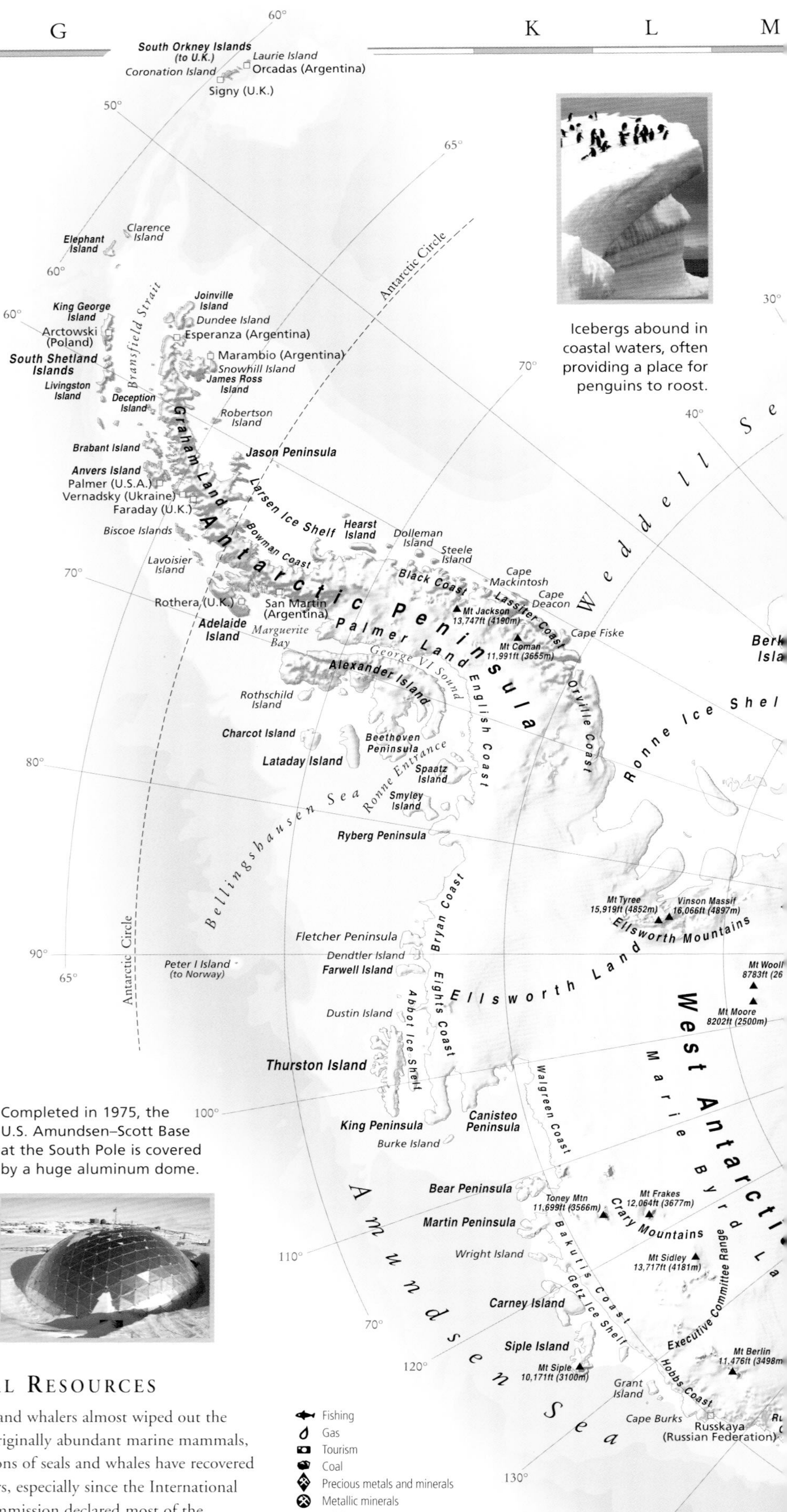

South Orkney Islands (to U.K.)
Laurie Island
Orcadas (Argentina)
Coronation Island
Signy (U.K.)
Elephant Island
Clarence Island
King George Island
Arctowski (Poland)
South Shetland Islands
Livingston Island
Deception Island
Bransfield Strait
Joinville Island
Dundee Island
Esperanza (Argentina)
Marambio (Argentina)
Snowhill Island
James Ross Island
Robertson Island
Antarctic Circle
Brabant Island
Anvers Island
Palmer (U.S.A.)
Vernadsky (Ukraine)
Faraday (U.K.)
Biscoe Islands
Graham Land
Jason Peninsula
Larsen Ice Shelf
Hearst Island
Dolleman Island
Steele Island
Bowman Coast
Lavoisier Island
Antarctic Peninsula
Black Coast
Cape Mackintosh
Cape Deacon
Lassiter Coast
Mt Jackson 13,747ft (4190m)
Mt Coman 11,991ft (3655m)
Cape Fiske
Rothera (U.K.)
San Martín (Argentina)
Adelaide Island
Marguerite Bay
Palmer Land
George VI Sound
Alexander Island
English Coast
Orville Coast
Weddell Sea
Rothschild Island
Charcot Island
Beethoven Peninsula
Lataday Island
Ronne Entrance
Spaatz Island
Smyley Island
Ronne Ice Shelf
Bellingshausen Sea
Ryberg Peninsula
Bryan Coast
Mt Tyree 15,919ft (4852m)
Vinson Massif 16,066ft (4897m)
Ellsworth Mountains
Fletcher Peninsula
Dendtler Island
Farwell Island
Peter I Island (to Norway)
Ellsworth Land
Eights Coast
Abbot Ice Shelf
Dustin Island
Thurston Island
Mt Moore 8202ft (2500m)
West Antarctica
Marie Byrd Land
Walgreen Coast
Canisteo Peninsula
King Peninsula
Burke Island
Amundsen Sea
Bear Peninsula
Toney Mtn 11,699ft (3566m)
Mt Frakes 12,064ft (3677m)
Crary Mountains
Martin Peninsula
Wright Island
Bakutis Coast
Mt Sidley 13,717ft (4181m)
Executive Committee Range
Carney Island
Getz Ice Shelf
Siple Island
Mt Siple 10,171ft (3100m)
Mt Berlin 11,476ft (3498m)
Hobbs Coast
Grant Island
Cape Burks
Russkaya (Russian Federation)

Icebergs abound in coastal waters, often providing a place for penguins to roost.

Completed in 1975, the U.S. Amundsen–Scott Base at the South Pole is covered by a huge aluminum dome.

THE ANTARCTIC TREATY

Seven countries—Argentina, Australia, Chile, France, New Zealand, Norway, and the United Kingdom—have at one time or other asserted sovereignty over parts of Antarctica. However, by becoming signatories to the Antarctic Treaty of 1959, they and 38 other nations have since agreed to suspend territorial claims and preserve the continent for nonmilitary scientific research. The Antarctic Treaty arose out of a worldwide scientific project called the International Geophysical Year, which began in 1957 and saw 12 nations establish numerous research stations across Antarctica.

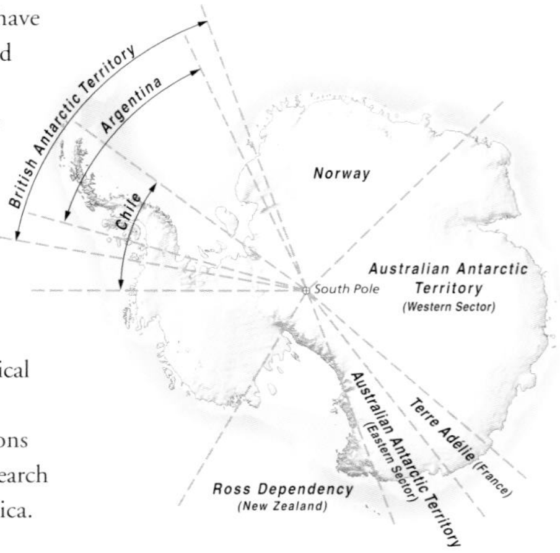

British Antarctic Territory
Argentina
Chile
Norway
Australian Antarctic Territory (Western Sector)
South Pole
Australian Antarctic Territory (Eastern Sector)
Terre Adélie (France)
Ross Dependency (New Zealand)

NATURAL RESOURCES

Early sealers and whalers almost wiped out the continent's originally abundant marine mammals, but populations of seals and whales have recovered in recent years, especially since the International Whaling Commission declared most of the Southern Ocean a whale sanctuary in 1994. Although 23 countries have agreed to manage Antarctic fisheries for sustainability, illegal fishing is steadily depleting stocks of Antarctic cod, finfish, and toothfish. Geologists concur that Antarctica may harbor great mineral wealth, including copper, gold, platinum, and oil. No economically exploitable reserves have been found, however, and, in any case, mining is banned under the Antarctic Treaty. Tourism is proving a more viable economic activity, with visitor numbers rising steadily.

Fishing
Gas
Tourism
Coal
Precious metals and minerals
Metallic minerals
Whales
Sanae (South Africa)
Syowa (Japan)
Neumayer (Germany)
Molodezhnaya (Russian Federation)
Palmer (U.S.A.)
Belgrano II (Argentina)
Mawson (Australia)
Rothera (U.K.)
Zhongshan (China)
Amundsen-Scott (U.S.A.)
Casey (Australia)
McMurdo (U.S.A)
Dumont d'Urville (France)
Marginal or nonproductive

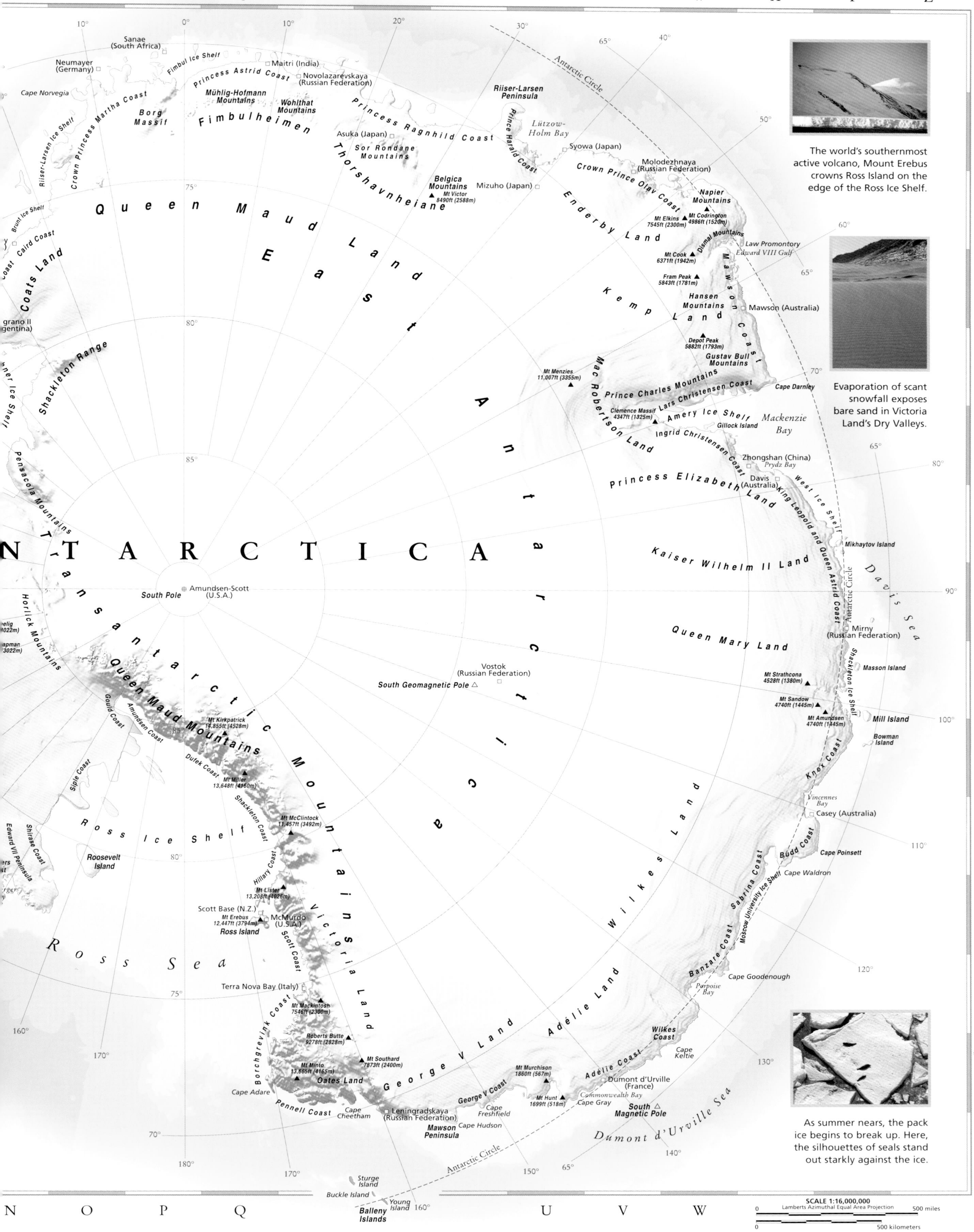
N O P Q R S T U V W X Y Z
1 2 3 4 5 6 7 8 9 10
Sanae (South Africa)
Neumayer (Germany)
Cape Norvegia
Fimbul Ice Shelf
Maitri (India)
Novolazarevskaya (Russian Federation)
Princess Astrid Coast
Mühlig-Hofmann Mountains
Wohlthat Mountains
Borg Massif
Fimbulheimen
Crown Princess Martha Coast
Riiser-Larsen Ice Shelf
Princess Ragnhild Coast
Asuka (Japan)
Sor Rondane Mountains
Thorshavnheiane
Belgica Mountains
Mt Victor 8490ft (2588m)
Mizuho (Japan)
Riiser-Larsen Peninsula
Prince Harald Coast
Lützow-Holm Bay
Syowa (Japan)
Antarctic Circle
Molodezhnaya (Russian Federation)
Crown Prince Olav Coast
Napier Mountains
Mt Codrington 4986ft (1520m)
Mt Elkins 7545ft (2300m)
Enderby Land
Dismal Mountains
Law Promontory
Edward VIII Gulf
Mt Cook 6371ft (1942m)
Fram Peak 5843ft (1781m)
Mawson Coast
Hansen Mountains
Mawson (Australia)
Kemp Land
Depot Peak 5882ft (1793m)
Gustav Bull Mountains
Cape Darnley
Queen Maud Land
East Antarctica
Brunt Ice Shelf
Caird Coast
Coats Land
Shackleton Range
Mt Menzies 11,007ft (3355m)
Mac Robertson Land
Prince Charles Mountains
Lars Christensen Coast
Clemence Massif 4347ft (1325m)
Amery Ice Shelf
Gillock Island
Mackenzie Bay
Ingrid Christensen Coast
Zhongshan (China)
Prydz Bay
Davis (Australia)
Princess Elizabeth Land
West Ice Shelf
King Leopold and Queen Astrid Coast
Mikhaytov Island
Pensacola Mountains
ANTARCTICA
Kaiser Wilhelm II Land
Davis Sea
Amundsen-Scott (U.S.A.)
South Pole
Horlick Mountains
Mirny (Russian Federation)
Queen Mary Land
Transantarctic Mountains
Vostok (Russian Federation)
South Geomagnetic Pole
Mt Strathcona 4528ft (1380m)
Masson Island
Shackleton Ice Shelf
Mt Sandow 4740ft (1445m)
Mt Amundsen 4740ft (1445m)
Mill Island
Bowman Island
Queen Maud Mountains
Gould Coast
Amundsen Coast
Mt Kirkpatrick 14,855ft (4528m)
Dufek Coast
Mt Miller 13,648ft (4160m)
Knox Coast
Siple Coast
Shackleton Coast
Vincennes Bay
Casey (Australia)
Mt McClintock 11,457ft (3492m)
Ross Ice Shelf
Roosevelt Island
Edward VII Peninsula
Shirase Coast
Budd Coast
Cape Poinsett
Cape Waldron
Hillary Coast
Mt Lister 13,208ft (4026m)
Wilkes Land
Sabrina Coast
Moscow University Ice Shelf
Scott Base (N.Z.)
Mt Erebus 12,447ft (3794m)
McMurdo (U.S.A.)
Ross Island
Victoria Land
Scott Coast
Ross Sea
Banzare Coast
Cape Goodenough
Terra Nova Bay (Italy)
Porpoise Bay
Mt Mackintosh 7546ft (2300m)
Borchgrevink Coast
Adélie Land
Roberts Butte 9278ft (2828m)
Wilkes Coast
Cape Keltie
Mt Southard 7873ft (2400m)
George V Land
Mt Minto 13,665ft (4165m)
Oates Land
Mt Murchison 1860ft (567m)
Adélie Coast
Dumont d'Urville (France)
Cape Adare
George V Coast
Mt Hunt 1699ft (518m)
Commonwealth Bay
Cape Gray
South Magnetic Pole
Pennell Coast
Cape Cheetham
Leningradskaya (Russian Federation)
Cape Freshfield
Mawson Peninsula
Cape Hudson
Dumont d'Urville Sea
Sturge Island
Buckle Island
Young Island
Balleny Islands
SCALE 1:16,000,000
Lamberts Azimuthal Equal Area Projection
500 miles
500 kilometers

The world's southernmost active volcano, Mount Erebus crowns Ross Island on the edge of the Ross Ice Shelf.

Evaporation of scant snowfall exposes bare sand in Victoria Land's Dry Valleys.

As summer nears, the pack ice begins to break up. Here, the silhouettes of seals stand out starkly against the ice.

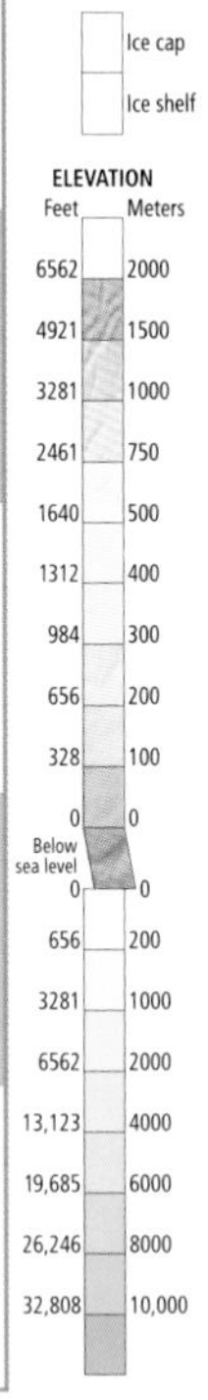
Ice cap
Ice shelf
ELEVATION
Feet Meters
6562 2000
4921 1500
3281 1000
2461 750
1640 500
1312 400
984 300
656 200
328 100
0 0
Below sea level
0 0
656 200
3281 1000
6562 2000
13,123 4000
19,685 6000
26,246 8000
32,808 10,000

Antarctica in Focus

Until the 20th century, Antarctica remained virtually unexplored. Although James Cook crossed the Antarctic Circle in 1773, he was blocked by ice, and it took another 65 years for the existence of a continent to be confirmed. The first human to set foot on this continent may have been the American John Davis in 1821, but it was 1899 before anyone spent a winter, and 1958 before a team crossed the icy expanse from one coast to the other.

The early 19th century saw sealers venture into the region, setting up bases on islands and almost destroying the fur seal populations. They were followed by 20th-century whalers, who killed 99 percent of blue whales, 97 percent of humpbacks, and 80 percent of fin whales before international agreements largely halted the practice.

The first permanent scientific bases were built in Antarctica in the 1950s. By studying the untouched ice layers, scientists have built up a picture of Earth's climate over the past 420,000 years. Fossil discoveries have shown that the continent was once lushly vegetated and had similar fauna to South America and Australia, providing evidence for the theory of continental drift, which states that Antarctica, Africa, India, South America, and Australia were once part of the supercontinent Gondwana. Current efforts are monitoring the ozone hole and the impact of global warming on Antarctic ice.

The lack of human impact that has made Antarctica a pristine laboratory for scientists has also made it a lure for adventurous tourists, whose numbers grew remarkably during the 1990s.

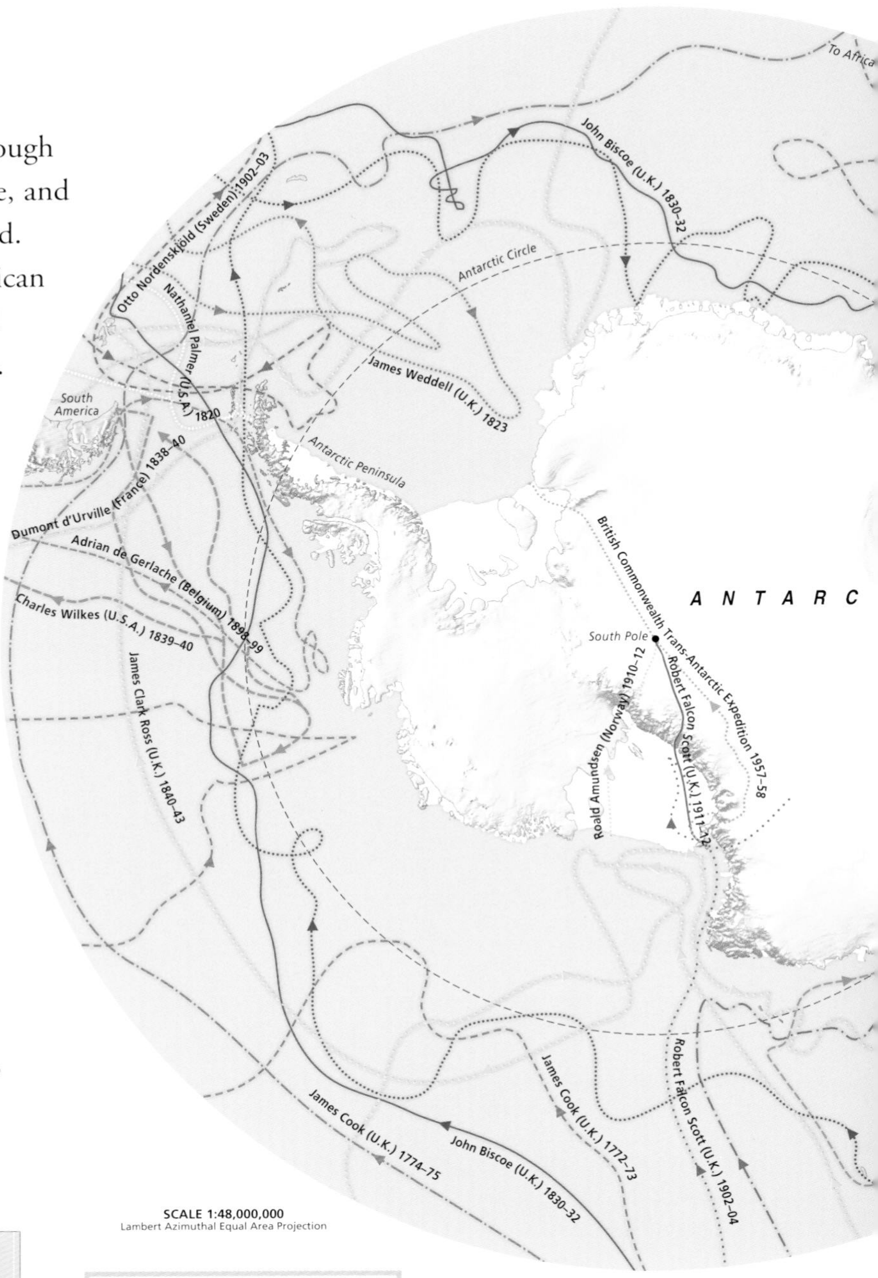

To Africa
John Biscoe (U.K.) 1830–32
Otto Nordenskjöld (Sweden) 1902–03
Nathaniel Palmer (U.S.A.) 1820
Antarctic Circle
James Weddell (U.K.) 1823
South America
Antarctic Peninsula
Dumont d'Urville (France) 1838–40
Adrian de Gerlache (Belgium) 1898–99
Charles Wilkes (U.S.A.) 1839–40
James Clark Ross (U.K.) 1840–43
British Commonwealth Trans-Antarctic Expedition 1957–58
ANTARC
South Pole
Roald Amundsen (Norway) 1910–12
Robert Falcon Scott (U.K.) 1911–12
James Cook (U.K.) 1774–75
John Biscoe (U.K.) 1830–32
James Cook (U.K.) 1772–73
Robert Falcon Scott (U.K.) 1902–04

SCALE 1:48,000,000
Lambert Azimuthal Equal Area Projection

Tourism Boom

In 1956, the first plane carrying tourists flew over Antarctica without landing, a method of viewing the icy continent that remains popular today. It was not until the late 1960s, however, that tourist cruise ships began regular visits. In 1991–92, tourists outnumbered scientific personnel for the first time, and tourist numbers continued to grow dramatically throughout the decade that followed. The vast majority of tourists visit by cruise ship, but several dozen fly to Antarctica for a land-based adventure.

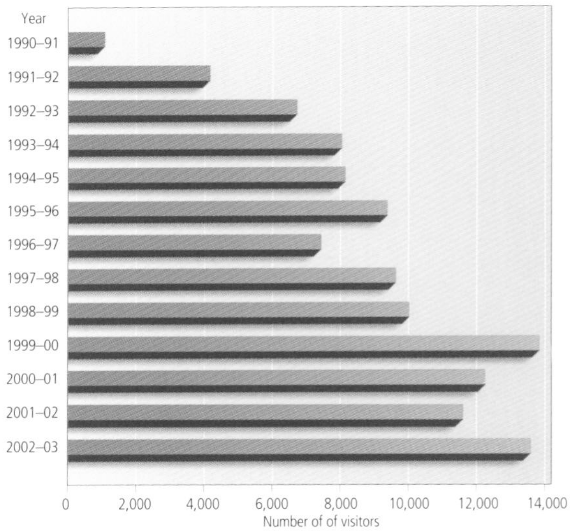

Year
1990–91
1991–92
1992–93
1993–94
1994–95
1995–96
1996–97
1997–98
1998–99
1999–00
2000–01
2001–02
2002–03
0
2,000
4,000
6,000
8,000
10,000
12,000
14,000
Number of of visitors

Most current tourism in Antarctica is ship-based, with visitors living aboard cruise liners and using inflatable craft to reach the shore. Land-based tourism would have a greater environmental impact.

The pristine layers of Antarctica's ice preserve a record of Earth's changing climate. Cores drilled out of the ice can reveal centuries of varying precipitation, temperature, and atmospheric composition.

ANNUAL MEAN TEMPERATURE

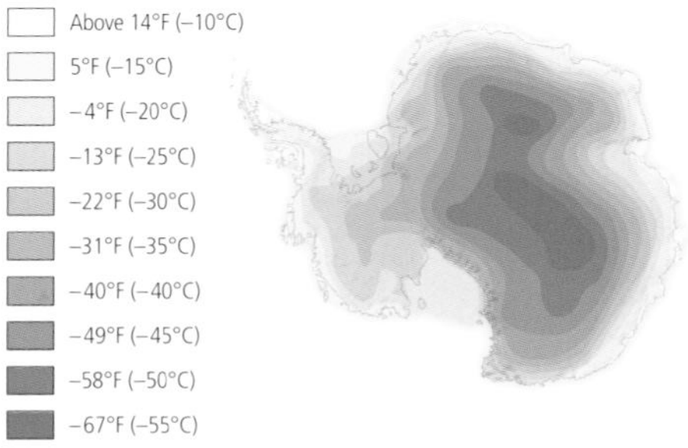

Above 14°F (−10°C)
5°F (−15°C)
−4°F (−20°C)
−13°F (−25°C)
−22°F (−30°C)
−31°F (−35°C)
−40°F (−40°C)
−49°F (−45°C)
−58°F (−50°C)
−67°F (−55°C)

ANNUAL MEAN SNOWFALL

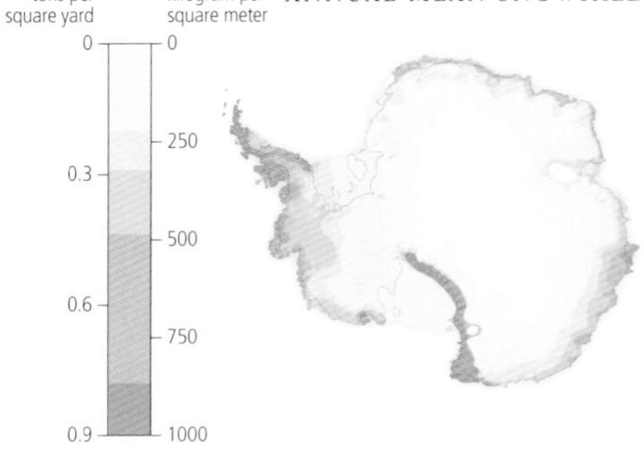

tons per square yard
kilogram per square meter
0
0.3
0.6
0.9
0
250
500
750
1000

KATABATIC WINDS

Wind

Cold, Dry, and Windy

Because of both its high elevation and its distance from the moderating effects of the ocean, Antarctica's eastern interior has by far the lowest temperatures. The continent receives little precipitation because the air is usually too cold to hold water vapor. Driven by gravity rather than pressure differences, katabatic winds blow constantly and become exceptionally strong near the coast.

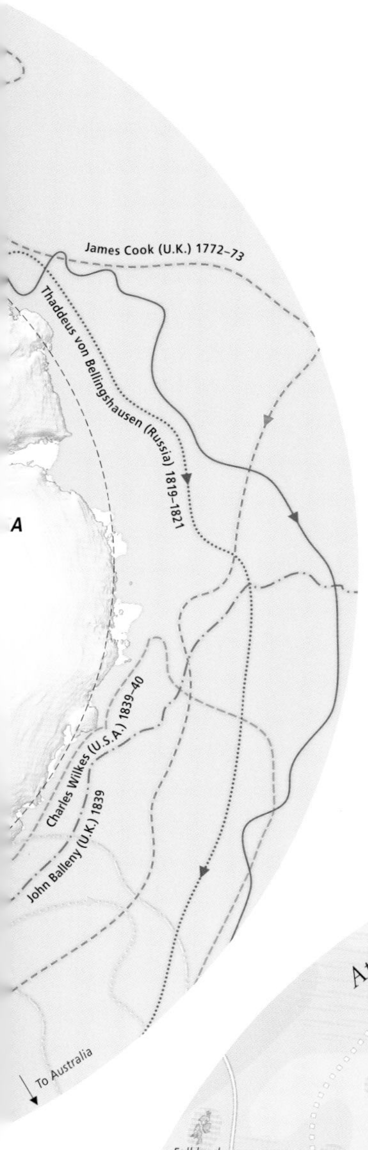
James Cook (U.K.) 1772–73
Thaddeus von Bellingshausen (Russia) 1819–1821
Charles Wilkes (U.S.A.) 1839–40
John Balleny (U.K.) 1839
To Australia
A

Antarctic Exploration

In search of a great southern land, James Cook crossed the Antarctic Circle three times on his voyage of 1772–75. Although he did not see land, his descriptions of the rich marine life encouraged sealers and explorers to follow him. In 1820, Bellingshausen and Palmer both investigated the Antarctic Peninsula region, while later explorers revealed more southerly areas of the continent. Scott and Amundsen raced each other to the South Pole, with Amundsen reaching it first in 1911. More than 45 years later, a joint Commonwealth team made the first overland crossing of Antarctica.

Led by Robert Falcon Scott, a British team reached the South Pole on January 17, 1912, only to discover that Roald Amundsen's Norwegian team had arrived a month earlier, on December 14, 1911. All members of Scott's team perished on the return journey.

The plankton-rich Antarctic waters support vast swarms of small crustaceans known as krill, which are the main food of baleen whales, three seal species, penguins and other birds, and many fishes.

The Ozone Hole

High in the stratosphere, a layer containing a small amount of the gas known as ozone absorbs most of the Sun's harmful ultraviolet rays. Since the 1980s, scientists have been monitoring Antarctica's ozone hole, an area of depleted ozone that forms every September. Their work showed that the hole was growing dramatically, and industrial pollutants such as chlorofluorocarbons (CFCs) were identified as the culprit. As each southern spring begins, the atmospheric conditions trap these ozone-destroying chlorine compounds above Antarctica. Most countries agreed to phase out the use of CFCs under the 1987 Montreal Protocol, but the pollutants linger in the atmosphere. The 2000 ozone hole (shown in the image below) was the largest ever recorded, measuring about 11 million square miles (29 million sq km)—roughly three times the size of the United States.

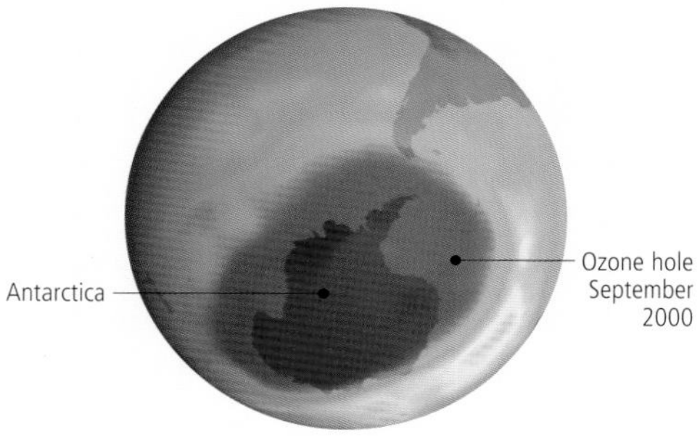
Antarctica
Ozone hole September 2000

Insulated by thick layers of blubber, the Weddell seal spends the many months of winter darkness under the ice, using sonar to locate its food and breathing holes. It breeds on sea ice or land in summer.

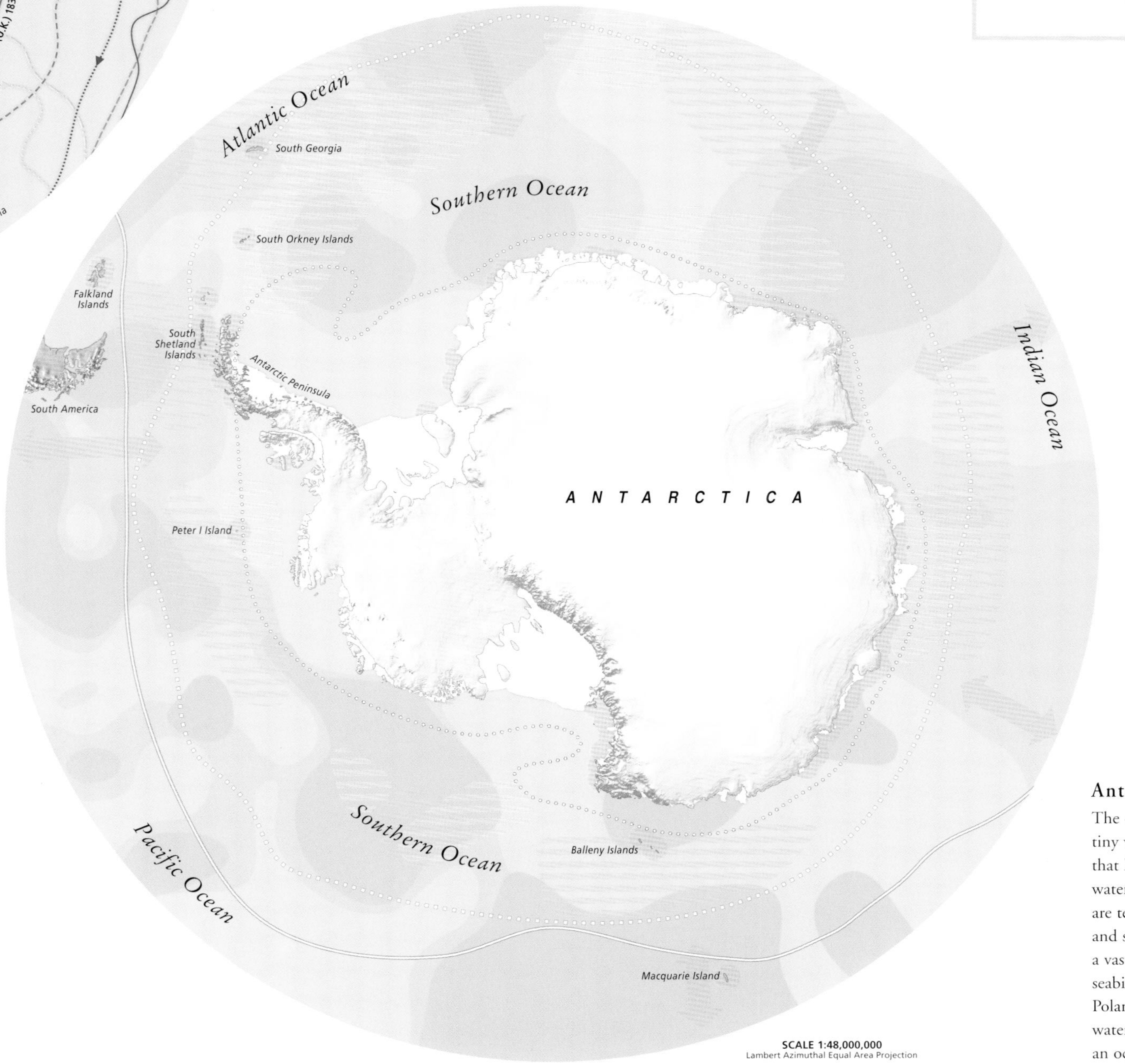
Atlantic Ocean
South Georgia
Southern Ocean
South Orkney Islands
Falkland Islands
South Shetland Islands
Antarctic Peninsula
South America
Indian Ocean
ANTARCTICA
Peter I Island
Southern Ocean
Pacific Ocean
Balleny Islands
Macquarie Island
SCALE 1:48,000,000
Lambert Azimuthal Equal Area Projection

POLAR OCEAN LIFE

- Antarctic Polar Frontal Zone
- Summer pack ice limit
- Winter pack ice limit
- Ice shelf
- High zooplankton concentration
- Medium zooplankton concentration
- Low zooplankton concentration
- Krill distribution
- Humpback whale migratory route
- Sei, blue, and fin whale distribution
- Penguin breeding colonies

Antarctic Animals

The only true land animals on Antarctica are tiny wingless midges and microscopic species that live in summer ponds. Some of the waters that surround the continent, however, are teeming, with blooms of phytoplankton and swarms of krill forming the center of a vast food web supporting fish, penguins, seabirds, seals, and whales. The Antarctic Polar Frontal Zone, where warm northern waters meet cold southern waters, acts as an oceanographic and biological barrier.

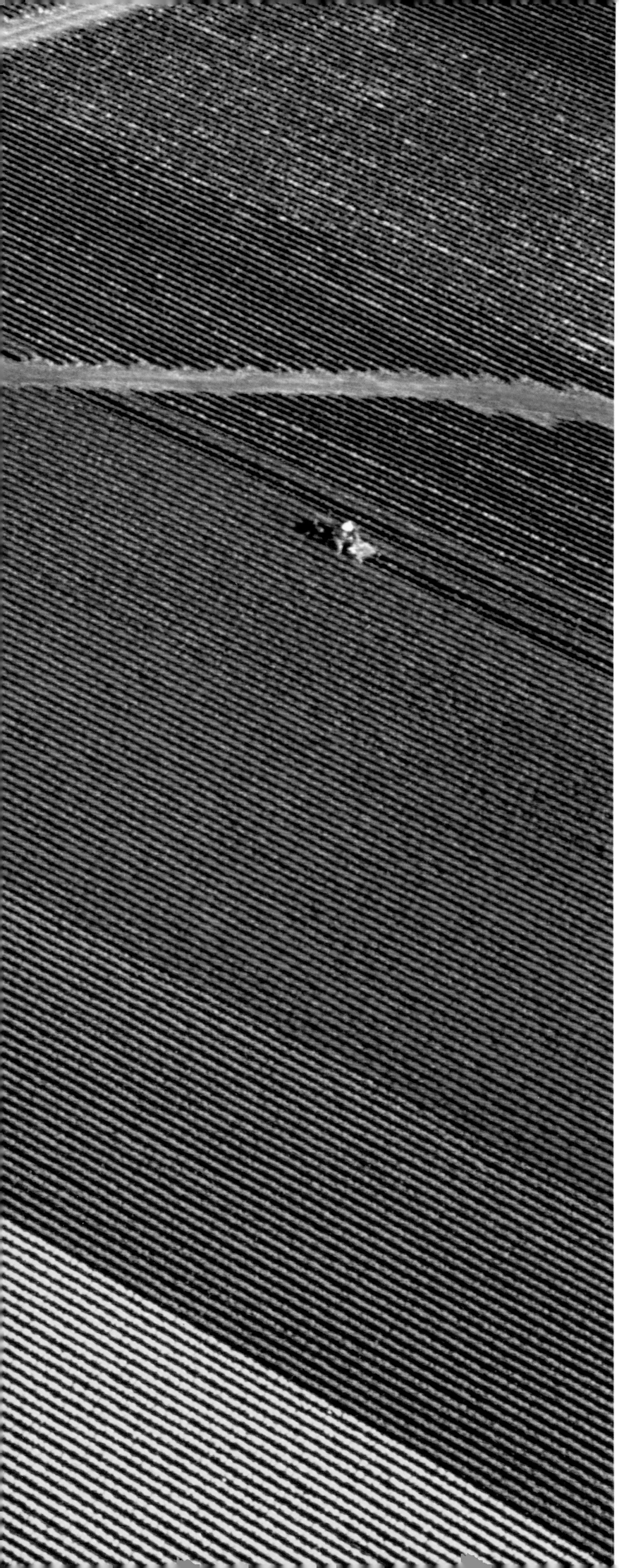

REFERENCE

These tulip fields, picturesque and colorful in April bloom, are located in the Skagit River delta, south of Mount Vernon in western Washington, U.S.A. The area boasts some of the state's most productive land, much of which, such as these agricultural flats, was reclaimed from swampland. The tractor gives perspective to the large scale of the tulip plantation.

Geographical Comparisons

Largest Islands

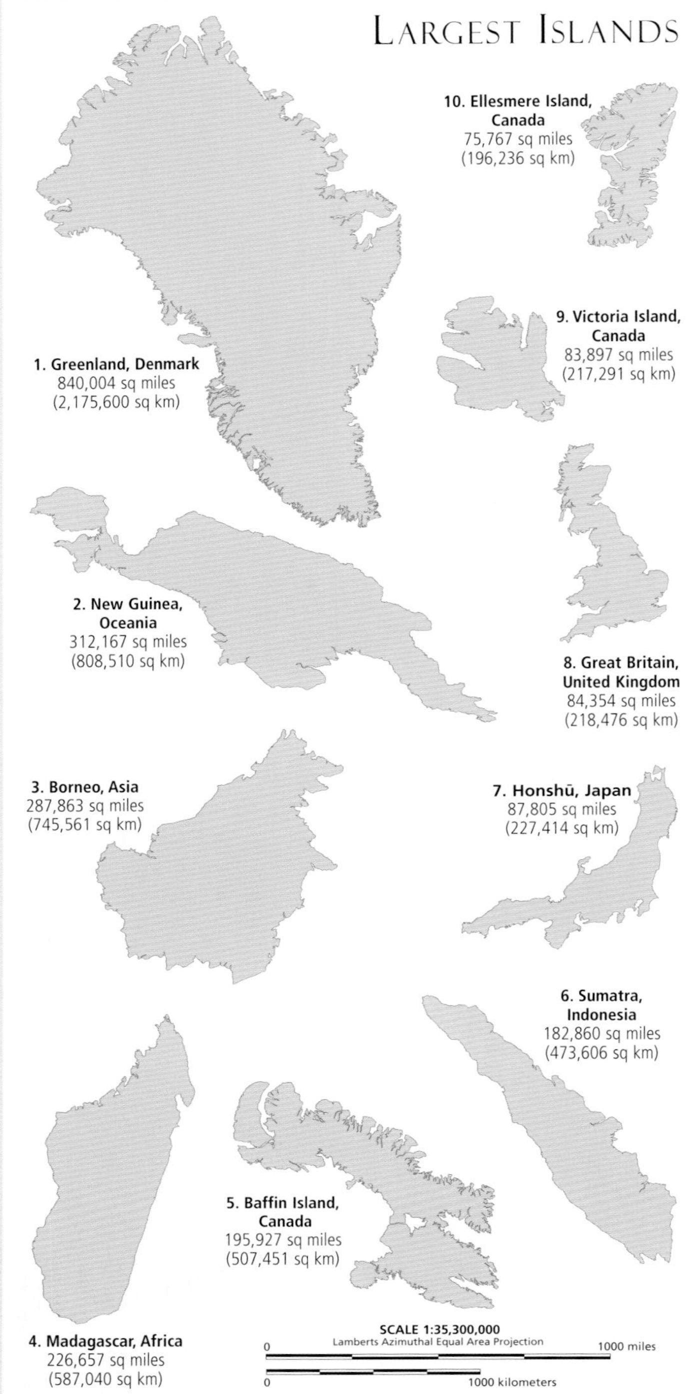

1. Greenland, Denmark
840,004 sq miles
(2,175,600 sq km)
2. New Guinea, Oceania
312,167 sq miles
(808,510 sq km)
3. Borneo, Asia
287,863 sq miles
(745,561 sq km)
4. Madagascar, Africa
226,657 sq miles
(587,040 sq km)
5. Baffin Island, Canada
195,927 sq miles
(507,451 sq km)
6. Sumatra, Indonesia
182,860 sq miles
(473,606 sq km)
7. Honshū, Japan
87,805 sq miles
(227,414 sq km)
8. Great Britain, United Kingdom
84,354 sq miles
(218,476 sq km)
9. Victoria Island, Canada
83,897 sq miles
(217,291 sq km)
10. Ellesmere Island, Canada
75,767 sq miles
(196,236 sq km)
SCALE 1:35,300,000
Lamberts Azimuthal Equal Area Projection
0
1000 miles
0
1000 kilometers

Largest Countries

1. Russian Federation
6,592,770 sq miles
(17,075,200 sq km)
3. United States of America
3,717,810 sq miles
(9,629,090 sq km)
6. Australia
2,967,910 sq miles
(7,686,850 sq km)
7. India
1,269,345 sq miles
(3,287,590 sq km)
8. Argentina
1,068,300 sq miles
(2,766,890 sq km)
SCALE 1:60,000,000
Lamberts Azimuthal Equal Area Projection
0
1500 miles
0
1500 kilometers

Longest Rivers

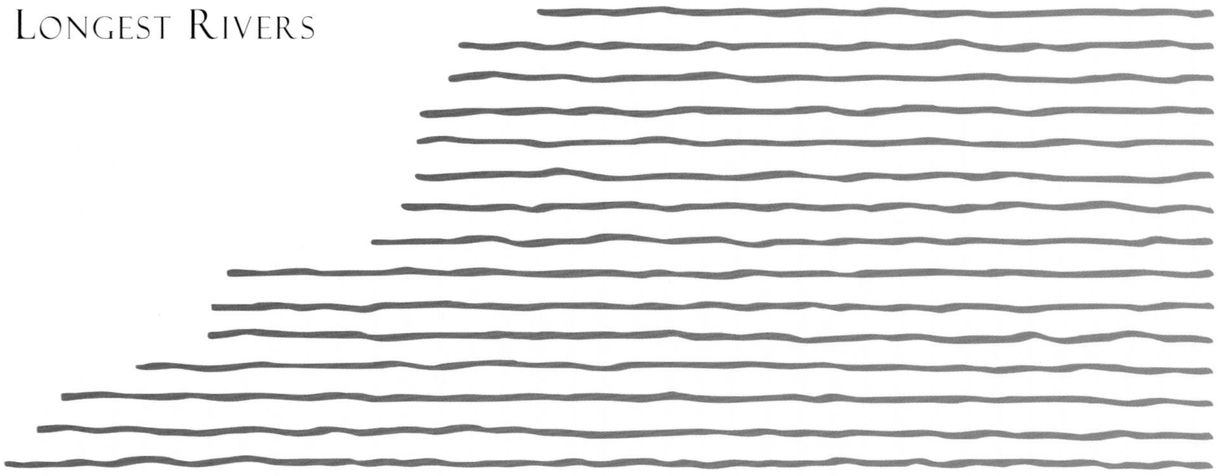

Murray–Darling, Australia 2,330 miles (3,750 km)
Niger, Africa 2,599 miles (4,184 km)
Mackenzie–Peace–Finlay, North America 2,635 miles (4,241 km)
Lena–Kirenga, Asia 2,734 miles (4,400 km)
Heilong Jiang (Amur)–Argun', Asia 2,744 miles (4,416 km)
Mekong, Asia 2,749 miles (4,425 km)
River Plate–Paraná, South America 2,796 miles (4,500 km)
Congo, Africa 2,900 miles (4,667 km)
Yellow, Asia 3,395 miles (5,464 km)
Yenisey–Angara–Selenga, Asia 3,448 miles (5,550 km)
Ob'– Irtysh, Asia 3,459 miles (5,568 km)
Mississippi–Missouri, North America 3,709 miles (5,969 km)
Yangtze, Asia 3,964 miles (6,380 km)
Amazon, South America 4,049 miles (6,516 km)
Nile, Africa 4,160 miles (6,695 km)

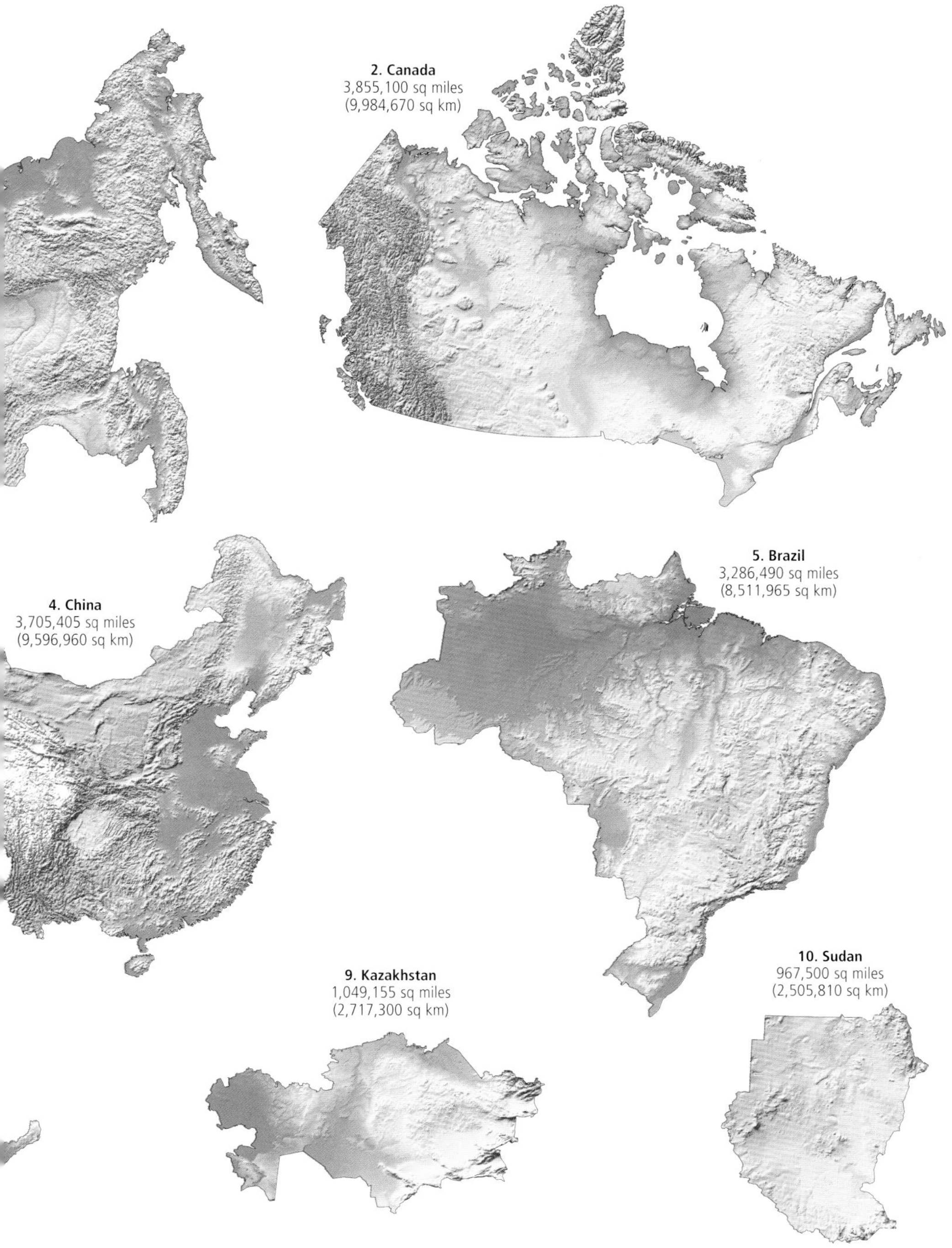
2. Canada
3,855,100 sq miles
(9,984,670 sq km)
4. China
3,705,405 sq miles
(9,596,960 sq km)
5. Brazil
3,286,490 sq miles
(8,511,965 sq km)
9. Kazakhstan
1,049,155 sq miles
(2,717,300 sq km)
10. Sudan
967,500 sq miles
(2,505,810 sq km)

Largest Lakes

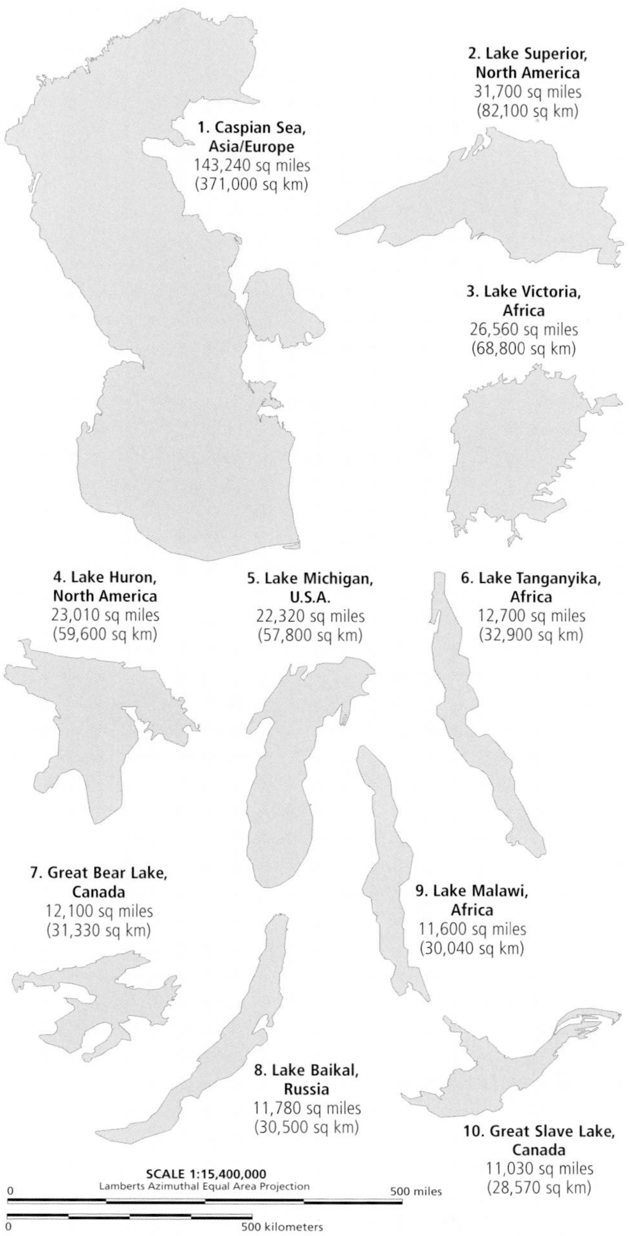
1. Caspian Sea, Asia/Europe
143,240 sq miles
(371,000 sq km)
2. Lake Superior, North America
31,700 sq miles
(82,100 sq km)
3. Lake Victoria, Africa
26,560 sq miles
(68,800 sq km)
4. Lake Huron, North America
23,010 sq miles
(59,600 sq km)
5. Lake Michigan, U.S.A.
22,320 sq miles
(57,800 sq km)
6. Lake Tanganyika, Africa
12,700 sq miles
(32,900 sq km)
7. Great Bear Lake, Canada
12,100 sq miles
(31,330 sq km)
8. Lake Baikal, Russia
11,780 sq miles
(30,500 sq km)
9. Lake Malawi, Africa
11,600 sq miles
(30,040 sq km)
10. Great Slave Lake, Canada
11,030 sq miles
(28,570 sq km)
SCALE 1:15,400,000
Lamberts Azimuthal Equal Area Projection
0
500 miles
0
500 kilometers

Major Mountains

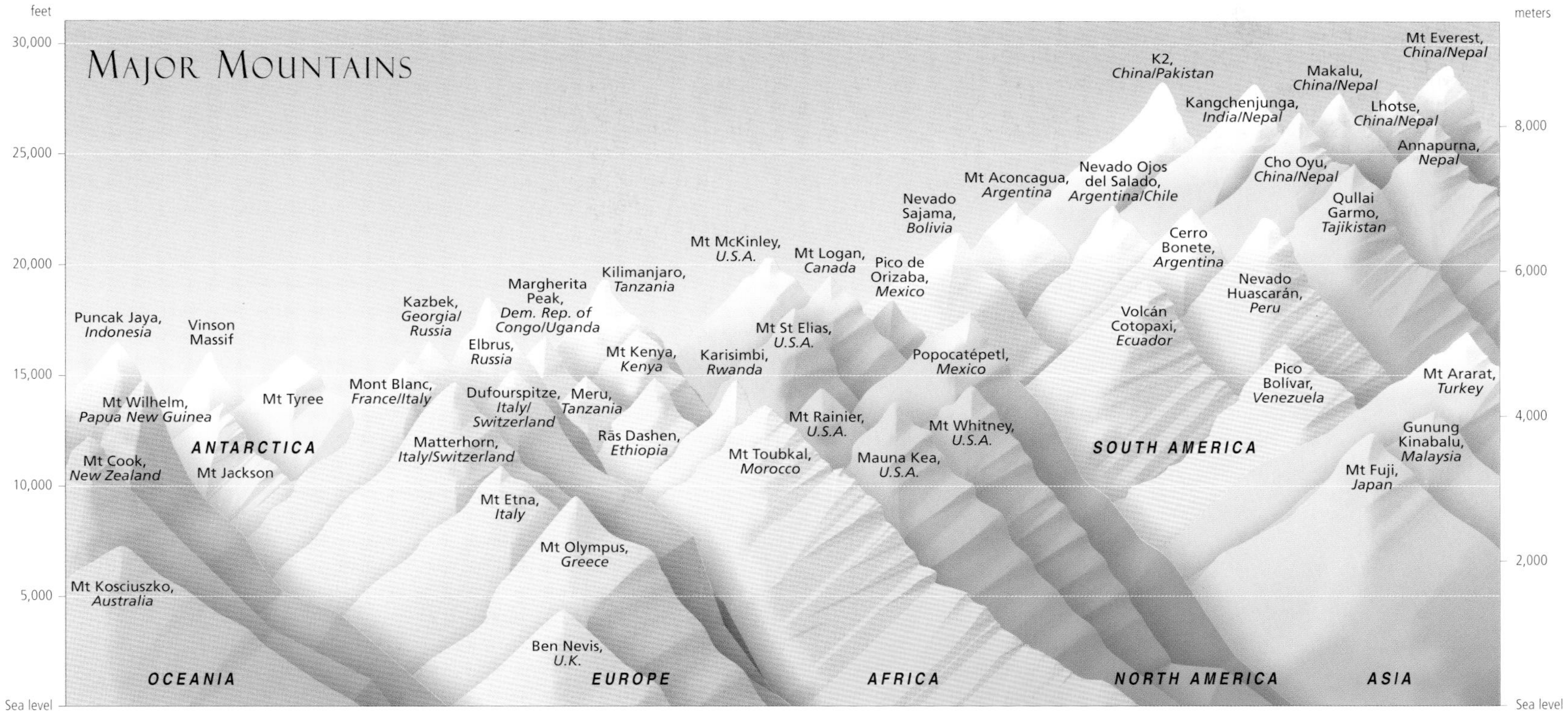
feet
30,000
25,000
20,000
15,000
10,000
5,000
Sea level
meters
8,000
6,000
4,000
2,000
Sea level
Mt Everest, China/Nepal
K2, China/Pakistan
Makalu, China/Nepal
Kangchenjunga, India/Nepal
Lhotse, China/Nepal
Annapurna, Nepal
Cho Oyu, China/Nepal
Qullai Garmo, Tajikistan
Mt Aconcagua, Argentina
Nevado Ojos del Salado, Argentina/Chile
Nevado Sajama, Bolivia
Cerro Bonete, Argentina
Nevado Huascarán, Peru
Volcán Cotopaxi, Ecuador
Pico Bolivar, Venezuela
Mt Ararat, Turkey
Gunung Kinabalu, Malaysia
Mt Fuji, Japan
Mt McKinley, U.S.A.
Mt Logan, Canada
Pico de Orizaba, Mexico
Mt St Elias, U.S.A.
Popocatépetl, Mexico
Mt Rainier, U.S.A.
Mt Whitney, U.S.A.
Mauna Kea, U.S.A.
Kilimanjaro, Tanzania
Mt Kenya, Kenya
Karisimbi, Rwanda
Margherita Peak, Dem. Rep. of Congo/Uganda
Meru, Tanzania
Ras Dashen, Ethiopia
Mt Toubkal, Morocco
Kazbek, Georgia/Russia
Elbrus, Russia
Mont Blanc, France/Italy
Dufourspitze, Italy/Switzerland
Matterhorn, Italy/Switzerland
Mt Etna, Italy
Mt Olympus, Greece
Ben Nevis, U.K.
Puncak Jaya, Indonesia
Vinson Massif
Mt Tyree
Mt Wilhelm, Papua New Guinea
ANTARCTICA
Mt Jackson
Mt Cook, New Zealand
Mt Kosciuszko, Australia
SOUTH AMERICA
OCEANIA
EUROPE
AFRICA
NORTH AMERICA
ASIA

Time Zones

-11
-10
-9
-8
-7
-6
-5
-4
-3
-2
-1
0
1
2
GREENLAND
(to Denmark)
KONG CHRISTIAN X LAND
JAN MAYEN
(to Norway)
SVALBARD
(to Norway)
Greenwich Meridian
Arctic Circle
ICELAND
U.S.A.
(Alaska)
CANADA
NEWFOUNDLAND
-3½
ST PIERRE AND MIQUELON
(to France)
UNITED STATES OF AMERICA
BERMUDA
(to U.K.)
AZORES
(to Portugal)
PORTUGAL
SPAIN
MADEIRA
(to Portugal)
CANARY ISLANDS
(to Spain)
MOROCCO
WESTERN SAHARA
Tropic of Cancer
THE BAHAMAS
CUBA
MEXICO
HAWAII
(U.S.A.)
HAITI
DOMINICAN REPUBLIC
JAMAICA
BELIZE
HONDURAS
GUATEMALA
EL SALVADOR
NICARAGUA
COSTA RICA
PANAMA
TRINIDAD AND TOBAGO
VENEZUELA
GUYANA
SURINAME
FRENCH GUIANA
(to France)
COLOMBIA
Equator
ECUADOR
GALAPAGOS ISLANDS
(to Ecuador)
KIRIBATI
12
-9½
MARQUESAS ISLANDS
(to France)
COOK ISLANDS
(to N.Z.)
FRENCH POLYNESIA
(to France)
BRAZIL
PERU
BOLIVIA
PARAGUAY
Tropic of Capricorn
PITCAIRN ISLANDS
(to U.K.)
-8½
EASTER ISLAND
(to Chile)
JUAN FERNANDEZ ISLANDS
(to Chile)
CHILE
URUGUAY
ARGENTINA
FALKLAND ISLANDS
(to U.K.)
SOUTH GEORGIA AND SOUTH SANDWICH ISLANDS
(to U.K.)
CAPE VERDE
ASCENSION
(to U.K.)
ST. HELENA
(to U.K.)
TRISTAN DA CUNHA
(to U.K.)
GOUGH ISLAND
(to U.K.)
NORWAY
SWEDEN
FINLAND
ESTONIA
LATVIA
LITH.
DENMARK
UNITED KINGDOM
REP. OF IRELAND
NETH.
BELG.
LUX.
GERMANY
POLAND
BELARUS
UKRAINE
CZECH.
SLOVAKIA
FRANCE
SWITZ.
AUST.
HUNGARY
MOL.
SLOV.
CRO.
BOS. HERZ.
SERB.
MONT.
ROMANIA
BULGARIA
MAC.
ALB.
ITALY
GREECE
TURKE
TUNISIA
MALTA
CYPRUS
LEBANON
ISRAEL
ALGERIA
LIBYA
EGYPT
MAURITANIA
MALI
NIGER
CHAD
SUDAN
SENEGAL
GAMBIA
GUINEA-BISSAU
GUINEA
BURKINA FASO
SIERRA LEONE
LIBERIA
CÔTE D'IVOIRE
GHANA
TOGO
BENIN
NIGERIA
CAMEROON
CENTRAL AFRICAN REPUBLIC
EQUATORIAL GUINEA
SÃO TOMÉ AND PRINCIPE
GABON
CONGO
DEMOCRATIC REPUBLIC OF CONGO
ANNOBÓN
(to Equatorial Guinea)
UGANDA
RWANDA
BURUNDI
TANZAN
ANGOLA
ZAMBIA
MALAWI
ZIMBABWE
NAMIBIA
BOTSWANA
SWAZI
REP. OF SOUTH AFRICA
LESOTHO
PRINC EDWA ISLAN
(to Sou Afric
SCALE 1:93,000,000
Miller Projection
01:00
02:00
03:00
04:00
05:00
06:00
07:00
08:00
09:00
10:00
11:00
12:00
13:00
14:00

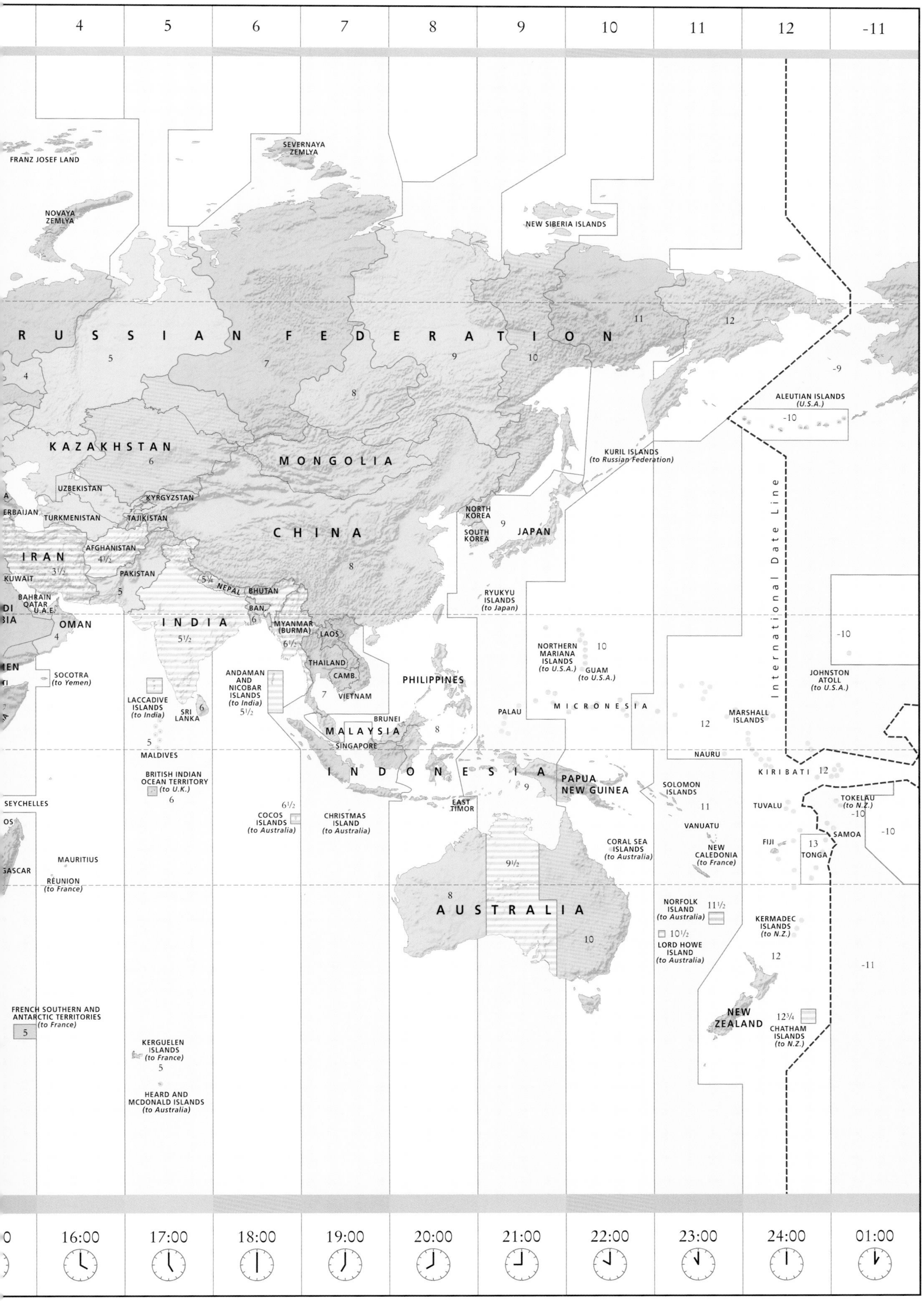
4
5
6
7
8
9
10
11
12
-11
FRANZ JOSEF LAND
SEVERNAYA ZEMLYA
NOVAYA ZEMLYA
NEW SIBERIA ISLANDS
RUSSIAN FEDERATION
KAZAKHSTAN
MONGOLIA
UZBEKISTAN
KYRGYZSTAN
TURKMENISTAN
TAJIKISTAN
AFGHANISTAN
IRAN
KUWAIT
PAKISTAN
NEPAL
BHUTAN
BAN.
BAHRAIN
QATAR
U.A.E.
OMAN
INDIA
CHINA
NORTH KOREA
SOUTH KOREA
JAPAN
KURIL ISLANDS (to Russian Federation)
ALEUTIAN ISLANDS (U.S.A.)
RYUKYU ISLANDS (to Japan)
MYANMAR (BURMA)
LAOS
THAILAND
CAMB.
VIETNAM
PHILIPPINES
SOCOTRA (to Yemen)
LACCADIVE ISLANDS (to India)
SRI LANKA
ANDAMAN AND NICOBAR ISLANDS (to India)
MALDIVES
BRITISH INDIAN OCEAN TERRITORY (to U.K.)
NORTHERN MARIANA ISLANDS (to U.S.A.)
GUAM (to U.S.A.)
MICRONESIA
PALAU
BRUNEI
MALAYSIA
SINGAPORE
INDONESIA
PAPUA NEW GUINEA
EAST TIMOR
MARSHALL ISLANDS
NAURU
KIRIBATI
JOHNSTON ATOLL (to U.S.A.)
SEYCHELLES
COCOS ISLANDS (to Australia)
CHRISTMAS ISLAND (to Australia)
SOLOMON ISLANDS
TUVALU
TOKELAU (to N.Z.)
SAMOA
VANUATU
FIJI
TONGA
CORAL SEA ISLANDS (to Australia)
NEW CALEDONIA (to France)
MAURITIUS
RÉUNION (to France)
AUSTRALIA
NORFOLK ISLAND (to Australia)
LORD HOWE ISLAND (to Australia)
KERMADEC ISLANDS (to N.Z.)
NEW ZEALAND
CHATHAM ISLANDS (to N.Z.)
FRENCH SOUTHERN AND ANTARCTIC TERRITORIES (to France)
KERGUELEN ISLANDS (to France)
HEARD AND MCDONALD ISLANDS (to Australia)
International Date Line
16:00
17:00
18:00
19:00
20:00
21:00
22:00
23:00
24:00
01:00

The standard time zone system is based on the theoretical division of the world into 24 zones of 15° of longitude. Each zone represents one hour of time. The middle meridian of each zone sets the time for that zone. The zero time zone is 7½° east and 7½° west of 0° longitude, the Greenwich (or prime) meridian. The time at this meridian is refered to as Greenwich mean time (GMT). Time zones to the west of the Greenwich meridian are earlier and zones to the east are later. The International Date Line has been designated at 180° longitude. The time is the same on both sides of this line but east of the International Date Line is one day earlier than it is to the west of the line.

Individual nations set their legal time based on this standard time zone system. For convenience certain islands or frontiers may be kept in a different time zone to the one in which they are physically located. For example, the South Island of New Zealand maintains the same time as the North Island despite its location in a different time zone. The time in certain nations or territories may differ from the rest of a zone by a fraction of an hour (for example India). This is indicated on the map by the striped areas. Some countries adjust the legal time for part of the year, particularly summer. They often advance their time by one hour to maximize the use of daylight hours.

On this map each zone is assigned a color. The numbers at the top of the map, and on each zone, signify the number of hours the zone is ahead or behind GMT. The 24-hour time and clocks at the bottom of the map indicate the time in each zone when it is 12:00 noon GMT.

The Greenwich meridian, located in London, England marks 0° longitude and the zero time zone.

FACT FILE

EUROPE

	Area sq miles (sq km)	Population	Capital	Currency	Official Languages	Other Languages	Main Religions	Life Expectancy	Literacy Rate	Economy	GDP US$
Albania	11,100 (28,750)	3,654,960	Tirana	lek (ALL)	Albanian (Tosk is the official dialect)	Greek	☪ 70%, ☦ 20%, ✝ 10%	72.1	86.5%,	⚘ 52%, ♜ 21%, ⚖ 27%	13.2 billion
Andorra	180 (470)	70,550	Andorra la Vella	euro (EUR)	Catalan	French, Castilian Spanish	✝	83.48	100%	NA	1.3 billion
Austria	32,380 (83,860)	8,221,260	Vienna	euro (EUR)	German		✝ 78%, ✚ 5%, ☪ and ✳ 17%	78	98%	⚘2%, ♜ 29%, ⚖ 69%	220 billion
Belarus	80,150 (207,600)	10,300,480	Minsk	Belarusian ruble (BYB/BYR)	Belarusian	Russian	☦ 80%, ✳ 20%	68.28	99.6%	⚘13%, ♜ 42%, ⚖ 45%	84.8 billion
Belgium	11,780 (30,510)	10,313,490	Brussels	euro (EUR)	Dutch, French, German		✝ 75%, ✚ or ✳ 25%	78.13	98%	⚘1.4%, ♜ 24%, ⚖ 74.6%	267.7 billion
Bosnia and Herzegovina	19,740 (51,130)	4,025,480	Sarajevo	marka (BAM)	Croatian, Serbian, Bosnian		☪ 40%, ☦ 31%, ✝ 15%, ✚ 4%, ✳ 10%	72.02	NA	⚘ 16%, ♜ 28%, ⚖ 56%	7 billion
Bulgaria	42,820 (110,910)	7,377,370	Sofia	lev (BGL)	Bulgarian		☦ 83.8%, ☪ 12.1%, ✝ 1.7%, ✡ 0.8%, ✚ and ✳ 1.6%	71.5	98.6%	⚘ 14.5%, ♜ 27.8%, ⚖ 57.7%	48 billion
Croatia	21,830 (56,540)	4,449,290	Zagreb	kuna (HRK)	Croatian	Italian, Hungarian, Czech, Slovak, German	✝ 76.5%, ☦ 11.1%, ☪ 1.2%, ✚ 0.4%, ✳ 10.8%	74.13	98.5%	⚘ 10%, ♜ 33%, ⚖ 57%	36.1 billion
Czech Republic	30,450 (78,870)	10,230,740	Prague	Czech koruna (CZK)	Czech		≡ 39.8%, ✝ 39.2%, ✚ 4.6%, ☦ 3%, ✳ 13.4%	74.95	99.9% (1999)	⚘ 5%, ♜ 41%, ⚖ 54%	147.9 billion
Denmark	16,640 (43,090)	5,413,720	Copenhagen	Danish krone (DKK)	Danish	English, Faroese, Greenlandic, German	✚ 95%, ∝ 3%, ☪ 2%	76.91	100%	⚘ 3%, ♜ 22%, ⚖ 75%	149.8 billion
Estonia	17,460 (45,230)	1,395,850	Tallinn	Estonian kroon (EEK)	Estonian	Russian, Ukrainian, Finnish, other	✚, ☦, ✝, ✡, ∝	70.02	99.8%	⚘ 6%, ♜ 28%, ⚖ 66%,	14.3 billion
Finland	130,130 (337,030)	5,203,940	Helsinki	euro (EUR)	Finnish	Swedish, Lapp, Russian	✚ 89%, ☦ 1%, ✳ 9%	77.75	100% (1980)	⚘ 3%, ♜ 28%, ⚖ 69%	133.5 billion
France	211,210 (547,030)	60,656,180	Paris	euro (EUR)	French	Provencal, Breton, Alsatian, Corsican, Basque, Flemish	✝ 83%-88%, ✚ 2%, ✡ 1%, ☪ 5%-10%, ✳ 4%	79.05	99% (1980)	⚘ 3.3%, ♜ 25.7%, ⚖ 71%	1.51 trillion
Germany	137,850 (357,020)	82,431,390	Berlin	euro (EUR)	German		✚ 34%, ✝ 34%, ☪ 3.7%, ✳ 28.3%	77.78	99% (1977)	⚘ 1%, ♜ 28%, ⚖ 71%	2.174 trillion
Greece	50,940 (131,940)	10,703,500	Athens	euro (EUR)	Greek	English, French	☦ 98%, ☪ 1.3%, ✳ 0.7%	78.74	97.5%	⚘ 8.3%, ♜ 27.3%, ⚖ 64.4%	189.7 billion
Hungary	35,920 (93,030)	9,986,520	Budapest	forint (HUF)	Hungarian		✝ 67.5%, ✚ 25%, ≡ and ✳ 7.5%	71.9	99.4%	⚘ 6%, ♜ 34%, ⚖ 60%	120.9 billion
Iceland	39,770 (103,000)	283,440	Reykjavík	Icelandic krona (ISK)	Icelandic		✚ 93%, ∝ and ✳ 7%	79.66	99.9% (1997)	⚘ 15% (includes fishing 13%), ♜ 21%, ⚖ 64%	6.85 billion
Ireland, Republic of	27,140 (70,280)	4,001,530	Dublin	euro (EUR)	English, Irish (Gaelic)		✝ 91.6%, ✚ 2.5%, ✳ 5.9%	77.17	98% (1981)	⚘ 4%, ♜ 38%, ⚖ 58%	104.7 billion
Italy	116,310 (301,230)	58,103,030	Rome	euro (EUR)	Italian	German, French, Slovene, Albanian, Greek, Italian	✝, ✚, ✡, ☪	79.25	98.6%	⚘ 2.4%, ♜ 30%, ⚖ 67.6%	1.402 trillion
Latvia	24,940 (64,590)	2,316,420	Rīga	Latvian lat (LVL)	Latvian	Lithuanian, Russian	✝, ✚, ☦	69	99.8%	⚘ 5%, ♜ 24%, ⚖ 71%	18.6 billion
Liechtenstein	62 (160)	33,720	Vaduz	Swiss franc (CHF)	German	Alemannic dialect	✝ 80%, ✚ 7.4%, ✳ 12.6%	79.1	100%	NA	730 million
Lithuania	25,170 (65,200)	3,577,950	Vilnius	litas (LTL)	Lithuanian	Polish, Russian	✝, ✚, ☦, ☪, ✡	69.42	99.6% (1981)	⚘ 9%, ♜ 32%, ⚖ 59%	27.4 billion
Luxembourg	1,000 (2,590)	465,250	Luxembourg	euro (EUR)	Luxembourgish	German, French	✝ (predominantly), ✚, ✡, ☪	77.48	100%	⚘ 1%, ♜ 30%, ⚖ 69%	19.2 billion
Macedonia (F.Y.R.O.M.)	9,780 (25,330)	2,079,060	Skopje	Macedonian denar (MKD)	Macedonian	Albanian, Turkish, Serbo-Croatian	☦ 67%, ☪ 30%, ✳ 3%	74.26	NA	⚘ 10%, ♜ 32%, ⚖ 58%	9 billion
Malta	122 (316)	406,260	Valletta	Maltese lira (MTL)	Maltese, English		✝ 91%	78.26	92.8%	⚘ 2.8%, ♜ 25.5%, ⚖ 71.7%	5.95 billion

Key to symbols: ∝ Christian ✝ Catholic ☦ Orthodox ✚ Protestant ☸ Buddhist ॐ Hindu ✡ Jewish ☪ Muslim ≡ Atheist ○ Indigenous ✳ Other ⚘ Agriculture ♜ Industry ⚖ Services NA Not Available
Note: All literacy statistics are for 2003 unless otherwise stated.

Area sq miles (sq km)	Population	Capital	Currency	Official Languages	Other Languages	Main Religions	Life Expectancy	Literacy Rate	Economy	GDP US$	
13,070 (33,840)	4,455,420	Chişinău	Moldovan leu (MDL)	Moldovan, Russian	Gagauz (a Turkish dialect)	☦ 98.5%, ✡ 1.5%	64.74	99.1%	⚘ 28%, ♜ 21%, ⚑ 51%	11.3 billion	Moldova
0.75 (1.95)	32,410	Monaco	euro (EUR)	French	English, Italian, Monegasque	✙ 90%	79.12	99%	NA	870 million	Monaco
16,030 (41,530)	16,304,210	Amsterdam, The Hague	euro (EUR)	Dutch		✙ 31%, ✝ 21%, ☪ 4.4%, ✱ 43.6%	78.58	99% (2000)	⚘ 3.3%, ♜ 26.3%, ⚑ 70.4%	413 billion	Netherlands
125,180 (324,220)	4,586,160	Oslo	Norwegian krone (NOK)	Norwegian	Saami, Finnish	✝ 86%, ∝ 3%, ✱ 11%	78.94	100%	⚘ 2%, ♜ 31%, ⚑ 67%	138.7 billion	Norway
120,730 (312,690)	38,635,140	Warsaw	zloty (PLN)	Polish		✙ 95%, ☦, ✝ and ✱ 5%	73.66	99.8%	⚘ 4%, ♜ 32%, ⚑ 64%	339.6 billion	Poland
35,670 (92,390)	10,135,380	Lisbon	euro (EUR)	Portuguese		✙ 94%, ✝	76.14	93.3%	⚘ 3.8%, ♜ 30.5%, ⚑ 65.7%	174.1 billion	Portugal
91,700 (237,500)	22,178,400	Bucharest	leu (ROL)	Romanian	Hungarian, German	☦ 70%, ✙ 6%, ✝ 6%, ✱ 18%	70.39	98.4%	⚘ 15%, ♜ 30%, ⚑ 55%	152.7 billion	Romania
24 (61)	28,880	San Marino	euro (EUR)	Italian		✙	81.33	96% (1976)	NA	940 million	San Marino
39,520 (102,350)	10,668,570	Belgrade	new Yugoslav dinar (YUM), euro (EUR)	Serbian, Albanian		☦ 65%, ☪ 19%, ✙ 4%, ✝ 1%, ✱ 11%	73.72	93% (1991)	⚘ 26%, ♜ 36%, ⚑ 38%	24 billion	Serbia and Montenegro
18,860 (48,850)	5,444,900	Bratislava	Slovak koruna (SKK)	Slovak	Hungarian	✙ 60.3%, ≡ 9.7%, ✝ 8.4%, ☦ 4.1%, ✱ 17.5%	74.2	NA	⚘ 4%, ♜ 32%, ⚑ 64%	62 billion	Slovakia
7,830 (20,720)	1,940,630	Ljubljana	tolar (SIT)	Slovenian, Serbo-Croatian		✙ 70.8%, ✝ 1%, ☪ 1%, ≡ 4.3%, ✱ 22.9%	75.29	99.7%	⚘ 4%, ♜ 35%, ⚑ 61%	31 billion	Slovenia
194,900 (504,780)	40,341,460	Madrid	euro (EUR)	Castilian Spanish	Catalan, Galician, Basque	✙ 94%, ✱ 6%	79.08	97.9%	⚘ 4%, ♜ 28%, ⚑ 68%	757 billion	Spain
173,730 (449,960)	8,879,790	Stockholm	Swedish krona (SEK)	Swedish	Saami, Finnish	✝ 87%, ✙, ☦, ☪, ✡, and ॐ 13%	79.84	99% (1979)	⚘ 2%, ♜ 28.7%, ⚑ 69.3%	219 billion	Sweden
15,940 (41,290)	7,346,070	Bern	Swiss franc (CHF)	German, French, Italian	Romansch, other	✙ 46.1%, ✝ 40%, ✱ 13.9%	79.86	99% (1980)	⚘ 2%, ♜ 34%, ⚑ 64%	226 billion	Switzerland
233,090 (603,700)	47,425,340	Kiev	hryvnia (UAH)	Ukrainian	Russian, Romanian, Polish, Hungarian	☦, ✙, ✝, ✡	66.33	99.7%	NA	205 billion	Ukraine
94,530 (244,820)	60,441,460	London	British pound (GBP)	English, Welsh, Scottish Gaelic		✙, ✝, ☪, ॐ, ✡, ✱	77.99	99% (2000)	⚘ 1.7%, ♜ 24.9%, ⚑ 73.4%	1.47 trillion	United Kingdom
0.17 (0.44)	900	Vatican City	euro (EUR)	Italian, Latin, French		✙		NA	NA	NA	Vatican City
171 (443)	68,720	Saint John's	East Caribbean dollar (XCD)	English	Local dialects	✝, ✙	71.02	89% (1960)	⚘ 3.9%, ♜ 19.1%, ⚑ 77%	674 million	Antigua and Barbuda
5,380 (13,940)	301,790	Nassau	Bahamian dollar (BSD)	English	Creole	✝ 70%, ✙ 19%, ∝ 6%, ✱ 5%	69.87	95.6%	⚘ 3%, ♜ 7%, ⚑ 90%	5 billion	The Bahamas
166 (431)	279,250	Bridgetown	Barbadian dollar (BBD)	English		✝ 67%, ✙ 4%, ✱ 29%	73.49	97.4% (1995)	⚘ 6%, ♜ 16%, ⚑ 78%	4 billion	Barbados
8,870 (22,970)	279,460	Belmopan	Belizean dollar (BZD)	English	Spanish, Mayan, Garifuna (Carib), Creole	✙ 49.6%, ✝ 27%, ✱ 23.4%	71.46	94.1%	⚘ 18%, ♜ 24%, ⚑ 58%	830 million	Belize
3,474,920 (9,984,670)	32,805,040	Ottawa	Canadian dollar (CAD)	English, French		✙ 46%, ✝ 36%, ✱ 18%	79.69	97% (1986)	⚘ 2%, ♜ 29%, ⚑ 69%	875 billion	Canada
19,730 (51,100)	4,016,170	San José	Costa Rican colon (CRC)	Spanish	English	✙ 76.3%, ✝ 15.7%, ✱ 8%	76.22	96%	⚘ 11%, ♜ 37%, ⚑ 52%	31.9 billion	Costa Rica
42,800 (110,860)	11,339,890	Havana	Cuban peso (CUP)	Spanish		✙, ✝, ✡, ✱	76.6	96.9%	⚘ 7.6%, ♜ 34.5%, ⚑ 57.9%	25.5 billion	Cuba
291 (754)	69,030	Roseau	East Caribbean dollar (XCD)	English	French patois	✙ 77%, ✝ 15%, ✱ 8%	73.86	94%	NA	262 million	Dominica

Key to symbols: ∝ Christian ✙ Catholic ☦ Orthodox ✝ Protestant ☸ Buddhist ॐ Hindu ✡ Jewish ☪ Muslim ≡ Atheist ○ Indigenous ✱ Other ⚘ Agriculture ♜ Industry ⚑ Services NA Not Available

Note: All literacy statistics are for 2003 unless otherwise stated.

Fact File

	Area sq miles (sq km)	Population	Capital	Currency	Official Languages	Other Languages	Main Religions	Life Expectancy	Literacy Rate	Economy	GDP US$
Dominican Republic	18,810 (48,730)	8,950,030	Santo Domingo	Dominican peso (DOP)	Spanish		✟ 95%	73.68	84.7%	Agriculture 11.1%, Industry 34.1%, Services 54.8%	50 billion
El Salvador	8,120 (21,040)	6,704,930	San Salvador	Salvadoran colon (SVC), U.S. dollar (USD)	Spanish	Nahua	✟ 83% ✝	70.32	80.2%	Agriculture 10%, Industry 30%, Services 60%	28.4 billion
Grenada	133 (344)	89,500	St George's	East Caribbean dollar (XCD)	English	French patois	✟ 53%, ✝ 47%	64.52	98% (1970)	Agriculture 7.7%, Industry 23.9%, Services 68.4%	424 million
Guatemala	42,040 (108,890)	14,655,190	Guatemala	quetzal (GTQ), U.S. dollar (USD)	Spanish	Amerindian languages	✟, ✝, ○	66.85	70.6%	Agriculture 23%, Industry 20%, Services 57%	48.3 billion
Haiti	10,710 (27,750)	7,790,340	Port-au-Prince	gourde (HTG)	French, Creole		✟ 80%, ✝ 16%, * 4%	49.55	52.9%	Agriculture 30%, Industry 20%, Services 50%	12 billion
Honduras	43,280 (112,090)	6,975,200	Tegucigalpa	lempira (HNL)	Spanish	Amerindian dialects	✟ 97%, ✝	68.77	76.2%	Agriculture 18%, Industry 32%, Services 50%	17 billion
Jamaica	4,240 (10,990)	2,731,830	Kingston	Jamaican dollar (JMD)	English	Patois English	✝ 61.3%, ✟ 4%, * 34.7%	75.64	87.9%	Agriculture 7%, Industry 28%, Services 65%	9.8 billion
Mexico	761,610 (1,972,550)	107,869,840	Mexico City	Mexican peso (MXN)	Spanish	Mayan, Nahuatl, other indigenous languages	✟ 89%, ✝ 6%, * 5%	72.03	92.2%	Agriculture 5%, Industry 26%, Services 69%	920 billion
Nicaragua	50,000 (129,490)	5,334,680	Managua	gold cordoba (NIO)	Spanish	English, indigenous languages	✟ 85%, ✝	69.37	67.5%	Agriculture 33%, Industry 23%, Services 44%	12.3 billion
Panama	30,190 (78,200)	3,039,150	Panama City	balboa (PAB), U.S. dollar (USD)	Spanish	English	✟ 85%, ✝ 15%	75.89	92.6%	Agriculture 7%, Industry 17%, Services 76%	16.9 billion
St Kitts and Nevis	101 (261)	38,960	Basseterre	East Caribbean dollar (XCD)	English		✝, ✟	71.29	97% (1980)	Agriculture 3.5%, Industry 25.8%, Services 70.7%	339 million
St Lucia	238 (616)	166,310	Castries	East Caribbean dollar (XCD)	English	French patois	✟ 90%, ✝ 10%	72.82	67% (1980)	Agriculture 7.9%, Industry 19.6%, Services 72.5%	700 million
St Vincent and the Grenadines	150 (389)	117,530	Kingstown	East Caribbean dollar (XCD)	English	French patois	✝ 75%, ✟ 13%, * 12%	72.82	96% (1970)	Agriculture 10%, Industry 26%, Services 64%	339 million
Trinidad and Tobago	1,980 (5,130)	1,088,640	Port of Spain	Trinidad and Tobago dollar (TTD)	English	Hindi, French, Spanish, Chinese	✟ 29.4%, ॐ 23.8%, ✝ 14.3%, ☪ 5.8%, * 26.7%	68.59	98.6%	Agriculture 1.6%, Industry 43.2%, Services 55.2%	10.6 billion
United States of America	3,717,810 (9,629,090)	295,734,130	Washington, D.C.	U.S. dollar (USD)	English	Spanish	✝ 56%, ✟ 28%, ✡ 2%, * 14%	77.4	97% (1979)	Agriculture 2%, Industry 18%, Services 80%	10.082 trillion
SOUTH AMERICA											
Argentina	1,068,300 (2,766,890)	39,537,940	Buenos Aires	Argentine peso (ARS)	Spanish	English, Italian, German, French	✟ 92%, ✝ 2%, ✡ 2%, * 4%	75.48	97.1%	Agriculture 6%, Industry 28%, Services 66%	453 billion
Bolivia	424,160 (1,098,580)	8,857,870	La Paz, Sucre	boliviano (BOB)	Spanish, Quechua, Aymara		✟ 95%, ✝	64.42	87.2%	Agriculture 14%, Industry 31%, Services 55%	21.4 billion
Brazil	3,286,490 (8,511,970)	186,112,790	Brasília	real (BRL)	Portuguese	Spanish, English, French	✟ 80%	63.55	86.4%	Agriculture 9%, Industry 32%, Services 59%	1.34 trillion
Chile	292,260 (756,950)	15,984,780	Santiago	Chilean peso (CLP)	Spanish		✟ 89%, ✝ 11%, ✡ less than 1%	76.14	96.2%	Agriculture 8%, Industry 38%, Services 54%	153 billion
Colombia	439,740 (1,138,910)	42,954,280	Bogotá	Colombian peso (COP)	Spanish		✟ 90%, * 10%	70.85	92.5%	Agriculture 19%, Industry 26%, Services 55%	255 billion
Ecuador	109,480 (283,560)	14,231,760	Quito	U.S. dollar (USD)	Spanish		✟ 95%, * 5%	71.61	92.5%	Agriculture 11%, Industry 25%, Services 64%	39.6 billion
Guyana	83,000 (214,970)	710,660	Georgetown	Guyanese dollar (GYD)	English	Amerindian dialects, Creole, Hindi, Urdu	∝ 50%, ॐ 35%, ☪ 10%, * 5%	62.59	98.8%	Agriculture 36.1%, Industry 31.8%, Services 32.1%	2.5 billion
Paraguay	157,050 (406,750)	6,347,880	Asunción	guarani (PYG)	Spanish, Guarani		✟ 90%, * 10%	74.16	94%	Agriculture 29%, Industry 26%, Services 45%	26.2 billion
Peru	496,230 (1,285,220)	29,309,290	Lima	nuevo sol (PEN)	Spanish, Quechua	Aymara	✟ 90%, * 10%	70.59	90.9%	Agriculture 10%, Industry 35%, Services 55%	132 billion
Suriname	63,040 (163,270)	438,140	Paramaribo	Surinamese guilder (SRG)	Dutch	English, Sranang Tongo, Hindustani, Javanese	ॐ 27.4%, ☪ 19.6%, ✟ 22.8%, ✝ 25.2%, ○ 5%	71.9	93% (1995)	Agriculture 13%, Industry 22%, Services 65%	1.5 billion

Key to symbols: ∝ Christian ✟ Catholic ☦ Orthodox ✝ Protestant ☸ Buddhist ॐ Hindu ✡ Jewish ☪ Muslim ≡ Atheist ○ Indigenous * Other Agriculture Industry Services **NA** Not Available

Note: All literacy statistics are for 2003 unless otherwise stated.

Area sq miles (sq km)	Population	Capital	Currency	Official Languages	Other Languages	Main Religions	Life Expectancy	Literacy Rate	Economy	GDP US$	
68,040 (176,220)	3,467,070	Montevideo	Uruguayan peso (UYU)	Spanish, Portunol, Brazilero		✟ 66%, ✝ 2%, ✡ 1%, ✱ 31%	75.66	98%	⚘ 6%, ♜ 29%, ⚑ 65%	31 billion	Uruguay
352,140 (912,050)	25,375,280	Caracas	bolivar (VEB)	Spanish	Indigenous dialects	✟ 96%, ✝ 2%, ✱ 2%	73.56	93.4%	⚘ 5%, ♜ 40%, ⚑ 55%	146.2 billion	Venezuela
250,000 (647,500)	30,241,190	Kabul	afghani (AFA)	Pashtu, Afghan Persian (Dari)	Turkic languages, other languages	☪ 99%, ✱ 1%	46.6	36% (1999)	⚘ 60%, ♜ 20%, ⚑ 20% (1990 est.)	21 billion	Afghanistan
11,510 (29,800)	3,326,830	Yerevan	dram (AMD)	Armenian, Russian		∝ 98%, ✱ 2%	66.59	98.6%	⚘ 29%, ♜ 32%, ⚑ 39%	11.2 billion	Armenia
33,440 (86,600)	7,911,970	Baku	Azerbaijani manat (AZM)	Azerbaijani (Azeri), Russian	Armenian, other	☪ 93.4%, ☦ 4.8%, ✱ 1.8%	63.06	97% (1989)	⚘ 22%, ♜ 33%, ⚑ 45%	24.3 billion	Azerbaijan
257 (665)	688,350	Al Manāmah	Bahraini dinar (BHD)	Arabic, English, Farsi, Urdu		☪ 100%	73.47	89.1%	⚘ 1%, ♜ 35%, ⚑ 64%	8.4 billion	Bahrain
55,600 (144,000)	144,319,630	Dacca	taka (BDT)	Bangla (also known as Bengali)	English	☪ 83%, ॐ 16%, ✱ 1%	60.92	43.1%	⚘ 30%, ♜ 18%, ⚑ 52%	230 billion	Bangladesh
18,147 (47,000)	2,232,290	Thimphu	ngultrum (BTN), Indian rupee (INR)	Dzongkha	Tibetan dialects, Nepalese dialects	☸ 75%, ॐ 25%	53.19	42.2% (1995)	⚘ 45%, ♜ 20%, ⚑ 35%	2.5 billion	Bhutan
2,230 (5,770)	372,360	Bandar Seri Begawan	Bruneian dollar (BND)	Malay	English, Chinese	☪ 67%, ☸ 13%, ∝ 10%, ○ and ✱ 10%	74.06	91.8%	⚘ 5%, ♜ 45%, ⚑ 50%	6.2 billion	Brunei
69,900 (181,040)	13,607,070	Phnom Penh	riel (KHR)	Khmer	French, English	☸ 95%, ✱ 5%	57.1	69.9%	⚘ 50%, ♜ 15%, ⚑ 35%	18.7 billion	Cambodia
3,705,410 (9,569,960)	1,302,207,990	Beijing	yuan (CNY)	Mandarin, Cantonese, Shanghaiese	Fuzhou, Hokkien-Taiwanese, Xiang, Gan, Hakka, other	☪ 1%-2%, ∝ 3%-4%, ☸, ✱	71.86	86%	⚘ 17.7%, ♜ 49.3%, ⚑ 33%	5.56 trillion	China
3,570 (9,250)	780,130	Nicosia	Cypriot pound (CYP), Turkish lira (TRL)	Greek, Turkish, English		☦ 78%, ☪ 18%, ✱ 4%	77.08	97.6%	Gr: ⚘4.6%, ♜19.9%, ⚑75.5%, Tk: ⚘8.3%, ♜20.7%, ⚑71.0%	10.2 billion	Cyprus
5,800 (15,010)	1,040,880	Dili	U.S. dollar (USD)	Tetum, Portuguese	Indonesian, English, Tetum, Galole, Mambae, Kemak	✟ 90%, ☪ 4%, ✝ 3%, ॐ 0.5%, ☸, ○	64.85	48% (2001)	⚘ 25.4%, ♜ 17.2%, ⚑ 57.4%	415 million	East Timor
26,910 (69,700)	4,886,720	T'bilisi	lari (GEL)	Georgian	Russian, Armenian, Azeri	☦ 75%, ☪ 11%, ✱ 14%	64.67	99% (1999)	⚘ 25%, ♜ 20%, ⚑ 55%	15.5 billion	Georgia
1,269,345 (3,287,590)	1,080,264,390	New Delhi	Indian rupee (INR)	Hindi	English, Bengali, Telugu, Marathi, Tamil, Urdu, other	ॐ 81.3%, ☪ 12%, ∝ 2.3%, ✱ 4.4%	63.23	59.5%	⚘ 25%, ♜ 26%, ⚑ 49%	2.5 trillion	India
741,100 (1,919,440)	241,973,880	Jakarta	Indonesian rupiah (IDR)	Bahasa Indonesia	English, Dutch, Javanese, local dialects	☪ 88%, ✝ 5%, ✟ 3%, ॐ 2%, ☸ 1%, ✱ 1%	68.63	88.5%	⚘ 17%, ♜ 41%, ⚑ 42%	687 billion	Indonesia
636,300 (1,648,000)	69,765,580	Tehran	Iranian rial (IRR)	Persian	Turkic, Kurdish, Luri, Balochi, Arabic, Turkish	☪ 99%, ✱ 1%	70.25	79.4%	⚘ 20%, ♜ 24%, ⚑ 56%	426 billion	Iran
168,750 (437,070)	26,074,910	Baghdad	Iraqi dinar (IQD)	Arabic, Kurdish	Assyrian, Armenian	☪ 97%, ∝ or ✱ 3%	67.38	40.4%	⚘ 6%, ♜ 13%, ⚑ 81% (1993 est.)	59 billion	Iraq
8,020 (20,070)	6,276,880	Jerusalem	new Israeli shekel (ILS)	Hebrew	Arabic, English	✡ 80.1%, ☪ 14.6%, ∝ 2.1%, ✱ 3.2%	78.86	95.4%	⚘ 4%, ♜ 37%, ⚑ 59%	119 billion	Israel
145,880 (377,840)	127,417,240	Tokyo	yen (JPY)	Japanese		☸ 84%, ✱ 16%	80.91	99% (1995)	⚘ 2%, ♜ 36%, ⚑ 62%	3.45 trillion	Japan
35,640 (92,300)	5,759,730	Ammān	Jordanian dinar (JOD)	Arabic	English	☪ 92%, ∝ 6%, ✱ 2%	77.71	91.3%	⚘ 3.7%, ♜ 26%, ⚑ 70.3%	21.6 billion	Jordan
1,049,155 (2,717,300)	16,846,390	Astana	tenge (KZT)	Kazakh, Russian		☪ 47%, ☦ 44%, ✝ 2%, ✱ 7%	63.38	98.4% (1999)	⚘ 10%, ♜ 30%, ⚑ 60%	98.1 billion	Kazakhstan
6,880 (17,820)	2,335,650	Kuwait	Kuwaiti dinar (KD)	Arabic	English	☪ 85%, ∝, ॐ, and ✱ 15%	76.46	83.5%	♜ 60%, ⚑ 39.7%, ⚘ 0.3%	30.9 billion	Kuwait
76,640 (198,500)	5,039,210	Bishkek	Kyrgyzstani som (KGS)	Kyrgyz, Russian		☪ 75%, ☦ 20%, ✱ 5%	63.56	97% (1989)	⚘ 38%, ♜ 27%, ⚑ 35%	13.5 billion	Kyrgyzstan
91,430 (236,800)	6,217,140	Vientiane	kip (LAK)	Lao	French, English, other	☸ 60%, ✱ 40%	53.88	52.8%	⚘ 53%, ♜ 22%, ⚑ 25%	9.2 billion	Laos

Key to symbols: ∝ Christian ✟ Catholic ☦ Orthodox ✝ Protestant ☸ Buddhist ॐ Hindu ✡ Jewish ☪ Muslim ≡ Atheist ○ Indigenous ✱ Other ⚘ Agriculture ♜ Industry ⚑ Services NA Not Available
Note: All literacy statistics are for 2003 unless otherwise stated.

Fact File

	Area sq miles (sq km)	Population	Capital	Currency	Official Languages	Other Languages	Main Religions	Life Expectancy	Literacy Rate	Economy	GDP US$
Lebanon	4,020 (10,400)	3,826,020	Beirut	Lebanese pound (LBP)	Arabic	French, English, Armenian	☪ 70%, ∝ 30%, ✡ less than 1%	71.79	87.4%	⚘ 12%, ▲ 21%, ⚇ 67%	18.8 billion
Malaysia	127,320 (329,750)	23,953,140	Kuala Lumpur	ringgit (MYR)	Bahasa Melayu	English, Chinese dialects, Iban, Kadazan	☪, ☸, ॐ, ∝, ✱	71.39	88.9%	⚘ 12%, ▲ 40%, ⚇ 48%	200 billion
Maldives	116 (300)	349,110	Male	rufiyaa (MVR)	Maldivian Dhivehi (dialect of Sinhala)	English	☪	62.93	97.2%	⚘ 20%, ▲ 18%, ⚇ 62%	1.2 billion
Mongolia	604,250 (1,565,000)	2,791,270	Ulaanbaatar	ogrog/tugrik (MNT)	Khalkha Mongol, Turkic, Russian		☸ 96%, ☪ and ∝ 4%	64.62	99.1%	⚘ 32%, ▲ 30%, ⚇ 38%	4.7 billion
Myanmar (Burma)	261,970 (678,500)	42,909,460	Rangoon	kyat (MMK)	Burmese	Minority ethnic groups have their own languages	☸ 89%, ∝ 4%, ☪ 4%, ✱ 3%	55.41	30% (1999)	⚘ 42%, ▲ 17%, ⚇ 41%	63 billion
Nepal	54,360 (140,800)	27,676,550	Kathmandu	Nepalese rupee (NPR)	Nepali	English, 12 other languages, about 30 major dialects	☸ 86.2%, ॐ 7.8%, ☪ 3.8%, ✱ 2.2%	58.61	45.2%	⚘ 41%, ▲ 22%, ⚇ 37%	35.6 billion
North Korea	46,540 (120,540)	22,912,180	P'yŏngyang	North Korean won (KPW)	Korean		☸, ∝, ✱	71.3	99%	⚘ 30%, ▲ 42%, ⚇ 28%	21.8 billion
Oman	82,030 (212,460)	3,001,580	Muscat	Omani rial (OMR)	Arabic	English, Baluchi, Urdu, Indian dialects	☪ 75%,	72.31	75.8%	⚘ 3%, ▲ 40%, ⚇ 57%	21.5 billion
Pakistan	310,400 (803,940)	156,689,150	Islamabad	Pakistani rupee (PKR)	Urdu, English	Punjabi, Sindhi, Siraiki, Pashtu, Balochi, other	☪ 97%, ∝, ॐ, ✱ 3%	61.82	45.7%	⚘ 26%, ▲ 24%, ⚇ 50%	299 billion
Philippines	115,830 (300,000)	87,857,470	Manila	Philippine peso (PHP)	Filipino (based on Tagalog), English	Tagalog, Cebuano, Ilocan, Hiligaynon, Bicol, Waray, other	☩ 83%, ✝ 9%, ☪ 5%, ☸ and ✱ 3%	68.12	95.9%	⚘ 17%, ▲ 30%, ⚇ 53%	335 billion
Qatar	4,420 (11,440)	863,050	Doha	Qatari rial (QAR)	Arabic	English	☪ 95%	72.88	82.5%	⚘ 1%, ▲ 49%, ⚇ 50%	16.3 billion
Russian Federation	6,592,770 (17,075,200)	143,736,790	Moscow	Russian ruble (RUR)	Russian		☦, ☪, ✱	67.5	99.6%	⚘ 7%, ▲ 37%, ⚇ 56%	1.2 trillion
Saudi Arabia	756,980 (1,960,580)	25,934,590	Riyadh	Saudi riyal (SAR)	Arabic		☪ 100%	68.4	78.8%	⚘ 7%, ▲ 48%, ⚇ 45%	241 billion
Singapore	268 (693)	4,930,860	Singapore	Singapore dollar (SGD)	Chinese, Malay, Tamil, English		☸, ☪, ∝, ॐ, ✱	80.29	93.2%	▲ 33%, ⚇ 67%	106.3 billion
South Korea	38,020 (98,480)	48,893,070	Seoul	South Korean won (KRW)	Korean	English	∝ 49%, ☸ 47%, ✱ 4%	74.88	98.1%	⚘ 5%, ▲ 44%, ⚇ 51%	865 billion
Sri Lanka	25,330 (65,610)	20,064,780	Colombo, Sri Jayewarden-epura Kotte	Sri Lankan rupee (LKR)	Sinhala	Tamil	☸ 70%, ॐ 15%, ∝ 8%, ☪ 7%	72.35	92.3%	⚘ 21%, ▲ 27%, ⚇ 52%	62.7 billion
Syria	71,500 (185,180)	18,448,750	Damascus	Syrian pound (SYP)	Arabic	Kurdish, Armenian, Aramaic, Circassian, French, English	☪ 90%, ∝ 10%, ✡ less than 1%	69.08	76.9%	⚘ 27%, ▲ 23%, ⚇ 50%	54.2 billion
Taiwan	13,980 (35,980)	22,894,380	Taipei	new Taiwan dollar (TWD)	Mandarin Chinese	Taiwanese (Min), Hakka dialects	☸ 93%, ∝ 4.5%, ✱ 2.5%	76.74	86% (1980)	⚘ 2%, ▲ 32%, ⚇ 66%	386 billion
Tajikistan	55,250 (143,100)	7,163,510	Dushanbe	somoni (TJS)	Tajik	Russian	☪ 90%	64.28	99.4%	⚘ 19%, ▲ 25%, ⚇ 56%	7.5 billion
Thailand	198,460 (514,000)	65,444,370	Bangkok	baht (THB)	Thai	English, ethnic and regional dialects	☸ 95%, ☪ 3.8%, ∝ 0.5%, ॐ 0.1%, ✱ 0.6%	69.18	96%	⚘ 11%, ▲ 40%, ⚇ 49%	410 billion
Turkey	301,380 (780,580)	69,660,560	Ankara	Turkish lira (TRL)	Turkish	Kurdish, Arabic, Armenian, Greek	☪ 99.8%, ✱ 0.2%	71.52	86.5%	⚘ 14.5%, ▲ 28.4%, ⚇ 57.1%	443 billion
Turkmenistan	188,460 (488,100)	4,952,080	Ashgabat	Turkmen manat (TMM)	Turkmen, Russian, Uzbek		☪ 89%, ☦ 9%, ✱ 2%	61.1	98%	⚘ 27%, ▲ 45%, ⚇ 28%	21.5 billion
United Arab Emirates	32,000 (82,880)	2,563,210	Abu Dhabi	Emirati dirham (AED)	Arabic	Persian, English, Hindi, Urdu	☪ 96%, ∝, ॐ, and ✱ 4%	74.52	77.9%	⚘ 3%, ▲ 46%, ⚇ 51%	51 billion
Uzbekistan	172,740 (447,400)	26,851,200	Tashkent	Uzbekistani sum (UZS)	Uzbek, Russian, Tajik		☪ 88%, ☦ 9%, ✱ 3%	63.9	99.3%	⚘ 33%, ▲ 24%, ⚇ 43%	62 billion
Vietnam	127,240 (329,560)	83,769,670	Hanoi	dong (VND)	Vietnamese	English, French, Chinese, Khmer	☸, ∝, ○, ☪	69.86	94%	⚘ 25%, ▲ 35%, ⚇ 40%	168.1 billion

Key to symbols: ∝ Christian ☩ Catholic ☦ Orthodox ✝ Protestant ☸ Buddhist ॐ Hindu ✡ Jewish ☪ Muslim ≡ Atheist ○ Indigenous ✱ Other ⚘ Agriculture ▲ Industry ⚇ Services **NA** Not Available
Note: All literacy statistics are for 2003 unless otherwise stated.

AREA SQ MILES (SQ KM)	POPULATION	CAPITAL	CURRENCY	OFFICIAL LANGUAGES	OTHER LANGUAGES	MAIN RELIGIONS	LIFE EXPECTANCY	LITERACY RATE	ECONOMY	GDP US$	
203,850 (527,970)	20,727,060	Ṣan'ā'	Yemeni rial (YER)	Arabic		☪, ✡, ∝, ॐ	60.59	50.2%	🌾 17%, 🏭 40%, 👥 43%	14.8 billion	Yemen
919,590 (2,381,740)	33,892,390	Algiers	Algerian dinar (DZD)	Arabic	French, Berber dialects	☪ 99%, ∝ and ✡ 1%	70.24	70%	🌾 17%, 🏭 33%, 👥 50%	177 billion	Algeria
481,350 (1,246,700)	11,190,790	Luanda	kwanza (AOA)	Portuguese	Bantu and African languages	O 47%, ✟ 38%, ✝ 15%	38.87	42% (1998)	🌾 6%, 🏭 70%, 👥 24%	13.3 billion	Angola
43,480 (112,620)	7,460,030	Porto-Novo	Communaute Financiere Africaine franc (XOF)	French	Fon, Yoruba, tribal languages	O 50%, ∝ 30%, ☪ 20%	49.69	40.9% (2000)	🌾 36%, 🏭 14%, 👥 50%	6.8 billion	Benin
231,800 (600,370)	1,545,290	Gaborone	pula (BWP)	English	Setswana	O 85%, ∝ 15%	35.29	79.8%	🌾 4%, 🏭 44% (including 36% mining), 👥 52%	12.4 billion	Botswana
105,870 (274,200)	13,925,310	Ouagadougou	Communaute Financiere Africaine franc (XOF)	French	African languages (belonging to Sudanic family)	O 40%, ☪ 50%, ∝ 10%	46.11	26.6%	🌾 31%, 🏭 28%, 👥 41%	12.8 billion	Burkina Faso
10,750 (27,830)	6,370,610	Bujumbura	Burundi franc (BIF)	Kirundi, French	Swahili	∝ 67%, O 23%, ☪ 10%	45.94	51.6%	🌾 50%, 🏭 18%, 👥 32%	3.7 billion	Burundi
183,570 (475,440)	16,380,010	Yaoundé	Communaute Financiere Africaine franc (XAF)	English, French	24 major African language groups	O 40%, ∝ 40%, ☪ 20%	54.36	79%	🌾 44%, 🏭 20%, 👥 36%	26.4 billion	Cameroon
1,560 (4,030)	418,220	Praia	Cape Verdean escudo (CVE)	Portuguese, Crioulo		✟, ✝	69.52	76.6%	🌾 11%, 🏭 17%, 👥 72%	600 million	Cape Verde
240,530 (622,980)	3,799,900	Bangui	Communaute Financiere Africaine franc (XAF)	French	Sangho, tribal languages	O 35%, ✝ 25%, ✟ 25%, ☪ 15%	43.58	51%	🌾 55%, 🏭 20%, 👥 25%	4.6 billion	Central African Republic
495,760 (1,284,000)	9,826,420	Ndjamena	Communaute Financiere Africaine franc (XAF)	French, Arabic	Sara, more than 120 languages and dialects	☪ 51%, ∝ 35%, ✱ 14%	51.27	47.5%	🌾 38%, 🏭 13%, 👥 49%	8.9 billion	Chad
838 (2,170)	671,250	Moroni	Comoran franc (KMF)	Arabic, French	Shikomoro (a blend of Swahili and Arabic)	☪ 98%, ✟ 2%	60.79	56.5%	🌾 40%, 🏭 4%, 👥 56%	424 million	Comoros
132,050 (342,000)	3,039,130	Brazzaville	Communaute Financiere Africaine franc (XAF)	French	Monokutuba, Lingala, other language/dialects	∝ 50%, O 48%, ☪ 2%	47.71	83.8%	🌾 10%, 🏭 48%, 👥 42%	2.5 billion	Congo
124,500 (322,460)	17,693,380	Yamoussoukro	Communaute Financiere Africaine franc (XOF)	French	60 native dialects (Dioula the most widely spoken)	∝ 20-30%, ☪ 35-40%, O 25-40%	44.72	50.9%	🌾 28%, 🏭 29%, 👥 43%	25.5 billion	Côte d'Ivoire
909,040 (2,354,410)	60,085,000	Kinshasa	Congolese franc (CDF)	French	Lingala, Kingwana, Kikongo, Tshiluba	✟ 50%, ✝ 20%, ✱ 10%, ☪ 10%, O 10%	49.13	65.5%	🌾 54%, 🏭 9%, 👥 37%	32 billion	Democratic Republic of Congo
8,880 (23,000)	476,700	Djibouti	Djiboutian franc (DJF)	French, Arabic	Somali, Afar	☪ 94%, ∝ 6%	51.6	67.9%	🌾 3%, 🏭 10%, 👥 87%	586 million	Djibouti
386,660 (1,001,450)	77,505,760	Cairo	Egyptian pound (EGP)	Arabic	English, French	☪ 94%, ∝ and ✱ 6%	64.05	57.7%	🌾 14%, 🏭 30%, 👥 56%	258 billion	Egypt
10,830 (28,050)	535,880	Malabo	Communaute Financiere Africaine franc (XAF)	Spanish, French	Pidgin English, Fang, Bubi, Ibo	∝, ✱	54.35	85.7%	🌾 20%, 🏭 60%, 👥 20%	1.04 billion	Equatorial Guinea
46,840 (121,320)	4,561,600	Asmara	nakfa (ERN)	Afar, Arabic, Tigre, Kunama, Tigrinya, Cushitic languages		☪, ∝, ✟, ✝	56.57	58.6%	🌾 17%, 🏭 29%, 👥 54%	3.2 billion	Eritrea
435,190 (1,127,130)	69,113,730	Addis Ababa	birr (ETB)	Amharic, Tigrinya, Oromigna, Somali Guaragigna, Arabic	English, other local languages	☪ 45%-50%, ☦ 35%-40%, O 12%, ✱ 3%-8%	44.21	42.7%	🌾 52.3%, 🏭 11.1%, 👥 36.6%	46 billion	Ethiopia
103,350 (267,670)	1,389,200	Libreville	Communaute Financiere Africaine franc (XAF)	French	Fang, Myene, Nzebi, Bapounou/Eschira, Bandjabi	∝ 55%-75%, O and ☪ less than 1%	49.11	63.2% (1995)	🌾 10%, 🏭 60%, 👥 30%	6.7 billion	Gabon
4,360 (11,300)	1,593,260	Banjul	dalasi (GMD)	English	Mandinka, Wolof, Fula, other indigenous languages	☪ 90%, ∝ 9%, O 1%	53.98	40.1%	🌾 21%, 🏭 12%, 👥 67%	2.5 billion	Gambia
92,460 (239,460)	21,029,850	Accra	cedi (GHC)	English	African languages (e.g. Akan, Moshi-Dagomba, Ewe, Ga)	O 21%, ☪ 16%, ∝ 63%	57.06	74.8%	🌾 36%, 🏭 25%, 👥 39%	39.4 billion	Ghana
94,930 (245,860)	9,467,870	Conakry	Guinean franc (GNF)	French	Each ethnic group has its own language	☪ 85%, ∝ 8%, O 7%	46.28	35.9% (1995)	🌾 24%, 🏭 38%, 👥 38%	15 billion	Guinea
13,950 (36,120)	1,416,030	Bissau	Communaute Financiere Africaine franc (XOF)	Portuguese	Crioulo, African languages	O 50%, ☪ 45%, ∝ 5%	49.8	42.4%	🌾 54%, 🏭 15%, 👥 31%	1.2 billion	Guinea-Bissau

Key to symbols: ∝ Christian ✟ Catholic ☦ Orthodox ✝ Protestant ☸ Buddhist ॐ Hindū ✡ Jewish ☪ Muslim ≡ Atheist O Indigenous ✱ Other 🌾 Agriculture 🏭 Industry 👥 Services **NA** Not Available
Note: All literacy statistics are for 2003 unless otherwise stated.

Fact File

	Area sq miles (sq km)	Population	Capital	Currency	Official Languages	Other Languages	Main Religions	Life Expectancy	Literacy Rate	Economy	GDP US$
Kenya	224,960 (582,650)	32,368,100	Nairobi	Kenyan shilling (KES)	English, Kiswahili	Indigenous languages	✝ 45%, ✠ 33%, ○ 10%, ☪ 10%, ✻ 2%	47.02	85.1%	⚘ 24%, ♜ 13%, ⚱ 63%	31 billion
Lesotho	11,720 (30,360)	1,867,040	Maseru	loti (LSL), South African rand (ZAR)	English	Sesotho (southern Sotho), Zulu, Xhosa	∝ 80%, ○ 20%	47	84.8%	⚘ 18%, ♜ 38%, ⚱ 44%	5.3 billion
Liberia	43,000 (111,370)	3,482,210	Monrovia	Liberian dollar (LRD)	English	20 ethnic group languages	○ 40%, ∝ 40%, ☪ 20%	51.8	57.5%	⚘ 60%, ♜ 10%, ⚱ 30%	3.6 billion
Libya	679,360 (1,759,540)	5,765,560	Tripoli	Libyan dinar (LYD)	Arabic, Italian, English		☪ 97%	75.86	82.6%	⚘ 7%, ♜ 47%, ⚱ 46%	40 billion
Madagascar	226,660 (587,040)	18,040,340	Antananarivo	Malagasy franc (MGF)	French, Malagasy		○ 52%, ∝ 41%, ☪ 7%	55.74	68.9%	⚘ 34%, ♜ 11%, ⚱ 55%	14 billion
Malawi	45,750 (118,480)	12,158,920	Lilongwe	Malawian kwacha (MWK)	English, Chichewa	Other regional languages	✝ 55%, ✠ 20%, ☪ 20%, ○ 3%, ✻ 2%	36.59	62.7%	⚘ 40%, ♜ 19%, ⚱ 41%	7 billion
Mali	478,770 (1,240,000)	12,291,530	Bamako	Communaute Financiere Africaine franc (XOF)	French	Bambara, African languages	☪ 90%, ○ 9%, ∝ 1%	47.39	46.4%	⚘ 45%, ♜ 17%, ⚱ 38%	9.2 billion
Mauritania	397,960 (1,030,700)	3,086,860	Nouakchott	ouguiya (MRO)	Hassaniya Arabic, Wolof	Pulaar, Soninke, French	☪ 100%	51.53	41.7%	⚘ 25%, ♜ 29%, ⚱ 46%	5 billion
Mauritius	788 (2,040)	1,230,600	Port Louis	Mauritian rupee (MUR)	English, French	Creole, Hindi, Urdu, Hakka, Bhojpuri	ॐ 52%, ∝ 28.3%, ☪ 16.6%, ✻ 3.1%	71.53	85.6%	⚘ 6%, ♜ 33%, ⚱ 61%	12.9 billion
Morocco	172,410 (446,550)	32,725,850	Rabat	Moroccan dirham (MAD)	Arabic	Berber dialects, French	☪ 98.7%, ∝ 1.1%, ✡ 0.2%	69.73	51.7%	⚘ 15%, ♜ 33%, ⚱ 52%	112 billion
Mozambique	309,500 (801,590)	17,710,040	Maputo	metical (MZM)	Portuguese	Indigenous dialects	○ 50%, ∝ 30%, ☪ 20%	35.46	47.8%	⚘ 33%, ♜ 25%, ⚱ 42%	17.5 billion
Namibia	318,700 (825,420)	1,975,850	Windhoek	Namibian dollar (NAD), South African rand (ZAR)	English	Afrikaans, German, Oshivambo, Herero, Nama	∝ 80%-90%, ○ 10%-20%	38.97	84%	⚘ 11%, ♜ 28%, ⚱ 61%	8.1 billion
Niger	489,190 (1,267,000)	11,665,940	Niamey	Communaute Financiere Africaine franc (XOF)	French	Hausa, Djerma	☪ 80%, ○ and ∝ 20%	41.91	17.6%	⚘ 41%, ♜ 17%, ⚱ 42%	8.4 billion
Nigeria	356,670 (923,770)	140,601,620	Abuja	naira (NGN)	English	Hausa, Yoruba, Igbo (Ibo), Fulani	☪ 50%, ∝ 40%, ○ 10%	50.59	68%	⚘ 39%, ♜ 33%, ⚱ 28%	105.9 billion
Rwanda	10,170 (26,340)	8,098,620	Kigali	Rwandan franc (RWF)	Kinyarwanda, French, English	Bantu, Kiswahili (Swahili)	✠ 56.5%, ✝ 37.1%, ☪ 4.6%, ○ 0.1%, ✻ 1.7%	38.66	70.4%	⚘ 46%, ♜ 20%, ⚱ 34%	7.2 billion
São Tomé and Príncipe	386 (1,000)	187,410	São Tomé	dobra (STD)	Portuguese		∝ 80%	65.93	79.3% (1991)	⚘ 25%, ♜ 10%, ⚱ 65%	189 million
Senegal	75,750 (196,190)	11,126,830	Dakar	Communaute Financiere Africaine franc (XOF)	French	Wolof, Pulaar, Jola, Mandinka	☪ 94%, ∝ 5%, ○ 1%	62.93	40.2%	⚘ 18.5%, ♜ 20.7%, ⚱ 60.8%	16.2 billion
Seychelles	176 (455)	81,190	Victoria	Seychelles rupee (SCR)	English, French	Creole	✠ 86.6%, ✝ 6.8%, ∝ 2.5%, ✻ 4.1%	70.97	58% (1971)	⚘ 3.1%, ♜ 26.3%, ⚱ 70.6%	605 million
Sierra Leone	27,700 (71,740)	6,017,640	Freetown	leone (SLL)	English	Mende, Temne, Krio	☪ 60%, ○ 30%, ∝ 10%	45.96	31.4% (1995)	⚘ 43%, ♜ 27%, ⚱ 30%	2.7 billion
Somalia	246,200 (637,660)	8,591,630	Mogadishu	Somali shilling (SOS)	Somali	Arabic, Italian, English	☪	46.96	37.8% (2001)	⚘ 65%, ♜ 10%, ⚱ 25%	4.1 billion
South Africa, Republic of	471,010 (1,219,910)	42,552,330	Bloemfontein, Cape Town, Pretoria	rand (ZAR)	Afrikaans, English, Ndebele, Pedi, Sotho, Swazi, Tsonga, Tswana,	Official: Venda, Xhosa, Zulu	∝ 68%, ☪ 2%, ॐ 1.5%, ○ 28.5%	45.43	86.4%	⚘ 3%, ♜ 31%, ⚱ 66%	412 billion
Sudan	967,500 (2,505,810)	40,187,490	Khartoum	Sudanese dinar (SDD)	Arabic	Nubian, Ta Bedawie, Nilotic, Nilo-Hamitic, Sudanic, English	☪ 70%, ○ 25%, ∝ 5%	57.33	61.1%	⚘ 43%, ♜ 17%, ⚱ 40%	49.3 billion
Swaziland	6,700 (17,360)	1,173,900	Mbabane	lilangeni (SZL)	English, siSwati		∝ and ○ 40%, ✠ 20%, ☪ 10%, ✝, ✡, and ✻ 30%	37	81.6%	⚘ 10%, ♜ 43%, ⚱ 47%	4.6 billion
Tanzania	364,900 (945,090)	37,322,700	Dodoma	Tanzanian shilling (TZS)	Kiswahili, Swahili	Kiunguju, English, Arabic	mainland: ∝ 30%, ☪ 35%, ○ 35%, Zanzibar: ☪ 99%	51.7	78.2%	⚘ 48.4%, ♜ 16.7%, ⚱ 34.9%	22.1 billion
Togo	21,930 (56,790)	5,681,520	Lomé	Communaute Financiere Africaine franc (XOF)	French	Ewe, Mina, Kabye, Dagomba	○ 51%, ∝ 29%, ☪ 20%	54.02	60.9%	⚘ 42%, ♜ 21%, ⚱ 37%	7.6 billion

Key to symbols: ∝ Christian ✠ Catholic ☦ Orthodox ✝ Protestant ☸ Buddhist ॐ Hindu ✡ Jewish ☪ Muslim ≡ Atheist ○ Indigenous ✻ Other ⚘ Agriculture ♜ Industry ⚱ Services **NA** Not Available
Note: All literacy statistics are for 2003 unless otherwise stated.

AREA SQ MILES (SQ KM)	POPULATION	CAPITAL	CURRENCY	OFFICIAL LANGUAGES	OTHER LANGUAGES	MAIN RELIGIONS	LIFE EXPECTANCY	LITERACY RATE	ECONOMY	GDP US$	
63,170 (163,610)	10,137,250	Tunis	Tunisian dinar (TND)	Arabic	French	☪ 98%, ∝ 1%, ✡ and ✱ 1%	74.16	74.2%	⚘ 13%, ⚒ 33%, ⛁ 54%	64.5 billion	Tunisia
91,140 (236,040)	27,202,150	Kampala	Ugandan shilling (UGX)	English	Niger-Congo/Nilo-Saharan languages Swahili, Arabic	✙ 33%, ✝ 33%, ☪ 16%, O 18%	43.81	69.9%	NA	29 billion	Uganda
290,580 (752,610)	10,613,620	Lusaka	Zambian kwacha (ZMK)	English	Bemba, Kaonda, Lozi, Lunda, Luvale, Nyanja, Tonga, other	∝ 50%-75%, ☪ and ॐ 24%-49%, O 1%	37.35	80.6%	⚘ 24%, ⚒ 25%, ⛁ 51%	8.5 billion	Zambia
150,800 (390,580)	12,746,990	Harare	Zimbabwean dollar (ZWD)	English	Shona, Sindebele, minor tribal dialects	syncretic (blend of ∝ and O) 50%, ∝ 25%, O 24%, ☪ and ✱ 1%	36.5	90.7%	⚘ 11%, ⚒ 14%, ⛁ 75%	28 billion	Zimbabwe

OCEANIA

AREA SQ MILES (SQ KM)	POPULATION	CAPITAL	CURRENCY	OFFICIAL LANGUAGES	OTHER LANGUAGES	MAIN RELIGIONS	LIFE EXPECTANCY	LITERACY RATE	ECONOMY	GDP US$	
2,967,910 (7,686,850)	20,090,440	Canberra	Australian dollar (AUD)	English	Indigenous languages	✝ 26.1%, ✙ 26%, ∝ 24.3%, ✱ 33.6%	80	100% (1980)	⚘ 3%, ⚒ 25%, ⛁ 72%	465.9 billion	Australia
7,050 (18,270)	893,350	Suva	Fijian dollar (FJD)	English	Fijian, Hindustani	∝ 52%, ॐ 38%, ☪ 8%, ✱ 2%	68.56	93.7%	⚘ 17%, ⚒ 25%, ⛁ 58%	4.4 billion	Fiji
313 (811)	103,090	Bairiki	Australian dollar (AUD)	English	I-Kiribati	✙ 52%, ✝ 40%, ☪ and ✱ 8%	60.54	NA	⚘ 30%, ⚒ 7%, ⛁ 63%	79 million	Kiribati
70 (181)	59,070	Majuro	U.S. dollar (USD)	Marshallese, English	Marshallese dialects (Malayo-Polynesian family), Japanese	∝	66.18	93.7% (1999)	⚘ 14%, ⚒ 16%, ⛁ 70%	115 million	Marshall Islands
271 (702)	138,740	Palikir	U.S. dollar (USD)	English	Trukese, Pohnpeian, Yapese, Kosrean, Ulithian, other	✙ 50%, ✝ 47%	NA	89% (1980)	⚘ 50%, ⚒ 4%, ⛁ 46%	269 million	Micronesia, Federated States of
8 (21)	13,050	Yaren	Australian dollar (AUD)	Nauruan	English	∝	61.57	NA	NA	60 million	Nauru
103,740 (268,680)	4,035,460	Wellington	New Zealand dollar (NZD)	English, Maori		✝ 52%, ✙ 15%, ✱ 33%	78.15	99% (1980)	⚘ 8%, ⚒ 23%, ⛁ 69%	75.4 billion	New Zealand
177 (458)	20,300	Koror	U.S. dollar (USD)	English, Palauan, Tobi, Angaur, Japanese, Sonsoralese		∝ 49%, O	69.19	92% (1980)	NA	174 million	Palau
178,700 (462,840)	5,545,270	Port Moresby	kina (PGK)	English, pidgin English, Motu	715 indigenous languages	✙ 22%, ✝ 44%, O 34%	63.83	66%	⚘ 30.4%, ⚒ 36.8%, ⛁ 32.8%	12.2 billion	Papua New Guinea
1,140 (2,940)	177,290	Apia	tala (WST)	Samoan (Polynesian), English		∝ 99.7%, ✱ 0.3%	69.8	99.7%	⚘ 16%, ⚒ 18%, ⛁ 66%	618 million	Samoa
10,980 (28,450)	538,030	Honiara	Solomon Islands dollar (SBD)	Melanesian pidgin, English	120 indigenous languages	✝ 78%, ✙ 18%, O 4%	71.82	NA	⚘ 42%, ⚒ 11%, ⛁ 47%	800 million	Solomon Islands
289 (748)	112,420	Nuku'alofa	pa'anga (TOP)	Tongan, English		∝	68.56	98.5% (1996)	⚘ 30%, ⚒ 10%, ⛁ 60%	225 million	Tonga
10 (26)	11,640	Vaiaku	Australian dollar (AUD), Tuvaluan dollar	Tuvaluan, English, Samoan, I-Kiribati		✝ 98.4%, ✱ 1.6%	66.98	NA	NA	12.2 million	Tuvalu
4,710 (12,200)	205,750	Port Vila	vatu (VUV)	English, French, Pidgin	more than 100 local languages	✝ 61.7%, ✙ 15%, O 7.6%, ✱ 15.7%	61.33	53% (1979)	⚘ 26%, ⚒ 12%, ⛁ 62%	257 million	Vanuatu

TERRITORIES AND DEPENDENCIES

AREA SQ MILES (SQ KM)	POPULATION	CAPITAL	CURRENCY	OFFICIAL LANGUAGES	OTHER LANGUAGES	MAIN RELIGIONS	LIFE EXPECTANCY	LITERACY RATE	ECONOMY	GDP US$	
77 (199)	73,320	Pago Pago	U.S. dollar (USD)	Samoan (Polynesian), English		∝ 50%, ✙ 20%, ✝ and ✱ 30%	75.53	97% (1980)	NA	500 million	American Samoa (U.S.A.)
39 (102)	13,250	The Valley	East Caribbean dollar (XCD)	English		✝ 85%, ✙ 3%, ✱ 12%	76.5	95%	⚘ 4%, ⚒ 18%, ⛁ 78%	104 million	Anguilla (U.K.)
75 (193)	71,570	Oranjestad	Aruban guilder/florin (AWG)	Dutch	Papiamento, English, Spanish	✙ 82%, ✝ 8%, ✱ 10%	78.67	97%	NA	1.94 billion	Aruba (Netherlands)
2 (5)	no indigenous inhabitants										Ashmore Reef and Cartier Islands (Australia)
0.54 (1.4)	no indigenous inhabitants										Baker Island (U.S.A.)
21 (53)	65,370	Hamilton	Bermudian dollar (BMD)	English	Portuguese	✝ 66%, ✙ 15%, ✱ 19%	77.3	98% (1970)	⚘ 1%, ⚒ 10%, ⛁ 89%	2.2 billion	Bermuda (U.K.)
23 (59)	uninhabited										Bouvetøya (Norway)

Key to symbols: ∝ Christian ✙ Catholic ☦ Orthodox ✝ Protestant ☸ Buddhist ॐ Hindu ✡ Jewish ☪ Muslim ≡ Atheist O Indigenous ✱ Other ⚘ Agriculture ⚒ Industry ⛁ Services NA Not Available
Note: All literacy statistics are for 2003 unless otherwise stated.

Fact File

	Area sq miles (sq km)	Population	Capital	Currency	Official Languages	Other Languages	Main Religions	Life Expectancy	Literacy Rate	Economy	GDP US$
British Indian Ocean Territory (U.K.)	23 (60)	no indigenous inhabitants									
British Virgin Islands (U.K.)	59 (153)	22,640	Road Town	U.S. dollar (USD)	English		✝ 86%, ✞ 10%, ✱ 4%	75.85	97.8% (1991)	⚘ 1.8%, ♜ 6.2%, ⚱ 92%	311 million
Cayman Islands (U.K.)	101 (262)	44,270	George Town	Caymanian dollar (KYD)	English		✝, ✞	79.18	98% (1970)	⚘ 1.4%, ♜ 3.2%, ⚱ 95.4%	1.18 billion
Christmas Island (Australia)	52 (135)	470	The Settlement	Australian dollar (AUD)	English	Chinese, Malay	☸ 36%, ☪ 25%, ∝ 18%, ✱ 21%	NA	NA	NA	NA
Clipperton Island (France)	2 (6)	uninhabited									
Cocos Islands (Australia)	5 (14)	630		Australian dollar (AUD)	Malay (Cocos dialect), English		☪ 80%, ✱ 20%	NA	NA	NA	NA
Cook Islands (N.Z.)	93 (240)	21,340	Avarua	New Zealand dollar (NZD)	English	Maori	∝	NA	95%	⚘ 17%, ♜ 7.8%, ⚱ 75.2%	105 million
Coral Sea Islands Territory (Australia)	1.1 (2.9)	no indigenous inhabitants									
Falkland Islands (U.K.)	4,700 (12,170)	2,970	Stanley	Falkland pound (FKP)	English		✝, ✞	NA	NA	NA	52 million
Faroe Islands (Denmark)	540 (1,400)	46,960	Torshavn	Danish krone (DKK)	Faroese, Danish		✝	78.74	NA	⚘ 27%, ♜ 11%, ⚱ 62%	910 million
French Guiana (France)	35,140 (91,000)	195,510	Cayenne	euro (EUR)	French		✞	76.69	83% (1982)	NA	2.26 billion
French Polynesia (France)	1,610 (4,170)	270,490	Papeete	Comptoirs Francais du Pacifique franc (XPF)	French, Tahitian		✝ 54%, ✞ 30%, ✱ 16%	75.23	98% (1977)	⚘ 6%, ♜ 18%, ⚱ 76%	1.3 billion
French Southern and Antarctic Lands (France)	3,020 (7,830)	no indigenous inhabitants									
Gibraltar (U.K.)	2.5 (6.5)	27,880	Gibraltar	Gibraltar pound (GIP)	English	Spanish, Italian, Portuguese, Russian	✞ 76.9%, ✝ 6.9%, ☪ 6.9%, ✡ 2.3%, ✱ 7%	79.23	above 80%	NA	500 million
Greenland (Denmark)	836,330 (2,166,090)	56,380	Nuuk	Danish krone (DKK)	Greenlandic (East Inuit), Danish, English		✝	68.69	NA	NA	1.1 billion
Guadeloupe (France)	690 (1,780)	448,710	Basse-Terre	euro (EUR)	French	Creole patois	✞ 95%, ॐ and ○ 4%, ✝ 1%	77.35	90% (1982)	NA	3.7 billion
Guam (U.S.A.)	212 (549)	169,970	Hagåtña	U.S. dollar (USD)	English, Chamorro, Japanese		✞ 85%, ✱ 15%	78.11	99% (1990)	⚘ 7%, ♜ 15%, ⚱ 78%	3.2 billion
Guernsey (U.K.)	30 (78)	65,230	St Peter Port	British pound (GBP), Guernsey pound	English, French, Norman-French dialect		✝, ✞	79.9	NA	⚘ 3%, ♜ 10%, ⚱ 87%	1.3 billion
Heard and McDonald Islands (Australia)	159 (412)	uninhabited									
Howland Island (U.S.A.)	0.6 (1.6)	uninhabited									
Isle of Man (U.K.)	221 (572)	75,050	Douglas	British pound (GBP), Manx pound	English, Manx Gaelic		✝, ✞, ∝	77.81	NA	⚘ 1%, ♜ 13%, ⚱ 86%	1.4 billion
Jan Mayen (Norway)	144 (373)	no indigenous inhabitants									
Jarvis Island (U.S.A.)	1.7 (4.5)	uninhabited									
Jersey (U.K.)	45 (116)	90,810	St Helier	British pound (GBP), Jersey pound	English, French	Norman-French dialect	✝, ✞	78.78	NA	⚘ 5%, ♜ 2%, ⚱ 93%	2.2 billion
Johnston Atoll (U.S.A.)	1.1 (2.8)	no indigenous inhabitants									

Key to symbols: ∝ Christian ✞ Catholic ☦ Orthodox ✝ Protestant ☸ Buddhist ॐ Hindu ✡ Jewish ☪ Muslim ≡ Atheist ○ Indigenous ✱ Other ⚘ Agriculture ♜ Industry ⚱ Services NA Not Available
Note: All literacy statistics are for 2003 unless otherwise stated.

Country	Area sq miles (sq km)	Population	Capital	Currency	Official Languages	Other Languages	Main Religions	Life Expectancy	Literacy Rate	Economy	GDP US$
Kingman Reef (U.S.A.)	0.4 (1.0)	uninhabited									
Martinique (France)	420 (1,100)	432,900	Fort-de-France	euro (EUR)	French, Creole patois		Catholic 95%, Hindu and Indigenous 5%	78.56	97.7%	Agriculture 6%, Industry 11%, Services 83%	4.39 billion
Mayotte (France)	140 (374)	193,630	Dzadaoudzi	euro (EUR)	French	Mahorian (a Swahili dialect)	Muslim 97%, Christian 3%	60.21	NA	NA	85 million
Midway Islands (U.S.A.)	2.4 (6.2)	no indigenous inhabitants									
Montserrat (U.K.)	39 (102)	9,340	Plymouth	East Caribbean dollar (XCD)	English		Protestant, Catholic, Christian	78.2	97% (1970)	Agriculture 5.4%, Industry 13.6%, Services 81%	31 million
Navassa Island (U.S.A.)	2.0 (5.2)	uninhabited									
Netherlands Antilles (Netherlands)	371 (960)	219,960	Willemstad	Netherlands Antillean guilder (ANG)	Dutch	Papiamento, English, Spanish	Catholic, Protestant, Jewish	75.15	96.7%	Agriculture 1%, Industry 15%, Services 84%	2.4 billion
New Caledonia (France)	7,360 (19,060)	216,490	Nouméa	Comptoirs Francais du Pacifique franc (XPF)	French	33 Melanesian-Polynesian dialects	Catholic 60%, Protestant 30%, Other 10%	73.27	91% (1976)	Agriculture 5%, Industry 30%, Services 65%	3.1 billion
Niue (N.Z.)	100 (260)	2,130	Alofi	New Zealand dollar (NZD)	Niuean, English		Protestant 85%, Other 15%	NA	95%	Agriculture NA, Industry NA, Services 55%	7.6 million
Norfolk Island (Australia)	13 (34)	1,870	Kingston	Australian dollar (AUD)	English	Norfolk (mixture of 18th century English and ancient Tahitian)	Protestant 55%, Catholic 11.5%, Other 33.5%	NA	NA	NA	NA
Northern Mariana Islands (U.S.A.)	184 (477)	85,370	Saipan	U.S. dollar (USD)	English, Chamorro, Carolinian		Christian	75.95	97% (1980)	NA	900 million
Palmyra Atoll (U.S.A.)	5 (12)	no indigenous inhabitants									
Paracel Islands (Occupied by China)	NA	no indigenous inhabitants									
Pitcairn Islands (U.K.)	18 (47)	50	Adamstown	New Zealand dollar (NZD)	English	Pitcairnese	Protestant 100%	NA	NA	NA	NA
Puerto Rico (U.S.A.)	3,510 (9,100)	3,929,510	San Juan	U.S. dollar (USD)	Spanish, English		Catholic 85%, Protestant and Other 15%	75.96	93.8% (2001)	Agriculture 1%, Industry 45%, Services 54%	43.9 billion
Réunion (France)	970 (2,520)	776,950	Saint-Denis	euro (EUR)	French	Creole widely used	Catholic 86%, Hindu, Muslim, Buddhist	73.18	88.9%	Agriculture 8%, Industry 19%, Services 73%	3.4 billion
St Helena (U.K.)	158 (410)	7,460	Jamestown	Saint Helenian pound (SHP)	English		Protestant, Catholic	77.2	97% (1987)	NA	18 million
St Pierre and Miquelon (France)	93 (242)	7,010	St-Pierre	euro (EUR)	French		Catholic 99%	77.93	99% (1982)	NA	74 million
South Georgia and Sandwich Islands (U.K.)	1,510 (3,900)	no indigenous inhabitants									
Svalbard (Norway)	1,510 (62,050)	2,870	Longyearbyen	Norwegian krone (NOK)	Russian, Norwegian		NA	NA	NA	NA	NA
Tokelau Islands (N.Z.)	4 (10)	1,430	administrative center on each atoll	New Zealand dollar (NZD)	Tokelauan (a Polynesian language), English		Protestant 70%, Catholic 28%, Other 2%	NA	NA	NA	1.5 million
Turks and Caicos Islands (U.K.)	166 (430)	20,560	Cockburn Town	U.S. dollar (USD)	English		Protestant 86%, Other 14%	73.76	98% (1970)	NA	128 million
U.S. Virgin Islands (U.S.A.)	136 (352)	127,310	Charlotte Amalie	U.S. dollar (USD)	English	Spanish, Creole	Protestant 59%, Catholic 34%, Other 7%	78.43	NA	NA	1.8 billion
Wake Atoll (U.S.A.)	2.5 (6.5)	no indigenous inhabitants									
Wallis and Futuna Islands (France)	106 (274)	16,030	Matā'Utu	Comptoirs Francais du Pacifique franc (XPF)	French, Wallisian (indigenous Polynesian language)		Catholic 100%	NA	50% (1969)	NA	30 million

Key to symbols: Christian, Catholic, Orthodox, Protestant, Buddhist, Hindu, Jewish, Muslim, Atheist, Indigenous, Other, Agriculture, Industry, Services, **NA** Not Available
Note: All literacy statistics are for 2003 unless otherwise stated.

Geographic Terms

A

Abyssal plain
Flat area of the ocean floor generally extending from the base of the continental slope to the mid-ocean ridge.

Acid rain
Wet and dry deposition of oxides of nitrogen and sulfur derived from burning fossil fuels, smelting metals, and motor vehicle exhaust fumes. Results in damage to the natural and built environment.

Air mass
A large body of air of relatively constant temperature and humidity.

Alluvial fan
A deposit that radiates downslope from the point where a stream leaves a confined channel. Typically found along mountain fronts.

Alpine
High-altitude, high-relative-relief terrain that is actively affected by frost action, lies above the tree line, and has been subjected to glacial erosion.

Altitude
Height above sea level.

Antarctic Circle
Line of latitude at 66.5ºS, poleward of which the Sun does not set at the summer solstice (21–22 December) and does not rise at the winter solstice (21–22 June).

Anticyclone
Area of high atmospheric pressure, generally stable and slow-moving, around which light winds spiral outward (clockwise in the Northern Hemisphere, anti clockwise in the Southern).

Arable
Strictly, a system of land use involving plowing. Usually refers to land that is tilled for crops.

Archipelago
Either a sea studded with islands or, nowadays, a group of islands.

Arctic Circle
Line of latitude at 66.5ºN, poleward of which the Sun does not set at the summer solstice (21–22 June) and does not rise at the winter solstice (21–22 December).

Arid
Dry, either because of low precipitation or high evapotranspiration with respect to precipitation.

Asthenosphere
Part of Earth's mantle extending from the base of the lithosphere (at depths of 30–185 miles [50–300 km]) to depths of around 430 miles (700 km). It is in a partially molten state and is less resistant to deformation than the over- and underlying zones.

Atmosphere
Layer of air that envelops Earth. Dry air contains roughly 78% nitrogen, 21% oxygen, 1% argon, and 0.03% carbon dioxide.

Atmospheric pressure
The pressure exerted by the weight of the atmosphere above a point.

Atoll
Low, subcircular coral reef enclosing a lagoon. Found mainly in the Indian and Pacific oceans.

Avalanche
Sudden and rapid movement of ice, snow, and/or debris down a slope.

Axis
An imaginary line connecting the North and South poles, tilted at about 66.5º to the plane of Earth's orbit, around which Earth rotates.

B

Basin
1. The total area of land drained by a river and its tributaries. 2. Depression within which deposition occurs, ranging from a small hollow to a major structural feature. 3. Hollow in the ground, with a multitude of possible origins including subsidence, glacial erosion, and tectonics.

Bedrock
Consolidated, relatively unweathered rock either exposed at the ground surface or underlying the regolith.

Biodiversity
The range of flora and fauna present in an ecosystem.

Biomass
The total mass of organisms in an area.

Biome
A major ecological community of plants and animals that occupies a particular terrestrial or, less commonly, marine environment.

Biosphere
The zone in which life occurs on Earth, normally conceived as a zone of interaction with the lithosphere, atmosphere, and hydrosphere.

Border
An imaginary line that separates one administrative and/or political unit from another.

Boreal forest
The Northern Hemisphere coniferous forest, lying between approximately 55ºN and 65ºN.

C

Caldera
A large crater-like, steep-walled basin created by the collapse of a volcano. May contain a crater lake and subsidiary volcanoes.

Canal
An artificial waterway cut to carry irrigation water or to provide a route for shipping.

Carbon cycle
The carbon occurring as carbon dioxide in the atmosphere is absorbed and stored by plants. The plants, some animals, and bacteria obtain nourishment from the carbon and return some back to the atmosphere as carbon dioxide.

Cash crop
A crop grown for sale, by contrast with a subsistence crop grown for use by the grower.

Channel
1. A natural or artificial course for running water. 2. A narrow stretch of water between two landmasses. 3. A natural or dredged navigable waterway in an area of generally shallower water.

City
A very large permanent settlement lacking self-sufficiency in the production of food and usually dependent on manufacturing and commerce. The combined population of a city and its suburbs is known as an urban agglomeration. All city population statistics quoted in this atlas are of urban agglomerations.

Climate
The average pattern of weather that occurs in a place over an extended period of time. Several schemes divide Earth into distinct climatic zones.

Coniferous forest
A forest comprised mainly of cone-bearing, often evergreen trees that usually have needle-shaped or scaly leaves.

Continent
1. One of Earth's seven principal landmasses: Africa, Antarctica, Asia, Australia, Europe, North America, South America. 2. That part of Earth's crust composed of ancient, thick, low-density material.

Continental drift
The theory that the present distribution of the continents is a result of the fragmentation of one or more pre-existing supercontinents that have drifted apart. Subsequently subsumed within the plate tectonics model.

Continental shelf
The part of the continental crust below sea level. Usually very gently sloping. Terminated by the steeper continental slope, which forms the true edge of the continents.

Coral
A porous, calcareous rock consisting of the continuous skeleton secreted by coral polyps, bottom-dwelling marine invertebrates common at shallow depth in clear intertropical seas.

Coral reef
An extensive, solidified accumulation of coral; divided into atolls, fringing, and barrier.

Cordillera
A linear mountain chain.

Core
The central part of Earth, 2,200 miles (3,500 km) in diameter. Composed of nickel–iron alloys, solid in the inner core (800 miles [1,300 km] in diameter) and liquid in the outer.

Coriolis effect
Earth's rotation means that bodies moving over its surface such as air (winds) and water (ocean currents) are deflected to the right in the Northern Hemisphere and to the left in the Southern.

Crust
The outermost layer of Earth, 3.75–43 miles (6–70 km) thick and composed of low-density rocks.

Cyclone
An area of relatively low atmospheric pressure, typically 620–1,200 miles (1,000–2,000 km) across, into which low-level winds spiral anti clockwise in the Northern Hemisphere and clockwise in the Southern.

D

Deciduous forest
An area dominated by woody perennial plants that shed their leaves at a particular time, season, or growth stage, such as before the cold or dry season.

Deforestation
The removal of trees from an area. May occur naturally, but the main cause is clearance for timber, agriculture, and urbanization. The practice may cause significant environmental damage.

Delta
An accumulation of river-borne sediment deposited where a stream enters a body of standing water and its strength is reduced by the sudden decrease in flow velocity.

Dependency
A territory and its population governed or held in trust by another nation.

Desert
An area of moisture deficiency where precipitation is low relative to losses by evapotranspiration.

Desertification
Land degradation in arid areas resulting from factors including climatic variation and human activities such as deforestation, overgrazing, and cultivation of marginal land.

Distributary
A stream channel that splits from the main line of flow.

Drainage basin
An area drained by a river system.

Drought
May be defined meteorologically as a relatively long period of relatively low precipitation or, in human terms, taking account of impacts on agriculture, water supply, etc.

Dune
A mound or ridge of windblown sand found most commonly in deserts and coastal environments.

E

Earthquake
A shock or series of shocks in Earth's crust caused by a sudden release of pressure in the crust or upper mantle.

Ecosystem
An interacting system of organisms and the environment to which they are adapted.

El Niño
The replacement of cold upwelling waters along the west coast of South America by warm currents from the west and north. Occurs irregularly at intervals of 2–7 years. Associated with changes in global atmospheric and ocean circulation that cause major shifts in climate worldwide.

Endangered species
A plant or animal species in danger of extinction whose survival is unlikely if the factors causing its vulnerability continue operating.

Environment
Simply, the surroundings. These may be natural (e.g. biological or physical environments) or artificial (e.g. built or social environments).

Eon
1. The longest period of geological time, such as the Phanerozoic, the last 590 million years. 2. A thousand million years.

Epicenter
The point on Earth's surface that lies directly above the focus of an earthquake.

Equator
An imaginary line that is at right angles to Earth's axis of rotation lying midway between the two poles. It divides the world into the Northern and Southern hemispheres.

Era
A division of geological time. The Phanerozoic (see Eon) is divided into three eras: Paleozoic, Mesozoic, and Cenozoic.

Erosion
The process whereby material is loosened or dissolved and moved from at or near Earth's surface.

Estuary
That section of a river where it enters the sea and is influenced by marine processes, such as tides and marine water quality.

Evapotranspiration
Total water loss from the soil, including evaporation and transpiration from plant surfaces.

Evergreen
A woody perennial plant that retains its foliage throughout the year by continuously shedding and replacing a few leaves at a time.

F

Fault
A planar fracture surface in rock along which relative motion has occurred. The fracturing is an adjustment to stresses in the rock.

Fauna
A group of animals particular to a region or a period of time.

Floodplain
That part of a river valley that is inundated in times of flood.

Flora
A group of plants particular to a region or a period of time.

Forest
A large area of trees whose crowns touch to form a continuous canopy.

Fossil
The remains of an organism preserved within rock.

Fossil fuel
Combustible material derived from the fossilized remains of plants and animals. Includes coal, gas, and oil.

G

Geothermal energy
Anomalously hot zones in Earth's crust may give rise to hot springs, steam, and hot rocks at the surface. Such energy may be employed for human use.

Geyser
A spring or fountain of geothermally heated water that erupts intermittently.

Glaciation
1. An episode of marked extension of ice sheets and glaciers. 2. The occupation of an area by ice sheets or glaciers. 3. The action of ice on the landscape.

Glacier
A mass of ice sufficiently large to deform and flow under its own weight.

Global warming
The possibility that Earth is warming as a consequence of human activity over the past century or more.

Grassland
A region in which the vegetation is dominated by grasses and other herbs.

Grazing
1. An area where livestock feed on growing grass or other herbs. 2. The act of feeding livestock on such areas.

Greenhouse effect
A natural phenomenon that occurs when short-wave solar radiation passes through Earth's atmosphere, is absorbed at the surface, and is re-radiated as longer wavelength thermal radiation. This maintains Earth's average temperature at a point warm enough to sustain life. It is argued that an increase in the incidence of greenhouse gases such as carbon dioxide, as a result of fossil fuel combustion, is enhancing the greenhouse effect and causing global temperatures to rise.

Greenwich mean time (GMT)
The official time at the Greenwich meridian (0º) in Greenwich, U.K. from which all time is calculated.

Greenwich meridian
A theoretical line, extending from the North to the South Pole, that

runs through Greenwich, U.K. This is the prime meridian, the 0° of longitude, from which all other meridians are measured.

H

Habitat
The environment in which an organism lives.

Hemisphere
Earth's surface is bisected by the Equator, producing the Northern and Southern hemispheres. Less precisely, the continents of North and South America are referred to as the Western Hemisphere.

High latitude
Broadly, the areas poleward of the Arctic and Antarctic circles.

Humidity
The water vapor content of the atmosphere.

Hurricane
An intense cyclonic vortex that occurs mainly over tropical oceans. Around 400 miles (650 km) in diameter and 90–185 miles (150–300 km) high, with maximum wind speeds of 330 feet per second (100 m/s). Also known in various parts of the world as typhoon, tropical cyclone, and cyclone.

Hydroelectricity
Electricity generated using the power of running water to turn turbines.

Hydrosphere
The component of Earth's system pertaining to water in its fresh or saline, and its solid, liquid, or gaseous state.

I

Ice age
A period in Earth's history when ice is found relatively extensively on the surface. There have been at least six ice ages. The present one, the Cenozoic, began perhaps 42 million years ago. The latest advance in the present ice age ended around 13,000 years ago.

Ice cap
A large, dome-shaped body of ice displaying a generally outward and radial flow.

Indigenous
Indigenous plants and animals are those that occur naturally in a region. Indigenous people are descendants of the people who inhabited a territory before the formation of modern nation states.

International Date Line
A theoretical line at approximately 180° of longitude. Places just west of the line are 12 hours ahead of GMT; points just east are 12 hours behind. East of the line the date is one day earlier than to the west.

Irrigation
The supply of water by artificial means to assist plant growth.

Island
A landmass smaller than a continent that is enclosed by water.

L

Latitude
The distance north and south of the Equator. Latitude is given by the angle formed between a line from the center of Earth to the Equator and a line from the center of Earth to the relevant point on Earth's surface. The latitude of the Equator is thus 0° and that of the North Pole is 90°N.

Lava
Magma that is extruded from volcanic fissures and vents. The term is also applied to the cooled and solidified form of this material.

Lithosphere
Earth's crust and part of the upper mantle form a strong layer relative to the underlying and more easily deformable asthenosphere. Varies from a few miles thick over the mid-ocean ridge to over 180 miles (300 km) thick below some continents.

Longitude
The distance east and west of the Greenwich meridian. Longitude is given by the angle formed between a line from the axis of Earth to the Greenwich meridian and a line from the axis of Earth to the relevant point on Earth's surface. The angles are measured both east and west of the Greenwich meridian. 180°W thus coincides with 180°E.

M

Magma
Molten or partly molten rock generated by partial melting within Earth's crust or upper mantle. Magma may be intruded into the crust where it cools and solidifies to form intrusive rock or it may be extruded onto Earth's surface where it cools and solidifies to form volcanic rock.

Mantle
That part of Earth's interior between the core and the crust.

Map projection
A means of allowing the whole or part of the spherical surface of Earth to be represented on a flat map. Earth's lines of latitude and longitude are transformed into a net on a plane surface, the map projection. There are many ways in which this may be undertaken, but all introduce some form of distortion onto the resultant map.

Meridian
A line of longitude linking the North and South poles.

Mesa
An isolated, flat-topped hill bounded by steep slopes or cliffs.

Midlatitudes
Broadly, those areas of Earth lying between the tropics and the poles.

Mid-ocean ridge
A linear mountain chain rising 0.5–1.75 miles (1–3 km) from the ocean floor, developed where upwelling basaltic magma forms new ocean crust along a margin between divergent tectonic plates.

Mineral
1. A natural, inorganic substance of definite chemical composition, almost always in crystalline form, that cannot be physically separated into simpler compounds. 2. A loose term for inorganic material.

Monsoon
A markedly seasonal wind. The term has been extended to cover the rains that accompany these winds.

Mountain
A high-altitude, high-relative-relief topographic feature with a summit small in proportion to its base.

N

Northern Hemisphere
Refers to the half of Earth north of the Equator (0°).

North Pole
The northernmost geographical point on Earth. It marks the northern axis of Earth's rotation.

O

Oasis
An area in a hot desert where there is sufficient water to sustain plant life.

Ocean
1. The body of salt water that covers 71% of Earth's surface. 2. One of Earth's large bodies of salt water (the Arctic, Atlantic, Indian, Pacific, and Southern oceans).

Ozone layer
An ozone-enriched region of the stratosphere 9–21 miles (15–35 km) above Earth's surface. Absorbs much of the Sun's ultraviolet radiation, preventing the damaging radiation from reaching Earth's surface.

P

Pangaea
The name given to the supercontinent postulated by continental drift theory. This split to produce the northern and southern continents of Laurasia and Gondwana.

Pasture
1. A place with growing grass or other herbs on which livestock are grazed. 2. The growing grass or other herbs on which livestock are grazed.

Peninsula
A narrow neck of land projecting into a body of water.

Plain
An area of flat or rolling land devoid of prominent elevations or depressions.

Plate tectonics
The theory that the lithosphere is divided into seven major (and several minor) segments or plates that are being formed along the mid-ocean ridges and reworked down into the mantle along the deep-sea trenches. The plates carry the continents on them, explaining their movement over time. The zones of interaction between plates are often characterized by earthquakes, volcanoes, and tectonic activity.

Plateau
A broad, elevated area of flat or rolling land.

R

Rain forest
Largely evergreen forest characteristic of permanently wet regions of the tropics and midlatitudes.

Rain shadow
The leeward side of a topographic barrier where precipitation is low. Moist air is forced upward on the windward slopes. This causes rain, reducing the moisture content of the air, which is warmed and dried further as it descends the leeward slopes.

Reef
1. A narrow area of rock or sediment (including coral) usually covered at high tide, but often exposed at low tide. 2. A coral reef.

Regolith
The mantle or layer of rock fragments, alluvium, soil, blown sand, etc, that rests on bedrock. It forms almost all of the surface of Earth's land.

Renewable energy
Energy from (in practical terms) inexhaustible sources. Includes hydroelectricity, solar and geothermal energy, and wind power.

Resource
An element of the environment that may be used to meet human needs. Resources may be natural (such as water or minerals) or human (such as the entrepreneurial talents of a population).

Rift valley
A long, linear trough formed by faulting due to tension in the lithosphere.

Ring of Fire
A belt of volcanoes and associated tectonic activity found around the perimeter of the Pacific Ocean. Also known as the Rim of Fire.

S

Savanna
An area of open grassland with some trees and shrubs found in the tropics and subtropics. Characterized by seasonal wet and dry climates.

Sea
1. The body of salt water that covers 71% of Earth's surface. 2. A large body of salt water wholly or partly enclosed by the land.

Sea ice
Ice that forms on the sea surface at temperatures below around 30°F (-2°C). Covers large areas of the polar oceans. Known as fast ice when attached to land and pack ice when floating free.

Sea level
The elevation of the ocean surface. The term is often used synonymously with mean sea level, which varies slightly from place to place.

Seamount
An isolated submarine hill or mountain, usually of volcanic origin.

Solstice
Either of the two times of the year (21–22 June or 21–22 December) when the Sun is at its greatest distance from the Equator. At these times of year, there are the longest hours of either day or night.

Southern Hemisphere
Refers to the half of Earth south of the Equator (0°).

South Pole
The southernmost geographical point on Earth. It marks the southern axis of Earth's rotation.

State
1. A territorial unit with clearly defined and internationally accepted boundaries, having an independent existence and responsible for its own legal system. 2. A unit of regional government with some independence in relation to internal affairs.

Steppe
A midlatitude grassland biome stretching from Austria to China.

Strait
A narrow passage of water connecting two larger water bodies.

Subduction
Where tectonic plates collide, one of the plates may be drawn down into the mantle in a process known as subduction. The subducted plate is almost invariably that composed of denser, ocean crust. Friction along the surface of the subducting slab may give rise to earthquakes or melting, and thus volcanic activity.

Subsistence agriculture
Farming in which the products grown or raised are primarily for the support of the farmer and dependents.

T

Tectonic plate
One of the seven large and several smaller segments into which the lithosphere is divided.

Temperate
A climate without extremes of temperature.

Territory
1. The land, sea, and air ruled by a sovereign authority. 2. An area dependent upon a sovereign state, but having some authority. 3. A large tract of land with undefined boundaries. 4. In Australia, Canada, and the U.S.A., an area without full rights as a state or province.

Time zone
A division of Earth's surface selected so that standard time is the same across the whole area. Adjacent time zones usually differ by an hour. Each time zone should theoretically cover 15° of longitude.

Topography
The surface features of an area. Strictly refers not only to physical, but also to human features.

Tornado
A violent rotating storm with winds of high speed circulating round a funnel cloud around 330 feet (100 m) in diameter.

Trench (deep-sea)
A narrow, elongated, steep-sided depression 10,000 feet (3,000 m) or more deeper than the adjacent deep-sea floor. Thought to mark the zone along which one tectonic plate is subducted beneath another.

Tributary
A stream or river that flows into a larger river.

Tropic of Cancer
An imaginary line encircling Earth at 23.5°N that marks the most northerly point at which the noonday Sun is directly overhead at some stage of the year (21–22 June, the summer solstice). Denotes the northern limit of the tropics.

Tropic of Capricorn
An imaginary line encircling Earth at 23.5°S that marks the most southerly point at which the noonday Sun is directly overhead at some stage of the year (21–22 December, the summer solstice). Denotes the southern limit of the tropics.

Tundra
Vast, level, treeless, marshy regions, usually with permanently frozen subsoil, supporting mosses, lichens, herbs, and dwarf shrubs. Classically the northern part of Eurasia, but the term has been expanded to include similar terrains in the Arctic, Antarctica, and at high altitude.

V

Vegetation
The plant cover of an area.

Volcano
1. An opening or vent in Earth's crust through which lava, gas, pumice, and ash is emitted. 2. The landform produced by the accumulation of lava and other volcanic materials around a vent.

W

Weathering
The in-situ alteration of materials at or near Earth's surface by physical, chemical, and biological processes.

Wilderness
An extensive area of land that exists in a natural or nearly natural state.

Woodland
A vegetation community of widely spaced, mature trees.

1

113 S 13 **100 Mile House**, British Columbia, Canada

A

80 H 1 **A Coruña**, Spain
80 J 1 **A Fonsagrada**, Spain
80 G 3 **A Guardia**, Spain
80 J 3 **A Gudiña**, Spain
87 B 17 **Aachen**, Germany
87 H 22 **Aalen**, Germany
83 E 18 **Aalst**, Luxembourg
83 J 16 **Aalst**, Netherlands
82 M 13 **Aalten**, Netherlands
83 D 17 **Aalter**, Belgium
88 F 6 **Aare**, Switzerland
83 H 18 **Aarschot**, Belgium
83 F 17 **Aartselaar**, Belgium
165 T 9 **Ab-i-Istada**, Afghanistan
193 R 14 **Aba**, Nigeria
195 Q 5 **Aba**, Democratic Republic of Congo
164 G 9 **Ābādān**, Iran
164 J 9 **Ābādeh**, Iran
188 J 8 **Abadla**, Algeria
214 D 2 **Abaiang**, Kiribati
193 R 12 **Abaji**, Nigeria
117 O 18 **Abajo Peak**, Utah, U.S.A.
193 R 13 **Abakaliki**, Nigeria
157 N 13 **Abakan**, Russian Federation
193 P 8 **Abala**, Niger
194 H 8 **Abala**, Congo
193 Q 8 **Abalak**, Niger
189 N 14 **Abalessa**, Algeria
141 F 17 **Abancay**, Peru
164 J 9 **Abarqū**, Iran
176 L 3 **Abashiri**, Japan
176 L 4 **Abashiri-ko**, Japan
212 F 7 **Abau**, Papua New Guinea
167 R 4 **Abay**, Kazakhstan
191 I 22 **Ābaya Hāyk'**, Ethiopia
157 N 13 **Abaza**, Russian Federation
194 H 4 **Abba**, Central African Republic
160 M 2 **Abbah**, Syria
91 B 17 **Abbasanta**, Italy
79 P 2 **Abbeville**, France
119 N 21 **Abbeville**, Louisiana, U.S.A.
123 N 7 **Abbeville**, Alabama, U.S.A.
123 P 7 **Abbeville**, Georgia, U.S.A.
123 Q 4 **Abbeville**, South Carolina, U.S.A.
77 B 20 **Abbeyfeale**, Republic of Ireland
218 J 8 **Abbot Ice Shelf**, Antarctica
113 S 15 **Abbotsford**, British Columbia, Canada
120 G 6 **Abbotsford**, Wisconsin, U.S.A.
165 X 7 **Abbottabad**, Pakistan
163 V 15 **'Abd al Kūrī**, Yemen
193 Y 9 **Abéché**, Chad
83 A 19 **Abele**, Belgium
214 D 2 **Abemama**, Kiribati
192 L 13 **Abengourou**, Côte d'Ivoire
85 B 26 **Åbenrå**, Denmark
193 P 13 **Abeokuta**, Nigeria
77 H 20 **Aberaeron**, United Kingdom
76 J 10 **Aberdeen**, United Kingdom
116 D 7 **Aberdeen**, Washington, U.S.A.
118 I 9 **Aberdeen**, South Dakota, U.S.A.
122 J 4 **Aberdeen**, Mississippi, U.S.A.
196 M 14 **Aberdeen**, Republic of South Africa
114 K 2 **Aberdeen Lake**, Nunavut, Canada
77 I 21 **Abergavenny**, United Kingdom
77 H 20 **Aberystwyth**, United Kingdom
90 E 9 **Abetone**, Italy
163 N 11 **Abhā**, Saudi Arabia
164 H 5 **Abhar**, Iran
193 R 13 **Abia**, Nigeria
192 K 14 **Abidjan**, Côte d'Ivoire
177 K 15 **Abiko**, Japan
119 I 20 **Abilene**, Texas, U.S.A.
121 N 15 **Abingdon**, Virginia, U.S.A.
190 E 10 **Abnûb**, Egypt
168 D 10 **Abohar**, India
192 L 13 **Aboisso**, Côte d'Ivoire
191 E 20 **Aboke**, Sudan
193 O 13 **Abomey**, Benin
193 U 14 **Abong Mbang**, Cameroon
163 V 11 **Aboot**, Oman
175 N 6 **Aborlan**, Philippines
193 Y 10 **Abou Déia**, Chad
163 T 5 **Abqaiq**, Saudi Arabia
144 I 5 **Abra Pampa**, Argentina
127 P 4 **Abraham's Bay**, The Bahamas
190 D 13 **'Abri**, Sudan
63 H 16 **Abrolhos Bank**, Atlantic Ocean
100 H 10 **Abrud**, Romania
98 D 8 **Abruka**, Estonia
90 I 13 **Abruzzo**, Italy
118 C 9 **Absaroka Range**, Montana, U.S.A.
89 R 6 **Abtenau**, Austria
160 I 3 **Abū aḍ Ḍuhūr**, Syria
161 R 7 **Abū al Jīr**, Iraq
163 W 6 **Abu al Jirab**, United Arab Emirates
163 O 11 **Abū 'Arīsh**, Saudi Arabia
163 W 6 **Abu Dhabi**, United Arab Emirates
190 D 8 **Abu Haggag**, Egypt
191 F 14 **Abu Hamed**, Sudan
161 O 5 **Abū Ḩardān**, Syria
161 O 5 **Abū Kamāl**, Syria
191 B 19 **Abu Matariq**, Sudan
164 K 13 **Abu Musa**, Iran
189 T 8 **Abū Nujaym**, Libya
189 T 8 **Abū Qurīn**, Libya
162 M 6 **Abū Rubayq**, Saudi Arabia
191 C 17 **Abu Shanab**, Sudan
190 E 12 **Abu Simbel**, Egypt
161 T 9 **Abū Şukhayr**, Iraq
191 D 18 **Abu Zabad**, Sudan
190 F 9 **Abu Zenīma**, Egypt
193 R 12 **Abuja**, Nigeria
194 L 5 **Abumombazi**, Democratic Republic of Congo
142 D 13 **Abunã**, Brazil
176 J 6 **Abuta**, Japan
191 C 17 **Abyad**, Sudan
191 C 20 **Abyei**, Sudan
142 K 11 **Açailândia**, Brazil
81 P 6 **Acalá de Henares**, Spain
125 Q 11 **Acambaro**, Mexico
124 M 10 **Acaponeta**, Mexico
125 Q 14 **Acapulco**, Mexico
142 K 10 **Acará**, Brazil
142 N 11 **Acaraú**, Brazil
142 F 9 **Acari Mountains**, Brazil
138 M 3 **Acarigua**, Venezuela
100 H 8 **Acâş**, Romania
125 S 13 **Acatlan**, Mexico
125 S 12 **Acatzingo**, Mexico
121 T 13 **Accomac**, Virginia, U.S.A.
192 M 13 **Accra**, Ghana
174 B 8 **Aceh**, Indonesia
91 K 16 **Acerno**, Italy
139 N 4 **Achaguas**, Venezuela
169 E 16 **Achalpur**, India
159 U 6 **Achaseli**, Georgia
89 N 6 **Achenkirch**, Austria
77 A 16 **Achill Island**, Republic of Ireland
157 N 12 **Achinsk**, Russian Federation
158 D 12 **Acipayam**, Turkey
91 K 22 **Acireale**, Italy
127 O 4 **Acklins Island**, The Bahamas
126 G 11 **Acoyapa**, Nicaragua
90 C 8 **Acqui Terme**, Italy
160 F 7 **Acre**, Israel
142 B 13 **Acre**, Brazil
91 M 18 **Acri**, Italy
125 R 11 **Actopan**, Mexico
142 O 12 **Açu**, Brazil
193 T 15 **Acurenam**, Equatorial Guinea
163 N 7 **Ad Dafinah**, Saudi Arabia
161 U 9 **Ad Daghgharah**, Iraq
163 P 4 **Ad Dahnā'**, Saudi Arabia
188 B 12 **Ad Dakhla**, Western Sahara
163 P 14 **Aḍ Ḍāli'**, Yemen
163 T 5 **Ad Dammām**, Saudi Arabia
163 N 11 **Ad Darb**, Saudi Arabia
163 P 6 **Ad Dawādimī**, Saudi Arabia
161 S 5 **Ad Dawr**, Iraq
161 Y 11 **Ad Dayr**, Iraq
163 R 6 **Ad Dilam**, Saudi Arabia
163 Q 6 **Ad Dir'īyah**, Saudi Arabia
161 U 9 **Ad Dīwānīyah**, Iraq
161 T 6 **Ad Dujayl**, Iraq
94 K 8 **Ada**, Serbia and Montenegro
119 K 18 **Ada**, Oklahoma, U.S.A.
112 A 8 **Adak**, Alaska, U.S.A.
112 A 8 **Adak Island**, Alaska, U.S.A.
163 Y 7 **Adam**, Oman
193 U 13 **Adamaoua**, Cameroon
97 H 23 **Adamas**, Greece
193 U 11 **Adamawa**, Nigeria
193 U 12 **Adamawa Highlands**, Cameroon
61 Y 15 **Adam's Rock**, Pitcairn Island
61 Y 14 **Adamstown**, Pitcairn Island
163 P 14 **Adan as Sughra**, Yemen
158 K 13 **Adana**, Turkey
176 K 13 **Adatara-san**, Japan
209 S 7 **Adavale**, Queensland, Australia
117 J 18 **Adaven**, Nevada, U.S.A.
167 N 4 **Aday**, Kazakhstan
191 I 20 **Addis Ababa**, Ethiopia
169 L 20 **Addu Atoll**, Maldives
123 P 7 **Adel**, Georgia, U.S.A.
209 P 12 **Adelaide**, South Australia, Australia
218 H 5 **Adelaide Island**, Antarctica
208 M 2 **Adelaide River**, Northern Territory, Australia
219 U 14 **Adélie Coast**, Antarctica
219 U 14 **Adélie Land**, Antarctica
167 S 11 **Adelunga Toghi**, Uzbekistan
81 S 7 **Ademuz**, Spain
163 P 14 **Aden**, Yemen
193 R 8 **Aderbissinat**, Niger
163 X 5 **Adh Dhayd**, United Arab Emirates
175 U 13 **Adi**, Indonesia
191 I 18 **Ādī Ārk'ay**, Ethiopia
191 I 17 **Adi Keyih**, Eritrea
191 I 17 **Ādīgrat**, Ethiopia
158 D 11 **Adigüzel Baraji**, Turkey
169 F 17 **Adilabad**, India
195 T 6 **Adilanga**, Uganda
159 S 10 **Adilcevaz**, Turkey
117 E 14 **Adin**, California, U.S.A.
83 A 18 **Adinkerke**, Belgium
189 S 11 **Adīrī**, Libya
121 T 7 **Adirondack Mountains**, New York, U.S.A.
191 H 18 **Ādīs Zemen**, Ethiopia
159 N 12 **Adiyaman**, Turkey
100 L 10 **Adjud**, Romania
88 G 7 **Adliswil**, Switzerland
116 D 6 **Admiralty Inlet**, Washington, U.S.A.
113 O 10 **Admiralty Island**, Alaska, U.S.A.
212 D 2 **Admiralty Islands**, Papua New Guinea
193 Q 12 **Ado-Ekiti**, Nigeria
191 D 21 **Adok**, Sudan
175 P 15 **Adonara**, Indonesia
169 E 19 **Adoni**, India
81 P 13 **Adra**, Spain
192 H 5 **Adrar**, Mauritania
188 K 11 **Adrar**, Algeria
189 R 13 **Adrar Mariou**, Algeria
188 B 14 **Adrar Souttouf**, Western Sahara
193 Z 9 **Adré**, Chad
119 G 17 **Adrian**, Texas, U.S.A.
120 M 9 **Adrian**, Michigan, U.S.A.
90 I 9 **Adriatic Sea**, Europe
195 P 7 **Adusa**, Democratic Republic of Congo
99 H 14 **Adutiškis**, Lithuania
191 I 17 **Ādwa**, Ethiopia
192 K 13 **Adzopé**, Côte d'Ivoire
97 I 17 **Aegean Sea**, Greece
98 G 6 **Aegviidu**, Estonia
161 V 9 **'Afak**, Iraq
97 O 24 **Afantou**, Greece
191 J 18 **Afar**, Ethiopia
191 J 17 **Afar Depression**, Ethiopia
165 R 8 **Afghanistan**, Asia
191 M 24 **Afgooye**, Somalia
163 O 6 **'Afif**, Saudi Arabia
193 R 13 **Afikpo**, Nigeria
188 M 7 **Aflou**, Algeria
191 K 25 **Afmadow**, Somalia
112 J 8 **Afognak Island**, Alaska, U.S.A.
142 M 13 **Afrânio**, Brazil
58 G 10 **Africana Seamount**, Indian Ocean
160 J 2 **'Afrīn**, Syria
158 L 11 **Afşin**, Turkey
82 I 8 **Afsluitdijk**, Netherlands
142 I 9 **Afuá**, Brazil
160 G 8 **'Afula**, Israel
158 F 10 **Afyon**, Turkey
193 S 6 **Agadez**, Niger
193 R 7 **Agadez**, Niger
188 F 9 **Agadir**, Morocco
62 K 9 **Agadir Canyon**, Atlantic Ocean
167 T 6 **Agadyr'**, Kazakhstan
169 M 14 **Agartala**, India
61 T 12 **Agassiz Fracture Zone**, Pacific Ocean
97 M 21 **Agathonisi**, Greece
175 X 13 **Agats**, Indonesia
169 B 22 **Agatti**, India
192 K 13 **Agboville**, Côte d'Ivoire
175 O 2 **Agbulu**, Philippines
159 W 9 **Ağcabädi**, Azerbaijan
159 W 9 **Ağdam**, Azerbaijan
159 W 8 **Ağdaş**, Azerbaijan
79 R 14 **Agde**, France
79 N 13 **Agen**, France
191 I 22 **Āgere Maryam**, Ethiopia
159 W 10 **Aghband**, Azerbaijan
97 M 22 **Agia Marina**, Greece
97 K 17 **Agia Paraskevi**, Greece
157 R 14 **Aginskoye**, Russian Federation
97 F 16 **Agiokampos**, Greece
97 H 14 **Ágion Óros**, Greece
97 I 16 **Agios Efstratios**, Greece
97 H 21 **Agios Georgios**, Greece
97 E 22 **Ágios Ilías**, Greece
97 L 21 **Agios Kirykos**, Greece
97 D 16 **Agnantero**, Greece
192 K 13 **Agnibilékrou**, Côte d'Ivoire
168 F 12 **Agra**, India
81 R 4 **Ágreda**, Spain
159 S 9 **Ağri**, Turkey
91 I 23 **Agrigento**, Italy
214 B 6 **Agrihan**, Northern Mariana Islands
97 C 18 **Agrinio**, Greece
91 K 17 **Agropoli**, Italy
159 X 8 **Ağsu**, Azerbaijan
124 J 3 **Agua Prieta**, Mexico
145 I 16 **Aguada Cecilio**, Argentina
127 T 7 **Aguadilla**, Puerto Rico
126 J 14 **Aguadulce**, Panama
125 O 10 **Aguascalientes**, Mexico
125 O 10 **Aguascalientes**, Mexico
193 N 6 **Aguelhok**, Mali
193 R 9 **Aguié**, Niger
214 B 8 **Aguijan**, Northern Mariana Islands
117 L 23 **Aguila**, Arizona, U.S.A.
81 N 2 **Aguilar de Campóo**, Spain
81 R 12 **Águilas**, Spain
125 O 12 **Aguililla**, Mexico
63 N 18 **Agulhas Bank**, Atlantic Ocean/Indian Ocean
63 O 19 **Agulhas Basin**, Atlantic Ocean
58 G 10 **Agulhas Basin Plateau**, Indian Ocean
143 L 18 **Agulhas Negras**, Brazil
58 H 10 **Agulhas Plateau**, Indian Ocean
63 M 19 **Agulhas Ridge**, Atlantic Ocean
177 N 24 **Aguni-jima**, Japan
164 G 3 **Ahar**, Iran
211 G 18 **Ahaura**, New Zealand
87 C 14 **Ahaus**, Germany
215 U 8 **Ahe**, French Polynesia
210 I 5 **Ahipara**, New Zealand
210 I 5 **Ahipara Bay**, New Zealand
210 J 12 **Ahititi**, New Zealand
159 R 11 **Ahlat**, Turkey
87 E 15 **Ahlen**, Germany
169 C 14 **Ahmadabad**, India
169 C 17 **Ahmadnagar**, India
165 W 11 **Ahmadpur East**, Pakistan
191 J 21 **Ahmar Mountains**, Ethiopia
124 J 7 **Ahome**, Mexico
164 G 9 **Āhū**, Iran
215 W 10 **Ahunui**, French Polynesia
164 G 9 **Ahvāz**, Iran
169 C 16 **Ahwa**, India
163 R 14 **Aḩwar**, Yemen
173 N 17 **Ai Yin Young**, Vietnam
212 A 5 **Aiambak**, Papua New Guinea
87 J 23 **Aichach**, Germany
89 S 2 **Aigen**, Austria
158 I 15 **Aigialousa**, Cyprus
97 G 21 **Aigina**, Greece
97 G 20 **Aigina**, Greece
97 E 14 **Aiginio**, Greece
97 D 19 **Aigio**, Greece
88 C 10 **Aigle**, Switzerland
144 O 12 **Aiguá**, Uruguay
176 I 13 **Aikawa**, Japan
209 N 6 **Aileron**, Northern Territory, Australia
215 W 1 **Ailinginae**, Marshall Islands
215 Y 3 **Ailinglaplap**, Marshall Islands
215 Y 2 **Ailuk**, Marshall Islands
144 H 8 **Aimogasta**, Argentina
189 P 6 **Aïn Beïda**, Algeria
192 I 2 **Aïn Ben Tili**, Mauritania
188 J 7 **Aïn Beni Mathar**, Morocco
188 M 5 **Aïn Defla**, Algeria
188 M 6 **Aïn Deheb**, Algeria
189 N 6 **Aïn el Hadjel**, Algeria
188 K 8 **Aïn Sefra**, Algeria
188 K 6 **Aïn Temouchent**, Algeria
98 F 9 **Ainaži**, Latvia
97 B 19 **Ainos**, Greece
81 U 3 **Ainsa**, Spain
141 K 20 **Aiquile**, Bolivia
174 G 9 **Air**, Indonesia
115 Q 1 **Air Force Island**, Nunavut, Canada
174 D 10 **Airbangis**, Indonesia
78 M 14 **Aire-sur-l'Adour**, France
88 G 9 **Airolo**, Switzerland
175 R 14 **Airpanas**, Indonesia
145 F 20 **Aisén**, Chile
81 T 9 **Aitana**, Spain
212 B 3 **Aitape**, Papua New Guinea
118 L 8 **Aitkin**, Minnesota, U.S.A.
215 P 10 **Aitutaki**, Cook Islands
100 I 10 **Aiud**, Romania
98 H 11 **Aiviekste**, Latvia
215 U 1 **Aiwo**, Nauru
79 U 14 **Aix-en-Provence**, France
79 V 10 **Aix-les-Bains**, France
169 N 14 **Aizawl**, India
98 G 11 **Aizkraukle**, Latvia
98 C 11 **Aizpute**, Latvia
176 K 13 **Aizu-Wakamatsu**, Japan
79 X 15 **Ajaccio**, France
168 G 13 **Ajaigarh**, India
169 D 16 **Ajanta**, India
169 D 16 **Ajanta Range**, India
189 W 8 **Ajdābiyā**, Libya
94 A 7 **Ajdovščina**, Slovenia
160 G 9 **'Ajlūn**, Jordan
163 X 5 **Ajman**, United Arab Emirates
168 D 12 **Ajmer**, India
117 L 24 **Ajo**, Arizona, U.S.A.
176 K 5 **Akabira**, Japan
188 L 11 **Akabli**, Algeria
191 I 20 **Āk'ak'ī**, Ethiopia
211 H 21 **Akaroa**, New Zealand
211 I 21 **Akaroa Harbour**, New Zealand
161 N 6 **Akāshat**, Iraq
177 G 18 **Akashi**, Japan
167 W 7 **Akbalyk**, Kazakhstan
167 T 7 **Akbulak**, Kazakhstan
159 N 11 **Akçadağ**, Turkey
159 O 13 **Akçakale**, Turkey
158 G 7 **Akçakoca**, Turkey
192 F 5 **Akchâr**, Mauritania
167 T 6 **Akchatau**, Kazakhstan
158 D 13 **Akdağlar**, Turkey
158 K 10 **Akdağmadeni**, Turkey
166 L 11 **Akdepe**, Turkmenistan
175 S 10 **Akelamo**, Indonesia
194 M 6 **Aketi**, Democratic Republic of Congo
159 S 7 **Akhalk'alak'i**, Georgia
166 L 13 **Akhalskiy Velayat**, Turkmenistan
159 S 7 **Akhalts'ikhe**, Georgia
158 C 10 **Akhisar**, Turkey
190 D 10 **Akhmîm**, Egypt
156 F 10 **Akhtubinsk**, Russian Federation
177 F 20 **Aki**, Japan
215 X 10 **Akiaki**, French Polynesia
194 G 8 **Akiéni**, Gabon
115 O 9 **Akimiski Island**, Québec, Canada
158 K 14 **Akinci Burnu**, Turkey
176 J 10 **Akita**, Japan
192 F 5 **Akjoujt**, Mauritania
188 G 9 **Akka**, Morocco
176 M 5 **Akkeshi**, Japan
176 M 5 **Akkeshi-wan**, Japan
167 S 10 **Akkol'**, Kazakhstan
167 S 3 **Akkol'**, Kazakhstan
158 B 12 **Akköy**, Turkey
167 V 3 **Akku**, Kazakhstan
167 O 9 **Akkum**, Kazakhstan
158 M 8 **Akkuş**, Turkey
193 O 12 **Aklampa**, Benin
113 O 4 **Aklavik**, Northwest Territories, Canada
167 R 4 **Akmola**, Kazakhstan
98 H 12 **Aknīste**, Latvia
177 F 18 **Akō**, Japan
191 F 21 **Akobo**, Sudan
169 E 14 **Akodia**, India
169 E 16 **Akola**, India
193 T 15 **Akom II**, Cameroon
191 H 16 **Akordat**, Eritrea
169 E 16 **Akot**, India
191 D 22 **Akot**, Sudan
115 S 5 **Akpatok Island**, Nunavut, Canada
170 H 5 **Akqi**, China
97 K 26 **Akra Agios Ioannis**, Greece
97 H 15 **Akra Akrathos**, Greece
97 H 14 **Akra Arapis**, Greece
97 C 19 **Akra Araxos**, Greece
97 H 15 **Akra Drepano**, Greece
97 I 19 **Akra Kafireas**, Greece
97 G 15 **Akra Kassandras**, Greece
97 I 26 **Akra Lithino**, Greece
97 F 23 **Akra Maleas**, Greece
97 K 19 **Akra Meston**, Greece
97 G 15 **Akra Paliouri**, Greece
97 M 25 **Akra Paraspori**, Greece
97 L 26 **Akra Sideros**, Greece
97 K 17 **Akra Sigri**, Greece
97 G 25 **Akra Spatha**, Greece
97 E 24 **Akra Tainaro**, Greece
193 S 7 **Akrérèb**, Niger
121 O 10 **Akron**, Ohio, U.S.A.
96 N 7 **Aksakovo**, Bulgaria
158 I 11 **Aksaray**, Turkey
166 J 4 **Aksay**, Kazakhstan
158 G 11 **Akşehir**, Turkey
158 F 11 **Akşehir Gölü**, Turkey
158 G 13 **Akseki**, Turkey
167 S 3 **Aksu**, Kazakhstan
167 U 3 **Aksu**, Kazakhstan
170 I 5 **Aksu**, China
167 T 6 **Aksu-Ayuly**, Kazakhstan
167 Y 6 **Aksuat**, Kazakhstan
167 U 9 **Aksuek**, Kazakhstan
191 I 17 **Āksum**, Ethiopia
167 P 12 **Aktash**, Uzbekistan
166 H 9 **Aktau**, Kazakhstan
167 U 3 **Aktogay**, Kazakhstan
167 U 6 **Aktogay**, Kazakhstan
167 W 7 **Aktogay**, Kazakhstan
99 K 20 **Aktsyabrski**, Belarus
166 L 6 **Aktyubinsk**, Kazakhstan
166 L 5 **Aktyubinsk**, Kazakhstan
194 K 6 **Akula**, Democratic Republic of Congo
115 P 5 **Akulivik**, Québec, Canada
177 B 23 **Akune**, Japan
193 Q 13 **Akure**, Nigeria
84 C 10 **Akureyri**, Iceland
177 B 26 **Akuseki-shima**, Japan
112 D 9 **Akutan Island**, Alaska, U.S.A.
193 R 14 **Akwa Ibom**, Nigeria
193 R 12 **Akwanga**, Nigeria
167 Y 6 **Akzhar**, Kazakhstan
159 O 12 **Akziyaret**, Turkey
189 W 7 **Al Abyār**, Libya
189 Y 7 **Al 'Adam**, Libya
163 S 3 **Al Aḩmadī**, Kuwait
163 O 4 **Al Ajfar**, Saudi Arabia
163 N 9 **Al 'Alayyah**, Saudi Arabia
161 S 1 **Al Amādīyah**, Iraq
161 Y 9 **Al 'Amārah**, Iraq
160 F 13 **Al 'Aqabah**, Jordan
163 N 9 **Al 'Aqīq**, Saudi Arabia
188 B 12 **Al Argoub**, Western Sahara
163 Q 4 **Al Arṭāwīyah**, Saudi Arabia
161 O 4 **Al 'Ashārah**, Syria
163 X 6 **Al 'Ayn**, United Arab Emirates
161 U 8 **Al 'Azīzīyah**, Iraq
189 S 8 **Al 'Azīzīyah**, Libya
161 P 2 **Al Ba'āj**, Iraq
160 J 2 **Al Bāb**, Syria
161 P 3 **Al Bādī**, Iraq
163 Q 8 **Al Badī'**, Saudi Arabia
163 N 9 **Al Bāḩah**, Saudi Arabia
160 H 3 **Al Bahlūlīyah**, Syria
189 Y 7 **Al Bardī**, Libya

Country · Internal administrative region: State/Province/Territory/Dependent territory · Capital city · Mountain range/Undersea ridge · Mountain peak/Volcano/Seamount · Geographic feature · Headland/Point/Cape/Peninsula · Desert · Island/Island group · Antarctic base · Ocean · Sea · Bay/Gulf/Channel/Strait · Lake · Salt pan/Dry/Intermittent lake · River

161 Z 11 Al Başrah, Iraq
163 Q 13 Al Bayḍā', Yemen
189 W 7 Al Bayḍā', Libya
162 M 7 Al Bi'ār, Saudi Arabia
162 K 3 Al Bi'r, Saudi Arabia
163 N 11 Al Birk, Saudi Arabia
163 O 5 Al Bukayrīyah, Saudi Arabia
163 X 6 Al Buraymī, Oman
161 N 4 Al Buşayrah, Syria
161 W 12 Al Buşayyah, Iraq
161 S 7 Al Fallūjah, Iraq
163 S 13 Al Fardah, Yemen
163 S 3 Al Farwānīyah, Kuwait
161 S 4 Al Fatḥah, Iraq
161 Z 12 Al Fāw, Iraq
163 O 13 Al Fāzih, Yemen
189 U 10 Al Fuqahā', Libya
161 U 10 Al Ghammās, Iraq
163 P 5 Al Ghāţ, Saudi Arabia
163 V 12 Al Ghayḍah, Yemen
161 S 7 Al Ḥabbānīyah, Iraq
161 Q 6 Al Ḥadīthah, Iraq
161 R 3 Al Ḥaḍr, Iraq
188 E 10 Al Haggounia, Western Sahara
163 X 6 Al Hajar'al Gharbī, Oman
163 R 12 Al Ḥajr, Yemen
161 Y 9 Al Ḥalfāyah, Iraq
162 L 1 Al Hamād, Saudi Arabia
189 Q 9 Al Ḥamādah al Ḥamrā', Libya
160 H 4 Al Ḥamīdīyah, Syria
162 M 6 Al Ḥanākīyah, Saudi Arabia
163 O 14 Al Ḥanīsh al Kabīr, Yemen
161 W 14 Al Haniyah, Iraq
163 O 11 Al Ḥaqū, Saudi Arabia
189 U 10 Al Haruj al Aswad, Libya
160 G 11 Al Ḥāsā, Jordan
161 O 2 Al Ḥasakah, Syria
161 U 9 Al Hāshimīyah, Iraq
161 O 2 Al Hawl, Syria
163 R 14 Al Ḥawrā, Yemen
161 W 9 Al Ḥayy, Iraq
163 P 12 Al Ḥazm al-Jawf, Yemen
163 V 9 Al Hibāk, Saudi Arabia
160 H 7 Al Hijānah, Syria
161 T 8 Al Ḥillah, Iraq
163 R 7 Al Ḥillah, Saudi Arabia
161 T 8 Al Hindīyah, Iraq
160 L 2 Al Hīshah, Syria
160 G 8 Al Ḥiṣn, Jordan
188 J 6 Al Hoceima, Morocco
163 O 13 Al Ḥudaydah, Yemen
163 T 5 Al Hufūf, Saudi Arabia
163 Q 14 Al Ḥumayshah, Yemen
163 X 8 Al Huwatsah, Oman
163 S 13 Al Ḥuwaymī, Yemen
162 L 1 Al 'Īsāwīyah, Saudi Arabia
189 W 7 Al Jabal al Akhḍar, Libya
160 H 12 Al Jafr, Jordan
189 Y 8 Al Jaghbūb, Libya
163 R 2 Al Jahrah, Kuwait
163 U 5 Al Jamalīyah, Qatar
162 M 2 Al Jawf, Saudi Arabia
189 Y 12 Al Jawf, Libya
161 N 2 Al Jazīrah, Syria
163 N 4 Al Jithāmīyah, Saudi Arabia
163 T 4 Al Jubayl, Saudi Arabia
162 M 8 Al Jumūm, Saudi Arabia
163 Z 9 Al Kalbān, Oman
160 G 11 Al Karak, Jordan
190 F 11 Al Karnak, Egypt
163 Y 6 Al Khābūrah, Oman
163 Z 9 Al Khalīf, Oman
161 U 6 Al Khāliş, Iraq
163 P 9 Al Khamāsīn, Saudi Arabia
163 Y 5 Al Khaşab, Oman
163 O 14 Al Khawkhah, Yemen
161 V 10 Al Khiḍr, Iraq
189 Y 12 Al Khufrah, Libya
189 T 7 Al Khums, Libya
161 T 9 Al Kifl, Iraq
163 U 5 Al Kir'ānah, Qatar
161 T 9 Al Kūfah, Iraq
161 X 9 Al Kumayt, Iraq
161 W 8 Al Kūt, Iraq
163 N 2 Al Labbah, Saudi Arabia
160 H 3 Al Lādhiqīyah, Syria
162 M 9 Al Līth, Saudi Arabia
161 R 11 Al Ma'ānīyah, Iraq
160 H 8 Al Mafraq, Jordan
188 F 10 Al Mahbas, Western Sahara
160 K 2 Al Mahdum, Syria
161 T 7 Al Maḥmūdīyah, Iraq
163 U 11 Al Mahrah, Yemen
163 O 12 Al Maḥwīt, Yemen
163 Q 5 Al Majma'ah, Saudi Arabia
161 Q 1 Al Mālikīyah, Syria
163 T 5 Al Manāmah, Bahrain
161 Z 11 Al Ma'qil, Iraq
163 O 13 Al Marāwi'ah, Yemen
189 W 7 Al Marj, Libya
163 Y 6 Al Masana'a, Oman
161 N 4 Al Mayādīn, Syria
160 G 10 Al Mazra'ah, Jordan
163 V 6 Al Mirfa, United Arab Emirates
163 T 5 Al Mubarrez, Saudi Arabia
160 G 14 Al Mudawwarah, Jordan
163 T 5 Al Muharraq, Bahrain
163 T 13 Al Mukallā, Yemen
189 X 7 Al Mukhaylī, Libya
161 U 6 Al Muqdādīyah, Iraq
162 L 6 Al Musayjīd, Saudi Arabia
161 W 9 Al Muwaffaqīyah, Iraq
163 N 7 Al Muwayh, Saudi Arabia
162 J 3 Al Muwayliḥ, Saudi Arabia
161 Y 11 Al Muzayri'ah, Iraq
160 H 4 Al Qadmūs, Syria
161 P 5 Al Qā'im, Iraq
163 O 6 Al Qā'īyah, Saudi Arabia
162 L 3 Al Qalībah, Saudi Arabia
161 O 1 Al Qāmishlī, Syria
160 H 3 Al Qardābah, Syria
160 I 5 Al Qaryatayn, Syria
163 S 12 Al Qaṭn, Yemen
160 H 10 Al Qaṭrānah, Jordan
189 T 12 Al Qaṭrūn, Libya
163 Q 3 Al Qayşūmah, Saudi Arabia
162 M 10 Al Qunfidhah, Saudi Arabia
161 Y 11 Al Qurnah, Iraq
161 W 11 Al Qusayr, Iraq
163 Q 6 Al Quwayi', Saudi Arabia
160 F 13 Al Quwayrah, Jordan
163 S 13 Al Quzah, Yemen
163 W 6 Al Samha, United Arab Emirates
163 S 5 Al 'Uḍaylīyah, Saudi Arabia
162 L 4 Al 'Ulā, Saudi Arabia
189 V 9 Al 'Uqaylah, Libya
189 R 12 Al 'Uwaynāt, Libya
189 Z 13 Al 'Uwaynāt, Libya
163 O 2 Al 'Uwayqīlah, Saudi Arabia
162 M 6 Al 'Uyūn, Saudi Arabia
163 O 4 Al 'Uyūn, Saudi Arabia
161 Y 10 Al 'Uzayr, Iraq
163 S 3 Al Wafrah, Kuwait
162 J 4 Al Wajh, Saudi Arabia
163 S 4 Al Wannān, Saudi Arabia
163 R 3 Al Wari'ah, Saudi Arabia
163 Y 6 Al Wāsiţ, Oman
189 T 12 Al Wīgh, Libya
163 R 6 Al Yamāmah, Saudi Arabia
167 S 11 Ala-Buka, Kyrgyzstan
158 G 11 Ala Dağl, Turkey
122 J 6 Alabama, U.S.A.
122 K 7 Alabama, Alabama, U.S.A.
158 J 9 Alaca, Turkey
158 K 7 Alaçam, Turkey
123 Q 9 Alachua, Florida, U.S.A.
142 O 13 Alagoas, Brazil
143 N 14 Alagoinhas, Brazil
81 S 4 Alagón, Spain
160 H 3 Alājah, Syria
126 G 13 Alajuela, Costa Rica
214 B 7 Alamagan, Northern Mariana Islands
163 P 5 Al'Amār, Saudi Arabia
191 I 18 Ālamat'ā, Ethiopia
126 H 10 Alamicamba, Nicaragua
117 J 19 Alamo, Nevada, U.S.A.
117 L 22 Alamo Dam, Arizona, U.S.A.
119 E 19 Alamogordo, New Mexico, U.S.A.
119 E 16 Alamosa, Colorado, U.S.A.
85 I 19 Åland, Finland
85 I 19 Ålands Hav, Finland
158 G 13 Alanya, Turkey
158 C 11 Alaşehir, Turkey
112 J 5 Alaska, U.S.A.
112 F 9 Alaska Peninsula, Alaska, U.S.A.
112 J 7 Alaska Range, Alaska, U.S.A.
159 Z 8 Älät, Azerbaijan
140 B 10 Alausí, Ecuador
159 T 8 Alaverdi, Armenia
85 K 16 Alavus, Finland
157 V 7 Alazeya, Russian Federation
81 R 9 Albacete, Spain
95 K 17 Albania, Europe
114 L 10 Albany, Ontario, Canada
120 K 15 Albany, Kentucky, U.S.A.
121 U 8 Albany, New York, U.S.A.
123 O 7 Albany, Georgia, U.S.A.
208 H 12 Albany, Western Australia, Australia
210 K 8 Albany, New Zealand
82 G 13 Albasserdam, Netherlands
209 R 1 Albatross Bay, Queensland, Australia
210 K 10 Albatross Point, New Zealand
123 W 1 Albemarle Sound, North Carolina, U.S.A.
90 B 9 Albenga, Italy
143 G 20 Alberdi, Paraguay
209 O 8 Alberga, South Australia, Australia
80 H 5 Albergaria-a-Velha, Portugal
79 Q 2 Albert, France
118 L 11 Albert Lea, Minnesota, U.S.A.
195 R 6 Albert Nile, Uganda
113 U 10 Alberta, Canada
121 R 14 Alberta, Virginia, U.S.A.
93 J 23 Albertirsa, Hungary
79 V 10 Albertville, France
122 M 4 Albertville, Alabama, U.S.A.
79 Q 13 Albi, France
81 O 14 Alboran Sea, Africa/Spain
85 C 23 Ålborg, Denmark
80 H 12 Albufeira, Portugal
88 I 9 Albula Alpen, Switzerland
119 E 17 Albuquerque, New Mexico, U.S.A.
80 J 8 Alburquerque, Spain
209 T 12 Albury, New South Wales, Australia
80 H 10 Alcácer do Sal, Portugal
80 L 13 Alcalá de los Gazules, Spain
81 O 12 Alcalá la Real, Spain
91 H 22 Alcamo, Italy
81 T 5 Alcañiz, Spain
80 J 8 Alcántara, Spain
81 Q 10 Alcaraz, Spain
81 N 12 Alcaudete, Spain
81 P 8 Alcázar de San Juan, Spain
101 Y 6 Alchevs'k, Ukraine
81 T 6 Alcorisa, Spain
144 K 12 Alcorta, Argentina
81 U 7 Alcossebre, Spain
118 E 11 Alcova, Wyoming, U.S.A.
81 T 9 Alcoy, Spain
81 Y 7 Alcúdia, Spain
58 K 5 Aldabra Islands, Indian Ocean
125 S 9 Aldama, Mexico
157 U 11 Aldan, Russian Federation
157 T 12 Aldan, Russian Federation
77 J 25 Alderney, United Kingdom
77 L 22 Aldershot, United Kingdom
192 F 7 Aleg, Mauritania
62 O 11 Alegranza, Canary Islands
143 M 18 Alegre, Brazil
143 G 21 Alegrete, Brazil
96 I 7 Aleksandrovo, Bulgaria
157 X 13 Aleksandrovsk-Sakhalinskiy, Russian Federation
94 N 13 Aleksinac, Serbia and Montenegro
79 N 5 Alençon, France
142 H 10 Alenquer, Brazil
117 D 25 Alenuihaha Channel, Hawaii, U.S.A.
160 J 2 Aleppo, Syria
79 Z 15 Aléria, France
141 G 15 Alerta, Peru
79 S 13 Alès, France
100 G 8 Aleşd, Romania
90 C 8 Alessandria, Italy
85 B 16 Ålesund, Norway
61 P 2 Aleutian Basin, Pacific Ocean
112 A 7 Aleutian Islands, Alaska, U.S.A.
112 G 9 Aleutian Range, Alaska, U.S.A.
61 O 2 Aleutian Trench, Pacific Ocean
113 N 10 Alexander Archipelago, Alaska, U.S.A.
196 I 12 Alexander Bay, Republic of South Africa
122 M 5 Alexander City, Alabama, U.S.A.
218 I 6 Alexander Island, Antarctica
211 D 23 Alexandra, New Zealand
100 J 13 Alexandria, Romania
118 K 9 Alexandria, Minnesota, U.S.A.
119 N 20 Alexandria, Louisiana, U.S.A.
121 S 12 Alexandria, Virginia, U.S.A.
190 D 7 Alexandria, Egypt
121 T 6 Alexandria Bay, New York, U.S.A.
96 K 13 Alexandroupoli, Greece
160 G 6 'Aley, Lebanon
156 L 13 Aleysk, Russian Federation
96 M 6 Alfatar, Bulgaria
90 G 9 Alfonsine, Italy
166 I 4 Algabas, Kazakhstan
80 G 12 Algarve, Portugal
80 L 14 Algeciras, Spain
191 I 15 Algena, Eritrea
188 K 11 Algeria, Africa
91 A 16 Alghero, Italy
188 M 5 Algiers, Algeria
81 T 9 Alginet, Spain
80 L 13 Algodonales, Spain
120 J 6 Algoma, Wisconsin, U.S.A.
118 L 11 Algona, Iowa, U.S.A.
161 V 8 'Alī, Iraq
161 X 8 'Ali al Gharbī, Iraq
159 Y 9 Äli Bayramli, Azerbaijan
165 V 7 'Alī Kheyl, Afghanistan
191 K 19 Ali Sabieh, Djibouti
158 B 10 Aliağa, Turkey
97 F 19 Aliartos, Greece
94 L 10 Alibunar, Serbia and Montenegro
81 T 10 Alicante, Spain
119 J 23 Alice, Texas, U.S.A.
126 K 9 Alice Shoal, Honduras
209 O 6 Alice Springs, Northern Territory, Australia
126 K 2 Alice Town, The Bahamas
122 K 5 Aliceville, Alabama, U.S.A.
167 U 14 Alichur, Tajikistan
168 F 11 Aligarh, India
97 N 24 Alimia, Greece
139 W 8 Alimimuni Peak, Suriname
165 W 11 Alipur, Pakistan
80 J 8 Aliseda, Spain
97 H 19 Aliveri, Greece
80 K 9 Aljucén, Spain
82 H 9 Alkmaar, Netherlands
168 G 13 Allahabad, India
112 K 4 Allakaket, Alaska, U.S.A.
157 V 10 Allakh-Yun', Russian Federation
197 O 9 Alldays, Republic of South Africa
121 P 13 Allegheny Mountains, West Virginia, U.S.A.
123 R 5 Allendale, South Carolina, U.S.A.
125 P 5 Allende, Mexico
125 Q 7 Allende, Mexico
121 T 10 Allentown, Pennsylvania, U.S.A.
169 D 23 Alleppey, India
87 H 26 Allgäuer Alpen, Germany/Austria
118 G 12 Alliance, Nebraska, U.S.A.
169 E 23 Allinagaram, India
120 L 7 Alma, Michigan, U.S.A.
123 Q 7 Alma, Georgia, U.S.A.
81 U 4 Almacelles, Spain
80 M 9 Almadén, Spain
81 O 9 Almagro, Spain
167 S 12 Almalyk, Uzbekistan
81 S 9 Almansa, Spain
80 M 7 Almanzor, Spain
143 K 14 Almas, Brazil
167 V 8 Almaty, Kazakhstan
167 V 10 Almaty, Kazakhstan
81 Q 4 Almazán, Spain
80 H 8 Almeirim, Portugal
142 I 10 Almeirim, Brazil
82 N 11 Almelo, Netherlands
81 Q 4 Almenar de Soria, Spain
80 K 9 Almendralejo, Spain
82 I 11 Almere, Netherlands
81 Q 13 Almería, Spain
85 F 24 Älmhult, Sweden
126 I 13 Almirante, Panama
80 H 11 Almodôvar, Portugal
80 J 12 Almonte, Spain
168 F 10 Almora, India
193 N 7 Almoustarat, Mali
81 O 13 Almuñécar, Spain
77 J 14 Alnwick, United Kingdom
214 J 10 Alofi, Niue
214 H 8 Alofi, Wallis and Futuna Islands
98 G 9 Aloja, Latvia
168 N 11 Along, India
97 G 17 Alonnisos, Greece
175 Q 15 Alor, Indonesia
174 D 7 Alor Setar, Malaysia
212 G 7 Alotau, Papua New Guinea
80 I 8 Alpalhao, Portugal
120 M 6 Alpena, Michigan, U.S.A.
209 T 7 Alpha, Queensland, Australia
65 R 7 Alpha Ridge, Arctic Ocean
82 G 12 Alphen, Netherlands
117 O 23 Alpine, Arizona, U.S.A.
79 V 12 Alps, Europe
209 P 5 Alpurrurulam, Northern Territory, Australia
79 W 5 Alsace, France
81 Q 2 Alsasua, Spain
87 G 17 Alsfeld, Germany
98 C 11 Alsunga, Latvia
84 K 7 Alta, Norway
144 J 10 Alta Gracia, Argentina
84 K 7 Altaelva, Norway
139 O 3 Altagracia de Orituco, Venezuela
170 L 2 Altai Mountains, China/Kazakhstan
123 Q 6 Altamaha, Georgia, U.S.A.
126 H 12 Altamira, Costa Rica
142 I 10 Altamira, Brazil
144 G 7 Altamira, Chile
91 M 16 Altamura, Italy
121 Q 14 Altavista, Virginia, U.S.A.
170 L 3 Altay, China
171 N 4 Altay, Mongolia
88 G 8 Altdorf, Switzerland
81 U 10 Altea, Spain
87 N 17 Altenberg, Germany
87 L 17 Altenburg, Germany
80 I 8 Alter do Chão, Portugal
84 I 8 Altevatnet, Norway
89 Q 4 Altheim, Austria
161 T 3 Altin Köprü, Iraq
141 H 20 Altiplano, Bolivia
143 H 16 Alto Araguaia, Brazil
196 J 3 Alto Chicapa, Angola
80 I 6 Alto da Torre, Portugal
138 I 4 Alto de Tamar, Colombia
143 H 16 Alto Garças, Brazil
197 T 6 Alto Molócuè, Mozambique
138 G 5 Alto Musinga, Colombia
142 K 13 Alto Parnaíba, Brazil
141 G 15 Alto Purús, Peru
145 G 19 Alto Río Senguerr, Argentina
119 N 16 Alton, Missouri, U.S.A.
121 Q 11 Altoona, Pennsylvania, U.S.A.
87 L 24 Altötting, Germany
170 K 7 Altun Shan, China
117 F 14 Alturas, California, U.S.A.
119 I 18 Altus, Oklahoma, U.S.A.
101 S 2 Altynivka, Ukraine
98 I 10 Alūksne, Latvia
101 U 13 Alupka, Ukraine
169 E 19 Alur, India
101 U 12 Alushta, Ukraine
119 J 16 Alva, Oklahoma, U.S.A.
125 T 12 Alvarado, Mexico
142 D 11 Alvarães, Brazil
85 D 17 Alvdal, Norway
85 E 18 Älvdalen, Sweden
85 F 18 Älvdalen, Sweden
85 A 18 Alvik, Norway
119 L 22 Alvin, Texas, U.S.A.
85 H 19 Alvkarleby, Sweden
84 J 12 Älvsbyn, Sweden
168 E 12 Alwar, India
99 F 16 Alytus, Lithuania
118 F 10 Alzada, Montana, U.S.A.
87 E 20 Alzey, Germany
193 Y 9 Am-Dam, Chad
193 Y 10 Am Timan, Chad
193 Z 8 Am-Zoer, Chad
191 D 22 Amadi, Sudan
161 S 1 Amādīyah, Iraq
115 Q 3 Amadjuak Lake, Nunavut, Canada
175 S 12 Amahai, Indonesia
177 A 23 Amakusa-nada, Japan
177 B 23 Amakusa-Shimo-shima, Japan
163 X 10 Amal, Oman
85 E 21 Åmål, Sweden
91 K 16 Amalfi, Italy
97 C 20 Amaliada, Greece
175 X 13 Amamapare, Indonesia
143 H 19 Amambai, Brazil
177 N 21 Amami-Ō-shima, Japan
177 N 23 Amami shotō, Japan
195 P 8 Amamula, Democratic Republic of Congo
212 A 3 Amanab, Papua New Guinea
90 I 12 Amandola, Italy
167 P 5 Amangel'dy, Kazakhstan
91 M 19 Amantea, Italy
215 W 9 Amanu, French Polynesia
197 P 13 Amanzimtoti, Republic of South Africa
142 I 9 Amapá, Brazil
142 I 8 Amapá, Brazil
172 D 11 Amarapura, Myanmar
117 I 19 Amargosa Valley, Nevada, U.S.A.
119 H 17 Amarillo, Texas, U.S.A.
169 H 15 Amarkantak, India
158 H 7 Amasra, Turkey
158 K 8 Amasya, Turkey
142 C 11 Amataurá, Brazil
83 I 20 Amay, Belgium
142 F 11 Amazon, South America
142 C 11 Amazon Basin, Brazil
62 F 13 Amazon Cone, Atlantic Ocean
140 C 11 Amazonas, Peru
142 D 11 Amazonas, Brazil
138 L 11 Amazonas, Colombia
139 O 8 Amazonas, Venezuela
168 E 10 Ambala, India
197 X 9 Ambalavao, Madgascar
197 Z 5 Ambanja, Madgascar
157 W 7 Ambarchik, Russian Federation
140 B 9 Ambato, Ecuador
197 X 6 Ambato Boeny, Madgascar
197 X 7 Ambatomainty, Madgascar
175 R 12 Ambelau, Indonesia
87 K 21 Amberg, Germany
120 J 5 Amberg, Wisconsin, U.S.A.
79 U 9 Ambérieu-en-Bugey, France
211 H 19 Amberley, New Zealand
192 G 8 Ambidédi, Mali
169 H 14 Ambikapur, India
197 Z 5 Ambilobe, Madgascar
141 D 15 Ambo, Peru
197 X 10 Amboasary, Madgascar
197 X 9 Ambohimahasoa, Madgascar
197 W 6 Ambohipaky, Madgascar
175 S 12 Ambon, Indonesia
175 S 12 Ambon, Indonesia
197 X 8 Ambositra, Madgascar
197 X 11 Ambovombe, Madgascar
117 J 22 Amboy, California, U.S.A.
196 F 2 Ambriz, Angola
213 R 10 Ambrym, Vanuatu
156 L 7 Amderma, Russian Federation
170 L 9 Amdo, China
125 N 11 Ameca, Mexico
82 K 5 Ameland, Netherlands
116 L 12 American Falls, Idaho, U.S.A.
215 Z 15 American Samoa, U.S.A.
63 J 22 American–Antarctic Ridge, Atlantic Ocean
123 N 6 Americus, Georgia, U.S.A.
82 J 12 Amersfoort, Netherlands
219 W 6 Amery Ice Shelf, Antarctica
118 L 12 Ames, Iowa, U.S.A.
97 C 18 Amfilochia, Greece
97 E 19 Amfissa, Greece
157 T 11 Amga, Russian Federation
157 U 11 Amga, Russian Federation
157 W 15 Amgu, Russian Federation
157 Z 6 Amguema, Russian Federation
189 O 11 Amguid, Algeria
157 V 13 Amgun, Russian Federation
191 I 19 Amhara, Ethiopia

Country · Internal administrative region: State/Province/Territory/Dependent territory · Capital city · Mountain range/Undersea ridge · Mountain peak/Volcano/Seamount · Geographic feature · Headland/Point/Cape/Peninsula · Desert · Island/Island group · Antarctic base · Ocean · Sea · Bay/Gulf/Channel/Strait · Lake · Salt pan/Dry/Intermittent lake · River

79 Q 2 Amiens, France
169 A 22 Amindivi Islands, India
169 B 22 Amini, India
191 K 23 Amino, Ethiopia
196 J 10 Aminuis, Namibia
58 K 5 Amirante Islands, Indian Ocean
58 K 5 Amirante Trench, Indian Ocean
113 Y 10 Amisk Lake, Saskatchewan, Canada
112 A 8 Amlia Island, Alaska, U.S.A.
160 H 9 Ammān, Jordan
84 H 12 Ammarnäs, Sweden
65 N 13 Ammassalik, Greenland
87 J 25 Ammersee, Germany
158 I 15 Ammóchostos, Cyprus
158 L 17 Amnat Charoen, Thailand
169 C 15 Amod, India
164 J 5 Amol, Iran
81 Q 1 Amorebieta, Spain
97 K 23 Amorgos, Greece
122 J 4 Amory, Mississippi, U.S.A.
115 P 12 Amos, Québec, Canada
85 B 20 Åmot, Norway
192 J 8 Amourj, Mauritania
197 Z 6 Ampanavoana, Madgascar
197 Z 5 Ampanefena, Madgascar
197 W 10 Ampanihy, Madgascar
169 H 25 Amparai, Sri Lanka
197 Z 8 Ampasimanolotra, Madgascar
62 K 9 Ampere Seamount, Atlantic Ocean
175 O 11 Ampoa, Indonesia
81 U 6 Amposta, Spain
163 P 12 Amrān, Yemen
169 E 16 Amravati, India
168 D 9 Amritsar, India
86 E 7 Amrum, Germany
82 H 11 Amstelveen, Netherlands
82 H 11 Amsterdam, Netherlands
59 N 10 Amsterdam Fracture Zone, Indian Ocean
59 O 10 Amsterdam Island, France
89 U 4 Amstetten, Austria
167 O 13 Amudar'ya, Turkmenistan
65 P 8 Amund Ringnes Island, Arctic Ocean
61 S 15 Amundsen Abyssal Plain, Pacific Ocean
219 P 9 Amundsen Coast, Antarctica
113 Q 3 Amundsen Gulf, Northwest Territories, Canada
219 Q 8 Amundsen-Scott, Antarctica
218 I 9 Amundsen Sea, Antarctica
174 L 12 Amuntai, Indonesia
157 U 14 Amur, Russian Federation
175 Q 10 Amurang, Indonesia
81 P 2 Amurrio, Spain
157 V 13 Amursk, Russian Federation
97 B 17 Amvrakikos Kolpos, Greece
101 Y 7 Amvrosiyivka, Ukraine
163 O 5 An Nabhānīyah, Saudi Arabia
160 I 6 An Nabk, Syria
162 L 2 An Nafūd, Saudi Arabia
161 T 9 An Najaf, Iraq
161 W 11 An Nāṣirīyah, Iraq
161 W 10 An Naṣr, Iraq
189 V 8 An Nawfalīyah, Libya
160 J 8 An Nimarah, Syria
163 N 10 An Nimāṣ, Saudi Arabia
163 S 4 An Nu'ayrīyah, Saudi Arabia
161 Q 9 An Nukhayb, Iraq
161 U 8 An Nu'mānīyah, Iraq
161 V 8 An Nu'mānīyah, Iraq
215 U 9 Anaa, French Polynesia
215 V 1 Anabar, Nauru
139 Q 3 Anaco, Venezuela
119 J 17 Anadarko, Oklahoma, U.S.A.
157 Z 7 Anadyr', Russian Federation
97 K 24 Anafi, Greece
143 M 15 Anagé, Brazil
91 I 14 Anagni, Italy
161 P 5 'Ānah, Iraq
117 H 23 Anaheim, California, U.S.A.
125 Q 6 Anáhuac, Mexico
169 D 23 Anai Mudi Peak, India
169 H 18 Anakapalle, India
197 Y 5 Analalava, Madgascar
142 E 11 Anamã, Brazil
193 R 13 Anambra, Nigeria
158 H 14 Anamur, Turkey
158 H 14 Anamur Burnu, Turkey
177 G 20 Anan, Japan
169 C 15 Anand, India
169 J 16 Anandapur, India
169 E 20 Anantapur, India
168 D 8 Anantnag, India
143 J 16 Anápolis, Brazil
164 K 10 Anār, Iran
164 K 8 Anārak, Iran
165 P 8 Anardara, Afghanistan
214 A 7 Anatahan, Northern Mariana Islands
158 D 10 Anatolia, Turkey
96 I 12 Anatoliki Makedonia Kai Thraki, Greece
213 S 13 Anatom, Vanuatu
144 K 8 Añatuya, Argentina
141 C 14 Ancash, Peru
78 L 7 Ancenis, France
193 R 11 Anchau, Nigeria
112 K 7 Anchorage, Alaska, U.S.A.
141 C 16 Ancón, Peru
90 I 11 Ancona, Italy
145 E 17 Ancud, Chile
171 W 3 Anda, China
141 E 17 Andahuaylas, Peru
144 I 8 Andalgalá, Argentina
80 L 12 Andalucía, Spain
122 L 7 Andalusia, Alabama, U.S.A.
169 O 23 Andaman and Nicobar Islands, India
59 R 3 Andaman Basin, Indian Ocean
169 O 21 Andaman Islands, India
173 D 18 Andaman Sea, Asia
209 P 9 Andamooka, South Australia, Australia
197 Z 5 Andapa, Madgascar
88 I 9 Andeer, Switzerland
83 I 21 Andenne, Belgium
193 O 8 Andéramboukane, Mali
83 F 21 Anderlues, Belgium
88 G 9 Andermatt, Switzerland
78 L 12 Andernos-les-Bains, France
113 P 5 Anderson, Northwest Territories, Canada
120 K 11 Anderson, Indiana, U.S.A.
123 P 3 Anderson, South Carolina, U.S.A.
141 G 19 Andes, South America
84 G 8 Andfjorden, Norway
169 F 19 Andhra Pradesh, India
167 T 12 Andijon Wiloyati, Uzbekistan
197 Y 7 Andilamena, Madgascar
197 Y 7 Andilanatoby, Madgascar
164 G 8 Andimeshk, Iran
167 T 12 Andizhan, Uzbekistan
165 R 5 Andkhvoy, Afghanistan
140 D 10 Andoas, Peru
171 Y 7 Andong, South Korea
81 W 2 Andorra, Europe
81 W 2 Andorra La Vella, Andorra
77 K 22 Andover, United Kingdom
84 G 8 Andøya, Norway
197 Z 4 Andranovondronina, Madgascar
197 W 10 Andranovory, Madgascar
81 X 8 Andratx, Spain
112 A 8 Andreanof Islands, Alaska, U.S.A.
58 K 3 Andrew Tablemount, Indian Ocean
119 G 20 Andrews, Texas, U.S.A.
167 X 7 Andreyevka, Kazakhstan
91 M 15 Andria, Italy
197 Y 7 Andriamena, Madgascar
101 X 8 Andriyivka, Ukraine
197 W 10 Androka, Madgascar
97 I 20 Andros, Greece
126 L 3 Andros Island, The Bahamas
126 L 3 Andros Town, The Bahamas
169 C 22 Andrott, India
84 I 8 Andselv, Norway
81 N 11 Andújar, Spain
196 H 4 Andulo, Angola
193 N 7 Anéfis, Mali
127 V 7 Anegada, Virgin Islands (U.K.)
193 N 13 Aného, Togo
81 U 2 Aneto, Spain
193 U 6 Aney, Niger
173 H 18 Ang Thong, Thailand
157 O 11 Angara, Russian Federation
157 P 13 Angarsk, Russian Federation
85 G 16 Ånge, Sweden
139 R 6 Angel Falls, Venezuela
175 O 3 Angeles, Philippines
85 E 24 Ängelholm, Sweden
86 N 12 Angermünde, Germany
78 M 7 Angers, France
85 J 15 Ängesön, Sweden
173 L 21 Ângk Tasaôm, Cambodia
77 H 18 Anglesey, United Kingdom
119 L 22 Angleton, Texas, U.S.A.
195 O 5 Ango, Democratic Republic of Congo
197 U 6 Angoche, Mozambique
164 M 13 Angohrān, Iran
145 F 15 Angol, Chile
196 H 3 Angola, Africa
63 M 16 Angola Basin, Atlantic Ocean
212 C 3 Angoram, Papua New Guinea
79 N 10 Angoulême, France
62 N 1 Angra do Heroismo, Azores
167 S 11 Angren, Uzbekistan
195 N 5 Angu, Democratic Republic of Congo
81 T 3 Angüés, Spain
127 W 7 Anguilla, U.K.
126 K 3 Anguilla Cays, The Bahamas
85 D 24 Anholt, Denmark
171 T 11 Anhua, China
171 U 9 Anhui, China
143 H 16 Anhumas, Brazil
176 J 10 Ani, Japan
112 H 6 Aniak, Alaska, U.S.A.
215 V 1 Anibare, Nauru
215 V 1 Anibare Bay, Nauru
119 C 20 Animas Peak, New Mexico, U.S.A.
197 Z 4 Anivorano Avaratra, Madgascar
213 S 12 Aniwa, Vanuatu
197 W 4 Anjouan, Comoros
171 X 6 Anju, North Korea
161 O 5 Anka, Iraq
171 S 10 Ankang, China
158 H 9 Ankara, Turkey
197 V 9 Ankazoabo, Madgascar
197 Y 7 Ankazobe, Madgascar
86 M 9 Anklam, Germany
169 C 20 Ankola, India
171 R 9 Ankou, China
193 R 13 Ankpa, Nigeria
193 N 13 Anloga, Ghana
120 M 9 Ann Arbor, Michigan, U.S.A.
156 F 9 Anna, Russian Federation
215 U 1 Anna Point, Nauru
189 P 5 Annaba, Algeria
173 M 15 Annam, Vietnam
173 K 14 Annam Highlands, Laos
121 S 12 Annapolis, Maryland, U.S.A.
168 I 11 Annapurna, Nepal
79 V 9 Annecy, France
122 M 4 Anniston, Alabama, U.S.A.
79 T 11 Annonay, France
97 J 26 Ano Viannos, Greece
171 V 10 Anqing, China
83 J 20 Ans, Belgium
87 I 21 Ansbach, Germany
58 A 10 Anse à la Mouche, Seychelles
58 B 10 Anse Royal, Seychelles
171 W 6 Anshan, China
171 Q 12 Anshun, China
144 N 11 Ansina, Uruguay
118 I 13 Ansley, Nebraska, U.S.A.
193 N 8 Ansongo, Mali
175 Y 11 Ansudu, Indonesia
141 F 18 Antabamba, Peru
197 Z 6 Antalaha, Madgascar
158 F 13 Antalya, Turkey
158 F 13 Antalya Körfezi, Turkey
197 Y 7 Antananarivo, Madgascar
197 X 7 Antananarivo, Madgascar
197 W 10 Antanimora Atsimo, Madgascar
218 H 4 Antarctic Peninsula, Antarctica
219 Q 7 Antarctica, 0
81 N 13 Antequera, Spain
119 E 20 Anthony, New Mexico, U.S.A.
188 F 9 Anti Atlas, Morocco
79 X 14 Antibes, France
120 H 5 Antigo, Wisconsin, U.S.A.
127 X 8 Antigua, Antigua and Barbuda
127 Y 7 Antigua and Barbuda, North America
97 F 25 Antikythira, Greece
97 H 23 Antimilos, Greece
158 L 14 Antioch, Turkey
138 H 5 Antioquia, Colombia
97 I 22 Antiparos, Greece
97 A 17 Antipaxoi, Greece
156 M 8 Antipayuta, Russian Federation
61 P 13 Antipodes Islands, Pacific Ocean
144 F 5 Antofagasta, Chile
144 F 5 Antofagasta, Chile
144 H 7 Antofagasta de la Sierra, Argentina
145 I 21 Antonio de Biedma, Argentina
77 F 15 Antrim, United Kingdom
90 H 13 Antrodoco, Italy
197 W 7 Antsalova, Madgascar
197 X 8 Antsirabe, Madgascar
197 Z 5 Antsiranana, Madgascar
197 Z 4 Antsiranana, Madgascar
98 H 9 Antsla, Estonia
197 Y 5 Antsohihy, Madgascar
145 F 14 Antuco, Chile
83 G 17 Antwerp, Belgium
83 G 17 Antwerpen, Belgium
169 I 16 Anugul, India
168 C 11 Anupgarh, India
169 G 24 Anuradhapura, Sri Lanka
213 S 8 Anuta, Solomon Islands
218 H 4 Anvers Island, Antarctica
171 N 6 Anxi, China
209 O 11 Anxious Bay, South Australia, Australia
171 T 8 Anyang, China
97 K 23 Anydro, Greece
171 O 8 A'nyêmaqên Shan, China
99 G 14 Anykščiai, Lithuania
83 D 19 Anzegem, Belgium
194 M 8 Anzi, Democratic Republic of Congo
91 H 15 Anzio, Italy
139 Q 4 Anzoátegui, Venezuela
173 G 23 Ao Ban Don, Thailand
173 F 24 Ao Luk, Thailand
173 G 22 Ao Sawi, Thailand
213 Q 10 Aoba, Vanuatu
177 L 20 Aoga-shima, Japan
212 M 7 Aola, Solomon Islands
176 J 9 Aomori, Japan
90 A 6 Aosta, Italy
188 C 11 Aoufist, Western Sahara
192 G 7 Aoukâr, Mauritania
188 L 11 Aoulef, Algeria
193 W 5 Aozou, Chad
195 S 6 Apac, Uganda
123 O 9 Apalachee Bay, Florida, U.S.A.
123 N 9 Apalachicola, Florida, U.S.A.
175 O 1 Aparri, Philippines
94 I 8 Apatin, Serbia and Montenegro
125 O 12 Apatzingán, Mexico
98 I 9 Ape, Latvia
82 L 12 Apeldoorn, Netherlands
90 D 9 Apennines, Italy
168 G 10 Api, Nepal
195 N 5 Api, Democratic Republic of Congo
215 V 15 Apia, Samoa
141 F 19 Aplao, Peru
142 N 12 Apodi, Brazil
139 V 6 Apoera, Suriname
209 R 14 Apollo Bay, Victoria, Australia
141 I 18 Apolo, Bolivia
120 H 3 Apostle Islands, Wisconsin, U.S.A.
64 M 14 Apostolens Tommefinger, Greenland
144 N 8 Apóstoles, Argentina
101 T 8 Apostolove, Ukraine
121 U 7 Appalachian Mountains, U.S.A.
90 I 13 Appennino Abruzzese, Italy
90 B 9 Appennino Ligure, Italy
91 L 16 Appennino Lucano, Italy
91 K 15 Appennino Napoletano, Italy
90 E 9 Appennino Tosco-Emiliano, Italy
90 H 11 Appennino Umbro-Marchigiano, Italy
88 I 7 Appenzell, Switzerland
82 N 6 Appingedam, Netherlands
120 I 6 Appleton, Wisconsin, U.S.A.
79 U 13 Apt, France
143 I 19 Apucarana, Brazil
139 N 5 Apure, Venezuela
139 N 4 Apure, Venezuela
141 F 18 Apurímac, Peru
141 E 16 Apurímac, Peru
165 S 5 Āqchah, Afghanistan
164 K 8 Āqdā, Iran
170 K 7 Aqqikkol Hu, China
160 G 9 'Aqraba, Israel
161 S 1 'Aqrah, Iraq
167 V 4 Aqtasty, Kazakhstan
143 G 18 Aquidauana, Brazil
78 L 12 Aquitaine, France
161 S 8 Ar Raḥḥālīyah, Iraq
161 S 7 Ar Ramādī, Iraq
160 G 13 Ar Ramlah, Jordan
160 H 8 Ar Ramtha, Jordan
160 L 3 Ar Raqqah, Syria
162 L 8 Ar Rās al Aswad, Saudi Arabia
163 O 5 Ar-Rass, Saudi Arabia
163 O 8 Ar Rawḍah, Saudi Arabia
163 R 13 Ar Rawḍah, Yemen
161 W 10 Ar Rifā'ī, Iraq
161 V 10 Ar Rihab, Iraq
163 P 5 Ar Rubay'iyah, Saudi Arabia
161 V 10 Ar Rumaythah, Iraq
160 L 3 Ar Ruṣāfah, Syria
160 H 9 Ar Ruṣayfah, Jordan
163 Z 6 Ar Rustāq, Oman
161 N 8 Ar Ruṭbah, Iraq
163 P 6 Ar Ruwayḍah, Saudi Arabia
191 J 22 Āra Ārba, Ethiopia
122 L 4 Arab, Alabama, U.S.A.
161 V 8 Arab Abdullah, Iraq
58 M 2 Arabian Basin, Indian Ocean
58 M 1 Arabian Sea, Indian Ocean
158 I 7 Araş, Turkey
143 O 14 Aracaju, Brazil
142 O 11 Aracati, Brazil
143 J 18 Araçatuba, Brazil
160 F 10 'Arad, Israel
100 F 10 Arad, Romania
193 Y 8 Arada, Chad
163 V 7 'Arādah, United Arab Emirates
161 Y 11 Aradah, Iraq
60 K 8 Arafura Sea, Pacific Ocean
60 K 9 Arafura Shelf, Pacific Ocean
159 T 8 Aragats Lerr, Armenia
81 S 5 Aragón, Spain
139 O 3 Aragua, Venezuela
143 J 14 Araguaçu, Brazil
142 J 13 Araguaia, Brazil
142 J 12 Araguaína, Brazil
143 J 17 Araguari, Brazil
177 I 14 Arai, Japan
164 H 7 Arāk, Iran
160 L 5 Arak, Syria
189 N 12 Arak, Algeria
172 B 13 Arakan, Myanmar
172 B 12 Arakan Yoma, Myanmar
166 L 9 Aral Sea, Kazakhstan/Uzbekistan
167 N 7 Aral'sk, Kazakhstan
209 S 6 Aramac, Queensland, Australia
212 B 6 Aramia, Papua New Guinea
77 A 18 Aran Islands, Republic of Ireland
81 O 4 Aranda de Duero, Spain
94 L 11 Aranđelovac, Serbia and Montenegro
81 O 7 Aranjuez, Spain
196 J 10 Aranos, Namibia
214 D 2 Aranuka, Kiribati
173 J 19 Aranyaprathet, Thailand
177 B 22 Arao, Japan
192 L 6 Araouane, Mali
211 J 16 Arapawa Island, New Zealand
142 O 13 Arapiraca, Brazil
159 N 10 Arapkir, Turkey
163 N 1 'Ar'ar, Saudi Arabia
138 K 10 Araracuara, Colombia
143 J 18 Araraquara, Brazil
142 H 12 Araras, Brazil
209 R 13 Ararat, Victoria, Australia
168 K 12 Araria, India
159 S 9 Aras, Azerbaijan/Turkey
159 R 9 Aras, Turkey
159 R 10 Aras Güneyi Dağlari, Turkey
215 U 8 Aratika, French Polynesia
159 N 12 Aratürk Baraji, Turkey
138 K 5 Arauca, Colombia
138 M 5 Arauca, Venezuela
138 L 5 Arauca, Colombia
145 F 15 Araucania, Chile
145 E 14 Arauco, Chile
168 C 13 Aravalli Range, India
143 K 17 Araxá, Brazil
159 W 10 Araz, Azerbaijan
191 H 22 Ārba Minch, Ethiopia
161 V 4 Arbat, Iraq
91 D 18 Arbatax, Italy
89 U 3 Arbesbach, Austria
161 T 2 Arbīl, Iraq
85 G 20 Arboga, Sweden
138 G 4 Arboletes, Colombia
88 I 6 Arbon, Switzerland
76 I 12 Arbroath, United Kingdom
78 L 12 Arcachon, France
123 R 12 Arcadia, Florida, U.S.A.
139 T 8 Arcarai Mountains, Guyana
117 C 14 Arcata, California, U.S.A.
125 Q 13 Arcelia, Mexico
126 I 4 Archipelago de los Canarreos, Cuba
208 I 12 Archipelago of the Recherche, Western Australia, Australia
126 K 4 Archipiélago de Camagüey, Cuba
145 E 23 Archipiélago de la Reina Adelaida, Chile
145 E 20 Archipiélago de los Chonos, Chile
126 K 5 Archipiélago de los Jardines de la Reina, Cuba
126 J 4 Archipiélago de Sabana, Cuba
126 L 13 Archipiélago de San Blas, Panama
61 W 2 Archipiélago Juan Fernández, Juan Fernández Islands
90 F 12 Arcidosso, Italy
116 L 12 Arco, Idaho, U.S.A.
80 L 13 Arcos de la Frontera, Spain
65 Q 8 Arctic Ocean,
218 G 3 Arctowski, Antarctica
159 U 8 Arcvašen, Armenia
160 I 11 Ard aş Şawwān, Jordan
96 J 11 Arda, Bulgaria
164 H 3 Ardabīl, Iran
164 H 3 Ardabīl, Iran
159 S 8 Ardahan, Turkey
164 K 8 Ardakān, Iran
77 E 17 Ardee, Republic of Ireland
83 H 23 Ardennes, Belgium
164 J 7 Ardestān, Iran
119 K 18 Ardmore, Oklahoma, U.S.A.
100 H 7 Ardusat, Romania
85 F 15 Åre, Sweden
195 Q 6 Arebi, Democratic Republic of Congo
127 T 7 Arecibo, Puerto Rico
143 G 15 Arenápolis, Brazil
80 M 7 Arenas de San Pedro, Spain
85 B 21 Arendal, Norway
83 H 16 Arendonk, Belgium
97 E 23 Areopoli, Greece
141 F 20 Arequipa, Peru
141 G 19 Arequipa, Peru
90 G 11 Arezzo, Italy
97 F 17 Argalasti, Greece
170 L 6 Argan, China
81 O 7 Arganda, Spain
79 N 4 Argentan, France
144 J 11 Argentina, South America
144 J 9 Argentina, Argentina
63 F 19 Argentine Abyssal Plain, Atlantic Ocean
63 G 18 Argentine Basin, Atlantic Ocean
165 S 9 Arghandab, Afghanistan

Country · Internal administrative region: State/Province/Territory/Dependent territory · Capital city · Mountain range/Undersea ridge · Mountain peak/Volcano/Seamount · Geographic feature · Headland/Point/Cape/Peninsula · Desert · Island/Island group · Antarctic base · Ocean · Sea · Bay/Gulf/Channel/Strait · Lake · Salt pan/Dry/Intermittent lake · River

97	E 21	**Argolikos Kolpos**, Greece ≈
97	E 21	**Argos**, Greece
97	C 14	**Argos Orestiko**, Greece
97	B 19	**Argostoli**, Greece
171	U 2	**Argun'**, China ∫
193	P 10	**Argungu**, Nigeria
171	P 3	**Arhangay**, Mongolia ▣
85	C 24	**Århus**, Denmark
169	L 18	**Ari Atoll**, Maldives ⛱
175	Q 8	**Ariaga**, Indonesia ⛱
196	J 12	**Ariamsvlei**, Namibia
144	J 12	**Arias**, Argentina
192	M 9	**Aribinda**, Burkina Faso
138	K 11	**Arica**, Colombia
140	D 9	**Arica**, Peru
144	F 2	**Arica**, Chile
177	G 19	**Arida**, Japan
160	I 3	**Arīḩā**, Syria
94	K 13	**Arilje**, Serbia and Montenegro
143	G 14	**Arinos**, Brazil ∫
142	F 12	**Aripuanã**, Brazil ∫
142	E 13	**Ariquemes**, Brazil
139	N 4	**Arismendi**, Venezuela
169	K 18	**Ariyaddu Channel**, Maldives ≈
81	Q 5	**Ariza**, Spain
117	L 22	**Arizona**, U.S.A. ▣
85	E 20	**Årjäng**, Sweden
84	H 12	**Arjeplog**, Sweden
119	M 18	**Arkadelphia**, Arkansas, U.S.A.
167	Q 5	**Arkalyk**, Kazakhstan
119	L 17	**Arkansas**, U.S.A. ▣
119	M 18	**Arkansas**, U.S.A. ∫
119	J 16	**Arkansas City**, Kansas, U.S.A.
156	I 6	**Arkhangel'sk**, Russian Federation
157	P 6	**Arkhipelag Nordenshel'da**, Russian Federation ⛱
97	F 18	**Arkitsa**, Greece
77	F 19	**Arklow**, Republic of Ireland
79	T 14	**Arles**, France
193	N 10	**Arli**, Burkina Faso
119	K 19	**Arlington**, Texas, U.S.A.
121	S 12	**Arlington**, Virginia, U.S.A.
193	Q 6	**Arlit**, Niger
83	K 25	**Arlon**, Belgium
208	G 11	**Armadale**, Western Australia, Australia
77	E 16	**Armagh**, United Kingdom
190	F 11	**Armant**, Egypt
97	M 26	**Armathia**, Greece ⛱
156	D 10	**Armavir**, Russian Federation
159	T 8	**Armenia**, Asia □
138	H 7	**Armenia**, Colombia
209	V 10	**Armidale**, New South Wales, Australia
114	L 10	**Armstrong**, Ontario, Canada
119	J 24	**Armstrong**, Texas, U.S.A.
97	G 14	**Arnaia**, Greece
115	R 5	**Arnaud**, Québec, Canada ∫
83	D 15	**Arnemuiden**, Netherlands
82	K 13	**Arnhem**, Netherlands
209	N 1	**Arnhem Land**, Northern Territory, Australia ◇
96	D 13	**Arnissa**, Greece
215	Z 3	**Arno**, Marshall Islands ⛱
90	E 10	**Arno**, Italy ∫
84	I 6	**Arnøya**, Norway ⛱
87	I 17	**Arnstadt**, Germany
196	K 11	**Aroab**, Namibia
114	M 11	**Aroland**, Ontario, Canada
191	H 16	**Aroma**, Sudan
62	M 12	**Arona**, Canary Islands
90	C 6	**Arona**, Italy
214	F 3	**Arorae**, Kiribati ⛱
88	I 8	**Arosa**, Switzerland
192	D 10	**Arquipélago dos Bijagós**, Guinea-Bissau ⛱
76	G 13	**Arran**, United Kingdom ⛱
79	Q 2	**Arras**, France
79	N 15	**Arreau**, France
62	O 11	**Arrecife**, Canary Islands
144	L 12	**Arrecifes**, Argentina
125	P 10	**Arriaga**, Mexico
125	V 14	**Arriaga**, Mexico
80	M 1	**Arriondas**, Spain
85	C 23	**Års**, Denmark
97	C 17	**Arta**, Greece
81	Z 8	**Artà**, Spain
159	U 9	**Artashat**, Armenia
125	O 13	**Arteaga**, Mexico
126	I 4	**Artemisa**, Cuba
101	X 6	**Artemivs'k**, Ukraine
91	H 14	**Artena**, Italy
87	J 16	**Artern**, Germany
81	V 4	**Artesa de Segre**, Spain
119	F 19	**Artesia**, New Mexico, U.S.A.
211	G 19	**Arthur's Pass**, New Zealand
113	P 5	**Artic Red**, Northwest Territories, Canada ∫
144	N 10	**Artigas**, Uruguay ▣
144	N 10	**Artigas**, Uruguay
159	T 8	**Art'ik**, Armenia
101	O 10	**Artsyz**, Ukraine
159	Q 7	**Artvin**, Turkey
195	R 6	**Aru**, Democratic Republic of Congo
195	R 6	**Arua**, Uganda
143	I 15	**Aruanã**, Brazil
127	R 11	**Aruba**, Netherlands ▣
142	E 11	**Arumã**, Brazil
168	N 11	**Arunachal Pradesh**, India ▣
195	V 10	**Arusha**, Tanzania ▣
195	V 10	**Arusha**, Tanzania
171	P 4	**Arvayheer**, Mongolia
114	L 4	**Arviat**, Nunavut, Canada
84	I 12	**Arvidsjaur**, Sweden
85	E 20	**Arvika**, Sweden
175	R 14	**Arwala**, Indonesia
171	V 3	**Arxan**, China
167	R 11	**Arys'**, Kazakhstan
91	C 15	**Arzachena**, Italy
156	G 9	**Arzamas**, Russian Federation
188	L 6	**Arzew**, Algeria
160	J 3	**As Sa'an**, Syria
160	M 3	**As Sabkhah**, Syria
160	G 11	**Aş Şafi**, Jordan
161	N 1	**Aş Şafiḩ**, Syria
160	J 2	**As Safīrah**, Syria
163	R 6	**As Salamiyah**, Saudi Arabia
161	U 12	**As Salmān**, Iraq
160	G 9	**As Salţ**, Jordan
161	V 10	**As Samāwah**, Iraq
160	H 7	**Aş Şanamayn**, Syria
162	J 3	**Aş Şawrah**, Saudi Arabia
161	O 5	**As Sayyāl**, Syria
189	V 8	**As Sidrah**, Libya
163	R 3	**Aş Şubayhīyah**, Kuwait
163	S 13	**As Sufāl**, Yemen
160	L 4	**As Sukhnah**, Syria
161	U 3	**As Sulaymānīyah**, Iraq
163	Q 9	**As Sulayyil**, Saudi Arabia
189	U 8	**As Sulţān**, Libya
163	O 8	**As Sūq**, Saudi Arabia
161	O 3	**Aş Şuwār**, Syria
160	H 8	**As Suwaydā'**, Syria
161	T 8	**As Suwayrah**, Iraq
164	G 6	**Asadābād**, Iran
165	V 7	**Asadābād**, Afghanistan
165	O 6	**Asadābād**, Iran
159	V 8	**Asaği**, Azerbaijan
176	K 4	**Asahi-dake**, Japan ▲
176	K 4	**Asahikawa**, Japan
164	H 4	**Asālem**, Iran
169	J 14	**Asansol**, India
191	J 19	**Āsayita**, Ethiopia
121	V 11	**Asbury Park**, New Jersey, U.S.A.
63	K 25	**Ascension**, U.K. ▣
124	L 3	**Ascensión**, Mexico
87	F 19	**Aschaffenburg**, Germany
90	I 12	**Ascoli Piceno**, Italy
91	L 15	**Ascoli Satriano**, Italy
191	I 21	**Āsela**, Ethiopia
85	H 14	**Åsele**, Sweden
96	I 10	**Asenovgrad**, Bulgaria
84	B 10	**Ásgarður**, Iceland
117	L 21	**Ash Fork**, Arizona, U.S.A.
161	S 11	**Ash Shabakah**, Iraq
161	O 2	**Ash Shaddādah**, Syria
163	X 5	**Ash Sha'm**, United Arab Emirates
161	V 12	**Ash Shāmīyah**, Iraq ◓
161	U 10	**Ash Shanāfīyah**, Iraq
163	P 6	**Ash Sha'rā'**, Saudi Arabia
163	R 11	**Ash Sharawrah**, Saudi Arabia
161	S 3	**Ash Sharqāţ**, Iraq
161	W 10	**Ash Shaţrah**, Iraq
160	G 11	**Ash Shawbak**, Jordan
163	P 14	**Ash Shaykh 'Uthman**, Yemen
163	T 13	**Ash Shiḩr**, Yemen
163	X 5	**Ash Şhināş**, Oman
163	P 3	**Ash Shu'bah**, Saudi Arabia
163	N 11	**Ash Shuqayq**, Saudi Arabia
189	T 9	**Ash Shuwayrif**, Libya
192	M 13	**Ashanti**, Ghana ▣
163	Q 5	**Asharat**, Saudi Arabia
211	G 21	**Ashburton**, New Zealand
160	E 9	**Ashdod**, Israel
123	Q 2	**Asheville**, North Carolina, U.S.A.
77	N 22	**Ashford**, United Kingdom
166	L 14	**Ashgabat**, Turkmenistan ⌂
176	K 5	**Ashibetsu**, Japan
177	J 15	**Ashikaga**, Japan
176	K 10	**Ashiro**, Japan
177	E 22	**Ashizuri-misaki**, Japan ▶
120	G 4	**Ashland**, Wisconsin, U.S.A.
121	N 13	**Ashland**, Kentucky, U.S.A.
121	Y 3	**Ashland**, Maine, U.S.A.
118	I 9	**Ashley**, North Dakota, U.S.A.
99	H 16	**Ashmyany**, Belarus
176	L 5	**Ashoro**, Japan
160	E 10	**Ashqelon**, Israel
121	O 9	**Ashtabula**, Ohio, U.S.A.
159	T 8	**Ashtarak**, Armenia
116	M 11	**Ashton**, Idaho, U.S.A.
169	F 17	**Asifabad**, India
169	I 17	**Asika**, India
188	I 6	**Asilah**, Morocco
156	M 12	**Asino**, Russian Federation
99	K 18	**Asipovichy**, Belarus
159	P 9	**Aşkale**, Turkey
85	D 20	**Askim**, Norway
85	A 18	**Askøy**, Norway ⛱
164	G 2	**Aşlāndūz**, Iran
191	I 17	**Asmara**, Eritrea ⌂
85	F 24	**Åsnen**, Sweden ◞
193	X 9	**Asnet**, Chad
177	C 22	**Aso-san**, Japan ▲
97	F 23	**Asopos**, Greece
191	G 20	**Āsosa**, Ethiopia
89	X 5	**Aspang-Markt**, Austria
119	E 14	**Aspen**, Colorado, U.S.A.
191	K 18	**Assab**, Eritrea
192	G 7	**Assaba**, Mauritania ▣
168	N 12	**Assam**, India ▣
193	Q 6	**Assamakka**, Niger
121	T 13	**Assateague Island**, Virginia, U.S.A. ⛱
83	F 18	**Asse**, Belgium
82	M 7	**Assen**, Netherlands
83	I 21	**Assesse**, Belgium
114	H 10	**Assiniboine**, Manitoba, Canada ∫
143	I 18	**Assis**, Brazil
143	B 14	**Assis Brasil**, Brazil
90	H 12	**Assisi**, Italy
85	D 18	**Åsta**, Norway ∫
97	M 25	**Astakida**, Greece ⛱
97	C 18	**Astakos**, Greece
167	R 4	**Astana**, Kazakhstan ⌂
164	H 3	**Āstārā**, Iran
83	K 16	**Asten**, Netherlands
90	B 8	**Asti**, Italy
141	H 17	**Astillero**, Peru
80	L 3	**Astorga**, Spain
156	F 11	**Astrakhan'**, Russian Federation
101	V 9	**Astrakhanka**, Ukraine
63	N 23	**Astrid Ridge**, Atlantic Ocean ⛰
212	D 4	**Astrolabe Bay**, Papua New Guinea ≈
97	E 21	**Astros**, Greece
99	F 18	**Astryna**, Belarus
80	L 1	**Asturias**, Spain ▣
97	L 23	**Astypalaia**, Greece ⛱
219	S 2	**Asuka**, Antarctica ⁙
214	A 5	**Asuncion**, Northern Mariana Islands ⛱
143	G 20	**Asunción**, Paraguay ⌂
141	I 16	**Asunción**, Bolivia
98	J 13	**Asvyeya**, Belarus
190	F 12	**Aswân**, Egypt
190	E 10	**Asyût**, Egypt
167	U 11	**At-Bashy**, Kyrgyzstan
160	G 11	**Aţ Ţafīlah**, Jordan
162	M 8	**Aţ Ţā'if**, Saudi Arabia
189	X 7	**At Tamīmī**, Libya
160	L 7	**Aţ Ţanf**, Syria
161	T 9	**Aţ Ţaqţaqānah**, Iraq
160	G 12	**Aţ Ţayyibah**, Jordan
161	N 3	**At Tibnī**, Syria
162	K 2	**Aţ Ţubayq**, Saudi Arabia ◇
163	O 14	**At Turbah**, Yemen
163	P 14	**At Turbah**, Yemen
214	H 11	**Ata**, Tonga ⛱
144	F 8	**Atacama**, Chile ▣
144	F 2	**Atacama Desert**, Chile ◓
214	J 6	**Atafu**, Tokelau Islands ⛱
193	N 12	**Atakpamé**, Togo
141	E 15	**Atalaya**, Peru
163	R 13	**'Ataq**, Yemen
192	G 5	**Atâr**, Mauritania
171	O 5	**Atas Bogd**, Mongolia ▲
167	S 6	**Atasu**, Kazakhstan
175	Q 15	**Atauro**, Indonesia ⛱
191	G 16	**Atbara**, Sudan ∫
191	F 15	**Atbara**, Sudan
167	Q 4	**Atbasar**, Kazakhstan
119	N 22	**Atchafalaya Bay**, Louisiana, U.S.A. ≈
192	M 12	**Atebubu**, Ghana
83	E 20	**Ath**, Belgium
113	U 11	**Athabasca**, Alberta, Canada ∫
97	G 20	**Athens**, Greece ⌂
119	K 19	**Athens**, Texas, U.S.A.
121	N 12	**Athens**, Ohio, U.S.A.
123	P 4	**Athens**, Georgia, U.S.A.
123	O 2	**Athens**, Tennessee, U.S.A.
158	H 15	**Athiénou**, Cyprus
77	D 18	**Athlone**, Republic of Ireland
121	W 8	**Athol**, Massachusetts, U.S.A.
97	H 15	**Athos**, Greece ▲
193	X 9	**Ati**, Chad
141	E 19	**Atico**, Peru
191	C 21	**Atiedo**, Sudan
81	P 5	**Atienza**, Spain
114	K 11	**Atikokan**, Ontario, Canada
215	Z 8	**Atimaono**, French Polynesia
215	P 10	**Atiu**, Cook Islands ⛱
112	A 8	**Atka**, Alaska, U.S.A.
157	X 10	**Atka**, Russian Federation
112	A 8	**Atka Island**, Alaska, U.S.A. ⛱
175	T 11	**Atkri**, Indonesia
116	J 11	**Atlanta**, Idaho, U.S.A.
119	L 19	**Atlanta**, Texas, U.S.A.
120	L 6	**Atlanta**, Michigan, U.S.A.
123	O 4	**Atlanta**, Georgia, U.S.A.
118	K 12	**Atlantic**, Iowa, U.S.A.
123	W 3	**Atlantic**, North Carolina, U.S.A.
121	U 11	**Atlantic City**, New Jersey, U.S.A.
62	G 10	**Atlantic Ocean**, ◎
138	H 2	**Atlantico**, Colombia ▣
63	K 20	**Atlantic–Indian Ridge**, Atlantic Ocean/Indian Ocean ⛰
58	J 14	**Atlantic–Indian–Antarctic Basin**, Southern Ocean ◇
62	F 9	**Atlantis Fracture Zone**, Atlantic Ocean ◇
188	H 9	**Atlas Mountains**, Morocco ⛰
188	L 7	**Atlas Saharien**, Algeria ⛰
113	O 9	**Atlin Lake**, British Columbia, Canada ◞
160	F 8	**'Atlit**, Israel
122	K 7	**Atmore**, Alabama, U.S.A.
141	J 22	**Atocha**, Bolivia
119	K 18	**Atoka**, Oklahoma, U.S.A.
173	N 17	**Atouat**, Laos ▲
164	M 4	**Atrak**, Iran ∫
177	K 16	**Atsugi**, Japan
176	J 12	**Atsumi**, Japan
177	I 18	**Atsumi**, Japan
176	J 5	**Atsuta**, Japan
173	N 18	**Attapu**, Laos
97	O 24	**Attavyros**, Greece ▲
114	M 10	**Attawapiskat**, Ontario, Canada ∫
115	O 9	**Attawapiskat**, Ontario, Canada
114	L 9	**Attawapiskat Lake**, Ontario, Canada ◞
89	R 5	**Attersee**, Austria ◞
83	K 25	**Attert**, Belgium
120	J 11	**Attica**, Indiana, U.S.A.
97	G 22	**Attiki**, Greece ▣
163	S 13	**Atūd**, Yemen
144	H 13	**Atuel**, Argentina ∫
215	X 6	**Atuona**, French Polynesia
166	I 7	**Atyrau**, Kazakhstan ▣
166	I 7	**Atyrau**, Kazakhstan
212	B 2	**Aua Island**, Papua New Guinea ⛱
83	K 26	**Aubange**, Belgium
79	S 12	**Aubenas**, France
79	Q 7	**Aubigny-sur-Nère**, France
79	Q 12	**Aubin**, France
116	E 7	**Auburn**, Washington, U.S.A.
117	E 17	**Auburn**, California, U.S.A.
120	G 11	**Auburn**, Illinois, U.S.A.
121	X 6	**Auburn**, Maine, U.S.A.
121	S 8	**Auburn**, New York, U.S.A.
122	M 6	**Auburn**, Alabama, U.S.A.
79	Q 9	**Aubusson**, France
98	D 12	**Auce**, Latvia
79	N 14	**Auch**, France
210	J 8	**Auckland**, New Zealand ▣
210	K 8	**Auckland**, New Zealand
61	O 13	**Auckland Islands**, New Zealand ⛱
78	H 5	**Audierne**, France
191	J 22	**Audo Range**, Ethiopia ⛰
87	L 18	**Aue**, Germany
87	L 18	**Auerbach**, Germany
209	T 7	**Augathella**, Queensland, Australia
87	I 24	**Augsburg**, Germany
98	H 13	**Augšzemes Augstiene**, Latvia ⛰
91	L 23	**Augusta**, Italy
120	G 6	**Augusta**, Wisconsin, U.S.A.
121	Y 6	**Augusta**, Maine, U.S.A.
123	Q 5	**Augusta**, Georgia, U.S.A.
208	F 12	**Augusta**, Western Australia, Australia
144	G 6	**Augusta Victoria**, Chile
92	N 9	**Augustów**, Poland
113	O 9	**Auke Bay**, Alaska, U.S.A.
212	M 6	**Auki**, Solomon Islands
193	P 11	**Auna**, Nigeria
115	S 6	**Aupaluk**, Québec, Canada
175	R 12	**Auponhia**, Indonesia
215	Z 3	**Aur**, Marshall Islands ⛱
174	F 9	**Aur**, Malaysia ⛱
168	F 12	**Auraiya**, India
169	D 16	**Aurangabad**, India
78	J 6	**Auray**, France
86	D 10	**Aurich**, Germany
79	Q 11	**Aurillac**, France
85	B 18	**Aurlandsvangen**, Norway
120	I 9	**Auroa**, Illinois, U.S.A.
119	F 14	**Aurora**, Colorado, U.S.A.
142	K 10	**Aurora do Pará**, Brazil
209	R 2	**Aurukun**, Queensland, Australia
196	I 11	**Aus**, Namibia
117	H 16	**Austin**, Nevada, U.S.A.
118	L 11	**Austin**, Minnesota, U.S.A.
119	J 21	**Austin**, Texas, U.S.A.
61	T 10	**Austral Fracture Zone**, Pacific Ocean ◇
61	S 10	**Austral Islands**, Pacific Ocean ⛱
215	R 12	**Austral Islands**, French Polynesia ⛱
209	N 6	**Australia**, Oceania □
209	U 12	**Australian Capital Territory**, Australia ▣
89	P 7	**Austria**, Europe □
84	G 9	**Austvågøy**, Norway ⛱
142	F 11	**Autazes**, Brazil
125	N 11	**Autlán**, Mexico
79	S 8	**Autun**, France
79	Q 10	**Auvergne**, France ▣
79	R 6	**Auxerre**, France
139	R 6	**Auyan Tepuí**, Venezuela ▲
79	S 7	**Avallon**, France
115	Z 10	**Avalon Peninsula**, Newfoundland and Labrador, Canada ▶
215	N 11	**Avarua**, Cook Islands ⌂
80	H 5	**Aveiro**, Portugal ▣
80	H 6	**Aveiro**, Portugal
142	H 11	**Aveiro**, Brazil
91	K 16	**Avellino**, Italy
91	J 16	**Aversa**, Italy
116	J 7	**Avery**, Idaho, U.S.A.
62	E 12	**Aves Ridge**, Atlantic Ocean ⛰
79	S 2	**Avesnes-sur-Helpe**, France
85	G 19	**Avesta**, Sweden
144	L 7	**Aviá Terai**, Argentina
76	H 10	**Aviemore**, United Kingdom
79	T 13	**Avignon**, France
81	N 6	**Ávila**, Spain
80	L 1	**Avilés**, Spain
98	I 6	**Avinurme**, Estonia
97	G 19	**Avlida**, Greece
91	K 23	**Avola**, Italy
77	J 20	**Avon**, United Kingdom ∫
123	R 12	**Avon Park**, Florida, U.S.A.
117	M 23	**Avondale**, Arizona, U.S.A.
78	L 4	**Avranches**, France
100	I 11	**Avrig**, Romania
191	L 24	**Aw Dheegle**, Somalia
176	J 12	**Awa-shima**, Japan ⛱
177	G 19	**Awaji-shima**, Japan ⛱
210	K 11	**Awakino**, New Zealand
163	T 5	**Awālī**, Bahrain
210	I 5	**Awanui**, New Zealand
191	L 21	**Āwarē**, Ethiopia
210	J 6	**Awarua**, New Zealand
211	B 21	**Awarua Point**, New Zealand ▶
191	I 21	**Āwasa**, Ethiopia
191	J 19	**Āwash**, Ethiopia ∫
191	J 20	**Āwash**, Ethiopia
211	I 17	**Awatere**, New Zealand ∫
189	S 11	**Awbārī**, Libya
191	C 20	**Aweil**, Sudan
122	L 7	**Awin**, Alabama, U.S.A.
189	X 9	**Awjilah**, Libya
188	C 13	**Awserd**, Western Sahara
65	P 8	**Axel Heiberg Island**, Arctic Ocean ⛱
192	L 14	**Axim**, Ghana
96	E 13	**Axios**, Greece ∫
141	E 18	**Ayacucho**, Peru ▣
141	E 17	**Ayacucho**, Peru
145	M 14	**Ayacucho**, Argentina
167	X 6	**Ayagoz**, Kazakhstan
170	L 7	**Ayakkum Hu**, China ◞
80	I 12	**Ayamonte**, Spain
157	V 12	**Ayan**, Russian Federation
158	J 7	**Ayancik**, Turkey
139	T 6	**Ayanganna Mountain**, Guyana ▲
193	R 12	**Ayangba**, Nigeria
141	G 18	**Ayaviri**, Peru
165	T 6	**Āybak**, Afghanistan
101	Y 5	**Aydar**, Ukraine ∫
158	C 11	**Aydin**, Turkey
158	B 11	**Aydin Dağlari**, Turkey
191	J 19	**Āyelu Terara**, Ethiopia ▲
81	S 3	**Ayerbe**, Spain
157	R 10	**Aykhal**, Russian Federation
211	H 20	**Aylesbury**, New Zealand
81	P 5	**Ayllón**, Spain
113	U 5	**Aylmer Lake**, Northwest Territories, Canada ◞
167	R 13	**Ayní**, Tajikistan
191	E 21	**Ayod**, Sudan
81	S 9	**Ayora**, Spain
193	N 8	**Ayorou**, Niger
192	H 7	**'Ayoûn el 'Atroûs**, Mauritania
77	G 14	**Ayr**, United Kingdom
209	U 5	**Ayr**, Queensland, Australia
158	I 12	**Ayranci**, Turkey
167	N 8	**Ayteke Bi**, Kazakhstan
96	M 9	**Aytos**, Bulgaria
163	W 11	**Ayun**, Oman
173	H 18	**Ayutthaya**, Thailand
158	A 9	**Ayvacik**, Turkey
158	B 9	**Ayvalik**, Turkey
160	H 6	**Az Zabadānī**, Syria
160	H 9	**Az Zarqā'**, Jordan
189	S 7	**Az Zāwīyah**, Libya
163	O 13	**Az Zaydīyah**, Yemen
163	P 5	**Az Zilfī**, Saudi Arabia
189	R 8	**Az Zintān**, Libya
161	Z 12	**Az Zubayr**, Iraq
163	O 12	**Az Zuhrah**, Yemen
163	O 14	**Az Zuqur**, Yemen ⛱
164	F 4	**Āzarbāyjān-e Gharbī**, Iran ▣
164	G 3	**Āzarbāyjān-e Sharqī**, Iran ▣
193	S 10	**Azare**, Nigeria
99	L 20	**Azarychy**, Belarus
160	J 1	**A'zāz**, Syria
188	G 7	**Azemmour**, Morocco
159	V 10	**Azerbaijan**, Asia □
191	H 18	**Āzezo**, Ethiopia
188	H 8	**Azilal**, Morocco
165	N 11	**'Azīzābād**, Iran
62	O 1	**Azores**, Portugal ▣
62	J 8	**Azores–Biscay Rise**, Atlantic Ocean ⛰
160	I 9	**Azraq ash Shīshān**, Jordan
188	I 7	**Azrou**, Morocco
117	K 24	**Aztec**, Arizona, U.S.A.
127	Q 7	**Azua**, Dominican Republic
80	L 10	**Azuaga**, Spain
140	B 10	**Azuay**, Ecuador ▣
145	L 14	**Azul**, Argentina
192	E 5	**Azzeffâl**, Mauritania ⛰

B

173	N 19	**Bâ Kêv**, Cambodia
175	P 15	**Baa**, Indonesia
160	H 5	**Ba'albek**, Lebanon
160	G 6	**Baaqline**, Lebanon
191	L 24	**Baardheere**, Somalia
191	K 17	**Bāb al Mandab**, Africa/Asia ≈
158	G 7	**Baba Burnu**, Turkey ▶
158	A 9	**Baba Burun**, Turkey ▶
101	N 12	**Babadag**, Romania
159	X 7	**Babadağ Dağl**, Azerbaijan ▲
166	L 14	**Babadurmaz**, Turkmenistan
158	B 7	**Babaeski**, Turkey
191	C 19	**Babanusa**, Sudan

□ Country ▣ Internal administrative region: State/Province/Territory/Dependent territory ⌂ Capital city ⛰ Mountain range/Undersea ridge ▲ Mountain peak/Volcano/Seamount ◇ Geographic feature ▶ Headland/Point/Cape/Peninsula ◓ Desert ⛱ Island/Island group ⁙ Antarctic base ◎ Ocean ◒ Sea ≈ Bay/Gulf/Channel/Strait ◞ Lake ⌗ Salt pan/Dry/Intermittent lake ∫ River

175 T 14 **Babar**, Indonesia
195 U 10 **Babati**, Tanzania
118 B 6 **Babb**, Montana, U.S.A.
113 Q 11 **Babine Lake**, British Columbia, Canada
175 U 12 **Babo**, Indonesia
164 J 5 **Bābol**, Iran
193 V 13 **Babongo**, Cameroon
117 N 25 **Baboquivari Peak**, Arizona, U.S.A.
194 G 4 **Baboua**, Central African Republic
99 L 19 **Babruysk**, Belarus
175 P 1 **Babuyan**, Philippines
175 O 1 **Babuyan Channel**, Philippines
175 P 1 **Babuyan Islands**, Philippines
172 M 11 **Băc Can**, Vietnam
172 M 12 **Băc Giang**, Vietnam
172 L 10 **Bac Lac**, Vietnam
173 M 23 **Bac Liêu**, Vietnam
172 M 12 **Băc Ninh**, Vietnam
172 L 11 **Băc Quang**, Vietnam
191 N 21 **Bacaadweyn**, Somalia
142 L 11 **Bacabal**, Brazil
142 I 11 **Bacajá**, Brazil
125 Z 12 **Bacalar**, Mexico
175 R 11 **Bacan**, Indonesia
100 L 9 **Bacău**, Romania
79 V 5 **Baccarat**, France
88 K 7 **Bach**, Austria
87 D 19 **Bacharach**, Germany
114 K 1 **Back**, Nunavut, Canada
94 J 9 **Bačka Palanka**, Serbia and Montenegro
94 J 8 **Bačka Topola**, Serbia and Montenegro
87 G 22 **Backnang**, Germany
175 P 5 **Bacolod**, Philippines
124 J 6 **Bácum**, Mexico
89 S 6 **Bad Aussee**, Austria
87 D 22 **Bad Bergzabern**, Germany
86 H 9 **Bad Bramstedt**, Germany
86 N 12 **Bad Freienwalde**, Germany
89 R 6 **Bad Goisern**, Austria
89 Q 7 **Bad Hofgastein**, Austria
87 E 14 **Bad Iburg**, Germany
89 R 5 **Bad Ischl**, Austria
89 S 8 **Bad Kleinkirchheim**, Austria
87 D 20 **Bad Kreuznach**, Germany
87 I 17 **Bad Langensalza**, Germany
89 T 3 **Bad Leonfelden**, Austria
87 H 21 **Bad Mergentheim**, Germany
87 H 19 **Bad Neustadt an der Saale**, Germany
86 H 10 **Bad Oldesloe**, Germany
89 X 8 **Bad Radkersburg**, Austria
87 L 25 **Bad Reichenhall**, Germany
87 H 17 **Bad Salzungen**, Germany
86 H 9 **Bad Segeberg**, Germany
89 U 7 **Bad St Leonhard**, Austria
87 J 25 **Bad Tölz**, Germany
87 G 25 **Bad Waldsee**, Germany
173 F 22 **Bada**, Myanmar
169 D 22 **Badagara**, India
171 O 7 **Badain Jaran Desert**, China
80 J 9 **Badajoz**, Spain
165 V 5 **Badakhshān**, Afghanistan
163 N 1 **Badanah**, Saudi Arabia
168 F 9 **Badarinath Peaks**, India
165 R 12 **Baddo**, Pakistan
89 X 4 **Baden**, Austria
87 E 22 **Baden Baden**, Germany
87 E 23 **Baden-wurttemberg**, Germany
89 Q 7 **Badgastein**, Austria
165 Q 7 **Bādghīs**, Afghanistan
82 H 11 **Badhoevedorp**, Netherlands
81 Z 7 **Badia d'Alcúdia**, Spain
81 X 8 **Badia de Palma**, Spain
165 U 15 **Badin**, Pakistan
118 F 9 **Badlands**, U.S.A.
193 N 12 **Badou**, Togo
162 L 6 **Badr Ḥunayn**, Saudi Arabia
161 W 7 **Badrah**, Iraq
209 R 1 **Badu Island**, Queensland, Australia
169 G 25 **Badulla**, Sri Lanka
81 N 12 **Baena**, Spain
81 O 11 **Baeza**, Spain
192 E 10 **Bafatá**, Guinea-Bissau
65 O 9 **Baffin Basin**, Arctic Ocean
65 N 10 **Baffin Bay**, Arctic Ocean
64 K 11 **Baffin Island**, Nunavut, Canada
193 T 14 **Bafia**, Cameroon
192 H 9 **Bafoulabé**, Mali
193 T 14 **Bafoussam**, Cameroon
164 L 9 **Bāfq**, Iran
158 K 7 **Bafra**, Turkey
158 L 7 **Bafra Burnu**, Turkey
195 P 7 **Bafwasende**, Democratic Republic of Congo
168 I 12 **Bagaha**, India
169 D 19 **Bagalkot**, India
195 W 11 **Bagamoyo**, Tanzania
196 K 7 **Bagani**, Namibia
174 D 9 **Bagansiapiapi**, Indonesia
193 P 9 **Bagaroua**, Niger
194 J 10 **Bagata**, Democratic Republic of Congo
117 L 22 **Bagdad**, Arizona, U.S.A.
143 H 22 **Bagé**, Brazil
168 G 10 **Bageshwar**, India
118 D 13 **Baggs**, Wyoming, U.S.A.
165 O 6 **Baghbaghū**, Iran
161 T 7 **Baghdad**, Iraq
91 I 21 **Bagheria**, Italy
164 L 10 **Bāghīn**, Iran
165 T 6 **Baghlān**, Afghanistan
165 U 6 **Baghlān**, Afghanistan
165 R 8 **Baghrān**, Afghanistan
175 P 5 **Bago**, Philippines
90 E 6 **Bagolino**, Italy
99 B 16 **Bagrationovsk**, Russian Federation
142 J 10 **Bagre**, Brazil
161 W 8 **Bagsaya**, Iraq
140 B 12 **Bagua**, Peru
193 P 10 **Bagudo**, Nigeria
175 O 3 **Baguio**, Philippines
126 L 2 **Bahamas, The**, North America
169 K 14 **Baharampur**, India
190 D 9 **Bahariya Oasis**, Egypt
101 W 7 **Bahatyr**, Ukraine
165 W 11 **Bahawalpur**, Pakistan
158 L 13 **Bahçe**, Turkey
143 M 14 **Bahia**, Brazil
145 K 16 **Bahía Anegada**, Argentina
124 G 6 **Bahía Asunción**, Mexico
145 K 15 **Bahía Blanca**, Argentina
145 J 15 **Bahía Blanca**, Argentina
145 I 19 **Bahía Bustamante**, Argentina
145 I 19 **Bahía Camarones**, Argentina
125 Z 12 **Bahía Chetumal**, Mexico
140 B 7 **Bahía de Ancón de Sardinas**, Ecuador
124 G 6 **Bahía de Ballenas**, Mexico
124 M 11 **Bahía de Banderas**, Mexico
125 V 11 **Bahía de Campeche**, Mexico
140 A 9 **Bahía de Caráquez**, Ecuador
145 G 26 **Bahía de Cook**, Chile
126 H 13 **Bahía de Coronado**, Costa Rica
125 Z 11 **Bahía de Espíritu Santo**, Mexico
125 Z 11 **Bahía de la Ascension**, Mexico
124 I 8 **Bahía de La Paz**, Mexico
124 G 4 **Bahía de los Ángeles**, Mexico
140 A 9 **Bahía de Mania**, Ecuador
125 P 13 **Bahía de Petacalco**, Mexico
127 R 7 **Bahía de Samaná**, Dominican Republic
126 H 12 **Bahía de San Juan del Norte**, Nicaragua
145 H 24 **Bahía de San Sebastián**, Argentina
140 A 9 **Bahía de Santa Elena**, Ecuador
124 K 7 **Bahía de Santa María**, Mexico
140 A 12 **Bahía de Sechura**, Peru
127 R 6 **Bahía Escocesa**, Dominican Republic
145 H 23 **Bahía Grande**, Argentina
124 I 4 **Bahía Kino**, Mexico
145 I 21 **Bahía Laura**, Argentina
124 H 8 **Bahía Magdalena**, Mexico
138 G 7 **Bahía Magdalena**, Colombia
145 I 26 **Bahía Nassau**, Chile
143 G 18 **Bahía Negra**, Paraguay
145 F 25 **Bahía Otway**, Chile
144 F 8 **Bahía Salada**, Chile
145 E 23 **Bahía Salvación**, Chile
144 N 13 **Bahía Samborombón**, Argentina
141 E 18 **Bahía San Nicolás**, Peru
124 G 5 **Bahia Sebastian Vizcaino**, Mexico
145 I 19 **Bahía Solano**, Argentina
124 F 5 **Bahía Tortugas**, Mexico
145 K 16 **Bahía Unión**, Argentina
191 H 19 **Bahir Dar**, Ethiopia
191 A 19 **Bahr el Arab**, Sudan
191 D 20 **Bahr el Ghazal**, Sudan
191 E 23 **Bahr el Jebel**, Sudan
168 H 12 **Bahraich**, India
163 U 4 **Bahrain**, Asia
165 P 14 **Bāhū Kālāt**, Iran
99 M 15 **Bahushewsk**, Belarus
172 L 13 **Bai Thurong**, Vietnam
101 N 12 **Baia**, Romania
142 J 10 **Baía de Marajó**, Brazil
197 U 5 **Baía de Memba**, Mozambique
197 U 4 **Baía de Pemba**, Mozambique
142 L 10 **Baía de São Marcos**, Brazil
196 F 6 **Baía dos Tigres**, Angola
196 F 4 **Baía Farta**, Angola
100 I 8 **Baia Mare**, Romania
142 J 10 **Baião**, Brazil
164 L 8 **Baiazeh**, Iran
193 W 12 **Baïbokoum**, Chad
171 W 4 **Baicheng**, China
100 K 12 **Băicoi**, Romania
115 T 11 **Baie-Comeau**, Québec, Canada
78 H 6 **Baie de Audierne**, France
78 K 7 **Baie de Bourgneuf**, France
78 H 5 **Baie de Douarnenez**, France
78 M 3 **Baie de Seine**, France
78 J 4 **Baie de St-Brieuc**, France
115 S 12 **Baie-St-Paul**, Québec, Canada
115 X 9 **Baie Verte**, Newfoundland and Labrador, Canada
171 Y 5 **Baihe**, China
100 K 10 **Băile Tuşnad**, Romania
81 O 11 **Bailén**, Spain
142 J 9 **Bailique**, Brazil
83 J 22 **Baillonville**, Belgium
196 H 4 **Bailundo**, Angola
212 C 5 **Baimuru**, Papua New Guinea
123 N 8 **Bainbridge**, Georgia, U.S.A.
175 O 15 **Baing**, Indonesia
160 I 11 **Bā'ir**, Jordan
170 I 8 **Bairab Co**, China
214 D 2 **Bairiki**, Kiribati
171 V 5 **Bairin Zuoqi**, China
167 Q 11 **Bairkum**, Kazakhstan
209 T 13 **Bairnsdale**, Victoria, Australia
171 X 5 **Baishan**, China
215 U 1 **Baiti**, Nauru
196 J 6 **Baixo-Longa**, Angola
191 F 15 **Baiyuda Desert**, Sudan
93 I 25 **Baja**, Hungary
124 F 2 **Baja California**, Mexico
124 F 4 **Baja California Norte**, Mexico
124 G 7 **Baja California Sur**, Mexico
174 G 9 **Bajau**, Indonesia
165 N 7 **Bajestān**, Iran
165 O 5 **Bājgīrān**, Iran
163 O 13 **Bājil**, Yemen
145 G 21 **Bajo Caracoles**, Argentina
193 T 11 **Bajoga**, Nigeria
167 V 8 **Bakanas**, Kazakhstan
193 Z 8 **Bakaoré**, Chad
192 G 8 **Bakel**, Senegal
118 F 9 **Baker**, Montana, U.S.A.
61 P 7 **Baker Island**, U.S.A.
114 K 3 **Baker Lake**, Nunavut, Canada
117 G 21 **Bakersfield**, California, U.S.A.
166 L 13 **Bakhardok**, Turkmenistan
101 T 12 **Bakhchysaray**, Ukraine
166 K 13 **Bakherden**, Turkmenistan
101 S 2 **Bakhmach**, Ukraine
157 N 10 **Bakhta**, Russian Federation
167 Y 7 **Bakhty**, Kazakhstan
158 D 7 **Bakirköy**, Turkey
96 O 13 **Bakiröy**, Turkey
84 D 10 **Bakkaflói**, Iceland
191 H 20 **Bako**, Ethiopia
192 I 11 **Bako**, Côte d'Ivoire
93 G 24 **Bakony**, Hungary
191 L 23 **Bakool**, Somalia
212 H 4 **Bakop**, Papua New Guinea
194 M 4 **Bakouma**, Central African Republic
159 Z 8 **Baku**, Azerbaijan
159 S 7 **Bakuriani**, Georgia
218 K 10 **Bakutis Coast**, Antarctica
158 H 10 **Balâ**, Turkey
165 Q 6 **Bālā Morghāb**, Afghanistan
174 M 7 **Balabac**, Philippines
101 U 7 **Balabyne**, Ukraine
161 T 6 **Balad**, Iraq
161 U 6 **Balad Rūz**, Iraq
169 G 15 **Balaghat**, India
169 D 17 **Balaghat Range**, India
81 V 4 **Balaguer**, Spain
159 V 6 **Balakän**, Azerbaijan
101 T 13 **Balaklava**, Ukraine
101 W 5 **Balakliya**, Ukraine
156 G 10 **Balakovo**, Russian Federation
174 M 7 **Balambangan**, Malaysia
175 O 3 **Balanga**, Philippines
169 H 16 **Balangir**, India
156 F 9 **Balashov**, Russian Federation
93 J 21 **Balassagyarmat**, Hungary
93 G 24 **Balaton**, Hungary
142 F 10 **Balbina**, Brazil
77 F 17 **Balbriggan**, Republic of Ireland
145 M 14 **Balcarce**, Argentina
96 N 7 **Balchik**, Bulgaria
211 E 25 **Balclutha**, New Zealand
119 H 22 **Balcones Escarpment**, Texas, U.S.A.
120 K 7 **Baldwin**, Michigan, U.S.A.
120 F 5 **Baldwin**, Wisconsin, U.S.A.
123 Q 9 **Baldwin**, Florida, U.S.A.
114 H 9 **Baldy Mountain**, Manitoba, Canada
118 D 7 **Baldy Mountain**, Montana, U.S.A.
117 O 22 **Baldy Peak**, Arizona, U.S.A.
192 H 10 **Baléa**, Mali
81 V 9 **Balearic Islands**, Spain
175 O 3 **Baler**, Philippines
175 P 3 **Baler Bay**, Philippines
169 K 16 **Baleshwar**, India
170 K 5 **Balguntay**, China
163 S 14 **Balḥaf**, Yemen
174 L 14 **Bali**, Indonesia
174 L 15 **Bali**, Indonesia
168 C 13 **Bali**, India
174 K 14 **Bali Sea**, Indonesia
174 D 9 **Balige**, Indonesia
158 C 9 **Balikesir**, Turkey
160 L 2 **Balīkh**, Syria
174 M 11 **Balikpapan**, Indonesia
175 N 8 **Balimbing**, Philippines
87 F 24 **Balingen**, Germany
175 O 1 **Balintang Channel**, Philippines
194 M 5 **Balitondo**, Central African Republic
163 N 9 **Baljurshī**, Saudi Arabia
82 J 8 **Balk**, Netherlands
96 F 8 **Balkan Mountains**, Bulgaria
166 J 12 **Balkanskiy Velayat**, Turkmenistan
167 Q 3 **Balkashino**, Kazakhstan
165 T 5 **Balkh**, Afghanistan
167 U 7 **Balkhash**, Kazakhstan
76 G 11 **Ballachulish**, United Kingdom
208 J 11 **Balladonia**, Western Australia, Australia
77 C 17 **Ballaghaderreen**, Republic of Ireland
169 F 17 **Ballalpur**, India
77 G 14 **Ballantrae**, United Kingdom
209 R 13 **Ballarat**, Victoria, Australia
219 S 15 **Balleny Islands**, Antarctica
77 B 16 **Ballina**, Republic of Ireland
209 W 9 **Ballina**, New South Wales, Australia
77 C 18 **Ballinasloe**, Republic of Ireland
119 I 20 **Ballinger**, Texas, U.S.A.
77 F 15 **Ballymena**, United Kingdom
77 C 16 **Ballysadare**, Republic of Ireland
145 G 20 **Balmaceda**, Chile
119 G 21 **Balmorhea**, Texas, U.S.A.
196 G 4 **Balombo**, Angola
168 B 13 **Balotra**, India
167 W 8 **Balpyk Bi**, Kazakhstan
209 R 11 **Balranald**, New South Wales, Australia
100 I 13 **Balş**, Romania
125 R 13 **Balsas**, Mexico
140 C 13 **Balsas**, Peru
142 K 12 **Balsas**, Brazil
88 E 7 **Balsthal**, Switzerland
101 O 7 **Balta**, Ukraine
94 O 13 **Balta Berilovac**, Serbia and Montenegro
100 M 8 **Bălţi**, Moldova
85 G 26 **Baltic Sea**, Europe
121 S 12 **Baltimore**, Maryland, U.S.A.
99 A 15 **Baltiysk**, Russian Federation
165 R 12 **Baluchistān**, Pakistan
168 K 13 **Balurghat**, India
98 I 10 **Balvi**, Latvia
167 V 10 **Balykchy**, Kyrgyzstan
166 I 7 **Balykshi**, Kazakhstan
165 N 11 **Bam**, Iran
193 U 10 **Bama**, Nigeria
209 R 1 **Bamaga**, Queensland, Australia
192 J 10 **Bamako**, Mali
192 M 7 **Bamba**, Mali
194 G 9 **Bambama**, Congo
196 K 6 **Bambangando**, Angola
194 K 4 **Bambari**, Central African Republic
87 I 20 **Bamberg**, Germany
123 R 5 **Bamberg**, South Carolina, U.S.A.
195 O 5 **Bambili**, Democratic Republic of Congo
194 I 5 **Bambio**, Central African Republic
191 G 19 **Bambudi**, Ethiopia
143 K 17 **Bambuí**, Brazil
171 N 10 **Bamda**, China
193 S 13 **Bamenda**, Cameroon
113 R 15 **Bamfield**, British Columbia, Canada
166 K 13 **Bami**, Turkmenistan
165 T 7 **Bāmīān**, Afghanistan
165 T 7 **Bāmīān**, Afghanistan
194 K 3 **Bamingui**, Central African Republic
194 K 2 **Bamingui-Bangoran**, Central African Republic
173 K 20 **Bâmnak**, Cambodia
165 O 13 **Bampūr**, Iran
172 K 13 **Ban Ban**, Laos
172 I 12 **Ban Boun Tai**, Laos
173 I 17 **Ban Bua Chum**, Thailand
173 J 21 **Ban Hat Lek**, Thailand
172 H 13 **Ban Houayxay**, Laos
173 G 21 **Ban Huai Yang**, Thailand
173 H 17 **Ban Khao Sai**, Thailand
173 E 24 **Ban Khok Kloi**, Thailand
173 G 24 **Ban Na San**, Thailand
173 I 14 **Ban Nalè**, Laos
173 L 15 **Ban Napè**, Laos
173 H 15 **Ban Pak Pat**, Thailand
173 K 15 **Ban Phaeng**, Laos
173 J 17 **Ban Phai**, Thailand
173 M 17 **Ban Phon**, Laos
173 J 15 **Ban Phu**, Thailand
173 G 19 **Ban Pong**, Thailand
173 G 18 **Ban Rai**, Thailand
173 F 15 **Ban Tha Song Yang**, Thailand
173 J 15 **Ban Thabôk**, Laos
173 M 17 **Ban Tôp**, Laos
173 K 14 **Ban Vang-An**, Laos
173 M 18 **Ban Xepian**, Laos
191 M 24 **Banaadir**, Somalia
214 C 3 **Banaba**, Kiribati
195 N 7 **Banalia**, Democratic Republic of Congo
192 I 9 **Banamba**, Mali
215 P 2 **Banana**, Kiribati
169 O 25 **Bananga**, India
96 M 13 **Banarli**, Turkey
168 D 13 **Banas**, India
158 E 10 **Banaz**, Turkey
170 M 10 **Banbar**, China
77 F 16 **Banbridge**, United Kingdom
77 K 20 **Banbury**, United Kingdom
125 Z 12 **Banco Chinchorro**, Mexico
126 I 9 **Banco Gorda**, Honduras
115 P 14 **Bancroft**, Ontario, Canada
168 G 13 **Banda**, India
193 U 12 **Banda**, Cameroon
195 P 5 **Banda**, Democratic Republic of Congo
174 B 8 **Banda Aceh**, Indonesia
175 S 13 **Banda Sea**, Indonesia
175 T 13 **Bandaneira**, Indonesia
164 L 12 **Bandar-e 'Abbās**, Iran
164 H 4 **Bandar-e Anzalī**, Iran
164 G 9 **Bandar-e Emām Khomeynī**, Iran
164 K 13 **Bandar-e Lengeh**, Iran
164 J 13 **Bandar-e Moghūyeh**, Iran
174 G 13 **Bandar Lampung**, Indonesia
174 L 8 **Bandar Seri Begawan**, Brunei
80 I 3 **Bande**, Spain
144 K 9 **Bandera**, Argentina
192 L 9 **Bandiagara**, Mali
168 D 7 **Bandipur**, India
158 C 8 **Bandirma**, Turkey
194 J 10 **Bandundu**, Democratic Republic of Congo
194 I 10 **Bandundu**, Democratic Republic of Congo
174 H 14 **Bandung**, Indonesia
100 M 13 **Băneasa**, Romania
127 N 5 **Banes**, Cuba
76 I 9 **Banff**, United Kingdom
192 K 11 **Banfora**, Burkina Faso
175 Q 7 **Banga**, Philippines
194 K 11 **Banga**, Democratic Republic of Congo
169 D 21 **Bangalore**, India
194 M 5 **Bangassou**, Central African Republic
175 P 11 **Banggai**, Indonesia
174 M 7 **Banggi**, Malaysia
189 W 7 **Banghāzī**, Libya
174 G 11 **Bangka**, Indonesia
175 Q 10 **Bangka**, Indonesia
174 K 14 **Bangkalan**, Indonesia
174 D 10 **Bangkinang**, Indonesia
174 F 11 **Bangko**, Indonesia
173 I 19 **Bangkok**, Thailand
168 K 13 **Bangladesh**, Asia
77 H 18 **Bangor**, United Kingdom
121 Y 5 **Bangor**, Maine, U.S.A.
175 O 2 **Bangued**, Philippines
194 J 5 **Bangui**, Central African Republic
175 O 1 **Bangui**, Philippines
194 I 6 **Bangui-Motaba**, Congo
195 P 7 **Banguru**, Democratic Republic of Congo
194 M 3 **Bani**, Central African Republic
163 O 10 **Banī Thawr**, Saudi Arabia
189 S 8 **Banī Walīd**, Libya
194 H 5 **Bania**, Central African Republic
212 G 7 **Baniara**, Papua New Guinea
193 O 10 **Banikoara**, Benin
160 H 4 **Bāniyās**, Syria
94 G 10 **Banja Luka**, Bosnia and Herzegovina
174 L 12 **Banjarmasin**, Indonesia
192 D 9 **Banjul**, Gambia
193 N 9 **Bankilaré**, Niger
193 T 13 **Bankim**, Cameroon
116 I 11 **Banks**, Idaho, U.S.A.
113 Q 1 **Banks Island**, Northwest Territories, Canada
213 R 9 **Banks Islands**, Vanuatu
116 G 6 **Banks Lake**, Washington, U.S.A.
211 I 20 **Banks Peninsula**, New Zealand
169 J 14 **Bankura**, India
165 V 8 **Bannu**, Pakistan
93 J 20 **Banská Bystrica**, Slovakia
96 G 11 **Bansko**, Bulgaria
169 C 14 **Banswara**, India
175 O 13 **Bantaeng**, Indonesia
193 O 12 **Bantè**, Benin
77 A 21 **Bantry Bay**, Republic of Ireland
193 U 13 **Banyo**, Cameroon
174 K 14 **Banyuwangi**, Indonesia
219 W 13 **Banzare Coast**, Antarctica
59 O 13 **Banzare Seamount**, Indian Ocean
173 N 21 **Bao Lôc**, Vietnam

Country; Internal administrative region: State/Province/Territory/Dependent territory; Capital city; Mountain range/Undersea ridge; Mountain peak/Volcano/Seamount; Geographic feature; Headland/Point/Cape/Peninsula; Desert; Island/Island group; Antarctic base; Ocean; Sea; Bay/Gulf/Channel/Strait; Lake; Salt pan/Dry/Intermittent lake; River

1 T 7 **Baoding**, China
1 R 9 **Baoji**, China
1 Y 3 **Baoqing**, China
4 H 4 **Baoro**, Central African Republic
1 O 13 **Baoshan**, China
1 S 6 **Baotou**, China
8 C 12 **Bap**, India
3 O 7 **Baqarah**, Saudi Arabia
1 U 6 **Ba'qūbah**, Iraq
I 17 **Bar**, Serbia and Montenegro
0 M 6 **Bar**, Ukraine
1 Z 6 **Bar Harbor**, Maine, U.S.A.
T 4 **Bar-le-Duc**, France
5 R 12 **Bara**, Indonesia
1 E 17 **Bara**, Sudan
1 T 11 **Bara**, Nigeria
1 L 25 **Baraawe**, Somalia
0 J 3 **Baradah**, Syria
4 L 12 **Baradero**, Argentina
7 Q 7 **Barahona**, Dominican Republic
9 I 15 **Barakot**, India
9 C 18 **Baramati**, India
H 19 **Baranavichy**, Belarus
3 N 10 **Baranof Island**, Alaska, U.S.A.
J 22 **Baraque de Fraiture**, Belgium
5 P 15 **Barate**, Indonesia
3 L 18 **Barbacena**, Brazil
7 Y 10 **Barbados**, North America
U 3 **Barbastro**, Spain
K 14 **Barbate**, Spain
M 10 **Barbezieux-St-Hilaire**, France
8 J 6 **Barbosa**, Colombia
7 X 7 **Barbuda**, Antigua and Barbuda
9 S 6 **Barcaldine**, Queensland, Australia
J 10 **Barcarrota**, Spain
X 5 **Barcelona**, Spain
9 P 3 **Barcelona**, Venezuela
2 E 10 **Barcelos**, Brazil
G 26 **Barcs**, Hungary
3 W 5 **Bardai**, Chad
9 N 15 **Bardarban**, Bangladesh
C 11 **Bárðarbunga**, Iceland
4 G 13 **Bardas Blancas**, Argentina
9 K 14 **Barddhaman**, India
L 19 **Bardejov**, Slovakia
A 7 **Bardonecchia**, Italy
G 19 **Bardsley Island**, United Kingdom
0 K 14 **Bardstown**, Kentucky, U.S.A.
8 F 11 **Bareilly**, India
T 10 **Barents Plain**, Arctic Ocean
V 11 **Barents Sea**, Arctic Ocean
U 13 **Barents Trough**, Arctic Ocean
1 H 17 **Barentu**, Eritrea
0 H 9 **Barga**, China
1 O 19 **Bargaal**, Somalia
9 I 16 **Bargarh**, India
1 O 19 **Bari**, Somalia
N 15 **Bari**, Italy
4 K 6 **Bari**, Democratic Republic of Congo
9 O 6 **Barika**, Algeria
5 W 7 **Barikoi**, Afghanistan
8 L 4 **Barinas**, Venezuela
8 L 4 **Barinas**, Venezuela
0 E 11 **Bârîs**, Egypt
9 M 15 **Barisal**, Bangladesh
9 L 15 **Barisal**, Bangladesh
4 L 11 **Barito**, Indonesia
3 Y 6 **Barkā**, Oman
1 P 10 **Barkam**, China
I 11 **Barkava**, Latvia
7 O 13 **Barkly East**, Republic of South Africa
9 P 5 **Barkly Homestead Roadhouse**, Northern Territory, Australia
9 O 3 **Barkly Tableland**, Northern Territory, Australia
0 M 5 **Barkol**, China
0 M 10 **Bârlad**, Romania
M 15 **Barletta**, Italy
E 11 **Barlinek**, Poland
8 B 13 **Barmer**, India
N 25 **Barn Long Point**, St Helena
6 M 13 **Barnaul**, Russian Federation
J 12 **Barneveld**, Netherlands
K 17 **Barnsley**, United Kingdom
121 X 9 **Barnstable**, Massachusetts, U.S.A.
77 H 22 **Barnstaple**, United Kingdom
123 R 5 **Barnwell**, South Carolina, U.S.A.
138 L 3 **Barquisimeto**, Venezuela
76 D 11 **Barra**, United Kingdom
143 L 14 **Barra**, Brazil
142 G 12 **Barra de São Manuel**, Brazil
143 G 15 **Barra do Bugres**, Brazil
142 L 12 **Barra do Corda**, Brazil
143 I 16 **Barra do Garças**, Brazil
125 S 8 **Barra Jesús Maria**, Mexico
62 F 11 **Barracuda Fracture Zone**, Atlantic Ocean
62 F 11 **Barracuda Ridge**, Atlantic Ocean
142 L 13 **Barragem de Sobradinho**, Brazil
143 J 17 **Barragen de São Simão**, Brazil
138 J 3 **Barranca**, Venezuela
141 C 15 **Barranca**, Peru
139 R 4 **Barrancas**, Venezuela
138 I 2 **Barranquilla**, Colombia
144 G 11 **Barreal**, Argentina
143 L 14 **Barreiras**, Brazil
142 E 12 **Barreirinha do Baeta**, Brazil
80 G 9 **Barreiro**, Portugal
169 O 21 **Barren Island**, India
143 J 18 **Barretos**, Brazil
115 U 14 **Barrington**, Nova Scotia, Canada
209 S 9 **Barringun**, New South Wales, Australia
77 E 19 **Barrow**, Republic of Ireland
112 K 2 **Barrow**, Alaska, U.S.A.
209 N 5 **Barrow Creek**, Northern Territory, Australia
77 I 16 **Barrow-in-Furness**, United Kingdom
208 E 6 **Barrow Island**, Western Australia, Australia
167 W 6 **Barshatas**, Kazakhstan
167 R 5 **Barshyn**, Kazakhstan
117 I 21 **Barstow**, California, U.S.A.
98 C 12 **Bārta**, Latvia
86 L 8 **Barth**, Germany
139 U 5 **Bartica**, Guyana
158 H 7 **Bartin**, Turkey
209 T 3 **Bartle Frere**, Queensland, Australia
119 K 16 **Bartlesville**, Oklahoma, U.S.A.
118 J 12 **Bartlett**, Nebraska, U.S.A.
121 V 6 **Barton**, Vermont, U.S.A.
92 K 8 **Bartoszyce**, Poland
123 R 11 **Bartow**, Florida, U.S.A.
163 S 13 **Barūm**, Yemen
174 K 15 **Barung**, Indonesia
174 M 10 **Barung**, Indonesia
174 C 9 **Barus**, Indonesia
171 T 4 **Baruun Urt**, Mongolia
169 C 15 **Barwani**, India
93 F 14 **Barycz**, Poland
99 K 16 **Barysaw**, Belarus
163 Z 7 **Barzamān**, Oman
194 H 11 **Bas-Congo**, Democratic Republic of Congo
167 P 14 **Basaga**, Turkmenistan
144 L 8 **Basail**, Argentina
117 G 18 **Basalt**, Nevada, U.S.A.
194 K 7 **Basankusu**, Democratic Republic of Congo
175 O 1 **Basco**, Philippines
88 D 6 **Basel**, Switzerland
164 H 10 **Bāsht**, Iran
101 S 8 **Bashtanka**, Ukraine
175 P 7 **Basilan**, Philippines
91 M 17 **Basilicata**, Italy
118 D 10 **Basin**, Wyoming, U.S.A.
77 K 22 **Basingstoke**, United Kingdom
94 C 10 **Baška**, Croatia
159 T 11 **Başkale**, Turkey
194 M 7 **Basoko**, Democratic Republic of Congo
209 S 14 **Bass Strait**, Tasmania, Australia
90 G 6 **Bassano del Grappa**, Italy
193 N 11 **Bassar**, Togo
197 U 8 **Bassas da India**, France
194 L 4 **Basse-Kotto**, Central African Republic
78 L 4 **Basse-Normandie**, France
127 X 8 **Basse-Terre**, Guadeloupe
173 C 16 **Bassein**, Myanmar
81 V 3 **Bassella**, Spain
127 W 8 **Basseterre**, St Kitts and Nevis
118 I 12 **Bassett**, Nebraska, U.S.A.
193 O 12 **Bassila**, Benin
193 Z 7 **Basso**, Chad
164 K 12 **Bastak**, Iran
164 G 3 **Bastānābād**, Iran
168 H 12 **Basti**, India
79 Z 14 **Bastia**, France
83 K 23 **Bastogne**, Belgium
119 N 19 **Bastrop**, Louisiana, U.S.A.
193 S 15 **Bata**, Equatorial Guinea
157 T 9 **Batagay**, Russian Federation
143 I 18 **Bataguassu**, Brazil
96 H 11 **Batak**, Bulgaria
174 L 13 **Batakan**, Indonesia
168 D 9 **Batala**, India
174 F 10 **Batam**, Indonesia
195 O 7 **Batama**, Democratic Republic of Congo
157 T 10 **Batamay**, Russian Federation
175 P 1 **Batan**, Philippines
175 P 1 **Batan Islands**, Philippines
194 D 8 **Batanga**, Gabon
175 O 4 **Batangas**, Philippines
121 R 8 **Batavia**, New York, U.S.A.
59 S 8 **Batavia Seamount**, Indian Ocean
208 M 1 **Batchelor**, Northern Territory, Australia
173 J 20 **Bătdâmbâng**, Cambodia
209 U 12 **Batemans Bay**, New South Wales, Australia
123 R 4 **Batesburg**, South Carolina, U.S.A.
119 N 16 **Batesville**, Arkansas, U.S.A.
122 I 4 **Batesville**, Mississippi, U.S.A.
77 J 22 **Bath**, United Kingdom
121 Y 6 **Bath**, Maine, U.S.A.
121 R 8 **Bath**, New York, U.S.A.
193 X 8 **Batha**, Chad
168 D 10 **Bathinda**, India
82 L 11 **Bathmen**, Netherlands
209 U 11 **Bathurst**, New South Wales, Australia
65 O 7 **Bathurst Island**, Arctic Ocean
113 T 3 **Bathurst Inlet**, Nunavut, Canada
113 T 4 **Bathurst Inlet**, Nunavut, Canada
208 L 1 **Bathurst Island**, Northern Territory, Australia
191 J 19 **Batī**, Ethiopia
158 E 13 **Bati Toroslar**, Turkey
159 Q 12 **Batman**, Turkey
189 O 6 **Batna**, Algeria
94 L 12 **Batočina**, Serbia and Montenegro
119 O 20 **Baton Rouge**, Louisiana, U.S.A.
168 D 8 **Batote**, India
193 V 14 **Batouri**, Cameroon
160 G 5 **Batroûn**, Lebanon
84 M 5 **Båtsfjord**, Norway
169 N 24 **Batti Malv**, India
169 G 24 **Batticaloa**, Sri Lanka
120 L 8 **Battle Creek**, Michigan, U.S.A.
117 I 15 **Battle Mountain**, Nevada, U.S.A.
191 J 21 **Batu**, Ethiopia
174 F 10 **Batu Pahat**, Malaysia
175 O 11 **Batudaka**, Indonesia
175 Q 8 **Batulaki**, Philippines
159 Q 7 **Bat'umi**, Georgia
174 F 13 **Baturaja**, Indonesia
101 R 2 **Baturyn**, Ukraine
174 I 10 **Bau**, Malaysia
175 P 13 **Baubau**, Indonesia
193 S 11 **Bauchi**, Nigeria
193 S 11 **Bauchi**, Nigeria
61 X 8 **Bauer Basin**, Pacific Ocean
175 R 15 **Baukau**, East Timor
212 M 6 **Baunani**, Solomon Islands
143 J 18 **Bauru**, Brazil
143 H 17 **Baús**, Brazil
98 F 12 **Bauska**, Latvia
87 O 16 **Bautzen**, Germany
87 L 25 **Bavarian Alps**, Germany
124 K 4 **Bavispe**, Mexico
174 I 12 **Bawal**, Indonesia
174 K 13 **Bawean**, Indonesia
190 D 9 **Bawiti**, Egypt
123 Q 7 **Baxley**, Georgia, U.S.A.
191 L 24 **Bay**, Somalia
119 L 22 **Bay City**, Texas, U.S.A.
120 M 7 **Bay City**, Michigan, U.S.A.
122 K 8 **Bay Minette**, Alabama, U.S.A.
169 I 19 **Bay of Bengal**, Asia
78 I 7 **Bay of Biscay**, France
115 U 14 **Bay of Fundy**, Nova Scotia, Canada
210 J 5 **Bay of Islands**, New Zealand
210 N 10 **Bay of Plenty**, New Zealand
210 N 11 **Bay of Plenty**, New Zealand
122 I 6 **Bay Springs**, Mississippi, U.S.A.
210 N 13 **Bay View**, New Zealand
126 M 6 **Bayamo**, Cuba
171 Q 6 **Bayan**, China
171 T 3 **Bayan**, Mongolia
171 S 6 **Bayan Obo**, China
170 L 2 **Bayan-Ölgiy**, Mongolia
171 N 4 **Bayan-Ovoo**, Mongolia
167 U 4 **Bayanaul**, Kazakhstan
170 J 5 **Bayanbulak**, China
194 H 6 **Bayanga**, Central African Republic
194 H 4 **Bayanga-Didi**, Central African Republic
171 O 4 **Bayanhongor**, Mongolia
171 P 4 **Bayanhongor**, Mongolia
119 D 19 **Bayard**, New Mexico, U.S.A.
175 P 6 **Bayawan**, Philippines
164 L 10 **Bayāẕ**, Iran
159 P 9 **Bayburt**, Turkey
156 L 7 **Baydaratskaya Guba**, Russian Federation
65 X 10 **Baydaratskaya Guba**, Arctic Ocean
191 L 23 **Baydhabo**, Somalia
193 Q 14 **Bayelsa**, Nigeria
87 L 22 **Bayerischer Wald**, Germany
87 J 22 **Bayern**, Germany
78 M 3 **Bayeux**, France
166 K 6 **Bayganin**, Kazakhstan
163 Q 13 **Bayḩan al Qişab**, Yemen
161 S 4 **Bayjī**, Iraq
157 O 11 **Baykit**, Russian Federation
167 N 8 **Baykonur**, Kazakhstan
78 K 14 **Bayonne**, France
140 A 12 **Bayóvar**, Peru
167 N 14 **Bayramaly**, Turkmenistan
87 J 20 **Bayreuth**, Germany
163 O 13 **Bayt al Faqīh**, Yemen
119 L 21 **Baytown**, Texas, U.S.A.
175 P 12 **Bayu**, Indonesia
174 F 12 **Bayunglincir**, Indonesia
81 P 12 **Baza**, Spain
101 O 2 **Bazar**, Ukraine
159 X 7 **Bazardüzü Dağl**, Azerbaijan
78 M 12 **Bazas**, France
165 S 13 **Bazdar**, Pakistan
171 R 10 **Bazhong**, China
100 F 12 **Baziaş**, Romania
165 O 12 **Bazmān**, Iran
160 H 5 **Bcharre**, Lebanon
118 G 8 **Beach**, North Dakota, U.S.A.
77 M 23 **Beachy Head**, United Kingdom
208 I 4 **Beagle Bay**, Western Australia, Australia
208 M 1 **Beagle Gulf**, Northern Territory, Australia
197 Z 5 **Bealanana**, Madgascar
116 M 13 **Bear Lake**, Idaho, U.S.A.
218 K 10 **Bear Peninsula**, Antarctica
120 G 11 **Beardstown**, Illinois, U.S.A.
81 P 10 **Beas de Segura**, Spain
118 K 13 **Beatrice**, Nebraska, U.S.A.
117 I 19 **Beatty**, Nevada, U.S.A.
115 Q 11 **Beattyville**, Québec, Canada
145 L 24 **Beauchene Island**, Falkland Islands
174 L 8 **Beaufort**, Malaysia
65 P 4 **Beaufort Sea**, Arctic Ocean
196 L 14 **Beaufort West**, Republic of South Africa
76 G 10 **Beauly**, United Kingdom
83 F 22 **Beaumont**, Belgium
119 M 21 **Beaumont**, Texas, U.S.A.
122 J 7 **Beaumont**, Mississippi, U.S.A.
79 O 13 **Beaumont-de-Lomagne**, France
79 T 8 **Beaune**, France
83 H 23 **Beauraing**, Belgium
79 P 3 **Beauvais**, France
113 W 10 **Beauval**, Saskatchewan, Canada
117 L 18 **Beaver**, Utah, U.S.A.
112 M 7 **Beaver Creek**, Yukon Territory, Canada
120 I 7 **Beaver Dam**, Wisconsin, U.S.A.
121 P 10 **Beaver Falls**, Pennsylvania, U.S.A.
120 L 5 **Beaver Island**, Michigan, U.S.A.
168 D 12 **Beawar**, India
193 W 12 **Béboto**, Chad
87 G 17 **Bebra**, Germany
94 K 8 **Bečej**, Serbia and Montenegro
80 J 2 **Becerreá**, Spain
188 J 8 **Béchar**, Algeria
121 O 14 **Beckley**, West Virginia, U.S.A.
100 I 8 **Beclean**, Romania
191 J 19 **Beda Hāyk'**, Ethiopia
191 H 21 **Bedelē**, Ethiopia
120 J 12 **Bedford**, Indiana, U.S.A.
120 K 13 **Bedford**, Kentucky, U.S.A.
121 Q 11 **Bedford**, Pennsylvania, U.S.A.
209 Q 7 **Bedourie**, Queensland, Australia
83 J 15 **Beek**, Netherlands
160 F 12 **Be'ér Menuha**, Israel
160 F 13 **Be'ér Ora**, Israel
160 F 10 **Be'ér Sheva'**, Israel
83 C 17 **Beernem**, Belgium
87 N 14 **Beeskow**, Germany
218 J 6 **Beethoven Peninsula**, Antarctica
119 J 23 **Beeville**, Texas, U.S.A.
194 K 7 **Befale**, Democratic Republic of Congo
197 Z 6 **Befandriana Avaratra**, Madgascar
194 L 7 **Befori**, Democratic Republic of Congo
209 U 13 **Bega**, New South Wales, Australia
164 H 9 **Behbahān**, Iran
164 K 5 **Behshahr**, Iran
165 T 7 **Behsūd**, Afghanistan
171 X 2 **Bei'an**, China
191 G 20 **Beigi**, Ethiopia
171 S 14 **Beihai**, China
171 T 6 **Beijing**, China
171 T 6 **Beijing Shi**, China
82 M 8 **Beilen**, Netherlands
87 J 22 **Beilngries**, Germany
170 M 8 **Beiluheyan**, China
171 V 5 **Beipiao**, China
84 B 10 **Bňir**, Iceland
197 R 8 **Beira**, Mozambique
160 G 6 **Beirut**, Lebanon
197 P 9 **Beitbridge**, Zimbabwe
100 G 9 **Beiuş**, Romania
80 H 11 **Beja**, Portugal
80 I 11 **Beja**, Portugal
189 Q 5 **Béja**, Tunisia
189 N 5 **Bejaïa**, Algeria
80 L 6 **Béjar**, Spain
80 M 12 **Beji**, Spain
166 H 11 **Bekdash**, Turkmenistan
93 L 24 **Békés**, Hungary
93 L 24 **Békéscsaba**, Hungary
197 W 10 **Bekily**, Madgascar
58 A 13 **Bel Ombre**, Mauritius
165 S 14 **Bela**, Pakistan
197 O 10 **Bela-Bela**, Republic of South Africa
94 M 10 **Bela Crkva**, Serbia and Montenegro
95 O 14 **Bela Palanka**, Serbia and Montenegro
193 U 14 **Bélabo**, Cameroon
167 W 4 **Bel'agash**, Kazakhstan
99 G 19 **Belarus**, Europe
174 C 9 **Belawan**, Indonesia
193 R 8 **Belbédji**, Niger
93 J 15 **Bełchatów**, Poland
115 O 7 **Belcher Islands**, Ontario, Canada
165 S 6 **Belchiragh**, Afghanistan
81 S 5 **Belchite**, Spain
158 L 9 **Belcik**, Turkey
117 E 15 **Belden**, California, U.S.A.
191 M 23 **Beledweyne**, Somalia
192 H 12 **Belefuanai**, Liberia
193 U 11 **Belel**, Nigeria
142 J 10 **Belém**, Brazil
158 L 14 **Belen**, Turkey
144 H 8 **Belén**, Argentina
192 H 11 **Bèlèya**, Guinea
77 F 15 **Belfast**, United Kingdom
121 Y 6 **Belfast**, Maine, U.S.A.
77 F 15 **Belfast Lough**, United Kingdom
191 G 19 **Bēlfodiyo**, Ethiopia
79 V 6 **Belfort**, France
169 C 19 **Belgaum**, India
219 T 3 **Belgica Mountains**, Antarctica
83 E 20 **Belgium**, Europe
156 E 9 **Belgorod**, Russian Federation
94 L 10 **Belgrade**, Serbia and Montenegro
219 N 5 **Belgrano II**, Antarctica
211 I 16 **Belgrove**, New Zealand
123 W 2 **Belhaven**, North Carolina, U.S.A.
189 O 9 **Belhirane**, Algeria
193 T 12 **Beli**, Nigeria
94 I 8 **Beli Manastir**, Croatia
174 F 13 **Belimbing**, Indonesia
194 F 7 **Bélinga**, Gabon
174 G 11 **Belinyu**, Indonesia
174 H 12 **Belitung**, Indonesia
126 E 7 **Belize**, North America
126 E 7 **Belize**, Belize
196 F 1 **Belize**, Angola
144 K 11 **Bell Ville**, Argentina
113 Q 13 **Bella Coola**, British Columbia, Canada
144 M 10 **Bella Unión**, Uruguay
144 M 9 **Bella Vista**, Argentina
145 G 24 **Bella Vista**, Argentina
79 O 9 **Bellac**, France
90 C 6 **Bellagio**, Italy
169 E 20 **Bellary**, India
118 G 10 **Belle Fourche**, South Dakota, U.S.A.
123 S 13 **Belle Glade**, Florida, U.S.A.
78 I 7 **Belle-Île**, France
115 X 8 **Belle Isle**, Newfoundland and Labrador, Canada
120 M 11 **Bellefontaine**, Ohio, U.S.A.
79 U 9 **Bellegarde-sur-Valserine**, France
119 J 14 **Belleville**, Kansas, U.S.A.
116 K 12 **Bellevue**, Idaho, U.S.A.
116 E 7 **Bellevue**, Washington, U.S.A.
139 Y 6 **Bellevue de L'Inini**, French Guiana
79 U 10 **Belley**, France
116 E 5 **Bellingham**, Washington, U.S.A.
218 H 8 **Bellingshausen Sea**, Antarctica
88 H 10 **Bellinzona**, Switzerland
212 L 8 **Bellona**, Solomon Islands
165 U 11 **Bellpat**, Pakistan
90 G 6 **Belluno**, Italy
126 E 8 **Belmopan**, Belize
143 L 18 **Belo Horizonte**, Brazil
157 U 14 **Belogorsk**, Russian Federation
96 F 7 **Belogradchik**, Bulgaria
197 W 11 **Beloha**, Madgascar
120 H 8 **Beloit**, Wisconsin, U.S.A.
156 H 6 **Belomorsk**, Russian Federation
169 M 14 **Belonia**, India
81 P 3 **Belorado**, Spain
156 I 11 **Beloretsk**, Russian Federation
96 F 7 **Belotintsi**, Bulgaria
167 Y 4 **Belousovka**, Kazakhstan
142 H 10 **Belterra**, Brazil
91 L 18 **Belvedere Marittimo**, Italy
156 M 11 **Belyy Yar**, Russian Federation
93 O 16 **Bełżec**, Poland
87 L 14 **Belzig**, Germany
196 G 1 **Bembe**, Angola
80 K 2 **Bembibre**, Spain
118 K 8 **Bemidji**, Minnesota, U.S.A.
82 K 13 **Bemmel**, Netherlands
175 T 12 **Bemu**, Indonesia
189 R 7 **Ben Guerdane**, Tunisia
76 G 8 **Ben Klibreck**, United Kingdom
76 H 11 **Ben Macdui**, United Kingdom
76 G 11 **Ben Nevis**, United Kingdom
188 H 7 **Ben Slimane**, Morocco
194 M 10 **Bena Dibele**, Democratic Republic of Congo
194 M 10 **Bena-Tshadi**, Democratic Republic of Congo
81 U 3 **Benabarre**, Spain
174 L 11 **Benagin**, Indonesia
209 S 13 **Benalla**, Victoria, Australia
80 L 3 **Benavente**, Spain

Country | Internal administrative region: State/Province/Territory/Dependent territory | Capital city | Mountain range/Undersea ridge | Mountain peak/Volcano/Seamount | Geographic feature | Headland/Point/Cape/Peninsula | Desert | Island/Island group | Antarctic base | Ocean | Sea | Bay/Gulf/Channel/Strait | Lake | Salt pan/Dry/Intermittent lake | River

76 E 10 Benbecula, United Kingdom
191 O 20 Bender-Bayla, Somalia
209 S 13 Bendigo, Victoria, Australia
197 Q 5 Bene, Mozambique
82 J 13 Beneden-Leeuwen, Netherlands
91 K 15 Benevento, Italy
195 N 7 Bengamisa, Democratic Republic of Congo
193 U 15 Bengbis, Cameroon
171 V 9 Bengbu, China
174 D 12 Bengkulu, Indonesia
174 E 12 Bengkulu, Indonesia
196 F 2 Bengo, Angola
196 G 5 Benguela, Angola
196 G 4 Benguela, Angola
190 E 8 Benha, Egypt
60 J 6 Benham Seamount, Pacific Ocean
141 J 18 Beni, Bolivia
141 J 17 Beni, Bolivia
195 Q 7 Beni, Democratic Republic of Congo
188 K 9 Beni-Abbès, Algeria
190 E 9 Benî Mazâr, Egypt
188 H 8 Beni Mellal, Morocco
188 K 8 Beni-Ounif, Algeria
188 K 6 Beni-Saf, Algeria
190 E 9 Beni Suef, Egypt
81 U 7 Benicasim, Spain
81 T 10 Benidorm, Spain
193 N 11 Benin, Africa
193 Q 13 Benin City, Nigeria
191 G 19 Benishangul, Ethiopia
145 L 14 Benito Juárez, Argentina
124 I 3 Benjamin Hill, Mexico
175 V 13 Benjina, Indonesia
176 I 6 Benkei-misaki, Japan
211 C 25 Benmore, New Zealand
63 N 25 Bennett's Point, St Helena
121 V 8 Bennington, Vermont, U.S.A.
117 O 25 Benson, Arizona, U.S.A.
175 O 14 Benteng, Indonesia
196 F 5 Bentiaba, Angola
209 Q 3 Bentinck Island, Queensland, Australia
173 F 21 Bentinck Island, Myanmar
191 D 20 Bentiu, Sudan
119 M 17 Benton, Arkansas, U.S.A.
120 H 13 Benton, Illinois, U.S.A.
120 J 9 Benton Harbor, Michigan, U.S.A.
174 H 10 Benua, Indonesia
193 R 12 Benue, Nigeria
171 W 5 Benxi, China
175 R 9 Beo, Indonesia
169 G 14 Beohari, India
192 J 12 Béoumi, Côte d'Ivoire
177 C 21 Beppu, Japan
197 X 10 Beraketa, Madgascar
95 K 15 Berane, Serbia and Montenegro
197 W 7 Beravina, Madgascar
191 F 15 Berber, Sudan
191 L 19 Berbera, Somalia
194 H 5 Berbérati, Central African Republic
87 M 25 Berchtesgaden, Germany
79 P 1 Berck, France
157 T 10 Berdigestyakh, Russian Federation
101 X 9 Berdyans'k, Ukraine
101 W 9 Berdyans'ka Kosa, Ukraine
101 W 9 Berdyans'ka Zatoka, Ukraine
101 N 4 Berdychiv, Ukraine
193 W 11 Béré, Chad
175 S 9 Berebere, Indonesia
100 H 6 Berehove, Ukraine
212 D 6 Bereina, Papua New Guinea
192 L 12 Berekum, Ghana
167 Z 4 Berel', Kazakhstan
190 G 12 Berenice, Egypt
114 I 9 Berens River, Manitoba, Canada
93 M 23 Berettyóújfalu, Hungary
100 J 5 Berezhany, Ukraine
101 Q 9 Berezivka, Ukraine
101 Q 2 Berezna, Ukraine
100 L 2 Berezne, Ukraine
156 I 7 Bereznik, Russian Federation
156 I 9 Berezniki, Russian Federation
156 K 9 Berezovo, Russian Federation
157 V 13 Berezovyy, Russian Federation
81 W 3 Berga, Spain
158 B 9 Bergama, Turkey
90 D 6 Bergamo, Italy
82 H 9 Bergen, Netherlands
85 A 18 Bergen, Norway
86 M 8 Bergen, Germany
83 F 15 Bergen op Zoom, Netherlands
79 N 11 Bergerac, France
87 C 17 Bergisch Gladbach, Germany
65 R 1 Bering Sea, Arctic Ocean
112 F 3 Bering Strait, Russian Federation/U.S.A.
83 K 16 Beringe, Netherlands
83 I 18 Beringen, Belgium
157 Z 7 Beringovskiy, Russian Federation
81 P 13 Berja, Spain
188 J 6 Berkane, Morocco
117 D 18 Berkeley, California, U.S.A.
218 M 5 Berkner Island, Antarctica
96 F 8 Berkovitsa, Bulgaria
84 M 5 Berlevåg, Norway
86 M 13 Berlin, Germany
86 M 13 Berlin, Germany
121 U 13 Berlin, Maryland, U.S.A.
125 N 7 Bermejillo, Mexico
144 K 6 Bermejo, Argentina/Bolivia
141 K 24 Bermejo, Bolivia
144 J 5 Bermejo, Argentina
144 K 6 Bermejo viejo, Argentina
80 L 5 Bermillo De Sayago, Spain
62 A 8 Bermuda, U.K.
62 E 10 Bermuda Rise, Atlantic Ocean
88 D 8 Bern, Switzerland
88 E 8 Bern, Switzerland
145 J 14 Bernasconi, Argentina
86 M 12 Bernau, Germany
79 O 4 Bernay, France
87 J 15 Bernburg, Germany
89 X 4 Berndorf, Austria
88 C 10 Bernese Alps, Switzerland
208 E 8 Bernier Island, Western Australia, Australia
89 X 6 Bernstein, Austria
197 W 9 Beroroha, Madgascar
96 F 11 Berovo, Macedonia (F.Y.R.O.M.)
188 H 7 Berrechid, Morocco
209 Q 11 Berri, South Australia, Australia
189 N 7 Berriane, Algeria
196 J 11 Berseba, Namibia
86 E 13 Bersenbrück, Germany
101 O 7 Bershad', Ukraine
142 L 12 Bertolinia, Brazil
193 V 14 Bertoua, Cameroon
214 E 3 Beru, Kiribati
142 E 11 Beruri, Brazil
76 J 13 Berwick-upon-Tweed, United Kingdom
101 T 9 Beryslav, Ukraine
197 W 6 Besalampy, Madgascar
79 V 7 Besançon, France
164 K 11 Beshneh, Iran
159 Q 12 Beşiri, Turkey
96 G 11 Beslet, Bulgaria
158 M 12 Besni, Turkey
122 L 5 Bessemer, Alabama, U.S.A.
83 J 15 Best, Netherlands
166 K 5 Bestamak, Kazakhstan
167 T 3 Bestobe, Kazakhstan
80 I 1 Betanzos, Spain
141 K 21 Betanzos, Bolivia
193 V 13 Bétaré Oya, Cameroon
167 Q 6 Betbulak, Kazakhstan
196 I 11 Bethanie, Namibia
119 L 13 Bethany, Missouri, U.S.A.
112 G 6 Bethel, Alaska, U.S.A.
120 L 12 Bethel, Ohio, U.S.A.
121 X 6 Bethel, Maine, U.S.A.
160 F 9 Bethlehem, Israel
197 O 12 Bethlehem, Republic of South Africa
197 W 10 Betioky, Madgascar
173 I 26 Betong, Thailand
209 Q 7 Betoota, Queensland, Australia
194 J 6 Bétou, Congo
167 Q 8 Betpak-Dala, Kazakhstan
197 X 10 Betroka, Madgascar
169 E 15 Betul, India
87 E 17 Betzdorf, Germany
120 K 6 Beulah, Michigan, U.S.A.
79 N 3 Beuzeville, France
87 G 15 Beverungen, Germany
82 G 10 Beverwijk, Netherlands
77 M 23 Bexhill, United Kingdom
159 N 10 Bey Dağl, Turkey
158 D 13 Bey Dağlari, Turkey
192 I 12 Beyla, Guinea
159 X 9 Beyläqan, Azerbaijan
191 K 18 Beylul, Eritrea
166 J 8 Beyneu, Kazakhstan
158 G 9 Beypazari, Turkey
191 N 21 Beyra, Somalia
158 G 12 Beyşehir, Turkey
158 F 12 Beyşehir Gölü, Turkey
159 S 12 Beytüşşebap, Turkey
79 R 14 Béziers, France
168 E 8 Bhadarwah, India
169 J 16 Bhadrakh, India
169 D 20 Bhadravati, India
168 J 13 Bhagalpur, India
169 M 14 Bhairab Bazar, Bangladesh
168 H 12 Bhairawa, Nepal
165 W 9 Bhakkar, Pakistan
172 E 9 Bhamo, Myanmar
169 F 16 Bhandara, India
168 E 12 Bharatpur, India
169 C 15 Bharuch, India
169 C 20 Bhatkal, India
169 K 15 Bhatpara, India
169 B 15 Bhavnagar, India
169 H 17 Bhawanipatna, India
165 X 8 Bhera, Pakistan
169 G 16 Bhilai, India
168 D 13 Bhilwara, India
169 G 19 Bhimavaram, India
168 F 12 Bhind, India
168 B 13 Bhinmal, India
169 C 17 Bhiwandi, India
168 E 11 Bhiwani, India
169 E 14 Bhopal, India
169 G 17 Bhopalpatnam, India
169 C 18 Bhor, India
169 J 16 Bhubaneshwar, India
168 A 14 Bhuj, India
173 G 15 Bhumiphol Dam, Thailand
169 D 16 Bhusawal, India
168 L 11 Bhutan, Asia
175 W 11 Biak, Indonesia
175 W 11 Biak, Indonesia
92 N 13 Biała Podlaska, Poland
92 F 9 Białogard, Poland
92 N 11 Białystok, Poland
194 K 5 Bianga, Central African Republic
192 I 12 Biankouma, Côte d'Ivoire
169 E 14 Biaora, India
164 L 6 Biārjmand, Iran
175 Q 10 Biaro, Indonesia
78 K 14 Biarritz, France
88 H 10 Biasca, Switzerland
190 E 9 Biba, Egypt
194 F 7 Bibas, Gabon
90 G 10 Bibbiena, Italy
87 G 24 Biberach, Germany
192 L 13 Bibiani, Ghana
100 K 9 Bicaz, Romania
209 T 15 Bicheno, Tasmania, Australia
159 P 5 Bichvint'a, Georgia
169 D 17 Bid, India
193 Q 12 Bida, Nigeria
78 L 14 Bidache, France
169 E 18 Bidar, India
121 X 7 Biddeford, Maine, U.S.A.
174 E 8 Bidor, Malaysia
196 I 5 Bié, Angola
117 E 14 Bieber, California, U.S.A.
92 M 10 Biebrza, Poland
93 L 18 Biecz, Poland
88 D 7 Biel, Switzerland
87 F 14 Bielefeld, Germany
88 C 7 Bieler See, Switzerland
90 B 7 Biella, Italy
92 N 11 Bielsk Podlaski, Poland
93 I 18 Bielsko-Biała, Poland
173 N 22 Biên Hoa, Vietnam
83 I 24 Bièvre, Belgium
194 E 8 Bifoun, Gabon
84 B 11 Bifröst, Iceland
211 B 22 Big Bay, New Zealand
118 L 7 Big Falls, Minnesota, U.S.A.
115 R 4 Big Island, Nunavut, Canada
117 G 14 Big Mountain, Nevada, U.S.A.
120 K 7 Big Rapids, Michigan, U.S.A.
118 D 8 Big Snow Mountain, Montana, U.S.A.
211 B 26 Big South Cape Island, New Zealand
119 H 20 Big Spring, Texas, U.S.A.
117 D 20 Big Sur, California, U.S.A.
118 D 9 Big Timber, Montana, U.S.A.
114 L 9 Big Trout Lake, Ontario, Canada
114 L 8 Big Trout Lake, Ontario, Canada
158 B 8 Biga, Turkey
158 C 9 Bigadiş, Turkey
208 J 2 Bigge Island, Western Australia, Australia
118 D 9 Bighorn, Wyoming, U.S.A.
118 D 10 Bighorn Basin, Wyoming, U.S.A.
118 D 9 Bighorn Lake, Montana, U.S.A.
118 E 10 Bighorn Mountains, Wyoming, U.S.A.
173 H 20 Bight of Bangkok, Thailand
193 O 14 Bight of Benin, Nigeria
193 Q 14 Bight of Biafra, Nigeria
192 D 9 Bignona, Senegal
94 D 10 Bihać, Bosnia and Herzegovina
169 I 14 Bihar, India
168 J 13 Bihar Sharif, India
100 H 9 Bihor Massif, Romania
169 D 19 Bijapur, India
164 G 5 Bījār, Iran
94 J 10 Bijeljina, Bosnia and Herzegovina
95 K 14 Bijelo Polje, Serbia and Montenegro
171 Q 12 Bijie, China
168 F 10 Bijnor, India
168 C 11 Bikaner, India
215 Z 1 Bikar, Marshall Islands
157 V 14 Bikin, Russian Federation
215 W 1 Bikini, Marshall Islands
189 W 13 Bikku Bitti, Libya
194 J 8 Bikoro, Democratic Republic of Congo
101 P 4 Bila Tserkva, Ukraine
169 H 15 Bilaspur, India
159 Y 9 Biläsuvar, Azerbaijan
173 F 19 Bilauktaung Range, Myanmar
81 P 1 Bilbao, Spain
93 G 20 Bílé Karpaty, Slovakia
95 H 15 Bileća, Bosnia and Herzegovina
158 E 8 Bilecik, Turkey
159 Z 8 Bilgjach, Azerbaijan
93 N 16 Biłgoraj, Poland
195 R 9 Bilharamulo, Tanzania
101 P 10 Bilhorod-Dnistrovs'kyy, Ukraine
195 N 5 Bili, Democratic Republic of Congo
157 X 7 Bilibino, Russian Federation
95 L 20 Bilisht, Albania
77 J 23 Bill of Portland, United Kingdom
208 K 5 Billiluna, Western Australia, Australia
118 D 9 Billings, Montana, U.S.A.
193 U 6 Bilma, Niger
209 V 7 Biloela, Queensland, Australia
101 U 12 Bilohirs'k, Ukraine
101 Y 4 Bilokurakyne, Ukraine
101 Z 4 Biloluts'k, Ukraine
101 T 2 Bilopillya, Ukraine
101 Z 5 Bilovods'k, Ukraine
122 J 8 Biloxi, Mississippi, U.S.A.
209 Q 7 Bilpa Morea Claypan, Queensland, Australia
82 I 12 Bilthoven, Netherlands
193 Y 8 Biltine, Chad
193 Y 8 Biltine, Chad
173 E 16 Bilugyun Island, Myanmar
126 H 9 Bilwascarma, Nicaragua
83 J 19 Bilzen, Belgium
193 N 12 Bimbila, Ghana
126 L 2 Bimini Islands, The Bahamas
193 Q 11 Bin-Yauri, Nigeria
83 F 21 Binche, Belgium
194 J 12 Bindu, Democratic Republic of Congo
197 P 6 Bindura, Zimbabwe
197 Q 7 Binga, Mozambique
169 B 22 Bingaram, India
87 D 19 Bingen, Germany
121 T 9 Binghamton, New York, U.S.A.
159 P 11 Bingöl, Turkey
173 O 17 Binh Son, Vietnam
174 C 9 Binjai, Indonesia
175 Q 13 Binongko, Indonesia
174 G 10 Bintan, Indonesia
174 F 13 Bintuhan, Indonesia
174 K 9 Bintulu, Malaysia
171 R 13 Binyang, China
171 U 7 Binzhou, China
145 F 14 Bío Bío, Chile
145 F 15 Biobío, Chile
94 D 12 Biograd na Moru, Croatia
188 C 12 Bir Anzarane, Western Sahara
188 A 14 Bir-Gandouz, Western Sahara
192 G 3 Bîr Mogreïn, Mauritania
162 L 6 Bi'r Nasīf, Saudi Arabia
161 S 9 Bi'r Sābil, Iraq
189 T 10 Birāk, Libya
194 M 1 Birao, Central African Republic
168 K 12 Biratnagar, Nepal
113 U 10 Birch Mountains, Alberta, Canada
191 L 21 Bircot, Ethiopia
93 N 18 Bircza, Poland
209 Q 7 Birdsville, Queensland, Australia
159 N 13 Birecik, Turkey
174 B 8 Bireun, Indonesia
165 N 8 Birjand, Iran
77 I 18 Birkenhead, United Kingdom
89 W 6 Birkfeld, Austria
161 U 1 Birkim, Iraq
167 T 9 Birlik, Kazakhstan
77 J 20 Birmingham, United Kingdom
122 L 5 Birmingham, Alabama, U.S.A.
214 J 4 Birnie, Kiribati
193 Q 11 Birnin-Gwari, Nigeria
193 P 10 Birnin-Kebbi, Nigeria
193 Q 9 Birnin Konni, Niger
193 S 10 Birnin Kudu, Nigeria
157 V 14 Birobidzhan, Russian Federation
77 D 18 Birr, Republic of Ireland
114 H 9 Birtle, Manitoba, Canada
98 F 12 Biržai, Lithuania
98 H 12 Birži, Latvia
117 O 25 Bisbee, Arizona, U.S.A.
62 K 7 Biscay Abyssal Plain, Atlantic Ocean
123 T 14 Biscayne Bay, Florida, U.S.A.
91 M 15 Bisceglie, Italy
89 Q 6 Bischofshofen, Austria
218 H 4 Biscoe Islands, Antarctica
96 L 6 Bisertsi, Bulgaria
95 E 14 Biševo, Croatia
167 U 10 Bishkek, Kyrgyzstan
169 K 14 Bishnupur, India
197 N 14 Bisho, Republic of South Africa
117 G 19 Bishop, California, U.S.A.
95 I 18 Bishti i Pallës, Albania
138 M 7 Bisinaca, Colombia
189 O 6 Biskra, Algeria
92 L 9 Biskupiec, Poland
175 R 6 Bislig, Philippines
118 H 8 Bismarck, North Dakota, U.S.A.
212 D 3 Bismarck Archipelago, Papua New Guinea
212 C 4 Bismarck Range, Papua New Guinea
212 D 3 Bismarck Sea, Papua New Guinea
159 Q 12 Bismil, Turkey
118 G 9 Bison, South Dakota, U.S.A.
192 E 10 Bissau, Guinea-Bissau
193 T 13 Bissaula, Nigeria
113 S 9 Bistcho Lake, Alberta, Canada
100 J 8 Bistrița, Romania
168 G 12 Biswan, India
194 E 6 Bitam, Gabon
87 B 19 Bitburg, Germany
116 J 8 Biteroot Range, Idaho, U.S.A.
166 H 4 Bitik, Kazakhstan
193 X 10 Bitkine, Chad
159 R 11 Bitlis, Turkey
96 C 13 Bitola, Macedonia (F.Y.R.O.M.)
91 M 15 Bitonto, Italy
196 J 14 Bitterfontein, Republic of South Africa
118 A 7 Bitteroot Range, Montana, U.S.A.
91 C 16 Bitti, Italy
175 Q 10 Bitung, Indonesia
193 U 11 Biu, Nigeria
88 I 9 Bivio, Switzerland
100 M 8 Bivolari, Romania
177 G 17 Biwa-ko, Japan
156 M 13 Biysk, Russian Federatic
177 F 19 Bizen, Japan
189 Q 5 Bizerte, Tunisia
94 F 8 Bjelovar, Croatia
85 I 15 Björna, Sweden
65 U 11 Bjørnøya, Norway
85 I 15 Bjurholm, Sweden
192 J 9 Bla, Mali
172 J 11 Black, Vietnam
218 J 5 Black Coast, Antarctica
87 D 25 Black Forest, Germany
118 G 10 Black Hills, South Dako U.S.A.
113 W 8 Black Lake, Saskatchew Canada
120 M 14 Black Mountain, Kentucky, U.S.A.
117 G 15 Black Rock Desert, Nevada, U.S.A.
211 B 26 Black Rock Point, New Zealand
158 G 6 Black Sea, Asia/Europe
115 X 8 Black Tickle, Newfoundland and Labrador, Canada
192 L 11 Black Volta, Burkina Faso
209 S 7 Blackall, Queensland, Australia
116 L 12 Blackfoot, Idaho, U.S.A.
77 I 17 Blackpool, United Kingdom
121 P 14 Blacksburg, Virginia, U.S.A.
123 Q 7 Blackshear, Georgia, U.S.A.
77 C 20 Blackwater, Republic of Ireland
209 U 6 Blackwater, Queenslan Australia
83 I 16 Bladel, Netherlands
96 G 11 Blagoevgrad, Bulgaria
96 F 10 Blagoevgrad, Bulgaria
157 U 14 Blagoveshchensk, Russi Federation
116 E 5 Blaine, Washington, U.S.A.
123 O 3 Blairsville, Georgia, U.S
120 I 2 Blake Point, Michigan, U.S.A.
123 N 7 Blakely, Georgia, U.S.A.
62 D 10 Blake–Bahama Ridge, Atlantic Ocean
141 L 17 Blanco, Bolivia
81 Y 4 Blanes, Spain
174 B 8 Blangkejeren, Indonesia
83 C 16 Blankenberge, Belgium
87 C 18 Blankenheim, Germany
197 R 5 Blantyre, Malawi
78 M 11 Blaye, France
94 B 6 Bled, Slovenia
83 C 20 Bléharies, Belgium
211 J 17 Blenheim, New Zealand
77 E 18 Blessington, Republic o Ireland
188 M 5 Blida, Algeria
211 A 22 Bligh Sound, New Zealand
116 J 12 Bliss, Idaho, U.S.A.
174 J 15 Blitar, Indonesia
193 N 12 Blitta, Togo
121 X 9 Block Island, Rhode Island, U.S.A.
197 N 12 Bloemfontein, Republic South Africa
196 M 12 Bloemhof, Republic of South Africa
79 O 7 Blois, France
84 B 10 Blönduós, Iceland
77 C 14 Bloody Foreland, Repub of Ireland
120 J 12 Bloomfield, Indiana, U.S.A.
120 H 10 Bloomington, Illinois, U.S.A.
120 J 12 Bloomington, Indiana, U.S.A.
123 N 8 Blountstown, Florida, U.S.A.
88 J 7 Bludenz, Austria
121 R 11 Blue Mountains, Pennsylvania, U.S.A.
209 O 2 Blue Mud Bay, Norther Territory, Australia
191 F 19 Blue Nile, Sudan
191 G 19 Blue Nile, Ethiopia/Sudan
123 O 3 Blue Ridge Mountains, Georgia, U.S.A.

Country · Internal administrative region: State/Province/Territory/Dependent territory · Capital city · Mountain range/Undersea ridge · Mountain peak/Volcano/Seamount · Geographic feature · Headland/Point/Cape/Peninsula · Desert · Island/Island group · Antarctic base · Ocean · Sea · Bay/Gulf/Channel/Strait · Lake · Salt pan/Dry/Intermittent lake

3 T 13 Blue River, British Columbia, Canada
1 O 14 Bluefield, Virginia, U.S.A.
6 H 11 Bluefields, Nicaragua
1 O 14 Bluestone Lake, West Virginia, U.S.A.
7 O 19 Bluff, Utah, U.S.A.
1 C 26 Bluff, New Zealand
3 J 20 Blumenau, Brazil
8 I 10 Blunt, South Dakota, U.S.A.
K 14 Blyth, United Kingdom
7 K 23 Blythe, California, U.S.A.
9 O 16 Blytheville, Arkansas, U.S.A.
2 G 12 Bo, Sierra Leone
1 V 7 Bo Hai, China
1 C 21 Bo River Post, Sudan
B 16 Boa Vista, Cape Verde
2 E 8 Boa Vista, Brazil
5 O 4 Boac, Philippines
6 G 11 Boaco, Nicaragua
4 J 5 Boali, Central African Republic
5 R 12 Boano, Indonesia
7 Z 4 Bobasakoa, Madgascar
D 8 Bobbio, Italy
I 24 Bobingen, Germany
2 L 10 Bobo-Dioulasso, Burkina Faso
F 9 Bobolice, Poland
7 O 9 Bobonong, Botswana
L 16 Bobr, Belarus
E 15 Bóbr, Poland
1 Q 3 Bobrovytsya, Ukraine
O 10 Bobrowniki, Poland
1 R 7 Bobrynets', Ukraine
7 X 9 Boby, Madgascar
2 C 13 Boca do Acre, Brazil
4 H 3 Bocaranga, Central African Republic
5 R 11 Bochart, Québec, Canada
C 14 Bocholt, Germany
C 16 Bochum, Germany
6 G 4 Bocoio, Angola
0 F 11 Bocşa, Romania
4 I 5 Boda, Central African Republic
H 23 Böda, Sweden
7 R 12 Bodaybo, Russian Federation
J 15 Bode Verde Fracture Zone, Atlantic Ocean
J 12 Boden, Sweden
G 26 Bodensee, Germany
G 23 Bodmin, United Kingdom
G 10 Bodø, Norway
8 B 12 Bodrum, Turkey
4 K 8 Boende, Democratic Republic of Congo
2 F 11 Boffa, Guinea
3 D 17 Bogale, Myanmar
9 O 20 Bogalusa, Louisiana, U.S.A.
4 J 4 Bogangolo, Central African Republic
8 K 10 Boğazliyan, Turkey
4 K 7 Bogbonga, Democratic Republic of Congo
0 L 4 Bogda Feng, China
0 L 4 Bogda Shan, China
E 12 Bogdanci, Macedonia (F.Y.R.O.M.)
2 C 3 Bogia, Papua New Guinea
L 23 Bognor Regis, United Kingdom
3 V 10 Bogo, Cameroon
7 R 2 Bogodukhovka, Kazakhstan
4 H 14 Bogor, Indonesia
8 I 7 Bogotá, Colombia
7 N 12 Bogotol, Russian Federation
7 O 12 Boguchany, Russian Federation
2 F 7 Bogué, Mauritania
1 W 7 Bohai Haixia, China
B 18 Bohemia, Czech Republic
L 21 Bohemian Forest, Germany/Czech Republic
D 19 Bohemian Massif, Czech Republic
E 13 Bohmte, Germany
1 V 4 Bohodukhiv, Ukraine
5 Q 6 Bohol, Philippines
0 M 5 Bois Blanc Island, Michigan, U.S.A.
6 I 11 Boise, Idaho, U.S.A.
9 G 16 Boise City, Oklahoma, U.S.A.
H 11 Boizenburg, Germany
J 15 Bojano, Italy
164 M 5 Bojnūrd, Iran
169 J 14 Bokaro, India
194 J 8 Bokatola, Democratic Republic of Congo
192 F 10 Boké, Guinea
85 A 20 Boknafjorden, Norway
194 G 10 Boko, Congo
194 G 10 Boko-Songho, Congo
194 J 5 Bokode, Democratic Republic of Congo
167 V 10 Bökönbaev, Kyrgyzstan
193 W 10 Bokoro, Chad
196 K 11 Bokspits, Botswana
212 J 5 Boku, Papua New Guinea
194 M 9 Bokwankusu, Democratic Republic of Congo
193 V 9 Bol, Chad
195 N 9 Bolaiti, Democratic Republic of Congo
79 N 3 Bolbec, France
100 L 11 Boldu, Romania
166 M 11 Boldumsaz, Turkmenistan
170 J 4 Bole, China
192 L 12 Bole, Ghana
194 K 8 Boleko, Democratic Republic of Congo
194 K 7 Bolena, Democratic Republic of Congo
93 E 15 Bolesławiec, Poland
192 M 11 Bolgatanga, Ghana
101 N 11 Bolhrad, Ukraine
171 Y 3 Boli, China
194 J 8 Bolia, Democratic Republic of Congo
175 N 3 Bolinao, Philippines
119 M 15 Bolivar, Missouri, U.S.A.
122 J 2 Bolivar, Tennessee, U.S.A.
140 B 9 Bolívar, Ecuador
138 I 4 Bolívar, Colombia
139 Q 5 Bolívar, Venezuela
141 J 19 Bolivia, South America
94 N 12 Boljevac, Serbia and Montenegro
79 T 13 Bollene, France
85 G 18 Bollnäs, Sweden
209 T 8 Bollon, Queensland, Australia
61 Q 13 Bollons Tablemount, Pacific Ocean
85 H 16 Bollstabruk, Sweden
85 E 24 Bolmen, Sweden
194 I 9 Bolobo, Democratic Republic of Congo
90 F 9 Bologna, Italy
140 F 13 Bolognesi, Peru
141 E 15 Bolognesi, Peru
156 F 7 Bologoye, Russian Federation
194 J 7 Bolomba, Democratic Republic of Congo
175 P 7 Bolong, Philippines
99 C 15 Bol'shakovo, Russian Federation
167 Z 5 Bol'shenarymskoye, Kazakhstan
156 J 7 Bol'shezemel'skaya Tundra, Russian Federation
157 O 9 Bol'shoy Porog, Russian Federation
82 J 7 Bolsward, Netherlands
81 T 3 Boltaña, Spain
77 J 17 Bolton, United Kingdom
158 G 8 Bolu, Turkey
212 G 6 Bolubolu, Papua New Guinea
84 A 9 Bolungarvik, Iceland
90 F 5 Bolzano, Italy
143 L 15 Bom Jesus da Lapa, Brazil
194 F 11 Boma, Democratic Republic of Congo
194 H 6 Bomassa, Congo
209 U 13 Bombala, New South Wales, Australia
80 G 8 Bombarral, Portugal
194 J 6 Bomboma, Democratic Republic of Congo
168 M 12 Bomdila, India
195 O 7 Bomili, Democratic Republic of Congo
85 A 19 Bømlo, Norway
164 F 4 Bonāb, Iran
127 S 11 Bonaire, Netherlands Antilles
126 G 10 Bonanza, Nicaragua
127 R 7 Bonao, Dominican Republic
208 I 3 Bonaparte Archipelago, Western Australia, Australia
115 Z 10 Bonavista, Newfoundland and Labrador, Canada
115 Y 10 Bonavista Bay, Newfoundland and Labrador, Canada
194 M 5 Bondo, Democratic Republic of Congo
192 L 12 Bondoukou, Côte d'Ivoire
192 L 10 Bondoukui, Burkina Faso
175 O 14 Bonerate, Indonesia
173 O 18 Bông Son, Vietnam
191 H 21 Bonga, Ethiopia
168 L 12 Bongaigaon, India
194 L 7 Bongandanga, Democratic Republic of Congo
193 V 11 Bongor, Chad
79 Y 15 Bonifacio, France
122 M 8 Bonifay, Florida, U.S.A.
60 L 5 Bonin Trench, Pacific Ocean
143 G 18 Bonito, Brazil
87 C 17 Bonn, Germany
79 P 9 Bonnat, France
116 I 5 Bonners Ferry, Idaho, U.S.A.
79 V 9 Bonneville, France
113 W 11 Bonnyville, Alberta, Canada
177 B 24 Bōno-misaki, Japan
173 O 21 Bonom Mhai, Vietnam
209 V 9 Bonshaw, New South Wales, Australia
174 M 11 Bontang, Indonesia
175 N 13 Bontosunggu, Indonesia
93 I 25 Bonyhád, Hungary
58 B 8 Booby Island, Seychelles
192 I 12 Boola, Guinea
123 Q 1 Boone, North Carolina, U.S.A.
122 J 3 Booneville, Mississippi, U.S.A.
121 T 7 Boonville, New York, U.S.A.
191 K 20 Boorama, Somalia
83 G 18 Boortmeerbeek, Belgium
191 O 19 Boosaaso, Somalia
64 M 8 Boothia Peninsula, Arctic Ocean
194 F 8 Booué, Gabon
87 D 19 Boppard, Germany
143 I 22 Boqueirão, Brazil
125 O 5 Boquillas del Carmen, Mexico
93 A 18 Bor, Czech Republic
94 N 12 Bor, Serbia and Montenegro
158 J 12 Bor, Turkey
191 E 22 Bor, Sudan
170 M 4 Bor-Üdzüür, Mongolia
215 S 9 Bora-Bora, French Polynesia
116 K 11 Borah Peak, Idaho, U.S.A.
85 E 22 Borås, Sweden
164 H 10 Borāzjān, Iran
142 F 11 Borba, Brazil
219 Q 14 Borchgrevink Coast, Antarctica
159 Q 7 Borçka, Turkey
78 M 11 Bordeaux, France
209 Q 12 Bordertown, South Australia, Australia
189 O 6 Bordj Bou Arréridj, Algeria
189 Q 9 Bordj Messaouda, Algeria
188 L 14 Bordj Mokhtar, Algeria
189 P 10 Bordj Omar Driss, Algeria
192 L 8 Boré, Mali
219 P 2 Borg Massif, Antarctica
84 D 10 Borgarfjördur, Iceland
84 A 11 Borgarnes, Iceland
82 N 8 Borger, Netherlands
119 H 17 Borger, Texas, U.S.A.
85 H 24 Borgholm, Sweden
91 M 20 Borgia, Italy
90 F 6 Borgo Valsugana, Italy
90 B 6 Borgomanero, Italy
156 F 9 Borisoglebsk, Russian Federation
197 Y 6 Boriziny, Madgascar
81 R 4 Borja, Spain
140 C 11 Borja, Peru
98 J 13 Borkavichy, Belarus
87 C 15 Borken, Germany
193 X 6 Borkou-Ennedi-Tibesti, Chad
86 C 10 Borkum, Germany
85 G 19 Borlänge, Sweden
90 E 5 Bormio, Italy
87 L 16 Borna, Germany
82 J 5 Borndiep, Netherlands
82 N 11 Borne, Netherlands
174 J 10 Borneo, Malaysia/Indonesia
85 F 26 Bornholm, Denmark
193 U 10 Borno, Nigeria
158 B 10 Bornova, Turkey
101 O 10 Borodino, Ukraine
101 O 3 Borodyanka, Ukraine
194 L 1 Boromata, Central African Republic
192 L 10 Boromo, Burkina Faso
175 Q 5 Borongan, Philippines
192 I 12 Borotou, Côte d'Ivoire
101 X 5 Borova, Ukraine
167 O 2 Borovskoy, Kazakhstan
209 O 3 Borroloola, Northern Territory, Australia
100 J 8 Borşa, Romania
84 K 6 Børselv, Norway
164 G 7 Borūjerd, Iran
101 Q 3 Boryspil', Ukraine
101 R 2 Borzna, Ukraine
157 S 14 Borzya, Russian Federation
91 B 17 Bosa, Italy
167 T 6 Bosaga, Kazakhstan
94 F 9 Bosanska Dubica, Bosnia and Herzegovina
94 F 9 Bosanska Gradiška, Bosnia and Herzegovina
94 E 11 Bosanski Petrovac, Bosnia and Herzegovina
171 R 13 Bose, China
94 H 10 Bosna, Bosnia and Herzegovina
94 G 11 Bosnia and Herzegovina, Europe
177 L 16 Bōsō-hantō, Japan
194 K 5 Bosobolo, Democratic Republic of Congo
158 D 7 Bosporus, Turkey
194 I 4 Bossangoa, Central African Republic
194 I 4 Bossembélé, Central African Republic
194 I 4 Bossentélé, Central African Republic
165 T 10 Bostan, Pakistan
170 K 5 Bosten Hu, China
77 L 18 Boston, United Kingdom
121 X 8 Boston, Massachusetts, U.S.A.
119 L 17 Boston Mountains, Arkansas, U.S.A.
169 B 15 Botad, India
209 V 12 Botany Bay, New South Wales, Australia
194 J 9 Botemola, Democratic Republic of Congo
96 I 9 Botev, Bulgaria
96 G 8 Botevgrad, Bulgaria
80 I 4 Boticas, Portugal
100 L 8 Botoşani, Romania
85 I 14 Botsmark, Sweden
196 K 9 Botswana, Africa
84 K 13 Bottenviken, Sweden
87 C 15 Bottrop, Germany
96 B 12 Botun, Macedonia (F.Y.R.O.M.)
189 P 7 Bou Aroua, Algeria
192 H 7 Boû Bleï'îne, Mauritania
188 F 9 Bou Izakarn, Morocco
189 N 6 Bou Saâda, Algeria
192 J 13 Bouaflé, Côte d'Ivoire
192 K 12 Bouaké, Côte d'Ivoire
194 H 4 Bouar, Central African Republic
188 K 8 Bouârfa, Morocco
194 J 4 Bouca, Central African Republic
194 I 5 Boudoua, Central African Republic
194 G 10 Bouenza, Congo
212 I 5 Bougainville, Papua New Guinea
193 O 6 Boughessa, Mali
192 I 10 Bougouni, Mali
188 L 7 Bougtob, Algeria
83 I 24 Bouillon, Belgium
189 N 5 Bouira, Algeria
188 C 11 Boujdour, Western Sahara
188 D 11 Boukra, Western Sahara
208 I 10 Boulder, Western Australia, Australia
117 J 20 Boulder City, Nevada, U.S.A.
188 I 7 Boulemane, Morocco
209 Q 6 Boulia, Queensland, Australia
79 O 1 Boulogne-sur-Mer, France
194 L 3 Boulouba, Central African Republic
188 H 8 Boumalne Dadès, Morocco
194 G 9 Boumango, Gabon
192 L 11 Bouna, Côte d'Ivoire
117 G 18 Boundary Peak, California, U.S.A.
192 J 11 Boundiali, Côte d'Ivoire
61 Y 14 Bounty Bay, Pitcairn Island
61 P 13 Bounty Islands, New Zealand
61 P 12 Bounty Trough, Pacific Ocean
213 P 14 Bourail, New Caledonia
79 U 9 Bourg-en-Bresse, France
79 W 10 Bourg-St-Maurice, France
79 P 10 Bourganeuf, France
79 Q 7 Bourges, France
79 R 7 Bourgogne, France
79 T 10 Bourgoin-Jallieu, France
209 S 9 Bourke, New South Wales, Australia
77 J 23 Bournemouth, United Kingdom
83 L 24 Bourscheid, Luxembourg
193 Z 10 Bourtoutou, Chad
117 K 23 Bouse, Arizona, U.S.A.
193 W 11 Bousso, Chad
83 H 18 Boutersem, Belgium
192 F 7 Boutilimit, Mauritania
63 M 21 Bouvetøya, Norway
193 Q 9 Bouza, Niger
116 I 8 Bovill, Idaho, U.S.A.
144 L 10 Bovril, Argentina
118 G 7 Bowbells, North Dakota, U.S.A.
209 U 5 Bowen, Queensland, Australia
117 O 24 Bowie, Arizona, U.S.A.
119 J 19 Bowie, Texas, U.S.A.
119 N 14 Bowling Green, Missouri, U.S.A.
120 J 14 Bowling Green, Kentucky, U.S.A.
120 M 10 Bowling Green, Ohio, U.S.A.
118 G 9 Bowman, North Dakota, U.S.A.
218 H 4 Bowman Coast, Antarctica
219 Y 10 Bowman Island, Antarctica
209 U 12 Bowral, New South Wales, Australia
83 K 15 Boxmeer, Netherlands
83 I 15 Boxtel, Netherlands
158 J 7 Boyabat, Turkey
138 J 6 Boyaca, Colombia
77 C 16 Boyle, Republic of Ireland
113 V 11 Boyle, Alberta, Canada
141 L 22 Boyuibe, Bolivia
158 B 11 Boz Dağlari, Turkey
158 C 13 Bozburun, Turkey
158 A 9 Bozcaada, Turkey
118 C 9 Bozeman, Montana, U.S.A.
171 U 9 Bozhou, China
158 G 13 Bozkir, Turkey
194 I 4 Bozoum, Central African Republic
159 N 12 Bozova, Turkey
158 E 9 Bozüyük, Turkey
90 E 8 Bozzolo, Italy
90 B 8 Bra, Italy
218 H 4 Brabant Island, Antarctica
83 F 19 Brabant Wallon, Belgium
94 E 13 Brač, Croatia
100 G 10 Brad, Romania
123 Q 12 Bradenton, Florida, U.S.A.
77 J 17 Bradford, United Kingdom
119 I 20 Brady, Texas, U.S.A.
76 J 4 Brae, United Kingdom
76 I 11 Braemar, United Kingdom
80 H 4 Braga, Portugal
80 H 4 Braga, Portugal
144 L 13 Bragado, Argentina
80 J 4 Bragança, Portugal
80 K 4 Bragança, Portugal
142 K 10 Bragança, Brazil
99 M 21 Brahin, Belarus
169 M 14 Brahmanbaria, Bangladesh
169 I 17 Brahmapur, India
168 M 12 Brahmaputra, India
77 G 19 Braich y Pwll, United Kingdom
100 M 11 Brăila, Romania
83 F 20 Braine-l'Alleud, Belgium
118 L 8 Brainerd, Minnesota, U.S.A.
86 E 11 Brake, Germany
192 F 7 Brâkna, Mauritania
86 E 13 Bramsche, Germany
63 A 16 Branco, Cape Verde
142 E 9 Branco, Brazil
196 G 9 Brandberg, Namibia
85 D 19 Brandbu, Norway
87 M 14 Brandenburg, Germany
86 L 13 Brandenburg, Germany
114 H 10 Brandon, Manitoba, Canada
196 K 13 Brandvlei, Republic of South Africa
123 P 9 Branford, Florida, U.S.A.
92 J 8 Braniewo, Poland
218 H 3 Bransfield Strait, Antarctica
92 N 11 Brańsk, Poland
122 M 7 Brantley, Alabama, U.S.A.
142 A 11 Brasil, Brazil
143 C 14 Brasiléia, Brazil
143 J 16 Brasília, Brazil
99 I 14 Braslaw, Belarus
100 K 11 Braşov, Romania
83 G 17 Brasschaat, Belgium
93 G 21 Bratislava, Slovakia
157 P 12 Bratsk, Russian Federation
157 P 12 Bratskoye Vodokhranilishche, Russian Federation
121 V 8 Brattleboro, Vermont, U.S.A.
101 O 11 Braţul Chilia, Romania
101 N 12 Braţul Sfântu Gheorghe, Romania
101 O 12 Braţul Sulina, Romania
89 Q 4 Braunau am Inn, Austria
87 I 15 Braunlage, Germany
86 I 13 Braunschweig, Germany
63 A 17 Brava, Cape Verde
117 J 24 Brawley, California, U.S.A.
115 P 1 Bray Island, Nunavut, Canada
142 H 13 Brazil, South America
120 J 11 Brazil, Indiana, U.S.A.
63 I 18 Brazil Basin, Atlantic Ocean
143 K 16 Brazilian Highlands, Brazil
119 J 19 Brazos, Texas, U.S.A.
194 H 10 Brazzaville, Congo
94 I 10 Brčko, Bosnia and Herzegovina
92 H 10 Brda, Poland
61 Y 15 Break im Hip, Pitcairn Island
211 A 24 Breaksea Island, New Zealand
210 K 6 Bream Bay, New Zealand
83 G 16 Brecht, Belgium
93 F 20 Břeclav, Czech Republic
83 H 15 Breda, Netherlands
196 K 15 Bredasdorp, Republic of South Africa
86 F 7 Bredstedt, Germany
83 J 17 Bree, Belgium
96 E 11 Bregalnica, Macedonia (F.Y.R.O.M.)
88 J 6 Bregenz, Austria
96 E 6 Bregovo, Bulgaria
84 A 10 Breida Fjörður, Iceland
84 D 11 Breiðdalsvik, Iceland
142 M 11 Brejo, Brazil
86 F 11 Bremen, Germany
86 F 11 Bremen, Germany
86 F 10 Bremerhaven, Germany
116 D 7 Bremerton, Washington, U.S.A.
86 G 10 Bremervörde, Germany
119 K 21 Brenham, Texas, U.S.A.
88 M 8 Brenner, Austria
90 E 6 Breno, Italy
77 M 21 Brentwood, United Kingdom
90 E 7 Brescia, Italy
83 D 16 Breskens, Netherlands
90 G 4 Bressanone, Italy
76 K 5 Bressay, United Kingdom
78 M 8 Bressuire, France
78 H 5 Brest, France
99 E 21 Brest, Belarus
99 G 20 Brestskaya Voblasts', Belarus
78 I 5 Bretagne, France
79 Q 3 Breteuil, France
119 O 21 Breton Sound, Louisiana, U.S.A.
87 F 22 Bretten, Germany
142 J 10 Breves, Brazil
209 T 9 Brewarrina, New South Wales, Australia
121 Z 5 Brewer, Maine, U.S.A.
116 G 6 Brewster, Washington, U.S.A.
122 L 8 Brewton, Alabama, U.S.A.
96 F 9 Breznik, Bulgaria
100 I 11 Brezoi, Romania

Country · Internal administrative region: State/Province/Territory/Dependent territory · Capital city · Mountain range/Undersea ridge · Mountain peak/Volcano/Seamount · Geographic feature · Headland/Point/Cape/Peninsula · Desert · Island/Island group · Antarctic base · Ocean · Sea · Bay/Gulf/Channel/Strait · Lake · Salt pan/Dry/Intermittent lake · River

194 L 4 **Bria**, Central African Republic
79 W 11 **Briançon**, France
126 I 13 **Bribri**, Costa Rica
100 M 7 **Briceni**, Moldova
77 I 22 **Bridgend**, United Kingdom
117 F 18 **Bridgeport**, California, U.S.A.
118 G 12 **Bridgeport**, Nebraska, U.S.A.
121 V 10 **Bridgeport**, Connecticut, U.S.A.
127 Y 10 **Bridgetown**, Barbados
208 G 12 **Bridgetown**, Western Australia, Australia
121 X 6 **Bridgton**, Maine, U.S.A.
77 I 22 **Bridgwater**, United Kingdom
77 L 16 **Bridlington**, United Kingdom
88 H 8 **Briel**, Switzerland
79 T 5 **Brienne-le-Château**, France
88 F 8 **Brienz**, Switzerland
91 L 16 **Brienza**, Italy
88 E 8 **Brienzer See**, Switzerland
88 E 10 **Brig**, Switzerland
117 M 14 **Brigham City**, Utah, U.S.A.
209 S 13 **Bright**, Victoria, Australia
77 L 23 **Brighton**, United Kingdom
123 R 12 **Brighton**, Florida, U.S.A.
211 E 25 **Brighton**, New Zealand
192 D 9 **Brikama**, Gambia
84 D 10 **Brimnes**, Iceland
91 O 16 **Brindisi**, Italy
79 R 11 **Brioude**, France
209 W 9 **Brisbane**, Queensland, Australia
77 J 22 **Bristol**, United Kingdom
123 N 8 **Bristol**, Florida, U.S.A.
123 Q 1 **Bristol**, Tennessee, U.S.A.
112 G 8 **Bristol Bay**, Alaska, U.S.A.
77 G 22 **Bristol Channel**, United Kingdom
113 Q 10 **British Columbia**, Canada
79 P 11 **Brive-la-Gaillarde**, France
81 P 2 **Briviesca**, Spain
93 F 19 **Brno**, Czech Republic
76 F 10 **Broadford**, United Kingdom
118 F 9 **Broadus**, Montana, U.S.A.
113 Z 12 **Broadview**, Saskatchewan, Canada
114 I 6 **Brochet**, Manitoba, Canada
115 Q 14 **Brockville**, Ontario, Canada
96 C 11 **Brod**, Macedonia (F.Y.R.O.M.)
92 J 10 **Brodnica**, Poland
100 J 4 **Brody**, Ukraine
209 R 10 **Broken Hill**, New South Wales, Australia
59 Q 8 **Broken Plateau**, Indian Ocean
139 X 6 **Brokopondo**, Suriname
85 C 23 **Brønderslev**, Denmark
192 M 12 **Brong-Ahafo**, Ghana
90 C 7 **Broni**, Italy
209 T 15 **Bronte Park**, Tasmania, Australia
174 M 6 **Brooke's Point**, Philippines
122 H 7 **Brookhaven**, Mississippi, U.S.A.
118 J 10 **Brookings**, South Dakota, U.S.A.
121 Q 14 **Brookneal**, Virginia, U.S.A.
112 J 3 **Brooks Range**, Alaska, U.S.A.
123 Q 10 **Brooksville**, Florida, U.S.A.
208 G 11 **Brookton**, Western Australia, Australia
208 I 4 **Broome**, Western Australia, Australia
100 K 8 **Broşteni**, Romania
169 N 22 **Brothers**, India
79 O 5 **Brou**, France
101 Q 3 **Brovary**, Ukraine
119 H 19 **Brownfield**, Texas, U.S.A.
118 B 7 **Browning**, Montana, U.S.A.
120 K 12 **Brownstown**, Indiana, U.S.A.
119 K 24 **Brownsville**, Texas, U.S.A.
119 J 20 **Brownwood**, Texas, U.S.A.
99 L 19 **Brozha**, Belarus
122 I 4 **Bruce**, Mississippi, U.S.A.
120 I 4 **Bruce Crossing**, Michigan, U.S.A.
87 F 22 **Bruchsal**, Germany
89 Q 7 **Bruck**, Austria
89 Y 4 **Bruck an der Leitha**, Austria
89 V 6 **Bruck an der Mur**, Austria
174 A 8 **Brueuh**, Indonesia
83 C 17 **Bruges**, Belgium
168 O 10 **Bruint**, India
120 G 4 **Brule**, Wisconsin, U.S.A.
83 G 24 **Brûly**, Belgium
143 M 15 **Brumado**, Brazil
82 L 12 **Brummen**, Netherlands
174 K 8 **Brunei**, Asia
174 L 8 **Brunei Bay**, Malaysia
90 G 4 **Brunico**, Italy
86 F 9 **Brunsbüttel**, Germany
119 M 14 **Brunswick**, Missouri, U.S.A.
121 X 6 **Brunswick**, Maine, U.S.A.
123 R 7 **Brunswick**, Georgia, U.S.A.
219 N 3 **Brunt Ice Shelf**, Antarctica
93 G 17 **Bruntál**, Czech Republic
209 T 15 **Bruny Island**, Tasmania, Australia
94 M 13 **Brus**, Serbia and Montenegro
118 G 13 **Brush**, Colorado, U.S.A.
88 K 10 **Brusio**, Switzerland
83 E 19 **Brussels**, Belgium
92 H 9 **Brusy**, Poland
101 O 4 **Brusyliv**, Ukraine
119 K 21 **Bryan**, Texas, U.S.A.
120 L 9 **Bryan**, Ohio, U.S.A.
218 J 8 **Bryan Coast**, Antarctica
101 Y 6 **Bryanka**, Ukraine
156 E 8 **Bryansk**, Russian Federation
210 J 7 **Brynderwyn**, New Zealand
123 P 2 **Bryson City**, North Carolina, U.S.A.
94 O 11 **Brza**, Serbia and Montenegro
93 G 15 **Brzeg**, Poland
191 K 25 **Bu'aale**, Somalia
215 U 1 **Buada Lagoon**, Nauru
212 L 6 **Buala**, Solomon Islands
189 T 8 **Bu'ayrāt al Hasūn**, Libya
192 E 10 **Buba**, Guinea-Bissau
163 S 2 **Bubiyān Island**, Kuwait
213 Y 11 **Buca**, Fiji
138 J 5 **Bucaramanga**, Colombia
91 K 16 **Buccino**, Italy
76 J 10 **Buchan Ness**, United Kingdom
121 P 14 **Buchanan**, Virginia, U.S.A.
192 H 13 **Buchanan**, Liberia
115 X 10 **Buchans**, Newfoundland and Labrador, Canada
100 J 13 **Bucharest**, Romania
121 Q 14 **Buckingham**, Virginia, U.S.A.
219 S 15 **Buckle Island**, Antarctica
93 G 19 **Bučovice**, Czech Republic
99 M 20 **Buda-Kashelyova**, Belarus
93 I 23 **Budapest**, Hungary
168 F 11 **Budaun**, India
219 X 11 **Budd Coast**, Antarctica
91 C 16 **Buddusò**, Italy
77 G 23 **Bude**, United Kingdom
122 H 7 **Bude**, Mississippi, U.S.A.
83 J 17 **Budel**, Netherlands
100 L 13 **Budeşti**, Romania
194 K 6 **Budjala**, Democratic Republic of Congo
95 I 16 **Budva**, Serbia and Montenegro
193 S 14 **Buea**, Cameroon
145 H 19 **Buen Pasto**, Argentina
144 I 12 **Buena Esperanza**, Argentina
119 E 14 **Buena Vista**, Colorado, U.S.A.
124 L 4 **Buenaventura**, Mexico
138 G 7 **Buenaventura**, Colombia
124 J 8 **Buenavista**, Mexico
144 M 12 **Buenos Aires**, Argentina
145 L 14 **Buenos Aires**, Argentina
124 M 6 **Búfalo**, Mexico
118 G 9 **Buffalo**, South Dakota, U.S.A.
118 E 10 **Buffalo**, Wyoming, U.S.A.
119 I 16 **Buffalo**, Oklahoma, U.S.A.
119 K 20 **Buffalo**, Texas, U.S.A.
121 Q 8 **Buffalo**, New York, U.S.A.
113 W 10 **Buffalo Narrows**, Saskatchewan, Canada
100 K 12 **Buftea**, Romania
92 N 12 **Bug**, Poland
138 H 7 **Buga**, Colombia
195 S 8 **Bugala Island**, Uganda
193 R 12 **Bugana**, Nigeria
166 I 13 **Bugdayli**, Turkmenistan
62 O 5 **Bugio**, Madeira
156 K 6 **Bugrino**, Russian Federation
160 K 2 **Buḥayrat al Asad**, Syria
161 S 8 **Buḥayrat ar Razāzah**, Iraq
161 S 6 **Buḥayrat ath Tharthār**, Iraq
160 I 5 **Buḥayrat Qaṭṭinah**, Syria
116 J 13 **Buhl**, Idaho, U.S.A.
100 L 9 **Buhuşi**, Romania
77 I 20 **Builth Wells**, United Kingdom
212 J 5 **Buin**, Papua New Guinea
171 U 3 **Buir Nur**, China
82 L 6 **Buitenpost**, Netherlands
196 K 9 **Buitepos**, Namibia
95 N 15 **Bujanovac**, Serbia and Montenegro
81 T 4 **Bujaraloz**, Spain
195 Q 10 **Bujumbura**, Burundi
212 B 6 **Buk**, Papua New Guinea
212 I 4 **Buka**, Papua New Guinea
195 O 13 **Bukama**, Democratic Republic of Congo
195 Q 9 **Bukavu**, Democratic Republic of Congo
167 O 12 **Bukhara**, Uzbekistan
167 O 12 **Bukhoro Wiloyati**, Uzbekistan
175 N 12 **Bukit Gandadiwata**, Indonesia
174 L 10 **Bukit Liangpran**, Indonesia
174 E 12 **Bukit Masurai**, Indonesia
174 K 11 **Bukit Raya**, Indonesia
174 D 11 **Bukittinggi**, Indonesia
195 S 8 **Bukoba**, Tanzania
175 T 12 **Bula**, Indonesia
88 G 6 **Bülach**, Switzerland
175 P 4 **Bulan**, Philippines
159 N 8 **Bulancak**, Turkey
193 S 10 **Bulangu**, Nigeria
159 R 10 **Bulanik**, Turkey
190 E 11 **Bûlâq**, Egypt
197 O 8 **Bulawayo**, Zimbabwe
167 R 1 **Bulayevo**, Kazakhstan
169 D 16 **Buldana**, India
171 P 3 **Bulgan**, Mongolia
171 O 5 **Bulgan**, Mongolia
171 P 3 **Bulgan**, Mongolia
171 Q 5 **Bulgan**, Mongolia
96 G 10 **Bulgaria**, Europe
175 S 10 **Buli**, Indonesia
191 L 19 **Bullaxaar**, Somalia
88 C 9 **Bulle**, Switzerland
211 G 17 **Buller**, New Zealand
211 K 14 **Bulls**, New Zealand
123 T 5 **Bulls Bay**, South Carolina, U.S.A.
212 D 5 **Bulolo**, Papua New Guinea
91 C 17 **Bultei**, Italy
194 L 8 **Bulukutu**, Democratic Republic of Congo
157 S 8 **Bulun**, Russian Federation
194 J 10 **Bulungu**, Democratic Republic of Congo
194 L 11 **Bulungu**, Democratic Republic of Congo
194 J 12 **Bumba**, Democratic Republic of Congo
194 L 6 **Bumba**, Democratic Republic of Congo
194 J 9 **Buna**, Democratic Republic of Congo
195 W 6 **Buna**, Kenya
195 R 8 **Bunazi**, Tanzania
208 G 12 **Bunbury**, Western Australia, Australia
195 T 9 **Bunda**, Tanzania
209 W 7 **Bundaberg**, Queensland, Australia
168 D 13 **Bundi**, India
191 D 22 **Bunduqiya**, Sudan
196 H 2 **Bungo**, Angola
177 D 21 **Bungo-suidō**, Japan
193 T 10 **Buni-Yadi**, Nigeria
195 R 7 **Bunia**, Democratic Republic of Congo
195 O 14 **Bunkeya**, Democratic Republic of Congo
119 N 20 **Bunkie**, Louisiana, U.S.A.
123 R 9 **Bunnell**, Florida, U.S.A.
193 S 11 **Bununu**, Nigeria
158 K 10 **Bünyan**, Turkey
193 P 10 **Bunza**, Nigeria
173 N 20 **Buôn Mê Thuôt**, Vietnam
157 S 7 **Buorkhaya Guba**, Russian Federation
190 G 10 **Bûr Safâga**, Egypt
191 N 19 **Buraan**, Somalia
191 B 19 **Buram**, Sudan
167 Z 5 **Buran**, Kazakhstan
191 M 20 **Burao**, Somalia
160 I 7 **Burāq**, Syria
163 P 5 **Buraydah**, Saudi Arabia
117 G 22 **Burbank**, California, U.S.A.
209 T 4 **Burdekin**, Queensland, Australia
83 I 20 **Burdinne**, Belgium
158 E 12 **Burdur**, Turkey
63 E 21 **Burdwood Bank**, Atlantic Ocean
191 G 21 **Burē**, Ethiopia
191 H 19 **Burē**, Ethiopia
165 X 10 **Burewala**, Pakistan
84 J 7 **Burfjord**, Norway
86 K 13 **Burg**, Germany
96 M 9 **Burgas**, Bulgaria
96 M 9 **Burgas**, Bulgaria
123 V 3 **Burgaw**, North Carolina, U.S.A.
88 E 7 **Burgdorf**, Switzerland
116 J 9 **Burgdorf**, Idaho, U.S.A.
89 X 8 **Burgenland**, Austria
115 X 11 **Burgeo**, Newfoundland and Labrador, Canada
83 D 14 **Burgh-Haamstede**, Netherlands
87 L 24 **Burghausen**, Germany
91 I 22 **Burgio**, Italy
81 O 3 **Burgos**, Spain
85 I 23 **Burgsvik**, Sweden
169 E 16 **Burhanpur**, India
175 P 4 **Burias**, Philippines
173 J 18 **Buriram**, Thailand
209 R 4 **Burke and Wills Roadhouse**, Queensland, Australia
218 J 9 **Burke Island**, Antarctica
209 Q 4 **Burketown**, Queensland, Australia
192 M10 **Burkina Faso**, Africa
166 I 4 **Burlin**, Kazakhstan
118 N 13 **Burlington**, Iowa, U.S.A.
119 G 14 **Burlington**, Colorado, U.S.A.
121 V 6 **Burlington**, Vermont, U.S.A.
211 H 17 **Burnbrae**, New Zealand
119 J 21 **Burnet**, Texas, U.S.A.
117 E 14 **Burney**, California, U.S.A.
209 S 15 **Burnie**, Tasmania, Australia
170 L 3 **Burqin**, China
209 P 11 **Burra**, South Australia, Australia
95 K 18 **Burrel**, Albania
81 T 7 **Burriana**, Spain
81 U 6 **Burriana**, Spain
158 D 8 **Bursa**, Turkey
175 Q 12 **Buru**, Indonesia
167 T 8 **Burulbaytal**, Kazakhstan
195 Q 9 **Burundi**, Africa
195 Q 10 **Bururi**, Burundi
77 M 20 **Bury St Edmunds**, United Kingdom
101 T 2 **Buryn'**, Ukraine
194 K 6 **Busa Modanda**, Democratic Republic of Congo
194 L 8 **Busanga**, Democratic Republic of Congo
164 I 11 **Būshehr**, Iran
164 H 11 **Būshehr**, Iran
195 Q 8 **Bushenyi**, Uganda
95 L 17 **Bushtricë**, Albania
194 L 6 **Businga**, Democratic Republic of Congo
93 K 16 **Busko-Zdrój**, Poland
208 F 12 **Busselton**, Western Australia, Australia
100 K 11 **Buşteni**, Romania
90 C 7 **Busto Arsizio**, Italy
175 N 4 **Busuanga**, Philippines
175 N 5 **Busuanga**, Philippines
86 F 9 **Büsum**, Germany
195 N 6 **Buta**, Democratic Republic of Congo
173 G 26 **Butang Group**, Thailand
195 Q 9 **Butare**, Rwanda
214 D 1 **Butaritari**, Kiribati
121 P 10 **Butler**, Pennsylvania, U.S.A.
122 J 6 **Butler**, Alabama, U.S.A.
123 O 6 **Butler**, Georgia, U.S.A.
175 P 13 **Buton**, Indonesia
76 F 8 **Butt of Lewis**, United Kingdom
118 B 9 **Butte**, Montana, U.S.A.
174 D 8 **Butterworth**, Malaysia
114 K 5 **Button Bay**, Manitoba, Canada
115 T 5 **Button Islands**, Nunavut, Canada
175 Q 6 **Butuan**, Philippines
168 H 12 **Butwal**, Nepal
87 F 18 **Butzbach**, Germany
191 M 23 **Buulobarde**, Somalia
191 K 26 **Buur Gaabo**, Somalia
191 L 24 **Buurhabaka**, Somalia
171 O 4 **Buyant**, Mongolia
99 K 21 **Buynavichy**, Belarus
96 M 12 **Büyükkarıştiran**, Turkey
100 L 12 **Buzău**, Romania
197 R 8 **Buzi**, Mozambique
156 H 10 **Buzuluk**, Russian Federation
167 P 4 **Buzuluk**, Kazakhstan
99 H 15 **Byahoml'**, Belarus
96 J 7 **Byala**, Bulgaria
96 N 8 **Byala**, Bulgaria
99 L 17 **Byalynichy**, Belarus
99 L 19 **Byarezina**, Belarus
99 G 20 **Byaroza**, Belarus
93 N 15 **Bychawa**, Poland
92 H 11 **Bydgoszcz**, Poland
99 J 15 **Byerazino**, Belarus
99 K 17 **Byerazino**, Belarus
99 L 15 **Byeshankovichy**, Belarus
85 J 14 **Bygdeå**, Sweden
85 B 21 **Bygland**, Norway
99 M 18 **Bykhaw**, Belarus
85 B 20 **Bykle**, Norway
117 O 23 **Bylas**, Arizona, U.S.A.
84 I 13 **Byskeälven**, Sweden
93 J 19 **Bystra**, Slovakia
93 I 17 **Bytom**, Poland
92 G 8 **Bytów**, Poland
195 Q 9 **Byumba**, Rwanda
92 K 12 **Bzura**, Poland

C

173 L 23 **Ca Mau**, Vietnam
196 H 4 **Caala**, Angola
143 G 20 **Caazapá**, Paraguay
141 D 18 **Caballas**, Peru
140 H 11 **Caballococha**, Peru
175 O 3 **Cabanatuan**, Philippines
94 C 8 **Čabar**, Slovenia
94 C 8 **Čabar**, Croatia
191 K 19 **Cabdul Qaadir**, Somalia
141 L 21 **Cabezas**, Bolivia
138 K 3 **Cabimas**, Venezuela
196 F 1 **Cabinda**, Angola
196 F 1 **Cabinda**, Angola
120 G 4 **Cable**, Wisconsin, U.S.A.
144 F 9 **Cabo Bascuñán**, Chile
127 Q 8 **Cabo Beata**, Dominican Republic
126 G 13 **Cabo Blanco**, Costa Rica
145 I 20 **Cabo Blanco**, Argentina
145 H 23 **Cabo Buen Tiempo**, Argentina
127 R 6 **Cabo Cabron**, Dominican Republic
126 G 9 **Cabo Camarón**, Honduras
80 F 8 **Cabo Carvoeiro**, Portugal
125 Z 9 **Cabo Catoche**, Mexico
124 F 3 **Cabo Colonet**, Mexico
145 M 15 **Cabo Corrientes**, Argentina
124 M 11 **Cabo Corrientes**, Mexico
126 H 5 **Cabo Corrientes**, Cuba
138 G 6 **Cabo Corrientes**, Colombia
126 L 6 **Cabo Cruz**, Cuba
145 I 22 **Cabo Dañoso**, Argentina
81 U 9 **Cabo de la Nao**, Spain
138 J 1 **Cabo de la Vela**, Colombia
81 T 11 **Cabo de Palos**, Spain
80 L 1 **Cabo de Penas**, Spain
81 U 9 **Cabo de San Antonio**, Spain
80 H 12 **Cabo de Santa Maria**, Portugal
197 Q 11 **Cabo de Santa Maria**, Mozambique
196 F 5 **Cabo de Santa Marta**, Angola
142 O 13 **Cabo de Santo Agostinho**, Brazil
143 M 18 **Cabo de São Tomé**, Brazil
80 G 12 **Cabo de São Vincent**, Portugal
80 G 11 **Cabo de Sines**, Portugal
197 U 3 **Cabo Delgado**, Mozambique
197 U 4 **Cabo Delgado**, Mozambique
145 I 19 **Cabo Dos Bahías**, Argentina
127 S 7 **Cabo Engaño**, Dominican Republic
80 G 10 **Cabo Espichel**, Portugal
127 P 8 **Cabo Falso**, Dominican Republic
80 G 2 **Cabo Fisterra**, Spain
126 I 9 **Cabo Gracias á Dios**, Nicaragua
81 T 10 **Cabo Huertas**, Spain
144 F 13 **Cabo Humos**, Chile
127 Q 6 **Cabo Isabela**, Dominican Republic
127 N 5 **Cabo Lucrecia**, Cuba
81 P 1 **Cabo Machichaco**, Spain
138 G 5 **Cabo Marzo**, Colombia
81 O 1 **Cabo Mayor**, Spain
142 J 8 **Cabo Norte**, Brazil
142 I 7 **Cabo Orange**, Brazil
80 I 1 **Cabo Ortegal**, Spain
140 E 9 **Cabo Pantoja**, Peru
145 F 24 **Cabo Pilar**, Chile
124 E 2 **Cabo Punta Banda**, Mexico
145 E 17 **Cabo Quedal**, Chile
145 E 18 **Cabo Quilán**, Chile
145 J 19 **Cabo Raso**, Argentina
61 Z 4 **Cabo Roggewein**, Easter Island
125 S 10 **Cabo Rojo**, Mexico
81 O 13 **Cabo Sacratif**, Spain
126 H 5 **Cabo San Antonio**, Cuba
145 I 25 **Cabo San Diego**, Argentina
145 H 22 **Cabo San Francisco de Paula**, Argentina
193 S 15 **Cabo San Juan**, Equator[ial] Guinea
124 H 8 **Cabo San Lázaro**, Mexico
124 J 9 **Cabo San Lucas**, Mexico
124 F 3 **Cabo San Quintín**, Mexico
126 F 12 **Cabo Santa Elena**, Costa Rica
145 E 23 **Cabo Santiago**, Chile
80 H 3 **Cabo Silleiro**, Spain
61 Y 5 **Cabo Sur**, Easter Island
80 K 14 **Cabo Trafalgar**, Spain
145 I 20 **Cabo Tres Puntas**, Argentina
145 H 24 **Cabo Vírgenes**, Argentina
209 W 8 **Caboolture**, Queensland, Australia
124 I 3 **Caborca**, Mexico
115 W 11 **Cabot Strait**, Nova Scoti[a], Canada
91 B 17 **Cabras**, Italy
81 Y 9 **Cabrera**, Spain
127 R 6 **Cabrera**, Dominican Republic
113 X 13 **Cabri**, Saskatchewan, Canada
142 N 13 **Cabrobó**, Brazil
139 O 5 **Cabruta**, Venezuela
94 K 12 **Čačak**, Serbia and Montenegro
143 H 22 **Cacapava do Sul**, Brazil
80 K 8 **Cáceres**, Spain
143 G 16 **Cáceres**, Brazil
192 D 9 **Cacheu**, Guinea-Bissau
144 I 6 **Cachi**, Argentina
142 H 13 **Cachimbo**, Brazil
196 I 4 **Cachingues**, Angola
142 H 11 **Cachoeirinha**, Brazil
143 M 18 **Cachoeiro de Itapemirim**, Brazil
141 J 15 **Cachuela Esperanza**, Bolivia
192 E 10 **Cacine**, Guinea-Bissau
196 J 3 **Cacolo**, Angola
196 F 1 **Cacongo**, Angola
143 I 17 **Caçu**, Brazil
196 G 2 **Cacuaco**, Angola
81 Y 3 **Cadaqués**, Spain
120 L 7 **Cadillac**, Michigan, U.S.A.
175 P 5 **Cadiz**, Philippines
80 K 13 **Cádiz**, Spain
78 M 4 **Caen**, France
77 H 18 **Caernarfon**, United Kingdom

Country · Internal administrative region: State/Province/Territory/Dependent territory · Capital city · Mountain range/Undersea ridge · Mountain peak/Volcano/Seamount · Geographic feature · Headland/Point/Cape/Peninsula · Desert · Island/Island group · Antarctic base · Ocean · Sea · Bay/Gulf/Channel/Strait · Lake · Salt pan/Dry/Intermittent lake · R

77 G 18 Caernarfon Bay, United Kingdom
143 M 15 Caetité, Brazil
144 I 7 Cafayate, Argentina
175 Q 6 Cagayan de Oro, Philippines
91 B 19 Cagliari, Italy
127 T 7 Caguas, Puerto Rico
196 G 6 Cahama, Angola
77 D 20 Caher, Republic of Ireland
77 A 20 Cahersiveen, Republic of Ireland
77 F 19 Cahore Point, Republic of Ireland
79 P 12 Cahors, France
140 C 12 Cahuapanas, Peru
101 N 10 Cahul, Moldova
173 L 24 Cai Nuoc, Vietnam
196 L 3 Caianda, Angola
143 I 16 Caiapônia, Brazil
126 K 4 Caibarién, Cuba
142 O 12 Caicó, Brazil
127 P 5 Caicos Islands, Turks and Caicos Islands
127 O 5 Caicos Passage, The Bahamas
208 K 10 Caiguna, Western Australia, Australia
142 H 11 Caima, Brazil
219 N 4 Caird Coast, Antarctica
209 T 3 Cairns, Queensland, Australia
190 F 8 Cairo, Egypt
120 H 14 Cairo, Illinois, U.S.A.
123 O 8 Cairo, Georgia, U.S.A.
196 G 5 Caitou, Angola
196 I 6 Caiundo, Angola
140 B 12 Cajamarca, Peru
140 B 13 Cajamarca, Peru
142 N 12 Cajazeiras, Brazil
94 K 12 Čajetina, Serbia and Montenegro
171 O 8 Caka, China
94 E 6 Čakovec, Croatia
193 R 14 Calabar, Nigeria
139 N 4 Calabozo, Venezuela
91 M 19 Calabria, Italy
141 I 20 Calacoto, Bolivia
100 G 13 Calafat, Romania
145 G 23 Calafate, Argentina
81 R 3 Calahorra, Spain
196 J 7 Calai, Angola
79 P 1 Calais, France
121 Z 5 Calais, Maine, U.S.A.
142 E 13 Calama, Brazil
144 G 5 Calama, Chile
138 I 3 Calamar, Colombia
138 J 8 Calamar, Colombia
100 H 10 Călan, Romania
196 H 2 Calandula, Angola
174 B 8 Calang, Indonesia
189 X 8 Calanscio Sand Sea, Libya
175 O 4 Calapan, Philippines
100 M 13 Călăraşi, Romania
101 N 8 Călăraşi, Moldova
81 R 5 Calatayud, Spain
175 P 4 Calauag, Philippines
175 O 1 Calayan, Philippines
175 Q 5 Calbayog, Philippines
87 J 14 Calbe, Germany
142 I 9 Calçoene, Brazil
142 I 8 Calçoene, Brazil
169 L 15 Calcutta, India
80 G 8 Caldas da Rainha, Portugal
144 F 8 Caldera, Chile
159 T 10 Caldiran, Turkey
119 J 16 Caldwell, Kansas, U.S.A.
122 L 5 Calera, Alabama, U.S.A.
144 F 3 Caleta Buena, Chile
144 F 4 Caleta Lobos, Chile
145 I 20 Caleta Olivia, Argentina
117 J 24 Calexico, California, U.S.A.
113 V 15 Calgary, Alberta, Canada
123 N 3 Calhoun, Georgia, U.S.A.
138 G 7 Cali, Colombia
169 D 22 Calicut, India
117 G 21 Caliente, California, U.S.A.
117 K 18 Caliente, Nevada, U.S.A.
117 E 20 California, U.S.A.
159 Y 9 Cälilabad, Azerbaijan
117 J 24 Calipatria, California, U.S.A.
91 L 16 Calitri, Italy
125 Y 11 Calkini, Mexico
141 C 16 Callao, Peru
209 W 8 Caloundra, Queensland, Australia
91 K 23 Caltagirone, Italy
91 J 22 Caltanissetta, Italy
196 G 3 Calulo, Angola
196 L 4 Calunda, Angola
196 J 6 Calunga, Angola
196 G 5 Caluquembe, Angola
191 O 18 Caluula, Somalia
79 Y 14 Calvi, France
196 K 14 Calvinia, Republic of South Africa
172 N 12 Câm Pha, Vietnam
173 O 20 Cam Ranh, Vietnam
143 N 15 Camaçari, Brazil
125 O 8 Camacho, Mexico
196 F 5 Camacuio, Angola
196 I 4 Camacupa, Angola
126 L 5 Camagüey, Cuba
143 N 15 Camamu, Brazil
141 F 19 Camaná, Peru
143 H 17 Camapuã, Brazil
143 I 22 Camaquã, Brazil
62 N 5 Câmara de Lobos, Madeira
145 I 19 Camarones, Argentina
115 U 12 Cambellton, New Brunswick, Canada
173 K 20 Cambodia, Asia
79 R 2 Cambrai, France
77 H 21 Cambrian Mtns, United Kingdom
77 M 20 Cambridge, United Kingdom
121 T 13 Cambridge, Maryland, U.S.A.
121 O 11 Cambridge, Ohio, U.S.A.
210 L 10 Cambridge, New Zealand
113 U 3 Cambridge Bay, Nunavut, Canada
196 K 1 Cambulo, Angola
119 M 18 Camden, Arkansas, U.S.A.
122 L 6 Camden, Alabama, U.S.A.
123 S 4 Camden, South Carolina, U.S.A.
209 U 12 Camden, New South Wales, Australia
196 K 3 Cameia, Angola
117 M 20 Cameron, Arizona, U.S.A.
119 M 21 Cameron, Louisiana, U.S.A.
120 F 5 Cameron, Wisconsin, U.S.A.
211 A 25 Cameron Mountains, New Zealand
193 T 14 Cameroon, Africa
142 J 10 Cametá, Brazil
158 B 12 Camiçi Gölü, Turkey
175 P 1 Camiguin, Philippines
175 Q 6 Camiguin, Philippines
123 O 7 Camilla, Georgia, U.S.A.
144 F 2 Camiña, Chile
80 H 3 Caminha, Portugal
141 L 22 Camiri, Bolivia
196 K 2 Camissombo, Angola
142 M 10 Camocim, Brazil
209 P 5 Camooweal, Queensland, Australia
169 O 24 Camorta, India
117 M 22 Camp Verde, Arizona, U.S.A.
126 F 10 Campamento, Honduras
91 K 15 Campania, Italy
120 M 11 Campbell Hill, Ohio, U.S.A.
61 O 13 Campbell Island, New Zealand
173 F 22 Campbell Island, Myanmar
61 O 12 Campbell Plateau, Pacific Ocean
113 R 14 Campbell River, British Columbia, Canada
120 K 14 Campbellsville, Kentucky, U.S.A.
77 F 14 Campbeltown, United Kingdom
125 Y 12 Campeche, Mexico
125 X 11 Campeche, Mexico
80 L 10 Campillo de Llerena, Spain
142 O 12 Campina Grande, Brazil
143 K 19 Campinas, Brazil
193 T 15 Campo, Cameroon
143 M 14 Campo Formoso, Brazil
144 K 7 Campo Gallo, Argentina
143 H 18 Campo Grande, Brazil
143 I 19 Campo Mourão, Brazil
143 G 15 Campo Novo de Parecis, Brazil
139 N 6 Campo Troco, Colombia
138 H 8 Campoalegre, Colombia
91 J 14 Campobasso, Italy
91 H 22 Campobello di Mazara, Italy
143 M 18 Campos, Brazil
143 K 15 Campos Belos, Brazil
100 J 11 Câmpulung, Romania
113 V 12 Camrose, Alberta, Canada
158 B 8 Can, Turkey
173 M 23 Cân Tho, Vietnam
113 Q 10 Canada, North America
65 O 4 Canada Basin, Arctic Ocean
119 H 17 Canadian, Texas, U.S.A.
119 I 17 Canadian, Texas, U.S.A.
65 P 4 Canadian Abyssal Plain, Arctic Ocean
158 A 8 Canakkale, Turkey
97 K 14 Çanakkale, Turkey
145 G 26 Canal Ballenero, Chile
142 I 9 Canal do Norte, Brazil
113 U 13 Canal Flats, British Columbia, Canada
141 A 18 Canal Isabela, Ecuador
145 E 22 Canal Ladrillero, Chile
145 F 19 Canal Moraleda, Chile
213 P 14 Canala, New Caledonia
144 I 13 Canalejas, Argentina
124 J 3 Cananea, Mexico
140 B 10 Cañar, Ecuador
140 B 10 Cañar, Ecuador
62 L 11 Canary Islands, Spain
125 N 8 Canatlán, Mexico
80 K 7 Cañaveral, Spain
143 N 16 Canavieiras, Brazil
90 G 5 Canazei, Italy
209 U 12 Canberra, Australian Capital Territory, Australia
117 E 14 Canby, California, U.S.A.
125 Z 10 Cancún, Mexico
158 I 9 Candir, Turkey
175 O 2 Candon, Philippines
144 N 13 Canelones, Uruguay
144 N 12 Canelones, Uruguay
81 R 7 Cañete, Spain
145 E 15 Cañete, Chile
141 E 17 Cangallo, Peru
196 J 5 Cangamba, Angola
196 H 3 Cangandala, Angola
80 K 1 Cangas del Narcea, Spain
196 J 5 Cangombe, Angola
196 J 4 Cangumbe, Angola
171 U 7 Cangzhou, China
115 S 8 Caniapiscau, Québec, Canada
91 J 23 Canicatti, Italy
158 K 7 Canik Dağlari, Turkey
142 N 11 Canindé, Brazil
218 K 9 Canisteo Peninsula, Antarctica
158 I 8 Cankiri, Turkey
209 U 13 Cann River, Victoria, Australia
76 E 11 Canna, United Kingdom
169 D 22 Cannanore, India
169 B 23 Cannanore Islands, India
79 W 14 Cannes, France
139 N 8 Caño Colorado, Colombia
143 I 22 Canoas, Brazil
143 I 20 Canoinhas, Brazil
119 F 15 Canon City, Colorado, U.S.A.
115 W 12 Canso, Nova Scotia, Canada
141 D 16 Canta, Peru
81 O 1 Cantabria, Spain
142 F 11 Cantagalo, Brazil
211 G 20 Canterbury, New Zealand
77 N 22 Canterbury, United Kingdom
211 H 21 Canterbury Bight, New Zealand
211 G 20 Canterbury Plains, New Zealand
175 R 6 Cantilan, Philippines
80 L 12 Cantillana, Spain
142 M 13 Canto do Buriti, Brazil
121 T 6 Canton, New York, U.S.A.
121 O 10 Canton, Ohio, U.S.A.
121 S 9 Canton, Pennsylvania, U.S.A.
122 I 5 Canton, Mississippi, U.S.A.
123 O 4 Canton, Georgia, U.S.A.
112 K 6 Cantwell, Alaska, U.S.A.
142 F 11 Canumã, Brazil
142 D 12 Canutama, Brazil
118 C 10 Canyon, Wyoming, U.S.A.
119 H 17 Canyon, Texas, U.S.A.
118 C 8 Canyon Ferry Lake, Montana, U.S.A.
172 M 10 Cao Bằng, Vietnam
196 H 2 Caombo, Angola
188 B 13 Cap Barbas, Western Sahara
192 E 11 Cap Boffa, Guinea
189 R 5 Cap Bon, Tunisia
189 O 5 Cap Bougaroûn, Algeria
81 Y 3 Cap de Creus, Spain
189 O 5 Cap de Fer, Algeria
81 Y 7 Cap de Formentor, Spain
78 K 2 Cap de la Hague, France
81 Y 8 Cap de ses Salines, Spain
81 Z 7 Cap des Freu, Spain
188 E 10 Cap Draâ, Morocco
78 K 4 Cap Fréhel, France
127 P 6 Cap-Haïtien, Haiti
115 R 5 Cap Hopes Advance, Québec, Canada
188 D 10 Cap Juby, Morocco
194 D 8 Cap Lopez, Gabon
188 F 8 Cap Rhir, Morocco
119 G 20 Cap Rock Escarpment, Texas, U.S.A.
192 E 11 Cap Verga, Guinea
192 D 8 Cap Vert, Senegal
115 P 4 Cap Wolstenholme, Québec, Canada
196 J 2 Capaia, Angola
143 J 19 Capão Bonito, Brazil
219 Q 14 Cape Adare, Antarctica
196 K 15 Cape Agulhas, Republic of South Africa
58 K 15 Cape Ann, Indian Ocean
158 J 15 Cape Apostolos Andreas, Cyprus
158 G 15 Cape Arnaoutis, Cyprus
209 P 1 Cape Arnhem, Northern Territory, Australia
113 R 3 Cape Baring, Northwest Territories, Canada
209 T 14 Cape Barren Island, Tasmania, Australia
210 L 7 Cape Barrier, New Zealand
63 M 18 Cape Basin, Atlantic Ocean
113 Q 3 Cape Bathurst, Northwest Territories, Canada
115 X 8 Cape Bauld, Newfoundland and Labrador, Canada
58 L 15 Cape Boothby, Indian Ocean
115 X 12 Cape Breton Island, Nova Scotia, Canada
210 J 5 Cape Brett, New Zealand
174 M 6 Cape Buliluyan, Philippines
218 L 12 Cape Burks, Antarctica
209 W 9 Cape Byron, New South Wales, Australia
175 O 4 Cape Calavite, Philippines
211 J 17 Cape Campbell, New Zealand
123 S 11 Cape Canaveral, Florida, U.S.A.
123 S 11 Cape Canaveral, Florida, U.S.A.
209 O 12 Cape Catastrophe, South Australia, Australia
121 T 14 Cape Charles, Virginia, U.S.A.
121 T 14 Cape Charles, Virginia, U.S.A.
219 R 14 Cape Cheetham, Antarctica
64 L 12 Cape Chidley, Arctic Ocean
169 G 19 Cape Chirala, India
114 L 6 Cape Churchill, Manitoba, Canada
77 B 21 Cape Clear, Republic of Ireland
192 M 14 Cape Coast, Ghana
121 Y 8 Cape Cod, Massachusetts, U.S.A.
121 X 8 Cape Cod Bay, Massachusetts, U.S.A.
65 Q 9 Cape Columbia, Arctic Ocean
196 J 14 Cape Columbine, Republic of South Africa
210 L 7 Cape Colville, New Zealand
169 E 24 Cape Comorin, India
112 G 8 Cape Constantine, Alaska, U.S.A.
113 Q 14 Cape Cook, British Columbia, Canada
123 Q 13 Cape Coral, Florida, U.S.A.
209 O 3 Cape Crawford, Northern Territory, Australia
212 E 5 Cape Cretin, Papua New Guinea
113 P 3 Cape Dalhousie, Northwest Territories, Canada
219 X 5 Cape Darnley, Antarctica
218 K 5 Cape Deacon, Antarctica
196 I 12 Cape Dernberg, Namibia
145 L 23 Cape Dolphin, Falkland Islands
115 P 3 Cape Dorset, Nunavut, Canada
115 T 1 Cape Dyer, Nunavut, Canada
211 H 15 Cape Farewell, New Zealand
123 V 4 Cape Fear, North Carolina, U.S.A.
218 K 5 Cape Fiske, Antarctica
116 C 5 Cape Flattery, Washington, U.S.A.
209 T 2 Cape Flattery, Queensland, Australia
208 L 2 Cape Ford, Northern Territory, Australia
211 F 17 Cape Foulwind, New Zealand
219 T 14 Cape Freshfield, Antarctica
196 F 7 Cape Fria, Namibia
158 H 15 Cape Gata, Cyprus
119 O 15 Cape Girardeau, Missouri, U.S.A.
212 C 3 Cape Girgir, Papua New Guinea
219 X 13 Cape Goodenough, Antarctica
219 U 14 Cape Gray, Antarctica
158 I 15 Cape Greko, Cyprus
209 S 1 Cape Grenville, Queensland, Australia
212 I 4 Cape Hanpan, Papua New Guinea
123 X 2 Cape Hatteras, North Carolina, U.S.A.
115 O 8 Cape Henrietta Maria, Ontario, Canada
145 I 26 Cape Horn, Chile
209 U 13 Cape Howe, New South Wales, Australia
219 T 15 Cape Hudson, Antarctica
209 Q 13 Cape Jaffa, South Australia, Australia
210 I 4 Cape Karikari, New Zealand
219 W 14 Cape Keltie, Antarctica
210 N 13 Cape Kidnappers, New Zealand
113 O 12 Cape Knox, British Columbia, Canada
158 H 15 Cape Kormakitis, Cyprus
115 T 5 Cape Labrador, Newfoundland and Labrador, Canada
208 G 12 Cape Leeuwin, Western Australia, Australia
208 I 3 Cape Leveque, Western Australia, Australia
112 I 2 Cape Lisburne, Alaska, U.S.A.
123 W 3 Cape Lookout, North Carolina, U.S.A.
218 K 5 Cape Mackintosh, Antarctica
58 B 11 Cape Malheureux, Mauritius
210 H 4 Cape Maria van Diemen, New Zealand
121 U 12 Cape May, New Jersey, U.S.A.
209 S 2 Cape Melville, Queensland, Australia
117 B 15 Cape Mendocino, California, U.S.A.
115 T 2 Cape Mercy, Nunavut, Canada
145 K 24 Cape Meredith, Falkland Islands
59 W 15 Cape Morse, Indian Ocean
212 F 6 Cape Nelson, Papua New Guinea
112 G 7 Cape Newenham, Alaska, U.S.A.
219 O 2 Cape Norvegia, Antarctica
196 J 15 Cape of Good Hope, Republic of South Africa
209 R 14 Cape Otway, Victoria, Australia
211 L 17 Cape Palliser, New Zealand
192 I 14 Cape Palmas, Côte d'Ivoire
113 Q 3 Cape Parry, Northwest Territories, Canada
208 J 11 Cape Pasley, Western Australia, Australia
215 T 14 Cape Pauva, Samoa
59 Q 15 Cape Penck, Indian Ocean
219 Y 11 Cape Poinsett, Antarctica
211 A 25 Cape Providence, New Zealand
197 N 15 Cape Recife, Republic of South Africa
210 H 4 Cape Reinga, New Zealand
123 T 5 Cape Romain, South Carolina, U.S.A.
123 R 14 Cape Romano, Florida, U.S.A.
210 O 10 Cape Runaway, New Zealand
123 R 15 Cape Sable, Florida, U.S.A.
62 E 8 Cape Sable, Nova Scotia, Canada
193 N 13 Cape Saint Paul, Ghana
175 R 7 Cape San Agustin, Philippines
113 P 14 Cape Scott, British Columbia, Canada
196 M 15 Cape Seal, Republic of South Africa
209 O 1 Cape Shield, Northern Territory, Australia
212 F 2 Cape Siemens, Papua New Guinea
212 I 8 Cape Siri, Papua New Guinea
115 N 4 Cape Southampton, Nunavut, Canada
209 P 12 Cape Spencer, South Australia, Australia
212 H 4 Cape St George, Papua New Guinea
211 J 15 Cape Stephens, New Zealand
114 L 7 Cape Tatnam, Manitoba, Canada
211 J 16 Cape Terawhiti, New Zealand
192 L 14 Cape Three Points, Ghana
196 J 15 Cape Town, Republic of South Africa
211 M 15 Cape Turnagain, New Zealand
115 U 6 Cape Uivak, Newfoundland and Labrador, Canada
63 A 16 Cape Verde, Atlantic Ocean
62 I 12 Cape Verde Basin, Atlantic Ocean
62 J 11 Cape Verde Plateau, Atlantic Ocean
219 X 12 Cape Waldron, Antarctica
212 E 6 Cape Ward Hunt, Papua New Guinea
209 O 1 Cape Wessel, Northern Territory, Australia
115 O 2 Cape Wilson, Nunavut, Canada
76 G 8 Cape Wrath, United Kingdom
209 R 1 Cape York, Queensland, Australia
209 R 1 Cape York Peninsula, Queensland, Australia
143 M 16 Capelinha, Brazil
209 U 6 Capella, Queensland, Australia
82 G 13 Capelle aan den IJssel, Netherlands
83 L 25 Capellen, Luxembourg
196 I 2 Capenda-Camulemba, Angola
90 I 13 Capestrano, Italy
119 F 18 Capitan Peak, New Mexico, U.S.A.
91 A 16 Capo Caccia, Italy
91 C 19 Capo Carbonara, Italy
91 N 19 Capo Colonna, Italy
91 D 16 Capo Comino, Italy
91 B 15 Capo del Falcone, Italy
91 B 18 Capo della Frasca, Italy
91 K 24 Capo delle Correnti, Italy
91 K 21 Capo di Milazzo, Italy
91 D 17 Capo di Monte Santu, Italy
91 K 21 Capo d'Orlando, Italy
91 I 21 Capo Gallo, Italy
91 H 22 Capo Granitola, Italy
91 L 23 Capo Murro di Porco, Italy
91 L 17 Capo Palinuro, Italy

Country · Internal administrative region: State/Province/Territory/Dependent territory · Capital city · Mountain range/Undersea ridge · Mountain peak/Volcano/Seamount · Geographic feature · Headland/Point/Cape/Peninsula · Desert · Island/Island group · Antarctic base · Ocean · Sea · Bay/Gulf/Channel/Strait · Lake · Salt pan/Dry/Intermittent lake · River

91 N 20 **Capo Rizzuto**, Italy
91 H 21 **Capo San Vito**, Italy
91 O 18 **Capo Santa Maria di Leuca**, Italy
91 J 24 **Capo Scaramia**, Italy
91 B 20 **Capo Spartivento**, Italy
91 N 17 **Capo Spulico**, Italy
91 N 18 **Capo Trionto**, Italy
91 L 20 **Capo Vaticano**, Italy
196 G 3 **Capolo**, Angola
158 J 11 **Cappadocia**, Turkey
91 J 16 **Capri**, Italy
196 L 7 **Caprivi**, Namibia
196 K 7 **Caprivi Strip**, Namibia
117 D 26 **Captain Cook**, Hawaii, U.S.A.
138 I 9 **Caquetá**, Colombia
138 I 10 **Caquetá**, Colombia
169 N 23 **Car Nicobar**, India
139 N 3 **Carabobo**, Venezuela
139 S 5 **Carabobo**, Venezuela
100 I 13 **Caracal**, Romania
142 E 8 **Caracaraí**, Brazil
139 O 2 **Caracas**, Venezuela
142 L 13 **Caracol**, Brazil
141 I 20 **Caracollo**, Bolivia
175 R 7 **Caraga**, Philippines
145 F 15 **Carahue**, Chile
100 G 11 **Caransebeş**, Romania
115 U 12 **Caraquet**, New Brunswick, Canada
140 A 9 **Caráquez**, Ecuador
126 H 9 **Caratasca**, Honduras
142 C 11 **Carauari**, Brazil
81 R 11 **Caravaca de la Cruz**, Spain
143 N 17 **Caravelas**, Brazil
80 H 1 **Caraballo**, Spain
119 E 14 **Carbondale**, Colorado, U.S.A.
120 H 13 **Carbondale**, Illinois, U.S.A.
121 T 9 **Carbondale**, Pennsylvania, U.S.A.
81 R 13 **Carboneras**, Spain
81 R 7 **Carboneras de Guadazaón**, Spain
79 Q 14 **Carcassonne**, France
140 B 8 **Carchi**, Ecuador
169 E 22 **Cardamom Hills**, India
125 T 12 **Cardel**, Mexico
81 N 10 **Cárdena**, Spain
125 V 13 **Cárdenas**, Mexico
126 J 4 **Cárdenas**, Cuba
77 I 22 **Cardiff**, United Kingdom
77 G 20 **Cardigan**, United Kingdom
77 G 19 **Cardigan Bay**, United Kingdom
173 J 21 **Cardomom Range**, Cambodia
144 M 12 **Cardona**, Uruguay
211 D 23 **Cardrona**, New Zealand
113 V 14 **Cardston**, Alberta, Canada
209 T 4 **Cardwell**, Queensland, Australia
100 G 7 **Carei**, Romania
78 L 3 **Carentan**, France
116 K 12 **Carey**, Idaho, U.S.A.
58 L 6 **Cargados Carajos Bank**, Indian Ocean
58 M 6 **Cargados Carajos Islands**, Indian Ocean
78 I 5 **Carhaix-Plouguer**, France
139 Q 2 **Cariaco**, Venezuela
140 B 11 **Cariamanga**, Ecuador
91 N 18 **Cariati**, Italy
126 K 12 **Caribbean Sea**, Atlantic Ocean
121 Y 3 **Caribou**, Maine, U.S.A.
113 T 9 **Caribou Mountains**, Alberta, Canada
81 S 5 **Cariñena**, Spain
143 L 15 **Carinhanha**, Brazil
139 R 3 **Caripito**, Venezuela
197 N 11 **Carletonville**, Republic of South Africa
117 I 15 **Carlin**, Nevada, U.S.A.
120 G 12 **Carlinville**, Illinois, U.S.A.
77 I 15 **Carlisle**, United Kingdom
121 R 11 **Carlisle**, Pennsylvania, U.S.A.
91 B 19 **Carloforte**, Italy
144 K 13 **Carlos Casares**, Argentina
77 E 19 **Carlow**, Republic of Ireland
119 F 19 **Carlsbad**, New Mexico, U.S.A.
58 K 2 **Carlsberg Ridge**, Indian Ocean
113 Z 12 **Carlyle**, Saskatchewan, Canada
120 H 12 **Carlyle Lake**, Illinois, U.S.A.
113 N 7 **Carmacks**, Yukon Territory, Canada
77 H 21 **Carmarthen**, United Kingdom
77 G 21 **Carmarthen Bay**, United Kingdom
79 P 13 **Carmaux**, France
77 G 18 **Carmel Head**, United Kingdom
126 D 7 **Carmelita**, Guatemala
144 M 12 **Carmelo**, Uruguay
138 I 3 **Carmen**, Colombia
144 G 7 **Carmen**, Chile
144 G 5 **Carmen Alto**, Chile
144 H 13 **Carmensa**, Argentina
120 I 13 **Carmi**, Illinois, U.S.A.
80 L 12 **Carmona**, Spain
76 G 10 **Carn Eighe**, United Kingdom
208 G 10 **Carnamah**, Western Australia, Australia
196 L 13 **Carnarvon**, Republic of South Africa
208 E 8 **Carnarvon**, Western Australia, Australia
218 K 11 **Carney Island**, Antarctica
194 H 4 **Carnot**, Central African Republic
76 I 12 **Carnoustie**, United Kingdom
77 F 20 **Carnsore Point**, Republic of Ireland
123 S 14 **Carol City**, Florida, U.S.A.
142 K 12 **Carolina**, Brazil
214 L 15 **Caroline Islands**, Federated States of Micronesia
91 J 21 **Caronia**, Italy
100 H 6 **Carpathian Mountains**, Europe
79 T 13 **Carpentras**, France
90 F 8 **Carpi**, Italy
123 N 9 **Carrabelle**, Florida, U.S.A.
90 D 9 **Carrara**, Italy
81 P 7 **Carrascosa del Campo**, Spain
77 A 20 **Carrauntuohil**, Republic of Ireland
125 N 6 **Carrillo**, Mexico
118 I 8 **Carrington**, North Dakota, U.S.A.
144 F 8 **Carrizal Bajo**, Chile
119 I 23 **Carrizo Springs**, Texas, U.S.A.
119 E 18 **Carrizozo**, New Mexico, U.S.A.
118 K 12 **Carroll**, Iowa, U.S.A.
123 N 5 **Carrollton**, Georgia, U.S.A.
158 L 8 **Carşamba**, Turkey
90 I 13 **Carsoli**, Italy
117 F 17 **Carson City**, Nevada, U.S.A.
81 S 12 **Cartagena**, Spain
138 H 2 **Cartagena**, Colombia
126 H 13 **Cartago**, Costa Rica
138 H 6 **Cartago**, Colombia
122 I 5 **Carthage**, Mississippi, U.S.A.
114 H 10 **Cartwright**, Manitoba, Canada
115 W 8 **Cartwright**, Newfoundland and Labrador, Canada
142 O 13 **Caruarú**, Brazil
139 Q 2 **Carúpano**, Venezuela
175 N 5 **Caruray**, Philippines
142 K 10 **Carutapera**, Brazil
117 H 17 **Carvers**, Nevada, U.S.A.
117 M 24 **Casa Grande**, Arizona, U.S.A.
188 H 7 **Casablanca**, Morocco
91 K 14 **Casacalenda**, Italy
90 B 7 **Casale**, Italy
138 K 6 **Casanare**, Colombia
126 F 12 **Casares**, Nicaragua
124 L 3 **Casas Grandes**, Mexico
81 R 9 **Casas Ibáñez**, Spain
58 A 9 **Cascade**, Seychelles
211 C 21 **Cascade Point**, New Zealand
61 U 3 **Cascadia Basin**, Pacific Ocean
142 N 11 **Cascavel**, Brazil
143 H 19 **Cascavel**, Brazil
91 J 15 **Caserta**, Italy
219 Y 11 **Casey**, Antarctica
175 P 3 **Casiguran**, Philippines
144 K 11 **Casilda**, Argentina
209 W 9 **Casino**, New South Wales, Australia
141 B 15 **Casma**, Peru
81 T 5 **Caspe**, Spain
118 E 11 **Casper**, Wyoming, U.S.A.
166 G 6 **Caspian Depression**, Kazakhstan/Russian Federation
166 G 8 **Caspian Sea**, Kazakhstan
120 M 7 **Cass City**, Michigan, U.S.A.
197 Q 5 **Cassacatiza**, Mozambique
196 J 4 **Cassamba**, Angola
113 P 9 **Cassiar**, British Columbia, Canada
113 O 8 **Cassiar Mountains**, Yukon Territory, Canada
143 I 17 **Cassilândia**, Brazil
196 H 5 **Cassinga**, Angola
91 I 15 **Cassino**, Italy
196 H 4 **Cassongue**, Angola
170 M 2 **Cast Uul**, Mongolia
90 D 11 **Castagneto Carducci**, Italy
142 F 12 **Castanha**, Brazil
142 K 10 **Castanhal**, Brazil
144 G 10 **Castaño**, Argentina
88 I 10 **Castasegna**, Switzerland
90 C 8 **Casteggio**, Italy
80 J 7 **Castel Branco**, Portugal
91 J 14 **Castél di Sangro**, Italy
79 V 13 **Castellane**, France
144 L 7 **Castelli**, Argentina
144 M 13 **Castelli**, Argentina
81 U 7 **Castelló de la Plana**, Spain
79 P 14 **Castelnaudary**, France
90 E 9 **Castelnovo ne' Monti**, Italy
80 I 7 **Castelo Branco**, Portugal
91 B 16 **Castelsardo**, Italy
91 I 22 **Casteltermini**, Italy
91 H 22 **Castelvetrano**, Italy
209 Q 13 **Casterton**, Victoria, Australia
90 E 12 **Castiglione della Pescaia**, Italy
144 F 8 **Castilla**, Chile
81 Q 8 **Castilla-La Mancha**, Spain
80 K 4 **Castilla Y León**, Spain
144 O 12 **Castillos**, Uruguay
117 N 17 **Castle Dale**, Utah, U.S.A.
117 K 24 **Castle Dome**, Arizona, U.S.A.
77 H 15 **Castle Douglas**, United Kingdom
62 B 7 **Castle Harbour**, Bermuda
63 N 26 **Castle Rock Point**, St Helena
77 B 17 **Castlebar**, Republic of Ireland
113 U 14 **Castlegar**, British Columbia, Canada
79 Q 14 **Castres**, France
127 Y 10 **Castries**, St Lucia
145 F 18 **Castro**, Chile
80 I 5 **Castro Daire**, Portugal
80 H 11 **Castro Verde**, Portugal
80 J 1 **Castropol**, Spain
91 M 18 **Castrovillari**, Italy
80 L 9 **Castuera**, Spain
211 A 23 **Caswell Sound**, New Zealand
159 Q 9 **Cat**, Turkey
127 N 3 **Cat Island**, The Bahamas
114 K 10 **Cat Lake**, Ontario, Canada
159 S 12 **Çatak**, Turkey
143 J 17 **Catalão**, Brazil
96 O 12 **Çatalca**, Turkey
81 W 4 **Cataluña**, Spain
158 J 6 **Catalzeytin**, Turkey
144 H 7 **Catamarca**, Argentina
144 I 8 **Catamarca**, Argentina
145 G 16 **Catán Lil**, Argentina
197 Q 7 **Catandica**, Mozambique
175 Q 4 **Catanduanes**, Philippines
91 K 22 **Catania**, Italy
91 M 20 **Catanzaro**, Italy
175 Q 4 **Catarman**, Philippines
197 Q 6 **Cataxa**, Mozambique
175 Q 5 **Catbalogan**, Philippines
175 R 7 **Cateel**, Philippines
192 E 10 **Catió**, Guinea-Bissau
211 D 25 **Catlins**, New Zealand
125 Q 8 **Catorce**, Mexico
145 H 15 **Catriel**, Argentina
144 J 13 **Catriló**, Argentina
121 U 8 **Catskill**, New York, U.S.A.
121 T 9 **Catskill Mountains**, New York, U.S.A.
175 O 6 **Cauayan**, Philippines
138 G 8 **Cauca**, Colombia
138 I 4 **Cauca**, Colombia
138 H 4 **Caucasia**, Colombia
159 Q 5 **Caucasus**, Asia
144 H 10 **Caucete**, Argentina
196 I 2 **Caungula**, Angola
144 F 13 **Cauquenes**, Chile
139 Q 6 **Caura**, Venezuela
118 J 7 **Cavalier**, North Dakota, U.S.A.
210 J 5 **Cavalli Islands**, New Zealand
192 I 13 **Cavally**, Liberia
77 D 16 **Cavan**, Republic of Ireland
158 E 13 **Cavdir**, Turkey
211 F 21 **Cave**, New Zealand
142 L 11 **Caxias**, Brazil
143 I 21 **Caxias do Sul**, Brazil
196 G 2 **Caxito**, Angola
158 F 11 **Cay**, Turkey
126 J 3 **Cay Sal**, The Bahamas
140 C 8 **Cayambe**, Ecuador
159 P 8 **Cayeli**, Turkey
139 Z 6 **Cayenne**, French Guiana
158 G 9 **Cayirhan**, Turkey
126 K 6 **Cayman Brac**, Cayman Islands
126 K 6 **Cayman Islands**, U.K.
126 I 7 **Cayman Trench**, Jamaica
62 B 11 **Cayman Trench**, Atlantic Ocean
191 M 20 **Caynabo**, Somalia
126 I 5 **Cayo del Rosario**, Cuba
126 J 5 **Cayo Largo**, Cuba
126 L 4 **Cayo Romano**, Cuba
126 M 5 **Cayo Sabinal**, Cuba
126 I 10 **Cayos Miskitos**, Nicaragua
100 L 12 **Căzănești**, Romania
79 O 14 **Cazères**, France
196 L 4 **Cazombo**, Angola
197 R 5 **Cazula**, Mozambique
142 N 12 **Ceará**, Brazil
63 H 14 **Ceara Abyssal Plain**, Atlantic Ocean
62 G 13 **Ceara Ridge**, Atlantic Ocean
125 N 6 **Ceballos**, Mexico
81 P 4 **Cebollera**, Spain
175 P 6 **Cebu**, Philippines
175 P 5 **Cebu**, Philippines
93 I 24 **Cece**, Hungary
118 M 11 **Cedar**, Iowa, U.S.A.
117 L 18 **Cedar City**, Utah, U.S.A.
123 P 10 **Cedar Key**, Florida, U.S.A.
114 H 8 **Cedar Lake**, Manitoba, Canada
118 M 12 **Cedar Rapids**, Iowa, U.S.A.
123 N 4 **Cedartown**, Georgia, U.S.A.
61 V 4 **Cedros Trench**, Pacific Ocean
209 N 10 **Ceduna**, South Australia, Australia
92 D 11 **Cedynia**, Poland
80 G 1 **Cée**, Spain
191 O 19 **Ceel Gaal**, Somalia
191 N 19 **Ceerigaabo**, Somalia
91 J 21 **Cefalù**, Italy
93 J 23 **Cegléd**, Hungary
171 Q 13 **Ceheng**, China
158 K 9 **Cekerek**, Turkey
125 Q 11 **Celaya**, Mexico
175 P 8 **Celebes Sea**, Asia
125 X 10 **Celestún**, Mexico
120 L 10 **Celina**, Ohio, U.S.A.
123 N 1 **Celina**, Tennessee, U.S.A.
94 D 7 **Celje**, Slovenia
86 H 13 **Celle**, Germany
83 D 20 **Celles**, Belgium
159 T 11 **Çelo Daglari**, Turkey
77 D 21 **Celtic Sea**, Republic of Ireland/U.K.
62 K 7 **Celtic Shelf**, Atlantic Ocean
122 M 2 **Center Hill Lake**, Tennessee, U.S.A.
122 L 5 **Centerville**, Alabama, U.S.A.
90 F 8 **Cento**, Italy
168 J 11 **Central**, Nepal
169 G 24 **Central**, Sri Lanka
195 V 8 **Central**, Kenya
197 N 9 **Central**, Botswana
197 Q 4 **Central**, Malawi
197 N 5 **Central**, Zambia
212 E 7 **Central**, Papua New Guinea
212 L 6 **Central**, Solomon Islands
192 M 14 **Central**, Ghana
194 H 4 **Central African Republic**, Africa
88 E 9 **Central Alps**, Switzerland
60 K 5 **Central Basin**, Pacific Ocean
165 T 12 **Central Brāhui Range**, Pakistan
98 H 11 **Central Highlands of Vidzemes**, Latvia
215 Q 5 **Central Line Islands**, Kiribati
165 Q 13 **Central Makran Range**, Pakistan
61 P 6 **Central Pacific Basin**, Pacific Ocean
88 D 7 **Central Plateau**, Switzerland
212 A 4 **Central Range**, Papua New Guinea
157 Q 9 **Central Siberian Plateau**, Russian Federation
145 F 14 **Central Valley**, Chile
117 E 15 **Central Valley**, California, U.S.A.
116 D 8 **Centralia**, Washington, U.S.A.
120 H 13 **Centralia**, Illinois, U.S.A.
79 P 7 **Centre**, France
193 U 13 **Centre**, Cameroon
58 B 12 **Centre de Flacq**, Mauritius
211 B 25 **Centre Island**, New Zealand
171 T 14 **Cenxi**, China
94 I 8 **Čepin**, Croatia
91 I 14 **Ceprano**, Italy
144 K 9 **Ceres**, Argentina
91 L 15 **Cerignola**, Italy
158 I 9 **Cerikli**, Turkey
158 H 8 **Cerkeş**, Turkey
96 N 12 **Cerkezköy**, Turkey
94 B 8 **Cerknica**, Slovenia
159 O 12 **Cermik**, Turkey
101 N 12 **Cerna**, Romania
100 M 13 **Cernavodă**, Romania
125 Q 7 **Cerralvo**, Mexico
95 K 19 **Cërrik**, Albania
125 Q 10 **Cerritos**, Mexico
144 G 11 **Cerro Amarillo**, Argentina
145 F 21 **Cerro Arenales**, Chile
141 A 19 **Cerro Azol**, Ecuador
125 S 10 **Cerro Azul**, Mexico
144 G 8 **Cerro Bonete**, Argentina
141 J 23 **Cerro Bonete**, Bolivia
145 F 23 **Cerro Cervantes**, Argentina
144 J 11 **Cerro Champaqui**, Argentina
126 H 13 **Cerro Chirripó Grande**, Costa Rica
145 H 20 **Cerro Cojudo Blanco**, Argentina
124 F 2 **Cerro de La Encantada**, Mexico
144 G 10 **Cerro de Olivares**, Chile
141 D 15 **Cerro de Pasco**, Peru
144 G 8 **Cerro de Petro**, Chile
144 H 6 **Cerro del Rincón**, Argentina
125 R 9 **Cerro del Tigre**, Mexico
139 P 7 **Cerro Duida**, Venezuela
138 I 7 **Cerro El Nevado**, Colombia
124 H 6 **Cerro Encantado**, Mexico
145 F 22 **Cerro Fitz Roy**, Argentina
144 H 7 **Cerro Galán**, Argentina
139 Q 6 **Cerro Guaiquinima**, Venezuela
145 F 20 **Cerro Hudson**, Chile
124 L 8 **Cerro Huehueto**, Mexico
144 O 11 **Cerro Largo**, Uruguay
126 E 9 **Cerro Las Minas**, Honduras
144 F 9 **Cerro Las Tórtolas**, Chile
145 F 22 **Cerro Lautaroŋ**, Chile
139 O 7 **Cerro Marahuaca**, Venezuela
145 F 21 **Cerro Mellizo Sur**, Chile
144 H 3 **Cerro Milliri**, Chile
145 F 22 **Cerro Murallón**, Chile
144 H 13 **Cerro Nevado**, Argentina
139 O 7 **Cerro Ovana**, Venezuela
145 F 23 **Cerro Paine**, Chile
139 O 6 **Cerro Paraque**, Venezuela
145 H 14 **Cerro Payún**, Argentina
125 R 8 **Cerro Peña Nevada**, Mexico
144 H 6 **Cerro Pular**, Chile
145 F 21 **Cerro San Lorenzo**, Argentina
143 G 20 **Cerro San Rafael**, Paraguay
145 F 20 **Cerro San Valentín**, Chile
126 G 10 **Cerro Saslaya**, Nicaragua
124 J 5 **Cerro Seberi**, Mexico
125 U 12 **Cerro Sta Martha**, Mexico
125 O 12 **Cerro Tancitaro**, Mexico
144 G 12 **Cerro Tupungato**, Argentina
124 H 3 **Cerro Viejo**, Mexico
141 C 15 **Cerro Yerupaja**, Peru
90 F 11 **Certaldo**, Italy
81 V 4 **Cervera**, Spain
90 H 9 **Cervia**, Italy
80 J 1 **Cervo**, Spain
138 J 3 **Cesar**, Colombia
90 G 9 **Cesena**, Italy
98 G 10 **Cēsis**, Latvia
93 D 16 **Česká Lípa**, Czech Republic
93 F 17 **Česká Třebová**, Czech Republic
93 C 19 **České Budějovice**, Czech Republic
93 C 20 **Český Krumlov**, Czech Republic
94 F 8 **Česma**, Croatia
158 A 11 **Çeşme**, Turkey
209 V 11 **Cessnock**, New South Wales, Australia
98 H 11 **Cesvaine**, Latvia
80 L 14 **Ceuta**, Spain
88 G 10 **Cevio**, Switzerland
158 K 13 **Ceyhan**, Turkey
159 P 13 **Ceylanpinar**, Turkey
59 P 4 **Ceylon Plain**, Indian Ocean
165 O 14 **Chābahār**, Iran
140 C 12 **Chachapoyas**, Peru
99 N 19 **Chachersk**, Belarus
144 K 7 **Chaco**, Argentina
193 W 8 **Chad**, Africa
123 U 4 **Chadbourn**, North Carolina, U.S.A.
145 I 14 **Chadileo**, Argentina
165 P 11 **Chagai Hills**, Pakistan
167 W 4 **Chagan**, Kazakhstan
165 R 7 **Chaghcharān**, Afghanistan
59 N 5 **Chagos Archipelago**, Indian Ocean
59 N 5 **Chagos Trench**, Indian Ocean
59 N 4 **Chagos–Laccadive Ridge**, Indian Ocean
164 I 8 **Chahār Mahall Va Bakhtīārī**, Iran
169 J 15 **Chaibasa**, India
58 K 4 **Chain Ridge**, Indian Ocean
173 H 18 **Chainat**, Thailand
145 F 18 **Chaitén**, Chile
173 I 17 **Chaiyaphum**, Thailand
144 M 10 **Chajarí**, Argentina
169 J 15 **Chakradharpur**, India
141 E 19 **Chala**, Peru
195 R 12 **Chala**, Tanzania
79 N 11 **Chalais**, France
197 T 6 **Chaláua**, Mozambique
195 V 6 **Chalbi Desert**, Kenya
115 U 11 **Chaleur Bay**, New Brunswick, Canada
97 N 24 **Chalki**, Greece
97 G 19 **Chalkida**, Greece
167 X 9 **Chalkudysu**, Kazakhstan
78 K 8 **Challans**, France
141 J 21 **Challapata**, Bolivia
60 L 6 **Challenger Deep**, Pacific Ocean
61 V 11 **Challenger Fracture Zone**, Pacific Ocean
61 O 12 **Challenger Plateau**, Pacific Ocean
116 K 10 **Challis**, Idaho, U.S.A.
79 T 8 **Chalon-sur-Saône**, France
79 S 4 **Châlons-en-Champagne**, France
164 I 5 **Chālūs**, Iran
87 L 21 **Cham**, Germany
197 Q 3 **Chama**, Zambia
165 S 10 **Chaman**, Pakistan
195 V 15 **Chamba**, Tanzania
118 I 11 **Chamberlain**, South Dakota, U.S.A.
121 R 11 **Chambersburg**, Pennsylvania, U.S.A.
79 V 10 **Chambéry**, France
197 P 3 **Chambeshi**, Zambia
161 U 3 **Chamchamāl**, Iraq

Country · Internal administrative region: State/Province/Territory/Dependent territory · Capital city · Mountain range/Undersea ridge · Mountain peak/Volcano/Seamount · Geographic feature · Headland/Point/Cape/Peninsula · Desert · Island/Island group · Antarctic base · Ocean · Sea · Bay/Gulf/Channel/Strait · Lake · Salt pan/Dry/Intermittent lake · River

144 I 10 **Chamical**, Argentina
79 W 9 **Chamonix-Mont-Blanc**, France
169 H 15 **Champa**, India
79 T 4 **Champagne-Ardenne**, France
173 L 18 **Champasak**, Laos
121 U 5 **Champlain**, New York, U.S.A.
125 X 12 **Champotón**, Mexico
169 D 22 **Chamrajnagar**, India
144 F 7 **Chañaral**, Chile
165 O 5 **Chanārān**, Iran
144 F 13 **Chanco**, Chile
169 J 16 **Chandbali**, India
168 E 13 **Chanderi**, India
168 E 10 **Chandigarh**, India
117 M 24 **Chandler**, Arizona, U.S.A.
169 M 14 **Chandpur**, Bangladesh
169 F 17 **Chandrapur**, India
197 Q 6 **Changara**, Mozambique
171 X 5 **Changbai Shan**, China
171 X 4 **Changchun**, China
171 T 11 **Changde**, China
171 W 13 **Changhua**, Taiwan
170 K 4 **Changji**, China
171 V 6 **Changli**, China
171 T 11 **Changsha**, China
171 W 10 **Changshu**, China
126 I 13 **Changuinola**, Panama
171 S 8 **Changzhi**, China
171 V 10 **Changzhou**, China
97 H 26 **Chania**, Greece
77 J 26 **Channel Islands**, United Kingdom
117 G 23 **Channel Islands**, California, U.S.A.
115 X 11 **Channel-Port-aux-Basques**, Newfoundland and Labrador, Canada
77 N 22 **Channel Tunnel**, United Kingdom/France
157 Z 6 **Chantal'skiy**, Russian Federation
173 I 20 **Chanthaburi**, Thailand
78 L 8 **Chantonnay**, France
169 N 24 **Chanumla**, India
141 B 14 **Chao**, Peru
171 V 10 **Chao Hu**, China
173 G 17 **Chao Phraya**, Thailand
188 I 6 **Chaouèn**, Morocco
171 V 13 **Chaozhou**, China
138 H 7 **Chaparral**, Colombia
166 I 4 **Chapayevo**, Kazakhstan
167 T 3 **Chapayevskoye**, Kazakhstan
143 H 20 **Chapecó**, Brazil
115 N 12 **Chapleau**, Ontario, Canada
113 Y 13 **Chaplin**, Saskatchewan, Canada
101 T 10 **Chaplynka**, Ukraine
121 N 13 **Chapmanville**, West Virginia, U.S.A.
141 L 22 **Charagua**, Bolivia
141 H 20 **Charana**, Bolivia
144 K 8 **Charata**, Argentina
125 P 9 **Charcas**, Mexico
218 I 6 **Charcot Island**, Antarctica
167 O 13 **Chardzhev**, Turkmenistan
193 W 10 **Chari-Baguirmi**, Chad
165 U 7 **Chārīkār**, Afghanistan
118 L 13 **Chariton**, Iowa, U.S.A.
139 U 5 **Charity**, Guyana
83 G 21 **Charleroi**, Belgium
118 M 11 **Charles City**, Iowa, U.S.A.
120 H 8 **Charles Mound**, Illinois, U.S.A.
121 O 13 **Charleston**, West Virginia, U.S.A.
123 T 5 **Charleston**, South Carolina, U.S.A.
211 F 17 **Charleston**, New Zealand
117 I 20 **Charleston Peak**, Nevada, U.S.A.
209 T 8 **Charleville**, Queensland, Australia
79 S 3 **Charleville-Mézières**, France
62 G 6 **Charlie–Gibbs Fracture Zone**, Atlantic Ocean
123 S 2 **Charlotte**, North Carolina, U.S.A.
127 V 7 **Charlotte Amalie**, Virgin Islands (U.S.A.)
123 Q 13 **Charlotte Harbor**, Florida, U.S.A.
121 R 13 **Charlottesville**, Virginia, U.S.A.
115 V 12 **Charlottetown**, Prince Edward Island, Canada
127 Y 12 **Charlotteville**, Trinidad and Tobago
209 R 12 **Charlton**, Victoria, Australia
115 O 10 **Charlton Island**, Ontario, Canada
79 V 5 **Charmes**, France
165 W 7 **Charsadda**, Pakistan
167 P 14 **Charshanga**, Turkmenistan
209 T 5 **Charters Towers**, Queensland, Australia
79 P 5 **Chartres**, France
167 X 9 **Charyn**, Kazakhstan
144 M 13 **Chascomús**, Argentina
99 K 15 **Chashniki**, Belarus
79 S 7 **Château-Chinon**, France
79 N 6 **Château-du-Loir**, France
79 R 4 **Château-Thierry**, France
78 L 6 **Châteaubriant**, France
79 O 6 **Châteaudun**, France
78 H 5 **Châteaulin**, France
79 P 8 **Châteauroux**, France
79 N 8 **Châtellerault**, France
77 M 21 **Chatham**, United Kingdom
115 N 15 **Chatham**, Ontario, Canada
61 P 12 **Chatham Islands**, New Zealand
113 O 10 **Chatham Strait**, Alaska, U.S.A.
79 O 8 **Châtillon-sur-Indre**, France
79 T 6 **Châtillon-sur-Seine**, France
123 N 3 **Chattanooga**, Tennessee, U.S.A.
173 I 17 **Chatturat**, Thailand
167 V 11 **Chatyr-Tash**, Kyrgyzstan
173 L 22 **Châu Đôc**, Vietnam
172 C 12 **Chauk**, Myanmar
79 T 5 **Chaumont**, France
169 G 23 **Chavakachcheri**, Sri Lanka
80 J 4 **Chaves**, Portugal
142 J 9 **Chaves**, Brazil
196 L 4 **Chavuma**, Zambia
99 N 17 **Chavusy**, Belarus
144 J 11 **Chazón**, Argentina
122 M 5 **Cheaha Mountain**, Alabama, U.S.A.
93 A 17 **Cheb**, Czech Republic
189 R 6 **Chebba**, Tunisia
156 G 9 **Cheboksary**, Russian Federation
120 L 5 **Cheboygan**, Michigan, U.S.A.
93 K 16 **Chęciny**, Poland
173 B 14 **Cheduba Island**, Myanmar
112 G 6 **Chefornak**, Alaska, U.S.A.
192 K 3 **Chegga**, Mauritania
116 D 8 **Chehalis**, Washington, U.S.A.
171 Y 8 **Cheju**, South Korea
171 X 8 **Cheju-do**, South Korea
166 I 12 **Cheleken**, Turkmenistan
145 I 15 **Chelforó**, Argentina
166 M 7 **Chelkar**, Kazakhstan
93 O 15 **Chełm**, Poland
92 I 10 **Chełmno**, Poland
77 M 21 **Chelmsford**, United Kingdom
92 I 11 **Chełmża**, Poland
77 J 21 **Cheltenham**, United Kingdom
211 L 14 **Cheltenham**, New Zealand
81 S 8 **Chelva**, Spain
169 G 18 **Chelvai**, India
156 I 11 **Chelyabinsk**, Russian Federation
157 Q 6 **Chelyuskin**, Russian Federation
188 G 8 **Chemaïa**, Morocco
167 N 15 **Chemenibit**, Turkmenistan
87 L 17 **Chemnitz**, Germany
188 I 11 **Chenachane**, Algeria
191 H 22 **Ch'ench'a**, Ethiopia
171 U 6 **Chengde**, China
171 Q 10 **Chengdu**, China
168 O 11 **Chengele**, India
169 G 21 **Chennai**, India
171 T 12 **Chenzhou**, China
96 I 11 **Chepelare**, Bulgaria
140 B 13 **Chepén**, Peru
144 I 10 **Chepes**, Argentina
123 S 3 **Cheraw**, South Carolina, U.S.A.
78 L 3 **Cherbourg**, France
156 M 12 **Cherepanovo**, Russian Federation
156 G 7 **Cherepovets**, Russian Federation
189 P 6 **Chéria**, Algeria
169 C 23 **Cheriyam**, India
101 R 5 **Cherkasy**, Ukraine
156 D 11 **Cherkessk**, Russian Federation
156 K 12 **Cherlak**, Russian Federation
96 F 9 **Cherni Vrŭkh**, Bulgaria
101 Q 2 **Chernihiv**, Ukraine
101 W 8 **Cherninivka**, Ukraine
100 K 7 **Chernivtsi**, Ukraine
101 P 2 **Chernobyl**, Ukraine
157 N 10 **Chernoostrovskoye**, Russian Federation
101 N 3 **Chernyakhiv**, Ukraine
99 C 16 **Chernyakhovsk**, Russian Federation
157 S 13 **Chernyshevsk**, Russian Federation
157 R 10 **Chernyshevskiy**, Russian Federation
118 K 11 **Cherokee**, Iowa, U.S.A.
168 M 13 **Cherrapunji**, India
121 U 11 **Cherry Hill**, New Jersey, U.S.A.
157 W 7 **Cherskiy**, Russian Federation
100 J 3 **Chervonohrad**, Ukraine
101 Y 5 **Chervonooskil's'ke Vodoskhovyshche**, Ukraine
101 P 9 **Chervonoznam"yanka**, Ukraine
99 K 18 **Chervyen'**, Belarus
99 N 18 **Cherykaw**, Belarus
121 T 15 **Chesapeake**, Virginia, U.S.A.
121 S 13 **Chesapeake Bay**, Maryland, U.S.A.
156 J 6 **Cheshskaya Guba**, Russian Federation
77 I 18 **Chester**, United Kingdom/United Kingdom
115 V 13 **Chester**, Nova Scotia, Canada
117 E 15 **Chester**, California, U.S.A.
118 C 7 **Chester**, Montana, U.S.A.
120 G 13 **Chester**, Illinois, U.S.A.
121 T 11 **Chester**, Pennsylvania, U.S.A.
121 S 14 **Chester**, Virginia, U.S.A.
123 R 3 **Chester**, South Carolina, U.S.A.
114 M 3 **Chesterfield Inlet**, Nunavut, Canada
121 X 4 **Chesuncook Lake**, Maine, U.S.A.
169 B 22 **Chetlat**, India
125 Z 12 **Chetumal**, Mexico
211 J 15 **Chetwode Islands**, New Zealand
113 S 11 **Chetwynd**, British Columbia, Canada
211 I 19 **Cheviot**, New Zealand
191 H 23 **Che'w Bahir**, Ethiopia
116 H 6 **Chewelah**, Washington, U.S.A.
118 G 10 **Cheyenne**, South Dakota, U.S.A.
118 F 13 **Cheyenne**, Wyoming, U.S.A.
119 H 14 **Cheyenne Wells**, Colorado, U.S.A.
168 F 13 **Chhatarpur**, India
169 I 17 **Chhatrapur**, India
169 F 15 **Chhindwara**, India
168 L 12 **Chhukha**, Bhutan
171 W 13 **Chiai**, Taiwan
173 I 15 **Chiang Khan**, Thailand
173 G 14 **Chiang Mai**, Thailand
172 H 13 **Chiang Rai**, Thailand
125 X 14 **Chiapas**, Mexico
159 S 6 **Chiat'ura**, Georgia
90 D 5 **Chiavenno**, Italy
177 L 16 **Chiba**, Japan
196 G 6 **Chibemba**, Angola
196 G 6 **Chibia**, Angola
115 R 11 **Chibougamau**, Québec, Canada
177 D 17 **Chibu**, Japan
177 D 17 **Chiburi-jima**, Japan
120 I 9 **Chicago**, Illinois, U.S.A.
113 N 10 **Chichagof Island**, Alaska, U.S.A.
188 G 8 **Chichaoua**, Morocco
77 L 23 **Chichester**, United Kingdom
139 N 2 **Chichiriviche**, Venezuela
119 J 17 **Chickasha**, Oklahoma, U.S.A.
112 M 6 **Chicken**, Alaska, U.S.A.
140 B 13 **Chiclayo**, Peru
145 H 19 **Chico**, Argentina
117 D 16 **Chico**, California, U.S.A.
196 H 5 **Chicomba**, Angola
197 Q 9 **Chicualacuala**, Mozambique
197 R 10 **Chidenguele**, Mozambique
87 L 25 **Chiemsee**, Germany
197 O 2 **Chiengi**, Zambia
173 F 23 **Chieo Lan Reservoir**, Thailand
90 B 8 **Chieri**, Italy
90 J 13 **Chieti**, Italy
171 V 5 **Chifeng**, China
112 G 9 **Chignik**, Alaska, U.S.A.
141 I 22 **Chiguana**, Bolivia
197 Q 9 **Chigubo**, Mozambique
124 M 5 **Chihuahua**, Mexico
124 M 5 **Chihuahua**, Mexico
167 Q 9 **Chiili**, Kazakhstan
169 C 21 **Chikmagalur**, India
169 C 19 **Chikodi**, India
197 Q 3 **Chikwa**, Zambia
176 J 7 **Chikyū-misaki**, Japan
196 G 4 **Chila**, Angola
165 Y 6 **Chilas**, Pakistan
169 F 24 **Chilaw**, Sri Lanka
209 V 7 **Childers**, Queensland, Australia
119 I 18 **Childress**, Texas, U.S.A.
145 F 15 **Chile**, South America
145 G 20 **Chile Chico**, Chile
144 H 9 **Chilecito**, Argentina
167 W 9 **Chilik**, Kazakhstan
197 N 4 **Chililabombwe**, Zambia
209 S 3 **Chillagoe**, Queensland, Australia
145 F 14 **Chillán**, Chile
145 L 14 **Chillar**, Argentina
120 H 10 **Chillicothe**, Illinois, U.S.A.
120 M 12 **Chillicothe**, Ohio, U.S.A.
141 H 20 **Chilliculco**, Peru
165 Y 5 **Chillinji**, Pakistan
125 R 13 **Chilpancingo**, Mexico
77 K 21 **Chiltern Hills**, United Kingdom
197 R 3 **Chilumba**, Malawi
171 X 12 **Chilung**, Taiwan
195 T 13 **Chimala**, Tanzania
197 Q 8 **Chimanimani**, Zimbabwe
83 F 23 **Chimay**, Belgium
140 B 9 **Chimborazo**, Ecuador
140 B 9 **Chimborazo**, Ecuador
141 B 14 **Chimbote**, Peru
212 C 5 **Chimbu**, Papua New Guinea
165 Y 10 **Chimian**, Pakistan
197 Q 7 **Chimoio**, Mozambique
172 B 11 **Chin**, Myanmar
170 K 8 **China**, Asia
125 R 7 **China**, Mexico
119 F 21 **Chinati Peak**, Texas, U.S.A.
167 R 12 **Chinaz**, Uzbekistan
141 D 17 **Chincha Alta**, Peru
113 S 10 **Chinchaga**, Alberta, Canada
209 V 8 **Chinchilla**, Queensland, Australia
197 S 7 **Chinde**, Mozambique
172 C 8 **Chindwin**, Myanmar
166 J 4 **Chingirlau**, Kazakhstan
197 N 4 **Chingola**, Zambia
196 H 4 **Chinguar**, Angola
192 G 5 **Chinguetti**, Mauritania
193 X 11 **Chinguil**, Chad
197 P 6 **Chinhoyi**, Zimbabwe
165 X 9 **Chiniot**, Pakistan
166 J 11 **Chink Kaplankyr**, Uzbekistan
117 O 20 **Chinle**, Arizona, U.S.A.
171 V 13 **Chinmen Tao**, Taiwan
169 F 17 **Chinnur**, India
177 I 16 **Chino**, Japan
79 N 7 **Chinon**, France
61 P 3 **Chinook Trough**, Pacific Ocean
197 Q 3 **Chinsali**, Zambia
169 E 21 **Chintamani**, India
90 G 7 **Chioggia**, Italy
97 K 19 **Chios**, Greece
97 K 19 **Chios**, Greece
197 Q 4 **Chipata**, Zambia
197 O 3 **Chipili**, Zambia
196 J 4 **Chipoia**, Angola
77 J 21 **Chippenham**, United Kingdom
120 G 5 **Chippewa Falls**, Wisconsin, U.S.A.
141 D 15 **Chiquian**, Peru
125 Z 10 **Chiquilá**, Mexico
126 D 9 **Chiquimula**, Guatemala
138 I 6 **Chiquinquira**, Colombia
169 G 19 **Chirala**, India
197 R 6 **Chiramba**, Mozambique
167 R 11 **Chirchik**, Uzbekistan
197 P 8 **Chiredzi**, Zimbabwe
193 T 5 **Chirfa**, Niger
117 O 25 **Chiricahua Peak**, Arizona, U.S.A.
138 J 3 **Chiriguana**, Colombia
112 H 9 **Chirikof Island**, Alaska, U.S.A.
126 I 13 **Chiriquí Grande**, Panama
169 H 15 **Chirmiri**, India
197 R 6 **Chiromo**, Mozambique
96 J 10 **Chirpan**, Bulgaria
197 O 6 **Chirundu**, Zambia
164 J 13 **Chirūyeh**, Iran
197 O 5 **Chisamba**, Zambia
115 P 9 **Chisasibi**, Québec, Canada
165 X 11 **Chishtian Mandi**, Pakistan
101 O 9 **Chişinău**, Moldova
100 F 9 **Chişineu-Criş**, Romania
167 Q 3 **Chistopol'ye**, Kazakhstan
157 R 14 **Chita**, Russian Federation
196 G 7 **Chitado**, Angola
197 P 4 **Chitambo**, Zambia
196 K 1 **Chitato**, Angola
112 L 8 **Chitina**, Alaska, U.S.A.
197 Q 2 **Chitipa**, Malawi
176 K 6 **Chitose**, Japan
169 D 20 **Chitradurga**, India
165 W 6 **Chitral**, Pakistan
126 J 14 **Chitré**, Panama
169 M 14 **Chittagong**, Bangladesh
169 M 15 **Chittagong**, Bangladesh
168 D 13 **Chittaurgarh**, India
169 F 21 **Chittoor**, India
197 O 7 **Chitungwiza**, Zimbabwe
196 K 5 **Chiume**, Angola
90 B 7 **Chivasso**, Italy
197 P 7 **Chivhu**, Zimbabwe
177 F 18 **Chizu**, Japan
167 R 2 **Chkalovo**, Kazakhstan
93 L 16 **Chmielnik**, Poland
173 L 18 **Chŏâm Khsant**, Cambodia
196 M 7 **Chobe**, Botswana
138 G 6 **Chocó**, Colombia
138 J 6 **Chocontá**, Colombia
92 G 11 **Chodzież**, Poland
145 I 15 **Choele Choel**, Argentina
197 Q 5 **Chofombo**, Mozambique
212 K 5 **Choiseul**, Solomon Islands
145 L 24 **Choiseul Sound**, Falkland Islands
124 K 6 **Choix**, Mexico
92 H 10 **Chojnice**, Poland
176 K 11 **Chōkai-san**, Japan
167 U 9 **Chokpar**, Kazakhstan
157 V 7 **Chokurdakh**, Russian Federation
197 Q 10 **Chókwe**, Mozambique
78 M 7 **Cholet**, France
145 G 18 **Cholila**, Argentina
167 V 10 **Cholpon-Ata**, Kyrgyzstan
126 F 10 **Choluteca**, Honduras
173 G 15 **Chom Thong**, Thailand
197 N 6 **Choma**, Zambia
93 B 16 **Chomutov**, Czech Republic
173 H 19 **Chon Buri**, Thailand
173 N 21 **Chon Thanh**, Vietnam
171 X 7 **Ch'ŏnan**, South Korea
140 A 9 **Chone**, Ecuador
171 Y 5 **Ch'ŏngjin**, North Korea
196 F 5 **Chongoroi**, Angola
171 R 11 **Chongqing**, China
171 R 11 **Chongqing**, China
197 O 5 **Chongwe**, Zambia
171 Y 7 **Chŏnju**, South Korea
171 T 4 **Chonogol**, Mongolia
100 G 6 **Chop**, Ukraine
100 K 6 **Chortkiv**, Ukraine
169 A 15 **Chorwad**, India
92 L 10 **Chorzele**, Poland
145 G 14 **Chos Malal**, Argentina
177 L 16 **Chōshi**, Japan
92 E 11 **Choszczno**, Poland
140 B 13 **Chota**, Peru
169 I 14 **Chota Nagpur**, India
118 C 7 **Choteau**, Montana, U.S.A.
188 L 6 **Chott ech Chergui**, Algeria
189 N 6 **Chott el Hodna**, Algeria
189 P 7 **Chott el Jerid**, Tunisia
189 O 7 **Chott Melrhir**, Algeria
192 G 5 **Choûm**, Mauritania
119 L 16 **Chouteau**, Oklahoma, U.S.A.
171 S 3 **Choybalsan**, Mongolia
171 R 4 **Choyr**, Mongolia
211 H 20 **Christchurch**, New Zealand
215 P 2 **Christmas Island**, Kiribati
174 G 15 **Christmas Island**, Australia
97 K 21 **Christos**, Greece
93 E 17 **Chrudim**, Czech Republic
96 I 13 **Chrysoupoli**, Greece
93 J 17 **Chrzanów**, Poland
167 R 9 **Chu**, Kazakhstan
167 T 9 **Chu-Iliyskiye Gory**, Kazakhstan
173 O 20 **Chu Yang Sin**, Vietnam
145 H 18 **Chubut**, Argentina
145 H 18 **Chubut**, Argentina
157 Z 5 **Chuckchi Sea**, Russian Federation/U.S.A.
101 N 4 **Chudniv**, Ukraine
99 I 20 **Chudzin**, Belarus
112 L 8 **Chugach Mountains**, Alaska, U.S.A.
177 D 19 **Chūgoku-sanchi**, Japan
101 W 4 **Chuhuyiv**, Ukraine
65 S 4 **Chukchi Abyssal Plain**, Arctic Ocean
65 R 5 **Chukchi Plateau**, Arctic Ocean
65 R 3 **Chukchi Sea**, Arctic Ocean
157 Z 6 **Chukotskiy Poluostrov**, Russian Federation
117 H 24 **Chula Vista**, California, U.S.A.
157 T 12 **Chul'man**, Russian Federation
156 L 12 **Chulym**, Russian Federation
173 I 16 **Chum Phae**, Thailand
191 I 23 **Chumba**, Ethiopia
144 I 9 **Chumbicha**, Argentina
157 V 12 **Chumikan**, Russian Federation
173 G 22 **Chumphon**, Thailand
173 H 17 **Chumsaeng**, Thailand
171 Y 6 **Ch'unch'ŏn**, South Korea
167 X 9 **Chundzha**, Kazakhstan
196 M 5 **Chunga**, Zambia
171 Y 7 **Ch'ungju**, South Korea
195 W 14 **Chungu**, Tanzania
195 S 13 **Chunya**, Tanzania
173 K 21 **Chuŏr Phnum Dâmrei**, Cambodia
173 K 18 **Chuŏr Phnum Dângrek**, Thailand
144 G 4 **Chuquicamata**, Chile
141 K 22 **Chuquisaca**, Bolivia
88 I 8 **Chur**, Switzerland
157 U 10 **Churapcha**, Russian Federation
121 S 14 **Church**, Virginia, U.S.A.
114 K 6 **Churchill**, Manitoba, Canada
115 U 8 **Churchill**, Newfoundland and Labrador, Canada
114 K 6 **Churchill**, Manitoba, Canada
115 U 8 **Churchill Falls**, Newfoundland and Labrador, Canada
168 D 11 **Churu**, India
138 M 2 **Churuguara**, Venezuela
176 L 6 **Chūrui**, Japan
168 F 8 **Chushul**, India
115 S 11 **Chute-des-Passes**, Québec, Canada
101 U 4 **Chutove**, Ukraine
215 O 15 **Chuuk**, Federated States of Micronesia
215 O 15 **Chuuk Islands**, Federated States of Micronesia
171 O 13 **Chuxiong**, China
167 U 10 **Chuyskaya Oblast'**, Kyrgyzstan
167 R 9 **Chyganak**, Kazakhstan
101 S 5 **Chyhyryn**, Ukraine
101 N 10 **Ciadîr-Lunga**, Moldova
174 H 14 **Ciamis**, Indonesia
174 H 14 **Cianjur**, Indonesia
94 M 12 **Ćićevac**, Serbia and Montenegro
213 Y 11 **Cicia**, Fiji
158 H 7 **Cide**, Turkey
92 K 11 **Ciechanów**, Poland
92 I 11 **Ciechocinek**, Poland
126 L 5 **Ciego de Ávila**, Cuba
138 I 2 **Ciénaga**, Colombia
126 K 5 **Cienfuegos**, Cuba
93 O 16 **Cieszanów**, Poland
93 I 18 **Cieszyn**, Poland
81 R 10 **Cieza**, Spain
158 H 11 **Cihanbeyli**, Turkey
125 N 12 **Cihuatlán**, Mexico
213 Y 10 **Cikobia**, Fiji
174 I 14 **Cilacap**, Indonesia
58 A 15 **Cilaos**, Réunion
159 S 8 **Cildir Gölö**, Turkey
171 S 11 **Cili**, China
81 O 2 **Cilleruelo de Bezana**, Spain

Country · Internal administrative region: State/Province/Territory/Dependent territory · Capital city · Mountain range/Undersea ridge · Mountain peak/Volcano/Seamount · Geographic feature · Headland/Point/Cape/Peninsula · Desert · Island/Island group · Antarctic base · Ocean · Sea · Bay/Gulf/Channel/Strait · Lake · Salt pan/Dry/Intermittent lake · River

159 Z 8 **Ciloy Adasi**, Azerbaijan
101 N 10 **Cimişlia**, Moldova
159 P 12 **Cinar**, Turkey
94 F 12 **Cincar**, Bosnia and Herzegovina
120 L 12 **Cincinnati**, Ohio, U.S.A.
158 C 12 **Cine**, Turkey
83 I 22 **Ciney**, Belgium
80 H 5 **Cinfães**, Portugal
90 F 12 **Cinigiano**, Italy
125 V 14 **Cintalapa**, Mexico
81 R 3 **Cintruénigo**, Spain
143 N 14 **Cipó**, Brazil
112 M 5 **Circle**, Alaska, U.S.A.
118 F 8 **Circle**, Montana, U.S.A.
117 M 18 **Circleville**, Utah, U.S.A.
120 M 12 **Circleville**, Ohio, U.S.A.
174 H 14 **Cirebon**, Indonesia
77 J 21 **Cirencester**, United Kingdom
90 A 7 **Cirie**, Italy
91 N 19 **Cirò Marina**, Italy
119 J 20 **Cisco**, Texas, U.S.A.
93 N 19 **Cisna**, Poland
91 H 14 **Cisterna di Latina**, Italy
80 M 2 **Cistierna**, Spain
196 K 14 **Citrusdal**, Republic of South Africa
90 G 12 **Città della Pieve**, Italy
90 G 11 **Città di Castello**, Italy
90 F 6 **Cittadella**, Italy
100 H 8 **Ciucea**, Romania
125 P 4 **Ciudad Acuña**, Mexico
125 P 13 **Ciudad Altamirano**, Mexico
139 Q 4 **Ciudad Bolívar**, Venezuela
124 M 6 **Ciudad Camargo**, Mexico
124 I 7 **Ciudad Constitución**, Mexico
125 W 14 **Ciudad Cuauhtémoc**, Mexico
144 J 8 **Ciudad de Loreto**, Argentina
125 R 10 **Ciudad de Valles**, Mexico
125 W 12 **Ciudad del Carmen**, Mexico
124 M 5 **Ciudad Delicias**, Mexico
139 R 4 **Ciudad Guayana**, Venezuela
125 O 11 **Ciudad Guzmán**, Mexico
124 L 3 **Ciudad Juárez**, Mexico
125 S 10 **Ciudad Madero**, Mexico
125 R 9 **Ciudad Mante**, Mexico
124 J 6 **Ciudad Obregón**, Mexico
139 Q 5 **Ciudad Piar**, Venezuela
81 N 9 **Ciudad Real**, Spain
80 K 6 **Ciudad Rodrigo**, Spain
125 Q 8 **Ciudad Victoria**, Mexico
81 Z 7 **Ciutadella de Menorca**, Spain
158 L 7 **Civa Burnu**, Turkey
90 G 13 **Civita Castellana**, Italy
90 I 11 **Civitanova Marche**, Italy
90 G 13 **Civitavecchia**, Italy
79 N 9 **Civray**, France
158 E 11 **Civril**, Turkey
171 W 10 **Cixi**, China
159 R 12 **Cizre**, Turkey
77 N 21 **Clacton-on-sea**, United Kingdom
79 R 7 **Clamecy**, France
122 M 5 **Clanton**, Alabama, U.S.A.
196 J 14 **Clanwilliam**, Republic of South Africa
173 F 22 **Clara Island**, Myanmar
120 L 7 **Clare**, Michigan, U.S.A.
77 A 17 **Clare Island**, Republic of Ireland
121 V 7 **Claremont**, New Hampshire, U.S.A.
211 I 18 **Clarence**, New Zealand
211 J 18 **Clarence**, New Zealand
63 K 26 **Clarence Bay**, Ascension
218 H 2 **Clarence Island**, Antarctica
113 O 11 **Clarence Strait**, Alaska, U.S.A.
127 N 4 **Clarence Town**, The Bahamas
115 Y 10 **Clarenville**, Newfoundland and Labrador, Canada
121 Q 10 **Clarion**, Pennsylvania, U.S.A.
61 S 6 **Clarion Fracture Zone**, Pacific Ocean
123 Q 4 **Clark Hill Reservoir**, South Carolina, U.S.A.
209 T 15 **Clarke Island**, Tasmania, Australia
121 P 12 **Clarksburg**, West Virginia, U.S.A.
122 H 4 **Clarksdale**, Mississippi, U.S.A.
116 H 8 **Clarkston**, Washington, U.S.A.
121 R 15 **Clarksville**, Virginia, U.S.A.
122 L 1 **Clarksville**, Tennessee, U.S.A.
211 E 25 **Clarksville**, New Zealand
123 Q 6 **Claxton**, Georgia, U.S.A.
117 N 22 **Clay Springs**, Arizona, U.S.A.
116 K 11 **Clayton**, Idaho, U.S.A.
119 N 20 **Clayton**, Louisiana, U.S.A.
119 G 16 **Clayton**, New Mexico, U.S.A.
113 S 10 **Clear Hills**, Alberta, Canada
117 C 17 **Clear Lake Reservoir**, California, U.S.A.
117 E 13 **Clear Lake Reservoir**, California, U.S.A.
116 J 9 **Clearwater**, Idaho, U.S.A.
113 T 13 **Clearwater**, British Columbia, Canada
123 P 11 **Clearwater**, Florida, U.S.A.
116 J 9 **Clearwater Mountains**, Idaho, U.S.A.
119 J 19 **Cleburne**, Texas, U.S.A.
219 V 6 **Clemence Massif**, Antarctica
79 Q 3 **Clermont**, France
209 U 6 **Clermont**, Queensland, Australia
79 R 10 **Clermont-Ferrand**, France
83 L 23 **Clervaux**, Luxembourg
90 F 5 **Cles**, Italy
119 L 21 **Cleveland**, Texas, U.S.A.
121 O 10 **Cleveland**, Ohio, U.S.A.
122 H 4 **Cleveland**, Mississippi, U.S.A.
123 O 3 **Cleveland**, Georgia, U.S.A.
123 N 3 **Cleveland**, Tennessee, U.S.A.
77 B 17 **Clew Bay**, Republic of Ireland
123 S 13 **Clewiston**, Florida, U.S.A.
77 A 17 **Clifden**, Republic of Ireland
211 J 17 **Clifford Bay**, New Zealand
117 O 24 **Clifton**, Arizona, U.S.A.
121 P 13 **Clifton Forge**, Virginia, U.S.A.
113 X 13 **Climax**, Saskatchewan, Canada
113 S 13 **Clinton**, British Columbia, Canada
118 N 12 **Clinton**, Iowa, U.S.A.
119 M 17 **Clinton**, Arkansas, U.S.A.
120 L 9 **Clinton**, Michigan, U.S.A.
122 H 6 **Clinton**, Mississippi, U.S.A.
123 U 3 **Clinton**, North Carolina, U.S.A.
123 Q 3 **Clinton**, South Carolina, U.S.A.
61 S 7 **Clipperton Fracture Zone**, Pacific Ocean
61 W 6 **Clipperton Island**, France
78 L 7 **Clisson**, France
77 B 21 **Clonakilty**, Republic of Ireland
209 Q 5 **Cloncurry**, Queensland, Australia
77 D 20 **Clonmel**, Republic of Ireland
86 D 12 **Cloppenburg**, Germany
144 M 6 **Clorinda**, Argentina
211 J 16 **Cloudy Bay**, New Zealand
117 C 17 **Cloverdale**, California, U.S.A.
119 G 18 **Clovis**, New Mexico, U.S.A.
100 H 9 **Cluj-Napoca**, Romania
79 S 9 **Cluny**, France
79 W 9 **Cluses**, France
90 D 6 **Clusone**, Italy
211 D 24 **Clutha**, New Zealand
76 H 13 **Clyde**, United Kingdom
113 V 11 **Clyde**, Alberta, Canada
211 D 25 **Clydevale**, New Zealand
172 K 12 **Co Nôi**, Vietnam
125 O 6 **Coahuila**, Mexico
117 H 18 **Coaldale**, Nevada, U.S.A.
142 D 12 **Coari**, Brazil
142 E 11 **Coari**, Brazil
195 X 9 **Coast**, Kenya
113 O 10 **Coast Moutains**, British Columbia, Canada
117 C 14 **Coast Ranges**, California, U.S.A.
115 O 4 **Coats Island**, Nunavut, Canada
219 N 4 **Coats Land**, Antarctica
125 U 13 **Coatzacoalcos**, Mexico
126 D 9 **Cobán**, Guatemala
209 S 10 **Cobar**, New South Wales, Australia
141 I 16 **Cobija**, Bolivia
121 U 8 **Cobleskill**, New York, U.S.A.
208 M 1 **Cobourg Peninsula**, Northern Territory, Australia
197 R 4 **Cóbuè**, Mozambique
87 I 19 **Coburg**, Germany
141 G 20 **Cocachacra**, Peru
143 I 15 **Cocalinho**, Brazil
141 J 19 **Cochabamba**, Bolivia
141 J 20 **Cochabamba**, Bolivia
145 F 17 **Cochamó**, Chile
87 C 19 **Cochem**, Germany
173 M 23 **Cochin**, Vietnam
169 D 23 **Cochin**, India
115 O 11 **Cochrane**, Ontario, Canada
145 F 21 **Cochrane**, Chile
209 Q 10 **Cockburn**, South Australia, Australia
127 Q 5 **Cockburn Harbour**, Turks and Caicos Islands
127 Q 5 **Cockburn Town**, Turks and Caicos Islands
126 J 13 **Coclé del Norte**, Panama
126 G 10 **Coco**, Nicaragua
169 N 20 **Coco Channel**, India
58 L 4 **Coco-de-Mer Seamounts**, Indian Ocean
123 S 11 **Cocoa Beach**, Florida, U.S.A.
194 D 7 **Cocobeach**, Gabon
143 L 15 **Cocos**, Brazil
59 Q 4 **Cocos Basin**, Indian Ocean
59 Z 1 **Cocos Islands**, Australia
125 N 11 **Cocula**, Mexico
115 U 6 **Cod Island**, Newfoundland and Labrador, Canada
142 E 11 **Codajás**, Brazil
211 B 26 **Codfish Island**, New Zealand
142 L 11 **Codó**, Brazil
127 W 7 **Codrington**, Antigua and Barbuda
118 D 10 **Cody**, Wyoming, U.S.A.
209 S 2 **Coen**, Queensland, Australia
87 D 14 **Coesfeld**, Germany
116 I 7 **Coeur d'Alene**, Idaho, U.S.A.
82 N 9 **Coevorden**, Netherlands
197 O 14 **Coffee Bay**, Republic of South Africa
122 J 7 **Coffeeville**, Alabama, U.S.A.
119 K 16 **Coffeyville**, Kansas, U.S.A.
209 O 11 **Coffin Bay**, South Australia, Australia
209 O 12 **Coffin Bay**, South Australia, Australia
209 O 11 **Coffin Bay Peninsula**, South Australia, Australia
209 W 10 **Coffs Harbour**, New South Wales, Australia
101 N 13 **Cogealac**, Romania
78 M 10 **Cognac**, France
193 T 15 **Cogo**, Equatorial Guinea
144 M 6 **Cogoi**, Argentina
145 F 20 **Coihaique**, Chile
169 E 22 **Coimbatore**, India
80 H 6 **Coimbra**, Portugal
80 H 7 **Coimbra**, Portugal
139 N 3 **Cojedes**, Venezuela
209 R 13 **Colac**, Victoria, Australia
211 B 25 **Colac**, New Zealand
143 M 17 **Colatina**, Brazil
77 M 20 **Colchester**, United Kingdom
112 F 9 **Cold Bay**, Alaska, U.S.A.
117 H 16 **Cold Spring**, Nevada, U.S.A.
119 N 15 **Coldwater**, Missouri, U.S.A.
120 L 9 **Coldwater**, Michigan, U.S.A.
121 W 5 **Colebrook**, New Hampshire, U.S.A.
120 I 5 **Coleman**, Wisconsin, U.S.A.
77 E 14 **Coleraine**, United Kingdom
116 H 8 **Colfax**, Washington, U.S.A.
90 D 6 **Colico**, Italy
83 E 15 **Colijnsplaat**, Netherlands
125 N 12 **Colima**, Mexico
125 N 12 **Colima**, Mexico
142 L 12 **Colinas**, Brazil
76 E 11 **Coll**, United Kingdom
81 O 6 **Collado Villalba**, Spain
90 F 11 **Colle di Val d'Elsa**, Italy
208 G 11 **Collie**, Western Australia, Australia
208 I 3 **Collier Bay**, Western Australia, Australia
211 I 15 **Collingwood**, New Zealand
122 I 7 **Collins**, Mississippi, U.S.A.
113 U 2 **Collinson Peninsula**, Nunavut, Canada
209 U 5 **Collinsville**, Queensland, Australia
145 F 15 **Collipulli**, Chile
79 W 5 **Colmar**, France
87 C 17 **Cologne**, Germany
138 I 8 **Colombia**, South America
62 D 12 **Colombian Basin**, Atlantic Ocean
169 F 25 **Colombo**, Sri Lanka
126 J 4 **Colón**, Cuba
126 K 13 **Colón**, Panama
144 K 12 **Colón**, Argentina
144 M 11 **Colón**, Argentina
127 O 4 **Colonel Hill**, The Bahamas
124 F 3 **Colonet**, Mexico
144 M 12 **Colonia**, Uruguay
214 K 14 **Colonia**, Federated States of Micronesia
144 M 12 **Colonia del Sacramento**, Uruguay
144 J 8 **Colonia Dora**, Argentina
145 H 20 **Colonia Las Heras**, Argentina
76 F 13 **Colonsay**, United Kingdom
119 D 14 **Colorado**, U.S.A.
145 H 14 **Colorado**, Argentina
117 L 20 **Colorado**, Mexico/U.S.A.
117 L 19 **Colorado City**, Arizona, U.S.A.
119 H 19 **Colorado City**, Texas, U.S.A.
117 I 23 **Colorado Desert**, California, U.S.A.
117 M 19 **Colorado Plateau**, Utah, U.S.A.
119 F 14 **Colorado Springs**, Colorado, U.S.A.
125 O 10 **Colotlán**, Mexico
123 N 7 **Colquitt**, Georgia, U.S.A.
117 N 16 **Colton**, Utah, U.S.A.
116 G 8 **Columbia**, Washington, U.S.A.
119 M 14 **Columbia**, Missouri, U.S.A.
122 I 7 **Columbia**, Mississippi, U.S.A.
122 L 2 **Columbia**, Tennessee, U.S.A.
123 W 1 **Columbia**, North Carolina, U.S.A.
123 R 4 **Columbia**, South Carolina, U.S.A.
116 H 8 **Columbia Basin**, Washington, U.S.A.
113 S 12 **Columbia Mountains**, British Columbia, Canada
63 I 16 **Columbia Seamount**, Atlantic Ocean
118 J 12 **Columbus**, Nebraska, U.S.A.
119 D 20 **Columbus**, New Mexico, U.S.A.
119 K 21 **Columbus**, Texas, U.S.A.
120 K 12 **Columbus**, Indiana, U.S.A.
120 M 11 **Columbus**, Ohio, U.S.A.
120 H 7 **Columbus**, Wisconsin, U.S.A.
122 J 5 **Columbus**, Mississippi, U.S.A.
123 N 6 **Columbus**, Georgia, U.S.A.
112 J 3 **Colville**, Alaska, U.S.A.
116 H 6 **Colville**, Washington, U.S.A.
210 L 8 **Colville**, New Zealand
210 K 7 **Colville Channel**, New Zealand
113 Q 5 **Colville Lake**, Northwest Territories, Canada
90 G 8 **Comacchio**, Italy
145 H 22 **Comandante Luis Piedra Buena**, Argentina
144 H 12 **Comandante Salas**, Argentina
100 L 10 **Comănești**, Romania
100 K 11 **Comarnic**, Romania
126 E 9 **Comayagua**, Honduras
144 F 10 **Combarbalá**, Chile
172 B 13 **Combermere Bay**, Myanmar
169 L 14 **Comilla**, Bangladesh
81 N 1 **Comillas**, Spain
125 W 14 **Comitán de Domínguez**, Mexico
62 A 7 **Commissioner's Point**, Bermuda
115 N 1 **Committee Bay**, Nunavut, Canada
219 V 14 **Commonwealth Bay**, Antarctica
90 C 6 **Como**, Italy
145 I 20 **Comodoro Rivadavia**, Argentina
124 I 7 **Comondú**, Mexico
197 V 3 **Comoros**, Africa
79 Q 3 **Compiègne**, France
101 N 10 **Comrat**, Moldova
61 R 3 **Comstock Seamount**, Pacific Ocean
173 M 24 **Côn Đao**, Vietnam
173 M 24 **Côn Son**, Vietnam
145 H 17 **Cona Niyeu**, Argentina
192 F 11 **Conakry**, Guinea
143 M 17 **Conceição da Barra**, Brazil
142 J 12 **Conceição do Araguaia**, Brazil
125 P 8 **Concepción**, Mexico
126 I 14 **Concepción**, Panama
141 J 16 **Concepción**, Bolivia
143 G 19 **Concepción**, Paraguay
144 I 8 **Concepción**, Argentina
145 E 14 **Concepción**, Chile
144 M 11 **Concepción del Uruguay**, Argentina
79 O 4 **Conches-en-Ouche**, France
144 G 4 **Conchi**, Chile
124 L 6 **Conchos**, Mexico
117 D 18 **Concord**, California, U.S.A.
121 W 7 **Concord**, New Hampshire, U.S.A.
140 E 11 **Concordia**, Peru
144 M 10 **Concordia**, Argentina
79 Q 11 **Condat**, France
126 F 10 **Condega**, Nicaragua
209 T 11 **Condobolin**, New South Wales, Australia
79 N 13 **Condom**, France
90 G 6 **Conegliano**, Italy
125 N 7 **Conejos**, Mexico
212 H 7 **Conflict Group**, Papua New Guinea
101 N 10 **Congaz**, Moldova
171 S 12 **Congjiang**, China
194 H 8 **Congo**, Africa
194 J 7 **Congo**, Democratic Republic of Congo/Angola
63 M 14 **Congo Cone**, Atlantic Ocean
117 L 22 **Congress**, Arizona, U.S.A.
113 V 10 **Conklin**, Alberta, Canada
77 B 17 **Connaught**, Republic of Ireland
121 P 9 **Conneaut**, Ohio, U.S.A.
121 V 9 **Connecticut**, U.S.A.
116 G 8 **Connell**, Washington, U.S.A.
58 K 12 **Conrad Rise**, Indian Ocean
119 L 21 **Conroe**, Texas, U.S.A.
101 N 13 **Constanța**, Romania
189 O 5 **Constantine**, Algeria
81 O 8 **Consuegra**, Spain
113 X 13 **Consul**, Saskatchewan, Canada
90 G 8 **Contarina**, Italy
140 B 13 **Contumazá**, Peru
113 U 5 **Contwoyto Lake**, Nunavut, Canada
91 N 16 **Conversano**, Italy
119 M 17 **Conway**, Arkansas, U.S.A.
121 W 6 **Conway**, New Hampshire, U.S.A.
123 T 4 **Conway**, South Carolina, U.S.A.
77 H 18 **Conwy**, United Kingdom
209 N 9 **Coober Pedy**, South Australia, Australia
118 L 7 **Cook**, Minnesota, U.S.A.
208 M 10 **Cook**, South Australia, Australia
112 I 8 **Cook Inlet**, Alaska, U.S.A.
215 O 10 **Cook Islands**, New Zealand
211 J 15 **Cook Strait**, New Zealand
123 N 1 **Cookeville**, Tennessee, U.S.A.
209 T 3 **Cooktown**, Queensland, Australia
209 W 9 **Coolangatta**, Queensland, Australia
208 I 10 **Coolgardie**, Western Australia, Australia
209 U 12 **Cooma**, New South Wales, Australia
209 Q 11 **Coombah**, New South Wales, Australia
209 T 10 **Coonabarabran**, New South Wales, Australia
209 U 10 **Coonamble**, New South Wales, Australia
169 C 20 **Coondapoor**, India
169 D 22 **Coonoor**, India
209 P 9 **Cooper**, South Australia, Australia
119 L 19 **Cooper**, Texas, U.S.A.
126 M 1 **Cooper's Town**, The Bahamas
144 H 8 **Copacabana**, Argentina
125 R 14 **Copala**, Mexico
85 D 25 **Copenhagen**, Denmark
144 F 8 **Copiapó**, Chile
120 I 3 **Copper Harbor**, Michigan, U.S.A.
197 N 4 **Copperbelt**, Zambia
170 J 9 **Coqên**, China
144 F 10 **Coquimbo**, Chile
144 F 10 **Coquimbo**, Chile
100 I 14 **Corabia**, Romania
141 E 18 **Coracora**, Peru
208 E 7 **Coral Bay**, Western Australia, Australia
123 S 14 **Coral Gables**, Florida, U.S.A.
115 O 3 **Coral Harbour**, Nunavut, Canada
60 M 9 **Coral Sea**, Pacific Ocean
60 M 9 **Coral Sea Basin**, Pacific Ocean
60 M 9 **Coral Sea Islands**, Pacific Ocean
120 L 14 **Corbin**, Kentucky, U.S.A.
145 G 18 **Corcovado**, Argentina
123 O 6 **Cordele**, Georgia, U.S.A.
80 J 2 **Cordillera Cantabrica**, Spain
126 I 14 **Cordillera Central**, Panama
138 H 8 **Cordillera Central**, Colombia
126 H 13 **Cordillera de Talamanca**, Costa Rica
144 G 6 **Cordillera Domeyko**, Chile
126 G 10 **Cordillera Entre Rios**, Honduras
126 G 10 **Cordillera Isabelia**, Nicaragua
125 Q 12 **Cordillera Neo-Volcánica**, Mexico
141 C 14 **Cordillera Occidental**, South America
141 D 15 **Cordillera Oriental**, Peru/Colombia
144 K 11 **Córdoba**, Argentina
138 H 4 **Córdoba**, Colombia
80 M 11 **Córdoba**, Spain
125 T 12 **Córdoba**, Mexico
144 J 10 **Córdoba**, Argentina
112 K 8 **Cordova**, Alaska, U.S.A.
97 A 16 **Corfu**, Greece
80 K 7 **Coria**, Spain
120 L 13 **Corinth**, Kentucky, U.S.A.
122 J 3 **Corinth**, Mississippi, U.S.A.
97 F 20 **Corinth Canal**, Greece
143 F 16 **Corixa Grande**, Brazil
77 C 21 **Cork**, Republic of Ireland
77 C 21 **Cork Harbour**, Republic of Ireland
91 I 22 **Corleone**, Italy
96 N 12 **Çorlu**, Turkey
120 G 5 **Cornell**, Wisconsin, U.S.A.
115 X 10 **Corner Brook**, Newfoundland and Labrador, Canada
62 G 8 **Corner Seamounts**, Atlantic Ocean
117 D 15 **Corning**, California, U.S.A.
121 S 9 **Corning**, New York, U.S.A.
115 R 14 **Cornwall**, Ontario, Canada
126 M 2 **Cornwall**, The Bahamas
138 M 2 **Coro**, Venezuela
141 I 19 **Coroico**, Bolivia
210 L 8 **Coromandel**, New Zealand
169 G 20 **Coromandel Coast**, India
210 L 8 **Coromandel Peninsula**, New Zealand
210 L 8 **Coromandel Range**, New Zealand
175 O 5 **Coron**, Philippines
119 E 18 **Corona**, New Mexico, U.S.A.
113 T 4 **Coronation Gulf**, Nunavut, Canada
218 H 1 **Coronation Island**, Antarctica

Country · Internal administrative region: State/Province/Territory/Dependent territory · Capital city · Mountain range/Undersea ridge · Mountain peak/Volcano/Seamount · Geographic feature · Headland/Point/Cape/Peninsula · Desert · Island/Island group · Antarctic base · Ocean · Sea · Bay/Gulf/Channel/Strait · Lake · Salt pan/Dry/Intermittent lake · River

145 K 15 **Coronel Dorrego**, Argentina
143 H 20 **Coronel Oviedo**, Paraguay
145 K 14 **Coronel Pringles**, Argentina
143 H 19 **Coronel Sapucaia**, Brazil
145 K 14 **Coronel Suárez**, Argentina
145 M 14 **Coronel Vidal**, Argentina
211 C 23 **Coronet Peak**, New Zealand
95 K 20 **Çorovodë**, Albania
209 S 12 **Corowa**, New South Wales, Australia
126 E 7 **Corozal**, Belize
145 H 22 **Corpen Aike**, Argentina
119 K 23 **Corpus Christi**, Texas, U.S.A.
141 I 21 **Corque**, Bolivia
62 O 11 **Corralejo**, Canary Islands
143 L 14 **Corrente**, Brazil
143 H 16 **Correntes**, Brazil
143 L 15 **Correntina**, Brazil
144 N 8 **Corrientes**, Argentina
144 M 8 **Corrientes**, Argentina
119 L 20 **Corrigan**, Texas, U.S.A.
208 G 11 **Corrigin**, Western Australia, Australia
79 X 14 **Corsica**, France
119 L 20 **Corsicana**, Texas, U.S.A.
80 J 11 **Cortegana**, Spain
90 B 8 **Cortemilia**, Italy
119 D 15 **Cortez**, Colorado, U.S.A.
90 H 5 **Cortina d'Ampezzo**, Italy
121 S 8 **Cortland**, New York, U.S.A.
90 G 11 **Cortona**, Italy
80 H 9 **Coruche**, Portugal
159 P 9 **Çoruh**, Turkey
158 J 8 **Çorum**, Turkey
143 G 17 **Corumbá**, Brazil
143 O 14 **Coruripe**, Brazil
62 L 1 **Corvo**, Azores
124 L 8 **Cosalá**, Mexico
125 T 12 **Cosamaloapan**, Mexico
144 G 3 **Coscaya**, Chile
91 M 19 **Cosenza**, Italy
121 O 11 **Coshocton**, Ohio, U.S.A.
79 R 7 **Cosne-cours-sur-Loire**, France
144 J 10 **Cosquín**, Argentina
81 T 11 **Costa Blanca**, Spain
81 X 4 **Costa Brava**, Spain
80 J 13 **Costa de la Luz**, Spain
81 T 8 **Costa del Azahar**, Spain
81 N 14 **Costa del Sol**, Spain
81 V 6 **Costa Dorada**, Spain
143 D 14 **Costa Marques**, Brazil
126 G 13 **Costa Rica**, North America
124 L 8 **Costa Rica**, Mexico
91 D 15 **Costa Smeralda**, Italy
81 N 1 **Costa Verde**, Spain
87 K 15 **Coswig**, Germany
175 Q 7 **Cotabato**, Philippines
141 J 22 **Cotagaita**, Bolivia
141 F 18 **Cotahuasi**, Peru
79 W 15 **Côte d'Azur**, France
192 K 12 **Côte d'Ivoire**, Africa
193 O 13 **Cotonou**, Benin
140 B 9 **Cotopaxi**, Ecuador
77 J 22 **Cotswold Hills**, United Kingdom
87 N 15 **Cottbus**, Germany
90 A 8 **Cottian Alps**, Italy
119 I 23 **Cotulla**, Texas, U.S.A.
121 Q 9 **Coudersport**, Pennsylvania, U.S.A.
116 G 7 **Coulee City**, Washington, U.S.A.
79 Q 4 **Coulommiers**, France
112 H 4 **Council**, Alaska, U.S.A.
116 I 10 **Council**, Idaho, U.S.A.
118 K 13 **Council Bluffs**, Iowa, U.S.A.
139 U 7 **Courantyne**, Suriname
77 F 21 **Courcelles**, Belgium
89 B 15 **Courland Lagoon**, Russian Federation
90 A 6 **Courmayeur**, Italy
58 B 8 **Cousin**, Seychelles
58 B 9 **Cousine**, Seychelles
78 L 4 **Coutances**, France
113 W 14 **Coutts**, Alberta, Canada
73 G 23 **Couvin**, Belgium
77 K 20 **Coventry**, United Kingdom
80 J 7 **Covilhã**, Portugal
120 L 12 **Covington**, Kentucky, U.S.A.
120 I 4 **Covington**, Michigan, U.S.A.
122 I 2 **Covington**, Tennessee, U.S.A.
123 O 5 **Covington**, Georgia, U.S.A.
209 P 11 **Cowell**, South Australia, Australia
77 K 23 **Cowes**, United Kingdom
209 T 11 **Cowra**, New South Wales, Australia
143 H 17 **Coxim**, Brazil
169 M 15 **Cox's Bazar**, Bangladesh
192 F 11 **Coyah**, Guinea
125 Z 10 **Cozumel**, Mexico
58 E 8 **Crab Island**, Rodrigues Island
197 N 14 **Cradock**, Republic of South Africa
210 K 7 **Cradock Channel**, New Zealand
113 O 11 **Craig**, Alaska, U.S.A.
118 E 13 **Craig**, Colorado, U.S.A.
116 I 8 **Craigmont**, Idaho, U.S.A.
87 H 22 **Crailsheim**, Germany
100 H 13 **Craiova**, Romania
114 H 7 **Cranberry Portage**, Manitoba, Canada
113 V 14 **Cranbrook**, British Columbia, Canada
218 L 10 **Crary Mountains**, Antarctica
212 H 4 **Crater Point**, Papua New Guinea
142 M 11 **Crateús**, Brazil
138 L 5 **Cravo Norte**, Colombia
118 G 12 **Crawford**, Nebraska, U.S.A.
63 K 18 **Crawford Seamount**, Atlantic Ocean
120 J 11 **Crawfordsville**, Indiana, U.S.A.
123 O 9 **Crawfordville**, Florida, U.S.A.
77 L 22 **Crawley**, United Kingdom
113 W 9 **Cree Lake**, Saskatchewan, Canada
124 L 5 **Creel**, Mexico
90 D 7 **Crema**, Italy
90 D 7 **Cremona**, Italy
122 H 3 **Crenshaw**, Mississippi, U.S.A.
94 B 10 **Cres**, Croatia
116 C 13 **Crescent City**, California, U.S.A.
123 R 9 **Crescent Lake**, Florida, U.S.A.
79 T 12 **Crest**, France
113 U 14 **Creston**, British Columbia, Canada
118 L 13 **Creston**, Iowa, U.S.A.
118 D 12 **Creston**, Wyoming, U.S.A.
122 L 8 **Crestview**, Florida, U.S.A.
97 I 26 **Crete**, Greece
121 R 14 **Crewe**, Virginia, U.S.A.
143 J 21 **Criciúma**, Brazil
76 H 12 **Crieff**, United Kingdom
94 C 9 **Crikvenica**, Croatia
101 U 11 **Crimea**, Ukraine
142 L 13 **Cristino Castro**, Brazil
101 O 8 **Criuleni**, Moldova
143 J 15 **Crixás**, Brazil
95 M 16 **Crna Gora**, Serbia and Montenegro/Macedonia (F.Y.R.O.M.)
94 E9 **Croatia**, Europe
119 L 20 **Crockett**, Texas, U.S.A.
77 N 18 **Cromer**, United Kingdom
211 D 23 **Cromwell**, New Zealand
127 O 4 **Crooked Island**, The Bahamas
127 N 5 **Crooked Island Passage**, The Bahamas
123 P 9 **Cross City**, Florida, U.S.A.
77 J 15 **Cross Fell**, United Kingdom
114 J 8 **Cross Lake**, Manitoba, Canada
193 R 13 **Cross River**, Nigeria
119 N 19 **Crossett**, Arkansas, U.S.A.
123 N 2 **Crossville**, Tennessee, U.S.A.
121 N 8 **Croswell**, Michigan, U.S.A.
91 N 19 **Crotone**, Italy
118 E 9 **Crow Agency**, Montana, U.S.A.
119 N 21 **Crowley**, Louisiana, U.S.A.
120 J 9 **Crown Point**, Indiana, U.S.A.
219 U 3 **Crown Prince Olav Coast**, Antarctica
219 O 3 **Crown Princess Martha Coast**, Antarctica
77 L 22 **Croydon**, United Kingdom
209 R 4 **Croydon**, Queensland, Australia
58 M 9 **Crozet Basin**, Indian Ocean
58 K 11 **Crozet Islands**, France
58 J 11 **Crozet Plateau**, Indian Ocean
78 H 5 **Crozon**, France
62 I 9 **Cruiser Tablemount**, Atlantic Ocean
142 A 13 **Cruzeiro do Sul**, Brazil
120 I 4 **Crystal Falls**, Michigan, U.S.A.
93 N 22 **Csenger**, Hungary
93 G 22 **Csorna**, Hungary
93 I 22 **Csóványos**, Hungary
173 O 17 **Cu Lao Cham**, Vietnam
173 O 17 **Cu Lao Re**, Vietnam
173 O 22 **Cu Lao Thu**, Vietnam
197 S 5 **Cuamba**, Mozambique
196 K 6 **Cuando Cubango**, Angola
196 J 7 **Cuangar**, Angola
196 G 2 **Cuanza Norte**, Angola
196 H 3 **Cuanza Sul**, Angola
125 O 6 **Cuatro Ciénegas**, Mexico
124 L 5 **Cuauhtémoc**, Mexico
126 K 5 **Cuba**, North America
119 E 17 **Cuba**, New Mexico, U.S.A.
196 G 4 **Cubal**, Angola
196 I 6 **Cubango**, Angola
158 H 9 **Cubuk**, Turkey
196 I 5 **Cuchi**, Angola
145 I 15 **Cuchillo-Có**, Argentina
142 C 9 **Cucuí**, Brazil
196 J 3 **Cucumbi**, Angola
138 J 4 **Cúcuta**, Colombia
169 F 22 **Cuddalore**, India
169 F 20 **Cuddapah**, India
208 G 9 **Cue**, Western Australia, Australia
81 N 5 **Cuéllar**, Spain
196 I 4 **Cuemba**, Angola
81 Q 7 **Cuenca**, Spain
140 B 10 **Cuenca**, Ecuador
125 N 8 **Cuencamé**, Mexico
125 R 12 **Cuernavaca**, Mexico
119 K 22 **Cuero**, Texas, U.S.A.
127 N 6 **Cueto**, Cuba
142 F 12 **Cuiaba**, Brazil
143 G 16 **Cuiabá**, Brazil
196 J 2 **Cuilo**, Angola
196 G 1 **Cuimba**, Angola
196 J 5 **Cuito Cuanavale**, Angola
100 G 13 **Cujmir**, Romania
174 F 9 **Cukai**, Malaysia
159 T 12 **Cukurca**, Turkey
175 O 5 **Culasi**, Philippines
118 G 7 **Culbertson**, Montana, U.S.A.
141 C 15 **Culebras**, Peru
82 I 13 **Culemborg**, Netherlands
159 V 10 **Culfa**, Azerbaijan
124 L 8 **Culiacán**, Mexico
175 N 5 **Culion**, Philippines
81 Q 12 **Cúllar-Baza**, Spain
81 T 9 **Cullera**, Spain
122 L 4 **Cullman**, Alabama, U.S.A.
121 R 13 **Culpeper**, Virginia, U.S.A.
139 Q 2 **Cumaná**, Venezuela
122 M 1 **Cumberland**, Tennessee, U.S.A.
121 Q 12 **Cumberland**, Maryland, U.S.A.
113 Y 10 **Cumberland Lake**, Saskatchewan, Canada
115 S 1 **Cumberland Peninsula**, Nunavut, Canada
122 K 5 **Cumberland Plateau**, Tennessee, U.S.A.
115 S 2 **Cumberland Sound**, Nunavut, Canada
142 H 9 **Cuminapanema**, Brazil
77 H 14 **Cumnock**, United Kingdom
124 J 4 **Cumpas**, Mexico
158 H 12 **Çumra**, Turkey
126 C 9 **Cunén**, Guatemala
196 H 6 **Cunene**, Angola
196 F 7 **Cunene**, Angola
90 A 9 **Cuneo**, Italy
173 O 19 **Cung Son**, Vietnam
209 T 9 **Cunnamulla**, Queensland, Australia
142 A 12 **Curaçá**, Brazil
142 N 13 **Curaçá**, Brazil
127 S 11 **Curaçao**, Netherlands Antilles
145 F 15 **Curacautín**, Chile
140 E 9 **Curaray**, Peru/Ecuador
58 B 12 **Curepipe**, Mauritius
144 F 13 **Curicó**, Chile
58 B 8 **Curieuse**, Seychelles
138 I 10 **Curiplaya**, Colombia
143 J 20 **Curitiba**, Brazil
63 C 16 **Curral Velho**, Cape Verde
117 J 17 **Currant**, Nevada, U.S.A.
117 J 15 **Currie**, Nevada, U.S.A.
209 R 14 **Currie**, Tasmania, Australia
123 X 1 **Currituck**, North Carolina, U.S.A.
112 J 7 **Curry**, Alaska, U.S.A.
209 V 7 **Curtis Island**, Queensland, Australia
142 H 9 **Curuá**, Brazil
142 I 10 **Curumu**, Brazil
141 G 17 **Cusco**, Peru
123 N 6 **Cusseta**, Georgia, U.S.A.
118 G 11 **Custer**, South Dakota, U.S.A.
123 N 7 **Cuthbert**, Georgia, U.S.A.
123 S 14 **Cutler Ridge**, Florida, U.S.A.
145 G 15 **Cutral-Co**, Argentina
169 J 16 **Cuttack**, India
196 H 6 **Cuvelai**, Angola
194 H 8 **Cuvette**, Congo
59 T 7 **Cuvier Basin**, Indian Ocean
59 S 7 **Cuvier Plateau**, Indian Ocean
86 F 9 **Cuxhaven**, Germany
144 F 2 **Cuya**, Chile
175 O 5 **Cuyo**, Philippines
175 O 5 **Cuyo**, Philippines
175 O 5 **Cuyo Islands**, Philippines
139 S 5 **Cuyuni**, Guyana
141 G 17 **Cuzco**, Peru
195 Q 9 **Cyangugu**, Rwanda
97 I 22 **Cyclades**, Greece
158 G 15 **Cyprus**, Asia
158 I 14 **Cyprus (Turkish Republic Of Northern Cyprus)**, Asia
92 F 10 **Czaplinek**, Poland
113 W 12 **Czar**, Alberta, Canada
92 F 11 **Czarnków**, Poland
93 C 18 **Czech Republic**, Europe
92 H 9 **Czersk**, Poland
93 I 16 **Częstochowa**, Poland
92 F 11 **Człopa**, Poland
92 G 10 **Człuchów**, Poland

D

171 V 3 **Da Hinggan Ling**, China
170 M 8 **Da Juh**, China
173 O 21 **Đa Lat**, Vietnam
173 O 17 **Đa Nẵng**, Vietnam
171 N 7 **Da Qaidam**, China
171 R 10 **Daba Shan**, China
138 L 2 **Dabajuro**, Venezuela
192 K 12 **Dabakala**, Côte d'Ivoire
93 J 23 **Dabas**, Hungary
191 H 18 **Dabat**, Ethiopia
138 G 5 **Dabeiba**, Colombia
169 C 18 **Dabhol**, India
192 G 11 **Dabola**, Guinea
192 K 14 **Dabou**, Côte d'Ivoire
93 J 17 **Dąbrowa Górnicza**, Poland
100 I 13 **Dăbuleni**, Romania
169 L 14 **Dacca**, Bangladesh
87 J 24 **Dachau**, Germany
171 R 10 **Dachaun**, China
62 J 10 **Dacia Seamount**, Atlantic Ocean
211 C 25 **Dacre**, New Zealand
160 K 1 **Dādāt**, Syria
191 K 18 **Daddato**, Djibouti
123 Q 10 **Dade City**, Florida, U.S.A.
169 C 16 **Dadra and Nagar Haveli**, India
165 T 13 **Dadu**, Pakistan
175 P 4 **Daet**, Philippines
163 V 7 **Dafir**, United Arab Emirates
191 L 21 **Daga Medo**, Ethiopia
98 I 13 **Dagda**, Latvia
171 U 7 **Dagu**, China
175 O 3 **Dagupan**, Philippines
162 L 8 **Dahabān**, Saudi Arabia
169 B 16 **Dahanu**, India
191 J 16 **Dahlak Archipelago**, Eritrea
87 M 14 **Dahme**, Germany
170 H 7 **Dahongliutan**, China
161 R 1 **Dahūk**, Iraq
212 M 6 **Dai**, Solomon Islands
171 T 7 **Dai Xian**, China
173 E 15 **Daik-u**, Myanmar
177 E 17 **Daimanji-san**, Japan
81 O 9 **Daimiel**, Spain
177 H 16 **Dainichiga-take**, Japan
177 I 18 **Daiō-zaki**, Japan
190 E 9 **Dairūt**, Egypt
120 F 4 **Dairyland**, Wisconsin, U.S.A.
209 Q 5 **Dajarra**, Queensland, Australia
165 P 8 **Dak**, Afghanistan
173 N 18 **Dak Kon**, Vietnam
192 D 8 **Dakar**, Senegal
190 D 11 **Dakhla Oasis**, Egypt
192 E 5 **Dakhlet Nouâdhibou**, Mauritania
169 O 25 **Dakoank**, India
169 C 15 **Dakor**, India
193 Q 9 **Dakoro**, Niger
95 L 16 **Đakovica**, Serbia and Montenegro
94 H 9 **Đakovo**, Croatia
196 J 3 **Dala**, Angola
192 G 11 **Dalaba**, Guinea
158 D 13 **Dalaman**, Turkey
171 Q 5 **Dalandzadgad**, Mongolia
171 P 5 **Dalay**, Mongolia
165 R 11 **Dalbandin**, Pakistan
209 V 8 **Dalby**, Queensland, Australia
123 N 1 **Dale Hollow Lake**, Tennessee, U.S.A.
101 S 11 **Daleke**, Ukraine
172 B 11 **Daletme**, Myanmar
119 G 17 **Dalhart**, Texas, U.S.A.
171 O 13 **Dali**, China
171 W 7 **Dalian**, China
119 K 19 **Dallas**, Texas, U.S.A.
94 D 12 **Dalmatia**, Croatia
157 W 15 **Dal'negorsk**, Russian Federation
192 J 13 **Daloa**, Côte d'Ivoire
169 I 14 **Daltenganj**, India
123 N 3 **Dalton**, Georgia, U.S.A.
175 O 1 **Dalupiri**, Philippines
84 C 10 **Dalvík**, Iceland
208 G 10 **Dalwallinu**, Western Australia, Australia
208 M 2 **Daly**, Northern Territory, Australia
209 N 3 **Daly Waters**, Northern Territory, Australia
169 B 16 **Daman**, India
169 B 16 **Daman and Diu**, India
190 E 7 **Damanhûr**, Egypt
175 S 14 **Damar**, Indonesia
194 J 5 **Damara**, Central African Republic
196 J 8 **Damaraland**, Namibia
193 U 9 **Damasak**, Nigeria
160 H 7 **Damascus**, Syria
193 T 10 **Damaturu**, Nigeria
196 G 1 **Damba**, Angola
193 R 10 **Dambatta**, Nigeria
193 U 10 **Damboa**, Nigeria
169 G 24 **Dambulla**, Sri Lanka
164 K 6 **Damghan**, Iran
169 F 14 **Damoh**, India
160 G 6 **Damour**, Lebanon
208 F 6 **Dampier**, Western Australia, Australia
212 E 4 **Dampier Strait**, Papua New Guinea
193 Q 10 **Dan-Gulbi**, Nigeria
192 I 13 **Danané**, Côte d'Ivoire
166 J 13 **Danata**, Turkmenistan
174 K 10 **Danau Luar**, Indonesia
175 O 10 **Danau Poso**, Indonesia
174 F 13 **Danau Ranau**, Indonesia
174 L 10 **Danau Semayang**, Indonesia
174 J 12 **Danau Sembulu**, Indonesia
174 C 9 **Danau Toba**, Indonesia
175 O 12 **Danau Towuti**, Indonesia
120 F 4 **Danbury**, Wisconsin, U.S.A.
121 V 9 **Danbury**, Connecticut, U.S.A.
117 J 22 **Danby Lake**, California, U.S.A.
191 H 23 **Dande**, Ethiopia
169 C 19 **Dandeli**, India
209 S 13 **Dandenong**, Victoria, Australia
171 X 6 **Dandong**, China
65 Q 12 **Daneborg**, Greenland
121 Z 4 **Danforth**, Maine, U.S.A.
196 G 2 **Dange**, Angola
167 R 14 **Danghara**, Tajikistan
191 H 19 **Dangila**, Ethiopia
126 E 8 **Dangriga**, Belize
171 U 9 **Dangshan**, China
191 G 19 **Dangur**, Ethiopia
118 C 11 **Daniel**, Wyoming, U.S.A.
115 X 9 **Daniel's Harbour**, Newfoundland and Labrador, Canada
95 I 15 **Danilovgrad**, Serbia and Montenegro
159 Z 8 **Dänizkänari**, Azerbaijan
177 A 23 **Danjo-guntō**, Japan
126 F 10 **Danlí**, Honduras
86 I 11 **Dannenberg**, Germany
191 M 21 **Danot**, Ethiopia
121 R 8 **Dansville**, New York, U.S.A.
96 K 6 **Danube**, Europe
173 D 16 **Danubyu**, Myanmar
120 I 11 **Danville**, Illinois, U.S.A.
120 L 14 **Danville**, Kentucky, U.S.A.
121 Q 15 **Danville**, Virginia, U.S.A.
171 S 15 **Danxian**, China
175 O 5 **Dao**, Philippines
172 N 12 **Đao Cai Bau**, Vietnam
172 M 12 **Đao Cat Ba**, Vietnam
173 K 22 **Đao Phu Quôc**, Vietnam
173 K 23 **Đao Thô Chur**, Vietnam
173 J 23 **Đao Vây**, Vietnam
171 T 12 **Daoxian**, China
193 N 11 **Dapaong**, Togo
175 P 6 **Dapitan**, Philippines
171 W 3 **Daqing**, China
161 T 4 **Dāqūq**, Iraq
195 W 12 **Dar Es Salaam**, Tanzania
160 H 8 **Dar'a**, Syria
192 E 8 **Dara**, Senegal
164 K 11 **Dārāb**, Iran
100 L 7 **Darabani**, Romania
189 R 9 **Daraj**, Libya
164 H 8 **Dārān**, Iran
95 K 15 **Đaravica**, Serbia and Montenegro
190 F 11 **Daraw**, Egypt
193 T 10 **Darazo**, Nigeria
164 M 9 **Darband**, Iran
168 J 13 **Darbhanga**, India
158 B 8 **Dardanelles**, Turkey
158 M 11 **Darende**, Turkey
191 A 18 **Darfur**, Sudan
167 N 12 **Darganata**, Turkmenistan
210 J 7 **Dargaville**, New Zealand
171 Q 3 **Darhan**, Mongolia
123 R 7 **Darien**, Georgia, U.S.A.
167 T 6 **Dar'inskiv**, Kazakhstan
126 F 11 **Darío**, Nicaragua
168 K 12 **Darjiling**, India
171 O 9 **Darlag**, China
209 S 10 **Darling**, New South Wales, Australia
77 J 15 **Darlington**, United Kingdom
92 F 8 **Darłowka**, Poland
87 F 20 **Darmstadt**, Germany
189 X 7 **Darnah**, Libya
113 Q 3 **Darnley Bay**, Northwest Territories, Canada
81 R 5 **Daroca**, Spain
165 O 5 **Darreh Gaz**, Iran
86 K 8 **Darss**, Germany
166 H 12 **Darta**, Turkmenistan
77 M 21 **Dartford**, United Kingdom
77 H 23 **Dartmoor**, United Kingdom
77 I 24 **Dartmouth**, United Kingdom
212 B 6 **Daru**, Papua New Guinea
175 S 10 **Daruba**, Indonesia
166 K 12 **Darvaza**, Turkmenistan
165 T 9 **Darwazgai**, Afghanistan
169 E 16 **Darwha**, India
145 L 23 **Darwin**, Falkland Islands
208 L 1 **Darwin**, Northern Territory, Australia
165 W 9 **Darya Khan**, Pakistan
164 J 11 **Daryācheh-ye Bakhtegan**, Iran
164 J 6 **Daryācheh-ye Namak**, Iran
165 P 10 **Daryācheh-ye Sīstau**, Iran
164 J 10 **Daryācheh-ye Tashk**, Iran
164 M 11 **Dārzīn**, Iran
166 M 11 **Dashkhovuz**, Turkmenistan
166 L 11 **Dashkhovuzskiy Velayat**, Turkmenistan
165 P 14 **Dasht**, Pakistan
164 M 5 **Dasht**, Iran
165 P 9 **Dasht-e Babus**, Afghanistan
164 J 7 **Dasht-e Kavir**, Iran
165 O 9 **Dasht-e Khāsh**, Afghanistan
164 M 8 **Dasht-e Lut**, Iran
165 P 10 **Dasht-i Margo**, Afghanistan
165 O 14 **Dashtiari**, Iran
168 D 6 **Dastegil Sar**, India
171 S 13 **Datang**, China
158 B 13 **Datça**, Turkey

Country | Internal administrative region: State/Province/Territory/Dependent territory | Capital city | Mountain range/Undersea ridge | Mountain peak/Volcano/Seamount | Geographic feature | Headland/Point/Cape/Peninsula | Desert | Island/Island group | Antarctic base | Ocean | Sea | Bay/Gulf/Channel/Strait | Lake | Salt pan/Dry/Intermittent lake | River

176 J 7 **Date**, Japan
171 V 12 **Datian**, China
119 D 18 **Datil**, New Mexico, U.S.A.
171 S 6 **Datong**, China
171 P 8 **Datong**, China
99 F 16 **Daugai**, Lithuania
98 H 13 **Daugavpils**, Latvia
169 C 17 **Daund**, India
173 F 20 **Daung Kyun**, Myanmar ⌓
114 H 9 **Dauphin**, Manitoba, Canada
122 J 9 **Dauphin Island**, Alabama, U.S.A. ⌓
193 R 9 **Daura**, Nigeria
159 Y 7 **Däväçi**, Azerbaijan
169 D 20 **Davangere**, India
175 Q 7 **Davao**, Philippines
175 R 7 **Davao Gulf**, Philippines ≈
116 H 7 **Davenport**, Washington, U.S.A.
118 N 12 **Davenport**, Iowa, U.S.A.
126 I 14 **David**, Panama
113 Y 12 **Davidson**, Saskatchewan, Canada
58 J 6 **Davie Ridge**, Indian Ocean ⛰
219 X 6 **Davis**, Antarctica ⁙
117 K 21 **Davis Dam**, Arizona, U.S.A.
115 V 7 **Davis Inlet**, Newfoundland and Labrador, Canada
219 Y 8 **Davis Sea**, Antarctica ◭
64 L 12 **Davis Strait**, Arctic Ocean ≈
88 J 8 **Davos**, Switzerland
113 W 8 **Davy Lake**, Saskatchewan, Canada ⌁
101 S 8 **Davydiv Brid**, Ukraine
163 Y 10 **Dawḩat Şawqirah**, Oman ≈
99 I 16 **Dawhinava**, Belarus
162 M 9 **Dawqah**, Saudi Arabia
163 W 10 **Dawqah**, Oman
188 D 10 **Dawra**, Western Sahara
113 N 6 **Dawson**, Yukon Territory, Canada
123 O 7 **Dawson**, Georgia, U.S.A.
113 S 11 **Dawson Creek**, British Columbia, Canada
163 Z 8 **Dawwah**, Oman
78 L 13 **Dax**, France
171 W 2 **Dayangshu**, China
171 P 13 **Dayao**, China
163 Y 6 **Dayl**, Oman
161 N 4 **Dayr az Zawr**, Syria
160 J 2 **Dayr Ḩāfir**, Syria
116 H 8 **Dayton**, Washington, U.S.A.
119 L 21 **Dayton**, Texas, U.S.A.
120 L 11 **Dayton**, Ohio, U.S.A.
123 N 2 **Dayton**, Tennessee, U.S.A.
123 S 10 **Daytona Beach**, Florida, U.S.A.
171 R 10 **Dazhu**, China
196 M 13 **De Aar**, Republic of South Africa
82 H 7 **De Cocksdorp**, Netherlands
122 M 8 **De Funiak Springs**, Florida, U.S.A.
83 B 16 **De Haan**, Belgium
120 H 9 **De Kalb**, Illinois, U.S.A.
157 W 13 **De-Kastri-Nysh**, Russian Federation
82 H 7 **De Koog**, Netherlands
82 O 11 **De Lutte**, Netherlands
83 A 17 **De Panne**, Belgium
120 I 6 **De Pere**, Wisconsin, U.S.A.
119 M 20 **De Ridder**, Louisiana, U.S.A.
120 M 5 **De Tour Village**, Michigan, U.S.A.
160 G 10 **Dead Sea**, Israel ⌁
127 N 4 **Deadman's**, The Bahamas
77 N 22 **Deal**, United Kingdom
120 M 9 **Dearborn**, Michigan, U.S.A.
113 P 9 **Dease Lake**, British Columbia, Canada
113 U 3 **Dease Strait**, Nunavut, Canada ≈
117 H 19 **Death Valley**, California, U.S.A. ◇
117 I 20 **Death Valley**, California, U.S.A.
174 J 10 **Debak**, Malaysia
101 Y 6 **Debal'tseve**, Ukraine
96 B 12 **Debar**, Macedonia (F.Y.R.O.M.)
93 L 17 **Dębica**, Poland
157 X 9 **Debin**, Russian Federation
93 M 14 **Dęblin**, Poland
92 D 11 **Dębno**, Poland
191 I 20 **Debre Birhan**, Ethiopia
191 H 19 **Debre Markos**, Ethiopia
191 I 19 **Debre Werk'**, Ethiopia
93 M 22 **Debrecen**, Hungary
95 K 15 **Dečani**, Serbia and Montenegro
118 K 12 **Decatur**, Nebraska, U.S.A.
120 H 11 **Decatur**, Illinois, U.S.A.
120 L 10 **Decatur**, Indiana, U.S.A.
122 L 3 **Decatur**, Alabama, U.S.A.
169 E 18 **Deccan Plateau**, India ◇
218 H 3 **Deception Island**, Antarctica ⌓
91 C 19 **Decimomannu**, Italy
79 R 8 **Decize**, France
118 M 11 **Decorah**, Iowa, U.S.A.
82 M 9 **Dedemsvaart**, Netherlands
191 J 20 **Deder**, Ethiopia
159 V 7 **Dedop'listsqaro**, Georgia
192 L 10 **Dédougou**, Burkina Faso
197 R 5 **Dedza**, Malawi
76 I 11 **Dee**, United Kingdom ∫
115 X 10 **Deer Lake**, Newfoundland and Labrador, Canada
116 H 6 **Deer Park**, Washington, U.S.A.
123 T 13 **Deerfield Beach**, Florida, U.S.A.
191 M 23 **Deeri**, Somalia
120 L 10 **Defiance**, Ohio, U.S.A.
191 L 21 **Degeh Bur**, Ethiopia
193 R 14 **Degema**, Nigeria
87 L 22 **Deggendorf**, Germany
164 J 10 **Deh Bīd**, Iran
165 Q 10 **Deh Shū**, Afghanistan
189 Q 8 **Dehiba**, Tunisia
164 F 7 **Dehlorān**, Iran
168 F 10 **Dehra Dun**, India
191 B 21 **Deim Zubeir**, Sudan
83 D 18 **Deinze**, Belgium
100 I 8 **Dej**, Romania
191 I 19 **Dejen**, Ethiopia
191 I 17 **Dekemhare**, Eritrea
194 L 10 **Dekese**, Democratic Republic of Congo
194 J 4 **Dékoa**, Central African Republic
58 I 11 **Del Cano Rise**, Indian Ocean ⛰
119 H 22 **Del Rio**, Texas, U.S.A.
117 F 21 **Delano**, California, U.S.A.
165 Q 9 **Delārām**, Afghanistan
196 M 11 **Delareyville**, Republic of South Africa
121 T 12 **Delaware**, U.S.A. ▣
121 T 10 **Delaware**, New Jersey, U.S.A. ∫
120 M 11 **Delaware**, Ohio, U.S.A.
121 T 12 **Delaware Bay**, Delaware, U.S.A. ≈
96 E 11 **Delčevo**, Macedonia (F.Y.R.O.M.)
88 D 6 **Delémont**, Switzerland
193 X 9 **Délép**, Chad
82 F 13 **Delft**, Netherlands
82 N 6 **Delfzijl**, Netherlands
191 E 14 **Delgo**, Sudan
168 E 11 **Delhi**, India ▣
168 E 11 **Delhi**, India
164 I 7 **Delījān**, Iran
113 R 6 **Déline**, Northwest Territories, Canada
87 K 15 **Delitzsch**, Germany
189 N 5 **Dellys**, Algeria
86 E 12 **Delmenhorst**, Germany
94 C 9 **Delnice**, Croatia
209 S 15 **Deloraine**, Tasmania, Australia
97 J 21 **Delos**, Greece ⌓
123 T 13 **Delray Beach**, Florida, U.S.A.
193 Q 13 **Delta**, Nigeria ▣
117 L 16 **Delta**, Utah, U.S.A.
119 D 14 **Delta**, Colorado, U.S.A.
139 S 3 **Delta Amacuro**, Venezuela ▣
112 L 6 **Delta Junction**, Alaska, U.S.A.
123 R 10 **Deltona**, Florida, U.S.A.
169 B 16 **Delvada**, India
194 L 11 **Demba**, Democratic Republic of Congo
191 G 20 **Dembī Dolo**, Ethiopia
195 N 5 **Dembia**, Central African Republic
62 G 12 **Demerara Abyssal Plain**, Atlantic Ocean ◇
62 F 12 **Demerara Plateau**, Atlantic Ocean ◇
119 D 19 **Deming**, New Mexico, U.S.A.
158 D 10 **Demirci**, Turkey
158 C 10 **Demirköprü Baraji**, Turkey ⌁
96 N 11 **Demirköy**, Turkey
86 L 9 **Demmin**, Germany
194 M 9 **Democratic Republic Of Congo**, Africa □
122 K 6 **Demopolis**, Alabama, U.S.A.
175 Y 12 **Demta**, Indonesia
82 H 7 **Den Burg**, Netherlands
173 H 15 **Den Chai**, Thailand
82 H 8 **Den Helder**, Netherlands
82 I 8 **Den Oever**, Netherlands
191 J 18 **Denakil Desert**, Ethiopia ∴
112 K 6 **Denali**, Alaska, U.S.A.
191 L 22 **Denan**, Ethiopia
167 Q 14 **Denau**, Uzbekistan
174 H 12 **Dendang**, Indonesia
192 J 8 **Dendâra**, Mauritania
83 E 19 **Denderleeuw**, Belgium
83 F 18 **Dendermonde**, Belgium
218 J 8 **Dendtler Island**, Antarctica ⌓
82 N 11 **Denekamp**, Netherlands
193 S 9 **Dengas**, Niger
193 Q 10 **Denge**, Nigeria
193 S 11 **Dengi**, Nigeria
208 E 8 **Denham**, Western Australia, Australia
81 U 9 **Denia**, Spain
215 U 1 **Denig**, Nauru
209 S 12 **Deniliquin**, New South Wales, Australia
116 G 13 **Denio**, Nevada, U.S.A.
118 K 12 **Denison**, Iowa, U.S.A.
158 D 12 **Denizli**, Turkey
85 C 25 **Denmark**, Europe □
208 G 12 **Denmark**, Western Australia, Australia
65 O 14 **Denmark Strait**, Arctic Ocean ≈
174 L 15 **Denpasar**, Indonesia
119 K 19 **Denton**, Texas, U.S.A.
212 G 6 **D'Entrecasteaux Islands**, Papua New Guinea ⌓
119 F 14 **Denver**, Colorado, U.S.A.
168 C 13 **Deogarh**, India
167 F 16 **Deoli**, India
169 F 14 **Deori**, India
168 I 12 **Deoria**, India
169 H 14 **Deosil**, India
115 Q 13 **Depot-Forbes**, Québec, Canada
219 W 5 **Depot Peak**, Antarctica ▲
193 Y 6 **Dépression Du Mourdi**, Chad ◇
157 U 8 **Deputatskiy**, Russian Federation
171 O 11 **Dêqên**, China
165 W 11 **Dera Ghazi Khan**, Pakistan
165 V 9 **Dera Ismail Khan**, Pakistan
100 M 5 **Derazhnya**, Ukraine
156 E 12 **Derbent**, Russian Federation
167 Q 14 **Derbent**, Uzbekistan
77 K 19 **Derby**, United Kingdom
208 I 4 **Derby**, Western Australia, Australia
193 Y 9 **Déréssa**, Chad
101 T 6 **Deriyivka**, Ukraine
101 Z 6 **Derkul**, Ukraine ∫
197 S 6 **Derre**, Mozambique
171 T 5 **Derst**, China
191 H 15 **Derudeb**, Sudan
94 H 10 **Derventa**, Bosnia and Herzegovina
167 P 4 **Derzhavinsk**, Kazakhstan
118 L 12 **Des Moines**, Iowa, U.S.A.
119 G 16 **Des Moines**, New Mexico, U.S.A.
144 H 11 **Desaguadero**, Argentina ∫
124 E 2 **Descanso**, Mexico
191 I 19 **Desē**, Ethiopia
145 H 20 **Deseado**, Argentina ∫
145 I 21 **Deseado**, Argentina
124 H 3 **Desemboque**, Mexico
117 J 23 **Desert Center**, California, U.S.A.
117 K 14 **Desert Peak**, Utah, U.S.A. ▲
62 O 5 **Deserta Grande**, Madeira ⌓
144 I 10 **Desiderio Tello**, Argentina
97 D 15 **Deskati**, Greece
101 Q 3 **Desna**, Ukraine ∫
94 M 12 **Despotovac**, Serbia and Montenegro
87 K 15 **Dessau**, Germany
83 E 18 **Destelbergen**, Belgium
100 E 11 **Deta**, Romania
197 N 7 **Dete**, Zimbabwe
87 F 14 **Detmold**, Germany
120 M 9 **Detroit**, Michigan, U.S.A.
115 U 10 **Détroit de Jacques-Cartier**, Québec, Canada ≈
115 U 11 **Détroit d'Honguedo**, Québec, Canada ≈
83 K 16 **Deurne**, Netherlands
89 Y 5 **Deutschkreutz**, Austria
89 V 8 **Deutschlandsberg**, Austria
100 H 10 **Deva**, Romania
158 K 9 **Deveci Dağlari**, Turkey
158 K 11 **Develi**, Turkey
82 L 11 **Deventer**, Netherlands
168 B 12 **Devikot**, India
211 H 15 **Devil River Peak**, New Zealand ▲
118 I 7 **Devil's Lake**, North Dakota, U.S.A. ⌁
118 I 7 **Devil's Lake**, North Dakota, U.S.A.
118 F 10 **Devil's Tower**, Wyoming, U.S.A. ▲
96 H 11 **Devin**, Bulgaria
209 S 15 **Deviot**, Tasmania, Australia
96 M 8 **Devnya**, Bulgaria
65 O 8 **Devon Island**, Arctic Ocean ⌓
209 S 15 **Devonport**, Tasmania, Australia
158 G 7 **Devrek**, Turkey
169 E 15 **Dewas**, India
171 Q 10 **Deyang**, China
164 M 8 **Deyhuk**, Iran
164 I 12 **Deyyer**, Iran
164 G 8 **Dezfūl**, Iran
171 U 7 **Dezhou**, China
163 T 5 **Dhahran**, Saudi Arabia
169 L 14 **Dhaka**, Bangladesh ▣
163 P 13 **Dhamār**, Yemen
169 G 16 **Dhamtari**, India
169 J 14 **Dhanbad**, India
169 D 15 **Dhar**, India
168 K 12 **Dharan Bazar**, Nepal
169 C 19 **Dharwad**, India
168 H 11 **Dhaulagiri**, Nepal ▲
160 G 10 **Dhībān**, Jordan
163 O 14 **Dhubāb**, Yemen
168 L 13 **Dhuburi**, India
169 D 16 **Dhule**, India
191 O 20 **Dhuudo**, Somalia
173 O 21 **Di Linh**, Vietnam
97 J 26 **Dia**, Greece ⌓
117 E 19 **Diablo Range**, California, U.S.A. ⛰
197 U 3 **Diaca**, Mozambique
192 K 9 **Diafarabé**, Mali
192 G 9 **Dialafara**, Mali
192 F 9 **Dialakoto**, Senegal
209 Q 7 **Diamantina**, Queensland, Australia ∫
59 S 9 **Diamantina Deep**, Indian Ocean ▲
59 R 9 **Diamantina Fracture Zone**, Indian Ocean ◇
118 D 13 **Diamond Peak**, Colorado, U.S.A. ▲
192 F 8 **Diamounguél**, Senegal
63 N 25 **Diana's Peak**, St Helena ▲
193 O 10 **Diapaga**, Burkina Faso
196 H 11 **Diaz Point**, Namibia ▶
163 X 5 **Dibā al Ḩişn**, Oman
194 M 11 **Dibaya**, Democratic Republic of Congo
194 K 10 **Dibaya-Lubwe**, Democratic Republic of Congo
191 A 18 **Dibbis**, Sudan
196 L 12 **Dibeng**, Republic of South Africa
168 O 11 **Dibrugarh**, India
160 K 3 **Dibsī**, Syria
118 G 8 **Dickinson**, North Dakota, U.S.A.
122 L 1 **Dickson**, Tennessee, U.S.A.
159 P 11 **Dicle Baraji**, Turkey ⌁
82 L 13 **Didam**, Netherlands
192 I 9 **Didiéni**, Mali
168 D 12 **Didwana**, India
96 L 12 **Didymoteicho**, Greece
79 U 12 **Die**, France
192 L 10 **Diébougou**, Burkina Faso
87 F 20 **Dieburg**, Germany
59 N 5 **Diego Garcia**, Indian Ocean ⌓
192 H 12 **Diéké**, Guinea
83 K 23 **Diekirch**, Luxembourg ▣
83 L 24 **Diekirch**, Luxembourg
192 I 9 **Diéma**, Mali
82 H 11 **Diemen**, Netherlands
172 J 12 **Điện Biên Phu**, Vietnam
173 L 14 **Diên Châu**, Vietnam
98 G 12 **Dienvidsusēja**, Latvia ∫
86 E 13 **Diepholz**, Germany
79 O 2 **Dieppe**, France
82 L 12 **Dieren**, Netherlands
83 I 18 **Diest**, Belgium
193 U 8 **Diffa**, Niger ▣
193 U 9 **Diffa**, Niger
195 O 5 **Digba**, Democratic Republic of Congo
115 U 13 **Digby**, Nova Scotia, Canada
79 V 13 **Digne-les-Baines**, France
79 S 9 **Digoin**, France
175 Q 7 **Digos**, Philippines
165 V 14 **Digri**, Pakistan
191 K 24 **Diinsoor**, Somalia
79 T 7 **Dijon**, France
84 G 13 **Dikanäs**, Sweden
191 K 19 **Dikhil**, Djibouti
158 B 10 **Dikili**, Turkey
157 S 11 **Dikimdya**, Russian Federation
192 J 12 **Dikodougou**, Côte d'Ivoire
83 B 18 **Diksmuide**, Belgium
157 N 6 **Dikson**, Russian Federation
193 V 10 **Dikwa**, Nigeria
191 I 22 **Dīla**, Ethiopia
175 Q 15 **Dili**, East Timor ⌂
195 O 5 **Dili**, Democratic Republic of Congo
159 U 8 **Dilijan**, Armenia
87 C 21 **Dilligen**, Germany
191 D 18 **Dilling**, Sudan
87 I 23 **Dillingen**, Germany
112 H 8 **Dillingham**, Alaska, U.S.A.
118 B 9 **Dillon**, Montana, U.S.A.
123 T 3 **Dillon**, South Carolina, U.S.A.
194 L 14 **Dilolo**, Democratic Republic of Congo
83 K 18 **Dilsen**, Belgium
161 T 6 **Diltāwa**, Iraq
168 N 12 **Dimapur**, India
194 M 11 **Dimbelenge**, Democratic Republic of Congo
192 K 13 **Dimbokro**, Côte d'Ivoire
95 O 14 **Dimitrovgrad**, Serbia and Montenegro
96 J 10 **Dimitrovgrad**, Bulgaria
175 Q 6 **Dinagat**, Philippines ⌓
168 K 13 **Dinajpur**, Bangladesh
78 K 5 **Dinan**, France
83 H 22 **Dinant**, Belgium
158 E 11 **Dinar**, Turkey
94 E 12 **Dinara**, Croatia ▲
94 E 11 **Dinaric Alps**, Bosnia and Herzegovina ⛰
191 G 18 **Dinder**, Sudan ∫
169 E 23 **Dindigul**, India
169 G 15 **Dindori**, India
194 I 11 **Dinga**, Democratic Republic of Congo
171 R 7 **Dingbian**, China
196 F 1 **Dinge**, Angola
168 K 12 **Dingla**, Nepal
77 A 20 **Dingle**, Republic of Ireland
77 A 20 **Dingle Bay**, Republic of Ireland ≈
87 L 23 **Dingolfing**, Germany
192 G 10 **Dinguiraye**, Guinea
115 W 12 **Dingwall**, Nova Scotia, Canada
171 Q 8 **Dingxi**, China
172 N 12 **Dinh Lâp**, Vietnam
87 H 22 **Dinkelsbühl**, Germany
83 F 15 **Dinteloord**, Netherlands
82 M 13 **Dinxperlo**, Netherlands
192 J 9 **Dioïla**, Mali
143 I 20 **Dioniso Cerqueira**, Brazil
192 D 9 **Diouloulou**, Senegal
192 I 8 **Dioumara**, Mali
193 P 10 **Dioundiou**, Niger
192 E 8 **Diourbel**, Senegal
168 N 13 **Diphu**, India
175 P 6 **Dipolog**, Philippines
83 L 25 **Dippach**, Luxembourg
192 L 8 **Diré**, Mali
191 K 20 **Dirē Dawa**, Ethiopia
59 Z 1 **Direction Island**, Cocos Islands ⌓
196 K 7 **Dirico**, Angola
208 E 8 **Dirk Hartog Island**, Western Australia, Australia ⌓
193 U 6 **Dirkou**, Niger
209 U 9 **Dirranbandi**, Queensland, Australia
163 N 10 **Ḑirs**, Saudi Arabia
209 Q 13 **Discovery Bay**, South Australia, Australia ≈
63 L 19 **Discovery Seamount**, Atlantic Ocean ▲
88 H 9 **Disentis**, Switzerland
65 N 11 **Disko**, Greenland ⌓
219 W 4 **Dismal Mountains**, Antarctica ⛰
169 A 16 **Diu**, India
164 G 5 **Dīvān Derreh**, Iran
194 F 9 **Divénié**, Congo
143 K 18 **Divinópolis**, Brazil
192 J 13 **Divo**, Côte d'Ivoire
159 N 10 **Divriği**, Turkey
165 T 14 **Diwana**, Pakistan
120 H 9 **Dixon**, Illinois, U.S.A.
113 N 12 **Dixon Entrance**, British Columbia, Canada ≈
127 N 3 **Dixon's**, The Bahamas
159 S 9 **Diyadin**, Turkey
159 P 12 **Diyarbakir**, Turkey
193 T 5 **Djado**, Niger
189 O 7 **Djamâa**, Algeria
194 H 9 **Djambala**, Congo
194 J 9 **Djampie**, Democratic Republic of Congo
189 Q 12 **Djanet**, Algeria
212 G 3 **Djaul Island**, Papua New Guinea ⌓
188 L 7 **Djebel Aïssa**, Algeria ▲
189 P 12 **Djebel Ounane**, Algeria ▲
189 P 13 **Djebel Telerhteba**, Algeria ▲
189 N 12 **Djebr**, Algeria ▲
193 X 10 **Djébrène**, Chad
193 X 9 **Djédaa**, Chad
188 K 11 **Djedid**, Algeria ⌁
188 M 6 **Djelfa**, Algeria
195 N 4 **Djéma**, Central African Republic
192 K 9 **Djenné**, Mali
194 L 9 **Djia**, Democratic Republic of Congo
192 M 9 **Djibo**, Burkina Faso
191 K 19 **Djibouti**, Djibouti ⌂
191 L 18 **Djibouti**, Africa □
192 I 8 **Djiguéni**, Mauritania
194 L 7 **Djolu**, Democratic Republic of Congo
193 O 11 **Djougou**, Benin
193 U 15 **Djoum**, Cameroon
84 D 11 **Djúpivogur**, Iceland
84 I 7 **Djupvik**, Norway
101 U 7 **Dmytrivka**, Ukraine
101 W 6 **Dmytrivka**, Ukraine
101 Q 4 **Dnieper**, Ukraine/Belarus ∫
100 K 6 **Dniester**, Moldova/Ukraine ∫
101 U 6 **Dniprodzerzhyns'k**, Ukraine
101 U 6 **Dnipropetrovs'k**, Ukraine
101 Q 9 **Dniprovs'kyy Lyman**, Ukraine ≈
101 P 10 **Dnistrov'kyy Lyman**, Ukraine ≈
99 F 21 **Dnyaprowski Buhski Kanal**, Belarus ∫
173 L 14 **Đô Lương**, Vietnam
172 M 12 **Đo Son**, Vietnam
174 M 13 **Doangdoangan Kecil**, Indonesia ⌓
193 W 12 **Doba**, Chad
99 L 19 **Dobasna**, Belarus ∫
98 E 11 **Dobele**, Latvia
87 L 16 **Döbeln**, Germany
89 V 7 **Dobersberg**, Austria
92 E 11 **Dobiegniew**, Poland
175 V 13 **Dobo**, Indonesia
94 H 10 **Doboj**, Bosnia and Herzegovina
92 K 9 **Dobre Miasto**, Poland
96 N 6 **Dobrich**, Bulgaria ▣
96 N 7 **Dobrich**, Bulgaria
99 D 15 **Dobrovol'sk**, Russian Federation
99 N 20 **Dobrush**, Belarus
101 Q 1 **Dobryanka**, Ukraine
208 L 7 **Docker River**, Northern Territory, Australia
169 D 22 **Dodda Betta**, India ▲
97 L 21 **Dodecanese**, Greece ⌓
119 I 15 **Dodge City**, Kansas, U.S.A.
120 G 8 **Dodgeville**, Wisconsin, U.S.A.
77 G 24 **Dodman Point**, United Kingdom ▶
195 U 11 **Dodoma**, Tanzania ⌂
195 U 12 **Dodoma**, Tanzania ▣
82 L 13 **Doesburg**, Netherlands
82 L 13 **Doetinchem**, Netherlands
123 O 9 **Dog Island**, Florida, U.S.A. ⌓
170 K 8 **Dogai Coring**, China ⌁
177 D 17 **Dōgo**, Japan ⌓
193 P 9 **Dogondoutchi**, Niger
193 W 11 **Dogoumbo**, Chad

□ Country ▣ Internal administrative region: State/Province/Territory/Dependent territory ⌂ Capital city ⛰ Mountain range/Undersea ridge ▲ Mountain peak/Volcano/Seamount ◇ Geographic feature ▶ Headland/Point/Cape/Peninsula ∴ Desert ⌓ Island/Island group ⁙ Antarctic base ∿ Ocean ◭ Sea ≈ Bay/Gulf/Channel/Strait ⌁ Lake ⛆ Salt pan/Dry/Intermittent lake ∫ Riv

159 O 8 **Doğu Karadeniz Dağlari**, Turkey ⛰
159 T 10 **Doğubeyazit**, Turkey
163 U 5 **Doha**, Qatar ⌂
173 F 14 **Doi Inthanon**, Thailand ▲
85 D 18 **Dokka**, Norway
82 K 6 **Dokkum**, Netherlands
99 J 15 **Dokshytsy**, Belarus
101 X 7 **Dokuchayevs'k**, Ukraine
145 I 18 **Dolavón**, Argentina
62 G 12 **Doldrums Fracture Zone**, Atlantic Ocean ◇
79 U 7 **Dôle**, France
77 H 19 **Dolgellau**, United Kingdom
157 X 14 **Dolinsk**, Russian Federation
95 N 14 **Doljevac**, Serbia and Montenegro
86 D 11 **Dollart**, Germany ≈
86 J 13 **Dolle**, Germany
218 J 4 **Dolleman Island**, Antarctica ⛱
93 J 19 **Dolný Kubín**, Slovakia
191 K 23 **Dolo Odo**, Ethiopia
90 F 5 **Dolomites**, Italy ⛰
171 Q 5 **Doloon**, Mongolia
126 D 8 **Dolores**, Guatemala
144 M 12 **Dolores**, Uruguay
113 R 3 **Dolphin and Union Strait**, Northwest Territories, Canada ≈
196 H 11 **Dolphin Head**, Namibia ▶
100 I 6 **Dolyna**, Ukraine
101 S 7 **Dolyns'ka**, Ukraine
93 M 18 **Domaradz**, Poland
93 B 18 **Domažlice**, Czech Republic
85 C 17 **Dombås**, Norway
197 Q 8 **Dombe**, Mozambique
93 H 25 **Dombóvár**, Hungary
13 S 12 **Dome Creek**, British Columbia, Canada
44 F 9 **Domeyko**, Chile
78 M 5 **Domfront**, France
27 X 9 **Dominica**, North America □
27 X 9 **Dominica Passage**, Guadeloupe ≈
27 R 8 **Dominican Republic**, North America □
91 M 21 **Domo**, Ethiopia
0 B 5 **Domodossola**, Italy
7 E 17 **Domokos**, Greece
75 N 15 **Dompu**, Indonesia
4 C 7 **Domžale**, Slovenia
6 I 10 **Don**, United Kingdom ∫
24 K 6 **Don**, Mexico
7 E 25 **Donaueschingen**, Germany
7 I 23 **Donauwörth**, Germany
7 K 17 **Doncaster**, United Kingdom
96 G 3 **Dondo**, Angola
97 R 7 **Dondo**, Mozambique
75 O 6 **Dondonay**, Philippines ⛱
7 D 15 **Donegal**, Republic of Ireland
7 C 15 **Donegal Bay**, Republic of Ireland ≈
01 X 7 **Donets'k**, Ukraine
73 N 16 **Đông Ha**, Vietnam
73 M 15 **Đông Hôi**, Vietnam
93 S 12 **Donga**, Nigeria
08 F 10 **Dongara**, Western Australia, Australia
71 P 12 **Dongchuan**, China
70 J 9 **Dongco**, China
71 S 15 **Dongfang**, China
75 N 11 **Donggala**, Indonesia
71 U 13 **Dongguan**, China
71 R 13 **Donglan**, China
94 J 6 **Dongo**, Democratic Republic of Congo
96 H 5 **Dongo**, Angola
91 E 14 **Dongola**, Sudan
91 E 23 **Dongotona Mountains**, Sudan ⛰
94 J 6 **Dongou**, Congo
1 S 7 **Dongsheng**, China
1 W 9 **Dongtai**, China
1 T 11 **Dongting Hu**, China ◣
1 V 7 **Dongying**, China
L 7 **Donkerbroek**, Netherlands
F 11 **Dønna**, Norway ⛱
B 6 **Donnas**, Italy
3 T 11 **Donnelly**, Alberta, Canada
T 6 **Donnersbach**, Austria
Q 1 **Donostia-San Sebastián**, Spain
K 22 **Donoussa**, Greece ⛱
J 23 **Dorchester**, United Kingdom
196 I 9 **Dordabis**, Namibia
79 N 12 **Dordogne**, France ∫
83 G 14 **Dordrecht**, Netherlands
193 N 9 **Dori**, Burkina Faso
88 J 6 **Dornbirn**, Austria
76 H 9 **Dornoch Firth**, United Kingdom ≈
171 T 3 **Dornod**, Mongolia ◘
171 R 5 **Dornogovi**, Mongolia ◘
192 M 8 **Doro**, Mali
93 I 22 **Dorog**, Hungary
85 H 14 **Dorotea**, Sweden
208 E 8 **Dorre Island**, Western Australia, Australia ⛱
209 V 10 **Dorrigo**, New South Wales, Australia
193 S 13 **Dorsale Camerounaise**, Cameroon ⛰
87 D 15 **Dortmund**, Germany
158 L 13 **Dörtyol**, Turkey
195 P 5 **Doruma**, Democratic Republic of Congo
164 M 7 **Dorūneh**, Iran
80 K 12 **Dos Hermanas**, Spain
145 I 18 **Dos Pozos**, Argentina
96 H 11 **Dospat**, Bulgaria
193 O 10 **Dosso**, Niger ◘
193 O 9 **Dosso**, Niger
166 I 6 **Dossor**, Kazakhstan
167 Y 8 **Dostyk**, Kazakhstan
123 N 7 **Dothan**, Alabama, U.S.A.
79 R 2 **Douai**, France
193 S 14 **Douala**, Cameroon
78 H 5 **Douarnenez**, France
211 D 23 **Double Cone**, New Zealand ▲
211 A 23 **Doubtful Sound**, New Zealand ≈
210 I 5 **Doubtless Bay**, New Zealand ≈
78 M 7 **Doué-la Fontaine**, France
192 L 8 **Douentza**, Mali
77 G 16 **Douglas**, United Kingdom
117 O 25 **Douglas**, Arizona, U.S.A.
123 P 7 **Douglas**, Georgia, U.S.A.
196 M 12 **Douglas**, Republic of South Africa
79 Q 2 **Doullens**, France
143 H 18 **Dourados**, Brazil
193 W 10 **Dourbali**, Chad
189 P 7 **Douz**, Tunisia
77 N 22 **Dover**, United Kingdom
121 T 12 **Dover**, Delaware, U.S.A.
121 X 7 **Dover**, New Hampshire, U.S.A.
121 U 10 **Dover**, New Jersey, U.S.A.
164 H 7 **Dow Rūd**, Iran
165 S 7 **Dowl at Yār**, Afghanistan
165 Q 8 **Dowlatābād**, Afghanistan
165 R 6 **Dowlatābād**, Afghanistan
116 M 13 **Downey**, Idaho, U.S.A.
165 U 6 **Dowshī**, Afghanistan
99 M 19 **Dowsk**, Belarus
177 D 17 **Dōzen**, Japan ⛱
101 R 4 **Drabiv**, Ukraine
82 L 7 **Drachten**, Netherlands
100 M 13 **Dragalina**, Romania
100 J 13 **Drăgănești-Vlașca**, Romania
97 K 26 **Dragonada**, Greece ⛱
99 G 21 **Drahichyn**, Belarus
145 G 26 **Drake Passage**, Chile ≈
63 D 21 **Drake Passage**, Atlantic Ocean ≈
197 N 14 **Drakensberg**, Republic of South Africa ⛰
96 H 12 **Drama**, Greece
85 D 20 **Drammen**, Norway
93 F 25 **Dráva**, Hungary ∫
94 F 7 **Drava**, Croatia ∫
94 C 6 **Dravograd**, Slovenia
92 E 10 **Drawa**, Poland ∫
113 U 12 **Drayton Valley**, Alberta, Canada
82 M 9 **Drenthe**, Netherlands ◘
87 N 17 **Dresden**, Germany
98 K 13 **Dretun'**, Belarus
79 O 4 **Dreux**, France
85 E 17 **Drevsjø**, Norway
211 L 15 **Dreyers Rock**, New Zealand
95 K 16 **Drin**, Albania ∫
94 I 11 **Drina**, Bosnia and Herzegovina ∫
95 K 17 **Drini i Zi**, Albania ∫
94 E 12 **Drniš**, Croatia
100 G 12 **Drobeta-Turnu Severin**, Romania
77 E 17 **Drogheda**, Republic of Ireland
100 I 5 **Drohobych**, Ukraine
90 A 9 **Dronero**, Italy
65 N 12 **Dronning Ingrid Land**, Greenland ◇
82 K 10 **Dronten**, Netherlands
89 V 2 **Drosendorf**, Austria
165 W 6 **Drosh**, Pakistan
113 V 13 **Drumheller**, Alberta, Canada
115 S 13 **Drummondville**, Québec, Canada
99 E 17 **Druskininkai**, Lithuania
99 L 17 **Druts'**, Belarus ∫
98 I 13 **Druya**, Belarus
157 V 8 **Druzhina**, Russian Federation
92 I 11 **Drwęca**, Poland ∫
123 P 15 **Dry Tortugas**, Florida, U.S.A. ⛱
96 J 8 **Dryanovo**, Bulgaria
114 J 11 **Dryden**, Ontario, Canada
98 K 13 **Drysa**, Belarus ∫
121 Q 10 **Du Bois**, Pennsylvania, U.S.A.
209 U 7 **Duaringa**, Queensland, Australia
162 J 4 **Ḍubā**, Saudi Arabia
163 X 5 **Dubai**, United Arab Emirates
101 O 8 **Dubăsari**, Moldova
101 O 8 **Dubăsari Reservoir**, Moldova ◣
114 J 3 **Dubawnt Lake**, Nunavut, Canada ◣
209 U 11 **Dubbo**, New South Wales, Australia
77 F 18 **Dublin**, Republic of Ireland ⌂
123 P 6 **Dublin**, Georgia, U.S.A.
100 K 3 **Dubno**, Ukraine
118 D 11 **Dubois**, Wyoming, U.S.A.
95 H 15 **Dubrovnik**, Croatia
100 L 2 **Dubrovytsya**, Ukraine
99 M 16 **Dubrowna**, Belarus
118 N 11 **Dubuque**, Iowa, U.S.A.
173 O 18 **Đuc Pho**, Vietnam
173 O 21 **Duc Trong**, Vietnam
117 N 15 **Duchesne**, Utah, U.S.A.
209 Q 5 **Duchess**, Queensland, Australia
101 T 8 **Dudchany**, Ukraine
83 L 26 **Dudelange**, Luxembourg
169 E 18 **Dudhani**, India
169 H 14 **Dudhi**, India
157 N 8 **Dudinka**, Russian Federation
77 J 19 **Dudley**, United Kingdom
192 I 13 **Duékoué**, Côte d'Ivoire
81 N 4 **Dueñas**, Spain
80 L 4 **Duero**, Spain ∫
219 P 10 **Dufek Coast**, Antarctica ◇
213 Q 7 **Duff Islands**, Solomon Islands ⛱
90 B 6 **Dufourspitze**, Italy/Switzerland ▲
94 C 12 **Dugi Otok**, Croatia ⛱
87 C 16 **Duisburg**, Germany
191 E 21 **Duk Faiwil**, Sudan
95 J 21 **Dukat i Ri**, Albania
197 N 13 **Dukathole**, Republic of South Africa
163 U 5 **Dukhān**, Qatar
163 O 5 **Dukhnah**, Saudi Arabia
165 U 11 **Duki**, Pakistan
99 H 14 **Dūkštas**, Lithuania
171 O 8 **Dulan**, China
144 K 9 **Dulce**, Argentina ∫
119 E 16 **Dulce**, New Mexico, U.S.A.
126 F 9 **Dulce Nombre de Culmí**, Honduras
96 M 8 **Dŭlgopol**, Bulgaria
87 D 15 **Dülmen**, Germany
96 M 6 **Dulovo**, Bulgaria
209 V 7 **Dululu**, Queensland, Australia
118 M 8 **Duluth**, Minnesota, U.S.A.
160 H 6 **Dūmā**, Syria
175 P 6 **Dumaguete**, Philippines
174 E 10 **Dumai**, Indonesia
175 N 5 **Dumaran**, Philippines ⛱
119 H 17 **Dumas**, Texas, U.S.A.
160 I 6 **Ḍumayr**, Syria
76 G 13 **Dumbarton**, United Kingdom
100 L 11 **Dumbrăveni**, Romania
168 F 8 **Dumchele**, India
77 H 15 **Dumfries**, United Kingdom
169 K 14 **Dumka**, India
219 V 14 **Dumont d'Urville**, Antarctica ⁜
219 U 15 **Dumont d'Urville Sea**, Antarctica ◒
190 F 7 **Dumyât**, Egypt
93 H 22 **Dunajská Streda**, Slovakia
93 I 26 **Dunaszekcső**, Hungary
93 I 24 **Dunaújváros**, Hungary
96 F 6 **Dunavtsi**, Bulgaria
100 L 6 **Dunayivtsi**, Ukraine
117 O 24 **Duncan**, Arizona, U.S.A.
119 J 18 **Duncan**, Oklahoma, U.S.A.
169 N 22 **Duncan Passage**, India ≈
76 J 7 **Duncansby Head**, United Kingdom ▶
98 D 9 **Dundaga**, Latvia
77 E 17 **Dundalk**, Republic of Ireland
121 S 12 **Dundalk**, Maryland, U.S.A.
77 E 17 **Dundalk Bay**, Republic of Ireland ≈
208 M 1 **Dundas Strait**, Northern Territory, Australia ≈
76 I 12 **Dundee**, United Kingdom
197 P 12 **Dundee**, Republic of South Africa
218 H 3 **Dundee Island**, Antarctica ⛱
171 Q 4 **Dundgovi**, Mongolia ◘
211 E 24 **Dunedin**, New Zealand
169 C 14 **Dungarpur**, India
77 D 20 **Dungarvan**, Republic of Ireland
77 N 22 **Dungeness**, United Kingdom ▶
195 P 5 **Dungu**, Democratic Republic of Congo
174 F 8 **Dungun**, Malaysia
190 H 13 **Dungunab**, Sudan
171 X 4 **Dunhua**, China
171 N 6 **Dunhuang**, China
158 E 10 **Dunilupinar**, Turkey
79 Q 1 **Dunkerque**, France
121 Q 9 **Dunkirk**, New York, U.S.A.
192 M 13 **Dunkwa**, Ghana
209 N 3 **Dunmarra**, Northern Territory, Australia
123 U 2 **Dunn**, North Carolina, U.S.A.
123 Q 10 **Dunnellon**, Florida, U.S.A.
211 D 24 **Dunrobin**, New Zealand
211 D 23 **Dunstan Mountains**, New Zealand ⛰
98 F 10 **Dunte**, Latvia
113 W 7 **Dunvegan Lake**, Northwest Territories, Canada ◣
96 F 10 **Dupnista**, Bulgaria
118 H 10 **Dupree**, South Dakota, U.S.A.
120 F 6 **Durand**, Wisconsin, U.S.A.
124 M 7 **Durango**, Mexico ◘
81 P 1 **Durango**, Spain
119 D 16 **Durango**, Colorado, U.S.A.
125 N 8 **Durango**, Mexico
96 O 6 **Durankulak**, Bulgaria
119 K 18 **Durant**, Oklahoma, U.S.A.
144 N 12 **Durazno**, Uruguay ◘
144 N 12 **Durazno**, Uruguay
197 P 13 **Durban**, Republic of South Africa
81 O 13 **Dúrcal**, Spain
87 B 17 **Düren**, Germany
169 G 16 **Durg**, India
169 K 14 **Durgapur**, India
77 J 15 **Durham**, United Kingdom
123 T 1 **Durham**, North Carolina, U.S.A.
174 E 10 **Duri**, Indonesia
101 N 9 **Durlești**, Moldova
95 J 14 **Durmitor**, Serbia and Montenegro ▲
76 G 8 **Durness**, United Kingdom
89 Y 3 **Dürnkrut**, Austria
95 J 18 **Durrës**, Albania
158 D 9 **Dursunbey**, Turkey
212 A 6 **Duru**, Papua New Guinea
191 M 20 **Durukhsi**, Somalia
96 O 12 **Durusu Gölü**, Turkey ◣
211 I 15 **D'Urville Island**, New Zealand ⛱
165 S 11 **Dushai**, Pakistan
166 M 14 **Dushak**, Turkmenistan
171 R 12 **Dushan**, China
167 R 13 **Dushanbe**, Tajikistan ⌂
121 S 9 **Dushore**, Pennsylvania, U.S.A.
211 A 24 **Dusky Sound**, New Zealand ≈
87 C 16 **Düsseldorf**, Germany
218 J 8 **Dustin Island**, Antarctica ⛱
174 F 11 **Dusunmudo**, Indonesia
112 D 9 **Dutch Harbor**, Alaska, U.S.A.
193 S 10 **Dutse**, Nigeria
193 R 10 **Dutsin-Ma**, Nigeria
169 F 20 **Duttaluru**, India
209 R 1 **Duyfken Point**, Queensland, Australia ▶
171 R 12 **Duyun**, China
93 M 15 **Duża**, Poland
158 G 8 **Düzce**, Turkey
96 K 7 **Dve Mogili**, Bulgaria
101 X 4 **Dvorichna**, Ukraine
169 A 15 **Dwarka**, India
120 I 10 **Dwight**, Illinois, U.S.A.
101 Z 7 **Dyakove**, Ukraine
122 I 1 **Dyersburg**, Tennessee, U.S.A.
157 T 10 **Dyeundyu**, Russian Federation
101 U 4 **Dykan'ka**, Ukraine
101 P 3 **Dymer**, Ukraine
101 X 6 **Dymytrov**, Ukraine
93 M 18 **Dynów**, Poland
209 U 6 **Dysart**, Queensland, Australia
97 D 20 **Dytiki Ellas**, Greece ◘
97 D 14 **Dytiki Makedonia**, Greece ◘
197 X 4 **Dzaoudzi**, France
159 Z 10 **Džarskij**, Azerbaijan
171 N 3 **Dzavhan**, Mongolia ◘
101 X 6 **Dzerzhyns'k**, Ukraine
167 O 9 **Dzhalagash**, Kazakhstan
167 T 11 **Dzhalal-Abadskaya Oblast'**, Kyrgyzstan ◘
166 H 5 **Dzhangala**, Kazakhstan
101 U 11 **Dzhankoy**, Ukraine
167 X 8 **Dzhansugurov**, Kazakhstan
166 F 5 **Dzhanybek**, Kazakhstan
101 S 10 **Dzharylhats'ka Zatoka**, Ukraine ≈
166 I 12 **Dzhebel**, Turkmenistan
167 T 14 **Dzhilandy**, Tajikistan
167 Q 12 **Dzhizak**, Uzbekistan
101 N 6 **Dzhuryn**, Ukraine
167 O 8 **Dzhusaly**, Kazakhstan
92 K 10 **Działdowo**, Poland
125 Y 10 **Dzilam de Bravo**, Mexico
189 O 7 **Dzioua**, Algeria
99 J 14 **Dzisna**, Belarus ∫
99 F 21 **Dzivin**, Belarus
171 N 2 **Dzur**, Mongolia
171 R 3 **Dzuunmod**, Mongolia
99 I 18 **Dzyarzhynsk**, Belarus
99 J 22 **Dzyarzhynsk**, Belarus
99 I 17 **Dzyarzhynskaya Hara**, Belarus ▲

E

173 O 19 **Ea Hleo**, Vietnam
117 O 22 **Eagar**, Arizona, U.S.A.
115 W 8 **Eagle**, Newfoundland and Labrador, Canada ∫
112 M 6 **Eagle**, Alaska, U.S.A.
117 F 15 **Eagle Lake**, California, U.S.A. ◣
121 X 3 **Eagle Lake**, Maine, U.S.A. ◣
121 Y 3 **Eagle Lake**, Maine, U.S.A.
119 I 22 **Eagle Pass**, Texas, U.S.A.
120 I 4 **Eagle River**, Wisconsin, U.S.A.
123 Q 3 **Easley**, South Carolina, U.S.A.
219 R 4 **East Antarctica**, Antarctica ◇
121 Q 8 **East Aurora**, New York, U.S.A.
119 O 22 **East Bay**, Louisiana, U.S.A. ≈
212 E 5 **East Bay**, Papua New Guinea ≈
127 Q 5 **East Caicos**, Turks and Caicos Islands ⛱
210 O 10 **East Cape**, New Zealand ▶
60 L 7 **East Caroline Basin**, Pacific Ocean ◇
60 K 4 **East China Sea**, Pacific Ocean ◒
77 M 19 **East Dereham**, United Kingdom
145 L 24 **East Falkland**, Falkland Islands ⛱
121 W 10 **East Hampton**, New York, U.S.A.
59 R 8 **East Indiaman Ridge**, Indian Ocean ⛰
76 H 13 **East Kilbride**, United Kingdom
121 O 10 **East Liverpool**, Ohio, U.S.A.
197 O 14 **East London**, Republic of South Africa
60 M 6 **East Mariana Basin**, Pacific Ocean ◇
212 H 4 **East New Britain**, Papua New Guinea ◘
63 N 16 **East Point**, Tristan da Cunha ▶
123 O 4 **East Point**, Georgia, U.S.A.
63 I 21 **East Scotia Basin**, Atlantic Ocean ◇
212 C 4 **East Sepik**, Papua New Guinea ◘
58 K 2 **East Sheba Ridge**, Indian Ocean ⛰
65 T 4 **East Siberian Sea**, Arctic Ocean ◒
120 G 12 **East St Louis**, Illinois, U.S.A.
175 R 15 **East Timor**, Asia □
77 M 23 **Eastbourne**, United Kingdom
61 X 3 **Easter Island**, Chile ◘
168 K 12 **Eastern**, Nepal ◘
169 G 24 **Eastern**, Sri Lanka ◘
192 G 12 **Eastern**, Sierra Leone ◘
195 W 7 **Eastern**, Kenya ◘
197 P 4 **Eastern**, Zambia ◘
192 M 13 **Eastern**, Ghana ◘
197 N 14 **Eastern Cape**, Republic of South Africa ◘
190 F 9 **Eastern Desert**, Egypt ◓
191 F 22 **Eastern Equatoria**, Sudan ◘
169 F 20 **Eastern Ghats**, India ⛰
212 D 5 **Eastern Highlands**, Papua New Guinea ◘
115 Q 10 **Eastmain**, Québec, Canada ∫
115 P 10 **Eastmain**, Québec, Canada
123 P 6 **Eastman**, Georgia, U.S.A.
121 T 10 **Easton**, Pennsylvania, U.S.A.
123 P 5 **Eatonton**, Georgia, U.S.A.
120 G 6 **Eau Claire**, Wisconsin, U.S.A.
214 L 15 **Eaurupik**, Federated States of Micronesia ⛱
193 P 11 **Eban**, Nigeria
125 R 10 **Ebano**, Mexico
193 T 15 **Ebebiyin**, Equatorial Guinea
89 S 5 **Ebensee**, Austria
158 G 11 **Eber Gölü**, Turkey ◣
86 M 12 **Eberswalde-Finow**, Germany
176 J 5 **Ebetsu**, Japan
171 P 11 **Ebian**, China
177 C 23 **Ebino**, Japan
170 J 4 **Ebinur Hu**, China ◣
91 K 16 **Eboli**, Italy
193 T 15 **Ebolowa**, Cameroon
215 Y 5 **Ebon**, Marshall Islands ⛱
196 H 9 **Ebony**, Namibia
193 R 13 **Ebonyi**, Nigeria ◘
81 T 5 **Ebro**, Spain ∫
97 L 15 **Eceabat**, Turkey
158 A 8 **Eceabat**, Turkey
188 L 6 **Ech Chélif**, Algeria
88 B 9 **Echallens**, Switzerland
96 I 12 **Echinos**, Greece
177 G 16 **Echizen-misaki**, Japan ▶
113 S 5 **Echo Bay**, Northwest Territories, Canada
83 K 17 **Echt**, Netherlands
83 M 24 **Echternach**, Luxembourg
209 S 12 **Echuca**, Victoria, Australia
80 M 12 **Écija**, Spain
86 H 8 **Eckernförde**, Germany
140 A 9 **Ecuador**, South America □
191 J 17 **Ed**, Eritrea
191 B 19 **Ed Da'ein**, Sudan
191 G 19 **Ed Damazin**, Sudan
191 F 15 **Ed Damer**, Sudan
191 E 15 **Ed Debba**, Sudan
191 E 17 **Ed Dueim**, Sudan
82 I 10 **Edam**, Netherlands
76 I 7 **Eday**, United Kingdom ⛱
120 I 14 **Eddyville**, Kentucky, U.S.A.
82 K 13 **Ede**, Netherlands
193 P 12 **Ede**, Nigeria
193 S 14 **Edéa**, Cameroon
77 I 15 **Eden**, United Kingdom ∫
209 U 13 **Eden**, New South Wales, Australia
211 C 25 **Edendale**, New Zealand
123 W 1 **Edenton**, North Carolina, U.S.A.
96 D 13 **Edessa**, Greece
210 M 10 **Edgecumbe**, New Zealand
118 G 11 **Edgemont**, South Dakota, U.S.A.
65 U 11 **Edgeoya**, Svalbard ⛱
76 I 13 **Edinburgh**, United Kingdom
100 M 7 **Edineț**, Moldova
96 M 11 **Edirne**, Turkey ◘
96 L 11 **Edirne**, Turkey
189 Q 10 **Edjeleh**, Algeria
113 V 12 **Edmonton**, Alberta, Canada

□ Country ◘ Internal administrative region: State/Province/Territory/Dependent territory ⌂ Capital city ⛰ Mountain range/Undersea ridge ▲ Mountain peak/Volcano/Seamount ◇ Geographic feature ▶ Headland/Point/Cape/Peninsula ◓ Desert ⛱ Island/Island group ⁜ Antarctic base ◎ Ocean ◒ Sea ≈ Bay/Gulf/Channel/Strait ◣ Lake ▚ Salt pan/Dry/Intermittent lake ∫ River

115 T 12 **Edmundston**, New Brunswick, Canada
193 Q 13 **Edo**, Nigeria
90 E 5 **Edolo**, Italy
158 B 9 **Edremit**, Turkey
158 A 9 **Edremit Körfezi**, Turkey
113 U 12 **Edson**, Alberta, Canada
144 J 13 **Eduardo Castex**, Argentina
219 N 11 **Edward VII Peninsula**, Antarctica
219 X 4 **Edward VIII Gulf**, Antarctica
119 G 21 **Edwards Plateau**, Texas, U.S.A.
194 H 9 **Edzouga**, Congo
83 D 17 **Eeklo**, Belgium
82 N 5 **Eemshaven**, Netherlands
213 R 11 **Éfaté**, Vanuatu
89 S 3 **Eferding**, Austria
120 H 12 **Effingham**, Illinois, U.S.A.
175 T 11 **Eftorobi**, Indonesia
171 S 3 **Eg**, Mongolia
112 H 8 **Egegik**, Alaska, U.S.A.
93 K 22 **Eger**, Hungary
63 M 26 **Egg Island**, St Helena
89 W 2 **Eggenburg**, Austria
87 L 24 **Eggenfelden**, Germany
83 H 20 **Eghezée**, Belgium
84 D 10 **Egilsstaðir**, Iceland
158 F 12 **Eğirdir**, Turkey
158 F 11 **Eğirdir Gölü**, Turkey
79 P 10 **Égletons**, France
157 Z 6 **Egvekinot**, Russian Federation
190 C 10 **Egypt**, Africa
87 G 24 **Ehingen**, Germany
177 C 24 **Ei**, Japan
215 W 6 **Eiao**, French Polynesia
82 M 12 **Eibergen**, Netherlands
89 V 8 **Eibiswald**, Austria
85 B 19 **Eidfjord**, Norway
87 B 19 **Eifel**, Germany
88 F 9 **Eiger**, Switzerland
76 F 11 **Eigg**, United Kingdom
169 B 25 **Eight Degree Channel**, Maldives
218 J 8 **Eights Coast**, Antarctica
208 H 5 **Eighty Mile Beach**, Western Australia, Australia
87 L 16 **Eilenburg**, Germany
160 F 11 **Ein Yahav**, Israel
209 S 4 **Einasleigh**, Queensland, Australia
87 H 15 **Einbeck**, Germany
83 J 16 **Eindhoven**, Netherlands
62 G 6 **Eirik Ridge**, Atlantic Ocean
84 B 11 **Eiriksjökull**, Iceland
142 B 12 **Eirunepé**, Brazil
87 H 17 **Eisenach**, Germany
89 U 6 **Eisenerz**, Austria
89 U 9 **Eisenkappel**, Austria
89 Y 5 **Eisenstadt**, Austria
87 I 18 **Eisfeld**, Germany
99 F 17 **Eišiškės**, Lithuania
87 J 15 **Eisleben Lutherstadt**, Germany
81 W 9 **Eivissa**, Spain
81 S 3 **Ejea de los Caballeros**, Spain
197 W 10 **Ejeda**, Madgascar
171 P 6 **Ejin Qi**, China
159 T 9 **Ejmiatsin**, Armenia
192 M 12 **Ejura**, Ghana
125 T 14 **Ejutla**, Mexico
118 F 9 **Ekalaka**, Montana, U.S.A.
211 K 15 **Eketahuna**, New Zealand
167 U 3 **Ekibastuz**, Kazakhstan
157 Q 9 **Ekonda**, Russian Federation
194 I 7 **Ekouamou**, Congo
85 F 23 **Eksjö**, Sweden
194 L 8 **Ekuku**, Democratic Republic of Congo
115 N 9 **Ekwan**, Ontario, Canada
189 Q 11 **El Adeb Larache**, Algeria
190 D 8 **El 'Alamein**, Egypt
189 O 8 **El Alia**, Algeria
80 L 12 **El Arahal**, Spain
124 H 5 **El Arco**, Mexico
188 K 7 **El Aricha**, Algeria
190 G 7 **El 'Arîsh**, Egypt
190 F 10 **El Balyana**, Egypt
124 L 3 **El Barreal**, Mexico
191 F 19 **El Barun**, Sudan
139 N 4 **El Baúl**, Venezuela
188 L 7 **El Bayadh**, Algeria
191 J 24 **El Beru Hagia**, Somalia
145 G 17 **El Bolsón**, Argentina
189 Q 8 **El Borma**, Tunisia
191 D 22 **El Buheyrat**, Sudan
145 H 17 **El Caín**, Argentina
117 H 24 **El Cajon**, California, U.S.A.
138 K 6 **El Campin**, Colombia
119 K 22 **El Campo**, Texas, U.S.A.
140 B 8 **El Carmen**, Ecuador
141 L 18 **El Carmen**, Bolivia
125 N 7 **El Casco**, Mexico
117 J 24 **El Centro**, California, U.S.A.
141 M 20 **El Cerro**, Bolivia
125 W 13 **El Chichónal**, Mexico
124 G 2 **El Chinero**, Mexico
125 Z 10 **El Cuyo**, Mexico
138 F 9 **El Diviso**, Colombia
119 M 18 **El Dorado**, Arkansas, U.S.A.
119 K 15 **El Dorado**, Kansas, U.S.A.
124 L 8 **El Dorado**, Mexico
138 K 9 **El Dorado**, Colombia
138 J 11 **El Encanto**, Colombia
190 E 9 **El Faiyûm**, Egypt
191 B 17 **El Fasher**, Sudan
190 E 9 **El Fashn**, Egypt
191 K 21 **El Fud**, Ethiopia
124 K 6 **El Fuerte**, Mexico
191 A 17 **El Geneina**, Sudan
191 F 17 **El Geteina**, Sudan
191 F 17 **El Gezira**, Sudan
190 E 8 **El Gîza**, Egypt
188 M 9 **El Goléa**, Algeria
124 G 2 **El Golfo de Santa Clara**, Mexico
192 G 4 **El Hammâmi**, Mauritania
192 J 4 **El Hank**, Mauritania
191 G 18 **El Hawata**, Sudan
62 L 12 **El Hierro**, Canary Islands
191 C 18 **El Hilla**, Sudan
188 M 9 **El Homr**, Algeria
188 G 7 **El Jadida**, Morocco
189 Q 6 **El Jem**, Tunisia
188 G 8 **El Kelaâ des Srarhna**, Morocco
191 K 22 **Ēl Kerē**, Ethiopia
191 E 15 **El Khandaq**, Sudan
190 E 11 **El Khârga**, Egypt
192 K 5 **El Khnâchich**, Mali
191 L 22 **Ēl K'oran**, Ethiopia
191 D 19 **El Lagowa**, Sudan
127 S 7 **El Macao**, Dominican Republic
190 E 8 **El Mansûra**, Egypt
139 R 5 **El Manteco**, Venezuela
189 O 7 **El Meghaïer**, Algeria
190 E 9 **El Minya**, Egypt
81 O 6 **El Molar**, Spain
192 I 6 **El Mreyyé**, Mauritania
191 C 19 **El Muglad**, Sudan
175 N 5 **El Nido**, Philippines
191 D 18 **El Obeid**, Sudan
191 C 18 **El Odaiya**, Sudan
140 A 11 **El Oro**, Ecuador
125 O 6 **El Oro**, Mexico
189 O 7 **El Oued**, Algeria
119 E 20 **El Paso**, Texas, U.S.A.
81 U 6 **El Perelló**, Spain
126 K 13 **El Porvenír**, Panama
126 D 9 **El Progreso**, Guatemala
141 L 19 **El Puente**, Bolivia
80 K 13 **El Puerto de Santa María**, Spain
190 D 11 **El Qasr**, Egypt
126 L 14 **El Real**, Panama
119 J 17 **El Reno**, Oklahoma, U.S.A.
190 F 11 **El Ridisîya Bahari**, Egypt
80 K 11 **El Ronquillo**, Spain
190 E 8 **El Saff**, Egypt
124 H 3 **El Sahuaro**, Mexico
145 H 21 **El Salado**, Argentina
124 M 8 **El Salto**, Mexico
126 D 10 **El Salvador**, North America
144 G 7 **El Salvador**, Chile
127 S 7 **El Seibo**, Dominican Republic
144 G 13 **El Sosneado**, Argentina
124 M 4 **El Sueco**, Mexico
80 K 3 **El Teleno**, Spain
139 Q 4 **El Tigre**, Venezuela
144 F 9 **El Toro**, Chile
190 F 9 **El Tûr**, Egypt
145 G 24 **El Turbio**, Argentina
81 W 5 **El Vendrell**, Spain
138 K 4 **El Vigía**, Venezuela
195 X 6 **El Wak**, Kenya
191 D 17 **El Wuz**, Sudan
97 F 23 **Elafonisos**, Greece
97 L 26 **Elasa**, Greece
97 E 15 **Elassona**, Greece
160 F 13 **Elat**, Israel
214 M 15 **Elato**, Federated States of Micronesia
159 O 11 **Elazığ**, Turkey
122 M 7 **Elba**, Alabama, U.S.A.
95 K 19 **Elbasan**, Albania
86 I 11 **Elbe**, Germany/Czech Republic
123 P 4 **Elberton**, Georgia, U.S.A.
158 M 11 **Elbistan**, Turkey
92 J 8 **Elbląg**, Poland
113 Y 12 **Elbow**, Saskatchewan, Canada
156 D 11 **Elbrus**, Russian Federation
82 K 10 **Elburg**, Netherlands
164 I 5 **Elburz Mountains**, Iran
81 S 10 **Elche**, Spain
81 R 10 **Elche de la Sierra**, Spain
81 S 10 **Elda**, Spain
157 U 11 **El'dikan**, Russian Federation
120 H 13 **Eldorado**, Illinois, U.S.A.
144 O 7 **Eldorado**, Argentina
142 J 12 **Eldorado dos Carajás**, Brazil
195 U 7 **Eldoret**, Kenya
97 G 20 **Elefsina**, Greece
98 E 12 **Eleja**, Latvia
195 U 4 **Elemi Triangle**, Kenya
96 K 8 **Elena**, Bulgaria
119 E 18 **Elephant Butte Reservoir**, New Mexico, U.S.A.
218 G 2 **Elephant Island**, Antarctica
126 M 2 **Eleuthera**, The Bahamas
76 I 9 **Elgin**, United Kingdom
118 H 9 **Elgin**, North Dakota, U.S.A.
120 I 9 **Elgin**, Illinois, U.S.A.
195 T 7 **Elgon**, Kenya
175 T 15 **Eliase**, Indonesia
119 G 18 **Elida**, New Mexico, U.S.A.
112 H 4 **Elim**, Alaska, U.S.A.
96 G 9 **Elin Pelin**, Bulgaria
195 N 8 **Elipa**, Democratic Republic of Congo
142 L 13 **Eliseu Martins**, Brazil
156 E 11 **Elista**, Russian Federation
121 U 10 **Elizabeth**, New Jersey, U.S.A.
123 W 1 **Elizabeth City**, North Carolina, U.S.A.
123 Q 1 **Elizabethton**, Tennessee, U.S.A.
120 K 14 **Elizabethtown**, Kentucky, U.S.A.
92 M 9 **Ełk**, Poland
116 J 9 **Elk City**, Idaho, U.S.A.
119 I 17 **Elk City**, Oklahoma, U.S.A.
113 W 11 **Elk Point**, Alberta, Canada
120 K 9 **Elkhart**, Indiana, U.S.A.
120 I 8 **Elkhorn**, Wisconsin, U.S.A.
96 L 10 **Elkhovo**, Bulgaria
121 P 12 **Elkins**, West Virginia, U.S.A.
113 V 14 **Elko**, British Columbia, Canada
117 J 15 **Elko**, Nevada, U.S.A.
121 Q 13 **Elkton**, Virginia, U.S.A.
123 O 6 **Ellaville**, Georgia, U.S.A.
65 P 7 **Ellef Ringnes Island**, Arctic Ocean
118 I 9 **Ellendale**, North Dakota, U.S.A.
116 F 7 **Ellensburg**, Washington, U.S.A.
65 O 8 **Ellesmere Island**, Arctic Ocean
123 O 3 **Ellijay**, Georgia, U.S.A.
197 O 14 **Elliot**, Republic of South Africa
115 O 13 **Elliot Lake**, Ontario, Canada
209 N 3 **Elliott**, Northern Territory, Australia
121 P 13 **Elliott Knob**, Virginia, U.S.A.
197 N 10 **Ellisras**, Republic of South Africa
209 O 11 **Elliston**, South Australia, Australia
76 J 10 **Ellon**, United Kingdom
120 F 5 **Ellsworth**, Wisconsin, U.S.A.
121 Z 5 **Ellsworth**, Maine, U.S.A.
218 J 8 **Ellsworth Land**, Antarctica
218 L 8 **Ellsworth Mountains**, Antarctica
87 H 22 **Ellwangen**, Germany
116 D 7 **Elma**, Washington, U.S.A.
158 E 13 **Elmali**, Turkey
88 K 7 **Elmen**, Austria
115 W 12 **Elmira**, Prince Edward Island, Canada
121 S 9 **Elmira**, New York, U.S.A.
86 G 10 **Elmshorn**, Germany
117 M 24 **Eloy**, Arizona, U.S.A.
82 K 13 **Elst**, Netherlands
87 M 16 **Elsterwerda**, Germany
61 S 13 **Eltanin Fracture Zone**, Pacific Ocean
210 J 13 **Eltham**, New Zealand
169 G 19 **Eluru**, India
98 H 8 **Elva**, Estonia
80 J 9 **Elvas**, Portugal
85 E 18 **Elverum**, Norway
142 A 12 **Elvira**, Brazil
117 J 17 **Ely**, Nevada, U.S.A.
121 N 10 **Elyria**, Ohio, U.S.A.
87 G 14 **Elze**, Germany
213 R 11 **Émaé**, Vanuatu
165 U 5 **Emām Şaḩēb**, Afghanistan
166 K 7 **Emba**, Kazakhstan
166 L 6 **Emba**, Kazakhstan
145 H 15 **Embalse Cerros Colorados**, Argentina
81 Q 8 **Embalse de Alarcón**, Spain
80 L 5 **Embalse de Almendra**, Spain
81 Q 6 **Embalse de Buendía**, Spain
80 M 8 **Embalse de Cíjara**, Spain
80 M 8 **Embalse de Garcia Sola**, Spain
139 R 4 **Embalse de Guri**, Venezuela
81 N 12 **Embalse de Iznajar**, Spain
80 L 9 **Embalse de Orellana**, Spain
80 K 8 **Embalse de Valdecañas**, Spain
80 M 9 **Embalse del Zújar**, Spain
145 H 15 **Embalse Ezequiel Ramos Mexia**, Argentina
145 H 18 **Embalse Florentino Ameghino**, Argentina
144 J 5 **Embarcación**, Argentina
194 K 8 **Embondo**, Democratic Republic of Congo
78 K 7 **Embouchure de la Loire**, France
195 V 8 **Embu**, Kenya
86 D 10 **Emden**, Germany
209 U 6 **Emerald**, Queensland, Australia
117 M 17 **Emery**, Utah, U.S.A.
158 D 10 **Emet**, Turkey
212 B 6 **Emeti**, Papua New Guinea
193 X 6 **Emi Koussi**, Chad
90 F 9 **Emilia-Romagna**, Italy
125 X 13 **Emiliano Zapata**, Mexico
170 J 3 **Emin**, China
212 F 2 **Emirau Island**, Papua New Guinea
158 F 10 **Emirdağ**, Turkey
209 T 14 **Emita**, Tasmania, Australia
86 C 13 **Emlichheim**, Germany
98 D 7 **Emmaste**, Estonia
82 K 9 **Emmeloord**, Netherlands
82 N 9 **Emmen**, Netherlands
87 B 14 **Emmerich**, Germany
209 S 7 **Emmet**, Queensland, Australia
112 G 5 **Emmonak**, Alaska, U.S.A.
119 G 22 **Emory Peak**, Texas, U.S.A.
124 I 5 **Empalme**, Mexico
144 M 8 **Empedrado**, Argentina
61 O 3 **Emperor Trough**, Pacific Ocean
90 E 10 **Empoli**, Italy
119 K 15 **Emporia**, Kansas, U.S.A.
121 R 15 **Emporia**, Virginia, U.S.A.
121 R 9 **Emporium**, Pennsylvania, U.S.A.
86 D 12 **Ems**, Germany
197 P 11 **Emzinoni**, Republic of South Africa
160 F 10 **En Gedi**, Israel
160 F 11 **'En Hazeva**, Israel
191 C 18 **En Nahud**, Sudan
175 W 12 **Enarotali**, Indonesia
143 G 20 **Encarnación**, Paraguay
117 H 24 **Encinitas**, California, U.S.A.
144 H 11 **Encón**, Argentina
93 L 21 **Encs**, Hungary
61 T 3 **Endeavour Seamount**, Pacific Ocean
175 O 15 **Endeh**, Indonesia
214 K 4 **Enderbury**, Kiribati
58 H 14 **Enderby Abyssal Plain**, Indian Ocean
219 U 3 **Enderby Land**, Antarctica
208 F 10 **Eneabba**, Western Australia, Australia
145 L 15 **Energia**, Argentina
96 K 13 **Enez**, Turkey
158 A 7 **Enez**, Turkey
121 W 9 **Enfield**, Connecticut, U.S.A.
123 V 1 **Enfield**, North Carolina, U.S.A.
212 B 4 **Enga**, Papua New Guinea
85 C 15 **Engan**, Norway
176 L 4 **Engaru**, Japan
88 G 8 **Engelberg**, Switzerland
89 R 3 **Engelhartszell**, Austria
156 F 10 **Engel's**, Russian Federation
82 H 6 **Engelschmangat**, Netherlands
82 L 5 **Engelsmanplaat**, Netherlands
174 E 13 **Enggano**, Indonesia
83 E 20 **Enghien**, Belgium
77 I 19 **England**, United Kingdom
115 X 9 **Englee**, Newfoundland and Labrador, Canada
63 K 25 **English Bay**, Ascension
77 J 24 **English Channel**, United Kingdom/France
62 L 7 **English Channel**, Atlantic Ocean
218 J 6 **English Coast**, Antarctica
98 E 10 **Engure**, Latvia
98 E 10 **Engures ezers**, Latvia
119 J 16 **Enid**, Oklahoma, U.S.A.
176 J 6 **Eniwa**, Japan
82 I 9 **Enkhuizen**, Netherlands
91 J 22 **Enna**, Italy
113 X 7 **Ennadai Lake**, Nunavut, Canada
77 B 19 **Ennis**, Republic of Ireland
77 E 19 **Enniscorthy**, Republic of Ireland
77 D 16 **Enniskillen**, United Kingdom
89 T 4 **Enns**, Austria
171 T 14 **Enping**, China
78 L 5 **Enree**, France
82 N 11 **Enschede**, Netherlands
124 F 2 **Ensenada**, Mexico
171 S 11 **Enshi**, China
177 I 18 **Enshū-nada**, Japan
195 S 8 **Entebbe**, Uganda
113 T 8 **Enterprise**, Northwest Territories, Canada
117 L 19 **Enterprise**, Utah, U.S.A.
113 T 12 **Entrance**, Alberta, Canada
144 M 10 **Entre Rios**, Argentina
80 H 8 **Entroncamento**, Portugal
193 R 13 **Enugu**, Nigeria
193 R 13 **Enugu**, Nigeria
157 Z 5 **Enurmino**, Russian Federation
142 B 12 **Envira**, Brazil
82 K 11 **Epe**, Netherlands
194 I 7 **Epéna**, Congo
79 S 4 **Épernay**, France
116 G 7 **Ephrata**, Washington, U.S.A.
121 T 11 **Ephrata**, Pennsylvania, U.S.A.
213 R 11 **Epi**, Vanuatu
79 V 5 **Épinal**, France
158 H 15 **Episkopi**, Cyprus
145 J 14 **Epu-pel**, Argentina
194 K 8 **Equateur**, Democratic Republic of Congo
169 L 20 **Equatorial Channel**, Maldives
193 R 15 **Equatorial Guinea**, Africa
188 I 8 **Er Rachidia**, Morocco
191 E 18 **Er Rahad**, Sudan
188 J 9 **Er Raoui**, Algeria
191 F 19 **Er Renk**, Sudan
212 C 5 **Erave**, Papua New Guinea
158 L 8 **Erbaa**, Turkey
159 T 11 **Erçek**, Turkey
159 S 10 **Erciş**, Turkey
158 K 11 **Erciyes Dağl**, Turkey
93 I 23 **Érd**, Hungary
158 C 8 **Erdek**, Turkey
158 J 13 **Erdemli**, Turkey
171 Q 3 **Erdenet**, Mongolia
171 Q 5 **Erdenetsogt**, Mongolia
87 K 24 **Erding**, Germany
171 T 2 **Ereentsav**, Mongolia
158 I 12 **Ereğli**, Turkey
158 G 7 **Ereğli**, Turkey
171 S 5 **Erenhot**, China
188 I 8 **Erfoud**, Morocco
87 I 17 **Erfurt**, Germany
192 K 5 **Erg Atouila**, Mali
188 H 13 **'Erg Chech**, Africa
193 W 8 **Erg du Djourab**, Chad
188 I 10 **Erg labès**, Algeria
188 G 11 **Erg Iguidi**, Algeria
159 O 11 **Ergani**, Turkey
171 S 5 **Ergel**, Mongolia
96 L 13 **Ergene**, Turkey
98 G 11 **Ērgļi**, Latvia
212 C 5 **Eri**, Papua New Guinea
63 N 18 **Erica Seamount**, Atlantic Ocean
80 F 9 **Ericeira**, Portugal
121 P 9 **Erie**, Pennsylvania, U.S.A.
97 A 15 **Eriekoussa**, Greece
192 K 5 **'Erîgât**, Mali
114 I 10 **Eriksdale**, Manitoba, Canada
176 L 6 **Erimo**, Japan
176 L 7 **Erimo-misaki**, Japan
76 E 11 **Eriskay**, United Kingdom
191 H 16 **Eritrea**, Africa
86 M 13 **Erkner**, Germany
87 I 20 **Erlangen**, Germany
209 N 7 **Erldunda**, Northern Territory, Australia
82 J 11 **Ermelo**, Netherlands
197 P 11 **Ermelo**, Republic of South Africa
158 H 13 **Ermenek**, Turkey
97 F 21 **Ermioni**, Greece
97 I 21 **Ermoupoli**, Greece
87 E 17 **Erndtebrück**, Germany
89 X 3 **Ernstbrunn**, Austria
169 E 22 **Erode**, India
209 R 8 **Eromanga**, Queensland, Australia
196 H 9 **Erongo**, Namibia
83 F 22 **Erquelinnes**, Belgium
77 B 16 **Erris Head**, Republic of Ireland
121 W 5 **Errol**, New Hampshire, U.S.A.
213 R 12 **Erromango**, Vanuatu
95 L 20 **Ersekë**, Albania
118 K 7 **Erskine**, Minnesota, U.S.A.
170 L 4 **Ertai**, China
159 R 12 **Eruh**, Turkey
143 H 22 **Erval**, Brazil
87 F 15 **Erwitte**, Germany
97 F 19 **Erythres**, Greece
157 O 14 **Erzin**, Russian Federation
158 L 13 **Erzin**, Turkey
159 O 9 **Erzincan**, Turkey
159 Q 9 **Erzurum**, Turkey
99 D 14 **Eržvilkas**, Lithuania
188 E 11 **Es Semara**, Western Sahara
191 F 18 **Es Suki**, Sudan
212 G 7 **Esa-ala**, Papua New Guinea
176 J 7 **Esan-misaki**, Japan
176 I 8 **Esashi**, Japan
176 K 3 **Esashi**, Japan
85 B 25 **Esbjerg**, Denmark
117 M 18 **Escalante**, Utah, U.S.A.
125 N 6 **Escalón**, Mexico
120 J 5 **Escanaba**, Michigan, U.S.A.
125 X 12 **Escárcega**, Mexico
175 P 1 **Escarpada Point**, Philippines
83 D 18 **Escaut**, Belgium
83 K 26 **Esch-sur-Alzette**, Luxembourg
87 H 16 **Eschwege**, Germany
141 H 19 **Escoma**, Bolivia
117 H 24 **Escondido**, California, U.S.A.
124 M 9 **Escuinapa**, Mexico
126 C 10 **Escuintla**, Guatemala
193 T 14 **Eséka**, Cameroon
158 D 13 **Esen**, Turkey
166 I 14 **Esenguly**, Turkmenistan
164 J 7 **Eşfahān**, Iran
164 I 8 **Eşfahān**, Iran
164 M 5 **Esfarāyen**, Iran
115 T 8 **Esker**, Newfoundland and Labrador, Canada
85 G 21 **Eskilstuna**, Sweden
158 F 9 **Eskişehir**, Turkey
164 F 6 **Eslāmābād-e Gharb**, Iran
126 L 5 **Esmeralda**, Cuba
140 A 8 **Esmeraldas**, Ecuador
140 B 7 **Esmeraldas**, Ecuador
165 O 13 **Espakeh**, Iran
79 Q 12 **Espalion**, France
86 F 13 **Espelkamp**, Germany

Country · Internal administrative region: State/Province/Territory/Dependent territory · Capital city · Mountain range/Undersea ridge · Mountain peak/Volcano/Seamount · Geographic feature · Headland/Point/Cape/Peninsula · Desert · Island/Island group · Antarctic base · Ocean · Sea · Bay/Gulf/Channel/Strait · Lake · Salt pan/Dry/Intermittent lake · River

208 I 12 **Esperance**, Western Australia, Australia
218 H 3 **Esperanza**, Antarctica
124 J 5 **Esperanza**, Mexico
141 G 15 **Esperanza**, Peru
145 G 23 **Esperanza**, Argentina
80 U 6 **Espiel**, Spain
138 I 7 **Espinal**, Colombia
80 G 5 **Espinho**, Portugal
143 M 17 **Espírito Santo**, Brazil
213 P 10 **Espiritu Santo**, Vanuatu
143 N 14 **Esplanada**, Brazil
85 L 19 **Espoo**, Finland
80 H 4 **Esposende**, Portugal
145 G 18 **Esquel**, Argentina
144 L 9 **Esquina**, Argentina
188 F 8 **Essaouira**, Morocco
87 C 15 **Essen**, Germany
139 U 6 **Essequibo**, Guyana
157 Y 10 **Esso**, Russian Federation
193 V 15 **Est**, Cameroon
143 N 14 **Estância**, Brazil
90 G 7 **Este**, Italy
144 K 9 **Esteban Rams**, Argentina
126 F 11 **Estelí**, Nicaragua
81 Q 2 **Estella**, Spain
80 M 14 **Estepona**, Spain
118 K 11 **Estherville**, Iowa, U.S.A.
123 R 6 **Estill**, South Carolina, U.S.A.
98 F 7 **Estonia**, Europe
145 I 26 **Estrecho de Le Maire**, Argentina
145 E 24 **Estrecho Nelson**, Chile
80 I 9 **Estremoz**, Portugal
194 D 7 **Estuaire**, Gabon
168 F 12 **Etah**, India
79 U 3 **Étain**, France
115 W 10 **Etamamoiu**, Québec, Canada
79 P 5 **Étampes**, France
168 F 12 **Etawah**, India
191 G 21 **Ethiopia**, Africa
191 G 20 **Ethiopian Highlands**, Ethiopia
158 H 9 **Etimesğut**, Turkey
112 F 5 **Etolin Strait**, Alaska, U.S.A.
194 H 7 **Etoumbi**, Congo
79 N 3 **Étretat**, France
96 H 9 **Etropole**, Bulgaria
78 M 15 **Etsaut**, France
83 L 24 **Ettelbruck**, Luxembourg
214 I 11 **Eua**, Tonga
208 L 10 **Eucla**, Western Australia, Australia
123 N 6 **Eufaula**, Alabama, U.S.A.
119 K 17 **Eufaula Lake**, Oklahoma, U.S.A.
209 S 9 **Eulo**, Queensland, Australia
119 G 19 **Eunice**, New Mexico, U.S.A.
83 L 20 **Eupen**, Belgium
160 L 3 **Euphrates**, Syria/Iraq
122 I 4 **Eupora**, Mississippi, U.S.A.
117 C 14 **Eureka**, California, U.S.A.
117 I 16 **Eureka**, Nevada, U.S.A.
117 M 16 **Eureka**, Utah, U.S.A.
118 A 6 **Eureka**, Montana, U.S.A.
82 F 13 **Europoort**, Netherlands
87 C 18 **Euskirchen**, Germany
123 R 10 **Eustis**, Florida, U.S.A.
122 K 5 **Eutaw**, Alabama, U.S.A.
113 Q 12 **Eutsuk Lake**, British Columbia, Canada
115 O 4 **Evans Strait**, Nunavut, Canada
118 C 12 **Evanston**, Wyoming, U.S.A.
120 I 9 **Evanston**, Illinois, U.S.A.
120 I 13 **Evansville**, Indiana, U.S.A.
197 O 11 **Evaton**, Republic of South Africa
164 J 12 **Evaz**, Iran
157 Y 9 **Evensk**, Russian Federation
116 E 6 **Everett**, Washington, U.S.A.
123 R 14 **Everglades**, Florida, U.S.A.
122 L 7 **Evergreen**, Alabama, U.S.A.
85 K 15 **Evijärvi**, Finland
85 B 21 **Evje**, Norway
80 I 10 **Evora**, Portugal
80 I 9 **Évora**, Portugal
79 O 4 **Évreux**, France
96 K 13 **Evros**, Greece
97 H 19 **Evvoia**, Greece
117 C 24 **Ewa Beach**, Hawaii, U.S.A.
63 M 16 **Ewing Seamount**, Atlantic Ocean
194 G 8 **Ewo**, Congo
218 L 11 **Executive Committee Range**, Antarctica
77 I 23 **Exeter**, United Kingdom
118 L 12 **Exira**, Iowa, U.S.A.
77 I 22 **Exmoor**, United Kingdom
121 T 14 **Exmore**, Virginia, U.S.A.
77 I 23 **Exmouth**, United Kingdom
208 E 6 **Exmouth**, Western Australia, Australia
59 T 7 **Exmouth Plateau**, Indian Ocean
80 K 8 **Extremadura**, Spain
193 V 11 **Extrême-Nord**, Cameroon
126 M 3 **Exuma Cays**, The Bahamas
191 O 21 **Eyl**, Somalia
79 P 10 **Eymoutiers**, France
209 O 11 **Eyre Peninsula**, South Australia, Australia
211 H 20 **Eyreton**, New Zealand
98 J 12 **Ezernieki**, Latvia
158 A 9 **Ezine**, Turkey

F

169 L 17 **Faadhippolhu Atoll**, Maldives
191 J 24 **Faafxadhuun**, Somalia
215 U 9 **Faaite**, French Polynesia
193 T 7 **Fachi**, Niger
145 G 19 **Facundo**, Argentina
193 Y 7 **Fada**, Chad
193 N 10 **Fada-Ngourma**, Burkina Faso
90 G 9 **Faenza**, Italy
215 U 14 **Fagamalo**, Samoa
100 J 10 **Făgăraș**, Romania
215 W 15 **Fagatogo**, American Samoa
85 G 20 **Fagersta**, Sweden
100 G 10 **Făget**, Romania
84 C 11 **Fagurhólsmýri**, Iceland
62 N 1 **Faial**, Azores
88 G 9 **Faido**, Switzerland
76 J 6 **Fair Isle**, United Kingdom
112 L 5 **Fairbanks**, Alaska, U.S.A.
116 J 2 **Fairfield**, Idaho, U.S.A.
117 D 17 **Fairfield**, California, U.S.A.
120 H 13 **Fairfield**, Illinois, U.S.A.
211 F 21 **Fairlie**, New Zealand
121 P 12 **Fairmont**, West Virginia, U.S.A.
119 E 14 **Fairplay**, Colorado, U.S.A.
165 X 9 **Faisalabad**, Pakistan
168 H 12 **Faizabad**, India
127 U 7 **Fajardo**, Puerto Rico
161 W 9 **Fajir**, Iraq
215 X 9 **Fakahina**, French Polynesia
214 J 6 **Fakaofo**, Tokelau Islands
215 U 9 **Fakarava**, French Polynesia
175 U 12 **Fakfak**, Indonesia
96 M 10 **Fakiya**, Bulgaria
85 D 26 **Fakse Bugt**, Denmark
78 M 4 **Falaise**, France
193 R 7 **Falaise de Tiguidit**, Niger
138 M 2 **Falcón**, Venezuela
90 I 10 **Falconara Marittima**, Italy
215 T 14 **Falealupo**, Samoa
215 V 15 **Falefa**, Samoa
100 M 8 **Fălești**, Moldova
86 L 13 **Falkensee**, Germany
76 H 13 **Falkirk**, United Kingdom
63 F 20 **Falkland Escarpment**, Atlantic Ocean
145 J 24 **Falkland Islands**, U.K.
63 F 20 **Falkland Plateau**, Atlantic Ocean
145 K 24 **Falkland Sound**, Falkland Islands
97 G 23 **Falkonera**, Greece
85 E 22 **Falköping**, Sweden
121 X 9 **Fall River**, Massachusetts, U.S.A.
117 G 16 **Fallon**, Nevada, U.S.A.
123 U 1 **Falls Lake Reserve**, North Carolina, U.S.A.
77 G 24 **Falmouth**, United Kingdom
126 L 7 **Falmouth**, Jamaica
196 J 15 **False Bay**, Republic of South Africa
112 E 9 **False Pass**, Alaska, U.S.A.
169 J 16 **False Point**, India
85 D 26 **Falster**, Denmark
100 L 8 **Fălticeni**, Romania
85 G 19 **Falun**, Sweden
144 H 9 **Famatina**, Argentina
164 H 6 **Famenin**, Iran
172 J 11 **Fan Si Pan**, Vietnam
197 Y 8 **Fandriana**, Madgascar
172 G 13 **Fang**, Thailand
191 E 20 **Fangak**, Sudan
215 W 9 **Fangatau**, French Polynesia
215 Y 11 **Fangataufa**, French Polynesia
171 X 3 **Fangzheng**, China
165 N 13 **Fannūj**, Iran
90 H 10 **Fano**, Italy
85 B 25 **Fanø**, Denmark
168 G 10 **Far Western**, Nepal
218 H 4 **Faraday**, Antarctica
195 Q 5 **Faradje**, Democratic Republic of Congo
197 Y 10 **Farafangana**, Madagascar
165 Q 8 **Farāh**, Afghanistan
165 P 9 **Farāh**, Afghanistan
214 A 8 **Farallon de Medinilla**, Northern Mariana Islands
214 A 5 **Farallon de Pajaros**, Northern Mariana Islands
192 H 11 **Faranah**, Guinea
163 X 10 **Fararah**, Oman
214 M 14 **Faraulep**, Federated States of Micronesia
211 H 15 **Farewell Spit**, New Zealand
167 S 12 **Farghona Wiloyati**, Uzbekistan
118 J 8 **Fargo**, North Dakota, U.S.A.
123 Q 8 **Fargo**, Georgia, U.S.A.
168 E 11 **Faridabad**, India
168 D 10 **Faridkot**, India
165 O 6 **Farīmān**, Iran
85 G 24 **Färjestaden**, Sweden
119 D 16 **Farmington**, New Mexico, U.S.A.
121 X 5 **Farmington**, Maine, U.S.A.
121 R 14 **Farmville**, Virginia, U.S.A.
80 H 12 **Faro**, Portugal
80 H 12 **Faro**, Portugal
113 O 7 **Faro**, Yukon Territory, Canada
65 R 15 **Faroe Islands**, Denmark
65 Q 15 **Faroe–Iceland Ridge**, Arctic Ocean
62 K 5 **Faroe–Shetland Trough**, Atlantic Ocean
85 I 22 **Fårösund**, Sweden
85 I 22 **Fårösund**, Sweden
58 K 6 **Farquhar Islands**, Indian Ocean
164 J 10 **Fārs**, Iran
97 E 17 **Farsala**, Greece
118 D 12 **Farson**, Wyoming, U.S.A.
119 G 18 **Farwell**, Texas, U.S.A.
218 J 8 **Farwell Island**, Antarctica
165 R 6 **Fāryāb**, Afghanistan
164 J 11 **Fasā**, Iran
91 N 16 **Fasano**, Italy
101 P 4 **Fastiv**, Ukraine
195 R 6 **Fataki**, Democratic Republic of Congo
168 D 10 **Fatehabad**, India
168 F 12 **Fatehgarh**, India
192 D 8 **Fatick**, Senegal
215 X 7 **Fatu Hiva**, French Polynesia
194 I 10 **Fatundu**, Democratic Republic of Congo
213 S 8 **Fatutaka**, Solomon Islands
84 G 10 **Fauske**, Norway
84 A 11 **Faxaflói**, Iceland
193 X 7 **Faya**, Chad
213 Q 13 **Fayaoué**, New Caledonia
122 K 4 **Fayette**, Alabama, U.S.A.
122 G 7 **Fayette**, Mississippi, U.S.A.
122 L 3 **Fayetteville**, Tennessee, U.S.A.
123 U 3 **Fayetteville**, North Carolina, U.S.A.
215 N 14 **Fayu**, Federated States of Micronesia
192 G 4 **Fdérik**, Mauritania
79 N 3 **Fécamp**, France
94 H 13 **Federacija Bosna Hercegovina**, Bosnia and Herzegovina
193 R 12 **Federal Capital Territory**, Nigeria
215 Q 14 **Federated States of Micronesia**, Oceania
161 O 3 **Fedghāmī**, Syria
167 O 2 **Fedorovka**, Kazakhstan
86 I 8 **Fehmarn**, Germany
86 I 7 **Fehmarnbelt**, Germany
89 X 8 **Fehring**, Austria
142 B 13 **Feijó**, Brazil
143 N 14 **Feira de Santana**, Brazil
158 K 12 **Feke**, Turkey
81 Y 8 **Felanitx**, Spain
89 X 8 **Feldbach**, Austria
88 I 7 **Feldkirch**, Austria
89 S 8 **Feldkirchen in Kärnten**, Austria
58 C 8 **Félicité**, Seychelles
169 L 18 **Felidhu Atoll**, Maldives
125 Z 11 **Felipe Carrillo Puerto**, Mexico
77 N 20 **Felixstowe**, United Kingdom
90 G 6 **Feltre**, Italy
85 E 17 **Femunden**, Norway
159 O 8 **Fener Burnu**, Turkey
97 J 14 **Fengari**, Greece
171 U 6 **Fengning**, China
171 V 1 **Fengshui Shan**, China
171 Q 9 **Fengxian**, China
212 I 3 **Feni Islands**, Papua New Guinea
112 B 9 **Fenimore Pass**, Alaska, U.S.A.
120 G 8 **Fennimore**, Wisconsin, U.S.A.
197 Z 7 **Fenoarivo Atsinanana**, Madgascar
77 M 19 **Fens, The**, United Kingdom
101 V 12 **Feodosiya**, Ukraine
120 J 13 **Ferdinand**, Indiana, U.S.A.
165 N 7 **Ferdows**, Iran
96 K 13 **Feres**, Greece
191 L 22 **Fērfēr**, Ethiopia
167 T 12 **Fergana**, Uzbekistan
167 S 12 **Fergana Valley**, Uzbekistan
118 K 9 **Fergus Falls**, Minnesota, U.S.A.
212 G 6 **Fergusson Island**, Papua New Guinea
189 P 6 **Fériana**, Tunisia
192 K 11 **Ferkessédougou**, Côte d'Ivoire
90 I 11 **Fermo**, Italy
80 K 5 **Fermoselle**, Spain
77 C 20 **Fermoy**, Republic of Ireland
144 J 8 **Fernández**, Argentina
123 R 8 **Fernandina Beach**, Florida, U.S.A.
63 I 14 **Fernando de Noronha**, Brazil
117 F 16 **Fernley**, Nevada, U.S.A.
91 M 16 **Ferrandina**, Italy
90 G 8 **Ferrara**, Italy
80 H 10 **Ferreira do Alentejo**, Portugal
80 I 1 **Ferrol**, Spain
188 I 7 **Fès**, Morocco
194 J 11 **Feshi**, Democratic Republic of Congo
119 N 14 **Festus**, Missouri, U.S.A.
100 M 13 **Fetești-Gara**, Romania
158 D 13 **Fethiye**, Turkey
166 I 10 **Fetisovo**, Kazakhstan
76 K 4 **Fetlar**, United Kingdom
87 H 22 **Feuchtwangen**, Germany
79 S 10 **Feurs**, France
165 V 5 **Feyzābād**, Afghanistan
144 H 8 **Fiambalá**, Argentina
197 X 9 **Fianarantsoa**, Madgascar
197 X 9 **Fianarantsoa**, Madgascar
193 V 11 **Fianga**, Chad
191 I 20 **Fichē**, Ethiopia
87 J 20 **Fichtelgebirge**, Germany
90 G 12 **Ficulle**, Italy
90 E 8 **Fidenza**, Italy
95 J 20 **Fier**, Albania
88 F 10 **Fiesch**, Switzerland
76 I 12 **Fife Ness**, United Kingdom
79 P 12 **Figeac**, France
80 G 7 **Figueira da Foz**, Portugal
81 Y 3 **Figueres**, Spain
188 K 8 **Figuig**, Morocco
193 V 11 **Figuil**, Cameroon
213 W 12 **Fiji**, Oceania
191 K 21 **Fīk'**, Ethiopia
197 O 8 **Filabusi**, Zimbabwe
126 G 12 **Filadelfia**, Costa Rica
143 F 18 **Filadélfia**, Paraguay
93 K 21 **Fiľakovo**, Slovakia
219 N 5 **Filchner Ice Shelf**, Antarctica
100 H 12 **Filiași**, Romania
97 C 22 **Filiatra**, Greece
193 P 9 **Filingué**, Niger
97 B 17 **Filippiada**, Greece
117 G 22 **Fillmore**, California, U.S.A.
117 L 17 **Fillmore**, Utah, U.S.A.
191 J 23 **Filtu**, Ethiopia
219 P 1 **Fimbul Ice Shelf**, Antarctica
219 P 2 **Fimbulheimen**, Antarctica
81 P 12 **Fiñana**, Spain
120 M 10 **Findlay**, Ohio, U.S.A.
121 R 8 **Finger Lakes**, New York, U.S.A.
197 P 5 **Fingoè**, Mozambique
158 E 14 **Finike**, Turkey
212 D 4 **Finisterre Range**, Papua New Guinea
209 O 7 **Finke**, Northern Territory, Australia
85 L 18 **Finland**, Europe
209 S 12 **Finley**, New South Wales, Australia
163 Z 7 **Fins**, Oman
212 E 5 **Finschhafen**, Papua New Guinea
88 F 9 **Finsteraarhorn**, Switzerland
211 A 25 **Fiordland**, New Zealand
113 V 9 **Firebag**, Alberta, Canada
90 F 9 **Firenzuola**, Italy
144 K 12 **Firmat**, Argentina
79 S 11 **Firminy**, France
168 F 12 **Firozabad**, India
168 D 9 **Firozpur**, India
77 G 14 **Firth of Clyde**, United Kingdom
76 I 12 **Firth of Forth**, United Kingdom
76 F 12 **Firth of Lorn**, United Kingdom
210 L 8 **Firth of Thames**, New Zealand
164 J 11 **Fīrūzābād**, Iran
164 J 6 **Fīrūzkūh**, Iran
59 Y 15 **Fisher Bay**, Indian Ocean
115 N 4 **Fisher Strait**, Nunavut, Canada
77 G 20 **Fishguard**, United Kingdom
79 R 3 **Fismes**, France
76 J 5 **Fitful Head**, United Kingdom
145 H 20 **Fitz Roy**, Argentina
141 F 16 **Fitzcarrald**, Peru
208 J 4 **Fitzroy**, Western Australia, Australia
208 J 4 **Fitzroy Crossing**, Western Australia, Australia
91 G 14 **Fiumicino**, Italy
90 D 9 **Fivizzano**, Italy
195 Q 10 **Fizi**, Democratic Republic of Congo
85 C 19 **Flå**, Norway
84 C 12 **Flaga**, Iceland
117 M 21 **Flagstaff**, Arizona, U.S.A.
63 N 25 **Flagstaff Bay**, St Helena
121 X 5 **Flagstaff Lake**, Maine, U.S.A.
115 P 8 **Flaherty Island**, Ontario, Canada
87 K 14 **Fläming**, Germany
118 D 12 **Flaming Gorge Reservoir**, Wyoming, U.S.A.
123 S 15 **Flamingo**, Florida, U.S.A.
83 C 19 **Flanders**, Belgium
85 G 14 **Flåsjön**, Sweden
58 B 11 **Flat Island**, Mauritius
118 B 7 **Flathead Lake**, Montana, U.S.A.
89 S 8 **Flattnitz**, Austria
62 B 7 **Flatts Village**, Bermuda
85 A 21 **Flekkefjord**, Norway
62 G 7 **Flemish Cap**, Atlantic Ocean
85 B 26 **Flensburg**, Denmark
86 G 7 **Flensburg**, Germany
78 M 4 **Flers**, France
218 I 8 **Fletcher Peninsula**, Antarctica
88 B 8 **Fleurier**, Switzerland
82 I 10 **Flevoland**, Netherlands
114 H 7 **Flin Flon**, Manitoba, Canada
209 R 5 **Flinders**, Queensland, Australia
209 T 14 **Flinders Island**, Tasmania, Australia
209 P 10 **Flinders Ranges**, South Australia, Australia
215 S 7 **Flint**, Kiribati
120 M 8 **Flint**, Michigan, U.S.A.
119 K 16 **Flint Hills**, Kansas, U.S.A.
85 E 18 **Flisa**, Norway
85 E 19 **Flisa**, Norway
120 H 12 **Flora**, Illinois, U.S.A.
79 S 12 **Florac**, France
122 M 8 **Florala**, Alabama, U.S.A.
90 F 10 **Florence**, Italy
117 N 24 **Florence**, Arizona, U.S.A.
121 P 11 **Florence**, Pennsylvania, U.S.A.
122 K 3 **Florence**, Alabama, U.S.A.
123 T 4 **Florence**, South Carolina, U.S.A.
138 H 9 **Florencia**, Colombia
83 G 22 **Florennes**, Belgium
83 J 25 **Florenville**, Belgium
62 M 1 **Flores**, Azores
175 O 15 **Flores**, Indonesia
144 M 12 **Flores**, Uruguay
126 D 8 **Flores**, Guatemala
175 N 15 **Flores Sea**, Indonesia
142 N 13 **Floresta**, Brazil
101 N 7 **Florești**, Moldova
142 L 12 **Floriano**, Brazil
143 J 21 **Florianópolis**, Brazil
123 R 11 **Florida**, U.S.A.
144 N 12 **Florida**, Uruguay
144 N 12 **Florida**, Uruguay
123 S 15 **Florida Bay**, Florida, U.S.A.
212 L 6 **Florida Islands**, Solomon Islands
123 R 15 **Florida Keys**, Florida, U.S.A.
96 C 13 **Florina**, Greece
85 A 17 **Florø**, Norway
119 H 18 **Floydada**, Texas, U.S.A.
82 J 8 **Fluessen**, Netherlands
175 S 12 **Fluk**, Indonesia
212 A 5 **Fly**, Papua New Guinea
214 I 10 **Foa**, Tonga
94 I 13 **Foča**, Bosnia and Herzegovina
100 L 11 **Focșani**, Romania
194 M 4 **Fodé**, Central African Republic
188 M 11 **Foggâret ez Zoûa**, Algeria
91 L 15 **Foggia**, Italy
63 A 17 **Fogo**, Cape Verde
115 Y 9 **Fogo Island**, Newfoundland and Labrador, Canada
175 Q 15 **Foho Tatamailau**, East Timor
86 F 7 **Föhr**, Germany
79 P 15 **Foix**, France
84 G 10 **Folda**, Norway
97 I 23 **Folegandros**, Greece
122 K 8 **Foley**, Alabama, U.S.A.
115 P 1 **Foley Island**, Nunavut, Canada
115 N 12 **Foleyet**, Ontario, Canada
90 H 12 **Foligno**, Italy
77 N 22 **Folkestone**, United Kingdom
90 E 12 **Follonica**, Italy
197 W 4 **Fomboni**, Comoros
120 I 7 **Fond du Luc**, Wisconsin, U.S.A.
91 I 15 **Fondi**, Italy
91 C 17 **Fonni**, Italy
138 J 2 **Fonseca**, Colombia
83 F 21 **Fontaine-l'Eveque**, Belgium
79 Q 5 **Fontainebleau**, France
142 D 10 **Fonte Boa**, Brazil
79 Q 4 **Fontenay-Trésigny**, France
84 D 9 **Fontur**, Iceland
214 I 10 **Fonualei**, Tonga
93 G 24 **Fonyód**, Hungary
209 T 11 **Forbes**, New South Wales, Australia
85 A 17 **Førde**, Norway
85 A 19 **Førde**, Norway
121 U 10 **Fords**, New Jersey, U.S.A.
119 M 18 **Fordyce**, Arkansas, U.S.A.
192 F 11 **Forécariah**, Guinea
122 I 6 **Forest**, Mississippi, U.S.A.
115 T 11 **Forestville**, Québec, Canada
76 I 11 **Forfar**, United Kingdom
116 C 6 **Forks**, Washington, U.S.A.
90 G 9 **Forlì**, Italy
81 W 9 **Formentera**, Spain
91 I 15 **Formia**, Italy
143 K 18 **Formiga**, Brazil
144 L 6 **Formosa**, Argentina
143 K 16 **Formosa**, Brazil
144 M 7 **Formosa**, Argentina

Country · Internal administrative region: State/Province/Territory/Dependent territory · Capital city · Mountain range/Undersea ridge · Mountain peak/Volcano/Seamount · Geographic feature · Headland/Point/Cape/Peninsula · Desert · Island/Island group · Antarctic base · Ocean · Sea · Bay/Gulf/Channel/Strait · Lake · Salt pan/Dry/Intermittent lake · River

143 K 14 **Formosa do Rio Preto**, Brazil
81 Z 7 **Fornells**, Spain
90 D 8 **Fornovo di Taro**, Italy
85 D 16 **Forolshogna**, Norway
208 K 10 **Forrest**, Western Australia, Australia
119 N 17 **Forrest City**, Arkansas, U.S.A.
209 S 4 **Forsayth**, Queensland, Australia
84 H 8 **Forsbakken**, Norway
85 L 18 **Forssa**, Finland
87 O 15 **Forst**, Germany
209 V 11 **Forster**, New South Wales, Australia
118 E 9 **Forsyth**, Montana, U.S.A.
123 O 5 **Forsyth**, Georgia, U.S.A.
165 X 11 **Fort Abbas**, Pakistan
115 O 10 **Fort Albany**, Ontario, Canada
76 G 10 **Fort Augustus**, United Kingdom
197 N 14 **Fort Beaufort**, Republic of South Africa
118 C 7 **Fort Benton**, Montana, U.S.A.
117 C 16 **Fort Bragg**, California, U.S.A.
113 V 9 **Fort Chipewyan**, Alberta, Canada
118 F 13 **Fort Collins**, Colorado, U.S.A.
127 X 9 **Fort-de-France**, Martinique
118 L 11 **Fort Dodge**, Iowa, U.S.A.
114 J 11 **Fort Frances**, Ontario, Canada
113 P 5 **Fort Good Hope**, Northwest Territories, Canada
123 T 13 **Fort Lauderdale**, Florida, U.S.A.
113 R 8 **Fort Liard**, Northwest Territories, Canada
127 P 6 **Fort Liberté**, Haiti
113 V 9 **Fort MacKay**, Alberta, Canada
113 V 10 **Fort McMurray**, Alberta, Canada
113 O 5 **Fort McPherson**, Northwest Territories, Canada
123 R 13 **Fort Myers**, Florida, U.S.A.
123 Q 13 **Fort Myers Beach**, Florida, U.S.A.
113 R 9 **Fort Nelson**, British Columbia, Canada
122 M 3 **Fort Payne**, Alabama, U.S.A.
118 E 7 **Fort Peck**, Montana, U.S.A.
118 E 7 **Fort Peck Reservoir**, Montana, U.S.A.
123 S 12 **Fort Pierce**, Florida, U.S.A.
195 R 7 **Fort Portal**, Uganda
113 T 8 **Fort Providence**, Northwest Territories, Canada
113 U 7 **Fort Resolution**, Northwest Territories, Canada
197 O 8 **Fort Rixon**, Zimbabwe
119 L 15 **Fort Scott**, Kansas, U.S.A.
114 M 7 **Fort Severn**, Ontario, Canada
166 G 8 **Fort-Shevchenko**, Kazakhstan
113 R 7 **Fort Simpson**, Northwest Territories, Canada
113 U 8 **Fort Smith**, Northwest Territories, Canada
119 L 17 **Fort Smith**, Arkansas, U.S.A.
113 R 12 **Fort St James**, British Columbia, Canada
113 S 10 **Fort St John**, British Columbia, Canada
119 G 21 **Fort Stockton**, Texas, U.S.A.
119 F 18 **Fort Sumner**, New Mexico, U.S.A.
123 O 6 **Fort Valley**, Georgia, U.S.A.
122 L 8 **Fort Walton Beach**, Florida, U.S.A.
120 L 10 **Fort Wayne**, Indiana, U.S.A.
76 G 11 **Fort William**, United Kingdom
119 J 19 **Fort Worth**, Texas, U.S.A.
112 M 5 **Fort Yukon**, Alaska, U.S.A.
142 N 11 **Fortaleza**, Brazil
141 O 22 **Forte Coimbra**, Bolivia
90 E 10 **Forte dei Marmi**, Italy
76 H 12 **Forth**, United Kingdom
141 N 21 **Fortín**, Bolivia
143 F 18 **Fortín Carlos Antonio López**, Paraguay
143 E 18 **Fortín Coronel Eugenio Garay**, Paraguay
143 F 17 **Fortín Galpón**, Paraguay
143 E 18 **Fortín Infante Rivarola**, Paraguay
143 F 18 **Fortín Madrejón**, Paraguay
144 L 5 **Fortín Pilcomayo**, Argentina
141 M 21 **Fortín Ravelo**, Bolivia
211 D 26 **Fortrose**, New Zealand
117 C 15 **Fortuna**, California, U.S.A.
118 G 7 **Fortuna**, North Dakota, U.S.A.
115 Y 11 **Fortune Bay**, Newfoundland and Labrador, Canada
164 J 13 **Forūr**, Iran
79 T 14 **Fos-sur-Mer**, France
171 T 13 **Foshan**, China
84 C 12 **Foss**, Iceland
90 A 8 **Fossano**, Italy
83 G 21 **Fosses-la-Ville**, Belgium
90 H 10 **Fossombrone**, Italy
194 E 8 **Fougamou**, Gabon
78 L 5 **Fougères**, France
190 G 12 **Foul Bay**, Egypt
76 J 5 **Foula**, United Kingdom
194 D 8 **Foulenzem**, Gabon
188 H 9 **Foum Zguid**, Morocco
193 T 13 **Foumban**, Cameroon
62 H 13 **Four North Fracture Zone**, Atlantic Ocean
97 L 21 **Fournoi**, Greece
192 G 10 **Fouta Djallon**, Guinea
211 B 26 **Foveaux Strait**, New Zealand
120 J 10 **Fowler**, Indiana, U.S.A.
209 N 10 **Fowlers Bay**, South Australia, Australia
113 T 11 **Fox Creek**, Alberta, Canada
211 D 20 **Fox Glacier**, New Zealand
112 C 9 **Fox Islands**, Alaska, U.S.A.
113 U 9 **Fox Lake**, Alberta, Canada
117 G 14 **Fox Mountain**, Nevada, U.S.A.
211 F 20 **Fox Peak**, New Zealand
64 K 9 **Foxe Basin**, Nunavut, Canada
115 O 2 **Foxe Channel**, Nunavut, Canada
115 P 3 **Foxe Peninsula**, Nunavut, Canada
85 D 20 **Foxen**, Sweden
211 K 15 **Foxton**, New Zealand
80 J 1 **Foz**, Spain
196 F 7 **Foz do Cunene**, Angola
143 H 20 **Foz do Iguaçu**, Brazil
81 U 4 **Fraga**, Spain
83 G 22 **Fraire**, Belgium
65 S 9 **Fram Basin**, Arctic Ocean
219 W 4 **Fram Peak**, Antarctica
143 J 18 **Franca**, Brazil
78 M 9 **France**, Europe
194 G 8 **Franceville**, Gabon
79 U 7 **Franche-Comté**, France
140 F 10 **Francisco de Orellana**, Peru
197 N 8 **Francistown**, Botswana
113 Q 12 **Francois Lake**, British Columbia, Canada
82 J 7 **Franeker**, Netherlands
120 L 13 **Frankfort**, Kentucky, U.S.A.
87 F 19 **Frankfurt am Main**, Germany
86 N 13 **Frankfurt an der Oder**, Germany
87 I 23 **Fränkische Alb**, Germany
120 K 12 **Franklin**, Indiana, U.S.A.
121 P 10 **Franklin**, Pennsylvania, U.S.A.
121 S 15 **Franklin**, Virginia, U.S.A.
121 Q 13 **Franklin**, West Virginia, U.S.A.
123 P 3 **Franklin**, North Carolina, U.S.A.
113 Q 3 **Franklin Bay**, Northwest Territories, Canada
116 H 6 **Franklin D. Roosevelt Lake**, Washington, U.S.A.
113 Q 5 **Franklin Mountains**, Northwest Territories, Canada
211 E 20 **Franz Josef Glacier**, New Zealand
156 N 3 **Franz Josef Land**, Russian Federation
113 R 12 **Fraser**, British Columbia, Canada
115 U 7 **Fraser**, Newfoundland and Labrador, Canada
209 W 8 **Fraser Island**, Queensland, Australia
113 R 12 **Fraser Lake**, British Columbia, Canada
113 R 12 **Fraser Plateau**, British Columbia, Canada
196 K 14 **Fraserburg**, Republic of South Africa
76 J 9 **Fraserburgh**, United Kingdom
115 O 11 **Fraserdale**, Ontario, Canada
210 N 12 **Frasertown**, New Zealand
83 D 20 **Frasnes-lez-Buissenal**, Belgium
88 H 6 **Frauenfeld**, Switzerland
144 M 11 **Fray Bentos**, Uruguay
120 F 4 **Frederic**, Wisconsin, U.S.A.
85 B 25 **Fredericia**, Denmark
119 I 18 **Frederick**, Oklahoma, U.S.A.
121 R 12 **Frederick**, Maryland, U.S.A.
119 J 21 **Fredericksburg**, Texas, U.S.A.
121 S 13 **Fredericksburg**, Virginia, U.S.A.
115 U 13 **Fredericton**, New Brunswick, Canada
85 C 23 **Frederikshavn**, Denmark
127 V 7 **Frederiksted**, Virgin Islands (U.S.A.)
117 L 19 **Fredonia**, Arizona, U.S.A.
85 I 14 **Fredrika**, Sweden
197 N 12 **Free State**, Republic of South Africa
119 L 22 **Freeport**, Texas, U.S.A.
120 H 8 **Freeport**, Illinois, U.S.A.
126 L 2 **Freeport**, The Bahamas
119 J 23 **Freer**, Texas, U.S.A.
192 F 12 **Freetown**, Sierra Leone
58 C 9 **Frégate**, Seychelles
80 J 10 **Fregenal de la Sierra**, Spain
87 M 17 **Freiberg**, Germany
87 D 25 **Freiburg im Breisgau**, Germany
87 D 18 **Freilingen**, Germany
87 K 23 **Freising**, Germany
89 T 3 **Freistadt**, Austria
208 G 11 **Fremantle**, Western Australia, Australia
117 D 18 **Fremont**, California, U.S.A.
120 K 7 **Fremont**, Michigan, U.S.A.
139 X 7 **French Guiana**, France
215 V 11 **French Polynesia**, French Polynesia
188 L 6 **Frenda**, Algeria
192 J 14 **Fresco**, Côte d'Ivoire
125 O 9 **Fresnillo**, Mexico
117 F 19 **Fresno**, California, U.S.A.
87 E 23 **Freudenstadt**, Germany
209 T 15 **Freycinet Peninsula**, Tasmania, Australia
79 V 4 **Freyming-Merlebach**, France
87 M 22 **Freyung**, Germany
192 F 11 **Fria**, Guinea
144 I 9 **Frías**, Argentina
88 D 8 **Fribourg**, Switzerland
88 F 6 **Frick**, Switzerland
89 X 6 **Friedberg**, Austria
87 G 25 **Friedrichshafen**, Germany
89 T 8 **Friesach**, Austria
82 K 7 **Friesland**, Netherlands
122 K 7 **Frisco City**, Alabama, U.S.A.
117 L 17 **Frisco Mountain**, Utah, U.S.A.
87 G 16 **Fritzlar**, Germany
90 H 5 **Friuli-Venezia Giulia**, Italy
115 S 3 **Frobisher Bay**, Nunavut, Canada
113 W 10 **Frobisher Lake**, Saskatchewan, Canada
85 D 14 **Frohavet**, Norway
89 V 7 **Frohnleiten**, Austria
121 Q 12 **Front Royal**, Virginia, U.S.A.
125 W 12 **Frontera**, Mexico
124 J 3 **Fronteras**, Mexico
91 I 14 **Frosinone**, Italy
85 C 14 **Frøya**, Norway
101 O 8 **Frunzivka**, Ukraine
94 J 9 **Fruška Gora**, Serbia and Montenegro
143 J 17 **Frutal**, Brazil
88 E 9 **Frutigen**, Switzerland
117 O 18 **Fry Canyon**, Utah, U.S.A.
169 L 20 **Fua Mulaku Island**, Maldives
177 E 19 **Fuchu**, Japan
171 W 11 **Fuding**, China
80 M 13 **Fuengirola**, Spain
62 N 11 **Fuerteventura**, Canary Islands
175 O 1 **Fuga**, Philippines
65 T 13 **Fugløya Bank**, Arctic Ocean
171 O 12 **Fugong**, China
170 L 3 **Fuhai**, China
161 Q 6 **Fuḥaymī**, Iraq
163 X 5 **Fujairah**, United Arab Emirates
177 J 17 **Fuji**, Japan
171 V 12 **Fujian**, China
177 J 17 **Fujieda**, Japan
171 Y 2 **Fujin**, China
177 J 17 **Fujinomiya**, Japan
177 J 16 **Fujiyoshida**, Japan
176 J 5 **Fukagawa**, Japan
170 K 4 **Fukang**, China
176 J 9 **Fukaura**, Japan
177 G 18 **Fukuchiyama**, Japan
177 A 22 **Fukue**, Japan
177 A 22 **Fukue-jima**, Japan
177 G 16 **Fukui**, Japan
177 B 21 **Fukuoka**, Japan
176 K 13 **Fukushima**, Japan
177 E 19 **Fukuyama**, Japan
192 D 10 **Fulacunda**, Guinea-Bissau
213 Z 12 **Fulaga**, Fiji
87 G 16 **Fulda**, Germany
87 G 18 **Fulda**, Germany
169 L 18 **Fulidhu Channel**, Maldives
171 R 11 **Fuling**, China
88 M 7 **Fulpmes**, Austria
119 M 14 **Fulton**, Missouri, U.S.A.
121 S 7 **Fulton**, New York, U.S.A.
79 O 12 **Fumel**, France
177 K 16 **Funabashi**, Japan
214 F 6 **Funafuti**, Tuvalu
85 E 16 **Funäsdalen**, Sweden
62 O 5 **Funchal**, Madeira
100 L 13 **Fundulea**, Romania
197 R 9 **Funhalouro**, Mozambique
171 Q 13 **Funing**, China
193 Q 10 **Funtua**, Nigeria
176 K 5 **Furano**, Japan
209 T 14 **Furneaux Group**, Tasmania, Australia
160 J 5 **Furqlus**, Syria
89 X 7 **Fürstenfeld**, Austria
86 N 13 **Fürstenwalde**, Germany
87 I 21 **Fürth**, Germany
176 K 12 **Furukawa**, Japan
138 I 7 **Fusagasugá**, Colombia
171 W 5 **Fushun**, China
88 G 9 **Fusio**, Switzerland
87 I 26 **Füssen**, Germany
177 C 21 **Futago-san**, Japan
145 F 18 **Futaleufú**, Chile
94 J 9 **Futog**, Serbia and Montenegro
177 K 16 **Futtsu**, Japan
214 H 8 **Futuna**, Wallis and Futuna Islands
213 S 12 **Futuna**, Vanuatu
171 S 8 **Fuxian**, China
171 W 5 **Fuxin**, China
176 J 12 **Fuya**, Japan
171 W 3 **Fuyu**, China
171 Z 2 **Fuyuan**, China
170 L 3 **Fuyun**, China
93 L 22 **Füzesabony**, Hungary
171 W 12 **Fuzhou**, China
159 W 9 **Füzuli**, Azerbaijan
85 C 25 **Fyn**, Denmark
97 C 18 **Fyteies**, Greece

G

191 N 21 **Gaalkacyo**, Somalia
117 H 17 **Gabbs**, Nevada, U.S.A.
196 G 3 **Gabela**, Angola
189 Q 7 **Gabès**, Tunisia
194 E 8 **Gabon**, Africa
196 M 10 **Gaborone**, Botswana
58 B 11 **Gabriel Island**, Mauritius
96 J 9 **Gabrovo**, Bulgaria
96 J 8 **Gabrovo**, Bulgaria
192 F 9 **Gabú**, Guinea-Bissau
95 H 14 **Gacko**, Bosnia and Herzegovina
159 V 8 **Gädäbäy**, Azerbaijan
169 D 19 **Gadag**, India
169 F 15 **Gadarwara**, India
169 A 16 **Gadhra**, India
122 M 4 **Gadsden**, Alabama, U.S.A.
169 E 19 **Gadwal**, India
100 J 12 **Găeşti**, Romania
91 I 15 **Gaeta**, Italy
214 M 14 **Gaferut**, Federated States of Micronesia
123 R 3 **Gaffney**, South Carolina, U.S.A.
189 P 7 **Gafsa**, Tunisia
175 T 11 **Gag**, Indonesia
193 V 12 **Gagal**, Chad
167 Q 12 **Gagarin**, Uzbekistan
91 O 17 **Gagliano del Capo**, Italy
192 J 13 **Gagnoa**, Côte d'Ivoire
115 T 9 **Gagnon**, Québec, Canada
171 O 7 **Gahe**, China
79 P 13 **Gaillac**, France
119 M 16 **Gainesville**, Missouri, U.S.A.
119 K 18 **Gainesville**, Texas, U.S.A.
123 Q 9 **Gainesville**, Florida, U.S.A.
123 O 4 **Gainesville**, Georgia, U.S.A.
98 G 11 **Gaiziņkalns**, Latvia
177 B 26 **Gaja-jima**, Japan
193 S 13 **Gakem**, Nigeria
165 X 6 **Gakuch**, Pakistan
61 T 8 **Galapagos Fracture Zone**, Pacific Ocean
141 A 17 **Galapagos Islands**, Ecuador
76 I 13 **Galashiels**, United Kingdom
96 N 8 **Galata**, Bulgaria
100 M 11 **Galați**, Romania
97 F 14 **Galatista**, Greece
62 M 12 **Gáldar**, Canary Islands
85 C 17 **Galdhøpiggen**, Norway
124 L 4 **Galeana**, Mexico
175 S 10 **Galela**, Indonesia
112 J 5 **Galena**, Alaska, U.S.A.
120 G 8 **Galena**, Illinois, U.S.A.
127 X 12 **Galeota Point**, Trinidad and Tobago
127 X 12 **Galera Point**, Trinidad and Tobago
120 G 10 **Galesburg**, Illinois, U.S.A.
120 G 6 **Galesville**, Wisconsin, U.S.A.
121 R 9 **Galeton**, Pennsylvania, U.S.A.
191 N 22 **Galguduud**, Somalia
100 H 13 **Galicea Mare**, Romania
80 I 2 **Galicia**, Spain
62 K 8 **Galicia Bank**, Atlantic Ocean
191 H 18 **Gallabat**, Sudan
90 C 6 **Gallarate**, Italy
122 L 1 **Gallatin**, Tennessee, U.S.A.
169 F 25 **Galle**, Sri Lanka
145 G 24 **Gallegos**, Argentina
91 O 17 **Gallipoli**, Italy
158 B 8 **Gallipoli**, Turkey
158 A 8 **Gallipoli Peninsula**, Turkey
121 N 12 **Gallipolis**, Ohio, U.S.A.
84 J 10 **Gällivare**, Sweden
119 D 17 **Gallup**, New Mexico, U.S.A.
188 D 12 **Galtat Zemmour**, Western Sahara
119 L 22 **Galveston**, Texas, U.S.A.
119 L 22 **Galveston Bay**, Texas, U.S.A.
144 K 11 **Gálvez**, Argentina
168 H 10 **Galwa**, Nepal
77 B 18 **Galway**, Republic of Ireland
77 B 18 **Galway Bay**, Republic of Ireland
194 D 9 **Gamba**, Gabon
191 F 21 **Gambēla**, Ethiopia
191 G 21 **Gambēla**, Ethiopia
192 D 9 **Gambia**, Africa
192 E 9 **Gambia**, Gambia
62 J 12 **Gambia Abyssal Plain**, Atlantic Ocean
215 W 11 **Gambier Islands**, French Polynesia
194 H 9 **Gamboma**, Congo
194 H 5 **Gamboula**, Central African Republic
159 W 8 **Gamiş Dağl**, Azerbaijan
117 O 20 **Ganado**, Arizona, U.S.A.
164 H 10 **Ganāveh**, Iran
159 V 8 **Gäncä**, Azerbaijan
196 G 5 **Ganda**, Angola
115 Y 10 **Gander**, Newfoundland and Labrador, Canada
81 U 5 **Gandesa**, Spain
169 A 14 **Gandhidham**, India
169 C 14 **Gandhinagar**, India
81 T 9 **Gandía**, Spain
145 H 17 **Gangán**, Argentina
168 D 10 **Ganganagar**, India
168 E 12 **Gangapur**, India
172 C 11 **Gangaw**, Myanmar
170 H 9 **Gangdise Shan**, China
87 B 17 **Gangelt**, Germany
168 K 13 **Ganges**, India
79 S 13 **Ganges**, France
59 P 1 **Ganges Cone**, Indian Ocean
168 G 12 **Gangetic Plain**, India
168 K 12 **Gangtok**, India
79 R 9 **Gannat**, France
118 D 11 **Gannett Peak**, Wyoming, U.S.A.
170 M 7 **Ganq**, China
89 Y 3 **Gänserndorf**, Austria
171 P 9 **Gansu**, China
159 P 5 **Gant'iadi**, Georgia
193 T 12 **Ganye**, Nigeria
166 G 7 **Ganyushkino**, Kazakhstan
171 U 12 **Ganzhou**, China
193 N 8 **Gao**, Mali
193 O 7 **Gao**, Mali
192 L 11 **Gaoua**, Burkina Faso
171 S 14 **Gaozhou**, China
79 V 12 **Gap**, France
170 H 9 **Gar**, China
191 O 21 **Garacad**, Somalia
191 M 20 **Garadag**, Somalia
192 I 10 **Garalo**, Mali
142 O 13 **Garanhuns**, Brazil
194 K 2 **Garba**, Central African Republic
195 W 7 **Garba Tula**, Kenya
191 K 23 **Garbahaarey**, Somalia
117 C 15 **Garberville**, California, U.S.A.
86 G 13 **Garbsen**, Germany
86 J 13 **Gardelegen**, Germany
119 H 15 **Garden City**, Kansas, U.S.A.
120 K 5 **Garden Corners**, Michigan, U.S.A.
165 U 8 **Gardez**, Afghanistan
123 R 12 **Gardner**, Florida, U.S.A.
61 Q 5 **Gardner Pinnacles**, Pacific Ocean
112 A 7 **Gareloi Island**, Alaska, U.S.A.
90 B 9 **Garessio**, Italy
189 O 12 **Garet El Djenoun**, Algeria
98 B 13 **Gargždai**, Lithuania
169 G 16 **Garhchiroli**, India
196 J 13 **Garies**, Republic of South Africa
195 X 8 **Garissa**, Kenya
119 K 19 **Garland**, Texas, U.S.A.
123 U 3 **Garland**, North Carolina, U.S.A.
99 E 15 **Garliava**, Lithuania
164 H 3 **Garmī**, Iran
87 I 26 **Garmisch-Partenkirchen**, Germany
164 J 6 **Garmsār**, Iran
209 R 11 **Garnpung Lake**, New South Wales, Australia
78 M 11 **Garonne**, France
191 N 20 **Garoowe**, Somalia
193 U 11 **Garoua**, Cameroon
193 V 13 **Garoua Boulai**, Cameroon
212 F 4 **Garove Island**, Papua New Guinea
118 B 8 **Garrison**, Montana, U.S.A.
114 K 1 **Garry Lake**, Nunavut, Canada
195 X 9 **Garsen**, Kenya
191 A 18 **Garsila**, Sudan
174 H 14 **Garut**, Indonesia
211 C 24 **Garvie Mountains**, New Zealand
169 I 14 **Garwa**, India
92 M 13 **Garwolin**, Poland
120 J 9 **Gary**, Indiana, U.S.A.
171 O 10 **Garzê**, China
138 H 8 **Garzón**, Colombia
78 M 13 **Gascony**, France
208 F 8 **Gascoyne**, Western Australia, Australia
208 F 8 **Gascoyne Junction**, Western Australia, Australia
59 S 7 **Gascoyne Plain**, Indian Ocean
165 P 12 **Gasht**, Iran
193 T 10 **Gashua**, Nigeria
212 G 5 **Gasmata**, Papua New Guinea
115 U 11 **Gaspé**, Québec, Canada
176 K 12 **Gassan**, Japan
193 T 12 **Gassol**, Nigeria
123 R 2 **Gastonia**, North Carolina, U.S.A.
97 C 20 **Gastouni**, Greece
145 G 17 **Gastre**, Argentina

Country · Internal administrative region: State/Province/Territory/Dependent territory · Capital city · Mountain range/Undersea ridge · Mountain peak/Volcano/Seamount · Geographic feature · Headland/Point/Cape/Peninsula · Desert · Island/Island group · Antarctic base · Ocean · Sea · Bay/Gulf/Channel/Strait · Lake · Salt pan/Dry/Intermittent lake · River

100 F 11 **Gătaia**, Romania
113 V 2 **Gateshead Island**, Nunavut, Canada
119 J 20 **Gatesville**, Texas, U.S.A.
213 Y 12 **Gau**, Fiji
213 Q 9 **Gaua**, Vanuatu
98 G 9 **Gauja**, Latvia
169 E 21 **Gauribidanur**, India
85 C 19 **Gausta**, Norway
197 O 11 **Gauteng**, Republic of South Africa
164 I 12 **Gāvbandī**, Iran
97 H 26 **Gavdopoula**, Greece
97 H 26 **Gavdos**, Greece
142 C 12 **Gaviãozinho**, Brazil
85 H 19 **Gävle**, Sweden
209 P 11 **Gawler**, South Australia, Australia
171 P 6 **Gaxun Nur**, China
168 I 13 **Gaya**, India
120 L 6 **Gaylord**, Michigan, U.S.A.
160 E 10 **Gaza**, Israel
197 Q 9 **Gaza**, Mozambique
160 E 10 **Gaza Strip**, Israel
166 J 13 **Gazandzhyk**, Turkmenistan
195 X 10 **Gazi**, Kenya
158 M 13 **Gaziantep**, Turkey
165 O 8 **Gazīk**, Iran
158 G 14 **Gazipaşa**, Turkey
167 O 12 **Gazli**, Uzbekistan
192 H 12 **Gbarnga**, Liberia
192 H 13 **Gbatala**, Liberia
193 S 12 **Gboko**, Nigeria
92 I 8 **Gdańsk**, Poland
92 I 8 **Gdynia**, Poland
175 S 11 **Gebe**, Indonesia
190 G 11 **Gebel Hamâta**, Egypt
190 F 9 **Gebel Katherina**, Egypt
191 I 20 **Gebre Guracha**, Ethiopia
158 E 8 **Gebze**, Turkey
191 G 21 **Gech'a**, Ethiopia
191 G 18 **Gedaref**, Sudan
191 G 17 **Gedaref**, Sudan
191 L 21 **Gedlegubē**, Ethiopia
191 K 24 **Gedo**, Somalia
85 D 26 **Gedser**, Denmark
83 H 17 **Geel**, Belgium
209 S 13 **Geelong**, Victoria, Australia
193 T 9 **Geidam**, Nigeria
113 X 9 **Geikie**, Saskatchewan, Canada
85 C 18 **Geilo**, Norway
195 S 9 **Geita**, Tanzania
171 P 13 **Gejiu**, China
91 J 23 **Gela**, Italy
170 L 9 **Geladaindong**, China
191 M 21 **Geladī**, Ethiopia
82 K 12 **Gelderland**, Netherlands
87 B 15 **Geldern**, Germany
83 J 16 **Geldrop**, Netherlands
83 K 18 **Geleen**, Netherlands
191 M 22 **Gelinsoor**, Somalia
83 G 20 **Gembloux**, Belgium
193 T 13 **Gembu**, Nigeria
194 K 6 **Gemena**, Democratic Republic of Congo
158 L 10 **Gemerek**, Turkey
158 D 8 **Gemlik**, Turkey
84 A 10 **Gemlufall**, Iceland
90 I 5 **Gemona del Friuli**, Italy
190 F 10 **Gemsa**, Egypt
145 J 14 **General Acha**, Argentina
144 H 13 **General Alvear**, Argentina
144 M 13 **General Belgrano**, Argentina
144 J 11 **General Cabrera**, Argentina
125 P 7 **General Cepeda**, Mexico
145 I 16 **General Conesa**, Argentina
144 L 7 **General José de San Martín**, Argentina
145 N 14 **General Juan Madariaga**, Argentina
145 K 14 **General La Madrid**, Argentina
144 G 1 **General Lagos**, Chile
145 M 14 **General Lavalle**, Argentina
144 I 6 **General Martín Miguel de Güemes**, Argentina
144 J 13 **General Pico**, Argentina
145 H 15 **General Roca**, Argentina
175 Q 8 **General Santos**, Philippines
96 N 6 **General-Toshevo**, Bulgaria
144 J 13 **General Villegas**, Argentina
120 G 9 **Geneseo**, Illinois, U.S.A.
191 I 20 **Genet**, Ethiopia
88 A 10 **Geneva**, Switzerland
121 S 8 **Geneva**, New York, U.S.A.
194 M 9 **Gengwa**, Democratic Republic of Congo
83 J 18 **Genk**, Belgium
90 C 9 **Genoa**, Italy
174 G 14 **Genteng**, Indonesia
86 K 13 **Genthin**, Germany
208 G 12 **Geographe Bay**, Western Australia, Australia
115 T 6 **George**, Québec, Canada
196 L 15 **George**, Republic of South Africa
63 N 26 **George Island**, St Helena
211 A 23 **George Sound**, New Zealand
126 J 6 **George Town**, Cayman Islands
127 N 4 **George Town**, The Bahamas
174 D 8 **George Town**, Malaysia
209 T 15 **George Town**, Tasmania, Australia
219 T 14 **George V Coast**, Antarctica
219 S 14 **George V Land**, Antarctica
218 I 5 **George VI Sound**, Antarctica
63 K 25 **Georgetown**, Ascension
139 U 5 **Georgetown**, Guyana
120 L 13 **Georgetown**, Kentucky, U.S.A.
121 T 12 **Georgetown**, Delaware, U.S.A.
123 T 5 **Georgetown**, South Carolina, U.S.A.
127 X 10 **Georgetown**, St Vincent and The Grenadines
192 E 9 **Georgetown**, Gambia
209 S 4 **Georgetown**, Queensland, Australia
159 T 6 **Georgia**, Asia
123 O 5 **Georgia**, U.S.A.
115 O 14 **Georgian Bay**, Ontario, Canada
209 P 5 **Georgina**, Queensland, Australia
167 X 5 **Georgiyevka**, Kazakhstan
86 D 10 **Georgsheil**, Germany
87 K 17 **Gera**, Germany
83 E 19 **Geraardsbergen**, Belgium
97 E 22 **Geraki**, Greece
208 F 10 **Geraldton**, Western Australia, Australia
159 Q 12 **Gercüş**, Turkey
158 H 8 **Gerede**, Turkey
165 R 9 **Gereshk**, Afghanistan
81 Q 12 **Gérgal**, Spain
117 G 15 **Gerlach**, Nevada, U.S.A.
93 K 19 **Gerlachovský štít**, Slovakia
87 H 17 **Germany**, Europe
177 I 16 **Gero**, Japan
158 K 7 **Gerze**, Turkey
85 I 19 **Geta**, Finland
81 O 7 **Getafe**, Spain
118 I 10 **Gettysburg**, South Dakota, U.S.A.
121 S 11 **Gettysburg**, Pennsylvania, U.S.A.
218 K 10 **Getz Ice Shelf Range**, Antarctica
159 S 11 **Gevaş**, Turkey
96 E 12 **Gevgelija**, Macedonia (F.Y.R.O.M.)
169 D 17 **Gevrai**, India
89 V 3 **Gföhl**, Austria
196 L 12 **Ghaap Plateau**, Republic of South Africa
189 Q 9 **Ghadāmis**, Libya
189 T 11 **Ghaddūwah**, Libya
168 H 12 **Ghaghara**, India
192 M12 **Ghana**, Africa
196 K 9 **Ghanzi**, Botswana
196 K 9 **Ghanzi**, Botswana
160 F 12 **Gharandal**, Jordan
189 N 8 **Ghardaïa**, Algeria
165 T 15 **Gharo**, Pakistan
189 S 8 **Gharyān**, Libya
189 R 12 **Ghāt**, Libya
188 K 6 **Ghazaouet**, Algeria
168 E 11 **Ghaziabad**, India
168 I 13 **Ghazipur**, India
165 T 9 **Ghazluna**, Pakistan
165 T 8 **Ghaznī**, Afghanistan
165 U 8 **Ghaznī**, Afghanistan
163 N 4 **Ghazzālah**, Saudi Arabia
83 D 18 **Ghent**, Belgium
100 K 9 **Gheorgheni**, Romania
100 I 8 **Gherla**, Romania
165 R 9 **Ghorak**, Afghanistan
165 V 12 **Ghotki**, Pakistan
165 R 8 **Ghowr**, Afghanistan
163 V 12 **Ghubbat al Qamar**, Yemen
161 O 2 **Ghūnā**, Syria
165 P 7 **Ghurian**, Afghanistan
173 N 22 **Gia Đinh**, Vietnam
173 L 23 **Gia Rai**, Vietnam
96 E 13 **Giannitsa**, Greece
91 L 22 **Giarre**, Italy
62 A 8 **Gibb's Hill**, Bermuda
196 I 10 **Gibeon**, Namibia
80 J 12 **Gibraleón**, Spain
80 L 14 **Gibraltar**, United Kingdom
80 L 14 **Gibraltar**, Gibraltar
208 J 7 **Gibson Desert**, Western Australia, Australia
85 H 14 **Gideälven**, Sweden
191 H 22 **Gīdolē**, Ethiopia
79 Q 6 **Gien**, France
87 F 18 **Giessen**, Germany
82 N 7 **Gieten**, Netherlands
116 H 6 **Gifford**, Washington, U.S.A.
86 H 13 **Gifhorn**, Germany
177 H 17 **Gifu**, Japan
80 L 1 **Gijón**, Spain
117 N 24 **Gila**, Arizona, U.S.A.
117 L 24 **Gila Bend**, Arizona, U.S.A.
117 N 23 **Gila Mountains**, Arizona, U.S.A.
164 H 4 **Gīlān**, Iran
100 H 9 **Gilău**, Romania
159 Y 7 **Giläzi**, Azerbaijan
214 D 1 **Gilbert Islands**, Kiribati
142 K 13 **Gilbués**, Brazil
197 T 6 **Gilé**, Mozambique
190 B 12 **Gilf Kebir Plateau**, Egypt
209 U 10 **Gilgandra**, New South Wales, Australia
165 Y 6 **Gilgit**, Pakistan
63 O 26 **Gill Point**, St Helena
114 K 7 **Gillam**, Manitoba, Canada
118 F 10 **Gillette**, Wyoming, U.S.A.
219 W 6 **Gillock Island**, Antarctica
120 I 10 **Gilman**, Illinois, U.S.A.
117 D 19 **Gilroy**, California, U.S.A.
191 G 20 **Gīmbī**, Ethiopia
175 Q 6 **Gingoog**, Philippines
191 J 21 **Gīnīr**, Ethiopia
97 H 17 **Gioura**, Greece
165 P 10 **Girdi**, Iran
76 J 11 **Girdle Ness**, United Kingdom
159 N 8 **Giresun**, Turkey
158 M 8 **Giresun Dağlari**, Turkey
190 F 10 **Girga**, Egypt
169 J 14 **Giridih**, India
81 Y 3 **Girona**, Spain
78 L 10 **Gironde**, France
77 G 14 **Girvan**, United Kingdom
210 O 11 **Gisborne**, New Zealand
210 O 12 **Gisborne**, New Zealand
195 Q 9 **Gisenyi**, Rwanda
85 E 23 **Gislaved**, Sweden
79 P 3 **Gisors**, France
83 B 17 **Gistel**, Belgium
90 J 12 **Giulianova**, Italy
100 K 14 **Giurgiu**, Romania
83 E 21 **Givry**, Belgium
197 P 9 **Giyani**, Republic of South Africa
191 I 20 **Giyon**, Ethiopia
167 P 12 **Gizhduvan**, Uzbekistan
157 Y 9 **Gizhiga**, Russian Federation
212 K 6 **Gizo**, Solomon Islands
92 M 9 **Giżycko**, Poland
95 I 17 **Gjiri i Drinit**, Albania
95 K 21 **Gjirokastër**, Albania
114 L 1 **Gjoa Haven**, Nunavut, Canada
84 B 10 **Gjögur**, Iceland
85 D 18 **Gjøvik**, Norway
115 X 12 **Glace Bay**, Nova Scotia, Canada
120 J 5 **Gladstone**, Michigan, U.S.A.
209 V 7 **Gladstone**, Queensland, Australia
209 P 11 **Gladstone**, South Australia, Australia
85 D 18 **Glåma**, Norway
82 O 12 **Glanerbrug**, Netherlands
88 H 7 **Glarus**, Switzerland
76 H 13 **Glasgow**, United Kingdom
120 K 14 **Glasgow**, Kentucky, U.S.A.
156 I 9 **Glazov**, Russian Federation
89 W 7 **Gleisdorf**, Austria
117 N 19 **Glen Canyon**, Utah, U.S.A.
117 M 19 **Glen Canyon**, Utah, U.S.A.
209 V 10 **Glen Innes**, New South Wales, Australia
211 F 23 **Glenavy**, New Zealand
117 M 23 **Glendale**, Arizona, U.S.A.
209 O 10 **Glendambo**, South Australia, Australia
209 U 5 **Glenden**, Queensland, Australia
118 F 8 **Glendive**, Montana, U.S.A.
139 T 6 **Glendor Mountains**, Guyana
112 L 7 **Glennallen**, Alaska, U.S.A.
123 Q 6 **Glennville**, Georgia, U.S.A.
211 C 22 **Glenorchy**, New Zealand
121 U 7 **Glens Falls**, New York, U.S.A.
77 C 15 **Glenties**, Republic of Ireland
118 K 13 **Glenwood**, Iowa, U.S.A.
119 C 19 **Glenwood**, New Mexico, U.S.A.
119 D 14 **Glenwood Springs**, Colorado, U.S.A.
88 F 9 **Gletsch**, Switzerland
92 K 11 **Glinojeck**, Poland
93 I 17 **Gliwice**, Poland
117 N 23 **Globe**, Arizona, U.S.A.
89 X 5 **Gloggnitz**, Austria
93 F 14 **Głogów**, Poland
84 F 11 **Glomfjord**, Norway
84 I 13 **Glommersträsk**, Sweden
77 J 21 **Gloucester**, United Kingdom
121 X 8 **Gloucester**, Massachusetts, U.S.A.
212 F 4 **Gloucester**, Papua New Guinea
167 X 4 **Glubokoye**, Kazakhstan
89 R 8 **Gmünd**, Austria
89 U 2 **Gmünd**, Austria
89 S 5 **Gmunden**, Austria
92 H 11 **Gniewkowo**, Poland
92 H 12 **Gniezno**, Poland
95 M 15 **Gnjilane**, Serbia and Montenegro
173 N 22 **Go Công**, Vietnam
169 C 20 **Goa**, India
168 L 12 **Goalpara**, India
192 L 13 **Goaso**, Ghana
191 J 21 **Goba**, Ethiopia
196 J 9 **Gobabis**, Namibia
62 K 7 **Goban Spur**, Atlantic Ocean
145 I 15 **Gobernador Duval**, Argentina
145 H 21 **Gobernador Gregores**, Argentina
145 G 23 **Gobernador Mayer**, Argentina
171 O 6 **Gobi Desert**, China
177 G 19 **Gobo**, Japan
87 B 15 **Goch**, Germany
196 J 10 **Gochas**, Namibia
169 F 17 **Godavari**, India
168 J 13 **Godda**, India
191 K 22 **Godē**, Ethiopia
191 M 22 **Godinlabe**, Somalia
93 J 22 **Gödöllő**, Hungary
114 K 7 **Gods**, Manitoba, Canada
114 J 8 **Gods Lake**, Manitoba, Canada
212 A 6 **Goe**, Papua New Guinea
83 E 15 **Goes**, Netherlands
89 V 2 **Göfritz**, Austria
193 O 11 **Gogounou**, Benin
191 C 20 **Gogrial**, Sudan
168 F 12 **Gohad**, India
143 J 16 **Goiânia**, Brazil
143 J 16 **Goiás**, Brazil
143 J 16 **Goiás**, Brazil
83 I 15 **Goirle**, Netherlands
158 A 8 **Gökçeada**, Turkey
158 B 12 **Gökova Körfezi**, Turkey
158 L 12 **Göksun**, Turkey
197 O 7 **Gokwe**, Zimbabwe
85 C 18 **Gol**, Norway
168 N 12 **Golaghat**, India
160 G 7 **Golan Heights**, Israel
165 U 7 **Golbahār**, Afghanistan
158 M 12 **Gölbasi**, Turkey
117 H 14 **Golconda**, Nevada, U.S.A.
158 E 8 **Gölcük**, Turkey
209 W 9 **Gold Coast**, Queensland, Australia
192 M 14 **Gold Coast**, Ghana
92 M 8 **Gołdap**, Poland
113 U 13 **Golden**, British Columbia, Canada
211 H 15 **Golden Bay**, New Zealand
59 R 8 **Golden Dragon Seamount**, Indian Ocean
116 F 9 **Goldendale**, Washington, U.S.A.
117 H 18 **Goldfield**, Nevada, U.S.A.
123 V 2 **Goldsboro**, North Carolina, U.S.A.
159 R 8 **Göle**, Turkey
92 D 10 **Goleniów**, Poland
164 L 4 **Golestān**, Iran
81 W 5 **Golf de Sant Jordi**, Spain
189 Q 7 **Golfe de Gabès**, Tunisia
189 R 5 **Golfe de Hammamet**, Tunisia
127 O 6 **Golfe de la Gonâve**, Haiti
78 J 4 **Golfe de St-Malo**, France
191 L 19 **Golfe de Tadjoura**, Djibouti
189 Q 5 **Golfe de Tunis**, Tunisia
81 Q 13 **Golfo de Almería**, Spain
145 F 17 **Golfo de Ancud**, Chile
145 E 14 **Golfo de Arauco**, Chile
126 I 4 **Golfo de Batabanó**, Cuba
80 J 12 **Golfo de Cádiz**, Portugal/Spain
126 I 14 **Golfo de Chiriquí**, Panama
145 E 18 **Golfo de Corcovado**, Chile
126 E 10 **Golfo de Fonseca**, Honduras
126 L 6 **Golfo de Guacanayabo**, Cuba
126 F 8 **Golfo de Honduras**, Honduras
126 J 13 **Golfo de los Mosquitos**, Panama
81 S 12 **Golfo de Mazarrón**, Spain
126 J 15 **Golfo de Montijo**, Panama
126 G 13 **Golfo de Nicoya**, Costa Rica
145 E 21 **Golfo de Penas**, Chile
145 I 20 **Golfo de San Jorge**, Argentina
125 U 14 **Golfo de Tehuantepec**, Mexico
138 G 4 **Golfo de Urabá**, Colombia/Panama
81 U 8 **Golfo de Valencia**, Spain
91 C 19 **Golfo di Cagliari**, Italy
91 H 21 **Golfo di Castellammare**, Italy
91 L 22 **Golfo di Catania**, Italy
91 B 15 **Golfo di dell'Asinara**, Italy
91 I 15 **Golfo di Gaeta**, Italy
91 L 20 **Golfo di Gioia**, Italy
91 M 14 **Golfo di Manfredonia**, Italy
91 I 16 **Golfo di Napoli**, Italy
91 L 24 **Golfo di Noto**, Italy
91 B 18 **Golfo di Oristano**, Italy
91 D 17 **Golfo di Orosei**, Italy
91 B 19 **Golfo di Palmas**, Italy
91 L 18 **Golfo di Policastro**, Italy
91 K 17 **Golfo di Salerno**, Italy
91 M 20 **Golfo di Santa Eufemia**, Italy
91 N 20 **Golfo di Squillace**, Italy
91 N 18 **Golfo di Taranto**, Italy
90 I 7 **Golfo di Trieste**, Italy
126 H 14 **Golfo Dulce**, Costa Rica
145 J 17 **Golfo Nuevo**, Argentina
145 J 17 **Golfo San José**, Argentina
145 J 17 **Golfo San Matías**, Argentina
145 E 23 **Golfo Trinidad**, Chile
171 N 8 **Golmud**, China
164 H 7 **Golpāyegān**, Iran
76 H 9 **Golspie**, United Kingdom
167 T 3 **Golubovka**, Kazakhstan
96 H 11 **Golyam Perelik**, Bulgaria
96 I 11 **Golyam Persenk**, Bulgaria
195 Q 9 **Goma**, Democratic Republic of Congo
168 G 12 **Gomati**, India
193 T 11 **Gombe**, Nigeria
193 T 11 **Gombe**, Nigeria
193 U 11 **Gombi**, Nigeria
58 E 8 **Gombrani Island**, Rodrigues Island
124 L 4 **Gómez Farías**, Mexico
125 N 7 **Gómez Palacio**, Mexico
127 O 6 **Gonaïves**, Haiti
164 L 5 **Gonbad-e Kavus**, Iran
168 H 12 **Gonda**, India
191 H 18 **Gonder**, Ethiopia
169 F 15 **Gondia**, India
158 C 8 **Gönen**, Turkey
170 L 11 **Gonggar**, China
171 P 8 **Gonghe**, China
170 J 4 **Gongliu**, China
171 N 6 **Gongpoquan**, China
193 T 10 **Goniri**, Nigeria
177 A 21 **Gōnoura**, Japan
175 P 2 **Gonzaga**, Philippines
117 E 19 **Gonzales**, California, U.S.A.
119 K 22 **Gonzales**, Texas, U.S.A.
212 G 6 **Goodenough Island**, Papua New Guinea
116 K 12 **Gooding**, Idaho, U.S.A.
58 B 11 **Goodlands**, Mauritius
209 S 11 **Goolgowi**, New South Wales, Australia
208 G 11 **Goomalling**, Western Australia, Australia
209 U 9 **Goondiwindi**, Queensland, Australia
82 M 11 **Goor**, Netherlands
145 L 24 **Goose Green**, Falkland Islands
116 F 13 **Goose Lake**, California, U.S.A.
168 F 10 **Gopeshwar**, India
93 F 14 **Góra**, Poland
166 J 12 **Gora Arlang**, Turkmenistan
167 P 14 **Gora Ayribaba**, Turkmenistan
156 M 14 **Gora Belukha**, Russian Federation
166 I 9 **Gora Besshoky**, Kazakhstan
166 J 13 **Gora Khasardag**, Turkmenistan
167 P 12 **Gora Khayatbashi**, Uzbekistan
167 V 7 **Gora Kotanemel'**, Kazakhstan
157 Z 8 **Gora Ledyanaya**, Russian Federation
157 X 13 **Gora Lopatina**, Russian Federation
167 S 10 **Gora Manas**, Kyrgyzstan
157 O 13 **Gora Munku Sardyk**, Russian Federation
170 K 3 **Gora Mustau**, China
156 K 8 **Gora Narodnaya**, Russian Federation
157 X 10 **Gora Nukh Yablonevyy**, Russian Federation
157 W 9 **Gora Pobeda**, Russian Federation
167 T 7 **Gora Shunak**, Kazakhstan
166 K 13 **Gora Tagarev**, Turkmenistan
157 V 14 **Gora Tardoki-Yani**, Russian Federation
156 J 8 **Gora Telposiz**, Russian Federation
168 H 12 **Gorakhpur**, India
94 I 13 **Goražde**, Bosnia and Herzegovina
121 R 13 **Gordonsville**, Virginia, U.S.A.
211 D 25 **Gore**, New Zealand
193 W 12 **Goré**, Chad
121 W 5 **Gore Mountain**, Vermont, U.S.A.
158 J 11 **Göreme**, Turkey
77 E 19 **Gorey**, Republic of Ireland
164 K 5 **Gorgān**, Iran
211 D 23 **Gorge Creek**, New Zealand
192 F 7 **Gorgol**, Mauritania
191 H 18 **Gorgora**, Ethiopia
159 T 6 **Gori**, Georgia
83 H 14 **Gorinchem**, Netherlands
159 V 9 **Goris**, Armenia
90 I 6 **Gorizia**, Italy
168 I 11 **Gorkha**, Nepal
93 L 18 **Gorlice**, Poland
87 O 16 **Görlitz**, Germany
96 H 7 **Gorni Dŭbnik**, Bulgaria
94 L 12 **Gornji Milanovac**, Serbia and Montenegro
156 M 13 **Gorno Altaysk**, Russian Federation
156 L 13 **Gornyak**, Russian Federation

Country · Internal administrative region: State/Province/Territory/Dependent territory · Capital city · Mountain range/Undersea ridge · Mountain peak/Volcano/Seamount · Geographic feature · Headland/Point/Cape/Peninsula · Desert · Island/Island group · Antarctic base · Ocean · Sea · Bay/Gulf/Channel/Strait · Lake · Salt pan/Dry/Intermittent lake · River

212 D 4 **Goroka**, Papua New Guinea
197 R 7 **Gorongosa**, Mozambique
175 P 10 **Gorontalo**, Indonesia
82 L 12 **Gorssel**, Netherlands
166 I 11 **Gory Akkyr**, Turkmenistan
167 N 12 **Gory Auminzatau**, Uzbekistan
167 Q 14 **Gory Baysuntau**, Uzbekistan
167 N 10 **Gory Bukantau**, Uzbekistan
157 P 7 **Gory Byrranga**, Russian Federation
167 O 11 **Gory Dzhetymtau**, Uzbekistan
157 P 8 **Gory Kamen'**, Russian Federation
166 J 11 **Gory Koymatdag**, Turkmenistan
166 L 7 **Gory Mugodzhary**, Kazakhstan
157 O 9 **Gory Putorana**, Russian Federation
93 K 15 **Góry Świętokrzyskie**, Poland
92 E 11 **Gorzów Wielkopolski**, Poland
209 V 11 **Gosford**, New South Wales, Australia
176 J 9 **Goshogawara**, Japan
87 H 14 **Goslar**, Germany
94 D 11 **Gospić**, Croatia
83 G 21 **Gosselies**, Belgium
85 B 15 **Gossen**, Norway
192 M 8 **Gossi**, Mali
96 C 11 **Gostivar**, Macedonia (F.Y.R.O.M.)
92 G 13 **Gostyń**, Poland
92 J 12 **Gostynin**, Poland
177 J 17 **Gotemba**, Japan
87 I 17 **Gotha**, Germany
85 D 22 **Gothenburg**, Sweden
193 O 9 **Gothèye**, Niger
85 I 23 **Gotland**, Sweden
177 A 23 **Gotō-rettō**, Japan
96 G 12 **Gotse Delchev**, Bulgaria
85 I 22 **Gotska Sandön**, Sweden
177 D 19 **Gōtsu**, Japan
87 H 15 **Göttingen**, Germany
82 G 13 **Gouda**, Netherlands
192 F 9 **Goudiri**, Senegal
193 T 9 **Goudoumaria**, Niger
63 I 19 **Gough Fracture Zone**, Atlantic Ocean
63 K 19 **Gough Island**, U.K.
209 U 12 **Goulburn**, New South Wales, Australia
209 N 1 **Goulburn Islands**, Northern Territory, Australia
219 O 9 **Gould Coast**, Antarctica
193 V 10 **Goulféy**, Cameroon
192 I 8 **Goumbou**, Mali
192 L 8 **Goundam**, Mali
193 X 11 **Goundi**, Chad
192 L 9 **Gourcy**, Burkina Faso
193 S 9 **Gouré**, Niger
79 P 3 **Gournay-en-Bray**, France
193 Y 6 **Gouro**, Chad
121 T 6 **Gouverneur**, New York, U.S.A.
143 M 17 **Governador Valadares**, Brazil
171 N 4 **Govi-Altay**, Mongolia
171 O 5 **Govi Altayn Nuruu**, Mongolia
169 H 14 **Govind Ballash Pant Sagar**, India
167 P 14 **Govurdak**, Turkmenistan
144 L 9 **Goya**, Argentina
159 X 8 **Göyçay**, Azerbaijan
158 F 8 **Göynük**, Turkey
159 Q 10 **Göynük**, Turkey
193 U 14 **Goyoum**, Cameroon
159 Y 10 **Göytäpä**, Azerbaijan
193 Z 10 **Goz-Beïda**, Chad
191 G 16 **Goz Regeb**, Sudan
170 I 8 **Gozha Co**, China
91 J 25 **Gozo**, Malta
196 M 14 **Graaf-Reinet**, Republic of South Africa
192 I 14 **Grabo**, Côte d'Ivoire
94 D 11 **Gračac**, Croatia
62 N 1 **Graciosa**, Azores
62 O 11 **Graciosa**, Canary Islands
94 H 10 **Gradačac**, Bosnia and Herzegovina
96 L 9 **Gradets**, Bulgaria
82 L 1 **Grado**, Spain
90 I 6 **Grado**, Italy
209 W 10 **Grafton**, New South Wales, Australia
113 O 12 **Graham Island**, British Columbia, Canada
218 H 3 **Graham Land**, Antarctica
197 N 15 **Grahamstown**, Republic of South Africa
142 K 12 **Grajaú**, Brazil
92 M 9 **Grajewo**, Poland
96 N 10 **Gramatikovo**, Bulgaria
76 H 11 **Grampian Mtns**, United Kingdom
86 N 11 **Gramzow**, Germany
145 G 21 **Gran Altiplanicie Central**, Argentina
62 M 12 **Gran Canaria**, Canary Islands
144 K 6 **Gran Chaco**, Argentina/Paraguay
141 E 15 **Gran Pajonal**, Peru
62 O 12 **Gran Tarajal**, Canary Islands
81 O 12 **Granada**, Spain
119 G 15 **Granada**, Colorado, U.S.A.
126 G 11 **Granada**, Nicaragua
138 J 7 **Granada**, Colombia
126 L 1 **Grand Bahama**, The Bahamas
62 F 7 **Grand Banks of Newfoundland**, Atlantic Ocean
192 K 14 **Grand-Bassam**, Côte d'Ivoire
127 Q 5 **Grand Caicos**, Turks and Caicos Islands
117 L 20 **Grand Canyon**, Arizona, U.S.A.
117 M 20 **Grand Canyon**, Arizona, U.S.A.
126 J 7 **Grand Cayman**, Cayman Islands
192 I 14 **Grand Cess**, Liberia
116 G 6 **Grand Coulee**, Washington, U.S.A.
193 T 7 **Grand Erg de Bilma**, Niger
188 J 9 **Grand Erg Occidental**, Algeria
189 N 10 **Grand Erg Oriental**, Algeria
118 J 7 **Grand Forks**, North Dakota, U.S.A.
120 K 8 **Grand Haven**, Michigan, U.S.A.
118 I 13 **Grand Island**, Nebraska, U.S.A.
119 D 14 **Grand Junction**, Colorado, U.S.A.
115 X 10 **Grand Lake**, Newfoundland and Labrador, Canada
118 M 7 **Grand Marais**, Minnesota, U.S.A.
120 K 4 **Grand Marais**, Michigan, U.S.A.
115 R 13 **Grand-Mère**, Québec, Canada
118 N 7 **Grand Portage**, Minnesota, U.S.A.
114 I 8 **Grand Rapids**, Manitoba, Canada
118 L 8 **Grand Rapids**, Minnesota, U.S.A.
120 K 8 **Grand Rapids**, Michigan, U.S.A.
118 C 10 **Grand Teton**, Wyoming, U.S.A.
127 Q 5 **Grand Turk**, Turks and Caicos Islands
116 J 12 **Grand View**, Idaho, U.S.A.
126 G 11 **Grande**, Nicaragua
141 L 21 **Grande**, Bolivia
58 B 11 **Grande Baie**, Mauritius
113 T 12 **Grande Cache**, Alberta, Canada
197 W 4 **Grande Comore**, Comoros
115 W 11 **Grande-Entrée**, Québec, Canada
113 T 11 **Grande Prairie**, Alberta, Canada
58 A 12 **Grande Rivière Noire**, Mauritius
58 C 12 **Grande Rivière Sud-Est**, Mauritius
80 G 10 **Grândola**, Portugal
116 F 8 **Grandview**, Washington, U.S.A.
116 I 9 **Grangeville**, Idaho, U.S.A.
118 K 10 **Granite Falls**, Minnesota, U.S.A.
118 D 9 **Granite Peak**, Montana, U.S.A.
218 L 11 **Grant Island**, Antarctica
77 L 19 **Grantham**, United Kingdom
119 D 17 **Grants**, New Mexico, U.S.A.
117 L 15 **Grantsville**, Utah, U.S.A.
78 L 4 **Granville**, France
116 J 13 **Grasmere**, Idaho, U.S.A.
85 I 19 **Gräsö**, Sweden
117 E 16 **Grass Valley**, California, U.S.A.
91 M 16 **Grassano**, Italy
79 W 13 **Grasse**, France
118 D 8 **Grassrange**, Montana, U.S.A.
118 G 8 **Grassy Butte**, North Dakota, U.S.A.
88 H 9 **Graubünden**, Switzerland
81 U 3 **Graus**, Spain
83 K 14 **Grave**, Netherlands
116 J 8 **Grave Peak**, Idaho, U.S.A.
90 D 5 **Gravedona**, Italy
79 U 7 **Gray**, France
89 W 7 **Graz**, Austria
126 M 2 **Great Abaco**, The Bahamas
208 K 11 **Great Australian Bight**, Western Australia, Australia
126 K 2 **Great Bahaman Bank**, The Bahamas
210 L 7 **Great Barrier Island**, New Zealand
209 S 1 **Great Barrier Reef**, Queensland, Australia
117 J 16 **Great Basin**, Nevada, U.S.A.
113 R 5 **Great Bear Lake**, Northwest Territories, Canada
119 I 15 **Great Bend**, Kansas, U.S.A.
77 J 14 **Great Britain**, United Kingdom
169 N 25 **Great Channel**, India
173 B 19 **Great Coco Island**, Myanmar
118 D 12 **Great Divide Basin**, Wyoming, U.S.A.
209 T 13 **Great Dividing Range**, Victoria, Australia
210 I 4 **Great Exhibition Bay**, New Zealand
127 N 3 **Great Exuma Island**, The Bahamas
118 C 7 **Great Falls**, Montana, U.S.A.
93 L 24 **Great Hungarian Plain**, Hungary
127 O 5 **Great Inagua Island**, The Bahamas
196 K 14 **Great Karoo**, Republic of South Africa
210 L 8 **Great Mercury Island**, New Zealand
62 I 10 **Great Meteor Tablemount**, Atlantic Ocean
169 O 25 **Great Nicobar**, India
77 L 20 **Great Ouse**, United Kingdom
115 Q 2 **Great Plain of the Koukdjuak**, Nunavut, Canada
119 H 20 **Great Plains**, U.S.A.
191 H 22 **Great Rift Valley**, Africa
121 U 7 **Great Sacandaga Lake**, New York, U.S.A.
117 L 14 **Great Salt Lake**, Utah, U.S.A.
117 K 16 **Great Salt Lake Desert**, Utah, U.S.A.
190 B 9 **Great Sand Sea**, Egypt/Libya
208 J 5 **Great Sandy Desert**, Western Australia, Australia
113 T 7 **Great Slave Lake**, Northwest Territories, Canada
123 O 2 **Great Smoky Mountains**, Tennessee, U.S.A.
113 R 10 **Great Snow Mountain**, British Columbia, Canada
62 A 7 **Great Sound**, Bermuda
208 L 8 **Great Victoria Desert**, Western Australia, Australia
173 E 21 **Great West Torres Islands**, Myanmar
77 N 19 **Great Yarmouth**, United Kingdom
161 S 2 **Great Zab**, Iraq
193 N 13 **Greater Accra**, Ghana
127 N 7 **Greater Antilles**, North America
59 S 4 **Greater Sunda Islands**, Indian Ocean
145 H 24 **Greec**, Chile
97 C 17 **Greece**, Europe
121 R 8 **Greece**, New York, U.S.A.
118 F 13 **Greeley**, Colorado, U.S.A.
117 N 16 **Green**, Utah, U.S.A.
120 I 6 **Green Bay**, Wisconsin, U.S.A.
123 R 9 **Green Cove Springs**, Florida, U.S.A.
212 I 4 **Green Islands**, Papua New Guinea
113 W 11 **Green Lake**, Saskatchewan, Canada
117 N 17 **Green River**, Utah, U.S.A.
118 D 12 **Green River**, Wyoming, U.S.A.
212 A 3 **Green River**, Papua New Guinea
120 J 11 **Greencastle**, Indiana, U.S.A.
123 P 1 **Greeneville**, Tennessee, U.S.A.
65 P 11 **Greenland**, Denmark
65 S 12 **Greenland Plain**, Arctic Ocean
65 R 13 **Greenland Sea**, Arctic Ocean
121 W 9 **Greenport**, New York, U.S.A.
123 S 1 **Greensboro**, North Carolina, U.S.A.
120 K 12 **Greensburg**, Indiana, U.S.A.
121 Q 11 **Greensburg**, Pennsylvania, U.S.A.
117 E 15 **Greenville**, California, U.S.A.
119 K 19 **Greenville**, Texas, U.S.A.
120 G 12 **Greenville**, Illinois, U.S.A.
120 L 11 **Greenville**, Ohio, U.S.A.
121 P 10 **Greenville**, Pennsylvania, U.S.A.
122 L 7 **Greenville**, Alabama, U.S.A.
122 G 4 **Greenville**, Mississippi, U.S.A.
123 O 8 **Greenville**, Florida, U.S.A.
123 V 2 **Greenville**, North Carolina, U.S.A.
123 Q 3 **Greenville**, South Carolina, U.S.A.
192 H 14 **Greenville**, Liberia
122 I 4 **Greenwood**, Mississippi, U.S.A.
123 Q 4 **Greenwood**, South Carolina, U.S.A.
209 R 4 **Gregory Range**, Queensland, Australia
86 M 9 **Greifswald**, Germany
86 M 8 **Greifswalder Bodden**, Germany
89 U 4 **Grein**, Austria
87 K 18 **Greiz**, Germany
156 I 6 **Gremikha**, Russian Federation
85 D 24 **Grenå**, Denmark
127 X 11 **Grenada**, North America
122 I 4 **Grenada**, Mississippi, U.S.A.
122 I 4 **Grenada Lake**, Mississippi, U.S.A.
127 X 11 **Grenadines, The**, St Vincent and The Grenadines
88 D 7 **Grenchen**, Switzerland
79 U 11 **Grenoble**, France
127 X 11 **Grenville**, Grenada
83 E 14 **Grevelingen**, Netherlands
87 D 14 **Greven**, Germany
97 C 15 **Grevena**, Greece
87 B 16 **Grevenbroich**, Germany
83 L 24 **Grevenmacher**, Luxembourg
83 M 25 **Grevenmacher**, Luxembourg
86 I 9 **Grevesmühlen**, Germany
211 F 18 **Grey**, New Zealand
115 X 9 **Grey Islands**, Newfoundland and Labrador, Canada
211 F 18 **Greymouth**, New Zealand
197 P 12 **Greytown**, Republic of South Africa
211 L 16 **Greytown**, New Zealand
89 S 4 **Grieskirchen**, Austria
123 O 5 **Griffin**, Georgia, U.S.A.
209 S 11 **Griffith**, New South Wales, Australia
159 Q 6 **Grigoleti**, Georgia
101 O 9 **Grigoriopol**, Moldova
194 K 4 **Grimari**, Central African Republic
87 L 16 **Grimma**, Germany
86 L 9 **Grimmen**, Germany
77 L 17 **Grimsby**, United Kingdom
84 C 9 **Grímsey**, Iceland
84 C 10 **Grímsstaðir**, Iceland
84 A 12 **Grindavík**, Iceland
88 F 9 **Grindelwald**, Switzerland
94 C 6 **Grintovec**, Slovenia
196 L 12 **Griquatown**, Republic of South Africa
94 E 10 **Grmeč**, Bosnia and Herzegovina
83 H 17 **Grobbendonk**, Belgium
98 B 11 **Grobiņa**, Latvia
89 S 6 **Gröbming**, Austria
93 G 16 **Grodków**, Poland
82 M 12 **Groenlo**, Netherlands
92 L 13 **Grójec**, Poland
63 I 15 **Groll Seamount**, Atlantic Ocean
85 E 14 **Grong**, Norway
82 M 6 **Groningen**, Netherlands
82 M 6 **Groningen**, Netherlands
196 I 12 **Groot Karas Berg**, Namibia
209 P 2 **Groote Eylandt**, Northern Territory, Australia
196 J 8 **Grootfontein**, Namibia
196 J 9 **Gross Ums**, Namibia
90 F 12 **Grosseto**, Italy
89 P 7 **Grossglockner**, Austria
115 W 7 **Groswater Bay**, Newfoundland and Labrador, Canada
215 Y 11 **Groupe Actéon**, French Polynesia
122 K 7 **Grove Hill**, Alabama, U.S.A.
117 E 21 **Grover Beach**, California, U.S.A.
156 E 11 **Groznyy**, Russian Federation
96 M 10 **Grudovo**, Bulgaria
92 I 10 **Grudziądz**, Poland
196 J 12 **Grünau**, Namibia
98 E 12 **Gruzdžiai**, Lithuania
88 D 9 **Gstaad**, Switzerland
144 I 7 **Guachipas**, Argentina
81 P 6 **Guadalajara**, Spain
125 O 11 **Guadalajara**, Mexico
212 K 7 **Guadalcanal**, Solomon Islands
212 M 7 **Guadalcanal**, Solomon Islands
144 H 12 **Guadales**, Argentina
80 L 12 **Guadalquivir**, Spain
61 V 4 **Guadalupe**, Mexico
80 M 8 **Guadalupe**, Spain
125 Q 7 **Guadalupe**, Mexico
125 N 8 **Guadalupe**, Mexico
119 F 20 **Guadalupe Peak**, Texas, U.S.A.
127 X 8 **Guadeloupe**, France
127 W 8 **Guadeloupe Passage**, Montserrat
81 N 9 **Guadiana**, Spain
81 P 12 **Guadix**, Spain
61 X 12 **Guafo Fracture Zone**, Pacific Ocean
138 M 8 **Guainía**, Colombia
138 M 8 **Guainía**, Colombia
143 D 14 **Guajará-Mirim**, Brazil
144 L 11 **Gualeguay**, Argentina
144 L 11 **Gualeguaychú**, Argentina
145 G 18 **Gualjaina**, Argentina
214 A 9 **Guam**, Guam
214 A 9 **Guam**, U.S.A.
145 K 14 **Guamini**, Argentina
124 K 7 **Guamúchil**, Mexico
171 P 10 **Guan Xian**, China
126 I 4 **Guanabacoa**, Cuba
126 G 8 **Guanaja**, Honduras
125 P 10 **Guanajuato**, Mexico
125 P 11 **Guanajuato**, Mexico
143 L 15 **Guanambi**, Brazil
138 M 4 **Guanare**, Venezuela
144 G 9 **Guandacol**, Argentina
126 H 4 **Guane**, Cuba
171 T 13 **Guangdong**, China
171 U 10 **Guangshui**, China
171 R 13 **Guangxi Zhuangzu**, China
171 Q 10 **Guangyuan**, China
171 T 13 **Guangzhou**, China
127 N 6 **Guantánamo**, Cuba
127 N 6 **Guantánamo Bay Naval Base**, Cuba
126 H 12 **Guápiles**, Costa Rica
143 E 15 **Guaporé**, Brazil
141 H 19 **Guaqui**, Bolivia
143 M 18 **Guarapari**, Brazil
143 I 20 **Guarapuava**, Brazil
141 I 17 **Guarayos**, Bolivia
80 J 5 **Guarda**, Portugal
80 J 6 **Guarda**, Portugal
139 O 4 **Guárico**, Venezuela
124 K 7 **Guasave**, Mexico
126 C 9 **Guatemala**, Guatemala
126 C 9 **Guatemala**, North America
61 X 7 **Guatemala Basin**, Pacific Ocean
139 O 2 **Guatire**, Venezuela
138 K 9 **Guaviare**, Colombia
138 M 7 **Guaviare**, Colombia
127 T 7 **Guayama**, Puerto Rico
140 A 10 **Guayaquil**, Ecuador
141 K 15 **Guayaramerín**, Bolivia
140 A 10 **Guayas**, Ecuador
124 I 5 **Guaymas**, Mexico
156 M 8 **Guba**, Russian Federation
191 G 19 **Guba**, Ethiopia
92 D 13 **Gubin**, Poland
193 U 10 **Gubio**, Nigeria
159 P 5 **Gudaut'a**, Georgia
163 O 1 **Gudayyidat 'Ar'ar**, Saudi Arabia
61 X 15 **Gudgeon Harbour**, Pitcairn Island
169 G 19 **Gudivada**, India
169 F 20 **Gudur**, India
192 H 12 **Guéckédou**, Guinea
193 V 10 **Guélengdeng**, Chad
189 P 5 **Guelma**, Algeria
188 F 9 **Guelmine**, Morocco
125 R 8 **Güémez**, Mexico
193 O 10 **Guéné**, Benin
193 X 10 **Guéra**, Chad
189 N 8 **Guerara**, Algeria
188 J 7 **Guercif**, Morocco
79 P 9 **Guéret**, France
77 J 25 **Guernsey**, United Kingdom
192 G 7 **Guérou**, Mauritania
125 Q 13 **Guerrero**, Mexico
125 Q 6 **Guerrero**, Mexico
124 G 5 **Guerrero Negro**, Mexico
192 J 13 **Guéyo**, Côte d'Ivoire
191 H 22 **Gugē**, Ethiopia
214 A 7 **Guguan**, Northern Mariana Islands
62 G 13 **Guiana Basin**, Atlantic Ocean
139 O 6 **Guiana Highlands**, Venezuela/Brazil
144 M 11 **Guichón**, Uruguay
193 W 11 **Guidari**, Chad
193 V 11 **Guider**, Cameroon
192 G 8 **Guidimaka**, Mauritania
171 S 14 **Guigang**, China
192 I 13 **Guiglo**, Côte d'Ivoire
80 L 6 **Guijuelo**, Spain
77 L 22 **Guildford**, United Kingdom
121 Y 5 **Guilford**, Maine, U.S.A.
171 S 13 **Guilin**, China
79 W 12 **Guillestre**, France
62 M 12 **Güímar**, Canary Islands
175 P 5 **Guimaras**, Philippines
122 K 4 **Guin**, Alabama, U.S.A.
192 F 10 **Guinea**, Africa
63 L 14 **Guinea Basin**, Atlantic Ocean
192 E 10 **Guinea-Bissau**, Africa
192 I 12 **Guinée-Forestière**, Guinea
192 F 10 **Guinée-Maritime**, Guinea
126 J 4 **Güines**, Cuba
78 J 5 **Guingamp**, France
80 I 1 **Guitiriz**, Spain
175 Q 5 **Guiuan**, Philippines
171 R 12 **Guiyang**, China
171 R 12 **Guizhou**, China
169 B 14 **Gujarat**, India
165 Y 9 **Gujranwala**, Pakistan
165 Y 8 **Gujrat**, Pakistan
171 P 8 **Gulang**, China
169 E 18 **Gulbarga**, India
98 I 10 **Gulbene**, Latvia
167 U 12 **Gülchö**, Kyrgyzstan
212 C 6 **Gulf**, Papua New Guinea
173 I 22 **Gulf of Thailand**, Thailand
58 J 2 **Gulf of Aden**, Indian Ocean
112 J 9 **Gulf of Alaska**, Alaska, U.S.A.
157 Z 6 **Gulf of Anadyr**, Russian Federation
160 E 14 **Gulf of Aqaba**, Africa/Asia
64 M 8 **Gulf of Boothia**, Nunavut, Canada

Country · Internal administrative region: State/Province/Territory/Dependent territory · Capital city · Mountain range/Undersea ridge · Mountain peak/Volcano/Seamount · Geographic feature · Headland/Point/Cape/Peninsula · Desert · Island/Island group · Antarctic base · Ocean · Sea · Bay/Gulf/Channel/Strait · Lake · Salt pan/Dry/Intermittent lake · River

5 I 19 Gulf of Bothnia, Europe
24 G 3 Gulf of California, Mexico
09 Q 2 Gulf of Carpentaria, Queensland, Australia
7 E 19 Gulf of Corinth, Greece
38 G 3 Gulf of Darién, Colombia/Panama
5 L 20 Gulf of Finland, Europe
2 J 7 Gulf of Gdańsk, Poland
0 C 10 Gulf of Genoa, Italy
40 A 10 Gulf of Guayaquil, Ecuador
93 R 15 Gulf of Guinea, Africa
69 A 14 Gulf of Kachchh, India
69 B 16 Gulf of Khambhat, India
21 Y 8 Gulf of Maine, Maine, U.S.A.
69 F 24 Gulf of Mannar, Sri Lanka
73 E 17 Gulf of Martaban, Myanmar
25 V 10 Gulf of Mexico, North America
63 Y 5 Gulf of Oman, Asia
26 K 14 Gulf of Panama, Panama
12 C 6 Gulf of Papua, Papua New Guinea
39 R 3 Gulf of Paria, Trinidad and Tobago/Venezuela
8 E 9 Gulf of Riga, Estonia/Latvia
90 C 7 Gulf of Salûm, Egypt/Libya
89 V 8 Gulf of Sirte, Libya
15 V 11 Gulf of St Lawrence, Québec, Canada
90 F 8 Gulf of Suez, Egypt
01 Y 9 Gulf of Taganrog, Russian Federation/Ukraine
9 S 3 Gulf of Thailand, Indian Ocean
0 I 5 Gulf of Tongking, Pacific Ocean
4 A 8 Gulf of Trieste, Slovenia
38 K 2 Gulf of Venezuela, Venezuela
0 H 7 Gulf of Venice, Italy
22 K 9 Gulf Shores, Alabama, U.S.A.
09 P 12 Gulf St Vincent, South Australia, Australia
22 I 8 Gulfport, Mississippi, U.S.A.
67 R 12 Gulistan, Uzbekistan
58 B 12 Güllük Körfezi, Turkey
58 A 9 Gülpinar, Turkey
59 Q 5 Gulrip'shi, Georgia
67 U 7 Gul'shad, Kazakhstan
95 S 6 Gulu, Uganda
6 K 10 Gülübovo, Bulgaria
6 I 7 Gulyantsi, Bulgaria
96 L 7 Gumare, Botswana
66 I 13 Gumdag, Turkmenistan
93 S 10 Gumel, Nigeria
69 I 15 Gumla, India
68 E 13 Guna, India
91 I 19 Guna Terara, Ethiopia
9 Q 4 Gundertshausen, Austria
58 L 12 Güney Doğu Toroslar, Turkey
94 J 11 Gungu, Democratic Republic of Congo
4 I 10 Gunja, Croatia
5 P 13 Gunnbjørn Fjeld, Greenland
09 U 10 Gunnedah, New South Wales, Australia
8 B 11 Gunners Quoin, Mauritius
17 M 17 Gunnison, Utah, U.S.A.
19 E 15 Gunnison, Colorado, U.S.A.
69 E 19 Guntakal, India
22 M 3 Guntersville Lake, Alabama, U.S.A.
69 G 19 Guntur, India
74 B 8 Gunung Abongabong, Indonesia
75 Q 10 Gunung Bulawa, Indonesia
75 W 12 Gunung Dom, Indonesia
74 D 11 Gunung Kerinci, Indonesia
75 U 11 Gunung Kwoka, Indonesia
75 O 10 Gunung Malino, Indonesia
175 V 11 Gunung Mebo, Indonesia
174 L 8 Gunung Murud, Malaysia
175 Q 15 Gunung Mutis, Indonesia
174 L 8 Gunung Pagon, Malaysia
174 K 15 Gunung Semeru, Indonesia
174 I 14 Gunung Slamet, Indonesia
174 E 8 Gunung Tahan, Malaysia
175 P 11 Gunung Tumpu, Indonesia
175 R 14 Gunungapi, Indonesia
174 C 10 Gunungsitoli, Indonesia
169 I 17 Gunupur, India
87 H 23 Günzburg, Germany
100 K 8 Gura Humorului, Romania
165 O 14 Gurdim, Iran
168 B 13 Gurha, India
89 T 8 Gurk, Austria
197 Q 6 Guro, Mozambique
197 S 5 Gurué, Mozambique
158 M 11 Gürün, Turkey
142 I 10 Gurupá, Brazil
143 J 14 Gurupi, Brazil
193 Q 10 Gusau, Nigeria
99 C 16 Gusev, Russian Federation
177 M 25 Gushikawa, Japan
91 B 18 Guspini, Italy
89 X 7 Güssing, Austria
89 V 5 Gusswerk, Austria
219 W 5 Gustav Bull Mountains, Antarctica
113 N 9 Gustavus, Alaska, U.S.A.
177 O 26 Gusukube, Japan
87 E 14 Gütersloh, Germany
119 I 18 Guthrie, Texas, U.S.A.
197 P 7 Gutu, Zimbabwe
168 M 13 Guwahati, India
161 S 2 Guwër, Iraq
139 S 6 Guyana, South America
171 R 6 Guyang, China
119 H 16 Guymon, Oklahoma, U.S.A.
171 R 8 Guyuan, China
167 P 13 Guzar, Uzbekistan
99 B 16 Gvardeysk, Russian Federation
173 C 15 Gwa, Myanmar
193 Q 9 Gwadabawa, Nigeria
165 P 14 Gwadar, Pakistan
168 F 13 Gwalior, India
197 O 8 Gwanda, Zimbabwe
195 O 5 Gwane, Democratic Republic of Congo
165 P 14 Gwatar Bay, Iran
195 Q 5 Gwawele, Democratic Republic of Congo
92 G 10 Gwda, Poland
197 O 7 Gweru, Zimbabwe
196 M 8 Gweta, Botswana
120 J 4 Gwinn, Michigan, U.S.A.
193 U 10 Gwoza, Nigeria
97 M 23 Gyali, Greece
170 K 6 Gyangzê, China
171 N 9 Gyaring Hu, China
97 I 21 Gyaros, Greece
157 N 7 Gyda, Russian Federation
157 N 7 Gydanskiy Poluostrov, Russian Federation
209 W 8 Gympie, Queensland, Australia
93 L 24 Gyomaendrőd, Hungary
93 K 22 Gyöngyös, Hungary
93 H 22 Győr, Hungary
114 I 9 Gypsumville, Manitoba, Canada
97 E 23 Gytheio, Greece
93 L 24 Gyula, Hungary
159 T 8 Gyumri, Armenia
166 J 13 Gyzylarbat, Turkmenistan
166 I 14 Gyzyletrek, Turkmenistan

H

172 N 12 Ha Côi, Vietnam
172 L 10 Ha Giang, Vietnam
173 L 22 Ha Tiên, Vietnam
173 M 15 Ha Tinh, Vietnam
98 F 8 Häädemeeste, Estonia
87 K 24 Haag in Oberbayern, Germany
82 N 12 Haaksbergen, Netherlands
214 I 10 Ha'apai Group, Tonga
85 L 15 Haapajärvi, Finland
215 Y 8 Haapiti, French Polynesia
98 E 7 Haapsalu, Estonia
82 G 11 Haarlem, Netherlands
211 D 21 Haast, New Zealand
163 X 5 Haba, United Arab Emirates
163 V 11 Ḩabarūt, Oman
195 X 7 Habaswein, Kenya
83 J 25 Habay-la-Neuve, Belgium
163 R 13 Ḩabbān, Yemen
171 U 5 Habirag, China
138 H 10 Hacha, Colombia
177 L 19 Hachijō-jima, Japan
176 K 9 Hachinohe, Japan
159 R 9 Haciömer, Turkey
121 U 10 Hackensack, New Jersey, U.S.A.
197 Q 8 Hacufera, Mozambique
193 S 10 Hadejia, Nigeria
160 F 8 Hadera, Israel
85 B 25 Haderslev, Denmark
169 E 17 Hadgaon, India
169 L 19 Hadhdhunmathi Atoll, Maldives
163 W 14 Hadīboh, Yemen
158 H 13 Hadim, Turkey
113 T 1 Hadley Bay, Nunavut, Canada
163 R 13 Ḩaḑramawt, Yemen
84 G 8 Hadseløy, Norway
85 C 24 Hadsund, Denmark
101 T 3 Hadyach, Ukraine
163 Q 3 Ḩafar al Bāţin, Saudi Arabia
158 M 9 Hafik, Turkey
162 L 4 Hafirat al'Aydā, Saudi Arabia
168 N 13 Haflong, India
84 A 11 Hafnarfjörður, Iceland
214 A 9 Hagåtña, Guam
112 G 8 Hagemeister Island, Alaska, U.S.A.
87 D 16 Hagen, Germany
116 J 12 Hagerman, Idaho, U.S.A.
121 R 12 Hagerstown, Maryland, U.S.A.
85 F 20 Hagfors, Sweden
177 C 20 Hagi, Japan
77 B 18 Hag's Head, Republic of Ireland
79 X 4 Haguenau, France
172 M 12 Hai Duong, Vietnam
172 M 12 Hai Phong, Vietnam
171 W 6 Haicheng, China
160 F 8 Haifa, Israel
171 S 14 Haikang, China
171 S 15 Haikou, China
163 N 4 Ḩā'il, Saudi Arabia
171 U 2 Hailar, China
84 L 13 Hailuoto, Finland
177 M 26 Haimi, Japan
171 S 15 Hainan, China
171 R 15 Hainan, China
171 S 15 Hainan Strait, China
83 E 21 Hainaut, Belgium
89 Z 4 Hainburg an der Donau, Austria
113 N 9 Haines, Alaska, U.S.A.
123 R 11 Haines City, Florida, U.S.A.
113 N 8 Haines Junction, Yukon Territory, Canada
89 W 4 Hainfeld, Austria
127 P 8 Haiti, North America
93 M 22 Hajdúböszörmény, Hungary
93 M 23 Hajdúszoboszló, Hungary
161 V 8 Ḩājī Muḩsin, Iraq
176 I 13 Hajiki-zaki, Japan
168 I 13 Hajipur, India
163 O 12 Ḩajjah, Yemen
164 L 12 Ḩājjīābād, Iran
92 O 11 Hajnówka, Poland
172 B 10 Haka, Myanmar
159 T 12 Hakkâri, Turkey
177 G 19 Hakken-san, Japan
176 K 9 Hakkōda-san, Japan
176 K 3 Hako-dake, Japan
176 J 8 Hakodate, Japan
177 H 15 Hakui, Japan
165 U 14 Hala, Pakistan
163 P 7 Halabān, Saudi Arabia
161 V 4 Halabja, Iraq
190 H 13 Halaib, Sudan
190 G 12 Halaib Triangle, Sudan
162 J 2 Ḩālat 'Ammār, Saudi Arabia
160 H 5 Halba, Lebanon
171 O 2 Halban, Mongolia
87 I 14 Halberstadt, Germany
85 D 20 Halden, Norway
168 F 11 Haldwani, India
117 F 18 Half Dome, California, U.S.A.
159 N 13 Halfeti, Turkey
211 C 26 Halfmoon Bay, New Zealand
82 H 11 Halfweg, Netherlands
115 P 13 Haliburton Highlands, Ontario, Canada
77 J 17 Halifax, United Kingdom
115 V 13 Halifax, Nova Scotia, Canada
115 O 1 Hall Beach, Nunavut, Canada
89 N 7 Hall in Tirol, Austria
215 O 14 Hall Islands, Federated States of Micronesia
115 S 3 Hall Peninsula, Nunavut, Canada
171 Y 9 Halla-san, South Korea
83 F 19 Halle, Belgium
87 K 16 Halle, Germany
89 Q 6 Hallein, Austria
219 N 3 Halley, Antarctica
208 K 4 Halls Creek, Western Australia, Australia
89 R 6 Hallstatt, Austria
88 F 7 Hallwiler See, Switzerland
175 S 10 Halmahera, Indonesia
175 S 11 Halmahera Sea, Indonesia
85 E 24 Halmstad, Sweden
83 F 15 Halsteren, Netherlands
172 L 11 Ham Yên, Vietnam
177 C 19 Hamada, Japan
164 G 6 Hamadān, Iran
164 G 6 Hamadān, Iran
189 R 12 Hamādat Murzuq, Libya
188 J 9 Hamaguir, Algeria
160 I 4 Ḩamāh, Syria
177 I 18 Hamamatsu, Japan
85 D 18 Hamar, Norway
177 F 17 Hamasaka, Japan
176 J 3 Hamatonbetsu, Japan
169 G 26 Hambantota, Sri Lanka
86 H 10 Hamburg, Germany
121 Q 8 Hamburg, New York, U.S.A.
163 O 10 Ḩamḑah, Saudi Arabia
162 M 9 Ḩamdānah, Saudi Arabia
85 L 18 Hämeenlinna, Finland
87 G 14 Hameln, Germany
208 F 6 Hamersley Range, Western Australia, Australia
171 X 6 Hamhŭng, North Korea
170 M 5 Hami, China
158 F 9 Hamidye, Turkey
62 A 7 Hamilton, Bermuda
76 H 13 Hamilton, United Kingdom
122 K 4 Hamilton, Alabama, U.S.A.
209 R 13 Hamilton, Victoria, Australia
210 K 10 Hamilton, New Zealand
62 F 6 Hamilton Bank, Atlantic Ocean
115 W 8 Hamilton Inlet, Newfoundland and Labrador, Canada
85 N 19 Hamina, Finland
123 T 3 Hamlet, North Carolina, U.S.A.
87 D 15 Hamm, Germany
188 G 10 Hammada du Drâa, Algeria
189 Q 10 Hammādat Tingharat, Libya
161 R 2 Ḩammān al 'Alīl, Iraq
85 G 16 Hammarstrand, Sweden
83 H 19 Hamme-Mille, Belgium
85 G 15 Hammerdal, Sweden
119 O 20 Hammond, Louisiana, U.S.A.
120 J 9 Hammond, Indiana, U.S.A.
121 U 11 Hammonton, New Jersey, U.S.A.
83 I 22 Hamois, Belgium
211 F 23 Hampden, New Zealand
119 M 18 Hampton, Arkansas, U.S.A.
121 X 7 Hampton, New Hampshire, U.S.A.
121 T 14 Hampton, Virginia, U.S.A.
123 R 5 Hampton, South Carolina, U.S.A.
191 C 17 Hamrat esh Sheikh, Sudan
165 N 12 Hāmūn-e Jaz Mūrīān, Iran
165 P 10 Hāmūn Helmand, Iran
165 P 9 Hāmūn Pu, Afghanistan
159 S 9 Hamur, Turkey
117 D 24 Hana, Hawaii, U.S.A.
162 K 5 Ḩanale, Saudi Arabia
176 K 10 Hanamaki, Japan
87 F 19 Hanau, Germany
171 S 8 Hancheng, China
121 R 11 Hancock, Maryland, U.S.A.
171 T 8 Handan, China
195 W 11 Handeni, Tanzania
93 I 20 Handlová, Slovakia
85 D 17 Hanestad, Norway
61 Y 5 Hanga Roa, Easter Island
171 O 3 Hangayn Nuruu, Mongolia
165 V 8 Hangu, Pakistan
171 P 11 Hangyuan, China
171 V 10 Hangzhou, China
159 P 11 Hani, Turkey
85 K 20 Hanko, Finland
117 N 17 Hanksville, Utah, U.S.A.
168 F 8 Hanle, India
158 L 10 Hanli, Turkey
211 H 18 Hanmer Springs, New Zealand
87 G 16 Hann-Münden, Germany
113 W 12 Hanna, Alberta, Canada
115 O 10 Hannah Bay, Ontario, Canada
118 N 13 Hannibal, Missouri, U.S.A.
86 G 13 Hannover, Germany
83 I 20 Hannut, Belgium
85 F 25 Hanöbukten, Sweden
172 L 12 Hanoi, Vietnam
219 W 4 Hansen Mountains, Antarctica
168 E 11 Hansi, India
99 H 20 Hantsavichy, Belarus
85 B 23 Hantsholm, Denmark
168 D 10 Hanumangarh, India
165 O 14 Hanzaram, Iran
171 R 9 Hanzhong, China
215 W 10 Hao, French Polynesia
169 K 15 Haora, India
189 O 8 Haoud el Hamra, Algeria
188 E 10 Haouza, Western Sahara
116 C 13 Happy Camp, California, U.S.A.
115 V 8 Happy Valley Goose Bay, Newfoundland and Labrador, Canada
162 J 2 Ḩaql, Saudi Arabia
171 P 6 Har Borog, China
171 N 7 Har Hu, China
160 G 7 Har Meron, Israel
171 N 3 Har Nuur, Mongolia
170 M 3 Har Us Nuur, Mongolia
191 K 18 Hara Alol, Djibouti
163 O 12 Ḩaraḑ, Yemen
163 S 6 Ḩaraḑh, Saudi Arabia
99 L 14 Haradok, Belarus
99 H 18 Haradzyeya, Belarus
215 V 9 Haraiki, French Polynesia
163 O 11 Ḩarajā, Saudi Arabia
176 L 13 Haramachi, Japan
165 R 10 Harappa Road, Pakistan
197 P 6 Harare, Zimbabwe
193 X 9 Haraz-Djombo, Chad
193 Y 11 Haraze Mangueigne, Chad
192 H 13 Harbel, Liberia
171 X 3 Harbin, China
115 Y 11 Harbour Breton, Newfoundland and Labrador, Canada
169 E 15 Harda Khas, India
85 A 19 Hardangerfjorden, Norway
196 I 10 Hardap, Namibia
123 R 6 Hardeeville, South Carolina, U.S.A.
82 J 11 Harderwijk, Netherlands
119 N 16 Hardy, Arkansas, U.S.A.
83 C 19 Harelbeke, Belgium
82 M 6 Haren, Netherlands
191 K 20 Hārer, Ethiopia
191 K 22 Hargele, Ethiopia
191 L 20 Hargeysa, Somalia
98 H 9 Hargla, Estonia
163 Q 13 Harīb, Yemen
168 F 10 Haridwar, India
169 D 20 Harihar, India
211 E 19 Harihari, New Zealand
83 F 14 Haringvliet, Netherlands
169 E 15 Harisal, India
120 M 15 Harlan, Kentucky, U.S.A.
82 J 7 Harlingen, Netherlands
119 J 24 Harlingen, Texas, U.S.A.
77 M 21 Harlow, United Kingdom
118 D 8 Harlowton, Montana, U.S.A.
158 D 9 Harmancik, Turkey
116 F12 Harney Basin, Oregon, U.S.A.
85 H 16 Härnösand, Sweden
81 P 2 Haro, Spain
192 I 14 Harper, Liberia
160 J 8 Ḩarrat ar Rujaylah, Jordan
160 J 9 Harrat ar Rujaylah, Jordan
162 M 6 Ḩarrat Rahaţ, Saudi Arabia
115 P 10 Harricanaw, Québec, Canada
123 O 2 Harriman, Tennessee, U.S.A.
62 B 7 Harrington Sound, Bermuda
76 E 9 Harris, United Kingdom
61 R 3 Harris Seamount, Pacific Ocean
120 H 13 Harrisburg, Illinois, U.S.A.
121 S 11 Harrisburg, Pennsylvania, U.S.A.
197 O 12 Harrismith, Republic of South Africa
118 G 11 Harrison, Nebraska, U.S.A.
119 M 16 Harrison, Arkansas, U.S.A.
121 Q 13 Harrisonburg, Virginia, U.S.A.
119 L 14 Harrisonville, Missouri, U.S.A.
120 M 6 Harrisville, Michigan, U.S.A.
77 K 17 Harrogate, United Kingdom
164 G 6 Harsīn, Iran
84 H 8 Harstad, Norway
120 K 7 Hart, Michigan, U.S.A.
89 X 6 Hartberg, Austria
85 B 19 Hårteigen, Norway
120 J 14 Hartford, Kentucky, U.S.A.
121 V 9 Hartford, Connecticut, U.S.A.
77 G 22 Hartland Point, United Kingdom
77 K 15 Hartlepool, United Kingdom
59 S 9 Hartog Ridge, Indian Ocean
209 O 6 Harts Range, Northern Territory, Australia
123 P 3 Hartwell Reservoir, Georgia, U.S.A.
118 I 8 Harvey, North Dakota, U.S.A.
120 I 9 Harvey, Illinois, U.S.A.
77 N 20 Harwich, United Kingdom
168 E 10 Haryana, India
87 H 15 Harz, Germany
158 J 11 Hasan Daği, Turkey
164 L 12 Ḩasan Langī, Iran
86 D 12 Haselünne, Germany
177 G 19 Hashimoto, Japan
164 I 5 Hashtgerd, Iran
163 X 11 Ḩāsik, Oman
169 D 21 Hassan, India
83 J 18 Hasselt, Belgium
87 I 19 Hassfurt, Germany
189 O 10 Hassi Bel Guebbour, Algeria
189 N 9 Hassi Inifel, Algeria
189 O 8 Hassi Messaoud, Algeria
85 E 25 Hässleholm, Sweden
77 M 22 Hastings, United Kingdom
118 J 13 Hastings, Nebraska, U.S.A.
120 K 8 Hastings, Michigan, U.S.A.
210 N 13 Hastings, New Zealand
163 V 12 Ḩaşwayl, Yemen
173 H 26 Hat Yai, Thailand
119 D 19 Hatch, New Mexico, U.S.A.
100 H 11 Haţeg, Romania
177 M 26 Hateruma-jima, Japan
171 P 2 Hatgal, Mongolia
168 E 12 Hathras, India
177 D 19 Hatsukaichi, Japan
169 F 14 Hatta, India
123 X 2 Hatteras, North Carolina, U.S.A.
62 D 10 Hatteras Abyssal Plain, Atlantic Ocean
123 X 2 Hatteras Island, North Carolina, U.S.A.
122 I 7 Hattiesburg, Mississippi, U.S.A.
62 J 6 Hatton Ridge, Atlantic Ocean
211 M 14 Hatuma, New Zealand
215 W 5 Hatutu, French Polynesia
93 J 22 Hatvan, Hungary
85 A 20 Haugesund, Norway
89 X 2 Haugsdorf, Austria
85 B 19 Haukeligrend, Norway
85 N 16 Haukivesi, Finland
210 K 8 Hauraki Gulf, New Zealand
87 D 24 Hausach, Germany
194 G 8 Haut-Ogooué, Gabon
192 H 10 Haute-Guinée, Guinea

Country · Internal administrative region: State/Province/Territory/Dependent territory · Capital city · Mountain range/Undersea ridge · Mountain peak/Volcano/Seamount · Geographic feature · Headland/Point/Cape/Peninsula · Desert · Island/Island group · Antarctic base · Ocean · Sea · Bay/Gulf/Channel/Strait · Lake · Salt pan/Dry/Intermittent lake · River

194 M 3 **Haute-Kotto**, Central African Republic
195 N 3 **Haute-Mbomou**, Central African Republic
79 O 3 **Haute-Normandie**, France
188 J 7 **Hauts Plateaux**, Morocco
126 I 4 **Havana**, Cuba
120 G 10 **Havana**, Illinois, U.S.A.
86 L 13 **Havel**, Germany
83 I 21 **Havelange**, Belgium
165 W 10 **Haveli**, Pakistan
123 W 3 **Havelock**, North Carolina, U.S.A.
211 I 16 **Havelock**, New Zealand
169 N 21 **Havelock Island**, India
82 L 9 **Havelte**, Netherlands
77 G 21 **Haverfordwest**, United Kingdom
83 I 22 **Haversin**, Belgium
171 T 4 **Havirga**, Mongolia
93 E 18 **Havlíčkův Brod**, Czech Republic
118 D 7 **Havre**, Montana, U.S.A.
115 W 12 **Havre Aubert**, Québec, Canada
115 U 10 **Havre-St-Pierre**, Québec, Canada
101 W 7 **Havrylivka**, Ukraine
96 L 12 **Havsa**, Turkey
158 B 6 **Havsa**, Turkey
158 K 8 **Havza**, Turkey
117 C 26 **Hawaii**, Hawaii, U.S.A.
117 C 26 **Hawaii**, U.S.A.
117 B 23 **Hawaiian Islands**, Hawaii, U.S.A.
163 S 2 **Ḩawallī**, Kuwait
210 J 13 **Hawera**, New Zealand
117 D 25 **Hawi**, Hawaii, U.S.A.
77 I 14 **Hawick**, United Kingdom
210 N 13 **Hawke Bay**, New Zealand
209 P 10 **Hawker**, South Australia, Australia
210 M 13 **Hawke's Bay**, New Zealand
115 X 9 **Hawkes Bay**, Newfoundland and Labrador, Canada
123 P 6 **Hawkinsville**, Georgia, U.S.A.
211 I 19 **Hawkswood**, New Zealand
161 S 7 **Hawr al Ḩabbānīyah**, Iraq
161 Y 11 **Hawr al Hammār**, Iraq
161 W 9 **Hawr as Sa'dīyah**, Iraq
163 S 12 **Ḩawra'**, Yemen
117 G 17 **Hawthorne**, Nevada, U.S.A.
209 S 12 **Hay**, New South Wales, Australia
113 T 8 **Hay River**, Northwest Territories, Canada
175 S 12 **Haya**, Indonesia
176 L 10 **Hayachine-san**, Japan
164 F 4 **Haydarābād**, Iran
117 N 24 **Hayden**, Arizona, U.S.A.
163 W 15 **Ḩayf**, Yemen
163 X 9 **Haymā'**, Oman
158 H 10 **Haymana**, Turkey
158 C 7 **Hayrabolu**, Turkey
118 D 7 **Hays**, Montana, U.S.A.
119 I 14 **Hays**, Kansas, U.S.A.
101 O 6 **Haysyn**, Ukraine
117 D 18 **Hayward**, California, U.S.A.
120 G 4 **Hayward**, Wisconsin, U.S.A.
120 M 14 **Hazard**, Kentucky, U.S.A.
169 I 14 **Hazaribag**, India
61 O 9 **Hazel Holme Bank**, Pacific Ocean
123 P 6 **Hazelhurst**, Georgia, U.S.A.
122 H 6 **Hazlehurst**, Mississippi, U.S.A.
120 H 5 **Heafford Junction**, Wisconsin, U.S.A.
59 O 12 **Heard Island**, Australia
119 K 21 **Hearne**, Texas, U.S.A.
115 N 11 **Hearst**, Ontario, Canada
218 J 4 **Hearst Island**, Antarctica
119 J 24 **Hebbronville**, Texas, U.S.A.
171 T 7 **Hebei**, China
209 T 9 **Hebel**, Queensland, Australia
117 N 22 **Heber**, Arizona, U.S.A.
160 F 10 **Hebron**, Israel
115 U 6 **Hebron**, Newfoundland and Labrador, Canada
118 J 13 **Hebron**, Nebraska, U.S.A.
113 P 12 **Hecate Strait**, British Columbia, Canada
125 Y 11 **Hecelchakán**, Mexico
171 R 13 **Hechi**, China
83 J 17 **Hechtel**, Belgium
171 R 11 **Hechuan**, China
85 F 16 **Hede**, Sweden
83 I 14 **Hedel**, Netherlands
82 G 10 **Heemskerk**, Netherlands
82 K 8 **Heerenveen**, Netherlands
82 H 9 **Heerhugowaard**, Netherlands
83 L 19 **Heerlen**, Netherlands
83 I 19 **Heers**, Belgium
83 J 14 **Heesh**, Netherlands
171 U 10 **Hefei**, China
171 S 11 **Hefeng**, China
171 Y 3 **Hegang**, China
86 F 8 **Heide**, Germany
87 F 21 **Heidelberg**, Germany
89 U 2 **Heidenreichstein**, Austria
171 X 2 **Heihe**, China
87 G 22 **Heilbronn**, Germany
89 Q 7 **Heiligenblut**, Austria
89 X 7 **Heiligenkreuz**, Austria
171 W 1 **Heilong Jiang**, China
171 W 3 **Heilongjiang**, China
84 B 12 **Heimaey**, Iceland
85 M 18 **Heinola**, Finland
87 B 16 **Heinsberg**, Germany
83 H 18 **Heist-op-den-Berg**, Belgium
159 N 11 **Hekimhan**, Turkey
84 B 11 **Hekla**, Iceland
92 I 8 **Hel**, Poland
168 N 12 **Helem**, India
118 C 8 **Helena**, Montana, U.S.A.
76 G 13 **Helensburgh**, United Kingdom
210 J 8 **Helensville**, New Zealand
86 E 9 **Helgoländer Bucht**, Germany
58 B 15 **Hell-Bourg**, Réunion
84 B 11 **Hella**, Iceland
85 A 21 **Helleland**, Norway
83 F 14 **Hellevoetsluis**, Netherlands
81 R 10 **Hellín**, Spain
116 I 10 **Hell's Canyon**, Idaho, U.S.A.
165 Q 11 **Helmand**, Afghanistan
165 P 10 **Helmand**, Afghanistan
196 H 11 **Helmeringhausen**, Namibia
83 J 15 **Helmond**, Netherlands
76 H 9 **Helmsdale**, United Kingdom
197 Z 6 **Helodrano Antongila**, Madgascar
85 E 25 **Helsingborg**, Sweden
85 M 19 **Helsinki**, Finland
190 E 8 **Helwân**, Egypt
86 G 10 **Hemmoor**, Germany
85 H 18 **Hemränge**, Sweden
210 K 7 **Hen and Chickens Islands**, New Zealand
171 T 9 **Henan**, China
176 J 9 **Henashi-zaki**, Japan
119 L 19 **Henderson**, Texas, U.S.A.
120 I 13 **Henderson**, Kentucky, U.S.A.
122 J 2 **Henderson**, Tennessee, U.S.A.
123 U 1 **Henderson**, North Carolina, U.S.A.
122 L 1 **Hendersonville**, Tennessee, U.S.A.
123 Q 2 **Hendersonville**, North Carolina, U.S.A.
77 L 21 **Hendon**, United Kingdom
164 J 13 **Hendorābī**, Iran
139 W 7 **Hendrik Top**, Suriname
212 C 5 **Henganofi**, Papua New Guinea
171 X 14 **Hengch'un**, Taiwan
171 N 11 **Hengduan Shan**, China
82 N 11 **Hengelo**, Netherlands
171 T 12 **Hengyang**, China
101 U 10 **Heniches'k**, Ukraine
86 L 12 **Hennigsdorf**, Germany
120 H 10 **Henry**, Illinois, U.S.A.
119 L 17 **Henryetta**, Oklahoma, U.S.A.
196 H 9 **Hentiesbaai**, Namibia
171 S 3 **Hentiy**, Mongolia
173 D 15 **Henzada**, Myanmar
165 P 7 **Herāt**, Afghanistan
165 P 7 **Herāt**, Afghanistan
191 H 15 **Herbagat**, Sudan
87 H 23 **Herbrechtingen**, Germany
95 I 16 **Herceg-Novi**, Serbia and Montenegro
84 C 10 **Herðubreið**, Iceland
77 I 20 **Hereford**, United Kingdom
119 G 18 **Hereford**, Texas, U.S.A.
215 V 10 **Hereheretue**, French Polynesia
210 I 5 **Herekino**, New Zealand
81 O 8 **Herencia**, Spain
83 H 17 **Herentals**, Belgium
87 F 14 **Herford**, Germany
88 H 6 **Herisau**, Switzerland
76 K 3 **Herma Ness**, United Kingdom
89 R 9 **Hermagor**, Austria
125 P 6 **Hermanas**, Mexico
209 N 7 **Hermannsburg**, Northern Territory, Australia
196 K 15 **Hermanus**, Republic of South Africa
212 C 2 **Hermit Islands**, Papua New Guinea
124 I 4 **Hermosillo**, Mexico
122 I 3 **Hernando**, Mississippi, U.S.A.
87 D 15 **Herne**, Germany
85 B 24 **Herning**, Denmark
87 F 23 **Herrenberg**, Germany
81 N 2 **Herrera de Pisuerga**, Spain
80 M 9 **Herrera del Duque**, Spain
113 N 3 **Herschel Island**, Yukon Territory, Canada
83 K 20 **Herve**, Belgium
209 W 7 **Hervey Bay**, Queensland, Australia
209 W 8 **Hervey Bay**, Queensland, Australia
87 H 15 **Herzberg**, Germany
87 M 15 **Herzberg**, Germany
160 F 9 **Herzliyya**, Israel
79 P 2 **Hesdin**, France
86 D 11 **Hesel**, Germany
171 S 13 **Heshan**, China
61 P 6 **Hess Tablemount**, Pacific Ocean
87 G 18 **Hessen**, Germany
93 K 22 **Heves**, Hungary
171 U 13 **Heyuan**, China
171 U 8 **Heze**, China
171 P 9 **Hezuo**, China
123 S 14 **Hialeah**, Florida, U.S.A.
123 R 2 **Hickory**, North Carolina, U.S.A.
176 K 6 **Hidaka**, Japan
176 K 6 **Hidaka-sanmyaku**, Japan
125 Q 11 **Hidalgo**, Mexico
124 M 6 **Hidalgo del Parral**, Mexico
86 L 7 **Hiddensee**, Germany
89 U 6 **Hieflau**, Austria
213 P 13 **Hienghène**, New Caledonia
177 D 19 **Higashi-Hiroshima**, Japan
177 G 18 **Higashi-ōsaka**, Japan
177 A 21 **Higashi-suidō**, Japan
120 L 6 **Higgins Lake**, Michigan, U.S.A.
188 H 8 **High Atlas**, Morocco
113 T 9 **High Level**, Alberta, Canada
119 G 17 **High Plains**, Texas, U.S.A.
121 U 9 **High Point**, New Jersey, U.S.A.
123 S 2 **High Point**, North Carolina, U.S.A.
123 Q 9 **High Springs**, Florida, U.S.A.
120 I 9 **Highland Park**, Illinois, U.S.A.
191 M 23 **Hiiraan**, Somalia
98 D 6 **Hiiumaa**, Estonia
162 K 3 **Hijaz**, Saudi Arabia
177 H 17 **Hikone**, Japan
215 V 9 **Hikueru**, French Polynesia
210 O 10 **Hikurangi**, New Zealand
210 J 6 **Hikurangi**, New Zealand
87 I 18 **Hildburghausen**, Germany
87 H 14 **Hildesheim**, Germany
116 J 12 **Hill City**, Idaho, U.S.A.
119 I 14 **Hill City**, Kansas, U.S.A.
219 Q 12 **Hillary Coast**, Antarctica
82 G 11 **Hillegom**, Netherlands
85 D 25 **Hillerød**, Denmark
209 S 11 **Hillston**, New South Wales, Australia
121 P 15 **Hillsville**, Virginia, U.S.A.
117 E 25 **Hilo**, Hawaii, U.S.A.
123 S 6 **Hilton Head Island**, South Carolina, U.S.A.
159 O 12 **Hilvan**, Turkey
82 I 11 **Hilversum**, Netherlands
168 F 9 **Himachal Pradesh**, India
168 F 8 **Himalaya**, Asia
95 K 21 **Himarë**, Albania
211 K 14 **Himatangi**, New Zealand
169 C 14 **Himatnagar**, India
177 F 18 **Himeji**, Japan
177 H 15 **Himi**, Japan
160 I 5 **Ḩimş**, Syria
101 N 9 **Hînceşti**, Moldova
127 P 7 **Hinche**, Haiti
209 T 4 **Hinchinbrook Island**, Queensland, Australia
194 F 10 **Hinda**, Congo
168 E 12 **Hindaun**, India
211 G 21 **Hinds**, New Zealand
165 U 6 **Hindu Kush**, Asia
169 E 20 **Hindupur**, India
169 F 16 **Hinganghat**, India
159 R 10 **Hinis**, Turkey
89 N 7 **Hintertux**, Austria
177 A 21 **Hirado**, Japan
169 H 15 **Hirakud Reservoir**, India
177 O 26 **Hirara**, Japan
169 E 20 **Hiriyur**, India
176 L 6 **Hiroo**, Japan
176 J 9 **Hirosaki**, Japan
177 D 19 **Hiroshima**, Japan
79 S 2 **Hirson**, France
168 D 11 **Hisar**, India
158 G 7 **Hisarönü**, Turkey
127 P 6 **Hispaniola**, Haiti
160 I 5 **Ḩisyah**, Syria
161 R 6 **Hīt**, Iraq
177 C 21 **Hita**, Japan
177 L 14 **Hitachi**, Japan
169 L 10 **Hitaddu**, Maldives
215 Z 8 **Hitiaa**, French Polynesia
177 C 23 **Hitoyoshi**, Japan
85 C 15 **Hitra**, Norway
213 P 9 **Hiu**, Vanuatu
177 J 14 **Hiuchiga-take**, Japan
215 X 6 **Hiva Oa**, French Polynesia
177 F 20 **Hiwasa**, Japan
113 U 7 **Hjalmar Lake**, Northwest Territories, Canada
85 G 21 **Hjälmaren**, Sweden
85 C 23 **Hjørring**, Denmark
172 F 5 **Hkakabo Razi**, Myanmar
197 P 11 **Hlatikulu**, Swaziland
101 S 5 **Hlobyne**, Ukraine
93 H 21 **Hlohovec**, Slovakia
101 T 1 **Hlukhiv**, Ukraine
99 K 19 **Hlusk**, Belarus
99 J 15 **Hlybokaye**, Belarus
193 N 13 **Ho**, Ghana
173 M 22 **Hô Chi Minh**, Vietnam
172 K 12 **Hô Sông Đa**, Vietnam
172 K 11 **Hô Thac Ba**, Vietnam
172 L 12 **Hoa Binh**, Vietnam
172 K 11 **Hoang Liên Son**, Vietnam
209 T 15 **Hobart**, Tasmania, Australia
119 G 19 **Hobbs**, New Mexico, U.S.A.
218 L 11 **Hobbs Coast**, Antarctica
123 T 12 **Hobe Sound**, Florida, U.S.A.
85 C 24 **Hobro**, Denmark
191 N 22 **Hobyo**, Somalia
89 R 8 **Hochalmspitze**, Austria
88 F 7 **Hochdorf**, Switzerland
196 I 9 **Hochfeld**, Namibia
89 T 6 **Hochreichart**, Austria
89 U 5 **Hochschwab**, Austria
90 F 4 **Hochwilde**, Austria/Italy
177 H 15 **Hodaka-dake**, Japan
192 I 7 **Hodh Ech Chargui**, Mauritania
192 I 7 **Hodh El Gharbi**, Mauritania
93 K 25 **Hódmezővásárhely**, Hungary
93 G 20 **Hodonín**, Czech Republic
171 O 3 **Hödrögö**, Mongolia
82 F 13 **Hoek van Holland**, Netherlands
83 K 18 **Hoensbroek**, Netherlands
171 Y 5 **Hoeryŏng**, North Korea
171 Y 6 **Hoeyang**, North Korea
87 K 18 **Hof**, Germany
84 D 11 **Höfn**, Iceland
84 C 11 **Hofsjökull**, Iceland
84 B 10 **Hofsós**, Iceland
177 C 20 **Hōfu**, Japan
189 O 14 **Hoggar**, Algeria
85 G 23 **Högsby**, Sweden
170 M 8 **Hoh Sai Hu**, China
89 O 7 **Hohe Tauern**, Austria
89 Y 2 **Hohenau an der March**, Austria
89 S 6 **Hoher Dachstein**, Austria
193 N 13 **Hohoe**, Ghana
101 Q 3 **Hoholiv**, Ukraine
173 O 17 **Hôi An**, Vietnam
172 L 13 **Hôi Xuân**, Vietnam
195 R 7 **Hoima**, Uganda
210 H 6 **Hokianga Harbour**, New Zealand
211 F 19 **Hokitika**, New Zealand
176 K 5 **Hokkaidō**, Japan
177 L 15 **Hokota**, Japan
159 T 9 **Hoktemberyan**, Armenia
195 X 9 **Hola**, Kenya
101 S 10 **Hola Prystan**, Ukraine
169 D 20 **Holalkere**, India
141 K 18 **Holanda**, Bolivia
116 L 13 **Holbrook**, Idaho, U.S.A.
117 O 21 **Holbrook**, Arizona, U.S.A.
117 M 17 **Holden**, Utah, U.S.A.
118 I 13 **Holdrege**, Nebraska, U.S.A.
126 M 5 **Holguín**, Cuba
93 G 20 **Holič**, Slovakia
85 E 18 **Höljes**, Sweden
89 X 2 **Hollabrunn**, Austria
120 K 8 **Holland**, Michigan, U.S.A.
83 G 14 **Hollands Diep**, Netherlands
83 K 24 **Hollange**, Belgium
82 J 5 **Hollum**, Netherlands
123 V 3 **Holly Ridge**, North Carolina, U.S.A.
122 I 3 **Holly Springs**, Mississippi, U.S.A.
123 T 14 **Hollywood**, Florida, U.S.A.
84 B 10 **Hólmavík**, Iceland
212 E 6 **Holnicote Bay**, Papua New Guinea
100 J 2 **Holoby**, Ukraine
160 F 9 **Ḩolon**, Israel
196 J 12 **Holoog**, Namibia
123 R 11 **Holopaw**, Florida, U.S.A.
85 B 24 **Holstebro**, Denmark
82 L 11 **Holten**, Netherlands
101 V 6 **Holubivka**, Ukraine
82 K 6 **Holwerd**, Netherlands
112 H 6 **Holy Cross**, Alaska, U.S.A.
76 J 13 **Holy Island**, United Kingdom
77 G 18 **Holyhead**, United Kingdom
118 G 13 **Holyoke**, Colorado, U.S.A.
121 V 8 **Holyoke**, Massachusetts, U.S.A.
87 J 25 **Holzkirchen**, Germany
87 G 15 **Holzminden**, Germany
195 T 8 **Homa Bay**, Kenya
172 C 9 **Homalin**, Myanmar
192 M 8 **Hombori**, Mali
192 L 8 **Hombori Toudo**, Mali
87 D 21 **Homburg**, Germany
115 R 1 **Home Bay**, Nunavut, Canada
59 Z 2 **Home Island**, Cocos Islands
59 Z 2 **Home Island Settlement**, Cocos Islands
99 L 20 **Homel'skaya Voblasts'**, Belarus
112 J 8 **Homer**, Alaska, U.S.A.
123 P 8 **Homerville**, Georgia, U.S.A.
123 S 14 **Homestead**, Florida, U.S.A.
84 F 12 **Hommelsto**, Norway
169 E 18 **Homnabad**, India
197 R 10 **Homoine**, Mozambique
99 N 20 **Homyel'**, Belarus
173 L 24 **Hon Khoai**, Vietnam
173 L 23 **Hon Rai**, Vietnam
138 I 6 **Honda**, Colombia
177 B 22 **Hondo**, Japan
126 F 9 **Honduras**, North America
85 D 19 **Hønefoss**, Norway
117 F 15 **Honey Lake**, California, U.S.A.
172 N 12 **Hông Gai**, Vietnam
171 U 14 **Hong Kong**, China
171 U 14 **Hong Kong**, China
171 S 12 **Hongjiang**, China
171 N 6 **Hongliuyuan**, China
171 S 4 **Hongor**, Mongolia
171 R 13 **Hongshui He**, China
177 H 19 **Hongū**, Japan
171 V 9 **Hongze Hu**, China
212 L 6 **Honiara**, Solomon Islands
176 J 11 **Honjō**, Japan
84 K 5 **Honningsvåg**, Norway
117 E 25 **Honokaa**, Hawaii, U.S.A.
117 D 25 **Honokohau**, Hawaii, U.S.A.
117 C 24 **Honolulu**, Hawaii, U.S.A.
177 H 17 **Honshū**, Japan
82 G 11 **Hoofddorp**, Netherlands
86 F 7 **Hooge**, Germany
82 M 8 **Hoogersmilde**, Netherlands
82 M 9 **Hoogeveen**, Netherlands
82 I 9 **Hoogkarspel**, Netherlands
77 E 20 **Hook Head**, Republic of Ireland
113 N 10 **Hoonah**, Alaska, U.S.A.
82 I 9 **Hoorn**, Netherlands
120 K 11 **Hoosier Hill**, Indiana, U.S.A.
171 P 4 **Höövör**, Mongolia
159 Q 7 **Hopa**, Turkey
113 S 14 **Hope**, British Columbia, Canada
119 M 18 **Hope**, Arkansas, U.S.A.
115 V 7 **Hopedale**, Newfoundland and Labrador, Canada
125 Y 11 **Hopelchén**, Mexico
208 I 12 **Hopetoun**, Western Australia, Australia
209 R 12 **Hopetoun**, Victoria, Australia
196 M 13 **Hopetown**, Republic of South Africa
172 E 8 **Hopin**, Myanmar
120 I 14 **Hopkinsville**, Kentucky, U.S.A.
172 E 12 **Hopong**, Myanmar
116 C 7 **Hoquiam**, Washington, U.S.A.
100 J 7 **Hora Hoverla**, Ukraine
159 R 9 **Horasan**, Turkey
81 N 8 **Horcajo de los Montes**, Spain
171 O 3 **Horgo**, Mongolia
101 N 12 **Horia**, Romania
61 P 10 **Horizon Deep**, Pacific Ocean
99 N 16 **Horki**, Belarus
219 N 8 **Horlick Mountains**, Antarctica
101 X 6 **Horlivka**, Ukraine
165 O 11 **Hormak**, Iran
164 L 13 **Hormoz**, Iran
164 L 12 **Hormozgān**, Iran
89 W 2 **Horn**, Austria
122 J 9 **Horn Island**, Mississippi, U.S.A.
209 R 1 **Horn Island**, Queensland, Australia
113 R 7 **Horn Mountains**, Northwest Territories, Canada
84 H 12 **Hornavan**, Sweden
121 R 9 **Hornell**, New York, U.S.A.
115 N 11 **Hornepayne**, Ontario, Canada
100 K 6 **Horodenka**, Ukraine
101 Q 1 **Horodnya**, Ukraine
101 Q 5 **Horodyshche**, Ukraine
176 J 3 **Horonobe**, Japan
176 K 6 **Horoshiri-dake**, Japan
210 K 10 **Horotiu**, New Zealand
171 W 5 **Horqin Zuoyi Houqi**, China
171 W 4 **Horqin Zuoyi Zhongqi**, China
169 L 17 **Horsburgh Atoll**, Maldives
59 Y 1 **Horsburgh Island**, Cocos Islands
85 C 25 **Horsens**, Denmark
116 I 11 **Horseshoe Bend**, Idaho, U.S.A.
62 J 9 **Horseshoe Seamounts**, Atlantic Ocean
77 L 22 **Horsham**, United Kingdom
209 R 13 **Horsham**, Victoria, Australia
83 L 16 **Horst**, Netherlands
62 N 1 **Horta**, Azores
113 Q 4 **Horton**, Northwest Territories, Canada
88 F 8 **Horw**, Switzerland
100 L 4 **Horyn**, Ukraine
191 I 21 **Hosa'ina**, Ethiopia
169 D 21 **Hosdrug**, India
193 U 12 **Hoséré Vokre**, Cameroon
165 R 14 **Hoshab**, Pakistan
169 E 15 **Hoshangabad**, India
168 E 9 **Hoshiarpur**, India
171 P 3 **Höshööt**, Mongolia
83 L 23 **Hosingen**, Luxembourg
212 G 4 **Hoskins**, Papua New Guinea

Country · Internal administrative region: State/Province/Territory/Dependent territory · Capital city · Mountain range/Undersea ridge · Mountain peak/Volcano/Seamount · Geographic feature · Headland/Point/Cape/Peninsula · Desert · Island/Island group · Antarctic base · Ocean · Sea · Bay/Gulf/Channel/Strait · Lake · Salt pan/Dry/Intermittent lake · Riv…

169 D 19 **Hospet**, India
118 G 11 **Hot Springs**, South Dakota, U.S.A.
119 M 18 **Hot Springs**, Arkansas, U.S.A.
85 F 14 **Hotagen**, Sweden
170 H 7 **Hotan**, China
85 G 14 **Hoting**, Sweden
63 H 15 **Hotspur Seamount**, Atlantic Ocean
113 S 6 **Hottah Lake**, Northwest Territories, Canada
213 P 13 **Houaïlu**, New Caledonia
83 K 23 **Houffalize**, Belgium
120 I 3 **Houghton**, Michigan, U.S.A.
120 L 6 **Houghton Lake**, Michigan, U.S.A.
210 I 4 **Houhora**, New Zealand
121 Z 4 **Houlton**, Maine, U.S.A.
119 O 21 **Houma**, Louisiana, U.S.A.
189 R 7 **Houmt Souk**, Tunisia
192 K 10 **Houndé**, Burkina Faso
210 N 10 **Houpoto**, New Zealand
113 Q 12 **Houston**, British Columbia, Canada
119 M 15 **Houston**, Missouri, U.S.A.
119 L 21 **Houston**, Texas, U.S.A.
122 J 4 **Houston**, Mississippi, U.S.A.
83 J 18 **Houthalen**, Belgium
208 E 9 **Houtman Abrolhos**, Western Australia, Australia
170 M 4 **Hovd**, Mongolia
170 M 3 **Hovd**, Mongolia
171 P 5 **Hovd**, Mongolia
171 O 2 **Hövsgöl**, Mongolia
171 P 2 **Hövsgöl Nuur**, Mongolia
120 L 8 **Howell**, Michigan, U.S.A.
118 H 10 **Howes**, South Dakota, U.S.A.
210 K 8 **Howick**, New Zealand
61 P 7 **Howland Island**, U.S.A.
113 U 13 **Howser**, British Columbia, Canada
87 G 15 **Höxter**, Germany
76 H 7 **Hoy**, United Kingdom
87 N 15 **Hoyerswerda**, Germany
80 J 7 **Hoyos**, Spain
85 O 15 **Höytiäinen**, Finland
93 E 17 **Hradec Králové**, Czech Republic
101 S 5 **Hradyz'k**, Ukraine
99 K 18 **Hradzyanka**, Belarus
94 H 12 **Hrasnica**, Bosnia and Herzegovina
159 U 8 **Hrazdan**, Armenia
101 R 4 **Hrebinka**, Ukraine
101 P 4 **Hrebinky**, Ukraine
99 E 18 **Hrodna**, Belarus
99 G 18 **Hrodzyenskaya Voblasts'**, Belarus
93 O 15 **Hrubieszów**, Poland
172 F 10 **Hsenwi**, Myanmar
172 E 13 **Hsi-hseng**, Myanmar
171 W 12 **Hsinchu**, Taiwan
173 H 20 **Hua Hin**, Thailand
141 C 16 **Huacho**, Peru
141 C 14 **Huacrachuco**, Peru
171 T 6 **Huade**, China
171 X 4 **Huadian**, China
215 S 9 **Huahine**, French Polynesia
171 T 6 **Huai'an**, China
171 S 12 **Huaihua**, China
171 V 9 **Huainan**, China
171 V 9 **Huaiyin**, China
125 S 13 **Huajuápan de León**, Mexico
117 K 21 **Hualapai Peak**, Arizona, U.S.A.
171 X 13 **Hualien**, Taiwan
141 D 14 **Huallaga**, Peru
140 C 13 **Huamachuco**, Peru
196 G 4 **Huambo**, Angola
196 H 4 **Huambo**, Angola
141 E 17 **Huancavelica**, Peru
141 E 17 **Huancavelica**, Peru
141 E 16 **Huancayo**, Peru
171 V 10 **Huangshan**, China
171 U 10 **Huangshi**, China
145 K 14 **Huanguelén**, Argentina
141 E 17 **Huanta**, Peru
141 D 15 **Huánuco**, Peru
141 D 15 **Huánuco**, Peru
141 J 20 **Huanuni**, Bolivia
141 C 15 **Huaráz**, Peru
141 C 15 **Huari**, Peru
141 C 15 **Huarmey**, Peru
144 F 9 **Huasco**, Chile
171 N 8 **Huashixia**, China
124 J 6 **Huatabampo**, Mexico
141 C 14 **Huaylas**, Peru
114 K 5 **Hubbart Point**, Manitoba, Canada
171 T 10 **Hubei**, China
169 D 19 **Hubli**, India
77 J 17 **Huddersfield**, United Kingdom
85 H 17 **Hudiksvall**, Sweden
121 U 8 **Hudson**, New York, U.S.A.
115 N 5 **Hudson Bay**, Québec, Canada
121 V 7 **Hudson Falls**, New York, U.S.A.
115 Q 4 **Hudson Strait**, Nunavut, Canada
173 N 16 **Huê**, Vietnam
100 H 9 **Huedin**, Romania
126 C 9 **Huehuetenango**, Guatemala
125 R 12 **Huejotzingo**, Mexico
125 N 9 **Huejuqilla**, Mexico
125 R 10 **Huejutla**, Mexico
81 O 11 **Huelma**, Spain
80 J 12 **Huelva**, Spain
144 F 11 **Huentelauquén**, Chile
81 Q 12 **Huércal-Overa**, Spain
81 T 3 **Huesca**, Spain
81 Q 11 **Huéscar**, Spain
125 P 12 **Huétamo**, Mexico
209 S 5 **Hughenden**, Queensland, Australia
119 L 18 **Hugo**, Oklahoma, U.S.A.
119 H 16 **Hugoton**, Kansas, U.S.A.
171 S 6 **Huhhot**, China
210 M 12 **Huiarau Range**, New Zealand
138 H 8 **Huila**, Colombia
196 G 5 **Huila**, Angola
196 H 6 **Huila Plateau**, Angola
171 P 12 **Huili**, China
144 I 5 **Huinahuaca**, Argentina
144 J 12 **Huinca Renancó**, Argentina
171 R 12 **Huishui**, China
85 K 18 **Huittinen**, Finland
125 W 15 **Huixtla**, Mexico
171 P 12 **Huize**, China
82 I 11 **Huizen**, Netherlands
171 Q 4 **Hujirt**, Mongolia
172 D 6 **Hukawng Valley**, Myanmar
196 K 10 **Hukuntsi**, Botswana
162 M 5 **Ḩulayfah**, Saudi Arabia
169 D 21 **Huliyar**, India
83 E 17 **Hulst**, Netherlands
171 U 3 **Hulun Nur**, China
101 W 7 **Hulyaypole**, Ukraine
171 W 1 **Huma**, China
127 U 7 **Humacao**, Puerto Rico
142 E 12 **Humaitá**, Brazil
77 L 17 **Humber**, United Kingdom
122 J 2 **Humboldt**, Tennessee, U.S.A.
93 M 19 **Humenné**, Slovakia
82 L 13 **Hummelo**, Netherlands
196 F 6 **Humpata**, Angola
116 L 10 **Humphrey**, Idaho, U.S.A.
117 M 21 **Humphreys Peak**, Arizona, U.S.A.
208 M 1 **Humpty Doo**, Northern Territory, Australia
189 U 9 **Hūn**, Libya
84 B 10 **Húnaflói**, Iceland
171 T 12 **Hunan**, China
100 G 10 **Hunedoara**, Romania
87 G 18 **Hünfeld**, Germany
93 H 24 **Hungary**, Europe
209 S 9 **Hungerford**, Queensland, Australia
171 X 6 **Hŭngnam**, North Korea
87 C 20 **Hunsrück**, Germany
213 T 14 **Hunter**, Pacific Ocean
209 S 14 **Hunter Island**, Tasmania, Australia
120 J 13 **Huntingburg**, Indiana, U.S.A.
120 K 10 **Huntington**, Indiana, U.S.A.
117 G 23 **Huntington Beach**, California, U.S.A.
76 I 10 **Huntly**, United Kingdom
115 P 13 **Huntsville**, Ontario, Canada
119 L 21 **Huntsville**, Texas, U.S.A.
122 L 3 **Huntsville**, Alabama, U.S.A.
213 N 12 **Huon**, New Caledonia
173 M 15 **Huong Khê**, Vietnam
209 S 15 **Huonville**, Tasmania, Australia
93 H 22 **Hurbanovo**, Slovakia
191 O 19 **Hurdiyo**, Somalia
190 F 10 **Hurghada**, Egypt
118 J 10 **Huron**, South Dakota, U.S.A.
123 N 6 **Hurtsboro**, Alabama, U.S.A.
84 C 10 **Húsavík**, Iceland
161 U 7 **Ḩusayn al Ghafūs**, Iraq
100 M 9 **Huşi**, Romania
85 F 22 **Huskvarna**, Sweden
112 J 4 **Huslia**, Alaska, U.S.A.
163 Q 12 **Ḩusn Al 'Abr**, Yemen
86 F 8 **Husum**, Germany
171 P 3 **Hutag**, Mongolia
119 J 15 **Hutchinson**, Kansas, U.S.A.
163 P 12 **Ḩūth**, Yemen
212 I 4 **Hutjena**, Papua New Guinea
88 E 7 **Huttwil**, Switzerland
83 I 21 **Huy**, Belgium
170 L 2 **Huyten Orgil**, Mongolia
171 V 10 **Huzhou**, China
84 C 11 **Hvannadalshnúkur**, Iceland
95 E 14 **Hvar**, Croatia
95 F 14 **Hvar**, Croatia
101 T 12 **Hvardiys'ke**, Ukraine
84 B 11 **Hveragerði**, Iceland
84 B 11 **Hvíta**, Iceland
197 N 7 **Hwange**, Zimbabwe
118 H 12 **Hyannis**, Nebraska, U.S.A.
171 N 3 **Hyargas Nuur**, Mongolia
208 H 11 **Hyden**, Western Australia, Australia
165 U 14 **Hyderabad**, Pakistan
169 F 18 **Hyderabad**, India
79 V 15 **Hyères**, France
171 Y 5 **Hyesan**, North Korea
177 D 22 **Hyūga**, Japan

I

189 O 15 **I-n-Guezzam**, Algeria
193 O 7 **I-n-Tebezas**, Mali
143 M 15 **Iaçu**, Brazil
101 N 9 **Ialoveni**, Moldova
100 M 9 **Iaşi**, Romania
142 B 9 **Iauaretê**, Brazil
175 N 3 **Iba**, Philippines
193 P 12 **Ibadan**, Nigeria
138 I 7 **Ibagué**, Colombia
95 L 15 **Ibar**, Serbia and Montenegro
140 C 8 **Ibarra**, Ecuador
144 L 6 **Ibarreta**, Argentina
163 P 13 **Ibb**, Yemen
191 D 23 **Ibba**, Sudan
86 D 13 **Ibbenbüren**, Germany
140 E 12 **Iberia**, Peru
84 H 8 **Ibestad**, Norway
193 Q 11 **Ibeto**, Nigeria
81 T 10 **Ibi**, Spain
193 S 12 **Ibi**, Nigeria
81 W 9 **Ibiza**, Spain
143 L 14 **Ibotirama**, Brazil
163 Z 7 **Ibrā'**, Oman
163 X 7 **Ibrī**, Oman
141 D 18 **Ica**, Peru
141 D 18 **Ica**, Peru
142 B 10 **Içá**, Brazil
142 C 9 **Içana**, Brazil
142 C 9 **Içana**, Brazil
84 C 10 **Iceland**, Europe
62 I 6 **Iceland Basin**, Atlantic Ocean
65 Q 14 **Icelandic Plateau**, Arctic Ocean
169 D 19 **Ichalkaranji**, India
177 L 16 **Ichihara**, Japan
176 K 11 **Ichinoseki**, Japan
101 R 3 **Ichnya**, Ukraine
83 B 17 **Ichtegem**, Belgium
142 N 12 **Icó**, Brazil
62 M 11 **Icod de Los Vinos**, Canary Islands
112 J 2 **Icy Cape**, Alaska, U.S.A.
191 O 22 **Idaan**, Somalia
119 L 18 **Idabel**, Oklahoma, U.S.A.
211 E 23 **Idaburn**, New Zealand
193 Q 13 **Idah**, Nigeria
116 J10 **Idaho**, U.S.A.
116 M 12 **Idaho Falls**, Idaho, U.S.A.
87 D 20 **Idar-Oberstein**, Germany
191 A 19 **Idd el Chanam**, Sudan
189 O 13 **Idelès**, Algeria
190 F 11 **Idfu**, Egypt
189 R 10 **Idhān Awbārī**, Libya
189 S 12 **Idhān Murzūq**, Libya
194 K 11 **Idiofa**, Democratic Republic of Congo
160 I 2 **Idlib**, Syria
177 N 24 **Ie-jima**, Japan
98 F 12 **Iecava**, Latvia
83 B 19 **Ieper**, Belgium
97 K 26 **Ierapetra**, Greece
100 I 9 **Iernut**, Romania
195 V 12 **Ifakara**, Tanzania
214 M 15 **Ifalik**, Federated States of Micronesia
197 Y 9 **Ifanadiana**, Madgascar
193 P 13 **Ife**, Nigeria
193 R 6 **Iferouâne**, Niger
189 N 12 **Ifetesene**, Algeria
93 H 25 **Igal**, Hungary
195 T 7 **Iganga**, Uganda
157 N 9 **Igarka**, Russian Federation
193 P 12 **Igboho**, Nigeria
159 T 9 **Iğdir**, Turkey
91 B 19 **Iglesias**, Italy
115 O 1 **Igloolik**, Nunavut, Canada
114 M 3 **Igluligaarjuk**, Nunavut, Canada
114 K 11 **Ignace**, Ontario, Canada
99 H 14 **Ignalina**, Lithuania
96 N 11 **Iğneada**, Turkey
158 C 6 **Iğneada**, Turkey
158 C 6 **Iğneada Burnu**, Turkey
169 N 22 **Ignoitijala**, India
97 A 16 **Igoumenitsa**, Greece
156 I 9 **Igra**, Russian Federation
156 K 9 **Igrim**, Russian Federation
143 H 20 **Iguaçu Falls**, Brazil
125 R 13 **Iguala**, Mexico
142 N 12 **Iguatu**, Brazil
194 D 9 **Iguéla**, Gabon
195 T 10 **Igunga**, Tanzania
197 Z 5 **Iharana**, Madgascar
169 L 16 **Ihavandhippolhu Atoll**, Maldives
171 R 5 **Ihbulag**, Mongolia
177 N 24 **Iheya-jima**, Japan
193 R 13 **Ihiala**, Nigeria
197 X 9 **Ihosy**, Madgascar
171 Q 3 **Ihsuuj**, Mongolia
177 I 17 **Iida**, Japan
84 L 12 **Iijoki**, Finland
85 M 15 **Iisalmi**, Finland
177 B 21 **Iizuka**, Japan
193 P 13 **Ijebu-Ode**, Nigeria
159 U 8 **Ijevan**, Armenia
82 G 10 **IJmuiden**, Netherlands
82 L 10 **IJssel**, Netherlands
82 I 8 **IJsselmeer**, Netherlands
143 H 21 **Ijuí**, Brazil
215 V 1 **Ijuw**, Nauru
83 B 17 **IJzer**, Belgium
113 Q 2 **Ikaahuk**, Northwest Territories, Canada
211 G 18 **Ikamatua**, New Zealand
193 Q 12 **Ikare**, Nigeria
97 K 21 **Ikaria**, Greece
211 F 23 **Ikawai**, New Zealand
176 L 5 **Ikeda**, Japan
177 F 20 **Ikeda**, Japan
194 M 8 **Ikela**, Democratic Republic of Congo
96 G 9 **Ikhtiman**, Bulgaria
177 A 21 **Iki**, Japan
177 A 21 **Iki-suidō**, Japan
193 P 13 **Ikire**, Nigeria
193 S 13 **Ikom**, Nigeria
197 X 9 **Ikongo**, Madgascar
193 P 13 **Ikorodu**, Nigeria
193 P 12 **Ila**, Nigeria
175 O 2 **Ilagan**, Philippines
195 V 7 **Ilaisamis**, Kenya
164 F 7 **Īlām**, Iran
164 F 7 **Īlām**, Iran
168 K 12 **Ilam**, Nepal
171 X 12 **Ilan**, Taiwan
101 V 6 **Ilarionove**, Ukraine
92 J 10 **Iława**, Poland
167 U 8 **Ile**, Kazakhstan
58 B 8 **Île Aride**, Seychelles
58 A 9 **Île au Cerf**, Seychelles
58 C 12 **Île aux Cerfs**, Mauritius
58 B 9 **Île aux Récifs**, Seychelles
58 D 7 **Île aux Sables**, Rodrigues Island
213 O 13 **Île Balabio**, New Caledonia
58 E 7 **Île Cocos**, Rodrigues Island
58 A 9 **Île Conception**, Seychelles
58 B 11 **Île d'Ambre**, Mauritius
115 U 10 **Île d'Anticosti**, Québec, Canada
79 P 5 **Île-de-France**, France
189 R 7 **Île de Jarba**, Tunisia
127 O 7 **Île de la Gonâve**, Haiti
127 P 6 **Île de la Tortue**, Haiti
78 K 8 **Île de Noirmoutier**, France
79 V 15 **Île de Porquerolles**, France
78 K 9 **Île de Ré**, France
213 Q 14 **Île des Pins**, New Caledonia
78 L 9 **Île d'Oléron**, France
78 G 5 **Île d'Ouessant**, France
78 J 8 **Île d'Yeu**, France
197 U 9 **Île Europa**, France
58 A 10 **Île Thérèse**, Seychelles
58 K 6 **Île Tromelin**, Indian Ocean
213 R 14 **Île Walpole**, New Caledonia
194 K 10 **Ilebo**, Democratic Republic of Congo
166 J 4 **Ilek**, Kazakhstan
195 U 5 **Ileret**, Kenya
213 O 13 **Îles Bélep**, New Caledonia
78 K 4 **Îles Chausey**, France
212 L 12 **Îles Chesterfield**, New Caledonia
78 H 6 **Îles de Glénan**, France
79 W 15 **Îles de Hyères**, France
115 W 11 **Îles de la Madeleine**, Québec, Canada
215 S 10 **Îles du Vent**, French Polynesia
197 Y 4 **Îles Glorieuses**, Seychelles
189 R 6 **Îles Kerkenah**, Tunisia
215 Q 11 **Îles Maria**, French Polynesia
215 U 8 **Îles Palliser**, French Polynesia
215 Q 9 **Îles Sous le Vent**, French Polynesia
193 P 12 **Ilesa**, Nigeria
77 M 21 **Ilford**, United Kingdom
77 H 22 **Ilfracombe**, United Kingdom
158 I 8 **Ilgaz**, Turkey
158 I 8 **Ilgaz Dağlari**, Turkey
158 G 11 **Ilgin**, Turkey
142 J 9 **Ilha Caviana**, Brazil
142 J 9 **Ilha Curuá**, Brazil
62 O 5 **Ilha da Madeira**, Madeira
63 I 16 **Ilha da Trindade**, Brazil
142 J 8 **Ilha de Maracá**, Brazil
142 J 9 **Ilha de Marajó**, Brazil
62 O 4 **Ilha de Porto Santo**, Madeira
143 J 21 **Ilha de Santa Catarina**, Brazil
143 J 20 **Ilha de São Francisco**, Brazil
143 K 19 **Ilha de São Sebastião**, Brazil
197 R 8 **Ilha do Bazaruto**, Mozambique
142 J 9 **Ilha Janaucu**, Brazil
142 J 9 **Ilha Mexiana**, Brazil
62 O 5 **Ilhas Desertas**, Madeira
63 I 16 **Ilhas Martin Vas**, Atlantic Ocean
143 N 15 **Ilhéus**, Brazil
100 G 10 **Ilia**, Romania
112 I 8 **Iliamna Lake**, Alaska, U.S.A.
159 N 10 **Ilic**, Turkey
175 Q 7 **Iligan**, Philippines
175 R 15 **Iliomar**, East Timor
159 R 12 **Ilisu Baraji**, Turkey
144 F 10 **Illapel**, Chile
87 H 24 **Illertissen**, Germany
101 Q 10 **Illichivs'k**, Ukraine
120 G 11 **Illinois**, U.S.A.
120 G 11 **Illinois**, Illinois, U.S.A.
101 O 6 **Illintsi**, Ukraine
189 Q 11 **Illizi**, Algeria
87 I 18 **Ilmenau**, Germany
141 G 20 **Ilo**, Peru
175 P 5 **Iloilo**, Philippines
193 P 12 **Ilorin**, Nigeria
94 B 11 **Ilovik**, Croatia
93 E 14 **Iłowa**, Poland
157 Y 9 **Il'pyrskiy**, Russian Federation
78 I 6 **Îls de Groix**, France
98 H 13 **Ilūkste**, Latvia
65 N 12 **Ilulissat**, Greenland
99 I 16 **Il'ya**, Belarus
177 D 20 **Imabari**, Japan
176 J 8 **Imabetsu**, Japan
161 U 9 **Imām al Ḩamzah**, Iraq
161 U 7 **Imām Ḩamīd**, Iraq
158 K 13 **Imamoğlu**, Turkey
177 B 21 **Imari**, Japan
62 F 6 **Imarssuak Seachannel**, Atlantic Ocean
141 G 19 **Imata**, Peru
85 O 18 **Imatra**, Finland
140 B 8 **Imbabura**, Ecuador
191 K 22 **Īmī**, Ethiopia
188 G 8 **Imi-n-Tanoute**, Morocco
159 X 9 **Imişli**, Azerbaijan
117 H 15 **Imlay**, Nevada, U.S.A.
188 B 12 **Imlili**, Western Sahara
87 H 26 **Immenstadt**, Germany
123 R 13 **Immokalee**, Florida, U.S.A.
193 R 13 **Imo**, Nigeria
90 G 9 **Imola**, Italy
212 A 3 **Imonda**, Papua New Guinea
142 K 11 **Imperatriz**, Brazil
90 B 10 **Imperia**, Italy
118 H 13 **Imperial**, Nebraska, U.S.A.
141 D 17 **Imperial**, Peru
194 J 7 **Impfondo**, Congo
168 O 13 **Imphal**, India
158 D 8 **Imrali**, Turkey
158 A 8 **Imroz**, Turkey
88 L 7 **Imst**, Austria
160 I 8 **Imtān**, Syria
124 I 3 **Imuris**, Mexico
189 Q 10 **In Aménas**, Algeria
189 O 13 **In Amguel**, Algeria
189 O 13 **In Ekker**, Algeria
188 M 11 **In Salah**, Algeria
177 I 16 **Ina**, Japan
63 N 16 **Inaccessible Island**, Tristan da Cunha
211 G 17 **Inangahua Junction**, New Zealand
175 U 12 **Inanwatan**, Indonesia
141 H 16 **Iñapari**, Peru
84 L 8 **Inari**, Finland
157 Q 10 **Inarigda**, Russian Federation
84 M 8 **Inarijärvi**, Finland
176 J 13 **Inawashiro-ko**, Japan
144 G 7 **Inca de Oro**, Chile
158 J 6 **Ince Burun**, Turkey
158 I 14 **Incekum Burnu**, Turkey
192 F 5 **Inchiri**, Mauritania
171 X 7 **Inch'ŏn**, South Korea
83 H 20 **Incourt**, Belgium
98 F 11 **Inčukalns**, Latvia
191 I 17 **Inda Silasē**, Ethiopia
85 F 15 **Indalsälven**, Sweden
172 E 12 **Indaw**, Myanmar
119 K 16 **Independence**, Kansas, U.S.A.
119 L 14 **Independence**, Missouri, U.S.A.
65 R 10 **Independence Fjord**, Greenland
166 I 6 **Inderborskiy**, Kazakhstan
168 D 13 **India**, Asia
115 W 7 **Indian Harbour**, Newfoundland and Labrador, Canada
59 P 7 **Indian Ocean**,
117 J 19 **Indian Springs**, Nevada, U.S.A.
117 O 21 **Indian Wells**, Arizona, U.S.A.
120 J 11 **Indiana**, U.S.A.
121 Q 10 **Indiana**, Pennsylvania, U.S.A.
120 K 11 **Indianapolis**, Indiana, U.S.A.
122 H 5 **Indianola**, Mississippi, U.S.A.
59 U 14 **Indian–Antarctic Basin**, Indian Ocean
59 U 12 **Indian–Antarctic Ridge**, Indian Ocean
157 U 7 **Indigirka**, Russian Federation
117 I 23 **Indio**, California, U.S.A.
212 M 6 **Indispensable Strait**, Solomon Islands
173 M 19 **Indochina Peninsula**, Cambodia
174 H 13 **Indonesia**, Asia
169 D 15 **Indore**, India
169 G 17 **Indravati**, India
99 E 18 **Indura**, Belarus
165 W 9 **Indus**, India/Pakistan
158 I 6 **Inebolu**, Turkey
158 E 9 **Inegöl**, Turkey
80 M 1 **Infiesto**, Spain
193 Q 7 **Ingal**, Niger
194 J 8 **Ingende**, Democratic Republic of Congo
144 K 5 **Ingeniero Guillermo Neuva Juárez**, Argentina
145 G 17 **Ingeniero Jacobacci**, Argentina
209 T 4 **Ingham**, Queensland, Australia
210 J 12 **Inglewood**, New Zealand
87 J 22 **Ingolstadt**, Germany

Country · Internal administrative region: State/Province/Territory/Dependent territory · Capital city · Mountain range/Undersea ridge · Mountain peak/Volcano/Seamount · Geographic feature · Headland/Point/Cape/Peninsula · Desert · Island/Island group · Antarctic base · Ocean · Sea · Bay/Gulf/Channel/Strait · Lake · Salt pan/Dry/Intermittent lake · River

219 W 6 **Ingrid Christensen Coast**, Antarctica
197 Q 9 **Inhambane**, Mozambique
197 R 10 **Inhambane**, Mozambique
197 R 7 **Inhaminga**, Mozambique
197 R 10 **Inharrime**, Mozambique
101 R 8 **Inhul**, Ukraine
101 S 8 **Inhulets**, Ukraine
77 A 17 **Inishbofin**, Republic of Ireland
77 B 18 **Inisheer**, Republic of Ireland
77 B 18 **Inishmore**, Republic of Ireland
77 A 17 **Inishturk**, Republic of Ireland
191 H 19 **Injibara**, Ethiopia
209 U 8 **Injune**, Queensland, Australia
116 L 12 **Inkom**, Idaho, U.S.A.
211 I 18 **Inland Kaikoura Range**, New Zealand
123 Q 3 **Inman**, South Carolina, U.S.A.
87 K 24 **Inn**, Germany
209 Q 8 **Innamincka**, South Australia, Australia
76 E 13 **Inner Hebrides**, United Kingdom
58 B 9 **Inner Islands**, Seychelles
171 S 5 **Inner Mongolia**, China
88 F 9 **Innerkirchen**, Switzerland
209 T 4 **Innisfail**, Queensland, Australia
88 M 7 **Innsbruck**, Austria
194 J 9 **Inongo**, Democratic Republic of Congo
92 H 11 **Inowrocław**, Poland
141 J 20 **Inquisivi**, Bolivia
88 C 7 **Ins**, Switzerland
100 M 12 **Insurăţei**, Romania
156 K 8 **Inta**, Russian Federation
88 E 9 **Interlaken**, Switzerland
118 L 7 **International Falls**, Minnesota, U.S.A.
169 N 21 **Interview Island**, India
144 L 9 **Intiyaco**, Argentina
100 K 11 **Întorsura Buzăului**, Romania
140 E 10 **Intutu**, Peru
177 L 15 **Inubō-zaki**, Japan
115 P 6 **Inukjuak**, Québec, Canada
113 O 4 **Inuvik**, Northwest Territories, Canada
76 G 12 **Inveraray**, United Kingdom
211 C 25 **Invercargill**, New Zealand
209 V 10 **Inverell**, New South Wales, Australia
76 H 10 **Inverness**, United Kingdom
123 Q 10 **Inverness**, Florida, U.S.A.
59 R 4 **Investigator Ridge**, Indian Ocean
156 M 13 **Inya**, Russian Federation
197 Q 7 **Inyangani**, Zimbabwe
195 S 12 **Inyonga**, Tanzania
177 C 25 **Iō-jima**, Japan
177 N 23 **Iō-Tori-jima**, Japan
97 B 16 **Ioannina**, Greece
119 K 15 **Iola**, Kansas, U.S.A.
76 E 12 **Iona**, United Kingdom
196 G 6 **Iona**, Angola
100 I 12 **Ioneşti**, Romania
97 A 17 **Ionian Islands**, Greece
97 C 21 **Ionian Sea**, Greece/Italy
97 B 17 **Ionioi Nisoi**, Greece
97 J 23 **Ios**, Greece
118 L 12 **Iowa**, U.S.A.
118 M 12 **Iowa City**, Iowa, U.S.A.
118 L 11 **Iowa Falls**, Iowa, U.S.A.
143 L 17 **Ipatinga**, Brazil
97 B 16 **Ipeiros**, Greece
93 I 21 **Ipel**, Slovakia
138 G 9 **Ipiales**, Colombia
143 I 19 **Ipiranga**, Brazil
142 A 13 **Ipixuna**, Brazil
174 E 8 **Ipoh**, Malaysia
194 L 4 **Ippy**, Central African Republic
158 B 7 **Ipsala**, Turkey
77 N 20 **Ipswich**, United Kingdom
209 W 9 **Ipswich**, Queensland, Australia
142 M 11 **Ipu**, Brazil
115 R 3 **Iqaluit**, Nunavut, Canada
171 N 7 **Iqe**, China
141 F 19 **Iquipi**, Peru
144 F 3 **Iquique**, Chile
140 F 11 **Iquitos**, Peru
194 L 4 **Ira Banda**, Central African Republic
177 N 26 **Irabu-jima**, Japan
177 I 18 **Irago-misaki**, Japan
97 J 23 **Irakleia**, Greece
96 F 13 **Irakleia**, Greece
97 J 26 **Irakleiou**, Greece
143 M 15 **Iramaia**, Brazil
164 K 7 **Iran**, Asia
164 K 9 **Iranian Plateau**, Iran
165 O 13 **Īrānshahr**, Iran
125 P 11 **Irapuato**, Mexico
161 R 8 **Iraq**, Asia
98 C 9 **Irbe Strait**, Estonia/Latvia
160 H 8 **Irbid**, Jordan
143 M 14 **Irecê**, Brazil
62 A 7 **Ireland Island**, Bermuda
167 N 6 **Irgiz**, Kazakhstan
188 H 8 **Irhil M'Goun**, Morocco
164 F 4 **Īrī Dāgh**, Iran
175 W 12 **Irian Jaya**, Indonesia
193 Z 8 **Iriba**, Chad
195 U 12 **Iringa**, Tanzania
195 U 12 **Iringa**, Tanzania
177 M 26 **Iriomote-jima**, Japan
142 H 11 **Iriri**, Brazil
77 G 17 **Irish Sea**, Republic of Ireland/United Kingdom
142 K 10 **Irituia**, Brazil
157 P 14 **Irkutsk**, Russian Federation
167 N 10 **Irlir Toghi**, Uzbekistan
158 I 9 **Irmak**, Turkey
62 H 5 **Irminger Basin**, Atlantic Ocean
177 J 18 **Irō-zaki**, Japan
121 N 13 **Ironton**, Ohio, U.S.A.
120 H 4 **Ironwood**, Michigan, U.S.A.
101 P 3 **Irpin'**, Ukraine
163 R 14 **Īrqah**, Yemen
173 C 17 **Irrawaddy**, Myanmar
172 C 13 **Irrawaddy**, Myanmar
101 N 3 **Irsha**, Ukraine
156 K 10 **Irtysh**, Russian Federation
167 U 2 **Irtyshsk**, Kazakhstan
177 K 16 **Iruma**, Japan
141 I 19 **Irupana**, Bolivia
119 K 19 **Irving**, Texas, U.S.A.
120 J 14 **Irvington**, Kentucky, U.S.A.
211 G 20 **Irwell**, New Zealand
193 Q 9 **Isa**, Nigeria
212 L 5 **Isabel**, Solomon Islands
175 O 7 **Isabela**, Philippines
101 N 11 **Isaccea**, Romania
84 A 10 **Ísafjörður**, Iceland
177 B 22 **Isahaya**, Japan
194 L 8 **Isanga**, Democratic Republic of Congo
193 Q 12 **Isanlu**, Nigeria
88 K 8 **Ischgl**, Austria
91 J 16 **Ischia**, Italy
177 H 18 **Ise**, Japan
177 H 18 **Ise-wan**, Japan
61 Q 15 **Iselin Seamount**, Pacific Ocean
195 N 7 **Isengi**, Democratic Republic of Congo
91 J 14 **Isernia**, Italy
193 P 12 **Iseyin**, Nigeria
167 R 12 **Isfana**, Kyrgyzstan
161 U 9 **Ishaq**, Iraq
177 N 26 **Ishigaki**, Japan
177 N 26 **Ishigaki-jima**, Japan
176 J 5 **Ishikari-wan**, Japan
177 N 24 **Ishikawa**, Japan
156 K 11 **Ishim**, Russian Federation
176 L 12 **Ishinomaki**, Japan
177 E 20 **Ishizuchi-san**, Japan
167 Q 12 **Ishtykhan**, Uzbekistan
156 K 11 **Isil'kul'**, Russian Federation
195 V 7 **Isiolo**, Kenya
195 P 6 **Isiro**, Democratic Republic of Congo
209 S 7 **Isisford**, Queensland, Australia
158 L 13 **Iskenderun**, Turkey
158 K 13 **Iskenderun Körfezi**, Turkey
158 J 8 **Iskilip**, Turkey
96 H 7 **Iskŭr**, Bulgaria
191 O 19 **Iskushuban**, Somalia
61 W 2 **Isla Alejandro Selkirk**, Juan Fernández Islands
124 H 4 **Isla Ángel de la Guarda**, Mexico
145 G 25 **Isla Aracena**, Chile
141 B 18 **Isla Baltra**, Ecuador
127 Q 8 **Isla Beata**, Dominican Republic
139 P 1 **Isla Blanquilla**, Venezuela
145 E 21 **Isla Campana**, Chile
124 I 7 **Isla Carmen**, Mexico
126 J 15 **Isla Cébaco**, Panama
124 F 5 **Isla Cedros**, Mexico
124 J 8 **Isla Cerralvo**, Mexico
145 F 23 **Isla Chatham**, Chile
145 G 25 **Isla Clarence**, Chile
139 Q 2 **Isla Coche**, Venezuela
126 I 15 **Isla Coiba**, Panama
145 F 24 **Isla Contreras**, Chile
125 W 12 **Isla de Aguada**, Mexico
81 P 15 **Isla de Alborán**, Spain
124 K 8 **Isla de Altamura**, Mexico
193 R 15 **Isla de Bioco**, Equatorial Guinea
145 E 18 **Isla de Chiloé**, Chile
125 Z 11 **Isla de Cozumel**, Mexico
126 G 8 **Isla de Guanaja**, Honduras
126 I 5 **Isla de la Juventud**, Cuba
145 J 26 **Isla de los Estados**, Argentina
139 Q 2 **Isla de Margarita**, Venezuela
126 G 12 **Isla de Ometepe**, Nicaragua
126 F 8 **Isla de Roatán**, Honduras
126 F 8 **Isla de Utila**, Honduras
126 L 14 **Isla del Rey**, Panama
145 F 25 **Isla Desolación**, Chile
145 E 23 **Isla Duque de York**, Chile
145 E 22 **Isla Esmeralda**, Chile
141 C 19 **Isla Española**, Ecuador
124 J 8 **Isla Espíritu Santo**, Mexico
141 A 19 **Isla Fernandina**, Ecuador
141 C 18 **Isla Genovesa**, Ecuador
145 H 26 **Isla Gordon**, Chile
145 H 25 **Isla Grande de Tierra del Fuego**, Chile
124 E 4 **Isla Guadalupe**, Mexico
145 E 18 **Isla Guafo**, Chile
145 E 19 **Isla Guamblin**, Chile
145 F 23 **Isla Hanover**, Chile
145 H 26 **Isla Hoste**, Chile
141 A 19 **Isla Isabela**, Ecuador
145 F 19 **Isla James**, Chile
145 F 21 **Isla Javier**, Chile
145 F 23 **Isla Jorge Montt**, Chile
139 P 2 **Isla La Tortuga**, Venezuela
145 I 26 **Isla Lennox**, Chile
145 G 26 **Isla Londonderry**, Chile
145 E 23 **Isla Madre de Dios**, Chile
145 F 19 **Isla Magdalena**, Chile
141 A 18 **Isla Marchena**, Ecuador
124 L 10 **Isla Maria Cleofas**, Mexico
124 L 10 **Isla María Madre**, Mexico
124 L 10 **Isla María Magdelena**, Mexico
145 F 19 **Isla Melchor**, Chile
145 E 15 **Isla Mocha**, Chile
127 S 7 **Isla Mona**, Puerto Rico
145 E 22 **Isla Mornington**, Chile
145 H 26 **Isla Navarino**, Chile
145 I 26 **Isla Nueva**, Chile
139 O 2 **Isla Orchila**, Venezuela
145 E 22 **Isla Patricio Lynch**, Chile
145 I 26 **Isla Picton**, Chile
141 B 17 **Isla Pinta**, Ecuador
145 E 21 **Isla Prat**, Chile
140 A 10 **Isla Puná**, Ecuador
145 G 24 **Isla Riesco**, Chile
61 Z 2 **Isla Robinson Crusoe**, Juan Fernández Islands
61 Z 10 **Isla San Ambrosio**, Pacific Ocean
141 C 19 **Isla San Cristóbal**, Ecuador
124 H 5 **Isla San Esteban**, Mexico
61 Y 10 **Isla San Felix**, Pacific Ocean
124 I 7 **Isla San José**, Mexico
126 K 14 **Isla San José de las Perlas**, Panama
124 L 10 **Isla San Juanito**, Mexico
124 H 4 **Isla San Lorenzo**, Mexico
141 B 18 **Isla San Salvador**, Ecuador
124 I 7 **Isla Santa Catalina**, Mexico
61 Y 2 **Isla Santa Clara**, Juan Fernández Islands
141 B 18 **Isla Santa Cruz**, Ecuador
141 B 19 **Isla Santa Fé**, Ecuador
145 G 25 **Isla Santa Inés**, Chile
124 H 8 **Isla Santa Margarita**, Mexico
141 B 19 **Isla Santa Maria**, Ecuador
127 S 7 **Isla Saona**, Dominican Republic
145 G 26 **Isla Stewart**, Chile
124 H 4 **Isla Tiburón**, Mexico
145 F 20 **Isla Victoria**, Chile
145 F 24 **Isla Vidal**, Chile
145 F 22 **Isla Wellington**, Chile
158 L 13 **Islahiye**, Turkey
165 Y 8 **Islamabad**, Pakistan
123 S 15 **Islamorada**, Florida, U.S.A.
114 J 8 **Island Lake**, Manitoba, Canada
114 J 8 **Island Lake**, Manitoba, Canada
112 C 9 **Islands of The Four Mountains**, Alaska, U.S.A.
81 V 7 **Islas Columbretes**, Spain
126 F 8 **Islas de la Bahía**, Honduras
126 I 11 **Islas del Maíz**, Nicaragua
145 H 26 **Islas Diego Ramirez**, Chile
139 O 2 **Islas Los Roques**, Venezuela
124 L 10 **Islas Marías**, Mexico
63 H 20 **Islas Orcadas Rise**, Atlantic Ocean
145 I 26 **Islas Wollaston**, Chile
76 E 13 **Islay**, United Kingdom
76 E 8 **Isle of Lewis**, United Kingdom
77 H 16 **Isle of Man**, United Kingdom
77 L 23 **Isle of Wight**, United Kingdom
120 I 2 **Isle Royale**, Michigan, U.S.A.
77 E 24 **Isles of Scilly**, United Kingdom
190 F 8 **Ismâ'iliya**, Egypt
159 X 7 **Ismayilli**, Azerbaijan
190 F 11 **Isna**, Egypt
197 Q 3 **Isoka**, Zambia
91 J 20 **Isola Alicudi**, Italy
91 B 15 **Isola Asinara**, Italy
91 C 15 **Isola Caprera**, Italy
90 D 12 **Isola d' Elba**, Italy
91 I 16 **Isola d' Ischia**, Italy
90 E 13 **Isola del Giglio**, Italy
90 D 12 **Isola di Capraia**, Italy
91 J 16 **Isola di Capri**, Italy
90 D 11 **Isola di Gorgona**, Italy
91 H 26 **Isola di Lampedusa**, Italy
91 G 26 **Isola di Lampione**, Italy
91 H 26 **Isola di Linosa**, Italy
90 E 13 **Isola di Montecristo**, Italy
91 G 24 **Isola di Pantelleria**, Italy
91 B 19 **Isola di San Pietro**, Italy
91 B 19 **Isola di Sant'Antioco**, Italy
91 I 20 **Isola di Ustica**, Italy
91 G 22 **Isola Favignana**, Italy
91 J 20 **Isola Filicudi**, Italy
91 G 21 **Isola Levanzo**, Italy
91 K 20 **Isola Lipari**, Italy
91 C 15 **Isola Maddalena**, Italy
91 G 21 **Isola Marettimo**, Italy
91 K 20 **Isola Panarea**, Italy
90 D 12 **Isola Pianosa**, Italy
91 K 20 **Isola Salina**, Italy
91 K 20 **Isola Stromboli**, Italy
91 K 21 **Isola Vulcano**, Italy
91 F 21 **Isole Egadi**, Italy
91 J 20 **Isole Lipari**, Italy
91 G 26 **Isole Pelagie**, Italy
90 L 13 **Isole Pianosa**, Italy
91 H 16 **Isole Ponziane**, Italy
90 L 13 **Isole San Domino**, Italy
90 L 13 **Isole Tremiti**, Italy
158 F 12 **Isparta**, Turkey
96 L 7 **Isperikh**, Bulgaria
160 F 11 **Israel**, Asia
208 J 11 **Israelite Bay**, Western Australia, Australia
192 J 13 **Issia**, Côte d'Ivoire
167 W 10 **Issyk-Kul'skaya Oblast'**, Kyrgyzstan
93 K 21 **Istállós-kő**, Hungary
96 O 12 **Istanbul**, Turkey
96 O 12 **Istanbul**, Turkey
164 H 7 **Īstgāh-e Eznā**, Iran
173 F 23 **Isthmus of Kra**, Thailand
126 K 13 **Isthmus of Panama**, Panama
97 F 18 **Istiaia**, Greece
159 V 9 **Istisu**, Azerbaijan
125 V 13 **Istmo de Tehuantepec**, Mexico
94 A 9 **Istra**, Croatia
167 W 9 **Isyk**, Kazakhstan
143 N 15 **Itabuna**, Brazil
142 F 10 **Itacoatiara**, Brazil
143 K 15 **Itaguari**, Brazil
142 G 11 **Itaituba**, Brazil
143 J 20 **Itajaí**, Brazil
90 F 10 **Italy**, Europe
197 W 10 **Itampolo**, Madgascar
168 N 12 **Itanagar**, India
143 M 16 **Itaobím**, Brazil
143 N 16 **Itapebi**, Brazil
142 L 11 **Itapecuru Mirim**, Brazil
143 M 18 **Itaperuna**, Brazil
143 J 19 **Itapetininga**, Brazil
142 B 12 **Itaquai**, Brazil
143 G 21 **Itaqui**, Brazil
169 E 15 **Itarsi**, India
142 I 9 **Itaupã**, Brazil
175 O 1 **Itbayat**, Philippines
141 G 20 **Ite**, Peru
97 E 19 **Itea**, Greece
195 P 9 **Itebero**, Democratic Republic of Congo
121 S 8 **Ithaca**, New York, U.S.A.
97 B 19 **Ithaki**, Greece
97 B 19 **Ithaki**, Greece
143 M 16 **Itinga**, Brazil
143 G 16 **Itiquira**, Brazil
177 K 17 **Itō**, Japan
177 I 15 **Itoigawa**, Japan
194 L 8 **Itoko**, Democratic Republic of Congo
65 Q 13 **Ittoqqortoormiit**, Greenland
142 B 11 **Itui**, Brazil
143 J 17 **Ituiutaba**, Brazil
195 P 10 **Itula**, Democratic Republic of Congo
143 J 17 **Itumbiara**, Brazil
139 U 6 **Ituni**, Guyana
143 J 17 **Iturama**, Brazil
144 N 8 **Ituzaingó**, Argentina
86 G 9 **Itzehoe**, Germany
157 Z 6 **Iul'tin**, Russian Federation
84 M 8 **Ivalo**, Finland
99 G 21 **Ivanava**, Belarus
94 F 7 **Ivanec**, Croatia
209 S 11 **Ivanhoe**, New South Wales, Australia
94 E 8 **Ivanić Grad**, Croatia
94 K 13 **Ivanjica**, Serbia and Montenegro
94 F 10 **Ivanjska**, Bosnia and Herzegovina
101 P 3 **Ivankiv**, Ukraine
100 J 6 **Ivano-Frankivs'k**, Ukraine
101 S 3 **Ivanytsya**, Ukraine
99 G 20 **Ivatsevichy**, Belarus
96 K 12 **Ivaylovgrad**, Bulgaria
156 J 9 **Ivdel'**, Russian Federation
100 M 11 **Iveşti**, Romania
64 L 13 **Ivittuut**, Greenland
197 X 9 **Ivohibe**, Madgascar
192 J 14 **Ivory Coast**, Côte d'Ivoire
90 B 7 **Ivrea**, Italy
115 P 4 **Ivujivik**, Québec, Canada
99 I 17 **Ivyanyets**, Belarus
121 O 13 **Ivydale**, West Virginia, U.S.A.
176 L 10 **Iwaizumi**, Japan
177 L 14 **Iwaki**, Japan
176 J 9 **Iwaki-san**, Japan
177 D 20 **Iwakuni**, Japan
176 J 5 **Iwamizawa**, Japan
176 I 6 **Iwanai**, Japan
176 K 10 **Iwate-san**, Japan
193 P 12 **Iwo**, Nigeria
99 G 17 **Iwye**, Belarus
141 I 17 **Ixiamas**, Bolivia
125 N 10 **Ixtlán**, Mexico
125 T 13 **Ixtlán**, Mexico
177 E 20 **Iyomishima**, Japan
195 U 12 **Izazi**, Tanzania
83 C 18 **Izegem**, Belgium
177 N 24 **Izena-jima**, Japan
156 I 9 **Izhevsk**, Russian Federation
101 N 11 **Izmayil**, Ukraine
158 B 10 **Izmir**, Turkey
158 A 10 **Izmir Körfezi**, Turkey
158 E 8 **Iznik Gölü**, Turkey
125 R 12 **Iztaccihuatl**, Mexico
177 K 17 **Izu-hantō**, Japan
177 K 18 **Izu-shotō**, Japan
60 L 4 **Izu Trench**, Pacific Ocean
125 R 12 **Izúcar de Matamoros**, Mexico
177 A 20 **Izuhara**, Japan
177 B 23 **Izumi**, Japan
177 D 18 **Izumo**, Japan
100 L 4 **Izyaslav**, Ukraine
101 X 5 **Izyum**, Ukraine

J

64 M 13 **J.A.D. Jenson Nunatakker**, Greenland
161 N 2 **Jabal 'Abd al 'Azīz**, Syria
161 N 2 **Jabal Abd al Azīz**, Syria
160 K 4 **Jabal Abū Raḥbah**, Syria
162 J 3 **Jabal ad Dubbagh**, Saudi Arabia
160 I 8 **Jabal ad Duruz**, Syria
160 J 3 **Jabal Aḥaṣ**, Syria
160 H 11 **Jabāl al 'Ādhiriyāt**, Jordan
160 I 2 **Jabal al Akr**, Syria
163 P 10 **Jabal al Amlaḥ**, Saudi Arabia
160 I 8 **Jabal al 'Arab**, Syria
160 F 13 **Jabal al Khashsh**, Jordan
162 J 3 **Jabal al Lawz**, Saudi Arabia
163 V 11 **Jabal al Qamar**, Oman
163 O 13 **Jabal an Nabī Shu'ayb**, Yemen
160 J 6 **Jabal an Niqniqīyah**, Syria
160 H 4 **Jabal an Nuṣayrīyah**, Syria
163 P 10 **Jabal ar Rubūṭ**, Saudi Arabia
189 Z 13 **Jabal Arkenu**, Libya
189 S 9 **Jabal as Sawdā'**, Libya
163 Y 7 **Jabal ash Shāms**, Oman
160 H 6 **Jabal ash Sharqī**, Lebanon
160 I 5 **Jabal ash Shawmariyah**, Syria
162 J 3 **Jabal ash Shifa**, Saudi Arabia
160 L 7 **Jabal aṭ Ṭanf**, Syria
160 F 13 **Jabal Bāqir**, Jordan
189 U 13 **Jabal Bin Ghanīmah**, Libya
160 L 4 **Jabal Bishrī**, Syria
163 X 6 **Jabal Ḥafīt**, United Arab Emirates
163 W 15 **Jabal Ḥajhir**, Yemen
161 S 4 **Jabal Hamrin**, Iraq
163 Z 7 **Jabal Khadar**, Oman
189 R 8 **Jabal Nafūsah**, Libya
162 L 5 **Jabal Nahr**, Saudi Arabia
189 W 14 **Jabal Nuqayy**, Libya
162 M 8 **Jabal Qarnayṭ**, Saudi Arabia
162 L 6 **Jabal Raḍwá**, Saudi Arabia
162 M 2 **Jabal Rāf**, Saudi Arabia
160 G 13 **Jabal Ramm**, Jordan
163 Z 7 **Jabal Salakh**, Oman
163 N 10 **Jabal Sawdā'**, Saudi Arabia
160 K 4 **Jabal Shā'īr**, Syria
161 O 2 **Jabal Sinjār**, Iraq
163 O 13 **Jabal Taqar**, Yemen
163 P 13 **Jabal Thamar**, Yemen
160 L 4 **Jabal Thulaythawat Gharbi**, Syria
163 Q 9 **Jabal Tuwayq**, Saudi Arabia
189 U 8 **Jabal Waddān**, Libya
189 V 9 **Jabal Zaltan**, Libya
169 G 15 **Jabalpur**, India
83 B 17 **Jabbeke**, Belgium
209 N 1 **Jabiru**, Northern Territory, Australia
160 H 3 **Jablah**, Syria
94 G 13 **Jablanica**, Bosnia and Herzegovina
93 E 16 **Jablonec nad Nisou**, Czech Republic
215 Y 3 **Jabwat**, Marshall Islands
81 T 2 **Jaca**, Spain

Country · Internal administrative region: State/Province/Territory/Dependent territory · Capital city · Mountain range/Undersea ridge · Mountain peak/Volcano/Seamount · Geographic feature · Headland/Point/Cape/Peninsula · Desert · Island/Island group · Antarctic base · Ocean · Sea · Bay/Gulf/Channel/Strait · Lake · Salt pan/Dry/Intermittent lake · River

125 R 11 Jacala, Mexico
142 G 12 Jacareacanga, Brazil
144 H 9 Jáchal, Argentina
142 D 13 Jaciparaná, Brazil
121 W 4 Jackman, Maine, U.S.A.
119 J 19 Jacksboro, Texas, U.S.A.
123 O 1 Jacksboro, Tennessee, U.S.A.
118 C 11 Jackson, Wyoming, U.S.A.
120 L 9 Jackson, Michigan, U.S.A.
121 N 12 Jackson, Ohio, U.S.A.
122 K 7 Jackson, Alabama, U.S.A.
122 H 6 Jackson, Mississippi, U.S.A.
122 J 2 Jackson, Tennessee, U.S.A.
123 O 5 Jackson, Georgia, U.S.A.
211 C 21 Jackson Bay, New Zealand
211 C 21 Jackson Bay, New Zealand
118 C 10 Jackson Lake, Wyoming, U.S.A.
211 G 19 Jacksons, New Zealand
119 L 20 Jacksonville, Texas, U.S.A.
120 G 11 Jacksonville, Illinois, U.S.A.
123 R 8 Jacksonville, Florida, U.S.A.
123 V 3 Jacksonville, North Carolina, U.S.A.
123 R 9 Jacksonville Beach, Florida, U.S.A.
127 P 7 Jacmel, Haiti
165 U 12 Jacobabad, Pakistan
142 J 11 Jacunda, Brazil
86 E 10 Jadebusen, Germany
163 V 12 Jādib, Yemen
81 P 6 Jadraque, Spain
81 O 11 Jaén, Spain
140 B 12 Jaén, Peru
169 F 23 Jaffna, Sri Lanka
169 H 17 Jagdalpur, India
171 W 2 Jagdaqi, China
161 O 1 Jāghir Bāzār, Syria
94 M 12 Jagodina, Serbia and Montenegro
169 F 17 Jagtial, India
143 H 22 Jaguarão, Brazil
143 H 23 Jaguarão, Brazil
144 H 8 Jagüé, Argentina
126 J 4 Jagüey Grande, Cuba
164 J 11 Jahrom, Iran
142 M 12 Jaicós, Brazil
168 D 12 Jaipur, India
168 B 12 Jaisalmer, India
94 G 11 Jajce, Bosnia and Herzegovina
168 L 12 Jakar, Bhutan
174 H 13 Jakarta, Indonesia
174 H 13 Jakarta Raya, Indonesia
113 O 9 Jakes Corner, Yukon Territory, Canada
165 P 13 Jakkī, Iran
84 H 11 Jäkkvik, Sweden
85 K 15 Jakobstad, Finland
163 Q 5 Jalājil, Saudi Arabia
167 T 11 Jalal-Abad, Kyrgyzstan
165 V 7 Jalālābād, Afghanistan
168 D 9 Jalandhar, India
126 D 9 Jalapa, Guatemala
126 F 10 Jalapa, Nicaragua
125 T 12 Jalapa Enríquez, Mexico
161 U 5 Jalawlā, Iraq
169 D 16 Jalgaon, India
161 X 11 Jalībah, Iraq
193 T 12 Jalingo, Nigeria
124 M 11 Jalisco, Mexico
169 D 17 Jalna, India
168 C 13 Jalor, India
125 O 10 Jalostotitlán, Mexico
125 O 10 Jalpa, Mexico
168 K 12 Jalpaiguri, India
189 X 9 Jālū, Libya
215 Y 4 Jaluit, Marshall Islands
191 K 25 Jamaame, Somalia
126 L 8 Jamaica, North America
127 N 7 Jamaica Channel, Jamaica
168 L 13 Jamalpur, Bangladesh
174 F 9 Jamaluang, Malaysia
174 E 11 Jambi, Indonesia
174 F 11 Jambi, Indonesia
118 I 8 James, North Dakota, U.S.A.
115 O 8 James Bay, Québec, Canada
218 H 3 James Ross Island, Antarctica
63 N 25 Jamestown, St Helena
118 I 8 Jamestown, North Dakota, U.S.A.
121 Q 9 Jamestown, New York, U.S.A.
168 D 8 Jammu, India
168 E 8 Jammu and Kashmir, India/Pakistan
169 A 15 Jamnagar, India
83 J 25 Jamoigne, Belgium
165 V 11 Jampur, Pakistan
85 L 17 Jämsä, Finland
169 J 15 Jamshedpur, India
193 T 12 Jamtari, Nigeria
168 J 13 Jamui, India
65 R 13 Jan Mayen, Norway
168 J 12 Janakpur, Nepal
143 L 16 Janaúba, Brazil
165 W 8 Jand, Pakistan
164 K 7 Jandaq, Iran
159 U 7 Jandari, Georgia
62 O 12 Jandía Playa, Canary Islands
120 H 8 Janesville, Wisconsin, U.S.A.
174 M 12 Jangeru, Indonesia
167 S 11 Jangy-Bazar, Kyrgyzstan
124 K 3 Janos, Mexico
93 N 15 Janów Lubelski, Poland
92 N 12 Janów Podlaski, Poland
143 L 16 Januária, Brazil
176 I 11 Japan, Asia
60 L 3 Japan Basin, Pacific Ocean
60 L 4 Japan Trench, Pacific Ocean
86 E 7 Japsand, Germany
142 B 10 Japurá, Brazil
126 L 15 Jaqué, Panama
160 K 1 Jarābulus, Syria
143 J 20 Jaraguá do Sul, Brazil
80 L 8 Jaraicejo, Spain
160 H 9 Jarash, Jordan
143 G 18 Jardim, Brazil
126 K 5 Jardines de la Reina, Cuba
142 H 9 Jari, Brazil
92 G 13 Jarocin, Poland
93 N 17 Jarosław, Poland
61 Q 8 Jarvis Island, U.S.A.
169 I 15 Jashpurnagar, India
99 G 16 Jašiūnai, Lithuania
164 M 14 Jāsk, Iran
93 M 18 Jasło, Poland
218 I 4 Jason Peninsula, Antarctica
113 T 12 Jasper, Alberta, Canada
119 M 20 Jasper, Texas, U.S.A.
120 J 13 Jasper, Indiana, U.S.A.
122 L 4 Jasper, Alabama, U.S.A.
123 P 8 Jasper, Florida, U.S.A.
123 O 3 Jasper, Georgia, U.S.A.
161 W 7 Jaşşān, Iraq
92 G 10 Jastrowie, Poland
93 I 18 Jastrzębie-Zdrój, Poland
93 K 23 Jászberény, Hungary
143 I 17 Jataí, Brazil
142 F 9 Jatapu, Brazil
165 U 15 Jati, Pakistan
143 J 18 Jaú, Brazil
141 D 16 Jauja, Peru
98 G 12 Jaunjelgava, Latvia
98 H 10 Jaunpiebalga, Latvia
98 D 11 Jaunpils, Latvia
168 H 13 Jaunpur, India
174 H 15 Java, Indonesia
59 R 5 Java Ridge, Indian Ocean
174 I 13 Java Sea, Indonesia
59 T 6 Java Trench, Indian Ocean
165 R 7 Javand, Afghanistan
171 S 3 Javarthushuu, Mongolia
93 E 19 Javořice, Czech Republic
93 H 19 Javorníky, Slovakia
174 G 14 Jawa Barat, Indonesia
174 I 14 Jawa Tengah, Indonesia
174 K 15 Jawa Timur, Indonesia
191 M 24 Jawhar, Somalia
140 B 13 Jayanca, Peru
175 Y 12 Jayapura, Indonesia
168 J 12 Jaynagar, India
169 H 17 Jaypur, India
160 I 6 Jayrūd, Syria
163 N 11 Jazā'ir Farasān, Saudi Arabia
175 U 11 Jazirah Doberai, Indonesia
163 Z 8 Jazīrat Maşīrah, Oman
161 N 3 Jazrah, Syria
160 G 5 Jbail, Lebanon
188 J 7 Jbel Bou Naceur, Morocco
188 F 10 Jdiriya, Western Sahara
160 J 2 Jebal Aḩaş, Syria
193 P 12 Jebba, Nigeria
100 E 10 Jebel, Romania
191 C 15 Jebel Abyad Plateau, Sudan
189 P 6 Jebel Chambi, Tunisia
160 G 6 Jebel Libnan, Lebanon
191 B 18 Jebel Marra, Sudan
191 H 14 Jebel Oda, Sudan
191 B 17 Jebel Teljo, Sudan
191 B 13 Jebel Uweinat, Sudan
165 S 13 Jebri, Pakistan
162 L 8 Jeddah, Saudi Arabia
93 K 16 Jędrzejów, Poland
119 M 14 Jefferson City, Missouri, U.S.A.
196 M 15 Jeffrey's Bay, Republic of South Africa
193 P 10 Jega, Nigeria
98 H 12 Jēkabpils, Latvia
191 K 20 Jeldēsa, Ethiopia
93 E 15 Jelenia Góra, Poland
98 E 12 Jelgava, Latvia
174 E 8 Jeli, Malaysia
114 L 11 Jellicoe, Ontario, Canada
210 K 7 Jellicoe Channel, New Zealand
174 G 9 Jemaja, Indonesia
174 K 15 Jember, Indonesia
83 G 21 Jemeppe, Belgium
167 Z 6 Jeminay, Kazakhstan
87 J 17 Jena, Germany
189 P 5 Jendouba, Tunisia
167 Y 10 Jengish Chokusu, Kyrgyzstan
159 Y 9 Jenikand, Azerbaijan
160 G 8 Jenin, Israel
121 N 14 Jenkins, Kentucky, U.S.A.
113 W 13 Jenner, Alberta, Canada
117 O 15 Jensen, Utah, U.S.A.
174 I 13 Jepara, Indonesia
143 M 15 Jequié, Brazil
191 E 22 Jerbar, Sudan
127 O 7 Jérémie, Haiti
125 O 9 Jerez, Mexico
80 K 13 Jerez de la Frontera, Spain
80 J 10 Jerez de los Caballeros, Spain
95 L 21 Jergucat, Albania
160 G 9 Jericho, Israel
209 T 6 Jericho, Queensland, Australia
209 S 12 Jerilderie, New South Wales, Australia
208 H 12 Jerramungup, Western Australia, Australia
165 U 14 Jerruck, Pakistan
77 J 26 Jersey, United Kingdom
121 U 10 Jersey City, New Jersey, U.S.A.
120 G 12 Jerseyville, Illinois, U.S.A.
160 G 9 Jerusalem, Israel
90 I 11 Jesi, Italy
169 L 15 Jessore, Bangladesh
123 Q 7 Jesup, Georgia, U.S.A.
144 J 10 Jesús María, Argentina
86 E 10 Jever, Germany
92 J 9 Jezioro Jeziorak, Poland
92 G 7 Jezioro Łebsko, Poland
92 L 9 Jezioro Mamry, Poland
92 L 9 Jezioro Sniardwy, Poland
92 J 12 Jezioro Włocławskie, Poland
92 L 12 Jezioro Zegrzyńskie, Poland
160 G 7 Jezzine, Lebanon
169 D 15 Jhabua, India
165 T 12 Jhal, Pakistan
165 R 14 Jhal Jhao, Pakistan
165 X 9 Jhang, Pakistan
168 F 13 Jhansi, India
169 I 15 Jharkhand, India
169 I 15 Jharsuguda, India
165 U 12 Jhatpat, Pakistan
165 X 8 Jhelum, Pakistan
169 K 14 Jhenida, Bangladesh
165 V 14 Jhudo, Pakistan
143 E 14 Ji-Paraná, Brazil
171 U 6 Ji Xian, China
171 Y 3 Jiamusi, China
171 U 12 Ji'an, China
171 V 12 Jiangle, China
171 T 14 Jiangmen, China
171 V 9 Jiangsu, China
171 U 11 Jiangxi, China
171 Q 10 Jiangyou, China
171 T 11 Jianli, China
171 T 8 Jiaozuo, China
171 W 10 Jiaxing, China
171 Y 2 Jiayin, China
171 O 6 Jiayuguan, China
100 H 8 Jibou, Romania
163 X 10 Jiddat al Ḩarāsīs, Oman
171 S 8 Jiexiu, China
171 U 13 Jieyang, China
99 F 16 Jieznas, Lithuania
193 S 10 Jigawa, Nigeria
171 P 9 Jigzhi, China
93 E 19 Jihlava, Czech Republic
189 O 5 Jijel, Algeria
191 K 20 Jijiga, Ethiopia
191 K 25 Jilib, Somalia
171 X 4 Jilin, China
171 X 4 Jilin, China
191 H 21 Jima, Ethiopia
100 E 10 Jimbolia, Romania
125 N 6 Jiménez, Mexico
171 U 8 Jinan, China
171 P 7 Jinchang, China
171 T 8 Jincheng, China
209 T 13 Jindabyne, New South Wales, Australia
93 D 19 Jindřichův Hradec, Czech Republic
171 V 11 Jingdezhen, China
170 J 4 Jinghe, China
171 T 10 Jingmen, China
171 T 10 Jingsha, China
171 Q 8 Jingtai, China
171 R 14 Jingxi, China
171 Q 8 Jingyuan, China
171 T 10 Jingzhou, China
171 V 2 Jinhe, China
171 W 11 Jinhua, China
171 T 6 Jining, China
171 U 8 Jining, China
195 S 7 Jinja, Uganda
191 H 22 Jinka, Ethiopia
126 F 11 Jinotepe, Nicaragua
171 T 11 Jinshi, China
171 V 6 Jinzhou, China
171 W 6 Jinzhou, China
140 A 9 Jipijapa, Ecuador
164 M 11 Jiroft, Iran
191 N 21 Jirriiban, Somalia
171 S 11 Jishou, China
160 H 2 Jisr Ash Shughūr, Syria
174 D 7 Jitra, Malaysia
100 H 12 Jiu, Romania
171 U 11 Jiujiang, China
171 P 11 Jiulong, China
171 O 7 Jiuquan, China
171 S 15 Jiusuo, China
165 P 14 Jiwani, Pakistan
171 Y 3 Jixi, China
163 O 11 Jīzān, Saudi Arabia
177 E 18 Jizō-zaki, Japan
167 Q 12 Jizzakh Wiloyati, Uzbekistan
142 O 12 João Pessoa, Brazil
143 K 17 João Pinheiro, Brazil
144 J 6 Joaquín V. González, Argentina
168 C 12 Jodhpur, India
85 O 16 Joensuu, Finland
177 I 14 Jōetsu, Japan
197 R 8 Jofane, Mozambique
168 J 12 Jogbani, India
168 G 11 Jogbura, Nepal
98 H 7 Jõgeva, Estonia
98 I 6 Jõgua, Estonia
117 H 21 Johannesburg, California, U.S.A.
197 O 11 Johannesburg, Republic of South Africa
76 I 8 John o'Groats, United Kingdom
119 H 15 Johnson, Kansas, U.S.A.
123 Q 1 Johnson City, Tennessee, U.S.A.
61 Q 6 Johnston Atoll, U.S.A.
174 F 10 Johor, Malaysia
174 F 10 Johor Bahru, Malaysia
98 I 6 Jõhvi, Estonia
79 T 5 Joinville, France
143 J 20 Joinville, Brazil
218 H 2 Joinville Island, Antarctica
84 I 11 Jokkmokk, Sweden
84 B 9 Jökulbunga, Iceland
164 F 3 Jolfa, Iran
120 I 9 Joliet, Illinois, U.S.A.
115 R 13 Joliette, Québec, Canada
175 O 8 Jolo, Philippines
175 O 8 Jolo, Philippines
168 H 11 Jomsom, Nepal
99 F 15 Jonava, Lithuania
119 N 16 Jonesboro, Arkansas, U.S.A.
119 M 19 Jonesboro, Louisiana, U.S.A.
123 R 3 Jonesville, South Carolina, U.S.A.
191 F 21 Jonglei, Sudan
191 E 21 Jonglei, Sudan
98 E 12 Joniškis, Lithuania
85 F 22 Jönköping, Sweden
119 L 16 Joplin, Missouri, U.S.A.
168 E 12 Jora, India
160 H 11 Jordan, Asia
160 G 9 Jordan, Israel
118 E 8 Jordan, Montana, U.S.A.
168 N 12 Jorhat, India
193 S 11 Jos, Nigeria
141 J 17 José Agustín Palacios, Bolivia
145 G 18 José de San Martin, Argentina
208 L 2 Joseph Bonaparte Gulf, Western Australia, Australia
212 C 4 Josephstaal, Papua New Guinea
160 G 7 Jouaiya, Lebanon
197 N 11 Jouberton, Republic of South Africa
82 K 8 Joure, Netherlands
84 M 11 Joutsijärvi, Finland
168 M 13 Jowai, India
165 S 5 Jowzjān, Afghanistan
116 D 6 Joyce, Washington, U.S.A.
192 E 6 Jreïda, Mauritania
116 C 5 Juan de Fuca Strait, Washington, U.S.A.
197 V 6 Juan de Nova, France
61 W 1 Juan Fernández Islands, Chile
140 D 13 Juanjuí, Peru
142 M 13 Juàzeiro, Brazil
142 N 12 Juàzeiro do Norte, Brazil
192 I 13 Juazohn, Liberia
191 K 24 Juba, Somalia
191 E 23 Juba, Sudan
191 K 25 Jubbada Dhexe, Somalia
191 K 26 Jubbada Hoose, Somalia
208 K 9 Jubilee Lake, Western Australia, Australia
81 Q 8 Júcar, Spain
125 U 14 Juchitán, Mexico
125 N 11 Juchitlán, Mexico
161 P 10 Judaidat al Hamir, Iraq
89 U 7 Judenburg, Austria
126 G 10 Juigalpa, Nicaragua
143 F 14 Juína, Brazil
86 C 10 Juist, Germany
143 L 18 Juiz de Fora, Brazil
144 I 5 Jujuy, Argentina
141 I 22 Julaca, Bolivia
174 J 10 Julau, Malaysia
141 H 19 Juli, Peru
209 R 5 Julia Creek, Queensland, Australia
141 H 19 Juliaca, Peru
94 A 6 Julian Alps, Slovenia
139 W 7 Juliana Top, Suriname
82 H 8 Julianadorp, Netherlands
87 B 17 Jülich, Germany
81 S 10 Jumilla, Spain
168 H 11 Jumla, Nepal
169 A 15 Junagadh, India
169 H 17 Junagarh, India
117 M 18 Junction, Utah, U.S.A.
119 I 21 Junction, Texas, U.S.A.
209 R 7 Jundah, Queensland, Australia
143 K 19 Jundiaí, Brazil
113 O 10 Juneau, Alaska, U.S.A.
88 F 9 Jungfrau, Switzerland
170 K 4 Junggar Desert, China
141 D 16 Junín, Peru
144 K 12 Junín, Argentina
85 H 15 Junsele, Sweden
99 G 16 Juozapinės kalnas, Lithuania
76 F 12 Jura, United Kingdom
88 B 8 Jura, Switzerland/France
138 F 5 Juradó, Colombia
99 D 15 Jurbarkas, Lithuania
160 G 11 Jurf ad Darāwīsh, Jordan
208 F 10 Jurien, Western Australia, Australia
101 N 12 Jurilovca, Romania
98 E 11 Jūrmala, Latvia
142 C 11 Juruá, Brazil
142 C 11 Juruá, Brazil
142 F 13 Juruena, Brazil
171 V 4 Jus Hua, China
144 I 12 Justo Daract, Argentina
142 C 11 Jutai, Brazil
142 C 10 Jutaí, Brazil
87 L 14 Jüterbog, Germany
143 H 19 Juti, Brazil
126 D 10 Jutiapa, Guatemala
126 F 9 Juticalpa, Honduras
85 N 17 Juva, Finland
165 P 9 Juwain, Afghanistan
164 J 12 Jūyom, Iran
85 C 24 Jylland, Denmark
85 M 16 Jyväskylä, Finland

K

165 Z 5 K2, Pakistan
117 D 26 Ka Lae, Hawaii, U.S.A.
84 L 8 Kaamanen, Finland
191 K 26 Kaambooni, Somalia
195 Y 9 Kaambooni, Kenya
175 O 13 Kabaena, Indonesia
167 N 12 Kabakly, Turkmenistan
192 G 11 Kabala, Sierra Leone
195 Q 8 Kabale, Uganda
195 O 11 Kabalo, Democratic Republic of Congo
195 P 10 Kabambare, Democratic Republic of Congo
174 C 9 Kabanjahe, Indonesia
213 Y 12 Kabara, Fiji
195 P 9 Kabare, Democratic Republic of Congo
84 I 12 Kåbdalis, Sweden
173 I 19 Kabin Buri, Thailand
195 N 11 Kabinda, Democratic Republic of Congo
177 M 26 Kabira, Japan
195 N 12 Kabongo, Democratic Republic of Congo
173 F 20 Kabosa Island, Myanmar
165 O 5 Kabūd Gonbad, Iran
164 G 6 Kabūd Rāhang, Iran
165 U 7 Kābul, Afghanistan
165 U 7 Kabul, Afghanistan
195 Q 15 Kabunda, Democratic Republic of Congo
175 R 9 Kaburuang, Indonesia
191 F 16 Kabushiya, Sudan
197 O 5 Kabwe, Zambia
95 M 16 Kačanik, Serbia and Montenegro
193 R 11 Kachia, Nigeria
172 E 8 Kachin, Myanmar
167 U 2 Kachiry, Kazakhstan
197 P 5 Kacholola, Zambia
157 Q 13 Kachug, Russian Federation
173 F 20 Kadan Kyun, Myanmar
213 W 12 Kadavu, Fiji
213 W 12 Kadavu Passage, Fiji
161 T 7 Kādhimain, Iraq
158 D 7 Kadiköy, Turkey
158 G 11 Kadinhani, Turkey
192 J 11 Kadiolo, Mali
169 E 20 Kadiri, India
158 L 12 Kadirli, Turkey
169 B 22 Kadmat, India
118 H 11 Kadoka, South Dakota, U.S.A.
197 P 7 Kadoma, Zimbabwe
191 D 19 Kadugli, Sudan
193 R 11 Kaduna, Nigeria
193 R 11 Kaduna, Nigeria
159 V 10 Kadžaran, Armenia
192 F 7 Kaédi, Mauritania
193 V 11 Kaélé, Cameroon
210 J 5 Kaeo, New Zealand
171 X 7 Kaesŏng, North Korea
162 K 1 Kāf, Saudi Arabia
194 M 13 Kafakumba, Democratic Republic of Congo
192 E 9 Kaffrine, Senegal
191 A 20 Kafia Kingi, Sudan
197 O 5 Kafue, Zambia
177 H 16 Kaga, Japan
194 K 3 Kaga Bandoro, Central African Republic
165 X 7 Kagan, Pakistan
167 O 13 Kagan, Uzbekistan
195 R 9 Kagera, Tanzania
159 S 9 Kağizman, Turkey
191 E 17 Kagmar, Sudan
177 C 24 Kagoshima, Japan
164 M 5 Kāhak, Iran
195 S 10 Kahama, Tanzania
101 Q 4 Kaharlyk, Ukraine
194 J 12 Kahemba, Democratic Republic of Congo
164 M 12 Kahnūj, Iran
192 I 14 Kahnwia, Liberia
210 I 5 Kahoe, New Zealand
117 C 25 Kahoolawe, Hawaii, U.S.A.
158 L 12 Kahramanmaraş, Turkey
159 N 12 Kahta, Turkey
175 U 13 Kai Besar, Indonesia
175 U 13 Kai Kecil, Indonesia
193 P 11 Kaiama, Nigeria
211 H 20 Kaiapoi, New Zealand
171 U 9 Kaifeng, China

Country · Internal administrative region: State/Province/Territory/Dependent territory · Capital city · Mountain range/Undersea ridge · Mountain peak/Volcano/Seamount · Geographic feature · Headland/Point/Cape/Peninsula · Desert · Island/Island group · Antarctic base · Ocean · Sea · Bay/Gulf/Channel/Strait · Lake · Salt pan/Dry/Intermittent lake · River

210 J 6 **Kaikohe**, New Zealand
211 I 18 **Kaikoura**, New Zealand
211 I 18 **Kaikoura Peninsula**, New Zealand
171 R 12 **Kaili**, China
117 D 24 **Kailua**, Hawaii, U.S.A.
175 V 12 **Kaimana**, Indonesia
98 D 7 **Käina**, Estonia
177 F 20 **Kainan**, Japan
212 D 5 **Kainantu**, Papua New Guinea
89 X 7 **Kaindorf**, Austria
193 P 11 **Kainji Reservoir**, Nigeria
84 K 10 **Kainulasjärvi**, Sweden
210 I 7 **Kaipara Harbour**, New Zealand
211 N 14 **Kairakau Beach**, New Zealand
212 B 3 **Kairiru**, Papua New Guinea
189 Q 6 **Kairouan**, Tunisia
212 D 6 **Kairuku**, Papua New Guinea
219 W 7 **Kaiser Wilhelm II Land**, Antarctica
87 D 21 **Kaiserslautern**, Germany
99 F 15 **Kaišiadorys**, Lithuania
211 E 25 **Kaitangata**, New Zealand
84 I 10 **Kaitumälven**, Sweden
117 B 25 **Kaiwi Channel**, Hawaii, U.S.A.
171 P 13 **Kaiyuan**, China
85 M 14 **Kajaani**, Finland
209 Q 5 **Kajabbi**, Queensland, Australia
165 R 9 **Kajaki**, Afghanistan
193 R 11 **Kajuru**, Nigeria
191 E 19 **Kaka**, Sudan
211 E 25 **Kaka Point**, New Zealand
175 P 14 **Kakabia**, Indonesia
196 K 12 **Kakamas**, Republic of South Africa
195 T 7 **Kakamega**, Kenya
169 N 23 **Kakana**, India
210 K 13 **Kakaramea**, New Zealand
192 H 13 **Kakata**, Liberia
210 K 13 **Kakatahi**, New Zealand
177 D 19 **Kake**, Japan
194 L 10 **Kakenge**, Democratic Republic of Congo
101 T 9 **Kakhovka Tavriys'k**, Ukraine
101 T 8 **Kakhovs'ke Vodoskhovyshche**, Ukraine
164 I 11 **Kākī**, Iran
169 H 18 **Kakinada**, India
113 S 8 **Kakisa Lake**, Northwest Territories, Canada
192 K 12 **Kakpin**, Côte d'Ivoire
112 M 3 **Kaktovik**, Alaska, U.S.A.
176 K 12 **Kakuda**, Japan
165 O 8 **Kāl-e Namakasār**, Afghanistan
195 R 12 **Kala**, Tanzania
165 V 8 **Kalabagh**, Pakistan
175 Q 15 **Kalabahi**, Indonesia
196 L 5 **Kalabo**, Zambia
115 Q 14 **Kaladar**, Ontario, Canada
196 K 9 **Kalahari Desert**, Botswana
85 L 14 **Kalajoki**, Finland
85 K 14 **Kalajoki**, Finland
193 P 11 **Kalalé**, Benin
165 W 6 **Kalam**, Pakistan
97 F 14 **Kalamaria**, Greece
97 D 22 **Kalamata**, Greece
120 K 9 **Kalamazoo**, Michigan, U.S.A.
169 E 17 **Kalamnuri**, India
97 B 18 **Kalamos**, Greece
97 D 16 **Kalampaka**, Greece
101 T 12 **Kalamyts'ka Zatoka**, Ukraine
192 I 10 **Kalana**, Mali
101 S 10 **Kalanchak**, Ukraine
195 T 11 **Kalangali**, Tanzania
175 O 14 **Kalao**, Indonesia
175 O 14 **Kalaotoa**, Indonesia
161 V 5 **Kalār**, Iraq
173 K 16 **Kalasin**, Thailand
165 T 11 **Kalat**, Pakistan
97 D 20 **Kalavryta**, Greece
208 F 9 **Kalbarri**, Western Australia, Australia
158 I 9 **Kalecik**, Turkey
175 Q 13 **Kaledupa**, Indonesia
195 N 10 **Kalema**, Democratic Republic of Congo
195 Q 11 **Kalémié**, Democratic Republic of Congo
172 C 10 **Kalemyo**, Myanmar
156 H 6 **Kalevala**, Russian Federation
172 C 10 **Kalewa**, Myanmar
208 I 10 **Kalgoorlie**, Western Australia, Australia
195 O 9 **Kalima**, Democratic Republic of Congo
174 I 11 **Kalimantan Barat**, Indonesia
174 M 12 **Kalimantan Selatan**, Indonesia
174 J 12 **Kalimantan Tengah**, Indonesia
174 L 10 **Kalimantan Timur**, Indonesia
169 I 16 **Kalinga**, India
99 B 15 **Kaliningrad**, Russian Federation
99 B 15 **Kaliningradskaya Oblast'**, Russian Federation
167 R 14 **Kalininobod**, Tajikistan
99 L 21 **Kalinkavichy**, Belarus
118 B 7 **Kalispell**, Montana, U.S.A.
93 H 14 **Kalisz**, Poland
92 F 10 **Kalisz Pomorski**, Poland
195 R 11 **Kaliua**, Tanzania
158 D 13 **Kalkan**, Turkey
208 M 4 **Kalkarindji**, Northern Territory, Australia
120 L 6 **Kalkaska**, Michigan, U.S.A.
196 I 8 **Kalkfeld**, Namibia
85 F 15 **Kallsjön**, Sweden
85 G 24 **Kalmar**, Sweden
98 F 11 **Kalnciems**, Latvia
93 I 25 **Kalocsa**, Hungary
197 N 6 **Kalomo**, Zambia
172 D 9 **Kalon**, Myanmar
168 F 9 **Kalpa**, India
169 C 23 **Kalpeni**, India
168 G 13 **Kalpi**, India
193 S 9 **Kalrguéri**, Niger
99 H 14 **Kaltanėnai**, Lithuania
156 F 8 **Kaluga**, Russian Federation
208 K 2 **Kalumburu**, Western Australia, Australia
85 D 25 **Kalundborg**, Denmark
100 I 5 **Kalush**, Ukraine
169 F 25 **Kalutara**, Sri Lanka
99 E 16 **Kalvarija**, Lithuania
156 F 8 **Kalyazin**, Russian Federation
97 M 22 **Kalymnos**, Greece
97 M 22 **Kalymnos**, Greece
101 N 5 **Kalynivka**, Ukraine
173 C 14 **Kama**, Myanmar
195 O 10 **Kama**, Democratic Republic of Congo
176 L 10 **Kamaishi**, Japan
177 J 16 **Kamakura**, Japan
192 G 11 **Kamakwie**, Sierra Leone
158 I 10 **Kaman**, Turkey
196 G 8 **Kamanjab**, Namibia
163 O 12 **Kamarān**, Yemen
192 G 11 **Kamaron**, Sierra Leone
208 I 10 **Kambalda**, Western Australia, Australia
195 O 14 **Kambove**, Democratic Republic of Congo
157 Y 9 **Kamchatka Peninsula**, Russian Federation
96 K 7 **Kamen**, Bulgaria
156 M 12 **Kamen'-na-Obi**, Russian Federation
195 N 11 **Kamende**, Democratic Republic of Congo
166 H 4 **Kamenka**, Kazakhstan
156 J 10 **Kamensk-Ural'skiy**, Russian Federation
177 H 18 **Kameyama**, Japan
177 B 23 **Kami-Koshiki-jima**, Japan
92 D 9 **Kamień Pomorski**, Poland
93 J 15 **Kamieńsk**, Poland
176 K 4 **Kamikawa**, Japan
113 X 6 **Kamilukuak Lake**, Nunavut, Canada
100 K 1 **Kamin'-Kashyrs'kyy**, Ukraine
195 N 13 **Kamina**, Democratic Republic of Congo
177 H 16 **Kamioka**, Japan
177 A 20 **Kamitsushima**, Japan
113 T 14 **Kamloops**, British Columbia, Canada
61 O 4 **Kammu Seamount**, Pacific Ocean
159 U 8 **Kamo**, Armenia
177 L 16 **Kamogawa**, Japan
195 S 7 **Kampala**, Uganda
174 E 8 **Kampar**, Malaysia
82 K 10 **Kampen**, Netherlands
195 O 10 **Kampene**, Democratic Republic of Congo
173 G 16 **Kamphaeng Phet**, Thailand
173 M 20 **Kâmpóng Cham**, Cambodia
173 L 20 **Kâmpóng Chhnăng**, Cambodia
173 K 19 **Kâmpóng Khleăng**, Cambodia
173 K 22 **Kâmpóng Saôm**, Cambodia
173 K 21 **Kâmpóng Spoe**, Cambodia
173 L 20 **Kâmpóng Thum**, Cambodia
173 K 22 **Kâmpôt**, Cambodia
192 L 11 **Kampti**, Burkina Faso
192 E 10 **Kamsar**, Guinea
191 K 25 **Kamsuuma**, Somalia
176 L 6 **Kamui-dake**, Japan
176 I 6 **Kamui-misaki**, Japan
195 S 7 **Kamuli**, Uganda
100 M 2 **Kam''yane**, Ukraine
100 L 6 **Kam''yanets'-Podil's'kyy**, Ukraine
101 U 8 **Kam''yanka**, Ukraine
99 E 20 **Kamyanyets**, Belarus
164 F 6 **Kāmyārān**, Iran
99 K 15 **Kamyen'**, Belarus
156 F 10 **Kamyshin**, Russian Federation
167 N 8 **Kamyshlybash**, Kazakhstan
172 C 11 **Kan**, Myanmar
117 L 19 **Kanab**, Utah, U.S.A.
112 A 8 **Kanaga Island**, Alaska, U.S.A.
115 U 8 **Kanairiktoktok**, Newfoundland and Labrador, Canada
97 B 17 **Kanallaki**, Greece
194 L 11 **Kananga**, Democratic Republic of Congo
177 H 15 **Kanazawa**, Japan
172 D 10 **Kanbalu**, Myanmar
177 J 17 **Kanbara**, Japan
173 G 19 **Kanchanaburi**, Thailand
169 F 21 **Kanchipuram**, India
165 S 10 **Kandahār**, Afghanistan
165 S 9 **Kandahār**, Afghanistan
156 I 5 **Kandalaksha**, Russian Federation
193 N 11 **Kandé**, Togo
165 V 12 **Kandhkot**, Pakistan
193 O 10 **Kandi**, Benin
165 U 13 **Kandiaro**, Pakistan
97 B 18 **Kandila**, Greece
158 F 7 **Kandira**, Turkey
169 A 14 **Kandla**, India
197 W 7 **Kandreho**, Madgascar
212 F 5 **Kandrian**, Papua New Guinea
169 G 25 **Kandy**, Sri Lanka
166 L 5 **Kandyagash**, Kazakhstan
121 Q 9 **Kane**, Pennsylvania, U.S.A.
62 G 10 **Kane Fracture Zone**, Atlantic Ocean
193 W 8 **Kanem**, Chad
117 C 24 **Kaneohe**, Hawaii, U.S.A.
98 I 9 **Kanepi**, Estonia
196 L 10 **Kang**, Botswana
64 M 12 **Kangaamiut**, Greenland
192 I 10 **Kangaba**, Mali
158 M 10 **Kangal**, Turkey
164 M 14 **Kangān**, Iran
174 E 7 **Kangar**, Malaysia
209 P 12 **Kangaroo Island**, South Australia, Australia
85 M 17 **Kangasniemi**, Finland
168 K 11 **Kangchenjunga**, India
115 S 1 **Kangeeak Point**, Nunavut, Canada
65 N 12 **Kangerlussaq**, Greenland
65 O 11 **Kangersuatsiaq**, Greenland
195 U 6 **Kangetet**, Kenya
171 X 5 **Kanggye**, North Korea
115 T 6 **Kangiqsualujjuaq**, Québec, Canada
115 R 4 **Kangiqsujuaq**, Québec, Canada
115 R 5 **Kangirsuk**, Québec, Canada
171 Y 6 **Kangnŭng**, South Korea
194 E 7 **Kango**, Gabon
168 E 9 **Kangra**, India
168 N 11 **Kangto**, India
173 C 16 **Kangyidaung**, Myanmar
172 C 11 **Kani**, Myanmar
192 J 12 **Kani**, Côte d'Ivoire
174 M 7 **Kanibongan**, Malaysia
156 J 6 **Kanin Nos**, Russian Federation
101 Q 4 **Kaniv**, Ukraine
169 F 15 **Kaniwara**, India
94 K 7 **Kanjiža**, Serbia and Montenegro
120 I 10 **Kankakee**, Illinois, U.S.A.
192 H 11 **Kankan**, Guinea
169 G 16 **Kanker**, India
173 F 21 **Kanmaw Kyun**, Myanmar
123 S 2 **Kannapolis**, North Carolina, U.S.A.
193 S 10 **Kano**, Nigeria
193 R 10 **Kano**, Nigeria
177 C 24 **Kanoya**, Japan
168 G 12 **Kanpur**, India
119 I 15 **Kansas**, U.S.A.
119 J 14 **Kansas**, Kansas, U.S.A.
119 L 14 **Kansas City**, Missouri, U.S.A.
157 O 12 **Kansk**, Russian Federation
173 G 25 **Kantang**, Thailand
193 N 10 **Kantchari**, Burkina Faso
169 K 15 **Kanthi**, India
214 J 4 **Kanton**, Kiribati
177 K 15 **Kanuma**, Japan
196 M 10 **Kanye**, Botswana
214 I 10 **Kao**, Tonga
175 S 10 **Kao**, Indonesia
173 J 21 **Kaôh Kŏng**, Cambodia
173 J 22 **Kaôh Rŭng**, Cambodia
171 W 13 **Kaohsiung**, Taiwan
196 G 7 **Kaokoveld**, Namibia
192 E 8 **Kaolack**, Senegal
196 M 5 **Kaoma**, Zambia
194 M 3 **Kaouadja**, Central African Republic
86 M 7 **Kap Arkona**, Germany
65 Q 13 **Kap Brewster**, Greenland
64 M 14 **Kap Farvel**, Greenland
65 R 9 **Kap Morris Jesup**, Greenland
159 V 10 **Kapan**, Armenia
194 M 13 **Kapanga**, Democratic Republic of Congo
197 P 2 **Kapatu**, Zambia
167 V 9 **Kapchagay**, Kazakhstan
167 W 9 **Kapchagayskoye Vodokhranilishche**, Kazakhstan
83 E 16 **Kapelle**, Netherlands
83 G 16 **Kapellen**, Belgium
85 I 20 **Kapellskär**, Sweden
195 U 7 **Kapenguria**, Kenya
89 V 6 **Kapfenberg**, Austria
158 C 8 **Kapidaği Peninsula**, Turkey
197 O 4 **Kapiri Mposhi**, Zambia
165 V 7 **Kāpīsā**, Afghanistan
174 K 10 **Kapit**, Malaysia
211 K 15 **Kapiti Island**, New Zealand
173 F 23 **Kapoe**, Thailand
191 F 23 **Kapoeta**, Sudan
93 H 25 **Kaposvár**, Hungary
87 D 19 **Kappel**, Germany
86 H 7 **Kappeln**, Germany
171 Y 5 **Kapsan**, North Korea
174 I 11 **Kapuas**, Indonesia
115 O 11 **Kapuskasing**, Ontario, Canada
195 U 6 **Kaputir**, Kenya
93 G 23 **Kapuvár**, Hungary
99 I 19 **Kapyl'**, Belarus
193 N 11 **Kara**, Togo
167 U 10 **Kara-Balta**, Kyrgyzstan
158 H 12 **Kara Dağ**, Turkey
159 O 8 **Kara Dağ**, Turkey
167 T 11 **Kara-Köl**, Kyrgyzstan
191 J 19 **Kara K'orē**, Ethiopia
167 W 11 **Kara-Say**, Kyrgyzstan
156 M 6 **Kara Sea**, Russian Federation
167 T 12 **Kara-Suu**, Kyrgyzstan
166 I 11 **Karabogazkel'**, Turkmenistan
158 H 7 **Karabük**, Turkey
167 W 8 **Karabulak**, Kazakhstan
158 A 10 **Karaburun**, Turkey
166 M 5 **Karabutak**, Kazakhstan
158 E 13 **Karaca Yarimadasi**, Turkey
158 D 8 **Karacabey**, Turkey
96 O 12 **Karacaköy**, Turkey
158 D 7 **Karacaköy**, Turkey
158 H 14 **Karaçal Tepe**, Turkey
165 T 15 **Karachi**, Pakistan
169 C 18 **Karad**, India
167 S 6 **Karaganda**, Kazakhstan
167 T 5 **Karaganda**, Kazakhstan
167 V 9 **Karagash**, Kazakhstan
167 U 5 **Karagayly**, Kazakhstan
157 Z 9 **Karaginskiy Zaliv**, Russian Federation
159 O 10 **Karagöl Dağlari**, Turkey
195 R 8 **Karagwe**, Tanzania
169 F 22 **Karaikal**, India
169 F 23 **Karaikkudi**, India
164 I 6 **Karaj**, Iran
174 E 9 **Karak**, Malaysia
166 K 9 **Karakalpakiya**, Uzbekistan
159 O 12 **Karakeçi**, Turkey
158 I 9 **Karakeçili**, Turkey
175 R 8 **Karakelong**, Indonesia
159 P 10 **Karakoçan**, Turkey
167 W 10 **Karakol**, Kyrgyzstan
165 Y 5 **Karakoram**, Pakistan
168 D 6 **Karakoram Range**, India
167 O 13 **Karakul'**, Uzbekistan
166 L 13 **Karakum Desert**, Turkmenistan
159 R 9 **Karakurt**, Turkey
193 V 9 **Karal**, Chad
98 C 8 **Karala**, Estonia
158 H 13 **Karaman**, Turkey
170 K 4 **Karamay**, China
211 G 16 **Karamea**, New Zealand
211 G 17 **Karamea Bight**, New Zealand
174 L 13 **Karamian**, Indonesia
210 K 10 **Karamu**, New Zealand
169 E 16 **Karanji**, India
96 M 7 **Karapelit**, Bulgaria
158 I 12 **Karapinar**, Turkey
196 I 12 **Karas**, Namibia
196 J 12 **Karasburg**, Namibia
84 L 7 **Kárášjohka**, Norway
158 F 7 **Karasu**, Turkey
156 L 12 **Karasuk**, Russian Federation
158 K 13 **Karataş**, Turkey
167 S 10 **Karatau**, Kazakhstan
166 J 5 **Karatobe**, Kazakhstan
167 V 8 **Karatol**, Kazakhstan
166 I 7 **Karaton**, Kazakhstan
84 I 11 **Karats**, Sweden
177 B 21 **Karatsu**, Japan
167 W 5 **Karaul**, Kazakhstan
89 S 9 **Karawanken**, Austria
167 S 6 **Karazhal**, Kazakhstan
161 T 8 **Karbalā'**, Iraq
85 G 17 **Kårböle**, Sweden
93 L 23 **Karcag**, Hungary
97 D 17 **Karditsa**, Greece
169 L 17 **Kardiva Channel**, Maldives
98 D 6 **Kärdla**, Estonia
169 F 15 **Kareli**, India
99 H 18 **Karelichy**, Belarus
195 R 12 **Karema**, Tanzania
173 F 16 **Karen**, Myanmar
168 E 13 **Karera**, India
84 J 8 **Karesuando**, Finland
156 M 11 **Kargasok**, Russian Federation
158 J 7 **Kargi**, Turkey
168 E 7 **Kargil**, India
156 H 7 **Kargopol'**, Russian Federation
92 E 13 **Kargowa**, Poland
193 T 10 **Kari**, Nigeria
197 O 6 **Kariba**, Zimbabwe
196 H 9 **Karibib**, Namibia
84 L 7 **Karigasniemi**, Finland
174 I 11 **Karimata**, Indonesia
169 F 18 **Karimnagar**, India
191 M 19 **Karin**, Somalia
195 Q 8 **Karisimbi**, Democratic Republic of Congo/Rwanda
177 I 17 **Kariya**, Japan
212 D 4 **Karkar Island**, Papua New Guinea
167 U 5 **Karkaralinsk**, Kazakhstan
159 U 9 **Karki**, Azerbaijan
101 R 11 **Karkinits'ka Zatoka**, Ukraine
98 G 8 **Karksi-Nuia**, Estonia
171 N 5 **Karlik Shan**, China
92 E 9 **Karlino**, Poland
159 Q 10 **Karliova**, Turkey
101 U 5 **Karlivka**, Ukraine
94 D 8 **Karlovac**, Croatia
96 I 9 **Karlovo**, Bulgaria
93 B 17 **Karlovy Vary**, Czech Republic
85 F 25 **Karlshamn**, Sweden
85 F 20 **Karlskoga**, Sweden
85 G 25 **Karlskrona**, Sweden
87 E 22 **Karlsruhe**, Germany
85 F 20 **Karlstad**, Sweden
118 J 7 **Karlstad**, Minnesota, U.S.A.
89 U 2 **Karlstift**, Austria
99 N 19 **Karma**, Belarus
168 E 10 **Karnal**, India
169 D 20 **Karnataka**, India
89 P 9 **Karnische Alpen**, Austria/Italy
96 M 9 **Karnobat**, Bulgaria
89 S 9 **Kärnten**, Austria
165 S 12 **Karodi**, Pakistan
168 N 13 **Karong**, India
197 R 2 **Karonga**, Malawi
165 W 9 **Karor**, Pakistan
191 I 15 **Karora**, Eritrea
175 N 11 **Karossa**, Indonesia
97 L 22 **Karpáthio Pélagos**, Greece
97 M 25 **Karpathos**, Greece
97 M 26 **Karpathos**, Greece
97 D 18 **Karpenisi**, Greece
208 F 6 **Karratha**, Western Australia, Australia
159 S 8 **Kars**, Turkey
85 L 14 **Kärsämäki**, Finland
98 J 11 **Kārsava**, Latvia
166 I 11 **Karshi**, Turkmenistan
167 P 13 **Karshi**, Uzbekistan
158 E 8 **Kartal**, Turkey
197 W 4 **Kartala**, Comoros
156 I 11 **Kartaly**, Russian Federation
92 H 8 **Kartuzy**, Poland
209 Q 3 **Karumba**, Queensland, Australia
165 O 12 **Kārvāndar**, Iran
169 C 20 **Karwar**, India
88 M 7 **Karwendelgebirge**, Austria
97 B 18 **Karya**, Greece
157 R 14 **Karymskoye**, Russian Federation
97 H 20 **Karystos**, Greece
158 D 15 **Kaş**, Turkey
114 L 9 **Kasabonika**, Ontario, Canada
194 J 10 **Kasai**, Democratic Republic of Congo
177 F 18 **Kasai**, Japan
194 L 11 **Kasai Occidental**, Democratic Republic of Congo
194 M 10 **Kasai Oriental**, Democratic Republic of Congo
194 M 14 **Kasaji**, Democratic Republic of Congo
197 P 3 **Kasama**, Zambia
196 M 7 **Kasane**, Botswana
169 C 21 **Kasaragod**, India
114 I 4 **Kasba Lake**, Nunavut, Canada
188 H 7 **Kasba Tadla**, Morocco
196 M 4 **Kasempa**, Zambia
195 P 14 **Kasenga**, Democratic Republic of Congo
195 Q 7 **Kasenye**, Democratic Republic of Congo
195 O 8 **Kasese**, Democratic Republic of Congo
195 Q 7 **Kasese**, Uganda
173 K 17 **Kaset Wisai**, Thailand
114 L 11 **Kashabowie**, Ontario, Canada
164 I 7 **Kāshān**, Iran
115 P 10 **Kashechewen**, Ontario, Canada
170 G 5 **Kashi**, China
177 H 18 **Kashihara**, Japan
177 L 14 **Kashima-nada**, Japan
177 I 14 **Kashiwazaki**, Japan
167 T 8 **Kashkanteniz**, Kazakhstan
165 N 6 **Kāshmar**, Iran
168 D 7 **Kashmir Valley**, India
175 N 11 **Kasimbar**, Indonesia
167 V 10 **Kaskelen**, Kazakhstan
156 I 10 **Kasli**, Russian Federation
113 U 14 **Kaslo**, British Columbia, Canada
195 O 10 **Kasongo**, Democratic Republic of Congo
194 I 12 **Kasongo-Lunda**, Democratic Republic of Congo
97 M 26 **Kasos**, Greece
159 T 6 **Kaspi**, Georgia
191 G 16 **Kassala**, Sudan
191 H 16 **Kassala**, Sudan
97 G 15 **Kassandreia**, Greece
87 G 16 **Kassel**, Germany
189 P 6 **Kasserine**, Tunisia
97 A 16 **Kassiopi**, Greece
158 I 7 **Kastamonu**, Turkey
97 G 26 **Kastelli**, Greece
97 J 26 **Kastelli**, Greece
83 H 17 **Kasterlee**, Belgium
97 C 14 **Kastoria**, Greece
97 B 18 **Kastos**, Greece

Country · Internal administrative region: State/Province/Territory/Dependent territory · Capital city · Mountain range/Undersea ridge · Mountain peak/Volcano/Seamount · Geographic feature · Headland/Point/Cape/Peninsula · Desert · Island/Island group · Antarctic base · Ocean · Sea · Bay/Gulf/Channel/Strait · Lake · Salt pan/Dry/Intermittent lake · River

99 O 18 **Kastsyukovichy**, Belarus
177 I 17 **Kasugai**, Japan
177 L 15 **Kasumiga-ura**, Japan ◣
197 Q 4 **Kasungu**, Malawi
165 Y 9 **Kasur**, Pakistan
208 M 7 **Kata Tjuta**, Northern Territory, Australia ▲
168 F 7 **Kataklik**, India
195 N 10 **Katako-Kombe**, Democratic Republic of Congo
195 T 6 **Katakwi**, Uganda
195 N 13 **Katanga**, Democratic Republic of Congo ▣
208 H 12 **Katanning**, Western Australia, Australia
97 B 20 **Katastari**, Greece
169 O 24 **Katchall**, India ≛
195 O 11 **Katea**, Democratic Republic of Congo
97 E 15 **Katerini**, Greece
197 Q 5 **Katete**, Zambia
172 E 9 **Katha**, Myanmar
208 M 2 **Katherine**, Northern Territory, Australia
169 A 15 **Kathiawar Peninsula**, India ▶
168 J 12 **Kathmandu**, Nepal ♜
192 I 9 **Kati**, Mali
168 K 13 **Katihar**, India
210 L 9 **Katikati**, New Zealand
192 K 12 **Katiola**, Côte d'Ivoire
215 V 9 **Katiu**, French Polynesia ≛
96 D 11 **Katlanovo**, Macedonia (F.Y.R.O.M.)
97 D 20 **Kato Achaïa**, Greece
96 H 12 **Kato Nevrokopi**, Greece
97 E 18 **Kato Tithorea**, Greece
167 Z 4 **Katon-Karagay**, Kazakhstan
209 U 11 **Katoomba**, New South Wales, Australia
93 I 17 **Katowice**, Poland
85 G 21 **Katrineholm**, Sweden
197 X 6 **Katsepy**, Madgascar
193 R 10 **Katsina**, Nigeria ▣
193 R 9 **Katsina**, Nigeria
193 S 13 **Katsina-Ala**, Nigeria
177 A 21 **Katsumoto**, Japan
177 L 16 **Katsuura**, Japan
97 N 24 **Kattavia**, Greece
85 D 23 **Kattegat**, Denmark ≈
84 H 13 **Kattisavan**, Sweden
210 I 6 **Katui**, New Zealand
173 F 22 **Kau-ye Kyun**, Myanmar ≛
117 B 23 **Kauai**, Hawaii, U.S.A. ≛
117 B 24 **Kauai Channel**, Hawaii, U.S.A. ≈
215 U 9 **Kauehi**, French Polynesia ≛
87 I 25 **Kaufbeuren**, Germany
85 K 17 **Kauhajoki**, Finland
84 L 10 **Kaukonen**, Finland
98 I 6 **Kauksi**, Estonia
117 C 24 **Kaunakakai**, Hawaii, U.S.A.
99 E 15 **Kaunas**, Lithuania
212 C 3 **Kaup**, Papua New Guinea
85 B 17 **Kaupanger**, Norway
193 Q 9 **Kaura-Namoda**, Nigeria
85 K 15 **Kaustinen**, Finland
84 K 8 **Kautokeino**, Norway
211 L 14 **Kauwhata**, New Zealand
96 D 12 **Kavadarci**, Macedonia (F.Y.R.O.M.)
95 J 19 **Kavajë**, Albania
158 B 8 **Kavak**, Turkey
96 H 13 **Kavala**, Greece
169 G 20 **Kavali**, India
164 I 11 **Kavār**, Iran
169 B 22 **Kavaratti**, India ≛
169 B 22 **Kavaratti**, India
96 O 7 **Kavarna**, Bulgaria
212 G 2 **Kavieng**, Papua New Guinea
177 G 19 **Kawachi-nagano**, Japan
210 J 6 **Kawakawa**, New Zealand
197 O 2 **Kawambwa**, Zambia
169 G 15 **Kawardha**, India
177 K 16 **Kawasaki**, Japan
177 B 20 **Kawashiri-misaki**, Japan ▶
210 K 7 **Kawau Island**, New Zealand ≛
210 M 12 **Kaweka**, New Zealand ▲
210 J 10 **Kawhia**, New Zealand
210 J 10 **Kawhia Harbour**, New Zealand ≈
117 I 18 **Kawich Peak**, Nevada, U.S.A. ▲
172 D 9 **Kawlin**, Myanmar
192 M 9 **Kaya**, Burkina Faso
174 E 13 **Kayaapu**, Indonesia
173 E 14 **Kayah**, Myanmar ▣
169 D 23 **Kayankulam**, India
194 M 13 **Kayembe-Mukulu**, Democratic Republic of Congo
117 N 19 **Kayenta**, Arizona, U.S.A.
192 G 9 **Kayes**, Mali
192 H 9 **Kayes**, Mali ▣
167 V 5 **Kaynar**, Kazakhstan
158 K 11 **Kayseri**, Turkey
174 G 12 **Kayuagung**, Indonesia
195 O 10 **Kayuyu**, Democratic Republic of Congo
157 O 8 **Kayyerkan**, Russian Federation
158 A 9 **Kaz Daği**, Turkey
157 T 7 **Kazach'ye**, Russian Federation
166 H 10 **Kazakhskiy Zaliv**, Kazakhstan ≈
167 Q 8 **Kazakhstan**, Asia □
114 J 4 **Kazan**, Nunavut, Canada ∿
156 H 9 **Kazan'**, Russian Federation
101 S 7 **Kazanka**, Ukraine
96 J 9 **Kazanlŭk**, Bulgaria
159 T 5 **Kazbek**, Georgia ▲
164 I 10 **Kāzerūn**, Iran
93 K 21 **Kazincbarcika**, Hungary
99 E 15 **Kazlu Rūda**, Lithuania
177 K 15 **Kazo**, Japan
113 X 6 **Kazon**, Nunavut, Canada ∿
166 G 5 **Kaztalovka**, Kazakhstan
194 L 11 **Kazumba**, Democratic Republic of Congo
92 G 11 **Kcynia**, Poland
97 H 21 **Kea**, Greece ≛
117 E 25 **Keaau**, Hawaii, U.S.A.
117 O 20 **Keams Canyon**, Arizona, U.S.A.
118 I 13 **Kearney**, Nebraska, U.S.A.
159 N 11 **Keban**, Turkey
159 O 10 **Keban Baraji**, Turkey ◣
193 P 10 **Kebbi**, Nigeria ▣
192 D 8 **Kébémèr**, Senegal
189 Q 7 **Kebili**, Tunisia
191 A 17 **Kebkabiya**, Sudan
84 I 9 **Kebnekaise**, Sweden ▲
191 L 21 **K'ebrī Dehar**, Ethiopia
93 J 24 **Kecskemét**, Hungary
174 D 8 **Kedah**, Malaysia ▣
99 E 14 **Kėdainiai**, Lithuania
193 W 10 **Kédédéssé**, Chad
192 F 6 **Kediet Ijill**, Mauritania ▲
174 J 14 **Kediri**, Indonesia
192 G 9 **Kédougou**, Senegal
93 H 17 **Kędzierzyn-Koźle**, Poland
113 P 7 **Keele Peak**, Yukon Territory, Canada ▲
196 J 11 **Keetmanshoop**, Namibia
97 A 19 **Kefallonia**, Greece ≛
97 M 23 **Kefalos**, Greece
175 Q 15 **Kefamenanu**, Indonesia
193 R 12 **Keffi**, Nigeria
84 A 11 **Keflavik**, Iceland
113 T 10 **Keg River**, Alberta, Canada
167 X 10 **Kegen**, Kazakhstan
191 F 14 **Keheili**, Sudan
87 D 23 **Kehl**, Germany
98 G 6 **Kehra**, Estonia
172 F 11 **Kehsi Mansam**, Myanmar
77 J 17 **Keighley**, United Kingdom
98 F 6 **Keila**, Estonia
196 K 12 **Keimoes**, Republic of South Africa
193 Q 8 **Keïta**, Niger
85 M 16 **Keitele**, Finland ◣
209 Q 12 **Keith**, South Australia, Australia
174 K 9 **Kejaman**, Malaysia
117 A 24 **Kekaha**, Hawaii, U.S.A.
211 J 17 **Kekerengu**, New Zealand
177 N 22 **Kekeroma-jima**, Japan ≛
93 K 22 **Kékes**, Hungary ▲
157 V 11 **Kekra**, Russian Federation
191 L 22 **K'elafo**, Ethiopia
175 R 12 **Kelang**, Indonesia ≛
174 D 9 **Kelang**, Malaysia
174 E 8 **Kelantan**, Malaysia ▣
189 R 5 **Kelibia**, Tunisia
158 M 8 **Kelkit**, Turkey ∿
159 O 9 **Kelkit**, Turkey
194 G 8 **Kéllé**, Congo
167 R 2 **Kellerovka**, Kazakhstan
116 I 7 **Kellogg**, Idaho, U.S.A.
84 N 10 **Kelloselkä**, Finland
77 E 17 **Kells**, Republic of Ireland
98 D 13 **Kelmė**, Lithuania
83 L 20 **Kelmis**, Belgium
193 W 11 **Kelo**, Chad
113 T 14 **Kelowna**, British Columbia, Canada
116 D 8 **Kelso**, Washington, U.S.A.
174 F 10 **Keluang**, Malaysia
174 F 11 **Kelume**, Indonesia
156 H 6 **Kem'**, Russian Federation
159 O 10 **Kemah**, Turkey
159 N 10 **Kemaliye**, Turkey
194 L 5 **Kembé**, Central African Republic
158 D 13 **Kemer**, Turkey
156 M 12 **Kemerovo**, Russian Federation
84 L 12 **Kemi**, Finland
84 M 11 **Kemijärvi**, Finland ◣
84 M 11 **Kemijärvi**, Finland
84 M 10 **Kemijoki**, Finland ∿
118 C 12 **Kemmerer**, Wyoming, U.S.A.
87 K 20 **Kemnath**, Germany
194 J 4 **Kémo**, Central African Republic ▣
219 U 4 **Kemp Land**, Antarctica ◇
126 M 3 **Kemp's Bay**, The Bahamas
209 V 10 **Kempsey**, New South Wales, Australia
87 H 25 **Kempten**, Germany
112 J 7 **Kenai**, Alaska, U.S.A.
112 J 8 **Kenai Peninsula**, Alaska, U.S.A. ▶
123 S 11 **Kenansville**, Florida, U.S.A.
77 I 16 **Kendal**, United Kingdom
123 S 14 **Kendall**, Florida, U.S.A.
120 K 10 **Kendallville**, Indiana, U.S.A.
175 P 12 **Kendari**, Indonesia
174 I 12 **Kendawangan**, Indonesia
193 X 11 **Kendégué**, Chad
169 J 16 **Kendraparha**, India
167 U 9 **Kendyktas**, Kazakhstan ▴
192 H 12 **Kenema**, Sierra Leone
166 L 11 **Keneurgench**, Turkmenistan
172 F 11 **Keng Lon**, Myanmar
172 F 12 **Keng Tawng**, Myanmar
194 I 10 **Kenge**, Democratic Republic of Congo
196 K 13 **Kenhardt**, Republic of South Africa
188 H 6 **Kénitra**, Morocco
77 B 20 **Kenmare**, Republic of Ireland
119 O 16 **Kennett**, Missouri, U.S.A.
116 G 8 **Kennewick**, Washington, U.S.A.
114 J 10 **Kenora**, Ontario, Canada
120 I 8 **Kenosha**, Wisconsin, U.S.A.
113 U 3 **Kent Peninsula**, Nunavut, Canada ▶
167 R 10 **Kentau**, Kazakhstan
120 J 10 **Kentland**, Indiana, U.S.A.
96 F 13 **Kentriki Makedonia**, Greece ▣
120 J 14 **Kentucky**, U.S.A. ▣
120 M 14 **Kentucky**, Kentucky, U.S.A. ∿
122 K 1 **Kentucky Lake**, Tennessee, U.S.A. ◣
172 G 12 **Kentung**, Myanmar
195 U 7 **Kenya**, Africa □
169 J 15 **Keonjhar**, India
174 F 12 **Kepahiang**, Indonesia
95 J 20 **Kepi i Gjuhëzës**, Albania ▶
95 J 18 **Kepi i Rodonit**, Albania ▶
93 H 15 **Kępno**, Poland
175 Q 14 **Kepulauan Alor**, Indonesia ≛
174 G 9 **Kepulauan Anambas**, Indonesia ≛
175 V 13 **Kepulauan Aru**, Indonesia ≛
175 U 10 **Kepulauan Asia**, Indonesia ≛
175 U 10 **Kepulauan Ayu**, Indonesia ≛
175 T 14 **Kepulauan Babar**, Indonesia ≛
175 T 13 **Kepulauan Banda**, Indonesia ≛
175 P 11 **Kepulauan Banggai**, Indonesia ≛
174 C 9 **Kepulauan Banyak**, Indonesia ≛
175 R 14 **Kepulauan Barat Daya**, Indonesia ≛
174 C 11 **Kepulauan Batu**, Indonesia ≛
175 O 14 **Kepulauan Bonerate**, Indonesia ≛
175 U 12 **Kepulauan Gorong**, Indonesia ≛
175 U 13 **Kepulauan Kai**, Indonesia ≛
174 L 14 **Kepulauan Kangean**, Indonesia ≛
174 J 13 **Kepulauan Karimunjawa**, Indonesia ≛
174 L 13 **Kepulauan Laut Kecil**, Indonesia ≛
175 S 14 **Kepulauan Leti**, Indonesia ≛
174 G 11 **Kepulauan Lingga**, Indonesia ≛
175 V 10 **Kepulauan Mapia**, Indonesia ≛
175 R 8 **Kepulauan Nanusa**, Indonesia ≛
174 H 8 **Kepulauan Natuna**, Indonesia ≛
175 R 11 **Kepulauan Obi**, Indonesia ≛
175 N 14 **Kepulauan Sabalana**, Indonesia ≛
175 R 9 **Kepulauan Sangir**, Indonesia ≛
175 P 14 **Kepulauan Solor**, Indonesia ≛
175 O 14 **Kepulauan Taka'Bonerate**, Indonesia ≛
175 R 8 **Kepulauan Talaud**, Indonesia ≛
174 H 10 **Kepulauan Tambelan**, Indonesia ≛
175 U 14 **Kepulauan Tanimbar**, Indonesia ≛
174 M 14 **Kepulauan Tengah**, Indonesia ≛
175 P 11 **Kepulauan Togian**, Indonesia ≛
175 Q 13 **Kepulauan Tukangbesi**, Indonesia ≛
175 U 13 **Kepulauan Watubela**, Indonesia ≛
169 D 23 **Kerala**, India ▣
209 R 12 **Kerang**, Victoria, Australia
97 H 20 **Keratea**, Greece
167 S 11 **Kerben**, Kyrgyzstan
101 W 11 **Kerch**, Ukraine
101 W 12 **Kerch Strait**, Ukraine ≈
191 H 22 **Kere**, Ethiopia
212 C 6 **Kerema**, Papua New Guinea
158 I 6 **Kerempe Burun**, Turkey ▶
191 I 16 **Keren**, Eritrea
59 N 11 **Kerguelen Islands**, France ≛
58 M 11 **Kerguelen Plateau**, Indian Ocean ◇
195 U 8 **Kericho**, Kenya
210 J 5 **Kerikeri**, New Zealand
167 P 14 **Kerki**, Turkmenistan
97 A 16 **Kerkyra**, Greece
191 E 14 **Kerma**, Sudan
61 P 11 **Kermadec Islands**, New Zealand ≛
61 P 11 **Kermadec Ridge**, Pacific Ocean ◇
61 P 11 **Kermadec Trench**, Pacific Ocean ◇
164 M 11 **Kermān**, Iran ▣
164 M 10 **Kermān**, Iran
164 F 6 **Kermānshāh**, Iran ▣
164 F 6 **Kermānshāh**, Iran
119 G 20 **Kermit**, Texas, U.S.A.
97 K 22 **Keros**, Greece ≛
193 O 11 **Kérou**, Benin
192 H 11 **Kérouané**, Guinea
113 X 12 **Kerrobert**, Saskatchewan, Canada
119 I 21 **Kerrville**, Texas, U.S.A.
77 A 19 **Kerry Head**, Republic of Ireland ▶
123 S 3 **Kershaw**, South Carolina, U.S.A.
174 I 11 **Kertamulia**, Indonesia
158 H 15 **Keryneia**, Cyprus
188 K 9 **Kerzaz**, Algeria
88 D 8 **Kerzers**, Switzerland
158 B 7 **Keşan**, Turkey
165 V 5 **Keshem**, Afghanistan
83 L 16 **Kessel**, Netherlands
77 I 15 **Keswick**, United Kingdom
93 G 24 **Keszthely**, Hungary
156 M 11 **Ket'**, Russian Federation ∿
174 I 11 **Ketapang**, Indonesia
113 P 11 **Ketchikan**, Alaska, U.S.A.
82 J 10 **Ketelmeer**, Netherlands ≈
92 L 9 **Kętrzyn**, Poland
194 H 7 **Ketta**, Congo
193 V 14 **Kétté**, Cameroon
120 L 12 **Kettering**, Ohio, U.S.A.
116 H 5 **Kettle Falls**, Washington, U.S.A.
85 L 16 **Keuruu**, Finland
175 P 15 **Kewapante**, Indonesia
120 I 3 **Keweenaw Bay**, Michigan, U.S.A. ≈
120 J 3 **Keweenaw Point**, Michigan, U.S.A. ▶
123 T 14 **Key Biscayne**, Florida, U.S.A.
123 T 15 **Key Largo**, Florida, U.S.A. ≛
123 S 15 **Key Largo**, Florida, U.S.A.
123 R 15 **Key West**, Florida, U.S.A.
191 F 23 **Keyala**, Sudan
121 Q 12 **Keyser**, West Virginia, U.S.A.
121 R 14 **Keysville**, Virginia, U.S.A.
197 O 8 **Kezi**, Zimbabwe
93 K 19 **Kežmarok**, Slovakia
196 K 10 **Kgalagadi**, Botswana ▣
197 N 10 **Kgatleng**, Botswana ▣
157 V 14 **Khabarovsk**, Russian Federation
163 X 6 **Khabb**, United Arab Emirates
101 P 9 **Khadzhybeys'kyy Lyman**, Ukraine ◣
168 J 13 **Khagaria**, India
169 M 14 **Khagrachari**, Bangladesh
165 U 12 **Khairpur**, Pakistan
165 X 11 **Khaïrpur**, Pakistan
190 D 7 **Khalîg el 'Arab**, Egypt ≈
163 Y 11 **Khalīj al Ḩalāniyāt**, Oman ≈
163 Z 9 **Khalīj Maşīrah**, Oman ≈
169 I 17 **Khallikot**, India
156 L 7 **Khal'mer-Yu**, Russian Federation
99 K 16 **Khalopyenichy**, Belarus
173 K 15 **Kham Ta Kla**, Thailand
169 D 16 **Khamgaon**, India
164 K 13 **Khamīr**, Iran
163 P 12 **Khamir**, Yemen
163 O 10 **Khamis**, Saudi Arabia
173 K 15 **Khamkkeut**, Laos
169 G 18 **Khammam**, India
157 S 10 **Khampa**, Russian Federation
157 R 11 **Khamra**, Russian Federation
161 Q 6 **Khān al Baghdādī**, Iraq
161 T 8 **Khan al Maḩāwīl**, Iraq
161 T 7 **Khān al Mashāhīdah**, Iraq
161 T 9 **Khān al Muşallá**, Iraq
161 T 10 **Khān ar Rahbah**, Iraq
161 P 2 **Khān as Sūr**, Iraq
161 U 9 **Khān Jadwal**, Iraq
160 I 3 **Khān Shaykhūn**, Syria
160 E 10 **Khān Yūnis**, Israel
165 U 5 **Khānābād**, Afghanistan
161 V 5 **Khānaqīn**, Iraq
169 E 15 **Khandwa**, India
157 U 10 **Khandyga**, Russian Federation
165 W 10 **Khanewal**, Pakistan
173 O 20 **Khanh Duong**, Vietnam
157 S 12 **Khani**, Russian Federation
168 E 9 **Khanna**, India
167 T 9 **Khantau**, Kazakhstan
156 K 10 **Khanty-Mansiysk**, Russian Federation
173 H 24 **Khao Chum Thong**, Thailand
173 I 18 **Khao Khiaw**, Thailand ▲
173 G 17 **Khao Laem Reservoir**, Thailand ◣
173 I 20 **Khao Sai Dao Tai**, Thailand ▲
156 F 11 **Kharabali**, Russian Federation
169 K 15 **Kharagpur**, India
165 S 12 **Kharan**, Pakistan
161 X 11 **Kharfiyah**, Iraq
164 H 10 **Khārg Islands**, Iran ≛
169 D 15 **Khargon**, India
169 H 16 **Khariar**, India
101 V 4 **Kharkiv**, Ukraine
96 K 11 **Kharmanli**, Bulgaria
156 G 7 **Kharovsk**, Russian Federation
191 F 16 **Khartoum**, Sudan ♜
191 F 16 **Khartoum**, Sudan ▣
156 E 12 **Khasav'yurt**, Russian Federation
165 P 12 **Khāsh**, Iran
156 L 8 **Khashgort**, Russian Federation
191 G 17 **Khashm el Girba**, Sudan
159 S 6 **Khashuri**, Georgia
96 K 11 **Khaskovo**, Bulgaria ▣
96 J 11 **Khaskovo**, Bulgaria
157 P 8 **Khatanga**, Russian Federation ∿
157 Q 8 **Khatanga**, Russian Federation
157 Q 7 **Khatangskiy Zaliv**, Russian Federation ≈
157 Z 7 **Khatyrka**, Russian Federation
169 A 14 **Khavda**, India
173 F 18 **Khawsa**, Myanmar
163 N 10 **Khawsh**, Saudi Arabia
162 L 5 **Khaybar**, Saudi Arabia
163 O 10 **Khaybar**, Saudi Arabia
196 K 15 **Khayelitsha**, Republic of South Africa
173 K 14 **Khê Bo**, Vietnam
173 N 16 **Khe Sanh**, Vietnam
168 G 10 **Khela**, India
188 I 7 **Khemisset**, Morocco
173 L 17 **Khemmarat**, Thailand
189 P 6 **Khenchela**, Algeria
188 I 7 **Khenifra**, Morocco
165 U 6 **Khenjan**, Afghanistan
101 S 9 **Kherson**, Ukraine
164 J 5 **Khezerābād**, Iran
157 R 14 **Khilok**, Russian Federation
160 K 4 **Khirbat Isrīyah**, Syria
173 G 17 **Khlong Khlung**, Thailand
100 M 5 **Khmel'nyts'kyy**, Ukraine
101 Q 6 **Khmel'ove**, Ukraine
101 N 5 **Khmil'nyk**, Ukraine
166 K 5 **Khobda**, Kazakhstan
159 R 6 **Khobi**, Georgia
101 O 4 **Khodorkiv**, Ukraine
167 O 13 **Khodzha Davlet**, Uzbekistan
191 C 22 **Khogali**, Sudan
173 H 18 **Khok Samrong**, Thailand
165 T 5 **Kholm**, Afghanistan
157 X 14 **Kholmsk**, Russian Federation
99 M 21 **Kholmyech**, Belarus
196 I 9 **Khomas**, Namibia ▣
164 H 7 **Khomeyn**, Iran
164 I 8 **Khomeynīshahr**, Iran
173 J 16 **Khon Kaen**, Thailand
164 J 12 **Khonj**, Iran
157 V 9 **Khonuu**, Russian Federation
157 V 14 **Khor**, Russian Federation
165 O 7 **Khorāsān**, Iran ▣
173 J 16 **Khorat Plateau**, Thailand ◇
157 Q 13 **Khorinsk**, Russian Federation
196 H 8 **Khorixas**, Namibia
101 T 10 **Khorly**, Ukraine
101 T 3 **Khorol**, Ukraine ∿
101 S 4 **Khorol**, Ukraine
164 G 7 **Khorramābād**, Iran
164 F 9 **Khorramshahr**, Iran
167 T 14 **Khorugh**, Tajikistan
165 T 10 **Khost**, Pakistan
100 L 6 **Khotyn**, Ukraine
188 H 7 **Khouribga**, Morocco
164 H 11 **Khowr-e Soltānī**, Iran ≈
165 V 8 **Khowst**, Afghanistan
99 M 21 **Khoyniki**, Belarus
157 U 9 **Khrebet Cherskogo**, Russian Federation ▴
157 U 12 **Khrebet Dzhugdzhur**, Russian Federation ▴
167 W 9 **Khrebet Dzhungarskiy Alatau**, Kazakhstan ▴
167 Q 9 **Khrebet Karatau**, Kazakhstan ◇
157 P 14 **Khrebet Khamar-Daban**, Russian Federation ▴
157 X 10 **Khrebet Kolymskiy**, Russian Federation ▴
167 P 12 **Khrebet Nuratau**, Uzbekistan ▴
157 T 8 **Khrebet Orulgan**, Russian Federation ▴
157 T 12 **Khrebet Synnagyn**, Russian Federation ▴
167 X 6 **Khrebet Tarbagatay**, Kazakhstan ▴
172 B 12 **Khreum**, Myanmar
166 L 5 **Khromtau**, Kazakhstan
173 K 18 **Khu Khan**, Thailand
163 P 6 **Khuff**, Saudi Arabia
167 R 12 **Khŭjand**, Tajikistan
162 L 7 **Khulays**, Saudi Arabia
169 L 15 **Khulna**, Bangladesh ▣
169 L 15 **Khulna**, Bangladesh
173 F 14 **Khun Yuam**, Thailand
169 J 14 **Khunti**, India
163 R 6 **Khurayş**, Saudi Arabia
165 W 9 **Khushab**, Pakistan
100 H 7 **Khust**, Ukraine
163 U 5 **Khuwayr**, Qatar
191 D 18 **Khuwei**, Sudan
165 T 12 **Khuzdar**, Pakistan
164 G 9 **Khūzestān**, Iran ▣
164 L 7 **Khvor**, Iran

□ Country ▣ Internal administrative region: State/Province/Territory/Dependent territory ♜ Capital city ▴ Mountain range/Undersea ridge ▲ Mountain peak/Volcano/Seamount ◇ Geographic feature ▶ Headland/Point/Cape/Peninsula ◓ Desert ≛ Island/Island group ⁞ Antarctic base ◎ Ocean ◒ Sea ≈ Bay/Gulf/Channel/Strait ◣ Lake ▚ Salt pan/Dry/Intermittent lake ∿ River

164 I 11 **Khvormūj**, Iran
164 F 3 **Khvoy**, Iran
165 V 7 **Khyber Pass**, Afghanistan ▲
212 L 5 **Kia**, Solomon Islands
209 U 12 **Kiama**, New South Wales, Australia
175 Q 8 **Kiamba**, Philippines
195 P 12 **Kiambi**, Democratic Republic of Congo
209 T 12 **Kiandra**, New South Wales, Australia
195 W 12 **Kibaha**, Tanzania
194 F 10 **Kibangou**, Congo
195 V 11 **Kibaya**, Tanzania
195 R 7 **Kiboga**, Uganda
195 O 10 **Kibombo**, Democratic Republic of Congo
195 R 10 **Kibondo**, Tanzania
191 I 22 **Kibre Mengist**, Ethiopia
96 C 12 **Kičevo**, Macedonia (F.Y.R.O.M.)
193 N 7 **Kidal**, Mali
193 O 6 **Kidal**, Mali ▣
77 I 20 **Kidderminster**, United Kingdom
192 G 8 **Kidira**, Senegal
86 H 8 **Kiel**, Germany
120 I 7 **Kiel**, Wisconsin, U.S.A.
93 K 15 **Kielce**, Poland
86 H 8 **Kieler Bucht**, Germany ≈
195 P 14 **Kienge**, Democratic Republic of Congo
212 J 5 **Kieta**, Papua New Guinea
101 P 3 **Kiev**, Ukraine ⌂
101 P 3 **Kiev Reservoir**, Ukraine ⌇
192 G 7 **Kiffa**, Mauritania
95 H 14 **Kifino Selo**, Bosnia and Herzegovina
97 G 20 **Kifisia**, Greece
97 E 18 **Kifisos**, Greece ∿
161 U 5 **Kifrī**, Iraq
195 Q 9 **Kigali**, Rwanda ⌂
192 J 10 **Kignan**, Mali
195 Q 10 **Kigoma**, Tanzania ▣
195 Q 11 **Kigoma**, Tanzania
117 D 25 **Kihei**, Hawaii, U.S.A.
210 L 10 **Kihikihi**, New Zealand
98 F 8 **Kihnu**, Estonia ⛬
177 H 19 **Kii-nagashima**, Japan
177 G 19 **Kii-sanchi**, Japan ▲▲
177 G 19 **Kii-suidō**, Japan ≈
167 T 7 **Kiik**, Kazakhstan
177 O 21 **Kikai**, Japan
177 O 21 **Kikai-jima**, Japan ⛬
94 L 8 **Kikinda**, Serbia and Montenegro
165 Q 14 **Kikki**, Pakistan
195 O 12 **Kikondja**, Democratic Republic of Congo
212 C 5 **Kikori**, Papua New Guinea ∿
212 C 5 **Kikori**, Papua New Guinea
194 J 11 **Kikwit**, Democratic Republic of Congo
117 B 23 **Kilauea**, Hawaii, U.S.A.
77 E 18 **Kilcock**, Republic of Ireland
77 E 18 **Kildare**, Republic of Ireland
194 K 11 **Kilembe**, Democratic Republic of Congo
215 Y 4 **Kili Island**, Marshall Islands ⛬
195 Q 10 **Kiliba**, Democratic Republic of Congo
195 X 10 **Kilifi**, Kenya
195 V 9 **Kilimanjaro**, Tanzania ▲
195 V 10 **Kilimanjaro**, Tanzania ▣
195 X 12 **Kilindoni**, Tanzania
98 F 8 **Kilingi-Nõmme**, Estonia
158 M 13 **Kilis**, Turkey
77 B 19 **Kilkee**, Republic of Ireland
77 D 19 **Kilkenny**, Republic of Ireland
96 F 13 **Kilkis**, Greece
77 B 20 **Killarney**, Republic of Ireland
119 J 20 **Killeen**, Texas, U.S.A.
115 T 5 **Killiniq**, Québec, Canada
76 G 13 **Kilmarnock**, United Kingdom
195 V 12 **Kilosa**, Tanzania
77 B 19 **Kilrush**, Republic of Ireland
169 B 22 **Kilttan**, India ⛬
195 P 13 **Kilwa**, Democratic Republic of Congo
195 W 13 **Kilwa Kivinje**, Tanzania
175 T 12 **Kilwo**, Indonesia
119 G 16 **Kim**, Colorado, U.S.A.
193 W 11 **Kim**, Chad
175 X 14 **Kimaan**, Indonesia
195 W 13 **Kimambi**, Tanzania
194 G 10 **Kimba**, Congo
209 O 11 **Kimba**, South Australia, Australia
212 G 4 **Kimbe**, Papua New Guinea
208 K 3 **Kimberley**, Western Australia, Australia ◇
196 M 12 **Kimberley**, Republic of South Africa
171 Y 5 **Kimch'aek**, North Korea
115 R 4 **Kimmirut**, Nunavut, Canada
97 I 23 **Kimolos**, Greece ⛬
192 K 10 **Kimparana**, Mali
194 G 11 **Kimpese**, Democratic Republic of Congo
176 I 13 **Kimpoku-san**, Japan ▲
194 H 11 **Kimvula**, Democratic Republic of Congo
195 W 10 **Kinango**, Kenya
97 L 22 **Kinaros**, Greece ⛬
115 O 14 **Kincardine**, Ontario, Canada
195 N 13 **Kinda**, Democratic Republic of Congo
113 X 12 **Kindersley**, Saskatchewan, Canada
192 F 11 **Kindia**, Guinea
195 O 9 **Kindu**, Democratic Republic of Congo
156 G 8 **Kineshma**, Russian Federation
117 E 20 **King City**, California, U.S.A.
145 K 23 **King George Bay**, Falkland Islands ≈
218 G 3 **King George Island**, Antarctica ⛬
115 P 7 **King George Islands**, Ontario, Canada ⛬
209 R 14 **King Island**, Tasmania, Australia ⛬
219 X 7 **King Leopold and Queen Astrid Coast**, Antarctica ◇
208 I 3 **King Leopold Ranges**, Western Australia, Australia ▲▲
113 P 10 **King Mountain**, British Columbia, Canada ▲
218 J 9 **King Peninsula**, Antarctica ▶
208 I 3 **King Sound**, Western Australia, Australia ≈
64 M 7 **King William Island**, Nunavut, Canada ⛬
209 W 8 **Kingaroy**, Queensland, Australia
156 F 6 **Kingisepp**, Russian Federation
117 K 21 **Kingman**, Arizona, U.S.A.
61 Q 7 **Kingman Reef**, U.S.A. ▣
165 V 10 **Kingri**, Pakistan
77 M 19 **King's**, United Kingdom
117 N 15 **Kings Peak**, Utah, U.S.A. ▲
209 P 12 **Kingscote**, South Australia, Australia
123 R 8 **Kingsland**, Georgia, U.S.A.
123 Q 1 **Kingsport**, Tennessee, U.S.A.
126 L 8 **Kingston**, Jamaica ⌂
121 U 9 **Kingston**, New York, U.S.A.
211 C 23 **Kingston**, New Zealand
209 Q 13 **Kingston S.E.**, South Australia, Australia
77 L 17 **Kingston upon Hull**, United Kingdom
77 L 21 **Kingston upon Thames**, United Kingdom
127 X 10 **Kingstown**, St Vincent and The Grenadines ⌂
119 J 23 **Kingsville**, Texas, U.S.A.
194 J 11 **Kingungi**, Democratic Republic of Congo
176 L 12 **Kinka-san**, Japan ▶
194 G 10 **Kinkala**, Congo
210 L 11 **Kinloch**, New Zealand
85 E 23 **Kinna**, Sweden
83 K 17 **Kinrooi**, Belgium
194 H 10 **Kinshasa**, Democratic Republic of Congo ⌂
194 H 10 **Kinshasa**, Democratic Republic of Congo ▣
123 V 2 **Kinston**, North Carolina, U.S.A.
192 M 12 **Kintampo**, Ghana
192 H 10 **Kintinian**, Guinea
175 P 11 **Kintom**, Indonesia
174 L 12 **Kintop**, Indonesia
77 F 14 **Kintyre**, United Kingdom ⛬
172 D 10 **Kinu**, Myanmar
195 T 10 **Kinyangiri**, Tanzania
191 F 23 **Kinyeti**, Sudan ▲
195 T 12 **Kipembawe**, Tanzania
195 R 12 **Kipili**, Tanzania
195 P 15 **Kipushi**, Democratic Republic of Congo
195 Q 15 **Kipushia**, Democratic Republic of Congo
213 N 7 **Kirakira**, Solomon Islands
169 G 17 **Kirandul**, India
192 H 8 **Kirané**, Mali
169 F 23 **Kiranur**, India
99 L 18 **Kirawsk**, Belarus
89 T 5 **Kirchdorf**, Austria
87 G 23 **Kirchheim**, Germany
157 Q 13 **Kirenga**, Russian Federation ∿
157 Q 12 **Kirensk**, Russian Federation
167 T 10 **Kirghiz Range**, Kyrgyzstan ▲▲
194 J 8 **Kiri**, Democratic Republic of Congo
214 I 4 **Kiribati**, Oceania □
159 Q 8 **Kirik**, Turkey
158 L 13 **Kirikhan**, Turkey
158 I 9 **Kirikkale**, Turkey
177 C 23 **Kirishima-yama**, Japan ▲
210 K 11 **Kiritehere**, New Zealand
212 G 6 **Kiriwina Island**, Papua New Guinea ⛬
76 I 12 **Kirkcaldy**, United Kingdom
84 M 6 **Kirkenes**, Norway
85 L 19 **Kirkkonummi**, Finland
115 O 12 **Kirkland Lake**, Ontario, Canada
96 N 11 **Kirklareli**, Turkey ▣
96 M 11 **Kirklareli**, Turkey
118 M 13 **Kirksville**, Missouri, U.S.A.
161 T 3 **Kirkūk**, Iraq
76 I 7 **Kirkwall**, United Kingdom
87 D 20 **Kirn**, Germany
156 H 9 **Kirov**, Russian Federation
156 F 8 **Kirov**, Russian Federation
101 V 8 **Kirove**, Ukraine
101 R 6 **Kirovohrad**, Ukraine
101 V 11 **Kirovs'ke**, Ukraine
158 J 10 **Kirşehir**, Turkey
165 T 12 **Kirthar Range**, Pakistan ▲▲
84 I 9 **Kiruna**, Sweden
195 N 8 **Kirundu**, Democratic Republic of Congo
85 G 22 **Kisa**, Sweden
195 N 7 **Kisangani**, Democratic Republic of Congo
175 R 14 **Kisar**, Indonesia ⛬
195 W 12 **Kisarawe**, Tanzania
177 K 16 **Kisarazu**, Japan
156 M 12 **Kiselevsk**, Russian Federation
94 H 12 **Kiseljak**, Bosnia and Herzegovina
168 K 12 **Kishanganj**, India
177 C 24 **Kishika-zaki**, Japan ▶
177 G 19 **Kishiwada**, Japan
167 S 2 **Kishkenekol'**, Kazakhstan
193 P 12 **Kisi**, Nigeria
195 T 8 **Kisii**, Kenya
93 J 25 **Kiskőrös**, Hungary
93 K 24 **Kiskunfélegyháza**, Hungary
93 J 25 **Kiskunhalas**, Hungary
191 K 26 **Kismaayo**, Somalia
177 I 17 **Kiso-sanmyaku**, Japan ▲▲
192 H 11 **Kissidougou**, Guinea
123 R 11 **Kissimmee**, Florida, U.S.A.
195 T 8 **Kisumu**, Kenya
93 N 21 **Kisvárda**, Hungary
119 G 15 **Kit Carson**, Colorado, U.S.A.
192 H 9 **Kita**, Mali
177 B 20 **Kita-Kyūshū**, Japan
177 L 14 **Kitaibaraki**, Japan
176 K 11 **Kitakami**, Japan
176 K 13 **Kitakata**, Japan
195 U 7 **Kitale**, Kenya
176 L 4 **Kitami**, Japan
176 J 3 **Kitami-sanchi**, Japan ▲▲
195 O 11 **Kitanda**, Democratic Republic of Congo
177 D 22 **Kitaura**, Japan
115 O 15 **Kitchener**, Ontario, Canada
195 S 6 **Kitgum**, Uganda
113 P 12 **Kitimat**, British Columbia, Canada
84 L 10 **Kitinen**, Finland ∿
97 E 14 **Kitros**, Greece
100 K 6 **Kitsman'**, Ukraine
84 K 10 **Kittilä**, Finland
123 X 1 **Kitty Hawk**, North Carolina, U.S.A.
195 S 12 **Kitunda**, Tanzania
197 O 4 **Kitwe**, Zambia
89 P 6 **Kitzbühel**, Austria
89 O 7 **Kitzbüheler Alpen**, Austria ▲▲
212 A 5 **Kiunga**, Papua New Guinea
85 L 15 **Kivijärvi**, Finland ⌇
98 I 6 **Kiviõli**, Estonia
212 C 6 **Kiwai Island**, Papua New Guinea ⛬
167 S 5 **Kiyevka**, Kazakhstan
158 C 6 **Kiyiköy**, Turkey
158 I 9 **Kizilirmak**, Turkey ∿
158 G 12 **Kizilören**, Turkey
159 P 13 **Kiziltepe**, Turkey
156 E 12 **Kizlyar**, Russian Federation
83 G 14 **Klaaswaal**, Netherlands
175 X 15 **Kladar**, Indonesia
93 C 17 **Kladno**, Czech Republic
94 O 10 **Kladovo**, Serbia and Montenegro
173 I 20 **Klaeng**, Thailand
89 T 9 **Klagenfurt**, Austria
98 B 13 **Klaipėda**, Lithuania
116 C 13 **Klamath**, California, U.S.A.
113 P 10 **Klappan**, British Columbia, Canada ∿
93 B 18 **Klatovy**, Czech Republic
82 N 9 **Klazienaveen**, Netherlands
196 I 13 **Kleinsee**, Republic of South Africa
94 E 11 **Klekovača**, Bosnia and Herzegovina ▲
101 N 7 **Klembivka**, Ukraine
197 N 11 **Klerksdorp**, Republic of South Africa
92 N 12 **Kleszczele**, Poland
100 L 3 **Klevan**, Ukraine
87 B 15 **Kleve**, Germany
99 L 18 **Klichaw**, Belarus
99 O 17 **Klimavichy**, Belarus
96 L 7 **Kliment**, Bulgaria
85 H 23 **Klintehamn**, Sweden
156 E 8 **Klintsy**, Russian Federation
95 O 15 **Klisura**, Serbia and Montenegro
94 F 11 **Ključ**, Bosnia and Herzegovina
93 I 15 **Kłobuck**, Poland
93 F 17 **Kłodzko**, Poland
85 D 19 **Kløfta**, Norway
83 E 16 **Kloosterzande**, Netherlands
88 J 8 **Klosters**, Switzerland
93 H 15 **Kluczbork**, Poland
99 I 19 **Klyetsk**, Belarus
157 Y 10 **Klyuchi**, Russian Federation
85 A 18 **Knarvik**, Norway
96 H 7 **Knezha**, Bulgaria
94 L 12 **Knić**, Serbia and Montenegro
94 E 12 **Knin**, Croatia
89 U 7 **Knittelfeld**, Austria
123 Q 13 **Knob Island**, Florida, U.S.A. ⛬
83 C 16 **Knokke-Heist**, Belgium
215 Z 4 **Knox**, Marshall Islands ⛬
120 J 10 **Knox**, Indiana, U.S.A.
219 X 10 **Knox Coast**, Antarctica ◇
118 L 12 **Knoxville**, Iowa, U.S.A.
123 O 6 **Knoxville**, Georgia, U.S.A.
123 P 2 **Knoxville**, Tennessee, U.S.A.
65 P 10 **Knud Rasmussen Land**, Greenland ◇
196 L 15 **Knysna**, Republic of South Africa
173 F 23 **Ko Chan**, Thailand ⛬
173 J 21 **Ko Chang**, Thailand ⛬
176 I 8 **Ko-jima**, Japan ⛬
173 J 21 **Ko Kut**, Thailand ⛬
173 F 25 **Ko Lanta**, Thailand ⛬
173 G 25 **Ko Lanta**, Thailand
173 G 25 **Ko Libong**, Thailand ⛬
173 H 23 **Ko Phangan**, Thailand ⛬
173 F 23 **Ko Phra Thong**, Thailand ⛬
173 F 25 **Ko Phuket**, Thailand ⛬
173 H 23 **Ko Samui**, Thailand ⛬
173 G 23 **Ko Tao**, Thailand ⛬
173 G 25 **Ko Yao Yai**, Thailand ⛬
195 W 11 **Koani**, Tanzania
174 G 12 **Koba**, Indonesia
94 A 7 **Kobarid**, Slovenia
177 F 18 **Kōbe**, Japan
175 R 10 **Kobe**, Indonesia
101 T 5 **Kobelyaky**, Ukraine
192 H 8 **Kobenni**, Mauritania
87 D 18 **Koblenz**, Germany
101 Q 9 **Kobleve**, Ukraine
191 I 18 **K'obo**, Ethiopia
195 R 6 **Koboko**, Uganda
175 V 13 **Kobroör**, Indonesia ⛬
99 F 21 **Kobryn**, Belarus
112 J 4 **Kobuk**, Alaska, U.S.A. ∿
159 Q 7 **K'obulet'i**, Georgia
158 E 8 **Kocaeli**, Turkey
96 E 11 **Kočani**, Macedonia (F.Y.R.O.M.)
94 K 11 **Koceljevo**, Serbia and Montenegro
94 C 8 **Kočevje**, Slovenia
168 L 12 **Koch Bihar**, India
177 E 20 **Kōchi**, Japan
167 V 10 **Kochkor**, Kyrgyzstan
156 E 11 **Kochubey**, Russian Federation
93 N 14 **Kock**, Poland
177 B 26 **Kodakara-jima**, Japan ⛬
169 J 14 **Kodarma**, India
112 I 9 **Kodiak**, Alaska, U.S.A.
112 I 9 **Kodiak Island**, Alaska, U.S.A. ⛬
169 A 16 **Kodinar**, India
157 P 12 **Kodinsk**, Russian Federation
191 E 20 **Kodok**, Sudan
176 J 8 **Kodomari-misaki**, Japan ▶
96 K 12 **Kodzhaele**, Greece ▲
196 J 11 **Koës**, Namibia
96 M 11 **Kofçaz**, Turkey
158 H 15 **Kofínou**, Cyprus
89 V 7 **Köflach**, Austria
192 M 13 **Koforidua**, Ghana
177 J 16 **Kōfu**, Japan
177 E 18 **Kōfu**, Japan
115 P 6 **Kogaluk**, Québec, Canada ∿
156 L 10 **Kogalym**, Russian Federation
85 D 25 **Køge**, Denmark
193 Q 12 **Kogi**, Nigeria ▣
165 R 8 **Koh-i-Sangān**, Afghanistan ▲
165 S 13 **Kohan**, Pakistan
165 W 8 **Kohat**, Pakistan
98 G 6 **Kohila**, Estonia
168 N 13 **Kohima**, India
164 H 9 **Kohkīlūyeh Va Būyeraḥmadī**, Iran ▣
165 P 7 **Kohsan**, Afghanistan
98 I 5 **Kohtla-Järve**, Estonia
161 T 2 **Koi Sanjaq**, Iraq
84 L 11 **Koivu**, Finland
208 G 12 **Kojonup**, Western Australia, Australia
167 V 12 **Kök-Aygy**, Kyrgyzstan
167 S 12 **Kokand**, Uzbekistan
192 E 8 **Koki**, Senegal
85 K 14 **Kokkola**, Finland
193 P 10 **Koko**, Nigeria
212 E 6 **Kokoda**, Papua New Guinea
192 H 9 **Kokofata**, Mali
120 K 11 **Kokomo**, Indiana, U.S.A.
211 E 23 **Kokonga**, New Zealand
212 H 4 **Kokopo**, Papua New Guinea
193 O 12 **Kokoro**, Benin
167 X 5 **Kokpekti**, Kazakhstan
167 Q 10 **Koksaray**, Kazakhstan
167 R 3 **Kokshetau**, Kazakhstan
83 A 17 **Koksijde**, Belgium
197 O 13 **Kokstad**, Republic of South Africa
167 X 9 **Koktal**, Kazakhstan
167 Y 7 **Koktuma**, Kazakhstan
177 C 23 **Kokubu**, Japan
156 I 5 **Kola Peninsula**, Russian Federation ▶
175 O 13 **Kolaka**, Indonesia
169 E 21 **Kolar**, India
168 E 13 **Kolaras**, India
84 K 10 **Kolari**, Finland
95 J 15 **Kolašin**, Serbia and Montenegro
168 C 11 **Kolayat**, India
192 E 9 **Kolda**, Senegal
194 M 10 **Kole**, Democratic Republic of Congo
195 N 6 **Kole**, Democratic Republic of Congo
98 H 7 **Kolga-Jaani**, Estonia
98 G 5 **Kolga laht**, Estonia ≈
169 C 18 **Kolhapur**, India
169 L 19 **Kolhumadulu Atoll**, Maldives ⛬
85 O 15 **Kolin**, Finland ▲
93 E 17 **Kolín**, Czech Republic
191 I 21 **K'olīto**, Ethiopia
214 H 8 **Koliu**, Wallis and Futuna Islands
98 D 9 **Kolkasrags**, Latvia ▶
167 R 14 **Kolkhozobod**, Tajikistan
100 K 2 **Kolky**, Ukraine
89 S 3 **Kollerschlag**, Austria
92 M 10 **Kolno**, Poland
92 I 13 **Koło**, Poland
92 E 8 **Kołobrzeg**, Poland
192 I 9 **Kolokani**, Mali
212 K 6 **Kolombangara**, Solomon Islands ⛬
156 F 8 **Kolomna**, Russian Federation
100 J 6 **Kolomyya**, Ukraine
192 J 10 **Kolondiéba**, Mali
215 Q 15 **Kolonia**, Federated States of Micronesia
175 P 13 **Kolono**, Indonesia
156 M 11 **Kolpashevo**, Russian Federation
97 H 15 **Kolpos Agiou Orous**, Greece ≈
97 H 25 **Kolpos Chanion**, Greece ≈
97 G 14 **Kolpos Ierissou**, Greece ≈
97 G 15 **Kolpos Kassandras**, Greece ≈
96 H 13 **Kolpos Kavalas**, Greece ≈
97 G 25 **Kolpos Kissamou**, Greece ≈
167 X 9 **Kol'shat**, Kazakhstan
167 R 4 **Koluton**, Kazakhstan
195 N 14 **Kolwezi**, Democratic Republic of Congo
99 M 22 **Kolyban**, Belarus
157 W 8 **Kolyma**, Russian Federation ∿
190 F 11 **Kôm Ombo**, Egypt
177 H 17 **Komaki**, Japan
195 Q 8 **Komanda**, Democratic Republic of Congo
93 H 22 **Komárno**, Slovakia
177 H 16 **Komatsu**, Japan
175 P 11 **Kombakomba**, Indonesia
192 M 10 **Kombissiri**, Burkina Faso
101 Q 9 **Kominternivs'ke**, Ukraine
93 H 25 **Komló**, Hungary
175 N 15 **Komodo**, Indonesia ⛬
192 H 11 **Komodou**, Guinea
177 J 15 **Komoro**, Japan
97 J 13 **Komotinì**, Greece
101 R 7 **Kompaniyivka**, Ukraine
196 M 14 **Kompasberg**, Republic of South Africa ▲
167 N 2 **Komsomolets**, Kazakhstan
157 W 13 **Komsomol'sk-na-Amure**, Russian Federation
157 Y 6 **Komsomol'skiy**, Russian Federation
166 M 5 **Komsomol'skoye**, Kazakhstan
96 J 11 **Komuniga**, Bulgaria
173 O 18 **Kon Plong**, Vietnam
173 O 18 **Kon Tum**, Vietnam
169 J 17 **Konarka**, India
169 H 17 **Kondagaon**, India
195 U 11 **Kondoa**, Tanzania
165 U 5 **Kondūz**, Afghanistan
213 P 13 **Koné**, New Caledonia
65 O 13 **Kong Christian IX Land**, Greenland ◇
65 P 12 **Kong Christian X Land**, Greenland ◇
65 N 12 **Kong Frederik IX Land**, Greenland ◇
65 Q 11 **Kong Frederik VIII Land**, Greenland ◇
65 Q 12 **Kong Wilhelm Land**, Greenland ◇
196 L 7 **Kongola**, Namibia
195 O 11 **Kongolo**, Democratic Republic of Congo
192 M 9 **Kongoussi**, Burkina Faso
85 D 20 **Kongsberg**, Norway
85 E 19 **Kongsvinger**, Norway
170 G 6 **Kongur Shan**, China ▲
195 U 11 **Kongwa**, Tanzania
87 M 25 **Königssee**, Germany ⌇
92 H 13 **Konin**, Poland
211 L 15 **Konini**, New Zealand
97 B 15 **Konitsa**, Greece
94 H 13 **Konjic**, Bosnia and Herzegovina
84 J 8 **Könkämäeno**, Finland ∿
192 K 8 **Konna**, Mali
192 M 13 **Konongo**, Ghana
212 G 3 **Konos**, Papua New Guinea
156 H 7 **Konosha**, Russian Federation
101 S 2 **Konotop**, Ukraine
93 K 15 **Końskie**, Poland
191 H 22 **Konso**, Ethiopia
87 F 25 **Konstanz**, Germany
169 G 18 **Konta**, India

□ Country ▣ Internal administrative region: State/Province/Territory/Dependent territory ⌂ Capital city ▲▲ Mountain range/Undersea ridge ▲ Mountain peak/Volcano/Seamount ◇ Geographic feature ▶ Headland/Point/Cape/Peninsula ◓ Desert ⛬ Island/Island group ⁙ Antarctic base ◎ Ocean ◒ Sea ≈ Bay/Gulf/Channel/Strait ⌇ Lake ▞ Salt pan/Dry/Intermittent lake ∿ River

193 Q 11 Kontagora, Nigeria
85 N 14 Kontiomäki, Finland
158 H 12 Konya, Turkey
175 U 11 Koor, Indonesia
208 G 10 Koorda, Western Australia, Australia
116 I 9 Kooskia, Idaho, U.S.A.
210 K 11 Kopaki, New Zealand
95 L 14 Kopaonik, Serbia and Montenegro
84 C 9 Kópasker, Iceland
167 V 7 Kopbirlik, Kazakhstan
94 A 8 Koper, Slovenia
164 L 4 Kopet Dag, Iran/Turkmenistan
95 J 16 Koplik, Albania
169 D 21 Koppa, India
85 D 17 Koppang, Norway
94 F 7 Koprivnica, Croatia
100 L 5 Kopychyntsi, Ukraine
95 L 17 Korab, Albania/Macedonia (F.Y.R.O.M.)
95 L 17 Korab, Albania
191 L 22 K'orahē, Ethiopia
169 E 18 Korangal, India
169 H 15 Korba, India
87 F 16 Korbach, Germany
193 X 11 Korbol, Chad
95 L 20 Korçë, Albania
95 F 15 Korčula, Croatia
95 E 15 Korčula, Croatia
95 E 14 Korčulanski Kanal, Croatia
167 U 10 Korday, Kazakhstan
164 F 5 Kordestān, Iran
171 W 6 Korea Bay, North Korea
171 Z 8 Korea Strait, South Korea
191 I 18 Korem, Ethiopia
210 J 7 Koremoa, New Zealand
100 L 3 Korets', Ukraine
157 Z 9 Korf, Russian Federation
158 E 8 Körfez, Turkey
170 I 4 Korgas, China
192 J 11 Korhogo, Côte d'Ivoire
97 F 20 Korinthos, Greece
93 H 23 Kōris-hegy, Hungary
176 K 13 Kōriyama, Japan
158 E 12 Korkuteli, Turkey
170 K 5 Korla, China
93 F 24 Körmend, Hungary
94 C 12 Kornat, Croatia
89 X 3 Korneuburg, Austria
213 Y 11 Koro, Fiji
192 L 9 Koro, Mali
213 X 12 Koro Sea, Fiji
193 X 8 Koro Toro, Chad
158 F 8 Köroğlu Dağlari, Turkey
158 G 8 Köroğlu Tepesi, Turkey
195 W 11 Korogwe, Tanzania
97 D 23 Koroni, Greece
214 I 15 Koror, Palau
93 K 24 Körös, Hungary
101 N 3 Korosten', Ukraine
101 O 4 Korostyshiv, Ukraine
85 M 17 Korpilahti, Finland
101 Q 5 Korsun'-Shevchenkivs'kyy, Ukraine
83 B 18 Kortemark, Belgium
191 E 15 Korti, Sudan
83 C 19 Kortrijk, Belgium
157 Y 9 Koryakskiy Khrebet, Russian Federation
92 N 10 Korycin, Poland
101 R 1 Koryukivka, Ukraine
97 M 23 Kos, Greece
97 M 22 Kos, Greece
101 U 10 Kosa Arabats'ka Strilka, Ukraine
101 V 10 Kosa Biryuchyy Ostriv, Ukraine
92 F 13 Kościan, Poland
92 H 9 Kościerzyna, Poland
122 I 5 Kosciusko, Mississippi, U.S.A.
98 G 6 Kose, Estonia
156 M 14 Kosh-Agach, Russian Federation
167 U 11 Kosh-Döbö, Kyrgyzstan
177 B 23 Koshiki-kaikyō, Japan
177 A 23 Koshikijima-rettō, Japan
165 P 7 Koshk, Afghanistan
93 L 20 Košice, Slovakia
100 J 7 Kosiv, Ukraine
94 K 12 Kosjerić, Serbia and Montenegro
167 Q 5 Koskol', Kazakhstan
171 Y 6 Kosŏng, North Korea
95 L 15 Kosovo, Serbia and Montenegro
95 L 15 Kosovska Mitrovica, Serbia and Montenegro
215 R 15 Kosrae, Federated States of Micronesia
215 R 15 Kosrae, Federated States of Micronesia
89 P 6 Kössen, Austria
167 O 4 Kostanay, Kazakhstan
167 O 3 Kostanay, Kazakhstan
96 H 10 Kostenets, Bulgaria
191 F 18 Kosti, Sudan
96 F 9 Kostinbrod, Bulgaria
100 L 3 Kostopil', Ukraine
92 D 12 Kostrzyn, Poland
101 X 6 Kostyantynivka, Ukraine
92 F 8 Koszalin, Poland
93 K 17 Koszyce, Poland
165 U 13 Kot Diji, Pakistan
168 E 11 Kot Putli, India
168 D 13 Kota, India
174 E 7 Kota Bharu, Malaysia
174 L 8 Kota Kinabalu, Malaysia
174 F 13 Kotaagung, Indonesia
174 M 12 Kotabaru, Indonesia
174 F 13 Kotabumi, Indonesia
175 Q 10 Kotamobagu, Indonesia
174 D 10 Kotapinang, Indonesia
210 K 12 Kotare, New Zealand
96 L 8 Kotel, Bulgaria
156 H 9 Kotel'nich, Russian Federation
156 E 10 Kotel'nikovo, Russian Federation
101 U 4 Kotel'va, Ukraine
195 T 6 Kotido, Uganda
85 N 18 Kotka, Finland
156 I 8 Kotlas, Russian Federation
112 H 5 Kotlik, Alaska, U.S.A.
95 I 16 Kotor, Serbia and Montenegro
94 G 10 Kotor Varoš, Bosnia and Herzegovina
193 R 10 Kotorkoshi, Nigeria
192 L 12 Kotouba, Côte d'Ivoire
101 O 8 Kotovs'k, Ukraine
99 F 13 Kotra, Belarus
165 U 14 Kotri, Pakistan
89 Q 9 Kötschach, Austria
169 G 18 Kottagudem, India
169 G 19 Kottapatnam, India
194 L 4 Kotto, Central African Republic
157 R 8 Kotuy, Russian Federation
112 I 3 Kotzebue, Alaska, U.S.A.
65 Q 2 Kotzebue Sound, Arctic Ocean
194 K 4 Kouango, Central African Republic
192 G 10 Koubia, Guinea
194 E 10 Kouilou, Congo
158 G 15 Koúklia, Cyprus
194 E 8 Koulamoutou, Gabon
192 I 9 Koulikoro, Mali
192 I 9 Koulikoro, Mali
213 O 13 Koumac, New Caledonia
192 F 10 Koumbia, Guinea
193 X 11 Koumra, Chad
192 F 9 Koúndâra, Guinea
192 E 9 Koungheul, Senegal
192 M 10 Koupéla, Burkina Faso
139 Y 6 Kourou, French Guiana
192 H 11 Kouroussa, Guinea
192 F 9 Koussanar, Senegal
193 V 10 Kousséri, Chad
192 J 10 Koutiala, Mali
97 D 16 Koutsochero, Greece
85 N 18 Kouvola, Finland
156 I 5 Kovdor, Russian Federation
100 J 2 Kovel', Ukraine
209 R 3 Kowanyama, Queensland, Australia
171 U 14 Kowloon, China
158 C 12 Köycegiz, Turkey
169 C 18 Koyna Reservoir, India
96 G 7 Koynare, Bulgaria
158 M 9 Koyulhisar, Turkey
158 K 12 Kozan, Turkey
97 D 15 Kozani, Greece
94 F 9 Kozara, Bosnia and Herzegovina
101 Q 3 Kozelets', Ukraine
157 R 7 Kozhevnikovo, Russian Federation
93 L 14 Kozienice, Poland
96 G 6 Kozloduy, Bulgaria
177 K 18 Kōzu-shima, Japan
101 O 5 Kozyatyn, Ukraine
193 N 13 Kpalimé, Togo
173 F 22 Kra Buri, Thailand
173 G 25 Krabi, Thailand
173 M 20 Krâchéh, Cambodia
94 L 12 Kragujevac, Serbia and Montenegro
174 G 14 Krakatau, Indonesia
93 K 17 Kraków, Poland
173 K 19 Krâlănh, Cambodia
127 S 11 Kralendijk, Netherlands Antilles
94 B 9 Kraljeviča, Croatia
94 L 12 Kraljevo, Serbia and Montenegro
93 B 17 Kralovice, Czech Republic
101 X 6 Kramators'k, Ukraine
83 F 15 Krammer, Netherlands
97 F 21 Kranidi, Greece
94 B 7 Kranj, Slovenia
166 K 4 Kransoyar, Kazakhstan
94 D 7 Krapina, Croatia
93 H 16 Krapkowice, Poland
156 K 6 Krasino, Russian Federation
98 I 13 Krāslava, Latvia
99 N 18 Krasnapollye, Belarus
99 I 19 Krasnaya Slabada, Belarus
101 O 8 Krasni Okny, Ukraine
93 M 15 Kraśnik, Poland
101 X 7 Krasnoarmiys'k, Ukraine
156 D 10 Krasnodar, Russian Federation
101 V 5 Krasnohrad, Ukraine
101 W 5 Krasnopavlivka, Ukraine
101 T 10 Krasnoperekops'k, Ukraine
101 U 3 Krasnopillya, Ukraine
157 N 9 Krasnosel'kup, Russian Federation
101 S 6 Krasnosillya, Ukraine
156 I 10 Krasnoufimsk, Russian Federation
166 H 12 Krasnovodskiy Zaliv, Turkmenistan
157 N 12 Krasnoyarsk, Russian Federation
93 O 15 Krasnystaw, Poland
101 Z 6 Krasnyy Luch, Ukraine
101 X 5 Krasnyy Lyman, Ukraine
96 E 10 Kratovo, Macedonia (F.Y.R.O.M.)
175 Y 12 Krau, Indonesia
87 B 16 Krefeld, Germany
101 T 6 Kremenchuk, Ukraine
101 S 5 Kremenchuts'ka Vodoskhovyshche, Ukraine
100 K 4 Kremenets', Ukraine
101 Y 5 Kreminna, Ukraine
100 J 6 Kremintsi, Ukraine
89 V 3 Krems an der Donau, Austria
96 F 11 Kresna, Bulgaria
97 D 21 Krestena, Greece
157 R 11 Krestyakh, Russian Federation
98 B 13 Kretinga, Lithuania
89 Q 8 Kreuzeck, Austria
88 H 6 Kreuzlingen, Switzerland
193 S 15 Kribi, Cameroon
89 W 6 Krieglach, Austria
97 C 18 Krikellos, Greece
89 O 7 Krimml, Austria
169 I 15 Krishna, India
169 E 21 Krishnagiri, India
169 K 14 Krishnanagar, India
169 D 21 Krishnaraja Sagara, India
85 B 22 Kristiansand, Norway
85 F 25 Kristianstad, Sweden
85 C 15 Kristiansund, Norway
85 J 17 Kristinestad, Finland
97 J 26 Kriti, Greece
96 E 10 Kriva Palanka, Macedonia (F.Y.R.O.M.)
94 F 7 Križevci, Croatia
94 B 9 Krk, Croatia
94 B 9 Krk, Croatia
94 E 12 Krka, Croatia
101 U 11 Krms'kyy Pivostriv, Ukraine
92 H 7 Krokowa, Poland
84 B 10 Króksfjarðarnes, Iceland
101 S 2 Krolevets', Ukraine
87 J 19 Kronach, Germany
173 J 21 Krŏng Kaôh Kŏng, Cambodia
157 Z 10 Kronotskiy Poluostrov, Russian Federation
157 Z 11 Kronotskiy Zaliv, Russian Federation
197 N 12 Kroonstad, Republic of South Africa
156 D 10 Kropotkin, Russian Federation
93 M 18 Krosno, Poland
93 G 14 Krotoszyn, Poland
94 D 7 Krško, Slovenia
96 J 12 Krumovgrad, Bulgaria
94 J 11 Krupanj, Serbia and Montenegro
93 I 21 Krupina, Slovakia
94 M 13 Kruševac, Serbia and Montenegro
99 N 17 Kryichaw, Belarus
101 T 13 Krymski Hori, Ukraine
93 L 18 Krynica, Poland
101 P 7 Kryve Ozero, Ukraine
101 T 7 Kryvyy Rih, Ukraine
101 N 7 Kryzhopil', Ukraine
93 I 15 Krzepice, Poland
188 K 10 Ksabi, Algeria
188 M 6 Ksar Chellala, Algeria
188 M 6 Ksar el Boukhari, Algeria
188 I 6 Ksar el Kebir, Morocco
174 E 8 Kuala Kangsar, Malaysia
174 E 8 Kuala Kerai, Malaysia
174 E 8 Kuala Lipis, Malaysia
174 E 9 Kuala Lumpur, Malaysia
174 L 8 Kuala Penyu, Malaysia
174 E 9 Kuala Selangor, Malaysia
174 F 8 Kuala Terengganu, Malaysia
174 K 11 Kualakurun, Indonesia
174 F 9 Kuantan, Malaysia
161 O 1 Kubaybāt, Syria
161 R 7 Kubaysah, Iraq
191 A 18 Kubbum, Sudan
212 B 5 Kubeai, Papua New Guinea
96 L 6 Kubrat, Bulgaria
94 M 11 Kučevo, Serbia and Montenegro
169 J 15 Kuchaiburi, India
174 I 10 Kuching, Malaysia
177 B 25 Kuchino-Erabu-shima, Japan
177 B 26 Kuchino-shima, Japan
177 B 22 Kuchinotsu, Japan
169 L 19 Kuda Huvadu Channel, Maldives
169 C 19 Kudal, India
163 N 10 Kudayd, Saudi Arabia
93 F 16 Kudowa-Zdrój, Poland
174 J 14 Kudus, Indonesia
89 O 6 Kufstein, Austria
113 S 4 Kugluktuk, Nunavut, Canada
113 O 3 Kugmallit Bay, Northwest Territories, Canada
165 N 12 Kūh-e Bazmān, Iran
164 F 5 Kūh-e Chehel Chashmeh, Iran
164 L 12 Kūh-e Fūrgun, Iran
164 H 8 Kūh-e Garbosh, Iran
161 T 2 Kūh-e Hājī Ebrāhīm, Iraq
164 F 5 Kūh-e-Haji Ebrahim, Iran
164 K 12 Kūh-e Hormoz, Iran
164 L 11 Kūh-e Ilazārān, Iran
164 M 8 Kūh-e Nāy Band, Iran
165 O 13 Kūh-e Nokhowch, Iran
165 O 9 Kūh-e Palangān, Iran
164 I 11 Kūh-e Shīb, Iran
165 P 12 Kūh-e Taftān, Iran
165 Q 13 Kūhak, Iran
164 H 3 Kuhha-ye Sabalan, Iran
85 N 14 Kuhmo, Finland
196 I 4 Kuito, Angola
177 K 14 Kuji, Japan
176 L 9 Kuji, Japan
177 C 21 Kujū-san, Japan
193 U 9 Kukawa, Nigeria
95 L 16 Kukës, Albania
94 J 8 Kula, Serbia and Montenegro
96 E 6 Kula, Bulgaria
158 C 10 Kula, Turkey
168 L 11 Kula Kangri, Bhutan
98 C 11 Kuldīga, Latvia
209 N 7 Kulgera, Northern Territory, Australia
167 O 10 Kulkuduk, Uzbekistan
87 J 19 Kulmbach, Germany
167 S 14 Kŭlob, Tajikistan
159 Q 11 Kulp, Turkey
166 J 7 Kul'sary, Kazakhstan
158 H 10 Kulu, Turkey
212 H 6 Kulumadau, Papua New Guinea
156 L 12 Kulunda, Russian Federation
177 K 15 Kumagaya, Japan
176 I 7 Kumaishi, Japan
177 C 22 Kumamoto, Japan
177 H 19 Kumano, Japan
96 D 10 Kumanovo, Macedonia (F.Y.R.O.M.)
211 E 18 Kumara Junction, New Zealand
208 H 7 Kumarina Roadhouse, Western Australia, Australia
192 L 13 Kumasi, Ghana
193 S 14 Kumba, Cameroon
169 F 22 Kumbakonam, India
175 Y 14 Kumbe, Indonesia
158 F 10 Kümbet, Turkey
163 P 9 Kumdah, Saudi Arabia
177 M 25 Kume-jima, Japan
156 H 11 Kumertau, Russian Federation
195 T 7 Kumi, Uganda
85 G 21 Kumla, Sweden
86 L 9 Kummerower See, Germany
193 T 11 Kumo, Nigeria
173 J 16 Kumphawapi, Thailand
169 C 20 Kumta, India
195 N 6 Kumu, Democratic Republic of Congo
170 L 5 Kümüx, China
165 V 6 Kunar, Afghanistan
98 H 5 Kunda, Estonia
196 I 2 Kunda-dia-Baze, Angola
174 M 7 Kundat, Malaysia
212 C 4 Kundiawa, Papua New Guinea
174 F 10 Kundur, Indonesia
165 U 5 Kunduz, Afghanistan
196 G 8 Kunene, Namibia
196 F 7 Kunene, Namibia
167 V 10 Kungei Alatau, Kyrgyzstan
113 P 13 Kunghit Island, British Columbia, Canada
166 L 10 Kungrad, Uzbekistan
85 D 23 Kungsbacka, Sweden
194 J 6 Kungu, Democratic Republic of Congo
156 I 10 Kungur, Russian Federation
172 F 12 Kunhing, Myanmar
177 D 21 Kunisaki, Japan
172 F 10 Kunlong, Myanmar
170 H 7 Kunlun Shan, China
171 P 13 Kunming, China
171 X 7 Kunsan, South Korea
93 K 24 Kunszentmárton, Hungary
212 I 4 Kunua, Papua New Guinea
208 K 3 Kununurra, Western Australia, Australia
194 H 10 Kunzulu, Democratic Republic of Congo
85 N 15 Kuopio, Finland
175 P 15 Kupang, Indonesia
212 E 7 Kupiano, Papua New Guinea
98 G 13 Kupiškis, Lithuania
113 O 10 Kupreanof Island, Alaska, U.S.A.
101 X 4 Kup''yans'k, Ukraine
170 J 5 Kuqa, China
159 V 7 Kür, Azerbaijan/Turkey
157 N 13 Kuragino, Russian Federation
177 E 19 Kurashiki, Japan
177 E 18 Kurayoshi, Japan
167 Y 5 Kurchum, Kazakhstan
161 R 1 Kurdistan, Asia
96 J 12 Kŭrdzhali, Bulgaria
96 J 11 Kŭrdzhali, Bulgaria
177 D 20 Kure, Japan
158 I 7 Küre, Turkey
158 H 7 Küre Dağlari, Turkey
98 D 8 Kuressaare, Estonia
167 R 5 Kurgal'dzhinskiy, Kazakhstan
156 J 11 Kurgan, Russian Federation
214 D 2 Kuria, Kiribati
163 Y 11 Kuria Muria, Oman
85 K 16 Kurikka, Finland
60 M 2 Kuril Basin, Pacific Ocean
157 Y 14 Kuril Islands, Russian Federation
60 M 3 Kuril Trench, Pacific Ocean
157 Y 14 Kuril'sk, Russian Federation
191 G 19 Kurmuk, Sudan
169 E 19 Kurnool, India
177 N 26 Kuro-shima, Japan
177 H 15 Kurobe, Japan
177 K 14 Kuroiso, Japan
211 E 22 Kurow, New Zealand
93 M 14 Kurów, Poland
98 E 13 Kuršėnai, Lithuania
98 D 12 Kursīši, Latvia
156 E 9 Kursk, Russian Federation
99 B 15 Kurskaya Kosa, Russian Federation
158 H 8 Kurşunlu, Turkey
159 R 12 Kurtalan, Turkey
170 K 5 Kuruktag, China
196 L 11 Kuruman, Republic of South Africa
177 B 21 Kurume, Japan
157 R 13 Kurumkan, Russian Federation
169 F 25 Kurunegala, Sri Lanka
139 U 7 Kurupukari, Guyana
166 H 10 Kuryk, Kazakhstan
158 C 8 Kuş Gölü, Turkey
158 B 11 Kuşadasi, Turkey
97 M 20 Kuşadasi Körfezi, Greece
158 B 11 Kusadasi Körfezi, Turkey
113 N 8 Kusawa Lake, Yukon Territory, Canada
177 C 24 Kushima, Japan
177 H 20 Kushimoto, Japan
176 M 5 Kushiro, Japan
167 O 3 Kushmurun, Kazakhstan
169 D 19 Kushtagi, India
166 I 4 Kushum, Kazakhstan
112 G 6 Kuskokwim, Alaska, U.S.A.
112 G 7 Kuskokwim Bay, Alaska, U.S.A.
112 H 7 Kuskokwim Mountains, Alaska, U.S.A.
176 M 4 Kussharo-ko, Japan
158 E 9 Kütahya, Turkey
159 R 6 K'ut'aisi, Georgia
210 N 10 Kutarere, New Zealand
176 J 6 Kutchan, Japan
94 F 8 Kutina, Croatia
172 F 10 Kutkai, Myanmar
92 J 13 Kutno, Poland
194 J 9 Kutu, Democratic Republic of Congo
191 B 17 Kutum, Sudan
115 S 6 Kuujjuaq, Québec, Canada
115 P 8 Kuujjuaraapik, Québec, Canada
98 G 5 Kuusalu, Estonia
84 N 11 Kuusamo, Finland
156 H 11 Kuvandyk, Russian Federation
196 H 5 Kuvango, Angola
163 S 3 Kuwait, Kuwait
163 R 2 Kuwait, Asia
101 Q 9 Kuyal'nyts'kyy Lyman, Ukraine
156 L 12 Kuybyshev, Russian Federation
101 W 8 Kuybysheve, Ukraine
167 Q 3 Kuybyshevskiy, Kazakhstan
167 U 8 Kuygan, Kazakhstan
170 K 4 Kuytun, China
156 G 10 Kuznetsk, Russian Federation
100 K 2 Kuznetsovs'k, Ukraine
156 I 6 Kuzomen', Russian Federation
176 K 10 Kuzumaki, Japan
84 H 7 Kvaløya, Norway
84 K 5 Kvaløya, Norway
84 K 6 Kvalsund, Norway
94 B 10 Kvarner, Croatia
94 B 10 Kvarnerić, Croatia
112 H 8 Kvichak Bay, Alaska, U.S.A.
197 P 13 Kwa Mashu, Republic of South Africa
195 U 11 Kwa Mtoro, Tanzania
173 F 18 Kwai, Thailand
215 X 2 Kwajalein, Marshall Islands
193 Q 13 Kwale, Nigeria
194 H 9 Kwamouth, Democratic Republic of Congo
171 Y 8 Kwangju, South Korea
193 P 11 Kwara, Nigeria
197 P 12 Kwazulu-Natal, Republic of South Africa
197 P 7 Kwekwe, Zimbabwe
196 M 9 Kweneng, Botswana
92 I 9 Kwidzyn, Poland
212 E 7 Kwikila, Papua New Guinea
193 X 11 Kyabé, Chad
173 E 16 Kyaikto, Myanmar
157 P 14 Kyakhta, Russian Federation
209 N 11 Kyancutta, South Australia, Australia
173 C 15 Kyangin, Myanmar
172 E 11 Kyaukme, Myanmar

Country · Internal administrative region: State/Province/Territory/Dependent territory · Capital city · Mountain range/Undersea ridge · Mountain peak/Volcano/Seamount · Geographic feature · Headland/Point/Cape/Peninsula · Desert · Island/Island group · Antarctic base · Ocean · Sea · Bay/Gulf/Channel/Strait · Lake · Salt pan/Dry/Intermittent lake · River

173 F 20 **Kyaukpya**, Myanmar
172 B 12 **Kyauktaw**, Myanmar
173 C 15 **Kyeintali**, Myanmar
195 T 13 **Kyela**, Tanzania
76 F 10 **Kyle of Lochalsh**, United Kingdom
87 B 19 **Kyll**, Germany
97 E 20 **Kyllini**, Greece
97 H 18 **Kymi**, Greece
209 R 5 **Kynuna**, Queensland, Australia
177 G 17 **Kyōga-misaki**, Japan
171 Z 7 **Kyŏngju**, South Korea
177 G 18 **Kyōto**, Japan
176 J 10 **Kyowa**, Japan
97 C 21 **Kyparissia**, Greece
97 C 21 **Kyparissiakos Kolpos**, Greece
157 R 14 **Kyra**, Russian Federation
97 H 17 **Kyra Panagia**, Greece
167 V 11 **Kyrgyzstan**, Asia
86 K 12 **Kyritz**, Germany
101 O 11 **Kyrnychky**, Ukraine
101 Q 2 **Kyselivka**, Ukraine
157 U 8 **Kytalyktakh**, Russian Federation
97 F 24 **Kythira**, Greece
97 F 24 **Kythira**, Greece
97 H 21 **Kythnos**, Greece
173 F 22 **Kyun Pila**, Myanmar
166 K 8 **Kyushe**, Kazakhstan
177 C 22 **Kyūshū**, Japan
96 F 10 **Kyustendil**, Bulgaria
96 F 10 **Kyustendil**, Bulgaria
85 L 15 **Kyyjärvi**, Finland
157 O 13 **Kyzyl**, Russian Federation
167 S 10 **Kyzyl-Adyr**, Kyrgyzstan
167 T 12 **Kyzyl-Kyya**, Kyrgyzstan
167 O 10 **Kyzylkum Desert**, Kazakhstan
167 O 9 **Kyzylorda**, Kazakhstan
167 P 9 **Kyzylorda**, Kazakhstan
166 I 9 **Kyzylsay**, Kazakhstan
167 R 6 **Kyzylzhar**, Kazakhstan

L

80 J 9 **La Albuera**, Spain
81 S 4 **La Almunia de Doña Godina**, Spain
139 Q 2 **La Asunción**, Venezuela
144 J 8 **La Banda**, Argentina
80 L 3 **La Bañeza**, Spain
118 C 12 **La Barge**, Wyoming, U.S.A.
78 J 7 **La Baule-Escoublac**, France
123 R 13 **La Belle**, Florida, U.S.A.
79 Q 10 **La Bourboule**, France
125 S 8 **La Carbonera**, Mexico
144 J 12 **La Carlota**, Argentina
81 O 10 **La Carolina**, Spain
126 F 9 **La Ceiba**, Honduras
79 R 7 **La Charité-sur-Loire**, France
79 P 8 **La Châtre**, France
88 C 7 **La-Chaux-de-Fonds**, Switzerland
124 M 8 **La Ciudad**, Mexico
144 I 8 **La Cocha**, Argentina
125 X 11 **La Costa**, Mexico
120 G 7 **La Crosse**, Wisconsin, U.S.A.
124 L 8 **La Cruz**, Mexico
126 G 12 **La Cruz**, Costa Rica
144 M 9 **La Cruz**, Argentina
58 C 9 **La Digue**, Seychelles
139 O 8 **La Esmeralda**, Venezuela
141 L 23 **La Esmeralda**, Bolivia
126 E 10 **La Esperanza**, Honduras
145 G 16 **La Esperanza**, Argentina
141 L 19 **La Estrella**, Bolivia
58 E 7 **La Ferme**, Rodrigues Island
79 N 6 **La Flèche**, France
213 P 14 **La Foa**, New Caledonia
80 K 5 **La Fuente de San Esteban**, Spain
189 P 5 **La Galite**, Tunisia
62 L 12 **La Gomera**, Canary Islands
139 S 6 **La Gran Sabana**, Venezuela
123 N 5 **La Grange**, Georgia, U.S.A.
138 K 1 **La Guajira**, Colombia
119 G 15 **La Junta**, Colorado, U.S.A.
145 F 14 **La Laja**, Chile
140 B 13 **La Libertad**, Peru
126 D 8 **La Libertad**, Guatemala
144 G 11 **La Ligua**, Chile
80 M 14 **La Línea de la Concepción**, Spain
113 V 10 **La Loche**, Saskatchewan, Canada
83 F 21 **La Louvière**, Belgium
91 D 15 **La Maddalena**, Italy
141 E 17 **La Mejorada**, Peru
141 E 16 **La Merced**, Peru
125 O 5 **La Mora**, Mexico
79 V 11 **La Mure**, France
80 M 8 **La Nava de Ricomalillo**, Spain
144 F 6 **La Negra**, Chile
141 D 16 **La Oroya**, Peru
62 L 11 **La Palma**, Canary Islands
126 L 14 **La Palma**, Panama
144 O 13 **La Paloma**, Uruguay
145 I 14 **La Pampa**, Argentina
141 I 19 **La Paz**, Bolivia
141 H 18 **La Paz**, Bolivia
124 J 8 **La Paz**, Mexico
144 H 12 **La Paz**, Argentina
144 L 10 **La Paz**, Argentina
138 M 11 **La Pedrera**, Colombia
125 N 5 **La Perla**, Mexico
176 I 2 **La Pérouse Strait**, Japan
125 S 8 **La Pesca**, Mexico
125 P 11 **La Piedad**, Mexico
144 M 13 **La Plata**, Argentina
58 A 14 **La Possession**, Réunion
144 I 4 **La Quiaca**, Argentina
81 Q 3 **La Rioja**, Spain
144 I 9 **La Rioja**, Argentina
144 H 9 **La Rioja**, Argentina
80 L 2 **La Robla**, Spain
80 K 9 **La Roca de la Sierra**, Spain
83 J 22 **La Roche-en-Ardenne**, Belgium
78 L 8 **La Roche-sur-Yon**, France
78 L 9 **La Rochelle**, France
81 Q 9 **La Roda**, Spain
127 S 7 **La Romana**, Dominican Republic
113 X 10 **La Ronge**, Saskatchewan, Canada
125 P 5 **La Rosita**, Mexico
120 H 9 **La Salle**, Illinois, U.S.A.
115 P 12 **La Sarre**, Québec, Canada
144 F 9 **La Serena**, Chile
81 W 3 **La Seu d'Urgell**, Spain
81 P 9 **La Solana**, Spain
90 D 9 **La Spezia**, Italy
138 I 10 **La Tagua**, Colombia
144 I 11 **La Toma**, Argentina
115 R 12 **La Tuque**, Québec, Canada
81 S 12 **La Unión**, Spain
125 P 13 **La Unión**, Mexico
126 E 10 **La Unión**, El Salvador
141 M 19 **La Unión**, Bolivia
125 O 6 **La Vibora**, Mexico
141 G 20 **La Yarada**, Peru
89 X 2 **Laa an der Thaya**, Austria
86 K 9 **Laage**, Germany
191 N 20 **Laascaanood**, Somalia
191 N 19 **Laasgoray**, Somalia
188 D 10 **Laâyoune**, Western Sahara
213 X 11 **Labasa**, Fiji
192 G 10 **Labé**, Guinea
115 R 13 **Labelle**, Québec, Canada
94 B 9 **Labin**, Croatia
175 P 3 **Labo**, Philippines
78 L 13 **Labouheyre**, France
144 J 12 **Laboulaye**, Argentina
115 U 7 **Labrador**, Newfoundland and Labrador, Canada
64 L 13 **Labrador Basin**, Arctic Ocean
115 T 9 **Labrador City**, Newfoundland and Labrador, Canada
64 L 12 **Labrador Sea**, Arctic Ocean
142 D 12 **Lábrea**, Brazil
174 F 11 **Labu**, Indonesia
174 K 8 **Labuan**, Malaysia
174 L 8 **Labuan**, Malaysia
175 R 11 **Labuan**, Indonesia
171 V 2 **Labudalin**, China
175 N 15 **Labuhanbajo**, Indonesia
174 D 9 **Labuhanbilik**, Indonesia
174 B 9 **Labuhanhaji**, Indonesia
174 G 13 **Labuhanmeringgai**, Indonesia
156 L 8 **Labytnangi**, Russian Federation
95 K 17 **Laç**, Albania
193 V 9 **Lac**, Chad
115 Q 8 **Lac à l'Eau Claire**, Québec, Canada
115 R 8 **Lac Bienville**, Québec, Canada
115 P 8 **Lac Burton**, Québec, Canada
115 S 8 **Lac Caniapiscau**, Québec, Canada
193 T 13 **Lac de Bamendjing**, Cameroon
192 I 13 **Lac de Buyo**, Côte d'Ivoire
192 J 12 **Lac de Kossou**, Côte d'Ivoire
193 V 12 **Lac de Ladgo**, Cameroon
192 H 9 **Lac de Manantali**, Mali
193 U 13 **Lac de Mbakaou**, Cameroon
88 C 8 **Lac de Neuchâtel**, Switzerland
115 Q 10 **Lac Evans**, Québec, Canada
192 K 7 **Lac Faguibine**, Mali
192 L 8 **Lac Garou**, Mali
115 Q 7 **Lac Guillaume-Delisle**, Québec, Canada
115 U 9 **Lac Joseph**, Newfoundland and Labrador, Canada
115 R 12 **Lac Kempt**, Québec, Canada
113 S 7 **Lac la Martre**, Northwest Territories, Canada
113 X 10 **Lac la Ronge**, Saskatchewan, Canada
194 J 9 **Lac Mai- Ndombe**, Democratic Republic of Congo
115 S 10 **Lac Manouane**, Québec, Canada
121 V 5 **Lac Memphrémagog**, Vermont, U.S.A.
115 Q 7 **Lac Minto**, Québec, Canada
115 Q 10 **Lac Mistassini**, Québec, Canada
192 L 8 **Lac Niangay**, Mali
194 J 8 **Lac Ntomba**, Democratic Republic of Congo
194 D 8 **Lac Onangue**, Gabon
115 Q 5 **Lac Payne**, Québec, Canada
114 K 10 **Lac Seul**, Ontario, Canada
115 R 12 **Lac St-Jean**, Québec, Canada
173 O 20 **Lac Thiên**, Vietnam
195 O 13 **Lac Upemba**, Democratic Republic of Congo
78 L 11 **Lacanau**, France
125 X 14 **Lacanja**, Mexico
94 J 10 **Lacarak**, Serbia and Montenegro
79 Q 14 **Lacaune**, France
169 A 22 **Laccadive Islands**, India
88 H 7 **Lachen**, Switzerland
209 S 11 **Lachlan**, New South Wales, Australia
168 K 12 **Lachung**, India
159 W 9 **Laçin**, Azerbaijan
91 C 18 **Laconi**, Italy
121 W 7 **Laconia**, New Hampshire, U.S.A.
101 N 12 **Lacul Razim**, Romania
101 N 13 **Lacul Sinoie**, Romania
168 E 7 **Ladakh Range**, India
99 A 16 **Ladushkin**, Russian Federation
209 T 14 **Lady Barron**, Tasmania, Australia
120 G 5 **Ladysmith**, Wisconsin, U.S.A.
197 P 12 **Ladysmith**, Republic of South Africa
101 P 6 **Ladyzhynka**, Ukraine
215 W 2 **Lae**, Marshall Islands
212 E 5 **Lae**, Papua New Guinea
85 D 23 **Laesø**, Denmark
84 L 7 **Laevvajåk**, Norway
119 N 21 **Lafayette**, Louisiana, U.S.A.
120 J 11 **Lafayette**, Indiana, U.S.A.
193 S 12 **Lafia**, Nigeria
193 Q 12 **Lafiagi**, Nigeria
156 F 11 **Lagan'**, Russian Federation
192 E 8 **Lagbar**, Senegal
85 C 17 **Lågen**, Norway
165 V 6 **Laghmān**, Afghanistan
188 M 7 **Laghouat**, Algeria
96 F 13 **Lagkadas**, Greece
145 F 22 **Lago Argentino**, Argentina
144 N 11 **Lago Artificial de Rincón del Bonete**, Uruguay
145 G 20 **Lago Buenos Aires**, Argentina
145 G 22 **Lago Cardiel**, Argentina
145 H 19 **Lago Colhué Huapi**, Argentina
197 Q 5 **Lago de Cahora Bassa**, Mozambique
126 D 9 **Lago de Izabal**, Guatemala
126 F 11 **Lago de Managua**, Nicaragua
141 I 21 **Lago de Poopó**, Bolivia
90 G 12 **Lago di Bolsena**, Italy
90 H 13 **Lago di Bracciano**, Italy
90 D 6 **Lago di Como**, Italy
90 E 7 **Lago di Garda**, Italy
91 L 14 **Lago di Lesina**, Italy
88 H 11 **Lago di Lugano**, Switzerland
91 L 14 **Lago di Varano**, Italy
90 E 6 **Lago d'Iseo**, Italy
145 H 25 **Lago Fagnano**, Argentina
126 K 13 **Lago Gatún**, Panama
145 G 20 **Lago General Carrera**, Chile
145 E 17 **Lago Llanquihué**, Chile
90 C 6 **Lago Maggiore**, Italy
144 J 10 **Lago Mar Chiquita**, Argentina
145 H 19 **Lago Musters**, Argentina
145 F 16 **Lago Nahuel Huapi**, Argentina
145 F 22 **Lago O'Higgins**, Chile
91 C 17 **Lago Omodeo**, Italy
145 H 15 **Lago Pellegrini**, Argentina
126 D 8 **Lago Petén Itzá**, Guatemala
145 F 16 **Lago Ranco**, Chile
145 F 16 **Lago Rupanco**, Chile
145 F 22 **Lago San Martin**, Argentina
90 G 11 **Lago Trasimeno**, Italy
145 F 22 **Lago Viedma**, Argentina
145 G 22 **Lago Viedma**, Argentina
80 G 12 **Lagoa**, Portugal
143 I 22 **Lagoa dos Patos**, Brazil
143 I 23 **Lagoa Mangueira**, Brazil
143 I 23 **Lagoa Mirim**, Brazil/Uruguay
159 V 6 **Lagodekhi**, Georgia
193 P 13 **Lagos**, Nigeria
80 G 12 **Lagos**, Portugal
193 O 13 **Lagos**, Nigeria
125 P 10 **Lagos de Moreno**, Mexico
195 Q 11 **Lagosa**, Tanzania
208 H 4 **Lagrange**, Western Australia, Australia
143 J 21 **Laguna**, Brazil
126 H 9 **Laguna Caratasca**, Honduras
125 O 11 **Laguna de Chapala**, Mexico
126 I 13 **Laguna de Chiriquí**, Panama
126 H 11 **Laguna de Perlas**, Nicaragua
126 H 11 **Laguna de Perlas**, Nicaragua
141 K 17 **Laguna de San Luis**, Bolivia
125 X 12 **Laguna de Términos**, Mexico
95 J 19 **Laguna e Karavastasë**, Albania
119 K 23 **Laguna Madre**, Texas, U.S.A.
125 S 8 **Laguna Madre**, Mexico
141 J 17 **Laguna Rogaguado**, Bolivia
125 U 14 **Laguna Superior**, Mexico
90 G 7 **Laguna Veneta**, Italy
144 G 4 **Lagunas**, Chile
175 N 8 **Lahad Datu**, Malaysia
117 D 24 **Lahaina**, Hawaii, U.S.A.
174 F 12 **Lahat**, Indonesia
172 D 7 **Lahe**, Myanmar
174 B 10 **Lahewa**, Indonesia
163 P 14 **Laḥij**, Yemen
87 E 18 **Lahn**, Germany
85 E 24 **Laholmsbukten**, Sweden
165 Y 9 **Lahore**, Pakistan
85 M 18 **Lahti**, Finland
193 W 11 **Laï**, Chad
172 J 11 **Lai Chau**, Vietnam
79 O 4 **L'Aigle**, France
196 L 15 **Laingsburg**, Republic of South Africa
84 J 8 **Lainioälven**, Sweden
174 E 12 **Lais**, Indonesia
171 W 7 **Laiyang**, China
171 T 7 **Laiyuan**, China
159 S 6 **Lajanurpekhi**, Georgia
143 I 21 **Lajes**, Brazil
62 O 1 **Lajes**, Azores
62 N 1 **Lajes do Pico**, Azores
94 K 11 **Lajkovac**, Serbia and Montenegro
191 J 19 **Lake Abbe**, Ethiopia
195 R 6 **Lake Albert**, Uganda/Democratic Republic of Congo
208 M 7 **Lake Amadeus**, Northern Territory, Australia
208 L 3 **Lake Argyle**, Western Australia, Australia
113 V 8 **Lake Athabasca**, Alberta, Canada
208 J 6 **Lake Auld**, Western Australia, Australia
208 G 9 **Lake Austin**, Western Australia, Australia
157 Q 13 **Lake Baikal**, Russian Federation
167 T 8 **Lake Balkhash**, Kazakhstan
208 I 9 **Lake Ballard**, Western Australia, Australia
197 O 3 **Lake Bangweulu**, Zambia
208 H 9 **Lake Barlee**, Western Australia, Australia
211 E 22 **Lake Benmore**, New Zealand
123 O 7 **Lake Blackshear**, Georgia, U.S.A.
209 Q 9 **Lake Blanche**, South Australia, Australia
94 B 6 **Lake Bled**, Slovenia
208 I 9 **Lake Carey**, Western Australia, Australia
209 T 11 **Lake Cargelligo**, New South Wales, Australia
208 I 8 **Lake Carnegie**, Western Australia, Australia
193 V 9 **Lake Chad**, Chad
121 V 6 **Lake Champlain**, Vermont, U.S.A.
119 M 21 **Lake Charles**, Louisiana, U.S.A.
116 F 6 **Lake Chelan**, Washington, U.S.A.
123 Q 9 **Lake City**, Florida, U.S.A.
123 T 4 **Lake City**, South Carolina, U.S.A.
113 U 9 **Lake Claire**, Alberta, Canada
211 G 19 **Lake Coleridge**, New Zealand
88 H 5 **Lake Constance**, Switzerland
208 I 10 **Lake Cowan**, Western Australia, Australia
209 T 5 **Lake Dalrymple**, Queensland, Australia
208 I 7 **Lake Disappointment**, Western Australia, Australia
77 I 15 **Lake District**, United Kingdom
208 I 6 **Lake Dora**, Western Australia, Australia
208 I 11 **Lake Dundas**, Western Australia, Australia
195 Q 8 **Lake Edward**, Democratic Republic of Congo/Uganda
211 H 21 **Lake Ellesmere**, New Zealand
118 C 7 **Lake Elwell**, Montana, U.S.A.
121 N 9 **Lake Erie**, Ohio, U.S.A.
195 U 10 **Lake Eyasi**, Tanzania
209 O 8 **Lake Eyre North**, South Australia, Australia
209 O 9 **Lake Eyre South**, South Australia, Australia
209 Q 10 **Lake Frome**, South Australia, Australia
209 O 10 **Lake Gairdner**, South Australia, Australia
88 B 9 **Lake Geneva**, Switzerland/France
121 U 7 **Lake George**, New York, U.S.A.
123 R 10 **Lake George**, Florida, U.S.A.
209 S 15 **Lake Gordon**, Tasmania, Australia
208 H 11 **Lake Grace**, Western Australia, Australia
208 K 5 **Lake Gregory**, Western Australia, Australia
211 B 25 **Lake Hauroko**, New Zealand
117 K 22 **Lake Havasu City**, Arizona, U.S.A.
211 D 22 **Lake Hawea**, New Zealand
208 I 11 **Lake Hope**, Western Australia, Australia
208 L 7 **Lake Hopkins**, Western Australia, Australia
121 N 5 **Lake Huron**, Canada/U.S.A.
197 O 6 **Lake Kariba**, Zimbabwe
171 Z 3 **Lake Khanka**, China
208 H 11 **Lake King**, Western Australia, Australia
195 Q 9 **Lake Kivu**, Rwanda/Democratic Republic of Congo
118 A 6 **Lake Koocanusa**, Montana, U.S.A.
195 S 7 **Lake Kyoga**, Uganda
156 G 6 **Lake Ladoga**, Russian Federation
175 Q 7 **Lake Lanao**, Philippines
208 I 10 **Lake Lefroy**, Western Australia, Australia
113 U 13 **Lake Louise**, Alberta, Canada
208 L 6 **Lake MacDonald**, Western Australia, Australia
208 L 6 **Lake Mackay**, Western Australia, Australia
208 E 7 **Lake MacLeod**, Western Australia, Australia
197 R 4 **Lake Malawi**, Malawi
211 B 24 **Lake Manapouri**, New Zealand
114 I 10 **Lake Manitoba**, Manitoba, Canada
195 U 10 **Lake Manyara**, Tanzania
138 K 3 **Lake Maracaibo**, Venezuela
123 S 5 **Lake Marion**, South Carolina, U.S.A.
208 I 10 **Lake Marmion**, Western Australia, Australia
122 M 5 **Lake Martin**, Alabama, U.S.A.
208 M 9 **Lake Maurice**, South Australia, Australia
117 K 20 **Lake Mead**, Nevada, U.S.A.
115 V 8 **Lake Melville**, Newfoundland and Labrador, Canada
120 J 8 **Lake Michigan**, Michigan, U.S.A.
208 J 9 **Lake Minigwal**, Western Australia, Australia
208 G 10 **Lake Moore**, Western Australia, Australia
123 S 5 **Lake Moultrie**, South Carolina, U.S.A.
123 Q 4 **Lake Murray**, South Carolina, U.S.A.
212 A 5 **Lake Murray**, Papua New Guinea
195 P 13 **Lake Mweru**, Democratic Republic of Congo/Zambia
190 F 12 **Lake Nasser**, Egypt
195 U 9 **Lake Natron**, Tanzania
208 L 7 **Lake Neale**, Northern Territory, Australia
126 G 12 **Lake Nicaragua**, Nicaragua
114 L 11 **Lake Nipigon**, Ontario, Canada
115 O 13 **Lake Nipissing**, Ontario, Canada
208 H 9 **Lake Noondie**, Western Australia, Australia
123 R 2 **Lake Norman**, North Carolina, U.S.A.
190 E 13 **Lake Nuba**, Sudan
118 I 9 **Lake Oahe**, South Dakota, U.S.A.
123 P 5 **Lake Oconee**, Georgia, U.S.A.
119 M 14 **Lake of the Ozarks**, Missouri, U.S.A.
114 J 11 **Lake of the Woods**, Canada/U.S.A.
211 D 21 **Lake Ohau**, New Zealand
96 B 13 **Lake Ohrid**, Macedonia (F.Y.R.O.M.)/Albania
123 S 12 **Lake Okeechobee**, Florida, U.S.A.
156 G 6 **Lake Onega**, Russian Federation
115 P 14 **Lake Ontario**, Ontario, Canada/U.S.A.
117 E 16 **Lake Oroville**, California, U.S.A.
119 M 17 **Lake Ouachita**, Arkansas, U.S.A.
209 S 15 **Lake Pedder**, Tasmania, Australia
98 I 7 **Lake Peipus**, Estonia

Country · Internal administrative region: State/Province/Territory/Dependent territory · Capital city · Mountain range/Undersea ridge · Mountain peak/Volcano/Seamount · Geographic feature · Headland/Point/Cape/Peninsula · Desert · Island/Island group · Antarctic base · Ocean · Sea · Bay/Gulf/Channel/Strait · Lake · Salt pan/Dry/Intermittent lake · Riv

21 U 6 **Lake Placid**, New York, U.S.A.
21 U 7 **Lake Pleasant**, New York, U.S.A.
11 B 25 **Lake Poteriteri**, New Zealand
17 N 19 **Lake Powell**, Arizona, U.S.A.
6 C 13 **Lake Prespa**, Europe
8 J 8 **Lake Pskov**, Estonia
11 E 21 **Lake Pukaki**, New Zealand
08 I 10 **Lake Rebecca**, Western Australia, Australia
10 M 10 **Lake Rotorua**, New Zealand
95 S 12 **Lake Rukwa**, Tanzania
18 H 7 **Lake Sakakawea**, North Dakota, U.S.A.
5 J 16 **Lake Scutari**, Serbia and Montenegro
23 N 8 **Lake Seminole**, Georgia, U.S.A.
23 O 3 **Lake Sidney Lanier**, Georgia, U.S.A.
23 P 5 **Lake Sinclair**, Georgia, U.S.A.
15 N 15 **Lake St Clair**, Canada/U.S.A.
14 K 10 **Lake St Joseph**, Ontario, Canada
97 Q 12 **Lake St Lucia**, Republic of South Africa
11 H 18 **Lake Sumner**, New Zealand
20 I 3 **Lake Superior**, Canada/U.S.A.
09 O 4 **Lake Sylvester**, Northern Territory, Australia
17 F 17 **Lake Tahoe**, California, U.S.A.
91 H 18 **Lake Tana**, Ethiopia
95 Q 11 **Lake Tanganyika**, Africa
10 M 11 **Lake Tarawera**, New Zealand
10 L 12 **Lake Taupo**, New Zealand
11 B 23 **Lake Te Anau**, New Zealand
11 F 21 **Lake Tekapo**, New Zealand
11 E 21 **Lake Tekapo**, New Zealand
60 G 8 **Lake Tiberias**, Israel
41 H 19 **Lake Titicaca**, Peru
09 P 10 **Lake Torrens**, South Australia, Australia
95 U 5 **Lake Turkana**, Ethiopia/Kenya
64 F 3 **Lake Urmia**, Iran
95 S 8 **Lake Victoria**, Africa
93 N 12 **Lake Volta**, Ghana
11 K 16 **Lake Wairarapa**, New Zealand
11 C 23 **Lake Wakatipu**, New Zealand
23 R 11 **Lake Wales**, Florida, U.S.A.
11 D 22 **Lake Wanaka**, New Zealand
08 I 8 **Lake Wells**, Western Australia, Australia
08 L 5 **Lake White**, Western Australia, Australia
20 I 6 **Lake Winnebago**, Wisconsin, U.S.A.
18 L 7 **Lake Winnibigoshish**, Minnesota, U.S.A.
14 I 9 **Lake Winnipeg**, Manitoba, Canada
14 H 8 **Lake Winnipegosis**, Manitoba, Canada
21 W 6 **Lake Winnipesaukee**, New Hampshire, U.S.A.
23 T 13 **Lake Worth**, Florida, U.S.A.
09 R 8 **Lake Yamma Yamma**, Queensland, Australia
13 Z 12 **Lakeba**, Fiji
23 R 11 **Lakeland**, Florida, U.S.A.
23 P 7 **Lakeland**, Georgia, U.S.A.
09 S 3 **Lakeland**, Queensland, Australia
09 T 13 **Lakes Entrance**, Victoria, Australia
19 E 14 **Lakewood**, Colorado, U.S.A.
21 U 11 **Lakewood**, New Jersey, U.S.A.
69 F 15 **Lakhnadon**, India
69 A 14 **Lakhpat**, India
65 V 8 **Lakki**, Pakistan
7 E 23 **Lakonikos Kolpos**, Greece
75 S 15 **Lakor**, Indonesia
92 J 13 **Lakota**, Côte d'Ivoire
4 L 5 **Laksefjorden**, Norway
84 K 6 **Lakselv**, Norway
169 A 22 **Lakshadweep**, India
94 G 10 **Lakaši**, Bosnia and Herzegovina
158 B 6 **Lalapaşa**, Turkey
96 L 11 **Lalapaşa**, Turkey
194 E 7 **Lalara**, Gabon
164 G 8 **Lālī**, Iran
191 I 19 **Lalībela**, Ethiopia
175 R 14 **Laliki**, Indonesia
80 I 2 **Lalín**, Spain
175 O 13 **Laloa**, Indonesia
173 K 16 **Lam Pao Reservoir**, Thailand
89 S 4 **Lambach**, Austria
78 J 5 **Lamballe**, France
194 E 8 **Lambaréné**, Gabon
140 A 13 **Lambayeque**, Peru
196 J 14 **Lambert's Bay**, Republic of South Africa
80 H 5 **Lamego**, Portugal
213 R 11 **Lamen**, Vanuatu
119 G 19 **Lamesa**, Texas, U.S.A.
91 M 20 **Lamezia**, Italy
97 E 18 **Lamia**, Greece
175 R 7 **Lamigan Point**, Philippines
213 Y 11 **Lamiti**, Fiji
175 T 10 **Lamlam**, Indonesia
175 P 3 **Lamon Bay**, Philippines
173 G 15 **Lampang**, Thailand
119 J 20 **Lampasas**, Texas, U.S.A.
125 Q 6 **Lampazos**, Mexico
173 G 14 **Lamphun**, Thailand
174 G 13 **Lampung**, Indonesia
195 X 9 **Lamu**, Kenya
117 C 24 **Lanai**, Hawaii, U.S.A.
117 C 24 **Lanai City**, Hawaii, U.S.A.
173 F 22 **Lanbi Kyun**, Myanmar
77 I 16 **Lancaster**, United Kingdom
117 G 22 **Lancaster**, California, U.S.A.
118 M 13 **Lancaster**, Missouri, U.S.A.
120 G 8 **Lancaster**, Wisconsin, U.S.A.
121 W 6 **Lancaster**, New Hampshire, U.S.A.
121 N 11 **Lancaster**, Ohio, U.S.A.
121 S 11 **Lancaster**, Pennsylvania, U.S.A.
123 S 3 **Lancaster**, South Carolina, U.S.A.
65 N 8 **Lancaster Sound**, Arctic Ocean
208 F 11 **Lancelin**, Western Australia, Australia
159 R 6 **Lanch'khut'i**, Georgia
90 J 13 **Lanciano**, Italy
145 F 16 **Lanco**, Chile
87 L 23 **Landau an der Isar**, Germany
87 E 21 **Landau in der Pfalz**, Germany
88 K 7 **Landeck**, Austria
118 D 11 **Lander**, Wyoming, U.S.A.
82 I 5 **Landerum**, Netherlands
169 N 20 **Landfall Island**, India
88 I 8 **Landquart**, Switzerland
77 F 24 **Land's End**, United Kingdom
87 I 24 **Landsberg**, Germany
87 K 23 **Landshut**, Germany
171 Q 6 **Lang Shan**, China
172 M 11 **Lang Son**, Vietnam
173 G 23 **Lang Suan**, Thailand
88 L 7 **Längenfeld**, Austria
89 W 3 **Langenlois**, Austria
88 E 7 **Langenthal**, Switzerland
86 D 10 **Langeoog**, Germany
156 L 10 **Langepas**, Russian Federation
171 U 7 **Langfang**, China
84 B 11 **Langjökull**, Iceland
174 D 7 **Langkawi**, Malaysia
174 M 7 **Langkon**, Malaysia
88 E 8 **Langnau**, Switzerland
79 R 12 **Langogne**, France
78 M 12 **Langon**, France
84 G 8 **Langøya**, Norway
79 U 6 **Langres**, France
174 C 8 **Langsa**, Indonesia
83 M 25 **Langsur**, Luxembourg
193 S 12 **Langtang**, Nigeria
79 Q 14 **Languedoc-Roussillon**, France
159 Y 10 **Länkäran**, Azerbaijan
78 I 4 **Lannion**, France
120 L 8 **Lansing**, Michigan, U.S.A.
84 J 11 **Lansjärv**, Sweden
91 C 18 **Lanusei**, Italy
62 O 11 **Lanzarote**, Canary Islands
171 Q 8 **Lanzhou**, China
172 K 11 **Lao Cai**, Vietnam
175 O 2 **Laoag**, Philippines
171 T 10 **Laohekou**, China
79 R 3 **Laon**, France
173 K 14 **Laos**, Asia
174 L 8 **Lapachito**, Argentina
193 Q 12 **Lapai**, Nigeria
79 S 9 **Lapalisse**, France
85 K 15 **Lappajärvi**, Finland
85 N 18 **Lappeenranta**, Finland
84 I 11 **Lappland**, Sweden
158 B 8 **Lâpseki**, Turkey
65 V 6 **Laptev Sea**, Arctic Ocean
85 K 16 **Lapua**, Finland
92 N 11 **Łapy**, Poland
90 I 13 **L'Aquila**, Italy
164 K 12 **Lār**, Iran
165 Q 9 **Lar Koh**, Afghanistan
138 L 2 **Lara**, Venezuela
188 H 6 **Larache**, Morocco
164 L 13 **Lārak**, Iran
118 F 12 **Laramie**, Wyoming, U.S.A.
118 E 11 **Laramie Mountains**, Wyoming, U.S.A.
175 P 15 **Larantuka**, Indonesia
175 U 14 **Larat**, Indonesia
81 P 1 **Laredo**, Spain
119 I 23 **Laredo**, Texas, U.S.A.
82 I 11 **Laren**, Netherlands
123 P 11 **Largo**, Florida, U.S.A.
76 G 13 **Largs**, United Kingdom
164 G 3 **Lāri**, Iran
97 E 16 **Larisa**, Greece
165 U 12 **Larkana**, Pakistan
158 I 15 **Larnaka**, Cyprus
77 F 15 **Larne**, United Kingdom
209 N 3 **Larrimah**, Northern Territory, Australia
219 W 5 **Lars Christensen Coast**, Antarctica
218 I 4 **Larsen Ice Shelf**, Antarctica
113 V 2 **Larsen Sound**, Nunavut, Canada
85 C 21 **Larvik**, Norway
119 G 15 **Las Animas**, Colorado, U.S.A.
139 P 4 **Las Bonitas**, Venezuela
119 E 19 **Las Cruces**, New Mexico, U.S.A.
144 L 13 **Las Flores**, Argentina
144 G 11 **Las Heras**, Argentina
124 M 7 **Las Herreras**, Mexico
145 G 21 **Las Horquetas**, Argentina
145 G 15 **Las Lajas**, Argentina
140 A 11 **Las Lomas**, Peru
144 L 6 **Las Lomitas**, Argentina
145 H 21 **Las Martinetas**, Argentina
62 N 12 **Las Palmas de Gran Canaria**, Canary Islands
81 Q 8 **Las Pedroñeras**, Spain
145 H 18 **Las Plumas**, Argentina
126 K 14 **Las Tablas**, Panama
144 I 8 **Las Termas**, Argentina
126 M 5 **Las Tunas**, Cuba
124 M 10 **Las Varas**, Mexico
117 J 20 **Las Vegas**, Nevada, U.S.A.
119 F 17 **Las Vegas**, New Mexico, U.S.A.
172 F 10 **Lashio**, Myanmar
165 R 9 **Lashkar Gāh**, Afghanistan
93 I 14 **Łask**, Poland
117 E 15 **Lassen Peak**, California, U.S.A.
218 K 5 **Lassiter Coast**, Antarctica
119 G 14 **Last Chance**, Colorado, U.S.A.
194 F 8 **Lastoursville**, Gabon
95 F 15 **Lastovo**, Croatia
95 E 15 **Lastovski Kanal**, Croatia
213 P 7 **Lata**, Solomon Islands
140 B 9 **Latacunga**, Ecuador
218 I 6 **Lataday Island**, Antarctica
214 I 10 **Late**, Tonga
169 I 14 **Latehar**, India
91 N 16 **Laterza**, Italy
91 H 15 **Latina**, Italy
90 H 6 **Latisana**, Italy
169 E 17 **Latur**, India
98 F 10 **Latvia**, Europe
84 B 10 **Laugarbakki**, Iceland
98 C 13 **Laukuva**, Lithuania
77 H 23 **Launceston**, United Kingdom
209 T 15 **Launceston**, Tasmania, Australia
172 F 7 **Launggyaung**, Myanmar
173 F 19 **Launglon Bok Islands**, Myanmar
209 S 3 **Laura**, Queensland, Australia
118 J 12 **Laurel**, Nebraska, U.S.A.
122 J 7 **Laurel**, Mississippi, U.S.A.
123 Q 3 **Laurens**, South Carolina, U.S.A.
115 R 11 **Laurentian Mountains**, Québec, Canada
91 L 17 **Lauria**, Italy
218 I 1 **Laurie Island**, Antarctica
123 T 3 **Laurinburg**, North Carolina, U.S.A.
91 K 17 **Laurino**, Italy
211 G 21 **Lauriston**, New Zealand
88 B 9 **Lausanne**, Switzerland
174 H 8 **Laut**, Indonesia
174 M 13 **Laut**, Indonesia
213 W 11 **Lautoka**, Fiji
82 L 5 **Lauwersmeer**, Netherlands
78 M 6 **Laval**, France
144 N 12 **Lavalleja**, Uruguay
89 U 8 **Lavamünd**, Austria
164 H 11 **Lāvar**, Iran
91 L 15 **Lavello**, Italy
208 I 9 **Laverton**, Western Australia, Australia
85 A 17 **Lavik**, Norway
218 H 5 **Lavoisier Island**, Antarctica
143 L 18 **Lavras**, Brazil
97 H 21 **Lavrio**, Greece
219 X 3 **Law Promontory**, Antarctica
172 E 8 **Lawa**, Myanmar
163 Q 14 **Lawdar**, Yemen
192 L 11 **Lawra**, Ghana
119 L 14 **Lawrence**, Kansas, U.S.A.
121 X 8 **Lawrence**, Massachusetts, U.S.A.
211 E 24 **Lawrence**, New Zealand
122 L 2 **Lawrenceburg**, Tennessee, U.S.A.
119 J 18 **Lawton**, Oklahoma, U.S.A.
163 R 7 **Laylā**, Saudi Arabia
61 P 5 **Laysan Island**, Pacific Ocean
117 C 16 **Laytonville**, California, U.S.A.
63 L 23 **Lazarev Sea**, Atlantic Ocean
125 O 13 **Lázaro Cárdenas**, Mexico
144 O 12 **Lazcano**, Uruguay
90 G 13 **Lazio**, Italy
157 U 9 **Lazo**, Russian Federation
101 S 10 **Lazurne**, Ukraine
79 O 8 **Le Blanc**, France
79 Q 15 **Le Boulou**, France
88 B 9 **Le Brassus**, Switzerland
58 A 15 **Le Gros Morne**, Réunion
79 N 3 **Le Havre**, France
189 P 5 **Le Kef**, Tunisia
88 C 7 **Le Locle**, Switzerland
79 N 6 **Le Mans**, France
118 K 11 **Le Mars**, Iowa, U.S.A.
78 L 5 **Le Mont-St-Michel**, France
91 M 15 **Le Murge**, Italy
78 J 7 **Le Palais**, France
58 A 14 **Le Port**, Réunion
79 S 11 **Le-Puy-en-Velay**, France
118 L 10 **Le Sueur**, Minnesota, U.S.A.
58 B 15 **Le Tampon**, Réunion
79 P 1 **Le Touquet-Paris-Plage**, France
79 O 2 **Le Tréport**, France
79 R 13 **Le Vigan**, France
113 W 13 **Leader**, Saskatchewan, Canada
114 I 7 **Leaf Rapids**, Manitoba, Canada
208 E 7 **Learmonth**, Western Australia, Australia
83 F 22 **L'Eau d'Heure**, Belgium
119 L 14 **Leavenworth**, Kansas, U.S.A.
92 H 7 **Łeba**, Poland
175 Q 7 **Lebak**, Philippines
95 N 14 **Lebane**, Serbia and Montenegro
160 H 6 **Lebanon**, Asia
120 J 11 **Lebanon**, Indiana, U.S.A.
121 W 7 **Lebanon**, New Hampshire, U.S.A.
121 N 15 **Lebanon**, Virginia, U.S.A.
122 M 1 **Lebanon**, Tennessee, U.S.A.
167 N 12 **Lebap**, Turkmenistan
167 O 14 **Lebapskiy Velayat**, Turkmenistan
117 G 21 **Lebec**, California, U.S.A.
101 T 3 **Lebedyn**, Ukraine
194 M 5 **Lebo**, Democratic Republic of Congo
92 H 8 **Lębork**, Poland
197 O 10 **Lebowakgomo**, Republic of South Africa
80 K 13 **Lebrija**, Spain
145 E 14 **Lebu**, Chile
91 O 17 **Lecce**, Italy
90 D 6 **Lecco**, Italy
88 J 7 **Lech**, Austria
97 C 20 **Lechaina**, Greece
88 K 7 **Lechtaler Alpen**, Austria
86 F 7 **Leck**, Germany
93 N 14 **Łęczna**, Poland
92 I 13 **Łęczyca**, Poland
80 K 5 **Ledesma**, Spain
77 B 21 **Lee**, Republic of Ireland
117 G 18 **Lee Vining**, California, U.S.A.
77 K 17 **Leeds**, United Kingdom
122 L 5 **Leeds**, Alabama, U.S.A.
86 D 11 **Leer**, Germany
82 I 13 **Leerdam**, Netherlands
121 R 12 **Leesburg**, Virginia, U.S.A.
123 R 10 **Leesburg**, Florida, U.S.A.
98 G 5 **Leesi**, Estonia
119 M 20 **Leesville**, Louisiana, U.S.A.
209 T 12 **Leeton**, New South Wales, Australia
196 L 14 **Leeu-Gamka**, Republic of South Africa
82 K 6 **Leeuwarden**, Netherlands
119 O 21 **Leeville**, Louisiana, U.S.A.
127 U 6 **Leeward Islands**, 0
158 H 15 **Lefka**, Cyprus
97 G 26 **Lefka Ori**, Greece
97 B 18 **Lefkada**, Greece
97 B 18 **Lefkada**, Greece
97 A 16 **Lefkimmi**, Greece
175 P 4 **Legaspi**, Philippines
117 C 15 **Leggett**, California, U.S.A.
83 J 24 **Léglise**, Belgium
90 F 7 **Legnago**, Italy
93 F 15 **Legnica**, Poland
195 N 6 **Leguga**, Democratic Republic of Congo
168 F 7 **Leh**, India
165 W 10 **Leiah**, Pakistan
89 W 8 **Leibnitz**, Austria
77 K 19 **Leicester**, United Kingdom
209 Q 4 **Leichhardt**, Queensland, Australia
82 G 12 **Leiden**, Netherlands
210 K 7 **Leigh**, New Zealand
209 P 9 **Leigh Creek**, South Australia, Australia
82 G 12 **Leimuiden**, Netherlands
87 G 14 **Leine**, Germany
87 H 16 **Leinefelde**, Germany
77 D 19 **Leinster**, Republic of Ireland
208 H 9 **Leinster**, Western Australia, Australia
97 L 21 **Leipsoi**, Greece
87 K 16 **Leipzig**, Germany
85 C 18 **Leira**, Norway
80 G 7 **Leiria**, Portugal
85 A 19 **Leirvik**, Norway
98 D 7 **Leisi**, Estonia
120 J 14 **Leitchfield**, Kentucky, U.S.A.
171 T 12 **Leiyang**, China
84 E 13 **Leka**, Norway
194 M 8 **Lekatero**, Democratic Republic of Congo
84 F 9 **Leknes**, Norway
194 G 9 **Lékoni**, Gabon
194 G 9 **Lékoumou**, Congo
85 G 19 **Leksand**, Sweden
82 J 10 **Lelystad**, Netherlands
212 I 4 **Lemankoa**, Papua New Guinea
158 H 15 **Lemesos**, Cyprus
87 F 14 **Lemgo**, Germany
115 T 3 **Lemieux Islands**, Nunavut, Canada
82 K 8 **Lemmer**, Netherlands
85 B 24 **Lemvig**, Denmark
173 C 15 **Lemyethna**, Myanmar
157 S 11 **Lena**, Russian Federation
143 M 15 **Lençóis**, Brazil
94 E 6 **Lendava**, Slovenia
170 M 7 **Lenghu**, China
167 T 12 **Lenin Peak**, Kyrgyzstan
101 W 11 **Lenine**, Ukraine
219 S 15 **Leningradskaya**, Antarctica
157 Y 5 **Leningradskiy**, Russian Federation
167 Y 4 **Leninogorsk**, Kazakhstan
167 U 3 **Leninskīy**, Kazakhstan
166 H 5 **Leninskoye**, Kazakhstan
167 P 2 **Leninskoye**, Kazakhstan
90 D 6 **Lenna**, Italy
87 E 16 **Lennestadt**, Germany
123 R 2 **Lenoir**, North Carolina, U.S.A.
79 Q 1 **Lens**, France
83 E 20 **Lens**, Belgium
157 R 11 **Lensk**, Russian Federation
159 S 5 **Lentekhi**, Georgia
93 F 24 **Lenti**, Hungary
99 G 16 **Lentvaris**, Lithuania
156 G 7 **Lent'yevo**, Russian Federation
173 G 21 **Lenya**, Myanmar
192 L 10 **Léo**, Burkina Faso
89 V 6 **Leoben**, Austria
89 X 4 **Leobersdorf**, Austria
77 I 20 **Leominster**, United Kingdom
80 L 2 **León**, Spain
126 F 11 **León**, Nicaragua
78 L 13 **Léon**, France
125 P 10 **León**, Mexico
215 W 15 **Leone**, American Samoa
97 F 22 **Leonidi**, Greece
208 I 9 **Leonora**, Western Australia, Australia
101 N 10 **Leova**, Moldova
197 N 9 **Lephepe**, Botswana
167 W 7 **Lepsy**, Kazakhstan
97 E 15 **Leptokarya**, Greece
91 I 22 **Lercara Friddi**, Italy
193 R 11 **Lere**, Nigeria
193 V 11 **Léré**, Chad
192 K 8 **Léré**, Mali
159 Y 10 **Lerik**, Azerbaijan
81 O 3 **Lerma**, Spain
88 L 6 **Lermoos**, Austria
97 M 22 **Leros**, Greece
76 J 4 **Lerwick**, United Kingdom
127 O 7 **Les Cayes**, Haiti
78 L 8 **Les Herbiers**, France
79 V 13 **Les Mées**, France
78 K 8 **Les Sables-d'Olonne**, France
58 C 8 **Les Sœurs**, Seychelles
79 S 12 **Les Vans**, France
97 J 17 **Lesbos**, Greece
171 P 11 **Leshan**, China
95 N 14 **Leskovac**, Serbia and Montenegro
95 L 21 **Leskovik**, Albania
116 K 11 **Leslie**, Idaho, U.S.A.
93 E 15 **Leśna**, Poland
157 O 12 **Lesosibirsk**, Russian Federation
197 N 13 **Lesotho**, Africa
157 V 15 **Lesozavodsk**, Russian Federation
78 L 11 **Lesparre-Médoc**, France
127 V 8 **Lesser Antilles**, North America
159 R 7 **Lesser Caucasus**, Georgia
113 U 11 **Lesser Slave Lake**, Alberta, Canada
59 T 5 **Lesser Sunda Islands**, Indian Ocean
83 E 20 **Lessines**, Belgium
85 L 15 **Lestijärvi**, Finland
85 K 14 **Lestijoki**, Finland
92 F 13 **Leszno**, Poland
113 W 14 **Lethbridge**, Alberta, Canada
139 T 7 **Lethem**, Guyana
175 R 15 **Leti**, Indonesia
138 L 13 **Leticia**, Colombia
142 B 11 **Letícia**, Brazil
173 D 15 **Letpadan**, Myanmar
173 F 21 **Letsok-aw Kyun**, Myanmar
196 J 4 **Léua**, Angola
87 H 25 **Leutkirch**, Germany
83 H 19 **Leuven**, Belgium
83 D 20 **Leuze-en-Hainaut**, Belgium
97 F 19 **Levadeia**, Greece
90 D 9 **Levanto**, Italy
87 C 17 **Leverkusen**, Germany
93 I 21 **Levice**, Slovakia
97 E 21 **Levidi**, Greece
97 L 22 **Levitha**, Greece
93 K 19 **Levoča**, Slovakia
96 J 7 **Levski**, Bulgaria
213 X 11 **Levuka**, Fiji
122 L 4 **Lewis Smith Lake**, Alabama, U.S.A.
120 J 14 **Lewisburg**, Kentucky, U.S.A.

Country · Internal administrative region: State/Province/Territory/Dependent territory · Capital city · Mountain range/Undersea ridge · Mountain peak/Volcano/Seamount · Geographic feature · Headland/Point/Cape/Peninsula · Desert · Island/Island group · Antarctic base · Ocean · Sea · Bay/Gulf/Channel/Strait · Lake · Salt pan/Dry/Intermittent lake · River

122 L 2 **Lewisburg**, Tennessee, U.S.A.
116 I 8 **Lewiston**, Idaho, U.S.A.
118 D 8 **Lewistown**, Montana, U.S.A.
121 R 10 **Lewistown**, Pennsylvania, U.S.A.
118 I 13 **Lexington**, Nebraska, U.S.A.
120 L 13 **Lexington**, Kentucky, U.S.A.
121 Q 14 **Lexington**, Virginia, U.S.A.
122 J 2 **Lexington**, Tennessee, U.S.A.
123 S 2 **Lexington**, North Carolina, U.S.A.
121 S 13 **Lexington Park**, Maryland, U.S.A.
175 Q 5 **Leyte**, Philippines
175 Q 5 **Leyte Gulf**, Philippines
93 N 17 **Leżajsk**, Poland
95 J 17 **Lezhë**, Albania
156 E 8 **L'gov**, Russian Federation
170 K 10 **Lhasa**, China
170 J 10 **Lhazê**, China
170 J 9 **Lhazhong**, China
174 C 8 **Lhokseumawe**, Indonesia
174 C 8 **Lhoksukon**, Indonesia
81 X 5 **L'Hospitalet de Llobregat**, Spain
175 R 6 **Lianga**, Philippines
171 N 13 **Lianghe**, China
171 T 12 **Lianhua**, China
171 T 13 **Lianshan**, China
171 V 6 **Lianshan**, China
171 V 8 **Lianyungang**, China
171 T 13 **Lianzhou**, China
171 V 5 **Liaoning**, China
171 W 5 **Liaoyang**, China
171 X 5 **Liaoyuan**, China
113 P 8 **Liard**, Yukon Territory, Canada
113 Q 9 **Liard Plateau**, British Columbia, Canada
165 S 14 **Liāri**, Pakistan
138 I 6 **Libano**, Colombia
118 A 7 **Libby**, Montana, U.S.A.
194 J 5 **Libenge**, Democratic Republic of Congo
119 H 16 **Liberal**, Kansas, U.S.A.
93 D 16 **Liberec**, Czech Republic
192 H 13 **Liberia**, Africa
126 G 12 **Liberia**, Costa Rica
138 M 4 **Libertad**, Venezuela
83 I 24 **Libin**, Belgium
78 M 11 **Libourne**, France
83 J 24 **Libramont**, Belgium
95 K 18 **Librazhd**, Albania
194 D 7 **Libreville**, Gabon
189 S 10 **Libya**, Africa
189 X 10 **Libyan Desert**, Africa
189 W 7 **Libyan Plateau**, Egypt/Libya
144 F 13 **Licantén**, Chile
91 J 23 **Licata**, Italy
159 Q 11 **Lice**, Turkey
197 R 4 **Lichinga**, Mozambique
197 N 11 **Lichtenburg**, Republic of South Africa
87 I 19 **Lichtenfels**, Germany
82 M 13 **Lichtenvoorde**, Netherlands
83 C 18 **Lichtervelde**, Belgium
99 G 17 **Lida**, Belarus
117 H 19 **Lida**, Nevada, U.S.A.
85 E 21 **Lidköping**, Sweden
91 G 14 **Lido di Ostia**, Italy
92 J 10 **Lidzbark**, Poland
92 K 9 **Lidzbark Warmiński**, Poland
88 I 7 **Liechtenstein**, Europe
83 K 21 **Liège**, Belgium
83 J 20 **Liège**, Belgium
85 O 15 **Lieksa**, Finland
89 P 8 **Lienz**, Austria
98 B 11 **Liepāja**, Latvia
83 G 17 **Lier**, Belgium
88 E 6 **Liestal**, Switzerland
85 M 16 **Lievestuore**, Finland
89 T 6 **Liezen**, Austria
194 M 6 **Lifanga**, Democratic Republic of Congo
77 E 18 **Liffey**, Republic of Ireland
213 Q 13 **Lifou**, New Caledonia
124 I 7 **Ligui**, Mexico
90 C 8 **Liguria**, Italy
90 A 12 **Ligurian Sea**, Europe
212 H 3 **Lihir Group**, Papua New Guinea
212 H 3 **Lihir Island**, Papua New Guinea
117 B 23 **Lihue**, Hawaii, U.S.A.
98 F 7 **Lihula**, Estonia
195 O 14 **Likasi**, Democratic Republic of Congo
194 M 6 **Likati**, Democratic Republic of Congo
215 Y 2 **Likiep**, Marshall Islands
194 K 8 **Likolia**, Democratic Republic of Congo
194 I 6 **Likouala**, Congo
174 I 10 **Liku**, Indonesia
79 R 1 **Lille**, France
83 H 17 **Lille**, Belgium
85 D 18 **Lillehammer**, Norway
113 S 14 **Lillooet**, British Columbia, Canada
197 R 5 **Lilongwe**, Malawi
58 C 9 **L'Îlot Frégate**, Seychelles
175 P 7 **Liloy**, Philippines
141 C 16 **Lima**, Peru
141 C 16 **Lima**, Peru
118 B 10 **Lima**, Montana, U.S.A.
120 L 10 **Lima**, Ohio, U.S.A.
143 G 19 **Lima**, Paraguay
163 X 5 **Limah**, Oman
145 G 16 **Limay**, Argentina
145 I 14 **Limay Mahuida**, Argentina
98 F 10 **Limbaži**, Latvia
83 I 18 **Limburg**, Belgium
83 K 16 **Limburg**, Netherlands
87 E 18 **Limburg**, Germany
85 F 18 **Limedsforsen**, Sweden
143 K 18 **Limeira**, Brazil
77 C 19 **Limerick**, Republic of Ireland
121 Z 3 **Limestone**, Maine, U.S.A.
85 B 23 **Limfjorden**, Denmark
84 L 13 **Liminka**, Finland
85 F 23 **Limmared**, Sweden
209 O 2 **Limmen Bight**, Northern Territory, Australia
97 G 18 **Limni**, Greece
97 D 14 **Limni Aliakmonas**, Greece
96 F 12 **Limni Kerkinitis**, Greece
97 D 18 **Limni Trichonida**, Greece
96 D 13 **Limni Vegoritis**, Greece
97 I 15 **Limnos**, Greece
79 O 10 **Limoges**, France
119 G 14 **Limon**, Colorado, U.S.A.
126 I 13 **Limón**, Costa Rica
126 G 9 **Limón**, Honduras
90 A 9 **Limone Piemonte**, Italy
79 O 10 **Limousin**, France
79 Q 15 **Limoux**, France
197 P 9 **Limpopo**, Mozambique/Botswana
175 N 5 **Linapacan**, Philippines
81 O 11 **Linares**, Spain
125 Q 8 **Linares**, Mexico
144 F 13 **Linares**, Chile
97 I 18 **Linaria**, Greece
171 O 13 **Lincang**, China
171 V 11 **Linchuan**, China
77 L 18 **Lincoln**, United Kingdom
118 K 13 **Lincoln**, Nebraska, U.S.A.
120 H 11 **Lincoln**, Illinois, U.S.A.
121 Y 4 **Lincoln**, Maine, U.S.A.
144 K 12 **Lincoln**, Argentina
211 H 20 **Lincoln**, New Zealand
87 G 26 **Lindau**, Germany
122 K 6 **Linden**, Alabama, U.S.A.
139 U 5 **Linden**, Guyana
195 W 13 **Lindi**, Tanzania
195 X 14 **Lindi**, Tanzania
97 O 24 **Lindos**, Greece
215 Q 1 **Line Islands**, Kiribati
171 S 8 **Linfen**, China
175 O 3 **Lingayen**, Philippines
175 O 2 **Lingayen Gulf**, Philippines
86 D 13 **Lingen**, Germany
174 F 11 **Lingga**, Indonesia
174 M 7 **Lingkabau**, Malaysia
194 L 7 **Lingomo**, Democratic Republic of Congo
171 R 14 **Lingshan**, China
171 S 15 **Lingshui**, China
192 E 8 **Linguère**, Senegal
171 U 6 **Lingyuan**, China
171 W 1 **Linhai**, China
171 W 11 **Linhai**, China
143 M 17 **Linhares**, Brazil
171 R 6 **Linhe**, China
85 G 22 **Linköping**, Sweden
171 Y 3 **Linkou**, China
98 F 12 **Linkuva**, Lithuania
87 B 17 **Linnich**, Germany
171 U 8 **Linqing**, China
88 H 8 **Linthal**, Switzerland
118 I 9 **Linton**, North Dakota, U.S.A.
120 J 12 **Linton**, Indiana, U.S.A.
171 U 5 **Linxi**, China
171 P 8 **Linxia**, China
171 V 8 **Linyi**, China
89 T 3 **Linz**, Austria
100 J 2 **Lioboml'**, Ukraine
91 L 16 **Lioni**, Italy
193 U 9 **Lioua**, Chad
194 H 7 **Liouesso**, Congo
175 O 4 **Lipa**, Philippines
100 L 7 **Lipcani**, Moldova
156 F 9 **Lipetsk**, Russian Federation
92 D 11 **Lipiany**, Poland
171 S 12 **Liping**, China
92 I 11 **Lipno**, Poland
100 F 10 **Lipova**, Romania
87 C 15 **Lippe**, Germany
87 E 15 **Lippstadt**, Germany
92 N 9 **Lipsk**, Poland
193 N 9 **Liptougou**, Burkina Faso
93 J 19 **Liptovský Mikuláš**, Slovakia
171 S 13 **Lipu**, China
195 S 6 **Lira**, Uganda
194 I 8 **Liranga**, Congo
167 N 3 **Lisakovsk**, Kazakhstan
194 L 6 **Lisala**, Democratic Republic of Congo
80 F 9 **Lisboa**, Portugal
80 G 9 **Lisbon**, Portugal
96 E 11 **Lisec**, Macedonia (F.Y.R.O.M.)
171 W 11 **Lishui**, China
79 N 4 **Lisieux**, France
156 E 9 **Liski**, Russian Federation
209 W 9 **Lismore**, New South Wales, Australia
77 B 19 **Listowel**, Republic of Ireland
120 G 12 **Litchfield**, Illinois, U.S.A.
97 B 21 **Lithakia**, Greece
209 U 11 **Lithgow**, New South Wales, Australia
99 C 14 **Lithuania**, Europe
89 U 1 **Litschau**, Austria
169 N 22 **Little Andaman**, India
126 K 6 **Little Cayman**, Cayman Islands
173 B 19 **Little Coco Island**, Myanmar
117 M 20 **Little Colorado**, Arizona, U.S.A.
118 L 9 **Little Falls**, Minnesota, U.S.A.
121 T 8 **Little Falls**, New York, U.S.A.
114 J 9 **Little Grand Rapids**, Manitoba, Canada
127 P 5 **Little Inagua Island**, The Bahamas
196 K 15 **Little Karoo**, Republic of South Africa
169 O 24 **Little Nicobar**, India
119 M 17 **Little Rock**, Arkansas, U.S.A.
208 I 7 **Little Sandy Desert**, Western Australia, Australia
161 S 3 **Little Zab**, Iraq
193 S 14 **Littoral**, Cameroon
101 N 5 **Lityn**, Ukraine
171 S 13 **Liuzhou**, China
100 H 7 **Livada**, Romania
98 H 12 **Līvāni**, Latvia
167 N 4 **Livanovka**, Kazakhstan
123 P 8 **Live Oak**, Florida, U.S.A.
77 I 18 **Liverpool**, United Kingdom
115 V 14 **Liverpool**, Nova Scotia, Canada
218 G 3 **Livingston Island**, Antarctica
197 N 7 **Livingstone**, Zambia
197 R 3 **Livingstonia**, Malawi
94 F 12 **Livno**, Bosnia and Herzegovina
90 E 11 **Livorno**, Italy
195 V 13 **Liwale**, Tanzania
92 M 12 **Liwiec**, Poland
171 P 10 **Lixian**, China
97 A 19 **Lixouri**, Greece
77 G 24 **Lizard Point**, United Kingdom
94 K 12 **Ljig**, Serbia and Montenegro
94 B 7 **Ljubljana**, Slovenia
94 J 11 **Ljubovija**, Serbia and Montenegro
85 I 23 **Ljugarn**, Sweden
85 G 16 **Ljungan**, Sweden
85 F 24 **Ljungby**, Sweden
85 G 17 **Ljusdal**, Sweden
85 G 17 **Ljusnan**, Sweden
77 H 21 **Llandovery**, United Kingdom
77 H 21 **Llanelli**, United Kingdom
81 N 1 **Llanes**, Spain
77 I 19 **Llangollen**, United Kingdom
125 N 5 **Llano de los Caballos Mesteños**, Mexico
119 G 19 **Llano Estacado**, Texas, U.S.A.
138 K 9 **Llanos**, Colombia
81 U 4 **Lleida**, Spain
80 K 10 **Llerena**, Spain
141 I 22 **Llica**, Bolivia
81 T 8 **Lliria**, Spain
81 W 3 **Llivia**, Spain
113 W 11 **Lloydminster**, Saskatchewan, Canada
81 Y 8 **Llucmajor**, Spain
117 M 17 **Loa**, Utah, U.S.A.
90 B 9 **Loano**, Italy
87 O 16 **Löbau**, Germany
194 I 5 **Lobaye**, Central African Republic
145 L 15 **Loberia**, Argentina
92 E 10 **Łobez**, Poland
196 G 4 **Lobito**, Angola
80 K 9 **Lobón**, Spain
62 O 11 **Lobos**, Canary Islands
144 L 13 **Lobos**, Argentina
173 M 21 **Lôc Ninh**, Vietnam
88 G 10 **Locarno**, Switzerland
76 G 12 **Loch Lomond**, United Kingdom
76 H 10 **Loch Ness**, United Kingdom
76 H 11 **Loch Rannoch**, United Kingdom
76 G 9 **Loch Shin**, United Kingdom
82 M 12 **Lochem**, Netherlands
79 O 7 **Loches**, France
76 F 13 **Lochgilphead**, United Kingdom
76 G 9 **Lochinver**, United Kingdom
92 M 12 **Łochów**, Poland
209 O 11 **Lock**, South Australia, Australia
121 R 10 **Lock Haven**, Pennsylvania, U.S.A.
77 I 14 **Lockerbie**, United Kingdom
209 S 1 **Lockhart River**, Queensland, Australia
91 M 21 **Locri**, Italy
160 F 9 **Lod**, Israel
79 R 13 **Lodève**, France
165 W 11 **Lodhran**, Pakistan
90 D 7 **Lodi**, Italy
117 E 18 **Lodi**, California, U.S.A.
84 G 9 **Lødingen**, Norway
194 M 10 **Lodja**, Democratic Republic of Congo
195 U 6 **Lodwar**, Kenya
93 J 14 **Łódź**, Poland
173 I 15 **Loei**, Thailand
89 P 6 **Lofer**, Austria
84 F 9 **Lofoten**, Norway
117 M 14 **Logan**, Utah, U.S.A.
121 N 13 **Logan**, West Virginia, U.S.A.
120 J 10 **Logansport**, Indiana, U.S.A.
193 V 10 **Logone Birni**, Cameroon
193 W 11 **Logone Occidental**, Chad
193 W 12 **Logone Oriental**, Chad
81 Q 3 **Logroño**, Spain
197 Y 5 **Lohatanjona Angadoka**, Madgascar
168 C 12 **Lohawat**, India
172 E 12 **Loi-lem**, Myanmar
172 E 11 **Loi Sang**, Myanmar
172 E 13 **Loikaw**, Myanmar
78 L 7 **Loire**, France
140 A 11 **Loja**, Ecuador
81 N 12 **Loja**, Spain
140 B 11 **Loja**, Ecuador
84 M 9 **Lokan tekojärvi**, Finland
83 E 17 **Lokeren**, Belgium
101 S 4 **Lokhvytsya**, Ukraine
195 U 6 **Lokichar**, Kenya
195 T 5 **Lokichokio**, Kenya
193 R 12 **Loko**, Nigeria
194 M 8 **Lokofe**, Democratic Republic of Congo
193 R 12 **Lokoja**, Nigeria
194 K 9 **Lokolama**, Democratic Republic of Congo
193 V 15 **Lokomo**, Cameroon
115 T 4 **Loks Land**, Nunavut, Canada
196 G 5 **Lola**, Angola
85 D 26 **Lolland**, Denmark
195 U 9 **Lollondo**, Tanzania
118 B 8 **Lolo**, Montana, U.S.A.
212 G 4 **Lolobau Island**, Papua New Guinea
193 T 15 **Lolodorf**, Cameroon
85 C 17 **Lom**, Norway
96 F 6 **Lom**, Bulgaria
173 I 16 **Lom Sak**, Thailand
192 H 11 **Loma Mountains**, Sierra Leone
141 E 19 **Lomas**, Peru
144 M 13 **Lomas de Zamora**, Argentina
208 I 3 **Lombadina**, Western Australia, Australia
90 E 6 **Lombardia**, Italy
175 P 15 **Lomblen**, Indonesia
174 L 15 **Lombok**, Indonesia
59 T 5 **Lombok Basin**, Indian Ocean
193 N 13 **Lomé**, Togo
194 M 9 **Lomela**, Democratic Republic of Congo
193 V 15 **Lomié**, Cameroon
83 I 17 **Lommel**, Belgium
65 R 9 **Lomonosov Ridge**, Arctic Ocean
117 E 22 **Lompoc**, California, U.S.A.
92 M 11 **Łomża**, Poland
145 G 15 **Loncopué**, Argentina
83 F 18 **Londerzeel**, Belgium
77 M 21 **London**, United Kingdom
115 O 15 **London**, Ontario, Canada
120 L 14 **London**, Kentucky, U.S.A.
77 D 15 **Londonderry**, United Kingdom
143 I 19 **Londrina**, Brazil
123 U 5 **Long Bay**, South Carolina, U.S.A.
117 G 23 **Long Beach**, California, U.S.A.
121 V 10 **Long Beach**, New York, U.S.A.
115 P 8 **Long Island**, Ontario, Canada
121 W 10 **Long Island**, New York, U.S.A.
127 N 4 **Long Island**, The Bahamas
209 V 6 **Long Island**, Queensland, Australia
212 E 4 **Long Island**, Papua New Guinea
121 V 9 **Long Island Sound**, New York, U.S.A.
114 I 8 **Long Point**, Manitoba, Canada
115 X 10 **Long Range Mountains**, Newfoundland and Labrador, Canada
117 L 18 **Long Valley Junction**, Utah, U.S.A.
173 L 22 **Long Xuyên**, Vietnam
97 D 22 **Longa**, Greece
196 I 5 **Longa**, Angola
174 L 9 **Longbawan**, Indonesia
171 R 11 **Longchang**, China
77 D 17 **Longford**, Republic of Ireland
195 V 9 **Longido**, Tanzania
174 L 11 **Longiram**, Indonesia
114 M 11 **Longlac**, Ontario, Canada
174 L 10 **Longnawan**, Indonesia
209 S 6 **Longreach**, Queensland, Australia
171 P 10 **Longriba**, China
79 U 3 **Longuyon**, France
116 D 8 **Longview**, Washington, U.S.A.
119 M 19 **Longview**, Texas, U.S.A.
63 N 25 **Longwood**, St Helena
83 K 26 **Longwy**, Belgium
171 V 12 **Longyan**, China
65 T 11 **Longyearbyen**, Svalbard
171 R 14 **Longzhou**, China
90 F 7 **Lonigo**, Italy
79 U 8 **Lons-le-Saunier**, France
175 S 13 **Lontar**, Indonesia
120 J 12 **Loogootee**, Indiana, U.S.A.
77 A 19 **Loop Head**, Republic of Ireland
173 H 18 **Lop Buri**, Thailand
170 L 6 **Lop Nur**, China
213 R 11 **Lopévi**, Vanuatu
84 I 6 **Lopphavet**, Norway
80 L 11 **Lora del Río**, Spain
121 N 10 **Lorain**, Ohio, U.S.A.
165 U 10 **Loralai**, Pakistan
81 R 11 **Lorca**, Spain
61 N 11 **Lord Howe Island**, Australia
173 F 22 **Lord Loughborough Island**, Myanmar
119 D 19 **Lordsburg**, New Mexico, U.S.A.
175 R 15 **Lore**, East Timor
212 E 2 **Lorengau**, Papua New Guinea
164 G 7 **Lorestān**, Iran
140 E 11 **Loreto**, Peru
124 I 7 **Loreto**, Mexico
141 K 19 **Loreto**, Bolivia
142 K 12 **Loreto**, Brazil
175 Q 5 **Loreto**, Philippines
138 H 3 **Lorica**, Colombia
78 I 6 **Lorient**, France
118 E 7 **Loring**, Montana, U.S.A.
123 U 4 **Loris**, South Carolina, U.S.A.
87 D 25 **Lörrach**, Germany
79 U 4 **Lorraine**, France
189 Q 8 **Lorzot**, Tunisia
117 F 22 **Los Alamos**, California, U.S.A.
119 E 17 **Los Alamos**, New Mexico, U.S.A.
144 L 8 **Los Amores**, Argentina
117 G 23 **Los Angeles**, California, U.S.A.
145 F 14 **Los Angeles**, Chile
117 E 19 **Los Banos**, California, U.S.A.
144 K 5 **Los Blancos**, Argentina
126 G 12 **Los Chiles**, Costa Rica
141 K 19 **Los Cusis**, Bolivia
145 E 16 **Los Lagos**, Chile
145 H 16 **Los Menucos**, Argentina
124 K 7 **Los Mochis**, Mexico
126 I 4 **Los Palacios**, Cuba
124 I 5 **Los Pocitos**, Mexico
140 B 10 **Los Rios**, Ecuador
144 J 9 **Los Telares**, Argentina
139 Q 2 **Los Testigos**, Venezuela
144 F 11 **Los Vilos**, Chile
215 O 15 **Losap**, Federated States of Micronesia
92 N 12 **Łosice**, Poland
94 B 11 **Lošinj**, Croatia
117 F 21 **Lost Hills**, California, U.S.A.
212 G 6 **Losuia**, Papua New Guinea
145 E 14 **Lota**, Chile
191 G 22 **Lotagipi Swamp**, Sudan
194 M 9 **Loto**, Democratic Republic of Congo
172 I 12 **Louang Namtha**, Laos
173 H 16 **Louang Phrabang Range**, Thailand
172 I 13 **Louangphrabang**, Laos
194 F 10 **Loubomo**, Congo
78 J 5 **Loudéac**, France
171 S 12 **Loudi**, China
79 N 8 **Loudun**, France
192 D 8 **Louga**, Senegal
77 D 16 **Lough Allen**, Republic of Ireland
77 C 16 **Lough Conn**, Republic of Ireland
77 C 18 **Lough Corrib**, Republic of Ireland
77 C 19 **Lough Derg**, Republic of Ireland
77 B 17 **Lough Mask**, Republic of Ireland
77 E 15 **Lough Neagh**, United Kingdom
77 C 17 **Lough Ree**, Republic of Ireland
77 K 19 **Loughborough**, United Kingdom
65 P 7 **Lougheed Island**, Arctic Ocean
77 C 18 **Loughrea**, Republic of Ireland
197 P 9 **Louis Trichardt**, Republic of South Africa
212 H 7 **Louisiade Archipelago**, Papua New Guinea
119 M 21 **Louisiana**, U.S.A.
120 K 13 **Louisville**, Kentucky, U.S.A.
122 J 5 **Louisville**, Mississippi, U.S.A.
194 H 8 **Loukoléla**, Congo
194 G 10 **Loukouo**, Congo
193 S 14 **Loum**, Cameroon
78 M 15 **Lourdes**, France
142 I 8 **Lourenço**, Brazil
80 G 9 **Loures**, Portugal
77 L 18 **Louth**, United Kingdom

Country · Internal administrative region: State/Province/Territory/Dependent territory · Capital city · Mountain range/Undersea ridge · Mountain peak/Volcano/Seamount · Geographic feature · Headland/Point/Cape/Peninsula · Desert · Island/Island group · Antarctic base · Ocean · Sea · Bay/Gulf/Channel/Strait · Lake · Salt pan/Dry/Intermittent lake · River

97 F 20 **Loutraki**, Greece
79 O 4 **Louviers**, France
85 J 14 **Lövånger**, Sweden
96 H 8 **Lovech**, Bulgaria □
96 I 8 **Lovech**, Bulgaria
118 F 13 **Loveland**, Colorado, U.S.A.
118 D 10 **Lovell**, Wyoming, U.S.A.
117 G 15 **Lovelock**, Nevada, U.S.A.
90 E 6 **Lovere**, Italy
93 C 16 **Lovosice**, Czech Republic
100 E 10 **Lovrin**, Romania
196 J 1 **Lóvua**, Angola
196 L 3 **Lôvua**, Angola
195 O 8 **Lowa**, Democratic Republic of Congo
121 W 8 **Lowell**, Massachusetts, U.S.A.
191 F 22 **Lowelli**, Sudan
86 L 12 **Löwenberg**, Germany
211 K 16 **Lower Hutt**, New Zealand
77 D 15 **Lower Lough Erne**, United Kingdom ◠
118 K 7 **Lower RedLake**, Minnesota, U.S.A. ◠
77 N 19 **Lowestoft**, United Kingdom
165 U 8 **Lowgar**, Afghanistan □
92 J 13 **Łowicz**, Poland
116 J 11 **Lowman**, Idaho, U.S.A.
121 T 7 **Lowville**, New York, U.S.A.
86 F 10 **Loxstedt**, Germany
213 R 13 **Loyalty Islands**, New Caledonia ✻
120 G 7 **Loyd**, Wisconsin, U.S.A.
99 N 21 **Loyew**, Belarus
94 J 11 **Loznica**, Serbia and Montenegro
96 L 7 **Loznitsa**, Bulgaria
101 W 6 **Lozova**, Ukraine
167 V 2 **Lozovoye**, Kazakhstan
81 O 5 **Lozoyuela**, Spain
142 G 11 **Lua Nova**, Brazil
196 K 3 **Luacano**, Angola
171 U 10 **Lu'an**, China
196 F 2 **Luanda**, Angola ♜
196 G 3 **Luanda**, Angola □
196 I 4 **Luando**, Angola
197 O 4 **Luanshya**, Zambia
195 P 13 **Luanza**, Democratic Republic of Congo
197 O 3 **Luapula**, Zambia □
80 K 1 **Luarca**, Spain
194 M 14 **Luashi**, Democratic Republic of Congo
196 K 3 **Luau**, Angola
193 S 15 **Luba**, Equatorial Guinea
93 O 17 **Lubaczów**, Poland
196 J 2 **Lubalo**, Angola
98 I 11 **Lubāna**, Latvia
98 I 11 **Lubānas ezers**, Latvia ◠
196 G 5 **Lubango**, Angola
195 O 11 **Lubao**, Democratic Republic of Congo
93 N 14 **Lubartów**, Poland
92 J 10 **Lubawa**, Poland
119 H 19 **Lubbock**, Texas, U.S.A.
121 Z 5 **Lubec**, Maine, U.S.A.
86 I 9 **Lübeck**, Germany
86 I 9 **Lübecker Bucht**, Germany ≈
195 N 10 **Lubefu**, Democratic Republic of Congo
93 F 14 **Lubin**, Poland
93 N 14 **Lublin**, Poland
93 I 16 **Lubliniec**, Poland
101 S 4 **Lubny**, Ukraine
195 O 14 **Lubudi**, Democratic Republic of Congo
195 P 14 **Lubumbashi**, Democratic Republic of Congo
197 N 5 **Lubungu**, Zambia
195 O 8 **Lubutu**, Democratic Republic of Congo
196 H 2 **Lucala**, Angola
196 K 2 **Lucapa**, Angola
90 E 10 **Lucca**, Italy
81 N 12 **Lucena**, Spain
175 O 4 **Lucena**, Philippines
93 J 21 **Lučenec**, Slovakia
91 K 14 **Lucera**, Italy
141 H 16 **Lucerna**, Peru
86 J 12 **Lüchow**, Germany
175 R 13 **Lucipara**, Indonesia ✻
196 F 5 **Lucira**, Angola
87 M 14 **Luckau**, Germany
87 M 14 **Luckenwalde**, Germany
168 G 12 **Lucknow**, India
78 L 8 **Luçon**, France
196 K 4 **Lucusse**, Angola
196 H 11 **Lüderitz**, Namibia
196 H 11 **Lüderitz Bay**, Namibia ≈
195 T 14 **Ludewa**, Tanzania
168 D 9 **Ludhiana**, India
120 K 7 **Ludington**, Michigan, U.S.A.
77 I 20 **Ludlow**, United Kingdom
117 I 22 **Ludlow**, California, U.S.A.
121 V 7 **Ludlow**, Vermont, U.S.A.
123 R 7 **Ludowici**, Georgia, U.S.A.
85 G 19 **Ludvika**, Sweden
87 F 22 **Ludwigsburg**, Germany
86 M 13 **Ludwigsfelde**, Germany
86 J 11 **Ludwigslust**, Germany
98 J 12 **Ludza**, Latvia
194 L 11 **Luebo**, Democratic Republic of Congo
195 O 10 **Lueki**, Democratic Republic of Congo
196 J 4 **Luena**, Angola
171 Q 9 **Lüeyang**, China
119 L 20 **Lufkin**, Texas, U.S.A.
156 F 7 **Luga**, Russian Federation
88 H 11 **Lugano**, Switzerland
213 Q 10 **Luganville**, Vanuatu
191 L 19 **Lughaye**, Somalia
80 J 1 **Lugo**, Spain
100 F 10 **Lugoj**, Romania
167 T 10 **Lugovoy**, Kazakhstan
101 Z 6 **Luhans'k**, Ukraine
195 V 13 **Luhombero**, Tanzania
171 O 10 **Luhuo**, China
196 L 6 **Luiana**, Angola
219 N 4 **Luitpold Coast**, Antarctica ◇
194 L 12 **Luiza**, Democratic Republic of Congo
144 G 11 **Luján de Cuyo**, Argentina
94 H 11 **Lukavac**, Bosnia and Herzegovina
96 I 11 **Lŭki**, Bulgaria
194 I 8 **Lukolela**, Democratic Republic of Congo
96 H 8 **Lukovit**, Bulgaria
92 M 13 **Łuków**, Poland
194 F 11 **Lukula**, Democratic Republic of Congo
196 L 5 **Lukulu**, Zambia
195 U 13 **Lukumburu**, Tanzania
84 J 12 **Luleå**, Sweden
84 J 11 **Luleälven**, Sweden ∫
96 M 12 **Lüleburgaz**, Turkey
158 C 7 **Lüleburgaz**, Turkey
195 P 10 **Lulimba**, Democratic Republic of Congo
194 J 7 **Lulonga**, Democratic Republic of Congo
215 Y 15 **Luma**, American Samoa
196 K 4 **Lumbala Kaquengue**, Angola
196 K 5 **Lumbala N'guimbo**, Angola
122 I 7 **Lumberton**, Mississippi, U.S.A.
123 T 3 **Lumberton**, North Carolina, U.S.A.
144 I 6 **Lumbrera**, Argentina
212 B 3 **Lumi**, Papua New Guinea
173 N 19 **Lumphăt**, Cambodia
211 C 24 **Lumsden**, New Zealand
196 I 2 **Lunda Norte**, Angola □
196 K 3 **Lunda Sul**, Angola □
197 Q 4 **Lundazi**, Zambia
77 G 22 **Lundy Island**, United Kingdom ✻
86 H 11 **Lüneburg**, Germany
87 D 15 **Lünen**, Germany
79 V 4 **Lunéville**, France
88 F 8 **Lungern**, Switzerland
170 I 9 **Lunggar**, China
192 F 12 **Lungi**, Sierra Leone
169 N 14 **Lunglei**, India
117 G 17 **Luning**, Nevada, U.S.A.
99 I 21 **Luninyets**, Belarus
168 D 11 **Lunkaransar**, India
192 F 12 **Lunsar**, Sierra Leone
89 U 5 **Lunz am See**, Austria
171 R 13 **Luodian**, China
171 T 9 **Luohe**, China
171 Q 13 **Luoping**, China
171 S 9 **Luoyang**, China
171 W 12 **Luoyuan**, China
194 G 11 **Luozi**, Democratic Republic of Congo
197 O 7 **Lupane**, Zimbabwe
171 P 12 **Lupanshui**, China
197 R 3 **Lupilichi**, Mozambique
171 P 9 **Luqu**, China
196 I 2 **Luremo**, Angola
77 F 16 **Lurgan**, United Kingdom
141 D 17 **Lurín**, Peru
195 R 9 **Lusahunga**, Tanzania
197 O 5 **Lusaka**, Zambia ♜
197 O 5 **Lusaka**, Zambia □
194 M 11 **Lusambo**, Democratic Republic of Congo
95 J 19 **Lushnjë**, Albania
195 W 10 **Lushoto**, Tanzania
171 O 12 **Lushui**, China
118 F 11 **Lusk**, Wyoming, U.S.A.
79 O 9 **Lussac-les-Châteaux**, France
88 I 6 **Lustenau**, Austria
87 L 14 **Lutherstadt Wittenberg**, Germany
195 Q 8 **Lutiba**, Democratic Republic of Congo
86 H 8 **Lütjenburg**, Germany
77 L 21 **Luton**, United Kingdom
113 U 7 **Lutselk'e**, Northwest Territories, Canada
100 K 3 **Luts'k**, Ukraine
101 Z 6 **Lutuhyne**, Ukraine
86 I 10 **Lützow**, Germany
219 U 2 **Lützow-Holm Bay**, Antarctica ≈
196 J 14 **Lutzville**, Republic of South Africa
191 K 23 **Luuq**, Somalia
195 O 12 **Luvua**, Democratic Republic of Congo ∫
196 K 4 **Luvuei**, Angola
195 S 7 **Luwero**, Uganda
175 P 11 **Luwuk**, Indonesia
83 L 25 **Luxembourg**, Luxembourg ♜
83 K 25 **Luxembourg**, Europe ■
83 I 23 **Luxembourg**, Belgium □
83 L 26 **Luxembourg**, Luxembourg □
79 V 6 **Luxeuil-les-Bains**, France
171 O 13 **Luxi**, China
190 F 11 **Luxor**, Egypt
156 I 8 **Luza**, Russian Federation
88 F 7 **Luzern**, Switzerland
171 Q 11 **Luzhou**, China
143 J 16 **Luziânia**, Brazil
175 O 2 **Luzon**, Philippines ✻
60 J 5 **Luzon Strait**, Pacific Ocean ◒
175 O 1 **Luzon Strait**, Philippines ◒
100 I 4 **L'viv**, Ukraine
65 V 5 **Lyakhovskiye Ostrova**, Arctic Ocean ✻
96 J 8 **Lyaskovets**, Bulgaria
85 I 14 **Lycksele**, Sweden
99 K 22 **Lyel'chytsy**, Belarus
99 K 15 **Lyepyel'**, Belarus
97 F 21 **Lygourio**, Greece
77 I 23 **Lyme Bay**, United Kingdom ≈
77 I 23 **Lyme Regis**, United Kingdom
92 K 8 **Łyna**, Poland ∫
121 Q 14 **Lynchburg**, Virginia, U.S.A.
85 A 21 **Lyngdal**, Norway
114 I 6 **Lynn Lake**, Manitoba, Canada
101 R 3 **Lynovytsya**, Ukraine
99 H 15 **Lyntupy**, Belarus
79 T 10 **Lyon**, France
123 Q 6 **Lyons**, Georgia, U.S.A.
99 M 15 **Lyozna**, Belarus
101 T 3 **Lypova Dolyna**, Ukraine
83 B 19 **Lys**, Belgium ∫
101 Y 5 **Lysychans'k**, Ukraine
77 I 17 **Lytham St Anne's**, United Kingdom
211 H 20 **Lyttelton**, New Zealand
113 S 14 **Lytton**, British Columbia, Canada
99 J 20 **Lyuban'**, Belarus
100 M 4 **Lyubar**, Ukraine
101 P 1 **Lyubech**, Ukraine
100 K 1 **Lyubeshiv**, Ukraine

M

169 B 26 **Maalhosmadulu Atoll**, Maldives ✻
197 N 6 **Maamba**, Zambia
160 G 12 **Ma'an**, Jordan
193 T 15 **Ma'an**, Cameroon
84 M 11 **Maaninkavaara**, Finland
83 J 16 **Maarheeze**, Netherlands
85 J 19 **Maarianhamina**, Finland
160 I 3 **Ma'arrat an Nu'man**, Syria
82 I 12 **Maarssen**, Netherlands
83 H 14 **Maas**, Netherlands ∫
83 K 18 **Maaseik**, Belgium
175 Q 6 **Maasin**, Philippines
82 F 13 **Maasland**, Netherlands
83 K 18 **Maasmechelen**, Belgium
83 K 19 **Maastricht**, Netherlands
175 S 10 **Maba**, Indonesia
197 Q 10 **Mabalane**, Mozambique
195 P 7 **Mabana**, Democratic Republic of Congo
172 E 10 **Mabein**, Myanmar
77 M 18 **Mablethorpe**, United Kingdom
197 R 9 **Mabote**, Mozambique
189 U 9 **Mabrūk**, Libya
219 V 5 **Mac Robertson Land**, Antarctica ◇
145 J 14 **Macachín**, Argentina
143 M 19 **Macaé**, Brazil
197 S 4 **Macaloge**, Mozambique
142 I 9 **Macapá**, Brazil
140 A 11 **Macará**, Ecuador
140 C 10 **Macas**, Ecuador
171 U 14 **Macau**, China
143 L 15 **Macaúbas**, Brazil
145 L 23 **Macbride Head**, Falkland Islands ▶
123 Q 8 **Macclenny**, Florida, U.S.A.
59 N 12 **MacDonald Islands**, Australia □
208 N 6 **MacDonnell Ranges**, Northern Territory, Australia ⛰
80 J 4 **Macedo de Cavaleiros**, Portugal
96 C 11 **Macedonia (F.Y.R.O.M.)**, Europe ■
142 O 13 **Maceió**, Brazil
90 I 11 **Macerata**, Italy
157 S 11 **Macha**, Russian Federation
140 B 8 **Machachi**, Ecuador
197 Q 9 **Machaila**, Mozambique
195 V 9 **Machakos**, Kenya
140 A 10 **Machala**, Ecuador
197 R 8 **Machanga**, Mozambique
191 F 20 **Machar Marshes**, Sudan ◇
141 L 22 **Machareti**, Bolivia
171 U 10 **Macheng**, China
169 J 16 **Machhagan**, India
121 Z 5 **Machias**, Maine, U.S.A.
62 O 5 **Machico**, Madeira
169 G 19 **Machilipatnam**, India
197 R 5 **Machinga**, Malawi
138 K 3 **Machiques**, Venezuela
197 Q 10 **Macia**, Mozambique
101 N 12 **Măcin**, Romania
116 K 11 **Mackay**, Idaho, U.S.A.
209 U 5 **Mackay**, Queensland, Australia
113 P 5 **Mackenzie**, Northwest Territories, Canada ∫
219 X 6 **Mackenzie Bay**, Antarctica ≈
113 O 3 **Mackenzie Bay**, Yukon Territory, Canada ≈
65 P 7 **Mackenzie King Island**, Arctic Ocean ✻
113 O 6 **Mackenzie Mountains**, Northwest Territories, Canada ⛰
120 L 5 **Mackinaw City**, Michigan, U.S.A.
113 W 12 **Macklin**, Saskatchewan, Canada
211 D 26 **Maclennan**, New Zealand
196 H 1 **Macocola**, Angola
120 F 10 **Macomb**, Illinois, U.S.A.
91 B 17 **Macomer**, Italy
197 U 4 **Macomia**, Mozambique
122 J 5 **Macon**, Mississippi, U.S.A.
123 P 5 **Macon**, Georgia, U.S.A.
79 T 9 **Mâcon**, France
196 L 4 **Macondo**, Angola
209 T 10 **Macquarie**, New South Wales, Australia ∫
61 N 13 **Macquarie Island**, Australia ✻
77 B 20 **Macroom**, Republic of Ireland
138 J 10 **Macuje**, Colombia
160 G 10 **Mādabā**, Jordan
197 P 12 **Madadeni**, Republic of South Africa
197 W 7 **Madagascar**, Africa ■
197 W 8 **Madagascar**, Madgascar ✻
58 K 8 **Madagascar Basin**, Indian Ocean ◇
58 J 8 **Madagascar Plateau**, Indian Ocean ◇
58 J 9 **Madagascar Ridge**, Indian Ocean ⛰
193 U 5 **Madama**, Niger
96 I 12 **Madan**, Bulgaria
212 D 4 **Madang**, Papua New Guinea □
212 D 4 **Madang**, Papua New Guinea
193 Q 9 **Madaoua**, Niger
166 I 13 **Madau**, Turkmenistan
121 Y 2 **Madawaska**, Maine, U.S.A.
62 N 4 **Madeira**, Portugal □
142 D 13 **Madeira**, Brazil ∫
62 J 10 **Madeira Ridge**, Atlantic Ocean ⛰
117 F 14 **Madeline**, California, U.S.A.
159 O 11 **Maden**, Turkey
167 W 6 **Madeniyet**, Kazakhstan
117 F 19 **Madera**, California, U.S.A.
124 K 4 **Madera**, Mexico
168 I 12 **Madhubani**, India
169 F 14 **Madhya Pradesh**, India □
169 C 21 **Madikeri**, India
194 H 11 **Madimba**, Democratic Republic of Congo
160 M 3 **Ma'din'**, Syria
160 K 3 **Madinat ath Thawrah**, Syria
194 E 10 **Madingo-Kayes**, Congo
141 I 17 **Madini**, Bolivia ∫
120 K 12 **Madison**, Indiana, U.S.A.
120 H 8 **Madison**, Wisconsin, U.S.A.
123 P 8 **Madison**, Florida, U.S.A.
123 P 4 **Madison**, Georgia, U.S.A.
119 L 20 **Madisonville**, Texas, U.S.A.
120 I 14 **Madisonville**, Kentucky, U.S.A.
174 J 14 **Madiun**, Indonesia
194 G 7 **Madjingo**, Gabon
98 G 11 **Madliena**, Latvia
195 W 7 **Mado Gashi**, Kenya
171 O 9 **Madoi**, China
98 H 11 **Madona**, Latvia
141 H 16 **Madre de Dios**, Peru □
141 G 17 **Madre de Dios**, Peru/Bolivia ∫
81 O 6 **Madrid**, Spain ♜
81 O 7 **Madrid**, Spain □
195 U 10 **Madukani**, Tanzania
174 K 14 **Madura**, Indonesia ✻
208 K 10 **Madura**, Western Australia, Australia
169 E 23 **Madurai**, India
173 F 14 **Mae Hong Son**, Thailand
173 F 15 **Mae Sariang**, Thailand
173 F 16 **Mae Sot**, Thailand
177 J 15 **Maebashi**, Japan
197 X 6 **Maevatanana**, Madgascar
213 R 10 **Maéwo**, Vanuatu ✻
114 H 8 **Mafeking**, Manitoba, Canada
197 N 13 **Mafeteng**, Lesotho
195 W 13 **Mafia Channel**, Tanzania ≈
195 X 12 **Mafia Island**, Tanzania ✻
196 M 11 **Mafikeng**, Republic of South Africa
195 U 12 **Mafinga**, Tanzania
157 X 10 **Magadan**, Russian Federation
195 V 9 **Magadi**, Kenya
145 F 24 **Magallanes**, Chile □
81 X 8 **Magalluf**, Spain
194 M 6 **Magbakele**, Democratic Republic of Congo
157 T 13 **Magdagachi**, Russian Federation
138 I 2 **Magdalena**, Colombia □
124 I 3 **Magdalena**, Mexico ∫
138 I 4 **Magdalena**, Colombia ∫
124 I 3 **Magdalena**, Mexico
141 L 17 **Magdalena**, Bolivia
144 M 13 **Magdalena**, Argentina
87 J 14 **Magdeburg**, Germany
177 C 25 **Mage-shima**, Japan ✻
90 C 7 **Magenta**, Italy
84 K 5 **Magerøya**, Norway ✻
190 E 9 **Maghâgha**, Egypt
192 F 8 **Maghama**, Mauritania
188 K 6 **Maghnia**, Algeria
81 O 11 **Magina**, Spain ▲
91 O 17 **Maglie**, Italy
212 F 4 **Magma Point**, Papua New Guinea ▶
209 T 4 **Magnetic Island**, Queensland, Australia ✻
156 I 11 **Magnitogorsk**, Russian Federation
119 M 19 **Magnolia**, Arkansas, U.S.A.
213 Y 11 **Mago**, Fiji ✻
197 P 6 **Màgoé**, Mozambique
192 F 7 **Magta' Lahjar**, Mauritania
197 Q 10 **Magude**, Mozambique
193 U 10 **Magumeri**, Nigeria
114 K 4 **Maguse Lake**, Nunavut, Canada ◠
172 C 13 **Magwe**, Myanmar □
172 C 13 **Magwe**, Myanmar
172 A 13 **Magyichaung**, Myanmar
173 J 17 **Maha Sarakham**, Thailand
164 F 4 **Mahābād**, Iran
197 W 6 **Mahabe**, Madgascar
168 H 11 **Mahabharat Range**, Nepal ⛰
169 B 18 **Mahad**, India
191 M 24 **Mahaddayweyne**, Somalia
195 R 6 **Mahagi Port**, Democratic Republic of Congo
197 X 7 **Mahajanga**, Madgascar □
197 X 6 **Mahajanga**, Madgascar
174 L 10 **Mahakam**, Indonesia ∫
164 H 7 **Mahallāt**, Iran
164 M 10 **Māhān**, Iran
169 I 16 **Mahanadi**, India ∫
197 Y 8 **Mahanoro**, Madgascar
169 D 17 **Maharashtra**, India □
160 H 10 **Maḩaţţat Dab'ah**, Jordan
191 D 18 **Mahbub**, Sudan
169 F 19 **Mahbubnagar**, India
189 R 6 **Mahdia**, Tunisia
169 D 22 **Mahe**, India
58 B 10 **Mahé**, Seychelles ✻
58 B 12 **Mahébourg**, Mauritius
195 V 13 **Mahenge**, Tanzania
211 F 23 **Maheno**, New Zealand
210 O 12 **Mahia**, New Zealand
210 O 12 **Mahia Peninsula**, New Zealand ▶
99 M 17 **Mahilyow**, Belarus
99 M 18 **Mahilyowskaya Voblasts'**, Belarus □
192 G 9 **Mahina**, Mali
86 M 13 **Mahlow**, Germany
164 J 5 **Mahmudabad**, Iran
210 K 11 **Mahoenui**, New Zealand
81 Z 7 **Mahon**, Spain
81 R 9 **Mahora**, Spain
192 K 10 **Mahou**, Burkina Faso
169 B 16 **Mahuva**, India
175 S 13 **Mai**, Indonesia ✻
215 Y 15 **Maia**, American Samoa
214 D 2 **Maiana**, Kiribati ✻
215 S 9 **Maiao**, French Polynesia ✻
138 K 2 **Maicao**, Colombia
142 H 9 **Maicuru**, Brazil ∫
77 M 22 **Maidstone**, United Kingdom
193 U 10 **Maiduguri**, Nigeria
169 G 14 **Maihar**, India
169 M 15 **Maijdi**, Bangladesh
169 G 12 **Maikala Range**, India ⛰
174 D 12 **Maileppe**, Indonesia
79 S 5 **Mailly-le-Camp**, France
87 F 20 **Main**, Germany ∫
63 K 26 **Main Base**, Ascension
87 K 23 **Mainburg**, Germany
121 X 5 **Maine**, U.S.A. □
76 H 7 **Mainland**, United Kingdom ✻
76 J 4 **Mainland**, United Kingdom ✻
197 W 7 **Maintirano**, Madgascar
87 E 19 **Mainz**, Germany
63 B 17 **Maio**, Cape Verde ✻
145 M 14 **Maipú**, Argentina
139 O 2 **Maiquetía**, Venezuela
89 W 2 **Maissau**, Austria
144 F 10 **Maitencillo**, Chile
197 N 8 **Maitengwe**, Botswana
209 V 11 **Maitland**, New South Wales, Australia
209 P 11 **Maitland**, South Australia, Australia
219 Q 1 **Maitri**, Antarctica ⁙
177 G 17 **Maizuru**, Japan
95 J 20 **Maja e Çikes**, Albania ▲
95 K 15 **Maja Jezercë**, Albania ▲
125 Z 12 **Majahual**, Mexico
94 N 11 **Majdanpek**, Serbia and Montenegro
175 N 12 **Majene**, Indonesia
94 H 10 **Majevica**, Bosnia and Herzegovina ⛰
81 X 8 **Majorca**, Spain ✻
215 Z 3 **Majuro**, Marshall Islands ♜
215 Z 3 **Majuro**, Marshall Islands ✻
193 T 14 **Makak**, Cameroon
175 N 12 **Makale**, Indonesia
195 Q 10 **Makamba**, Burundi
167 Y 7 **Makanchi**, Kazakhstan
194 J 7 **Makanza**, Democratic Republic of Congo
210 O 12 **Makaraka**, New Zealand
101 O 3 **Makariv**, Ukraine
157 X 14 **Makarov**, Russian Federation
65 R 8 **Makarov Basin**, Arctic Ocean ◇
60 M 5 **Makarov Seamount**, Pacific Ocean ▲
95 F 14 **Makarska**, Croatia
175 N 11 **Makassar Strait**, Indonesia ≈
166 J 6 **Makat**, Kazakhstan

■ Country □ Internal administrative region: State/Province/Territory/Dependent territory ♜ Capital city ⛰ Mountain range/Undersea ridge ▲ Mountain peak/Volcano/Seamount ◇ Geographic feature ▶ Headland/Point/Cape/Peninsula ◢ Desert ✻ Island/Island group ⁙ Antarctic base ◎ Ocean ◒ Sea ≈ Bay/Gulf/Channel/Strait ◠ Lake ◌ Salt pan/Dry/Intermittent lake ∫ River

215 T 9 **Makatea**, French Polynesia ⩩
172 E 7 **Makaw**, Myanmar
215 V 9 **Makemo**, French Polynesia ⩩
192 G 11 **Makeni**, Sierra Leone
156 E 12 **Makhachkala**, Russian Federation
166 I 6 **Makhambet**, Kazakhstan
161 S 3 **Makhmūr**, Iraq
211 F 22 **Makikihi**, New Zealand
214 D 1 **Makin**, Kiribati ⩩
195 V 9 **Makindu**, Kenya
167 R 3 **Makinsk**, Kazakhstan
213 N 7 **Makira**, Solomon Islands ▣
115 V 7 **Makkovik**, Newfoundland and Labrador, Canada
93 L 25 **Makó**, Hungary
194 F 7 **Makokou**, Gabon
195 S 13 **Makongolosi**, Tanzania
195 Q 6 **Makoro**, Democratic Republic of Congo
194 H 9 **Makotipoko**, Congo
194 H 7 **Makoua**, Congo
97 K 24 **Makra**, Greece ⩩
97 D 18 **Makrakomi**, Greece
165 O 13 **Makran**, Iran ◇
165 N 14 **Makran Coast**, Iran ◇
97 H 20 **Makronisi**, Greece ⩩
164 E 2 **Mākū**, Iran
195 T 13 **Makumbako**, Tanzania
194 K 11 **Makumbi**, Democratic Republic of Congo
195 V 14 **Makunguwiro**, Tanzania
169 L 16 **Makunudhoo Atoll**, Maldives ⩩
177 B 24 **Makurazaki**, Japan
193 S 12 **Makurdi**, Nigeria
112 D 9 **Makushin Volcano**, Alaska, U.S.A. ▲
191 K 25 **Makuungo**, Somalia
141 C 17 **Mala**, Peru
94 C 10 **Mala Kapela**, Croatia ⛰
175 Q 7 **Malabang**, Philippines
169 C 21 **Malabar Coast**, India ◇
193 S 14 **Malabo**, Equatorial Guinea ⌂
93 G 21 **Malacky**, Slovakia
99 I 16 **Maladzyechna**, Belarus
81 N 13 **Málaga**, Spain
81 O 9 **Malagón**, Spain
197 X 8 **Malaimbandy**, Madgascar
212 M 6 **Malaita**, Solomon Islands ⩩
213 N 6 **Malaita**, Solomon Islands ▣
191 E 20 **Malakal**, Sudan
168 G 11 **Malakheti**, Nepal
213 P 11 **Malakula**, Vanuatu ⩩
212 D 4 **Malalamai**, Papua New Guinea
212 B 6 **Malam**, Papua New Guinea
175 O 12 **Malamala**, Indonesia
174 J 14 **Malang**, Indonesia
196 H 2 **Malanje**, Angola ▣
196 H 3 **Malanje**, Angola
144 H 10 **Malanzán**, Argentina
85 H 20 **Mälaren**, Sweden ◢
144 G 13 **Malargüe**, Argentina
99 E 22 **Malaryta**, Belarus
159 N 11 **Malatya**, Turkey
169 E 21 **Malavalli**, India
197 Q 4 **Malawi**, Africa □
191 H 17 **Malawiya**, Sudan
175 Q 7 **Malaybalay**, Philippines
164 G 6 **Malāyer**, Iran
174 F 8 **Malaysia**, Asia □
159 R 10 **Malazgirt**, Turkey
92 I 9 **Malbork**, Poland
86 L 10 **Malchin**, Germany
86 K 10 **Malchow**, Germany
83 D 17 **Maldegem**, Belgium
83 K 14 **Malden**, Netherlands
215 Q 4 **Malden Island**, Kiribati ⩩
169 K 19 **Maldives**, Asia □
144 O 13 **Maldonado**, Uruguay ▣
169 L 18 **Male**, Maldives ⌂
169 L 17 **Male Atoll**, Maldives ⩩
93 G 21 **Malé Karpaty**, Slovakia ⛰
169 E 17 **Malegaon**, India
169 C 16 **Malegaon**, India
195 O 9 **Malela**, Democratic Republic of Congo
195 O 13 **Malemba Nkulu**, Democratic Republic of Congo
165 T 8 **Mālestān**, Afghanistan
191 B 17 **Malha**, Sudan
161 R 5 **Malḩāt**, Iraq
192 F 10 **Mali**, Africa □
195 O 9 **Mali**, Democratic Republic of Congo
173 F 20 **Mali Kyun**, Myanmar ⩩
77 E 14 **Malin**, Republic of Ireland
77 D 14 **Malin Head**, Republic of Ireland ▶
195 X 9 **Malindi**, Kenya
194 F 9 **Malinga**, Gabon
171 Q 14 **Malipo**, China
95 L 20 **Maliq**, Albania
175 Q 7 **Malita**, Philippines
96 L 13 **Malkara**, Turkey
76 F 11 **Mallaig**, United Kingdom
190 E 9 **Mallawi**, Egypt
114 K 3 **Mallery Lake**, Nunavut, Canada ◢
77 C 20 **Mallow**, Republic of Ireland
212 G 4 **Malmal**, Papua New Guinea
83 L 21 **Malmédy**, Belgium
196 J 15 **Malmesbury**, Republic of South Africa
85 E 25 **Malmö**, Sweden
156 H 9 **Malmyzh**, Russian Federation
100 K 10 **Malnaş**, Romania
213 Q 10 **Malo**, Vanuatu ⩩
142 G 9 **Maloca**, Brazil
215 Z 2 **Maloelap**, Marshall Islands ⩩
121 U 6 **Malone**, New York, U.S.A.
194 M 14 **Malonga**, Democratic Republic of Congo
85 A 16 **Måløy**, Norway
156 I 7 **Malozemel'skaya Tundra**, Russian Federation ◇
168 D 12 **Malpura**, India
91 I 25 **Malta**, Europe □
91 K 25 **Malta**, Malta ⩩
98 I 12 **Malta**, Latvia
118 E 7 **Malta**, Montana, U.S.A.
91 I 24 **Malta Channel**, Italy/Malta ≈
196 I 10 **Maltahöhe**, Namibia
175 R 13 **Maluku**, Indonesia ▣
85 F 19 **Malung**, Sweden
212 M 6 **Malu'u**, Solomon Islands
169 B 19 **Malvan**, India
101 O 3 **Malyn**, Ukraine
195 Q 7 **Mambasa**, Democratic Republic of Congo
194 H 5 **Mambéré-Kadéï**, Central African Republic ▣
175 N 4 **Mamburao**, Philippines
58 B 9 **Mamelles**, Seychelles ⩩
197 O 11 **Mamelodi**, Republic of South Africa
193 S 13 **Mamfé**, Cameroon
144 G 3 **Mamiña**, Chile
167 Q 1 **Mamlyutka**, Kazakhstan
159 W 10 **Mammadbajli**, Azerbaijan
117 N 24 **Mammoth**, Arizona, U.S.A.
99 A 16 **Mamonovo**, Russian Federation
141 K 17 **Mamoré**, Bolivia ∿
142 C 10 **Mamori**, Brazil
142 C 12 **Mamoriá**, Brazil
192 G 11 **Mamou**, Guinea
192 M 13 **Mampong**, Ghana
175 N 12 **Mamuju**, Indonesia
163 X 10 **Ma'mūl**, Oman
192 I 12 **Man**, Côte d'Ivoire
140 A 9 **Manabí**, Ecuador ▣
142 F 11 **Manacapuru**, Brazil
81 Y 8 **Manacor**, Spain
175 Q 10 **Manado**, Indonesia
126 F 11 **Managua**, Nicaragua ⌂
197 Y 9 **Manakara**, Madgascar
163 P 13 **Manākhah**, Yemen
212 C 3 **Manam**, Papua New Guinea ⩩
197 X 10 **Manambondro**, Madgascar
197 Z 6 **Mananara Avaratra**, Madgascar
197 Y 9 **Mananjary**, Madgascar
192 I 11 **Manankoro**, Mali
197 X 10 **Manantenina**, Madgascar
211 C 24 **Manapouri**, New Zealand
170 K 3 **Manas Hu**, China ◢
63 N 26 **Manati Bay**, St Helena ≈
142 F 10 **Manaus**, Brazil
158 F 13 **Manavgat**, Turkey
191 B 18 **Manawashei**, Sudan
210 L 13 **Manawatu-Wanganui**, New Zealand ▣
160 K 2 **Manbij**, Syria
77 J 18 **Manchester**, United Kingdom
120 L 14 **Manchester**, Kentucky, U.S.A.
121 W 7 **Manchester**, New Hampshire, U.S.A.
121 V 7 **Manchester**, Vermont, U.S.A.
122 M 2 **Manchester**, Tennessee, U.S.A.
158 M 10 **Mancilik**, Turkey
165 P 14 **Mand**, Pakistan
197 W 8 **Mandabe**, Madgascar
165 P 8 **Mandal**, Afghanistan
172 C 12 **Mandalay**, Myanmar ▣
172 D 11 **Mandalay**, Myanmar
171 Q 4 **Mandalgovi**, Mongolia
161 V 6 **Mandalī**, Iraq
118 H 8 **Mandan**, North Dakota, U.S.A.
175 P 5 **Mandaon**, Philippines
91 C 18 **Mandas**, Italy
195 Y 5 **Mandera**, Kenya
126 M 7 **Mandeville**, Jamaica
168 B 12 **Mandha**, India
191 L 20 **Mandheera**, Somalia
168 E 9 **Mandi**, India
197 Q 6 **Mandié**, Mozambique
197 S 5 **Mandimba**, Mozambique
194 E 9 **Mandji**, Gabon
169 G 15 **Mandla**, India
85 B 25 **Mandø**, Denmark ⩩
197 Z 6 **Mandritsara**, Madgascar
169 D 14 **Mandsaur**, India
208 G 11 **Mandurah**, Western Australia, Australia
91 O 17 **Manduria**, Italy
169 A 14 **Mandvi**, India
169 E 21 **Mandya**, India
190 E 10 **Manfalût**, Egypt
91 L 14 **Manfredonia**, Italy
212 H 3 **Manga**, Papua New Guinea
194 K 10 **Mangai**, Democratic Republic of Congo
212 G 3 **Mangai**, Papua New Guinea
215 P 11 **Mangaia**, Cook Islands ⩩
210 L 11 **Mangakino**, New Zealand
101 N 14 **Mangalia**, Romania
193 Y 10 **Mangalmé**, Chad
169 C 21 **Mangalore**, India
210 I 5 **Mangamuka**, New Zealand
215 Z 12 **Mangareva**, French Polynesia ⩩
197 N 12 **Mangaung**, Republic of South Africa
210 M 13 **Mangaweka**, New Zealand
210 K 7 **Mangawhai**, New Zealand
87 J 26 **Mangfallgebirge**, Germany ⛰
174 H 12 **Manggar**, Indonesia
212 M 8 **Manggautu**, Solomon Islands
166 J 10 **Mangistau**, Kazakhstan ▣
165 X 8 **Mangla Reservoir**, Pakistan ◢
170 L 7 **Mangnai**, China
193 N 11 **Mango**, Togo
197 R 5 **Mangochi**, Malawi
175 R 11 **Mangole**, Indonesia ⩩
210 I 5 **Mangonui**, New Zealand
126 M 3 **Mangrove Cay**, The Bahamas
80 J 6 **Mangualde**, Portugal
171 V 1 **Mangui**, China
166 G 8 **Mangyshlakskiy Zaliv**, Kazakhstan ≈
119 K 14 **Manhattan**, Kansas, U.S.A.
83 K 22 **Manhay**, Belgium
90 H 6 **Maniago**, Italy
197 Q 7 **Manica**, Mozambique ▣
197 P 7 **Manicaland**, Zimbabwe ▣
142 E 12 **Manicoré**, Brazil
115 T 10 **Manicouagan**, Québec, Canada
195 O 9 **Maniema**, Democratic Republic of Congo ▣
163 S 4 **Manīfah**, Saudi Arabia
114 J 10 **Manigotagan**, Manitoba, Canada
215 U 8 **Manihi**, French Polynesia ⩩
215 O 7 **Manihiki**, Cook Islands ⩩
61 Q 9 **Manihiki Plateau**, Pacific Ocean ◇
64 M 12 **Maniitsoq**, Greenland
175 O 4 **Manila**, Philippines ⌂
117 O 14 **Manila**, Utah, U.S.A.
175 V 11 **Manim**, Indonesia ⩩
209 N 1 **Maningrida**, Northern Territory, Australia
175 R 12 **Manipa**, Indonesia ⩩
168 N 13 **Manipur**, India ▣
169 N 14 **Manipur Hills**, India ⛰
158 B 10 **Manisa**, Turkey
143 H 14 **Manissauá-Miçu**, Brazil ∿
120 K 6 **Manistee**, Michigan, U.S.A. ∿
120 K 6 **Manistee**, Michigan, U.S.A.
120 K 5 **Manistique**, Michigan, U.S.A.
120 K 4 **Manistique Lake**, Michigan, U.S.A. ◢
114 I 7 **Manitoba**, Canada ▣
120 K 5 **Manitou Islands**, Michigan, U.S.A. ⩩
115 O 13 **Manitoulin Island**, Ontario, Canada ⩩
114 M 11 **Manitouwadge**, Ontario, Canada
115 Q 13 **Maniwaki**, Québec, Canada
175 W 12 **Maniwori**, Indonesia
138 H 6 **Manizales**, Colombia
197 W 9 **Manja**, Madgascar
164 H 5 **Manjil**, Iran
208 G 12 **Manjimup**, Western Australia, Australia
118 L 10 **Mankato**, Minnesota, U.S.A.
193 U 14 **Mankim**, Cameroon
192 J 12 **Mankono**, Côte d'Ivoire
169 G 24 **Mankulam**, Sri Lanka
169 C 16 **Manmad**, India
174 E 13 **Manna**, Indonesia
169 F 24 **Mannar**, Sri Lanka
169 F 24 **Mannar Island**, Sri Lanka ⩩
87 F 21 **Mannheim**, Germany
123 S 4 **Manning**, South Carolina, U.S.A.
192 G 12 **Mano**, Sierra Leone
192 G 12 **Mano River**, Liberia
175 V 11 **Manokwari**, Indonesia
100 L 7 **Manoleasa**, Romania
195 P 12 **Manono**, Democratic Republic of Congo
79 V 13 **Manosque**, France
171 X 5 **Manp'o**, North Korea
214 K 4 **Manra**, Kiribati ⩩
81 W 4 **Manresa**, Spain
197 O 3 **Mansa**, Zambia
192 E 9 **Mansa Konko**, Gambia
192 E 9 **Mansabá**, Guinea-Bissau
165 X 7 **Mansehra**, Pakistan
115 P 4 **Mansel Island**, Nunavut, Canada ⩩
77 K 18 **Mansfield**, United Kingdom
119 M 20 **Mansfield**, Louisiana, U.S.A.
121 N 10 **Mansfield**, Ohio, U.S.A.
121 S 9 **Mansfield**, Pennsylvania, U.S.A.
172 D 9 **Mansi**, Myanmar
192 E 10 **Mansôa**, Guinea-Bissau
158 K 12 **Mansurlu**, Turkey
140 A 9 **Manta**, Ecuador
117 E 18 **Manteca**, California, U.S.A.
138 M 5 **Mantecal**, Venezuela
123 X 1 **Manteo**, North Carolina, U.S.A.
79 P 4 **Mantes-la-Jolie**, France
117 M 16 **Manti**, Utah, U.S.A.
97 G 18 **Mantoudi**, Greece
90 E 7 **Mantova**, Italy
215 Y 15 **Manua Islands**, American Samoa ⩩
215 P 10 **Manuae**, Cook Islands ⩩
215 Q 9 **Manuae**, French Polynesia ⩩
142 H 12 **Manuelzinho**, Brazil
215 W 10 **Manuhangi**, French Polynesia ⩩
175 P 12 **Manui**, Indonesia ⩩
164 M 12 **Manūjān**, Iran
210 K 8 **Manukau**, New Zealand
210 J 9 **Manukau Harbour**, New Zealand ≈
212 D 2 **Manus**, Papua New Guinea ▣
212 D 2 **Manus Island**, Papua New Guinea ⩩
195 T 11 **Manyoni**, Tanzania
81 P 9 **Manzanares**, Spain
125 N 12 **Manzanillo**, Mexico
164 I 6 **Manzariyeh**, Iran
171 U 2 **Manzhouli**, China
90 G 13 **Manziana**, Italy
197 P 11 **Manzini**, Swaziland
193 V 9 **Mao**, Chad
171 T 14 **Maoming**, China
197 Q 9 **Mapai**, Mozambique
125 W 15 **Mapastepec**, Mexico
175 Y 14 **Mapi**, Indonesia ∿
175 Y 14 **Mapi**, Indonesia
175 N 7 **Mapin**, Philippines ⩩
197 R 9 **Mapinhane**, Mozambique
113 X 13 **Maple Creek**, Saskatchewan, Canada
122 L 5 **Maplesville**, Alabama, U.S.A.
212 B 3 **Maprik**, Papua New Guinea
211 H 16 **Mapua**, New Zealand
142 G 9 **Mapuera**, Brazil ∿
197 Q 11 **Maputo**, Mozambique ⌂
197 Q 10 **Maputo**, Mozambique ▣
81 N 7 **Maqueda**, Spain
196 G 1 **Maquela do Zombo**, Angola
145 H 17 **Maquinchao**, Argentina
145 M 15 **Mar del Plata**, Argentina
195 T 9 **Mara**, Tanzania ▣
142 D 10 **Maraã**, Brazil
142 J 11 **Marabá**, Brazil
138 J 2 **Maracaibo**, Venezuela
143 H 18 **Maracaju**, Brazil
139 N 3 **Maracay**, Venezuela
189 W 9 **Marādah**, Libya
193 R 9 **Maradi**, Niger ▣
193 R 9 **Maradi**, Niger
164 F 4 **Marāgheh**, Iran
214 D 2 **Marakei**, Kiribati ⩩
195 V 7 **Maralal**, Kenya
194 J 4 **Marali**, Central African Republic
218 H 3 **Marambio**, Antarctica ⌗
117 N 24 **Marana**, Arizona, U.S.A.
81 Q 5 **Maranchón**, Spain
164 F 3 **Marand**, Iran
142 K 12 **Maranhão**, Brazil ▣
140 C 11 **Marañon**, Peru ∿
100 L 10 **Mărășești**, Romania
91 L 17 **Maratea**, Italy
114 M 12 **Marathon**, Ontario, Canada
119 G 21 **Marathon**, Texas, U.S.A.
123 S 15 **Marathon**, Florida, U.S.A.
210 O 11 **Marau Point**, New Zealand ▶
163 U 12 **Mar'ayt**, Yemen
159 Y 8 **Mărază**, Azerbaijan
80 M 14 **Marbella**, Spain
208 H 6 **Marble Bar**, Western Australia, Australia
117 M 20 **Marble Canyon**, Arizona, U.S.A. ◇
197 O 10 **Marble Hall**, Republic of South Africa
87 F 17 **Marburg**, Germany
143 H 14 **Marcelândia**, Brazil
89 Z 3 **March**, Austria ∿
90 I 11 **Marche**, Italy ▣
83 J 22 **Marche-en-Famenne**, Belgium
89 Z 3 **Marchegg**, Austria
80 L 12 **Marchena**, Spain
141 E 18 **Marcona**, Peru
144 K 11 **Marcos Juárez**, Argentina
165 W 7 **Mardan**, Pakistan
159 P 12 **Mardin**, Turkey
159 P 12 **Mardin Dağlari**, Turkey ⛰
213 R 14 **Maré**, New Caledonia ⩩
125 V 14 **Mare Muerto**, Mexico ◢
209 T 3 **Mareeba**, Queensland, Australia
144 H 10 **Mareyes**, Argentina
119 F 21 **Marfa**, Texas, U.S.A.
208 F 12 **Margaret River**, Western Australia, Australia
77 N 21 **Margate**, United Kingdom
123 S 13 **Margate**, Florida, U.S.A.
197 P 13 **Margate**, Republic of South Africa
168 O 12 **Margherita**, India
195 R 7 **Margherita Peak**, Uganda ▲
100 G 8 **Marghita**, Romania
218 I 5 **Marguerite Bay**, Antarctica ≈
161 X 9 **Marhaj Kahlīl**, Iraq
101 U 8 **Marhanets'**, Ukraine
188 L 6 **Marhoum**, Algeria
212 A 6 **Mari**, Papua New Guinea
215 Y 11 **Maria**, French Polynesia ⩩
144 G 5 **Maria Elena**, Chile
209 T 15 **Maria Island**, Tasmania, Australia ⩩
89 P 8 **Maria Luggau**, Austria
214 A 8 **Mariana Islands**, Northern Mariana Islands ⩩
60 L 6 **Mariana Trench**, Pacific Ocean ◇
126 I 4 **Marianao**, Cuba
123 N 8 **Marianna**, Florida, U.S.A.
58 C 8 **Marianne**, Seychelles ⩩
85 G 23 **Mariannelund**, Sweden
144 M 9 **Mariano Loza**, Argentina
93 A 17 **Marianské Lázně**, Czech Republic
89 V 5 **Mariazell**, Austria
163 Q 12 **Ma'rib**, Yemen
94 D 6 **Maribor**, Slovenia
117 F 21 **Maricopa**, California, U.S.A.
191 D 22 **Maridi**, Sudan
218 L 9 **Marie Byrd Land**, Antarctica ◇
61 T 15 **Marie Byrd Seamount**, Pacific Ocean ▲
127 X 8 **Marie-Galante**, Guadeloupe ⩩
126 I 4 **Mariel**, Cuba
83 G 23 **Mariembourg**, Belgium
87 M 18 **Marienberg**, Germany
196 J 10 **Mariental**, Namibia
85 F 21 **Mariestad**, Sweden
121 O 12 **Marietta**, Ohio, U.S.A.
123 O 4 **Marietta**, Georgia, U.S.A.
99 E 16 **Marijampolė**, Lithuania
143 J 18 **Marília**, Brazil
196 H 2 **Marimba**, Angola
117 D 19 **Marina**, California, U.S.A.
90 D 10 **Marina di Carrara**, Italy
99 J 18 **Mar''ina Horka**, Belarus
175 O 4 **Marinduque**, Philippines ⩩
120 J 5 **Marinette**, Wisconsin, U.S.A.
143 I 19 **Maringá**, Brazil
80 G 7 **Marinha Grande**, Portugal
120 K 10 **Marion**, Indiana, U.S.A.
120 M 11 **Marion**, Ohio, U.S.A.
121 O 15 **Marion**, Virginia, U.S.A.
123 T 4 **Marion**, South Carolina, U.S.A.
139 X 7 **Maripasoula**, French Guiana
117 F 18 **Mariposa**, California, U.S.A.
175 P 10 **Marisa**, Indonesia
80 K 12 **Marismas del Guadalquivir**, Spain ◇
96 K 11 **Maritsa**, Bulgaria ∿
101 X 8 **Mariupol'**, Ukraine
98 F 7 **Märjamaa**, Estonia
160 G 7 **Marjayoun**, Lebanon
191 L 24 **Marka**, Somalia
192 J 9 **Markala**, Mali
171 O 11 **Markam**, China
169 F 19 **Markapur**, India
164 H 7 **Markazī**, Iran ▣
82 M 12 **Markelo**, Netherlands
82 I 10 **Markermeer**, Netherlands ≈
170 H 6 **Markit**, China
101 Z 4 **Markivka**, Ukraine
82 K 9 **Marknesse**, Netherlands
194 I 3 **Markounda**, Central African Republic
157 Y 7 **Markovo**, Russian Federation
193 N 9 **Markoye**, Burkina Faso
87 K 19 **Marktredwitz**, Germany
209 N 8 **Marla**, South Australia, Australia
211 I 17 **Marlborough**, New Zealand ▣
209 V 6 **Marlborough**, Queensland, Australia
169 C 19 **Marmagao**, India
79 N 12 **Marmande**, France
158 C 8 **Marmara**, Turkey ⩩
158 C 8 **Marmara**, Turkey
96 N 13 **Marmaraereğlisi**, Turkey
158 C 13 **Marmaris**, Turkey
90 G 5 **Marmolada**, Italy ▲
86 F 9 **Marne**, Germany
159 U 7 **Marneuli**, Georgia
193 X 12 **Maro**, Chad
139 N 8 **Maroa**, Venezuela
197 Z 6 **Maroantsetra**, Madgascar
215 W 10 **Marokau**, French Polynesia ⩩
197 Z 5 **Maromokotro**, Madgascar ▲
197 P 7 **Marondera**, Zimbabwe
139 X 8 **Maroni**, French Guiana ∿
209 W 8 **Maroochydore**, Queensland, Australia
210 I 6 **Maropiu**, New Zealand
175 N 13 **Maros**, Indonesia
215 V 14 **Marotiri**, French Polynesia ⩩
193 V 11 **Maroua**, Cameroon
197 X 6 **Marovoay**, Madgascar
61 S 9 **Marquesas Fracture Zone**, Pacific Ocean ◇
61 T 8 **Marquesas Islands**, Pacific Ocean ⩩

□ Country ▣ Internal administrative region: State/Province/Territory/Dependent territory ⌂ Capital city ⛰ Mountain range/Undersea ridge ▲ Mountain peak/Volcano/Seamount ◇ Geographic feature ▶ Headland/Point/Cape/Peninsula ◠ Desert ⩩ Island/Island group ⌗ Antarctic base ◎ Ocean ◣ Sea ≈ Bay/Gulf/Channel/Strait ◢ Lake ◤ Salt pan/Dry/Intermittent lake ∿ River

215 V 5 **Marquesas Islands**, French Polynesia ✱
123 Q 15 **Marquesas Keys**, Florida, U.S.A. ✱
120 J 4 **Marquette**, Michigan, U.S.A.
191 A 17 **Marra Plateau**, Sudan ◇
90 G 10 **Marradi**, Italy
188 G 8 **Marrakech**, Morocco
209 S 15 **Marrawah**, Tasmania, Australia
209 P 9 **Marree**, South Australia, Australia
197 S 7 **Marromeu**, Mozambique
197 S 4 **Marrupa**, Mozambique
189 W 8 **Marsa al Burayqah**, Libya
190 G 11 **Marsa Alam**, Egypt
190 C 7 **Marsa Matrûh**, Egypt
195 V 6 **Marsabit**, Kenya
91 G 22 **Marsala**, Italy
82 H 8 **Marsdiep**, Netherlands ≈
79 U 14 **Marseille**, France
126 M 1 **Marsh Harbour**, The Bahamas
119 N 21 **Marsh Island**, Louisiana, U.S.A. ✱
118 K 10 **Marshall**, Minnesota, U.S.A.
119 L 19 **Marshall**, Texas, U.S.A.
215 W 4 **Marshall Islands**, Oceania ◘
118 L 12 **Marshalltown**, Iowa, U.S.A.
120 H 6 **Marshfield**, Wisconsin, U.S.A.
174 L 12 **Martapura**, Indonesia
174 F 13 **Martapura**, Indonesia
83 K 24 **Martelange**, Belgium
115 O 13 **Marten River**, Ontario, Canada
121 X 9 **Martha's Vineyard**, Massachusetts, U.S.A. ✱
88 C 10 **Martigny**, Switzerland
93 I 19 **Martin**, Slovakia
118 H 11 **Martin**, South Dakota, U.S.A.
122 J 1 **Martin**, Tennessee, U.S.A.
218 K 10 **Martin Peninsula**, Antarctica ▶
91 N 16 **Martina Franca**, Italy
211 L 16 **Martinborough**, New Zealand
125 S 11 **Martínez**, Mexico
127 X 9 **Martinique**, France ▣
127 X 9 **Martinique Passage**, Dominica ≈
97 F 19 **Martino**, Greece
121 R 12 **Martinsburg**, West Virginia, U.S.A.
120 J 12 **Martinsville**, Indiana, U.S.A.
121 P 15 **Martinsville**, Virginia, U.S.A.
211 L 14 **Marton**, New Zealand
166 K 4 **Martuk**, Kazakhstan
159 U 9 **Martuni**, Armenia
177 E 19 **Marugame**, Japan
143 O 14 **Maruim**, Brazil
215 V 9 **Marutea**, French Polynesia ✱
215 Y 11 **Marutea**, French Polynesia ✱
167 N 14 **Mary**, Turkmenistan
209 W 8 **Maryborough**, Queensland, Australia
121 S 12 **Maryland**, U.S.A. ▣
117 M 17 **Marysvale**, Utah, U.S.A.
116 E 6 **Marysville**, Washington, U.S.A.
117 E 17 **Marysville**, California, U.S.A.
119 K 14 **Marysville**, Kansas, U.S.A.
120 M 11 **Marysville**, Ohio, U.S.A.
118 L 13 **Maryville**, Missouri, U.S.A.
123 O 2 **Maryville**, Tennessee, U.S.A.
167 N 15 **Maryyskiy Velayat**, Turkmenistan ▣
195 R 8 **Masaka**, Uganda
174 L 13 **Masalembu Besar**, Indonesia ✱
174 L 13 **Masalembu Kecil**, Indonesia ✱
159 Y 10 **Masalli**, Azerbaijan
175 O 12 **Masamba**, Indonesia
171 Y 7 **Masan**, South Korea
195 W 14 **Masasi**, Tanzania
141 L 21 **Masavi**, Bolivia
175 P 5 **Masbate**, Philippines ✱
175 P 5 **Masbate**, Philippines
58 L 6 **Mascarene Basin**, Indian Ocean ◇
58 K 7 **Mascarene Plain**, Indian Ocean ◇
58 L 5 **Mascarene Ridge**, Indian Ocean ⛰
197 N 12 **Maseru**, Lesotho ♜
165 O 6 **Mashhad**, Iran
164 L 10 **Mashīz**, Iran
197 P 6 **Mashonaland Central**, Zimbabwe ▣
197 Q 6 **Mashonaland East**, Zimbabwe ▣
197 O 6 **Mashonaland West**, Zimbabwe ▣
84 K 7 **Masi**, Norway
194 J 10 **Masi-Manimba**, Democratic Republic of Congo
124 J 6 **Masiáca**, Mexico
195 R 7 **Masindi**, Uganda
159 T 9 **Masis**, Armenia
141 E 14 **Masisea**, Peru
164 G 8 **Masjed Soleymān**, Iran
94 D 11 **Maslenica**, Croatia
163 S 13 **Masna'ah**, Yemen
197 W 7 **Masoarivo**, Madgascar
119 I 21 **Mason**, Texas, U.S.A.
211 B 26 **Mason Bay**, New Zealand ≈
118 L 11 **Mason City**, Iowa, U.S.A.
62 N 12 **Maspalomas**, Canary Islands
90 E 10 **Massa**, Italy
90 F 12 **Massa Marittimo**, Italy
121 V 8 **Massachusetts**, U.S.A. ▣
121 X 8 **Massachusetts Bay**, Massachusetts, U.S.A. ≈
193 V 10 **Massaguet**, Chad
193 W 9 **Massakory**, Chad
197 Q 9 **Massangena**, Mozambique
197 R 4 **Massangulo**, Mozambique
191 I 16 **Massawa**, Eritrea
191 I 16 **Massawa Channel**, Eritrea ≈
121 T 6 **Massena**, New York, U.S.A.
193 W 10 **Massenya**, Chad
113 O 12 **Masset**, British Columbia, Canada
79 R 11 **Massif Central**, France ⛰
127 O 7 **Massif de la Hotte**, Haiti ⛰
193 S 6 **Massif de L'aïr**, Niger ⛰
194 L 3 **Massif des Bongo**, Central African Republic ⛰
193 Z 8 **Massif du Kapka**, Chad ⛰
192 G 10 **Massif du Tamgué**, Guinea ▲
194 H 4 **Massif du Yadé**, Central African Republic ⛰
193 Z 7 **Massif Ennedi**, Chad ⛰
192 J 10 **Massigui**, Mali
197 R 9 **Massinga**, Mozambique
197 Q 10 **Massingir**, Mozambique
219 Y 9 **Masson Island**, Antarctica ✱
162 L 8 **Mastābah**, Saudi Arabia
159 Z 8 **Mastağa**, Azerbaijan
211 L 15 **Masterton**, New Zealand
126 L 2 **Mastic Point**, The Bahamas
165 W 5 **Mastuj**, Pakistan
165 T 11 **Mastung**, Pakistan
162 L 7 **Mastūrah**, Saudi Arabia
177 C 19 **Masuda**, Japan
197 P 8 **Masvingo**, Zimbabwe ▣
197 P 8 **Masvingo**, Zimbabwe
160 H 4 **Maşyāf**, Syria
99 E 21 **Masyevichy**, Belarus
214 H 8 **Matā 'Utu**, Wallis and Futuna Islands ♜
197 N 7 **Matabeleland North**, Zimbabwe ▣
197 O 8 **Matabeleland South**, Zimbabwe ▣
194 G 11 **Matadi**, Democratic Republic of Congo
126 G 11 **Matagalpa**, Nicaragua
115 P 11 **Matagami**, Québec, Canada
119 L 22 **Matagorda**, Texas, U.S.A.
119 K 23 **Matagorda Island**, Texas, U.S.A. ✱
215 T 8 **Mataiva**, French Polynesia ✱
174 G 9 **Matak**, Indonesia ✱
167 U 5 **Matak**, Kazakhstan
210 M 9 **Matakana Island**, New Zealand ✱
210 O 10 **Matakaoa Point**, New Zealand ▶
196 H 5 **Matala**, Angola
192 F 8 **Matam**, Senegal
210 L 10 **Matamata**, New Zealand
193 R 9 **Matamey**, Niger
125 S 7 **Matamoros**, Mexico
115 T 11 **Matane**, Québec, Canada
126 J 4 **Matanzas**, Cuba
169 G 25 **Matara**, Sri Lanka
97 C 19 **Mataragka**, Greece
174 L 15 **Mataram**, Indonesia
209 N 2 **Mataranka**, Northern Territory, Australia
81 X 4 **Mataró**, Spain
210 M 10 **Matata**, New Zealand
211 C 24 **Mataura**, New Zealand ∿
211 D 25 **Mataura**, New Zealand
215 V 15 **Matautu**, Samoa
61 Y 5 **Mataveri**, Easter Island
210 N 11 **Matawai**, New Zealand
167 W 8 **Matay**, Kazakhstan
141 L 17 **Mategua**, Bolivia
125 Q 9 **Matehuala**, Mexico
195 V 14 **Matemanga**, Tanzania
91 M 16 **Matera**, Italy
93 N 21 **Mátészalka**, Hungary
189 Q 5 **Mateur**, Tunisia
115 O 12 **Matheson**, Ontario, Canada
121 T 14 **Mathews**, Virginia, U.S.A.
119 J 23 **Mathis**, Texas, U.S.A.
168 E 12 **Mathura**, India
175 R 7 **Mati**, Philippines
143 L 15 **Matias Cardoso**, Brazil
115 T 8 **Matimekosh**, Québec, Canada
98 G 9 **Matīši**, Latvia
165 U 14 **Matli**, Pakistan
143 H 14 **Mato Grosso**, Brazil ▣
143 H 17 **Mato Grosso do Sul**, Brazil ▣
80 H 5 **Matosinhos**, Portugal
89 P 8 **Matrei in Osttirol**, Austria
196 J 15 **Matroosberg**, Republic of South Africa ▲
171 W 12 **Matsu Tao**, Taiwan ✱
177 D 18 **Matsue**, Japan
176 I 8 **Matsumae**, Japan
177 I 16 **Matsumoto**, Japan
177 H 18 **Matsusaka**, Japan
177 D 20 **Matsuyama**, Japan
88 D 11 **Matterhorn**, Switzerland/Italy ▲
117 J 14 **Matterhorn**, Nevada, U.S.A. ▲
89 Y 5 **Mattersburg**, Austria
213 S 14 **Matthew Island**, Vanuatu ✱
127 O 5 **Matthew Town**, The Bahamas
89 Q 4 **Mattighofen**, Austria
120 I 11 **Mattoon**, Illinois, U.S.A.
141 D 16 **Matucana**, Peru
213 Y 12 **Matuku**, Fiji ✱
196 I 4 **Matumbo**, Angola
139 R 3 **Maturín**, Venezuela
175 Q 8 **Matutuang**, Indonesia ✱
168 I 13 **Mau**, India
168 F 13 **Mau Rampur**, India
197 S 5 **Maúa**, Mozambique
79 S 2 **Maubeuge**, France
173 D 16 **Maubin**, Myanmar
63 L 23 **Maud Rise**, Atlantic Ocean ⛰
142 G 11 **Maués**, Brazil
214 A 5 **Maug Islands**, Northern Mariana Islands ✱
117 D 24 **Maui**, Hawaii, U.S.A. ✱
215 P 10 **Mauke**, Cook Islands ✱
144 F 13 **Maule**, Chile ▣
145 F 17 **Maullín**, Chile
120 M 9 **Maumee**, Ohio, U.S.A.
196 L 8 **Maun**, Botswana
117 E 25 **Mauna Kea**, Hawaii, U.S.A. ▲
117 E 26 **Mauna Loa**, Hawaii, U.S.A. ▲
210 J 6 **Maungatapere**, New Zealand
173 F 19 **Maungmagan Islands**, Myanmar ✱
215 R 9 **Maupihaa**, French Polynesia ✱
215 R 9 **Maupiti**, French Polynesia ✱
79 Q 11 **Mauriac**, France
192 F 6 **Mauritania**, Africa ◘
58 A 11 **Mauritius**, Indian Ocean ◘
58 K 8 **Mauritius Trench**, Indian Ocean ◇
62 I 6 **Maury Seachannel**, Atlantic Ocean ≈
120 H 7 **Mauston**, Wisconsin, U.S.A.
89 R 7 **Mauterndorf**, Austria
195 O 6 **Mava**, Democratic Republic of Congo
197 S 4 **Mavago**, Mozambique
196 J 6 **Mavengue**, Angola
196 K 6 **Mavinga**, Angola
194 I 11 **Mawanga**, Democratic Republic of Congo
219 X 4 **Mawson**, Antarctica ⁙
219 W 4 **Mawson Coast**, Antarctica ◇
219 T 15 **Mawson Peninsula**, Antarctica ▶
144 I 8 **Maxán**, Argentina
125 Y 10 **Maxcanú**, Mexico
85 K 15 **Maxmo**, Finland
174 I 11 **Maya**, Indonesia ✱
157 U 11 **Maya**, Russian Federation ∿
126 D 8 **Maya Mountains**, Belize/Guatemala ⛰
127 P 4 **Mayaguana Island**, The Bahamas ✱
127 T 7 **Mayagüez**, Puerto Rico
193 R 9 **Mayahi**, Niger
167 T 14 **Mayakovskogo**, Tajikistan ▲
194 H 10 **Mayama**, Congo
164 L 5 **Mayamey**, Iran
191 I 18 **Maych'ew**, Ethiopia
191 M 19 **Maydh**, Somalia
78 M 5 **Mayenne**, France
120 H 14 **Mayfield**, Kentucky, U.S.A.
211 F 21 **Mayfield**, New Zealand
96 M 11 **Mayha Dağl**, Turkey ▲
167 U 4 **Maykain**, Kazakhstan
156 D 10 **Maykop**, Russian Federation
167 T 11 **Mayluu-Suu**, Kyrgyzstan
167 N 8 **Maylybas**, Kazakhstan
172 E 11 **Maymyo**, Myanmar
113 O 7 **Mayo**, Yukon Territory, Canada
123 P 9 **Mayo**, Florida, U.S.A.
193 T 12 **Mayo-Belwa**, Nigeria
193 V 11 **Mayo-Kébbi**, Chad ▣
194 F 9 **Mayoko**, Congo
145 K 15 **Mayor Buratovich**, Argentina
210 M 9 **Mayor Island**, New Zealand ✱
143 F 17 **Mayor Pablo Lagerenza**, Paraguay
197 X 4 **Mayotte**, France ▣
89 N 7 **Mayrhofen**, Austria
157 U 13 **Mayskiy**, Russian Federation
167 V 4 **Mayskoye**, Kazakhstan
120 M 13 **Maysville**, Kentucky, U.S.A.
175 R 10 **Mayu**, Indonesia ✱
194 E 10 **Mayumba**, Gabon
118 J 8 **Mayville**, North Dakota, U.S.A.
197 N 5 **Mazabuka**, Zambia
116 F 5 **Mazama**, Washington, U.S.A.
79 Q 14 **Mazamet**, France
140 F 10 **Mazán**, Peru
164 J 5 **Māzandarān**, Iran ▣
170 G 7 **Mazar**, China
165 T 5 **Mazār-e Sharīf**, Afghanistan
91 G 22 **Mazara del Vallo**, Italy
81 R 12 **Mazarrón**, Spain
124 J 4 **Mazatán**, Mexico
124 L 9 **Mazatlán**, Mexico
117 M 22 **Mazatzal Peak**, Arizona, U.S.A. ▲
98 D 12 **Mažeikiai**, Lithuania
98 D 9 **Mazirbe**, Latvia
124 J 4 **Mazocahui**, Mexico
195 W 12 **Mazomora**, Tanzania
197 P 9 **Mazunga**, Zimbabwe
99 L 21 **Mazyr**, Belarus
197 P 11 **Mbabane**, Swaziland ♜
192 K 12 **Mbahiakro**, Côte d'Ivoire
194 J 5 **Mbaïki**, Central African Republic
193 V 15 **Mbalam**, Cameroon
195 T 7 **Mbale**, Uganda
193 T 15 **Mbalmayo**, Cameroon
212 M 7 **Mbalo**, Solomon Islands
195 T 14 **Mbamba Bay**, Tanzania
194 J 8 **Mbandaka**, Democratic Republic of Congo
193 S 14 **Mbanga**, Cameroon
196 G 1 **M'banza Congo**, Angola
194 H 11 **Mbanza-Ngungu**, Democratic Republic of Congo
195 R 8 **Mbarara**, Uganda
194 J 5 **Mbata**, Central African Republic
195 S 12 **Mbeya**, Tanzania ▣
195 T 13 **Mbeya**, Tanzania
194 F 9 **Mbigou**, Gabon
195 U 14 **Mbinga**, Tanzania
197 P 8 **Mbizi**, Zimbabwe
195 O 4 **Mboki**, Central African Republic
194 G 7 **Mbomo**, Congo
194 M 4 **Mbomou**, Central African Republic ▣
192 D 8 **Mbour**, Senegal
192 G 8 **Mbout**, Mauritania
195 S 13 **Mbozi**, Tanzania
194 M 11 **Mbuji-Mayi**, Democratic Republic of Congo
195 U 10 **Mbulu**, Tanzania
195 U 12 **Mbuyuni**, Tanzania
119 K 17 **McAlester**, Oklahoma, U.S.A.
119 J 24 **McAllen**, Texas, U.S.A.
123 S 3 **McBee**, South Carolina, U.S.A.
113 T 12 **McBride**, British Columbia, Canada
116 I 10 **McCall**, Idaho, U.S.A.
119 G 21 **McCamey**, Texas, U.S.A.
116 L 13 **McCammon**, Idaho, U.S.A.
65 N 7 **McClintock Channel**, Nunavut, Canada ≈
65 O 6 **McClure Strait Gulf**, Arctic Ocean ≈
122 H 7 **McComb**, Mississippi, U.S.A.
118 H 13 **McCook**, Nebraska, U.S.A.
116 H 13 **McDermitt**, Nevada, U.S.A.
117 J 16 **McGill**, Nevada, U.S.A.
112 I 6 **McGrath**, Alaska, U.S.A.
195 X 13 **Mchinga**, Tanzania
197 Q 4 **Mchinji**, Malawi
118 H 9 **McIntosh**, South Dakota, U.S.A.
214 I 4 **McKean**, Kiribati ✱
214 I 4 **McKean**, Kiribati ✱
122 J 1 **McKenzie**, Tennessee, U.S.A.
112 K 6 **McKinley Park**, Alaska, U.S.A.
119 K 19 **McKinney**, Texas, U.S.A.
113 R 11 **McLeod Lake**, British Columbia, Canada
173 F 21 **McLeods Island**, Myanmar ✱
120 K 4 **McMillan**, Michigan, U.S.A.
122 M 2 **McMinnville**, Tennessee, U.S.A.
219 R 12 **McMurdo**, Antarctica ⁙
119 J 15 **Mcpherson**, Kansas, U.S.A.
123 P 6 **McRae**, Georgia, U.S.A.
197 O 14 **Mdantsane**, Republic of South Africa
113 X 11 **Meadow Lake**, Saskatchewan, Canada
121 P 9 **Meadville**, Pennsylvania, U.S.A.
80 H 6 **Mealhada**, Portugal
115 V 8 **Mealy Mountains**, Newfoundland and Labrador, Canada ⛰
79 Q 4 **Meaux**, France
162 M 8 **Mecca**, Saudi Arabia
83 G 18 **Mechelen**, Belgium
188 L 7 **Mecheria**, Algeria
158 K 8 **Mecitözü**, Turkey
86 K 10 **Mecklenburg-Vorpommern**, Germany ▣
86 J 8 **Mecklenburger Bucht**, Germany ≈
197 T 4 **Mecula**, Mozambique
174 C 9 **Medan**, Indonesia
145 K 15 **Médanos**, Argentina
188 M 5 **Médéa**, Algeria
138 G 5 **Medellín**, Colombia
82 I 9 **Medemblik**, Netherlands
189 R 7 **Medenine**, Tunisia
192 E 7 **Mederdra**, Mauritania
120 G 5 **Medford**, Wisconsin, U.S.A.
144 I 12 **Media Luna**, Argentina
100 I 10 **Mediaş**, Romania
90 G 9 **Medicina**, Italy
118 E 12 **Medicine Bow**, Wyoming, U.S.A.
113 W 13 **Medicine Hat**, Alberta, Canada
119 J 16 **Medicine Lodge**, Kansas, U.S.A.
118 I 8 **Medina**, North Dakota, U.S.A.
121 Q 8 **Medina**, New York, U.S.A.
162 M 6 **Medina**, Saudi Arabia
80 M 4 **Medina de Rioseco**, Spain
80 M 5 **Medina del Campo**, Spain
192 F 9 **Medina Gounas**, Senegal
81 Q 5 **Medinaceli**, Spain
62 L 9 **Mediterranean Sea**, Africa/Asia/Europe ◒
99 G 16 **Medninkai**, Lithuania
194 E 7 **Médouneu**, Gabon
95 M 15 **Medveda**, Serbia and Montenegro
156 H 6 **Medvezh'yegorsk**, Russian Federation
208 G 8 **Meekatharra**, Western Australia, Australia
83 H 16 **Meer**, Belgium
82 I 13 **Meerkerk**, Netherlands
83 J 19 **Meerssen**, Belgium
168 E 11 **Meerut**, India
191 I 23 **Mēga**, Ethiopia
191 H 23 **Mega Escarpment**, Ethiopia ⛰
191 J 21 **Megalo**, Ethiopia
97 D 21 **Megalopoli**, Greece
97 B 18 **Meganisi**, Greece ✱
97 G 20 **Megara**, Greece
168 M 13 **Meghalaya**, India ▣
159 V 10 **Meghri**, Azerbaijan
158 D 14 **Megisti**, Greece ✱
100 G 12 **Mehadica**, Romania
84 L 5 **Mehamn**, Norway
165 U 13 **Mehar**, Pakistan
215 T 9 **Mehetia**, French Polynesia ✱
164 L 8 **Mehr Jān**, Iran
164 F 7 **Mehrān**, Iran
193 U 13 **Meiganga**, Cameroon
171 X 5 **Meihekou**, China
172 D 12 **Meiktila**, Myanmar
87 H 18 **Meiningen**, Germany
87 M 16 **Meissen**, Germany
171 V 13 **Meizhou**, China
144 H 9 **Mejicana**, Argentina ▲
144 F 5 **Mejillones**, Chile
215 Z 2 **Mejit Island**, Marshall Islands ✱
194 G 7 **Mékambo**, Gabon
191 I 18 **Mek'elē**, Ethiopia
192 D 8 **Mékhé**, Senegal
165 U 10 **Mekhtar**, Pakistan
188 I 7 **Meknès**, Morocco
173 L 20 **Mekong**, Asia ∿
174 E 9 **Melaka**, Malaysia ▣
174 E 9 **Melaka**, Malaysia
212 H 2 **Melanesia**, Oceania ◇
60 M 7 **Melanesian Basin**, Pacific Ocean ◇
123 S 11 **Melbourne**, Florida, U.S.A.
209 S 13 **Melbourne**, Victoria, Australia
193 X 10 **Mélfi**, Chad
113 Y 11 **Melfort**, Saskatchewan, Canada
80 I 2 **Melide**, Spain
97 D 22 **Meligalas**, Greece
81 P 15 **Melilla**, Spain
144 F 12 **Melipilla**, Chile
114 H 10 **Melita**, Manitoba, Canada
91 L 22 **Melito di Porto Salvo**, Italy
101 V 9 **Melitopol'**, Ukraine
96 I 12 **Melivoia**, Greece
89 V 4 **Melk**, Austria
191 I 23 **Melka Guba**, Ethiopia
88 J 7 **Mellau**, Austria
83 E 18 **Melle**, Belgium
85 E 21 **Mellerud**, Sweden
86 E 10 **Mellum**, Germany ✱
93 D 17 **Mělník**, Czech Republic
144 O 11 **Melo**, Uruguay
84 L 10 **Meltaus**, Finland
209 S 13 **Melton**, Victoria, Australia
79 Q 5 **Melun**, France
191 E 19 **Melut**, Sudan
113 Z 12 **Melville**, Saskatchewan, Canada
208 M 1 **Melville Island**, Northern Territory, Australia ✱
65 O 6 **Melville Island**, Arctic Ocean ✱
115 O 1 **Melville Peninsula**, Nunavut, Canada ▶
174 J 11 **Memala**, Indonesia
197 U 5 **Memba**, Mozambique
175 X 11 **Memberamo**, Indonesia ∿
87 H 25 **Memmingen**, Germany
174 I 10 **Mempawah**, Indonesia
119 I 18 **Memphis**, Texas, U.S.A.
122 I 2 **Memphis**, Tennessee, U.S.A.
101 R 2 **Mena**, Ukraine
119 L 18 **Mena**, Arkansas, U.S.A.
193 O 8 **Ménaka**, Mali
175 Q 11 **Menanga**, Indonesia
61 T 12 **Menard Fracture Zone**, Pacific Ocean ◇
79 R 12 **Mende**, France
191 I 22 **Mendebo Mountains**, Ethiopia ⛰
191 I 17 **Mendefera**, Eritrea

◘ Country ▣ Internal administrative region: State/Province/Territory/Dependent territory ♜ Capital city ⛰ Mountain range/Undersea ridge ▲ Mountain peak/Volcano/Seamount ◇ Geographic feature ▶ Headland/Point/Cape/Peninsula ◭ Desert ✱ Island/Island group ⁙ Antarctic base ◎ Ocean ◒ Sea ≈ Bay/Gulf/Channel/Strait ⌒ Lake ◩ Salt pan/Dry/Intermittent lake ∿ River

65 S 6 Mendeleyev Ridge, Arctic Ocean
122 I 6 Mendenhall, Mississippi, U.S.A.
125 R 7 Méndez, Mexico
191 G 20 Mendī, Ethiopia
212 B 5 Mendi, Papua New Guinea
117 C 16 Mendocino, California, U.S.A.
61 Q 4 Mendocino Fracture Zone, Pacific Ocean
120 H 9 Mendota, Illinois, U.S.A.
144 H 12 Mendoza, Argentina
144 H 11 Mendoza, Argentina
83 B 19 Menen, Belgium
215 U 1 Meneng Point, Nauru
91 H 22 Menfi, Italy
174 G 13 Menggala, Indonesia
171 O 14 Menghai, China
209 R 10 Menindee, New South Wales, Australia
209 R 10 Menindee Lake, New South Wales, Australia
157 S 9 Menkere, Russian Federation
120 I 8 Menomonee Falls, Wisconsin, U.S.A.
196 I 5 Menongue, Angola
174 G 12 Mentok, Indonesia
121 O 9 Mentor, Ohio, U.S.A.
171 P 7 Menyuan, China
208 I 10 Menzies, Western Australia, Australia
82 L 9 Meppel, Netherlands
86 D 12 Meppen, Germany
78 G 5 Mer d'Iroise, France
174 G 13 Merak, Indonesia
90 F 5 Merano, Italy
175 Y 15 Merauke, Indonesia
138 F 8 Mercaderes, Colombia
117 E 19 Merced, California, U.S.A.
144 I 12 Mercedes, Argentina
144 M 9 Mercedes, Argentina
144 M 12 Mercedes, Uruguay
121 P 10 Mercer, Pennsylvania, U.S.A.
210 L 8 Mercury Bay, New Zealand
210 L 8 Mercury Islands, New Zealand
213 R 9 Mere Lava, Vanuatu
191 N 23 Mereeg, Somalia
210 K 9 Meremere, New Zealand
173 F 20 Mergui, Myanmar
173 E 21 Mergui Archipelago, Myanmar
96 L 12 Meriş, Turkey
138 K 4 Mérida, Venezuela
80 K 9 Mérida, Spain
125 Y 10 Mérida, Mexico
138 L 4 Mérida, Venezuela
121 V 9 Meriden, Connecticut, U.S.A.
122 J 6 Meridian, Mississippi, U.S.A.
188 J 8 Meridja, Algeria
85 J 17 Merikarvia, Finland
87 I 24 Mering, Germany
214 I 15 Merir, Palau
167 T 10 Merke, Kazakhstan
99 F 17 Merkinė, Lithuania
191 E 15 Merowe, Sudan
208 H 11 Merredin, Western Australia, Australia
120 H 5 Merrill, Wisconsin, U.S.A.
118 H 11 Merriman, Nebraska, U.S.A.
113 T 14 Merritt, British Columbia, Canada
191 J 17 Mersa Fatma, Eritrea
191 I 16 Mersa Gulbub, Eritrea
83 L 25 Mersch, Luxembourg
77 I 18 Mersey, United Kingdom
158 J 13 Mersin, Turkey
98 E 10 Mērsrags, Latvia
168 C 12 Merta, India
77 I 21 Merthyr Tydfil, United Kingdom
195 W 7 Merti, Kenya
80 I 11 Mértola, Portugal
195 V 9 Meru, Tanzania
195 V 7 Meru, Kenya
158 K 8 Merzifon, Turkey
87 B 21 Merzig, Germany
117 M 23 Mesa, Arizona, U.S.A.
125 P 9 Mesa Central, Mexico
91 O 16 Mesagne, Italy
87 E 16 Meschede, Germany
97 F 14 Mesimeri, Greece
88 H 10 Mesocco, Switzerland
97 C 19 Mesolongi, Greece
144 L 11 Mesopotamia, Argentina
117 K 19 Mesquite, Nevada, U.S.A.
189 N 7 Messaad, Algeria
91 L 21 Messina, Italy
197 P 9 Messina, Republic of South Africa
97 D 22 Messiniakos Kolpos, Greece
96 G 11 Mesta, Bulgaria
90 G 7 Mestre, Italy
138 J 7 Meta, Colombia
138 M 6 Meta, Colombia
115 R 3 Meta Incognita Peninsula, Nunavut, Canada
119 O 21 Metairie, Louisiana, U.S.A.
144 I 6 Metán, Argentina
197 R 4 Metangula, Mozambique
197 S 5 Metarica, Mozambique
191 H 18 Metema, Ethiopia
212 G 3 Meteran, Papua New Guinea
211 G 20 Methven, New Zealand
95 G 14 Metković, Croatia
189 P 7 Metlaoui, Tunisia
197 U 4 Metoro, Mozambique
174 G 13 Metro, Indonesia
120 H 14 Metropolis, Illinois, U.S.A.
97 C 16 Metsovo, Greece
191 G 21 Metu, Ethiopia
79 V 4 Metz, France
83 H 21 Meuse, Belgium
124 F 2 Mexicali, Mexico
117 O 19 Mexican Hat, Utah, U.S.A.
125 N 8 Mexico, North America
125 Q 12 México, Mexico
125 R 12 Mexico City, Mexico
165 R 6 Meymaneh, Afghanistan
164 I 7 Meymeh, Iran
125 V 13 Mezcalapa, Mexico
96 G 8 Mezdra, Bulgaria
156 I 7 Mezen', Russian Federation
125 S 7 Mezquital, Mexico
197 Q 4 Mfuwe, Zambia
91 K 25 Mgarr, Malta
197 Q 11 Mhlume, Swaziland
177 C 19 Mi-shima, Japan
125 T 14 Miahuatlán, Mexico
80 L 9 Miajadas, Spain
119 K 16 Miami, Oklahoma, U.S.A.
123 T 14 Miami, Florida, U.S.A.
123 T 14 Miami Beach, Florida, U.S.A.
165 X 10 Mian Chanmum, Pakistan
164 F 4 Miandowāb, Iran
197 X 8 Miandrivazo, Madgascar
164 G 4 Mīāneh, Iran
175 R 8 Miangas, Indonesia
171 P 11 Mianning, China
92 G 8 Mianowice, Poland
165 W 8 Mianwali, Pakistan
171 Q 10 Mianyang, China
197 Y 8 Miarinarivo, Madgascar
156 I 11 Miass, Russian Federation
92 G 9 Miastko, Poland
93 M 20 Michalovce, Slovakia
120 K 8 Michigan, U.S.A.
120 J 9 Michigan City, Indiana, U.S.A.
114 M 12 Michipicoten Island, Ontario, Canada
125 O 12 Michoacán, Mexico
156 F 9 Michurinsk, Russian Federation
127 X 10 Micoud, St Lucia
59 P 5 Mid-Indian Basin, Indian Ocean
58 L 3 Mid-Indian Ridge, Indian Ocean
168 H 11 Mid Western, Nepal
174 H 9 Midai, Indonesia
83 D 15 Middelburg, Netherlands
196 M 14 Middelburg, Republic of South Africa
82 H 8 Middenmeer, Netherlands
61 X 6 Middle America Trench, Pacific Ocean
169 N 21 Middle Andaman, India
63 O 16 Middle Island, Tristan da Cunha
211 E 24 Middlemarch, New Zealand
209 U 6 Middlemount, Queensland, Australia
120 M 15 Middlesboro, Kentucky, U.S.A.
77 K 15 Middlesbrough, United Kingdom
209 Q 6 Middleton, Queensland, Australia
121 U 10 Middletown, New Jersey, U.S.A.
121 U 9 Middletown, New York, U.S.A.
188 I 7 Midelt, Morocco
79 O 14 Midi-Pyrénées, France
120 M 7 Midland, Michigan, U.S.A.
197 O 7 Midlands, Zimbabwe
197 X 10 Midongy Atsimo, Madgascar
63 K 20
61 P 5 Midway Islands, U.S.A.
118 E 11 Midwest, Wyoming, U.S.A.
159 Q 12 Midyat, Turkey
96 F 7 Midzhur, Bulgaria
177 D 21 Mie, Japan
92 F 12 Międzychód, Poland
92 N 13 Międzyrzec Podlaski, Poland
92 E 12 Międzyrzecz, Poland
93 L 17 Mielec, Poland
195 V 13 Miembwe, Tanzania
80 L 1 Mieres, Spain
83 J 16 Mierlo, Netherlands
92 I 7 Mierzeja Helska, Poland
92 I 8 Mierzeja Wiślana, Poland
168 N 10 Miging, India
90 G 8 Migliarino, Italy
125 O 8 Miguel Auza, Mexico
172 C 13 Migyaunye, Myanmar
177 E 19 Mihara, Japan
82 H 12 Mijdrecht, Netherlands
99 I 21 Mikashevichy, Belarus
156 F 10 Mikhaylovka, Russian Federation
167 U 2 Mikhaylovka, Kazakhstan
156 L 13 Mikhaylovskiy, Russian Federation
219 Y 7 Mikhaytov Island, Antarctica
85 N 17 Mikkeli, Finland
195 V 12 Mikumi, Tanzania
156 I 8 Mikun', Russian Federation
177 L 18 Mikura-jima, Japan
169 B 25 Miladhunmadulu Atoll, Maldives
90 C 7 Milan, Italy
122 J 2 Milan, Tennessee, U.S.A.
197 S 6 Milange, Mozambique
94 N 11 Milanovac, Serbia and Montenegro
158 B 12 Milas, Turkey
99 H 19 Milavidy, Belarus
121 Z 5 Milbridge, Maine, U.S.A.
209 R 11 Mildura, Victoria, Australia
191 J 19 Mīlē, Ethiopia
171 P 13 Mile, China
209 V 8 Miles, Queensland, Australia
118 F 9 Miles City, Montana, U.S.A.
117 L 18 Milford, Utah, U.S.A.
121 W 8 Milford, Massachusetts, U.S.A.
121 U 10 Milford, Pennsylvania, U.S.A.
77 G 21 Milford Haven, United Kingdom
211 A 22 Milford Sound, New Zealand
211 B 22 Milford Sound, New Zealand
215 Z 4 Mili, Marshall Islands
93 G 14 Milicz, Poland
208 M 1 Milikapiti, Northern Territory, Australia
157 Z 11 Mil'kovo, Russian Federation
115 P 3 Mill Island, Nunavut, Canada
219 Y 10 Mill Island, Antarctica
79 R 13 Millau, France
118 L 8 Mille Lacs, Minnesota, U.S.A.
123 P 5 Milledgeville, Georgia, U.S.A.
215 S 6 Millennium, Kiribati
156 E 10 Millerovo, Russian Federation
121 S 10 Millersburg, Pennsylvania, U.S.A.
90 B 9 Millesimo, Italy
209 Q 13 Millicent, South Australia, Australia
121 Y 4 Millinocket, Maine, U.S.A.
122 K 4 Millport, Alabama, U.S.A.
113 S 8 Mills Lake, Northwest Territories, Canada
77 B 19 Milltown Malbay, Republic of Ireland
121 U 12 Millville, New Jersey, U.S.A.
212 G 7 Milne Bay, Papua New Guinea
212 H 7 Milne Bay, Papua New Guinea
121 Y 5 Milo, Maine, U.S.A.
97 H 23 Milos, Greece
101 Z 4 Milove, Ukraine
121 S 10 Milton, Pennsylvania, U.S.A.
122 L 8 Milton, Florida, U.S.A.
211 E 25 Milton, New Zealand
77 L 20 Milton Keynes, United Kingdom
119 J 14 Miltonvale, Kansas, U.S.A.
120 I 8 Milwaukee, Wisconsin, U.S.A.
62 E 11 Milwaukee Deep, Atlantic Ocean
78 L 13 Mimizan, France
194 F 8 Mimongo, Gabon
117 H 17 Mina, Nevada, U.S.A.
163 W 5 Mina Jebel Ali, United Arab Emirates
163 S 3 Minā' Sa'ūd, Kuwait
164 M 13 Mīnāb, Iran
177 B 23 Minamata, Japan
126 M 5 Minas, Cuba
144 N 12 Minas, Uruguay
126 H 4 Minas de Matahambre, Cuba
143 L 16 Minas Gerais, Brazil
125 V 13 Minatitlán, Mexico
172 C 13 Minbu, Myanmar
76 F 9 Minch, The, United Kingdom
145 F 18 Minchinmávida, Chile
175 Q 7 Mindanao, Philippines
87 H 24 Mindelheim, Germany
63 A 15 Mindelo, Cape Verde
86 F 13 Minden, Germany
119 M 19 Minden, Louisiana, U.S.A.
175 O 4 Mindoro, Philippines
177 C 20 Mine, Japan
77 D 20 Mine Head, Republic of Ireland
77 I 22 Minehead, United Kingdom
119 L 19 Mineola, Texas, U.S.A.
119 J 19 Mineral Wells, Texas, U.S.A.
117 L 18 Minersville, Utah, U.S.A.
91 M 15 Minervino Murge, Italy
195 P 14 Minga, Democratic Republic of Congo
159 W 8 Mingäçevir, Azerbaijan
159 W 7 Mingäçevir Su Anbari, Azerbaijan
194 L 4 Mingala, Central African Republic
208 G 10 Mingenew, Western Australia, Australia
172 D 9 Mingin Range, Myanmar
171 W 3 Mingshui, China
76 D 11 Mingulay, United Kingdom
173 D 15 Minhla, Myanmar
169 B 24 Minicoy Island, India
208 F 7 Minilya Bridge Roadhouse, Western Australia, Australia
192 I 11 Mininian, Côte d'Ivoire
171 P 7 Minle, China
193 Q 11 Minna, Nigeria
118 K 10 Minneapolis, Minnesota, U.S.A.
119 I 16 Minneola, Kansas, U.S.A.
118 J 8 Minnesota, U.S.A.
81 Z 7 Minorca, Spain
118 H 7 Minot, North Dakota, U.S.A.
99 J 17 Minsk, Belarus
92 L 13 Mińsk Mazowiecki, Poland
99 J 18 Minskaya Voblasts', Belarus
193 U 14 Minta, Cameroon
112 K 5 Minto, Alaska, U.S.A.
113 R 2 Minto Inlet, Northwest Territories, Canada
113 Z 13 Minton, Saskatchewan, Canada
91 J 15 Minturno, Italy
194 F 6 Minvoul, Gabon
171 Q 9 Minxian, China
172 C 11 Minywa, Myanmar
168 O 11 Minzong, India
120 M 6 Mio, Michigan, U.S.A.
99 H 18 Mir, Belarus
80 H 6 Mira, Portugal
142 J 13 Miracema do Tocantins, Brazil
165 V 8 Miram Shah, Pakistan
79 N 12 Miramont-de-Guyenne, France
139 O 3 Miranda, Venezuela
143 G 17 Miranda, Brazil
81 P 2 Miranda de Ebro, Spain
80 J 4 Mirandela, Portugal
95 M 20 Miras, Albania
163 X 11 Mirbāṭ, Oman
174 K 8 Miri, Malaysia
209 V 7 Miriam Vale, Queensland, Australia
165 P 11 Mīrjāveh, Iran
219 Y 8 Mirny, Antarctica
157 R 11 Mirnyy, Russian Federation
92 F 10 Mirosławiec, Poland
165 U 14 Mirpur Khas, Pakistan
165 U 15 Mirpur Sakro, Pakistan
191 N 22 Mirsale, Somalia
97 F 22 Mirtoö Pelagos, Greece
168 H 13 Mirzapur, India
177 D 21 Misaki, Japan
176 K 9 Misawa, Japan
115 V 11 Miscou Island, New Brunswick, Canada
165 Y 5 Misgar, Pakistan
169 O 24 Misha, India
171 Y 3 Mishan, China
168 O 11 Mishmi Hills, India
212 C 5 Misiki, Papua New Guinea
144 O 8 Misiones, Argentina
163 O 6 Miskah, Saudi Arabia
93 L 21 Miskolc, Hungary
175 T 11 Misoöl, Indonesia
189 T 7 Mişrātah, Libya
118 H 11 Mission, South Dakota, U.S.A.
115 N 9 Missisa Lake, Ontario, Canada
122 H 5 Mississippi, U.S.A.
119 N 14 Mississippi, U.S.A.
122 I 8 Mississippi Sound, Mississippi, U.S.A.
118 B 8 Missoula, Montana, U.S.A.
188 J 7 Missour, Morocco
119 L 15 Missouri, U.S.A.
118 I 10 Missouri, South Dakota, U.S.A.
119 L 22 Missouri City, Texas, U.S.A.
115 R 11 Mistassini, Québec, Canada
89 Y 2 Mistelbach, Austria
126 H 7 Misteriosa Bank, Guatemala
101 Y 5 Mistky, Ukraine
142 H 8 Mitaraka, Brazil
209 R 3 Mitchell, Queensland, Australia
118 J 11 Mitchell, South Dakota, U.S.A.
209 T 8 Mitchell, Queensland, Australia
77 C 20 Mitchelstown, Republic of Ireland
165 V 15 Mithi, Pakistan
215 P 10 Mitiaro, Cook Islands
177 L 15 Mito, Japan
195 W 13 Mitole, Tanzania
176 K 6 Mitsuishi, Japan
177 A 20 Mitsushima, Japan
88 J 7 Mittelberg, Austria
88 L 8 Mittelberg, Austria
89 P 7 Mittersill, Austria
87 M 26 Mittlespitze, Germany
138 L 9 Mitú, Colombia
195 P 13 Mitwaba, Democratic Republic of Congo
194 E 7 Mitzic, Gabon
177 K 17 Miura, Japan
177 L 18 Miyake-jima, Japan
176 L 10 Miyako, Japan
177 O 26 Miyako-jima, Japan
177 N 26 Miyako-rettō, Japan
177 C 23 Miyakonojō, Japan
166 J 5 Miyaly, Kazakhstan
177 D 23 Miyazaki, Japan
177 G 17 Miyazu, Japan
177 D 19 Miyoshi, Japan
171 U 6 Miyun, China
191 G 21 Mīzan Teferī, Ethiopia
189 S 8 Mizdah, Libya
77 A 21 Mizen Head, Republic of Ireland
100 I 6 Mizhhir"ya, Ukraine
100 L 12 Mizil, Romania
96 G 7 Miziya, Bulgaria
169 N 14 Mizoram, India
160 E 11 Mizpe Ramon, Israel
219 T 3 Mizuho, Antarctica
85 F 22 Mjölby, Sweden
195 W 11 Mkata, Tanzania
195 W 10 Mkomazi, Tanzania
197 O 4 Mkushi, Zambia
93 D 16 Mladá Boleslav, Czech Republic
94 L 11 Mladenovac, Serbia and Montenegro
92 K 11 Mława, Poland
95 G 15 Mljet, Croatia
95 F 15 Mljetski Kanal, Croatia
84 F 11 Mo i Rana, Norway
175 S 14 Moa, Indonesia
127 O 6 Moa, Cuba
209 R 1 Moa Island, Queensland, Australia
117 O 17 Moab, Utah, U.S.A.
213 Y 12 Moala, Fiji
197 Q 10 Moamba, Mozambique
211 G 18 Moana, New Zealand
194 F 8 Moanda, Gabon
164 I 8 Mobārakeh, Iran
194 L 5 Mobaye, Central African Republic
194 L 5 Mobayi-Mbongo, Democratic Republic of Congo
119 M 14 Moberly, Missouri, U.S.A.
122 K 8 Mobile, Alabama, U.S.A.
122 K 8 Mobile Bay, Alabama, U.S.A.
118 H 9 Mobridge, South Dakota, U.S.A.
172 L 12 Môc Châu, Vietnam
127 Q 6 Moca, Dominican Republic
197 U 5 Moçambique, Mozambique
163 O 14 Mocha, Yemen
61 X 12 Mocha Fracture Zone, Pacific Ocean
197 U 3 Mocimboa da Praia, Mozambique
196 H 4 Môco, Angola
138 G 9 Mocoa, Colombia
124 M 4 Moctezuma, Mexico
197 S 6 Mocuba, Mozambique
79 W 11 Modane, France
90 F 8 Modena, Italy
117 K 18 Modena, Utah, U.S.A.
117 E 18 Modesto, California, U.S.A.
91 K 24 Modica, Italy
89 X 4 Mödling, Austria
171 R 3 Modot, Mongolia
94 H 10 Modriča, Bosnia and Herzegovina
209 S 13 Moe, Victoria, Australia
210 K 7 Moehau, New Zealand
139 X 6 Moengo, Suriname
87 C 15 Moers, Germany
168 D 9 Moga, India
191 M 24 Mogadishu, Somalia
194 J 6 Mogalo, Democratic Republic of Congo
176 J 12 Mogami, Japan
172 E 8 Mogaung, Myanmar
96 C 12 Mogila, Macedonia (F.Y.R.O.M.)
92 H 12 Mogilno, Poland
197 U 5 Mogincual, Mozambique
157 S 13 Mogocha, Russian Federation
191 E 20 Mogogh, Sudan
172 E 10 Mogok, Myanmar
93 I 26 Mohács, Hungary
188 H 7 Mohammedia, Morocco
171 V 1 Mohe, China
197 W 4 Mohéli, Comoros
196 K 7 Mohembo, Botswana
65 R 13 Mohns Ridge, Arctic Ocean
172 E 9 Mohnyin, Myanmar
141 H 18 Moho, Peru
195 W 13 Mohoro, Tanzania
100 M 6 Mohyliv-Podil's'kyy, Ukraine
168 N 13 Moirang, India
97 I 26 Moires, Greece
144 K 10 Moisés Ville, Argentina
193 X 12 Moïssala, Chad
117 G 21 Mojave, California, U.S.A.
117 H 22 Mojave Desert, California, U.S.A.
177 C 20 Mojikō, Japan
95 J 14 Mojkovac, Serbia and Montenegro
168 N 12 Mokokchung, India
211 D 25 Mokoreta, New Zealand
171 Y 8 Mokp'o, South Korea
193 P 11 Mokwa, Nigeria
83 I 17 Mol, Belgium
91 N 15 Mola di Bari, Italy

Country · Internal administrative region: State/Province/Territory/Dependent territory · Capital city · Mountain range/Undersea ridge · Mountain peak/Volcano/Seamount · Geographic feature · Headland/Point/Cape/Peninsula · Desert · Island/Island group · Antarctic base · Ocean · Sea · Bay/Gulf/Channel/Strait · Lake · Salt pan/Dry/Intermittent lake · River

125 R 11 Molango, Mexico
97 F 23 Molaoi, Greece
94 B 11 Molat, Croatia
85 B 15 Molde, Norway
101 N 9 Moldova, Europe
194 K 5 Molegbe, Democratic Republic of Congo
196 M 10 Molepolole, Botswana
99 G 14 Molėtai, Lithuania
91 M 15 Molfetta, Italy
81 R 6 Molina de Aragón, Spain
119 K 15 Moline, Kansas, U.S.A.
120 G 9 Moline, Illinois, U.S.A.
195 R 12 Moliro, Democratic Republic of Congo
91 K 14 Molise, Italy
91 L 17 Moliterno, Italy
89 Q 8 Möll, Austria
141 F 20 Mollendo, Peru
81 V 4 Mollerussa, Spain
86 I 10 Mölln, Germany
101 V 8 Molochans'k, Ukraine
101 V 9 Molochnyy Lyman, Ukraine
219 V 2 Molodezhnaya, Antarctica
167 T 4 Molodezhnyy, Kazakhstan
117 C 24 Molokai, Hawaii, U.S.A.
61 R 5 Molokai Fracture Zone, Pacific Ocean
97 E 18 Molos, Greece
193 V 15 Moloundou, Cameroon
197 N 13 Molteno, Republic of South Africa
175 U 14 Molu, Indonesia
175 Q 11 Molucca Sea, Indonesia
175 T 10 Moluccas, Indonesia
197 S 5 Molumbo, Mozambique
197 T 6 Moma, Mozambique
195 X 10 Mombasa, Kenya
169 N 14 Mombi New, India
96 J 12 Momchilgrad, Bulgaria
194 L 8 Mompono, Democratic Republic of Congo
138 I 3 Mompós, Colombia
157 U 8 Momskiy Khrebet, Russian Federation
173 E 16 Mon, Myanmar
85 E 26 Møn, Denmark
79 X 13 Monaco, Monaco
79 W 13 Monaco, Europe
62 J 9 Monaco Basin, Atlantic Ocean
139 R 3 Monagas, Venezuela
197 U 5 Monapo, Mozambique
91 B 19 Monastir, Italy
189 R 6 Monastir, Tunisia
176 K 3 Monbetsu, Japan
176 K 6 Monbetsu, Japan
193 U 11 Monboré, Cameroon
156 I 5 Monchegorsk, Russian Federation
87 B 16 Mönchengladbach, Germany
89 Y 4 Mönchhof, Austria
123 S 5 Moncks Corner, South Carolina, U.S.A.
125 P 6 Monclova, Mexico
115 V 13 Moncton, New Brunswick, Canada
91 I 21 Mondello, Italy
194 L 6 Mondjamboli, Democratic Republic of Congo
193 V 9 Mondo, Chad
80 J 1 Mondoñedo, Spain
90 A 9 Mondovi, Italy
91 I 15 Mondragone, Italy
89 R 5 Mondsee, Austria
97 F 23 Monemvasia, Greece
80 I 9 Monforte, Portugal
80 J 2 Monforte, Spain
172 N 11 Mong Cai, Vietnam
172 F 13 Mong Hang, Myanmar
172 H 12 Mong Hpayak, Myanmar
172 F 11 Mong Hsu, Myanmar
172 F 11 Mong Kung, Myanmar
172 E 10 Möng Mir, Myanmar
172 F 13 Mong Pan, Myanmar
172 G 12 Mong Ping, Myanmar
172 G 12 Mong Pu, Myanmar
172 F 11 Mong Yai, Myanmar
194 M 5 Monga, Democratic Republic of Congo
191 E 22 Mongalla, Sudan
168 M 12 Mongar, Bhutan
195 Q 6 Mongbwalu, Democratic Republic of Congo
90 A 9 Mongioie, Italy
193 X 10 Mongo, Chad
171 N 4 Mongolia, Asia
193 T 15 Mongomo, Equatorial Guinea
193 U 10 Mongonu, Nigeria
165 W 7 Mongora, Pakistan
193 Z 10 Mongororo, Chad
196 L 5 Mongu, Zambia
120 H 5 Monico, Wisconsin, U.S.A.
208 E 8 Monkey Mia, Western Australia, Australia
92 N 10 Mońki, Poland
194 L 9 Monkoto, Democratic Republic of Congo
77 I 21 Monmouth, United Kingdom
120 G 10 Monmouth, Illinois, U.S.A.
117 G 18 Mono Lake, California, U.S.A.
91 N 15 Monopoli, Italy
93 J 23 Monor, Hungary
193 Z 7 Monou, Chad
79 O 12 Monpazier, France
81 S 6 Monreal del Campo, Spain
119 N 19 Monroe, Louisiana, U.S.A.
120 M 9 Monroe, Michigan, U.S.A.
123 S 3 Monroe, North Carolina, U.S.A.
120 J 12 Monroe Lake, Indiana, U.S.A.
122 K 7 Monroeville, Alabama, U.S.A.
192 G 13 Monrovia, Liberia
83 E 21 Mons, Belgium
87 B 18 Monschau, Germany
82 F 13 Monster, Netherlands
90 A 6 Mont Blanc, Europe
193 S 14 Mont Cameroun, Cameroon
58 B 12 Mont Cocotte, Mauritius
115 S 10 Mont de Babel, Québec, Canada
78 M 13 Mont-de-Marsan, France
65 O 13 Mont Forel, Greenland
194 E 8 Mont Iboundji, Gabon
115 T 11 Mont-Joli, Québec, Canada
79 W 12 Mont Pelat, France
139 Y 8 Mont St-Marcel, French Guiana
189 O 13 Mont Tahat, Algeria
79 W 11 Mont Thabor, France
194 M 2 Mont Toussoro, Central African Republic
79 U 13 Mont Ventoux, France
115 T 9 Mont Wright, Québec, Canada
115 R 9 Mont Yapeitso, Québec, Canada
112 K 8 Montague Island, Alaska, U.S.A.
78 L 8 Montaigu, France
81 S 6 Montalbán, Spain
90 F 13 Montalto di Castro, Italy
140 C 10 Montalvo, Ecuador
96 G 7 Montana, Bulgaria
118 C 8 Montana, U.S.A.
96 F 7 Montana, Bulgaria
79 Q 6 Montargis, France
79 O 13 Montauban, France
121 W 10 Montauk Point, New York, U.S.A.
79 S 6 Montbard, France
79 V 6 Montbéliard, France
81 V 5 Montblanc, Spain
79 S 8 Montceau-les-Mines, France
142 H 10 Monte Alegre, Brazil
90 J 13 Monte Amaro, Italy
143 M 16 Monte Azul, Brazil
140 E 12 Monte Bello, Peru
145 F 24 Monte Burney, Chile
79 X 13 Monte Carlo, Monaco
90 I 13 Monte Carno, Italy
144 M 9 Monte Caseros, Argentina
79 Y 14 Monte Cinto, France
127 Q 6 Monte Cristi, Dominican Republic
145 H 25 Monte Darwin, Chile
145 H 24 Monte Dinero, Argentina
79 Y 15 Monte Incudine, France
145 F 19 Monte Macá, Chile
145 F 18 Monte Melimoyu, Chile
91 J 15 Monte Miletto, Italy
143 N 16 Monte Pascoal, Brazil
144 K 7 Monte Quemado, Argentina
79 Y 15 Monte Rotondo, France
91 L 14 Monte Sant'Angelo, Italy
143 N 14 Monte Santo, Brazil
90 A 8 Monte Viso, Italy
119 E 15 Monte Vista, Colorado, U.S.A.
208 F 6 Montebello Islands, Western Australia, Australia
90 F 13 Montefiascone, Italy
126 L 7 Montego Bay, Jamaica
79 T 12 Montélimar, France
80 H 9 Montemor-o-nova, Portugal
125 Q 7 Montemorelos, Mexico
95 I 15 Montenegro, Serbia and Montenegro
197 T 4 Montepuez, Mozambique
117 D 19 Monterey, California, U.S.A.
121 Q 13 Monterey, Virginia, U.S.A.
117 D 19 Monterey Bay, California, U.S.A.
138 H 4 Montería, Colombia
141 L 20 Montero, Bolivia
125 Q 7 Monterrey, Mexico
143 L 16 Montes Claros, Brazil
144 N 13 Montevideo, Uruguay
122 M 6 Montgomery, Alabama, U.S.A.
88 C 10 Monthey, Switzerland
117 O 18 Monticello, Utah, U.S.A.
119 N 18 Monticello, Arkansas, U.S.A.
120 L 15 Monticello, Kentucky, U.S.A.
121 U 9 Monticello, New York, U.S.A.
122 H 7 Monticello, Mississippi, U.S.A.
80 G 9 Montijo, Portugal
79 P 9 Montluçon, France
79 R 4 Montmirail, France
209 V 7 Monto, Queensland, Australia
81 N 11 Montoro, Spain
116 M 13 Montpelier, Idaho, U.S.A.
121 V 6 Montpelier, Vermont, U.S.A.
79 S 14 Montpellier, France
115 R 13 Montréal, Québec, Canada
113 X 10 Montreal Lake, Saskatchewan, Canada
113 X 11 Montreal Lake, Saskatchewan, Canada
115 N 12 Montreal River, Ontario, Canada
88 C 9 Montreux, Switzerland
76 J 11 Montrose, United Kingdom
119 D 15 Montrose, Colorado, U.S.A.
121 T 9 Montrose, Pennsylvania, U.S.A.
193 S 7 Monts Bagzane, Niger
189 Q 7 Monts des Ksour, Tunisia
189 N 12 Monts du Mouydir, Algeria
195 Q 12 Monts Mitumba, Democratic Republic of Congo
195 O 13 Monts Mulumbe, Democratic Republic of Congo
115 S 13 Monts Notre Dame, Québec, Canada
127 W 8 Montserrat, U.K.
81 N 5 Montuenga, Spain
117 N 19 Monument Valley, Arizona, U.S.A.
194 L 6 Monveda, Democratic Republic of Congo
172 D 11 Monywa, Myanmar
90 C 6 Monza, Italy
81 U 4 Monzón, Spain
141 D 14 Monzón, Peru
197 N 10 Mookane, Botswana
209 Q 9 Moolawatana, South Australia, Australia
209 Q 9 Moomba, South Australia, Australia
209 U 9 Moonie, Queensland, Australia
208 G 10 Moora, Western Australia, Australia
116 K 11 Moore, Idaho, U.S.A.
118 D 8 Moore, Montana, U.S.A.
119 I 22 Moore, Texas, U.S.A.
215 S 9 Moorea, French Polynesia
215 Y 7 Moorea, French Polynesia
121 Q 12 Moorefield, West Virginia, U.S.A.
118 J 8 Moorhead, Minnesota, U.S.A.
115 O 10 Moose, Ontario, Canada
121 X 4 Moosehead Lake, Maine, U.S.A.
115 O 10 Moosonee, Ontario, Canada
197 S 7 Mopeia, Mozambique
192 K 9 Mopti, Mali
192 L 9 Mopti, Mali
165 T 8 Moqor, Afghanistan
141 H 19 Moquegua, Peru
141 G 20 Moquegua, Peru
93 H 23 Mór, Hungary
80 H 9 Mora, Portugal
81 O 8 Mora, Spain
85 F 18 Mora, Sweden
193 V 10 Mora, Cameroon
168 F 11 Moradabad, India
197 W 7 Morafenobe, Madgascar
92 J 9 Morąg, Poland
126 E 9 Morales, Guatemala
197 Y 8 Moramanga, Madgascar
209 U 6 Moranbah, Queensland, Australia
215 X 12 Morane, French Polynesia
169 F 25 Moratuwa, Sri Lanka
94 M 11 Morava, Serbia and Montenegro/Czech Republic
93 E 19 Moravia, Czech Republic
93 E 19 Moravské Budějovice, Czech Republic
208 F 10 Morawa, Western Australia, Australia
76 H 9 Moray Firth, United Kingdom
87 C 20 Morbach, Germany
169 B 14 Morbi, India
89 Y 5 Mörbisch, Austria
91 J 15 Morcone, Italy
209 U 9 Moree, New South Wales, Australia
120 M 13 Morehead, Kentucky, U.S.A.
212 A 6 Morehead, Papua New Guinea
123 W 3 Morehead City, North Carolina, U.S.A.
125 P 11 Morelia, Mexico
81 T 6 Morella, Spain
125 R 12 Morelos, Mexico
168 E 12 Morena, India
113 P 13 Moresby Island, British Columbia, Canada
209 W 8 Moreton Island, Queensland, Australia
79 V 8 Morez, France
158 H 15 Morfou, Cyprus
158 G 15 Morfou Bay, Cyprus
209 Q 11 Morgan, South Australia, Australia
119 O 21 Morgan City, Louisiana, U.S.A.
123 R 2 Morganton, North Carolina, U.S.A.
121 P 12 Morgantown, West Virginia, U.S.A.
88 B 9 Morges, Switzerland
176 J 7 Mori, Japan
119 E 17 Moriarty, New Mexico, U.S.A.
192 H 11 Moribaya, Guinea
138 L 8 Morichal, Colombia
176 K 10 Morioka, Japan
78 I 4 Morlaix, France
91 M 18 Mormanno, Italy
58 A 9 Morne Seychellois, Seychelles
61 X 13 Mornington Abyssal Plain, Pacific Ocean
209 P 3 Mornington Island, Queensland, Australia
165 U 13 Moro, Pakistan
175 P 7 Moro Gulf, Philippines
212 E 5 Morobe, Papua New Guinea
212 E 5 Morobe, Papua New Guinea
188 F 8 Morocco, Africa
120 J 10 Morocco, Indiana, U.S.A.
100 K 1 Morochne, Ukraine
195 V 12 Morogoro, Tanzania
195 V 12 Morogoro, Tanzania
125 P 11 Moroleón, Mexico
175 Q 14 Moromaho, Indonesia
197 V 9 Morombe, Madgascar
126 L 5 Morón, Cuba
171 P 2 Mörön, Mongolia
140 C 10 Morona, Ecuador
140 C 10 Morona-Santiago, Ecuador
197 W 8 Morondava, Madgascar
192 J 11 Morondo, Côte d'Ivoire
197 W 4 Moroni, Comoros
175 S 9 Morotai, Indonesia
195 T 6 Moroto, Uganda
195 T 6 Moroto, Uganda
156 E 10 Morozovsk, Russian Federation
143 L 14 Morpara, Brazil
210 L 10 Morrinsville, New Zealand
114 I 11 Morris, Manitoba, Canada
118 K 9 Morris, Minnesota, U.S.A.
120 H 10 Morris, Illinois, U.S.A.
123 P 1 Morristown, Tennessee, U.S.A.
117 E 21 Morro Bay, California, U.S.A.
143 M 14 Morro do Chapéu, Brazil
84 G 10 Mørsvikbotn, Norway
79 N 5 Mortagne-au-Perche, France
144 K 10 Morteros, Argentina
127 N 4 Mortimer's, The Bahamas
215 P 15 Mortlock Islands, Federated States of Micronesia
116 E 8 Morton, Washington, U.S.A.
195 T 5 Morungole, Uganda
209 T 8 Morven, Queensland, Australia
118 E 8 Mosby, Montana, U.S.A.
156 F 8 Moscow, Russian Federation
116 I 8 Moscow, Idaho, U.S.A.
219 X 12 Moscow University Ice Shelf, Antarctica
87 C 19 Mosel, Germany
195 V 10 Moshi, Tanzania
101 R 5 Moshny, Ukraine
92 G 13 Mosina, Poland
84 F 12 Mosjøen, Norway
84 F 9 Moskenesøy, Norway
93 G 22 Moson-magyaróvár, Hungary
115 P 5 Mosquito Bay, Québec, Canada
126 H 11 Mosquito Coast, Nicaragua
85 D 20 Moss, Norway
211 C 24 Mossburn, New Zealand
196 L 15 Mossel Bay, Republic of South Africa
194 F 9 Mossendjo, Congo
142 O 12 Mossoró, Brazil
188 L 6 Mostaganem, Algeria
95 G 14 Mostar, Bosnia and Herzegovina
143 I 22 Mostardas, Brazil
101 Q 8 Mostove, Ukraine
100 H 4 Mostys'ka, Ukraine
161 R 2 Mosul, Iraq
191 I 19 Mot'a, Ethiopia
81 P 8 Mota del Cuervo, Spain
213 Q 9 Mota Lava, Vanuatu
99 G 21 Motal', Belarus
85 F 21 Motala, Sweden
168 F 13 Moth, India
81 R 8 Motilla del Palancar, Spain
210 M 10 Motiti Island, New Zealand
81 Q 1 Motrico, Spain
100 G 12 Motru, Romania
176 I 7 Motsuta-misaki, Japan
210 N 11 Motu, New Zealand
61 X 5 Motu Nui, Easter Island
215 R 9 Motu One, French Polynesia
211 H 16 Motueka, New Zealand
210 J 12 Motunui, New Zealand
212 I 5 Motupena Point, Papua New Guinea
194 I 6 Mouali Gbangba, Congo
192 G 7 Moudjéria, Mauritania
85 K 17 Mouhijärvi, Finland
194 E 9 Mouila, Gabon
191 K 18 Moulhoulê, Djibouti
79 R 8 Moulins, France
173 F 16 Moulmein, Myanmar
122 L 3 Moulton, Alabama, U.S.A.
123 O 7 Moultrie, Georgia, U.S.A.
193 W 12 Moundou, Chad
121 P 11 Moundsville, West Virginia, U.S.A.
144 G 11 Mount Aconcagua, Argentina
145 K 23 Mt Adam, Falkland Islands
116 E 8 Mt Adams, Washington, U.S.A.
123 S 1 Mount Airy, North Carolina, U.S.A.
212 E 6 Mt Albert Edward, Papua New Guinea
219 Y 10 Mt Amundsen, Antarctica
211 C 26 Mt Anglem, New Zealand
175 Q 7 Mount Apo, Philippines
159 T 9 Mt Ararat, Turkey
211 F 20 Mt Arrowsmith, New Zealand
211 C 22 Mt Aspiring, New Zealand
113 U 13 Mt Assiniboine, British Columbia, Canada
208 F 7 Mt Augustus, Western Australia, Australia
116 F 5 Mt Baker, Washington, U.S.A.
212 I 4 Mt Balbi, Papua New Guinea
212 E 5 Mt Bangeta, Papua New Guinea
117 K 19 Mt Bangs, Arizona, U.S.A.
208 H 12 Mount Barker, Western Australia, Australia
208 K 3 Mount Barnett Roadhouse, Western Australia, Australia
209 V 10 Mt Barrington, New South Wales, Australia
115 V 7 Mt Benedict, Newfoundland and Labrador, Canada
218 M 11 Mt Berlin, Antarctica
194 F 9 Mt Berongou, Congo
112 L 7 Mt Blackburn, Alaska, U.S.A.
209 T 12 Mt Bogong, Victoria, Australia
112 M 8 Mt Bona, Alaska, U.S.A.
212 B 5 Mt Bosavi, Papua New Guinea
208 J 4 Mt Broome, Western Australia, Australia
211 C 22 Mt Cardrona, New Zealand
115 U 12 Mount Carleton, New Brunswick, Canada
160 F 8 Mt Carmel, Israel
115 U 5 Mt Caubvick, Newfoundland and Labrador, Canada
219 N 9 Mt Chapman, Antarctica
219 W 3 Mt Codrington, Antarctica
113 T 13 Mt Columbia, British Columbia, Canada
218 K 5 Mt Coman, Antarctica
211 E 20 Mount Cook, New Zealand
219 W 4 Mt Cook, Antarctica
211 E 20 Mt Cook, New Zealand
120 I 4 Mt Curwood, Michigan, U.S.A.
175 P 6 Mount Dapiak, Philippines
197 P 6 Mount Darwin, Zimbabwe
121 Q 11 Mt Davis, Pennsylvania, U.S.A.
121 Z 6 Mount Desert Island, Maine, U.S.A.
112 K 4 Mt Doonerak, Alaska, U.S.A.
112 I 8 Mt Douglas, Alaska, U.S.A.
212 E 2 Mt Dremsel, Papua New Guinea
211 C 22 Mt Earnslaw, New Zealand
219 W 3 Mt Elkins, Antarctica
117 M 18 Mt Ellen, Utah, U.S.A.
219 Q 12 Mt Erebus, Antarctica
212 D 5 Mt Eruki, Papua New Guinea
91 K 22 Mount Etna, Italy
118 B 8 Mt Evans, Montana, U.S.A.
168 J 11 Mt Everest, China/Nepal
113 N 9 Mt Fairweather, Alaska, U.S.A.
215 V 15 Mt Fito, Samoa
63 A 17 Mt Fogo, Cape Verde
218 L 10 Mt Frakes, Antarctica
177 J 16 Mt Fuji, Japan
209 Q 13 Mount Gambier, South Australia, Australia
212 C 5 Mt Giluwe, Papua New Guinea
117 O 24 Mt Graham, Arizona, U.S.A.
123 P 2 Mt Guyot, North Carolina, U.S.A.
212 C 4 Mount Hagen, Papua New Guinea
112 M 6 Mt Harper, Alaska, U.S.A.
119 E 14 Mt Harvard, Colorado, U.S.A.

Country · Internal administrative region: State/Province/Territory/Dependent territory · Capital city · Mountain range/Undersea ridge · Mountain peak/Volcano/Seamount · Geographic feature · Headland/Point/Cape/Peninsula · Desert · Island/Island group · Antarctic base · Ocean · Sea · Bay/Gulf/Channel/Strait · Lake · Salt pan/Dry/Intermittent lake · River

113 N 9 **Mt Hay**, British Columbia, Canada
112 L 6 **Mt Hayes**, Alaska, U.S.A.
211 K 15 **Mt Hector**, New Zealand
195 Q 10 **Mt Heha̧n**, Burundi
211 H 20 **Mt Herbert**, New Zealand
160 H 7 **Mt Hermon**, Syria
120 H 7 **Mount Horeb**, Wisconsin, U.S.A.
213 Q 14 **Mt Humboldt**, New Caledonia
219 U 14 **Mt Hunt**, Antarctica
211 G 20 **Mount Hutt**, New Zealand
211 F 20 **Mt Hutt**, New Zealand
209 Q 5 **Mount Isa**, Queensland, Australia
218 K 5 **Mt Jackson**, Antarctica
117 I 17 **Mt Jefferson**, Nevada, U.S.A.
121 Y 4 **Mt Katahdin**, Maine, U.S.A.
112 I 8 **Mt Katmai**, Alaska, U.S.A.
195 V 8 **Mt Kenya**, Kenya
174 M 7 **Mt Kinabalu**, Malaysia
219 Q 10 **Mt Kirkpatrick**, Antarctica
209 T 13 **Mt Kosciuszko**, New South Wales, Australia
219 Q 12 **Mt Lister**, Antarctica
119 F 21 **Mt Livermore**, Texas, U.S.A.
112 M 8 **Mt Logan**, Yukon Territory, Canada
211 B 23 **Mt Lyall**, New Zealand
219 R 13 **Mt Mackintosh**, Antarctica
208 G 9 **Mount Magnet**, Western Australia, Australia
121 V 6 **Mt Mansfield**, Vermont, U.S.A.
112 K 7 **Mt Marcus Baker**, Alaska, U.S.A.
121 U 6 **Mt Marcy**, New York, U.S.A.
117 M 17 **Mt Marvine**, Utah, U.S.A.
210 M 10 **Mount Maunganui**, New Zealand
219 R 11 **Mt McClintock**, Antarctica
112 J 6 **Mt McKinley**, Alaska, U.S.A.
208 G 7 **Mt Meharry**, Western Australia, Australia
219 U 5 **Mt Menzies**, Antarctica
112 M 3 **Mt Michelson**, Alaska, U.S.A.
219 Q 10 **Mt Miller**, Antarctica
219 R 14 **Mt Minto**, Antarctica
123 Q 2 **Mt Mitchell**, North Carolina, U.S.A.
218 M 8 **Mt Moore**, Antarctica
219 U 14 **Mt Murchison**, Antarctica
113 P 8 **Mt Murray**, Yukon Territory, Canada
210 L 12 **Mt Ngauruhoe**, New Zealand
97 E 15 **Mt Olympus**, Greece
116 D 6 **Mt Olympus**, Washington, U.S.A.
211 F 22 **Mt Orr**, New Zealand
209 S 15 **Mt Ossa**, Tasmania, Australia
213 P 13 **Mt Panié**, New Caledonia
117 F 22 **Mt Pinos**, California, U.S.A.
117 M 16 **Mount Pleasant**, Utah, U.S.A.
121 Q 11 **Mount Pleasant**, Pennsylvania, U.S.A.
123 T 5 **Mount Pleasant**, South Carolina, U.S.A.
118 M 12 **Mt Pleasant**, Iowa, U.S.A.
119 L 19 **Mt Pleasant**, Texas, U.S.A.
212 M 7 **Mt Popomanaseu**, Solomon Islands
175 O 2 **Mt Pulog**, Philippines
113 R 13 **Mt Queen Bess**, British Columbia, Canada
175 Q 7 **Mount Ragang**, Philippines
208 J 11 **Mt Ragged**, Western Australia, Australia
116 E 7 **Mt Rainier**, Washington, U.S.A.
113 O 10 **Mt Ratz**, British Columbia, Canada
113 T 12 **Mt Robson**, British Columbia, Canada
121 O 15 **Mt Rogers**, Virginia, U.S.A.
211 F 19 **Mt Rolleston**, New Zealand
139 S 6 **Mt Roraima**, Guyana
211 L 16 **Mt Ross**, New Zealand
210 K 12 **Mt Ruapehu**, New Zealand
118 G 11 **Mt Rushmore**, South Dakota, U.S.A.
219 X 9 **Mt Sandow**, Antarctica
113 Q 13 **Mt Saugstad**, British Columbia, Canada
219 N 8 **Mt Seelig**, Antarctica
117 D 14 **Mt Shasta**, California, U.S.A.
218 L 10 **Mt Sidley**, Antarctica
215 U 15 **Mt Silisili**, Samoa
212 G 7 **Mt Simpson**, Papua New Guinea
212 H 4 **Mt Sinewit**, Papua New Guinea
218 K 11 **Mt Siple**, Antarctica
212 B 5 **Mt Sisa**, Papua New Guinea
211 B 24 **Mt Solitary**, New Zealand
219 S 14 **Mt Southard**, Antarctica
112 M 8 **Mt St Elias**, Alaska, U.S.A.
116 E 8 **Mt St Helens**, Washington, U.S.A.
211 D 22 **Mt St Mary**, New Zealand
211 J 16 **Mt Stokes**, New Zealand
219 X 9 **Mt Strathcona**, Antarctica
212 E 5 **Mt Strong**, Papua New Guinea
191 H 16 **Mount Suara**, Eritrea
113 Q 10 **Mt Sylvia**, British Columbia, Canada
212 D 5 **Mt Tabletop**, Papua New Guinea
213 P 10 **Mt Tabwemasana**, Vanuatu
212 J 5 **Mt Takuan**, Papua New Guinea
210 J 12 **Mt Taranaki (Mt Egmont)**, New Zealand
119 D 17 **Mt Taylor**, New Mexico, U.S.A.
117 K 21 **Mt Tipton**, Arizona, U.S.A.
210 L 12 **Mt Tongariro**, New Zealand
112 J 7 **Mt Torbert**, Alaska, U.S.A.
188 G 8 **Mt Toubkal**, Morocco
158 G 15 **Mount Troödos**, Cyprus
117 L 20 **Mt Trumbull**, Arizona, U.S.A.
218 L 7 **Mt Tyree**, Antarctica
212 G 4 **Mt Ulawun**, Papua New Guinea
211 H 18 **Mt Una**, New Zealand
121 R 11 **Mt Union**, Pennsylvania, U.S.A.
145 L 23 **Mt Usborne**, Falkland Islands
112 F 9 **Mt Veniaminof**, Alaska, U.S.A.
116 E 5 **Mount Vernon**, Washington, U.S.A.
120 H 13 **Mount Vernon**, Illinois, U.S.A.
122 K 7 **Mount Vernon**, Alabama, U.S.A.
121 N 11 **Mt Vernon**, Ohio, U.S.A.
219 T 3 **Mt Victor**, Antarctica
172 C 12 **Mt Victoria**, Myanmar
212 E 6 **Mt Victoria**, Papua New Guinea
213 X 11 **Mt Victoria**, Fiji
212 F 6 **Mt Victory**, Papua New Guinea
113 Q 13 **Mt Waddington**, British Columbia, Canada
121 X 6 **Mt Washington**, New Hampshire, U.S.A.
117 G 19 **Mt Whitney**, California, U.S.A.
120 G 4 **Mt Whittlesey**, Wisconsin, U.S.A.
212 C 4 **Mt Wilhelm**, Papua New Guinea
113 P 10 **Mt Will**, British Columbia, Canada
119 D 15 **Mt Wilson**, Colorado, U.S.A.
208 M 8 **Mt Woodroffe**, South Australia, Australia
218 M 8 **Mt Woollard**, Antarctica
112 L 7 **Mt Wrangell**, Alaska, U.S.A.
208 M 6 **Mt Zeil**, Northern Territory, Australia
118 E 13 **Mt Zirkel**, Colorado, U.S.A.
116 J 12 **Mountain Home**, Idaho, U.S.A.
189 T 13 **Mountains of Tummo**, Libya
77 F 24 **Mount's Bay**, United Kingdom
80 I 10 **Moura**, Portugal
142 E 10 **Moura**, Brazil
209 V 7 **Moura**, Queensland, Australia
193 Z 10 **Mouraya**, Chad
192 I 9 **Mourdiah**, Mali
210 M 10 **Mourea**, New Zealand
83 C 19 **Mouscron**, Belgium
193 W 10 **Mousgougou**, Chad
191 K 18 **Moussa Ali**, Djibouti
193 W 9 **Moussoro**, Chad
81 V 6 **Mouth of the Ebro**, Spain
77 A 19 **Mouth of the Shannon**, Republic of Ireland
171 W 9 **Mouth of the Yangtze**, China
142 J 9 **Mouths of the Amazon**, Brazil
169 K 16 **Mouths of the Ganges**, India
169 H 19 **Mouths of the Godavari**, India
165 T 15 **Mouths of the Indus**, Pakistan
173 B 17 **Mouths of the Irrawaddy**, Myanmar
169 G 19 **Mouths of the Krishna**, India
173 M 23 **Mouths of the Mekong**, Vietnam
193 Q 14 **Mouths of the Niger**, Nigeria
88 D 7 **Moutier**, Switzerland
79 V 10 **Moûtiers**, France
97 D 17 **Mouzaki**, Greece
196 J 5 **Moxico**, Angola
191 I 23 **Moyale**, Ethiopia
188 H 8 **Moyen Atlas**, Morocco
193 X 11 **Moyen-Chari**, Chad
194 D 8 **Moyen-Ogooué**, Gabon
197 N 13 **Moyeni**, Lesotho
192 F 10 **Moyenne-Guinée**, Guinea
174 M 15 **Moyo**, Indonesia
195 R 5 **Moyo**, Uganda
140 C 12 **Moyobamba**, Peru
84 G 9 **Møysalen**, Norway
167 T 9 **Moyynkum**, Kazakhstan
167 T 7 **Moyynty**, Kazakhstan
197 Q 9 **Mozambique**, Africa
197 T 8 **Mozambique Channel**, Africa
58 I 10 **Mozambique Escarpment**, Indian Ocean
58 I 9 **Mozambique Ridge**, Indian Ocean
156 F 8 **Mozhaysk**, Russian Federation
195 Q 12 **Mpala**, Democratic Republic of Congo
195 R 11 **Mpanda**, Tanzania
196 M 7 **Mpandamatenga**, Botswana
194 H 9 **Mpé**, Congo
195 S 7 **Mpigi**, Uganda
197 P 3 **Mpika**, Zambia
197 P 2 **Mporokoso**, Zambia
194 H 9 **Mpouya**, Congo
197 O 10 **Mpumalanga**, Republic of South Africa
195 U 11 **Mpwapwa**, Tanzania
92 L 9 **Mrągowo**, Poland
96 D 12 **Mrešičko**, Macedonia (F.Y.R.O.M.)
94 F 11 **Mrkonjić-Grad**, Bosnia and Herzegovina
101 Q 2 **Mryn**, Ukraine
189 N 6 **M'sila**, Algeria
99 N 17 **Mstsislaw**, Belarus
195 W 14 **Mtama**, Tanzania
159 T 6 **Mts'khet'a**, Georgia
195 W 14 **Mtwara**, Tanzania
195 X 14 **Mtwara**, Tanzania
194 F 11 **Muanda**, Democratic Republic of Congo
173 L 15 **Muang Khammouan**, Laos
173 M 18 **Muang Không**, Laos
173 L 17 **Muang Khôngxédôn**, Laos
172 J 12 **Muang Khoua**, Laos
172 J 12 **Muang Ngoy**, Laos
172 I 11 **Muang Ou Nua**, Laos
172 H 13 **Muang Pakbeng**, Laos
173 K 14 **Muang Pakxan**, Laos
173 L 16 **Muang Phalan**, Laos
173 M 16 **Muang Phin**, Laos
173 I 14 **Muang Phôn-Hông**, Laos
172 H 12 **Muang Sing**, Laos
172 J 13 **Muang Souy**, Laos
173 I 14 **Muang Xaignabouri**, Laos
172 I 12 **Muang Xay**, Laos
174 E 12 **Muaraaman**, Indonesia
174 F 12 **Muarabeliti**, Indonesia
174 E 11 **Muarabungo**, Indonesia
174 F 13 **Muaradua**, Indonesia
174 F 12 **Muaraenim**, Indonesia
174 C 11 **Muarasiberut**, Indonesia
167 P 13 **Mubarek**, Uzbekistan
193 U 11 **Mubi**, Nigeria
208 G 11 **Muchea**, Western Australia, Australia
76 F 11 **Muck**, United Kingdom
197 U 4 **Mucojo**, Mozambique
196 K 3 **Muconda**, Angola
196 H 6 **Mucope**, Angola
158 J 10 **Mucur**, Turkey
143 N 17 **Mucuri**, Brazil
118 G 10 **Mud Butte**, South Dakota, U.S.A.
171 Y 4 **Mudanjiang**, China
158 D 8 **Mudanya**, Turkey
118 E 12 **Muddy Gap**, Wyoming, U.S.A.
169 D 19 **Mudhol**, India
173 F 17 **Mudon**, Myanmar
191 N 21 **Mudug**, Somalia
197 U 3 **Mueda**, Mozambique
197 O 4 **Mufulira**, Zambia
196 M 4 **Mufumbwe**, Zambia
159 Y 9 **Muğan Düzü**, Azerbaijan
197 S 6 **Mugeba**, Mozambique
164 J 7 **Mūghār**, Iran
158 C 12 **Muğla**, Turkey
191 B 18 **Muhagiriya**, Sudan
190 G 13 **Muhammad Qol**, Sudan
161 O 7 **Muḩaywīr**, Iraq
219 Q 2 **Mühlig-Hofmann Mountains**, Antarctica
89 S 3 **Mühlviertel**, Austria
160 H 4 **Muḩradah**, Syria
98 E 7 **Muhu**, Estonia
195 P 8 **Muhulu**, Democratic Republic of Congo
191 G 22 **Mui**, Ethiopia
173 L 24 **Mui Ca Mau**, Vietnam
197 T 5 **Muite**, Mozambique
100 H 6 **Mukacheve**, Ukraine
174 J 9 **Mukah**, Malaysia
173 L 16 **Mukdahan**, Thailand
208 G 10 **Mukinbudin**, Western Australia, Australia
174 E 12 **Mukomuko**, Indonesia
169 L 18 **Mulakatholhu Atoll**, Maldives
197 S 5 **Mulanje**, Malawi
197 R 6 **Mulanje**, Malawi
161 W 8 **Mūlat al Mashkhūr**, Iraq
145 F 14 **Mulchén**, Chile
195 S 9 **Muleba**, Tanzania
124 I 6 **Mulegé**, Mexico
81 P 12 **Mulhacén**, Spain
79 W 6 **Mulhouse**, France
76 F 12 **Mull**, United Kingdom
77 G 15 **Mull of Galloway**, United Kingdom
77 F 14 **Mull of Kintyre**, United Kingdom
76 F 13 **Mull of Oa**, United Kingdom
208 F 9 **Mullewa**, Western Australia, Australia
87 D 25 **Müllheim**, Germany
77 D 17 **Mullingar**, Republic of Ireland
196 M 6 **Mulobezi**, Zambia
169 F 15 **Multai**, India
165 W 10 **Multan**, Pakistan
194 M 5 **Muma**, Democratic Republic of Congo
165 O 14 **Mūmān**, Iran
169 B 17 **Mumbai**, India
196 L 5 **Mumbeji**, Zambia
196 G 3 **Mumbondo**, Angola
197 N 5 **Mumbwa**, Zambia
212 E 5 **Mumeng**, Papua New Guinea
175 P 13 **Muna**, Indonesia
125 Y 11 **Muna**, Mexico
168 A 12 **Munabao**, India
170 O 14 **Munai**, China
177 B 21 **Munakata**, Japan
166 H 9 **Munayshy**, Kazakhstan
113 Q 9 **Muncho Lake**, British Columbia, Canada
120 K 11 **Muncie**, Indiana, U.S.A.
121 S 10 **Muncy**, Pennsylvania, U.S.A.
165 W 10 **Munda**, Pakistan
143 M 14 **Mundo Novo**, Brazil
208 K 10 **Mundrabilla**, Western Australia, Australia
209 V 8 **Mundubbera**, Queensland, Australia
81 Q 9 **Munera**, Spain
120 K 14 **Munfordville**, Kentucky, U.S.A.
197 Q 6 **Mungári**, Mozambique
195 P 6 **Mungbere**, Democratic Republic of Congo
168 J 13 **Munger**, India
209 P 8 **Mungerannie Hotel**, South Australia, Australia
209 U 9 **Mungindi**, New South Wales, Australia
87 J 24 **Munich**, Germany
85 D 21 **Munkedal**, Sweden
77 B 20 **Munster**, Republic of Ireland
86 H 12 **Münster**, Germany
87 D 14 **Münster**, Germany
88 F 9 **Münster**, Switzerland
84 N 11 **Muojärvi**, Finland
172 K 12 **Muong Het**, Laos
84 K 9 **Muonio**, Finland
160 K 8 **Muqāţ**, Jordan
163 Q 14 **Muqaybirah**, Yemen
159 T 10 **Muradiye**, Turkey
176 J 13 **Murakami**, Japan
195 Q 9 **Muramvya**, Burundi
156 H 8 **Murashi**, Russian Federation
159 R 10 **Murat**, Turkey
79 Q 11 **Murat**, France
96 M 12 **Muratli**, Turkey
89 T 7 **Murau**, Austria
91 C 18 **Muravera**, Italy
164 I 8 **Murchek-Khort**, Iran
208 F 9 **Murchison**, Western Australia, Australia
211 H 17 **Murchison**, New Zealand
208 F 9 **Murchison Roadhouse**, Western Australia, Australia
81 R 11 **Murcia**, Spain
81 S 11 **Murcia**, Spain
118 H 11 **Murdo**, South Dakota, U.S.A.
89 W 8 **Mureck**, Austria
100 J 9 **Mureş**, Romania
79 O 14 **Muret**, France
122 L 2 **Murfreesboro**, Tennessee, U.S.A.
123 V 1 **Murfreesboro**, North Carolina, U.S.A.
167 U 13 **Murghob**, Tajikistan
209 V 8 **Murgon**, Queensland, Australia
88 F 7 **Muri**, Switzerland
196 K 3 **Muriege**, Angola
215 O 14 **Murilo Atoll**, Federated States of Micronesia
159 P 10 **Mürit Dağlari**, Turkey
86 L 10 **Müritz**, Germany
210 O 12 **Muriwai**, New Zealand
156 I 5 **Murmansk**, Russian Federation
65 U 12 **Murmansk Rise**, Arctic Ocean
156 G 9 **Murom**, Russian Federation
195 R 8 **Murongo**, Tanzania
176 J 7 **Muroran**, Japan
177 F 20 **Muroto**, Japan
177 F 21 **Muroto-zaki**, Japan
123 O 3 **Murphy**, North Carolina, U.S.A.
209 R 12 **Murray**, New South Wales, Australia
120 H 15 **Murray**, Kentucky, U.S.A.
209 Q 12 **Murray Bridge**, South Australia, Australia
61 R 4 **Murray Fracture Zone**, Pacific Ocean
58 M 2 **Murray Ridge**, Indian Ocean
120 G 11 **Murrayville**, Illinois, U.S.A.
165 X 7 **Murree**, Pakistan
197 T 5 **Murrupula**, Mozambique
94 E 6 **Murska Sobota**, Slovenia
113 S 13 **Murtle Lake**, British Columbia, Canada
169 B 17 **Murud**, India
210 M 11 **Murupara**, New Zealand
215 X 11 **Mururoa**, French Polynesia
169 G 14 **Murwara**, India
209 W 9 **Murwillumbah**, New South Wales, Australia
189 S 11 **Murzūq**, Libya
89 W 5 **Mürzzuschlag**, Austria
159 Q 11 **Muş**, Turkey
98 E 12 **Mūša**, Lithuania
165 R 9 **Musa Qala**, Afghanistan
194 M 9 **Musadi**, Democratic Republic of Congo
96 G 10 **Musala**, Bulgaria
161 X 9 **Musallam**, Iraq
171 Y 5 **Musan**, North Korea
163 X 4 **Musandam Peninsula**, Oman
163 P 14 **Musaymir**, Yemen
163 Z 6 **Muscat**, Oman
115 Y 9 **Musgrave Harbour**, Newfoundland and Labrador, Canada
208 L 8 **Musgrave Ranges**, South Australia, Australia
165 U 8 **Mūshakī**, Afghanistan
160 I 10 **Mushāsh Ḩadraj**, Jordan
194 I 9 **Mushie**, Democratic Republic of Congo
212 C 3 **Mushu**, Papua New Guinea
120 K 8 **Muskegon**, Michigan, U.S.A.
119 K 17 **Muskogee**, Oklahoma, U.S.A.
113 R 9 **Muskwa**, British Columbia, Canada
191 G 15 **Musmar**, Sudan
195 T 8 **Musoma**, Tanzania
195 T 12 **Musombe**, Tanzania
115 W 10 **Musquaro**, Québec, Canada
212 F 2 **Mussau Island**, Papua New Guinea
196 H 3 **Mussende**, Angola
79 N 11 **Mussidan**, France
158 C 9 **Mustafakemalpaşa**, Turkey
191 L 22 **Mustahīl**, Ethiopia
88 K 9 **Müstair**, Switzerland
127 X 11 **Mustique**, St Vincent and The Grenadines
98 D 7 **Mustjala**, Estonia
98 H 8 **Mustla**, Estonia
98 I 7 **Mustvee**, Estonia
209 V 11 **Muswellbrook**, New South Wales, Australia
158 I 13 **Mut**, Turkey
190 D 11 **Mut**, Egypt
197 Q 7 **Mutare**, Zimbabwe
138 G 5 **Mutis**, Colombia
197 W 4 **Mutsamudu**, Comoros
195 N 14 **Mutshatsha**, Democratic Republic of Congo
176 K 8 **Mutsu**, Japan
176 J 8 **Mutsu-wan**, Japan
209 S 6 **Muttaburra**, Queensland, Australia
211 B 26 **Muttonbird Islands**, New Zealand
169 F 20 **Muttukuru**, India
197 S 5 **Mutuali**, Mozambique
193 T 12 **Mutum Biyu**, Nigeria
169 G 24 **Mutur**, Sri Lanka
170 K 8 **Mutztag Feng**, China
196 H 2 **Muxaluando**, Angola
196 F 3 **Muxima**, Angola
193 S 10 **Muya**, Nigeria
195 R 9 **Muyinga**, Burundi
166 L 10 **Muynak**, Uzbekistan
195 O 12 **Muyumba**, Democratic Republic of Congo
165 X 7 **Muzaffarabad**, Pakistan
165 W 10 **Muzaffargarh**, Pakistan
168 E 10 **Muzaffarnagar**, India
168 J 13 **Muzaffarpur**, India
78 J 6 **Muzillac**, France
125 P 5 **Múzquiz**, Mexico
193 T 15 **Mvangan**, Cameroon
191 D 22 **Mvolo**, Sudan
195 V 12 **Mvomero**, Tanzania
197 P 7 **Mvuma**, Zimbabwe
195 S 9 **Mwanza**, Tanzania
195 S 9 **Mwanza**, Tanzania
194 L 10 **Mweka**, Democratic Republic of Congo
197 O 3 **Mwenda**, Zambia
194 M 12 **Mwene-Ditu**, Democratic Republic of Congo
197 P 8 **Mwenezi**, Zimbabwe
195 P 9 **Mwenga**, Democratic Republic of Congo
194 M 13 **Mwimba**, Democratic Republic of Congo
196 M 3 **Mwinilunga**, Zambia
215 Q 15 **Mwokil**, Federated States of Micronesia
173 M 22 **My Tho**, Vietnam
99 I 15 **Myadzyel**, Belarus
123 Q 12 **Myakka City**, Florida, U.S.A.
172 C 12 **Myanmar (Burma)**, Asia

Country · Internal administrative region: State/Province/Territory/Dependent territory · Capital city · Mountain range/Undersea ridge · Mountain peak/Volcano/Seamount · Geographic feature · Headland/Point/Cape/Peninsula · Desert · Island/Island group · Antarctic base · Ocean · Sea · Bay/Gulf/Channel/Strait · Lake · Salt pan/Dry/Intermittent lake · River

C 16 **Myaungmya**, Myanmar
D 12 **Myingyan**, Myanmar
F 19 **Myinmoletkat**, Myanmar
E 8 **Myitkyina**, Myanmar
F 19 **Myitta**, Myanmar
D 12 **Myittha**, Myanmar
V 8 **Mykhaylivka**, Ukraine
I 5 **Mykolayiv**, Ukraine
R 9 **Mykolayiv**, Ukraine
J 21 **Mykonos**, Greece
J 21 **Mykonos**, Greece
J 7 **Myla**, Russian Federation
T 8 **Mynaral**, Kazakhstan
B 12 **Myohaung**, Myanmar
J 13 **Myory**, Belarus
B 12 **Myrdalsjökull**, Iceland
T 4 **Myrhorod**, Ukraine
I 15 **Myrina**, Greece
Q 4 **Myrne**, Ukraine
X 8 **Myrne**, Ukraine
U 4 **Myrtle Beach**, South Carolina, U.S.A.
X 10 **Mys Alevina**, Russian Federation
X 14 **Mys Aniva**, Russian Federation
T 13 **Mys Ayya**, Ukraine
Y 5 **Mys Blossom**, Russian Federation
W 12 **Mys Chauda**, Ukraine
R 5 **Mys Chelyuskin**, Russian Federation
W 10 **Mys Duga-Zapadnaya**, Russian Federation
W 12 **Mys Elizavety**, Russian Federation
Z 9 **Mys Govena**, Russian Federation
J 6 **Mys Kanin Nos**, Russian Federation
W 11 **Mys Kazantip**, Ukraine
S 13 **Mys Khersones**, Ukraine
X 14 **Mys Kril'on**, Russian Federation
Y 5 **Mys Litke**, Russian Federation
V 7 **Mys Lopatka**, Russian Federation
Z 12 **Mys Lopatka**, Russian Federation
Z 7 **Mys Navarin**, Russian Federation
H 10 **Mys Peschanyy**, Kazakhstan
H 10 **Mys Sengirli**, Kazakhstan
X 6 **Mys Shelagskiy**, Russian Federation
Y 5 **Mys Shmidta**, Russian Federation
H 11 **Mys Suz**, Kazakhstan
X 13 **Mys Terpeniya**, Russian Federation
X 10 **Mys Tolstoy**, Russian Federation
G 8 **Mys Tyub-Karagan**, Kazakhstan
S 12 **Mys Yevpatoriys'kyy**, Ukraine
Y 10 **Mys Yuzhnyy**, Russian Federation
N 5 **Mys Zhelaniya**, Russian Federation
K 18 **Myślenice**, Poland
D 11 **Myślibórz**, Poland
D 21 **Mysore**, India
L 17 **Mytilini**, Greece
N 15 **Myton**, Utah, U.S.A.
Q 3 **Mzimba**, Malawi
Q 3 **Mzuzu**, Malawi

F 10 **Na-lang**, Myanmar
F 13 **Naaldwijk**, Netherlands
D 26 **Naalehu**, Hawaii, U.S.A.
K 7 **Naama**, Algeria
K 19 **Naantali**, Finland
I 11 **Naarden**, Netherlands
P 5 **Nabas**, Philippines
V 10 **Naberera**, Tanzania
H 10 **Naberezhnyye Chelny**, Russian Federation
M 7 **Nabesna**, Alaska, U.S.A.
Q 5 **Nabeul**, Tunisia
W 12 **Nabire**, Indonesia
G 9 **Nāblus**, Israel
M 11 **Nabolo**, Ghana
X 11 **Nabouwalu**, Fiji
U 5 **Nacala**, Mozambique
F 10 **Nacaome**, Honduras
U 5 **Nacaroa**, Mozambique
W 14 **Nachingwea**, Tanzania
B 11 **Nachna**, India
93 F 16 **Náchod**, Czech Republic
169 N 22 **Nachuge**, India
119 L 20 **Nacogdoches**, Texas, U.S.A.
124 J 3 **Nacozari de García**, Mexico
213 W 11 **Nadi**, Fiji
169 C 15 **Nadiad**, India
159 V 9 **Nadirchanly**, Azerbaijan
100 E 10 **Nădlac**, Romania
188 J 6 **Nador**, Morocco
100 J 6 **Nadvirna**, Ukraine
156 L 8 **Nadym**, Russian Federation
85 D 26 **Naestved**, Denmark
97 D 19 **Nafpaktos**, Greece
97 F 21 **Nafplio**, Greece
163 P 5 **Nafy**, Saudi Arabia
190 F 11 **Nag' Hammadi**, Egypt
175 P 4 **Naga**, Philippines
168 O 13 **Naga Hills**, India
177 D 20 **Nagahama**, Japan
177 H 17 **Nagahama**, Japan
169 D 18 **Nagaj**, India
168 O 12 **Nagaland**, India
177 I 15 **Nagano**, Japan
177 J 14 **Nagaoka**, Japan
168 N 12 **Nagaon**, India
169 F 22 **Nagappattinam**, India
169 F 19 **Nagarjuna Sagar**, India
177 B 22 **Nagasaki**, Japan
177 C 20 **Nagato**, Japan
168 C 12 **Nagaur**, India
169 E 24 **Nagercoil**, India
165 R 13 **Nagha Kalat**, Pakistan
168 F 10 **Nagina**, India
177 N 24 **Nago**, Japan
87 F 23 **Nagold**, Germany
177 H 17 **Nagoya**, Japan
169 F 16 **Nagpur**, India
170 L 10 **Nagqu**, China
156 M 3 **Nagurskoye**, Russian Federation
93 G 25 **Nagyatád**, Hungary
93 M 21 **Nagyhalász**, Hungary
93 G 25 **Nagykanizsa**, Hungary
93 J 23 **Nagykáta**, Hungary
177 N 25 **Naha**, Japan
160 F 7 **Nahariyya**, Israel
160 H 3 **Nahr al Āşī**, Syria
161 U 7 **Nahr Diyālá**, Iraq
124 M 5 **Naica**, Mexico
100 F 12 **Naidăş**, Romania
171 V 5 **Naiman Qi**, China
164 J 8 **Nā'īn**, Iran
115 U 7 **Nain**, Newfoundland and Labrador, Canada
169 G 15 **Nainpur**, India
76 H 10 **Nairn**, United Kingdom
195 V 8 **Nairobi**, Kenya
98 F 5 **Naissaar**, Estonia
195 U 8 **Naivasha**, Kenya
164 I 8 **Najafābād**, Iran
171 Y 5 **Najin**, North Korea
163 P 11 **Najrān**, Saudi Arabia
177 A 22 **Nakadōri-shima**, Japan
177 E 21 **Nakamura**, Japan
177 I 15 **Nakano**, Japan
177 B 26 **Nakano-shima**, Japan
177 D 17 **Nakano-shima**, Japan
176 M 4 **Nakashibetsu**, Japan
195 S 7 **Nakasongola**, Uganda
177 C 21 **Nakatsu**, Japan
177 I 17 **Nakatsugawa**, Japan
191 I 16 **Nakfa**, Eritrea
190 F 8 **Nakhl**, Egypt
164 I 12 **Nakhl-e Taqī**, Iran
157 V 15 **Nakhodka**, Russian Federation
173 I 19 **Nakhon Nayok**, Thailand
173 K 15 **Nakhon Phanom**, Thailand
173 I 18 **Nakhon Ratchasima**, Thailand
173 G 17 **Nakhon Sawan**, Thailand
173 H 24 **Nakhon Si Thammarat**, Thailand
169 A 14 **Nakhtarana**, India
92 G 11 **Nakło nad Notecią**, Poland
112 H 8 **Naknek**, Alaska, U.S.A.
197 Q 2 **Nakonde**, Zambia
85 D 26 **Nakskov**, Denmark
85 F 16 **Näkten**, Sweden
195 U 8 **Nakuru**, Kenya
113 U 14 **Nakusp**, British Columbia, Canada
165 S 12 **Nal**, Pakistan
156 E 11 **Nal'chik**, Russian Federation
169 A 14 **Naliya**, India
158 G 9 **Nallihan**, Turkey
189 R 8 **Nālūt**, Libya
170 L 10 **Nam Co**, China
172 M 13 **Nam Đinh**, Vietnam
173 J 14 **Nam Ngum Reservoir**, Laos
173 J 16 **Nam Phong**, Thailand
196 H 7 **Namacunde**, Angola
197 S 6 **Namacurra**, Mozambique
168 H 11 **Namai**, Nepal
169 E 22 **Namakkal**, India
195 V 9 **Namanga**, Kenya
167 S 11 **Namangan**, Uzbekistan
167 S 11 **Namangan Wiloyati**, Uzbekistan
197 U 5 **Namapa**, Mozambique
196 J 11 **Namaqualand**, Namibia
212 G 3 **Namatanai**, Papua New Guinea
209 W 10 **Nambucca Heads**, New South Wales, Australia
196 G 8 **Namib Desert**, Namibia
196 F 6 **Namibe**, Angola
196 F 6 **Namibe**, Angola
196 H 9 **Namibia**, Africa
63 M 17 **Namibia Abyssal Plain**, Atlantic Ocean
197 S 7 **Namidobe**, Mozambique
170 M 10 **Namjagbarwa**, China
172 E 11 **Namlan**, Myanmar
175 R 12 **Namlea**, Indonesia
209 T 10 **Namoi**, New South Wales, Australia
215 O 15 **Namoluk**, Federated States of Micronesia
215 N 14 **Namonuito**, Federated States of Micronesia
215 X 4 **Namorik**, Marshall Islands
116 I 12 **Nampa**, Idaho, U.S.A.
192 K 8 **Nampala**, Mali
171 X 6 **Namp'o**, North Korea
197 T 5 **Nampula**, Mozambique
197 U 5 **Nampula**, Mozambique
172 F 12 **Namsang**, Myanmar
85 E 14 **Namsos**, Norway
157 T 10 **Namtsy**, Russian Federation
172 E 10 **Namtu**, Myanmar
215 X 3 **Namu**, Marshall Islands
197 S 5 **Namuli**, Mozambique
197 T 4 **Namuno**, Mozambique
83 H 22 **Namur**, Belgium
83 H 21 **Namur**, Belgium
196 I 7 **Namutoni**, Namibia
197 N 6 **Namwala**, Zambia
171 Y 8 **Namwŏn**, South Korea
172 E 6 **Namya Ra**, Myanmar
93 H 15 **Namysłów**, Poland
173 H 14 **Nan**, Thailand
194 J 3 **Nana-Grébizi**, Central African Republic
194 H 4 **Nana-Mambéré**, Central African Republic
113 R 15 **Nanaimo**, British Columbia, Canada
177 H 15 **Nanao**, Japan
171 Q 10 **Nanbu**, China
171 X 3 **Nancha**, China
171 U 11 **Nanchang**, China
171 Q 10 **Nanchong**, China
169 O 24 **Nancowry**, India
79 V 4 **Nancy**, France
168 F 10 **Nanda Devi**, India
169 E 17 **Nanded**, India
169 C 15 **Nandurbar**, India
169 F 19 **Nandyal**, India
171 V 12 **Nanfeng**, China
170 L 11 **Nang**, China
193 U 14 **Nanga Eboko**, Cameroon
165 Y 6 **Nanga Parbat**, Pakistan
165 V 7 **Nangarhār**, Afghanistan
174 J 11 **Nangatayap**, Indonesia
171 U 8 **Nangong**, China
171 N 10 **Nangqên**, China
195 W 13 **Nangulangwa**, Tanzania
169 E 21 **Nanjangud**, India
171 V 9 **Nanjing**, China
177 F 20 **Nankoku**, Japan
196 J 6 **Nankova**, Angola
171 R 14 **Nanning**, China
64 M 14 **Nanortalik**, Greenland
171 V 12 **Nanping**, China
65 T 9 **Nansen Basin**, Arctic Ocean
65 S 10 **Nansen Cordillera**, Arctic Ocean
195 S 9 **Nansio**, Tanzania
78 L 7 **Nantes**, France
113 V 13 **Nanton**, Alberta, Canada
171 W 9 **Nantong**, China
121 Y 9 **Nantucket**, Massachusetts, U.S.A.
121 Y 9 **Nantucket Island**, Massachusetts, U.S.A.
121 Y 9 **Nantucket Sound**, Massachusetts, U.S.A.
214 E 5 **Nanumanga**, Tuvalu
214 E 5 **Nanumea**, Tuvalu
208 E 6 **Nanutarra Roadhouse**, Western Australia, Australia
171 U 13 **Nanxiong**, China
171 T 9 **Nanyang**, China
176 K 13 **Nanyo**, Japan
195 V 7 **Nanyuki**, Kenya
168 C 8 **Naoshera**, India
117 D 17 **Napa**, California, U.S.A.
113 T 5 **Napaktulik Lake**, Nunavut, Canada
210 N 13 **Napier**, New Zealand
219 W 3 **Napier Mountains**, Antarctica
91 J 16 **Naples**, Italy
116 I 6 **Naples**, Idaho, U.S.A.
123 R 13 **Naples**, Florida, U.S.A.
140 B 8 **Napo**, Ecuador
140 D 9 **Napo**, Ecuador/Peru
120 L 10 **Napoleon**, Ohio, U.S.A.
215 W 8 **Napuka**, French Polynesia
163 Q 13 **Naqūb**, Yemen
177 H 18 **Nara**, Japan
192 J 8 **Nara**, Mali
119 G 17 **Nara Visa**, New Mexico, U.S.A.
99 I 15 **Narach**, Belarus
209 Q 13 **Naracoorte**, South Australia, Australia
169 G 17 **Narainpur**, India
171 T 5 **Naran Bulag**, China
140 B 10 **Naranjal**, Ecuador
140 D 11 **Naranjal**, Peru
125 S 10 **Naranjos**, Mexico
177 A 22 **Narao**, Japan
169 I 18 **Narasannapeta**, India
173 I 26 **Narathiwat**, Thailand
79 R 15 **Narbonne**, France
169 O 20 **Narcondam Island**, India
62 D 10 **Nares Abyssal Plain**, Atlantic Ocean
62 F 10 **Nares Deep**, Atlantic Ocean
65 O 9 **Nares Strait**, Arctic Ocean
92 L 11 **Narew**, Poland
169 D 19 **Nargund**, India
196 J 10 **Narib**, Namibia
165 U 6 **Narin**, Afghanistan
138 F 9 **Nariño**, Colombia
177 L 16 **Narita**, Japan
169 D 15 **Narmada**, India
213 Y 12 **Naro**, Fiji
195 U 8 **Narok**, Kenya
209 U 13 **Narooma**, New South Wales, Australia
209 U 10 **Narrabri**, New South Wales, Australia
209 T 12 **Narrandera**, New South Wales, Australia
208 G 11 **Narrogin**, Western Australia, Australia
209 T 11 **Narromine**, New South Wales, Australia
64 M 13 **Narsarsuaq**, Greenland
169 L 14 **Narsingdi**, Bangladesh
171 U 5 **Nart**, China
177 F 19 **Naruto**, Japan
98 J 5 **Narva**, Estonia
98 J 5 **Narva Bay**, Estonia
84 H 9 **Narvik**, Norway
156 K 7 **Nar'yan-Mar**, Russian Federation
167 T 11 **Naryn**, Kyrgyzstan
167 V 11 **Naryn**, Kyrgyzstan
167 V 11 **Narynskaya Oblast'**, Kyrgyzstan
213 Y 11 **Nasau**, Fiji
116 D 8 **Naselle**, Washington, U.S.A.
169 C 16 **Nashik**, India
121 W 8 **Nashua**, New Hampshire, U.S.A.
120 H 13 **Nashville**, Illinois, U.S.A.
122 L 1 **Nashville**, Tennessee, U.S.A.
62 F 10 **Nashville Seamount**, Atlantic Ocean
94 H 8 **Našice**, Croatia
191 F 20 **Nasir**, Sudan
115 U 8 **Naskaupi**, Newfoundland and Labrador, Canada
168 I 13 **Nasmganj**, India
91 K 21 **Naso**, Italy
195 N 14 **Nasondoye**, Democratic Republic of Congo
193 R 12 **Nassarawa**, Nigeria
126 M 3 **Nassau**, The Bahamas
214 M 7 **Nassau**, Cook Islands
85 F 23 **Nässjö**, Sweden
115 Q 7 **Nastapoca**, Québec, Canada
115 P 7 **Nastapoka Islands**, Ontario, Canada
177 K 14 **Nasu-dake**, Japan
197 N 8 **Nata**, Botswana
138 H 7 **Natagaima**, Colombia
142 O 12 **Natal**, Brazil
174 C 10 **Natal**, Indonesia
58 I 9 **Natal Basin**, Indian Ocean
58 H 9 **Natal Valley**, Indian Ocean
164 I 7 **Naţanz**, Iran
115 V 10 **Natashquan**, Québec, Canada
122 G 7 **Natchez**, Mississippi, U.S.A.
119 M 20 **Natchitoches**, Louisiana, U.S.A.
212 D 7 **National Capital District**, Papua New Guinea
193 N 11 **Natitingou**, Benin
176 K 12 **Natori**, Japan
169 E 23 **Nattam**, India
173 E 14 **Nattaung**, Myanmar
174 H 9 **Natuna Besar**, Indonesia
59 S 9 **Naturaliste Fracture Zone**, Indian Ocean
59 T 9 **Naturaliste Plateau**, Indian Ocean
196 I 10 **Nauchas**, Namibia
88 K 8 **Nauders**, Austria
86 L 13 **Nauen**, Germany
168 C 11 **Naukh**, India
215 U 1 **Nauru**, Oceania
140 E 11 **Nauta**, Peru
125 T 11 **Nautla**, Mexico
165 R 9 **Nauzad**, Afghanistan
81 N 8 **Navahermosa**, Spain
99 H 18 **Navahrudak**, Belarus
175 Q 5 **Naval**, Philippines
80 L 7 **Navalmoral de la Mata**, Spain
99 K 14 **Navapolatsk**, Belarus
81 R 2 **Navarra**, Spain
127 N 7 **Navassa Island**, U.S.A.
99 G 18 **Navavel'nya**, Belarus
144 F 12 **Navidad**, Chile
169 A 14 **Navlakhi**, India
167 P 12 **Navoi**, Uzbekistan
124 J 6 **Navojoa**, Mexico
169 C 16 **Navsari**, India
213 W 12 **Navua**, Fiji
160 H 8 **Nawá**, Syria
165 U 13 **Nawabshah**, Pakistan
168 J 13 **Nawada**, India
165 T 9 **Nāwah**, Afghanistan
168 D 11 **Nawalgarh**, India
169 H 16 **Nawapara**, India
172 F 10 **Nawngleng**, Myanmar
167 O 10 **Nawoiy Wiloyati**, Uzbekistan
159 V 10 **Naxçivan**, Azerbaijan
97 J 22 **Naxos**, Greece
97 J 22 **Naxos**, Greece
138 G 7 **Naya**, Colombia
165 T 7 **Nayak**, Afghanistan
125 N 10 **Nayar**, Mexico
124 M 10 **Nayarit**, Mexico
176 K 4 **Nayoro**, Japan
169 F 20 **Nayudupeta**, India
160 G 8 **Nazareth**, Israel
58 L 6 **Nazareth Bank**, Indian Ocean
141 E 18 **Nazca**, Peru
177 O 22 **Naze**, Japan
158 C 11 **Nazilli**, Turkey
191 I 20 **Nazrēt**, Ethiopia
163 Y 7 **Nazwá**, Oman
197 O 2 **Nchelenge**, Zambia
196 K 9 **Ncojane**, Botswana
193 T 15 **Ncue**, Equatorial Guinea
196 G 3 **N'dalatando**, Angola
193 O 11 **Ndali**, Benin
194 K 3 **Ndélé**, Central African Republic
193 V 14 **Ndélélé**, Cameroon
194 E 9 **Ndendé**, Gabon
213 P 7 **Ndeni**, Solomon Islands
193 V 10 **Ndjamena**, Chad
194 E 8 **Ndjolé**, Gabon
194 G 8 **Ndjounou**, Gabon
197 O 4 **Ndola**, Zambia
195 Q 6 **Nduye**, Democratic Republic of Congo
97 F 17 **Nea Anchialos**, Greece
97 F 15 **Nea Moudania**, Greece
96 G 13 **Nea Zichni**, Greece
116 C 6 **Neah Bay**, Washington, U.S.A.
97 F 23 **Neapoli**, Greece
97 K 26 **Neapoli**, Greece
77 H 21 **Neath**, United Kingdom
195 R 6 **Nebbi**, Uganda
192 M 10 **Nebbou**, Burkina Faso
166 I 12 **Nebitdag**, Turkmenistan
118 G 12 **Nebraska**, U.S.A.
118 K 13 **Nebraska City**, Nebraska, U.S.A.
87 F 21 **Neckar**, Germany
145 L 15 **Necochea**, Argentina
193 X 8 **Nédéley**, Chad
83 K 17 **Nederweert**, Netherlands
101 T 3 **Nedryhayliv**, Ukraine
117 K 22 **Needles**, California, U.S.A.
114 H 10 **Neepawa**, Manitoba, Canada
159 Z 9 **Neftçala**, Azerbaijan
156 H 10 **Neftekamsk**, Russian Federation
156 L 10 **Nefteyugansk**, Russian Federation
196 G 2 **Negage**, Angola
174 L 15 **Negara**, Indonesia
191 I 21 **Negēlē**, Ethiopia
191 I 22 **Negēlē**, Ethiopia
174 E 9 **Negeri Sembilan**, Malaysia
160 E 12 **Negev**, Israel
195 W 15 **Negomane**, Tanzania
169 F 25 **Negombo**, Sri Lanka
94 O 11 **Negotin**, Serbia and Montenegro
100 I 12 **Negreni**, Romania
140 A 11 **Negritos**, Peru
142 E 9 **Negro**, South America
175 P 6 **Negros**, Philippines
101 N 14 **Negru Vodă**, Romania
165 O 9 **Nehbandān**, Iran
171 W 2 **Nehe**, China
100 K 11 **Nehoiu**, Romania
196 H 6 **Nehone**, Angola
214 J 10 **Neiafu**, Tonga
127 Q 7 **Neiba**, Dominican Republic
171 Q 11 **Neijiang**, China
169 N 22 **Neill Island**, India
138 H 8 **Neiva**, Colombia
125 T 14 **Nejapa Tequisistlán**, Mexico
191 H 20 **Nek'emtē**, Ethiopia
169 G 20 **Nellore**, India
211 I 16 **Nelson**, New Zealand
113 U 14 **Nelson**, British Columbia, Canada
211 I 16 **Nelson**, New Zealand
209 V 11 **Nelson Bay**, New South Wales, Australia
197 P 10 **Nelspruit**, Republic of South Africa
192 J 7 **Néma**, Mauritania
99 D 15 **Neman**, Lithuania
99 C 15 **Neman**, Russian Federation
193 Q 14 **Nembe**, Nigeria
97 E 20 **Nemea**, Greece
99 G 15 **Nemenčinė**, Lithuania
176 N 4 **Nemuro**, Japan
176 N 4 **Nemuro-hantō**, Japan
176 M 3 **Nemuro-kaikyō**, Japan
176 N 4 **Nemuro-wan**, Japan
101 N 6 **Nemyriv**, Ukraine
215 W 10 **Nengonengo**, French Polynesia
171 W 2 **Nenjiang**, China
177 H 17 **Neo**, Japan
97 L 20 **Neo Karlovasi**, Greece
168 H 11 **Nepal**, Asia
168 H 11 **Nepalganj**, Nepal
117 M 16 **Nephi**, Utah, U.S.A.
93 B 18 **Nepomuk**, Czech Republic
157 S 14 **Nerchinsk**, Russian Federation
98 G 12 **Nereta**, Latvia
95 G 14 **Neretva**, Bosnia and Herzegovina
196 K 6 **Neriquinha**, Angola
99 F 15 **Neris**, Lithuania
81 N 13 **Nerja**, Spain
157 T 12 **Neryungri**, Russian Federation
82 K 5 **Nes**, Netherlands
96 N 9 **Nesebŭr**, Bulgaria
119 I 15 **Ness City**, Kansas, U.S.A.
99 D 15 **Nesterov**, Russian Federation
114 J 11 **Nestor Falls**, Ontario, Canada
96 H 12 **Nestos**, Greece
160 F 8 **Netanya**, Israel
82 H 10 **Netherlands**, Europe

Country · Internal administrative region: State/Province/Territory/Dependent territory · Capital city · Mountain range/Undersea ridge · Mountain peak/Volcano/Seamount · Geographic feature · Headland/Point/Cape/Peninsula · Desert · Island/Island group · Antarctic base · Ocean · Sea · Bay/Gulf/Channel/Strait · Lake · Salt pan/Dry/Intermittent lake · River

127 S 11 **Netherlands Antilles**, Netherlands ▣
115 Q 2 **Nettilling Lake**, Nunavut, Canada ∽
87 J 23 **Neuberg**, Germany
86 M 10 **Neubrandenburg**, Germany
86 J 9 **Neubukow**, Germany
88 C 7 **Neuchâtel**, Switzerland
86 M 13 **Neuenhagen**, Germany
79 U 5 **Neufchâteau**, France
83 J 24 **Neufchâteau**, Belgium
79 O 2 **Neufchâtel-en-Bray**, France
89 S 3 **Neufelden**, Austria
89 W 4 **Neulengbach**, Austria
87 J 21 **Neumarkt**, Germany
219 O 1 **Neumayer**, Antarctica ⁙
86 H 9 **Neumünster**, Germany
79 P 6 **Neung-sur-Beuvron**, France
87 C 21 **Neunkirchen**, Germany
89 W 5 **Neunkirchen**, Austria
145 G 15 **Neuquén**, Argentina ▣
145 G 14 **Neuquén**, Argentina ∿
145 H 15 **Neuquén**, Argentina
86 L 12 **Neuruppin**, Germany
89 Y 5 **Neusiedler See**, Austria ∽
87 C 16 **Neuss**, Germany
86 G 13 **Neustadt**, Germany
86 I 9 **Neustadt**, Germany
87 E 21 **Neustadt**, Germany
87 J 17 **Neustadt**, Germany
87 K 22 **Neustadt**, Germany
87 I 20 **Neustadt an der Aisch**, Germany
86 L 11 **Neustrelitz**, Germany
86 F 9 **Neuwerk**, Germany 🏝
87 D 18 **Neuwied**, Germany
117 G 17 **Nevada**, U.S.A. ▣
119 L 15 **Nevada**, Missouri, U.S.A.
125 N 12 **Nevada de Colima**, Mexico ▲
141 F 19 **Nevado Ampato**, Peru ▲
144 G 13 **Nevado Campanario**, Argentina ▲
141 F 18 **Nevado Coropuna**, Peru ▲
144 H 5 **Nevado de Chañi**, Argentina ▲
144 H 5 **Nevado de Poquis**, Chile ▲
125 Q 12 **Nevado de Tolúca**, Mexico ▲
138 H 8 **Nevado del Huila**, Colombia ▲
138 I 6 **Nevado del Ruiz**, Colombia ▲
141 C 14 **Nevado Huascarán**, Peru ▲
141 I 19 **Nevado Illampu**, Bolivia ▲
144 H 8 **Nevado Ojos del Salado**, Argentina ▲
141 I 20 **Nevado Sajama**, Bolivia ▲
144 H 6 **Nevados de Cachi**, Argentina ▲
79 R 8 **Nevers**, France
156 D 11 **Nevinnomyssk**, Russian Federation
127 W 8 **Nevis**, St Kitts and Nevis 🏝
158 J 11 **Nevşehir**, Turkey
120 K 13 **New Albany**, Indiana, U.S.A.
122 J 3 **New Albany**, Mississippi, U.S.A.
139 V 5 **New Amsterdam**, Guyana
121 X 9 **New Bedford**, Massachusetts, U.S.A.
123 W 2 **New Bern**, North Carolina, U.S.A.
119 L 18 **New Boston**, Texas, U.S.A.
212 F 4 **New Britain**, Papua New Guinea 🏝
115 U 12 **New Brunswick**, Canada ▣
213 N 14 **New Caledonia**, New Caledonia 🏝
213 O 15 **New Caledonia**, France ▣
61 N 10 **New Caledonia Trough**, Pacific Ocean ◇
120 L 13 **New Castle**, Kentucky, U.S.A.
121 P 10 **New Castle**, Pennsylvania, U.S.A.
168 E 11 **New Delhi**, India ⌂
123 R 5 **New Ellenton**, South Carolina, U.S.A.
121 W 9 **New England**, Massachusetts, U.S.A. ◇
62 E 8 **New England Seamounts**, Atlantic Ocean ⛰
212 K 6 **New Georgia**, Solomon Islands 🏝
212 J 6 **New Georgia Islands**, Solomon Islands 🏝
212 K 5 **New Georgia Sound**, Solomon Islands ≈
115 W 12 **New Glasgow**, Nova Scotia, Canada
59 X 5 **New Guinea**, Indian Ocean 🏝
121 W 7 **New Hampshire**, U.S.A. ▣
212 G 2 **New Hanover**, Papua New Guinea 🏝
121 V 9 **New Haven**, Connecticut, U.S.A.
113 Q 11 **New Hazelton**, British Columbia, Canada
61 O 10 **New Hebrides Trench**, Pacific Ocean ◇
119 N 21 **New Iberia**, Louisiana, U.S.A.
212 G 3 **New Ireland**, Papua New Guinea 🏝
212 H 2 **New Ireland**, Papua New Guinea ▣
121 U 11 **New Jersey**, U.S.A. ▣
115 O 12 **New Liskeard**, Ontario, Canada
120 I 6 **New London**, Wisconsin, U.S.A.
121 W 9 **New London**, Connecticut, U.S.A.
116 I 10 **New Meadows**, Idaho, U.S.A.
119 D 18 **New Mexico**, U.S.A. ▣
209 S 15 **New Norfolk**, Tasmania, Australia
119 O 21 **New Orleans**, Louisiana, U.S.A.
116 F 13 **New Pine Creek**, California, U.S.A.
210 J 12 **New Plymouth**, New Zealand
126 M 2 **New Providence**, The Bahamas 🏝
115 U 11 **New Richmond**, Québec, Canada
121 V 10 **New Rochelle**, New York, U.S.A.
77 E 20 **New Ross**, Republic of Ireland
157 T 6 **New Siberia Islands**, Russian Federation 🏝
123 S 10 **New Smyrna Beach**, Florida, U.S.A.
209 T 10 **New South Wales**, Australia ▣
118 L 10 **New Ulm**, Minnesota, U.S.A.
121 S 8 **New York**, U.S.A. ▣
121 U 10 **New York**, New York, U.S.A.
211 I 14 **New Zealand**, Oceania □
195 W 14 **Newala**, Tanzania
121 T 11 **Newark**, Delaware, U.S.A.
121 U 10 **Newark**, New Jersey, U.S.A.
121 R 8 **Newark**, New York, U.S.A.
121 N 11 **Newark**, Ohio, U.S.A.
123 R 4 **Newberry**, South Carolina, U.S.A.
121 U 9 **Newburgh**, New York, U.S.A.
77 K 22 **Newbury**, United Kingdom
77 F 16 **Newcastle**, United Kingdom
115 U 12 **Newcastle**, New Brunswick, Canada
118 F 11 **Newcastle**, Wyoming, U.S.A.
209 V 11 **Newcastle**, New South Wales, Australia
77 J 15 **Newcastle upon Tyne**, United Kingdom
115 X 10 **Newfoundland**, Newfoundland and Labrador, Canada 🏝
115 V 9 **Newfoundland and Labrador**, Canada ▣
62 F 8 **Newfoundland Ridge**, Atlantic Ocean ⛰
62 G 8 **Newfoundland Seamounts**, Atlantic Ocean ⛰
120 I 11 **Newman**, Illinois, U.S.A.
208 H 7 **Newman**, Western Australia, Australia
123 N 5 **Newnan**, Georgia, U.S.A.
77 I 21 **Newport**, United Kingdom
77 K 23 **Newport**, United Kingdom
116 I 6 **Newport**, Washington, U.S.A.
121 W 7 **Newport**, New Hampshire, U.S.A.
121 X 9 **Newport**, Rhode Island, U.S.A.
121 V 5 **Newport**, Vermont, U.S.A.
123 P 2 **Newport**, Tennessee, U.S.A.
121 S 14 **Newport News**, Virginia, U.S.A.
77 F 16 **Newry**, United Kingdom
119 J 15 **Newton**, Kansas, U.S.A.
122 J 6 **Newton**, Mississippi, U.S.A.
77 G 15 **Newton Stewart**, United Kingdom
77 I 19 **Newtown**, United Kingdom
164 J 8 **Neyestānak**, Iran
165 N 6 **Neyshābūr**, Iran
169 E 24 **Neyyattinkara**, India
174 I 10 **Ngabang**, Indonesia
194 H 10 **Ngabé**, Congo
172 E 7 **Ngagahtawng**, Myanmar
214 J 14 **Ngajangel**, Palau 🏝
193 V 10 **Ngala**, Nigeria
193 W 11 **Ngam**, Chad
193 W 10 **Ngama**, Chad
196 L 8 **Ngamiland**, Botswana ▣
191 E 23 **Ngangala**, Sudan
170 I 8 **Nganglong Kangri**, China ▲
173 H 14 **Ngao**, Thailand
193 U 13 **Ngaoundal**, Cameroon
193 U 12 **Ngaoundéré**, Cameroon
195 R 9 **Ngara**, Tanzania
194 H 6 **Ngbala**, Congo
215 P 15 **Ngetik Atoll**, Federated States of Micronesia 🏝
212 L 6 **Nggatokae**, Solomon Islands 🏝
194 H 9 **Ngo**, Congo
173 O 18 **Ngoc Linh**, Vietnam ▲
193 U 12 **Ngong**, Cameroon
194 I 5 **Ngoto**, Central African Republic
194 E 9 **Ngounié**, Gabon ▣
193 W 9 **Ngoura**, Chad
193 U 8 **Ngourti**, Niger
195 N 4 **Ngouyo**, Central African Republic
194 H 5 **Nguia Bouar**, Central African Republic
193 U 9 **Nguigmi**, Niger
208 L 1 **Nguiu**, Northern Territory, Australia
209 O 2 **Ngukurr**, Northern Territory, Australia
214 J 14 **Ngulu**, Federated States of Micronesia 🏝
197 P 8 **Ngundu**, Zimbabwe
193 S 9 **Nguru**, Nigeria
172 M 11 **Nguyên**, Vietnam
173 O 20 **Nha Trang**, Vietnam
197 R 7 **Nhamatanda**, Mozambique
142 G 10 **Nhamundá**, Brazil
196 I 4 **N'harea**, Angola
209 R 12 **Nhill**, Victoria, Australia
209 O 1 **Nhulunbuy**, Northern Territory, Australia
195 P 7 **Nia-Nia**, Democratic Republic of Congo
115 P 15 **Niagara Falls**, Ontario, Canada
121 Q 8 **Niagara Falls**, New York, U.S.A.
174 K 9 **Niah**, Malaysia
168 I 11 **Niak**, Nepal
193 P 9 **Niamey**, Niger ⌂
195 P 5 **Niangara**, Democratic Republic of Congo
192 K 11 **Niangoloko**, Burkina Faso
194 F 9 **Niari**, Congo ▣
174 B 10 **Nias**, Indonesia 🏝
197 S 4 **Niassa**, Mozambique ▣
215 U 9 **Niau**, French Polynesia 🏝
215 U 1 **Nibok**, Nauru
126 G 11 **Nicaragua**, North America □
62 C 11 **Nicaraguan Rise**, Atlantic Ocean ⛰
91 M 19 **Nicastro**, Italy
79 X 13 **Nice**, France
122 L 8 **Niceville**, Florida, U.S.A.
177 D 23 **Nichinan**, Japan
123 T 4 **Nichols**, South Carolina, U.S.A.
169 N 24 **Nicobar Islands**, India 🏝
158 H 15 **Nicosia**, Cyprus ⌂
91 J 22 **Nicosia**, Italy
93 K 16 **Nida**, Poland ∿
99 B 14 **Nida**, Lithuania
96 D 13 **Nidže Kožuf**, Macedonia (F.Y.R.O.M.) ⛰
92 K 10 **Nidzica**, Poland
86 F 7 **Niebüll**, Germany
83 M 25 **Niederanven**, Luxembourg
89 U 3 **Niederösterreich**, Austria ▣
86 F 12 **Niedersachsen**, Germany ▣
93 M 15 **Niedrzwica**, Poland
194 H 4 **Niem**, Central African Republic
86 G 13 **Nienburg**, Germany
87 O 16 **Niesky**, Germany
82 K 11 **Nieuw-Milligen**, Netherlands
139 V 6 **Nieuw Nickerie**, Suriname
82 I 13 **Nieuwegein**, Netherlands
83 E 15 **Nieuwerkerk**, Netherlands
82 G 13 **Nieuwerkerk aan den IJssel**, Netherlands
82 N 6 **Nieuwolda**, Netherlands
83 A 17 **Nieuwpoort**, Belgium
158 J 12 **Niğde**, Turkey
193 R 8 **Niger**, Africa □
193 Q 11 **Niger**, Nigeria ▣
193 Q 12 **Niger**, Africa ∿
62 M 13 **Niger Cone**, Atlantic Ocean ◇
193 R 11 **Nigeria**, Africa □
63 O 17 **Nightingale Island**, Tristan da Cunha 🏝
215 V 9 **Nihiru**, French Polynesia 🏝
176 K 13 **Nihonmatsu**, Japan
177 K 18 **Nii-jima**, Japan 🏝
176 J 13 **Niigata**, Japan
177 I 15 **Niigata-yake-yama**, Japan ▲
177 E 20 **Niihama**, Japan
117 A 24 **Niihau**, Hawaii, U.S.A. 🏝
177 E 18 **Niimi**, Japan
176 J 13 **Niitsu**, Japan
81 Q 13 **Níjar**, Spain
82 J 12 **Nijkerk**, Netherlands
83 K 14 **Nijmegen**, Netherlands
82 M 11 **Nijverdal**, Netherlands
97 E 16 **Nikaia**, Greece
156 I 5 **Nikel'**, Russian Federation
84 I 9 **Nikkaluokta**, Sweden
193 O 11 **Nikki**, Benin
177 K 14 **Nikkō**, Japan
157 W 12 **Nikolayevsk-na-Amure**, Russian Federation
96 I 7 **Nikopol**, Bulgaria
101 U 8 **Nikopol'**, Ukraine
158 M 8 **Niksar**, Turkey
165 O 13 **Nīkshahr**, Iran
95 I 15 **Nikšić**, Serbia and Montenegro
214 I 4 **Nikumaroro**, Kiribati 🏝
214 E 3 **Nikunau**, Kiribati 🏝
175 T 14 **Nila**, Indonesia 🏝
169 L 18 **Nilandhoo Atoll**, Maldives 🏝
191 F 16 **Nile**, Sudan ▣
190 E 10 **Nile**, Egypt/Sudan ∿
190 E 7 **Nile Delta**, Egypt ◇
120 K 9 **Niles**, Michigan, U.S.A.
125 U 14 **Niltepec**, Mexico
192 I 12 **Nimba Mountains**, Côte d'Ivoire/Guinea ▲
79 S 13 **Nîmes**, France
165 Q 10 **Nīmrūz**, Afghanistan ▣
191 E 23 **Nimule**, Sudan
196 K 5 **Ninda**, Angola
169 A 23 **Nine Degree Channel**, India ≈
59 Q 8 **Ninetyeast Ridge**, Indian Ocean ⛰
171 Y 4 **Ning'an**, China
171 W 10 **Ningbo**, China
171 U 12 **Ningdu**, China
171 W 10 **Ninghai**, China
171 R 14 **Ningming**, China
171 Q 8 **Ningxia**, China ▣
172 M 13 **Ninh Binh**, Vietnam
173 O 20 **Ninh Hoa**, Vietnam
212 C 2 **Ninigo Group**, Papua New Guinea 🏝
176 K 9 **Ninohe**, Japan
192 J 9 **Niono**, Mali
192 H 8 **Nioro**, Mali
78 M 9 **Niort**, France
113 Y 11 **Nipawin**, Saskatchewan, Canada
114 L 11 **Nipigon**, Ontario, Canada
169 F 17 **Nirmal**, India
94 N 13 **Niš**, Serbia and Montenegro
161 U 14 **Nişāb**, Iraq
163 Q 13 **Nişab**, Yemen
177 C 25 **Nishino-omote**, Japan
177 F 18 **Nishiwaki**, Japan
177 C 22 **Nisi-mera**, Japan
93 M 16 **Nisko**, Poland
85 E 24 **Nissan**, Sweden ∿
212 I 4 **Nissan Island**, Papua New Guinea 🏝
85 B 20 **Nisser**, Norway ∽
97 M 23 **Nisyros**, Greece 🏝
177 E 18 **Nita**, Japan
93 H 21 **Nitra**, Slovakia
214 I 9 **Niua Group**, Tonga 🏝
214 I 9 **Niuafo'ou**, Tonga 🏝
214 I 9 **Niuatoputapu**, Tonga 🏝
214 K 10 **Niue**, Niue 🏝
214 K 10 **Niue**, New Zealand ▣
214 G 7 **Niulakita**, Tuvalu 🏝
214 F 5 **Niutao**, Tuvalu 🏝
83 F 20 **Nivelles**, Belgium
169 E 17 **Nizam Sagar**, India ∽
169 F 17 **Nizamabad**, India
157 O 13 **Nizhneudinsk**, Russian Federation
156 L 10 **Nizhnevartovsk**, Russian Federation
157 T 7 **Nizhneyyansk**, Russian Federation
156 H 8 **Nizhniy Novgorod**, Russian Federation
156 J 10 **Nizhniy Tagil**, Russian Federation
157 N 9 **Nizhnyaya Tunguska**, Russian Federation ∿
101 R 2 **Nizhyn**, Ukraine
158 M 13 **Nizip**, Turkey
95 I 14 **Njegoš**, Serbia and Montenegro ▲
197 P 12 **Njesuthi**, Lesotho ▲
195 W 13 **Njinjo**, Tanzania
195 T 13 **Njombe**, Tanzania
195 R 12 **Nkasi**, Tanzania
197 O 7 **Nkayi**, Zimbabwe
197 R 3 **Nkhata Bay**, Malawi
197 R 4 **Nkhotakota**, Malawi
195 R 11 **Nkondwe**, Tanzania
193 S 14 **Nkongsamba**, Cameroon
196 J 7 **Nkurenkuru**, Namibia
172 F 8 **Nmai Hka**, Myanmar ∿
169 J 15 **Noamundi**, India
177 D 22 **Nobeoka**, Japan
176 J 7 **Noboribetsu**, Japan
143 G 15 **Nobres**, Brazil
209 R 8 **Noccundra**, Queensland, Australia
125 S 13 **Nochixtlán**, Mexico
91 N 16 **Noci**, Italy
177 K 15 **Noda**, Japan
117 N 26 **Nogales**, Arizona, U.S.A.
124 I 3 **Nogales**, Mexico
79 O 5 **Nogent-le-Rotrou**, France
157 O 10 **Noginsk**, Russian Federation
87 C 20 **Nohfelden**, Germany
80 H 2 **Noia**, Spain
78 K 7 **Noirmoutier-en-l'Île**, France
177 L 17 **Nojima-zaki**, Japan ▶
165 Q 12 **Nok Kundi**, Pakistan
168 C 11 **Nokha**, India
85 L 18 **Nokia**, Finland
193 V 9 **Nokou**, Chad
91 J 16 **Nola**, Italy
194 H 5 **Nola**, Central African Republic
177 B 24 **Noma-misaki**, Japan ▶
112 H 4 **Nome**, Alaska, U.S.A.
177 B 22 **Nomo-zaki**, Japan ▶
214 I 10 **Nomuka Group**, Tonga 🏝
215 O 14 **Nomwin**, Federated States of Micronesia 🏝
173 I 16 **Nong Bua Lamphu**, Thailand
173 J 15 **Nong Khai**, Thailand
171 W 4 **Nong'an**, China
214 E 3 **Nonouti**, Kiribati 🏝
173 H 19 **Nonthaburi**, Thailand
79 N 10 **Nontron**, France
82 G 8 **Nooderhaaks**, Netherlands 🏝
83 I 15 **Noord-Brabant**, Netherlands ▣
82 H 9 **Noord-Holland**, Netherlands ▣
112 I 3 **Noorvik**, Alaska, U.S.A.
209 W 8 **Noosa Heads**, Queensland, Australia
167 R 13 **Norak**, Tajikistan
193 U 12 **Nord**, Cameroon ▣
84 I 6 **Nord-Kvaløy**, Norway 🏝
193 T 13 **Nord-Ouest**, Cameroon ▣
79 Q 1 **Nord-pas-de-Calais**, France ▣
65 U 11 **Nordaustlandet**, Svalbard 🏝
86 D 10 **Norden**, Germany
86 C 10 **Norderney**, Germany 🏝
86 F 8 **Norderoogsand**, Germany 🏝
85 B 17 **Nordfjordeid**, Norway
84 G 10 **Nordfold**, Norway
86 E 8 **Nordfriesische Inseln**, Germany ◇
87 I 15 **Nordhausen**, Germany
86 C 13 **Nordhorn**, Germany
84 K 5 **Nordkapp**, Norway ▶
195 P 8 **Nordkivu**, Democratic Republic of Congo ▣
85 F 14 **Nordli**, Norway
87 I 22 **Nördlingen**, Germany
85 I 15 **Nordmaling**, Sweden
85 B 15 **Nordmøre**, Norway 🏝
85 B 16 **Nordøyane**, Norway 🏝
87 E 15 **Nordrhein-Westfalen**, Germany ▣
86 F 8 **Nordstrand**, Germany 🏝
157 R 7 **Nordvik**, Russian Federation
85 C 19 **Noresund**, Norway
118 J 12 **Norfolk**, Nebraska, U.S.A.
121 T 14 **Norfolk**, Virginia, U.S.A.
61 O 10 **Norfolk Island**, Australia 🏝
112 F 4 **Norhtwest Cape**, Alaska, U.S.A. ▶
157 O 8 **Noril'sk**, Russian Federation
209 R 4 **Norman**, Queensland, Australia ∿
119 K 17 **Norman**, Oklahoma, U.S.A.
113 Q 6 **Norman Wells**, Northwest Territories, Canada
212 G 7 **Normanby Island**, Papua New Guinea 🏝
212 H 7 **Normanby Island**, Papua New Guinea 🏝
78 L 4 **Normandy**, France ▣
209 R 4 **Normanton**, Queensland, Australia
145 G 17 **Ñorquinco**, Argentina
85 F 19 **Norra Ny**, Sweden
84 G 12 **Norra Storfjället**, Sweden ▲
85 G 14 **Norråker**, Sweden
85 C 23 **Nørresundby**, Denmark
85 G 21 **Norrköping**, Sweden
85 I 20 **Norrtälje**, Sweden
208 I 11 **Norseman**, Western Australia, Australia
85 C 20 **Norsjø**, Norway ∽
213 Q 10 **Norsup**, Vanuatu
138 J 4 **Norte de Santander**, Colombia ▣
121 V 8 **North Adams**, Massachusetts, U.S.A.
62 E 10 **North American Basin**, Atlantic Ocean ◇
169 N 20 **North Andaman**, India 🏝
123 Q 5 **North Augusta**, South Carolina, U.S.A.
59 U 6 **North Australian Basin**, Indian Ocean ◇
113 X 11 **North Battleford**, Saskatchewan, Canada
115 P 13 **North Bay**, Ontario, Canada
115 O 7 **North Belcher Islands**, Ontario, Canada 🏝
127 P 5 **North Caicos**, Turks and Caicos Islands 🏝
210 I 4 **North Cape**, New Zealand ▶
123 U 2 **North Carolina**, U.S.A. ▣
169 G 24 **North Central**, Sri Lanka ▣
115 N 13 **North Channel**, Ontario, Canada ≈
77 E 14 **North Channel**, Republic of Ireland/United Kingdom ≈
118 G 8 **North Dakota**, U.S.A. ▣
197 N 8 **North East**, Botswana ▣
121 P 9 **North East**, Pennsylvania, U.S.A.
195 X 6 **North-Eastern**, Kenya ▣
61 O 9 **North Fiji Basin**, Pacific Ocean ◇
77 N 21 **North Foreland**, United Kingdom ▶
116 K 9 **North Fork**, Idaho, U.S.A.
117 J 14 **North Fork**, Nevada, U.S.A.
210 J 7 **North Head**, New Zealand ▶
195 V 6 **North Horr**, Kenya
169 L 20 **North Huvadhu Atoll**, Maldives 🏝
58 A 9 **North Island**, Seychelles 🏝
210 M 11 **North Island**, New Zealand 🏝
169 B 23 **North Island**, India 🏝

□ Country ▣ Internal administrative region: State/Province/Territory/Dependent territory ⌂ Capital city ⛰ Mountain range/Undersea ridge ▲ Mountain peak/Volcano/Seamount ◇ Geographic feature ▶ Headland/Point/Cape/Peninsula ◭ Desert 🏝 Island/Island group ⁙ Antarctic base ◎ Ocean ◑ Sea ≈ Bay/Gulf/Channel/Strait ∽ Lake ⚑ Salt pan/Dry/Intermittent lake ∿ River

5 P 1 **North Island**, Philippines
Q 5 **North Keeling Island**, Cocos Islands
1 Z 6 **North Korea**, Asia
8 N 12 **North Lakhimpur**, India
9 L 17 **North Maalhosmadulu Atoll**, Maldives
9 L 16 **North Miladunmadulu Atoll**, Maldives
8 G 12 **North Platte**, Nebraska, U.S.A.
8 H 13 **North Platte**, Nebraska, U.S.A.
A 9 **North Point**, Seychelles
20 M 6 **North Point**, Michigan, U.S.A.
K 25 **North Point**, Ascension
N 16 **North Point**, Tristan da Cunha
5 S 8 **North Pole**, Arctic Ocean
12 L 6 **North Pole**, Alaska, U.S.A.
59 N 21 **North Reef Island**, India
I 6 **North Ronaldsay**, United Kingdom
13 W 11 **North Saskatchewan**, Alberta, Canada
2 M 6 **North Sea**, Atlantic Ocean
69 N 22 **North Sentinel Island**, India
12 J 4 **North Solomons**, Papua New Guinea
09 W 9 **North Stradbroke Island**, Queensland, Australia
10 J 12 **North Taranaki Bight**, New Zealand
15 O 9 **North Twin Island**, Québec, Canada
6 E 10 **North Uist**, United Kingdom
96 L 11 **North West**, Republic of South Africa
08 E 6 **North West Cape**, Western Australia, Australia
65 W 6 **North West Frontier**, Pakistan
6 G 11 **North West Highlands**, United Kingdom
69 F 24 **North Western**, Sri Lanka
96 M 4 **North-Western**, Zambia
208 G 11 **Northam**, Western Australia, Australia
7 L 20 **Northampton**, United Kingdom
208 E 9 **Northampton**, Western Australia, Australia
12 G 4 **Northeast Cape**, Alaska, U.S.A.
51 R 3 **Northeast Pacific Basin**, Pacific Ocean
37 H 15 **Northeim**, Germany
191 D 14 **Northern**, Sudan
169 G 23 **Northern**, Sri Lanka
192 G 11 **Northern**, Sierra Leone
197 Q 3 **Northern**, Malawi
197 O 10 **Northern**, Republic of South Africa
197 P 3 **Northern**, Zambia
212 F 6 **Northern**, Papua New Guinea
192 M 12 **Northern**, Ghana
191 C 20 **Northern Bahr el Ghazal**, Sudan
196 K 13 **Northern Cape**, Republic of South Africa
214 L 7 **Northern Cook Islands**, Cook Islands
191 B 15 **Northern Darfur**, Sudan
77 E 15 **Northern Ireland**, United Kingdom
191 D 16 **Northern Kordofan**, Sudan
213 Y 11 **Northern Lau Group**, Fiji
214 A 6 **Northern Mariana Islands**, U.S.A.
90 D 8 **Northern Plain**, Italy
209 N 4 **Northern Territory**, Australia
118 L 10 **Northfield**, Minnesota, U.S.A.
210 J 6 **Northland**, New Zealand
115 V 12 **Northumberland Strait**, Prince Edward Island, Canada
121 U 7 **Northville**, New York, U.S.A.
62 E 5 **Northwest Atlantic Mid-Ocean Channel**, Atlantic Ocean
61 N 3 **Northwest Pacific Basin**, Pacific Ocean
113 T 6 **Northwest Territories**, Canada
65 R 4 **Northwind Plain**, Arctic Ocean
65 Q 1 **Norton Sound**, Arctic Ocean
121 N 10 **Norwalk**, Ohio, U.S.A.
85 B 19 **Norway**, Europe
114 J 8 **Norway House**, Manitoba, Canada
65 S 15 **Norwegian Basin**, Arctic Ocean
65 T 14 **Norwegian Sea**, Arctic Ocean
77 N 19 **Norwich**, United Kingdom
121 W 9 **Norwich**, Connecticut, U.S.A.
96 N 9 **Nos Emine**, Bulgaria
96 O 7 **Nos Kaliakra**, Bulgaria
96 O 7 **Nos Shabla**, Bulgaria
176 N 4 **Nosapu-misaki**, Japan
176 I 2 **Noshappu-misaki**, Japan
176 J 10 **Noshiro**, Japan
156 K 7 **Nosovaya**, Russian Federation
165 O 11 **Noşratābād**, Iran
76 I 8 **Noss Head**, United Kingdom
192 I 9 **Nossombougou**, Mali
197 Y 5 **Nosy Bé**, Madgascar
197 Z 7 **Nosy Boraha**, Madgascar
197 Y 8 **Nosy-Varika**, Madgascar
117 L 16 **Notch Peak**, Utah, U.S.A.
92 E 11 **Noteć**, Poland
97 J 23 **Notio Aigaio**, Greece
97 A 16 **Notio Steno Kerkyras**, Greece
97 G 19 **Notios Evvoïkos Kolpos**, Greece
91 K 24 **Noto**, Italy
177 H 15 **Noto-hantō**, Japan
176 M 3 **Notoro-ko**, Japan
115 Y 9 **Notre Dame Bay**, Newfoundland and Labrador, Canada
115 P 10 **Nottaway**, Québec, Canada
77 K 18 **Nottingham**, United Kingdom
115 P 4 **Nottingham Island**, Nunavut, Canada
188 A 14 **Nouâdhibou**, Western Sahara
192 D 5 **Nouâdhibou**, Mauritania
192 E 6 **Nouakchott**, Mauritania
192 E 6 **Nouâmghâr**, Mauritania
173 N 17 **Nouei**, Vietnam
213 Q 14 **Nouméa**, New Caledonia
167 R 12 **Nov**, Tajikistan
143 J 15 **Nova**, Brazil
196 F 2 **Nova Caipemba**, Angola
143 L 18 **Nova Friburgo**, Brazil
94 G 9 **Nova Gradiška**, Croatia
143 L 19 **Nova Iguaçu**, Brazil
197 R 8 **Nova Mambone**, Mozambique
197 T 6 **Nova Nabúri**, Mozambique
101 R 8 **Nova Odesa**, Ukraine
115 V 14 **Nova Scotia**, Canada
61 P 8 **Nova Trough**, Pacific Ocean
94 K 13 **Nova Varoš**, Serbia and Montenegro
96 K 9 **Nova Zagora**, Bulgaria
90 B 7 **Novara**, Italy
117 D 18 **Novato**, California, U.S.A.
156 L 6 **Novaya Zemlya**, Russian Federation
93 H 22 **Nové Zámky**, Slovakia
101 S 1 **Novhorod-Sivers'kyy**, Ukraine
101 S 7 **Novhorodka**, Ukraine
94 K 8 **Novi Bečej**, Serbia and Montenegro
96 G 9 **Novi-Iskŭr**, Bulgaria
90 C 8 **Novi Ligure**, Italy
95 L 14 **Novi Pazar**, Serbia and Montenegro
96 M 7 **Novi Pazar**, Bulgaria
94 K 9 **Novi Sad**, Serbia and Montenegro
142 E 10 **Novo Airão**, Brazil
142 F 11 **Novo Aripuanã**, Brazil
143 I 21 **Novo Hamburgo**, Brazil
94 C 8 **Novo Mesto**, Slovenia
96 F 12 **Novo Selo**, Macedonia (F.Y.R.O.M.)
101 Q 6 **Novoarkhanhel's'k**, Ukraine
101 Y 8 **Novoazovs'k**, Ukraine
167 S 13 **Novobod**, Tajikistan
166 H 6 **Novobogatinskoye**, Kazakhstan
101 V 8 **Novobohdanivka**, Ukraine
156 E 10 **Novocherkassk**, Russian Federation
156 I 7 **Novodvinsk**, Russian Federation
100 M 3 **Novohrad-Volyns'kyy**, Ukraine
156 M 13 **Novokuznetsk**, Russian Federation
219 R 1 **Novolazarevskaya**, Antarctica
101 V 6 **Novomoskovs'k**, Ukraine
156 F 8 **Novomoskovsk**, Russian Federation
101 U 10 **Novoolekisiyivka**, Ukraine
101 U 7 **Novopokrovka**, Ukraine
101 Z 4 **Novopskov**, Ukraine
156 D 10 **Novorossiysk**, Russian Federation
157 Q 7 **Novorybnaya**, Russian Federation
101 T 11 **Novoselivs'ke**, Ukraine
156 M 12 **Novosibirsk**, Russian Federation
101 U 10 **Novotroyits'ke**, Ukraine
101 Q 7 **Novoukrayinka**, Ukraine
99 M 18 **Novy Bykhaw**, Belarus
93 H 18 **Nový Jičín**, Czech Republic
101 S 8 **Novyy Buh**, Ukraine
101 R 3 **Novyy Bykiv**, Ukraine
156 M 8 **Novyy Port**, Russian Federation
156 M 9 **Novyy Urengoy**, Russian Federation
157 V 13 **Novyy Urgal**, Russian Federation
93 I 15 **Nowa**, Poland
93 M 16 **Nowa Dęba**, Poland
93 F 16 **Nowa Ruda**, Poland
92 E 10 **Nowogard**, Poland
209 U 12 **Nowra**, New South Wales, Australia
165 W 6 **Nowshak**, Pakistan
165 W 7 **Nowshera**, Pakistan
92 K 12 **Nowy Dwór Mazowiecki**, Poland
93 L 18 **Nowy Sącz**, Poland
93 K 18 **Nowy Targ**, Poland
156 M 9 **Noyabr'sk**, Russian Federation
79 R 3 **Noyon**, France
78 K 6 **Nozay**, France
194 I 8 **Nsambi**, Democratic Republic of Congo
197 R 6 **Nsanje**, Malawi
193 T 15 **Nsoc**, Equatorial Guinea
197 P 3 **Nsombo**, Zambia
193 Q 13 **Nsukka**, Nigeria
194 I 9 **Ntandembele**, Democratic Republic of Congo
197 R 5 **Ntcheu**, Malawi
194 D 7 **Ntoum**, Gabon
195 R 8 **Ntungamo**, Uganda
196 M 8 **Ntwetwe Pan**, Botswana
191 E 18 **Nuba Mountains**, Sudan
191 G 14 **Nubian Desert**, Sudan
213 Y 10 **Nubu**, Fiji
125 U 13 **Nudo de Zempoaltépetl**, Mexico
114 J 4 **Nueltin Lake**, Nunavut, Canada
126 D 9 **Nueva Arcadia**, Honduras
138 L 3 **Nueva Bolivia**, Venezuela
125 X 12 **Nueva Coahuila**, Mexico
139 P 2 **Nueva Esparta**, Venezuela
144 I 13 **Nueva Galia**, Argentina
126 I 5 **Nueva Gerona**, Cuba
140 C 8 **Nueva Loja**, Ecuador
145 G 19 **Nueva Lubecka**, Argentina
126 D 9 **Nueva Ocotepeque**, Honduras
144 L 6 **Nueva Pompeya**, Argentina
125 P 5 **Nueva Rosita**, Mexico
126 D 10 **Nueva San Salvador**, El Salvador
125 R 8 **Nueva Villa de Padilla**, Mexico
144 L 13 **Nueve de Julio**, Argentina
126 M 5 **Nuevitas**, Cuba
125 Q 6 **Nuevo Laredo**, Mexico
125 R 7 **Nuevo León**, Mexico
191 O 20 **Nugaal**, Somalia
212 J 3 **Nuguria Islands**, Papua New Guinea
210 O 12 **Nuhaka**, New Zealand
214 F 5 **Nui**, Tuvalu
112 L 2 **Nuiqsut**, Alaska, U.S.A.
212 J 5 **Nukiki**, Solomon Islands
212 B 3 **Nuku**, Papua New Guinea
215 W 6 **Nuku Hiva**, French Polynesia
214 I 11 **Nuku'alofa**, Tonga
214 F 6 **Nukufetau**, Tuvalu
214 G 6 **Nukulaelae**, Tuvalu
212 L 4 **Nukumanu Islands**, Papua New Guinea
214 K 6 **Nukunonu**, Tokelau Islands
214 J 6 **Nukunonu**, Tokelau Islands
215 P 15 **Nukuoro**, Federated States of Micronesia
166 M 10 **Nukus**, Uzbekistan
208 H 6 **Nullagine**, Western Australia, Australia
208 M 10 **Nullarbor**, South Australia, Australia
208 L 10 **Nullarbor Plain**, Western Australia, Australia
175 V 11 **Num**, Indonesia
193 U 11 **Numan**, Nigeria
83 G 14 **Numansdorp**, Netherlands
177 J 15 **Numata**, Japan
177 K 17 **Numazu**, Japan
209 O 2 **Numbulwar**, Northern Territory, Australia
114 J 2 **Nunavut**, Canada
171 V 4 **Nungnain Sum**, China
112 F 6 **Nunivak Island**, Alaska, U.S.A.
157 Z 6 **Nunligran**, Russian Federation
82 K 11 **Nunspeet**, Netherlands
91 C 17 **Nuoro**, Italy
213 P 7 **Nupani**, Solomon Islands
163 N 5 **Nuqrah**, Saudi Arabia
138 G 6 **Nuquí**, Colombia
167 N 6 **Nura**, Kazakhstan
164 I 10 **Nūrābād**, Iran
167 P 12 **Nurata**, Uzbekistan
87 I 21 **Nuremberg**, Germany
124 J 5 **Nuri**, Mexico
85 N 14 **Nurmes**, Finland
165 W 9 **Nurpur**, Pakistan
168 E 8 **Nurpur**, India
174 M 14 **Nusa Tenggara Barat**, Indonesia
175 O 15 **Nusa Tenggara Timur**, Indonesia
159 Q 13 **Nusaybin**, Turkey
165 S 11 **Nushki**, Pakistan
65 O 11 **Nuugaatsiaq**, Greenland
64 M 12 **Nuuk**, Greenland
65 N 11 **Nuussuaq**, Greenland
65 O 10 **Nuussuaq**, Greenland
156 K 9 **Nyagan'**, Russian Federation
195 U 7 **Nyahururu**, Kenya
170 K 10 **Nyainqêntanglha**, China
170 L 10 **Nyainqêntanglha Shan**, China
195 S 9 **Nyakaliro**, Tanzania
191 A 18 **Nyala**, Sudan
197 O 8 **Nyamandhiovu**, Zimbabwe
191 C 20 **Nyamlell**, Sudan
194 E 10 **Nyanga**, Gabon
194 F 9 **Nyanga**, Congo
195 T 8 **Nyanza**, Kenya
99 I 19 **Nyasvizh**, Belarus
197 O 7 **Nyathi**, Zimbabwe
173 E 15 **Nyaunglebin**, Myanmar
85 E 18 **Nybergsund**, Norway
85 C 25 **Nyborg**, Denmark
85 G 24 **Nybro**, Sweden
195 V 8 **Nyeri**, Kenya
191 E 20 **Nyerol**, Sudan
170 M 11 **Nyingchi**, China
93 N 22 **Nyírbátor**, Hungary
93 M 22 **Nyíregyháza**, Hungary
85 D 26 **Nykøbing**, Denmark
85 H 21 **Nyköping**, Sweden
85 H 21 **Nynäshamn**, Sweden
209 T 10 **Nyngan**, New South Wales, Australia
99 G 18 **Nyoman**, Belarus
88 A 9 **Nyon**, Switzerland
79 U 12 **Nyons**, France
156 J 9 **Nyrob**, Russian Federation
93 G 16 **Nysa**, Poland
176 J 10 **Nyūdō-zaki**, Japan
195 P 11 **Nyunzu**, Democratic Republic of Congo
174 M 9 **Nyurang**, Indonesia
157 S 10 **Nyurba**, Russian Federation
157 S 11 **Nyuya**, Russian Federation
101 U 9 **Nyzhni Sirohozy**, Ukraine
101 U 9 **Nyzhni Torhayi**, Ukraine
101 U 11 **Nyzhn'ohirs'kyy**, Ukraine
194 E 10 **Nzambi**, Congo
195 S 10 **Nzega**, Tanzania
192 H 12 **Nzérékoré**, Guinea
196 F 2 **N'zeto**, Angola
195 P 10 **Nzingu**, Democratic Republic of Congo

O

176 H 8 **Ō-shima**, Japan
177 K 17 **Ō-shima**, Japan
117 C 24 **Oahu**, Hawaii, U.S.A.
117 M 16 **Oak City**, Utah, U.S.A.
120 I 8 **Oak Creek**, Wisconsin, U.S.A.
116 E 6 **Oak Harbor**, Washington, U.S.A.
123 O 1 **Oak Ridge**, Tennessee, U.S.A.
117 F 19 **Oakhurst**, California, U.S.A.
117 D 18 **Oakland**, California, U.S.A.
121 Q 12 **Oakland**, Maryland, U.S.A.
116 K 13 **Oakley**, Idaho, U.S.A.
119 H 14 **Oakley**, Kansas, U.S.A.
208 H 5 **Oakover**, Western Australia, Australia
210 J 12 **Oakura**, New Zealand
210 J 6 **Oakura**, New Zealand
211 F 23 **Oamaru**, New Zealand
177 D 19 **Ōasa**, Japan
117 K 14 **Oasis**, Nevada, U.S.A.
219 R 14 **Oates Land**, Antarctica
125 S 14 **Oaxaca**, Mexico
125 T 14 **Oaxaca**, Mexico
156 L 10 **Ob'**, Russian Federation
193 T 14 **Obala**, Cameroon
76 F 12 **Oban**, United Kingdom
211 D 23 **Obelisk**, New Zealand
144 O 8 **Oberá**, Argentina
89 Q 8 **Oberdrauburg**, Austria
119 H 14 **Oberlin**, Kansas, U.S.A.
89 Q 5 **Oberndorf**, Austria
89 Q 4 **Oberösterreich**, Austria
87 K 20 **Oberpfälzer Wald**, Germany
89 Y 6 **Oberpullendorf**, Austria
87 H 26 **Oberstdorf**, Germany
89 R 8 **Obervellach**, Austria
89 X 6 **Oberwart**, Austria
175 S 11 **Obi**, Indonesia
142 G 10 **Óbidos**, Brazil
176 L 5 **Obihiro**, Japan
157 U 14 **Obluch'ye**, Russian Federation
195 O 4 **Obo**, Central African Republic
195 O 8 **Obokote**, Democratic Republic of Congo
99 K 14 **Obol'**, Belarus
101 S 5 **Obolon'**, Ukraine
92 G 12 **Oborniki**, Poland
194 H 8 **Obouya**, Congo
92 E 12 **Obra**, Poland
94 K 11 **Obrenovac**, Serbia and Montenegro
96 N 7 **Obrochishte**, Bulgaria
158 H 11 **Obruk**, Turkey
156 L 8 **Obskaya**, Russian Federation
65 X 10 **Obskaya Guba**, Arctic Ocean
192 L 13 **Obuasi**, Ghana
101 P 4 **Obukhiv**, Ukraine
156 I 8 **Ob''yachevo**, Russian Federation
101 W 9 **Obytichna Kosa**, Ukraine
101 V 10 **Obytichna Zatoka**, Ukraine
123 Q 10 **Ocala**, Florida, U.S.A.
210 K 6 **Ocean Beach**, New Zealand
121 U 13 **Ocean City**, Maryland, U.S.A.
116 C 8 **Ocean Park**, Washington, U.S.A.
122 J 8 **Ocean Springs**, Mississippi, U.S.A.
62 G 9 **Oceanographer Fracture Zone**, Atlantic Ocean
117 H 24 **Oceanside**, California, U.S.A.
101 Q 9 **Ochakiv**, Ukraine
159 Q 6 **Och'amch'ire**, Georgia
176 N 4 **Ochiishi-misaki**, Japan
126 M 7 **Ocho Rios**, Jamaica
123 R 14 **Ochopee**, Florida, U.S.A.
87 H 20 **Ochsenfurt**, Germany
123 P 7 **Ocilla**, Georgia, U.S.A.
123 P 6 **Ocmulgee**, Georgia, U.S.A.
125 W 13 **Ocosingo**, Mexico
123 X 2 **Ocracoke Island**, North Carolina, U.S.A.
141 J 21 **Ocuri**, Bolivia
177 D 18 **Ōda**, Japan
192 M 13 **Oda**, Ghana
176 J 9 **Ōdate**, Japan
177 K 17 **Odawara**, Japan
80 G 11 **Odemira**, Portugal
158 C 11 **Ödemiş**, Turkey
85 C 25 **Odense**, Denmark
86 N 12 **Oder**, Germany/Poland
86 M 9 **Oderhaff**, Germany
90 H 6 **Oderzo**, Italy
101 Q 10 **Odesa**, Ukraine
119 G 20 **Odessa**, Texas, U.S.A.
192 I 11 **Odienné**, Côte d'Ivoire
173 L 21 **Ôdôngk**, Cambodia
82 N 8 **Odoorn**, Netherlands
100 K 10 **Odorheiu Secuiesc**, Romania
93 K 14 **Odrzywół**, Poland
94 J 9 **Odžaci**, Serbia and Montenegro
142 M 12 **Oeiras**, Brazil
87 K 18 **Oelsnitz**, Germany
209 N 1 **Oenpelli**, Northern Territory, Australia
159 P 8 **Of**, Turkey
160 E 10 **Ofaqim**, Israel
193 P 12 **Offa**, Nigeria
87 F 19 **Offenbach**, Germany
87 D 23 **Offenburg**, Germany
97 K 23 **Ofidoussa**, Greece
215 Y 15 **Ofu**, American Samoa
176 L 11 **Ōfunato**, Japan
176 J 10 **Oga**, Japan
176 K 11 **Ogachi**, Japan
191 M 21 **Ogadēn**, Ethiopia
177 H 17 **Ogaki**, Japan
118 H 13 **Ogallala**, Nebraska, U.S.A.
176 K 9 **Ogawara-ko**, Japan
193 P 12 **Ogbomoso**, Nigeria
117 M 14 **Ogden**, Utah, U.S.A.
123 R 6 **Ogeechee**, Georgia, U.S.A.
176 I 13 **Ogi**, Japan
113 N 5 **Ogilvie Mountains**, Yukon Territory, Canada
193 S 13 **Ogoja**, Nigeria
114 M 10 **Ogoki**, Ontario, Canada
194 G 7 **Ogooué-Ivindo**, Gabon
194 F 8 **Ogooué-Lolo**, Gabon
194 D 8 **Ogooué-Maritime**, Gabon
96 F 11 **Ograzden**, Macedonia (F.Y.R.O.M.)
98 F 11 **Ogre**, Latvia
94 C 9 **Ogulin**, Croatia
193 O 13 **Ogun**, Nigeria
159 W 7 **Oğuz**, Azerbaijan
61 X 15 **Oh Dear**, Pitcairn Island
210 L 13 **Ohakune**, New Zealand
189 Q 10 **Ohanet**, Algeria
196 I 7 **Ohangwena**, Namibia
211 K 15 **Ohau**, New Zealand
210 K 10 **Ohaupo**, New Zealand
144 F 12 **O'Higgins**, Chile
121 N 11 **Ohio**, U.S.A.
121 O 12 **Ohio**, U.S.A.
93 B 16 **Ohře**, Czech Republic
96 B 12 **Ohrid**, Macedonia (F.Y.R.O.M.)
210 K 12 **Ohura**, New Zealand
139 Y 8 **Oiapoque**, French Guiana/Brazil
142 I 8 **Oiapoque**, Brazil
115 S 1 **Oikiqtarjuaq**, Nunavut, Canada
83 I 15 **Oirschot**, Netherlands
177 C 21 **Ōita**, Japan
97 E 18 **Oiti**, Greece
120 G 5 **Ojibwa**, Wisconsin, U.S.A.
177 A 22 **Ojika-jima**, Japan
125 N 4 **Ojinaga**, Mexico
177 J 14 **Ojiya**, Japan
124 M 4 **Ojo de Laguna**, Mexico
212 A 4 **Ok Tedi**, Papua New Guinea
175 Y 14 **Okaba**, Indonesia
196 I 9 **Okahandja**, Namibia
210 I 5 **Okaihau**, New Zealand
115 U 6 **Okak Islands**, Newfoundland and Labrador, Canada
196 I 8 **Okakarara**, Namibia

Country · Internal administrative region: State/Province/Territory/Dependent territory · Capital city · Mountain range/Undersea ridge · Mountain peak/Volcano/Seamount · Geographic feature · Headland/Point/Cape/Peninsula · Desert · Island/Island group · Antarctic base · Ocean · Sea · Bay/Gulf/Channel/Strait · Lake · Salt pan/Dry/Intermittent lake · River

196 I 8 **Okaputa**, Namibia
165 X 10 **Okara**, Pakistan
166 I 13 **Okarem**, Turkmenistan
211 E 19 **Okarito Lagoon**, New Zealand
196 H 8 **Okaukuejo**, Namibia
196 J 7 **Okavango**, Namibia
196 K 7 **Okavango**, Botswana
196 L 7 **Okavango Delta**, Botswana
177 I 16 **Okaya**, Japan
177 F 19 **Okayama**, Japan
177 I 17 **Okazaki**, Japan
123 S 12 **Okeechobee**, Florida, U.S.A.
77 H 23 **Okehampton**, United Kingdom
157 W 12 **Okha**, Russian Federation
157 W 11 **Okhotsk**, Russian Federation
101 V 9 **Okhrimivka**, Ukraine
101 U 4 **Okhtyrka**, Ukraine
177 D 17 **Oki-shotō**, Japan
177 O 24 **Okinawa**, Japan
177 O 25 **Okinawa-shotō**, Japan
177 E 22 **Okino-shima**, Japan
177 N 23 **Okinoerabu-jima**, Japan
119 I 17 **Oklahoma**, U.S.A.
119 J 17 **Oklahoma City**, Oklahoma, U.S.A.
194 G 8 **Okondja**, Gabon
194 H 8 **Okoyo**, Congo
173 D 15 **Okpo**, Myanmar
84 J 6 **Øksfjord**, Norway
156 H 10 **Oktyabr'skiy**, Russian Federation
157 Z 11 **Oktyabr'skiy**, Russian Federation
177 N 24 **Oku**, Japan
176 H 7 **Okushiri-tō**, Japan
193 O 12 **Okuta**, Nigeria
98 F 11 **Olaine**, Latvia
117 G 20 **Olancha**, California, U.S.A.
85 H 24 **Öland**, Sweden
209 Q 10 **Olary**, South Australia, Australia
145 L 14 **Olavarria**, Argentina
93 G 15 **Oława**, Poland
91 C 16 **Olbia**, Italy
113 N 4 **Old Crow**, Yukon Territory, Canada
118 C 10 **Old Faithful**, Wyoming, U.S.A.
121 T 7 **Old Forge**, New York, U.S.A.
112 I 9 **Old Harbor**, Alaska, U.S.A.
77 C 21 **Old Head of Kinsale**, Republic of Ireland
121 Y 5 **Old Town**, Maine, U.S.A.
113 Y 13 **Old Wives Lake**, Saskatchewan, Canada
82 K 10 **Oldebroek**, Netherlands
86 E 11 **Oldenburg**, Germany
86 I 8 **Oldenburg in Holstein**, Germany
82 N 11 **Oldenzaal**, Netherlands
84 K 6 **Olderfjord**, Norway
77 J 17 **Oldham**, United Kingdom
121 Q 9 **Olean**, New York, U.S.A.
92 M 9 **Olecko**, Poland
157 S 11 **Olekminsk**, Russian Federation
101 R 6 **Oleksandrivka**, Ukraine
101 W 7 **Oleksandrivka**, Ukraine
101 S 6 **Oleksandriya**, Ukraine
157 R 8 **Olenëk**, Russian Federation
157 S 7 **Olenekskiy Zaliv**, Russian Federation
101 S 11 **Olenevka**, Ukraine
93 G 15 **Oleśnica**, Poland
93 I 16 **Olesno**, Poland
100 M 2 **Olevs'k**, Ukraine
84 G 11 **Ølfjellet**, Norway
170 M 2 **Ölgiy**, Mongolia
80 I 12 **Olhão**, Portugal
94 C 11 **Olib**, Croatia
120 M 13 **Olive Hill**, Kentucky, U.S.A.
143 K 18 **Oliveira**, Brazil
80 J 9 **Olivenza**, Spain
113 X 9 **Oliver Lake**, Saskatchewan, Canada
93 J 17 **Olkusz**, Poland
144 H 4 **Ollagüe**, Chile
194 H 8 **Ollombo**, Congo
81 N 5 **Olmedo**, Spain
140 B 12 **Olmos**, Peru
120 I 12 **Olney**, Illinois, U.S.A.
93 G 18 **Olomouc**, Czech Republic
156 G 6 **Olonets**, Russian Federation
175 O 3 **Olongapo**, Philippines
78 M 14 **Oloron-Ste-Marie**, France
215 Y 15 **Olosega**, American Samoa
81 X 3 **Olot**, Spain
157 R 14 **Olovyannaya**, Russian Federation
99 K 18 **Ol'sa**, Belarus
92 K 9 **Olsztyn**, Poland
92 K 10 **Olsztynek**, Poland
100 I 10 **Olt**, Romania
88 E 6 **Olten**, Switzerland
100 L 13 **Oltenița**, Romania
159 R 8 **Oltu**, Turkey
116 D 7 **Olympia**, Washington, U.S.A.
157 Z 8 **Olyutorskiy**, Russian Federation
157 Z 9 **Olyutorskiy Zaliv**, Russian Federation
191 H 17 **Om Hajêr**, Eritrea
176 J 8 **Ōma**, Japan
176 J 8 **Ōma-zaki**, Japan
177 J 18 **Omae-zaki**, Japan
176 K 11 **Ōmagari**, Japan
77 E 15 **Omagh**, United Kingdom
140 F 11 **Omaguas**, Peru
118 K 12 **Omaha**, Nebraska, U.S.A.
196 J 9 **Omaheke**, Namibia
116 G 6 **Omak**, Washington, U.S.A.
211 D 23 **Omakau**, New Zealand
211 M 14 **Omakere**, New Zealand
159 U 6 **Omalo**, Georgia
163 Y 8 **Oman**, Asia
211 E 22 **Omarama**, New Zealand
196 I 9 **Omaruru**, Namibia
194 I 4 **Ombella-Mpoko**, Central African Republic
194 D 9 **Omboué**, Gabon
191 F 16 **Omdurman**, Sudan
101 T 5 **Omel'nyk**, Ukraine
125 R 14 **Ometepec**, Mexico
164 G 9 **Omīdīyeh**, Iran
94 F 13 **Omiš**, Croatia
82 M 10 **Ommen**, Netherlands
171 Q 5 **Ömnögövi**, Mongolia
191 G 22 **Omo Wenz**, Ethiopia
215 X 7 **Omoa**, French Polynesia
157 X 8 **Omolon**, Russian Federation
157 X 8 **Omolon**, Russian Federation
156 K 11 **Omsk**, Russian Federation
157 X 9 **Omsukchan**, Russian Federation
176 K 3 **Ōmū**, Japan
177 B 22 **Ōmura**, Japan
96 L 8 **Omurtag**, Bulgaria
196 G 7 **Omusati**, Namibia
177 B 22 **Ōmuta**, Japan
120 G 6 **Onalaska**, Wisconsin, U.S.A.
120 L 5 **Onaway**, Michigan, U.S.A.
176 M 5 **Onbetsu**, Japan
196 G 6 **Oncócua**, Angola
196 H 7 **Ondangwa**, Namibia
93 M 19 **Ondava**, Slovakia
169 F 14 **Onder**, India
196 H 6 **Ondjiva**, Angola
193 Q 13 **Ondo**, Nigeria
193 P 13 **Ondo**, Nigeria
171 S 4 **Öndörhaan**, Mongolia
169 K 20 **One and a Half Degree Channel**, Maldives
156 H 6 **Onega**, Russian Federation
121 T 8 **Oneida**, New York, U.S.A.
121 T 7 **Oneida Lake**, New York, U.S.A.
118 I 12 **O'Neill**, Nebraska, U.S.A.
121 T 8 **Oneonta**, New York, U.S.A.
122 M 4 **Oneonta**, Alabama, U.S.A.
100 L 10 **Onești**, Romania
194 G 8 **Onga**, Gabon
211 K 12 **Ongarue**, New Zealand
171 Q 4 **Ongi**, Mongolia
169 G 19 **Ongole**, India
159 S 6 **Oni**, Georgia
193 Q 13 **Onitsha**, Nigeria
157 U 11 **Onnes**, Russian Federation
213 X 12 **Ono**, Fiji
177 H 16 **Ono**, Japan
213 Z 13 **Ono-i-lau**, Fiji
177 B 21 **Ōnojō**, Japan
177 E 19 **Onomichi**, Japan
214 E 3 **Onotoa**, Kiribati
196 J 12 **Onseepkans**, Republic of South Africa
208 E 6 **Onslow**, Western Australia, Australia
123 V 4 **Onslow Bay**, North Carolina, U.S.A.
114 K 10 **Ontario**, Canada
116 I 11 **Ontario**, Idaho, U.S.A.
81 T 9 **Ontinyent**, Spain
120 H 3 **Ontonagon**, Michigan, U.S.A.
212 L 4 **Ontong Java Atoll**, Solomon Islands
209 O 8 **Oodnadatta**, South Australia, Australia
191 L 20 **Oodweyne**, Somalia
208 M 10 **Ooldea**, South Australia, Australia
119 K 16 **Oologah Lake**, Oklahoma, U.S.A.
83 D 18 **Oost-Vlaanderen**, Belgium
82 I 6 **Oost-Vlieland**, Netherlands
83 B 17 **Oostende**, Belgium
82 J 5 **Oosterend**, Netherlands
83 H 15 **Oosterhout**, Netherlands
83 E 15 **Oosterschelde**, Netherlands
83 C 15 **Oostersscheldekering**, Netherlands
82 L 7 **Oosterwolde**, Netherlands
83 C 17 **Oostkamp**, Belgium
83 A 18 **Oostvleteren**, Belgium
173 L 23 **Ôp Luc**, Vietnam
195 N 8 **Opala**, Democratic Republic of Congo
93 L 16 **Opatów**, Poland
93 H 17 **Opava**, Czech Republic
123 N 6 **Opelika**, Alabama, U.S.A.
119 N 21 **Opelousas**, Louisiana, U.S.A.
212 G 4 **Open Bay**, Papua New Guinea
118 E 7 **Opheim**, Montana, U.S.A.
82 J 13 **Opheusden**, Netherlands
195 P 7 **Opienge**, Democratic Republic of Congo
101 U 4 **Opishnya**, Ukraine
93 K 14 **Opoczno**, Poland
93 H 16 **Opole**, Poland
166 J 8 **Opornyy**, Kazakhstan
210 N 10 **Opotiki**, New Zealand
122 M 7 **Opp**, Alabama, U.S.A.
85 D 16 **Oppdal**, Norway
91 M 21 **Oppido Mamertina**, Italy
210 J 13 **Opunake**, New Zealand
196 G 7 **Opuwo**, Namibia
117 N 24 **Oracle**, Arizona, U.S.A.
100 G 8 **Oradea**, Romania
117 N 20 **Oraibi**, Arizona, U.S.A.
188 K 6 **Oran**, Algeria
144 J 5 **Orán**, Argentina
101 P 2 **Orane**, Ukraine
196 M 13 **Orange**, Republic of South Africa
79 T 13 **Orange**, France
209 U 11 **Orange**, New South Wales, Australia
63 N 16 **Orange Cone**, Atlantic Ocean
126 E 7 **Orange Walk**, Belize
123 R 5 **Orangeburg**, South Carolina, U.S.A.
212 F 7 **Orangerie Bay**, Papua New Guinea
86 L 12 **Oranienburg**, Germany
196 I 12 **Oranjemund**, Namibia
127 R 11 **Oranjestad**, Aruba
196 M 8 **Orapa**, Botswana
100 H 10 **Orăștie**, Romania
93 J 19 **Orava**, Slovakia
100 F 11 **Oravița**, Romania
211 B 25 **Orawia**, New Zealand
90 F 13 **Orbetello**, Italy
209 T 13 **Orbost**, Victoria, Australia
218 I 1 **Orcadas**, Antarctica
81 Q 10 **Orcera**, Spain
208 L 4 **Ord**, Western Australia, Australia
80 H 1 **Ordes**, Spain
158 M 8 **Ordu**, Turkey
167 N 3 **Ordzhonikidze**, Kazakhstan
159 X 9 **Ordzonikidze**, Azerbaijan
93 A 17 **Ore Mountains**, Czech Republic/Germany
85 G 20 **Örebro**, Sweden
116 E 11 **Oregon**, U.S.A.
120 H 8 **Oregon**, Wisconsin, U.S.A.
101 T 6 **Orel**, Ukraine
156 E 8 **Orel**, Russian Federation
140 D 13 **Orellana**, Peru
158 C 12 **Ören**, Turkey
156 H 11 **Orenburg**, Russian Federation
96 L 12 **Orestiada**, Greece
211 C 25 **Oreti**, New Zealand
210 K 8 **Orewa**, New Zealand
119 E 19 **Organ Peak**, New Mexico, U.S.A.
139 Y 6 **Organabo**, French Guiana
165 U 8 **Orgūn**, Afghanistan
101 N 8 **Orhei**, Moldova
81 S 2 **Orhi**, Spain
117 C 14 **Orick**, California, U.S.A.
195 O 6 **Orientale**, Democratic Republic of Congo
145 K 15 **Oriente**, Argentina
81 S 11 **Orihuela**, Spain
101 V 8 **Orikhiv**, Ukraine
101 V 5 **Oril'**, Ukraine
101 V 5 **Oril'ka**, Ukraine
115 P 14 **Orillia**, Ontario, Canada
118 F 12 **Orin**, Wyoming, U.S.A.
139 O 4 **Orinoco**, Venezuela
212 B 6 **Oriomo**, Papua New Guinea
169 I 16 **Orissa**, India
98 E 7 **Orissaare**, Estonia
91 B 18 **Oristano**, Italy
85 O 16 **Orivesi**, Finland
142 G 10 **Oriximiná**, Brazil
125 S 12 **Orizaba**, Mexico
85 E 24 **Örkelljunga**, Sweden
76 H 7 **Orkney Islands**, United Kingdom
119 F 20 **Orla**, Texas, U.S.A.
123 R 11 **Orlando**, Florida, U.S.A.
117 C 14 **Orleans**, California, U.S.A.
121 Y 9 **Orleans**, Massachusetts, U.S.A.
79 P 6 **Orléans**, France
79 Q 4 **Orly**, France
165 R 14 **Ormara**, Pakistan
175 Q 5 **Ormoc**, Philippines
123 R 10 **Ormond Beach**, Florida, U.S.A.
97 G 14 **Ormylia**, Greece
92 K 9 **Orneta**, Poland
85 I 21 **Ornö**, Sweden
118 E 13 **Orno Peak**, Colorado, U.S.A.
85 I 15 **Örnsköldsvik**, Sweden
192 K 10 **Orodara**, Burkina Faso
116 I 8 **Orofino**, Idaho, U.S.A.
171 P 4 **Orog Nuur**, Mongolia
215 P 15 **Oroluk**, Federated States of Micronesia
191 H 20 **Oromia**, Ethiopia
160 F 11 **Oron**, Israel
193 S 14 **Oron**, Nigeria
214 J 4 **Orona**, Kiribati
97 J 26 **Oros Kofinas**, Greece
91 D 17 **Orosei**, Italy
93 L 25 **Orosháza**, Hungary
117 H 14 **Orovada**, Nevada, U.S.A.
117 E 16 **Oroville**, California, U.S.A.
62 G 7 **Orphan Knoll**, Atlantic Ocean
99 M 16 **Orsha**, Belarus
88 D 11 **Orsières**, Switzerland
156 H 11 **Orsk**, Russian Federation
100 G 12 **Orșova**, Romania
158 H 13 **Orta Toroslar**, Turkey
158 I 12 **Ortaköy**, Turkey
89 Y 3 **Orth an der Donau**, Austria
78 L 14 **Orthez**, France
141 I 16 **Orthon**, Bolivia
80 I 1 **Ortigueira**, Spain
124 J 5 **Ortiz**, Mexico
90 J 13 **Ortona**, Italy
118 K 9 **Ortonville**, Minnesota, U.S.A.
164 F 3 **Orūmīyeh**, Iran
141 I 21 **Oruro**, Bolivia
141 J 20 **Oruro**, Bolivia
85 D 22 **Orust**, Sweden
90 G 12 **Orvieto**, Italy
218 K 6 **Orville Coast**, Antarctica
121 O 9 **Orwell**, Ohio, U.S.A.
96 H 6 **Oryakhovo**, Bulgaria
90 D 7 **Orzinuovi**, Italy
62 O 11 **Orzola**, Canary Islands
92 M 9 **Orzysz**, Poland
177 G 18 **Ōsaka**, Japan
177 G 18 **Ōsaka-wan**, Japan
167 S 4 **Osakarovka**, Kazakhstan
59 P 6 **Osborn Plateau**, Indian Ocean
91 C 16 **Oschiri**, Italy
120 M 6 **Oscoda**, Michigan, U.S.A.
94 J 11 **Osečina**, Serbia and Montenegro
167 T 12 **Osh**, Kyrgyzstan
196 H 7 **Oshakati**, Namibia
176 I 7 **Oshamambe**, Japan
196 H 7 **Oshana**, Namibia
115 P 14 **Oshawa**, Ontario, Canada
176 L 12 **Oshika-hantō**, Japan
196 H 7 **Oshikango**, Namibia
196 I 7 **Oshikoto**, Namibia
176 I 7 **Oshima-hantō**, Japan
118 G 13 **Oshkosh**, Nebraska, U.S.A.
120 H 7 **Oshkosh**, Wisconsin, U.S.A.
193 P 12 **Oshogbo**, Nigeria
167 T 12 **Oshskaya Oblast'**, Kyrgyzstan
194 K 10 **Oshwe**, Democratic Republic of Congo
94 I 8 **Osijek**, Croatia
118 M 12 **Oskaloosa**, Iowa, U.S.A.
85 G 23 **Oskarshamn**, Sweden
101 X 4 **Oskol**, Ukraine
85 D 20 **Oslo**, Norway
85 C 21 **Oslofjorden**, Norway
158 J 8 **Osmancik**, Turkey
158 E 8 **Osmaneli**, Turkey
158 L 13 **Osmaniye**, Turkey
98 E 6 **Osmussaar**, Estonia
86 E 13 **Osnabrück**, Germany
96 D 10 **Osogovske Planine**, Macedonia (F.Y.R.O.M.)
143 J 22 **Osório**, Brazil
81 N 3 **Osorno**, Spain
145 E 16 **Osorno**, Chile
113 T 14 **Osoyoos**, British Columbia, Canada
85 A 19 **Osøyra**, Norway
83 J 14 **Oss**, Netherlands
157 Y 9 **Ossora**, Russian Federation
101 P 3 **Oster**, Ukraine
86 J 12 **Osterburg**, Germany
85 F 16 **Östersund**, Sweden
86 C 10 **Ostfriesische Inseln**, Germany
85 I 19 **Östhammar**, Sweden
90 F 8 **Ostiglia**, Italy
93 H 18 **Ostrava**, Czech Republic
92 J 9 **Ostróda**, Poland
100 L 4 **Ostroh**, Ukraine
92 L 11 **Ostrołęka**, Poland
157 Q 5 **Ostrov**, Russian Federation
156 F 7 **Ostrov**, Russian Federation
157 N 6 **Ostrov Arkitcheskogo Instituta**, Russian Federation
157 X 6 **Ostrov Ayon**, Russian Federation
157 T 6 **Ostrov Bel'kovskiy**, Russian Federation
156 M 6 **Ostrov Belyy**, Russian Federation
157 U 5 **Ostrov Bennetta**, Russian Federation
157 Z 10 **Ostrov Beringa**, Russian Federation
157 U 6 **Ostrov Bol'shaya Lyakhovskiy**, Russian Federation
157 R 7 **Ostrov Bol'shoy Begichev**, Russian Federation
159 Z 8 **Ostrov Bulla**, Azerbaijan
157 N 4 **Ostrov Dzheksona**, Russian Federation
157 O 3 **Ostrov Greem-Bell**, Russian Federation
157 O 5 **Ostrov Isachenko**, Russian Federation
157 Y 14 **Ostrov Iturup**, Russian Federation
157 Z 9 **Ostrov Karaginskiy**, Russian Federation
156 K 6 **Ostrov Kolguyev**, Russian Federation
157 P 4 **Ostrov Komsomolets**, Russian Federation
157 T 6 **Ostrov Kotel'nyy**, Russian Federation
166 G 8 **Ostrov Kulaly**, Kazakhstan
157 Y 14 **Ostrov Kunashir**, Russian Federation
157 U 6 **Ostrov Malyy Lyakhovskiy**, Russian Federation
157 R 5 **Ostrov Malyy Taymyr**, Russian Federation
157 Z 10 **Ostrov Mednyy**, Russian Federation
156 K 6 **Ostrov Mezhdusharskiy**, Russian Federation
157 U 6 **Ostrov Novaya Sibir'**, Russian Federation
166 H 12 **Ostrov Ogurchinskiy**, Turkmenistan
157 P 5 **Ostrov Oktyabr'skoy Revolyutsii**, Russian Federation
157 N 7 **Ostrov Oleniy**, Russian Federation
157 Z 12 **Ostrov Onekotan**, Russian Federation
157 Z 12 **Ostrov Paramushir**, Russian Federation
157 P 4 **Ostrov Pioner**, Russian Federation
157 N 3 **Ostrov Rudol'fa**, Russian Federation
157 Z 13 **Ostrov Shiashkotan**, Russian Federation
157 P 4 **Ostrov Shmidta**, Russian Federation
157 N 7 **Ostrov Sibiryakova**, Russian Federation
157 Z 13 **Ostrov Simushir**, Russian Federation
157 T 6 **Ostrov Stolbovoy**, Russian Federation
157 Y 14 **Ostrov Urup**, Russian Federation
157 O 4 **Ostrov Ushakova**, Russian Federation
157 O 5 **Ostrov Uyedineniya**, Russian Federation
156 L 7 **Ostrov Vaygach**, Russian Federation
157 N 6 **Ostrov Vil'kitskogo**, Russian Federation
157 O 4 **Ostrov Vise**, Russian Federation
166 L 9 **Ostrov Vozrozhdeniya**, Uzbekistan
157 V 5 **Ostrov Zhokhova**, Russian Federation
157 U 5 **Ostrova De-Longa**, Russian Federation
157 O 6 **Ostrova Izvestiy Ts. I. K.**, Russian Federation
157 W 6 **Ostrova Medvezh'i**, Russian Federation
166 H 8 **Ostrova Tyulen'i**, Kazakhstan
92 M 11 **Ostrów Mazowiecki**, Poland
93 H 14 **Ostrów Wielkopolski**, Poland
93 L 15 **Ostrowiec Świętokrzyski**, Poland
93 H 14 **Ostrzeszów**, Poland
86 M 8 **Ostseebad Göhren**, Germany
89 O 8 **Osttirol**, Austria
91 O 16 **Ostuni**, Italy
96 I 8 **Osŭm**, Bulgaria
177 C 24 **Ōsumi-hantō**, Japan
177 C 24 **Ōsumi-kaikyō**, Japan
177 B 25 **Ōsumi-shotō**, Japan
193 P 13 **Osun**, Nigeria
80 M 12 **Osuna**, Spain
121 S 7 **Oswego**, New York, U.S.A.
77 I 19 **Oswestry**, United Kingdom
101 W 9 **Osypenko**, Ukraine
211 E 22 **Otago**, New Zealand
211 F 24 **Otago Peninsula**, New Zealand
210 J 6 **Otaika**, New Zealand
211 K 15 **Otaki**, New Zealand
167 U 9 **Otar**, Kazakhstan
176 J 5 **Otaru**, Japan
140 B 8 **Otavalo**, Ecuador
196 I 8 **Otavi**, Namibia
177 K 14 **Ōtawara**, Japan
211 E 22 **Otematata**, New Zealand
98 H 8 **Otepää**, Estonia
116 G 8 **Othello**, Washington, U.S.A.
97 A 15 **Othonoi**, Greece
211 G 19 **Otira**, New Zealand
196 I 8 **Otjiwarongo**, Namibia
196 J 8 **Otjozondjupa**, Namibia
171 R 7 **Otog Qi**, China
176 J 3 **Otoineppu**, Japan
210 K 11 **Otorohanga**, New Zealand
211 E 20 **Otorokua Point**, New Zealand
85 B 20 **Otra**, Norway
91 O 17 **Otranto**, Italy
157 Y 7 **Otrozhnyy**, Russian Federation
120 K 8 **Otsego**, Michigan, U.S.A.
177 G 18 **Ōtsu**, Japan
85 D 17 **Otta**, Norway
115 Q 13 **Ottawa**, Ontario, Canada
115 P 13 **Ottawa**, Québec, Canada
119 K 15 **Ottawa**, Kansas, U.S.A.
115 O 6 **Ottawa Islands**, Ontario, Canada
85 G 25 **Ottenby**, Sweden
89 V 3 **Ottenschlag**, Austria
86 F 10 **Otterndorf**, Germany
90 D 8 **Ottone**, Italy
118 M 13 **Ottumwa**, Iowa, U.S.A.

Country · Internal administrative region: State/Province/Territory/Dependent territory · Capital city · Mountain range/Undersea ridge · Mountain peak/Volcano/Seamount · Geographic feature · Headland/Point/Cape/Peninsula · Desert · Island/Island group · Antarctic base · Ocean · Sea · Bay/Gulf/Channel/Strait · Lake · Salt pan/Dry/Intermittent lake · River

3 R 13 Otukpa, Nigeria
3 R 13 Otukpo, Nigeria
4 K 8 Otumpa, Argentina
L 13 Otwock, Poland
K 8 Ötztaler Alpen, Austria
76 K 10 Ōu-sanmyaku, Japan
9 K 18 Ouachita Mountains, Oklahoma, U.S.A.
92 G 5 Ouadâne, Mauritania
94 L 3 Ouadda, Central African Republic
93 Y 9 Ouaddaï, Chad
92 M 10 Ouagadougou, Burkina Faso
92 L 9 Ouahigouya, Burkina Faso
94 K 4 Ouaka, Central African Republic
92 J 7 Oualâta, Mauritania
93 O 9 Ouallam, Niger
39 Z 7 Ouanary, French Guiana
95 O 4 Ouanda, Central African Republic
94 J 3 Ouandago, Central African Republic
94 M 2 Ouandja, Central African Republic
94 L 5 Ouango, Central African Republic
92 K 11 Ouangolodougou, Côte d'Ivoire
93 N 10 Ouargaye, Burkina Faso
89 O 8 Ouargla, Algeria
3 F 14 Oude-Tonge, Netherlands
3 D 19 Oudenaarde, Belgium
96 L 15 Oudtshoorn, Republic of South Africa
88 H 7 Oued Zem, Morocco
92 I 10 Ouéléssébougou, Mali
94 H 7 Ouésso, Congo
93 T 13 Ouest, Cameroon
94 I 3 Ouham, Central African Republic
94 H 3 Ouham-Pendé, Central African Republic
88 K 6 Oujda, Morocco
92 G 5 Oujeft, Mauritania
88 G 9 Oulad Teïma, Morocco
92 G 8 Ould Yenjé, Mauritania
89 N 7 Ouled Djellal, Algeria
84 L 13 Oulu, Finland
85 M 14 Oulujärvi, Finland
84 L 13 Oulujoki, Finland
193 Y 8 Oum-Chalouba, Chad
189 O 6 Oum el Bouaghi, Algeria
193 Y 9 Oum-Hadjer, Chad
188 F 8 Ounara, Morocco
84 K 10 Ounasjoki, Finland
193 X 6 Ounianga Kébir, Chad
193 Y 6 Ounianga Sérir, Chad
171 W 1 Oupu, China
85 C 18 Øure Ardel, Norway
80 I 3 Ourense, Spain
142 N 13 Ouricurí, Brazil
143 J 19 Ourinhos, Brazil
83 J 22 Ourthe, Belgium
77 K 17 Ouse, United Kingdom
77 D 10 Outer Hebrides, United Kingdom
196 I 8 Outjo, Namibia
211 E 24 Outram, New Zealand
213 Q 13 Ouvéa, New Caledonia
209 R 12 Ouyen, Victoria, Australia
158 I 14 Ovacik, Turkey
213 X 11 Ovalau, Fiji
144 F 10 Ovalle, Chile
196 G 7 Ovamboland, Namibia
194 F 7 Ovan, Gabon
80 H 5 Ovar, Portugal
193 U 15 Oveng, Cameroon
83 G 19 Overijse, Belgium
82 M 11 Overijssel, Netherlands
84 K 11 Överkalix, Sweden
119 L 14 Overland Park, Kansas, U.S.A.
208 F 8 Overlander Roadhouse, Western Australia, Australia
83 J 17 Overpelt, Belgium
117 K 20 Overton, Nevada, U.S.A.
101 N 13 Ovidiu, Romania
80 L 1 Oviedo, Spain
127 Q 7 Oviedo, Dominican Republic
98 C 9 Ovišrags, Latvia
171 P 4 Övörhangay, Mongolia
84 J 9 Övre Soppero, Sweden
101 O 2 Ovruch, Ukraine
211 E 25 Owaka, New Zealand
194 H 8 Owando, Congo
177 H 19 Owase, Japan
211 C 26 Owen Head, New Zealand
173 F 21 Owen Island, Myanmar
211 H 17 Owen River, New Zealand
115 O 14 Owen Sound, Ontario, Canada
212 E 6 Owen Stanley Range, Papua New Guinea
117 H 20 Owens Lake, California, U.S.A.
120 J 14 Owensboro, Kentucky, U.S.A.
193 R 14 Owerri, Nigeria
193 Q 13 Owo, Nigeria
120 L 8 Owosso, Michigan, U.S.A.
116 I 13 Owyhee, Nevada, U.S.A.
113 Z 12 Oxbow, Saskatchewan, Canada
85 H 21 Oxelösund, Sweden
77 K 21 Oxford, United Kingdom
121 S 8 Oxford, New York, U.S.A.
122 I 3 Oxford, Mississippi, U.S.A.
211 G 20 Oxford, New Zealand
117 F 22 Oxnard, California, U.S.A.
167 U 12 Oy Tal, Kyrgyzstan
177 H 15 Oyabe, Japan
177 K 15 Oyama, Japan
194 E 7 Oyem, Gabon
113 W 13 Oyen, Alberta, Canada
85 D 20 Øyeren, Norway
193 P 12 Oyo, Nigeria
193 P 12 Oyo, Nigeria
194 H 8 Oyo, Congo
141 C 15 Oyón, Peru
172 A 13 Oyster Island, Myanmar
159 T 11 Özalp, Turkey
119 L 16 Ozark Plateau, Missouri, U.S.A.
61 Q 10 Ozbourn Seamount, Pacific Ocean
93 K 21 Ózd, Hungary
157 Z 12 Ozernovskiy, Russian Federation
167 Q 9 Ozero Akzhaykyn, Kazakhstan
167 X 7 Ozero Alakol', Kazakhstan
166 G 5 Ozero Aralsor, Kazakhstan
167 Q 12 Ozero Aydarkul', Uzbekistan
166 I 6 Ozero Inder, Kazakhstan
166 I 5 Ozero Itmurinkol', Kazakhstan
167 R 8 Ozero Karakoyyn, Kazakhstan
167 U 5 Ozero Karasor, Kazakhstan
167 P 3 Ozero Kusmurun, Kazakhstan
167 Z 5 Ozero Markakol', Kazakhstan
167 X 7 Ozero Sasykkol, Kazakhstan
157 Y 14 Ozero Shikotan, Russian Federation
167 S 2 Ozero Siletiteniz, Kazakhstan
167 P 8 Ozero Solonchak, Kazakhstan
157 Q 6 Ozero Taymyr, Russian Federation
167 S 2 Ozero Teke, Kazakhstan
167 Q 5 Ozero Tengiz, Kazakhstan
167 S 2 Ozero Ul'ken Karoy, Kazakhstan
101 N 11 Ozero Yalpuh, Ukraine
167 Y 6 Ozero Zaysan, Kazakhstan
99 C 16 Ozersk, Russian Federation
167 T 12 Özgön, Kyrgyzstan
91 C 16 Ozieri, Italy
93 H 16 Ozimek, Poland
92 J 13 Ozorków, Poland
177 D 21 Ōzu, Japan
125 S 10 Ozuluama, Mexico
159 R 7 Ozurget'i, Georgia

P

173 F 16 Pa-an, Myanmar
213 R 11 Paama, Vanuatu
64 M 13 Paamiut, Greenland
196 J 15 Paarl, Republic of South Africa
93 J 14 Pabianice, Poland
169 K 14 Pabna, Bangladesh
99 G 15 Pabradė, Lithuania
140 B 13 Pacasmayo, Peru
97 K 24 Pachia, Greece
91 K 24 Pachino, Italy
141 E 14 Pachitea, Peru
97 H 26 Páchnes, Greece
125 R 11 Pachuca, Mexico
61 R 7 Pacific Ocean, 0
209 R 10 Packsaddle, New South Wales, Australia
116 E 8 Packwood, Washington, U.S.A.
174 D 11 Padang, Indonesia
174 D 10 Padangsidimpuan, Indonesia
174 I 11 Padangtikar, Indonesia
141 K 23 Padcaya, Bolivia
87 F 15 Paderborn, Germany
141 K 21 Padilla, Bolivia
100 L 12 Padina, Romania
90 G 7 Padova, Italy
119 K 24 Padre Island, Texas, U.S.A.
91 D 16 Padru, Italy
120 H 14 Paducah, Kentucky, U.S.A.
168 E 8 Padum, India
215 Z 8 Paea, French Polynesia
171 X 5 Paektu-san, North Korea
210 L 9 Paeroa, New Zealand
158 G 15 Pafos, Cyprus
197 P 9 Pafuri, Mozambique
94 C 11 Pag, Croatia
94 C 11 Pag, Croatia
142 H 11 Paga-Conta, Brazil
175 P 7 Pagadian, Philippines
174 D 12 Pagai Selatan, Indonesia
174 D 12 Pagai Utara, Indonesia
214 B 6 Pagan, Northern Mariana Islands
97 F 17 Pagasitikos Kolpos, Greece
174 L 12 Pagatan, Indonesia
96 L 13 Pağayiğit, Turkey
117 M 19 Page, Arizona, U.S.A.
99 C 14 Pagėgiai, Lithuania
215 W 15 Pago Pago, American Samoa
170 K 11 Pagri, China
174 E 9 Pahang, Malaysia
211 L 15 Pahiatua, New Zealand
169 N 21 Pahlagaon, India
173 F 14 Pai, Thailand
98 G 7 Paide, Estonia
210 J 5 Paihia, New Zealand
85 M 17 Päijänne, Finland
173 J 20 Pailin, Cambodia
145 F 16 Paillaco, Chile
78 J 4 Paimpol, France
174 D 11 Painan, Indonesia
117 M 20 Painted Desert, Arizona, U.S.A.
121 N 14 Paintsville, Kentucky, U.S.A.
81 Q 2 País Vasco, Spain
140 A 12 Paita, Peru
84 K 10 Pajala, Sweden
173 I 18 Pak Thong Chai, Thailand
139 Q 7 Pakaraima Mountains, Venezuela/Brazil
193 R 10 Paki, Nigeria
165 U 12 Pakistan, Asia
172 C 12 Pakokku, Myanmar
93 I 25 Paks, Hungary
165 U 8 Paktīā, Afghanistan
165 U 9 Paktīkā, Afghanistan
173 L 18 Pakxé, Laos
193 V 11 Pala, Chad
119 K 22 Palacios, Texas, U.S.A.
141 K 17 Palacios, Bolivia
81 Y 4 Palafrugell, Spain
158 H 15 Palaichóri, Cyprus
97 G 26 Palaiochora, Greece
97 B 18 Palairos, Greece
97 D 16 Palamas, Greece
81 Y 4 Palamós, Spain
157 Y 9 Palana, Russian Federation
175 P 2 Palanan, Philippines
175 P 2 Palanan Point, Philippines
98 B 13 Palanga, Lithuania
174 K 12 Palangkaraya, Indonesia
169 B 14 Palanpur, India
197 N 9 Palapye, Botswana
165 X 6 Palas, Pakistan
123 R 9 Palatka, Florida, U.S.A.
157 X 10 Palatka, Russian Federation
214 I 15 Palau, Oceania
214 I 15 Palau, Palau
91 C 15 Palau, Italy
60 K 7 Palau Trench, Pacific Ocean
173 F 19 Palauk, Myanmar
215 U 15 Palauli Bay, Samoa
173 F 20 Palaw, Myanmar
175 N 6 Palawan, Philippines
174 M 6 Palawan Passage, Philippines
60 I 7 Palawan Trough, Pacific Ocean
98 F 6 Paldiski, Estonia
175 O 10 Paleleh, Indonesia
174 G 12 Palembang, Indonesia
117 J 23 Palen Dry Lake, California, U.S.A.
145 F 18 Palena, Chile
81 N 3 Palencia, Spain
91 I 21 Palermo, Italy
160 F 10 Palestine, Israel
119 L 20 Palestine, Texas, U.S.A.
172 B 12 Paletwa, Myanmar
169 D 22 Palghat, India
196 G 8 Palgrave Point, Namibia
168 C 13 Pali, India
215 P 15 Palikir, Federated States of Micronesia
83 I 24 Paliseul, Belgium
169 B 15 Palitana, India
169 F 23 Palk Strait, Sri Lanka
169 I 17 Palkonda, India
169 G 21 Pallavaram, India
195 T 7 Pallisa, Uganda
211 K 16 Palliser Bay, New Zealand
117 I 23 Palm Springs, California, U.S.A.
81 Y 8 Palma, Spain
80 M 11 Palma del Río, Spain
127 N 6 Palma Soriano, Cuba
142 K 13 Palmas, Brazil
117 G 22 Palmdale, California, U.S.A.
142 L 12 Palmeiras, Brazil
218 H 4 Palmer, Antarctica
112 K 7 Palmer, Alaska, U.S.A.
218 I 5 Palmer Land, Antarctica
126 H 13 Palmer Sur, Costa Rica
215 N 10 Palmerston, Cook Islands
208 L 1 Palmerston, Northern Territory, Australia
211 F 24 Palmerston, New Zealand
211 L 15 Palmerston North, New Zealand
91 L 21 Palmi, Italy
138 H 7 Palmira, Colombia
160 K 5 Palmyra, Syria
61 Q 7 Palmyra Atoll, U.S.A.
117 D 18 Palo Alto, California, U.S.A.
126 M 14 Palo de las Letras, Panama
138 G 4 Palo de las Letras, Colombia
144 M 7 Palo Santo, Argentina
191 F 19 Paloich, Sudan
84 K 9 Palojoensuu, Finland
141 H 18 Palomani, Peru
125 U 13 Palomares, Mexico
175 O 12 Palopo, Indonesia
141 E 18 Palpa, Peru
175 O 15 Palu, Indonesia
159 P 11 Palu, Turkey
175 N 11 Palu, Indonesia
174 H 14 Pamanukan, Indonesia
175 X 12 Pamdai, Indonesia
169 H 15 Pamgarh, India
89 Z 5 Pamhagen, Austria
79 P 15 Pamiers, France
167 U 14 Pamir, Tajikistan
123 W 2 Pamlico Sound, North Carolina, U.S.A.
119 H 17 Pampa, Texas, U.S.A.
144 K 7 Pampa de los Guanacos, Argentina
141 K 20 Pampa Grande, Bolivia
144 I 13 Pampas, Argentina
81 R 2 Pamplona, Spain
138 J 5 Pamplona, Colombia
158 E 8 Pamukova, Turkey
120 H 12 Pana, Illinois, U.S.A.
194 F 9 Pana, Gabon
125 Z 10 Panabá, Mexico
117 K 18 Panaca, Nevada, U.S.A.
96 H 9 Panagyurishte, Bulgaria
174 G 14 Panaitan, Indonesia
169 C 19 Panaji, India
126 K 13 Panama, North America
61 Y 7 Panama Basin, Pacific Ocean
126 K 13 Panama Canal, Panama
126 K 14 Panama City, Panama
122 M 9 Panama City, Florida, U.S.A.
175 P 5 Panay, Philippines
175 P 6 Panay Gulf, Philippines
94 L 10 Pančevo, Serbia and Montenegro
100 F 9 Pâncota, Romania
197 R 10 Panda, Mozambique
174 L 11 Pandang, Indonesia
174 G 14 Pandeglang, Indonesia
98 G 13 Pandėlys, Lithuania
169 D 18 Pandharpur, India
169 F 15 Pandhurna, India
141 I 16 Pando, Bolivia
194 J 5 Pandu, Democratic Republic of Congo
98 F 13 Panevėžys, Lithuania
173 G 15 Pang, Thailand
195 O 6 Panga, Democratic Republic of Congo
214 I 10 Pangai, Tonga
195 W 11 Pangani, Tanzania
195 O 9 Pangi, Democratic Republic of Congo
174 C 9 Pangkalanbrandan, Indonesia
174 J 12 Pangkalanbuun, Indonesia
174 G 12 Pangkalpinang, Indonesia
115 S 2 Pangnirtung, Nunavut, Canada
194 L 3 Pangonda, Central African Republic
145 F 16 Panguipulli, Chile
117 L 18 Panguitch, Utah, U.S.A.
212 J 5 Panguna, Papua New Guinea
175 O 7 Pangutaran, Philippines
195 P 12 Pania-Mwanga, Democratic Republic of Congo
167 R 14 Panj, Tajikistan
165 T 7 Panjāb, Afghanistan
167 Q 13 Panjakent, Tajikistan
165 R 13 Panjgur, Pakistan
171 W 6 Panjin, China
193 S 11 Pankshin, Nigeria
208 F 6 Pannawonica, Western Australia, Australia
143 G 17 Pantanal, Brazil
175 Q 15 Pantar, Indonesia
91 G 24 Pantelleria, Italy
175 Q 15 Pantemakassar, East Timor
172 C 9 Pantha, Myanmar
174 D 10 Panti, Indonesia
125 R 10 Pánuco, Mexico
125 S 10 Pánuco, Mexico
171 O 12 Panzhihua, China
194 J 12 Panzi, Democratic Republic of Congo
126 D 9 Panzos, Guatemala
91 M 19 Paola, Italy
120 J 13 Paoli, Indiana, U.S.A.
93 G 23 Pápa, Hungary
76 I 6 Papa Westray, United Kingdom
143 F 14 Papagaio, Brazil
210 L 12 Papakai, New Zealand
210 J 7 Paparoa, New Zealand
215 Z 8 Papeete, French Polynesia
86 D 11 Papenburg, Germany
215 Y 7 Papetoai, French Polynesia
98 G 13 Papilys, Lithuania
144 F 6 Paposo, Chile
169 H 17 Pappadahandi, India
212 H 5 Papua New Guinea, Oceania
173 E 15 Papun, Myanmar
142 I 11 Pará, Brazil
208 G 7 Paraburdoo, Western Australia, Australia
165 V 8 Parachinar, Pakistan
94 M 12 Paraćin, Serbia and Montenegro
142 N 11 Paracuru, Brazil
169 J 16 Paradwip, India
142 K 10 Paragominas, Brazil
141 M 18 Paragua, Bolivia
143 F 19 Paraguay, South America
143 G 19 Paraguay, Paraguay
142 O 13 Paraiba, Brazil
85 K 19 Parainen, Finland
125 V 12 Paraíso, Mexico
125 W 12 Paraíso, Mexico
193 O 11 Parakou, Benin
139 X 6 Paramaribo, Suriname
97 B 16 Paramythia, Greece
143 I 19 Paraná, Brazil
144 L 10 Paraná, Argentina/Brazil
144 L 10 Paraná, Argentina
143 K 14 Paranã, Brazil
143 J 20 Paranaguá, Brazil
143 I 17 Paranaíba, Brazil
143 I 18 Paranapanema, Brazil
143 H 19 Paranavaí, Brazil
215 W 10 Paraoa, French Polynesia
143 L 17 Paraopeba, Brazil
161 T 4 Pārapāra, Iraq
142 I 12 Parauapebas, Brazil
169 E 17 Parbhani, India
86 J 10 Parchim, Germany
93 N 14 Parczew, Poland
208 G 5 Pardoo Roadhouse, Western Australia, Australia
93 E 17 Pardubice, Czech Republic
164 F 2 Pareh, Iran
210 H 4 Parengarenga Harbour, New Zealand
115 Q 12 Parent, Québec, Canada
211 F 22 Pareora, New Zealand
175 N 12 Parepare, Indonesia
97 B 17 Parga, Greece
175 O 11 Parigi, Indonesia
142 G 10 Parintins, Brazil
79 Q 4 Paris, France
119 L 18 Paris, Texas, U.S.A.
120 L 13 Paris, Kentucky, U.S.A.
122 K 1 Paris, Tennessee, U.S.A.
164 L 10 Pārīz, Iran
120 G 4 Park Falls, Wisconsin, U.S.A.
118 K 8 Park Rapids, Minnesota, U.S.A.
85 K 17 Parkano, Finland
117 K 23 Parker, Arizona, U.S.A.
121 O 12 Parkersburg, West Virginia, U.S.A.
209 T 11 Parkes, New South Wales, Australia
169 I 17 Parlakimidi, India
169 D 17 Parli, India
90 D 8 Parma, Italy
142 K 13 Parnaíba, Brazil
142 M 11 Parnaíba, Brazil
97 E 18 Parnassos, Greece
89 Z 4 Parndorf, Austria
97 E 22 Parnon, Greece
98 F 8 Pärnu, Estonia
98 F 7 Pärnu-Jaagupi, Estonia
98 F 8 Pärnu laht, Estonia
168 L 12 Paro, Bhutan
97 J 22 Paros, Greece
97 J 22 Paros, Greece
117 L 18 Parowan, Utah, U.S.A.
125 P 7 Parras, Mexico
126 H 13 Parrita, Costa Rica
115 O 1 Parry Bay, Nunavut, Canada
65 O 8 Parry Islands, Arctic Ocean
115 O 13 Parry Sound, Ontario, Canada
92 F 9 Parsęta, Poland
119 K 15 Parsons, Kansas, U.S.A.
88 J 8 Partenen, Austria
78 M 8 Parthenay, France
93 I 20 Partizánske, Slovakia
142 H 9 Paru, Brazil
142 G 10 Paru de Oeste, Brazil
168 D 12 Parvatsar, India
165 U 7 Parwān, Afghanistan
99 L 19 Parychy, Belarus
117 G 22 Pasadena, California, U.S.A.
119 L 21 Pasadena, Texas, U.S.A.
158 B 8 Paşalimani, Turkey
174 D 12 Pasapuat, Indonesia
122 J 8 Pascagoula, Mississippi, U.S.A.
100 L 8 Paşcani, Romania
141 D 15 Pasco, Peru
116 G 8 Pasco, Washington, U.S.A.
86 N 10 Pasewalk, Germany
113 W 8 Pasfield Lake, Saskatchewan, Canada
168 O 11 Pasighat, India
159 Q 9 Pasinler, Turkey
174 E 8 Pasir Putih, Malaysia
165 P 12 Paskūh, Iran
92 J 9 Pasłęk, Poland
92 J 8 Pasłęka, Poland
165 Q 14 Pasni, Pakistan
145 H 18 Paso de Indios, Argentina
144 M 9 Paso de los Libres, Argentina
144 N 11 Paso de los Toros, Uruguay
145 H 19 Paso Río Mayo, Argentina
117 E 21 Paso Robles, California, U.S.A.
113 S 1 Passage Point, Northwest Territories, Canada
89 W 6 Passail, Austria
87 M 23 Passau, Germany

Country · Internal administrative region: State/Province/Territory/Dependent territory · Capital city · Mountain range/Undersea ridge · Mountain peak/Volcano/Seamount · Geographic feature · Headland/Point/Cape/Peninsula · Desert · Island/Island group · Antarctic base · Ocean · Sea · Bay/Gulf/Channel/Strait · Lake · Salt pan/Dry/Intermittent lake · River

175 P 5 Passi, Philippines
143 I 21 Passo Fundo, Brazil
99 I 15 Pastavy, Belarus
140 C 9 Pastaza, Ecuador
138 G 9 Pasto, Colombia
165 Y 5 Pasu, Pakistan
174 K 14 Pasuruan, Indonesia
98 F 13 Pasvalys, Lithuania
194 L 3 Pata, Central African Republic
145 G 22 Patagonia, Argentina
168 J 12 Patan, Nepal
169 B 14 Patan, India
169 F 14 Patan, India
175 S 10 Patani, Indonesia
210 J 13 Patea, New Zealand
193 Q 12 Pategi, Nigeria
89 R 8 Paternion, Austria
91 K 22 Paterno, Italy
121 U 10 Paterson, New Jersey, U.S.A.
168 D 9 Pathankot, India
118 E 12 Pathfinder Reservoir, Wyoming, U.S.A.
173 G 22 Pathiu, Thailand
168 E 10 Patiala, India
160 O 12 Patkoo Range, India
97 L 21 Patmos, Greece
168 I 13 Patna, India
159 S 10 Patnos, Turkey
120 J 13 Patoka Lake, Indiana, U.S.A.
142 O 12 Patos, Brazil
143 K 17 Patos de Minas, Brazil
144 H 9 Patquía, Argentina
97 D 19 Patra, Greece
97 C 19 Patraïkos Kolpos, Greece
84 A 10 Patreksfjörður, Iceland
173 I 26 Pattani, Thailand
173 H 20 Pattaya, Thailand
121 Y 4 Patten, Maine, U.S.A.
61 R 2 Patton Seamount, Pacific Ocean
169 L 15 Patuakhali, Bangladesh
125 P 12 Pátzcuaro, Mexico
78 M 14 Pau, France
142 C 13 Pauini, Brazil
172 C 12 Pauk, Myanmar
113 Q 4 Paulatuk, Northwest Territories, Canada
117 L 22 Paulden, Arizona, U.S.A.
142 O 13 Paulista, Brazil
142 N 13 Paulo Afonso, Brazil
119 J 18 Pauls Valley, Oklahoma, U.S.A.
172 C 9 Paungbyin, Myanmar
173 D 14 Paungde, Myanmar
169 E 20 Pavagada, India
90 C 7 Pavia, Italy
98 C 11 Pāvilosta, Latvia
96 J 8 Pavlikeni, Bulgaria
100 J 3 Pavlivka, Ukraine
167 U 4 Pavlodar, Kazakhstan
167 U 3 Pavlodar, Kazakhstan
101 V 6 Pavlohrad, Ukraine
94 F 8 Pavlovac, Croatia
156 D 10 Pavlovskaya, Russian Federation
90 F 9 Pavullo nel Frignano, Italy
97 H 26 Paximadia, Greece
97 A 17 Paxoi, Greece
112 L 7 Paxson, Alaska, U.S.A.
173 E 15 Payagyi, Myanmar
174 D 11 Payakumbuh, Indonesia
88 C 8 Payerne, Switzerland
208 G 10 Paynes Find, Western Australia, Australia
78 L 6 Pays de la Loire, France
144 M 11 Paysandu, Uruguay
144 M 11 Paysandú, Uruguay
117 N 22 Payson, Arizona, U.S.A.
174 G 12 Payung, Indonesia
138 K 6 Paz de Ariporo, Colombia
159 Q 7 Pazar, Turkey
158 F 7 Pazarbaşi Burnu, Turkey
158 M 12 Pazarcik, Turkey
96 H 10 Pazardzhik, Bulgaria
96 H 10 Pazardzhik, Bulgaria
94 A 9 Pazin, Croatia
113 U 9 Peace, Alberta, Canada
113 T 10 Peace River, Alberta, Canada
117 L 21 Peach Springs, Arizona, U.S.A.
117 C 15 Peanut, California, U.S.A.
117 O 25 Pearce, Arizona, U.S.A.
122 H 6 Pearl, Mississippi, U.S.A.
117 C 24 Pearl City, Hawaii, U.S.A.
117 B 24 Pearl Harbor, Hawaii, U.S.A.
123 P 7 Pearson, Georgia, U.S.A.
65 R 10 Peary Land, Greenland
115 N 8 Peawanuck, Ontario, Canada
197 T 6 Pebane, Mozambique
140 G 10 Pebas, Peru
145 L 23 Pebble Island, Falkland Islands
95 K 15 Peć, Serbia and Montenegro
156 J 7 Pechora, Russian Federation
156 J 8 Pechora, Russian Federation
156 K 6 Pechorskoye More, Russian Federation
119 G 20 Pecos, U.S.A.
119 G 20 Pecos, Texas, U.S.A.
83 C 20 Pecq, Belgium
93 H 26 Pécs, Hungary
126 K 14 Pedasí, Panama
127 Q 7 Pedernales, Dominican Republic
196 F 6 Pediva, Angola
143 M 16 Pedra Azul, Brazil
63 B 17 Pedra Badejo, Cape Verde
143 E 14 Pedras Negras, Brazil
125 N 7 Pedriceña, Mexico
142 K 13 Pedro Afonso, Brazil
126 L 8 Pedro Bank, Honduras
144 G 5 Pedro de Valdivia, Chile
143 G 18 Pedro Juan Caballero, Paraguay
120 M 12 Peebles, Ohio, U.S.A.
121 U 9 Peekskill, New York, U.S.A.
113 N 5 Peel, Yukon Territory, Canada
77 G 16 Peel, United Kingdom
86 M 9 Peene, Germany
86 M 8 Peenemünde, Germany
211 I 20 Pegasus Bay, New Zealand
87 J 20 Pegnitz, Germany
173 D 15 Pegu, Myanmar
173 E 16 Pegu, Myanmar
173 D 14 Pegu Yoma, Myanmar
174 B 8 Pegunungan Barisan, Indonesia
174 L 10 Pegunungan Iran, Indonesia
175 X 12 Pegunungan Maoke, Indonesia
174 K 11 Pegunungan Muller, Indonesia
174 J 11 Pegunungan Schwaner, Indonesia
144 K 13 Pehuajó, Argentina
97 G 20 Peiraias, Greece
143 J 14 Peixe, Brazil
174 H 10 Pejantan, Indonesia
174 F 9 Pekan, Malaysia
174 E 10 Pekanbaru, Indonesia
174 M 10 Pelawanbesar, Indonesia
175 P 11 Peleng, Indonesia
93 D 18 Pelhřimov, Czech Republic
126 L 2 Pelican Point, The Bahamas
96 C 13 Pelister, Macedonia (F.Y.R.O.M.)
122 M 4 Pell City, Alabama, U.S.A.
84 K 11 Pello, Finland
86 F 8 Pellworm, Germany
113 N 7 Pelly, Yukon Territory, Canada
114 M 1 Pelly Bay, Nunavut, Canada
113 N 7 Pelly Crossing, Yukon Territory, Canada
119 D 18 Pelona Mountain, New Mexico, U.S.A.
97 D 21 Peloponnese, Greece
97 E 22 Peloponnisos, Greece
143 I 22 Pelotas, Brazil
174 I 10 Pemangkat, Indonesia
174 C 9 Pematangsiantar, Indonesia
197 U 4 Pemba, Mozambique
197 N 6 Pemba, Zambia
195 W 11 Pemba Channel, Tanzania
195 X 11 Pemba Island, Tanzania
113 S 14 Pemberton, British Columbia, Canada
208 G 12 Pemberton, Western Australia, Australia
118 J 7 Pembina, Minnesota, U.S.A.
118 J 7 Pembina, North Dakota, U.S.A.
120 I 5 Pembine, Wisconsin, U.S.A.
175 X 14 Pembre, Indonesia
77 G 21 Pembroke, United Kingdom
115 Q 13 Pembroke, Ontario, Canada
81 N 1 Pena Prieta, Spain
80 I 5 Penafiel, Portugal
81 N 4 Peñafiel, Spain
81 O 5 Peñalara, Spain
142 L 11 Penalva, Brazil
80 M 6 Peñaranda de Bracamonte, Spain
80 L 10 Peñarroya-Pueblonuevo, Spain
116 I 6 Pend Oreille Lake, Idaho, U.S.A.
195 N 11 Penge, Democratic Republic of Congo
171 W 7 Penglai, China
172 B 12 Pengwa, Myanmar
174 L 15 Penida, Indonesia
145 G 25 Península Brecknock, Chile
126 J 14 Península de Azuero, Panama
145 G 25 Península de Brunswick, Chile
126 H 14 Península de Osa, Costa Rica
145 E 20 Península de Taitao, Chile
145 H 26 Peninsula Hardy, Chile
145 I 25 Península Mitre, Argentina
141 D 18 Peninsula Paracas, Peru
138 L 1 Peninsula Paraguaná, Venezuela
145 E 21 Península Tres Montes, Chile
145 J 17 Peninsula Valdés, Argentina
145 K 15 Península Verde, Argentina
145 E 22 Península Wharton, Chile
115 U 11 Péninsule de Gaspé, Québec, Canada
115 P 5 Pèninsule d'Ungava, Québec, Canada
81 U 7 Peñíscola, Spain
161 V 3 Penjwin, Iraq
78 H 6 Penmarch, France
90 J 13 Penne, Italy
219 Q 14 Pennell Coast, Antarctica
77 I 14 Pennines, United Kingdom
121 T 11 Pennsville, New Jersey, U.S.A.
121 P 10 Pennsylvania, U.S.A.
209 N 10 Penong, South Australia, Australia
126 J 14 Penonomé, Panama
61 R 8 Penrhyn Basin, Pacific Ocean
77 I 15 Penrith, United Kingdom
122 L 8 Pensacola, Florida, U.S.A.
219 N 6 Pensacola Mountains, Antarctica
141 M 18 Pensamiento, Bolivia
213 R 10 Pentecost, Vanuatu
113 T 14 Penticton, British Columbia, Canada
209 T 5 Pentland, Queensland, Australia
76 H 7 Pentland Firth, United Kingdom
169 E 20 Penukonda, India
156 G 9 Penza, Russian Federation
77 F 24 Penzance, United Kingdom
87 J 25 Penzberg, Germany
157 Y 9 Penzhinskaya Guba, Russian Federation
120 H 10 Peoria, Illinois, U.S.A.
210 K 9 Pepepe, New Zealand
174 D 8 Perak, Malaysia
81 S 6 Perales del Alfambra, Spain
97 I 26 Perama, Greece
169 F 22 Perambalur, India
84 N 12 Peranka, Finland
89 X 4 Perchtoldsdorf, Austria
208 J 5 Percival Lakes, Western Australia, Australia
100 H 6 Perechyn, Ukraine
138 H 6 Pereira, Colombia
143 I 18 Pereira Barreto, Brazil
100 J 4 Peremyshlyany, Ukraine
101 V 5 Pereshchepyne, Ukraine
101 Q 4 Pereyaslav-Khmel'nyts'kyy, Ukraine
116 E 13 Perez, California, U.S.A.
89 T 4 Perg, Austria
144 K 12 Pergamino, Argentina
85 K 15 Perhonjoki, Finland
115 S 10 Péribonca, Québec, Canada
144 I 6 Perico, Argentina
124 L 7 Pericos, Mexico
79 O 11 Périgueux, France
97 H 17 Peristera, Greece
145 G 20 Perito Moreno, Argentina
86 K 11 Perleberg, Germany
174 D 7 Perlis, Malaysia
156 I 9 Perm', Russian Federation
95 L 21 Përmet, Albania
94 B 11 Permuda, Croatia
142 O 13 Pernambuco, Brazil
63 J 14 Pernambuco Abyssal Plain, Atlantic Ocean
63 I 14 Pernambuco Seamounts, Atlantic Ocean
96 F 9 Pernik, Bulgaria
96 F 9 Pernik, Bulgaria
89 W 5 Pernitz, Austria
125 S 12 Perote, Mexico
79 R 15 Perpignan, France
123 P 9 Perry, Florida, U.S.A.
123 O 6 Perry, Georgia, U.S.A.
119 H 16 Perryton, Texas, U.S.A.
141 L 18 Perseverancia, Bolivia
163 T 3 Persian Gulf, Asia
76 I 12 Perth, United Kingdom
115 Q 14 Perth, Ontario, Canada
208 G 11 Perth, Western Australia, Australia
59 T 8 Perth Basin, Indian Ocean
78 L 9 Pertuis Breton, France
78 L 9 Pertuis d'Antioche, France
141 E 15 Peru, South America
141 J 16 Perú, Bolivia
61 Y 9 Peru Basin, Pacific Ocean
90 G 11 Perugia, Italy
61 Z 7 Peru–Chile Trench, Pacific Ocean
83 D 21 Peruwelz, Belgium
101 Q 7 Pervomays'k, Ukraine
101 T 11 Pervomays'ke, Ukraine
101 V 5 Pervomays'kyy, Ukraine
157 Y 8 Pervorechenskiy, Russian Federation
156 I 10 Pervoural'sk, Russian Federation
90 H 10 Pesaro, Italy
90 J 13 Pescara, Italy
165 W 7 Peshawar, Pakistan
95 L 17 Peshkopi, Albania
96 H 10 Peshtera, Bulgaria
167 R 9 Peski Muyunkum, Kazakhstan
167 V 8 Peski Saryyesik-Atyrau, Kazakhstan
167 U 9 Peski Taukum, Kazakhstan
160 F 9 Petah Tiqwa, Israel
97 D 22 Petalidi, Greece
117 D 17 Petaluma, California, U.S.A.
83 K 26 Pètange, Luxembourg
125 P 13 Petatlán, Mexico
197 P 5 Petauke, Zambia
120 G 6 Petenwell Lake, Wisconsin, U.S.A.
218 H 8 Peter I Island, Norway
113 W 10 Peter Pond Lake, Saskatchewan, Canada
115 N 12 Peterbell, Ontario, Canada
77 L 19 Peterborough, United Kingdom
115 P 14 Peterborough, Ontario, Canada
209 P 11 Peterborough, South Australia, Australia
76 J 10 Peterhead, United Kingdom
65 P 12 Petermann Bjerg, Greenland
113 O 10 Petersburg, Alaska, U.S.A.
121 S 14 Petersburg, Virginia, U.S.A.
113 R 9 Petitot, British Columbia, Canada
125 Z 11 Peto, Mexico
120 L 5 Petoskey, Michigan, U.S.A.
160 G 12 Petra, Jordan
96 F 12 Petrich, Bulgaria
101 P 9 Petrivka, Ukraine
101 U 9 Petrivka, Ukraine
138 J 4 Petrólea, Colombia
142 N 13 Petrolina, Brazil
167 R 1 Petropavlovsk, Kazakhstan
157 Z 11 Petropavlovsk-Kamchatskiy, Russian Federation
100 H 11 Petroşani, Romania
157 Q 14 Petrovsk-Zabaykal'skiy, Russian Federation
156 G 6 Petrozavodsk, Russian Federation
100 M 7 Petruşeni, Moldova
101 U 6 Petrykivka, Ukraine
82 G 9 Petten, Netherlands
156 J 11 Petukhovo, Russian Federation
89 S 3 Peuerbach, Austria
174 C 8 Peureula, Indonesia
157 X 6 Pevek, Russian Federation
93 G 21 Pezinok, Slovakia
165 V 9 Pezu, Pakistan
87 J 23 Pfaffenhofen an der Ilm, Germany
87 F 22 Pforzheim, Germany
87 G 25 Pfullendorf, Germany
88 K 8 Pfunds, Austria
197 P 10 Phalaborwa, Republic of South Africa
165 X 8 Phalia, Pakistan
168 C 12 Phalodi, India
173 O 21 Phan Rang, Vietnam
173 O 21 Phan Ri, Vietnam
173 O 22 Phan Thiêt, Vietnam
173 K 15 Phang Khon, Thailand
173 F 24 Phangnga, Thailand
168 J 12 Phaplu, Nepal
173 H 25 Phatthalung, Thailand
173 H 14 Phayao, Thailand
123 N 6 Phenix City, Alabama, U.S.A.
173 H 20 Phet Buri, Thailand
173 I 16 Phetchabun, Thailand
173 H 17 Phichit, Thailand
121 T 11 Philadelphia, Pennsylvania, U.S.A.
122 J 5 Philadelphia, Mississippi, U.S.A.
83 G 22 Philippeville, Belgium
60 K 6 Philippine Basin, Pacific Ocean
60 K 6 Philippine Sea, Pacific Ocean
60 J 5 Philippine Trench, Pacific Ocean
175 N 6 Philippines, Asia
119 I 14 Phillipsburg, Kansas, U.S.A.
173 J 18 Phimai, Thailand
173 H 16 Phitsanulok, Thailand
173 L 21 Phnom Penh, Cambodia
173 K 21 Phnum Aôral, Cambodia
173 J 20 Phnum Tumpôr, Cambodia
214 K 4 Phoenix, Kiribati
117 M 23 Phoenix, Arizona, U.S.A.
214 H 4 Phoenix Islands, Kiribati
173 J 17 Phon, Thailand
172 K 11 Phong Thô, Vietnam
172 I 11 Phôngsali, Laos
173 J 14 Phou Bia, Laos
173 L 15 Phou Cô Pi, Laos
172 I 13 Phou Houie Moc, Laos
172 J 13 Phou San, Laos
173 M 17 Phou Set, Laos
173 K 14 Phou Xai Lai Leng, Laos/Vietnam
173 H 15 Phrae, Thailand
173 K 22 Phsar Ream, Cambodia
173 N 16 Phu Lôc, Vietnam
172 M 12 Phu Ly, Vietnam
173 O 18 Phu My, Vietnam
173 O 19 Phu Nhon, Vietnam
172 L 12 Phu Tho, Vietnam
173 F 25 Phuket, Thailand
173 L 21 Phumi Banam, Cambodia
173 J 21 Phumi Kaôh Kŏng, Cambodia
173 M 21 Phumi Krêk, Cambodia
173 L 19 Phumi Mlu Prey, Cambodia
173 K 19 Phumi Moŭng, Cambodia
173 K 20 Phumi Prâmaôy, Cambodia
173 K 19 Phumi Sâmraông, Cambodia
173 K 22 Phumi Veal Renh, Cambodia
173 L 23 Phuoc Long, Vietnam
90 D 8 Piacenza, Italy
90 E 8 Piadena, Italy
92 L 13 Piaseczno, Poland
93 N 15 Piaski, Poland
100 L 9 Piatra Neamţ, Romania
142 L 13 Piauí, Brazil
142 L 13 Piaui, Brazil
191 F 21 Pibor Post, Sudan
127 P 7 Pic de la Selle, Haiti
192 H 12 Pic de Tibé, Guinea
79 O 15 Pic d'Estats, France/Spain
78 L 15 Pic d'Orhy, France
144 G 3 Pica, Chile
125 O 4 Picacho del Centinela, Mexico
79 Q 3 Picardie, France
122 I 8 Picayune, Mississippi, U.S.A.
144 J 5 Pichanal, Argentina
145 J 15 Pichi Mahuida, Argentina
144 F 12 Pichilemu, Chile
124 J 8 Pichilingue, Mexico
140 B 8 Pichincha, Ecuador
114 L 10 Pickle Lake, Ontario, Canada
118 I 11 Pickstown, South Dakota, U.S.A.
62 N 2 Pico, Azores
62 M 1 Pico, Azores
193 S 15 Pico Basile, Equatorial Guinea
138 K 4 Pico Bolívar, Venezuela
138 I 2 Pico Cristóbal Colón, Colombia
139 O 9 Pico da Neblina, Venezuela
143 L 17 Pico de Itambé, Brazil
62 M 12 Pico de las Nieves, Canary Islands
125 S 12 Pico de Orizaba, Mexico
194 B 7 Pico de São Tomé, São Tomé and Príncipe
62 L 12 Pico del Teide, Canary Islands
127 Q 7 Pico Duarte, Dominican Republic
126 F 10 Pico Mogotón, Nicaragua
62 O 4 Pico Ruivo, Madeira
126 K 4 Pico San Juan, Cuba
142 D 9 Pico Tamacuari, Brazil
145 H 20 Pico Truncado, Argentina
126 M 6 Pico Turquino, Cuba
142 M 12 Picos, Brazil
140 D 13 Picota, Peru
211 J 16 Picton, New Zealand
145 G 15 Picún Leufú, Argentina
165 Q 14 Pidarak, Pakistan
100 J 5 Pidhaytsi, Ukraine
169 G 25 Pidurutalagala, Sri Lanka
123 O 5 Piedmont, Georgia, U.S.A.
122 M 4 Piedmont, Alabama, U.S.A.
80 L 6 Piedrahita, Spain
125 Q 5 Piedras Negras, Mexico
85 N 16 Pieksämäki, Finland
85 O 15 Pielinen, Finland
90 B 8 Piemonte, Italy
92 J 8 Pieniężno, Poland
118 H 10 Pierre, South Dakota, U.S.A.
58 E 8 Pierrot Island, Rodrigues Island
93 H 20 Piešťany, Slovakia
197 P 11 Piet Retief, Republic of South Africa
58 B 11 Pieter Both, Mauritius
197 P 12 Pietermaritzburg, Republic of South Africa
197 O 10 Pietersburg, Republic of South Africa
90 H 5 Pieve di Cadóre, Italy
145 K 14 Pigüé, Argentina
85 L 15 Pihtipudas, Finland
125 V 14 Pijijiapan, Mexico
167 W 11 Pik Dankova, Kyrgyzstan
167 Y 10 Pik Khan-Tengri, Kazakhstan/Kyrgyzstan
196 J 15 Piketberg, Republic of South Africa
121 N 14 Pikeville, Kentucky, U.S.A.
171 W 6 Pikou, China
194 I 7 Pikounda, Congo
144 M 13 Pila, Argentina
92 G 11 Piła, Poland
143 G 20 Pilar, Paraguay
144 L 12 Pilar, Argentina
208 H 6 Pilbara, Western Australia, Australia
145 G 17 Pilcaniyeu, Argentina
144 K 5 Pilcomayo, Argentina
169 F 21 Pileru, India
168 G 11 Pilibhit, India
93 K 14 Pilica, Poland
63 L 26 Pillar Bay, Ascension

Country · Internal administrative region: State/Province/Territory/Dependent territory · Capital city · Mountain range/Undersea ridge · Mountain peak/Volcano/Seamount · Geographic feature · Headland/Point/Cape/Peninsula · Desert · Island/Island group · Antarctic base · Ocean · Sea · Bay/Gulf/Channel/Strait · Lake · Salt pan/Dry/Intermittent lake · River

1 G 17 **Pillcopata**, Peru
6 M 6 **Pilón**, Cuba
2 H 8 **Pilot Point**, Alaska, U.S.A.
L 17 **Pilzno**, Poland
3 E 14 **Pimenta Bueno**, Brazil
T 4 **Pina**, Spain
5 X 10 **Pinaki**, French Polynesia
4 D 8 **Pinang**, Malaysia
4 D 8 **Pinang**, Malaysia
6 H 4 **Pinar del Río**, Cuba
8 L 11 **Pinarbaşi**, Turkey
8 C 6 **Pinarhisar**, Turkey
3 V 14 **Pincher Creek**, Alberta, Canada
5 X 9 **Pindi Bhattian**, Pakistan
5 W 8 **Pindi Gheb**, Pakistan
B 15 **Pindus Mountains**, Greece
8 B 13 **Pindwara**, India
9 N 18 **Pine Bluff**, Arkansas, U.S.A.
8 M 2 **Pine Creek**, Northern Territory, Australia
4 I 9 **Pine Dock**, Manitoba, Canada
4 I 10 **Pine Falls**, Manitoba, Canada
3 R 11 **Pine Hills**, Florida, U.S.A.
3 U 8 **Pine Point**, Northwest Territories, Canada
8 G 11 **Pine Ridge**, South Dakota, U.S.A.
66 I 7 **Pinega**, Russian Federation
13 X 10 **Pinehouse Lake**, Saskatchewan, Canada
7 E 16 **Pineios**, Greece
) A 8 **Pinerolo**, Italy
71 P 8 **Ping'an**, China
71 S 9 **Pingdingshan**, China
15 R 15 **Pingelap**, Federated States of Micronesia
71 S 10 **Pingli**, China
71 R 8 **Pingliang**, China
71 X 13 **P'ingtung**, Taiwan
71 U 12 **Pingxiang**, China
42 L 10 **Pinheiro**, Brazil
0 J 6 **Pinhel**, Portugal
74 C 10 **Pini**, Indonesia
08 G 11 **Pinjarra**, Western Australia, Australia
72 D 9 **Pinlebu**, Myanmar
09 Q 12 **Pinnaroo**, South Australia, Australia
1 S 10 **Pinoso**, Spain
25 S 14 **Pinotepa Nacional**, Mexico
9 H 21 **Pinsk**, Belarus
44 G 3 **Pintados**, Chile
44 K 9 **Pinto**, Argentina
95 N 12 **Piodi**, Democratic Republic of Congo
0 E 12 **Piombino**, Italy
10 K 11 **Piopio**, New Zealand
3 J 14 **Piotrków Trybunalski**, Poland
7 H 17 **Piperi**, Greece
18 K 10 **Pipestone**, Minnesota, U.S.A.
10 K 13 **Pipiriki**, New Zealand
20 L 11 **Piqua**, Ohio, U.S.A.
68 C 7 **Pir Panjal Range**, India
43 K 19 **Piracicaba**, Brazil
44 M 7 **Pirané**, Argentina
43 I 16 **Piranhas**, Brazil
43 L 16 **Pirapora**, Brazil
42 M 11 **Piripiri**, Brazil
37 D 21 **Pirmasens**, Germany
95 O 14 **Pirot**, Serbia and Montenegro
75 S 12 **Piru**, Indonesia
165 R 9 **Pirzada**, Afghanistan
90 E 10 **Pisa**, Italy
144 F 3 **Pisagua**, Chile
91 K 17 **Pisciotta**, Italy
141 D 17 **Pisco**, Peru
93 C 19 **Písek**, Czech Republic
141 M 17 **Piso Firme**, Bolivia
125 Z 10 **Pisté**, Mexico
91 M 17 **Pisticci**, Italy
90 F 10 **Pistoia**, Italy
92 M 10 **Pisz**, Poland
192 G 10 **Pita**, Guinea
115 U 9 **Pitaga**, Newfoundland and Labrador, Canada
143 I 19 **Pitanga**, Brazil
61 W 14 **Pitcairn Island**, U.K.
84 J 13 **Piteå**, Sweden
84 I 12 **Piteälven**, Sweden
100 I 12 **Pitești**, Romania
79 Q 6 **Pithiviers**, France
168 G 10 **Pithoragarh**, India
76 H 11 **Pitlochry**, United Kingdom
94 F 7 **Pitomača**, Croatia
58 C 15 **Piton de la Fournaise**, Réunion
58 A 12 **Piton de la Petite Rivière Noire**, Mauritius
58 A 14 **Piton des Neiges**, Réunion
145 F 15 **Pitrufquén**, Chile
113 P 12 **Pitt Island**, British Columbia, Canada
83 C 18 **Pittem**, Belgium
169 B 22 **Pitti**, India
121 P 11 **Pittsburgh**, Pennsylvania, U.S.A.
121 Y 5 **Pittsfield**, Maine, U.S.A.
121 V 8 **Pittsfield**, Massachusetts, U.S.A.
142 J 13 **Pium**, Brazil
140 A 12 **Piura**, Peru
140 A 12 **Piura**, Peru
101 Q 8 **Pivdennyy Buh**, Ukraine
94 B 8 **Pivka**, Slovenia
88 J 9 **Piz Bernina**, Switzerland/Italy
141 H 20 **Pizacoma**, Peru
193 Q 11 **Pizhi**, Nigeria
115 Y 11 **Placentia Bay**, Newfoundland and Labrador, Canada
175 Q 5 **Placer**, Philippines
117 E 17 **Placerville**, California, U.S.A.
188 L 11 **Plaine du Tidikelt**, Algeria
119 H 18 **Plainview**, Texas, U.S.A.
174 M 15 **Plampang**, Indonesia
95 H 14 **Plana**, Bosnia and Herzegovina
142 H 9 **Planalto de Maracanaquara**, Brazil
196 I 5 **Planalto do Bié**, Angola
143 H 15 **Planalto do Mato Grosso**, Brazil
197 T 4 **Planalto Moçambicano**, Mozambique
119 K 19 **Plano**, Texas, U.S.A.
80 K 7 **Plasencia**, Spain
97 D 20 **Platanos**, Greece
193 S 12 **Plateau**, Nigeria
195 O 14 **Plateau de La Manika**, Democratic Republic of Congo
173 M 18 **Plateau des Bolovens**, Laos
193 U 5 **Plateau du Djado**, Niger
189 P 11 **Plateau du Fadnoun**, Algeria
194 M 12 **Plateau du Kasai**, Democratic Republic of Congo
193 T 4 **Plateau du Manguéni**, Niger
188 M 10 **Plateau du Tademaït**, Algeria
189 O 11 **Plateau du Tinrhert**, Algeria
194 G 9 **Plateaux**, Congo
94 K 10 **Platičevo**, Serbia and Montenegro
138 I 3 **Plato**, Colombia
118 J 13 **Platte**, Nebraska, U.S.A.
120 G 8 **Platteville**, Wisconsin, U.S.A.
121 U 6 **Plattsburgh**, New York, U.S.A.
87 K 18 **Plauen**, Germany
86 K 10 **Plauer See**, Germany
95 K 15 **Plav**, Serbia and Montenegro
156 F 8 **Plavsk**, Russian Federation
173 O 19 **Plây Cu**, Vietnam
62 O 11 **Playa Blanca**, Canary Islands
125 S 7 **Playa Lauro Villar**, Mexico
93 C 20 **Plechý**, Czech Republic
118 F 7 **Plentywood**, Montana, U.S.A.
156 H 7 **Plesetsk**, Russian Federation
92 H 13 **Pleszew**, Poland
96 I 7 **Pleven**, Bulgaria
96 I 7 **Pleven**, Bulgaria
94 D 10 **Plitvica Selo**, Croatia
94 J 13 **Pljevlja**, Serbia and Montenegro
92 J 12 **Płock**, Poland
94 G 13 **Pločno**, Bosnia and Herzegovina
78 K 6 **Ploërmel**, France
100 K 12 **Ploiești**, Romania
97 L 18 **Plomari**, Greece
86 H 9 **Plön**, Germany
92 K 12 **Płońsk**, Poland
99 H 21 **Plotnitsa**, Belarus
92 E 9 **Płoty**, Poland
78 H 4 **Ploudalmézeau**, France
96 I 10 **Plovdiv**, Bulgaria
96 I 10 **Plovdiv**, Bulgaria
90 G 7 **Plove di Sacco**, Italy
116 I 7 **Plummer**, Idaho, U.S.A.
197 O 8 **Plumtree**, Zimbabwe
98 C 13 **Plungė**, Lithuania
95 I 14 **Plužine**, Serbia and Montenegro
99 J 16 **Plyeshchanitsy**, Belarus
127 W 8 **Plymouth**, Montserrat
77 H 24 **Plymouth**, United Kingdom
120 K 10 **Plymouth**, Indiana, U.S.A.
121 X 8 **Plymouth**, Massachusetts, U.S.A.
93 B 18 **Plzeň**, Czech Republic
92 F 12 **Pniewy**, Poland
90 E 8 **Po**, Italy
192 M 10 **Pô**, Burkina Faso
90 H 8 **Po Delta**, Italy
116 L 12 **Pocatello**, Idaho, U.S.A.
87 M 23 **Pocking**, Germany
121 T 13 **Pocomoke City**, Maryland, U.S.A.
143 G 16 **Poconé**, Brazil
143 K 18 **Poços de Caldas**, Brazil
94 N 12 **Podgorac**, Serbia and Montenegro
95 J 16 **Podgorica**, Serbia and Montenegro
157 N 11 **Podkamennaya Tunguska**, Russian Federation
192 E 7 **Podor**, Senegal
95 M 14 **Podujevo**, Serbia and Montenegro
93 G 22 **Podunajská nížina**, Slovakia
196 K 13 **Pofadder**, Republic of South Africa
90 F 8 **Poggio Rusco**, Italy
95 L 19 **Pogradec**, Albania
171 Z 7 **P'ohang**, South Korea
84 L 13 **Pohjois-li**, Finland
215 P 15 **Pohnpei**, Federated States of Micronesia
215 P 15 **Pohnpei**, Federated States of Micronesia
117 C 16 **Point Arena**, California, U.S.A.
117 C 17 **Point Arena**, California, U.S.A.
117 E 22 **Point Arguello**, California, U.S.A.
112 K 1 **Point Barrow**, Alaska, U.S.A.
61 X 15 **Point Christian**, Pitcairn Island
117 E 22 **Point Conception**, California, U.S.A.
120 K 5 **Point Detour**, Michigan, U.S.A.
112 K 1 **Point Franklin**, Alaska, U.S.A.
112 H 2 **Point Hope**, Alaska, U.S.A.
169 G 23 **Point Pedro**, Sri Lanka
117 C 18 **Point Reyes**, California, U.S.A.
208 F 5 **Point Samson**, Western Australia, Australia
116 C 13 **Point St George**, California, U.S.A.
120 J 5 **Point Sturgeon**, Wisconsin, U.S.A.
127 X 8 **Pointe-à-Pitre**, Guadeloupe
121 N 7 **Pointe Aux Barques**, Michigan, U.S.A.
139 Z 6 **Pointe Béhague**, French Guiana
58 F 7 **Pointe Cotton**, Rodrigues Island
78 L 3 **Pointe de Barfleur**, France
58 B 15 **Pointe de Langevin**, Réunion
78 H 6 **Pointe de Penmarch**, France
78 K 7 **Pointe de St-Gildas**, France
78 G 5 **Pointe de St-Mathieu**, France
58 C 15 **Pointe des Cascades**, Réunion
58 A 14 **Pointe des Galets**, Réunion
78 G 5 **Pointe du Raz**, France
58 B 10 **Pointe du Sud**, Seychelles
194 E 10 **Pointe-Noire**, Congo
58 A 12 **Pointe Sud Ouest**, Mauritius
90 B 8 **Poirino**, Italy
79 N 8 **Poitiers**, France
78 M 9 **Poitou-Charentes**, France
79 P 3 **Poix-de-Picardie**, France
92 K 10 **Pojezierze Mazurskie**, Poland
141 K 20 **Pojo**, Bolivia
168 B 12 **Pokaran**, India
210 K 9 **Pokeno**, New Zealand
84 L 9 **Pokka**, Finland
195 O 6 **Poko**, Democratic Republic of Congo
157 T 11 **Pokrovsk**, Russian Federation
164 J 10 **Pol-e Fāsā**, Iran
165 U 6 **Pol-e Khomrī**, Afghanistan
93 J 20 **Polana**, Slovakia
92 F 11 **Poland**, Europe
92 G 9 **Polanów**, Poland
158 G 9 **Polatli**, Turkey
99 K 14 **Polatsk**, Belarus
65 R 9 **Pole Plain**, Arctic Ocean
175 N 12 **Polewali**, Indonesia
193 U 12 **Poli**, Cameroon
92 D 10 **Police**, Poland
97 K 17 **Polichnitos**, Greece
79 U 8 **Poligny**, France
175 P 3 **Polillo Islands**, Philippines
158 G 15 **Polis**, Cyprus
101 O 2 **Polis'ke**, Ukraine
169 E 22 **Pollachi**, India
81 Y 7 **Pollença**, Spain
210 J 9 **Pollok**, New Zealand
101 W 8 **Polohy**, Ukraine
169 G 24 **Polonnaruwa**, Sri Lanka
100 M 4 **Polonne**, Ukraine
100 H 12 **Polovragi**, Romania
96 J 7 **Polski Trŭmbesh**, Bulgaria
101 U 5 **Poltava**, Ukraine
98 H 7 **Põltsamaa**, Estonia
156 J 6 **Poluostrov Kanin**, Russian Federation
156 I 5 **Poluostrov Rybachiy**, Russian Federation
157 O 7 **Poluostrov Taymyr**, Russian Federation
156 M 7 **Poluostrov Yamal**, Russian Federation
98 I 8 **Põlva**, Estonia
97 I 23 **Polyaigos**, Greece
97 G 14 **Polygyros**, Greece
96 E 13 **Polykastro**, Greece
214 F 3 **Polynesia**, Oceania
80 H 7 **Pombal**, Portugal
197 R 9 **Pomene**, Mozambique
92 F 9 **Pomerania**, Poland
212 G 4 **Pomio**, Papua New Guinea
86 N 9 **Pommersche Bucht**, Germany
117 G 23 **Pomona**, California, U.S.A.
96 N 9 **Pomorie**, Bulgaria
123 T 13 **Pompano Beach**, Florida, U.S.A.
91 J 16 **Pompei**, Italy
119 K 16 **Ponca City**, Oklahoma, U.S.A.
127 T 7 **Ponce**, Puerto Rico
119 J 16 **Pond Creek**, Oklahoma, U.S.A.
169 D 22 **Pondicherry**, India
169 F 22 **Pondicherry**, India
169 H 19 **Pondicherry**, India
169 F 22 **Pondicherry**, India
80 K 2 **Ponferrada**, Spain
93 M 15 **Poniatowa**, Poland
83 F 21 **Pont-à-Celles**, Belgium
79 U 4 **Pont-à-Mousson**, France
90 A 7 **Pont-Canavese**, Italy
143 N 17 **Ponta da Baleia**, Brazil
197 R 10 **Ponta da Barra**, Mozambique
197 R 9 **Ponta da Barra Falsa**, Mozambique
196 F 2 **Ponta das Palmeirinhas**, Angola
196 F 4 **Ponta das Salinas**, Angola
62 O 2 **Ponta Delgada**, Azores
196 F 6 **Ponta do Enfião**, Angola
62 N 5 **Ponta do Sol**, Madeira
63 A 15 **Ponta do Sol**, Cape Verde
143 J 19 **Ponta Grossa**, Brazil
143 J 21 **Ponta Imbituba**, Brazil
143 H 18 **Ponta Porã**, Brazil
197 S 7 **Ponta Timbué**, Mozambique
79 V 8 **Pontarlier**, France
78 K 7 **Pontchâteau**, France
143 K 14 **Ponte Alta do Tocantins**, Brazil
80 H 4 **Ponte da Barca**, Portugal
80 H 4 **Ponte de Lima**, Portugal
80 H 8 **Ponte de Sor**, Portugal
80 H 3 **Ponteareas**, Spain
90 I 5 **Pontebba**, Italy
77 K 17 **Pontefract**, United Kingdom
143 F 15 **Pontes e Lacerda**, Brazil
80 H 2 **Pontevedra**, Spain
120 I 10 **Pontiac**, Illinois, U.S.A.
174 I 11 **Pontianak**, Indonesia
78 J 5 **Pontivy**, France
79 P 4 **Pontoise**, France
114 I 8 **Ponton**, Manitoba, Canada
122 J 4 **Pontotoc**, Mississippi, U.S.A.
90 D 9 **Pontremoli**, Italy
81 V 4 **Ponts**, Spain
77 I 21 **Pontypridd**, United Kingdom
99 J 15 **Ponya**, Belarus
209 O 11 **Poochera**, South Australia, Australia
194 H 9 **Pool**, Congo
77 J 23 **Poole**, United Kingdom
209 R 11 **Pooncarie**, New South Wales, Australia
210 K 6 **Poor Knights Islands**, New Zealand
101 V 6 **Popasne**, Ukraine
138 G 8 **Popayán**, Colombia
98 C 10 **Pope**, Latvia
83 A 19 **Poperinge**, Belgium
119 N 16 **Poplar Bluff**, Missouri, U.S.A.
122 I 8 **Poplarville**, Mississippi, U.S.A.
125 R 12 **Popocatépetl**, Mexico
194 I 11 **Popokabaka**, Democratic Republic of Congo
90 I 13 **Popoli**, Italy
212 E 6 **Popondetta**, Papua New Guinea
96 L 7 **Popovo**, Bulgaria
93 K 19 **Poprad**, Slovakia
211 M 14 **Porangahau**, New Zealand
143 J 15 **Porangatu**, Brazil
169 A 15 **Porbandar**, India
62 J 6 **Porcupine Abyssal Plain**, Atlantic Ocean
90 H 6 **Pordenone**, Italy
94 A 9 **Porec**, Croatia
212 B 4 **Porgera**, Papua New Guinea
85 J 18 **Pori**, Finland
211 K 16 **Porirua**, New Zealand
84 I 11 **Porjus**, Sweden
156 F 7 **Porkhov**, Russian Federation
209 R 2 **Pormpuraaw**, Queensland, Australia
78 K 7 **Pornic**, France
157 X 13 **Poronaysk**, Russian Federation
97 G 21 **Poros**, Greece
99 F 19 **Porozava**, Belarus
219 W 13 **Porpoise Bay**, Antarctica
63 L 25 **Porpoise Point**, Ascension
88 C 6 **Porrentruy**, Switzerland
90 E 9 **Porreta Terme**, Italy
84 K 6 **Porsangen**, Norway
85 C 20 **Porsgrunn**, Norway
127 O 7 **Port-à-Piment**, Haiti
113 R 15 **Port Alberni**, British Columbia, Canada
197 N 15 **Port Alfred**, Republic of South Africa
116 D 6 **Port Angeles**, Washington, U.S.A.
126 M 7 **Port Antonio**, Jamaica
119 M 21 **Port Arthur**, Texas, U.S.A.
209 T 15 **Port Arthur**, Tasmania, Australia
127 Q 7 **Port-au-Prince**, Haiti
209 P 10 **Port Augusta**, South Australia, Australia
196 K 15 **Port Beaufort**, Republic of South Africa
195 S 7 **Port Bell**, Uganda
169 N 22 **Port Blair**, India
169 L 15 **Port Canning**, India
211 F 24 **Port Chalmers**, New Zealand
123 Q 12 **Port Charlotte**, Florida, U.S.A.
127 P 6 **Port-de-Paix**, Haiti
174 E 9 **Port Dickson**, Malaysia
209 T 3 **Port Douglas**, Queensland, Australia
197 P 13 **Port Edward**, Republic of South Africa
197 N 15 **Port Elizabeth**, Republic of South Africa
210 L 7 **Port Fitzroy**, New Zealand
194 D 8 **Port-Gentil**, Gabon
122 G 6 **Port Gibson**, Mississippi, U.S.A.
76 G 13 **Port Glasgow**, United Kingdom
193 R 14 **Port Harcourt**, Nigeria
113 Q 14 **Port Hardy**, British Columbia, Canada
115 W 12 **Port Hawkesbury**, Nova Scotia, Canada
208 G 5 **Port Hedland**, Western Australia, Australia
112 G 8 **Port Heiden**, Alaska, U.S.A.
115 X 8 **Port Hope Simpson**, Newfoundland and Labrador, Canada
127 N 3 **Port Howe**, The Bahamas
121 N 8 **Port Huron**, Michigan, U.S.A.
119 K 24 **Port Isabel**, Texas, U.S.A.
119 K 22 **Port Lavaca**, Texas, U.S.A.
209 O 12 **Port Lincoln**, South Australia, Australia
192 F 11 **Port Loko**, Sierra Leone
58 B 12 **Port Louis**, Mauritius
209 V 10 **Port Macquarie**, New South Wales, Australia
58 E 7 **Port Mathurin**, Rodrigues Island
115 U 10 **Port-Menier**, Québec, Canada
212 E 6 **Port Moresby**, Papua New Guinea
127 N 4 **Port Nelson**, The Bahamas
196 I 13 **Port Nolloth**, Republic of South Africa
76 F 8 **Port of Ness**, United Kingdom
127 X 12 **Port of Spain**, Trinidad and Tobago
211 B 26 **Port Pegasus**, New Zealand
209 P 11 **Port Pirie**, South Australia, Australia
123 S 6 **Port Royal Sound**, South Carolina, U.S.A.
190 F 7 **Port Said**, Egypt
197 P 13 **Port Shepstone**, Republic of South Africa
123 N 9 **Port St Joe**, Florida, U.S.A.
197 O 14 **Port St Johns**, Republic of South Africa
145 K 24 **Port Stephens**, Falkland Islands
191 H 14 **Port Sudan**, Sudan
79 R 15 **Port-Vendres**, France
213 Q 11 **Port Vila**, Vanuatu
210 K 9 **Port Waikato**, New Zealand
209 P 11 **Port Wakefield**, South Australia, Australia
209 S 14 **Port Welshpool**, Victoria, Australia
77 E 16 **Portadown**, United Kingdom
120 H 7 **Portage**, Wisconsin, U.S.A.
114 I 10 **Portage la Praire**, Manitoba, Canada
80 I 9 **Portalegre**, Portugal
80 I 8 **Portalegre**, Portugal
119 G 18 **Portales**, New Mexico, U.S.A.
81 Y 3 **Portbou**, Spain
143 L 16 **Porteirinha**, Brazil
80 I 10 **Portel**, Portugal
142 I 10 **Portel**, Brazil
117 G 20 **Porterville**, California, U.S.A.
97 B 20 **Porthmos Zakynthou**, Greece
81 W 9 **Portinatx**, Spain
120 L 11 **Portland**, Indiana, U.S.A.
121 X 7 **Portland**, Maine, U.S.A.
209 Q 13 **Portland**, Victoria, Australia
210 O 13 **Portland Island**, New Zealand
63 K 26 **Portland Point**, Ascension
77 D 18 **Portlaoise**, Republic of Ireland
80 H 5 **Porto**, Portugal
80 H 5 **Porto**, Portugal
142 I 11 **Porto Alegre**, Brazil
143 I 22 **Porto Alegre**, Brazil
196 G 3 **Porto Amboim**, Angola
143 H 15 **Porto Artur**, Brazil
143 J 20 **Porto Belo**, Brazil
142 I 10 **Pôrto de Moz**, Brazil
143 G 14 **Porto dos Gaúchos**, Brazil

Country · Internal administrative region: State/Province/Territory/Dependent territory · Capital city · Mountain range/Undersea ridge · Mountain peak/Volcano/Seamount · Geographic feature · Headland/Point/Cape/Peninsula · Desert · Island/Island group · Antarctic base · Ocean · Sea · Bay/Gulf/Channel/Strait · Lake · Salt pan/Dry/Intermittent lake · River

91 I 23 Porto Empedocle, Italy
143 F 16 Porto Esperidião, Brazil
142 K 12 Porto Franco, Brazil
142 I 9 Porto Grande, Brazil
63 B 17 Porto Inglês, Cape Verde
143 G 16 Porto Jofre, Brazil
62 N 4 Porto Moniz, Madeira
143 G 18 Porto Murtinho, Brazil
63 A 15 Porto Novo, Cape Verde
193 O 13
90 I 11 Porto Recanati, Italy
63 B 17 Porto Rincão, Cape Verde
90 I 11 Porto San Giorgio, Italy
62 O 4 Porto Santo, Madeira
143 N 16 Porto Seguro, Brazil
91 B 16 Porto Torres, Italy
79 Y 15
142 D 13 Porto Velho, Brazil
126 K 13 Portobelo, Panama
90 E 12 Portoferraio, Italy
117 F 16 Portola, California, U.S.A.
140 B 9 Portoviejo, Ecuador
76 F 10 Portree, United Kingdom
77 K 23 Portsmouth, United Kingdom
120 M 12 Portsmouth, Ohio, U.S.A.
121 X 7 Portsmouth, New Hampshire, U.S.A.
121 T 14 Portsmouth, Virginia, U.S.A.
127 X 9 Portsmouth, Dominica
84 L 9 Porttipahdan tekojärvi, Finland
80 G 12 Portugal, Europe
138 M 3 Portuguesa, Venezuela
145 H 25 Porvenir, Chile
85 M 19 Porvoo, Finland
144 N 8 Posadas, Argentina
88 J 10 Poschiavo, Switzerland
164 L 8 Posht-e Badam, Iran
84 M 11 Posio, Finland
175 O 11 Poso, Indonesia
159 R 7 Posof, Turkey
140 A 10 Posorja, Ecuador
143 K 15 Posse, Brazil
188 L 13 Post Weygand, Algeria
94 B 8 Postojna, Slovenia
94 G 13 Posušje, Bosnia and Herzegovina
119 L 17 Poteau, Oklahoma, U.S.A.
119 J 22 Poteet, Texas, U.S.A.
91 L 16 Potenza, Italy
81 N 1 Potes, Spain
159 Q 6 P'ot'i, Georgia
193 T 10 Potiskum, Nigeria
116 I 8 Potlatch, Idaho, U.S.A.
121 S 13 Potomac, Virginia, U.S.A.
141 J 23 Potosí, Bolivia
141 J 21 Potosí, Bolivia
86 M 13 Potsdam, Germany
121 U 6 Potsdam, New York, U.S.A.
121 T 11 Pottstown, Pennsylvania, U.S.A.
121 S 10 Pottsville, Pennsylvania, U.S.A.
169 H 25 Pottuvil, Sri Lanka
165 W 8 Potwar Plateau, Pakistan
121 U 9 Poughkeepsie, New York, U.S.A.
210 M 13 Poukawa, New Zealand
213 O 13 Poum, New Caledonia
173 K 20 Poŭthĭsăt, Cambodia
210 O 12 Poverty Bay, New Zealand
80 H 4 Póvoa de Varzim, Portugal
118 E 10 Powder, Montana, U.S.A.
63 G 22 Powell Basin, Atlantic Ocean
113 R 14 Powell River, British Columbia, Canada
120 J 5 Powers, Michigan, U.S.A.
171 U 11 Poyang Hu, China
89 Y 2 Poysdorf, Austria
125 S 11 Poza Rica, Mexico
158 J 12 Pozanti, Turkey
94 M 10 Požarevac, Serbia and Montenegro
94 K 12 Požega, Serbia and Montenegro
94 G 9 Požega, Croatia
92 G 12 Poznań, Poland
81 P 11 Pozo Alcón, Spain
143 G 19 Pozo Colorado, Paraguay
141 M 20 Pozo del Tigre, Bolivia
144 J 8 Pozo Hondo, Argentina
80 M 10 Pozoblanco, Spain
91 K 24 Pozzallo, Italy
174 F 12 Prabumulih, Indonesia
173 G 21 Prachuap Khiri Khan, Thailand
93 G 17 Praděd, Czech Republic
79 Q 15 Prades, France
143 N 16 Prado, Brazil
89 O 7 Prägraten, Austria
93 C 17 Prague, Czech Republic
63 B 17 Praia, Cape Verde
142 H 10 Prainha, Brazil
173 J 18 Prakhon Chai, Thailand
98 G 5 Prangli, Estonia
174 D 9 Prapat, Indonesia
173 J 18 Prasat, Thailand
58 B 9 Praslin, Seychelles
90 F 10 Prato, Italy
119 I 15 Pratt, Kansas, U.S.A.
61 S 2 Pratt Seamount, Pacific Ocean
122 L 6 Prattville, Alabama, U.S.A.
174 L 15 Praya, Indonesia
99 J 14 Prazaroki, Belarus
89 S 7 Predlitz, Austria
89 T 3 Pregarten, Austria
98 I 12 Preiļi, Latvia
120 H 5 Prentice, Wisconsin, U.S.A.
86 M 11 Prenzlau, Germany
173 B 18 Preparis Island, Myanmar
173 B 17 Preparis North Channel, Myanmar
173 B 18 Preparis South Channel, Myanmar
93 G 18 Přerov, Czech Republic
125 W 14 Presa de la Angostura, Mexico
125 P 12 Presa del Infiernillo, Mexico
125 T 13 Presa Miguel Alemán, Mexico
125 V 13 Presa Nezahualcóyotl, Mexico
117 L 22 Prescott, Arizona, U.S.A.
211 A 25 Preservation Inlet, New Zealand
95 N 16 Preševo, Serbia and Montenegro
144 L 7 Presidencia Roque Sáenz Peña, Argentina
61 S 10 President Thiers Seamount, Pacific Ocean
142 L 11 Presidente Dutra, Brazil
143 I 18 Presidente Prudente, Brazil
119 F 22 Presidio, Texas, U.S.A.
167 Q 2 Presnovka, Kazakhstan
93 L 19 Prešov, Slovakia
121 Y 3 Presque Isle, Maine, U.S.A.
192 L 13 Prestea, Ghana
77 I 17 Preston, United Kingdom
116 M 13 Preston, Idaho, U.S.A.
121 N 14 Prestonburg, Kentucky, U.S.A.
197 O 10 Pretoria, Republic of South Africa
97 B 17 Preveza, Greece
112 D 7 Pribilof Islands, Alaska, U.S.A.
94 J 13 Priboj, Serbia and Montenegro
93 C 18 Příbram, Czech Republic
117 N 16 Price, Utah, U.S.A.
99 E 16 Prienai, Lithuania
196 L 13 Prieska, Republic of South Africa
93 I 20 Prievidza, Slovakia
94 F 10 Prijedor, Bosnia and Herzegovina
94 J 13 Prijepolje, Serbia and Montenegro
96 D 12 Prilep, Macedonia (F.Y.R.O.M.)
99 A 15 Primorsk, Russian Federation
96 N 10 Primorsko, Bulgaria
113 W 10 Primrose Lake, Saskatchewan, Canada
113 X 11 Prince Albert, Saskatchewan, Canada
196 L 15 Prince Albert, Republic of South Africa
113 S 2 Prince Albert Peninsula, Northwest Territories, Canada
113 R 3 Prince Albert Sound, Northwest Territories, Canada
115 P 1 Prince Charles Island, Nunavut, Canada
219 V 5 Prince Charles Mountains, Antarctica
58 H 12 Prince Edward Fracture Zone, Indian Ocean
115 V 12 Prince Edward Island, Prince Edward Island, Canada
115 V 12 Prince Edward Island, Canada
58 I 11 Prince Edward Islands, South Africa
113 S 12 Prince George, British Columbia, Canada
219 U 2 Prince Harald Coast, Antarctica
113 O 11 Prince of Wales Island, Alaska, U.S.A.
209 R 1 Prince of Wales Island, Queensland, Australia
113 U 1 Prince of Wales Island, Nunavut, Canada
113 R 2 Prince of Wales Strait, Northwest Territories, Canada
65 P 6 Prince Patrick Island, Arctic Ocean
113 P 12 Prince Rupert, British Columbia, Canada
112 K 8 Prince William Sound, Alaska, U.S.A.
219 P 2 Princess Astrid Coast, Antarctica
209 S 2 Princess Charlotte Bay, Queensland, Australia
219 V 7 Princess Elizabeth Land, Antarctica
219 R 2 Princess Ragnhild Coast, Antarctica
113 P 12 Princess Royal Island, British Columbia, Canada
120 H 9 Princeton, Illinois, U.S.A.
121 O 14 Princeton, West Virginia, U.S.A.
194 C 7 Príncipe, São Tomé and Príncipe
83 G 15 Prinsenbeek, Netherlands
126 H 10 Prinzapolca, Nicaragua
99 L 22 Pripet, Belarus
99 H 21 Pripet Marshes, Belarus
94 E 9 Priseka, Croatia
95 M 15 Priština, Serbia and Montenegro
86 K 11 Pritzwalk, Germany
79 T 12 Privas, France
94 C 11 Privlaka, Croatia
95 L 16 Prizren, Serbia and Montenegro
91 I 22 Prizzi, Italy
94 G 10 Prnjavor, Bosnia and Herzegovina
174 K 14 Probolinggo, Indonesia
139 W 6 Professor van Blommestein Meer, Suriname
83 G 21 Profondeville, Belgium
125 Y 10 Progreso, Mexico
126 E 9 Progreso, Honduras
95 J 16 Prokletije, Albania
95 N 14 Prokuplje, Serbia and Montenegro
157 T 7 Proliv Dmitriya Lapteva, Russian Federation
156 K 6 Proliv Karskiye Vorota, Russian Federation
157 X 5 Proliv Longa, Russian Federation
157 P 5 Proliv Vil'kitskogo, Russian Federation
91 L 14 Promontorio del Gargano, Italy
99 N 18 Pronya, Belarus
209 T 5 Proserpine, Queensland, Australia
92 H 13 Prosna, Poland
63 N 25 Prosperous Bay, St Helena
93 G 18 Prostějov, Czech Republic
63 N 18 Protea Seamount, Atlantic Ocean/Indian Ocean
96 M 8 Provadiya, Bulgaria
79 U 14 Provence, France
79 V 13 Provence-Alpes-Côte-d'Azur, France
121 X 9 Providence, Rhode Island, U.S.A.
157 Z 6 Provideniya, Russian Federation
79 R 5 Provins, France
117 M 15 Provo, Utah, U.S.A.
112 L 3 Prudhoe Bay, Alaska, U.S.A.
93 H 17 Prudnik, Poland
87 B 19 Prüm, Germany
100 I 12 Prundeni, Romania
92 K 13 Pruszków, Poland
100 L 7 Prut, Moldova
88 L 7 Prutz, Austria
99 F 20 Pruzhany, Belarus
101 V 9 Pryazovs'ke, Ukraine
219 X 6 Prydz Bay, Antarctica
101 R 3 Pryluky, Ukraine
101 W 9 Prymors'k, Ukraine
101 O 11 Prymors'ke, Ukraine
101 V 11 Prymors'kyy, Ukraine
101 P 2 Pryp"yat, Ukraine
92 L 11 Przasnysz, Poland
93 J 15 Przedbórz, Poland
93 N 17 Przemyśl, Poland
93 N 17 Przeworsk, Poland
97 G 19 Psachna, Greece
97 J 18 Psara, Greece
156 F 6 Pskov, Russian Federation
167 N 4 Pskovskiy, Kazakhstan
101 T 3 Ps'ol, Ukraine
97 D 14 Ptolemaïda, Greece
99 K 21 Ptsich, Belarus
99 K 21 Ptsich, Belarus
94 D 6 Ptuj, Slovenia
173 H 14 Pua, Thailand
171 Q 12 Pu'an, China
215 U 14 Pu'apu'a, Samoa
140 G 10 Puca Urco, Peru
141 E 14 Pucallpa, Peru
171 V 11 Pucheng, China
171 Y 7 Puch'ŏn, South Korea
100 J 12 Pucioasa, Romania
145 F 15 Pucón, Chile
84 M 12 Pudasjärvi, Finland
156 H 7 Pudozh, Russian Federation
125 S 13 Puebla, Mexico
125 R 12 Puebla, Mexico
80 K 3 Puebla de Sanabria, Spain
119 F 15 Pueblo, Colorado, U.S.A.
81 Q 11 Pueblo de Don Fadrique, Spain
145 I 15 Puelches, Argentina
145 H 14 Puelén, Argentina
171 O 14 Pu'er, China
124 G 3 Puertecitos, Mexico
145 F 20 Puerto Aisen, Chile
138 L 11 Puerto Alfonso, Colombia
125 T 15 Puerto Ángel, Mexico
126 I 14 Puerto Armuelles, Panama
138 H 9 Puerto Asís, Colombia
139 N 6 Puerto Ayacucho, Venezuela
141 B 19 Puerto Ayora, Ecuador
141 C 19 Puerto Baquerizo Moreno, Ecuador
126 E 9 Puerto Barrios, Guatemala
138 I 5 Puerto Berrío, Colombia
139 N 2 Puerto Cabello, Venezuela
126 H 10 Puerto Cabezas, Nicaragua
139 N 6 Puerto Carreño, Colombia
141 J 16 Puerto Cavinas, Bolivia
145 F 19 Puerto Cisnes, Chile
145 H 23 Puerto Coig, Argentina
126 H 13 Puerto Cortés, Costa Rica
126 E 8 Puerto Cortés, Honduras
124 H 3 Puerto de Lobos, Mexico
62 O 11 Puerto del Rosario, Canary Islands
125 S 14 Puerto Escondido, Mexico
140 D 9 Puerto Francisco de Orellana, Ecuador
141 K 16 Puerto Génova, Bolivia
141 K 20 Puerto Grether, Bolivia
145 I 26 Puerto Harberton, Argentina
141 I 17 Puerto Heath, Bolivia
139 N 7 Puerto Inírida, Colombia
144 K 5 Puerto Irigoyen, Argentina
126 G 13 Puerto Jesus, Costa Rica
138 I 10 Puerto Leguízamo, Colombia
126 H 9 Puerto Lempira, Honduras
124 H 4 Puerto Libertad, Mexico
145 I 17 Puerto Lobos, Argentina
138 K 1 Puerto Lopez, Colombia
140 A 9 Puerto López, Ecuador
125 W 15 Puerto Madero, Mexico
145 I 18 Puerto Madryn, Argentina
141 H 16 Puerto Maldonado, Peru
140 A 11 Puerto Máncora, Peru
145 F 17 Puerto Montt, Chile
141 B 14 Puerto Morin, Peru
145 F 24 Puerto Natáles, Chile
138 L 6 Puerto Nuevo, Colombia
126 L 14 Puerto Obaldia, Panama
126 M 5 Puerto Padre, Cuba
139 N 5 Puerto Páez, Venezuela
140 D 11 Puerto Pardo, Peru
124 G 2 Puerto Peñasco, Mexico
138 J 10 Puerto Pizarro, Colombia
127 Q 6 Puerto Plata, Dominican Republic
141 F 15 Puerto Portillo, Peru
175 N 6 Puerto Princesa, Philippines
127 T 8 Puerto Rico, U.S.A.
144 O 8 Puerto Rico, Argentina
62 D 11 Puerto Rico Trench, Atlantic Ocean
145 H 22 Puerto San Julián, Argentina
145 H 22 Puerto Santa Cruz, Argentina
143 G 18 Puerto Sastre, Paraguay
141 K 17 Puerto Siles, Bolivia
140 H 10 Puerto Socorro, Peru
141 O 21 Puerto Suárez, Bolivia
124 M 11 Puerto Vallarta, Mexico
141 E 15 Puerto Victoria, Peru
141 A 19 Puerto Villamil, Ecuador
145 I 19 Puerto Visser, Argentina
145 H 25 Puerto Yartou, Chile
81 N 10 Puertollano, Spain
116 E 6 Puget Sound, Washington, U.S.A.
91 M 15 Puglia, Italy
85 O 16 Puhos, Finland
81 W 3 Puigcerdà, Spain
79 P 15 Puigmal, France/Spain
192 G 12 Pujehun, Sierra Leone
214 M 7 Pukapuka, Cook Islands
215 X 8 Pukapuka, French Polynesia
215 Y 10 Pukarua, French Polynesia
114 H 7 Pukatawagan, Manitoba, Canada
95 K 16 Pukë, Albania
210 K 9 Pukekohe, New Zealand
211 E 19 Pukekura, New Zealand
91 C 19 Pula, Italy
94 A 10 Pula, Croatia
141 J 22 Pulacayo, Bolivia
175 N 10 Pulai, Indonesia
174 L 12 Pulangpisau, Indonesia
215 N 15 Pulap, Federated States of Micronesia
121 S 7 Pulaski, New York, U.S.A.
121 P 14 Pulaski, Virginia, U.S.A.
122 L 3 Pulaski, Tennessee, U.S.A.
175 X 14 Pulau Dolak, Indonesia
175 N 9 Pulau Maratua, Indonesia
215 N 15 Pulawat, Federated States of Micronesia
93 M 14 Puławy, Poland
85 M 14 Pulkkila, Finland
116 I 8 Pullman, Washington, U.S.A.
214 I 15 Pulo Anna, Palau
92 L 12 Pułtusk, Poland
170 I 7 Pulu, China
59 Z 2 Pulu Capelok, Cocos Islands
59 Z 2 Pulu Pandang, Cocos Islands
159 P 10 Pülümür, Turkey
215 N 15 Pulusuk, Federated States of Micronesia
144 H 6 Puna de Atacama, Argentina
211 F 18 Punakaiki, New Zealand
168 L 12 Punakha, Bhutan
141 J 20 Punata, Bolivia
175 W 12 Puncak Jaya, Indonesia
175 Y 13 Puncak Mandala, Indonesia
175 X 13 Puncak Trikora, Indonesia
168 E 10 Pundri, India
169 C 17 Pune, India
195 O 8 Punia, Democratic Republic of Congo
165 X 10 Punjab, Pakistan
168 D 10 Punjab, India
141 G 18 Puno, Peru
141 H 19 Puno, Peru
124 G 6 Punta Abreojos, Mexico
91 N 19 Punta Alice, Italy
125 Z 11 Punta Allen, Mexico
80 L 15 Punta Almina, Spain
145 K 15 Punta Alta, Argentina
124 J 9 Punta Arena, Mexico
145 G 25 Punta Arenas, Chile
141 E 19 Punta Atico, Peru
61 Y 5 Punta Baja, Easter Island
124 F 3 Punta Baja, Mexico
145 J 17 Punta Bermeja, Argentina
126 I 14 Punta Burica, Costa Rica
138 H 2 Punta Canoas, Colombia
91 B 15 Punta Caprara, Italy
138 F 7 Punta Chirambirá, Colombia
126 E 11 Punta Cosigüina, Honduras
61 Z 5 Punta Cuidado, Easter Island
144 F 12 Punta Curaumilla, Chile
145 H 24 Punta de Arenas, Argentina
81 P 13 Punta de las Entinas, Spain
124 M 11 Punta de Mita, Mexico
126 H 11 Punta de Perlas, Nicaragua
127 O 6 Punta de Quemado, Cuba
126 H 12 Punta del Mono, Nicaragua
145 J 18 Punta Delgada, Argentina
145 H 22 Punta Desengaño, Argentina
124 F 5 Punta Eugenia, Mexico
145 E 16 Punta Galera, Chile
140 A 8 Punta Galera, Ecuador
138 K 1 Punta Gallinas, Colombia
144 F 2 Punta Gorda, Chile
126 E 8 Punta Gorda, Belize
126 H 12 Punta Gorda, Nicaragua
125 Z 11 Punta Herrero, Mexico
144 F 5 Punta Jorjino, Chile
145 E 14 Punta Lavapié, Chile
144 F 10 Punta Lengua de Vaca, Chile
145 H 23 Punta León, Argentina
126 K 15 Punta Mala, Panama
138 E 9 Punta Manglares, Colombia
126 J 15 Punta Mariato, Panama
80 L 14 Punta Marroquí, Spain
145 I 21 Punta Medanosa, Argentina
140 A 12 Punta Negro, Peru
145 J 18 Punta Ninfas, Argentina
145 J 17 Punta Norte, Argentina
145 J 17 Punta Norte, Argentina
140 A 11 Punta Pariñas, Peru
126 H 9 Punta Patuca, Honduras
124 G 4 Punta Prieta, Mexico
145 K 16 Punta Rasa, Argentina
138 F 8 Punta Reyes, Colombia
125 U 12 Punta Roca Partida, Mexico
124 J 6 Punta Rosa, Mexico
61 Z 4 Punta Rosalia, Easter Island
141 C 16 Punta Salinasó Lachay, Peru
124 G 6 Punta San Hipólito, Mexico
61 Y 4 Punta San Juan, Easter Island
126 H 14 Punta San Pedro, Costa Rica
140 A 10 Punta Santa Elena, Ecuador
141 D 18 Punta Santa Maria, Peru
125 N 13 Punta Tejupan, Mexico
144 F 12 Punta Topocalma, Chile
126 G 13 Puntarenas, Costa Rica
138 L 2 Punto Fijo, Venezuela
84 M 13 Puolanka, Finland
211 H 15 Puponga, New Zealand
171 T 11 Puqi, China
141 E 18 Puquio, Peru
144 G 8 Puquios, Chile
212 C 6 Puratu Island, Papua New Guinea
89 Y 4 Purbach, Austria
98 G 5 Purekkari neem, Estonia
145 F 15 Purén, Chile
169 J 17 Puri, India
89 X 3 Purkersdorf, Austria
82 H 10 Purmerend, Netherlands
145 E 17 Purranque, Chile
125 P 12 Puruarán, Mexico
174 L 11 Purukcahu, Indonesia
169 J 14 Puruliya, India
142 D 12 Purus, Brazil
85 O 16 Puruvesi, Finland
96 J 10 Pŭrvomay, Bulgaria
174 H 14 Purwakarta, Indonesia
171 Z 8 Pusan, South Korea
171 W 13 Putai, Taiwan
172 F 6 Putao, Myanmar
210 L 10 Putaruru, New Zealand
171 W 12 Putian, China

Country · Internal administrative region: State/Province/Territory/Dependent territory · Capital city · Mountain range/Undersea ridge · Mountain peak/Volcano/Seamount · Geographic feature · Headland/Point/Cape/Peninsula · Desert · Island/Island group · Antarctic base · Ocean · Sea · Bay/Gulf/Channel/Strait · Lake · Salt pan/Dry/Intermittent lake · River

1 H 18 Putina, Peru
0 N 12 Putorino, New Zealand
4 G 2 Putre, Chile
9 F 24 Puttalam, Sri Lanka
J 11 Putten, Netherlands
I 8 Puttgarden, Germany
9 D 21 Puttur, India
8 H 9 Putumayo, Colombia
8 J 11 Putumayo, Colombia
4 K 10 Putusibau, Indonesia
1 T 2 Putyvl', Ukraine
M 17 Puula, Finland
N 17 Puumala, Finland
5 P 5 Puvurnituq, Québec, Canada
5 F 16 Puyehue, Chile
0 C 9 Puyo, Ecuador
1 A 25 Puysegur Point, New Zealand
5 W 12 Pwani, Tanzania
5 Q 13 Pweto, Democratic Republic of Congo
H 19 Pwllheli, United Kingdom
3 D 17 Pyapon, Myanmar
7 O 6 Pyasinskiy Zaliv, Russian Federation
6 E 11 Pyatigorsk, Russian Federation
1 T 6 P''yatykhatky, Ukraine
2 D 12 Pyawbwe, Myanmar
3 C 14 Pyè, Myanmar
K 21 Pyetrykaw, Belarus
L 14 Pyhäjoki, Finland
M 15 Pyhäsalmi, Finland
O 16 Pyhäselkä, Finland
M 10 Pyhätunturin, Finland
2 D 13 Pyinmana, Myanmar
D 22 Pylos, Greece
1 X 6 P'yŏngyang, North Korea
7 F 15 Pyramid Lake, Nevada, U.S.A.
R 2 Pyrenees, Spain/France
E 15 Pyrgetos, Greece
K 19 Pyrgi, Greece
C 21 Pyrgos, Greece
01 R 4 Pyryatyn, Ukraine
2 D 11 Pyrzyce, Poland
J 15 Pyshna, Belarus
01 V 7 Pys'menne, Ukraine
5 C 16 Pyttegga, Norway
73 D 14 Pyu, Myanmar

Q

62 L 7 Qaḑīmah, Saudi Arabia
61 U 4 Qādir Karam, Iraq
65 R 6 Qaisar, Afghanistan
61 U 2 Qalā Diza, Iraq
71 S 13 Qal'aikhum, Tajikistan
63 W 14 Qalansīyah, Yemen
65 T 9 Qalāt, Afghanistan
61 W 12 Qal'at Abū Ghar, Iraq
62 J 4 Qal'at al Aẓlam, Saudi Arabia
60 H 4 Qal'at al Ḥiṣn, Syria
63 O 9 Qal'at Bīshah, Saudi Arabia
61 Y 10 Qal'at Ṣāliḥ, Iraq
61 W 9 Qal'at Sukkār, Iraq
65 Q 7 Qal'eh-ye, Afghanistan
60 F 9 Qalqilya, Israel
13 Y 4 Qamanittuaq, Nunavut, Canada
71 N 10 Qamdo, China
89 W 8 Qamīnis, Libya
91 O 18 Qandala, Somalia
59 V 10 Qapiciğ Dağl, Armenia
61 U 5 Qara Tepe, Iraq
162 M 2 Qārah, Saudi Arabia
161 Q 1 Qaratshuk, Syria
191 N 20 Qardho, Somalia
167 U 13 Qarokŭl, Tajikistan
167 P 13 Qashqadaryo Wiloyati, Uzbekistan
160 I 9 Qaṣr al Azraq, Jordan
160 H 10 Qaṣr al Kharānah, Jordan
163 S 2 Qaṣr aṣ Ṣabiyah, Kuwait
190 D 10 Qasr Farafra, Egypt
163 Q 8 Qaṣr Ḥimām, Saudi Arabia
189 S 11 Qaṣr Larocu, Libya
160 H 7 Qatanā, Syria
163 U 5 Qatar, Asia
164 K 11 Qaṭrūyeh, Iran
190 C 9 Qattâra Depression, Egypt
159 W 7 Qax, Azerbaijan
165 N 8 Qāyen, Iran
161 S 3 Qayyārah, Iraq
159 U 7 Qazax, Azerbaijan
159 Y 8 Qazimämmäd, Azerbaijan
164 H 5 Qazvīn, Iran
164 H 5 Qazvīn, Iran
190 F 10 Qena, Egypt
65 N 12 Qeqertarsuaq, Greenland
164 L 13 Qeshm, Iran
164 L 13 Qeshm, Iran
164 J 13 Qeys, Iran
160 E 11 Qeẓi'ot, Israel
171 N 9 Qidukou, China
170 J 7 Qiemo, China
171 R 11 Qijiang, China
170 M 5 Qijiaojing, China
165 Q 12 Qila Ladgasht, Pakistan
165 P 11 Qila Safed, Pakistan
165 U 10 Qila Saifullah, Pakistan
171 N 7 Qilian Shan, China
171 W 8 Qingdao, China
171 N 8 Qinghai, China
171 O 8 Qinghai Hu, China
171 R 8 Qingyang, China
171 T 13 Qingyuan, China
171 V 8 Qingzhou, China
171 V 6 Qinhuangdao, China
171 S 14 Qinzhou, China
171 T 15 Qionghai, China
171 W 3 Qiqihar, China
164 J 11 Qīr, Iran
160 F 10 Qiryat Gat, Israel
163 U 12 Qishn, Yemen
170 L 5 Qitai, China
167 V 14 Qizilrabot, Tajikistan
164 J 5 Qolleh-ye Damāvand, Iran
164 I 6 Qom, Iran
164 I 6 Qom, Iran
191 O 21 Qooriga Neegro, Somalia
166 L 10 Qoraqalpoghiston Respublikasi, Uzbekistan
160 H 5 Qornet es Saouda, Lebanon
161 T 2 Qosh Tepe, Iraq
86 E 12 Quakenbrück, Germany
173 K 23 Quân Đao Nam Du, Vietnam
173 O 17 Quang Ngai, Vietnam
173 N 16 Quang Tri, Vietnam
171 W 12 Quanzhou, China
171 T 12 Quanzhou, China
115 R 5 Quaqtaq, Québec, Canada
143 G 22 Quaraí, Brazil
59 Y 3 Quarantine Station, Cocos Islands
211 D 25 Quarry Hills, New Zealand
58 B 12 Quartier Militaire, Mauritius
91 C 19 Quartu Sant'Elena, Italy
117 I 19 Quartzite Mountain, Nevada, U.S.A.
117 K 23 Quartzsite, Arizona, U.S.A.
159 X 7 Quba, Azerbaijan
165 N 5 Quchan, Iran
160 K 4 Qudaym, Syria
209 U 12 Queanbeyan, New South Wales, Australia
115 Q 9 Québec, Canada
115 S 12 Québec, Québec, Canada
87 I 15 Quedlinburg, Germany
113 O 12 Queen Charlotte, British Columbia, Canada
145 J 23 Queen Charlotte Bay, Falkland Islands
113 O 12 Queen Charlotte Islands, British Columbia, Canada
113 Q 13 Queen Charlotte Sound, British Columbia, Canada
65 P 6 Queen Elizabeth Islands, Arctic Ocean
219 W 8 Queen Mary Land, Antarctica
63 O 15 Queen Mary's Peak, Tristan da Cunha
114 J 1 Queen Maud Gulf, Nunavut, Canada
219 O 3 Queen Maud Land, Antarctica
219 O 9 Queen Maud Mountains, Antarctica
209 R 6 Queensland, Australia
209 S 15 Queenstown, Tasmania, Australia
211 C 23 Queenstown, New Zealand
116 C 7 Queets, Washington, U.S.A.
196 I 2 Quela, Angola
197 S 7 Quelimane, Mozambique
145 F 18 Quellón, Chile
119 D 18 Quemado, New Mexico, U.S.A.
145 F 17 Quemchi, Chile
125 Q 11 Querétaro, Mexico
125 Q 11 Querétaro, Mexico
87 J 16 Querfurt, Germany
81 P 11 Quesada, Spain
113 S 12 Quesnel, British Columbia, Canada
113 S 12 Quesnel Lake, British Columbia, Canada
165 T 10 Quetta, Pakistan
145 F 16 Queule, Chile
140 A 9 Quevedo, Ecuador
174 M 6 Quezon, Philippines
175 O 3 Quezon City, Philippines
188 I 6 Quezzane, Morocco
171 U 8 Qufu, China
172 L 13 Qui Châu, Vietnam
173 O 19 Qui Nhon, Vietnam
196 G 2 Quibaxe, Angola
138 G 6 Quibdó, Colombia
78 J 6 Quiberon, France
86 H 10 Quickborn, Germany
83 D 21 Quiévrechain, Belgium
143 G 20 Quiindy, Paraguay
196 G 5 Quilengues, Angola
113 Y 11 Quill Lakes, Saskatchewan, Canada
141 F 17 Quillabamba, Peru
144 G 4 Quillagua, Chile
79 Q 15 Quillan, France
169 D 24 Quilon, India
209 S 8 Quilpie, Queensland, Australia
144 F 11 Quilpue, Chile
196 H 1 Quimbele, Angola
144 K 8 Quimili, Argentina
78 H 6 Quimper, France
78 I 6 Quimperlé, France
116 D 7 Quinault, Washington, U.S.A.
141 G 17 Quince Mil, Peru
117 E 16 Quincy, California, U.S.A.
120 F 11 Quincy, Illinois, U.S.A.
123 N 8 Quincy, Florida, U.S.A.
144 I 11 Quines, Argentina
197 U 6 Quinga, Mozambique
112 G 7 Quinhagak, Alaska, U.S.A.
125 Z 11 Quintana Roo, Mexico
81 P 8 Quintanar, Spain
196 F 1 Quinzau, Angola
197 U 3 Quionga, Mozambique
196 G 5 Quipungo, Angola
145 F 14 Quirihue, Chile
141 K 21 Quiroga, Bolivia
196 I 3 Quitapa, Angola
196 H 6 Quiteve, Angola
122 J 6 Quitman, Mississippi, U.S.A.
123 O 8 Quitman, Georgia, U.S.A.
140 B 8 Quito, Ecuador
142 N 11 Quixadá, Brazil
171 Q 13 Qujing, China
167 Q 13 Qullai Chimtarha, Tajikistan
167 S 13 Qullai Garmo, Tajikistan
167 T 14 Qullai Karl Marks, Tajikistan
209 P 10 Quorn, South Australia, Australia
163 Z 6 Qurayat, Oman
167 R 14 Qŭrghonteppa, Tajikistan
159 X 7 Qusar, Azerbaijan
163 T 13 Qusāy'ir, Yemen
190 G 10 Quseir, Egypt
171 V 11 Quzhou, China
159 V 6 Qvareli, Georgia

R

89 V 2 Raabs an der Thaya, Austria
84 L 13 Raahe, Finland
82 L 11 Raalte, Netherlands
174 L 14 Raas, Indonesia
94 C 10 Rab, Croatia
94 C 10 Rab, Croatia
93 K 18 Raba, Poland
175 N 15 Raba, Indonesia
93 G 23 Rába, Hungary
191 F 18 Rabak, Sudan
188 H 7 Rabat, Morocco
91 J 26 Rabat, Malta
212 H 3 Rabaul, Papua New Guinea
208 L 5 Rabbit Flat Roadhouse, Northern Territory, Australia
174 B 9 Rabi, Indonesia
213 Y 11 Rabi, Fiji
162 L 7 Rābigh, Saudi Arabia
93 K 18 Rabka, Poland
173 L 23 Rach Gia, Vietnam
119 J 24 Rachal, Texas, U.S.A.
93 H 17 Racibórz, Poland
120 I 8 Racine, Wisconsin, U.S.A.
120 L 4 Raco, Michigan, U.S.A.
163 P 13 Radā', Yemen
99 I 17 Radashkovichy, Belarus
100 J 4 Radekhiv, Ukraine
121 P 14 Radford, Virginia, U.S.A.
169 B 14 Radhanpur, India
115 P 9 Radisson, Québec, Canada
138 E 8 Rado de Tumaco, Colombia
93 L 14 Radom, Poland
191 B 19 Radom, Sudan
96 F 9 Radomir, Bulgaria
93 J 15 Radomsko, Poland
96 L 11 Radovets, Bulgaria
96 E 11 Radoviš, Macedonia (F.Y.R.O.M.)
89 R 6 Radstadt, Austria
99 F 17 Radun', Belarus
98 E 13 Radviliškis, Lithuania
92 N 13 Radzyń Podlaski, Poland
168 G 12 Rae Bareli, India
113 T 7 Rae-Edzo, Northwest Territories, Canada
113 S 6 Rae Lakes, Northwest Territories, Canada
123 T 3 Raeford, North Carolina, U.S.A.
211 D 24 Raes Junction, New Zealand
210 K 13 Raetihi, New Zealand
144 K 10 Rafaela, Argentina
163 O 2 Rafḩā', Saudi Arabia
97 H 20 Rafina, Greece
164 L 10 Rafsanjān, Iran
191 B 20 Raga, Sudan
210 K 10 Raglan, New Zealand
91 K 23 Ragusa, Italy
175 P 13 Raha, Indonesia
99 M 19 Rahachow, Belarus
191 F 17 Rahad Canal, Sudan
193 S 11 Rahama, Nigeria
165 V 12 Rahimyar Khan, Pakistan
164 H 6 Rāhjerd, Iran
215 S 9 Raiatea, French Polynesia
169 E 19 Raichur, India
169 H 15 Raigarh, India
175 O 15 Raijua, Indonesia
113 S 9 Rainbow Lake, Alberta, Canada
118 L 6 Rainy Lake, Minnesota, U.S.A.
85 J 15 Raippaluoto, Finland
169 G 16 Raipur, India
215 T 12 Raivavae, French Polynesia
169 G 16 Raj-Nandgaon, India
169 I 15 Rajagangapur, India
169 H 18 Rajahmundry, India
174 J 9 Rajang, Malaysia
165 V 11 Rajanpur, Pakistan
169 E 23 Rajapalaiyam, India
169 C 18 Rajapur, India
168 C 11 Rajasthan, India
168 D 11 Rajgarh, India
169 B 15 Rajkot, India
169 D 15 Rajpur, India
168 L 13 Rajshahi, Bangladesh
169 K 14 Rajshahi, Bangladesh
215 O 6 Rakahanga, Cook Islands
195 R 8 Rakai, Uganda
211 F 20 Rakaia, New Zealand
211 G 21 Rakaia, New Zealand
100 I 7 Rakhiv, Ukraine
167 P 6 Rakhmet, Kazakhstan
93 C 17 Rakovnik, Czech Republic
98 H 6 Rakvere, Estonia
123 U 2 Raleigh, North Carolina, U.S.A.
123 W 3 Raleigh Bay, North Carolina, U.S.A.
215 W 2 Ralik Chain, Marshall Islands
164 I 5 Rām-Sar, Iran
160 G 7 Rama, Israel
126 H 11 Rama, Nicaragua
160 F 9 Ramallah, Israel
169 F 23 Ramanathapuram, India
169 H 14 Ramanuj Ganj, India
212 E 2 Rambutyo Island, Papua New Guinea
169 I 14 Ramgarh, India
164 H 9 Rāmhormoz, Iran
209 O 1 Ramingining, Northern Territory, Australia
160 F 9 Ramla, Israel
163 Q 13 Ramlat as Sab'atayn, Yemen
163 P 11 Ramlat Dahm, Yemen
160 G 13 Ramm, Jordan
100 L 11 Râmnicu Sărat, Romania
100 I 11 Râmnicu Vâlcea, Romania
168 F 11 Rampur, India
168 E 9 Rampur, India
169 I 16 Rampur, India
173 B 14 Ramree Island, Myanmar
77 H 16 Ramsey, United Kingdom
77 N 21 Ramsgate, United Kingdom
164 G 9 Rāmshir, Iran
85 G 17 Ramsjö, Sweden
212 C 4 Ramu, Papua New Guinea
168 D 13 Rana Pratap Sagar, India
144 G 12 Rancagua, Chile
83 F 23 Rance, Belgium
169 I 14 Ranchi, India
125 O 9 Rancho Grande, Mexico
91 K 22 Randazzo, Italy
85 C 24 Randers, Denmark
84 H 11 Randijaure, Sweden
192 F 8 Ranérou, Senegal
211 E 23 Ranfurly, New Zealand
173 I 26 Rangae, Thailand
169 M 15 Rangamati, Bangladesh
210 I 5 Rangaunu Bay, New Zealand
121 X 5 Rangeley, Maine, U.S.A.
118 D 13 Rangely, Colorado, U.S.A.
168 M 12 Rangia, India
210 L 12 Rangipo, New Zealand
210 K 9 Rangiriri, New Zealand
215 T 8 Rangiroa, French Polynesia
210 M 12 Rangitaiki, New Zealand
211 F 21 Rangitata, New Zealand
210 L 13 Rangitikei, New Zealand
173 E 16 Rangoon, Myanmar
168 L 13 Rangpur, Bangladesh
169 D 20 Ranibennur, India
114 L 4 Rankin Inlet, Nunavut, Canada
169 A 14 Rann of Kachchh, India
197 W 9 Ranohira, Madgascar
173 F 23 Ranong, Thailand
212 J 6 Ranongga, Solomon Islands
173 H 25 Ranot, Thailand
175 V 11 Ransiki, Indonesia
174 L 12 Rantau, Indonesia
84 M 12 Ranua, Finland
161 U 2 Rānya, Iraq
215 V 14 Rapa, French Polynesia
90 C 9 Rapallo, Italy
169 A 14 Rapar, India
118 G 10 Rapid City, South Dakota, U.S.A.
98 I 8 Rāpina, Estonia
98 G 6 Rapla, Estonia
88 H 7 Rapperswil, Switzerland
215 V 9 Raraka, French Polynesia
215 W 9 Raroia, French Polynesia
215 O 11 Rarotonga, Cook Islands
190 F 9 Rās, Egypt
162 K 6 Rās Abū Madd, Saudi Arabia
190 H 13 Rās Abu Shagara, Sudan
163 Z 9 Rās ad Daqm, Oman
161 N 1 Ra's al 'Ayn, Syria
160 H 3 Rās al Basīṭ, Syria
163 Z 7 Rās al Ḥadd, Oman
163 Z 7 Rās al Ḥadd, Oman
163 S 13 Rās al Kalb, Yemen
163 X 5 Rās al Khaimah, United Arab Emirates
163 Z 10 Rās al Madrakah, Oman
163 S 3 Ras al Mish'āb, Saudi Arabia
189 Y 7 Rās al Muraysah, Libya
160 G 12 Rās an Naqb, Jordan
162 I 3 Rās ash Shaykh Humayd, Saudi Arabia
189 X 7 Rās at Tīn, Libya
163 S 4 Rās az Zawr, Saudi Arabia
163 O 15 Rās Bāb al Mandab, Yemen
190 G 12 Rās Banâs, Egypt
162 K 6 Rās Barīdī, Saudi Arabia
191 O 22 Rās Cabaad, Somalia
191 O 18 Rās Caluula, Somalia
191 O 18 Rās Caseyr, Somalia
191 I 18 Rās Dashen, Ethiopia
191 O 20 Rās Durdura, Somalia
164 G 10 Rās-e Barkan, Iran
164 H 11 Rās-e Halīleh, Iran
165 N 14 Rās-e Meydanī, Iran
190 D 7 Rās el Kanâyis, Egypt
192 K 7 Rās el Mâ, Mali
163 V 12 Rās Fartak, Yemen
191 O 20 Rās Gabbac, Somalia
190 H 13 Rās Hardârba, Sudan
162 L 8 Rās Ḥāṭibah, Saudi Arabia
191 O 21 Rās Ilig, Somalia
163 O 13 Rās 'Īsá, Yemen
165 Q 14 Rās Jaddi, Pakistan
164 M 14 Rās Jagīn, Iran
162 K 5 Rās Karkūmā, Saudi Arabia
191 I 15 Rās Kasar, Sudan/Eritrea
191 M 19 Rās Khansiir, Somalia
191 O 20 Rās Macbar, Somalia
163 X 11 Rās Mirbāṭ, Oman
163 X 14 Rās Momi, Yemen
165 T 15 Ras Muari, Pakistan
190 G 10 Rās Muhammad, Egypt
163 X 11 Rās Naws, Oman
188 A 14 Rās Nouâdhibou, Western Sahara
192 E 5 Rās Nouâdhibou, Mauritania
165 P 14 Ras Nuh, Pakistan
165 R 14 Ras Ormara, Pakistan
164 H 11 Rās osh Shaṭṭ, Iran
163 W 11 Rās Sājir, Oman
163 Y 10 Rās Ṣawqirah, Oman
195 X 9 Ras Shaka, Kenya
163 Y 10 Rās Sharbithāt, Oman
163 V 14 Rās Shu'ab, Yemen
163 Z 9 Rās Ṣirāb, Oman
191 N 19 Rās Surud, Somalia
163 S 3 Rās Tanāqib, Saudi Arabia
163 T 4 Rās Tannūrah, Saudi Arabia
192 E 6 Rās Timirist, Mauritania
191 O 19 Rās Xaafuun, Somalia
99 D 14 Raseiniai, Lithuania
191 E 19 Rashad, Sudan
101 T 4 Rashivka, Ukraine
164 K 6 Rashm, Iran
164 H 4 Rasht, Iran
173 K 17 Rasi Salai, Thailand
95 L 14 Raška, Serbia and Montenegro
165 Q 11 Raskoh, Pakistan
114 L 1 Rasmussen Basin, Nunavut, Canada
113 W 2 Rasmussen Bay, Nunavut, Canada
99 L 16 Rasna, Belarus
100 J 11 Râşnov, Romania
63 A 16 Raso, Cape Verde
87 E 22 Rastatt, Germany
84 L 6 Rásttigáisa, Norway
173 G 19 Rat Buri, Thailand
211 L 14 Rata, New Zealand
215 X 2 Ratak Chain, Marshall Islands
168 D 11 Ratangarh, India
85 F 16 Rätansbyn, Sweden
172 A 12 Rathedaung, Myanmar
86 K 13 Rathenow, Germany
169 D 14 Ratlam, India
169 C 18 Ratnagiri, India
169 G 25 Ratnapura, Sri Lanka
100 J 1 Ratne, Ukraine
165 U 12 Rato Dero, Pakistan
119 F 16 Raton, New Mexico, U.S.A.
89 N 6 Rattenberg, Austria
174 E 9 Raub, Malaysia
145 L 14 Rauch, Argentina
163 R 2 Raudhatain, Kuwait
210 O 11 Raukumara Range, New Zealand
85 J 18 Rauma, Finland
169 I 15 Raurkela, India
176 M 3 Rausu, Japan
210 O 10 Rautoria, New Zealand
100 I 3 Rava-Rus'ka, Ukraine
215 W 10 Ravahere, French Polynesia
118 B 7 Ravalli, Montana, U.S.A.
164 M 9 Rāvar, Iran
83 H 16 Ravels, Belgium
117 F 15 Ravendale, California, U.S.A.
90 G 9 Ravenna, Italy
87 G 25 Ravensburg, Germany
209 T 4 Ravenshoe, Queensland, Australia
208 H 11 Ravensthorpe, Western Australia, Australia
165 X 10 Ravi, Pakistan
167 N 14 Ravnina, Turkmenistan
161 Q 5 Rāwah, Iraq

Country · Internal administrative region: State/Province/Territory/Dependent territory · Capital city · Mountain range/Undersea ridge · Mountain peak/Volcano/Seamount · Geographic feature · Headland/Point/Cape/Peninsula · Desert · Island/Island group · Antarctic base · Ocean · Sea · Bay/Gulf/Channel/Strait · Lake · Salt pan/Dry/Intermittent lake · River

165 W 8 **Rawalpindi**, Pakistan
161 T 1 **Rawāndiz**, Iraq
175 U 11 **Rawas**, Indonesia
93 G 14 **Rawicz**, Poland
208 K 10 **Rawlinna**, Western Australia, Australia
118 E 12 **Rawlins**, Wyoming, U.S.A.
145 I 18 **Rawson**, Argentina
171 N 11 **Rawu**, China
160 H 6 **Rayak**, Lebanon
157 U 14 **Raychikhinsk**, Russian Federation
163 P 12 **Raydah**, Yemen
116 D 8 **Raymond**, Washington, U.S.A.
173 I 20 **Rayong**, Thailand
165 V 8 **Razani**, Pakistan
96 L 7 **Razgrad**, Bulgaria ▣
96 L 7 **Razgrad**, Bulgaria
96 G 11 **Razlog**, Bulgaria
77 K 21 **Reading**, United Kingdom
121 T 11 **Reading**, Pennsylvania, U.S.A.
120 F 7 **Readstown**, Wisconsin, U.S.A.
144 J 13 **Realicó**, Argentina
173 J 20 **Reăng Kesei**, Cambodia
215 Y 10 **Réao**, French Polynesia ⛱
189 Q 8 **Rebaa**, Algeria
84 I 7 **Rebbenesøy**, Norway ⛱
189 W 12 **Rebiana Sand Sea**, Libya ◇
176 I 3 **Rebun-tō**, Japan ⛱
99 M 20 **Rechytsa**, Belarus
142 O 13 **Recife**, Brazil
145 F 14 **Recinto**, Chile
144 L 9 **Reconquista**, Argentina
144 I 9 **Recreo**, Argentina
118 J 7 **Red**, Minnesota, U.S.A. ∿
119 M 18 **Red**, Various, U.S.A. ∿
172 K 11 **Red**, Vietnam ∿
115 X 8 **Red Bay**, Newfoundland and Labrador, Canada
117 D 15 **Red Bluff**, California, U.S.A.
113 V 12 **Red Deer**, Alberta, Canada
117 D 25 **Red Hill**, Hawaii, U.S.A. ▲
119 I 16 **Red Hills**, Kansas, U.S.A. ◇
114 J 10 **Red Lake**, Ontario, Canada
118 D 9 **Red Lodge**, Montana, U.S.A.
191 G 14 **Red Sea**, Sudan ▣
162 J 6 **Red Sea**, Africa/Asia ⌓
118 M 10 **Red Wing**, Minnesota, U.S.A.
77 K 15 **Redcar**, United Kingdom
117 D 15 **Redding**, California, U.S.A.
77 J 20 **Redditch**, United Kingdom
142 J 12 **Redenção**, Brazil
142 L 13 **Redenção do Gurguéia**, Brazil
118 I 10 **Redfield**, South Dakota, U.S.A.
117 H 23 **Redlands**, California, U.S.A.
117 C 16 **Redwood Valley**, California, U.S.A.
120 K 7 **Reed City**, Michigan, U.S.A.
121 T 13 **Reedville**, Virginia, U.S.A.
211 G 17 **Reefton**, New Zealand
87 B 15 **Rees**, Germany
159 N 9 **Refahiye**, Turkey
122 K 5 **Reform**, Alabama, U.S.A.
92 E 9 **Rega**, Poland ∿
87 M 22 **Regen**, Germany
87 K 22 **Regensburg**, Germany
188 L 11 **Reggane**, Algeria
90 E 8 **Reggio**, Italy
91 L 21 **Reggio di Calabria**, Italy
100 J 9 **Reghin**, Romania
113 Y 12 **Regina**, Saskatchewan, Canada
165 R 10 **Registan**, Afghanistan ◇
143 J 19 **Registro**, Brazil
168 N 11 **Regong**, India
80 I 10 **Reguengos de Monsaraz**, Portugal
196 I 10 **Rehoboth**, Namibia
123 T 1 **Reidsville**, North Carolina, U.S.A.
77 L 22 **Reigate**, United Kingdom
79 S 3 **Reims**, France
88 F 7 **Reinach**, Switzerland
113 X 10 **Reindeer**, Saskatchewan, Canada ∿
113 X 8 **Reindeer Lake**, Saskatchewan, Canada ◣
81 N 2 **Reinosa**, Spain
89 Y 2 **Reinthal**, Austria
215 V 10 **Reitoru**, French Polynesia ⛱
113 V 6 **Reliance**, Northwest Territories, Canada
188 L 6 **Relizane**, Algeria
189 Q 8 **Remada**, Tunisia
87 C 18 **Remagen**, Germany
174 J 14 **Rembang**, Indonesia
189 Q 8 **Remel el Abiod**, Tunisia ⛰
83 M 26 **Remich**, Luxembourg
79 V 6 **Remiremont**, France
87 C 16 **Remscheid**, Germany
172 F 6 **Renam**, Myanmar
120 H 13 **Rend Lake**, Illinois, U.S.A. ◣
212 K 6 **Rendova**, Solomon Islands ⛱
86 G 8 **Rendsburg**, Germany
174 E 11 **Rengat**, Indonesia
144 G 12 **Rengo**, Chile
101 N 11 **Reni**, Ukraine
209 Q 11 **Renmark**, South Australia, Australia
212 L 8 **Rennell**, Solomon Islands ⛱
78 L 5 **Rennes**, France
114 J 10 **Rennie**, Manitoba, Canada
117 F 16 **Reno**, Nevada, U.S.A.
171 U 7 **Renqiu**, China
175 O 15 **Reo**, Indonesia
167 N 13 **Repetek**, Turkmenistan
142 F 10 **Represa de Balbina**, Brazil ◣
143 H 19 **Represa de Itaipu**, Paraguay ◣
143 I 18 **Represa Porto Primavera**, Brazil ◣
143 J 15 **Represa Serra da Mesa**, Brazil ◣
143 L 17 **Represa Três Marias**, Brazil ◣
142 J 11 **Represa Tucuruí**, Brazil ◣
116 G 6 **Republic**, Washington, U.S.A.
77 D 17 **Republic of Ireland**, Europe □
196 M 12 **Republic of South Africa**, Africa □
94 F 10 **Republica Srpska**, Bosnia and Herzegovina ▣
115 N 2 **Repulse Bay**, Nunavut, Canada
81 S 8 **Requena**, Spain
140 E 12 **Requena**, Peru
79 Q 13 **Réquista**, France
158 M 9 **Reşadiye**, Turkey
159 S 11 **Reşadiye**, Turkey
96 C 12 **Resen**, Macedonia (F.Y.R.O.M.)
115 Q 13 **Réservoir Baskatong**, Québec, Canada ◣
115 Q 12 **Réservoir Cabonga**, Québec, Canada ◣
115 Q 11 **Réservoir Gouin**, Québec, Canada ◣
115 P 9 **Réservoir la Grande Deux**, Québec, Canada ◣
115 Q 9 **Réservoir la Grande Trois**, Québec, Canada ◣
115 S 10 **Réservoir Manicouagan**, Québec, Canada ◣
115 Q 9 **Réservoir Opinaca**, Québec, Canada ◣
115 S 11 **Réservoir Pipmuacan**, Québec, Canada ◣
101 T 5 **Reshetylivka**, Ukraine
144 M 8 **Resistencia**, Argentina
100 F 11 **Reșița**, Romania
92 E 9 **Resko**, Poland
115 T 4 **Resolution Island**, Nunavut, Canada ⛱
211 A 24 **Resolution Island**, New Zealand ⛱
156 M 13 **Respublika Altay**, Russian Federation ▣
157 R 13 **Respublika Buryatiya**, Russian Federation ▣
156 H 5 **Respublika Kareliya**, Russian Federation ▣
157 N 13 **Respublika Khakasiya**, Russian Federation ▣
156 J 8 **Respublika Komi**, Russian Federation ▣
157 R 10 **Respublika Sakha**, Russian Federation ▣
157 O 13 **Respublika Tyva**, Russian Federation ▣
144 F 13 **Retén Llico**, Chile
79 S 3 **Rethel**, France
97 H 26 **Rethymno**, Greece
89 W 2 **Retz**, Austria
58 B 14 **Réunion**, France ▣
87 G 23 **Reutlingen**, Germany
88 L 6 **Reutte**, Austria
79 P 14 **Revel**, France
113 T 13 **Revelstoke**, British Columbia, Canada
140 A 12 **Reventazón**, Peru
61 V 5 **Revillagigedo Islands**, Mexico ⛱
160 E 11 **Revivim**, Israel
169 G 14 **Rewa**, India
116 M 11 **Rexburg**, Idaho, U.S.A.
141 I 18 **Reyes**, Bolivia
84 A 11 **Reykanestá**, Iceland ▶
65 N 14 **Reykjanes Basin**, Arctic Ocean ◇
65 N 15 **Reykjanes Ridge**, Arctic Ocean ⛰
84 B 11 **Reykjavík**, Iceland ♜
125 R 7 **Reynosa**, Mexico
98 I 12 **Rēzekne**, Latvia
101 N 8 **Rezina**, Moldova
94 N 12 **Rgotina**, Serbia and Montenegro
86 D 13 **Rheine**, Germany
88 E 6 **Rheinfelden**, Switzerland
87 D 20 **Rheinland-Pfalz**, Germany ▣
88 H 9 **Rheinwaldhorn**, Switzerland ▲
87 C 18 **Rhine**, Europe ∿
195 R 6 **Rhino Camp**, Uganda
86 K 12 **Rhinow**, Germany
83 H 21 **Rhisnes**, Belgium
121 W 9 **Rhode Island**, U.S.A. ▣
121 X 9 **Rhode Island Sound**, Rhode Island, U.S.A. ≈
97 O 24 **Rhodes**, Greece ⛱
96 G 11 **Rhodope Mountains**, Bulgaria ⛰
87 G 19 **Rhön**, Germany ⛰
79 T 12 **Rhône**, France/Switzerland ∿
79 U 11 **Rhône-Alpes**, France ▣
77 I 18 **Rhyl**, United Kingdom
193 S 15 **Riaba**, Equatorial Guinea
142 K 12 **Riachão**, Brazil
143 L 14 **Riachão das Neves**, Brazil
143 J 15 **Rialma**, Brazil
80 G 2 **Rías Bajas**, Spain ◇
174 E 10 **Riau**, Indonesia ▣
81 O 5 **Riaza**, Spain
143 H 18 **Ribas do Rio Pardo**, Brazil
197 T 5 **Ribáuè**, Mozambique
77 J 17 **Ribble**, United Kingdom ∿
85 B 25 **Ribe**, Denmark
80 G 2 **Ribeira**, Spain
62 O 2 **Ribeira Grande**, Azores
143 J 18 **Ribeirão Preto**, Brazil
141 J 16 **Riberalta**, Bolivia
81 X 3 **Ribes de Freser**, Spain
94 C 8 **Ribnica**, Slovenia
101 O 8 **Rîbnița**, Moldova
86 K 8 **Ribnitz-Damgarten**, Germany
124 L 4 **Ricardo Flores Magón**, Mexico
90 H 10 **Riccione**, Italy
123 P 4 **Richard B. Russell Lake**, Georgia, U.S.A. ◣
192 E 7 **Richard Toll**, Senegal
197 Q 12 **Richards Bay**, Republic of South Africa
116 K 12 **Richfield**, Idaho, U.S.A.
120 G 7 **Richland Center**, Wisconsin, U.S.A.
120 L 11 **Richmond**, Indiana, U.S.A.
120 L 14 **Richmond**, Kentucky, U.S.A.
121 R 14 **Richmond**, Virginia, U.S.A.
196 L 13 **Richmond**, Republic of South Africa
209 S 5 **Richmond**, Queensland, Australia
211 I 16 **Richmond**, New Zealand
123 R 6 **Richmond Hill**, Georgia, U.S.A.
211 H 17 **Richmond Range**, New Zealand ⛰
117 H 21 **Ridgecrest**, California, U.S.A.
123 R 6 **Ridgeland**, South Carolina, U.S.A.
89 R 4 **Ried im Innkreis**, Austria
87 G 24 **Riedlingen**, Germany
87 M 16 **Riesa**, Germany
98 C 13 **Rietavas**, Lithuania
90 H 13 **Rieti**, Italy
84 C 9 **Rifstangi**, Iceland ▶
195 U 6 **Rift Valley**, Kenya ▣
193 V 9 **Rig-Rig**, Chad
98 F 11 **Rīga**, Latvia ♜
116 I 9 **Riggins**, Idaho, U.S.A.
98 E 6 **Riguldi**, Estonia
219 N 3 **Riiser-Larsen Ice Shelf**, Antarctica ◇
219 U 2 **Riiser-Larsen Peninsula**, Antarctica ▶
63 N 23 **Riiser-Larsen Sea**, Atlantic Ocean ⌓
98 F 6 **Riisipere**, Estonia
193 Q 10 **Rijau**, Nigeria
94 B 9 **Rijeka**, Croatia
82 M 11 **Rijssen**, Netherlands
176 L 4 **Rikubetsu**, Japan
96 G 10 **Rila**, Bulgaria ⛰
83 F 16 **Rilland**, Netherlands
215 R 11 **Rimatara**, French Polynesia ⛱
93 K 21 **Rimavská Sobota**, Slovakia
90 H 10 **Rimini**, Italy
175 N 15 **Rinca**, Indonesia ⛱
97 J 21 **Rineia**, Greece ⛱
168 D 12 **Ringas**, India
193 S 10 **Ringim**, Nigeria
85 B 24 **Ringkøbing**, Denmark
118 C 9 **Ringling**, Montana, U.S.A.
85 D 25 **Ringsted**, Denmark
84 I 7 **Ringvassøy**, Norway ⛱
142 C 13 **Rio Branco**, Brazil
143 H 18 **Rio Brilhante**, Brazil
145 F 16 **Río Bueno**, Chile
127 X 12 **Rio Claro**, Trinidad and Tobago
145 J 15 **Río Colorado**, Argentina
144 J 11 **Río Cuarto**, Argentina
143 M 19 **Rio de Janeiro**, Brazil ▣
143 L 19 **Rio de Janeiro**, Brazil
143 J 21 **Rio do Sul**, Brazil
145 H 23 **Río Gallegos**, Argentina
125 N 3 **Rio Grande**, Mexico/U.S.A. ∿
143 I 23 **Rio Grande**, Brazil
125 O 8 **Río Grande**, Mexico
145 I 25 **Río Grande**, Argentina
119 J 24 **Rio Grande City**, Texas, U.S.A.
125 N 10 **Rio Grande de Santiago**, Mexico ∿
142 O 12 **Rio Grande do Norte**, Brazil ▣
143 H 21 **Rio Grande do Sul**, Brazil ▣
63 J 17 **Rio Grande Fracture Zone**, Atlantic Ocean ◇
63 H 17 **Rio Grande Gap**, Atlantic Ocean ⛰
63 H 17 **Rio Grande Rise**, Atlantic Ocean ⛰
126 K 14 **Río Hato**, Panama
125 Z 10 **Río Lagartos**, Mexico
80 G 8 **Rio Maior**, Portugal
141 J 21 **Río Mulatos**, Bolivia
144 M 11 **Río Negro**, Uruguay ▣
145 I 16 **Río Negro**, Argentina ▣
140 D 10 **Río Tigre**, Peru
174 M 6 **Rio Tuba**, Philippines
143 I 17 **Rio Verde**, Brazil
145 G 24 **Rio Verde**, Chile
125 Q 10 **Río Verde**, Mexico
140 B 9 **Riobamba**, Ecuador
138 J 2 **Ríohacha**, Colombia
140 C 12 **Rioja**, Peru
79 R 10 **Riom**, France
81 Q 10 **Riópar**, Spain
101 Q 1 **Ripky**, Ukraine
120 M 13 **Ripley**, Ohio, U.S.A.
121 O 12 **Ripley**, West Virginia, U.S.A.
122 I 2 **Ripley**, Tennessee, U.S.A.
81 X 3 **Ripoll**, Spain
83 K 15 **Rips**, Netherlands
100 M 7 **Rîșcani**, Moldova
176 I 3 **Rishiri-tō**, Japan ⛱
176 I 3 **Rishiri-yama**, Japan ▲
160 F 9 **Rishon Le Ẕiyyon**, Israel
85 D 15 **Rissa**, Norway
85 N 17 **Ristiina**, Finland
84 N 13 **Ristijärvi**, Finland
98 C 6 **Ristna**, Estonia
169 N 21 **Ritchie's Archipelago**, India ⛱
116 H 7 **Ritzville**, Washington, U.S.A.
90 F 6 **Riva del Garda**, Italy
144 J 13 **Rivadavia**, Argentina
144 K 6 **Rivadavia**, Argentina
144 G 9 **Rivadavia**, Chile
126 G 12 **Rivas**, Nicaragua
192 H 13 **River Cess**, Liberia
144 M 13 **River Plate**, Uruguay ∿
144 N 10 **Rivera**, Uruguay ▣
144 N 10 **Rivera**, Uruguay
145 J 14 **Rivera**, Argentina
121 V 10 **Riverhead**, New York, U.S.A.
193 Q 14 **Rivers**, Nigeria ▣
211 D 24 **Riversdale**, New Zealand
211 L 16 **Riversdale Beach**, New Zealand
117 H 23 **Riverside**, California, U.S.A.
115 Q 7 **Rivière aux Feuilles**, Québec, Canada ∿
115 R 7 **Rivière aux Mélèzes**, Québec, Canada ∿
115 W 10 **Rivière-aux-Saumons**, Québec, Canada
115 T 12 **Rivière-du-Loup**, Québec, Canada
58 B 11 **Rivière du Rempart**, Mauritius
115 T 11 **Rivière-Pentecôte**, Québec, Canada
127 X 9 **Rivière-Pilote**, Martinique
100 L 3 **Rivne**, Ukraine
90 A 7 **Rivoli**, Italy
196 K 6 **Rivungo**, Angola
163 R 6 **Riyadh**, Saudi Arabia ♜
159 P 8 **Rize**, Turkey
171 V 8 **Rizhao**, China
158 J 15 **Rizokarpason**, Cyprus
127 V 7 **Road Town**, Virgin Islands (U.K.) ♜
117 N 15 **Roan Plateau**, Utah, U.S.A. ◇
79 S 9 **Roanne**, France
121 P 14 **Roanoke**, Virginia, U.S.A.
123 N 5 **Roanoke**, Alabama, U.S.A.
123 X 1 **Roanoke Island**, North Carolina, U.S.A. ⛱
123 V 1 **Roanoke Rapids**, North Carolina, U.S.A.
126 F 8 **Roatán**, Honduras
209 S 14 **Robbins Island**, Tasmania, Australia ⛱
219 R 14 **Roberts Butte**, Antarctica ▲
218 I 3 **Robertson Island**, Antarctica ⛱
192 G 13 **Robertsport**, Liberia
115 R 12 **Roberval**, Québec, Canada
209 R 12 **Robinvale**, Victoria, Australia
81 Q 9 **Robledo**, Spain
114 H 9 **Roblin**, Manitoba, Canada
141 N 21 **Robore**, Bolivia
119 J 23 **Robstown**, Texas, U.S.A.
91 J 14 **Roccaraso**, Italy
144 O 12 **Rocha**, Uruguay ▣
144 O 12 **Rocha**, Uruguay
79 O 10 **Rochechouart**, France
143 H 17 **Rochedo**, Brazil
78 L 9 **Rochefort**, France
83 I 23 **Rochefort**, Belgium
118 M 10 **Rochester**, Minnesota, U.S.A.
120 K 10 **Rochester**, Indiana, U.S.A.
121 X 7 **Rochester**, New Hampshire, U.S.A.
121 R 8 **Rochester**, New York, U.S.A.
211 D 24 **Rock and Pillar Range**, New Zealand ⛰
123 R 3 **Rock Hill**, South Carolina, U.S.A.
118 D 12 **Rock Springs**, Wyoming, U.S.A.
62 J 6 **Rockall Bank**, Atlantic Ocean ◇
62 J 6 **Rockall Trough**, Atlantic Ocean ◇
120 H 9 **Rockford**, Illinois, U.S.A.
209 V 7 **Rockhampton**, Queensland, Australia
123 T 3 **Rockingham**, North Carolina, U.S.A.
118 I 7 **Rocklake**, North Dakota, U.S.A.
121 Y 6 **Rockland**, Maine, U.S.A.
116 E 6 **Rockport**, Washington, U.S.A.
119 I 21 **Rocksprings**, Texas, U.S.A.
123 V 1 **Rocky Mount**, North Carolina, U.S.A.
113 U 12 **Rocky Mountain House**, Alberta, Canada
113 S 11 **Rocky Mountains**, Canada/U.S.A. ⛰
196 G 8 **Rocky Point**, Namibia ▶
144 G 10 **Rodeo**, Argentina
79 Q 12 **Rodez**, France
87 L 21 **Roding**, Germany
100 J 8 **Rodna**, Romania
96 H 13 **Rodolivos**, Greece
97 O 23 **Rodos**, Greece
58 E 7 **Rodrigues Island**, Mauritius ▣
208 F 6 **Roebourne**, Western Australia, Australia
208 I 4 **Roebuck Bay**, Western Australia, Australia ≈
208 I 4 **Roebuck Plains Roadhouse**, Western Australia, Australia
83 K 17 **Roermond**, Netherlands
115 N 3 **Roes Welcome Sound**, Nunavut, Canada ≈
83 A 18 **Roesbrugge-Haringe**, Belgium
83 B 18 **Roeselare**, Belgium
91 L 17 **Rofrano**, Italy
94 I 13 **Rogatica**, Bosnia and Herzegovina
119 L 16 **Rogers**, Arkansas, U.S.A.
120 M 5 **Rogers City**, Michigan, U.S.A.
116 J 13 **Rogerson**, Idaho, U.S.A.
61 X 11 **Roggeveen Basin**, Pacific Ocean ◇
79 Y 14 **Rogliano**, France
91 M 19 **Rogliano**, Italy
100 J 5 **Rohatyn**, Ukraine
89 S 3 **Rohrbach**, Austria
165 U 12 **Rohri**, Pakistan
168 E 11 **Rohtak**, India
98 E 6 **Rohuküla**, Estonia
173 K 17 **Roi Et**, Thailand
168 O 11 **Roing**, India
98 D 10 **Roja**, Latvia
144 K 12 **Rojas**, Argentina
98 G 13 **Rokiškis**, Lithuania
176 K 8 **Rokkasho**, Japan
177 H 14 **Rokkō-zaki**, Japan ▶
100 M 2 **Rokytne**, Ukraine
85 A 19 **Røldal**, Norway
119 M 15 **Rolla**, Missouri, U.S.A.
88 B 9 **Rolle**, Switzerland
209 U 7 **Rolleston**, Queensland, Australia
84 K 5 **Rolvsøya**, Norway ⛱
175 R 14 **Roma**, Indonesia ⛱
209 U 8 **Roma**, Queensland, Australia
63 J 14 **Romanche Gap**, Atlantic Ocean ◇
100 G 10 **Romania**, Europe □
157 R 13 **Romanovka**, Russian Federation
175 P 4 **Romblon**, Philippines
91 H 14 **Rome**, Italy ♜
121 T 7 **Rome**, New York, U.S.A.
123 N 4 **Rome**, Georgia, U.S.A.
79 R 5 **Romilly-sur-Seine**, France
121 Q 12 **Romney**, West Virginia, U.S.A.
101 S 3 **Romny**, Ukraine
85 B 25 **Rømø**, Denmark ⛱
79 P 7 **Romorantin-Lanthenay**, France
173 M 15 **Ron**, Vietnam
80 M 13 **Ronda**, Spain
138 K 5 **Rondón**, Colombia
143 E 14 **Rondônia**, Brazil ▣
143 H 16 **Rondonópolis**, Brazil
171 R 13 **Rong'an**, China
215 W 1 **Rongelap Atoll**, Marshall Islands ⛱
215 X 1 **Rongrik**, Marshall Islands ⛱
85 F 26 **Rønne**, Denmark
218 I 7 **Ronne Entrance**, Antarctica ≈
218 L 7 **Ronne Ice Shelf**, Antarctica ◇
85 G 24 **Ronneby**, Sweden
85 F 15 **Rönnöfors**, Sweden
83 D 19 **Ronse**, Belgium
63 O 15 **Rookery Point**, Tristan da Cunha ▶
168 F 10 **Roorkee**, India
83 G 15 **Roosendaal**, Netherlands
117 N 23 **Roosevelt**, Arizona, U.S.A.
219 O 11 **Roosevelt Island**, Antarctica ⛱
93 M 17 **Ropczyce**, Poland
209 N 2 **Roper Bar**, Northern Territory, Australia
78 M 13 **Roquefort**, France
142 E 8 **Roraima**, Brazil ▣
85 E 16 **Røros**, Norway
101 Q 5 **Ros'**, Ukraine ∿
140 B 8 **Rosa Zárate**, Ecuador
126 J 8 **Rosalind Bank**, Honduras ≈
124 M 9 **Rosario**, Mexico
138 K 3 **Rosario**, Venezuela
144 L 11 **Rosario**, Argentina
126 G 7 **Rosario Bank**, Guatemala ≈
144 J 7 **Rosario de la Frontera**, Argentina
143 H 22 **Rosário do Sul**, Brazil
124 E 2 **Rosarito**, Mexico
124 G 5 **Rosarito**, Mexico
124 I 6 **Rosarito**, Mexico

□ Country ▣ Internal administrative region: State/Province/Territory/Dependent territory ♜ Capital city ⛰ Mountain range/Undersea ridge ▲ Mountain peak/Volcano/Seamount ◇ Geographic feature ▶ Headland/Point/Cape/Peninsula ◢ Desert ⛱ Island/Island group ⁙ Antarctic base ≋ Ocean ⌓ Sea ≈ Bay/Gulf/Channel/Strait ◣ Lake ◳ Salt pan/Dry/Intermittent lake ∿ River

91 L 20 **Rosarno**, Italy
77 C 17 **Roscommon**, Republic of Ireland
77 D 19 **Roscrea**, Republic of Ireland
214 L 8 **Rose**, American Samoa
58 B 12 **Rose Belle**, Mauritius
58 B 12 **Rose Hill**, Mauritius
117 O 23 **Rose Peak**, Arizona, U.S.A.
127 X 9 **Roseau**, Dominica
83 H 22 **Rosée**, Belgium
191 G 19 **Roseires Reservoir**, Sudan
87 K 25 **Rosenheim**, Germany
81 Y 3 **Roses**, Spain
90 J 12 **Roseto degli Abruzzi**, Italy
113 X 12 **Rosetown**, Saskatchewan, Canada
120 G 10 **Roseville**, Illinois, U.S.A.
196 I 12 **Rosh Pinah**, Namibia
90 E 11 **Rosignano Marittimo**, Italy
100 J 13 **Roşiori de Vede**, Romania
156 E 8 **Roslavl'**, Russian Federation
209 T 15 **Ross**, Tasmania, Australia
211 F 19 **Ross**, New Zealand
122 I 6 **Ross Barnett Reservoir**, Mississippi, U.S.A.
219 O 11 **Ross Ice Shelf**, Antarctica
219 Q 12 **Ross Island**, Antarctica
113 O 8 **Ross River**, Yukon Territory, Canada
219 N 12 **Ross Sea**, Antarctica
77 C 15 **Rossan Point**, Republic of Ireland
212 I 7 **Rossel Island**, Papua New Guinea
77 E 20 **Rosslare**, Republic of Ireland
192 E 7 **Rosso**, Mauritania
156 E 9 **Rossosh'**, Russian Federation
84 F 12 **Røssvatnet**, Norway
164 J 13 **Rostāq**, Iran
86 J 9 **Rostock**, Germany
156 E 10 **Rostov-na-Donu**, Russian Federation
119 F 19 **Roswell**, New Mexico, U.S.A.
123 O 4 **Roswell**, Georgia, U.S.A.
214 A 9 **Rota**, Northern Mariana Islands
175 P 15 **Rote**, Indonesia
86 G 11 **Rotenburg**, Germany
87 E 17 **Rothaargebirge**, Germany
87 H 21 **Rothenburg ob der Tauber**, Germany
218 H 5 **Rothera**, Antarctica
77 K 18 **Rotherham**, United Kingdom
218 I 6 **Rothschild Island**, Antarctica
175 P 15 **Roti**, Indonesia
211 G 19 **Rotomanu**, New Zealand
91 N 17 **Rotondella**, Italy
210 M 11 **Rotorua**, New Zealand
89 T 6 **Rottenmann**, Austria
82 G 13 **Rotterdam**, Netherlands
82 M 5 **Rottumeroog**, Netherlands
82 L 4 **Rottumerplaat**, Netherlands
87 F 24 **Rottweil**, Germany
213 W 8 **Rotuma**, Fiji
79 Q 1 **Roubaix**, France
79 O 3 **Rouen**, France
58 C 11 **Round Island**, Mauritius
117 O 19 **Round Rock**, Arizona, U.S.A.
119 J 21 **Round Rock**, Texas, U.S.A.
118 D 9 **Roundup**, Montana, U.S.A.
76 I 6 **Rousay**, United Kingdom
115 P 12 **Rouyn**, Québec, Canada
84 L 11 **Rovaniemi**, Finland
101 Z 7 **Roven'ky**, Ukraine
88 H 10 **Roveredo**, Switzerland
90 F 6 **Rovereto**, Italy
173 L 19 **Rôvieng Tbong**, Cambodia
90 G 8 **Rovigo**, Italy
100 H 12 **Rovinari**, Romania
94 A 9 **Rovinj**, Croatia
115 O 1 **Rowley Island**, Nunavut, Canada
59 U 7 **Rowley Shoals**, Indian Ocean
175 P 5 **Roxas**, Philippines
175 N 6 **Roxas**, Philippines
123 T 1 **Roxboro**, North Carolina, U.S.A.
209 P 10 **Roxby Downs**, South Australia, Australia
119 F 17 **Roy**, New Mexico, U.S.A.
121 V 7 **Royalton**, Vermont, U.S.A.
78 L 10 **Royan**, France
79 Q 3 **Roye**, France
123 P 4 **Royston**, Georgia, U.S.A.
95 L 15 **Rožaje**, Serbia and Montenegro
92 L 11 **Różan**, Poland
101 T 11 **Rozdol'ne**, Ukraine
93 K 20 **Rožňava**, Slovakia
82 F 13 **Rozenburg**, Netherlands
82 K 13 **Rozendaal**, Netherlands
100 K 3 **Rozhyshche**, Ukraine
95 K 17 **Rrëshen**, Albania
156 F 9 **Rtishchevo**, Russian Federation
196 G 7 **Ruacana**, Namibia
211 L 14 **Ruahine Range**, New Zealand
210 J 6 **Ruakaka**, New Zealand
211 C 26 **Ruapuke Island**, New Zealand
210 M 11 **Ruatahuna**, New Zealand
210 J 7 **Ruawai**, New Zealand
163 Q 10 **Rub' al Khālī**, Saudi Arabia
101 Y 5 **Rubizhne**, Ukraine
156 L 13 **Rubtsovsk**, Russian Federation
112 J 5 **Ruby**, Alaska, U.S.A.
117 J 16 **Ruby Mountains**, Nevada, U.S.A.
100 J 11 **Rucăr**, Romania
98 B 12 **Rucava**, Latvia
165 Q 11 **Rudbar**, Afghanistan
167 O 3 **Rudnyy**, Kazakhstan
87 J 17 **Rudolstadt**, Germany
79 P 2 **Rue**, France
191 F 17 **Rufa'a**, Sudan
79 N 9 **Ruffec**, France
144 J 12 **Rufino**, Argentina
197 O 5 **Rufunsa**, Zambia
77 K 20 **Rugby**, United Kingdom
118 I 7 **Rugby**, North Dakota, U.S.A.
86 L 8 **Rügen**, Germany
195 Q 8 **Ruhengeri**, Rwanda
98 E 9 **Ruhnu**, Estonia
171 W 11 **Rui'an**, China
171 V 12 **Ruijin**, China
171 N 13 **Ruili**, China
195 U 12 **Ruipa**, Tanzania
124 M 10 **Ruiz**, Mexico
98 G 9 **Rūjiena**, Latvia
84 N 11 **Ruka**, Finland
195 R 12 **Rukwa**, Tanzania
76 E 11 **Rum**, United Kingdom
127 N 3 **Rum Cay**, The Bahamas
94 K 10 **Ruma**, Serbia and Montenegro
163 R 5 **Rumāh**, Saudi Arabia
161 Y 12 **Rumaila**, Iraq
191 D 21 **Rumbek**, Sudan
212 A 4 **Rumginae**, Papua New Guinea
176 J 4 **Rumoi**, Japan
197 R 3 **Rumphi**, Malawi
196 J 7 **Rundu**, Namibia
195 P 6 **Rungu**, Democratic Republic of Congo
195 T 12 **Rungwa**, Tanzania
85 O 17 **Ruokolahti**, Finland
170 K 6 **Ruoqiang**, China
84 M 6 **Ruostefjelbma**, Norway
174 E 10 **Rupat**, Indonesia
100 J 10 **Rupea**, Romania
121 P 13 **Rupert**, West Virginia, U.S.A.
218 M 12 **Ruppert Coast**, Antarctica
141 I 18 **Rurrenabaque**, Bolivia
215 S 11 **Rurutu**, French Polynesia
197 Q 7 **Rusape**, Zimbabwe
100 I 7 **Ruscova**, Romania
96 K 6 **Ruse**, Bulgaria
96 K 6 **Ruse**, Bulgaria
120 G 11 **Rushville**, Illinois, U.S.A.
99 C 14 **Rusnė**, Lithuania
98 I 12 **Rušonu ezers**, Latvia
212 L 6 **Russell Islands**, Solomon Islands
119 M 17 **Russellville**, Arkansas, U.S.A.
120 J 15 **Russellville**, Kentucky, U.S.A.
122 K 3 **Russellville**, Alabama, U.S.A.
156 J 9 **Russian Federation**, Asia
218 M 12 **Russkaya**, Antarctica
157 V 7 **Russkoye Ust'ye**, Russian Federation
159 U 7 **Rust'avi**, Georgia
197 N 11 **Rustenburg**, Republic of South Africa
119 M 19 **Ruston**, Louisiana, U.S.A.
85 C 17 **Ruten**, Norway
175 O 15 **Ruteng**, Indonesia
117 J 16 **Ruth**, Nevada, U.S.A.
123 R 2 **Rutherfordton**, North Carolina, U.S.A.
121 V 7 **Rutland**, Vermont, U.S.A.
169 N 22 **Rutland Island**, India
170 H 8 **Rutog**, China
82 M 12 **Ruurlo**, Netherlands
195 U 14 **Ruvuma**, Tanzania
197 S 3 **Ruvuma**, Mozambique/Tanzania
163 V 6 **Ruweis**, United Arab Emirates
99 F 19 **Ruzhany**, Belarus
93 J 19 **Ružomberok**, Slovakia
195 Q 9 **Rwanda**, Africa
156 F 8 **Ryazan'**, Russian Federation
218 J 7 **Ryberg Peninsula**, Antarctica
156 G 8 **Rybinsk**, Russian Federation
93 I 17 **Rybnik**, Poland
209 S 13 **Rye**, Victoria, Australia
93 M 14 **Ryki**, Poland
176 I 13 **Ryōtsu**, Japan
92 J 11 **Rypin**, Poland
177 N 24 **Ryukyu Islands**, Japan
60 K 5 **Ryukyu Trench**, Pacific Ocean
92 D 12 **Rzepin**, Poland
93 M 17 **Rzeszów**, Poland
156 F 7 **Rzhev**, Russian Federation

S

82 L 13 **'s-Heerenberg**, Netherlands
83 I 14 **'s-Hertogenbosch**, Netherlands
173 M 22 **Sa Đec**, Vietnam
173 I 19 **Sa Kaeo**, Thailand
191 K 24 **Saacow**, Somalia
87 J 15 **Saale**, Germany
87 J 18 **Saalfeld**, Germany
89 Q 6 **Saalfelden**, Austria
87 C 21 **Saarbrücken**, Germany
87 B 20 **Saarburg**, Germany
98 D 9 **Sääre**, Estonia
98 D 8 **Saaremaa**, Estonia
85 L 16 **Saarijärvi**, Finland
87 C 21 **Saarland**, Germany
88 E 10 **Saas Fee**, Switzerland
160 J 6 **Sab' Ābār**, Syria
127 V 7 **Saba**, Netherlands Antilles
94 J 10 **Šabac**, Serbia and Montenegro
81 W 4 **Sabadell**, Spain
177 G 16 **Sabae**, Japan
174 M 8 **Sabah**, Malaysia
168 E 12 **Sabalgarh**, India
138 L 3 **Sabana Grande**, Venezuela
138 I 2 **Sabanalarga**, Colombia
138 L 3 **Sabaneta**, Venezuela
174 B 8 **Sabang**, Indonesia
100 L 9 **Săbăoani**, Romania
169 G 25 **Sabaragamuwa**, Sri Lanka
91 H 15 **Sabaudia**, Italy
141 I 21 **Sabaya**, Bolivia
160 H 9 **Şabḩā**, Jordan
189 T 11 **Sabhā**, Libya
81 T 3 **Sabiñánigo**, Spain
125 Q 6 **Sabinas Hidalgo**, Mexico
189 T 8 **Sabkhat al Hayshah**, Libya
189 X 9 **Sabkhat al Qunayyin**, Libya
189 W 9 **Sabkhat Ghuzayyil**, Libya
175 O 4 **Sablayan**, Philippines
193 S 9 **Sabon Kafi**, Niger
78 M 13 **Sabres**, France
219 X 12 **Sabrina Coast**, Antarctica
175 O 1 **Sabtang**, Philippines
80 J 6 **Sabugal**, Portugal
175 N 11 **Sabulu**, Indonesia
163 O 11 **Şabyā**, Saudi Arabia
164 M 6 **Sabzevār**, Iran
81 Q 6 **Sacedón**, Spain
87 M 16 **Sachsen**, Germany
86 J 12 **Sachsen-Anhalt**, Germany
121 S 7 **Sackets Harbor**, New York, U.S.A.
117 E 17 **Sacramento**, California, U.S.A.
117 D 15 **Sacramento Valley**, California, U.S.A.
160 I 5 **Şadad**, Syria
163 O 11 **Şa'dah**, Yemen
173 H 26 **Sadao**, Thailand
169 E 18 **Sadaseopet**, India
161 V 4 **Sadd Darband-i Khān**, Iraq
161 T 8 **Saddat al Hindīyah**, Iraq
163 X 11 **Şadḩ**, Oman
191 G 20 **Sadi**, Ethiopia
165 V 12 **Sadiqabad**, Pakistan
168 O 11 **Sadiya**, India
176 I 13 **Sadoga-shima**, Japan
101 U 11 **Sadove**, Ukraine
165 V 4 **Safed Khirs**, Afghanistan
165 P 7 **Safed Koh**, Afghanistan
85 E 21 **Säffle**, Sweden
117 O 24 **Safford**, Arizona, U.S.A.
188 G 8 **Safi**, Morocco
165 O 10 **Safidabeh**, Iran
160 H 4 **Şāfītā**, Syria
161 Z 12 **Safwān**, Iraq
212 E 4 **Sag Sag**, Papua New Guinea
170 I 10 **Saga**, China
177 B 21 **Saga**, Japan
177 E 21 **Saga**, Japan
176 K 12 **Sagae**, Japan
172 C 10 **Sagaing**, Myanmar
172 D 11 **Sagaing**, Myanmar
177 K 17 **Sagami-nada**, Japan
177 K 16 **Sagami-wan**, Japan
173 F 21 **Saganthif Kyun**, Myanmar
169 F 14 **Sagar**, India
157 S 7 **Sagastyr**, Russian Federation
168 I 12 **Sagauli**, India
164 L 8 **Saghand**, Iran
120 M 7 **Saginaw**, Michigan, U.S.A.
120 M 7 **Saginaw Bay**, Michigan, U.S.A.
166 J 6 **Sagiz**, Kazakhstan
81 P 11 **Sagra**, Spain
80 G 12 **Sagres**, Portugal
172 C 13 **Sagu**, Myanmar
127 N 6 **Sagua de Tánamo**, Cuba
126 K 4 **Sagua la Grande**, Cuba
119 E 15 **Saguache**, Colorado, U.S.A.
115 S 12 **Saguenay**, Québec, Canada
115 S 11 **Saguenay**, Québec, Canada
81 T 8 **Sagunto**, Spain
112 L 3 **Sagwon**, Alaska, U.S.A.
160 H 9 **Saḩāb**, Jordan
188 I 13 **Sahara**, Africa
62 J 10 **Saharan Seamounts**, Atlantic Ocean
168 E 10 **Saharanpur**, India
159 V 10 **Şahbuz**, Azerbaijan
192 M 9 **Sahel**, Burkina Faso
165 X 10 **Sahiwal**, Pakistan
165 W 9 **Sahiwal**, Pakistan
165 O 9 **Sahlābād**, Iran
161 T 12 **Şaḩrā' al Ḩijāra**, Iraq
124 J 4 **Sahuaripa**, Mexico
125 O 11 **Sahuayo**, Mexico
59 V 6 **Sahul Shelf**, Indian Ocean
191 B 20 **Sa'id Bundas**, Sudan
160 G 6 **Saïda**, Lebanon
188 L 6 **Saïda**, Algeria
212 D 4 **Saidor**, Papua New Guinea
168 K 13 **Saidpur**, Bangladesh
177 E 17 **Saigō**, Japan
177 E 20 **Saijō**, Japan
177 D 21 **Saiki**, Japan
85 N 17 **Saimaa**, Finland
165 P 11 **Saindak**, Pakistan
76 J 13 **St Abb's Head**, United Kingdom
89 W 5 **St Aegyd am Neuwalde**, Austria
79 O 7 **St-Aignan**, France
115 Y 10 **St Alban's**, Newfoundland and Labrador, Canada
77 L 21 **St Albans**, United Kingdom
121 N 13 **St Albans**, West Virginia, U.S.A.
79 Q 8 **St-Amand-Montrond**, France
79 U 9 **St-Amour**, France
89 U 8 **St Andrä**, Austria
58 B 14 **St-André**, Réunion
123 R 7 **St Andrew Sound**, Georgia, U.S.A.
76 I 12 **St Andrews**, United Kingdom
58 B 9 **Ste Anne**, Seychelles
115 X 9 **St Anthony**, Newfoundland and Labrador, Canada
88 K 7 **St Anton am Arlberg**, Austria
209 R 13 **St Arnaud**, Victoria, Australia
211 H 17 **St Arnaud**, New Zealand
115 W 9 **St-Augustin**, Québec, Canada
123 R 9 **St Augustine**, Florida, U.S.A.
77 G 24 **St Austell**, United Kingdom
127 W 7 **St Barthélémy**, France
79 N 15 **St-Béat**, France
58 B 14 **St-Benoit**, Réunion
78 J 5 **St-Brieuc**, France
79 O 6 **St-Calais**, France
115 P 15 **St Catharines**, Ontario, Canada
62 B 6 **St Catherine Point**, Bermuda
77 K 23 **St Catherine's Point**, United Kingdom
79 P 12 **St-Céré**, France
118 L 9 **St Cloud**, Minnesota, U.S.A.
127 U 7 **St Croix**, Virgin Islands (U.S.A.)
120 F 4 **St Croix**, Wisconsin, U.S.A.
120 F 5 **St Croix Falls**, Wisconsin, U.S.A.
77 G 21 **St David's**, United Kingdom
77 F 21 **St David's Head**, United Kingdom
62 B 7 **St David's Island**, Bermuda
58 A 14 **St-Denis**, Réunion
79 W 5 **St-Dié**, France
79 T 5 **St Dizier**, France
79 T 10 **St-Étienne**, France
127 W 8 **St Eusatius**, Netherlands Antilles
79 S 6 **St-Florentin**, France
79 R 11 **St-Flour**, France
119 H 14 **St Francis**, Kansas, U.S.A.
88 I 6 **St Gallen**, Switzerland
79 N 15 **St-Gaudens**, France
62 C 7 **St George**, Bermuda
117 K 19 **St George**, Utah, U.S.A.
123 S 5 **St George**, South Carolina, U.S.A.
209 U 9 **St George**, Queensland, Australia
115 U 13 **St-George**, New Brunswick, Canada
112 D 7 **St George Island**, Alaska, U.S.A.
123 N 9 **St George Island**, Florida, U.S.A.
89 U 3 **St Gergen**, Austria
127 X 11 **St George's**, Grenada
115 S 13 **St Georges**, Québec, Canada
139 Y 7 **St Georges**, French Guiana
115 W 11 **St Georges Bay**, Newfoundland and Labrador, Canada
77 E 21 **St George's Channel**, Republic of Ireland/United Kingdom
212 H 3 **St George's Channel**, Papua New Guinea
62 B 7 **St George's Island**, Bermuda
89 R 5 **St Gilgen**, Austria
83 F 17 **St-Gillis-Waas**, Belgium
79 O 15 **St-Girons**, France
77 G 21 **St Govan's Head**, United Kingdom
63 M 25 **St Helena**, U.K.
196 J 14 **Saint Helena Bay**, Republic of South Africa
63 J 16 **Saint Helena Fracture Zone**, Atlantic Ocean
123 S 6 **St Helena Sound**, South Carolina, U.S.A.
77 J 18 **St Helens**, United Kingdom
209 T 15 **St Helens**, Tasmania, Australia
77 J 26 **St Helier**, United Kingdom
83 J 23 **St-Hubert**, Belgium
120 L 5 **St Ignace**, Michigan, U.S.A.
77 F 24 **St Ives**, United Kingdom
82 J 6 **St Jacobiparochie**, Netherlands
89 O 8 **St Jakob**, Austria
78 K 14 **St-Jean-de-Luz**, France
79 V 11 **St-Jean-de-Maurienne**, France
78 K 8 **St-Jean-de-Monts**, France
115 R 13 **St-Jean-sur-Richelieu**, Québec, Canada
89 P 6 **St Johann in Tirol**, Austria
121 X 3 **St John**, Maine, U.S.A.
115 U 13 **St John**, New Brunswick, Canada
127 W 8 **St John's**, Antigua and Barbuda
115 Z 10 **St John's**, Newfoundland and Labrador, Canada
117 O 22 **St Johns**, Arizona, U.S.A.
119 L 14 **St Joseph**, Missouri, U.S.A.
58 B 15 **St-Joseph**, Réunion
119 K 23 **St Joseph Island**, Texas, U.S.A.
79 O 10 **St-Junien**, France
127 W 7 **St Kitts**, St Kitts and Nevis
127 V 8 **St Kitts and Nevis**, North America
139 X 6 **St-Laurent-du-Maroni**, French Guiana
115 T 12 **St Lawrence**, Canada/U.S.A.
115 Y 11 **St Lawrence**, Newfoundland and Labrador, Canada
112 F 4 **St Lawrence Island**, Alaska, U.S.A.
83 K 25 **St-Léger**, Belgium
58 A 15 **St Leu**, Réunion
78 L 4 **St-Lô**, France
119 N 14 **St Louis**, Missouri, U.S.A.
58 A 15 **St-Louis**, Réunion
192 D 7 **St-Louis**, Senegal
127 X 10 **St Lucia**, North America
127 V 7 **St Maarten**, Netherlands Antilles
78 K 4 **St-Malo**, France
127 P 7 **St Marc**, Haiti
79 P 8 **St-Marcel**, France
83 E 19 **St-Maria-Lierde**, Belgium
58 B 14 **Ste-Marie**, Réunion
123 O 9 **St Marks**, Florida, U.S.A.
127 W 7 **St Martin**, France
209 P 10 **St Mary Peak**, South Australia, Australia
115 Z 11 **St Mary's Bay**, Newfoundland and Labrador, Canada
112 E 5 **St Matthew Island**, Alaska, U.S.A.
212 F 2 **St Matthias Group**, Papua New Guinea
78 M 9 **St-Maxient-l'École**, France
79 W 14 **Ste-Maxime**, France
89 R 7 **St Michael**, Austria
89 U 6 **St Michael**, Austria
88 J 9 **St Moritz**, Switzerland
78 K 7 **St-Nazaire**, France
83 F 17 **St-Niklaas**, Belgium
88 E 10 **St Niklaus**, Switzerland
89 S 6 **St Nikolai**, Austria
79 Q 1 **St-Omer**, France
78 L 14 **St-Palais**, France
58 A 14 **St Paul**, Réunion
118 L 10 **St Paul**, Minnesota, U.S.A.
62 H 13 **Saint Paul Fracture Zone**, Atlantic Ocean
59 O 10 **St Paul Island**, France
112 D 7 **St Paul Island**, Alaska, U.S.A.
61 Y 15 **St Paul's Point**, Pitcairn Island
86 F 8 **St Peter-Ording**, Germany
77 J 25 **St Peter Port**, United Kingdom
115 W 12 **St Peter's**, Nova Scotia, Canada
123 Q 12 **St Petersburg**, Florida, U.S.A.
156 F 6 **St Petersburg**, Russian Federation
58 A 15 **St-Pierre**, Réunion
115 Y 11 **St-Pierre**, France, Canada
115 X 11 **St Pierre and Miquelon**, France
78 L 9 **St-Pierre-d'Oléron**, France
78 I 4 **St-Pol-de-Léon**, France
89 W 4 **St Pölten**, Austria
79 Q 14 **St-Pons-de-Thomières**, France
79 R 9 **St-Pourçain-sur-Sioule**, France

Country · Internal administrative region: State/Province/Territory/Dependent territory · Capital city · Mountain range/Undersea ridge · Mountain peak/Volcano/Seamount · Geographic feature · Headland/Point/Cape/Peninsula · Desert · Island/Island group · Antarctic base · Ocean · Sea · Bay/Gulf/Channel/Strait · Lake · Salt pan/Dry/Intermittent lake · River

79 R 2 **St-Quentin**, France
79 W 14 **St-Raphaël**, France
58 B 15 **Ste-Rose**, Réunion
115 S 12 **St Siméon**, Québec, Canada
123 T 5 **St Stephen**, South Carolina, U.S.A.
79 W 14 **St-Tropez**, France
83 I 19 **St-Truiden**, Belgium
79 O 2 **St-Valery-en-Caux**, France
89 T 8 **St Veit an der Glan**, Austria
127 Y 11 **St Vincent and The Grenadines**, North America
123 N 9 **St Vincent Island**, Florida, U.S.A.
127 X 10 **St Vincent Passage**, St Lucia
113 W 11 **St Walburg**, Saskatchewan, Canada
127 X 9
127 X 8
78 M 10 **Saintes**, France
214 A 8 **Saipan**, Northern Mariana Islands
214 A 8 **Saipan**, Northern Mariana Islands
172 B 11 **Saitlai**, Myanmar
177 C 23 **Saito**, Japan
141 H 20 **Sajama**, Bolivia
188 J 6 **Saka**, Morocco
177 G 18 **Sakai**, Japan
177 F 19 **Sakaide**, Japan
177 E 18 **Sakaiminato**, Japan
162 M 2 **Sakākah**, Saudi Arabia
197 W 9 **Sakaraha**, Madgascar
192 K 12 **Sakassou**, Côte d'Ivoire
176 J 12 **Sakata**, Japan
157 X 13 **Sakhalin**, Russian Federation
159 W 7 **Şäki**, Azerbaijan
193 O 12 **Saki**, Nigeria
99 D 15 **Šakiai**, Lithuania
177 M 26 **Sakishima-shotō**, Japan
173 K 16 **Sakon Nakhon**, Thailand
165 U 14 **Sakrand**, Pakistan
196 K 13 **Sakrivier**, Republic of South Africa
177 J 15 **Saku**, Japan
177 L 16 **Sakura**, Japan
101 T 12 **Saky**, Ukraine
63 B 16 **Sal**, Cape Verde
85 H 20 **Sala**, Sweden
61 W 10 **Sala y Gómez**, Chile
98 F 9 **Salacgrīva**, Latvia
144 M 8 **Saladas**, Argentina
144 L 13 **Saladillo**, Argentina
144 L 9 **Salado**, Argentina
125 P 5 **Salado**, Mexico
192 I 11 **Saladou**, Guinea
192 M 12 **Salaga**, Ghana
161 T 2 **Salahuddin**, Iraq
215 U 15 **Sala'ilua**, Samoa
193 W 8 **Salal**, Chad
190 H 13 **Salāla**, Sudan
163 W 11 **Şalālah**, Oman
126 D 9 **Salamá**, Guatemala
80 L 5 **Salamanca**, Spain
144 F 11 **Salamanca**, Chile
193 Y 10 **Salamat**, Chad
160 I 4 **Salamīyah**, Syria
215 V 15 **Salani**, Samoa
98 C 12 **Salantai**, Lithuania
144 H 6 **Salar de Arizaro**, Argentina
144 H 4 **Salar de Ascotán**, Chile
144 G 5 **Salar de Atacama**, Chile
141 I 21 **Salar de Coipasa**, Bolivia
141 I 22 **Salar de Uyuni**, Bolivia
81 O 3 **Salas de los Infantes**, Spain
174 J 14 **Salatiga**, Indonesia
175 T 11 **Salawati**, Indonesia
169 A 15 **Salaya**, India
175 O 13 **Salayar**, Indonesia
196 J 15 **Saldanha**, Republic of South Africa
98 D 11 **Saldus**, Latvia
209 T 13 **Sale**, Victoria, Australia
156 L 8 **Salekhard**, Russian Federation
215 U 15 **Salelologa**, Samoa
117 M 15 **Salem**, Utah, U.S.A.
120 H 12 **Salem**, Illinois, U.S.A.
121 X 8 **Salem**, Massachusetts, U.S.A.
169 E 22 **Salem**, India
91 H 22 **Salemi**, Italy
91 O 16 **Salentina Peninsula**, Italy
91 K 16 **Salerno**, Italy
93 J 21 **Salgótarján**, Hungary
142 N 13 **Salgueiro**, Brazil
188 L 11 **Sali**, Algeria
175 R 9 **Salibabu**, Indonesia
119 E 15 **Salida**, Colorado, U.S.A.
99 J 20 **Salihorsk**, Belarus
197 R 4 **Salima**, Malawi
117 M 17 **Salina**, Utah, U.S.A.
119 J 14 **Salina**, Kansas, U.S.A.
125 U 14 **Salina Cruz**, Mexico
145 I 16 **Salina Gualicho**, Argentina
117 D 19 **Salinas**, California, U.S.A.
125 P 9 **Salinas**, Mexico
140 A 10 **Salinas**, Ecuador
144 I 5 **Salinas Grandes**, Argentina
142 K 9 **Salinópolis**, Brazil
77 K 22 **Salisbury**, United Kingdom
121 T 13 **Salisbury**, Maryland, U.S.A.
123 S 2 **Salisbury**, North Carolina, U.S.A.
115 P 3 **Salisbury Island**, Nunavut, Canada
77 I 22 **Salisbury Plain**, United Kingdom
100 I 11 **Sălişte**, Romania
160 I 8 **Şalkhad**, Syria
81 W 4 **Sallent**, Spain
119 L 17 **Sallisaw**, Oklahoma, U.S.A.
115 Q 4 **Salluit**, Québec, Canada
161 U 7 **Salmān Pāk**, Iraq
164 E 3 **Salmās**, Iran
98 D 8 **Salme**, Estonia
116 J 10 **Salmon**, Idaho, U.S.A.
113 T 13 **Salmon Arm**, British Columbia, Canada
61 P 5 **Salmon Bank**, Pacific Ocean
116 J 10 **Salmon River Mountains**, Idaho, U.S.A.
85 L 19 **Salo**, Finland
90 E 6 **Salò**, Italy
79 U 14 **Salon-de-Provence**, France
100 F 9 **Salonta**, Romania
144 I 10 **Salsacate**, Argentina
156 E 10 **Sal'sk**, Russian Federation
117 N 23 **Salt**, Arizona, U.S.A.
119 F 20 **Salt Flat**, Texas, U.S.A.
117 M 15 **Salt Lake City**, Utah, U.S.A.
165 W 8 **Salt Range**, Pakistan
144 I 6 **Salta**, Argentina
144 I 6 **Salta**, Argentina
125 P 7 **Saltillo**, Mexico
144 N 10 **Salto**, Uruguay
144 L 12 **Salto**, Argentina
144 M 10 **Salto**, Uruguay
143 H 19 **Salto del Guairá**, Paraguay
117 J 23 **Salton Sea**, California, U.S.A.
85 J 19 **Saltvik**, Finland
123 Q 4 **Saluda**, South Carolina, U.S.A.
160 M 2 **Salūq**, Syria
143 N 15 **Salvador**, Brazil
144 J 4 **Salvador Mazza**, Argentina
163 T 6 **Salwah**, Saudi Arabia
172 F 13 **Salween**, Myanmar
117 C 14 **Salyer**, California, U.S.A.
89 Q 7 **Salzburg**, Austria
89 Q 5 **Salzburg**, Austria
87 H 14 **Salzgitter**, Germany
89 Q 5 **Salzkammergut**, Austria
86 I 12 **Salzwedel**, Germany
173 G 16 **Sam Ngao**, Thailand
172 M 13 **Sâm Son**, Vietnam
141 K 21 **Samaipata**, Bolivia
190 E 9 **Samâlût**, Egypt
127 R 7 **Samaná**, Dominican Republic
165 T 6 **Samangān**, Afghanistan
175 Q 4 **Samar**, Philippines
156 G 10 **Samara**, Russian Federation
212 G 7 **Samarai**, Papua New Guinea
174 M 11 **Samarinda**, Indonesia
167 Q 13 **Samarkand**, Uzbekistan
167 P 12 **Samarqand Wiloyati**, Uzbekistan
161 S 6 **Sāmarrā'**, Iraq
167 Y 5 **Samarskoye**, Kazakhstan
159 Y 8 **Şamaxi**, Azerbaijan
195 O 10 **Samba**, Democratic Republic of Congo
196 H 2 **Samba Cajú**, Angola
169 I 16 **Sambalpur**, India
174 I 10 **Sambas**, Indonesia
197 Z 5 **Sambava**, Madgascar
100 H 5 **Sambir**, Ukraine
83 E 22 **Sambre**, Belgium
197 O 3 **Samfya**, Zambia
171 Y 5 **Samjiyŏn**, North Korea
159 V 8 **Şämkir**, Azerbaijan
189 T 11 **Samnū**, Libya
215 W 15 **Samoa**, Oceania
61 Q 9 **Samoa Basin**, Pacific Ocean
214 J 8 **Samoan Islands**, Oceania
94 D 8 **Samobor**, Croatia
96 G 10 **Samokov**, Bulgaria
93 G 21 **Šamorín**, Slovakia
97 L 20 **Samos**, Greece
97 M 20 **Samos**, Greece
97 I 14 **Samotharaki**, Greece
174 K 12 **Sampit**, Indonesia
212 H 4 **Sampun**, Papua New Guinea
195 P 13 **Sampwe**, Democratic Republic of Congo
85 D 25 **Samsø**, Denmark
173 H 19 **Samut Prakan**, Thailand
173 H 19 **Samut Sakhon**, Thailand
173 H 19 **Samut Songkhram**, Thailand
93 N 19 **San**, Poland
192 K 9 **San**, Mali
144 H 10 **San Agustín de Valle Fértil**, Argentina
117 E 18 **San Andreas**, California, U.S.A.
141 K 18 **San Andrés**, Bolivia
125 U 12 **San Andrés Tuxtla**, Mexico
119 I 20 **San Angelo**, Texas, U.S.A.
119 J 22 **San Antonio**, Texas, U.S.A.
126 E 8 **San Antonio**, Belize
139 N 8 **San Antonio**, Venezuela
139 Q 3 **San Antonio**, Venezuela
144 H 11 **San Antonio**, Argentina
144 I 9 **San Antonio**, Argentina
144 F 12 **San Antonio**, Chile
81 W 9 **San Antonio Abad**, Spain
144 I 6 **San Antonio de los Cobres**, Argentina
145 J 16 **San Antonio Oeste**, Argentina
90 J 12 **San Benedetto del Tronto**, Italy
88 H 9 **San Bernadino**, Switzerland
117 H 22 **San Bernardino**, California, U.S.A.
117 H 22 **San Bernardino Mountains**, California, U.S.A.
144 G 12 **San Bernardo**, Chile
124 K 7 **San Blas**, Mexico
141 J 18 **San Borja**, Bolivia
144 K 6 **San Camilo**, Argentina
124 H 7 **San Carlos**, Mexico
126 G 12 **San Carlos**, Nicaragua
139 O 9 **San Carlos**, Venezuela
141 L 20 **San Carlos**, Bolivia
144 N 13 **San Carlos**, Uruguay
145 F 14 **San Carlos**, Chile
175 N 3 **San Carlos**, Philippines
145 G 17 **San Carlos de Bariloche**, Argentina
144 K 13 **San Carlos de Bolívar**, Argentina
91 O 16 **San Cataldo**, Italy
117 H 23 **San Clemente**, California, U.S.A.
144 F 13 **San Clemente**, Chile
117 G 24 **San Clemente Island**, California, U.S.A.
213 N 7 **San Cristobal**, Solomon Islands
138 J 11 **San Cristóbal**, Colombia
138 K 4 **San Cristóbal**, Venezuela
144 K 9 **San Cristóbal**, Argentina
62 M 11 **San Cristóbal de la Laguna**, Canary Islands
125 W 13 **San Cristóbal de las Casas**, Mexico
117 H 24 **San Diego**, California, U.S.A.
90 H 7 **San Donà di Piave**, Italy
124 G 3 **San Felipe**, Mexico
125 P 10 **San Felipe**, Mexico
138 M 2 **San Felipe**, Venezuela
144 G 11 **San Felipe**, Chile
80 K 13 **San Fernando**, Spain
117 G 22 **San Fernando**, California, U.S.A.
124 G 4 **San Fernando**, Mexico
125 S 8 **San Fernando**, Mexico
127 X 12 **San Fernando**, Trinidad and Tobago
144 M 12 **San Fernando**, Argentina
144 G 12 **San Fernando**, Chile
175 O 3 **San Fernando**, Philippines
175 O 2 **San Fernando**, Philippines
139 N 4 **San Fernando de Apure**, Venezuela
139 N 7 **San Fernando de Atabapo**, Venezuela
117 D 18 **San Francisco**, California, U.S.A.
144 K 10 **San Francisco**, Argentina
117 D 18 **San Francisco Bay**, California, U.S.A.
144 J 9 **San Francisco del Chañar**, Argentina
81 W 10 **San Francisco Javier**, Spain
140 C 8 **San Gabriel**, Ecuador
127 T 7 **San Germán**, Puerto Rico
90 E 11 **San Gimignano**, Italy
91 N 19 **San Giovanni in Fiore**, Italy
124 H 6 **San Ignacio**, Mexico
126 E 8 **San Ignacio**, Belize
140 B 12 **San Ignacio**, Peru
141 J 18 **San Ignacio**, Bolivia
141 M 19 **San Ignacio**, Bolivia
141 K 18 **San Javier**, Bolivia
144 L 10 **San Javier**, Argentina
117 E 18 **San Joaquin**, California, U.S.A.
117 E 19 **San Joaquin Valley**, California, U.S.A.
117 D 19 **San Jose**, California, U.S.A.
175 O 3 **San Jose**, Philippines
175 O 4 **San Jose**, Philippines
214 A 8 **San Jose**, Northern Mariana Islands
126 H 13 **San José**, Costa Rica
144 N 12 **San José**, Uruguay
126 C 10 **San José**, Guatemala
144 M 12 **San José**, Uruguay
141 N 20 **San José de Chiquitos**, Bolivia
144 M 10 **San José de Feliciano**, Argentina
124 J 4 **San José de Gracia**, Mexico
144 H 10 **San José de Jáchal**, Argentina
144 J 10 **San José de la Dormida**, Argentina
141 D 16 **San José de Quero**, Peru
125 Q 8 **San José de Raíces**, Mexico
124 J 9 **San José del Cabo**, Mexico
138 J 8 **San José del Guaviare**, Colombia
127 T 7 **San Juan**, Puerto Rico
144 G 10 **San Juan**, Argentina
126 H 12 **San Juan**, Nicaragua
125 T 13 **San Juan**, Mexico
127 Q 7 **San Juan**, Dominican Republic
144 H 10 **San Juan**, Argentina
61 Z 1 **San Juan Bautista**, Juan Fernández Islands
143 G 20 **San Juan Bautista**, Paraguay
139 N 3 **San Juan de los Morros**, Venezuela
145 J 25 **San Juan de Salvamento**, Argentina
126 H 12 **San Juan del Norte**, Nicaragua
125 Q 11 **San Juan del Río**, Mexico
126 G 12 **San Juan del Sur**, Nicaragua
119 E 15 **San Juan Mountains**, Colorado, U.S.A.
124 H 6 **San Juanico**, Mexico
144 L 10 **San Justo**, Argentina
140 B 7 **San Lorenzo**, Ecuador
141 J 18 **San Lorenzo**, Bolivia
141 H 16 **San Lorenzo**, Peru
144 K 11 **San Lorenzo**, Argentina
124 H 6 **San Lucas**, Mexico
124 J 9 **San Lucas**, Mexico
141 K 22 **San Lucas**, Bolivia
144 I 12 **San Luis**, Argentina
144 I 11 **San Luis**, Argentina
125 Q 10 **San Luis de la Paz**, Mexico
117 E 21 **San Luis Obispo**, California, U.S.A.
125 P 9 **San Luis Potosí**, Mexico
125 P 10 **San Luis Potosí**, Mexico
124 G 1 **San Luis Río Colorado**, Mexico
124 H 3 **San Luisito**, Mexico
119 J 21 **San Marcos**, Texas, U.S.A.
125 R 14 **San Marcos**, Mexico
90 H 10 **San Marino**, Europe
218 I 5 **San Martin**, Antarctica
140 C 13 **San Martín**, Peru
141 L 18 **San Martín**, Bolivia
144 H 11 **San Martín**, Argentina
144 I 9 **San Martín**, Argentina
145 G 16 **San Martín de Los Andes**, Argentina
81 N 6 **San Martín de Valdeiglesias**, Spain
117 D 18 **San Mateo**, California, U.S.A.
141 O 19 **San Matías**, Bolivia
141 L 18 **San Miguel**, Bolivia
126 E 10 **San Miguel**, El Salvador
126 K 14 **San Miguel**, Panama
141 M 20 **San Miguel**, Bolivia
141 J 19 **San Miguel de Huachi**, Bolivia
144 J 7 **San Miguel de Tucumán**, Argentina
144 M 13 **San Miguel del Monte**, Argentina
117 E 22 **San Miguel Island**, California, U.S.A.
126 K 13 **San Miguelito**, Panama
144 L 12 **San Nicolás de los Arroyos**, Argentina
117 F 23 **San Nicolas Island**, California, U.S.A.
91 C 18 **San Nicolò Gerrei**, Italy
141 L 19 **San Pablo**, Bolivia
175 O 4 **San Pablo**, Philippines
124 J 8 **San Pedro**, Mexico
126 E 7 **San Pedro**, Belize
144 I 6 **San Pedro**, Argentina
144 L 12 **San Pedro**, Argentina
192 J 14 **San-Pédro**, Côte d'Ivoire
125 O 7 **San Pedro de las Colonias**, Mexico
127 R 7 **San Pedro de Macoris**, Dominican Republic
81 S 11 **San Pedro del Pinatar**, Spain
126 E 9 **San Pedro Sula**, Honduras
124 F 3 **San Quintín**, Mexico
144 H 12 **San Rafael**, Argentina
141 K 17 **San Ramón**, Bolivia
141 M 20 **San Ramón**, Bolivia
90 A 10 **San Remo**, Italy
126 D 10 **San Salvador**, El Salvador
127 O 3 **San Salvador**, The Bahamas
144 M 10 **San Salvador**, Argentina
144 I 5 **San Salvador de Jujuy**, Argentina
145 H 25 **San Sebastián**, Argentina
62 L 12 **San Sebastián de la Gomera**, Canary Islands
91 L 14 **San Severo**, Italy
117 E 21 **San Simeon**, California, U.S.A.
124 F 2 **San Vicente**, Mexico
126 E 10 **San Vicente**, El Salvador
141 D 17 **San Vicente de Cañete**, Peru
138 I 8 **San Vicente del Caguán**, Colombia
163 P 13 **Şan'ā'**, Yemen
191 N 19 **Sanaag**, Somalia
219 P 1 **Sanae**, Antarctica
164 F 5 **Sanandaj**, Iran
163 U 11 **Sanaw**, Yemen
170 H 5 **Sanchakou**, China
168 B 13 **Sanchor**, India
79 Q 8 **Sancoins**, France
126 K 5 **Sancti Spíritus**, Cuba
169 B 22 **Sand Cay**, India
177 G 18 **Sanda**, Japan
174 I 11 **Sandai**, Indonesia
174 M 8 **Sandakan**, Malaysia
173 M 20 **Sândân**, Cambodia
96 G 12 **Sandanski**, Bulgaria
192 H 8 **Sandaré**, Mali
212 A 4 **Sandaun**, Papua New Guinea
76 I 6 **Sanday**, United Kingdom
117 O 21 **Sanders**, Arizona, U.S.A.
119 G 21 **Sanderson**, Texas, U.S.A.
208 H 5 **Sandfire Roadhouse**, Western Australia, Australia
89 U 3 **Sandl**, Austria
85 A 20 **Sandnes**, Norway
194 M 13 **Sandoa**, Democratic Republic of Congo
93 M 16 **Sandomierz**, Poland
84 K 12 **Sandön**, Sweden
173 C 14 **Sandoway**, Myanmar
116 I 6 **Sandpoint**, Idaho, U.S.A.
118 L 9 **Sandstone**, Minnesota, U.S.A.
208 H 9 **Sandstone**, Western Australia, Australia
121 N 7 **Sandusky**, Michigan, U.S.A.
121 N 10 **Sandusky**, Ohio, U.S.A.
85 E 15 **Sandvika**, Norway
196 H 10 **Sandwich Bay**, Namibia
63 N 26 **Sandy Bay**, St Helena
209 W 7 **Sandy Cape**, Queensland, Australia
114 K 9 **Sandy Lake**, Ontario, Canada
114 K 9 **Sandy Lake**, Ontario, Canada
167 N 15 **Sandykachi**, Turkmenistan
121 X 7 **Sanford**, Maine, U.S.A.
123 R 10 **Sanford**, Florida, U.S.A.
123 T 2 **Sanford**, North Carolina, U.S.A.
169 C 17 **Sangamner**, India
165 O 7 **Sangan**, Iran
157 T 10 **Sangar**, Russian Federation
79 P 1 **Sangatte**, France
175 N 15 **Sangeang**, Indonesia
87 J 16 **Sangerhausen**, Germany
174 J 10 **Sanggau**, Indonesia
194 H 7 **Sangha**, Congo
193 N 10 **Sangha**, Burkina Faso
194 H 5 **Sangha-Mbaéré**, Central African Republic
165 U 14 **Sanghar**, Pakistan
97 E 23 **Sangiás**, Greece
175 Q 9 **Sangir**, Indonesia
171 Y 7 **Sangju**, South Korea
169 C 18 **Sangli**, India
193 U 15 **Sangmélima**, Cameroon
197 P 9 **Sango**, Zimbabwe
119 E 15 **Sangre de Cristo Range**, Colorado, U.S.A.
127 X 12 **Sangre Grande**, Trinidad and Tobago
168 E 10 **Sangrur**, India
143 G 14 **Sangue**, Brazil
81 S 3 **Sangüesa**, Spain
78 L 12 **Sanguinet**, France
123 Q 13 **Sanibel Island**, Florida, U.S.A.
115 P 7 **Sanikiluaq**, Ontario, Canada
161 R 6 **Saniyah**, Iraq
164 G 4 **Sanjbod**, Iran
176 J 13 **Sanjō**, Japan
80 K 13 **Sanlúcar de Barrameda**, Spain
91 C 18 **Sanluri**, Italy
171 S 9 **Sanmenxia**, China
171 V 12 **Sanming**, China
92 J 12 **Sanniki**, Poland
93 N 18 **Sanok**, Poland
90 G 11 **Sansepolcro**, Italy
94 F 10 **Sanski Most**, Bosnia and Herzegovina
171 S 12 **Sansui**, China
81 U 6 **Sant Carles de la Ràpita**, Spain
81 Y 4 **Sant Feliu de Guíxols**, Spain
116 I 7 **Santa**, Idaho, U.S.A.
141 B 14 **Santa**, Peru
117 H 23 **Santa Ana**, California, U.S.A.
124 I 3 **Santa Ana**, Mexico
126 D 10 **Santa Ana**, El Salvador
141 K 17 **Santa Ana de Yacuma**, Bolivia
117 F 22 **Santa Barbara**, California, U.S.A.
138 L 4 **Santa Barbara**, Venezuela
117 F 23 **Santa Barbara Island**, California, U.S.A.
144 G 6 **Santa Catalina**, Chile
117 G 23 **Santa Catalina Island**, California, U.S.A.
143 I 20 **Santa Catarina**, Brazil
124 F 4 **Santa Catarina**, Mexico
117 D 19 **Santa Clara**, California, U.S.A.
126 K 4 **Santa Clara**, Cuba
138 L 12 **Santa Clara**, Colombia
140 E 10 **Santa Clotilde**, Peru
145 H 22 **Santa Cruz**, Argentina
141 L 21 **Santa Cruz**, Bolivia
145 G 23 **Santa Cruz**, Argentina
117 D 19 **Santa Cruz**, California, U.S.A.
141 L 20 **Santa Cruz**, Bolivia
175 O 4 **Santa Cruz**, Philippines
62 L 11 **Santa Cruz de la Palma**, Canary Islands
81 O 10 **Santa Cruz de Mudela**, Spain
62 M 11 **Santa Cruz de Tenerife**, Canary Islands

Country · Internal administrative region: State/Province/Territory/Dependent territory · Capital city · Mountain range/Undersea ridge · Mountain peak/Volcano/Seamount · Geographic feature · Headland/Point/Cape/Peninsula · Desert · Island/Island group · Antarctic base · Ocean · Sea · Bay/Gulf/Channel/Strait · Lake · Salt pan/Dry/Intermittent lake · River

O 7 Santa Cruz del al Zarza, Spain
N 7 Santa Cruz del Retamar, Spain
26 L 5 Santa Cruz del Sur, Cuba
43 I 22 Santa Cruz do Sul, Brazil
17 F 22 Santa Cruz Island, California, U.S.A.
13 P 7 Santa Cruz Islands, Solomon Islands
39 S 6 Santa Elena de Uairén, Venezuela
19 F 17 Santa Fe, New Mexico, U.S.A.
44 K 8 Santa Fé, Argentina
26 I 5 Santa Fé, Cuba
44 L 10 Santa Fé, Argentina
24 I 9 Santa Genoveva, Mexico
42 L 11 Santa Inês, Brazil
12 L 6 Santa Isabel, Solomon Islands
43 F 15 Santa Isabel, Brazil
44 H 13 Santa Isabel, Argentina
42 D 9 Santa Isabel do Rio Negro, Brazil
44 M 9 Santa Lucia, Argentina
17 D 19 Santa Lucia Range, California, U.S.A.
63 A 15 Santa Luzia, Cape Verde
42 K 11 Santa Luzia, Brazil
62 O 2 Santa Maria, Azores
63 B 16 Santa Maria, Cape Verde
117 E 21 Santa Maria, California, U.S.A.
142 G 10 Santa Maria, Brazil
143 H 22 Santa Maria, Brazil
125 X 12 Santa María, Mexico
144 I 7 Santa María, Argentina
142 J 13 Santa Maria das Barreiras, Brazil
142 E 9 Santa Maria do Boiaçu, Brazil
138 I 2 Santa Marta, Colombia
117 G 22 Santa Monica, California, U.S.A.
80 K 11 Santa Ollala del Cala, Spain
117 D 17 Santa Rosa, California, U.S.A.
119 F 17 Santa Rosa, New Mexico, U.S.A.
125 Y 11 Santa Rosa, Mexico
141 J 18 Santa Rosa, Bolivia
141 G 18 Santa Rosa, Peru
144 H 12 Santa Rosa, Argentina
145 I 16 Santa Rosa, Argentina
145 J 14 Santa Rosa, Argentina
126 E 9 Santa Rosa de Copán, Honduras
141 M 19 Santa Rosa de la Roca, Bolivia
142 B 13 Santa Rosa do Purus, Brazil
117 F 23 Santa Rosa Island, California, U.S.A.
124 H 6 Santa Rosalía, Mexico
144 L 8 Santa Sylvina, Argentina
143 H 23 Santa Vitória do Palmar, Brazil
170 J 4 Santai, China
143 L 15 Santana, Brazil
142 I 13 Santana do Araguaia, Brazil
138 J 5 Santander, Colombia
81 O 1 Santander, Spain
91 B 19 Sant'Antioco, Italy
81 Y 8 Santanyi, Spain
80 H 8 Santarém, Portugal
80 G 8 Santarém, Portugal
142 H 10 Santarém, Brazil
126 K 2 Santaren Channel, The Bahamas
123 T 5 Santee, South Carolina, U.S.A.
144 F 12 Santiago, Chile
144 F 12 Santiago, Chile
124 J 9 Santiago, Mexico
126 J 14 Santiago, Panama
127 Q 6 Santiago, Dominican Republic
143 H 21 Santiago, Brazil
175 O 2 Santiago, Philippines
125 U 14 Santiago Astata, Mexico
127 N 6 Santiago de Cuba, Cuba
80 H 1 Santiago del Compostela, Spain
144 J 7 Santiago del Estero, Argentina
144 J 8 Santiago del Estero, Argentina
80 G 11 Santiago do Cacém, Portugal
119 G 21 Santiago Peak, Texas, U.S.A.
175 O 10 Santigi, Indonesia
88 I 7 Säntis, Switzerland
81 P 10 Santisteban del Puerto, Spain
143 M 18 Santo Amaro de Campos, Brazil
63 A 15 Santo Antão, Cape Verde
141 N 20 Santo Corazón, Bolivia
127 R 7 Santo Domingo, Dominican Republic
124 H 7 Santo Domingo, Mexico
126 G 11 Santo Domingo, Nicaragua
141 H 17 Santo Domingo, Peru
80 H 4 Santo Tirso, Portugal
124 F 2 Santo Tomás, Mexico
141 G 18 Santo Tomás, Peru
144 N 9 Santo Tomé, Argentina
143 K 19 Santos, Brazil
63 H 17 Santos Plateau, Atlantic Ocean
171 S 15 Sanya, China
196 H 1 Sanza Pombo, Angola
143 H 21 São Borja, Brazil
143 J 18 São Carlos, Brazil
143 I 14 São Félix do Araguaia, Brazil
142 I 12 São Félix do Xingu, Brazil
63 A 17 São Filipe, Cape Verde
143 L 15 São Francisco, Brazil
143 H 22 São Gabriel, Brazil
142 C 9 São Gabriel da Cachoeira, Brazil
143 L 19 São Gonçalo, Brazil
142 C 9 São João, Brazil
143 J 15 São João d'Aliança, Brazil
142 J 12 São João do Araguaia, Brazil
142 M 13 São João do Piauí, Brazil
62 N 1 São Jorge, Azores
143 J 21 São José, Brazil
143 I 22 São José do Norte, Brazil
143 J 18 São José do Rio Preto, Brazil
142 L 10 São Luís, Brazil
143 H 21 São Luís Gonzaga, Brazil
143 G 15 São Manuel, Brazil
143 M 17 São Mateus, Brazil
62 O 2 São Miguel, Azores
143 I 15 São Miguel do Araguaia, Brazil
143 H 20 São Miguel d'Oeste, Brazil
63 A 16 São Nicolau, Cape Verde
143 J 18 São Paulo, Brazil
143 K 19 São Paulo, Brazil
62 I 13 São Pedro e São Paulo, Atlantic Ocean
143 K 16 São Romão, Brazil
143 K 18 São Sebastião do Paraíso, Brazil
143 I 17 São Simão, Brazil
63 B 17 São Tiago, Cape Verde
194 B 7 São Tomé, São Tomé and Príncipe
194 B 8 São Tomé, São Tomé and Príncipe
194 B 7 São Tomé and Príncipe, Africa
63 A 15 São Vicente, Cape Verde
62 N 5 São Vicente, Madeira
143 K 19 São Vicente, Brazil
79 U 7 Saône, France
158 F 8 Sapanca, Turkey
193 Q 13 Sapele, Nigeria
97 J 13 Sapes, Greece
176 J 6 Sapporo, Japan
91 L 17 Sapri, Italy
174 K 14 Sapudi, Indonesia
119 K 17 Sapulpa, Oklahoma, U.S.A.
174 M 8 Sapulut, Malaysia
164 F 5 Saqqez, Iran
164 F 5 Sar Dasht, Iran
165 S 6 Sar-e Pol, Afghanistan
165 S 6 Sar-e Pol, Afghanistan
161 T 1 Sar i Kōrāwa, Iraq
165 S 6 Sar-i-Pul, Afghanistan
95 L 17 Šar Planina, Serbia and Montenegro
96 B 11 Šar Planina, Macedonia (F.Y.R.O.M.)
173 H 18 Sara Buri, Thailand
164 G 4 Sarāb, Iran
161 U 7 Sarābādī, Iraq
140 B 11 Saraguro, Ecuador
169 H 16 Saraipali, India
94 H 12 Sarajevo, Bosnia and Herzegovina
166 M 15 Sarakhs, Turkmenistan
172 D 8 Saramati, Myanmar
140 C 11 Sarameriza, Peru
167 T 5 Saran', Kazakhstan
95 K 22 Sarandë, Albania
143 I 21 Sarandi, Brazil
175 Q 8 Sarangani Islands, Philippines
169 H 16 Sarangarh, India
169 E 14 Sarangpur, India
156 G 9 Saransk, Russian Federation
156 I 10 Sarapul, Russian Federation
160 I 3 Sarāqib, Syria
123 Q 12 Sarasota, Florida, U.S.A.
101 O 10 Sarata, Ukraine
174 J 10 Saratok, Malaysia
156 F 10 Saratov, Russian Federation
165 P 13 Saravan, Iran
173 M 17 Saravan, Laos
174 J 9 Sarawak, Malaysia
158 C 7 Saray, Turkey
160 H 3 Şarāyā, Syria
192 G 9 Saraya, Senegal
158 D 11 Sarayköy, Turkey
158 H 11 Sarayönü, Turkey
165 P 13 Sarbāz, Iran
165 O 9 Sarbīsheh, Iran
93 I 24 Sárbogárd, Hungary
144 F 9 Sarco, Chile
168 D 11 Sardarshahr, India
91 C 17 Sardegna, Italy
91 C 17 Sardinia, Italy
122 I 3 Sardis Lake, Mississippi, U.S.A.
88 I 7 Sargans, Switzerland
62 E 10 Sargasso Sea, Atlantic Ocean
165 X 9 Sargodha, Pakistan
193 X 11 Sarh, Chad
164 K 5 Sārī, Iran
97 M 25 Saria, Greece
214 A 7 Sarigan, Northern Mariana Islands
159 R 9 Sarikamiş, Turkey
174 J 9 Sarikei, Malaysia
209 U 6 Sarina, Queensland, Australia
81 T 4 Sariñena, Spain
189 V 13 Sarir Tibesti, Libya
171 X 6 Sariwŏn, North Korea
158 D 7 Sariyer, Turkey
158 L 11 Sariz, Turkey
77 J 25 Sark, United Kingdom
167 X 8 Sarkand, Kazakhstan
158 F 11 Şarkikaraagaç, Turkey
85 O 17 Särkisalmi, Finland
158 L 10 Şarkişla, Turkey
97 M 14 Şarköy, Turkey
175 X 11 Sarmi, Indonesia
85 E 17 Särna, Sweden
88 F 8 Sarnen, Switzerland
115 N 15 Sarnia, Ontario, Canada
100 L 2 Sarny, Ukraine
176 L 3 Saroma-ko, Japan
97 G 20 Saronic Gulf, Greece
158 A 8 Saros Körfezi, Turkey
93 M 21 Sárospatak, Hungary
165 V 7 Sarowbī, Afghanistan
79 W 4 Sarrebourg, France
79 W 4 Sarreguemines, France
165 V 13 Sartanahu, Pakistan
79 Y 15 Sartène, France
97 H 15 Sarti, Greece
176 K 6 Saru, Japan
159 U 9 Sārur, Azerbaijan
93 G 23 Sárvár, Hungary
164 I 11 Sarvestān, Iran
167 U 12 Sary-Tash, Kyrgyzstan
166 I 8 Sarykamys, Kazakhstan
166 L 11 Sarykamyshkoye Ozero, Turkmenistan
167 W 9 Saryozek, Kazakhstan
167 T 8 Saryshagan, Kazakhstan
167 Q 8 Sarysu, Kazakhstan
167 W 5 Sarzhal, Kazakhstan
174 D 10 Sasak, Indonesia
212 K 5 Sasamungga, Solomon Islands
168 H 13 Sasaram, India
177 A 22 Sasebo, Japan
168 F 7 Saser Kangri, India
113 X 9 Saskatchewan, Canada
113 X 12 Saskatoon, Saskatchewan, Canada
157 R 8 Saskylakh, Russian Federation
197 O 11 Sasolburg, Republic of South Africa
192 I 14 Sass Town, Liberia
192 J 14 Sassandra, Côte d'Ivoire
91 C 16 Sassari, Italy
82 G 12 Sassenheim, Netherlands
86 M 8 Sassnitz, Germany
90 F 9 Sassuolo, Italy
177 C 24 Sata-misaki, Japan
169 C 18 Satara, India
141 E 16 Satipo, Peru
169 G 14 Satna, India
93 M 21 Sátoraljaújhely, Hungary
167 Q 7 Satpayev, Kazakhstan
169 D 15 Satpura Range, India
177 C 24 Satsuma-hantō, Japan
173 H 20 Sattahip, Thailand
168 F 7 Satti, India
100 H 7 Satu Mare, Romania
173 H 26 Satun, Thailand
174 L 14 Saubi, Indonesia
144 M 9 Sauce, Argentina
167 R 9 Saudakent, Kazakhstan
163 S 8 Saudi Arabia, Asia
87 G 24 Saulgau, Germany
79 S 7 Saulieu, France
98 F 10 Saulkrasti, Latvia
115 N 13 Sault Sainte Marie, Ontario, Canada
120 M 4 Sault Sainte Marie, Michigan, U.S.A.
175 U 14 Saumlakki, Indonesia
79 N 7 Saumur, France
219 N 11 Saunders Coast, Antarctica
196 J 2 Saurimo, Angola
139 T 8 Sauriwaunawa, Guyana
94 H 10 Sava, Europe
126 F 9 Savá, Honduras
215 U 14 Savai'i, Samoa
193 O 12 Savalou, Benin
126 L 7 Savanna-la-Mar, Jamaica
123 Q 5 Savannah, South Carolina, U.S.A.
122 K 2 Savannah, Tennessee, U.S.A.
123 R 6 Savannah, Georgia, U.S.A.
173 L 16 Savannakhét, Laos
114 K 11 Savant Lake, Ontario, Canada
158 C 9 Savaştepe, Turkey
164 I 6 Sāveh, Iran
192 M 11 Savelugu, Ghana
79 W 4 Saverne, France
99 M 22 Savichy, Belarus
90 A 8 Savigliano, Italy
95 I 14 Šavnik, Serbia and Montenegro
90 B 9 Savona, Italy
85 O 17 Savonlinna, Finland
112 F 4 Savoonga, Alaska, U.S.A.
159 R 7 Şavşat, Turkey
175 P 15 Savu, Indonesia
84 M 10 Savukoski, Finland
213 X 11 Savusavu, Fiji
172 F 7 Sawan, Myanmar
173 G 16 Sawankhalok, Thailand
177 L 15 Sawara, Japan
176 I 13 Sawasaki-bana, Japan
209 W 10 Sawtell, New South Wales, Australia
175 O 15 Sawu Sea, Indonesia
193 O 9 Say, Niger
166 I 9 Say-Utes, Kazakhstan
160 H 4 Şāyā, Syria
167 V 7 Sayak, Kazakhstan
141 C 16 Sayán, Peru
175 I 10 Sayang, Indonesia
167 O 13 Sayat, Turkmenistan
126 D 8 Sayaxché, Guatemala
163 U 13 Sayḥūt, Yemen
166 F 5 Saykhin, Kazakhstan
191 K 19 Sāylac, Somalia
171 N 3 Sayn-Ust, Mongolia
171 S 4 Saynshand, Mongolia
170 I 4 Sayram Hu, China
125 N 11 Sayula, Mexico
125 U 13 Sayula, Mexico
163 S 12 Say'ūn, Yemen
95 J 20 Sazan, Albania
165 X 6 Sazin, Pakistan
188 L 10 Sbaa, Algeria
112 G 5 Scammon Bay, Alaska, U.S.A.
90 F 12 Scansano, Italy
100 M 12 Scânteia, Romania
76 I 7 Scapa Flow, United Kingdom
77 L 16 Scarborough, United Kingdom
127 Y 12 Scarborough, Trinidad and Tobago
211 H 19 Scargill, New Zealand
76 E 9 Scarp, United Kingdom
83 F 19 Schaerbeek, Belgium
88 G 5 Schaffhausen, Switzerland
82 H 9 Schagen, Netherlands
89 R 3 Schärding, Austria
83 E 14 Scharendijke, Netherlands
86 E 9 Scharhörn, Germany
88 M 6 Scharnitz, Austria
82 N 6 Scheemda, Netherlands
115 T 8 Schefferville, Québec, Canada
89 V 4 Scheibbs, Austria
89 T 7 Scheifling, Austria
117 J 18 Schell Creek Range, Nevada, U.S.A.
121 U 8 Schenectady, New York, U.S.A.
82 F 12 Scheveningen, Netherlands
82 G 13 Schiedam, Netherlands
82 L 5 Schiermonnikoog, Netherlands
88 I 8 Schiers, Switzerland
83 G 17 Schilde, Belgium
90 F 6 Schio, Italy
100 M 9 Schitu Duca, Romania
87 K 16 Schkeuditz, Germany
89 S 6 Schladming, Austria
87 B 18 Schleiden, Germany
87 K 18 Schleiz, Germany
86 G 8 Schleswig, Germany
86 G 9 Schleswig-Holstein, Germany
89 S 4 Schlierbach, Austria
63 N 18 Schmidt-Ott Seamount, Atlantic Ocean
87 I 25 Schongau, Germany
83 D 16 Schoondijke, Netherlands
87 D 25 Schopfheim, Germany
83 G 17 Schoten, Belgium
212 C 3 Schouten Islands, Papua New Guinea
196 J 12 Schroffenstein, Namibia
88 J 7 Schruns, Austria
77 B 21 Schull, Republic of Ireland
117 G 17 Schurz, Nevada, U.S.A.
87 I 21 Schwabach, Germany
87 G 22 Schwäbisch, Germany
87 G 23 Schwäbisch Gmünd, Germany
87 G 17 Schwalmstadt, Germany
87 K 21 Schwandorf, Germany
89 N 7 Schwaz, Austria
86 N 11 Schwedt, Germany
87 H 19 Schweinfurt, Germany
86 J 10 Schwerin, Germany
86 J 10 Schweriner See, Germany
88 G 8 Schwyz, Switzerland
91 H 22 Sciacca, Italy
118 F 7 Scobey, Montana, U.S.A.
63 E 21 Scotia Ridge, Atlantic Ocean
63 G 21 Scotia Sea, Atlantic Ocean
76 G 12 Scotland, United Kingdom
123 V 1 Scotland Neck, North Carolina, U.S.A.
219 Q 12 Scott Base, Antarctica
219 Q 12 Scott Coast, Antarctica
113 W 8 Scott Lake, Saskatchewan, Canada
197 P 13 Scottburgh, Republic of South Africa
118 G 12 Scottsbluff, Nebraska, U.S.A.
122 M 3 Scottsboro, Alabama, U.S.A.
120 K 13 Scottsburg, Indiana, U.S.A.
117 M 23 Scottsdale, Arizona, U.S.A.
209 T 15 Scottsdale, Tasmania, Australia
117 H 19 Scotty's Junction, Nevada, U.S.A.
121 T 9 Scranton, Pennsylvania, U.S.A.
77 K 17 Scunthorpe, United Kingdom
88 K 8 Scuol, Switzerland
101 W 10 Sea of Azov, Russian Federation/Ukraine
97 H 24 Sea of Crete, Greece
60 L 3 Sea of Japan, Pacific Ocean
158 C 8 Sea of Marmara, Turkey
157 X 11 Sea of Okhotsk, Russian Federation
76 E 10 Sea of the Hebrides, United Kingdom
121 T 12 Seaford, Delaware, U.S.A.
63 O 16 Seal Bay, Tristan da Cunha
117 J 21 Searchlight, Nevada, U.S.A.
119 N 17 Searcy, Arkansas, U.S.A.
116 E 7 Seattle, Washington, U.S.A.
211 I 18 Seaward Kaikoura Range, New Zealand
121 X 6 Sebago Lake, Maine, U.S.A.
123 S 11 Sebastian, Florida, U.S.A.
193 N 9 Sebba, Burkina Faso
188 K 6 Sebdou, Algeria
192 I 9 Sébékoro, Mali
174 E 11 Seberida, Indonesia
100 H 10 Sebeş, Romania
159 N 9 Sebinkarahisar, Turkey
100 G 9 Sebiş, Romania
188 L 12 Sebkha Azzel Matti, Algeria
188 L 12 Sebkha Mekerrhane, Algeria
192 E 6 Sebkha Narhamcha, Mauritania
192 H 3 Sebkha Oumm ed Droûs Telli, Mauritania
192 G 5 Sebkhet Chemchâm, Mauritania
192 H 3 Sebkhet Oumm ed Droûs Guebli, Mauritania
192 J 4 Sebkhet Ti-n-Bessaïs, Mauritania
123 R 12 Sebring, Florida, U.S.A.
174 M 12 Sebuku, Indonesia
140 A 12 Sechura, Peru
211 A 23 Secretary Island, New Zealand
169 F 18 Secunderabad, India
98 C 12 Seda, Lithuania
119 M 14 Sedalia, Missouri, U.S.A.
169 E 18 Sedam, India
79 T 3 Sedan, France
81 O 2 Sedano, Spain
211 J 17 Seddon, New Zealand
160 F 11 Sede Boqer, Israel
165 N 8 Sedeh, Iran
160 E 10 Sederot, Israel
160 F 10 Sedom, Israel
88 M 7 Seefeld in Tirol, Austria
196 J 11 Seeheim, Namibia
86 N 13 Seelow, Germany
79 N 5 Sées, France
87 H 15 Seesen, Germany
89 V 6 Seewiesen, Austria
192 G 12 Sefadu, Sierra Leone
192 G 8 Ségala, Mali
174 F 9 Segamat, Malaysia
193 P 11 Ségbana, Benin
156 H 6 Segezha, Russian Federation
91 H 14 Segni, Italy
192 J 9 Ségou, Mali
192 J 9 Ségou, Mali
81 N 5 Segovia, Spain
138 I 5 Segovia, Colombia
78 M 6 Segré, France
112 B 8 Seguam Island, Alaska, U.S.A.
193 U 5 Séguédine, Niger
192 J 12 Séguéla, Côte d'Ivoire
119 J 22 Seguin, Texas, U.S.A.
196 L 8 Sehithwa, Botswana
169 E 14 Sehore, India
212 G 7 Sehulea, Papua New Guinea
165 T 13 Sehwan, Pakistan
88 C 7 Seignelégier, Switzerland
84 J 6 Seiland, Norway
119 I 16 Seiling, Oklahoma, U.S.A.
85 K 16 Seinäjoki, Finland
79 O 3 Seine, France
92 N 8 Sejny, Poland
174 F 12 Sekayu, Indonesia
177 I 17 Seki, Japan
174 D 9 Selangor, Malaysia
173 K 17 Selaphum, Thailand
175 T 15 Selaru, Indonesia
174 L 15 Selat Alas, Indonesia
174 L 15 Selat Bali, Indonesia
174 F 11 Selat Berhala, Indonesia
174 C 11 Selat Bungalaut, Indonesia
175 T 11 Selat Dampir, Indonesia
175 S 11 Selat Jailolo, Indonesia
174 H 11 Selat Karimata, Indonesia
174 L 13 Selat Laut, Indonesia
174 L 15 Selat Lombok, Indonesia
174 K 14 Selat Madura, Indonesia
175 R 12 Selat Manipa, Indonesia
174 D 11 Selat Mentawai, Indonesia

Country · Internal administrative region: State/Province/Territory/Dependent territory · Capital city · Mountain range/Undersea ridge · Mountain peak/Volcano/Seamount · Geographic feature · Headland/Point/Cape/Peninsula · Desert · Island/Island group · Antarctic base · Ocean · Sea · Bay/Gulf/Channel/Strait · Lake · Salt pan/Dry/Intermittent lake · River

175 R 11 **Selat Obi**, Indonesia ≈
175 Q 15 **Selat Ombai**, Indonesia ≈
175 P 11 **Selat Peleng**, Indonesia ≈
175 P 15 **Selat Rote**, Indonesia ≈
174 M 15 **Selat Sape**, Indonesia ≈
175 N 14 **Selat Selayar**, Indonesia ≈
174 H 9 **Selat Serasan**, Indonesia ≈
174 C 11 **Selat Siberut**, Indonesia ≈
175 N 15 **Selat Sumba**, Indonesia ≈
175 O 11 **Selat Walea**, Indonesia ≈
175 R 15 **Selat Wetar**, Indonesia ≈
175 W 11 **Selat Yapen**, Indonesia ≈
87 K 19 **Selb**, Germany
118 I 9 **Selby**, South Dakota, U.S.A.
121 U 13 **Selbyville**, Delaware, U.S.A.
175 T 11 **Sele**, Indonesia
171 P 3 **Selenga**, Mongolia ∿
171 Q 2 **Selenge**, Mongolia ◘
194 J 9 **Selenge**, Democratic Republic of Congo
79 W 5 **Sélestat**, France
118 H 9 **Selfridge**, North Dakota, U.S.A.
192 G 8 **Sélibabi**, Mauritania
117 L 21 **Seligman**, Arizona, U.S.A.
114 I 10 **Selkirk**, Manitoba, Canada
117 M 25 **Sells**, Arizona, U.S.A.
117 F 20 **Selma**, California, U.S.A.
122 L 6 **Selma**, Alabama, U.S.A.
122 J 2 **Selmer**, Tennessee, U.S.A.
79 T 6 **Selongey**, France
113 W 7 **Selwyn Lake**, Saskatchewan, Canada ◣
113 O 6 **Selwyn Mountains**, Yukon Territory, Canada ⛰
100 J 7 **Selyatyn**, Ukraine
142 H 11 **Sem-Tripa**, Brazil
174 I 13 **Semarang**, Indonesia
174 L 12 **Semaras**, Indonesia
174 I 10 **Sematan**, Malaysia
194 G 7 **Sembé**, Congo
159 U 12 **Şemdinli**, Turkey
175 U 12 **Semenanjung Bomberai**, Indonesia ▶
194 J 9 **Semendua**, Democratic Republic of Congo
101 R 1 **Semenivka**, Ukraine
119 G 19 **Seminole**, Texas, U.S.A.
167 O 3 **Semiozernoye**, Kazakhstan
167 W 4 **Semipalatinsk**, Kazakhstan
175 O 5 **Semirara Islands**, Philippines ✱
174 J 10 **Semitau**, Indonesia
164 L 6 **Semnān**, Iran ◘
164 K 6 **Semnān**, Iran
83 H 24 **Semois**, Belgium ∿
175 N 8 **Semporna**, Malaysia
174 K 12 **Semuda**, Indonesia
142 B 13 **Sena Madureira**, Brazil
142 N 12 **Senador Pompeu**, Brazil
159 R 6 **Senaki**, Georgia
196 L 6 **Senanga**, Zambia
176 K 12 **Sendai**, Japan
177 B 23 **Sendai**, Japan
176 L 12 **Sendai-wan**, Japan ≈
93 G 21 **Senec**, Slovakia
83 F 21 **Seneffe**, Belgium
192 E 8 **Senegal**, Africa □
192 E 7 **Sénégal**, Mauritania ∿
87 N 15 **Senftenberg**, Germany
197 P 2 **Senga Hill**, Zambia
195 S 9 **Sengerema**, Tanzania
90 I 10 **Senigallia**, Italy
94 C 10 **Senj**, Croatia
84 H 7 **Senja**, Norway ✱
192 I 12 **Senko**, Guinea
79 Q 4 **Senlis**, France
173 N 20 **Senmonorom**, Cambodia
177 G 19 **Sennan**, Japan
191 G 18 **Sennar**, Sudan ◘
191 F 18 **Sennar**, Sudan
145 G 25 **Seno Otway**, Chile ◣
145 F 24 **Seno Skyring**, Chile ◣
79 R 5 **Sens**, France
94 K 7 **Senta**, Serbia and Montenegro
118 F 8 **Sentinel Butte**, North Dakota, U.S.A. ▲
169 F 15 **Seoni**, India
171 Y 7 **Seoul**, South Korea ⌂
174 L 14 **Sepanjang**, Indonesia ✱
211 H 15 **Separation Point**, New Zealand ▶
174 M 10 **Sepasu**, Indonesia
212 B 3 **Sepik**, Papua New Guinea ∿
115 U 10 **Sept-Îles**, Québec, Canada
96 H 10 **Septemvri**, Bulgaria
83 J 20 **Seraing**, Belgium
175 S 12 **Seram**, Indonesia ✱
175 S 12 **Seram Sea**, Indonesia ◓
174 G 13 **Serang**, Indonesia
174 I 9 **Serasan**, Indonesia ✱
94 L 12 **Serbia**, Serbia and Montenegro ◘
94 L 13 **Serbia and Montenegro**, Europe □
191 J 18 **Serdo**, Ethiopia
167 Y 4 **Serebryansk**, Kazakhstan
93 H 21 **Sereď**, Slovakia
158 I 10 **Şereflikoçhisar**, Turkey
174 E 9 **Seremban**, Malaysia
195 T 9 **Serengeti Plain**, Tanzania ◇
197 P 4 **Serenje**, Zambia
100 K 5 **Seret**, Ukraine ∿
171 S 4 **Sergelen**, Mongolia
167 Q 2 **Sergeyevka**, Kazakhstan
143 N 14 **Sergipe**, Brazil ◘
97 I 22 **Serifos**, Greece ✱
158 F 13 **Serik**, Turkey
212 A 6 **Serki**, Papua New Guinea
175 S 14 **Sermata**, Indonesia ✱
81 Q 12 **Serón**, Spain
196 K 7 **Seronga**, Botswana
156 J 9 **Serov**, Russian Federation
197 N 9 **Serowe**, Botswana
80 I 11 **Serpa**, Portugal
127 X 13 **Serpent's Mouth**, Trinidad and Tobago ≈
156 F 8 **Serpukhov**, Russian Federation
143 M 18 **Serra**, Brazil
196 G 6 **Serra da Chela**, Angola ⛰
142 M 11 **Serra da Ibiapaba**, Brazil ⛰
142 G 12 **Serra do Cachimbo**, Brazil ⛰
143 L 17 **Serra do Espinhaço**, Brazil ⛰
143 J 20 **Serra do Mar**, Brazil ⛰
143 H 15 **Serra do Roncador**, Brazil ⛰
143 D 14 **Serra dos Parecis**, Brazil ⛰
143 I 21 **Serra Geral**, Brazil ⛰
91 M 20 **Serra San Bruno**, Italy
139 Q 5 **Serranía Turagua**, Venezuela ▲
126 K 9 **Serranilla Bank**, Honduras ≈
143 I 17 **Serranópolis**, Brazil
96 G 13 **Serres**, Greece
144 I 10 **Serrezuela**, Argentina
143 N 14 **Serrinha**, Brazil
175 T 14 **Serua**, Indonesia ✱
175 W 11 **Serui**, Indonesia
97 D 15 **Servia**, Greece
175 S 11 **Sesepe**, Indonesia
196 H 8 **Sesfontein**, Namibia
196 M 6 **Sesheke**, Zambia
80 F 10 **Sesimbra**, Portugal
84 K 12 **Seskar Furö**, Sweden ✱
196 K 5 **Sessa**, Angola
90 D 9 **Sestri Levante**, Italy
90 A 8 **Sestriere**, Italy
94 E 8 **Sesvete**, Croatia
176 I 7 **Setana**, Japan
79 S 14 **Sète**, France
143 L 17 **Sete Lagoas**, Brazil
177 O 22 **Seteuchi**, Japan
189 O 5 **Sétif**, Algeria
177 I 17 **Seto**, Japan
177 E 20 **Seto naikai**, Japan ◓
188 H 7 **Settat**, Morocco
194 D 9 **Setté Cama**, Gabon
63 O 15 **Settlement of Edinburgh**, Tristan da Cunha ⌂
80 G 10 **Setubal**, Portugal ◘
80 G 9 **Setúbal**, Portugal
159 U 8 **Sevana Lich**, Armenia ◣
101 T 12 **Sevastopol'**, Ukraine
113 Q 11 **Seven Sisters Peaks**, British Columbia, Canada ▲
114 M 8 **Severn**, Ontario, Canada ∿
77 J 20 **Severn**, United Kingdom ∿
114 K 8 **Severn Lake**, Ontario, Canada ◣
157 Q 4 **Severnaya Zemlya**, Russian Federation ✱
157 X 6 **Severnyy Anyuyskiy Khrebet**, Russian Federation ⛰
167 Q 2 **Severnyy Kazakhstan**, Kazakhstan ◘
157 Z 12 **Severo-Kuril'sk**, Russian Federation
157 P 7 **Severo-Sibirskaya Nizmennost'**, Russian Federation ◇
157 O 11 **Severo-Yeniseyskiy**, Russian Federation
157 R 12 **Severobaykal'sk**, Russian Federation
156 I 6 **Severodvinsk**, Russian Federation
156 I 5 **Severomorsk**, Russian Federation
117 L 17 **Sevier**, Utah, U.S.A. ∿
117 L 17 **Sevier Lake**, Utah, U.S.A. ◣
138 H 7 **Sevilla**, Colombia
80 K 12 **Seville**, Spain
96 I 8 **Sevlievo**, Bulgaria
94 D 7 **Sevnica**, Slovenia
112 J 8 **Seward**, Alaska, U.S.A.
112 H 4 **Seward Peninsula**, Alaska, U.S.A. ▶
156 M 7 **Seyakha**, Russian Federation
125 X 11 **Seybaplaya**, Mexico
58 A 8 **Seychelles**, Indian Ocean □
167 N 13 **Seydi**, Turkmenistan
158 G 12 **Seydisehir**, Turkey
84 D 10 **Seyðisfjörður**, Iceland
158 K 12 **Seyhan**, Turkey ∿
101 S 2 **Seym**, Ukraine ∿
119 I 19 **Seymour**, Texas, U.S.A.
209 S 13 **Seymour**, Victoria, Australia
165 U 7 **Seyyedābād**, Afghanistan
79 R 5 **Sézanne**, France
91 H 15 **Sezze**, Italy
97 H 26 **Sfakia**, Greece
189 R 6 **Sfax**, Tunisia
171 R 9 **Shaanxi**, China ◘
191 M 23 **Shabeellaha Dhexe**, Somalia ◘
191 L 24 **Shabeellaha Hoose**, Somalia ◘
96 O 7 **Shabla**, Bulgaria
195 P 9 **Shabunda**, Democratic Republic of Congo
163 R 13 **Shabwah**, Yemen
170 H 6 **Shache**, China
219 Q 11 **Shackleton Coast**, Antarctica ◇
219 Y 9 **Shackleton Ice Shelf**, Antarctica ◇
219 N 6 **Shackleton Range**, Antarctica ⛰
211 F 24 **Shag Point**, New Zealand ▶
63 H 21 **Shag Rocks**, Atlantic Ocean ⛰
165 T 9 **Shāh Jūy**, Afghanistan
160 I 8 **Shahbā'**, Syria
165 U 14 **Shahdapur**, Pakistan
169 G 14 **Shahdol**, India
168 G 11 **Shahjahanpur**, India
169 E 19 **Shahpur**, India
164 H 8 **Shahr-e Kord**, Iran
165 S 9 **Shahr-i-Safa**, Afghanistan
165 R 7 **Shahrak**, Afghanistan
165 O 8 **Shāhrakht**, Iran
164 I 8 **Shahrezā**, Iran
167 R 14 **Shahrtuz**, Tajikistan
164 L 5 **Shāhrūd**, Iran
167 R 14 **Shakh**, Tajikistan
167 Q 13 **Shakhrisabz**, Uzbekistan
167 S 5 **Shakhtinsk**, Kazakhstan
156 E 10 **Shakhty**, Russian Federation
166 L 6 **Shakhty**, Kazakhstan
176 I 6 **Shakotan-hantō**, Japan ▶
176 I 5 **Shakotan-misaki**, Japan ▶
167 V 3 **Shalday**, Kazakhstan
123 U 4 **Shallotte**, North Carolina, U.S.A.
171 O 10 **Shaluli Shan**, China ⛰
114 L 7 **Shamattawa**, Manitoba, Canada
163 W 6 **Shamis**, United Arab Emirates
119 I 17 **Shamrock**, Texas, U.S.A.
172 F 12 **Shan**, Myanmar ◘
172 E 12 **Shan Plateau**, Myanmar ◇
171 V 8 **Shandong**, China ◘
161 V 7 **Shandrūkh**, Iraq
171 X 10 **Shanghai**, China ◘
171 W 10 **Shanghai**, China
171 V 12 **Shanghang**, China
196 L 6 **Shangombo**, Zambia
171 U 9 **Shangqiu**, China
171 V 11 **Shangrao**, China
171 X 3 **Shangzhi**, China
193 T 11 **Shani**, Nigeria
77 D 17 **Shannon**, Republic of Ireland ∿
211 L 15 **Shannon**, New Zealand
157 V 12 **Shantarskiye Ostrova**, Russian Federation ✱
171 V 13 **Shantou**, China
171 S 8 **Shanxi**, China ◘
171 S 9 **Shanyang**, China
171 U 13 **Shaoguan**, China
171 W 10 **Shaoxing**, China
171 T 12 **Shaoyang**, China
76 I 7 **Shapinsay**, United Kingdom ✱
163 Q 5 **Shaqrā'**, Saudi Arabia
167 X 5 **Shar**, Kazakhstan
191 C 18 **Sharafa**, Sudan
167 Q 11 **Shardara**, Kazakhstan
171 N 4 **Sharga**, Mongolia
176 M 4 **Shari**, Japan
163 X 5 **Sharjah**, United Arab Emirates
208 E 8 **Shark Bay**, Western Australia, Australia ≈
99 I 14 **Sharkawshchyna**, Belarus
163 U 13 **Sharkhāt**, Yemen
190 G 9 **Sharm el Sheikh**, Egypt
191 I 21 **Shashemenē**, Ethiopia
117 D 14 **Shasta Lake**, California, U.S.A. ◣
161 Z 12 **Shaţţ al 'Arab**, Iraq ∿
120 I 6 **Shawano**, Wisconsin, U.S.A.
119 K 17 **Shawnee**, Oklahoma, U.S.A.
167 R 10 **Shayan**, Kazakhstan
162 K 5 **Shaybārā**, Saudi Arabia ✱
161 X 8 **Shaykh Jūwī**, Iraq
161 W 8 **Shaykh Sa'd**, Iraq
167 T 14 **Shazud**, Tajikistan
101 Z 5 **Shchastya**, Ukraine
167 V 3 **Shcherbakty**, Kazakhstan
101 R 1 **Shchors**, Ukraine
167 R 3 **Shchuchinsk**, Kazakhstan
99 F 18 **Shchuchyn**, Belarus
191 L 25 **Shebeli**, Somalia/Ethiopia ∿
120 J 7 **Sheboygan**, Wisconsin, U.S.A.
115 W 13 **Sheet Harbour**, Nova Scotia, Canada
160 F 8 **Shefar'am**, Israel
77 K 18 **Sheffield**, United Kingdom
122 K 3 **Sheffield**, Alabama, U.S.A.
165 Y 9 **Shekhupura**, Pakistan
118 C 7 **Shelby**, Montana, U.S.A.
120 H 12 **Shelbyville**, Illinois, U.S.A.
120 K 12 **Shelbyville**, Indiana, U.S.A.
122 M 2 **Shelbyville**, Tennessee, U.S.A.
115 U 10 **Sheldrake**, Québec, Canada
112 H 9 **Shelikof Strait**, Alaska, U.S.A. ≈
116 D 7 **Shelton**, Washington, U.S.A.
167 X 4 **Shemonaikha**, Kazakhstan
118 K 13 **Shenandoah**, Iowa, U.S.A.
193 S 12 **Shendam**, Nigeria
191 F 16 **Shendi**, Sudan
156 H 7 **Shenkursk**, Russian Federation
171 W 5 **Shenyang**, China
171 U 14 **Shenzhen**, China
100 M 4 **Shepetivka**, Ukraine
213 R 11 **Shepherd Islands**, Vanuatu ✱
209 S 12 **Shepparton**, Victoria, Australia
192 F 12 **Sherbro Island**, Sierra Leone ✱
115 S 13 **Sherbrooke**, Québec, Canada
191 F 15 **Shereiq**, Sudan
168 B 12 **Shergarh**, India
118 E 10 **Sheridan**, Wyoming, U.S.A.
119 K 18 **Sherman**, Texas, U.S.A.
121 Z 4 **Sherman Mills**, Maine, U.S.A.
76 J 4 **Shetland Islands**, United Kingdom ✱
166 H 9 **Shetpe**, Kazakhstan
191 G 21 **Shewa Gīmīra**, Ethiopia
164 J 13 **Sheykh Sho'eyb**, Iran ✱
76 F 9 **Shiant Islands**, United Kingdom ✱
163 S 12 **Shibām**, Yemen
176 J 13 **Shibata**, Japan
176 M 4 **Shibecha**, Japan
176 K 4 **Shibetsu**, Japan
176 M 4 **Shibetsu**, Japan
190 E 8 **Shibîn el Kôm**, Egypt
171 W 7 **Shidao**, China
170 K 4 **Shihezi**, China
176 L 5 **Shihoro**, Japan
177 C 22 **Shiiba**, Japan
171 T 7 **Shijiazhuang**, China
176 J 7 **Shikabe**, Japan
165 U 12 **Shikarpur**, Pakistan
177 K 18 **Shikine-shima**, Japan ✱
177 E 20 **Shikoku**, Japan ✱
60 L 4 **Shikoku Basin**, Pacific Ocean ◇
177 E 21 **Shikoku-sanchi**, Japan ⛰
176 J 6 **Shikotsu-ko**, Japan ◣
168 M 13 **Shillong**, India
177 B 22 **Shimabara**, Japan
157 U 13 **Shimanovsk**, Russian Federation
191 M 19 **Shimbiris**, Somalia ▲
177 J 17 **Shimizu**, Japan
168 E 9 **Shimla**, India
177 B 24 **Shimo-Koshiki-jima**, Japan ✱
177 K 17 **Shimoda**, Japan
169 C 20 **Shimoga**, India
176 J 8 **Shimokita-hantō**, Japan ▶
177 B 20 **Shimonoseki**, Japan
165 Y 5 **Shimshal**, Pakistan
165 Q 8 **Shīndand**, Afghanistan
172 E 7 **Shingbwiyang**, Myanmar
177 H 19 **Shingū**, Japan
176 K 12 **Shinjō**, Japan
176 K 5 **Shintoku**, Japan
195 T 10 **Shinyanga**, Tanzania ◘
195 T 10 **Shinyanga**, Tanzania
176 K 12 **Shiogama**, Japan
177 I 16 **Shiojiri**, Japan
177 N 26 **Shiokawa**, Japan
177 H 20 **Shiono-misaki**, Japan ▶
177 L 14 **Shioya-zaki**, Japan ▶
119 D 16 **Ship Rock**, New Mexico, U.S.A. ▲
119 D 16 **Shiprock**, New Mexico, U.S.A.
164 J 9 **Shīr Kūh**, Iran ▲
176 J 8 **Shirakami-misaki**, Japan ▶
177 K 14 **Shirakawa**, Japan
176 M 5 **Shiranuka**, Japan
219 N 11 **Shirase Coast**, Antarctica ◇
164 I 10 **Shīrāz**, Iran
176 M 3 **Shiretoko-hantō**, Japan ▶
176 M 3 **Shiretoko-misaki**, Japan ▶
176 K 8 **Shiriya-zaki**, Japan ▶
121 V 10 **Shirley**, New York, U.S.A.
176 K 12 **Shiroishi**, Japan
193 R 11 **Shiroro Reservoir**, Nigeria ◣
165 N 5 **Shīrvān**, Iran
171 W 1 **Shisanzhan**, China
112 E 9 **Shishaldin Volcano**, Alaska, U.S.A. ▲
168 B 12 **Shiv**, India
168 E 13 **Shivpuri**, India
171 U 1 **Shiwei**, China
171 S 9 **Shiyan**, China
176 L 11 **Shizugawa**, Japan
171 R 7 **Shizuishan**, China
177 J 17 **Shizuoka**, Japan
99 M 16 **Shklow**, Belarus
95 J 16 **Shkodër**, Albania
95 J 19 **Shkumbin**, Albania ∿
177 D 19 **Shōbara**, Japan
177 F 19 **Shodo-shima**, Japan ✱
176 J 5 **Shokanbetsu-dake**, Japan ▲
167 O 4 **Sholaksay**, Kazakhstan
167 R 9 **Shollakorgan**, Kazakhstan
63 M 20 **Shona Ridge**, Atlantic Ocean ⛰
165 S 14 **Shorap**, Pakistan
212 J 5 **Shortland Island**, Solomon Islands ✱
176 J 4 **Shosanbetsu**, Japan
117 I 21 **Shoshone**, California, U.S.A.
117 H 17 **Shoshone Mountains**, Nevada, U.S.A. ⛰
118 D 11 **Shoshoni**, Wyoming, U.S.A.
101 S 1 **Shostka**, Ukraine
117 O 22 **Show Low**, Arizona, U.S.A.
191 G 17 **Showak**, Sudan
119 M 19 **Shreveport**, Louisiana, U.S.A.
77 I 19 **Shrewsbury**, United Kingdom
167 T 10 **Shu**, Kazakhstan
161 Y 11 **Shu'aiba**, Iraq
171 W 5 **Shuangliao**, China
171 Y 3 **Shuangyashan**, China
166 L 6 **Shubarkuduk**, Kazakhstan
171 U 10 **Shucheng**, China
101 Y 5 **Shul'hynka**, Ukraine
112 G 9 **Shumagin Islands**, Alaska, U.S.A. ✱
166 L 10 **Shumanay**, Uzbekistan
96 M 7 **Shumen**, Bulgaria ◘
96 L 8 **Shumen**, Bulgaria
156 I 11 **Shumikha**, Russian Federation
99 L 14 **Shumilina**, Belarus
112 J 4 **Shungnak**, Alaska, U.S.A.
163 Q 14 **Shuqrah**, Yemen
164 I 7 **Shūr Āb**, Iran
165 N 11 **Shūr Gaz**, Iran
164 M 7 **Shūrāb**, Iran
197 P 7 **Shurugwi**, Zimbabwe
165 O 9 **Shusf**, Iran
164 G 8 **Shūsh**, Iran
164 G 8 **Shushtar**, Iran
172 D 11 **Shwebo**, Myanmar
167 R 11 **Shymkent**, Kazakhstan
101 S 8 **Shyroke**, Ukraine
101 T 4 **Shyshaky**, Ukraine
99 J 19 **Shyshchytsy**, Belarus
173 G 18 **Si Nakarin Reservoir**, Thailand ◣
173 H 20 **Si Racha**, Thailand
175 V 14 **Sia**, Indonesia
165 Q 13 **Siahan Range**, Pakistan ⛰
165 Y 8 **Sialkot**, Pakistan
212 E 5 **Sialum**, Papua New Guinea
174 G 9 **Siantan**, Indonesia ✱
175 R 6 **Siargao**, Philippines ✱
175 O 8 **Siasi**, Philippines ✱
175 O 8 **Siasi**, Philippines
212 E 4 **Siassi**, Papua New Guinea
97 D 15 **Siatista**, Greece
175 P 6 **Siaton**, Philippines
175 Q 9 **Siau**, Indonesia ✱
98 E 13 **Šiaulėnai**, Lithuania
98 E 13 **Šiauliai**, Lithuania
175 P 1 **Siayan**, Philippines ✱
91 M 18 **Sibari**, Italy
94 D 13 **Šibenik**, Croatia
157 N 9 **Siberia**, Russian Federation ◇
174 C 11 **Siberut**, Indonesia ✱
165 T 11 **Sibi**, Pakistan
212 B 6 **Sibidiri**, Papua New Guinea
194 G 10 **Sibiti**, Congo
100 I 10 **Sibiu**, Romania
175 N 10 **Siboa**, Indonesia
174 C 10 **Sibolga**, Indonesia
168 O 12 **Sibsagar**, India
174 J 9 **Sibu**, Malaysia
175 P 7 **Sibuco**, Philippines
194 J 4 **Sibut**, Central African Republic
175 N 8 **Sibutu Group**, Philippines ✱
175 P 4 **Sibuyan**, Philippines ✱
141 I 20 **Sicasica**, Bolivia
173 G 24 **Sichon**, Thailand
171 P 11 **Sichuan**, China ◘
171 Q 10 **Sichuan Basin**, China ◇
91 J 23 **Sicilia**, Italy ◘
91 F 21 **Sicilian Channel**, Africa/Europe ≈
91 I 22 **Sicily**, Italy ✱
94 J 9 **Šid**, Serbia and Montenegro
188 L 6 **Sid**, Algeria
91 M 21 **Siderno**, Italy
169 H 14 **Sidhi**, India
188 L 6 **Sidi Ali**, Algeria
190 C 7 **Sidi Barrani**, Egypt
188 K 6 **Sidi Bel Abbès**, Algeria
188 G 7 **Sidī-Bennour**, Morocco
189 Q 6 **Sidi Bouzid**, Tunisia
188 F 9 **Sidi Ifni**, Morocco
188 I 6 **Sidi Kacem**, Morocco
188 G 7 **Sidi-Smaïl**, Morocco
174 C 9 **Sidikalang**, Indonesia
96 G 12 **Sidirokastro**, Greece
118 G 8 **Sidney**, Montana, U.S.A.
192 I 10 **Sido**, Mali
143 H 18 **Sidrolândia**, Brazil
92 M 13 **Siedlce**, Poland
87 E 17 **Siegen**, Germany
173 K 19 **Siem Reap**, Cambodia
92 N 12 **Siemiatycze**, Poland
173 M 19 **Siempang**, Cambodia
90 F 11 **Siena**, Italy
93 I 14 **Sieradz**, Poland
92 J 11 **Sierpc**, Poland
119 E 20 **Sierra Blanca**, Texas, U.S.A. ▲
119 F 20 **Sierra Blanca**, Texas, U.S.A.
145 H 16 **Sierra Colorada**, Argentina

□ Country ◘ Internal administrative region: State/Province/Territory/Dependent territory ⌂ Capital city ⛰ Mountain range/Undersea ridge ▲ Mountain peak/Volcano/Seamount ◇ Geographic feature ▶ Headland/Point/Cape/Peninsula ◭ Desert ✱ Island/Island group ⁙ Antarctic base ◎ Ocean ◓ Sea ≈ Bay/Gulf/Channel/Strait ◣ Lake ▚ Salt pan/Dry/Intermittent lake ∿ River

145 H 14 **Sierra de Auca Mahuida**, Argentina
124 G 5 **Sierra de Camalli**, Mexico
124 F 2 **Sierra de Juárez**, Mexico
125 S 14 **Sierra de Miahuatlán**, Mexico
145 I 17 **Sierra Grande**, Argentina
192 G 11 **Sierra Leone**, Africa
62 K 13 **Sierra Leone Basin**, Atlantic Ocean
62 J 13 **Sierra Leone Rise**, Atlantic Ocean
125 V 14 **Sierra Madre**, Mexico
175 O 3 **Sierra Madre**, Philippines
125 P 13 **Sierra Madre del Sur**, Mexico
124 K 4 **Sierra Madre Occidental**, Mexico
125 P 5 **Sierra Madre Oriental**, Mexico
126 M 6 **Sierra Maestra**, Cuba
139 N 6 **Sierra Maigualida**, Venezuela
80 K 11 **Sierra Morena**, Spain
144 H 7 **Sierra Nevada**, Argentina
117 E 16 **Sierra Nevada**, California, U.S.A.
139 P 6 **Sierra Parima**, Venezuela
124 F 2 **Sierra San Pedro Martir**, Mexico
139 O 10 **Sierra Tapirapecó**, Venezuela
117 O 25 **Sierra Vista**, Arizona, U.S.A.
144 I 11 **Sierras de Córdoba**, Argentina
88 D 10 **Sierre**, Switzerland
85 L 14 **Sievi**, Finland
97 I 22 **Sifnos**, Greece
213 W 12 **Sigatoka**, Fiji
65 N 11 **Sigguup Nunaa**, Greenland
100 I 7 **Sighetu Marmației**, Romania
100 J 10 **Sighișoara**, Romania
174 B 8 **Sigli**, Indonesia
84 C 9 **Siglufjörður**, Iceland
87 F 24 **Sigmaringen**, Germany
83 L 20 **Signal de Botrange**, Belgium
117 K 19 **Signal Peak**, Utah, U.S.A.
218 H 1 **Signy**, Antarctica
81 S 2 **Sigüés**, Spain
192 H 10 **Siguiri**, Guinea
98 G 10 **Sigulda**, Latvia
169 G 14 **Sihora**, India
141 C 14 **Sihuas**, Peru
85 N 15 **Siilinjärvi**, Finland
159 R 12 **Siirt**, Turkey
213 N 6 **Sikaiana**, Solomon Islands
168 D 11 **Sikar**, India
192 J 10 **Sikasso**, Mali
192 J 10 **Sikasso**, Mali
172 E 9 **Sikaw**, Myanmar
119 O 15 **Sikeston**, Missouri, U.S.A.
157 W 15 **Sikhote-Alin'**, Russian Federation
97 J 23 **Sikinos**, Greece
168 K 12 **Sikkim**, India
93 H 26 **Siklós**, Hungary
157 S 8 **Siktyakh**, Russian Federation
90 E 5 **Silandro**, Italy
175 P 5 **Silay**, Philippines
94 B 11 **Silba**, Croatia
168 N 13 **Silchar**, India
93 D 14 **Silesia**, Poland
189 N 14 **Silet**, Algeria
58 A 9 **Silhouette**, Seychelles
158 I 14 **Silifke**, Turkey
168 K 12 **Siliguri**, India
170 K 9 **Siling Co**, China
96 M 6 **Silistra**, Bulgaria
96 M 6 **Silistra**, Bulgaria
158 D 7 **Silivri**, Turkey
85 F 18 **Siljan**, Sweden
81 T 8 **Silla**, Spain
98 J 6 **Sillamäe**, Estonia
89 P 9 **Sillian**, Austria
99 C 14 **Šilutė**, Lithuania
159 Q 11 **Silvan**, Turkey
159 Q 11 **Silvan Baraji**, Turkey
169 C 16 **Silvassa**, India
118 M 8 **Silver Bay**, Minnesota, U.S.A.
119 D 19 **Silver City**, New Mexico, U.S.A.
210 K 8 **Silverdale**, New Zealand
80 H 12 **Silves**, Portugal
125 Y 12 **Silvituc**, Mexico
88 J 8 **Silvretta Gruppe**, Switzerland
171 O 14 **Simao**, China
158 D 10 **Simav**, Turkey
194 M 7 **Simba**, Democratic Republic of Congo
212 C 4 **Simbai**, Papua New Guinea
191 I 18 **Simēn Mountains**, Ethiopia
174 A 9 **Simeuluë**, Indonesia
101 U 12 **Simferopol'**, Ukraine
169 H 15 **Simga**, India
117 G 22 **Simi Valley**, California, U.S.A.
168 H 10 **Simikot**, Nepal
99 E 16 **Simnas**, Lithuania
84 M 11 **Simojärvi**, Finland
142 M 13 **Simplício Mendes**, Brazil
88 F 10 **Simplon**, Switzerland
209 P 7 **Simpson Desert**, Northern Territory, Australia
113 X 1 **Simpson Peninsula**, Nunavut, Canada
168 I 12 **Simra**, Nepal
85 F 25 **Simrishamn**, Sweden
191 M 22 **Sina Dhaqa**, Somalia
174 B 9 **Sinabang**, Indonesia
190 F 9 **Sinai**, Egypt
124 K 6 **Sinaloa**, Mexico
189 R 8 **Sīnāwin**, Libya
172 E 8 **Sinbo**, Myanmar
172 C 12 **Sinbyugyun**, Myanmar
158 M 10 **Sincan**, Turkey
138 H 3 **Sincelejo**, Colombia
165 U 13 **Sind**, Pakistan
168 E 13 **Sind**, India
165 W 10 **Sind Sāgar Doāb**, Pakistan
174 H 14 **Sindangbarang**, Indonesia
98 F 8 **Sindi**, Estonia
80 G 10 **Sines**, Portugal
192 J 13 **Sinfra**, Côte d'Ivoire
173 H 18 **Sing Buri**, Thailand
191 F 18 **Singa**, Sudan
174 F 10 **Singapore**, Singapore
174 F 10 **Singapore**, Asia
174 L 15 **Singaraja**, Indonesia
169 G 20 **Singaray-akonda**, India
87 F 25 **Singen**, Germany
101 N 8 **Sîngerei**, Moldova
195 T 12 **Singida**, Tanzania
195 T 10 **Singida**, Tanzania
172 D 7 **Singkaling Hkamti**, Myanmar
175 O 13 **Singkang**, Indonesia
174 I 10 **Singkawang**, Indonesia
174 F 11 **Singkep**, Indonesia
209 V 11 **Singleton**, New South Wales, Australia
91 D 16 **Siniscola**, Italy
94 E 13 **Sinj**, Croatia
175 O 13 **Sinjai**, Indonesia
161 P 2 **Sinjār**, Iraq
172 E 9 **Sinkan**, Myanmar
191 H 15 **Sinkat**, Sudan
143 H 14 **Sinop**, Brazil
158 K 6 **Sinop**, Turkey
158 K 6 **Sinop Burnu**, Turkey
171 Y 6 **Sinp'o**, North Korea
174 J 10 **Sintang**, Indonesia
119 K 23 **Sinton**, Texas, U.S.A.
80 F 9 **Sintra**, Portugal
171 X 6 **Sinŭiju**, North Korea
191 O 20 **Sinujiif**, Somalia
175 P 7 **Siocon**, Philippines
93 H 24 **Siófok**, Hungary
88 D 10 **Sion**, Switzerland
118 K 12 **Sioux City**, Iowa, U.S.A.
118 J 11 **Sioux Falls**, South Dakota, U.S.A.
114 K 10 **Sioux Lookout**, Ontario, Canada
175 P 6 **Sipalay**, Philippines
171 W 5 **Siping**, China
114 J 7 **Sipiwesk**, Manitoba, Canada
219 O 11 **Siple Coast**, Antarctica
218 K 11 **Siple Island**, Antarctica
174 D 12 **Sipura**, Indonesia
175 P 6 **Siquijor**, Philippines
209 P 2 **Sir Edward Pellew Group**, Northern Territory, Australia
85 A 21 **Sira**, Norway
169 E 20 **Sira**, India
167 R 12 **Sirdaryo Wiloyati**, Uzbekistan
100 L 7 **Siret**, Romania
164 L 13 **Sīrīk**, Iran
173 H 15 **Sirikit Reservoir**, Thailand
164 L 11 **Sīrjān**, Iran
159 R 12 **Şirnak**, Turkey
164 J 13 **Sīrrī**, Iran
168 D 10 **Sirsa**, India
169 D 20 **Sirsi**, India
169 F 17 **Sirsilla**, India
189 U 8 **Sirte**, Libya
99 G 15 **Širvintos**, Lithuania
161 V 4 **Sirwan**, Iraq
94 E 8 **Sisak**, Croatia
173 K 18 **Sisaket**, Thailand
159 V 9 **Sisian**, Armenia
173 J 19 **Sisŏphŏn**, Cambodia
212 B 3 **Sissano**, Papua New Guinea
118 J 9 **Sisseton**, South Dakota, U.S.A.
165 P 13 **Sīstān Va Balūchestān**, Iran
80 L 7 **Sistema Central**, Spain
81 O 4 **Sistema Ibérico**, Spain
81 N 12 **Sistemas Béticos**, Spain
79 V 13 **Sisteron**, France
169 N 22 **Sisters**, India
168 G 12 **Sitapur**, India
97 K 26 **Siteia**, Greece
81 W 5 **Sitges**, Spain
113 N 10 **Sitka**, Alaska, U.S.A.
173 D 14 **Sittang**, Myanmar
83 K 18 **Sittard**, Netherlands
172 B 13 **Sittwe**, Myanmar
215 V 15 **Si'umu**, Samoa
126 G 10 **Siuna**, Nicaragua
169 K 14 **Siuri**, India
169 F 23 **Sivaganga**, India
164 J 10 **Sīvand**, Iran
158 M 9 **Sivas**, Turkey
159 O 12 **Siverek**, Turkey
101 Y 5 **Sivers'k**, Ukraine
158 G 10 **Sivrihisar**, Turkey
175 O 12 **Siwa**, Indonesia
190 B 9 **Siwa**, Egypt
190 B 8 **Siwa Oasis**, Egypt
168 E 9 **Siwalik Range**, India
159 Y 7 **Siyäzän**, Azerbaijan
85 D 25 **Sjaelland**, Denmark
95 K 14 **Sjenica**, Serbia and Montenegro
101 S 10 **Skadovs'k**, Ukraine
85 C 22 **Skagen**, Denmark
85 B 23 **Skagerrak**, Denmark
113 O 9 **Skagway**, Alaska, U.S.A.
97 E 22 **Skala**, Greece
100 L 6 **Skala-Podil's'ka**, Ukraine
85 E 24 **Skälderviken**, Sweden
97 H 17 **Skantzoura**, Greece
165 Y 6 **Skardu**, Pakistan
85 A 19 **Skare**, Norway
93 L 15 **Skarżysko-Kamienna**, Poland
188 C 12 **Skaymat**, Western Sahara
77 M 18 **Skegness**, United Kingdom
84 J 13 **Skellefteå**, Sweden
85 D 20 **Ski**, Norway
97 F 17 **Skiathos**, Greece
97 G 17 **Skiathos**, Greece
84 I 7 **Skibotn**, Norway
99 F 18 **Skidal'**, Belarus
85 C 20 **Skien**, Norway
92 K 13 **Skierniewice**, Poland
189 O 5 **Skikda**, Algeria
85 B 24 **Skive**, Denmark
97 F 16 **Sklithro**, Greece
100 I 5 **Skole**, Ukraine
97 G 17 **Skopelos**, Greece
97 G 17 **Skopelos**, Greece
96 D 10 **Skopje**, Macedonia (F.Y.R.O.M.)
85 F 22 **Skövde**, Sweden
157 T 13 **Skovorodino**, Russian Federation
121 Y 5 **Skowhegan**, Maine, U.S.A.
85 D 20 **Skrimfjell**, Norway
98 C 11 **Skrunda**, Latvia
85 A 20 **Skudeneshavn**, Norway
197 P 10 **Skukuza**, Republic of South Africa
98 C 12 **Skuodas**, Lithuania
101 O 5 **Skvyra**, Ukraine
92 E 12 **Skwierzyna**, Poland
76 F 10 **Skye**, United Kingdom
97 H 18 **Skyropoula**, Greece
97 H 18 **Skyros**, Greece
97 I 18 **Skyros**, Greece
85 D 25 **Slagelse**, Denmark
77 E 19 **Slaney**, Republic of Ireland
100 I 13 **Slatina**, Romania
94 G 8 **Slatina**, Croatia
157 Y 8 **Slautnoye**, Russian Federation
113 U 8 **Slave**, Northwest Territories, Canada
193 O 13 **Slave Coast**, Nigeria
113 U 11 **Slave Lake**, Alberta, Canada
94 G 8 **Slavonija**, Croatia
94 H 9 **Slavonski Brod**, Croatia
99 N 18 **Slawharad**, Belarus
92 G 8 **Sławno**, Poland
115 O 7 **Sleeper Island**, Ontario, Canada
92 H 12 **Ślesin**, Poland
121 U 8 **Slide Mountain**, New York, U.S.A.
119 O 21 **Slidell**, Louisiana, U.S.A.
77 C 16 **Sligo**, Republic of Ireland
77 C 16 **Sligo Bay**, Republic of Ireland
96 L 9 **Sliven**, Bulgaria
96 K 9 **Sliven**, Bulgaria
96 K 6 **Slivo Pole**, Bulgaria
94 E 7 **Sljeme**, Croatia
101 O 7 **Slobidka**, Ukraine
100 M 13 **Slobozia**, Romania
82 N 6 **Slochteren**, Netherlands
85 B 16 **Slogen**, Norway
93 K 17 **Słomniki**, Poland
99 G 19 **Slonim**, Belarus
82 J 8 **Slotermeer**, Netherlands
77 L 21 **Slough**, United Kingdom
93 I 21 **Slovak Ore Mountains**, Slovakia
93 I 20 **Slovakia**, Europe
101 N 2 **Slovechne**, Ukraine
94 C 7 **Slovenia**, Europe
94 D 6 **Slovenska Bistrica**, Slovenia
101 X 5 **Slov"yans'k**, Ukraine
99 L 22 **Slovyechna**, Belarus
92 D 12 **Słubice**, Poland
100 L 2 **Sluch**, Ukraine
83 C 16 **Sluis**, Netherlands
92 H 13 **Słupca**, Poland
92 G 8 **Słupsk**, Poland
84 H 13 **Slussfors**, Sweden
99 J 19 **Slutsk**, Belarus
77 A 17 **Slyne Head**, Republic of Ireland
157 P 14 **Slyudyanka**, Russian Federation
121 Y 6 **Small Point**, Maine, U.S.A.
115 U 8 **Smallwood Reservoir**, Newfoundland and Labrador, Canada
99 J 17 **Smalyavichy**, Belarus
99 H 16 **Smarhon'**, Belarus
94 L 10 **Smederevo**, Serbia and Montenegro
94 M 11 **Smederevska Palanka**, Serbia and Montenegro
101 R 5 **Smila**, Ukraine
99 J 17 **Smilavichy**, Belarus
98 H 10 **Smiltene**, Latvia
115 P 5 **Smith Island**, Nunavut, Canada
116 C 13 **Smith River**, California, U.S.A.
115 Q 14 **Smiths Falls**, Ontario, Canada
119 I 14 **Smoky Hills**, Kansas, U.S.A.
85 C 15 **Smøla**, Norway
156 E 7 **Smolensk**, Russian Federation
97 C 15 **Smolikas**, Greece
96 I 11 **Smolyan**, Bulgaria
96 I 12 **Smolyan**, Bulgaria
96 L 8 **Smyadovo**, Bulgaria
218 J 7 **Smyley Island**, Antarctica
84 D 10 **Snaefell**, Iceland
84 C 11 **Snaekollur**, Iceland
116 G 8 **Snake**, U.S.A.
116 K 12 **Snake River Plain**, Idaho, U.S.A.
85 E 14 **Snåsvatn**, Norway
82 J 7 **Sneek**, Netherlands
82 K 7 **Sneekermeer**, Netherlands
84 A 11 **Snæfellsjökull**, Iceland
157 O 8 **Snezhnogorsk**, Russian Federation
93 E 16 **Sněžka**, Czech Republic
101 S 9 **Snihurivka**, Ukraine
93 M 19 **Snina**, Slovakia
85 C 16 **Snöhetta**, Norway
85 B 20 **Snønuten**, Norway
85 C 16 **Snota**, Norway
113 W 7 **Snowbird Lake**, Northwest Territories, Canada
77 H 18 **Snowdon**, United Kingdom
117 O 22 **Snowflake**, Arizona, U.S.A.
218 I 3 **Snowhill Island**, Antarctica
127 O 4 **Snug Corner**, The Bahamas
115 X 8 **Snug Harbour**, Newfoundland and Labrador, Canada
173 M 20 **Snuŏl**, Cambodia
100 K 6 **Snyatyn**, Ukraine
119 H 19 **Snyder**, Texas, U.S.A.
197 X 6 **Soalala**, Madgascar
197 Z 6 **Soanierana-Ivongo**, Madgascar
191 E 20 **Sobat**, Sudan
93 C 19 **Soběslav**, Czech Republic
142 M 11 **Sobral**, Brazil
173 M 23 **Soc Trăng**, Vietnam
92 K 13 **Sochaczew**, Poland
156 D 11 **Sochi**, Russian Federation
96 G 13 **Sochos**, Greece
61 R 9 **Society Archipelago**, Pacific Ocean
215 Q 9 **Society Archipelago**, French Polynesia
144 H 6 **Socompa**, Argentina
119 E 18 **Socorro**, New Mexico, U.S.A.
138 I 5 **Socorro**, Colombia
163 W 14 **Socotra**, Yemen
116 M 12 **Soda Springs**, Idaho, U.S.A.
84 L 10 **Sodankylä**, Finland
85 H 18 **Söderhamn**, Sweden
191 D 17 **Sodiri**, Sudan
191 H 21 **Sodo**, Ethiopia
175 Q 15 **Soë**, Indonesia
197 P 9 **Soekmekaar**, Republic of South Africa
98 D 7 **Soela Väin**, Estonia
82 I 12 **Soest**, Netherlands
97 D 17 **Sofades**, Greece
197 R 7 **Sofala**, Mozambique
96 G 9 **Sofia**, Bulgaria
97 F 20 **Sofiko**, Greece
96 H 9 **Sofiya**, Bulgaria
101 T 7 **Sofiyivka**, Ukraine
170 M 10 **Sog**, China
138 J 6 **Sogamoso**, Colombia
85 A 17 **Sognefjorden**, Norway
175 Q 5 **Sogod**, Philippines
190 E 10 **Sohâg**, Egypt
169 I 16 **Sohapur**, India
165 X 8 **Sohawa**, Pakistan
83 J 21 **Soheit-Tinlot**, Belgium
62 F 9 **Sohm Abyssal Plain**, Atlantic Ocean
83 F 20 **Soignies**, Belgium
79 R 3 **Soissons**, France
177 E 19 **Sōja**, Japan
171 Y 6 **Sokch'o**, South Korea
158 B 11 **Söke**, Turkey
167 S 12 **Sokh**, Uzbekistan
159 Q 5 **Sokhumi**, Georgia
94 N 13 **Sokobanja**, Serbia and Montenegro
193 N 12 **Sokodé**, Togo
94 I 12 **Sokolac**, Bosnia and Herzegovina
101 P 6 **Sokolivka**, Ukraine
92 O 10 **Sokółka**, Poland
192 J 8 **Sokolo**, Mali
101 U 9 **Sokolohirne**, Ukraine
92 M 12 **Sokołów Podlaski**, Poland
193 P 9 **Sokoto**, Nigeria
193 P 9 **Sokoto**, Nigeria
156 H 11 **Sol'-Iletsk**, Russian Federation
211 A 26 **Solander Island**, New Zealand
169 D 18 **Solapur**, India
101 N 7 **Soldănești**, Moldova
88 L 8 **Sölden**, Austria
117 E 20 **Soledad**, California, U.S.A.
138 I 2 **Soledad**, Colombia
79 Y 15 **Solenzara**, France
159 Q 10 **Solhan**, Turkey
156 J 9 **Solikamsk**, Russian Federation
142 D 11 **Solimões**, Brazil
87 C 16 **Solingen**, Germany
159 Y 6 **Şollar**, Azerbaijan
85 H 15 **Sollefteå**, Sweden
81 Y 7 **Soller**, Spain
100 L 5 **Soloblovtsi**, Ukraine
174 D 11 **Solok**, Indonesia
126 C 9 **Sololá**, Guatemala
213 O 6 **Solomon Islands**, Oceania
212 G 6 **Solomon Sea**, Solomon Islands/Papua New Guinea
120 F 4 **Solon Springs**, Wisconsin, U.S.A.
175 P 15 **Solor**, Indonesia
88 E 7 **Solothurn**, Switzerland
93 I 24 **Solt**, Hungary
94 E 13 **Šolta**, Croatia
164 I 6 **Soltānābād**, Iran
165 N 5 **Soltānābād**, Iran
86 G 12 **Soltau**, Germany
77 H 15 **Solway Firth**, United Kingdom
197 N 4 **Solwezi**, Zambia
176 L 13 **Sōma**, Japan
158 C 9 **Soma**, Turkey
191 M 22 **Somali**, Ethiopia
58 J 5 **Somali Basin**, Indian Ocean
191 K 24 **Somalia**, Africa
196 K 2 **Sombo**, Angola
94 I 8 **Sombor**, Serbia and Montenegro
83 G 21 **Sombreffe**, Belgium
125 N 9 **Sombrerete**, Mexico
145 H 24 **Sombrero**, Chile
100 H 8 **Şomcuta Mare**, Romania
168 C 12 **Somdari**, India
83 K 16 **Someren**, Netherlands
62 A 7 **Somerset**, Bermuda
120 L 14 **Somerset**, Kentucky, U.S.A.
62 A 7 **Somerset Island**, Bermuda
65 N 8 **Somerset Island**, Arctic Ocean
161 Y 9 **Someydeh**, Iraq
87 I 16 **Sömmerda**, Germany
84 E 12 **Sømna**, Norway
213 Y 11 **Somosomo**, Fiji
126 F 11 **Somotillo**, Nicaragua
126 F 10 **Somoto**, Nicaragua
169 I 17 **Sompeta**, India
169 H 14 **Son**, India
83 J 15 **Son**, Netherlands
172 K 12 **Son La**, Vietnam
126 J 14 **Soná**, Panama
85 C 26 **Sønderborg**, Denmark
87 I 16 **Sonderhausen**, Germany
90 D 5 **Sondrio**, Italy
174 K 10 **Song**, Malaysia
173 O 19 **Sông Cau**, Vietnam
173 L 24 **Sông Đôc**, Vietnam
195 U 14 **Songea**, Tanzania
173 H 25 **Songkhla**, Thailand
171 X 6 **Songnim**, North Korea
196 G 1 **Songo**, Angola
197 Q 5 **Songo**, Mozambique
171 T 9 **Songxian**, China
171 W 4 **Songyuan**, China
171 T 5 **Sonid Zuoqi**, China
165 T 14 **Sonmiani**, Pakistan
165 S 14 **Sonmiani Bay**, Pakistan
124 H 2 **Sonoita**, Mexico
124 I 4 **Sonora**, Mexico
124 I 4 **Sonora**, Mexico
117 F 18 **Sonora**, California, U.S.A.
119 H 21 **Sonora**, Texas, U.S.A.
117 J 24 **Sonoran Desert**, California, U.S.A.
214 I 15 **Sonsorol Islands**, Palau
157 Z 10 **Sopka Klyuchevskaya**, Russian Federation
157 Z 11 **Sopka Koryakskaya**, Russian Federation
157 Z 10 **Sopka Shiveluch**, Russian Federation
92 I 8 **Sopot**, Poland
93 F 22 **Sopron**, Hungary
101 T 1 **Sopych**, Ukraine
219 S 2 **Sor Rondane Mountains**, Antarctica
91 I 14 **Sora**, Italy
81 Q 13 **Sorbas**, Spain
115 R 13 **Sorel**, Québec, Canada
158 K 9 **Sorgun**, Turkey
81 Q 4 **Soria**, Spain
144 M 12 **Soriano**, Uruguay
169 J 16 **Soro**, India
143 K 19 **Sorocaba**, Brazil
214 K 15 **Sorol**, Federated States of Micronesia
175 T 11 **Sorong**, Indonesia
195 T 7 **Soroti**, Uganda
84 J 6 **Sørøya**, Norway
84 J 6 **Sørøysundet**, Norway
91 J 16 **Sorrento**, Italy
84 N 9 **Sorsatunturi**, Finland
84 H 12 **Sorsele**, Sweden
175 Q 4 **Sorsogon**, Philippines

Country · Internal administrative region: State/Province/Territory/Dependent territory · Capital city · Mountain range/Undersea ridge · Mountain peak/Volcano/Seamount · Geographic feature · Headland/Point/Cape/Peninsula · Desert · Island/Island group · Antarctic base · Ocean · Sea · Bay/Gulf/Channel/Strait · Lake · Salt pan/Dry/Intermittent lake · River

156 G 6 **Sortavala**, Russian Federation
84 G 8 **Sortland**, Norway
84 F 9 **Sørvågen**, Norway
197 O 10 **Soshanguve**, Republic of South Africa
156 I 6 **Sosnovka**, Russian Federation
93 J 17 **Sosnowiec**, Poland
101 R 2 **Sosnytsya**, Ukraine
156 J 10 **Sos'va**, Russian Federation
85 N 14 **Sotkamo**, Finland
144 I 10 **Soto**, Argentina
125 R 9 **Soto la Marina**, Mexico
85 A 18 **Sotra**, Norway
125 Y 10 **Sotuta**, Mexico
194 G 6 **Souanké**, Congo
192 J 13 **Soubré**, Côte d'Ivoire
97 H 26 **Souda**, Greece
96 K 12 **Soufli**, Greece
192 G 11 **Souguéta**, Guinea
58 B 13 **Souillac**, Mauritius
79 P 11 **Souillac**, France
189 P 5 **Souk Ahras**, Algeria
188 I 6 **Souk el Arbaâ du Rharb**, Morocco
78 L 10 **Soulac-sur-Mer**, France
160 F 7 **Soûr**, Lebanon
141 G 18 **Source of the Amazon**, Peru
142 J 10 **Soure**, Brazil
142 N 12 **Sousa**, Brazil
189 Q 6 **Sousse**, Tunisia
169 N 22 **South Andaman**, India
209 O 9 **South Australia**, Australia
59 U 10 **South Australian Basin**, Indian Ocean
59 W 11 **South Australian Plain**, Indian Ocean
119 D 18 **South Baldy**, New Mexico, U.S.A.
120 K 9 **South Bend**, Indiana, U.S.A.
123 S 4 **South Carolina**, U.S.A.
126 I 9 **South Cay**, Honduras
60 I 6 **South China Sea**, Pacific Ocean
118 H 10 **South Dakota**, U.S.A.
77 K 22 **South Downs**, United Kingdom
196 M 10 **South East**, Botswana
63 L 26 **South East Bay**, Ascension
209 S 15 **South East Cape**, Tasmania, Australia
61 O 10 **South Fiji Basin**, Pacific Ocean
219 T 9 **South Geomagnetic Pole**, Antarctica
63 H 21 **South Georgia**, U.K.
120 J 8 **South Haven**, Michigan, U.S.A.
114 K 4 **South Henik Lake**, Nunavut, Canada
121 R 15 **South Hill**, Virginia, U.S.A.
195 V 6 **South Horr**, Kenya
169 L 20 **South Huvadhu Atoll**, Maldives
59 V 13 **South Indian Basin**, Indian Ocean
59 Z 3 **South Island**, Cocos Islands
211 G 19 **South Island**, New Zealand
169 B 23 **South Island**, India
114 I 11 **South Junction**, Manitoba, Canada
171 X 8 **South Korea**, Asia
117 F 17 **South Lake Tahoe**, California, U.S.A.
169 M 17 **South Maalhosmadulu Atoll**, Maldives
219 V 14 **South Magnetic Pole**, Antarctica
169 L 18 **South Male Atoll**, Maldives
169 L 17 **South Miladunmadulu Atoll**, Maldives
113 Q 8 **South Nahanni**, Northwest Territories, Canada
126 L 7 **South Negril Point**, Jamaica
218 H 1 **South Orkney Islands**, U.K.
63 G 22 **South Orkney Rise**, Atlantic Ocean
118 F 13 **South Platte**, Colorado, U.S.A.
63 K 26 **South Point**, Ascension
219 P 8 **South Pole**, Antarctica
76 I 7 **South Ronaldsay**, United Kingdom
63 I 22 **South Sandwich Islands**, U.K.
63 I 21 **South Sandwich Trench**, Atlantic Ocean
113 W 13 **South Saskatchewan**, Saskatchewan, Canada
218 G 3 **South Shetland Islands**, U.K.
63 E 22 **South Shetland Trough**, Atlantic Ocean
77 K 15 **South Shields**, United Kingdom
61 N 9 **South Solomon Trench**, Pacific Ocean
115 P 1 **South Spicer Island**, Nunavut, Canada
210 J 13 **South Taranaki Bight**, New Zealand
59 Y 11 **South Tasman Rise**, Indian Ocean
115 P 9 **South Twin Island**, Québec, Canada
76 D 10 **South Uist**, United Kingdom
63 K 26 **South West Bay**, Ascension
211 B 26 **South West Cape**, New Zealand
63 M 26 **South West Point**, St Helena
77 K 22 **Southampton**, United Kingdom
121 W 10 **Southampton**, New York, U.S.A.
115 N 3 **Southampton Island**, Nunavut, Canada
121 W 8 **Southbridge**, Massachusetts, U.S.A.
59 O 10 **Southeast Indian Ridge**, Indian Ocean
61 U 14 **Southeast Pacific Basin**, Pacific Ocean
113 X 9 **Southend**, Saskatchewan, Canada
77 M 21 **Southend-on-Sea**, United Kingdom
191 G 22 **Southern**, Ethiopia
169 G 26 **Southern**, Sri Lanka
192 G 12 **Southern**, Sierra Leone
196 L 10 **Southern**, Botswana
197 R 5 **Southern**, Malawi
197 N 6 **Southern**, Zambia
211 C 22 **Southern Alps**, New Zealand
215 O 10 **Southern Cook Islands**, Cook Islands
208 H 10 **Southern Cross**, Western Australia, Australia
191 A 19 **Southern Darfur**, Sudan
212 B 5 **Southern Highlands**, Papua New Guinea
114 J 6 **Southern Indian Lake**, Manitoba, Canada
114 J 6 **Southern Indian Lake**, Manitoba, Canada
191 E 19 **Southern Kordofan**, Sudan
213 Y 12 **Southern Lau Group**, Fiji
215 R 6 **Southern Line Islands**, Kiribati
59 U 14 **Southern Ocean**, Indian Ocean
77 H 14 **Southern Uplands**, United Kingdom
113 Y 12 **Southey**, Saskatchewan, Canada
211 C 24 **Southland**, New Zealand
77 I 17 **Southport**, United Kingdom
123 V 4 **Southport**, North Carolina, U.S.A.
209 S 15 **Southport**, Tasmania, Australia
58 I 10 **Southwest Indian Ridge**, Indian Ocean
61 P 12 **Southwest Pacific Basin**, Pacific Ocean
212 D 2 **Southwest Point**, Papua New Guinea
91 M 20 **Soverato**, Italy
91 M 19 **Soveria Mannelli**, Italy
99 C 15 **Sovetsk**, Russian Federation
156 J 9 **Sovetskiy**, Russian Federation
197 N 8 **Sowa Pan**, Botswana
197 N 11 **Soweto**, Republic of South Africa
176 J 2 **Sōya-misaki**, Japan
176 J 2 **Sōya-wan**, Japan
125 W 13 **Soyaló**, Mexico
196 F 1 **Soyo**, Angola
99 N 18 **Sozh**, Belarus
96 N 9 **Sozopol**, Bulgaria
83 K 21 **Spa**, Belgium
218 J 6 **Spaatz Island**, Antarctica
167 O 8 **Space Launching Center**, Kazakhstan
81 Q 8 **Spain**, Europe
117 F 16 **Sparks**, Nevada, U.S.A.
123 R 1 **Sparta**, North Carolina, U.S.A.
123 N 2 **Sparta**, Tennessee, U.S.A.
123 Q 3 **Spartanburg**, South Carolina, U.S.A.
97 E 22 **Sparti**, Greece
113 V 14 **Sparwood**, British Columbia, Canada
157 V 15 **Spassk-Dal'niy**, Russian Federation
63 N 26 **Speery Island**, St Helena
127 Y 10 **Speightstown**, Barbados
116 L 11 **Spencer**, Idaho, U.S.A.
118 K 11 **Spencer**, Iowa, U.S.A.
209 O 11 **Spencer Gulf**, South Australia, Australia
211 C 24 **Spencer Peak**, New Zealand
97 F 22 **Spetses**, Greece
97 F 22 **Spetses**, Greece
76 H 10 **Spey**, United Kingdom
87 E 21 **Speyer**, Germany
86 D 9 **Spiekeroog**, Germany
89 W 8 **Spielfeld**, Austria
63 L 21 **Spiess Seamount**, Atlantic Ocean
88 E 9 **Spiez**, Switzerland
97 I 26 **Spili**, Greece
165 S 10 **Spin**, Afghanistan
91 M 16 **Spinazzola**, Italy
210 H 4 **Spirits Bay**, New Zealand
113 X 11 **Spiritwood**, Saskatchewan, Canada
159 T 8 **Spitak**, Armenia
65 U 11 **Spitsbergen**, Svalbard
89 R 8 **Spittal**, Austria
89 V 3 **Spitz**, Austria
94 E 13 **Split**, Croatia
88 I 9 **Splügen**, Switzerland
98 I 13 **Špoģi**, Latvia
116 H 7 **Spokane**, Washington, U.S.A.
90 H 12 **Spoleto**, Italy
120 F 4 **Spooner**, Wisconsin, U.S.A.
116 H 7 **Sprague**, Washington, U.S.A.
94 H 10 **Spreča**, Bosnia and Herzegovina
83 J 21 **Sprimont**, Belgium
123 Q 11 **Spring Hill**, Florida, U.S.A.
196 J 13 **Springbok**, Republic of South Africa
115 X 10 **Springdale**, Newfoundland and Labrador, Canada
120 L 12 **Springdale**, Ohio, U.S.A.
119 F 16 **Springer**, New Mexico, U.S.A.
119 G 16 **Springfield**, Colorado, U.S.A.
119 M 15 **Springfield**, Missouri, U.S.A.
120 G 11 **Springfield**, Illinois, U.S.A.
120 M 11 **Springfield**, Ohio, U.S.A.
121 V 8 **Springfield**, Massachusetts, U.S.A.
121 V 7 **Springfield**, Vermont, U.S.A.
122 L 1 **Springfield**, Tennessee, U.S.A.
211 G 18 **Springs Junction**, New Zealand
209 U 7 **Springsure**, Queensland, Australia
121 Q 12 **Spruce Knob**, West Virginia, U.S.A.
117 K 15 **Spruce Mountain**, Nevada, U.S.A.
83 G 15 **Sprundel**, Netherlands
77 L 17 **Spurn Head**, United Kingdom
211 I 18 **Spy Glass Point**, New Zealand
113 S 14 **Squamish**, British Columbia, Canada
94 J 8 **Srbobran**, Serbia and Montenegro
173 K 22 **Srê Âmbel**, Cambodia
157 Y 9 **Sredinnyy Khrebet**, Russian Federation
96 M 6 **Sredishte**, Bulgaria
157 W 8 **Srednekolymsk**, Russian Federation
96 H 9 **Srednogorie**, Bulgaria
92 G 13 **Śrem**, Poland
157 S 13 **Sretensk**, Russian Federation
174 J 10 **Sri Aman**, Malaysia
169 F 25 **Sri Jayewardenepura Kotte**, Sri Lanka
169 H 23 **Sri Lanka**, Asia
169 I 18 **Srikakulam**, India
168 D 7 **Srinagar**, India
92 G 13 **Środa Wielkopolska**, Poland
86 G 10 **Stade**, Germany
85 A 16 **Stadlandet**, Norway
82 N 7 **Stadskanaal**, Netherlands
77 J 19 **Stafford**, United Kingdom
89 S 6 **Stainach**, Austria
89 V 8 **Stainz**, Austria
101 Y 6 **Stakhanov**, Ukraine
89 Q 8 **Stall**, Austria
93 M 16 **Stalowa Wola**, Poland
119 I 19 **Stamford**, Texas, U.S.A.
121 V 10 **Stamford**, Connecticut, U.S.A.
196 J 10 **Stampriet**, Namibia
88 L 7 **Stams**, Austria
197 O 11 **Standerton**, Republic of South Africa
120 M 7 **Standish**, Michigan, U.S.A.
197 P 12 **Stanger**, Republic of South Africa
101 R 9 **Stanislav**, Ukraine
145 L 24 **Stanley**, Falkland Islands
116 J 11 **Stanley**, Idaho, U.S.A.
157 S 12 **Stanovoy Khrebet**, Russian Federation
157 R 12 **Stanovoye Nagor'ye**, Russian Federation
209 V 9 **Stanthorpe**, Queensland, Australia
82 L 9 **Staphorst**, Netherlands
93 L 19 **Stará-Lubovna**, Slovakia
96 J 9 **Stara Zagora**, Bulgaria
96 J 9 **Stara-Zagora**, Bulgaria
93 L 15 **Starachowice**, Poland
215 Q 5 **Starbuck Island**, Kiribati
92 E 10 **Stargard-Szczeciński**, Poland
123 Q 9 **Starke**, Florida, U.S.A.
122 J 4 **Starkville**, Mississippi, U.S.A.
87 I 25 **Starnberger See**, Germany
96 N 8 **Staro Oryakhovo**, Bulgaria
101 Y 5 **Starobil's'k**, Ukraine
92 I 9 **Starogard Gdański**, Poland
100 M 4 **Starokostyantyniv**, Ukraine
101 V 5 **Starovirivka**, Ukraine
77 H 24 **Start Point**, United Kingdom
101 V 12 **Staryy Krym**, Ukraine
156 L 9 **Staryy Nadym**, Russian Federation
156 E 9 **Staryy Oskol**, Russian Federation
101 W 4 **Staryy Saltiv**, Ukraine
99 K 19 **Staryya Darohi**, Belarus
93 L 16 **Staszów**, Poland
121 R 10 **State College**, Pennsylvania, U.S.A.
123 Q 6 **Statesboro**, Georgia, U.S.A.
123 R 2 **Statesville**, North Carolina, U.S.A.
65 R 10 **Station Nord**, Greenland
121 Q 13 **Staunton**, Virginia, U.S.A.
85 A 20 **Stavanger**, Norway
211 F 20 **Staveley**, New Zealand
83 E 15 **Stavenisse**, Netherlands
156 E 11 **Stavropol'**, Russian Federation
97 G 14 **Stavros**, Greece
92 M 10 **Stawiski**, Poland
92 H 13 **Stawiszyn**, Poland
118 E 13 **Steamboat Springs**, Colorado, U.S.A.
120 L 15 **Stearns**, Kentucky, U.S.A.
112 H 5 **Stebbins**, Alaska, U.S.A.
218 J 5 **Steele Island**, Antarctica
113 T 9 **Steen River**, Alberta, Canada
83 F 15 **Steenbergen**, Netherlands
82 K 9 **Steenwijk**, Netherlands
208 E 8 **Steep Point**, Western Australia, Australia
113 T 1 **Stefansson Island**, Nunavut, Canada
89 X 7 **Stegersbach**, Austria
100 G 9 **Ştei**, Romania
89 V 7 **Steiermark**, Austria
114 I 10 **Steinbach**, Manitoba, Canada
83 K 25 **Steinfort**, Luxembourg
87 D 14 **Steinfurt**, Germany
196 J 13 **Steinkopf**, Republic of South Africa
83 E 14 **Stellendam**, Netherlands
79 T 3 **Stenay**, France
86 K 13 **Stendal**, Germany
98 D 10 **Stende**, Latvia
97 F 25 **Steno Antikythiro**, Greece
97 F 23 **Steno Elafonisou**, Greece
97 M 24 **Steno Karpathou**, Greece
100 L 2 **Stepan'**, Ukraine
115 X 10 **Stephenville**, Newfoundland and Labrador, Canada
119 J 20 **Stephenville**, Texas, U.S.A.
167 S 3 **Stepnogorsk**, Kazakhstan
94 K 11 **Stepojevac**, Serbia and Montenegro
97 F 19 **Sterea Ellas**, Greece
118 G 13 **Sterling**, Colorado, U.S.A.
120 G 9 **Sterling**, Illinois, U.S.A.
120 M 8 **Sterling Heights**, Michigan, U.S.A.
156 H 10 **Sterlitamak**, Russian Federation
113 V 12 **Stettler**, Alberta, Canada
121 O 11 **Steubenville**, Ohio, U.S.A.
77 L 20 **Stevenage**, United Kingdom
120 H 6 **Stevens Point**, Wisconsin, U.S.A.
112 L 5 **Stevens Village**, Alaska, U.S.A.
122 M 3 **Stevenson**, Alabama, U.S.A.
113 P 11 **Stewart**, Alaska, U.S.A.
211 C 26 **Stewart Island**, New Zealand
89 T 4 **Steyr**, Austria
82 K 6 **Stiens**, Netherlands
119 J 16 **Stillwater**, Oklahoma, U.S.A.
117 G 16 **Stillwater Range**, Nevada, U.S.A.
94 G 12 **Štilt**, Bosnia and Herzegovina
96 E 11 **Štip**, Macedonia (F.Y.R.O.M.)
76 H 12 **Stirling**, United Kingdom
84 J 6 **Stjernøya**, Norway
87 F 25 **Stockach**, Germany
89 X 3 **Stockerau**, Austria
85 H 21 **Stockholm**, Sweden
77 J 18 **Stockport**, United Kingdom
63 I 15 **Stocks Seamount**, Atlantic Ocean
117 E 18 **Stockton**, California, U.S.A.
92 M 13 **Stoczek**, Poland
93 B 18 **Stod**, Czech Republic
173 M 19 **Stœng Trêng**, Cambodia
77 J 18 **Stoke-on-Trent**, United Kingdom
94 N 11 **Stol**, Serbia and Montenegro
156 L 5 **Stolbovoy**, Russian Federation
99 I 21 **Stolin**, Belarus
63 O 16 **Stoltenhoff Island**, Tristan da Cunha
115 P 13 **Stonecliffe**, Ontario, Canada
76 J 11 **Stonehaven**, United Kingdom
113 W 8 **Stony Rapids**, Saskatchewan, Canada
63 O 16 **Stonyhill Point**, Tristan da Cunha
84 I 12 **Storavan**, Sweden
85 A 19 **Stord**, Norway
85 C 25 **Store Baelt**, Denmark
85 D 15 **Støren**, Norway
84 G 11 **Storjord**, Norway
113 T 1 **Storkerson Peninsula**, Nunavut, Canada
85 E 15 **Storlien**, Norway
118 K 11 **Storm Lake**, Iowa, U.S.A.
76 F 8 **Stornoway**, United Kingdom
100 K 7 **Storozhynets'**, Ukraine
85 F 15 **Storsjön**, Sweden
82 H 6 **Stortemelk**, Netherlands
84 H 13 **Storuman**, Sweden
84 H 13 **Storuman**, Sweden
77 M 20 **Stour**, United Kingdom
114 J 9 **Stout Lake**, Ontario, Canada
99 I 18 **Stowbtsy**, Belarus
77 D 15 **Strabane**, United Kingdom
209 S 15 **Strahan**, Tasmania, Australia
83 J 25 **Straimont**, Belgium
115 X 9 **Strait of Belle Isle**, Newfoundland and Labrador, Canada
91 C 15 **Strait of Bonifacio**, Italy
77 N 22 **Strait of Dover**, France/United Kingdom
113 R 14 **Strait of Georgia**, British Columbia, Canada
80 K 15 **Strait of Gibraltar**, Africa/Europe
163 X 4 **Strait of Hormuz**, Asia
145 G 25 **Strait of Magellan**, Chile
174 C 7 **Strait of Malacca**, Asia
126 I 3 **Straits of Florida**, North America
93 C 19 **Strakonice**, Czech Republic
86 L 8 **Stralsund**, Germany
77 F 16 **Strangford Lough**, United Kingdom
85 H 20 **Strängnäs**, Sweden
77 G 15 **Stranraer**, United Kingdom
79 X 4 **Strasbourg**, France
89 R 5 **Strasswalchen**, Austria
119 H 16 **Stratford**, Texas, U.S.A.
210 J 13 **Stratford**, New Zealand
77 K 20 **Stratford-upon-Avon**, United Kingdom
209 S 15 **Strathgordon**, Tasmania, Australia
121 X 5 **Stratton**, Maine, U.S.A.
121 V 7 **Stratton Mountain**, Vermont, U.S.A.
87 L 22 **Straubing**, Germany
84 A 9 **Straumnes**, Iceland
209 N 11 **Streaky Bay**, South Australia, Australia
100 G 12 **Strehaia**, Romania
98 G 9 **Strenči**, Latvia
90 C 6 **Stresa**, Italy
91 L 22 **Stretta di Messina**, Italy
116 L 13 **Strevell**, Idaho, U.S.A.
93 B 18 **Stříbro**, Czech Republic
212 A 5 **Strickland**, Papua New Guinea
145 J 16 **Stroeder**, Argentina
91 L 20 **Stromboli**, Italy
76 I 7 **Stromness**, United Kingdom
85 D 21 **Strömstad**, Sweden
85 G 15 **Strömsund**, Sweden
76 I 7 **Stronsay**, United Kingdom
121 T 10 **Stroudsburg**, Pennsylvania, U.S.A.
85 B 24 **Struer**, Denmark
96 B 12 **Struga**, Macedonia (F.Y.R.O.M.)
96 F 11 **Struma**, Bulgaria
96 E 12 **Strumica**, Macedonia (F.Y.R.O.M.)
100 I 5 **Stryy**, Ukraine
93 H 16 **Strzelce Opolskie**, Poland
93 G 16 **Strzelin**, Poland
92 H 12 **Strzelno**, Poland
123 T 12 **Stuart**, Florida, U.S.A.
88 L 7 **Stubaier Alpen**, Austria
219 S 15 **Sturge Island**, Antarctica
120 J 6 **Sturgeon Bay**, Wisconsin, U.S.A.
118 G 10 **Sturgis**, South Dakota, U.S.A.
93 I 22 **Štúrovo**, Slovakia
209 Q 8 **Sturt Stony Desert**, South Australia, Australia
197 N 14 **Stutterheim**, Republic of South Africa
87 F 23 **Stuttgart**, Germany
119 N 17 **Stuttgart**, Arkansas, U.S.A.
84 A 10 **Stykkishólmur**, Iceland
97 E 18 **Stylida**, Greece
100 K 3 **Styr**, Ukraine/Belarus
191 H 14 **Suakin**, Sudan
194 K 12 **Suana**, Democratic Republic of Congo
174 H 9 **Subi Besar**, Indonesia
91 H 14 **Subiaco**, Italy
94 J 7 **Subotica**, Serbia and Montenegro
100 L 8 **Suceava**, Romania
100 K 7 **Suceviţa**, Romania
92 N 10 **Suchowola**, Poland
141 K 21 **Sucre**, Bolivia
138 I 4 **Sucre**, Colombia

Country · Internal administrative region: State/Province/Territory/Dependent territory · Capital city · Mountain range/Undersea ridge · Mountain peak/Volcano/Seamount · Geographic feature · Headland/Point/Cape/Peninsula · Desert · Island/Island group · Antarctic base · Ocean · Sea · Bay/Gulf/Channel/Strait · Lake · Salt pan/Dry/Intermittent lake · River

9 Q 3 **Sucre**, Venezuela
0 C 8 **Sucumbíos**, Ecuador
2 F 11 **Sucunduri**, Brazil
3 T 15 **Sud**, Cameroon
5 P 9 **Sud-Kivu**, Democratic Republic of Congo
3 S 14 **Sud-Ouest**, Cameroon
1 V 12 **Sudak**, Ukraine
1 B 19 **Sudan**, Africa
5 O 13 **Sudbury**, Ontario, Canada
1 D 21 **Sudd**, Sudan
E 8 **Süderoogsand**, Germany
E 16 **Sudeten**, Czech Republic
T 8 **Sueca**, Spain
0 F 8 **Suez**, Egypt
0 F 8 **Suez Canal**, Egypt
1 S 15 **Suffolk**, Virginia, U.S.A.
N 25 **Sugar Loaf Point**, St Helena
0 H 5 **Sugun**, China
1 Q 7 **Suhait**, China
3 Y 6 **Şuḩār**, Oman
1 S 4 **Sühbaatar**, Mongolia
1 Q 2 **Sühbaatar**, Mongolia
I 18 **Suhl**, Germany
F 12 **Šuica**, Bosnia and Herzegovina
71 U 12 **Suichuan**, China
71 S 7 **Suide**, China
69 B 14 **Suigam**, India
71 X 3 **Suihua**, China
71 R 10 **Suining**, China
9 T 4 **Suippes**, France
7 D 20 **Suir**, Republic of Ireland
71 V 6 **Suizhong**, China
71 T 10 **Suizhou**, China
65 U 15 **Sujawal**, Pakistan
74 H 14 **Sukabumi**, Indonesia
74 I 11 **Sukadana**, Indonesia
77 K 14 **Sukagawa**, Japan
74 J 12 **Sukaramai**, Indonesia
75 N 8 **Sukau**, Malaysia
5 M 14 **Sukeva**, Finland
73 G 16 **Sukhothai**, Thailand
65 U 12 **Sukkur**, Pakistan
89 U 10 **Sūknah**, Libya
96 I 8 **Sukses**, Namibia
77 E 21 **Sukumo**, Japan
5 A 17 **Sula**, Norway
01 S 4 **Sula**, Ukraine
75 R 12 **Sulabesi**, Indonesia
65 U 12 **Sulaiman Ranges**, Pakistan
75 O 12 **Sulawesi**, Indonesia
75 N 13 **Sulawesi Selatan**, Indonesia
75 P 12 **Sulawesi Tengah**, Indonesia
75 P 14 **Sulawesi Tenggara**, Indonesia
75 P 10 **Sulawesi Utara**, Indonesia
61 U 4 **Sulaymān Beg**, Iraq
2 E 13 **Sulechów**, Poland
93 R 12 **Suleja**, Nigeria
3 J 15 **Sulejów**, Poland
6 F 12 **Sulingen**, Germany
140 A 12 **Sullana**, Peru
122 K 4 **Sulligent**, Alabama, U.S.A.
119 N 15 **Sullivan**, Missouri, U.S.A.
96 L 11 **Süloğlu**, Turkey
119 K 18 **Sulphur**, Oklahoma, U.S.A.
115 N 12 **Sultan**, Ontario, Canada
189 W 8 **Sultan**, Libya
158 I 11 **Sultanhani**, Turkey
168 H 12 **Sultanpur**, India
175 O 8 **Sulu Archipelago**, Philippines
175 O 7 **Sulu Sea**, Malaysia/Philippines
158 G 10 **Sülüklü**, Turkey
167 R 12 **Sülüktü**, Kyrgyzstan
189 W 7 **Sulunḩah**, Libya
189 W 7 **Sulūq**, Libya
87 K 20 **Sulzbach-Rosenberg**, Germany
219 N 12 **Sulzberger Bay**, Antarctica
174 D 11 **Sumatera Barat**, Indonesia
174 F 12 **Sumatera Selatan**, Indonesia
174 D 9 **Sumatera Utara**, Indonesia
174 F 10 **Sumatra**, Indonesia
175 N 15 **Sumba**, Indonesia
175 N 14 **Sumbawa**, Indonesia
174 M 15 **Sumbawabesar**, Indonesia
195 R 12 **Sumbawanga**, Tanzania
196 G 4 **Sumbe**, Angola
197 O 2 **Sumbu**, Zambia
76 J 5 **Sumburgh Head**, United Kingdom
164 H 4 **Sume'eh Sarā**, Iran
191 C 20 **Sumeih**, Sudan
174 K 14 **Sumenep**, Indonesia
177 O 22 **Sumiyō**, Japan
161 R 1 **Summēl**, Iraq
123 N 3 **Summerville**, Georgia, U.S.A.
123 S 5 **Summerville**, South Carolina, U.S.A.
113 R 9 **Summit Lake**, British Columbia, Canada
177 G 19 **Sumoto**, Japan
93 G 17 **Šumperk**, Czech Republic
172 F 7 **Sumprabum**, Myanmar
159 Z 8 **Sumqayit**, Azerbaijan
123 S 4 **Sumter**, South Carolina, U.S.A.
101 U 3 **Sumy**, Ukraine
117 H 23 **Sun City**, California, U.S.A.
176 J 5 **Sunagawa**, Japan
163 X 6 **Şunaynah**, Oman
144 K 10 **Sunchales**, Argentina
171 Y 8 **Sunch'ŏn**, South Korea
59 S 3 **Sunda Shelf**, Indian Ocean
174 G 13 **Sunda Strait**, Indonesia
118 F 10 **Sundance**, Wyoming, U.S.A.
77 K 15 **Sunderland**, United Kingdom
158 F 9 **Sündiken Dağlari**, Turkey
85 H 17 **Sundsvall**, Sweden
195 W 10 **Sunga**, Tanzania
174 D 8 **Sungai Petani**, Malaysia
174 E 11 **Sungaidareh**, Indonesia
174 E 11 **Sungaipenuh**, Indonesia
194 I 8 **Sungu**, Democratic Republic of Congo
158 J 9 **Sungurlu**, Turkey
138 H 6 **Sunia**, Colombia
85 E 20 **Sunne**, Sweden
116 F 8 **Sunnyside**, Washington, U.S.A.
117 D 18 **Sunnyvale**, California, U.S.A.
209 W 8 **Sunshine Coast**, Queensland, Australia
157 S 11 **Suntar**, Russian Federation
165 P 14 **Suntsar**, Pakistan
171 X 2 **Sunwu**, China
192 L 12 **Sunyani**, Ghana
177 C 20 **Suō-nada**, Japan
84 N 13 **Suomussalmi**, Finland
173 L 21 **Suŏng**, Cambodia
156 G 6 **Suoyarvi**, Russian Federation
117 N 23 **Superior**, Arizona, U.S.A.
120 F 3 **Superior**, Wisconsin, U.S.A.
159 R 10 **Süphan Dağt**, Turkey
175 W 11 **Supiori**, Indonesia
161 X 11 **Sūq ash Shuyūkh**, Iraq
171 V 9 **Suqian**, China
163 Z 7 **Şūr**, Oman
159 Z 7 **Şuraabad**, Azerbaijan
165 S 12 **Surab**, Pakistan
174 K 14 **Surabaya**, Indonesia
174 J 14 **Surakarta**, Indonesia
169 C 15 **Surat**, India
209 U 8 **Surat**, Queensland, Australia
173 G 23 **Surat Thani**, Thailand
168 C 10 **Suratgarh**, India
99 M 14 **Surazh**, Belarus
161 U 3 **Sūrdāsh**, Iraq
100 M 12 **Surdila-Greci**, Romania
95 N 15 **Surdulica**, Serbia and Montenegro
169 B 15 **Surendranagar**, India
209 W 9 **Surfers Paradise**, Queensland, Australia
126 J 4 **Surgidero de Batabanó**, Cuba
156 L 10 **Surgut**, Russian Federation
169 F 18 **Suriapet**, India
175 Q 6 **Surigao**, Philippines
173 K 18 **Surin**, Thailand
139 V 7 **Suriname**, South America
168 G 11 **Surkhet**, Nepal
167 Q 14 **Surkhondaryo Wiloyati**, Uzbekistan
159 O 8 **Sürmene**, Turkey
88 F 7 **Sursee**, Switzerland
84 B 12 **Surtsey**, Iceland
159 N 13 **Sürüş**, Turkey
177 J 17 **Suruga-wan**, Japan
174 E 12 **Surulangun**, Indonesia
159 W 9 **Şuşa**, Azerbaijan
90 A 7 **Susa**, Italy
177 C 19 **Susa**, Japan
95 E 15 **Sušac**, Croatia
94 B 11 **Susak**, Croatia
177 E 21 **Susaki**, Japan
177 G 20 **Susami**, Japan
164 G 8 **Süsangerd**, Iran
117 F 15 **Susanville**, California, U.S.A.
88 J 8 **Susch**, Switzerland
159 N 9 **Suşehri**, Turkey
173 G 25 **Suso**, Thailand
144 I 5 **Susques**, Argentina
113 Q 11 **Sustut Peak**, British Columbia, Canada
157 W 9 **Susuman**, Russian Federation
170 M 3 **Sutay Uul**, Mongolia
196 K 14 **Sutherland**, Republic of South Africa
165 W 11 **Sutlej**, Pakistan
121 P 13 **Sutton**, West Virginia, U.S.A.
115 N 8 **Sutton Ridges**, Ontario, Canada
176 I 6 **Suttsu**, Japan
171 Q 3 **Süüj**, Mongolia
98 H 9 **Suur Munamägi**, Estonia
167 U 11 **Suusamyr**, Kyrgyzstan
213 X 12 **Suva**, Fiji
101 O 11 **Suvorove**, Ukraine
92 N 8 **Suwałki**, Poland
173 K 17 **Suwannaphum**, Thailand
177 B 26 **Suwanose-jima**, Japan
215 N 8 **Suwarrow**, Cook Islands
160 G 9 **Suwaylih**, Jordan
171 X 7 **Suwon**, South Korea
167 R 9 **Suzak**, Kazakhstan
177 I 15 **Suzaka**, Japan
171 W 10 **Suzhou**, China
171 V 9 **Suzhou**, China
177 H 14 **Suzu**, Japan
177 H 14 **Suzu-misaki**, Japan
177 H 18 **Suzuka**, Japan
65 S 10 **Svalbard**, Norway
85 F 26 **Svaneke**, Denmark
84 J 10 **Svappavaara**, Sweden
84 J 12 **Svartlå**, Sweden
101 Y 5 **Svatove**, Ukraine
173 M 21 **Svay Rieng**, Cambodia
98 G 13 **Svėdasai**, Lithuania
85 F 17 **Sveg**, Sweden
99 C 14 **Švėkšna**, Lithuania
85 C 26 **Svendborg**, Denmark
85 F 16 **Svenstavik**, Sweden
101 Z 6 **Sverdlovs'k**, Ukraine
96 E 11 **Sveti Nikole**, Macedonia (F.Y.R.O.M.)
157 W 14 **Svetlaya**, Russian Federation
99 A 15 **Svetlyy**, Russian Federation
84 C 11 **Sviahnúkar**, Iceland
93 M 19 **Svidnik**, Slovakia
96 K 11 **Svilengrad**, Bulgaria
99 H 15 **Svir**, Belarus
96 J 7 **Svishtov**, Bulgaria
99 F 19 **Svislach**, Belarus
93 F 18 **Svitavy**, Czech Republic
157 U 13 **Svobodnyy**, Russian Federation
96 G 8 **Svoge**, Bulgaria
94 N 13 **Svrljig**, Serbia and Montenegro
99 L 20 **Svyetlahorsk**, Belarus
87 F 24 **Swabian Alp**, Germany
214 K 7 **Swains**, American Samoa
123 Q 6 **Swainsboro**, Georgia, U.S.A.
196 H 9 **Swakopmund**, Namibia
213 Q 7 **Swallow Islands**, Solomon Islands
209 R 12 **Swan Hill**, Victoria, Australia
114 H 9 **Swan River**, Manitoba, Canada
77 J 23 **Swanage**, United Kingdom
123 W 2 **Swanquarter**, North Carolina, U.S.A.
77 H 21 **Swansea**, United Kingdom
209 V 11 **Swansea**, New South Wales, Australia
209 T 15 **Swansea**, Tasmania, Australia
92 G 12 **Swarzędz**, Poland
197 P 11 **Swaziland**, Africa
85 F 22 **Sweden**, Europe
119 I 19 **Sweetwater**, Texas, U.S.A.
123 O 2 **Sweetwater**, Tennessee, U.S.A.
196 K 15 **Swellendam**, Republic of South Africa
93 N 15 **Świdnik**, Poland
92 E 9 **Świdwin**, Poland
92 E 13 **Świebodzin**, Poland
92 I 10 **Świecie**, Poland
113 X 13 **Swift Current**, Saskatchewan, Canada
77 K 21 **Swindon**, United Kingdom
92 D 9 **Świnoujście**, Poland
88 B 8 **Switzerland**, Europe
99 L 15 **Syanno**, Belarus
93 H 15 **Syców**, Poland
115 X 12 **Sydney**, Nova Scotia, Canada
209 V 11 **Sydney**, New South Wales, Australia
101 Y 5 **Syeverodonets'k**, Ukraine
86 F 12 **Syke**, Germany
156 I 8 **Syktyvkar**, Russian Federation
122 M 5 **Sylacauga**, Alabama, U.S.A.
168 M 13 **Sylhet**, Bangladesh
86 E 7 **Sylt**, Germany
123 R 6 **Sylvania**, Georgia, U.S.A.
123 O 7 **Sylvester**, Georgia, U.S.A.
97 N 23 **Symi**, Greece
101 V 6 **Synel'nykove**, Ukraine
85 C 18 **Synnfjell**, Norway
219 U 2 **Syowa**, Antarctica
91 L 23 **Syracuse**, Italy
119 H 15 **Syracuse**, Kansas, U.S.A.
121 S 8 **Syracuse**, New York, U.S.A.
167 Q 10 **Syrdar'ya**, Kazakhstan
160 K 4 **Syria**, Asia
173 D 16 **Syriam**, Myanmar
160 K 8 **Syrian Desert**, Jordan
97 L 24 **Syrna**, Greece
97 I 21 **Syros**, Greece
85 N 15 **Syväri**, Finland
156 G 10 **Syzran'**, Russian Federation
92 F 12 **Szamotuły**, Poland
92 D 10 **Szczecin**, Poland
92 F 9 **Szczecinek**, Poland
93 J 16 **Szczekociny**, Poland
92 M 10 **Szczuczyn**, Poland
92 L 10 **Szczytno**, Poland
93 K 25 **Szeged**, Hungary
93 L 24 **Szeghalom**, Hungary
93 I 23 **Székesfehervár**, Hungary
93 I 25 **Szekszárd**, Hungary
93 K 24 **Szentes**, Hungary
93 H 26 **Szentőrinc**, Hungary
93 L 21 **Szerencs**, Hungary
93 K 23 **Szolnok**, Hungary
93 F 23 **Szombathely**, Hungary
93 E 14 **Szprotawa**, Poland
92 H 11 **Szubin**, Poland

T

172 F 12 **Ta-Kaw**, Myanmar
172 I 11 **Ta Loung San**, Laos
175 P 4 **Tabaco**, Philippines
212 H 3 **Tabar Islands**, Papua New Guinea
164 M 8 **Ţabas**, Iran
125 V 12 **Tabasco**, Mexico
164 M 10 **Tabāsīn**, Iran
142 B 11 **Tabatinga**, Brazil
188 J 10 **Tabelbala**, Algeria
113 W 13 **Taber**, Alberta, Canada
195 P 7 **Tabili**, Democratic Republic of Congo
214 E 3 **Tabiteuea**, Kiribati
175 O 4 **Tablas**, Philippines
119 M 16 **Table Rock Lake**, Missouri, U.S.A.
93 D 19 **Tábor**, Czech Republic
195 S 11 **Tabora**, Tanzania
195 S 11 **Tabora**, Tanzania
167 R 12 **Taboshar**, Tajikistan
192 I 14 **Tabou**, Côte d'Ivoire
164 G 4 **Tabrīz**, Iran
215 P 1 **Tabuaeran**, Kiribati
212 A 4 **Tabubil**, Papua New Guinea
162 K 3 **Tabūk**, Saudi Arabia
170 J 3 **Tacheng**, China
138 K 5 **Tachira**, Venezuela
175 Q 5 **Tacloban**, Philippines
141 H 20 **Tacna**, Peru
138 L 11 **Tacna**, Colombia
141 H 20 **Tacna**, Peru
144 J 6 **Taco Pozo**, Argentina
116 E 7 **Tacoma**, Washington, U.S.A.
144 N 11 **Tacuarembo**, Uruguay
144 N 11 **Tacuarembó**, Uruguay
213 Q 14 **Tadine**, New Caledonia
189 N 12 **Tadjmout**, Algeria
191 K 19 **Tadjoura**, Djibouti
188 M 7 **Tadjrouna**, Algeria
169 E 20 **Tadpatri**, India
171 Y 7 **Taegu**, South Korea
171 Y 7 **Taejŏn**, South Korea
81 R 3 **Tafalla**, Spain
144 I 7 **Tafi Viejo**, Argentina
188 F 9 **Tafraoute**, Morocco
164 K 9 **Taft**, Iran
169 O 24 **Tafwap**, India
215 U 15 **Taga**, Samoa
191 E 14 **Tagab**, Sudan
192 H 6 **Tagant**, Mauritania
177 C 21 **Tagawa**, Japan
175 Q 6 **Tagbilaran**, Philippines
188 K 9 **Taghit**, Algeria
113 O 9 **Tagish Lake**, Canada
167 O 15 **Tagtabazar**, Turkmenistan
143 K 14 **Taguatinga**, Brazil
212 H 8 **Tagula**, Papua New Guinea
212 H 8 **Tagula Island**, Papua New Guinea
175 Q 7 **Tagum**, Philippines
62 K 9 **Tagus Abyssal Plain**, Atlantic Ocean
215 S 9 **Tahaa**, French Polynesia
215 V 9 **Tahanea**, French Polynesia
171 W 1 **Tahe**, China
215 Z 8 **Tahiti**, French Polynesia
117 F 16 **Tahoe City**, California, U.S.A.
116 C 7 **Taholah**, Washington, U.S.A.
210 K 12 **Tahora**, New Zealand
193 Q 8 **Tahoua**, Niger
193 Q 8 **Tahoua**, Niger
161 V 9 **Taḩrīr**, Iraq
164 M 11 **Tahrūd**, Iran
190 E 10 **Tahta**, Egypt
158 K 13 **Tahtali Dağlari**, Turkey
141 I 16 **Tahuamanu**, Bolivia
215 X 6 **Tahuatu**, French Polynesia
175 Q 9 **Tahulandang**, Indonesia
175 Q 9 **Tahuna**, Indonesia
210 L 9 **Tahuna**, New Zealand
192 I 13 **Taï**, Côte d'Ivoire
171 U 8 **Tai'an**, China
171 X 13 **T'aichung**, Taiwan
211 E 24 **Taieri**, New Zealand
97 E 22 **Taigetos**, Greece
210 L 13 **Taihape**, New Zealand
173 D 16 **Taikkyi**, Myanmar
209 Q 12 **Tailem Bend**, South Australia, Australia
76 H 9 **Tain**, United Kingdom
171 W 13 **T'ainan**, Taiwan
215 X 6 **Taiohae**, French Polynesia
171 X 12 **Taipei**, Taiwan
174 D 8 **Taiping**, Malaysia
177 B 26 **Taira-jima**, Japan
210 L 9 **Tairua**, New Zealand
164 E 6 **Tairuq**, Iran
174 E 13 **Tais**, Indonesia
171 X 13 **T'aitung**, Taiwan
84 M 12 **Taivalkoski**, Finland
171 X 13 **Taiwan**, Asia
171 W 13 **Taiwan Strait**, Asia
171 T 7 **Taiyuan**, China
171 W 11 **Taizhou**, China
171 W 9 **Taizhou**, China
163 P 14 **Ta'izz**, Yemen
189 T 12 **Tajarḩī**, Libya
167 S 13 **Tajikistan**, Asia
177 K 14 **Tajima**, Japan
124 I 3 **Tajitos**, Mexico
80 L 7 **Tajo**, Spain
173 G 16 **Tak**, Thailand
164 G 5 **Takāb**, Iran
195 X 6 **Takabba**, Kenya
211 I 15 **Takaka**, New Zealand
177 F 19 **Takamatsu**, Japan
177 D 23 **Takanabe**, Japan
177 H 15 **Takaoka**, Japan
215 U 8 **Takapoto**, French Polynesia
210 J 8 **Takapuna**, New Zealand
177 B 26 **Takara-jima**, Japan
215 U 8 **Takaroa**, French Polynesia
177 J 15 **Takasaki**, Japan
196 M 10 **Takatokwane**, Botswana
177 G 18 **Takatsuki**, Japan
177 E 21 **Takatsuki-yama**, Japan
177 H 16 **Takayama**, Japan
177 C 25 **Take-shima**, Japan
177 G 17 **Takefu**, Japan
174 B 8 **Takengon**, Indonesia
177 B 21 **Takeo**, Japan
164 H 5 **Tākestān**, Iran
177 C 22 **Taketa**, Japan
173 L 22 **Takêv**, Cambodia
165 V 6 **Takhār**, Afghanistan
165 S 10 **Takhta Pul Post**, Afghanistan
176 J 5 **Takikawa**, Japan
176 K 4 **Takinoue**, Japan
212 G 3 **Takis**, Papua New Guinea
113 Q 11 **Takla Lake**, British Columbia, Canada
170 H 6 **Taklimakan Desert**, China
192 M 14 **Takoradi**, Ghana
157 R 12 **Taksimo**, Russian Federation
173 F 24 **Takua Pa**, Thailand
193 S 12 **Takum**, Nigeria
215 W 9 **Takume**, French Polynesia
215 P 10 **Takutea**, Cook Islands
212 K 4 **Takuu Islands**, Papua New Guinea
144 H 10 **Talacasto**, Argentina
99 L 16 **Talachyn**, Belarus
165 W 8 **Talagang**, Pakistan
169 F 23 **Talaimannar**, Sri Lanka
174 G 12 **Talangbatu**, Indonesia
140 A 11 **Talara**, Peru
167 T 10 **Talas**, Kyrgyzstan
212 F 4 **Talasea**, Papua New Guinea
167 T 11 **Talasskaya Oblast'**, Kyrgyzstan
80 M 7 **Talavera de la Reina**, Spain
144 F 13 **Talca**, Chile
145 E 14 **Talcahuano**, Chile
169 J 16 **Talcher**, India
167 W 8 **Taldykorgan**, Kazakhstan
167 V 10 **Talgar**, Kazakhstan
191 E 22 **Tali Post**, Sudan
175 Q 11 **Taliabu**, Indonesia
169 D 19 **Talikota**, India
167 P 13 **Talimardzhan**, Uzbekistan
159 W 10 **Talish Mountains**, Azerbaijan
174 L 15 **Taliwang**, Indonesia
161 Q 2 **Tall 'Afar**, Iraq
160 K 1 **Tall al Aḩmar**, Syria
161 W 11 **Tall al Laḩm**, Iraq
161 O 1 **Tall Baydar**, Syria
160 J 7 **Tall Ghāb**, Syria
161 Q 2 **Tall Ḩuqnah**, Iraq
161 R 2 **Tall Kayf**, Iraq
161 Q 1 **Tall Kūjik**, Syria
160 L 7 **Tall Salāh**, Jordan
161 N 1 **Tall Tamir**, Syria
161 Q 1 **Tall 'Uwaynāt**, Iraq
123 O 8 **Tallahassee**, Florida, U.S.A.
98 F 5 **Tallinn**, Estonia
100 I 11 **Tălmaciu**, Romania
188 G 8 **Talmest**, Morocco
101 P 6 **Tal'ne**, Ukraine
191 E 19 **Talodi**, Sudan
165 V 5 **Tāloqān**, Afghanistan
171 O 4 **Talshand**, Mongolia
98 D 10 **Talsi**, Latvia
144 F 7 **Taltal**, Chile
175 P 10 **Taludaa**, Indonesia
174 E 11 **Taluk**, Indonesia
173 O 17 **Tam Ky**, Vietnam
192 M 11 **Tamale**, Ghana
214 E 3 **Tamana**, Kiribati
188 F 8 **Tamanar**, Morocco
189 T 11 **Tamanhint**, Libya
189 O 14 **Tamanrasset**, Algeria
172 D 8 **Tamanthi**, Myanmar
77 H 23 **Tamar**, United Kingdom
93 H 25 **Tamási**, Hungary
125 R 9 **Tamaulipas**, Mexico
125 R 10 **Tamazunchale**, Mexico
192 F 9 **Tambacounda**, Senegal
174 H 10 **Tambelan Besar**, Indonesia
156 M 7 **Tambey**, Russian Federation
141 G 20 **Tambo**, Peru
209 T 7 **Tambo**, Queensland, Australia
140 A 12 **Tambo Grande**, Peru
197 W 7 **Tambohorano**, Madgascar
195 N 4 **Tamboura**, Central African Republic
156 F 9 **Tambov**, Russian Federation
191 C 22 **Tambura**, Sudan

Country · Internal administrative region: State/Province/Territory/Dependent territory · Capital city · Mountain range/Undersea ridge · Mountain peak/Volcano/Seamount · Geographic feature · Headland/Point/Cape/Peninsula · Desert · Island/Island group · Antarctic base · Ocean · Sea · Bay/Gulf/Channel/Strait · Lake · Salt pan/Dry/Intermittent lake · River

192 H 7 **Tâmchekket**, Mauritania
169 F 22 **Tamil Nadu**, India ▣
88 I 8 **Tamins**, Switzerland
94 L 10 **Tamiš**, Serbia and Montenegro ∿
85 L 20 **Tammisaari**, Finland
123 Q 11 **Tampa**, Florida, U.S.A.
123 P 12 **Tampa Bay**, Florida, U.S.A. ≈
85 L 17 **Tampere**, Finland
125 S 10 **Tampico**, Mexico
163 Q 9 **Tamrah**, Saudi Arabia
140 F 11 **Tamshiyacu**, Peru
89 S 7 **Tamsweg**, Austria
209 U 10 **Tamworth**, New South Wales, Australia
173 M 22 **Tân An**, Vietnam
188 E 10 **Tan-Tan**, Morocco
84 M 6 **Tana Bru**, Norway
177 G 20 **Tanabe**, Japan
174 C 11 **Tanahbala**, Indonesia ⛱
174 M 11 **Tanahgrogot**, Indonesia
175 O 14 **Tanahjampea**, Indonesia ⛱
174 C 11 **Tanahmasa**, Indonesia ⛱
208 M 5 **Tanami Desert**, Northern Territory, Australia ◭
112 K 5 **Tanana**, Alaska, U.S.A.
168 H 12 **Tanda**, India
192 L 12 **Tanda**, Côte d'Ivoire
175 R 6 **Tandag**, Philippines
100 M 12 **Tăndărei**, Romania
145 L 14 **Tandil**, Argentina
193 W 11 **Tandjilé**, Chad ▣
165 U 14 **Tando Adam**, Pakistan
177 C 25 **Tanega-shima**, Japan ⛱
93 N 16 **Tanew**, Poland ∿
188 K 15 **Tanezrouft**, Algeria ⛰
195 W 11 **Tanga**, Tanzania ▣
195 W 11 **Tanga**, Tanzania
212 H 3 **Tanga Islands**, Papua New Guinea ⛱
170 K 9 **Tanggula Shan**, China ⛰
188 I 6 **Tangier**, Morocco
177 F 17 **Tango**, Japan
210 N 13 **Tangoio**, New Zealand
170 J 9 **Tangra Yumco**, China ◣
174 B 8 **Tangse**, Indonesia
171 V 6 **Tangshan**, China
197 V 9 **Tanjona Ankaboa**, Madgascar ▶
197 Z 4 **Tanjona Bobaomby**, Madgascar ▶
197 Z 6 **Tanjona Masoala**, Madgascar ▶
197 W 6 **Tanjona Vilanandro**, Madgascar ▶
197 W 11 **Tanjona Vohimena**, Madgascar ▶
174 L 11 **Tanjung**, Indonesia
175 O 10 **Tanjung Arus**, Indonesia ▶
174 J 14 **Tanjung Bugel**, Indonesia ▶
174 F 13 **Tanjung Cina**, Indonesia ▶
175 X 11 **Tanjung d'Urville**, Indonesia ▶
174 G 14 **Tanjung Guhakolak**, Indonesia ▶
175 O 10 **Tanjung Kandi**, Indonesia ▶
175 O 13 **Tanjung Koku**, Indonesia ▶
174 L 13 **Tanjung Layar**, Indonesia ▶
175 S 11 **Tanjung Libobo**, Indonesia ▶
174 G 12 **Tanjung Lumut**, Indonesia ▶
175 N 10 **Tanjung Mangkalihat**, Indonesia ▶
174 L 15 **Tanjung Mebulu**, Indonesia ▶
174 I 10 **Tanjung Munggguresak**, Indonesia ▶
175 R 12 **Tanjung Palpetu**, Indonesia ▶
174 J 12 **Tanjung Puting**, Indonesia ▶
174 I 12 **Tanjung Sambar**, Indonesia ▶
174 L 13 **Tanjung Selatan**, Indonesia ▶
174 J 9 **Tanjung Sirik**, Malaysia ▶
175 S 9 **Tanjung Sopi**, Indonesia ▶
175 X 15 **Tanjung Vals**, Indonesia ▶
175 R 12 **Tanjung Waka**, Indonesia ▶
174 H 12 **Tanjungpandan**, Indonesia
174 F 10 **Tanjungpinang**, Indonesia
174 L 9 **Tanjungredeb**, Indonesia
174 M 9 **Tanjungselor**, Indonesia
165 V 9 **Tank**, Pakistan
168 F 7 **Tankse**, India
213 R 12 **Tanna**, Vanuatu ⛱
193 S 8 **Tanout**, Niger
190 E 8 **Tanta**, Egypt
160 F 8 **Tantura**, Israel
195 S 11 **Tanzania**, Africa □
91 L 21 **Taormina**, Italy
119 F 16 **Taos**, New Mexico, U.S.A.
192 L 4 **Taoudenni**, Mali
188 I 6 **Taounate**, Morocco
188 J 6 **Taourirt**, Morocco
188 J 9 **Taouz**, Morocco
171 X 12 **T'aoyüan**, Taiwan
98 H 6 **Tapa**, Estonia
125 W 15 **Tapachula**, Mexico
142 G 11 **Tapajós**, Brazil ∿
174 C 9 **Tapaktuan**, Indonesia
174 D 12 **Tapan**, Indonesia
211 D 24 **Tapanui**, New Zealand
142 C 12 **Tapauá**, Brazil ∿
142 E 12 **Tapauá**, Brazil
192 H 13 **Tapeta**, Liberia
145 G 23 **Tapi Aike**, Argentina
80 K 1 **Tapia de Casariego**, Spain
93 G 24 **Tapolca**, Hungary
121 S 13 **Tappahannock**, Virginia, U.S.A.
176 J 8 **Tappi-zaki**, Japan ▶
161 T 3 **Ţaqţaq**, Iraq
143 G 17 **Taquari**, Brazil ∿
193 T 12 **Taraba**, Nigeria ▣
161 W 9 **Tarād al Kahf**, Iraq
210 M 13 **Taradale**, New Zealand
189 T 11 **Tarāghin**, Libya
174 M 9 **Tarakan**, Indonesia
177 N 26 **Tarana-jima**, Japan ⛱
210 J 12 **Taranaki**, New Zealand ▣
81 P 7 **Tarancón**, Spain
76 E 9 **Taransay**, United Kingdom ⛱
91 N 17 **Taranto**, Italy
144 G 3 **Tarapacá**, Chile ▣
138 M 12 **Tarapacá**, Colombia
140 D 13 **Tarapoto**, Peru
142 B 9 **Taraquá**, Brazil
79 T 9 **Tarare**, France
101 P 5 **Tarashcha**, Ukraine
189 Q 12 **Tarat**, Algeria
141 H 20 **Tarata**, Peru
142 B 13 **Tarauacá**, Brazil ∿
142 B 13 **Tarauacá**, Brazil
215 Z 8 **Taravao**, French Polynesia
214 D 2 **Tarawa**, Kiribati ⛱
210 M 12 **Tarawera**, New Zealand
167 S 10 **Taraz**, Kazakhstan
81 R 4 **Tarazona**, Spain
167 X 6 **Tarbagatay**, Kazakhstan
76 H 9 **Tarbat Ness**, United Kingdom ▶
165 X 7 **Tarbela Reservoir**, Pakistan ◣
76 E 9 **Tarbert**, United Kingdom
76 F 13 **Tarbert**, United Kingdom
77 B 19 **Tarbert**, Republic of Ireland
79 N 14 **Tarbes**, France
94 H 12 **Tarčin**, Bosnia and Herzegovina
209 O 10 **Tarcoola**, South Australia, Australia
209 V 11 **Taree**, New South Wales, Australia
157 O 7 **Tareya**, Russian Federation
188 D 10 **Tarfaya**, Morocco
100 J 12 **Târgovişte**, Romania
100 H 11 **Târgu Jiu**, Romania
100 J 9 **Târgu Mureş**, Romania
100 K 10 **Târgu Secuiesc**, Romania
189 S 8 **Tarhūnah**, Libya
163 W 6 **Tarif**, United Arab Emirates
80 L 14 **Tarifa**, Spain
141 K 23 **Tarija**, Bolivia ▣
141 K 23 **Tarija**, Bolivia ∿
141 K 23 **Tarija**, Bolivia
170 I 6 **Tarim Basin**, China ◇
170 I 5 **Tarim He**, China ∿
195 T 8 **Tarime**, Tanzania
165 S 8 **Tarīn Kowt**, Afghanistan
175 X 12 **Taritatu**, Indonesia ∿
156 M 9 **Tarko-Sale**, Russian Federation
192 L 14 **Tarkwa**, Ghana
175 O 3 **Tarlac**, Philippines
93 M 16 **Tarnobrzeg**, Poland
93 N 16 **Tarnogród**, Poland
93 L 17 **Tarnów**, Poland
85 H 19 **Tärnsjö**, Sweden
164 L 12 **Ţārom**, Iran
209 U 8 **Taroom**, Queensland, Australia
188 G 9 **Taroudannt**, Morocco
123 P 11 **Tarpon Springs**, Florida, U.S.A.
127 N 3 **Tarpum Bay**, The Bahamas
90 G 13 **Tarquinia**, Italy
209 N 4 **Tarrabool Lake**, Northern Territory, Australia ⚑
81 V 5 **Tarragona**, Spain
193 X 5 **Tarso Emissi**, Chad ▲
158 J 13 **Tarsus**, Turkey
144 J 5 **Tartagal**, Argentina
98 I 8 **Tartu**, Estonia
160 H 4 **Ţarţūs**, Syria
176 J 6 **Tarumae-san**, Japan ▲
177 C 24 **Tarumizu**, Japan
174 C 9 **Tarutung**, Indonesia
101 O 10 **Tarutyne**, Ukraine
90 I 5 **Tarvisio**, Italy
157 T 10 **Tas-Tumas**, Russian Federation
167 P 9 **Tasbuget**, Kazakhstan
167 T 11 **Tash-Kömür**, Kyrgyzstan
159 T 7 **Tashir**, Armenia
167 R 11 **Tashkent**, Uzbekistan ⌂
167 N 15 **Tashkepri**, Turkmenistan
174 E 8 **Tasik Kenyir**, Malaysia ◣
115 R 6 **Tasiujaq**, Québec, Canada
65 O 11 **Tasiusaq**, Greenland
193 T 8 **Tasker**, Niger
167 X 6 **Taskesken**, Kazakhstan
158 J 7 **Taşköprü**, Turkey
212 G 2 **Taskul**, Papua New Guinea
159 S 10 **Taşliçay**, Turkey
211 H 16 **Tasman**, New Zealand ▣
61 N 12 **Tasman Basin**, Pacific Ocean ◇
211 I 15 **Tasman Bay**, New Zealand ≈
209 T 15 **Tasman Peninsula**, Tasmania, Australia ▶
61 N 11 **Tasman Sea**, Pacific Ocean ◗
209 R 15 **Tasmania**, Australia, Australia ▣
158 L 8 **Taşova**, Turkey
193 Q 7 **Tassara**, Niger
189 N 15 **Tassili du Hoggar**, Algeria ◇
189 O 11 **Tassili n'Ajjer**, Algeria ◇
142 L 13 **Tasso Fragoso**, Brazil
93 I 22 **Tata**, Hungary
188 G 9 **Tata**, Morocco
93 I 22 **Tatabánya**, Hungary
215 X 9 **Tatakoto**, French Polynesia ⛱
189 Q 7 **Tataouine**, Tunisia
101 O 11 **Tatarbunary**, Ukraine
156 L 12 **Tatarsk**, Russian Federation
157 W 13 **Tatarskiy Proliv**, Russian Federation ≈
174 K 9 **Tatau**, Malaysia
177 L 17 **Tateyama**, Japan
113 T 8 **Tathlina Lake**, Northwest Territories, Canada ◣
163 O 9 **Tathlīth**, Saudi Arabia
172 D 13 **Tatkon**, Myanmar
113 R 13 **Tatla Lake**, British Columbia, Canada
158 I 15 **Tatlisu**, Cyprus
93 J 19 **Tatra Mountains**, Slovakia ⛰
165 U 15 **Tatta**, Pakistan
167 T 10 **Tatti**, Kazakhstan
119 G 19 **Tatum**, New Mexico, U.S.A.
159 R 11 **Tatvan**, Turkey
215 Y 15 **Tau**, American Samoa ⛱
142 N 12 **Taua**, Brazil
143 K 19 **Taubaté**, Brazil
166 H 9 **Tauchik**, Kazakhstan
215 W 9 **Tauere**, French Polynesia ⛱
87 F 18 **Taufstein**, Germany ▲
210 K 12 **Taumarunui**, New Zealand
172 E 12 **Taunggyi**, Myanmar
172 F 11 **Taunglau**, Myanmar
172 D 12 **Taungtha**, Myanmar
173 C 14 **Taunqup**, Myanmar
165 V 10 **Taunsa**, Pakistan
77 I 22 **Taunton**, United Kingdom
87 D 19 **Taunus**, Germany ◇
210 K 10 **Taupiri**, New Zealand
210 M 11 **Taupo**, New Zealand
99 C 14 **Tauragė**, Lithuania
210 M 10 **Tauranga**, New Zealand
91 M 21 **Taurianova**, Italy
210 H 5 **Tauroa Point**, New Zealand ▶
158 F 13 **Taurus Mountains**, Turkey ⛰
81 S 4 **Tauste**, Spain
61 Y 15 **Tautama**, Pitcairn Island ▶
215 Z 8 **Tautira**, French Polynesia
157 X 10 **Tauyskaya Guba**, Russian Federation ≈
158 D 12 **Tavas**, Turkey
156 J 10 **Tavda**, Russian Federation
81 T 9 **Tavernes de la Valldigna**, Spain
213 Y 11 **Taveuni**, Fiji ⛱
80 I 12 **Tavira**, Portugal
77 H 23 **Tavistock**, United Kingdom
173 F 19 **Tavoy**, Myanmar
173 F 19 **Tavoy Point**, Myanmar ▶
158 E 9 **Tavşanli**, Turkey
169 E 15 **Tawa Reservoir**, India ◣
120 M 7 **Tawas City**, Michigan, U.S.A.
174 M 8 **Tawau**, Malaysia
175 N 8 **Tawitawi**, Philippines ⛱
125 Q 12 **Taxco**, Mexico
170 G 6 **Taxkorgan**, China
76 H 12 **Tay**, United Kingdom ∿
173 M 21 **Tây Ninh**, Vietnam
191 L 23 **Tayeeglow**, Somalia
171 O 4 **Taygan**, Mongolia
118 I 12 **Taylor**, Nebraska, U.S.A.
162 L 4 **Taymā'**, Saudi Arabia
166 I 5 **Taypak**, Kazakhstan
157 O 12 **Tayshet**, Russian Federation
175 N 5 **Taytay**, Philippines
165 O 7 **Tayyebād**, Iran
167 R 2 **Tayynsha**, Kazakhstan
157 N 8 **Taz**, Russian Federation ∿
188 J 7 **Taza**, Morocco
161 T 4 **Tāza Khurmātū**, Iraq
188 H 9 **Tazenakht**, Morocco
113 V 8 **Tazin Lake**, Saskatchewan, Canada ◣
189 X 11 **Tāzirbū**, Libya
156 M 8 **Tazovskiy**, Russian Federation
188 H 9 **Tazzarine**, Morocco
188 J 8 **Tazzouguert**, Morocco
159 U 7 **T'Bilisi**, Georgia ⌂
193 T 12 **Tchabal Mbabo**, Cameroon ▲
194 E 9 **Tchibanga**, Gabon
193 Q 8 **Tchin-Tabaradene**, Niger
193 V 12 **Tcholliré**, Cameroon
92 I 9 **Tczew**, Poland
211 B 24 **Te Anau**, New Zealand
210 O 10 **Te Araroa**, New Zealand
210 N 10 **Te Kaha**, New Zealand
210 H 4 **Te Kao**, New Zealand
210 O 12 **Te Kapu**, New Zealand ▲
210 O 11 **Te Karaka**, New Zealand
211 L 17 **Te Kaukau Point**, New Zealand ▶
210 K 11 **Te Kuiti**, New Zealand
210 M 12 **Te Pohue**, New Zealand
210 M 10 **Te Puke**, New Zealand
210 I 6 **Te Raupa**, New Zealand ▲
210 N 10 **Te Teko**, New Zealand
211 B 25 **Te Waewae**, New Zealand
211 A 25 **Te Waewae Bay**, New Zealand ≈
124 M 9 **Teacapán**, Mexico
215 Z 8 **Teahupoo**, French Polynesia
125 W 13 **Teapa**, Mexico
175 X 11 **Teba**, Indonesia
189 P 6 **Tébessa**, Algeria
159 U 6 **Tebulos Mt'a**, Georgia ▲
124 F 2 **Tecate**, Mexico
192 L 12 **Techiman**, Ghana
101 N 13 **Techirghiol**, Romania
97 C 17 **Techniti Limni Kremaston**, Greece ◣
145 G 18 **Tecka**, Argentina
125 N 12 **Tecomán**, Mexico
124 J 5 **Tecoripa**, Mexico
125 Q 13 **Técpan**, Mexico
100 M 11 **Tecuci**, Romania
191 L 23 **Ted**, Somalia
166 M 14 **Tedzhen**, Turkmenistan
117 O 19 **Teec Nos Pas**, Arizona, U.S.A.
157 N 14 **Teeli**, Russian Federation
77 J 16 **Tees**, United Kingdom ∿
142 D 11 **Tefé**, Brazil
174 I 14 **Tegal**, Indonesia
83 L 16 **Tegelen**, Netherlands
193 Q 11 **Tegina**, Nigeria
213 Q 9 **Tégua**, Vanuatu ⛱
126 F 10 **Tegucigalpa**, Honduras ⌂
164 I 5 **Tehrān**, Iran ▣
164 I 6 **Tehran**, Iran ⌂
125 S 12 **Tehuacán**, Mexico
215 W 9 **Tehuata**, French Polynesia ⛱
191 B 16 **Teiga Plateau**, Sudan ◇
100 H 10 **Teiuş**, Romania
167 W 8 **Tekeli**, Kazakhstan
167 X 10 **Tekes**, Kazakhstan
170 H 7 **Tekilitag**, China ▲
96 N 13 **Tekirdağ**, Turkey ▣
96 M 13 **Tekirdağ**, Turkey
175 P 11 **Teku**, Indonesia
160 E 9 **Tel Aviv-Jaffa**, Israel
126 F 9 **Tela**, Honduras
188 K 6 **Télagh**, Algeria
193 O 8 **Télataï**, Mali
159 U 6 **T'elavi**, Georgia
125 Y 10 **Telchac Puerto**, Mexico
100 I 8 **Telciu**, Romania
62 N 12 **Telde**, Canary Islands
212 A 4 **Telefomin**, Papua New Guinea
101 N 8 **Teleneşti**, Moldova
142 G 13 **Teles Pires**, Brazil ∿
117 H 20 **Telescope Peak**, California, U.S.A. ▲
208 I 6 **Telfer**, Western Australia, Australia
77 J 19 **Telford**, United Kingdom
88 L 7 **Telfs**, Austria
112 H 4 **Teller**, Alaska, U.S.A.
161 W 10 **Telloh**, Iraq
119 D 15 **Telluride**, Colorado, U.S.A.
101 Y 8 **Tel'manove**, Ukraine
145 I 17 **Telsen**, Argentina
98 C 13 **Telšiai**, Lithuania
174 D 9 **Teluk Anson**, Malaysia
175 U 12 **Teluk Beru**, Indonesia ≈
175 O 12 **Teluk Bone**, Indonesia ≈
175 W 12 **Teluk Cenderawasih**, Indonesia ≈
174 I 9 **Teluk Datu**, Malaysia ≈
175 V 12 **Teluk Kamrau**, Indonesia ≈
174 J 12 **Teluk Kumai**, Indonesia ≈
174 G 14 **Teluk Palabuhanratu**, Indonesia ≈
175 O 11 **Teluk Poso**, Indonesia ≈
174 K 12 **Teluk Sampit**, Indonesia ≈
174 I 11 **Teluk Sukadana**, Indonesia ≈
175 O 11 **Teluk Tomini**, Indonesia ≈
174 I 11 **Telukbatang**, Indonesia
174 C 10 **Telukdalam**, Indonesia
193 N 13 **Tema**, Ghana
215 W 11 **Tematangi**, French Polynesia ⛱
175 W 13 **Tembagapura**, Indonesia
174 F 11 **Tembilahan**, Indonesia
197 O 11 **Tembisa**, Republic of South Africa
81 O 8 **Tembleque**, Spain
196 H 2 **Tembo Aluma**, Angola
117 H 23 **Temecula**, California, U.S.A.
192 M 7 **Téméra**, Mali
94 K 9 **Temerin**, Serbia and Montenegro
174 E 9 **Temerloh**, Malaysia
167 T 5 **Temirtau**, Kazakhstan
209 T 12 **Temora**, New South Wales, Australia
124 L 4 **Temósachic**, Mexico
213 Q 7 **Temotu**, Solomon Islands ▣
117 M 23 **Tempe**, Arizona, U.S.A.
119 K 20 **Temple**, Texas, U.S.A.
196 I 5 **Tempué**, Angola
101 X11 **Temryukskiy Zaliv**, Ukraine ≈
145 F 15 **Temuco**, Chile
211 F 21 **Temuka**, New Zealand
169 M 23 **Ten Degree Channel**, India ≈
123 R 14 **Ten Thousand Islands**, Florida, U.S.A. ⛱
140 C 9 **Tena**, Ecuador
192 K 11 **Téna Kourou**, Burkina Faso ▲
169 G 19 **Tenali**, India
215 Y 11 **Tenararo**, French Polynesia ⛱
173 F 20 **Tenasserim**, Myanmar ▣
191 J 19 **Tendaho**, Ethiopia
191 E 18 **Tendelti**, Sudan
176 K 12 **Tendō**, Japan
116 K 10 **Tendoy**, Idaho, U.S.A.
188 K 7 **Tendrara**, Morocco
192 K 9 **Ténenkou**, Mali
193 T 5 **Ténéré du Tafassâsset**, Niger ◇
62 M 12 **Tenerife**, Canary Islands ⛱
188 L 5 **Ténès**, Algeria
192 J 11 **Tengréla**, Côte d'Ivoire
123 P 9 **Tenille**, Florida, U.S.A.
195 O 14 **Tenke**, Democratic Republic of Congo
209 O 5 **Tennant Creek**, Northern Territory, Australia
122 L 2 **Tennessee**, U.S.A. ▣
122 K 2 **Tennessee**, Tennessee, U.S.A. ∿
83 J 23 **Tenneville**, Belgium
84 M 10 **Tenniöjoki**, Finland ∿
84 L 7 **Tenojoki**, Finland ∿
125 X 13 **Tenosique**, Mexico
177 I 17 **Tenryū**, Japan ∿
177 I 17 **Tenryū**, Japan
209 V 9 **Tenterfield**, New South Wales, Australia
143 M 17 **Teófilo Otôni**, Brazil
175 T 14 **Tepa**, Indonesia
125 O 11 **Tepatitlán**, Mexico
95 K 21 **Tepelenë**, Albania
124 M 10 **Tepic**, Mexico
93 C 16 **Teplice**, Czech Republic
215 W 8 **Tepoto**, French Polynesia ⛱
125 N 11 **Tequila**, Mexico
82 O 8 **Ter Apel**, Netherlands
193 N 9 **Téra**, Niger
215 O 1 **Teraina**, Kiribati ⛱
90 I 12 **Teramo**, Italy
82 M 13 **Terborg-Silvolde**, Netherlands
159 P 9 **Tercan**, Turkey
62 O 1 **Terceira**, Azores ⛱
100 G 11 **Teregova**, Romania
167 Z 5 **Terekty**, Kazakhstan
174 F 8 **Terengganu**, Malaysia ▣
167 P 9 **Terenozek**, Kazakhstan
142 M 11 **Teresina**, Brazil
92 O 13 **Terespol**, Poland
169 N 24 **Teressa Island**, India ⛱
79 R 3 **Tergnier**, France
119 F 22 **Terlingua**, Texas, U.S.A.
158 M 8 **Terme**, Turkey
167 Q 14 **Termez**, Uzbekistan
91 I 21 **Termini Imerese**, Italy
193 T 8 **Termit-Kaoboul**, Niger
175 R 10 **Ternate**, Indonesia
83 E 16 **Terneuzen**, Netherlands
90 H 13 **Terni**, Italy
101 P 6 **Ternivka**, Ukraine
100 K 5 **Ternopil'**, Ukraine
101 T 2 **Terny**, Ukraine
196 L 11 **Terra Firma**, Republic of South Africa
219 R 13 **Terra Nova Bay**, Antarctica ⠿
113 Q 12 **Terrace**, British Columbia, Canada
114 M 12 **Terrace Bay**, Ontario, Canada
91 H 15 **Terracina**, Italy
84 E 13 **Terråk**, Norway
91 B 18 **Terralba**, Italy
120 I 12 **Terre Haute**, Indiana, U.S.A.
116 L 11 **Terreton**, Idaho, U.S.A.
118 F 8 **Terry**, Montana, U.S.A.
122 H 6 **Terry**, Mississippi, U.S.A.
82 I 5 **Terschelling**, Netherlands ⛱
167 V 11 **Terskey Ala-Too**, Kyrgyzstan ⛰
91 D 18 **Tertenia**, Italy
81 S 7 **Teruel**, Spain
173 G 26 **Terutao**, Thailand ⛱
96 M 6 **Tervel**, Bulgaria
191 H 17 **Teseney**, Eritrea
176 M 4 **Teshikaga**, Japan
176 J 3 **Teshio**, Japan ∿
176 J 3 **Teshio**, Japan
176 J 3 **Teshio-sanchi**, Japan ⛰
113 O 9 **Teslin Lake**, British Columbia, Canada ◣
188 L 15 **Tessalit**, Algeria
193 N 6 **Tessalit**, Mali
193 R 9 **Tessaoua**, Niger
86 K 9 **Tessin**, Germany
197 Q 5 **Tete**, Mozambique ▣
197 R 6 **Tete**, Mozambique
113 T 12 **Tête Jaune Cache**, British Columbia, Canada
212 K 6 **Tetepare**, Solomon Islands ⛱
101 P 3 **Teteriv**, Ukraine ∿
86 K 9 **Teterow**, Germany
215 T 9 **Tetiaroa**, French Polynesia ⛱
81 Q 12 **Tetica de Becares**, Spain ▲
101 O 5 **Tetiyiv**, Ukraine
118 C 11 **Teton Range**, Wyoming, U.S.A. ⛰
188 I 6 **Tétouan**, Morocco

□ Country ▣ Internal administrative region: State/Province/Territory/Dependent territory ⌂ Capital city ⛰ Mountain range/Undersea ridge ▲ Mountain peak/Volcano/Seamount ◇ Geographic feature ▶ Headland/Point/Cape/Peninsula ◭ Desert ⛱ Island/Island group ⠿ Antarctic base ◎ Ocean ◗ Sea ≈ Bay/Gulf/Channel/Strait ◣ Lake ⚑ Salt pan/Dry/Intermittent lake ∿ River

96	C 10	**Tetovo**, Macedonia (F.Y.R.O.M.)
215	Z 8	**Tetufera**, French Polynesia ▲
177	B 24	**Teuchi**, Japan
175	S 14	**Teun**, Indonesia ⁂
176	J 4	**Teuri-tō**, Japan ⁂
171	P 9	**Tēwo**, China
119	L 18	**Texarkana**, Texas, U.S.A.
119	H 20	**Texas**, U.S.A. ▣
209	V 9	**Texas**, Queensland, Australia
82	H 7	**Texel**, Netherlands ⁂
168	N 12	**Tezpur**, India
168	O 11	**Tezu**, India
188	F 11	**Tfaritiy**, Western Sahara
173	K 18	**Tha Tum**, Thailand
197	O 12	**Thabana-Ntlenyana**, Lesotho ▲
197	N 10	**Thabazimbi**, Republic of South Africa
172	M 12	**Thai Binh**, Vietnam
172	L 11	**Thai Nguyên**, Vietnam
173	G 17	**Thailand**, Asia □
165	V 8	**Thal**, Pakistan
173	H 25	**Thale Luang**, Thailand ◣
209	U 9	**Thallon**, Queensland, Australia
163	W 11	**Thamarīt**, Oman
77	K 21	**Thames**, United Kingdom ∫
210	L 9	**Thames**, New Zealand
173	F 23	**Than Kyun**, Myanmar ⁂
173	F 17	**Thanbyuzayat**, Myanmar
169	B 17	**Thane**, India
172	M 13	**Thanh Hoa**, Vietnam
169	F 22	**Thanjavur**, India
173	G 21	**Thap Sakae**, Thailand
165	U 13	**Thar Desert**, Pakistan ◠
209	S 9	**Thargomindah**, Queensland, Australia
161	R 6	**Tharthar**, Iraq/Pakistan
163	W 7	**Tharwānīyyah**, United Arab Emirates
97	I 14	**Thasos**, Greece ⁂
96	I 13	**Thasos**, Greece
173	E 16	**Thaton**, Myanmar
173	F 20	**Thayawthadangyi Kyun**, Myanmar ⁂
173	C 14	**Thayetmyo**, Myanmar
190	E 11	**The Great Oasis**, Egypt ◇
82	F 12	**The Hague**, Netherlands ■
211	E 21	**The Hunters Hills**, New Zealand ⛰
114	H 8	**The Pas**, Manitoba, Canada
63	L 26	**The Peak**, Ascension ▲
127	X 10	**The Pitons**, St Lucia ▲
172	F 7	**The Triangle**, Myanmar ◇
127	W 7	**The Valley**, Anguilla ■
118	H 12	**Thedford**, Nebraska, U.S.A.
173	F 21	**Theinkun**, Myanmar
117	N 23	**Theodore Roosevelt Lake**, Arizona, U.S.A. ◣
97	F 15	**Thermaïkos Kolpos**, Greece ≈
97	E 18	**Thermopyles**, Greece
113	Q 2	**Thesiger Bay**, Northwest Territories, Canada ≈
97	E 17	**Thessalia**, Greece ▣
97	F 14	**Thessaloniki**, Greece
77	M 19	**Thetford**, United Kingdom
118	K 7	**Thief River Falls**, Minnesota, U.S.A.
79	R 10	**Thiers**, France
192	D 8	**Thiès**, Senegal
195	V 8	**Thika**, Kenya
169	L 16	**Thiladhunmathee Atoll**, Maldives ⁂
168	L 12	**Thimphu**, Bhutan ■
213	P 14	**Thio**, New Caledonia
79	V 3	**Thionville**, France
97	J 24	**Thira**, Greece ⁂
97	J 23	**Thira**, Greece
97	J 23	**Thirasia**, Greece ⁂
77	K 16	**Thirsk**, United Kingdom
85	B 23	**Thisted**, Denmark
97	G 19	**Thiva**, Greece
79	O 10	**Thiviers**, France
173	G 15	**Thoen**, Thailand
172	H 13	**Thoeng**, Thailand
197	P 9	**Thohoyandou**, Republic of South Africa
121	Q 12	**Thomas**, West Virginia, U.S.A.
123	O 5	**Thomaston**, Georgia, U.S.A.
122	K 6	**Thomasville**, Alabama, U.S.A.
123	O 8	**Thomasville**, Georgia, U.S.A.
83	L 22	**Thommen**, Belgium
114	J 7	**Thompson**, Manitoba, Canada
117	O 17	**Thompson**, Utah, U.S.A.
118	A 7	**Thompson Falls**, Montana, U.S.A.
209	R 7	**Thomson**, Queensland, Australia ∫
123	Q 5	**Thomson**, Georgia, U.S.A.
79	V 9	**Thonon-les-Bains**, France
77	H 14	**Thornhill**, United Kingdom
219	R 2	**Thorshavnheiane**, Antarctica ⛰
78	M 8	**Thouars**, France
117	K 14	**Thousand Springs**, Nevada, U.S.A.
97	I 14	**Thrakiko Pelagos**, Greece ◒
118	C 9	**Three Forks**, Montana, U.S.A.
171	R 10	**Three Gorges Dam**, China ◣
209	S 14	**Three Hummock Island**, Tasmania, Australia ⁂
210	G 3	**Three Kings Islands**, New Zealand ⁂
173	F 18	**Three Pagodas Pass**, Thailand ◇
119	J 22	**Three Rivers**, Texas, U.S.A.
120	K 9	**Three Rivers**, Michigan, U.S.A.
119	I 19	**Throckmorton**, Texas, U.S.A.
173	M 21	**Thu Dâu Môt**, Vietnam
83	F 21	**Thuin**, Belgium
65	P 9	**Thule**, Greenland
197	O 9	**Thuli**, Zimbabwe
88	E 8	**Thun**, Switzerland
114	L 12	**Thunder Bay**, Ontario, Canada
88	E 8	**Thuner See**, Switzerland ◣
173	G 24	**Thung Song**, Thailand
87	J 17	**Thüringen**, Germany ▣
87	H 17	**Thüringer Wald**, Germany ◇
77	D 19	**Thurles**, Republic of Ireland
209	R 1	**Thursday Island**, Queensland, Australia ⁂
76	H 8	**Thurso**, United Kingdom
218	J 9	**Thurston Island**, Antarctica ⁂
88	I 9	**Thusis**, Switzerland
209	N 6	**Ti Tree**, Northern Territory, Australia
170	H 5	**Tian Shan**, China ⛰
171	R 13	**Tian'e**, China
171	U 7	**Tianjin**, China
171	U 7	**Tianjin Shi**, China ▣
171	O 8	**Tianjun**, China
171	R 13	**Tianlin**, China
171	Q 9	**Tianshui**, China
171	R 13	**Tianyang**, China
188	L 6	**Tiaret**, Algeria
213	O 13	**Tiari**, New Caledonia
192	K 13	**Tiassalé**, Côte d'Ivoire
193	U 13	**Tibati**, Cameroon
160	G 8	**Tiberias**, Israel
193	W 5	**Tibesti**, Chad ⛰
170	J 8	**Tibet**, China ▣
209	R 9	**Tibooburra**, New South Wales, Australia
192	I 6	**Tichît**, Mauritania
188	C 14	**Tichla**, Western Sahara
88	G 10	**Ticino**, Switzerland ▣
121	U 7	**Ticonderoga**, New York, U.S.A.
125	Y 11	**Ticul**, Mexico
209	S 14	**Tidal River**, Victoria, Australia
172	B 10	**Tiddim**, Myanmar
169	O 24	**Tiden**, India
192	G 6	**Tidjikja**, Mauritania
88	I 9	**Tiefencastel**, Switzerland
82	J 13	**Tiel**, Netherlands
171	X 3	**Tieli**, China
171	W 5	**Tieling**, China
170	I 7	**Tielongtan**, China
172	N 11	**Tiên Yên**, Vietnam
83	H 19	**Tienen**, Belgium
87	E 25	**Tiengen**, Germany
85	H 19	**Tierp**, Sweden
125	R 13	**Tierra Colorada**, Mexico
145	I 25	**Tierra del Fuego**, Argentina ▣
143	J 18	**Tietê**, Brazil ∫
120	M 10	**Tiffin**, Ohio, U.S.A.
175	R 10	**Tifore**, Indonesia ⁂
123	P 7	**Tifton**, Georgia, U.S.A.
175	R 12	**Tifu**, Indonesia
213	Q 13	**Tiga**, New Caledonia ⁂
116	H 6	**Tiger**, Washington, U.S.A.
101	O 9	**Tighina**, Moldova
193	U 12	**Tignère**, Cameroon
115	V 12	**Tignish**, Prince Edward Island, Canada
191	H 17	**Tigray**, Ethiopia ▣
140	D 10	**Tigre**, Peru ∫
159	P 12	**Tigris**, Asia ∫
192	E 7	**Tiguent**, Mauritania
210	L 11	**Tihoi**, New Zealand
189	R 8	**Tījī**, Libya
124	E 1	**Tijuana**, Mexico
215	T 8	**Tikehau**, French Polynesia ⁂
215	V 8	**Tikei**, French Polynesia ⁂
156	G 7	**Tikhvin**, Russian Federation
61	T 9	**Tiki Basin**, Pacific Ocean ◇
210	O 10	**Tikitiki**, New Zealand
213	R 8	**Tikopia**, Solomon Islands ⁂
161	S 5	**Tikrīt**, Iraq
157	S 7	**Tiksi**, Russian Federation
83	I 15	**Tilburg**, Netherlands
144	I 5	**Tilcara**, Argentina
193	P 8	**Tilemsès**, Niger
193	O 9	**Tillabéri**, Niger ▣
193	O 9	**Tillabéri**, Niger
169	O 24	**Tillanchong Island**, India ⁂
113	W 13	**Tilley**, Alberta, Canada
193	P 8	**Tillia**, Niger
122	J 8	**Tillmans Corner**, Alabama, U.S.A.
193	O 8	**Tiloa**, Niger
144	H 5	**Tilomonte**, Chile
97	N 23	**Tilos**, Greece ⁂
189	N 7	**Tilrhemt**, Algeria
190	E 10	**Tima**, Egypt
62	O 11	**Timanfaya**, Canary Islands ▲
159	S 10	**Timar**, Turkey
211	F 22	**Timaru**, New Zealand
119	N 22	**Timbalier Bay**, Louisiana, U.S.A. ≈
192	I 8	**Timbedgha**, Mauritania
208	M 3	**Timber Creek**, Northern Territory, Australia
192	L 7	**Timbuktu**, Mali
192	M 6	**Timétrine**, Mali
193	R 7	**Timia**, Niger
188	L 10	**Timimoun**, Algeria
167	P 2	**Timiryazevo**, Kazakhstan
100	G 11	**Timiș**, Romania ∫
100	F 10	**Timișoara**, Romania
61	X 15	**Timiti's Crack**, Pitcairn Island ▶
115	O 12	**Timmins**, Ontario, Canada
120	H 5	**Timms Hill**, Wisconsin, U.S.A. ▲
215	Z 12	**Timoé**, French Polynesia ⁂
175	Q 15	**Timor**, Indonesia ⁂
59	V 6	**Timor Sea**, Indian Ocean ◒
59	V 6	**Timor Trough**, Indian Ocean ◇
144	K 13	**Timote**, Argentina
188	K 10	**Timoudi**, Algeria
85	H 16	**Timrå**, Sweden
139	N 3	**Tinaco**, Venezuela
160	L 2	**Tinah**, Syria
169	F 21	**Tindivanam**, India
188	G 10	**Tindouf**, Algeria
80	K 1	**Tineo**, Spain
188	I 8	**Tinerhir**, Morocco
188	H 10	**Tinfouchy**, Algeria
141	D 14	**Tingo Maria**, Peru
214	A 8	**Tinian**, Northern Mariana Islands ⁂
144	H 8	**Tinogasta**, Argentina
97	J 21	**Tinos**, Greece ⁂
97	J 21	**Tinos**, Greece
168	O 11	**Tinsukia**, India
113	R 12	**Tintagel**, British Columbia, Canada
192	H 7	**Tintâne**, Mauritania
144	K 7	**Tintina**, Argentina
174	F 9	**Tioman**, Malaysia ⁂
90	E 6	**Tione di Trento**, Italy
114	M 12	**Tip Top Hill**, Ontario, Canada ▲
126	F 11	**Tipitapa**, Nicaragua
77	C 19	**Tipperary**, Republic of Ireland
169	D 21	**Tiptur**, India
125	Q 12	**Tiquicheo**, Mexico
95	K 18	**Tirana**, Albania ■
90	E 5	**Tirano**, Italy
101	O 9	**Tiraspol**, Moldova
210	L 10	**Tirau**, New Zealand
211	L 15	**Tiraumea**, New Zealand
159	N 8	**Tirebolu**, Turkey
76	E 12	**Tiree**, United Kingdom ⁂
192	I 3	**Tiris Zemmour**, Mauritania ▣
88	K 7	**Tirol**, Austria ▣
194	L 2	**Tiroungoulou**, Central African Republic
210	K 11	**Tirua Point**, New Zealand ▶
169	E 24	**Tiruchchendur**, India
169	F 22	**Tiruchchirappalli**, India
169	E 24	**Tirunelveli**, India
169	F 21	**Tirupati**, India
169	E 22	**Tiruppur**, India
169	E 22	**Tiruvannamalai**, India
169	G 21	**Tiruvottiyur**, India
94	K 8	**Tisa**, Serbia and Montenegro ∫
169	E 24	**Tisaiyanvilai**, India
188	M 6	**Tissemsilt**, Algeria
93	L 22	**Tiszafüred**, Hungary
93	L 22	**Tiszaújváros**, Hungary
93	M 21	**Tiszavasvári**, Hungary
189	O 13	**Tit**, Algeria
157	S 7	**Tit-Ary**, Russian Federation
169	H 16	**Titlagarh**, India
94	E 11	**Titov Drvar**, Bosnia and Herzegovina
94	D 10	**Titova Korenica**, Croatia
87	L 24	**Tittmoning**, Germany
100	J 12	**Titu**, Romania
123	S 11	**Titusville**, Florida, U.S.A.
168	C 12	**Tivari**, India
77	I 23	**Tiverton**, United Kingdom
160	K 5	**Tiyās**, Syria
189	N 5	**Tizi Ouzou**, Algeria
125	Z 10	**Tizimín**, Mexico
188	F 9	**Tiznit**, Morocco
82	K 8	**Tjeukemeer**, Netherlands ◣
85	D 22	**Tjörn**, Sweden ⁂
84	E 12	**Tjøtta**, Norway
208	J 8	**Tjukayirla Roadhouse**, Western Australia, Australia
125	T 13	**Tlacolula**, Mexico
125	R 12	**Tlalnepantla**, Mexico
125	R 12	**Tlaxcala**, Mexico ▣
125	S 13	**Tlaxiaco**, Mexico
188	K 6	**Tlemcen**, Algeria
197	N 10	**Tlokweng**, Botswana
189	U 11	**Tmassah**, Libya
192	F 5	**Tmeïmîchât**, Mauritania
177	K 17	**To-shima**, Japan ⁂
197	Y 7	**Toamasina**, Madgascar ▣
197	Z 7	**Toamasina**, Madgascar
215	U 9	**Toau**, French Polynesia ⁂
165	T 10	**Toba and Kakar Ranges**, Pakistan ⛰
127	X 12	**Tobago**, Trinidad and Tobago ⁂
81	R 10	**Tobarra**, Spain
209	P 6	**Tobermorey**, Northern Territory, Australia
76	E 11	**Tobermory**, United Kingdom
113	Y 10	**Tobin Lake**, Saskatchewan, Canada ◣
174	G 12	**Toboali**, Indonesia
167	N 3	**Tobol**, Kazakhstan
156	K 10	**Tobol'sk**, Russian Federation
189	Y 7	**Tobruk**, Libya
143	J 14	**Tocantins**, Brazil ▣
142	J 11	**Tocantins**, Brazil ∫
123	P 3	**Toccoa**, Georgia, U.S.A.
144	G 4	**Toco**, Chile
144	H 5	**Toconao**, Chile
144	F 4	**Tocopilla**, Chile
90	H 12	**Todi**, Italy
176	J 7	**Todohokke**, Japan
124	J 9	**Todos Santos**, Mexico
141	K 19	**Todos Santos**, Bolivia
211	C 26	**Toetoes Bay**, New Zealand ≈
215	R 15	**Tofol**, Federated States of Micronesia
214	I 10	**Tofua**, Tonga ⁂
213	Q 9	**Toga**, Vanuatu ⁂
177	L 16	**Tōgane**, Japan
191	M 20	**Togdheer**, Somalia ▣
177	H 15	**Togi**, Japan
112	G 7	**Togiak**, Alaska, U.S.A.
175	P 11	**Togian**, Indonesia ⁂
193	N 12	**Togo**, Africa □
170	M 3	**Tögrög**, Mongolia
166	M 7	**Toguz**, Kazakhstan
215	Z 8	**Tohiea**, French Polynesia ▲
177	J 17	**Toi**, Japan
177	D 24	**Toi-misaki**, Japan ▶
177	E 18	**Tōjō**, Japan
112	M 6	**Tok**, Alaska, U.S.A.
177	I 18	**Tōkai**, Japan
177	J 14	**Tōkamachi**, Japan
191	H 15	**Tokar**, Sudan
177	B 26	**Tokara-rettō**, Japan ⁂
211	F 23	**Tokarahi**, New Zealand
177	N 25	**Tokasiki-jima**, Japan ⁂
158	L 9	**Tokat**, Turkey
214	J 5	**Tokelau Islands**, New Zealand ▣
210	K 12	**Tokirima**, New Zealand
176	L 5	**Tokkachi**, Japan ∫
101	V 8	**Tokmak**, Ukraine
210	O 11	**Tokomaru Bay**, New Zealand
176	L 4	**Tokoro**, Japan ∫
210	L 11	**Tokoroa**, New Zealand
192	H 11	**Tokounuo**, Guinea
167	T 11	**Toktogul**, Kyrgyzstan
214	I 10	**Toku**, Tonga ⁂
177	N 22	**Toku-no-shima**, Japan ⁂
177	N 22	**Tokunoshima**, Japan
177	F 19	**Tokushima**, Japan
177	D 20	**Tokuyama**, Japan
177	K 16	**Tokyo**, Japan ■
177	K 16	**Tōkyō-wan**, Japan ≈
165	S 6	**Tokzār**, Afghanistan
210	O 11	**Tolaga Bay**, New Zealand
197	X 11	**Tôlanaro**, Madgascar
170	M 3	**Tolbo**, Mongolia
126	I 14	**Tolé**, Panama
167	T 9	**Tole Bi**, Kazakhstan
81	O 7	**Toledo**, Spain
120	M 9	**Toledo**, Ohio, U.S.A.
143	H 19	**Toledo**, Brazil
119	M 20	**Toledo Bend Reservoir**, Louisiana, U.S.A. ◣
170	J 3	**Toli**, China
197	W 9	**Toliara**, Madgascar ▣
197	V 10	**Toliara**, Madgascar
138	H 7	**Tolima**, Colombia ▣
175	O 10	**Tolitoli**, Indonesia
167	U 10	**Tolmak**, Kyrgyzstan
90	H 5	**Tolmezzo**, Italy
94	A 7	**Tolmin**, Slovenia
93	I 25	**Tolna**, Hungary
194	J 9	**Tolo**, Democratic Republic of Congo
81	R 1	**Tolosa**, Spain
125	Q 12	**Toluca**, Mexico
91	M 16	**Tolve**, Italy
156	G 10	**Tol'yatti**, Russian Federation
197	O 9	**Tom Burke**, Republic of South Africa
208	G 6	**Tom Price**, Western Australia, Australia
120	G 6	**Tomah**, Wisconsin, U.S.A.
176	K 6	**Tomakomai**, Japan
176	J 4	**Tomamae**, Japan
167	U 7	**Tomar**, Kazakhstan
158	K 11	**Tomarza**, Turkey
93	O 16	**Tomaszów Lubelski**, Poland
93	K 14	**Tomaszów Mazowiecki**, Poland
124	M 11	**Tomatlán**, Mexico
122	K 6	**Tombigbee**, Alabama, U.S.A. ∫
196	F 1	**Tomboco**, Angola
192	L 7	**Tombouctou**, Mali ▣
117	O 25	**Tombstone**, Arizona, U.S.A.
196	F 6	**Tombua**, Angola
145	F 14	**Tomé**, Chile
175	Q 13	**Tomea**, Indonesia ⁂
81	P 9	**Tomelloso**, Spain
167	Q 9	**Tomenaryk**, Kazakhstan
176	L 13	**Tomioka**, Japan
138	M 6	**Tomo**, Colombia ∫
194	H 6	**Tomori**, Central African Republic
156	M 12	**Tomsk**, Russian Federation
157	V 9	**Tomtor**, Russian Federation
175	U 12	**Tomu**, Indonesia
177	N 25	**Tonaki-jima**, Japan ⁂
125	V 14	**Tonalá**, Mexico
142	C 11	**Tonantins**, Brazil
116	G 5	**Tonasket**, Washington, U.S.A.
121	Q 8	**Tonawanda**, New York, U.S.A.
175	Q 10	**Tondano**, Indonesia
85	B 26	**Tønder**, Denmark
218	K 10	**Toney Mountain**, Antarctica ▲
214	I 9	**Tonga**, Oceania □
61	P 10	**Tonga Trench**, Pacific Ocean ◇
215	P 6	**Tongareva**, Cook Islands ⁂
214	I 11	**Tongatapu**, Tonga ⁂
214	H 12	**Tongatapu Group**, Tonga ⁂
171	R 9	**Tongchuan**, China
171	S 12	**Tongdao**, China
83	J 19	**Tongeren**, Belgium
171	Z 7	**Tonghae**, South Korea
171	X 5	**Tonghua**, China
171	W 5	**Tongliao**, China
213	R 11	**Tongoa**, Vanuatu ⁂
175	O 8	**Tongquil**, Philippines ⁂
171	S 12	**Tongren**, China
171	S 15	**Tongshi**, China
76	H 8	**Tongue**, United Kingdom
171	Q 8	**Tongxin**, China
171	R 11	**Tongzi**, China
124	J 5	**Tónichi**, Mexico
191	D 21	**Tonj**, Sudan
168	D 12	**Tonk**, India
164	I 5	**Tonkābon**, Iran
172	L 11	**Tonkin**, Vietnam ◇
173	K 20	**Tônlé Sab**, Cambodia ◣
79	S 6	**Tonnerre**, France
86	F 8	**Tönning**, Germany
117	H 18	**Tonopah**, Nevada, U.S.A.
126	J 15	**Tonosí**, Panama
85	D 20	**Tønsberg**, Norway
117	L 15	**Tooele**, Utah, U.S.A.
209	V 9	**Toowoomba**, Queensland, Australia
191	O 18	**Tooxin**, Somalia
208	M 3	**Top Springs**, Northern Territory, Australia
119	K 14	**Topeka**, Kansas, U.S.A.
100	J 9	**Toplița**, Romania
62	N 1	**Topo**, Azores
117	K 22	**Topock**, California, U.S.A.
96	C 12	**Topolčani**, Macedonia (F.Y.R.O.M.)
124	K 7	**Topolobampo**, Mexico
96	K 10	**Topolovgrad**, Bulgaria
101	N 3	**Toporyshche**, Ukraine
210	J 7	**Topuni**, New Zealand
158	B 11	**Torbali**, Turkey
165	O 7	**Torbat-e Heydarīyeh**, Iran
165	O 6	**Torbat-e Jām**, Iran
80	M 4	**Tordesillas**, Spain
84	K 12	**Töre**, Sweden
101	Y 7	**Torez**, Ukraine
87	L 15	**Torgau**, Germany
86	N 10	**Torgelow**, Germany
167	O 5	**Torghay**, Kazakhstan
83	B 18	**Torhout**, Belgium
191	E 23	**Torit**, Sudan
84	I 9	**Torneälven**, Sweden ∫
84	I 9	**Torneträsk**, Sweden ◣
84	I 9	**Torneträsk**, Sweden
115	T 5	**Torngat Mountains**, Québec, Canada ⛰
84	K 12	**Tornio**, Finland
145	K 15	**Tornquist**, Argentina
80	M 4	**Toro**, Spain
193	S 11	**Toro**, Nigeria
117	I 23	**Toro Peak**, California, U.S.A. ▲
193	O 9	**Torodi**, Niger
212	J 5	**Torokina**, Papua New Guinea
93	K 23	**Törökszentmiklós**, Hungary
115	P 14	**Toronto**, Ontario, Canada
195	T 7	**Tororo**, Uganda
77	I 23	**Torquay**, United Kingdom
81	N 3	**Torquemada**, Spain
117	G 23	**Torrance**, California, U.S.A.
80	H 10	**Torrão**, Portugal
81	V 3	**Torre de Cadi**, Spain
80	J 5	**Torre de Moncorvo**, Portugal
80	M 13	**Torrecilla**, Spain ▲
81	O 1	**Torrelavega**, Spain
125	O 7	**Torreón**, Mexico
143	J 21	**Torres**, Brazil
213	P 9	**Torres Islands**, Vanuatu ⁂
80	H 8	**Torres Novas**, Portugal
60	L 9	**Torres Strait**, Pacific Ocean ≈
80	G 8	**Torres Vedras**, Portugal
81	T 11	**Torrevieja**, Spain
212	A 3	**Torricelli Mountains**, Papua New Guinea ⛰
90	C 9	**Torriglia**, Italy
118	F 12	**Torrington**, Wyoming, U.S.A.
85	F 14	**Torrön**, Sweden ◣
85	E 19	**Torsby**, Sweden
145	F 14	**Tortel**, Chile
167	T 4	**Tortkuduk**, Kazakhstan
159	Q 9	**Tortum**, Turkey
164	L 6	**Ţorūd**, Iran
159	O 8	**Torul**, Turkey
92	H 11	**Toruń**, Poland
98	H 9	**Tõrva**, Estonia
156	F 7	**Torzhok**, Russian Federation
177	E 20	**Tosa**, Japan

□ Country ▣ Internal administrative region: State/Province/Territory/Dependent territory ■ Capital city ⛰ Mountain range/Undersea ridge ▲ Mountain peak/Volcano/Seamount ◇ Geographic feature ▶ Headland/Point/Cape/Peninsula ◠ Desert ⁂ Island/Island group ⁙ Antarctic base ◌ Ocean ◒ Sea ≈ Bay/Gulf/Channel/Strait ◣ Lake ◤ Salt pan/Dry/Intermittent lake ∫ River

177 F 21 **Tosa-wan**, Japan
177 E 21 **Tosashimizu**, Japan
84 F 13 **Tosbotn**, Norway
196 M 11 **Tosca**, Republic of South Africa
90 F 11 **Toscana**, Italy
167 R 11 **Toshkent Wiloyati**, Uzbekistan
144 K 9 **Tostado**, Argentina
98 F 8 **Tõstamaa**, Estonia
86 G 11 **Tostedt**, Germany
158 J 8 **Tosya**, Turkey
81 R 11 **Totana**, Spain
139 V 6 **Totness**, Suriname
144 F 8 **Totoral**, Chile
213 Y 12 **Totoya**, Fiji
177 F 17 **Tottori**, Japan
192 I 12 **Touba**, Côte d'Ivoire
192 E 8 **Touba**, Senegal
193 V 12 **Touboro**, Cameroon
192 L 9 **Tougan**, Burkina Faso
189 O 7 **Touggourt**, Algeria
192 G 10 **Tougué**, Guinea
213 P 13 **Touho**, New Caledonia
192 H 8 **Touil**, Mauritania
192 H 9 **Toukoto**, Mali
79 U 4 **Toul**, France
79 V 15 **Toulon**, France
79 P 14 **Toulouse**, France
192 J 13 **Toumodi**, Côte d'Ivoire
193 U 12 **Toungo**, Nigeria
173 E 14 **Toungoo**, Myanmar
193 V 9 **Tourba**, Chad
83 C 20 **Tournai**, Belgium
141 E 14 **Tournavista**, Peru
79 T 11 **Tournon-sur-Rhône**, France
79 T 8 **Tournus**, France
142 O 12 **Touros**, Brazil
79 N 7 **Tours**, France
171 Q 3 **Töv**, Mongolia
159 U 7 **Tovuz**, Azerbaijan
176 K 9 **Towada**, Japan
176 K 9 **Towada-ko**, Japan
121 S 9 **Towanda**, Pennsylvania, U.S.A.
209 T 4 **Townsville**, Queensland, Australia
191 G 22 **Towot**, Sudan
121 S 12 **Towson**, Maryland, U.S.A.
176 J 6 **Tōya-ko**, Japan
177 H 15 **Toyama**, Japan
177 H 14 **Toyama-wan**, Japan
156 I 7 **Toyma**, Russian Federation
177 I 18 **Toyohashi**, Japan
177 F 17 **Toyooka**, Japan
177 I 17 **Toyota**, Japan
189 P 7 **Tozeur**, Tunisia
159 S 6 **Tqibuli**, Georgia
159 Q 5 **Tqvarch'eli**, Georgia
173 M 23 **Tra Vinh**, Vietnam
80 K 4 **Trabazos**, Spain
159 O 8 **Trabzon**, Turkey
89 W 4 **Traisen**, Austria
77 B 20 **Tralee**, Republic of Ireland
85 F 22 **Tranås**, Sweden
144 I 7 **Trancas**, Argentina
173 G 25 **Trang**, Thailand
175 V 14 **Trangan**, Indonesia
144 N 10 **Tranqueras**, Uruguay
219 N 7 **Transantarctic Mountains**, Antarctica
58 H 9 **Transkei Basin**, Indian Ocean
100 G 10 **Transylvania**, Romania
100 G 11 **Transylvanian Alps**, Romania
100 H 8 **Transylvanian Basin**, Romania
91 H 21 **Trapani**, Italy
192 F 6 **Trarza**, Mauritania
168 M 12 **Trashigang**, Bhutan
173 J 20 **Trat**, Thailand
89 T 4 **Traun**, Austria
89 S 5 **Traunsee**, Austria
86 I 9 **Travemünde**, Germany
120 K 6 **Travers City**, Michigan, U.S.A.
90 D 8 **Travo**, Italy
212 J 5 **Treasury Islands**, Solomon Islands
93 E 19 **Třebíč**, Czech Republic
95 H 15 **Trebinje**, Bosnia and Herzegovina
93 M 20 **Trebišov**, Slovakia
211 C 22 **Treble Cone**, New Zealand
94 C 8 **Trebnje**, Slovenia
169 B 22 **Tree Island**, India
144 O 11 **Treinta y Tres**, Uruguay
144 O 12 **Treinta y Tres**, Uruguay
145 I 18 **Trelew**, Argentina
85 E 26 **Trelleborg**, Sweden
58 B 15 **Tremblet**, Réunion
120 J 4 **Trenary**, Michigan, U.S.A.
93 H 20 **Trenčín**, Slovakia
144 K 13 **Trenque Lauquen**, Argentina
77 K 18 **Trent**, United Kingdom
90 F 5 **Trentino-Alto Adige**, Italy
90 F 6 **Trento**, Italy
115 Q 14 **Trenton**, Ontario, Canada
121 U 11 **Trenton**, New Jersey, U.S.A.
115 Z 11 **Trepassey**, Newfoundland and Labrador, Canada
145 L 15 **Tres Arroyos**, Argentina
142 E 12 **Três Casas**, Brazil
145 H 21 **Tres Cerros**, Argentina
138 H 9 **Tres Esquinas**, Colombia
143 I 18 **Três Lagoas**, Brazil
145 G 22 **Tres Lagos**, Argentina
125 V 14 **Tres Picos**, Mexico
119 E 16 **Tres Piedras**, New Mexico, U.S.A.
85 D 18 **Tretten**, Norway
90 D 7 **Treviglio**, Italy
90 G 6 **Treviso**, Italy
77 G 23 **Trevose Head**, United Kingdom
95 N 16 **Trgovište**, Serbia and Montenegro
97 M 24 **Tria Nisia**, Greece
119 H 15 **Tribune**, Kansas, U.S.A.
169 D 22 **Trichur**, India
89 T 6 **Trieben**, Austria
87 B 20 **Trier**, Germany
90 I 7 **Trieste**, Italy
94 A 6 **Triglav**, Slovenia
97 D 16 **Trikala**, Greece
169 G 24 **Trincomalee**, Sri Lanka
127 X 12 **Trinidad**, Trinidad and Tobago
119 F 16 **Trinidad**, Colorado, U.S.A.
126 K 5 **Trinidad**, Cuba
141 K 18 **Trinidad**, Bolivia
144 M 12 **Trinidad**, Uruguay
127 Y 12 **Trinidad and Tobago**, North America
115 Z 10 **Trinity Bay**, Newfoundland and Labrador, Canada
112 H 9 **Trinity Islands**, Alaska, U.S.A.
58 B 11 **Triolet**, Mauritius
160 G 5 **Tripoli**, Lebanon
189 S 7 **Tripoli**, Libya
97 E 21 **Tripoli**, Greece
169 M 14 **Tripura**, India
86 F 9 **Trischen**, Germany
63 O 15 **Tristan da Cunha**, Tristan da Cunha
63 N 15 **Tristan da Cunha**, U.K.
63 I 18 **Tristan da Cunha Fracture Zone**, Atlantic Ocean
169 D 24 **Trivandrum**, India
91 K 14 **Trivento**, Italy
93 G 21 **Trnava**, Slovakia
212 G 6 **Trobriand Islands**, Papua New Guinea
167 P 2 **Troebratskây**, Kazakhstan
84 F 12 **Trofors**, Norway
94 E 13 **Trogir**, Croatia
94 E 12 **Troglav**, Bosnia and Herzegovina
94 F 12 **Troglav**, Croatia
91 L 15 **Troia**, Italy
83 K 21 **Trois-Ponts**, Belgium
115 R 13 **Trois-Rivières**, Québec, Canada
156 I 11 **Troitsk**, Russian Federation
85 E 22 **Trollhättan**, Sweden
142 G 9 **Trombetas**, Brazil
197 N 13 **Trompsburg**, Republic of South Africa
84 I 7 **Tromsø**, Norway
85 D 15 **Trondheim**, Norway
85 D 15 **Trondheimsfjorden**, Norway
168 L 12 **Trongsa**, Bhutan
77 G 14 **Troon**, United Kingdom
97 D 20 **Tropaia**, Greece
91 L 20 **Tropea**, Italy
62 J 11 **Tropic Seamount**, Atlantic Ocean
101 U 3 **Trostyanets'**, Ukraine
114 K 10 **Trout Lake**, Ontario, Canada
113 R 8 **Trout Lake**, Northwest Territories, Canada
121 U 8 **Troy**, New York, U.S.A.
122 M 7 **Troy**, Alabama, U.S.A.
117 J 17 **Troy Peak**, Nevada, U.S.A.
96 I 8 **Troyan**, Bulgaria
79 S 5 **Troyes**, France
101 Y 4 **Troyits'ke**, Ukraine
119 F 17 **Truchas Peak**, New Mexico, U.S.A.
117 F 16 **Truckee**, California, U.S.A.
138 L 3 **Trujillo**, Venezuela
80 L 8 **Trujillo**, Spain
126 G 9 **Trujillo**, Honduras
141 B 14 **Trujillo**, Peru
96 E 9 **Trŭn**, Bulgaria
77 G 24 **Truro**, United Kingdom
115 V 13 **Truro**, Nova Scotia, Canada
113 R 10 **Trutch**, British Columbia, Canada
119 D 19 **Truth Or Consequences**, New Mexico, U.S.A.
96 J 9 **Tryavna**, Bulgaria
94 D 10 **Tržac**, Bosnia and Herzegovina
92 F 11 **Trzcianka**, Poland
92 E 12 **Trzciel**, Poland
93 G 15 **Trzebnica**, Poland
94 B 6 **Tržič**, Slovenia
171 U 3 **Tsagaannuur**, Mongolia
84 I 9 **Tsåktso**, Sweden
159 T 7 **Ts'alka**, Georgia
96 N 10 **Tsarevo**, Bulgaria
101 U 6 **Tsarychanka**, Ukraine
171 N 4 **Tseel**, Mongolia
196 J 11 **Tses**, Namibia
196 L 9 **Tsetseng**, Botswana
193 N 13 **Tsévié**, Togo
196 L 11 **Tshabong**, Botswana
196 L 10 **Tshane**, Botswana
194 F 11 **Tshela**, Democratic Republic of Congo
194 L 12 **Tshibala**, Democratic Republic of Congo
194 L 13 **Tshibwika**, Democratic Republic of Congo
194 K 11 **Tshikapa**, Democratic Republic of Congo
195 P 12 **Tshimbo**, Democratic Republic of Congo
197 Q 10 **Tshokwane**, Republic of South Africa
196 K 9 **Tshootsha**, Botswana
113 O 5 **Tsiigehtchic**, Northwest Territories, Canada
196 L 11 **Tsineng**, Republic of South Africa
197 W 11 **Tsiombe**, Madgascar
197 W 7 **Tsiroanomandidy**, Madgascar
159 T 6 **Ts'khinvali**, Georgia
159 V 7 **Tsnori**, Georgia
197 O 13 **Tsolo**, Republic of South Africa
159 R 6 **Tsqaltubo**, Georgia
177 H 18 **Tsu**, Japan
177 L 15 **Tsuchiura**, Japan
176 J 8 **Tsugarū-kaikyō**, Japan
177 D 21 **Tsukumi**, Japan
196 I 7 **Tsumeb**, Namibia
196 I 10 **Tsumis Park**, Namibia
196 J 8 **Tsumkwe**, Namibia
177 G 17 **Tsuruga**, Japan
177 F 20 **Tsurugi-san**, Japan
176 J 12 **Tsuruoka**, Japan
177 A 20 **Tsushima**, Japan
177 F 18 **Tsuyama**, Japan
197 N 11 **Tswelelang**, Republic of South Africa
99 N 20 **Tsyerakhowka**, Belarus
101 S 9 **Tsyurupyns'k**, Ukraine
113 R 8 **Tthenaagoo**, Northwest Territories, Canada
210 N 12 **Tuai**, New Zealand
210 K 9 **Tuakau**, New Zealand
77 C 17 **Tuam**, Republic of Ireland
215 T 8 **Tuamotu Archipelago**, French Polynesia
61 T 9 **Tuamotu Fracture Zone**, Pacific Ocean
172 J 11 **Tuân Giao**, Vietnam
156 D 10 **Tuapse**, Russian Federation
214 J 8 **Tuasivi**, Samoa
117 N 20 **Tuba City**, Arizona, U.S.A.
117 N 25 **Tubac**, Arizona, U.S.A.
175 S 11 **Tubalai**, Indonesia
174 J 14 **Tuban**, Indonesia
160 G 8 **Tūbās**, Israel
87 F 23 **Tübingen**, Germany
83 F 20 **Tubize**, Belgium
192 G 13 **Tubmanburg**, Liberia
215 T 12 **Tubuai**, French Polynesia
61 T 10 **Tubuai Island**, Pacific Ocean
141 O 21 **Tucavaca**, Bolivia
92 H 10 **Tuchola**, Poland
123 O 4 **Tucker**, Georgia, U.S.A.
62 B 7 **Tucker's Town**, Bermuda
117 N 25 **Tucson**, Arizona, U.S.A.
144 I 8 **Tucumán**, Argentina
119 G 17 **Tucumcari**, New Mexico, U.S.A.
144 H 10 **Tucunuco**, Argentina
142 J 11 **Tucuruí**, Brazil
81 R 3 **Tudela**, Spain
98 I 6 **Tudu**, Estonia
168 O 12 **Tuensang**, India
163 S 4 **Ţufayḩ**, Saudi Arabia
212 F 6 **Tufi**, Papua New Guinea
61 S 2 **Tufts Abyssal Plain**, Pacific Ocean
175 O 2 **Tuguegarao**, Philippines
157 V 13 **Tugur**, Russian Federation
210 K 12 **Tuhua**, New Zealand
80 H 3 **Tui**, Spain
62 N 12 **Tuineje**, Canary Islands
191 M 21 **Tukayel**, Ethiopia
100 H 6 **Tukhol'ka**, Ukraine
167 U 14 **Tŭkhtamish**, Tajikistan
189 W 7 **Tūkrah**, Libya
113 O 4 **Tuktoyaktuk**, Northwest Territories, Canada
98 E 11 **Tukums**, Latvia
195 T 13 **Tukuyu**, Tanzania
125 Q 9 **Tula**, Mexico
156 F 8 **Tula**, Russian Federation
215 X 15 **Tula**, American Samoa
212 M 6 **Tulaghi**, Solomon Islands
165 Q 8 **Tulak**, Afghanistan
125 R 11 **Tulancingo**, Mexico
117 F 20 **Tulare**, California, U.S.A.
140 B 8 **Tulcán**, Ecuador
101 N 12 **Tulcea**, Romania
119 H 18 **Tulia**, Texas, U.S.A.
113 Q 6 **Tulít'a**, Northwest Territories, Canada
122 M 2 **Tullahoma**, Tennessee, U.S.A.
77 D 18 **Tullamore**, Republic of Ireland
79 P 11 **Tulle**, France
89 X 3 **Tulln**, Austria
119 N 20 **Tullos**, Louisiana, U.S.A.
209 T 4 **Tully**, Queensland, Australia
100 L 10 **Tulnici**, Romania
84 M 9 **Tulppio**, Finland
119 K 16 **Tulsa**, Oklahoma, U.S.A.
157 P 13 **Tulun**, Russian Federation
212 J 4 **Tulun Islands**, Papua New Guinea
138 F 8 **Tumaco**, Colombia
194 M 9 **Tumba**, Democratic Republic of Congo
174 K 11 **Tumbangsamba**, Indonesia
140 A 11 **Tumbes**, Peru
113 S 11 **Tumbler Ridge**, British Columbia, Canada
209 O 11 **Tumby Bay**, South Australia, Australia
139 S 5 **Tumeremo**, Venezuela
169 E 21 **Tumkur**, India
192 L 11 **Tumu**, Ghana
142 H 8 **Tumuc-Humac Mountains**, Brazil/Suriname
159 O 10 **Tunceli**, Turkey
193 R 10 **Tundun-Wada**, Nigeria
195 V 14 **Tunduru**, Tanzania
96 J 9 **Tundzha**, Bulgaria
193 S 12 **Tunga**, Nigeria
169 D 20 **Tungabhadra Reservoir**, India
191 E 19 **Tungaru**, Sudan
175 P 7 **Tungawan**, Philippines
140 C 9 **Tungurahua**, Ecuador
169 H 18 **Tuni**, India
122 H 3 **Tunica**, Mississippi, U.S.A.
189 Q 5 **Tunis**, Tunisia
189 P 6 **Tunisia**, Africa
138 J 6 **Tunja**, Colombia
84 F 13 **Tunnsjøen**, Norway
112 F 6 **Tununak**, Alaska, U.S.A.
144 G 12 **Tunuyán**, Argentina
167 W 10 **Tŭp**, Kyrgyzstan
215 R 9 **Tupai**, French Polynesia
143 H 21 **Tupanciretã**, Brazil
122 J 4 **Tupelo**, Mississippi, U.S.A.
142 J 13 **Tupiratins**, Brazil
141 J 23 **Tupiza**, Bolivia
157 P 10 **Tura**, Russian Federation
167 S 10 **Tura-Ryskulova**, Kazakhstan
163 N 8 **Turabah**, Saudi Arabia
211 K 14 **Turakina**, New Zealand
211 K 16 **Turakirae Head**, New Zealand
212 B 5 **Turama**, Papua New Guinea
166 K 13 **Turan Lowland**, Turkmenistan
210 L 12 **Turangi**, New Zealand
99 J 21 **Turaw**, Belarus
162 L 1 **Turayf**, Saudi Arabia
165 Q 14 **Turbat**, Pakistan
138 G 4 **Turbo**, Colombia
100 I 9 **Turda**, Romania
215 X 11 **Tureia**, French Polynesia
92 I 13 **Turek**, Poland
167 T 4 **Turgay**, Kazakhstan
96 L 8 **Tŭrgovishte**, Bulgaria
96 L 8 **Tŭrgovishte**, Bulgaria
158 B 11 **Turgutlu**, Turkey
158 L 9 **Turhal**, Turkey
144 G 4 **Turi**, Chile
98 G 7 **Türi**, Estonia
81 S 8 **Turia**, Spain
142 L 10 **Turiaçu**, Brazil
90 A 7 **Turin**, Italy
100 J 2 **Turiys'k**, Ukraine
100 H 5 **Turka**, Ukraine
158 B 8 **Türkeli**, Turkey
167 Q 10 **Turkestan**, Kazakhstan
167 Q 12 **Turkestan Range**, Uzbekistan
158 M 10 **Turkey**, Asia
166 H 12 **Turkmenbashi**, Turkmenistan
166 M 12 **Turkmenistan**, Asia
166 I 13 **Turkmenskiy Zaliv**, Turkmenistan
158 L 12 **Türkoğlu**, Turkey
127 Q 4 **Turks and Caicos Islands**, U.K.
127 Q 5 **Turks Islands**, Turks and Caicos Islands
85 K 19 **Turku**, Finland
117 E 18 **Turlock**, California, U.S.A.
126 E 8 **Turneffe Islands**, Belize
83 H 16 **Turnhout**, Belgium
89 W 4 **Türnitz**, Austria
113 V 9 **Turnor Lake**, Saskatchewan, Canada
100 J 14 **Turnu Măgurele**, Romania
170 L 5 **Turpan**, China
170 L 5 **Turpan Depression**, China
89 S 8 **Turrach**, Austria
161 V 7 **Tursāq**, Iraq
166 M 11 **Turtkul'**, Uzbekistan
157 N 9 **Turukhansk**, Russian Federation
122 K 5 **Tuscaloosa**, Alabama, U.S.A.
90 D 9 **Tuscan Archipelago**, Italy
159 S 10 **Tutak**, Turkey
169 E 24 **Tuticorin**, India
96 L 6 **Tutrakan**, Bulgaria
87 F 24 **Tuttlingen**, Germany
175 R 15 **Tutuala**, East Timor
215 X 15 **Tutuila**, American Samoa
197 N 8 **Tutume**, Botswana
211 L 16 **Tuturumuri**, New Zealand
85 N 15 **Tuusniemi**, Finland
214 G 5 **Tuvalu**, Oceania
162 L 7 **Tuwwal**, Saudi Arabia
125 O 12 **Tuxpan**, Mexico
125 S 11 **Tuxpan**, Mexico
125 V 14 **Tuxtla Gutiérrez**, Mexico
173 N 20 **Tuy Duc**, Vietnam
173 O 19 **Tuy Hoa**, Vietnam
172 L 11 **Tuyên Quang**, Vietnam
158 I 11 **Tuz Gölü**, Turkey
161 U 4 **Tūz Khurmātū**, Iraq
94 I 11 **Tuzla**, Bosnia and Herzegovina
101 N 13 **Tuzla**, Romania
158 J 13 **Tuzla**, Turkey
156 F 7 **Tver'**, Russian Federation
93 J 19 **Tvrdošin**, Slovakia
96 K 9 **Tvŭrdista**, Bulgaria
76 J 13 **Tweed**, United Kingdom
117 I 22 **Twentynine Palms**, California, U.S.A.
123 Q 6 **Twin City**, Georgia, U.S.A.
116 K 13 **Twin Falls**, Idaho, U.S.A.
116 F 6 **Twisp**, Washington, U.S.A.
211 E 21 **Twizel**, New Zealand
63 L 26 **Two Boats Village**, Ascension
120 J 6 **Two Rivers**, Wisconsin, U.S.A.
93 I 17 **Tychy**, Poland
119 L 19 **Tyler**, Texas, U.S.A.
122 H 7 **Tylertown**, Mississippi, U.S.A.
97 I 26 **Tympaki**, Greece
157 T 13 **Tynda**, Russian Federation
77 I 15 **Tyne**, United Kingdom
85 D 16 **Tynset**, Norway
85 D 19 **Tyrifjorden**, Norway
97 E 16 **Tyrnavos**, Greece
121 R 10 **Tyrone**, Pennsylvania, U.S.A.
91 E 15 **Tyrrhenian Sea**, Europe
156 K 11 **Tyukalinsk**, Russian Federation
156 J 10 **Tyumen'**, Russian Federation

U

215 X 6 **Ua Huka**, French Polynesia
215 W 6 **Ua Pou**, French Polynesia
142 D 11 **Uarini**, Brazil
142 F 10 **Uatumã**, Brazil
142 N 13 **Uauá**, Brazil
126 D 7 **Uaxactún**, Guatemala
143 L 18 **Ubá**, Brazil
143 N 15 **Ubaitaba**, Brazil
194 J 5 **Ubangi**, Central African Republic
161 N 7 **Ubaylah**, Iraq
177 C 20 **Ube**, Japan
81 O 11 **Úbeda**, Spain
143 J 17 **Uberaba**, Brazil
143 J 17 **Uberlândia**, Brazil
87 F 25 **Überlingen**, Germany
173 I 16 **Ubolratna Reservoir**, Thailand
197 Q 12 **Ubombo**, Republic of South Africa
173 L 17 **Ubon Ratchathani**, Thailand
195 N 8 **Ubundu**, Democratic Republic of Congo
141 E 14 **Ucayali**, Peru
141 E 14 **Ucayali**, Peru
83 F 19 **Uccle**, Belgium
157 P 10 **Uchami**, Russian Federation
167 X 7 **Ucharal**, Kazakhstan
177 C 24 **Uchinoura**, Japan
176 I 7 **Uchiura-wan**, Japan
167 O 11 **Uchkuduk**, Uzbekistan
157 U 13 **Uda**, Russian Federation
157 R 9 **Udachnyy**, Russian Federation
168 C 13 **Udaipur**, India
101 S 3 **Uday**, Ukraine
94 D 11 **Udbina**, Croatia
85 D 22 **Uddevalla**, Sweden
84 H 12 **Uddjaure**, Sweden
83 J 15 **Uden**, Netherlands
90 I 6 **Udine**, Italy
61 S 13 **Udintsev Fracture Zone**, Pacific Ocean
169 C 21 **Udipi**, India
173 J 15 **Udon Thani**, Thailand
86 M 10 **Uecker**, Germany
177 I 15 **Ueda**, Japan
194 L 5 **Uele**, Democratic Republic of Congo
157 Z 5 **Uelen**, Russian Federation
157 Z 6 **Uel'kal'**, Russian Federation
86 I 12 **Uelzen**, Germany
177 H 18 **Ueno**, Japan
156 I 10 **Ufa**, Russian Federation
98 D 10 **Ugāle**, Latvia
195 R 6 **Uganda**, Africa
91 O 18 **Ugento**, Italy
157 W 13 **Uglegorsk**, Russian Federation
94 C 12 **Ugljan**, Croatia
157 Z 6 **Ugol'nyye**, Russian Federation
93 G 19 **Uherské Hradiště**, Czech Republic
76 F 10 **Uig**, United Kingdom
196 G 1 **Uíge**, Angola
196 G 2 **Uíge**, Angola
166 J 5 **Uil**, Kazakhstan
117 M 15 **Uinta Mountains**, Utah, U.S.A.
196 H 9 **Uis**, Namibia
82 H 11 **Uithoorn**, Netherlands
215 W 2 **Ujae**, Marshall Islands
93 M 22 **Újfehértó**, Hungary
177 G 18 **Uji**, Japan
177 B 24 **Uji-guntō**, Japan
177 K 14 **Ujiie**, Japan
169 D 14 **Ujjain**, India
175 N 13 **Ujung Pandang**, Indonesia
174 C 8 **Ujung Tamiang**, Indonesia
193 Q 11 **Ukata**, Nigeria
177 O 22 **Uke-jima**, Japan
195 S 9 **Ukerewe Island**, Tanzania
156 J 8 **Ukhta**, Russian Federation

Country · Internal administrative region: State/Province/Territory/Dependent territory · Capital city · Mountain range/Undersea ridge · Mountain peak/Volcano/Seamount · Geographic feature · Headland/Point/Cape/Peninsula · Desert · Island/Island group · Antarctic base · Ocean · Sea · Bay/Gulf/Channel/Strait · Lake · Salt pan/Dry/Intermittent lake · River

13 N 7 **Uki**, Solomon Islands ⁂
17 C 16 **Ukiah**, California, U.S.A.
9 F 14 **Ukmergė**, Lithuania
01 O 6 **Ukraine**, Europe □
96 G 4 **Uku**, Angola
77 A 21 **Uku-jima**, Japan ⁂
71 R 3 **Ulaanbaatar**, Mongolia ⌂
70 M 2 **Ulaangom**, Mongolia
57 Q 14 **Ulan-Ude**, Russian Federation
70 L 8 **Ulan Ul Hu**, China ∽
67 S 9 **Ulanbel'**, Kazakhstan
71 V 4 **Ulanhot**, China
58 C 7 **Ulaş**, Turkey
58 M 10 **Ulaş**, Turkey
13 N 7 **Ulawa**, Solomon Islands ⁂
5 J 17 **Ulcinj**, Serbia and Montenegro
71 T 2 **Uldz**, Mongolia ∿
71 S 3 **Uldz**, Mongolia
69 C 17 **Ulhasnagar**, India
71 O 3 **Uliastay**, Mongolia
14 K 14 **Ulithi**, Federated States of Micronesia ⁂
67 N 5 **Ul'kayak**, Kazakhstan ∿
209 U 12 **Ulladulla**, New South Wales, Australia
76 G 9 **Ullapool**, United Kingdom
171 Z 6 **Ullŭng-do**, South Korea ⁂
87 H 24 **Ulm**, Germany
100 H 8 **Ulmeni**, Romania
94 H 13 **Ulog**, Bosnia and Herzegovina
197 R 5 **Ulongue**, Mozambique
171 Z 7 **Ulsan**, South Korea
85 D 16 **Ulsberg**, Norway
77 D 15 **Ulster**, United Kingdom □
158 D 8 **Ulubat Gölü**, Turkey ∽
158 D 9 **Uludağ**, Turkey ▲
170 G 5 **Ulugqat**, China
158 J 12 **Ulukişla**, Turkey
215 N 14 **Ulul**, Federated States of Micronesia ⁂
197 P 12 **Ulundi**, Republic of South Africa
170 L 3 **Ulungur Hu**, China ∽
113 R 3 **Uluqsaqtuuq**, Northwest Territories, Canada
208 M 7 **Uluru**, Northern Territory, Australia ⛰
101 P 7 **Ul'yanovka**, Ukraine
156 G 9 **Ul'yanovsk**, Russian Federation
167 T 5 **Ul'yanovskiy**, Kazakhstan
167 Q 6 **Ulytau**, Kazakhstan
94 A 8 **Umag**, Croatia
101 P 6 **Uman'**, Ukraine
165 V 14 **Umarkot**, Pakistan
90 G 11 **Umbertide**, Italy
212 E 4 **Umboi Island**, Papua New Guinea ⁂
90 H 12 **Umbria**, Italy □
212 F 2 **Umbukul**, Papua New Guinea
85 J 15 **Umeå**, Sweden
85 I 14 **Umeälven**, Sweden ∿
163 R 3 **Umgharah**, Kuwait
112 L 3 **Umiat**, Alaska, U.S.A.
113 U 4 **Umingmaktok**, Nunavut, Canada
197 P 13 **Umlazi**, Republic of South Africa
163 X 5 **Umm al Qaiwain**, United Arab Emirates
161 R 5 **Umm al Tūz**, Iraq
191 C 17 **Umm Bel**, Sudan
162 K 5 **Umm Lajj**, Saudi Arabia
161 Z 12 **Umm Qaşr**, Iraq
191 E 18 **Umm Ruwaba**, Sudan
189 Y 7 **Umm Sa'ad**, Libya
163 U 6 **Umm Sa'id**, Qatar
191 E 17 **Umm Saiyala**, Sudan
162 J 5 **Umm Urūmah**, Saudi Arabia ⁂
65 O 9 **Ummannaq**, Greenland
112 C 9 **Umnak Island**, Alaska, U.S.A. ⁂
196 I 4 **Umpulo**, Angola
197 O 14 **Umtata**, Republic of South Africa
193 R 13 **Umuahia**, Nigeria
143 H 19 **Umuarama**, Brazil
94 E 10 **Una**, Bosnia and Herzegovina/Croatia ∿
143 N 16 **Una**, Brazil
112 D 9 **Unalaska Island**, Alaska, U.S.A. ⁂
84 L 10 **Unari**, Finland ∽
84 L 10 **Unari**, Finland
175 O 11 **Unauna**, Indonesia ⁂
160 G 12 **'Unayzah**, Jordan
163 P 5 **'Unayzah**, Saudi Arabia
118 H 8 **Underwood**, North Dakota, U.S.A.
212 F 4 **Unea Island**, Papua New Guinea ⁂
115 S 5 **Ungava Bay**, Québec, Canada ≈
195 X 9 **Ungwana Bay**, Kenya ≈
143 I 20 **União da Vitória**, Brazil
63 L 26 **Unicorn Point**, Ascension ▶
94 B 10 **Unije**, Croatia ⁂
112 E 9 **Unimak Island**, Alaska, U.S.A. ⁂
142 D 10 **Unini**, Brazil ∿
121 P 9 **Union City**, Pennsylvania, U.S.A.
122 J 1 **Union City**, Tennessee, U.S.A.
122 M 6 **Union Springs**, Alabama, U.S.A.
121 P 11 **Uniontown**, Pennsylvania, U.S.A.
163 W 6 **United Arab Emirates**, Asia □
77 J 16 **United Kingdom**, Europe □
117 H 13
89 P 6 **Unken**, Austria
76 K 3 **Unst**, United Kingdom ⁂
139 R 4 **Upata**, Venezuela
196 K 12 **Upington**, Republic of South Africa
169 A 15 **Upleta**, India
215 V 15 **Upolu**, Samoa ⁂
192 M 11 **Upper East**, Ghana □
211 K 16 **Upper Hutt**, New Zealand
191 F 20 **Upper Nile**, Sudan □
118 K 7 **Upper Red Lake**, Minnesota, U.S.A. ∽
120 M 10 **Upper Sandusky**, Ohio, U.S.A.
192 L 11 **Upper West**, Ghana □
85 H 20 **Uppsala**, Sweden
114 K 11 **Upsala**, Ontario, Canada
163 N 5 **'Uqlat aş Şuqūr**, Saudi Arabia
161 N 6 **Uqlat Şawāb**, Iraq
171 R 6 **Urad Houqi**, China
176 L 5 **Urahoro**, Japan
176 L 6 **Urakawa**, Japan
166 I 5 **Ural**, Kazakhstan ∿
156 I 11 **Ural Mountains**, Russian Federation ⛰
166 I 4 **Ural'sk**, Kazakhstan
160 I 2 **Urām aş Şughrá**, Syria
195 S 11 **Urambo**, Tanzania
209 P 5 **Urandangi**, Queensland, Australia
143 L 15 **Urandi**, Brazil
177 K 16 **Urawa**, Japan
156 J 9 **Uray**, Russian Federation
163 S 5 **Uray'irah**, Saudi Arabia
120 I 11 **Urbana**, Illinois, U.S.A.
90 G 10 **Urbania**, Italy
90 G 10 **Urbino**, Italy
141 G 17 **Urcos**, Peru
170 M 3 **Urdgol**, Mongolia
167 X 7 **Urdzhar**, Kazakhstan
156 M 9 **Urengoy**, Russian Federation
213 Q 9 **Uréparapara**, Vanuatu ⁂
166 M 11 **Urgench**, Uzbekistan
170 K 3 **Urho**, China
168 D 7 **Uri**, India
167 P 3 **Uritskiy**, Kazakhstan
82 J 9 **Urk**, Netherlands
158 A 10 **Urla**, Turkey
193 Q 13 **Uromi**, Nigeria
95 M 16 **Uroševac**, Serbia and Montenegro
167 R 12 **Üroteppa**, Tajikistan
171 P 5 **Urt**, Mongolia
124 K 5 **Uruáchic**, Mexico
143 J 15 **Uruaçu**, Brazil
125 P 12 **Uruapan**, Mexico
142 G 10 **Urucará**, Brazil
142 L 12 **Uruçui**, Brazil
143 G 21 **Uruguaiana**, Brazil
144 N 12 **Uruguay**, South America □
144 O 8 **Uruguay**, South America ∿
170 K 5 **Ürümqi**, China
165 T 8 **Urūzgān**, Afghanistan □
100 L 12 **Urziceni**, Romania
101 X 9 **Urzuf**, Ukraine
177 C 21 **Usa**, Japan
158 D 10 **Uşak**, Turkey
94 L 13 **Ušće**, Serbia and Montenegro
162 L 8 **'Usfān**, Saudi Arabia
162 M 8 **'Ushayrah**, Saudi Arabia
177 B 23 **Ushibuka**, Japan
167 W 8 **Ushtobe**, Kazakhstan
145 H 25 **Ushuaia**, Argentina
212 D 4 **Usino**, Papua New Guinea
156 K 7 **Usinsk**, Russian Federation
158 D 7 **Usküdar**, Turkey
87 G 15 **Uslar**, Germany
98 C 10 **Usmas ezers**, Latvia ∽
156 I 7 **Usogorsk**, Russian Federation
157 Q 13 **Usol'ye-Sibirskoye**, Russian Federation
101 W 7 **Uspenivka**, Ukraine
167 V 3 **Uspenka**, Kazakhstan
79 Q 10 **Ussel**, France
157 V 15 **Ussuriysk**, Russian Federation
157 Q 13 **Ust'-Barguzin**, Russian Federation
157 P 12 **Ust'-Ilimsk**, Russian Federation
157 Z 10 **Ust'-Kamchatsk**, Russian Federation
167 X 4 **Ust'-Kamenogorsk**, Kazakhstan
157 P 12 **Ust'-Kut**, Russian Federation
157 T 8 **Ust'-Kuyga**, Russian Federation
157 U 11 **Ust'-Maya**, Russian Federation
157 V 9 **Ust'-Nera**, Russian Federation
157 R 7 **Ust'-Olenek**, Russian Federation
157 W 10 **Ust'-Omchug**, Russian Federation
157 O 8 **Ust'-Port**, Russian Federation
156 J 7 **Ust'-Tsil'ma**, Russian Federation
167 O 2 **Ust'-Uyskoye**, Kazakhstan
93 C 16 **Ústí nad Labem**, Czech Republic
92 G 8 **Ustka**, Poland
96 L 10 **Ustrem**, Bulgaria
92 F 8 **Ustronie Morskie**, Poland
93 N 18 **Ustrzyki Dolne**, Poland
166 J 9 **Ustyurt Plateau**, Kazakhstan ◇
126 E 10 **Usulután**, El Salvador
125 X 13 **Usumacinta**, Mexico ∿
175 W 13 **Uta**, Indonesia
117 N16 **Utah**, U.S.A. □
117 M 15 **Utah Lake**, Utah, U.S.A. ∽
99 G 14 **Utena**, Lithuania
195 W 12 **Utete**, Tanzania
173 H 17 **Uthai Thani**, Thailand
165 T 14 **Uthal**, Pakistan
121 T 8 **Utica**, New York, U.S.A.
177 B 22 **Uto**, Japan
168 H 12 **Utraula**, India
82 H 12 **Utrecht**, Netherlands □
82 I 12 **Utrecht**, Netherlands
215 Y 1 **Utrik**, Marshall Islands ⁂
84 L 7 **Utsjoki**, Finland
177 K 15 **Utsunomiya**, Japan
168 G 12 **Uttar Pradesh**, India □
173 H 15 **Uttaradit**, Thailand
168 F 10 **Uttaranchal**, India □
168 F 10 **Uttarkashi**, India
170 K 3 **Utubulak**, China
213 Q 8 **Utupua**, Solomon Islands ⁂
215 S 9 **Uturoa**, French Polynesia
85 L 16 **Uurainen**, Finland
85 J 19 **Uusikaupunki**, Finland
169 G 25 **Uva**, Sri Lanka □
94 J 13 **Uvac**, Serbia and Montenegro ∿
119 I 22 **Uvalde**, Texas, U.S.A.
99 M 20 **Uvaravichy**, Belarus
195 R 11 **Uvinza**, Tanzania
212 G 5 **Uvol**, Papua New Guinea
171 N 2 **Uvs**, Mongolia □
171 N 2 **Uvs Nuur**, Mongolia ∽
177 D 21 **Uwajima**, Japan
163 Y 7 **'Uwayfi**, Oman
189 S 10 **'Uwaynāt Wannīn**, Libya
157 O 12 **Uyar**, Russian Federation
171 R 5 **Üydzin**, Mongolia
193 R 14 **Uyo**, Nigeria
167 S 10 **Uyuk**, Kazakhstan
167 O 11 **Uzbekistan**, Asia □
99 I 18 **Uzda**, Belarus
79 P 10 **Uzerche**, France
79 T 13 **Uzès**, France
101 N 3 **Uzh**, Ukraine ∿
100 G 6 **Uzhhorod**, Ukraine
94 K 12 **Užice**, Serbia and Montenegro
167 V 10 **Uzunaghach**, Kazakhstan
158 B 7 **Uzunköprü**, Turkey
98 D 13 **Užventis**, Lithuania

V

196 M 12 **Vaal**, Republic of South Africa ∿
84 M 13 **Vaala**, Finland
83 L 19 **Vaals**, Netherlands
85 J 16 **Vaasa**, Finland
82 K 11 **Vaassen**, Netherlands
98 F 13 **Vabalninkas**, Lithuania
93 J 22 **Vác**, Hungary
143 I 21 **Vacaria**, Brazil
117 D 17 **Vacaville**, California, U.S.A.
58 B 12 **Vacoas**, Mauritius
169 C 15 **Vadodara**, India
84 M 6 **Vadsø**, Norway
88 I 7 **Vaduz**, Liechtenstein ⌂
212 K 5 **Vaghena**, Solomon Islands ⁂
84 H 8 **Vågsfjorden**, Norway ≈
93 H 19 **Váh**, Slovakia ∿
215 X 10 **Vahitahi**, French Polynesia ⁂
214 G 6 **Vaiaku**, Tuvalu ⌂
119 E 14 **Vail**, Colorado, U.S.A.
215 X 10 **Vairaatea**, French Polynesia ⁂
98 E 6 **Väiri**, Estonia ≈
214 F 5 **Vaitupu**, Tuvalu ⁂
194 M 2 **Vakaga**, Central African Republic □
79 W 10 **Val d'Isere**, France
115 P 12 **Val-d'Or**, Québec, Canada
113 Y 13 **Val Marie**, Saskatchewan, Canada
88 D 10 **Valais**, Switzerland □
96 E 12 **Valandovo**, Macedonia (F.Y.R.O.M.)
97 H 18 **Valaxa**, Greece ⁂
145 I 16 **Valcheta**, Argentina
156 F 7 **Valday**, Russian Federation
81 P 9 **Valdepeñas**, Spain
80 M 3 **Valderas**, Spain
112 K 7 **Valdez**, Alaska, U.S.A.
145 F 16 **Valdivia**, Chile
63 M 17 **Valdivia Seamount**, Atlantic Ocean ▲
123 P 8 **Valdosta**, Georgia, U.S.A.
85 C 18 **Valdres**, Norway ⛰
159 S 7 **Vale**, Georgia
100 G 8 **Valea lui Mihai**, Romania
143 N 15 **Valença**, Brazil
142 M 12 **Valença do Piauí**, Brazil
79 T 11 **Valence**, France
81 S 8 **Valencia**, Spain □
81 T 8 **Valencia**, Spain
139 N 3 **Valencia**, Venezuela
80 J 8 **Valencia de Alcántara**, Spain
80 L 3 **Valencia de Don Juan**, Spain
79 R 1 **Valenciennes**, France
118 H 11 **Valentine**, Nebraska, U.S.A.
90 C 8 **Valenza**, Italy
175 O 3 **Valenzuela**, Philppines
61 Q 12 **Valerie Guyot**, Pacific Ocean ▲
98 H 9 **Valga**, Estonia
94 K 11 **Valjevo**, Serbia and Montenegro
98 H 9 **Valka**, Latvia
83 J 16 **Valkenswaard**, Netherlands
101 V 4 **Valky**, Ukraine
81 N 4 **Valladolid**, Spain
125 Z 10 **Valladolid**, Mexico
91 L 15 **Vallata**, Italy
90 A 6 **Valle D'Aosta**, Italy □
139 N 3 **Valle de La Pascua**, Venezuela
138 G 7 **Valle Del Cauca**, Colombia □
125 T 13 **Valle Nacional**, Mexico
138 J 2 **Valledupar**, Colombia
117 D 17 **Vallejo**, California, U.S.A.
144 F 9 **Vallenar**, Chile
91 K 26 **Valletta**, Malta ⌂
118 J 8 **Valley City**, North Dakota, U.S.A.
113 T 11 **Valleyview**, Alberta, Canada
90 G 9 **Valli di Comacchio**, Italy ∽
91 K 17 **Vallo della Lucania**, Italy
88 B 8 **Vallorbe**, Switzerland
81 V 5 **Valls**, Spain
98 G 9 **Valmiera**, Latvia
78 L 3 **Valognes**, France
99 H 17 **Valozhyn**, Belarus
169 E 23 **Valparai**, India
144 F 11 **Valparaíso**, Chile □
144 F 11 **Valparaíso**, Chile
94 H 8 **Valpovo**, Croatia
88 H 9 **Vals**, Switzerland
169 C 16 **Valsad**, India
85 F 14 **Valsjöbyn**, Sweden
62 K 12 **Valverde**, Canary Islands
80 J 11 **Valverde del Camino**, Spain
85 K 18 **Vammala**, Finland
159 S 11 **Van**, Turkey
119 N 15 **Van Buren**, Missouri, U.S.A.
121 Y 3 **Van Buren**, Maine, U.S.A.
173 O 19 **Vân Canh**, Vietnam
208 M 1 **Van Diemen Gulf**, Northern Territory, Australia ≈
159 S 11 **Van Gölü**, Turkey ∽
120 L 10 **Van Wert**, Ohio, U.S.A.
159 T 8 **Vanadzor**, Armenia
215 X 11 **Vanavana**, French Polynesia ⁂
157 P 11 **Vanavara**, Russian Federation
113 S 14 **Vancouver**, British Columbia, Canada
116 D 9 **Vancouver**, Washington, U.S.A.
113 Q 14 **Vancouver Island**, British Columbia, Canada ⁂
120 H 12 **Vandalia**, Illinois, U.S.A.
209 P 3 **Vanderlin Island**, Northern Territory, Australia ⁂
169 F 21 **Vandivasi**, India
98 G 7 **Vändra**, Estonia
85 E 21 **Vänern**, Sweden ∽
85 E 22 **Vänersborg**, Sweden
197 Y 10 **Vangaindrano**, Madgascar
212 K 6 **Vangunu**, Solomon Islands ⁂
213 Q 8 **Vanikoro Islands**, Solomon Islands ⁂
212 A 3 **Vanimo**, Papua New Guinea
157 W 14 **Vanino**, Russian Federation
100 G 12 **Vânju Mare**, Romania
157 Z 5 **Vankarem**, Russian Federation
84 I 6 **Vanna**, Norway ⁂
78 J 6 **Vannes**, France
196 J 14 **Vanrhynsdorp**, Republic of South Africa
115 O 2 **Vansittart Island**, Nunavut, Canada ⁂
85 L 19 **Vantaa**, Finland
213 Z 11 **Vanua Balavu**, Fiji ⁂
213 Q 9 **Vanua Lava**, Vanuatu ⁂
213 X 10 **Vanua Levu**, Fiji ⁂
213 S 11 **Vanuatu**, Oceania □
192 L 11 **Varalé**, Côte d'Ivoire
90 B 6 **Varallo**, Italy
164 I 6 **Varāmīn**, Iran
168 H 13 **Varanasi**, India
84 M 6 **Varangerfjorden**, Norway ≈
84 M 6 **Varangerhalvøya**, Norway ▶
99 I 14 **Varapayeva**, Belarus
94 E 7 **Varaždin**, Croatia
85 D 23 **Varberg**, Sweden
97 C 20 **Varda**, Greece
96 D 11 **Vardar**, Macedonia (F.Y.R.O.M.) ∿
85 B 25 **Varde**, Denmark
159 V 9 **Vardenis**, Armenia
84 N 6 **Vardø**, Norway
86 E 10 **Varel**, Germany
99 F 16 **Varėna**, Lithuania
90 C 6 **Varese**, Italy
100 J 8 **Vârful Ineu**, Romania ▲
100 J 11 **Vârful Moldoveanu**, Romania ▲
100 J 11 **Vârful Omu**, Romania ▲
100 G 11 **Vârful Peleaga**, Romania ▲
100 I 8 **Vârful Pietrosu**, Romania ▲
100 G 12 **Vârful Svinecea Mare**, Romania ▲
100 K 9 **Vârful Toaca**, Romania ▲
144 F 6 **Varillas**, Chile
85 N 16 **Varkaus**, Finland
97 G 20 **Varkiza**, Greece
85 E 20 **Värmeln**, Sweden ∽
96 N 8 **Varna**, Bulgaria □
96 N 8 **Varna**, Bulgaria
85 F 23 **Värnamo**, Sweden
98 D 13 **Varniai**, Lithuania
99 H 15 **Varnyany**, Belarus
159 Q 10 **Varto**, Turkey
90 C 8 **Varzi**, Italy
93 N 21 **Vásárosnamény**, Hungary
99 L 21 **Vasilyevichy**, Belarus
100 M 9 **Vaslui**, Romania
120 M 8 **Vassar**, Michigan, U.S.A.
84 G 12 **Västansjö**, Sweden
85 G 17 **Västbäcka**, Sweden
85 G 20 **Västerås**, Sweden
85 E 18 **Västerdalälven**, Sweden ∿
85 G 23 **Västervik**, Sweden
90 K 13 **Vasto**, Italy
85 E 20 **Västra Silen**, Sweden ∽
93 F 24 **Vasvár**, Hungary
101 V 8 **Vasylivka**, Ukraine
101 P 4 **Vasyl'kiv**, Ukraine
101 V 7 **Vasyl'kivka**, Ukraine
79 P 7 **Vatan**, France
76 D 11 **Vatersay**, United Kingdom ⁂
91 H 14 **Vatican City**, Europe □
84 C 11 **Vatnajökull**, Iceland ◇
197 Y 8 **Vatomandry**, Madgascar
100 J 8 **Vatra Dornei**, Romania
85 F 22 **Vättern**, Sweden ∽
213 W 12 **Vatulele**, Fiji ⁂
88 B 9 **Vaud**, Switzerland □
119 F 18 **Vaughn**, New Mexico, U.S.A.
138 L 9 **Vaupés**, Colombia □
79 S 14 **Vauvert**, France
214 J 10 **Vava'u Group**, Tonga ⁂
169 G 24 **Vavuniya**, Sri Lanka
99 M 17 **Vawkavichy**, Belarus
99 F 19 **Vawkavysk**, Belarus
85 F 24 **Växjö**, Sweden
159 U 9 **Vayk**, Armenia
86 E 12 **Vechta**, Germany
169 F 23 **Vedaranniyam**, India
100 K 14 **Vedea**, Romania
144 K 12 **Vedia**, Argentina
99 M 21 **Vedrych**, Belarus ∿
82 N 7 **Veendam**, Netherlands
82 J 13 **Veenendaal**, Netherlands
84 E 12 **Vega**, Norway ⁂
83 J 15 **Veghel**, Netherlands
169 L 19 **Veimandu Channel**, Maldives ≈
85 B 25 **Vejle**, Denmark
95 F 14 **Vela Luka**, Croatia
62 N 1 **Velas**, Azores
87 C 16 **Velbert**, Germany
89 S 9 **Velden**, Austria
94 C 10 **Velebit**, Croatia ⛰
94 C 6 **Velenje**, Slovenia
96 D 11 **Veles**, Macedonia (F.Y.R.O.M.)
81 Q 11 **Vélez Rubio**, Spain
94 M 10 **Velika**, Serbia and Montenegro ∿
94 D 8 **Velika Gorica**, Croatia
94 C 9 **Velika Kapela**, Croatia ⛰
94 D 9 **Velika Kladuša**, Bosnia and Herzegovina
156 F 7 **Velikiy Novgorod**, Russian Federation
156 F 7 **Velikiye Luki**, Russian Federation
96 J 8 **Veliko Tŭrnovo**, Bulgaria □
96 J 8 **Veliko Tŭrnovo**, Bulgaria
192 F 9 **Vélingara**, Senegal
96 H 10 **Velingrad**, Bulgaria
93 F 19 **Velká Biteš**, Czech Republic
212 J 5 **Vella Lavella**, Solomon Islands ⁂
169 F 21 **Vellore**, India
97 G 22 **Velopoula**, Greece ⁂
156 H 7 **Vel'sk**, Russian Federation
101 R 9 **Velyka Korenykha**, Ukraine
101 T 8 **Velyka Lepetykha**, Ukraine
101 X 4 **Velykyy Burluk**, Ukraine
62 G 12 **Vema Fracture Zone**, Atlantic Ocean ◇
63 M 17 **Vema Seamount**, Atlantic Ocean ▲
144 K 12 **Venado Tuerto**, Argentina
80 H 9 **Vendas Novas**, Portugal
156 I 7 **Vendinga**, Russian Federation
79 O 6 **Vendôme**, France
90 G 7 **Veneto**, Italy □
139 N 5 **Venezuela**, South America □
62 E 12 **Venezuelan Basin**, Atlantic Ocean ◇
90 G 7 **Venice**, Italy
119 O 21 **Venice**, Louisiana, U.S.A.
123 Q 12 **Venice**, Florida, U.S.A.
83 L 16 **Venlo**, Netherlands
83 K 15 **Venray**, Netherlands
98 C 11 **Venta**, Latvia/Lithuania ∿

□ Country □ Internal administrative region: State/Province/Territory/Dependent territory ⌂ Capital city ⛰ Mountain range/Undersea ridge ▲ Mountain peak/Volcano/Seamount ◇ Geographic feature ▶ Headland/Point/Cape/Peninsula ◭ Desert ⁂ Island/Island group ⁙ Antarctic base ≋ Ocean ◗ Sea ≈ Bay/Gulf/Channel/Strait ∽ Lake ◪ Salt pan/Dry/Intermittent lake ∿ River

197 N 13 **Venterstad**, Republic of South Africa
90 A 10 **Ventimiglia**, Italy
145 F 17 **Ventisquero**, Argentina
98 C 10 **Ventspils**, Latvia
117 F 22 **Ventura**, California, U.S.A.
81 R 12 **Vera**, Spain
144 L 9 **Vera**, Argentina
125 R 10 **Veracruz**, Mexico
125 T 12 **Veracruz**, Mexico
169 A 16 **Veraval**, India
90 C 6 **Verbania**, Italy
90 B 7 **Vercelli**, Italy
85 E 14 **Verdalsøra**, Norway
117 M 22 **Verde**, Arizona, U.S.A.
79 T 4 **Verdun**, France
144 O 12 **Vergara**, Uruguay
101 U 8 **Verkhiniy Rohachyk**, Ukraine
157 T 7 **Verkhoyanskiy Khrebet**, Russian Federation
113 W 11 **Vermilion**, Alberta, Canada
118 L 7 **Vermilion Lake**, Minnesota, U.S.A.
118 J 11 **Vermillion**, Nebraska, U.S.A.
121 V 6 **Vermont**, U.S.A.
218 H 4 **Vernadsky**, Antarctica
117 O 15 **Vernal**, Utah, U.S.A.
79 O 4 **Verneuil-sur-Avre**, France
113 T 14 **Vernon**, British Columbia, Canada
117 L 15 **Vernon**, Utah, U.S.A.
119 I 18 **Vernon**, Texas, U.S.A.
122 K 4 **Vernon**, Alabama, U.S.A.
123 S 12 **Vero Beach**, Florida, U.S.A.
97 E 14 **Veroia**, Greece
90 F 7 **Verona**, Italy
79 P 4 **Versailles**, France
120 K 12 **Versailles**, Indiana, U.S.A.
88 A 10 **Versoix**, Switzerland
126 L 5 **Vertientes**, Cuba
101 R 2 **Vertiyivka**, Ukraine
83 K 20 **Verviers**, Belgium
79 S 2 **Vervins**, France
113 Y 13 **Verwood**, Saskatchewan, Canada
79 Z 14 **Vescovato**, France
101 U 9 **Vesele**, Ukraine
79 V 6 **Vesoul**, France
122 L 5 **Vestavia Hills**, Alabama, U.S.A.
85 A 21 **Vestbygd**, Norway
84 G 8 **Vesterålen**, Norway
84 G 9 **Vestfjorden**, Norway
84 G 9 **Vestvågøy**, Norway
91 J 16 **Vesuvius**, Italy
93 H 24 **Veszprém**, Hungary
85 G 23 **Vetlanda**, Sweden
156 H 8 **Vetluzhskiy**, Russian Federation
96 K 6 **Vetovo**, Bulgaria
90 G 13 **Vetralla**, Italy
96 M 9 **Vetren**, Bulgaria
83 A 17 **Veurne**, Belgium
88 C 9 **Vevey**, Switzerland
79 U 12 **Veynes**, France
158 K 8 **Vezirköprü**, Turkey
80 H 3 **Viana do Castelo**, Portugal
80 H 4 **Viana do Castelo**, Portugal
83 L 24 **Vianden**, Luxembourg
82 I 13 **Vianen**, Netherlands
172 H 12 **Viangphoukha**, Laos
90 E 10 **Viareggio**, Italy
91 M 20 **Vibo Valentia**, Italy
85 C 24 **Viborg**, Denmark
81 X 4 **Vic**, Spain
78 M 14 **Vic-en-Bigorre**, France
90 F 7 **Vicenza**, Italy
138 M 6 **Vichada**, Colombia
138 L 7 **Vichada**, Colombia
79 R 9 **Vichy**, France
122 H 6 **Vicksburg**, Mississippi, U.S.A.
116 M 11 **Victor**, Idaho, U.S.A.
209 P 12 **Victor Harbor**, South Australia, Australia
58 A 9 **Victoria**, Seychelles
209 T 13 **Victoria**, Australia
208 M 3 **Victoria**, Northern Territory, Australia
113 S 15 **Victoria**, British Columbia, Canada
119 K 22 **Victoria**, Texas, U.S.A.
144 L 11 **Victoria**, Argentina
196 M 7 **Victoria Falls**, Zimbabwe
113 T 2 **Victoria Island**, Northwest Territories, Canada
219 R 12 **Victoria Land**, Antarctica
126 E 8 **Victoria Peak**, Belize
208 M 3 **Victoria River**, Northern Territory, Australia
196 L 14 **Victoria West**, Republic of South Africa
115 S 13 **Victoriaville**, Québec, Canada
144 I 13 **Victorica**, Argentina
117 H 22 **Victorville**, California, U.S.A.
144 J 12 **Vicuña Mackenna**, Argentina
117 J 22 **Vidal Junction**, California, U.S.A.
100 J 13 **Videle**, Romania
80 I 10 **Vidigueira**, Portugal
96 E 6 **Vidin**, Bulgaria
96 F 6 **Vidin**, Bulgaria
95 H 14 **Viduša**, Bosnia and Herzegovina
99 H 14 **Vidzy**, Belarus
145 J 16 **Viedma**, Argentina
98 D 12 **Viekšniai**, Lithuania
81 V 2 **Vielha**, Spain
83 K 22 **Vielsalm**, Belgium
89 X 3 **Vienna**, Austria
79 T 10 **Vienne**, France
173 J 15 **Vientiane**, Laos
87 B 16 **Viersen**, Germany
88 F 8 **Vierwaldstätter See**, Switzerland
79 P 7 **Vierzon**, France
98 G 12 **Viesīte**, Latvia
91 M 14 **Vieste**, Italy
172 L 12 **Viêt Tri**, Vietnam
84 I 10 **Vietas**, Sweden
172 L 13 **Vietnam**, Asia
127 X 10 **Vieux Fort**, St Lucia
175 O 2 **Vigan**, Philippines
90 C 7 **Vigevano**, Italy
125 Z 11 **Vigía Chico**, Mexico
81 T 2 **Vignemale**, Spain/France
80 H 3 **Vigo**, Spain
165 X 10 **Vihari**, Pakistan
85 L 19 **Vihti**, Finland
98 I 10 **Viļaka**, Latvia
98 I 11 **Viļāni**, Latvia
85 M 15 **Viitasaari**, Finland
98 H 5 **Viitna**, Estonia
169 G 19 **Vijayawada**, India
84 E 13 **Vik**, Norway
84 C 12 **Vík**, Iceland
96 G 11 **Vikhren**, Bulgaria
113 V 12 **Viking**, Alberta, Canada
84 E 13 **Vikna**, Norway
143 F 15 **Vila Bela da Santissima Trindade**, Brazil
142 B 10 **Vila Bittencourt**, Brazil
63 A 16 **Vila da Ribeira Brava**, Cape Verde
63 B 16 **Vila da Sal Rei**, Cape Verde
197 R 6 **Vila de Sena**, Mozambique
80 G 12 **Vila do Bispo**, Portugal
63 B 17 **Vila do Tarrafal**, Cape Verde
80 G 9 **Vila Franca de Xira**, Portugal
80 J 5 **Vila Nova de Foz Coa**, Portugal
80 H 5 **Vila Nova de Gaia**, Portugal
63 A 17 **Vila Nova Sintra**, Cape Verde
142 F 9 **Vila Novo Paraíso**, Brazil
80 I 5 **Vila Real**, Portugal
80 I 5 **Vila Real**, Portugal
142 I 8 **Vila Velha**, Brazil
141 K 22 **Vilacaya**, Bolivia
80 J 1 **Vilalba**, Spain
197 R 9 **Vilanculos**, Mozambique
169 E 23 **Vilatikkulam**, India
85 H 14 **Vilhelmina**, Sweden
143 F 14 **Vilhena**, Brazil
101 T 12 **Viline**, Ukraine
98 G 8 **Viljandi**, Estonia
99 D 15 **Vilkaviškis**, Lithuania
99 E 15 **Vilkija**, Lithuania
144 L 8 **Villa**, Argentina
141 K 22 **Villa Abecia**, Bolivia
124 M 3 **Villa Ahumada**, Mexico
144 L 11 **Villa Constitución**, Argentina
144 J 10 **Villa del Rosario**, Argentina
144 I 11 **Villa Dolores**, Argentina
125 W 14 **Villa Flores**, Mexico
124 I 7 **Villa Insurgentes**, Mexico
145 J 15 **Villa Iris**, Argentina
91 J 16 **Villa Literno**, Italy
144 J 11 **Villa María**, Argentina
141 I 22 **Villa Martín**, Bolivia
141 L 23 **Villa Montes**, Bolivia
124 M 6 **Villa Ocampo**, Mexico
144 L 8 **Villa Ocampo**, Argentina
144 J 9 **Villa Ojo de Agua**, Argentina
124 M 9 **Villa Unión**, Mexico
125 N 8 **Villa Unión**, Mexico
144 H 9 **Villa Unión**, Argentina
144 I 12 **Villa Valeria**, Argentina
80 L 1 **Villablino**, Spain
81 P 11 **Villacarrillo**, Spain
81 N 6 **Villacastín**, Spain
89 S 9 **Villach**, Austria
80 M 3 **Villada**, Spain
80 J 2 **Villafranca del Bierzo**, Spain
91 I 22 **Villafrati**, Italy
125 Q 8 **Villagrán**, Mexico
144 L 11 **Villaguay**, Argentina
125 W 13 **Villahermosa**, Mexico
81 T 10 **Villajoyosa**, Spain
145 J 16 **Villalonga**, Argentina
80 M 4 **Villalpando**, Spain
91 B 16 **Villanova Monteleone**, Italy
81 P 10 **Villanueva de los Infantes**, Spain
93 I 26 **Villány**, Hungary
80 M 4 **Villardefrades**, Spain
145 F 15 **Villarrica**, Chile
81 Q 8 **Villarrobledo**, Spain
91 C 19 **Villasimius**, Italy
138 J 7 **Villavicencio**, Colombia
80 M 1 **Villaviciosa de Asturias**, Spain
141 K 23 **Villazon**, Bolivia
79 P 12 **Villefranche-de-Rouergue**, France
79 T 9 **Villefranche-sur-Saône**, France
81 S 10 **Villena**, Spain
99 G 16 **Vilnius**, Lithuania
87 L 23 **Vilsbiburg**, Germany
87 M 23 **Vilshofen**, Germany
83 G 18 **Vilvoorde**, Belgium
99 I 16 **Vilyeyka**, Belarus
157 S 10 **Vilyuy**, Russian Federation
157 Q 10 **Vilyuyskoye Vodokhranilishche**, Russian Federation
80 G 1 **Vimianzo**, Spain
79 N 4 **Vimoutiers**, France
144 E 11 **Viña del Mar**, Chile
197 Z 6 **Vinanivao**, Madgascar
81 U 6 **Vinarós**, Spain
120 I 12 **Vincennes**, Indiana, U.S.A.
219 Y 11 **Vincennes Bay**, Antarctica
169 C 15 **Vindhya Ranges**, India
100 F 10 **Vinga**, Romania
173 L 14 **Vinh**, Vietnam
173 N 16 **Vinh Linh**, Vietnam
173 M 22 **Vinh Long**, Vietnam
173 L 23 **Vinh Rach Gia**, Vietnam
80 J 4 **Vinhais**, Portugal
96 E 11 **Vinica**, Macedonia (F.Y.R.O.M.)
119 L 16 **Vinita**, Oklahoma, U.S.A.
94 I 9 **Vinkovci**, Croatia
101 N 5 **Vinnytsya**, Ukraine
218 L 7 **Vinson Massif**, Antarctica
194 G 10 **Vinza**, Congo
90 F 4 **Vipiteno**, Italy
175 Q 4 **Virac**, Philippines
169 B 14 **Viramgam**, India
159 P 13 **Viranşehir**, Turkey
165 W 15 **Virawah**, Pakistan
114 H 10 **Virden**, Manitoba, Canada
78 M 4 **Vire**, France
196 G 6 **Virei**, Angola
127 U 6 **Virgin Islands**, U.K.
127 U 8 **Virgin Islands**, U.S.A.
121 Q 13 **Virginia**, U.S.A.
118 L 7 **Virginia**, Minnesota, U.S.A.
197 N 12 **Virginia**, Republic of South Africa
121 T 14 **Virginia Beach**, Virginia, U.S.A.
117 F 16 **Virginia City**, Nevada, U.S.A.
85 N 18 **Virojoki**, Finland
94 G 8 **Virovitica**, Croatia
83 J 26 **Virton**, Belgium
98 E 7 **Virtsu**, Estonia
141 B 14 **Virú**, Peru
95 E 14 **Vis**, Croatia
117 F 20 **Visalia**, California, U.S.A.
85 H 23 **Visby**, Sweden
142 B 11 **Visconde do Rio Branco**, Brazil
65 O 7 **Viscount Melville Sound**, Arctic Ocean
83 K 19 **Visé**, Belgium
94 J 12 **Višegrad**, Bosnia and Herzegovina
80 I 6 **Viseu**, Portugal
80 I 6 **Viseu**, Portugal
169 H 18 **Vishakhapatnam**, India
96 L 11 **Vishegrad**, Bulgaria
167 S 4 **Vishnevka**, Kazakhstan
88 E 10 **Visp**, Switzerland
92 J 12 **Vistula**, Poland
99 A 16 **Vistula Lagoon**, Russian Federation
101 S 8 **Visun'**, Ukraine
96 I 7 **Vit**, Bulgaria
90 G 13 **Viterbo**, Italy
213 W 11 **Viti Levu**, Fiji
80 K 5 **Vitigudino**, Spain
143 M 18 **Vitória**, Brazil
143 M 16 **Vitória da Conquista**, Brazil
142 I 10 **Vitória do Xingu**, Brazil
81 Q 2 **Vitoria-Gasteiz**, Spain
63 H 16 **Vitória Seamount**, Atlantic Ocean
96 F 9 **Vitosha**, Bulgaria
78 L 5 **Vitré**, France
79 T 4 **Vitry-le-François**, France
99 M 14 **Vitsyebsk**, Belarus
99 L 15 **Vitsyebskaya Voblasts'**, Belarus
84 J 10 **Vittangi**, Sweden
79 U 5 **Vittel**, France
91 J 23 **Vittoria**, Italy
61 P 6 **Vityaz Seamount**, Pacific Ocean
80 J 1 **Viveiro**, Spain
81 T 7 **Viver**, Spain
197 O 9 **Vivo**, Republic of South Africa
79 N 9 **Vivonne**, France
96 N 11 **Vize**, Turkey
169 H 18 **Vizianagaram**, India
100 M 12 **Viziru**, Romania
95 K 20 **Vjosë**, Albania
83 I 19 **Vlaams Brabant**, Belgium
82 F 13 **Vlaardingen**, Netherlands
95 N 15 **Vladičin Han**, Serbia and Montenegro
156 G 8 **Vladimir**, Russian Federation
96 G 7 **Vladimirovo**, Bulgaria
157 V 15 **Vladivostok**, Russian Federation
82 O 7 **Vlagtwedde**, Netherlands
94 I 12 **Vlasenica**, Bosnia and Herzegovina
94 G 11 **Vlašić**, Bosnia and Herzegovina
93 D 18 **Vlašim**, Czech Republic
95 N 14 **Vlasotince**, Serbia and Montenegro
82 H 6 **Vlieland**, Netherlands
83 D 16 **Vlissingen**, Netherlands
95 J 20 **Vlorë**, Albania
93 C 18 **Vltava**, Czech Republic
89 R 4 **Vöcklabruck**, Austria
193 T 12 **Vogel Peak**, Nigeria
87 F 18 **Vogelsberg**, Germany
197 Y 9 **Vohilava**, Madgascar
98 D 7 **Võhma**, Estonia
98 G 7 **Võhma**, Estonia
195 W 10 **Voi**, Kenya
100 I 11 **Voineasa**, Romania
192 H 12 **Voinjama**, Liberia
79 U 10 **Voiron**, France
89 V 7 **Voitsberg**, Austria
94 D 9 **Vojnić**, Croatia
94 J 9 **Vojvodina**, Serbia and Montenegro
193 U 12 **Voko**, Cameroon
126 C 9 **Volcán Agua**, Guatemala
144 G 6 **Volcán Antofalla**, Argentina
144 H 4 **Volcán Apagado**, Chile
126 I 13 **Volcán Barú**, Panama
144 G 8 **Volcán Copiapó**, Chile
145 F 18 **Volcán Corcovado**, Chile
140 B 9 **Volcán Cotopaxi**, Ecuador
141 A 18 **Volcán Darwin**, Ecuador
125 W 15 **Volcán de Tacaná**, Mexico
145 G 14 **Volcán Domuyo**, Argentina
144 G 2 **Volcán Guallatiri**, Chile
126 H 13 **Volcán Irazu**, Costa Rica
141 A 18 **Volcán La Cumbre**, Ecuador
145 F 16 **Volcán Lanin**, Argentina
124 H 5 **Volcán Las Tres Virgenes**, Mexico
144 H 5 **Volcán Licancábur**, Chile
144 G 6 **Volcán Llullaillaco**, Chile
126 G 12 **Volcán Miravalles**, Costa Rica
141 G 19 **Volcán Misti**, Peru
141 I 23 **Volcán Ollagüe**, Bolivia
126 G 12 **Volcán Poás**, Costa Rica
144 G 12 **Volcán San José**, Chile
140 B 10 **Volcán Sangay**, Ecuador
138 G 8 **Volcán Sotará**, Colombia
144 F 1 **Volcán Tacora**, Chile
126 C 9 **Volcán Tajumulco**, Guatemala
145 G 14 **Volcán Tromen**, Argentina
145 F 16 **Volcán Villarrica**, Chile
141 A 18 **Volcán Wolf**, Ecuador
82 I 10 **Volendam**, Netherlands
156 F 10 **Volga**, Russian Federation
156 F 10 **Volgograd**, Russian Federation
89 T 9 **Völkermarkt**, Austria
156 G 7 **Volkhov**, Russian Federation
101 X 7 **Volnovakha**, Ukraine
157 P 8 **Volochanka**, Russian Federation
100 L 5 **Volochys'k**, Ukraine
101 P 5 **Volodarka**, Ukraine
101 X 8 **Volodars'ke**, Ukraine
100 J 3 **Volodymyr-Volyns'kyy**, Ukraine
100 L 2 **Volodymyrets'**, Ukraine
156 G 8 **Vologda**, Russian Federation
101 W 5 **Volokhiv Yar**, Ukraine
156 F 8 **Volokolamsk**, Russian Federation
97 F 17 **Volos**, Greece
101 Z 5 **Voloshino**, Ukraine
193 N 12 **Volta**, Ghana
193 N 13 **Volta**, Ghana
90 E 11 **Volterra**, Italy
197 X 10 **Vondrozo**, Madgascar
97 B 18 **Vonitsa**, Greece
98 I 8 **Võnnu**, Estonia
82 J 12 **Voorhuizen**, Netherlands
82 G 12 **Voorschoten**, Netherlands
84 D 10 **Vopnafjörður**, Iceland
99 G 17 **Voranava**, Belarus
89 S 5 **Vorchdorf**, Austria
82 L 12 **Vorden**, Netherlands
85 D 26 **Vordingborg**, Denmark
97 K 18 **Voreio Aigaio**, Greece
97 G 18 **Voreioi Sporades**, Greece
97 F 18 **Voreios Evvoïkos Kolpos**, Greece
65 T 15 **Voring Plateau**, Arctic Ocean
156 L 8 **Vorkuta**, Russian Federation
98 E 6 **Vormsi**, Estonia
156 F 9 **Voronezh**, Russian Federation
101 U 4 **Vorskla**, Ukraine
98 G 8 **Võrtsjärv**, Estonia
98 I 9 **Võru**, Estonia
167 S 12 **Vorukh**, Tajikistan
196 L 13 **Vosburg**, Republic of South Africa
167 R 14 **Vose**, Tajikistan
79 W 6 **Vosges**, France
85 A 18 **Voss**, Norway
167 X 5 **Vostochnyy Kazakhstan**, Kazakhstan
157 N 13 **Vostochnyy Sayan**, Russian Federation
219 T 9 **Vostok**, Antarctica
215 R 6 **Vostok**, Kiribati
79 T 3 **Vouziers**, France
101 W 7 **Vovcha**, Ukraine
101 W 3 **Vovchans'k**, Ukraine
156 J 8 **Voyvozh**, Russian Federation
101 Q 8 **Voznesens'k**, Ukraine
101 R 8 **Vozsiyats'ke**, Ukraine
99 J 20 **Vozyera Chyrvonaye**, Belarus
101 P 8 **Vradiyivka**, Ukraine
95 N 15 **Vranjska Banja**, Serbia and Montenegro
93 M 20 **Vranov nad Toplou**, Slovakia
96 G 8 **Vratsa**, Bulgaria
96 G 8 **Vratsa**, Bulgaria
94 B 7 **Vrhnika**, Slovenia
83 D 15 **Vrouwenpolder**, Netherlands
94 M 9 **Vršac**, Serbia and Montenegro
94 E 10 **Vrtoče**, Bosnia and Herzegovina
196 M 11 **Vryburg**, Republic of South Africa
197 P 12 **Vryheid**, Republic of South Africa
93 H 19 **Vsetín**, Czech Republic
95 M 15 **Vučitrn**, Serbia and Montenegro
83 I 15 **Vught**, Netherlands
101 X 7 **Vuhledar**, Ukraine
94 I 9 **Vukovar**, Croatia
156 J 8 **Vuktyl'**, Russian Federation
197 P 11 **Vukuzakhe**, Republic of South Africa
157 Y 10 **Vulkan Ichinskiy**, Russian Federation
173 N 22 **Vung Tau**, Vietnam
213 X 12 **Vunisea**, Fiji
85 M 18 **Vuohijarvi**, Finland
84 J 11 **Vuollerim**, Sweden
84 H 11 **Vuolvojaure**, Sweden
84 L 9 **Vuotso**, Finland
156 F 8 **Vyaz'ma**, Russian Federation
156 G 6 **Vyborg**, Russian Federation
98 J 13 **Vyerkhnyadzvinsk**, Belarus
99 N 20 **Vyetka**, Belarus
99 K 14 **Vyetryna**, Belarus
99 H 20 **Vyhanashchy**, Belarus
101 O 11 **Vylkove**, Ukraine
100 H 7 **Vylok**, Ukraine
100 K 4 **Vyshnivets'**, Ukraine
93 G 19 **Vyškov**, Czech Republic
99 E 20 **Vysokaye**, Belarus
101 O 2 **Vystupovychi**, Ukraine
156 G 7 **Vytegra**, Russian Federation

W

192 L 11 **Wa**, Ghana
119 I 14 **Wa Keeney**, Kansas, U.S.A.
83 I 14 **Waal**, Netherlands
83 I 14 **Waalwijk**, Netherlands
191 E 21 **Waat**, Sudan
212 C 4 **Wabag**, Papua New Guinea
113 U 9 **Wabasca**, Alberta, Canada
113 U 10 **Wabasca-Desmarais**, Alberta, Canada
120 I 13 **Wabash**, U.S.A.
120 K 10 **Wabash**, Indiana, U.S.A.
123 P 10 **Waccasassa Bay**, Florida, U.S.A.
119 K 20 **Waco**, Texas, U.S.A.
165 S 13 **Wad**, Pakistan
191 C 18 **Wad Banda**, Sudan
191 F 16 **Wad Hamid**, Sudan
191 F 17 **Wad Medani**, Sudan
189 U 9 **Waddān**, Libya
82 H 6 **Waddeneilanden**, Netherlands
82 H 8 **Waddenzee**, Netherlands
118 K 8 **Wadena**, Minnesota, U.S.A.
88 G 7 **Wädenswil**, Switzerland
161 X 14 **Wādī al Bāṭin**, Iraq
163 T 12 **Wādī al Masīlah**, Yemen
160 G 9 **Wādī as Sīr**, Jordan
161 R 3 **Wādī ath Tharthār**, Iraq
190 E 13 **Wadi Halfa**, Sudan
161 O 7 **Wādī Ḥawrān**, Iraq
160 G 12 **Wādī Mūsā**, Jordan
123 Q 5 **Wadley**, Georgia, U.S.A.
177 N 23 **Wadomari**, Japan
82 K 13 **Wageningen**, Netherlands
114 M 2 **Wager Bay**, Nunavut, Canada
209 T 12 **Wagga Wagga**, New South Wales, Australia
208 G 11 **Wagin**, Western Australia, Australia
88 G 7 **Wägiteler See**, Switzerland
92 G 11 **Wągrowiec**, Poland
165 X 8 **Wah**, Pakistan

Country · Internal administrative region: State/Province/Territory/Dependent territory · Capital city · Mountain range/Undersea ridge · Mountain peak/Volcano/Seamount · Geographic feature · Headland/Point/Cape/Peninsula · Desert · Island/Island group · Antarctic base · Ocean · Sea · Bay/Gulf/Channel/Strait · Lake · Salt pan/Dry/Intermittent lake · River

17 K 17 Wah Wah Mountains, Utah, U.S.A.
75 S 12 Wahai, Indonesia
10 L 10 Waharoa, New Zealand
91 D 20 Wahda, Sudan
17 C 24 Wahiawa, Hawaii, U.S.A.
18 J 9 Wahpeton, North Dakota, U.S.A.
11 H 18 Waiau, New Zealand
11 H 19 Waiau, New Zealand
9 U 4 Waidhofen an der Ybbs, Austria
75 T 11 Waigeo, Indonesia
10 I 5 Waiharara, New Zealand
10 O 11 Waihau Bay, New Zealand
10 K 8 Waiheke Island, New Zealand
10 L 9 Waihi, New Zealand
10 O 11 Waihirere, New Zealand
11 E 25 Waihola, New Zealand
75 N 15 Waikabubak, Indonesia
11 K 15 Waikanae, New Zealand
11 H 19 Waikari, New Zealand
10 K 11 Waikato, New Zealand
11 F 24 Waikouaiti, New Zealand
17 D 24 Wailuku, Hawaii, U.S.A.
11 H 17 Waimarie, New Zealand
11 G 22 Waimate, New Zealand
17 C 24 Waimea, Hawaii, U.S.A.
17 D 25 Waimea, Hawaii, U.S.A.
75 O 15 Waingapu, Indonesia
11 L 16 Wainuioru, New Zealand
12 K 2 Wainwright, Alaska, U.S.A.
13 W 12 Wainwright, Alberta, Canada
10 M 11 Waiotapu, New Zealand
10 L 13 Waiouru, New Zealand
11 D 25 Waipahi, New Zealand
11 H 19 Waipara, New Zealand
11 M 14 Waipawa, New Zealand
10 J 7 Waipu, New Zealand
11 M 14 Waipukurau, New Zealand
11 I 17 Wairau, New Zealand
11 I 17 Wairau Valley, New Zealand
10 N 12 Wairoa, New Zealand
10 M 12 Waitahanui, New Zealand
10 L 9 Waitakaruru, New Zealand
10 J 8 Waitakere, New Zealand
11 E 22 Waitaki, New Zealand
11 F 24 Waitati, New Zealand
10 K 13 Waitotara, New Zealand
10 J 9 Waiuku, New Zealand
177 H 14 Wajima, Japan
194 K 7 Waka, Democratic Republic of Congo
177 G 17 Wakasa-wan, Japan
177 G 19 Wakayama, Japan
177 F 19 Waki, Japan
176 J 8 Wakinosawa, Japan
176 J 3 Wakkanai, Japan
196 H 4 Waku-Kungo, Angola
212 J 4 Wakunai, Papua New Guinea
93 F 16 Wałbrzych, Poland
209 V 10 Walcha, New South Wales, Australia
92 F 10 Wałcz, Poland
87 D 24 Waldkirch, Germany
121 S 13 Waldorf, Maryland, U.S.A.
87 E 25 Waldshut, Germany
175 P 11 Waleabahi, Indonesia
77 H 21 Wales, United Kingdom
112 G 3 Wales, Alaska, U.S.A.
83 L 25 Walferdange, Luxembourg
209 T 9 Walgett, New South Wales, Australia
218 K 9 Walgreen Coast, Antarctica
195 P 8 Walikale, Democratic Republic of Congo
117 G 17 Walker Lake, Nevada, U.S.A.
116 H 9 Walla Walla, Washington, U.S.A.
59 S 7 Wallaby Plateau, Indian Ocean
116 I 7 Wallace, Idaho, U.S.A.
123 V 3 Wallace, North Carolina, U.S.A.
113 T 11 Wallace Mountain, Alberta, Canada
209 P 11 Wallaroo, South Australia, Australia
87 G 20 Walldürn, Germany
88 H 7 Wallensee, Switzerland
214 I 8 Wallis, Wallis and Futuna Islands
214 H 7 Wallis and Futuna Islands, France
88 D 10 Walliser Alpen, Switzerland
208 G 12 Walpole, Western Australia, Australia
119 F 15 Walsenburg, Colorado, U.S.A.
169 H 18 Waltair, India
123 N 7 Walter F. George Reservoir, Georgia, U.S.A.
123 S 5 Walterboro, South Carolina, U.S.A.
58 J 9 Walters Shoal, Indian Ocean
196 H 9 Walvis Bay, Namibia
196 H 10 Walvis Bay, Namibia
63 L 17 Walvis Ridge, Atlantic Ocean
175 Y 14 Wamal, Indonesia
194 L 8 Wamba, Democratic Republic of Congo
195 P 6 Wamba, Democratic Republic of Congo
165 V 9 Wana, Pakistan
209 R 9 Wanaaring, New South Wales, Australia
211 D 22 Wanaka, New Zealand
175 W 13 Wanapiri, Indonesia
175 W 12 Wandai, Indonesia
65 S 10 Wandel Sea, Arctic Ocean
173 G 14 Wang Nua, Thailand
173 I 16 Wang Saphung, Thailand
210 K 13 Wanganui, New Zealand
211 K 14 Wanganui, New Zealand
209 S 12 Wangaratta, Victoria, Australia
87 G 25 Wangen, Germany
86 E 9 Wangerooge, Germany
175 P 13 Wangiwangi, Indonesia
171 Y 4 Wangqing, China
113 T 11 Wanham, Alberta, Canada
195 N 7 Wanie-Rukula, Democratic Republic of Congo
191 L 24 Wanlaweyn, Somalia
171 S 15 Wanning, China
171 R 10 Wanxian, China
171 R 10 Wanyuan, China
120 L 10 Wapakoneta, Ohio, U.S.A.
116 F 8 Wapato, Washington, U.S.A.
82 L 11 Wapenveld, Netherlands
191 D 21 Warab, Sudan
191 D 21 Warab, Sudan
208 K 7 Warakurna Roadhouse, Western Australia, Australia
191 L 21 Warandab, Ethiopia
169 F 18 Warangal, India
87 F 15 Warburg, Germany
209 P 8 Warburton, South Australia, Australia
208 K 8 Warburton, Western Australia, Australia
165 U 7 Wardag, Afghanistan
169 F 16 Wardha, India
161 P 2 Wardīyah, Iraq
83 C 19 Waregem, Belgium
83 I 20 Waremme, Belgium
86 L 10 Waren, Germany
87 E 14 Warendorf, Germany
209 V 6 Warginburra Peninsula, Queensland, Australia
209 V 9 Warialda, New South Wales, Australia
92 L 13 Warka, Poland
210 K 7 Warkworth, New Zealand
117 I 18 Warm Springs, Nevada, U.S.A.
175 U 11 Warmandi, Indonesia
196 J 12 Warmbad, Namibia
77 J 22 Warminster, United Kingdom
208 K 3 Warmun, Western Australia, Australia
86 K 8 Warnemünde, Germany
123 P 6 Warner Robins, Georgia, U.S.A.
83 B 19 Warneton, Belgium
169 F 16 Warora, India
209 Q 12 Warracknabeal, Victoria, Australia
209 S 9 Warrego, Queensland, Australia
120 M 8 Warren, Michigan, U.S.A.
121 O 10 Warren, Ohio, U.S.A.
121 Q 9 Warren, Pennsylvania, U.S.A.
121 R 13 Warrenton, Virginia, U.S.A.
196 M 12 Warrenton, Republic of South Africa
193 Q 14 Warri, Nigeria
77 J 18 Warrington, United Kingdom
122 K 8 Warrington, Florida, U.S.A.
122 L 4 Warrior, Alabama, U.S.A.
209 R 13 Warrnambool, Victoria, Australia
118 K 7 Warroad, Minnesota, U.S.A.
92 L 12 Warsaw, Poland
119 M 15 Warsaw, Missouri, U.S.A.
120 K 10 Warsaw, Indiana, U.S.A.
121 R 8 Warsaw, New York, U.S.A.
123 U 3 Warsaw, North Carolina, U.S.A.
191 M 24 Warshiikh, Somalia
93 I 14 Warta, Poland
169 F 16 Warud, India
77 K 20 Warwick, United Kingdom
121 W 9 Warwick, Rhode Island, U.S.A.
209 V 9 Warwick, Queensland, Australia
117 M 14 Wasatch Range, Utah, U.S.A.
77 M 18 Wash, The, United Kingdom
165 Q 13 Washap, Pakistan
120 G 3 Washburn, Wisconsin, U.S.A.
169 E 16 Washim, India
116 E 7 Washington, U.S.A.
121 P 11 Washington, Pennsylvania, U.S.A.
123 V 2 Washington, North Carolina, U.S.A.
121 S 12 Washington, D.C., District of Columbia, U.S.A.
120 J 5 Washington Island, Wisconsin, U.S.A.
115 P 10 Waskaganish, Québec, Canada
113 X 10 Waskesiu Lake, Saskatchewan, Canada
126 H 10 Waspán, Nicaragua
83 H 14 Waspik, Netherlands
192 F 9 Wassadou, Senegal
87 K 24 Wasserburg, Germany
87 G 18 Wasserkuppe, Germany
212 E 4 Wasu, Papua New Guinea
212 B 6 Wasua, Papua New Guinea
175 O 13 Watampone, Indonesia
169 L 18 Wataru Channel, Maldives
121 V 9 Waterbury, Connecticut, U.S.A.
77 D 20 Waterford, Republic of Ireland
83 G 20 Waterloo, Belgium
118 M 11 Waterloo, Iowa, U.S.A.
120 I 4 Watersmeet, Michigan, U.S.A.
118 J 10 Watertown, South Dakota, U.S.A.
121 S 7 Watertown, New York, U.S.A.
77 A 21 Waterville, Republic of Ireland
116 F 7 Waterville, Washington, U.S.A.
77 L 21 Watford, United Kingdom
195 Q 6 Watsa, Democratic Republic of Congo
194 K 8 Watsi Kengo, Democratic Republic of Congo
113 Y 11 Watson, Saskatchewan, Canada
113 P 9 Watson Lake, Yukon Territory, Canada
117 D 19 Watsonville, California, U.S.A.
123 N 2 Watts Bar Lake, Tennessee, U.S.A.
88 H 7 Wattwil, Switzerland
191 C 21 Wau, Sudan
212 E 5 Wau, Papua New Guinea
209 N 5 Wauchope, Northern Territory, Australia
123 R 12 Wauchula, Florida, U.S.A.
120 I 8 Waukegan, Illinois, U.S.A.
120 I 8 Waukesha, Wisconsin, U.S.A.
120 H 6 Waupaca, Wisconsin, U.S.A.
120 H 5 Wausau, Wisconsin, U.S.A.
120 H 7 Wautoma, Wisconsin, U.S.A.
208 M 3 Wave Hill, Northern Territory, Australia
121 S 9 Waverly, New York, U.S.A.
122 K 1 Waverly, Tennessee, U.S.A.
83 G 20 Wavre, Belgium
189 U 11 Wāw al Kabīr, Libya
115 N 12 Wawa, Ontario, Canada
193 P 11 Wawa, Nigeria
212 B 5 Wawoi, Papua New Guinea
119 K 19 Waxahachie, Texas, U.S.A.
175 S 9 Wayabula, Indonesia
175 T 10 Wayag, Indonesia
123 Q 7 Waycross, Georgia, U.S.A.
122 J 7 Waynesboro, Mississippi, U.S.A.
122 K 2 Waynesboro, Tennessee, U.S.A.
123 R 5 Waynesboro, Georgia, U.S.A.
193 V 10 Waza, Cameroon
165 T 9 Wazi Khwa, Afghanistan
165 Y 8 Wazirabad, Pakistan
92 H 10 Wda, Poland
213 Q 13 Wé, New Caledonia
119 J 17 Weatherford, Oklahoma, U.S.A.
117 D 15 Weaverville, California, U.S.A.
114 M 9 Webequie, Ontario, Canada
60 K 8 Weber Basin, Pacific Ocean
212 G 7 Wedau, Papua New Guinea
63 H 23 Weddel Abyssal Plain, Atlantic Ocean
145 K 24 Weddell Island, Falkland Islands
218 K 5 Weddell Sea, Antarctica
209 U 10 Wee Waa, New South Wales, Australia
117 D 14 Weed, California, U.S.A.
83 I 16 Weelde, Belgium
83 K 17 Weert, Netherlands
82 H 11 Weesp, Netherlands
92 L 8 Węgorzewo, Poland
92 M 12 Węgrów, Poland
174 B 8 Weh, Indonesia
171 U 6 Weichang, China
87 K 20 Weiden, Germany
171 V 7 Weifang, China
171 W 7 Weihai, China
87 J 17 Weimar, Germany
171 S 9 Weinan, China
171 Q 12 Weining, China
209 R 1 Weipa, Queensland, Australia
116 I 11 Weiser, Idaho, U.S.A.
122 M 4 Weiss Lake, Alabama, U.S.A.
87 I 22 Weissenburg in Bayern, Germany
87 N 15 Weisswasser, Germany
83 L 23 Weiswampach, Luxembourg
89 U 2 Weitra, Austria
89 W 7 Weiz, Austria
92 H 8 Wejherowo, Poland
211 G 15 Wekakura Point, New Zealand
121 N 14 Welch, West Virginia, U.S.A.
191 I 19 Weldiya, Ethiopia
117 G 21 Weldon, California, U.S.A.
61 T 2 Welker Seamount, Pacific Ocean
191 H 21 Welk'īt'ē, Ethiopia
197 N 12 Welkom, Republic of South Africa
169 G 25 Wellawaya, Sri Lanka
209 Q 3 Wellesley Islands, Queensland, Australia
83 I 23 Wellin, Belgium
211 L 16 Wellington, New Zealand
211 L 16 Wellington, New Zealand
209 U 11 Wellington, New South Wales, Australia
117 J 14 Wells, Nevada, U.S.A.
210 K 7 Wellsford, New Zealand
89 S 4 Wels, Austria
77 I 19 Welshpool, United Kingdom
115 P 9 Wemindji, Québec, Canada
116 F 7 Wenatchee, Washington, U.S.A.
171 T 15 Wenchang, China
192 L 12 Wenchi, Ghana
87 E 17 Wenden, Germany
117 L 23 Wenden, Arizona, U.S.A.
117 K 15 Wendover, Nevada, U.S.A.
88 E 9 Wengen, Switzerland
215 O 15 Weno, Federated States of Micronesia
170 J 4 Wenquan, China
170 L 9 Wenquan, China
209 R 11 Wentworth, New South Wales, Australia
171 Q 9 Wenxian, China
171 W 11 Wenzhou, China
83 K 21 Werbomont, Belgium
196 L 10 Werda, Botswana
191 L 21 Werdēr, Ethiopia
89 R 6 Werfen, Austria
87 E 15 Werl, Germany
87 K 21 Wernberg-Köblitz, Germany
87 I 15 Wernigerode, Germany
191 H 19 Werota, Ethiopia
87 H 16 Werra, Germany
87 G 20 Wertheim, Germany
82 I 9 Wervershoof, Netherlands
87 B 15 Wesel, Germany
87 G 15 Weser, Germany
121 Z 5 Wesley, Maine, U.S.A.
209 O 1 Wessel Islands, Northern Territory, Australia
218 L 7 West Antarctica, Antarctica
160 G 9 West Bank, Israel
122 M 9 West Bay, Florida, U.S.A.
169 K 15 West Bengal, India
118 C 6 West Butte, Montana, U.S.A.
211 A 25 West Cape, New Zealand
60 K 7 West Caroline Basin, Pacific Ocean
211 E 19 West Coast, New Zealand
145 J 23 West Falkland, Falkland Islands
214 M 15 West Fayu, Federated States of Micronesia
121 Z 5 West Grand Lake, Maine, U.S.A.
219 X 6 West Ice Shelf, Antarctica
59 Y 2 West Island, Cocos Islands
59 Y 3 West Island Settlement, Cocos Islands
60 K 6 West Mariana Basin, Pacific Ocean
212 F 5 West New Britain, Papua New Guinea
197 P 8 West Nicholson, Zimbabwe
123 T 13 West Palm Beach, Florida, U.S.A.
119 M 16 West Plains, Missouri, U.S.A.
121 S 14 West Point, Virginia, U.S.A.
122 M 5 West Point Lake, Alabama, U.S.A.
63 E 22 West Scotia Ridge, Atlantic Ocean
58 J 2 West Sheba Ridge, Indian Ocean
156 L 9 West Siberian Plain, Russian Federation
82 I 6 West-Terschelling, Netherlands
121 O 13 West Virginia, U.S.A.
83 A 18 West-Vlaanderen, Belgium
209 T 11 West Wyalong, New South Wales, Australia
120 G 7 Westby, Wisconsin, U.S.A.
82 M 8 Westerbork, Netherlands
168 I 11 Western, Nepal
169 F 25 Western, Sri Lanka
195 T 7 Western, Kenya
196 L 6 Western, Zambia
212 B 5 Western, Papua New Guinea
212 J 6 Western, Solomon Islands
192 L 13 Western, Ghana
192 F 12 Western Area, Sierra Leone
208 J 7 Western Australia, Australia
191 C 21 Western Bahr el Ghazal, Sudan
196 L 14 Western Cape, Republic of South Africa
191 A 17 Western Darfur, Sudan
190 C 9 Western Desert, Egypt
98 F 11 Western Dvina, Belarus/Latvia
191 D 22 Western Equatoria, Sudan
169 C 17 Western Ghats, India
61 X 14 Western Harbour, Pitcairn Island
212 C 4 Western Highlands, Papua New Guinea
191 D 19 Western Kordofan, Sudan
188 C 12 Western Sahara, Africa
83 D 16 Westerschelde, Netherlands
121 P 9 Westfield, New York, U.S.A.
82 K 5 Westgat, Netherlands
118 H 7 Westhope, North Dakota, U.S.A.
83 G 16 Westmalle, Belgium
121 S 11 Westminster, Maryland, U.S.A.
121 P 12 Weston, West Virginia, U.S.A.
77 I 22 Weston-super-Mare, United Kingdom
77 B 17 Westport, Republic of Ireland
116 C 7 Westport, Washington, U.S.A.
211 G 17 Westport, New Zealand
76 I 6 Westray, United Kingdom
114 H 8 Westray, Manitoba, Canada
115 O 12 Westree, Ontario, Canada
175 R 14 Wetar, Indonesia
113 V 12 Wetaskiwin, Alberta, Canada
195 X 11 Wete, Tanzania
87 E 18 Wetzlar, Germany
83 C 19 Wevelgem, Belgium
112 I 2 Wevok, Alaska, U.S.A.
123 N 9 Wewahitchka, Florida, U.S.A.
212 C 3 Wewak, Papua New Guinea
77 E 20 Wexford, Republic of Ireland
113 Z 12 Weyburn, Saskatchewan, Canada
89 U 5 Weyer Markt, Austria
87 D 17 Weyerbusch, Germany
77 J 23 Weymouth, United Kingdom
113 S 7 Wha Ti, Northwest Territories, Canada
210 M 11 Whakamaru, New Zealand
210 J 6 Whakapara, New Zealand
211 M 15 Whakataki, New Zealand
210 N 10 Whakatane, New Zealand
210 N 13 Whakatu, New Zealand
114 L 4 Whale Cove, Nunavut, Canada
76 K 4 Whalsay, United Kingdom
210 M 9 Whangamata, New Zealand
210 K 12 Whangamomona, New Zealand
211 H 15 Whanganui Inlet, New Zealand
210 O 10 Whangaparaoa, New Zealand
210 O 11 Whangara, New Zealand
210 J 6 Whangarei, New Zealand
59 R 7 Wharton Basin, Indian Ocean
122 K 3 Wheeler Lake, Alabama, U.S.A.
119 E 16 Wheeler Peak, New Mexico, U.S.A.
121 P 11 Wheeling, West Virginia, U.S.A.
210 L 8 Whenuakite, New Zealand
77 J 16 Whernside, United Kingdom
210 I 6 Whirinaki, New Zealand
113 S 14 Whistler, British Columbia, Canada
77 L 16 Whitby, United Kingdom
117 J 19 White, Nevada, U.S.A.
120 J 12 White, Indiana, U.S.A.
115 X 10 White Bay, Newfoundland and Labrador, Canada
118 G 9 White Butte, North Dakota, U.S.A.
121 Y 4 White Cap Mountain, Maine, U.S.A.
209 R 10 White Cliffs, New South Wales, Australia
115 W 12 White Hill, Nova Scotia, Canada
210 N 9 White Island, New Zealand
119 N 21 White Lake, Louisiana, U.S.A.
117 G 18 White Mountain, California, U.S.A.
121 W 7 White Mountains, Vermont, U.S.A.
191 F 18 White Nile, Sudan
191 D 21 White Nile, Sudan

Country · Internal administrative region: State/Province/Territory/Dependent territory · Capital city · Mountain range/Undersea ridge · Mountain peak/Volcano/Seamount · Geographic feature · Headland/Point/Cape/Peninsula · Desert · Island/Island group · Antarctic base · Ocean · Sea · Bay/Gulf/Channel/Strait · Lake · Salt pan/Dry/Intermittent lake · River

156 H 6 **White Sea**, Russian Federation
121 P 14 **White Sulpher Springs**, West Virginia, U.S.A.
192 M 10 **White Volta**, Ghana
113 U 11 **Whitecourt**, Alberta, Canada
120 L 4 **Whitefish Bay**, Michigan, U.S.A.
120 G 6 **Whitehall**, Wisconsin, U.S.A.
121 V 7 **Whitehall**, New York, U.S.A.
77 H 15 **Whitehaven**, United Kingdom
113 O 8 **Whitehorse**, Yukon Territory, Canada
123 U 3 **Whiteville**, North Carolina, U.S.A.
119 D 19 **Whitewater Baldy**, New Mexico, U.S.A.
77 H 15 **Whithorn**, United Kingdom
123 R 3 **Whitmire**, South Carolina, U.S.A.
115 P 14 **Whitney**, Ontario, Canada
209 U 5 **Whitsunday Group**, Queensland, Australia
112 K 8 **Whittier**, Alaska, U.S.A.
113 W 7 **Wholdaia Lake**, Northwest Territories, Canada
209 P 11 **Whyalla**, South Australia, Australia
173 G 14 **Wiang Pa Pao**, Thailand
172 G 13 **Wiang Phran**, Thailand
119 J 15 **Wichita**, Kansas, U.S.A.
119 J 18 **Wichita Falls**, Texas, U.S.A.
76 I 8 **Wick**, United Kingdom
117 M 23 **Wickenburg**, Arizona, U.S.A.
77 F 19 **Wicklow Head**, Republic of Ireland
87 E 15 **Wiedenbrück**, Germany
87 D 17 **Wiehl**, Germany
86 L 7 **Wiek**, Germany
92 L 10 **Wielbark**, Poland
93 I 15 **Wieluń**, Poland
89 X 5 **Wiener Neustadt**, Austria
93 M 14 **Wieprz**, Poland
87 E 19 **Wiesbaden**, Germany
87 C 18 **Wiesemscheid**, Germany
87 F 21 **Wiesloch**, Germany
122 I 8 **Wiggins**, Mississippi, U.S.A.
83 K 14 **Wijchen**, Netherlands
82 J 13 **Wijk bij Duurstede**, Netherlands
191 I 17 **Wik'ro**, Ethiopia
88 H 6 **Wil**, Switzerland
116 G 7 **Wilbur**, Washington, U.S.A.
209 R 10 **Wilcannia**, New South Wales, Australia
86 E 12 **Wildeshausen**, Germany
88 D 9 **Wildhorn**, Switzerland
89 W 8 **Wildon**, Austria
88 L 8 **Wildspitze**, Austria
113 U 12 **Wildwood**, Alberta, Canada
139 V 7 **Wilhelmina Gebergte**, Suriname
86 E 10 **Wilhelmshaven**, Germany
121 T 10 **Wilkes Barre**, Pennsylvania, U.S.A.
219 W 13 **Wilkes Coast**, Antarctica
219 V 12 **Wilkes Land**, Antarctica
123 R 1 **Wilkesboro**, North Carolina, U.S.A.
116 C 7 **Willapa Bay**, Washington, U.S.A.
119 E 18 **Willard**, New Mexico, U.S.A.
121 N 10 **Willard**, Ohio, U.S.A.
117 O 24 **Willcox**, Arizona, U.S.A.
83 F 18 **Willebroek**, Belgium
127 S 11 **Willemstad**, Netherlands Antilles
209 O 9 **William Creek**, South Australia, Australia
117 M 21 **Williams**, Arizona, U.S.A.
117 D 16 **Williams**, California, U.S.A.
208 G 11 **Williams**, Western Australia, Australia
113 S 13 **Williams Lake**, British Columbia, Canada
120 L 15 **Williamsburg**, Kentucky, U.S.A.
121 S 10 **Williamsport**, Pennsylvania, U.S.A.
123 V 2 **Williamston**, North Carolina, U.S.A.
118 G 7 **Williston**, North Dakota, U.S.A.
123 Q 10 **Williston**, Florida, U.S.A.
196 K 14 **Williston**, Republic of South Africa
113 R 11 **Williston Lake**, British Columbia, Canada
117 C 16 **Willits**, California, U.S.A.
118 K 9 **Willmar**, Minnesota, U.S.A.
196 M 15 **Willowmore**, Republic of South Africa
117 D 16 **Willows**, California, U.S.A.
120 M 12 **Wilmington**, Ohio, U.S.A.
121 T 11 **Wilmington**, Delaware, U.S.A.
123 V 4 **Wilmington**, North Carolina, U.S.A.
123 V 2 **Wilson**, North Carolina, U.S.A.
209 S 14 **Wilsons Promontory**, Victoria, Australia
83 K 24 **Wiltz**, Luxembourg
208 H 8 **Wiluna**, Western Australia, Australia
211 M 15 **Wimbledon**, New Zealand
197 N 12 **Winburg**, Republic of South Africa
77 K 22 **Winchester**, United Kingdom
120 L 13 **Winchester**, Kentucky, U.S.A.
121 R 12 **Winchester**, West Virginia, U.S.A.
122 M 3 **Winchester**, Tennessee, U.S.A.
118 C 11 **Wind River Range**, Wyoming, U.S.A.
123 O 4 **Winder**, Georgia, U.S.A.
196 I 9 **Windhoek**, Namibia
114 K 9 **Windigo Lake**, Ontario, Canada
89 T 5 **Windischgarsten**, Austria
118 K 10 **Windom**, Minnesota, U.S.A.
209 R 7 **Windorah**, Queensland, Australia
115 V 13 **Windsor**, Nova Scotia, Canada
115 N 15 **Windsor**, Ontario, Canada
123 W 1 **Windsor**, North Carolina, U.S.A.
127 Y 8 **Windward Islands**, 0
127 O 6 **Windward Passage**, Cuba
114 M 9 **Winisk**, Ontario, Canada
115 N 8 **Winisk**, Ontario, Canada
173 F 17 **Winkana**, Myanmar
89 Q 8 **Winklern**, Austria
192 M 14 **Winneba**, Ghana
117 H 14 **Winnemucca**, Nevada, U.S.A.
117 G 15 **Winnemucca Lake**, Nevada, U.S.A.
118 I 11 **Winner**, South Dakota, U.S.A.
114 J 10 **Winnipeg**, Manitoba, Canada
117 M 21 **Winona**, Arizona, U.S.A.
122 I 5 **Winona**, Mississippi, U.S.A.
82 O 7 **Winschoten**, Netherlands
86 H 11 **Winsen**, Germany
117 N 21 **Winslow**, Arizona, U.S.A.
121 Y 6 **Winslow**, Maine, U.S.A.
121 V 9 **Winsted**, Connecticut, U.S.A.
123 S 1 **Winston-Salem**, North Carolina, U.S.A.
123 R 10 **Winter Park**, Florida, U.S.A.
82 N 13 **Winterswijk**, Netherlands
88 G 6 **Winterthur**, Switzerland
209 R 6 **Winton**, Queensland, Australia
211 C 25 **Winton**, New Zealand
120 F 6 **Wisconsin**, U.S.A.
120 H 6 **Wisconsin Rapids**, Wisconsin, U.S.A.
112 L 4 **Wiseman**, Alaska, U.S.A.
93 I 18 **Wisła**, Poland
86 J 9 **Wismar**, Germany
79 X 4 **Wissembourg**, France
92 O 13 **Wisznice**, Poland
86 J 12 **Wittenberge**, Germany
86 I 10 **Wittenburg**, Germany
208 G 6 **Wittenoom**, Western Australia, Australia
87 C 19 **Wittlich**, Germany
86 K 11 **Wittstock**, Germany
212 F 4 **Witu Islands**, Papua New Guinea
196 J 9 **Witvlei**, Namibia
87 G 16 **Witzenhausen**, Germany
92 J 11 **Wkra**, Poland
92 H 7 **Władysławowo**, Poland
92 I 12 **Włocławek**, Poland
93 O 14 **Włodawa**, Poland
93 J 15 **Włoszczowa**, Poland
209 T 12 **Wodonga**, Victoria, Australia
93 K 16 **Wodzisław**, Poland
93 I 17 **Wodzisław Śląski**, Poland
82 H 12 **Woerden**, Netherlands
88 F 6 **Wohlen**, Switzerland
219 R 2 **Wohlthat Mountains**, Antarctica
175 V 13 **Wokam**, Indonesia
86 M 10 **Woldegk**, Germany
214 L 15 **Woleai**, Federated States of Micronesia
194 F 6 **Woleu-Ntem**, Gabon
118 C 8 **Wolf Creek**, Montana, U.S.A.
112 J 5 **Wolf Mountain**, Alaska, U.S.A.
118 F 7 **Wolf Point**, Montana, U.S.A.
89 U 8 **Wolfsberg**, Austria
86 I 13 **Wolfsburg**, Germany
86 M 9 **Wolgast**, Germany
88 F 7 **Wolhusen**, Switzerland
92 D 9 **Wolin**, Poland
113 X 8 **Wollaston Lake**, Saskatchewan, Canada
113 T 3 **Wollaston Peninsula**, Nunavut, Canada
209 P 3 **Wollogorang Roadhouse**, Northern Territory, Australia
209 U 12 **Wollongong**, New South Wales, Australia
93 F 14 **Wołów**, Poland
118 I 10 **Wolsey**, South Dakota, U.S.A.
92 F 13 **Wolsztyn**, Poland
82 K 8 **Wolvega**, Netherlands
77 J 19 **Wolverhampton**, United Kingdom
208 G 10 **Wongan Hills**, Western Australia, Australia
113 S 10 **Wonowon**, British Columbia, Canada
171 Y 6 **Wŏnsan**, North Korea
209 S 14 **Wonthaggi**, Victoria, Australia
122 J 3 **Woodall Mountain**, Mississippi, U.S.A.
123 R 8 **Woodbine**, Georgia, U.S.A.
211 H 20 **Woodend**, New Zealand
117 D 17 **Woodland**, California, U.S.A.
121 Z 5 **Woodland**, Maine, U.S.A.
212 H 6 **Woodlark Island**, Papua New Guinea
120 H 5 **Woodruff**, Wisconsin, U.S.A.
121 O 12 **Woodsfield**, Ohio, U.S.A.
120 I 8 **Woodstock**, Illinois, U.S.A.
211 H 16 **Woodstock**, New Zealand
122 G 7 **Woodville**, Mississippi, U.S.A.
211 L 14 **Woodville**, New Zealand
119 I 16 **Woodward**, Oklahoma, U.S.A.
175 W 11 **Woöi**, Indonesia
209 P 10 **Woomera**, South Australia, Australia
121 W 8 **Woonsocket**, Rhode Island, U.S.A.
208 F 8 **Wooramel Roadhouse**, Western Australia, Australia
121 N 10 **Wooster**, Ohio, U.S.A.
191 L 19 **Woqooyi Galbeed**, Somalia
77 J 20 **Worcester**, United Kingdom
121 X 8 **Worcester**, Massachusetts, U.S.A.
196 K 15 **Worcester**, Republic of South Africa
89 O 6 **Wörgl**, Austria
175 V 14 **Workai**, Indonesia
77 H 15 **Workington**, United Kingdom
82 J 8 **Workum**, Netherlands
118 D 10 **Worland**, Wyoming, U.S.A.
87 E 20 **Worms**, Germany
77 L 23 **Worthing**, United Kingdom
118 J 11 **Worthington**, Minnesota, U.S.A.
215 W 2 **Wotho**, Marshall Islands
215 Y 2 **Wotje**, Marshall Islands
175 O 12 **Wotu**, Indonesia
175 P 13 **Wowoni**, Indonesia
157 Y 5 **Wrangel Island**, Russian Federation
65 T 5 **Wrangel Sea**, Arctic Ocean
113 O 11 **Wrangell**, Alaska, U.S.A.
196 I 13 **Wreck Point**, Republic of South Africa
123 Q 5 **Wrens**, Georgia, U.S.A.
77 I 18 **Wrexham**, United Kingdom
118 F 11 **Wright**, Wyoming, U.S.A.
218 K 10 **Wright Island**, Antarctica
169 N 21 **Wrightmyo**, India
113 R 7 **Wrigley**, Northwest Territories, Canada
93 G 15 **Wrocław**, Poland
92 F 12 **Wronki**, Poland
92 H 12 **Września**, Poland
92 F 13 **Wschowa**, Poland
208 G 10 **Wubin**, Western Australia, Australia
163 R 11 **Wuday'ah**, Saudi Arabia
193 S 10 **Wudil**, Nigeria
171 Q 9 **Wudu**, China
171 R 7 **Wuhai**, China
171 U 10 **Wuhan**, China
171 V 10 **Wuhu**, China
193 S 12 **Wukari**, Nigeria
175 T 14 **Wuliaru**, Indonesia
89 T 2 **Wullowitz**, Austria
193 S 13 **Wum**, Cameroon
191 C 20 **Wun Rog**, Sudan
87 C 16 **Wuppertal**, Germany
87 H 20 **Würzburg**, Germany
87 L 16 **Wurzen**, Germany
63 L 18 **Wüst Seamount**, Atlantic Ocean
171 T 7 **Wutai Shan**, China
83 G 16 **Wuustwezel**, Belgium
212 B 2 **Wuvulu Island**, Papua New Guinea
171 V 10 **Wuxi**, China
171 S 10 **Wuxi**, China
171 X 2 **Wuyiling**, China
171 Q 7 **Wuzhong**, China
171 S 13 **Wuzhou**, China
209 T 8 **Wyandra**, Queensland, Australia
77 I 20 **Wye**, United Kingdom
208 K 3 **Wyndham**, Western Australia, Australia
119 N 17 **Wynne**, Arkansas, U.S.A.
118 E 10 **Wyola**, Montana, U.S.A.
118 D 11 **Wyoming**, U.S.A.
120 K 8 **Wyoming**, Michigan, U.S.A.
118 C 11 **Wyoming Range**, Wyoming, U.S.A.
92 L 12 **Wyszków**, Poland
92 K 12 **Wyszogród**, Poland
121 O 14 **Wytheville**, Virginia, U.S.A.
93 M 15 **Wyżyna Lubelska**, Poland
93 J 17 **Wyżyna Małopolska**, Poland

X

125 Z 10 **X-Can**, Mexico
196 I 3 **Xá-Muteba**, Angola
191 O 19 **Xaafuun**, Somalia
159 Y 7 **Xaçmaz**, Azerbaijan
197 Q 10 **Xai-Xai**, Mozambique
170 K 10 **Xainza**, China
172 K 13 **Xam Hua**, Laos
142 K 12 **Xambioá**, Brazil
196 G 6 **Xangongo**, Angola
159 W 9 **Xankändi**, Azerbaijan
87 B 15 **Xanten**, Germany
96 I 13 **Xanthi**, Greece
191 N 23 **Xarardheere**, Somalia
81 T 9 **Xàtiva**, Spain
170 J 11 **Xêgar**, China
120 M 12 **Xenia**, Ohio, U.S.A.
196 M 8 **Xhumo**, Botswana
171 U 4 **Xi Ujimqin Qi**, China
171 V 13 **Xiamen**, China
171 R 9 **Xi'an**, China
171 T 12 **Xiang**, China
171 O 11 **Xiangcheng**, China
171 T 10 **Xiangfan**, China
173 J 14 **Xiangkhoang**, Laos
173 J 14 **Xiangkhoang Plateau**, Laos
171 T 11 **Xiangtan**, China
171 U 11 **Xianning**, China
171 T 10 **Xiantao**, China
171 R 9 **Xianyang**, China
171 W 1 **Xiao Higgan Ling**, China
171 W 12 **Xiapu**, China
171 P 12 **Xichang**, China
171 R 12 **Xifeng**, China
170 K 10 **Xigazê**, China
171 U 5 **Xilinhot**, China
171 O 6 **Ximiao**, China
171 U 3 **Xin Barag Zuoqi**, China
171 U 13 **Xingning**, China
171 T 8 **Xingtai**, China
142 I 13 **Xingu**, Brazil
142 J 12 **Xinguara**, Brazil
171 Q 13 **Xingyi**, China
171 P 8 **Xining**, China
170 I 6 **Xinjiang Uygur**, China
171 V 8 **Xintai**, China
171 T 8 **Xinxiang**, China
171 T 10 **Xinyang**, China
170 J 4 **Xinyuan**, China
171 R 6 **Xinzhoa**, China
171 T 7 **Xinzhou**, China
143 M 14 **Xique-Xique**, Brazil
192 E 10 **Xitole**, Guinea-Bissau
171 T 11 **Xiushui**, China
171 T 9 **Xixia**, China
171 R 9 **Xixiang**, China
191 M 19 **Xjis**, Somalia
159 U 10 **Xok**, Azerbaijan
173 N 21 **Xom Duc Hanh**, Vietnam
170 L 7 **Xorkol**, China
171 T 9 **Xuchang**, China
191 L 23 **Xuddur**, Somalia
191 N 20 **Xudun**, Somalia
171 S 15 **Xuwen**, China
171 Q 11 **Xuyong**, China
171 V 9 **Xuzhou**, China
97 F 20 **Xylokastro**, Greece

Y

171 P 11 **Ya'an**, China
191 I 23 **Yabēlo**, Ethiopia
96 H 8 **Yablanitsa**, Bulgaria
193 P 10 **Yabo**, Nigeria
160 I 6 **Yabrūd**, Syria
141 L 23 **Yacuiba**, Bolivia
141 J 18 **Yacuma**, Bolivia
177 M 26 **Yaeyama-rettō**, Japan
189 S 8 **Yafran**, Libya
63 E 21 **Yaghan Basin**, Atlantic Ocean
176 J 4 **Yagishiri-tō**, Japan
157 W 9 **Yagodnoye**, Russian Federation
113 U 14 **Yahk**, British Columbia, Canada
101 R 4 **Yahotyn**, Ukraine
194 M 7 **Yahuma**, Democratic Republic of Congo
177 J 17 **Yaizu**, Japan
171 O 11 **Yajiang**, China
194 J 5 **Yaka**, Central African Republic
171 V 2 **Yakeshi**, China
116 F 8 **Yakima**, Washington, U.S.A.
165 Q 12 **Yakmach**, Pakistan
192 L 9 **Yako**, Burkina Faso
96 G 11 **Yakoruda**, Bulgaria
177 D 25 **Yaku-shima**, Japan
176 I 7 **Yakumo**, Japan
112 M 9 **Yakutat**, Alaska, U.S.A.
157 T 10 **Yakutsk**, Russian Federation
101 V 9 **Yakymivka**, Ukraine
173 I 26 **Yala**, Thailand
195 N 8 **Yaleko**, Democratic Republic of Congo
194 M 4 **Yalinga**, Central African Republic
194 I 4 **Yaloké**, Central African Republic
158 E 8 **Yalova**, Turkey
101 U 13 **Yalta**, Ukraine
171 X 5 **Yalu**, China
156 J 11 **Yalutorovsk**, Russian Federation
158 F 11 **Yalvaş**, Turkey
176 L 10 **Yamada**, Japan
177 C 22 **Yamaga**, Japan
176 K 12 **Yamagata**, Japan
177 C 20 **Yamaguchi**, Japan
177 N 22 **Yamato**, Japan
191 C 23 **Yambio**, Sudan
96 L 10 **Yambol**, Bulgaria
96 L 9 **Yambol**, Bulgaria
156 M 8 **Yamburg**, Russian Federation
175 T 14 **Yamdena**, Indonesia
192 K 13 **Yamoussoukro**, Côte d'Ivoire
101 N 7 **Yampil'**, Ukraine
101 T 1 **Yampil'**, Ukraine
170 L 11 **Yamzho Yumco**, China
171 U 6 **Yan Shan**, China
157 T 8 **Yana**, Russian Federation
212 H 7 **Yanaba Island**, Papua New Guinea
177 E 20 **Yanadani**, Japan
177 D 20 **Yanai**, Japan
169 H 19 **Yanam**, India
171 R 8 **Yan'an**, China
162 K 6 **Yanbu' al Baḩr**, Saudi Arabia
171 W 9 **Yancheng**, China
171 N 7 **Yanchiwan**, China
194 I 9 **Yandja**, Democratic Republic of Congo
194 K 3 **Yangalia**, Central African Republic
195 N 7 **Yangambi**, Democratic Republic of Congo
192 J 9 **Yangasso**, Mali
170 L 10 **Yangbajain**, China
171 T 14 **Yangjiang**, China
171 T 7 **Yangquan**, China
171 T 13 **Yangshan**, China
171 P 12 **Yangtze**, China
171 V 9 **Yangzhou**, China
171 Y 4 **Yanji**, China
171 Q 12 **Yanjin**, China
118 J 11 **Yankton**, South Dakota, U.S.A.
171 Q 13 **Yanshan**, China
157 T 7 **Yanskiy Zaliv**, Russian Federation
171 W 7 **Yantai**, China
99 A 15 **Yantarnyy**, Russian Federation
96 J 6 **Yantra**, Bulgaria
171 P 12 **Yanyuan**, China
193 T 14 **Yaoundé**, Cameroon
214 K 14 **Yap**, Federated States of Micronesia
214 L 15 **Yap**, Federated States of Micronesia
60 K 7 **Yap Trench**, Pacific Ocean
175 W 11 **Yapen**, Indonesia
124 J 5 **Yaqui**, Mexico
138 M 3 **Yaracuy**, Venezuela
158 E 14 **Yardimci Burnu**, Turkey
159 Y 10 **Yardimli**, Azerbaijan
77 N 19 **Yare**, United Kingdom
215 U 1 **Yaren**, Nauru
138 J 10 **Yari**, Colombia
163 P 13 **Yarim**, Yemen
142 H 9 **Yaripo**, Brazil
170 H 6 **Yarkant He**, China
158 H 12 **Yarma**, Turkey
115 U 14 **Yarmouth**, Nova Scotia, Canada
156 G 8 **Yaroslavl'**, Russian Federation
138 H 5 **Yarumal**, Colombia
213 W 11 **Yasawa Group**, Fiji
193 R 10 **Yashi**, Nigeria
193 P 11 **Yashikera**, Nigeria
100 I 7 **Yasinya**, Ukraine
99 C 14 **Yasnoye**, Russian Federation
173 K 17 **Yasothon**, Thailand
209 U 12 **Yass**, New South Wales, Australia
164 I 9 **Yāsūj**, Iran
158 M 7 **Yasun Burnu**, Turkey
158 C 12 **Yatağan**, Turkey
213 Q 14 **Yaté**, New Caledonia
119 K 15 **Yates Center**, Kansas, U.S.A.
114 K 3 **Yathkyed Lake**, Nunavut, Canada
195 N 7 **Yatolema**, Democratic Republic of Congo
177 C 22 **Yatsushiro**, Japan
160 F 10 **Yatta**, Israel
141 E 19 **Yauca**, Peru
141 G 18 **Yauri**, Peru
140 F 11 **Yavari**, Peru/Brazil
124 J 6 **Yávaros**, Mexico
169 F 16 **Yavatmal**, India
167 Q 2 **Yavlenka**, Kazakhstan
100 I 4 **Yavoriv**, Ukraine
177 D 21 **Yawatahama**, Japan
164 L 9 **Yazd**, Iran
164 K 9 **Yazd**, Iran
164 I 9 **Yazd-e Khast**, Iran
165 O 8 **Yazdan**, Iran
159 N 11 **Yazihan**, Turkey
122 H 5 **Yazoo City**, Mississippi, U.S.A.
89 U 4 **Ybbs an der Donau**, Austria
97 G 22 **Ydra**, Greece
97 G 21 **Ydra**, Greece
173 F 18 **Ye**, Myanmar
193 X 5 **Yebbi-Bou**, Chad
170 H 6 **Yecheng**, China
81 S 10 **Yecla**, Spain
124 K 5 **Yécora**, Mexico

Country · Internal administrative region: State/Province/Territory/Dependent territory · Capital city · Mountain range/Undersea ridge · Mountain peak/Volcano/Seamount · Geographic feature · Headland/Point/Cape/Peninsula · Desert · Island/Island group · Antarctic base · Ocean · Sea · Bay/Gulf/Channel/Strait · Lake · Salt pan/Dry/Intermittent lake · River

173 D 14 **Yedashe**, Myanmar
99 I 14 **Yedy**, Belarus
191 K 23 **Yeed**, Somalia
123 R 12 **Yeehaw Junction**, Florida, U.S.A.
159 U 9 **Yeghegnadzor**, Armenia
167 V 5 **Yegindybulak**, Kazakhstan
193 N 12 **Yégué**, Togo
173 C 15 **Yegyi**, Myanmar
191 D 22 **Yei**, Sudan
191 E 23 **Yei**, Sudan
192 M 12 **Yeji**, Ghana
156 J 10 **Yekaterinburg**, Russian Federation
101 R 8 **Yelanets'**, Ukraine
156 F 9 **Yelets**, Russian Federation
192 H 8 **Yélimané**, Mali
76 J 4 **Yell**, United Kingdom
171 S 8 **Yellow**, China
116 J 10 **Yellow Pine**, Idaho, U.S.A.
171 X 8 **Yellow Sea**, Asia
113 T 7 **Yellowknife**, Northwest Territories, Canada
118 D 9 **Yellowstone**, Montana, U.S.A.
118 C 10 **Yellowstone Lake**, Wyoming, U.S.A.
167 N 14 **Yeloten**, Turkmenistan
99 L 21 **Yel'sk**, Belarus
193 P 11 **Yelwa**, Nigeria
163 T 12 **Yemen**, Asia
100 M 3 **Yemil'chyne**, Ukraine
172 L 11 **Yên Bai**, Vietnam
172 C 13 **Yenangyaung**, Myanmar
193 N 11 **Yendi**, Ghana
194 F 10 **Yénéganou**, Congo
170 G 6 **Yengisar**, China
194 H 7 **Yengo**, Congo
158 E 8 **Yenişehir**, Turkey
157 N 10 **Yenisey**, Russian Federation
65 X 9 **Yeniseyky Zaliv**, Arctic Ocean
157 N 11 **Yeniseyskiy Kryazh**, Russian Federation
77 J 23 **Yeovil**, United Kingdom
124 K 5 **Yepachi**, Mexico
209 V 6 **Yeppoon**, Queensland, Australia
166 L 13 **Yerbent**, Turkmenistan
157 Q 11 **Yerbogachen**, Russian Federation
159 T 9 **Yerevan**, Armenia
167 T 4 **Yereymentau**, Kazakhstan
117 G 17 **Yerington**, Nevada, U.S.A.
158 J 9 **Yerköy**, Turkey
169 D 17 **Yermala**, India
157 T 13 **Yerofey**, Russian Federation
160 F 11 **Yeroham**, Israel
172 C 11 **Yesagyo**, Myanmar
167 P 4 **Yesil'**, Kazakhstan
158 J 11 **Yeşilhisar**, Turkey
158 E 12 **Yeşilova**, Turkey
159 W 8 **Yevlax**, Azerbaijan
101 T 12 **Yevpatoriya**, Ukraine
98 L 13 **Yezyaryshcha**, Belarus
171 Q 11 **Yibin**, China
171 S 10 **Yichang**, China
171 X 2 **Yichun**, China
171 U 11 **Yichun**, China
171 Y 3 **Yilan**, China
158 L 9 **Yildizeli**, Turkey
171 U 1 **Yimuhe**, China
171 Q 7 **Yinchuan**, China
171 W 6 **Yingkou**, China
171 V 11 **Yingtan**, China
170 J 4 **Yining**, China
191 E 22 **Yirol**, Sudan
171 V 8 **Yishui**, China
171 N 5 **Yiwu**, China
171 T 11 **Yiyang**, China
98 C 12 **Ylakiai**, Lithuania
84 L 12 **Yli-Kärppä**, Finland
84 K 11 **Ylitornio**, Finland
65 Q 11 **Ymer Nunatak**, Greenland
157 V 11 **Ynykchanskiy**, Russian Federation
193 T 10 **Yobe**, Nigeria
176 I 6 **Yobetsu-dake**, Japan
191 K 19 **Yoboki**, Djibouti
174 I 15 **Yogyakarta**, Indonesia
174 I 14 **Yogyakarta**, Indonesia
177 F 17 **Yōka**, Japan
193 V 14 **Yokadouma**, Cameroon
177 N 21 **Yokate-jima**, Japan
177 H 18 **Yokkaichi**, Japan
193 U 13 **Yoko**, Cameroon
177 K 16 **Yokohama**, Japan
177 K 16 **Yokosuka**, Japan
176 K 11 **Yokote**, Japan
193 U 12 **Yola**, Nigeria
194 M 9 **Yolombo**, Democratic Republic of Congo
177 E 18 **Yonago**, Japan
177 L 26 **Yonaguni-jima**, Japan
176 K 13 **Yonezawa**, Japan
171 V 12 **Yong'an**, China
171 U 11 **Yongfeng**, China
171 P 12 **Yongren**, China
171 O 12 **Yongsheng**, China
171 S 11 **Yongshun**, China
171 T 12 **Yongzhou**, China
121 V 10 **Yonkers**, New York, U.S.A.
77 K 17 **York**, United Kingdom
121 S 11 **York**, Pennsylvania, U.S.A.
122 J 6 **York**, Alabama, U.S.A.
208 G 11 **York**, Western Australia, Australia
209 P 11 **Yorke Peninsula**, South Australia, Australia
209 O 12 **Yorketown**, South Australia, Australia
113 Z 11 **Yorkton**, Saskatchewan, Canada
121 S 14 **Yorktown**, Virginia, U.S.A.
126 F 9 **Yoro**, Honduras
177 N 22 **Yoro-jima**, Japan
177 O 23 **Yoron-tō**, Japan
117 F 18 **Yosemite Village**, California, U.S.A.
156 H 9 **Yoshkar-Ola**, Russian Federation
160 F 12 **Yotvata**, Israel
77 C 20 **Youghal**, Republic of Ireland
77 D 21 **Youghal Bay**, Republic of Ireland
144 M 11 **Young**, Uruguay
209 T 12 **Young**, New South Wales, Australia
219 S 15 **Young Island**, Antarctica
61 X 14 **Young's Rock**, Pitcairn Island
121 P 10 **Youngstown**, Ohio, U.S.A.
188 G 7 **Youssoufia**, Morocco
171 S 11 **Youyang**, China
156 M 14 **Youyi Feng**, Russian Federation
158 J 9 **Yozgat**, Turkey
116 D 13 **Yreka**, California, U.S.A.
212 F 2 **Ysabel Channel**, Papua New Guinea
85 E 26 **Ystad**, Sweden
167 V 10 **Ysyk-Köl**, Kyrgyzstan
175 T 11 **Yu**, Indonesia
171 X 13 **Yü-Shan**, Taiwan
171 P 13 **Yuan**, China
171 O 13 **Yuanjiang**, China
117 E 16 **Yuba City**, California, U.S.A.
176 K 5 **Yūbari-sanchi**, Japan
125 Y 10 **Yucatán**, Mexico
125 Y 9 **Yucatan Channel**, Mexico
125 Y 11 **Yucatan Peninsula**, Mexico
171 T 7 **Yuci**, China
208 M 6 **Yuendumu**, Northern Territory, Australia
171 T 11 **Yueyang**, China
157 X 7 **Yukagirskoye Ploskogor'ye**, Russian Federation
98 K 13 **Yukhavichy**, Belarus
194 K 10 **Yuki**, Democratic Republic of Congo
112 I 5 **Yukon**, U.S.A./Canada
113 O 8 **Yukon Territory**, Canada
159 T 12 **Yüksekova**, Turkey
177 C 20 **Yukuhashi**, Japan
208 M 7 **Yulara**, Northern Territory, Australia
123 R 8 **Yulee**, Florida, U.S.A.
171 S 14 **Yulin**, China
171 S 7 **Yulin**, China
117 K 24 **Yuma**, Arizona, U.S.A.
194 I 9 **Yumbi**, Democratic Republic of Congo
195 O 8 **Yumbi**, Democratic Republic of Congo
171 O 7 **Yumen**, China
158 G 10 **Yunak**, Turkey
112 B 8 **Yunaska Island**, Alaska, U.S.A.
141 J 20 **Yungas**, Bolivia
171 U 10 **Yunmeng**, China
171 O 13 **Yunnan**, China
209 Q 11 **Yunta**, South Australia, Australia
171 V 13 **Yunxiao**, China
61 X 9 **Yupanqui Basin**, Pacific Ocean
141 J 22 **Yura**, Bolivia
99 H 17 **Yuratsishki**, Belarus
156 M 12 **Yurga**, Russian Federation
140 D 12 **Yurimaguas**, Peru
101 V 6 **Yur''yivka**, Ukraine
171 N 9 **Yushu**, China
171 X 4 **Yushu**, China
159 Q 8 **Yusufeli**, Turkey
177 E 21 **Yusuhara**, Japan
170 I 7 **Yutian**, China
177 N 22 **Yuwan-dake**, Japan
171 P 13 **Yuxi**, China
157 Y 14 **Yuzhno-Kuril'sk**, Russian Federation
157 X 14 **Yuzhno-Sakhalinsk**, Russian Federation
101 Q 7 **Yuzhnoukrayinsk**, Ukraine
167 R 9 **Yuzhnyy Kazakhstan**, Kazakhstan
88 B 8 **Yverdon**, Switzerland
79 O 3 **Yvetot**, France
172 D 13 **Ywamun**, Myanmar
172 D 10 **Ywathit**, Myanmar

Z

82 H 10 **Zaandam**, Netherlands
157 S 14 **Zabaykal'sk**, Russian Federation
195 O 6 **Zabia**, Democratic Republic of Congo
163 O 13 **Zabīd**, Yemen
165 P 10 **Zābol**, Iran
93 I 17 **Zabrze**, Poland
165 T 8 **Zābul**, Afghanistan
125 P 12 **Zacapu**, Mexico
125 O 8 **Zacatecas**, Mexico
125 O 9 **Zacatecas**, Mexico
125 S 11 **Zacatlán**, Mexico
97 D 21 **Zacharo**, Greece
101 U 5 **Zachepylivka**, Ukraine
94 C 12 **Zadar**, Croatia
173 F 22 **Zadetkale Kyun**, Myanmar
173 F 23 **Zadetkyi Kyun**, Myanmar
170 M 9 **Zadoi**, China
97 L 24 **Zafora**, Greece
80 K 10 **Zafra**, Spain
188 F 10 **Zag**, Morocco
93 E 14 **Żagań**, Poland
190 E 8 **Zagazig**, Egypt
189 Q 5 **Zaghouan**, Tunisia
94 D 8 **Zagreb**, Croatia
164 G 6 **Zagros Mountains**, Iran
94 M 11 **Žagubica**, Serbia and Montenegro
170 K 9 **Za'gya**, China
165 O 11 **Zāhedān**, Iran
160 H 6 **Zahlé**, Lebanon
163 O 11 **Zahrān**, Saudi Arabia
161 T 13 **Zahrat al Baṭn**, Iraq
196 F 1 **Zaire**, Angola
94 N 12 **Zaječar**, Serbia and Montenegro
161 R 1 **Zākhō**, Iraq
156 I 5 **Zakhrebetnoye**, Russian Federation
93 J 19 **Zakopane**, Poland
193 Y 10 **Zakouma**, Chad
97 B 20 **Zakynthos**, Greece
97 B 20 **Zakynthos**, Greece
161 N 3 **Zalābiyah**, Syria
93 F 24 **Zalaegerszeg**, Hungary
193 S 11 **Zalanga**, Nigeria
171 V 3 **Zalantun**, China
100 H 8 **Zalău**, Romania
92 D 9 **Zalew Szczeciński**, Poland
92 J 8 **Zalew Wiślany**, Poland
163 N 7 **Zalim**, Saudi Arabia
191 A 18 **Zalingei**, Sudan
100 K 6 **Zalishchyky**, Ukraine
157 X 14 **Zaliv Aniva**, Russian Federation
166 I 11 **Zaliv Kara-Bogaz-Gol**, Turkmenistan
166 I 8 **Zaliv Komsomolets**, Kazakhstan
157 Z 6 **Zaliv Kresta**, Russian Federation
157 Y 9 **Zaliv Shelikhova**, Russian Federation
157 X 13 **Zaliv Terpeniya**, Russian Federation
101 R 10 **Zaliznyy Port**, Ukraine
83 I 14 **Zaltbommel**, Netherlands
113 S 9 **Zama Lake**, Alberta, Canada
163 R 12 **Zamakh**, Yemen
197 R 6 **Zambezi**, Africa
196 L 4 **Zambezi**, Zambia
197 S 6 **Zambézia**, Mozambique
196 M 5 **Zambia**, Africa
175 P 7 **Zamboanga**, Philippines
92 M 11 **Zambrów**, Poland
197 P 5 **Zambue**, Mozambique
193 Q 10 **Zamfara**, Nigeria
140 B 11 **Zamora**, Ecuador
80 L 4 **Zamora**, Spain
140 B 11 **Zamora**, Ecuador
140 B 11 **Zamora-Chinchipe**, Ecuador
125 O 11 **Zamora de Hidalgo**, Mexico
93 O 15 **Zamość**, Poland
194 G 9 **Zanaga**, Congo
121 N 11 **Zanesville**, Ohio, U.S.A.
192 J 10 **Zangasso**, Mali
164 G 5 **Zanjān**, Iran
164 G 5 **Zanjān**, Iran
195 W 11 **Zanzibar**, Tanzania
195 W 11 **Zanzibar Channel**, Tanzania
195 X 11 **Zanzibar Island**, Tanzania
189 Q 12 **Zaouatallaz**, Algeria
167 S 3 **Zaozernyy**, Kazakhstan
171 U 8 **Zaozhuang**, China
94 L 13 **Zapadna Morava**, Serbia and Montenegro
156 F 7 **Zapadnaya Dvina**, Russian Federation
166 I 4 **Zapadnyy Kazakhstan**, Kazakhstan
156 M 13 **Zapadnyy Sayan**, Russian Federation
145 G 15 **Zapala**, Argentina
119 I 24 **Zapata**, Texas, U.S.A.
63 G 19 **Zapiola Ridge**, Atlantic Ocean
63 I 18 **Zapiola Seamount**, Atlantic Ocean
101 V 7 **Zaporizhzhya**, Ukraine
159 V 7 **Zaqatala**, Azerbaijan
158 M 9 **Zara**, Turkey
167 O 11 **Zarafshan**, Uzbekistan
81 S 4 **Zaragoza**, Spain
164 L 10 **Zarand**, Iran
165 P 10 **Zaranj**, Afghanistan
98 H 13 **Zarasai**, Lithuania
159 Y 7 **Zarat**, Azerbaijan
144 L 12 **Zárate**, Argentina
139 P 3 **Zaraza**, Venezuela
165 U 8 **Zarghūn Shahr**, Afghanistan
193 R 10 **Zaria**, Nigeria
93 I 21 **Žarnovica**, Slovakia
93 D 14 **Żary**, Poland
189 Q 10 **Zarzaïtine**, Algeria
189 R 7 **Zarzis**, Tunisia
168 E 8 **Zaskar Mountains**, India
99 I 17 **Zaslawye**, Belarus
93 B 16 **Žatec**, Czech Republic
101 P 10 **Zatoka**, Ukraine
92 D 9 **Zatoka Pomorska**, Poland
83 G 19 **Zaventem**, Belgium
93 J 16 **Zawiercie**, Poland
189 T 11 **Zawīlah**, Libya
189 W 8 **Zāwiyat Masūs**, Libya
167 Z 6 **Zaysan**, Kazakhstan
171 N 11 **Zayü**, China
167 O 6 **Zban**, Kazakhstan
100 K 4 **Zbarazh**, Ukraine
92 H 9 **Zblewo**, Poland
100 K 4 **Zboriv**, Ukraine
93 I 14 **Zduńska Wola**, Poland
214 B 7 **Zealandia Bank**, Northern Mariana Islands
165 V 5 **Zēbāk**, Afghanistan
161 T 1 **Zēbār**, Iraq
83 D 15 **Zeeland**, Netherlands
160 F 10 **Ze'elim**, Israel
86 M 11 **Zehdenick**, Germany
82 I 12 **Zeist**, Netherlands
87 K 17 **Zeitz**, Germany
94 H 13 **Zelena Gora**, Bosnia and Herzegovina
99 A 14 **Zelenogradsk**, Russian Federation
94 E 7 **Zelina**, Croatia
89 Q 7 **Zell am See**, Austria
89 N 7 **Zell am Ziller**, Austria
98 I 10 **Zeltiņi**, Latvia
99 F 19 **Zel'va**, Belarus
83 E 17 **Zelzate**, Belgium
195 N 5 **Zémio**, Central African Republic
156 M 3 **Zemlya Aleksandry**, Russian Federation
156 M 3 **Zemlya Georga**, Russian Federation
94 H 12 **Zenica**, Bosnia and Herzegovina
94 H 11 **Žepče**, Bosnia and Herzegovina
167 R 13 **Zerafshon**, Tajikistan
87 K 14 **Zerbst**, Germany
167 R 3 **Zerenda**, Kazakhstan
189 O 6 **Zeribet el Oued**, Algeria
88 E 11 **Zermatt**, Switzerland
88 J 9 **Zernez**, Switzerland
86 G 11 **Zeven**, Germany
82 L 13 **Zevenaar**, Netherlands
83 G 15 **Zevenbergen**, Netherlands
157 T 13 **Zeya**, Russian Federation
157 U 13 **Zeya**, Russian Federation
157 U 13 **Zeyskoye Vodokhranilishche**, Russian Federation
160 H 5 **Zgharta**, Lebanon
92 J 13 **Zgierz**, Poland
93 D 15 **Zgorzelec**, Poland
101 R 1 **Zhadove**, Ukraine
167 Q 4 **Zhaksy**, Kazakhstan
166 H 5 **Zhalpaktal**, Kazakhstan
167 T 9 **Zhambyl**, Kazakhstan
167 S 7 **Zhambyl**, Kazakhstan
167 Q 10 **Zhanakorgan**, Kazakhstan
167 U 6 **Zhanaortalyk**, Kazakhstan
166 I 10 **Zhanaozen**, Kazakhstan
167 R 10 **Zhanatas**, Kazakhstan
166 H 7 **Zhanbay**, Kazakhstan
171 X 4 **Zhangguangcai Ling**, China
167 X 5 **Zhangiztobe**, Kazakhstan
171 T 6 **Zhangjiakou**, China
171 P 7 **Zhangye**, China
171 V 13 **Zhangzhou**, China
171 S 14 **Zhanjiang**, China
166 J 6 **Zhanterek**, Kazakhstan
171 P 11 **Zhaojue**, China
171 T 13 **Zhaoqing**, China
171 Q 12 **Zhaotong**, China
171 W 4 **Zhaoyuan**, China
170 J 10 **Zhari Namco**, China
166 K 6 **Zharkamys**, Kazakhstan
167 X 9 **Zharkent**, Kazakhstan
167 X 5 **Zharma**, Kazakhstan
101 P 5 **Zhashkiv**, Ukraine
170 H 8 **Zhaxigang**, China
171 V 10 **Zhejiang**, China
167 U 2 **Zhelezinka**, Kazakhstan
99 B 16 **Zheleznodorozhnyy**, Russian Federation
171 T 9 **Zhengzhou**, China
171 W 9 **Zhenjiang**, China
167 Q 7 **Zhezkazgan**, Kazakhstan
157 S 9 **Zhigansk**, Russian Federation
157 R 8 **Zhilinda**, Russian Federation
167 N 3 **Zhitikara**, Kazakhstan
99 M 19 **Zhlobin**, Belarus
101 N 6 **Zhmerynka**, Ukraine
165 U 10 **Zhob**, Pakistan
165 U 10 **Zhob**, Pakistan
99 K 17 **Zhodzina**, Belarus
171 P 11 **Zhongdian**, China
171 Q 8 **Zhongning**, China
219 X 6 **Zhongshan**, Antarctica
100 I 4 **Zhovkva**, Ukraine
101 P 8 **Zhovten'**, Ukraine
101 T 7 **Zhovti Vody**, Ukraine
171 V 8 **Zhucheng**, China
171 T 14 **Zhuhai**, China
171 T 9 **Zhumadian**, China
166 L 5 **Zhuryn**, Kazakhstan
171 T 11 **Zhuzhou**, China
166 I 4 **Zhympity**, Kazakhstan
99 J 21 **Zhytkavichy**, Belarus
101 N 4 **Zhytomyr**, Ukraine
93 I 20 **Žiar nad Hronom**, Slovakia
161 S 1 **Zībār**, Iraq
171 U 8 **Zibo**, China
171 S 8 **Zichang**, China
167 R 13 **Ziddí**, Tajikistan
93 G 16 **Ziębice**, Poland
92 E 13 **Zielona Góra**, Poland
83 E 15 **Zierikzee**, Netherlands
172 B 13 **Zigaing**, Myanmar
189 X 11 **Zighan**, Libya
173 D 14 **Zigon**, Myanmar
171 Q 11 **Zigong**, China
193 V 8 **Ziguey**, Chad
192 D 9 **Ziguinchor**, Senegal
125 P 13 **Zihuatanejo**, Mexico
158 K 9 **Zile**, Turkey
93 I 19 **Žilina**, Slovakia
189 V 10 **Zillah**, Libya
89 N 7 **Zillertaler Alpen**, Austria
98 J 12 **Zilupe**, Latvia
157 P 13 **Zima**, Russian Federation
197 N 6 **Zimba**, Zambia
197 O 7 **Zimbabwe**, Africa
192 G 12 **Zimmi**, Sierra Leone
100 J 14 **Zimnicea**, Romania
193 T 9 **Zinder**, Niger
193 S 9 **Zinder**, Niger
163 Q 14 **Zinjibār**, Yemen
93 H 23 **Zirc**, Hungary
86 N 9 **Zirchow**, Germany
94 D 13 **Žirje**, Croatia
168 N 11 **Ziro**, India
125 Q 12 **Zitácuaro**, Mexico
87 O 17 **Zittau**, Germany
94 I 11 **Živinice**, Bosnia and Herzegovina
191 I 21 **Ziway Hāyk'**, Ethiopia
96 I 12 **Zlatograd**, Bulgaria
156 I 10 **Zlatoust**, Russian Federation
93 H 19 **Zlín**, Czech Republic
189 S 7 **Zlīṭan**, Libya
93 I 14 **Złoczew**, Poland
92 G 10 **Złotów**, Poland
93 G 14 **Żmigród**, Poland
101 W 4 **Zmiyiv**, Ukraine
167 W 4 **Znamenka**, Kazakhstan
92 H 11 **Żnin**, Poland
93 F 20 **Znojmo**, Czech Republic
82 G 12 **Zoetermeer**, Netherlands
171 O 10 **Zogqên**, China
171 P 9 **Zoigê**, China
83 I 18 **Zolder**, Belgium
101 V 3 **Zolochiv**, Ukraine
101 Y 6 **Zolote**, Ukraine
101 R 5 **Zolotonosha**, Ukraine
194 J 5 **Zongo**, Democratic Republic of Congo
158 G 7 **Zonguldak**, Turkey
83 B 19 **Zonnebeke**, Belgium
80 L 8 **Zorita**, Spain
96 L 10 **Zornitsa**, Bulgaria
140 A 11 **Zorritos**, Peru
192 H 12 **Zorzor**, Liberia
83 E 19 **Zottegem**, Belgium
193 W 5 **Zouar**, Chad
192 G 4 **Zouérat**, Mauritania
94 K 9 **Zrenjanin**, Serbia and Montenegro
87 L 17 **Zschopau**, Germany
63 M 16 **Zubov Seamount**, Atlantic Ocean
192 J 12 **Zuénoula**, Côte d'Ivoire
81 S 4 **Zuera**, Spain
163 V 10 **Ẓufār**, Oman
88 G 7 **Zug**, Switzerland
159 R 6 **Zugdidi**, Georgia
88 G 7 **Zuger See**, Switzerland
88 L 6 **Zugspitze**, Austria/Germany
193 Q 10 **Zugu**, Nigeria
83 F 14 **Zuid-Holland**, Netherlands
82 M 6 **Zuidhorn**, Netherlands
82 M 7 **Zuidlaardermeer**, Netherlands
138 K 3 **Zulia**, Venezuela
87 B 17 **Zülpich**, Germany
140 B 11 **Zumba**, Ecuador
197 P 5 **Zumbo**, Mozambique
119 C 17 **Zuni Mountains**, New Mexico, U.S.A.
171 R 12 **Zunyi**, China
88 J 9 **Zuoz**, Switzerland
94 I 9 **Županja**, Croatia
95 L 16 **Žur**, Serbia and Montenegro
165 P 6 **Zūrābād**, Iran
82 J 7 **Zurich**, Netherlands
88 G 6 **Zürich**, Switzerland
88 G 7 **Zürich See**, Switzerland
193 Q 10 **Zuru**, Nigeria
82 L 12 **Zutphen**, Netherlands
189 R 7 **Zuwārah**, Libya
101 Q 6 **Zvenyhorodka**, Ukraine
96 M 10 **Zvezdets**, Bulgaria
197 P 8 **Zvishavane**, Zimbabwe
93 J 20 **Zvolen**, Slovakia
94 I 11 **Zvornik**, Serbia and Montenegro
192 I 13 **Zwedru**, Liberia
88 D 9 **Zweisimmen**, Switzerland
89 V 3 **Zwettl**, Austria
87 L 17 **Zwickau**, Germany
93 N 16 **Zwierzyniec**, Poland
83 F 17 **Zwijndrecht**, Belgium
93 M 14 **Zwoleń**, Poland
82 L 10 **Zwolle**, Netherlands
99 J 16 **Zyembin**, Belarus
92 K 13 **Żyrardów**, Poland
157 W 8 **Zyryanka**, Russian Federation
157 N 10 **Zyryanovo**, Russian Federation
167 Y 4 **Zyryanovsk**, Kazakhstan
93 J 18 **Żywiec**, Poland

Country · Internal administrative region: State/Province/Territory/Dependent territory · Capital city · Mountain range/Undersea ridge · Mountain peak/Volcano/Seamount · Geographic feature · Headland/Point/Cape/Peninsula · Desert · Island/Island group · Antarctic base · Ocean · Sea · Bay/Gulf/Channel/Strait · Lake · Salt pan/Dry/Intermittent lake · River

ACKNOWLEDGMENTS

Weldon Owen would like to thank the following people for their assistance in the production of this book: Tony Burton (Flag Society of Australia), Melanie Calabretta, Brendan Cotter, Jess Cox, Janine Flew, Helen Flint, Angela Handley, Emma Hutchinson, Tessy Grabo, Global Forest Watch, Matthew Hall, Ralph Kelly (Flag Society of Australia), Professor Kim Lowell (Département des sciences du bois et de la forêt, Université Laval, Canada), Rory Moore, Michael Nahas, Grace Newell, Sarah Plant (Puddingburn Publishing Services), Deborah Smith, Kiren Thandi, Shannon Tufui. **Text**: Jenni Bruce (thematic map pages), Scott Forbes (regional map pages), Dr Stephen Gale (Geographic Terms), Margaret McPhee (satellite image pages).

NOTES

1. All population statistics quoted in this atlas are projected 2005 figures. National population statistics have been sourced from the U.S. Census Bureau. City Population statistics have been sourced from the United Nations Population Division,World Urbanization Prospects: The 2001 Revision.
2. All city population statistics quoted in this atlas are of urban agglomerations. The combined population of a city and its suburbs is known as an urban agglomeration.
3. All statistics for the Fact File have been sourced from the CIA World Factbook

PHOTO CREDITS

Key t=top; l=left; r=right; tl=top left; tcl=top center left; tc=top center; tcr=top center right; tr=top right; cl=center left; c=center; cr=center right; b=bottom; bl=bottom left; bc=bottom center; bcl=bottom center left; bcr=bottom center right; br=bottom right

AAP = Australian Associated Press; APL/Corbis = Australian Picture Library/Corbis; COR = Corel Corp.; DS = Digital Stock; GI = Getty Images; IOT = Images on Tap; N_E = NASA/Earth Observatory; N_ES = NASA/Earth from Space; N_J = NASA/Jet Propulsion Laboratory; N_T = NASA/TOMS; N_V = NASA/Visible Earth; NASA = National Aeronautics and Space Administration; NHM = The Natural History Museum, London; PD = Photodisc; PE = PhotoEssentials; PL = photolibrary.com/Science Photo Library; PPB = pacific-picture Bildagentur; REU = Reuters.

2t Craig Mahew/Robert Simmon/NASA/GSFC **5**bl Serg Andrefouet/Frank Muller-Karger/Institute for Marine Remote Sensing/University of South Florida; br DS **6**tc, tc, tr N_V; tl PL **7**tc, tc, tl N_V; tr Jerry Stebbins **8**bl Jacques Descloitres/MODIS Rapid Response Team/NASA/GSFC; br NASA/GSFC/METI/ERSDAC/JAROS/US/Japan ASTER Science Team; c N_J; cr N_J/NIMA; cl N_J/GSFC/LaRC/MISR Team; tr NASA/GSFC/METI/ERSDAC/JAROS/US/Japan ASTER Science Team **14**t PL **16**cr NASA/GSFC; tr PL **17**cr NASA/GSFC/METI/ERSDAC/JAROS/US/Japan ASTER Science Team **19**b APL/Corbis; br, cr, tr GI **20**c NASA; cl APL/Corbis; tr DS **21**cr AAP/AFP AFP; tr APL/Corbis **22**bcl DS; bcr, bl, br APL/Corbis **23**tc, tl COR; tr APL/Corbis **24**cr APL/Corbis; tr PL **25**br PL; cr NHM **26**cl APL/Corbis **27**br, cr APL/Corbis; tr PL **28**c, br APL/Corbis **29**tr REU **30**br, tr APL/Corbis **31**cl APL/Corbis **32**bl COR **33**tc NASA; tr APL/Corbis **34**c, tr APL/Corbis **35**br, cr APL/Corbis **36**br, cl GI; tc AAP/Associated Press AP **37**br, cr, tr GI **38**tc GI; tr APL/Corbis **39**bl AAP; tcl APL/Corbis; tl, tcr, tr GI **40**tr APL/Corbis **41**br, tc, tr APL/Corbis **42**bl, c APL/Corbis **43**bc, cr APL/Corbis cl GI **44**c APL/Corbis **45**br APL/Corbis; tr PL **46**tc AFP AFP **47**bl, cr APL/Corbis **48**t PL **52**bl APL/Corbis **53**br, tc, tl APL/Corbis **54**c APL/Corbis **56**bl Liam Gumley/MODIS Atmosphere Team/University of Wisconsin-Madison cr COR **57**c APL/Corbis **58**cl APL/Corbis **59**tr APL/Corbis **60**bc, br, tc, tr APL/Corbis; c AAP Image **62**br, bl, tl APL/Corbis **63**bl APL/Corbis **64**bc, br, c, cr, tr APL/Corbis **66**c Craig Mayhew/Robert Simmon/NASA/GSFC **68**bl NASA/GSFC/MITI/ERSDAC/JAROS/US/Japan ASTER Science Team; br, t NASA/GSFC/METI/ERSDAC/JAROS/US/Japan ASTER Science Team **69**br Our Earth as Art/USGC/NASA **70**bc APL/Corbis; cl Jacques Descloitres/MODIS Rapid Response Team/NASA/GSFC; tl PL **71**bl NASA/GSFC/LaRC/JPL/MISR Team; c Earth Sciences and Image Analysis/NASA-Johnson Space Center **72**cr PL **75**c APL/Corbis; cr APL/Corbis; tr Associated Press AP **76**bc PD; br GI; **77**tl GI **79**br, cr GI; t PD; tr APL/Corbis **80**cl IOT; c COR **82**bl APL/Corbis; cl COR; tl GI **83**tc APL/Corbis; tl IOT **85**c PE; cr GI **86**br GI **87**br APL/Corbis; tr GI **88**tc, tr GI **89**tl GI **91**tc, tr APL/Corbis **92**bc Georg Gerster; br GI **93**tr PD **95**c, cl, tc, tr APL/Corbis; tl GI **97**tc APL/Corbis; tl Guido Alberto Rossi **99**bc, cr APL/Corbis; tr GI **100**br APL/Corbis **101**tc, tr APL/Corbis **102**c Craig Mahew/Robert Simmon/NASA/GSFC **104**br NASA/GSFC/MITI/ERSDAC/JAROS/US/Japan ASTER Science Team; c APL/Corbis; tr Professor Stanley Herwitz/Clark University/NASA **105**t SRTM Team/N_J/NIMA **106**bl DS; br NASA/GSFC/LaRC/JPL/MISR Team; c Jacques Descloitres/MODIS Land Rapid Response Team/NASA/GSFC **107**bl N_J; cl Jeff Schmaltz/MODIS Rapid Response Team/NASA/GSFC **108**cl GI **111**br NASA; bc, c, cl, tc APL/Corbis **112**cr PD **113**bl PD; tl APL/Corbis **114**cl COR; c GI **115**br APL/Corbis; cr COR **116**bc COR; br PD; tr GI **117**bc GI; bl PD **119**bl, cr GI; tr PD **121**tl, tcl GI; tcr PD; tr APL/Corbis **122**br, c DS; cr APL/Corbis **123**bl GI **124**bc, br, c APL/Corbis **125**tc GI tl GI **127**bl, bcl, br GI; bc, bcr APL/Corbis **128**c Craig Mahew/Robert Simmon/NASA/GSFC **130**bl, tr GI; br GI **131**c Sea WiFS Project/NASA/GSFC/ORBIMAGE **132**br APL/Corbis; c NASA/GSFC/MITI/ERSDAC/JAROS/US/Japan Aster Science Team cl GI **133**bl APL/Corbis; cl Sea WiFS Project/NASA/GSFC/ORBIMAGE; tr NASA/EFS **134**cl PD **137**br, c, cl, tr APL/Corbis tl GI **138**bc APL/Corbis; br PD **139**bc, bl APL/Corbis; c GI **140**c GI; cl APL/Corbis **141**cr, tl PD; tr PE **143**bc GI; bl, cl Pd; cr, tc APL/Corbis **144**cr APL/Corbis; br GI **145**tl GI; tr GI **146**c Craig Mahew/Robert Simmon/NASA/GSFC **148**b, c N_J cr NASA/GSFC/METI/ERSDAC/JAROS/US/Japan Aster Science Team **149**br N_J **150**bc Jacques Descloitres/MODIS Land Rapid Response Team bl APL/ Corbis cr Jeff Schmaltz/MODIS Rapid Response Team/NASA/GSFC **151**bl Jacques Descloitres/MODIS Land Rapid Response Team/NASA/GSFC; cl Jacques Descloitres/MODIS Land Rapid Response Team/NASA/GSFC **154**bl APL/Corbis **155**tl, tr APL/Corbis; tc AFP AFP **156**cl, tr APL/Corbis; tc GI **158**bl APL/Corbis **159**bc, bl APL/Corbis **160**br, cr GI **161**br, tr APL/Corbis; cr GI **162**br APL/Corbis **163**br, tr APL/Corbis; tc GI **164**c, cl, tc, tr APL/Corbis **165**br APL/Corbis **166**tc, tr APL/Corbis **167**tr APL/Corbis **168**bc EPA AFPI; c APL/Corbis **169**c APL/Corbis **170**br, cl APL/Corbis; bc Associated Press/XINHUA News Agency; c PD **171**br PD **172**c, cl, cr APL/Corbis **173**tr APL/Corbis; cr PD **174**bl Associated Press AP; bc GI; cr APL/Corbis **176**tc GI; tr APL/Corbis **177**bl, tl GI; cr, tc APL/Corbis **178**c Craig Mahew/Robert Simmon/NASA/GSFC **180**b N_J; tr N_J **181**br N_J; t Jacques Descloitres/MODIS Rapid Response Team/NASA/GSFC **182**br APL/Corbis; c Jacques Descloitres/MODIS Land Rapid Response Team/NASA/GSFC; cl Jacques Descloitres/MODIS Land Science Team; cr APL/Corbis **183**br, tl APL/Corbis; c Jacques Descloitres/MODIS Land Rapid Response Team/NASA/GSFC **184**cr GI **187**tc, tl, tr APL/Corbis **188**c, cl APL/Corbis **189**bc Associated Press AP; c APL/Corbis **190**c APL/Corbis **191**cl, tl, tr APL/Corbis **192**cl APL/Corbis **193**br APL/Corbis **194**cl PL **195**br, cr APL/Corbis **197**bc, bl, c, tr APL/Corbis **198**c Craig Mahew/Robert Simmon/NASA/GSFC **200**cr Jacques Descloitres/MODIS Rapid Response Team/NASA/GSFC; tl NASA/GSFC/MITI/ERSDAC/JAROS/US/Japan Aster Science Team **201**cr Jacques Descloitres/MODIS Land Science Team; tr GSFC Landsat Team/Australian Ground Receiving Station Teams/NASA **202**bl APL/Corbis; br, c N_ES **203**c, cr N_ES **206**bl, br APL/Corbis **207**br PL; c Paul Hoehenberger/PPB; cl, cr APL/Corbis **208**br APL/Corbis **209**bl, cr, tr APL/Corbis **210**c, cr APL/Corbis **211**bc, bl, cl, c APL/Corbis **212**bc, br, cr, tr APL/Corbis **214**br, cl, tr APL/Corbis **215**bl, tc APL/Corbis **216**c PL **218**c, tr APL/Corbis **219**br, cr, tr APL/Corbis **220**c APL/Corbis; cr PL **221**c, cr, tc APL/Corbis; tr N_T **222**c Jerry Stebbins **227**br APL/Corbis

ILLUSTRATION CREDITS

Richard Bonson/Tom Connell/Wildlife Art Ltd: 20 **John Bull:** 1 **Andrew Davies/Creative Communication:** 18, 20, 22, 24, 26, 28, 29, 30, 32, 34, 36, 38, 40, 41, 42, 43, 44, 45, 46, 47, 56, 57, 64, 72, 76, 78, 80, 82, 84, 86, 88, 90, 92, 94, 96, 98, 100, 108, 110, 112, 114, 116, 118, 120, 122, 124, 126, 133, 134, 136, 138, 140, 142, 144, 152, 153, 154, 155, 156, 158, 160, 162, 165, 166, 168, 170, 172, 175, 176, 184, 188, 189, 190, 193, 195, 196, 208, 209, 211, 213, 218, 220, 221, 226 **Chris Forsey:** 150 **Mark A. Garlick/space-art.co.uk:** 16 **Rob Mancini:** 26, 44, 45 **Map Illustrations:** 20, 22, 50, 52, 53, 56, 57, 58, 59, 60, 61, 62, 63, 64, 70, 71, 72, 73, 74, 75, 76, 78, 80, 81, 82, 84, 85, 86, 88, 90, 92, 94, 96, 98, 100, 106, 107, 108, 110, 111, 112, 114, 116, 118, 120, 122, 124, 126, 132, 133, 134, 136, 137, 138, 140, 142, 144, 150, 151, 153, 154, 155, 156, 158, 160, 162, 164, 166, 168, 169, 170, 172, 174, 176, 182, 183, 184, 185, 186, 187, 188, 189, 190, 192, 194, 196, 202, 203, 204, 205, 206, 208, 210, 212, 214, 215, 218, 224, 225 **Edwina Riddell:** 24 **Guido Alberto Rossi:** 97 **Peter Scott/Wildlife Art Ltd:** 22 **Suzanne Tawansi:** 12, 13, 51, 186, 187, 204, 20, 207 **Richard Bonson/Wildlife Art Ltd:** 18 **Rod Westblade:** 106 **Murray Zanoni:** 78, 82, 87, 88, 90, 92, 94, 96, 98, 101, 114, 121, 123, 125, 126, 139, 143, 144, 156, 158, 160, 162, 167, 173, 175, 188, 191, 192, 194, 197, 209, 210

Flags of the World

EUROPE
Repubic of Ireland
United Kingdom
Denmark
Finland
Iceland
Norway
Sweden
Germany
Austria
Liechtenstein
Slovakia
Albania
Bosnia and Herzegovina
Croatia
Serbia and Montenegro
Slovenia
Bulgaria
Macedonia
NORTH AMERICA
Canada
United States of America
Mexico
Antigua and Barbuda
The Bahamas
Barbados
Belize
Honduras
Jamaica
Nicaragua
Panama
St Kitts and Nevis
St Lucia
St Vincent and the Grenadines
Trinidad and Tobago
Brazil
Paraguay
Argentina
Chile
Uruguay
ASIA
Russian Federation
Armenia
Syria
Bahrain
Kuwait
Oman
Qatar
Saudi Arabia
United Arab Emirates
Yemen
Bangladesh
Bhutan
India
Maldives
Nepal
Sri Lanka
China
Mongolia
Brunei
East Timor
Indonesia
Malaysia
Philippines
Singapore
Japan
AFRICA
Somalia
Sudan
Benin
Burkina Faso
Cameroon
Chad
Côte d'Ivoire
Equatorial Guinea
Nigeria
Senegal
Sierra Leone
Togo
Burundi
Central Africa Republic
Congo
Democratic Republic of Congo
Comoros
Lesotho
Madagascar
Malawi
Mozambique
Namibia
Republic of South Africa
Swaziland
Fiji
Papua New Guinea
Solomon Islands
Vanuatu
Federated States of Micronesia
Kiribati
Marshall Islands
Nauru